MERRIAM-WEBSTER'S
DESK
DICTIONARY

MERRIAM-WEBSTER'S
DESK
DICTIONARY

A GENUINE MERRIAM-WEBSTER

The name *Webster* alone is no guarantee of excellence. It is used by a number of publishers and may serve mainly to mislead an unwary buyer.

Merriam-Webster™ is the name you should look for when you consider the purchase of dictionaries or other fine reference books. It carries the reputation of a company that has been publishing since 1831 and is your assurance of quality and authority.

Library of Congress Cataloging in Publication Data
Main entry under title:
Merriam-Webster's desk dictionary.
    p.   cm.
  ISBN 0-87779-549-5
  1. English language — Dictionaries.   I. Merriam-Webster, Inc.
PE1628.M365   1995
423 — dc20   95-5824
                                                                            CIP

Made in the United States of America

14QP/WV05

Contents

Preface

MERRIAM-WEBSTER'S DESK DICTIONARY is the most recent in a series of Merriam-Webster® concise dictionaries that extends back more than 130 years. Over the years, books in this series have carried varied titles, such as Webster's Condensed Dictionary, Webster's Practical Dictionary, and Webster's Ideal Dictionary, but all have shared in being designed to meet the day-to-day needs of dictionary users in the home or office. This new work is firmly within the tradition of those previous books in its emphasis on practicality, range of material offered, and ease of use, but it also draws much new information—including new vocabulary—from Merriam-Webster's Collegiate Dictionary, Tenth Edition, the latest in our Collegiate® line of dictionaries.

The heart of Merriam-Webster's Desk Dictionary is the A-Z vocabulary. Within this section, one finds the core of the English vocabulary; obsolete, rare, and highly technical words and obsolete meanings of common words have been omitted. The vocabulary is thus a compilation of the words most likely to be looked up by any person searching for a meaning, pronunciation, or end-of-line division point. Every definition in this section is based on examples of actual usage found among the more than 14,500,000 citations in the Merriam-Webster files.

The A-Z vocabulary is followed by several sections that dictionary users have long found helpful: Common English Given Names; Foreign Words and Phrases that often occur in English texts but that have not yet become part of the English vocabulary; thousands of proper names brought together under the separate headings Biographical Names and Geographical Names; Nations of the World; a list of places in the United States having 19,000 or more inhabitants in the most recent census, with a list of State Facts such as states' nicknames, areas, and mottoes; a similar list of places in Canada, with a summary by provinces and territories; a section devoted to widely used Signs and Symbols; a Handbook of Style section that summarizes common conventions of punctuation, capitalization, and the use of italics; a section on the Documentation of Sources, with information on footnotes and other kinds of bibliographical references; and finally, a list of the Forms of Address for governmental, diplomatic, religious, and military officials. All are listed on the Contents page.

The A-Z vocabulary is preceded by a section of Explanatory Notes that should be read carefully by every user of the dictionary. An understanding of the information contained in these notes will add markedly to the satisfaction and pleasure that come from looking into the pages of the dictionary. Following these notes is a page that lists and explains the pronunciation symbols used in this dictionary.

Merriam-Webster's Desk Dictionary is the product of a company that has been publishing dictionaries for 150 years. It has been edited by an experienced staff of professional lexicographers, who believe that it will serve well those who want an easy-to-read record of today's English words.

Explanatory Notes

Entries

A boldface letter or a combination of such letters, including punctuation marks and diacritics where needed, that is set flush with the left-hand margin of each column of type is a main entry. The main entry may consist of letters set solid, of letters joined by a hyphen or a diagonal, or of letters separated by one or more spaces:

> **alone** . . . *adj*
>
> **avant–garde** . . . *n*
>
> **and/or** . . . *conj*
>
> **assembly language** . . . *n*

The material in lightface type that follows each main entry on the same line and on succeeding indented lines presents information about the main entry.

The main entries follow one another in alphabetical order letter by letter: *bill of health* follows *billion; Day of Atonement* follows *daylight saving time*. Those containing an Arabic numeral are alphabetized as if the numeral were spelled out: *4-H* comes between *fourfold* and *Four Hundred; 3-D* comes between *three* and *three-dimensional*. Those that often begin with the abbreviation *St.* in common usage have the abbreviation spelled out: *Saint Valentine's Day*.

A pair of guide words is printed at the top of each page. These indicate that the entries falling alphabetically between the words at the top of the outer column of each page are found on that page.

The guide words are usually the alphabetically first and the alphabetically last entries on the page:

> ### airbrush • albumin

Occasionally the last printed entry is not the alphabetically last entry. On page 108, for example, *combings* is the last main entry, but *combining*, an inflected form at *¹combine*, is the alphabetically last entry and is therefore the second guide word. The alphabetically last entry is not used, however, if it follows alphabetically the first guide word on the succeeding page. Thus on page 129 *craving* is not a guide word because it follows alphabetically the entry *craven* which is the first guide word on page 130.

Any boldface word—a main entry with definition, a variant, an inflected form, a defined or undefined run-on, or a run-in entry—may be used as a guide word.

When one main entry has exactly the same written form as another, the two are distinguished by superscript numerals preceding each word:

> **¹melt** . . . *vb*   **¹pine** . . . *n*
>
> **²melt** *n*   **²pine** *vb*

Full words come before parts of words made up of the same letters; solid compounds come before hyphenated compounds; hyphenated compounds come before open compounds; and lowercase entries come before those with an initial capital:

> **²super** . . . *adj*
>
> **super-** . . . *prefix*
>
> **run·down** . . . *n*
>
> **run–down** . . . *adj*
>
> **run down** *vb*
>
> **dutch** . . . *adv*
>
> **Dutch** . . . *n*

The centered dots within entry words indicate division points at which a hyphen may be put at the end of a line of print or writing. Thus the noun *cap·puc·ci·no* may be ended on one line and continued on the next in this manner:

> cap-
>
> *puccino*
>
> cappuc-
>
> *cino*
>
> cappucci-
>
> *no*

Centered dots are not shown after a single initial letter or before a single terminal letter because typesetters seldom cut off a single letter:

> **abyss** . . . *n*
>
> **flighty** . . . *adj*
>
> **idea** . . . *n*

Nor are they usually shown at the second and succeeding homographs unless they differ among themselves:

> **¹sig·nal** . . . *n*
>
> **²signal** *vb*
>
> **³signal** *adj*
>
> **¹min·ute** . . . *n*
>
> **²mi·nute** . . . *adj*

There are acceptable alternative end-of-line divisions just as there are acceptable variant spellings and pronunciations, but no more than one division is shown for any entry in this dictionary.

A double hyphen at the end of a line in this dictionary (as in the definition at **accelerator**) stands for a hyphen that is retained when the word is written as a unit on one line. This kind of fixed hyphen is always represented in boldface words in this dictionary with an en dash.

When a main entry is followed by the word *or* and another spelling, the two spellings are equal variants. Both are standard, and either one may be used according to personal inclination:

> **ocher** *or* **ochre**

If two variants joined by *or* are out of alphabetical order, they remain equal variants. The one printed first is, however, slightly more common than the second:

> **¹plow** *or* **plough**

When another spelling is joined to the main entry by the word *also*, the spelling after *also* is a secondary variant and occurs less frequently than the first:

absinthe *also* **absinth**

Secondary variants belong to standard usage and may be used according to personal inclination. Once the word *also* is used to signal a secondary variant, all following variants are joined by *or:*

²**wool·ly** *also* **wool·ie** *or* **wooly**

Variants whose spelling puts them alphabetically more than a column away from the main entry are entered at their own alphabetical places and usually not at the main entry:

li·chee *var of* LITCHI

Variants having a usage label appear only at their own alphabetical places:

me·tre . . . *chiefly Brit var of* METER

To show all the stylings that are found for English compounds would require space that can be better used for other information. So this dictionary limits itself to a single styling for a compound:

peace·mak·er

pell–mell

boom box

When a compound is widely used and one styling predominates, that styling is shown. When a compound is uncommon or when the evidence indicates that two or three stylings are approximately equal in frequency, the styling shown is based on the comparison of other similar compounds.

A main entry may be followed by one or more derivatives or by a homograph with a different functional label. These are run-on entries. Each is introduced by a boldface dash and each has a functional label. They are not defined, however, since their meanings are readily understood from the meaning of the root word:

fear·less . . . *adj* . . . — **fear·less·ly** *adv*
— **fear·less·ness** *n*

hic·cup . . . *n* . . . — **hiccup** *vb*

A main entry may be followed by one or more phrases containing the entry word or an inflected form of it. These are also run-on entries. Each is introduced by a boldface dash but there is no functional label. They are, however, defined since their meanings are more than the sum of the meanings of their elements:

¹**set** . . . *vb* . . . — **set sail** : . . .

¹**hand** . . . *n* . . . — **at hand** : . . .

Defined phrases of this sort are run on at the entry defining the first major word in the phrase. When there are variants, however, the run-on appears at the entry defining the first major word which is invariable in the phrase:

¹**seed** . . . *n* . . . — **go to seed** *or* **run to seed** 1 : . . .

Boldface words that appear within parentheses (as

co·ca at co·caine and jet engine and jet propulsion at jet–propelled) are run-in entries.

Attention is called to the definition of *vocabulary entry* on page 615. The term *dictionary entry* includes all vocabulary entries as well as all boldface entries in the section headed "Foreign Words and Phrases."

Pronunciation

The matter between a pair of reversed virgules \ \ following the entry word indicates the pronunciation. The symbols used are explained in the chart printed inside the back cover.

A hyphen is used in the pronunciation to show syllabic division. These hyphens sometimes coincide with the centered dots in the entry word that indicate end-of-line division:

ab·sen·tee \ˌab-sən-ˈtē\

Sometimes they do not:

met·ric \ˈme-trik\

A high-set mark ˈ indicates major (primary) stress or accent; a low-set mark ˌ indicates minor (secondary) stress or accent:

heart·beat \ˈhärt-ˌbēt\

The stress mark stands at the beginning of the syllable that receives the stress.

A syllable with neither a high-set mark nor a low-set mark is unstressed:

¹**struc·ture** \ˈstrək-chər\

The presence of variant pronunciations indicates that not all educated speakers pronounce words the same way. A second-place variant is not to be regarded as less acceptable than the pronunciation that is given first. It may, in fact, be used by as many educated speakers as the first variant, but the requirements of the printed page are such that one must precede the other:

apri·cot \ˈa-prə-ˌkät, ˈā-\

pro·vost \ˈprō-ˌvōst, ˈprä-vəst\

Symbols enclosed by parentheses represent elements that are present in the pronunciation of some speakers but are absent from the pronunciation of other speakers, or elements that are present in some but absent from other utterances of the same speaker:

¹**om·ni·bus** \ˈäm-ni-(ˌ)bəs\

ad·di·tion·al \ə-ˈdi-sh(ə-)nəl\

Thus, the above parentheses indicate that some people say \ˈäm-ni-ˌbəs\ and others say \ˈäm-ni-bəs\; some \ə-ˈdi-shə-nəl\, others \ə-ˈdi-shnəl\.

When a main entry has less than a full pronunciation, the missing part is to be supplied from a pronunciation in a preceding entry or within the same pair of reversed virgules:

cham·pi·on·ship \-ˌship\

pa·la·ver \pə-ˈla-vər, -ˈlä-\

The pronunciation of the first three syllables of *cham-*

pionship is found at the main entry *champion*. The hyphens before and after \ˈlä\ in the second pronunciation of *palaver* indicate that both the first and the last parts of the pronunciation are to be taken from the immediately preceding pronunciation.

In general, no pronunciation is indicated for open compounds consisting of two or more English words that have own-place entry:

witch doctor *n*

Only the first entry in a sequence of numbered homographs is given a pronunciation if their pronunciations are the same:

¹**re·ward** \ri-ˈwȯrd\ *vb*

²**reward** *n*

The absent but implied pronunciation of derivatives and compounds run on after a main entry is a combination of the pronunciation at the main entry and the pronunciation of the other element as given at its alphabetical place in the vocabulary:

— **quick·ness** *n*

— **hold forth**

Thus, the pronunciation of *quickness* is the sum of the pronunciations given at *quick* and *-ness;* that of *hold forth*, the sum of the pronunciations of the two elements that make up the phrase.

Functional Labels

An italic label indicating a part of speech or another functional classification follows the pronunciation or, if no pronunciation is given, the main entry. The eight traditional parts of speech are indicated as follows:

bold . . . *adj*

forth·with . . . *adv*

¹**but** . . . *conj*

ge·sund·heit . . . *interj*

bo·le·ro . . . *n*

²**un·der** . . . *prep*

¹**it** . . . *pron*

slap . . . *vb*

Other italicized labels used to indicate functional classifications that are not traditional parts of speech include:

ATM *abbr*

self- *comb form*

un- . . . *prefix*

-ial *adj suffix*

²**-ly** *adv suffix*

²**-er** . . . *n suffix*

-ize . . . *vb suffix*

Fe *symbol*

may . . . *verbal auxiliary*

Functional labels are sometimes combined:

afloat . . . *adj or adv*

Inflected Forms

Nouns

The plurals of nouns are shown in this dictionary when suffixation brings about a change of final *-y* to *-i-*, when the noun ends in a consonant plus *-o* or in *-ey*, when the noun ends in *-oo*, when the noun has an irregular plural or a zero plural or a foreign plural, when the noun is a compound that pluralizes any element but the last, when a final consonant is doubled, when the noun has variant plurals, and when it is believed that the dictionary user might have reasonable doubts about the spelling of the plural or when the plural is spelled in a way contrary to what is expected:

²**spy** *n, pl* **spies**

si·lo . . . *n, pl* **silos**

val·ley . . . *n, pl* **valleys**

²**shampoo** *n, pl* **shampoos**

¹**quiz** . . . *n, pl* **quiz·zes**

¹**fish** . . . *n, pl* **fish** *or* **fishes**

mouse . . . *n, pl* **mice**

moose . . . *n, pl* **moose**

cri·te·ri·on . . . *n, pl* **-ria**

son–in–law . . . *n, pl* **sons–in–law**

pi . . . *n, pl* **pis**

³**dry** *n, pl* **drys**

Cutback inflected forms are used when the noun has three or more syllables:

ame·ni·ty . . . *n, pl* **-ties**

The plurals of nouns are usually not shown when the base word is unchanged by suffixation, when the noun is a compound whose second element is readily recognizable as a regular free form entered at its own place, or when the noun is unlikely to occur in the plural:

night . . . *n*

fore·foot . . . *n*

mo·nog·a·my . . . *n*

Nouns that are plural in form and that regularly occur in plural construction are labeled *n pl*:

munch·ies . . . *n pl*

Nouns that are plural in form but that are not always construed as plurals are appropriately labeled:

lo·gis·tics . . . *n sing or pl*

Verbs

The principal parts of verbs are shown in this dictionary when suffixation brings about a doubling of a final consonant or an elision of a final *-e* or a change of final *-y* to *-i-*, when final *-c* changes to *-ck* in suffixation, when the verb ends in *-ey*, when the inflection is irregular, when there are variant inflected forms, and when it is believed that the dictionary user might have reasonable doubts about the spelling of an inflected form or when the inflected form is spelled in a way contrary to what is expected:

²snag *vb* snagged; snag·ging
¹move . . . *vb* moved; mov·ing
¹cry . . . *vb* cried; cry·ing
¹frol·ic . . . *vb* frol·icked; frol·ick·ing
sur·vey . . . *vb* sur·veyed; sur·vey·ing
¹drive . . . *vb* drove . . .; driv·en . . .; driv·ing
²bus *vb* bused *or* bussed; bus·ing *or* bus·sing
²visa *vb* vi·saed . . .; vi·sa·ing
²chagrin *vb* cha·grined . . .; cha·grin·ing

The principal parts of a regularly inflected verb are shown when it is desirable to indicate the pronunciation of one of the inflected forms:

learn . . . *vb* learned \ˈlərnd, ˈlərnt\; learn·ing
¹al·ter \ˈȯl-tər\ *vb* al·tered; al·ter·ing \-t(ə-)riŋ\

Cutback inflected forms are usually used when the verb has three or more syllables, when it is a two-syllable word that ends in *-l* and has variant spellings, and when it is a compound whose second element is readily recognized as an irregular verb:

elim·i·nate . . . *vb* -nated; -nat·ing
²quarrel *vb* -reled *or* -relled; -rel·ing *or* -rel·ling
¹re·take . . . *vb* -took . . .; -tak·en . . .; -tak·ing

The principal parts of verbs are usually not shown when the base word is unchanged by suffixation or when the verb is a compound whose second element is readily recognizable as a regular free form entered at its own place:

¹jump . . . *vb*
pre·judge . . . *vb*

Another inflected form of English verbs is the third person singular of the present tense, which is regularly formed by the addition of *-s* or *-es* to the base form of the verb. This inflected form is not shown except at a handful of entries (as *have* and *do*) for which it is in some way anomalous.

Adjectives & Adverbs

The comparative and superlative forms of adjectives and adverbs are shown in this dictionary when suffixation brings about a doubling of a final consonant or an elision of a final *-e* or a change of final *-y* to *-i-*, when the word ends in *-ey*, when the inflection is irregular, and when there are variant inflected forms:

¹red . . . *adj* red·der; red·dest
¹tame . . . *adj* tam·er; tam·est
¹kind·ly . . . *adj* kind·li·er; -est
hors·ey *or* horsy . . . *adj* hors·i·er; -est
¹good . . . *adj* bet·ter . . .; best
¹far . . . *adv* far·ther . . . *or* fur·ther . . .;
    far·thest *or* fur·thest

The superlative forms of adjectives and adverbs of two or more syllables are usually cut back:

³fancy *adj* fan·ci·er; -est
¹ear·ly . . . *adv* ear·li·er; -est

The comparative and superlative forms of regularly inflected adjectives and adverbs are shown when it is desirable to indicate the pronunciation of the inflected forms:

¹young \ˈyəŋ\ *adj* youn·ger \ˈyəŋ-gər\; youn·gest
\ˈyəŋ-gəst\

The inclusion of inflected forms in *-er* and *-est* at adjective and adverb entries means nothing more about the use of *more* and *most* with these adjectives and adverbs than that their comparative and superlative degrees may be expressed in either way: *lazier* or *more lazy; laziest* or *most lazy*.

At a few adjective entries only the superlative form is shown:

²mere *adj, superlative* mer·est

The absence of the comparative form indicates that there is no evidence of its use.

The comparative and superlative forms of adjectives and adverbs are usually not shown when the base word is unchanged by suffixation, when the inflected forms of the word are identical with those of a preceding homograph, or when the word is a compound whose second element is readily recognizable as a regular free form entered at its own place:

¹near *adv*
³good *adv*
un·wor·thy . . . *adj*

Inflected forms are not shown at undefined run-ons.

Capitalization

Most entries in this dictionary begin with a lowercase letter. A few of these have an italicized label *often cap*, which indicates that the word is as likely to be capitalized as not and that it is as acceptable with an uppercase initial as it is with one in lowercase. Some entries begin with an uppercase letter, which indicates that the word is usually capitalized. The absence of an initial capital or of an *often cap* label indicates that the word is not ordinarily capitalized:

salm·on . . . *n*
gar·gan·tuan . . . *adj, often cap*
Mo·hawk . . . *n*

The capitalization of entries that are open or hyphenated compounds is similarly indicated by the form of the entry or by an italicized label:

dry goods . . . *n pl*
french fry *vb, often cap 1st F*
un–Amer·i·can . . . *adj*
Par·kin·son's disease . . . *n*
lazy Su·san . . . *n*
Jack Frost *n*

A word that is capitalized in some senses and lowercase in others shows variations from the form of the main entry by the use of italicized labels at the appropriate senses:

Trin·i·ty . . . *n* . . . **2** *not cap*
To·ry . . . *n* . . . **3** *often not cap*
ti·tan . . . *n* **1** *cap*
re·nais·sance . . . *n* . . . **1** *cap* . . . **2** *often cap*

Etymology

This dictionary gives the etymologies for a number of the vocabulary entries. These etymologies are in bold-face square brackets preceding the definition. Meanings given in roman type within these brackets are not definitions of the entry, but are meanings of the Middle English, Old English, or non-English words within the brackets.

The etymology gives the language from which words borrowed into English have come. It also gives the form of the word in that language or a representation of the word in our alphabet if the form in that language differs from that in English:

philo·den·dron . . . [NL, fr. Gk, neut. of *philo-dendros* loving trees . . .]
¹sav·age . . . [ME *sauvage*, fr. MF, fr. ML *salvaticus*, alter. of L *silvaticus* of the woods, wild . . .]

An etymology beginning with the name of a language (including ME or OE) and not giving the foreign (or Middle English or Old English) form indicates that this form is the same as the form of the entry word:

le·gume . . . [F]
¹jour·ney . . . [ME, fr. OF . . .]

An etymology beginning with the name of a language (including ME or OE) and not giving the foreign (or Middle English or Old English) meaning indicates that this meaning is the same as the meaning expressed in the first definition in the entry:

ug·ly . . . *adj* . . . [ME, fr. ON *uggligr* . . .] **1**
: FRIGHTFUL, DIRE

Usage

Three types of status labels are used in this dictionary—temporal, regional, and stylistic—to signal that a word or a sense of a word is not part of the standard vocabulary of English.

The temporal label *obs* for "obsolete" means that there is no evidence of use since 1755:

³post *n* **1** *obs*

The label *obs* is a comment on the word being defined. When a thing, as distinguished from the word used to designate it, is obsolete, appropriate orientation is usually given in the definition:

cat·a·pult . . . *n* **1** : an ancient military machine for hurling missiles

The temporal label *archaic* means that a word or sense once in common use is found today only sporadically or in special contexts:

¹mete . . . *vb* . . . **1** *archaic*
¹thou . . . *pron, archaic*

A word or sense limited in use to a specific region of the U.S. has an appropriate label. The adverb *chiefly* precedes a label when the word has some currency outside the specified region, and a double label is used to indicate considerable currency in each of two specific regions:

²wash *n* . . . **5** *West*
do·gie . . . *n, chiefly West*
crul·ler . . . *n* . . . **2** *Northern & Midland*

Words current in all regions of the U.S. have no label.

A word or sense limited in use to one of the other countries of the English-speaking world has an appropriate regional label:

chem·ist . . . *n* . . . **2** *Brit*
loch . . . *n, Scot*
²wireless *n* . . . **2** *chiefly Brit*

The label *dial* for "dialect" indicates that the pattern of use of a word or sense is too complex for summary labeling: it usually includes several regional varieties of American English or of American and British English:

²mind *vb* **1** *chiefly dial*

The stylistic label *slang* is used with words or senses that are especially appropriate in contexts of extreme informality:

³can . . . *vb* . . . **2** *slang*
²grand *n, slang*

There is no satisfactory objective test for slang, especially with reference to a word out of context. No word, in fact, is invariably slang, and many standard words can be given slang applications.

Definitions are sometimes followed by verbal illustrations that show a typical use of the word in context. These illustrations are enclosed in angle brackets, and the word being illustrated is usually replaced by a lightface swung dash. The swung dash stands for the boldface entry word, and it may be followed by an italicized suffix:

¹jump . . . *vb* . . . **5** . . . ⟨∼ the gun⟩
all–around . . . *adj* **1** . . . ⟨best ∼ performance⟩
¹can·on . . . *n* . . . **3** . . . ⟨the ∼s of good taste⟩
en·joy . . . *vb* . . . **2** . . . ⟨∼ed the concert⟩

The swung dash is not used when the form of the boldface entry word is changed in suffixation, and it is not used for open compounds:

²deal *vb* . . . **2** . . . ⟨dealt him a blow⟩
drum up *vb* **1** . . . ⟨drum up business⟩

Definitions are sometimes followed by usage notes that give supplementary information about such matters as idiom, syntax, and semantic relationship. A usage note is introduced by a lightface dash:

²cry *n* . . . **5** . . . — usu. used in the phrase *a far cry*
²drum *vb* . . . **4** . . . — usu. used with *out*
¹jaw . . . *n* . . . **2** . . . — usu. used in pl.

¹**ada·gio** . . . *adv or adj* . . . — used as a direction in music

hajji . . . *n* . . . — often used as a title

Sometimes a usage note is used in place of a definition. Some function words (as conjunctions and prepositions) have chiefly grammatical meaning and little or no lexical meaning; most interjections express feelings but are otherwise untranslatable into lexical meaning; and some other words (as honorific titles) are more amenable to comment than to definition:

or . . . *conj* — used as a function word to indicate an alternative

¹**at** . . . *prep* 1 — used to indicate a point in time or space

auf Wie·der·seh·en . . . *interj* . . . — used to express farewell

sir . . . *n* . . . 2 — used as a usu. respectful form of address

Sense Division

A boldface colon is used in this dictionary to introduce a definition:

equine . . . *adj* . . . : of or relating to the horse

It is also used to separate two or more definitions of a single sense:

no·ti·fy . . . *vb* . . . 1 : to give notice of : report the occurrence of

Boldface Arabic numerals separate the senses of a word that has more than one sense:

add . . . *vb* 1 : to join something else so as to increase in number or amount 2 : to say further . . . 3 : to combine (numbers) into one sum

A particular semantic relationship between senses is sometimes suggested by the use of one of the two italic sense dividers *esp* or *also*.

The sense divider *esp* (for *especially*) is used to introduce the most common meaning included in the more general preceding definition:

crys·tal . . . *n* . . . 2 : something resembling crystal (as in transparency); *esp* : a clear glass used for table articles

The sense divider *also* is used to introduce a meaning related to the preceding sense by an easily understood extension of that sense:

chi·na . . . *n* : porcelain ware; *also* : domestic pottery in general

The order of senses is historical: the sense known to have been first used in English is entered first. This is not to be taken to mean, however, that each sense of a multisense word developed from the immediately preceding sense. It is altogether possible that sense 1 of a word has given rise to sense 2 and sense 2 to sense 3, but frequently sense 2 and sense 3 may have developed independently of one another from sense 1.

When an italicized label follows a boldface numeral, the label applies only to that specific numbered sense. It

does not apply to any other boldface numbered senses:

craft . . . *n* . . . 3 *pl usu* **craft**
¹**fa·ther** . . . *n* . . . 2 *cap* . . . 5 *often cap*
dul·ci·mer . . . *n* . . . 2 *or* **dul·ci·more** \-₁mōr\
²**lift** *n* . . . 5 *chiefly Brit*

At *craft* the *pl* label applies to sense **3** but to none of the other numbered senses. At *father* the *cap* label applies only to sense **2** and the *often cap* label only to sense **5**. At *dulcimer* the variant spelling and pronunciation apply only to sense **2**, and the *chiefly Brit* label at *lift* applies only to sense **5**.

Cross-Reference

Four different kinds of cross-references are used in this dictionary: directional, synonymous, cognate, and inflectional. In each instance the cross-reference is readily recognized by the lightface small capitals in which it is printed.

A cross-reference following a lightface dash and beginning with *see* is a directional cross-reference. It directs the dictionary user to look elsewhere for further information:

ri·al . . . *n* — see MONEY table

A cross-reference following a boldface colon is a synonymous cross-reference. It may stand alone as the only definition for an entry or for a sense of an entry; it may follow an analytical definition; it may be one of two or more synonymous cross-references separated by commas:

pa·pa . . . *n* : FATHER
¹**par·tic·u·lar** . . . *adj* . . . 4 : attentive to details : PRECISE
²**main** *adj* 1 : CHIEF, PRINCIPAL
¹**fig·ure** . . . *n* . . . 6 : SHAPE, FORM, OUTLINE

A synonymous cross-reference indicates that an entry, a definition at the entry, or a specific sense at the entry cross-referred to can be substituted as a definition for the entry or the sense in which the cross-reference appears.

A cross-reference following an italic *var of* ("variant of") is a cognate cross-reference:

pick·a·back . . . *var of* PIGGYBACK

Occasionally a cognate cross-reference has a limiting label preceding *var of* as an indication that the variant is not standard English:

aero·plane . . . *chiefly Brit var of* AIRPLANE

A cross-reference following an italic label that identifies an entry as an inflected form (as of a noun or verb) is an inflectional cross-reference:

calves *pl of* CALF
woven *past part of* WEAVE

Inflectional cross-references appear only when the inflected form falls at least a column away from the entry cross-referred to.

Synonyms

A boldface **syn** near the end of an entry introduces words that are synonymous with the word being defined:

> **alone** . . . *adj* . . . **syn** lonely, lonesome, lone, solitary

Synonyms are not definitions although they may often be substituted for each other in context.

Combining Forms, Prefixes, & Suffixes

An entry that begins or ends with a hyphen is a word element that forms part of an English compound:

> **-wise** . . . *adv comb form* . . . ⟨slant*wise*⟩
> **ex-** . . . *prefix* . . . ⟨*ex*-president⟩
> **-let** . . . *n suffix* **1** . . . ⟨book*let*⟩

Combining forms, prefixes, and suffixes are entered in this dictionary for two reasons: to make understandable the meaning of many undefined run-ons and to make recognizable the meaningful elements of words that are not entered in the dictionary.

Lists of Undefined Words

Lists of undefined words occur after the entries *anti-*, *in-*, *non-*, *over-*, *re-*, *self-*, *semi-*, *sub-*, *super-*, and *un-*. These words are undefined because they are self-explanatory: their meanings are simply the sum of a meaning of the prefix or combining form and a meaning of the root word.

Abbreviations & Symbols

Abbreviations and symbols for chemical elements are included as main entries in the vocabulary:

> **RSVP** *abbr* . . . please reply
> **Ca** *symbol* calcium

Abbreviations have been normalized to one form. In practice, however, there is considerable variation in the use of periods and in capitalization (as *vhf*, *v.h.f.*, *VHF*, and *V.H.F.*), and stylings other than those given in this dictionary are often acceptable.

Symbols that are not capable of being alphabetized are included in a separate section of the back matter headed "Signs and Symbols."

Abbreviations Used in This Work

ab	about	*Heb*	Hebrew	*OPer*	Old Persian
abbr	abbreviation	*Hung*	Hungarian	*OProv*	Old Provençal
abl	ablative	*Icel*	Icelandic	*orig*	originally
acc	accusative	*imit*	imitative	*part*	participle
A.D.	anno Domini	*imper*	imperative	*Per*	Persian
adj	adjective	*interj*	interjection	*perh*	perhaps
adv	adverb	*Ir*	Irish	*Pg*	Portuguese
alter	alteration	*irreg*	irregular	*pl*	plural
Am	American	*It, Ital*	Italian	*Pol*	Polish
AmerF	American French	*Jp*	Japanese	*pp*	past participle
AmerInd	American Indian	*K*	Kelvin	*prep*	preposition
AmerSp	American Spanish	*L*	Latin	*pres*	present
Ar	Arabic	*LaF*	Louisiana French	*prob*	probably
Aram	Aramaic	*LG*	Low German	*pron*	pronoun, pronunciation
B.C.	before Christ	*LGk*	Late Greek	*Prov*	Provençal
Brit	British	*LHeb*	Late Hebrew	*prp*	present participle
C	Celsius	*lit*	literally	*Russ*	Russian
Calif	California	*LL*	Late Latin	*Sc*	Scotch, Scots
CanF	Canadian French	*masc*	masculine	*Scand*	Scandinavian
cap	capital, capitalized	*MD*	Middle Dutch	*ScGael*	Scottish Gaelic
Celt	Celtic	*ME*	Middle English	*Scot*	Scottish
cent	century	*MexSp*	Mexican Spanish	*sing*	singular
Chin	Chinese	*MF*	Middle French	*Skt*	Sanskrit
comb	combining	*MGk*	Middle Greek	*Slav*	Slavic
compar	comparative	*ML*	Medieval Latin	*So*	South
conj	conjunction	*modif*	modification	*Sp*	Spanish
D	Dutch	*MS*	manuscript	*St*	Saint
Dan	Danish	*n*	noun	*superl*	superlative
dat	dative	*neut*	neuter	*Sw*	Swedish
deriv	derivative	*NewEng*	New England	*syn*	synonym, synonymy
dial	dialect	*NGk*	New Greek	*trans*	translation
dim	diminutive	*NHeb*	New Hebrew	*Turk*	Turkish
E	English	*NL*	New Latin	*US*	United States
Egypt	Egyptian	*No*	North	*USSR*	Union of Soviet
Eng	English	*Norw*	Norwegian		Socialist Republics
esp	especially	*n pl*	noun plural	*usu*	usually
F	Fahrenheit, French	*obs*	obsolete	*var*	variant
fem	feminine	*OE*	Old English	*vb*	verb
fr	from	*OF*	Old French	*vi*	verb intransitive
G	German	*OIr*	Old Irish	*VL*	Vulgar Latin
Gk	Greek	*OIt*	Old Italian	*vt*	verb transitive
Gmc	Germanic	*ON*	Old Norse	*W*	Welsh

Pronunciation Symbols

ə . . . . **a**but, c**o**llect, s**u**ppose

'ə, ,ə . . . . h**u**mdr**u**m

ᵊ . . . . (in ᵊl, ᵊn) batt**le**, cott**on**; (in lᵊ, mᵊ, rᵊ) French tab**le**, pris**me**, ti**tre**

ər . . . . op**era**tion, furth**er**

a . . . . m**a**p, p**a**tch

ā . . . . d**ay**, f**a**te

ä . . . . b**o**ther, c**o**t, f**a**ther

à . . . . a sound between \a\ and \ä\, as in an Eastern New England pronunciation of **au**nt, **a**sk

aů . . . . n**ow**, **ou**t

b . . . . **b**a**b**y, ri**b**

ch . . . . **ch**in, cat**ch**

d . . . . **d**i**d**, a**dd**er

e . . . . s**e**t, r**e**d

ē . . . . b**ea**t, **ea**sy

f . . . . **f**i**f**ty, cu**ff**

g . . . . **g**o, bi**g**

h . . . . **h**at, a**h**ead

hw . . . . **wh**ale

i . . . . t**i**p, ban**i**sh

ī . . . . s**i**te, b**uy**

j . . . . **j**ob, e**dg**e

k . . . . **k**in, **c**ook

k̲ . . . . German Ba**ch**, Scots lo**ch**

l . . . . **l**i**l**y, coo**l**

m . . . . **m**ur**m**ur, di**m**

n . . . . **n**i**n**e, ow**n**

ⁿ . . . . indicates that a preceding vowel is pronounced through both nose and mouth, as in French bon \bōⁿ\

ŋ . . . . si**ng**, si**ng**er, fi**ng**er, i**n**k

ō . . . . b**o**ne, holl**ow**

ȯ . . . . s**aw**

Œ . . . . French b**œu**f, German H**ö**lle

Œ̄ . . . . French f**eu**, German H**öh**le

ȯi . . . . t**oy**

p . . . . **p**e**p**per, li**p**

r . . . . **r**a**r**ity

s . . . . **s**ource, le**ss**

sh . . . . **sh**y, mi**ss**ion

t . . . . **t**ie, a**tt**ack

th . . . . **th**in, e**th**er

th̲ . . . . **th**en, ei**th**er

ü . . . . b**oo**t, few \'fyü\

ů . . . . p**u**t, pure \'pyůr\

ŭe . . . . German f**ü**llen

ū̲e . . . . French r**u**e, German f**üh**len

v . . . . **v**i**v**id, gi**v**e

w . . . . **w**e, a**w**ay

y . . . . **y**ard, cue \'kyü\

ʸ . . . . indicates that a preceding \l\, \n\, or \w\ is modified by having the tongue approximate the position for \y\, as in French di**gne** \dēnʸ\

z . . . . **z**one, rai**s**e

zh . . . . vi**s**ion, plea**s**ure

\ . . . . slant line used in pairs to mark the beginning and end of a transcription: \'pen\

' . . . . mark at the beginning of a syllable that has primary (strongest) stress: \'bar-ē-ər\

ˌ . . . . mark at the beginning of a syllable that has secondary (next-strongest) stress: \'shəf-əl-ˌbōrd\

- . . . . mark of a syllable division in pronunciations (the mark of end-of-line division in boldface entries is a centered dot •)

() . . . . indicate that what is symbolized between sometimes occurs and sometimes does not occur in the pronunciation of the word: **bakery** \'bā-k(ə-)rē\ = \'bā-kə-rē, 'bā-krē\

A

¹**a** \ˈā\ *n, pl* **a's** *or* **as** \ˈāz\ *often cap* **1** : the 1st letter of the English alphabet **2** : a grade rating a student's work as superior

²**a** \ə, (ˈ)ā\ *indefinite article* : ONE, SOME — used to indicate an unspecified or unidentified individual ⟨there's ∼ man outside⟩

³**a** *abbr, often cap* **1** absent **2** acre **3** alto **4** answer **5** are **6** area

AA *abbr* **1** Alcoholics Anonymous **2** antiaircraft **3** associate in arts

AAA *abbr* American Automobile Association

A and M *abbr* agricultural and mechanical

A and R *abbr* artists and repertory

aard·vark \ˈärd-ˌvärk\ *n* [obs. Afrikaans, fr. Afrikaans *aard* earth + *vark* pig] : a large burrowing African ungulate mammal that feeds on ants and termites with its sticky tongue

ab *abbr* about

Ab \ˈäb, ˈäv, ˈȯv\ *n* [Heb *Āḇh*] : the 11th month of the civil year or the 5th month of the ecclesiastical year in the Jewish calendar

AB *abbr* **1** able-bodied seaman **2** airman basic **3** [NL *artium baccalaureus*] bachelor of arts

ABA *abbr* American Bar Association

aback \ə-ˈbak\ *adv* : by surprise ⟨taken ∼⟩

aba·cus \ˈa-bə-kəs\ *n, pl* **aba·ci** \-ˌsī, -ˌkē\ *or* **aba·cus·es** : an instrument for making calculations by sliding counters along rods or grooves

abacus

¹**abaft** \ə-ˈbaft\ *prep* : to the rear of

²**abaft** *adv* : toward or at the stern : AFT

ab·a·lo·ne \ˌa-bə-ˈlō-nē, ˈa-bə-ˌ\ *n* : a large edible sea mollusk with a flattened slightly spiral shell with holes along the edge

¹**aban·don** \ə-ˈban-dən\ *vb* [ME *abandounen*, fr. MF *abandoner*, fr. *abandon*, n., surrender, fr. *a bandon* in one's power] : to give up completely : FORSAKE, DESERT — **aban·don·ment** *n*

²**abandon** *n* : a thorough yielding to natural impulses; *esp* : EXUBERANCE

aban·doned \ə-ˈban-dənd\ *adj* : morally unrestrained **syn** profligate, dissolute, reprobate

abase \ə-ˈbās\ *vb* **abased; abas·ing** : HUMBLE, DEGRADE — **abase·ment** *n*

abash \ə-ˈbash\ *vb* : to destroy the composure of : EMBARRASS — **abash·ment** *n*

abate \ə-ˈbāt\ *vb* **abat·ed; abat·ing** **1** : to put an end to ⟨∼ a nuisance⟩ **2** : to decrease in amount, number, or degree

abate·ment \ə-ˈbāt-mənt\ *n* **1** : DECREASE **2** : an amount abated; *esp* : a deduction from a tax

ab·at·toir \ˈa-bə-ˌtwär\ *n* [F] : SLAUGHTERHOUSE

ab·ba·cy \ˈa-bə-sē\ *n, pl* **-cies** : the office or term of office of an abbot or abbess

ab·bé \a-ˈbā, ˈa-ˌ\ *n* : a member of the French secular clergy — used as a title

ab·bess \ˈa-bəs\ *n* : the superior of a convent for nuns

ab·bey \ˈa-bē\ *n, pl* **abbeys** **1** : MONASTERY **2** : CONVENT **3** : an abbey church

ab·bot \ˈa-bət\ *n* [ME *abbod*, fr. OE, fr. LL *abbat-*, *abbas*, fr. LGk *abbas*, fr. Aramaic *abbā* father] : the superior of a monastery for men

abbr *abbr* abbreviation

ab·bre·vi·ate \ə-ˈbrē-vē-ˌāt\ *vb* **-at·ed; -at·ing** : SHORTEN, CURTAIL; *esp* : to reduce to an abbreviation

ab·bre·vi·a·tion \ə-ˌbrē-vē-ˈā-shən\ *n* **1** : the act or result of abbreviating **2** : a shortened form of a word or phrase used for brevity esp. in writing

¹**ABC** \ˌā-(ˌ)bē-ˈsē\ *n, pl* **ABC's** *or* **ABCs** \-ˈsēz\ **1** : ALPHABET — usu. used in pl. **2** : RUDIMENTS

²**ABC** *abbr* American Broadcasting Company

ABD \ˌā-bē-ˈdē\ *n, pl* **ABDs** *also* **ABD's** [all but dissertation] : a doctoral candidate who has completed required courses and examinations but not a dissertation

Ab·di·as \ab-ˈdī-əs\ *n* : OBADIAH

ab·di·cate \ˈab-di-ˌkāt\ *vb* **-cat·ed; -cat·ing** : to give up (as a throne) formally — **ab·di·ca·tion** \ˌab-di-ˈkā-shən\ *n*

ab·do·men \ˈab-də-mən, ab-ˈdō-\ *n* **1** : the cavity in or area of the body between the chest and the pelvis **2** : the part of the body posterior to the thorax in an arthropod — **ab·dom·i·nal** \ab-ˈdä-mən-ᵊl\ *adj* — **ab·dom·i·nal·ly** *adv*

ab·duct \ab-ˈdəkt\ *vb* : to take away (a person) by force : KIDNAP — **ab·duc·tion** \-ˈdək-shən\ *n* — **ab·duc·tor** \-tər\ *n*

abeam \ə-ˈbēm\ *adv or adj* : on a line at right angles to a ship's keel

abed \ə-ˈbed\ *adv or adj* : in bed

Abe·na·ki \ˌa-bə-ˈnä-kē\ *n, pl* **Abenaki** *or* **Abenakis** : a member of a group of American Indian peoples of northern New England and southern Quebec

ab·er·ra·tion \ˌa-bə-ˈrā-shən\ *n* **1** : deviation esp. from a moral standard or normal state **2** : failure of a mirror or lens to produce exact point-to-point correspondence between an object and its image **3** : unsoundness of mind : DERANGEMENT — **ab·er·rant** \a-ˈber-ənt\ *adj*

abet \ə-ˈbet\ *vb* **abet·ted; abet·ting** [ME *abetten*, fr. MF *abeter*, fr. OF *beter* to bait] **1** : INCITE, ENCOURAGE **2** : to assist or support in the achievement of a purpose — **abet·tor** *or* **abet·ter** \-ˈbe-tər\ *n*

abey·ance \ə-ˈbā-əns\ *n* : a condition of suspended activity

ab·hor \əb-ˈhȯr, ab-\ *vb* **ab·horred; ab·hor·ring** [ME *abhorren*, fr. L *abhorrēre*, fr. *ab-* + *horrēre* to shudder] : LOATHE, DETEST — **ab·hor·rence** \-əns\ *n*

ab·hor·rent \-ənt\ *adj* : LOATHSOME, DETESTABLE

Abib \ä-ˈvēv\ *n* [Heb *Āḇhībh*, lit., ear of grain] : the first month of the ancient Hebrew calendar corresponding to Nisan

abide \ə-ˈbīd\ *vb* **abode** \-ˈbōd\ *or* **abid·ed; abid·ing** **1** : BEAR, ENDURE **2** : DWELL, REMAIN, LAST

abil·i·ty \ə-ˈbi-lə-tē\ *n, pl* **-ties** : the quality of being able : POWER, SKILL

-ability *also* **-ibility** *n suffix* : capacity, fitness, or ten-

---

\ə\abut \ᵊ\kitten \ər\further \a\ash \ā\ace \ä\mop, mar \au̇\out \ch\chin \e\bet \ē\easy \g\go \i\hit \ī\ice \j\job \ŋ\sing \ō\go \ȯ\law \ȯi\boy \th\thin \t͟h\the \ü\loot \u̇\foot \y\yet \zh\vision *see also* Pronunciation Symbols page

dency to act or be acted on in a (specified) way ⟨flamm*ability*⟩

ab·ject \'ab-ˌjekt, ab-'jekt\ *adj* : low in spirit or hope : CRINGING — **ab·jec·tion** \ab-'jek-shən\ *n* — **ab·ject·ly** *adv* — **ab·ject·ness** *n*

ab·jure \ab-'jür\ *vb* **ab·jured; ab·jur·ing 1** : to renounce solemnly : RECANT **2** : to abstain from — **ab·ju·ra·tion** \ˌab-jə-'rā-shən\ *n*

abl *abbr* ablative

ab·late \a-'blāt\ *vb* **ab·lat·ed; ab·lat·ing** : to remove or become removed esp. by cutting, abrading, or vaporizing

ab·la·tion \a-'blā-shən\ *n* **1** : surgical cutting and removal **2** : loss of a part (as the outside of a nose cone) by melting or vaporization

ab·la·tive \'ab-lə-tiv\ *adj* : of, relating to, or constituting a grammatical case (as in Latin) expressing typically the relation of separation and source — **ablative** *n*

ablaze \ə-'blāz\ *adj or adv* : being on fire : BLAZING

able \'ā-bəl\ *adj* **abler** \-b(ə-)lər\; **ablest** \-b(ə-)ləst\ **1** : having sufficient power, skill, or resources to accomplish an object **2** : marked by skill or efficiency — **ably** \-blē\ *adv*

-able *also* **-ible** *adj suffix* **1** : capable of, fit for, or worthy of (being so acted upon or toward) ⟨break*able*⟩ ⟨collect*ible*⟩ **2** : tending, given, or liable to ⟨knowledge*able*⟩ ⟨perish*able*⟩

able–bod·ied \ˌā-bəl-'bä-dēd\ *adj* : having a sound strong body

abloom \ə-'blüm\ *adj* : BLOOMING

ab·lu·tion \ə-'blü-shən, a-\ *n* : the washing of one's body or part of it

ABM \ˌā-(ˌ)bē-'em\ *n, pl* **ABM's** *or* **ABMs** : ANTIBALLISTIC MISSILE

Ab·na·ki \ab-'nä-kē\ *var of* ABENAKI

ab·ne·gate \'ab-ni-ˌgāt\ *vb* **-gat·ed; -gat·ing 1** : DENY, RENOUNCE **2** : SURRENDER, RELINQUISH — **ab·ne·ga·tion** \ˌab-ni-'gā-shən\ *n*

ab·nor·mal \ab-'nòr-məl\ *adj* : deviating from the normal or average — **ab·nor·mal·i·ty** \ˌab-nòr-'ma-lə-tē\ *n* — **ab·nor·mal·ly** *adv*

¹aboard \ə-'bòrd\ *adv* **1** : ALONGSIDE **2** : on, onto, or within a car, ship, or aircraft **3** : in or into a group or association ⟨welcome new workers ∼⟩

²aboard *prep* : ON, ONTO, WITHIN

abode \ə-'bōd\ *n* **1** : STAY, SOJOURN **2** : HOME, RESIDENCE

abol·ish \ə-'bä-lish\ *vb* : to do away with : ANNUL — **ab·o·li·tion** \ˌa-bə-'li-shən\ *n*

ab·o·li·tion·ism \ˌa-bə-'li-shə-ˌni-zəm\ *n* : advocacy of the abolition of slavery — **ab·o·li·tion·ist** \-'li-sh(ə-)nist\ *n or adj*

A–bomb \'ā-ˌbäm\ *n* : ATOMIC BOMB — **A–bomb** *vb*

abom·i·na·ble \ə-'bä-mə-nə-bəl\ *adj* : ODIOUS, LOATHSOME, DETESTABLE

abominable snow·man \-'snō-mən, -ˌman\ *n, often cap A&S* : a mysterious creature with human or apelike characteristics reported to exist in the high Himalayas

abom·i·nate \ə-'bä-mə-ˌnāt\ *vb* **-nat·ed; -nat·ing** [L *abominari,* lit., to deprecate as an ill omen, fr. *ab-* away + *omen* omen] : LOATHE, DETEST

abom·i·na·tion \ə-ˌbä-mə-'nā-shən\ *n* **1** : something abominable **2** : DISGUST, LOATHING

ab·orig·i·nal \ˌa-bə-'ri-jə-nəl\ *adj* : ORIGINAL, INDIGENOUS, PRIMITIVE

ab·orig·i·ne \ˌa-bə-'ri-jə-nē\ *n* : a member of the original race of inhabitants of a region : NATIVE

aborn·ing \ə-'bòr-niŋ\ *adv* : while being born or produced

¹abort \ə-'bòrt\ *vb* **1** : to cause or undergo abortion **2** : to terminate prematurely ⟨∼ a spaceflight⟩ — **abor·tive** \-'bòr-tiv\ *adj*

²abort *n* : the premature termination of a mission of or a procedure relating to an aircraft or spacecraft

abor·tion \ə-'bòr-shən\ *n* : the spontaneous or induced termination of a pregnancy after, accompanied by, resulting in, or closely followed by the death of the embryo or fetus

abor·tion·ist \-sh(ə-)nist\ *n* : one who induces abortions

abound \ə-'baund\ *vb* **1** : to be plentiful : TEEM **2** : to be fully supplied

¹about \ə-'baut\ *adv* **1** : reasonably close to; *also* : on the verge of ⟨∼ to join the army⟩ **2** : on all sides **3** : NEARBY

²about *prep* **1** : on every side of **2** : near to **3** : CONCERNING

about–face \-'fās\ *n* : a reversal of direction or attitude — **about–face** *vb*

¹above \ə-'bəv\ *adv* **1** : in the sky; *also* : in or to heaven **2** : in or to a higher place; *also* : higher on the same page or on a preceding page

²above *prep* **1** : in or to a higher place than : OVER ⟨storm clouds ∼ the bay⟩ **2** : superior to ⟨he thought her far ∼ him⟩ **3** : more than : EXCEEDING **4** : as distinct from ⟨∼ the noise⟩

above·board \-ˌbōrd\ *adv or adj* : without concealment or deception : OPENLY

abp *abbr* archbishop

abr *abbr* abridged; abridgment

ab·ra·ca·dab·ra \ˌa-brə-kə-'da-brə\ *n* **1** : a magical charm or incantation against calamity **2** : GIBBERISH

abrade \ə-'brād\ *vb* **abrad·ed; abrad·ing 1** : to wear away by friction **2** : to wear down in spirit : IRRITATE — **abra·sion** \-'brā-zhən\ *n*

¹abra·sive \ə-'brā-siv\ *n* : a substance (as pumice) for abrading, smoothing, or polishing

²abrasive *adj* : tending to abrade : causing irritation ⟨∼ relationships⟩ — **abra·sive·ly** *adv* — **abra·sive·ness** *n*

abreast \ə-'brest\ *adv or adj* **1** : side by side **2** : up to a standard or level esp. of knowledge

abridge \ə-'brij\ *vb* **abridged; abridg·ing** [ME *abregen,* fr. MF *abregier,* fr. LL *abbreviare,* fr. L *ad* to + *brevis* short] : to lessen in length or extent : SHORTEN — **abridg·ment** *or* **abridge·ment** *n*

abroad \ə-'bròd\ *adv or adj* **1** : over a wide area **2** : away from one's home **3** : outside one's country

ab·ro·gate \'a-brə-ˌgāt\ *vb* **-gat·ed; -gat·ing** : ANNUL, REVOKE — **ab·ro·ga·tion** \ˌa-brə-'gā-shən\ *n*

abrupt \ə-'brəpt\ *adj* **1** : broken or as if broken off **2** : SUDDEN, HASTY **3** : so quick as to seem rude **4** : DISCONNECTED **5** : STEEP — **abrupt·ly** *adv*

abs *abbr* absolute

ab·scess \'ab-ˌses\ *n, pl* **ab·scess·es** [L *abscessus,* lit., act of going away, fr. *abscedere* to go away, fr. *abs-, ab-* away + *cedere* to go] : a localized collection of pus surrounded by inflamed tissue — **ab·scessed** \-ˌsest\ *adj*

ab·scis·sa \ab-'si-sə\ *n, pl* **abscissas** *also* **ab·scis·sae** \-'si-(ˌ)sē\ : the horizontal coordinate of a point in a plane coordinate system obtained by measuring parallel to the x-axis

ab·scis·sion \ab-'si-zhən\ *n* **1** : the act or process of cutting off **2** : the natural separation of flowers, fruits, or leaves from plants — **ab·scise** \ab-'sīz\ *vb*

ab·scond \ab-'skänd\ *vb* : to depart secretly and hide oneself

ab·sence \'ab-səns\ *n* **1** : the state or time of being absent **2** : WANT, LACK **3** : INATTENTION

¹ab·sent \'ab-sənt\ *adj* **1** : not present **2** : LACKING **3** : INATTENTIVE

²ab·sent \ab-'sent\ *vb* : to keep (oneself) away

³ab·sent \'ab-sənt\ *prep* : in the absence of : WITHOUT

ab·sen·tee \ˌab-sən-'tē\ *n* : one that is absent or keeps away

absentee ballot *n* : a ballot submitted (as by mail) in advance of an election by a voter who is unable to be present at the polls

ab·sen·tee·ism \ˌab-sən-'tē-ˌi-zəm\ *n* : chronic absence (as from work or school)

ab·sent·mind·ed \\ˌab-sənt-'mīn-dəd\ *adj* : unaware of one's surroundings or actions : INATTENTIVE — **ab·sent·mind·ed·ly** *adv* — **ab·sent·mind·ed·ness** *n*

ab·sinthe *also* **ab·sinth** \'ab-ˌsinth\ *n* [F] : a liqueur flavored esp. with wormwood and anise

ab·so·lute \'ab-sə-ˌlüt, ˌab-sə-'lüt\ *adj* **1** : free from imperfection or mixture **2** : free from control, restriction, or qualification **3** : lacking grammatical connection with any other word in a sentence ⟨∼ construction⟩ **4** : POSITIVE ⟨∼ proof⟩ **5** : relating to the fundamental units of length, mass, and time **6** : FUNDAMENTAL, ULTIMATE — **ab·so·lute·ly** *adv*

absolute pitch *n* **1** : the position of a tone in a standard scale independently determined by its rate of vibration **2** : the ability to sing a note asked for or to name a note heard

absolute value *n* : the numerical value of a real number that for a positive number or zero is equal to the number itself and for a negative number is equal to the positive number which when added to it is equal to zero

absolute zero *n* : a theoretical temperature marked by a complete absence of heat and equivalent to exactly −273.15°C or −459.67°F

ab·so·lu·tion \ˌab-sə-'lü-shən\ *n* : the act of absolving; *esp* : a remission of sins pronounced by a priest in the sacrament of reconciliation

ab·so·lut·ism \'ab-sə-ˌlü-ˌti-zəm\ *n* **1** : the theory that a ruler or government should have unlimited power **2** : government by an absolute ruler or authority

ab·solve \əb-'zälv, -'sälv\ *vb* **ab·solved; ab·solv·ing** : to set free from an obligation or the consequences of guilt

ab·sorb \əb-'sòrb, -'zòrb\ *vb* **1** : to take in and make part of an existent whole **2** : to suck up or take in in the manner of a sponge **3** : to engage (one's attention) : ENGROSS **4** : to receive without recoil or echo ⟨a ceiling that ∼s sound⟩ **5** : ASSUME, BEAR ⟨∼ all costs⟩ **6** : to transform (radiant energy) into a different form usu. with a resulting rise in temperature — **ab·sorb·ing** *adj* — **ab·sorb·ing·ly** *adv*

ab·sor·bent *also* **ab·sor·bant** \əb-'sòr-bənt, -'zòr-\ *adj* : able to absorb ⟨∼ cotton⟩ — **ab·sor·ben·cy** \-bən-sē\ *n* — **absorbent** *also* **absorbant** *n*

ab·sorp·tion \əb-'sòrp-shən, -'zòrp-\ *n* **1** : a process of absorbing or being absorbed **2** : concentration of attention — **ab·sorp·tive** \-tiv\ *adj*

ab·stain \əb-'stān\ *vb* : to refrain from an action or practice — **ab·stain·er** *n* — **ab·sten·tion** \-'sten-chən\ *n*

ab·ste·mi·ous \ab-'stē-mē-əs\ *adj* : sparing in use of food or drink : TEMPERATE — **ab·ste·mi·ous·ly** *adv* — **ab·ste·mi·ous·ness** *n*

ab·sti·nence \'ab-stə-nəns\ *n* : voluntary refraining esp. from eating certain foods or drinking liquor — **ab·sti·nent** \-nənt\ *adj*

abstr *abbr* abstract

¹**ab·stract** \ab-'strakt, 'ab-ˌstrakt\ *adj* **1** : considered apart from a particular instance **2** : expressing a quality apart from an object ⟨*whiteness* is an ∼ word⟩ **3** : having only intrinsic form with little or no pictorial representation ⟨∼ painting⟩ — **ab·stract·ly** *adv* — **ab·stract·ness** *n*

²**ab·stract** \'ab-ˌstrakt; *2 also* ab-'strakt\ *n* **1** : SUMMARY, EPITOME **2** : an abstract thing or state

³**ab·stract** \ab-'strakt, 'ab-ˌstrakt; *2 usu* 'ab-ˌstrakt\ *vb* **1** : REMOVE, SEPARATE **2** : to make an abstract of : SUMMARIZE **3** : to draw away the attention of **4** : STEAL — **ab·stract·ed·ly** \ab-'strak-təd-lē, 'ab-ˌstrak-\ *adv*

abstract expressionism *n* : art that expresses the artist's attitudes and emotions through abstract forms — **abstract expressionist** *n*

ab·strac·tion \ab-'strak-shən\ *n* **1** : the act of abstracting : the state of being abstracted **2** : an abstract idea **3** : an abstract work of art

ab·struse \ab-'strüs\ *adj* : hard to understand : RECONDITE — **ab·struse·ly** *adv* — **ab·struse·ness** *n*

ab·surd \əb-'sərd, -'zərd\ *adj* [MF *absurde*, fr. L *absurdus*, fr. *ab-* from + *surdus* deaf, stupid] : RIDICULOUS, UNREASONABLE — **ab·sur·di·ty** \-'sər-də-tē, -'zər-\ *n* — **ab·surd·ly** *adv*

abun·dant \ə-'bən-dənt\ *adj* [ME, fr. MF, fr. L *abundant-, abundans,* prp. of *abundare* to abound, fr. *ab-* from + *unda* wave] : more than enough : amply sufficient **syn** copious, plentiful, ample, bountiful — **abun·dance** \-dəns\ *n* — **abun·dant·ly** *adv*

¹**abuse** \ə-'byüs\ *n* **1** : a corrupt practice **2** : MISUSE ⟨drug ∼⟩ **3** : coarse and insulting speech **4** : MISTREATMENT ⟨child ∼⟩

²**abuse** \ə-'byüz\ *vb* **abused; abus·ing 1** : to put to a wrong use : MISUSE **2** : MISTREAT **3** : to attack in words : REVILE — **abus·er** *n* — **abu·sive** \-'byü-siv\ *adj* — **abu·sive·ly** *adv* — **abu·sive·ness** *n*

abut \ə-'bət\ *vb* **abut·ted; abut·ting** : to touch along a border : border on

abut·ment \ə-'bət-mənt\ *n* : the part of a structure (as a bridge) that supports weight or withstands lateral pressure

abut·ter \ə-'bə-tər\ *n* : one that abuts; *esp* : the owner of a contiguous property

abys·mal \ə-'biz-məl\ *adj* **1** : immeasurably deep : BOTTOMLESS **2** : absolutely wretched ⟨∼ living conditions of the poor⟩ — **abys·mal·ly** *adv*

abyss \ə-'bis\ *n* **1** : the bottomless pit in old accounts of the universe **2** : an immeasurable depth

abys·sal \ə-'bi-səl\ *adj* : of or relating to the bottom waters of the ocean depths

ac *abbr* account

-ac *n suffix* : one affected with ⟨hypochondri*ac*⟩

Ac *symbol* actinium

AC *abbr* **1** air-conditioning **2** alternating current **3** [L *ante Christum*] before Christ **4** [L *ante cibum*] before meals **5** area code

aca·cia \ə-'kā-shə\ *n* : any of numerous leguminous trees or shrubs with round white or yellow flower clusters and often fernlike leaves

acad *abbr* academic; academy

ac·a·deme \'a-kə-ˌdēm, ˌa-kə-'\ *n* : SCHOOL; *also* : academic environment

¹**ac·a·dem·ic** \ˌa-kə-'de-mik\ *n* : a person who is academic in background, outlook, or methods

²**academic** *adj* **1** : of, relating to, or associated with schools or colleges **2** : literary or general rather than technical **3** : theoretical rather than practical — **ac·a·dem·i·cal·ly** \-mi-k(ə-)lē\ *adv*

ac·a·de·mi·cian \ˌa-kə-də-'mi-shən, ə-ˌka-də-\ *n* **1** : a member of a society of scholars or artists **2** : ACADEMIC

ac·a·dem·i·cism \ˌa-kə-'de-mə-ˌsi-zəm\ *also* **acad·e·mism** \ə-'ka-də-ˌmi-zəm\ *n* **1** : a formal academic quality **2** : purely speculative thinking

acad·e·my \ə-'ka-də-mē\ *n, pl* **-mies** [Gk *Akadēmeia,* school of philosophy founded by Plato, fr. *Akadēmeia,* gymnasium where Plato taught, fr. *Akadēmos* Greek mythological hero] **1** : a school above the elementary level; *esp* : a private high school **2** : a society of scholars or artists

acan·thus \ə-'kan-thəs\ *n, pl* **acanthus 1** : any of a genus of prickly herbs of the Mediterranean region **2** : an ornamentation (as on a column) representing the leaves of the acanthus

a cap·pel·la *also* **a ca·pel·la** \ˌä-kə-'pe-lə\ *adv or adj* [It *a cappella* in chapel style] : without instrumental accompaniment

---

\ə\abut \ʲ\kitten \ər\further \a\ash \ā\ace \ä\mop, mar \aů\out \ch\chin \e\bet \ē\easy \g\go \i\hit \ī\ice \j\job \ŋ\sing \ō\go \ò\law \òi\boy \th\thin \t̲h̲\the \ü\loot \ů\foot \y\yet \zh\vision *see also* Pronunciation Symbols page

acc *abbr* accusative

ac·cede \ak-ˈsēd\ *vb* **ac·ced·ed; ac·ced·ing 1** : to become a party to an agreement **2** : to express approval **3** : to enter upon an office **syn** agree, acquiesce, assent, consent, subscribe

ac·cel·er·ate \ik-ˈse-lə-ˌrāt, ak-\ *vb* **-at·ed; -at·ing 1** : to bring about earlier **2** : to speed up : QUICKEN — **ac·cel·er·a·tion** \-ˌse-lə-ˈrā-shən\ *n*

ac·cel·er·a·tor \ik-ˈse-lə-ˌrā-tər, ak-\ *n* **1** : one that accelerates **2** : a pedal for controlling the speed of a motor-vehicle engine **3** : an apparatus for imparting high velocities to charged particles

ac·cel·er·om·e·ter \ik-ˌse-lə-ˈrä-mə-tər, ak-\ *n* : an instrument for measuring acceleration or vibrations

¹ac·cent \ˈak-ˌsent, ak-ˈsent\ *vb* : STRESS, EMPHASIZE

²ac·cent \ˈak-ˌsent\ *n* **1** : a distinctive manner of pronunciation ⟨a foreign ∼⟩ **2** : prominence given to one syllable of a word esp. by stress **3** : a mark (as ´, `, ^) over a vowel used usu. to indicate a difference in pronunciation from a vowel not so marked — **ac·cen·tu·al** \ak-ˈsen-chə-wəl\ *adj*

ac·cen·tu·ate \ak-ˈsen-chə-ˌwāt\ *vb* **-at·ed; -at·ing** : ACCENT — **ac·cen·tu·a·tion** \-ˌsen-chə-ˈwā-shən\ *n*

ac·cept \ik-ˈsept, ak-\ *vb* **1** : to receive willingly **2** : to agree to **3** : to assume an obligation to pay

ac·cept·able \ik-ˈsep-tə-bəl, ak-\ *adj* : capable or worthy of being accepted — **ac·cept·abil·i·ty** \ik-ˌsep-tə-ˈbi-lə-tē, ak-\ *n*

ac·cep·tance \ik-ˈsep-təns, ak-\ *n* **1** : the act of accepting **2** : the state of being accepted or acceptable **3** : an accepted bill of exchange

ac·cep·ta·tion \ˌak-ˌsep-ˈtā-shən\ *n* : the generally understood meaning of a word

¹ac·cess \ˈak-ˌses\ *n* **1** : capacity to enter or approach **2** : a way of approach : ENTRANCE

²access *vb* : to get at : gain access to

ac·ces·si·ble \ik-ˈse-sə-bəl, ak-, ek-\ *adj* **1** : capable of being reached ⟨∼ by train⟩ **2** : capable of being used, seen, or known : OBTAINABLE ⟨∼ information⟩ — **ac·ces·si·bil·i·ty** \-ˌse-sə-ˈbi-lə-tē\ *n*

ac·ces·sion \ik-ˈse-shən, ak-\ *n* **1** : increase by something added **2** : something added **3** : the act of coming to a high office or position

ac·ces·so·ry *also* **ac·ces·sa·ry** \ik-ˈse-sə-rē, ak-\ *n, pl* **-ries 1** : a person who though not present abets or assists in the commission of an offense **2** : something helpful but not essential **syn** appurtenance, adjunct, appendage, appendix — **accessory** *adj*

ac·ci·dent \ˈak-sə-dənt\ *n* **1** : an event occurring by chance or unintentionally **2** : CHANCE ⟨met by ∼⟩ **3** : a nonessential property

¹ac·ci·den·tal \ˌak-sə-ˈdent-ᵊl\ *adj* **1** : happening unexpectedly or by chance **2** : happening without intent or through carelessness **syn** casual, fortuitous, incidental, chance — **ac·ci·den·tal·ly** \-ˈden-tə-lē\ *also* **ac·ci·dent·ly** \-ˈdent-lē\ *adv*

²accidental *n* : a musical note foreign to a key indicated by a signature

ac·claim \ə-ˈklām\ *vb* **1** : APPLAUD, PRAISE **2** : to declare by acclamation **syn** extol, laud, commend, hail — **acclaim** *n*

ac·cla·ma·tion \ˌa-klə-ˈmā-shən\ *n* **1** : loud eager applause **2** : an overwhelming affirmative vote by shouting or applause rather than by ballot

ac·cli·mate \ˈa-klə-ˌmāt, ə-ˈklī-mət\ *vb* **-mat·ed; -mat·ing** : ACCLIMATIZE — **ac·cli·ma·tion** \ˌa-klə-ˈmā-shən, -ˌklī-\ *n*

ac·cli·ma·tize \ə-ˈklī-mə-ˌtīz\ *vb* **-tized; -tiz·ing** : to accustom or become accustomed to a new climate or situation — **ac·cli·ma·ti·za·tion** \-ˌklī-mə-tə-ˈzā-shən\ *n*

ac·cliv·i·ty \ə-ˈkli-və-tē\ *n, pl* **-ties** : an ascending slope

ac·co·lade \ˈa-kə-ˌlād\ *n* [F, fr. *accoler* to embrace, fr. L

ad- to + *collum* neck] : an expression of praise : AWARD

ac·com·mo·date \ə-ˈkä-mə-ˌdāt\ *vb* **-dat·ed; -dat·ing 1** : to make fit or suitable : ADAPT, ADJUST **2** : HARMONIZE, RECONCILE **3** : to provide with something needed **4** : to hold without crowding **5** : to undergo visual accommodation

ac·com·mo·dat·ing *adj* : OBLIGING

ac·com·mo·da·tion \ə-ˌkä-mə-ˈdā-shən\ *n* **1** : something supplied to satisfy a need; *esp* : LODGINGS — usu. used in pl. **2** : the act of accommodating : ADJUSTMENT **3** : the automatic adjustment of the eye for seeing at different distances

ac·com·pa·ni·ment \ə-ˈkəm-pə-nē- mənt, -ˈkəmp-nē-\ *n* : something that accompanies another; *esp* : subordinate music to support a principal voice or instrument

ac·com·pa·ny \-nē\ *vb* **-nied; -ny·ing 1** : to go or occur with : ATTEND **2** : to play an accompaniment for — **ac·com·pa·nist** \-nist\ *n*

ac·com·plice \ə-ˈkäm-pləs, -ˈkəm-\ *n* : an associate in crime

ac·com·plish \ə-ˈkäm-plish, -ˈkəm-\ *vb* : to bring to completion **syn** achieve, effect, execute, perform — **ac·com·plish·er** *n*

ac·com·plished *adj* **1** : EXPERT, SKILLED **2** : established beyond doubt

ac·com·plish·ment \ə-ˈkäm-plish-mənt, -ˈkəm-\ *n* **1** : COMPLETION **2** : something completed or effected **3** : an acquired excellence or skill

¹ac·cord \ə-ˈkórd\ *vb* [ME, fr. OF *acorder,* fr. L *ad-* to + *cord-, cor* heart] **1** : GRANT, CONCEDE **2** : AGREE, HARMONIZE — **ac·cor·dant** \-ˈkórd-ᵊnt\ *adj*

²accord *n* **1** : AGREEMENT, HARMONY **2** : willingness to act ⟨gave of their own ∼⟩

ac·cor·dance \ə-ˈkórd-ᵊns\ *n* **1** : ACCORD **2** : the act of granting

ac·cord·ing·ly \ə-ˈkór-diŋ-lē\ *adv* **1** : in accordance **2** : CONSEQUENTLY, SO

according to *prep* **1** : in conformity with ⟨paid *according to* ability⟩ **2** : as stated or attested by ⟨*according to* you⟩

¹ac·cor·di·on \ə-ˈkór-dē-ən\ *n* [G *Akkordion,* fr. *Akkord* chord] : a portable keyboard instrument with a bellows and reeds — **ac·cor·di·on·ist** \-ə-nist\ *n*

accordion

²accordion *adj* : folding like the bellows of an accordion ⟨∼ pleats⟩

ac·cost \ə-ˈkóst\ *vb* [MF *accoster,* ultim. fr. L *ad-* to + *costa* rib, side] : to approach and speak to esp. aggressively

¹ac·count \ə-ˈkaunt\ *n* **1** : a statement of business transactions **2** : an arrangement with a vendor to supply credit **3** : a statement of reasons, causes, or motives **4** : VALUE, IMPORTANCE **5** : a sum of money deposited in a bank and subject to withdrawal by the depositor — **on account of** : BECAUSE OF — **on no account** : under no circumstances — **on one's own account :** on one's own behalf

²**account** *vb* **1 :** CONSIDER ⟨I ∼ him lucky⟩ **2 :** to give an explanation — used with *for*

ac·count·able \ə-'kaún-tə-bəl\ *adj* **1 :** ANSWERABLE, RESPONSIBLE **2 :** EXPLICABLE — **ac·count·abil·i·ty** \-ˌkaún-tə-'bi-lə-tē\ *n*

ac·coun·tant \ə-'kaúnt-ᵊnt\ *n* **:** a person skilled in accounting — **ac·coun·tan·cy** \-ᵊn-sē\ *n*

account executive *n* **:** a business executive in charge of a client's account

ac·count·ing \ə-'kaún-tiŋ\ *n* **:** the art or system of keeping and analyzing financial records

ac·cou·tre *or* **ac·cou·ter** \ə-'kü-tər\ *vb* **-cou·tred** *or* **-cou·tered; -cou·tring** *or* **-cou·ter·ing** \-'kü-t(ə-)riŋ\ **:** EQUIP, OUTFIT

ac·cou·tre·ment *or* **ac·cou·ter·ment** \ə-'kü-trə-mənt, -'kü-tər-\ *n* [F] **1 :** an accessory item — usu. used in pl. **2 :** an identifying characteristic

ac·cred·it \ə-'kre-dət\ *vb* **1 :** to endorse or approve officially **2 :** CREDIT — **ac·cred·i·ta·tion** \-ˌkre-də-'tā-shən\ *n*

ac·cre·tion \ə-'krē-shən\ *n* **1 :** growth or enlargement esp. by addition from without **2 :** a product of accretion

ac·crue \ə-'krü\ *vb* **ac·crued; ac·cru·ing 1 :** to come by way of increase **2 :** to be added by periodic growth — **ac·cru·al** \-əl\ *n*

acct *abbr* account; accountant

ac·cul·tur·a·tion \ə-ˌkəl-chə-'rā-shən\ *n* **:** cultural modification of an individual or group by borrowing and adapting traits from another culture

ac·cu·mu·late \ə-'kyü-myə-ˌlāt\ *vb* **-lat·ed; -lat·ing** [L *accumulare,* fr. *ad*- to + *cumulare* to heap up] **:** to heap or pile up **syn** amass, gather, collect, stockpile — **ac·cu·mu·la·tion** \-ˌkyü-myə-'lā-shən\ *n* — **ac·cu·mu·la·tive** \-'kyü-myə-lə-tiv\ *adj* — **ac·cu·mu·la·tor** \-'kyü-myə-ˌlā-tər\ *n*

ac·cu·rate \'a-kyə-rət\ *adj* **:** free from error **:** EXACT, PRECISE — **ac·cu·ra·cy** \-rə-sē\ *n* — **ac·cu·rate·ly** *adv* — **ac·cu·rate·ness** *n*

ac·cursed \ə-'kərst, -'kər-səd\ *or* **ac·curst** \ə-'kərst\ *adj* **1 :** being under a curse **2 :** DAMNABLE, EXECRABLE

ac·cus·al \ə-'kyü-zəl\ *n* **:** ACCUSATION

ac·cu·sa·tive \ə-'kyü-zə-tiv\ *adj* **:** of, relating to, or being a grammatical case marking the direct object of a verb or the object of a preposition — **accusative** *n*

ac·cuse \ə-'kyuz\ *vb* **ac·cused; ac·cus·ing :** to charge with an offense **:** BLAME — **ac·cu·sa·tion** \ˌa-kyə-'zā-shən\ *n* — **ac·cus·er** *n*

ac·cused \ə-'kyüzd\ *n, pl* **accused :** the defendant in a criminal case

ac·cus·tom \ə-'kəs-təm\ *vb* **:** to make familiar through use or experience

ac·cus·tomed \ə-'kəs-təmd\ *adj* **:** USUAL, CUSTOMARY

¹**ace** \'ās\ *n* [ME *as* a die face marked with one spot, fr. OF, fr. L, unit, a copper coin] **1 :** a playing card bearing a single large pip in its center **2 :** a point (as in tennis) won on a serve that goes untouched **3 :** a golf score of one stroke on a hole **4 :** a combat pilot who has downed five or more enemy planes **5 :** one that excels

²**ace** *vb* **aced; ac·ing 1 :** to score an ace against (an opponent) or on (a golf hole) **2 :** to defeat decisively

³**ace** *adj* **:** of first rank or quality

acer·bic \ə-'sər-bik, a-\ *adj* **:** acid in temper, mood, or tone

acer·bi·ty \ə-'sər-bə-tē\ *n, pl* **-ties :** SOURNESS, BITTERNESS

acet·amin·o·phen \ə-ˌsē-tə-'mi-nə-fən\ *n* **:** a crystalline compound used in chemical synthesis and in medicine to relieve pain and fever

ac·e·tate \'a-sə-ˌtāt\ *n* **1 :** a salt or ester of acetic acid **2 :** a textile fiber made from cellulose and acetic acid; *also* **:** a fabric or plastic made of this fiber

ace·tic acid \ə-'sē-tik-\ *n* **:** a colorless pungent liquid acid that is the chief acid of vinegar and is used esp. in making chemical compounds

ace·tone \'a-sə-ˌtōn\ *n* **:** a volatile flammable fragrant liquid compound used in making other chemical compounds and as a solvent

ace·tyl·cho·line \ə-ˌsēt-ᵊl-'kō-ˌlēn\ *n* **:** a compound that is released at nerve endings of the autonomic nervous system and is active in the transmission of nerve impulses

acet·y·lene \ə-'set-ᵊl-ən, -ᵊl-ˌēn\ *n* **:** a colorless flammable gas used as a fuel (as in welding and soldering)

ace·tyl·sal·i·cyl·ic acid \ə-ˌsēt-ᵊl-ˌsa-lə-ˌsi-lik-\ *n* **:** ASPIRIN 1

ache \'āk\ *vb* **ached; ach·ing 1 :** to suffer a usu. dull persistent pain **2 :** LONG, YEARN — **ache** *n*

achieve \ə-'chēv\ *vb* **achieved; achiev·ing** [ME *acheven,* fr. MF *achever* to finish, fr. *a-* to (fr. L *ad*-) + *chief* end, head, fr. L *caput*] **:** to gain by work or effort **syn** accomplish, attain, realize — **achiev·able** \-'chē-və-bəl\ *adj* — **achieve·ment** *n* — **achiev·er** *n*

Achil·les' heel \ə-ˌki-lēz-\ *n* [fr. the story that the Greek warrior Achilles was vulnerable only in the heel] **:** a vulnerable point

Achil·les tendon \ə-ˌki-lēz-\ *n* **:** the tendon joining the muscles in the calf of the leg to the bone of the heel

ach·ro·mat·ic \ˌa-krə-'ma-tik\ *adj* **:** giving an image almost free from extraneous colors ⟨∼ lens⟩

achy \'ā-kē\ *adj* **ach·i·er; ach·i·est :** afflicted with aches — **ach·i·ness** *n*

¹**ac·id** \'a-səd\ *adj* **1 :** sour or biting to the taste; *also* **:** sharp or sour in manner **2 :** of or relating to an acid — **acid·i·ty** \ə-'si-də-tē\ *n* — **acid·ly** *adv*

²**acid** *n* **1 :** a sour substance **2 :** a usu. water-soluble chemical compound that has a sour taste, reacts with a base to form a salt, and reddens litmus **3 :** LSD — **acid·ic** \ə-'si-dik\ *adj*

acid·i·fy \ə-'si-də-ˌfī\ *vb* **-fied; -fy·ing 1 :** to make or become acid **2 :** to change into an acid — **acid·i·fi·ca·tion** \-ˌsi-də-fə-'kā-shən\ *n*

ac·i·do·sis \ˌa-sə-'dō-səs\ *n, pl* **-do·ses** \-ˌsēz\ **:** an abnormal state of reduced alkalinity of the blood and body tissues

acid precipitation *n* **:** precipitation with above normal acidity that is caused esp. by atmospheric pollutants

acid rain *n* **:** acid precipitation in the form of rain

acid test *n* **:** a severe or crucial test

acid·u·lous \ə-'si-jə-ləs\ *adj* **:** somewhat acid or harsh in taste or manner

ack *abbr* acknowledge; acknowledgment

ac·knowl·edge \ik-'nä-lij, ak-\ *vb* **-edged; -edg·ing 1 :** to recognize the rights or authority of **2 :** to admit as true **3 :** to express thanks for; *also* **:** to report receipt of **4 :** to recognize as valid — **ac·knowl·edg·ment** *or* **ac·knowl·edge·ment** *n*

ACLU *abbr* American Civil Liberties Union

ac·me \'ak-mē\ *n* [Gk *akmē*] **:** the highest point

ac·ne \'ak-nē\ *n* [Gk *aknē,* MS var. of *akmē,* lit., point] **:** a skin disorder marked by inflammation of skin glands and hair follicles and by pimple formation esp. on the face

ac·o·lyte \'a-kə-ˌlīt\ *n* **1 :** one who assists a member of the clergy in a liturgical service **2 :** FOLLOWER

ac·o·nite \'a-kə-ˌnīt\ *n* **1 :** MONKSHOOD **2 :** a drug obtained from a common Old World monkshood

acorn \'ā-ˌkȯrn, -kərn\ *n* **:** the nut of the oak

acorn squash *n* **:** an acorn-shaped dark green winter squash with a ridged surface

---

\ə\abut \ᵊ\kitten \ər\further \a\ash \ā\ace \ä\mop, mar \aú\out \ch\chin \e\bet \ē\easy \g\go \i\hit \ī\ice \j\job \ŋ\sing \ō\go \ȯ\law \ȯi\boy \th\thin \t͟h\the \ü\loot \ú\foot \y\yet \zh\vision *see also* Pronunciation Symbols page

acous·tic \ə-'kü-stik\ *or* **acous·ti·cal** \-sti-kəl\ *adj* **1** : of or relating to the sense or organs of hearing, to sound, or to the science of sounds **2** : deadening sound ⟨∼ tile⟩ **3** : operated by or utilizing sound waves — **acous·ti·cal·ly** \-k(ə-)lē\ *adv*

acous·tics \ə-'kü-stiks\ *n sing or pl* **1** : the science of sound **2** : the qualities in a room that make it easy or hard for a person in it to hear distinctly

ac·quaint \ə-'kwānt\ *vb* [ME, ultim. fr. L *ad-* + *cognoscere* to know] **1** : to cause to know personally **2** : INFORM

ac·quain·tance \ə-'kwānt-ᵊns\ *n* **1** : personal knowledge **2** : a person with whom one is acquainted — **ac·quain·tance·ship** *n*

ac·qui·esce \ₐa-kwē-'es\ *vb* **-esced; -esc·ing** : to accept, comply, or submit without open opposition **syn** consent, agree, assent, accede — **ac·qui·es·cence** \-'es-ᵊns\ *n* — **ac·qui·es·cent** \-ᵊnt\ *adj* — **ac·qui·es·cent·ly** *adv*

ac·quire \ə-'kwīr\ *vb* **ac·quired; ac·quir·ing** : to gain possession of : GET — **ac·quir·able** \-'kwī-rə-bəl\ *adj*

ac·quired \ə-'kwīrd\ *adj* **1** : gained by or as a result of effort or experience **2** : caused by environmental forces and not passed from parent to offspring in the genes ⟨∼ characteristics⟩

acquired immune deficiency syndrome *n* : AIDS

acquired immunodeficiency syndrome *n* : AIDS

ac·quire·ment *n* **1** : ATTAINMENT, ACCOMPLISHMENT **2** : the act of acquiring

ac·qui·si·tion \ₐa-kwə-'zi-shən\ *n* **1** : ACQUIREMENT **2** : something acquired

ac·quis·i·tive \ə-'kwi-zə-tiv\ *adj* : eager to acquire : GREEDY — **ac·quis·i·tive·ly** *adv* — **ac·quis·i·tive·ness** *n*

ac·quit \ə-'kwit\ *vb* **ac·quit·ted; ac·quit·ting 1** : to pronounce not guilty **2** : to conduct (oneself) usu. satisfactorily — **ac·quit·tal** \-ᵊl\ *n*

acre \'ā-kər\ *n* **1** *pl* : LANDS, ESTATE **2** — see WEIGHT table

acre·age \'ā-k(ə-)rij\ *n* : area in acres

ac·rid \'a-krəd\ *adj* **1** : sharp and biting in taste or odor **2** : deeply bitter : CAUSTIC — **acrid·i·ty** \a-'kri-də-tē\ *n* — **ac·rid·ly** *adv* — **ac·rid·ness** *n*

ac·ri·mo·ny \'a-krə-ₘmō-nē\ *n, pl* **-nies** : harsh or biting sharpness of language or feeling — **ac·ri·mo·ni·ous** \ₐa-krə-'mō-nē-əs\ *adj* — **ac·ri·mo·ni·ous·ly** *adv* — **ac·ri·mo·ni·ous·ness** *n*

ac·ro·bat \'a-krə-ₘbat\ *n* [F *acrobate*, fr. Gk *akrobatēs*, fr. *akros* topmost + *bainein* to go] : a performer of gymnastic feats — **ac·ro·bat·ic** \ₐa-krə-'ba-tik\ *adj* — **ac·ro·bat·i·cal·ly** \-ti-k(ə-)lē\ *adv*

ac·ro·bat·ics \ₐa-krə-'ba-tiks\ *n sing or pl* : the performance of an acrobat

ac·ro·nym \'a-krə-ₘnim\ *n* : a word (as *radar*) formed from the initial letter or letters of each of the successive parts or major parts of a compound term

ac·ro·pho·bia \ₐa-krə-'fō-bē-ə\ *n* : abnormal dread of being at a great height

acrop·o·lis \ə-'krä-pə-ləs\ *n* [Gk *akropolis*, fr. *akros* topmost + *polis* city] : the upper fortified part of an ancient Greek city

¹**across** \ə-'krôs\ *adv* **1** : to or on the opposite side **2** : so as to be understandable ⟨get the point ∼⟩

²**across** *prep* **1** : to or on the opposite side of ⟨ran ∼ the street⟩ **2** : on so as to cross or pass at an angle ⟨a log ∼ the road⟩

across–the–board *adj* **1** : placed to win if a competitor wins, places, or shows ⟨an ∼ bet⟩ **2** : including all classes or categories ⟨an ∼ wage increase⟩

acros·tic \ə-'krôs-tik\ *n* : a composition usu. in verse in which the initial or final letters of the lines taken in order form a word or phrase — **acrostic** *adj*

acryl·ic \ə-'kri-lik\ *n* **1** : ACRYLIC RESIN **2** : a paint in

which the vehicle is acrylic resin **3** : a quick-drying synthetic textile fiber

acrylic resin *n* : a glassy thermoplastic used for cast and molded parts or as coatings and adhesives

¹**act** \'akt\ *n* **1** : a thing done : DEED **2** : STATUTE, DECREE **3** : a main division of a play; *also* : an item on a variety program **4** : an instance of insincere behavior : PRETENSE

²**act** *vb* **1** : to perform by action esp. on the stage; *also* : FEIGN, SIMULATE, PRETEND **2** : to take action **3** : to conduct oneself : BEHAVE **4** : to perform a specified function **5** : to produce an effect

³**act** *abbr* **1** active **2** actual

ACT *abbr* Australian Capital Territory

actg *abbr* acting

ACTH \ₐā-(ₚ)sē-(ₚ)tē-'āch\ *n* : a protein hormone of the pituitary gland that stimulates the adrenal cortex

act·ing \'ak-tiŋ\ *adj* : doing duty temporarily or for another ⟨∼ president⟩

ac·ti·nide series \'ak-tə-ₘnīd-\ *n* : the series of chemical elements in the periodic table that begins with actinium or thorium and ends with lawrencium

ac·tin·i·um \ak-'ti-nē-əm\ *n* : a radioactive metallic chemical element — see ELEMENT table

ac·tion \'ak-shən\ *n* **1** : a legal proceeding **2** : the manner or method of performing **3** : ACTIVITY **4** : ACT, DEED **5** : the accomplishment of a thing usu. over a period of time, in stages, or with the possibility of repetition **6** *pl* : CONDUCT **7** : COMBAT, BATTLE **8** : the events of a literary plot **9** : an operating mechanism ⟨the ∼ of a gun⟩; *also* : the way it operates ⟨stiff ∼⟩

ac·tion·able \'ak-sh(ə-)nə-bəl\ *adj* : affording ground for an action or suit at law — **ac·tion·ably** \-blē\ *adv*

ac·ti·vate \'ak-tə-ₘvāt\ *vb* **-vat·ed; -vat·ing 1** : to spur into action; *also* : to make active, reactive, or radioactive **2** : to treat (as carbon) so as to improve adsorptive properties **3** : to set up (a military unit) formally; *also* : to call to active duty — **ac·ti·va·tion** \ₐak-tə-'vā-shən\ *n* — **ac·ti·va·tor** \'ak-tə-ₘvā-tər\ *n*

ac·tive \'ak-tiv\ *adj* **1** : causing or involving action or change **2** : asserting that the grammatical subject performs the action represented by the verb ⟨∼ voice⟩ **3** : BRISK, LIVELY **4** : erupting or likely to erupt ⟨∼ volcano⟩ **5** : presently in operation or use **6** : tending to progress or to cause degeneration ⟨∼ tuberculosis⟩ — **active** *n* — **ac·tive·ly** *adv* — **ac·tive·ness** *n*

ac·tiv·ism \'ak-ti-ₚvi-zəm\ *n* : a doctrine or practice that emphasizes vigorous action for political ends — **ac·tiv·ist** \-vist\ *n or adj*

ac·tiv·i·ty \ak-'ti-və-tē\ *n, pl* **-ties 1** : the quality or state of being active **2** : forceful or energetic action **3** : an occupation in which one is engaged

ac·tor \'ak-tər\ *n* : a person who acts in a play or motion picture

ac·tress \'ak-trəs\ *n* : a woman who is an actor

Acts \'akts\ *or* **Acts of the Apostles** *n* — see BIBLE table

ac·tu·al \'ak-chə-wəl, -shə-\ *adj* : really existing : REAL — **ac·tu·al·i·ty** \ₐak-chə-'wa-lə-tē, -shə-\ *n* — **ac·tu·al·iza·tion** \ₐak-chə-wə-lə-'zā-shən, -shə-\ *n* — **ac·tu·al·ize** \'ak-chə-wə-ₚlīz, -shə-\ *vb*

ac·tu·al·ly \'ak-chə-wə-lē, -shə-\ *adv* : in fact or in truth : REALLY

ac·tu·ary \'ak-chə-ₚwer-ē, -shə-\ *n, pl* **-ar·ies** : a person who calculates insurance risks and premiums — **ac·tu·ar·i·al** \ₐak-chə-'wer-ē-əl, -shə-\ *adj*

ac·tu·ate \'ak-chə-ₚwāt\ *vb* **-at·ed; -at·ing 1** : to put into action **2** : to move to action — **ac·tu·a·tion** \ₐak-chə-'wā-shən, -shə-\ *n* — **ac·tu·a·tor** \'ak-chə-ₚwā-tər, -shə-\ *n*

act up *vb* **1** : MISBEHAVE **2** : to function improperly

acu·ity \ə-'kyü-ə-tē\ *n, pl* **-ities** : keenness of perception

acu·men \ə-'kyü-mən\ *n* : mental keenness and penetration **syn** discernment, insight, percipience, perspicacity

acu·pres·sure \'a-kyu̇-ˌpre-shər\ *n* : SHIATSU

acu·punc·ture \-ˌpəŋk-chər\ *n* : an orig. Chinese practice of puncturing the body (as with needles) at specific points to cure disease or relieve pain — **acu·punc·tur·ist** \ˌa-kyu̇-ˈpəŋk-chə-rist\ *n*

acute \ə-ˈkyüt\ *adj* **acut·er; acut·est** [L *acutus,* pp. of *acuere* to sharpen, fr. *acus* needle] **1** : SHARP, POINTED **2** : containing less than 90 degrees ⟨an ∼ angle⟩ **3** : sharply perceptive; *esp* : mentally keen **4** : SEVERE ⟨∼ distress⟩; *also* : having a sudden onset, sharp rise, and short duration ⟨∼ inflammation⟩ **5** : of, marked by, or being an accent mark having the form ´ — **acute·ly** *adv* — **acute·ness** *n*

acy·clo·vir \(ˌ)ā-ˈsī-klō-ˌvir\ *n* : a drug used esp. to treat the genital form of herpes simplex

ad \'ad\ *n* : ADVERTISEMENT

AD *abbr* **1** after date **2** [L *anno Domini*] in the year of our Lord — often printed in small capitals and often punctuated **3** assistant director **4** athletic director

ad·age \'a-dij\ *n* : an old familiar saying : PROVERB, MAXIM

¹ada·gio \ə-ˈdä-j(ē-ˌ)ō, -zh(ē-ˌ)ō\ *adv or adj* [It] : at a slow tempo — used as a direction in music

²adagio *n, pl* **-gios 1** : an adagio movement **2** : a ballet duet or trio displaying feats of lifting and balancing

¹ad·a·mant \'a-də-mənt, -ˌmant\ *n* [ME, fr. OF, fr. L *adamant-, adamas* hardest metal, diamond, fr. Gk] : a stone imagined to be impenetrably hard — **ad·a·man·tine** \ˌa-də-ˈman-ˌtēn, -ˌtīn\ *adj*

²adamant *adj* : INFLEXIBLE, UNYIELDING — **ad·a·mant·ly** *adv*

Ad·am's apple \'a-dəmz-\ *n* : the projection in front of the neck formed by the largest cartilage of the larynx

adapt \ə-ˈdapt\ *vb* : to make suitable or fit (as for a new use or for different conditions) **syn** adjust, accommodate, conform — **adapt·abil·i·ty** \ə-ˌdap-tə-ˈbi-lə-tē\ *n* — **adapt·able** *adj* — **ad·ap·ta·tion** \ˌa-ˌdap-ˈtā-shən\ *n* — **ad·ap·ta·tion·al** \-sh(ə-)nəl\ *adj* — **adap·tive** \ə-ˈdap-tiv\ *adj* — **ad·ap·tiv·i·ty** \ˌa-ˌdap-ˈti-və-tē\ *n*

adapt·er *also* **adap·tor** \ə-ˈdap-tər\ *n* **1** : one that adapts **2** : a device for connecting two dissimilar parts of an apparatus **3** : an attachment for adapting apparatus for uses not orig. intended

Adar \ä-ˈdär, ˈä-ˌdär\ *n* [ME, fr. Heb *Ădhār*] : the 6th month of the civil year or the 12th month of the ecclesiastical year in the Jewish calendar

Adar Sheni \ä-ˌdär-shä-ˈnē\ *n* [Heb *Ădhār Shēnī,* second Adar] : VEADAR

ADC *abbr* **1** aide-de-camp **2** Aid to Dependent Children

add \'ad\ *vb* **1** : to join to something else so as to increase in number or amount **2** : to say further ⟨let me ∼ this⟩ **3** : to combine (numbers) into one sum

ad·dend \'a-ˌdend\ *n* : a number to be added to another

ad·den·dum \ə-ˈden-dəm\ *n, pl* **-da** \-də\ [L] : something added; *esp* : a supplement to a book

¹ad·der \'a-dər\ *n* **1** : a poisonous European viper or a related snake **2** : any of various harmless No. American snakes (as the hognose snake)

²add·er \'a-dər\ *n* : one that adds; *esp* : a device that performs addition

¹ad·dict \ə-ˈdikt\ *vb* **1** : to devote or surrender (oneself) to something habitually or excessively **2** : to cause addiction to a substance in (as a person) — **ad·dic·tive** \-ˈdik-tiv\ *adj*

²ad·dict \'a-(ˌ)dikt\ *n* : one who is addicted to a substance

ad·dic·tion \ə-ˈdik-shən\ *n* **1** : the quality or state of being addicted **2** : compulsive need for and use of a habit=forming substance (as heroin, nicotine, or alcohol) characterized by well-defined physiological symptoms upon withdrawal; *also* : persistent compulsive use of a substance known by the user to be harmful

ad·di·tion \ə-ˈdi-shən\ *n* **1** : the act or process of adding; *also* : something added **2** : the operation of combining numbers to obtain their sum **syn** accretion, increment, accession, augmentation

ad·di·tion·al \ə-ˈdi-sh(ə-)nəl\ *adj* : coming by way of addition : ADDED, EXTRA

ad·di·tion·al·ly \ə-ˈdi-sh(ə-)nə-lē\ *adv* : in or by way of addition : FURTHERMORE

¹ad·di·tive \'a-də-tiv\ *adj* **1** : of, relating to, or characterized by addition **2** : produced by addition — **ad·di·tiv·i·ty** \ˌa-də-ˈti-və-tē\ *n*

²additive *n* : a substance added to another in small quantities to effect a desired change in properties ⟨food ∼s⟩

ad·dle \'ad-ᵊl\ *vb* **ad·dled; ad·dling 1** : to throw into confusion : MUDDLE **2** : to become rotten ⟨addled eggs⟩

addn *abbr* addition

addnl *abbr* additional

add–on \'ad-ˌȯn, -ˌän\ *n* : something (as a feature or accessory) added esp. as an enhancement

¹ad·dress \ə-ˈdres\ *vb* **1** : to direct the attention of (oneself) **2** : to direct one's remarks to : deliver an address to **3** : to mark directions for delivery on **4** : to identify (as a memory location) by an address

²ad·dress \ə-ˈdres, 'a-ˌdres\ *n* **1** : skillful management **2** : a formal speech : LECTURE **3** : the place where a person or organization may be communicated with **4** : the directions for delivery placed on mail **5** : a location (as in a computer's memory) where particular data is stored

ad·dress·ee \ˌa-ˌdre-ˈsē, ə-ˌdre-ˈsē\ *n* : one to whom something is addressed

ad·duce \ə-ˈdüs, -ˈdyüs\ *vb* **ad·duced; ad·duc·ing** : to offer as argument, reason, or proof **syn** advance, allege, cite, submit — **ad·duc·er** *n*

-ade *n suffix* **1** : act : action ⟨blockade⟩ **2** : product; *esp* : sweet drink ⟨limeade⟩

ad·e·nine \'ad-ᵊn-ˌēn\ *n* : one of the purine bases that make up the genetic code of DNA and RNA

ad·e·noid \'ad-ˌnȯid, -ᵊn-ˌȯid\ *n* : an enlarged mass of tissue near the opening of the nose into the throat — usu. used in pl. — **adenoid** *or* **ad·e·noi·dal** \ˌad-ˈnȯi-dəl, -ᵊn-ˈȯi-\ *adj*

aden·o·sine tri·phos·phate \ə-ˈde-nə-ˌsēn-trī-ˈfäs-ˌfāt\ *n* : ATP

¹ad·ept \'a-ˌdept\ *n* : EXPERT

²adept \ə-ˈdept\ *adj* : highly skilled : EXPERT — **adept·ly** *adv* — **adept·ness** *n*

ad·e·quate \'a-di-kwət\ *adj* : equal to or sufficient for a specific requirement — **ad·e·qua·cy** \-kwə-sē\ *n* — **ad·e·quate·ly** *adv* — **ad·e·quate·ness** *n*

ad·here \ad-ˈhir\ *vb* **ad·hered; ad·her·ing 1** : to give support : maintain loyalty **2** : to stick fast : CLING — **ad·her·ence** \-ˈhir-əns\ *n* — **ad·her·ent** \-ənt\ *adj or n*

ad·he·sion \ad-ˈhē-zhən\ *n* **1** : the act or state of adhering **2** : the union of bodily tissues abnormally grown together after inflammation; *also* : the newly formed uniting tissue **3** : the molecular attraction between the surfaces of bodies in contact

¹ad·he·sive \-ˈhē-siv, -ziv\ *adj* **1** : tending to adhere : STICKY **2** : prepared for adhering

²adhesive *n* : an adhesive substance

adhesive tape *n* : tape coated on one side with an adhesive mixture; *esp* : one used for covering wounds

¹ad hoc \'ad-ˈhäk, -ˈhōk\ *adv* [L, for this] : for the case at hand apart from other applications

²ad hoc *adj* : concerned with or formed for a particular purpose ⟨an *ad hoc* committee⟩ ⟨*ad hoc* solutions⟩

adi·a·bat·ic \ˌa-dē-ə-ˈba-tik\ *adj* : occurring without loss or gain of heat — **adi·a·bat·i·cal·ly** \-ti-k(ə-)lē\ *adv*

---

adieu \ə-'dü, -'dyü\ *n, pl* **adieus** *or* **adieux** \ə-'düz, -'dyüz\ : FAREWELL — often used interjectionally

ad·in·fi·ni·tum \ˌad-ˌin-fə-'nī-təm\ *adv or adj* : without end or limit

ad in·ter·im \ad-'in-tə-rəm, -ˌrim\ *adv* : for the intervening time — **ad interim** *adj*

adi·os \ˌä-dē-'ōs, ˌä-\ *interj* [Sp *adiós*, lit., to God] — used to express farewell

ad·i·pose \'a-də-ˌpōs\ *adj* : of or relating to animal fat : FATTY

adj *abbr* **1** adjective **2** adjutant

ad·ja·cent \ə-'jās-ənt\ *adj* : situated near or next **syn** adjoining, contiguous, abutting, juxtaposed, conterminous — **ad·ja·cent·ly** *adv*

ad·jec·tive \'a-jik-tiv\ *n* : a word that typically serves as a modifier of a noun — **ad·jec·ti·val** \ˌa-jik-'tī-vəl\ *adj* — **ad·jec·ti·val·ly** *adv*

ad·join \ə-'join\ *vb* : to be situated next to

ad·join·ing *adj* : touching or bounding at a point or line

ad·journ \ə-'jərn\ *vb* **1** : to suspend indefinitely or until a stated time **2** : to transfer to another place — **ad·journ·ment** *n*

ad·judge \ə-'jəj\ *vb* **ad·judged; ad·judg·ing 1** : JUDGE, ADJUDICATE **2** : to hold or pronounce to be : DEEM **3** : to award by judicial decision

ad·ju·di·cate \ə-'jü-di-ˌkāt\ *vb* **-cat·ed; -cat·ing** : to settle judicially — **ad·ju·di·ca·tion** \ə-ˌjü-di-'kā-shən\ *n*

ad·junct \'a-ˌjəŋkt\ *n* : something joined or added to another but not essentially a part of it **syn** appendage, appurtenance, accessory, appendix

ad·jure \ə-'jür\ *vb* **ad·jured; ad·jur·ing** : to command solemnly : urge earnestly **syn** beg, beseech, implore — **ad·ju·ra·tion** \ˌa-jə-'rā-shən\ *n*

ad·just \ə-'jəst\ *vb* **1** : to bring to agreement : SETTLE **2** : to cause to conform : ADAPT, FIT **3** : REGULATE ⟨∼ a watch⟩ — **ad·just·able** *adj* — **ad·just·er** *also* **ad·jus·tor** \ə-'jəs-tər\ *n* — **ad·just·ment** \ə-'jəst-mənt\ *n*

ad·ju·tant \'a-jə-tənt\ *n* : one who assists; *esp* : an officer who assists a commanding officer by handling correspondence and keeping records

ad·ju·vant \'a-jə-vənt\ *n* : one that helps or facilitates; *esp* : something that enhances the effectiveness of medical treatment — **adjuvant** *adj*

¹ad–lib \'ad-'lib\ *vb* **ad–libbed; ad–lib·bing** : IMPROVISE — **ad–lib** *n*

²ad–lib *adj* : spoken, composed, or performed without preparation

ad lib \'ad-'lib\ *adv* [NL *ad libitum*] **1** : at one's pleasure **2** : without limit

adm *abbr* administration; administrative

ADM *abbr* admiral

ad·man \'ad-ˌman\ *n* : one who writes, solicits, or places advertisements

admin *abbr* administration; administrative

ad·min·is·ter \əd-'mi-nə-stər\ *vb* **1** : MANAGE, SUPERINTEND **2** : to mete out : DISPENSE **3** : to give ritually or remedially ⟨∼ quinine for malaria⟩ **4** : to perform the office of administrator — **ad·min·is·tra·ble** \-strə-bəl\ *adj* — **ad·min·is·trant** \-strənt\ *n*

ad·min·is·tra·tion \ad-ˌmi-nə-'strā-shən\ *n* **1** : the act or process of administering **2** : MANAGEMENT **3** : the officials directing the government of a country **4** : the term of office of an administrative officer or body — **ad·min·is·tra·tive** \ad-'mi-nə-ˌstrā-tiv\ *adj* — **ad·min·is·tra·tive·ly** *adv*

ad·min·is·tra·tor \ad-'mi-nə-ˌstrā-tər\ *n* : one that administers; *esp* : one who settles an intestate estate

ad·mi·ra·ble \'ad-m(ə-)rə-bəl\ *adj* : worthy of admiration : EXCELLENT — **ad·mi·ra·bil·i·ty** \ˌad-m(ə-)rə-'bi-lə-tē\ *n* — **ad·mi·ra·ble·ness** *n* — **ad·mi·ra·bly** \-blē\ *adv*

ad·mi·ral \'ad-m(ə-)rəl\ *n* [ME, ultim. fr. Ar *amīr-al-* commander of the (as in *amīr-al-bahr* commander of

the sea)] : a commissioned officer in the navy ranking next below a fleet admiral

ad·mi·ral·ty \'ad-m(ə-)rəl-tē\ *n* **1** *cap* : a British government department formerly having authority over naval affairs **2** : the court having jurisdiction over questions of maritime law

ad·mire \əd-'mīr\ *vb* **ad·mired; ad·mir·ing** [MF *admirer*, fr. L *admirari*, fr. *ad-* to + *mirari* to wonder] : to regard with high esteem — **ad·mi·ra·tion** \ˌad-mə-'rā-shən\ *n* — **ad·mir·er** *n* — **ad·mir·ing·ly** \-'mī-riŋ-lē\ *adv*

ad·mis·si·ble \əd-'mi-sə-bəl\ *adj* : that can be or is worthy to be admitted or allowed : ALLOWABLE ⟨∼ evidence⟩ — **ad·mis·si·bil·i·ty** \-ˌmi-sə-'bi-lə-tē\ *n*

ad·mis·sion \əd-'mi-shən\ *n* **1** : the act of admitting **2** : the privilege of being admitted **3** : a fee paid for admission **4** : the granting of an argument **5** : the acknowledgment of a fact

ad·mit \əd-'mit\ *vb* **ad·mit·ted; ad·mit·ting 1** : PERMIT, ALLOW **2** : to recognize as genuine or valid **3** : to allow to enter

ad·mit·tance \əd-'mit-ᵊns\ *n* : permission to enter

ad·mit·ted·ly \əd-'mi-təd-lē\ *adv* **1** : as has been or must be admitted **2** : it must be admitted

ad·mix \ad-'miks\ *vb* : to mix in

ad·mix·ture \ad-'miks-chər\ *n* **1** : something added in mixing **2** : MIXTURE

ad·mon·ish \ad-'mä-nish\ *vb* : to warn gently : reprove with a warning **syn** chide, reproach, rebuke, reprimand, reprove — **ad·mon·ish·er** *n* — **ad·mon·ish·ing·ly** *adv* — **ad·mon·ish·ment** *n* — **ad·mo·ni·tion** \ˌad-mə-'ni-shən\ *n* — **ad·mon·i·to·ry** \ad-'mä-nə-ˌtōr-ē\ *adj*

ad nau·se·am \ad-'nȯ-zē-əm\ *adv* [L] : to a sickening or excessive degree

ado \ə-'dü\ *n* **1** : bustling excitement : FUSS **2** : TROUBLE

ado·be \ə-'dō-bē\ *n* **1** : sun-dried brick; *also* : clay for making such bricks **2** : a structure made of adobe bricks

ad·o·les·cence \ˌad-ᵊl-'es-ᵊns\ *n* : the process or period of growth between childhood and maturity — **ad·o·les·cent** \-ᵊnt\ *adj or n*

adopt \ə-'däpt\ *vb* **1** : to take (a child of other parents) as one's own child **2** : to take up and practice as one's own **3** : to accept formally and put into effect — **adopt·able** \-'däp-tə-bəl\ *adj* — **adopt·er** *n* — **adop·tion** \-'däp-shən\ *n*

adop·tive \ə-'däp-tiv\ *adj* : made or acquired by adoption ⟨∼ father⟩ — **adop·tive·ly** *adv*

ador·able \ə-'dȯr-ə-bəl\ *adj* **1** : worthy of adoration **2** : extremely charming — **ador·able·ness** *n* — **ador·ably** \-blē\ *adv*

adore \ə-'dȯr\ *vb* **adored; ador·ing** [ME *adouren*, fr. MF *adorer*, fr. L *adorare*, fr. *ad-* to + *orare* to speak, pray] **1** : WORSHIP **2** : to regard with loving admiration **3** : to be extremely fond of — **ad·o·ra·tion** \ˌa-də-'rā-shən\ *n*

adorn \ə-'dȯrn\ *vb* : to enhance the appearance of esp. with ornaments — **adorn·ment** *n*

ad·re·nal \ə-'drēn-ᵊl\ *adj* : of, relating to, or being a pair of endocrine organs (**adrenal glands**) that are located near the kidneys and produce several hormones and esp. epinephrine

adren·a·line \ə-'dren-ᵊl-ən\ *n* : EPINEPHRINE

adrift \ə-'drift\ *adv or adj* **1** : afloat without motive power or moorings **2** : without guidance or purpose

adroit \ə-'drȯit\ *adj* [F, fr. OF, fr. *a-* to + *droit* right] **1** : dexterous with one's hands **2** : SHREWD, RESOURCEFUL **syn** canny, clever, cunning, ingenious — **adroit·ly** *adv* — **adroit·ness** *n*

ad·sorb \ad-'sȯrb, -'zȯrb\ *vb* : to take up (as molecules of gases) and hold on the surface of a solid or liquid — **ad·sorp·tion** \-'sȯrp-shən, -'zȯrp-\ *n*

ad·u·late \'a-jə-ˌlāt\ *vb* **-lat·ed; -lat·ing** : to flatter or admire excessively — **ad·u·la·tion** \ˌa-jə-ˈlā-shən\ n — **ad·u·la·tor** \ˈa-jə-ˌlā-tər\ n — **ad·u·la·to·ry** \-lə-ˌtōr-ē\ adj

¹**adult** \ə-ˈdəlt, ˈa-ˌ\ adj [L adultus, pp. of adolescere to grow up, fr. ad- to + alescere to grow] : fully developed and mature — **adult·hood** n

²**adult** n : one that is adult; esp : a human being after an age (as 18) specified by law

adul·ter·ant \ə-ˈdəl-tə-rənt\ n : something used to adulterate another

adul·ter·ate \ə-ˈdəl-tə-ˌrāt\ vb **-at·ed; -at·ing** [L adulterare, fr. ad- to + alter other] : to make impure by mixing in a foreign or inferior substance — **adul·ter·a·tion** \-ˌdəl-tə-ˈrā-shən\ n

adul·tery \ə-ˈdəl-t(ə-)rē\ n, pl **-ter·ies** : sexual unfaithfulness of a married person — **adul·ter·er** \-tər-ər\ n — **adul·ter·ess** \-t(ə-)rəs\ n — **adul·ter·ous** \-t(ə-)rəs\ adj

ad·um·brate \ˈa-dəm-ˌbrāt\ vb **-brat·ed; -brat·ing 1** : to foreshadow vaguely : INTIMATE **2** : to suggest or disclose partially **3** : SHADE, OBSCURE — **ad·um·bra·tion** \ˌa-dəm-ˈbrā-shən\ n

adv abbr **1** adverb **2** advertisement

ad va·lor·em \ˌad-və-ˈlōr-əm\ adj [L, according to the value] : imposed at a percentage of the value ⟨an ad valorem tax⟩

¹**ad·vance** \əd-ˈvans\ vb **ad·vanced; ad·vanc·ing 1** : to assist the progress of **2** : to bring or move forward **3** : to promote in rank **4** : to make earlier in time **5** : PROPOSE **6** : LEND **7** : to raise in rate : INCREASE — **ad·vance·ment** n

²**advance** n **1** : a forward movement **2** : IMPROVEMENT **3** : a rise esp. in price or value **4** : OFFER — **in advance** : BEFOREHAND

³**advance** adj : made, sent, or furnished ahead of time

ad·van·tage \əd-ˈvan-tij\ n **1** : superiority of position **2** : BENEFIT, GAIN **3** : the 1st point won in tennis after deuce — **ad·van·ta·geous** \ˌad-van-ˈtā-jəs\ adj — **ad·van·ta·geous·ly** adv

ad·vent \ˈad-ˌvent\ n **1** cap : a penitential period beginning four Sundays before Christmas **2** cap : the coming of Christ **3** : a coming into being or use

ad·ven·ti·tious \ˌad-vən-ˈti-shəs\ adj **1** : ACCIDENTAL, INCIDENTAL **2** : arising or occurring sporadically or in other than the usual location ⟨∼ buds⟩ — **ad·ven·ti·tious·ly** adv

²**ad·ven·ture** \əd-ˈven-chər\ n **1** : a risky undertaking **2** : a remarkable and exciting experience — **ad·ven·tur·ous** \-ch(ə-)rəs\ adj

²**adventure** vb **-ven·tured; -ven·tur·ing** \-ˈven-ch(ə-)riŋ\ : RISK, HAZARD

ad·ven·tur·er \əd-ˈven-ch(ə-)rər\ n **1** : a person who engages in new and risky undertakings **2** : a person who follows a military career for adventure or profit **3** : a person who tries to gain wealth by questionable means

ad·ven·ture·some \əd-ˈven-chər-səm\ adj : inclined to take risks

ad·ven·tur·ess \əd-ˈven-ch(ə-)rəs\ n : a female adventurer

ad·verb \ˈad-ˌvərb\ n : a word that typically serves as a modifier of a verb, an adjective, or another adverb — **ad·ver·bi·al** \ad-ˈvər-bē-əl\ adj — **ad·ver·bi·al·ly** adv

¹**ad·ver·sary** \ˈad-vər-ˌser-ē\ n, pl **-sar·ies** : FOE

²**adversary** adj : involving antagonistic parties or interests

ad·verse \ad-ˈvərs, ˈad-ˌvərs\ adj **1** : acting against or in a contrary direction **2** : UNFAVORABLE — **ad·verse·ly** adv

ad·ver·si·ty \ad-ˈvər-sə-tē\ n, pl **-ties** : hard times : MISFORTUNE

ad·vert \ad-ˈvərt\ vb : REFER

ad·ver·tise \ˈad-vər-ˌtīz\ vb **-tised; -tis·ing 1** : INFORM, NOTIFY **2** : to call public attention to esp. in order to sell — **ad·ver·tis·er** n

ad·ver·tise·ment \ˌad-vər-ˈtīz-mənt; əd-ˈvər-təs-mənt\ n **1** : the act of advertising **2** : a public notice intended to advertise something

ad·ver·tis·ing \ˈad-vər-ˌtī-ziŋ\ n : the business of preparing advertisements

ad·vice \əd-ˈvīs\ n **1** : recommendation with regard to a course of action : COUNSEL **2** : INFORMATION, REPORT

ad·vis·able \əd-ˈvī-zə-bəl\ adj : proper to be done : EXPEDIENT — **ad·vis·abil·i·ty** \-ˌvī-zə-ˈbi-lə-tē\ n

ad·vise \əd-ˈvīz\ vb **ad·vised; ad·vis·ing 1** : to give advice to : COUNSEL **2** : INFORM, NOTIFY **3** : CONSULT, CONFER — **ad·vis·er** or **ad·vi·sor** \-ˈvī-zər\ n

ad·vised \əd-ˈvīzd\ adj : thought out : CONSIDERED ⟨well-advised⟩ — **ad·vis·ed·ly** \-ˈvī-zəd-lē\ adv

ad·vise·ment \əd-ˈvīz-mənt\ n **1** : careful consideration **2** : the act of advising

ad·vi·so·ry \əd-ˈvī-zə-rē\ adj **1** : having or exercising power to advise **2** : containing advice

¹**ad·vo·cate** \ˈad-və-kət, -ˌkāt\ n [ultim. fr. L advocare to summon, fr. ad- to + vocare to call] **1** : one who pleads another's cause **2** : one who argues or pleads for a cause or proposal — **ad·vo·ca·cy** \-və-kə-sē\ n

²**ad·vo·cate** \-ˌkāt\ vb **-cat·ed; -cat·ing** : to plead in favor of — **ad·vo·ca·tion** \ˌad-və-ˈkā-shən\ n

advt abbr advertisement

adze also **adz** \ˈadz\ n : a tool with a curved blade set at right angles to the handle that is used in shaping wood

adze

AEC abbr Atomic Energy Commission

ae·gis \ˈē-jəs\ n **1** : SHIELD, PROTECTION **2** : PATRONAGE, SPONSORSHIP

ae·o·li·an harp \ē-ˈō-lē-ən-\ n : a box with strings that produce musical sounds when the wind blows on them

ae·on \ˈē-ən, -ˌän\ n **1** : an indefinitely long time : AGE **2** usu eon : a very large division of geologic time usu. longer than an era

aer·ate \ˈa(-ə)r-ˌāt\ vb **aer·at·ed; aer·at·ing 1** : to supply (blood) with oxygen by respiration **2** : to supply, impregnate, or combine with a gas and esp. air — **aer·a·tion** \ˌa(-ə)r-ˈā-shən\ n — **aer·a·tor** \ˈa(-ə)r-ˌā-tər\ n

¹**ae·ri·al** \ˈar-ē-əl\ adj **1** : inhabiting, occurring in, or done in the air **2** : AIRY **3** : of or relating to aircraft

²**aer·i·al** \ˈar-ē-əl\ n : ANTENNA 2

ae·ri·al·ist \ˈar-ē-ə-list\ n : a performer of feats above the ground esp. on a trapeze

ae·rie \ˈar-ē, ˈir-ē\ n : a highly placed nest (as of an eagle)

aer·o·bat·ics \ˌar-ə-ˈba-tiks\ n sing or pl : spectacular flying feats and maneuvers

aer·o·bic \ˌa(-ə)r-ˈrō-bik\ adj **1** : living or active only in the presence of oxygen ⟨∼ bacteria⟩ **2** : of or relating to aerobics — **aer·o·bi·cal·ly** \-bi-k(ə-)lē\ adv

aer·o·bics \-biks\ n sing or pl : strenuous exercises that produce a marked temporary increase in respiration and heart rate; also : a system of physical conditioning involving these

aero·drome \ˈar-ə-ˌdrōm\ n, chiefly Brit : AIRPORT

aero·dy·nam·ics \ˌar-ō-dī-ˈna-miks\ n : the science dealing with the forces acting on bodies in motion in a gas

---

\ə\abut \ᵊ\kitten \ər\further \a\ash \ā\ace \ä\mop, mar
\au̇\out \ch\chin \e\bet \ē\easy \g\go \i\hit \ī\ice \j\job
\ŋ\sing \ō\go \ȯ\law \oi̇\boy \th\thin \t̲h̲\the \ü\loot \u̇\foot
\y\yet \zh\vision see also Pronunciation Symbols page

(as air) — **aero·dy·nam·ic** \-mik\ *also* **aero·dy·nam·i·cal** \-mi-kəl\ *adj* — **aero·dy·nam·i·cal·ly** \-mi-k(ə-)lē\ *adv*

aero·naut \'ar-ə-ˌnȯt\ *n* : one who operates or travels in an airship or balloon

aero·nau·tics \ˌar-ə-'nȯ-tiks\ *n* : the science of aircraft operation — **aero·nau·ti·cal** \-ti-kəl\ *also* **aero·nau·tic** \-tik\ *adj*

aero·plane \'ar-ə-ˌplān\ *chiefly Brit var of* AIRPLANE

aero·sol \'ar-ə-ˌsäl, -ˌsȯl\ *n* **1** : a suspension of fine solid or liquid particles in a gas **2** : a substance (as an insecticide) dispensed from a pressurized container as an aerosol

aero·space \'ar-ō-ˌspās\ *n* : the earth's atmosphere and the space beyond — **aerospace** *adj*

aery \'ar-ē\ *adj* **aer·i·er; -est** : having an aerial quality : ETHEREAL

aes·thete \'es-ˌthēt\ *n* : a person having or affecting sensitivity to beauty esp. in art

aes·thet·ic \es-'the-tik\ *adj* **1** : of or relating to aesthetics : ARTISTIC **2** : appreciative of the beautiful — **aes·thet·i·cal·ly** \-ti-k(ə-)lē\ *adv*

aes·thet·ics \-tiks\ *n* : a branch of philosophy dealing with the nature, creation, and appreciation of beauty

AF *abbr* **1** air force **2** audio frequency

¹afar \ə-'fär\ *adv* : from, at, or to a great distance

²afar *n* : a great distance

AFB *abbr* air force base

AFC *abbr* **1** American Football Conference **2** automatic frequency control

AFDC *abbr* Aid to Families with Dependent Children

af·fa·ble \'a-fə-bəl\ *adj* : courteous and agreeable in conversation — **af·fa·bil·i·ty** \ˌa-fə-'bi-lə-tē\ *n* — **af·fa·bly** \'a-fə-blē\ *adv*

af·fair \ə-'far\ *n* [ME *affaire*, fr. MF, fr. *a faire* to do] **1** : something that relates to or involves one : CONCERN **2** : a romantic or sexual attachment of limited duration

¹af·fect \ə-'fekt, a-\ *vb* **1** : to be fond of using or wearing **2** : SIMULATE, ASSUME, PRETEND

²affect *vb* : to produce an effect on : INFLUENCE

af·fec·ta·tion \ˌa-fek-'tā-shən\ *n* : an attitude or behavior that is assumed by a person but not genuinely felt

af·fect·ed \a-'fek-təd\ *adj* **1** : given to affectation **2** : artificially assumed to impress others — **af·fect·ed·ly** *adv*

af·fect·ing \a-'fek-tiŋ\ *adj* : arousing pity, sympathy, or sorrow ⟨an ~ story⟩ — **af·fect·ing·ly** *adv*

af·fec·tion \ə-'fek-shən\ *n* : tender attachment — **af·fec·tion·ate** \-sh(ə-)nət\ *adj* — **af·fec·tion·ate·ly** *adv*

af·fer·ent \'a-fə-rənt, -ˌfer-ənt\ *adj* : bearing or conducting inward toward a more central part and esp. a nerve center (as the brain or spinal cord)

af·fi·ance \ə-'fī-əns\ *vb* **-anced; -anc·ing** : BETROTH, ENGAGE

af·fi·da·vit \ˌa-fə-'dā-vət\ *n* [ML, he has made an oath] : a sworn statement in writing

¹af·fil·i·ate \ə-'fi-lē-ˌāt\ *vb* **-at·ed; -at·ing** : to associate as a member or branch — **af·fil·i·a·tion** \-ˌfi-lē-'ā-shən\ *n*

²af·fil·i·ate \ə-'fi-lē-ət\ *n* : an affiliated person or organization

af·fin·i·ty \ə-'fi-nə-tē\ *n, pl* **-ties 1** : KINSHIP, RELATIONSHIP **2** : attractive force : ATTRACTION, SYMPATHY

af·firm \ə-'fərm\ *vb* **1** : CONFIRM **2** : to assert positively **3** : to make a solemn and formal declaration or assertion in place of an oath **syn** aver, avow, avouch, declare, assert — **af·fir·ma·tion** \ˌa-fər-'mā-shən\ *n*

¹af·fir·ma·tive \ə-'fər-mə-tiv\ *adj* : asserting that the fact is so : POSITIVE

²affirmative *n* **1** : an expression of affirmation or assent **2** : the side that upholds the proposition stated in a debate

affirmative action *n* : an active effort to improve the employment or educational opportunities of members of minority groups and women

¹af·fix \ə-'fiks\ *vb* : ATTACH, ADD

²af·fix \'a-ˌfiks\ *n* : one or more sounds or letters attached to the beginning or end of a word that produce a derivative word or an inflectional form

af·fla·tus \ə-'flā-təs\ *n* : divine inspiration

af·flict \ə-'flikt\ *vb* : to cause pain and distress to **syn** rack, try, torment, torture — **af·flic·tion** \-'flik-shən\ *n*

af·flic·tive \ə-'flik-tiv\ *adj* : causing affliction : DISTRESSING — **af·flic·tive·ly** *adv*

af·flu·ence \'a-ˌflü-ən(t)s, a-'flü-\ *n* : abundant supply; *also* : WEALTH, RICHES — **af·flu·ent** \-ənt\ *adj*

af·ford \ə-'fōrd\ *vb* **1** : to manage to bear or bear the cost of without serious harm or loss **2** : PROVIDE, FURNISH

af·for·es·ta·tion \a-ˌfȯr-ə-'stā-shən\ *n* : the act or process of establishing a forest — **af·for·est** \a-'fȯr-əst, -'fär-\ *vb*

af·fray \ə-'frā\ *n* : FIGHT, FRAY

af·fright \ə-'frīt\ *vb* : FRIGHTEN, ALARM — **affright** *n*

af·front \ə-'frənt\ *vb* **1** : INSULT **2** : CONFRONT — **affront** *n*

af·ghan \'af-ˌgan\ *n* **1** *cap* : a native or inhabitant of Afghanistan **2** : a blanket or shawl of colored wool knitted or crocheted in sections — **Afghan** *adj*

Afghan hound *n* : any of a breed of tall slim swift hunting dogs with a coat of silky thick hair and a long silky top knot

af·ghani \af-'ga-nē\ *n* — see MONEY table

afi·cio·na·do \ə-ˌfi-sh(ē-)ə-'nä-dō, -sē-ə-\ *n, pl* **-dos** [Sp, fr. pp. of *aficionar* to inspire affection] : DEVOTEE, FAN

afield \ə-'fēld\ *adv or adj* **1** : to, in, or on the field **2** : away from home **3** : out of the way : ASTRAY

afire \ə-'fīr\ *adj or adv* : being on fire : BURNING

AFL *abbr* American Football League

aflame \ə-'flām\ *adj or adv* : FLAMING

AFL–CIO *abbr* American Federation of Labor and Congress of Industrial Organizations

afloat \ə-'flōt\ *adj or adv* **1** : borne on or as if on the water **2** : CIRCULATING ⟨rumors were ~⟩ **3** : ADRIFT

aflut·ter \ə-'flə-tər\ *adj* **1** : FLUTTERING **2** : nervously excited

afoot \ə-'fút\ *adv or adj* **1** : on foot **2** : in action : in progress

afore·men·tioned \ə-'fōr-ˌmen-chənd\ *adj* : mentioned previously

afore·said \-ˌsed\ *adj* : said or named before

afore·thought \-ˌthȯt\ *adj* : PREMEDITATED ⟨with malice ~⟩

a for·ti·o·ri \ˌä-ˌfȯr-tē-'ȯr-ē\ *adv* [NL, lit., from the stronger (argument)] : with even greater reason

afoul of \ə-'faül-əv\ *prep* **1** : in or into conflict with **2** : in or into collision or entanglement with

Afr *abbr* Africa; African

afraid \ə-'frād\ *adj* : FRIGHTENED, FEARFUL

A–frame \'ā-ˌfrām\ *n* : a building having triangular front and rear walls with the roof reaching to the ground

afresh \ə-'fresh\ *adv* : ANEW, AGAIN

Af·ri·can \'a-fri-kən\ *n* **1** : a native or inhabitant of Africa **2** : a person of African ancestry — **African** *adj*

A·fri·can–Amer·i·can \-ə-'mer-ə-kən\ *n* : AFRO-AMERICAN — **African–American** *adj*

Af·ri·can·ized bee \'a-frə-kə-ˌnīzd-\ *n* : a highly aggressive hybrid honeybee accidentally produced from Brazilian and African stocks that has spread from So. America into Mexico and the southern U.S.

Africanized honeybee *n* : AFRICANIZED BEE

African violet *n* : a tropical African plant widely grown indoors for its velvety fleshy leaves and showy purple, pink, or white flowers

Af·ri·kaans \ˌa-fri-'käns\ *n* : a language developed from 17th century Dutch that is one of the official languages of the Republic of So. Africa

¹Af·ro \'a-frō\ *adj* : having the hair shaped into a round bushy mass

²Afro *n, pl* **Afros** : an Afro hairstyle

Af·ro–Amer·i·can \₁a-frō-ə-'mer-ə-kən\ *n* : an American of African and esp. of black African descent — **Afro–American** *adj*

aft \'aft\ *adv* : near, toward, or in the stern of a ship or the tail of an aircraft

AFT *abbr* American Federation of Teachers

¹af·ter \'af-tər\ *adv* : AFTERWARD, SUBSEQUENTLY

²after *prep* **1** : behind in place **2** : later than **3** : in pursuit or search of ⟨he's ~ your job⟩

³after *conj* : following the time when

⁴after *adj* **1** : LATER **2** : located toward the rear

af·ter·birth \'af-tər-₁bərth\ *n* : the placenta and membranes of the fetus that are expelled after childbirth

af·ter·burn·er \-₁bər-nər\ *n* : a device incorporated in the tail pipe of a turbojet engine for injecting fuel into the hot exhaust gases and burning it to provide extra thrust

af·ter·care \-₁ker\ *n* : the care, nursing, or treatment of a convalescent patient

af·ter·deck \-₁dek\ *n* : the rear half of the deck of a ship

af·ter·ef·fect \-ə-₁fekt\ *n* : an effect that follows its cause after an interval

af·ter·glow \-₁glō\ *n* : a glow remaining where a light has disappeared

af·ter·im·age \-₁im-ij\ *n* : a usu. visual sensation continuing after the stimulus causing it has ended

af·ter·life \-₁līf\ *n* : an existence after death

af·ter·math \-₁math\ *n* **1** : a second-growth crop esp. of hay **2** : CONSEQUENCES, EFFECTS **syn** aftereffect, upshot, result, outcome

af·ter·noon \₁af-tər-'nün\ *n* : the time between noon and evening

af·ter·shave \'af-tər-₁shāv\ *n* : a usu. scented lotion for the face after shaving

af·ter·taste \-₁tāst\ *n* : a sensation (as of flavor) continuing after the stimulus causing it has ended

af·ter–tax \'af-tər-'taks\ *adj* : remaining after payment of taxes and esp. of income tax ⟨an ~ profit⟩

af·ter·thought \-₁thȯt\ *n* : a later thought; *also* : something thought of later

af·ter·ward \-wərd\ *or* **af·ter·wards** \-wərdz\ *adv* : at a later time

Ag *symbol* [L *argentum*] silver

AG *abbr* **1** adjutant general **2** attorney general

again \ə-'gen, -'gin\ *adv* **1** : once more : ANEW **2** : on the other hand **3** : in addition : BESIDES

against \ə-'genst\ *prep* **1** : in opposition to **2** : directly opposite to : FACING **3** : as defense from **4** : so as to touch or strike ⟨threw him ~ the wall⟩; *also* : TOUCHING

¹aga·pe \ä-'gä-pā, 'ä-gə-₁pā\ *n* [Gk, lit., love] : unselfish unconditional love for another

²agape \ə-'gāp\ *adj or adv* : having the mouth open in wonder or surprise : GAPING

agar \'ä-gär\ *n* **1** : a jellylike substance extracted from a red alga and used esp. as a gelling and stabilizing agent in foods **2** : a culture medium containing agar

agar–agar \₁ä-gär-'ä-₁gär\ *n* : AGAR

ag·ate \'a-gət\ *n* **1** : a striped or clouded quartz **2** : a playing marble of agate or of glass

aga·ve \ə-'gä-vē\ *n* : any of a genus of spiny-leaved plants (as a century plant) related to the amaryllis

agcy *abbr* agency

¹age \'āj\ *n* **1** : the length of time during which a being or thing has lived or existed **2** : the time of life at which some particular qualification is achieved; *esp* : MAJORITY **3** : the latter part of life **4** : a long time **5** : a period in history

²age *vb* **aged**; **ag·ing** *or* **age·ing** **1** : to grow old or cause

to grow old **2** : to become or cause to become mature or mellow

-age *n suffix* **1** : aggregate : collection ⟨track*age*⟩ **2** : action : process ⟨haul*age*⟩ **3** : cumulative result of ⟨break*age*⟩ **4** : rate of ⟨dos*age*⟩ **5** : house or place of ⟨orphan*age*⟩ **6** : state : rank ⟨vassal*age*⟩ **7** : fee : charge ⟨post*age*⟩

aged \'ā-jəd *for 1*; 'ājd *for 2*\ *adj* **1** : of advanced age **2** : having attained a specified age ⟨a man ~ 40 years⟩

age·less \'āj-ləs\ *adj* **1** : not growing old or showing the effects of age **2** : TIMELESS, ETERNAL ⟨~ truths⟩

agen·cy \'ā-jən-sē\ *n, pl* **-cies** **1** : one through which something is accomplished : INSTRUMENTALITY **2** : the office or function of an agent **3** : an establishment doing business for another **4** : an administrative division (as of a government) **syn** means, medium, vehicle

agen·da \ə-'jen-də\ *n* : a list of things to be done : PROGRAM

agent \'ā-jənt\ *n* **1** : one that acts **2** : MEANS, INSTRUMENT **3** : a person acting or doing business for another **syn** attorney, deputy, proxy, delegate

Agent Orange *n* : an herbicide widely used in the Vietnam War that is composed of 2,4-D and 2,4,5-T and contains a toxic contaminant

agent pro·vo·ca·teur \'ä-₁zhän-prō-₁vä-kə-'tər, 'ä-jənt-\ *n, pl* **agents provocateurs** \'ä-₁zhän-prō-₁väk-ə-'tər, 'ä-jənts-prō-\ [F] : a person hired to infiltrate a group and incite its members to illegal action

age of consent : the age at which one is legally competent to give consent esp. to marriage or to sexual intercourse

age–old \'āj-'ōld\ *adj* : having existed for ages : ANCIENT

ag·er·a·tum \₁a-jə-'rā-təm\ *n, pl* **-tum** *also* **-tums** : any of a large genus of tropical American plants that are related to the daisies and have small showy heads of blue or white flowers

Ag·ge·us \a-'gē-əs\ *n* : HAGGAI

¹ag·glom·er·ate \ə-'glä-mə-₁rāt\ *vb* **-at·ed; -at·ing** [L *agglomerare* to heap up, join, fr. *ad-* to + *glomer-, glomus* ball] : to gather into a mass : CLUSTER — **ag·glom·er·a·tion** \-₁glä-mə-'rā-shən\ *n*

²ag·glom·er·ate \-rət\ *n* : rock composed of volcanic fragments

ag·glu·ti·nate \ə-'glüt-ᵊn-₁āt\ *vb* **-nat·ed; -nat·ing** **1** : to cause to adhere : gather into a group or mass **2** : to cause (as red blood cells or bacteria) to collect into clumps — **ag·glu·ti·na·tion** \-₁glüt-ᵊn-'ā-shən\ *n*

ag·gran·dize \ə-'gran-₁dīz, 'a-grən-\ *vb* **-dized; -diz·ing** : to make great or greater — **ag·gran·dize·ment** \ə-'gran-dəz-mənt, -₁dīz-; ₁a-grən-'dīz-\ *n*

ag·gra·vate \'a-grə-₁vāt\ *vb* **-vat·ed; -vat·ing** **1** : to make more severe : INTENSIFY **2** : IRRITATE — **ag·gra·va·tion** \₁a-grə-'vā-shən\ *n*

¹ag·gre·gate \'a-gri-gət\ *adj* : formed by the gathering of units into one mass

²ag·gre·gate \-₁gāt\ *vb* **-gat·ed; -gat·ing** : to collect into one mass

³ag·gre·gate \-gət\ *n* : a mass or body of units or parts somewhat loosely associated with one another; *also* : the whole amount

ag·gre·ga·tion \₁a-gri-'gā-shən\ *n* **1** : a group, body, or mass composed of many distinct parts **2** : the collecting of units or parts into a mass or whole

ag·gres·sion \ə-'gre-shən\ *n* **1** : an unprovoked attack **2** : the practice of making attacks **3** : hostile, injurious, or destructive behavior or outlook esp. when caused by frustration — **ag·gres·sor** \-'gre-sər\ *n*

\ə\abut \ᵊ\kitten \ər\further \a\ash \ā\ace \ä\mop, mar \au̇\out \ch\chin \e\bet \ē\easy \g\go \i\hit \ī\ice \j\job \ŋ\sing \ō\go \ȯ\law \ȯi\boy \th\thin \t͟h\the \ü\loot \u̇\foot \y\yet \zh\vision *see also* Pronunciation Symbols page

ag·gres·sive \ə-'gre-siv\ adj 1 : tending toward or exhibiting aggression; *esp* : marked by combative readiness 2 : marked by driving energy or initiative : ENTERPRISING 3 : more intensive or comprehensive esp. in dosage or extent — **ag·gres·sive·ly** adv — **ag·gres·sive·ness** n

ag·grieve \ə-'grēv\ vb **ag·grieved; ag·griev·ing** 1 : to cause grief to 2 : to inflict injury on : WRONG

aghast \ə-'gast\ adj : struck with amazement or horror

ag·ile \'a-jəl\ adj : able to move quickly and easily — **agil·i·ty** \ə-'ji-lə-tē\ n

ag·i·tate \'a-jə-ˌtāt\ vb **-tat·ed; -tat·ing** 1 : to move with an irregular rapid motion 2 : to stir up : EXCITE 3 : to discuss earnestly 4 : to attempt to arouse public feeling — **ag·i·ta·tion** \ˌa-jə-'tā-shən\ n — **ag·i·ta·tor** \'a-jə-ˌtā-tər\ n

ag·it·prop \'a-jət-ˌpräp\ n [Russ] : political propaganda promulgated esp. through the arts

agleam \ə-'glēm\ adj : GLEAMING

aglit·ter \ə-'gli-tər\ adj : GLITTERING

aglow \ə-'glō\ adj : GLOWING

ag·nos·tic \ag-'näs-tik\ adj [Gk *agnōstos* unknown, unknowable, fr. *a-* un- + *gnōstos* known] : of or relating to the belief that the existence of any ultimate reality (as God) is unknown and prob. unknowable — **agnostic** n — **ag·nos·ti·cism** \-'näs-tə-ˌsi-zəm\ n

ago \ə-'gō\ adj or adv : earlier than the present time

agog \ə-'gäg\ adj [MF *en gogues* in mirth] : full of excitement : EAGER

a–go–go \ä-'gō-ˌgō\ adj [*Whisky à Gogo*, café and disco in Paris, France, fr. F *à gogo* galore] : GO-GO

ag·o·nize \'a-gə-ˌnīz\ vb **-nized; -niz·ing** : to suffer or cause to suffer agony — **ag·o·niz·ing·ly** adv

ag·o·ny \'a-gə-nē\ n, pl **-nies** [ME *agonie*, fr. L *agonia*, fr. Gk *agōnia* struggle, anguish, fr. *agōn* gathering, contest for a prize] : extreme pain of mind or body **syn** suffering, distress, misery

ago·ra \ˌä-gə-'rä\ n, pl **ago·rot** \-'rōt\ — see *shekel* at MONEY table

ag·o·ra·pho·bia \ˌa-gə-rə-'fō-bē-ə\ n : abnormal fear of being in a helpless, embarrassing, or inescapable situation characterized esp. by avoidance of open or public places — **ag·o·ra·pho·bic** \-'fō-bik, -'fä-\ adj or n

agr abbr agricultural; agriculture

agrar·i·an \ə-'grer-ē-ən\ adj 1 : of or relating to land or its ownership ⟨∼ reforms⟩ 2 : of or relating to farmers or farming interests — **agrarian** n — **agrar·i·an·ism** n

agree \ə-'grē\ vb **agreed; agree·ing** 1 : ADMIT, CONCEDE 2 : to be similar : CORRESPOND 3 : to express agreement or approval 4 : to be in harmony 5 : to settle by common consent 6 : to be fitting or healthful : SUIT

agree·able \ə-'grē-ə-bəl\ adj 1 : PLEASING, PLEASANT 2 : ready to consent 3 : being in harmony : CONSONANT — **agree·able·ness** n — **agree·ably** \-blē\ adv

agree·ment \ə-'grē-mənt\ n 1 : harmony of opinion or action 2 : mutual understanding or arrangement; *also* : a document containing such an arrangement

ag·ri·busi·ness \'a-grə-ˌbiz-nəs, -nəz\ n : an industry engaged in the manufacture and sale of farm equipment and supplies and in the production, processing, storage, and sale of farm commodities

agric abbr agricultural; agriculture

ag·ri·cul·ture \'a-gri-ˌkəl-chər\ n : FARMING, HUSBANDRY — **ag·ri·cul·tur·al** \ˌa-gri-'kəl-ch(ə-)rəl\ adj — **ag·ri·cul·tur·ist** \-ch(ə-)rist\ or **ag·ri·cul·tur·al·ist** \-ch(ə-)rə-list\ n

agron·o·my \ə-'grä-nə-mē\ n : a branch of agriculture that deals with the raising of crops and the care of the soil — **ag·ro·nom·ic** \ˌa-grə-'nä-mik\ adj — **agron·o·mist** \ə-'grä-nə-mist\ n

aground \ə-'graund\ adv or adj : on or onto the bottom or shore ⟨ran ∼⟩

agt abbr agent

ague \'ā-gyü\ n : a fever (as malaria) with recurrent chills and sweating

ahead \ə-'hed\ adv or adj 1 : in or toward the front 2 : into or for the future ⟨plan ∼⟩ 3 : in or toward a more advantageous position

ahead of prep 1 : in front or advance of 2 : in excess of : ABOVE

AH abbr anno hegirae

AHL abbr American Hockey League

ahoy \ə-'hȯi\ interj — used in hailing ⟨ship ∼⟩

AI abbr artificial intelligence

¹aid \'ād\ vb : to provide with what is useful in achieving an end : ASSIST

²aid n 1 : ASSISTANCE 2 : ASSISTANT

AID abbr Agency for International Development

aide \'ād\ n : a person who acts as an assistant; *esp* : a military officer assisting a superior

aide–de–camp \ˌād-di-'kamp, -'käᵐ\ n, pl **aides–de–camp** \ˌādz-di-\ [F] : AIDE

AIDS \'ādz\ n [acquired *i*mmuno*d*eficiency *s*yndrome] : a serious disease of the human immune system that is caused by infection with HIV, that is characterized by severe reduction in the numbers of helper T cells, that in modern industrialized nations occurs esp. in intravenous users of illicit drugs and in homosexual and bisexual men, and that is transmitted esp. in blood and bodily secretions (as semen)

AIDS–related complex n : a group of symptoms (as fever, weight loss, and lymphadenopathy) that is associated with the presence of antibodies to HIV and is followed by the development of AIDS in a certain proportion of cases

AIDS virus n : HIV

ai·grette \ā-'gret, 'ā-ˌ\ n [F, plume, egret] : a plume or decorative tuft for the head

ail \'āl\ vb 1 : to be the matter with : TROUBLE 2 : to be unwell

ai·lan·thus \ā-'lan-thəs\ n : any of a genus of Asian trees or shrubs with pinnate leaves and ill-scented greenish flowers

ai·le·ron \'ā-lə-ˌrän\ n : a movable part of an airplane wing used in banking

ail·ment \'āl-mənt\ n : a bodily disorder

¹aim \'ām\ vb [ME, fr. MF *aesmer* & *esmer*; MF *aesmer*, fr. OF, fr. *a-* to (fr. L *ad-*) + *esmer* to estimate, fr. L *aestimare*] 1 : to point a weapon at an object 2 : to direct one's efforts : ASPIRE 3 : to direct to or toward a specified object or goal

²aim n 1 : the pointing of a weapon at an object 2 : the ability to hit a target 3 : OBJECT, PURPOSE — **aim·less** \-ləs\ adj — **aim·less·ly** adv — **aim·less·ness** n

AIM abbr American Indian Movement

ain't \'ānt\ 1 : are not 2 : is not 3 : am not — though disapproved by many and more common in less educated speech, used orally in most parts of the U.S. by many educated speakers esp. in the phrase *ain't I*

Ai·nu \'ī-nü\ n, pl **Ainu** or **Ainus** 1 : a member of an indigenous people of northern Japan 2 : the language of the Ainu people

¹air \'ar\ n 1 : the gaseous mixture surrounding the earth 2 : a light breeze 3 : MELODY, TUNE 4 : the outward appearance of a person or thing : MANNER 5 : an artificial manner 6 : COMPRESSED AIR ⟨∼ sprayer⟩ 7 : AIRCRAFT ⟨∼ patrol⟩ 8 : AVIATION ⟨∼ safety⟩ 9 : the medium of transmission of radio waves; *also* : RADIO, TELEVISION

²air vb 1 : to expose to the air 2 : to expose to public view

air bag n : a bag designed to inflate automatically to protect automobile occupants in case of collision

air·boat \'ar-ˌbōt\ n : a shallow-draft boat driven by an airplane propeller

air·borne \-ˌbȯrn\ adj : done or being in the air

air brake n 1 : a brake operated by a piston driven by

compressed air **2** : a surface projected into the airflow to lower an airplane's speed

air·brush \'ar-ˌbrəsh\ *n* : a device for applying a fine spray (as of paint) by compressed air — **airbrush** *vb*

air–con·di·tion \ˌar-kən-ˈdi-shən\ *vb* : to equip with an apparatus for filtering air and controlling its humidity and temperature — **air con·di·tion·er** \-ˈdi-sh(ə-)nər\ *n*

air·craft \'ar-ˌkraft\ *n, pl* **aircraft** : a vehicle for travel-ing through the air

aircraft carrier *n* : a warship with a deck on which air-planes can be launched and landed

air·drop \'ar-ˌdräp\ *n* : delivery of cargo or personnel by parachute from an airplane in flight — **air–drop** *vb*

Aire·dale terrier \'ar-ˌdāl-\ *n* : any of a breed of large terriers with a hard wiry coat

air·fare \'ar-ˌfar\ *n* : fare for travel by airplane

air·field \-ˌfēld\ *n* : AIRPORT

air·flow \-ˌflō\ *n* : the motion of air relative to a body in it

air·foil \-ˌföil\ *n* : an airplane surface designed to pro-duce reaction forces from the air through which it moves

air force *n* : the military organization of a nation for air warfare

air·frame \'ar-ˌfrām\ *n* : the structure of an aircraft, rocket, or missile without the power plant

air·freight \-ˈfrāt\ *n* : freight transport by aircraft in vol-ume; *also* : the charge for this service

air gun *n* **1** : a gun operated by compressed air **2** : a hand tool that works by compressed air; *esp* : AIRBRUSH

air·head \'ar-ˌhed\ *n* : a mindless or stupid person

air lane *n* : AIRWAY 1

air·lift \'ar-ˌlift\ *n* : transportation (as of supplies or passengers) by aircraft — **airlift** *vb*

air·line \-ˌlīn\ *n* : a transportation system using airplanes

air·lin·er \-ˌlī-nər\ *n* : a large passenger airplane oper-ated by an airline

air lock *n* : an airtight chamber separating areas of dif-ferent pressure

air·mail \'ar-ˌmāl\ *n* : the system of transporting mail by aircraft; *also* : mail so transported — **airmail** *vb*

air·man \-mən\ *n* **1** : AVIATOR, PILOT **2** : an enlisted man in the air force in one of the three ranks below sergeant

airman basic *n* : an enlisted man of the lowest rank in the air force

airman first class *n* : an enlisted man in the air force with a rank just below that of sergeant

air mass *n* : a large horizontally homogeneous body of air

air·mo·bile \'ar-ˌmō-bəl, -ˌbēl\ *adj* : of, relating to, or being a military unit whose members are transported to combat areas usu. by helicopter

air·plane \-ˌplān\ *n* : a powered heavier-than-air aircraft that has fixed wings from which it derives lift

air·play \-ˌplā\ *n* : the playing of a musical recording on the air by a radio station

air pocket *n* : a condition of the atmosphere that causes an airplane to drop suddenly

air police *n* : the military police of an air force

air·port \'ar-ˌpōrt\ *n* : a place from which aircraft op-erate that usu. has paved runways and a terminal

air raid *n* : an attack by armed airplanes on a surface target

air·ship \'ar-ˌship\ *n* : a lighter-than-air aircraft having propulsion and steering systems

air·sick \-ˌsik\ *adj* : affected with motion sickness asso-ciated with flying — **air·sick·ness** *n*

air·space \-ˌspās\ *n* : the space above a nation and under its jurisdiction

air·speed \-ˌspēd\ *n* : the speed of an object (as an airplane) with relation to the surrounding air

air·strip \-ˌstrip\ *n* : a runway without normal airport fa-cilities

air·tight \'ar-ˈtīt\ *adj* **1** : so tightly sealed that no air can enter or escape **2** : leaving no opening for attack

air–to–air *adj* : launched from one airplane in flight at another; *also* : involving aircraft in flight

air·waves \'ar-ˌwāvz\ *n pl* : AIR 9

air·way \-ˌwā\ *n* **1** : a regular route for airplanes **2** : AIR-LINE

air·wor·thy \-ˌwər-thē\ *adj* : fit for operation in the air ⟨an ∼ plane⟩ — **air·wor·thi·ness** *n*

airy \'ar-ē\ *adj* **air·i·er; -est** **1** : LOFTY **2** : lacking in re-ality : EMPTY **3** : DELICATE **4** : BREEZY

aisle \'īl\ *n* [ME *ile*, fr. MF *ele* wing, fr. L *ala*] **1** : the side of a church nave separated by piers from the nave proper **2** : a passage between sections of seats

ajar \ə-ˈjär\ *adj or adv* : partly open

AK *abbr* Alaska

aka *abbr* also known as

AKC *abbr* American Kennel Club

akim·bo \ə-ˈkim-bō\ *adj or adv* : having the hand on the hip and the elbow turned outward

akin \ə-ˈkin\ *adj* **1** : related by blood **2** : similar in kind

Al *symbol* aluminum

AL *abbr* **1** Alabama **2** American League **3** American Le-gion

¹-al *adj suffix* : of, relating to, or characterized by ⟨direc-tion*al*⟩

²-al *n suffix* : action : process ⟨rehears*al*⟩

Ala *abbr* Alabama

al·a·bas·ter \'a-lə-ˌbas-tər\ *n* **1** : a compact fine-textured usu. white and translucent gypsum often carved into objects (as vases) **2** : a hard translucent cal-cite

à la carte \ˌa-lə-ˈkärt, ˌä-\ *adv or adj* [F] : with a sep-arate price for each item on the menu

alac·ri·ty \ə-ˈla-krə-tē\ *n* : cheerful readiness : BRISK-NESS

à la mode \ˌa-lə-ˈmōd, ˌä-\ *adj* [F, according to the fash-ion] **1** : FASHIONABLE, STYLISH **2** : topped with ice cream

¹alarm \ə-ˈlärm\ *also* **ala·rum** \ə-ˈlär-əm, -ˈlar-\ *n* [ME *alarme*, fr. MF, fr. OIt *all'arme*, lit., to the weapon] **1** : a warning signal or device **2** : the terror caused by sud-den danger

²alarm *also* **alarum** *vb* **1** : to warn of danger **2** : FRIGHTEN

alarm·ist \ə-ˈlär-mist\ *n* : a person who alarms others esp. needlessly

alas \ə-ˈlas\ *interj* — used to express unhappiness, pity, or concern

al·ba·core \'al-bə-ˌkōr\ *n, pl* **-core** *or* **-cores** : a large tuna that is a source of canned tuna

Al·ba·nian \al-ˈbā-nē-ən\ *n* : a native or inhabitant of Al-bania

al·ba·tross \'al-bə-ˌtròs, -ˌträs\ *n, pl* **-tross** *or* **-tross·es** : any of a family of large web-footed seabirds

al·be·do \al-ˈbē-(ˌ)dō\ *n, pl* **-dos** : the fraction of incident radiation that is reflected by a body or surface

al·be·it \òl-ˈbē-ət, al-\ *conj* : even though : ALTHOUGH

al·bi·no \al-ˈbī-nō\ *n, pl* **-nos** : a person or nonhuman mammal lacking coloring matter in the skin, hair, and eyes — **al·bi·nism** \'al-bə-ˌni-zəm\ *n*

al·bum \'al-bəm\ *n* **1** : a book with blank pages used for making a collection (as of stamps) **2** : one or more re-cordings (as on tape or disk) produced as a single unit

al·bu·men \al-ˈbyü-mən\ *n* **1** : the white of an egg **2** : ALBUMIN

al·bu·min \al-ˈbyü-mən\ *n* : any of numerous water-soluble proteins of blood, milk, egg white, and plant and animal tissues

---

\ə\abut \ˈə\kitten \ər\further \a\ash \ā\ace \ä\mop, mar \au̇\out \ch\chin \e\bet \ē\easy \g\go \i\hit \ī\ice \j\job \ŋ\sing \ō\go \ò\law \ói\boy \th\thin \t̲h̲\the \ü\loot \u̇\foot \y\yet \zh\vision *see also* Pronunciation Symbols page

al·bu·min·ous \al-ᵇbyü-mə-nəs\ *adj* : containing or resembling albumen or albumin

alc *abbr* alcohol

al·cal·de \al-ᵇkäl-dē\ *n* : the chief administrative and judicial officer of a Spanish or Spanish-American town

al·ca·zar \al-ᵇkä-zər, -ᵇka-\ *n* [Sp *alcázar*, fr. Ar *al-qaṣr* the castle] : a Spanish fortress or palace

al·che·my \ᵇal-kə-mē\ *n* : medieval chemistry chiefly concerned with efforts to turn base metals into gold — **al·che·mist** \ᵇal-kə-mist\ *n*

al·co·hol \ᵇal-kə-ˌhȯl\ *n* [NL, fr. ML, powdered antimony, fr. Sp, fr. Ar *al-kuḥul* the powdered antimony] 1 : a colorless flammable liquid that is the intoxicating agent in fermented and distilled liquors 2 : any of various carbon compounds similar to alcohol 3 : beverages containing alcohol

¹**al·co·hol·ic** \ˌal-kə-ᵇhȯ-lik, -ᵇhä-\ *adj* 1 : of, relating to, caused by, or containing alcohol 2 : affected with alcoholism — **al·co·hol·i·cal·ly** \-li-k(ə-)lē\ *adv*

²**alcoholic** *n* : a person affected with alcoholism

al·co·hol·ism \ᵇal-kə-ˌhȯ-ˌli-zəm\ *n* : continued excessive and usu. uncontrollable use of alcoholic drinks; *also* : a complex chronic psychological and nutritional disorder associated with such use

al·cove \ᵇal-ˌkōv\ *n* 1 : a nook or small recess opening off a larger room 2 : a niche or arched opening (as in a wall)

ald *abbr* alderman

al·der \ᵇȯl-dər\ *n* : a tree or shrub related to the birches and growing in wet areas

al·der·man \ᵇȯl-dər-mən\ *n* : a member of a city legislative body

ale \ᵇāl\ *n* : an alcoholic beverage brewed from malt and hops that is usu. more bitter than beer

ale·a·tor·ic \ˌā-lē-ə-ᵇtȯr-ik\ *adj* : characterized by chance or random elements ⟨∼ music⟩

ale·a·to·ry \ᵇā-lē-ə-ˌtȯr-ē\ *adj* : ALEATORIC

alee \ə-ᵇlē\ *adv* : on or toward the lee

ale·house \ᵇāl-ˌhau̇s\ *n* : a place where ale is sold to be drunk on the premises

¹**alert** \ə-ᵇlərt\ *adj* [It *all' erta*, lit., on the ascent] 1 : watchful against danger 2 : quick to perceive and act — **alert·ly** *adv* — **alert·ness** *n*

²**alert** *n* 1 : ALARM 1 2 : the period during which an alert is in effect

³**alert** *vb* 1 : WARN 2 : to make aware of

Aleut \ə-lē-ᵇüt, ə-ᵇlüt\ *n* 1 : a member of a people of the Aleutian and Shumagin islands and the western part of Alaska peninsula 2 : the language of the Aleuts

ale·wife \ᵇāl-ˌwīf\ *n* : a food fish of the herring family abundant esp. on the Atlantic coast

Al·ex·an·dri·an \ˌa-lig-ᵇzan-drē-ən\ *adj* 1 : of or relating to Alexander the Great 2 : HELLENISTIC

al·ex·an·drine \-ᵇzan-drən\ *n, often cap* : a line of six iambic feet

al·fal·fa \al-ᵇfal-fə\ *n* : a leguminous plant widely grown for hay and forage

al·fres·co \al-ᵇfres-kō\ *adj or adv* [It] : taking place in the open air

alg *abbr* algebra

al·ga \ᵇal-gə\ *n, pl* **al·gae** \ᵇal-(ˌ)jē\ : any of a group of lower plants having chlorophyll but no vascular system and including seaweeds and related freshwater plants — **al·gal** \-gəl\ *adj*

al·ge·bra \ᵇal-jə-brə\ *n* [ML, fr. Ar *al-jabr*] : a branch of mathematics using symbols (as letters) to explore the relationships between numbers and the operations used to work with them — **al·ge·bra·ic** \ˌal-jə-ᵇbrā-ik\ *adj* — **al·ge·bra·i·cal·ly** \-ᵇbrā-ə-k(ə-)lē\ *adv*

Al·ge·ri·an \al-ᵇjir-ē-ən\ *n* : a native or inhabitant of Algeria — **Algerian** *adj*

Al·gon·quin \al-ᵇgän-kwən, -ᵇgäŋ-\ *n* : a member of an American Indian people of the Ottawa River valley

al·go·rithm \ᵇal-gə-ˌri-thəm\ *n* : a procedure for solving a problem esp. in mathematics or computing — **al·go·rith·mic** \ˌal-gə-ᵇrith-mik\ *adj* — **al·go·rith·mi·cal·ly** \-mi-k(ə-)lē\ *adv*

¹**alias** \ᵇā-lē-əs, ᵇāl-yəs\ *adv* [L, otherwise, fr. *alius* other] : otherwise called

²**alias** *n* : an assumed name

¹**al·i·bi** \ᵇa-lə-ˌbī\ *n* [L, elsewhere, fr. *alius* other] 1 : a plea offered by an accused person of not having been at the scene of an offense 2 : an excuse (as for failure)

²**alibi** *vb* **-bied; -bi·ing** 1 : to furnish an excuse for 2 : to offer an excuse

¹**alien** \ᵇā-lē-ən, ᵇāl-yən\ *adj* : belonging to another : FOREIGN

²**alien** *n* 1 : a foreign-born resident who has not been naturalized 2 : EXTRATERRESTRIAL

alien·able \ᵇāl-yə-nə-bəl, ᵇā-lē-ə-nə-\ *adj* : transferable to the ownership of another ⟨∼ property⟩

alien·ate \ᵇā-lē-ə-ˌnāt, ᵇāl-yə-\ *vb* **-at·ed; -at·ing** 1 : to make hostile : ESTRANGE 2 : to transfer (property) to another — **alien·ation** \ˌā-lē-ə-ᵇnā-shən, ˌāl-yə-\ *n*

alien·ist \ᵇā-lē-ə-nist, ᵇāl-yə-\ *n* : PSYCHIATRIST

¹**alight** \ə-ᵇlīt\ *vb* **alight·ed** *also* **alit** \ə-ᵇlit\ **alight·ing** 1 : to get down (as from a vehicle) 2 : to come to rest from the air **syn** settle, land, perch

²**alight** *adj* : lighted up

align *also* **aline** \ə-ᵇlīn\ *vb* 1 : to bring into line 2 : to array on the side of or against a cause — **align·er** *n* — **align·ment** *also* **aline·ment** *n*

¹**alike** \ə-ᵇlīk\ *adv* : EQUALLY

²**alike** *adj* : LIKE **syn** akin, analogous, similar, comparable

al·i·ment \ᵇa-lə-mənt\ *n* : NOURISHMENT 1 — **aliment** *vb*

al·i·men·ta·ry \ˌa-lə-ᵇmen-t(ə-)rē\ *adj* : of, relating to, or functioning in nourishment or nutrition

alimentary canal *n* : the tube that extends from the mouth to the anus and functions in the digestion and absorption of food and the elimination of residues

al·i·mo·ny \ᵇa-lə-ˌmō-nē\ *n, pl* **-nies** [L *alimonia* sustenance, fr. *alere* to nourish] : an allowance made to one spouse by the other for support pending or after legal separation or divorce

A–line \ᵇā-ˌlīn\ *adj* : having a flared bottom and a close-fitting top ⟨an ∼ skirt⟩

alive \ə-ᵇlīv\ *adj* 1 : having life 2 : being in force or operation 3 : SENSITIVE ⟨∼ to the danger⟩ 4 : ALERT, BRISK 5 : ANIMATED ⟨streets ∼ with traffic⟩ — **alive·ness** *n*

alk *abbr* alkaline

al·ka·li \ᵇal-kə-ˌlī\ *n, pl* **-lies** *or* **-lis** 1 : a substance (as a hydroxide) that has a bitter taste and neutralizes acids 2 : a mixture of salts in the soil of some dry regions in such amount as to make ordinary farming impossible — **al·ka·line** \-kə-lən, -ˌlīn\ *adj* — **al·ka·lin·i·ty** \ˌal-kə-ᵇli-nə-tē\ *n*

al·ka·loid \ᵇal-kə-ˌlȯid\ *n* : any of various usu. basic and bitter organic compounds found esp. in seed plants

al·kane \ᵇal-ˌkān\ *n* : a hydrocarbon in which each carbon atom is bonded to 4 other atoms

al·kyd \ᵇal-kəd\ *n* : any of numerous synthetic resins used esp. for protective coatings and in paint

¹**all** \ᵇȯl\ *adj* 1 : the whole of 2 : every member of 3 : EVERY ⟨∼ manner of problems⟩ 4 : any whatever ⟨beyond ∼ doubt⟩ 5 : nothing but ⟨∼ ears⟩ 6 : being more than one person or thing ⟨who ∼ is coming⟩

²**all** *adv* 1 : WHOLLY 2 : selected as the best — used in combination ⟨*all*-state champs⟩ 3 : so much ⟨∼ the better for it⟩ 4 : for each side ⟨the score is two ∼⟩

³**all** *pron* 1 : the whole number, quantity, or amount ⟨∼ of it is gone⟩ 2 : EVERYBODY, EVERYTHING ⟨that is ∼⟩

⁴**all** *n* : the whole of one's resources ⟨gave his ∼⟩

Al·lah \ᵇä-lä, ᵇa-; ä-ᵇlä\ *n* [Ar] : GOD 1 — used in Islam

all along *adv* : all the time ⟨knew it *all along*⟩

all–Amer·i·can \ˌȯl-ə-ᵇmer-ə-kən\ *adj* 1 : selected as the best in the U.S. 2 : composed wholly of American elements 3 : typical of the U.S. — **all–American** *n*

all–around \ˌȯl-ə-ˈrau̇nd\ *adj* **1** : considered in all aspects ⟨best ∼ performance⟩ **2** : competent in many fields : VERSATILE ⟨an ∼ athlete⟩

al·lay \ə-ˈlā\ *vb* **1** : ALLEVIATE **2** : CALM **syn** lighten, relieve, ease, assuage

all clear *n* : a signal that a danger has passed

al·lege \ə-ˈlej\ *vb* **al·leged; al·leg·ing 1** : to assert without proof **2** : to offer as a reason — **al·le·ga·tion** \ˌa-li-ˈgā-shən\ *n* — **al·leg·ed·ly** \ə-ˈle-jəd-lē\ *adv*

al·le·giance \ə-ˈlē-jəns\ *n* **1** : loyalty owed by a citizen to a government **2** : loyalty to a person or cause

al·le·go·ry \ˈa-lə-ˌgȯr-ē\ *n, pl* **-ries** : the expression through symbolism of truths or generalizations about human experience — **al·le·gor·i·cal** \ˌa-lə-ˈgȯr-i-kəl\ *adj* — **al·le·gor·i·cal·ly** \-k(ə-)lē\ *adv*

[1]**al·le·gro** \ə-ˈle-grō, -ˈlā-\ *n, pl* **-gros** : an allegro movement

[2]**allegro** *adv or adj* [It, merry] : at a brisk lively tempo — used as a direction in music

al·le·lu·ia \ˌa-lə-ˈlü-yə\ *interj* : HALLELUJAH

Al·len wrench \ˈa-lən-\ *n* [*Allen* Manufacturing Company, Hartford, Conn.] : an L-shaped hexagonal metal bar of which either end fits the socket of a screw or bolt

al·ler·gen \ˈa-lər-jən\ *n* : something that causes allergy — **al·ler·gen·ic** \ˌa-lər-ˈje-nik\ *adj*

al·ler·gist \ˈa-lər-jist\ *n* : a specialist in allergies

al·ler·gy \ˈa-lər-jē\ *n, pl* **-gies** [G *Allergie,* fr. Gk *allos* other + *ergon* work] : exaggerated or abnormal reaction (as by sneezing) to substances or situations harmless to most people — **al·ler·gic** \ə-ˈlər-jik\ *adj*

al·le·vi·ate \ə-ˈlē-vē-ˌāt\ *vb* **-at·ed; -at·ing** : RELIEVE, LESSEN **syn** lighten, mitigate, allay — **al·le·vi·a·tion** \ə-ˌlē-vē-ˈā-shən\ *n*

al·ley \ˈa-lē\ *n, pl* **alleys 1** : a garden or park walk **2** : a place for bowling **3** : a narrow passageway esp. between buildings

al·ley–oop \ˌa-lē-ˈyüp\ *n* : a basketball play in which a player catches a pass above the basket and immediately dunks the ball

al·ley·way \ˈa-lē-ˌwā\ *n* : ALLEY 3

All·hal·lows \ȯl-ˈha-lōz\ *n, pl* **Allhallows** : ALL SAINTS' DAY

al·li·ance \ə-ˈlī-əns\ *n* : a union to promote common interests **syn** league, coalition, confederacy, federation

al·li·ga·tor \ˈa-lə-ˌgā-tər\ *n* [Sp *el lagarto* the lizard] : either of two large short-legged reptiles resembling crocodiles but having a shorter and broader snout

alligator

alligator pear *n* : AVOCADO

al·lit·er·ate \ə-ˈli-tə-ˌrāt\ *vb* **-at·ed; -at·ing 1** : to form an alliteration **2** : to arrange so as to make alliteration

al·lit·er·a·tion \ə-ˌli-tə-ˈrā-shən\ *n* : the repetition of initial sounds in adjacent words or syllables — **al·lit·er·a·tive** \-ˈli-tə-ˌrā-tiv\ *adj*

al·lo·cate \ˈa-lə-ˌkāt\ *vb* **-cat·ed; -cat·ing** : ALLOT, ASSIGN — **al·lo·ca·tion** \ˌa-lə-ˈkā-shən\ *n*

al·lot \ə-ˈlät\ *vb* **al·lot·ted; al·lot·ting** : to distribute as a share **syn** assign, apportion, allocate — **al·lot·ment** *n*

all–out \ˈȯl-ˈau̇t\ *adj* : made with maximum effort

all over *adv* : EVERYWHERE

al·low \ə-ˈlau̇\ *vb* **1** : to assign as a share ⟨∼ time for rest⟩ **2** : to count as a deduction **3** : to make allowance ⟨∼

for expansion⟩ **4** : ADMIT, CONCEDE **5** : PERMIT ⟨∼s the dog to roam⟩ — **al·low·able** *adj*

al·low·ance \-əns\ *n* **1** : an allotted share **2** : money given regularly for expenses **3** : a taking into account of extenuating circumstances

al·loy \ˈa-ˌlȯi, ə-ˈlȯi\ *n* **1** : a substance composed of metals melted together **2** : an admixture that lessens value — **al·loy** \ə-ˈlȯi, ˈa-ˌlȯi\ *vb*

all right *adv* **1** : very well ⟨all right, let's go⟩ **2** : beyond doubt **3** : SATISFACTORILY — **all right** *adj*

All Saints' Day *n* : a Christian feast on November 1 in honor of all the saints

All Souls' Day *n* : a day of prayer observed by some Christian churches on November 2 for the souls of the faithful departed

all·spice \ˈȯl-ˌspīs\ *n* : the berry of a West Indian tree related to the European myrtle; *also* : the mildly pungent and aromatic spice made from it

all–star \ˈȯl-ˌstär\ *n* : a member of a team of star performers — **all–star** *adj*

all told *adv* : with everything counted

al·lude \ə-ˈlüd\ *vb* **al·lud·ed; al·lud·ing** [L *alludere,* lit., to play with] : to refer indirectly — **al·lu·sion** \-ˈlü-zhən\ *n* — **al·lu·sive** \-ˈlü-siv\ *adj* — **al·lu·sive·ly** *adv* — **al·lu·sive·ness** *n*

al·lure \ə-ˈlu̇r\ *vb* **al·lured; al·lur·ing** : CHARM, ENTICE — **allure** *n* — **al·lur·ing·ly** *adv*

al·lu·vi·um \ə-ˈlü-vē-əm\ *n, pl* **-vi·ums** *or* **-via** \-vē-ə\ : soil material (as clay) deposited by running water — **al·lu·vi·al** \-vē-əl\ *adj or n*

al·ly \ə-ˈlī, ˈa-ˌlī\ *vb* **al·lied; al·ly·ing** : to enter into an alliance — **al·ly** \ˈa-ˌlī, ə-ˈlī\ *n*

-ally *adv suffix* : [2]-LY ⟨specifi*cally*⟩

al·ma ma·ter \ˌal-mə-ˈmä-tər\ *n* [L, fostering mother] **1** : an educational institute that one has attended **2** : the song or hymn of an alma mater

al·ma·nac \ˈȯl-mə-ˌnak, ˈal-\ *n* **1** : a publication esp. of astronomical and meteorological data **2** : a usu. annual publication of miscellaneous information

al·man·dite \ˈal-mən-ˌdīt\ *n* : a deep red garnet

al·mighty \ȯl-ˈmī-tē\ *adj* **1** *often cap* : having absolute power over all ⟨*Almighty* God⟩ **2** : relatively unlimited in power — **al·might·i·ness** *n*

Almighty *n* : GOD 1

al·mond \ˈä-mənd, ˈa-; ˈal-\ *n* : a small tree related to the peach; *also* : the edible nutlike kernel of its fruit

al·mo·ner \ˈal-mə-nər, ˈä-mə-\ *n* : a person who distributes alms

al·most \ˈȯl-ˌmōst, ȯl-ˈmōst\ *adv* : very nearly but not exactly

alms \ˈämz, ˈälmz\ *n, pl* **alms** [ME *almesse, almes,* fr. OE *ælmesse, ælms,* fr. L *eleemosyna* alms, fr. Gk *eleēmosynē* pity, alms, fr. *eleēmōn* merciful] : something given freely to relieve the poor

alms·house \-ˌhau̇s\ *n* : POORHOUSE

al·oe \ˈa-lō\ *n* **1** : any of a large genus of succulent chiefly southern African plants related to the lilies **2** *pl* : the dried juice of the leaves of an aloe used esp. formerly as a laxative

aloft \ə-ˈlȯft\ *adv* **1** : high in the air **2** : in flight

alo·ha \ə-ˈlō-ə, ä-ˈlō-hä\ *interj* [Hawaiian] — used to greet or bid farewell

alone \ə-ˈlōn\ *adj* **1** : separated from others **2** : not including anyone or anything else : ONLY **syn** lonely, lonesome, lone, solitary — **alone** *adv*

[1]**along** \ə-ˈlȯŋ\ *prep* **1** : in line with the direction of ⟨sail ∼ the coast⟩ **2** : at a point on or during ⟨stopped ∼ the way⟩

\ə\abut \ᵊ\kitten \ər\further \a\ash \ā\ace \ä\mop, mar \au̇\out \ch\chin \e\bet \ē\easy \g\go \i\hit \ī\ice \j\job \ŋ\sing \ō\go \ȯ\law \ȯi\boy \th\thin \t͟h\the \ü\loot \u̇\foot \y\yet \zh\vision *see also* Pronunciation Symbols page

²**along** *adv* **1** : FORWARD, ON **2** : as a companion ⟨bring her ∼⟩ **3** : at an advanced point ⟨plans are far ∼⟩

along·shore \ə-ˈlȯŋ-ˈshȯr\ *adv or adj* : along the shore or coast

¹**along·side** \-ˌsīd\ *adv* : along or by the side

²**alongside** *prep* **1** : along or by the side of **2** : in association with

alongside of *prep* : ALONGSIDE

aloof \ə-ˈlüf\ *adj* : removed or distant physically or emotionally — **aloof·ness** *n*

al·o·pe·cia \ˌa-lə-ˈpē-sh(ē-)ə\ *n* : BALDNESS

aloud \ə-ˈlau̇d\ *adv* : with a loud voice

alp \ˈalp\ *n* : a high rugged mountain

al·pa·ca \al-ˈpa-kə\ *n* : a domesticated mammal esp. of Peru that is related to the llama; *also* : its woolly hair or cloth made from this

al·pha \ˈal-fə\ *n* **1** : the 1st letter of the Greek alphabet — A or α **2** : something first : BEGINNING

al·pha·bet \ˈal-fə-ˌbet\ *n* : the set of letters or characters used in writing a language

al·pha·bet·i·cal \ˌal-fə-ˈbe-ti-kəl\ *or* **al·pha·bet·ic** \-ˈbe-tik\ *adj* **1** : arranged in the order of the letters of the alphabet **2** : of or employing an alphabet — **al·pha·bet·i·cal·ly** \-ti-k(ə-)lē\ *adv*

al·pha·bet·ize \ˈal-fə-bə-ˌtīz\ *vb* **-ized; -iz·ing** : to arrange in alphabetical order — **al·pha·bet·iz·er** *n*

al·pha·nu·mer·ic \ˌal-fə-nù-ˈmer-ik, -nyù-\ *adj* : consisting of letters and numbers and often other symbols ⟨an ∼ code⟩; *also* : being a character in an alphanumeric system

alpha particle *n* : a positively charged particle identical with the nucleus of a helium atom that is ejected at high speed in certain radioactive transformations

alpha rhythm *n* : ALPHA WAVE

alpha wave *n* : an electrical rhythm of the brain often associated with a state of wakeful relaxation

Al·pine \ˈal-ˌpīn\ *adj* **1** : relating to, located in, or resembling the Alps mountains **2** *often not cap* : of, relating to, or growing on upland slopes above timberline **3** : of or relating to competitive ski events consisting of slalom and downhill racing

al·ready \ȯl-ˈre-dē\ *adv* : by this time : PREVIOUSLY

al·right \ȯl-ˈrīt\ *adv* : ALL RIGHT

al·so \ˈȯl-sō\ *adv* : in addition : TOO

al·so–ran \-ˌran\ *n* **1** : a horse or dog that finishes out of the money in a race **2** : a contestant that does not win

alt *abbr* **1** alternate **2** altitude

Alta *abbr* Alberta

al·tar \ˈȯl-tər\ *n* **1** : a structure on which sacrifices are offered or incense is burned **2** : a table used as a center of ritual or worship

altar boy *n* : a boy who assists the celebrant at a church service

¹**al·ter** \ˈȯl-tər\ *vb* **al·tered; al·ter·ing** \-t(ə-)riŋ\ **1** : to make or become different **2** : CASTRATE, SPAY — **al·ter·a·tion** \ˌȯl-tə-ˈrā-shən\ *n*

²**alter** *abbr* alteration

al·ter·ca·tion \ˌȯl-tər-ˈkā-shən\ *n* : a noisy or angry dispute

al·ter ego \ˌȯl-tər-ˈē-gō\ *n* [L, lit., second I] : a second self; *esp* : a trusted friend

¹**al·ter·nate** \ˈȯl-tər-nət, ˈal-\ *adj* **1** : arranged or succeeding by turns **2** : every other **3** : being an alternative ⟨an ∼ route⟩ — **al·ter·nate·ly** *adv*

²**al·ter·nate** \-ˌnāt\ *vb* **-nat·ed; -nat·ing** : to occur or cause to occur by turns — **al·ter·na·tion** \ˌȯl-tər-ˈnā-shən, ˌal-\ *n*

³**alternate** *n* : SUBSTITUTE

alternating current *n* : an electric current that reverses its direction at regular intervals

al·ter·na·tive \ȯl-ˈtər-nə-tiv, al-\ *adj* : offering a choice — **alternative** *n*

al·ter·na·tor \ˈȯl-tər-ˌnā-tər, ˈal-\ *n* : an electric generator for producing alternating current

al·though *also* **al·tho** \ȯl-ˈthō\ *conj* : in spite of the fact that : even though

al·tim·e·ter \al-ˈti-mə-tər, ˈal-tə-ˌmē-tər\ *n* : an instrument for measuring altitude

al·ti·tude \ˈal-tə-ˌtüd, -ˌtyüd\ *n* **1** : angular distance above the horizon **2** : vertical distance : HEIGHT **3** : the perpendicular distance in a geometric figure from the vertex to the base, from the vertex of an angle to the side opposite, or from the base to a parallel side or face

al·to \ˈal-tō\ *n, pl* **altos** [It, lit., high, fr. L *altus*] : the lower female voice part in a 4-part chorus; *also* : a singer having this voice or part

¹**al·to·geth·er** \ˌȯl-tə-ˈge-thər\ *adv* **1** : WHOLLY **2** : in all **3** : on the whole

²**altogether** *n* : NUDE ⟨posed in the ∼⟩

al·tru·ism \ˈal-trü-ˌi-zəm\ *n* : unselfish interest in the welfare of others — **al·tru·ist** \-ist\ *n* — **al·tru·is·tic** \ˌal-trü-ˈis-tik\ *adj* — **al·tru·is·ti·cal·ly** \-ti-k(ə-)lē\ *adv*

al·um \ˈa-ləm\ *n* : either of two colorless crystalline aluminum-containing compounds used esp. as an emetic or as an astringent and styptic

alu·mi·na \ə-ˈlü-mə-nə\ *n* : the oxide of aluminum occurring in nature as corundum and in bauxite

al·u·min·i·um \ˌal-yə-ˈmi-nē-əm\ *n, chiefly Brit* : ALUMINUM

alu·mi·nize \ə-ˈlü-mə-ˌnīz\ *vb* **-nized; -niz·ing** : to treat with aluminum

alu·mi·num \ə-ˈlü-mə-nəm\ *n* : a silver-white malleable ductile light metallic element that is the most abundant metal in the earth's crust — see ELEMENT table

alum·na \ə-ˈləm-nə\ *n, pl* **-nae** \-(ˌ)nē\ : a woman graduate or former student of a college or school

alum·nus \ə-ˈləm-nəs\ *n, pl* **-ni** \-ˌnī\ [L, foster son, pupil, fr. *alere* to nourish] : a graduate or former student of a college or school

al·ways \ˈȯl-wēz, -wəz, -(ˌ)wāz\ *adv* **1** : at all times : INVARIABLY **2** : FOREVER

Alz·hei·mer's disease \ˈälts-ˌhī-mərz-, ˈalts-\ *n* : a degenerative disease of the central nervous system characterized esp. by premature senile mental deterioration

am *pres 1st sing of* BE

¹**Am** *abbr* America; American

²**Am** *symbol* americium

¹**AM** \ˈā-ˌem\ *n* : a broadcasting system using amplitude modulation; *also* : a radio receiver for broadcasts made by such a system

²**AM** *abbr* **1** ante meridiem — often not cap. and often punctuated **2** [NL *artium magister*] master of arts

AMA *abbr* American Medical Association

amah \ˈä-(ˌ)mä\ *n* : an Oriental female servant; *esp* : a Chinese nursemaid

amain \ə-ˈmān\ *adv, archaic* : with full force or speed

amal·gam \ə-ˈmal-gəm\ *n* **1** : an alloy of mercury with another metal used in making dental cements **2** : a mixture of different elements

amal·gam·ate \ə-ˈmal-gə-ˌmāt\ *vb* **-at·ed; -at·ing** : to unite or merge into one body — **amal·ga·ma·tion** \-ˌmal-gə-ˈmā-shən\ *n*

aman·u·en·sis \ə-ˌman-yə-ˈwen-səs\ *n, pl* **-en·ses** \-ˌsēz\ : one employed to write from dictation or to copy what another has written : SECRETARY

am·a·ranth \ˈa-mə-ˌranth\ *n* **1** : any of a large genus of coarse herbs sometimes grown for their showy flowers **2** : a flower that never fades

am·a·ran·thine \ˌa-mə-ˈran-thən, -ˌthīn\ *adj* **1** : relating to or resembling an amaranth **2** : UNDYING

am·a·ryl·lis \ˌa-mə-ˈri-ləs\ *n* : any of various plants related to the lilies; *esp* : any of several African herbs having bulbs and grown for their clusters of large showy flowers

amass \ə-'mas\ *vb* : ACCUMULATE

am·a·teur \'a-mə-(ˌ)tər, -ˌtůr, -ˌtyůr, -ˌchůr, -chər\ *n* [F, fr. L *amator* lover, fr. *amare* to love] **1** : a person who engages in a pursuit for pleasure and not as a profession **2** : a person who is not expert — **am·a·teur·ish** \ˌa-mə-'tər-ish, -ˌtůr-, -ˌtyůr-, -ˌchůr-, -ˌchər-\ *adj* — **am·a·teur·ism** \'a-mə-(ˌ)tər-i-ˌzəm, -ˌtůr-, -ˌtyůr-, -ˌchůr-, -ˌchər-\ *n*

am·a·tive \'a-mə-tiv\ *adj* : indicative of love : AMOROUS — **am·a·tive·ly** *adv* — **am·a·tive·ness** *n*

am·a·to·ry \'a-mə-ˌtōr-ē\ *adj* : of or expressing sexual love

amaze \ə-'māz\ *vb* **amazed; amaz·ing** : to fill with wonder : ASTOUND **syn** astonish, surprise, dumbfound — **amaze·ment** *n* — **amaz·ing·ly** *adv*

am·a·zon \'a-mə-ˌzän, -zən\ *n* **1** *cap* : a member of a race of female warriors of Greek mythology **2** : a tall strong often masculine woman — **am·a·zo·ni·an** \ˌa-mə-'zō-nē-ən\ *adj, often cap*

amb *abbr* ambassador

am·bas·sa·dor \am-'ba-sə-dər\ *n* : a representative esp. of a government — **am·bas·sa·do·ri·al** \-ˌba-sə-'dōr-ē-əl\ *adj* — **am·bas·sa·dor·ship** *n*

am·ber \'am-bər\ *n* : a yellowish or brownish fossil resin used esp. for ornamental objects; *also* : the color of this resin

am·ber·gris \'am-bər-ˌgris, -ˌgrēs\ *n* : a waxy substance from the sperm whale used in making perfumes

am·bi·dex·trous \ˌam-bi-'dek-strəs\ *adj* : using both hands with equal ease — **am·bi·dex·trous·ly** *adv*

am·bi·ence *or* **am·bi·ance** \'am-bē-əns, än-'byäⁿs\ *n* : a pervading atmosphere

am·bi·ent \'am-bē-ənt\ *adj* : existing on all sides

am·big·u·ous \am-'bi-gyə-wəs\ *adj* : capable of being understood in more than one way — **am·bi·gu·i·ty** \ˌam-bə-'gyü-ə-tē\ *n* — **am·big·u·ous·ly** *adv*

am·bi·tion \am-'bi-shən\ *n* [ME, fr. MF or L; MF, fr. L *ambition-, ambitio*, lit., act of soliciting for votes, fr. *ambire* to go around] : eager desire for success or power

am·bi·tious \-shəs\ *adj* : characterized by ambition — **am·bi·tious·ly** *adv*

am·biv·a·lence \am-'bi-və-ləns\ *n* : simultaneous attraction toward and repulsion from a person, object, or action — **am·biv·a·lent** \-lənt\ *adj*

¹am·ble \'am-bəl\ *vb* **am·bled; am·bling** \-b(ə-)liŋ\ : to go at an amble

²amble *n* : an easy gait esp. of a horse

am·bro·sia \am-'brō-zh(ē-)ə\ *n* : the food of the Greek and Roman gods — **am·bro·sial** \-zh(ē-)əl\ *adj*

am·bu·lance \'am-byə-ləns\ *n* : a vehicle equipped for carrying the injured or sick

am·bu·lant \'am-byə-lənt\ *adj* : AMBULATORY

¹am·bu·la·to·ry \'am-byə-lə-ˌtōr-ē\ *adj* **1** : of, relating to, or adapted to walking **2** : able to walk or move about

²ambulatory *n, pl* **-ries** : a sheltered place (as in a cloister) for walking

am·bus·cade \'am-bə-ˌskād\ *n* : AMBUSH

am·bush \'am-ˌbůsh\ *n* : a trap in which concealed persons wait to attack by surprise — **ambush** *vb*

amdt *abbr* amendment

ame·ba, ame·boid *var of* AMOEBA, AMOEBOID

ame·lio·rate \ə-'mēl-yə-ˌrāt\ *vb* **-rat·ed; -rat·ing** : to make or grow better : IMPROVE — **ame·lio·ra·tion** \-ˌmēl-yə-'rā-shən\ *n*

amen \(ˌ)ā-'men, (ˌ)ä-\ *interj* — used esp. at the end of prayers to affirm or express approval

ame·na·ble \ə-'mē-nə-bəl, -'me-\ *adj* **1** : ANSWERABLE **2** : COMPLIANT

amend \ə-'mend\ *vb* **1** : to change for the better : IMPROVE **2** : to alter formally in phraseology — **amend·able** \-'men-də-bəl\ *adj*

amend·ment \ə-'mend-mənt\ *n* **1** : correction of faults **2** : the process of amending a parliamentary motion or a constitution; *also* : the alteration so proposed or made

amends \ə-'mendz\ *n sing or pl* : compensation for injury or loss

ame·ni·ty \ə-'me-nə-tē, -'mē-\ *n, pl* **-ties 1** : AGREEABLENESS **2** : a gesture observed in social relationships **3** : something that serves as a comfort or convenience

Amer *abbr* America; American

amerce \ə-'mərs\ *vb* **amerced; amerc·ing 1** : to penalize by a fine determined by the court **2** : PUNISH — **amerce·ment** *n*

Amer·i·can \ə-'mer-ə-kən\ *n* **1** : a native or inhabitant of No. or So. America **2** : a citizen of the U.S. — **American** *adj* — **Amer·i·can·ism** \-ə-kə-ˌni-zəm\ *n* — **Amer·i·can·iza·tion** \ə-ˌmer-ə-kə-nə-'zā-shən\ *n* — **Amer·i·can·ize** \ə-'mer-ə-kə-ˌnīz\ *vb* — **Amer·i·can·ness** *n*

Amer·i·ca·na \ə-ˌmer-ə-'ka-nə, -'kä-\ *n pl* : materials concerning or characteristic of America, its civilization, or its culture

American Indian *n* : a member of any of the aboriginal peoples of No. and So. America except the Eskimos

American plan *n* : a hotel plan whereby the daily rates cover the cost of room and three meals

American Sign Language *n* : a sign language for the deaf in which meaning is conveyed by a system of hand gestures and placement

am·er·i·ci·um \ˌam-ə-'rish-ē-əm, -'ris-\ *n* : a radioactive metallic chemical element produced artificially from plutonium — see ELEMENT table

AmerInd *abbr* American Indian

Am·er·in·di·an \ˌa-mə-'rin-dē-ən\ *n* : AMERICAN INDIAN — **Amerindian** *adj*

am·e·thyst \'a-mə-thəst\ *n* [ME *amatiste*, fr. OF & L; OF, fr. L *amethystus*, fr. Gk *amethystos*, lit., remedy against drunkenness, fr. *a-* not + *methyein* to be drunk, fr. *methy* wine] : a gemstone consisting of clear purple or bluish violet quartz

ami·a·ble \'ā-mē-ə-bəl\ *adj* **1** : AGREEABLE **2** : having a friendly and sociable disposition — **ami·a·bil·i·ty** \ˌā-mē-ə-'bi-lə-tē\ *n* — **ami·a·ble·ness** *n* — **ami·a·bly** \'ā-mē-ə-blē\ *adv*

am·i·ca·ble \'a-mi-kə-bəl\ *adj* : FRIENDLY, PEACEABLE — **am·i·ca·bil·i·ty** \ˌa-mi-kə-'bi-lə-tē\ *n* — **am·i·ca·bly** \'a-mi-kə-blē\ *adv*

amid \ə-'mid\ *or* **amidst** \-'midst\ *prep* : in or into the middle of : AMONG

amid·ships \ə-'mid-ˌships\ *adv* : in or near the middle of a ship

ami·no acid \ə-'mē-nō-\ *n* : any of numerous nitrogen-containing acids that include some which are used by cells to build proteins

¹amiss \ə-'mis\ *adv* **1** : WRONGLY **2** : ASTRAY **3** : IMPERFECTLY

²amiss *adj* **1** : WRONG **2** : out of place

am·i·ty \'a-mə-tē\ *n, pl* **-ties** : FRIENDSHIP; *esp* : friendly relations between nations

am·me·ter \'a-ˌmē-tər\ *n* : an instrument for measuring electric current in amperes

am·mo \'a-mō\ *n* : AMMUNITION

am·mo·nia \ə-'mō-nyə\ *n* [NL, fr. L *sal ammoniacus* sal ammoniac (ammonium chloride), lit., salt of Ammon, fr. Gk *ammōniakos* of Ammon, fr. *Ammōn* Ammon, Amen, an Egyptian god near one of whose temples it was prepared] **1** : a colorless gaseous compound of nitrogen and hydrogen used in refrigeration and in the making of fertilizers and explosives **2** : a solution (**ammonia water**) of ammonia in water

am·mo·ni·um \ə-'mō-nē-əm\ *n* : an ion or chemical

\ə\abut \ᵊ\kitten \ər\further \a\ash \ā\ace \ä\mop, mar \aů\out \ch\chin \e\bet \ē\easy \g\go \i\hit \ī\ice \j\job \ŋ\sing \ō\go \ȯ\law \ȯi\boy \th\thin \t̲h̲\the \ü\loot \ů\foot \y\yet \zh\vision   *see also* Pronunciation Symbols page

group derived from ammonia by combination with hydrogen

ammonium chloride *n* : a white crystalline volatile salt used in batteries and as an expectorant

am·mu·ni·tion \,am-yə-'ni-shən\ *n* **1** : projectiles fired from guns **2** : explosive items used in war **3** : material for use in attack or defense

Amn *abbr* airman

am·ne·sia \am-'nē-zhə\ *n* **1** : abnormal loss of memory **2** : the selective overlooking of events or acts not favorable to one's purpose — **am·ne·si·ac** \-zhē-,ak, -zē-\ *or* **am·ne·sic** \-zik, -sik\ *adj or n*

am·nes·ty \'am-nə-stē\ *n, pl* **-ties** : an act granting a pardon to a group of individuals — **amnesty** *vb*

am·nio·cen·te·sis \,am-nē-ō-,sen-'tē-səs\ *n, pl* **-te·ses** \-,sēz\ : the surgical insertion of a hollow needle through the abdominal wall and uterus of a pregnant female esp. to obtain fluid used to check the fetus for chromosomal abnormality and to determine sex

amoe·ba \ə-'mē-bə\ *n, pl* **-bas** *or* **-bae** \-(,)bē\ : any of various tiny one-celled protozoans that lack permanent cell organs and occur esp. in water and soil — **amoe·bic** \-bik\ *adj*

amoe·boid \-,bȯid\ *adj* : resembling an amoeba esp. in moving or readily changing shape

amok \ə-'mək, -'mäk\ *or* **amuck** \-'mək\ *adv* : in a violent, frenzied, or uncontrolled manner ⟨run ∼⟩

among \ə-'məŋ\ *also* **amongst** \-'məŋst\ *prep* **1** : in or through the midst of **2** : in the number, class, or company of **3** : in shares to each of **4** : by common action of

amon·til·la·do \ə-,män-tə-'lä-dō\ *n, pl* **-dos** [Sp] : a medium dry sherry

amor·al \ā-'mȯr-əl\ *adj* **1** : neither moral nor immoral; *esp* : being outside the sphere to which moral judgments apply **2** : lacking moral sensibility — **amor·al·ly** *adv*

am·o·rous \'a-mə-rəs\ *adj* **1** : inclined to love **2** : being in love **3** : of or indicative of love — **am·o·rous·ly** *adv* — **am·o·rous·ness** *n*

amor·phous \ə-'mȯr-fəs\ *adj* **1** : SHAPELESS, FORMLESS **2** : not crystallized

am·or·tize \'a-mər-,tīz, ə-'mȯr-\ *vb* **-tized; -tiz·ing** : to extinguish (as a mortgage) usu. by payment on the principal at the time of each periodic interest payment — **amor·ti·za·tion** \,a-mər-tə-'zā-shən, ə-,mȯr-\ *n*

Amos \'ā-məs\ — see BIBLE table

¹amount \ə-'maůnt\ *vb* **1** : to be equivalent **2** : to reach a total : add up

²amount *n* **1** : the total number or quantity **2** : a principal sum plus the interest on it

amour \ə-'műr, ä-, a-\ *n* **1** : a love affair esp. when illicit **2** : LOVER

amour pro·pre \,a-,műr-'prōprᵊ, ,ä-, -'prȯprᵊ\ *n* [F] : SELF-ESTEEM

¹amp \'amp\ *n* : AMPLIFIER; *also* : a unit consisting of an electronic amplifier and a loudspeaker

²amp *abbr* ampere

am·per·age \'am-p(ə-)rij\ *n* : the strength of a current of electricity expressed in amperes

am·pere \'am-,pir\ *n* : a unit of electric current equivalent to a steady current produced by one volt applied across a resistance of one ohm

am·per·sand \'am-pər-,sand\ *n* [alter. of *and per se and*, spoken form of the phrase & *per se and*, lit., (the character) & by itself (stands for the word) *and*] : a character & used for the word *and*

am·phet·amine \am-'fe-tə-,mēn, -mən\ *n* : a compound or one of its derivatives that stimulates the central nervous system and is used esp. to treat hyperactive children and to suppress appetite

am·phib·i·an \am-'fi-bē-ən\ *n* **1** : an amphibious organism; *esp* : any of a class of animals (as frogs and salamanders) intermediate between fishes and reptiles **2** : an airplane that can land on and take off from either land or water

am·phib·i·ous \am-'fi-bē-əs\ *adj* [Gk *amphibios,* lit., living a double life, fr. *amphi-* on both sides + *bios* mode of life] **1** : able to live both on land and in water **2** : adapted for both land and water **3** : made by joint action of land, sea, and air forces invading from the sea; *also* : trained for such action

am·phi·bole \'am-fə-,bōl\ *n* : any of a group of rock-forming minerals of similar crystal structure

am·phi·the·ater \'am-fə-,thē-ə-tər\ *n* **1** : an oval or circular structure with rising tiers of seats around an arena **2** : a very large auditorium

am·pho·ra \'am-fə-rə\ *n, pl* **-rae** \-,rē\ *or* **-ras** : an ancient Greek jar or vase with two handles that rise almost to the level of the mouth

am·ple \'am-pəl\ *adj* **am·pler** \-plər\ **am·plest** \-pləst\ **1** : LARGE, CAPACIOUS **2** : enough to satisfy : ABUNDANT — **am·ply** \-plē\ *adv*

am·pli·fy \'am-plə-,fī\ *vb* **-fied; -fy·ing 1** : to expand by extended treatment **2** : to increase in magnitude or strength; *esp* : to make louder — **am·pli·fi·ca·tion** \,am-plə-fə-'kā-shən\ *n* — **am·pli·fi·er** \'am-plə-,fī-(-ə)r\ *n*

am·pli·tude \-,tüd, -,tyüd\ *n* **1** : ample extent : FULLNESS **2** : the extent of a vibratory movement (as of a pendulum) or of an oscillation (as of an alternating current or a radio wave)

amplitude modulation *n* : modulation of the amplitude of a radio carrier wave in accordance with the strength of the signal; *also* : a broadcasting system using such modulation

am·poule *or* **am·pule** *also* **am·pul** \'am-,pyül, -,pül\ *n* : a small sealed bulbous glass vessel used to hold a solution for hypodermic injection

am·pu·tate \'am-pyə-,tāt\ *vb* **-tat·ed; -tat·ing** : to cut off ⟨∼ a leg⟩ — **am·pu·ta·tion** \,am-pyə-'tā-shən\ *n*

am·pu·tee \,am-pyə-'tē\ *n* : one who has had a limb amputated

AMSLAN *abbr* American Sign Language

amt *abbr* amount

amuck \ə-'mək\ *var of* AMOK

am·u·let \'am-yə-lət\ *n* : an ornament worn as a charm against evil

amuse \ə-'myüz\ *vb* **amused; amus·ing** : to entertain in a light or playful manner : DIVERT — **amuse·ment** *n*

AM·VETS \'am-,vets\ *abbr* American Veterans (of World War II)

am·y·lase \'a-mə-,lās, -,lāz\ *n* : any of several enzymes that accelerate the breakdown of starch and glycogen

an \ən, (')an\ *indefinite article* : A — used before words beginning with a vowel sound

¹-an *or* **-ian** *also* **-ean** *n suffix* **1** : one that belongs to ⟨Americ*an*⟩ ⟨crustac*ean*⟩ **2** : one skilled in or specializing in ⟨phonetic*ian*⟩

²-an *or* **-ian** *also* **-ean** *adj suffix* **1** : of or belonging to ⟨Americ*an*⟩ **2** : characteristic of : resembling ⟨Mozarte*an*⟩

AN *abbr* airman (Navy)

an·a·bol·ic steroid \,a-nə-'bä-lik-\ *n* : any of a group of synthetic steroid hormones sometimes abused by athletes in training to increase temporarily the size of their muscles

anach·ro·nism \ə-'na-krə-,ni-zəm\ *n* **1** : the error of placing a person or thing in the wrong period **2** : one that is chronologically out of place — **anach·ro·nis·tic** \ə-,na-krə-'nis-tik\ *adj* — **anach·ro·nous** \-'na-krə-nəs\ *adj*

an·a·con·da \,a-nə-'kän-də\ *n* : a large So. American snake that suffocates and kills its prey by constriction

anae·mia, anae·mic *chiefly Brit var of* ANEMIA, ANEMIC

an·aer·obe \'a-nə-,rōb\ *n* : an anaerobic organism

an·aer·o·bic \ˌa-nə-ˈrō-bik\ adj : living, active, occurring, or existing in the absence of free oxygen

an·aes·the·sia, an·aes·thet·ic chiefly Brit var of ANESTHESIA, ANESTHETIC

ana·gram \ˈa-nə-ˌgram\ n : a word or phrase made by transposing the letters of another word or phrase

¹**anal** \ˈān-ᵊl\ adj 1 : of, relating to, or situated near the anus 2 : of, relating to, or characterized by the stage of psychosexual development in psychoanalytic theory during which one is concerned esp. with feces 3 : of, relating to, or characterized by personality traits (as parsimony and ill humor) considered typical of fixation at the anal stage of development — **anal·ly** adv

²**anal** abbr 1 analogy 2 analysis; analytic

an·al·ge·sia \ˌan-ᵊl-ˈjē-zhə\ n : insensibility to pain — **an·al·ge·sic** \-ˈjē-zik, -sik\ adj

an·al·ge·sic \-ˈjē-zik, -sik\ n : an agent for producing analgesia

analog computer \ˈan-ᵊl-ˌȯg, -ˌäg-\ n : a computer that operates with numbers represented by directly measurable quantities (as voltages)

anal·o·gous \ə-ˈna-lə-gəs\ adj : similar in one or more respects

an·a·logue or **an·a·log** \ˈan-ᵊl-ˌȯg, -ˌag\ n 1 : something that is analogous to something else 2 : an organ similar in function to one of another animal or plant but different in structure or origin

anal·o·gy \ə-ˈna-lə-jē\ n, pl **-gies** 1 : inference that if two or more things agree in some respects they will probably agree in others 2 : a likeness in one or more ways between things otherwise unlike — **an·a·log·i·cal** \ˌan-ᵊl-ˈä-ji-kəl\ adj — **an·a·log·i·cal·ly** \-k(ə-)lē\ adv

an·a·lyse chiefly Brit var of ANALYZE

anal·y·sis \ə-ˈna-lə-səs\ n, pl **-y·ses** \-ˌsēz\ [NL, fr. Gk, fr. analyein to break up, fr. ana- up + lyein to loosen] 1 : separation of a thing into the parts or elements of which it is composed 2 : an examination of a thing to determine its parts or elements; also : a statement showing the results of such an examination 3 : PSYCHOANALYSIS — **an·a·lyst** \ˈan-ᵊl-ist\ n — **an·a·lyt·ic** \ˌan-ᵊl-ˈi-tik\ or **an·a·lyt·i·cal** \-ti-kəl\ adj — **an·a·lyt·i·cal·ly** adv

an·a·lyze \ˈan-ᵊl-ˌīz\ vb **-lyzed; -lyz·ing** : to make an analysis of

an·a·pest \ˈa-nə-ˌpest\ n : a metrical foot of two unaccented syllables followed by one accented syllable — **an·a·pes·tic** \ˌa-nə-ˈpes-tik\ adj or n

an·ar·chism \ˈa-nər-ˌki-zəm\ n : the theory that all government is undesirable — **an·ar·chist** \-kist\ n or adj — **an·ar·chis·tic** \ˌa-nər-ˈkis-tik\ adj

an·ar·chy \ˈan-ər-kē\ n 1 : a social structure without government or law and order 2 : utter confusion — **an·ar·chic** \a-ˈnär-kik\ adj — **an·ar·chi·cal·ly** \-ki-k(ə-)lē\ adv

anas·to·mo·sis \ə-ˌnas-tə-ˈmō-səs\ n, pl **-mo·ses** \-ˌsēz\ 1 : the union of parts or branches (as of blood vessels) 2 : NETWORK

anat abbr anatomical; anatomy

anath·e·ma \ə-ˈna-thə-mə\ n 1 : a solemn curse 2 : a person or thing accursed; also : one intensely disliked

anath·e·ma·tize \-ˌtīz\ vb **-tized; -tiz·ing** : to pronounce an anathema against : CURSE

anat·o·mize \ə-ˈna-tə-ˌmīz\ vb **-mized; -miz·ing** : to dissect so as to examine the structure and parts; also : ANALYZE

anat·o·my \ə-ˈna-tə-mē\ n, pl **-mies** [LL anatomia dissection, fr. Gk anatomē, fr. anatemnein to dissect, fr. ana- up + temnein to cut] 1 : a branch of science dealing with the structure of organisms 2 : structural makeup esp. of an organism or any of its parts 3 : a separating into parts for detailed study : ANALYSIS — **an·a·tom·ic** \ˌa-nə-ˈtä-mik\ or **an·a·tom·i·cal** \-mi-kəl\

adj — **an·a·tom·i·cal·ly** \-mi-k(ə-)lē\ adv — **anat·o·mist** \ə-ˈna-tə-mist\ n

anc abbr ancient

-ance n suffix 1 : action or process ⟨furtherance⟩ : instance of an action or process ⟨performance⟩ 2 : quality or state : instance of a quality or state ⟨protuberance⟩ 3 : amount or degree ⟨conductance⟩

an·ces·tor \ˈan-ˌses-tər\ n [ME ancestre, fr. OF, fr. L antecessor predecessor, fr. antecedere to go before, fr. ante- before + cedere to go] : one from whom an individual is descended

an·ces·tress \ˈan-ˌses-trəs\ n : a female ancestor

an·ces·try \ˈan-ˌses-trē\ n 1 : line of descent : LINEAGE 2 : ANCESTORS — **an·ces·tral** \an-ˈses-trəl\ adj

¹**an·chor** \ˈaŋ-kər\ n 1 : a heavy metal device attached to a ship that catches hold of the bottom and holds the ship in place 2 : ANCHORPERSON

²**anchor** vb : to hold or become held in place by or as if by an anchor

an·chor·age \ˈaŋ-k(ə-)rij\ n : a place suitable for ships to anchor

an·cho·rite \ˈaŋ-kə-ˌrīt\ n : HERMIT

an·chor·man \ˈaŋ-kər-ˌman\ n 1 : the member of a team who competes last 2 : an anchorperson who is a man

an·chor·per·son \-ˌpər-sən\ n : a broadcaster who reads the news and introduces the reports of other broadcasters

an·chor·wom·an \-ˌwu̇-mən\ n 1 : a woman who competes last 2 : an anchorperson who is a woman

an·cho·vy \ˈan-ˌchō-vē, an-ˈchō-\ n, pl **-vies** or **-vy** : a small herringlike fish used esp. for sauces and relishes

an·cien ré·gime \äⁿs-yaⁿ-rā-ˈzhēm\ n 1 : the political and social system of France before the Revolution of 1789 2 : a system no longer prevailing

¹**an·cient** \ˈān-shənt\ adj 1 : having existed for many years 2 : belonging to times long past; esp : belonging to the period before the Middle Ages

²**ancient** n 1 : an aged person 2 pl : the peoples of ancient Greece and Rome; esp : the classical authors of Greece and Rome

an·cil·lary \ˈan-sə-ˌler-ē\ adj 1 : SUBORDINATE, SUBSIDIARY 2 : AUXILIARY, SUPPLEMENTARY — **ancillary** n

-ancy n suffix : quality or state ⟨flamboyancy⟩

and \ənd, (ˈ)and\ conj 1 — used to indicate connection or addition esp. of items within the same class or type or to join words or phrases of the same grammatical rank or function 2 — used to join one finite verb to another so that together they are equivalent to an infinitive of purpose ⟨come ~ see me⟩

¹**an·dan·te** \än-ˈdän-ˌtā, -ˌtē\ adv or adj [It, lit., going, prp. of andare to go] : moderately slow — used as a direction in music

²**andante** n : an andante movement

and·iron \ˈan-ˌdī(-ə)rn\ n : one of a pair of metal supports for firewood in a fireplace

and/or \ˈand-ˈȯr\ conj — used to indicate that either and or or may apply ⟨men ~ women means men and women or men or women⟩

An·dor·ran \an-ˈdȯr-ən\ n : a native or inhabitant of Andorra

an·dro·gen \ˈan-drə-jən\ n : a male sex hormone

an·drog·y·nous \an-ˈdrä-jə-nəs\ adj 1 : having the characteristics of both male and female 2 : suitable for either sex ⟨~ clothing⟩

an·droid \ˈan-ˌdrȯid\ n : a mobile robot usu. with a human form

an·ec·dot·al \ˌa-nik-ˈdōt-ᵊl\ adj 1 : relating to or consisting of anecdotes **2** : based on reports of an unscientific nature — **an·ec·dot·al·ly** *adv*

an·ec·dote \'an-ik-ˌdōt\ *n*, *pl* **-dotes** *also* **-dota** \ə-nik-'dō-tə\ [F, fr. Gk *anekdota* unpublished items, fr. *a-* not + *ekdidonai* to publish] : a brief story of an interesting, amusing, or biographical incident

ane·mia \ə-'nē-mē-ə\ *n* **1** : a condition in which blood is deficient in quantity, in red blood cells, or in hemoglobin and which is marked by pallor, weakness, and irregular heart action **2** : lack of vitality — **ane·mic** \ə-'nē-mik\ *adj*

an·e·mom·e·ter \ˌa-nə-'mä-mə-tər\ *n* : an instrument for measuring the force or speed of the wind

anem·o·ne \ə-'ne-mə-nē\ *n* : any of a large genus of herbs related to the buttercups that have showy flowers without petals but with conspicuous often colored sepals

anent \ə-'nent\ *prep* : CONCERNING

an·es·the·sia \ˌa-nəs-'thē-zhə\ *n* : loss of bodily sensation

an·es·the·si·ol·o·gy \-ˌthē-zē-'ä-lə-jē\ *n* : a branch of medical science dealing with anesthesia and anesthetics — **an·es·the·si·ol·o·gist** \-jist\ *n*

¹an·es·thet·ic \ˌa-nəs-'the-tik\ *adj* : of, relating to, or capable of producing anesthesia

²anesthetic *n* : an agent that produces anesthesia — **anes·the·tist** \ə-'nes-thə-tist\ *n* — **anes·the·tize** \-thə-ˌtīz\ *vb*

anew \ə-'nü, -'nyü\ *adv* **1** : over again **2** : in a new form

an·gel \'ān-jəl\ *n* [ME, fr. OF *angele*, fr. L *angelus*, fr. Gk *angelos*, lit., messenger] **1** : a spiritual being superior to man **2** : an attendant spirit **3** : a winged figure of human form in art **4** : MESSENGER, HARBINGER **5** : a person held to resemble an angel **6** : a financial backer — **an·gel·ic** \an-'je-lik\ *or* **an·gel·i·cal** \-li-kəl\ *adj* — **an·gel·i·cal·ly** \-k(ə-)lē\ *adv*

an·gel·fish \'ān-jəl-ˌfish\ *n* : any of several bright‑colored tropical fishes that are flattened from side to side

an·gel·i·ca \an-'je-li-kə\ *n* : a biennial herb related to the carrot whose roots and fruit furnish a flavoring oil

¹an·ger \'aŋ-gər\ *vb* : to make angry

²anger *n* [ME, affliction, anger, fr. ON *angr* grief] : a strong feeling of displeasure **syn** wrath, ire, rage, fury, indignation

an·gi·na \an-'jī-nə\ *n* : a disorder (as of the heart) marked by attacks of intense pain; *esp* : ANGINA PECTORIS — **an·gi·nal** \an-'jīn-°l\ *adj*

angina pec·to·ris \-'pek-t(ə-)rəs\ *n* : a heart disease marked by brief attacks of sharp chest pain caused by deficient oxygenation of heart muscles

an·gio·gram \'an-jē-ə-ˌgram\ *n* : an X-ray photograph made by angiography

an·gi·og·ra·phy \ˌan-jē-'ä-grə-fē\ *n* : the use of X rays to make blood vessels visible (as by photography) after injection of a substance opaque to radiation

an·gio·plas·ty \'an-jē-ə-ˌplas-tē\ *n* : surgical repair of a blood vessel esp. by using an inflatable catheter to unblock arteries clogged by atherosclerotic deposits

an·gio·sperm \-ˌspərm\ *n* : FLOWERING PLANT

¹an·gle \'aŋ-gəl\ *n* **1** : a sharp projecting corner **2** : the figure formed by the meeting of two lines in a point **3** : a point of view **4** : a special technique or plan : GIMMICK — **an·gled** *adj*

²angle *vb* **an·gled; an·gling** \-g(ə-)liŋ\ : to turn, move, or direct at an angle

³angle *vb* **an·gled; an·gling** \-g(ə-)liŋ\ : to fish with a hook and line — **an·gler** \-glər\ *n* — **an·gling** \-gliŋ\ *n*

an·gle·worm \'aŋ-gəl-ˌwərm\ *n* : EARTHWORM

An·gli·can \'aŋ-gli-kən\ *adj* **1** : of or relating to the established episcopal Church of England **2** : of or relating to England or the English nation — **Anglican** *n* — **An·gli·can·ism** \-kə-ˌni-zəm\ *n*

an·gli·cize \'aŋ-glə-ˌsīz\ *vb* **-cized; -ciz·ing** *often cap* **1** : to make English (as in habits, speech, character, or outlook) **2** : to borrow (a foreign word or phrase) into English without changing form or spelling and sometimes without changing pronunciation — **an·gli·ci·za·tion** \ˌaŋ-glə-sə-'zā-shən\ *n*, *often cap*

An·glo \'aŋ-glō\ *n*, *pl* **Anglos** : a non-Hispanic white inhabitant of the U.S.; *esp* : one of English origin and descent

An·glo–French \ˌaŋ-glō-'french\ *n* : the French language used in medieval England

An·glo·phile \'aŋ-glə-ˌfīl\ *also* **An·glo·phil** \-ˌfil\ *n* : one who greatly admires England and things English

An·glo·phobe \'aŋ-glə-ˌfōb\ *n* : one who is averse to England and things English

An·glo–Sax·on \ˌaŋ-glō-'sak-sən\ *n* **1** : a member of any of the Germanic peoples who invaded England in the 5th century A.D. **2** : a member of the English people **3** : Old English — **Anglo–Saxon** *adj*

an·go·ra \aŋ-'gōr-ə, an-\ *n* **1** : yarn or cloth made from the hair of an Angora goat or rabbit **2** *cap* : any of a breed of cats, goats, or rabbits with a long silky coat

an·gry \'aŋ-grē\ *adj* **an·gri·er; -est** : feeling or showing anger **syn** enraged, wrathful, irate, indignant, mad — **an·gri·ly** \-grə-lē\ *adv*

angst \'äŋst\ *n* [G] : a feeling of anxiety

ang·strom \'aŋ-strəm\ *n* : a unit of length equal to one ten-billionth of a meter

an·guish \'aŋ-gwish\ *n* : extreme pain or distress esp. of mind — **an·guished** \-gwisht\ *adj*

an·gu·lar \'aŋ-gyə-lər\ *adj* **1** : sharp-cornered **2** : having one or more angles **3** : being thin and bony — **an·gu·lar·i·ty** \ˌaŋ-gyə-'lar-ə-tē\ *n*

An·gus \'aŋ-gəs\ *n* : any of a breed of usu. black hornless beef cattle originating in Scotland

an·hy·drous \an-'hī-drəs\ *adj* : free from water

an·i·line \'an-°l-ən\ *n* : an oily poisonous liquid used in making dyes, medicines, and explosives

an·i·mad·vert \ˌa-nə-ˌmad-'vərt\ *vb* : to remark critically : express censure — **an·i·mad·ver·sion** \-'vər-zhən\ *n*

¹an·i·mal \'a-nə-məl\ *n* **1** : any of a kingdom of living things typically differing from plants in capacity for active movement, in rapid response to stimulation, and in lack of cellulose cell walls **2** : a lower animal as distinguished from human beings; *also* : MAMMAL

²animal *adj* **1** : of, relating to, or derived from animals **2** : of or relating to the physical as distinguished from the mental or spiritual **syn** carnal, fleshly, sensual

an·i·mal·cule \ˌa-nə-'mal-kyül\ *n* : a tiny animal usu. invisible to the naked eye

¹an·i·mate \'a-nə-mət\ *adj* : having life

²an·i·mate \-ˌmāt\ *vb* **-mat·ed; -mat·ing** **1** : to impart life to **2** : to give spirit and vigor to **3** : to make appear to move ⟨~ a cartoon for motion pictures⟩ — **an·i·mat·ed** *adj*

an·i·ma·tion \ˌa-nə-'mā-shən\ *n* **1** : VIVACITY, LIVELINESS **2** : a motion picture made from a series of drawings simulating motions by means of slight progressive changes

an·i·mism \'a-nə-ˌmi-zəm\ *n* : attribution of conscious life to objects in and phenomena of nature or to inanimate objects — **an·i·mist** \-mist\ *n* — **an·i·mis·tic** \ˌa-nə-'mis-tik\ *adj*

angle 2: *1* obtuse, *2* right, *3* acute

an·i·mos·i·ty \ˌa-nə-'mä-sə-tē\ *n, pl* **-ties** : ILL WILL, RESENTMENT

an·i·mus \'a-nə-məs\ *n* : deep-seated resentment and hostility

an·ion \'a-ˌnī-ən, -ˌnī-ˌän\ *n* : a negatively charged ion

an·ise \'a-nəs\ *n* : an herb related to the carrot with aromatic seeds (**aniseed** \-ˌsēd\) used in flavoring

an·is·ette \ˌa-nə-'set, -'zet\ *n* [F] : a usu. colorless sweet liqueur flavored with aniseed

ankh \'äŋk\ *n* : a cross having a loop for its upper vertical arm and serving esp. in ancient Egypt as an emblem of life

an·kle \'aŋ-kəl\ *n* : the joint or region between the foot and the leg

an·kle·bone \'aŋ-kəl-ˌbōn\ *n* : the bone that in human beings bears the weight of the body and with the tibia and fibula forms the ankle joint

an·klet \'aŋ-klət\ *n* **1** : something (as an ornament) worn around the ankle **2** : a short sock reaching slightly above the ankle

ann *abbr* **1** annals **2** annual

an·nals \'an-°lz\ *n pl* **1** : a record of events in chronological order **2** : historical records — **an·nal·ist** \-°l-ist\ *n*

an·neal \ə-'nēl\ *vb* **1** : to make (as glass or steel) less brittle by heating and then cooling **2** : STRENGTHEN, TOUGHEN

¹an·nex \ə-'neks, 'a-ˌneks\ *vb* **1** : to attach as an addition **2** : to incorporate (as a territory) within a political domain — **an·nex·a·tion** \ˌa-nek-'sā-shən\ *n*

²an·nex \'a-ˌneks, -niks\ *n* : a subsidiary or supplementary structure

an·nexe *chiefly Brit var of* ANNEX

an·ni·hi·late \ə-'nī-ə-ˌlāt\ *vb* **-lat·ed; -lat·ing** : to destroy completely — **an·ni·hi·la·tion** \-ˌnī-ə-'lā-shən\ *n*

an·ni·ver·sa·ry \ˌa-nə-'vər-sə-rē\ *n, pl* **-ries** : the annual return of the date of a notable event and esp. a wedding

an·no Do·mi·ni \ˌa-nō-'dä-mə-nē, -'dō-, -ˌnī\ *adv, often cap A* [ML, in the year of the Lord] — used to indicate that a time division falls within the Christian era

anno he·gi·rae \ˌa-nō-hi-'jī-(ˌ)rē, -'he-jə-ˌrē\ *adv, often cap A&H* [NL, in the year of the Hegira] — used to indicate that a time division falls within the Islamic era

an·no·tate \'a-nə-ˌtāt\ *vb* **-tat·ed; -tat·ing** : to furnish with notes — **an·no·ta·tion** \ˌa-nə-'tā-shən\ *n* — **an·no·ta·tor** \'a-nə-ˌtā-tər\ *n*

an·nounce \ə-'naůns\ *vb* **an·nounced; an·nounc·ing 1** : to make known publicly **2** : to give notice of the arrival or presence of — **an·nounce·ment** *n*

an·nounc·er \ə-'naůn-sər\ *n* : a person who introduces radio or television programs, makes commercial announcements, or gives station identification

an·noy \ə-'nói\ *vb* : to disturb or irritate esp. by repeated acts : VEX **syn** irk, bother, pester, tease, harass — **an·noy·ing·ly** *adv*

an·noy·ance \ə-'nói-əns\ *n* **1** : the act of annoying **2** : the state of being annoyed **3** : NUISANCE

¹an·nu·al \'an-yə-wəl\ *adj* **1** : covering the period of a year **2** : occurring once a year : YEARLY **3** : completing the life cycle in one growing season ⟨∼ plants⟩ — **an·nu·al·ly** *adv*

²annual *n* **1** : a publication appearing once a year **2** : an annual plant

annual ring *n* : the layer of wood produced by a single year's growth of a woody plant

an·nu·i·tant \ə-'nü-ə-tənt, -'nyü-\ *n* : a beneficiary of an annuity

an·nu·i·ty \ə-'nü-ə-tē, -'nyü-\ *n, pl* **-i·ties** : an amount payable annually; *also* : the right to receive such a payment

an·nul \ə-'nəl\ *vb* **an·nulled; an·nul·ling** : to make legally void — **an·nul·ment** *n*

an·nu·lar \'an-yə-lər\ *adj* : ring-shaped

an·nun·ci·ate \ə-'nən-sē-ˌāt\ *vb* **-at·ed; -at·ing** : ANNOUNCE

an·nun·ci·a·tion \ə-ˌnən-sē-'ā-shən\ *n* **1** : ANNOUNCEMENT **2** *cap* : March 25 observed as a church festival commemorating the announcement of the Incarnation

an·nun·ci·a·tor \ə-'nən-sē-ˌā-tər\ *n* : one that annunciates; *specif* : a usu. electrically controlled signal board or indicator

an·ode \'a-ˌnōd\ *n* **1** : the positive electrode of an electrolytic cell **2** : the negative terminal of a battery **3** : the electron-collecting electrode of an electron tube — **an·od·ic** \a-'nä-dik\ *also* **an·od·al** \-'nōd-°l\ *adj*

an·od·ize \'a-nə-ˌdīz\ *vb* **-ized; -iz·ing** : to subject (a metal) to electrolytic action as the anode of a cell in order to coat with a protective or decorative film

an·o·dyne \'a-nə-ˌdīn\ *n* : something that relieves pain : a soothing agent

anoint \ə-'nóint\ *vb* **1** : to apply oil to esp. as a sacred rite **2** : CONSECRATE — **anoint·ment** *n*

anom·a·lous \ə-'nä-mə-ləs\ *adj* : deviating from a general rule : ABNORMAL

anom·a·ly \ə-'nä-mə-lē\ *n, pl* **-lies** : something anomalous : IRREGULARITY

¹anon \ə-'nän\ *adv, archaic* : SOON

²anon *abbr* anonymous; anonymously

anon·y·mous \ə-'nä-nə-məs\ *adj* : of unknown or undeclared origin or authorship — **an·o·nym·i·ty** \ˌa-nə-'ni-mə-tē\ *n* — **anon·y·mous·ly** *adv*

anoph·e·les \ə-'nä-fə-ˌlēz\ *n* [NL, genus name, fr. Gk *anōphelēs* useless, fr. *a-* not + *ophelos* advantage, help] : any of a genus of mosquitoes that includes all mosquitoes which transmit malaria to human beings

an·o·rec·tic \ˌa-nə-'rek-tik\ *adj* : ANOREXIC — **anorectic** *n*

an·orex·ia \ˌa-nə-'rek-sē-ə\ *n* **1** : loss of appetite esp. when prolonged **2** : ANOREXIA NERVOSA

anorexia ner·vo·sa \-nər-'vō-sə\ *n* : a serious disorder in eating behavior marked esp. by a pathological fear of weight gain leading to faulty eating patterns, malnutrition, and usu. excessive weight loss

an·orex·ic \ˌa-nə-'rek-sik\ *adj* **1** : lacking or causing loss of appetite **2** : affected with or as if with anorexia nervosa — **anorexic** *n*

¹an·oth·er \ə-'nə-thər\ *adj* **1** : some other **2** : being one in addition : one more

²another *pron* **1** : an additional one : one more **2** : one that is different from the first or present one

ans *abbr* answer

¹an·swer \'an-sər\ *n* **1** : something spoken or written in reply to a question **2** : a solution of a problem

²answer *vb* **1** : to speak or write in reply to **2** : to be responsible **3** : to be adequate — **an·swer·er** *n*

an·swer·able \'an-sə-rə-bəl\ *adj* **1** : subject to taking blame or responsibility **2** : capable of being refuted

answering machine *n* : a machine that receives telephone calls by playing a recorded message and usu. by recording messages from callers

answering service *n* : a commercial service that answers telephone calls for its clients

¹ant \'ant\ *n* : any of a family of small social insects related to the bees and living in communities usu. in earth or wood

²ant *abbr* antonym

Ant *abbr* Antarctica

ant- — see ANTI-

¹-ant *n suffix* **1** : one that performs or promotes (a specified action) ⟨coolant⟩ **2** : thing that is acted upon (in a specified manner) ⟨inhalant⟩

\ə\abut \ə\kitten \ər\further \a\ash \ā\ace \ä\mop, mar \aů\out \ch\chin \e\bet \ē\easy \g\go \i\hit \ī\ice \j\job \ŋ\sing \ō\go \ó\law \ói\boy \th\thin \th\the \ü\loot \ů\foot \y\yet \zh\vision *see also* Pronunciation Symbols page

²**-ant** *adj suffix* **1** : performing (a specified action) or being (in a specified condition) ⟨propell*ant*⟩ **2** : promoting (a specified action or process) ⟨expector*ant*⟩

ant·ac·id \ant-'a-səd\ *n* : an agent that counteracts acidity — **antacid** *adj*

an·tag·o·nism \an-'ta-gə-ˌni-zəm\ *n* **1** : active opposition or hostility **2** : opposition in physiological action — **an·tag·o·nis·tic** \-ˌta-gə-'nis-tik\ *adj*

an·tag·o·nist \-nist\ *n* : ADVERSARY, OPPONENT

an·tag·o·nize \an-'ta-gə-ˌnīz\ *vb* **-nized; -niz·ing** : to provoke the hostility of

ant·arc·tic \ant-'ärk-tik, -'är-tik\ *adj, often cap* : of or relating to the south pole or the region near it

antarctic circle *n, often cap A&C* : the parallel of latitude that is approximately 66½ degrees south of the equator

¹**an·te** \'an-tē\ *n* : a poker stake put up before the deal to build the pot; *also* : an amount paid : PRICE

²**ante** *vb* **an·ted; an·te·ing 1** : to put up (an ante) **2** : PAY

ant·eat·er \'ant-ˌē-tər\ *n* : any of several mammals (as an aardvark) that feed mostly on ants or termites

an·te·bel·lum \ˌan-ti-'be-ləm\ *adj* : existing before a war; *esp* : existing before the U.S. Civil War of 1861-65

an·te·ced·ent \ˌan-tə-'sēd-ᵊnt\ *n* **1** : a noun, pronoun, phrase, or clause referred to by a personal or relative pronoun **2** : a preceding event or cause **3** *pl* : the significant conditions of one's earlier life **4** *pl* : ANCESTORS — **antecedent** *adj*

an·te·cham·ber \'an-ti-ˌchām-bər\ *n* : ANTEROOM

an·te·date \'an-ti-ˌdāt\ *vb* **1** : to date (a paper) as of an earlier day than that on which the actual writing or signing is done **2** : to precede in time

an·te·di·lu·vi·an \ˌan-ti-də-'lü-vē-ən, -dī-\ *adj* **1** : of the period before the biblical flood **2** : ANTIQUATED

an·te·lope \'ant-ᵊl-ˌōp\ *n, pl* **-lope** *or* **-lopes** [ME, fabulous heraldic beast, prob. fr. MF *antelop* savage animal with sawlike horns, fr. ML *anthalopus*, fr. LGk *antholops*] **1** : any of various Old World cud-chewing mammals related to the oxen but with smaller lighter bodies and horns that extend upward and backward **2** : PRONGHORN

an·te me·ri·di·em \'an-ti-mə-'ri-dē-əm\ *adj* [L] : being before noon

an·ten·na \an-'te-nə\ *n, pl* **-nae** \-(ˌ)nē\ *or* **-nas** [ML, fr. L, sail yard] **1** : one of the long slender paired segmented sensory organs on the head of an arthropod (as an insect or crab) **2** *pl usu* **-nas** : a metallic device (as a rod or wire) for sending out or receiving radio waves

an·te·pe·nult \ˌan-ti-'pē-ˌnəlt\ *also* **an·te·pen·ul·ti·ma** \-pi-'nəl-tə-mə\ *n* : the 3d syllable of a word counting from the end — **an·te·pen·ul·ti·mate** \-pi-'nəl-tə-mət\ *adj or n*

an·te·ri·or \an-'tir-ē-ər\ *adj* **1** : situated before or toward the front **2** : situated near or nearer to the head **3** : coming before in time **syn** preceding, previous, prior, antecedent

an·te·room \'an-ti-ˌrüm, -ˌrum\ *n* : a room forming the entrance to another and often used as a waiting room

an·them \'an-thəm\ *n* **1** : a sacred vocal composition **2** : a song or hymn of praise or gladness

an·ther \'an-thər\ *n* : the part of a stamen of a seed plant that produces and contains pollen

ant·hill \'ant-ˌhil\ *n* : a mound thrown up by ants or termites in digging their nest

an·thol·o·gy \an-'thä-lə-jē\ *n, pl* **-gies** [NL *anthologia* collection of epigrams, fr. MGk, fr. Gk, flower gathering, fr. *anthos* flower + *logia* collecting, fr. *legein* to gather] : a collection of literary selections — **an·thol·o·gist** \-jist\ *n* — **an·thol·o·gize** \-ˌjīz\ *vb*

an·thra·cite \'an-thrə-ˌsīt\ *n* : a hard glossy coal that burns without much smoke

an·thrax \'an-ˌthraks\ *n* : an infectious and usu. fatal bacterial disease of warm-blooded animals (as cattle and sheep) that is transmissible to humans; *also* : a bacterium causing anthrax

an·thro·po·cen·tric \ˌan-thrə-pə-'sen-trik\ *adj* : interpreting or regarding the world in terms of human values and experiences

an·thro·poid \'an-thrə-ˌpoid\ *n* **1** : any of several large tailless apes (as a gorilla) **2** : a person resembling an ape — **anthropoid** *adj*

an·thro·pol·o·gy \ˌan-thrə-'pä-lə-jē\ *n* : the science of human beings and esp. of their physical characteristics, their origin and the distribution of races, their environment and social relations, and their culture — **an·thro·po·log·i·cal** \-pə-'lä-ji-kəl\ *adj* — **an·thro·pol·o·gist** \-'pä-lə-jist\ *n*

an·thro·po·mor·phism \ˌan-thrə-pə-'mor-ˌfi-zəm\ *n* : an interpretation of what is not human or personal in terms of human or personal characteristics : HUMANIZATION — **an·thro·po·mor·phic** \-fik\ *adj*

an·ti \'an-ˌtī, -tē\ *n, pl* **antis** : one who is opposed

anti- \ˌan-ti, -tē, -ˌtē\ *or* **ant-** *or* **anth-** *prefix* **1** : opposite in kind, position, or action **2** : opposing : hostile toward **3** : counteractive **4** : preventive of : curative of

antiaging	antigovernment
anti-AIDS	anti-imperialism
antiaircraft	anti-imperialist
antialcohol	antiknock
anti-American	antilabor
antiapartheid	antimalarial
antibacterial	antimicrobial
anticapitalist	antinausea
anti-Catholic	antipoverty
anticholesterol	antislavery
anticlerical	antispasmodic
anticolonial	antistatic
anticommunism	antisubmarine
anticommunist	antitank
antidemocratic	antitumor
antiestablishment	antiviral
antifascist	

an·ti·abor·tion \ˌan-tē-ə-'bor-shən, ˌan-ˌtī-\ *adj* : opposed to abortion

an·ti·bal·lis·tic missile \ˌan-ti-bə-'lis-tik-, ˌan-ˌtī-\ *n* : a missile for intercepting and destroying ballistic missiles

an·ti·bi·ot·ic \-bī-'ä-tik, -bē-\ *n* : a substance produced by or derived by chemical alteration of a substance produced by a microorganism (as a fungus or bacterium) that in dilute solution inhibits or kills another microorganism — **antibiotic** *adj*

an·ti·body \'an-ti-ˌbä-dē\ *n* : any of a large number of proteins of high molecular weight produced normally by specialized B cells after stimulation by an antigen and acting specifically against the antigen in an immune response

¹**an·tic** \'an-tik\ *n* : an often wildly playful or funny act or action

²**antic** *adj* [It *antico* ancient, fr. L *antiquus*] **1** *archaic* : GROTESQUE **2** : PLAYFUL

an·ti·can·cer \ˌan-ti-'kan-sər, ˌan-ˌtī-\ *adj* : used against or tending to arrest cancer ⟨∼ drugs⟩

An·ti·christ \'an-ti-ˌkrīst\ *n* **1** : one who denies or opposes Christ **2** : a false Christ

an·tic·i·pate \an-'ti-sə-ˌpāt\ *vb* **-pat·ed; -pat·ing 1** : to foresee and provide for beforehand **2** : to look forward to — **an·tic·i·pa·tion** \-ˌti-sə-'pā-shən\ *n* — **an·tic·i·pa·to·ry** \-'ti-sə-pə-ˌtor-ē\ *adj*

an·ti·cli·max \ˌan-ti-'klī-ˌmaks\ *n* : something closing a series that is strikingly less important than what has preceded it — **an·ti·cli·mac·tic** \-klī-'mak-tik\ *adj*

an·ti·cline \'an-ti-ˌklīn\ *n* : an arch of layers of rock in the earth's crust

an·ti·co·ag·u·lant \ˌan-ti-kō-'a-gyə-lənt\ *n* : a substance that hinders the clotting of blood — **anticoagulant** *adj*

an·ti·cy·clone \ˌan-ti-'sī-ˌklōn\ *n* : a system of winds that rotates about a center of high atmospheric pressure — **an·ti·cy·clon·ic** \-sī-ˈklä-nik\ *adj*

¹an·ti·de·pres·sant \ˌan-ti-di-ˈpres-ᵊnt, ˌan-ˌtī-\ *adj* : used or tending to relieve psychic depression ⟨∼ drugs⟩

²antidepressant *n* : an antidepressant drug

an·ti·dote \ˈan-ti-ˌdōt\ *n* : a remedy to counteract the effects of poison

an·ti·drug \ˈan-ˌtī-ˌdrəg\ *adj* : acting against or opposing illicit drugs

an·ti·fer·til·i·ty \ˌan-ti-fər-ˈti-lə-tē\ *adj* : tending to control excess or unwanted fertility : CONTRACEPTIVE ⟨∼ agents⟩

an·ti·freeze \ˈan-ti-ˌfrēz\ *n* : a substance added to a liquid to lower its freezing temperature

an·ti·gen \ˈan-ti-jən\ *n* : a usu. protein or carbohydrate substance (as a toxin or an enzyme) capable of stimulating an immune response — **an·ti·gen·ic** \ˌan-ti-ˈje-nik\ *adj* — **an·ti·ge·nic·i·ty** \-jə-ˈni-sə-tē\ *n*

an·ti·grav·i·ty \ˌan-ti-ˈgra-və-tē, ˌan-ˌtī-\ *adj* : reducing or canceling the effect of gravity

an·ti·he·ro \ˈan-ti-ˌhē-rō, ˈan-ˌtī-\ *n* : a protagonist who is notably lacking in heroic qualities (as courage)

an·ti·his·ta·mine \ˌan-ti-ˈhis-tə-ˌmēn, ˌan-ˌtī-, -mən\ *n* : any of various drugs used in treating allergies and colds

an·ti·hy·per·ten·sive \-ˌhī-pər-ˈten-siv\ *n* : a substance that is effective against high blood pressure — **anti·hypertensive** *adj*

an·ti–in·flam·ma·to·ry \-in-ˈfla-mə-ˌtōr-ē\ *adj* : counteracting inflammation — **anti–inflammatory** *n*

an·ti–in·tel·lec·tu·al \-ˌint-ᵊl-ˈek-chə-wəl\ *adj* : opposing or hostile to intellectuals or to an intellectual view or approach

an·ti·lock \ˈan-ti-ˌläk, ˈan-ˌtī-\ *adj* : being a braking system designed to prevent the wheels from locking

an·ti·log·a·rithm \ˌan-ti-ˈlȯ-gə-ˌri-thəm, ˌan-ˌtī-, -ˈlä-\ *n* : the number corresponding to a given logarithm

an·ti·ma·cas·sar \ˌan-ti-mə-ˈka-sər\ *n* : a cover to protect the back or arms of furniture

an·ti·mat·ter \ˈan-ti-ˌma-tər, ˈan-ˌtī-\ *n* : matter composed of antiparticles

an·ti·mo·ny \ˈan-tə-ˌmō-nē\ *n* : a brittle silvery white metallic chemical element used esp. in alloys — see ELEMENT table

an·ti·neu·tron \ˌan-ti-ˈnü-ˌträn, ˌan-ˌtī-, -ˈnyü-\ *n* : the antiparticle of the neutron

an·ti·no·mi·an \ˌan-ti-ˈnō-mē-ən\ *n* : one who denies the validity of moral laws

an·tin·o·my \an-ˈti-nə-mē\ *n, pl* **-mies** : a contradiction between two seemingly true statements

an·ti·nov·el \ˈan-ti-ˌnä-vəl, ˈan-ˌtī-\ *n* : a work of fiction that lacks all or most of the traditional features of the novel

an·ti·nu·cle·ar \ˌan-ti-ˈnü-klē-ər, -ˈnyü-\ *adj* : opposing the use or production of nuclear power plants

an·ti·ox·i·dant \ˌan-tē-ˈäk-sə-dənt, ˌan-ˌtī-\ *n* : a substance that inhibits oxidation — **antioxidant** *adj*

an·ti·par·ti·cle \ˈan-ti-ˌpär-ti-kəl, ˈan-ˌtī-\ *n* : a subatomic particle identical to another subatomic particle in mass but opposite to it in electric and magnetic properties

an·ti·pas·to \ˌan-ti-ˈpas-tō, ˌän-ti-ˈpäs-\ *n, pl* **-ti** \-(ˌ)tē\ : any of various typically Italian hors d'oeuvres

an·tip·a·thy \an-ˈti-pə-thē\ *n, pl* **-thies 1** : settled aversion or dislike **2** : an object of aversion — **an·ti·pa·thet·ic** \ˌan-ti-pə-ˈthe-tik\ *adj*

an·ti·per·son·nel \ˌan-ti-ˌpərs-ᵊn-ˈel, ˌan-ˌtī-\ *adj* : designed for use against military personnel ⟨∼ mine⟩

an·ti·per·spi·rant \-ˈpər-spə-rənt\ *n* : a preparation used to check perspiration

an·tiph·o·nal \an-ˈti-fən-ᵊl\ *adj* : performed by two alternating groups — **an·tiph·o·nal·ly** *adv*

an·ti·pode \ˈan-tə-ˌpōd\ *n, pl* **an·tip·o·des** \an-ˈti-pə-ˌdēz\ [ME *antipodes*, pl., persons dwelling at opposite points on the globe, fr. L, fr. Gk, fr. pl. of *antipod-*, *antipous* with feet opposite, fr. *anti-* against + *pod-*, *pous* foot] : the parts of the earth diametrically opposite — usu. used in pl. — **an·tip·o·dal** \an-ˈti-pəd-ᵊl\ *adj* — **an·tip·o·de·an** \(ˌ)an-ˌti-pə-ˈdē-ən\ *adj*

an·ti·pol·lu·tion \ˌan-ti-pə-ˈlü-shən\ *adj* : designed to prevent, reduce, or eliminate pollution ⟨∼ laws⟩

an·ti·pope \ˈan-ti-ˌpōp\ *n* : one elected or claiming to be pope in opposition to the pope canonically chosen

an·ti·pro·ton \ˌan-ti-ˈprō-ˌtän\ *n* : the antiparticle of the proton

an·ti·quar·i·an \ˌan-tə-ˈkwer-ē-ən\ *adj* **1** : of or relating to antiquities **2** : dealing in old books — **antiquarian** *n* — **an·ti·quar·i·an·ism** *n*

an·ti·quary \ˈan-tə-ˌkwer-ē\ *n, pl* **-quar·ies** : a person who collects or studies antiquities

an·ti·quat·ed \ˈan-tə-ˌkwā-təd\ *adj* : OUT-OF-DATE, OLD-FASHIONED

¹an·tique \an-ˈtēk\ *n* : an object made in a bygone period

²antique *adj* **1** : belonging to antiquity **2** : OLD-FASHIONED **3** : of a bygone style or period

³antique *vb* **-tiqued; -tiqu·ing 1** : to finish or refinish in antique style : give an appearance of age to **2** : to shop around for antiques — **an·tiqu·er** *n*

an·tiq·ui·ty \an-ˈti-kwə-tē\ *n, pl* **-ties 1** : ancient times **2** : great age **3** *pl* : relics of ancient times **4** *pl* : matters relating to ancient culture

an·tis *pl of* ANTI

an·ti–Sem·i·tism \ˌan-ti-ˈse-mə-ˌti-zəm, ˌan-ˌtī-\ *n* : hostility toward Jews as a religious or social minority — **an·ti–Se·mit·ic** \-sə-ˈmi-tik\ *adj*

an·ti·sep·tic \ˌan-tə-ˈsep-tik\ *adj* **1** : killing or checking the growth of germs that cause decay or infection **2** : scrupulously clean : ASEPTIC — **antiseptic** *n* — **an·ti·sep·ti·cal·ly** *adv*

an·ti·se·rum \ˈan-ti-ˌsir-əm, ˈan-ˌtī-\ *n* : a serum containing antibodies

an·ti·so·cial \ˌan-ti-ˈsō-shəl\ *adj* **1** : disliking the society of others **2** : contrary or hostile to the well-being of society ⟨crime is ∼⟩ — **an·ti·so·cial·ly** *adv*

an·tith·e·sis \an-ˈti-thə-səs\ *n, pl* **-e·ses** \-ˌsēz\ **1** : the opposition or contrast of ideas **2** : the direct opposite

an·ti·thet·i·cal \ˌan-tə-ˈthe-ti-kəl\ *also* **an·ti·thet·ic** \-tik\ *adj* : constituting or marked by antithesis — **an·ti·thet·i·cal·ly** \-ti-k(ə-)lē\ *adv*

an·ti·tox·in \ˌan-ti-ˈtäk-sən\ *n* : an antibody that is able to neutralize a particular toxin or disease-causing agent; *also* : an antiserum containing an antitoxin

an·ti·trust \ˌan-ti-ˈtrəst\ *adj* : of or relating to legislation against trusts; *also* : consisting of laws to protect trade and commerce from unlawful restraints and monopolies or unfair business practices

an·ti·ven·in \-ˈve-nən\ *n* : an antitoxin to a venom; *also* : a serum containing such antitoxin

ant·ler \ˈant-lər\ *n* [ME *aunteler*, fr. MF *antoillier*, fr. (assumed) VL *anteocularis* located before the eye, fr. L *ante-* before + *oculus* eye] : one of the paired deciduous solid bone processes on the head of a deer; *also* : a branch of this — **ant·lered** \-lərd\ *adj*

ant lion *n* : any of various insects having a long-jawed larva that digs a conical pit in which it lies in wait for insects (as ants) on which it feeds

an·to·nym \ˈan-tə-ˌnim\ *n* : a word of opposite meaning

anus \ˈā-nəs\ *n* [L] : the lower or posterior opening of the alimentary canal

an·vil \ˈan-vəl\ *n* **1** : a heavy iron block on which metal is shaped **2** : INCUS

\ə\abut \ᵊ\kitten \ər\further \a\ash \ā\ace \ä\mop, mar
\au̇\out \ch\chin \e\bet \ē\easy \g\go \i\hit \ī\ice \j\job
\ŋ\sing \ō\go \o\law \oi\boy \th\thin \th\the \ü\loot \u̇\foot
\y\yet \zh\vision *see also* Pronunciation Symbols page

anx·i·ety \aŋ-ˈzī-ə-tē\ n, pl **-et·ies** 1 : painful uneasiness of mind usu. over an anticipated ill 2 : abnormal apprehension and fear often accompanied by physiological signs (as sweating and increased pulse), by doubt about the nature and reality of the threat itself, and by self-doubt

anx·ious \ˈaŋk-shəs\ adj 1 : uneasy in mind : WORRIED 2 : earnestly wishing : EAGER — **anx·ious·ly** adv

¹**any** \ˈe-nē\ adj 1 : one chosen at random 2 : of whatever number or quantity

²**any** pron 1 : any one or ones ⟨take ∼ of the books you like⟩ 2 : any amount ⟨∼ of the money not used is to be returned⟩

³**any** adv : to any extent or degree : AT ALL ⟨could not walk ∼ farther⟩

any·body \-ˌbä-dē, -bə-\ pron : ANYONE

any·how \-ˌhau̇\ adv 1 : in any way 2 : NEVERTHELESS; also : in any case

any·more \ˌe-nē-ˈmȯr\ adv 1 : any longer 2 : at the present time

any·one \ˈe-nē-(ˌ)wən\ pron : any person

any·place \-ˌplās\ adv : ANYWHERE

any·thing \-ˌthiŋ\ pron : any thing whatever

any·time \ˈe-nē-ˌtīm\ adv : at any time whatever

any·way \-ˌwā\ adv : ANYHOW

any·where \-ˌhwer\ adv : in or to any place

any·wise \-ˌwīz\ adv : in any way whatever

A–OK \ˌā-ō-ˈkā\ adv or adj : very definitely OK

A1 \ˈā-ˈwən\ adj : of the finest quality

aor·ta \ā-ˈȯr-tə\ n, pl **-tas** or **-tae** \-tē\ : the main artery that carries blood from the heart — **aor·tic** \-tik\ adj

ap abbr 1 apostle 2 apothecaries'

AP abbr 1 American plan 2 Associated Press

apace \ə-ˈpās\ adv : SWIFTLY

Apache \ə-ˈpa-chē\ n, pl **Apache** or **Apach·es** \-ˈpa-chēz, -ˈpa-shəz\ : a member of an American Indian people of the southwestern U.S.; also : any of the languages of the Apache people — **Apach·e·an** \ə-ˈpa-chē-ən\ adj or n

ap·a·nage var of APPANAGE

apart \ə-ˈpärt\ adv 1 : separately in place or time 2 : ASIDE 3 : in two or more parts : to pieces

apart·heid \ə-ˈpär-ˌtāt, -ˌtīt\ n [Afrikaans] : a policy of racial segregation practiced in the Republic of So. Africa

apart·ment \ə-ˈpärt-mənt\ n : a room or set of rooms occupied as a dwelling; also : a building divided into individual dwelling units

ap·a·thy \ˈa-pə-thē\ n 1 : lack of emotion 2 : lack of interest : INDIFFERENCE — **ap·a·thet·ic** \ˌa-pə-ˈthe-tik\ adj — **ap·a·thet·i·cal·ly** \-ti-k(ə-)lē\ adv

ap·a·tite \ˈa-pə-ˌtīt\ n : any of a group of minerals that are phosphates of calcium and occur esp. in phosphate rock and in bones and teeth

APB abbr all points bulletin

¹**ape** \ˈāp\ n 1 : any of the larger tailless primates (as a baboon or gorilla); also : MONKEY 2 : MIMIC, IMITATOR; also : a large uncouth person

²**ape** vb **aped; ap·ing** : IMITATE, MIMIC

ape–man \ˈāp-ˌman\ n : a primate intermediate in character between Homo sapiens and the higher apes

aper·çu \ˌa-per-ˈsu̅e̅, ˌa-pər-ˈsü\ n, pl **aperçus** \-ˈsu̅e̅(z), -ˈsüz\ : an immediate impression; esp : INSIGHT

aper·i·tif \ˌä-ˌper-ə-ˈtēf\ n : an alcoholic drink taken as an appetizer

ap·er·ture \ˈa-pər-ˌchu̇r, -chər\ n : OPENING, HOLE

apex \ˈā-ˌpeks\ n, pl **apex·es** or **api·ces** \ˈā-pə-ˌsēz, ˈa-\ : the highest point : PEAK

apha·sia \ə-ˈfā-zh(ē-)ə\ n : loss or impairment of the power to use or comprehend words — **apha·sic** \-zik\ adj or n

aph·elion \a-ˈfēl-yən\ n, pl **-elia** \-yə\ [NL, fr. apo- away

from + Gk *hēlios* sun] : the point in an object's orbit most distant from the sun

aphid \ˈā-fəd\ n : any of numerous small insects that suck the juices of plants

aphis \ˈā-fəs, ˈa-\ n, pl **aphi·des** \-fə-ˌdēz\ : APHID

aph·o·rism \ˈa-fə-ˌri-zəm\ n : a short saying stating a general truth : MAXIM — **aph·o·ris·tic** \ˌa-fə-ˈris-tik\ adj

aph·ro·di·si·ac \ˌa-frə-ˈdi-zē-ˌak, -ˈdē-zē-\ n : an agent that excites sexual desire — **aphrodisiac** adj

api·ary \ˈā-pē-ˌer-ē\ n, pl **-ar·ies** : a place where bees are kept — **api·a·rist** \-pē-ə-rist\ n

api·cal \ˈā-pi-kəl, ˈa-\ adj : of, relating to, or situated at an apex — **api·cal·ly** \-k(ə-)lē\ adv

apiece \ə-ˈpēs\ adv : for each one

aplen·ty \ə-ˈplen-tē\ adj : being in plenty or abundance

aplomb \ə-ˈpläm, -ˈpləm\ n [F, lit., perpendicularity, fr. MF, fr. *a plomb*, lit., according to the plummet] : complete composure or self-assurance

APO abbr army post office

Apoc abbr 1 Apocalypse 2 Apocrypha

apoc·a·lypse \ə-ˈpä-kə-ˌlips\ n 1 : a writing prophesying a cataclysm in which evil forces are destroyed 2 cap — see BIBLE table — **apoc·a·lyp·tic** \-ˌpä-kə-ˈlip-tik\ also **apoc·a·lyp·ti·cal** \-ti-kəl\ adj

Apoc·ry·pha \ə-ˈpä-krə-fə\ n 1 not cap : writings of dubious authenticity 2 : books included in the Septuagint and Vulgate but excluded from the Jewish and Protestant canons of the Old Testament — see BIBLE table 3 : early Christian writings not included in the New Testament

apoc·ry·phal \-fəl\ adj 1 : not canonical : SPURIOUS 2 often cap : of or resembling the Apocrypha — **apoc·ry·phal·ly** adv — **apoc·ry·phal·ness** n

apo·gee \ˈa-pə-(ˌ)jē\ n [F apogée, fr. NL apogaeum, fr. Gk apogaion, fr. apo away from + gē earth] : the point at which an orbiting object is farthest from the body being orbited

apo·lit·i·cal \ˌā-pə-ˈli-ti-kəl\ adj 1 : having an aversion for or no interest in political affairs 2 : having no political significance — **apo·lit·i·cal·ly** \-k(ə-)lē\ adv

apol·o·get·ic \ə-ˌpä-lə-ˈje-tik\ adj : expressing apology — **apol·o·get·i·cal·ly** \-ti-k(ə-)lē\ adv

ap·o·lo·gia \ˌa-pə-ˈlō-j(ē-)ə\ n : APOLOGY; esp : an argument in support or justification

apol·o·gize \ə-ˈpä-lə-ˌjīz\ vb : to make an apology : express regret — **apol·o·gist** \-jist\ n

apol·o·gy \ə-ˈpä-lə-jē\ n, pl **-gies** 1 : a formal justification : DEFENSE 2 : an expression of regret for a wrong

ap·o·plexy \ˈa-pə-ˌplek-sē\ n : STROKE 3 — **ap·o·plec·tic** \ˌa-pə-ˈplek-tik\ adj

aport \ə-ˈpȯrt\ adv : on or toward the left side of a ship

apos·ta·sy \ə-ˈpäs-tə-sē\ n, pl **-sies** : a renunciation or abandonment of a former loyalty (as to a religion) — **apos·tate** \ə-ˈpäs-ˌtāt, -tət\ adj or n

a pos·te·ri·o·ri \ˌä-pō-ˌstir-ē-ˈōr-ē\ adj [L, lit., from the latter] : relating to or derived by reasoning from observed facts — **a posteriori** adv

apos·tle \ə-ˈpä-səl\ n 1 : one of the group composed of Jesus' 12 original disciples and Paul 2 : the first prominent missionary to a region or group 3 : a person who initiates or first advocates a great reform — **apos·tle·ship** n

ap·os·tol·ic \ˌa-pə-ˈstä-lik\ adj 1 : of or relating to an apostle or to the New Testament apostles 2 : of or relating to a succession of spiritual authority from the apostles 3 : PAPAL

¹**apos·tro·phe** \ə-ˈpäs-trə-(ˌ)fē\ n : the rhetorical addressing of a usu. absent person or a usu. personified thing (as in "O grave, where is thy victory?")

²**apostrophe** n : a punctuation mark ' used esp. to indicate the possessive case or the omission of a letter or figure

apos·tro·phize \ə-ˈpäs-trə-ˌfīz\ vb **-phized; -phiz·ing** : to address as if present or capable of understanding

apothecaries' weight n : a system of weights based on the troy pound and ounce and used chiefly by pharmacists — see WEIGHT table

apoth·e·cary \ə-ˈpä-thə-ˌker-ē\ n, pl **-car·ies** [ME apothecarie, fr. ML apothecarius, fr. LL. shopkeeper, fr. L apotheca storehouse, fr. Gk apothēkē, fr. apotithenai to put away] : DRUGGIST

ap·o·thegm \ˈa-pə-ˌthem\ n : APHORISM

apo·the·o·sis \ə-ˌpä-thē-ˈō-səs, ˌa-pə-ˈthē-ə-səs\ n, pl **-o·ses** \-ˌsēz\ 1 : DEIFICATION 2 : the perfect example

app abbr 1 apparatus 2 appendix

ap·pall also **ap·pal** \ə-ˈpȯl\ vb **ap·palled; ap·pall·ing** : to overcome with horror : DISMAY

Ap·pa·loo·sa \ˌa-pə-ˈlü-sə\ n : any of a breed of saddle horses developed in western No. America and usu. having a white or solid-colored coat with small spots

Appaloosa

ap·pa·nage \ˈa-pə-nij\ n 1 : provision (as a grant of land) made by a sovereign or legislative body for dependent members of the royal family 2 : a rightful adjunct

ap·pa·ra·tus \ˌa-pə-ˈra-təs, -ˈrā-\ n, pl **-tus·es** or **-tus** [L] 1 : a set of materials or equipment for a particular use 2 : a complex machine or device : MECHANISM 3 : the organization of a political party or underground movement

¹**ap·par·el** \ə-ˈpar-əl\ vb **-eled** or **-elled; -el·ing** or **-el·ling** 1 : CLOTHE 2 : ADORN

²**apparel** n : CLOTHING, DRESS

ap·par·ent \ə-ˈpar-ənt\ adj 1 : open to view : VISIBLE 2 : EVIDENT, OBVIOUS 3 : appearing as real or true : SEEMING

ap·par·ent·ly \-lē\ adv : it seems apparent

ap·pa·ri·tion \ˌa-pə-ˈri-shən\ n : a supernatural appearance : GHOST

ap·peal \ə-ˈpēl\ vb 1 : to take steps to have (a case) reheard in a higher court 2 : to plead for help, corroboration, or decision 3 : to arouse a sympathetic response — **appeal** n

ap·pear \ə-ˈpir\ vb 1 : to become visible 2 : to come formally before an authority 3 : SEEM 4 : to become evident 5 : to come before the public

ap·pear·ance \ə-ˈpir-əns\ n 1 : outward aspect : LOOK 2 : the act of appearing 3 : PHENOMENON

ap·pease \ə-ˈpēz\ vb **ap·peased; ap·peas·ing** 1 : to cause to subside : ALLAY 2 : PACIFY, CONCILIATE; esp : to buy off by concessions — **ap·pease·ment** n — **ap·peas·able** \-ˈpē-zə-bəl\ adj

ap·pel·lant \ə-ˈpe-lənt\ n : one who appeals esp. from a judicial decision

ap·pel·late \ə-ˈpe-lət\ adj : having power to review decisions of a lower court

ap·pel·la·tion \ˌa-pə-ˈlā-shən\ n : NAME, DESIGNATION

ap·pel·lee \ˌa-pə-ˈlē\ n : one against whom an appeal is taken

ap·pend \ə-ˈpend\ vb : to attach esp. as something additional : AFFIX

ap·pend·age \ə-ˈpen-dij\ n 1 : something appended to a principal or greater thing 2 : a projecting part of the body (as an antenna) esp. when paired with one on each side **syn** accessory, adjunct, appendix, appurtenance

ap·pen·dec·to·my \ˌa-pən-ˈdek-tə-mē\ n, pl **-mies** : surgical removal of the intestinal appendix

ap·pen·di·ci·tis \ə-ˌpen-də-ˈsī-təs\ n : inflammation of the intestinal appendix

ap·pen·dix \ə-ˈpen-diks\ n, pl **-dix·es** or **-di·ces** \-də-ˌsēz\ [L] 1 : supplementary matter added at the end of a book 2 : a narrow blind tube usu. about three or four inches long that extends from the cecum in the lower right-hand part of the abdomen

ap·per·tain \ˌa-pər-ˈtān\ vb : to belong as a rightful part or privilege

ap·pe·tite \ˈa-pə-ˌtīt\ n [ME apetit, fr. MF, fr. L appetitus, fr. appetere to strive after, fr. ad- to + petere to go to] 1 : natural desire for satisfying some want or need esp. for food 2 : TASTE, PREFERENCE

ap·pe·tiz·er \ˈa-pə-ˌtī-zər\ n : a food or drink taken just before a meal to stimulate the appetite

ap·pe·tiz·ing \-ziŋ\ adj : tempting to the appetite — **ap·pe·tiz·ing·ly** adv

appl abbr applied

ap·plaud \ə-ˈplȯd\ vb : to show approval esp. by clapping

ap·plause \ə-ˈplȯz\ n : approval publicly expressed (as by clapping)

ap·ple \ˈa-pəl\ n : a rounded fruit with firm white flesh and a seedy core; also : a tree that bears this fruit

ap·ple·jack \-ˌjak\ n : a liquor distilled from fermented cider

ap·pli·ance \ə-ˈplī-əns\ n 1 : INSTRUMENT, DEVICE 2 : a piece of household equipment (as a stove or toaster) operated by gas or electricity

ap·pli·ca·ble \ˈa-pli-kə-bəl, ə-ˈpli-kə-\ adj : capable of being applied : RELEVANT — **ap·pli·ca·bil·i·ty** \ˌa-pli-kə-ˈbi-lə-tē, ə-ˌpli-kə-\ n

ap·pli·cant \ˈa-pli-kənt\ n : one who applies

ap·pli·ca·tion \ˌa-plə-ˈkā-shən\ n 1 : the act of applying 2 : assiduous attention 3 : REQUEST; also : a form used in making a request 4 : something placed or spread on a surface 5 : capacity for use

ap·pli·ca·tor \ˈa-plə-ˌkā-tər\ n : a device for applying a substance (as medicine or polish)

ap·plied \ə-ˈplīd\ adj : put to practical use 〈~ art〉

ap·pli·qué \ˌa-plə-ˈkā\ n [F] : a fabric decoration cut out and fastened to a larger piece of material — **appliqué** vb

ap·ply \ə-ˈplī\ vb **ap·plied; ap·ply·ing** 1 : to put to practical use 2 : to place in contact : put or spread on a surface 3 : to employ with close attention 4 : to have reference or connection 5 : to submit a request

ap·point \ə-ˈpȯint\ vb 1 : to fix or set officially 〈~ a day for trial〉 2 : to name officially 3 : to fit out : EQUIP

ap·poin·tee \ə-ˌpȯin-ˈtē, ˌa-\ n : a person appointed

ap·point·ive \ə-ˈpȯin-tiv\ adj : subject to appointment

ap·point·ment \ə-ˈpȯint-mənt\ n 1 : the act of appointing 2 : an arrangement for a meeting 3 pl : FURNISHINGS, EQUIPMENT 4 : a nonelective office or position

ap·por·tion \ə-ˈpȯr-shən\ vb : to distribute proportionately : ALLOT — **ap·por·tion·ment** n

ap·po·site \ˈa-pə-zət\ adj : APPROPRIATE, RELEVANT — **ap·po·site·ly** adv — **ap·po·site·ness** n

ap·po·si·tion \ˌa-pə-ˈzi-shən\ n : a grammatical construction in which a noun or pronoun is followed by another that has the same referent (as the poet and Burns in "a biography of the poet Burns")

\ə\abut \ᵊ\kitten \ər\further \a\ash \ā\ace \ä\mop, mar
\aù\out \ch\chin \e\bet \ē\easy \g\go \i\hit \ī\ice \j\job
\ŋ\sing \ō\go \ȯ\law \ȯi\boy \th\thin \t̷h\the \ü\loot \ù\foot
\y\yet \zh\vision see also Pronunciation Symbols page

ap·pos·i·tive \ə-'pä-zə-tiv, a-\ *adj* : of, relating to, or standing in grammatical apposition — **appositive** *n*

ap·praise \ə-'prāz\ *vb* **ap·praised; ap·prais·ing** : to set a value on — **ap·prais·al** \-'prā-zəl\ *n* — **ap·prais·er** *n*

ap·pre·cia·ble \ə-'prē-shə-bəl\ *adj* : large enough to be recognized and measured — **ap·pre·cia·bly** *adv*

ap·pre·ci·ate \ə-'prē-shē-ˌāt\ *vb* **-at·ed; -at·ing 1** : to value justly **2** : to be aware of **3** : to be grateful for **4** : to increase in value — **ap·pre·ci·a·tion** \-ˌprē-shē-'ā-shən\ *n*

ap·pre·cia·tive \ə-'prē-shə-tiv, -shē-ˌāt-\ *adj* : having or showing appreciation — **ap·pre·cia·tive·ly** *adv*

ap·pre·hend \ˌa-pri-'hend\ *vb* **1** : ARREST **2** : to become aware of **3** : to look forward to with dread **4** : UNDERSTAND — **ap·pre·hen·sion** \-'hen-chən\ *n*

ap·pre·hen·sive \-'hen-siv\ *adj* : viewing the future with anxiety — **ap·pre·hen·sive·ly** *adv* — **ap·pre·hen·sive·ness** *n*

¹**ap·pren·tice** \ə-'pren-təs\ *n* **1** : a person learning a craft under a skilled worker **2** : BEGINNER — **ap·pren·tice·ship** *n*

²**apprentice** *vb* **-ticed; -tic·ing** : to bind or set at work as an apprentice

ap·prise \ə-'prīz\ *vb* **ap·prised; ap·pris·ing** : INFORM

ap·proach \ə-'prōch\ *vb* **1** : to move nearer to **2** : to be almost the same as **3** : to make advances to esp. for the purpose of creating a desired result **4** : to take preliminary steps toward — **approach** *n* — **ap·proach·able** *adj*

ap·pro·ba·tion \ˌa-prə-'bā-shən\ *n* : APPROVAL

¹**ap·pro·pri·ate** \ə-'prō-prē-ˌāt\ *vb* **-at·ed; -at·ing 1** : to take possession of **2** : to set apart for a particular use

²**ap·pro·pri·ate** \ə-'prō-prē-ət\ *adj* : fitted to a purpose or use : SUITABLE **syn** proper, fit, apt, befitting — **ap·pro·pri·ate·ly** *adv* — **ap·pro·pri·ate·ness** *n*

ap·pro·pri·a·tion \ə-ˌprō-prē-'ā-shən\ *n* : something (as money) set aside by formal action for a specific use

ap·prov·al \ə-'prü-vəl\ *n* : an act of approving — **on approval** : subject to a prospective buyer's acceptance or refusal

ap·prove \ə-'prüv\ *vb* **ap·proved; ap·prov·ing 1** : to have or express a favorable opinion of **2** : to accept as satisfactory : RATIFY

approx *abbr* approximate; approximately

¹**ap·prox·i·mate** \ə-'präk-sə-mət\ *adj* : nearly correct or exact — **ap·prox·i·mate·ly** *adv*

²**ap·prox·i·mate** \-ˌmāt\ *vb* **-mat·ed; -mat·ing** : to come near : APPROACH — **ap·prox·i·ma·tion** \ə-ˌpräk-sə-'mā-shən\ *n*

appt *abbr* appoint; appointed; appointment

ap·pur·te·nance \ə-'pərt-nəns, -ᵊn-əns\ *n* : something that belongs to or goes with another thing **syn** accessory, adjunct, appendage, appendix — **ap·pur·te·nant** \ə-'pərt-nənt, -ᵊn-ənt\ *adj*

Apr *abbr* April

APR *abbr* annual percentage rate

apri·cot \'a-prə-ˌkät, 'ā-\ *n* [deriv. of Ar *al-birqûq*] : an oval orange-colored fruit resembling the related peach and plum in flavor; *also* : a tree bearing apricots

April \'ā-prəl\ *n* [ME, fr. OF & L; OF *avrill*, fr. L *Aprilis*] : the 4th month of the year having 30 days

a pri·o·ri \ˌä-prē-'ōr-ē\ *adj* [L, from the former] **1** : characterized by or derived by reasoning from self-evident propositions **2** : independent of experience — **a priori** *adv*

apron \'ā-prən\ *n* [ME, alter. (resulting fr. misdivision of *a napron*) of *napron*, fr. MF *naperon*, dim. of *nape* cloth, modif. of L *mappa* napkin] **1** : a garment tied over the front of the body to protect the clothes **2** : a paved area for parking or handling airplanes — **aproned** *adj*

¹**ap·ro·pos** \ˌa-prə-'pō, 'a-prə-ˌpō\ *adv* [F *à propos*, lit.,

to the purpose] **1** : OPPORTUNELY **2** : in passing : INCIDENTALLY

²**apropos** *adj* : being to the point

apropos of *prep* : with regard to

apse \'aps\ *n* : a projecting usu. semicircular and vaulted part of a building (as a church)

¹**apt** \'apt\ *adj* **1** : well adapted : SUITABLE **2** : having an habitual tendency : LIKELY **3** : quick to learn — **apt·ly** *adv* — **apt·ness** \'apt-nəs\ *n*

²**apt** *abbr* **1** apartment **2** aptitude

ap·ti·tude \'ap-tə-ˌtüd, -ˌtyüd\ *n* **1** : natural ability : TALENT **2** : capacity for learning **3** : APPROPRIATENESS

aqua \'a-kwə, 'ä-\ *n* : a light greenish blue color

aqua·cul·ture *also* **aqui·cul·ture** \'a-kwə-ˌkəl-chər, 'ä-\ *n* : the cultivation of aquatic plants or animals (as fish or shellfish) for human use

aqua·ma·rine \ˌa-kwə-mə-'rēn, ˌä-\ *n* **1** : a bluish green gem **2** : a pale blue to light greenish blue

aqua·naut \'a-kwə-ˌnȯt, 'ä-\ *n* : a person who lives in an underwater shelter for an extended period

aqua·plane \-ˌplān\ *n* : a board towed behind a motorboat and ridden by a person standing on it — **aquaplane** *vb*

aqua re·gia \ˌa-kwə-'rē-j(ē-)ə\ *n* [NL, lit., royal water] : a mixture of nitric and hydrochloric acids that dissolves gold or platinum

aquar·i·um \ə-'kwar-ē-əm\ *n, pl* **-i·ums** *or* **-ia** \-ē-ə\ **1** : a container (as a glass tank) in which living aquatic animals or plants are kept **2** : a place where aquatic animals and plants are kept and shown

Aquar·i·us \ə-'kwar-ē-əs\ *n* [L, lit., water carrier] **1** : a zodiacal constellation between Capricorn and Pisces usu. pictured as a man pouring water **2** : the 11th sign of the zodiac in astrology; *also* : one born under this sign

¹**aquat·ic** \ə-'kwä-tik, -'kwa-\ *adj* **1** : growing or living in or frequenting water **2** : performed in or on water

²**aquatic** *n* : an aquatic animal or plant

aqua·vit \'ä-kwə-ˌvēt\ *n* : a clear liquor flavored with caraway seeds

aqua vi·tae \ˌa-kwə-'vī-tē, ˌä-\ *n* [ME, fr. ML, lit., water of life] : a strong alcoholic liquor (as brandy)

aq·ue·duct \'a-kwə-ˌdəkt\ *n* **1** : a conduit for carrying running water **2** : a structure carrying a canal over a river or hollow **3** : a passage in a bodily part

aqueduct 1

aque·ous \'ā-kwē-əs, 'a-\ *adj* **1** : WATERY **2** : made of, by, or with water

aqueous humor *n* : a clear fluid occupying the space between the lens and the cornea of the eye

aqui·fer \'a-kwə-fər, 'ä-\ *n* : a water-bearing stratum of permeable rock, sand, or gravel

aq·ui·line \'a-kwə-ˌlīn, -lən\ *adj* **1** : of or resembling an eagle **2** : hooked like an eagle's beak ⟨an ∼ nose⟩

ar *abbr* arrival; arrive

Ar *symbol* argon

AR *abbr* Arkansas

-ar *adj suffix* : of or relating to ⟨molecul*ar*⟩ : being ⟨spectacul*ar*⟩ : resembling ⟨oracul*ar*⟩

Ar·ab \'ar-əb\ *n* **1** : a member of a Semitic people of the Arabian peninsula in southwestern Asia **2** : a member of an Arabic-speaking people — **Arab** *adj* — **Ara·bi·an** \ə-'rā-bē-ən\ *adj or n*

ar·a·besque \ˌar-ə-'besk\ *n* : a design of interlacing lines forming figures of flowers, foliage, and sometimes animals — **arabesque** *adj*

¹**Ar·a·bic** \'ar-ə-bik\ *n* : a Semitic language of southwestern Asia and northern Africa

²**Arabic** *adj* **1** : of or relating to the Arabs, Arabic, or the Arabian peninsula in southwestern Asia **2** : expressed in or making use of Arabic numerals

Arabic numeral *n* : any of the number symbols 0, 1, 2, 3, 4, 5, 6, 7, 8, 9

ar·a·ble \'ar-ə-bəl\ *adj* : fit for or used for the growing of crops

arach·nid \ə-'rak-nəd\ *n* : any of a class of usu. 8-legged arthropods comprising the spiders, scorpions, mites, and ticks — **arachnid** *adj*

Ar·a·ma·ic \ˌar-ə-'mā-ik\ *n* : an ancient Semitic language

ar·a·mid \'ar-ə-məd, -ˌmid\ *n* : any of several light but very strong heat-resistant synthetic materials used esp. in textiles and plastics

Arap·a·ho *or* **Arap·a·hoe** \ə-'ra-pə-ˌhō\ *n, pl* **-ho** *or* **-hos** *or* **-hoe** *or* **-hoes** : a member of an American Indian people of the western U.S.

ar·bi·ter \'är-bə-tər\ *n* : one having power to decide : JUDGE

ar·bi·trage \'är-bə-ˌträzh\ *n* [F, fr. MF, arbitration] : the purchase and sale of the same or equivalent securities in different markets in order to profit from price discrepancies

ar·bi·tra·geur \ˌär-bə-(ˌ)trä-'zhər\ *or* **ar·bi·trag·er** \'är-bə-ˌträ-zhər\ *n* : one who practices arbitrage

ar·bit·ra·ment \är-'bi-trə-mənt\ *n* **1** : the act of deciding a dispute **2** : the judgment given by an arbitrator

ar·bi·trary \'är-bə-ˌtrer-ē\ *adj* **1** : AUTOCRATIC, DESPOTIC **2** : determined by will or caprice : selected at random — **ar·bi·trari·ly** \ˌär-bə-'trer-ə-lē\ *adv* — **ar·bi·trari·ness** \'är-bə-ˌtrer-ē-nəs\ *n*

ar·bi·trate \'är-bə-ˌtrāt\ *vb* **-trat·ed; -trat·ing** **1** : to act as arbitrator **2** : to act on as arbitrator **3** : to submit for decision to an arbitrator — **ar·bi·tra·tion** \ˌär-bə-'trā-shən\ *n*

ar·bi·tra·tor \'är-bə-ˌtrā-tər\ *n* : one chosen to settle differences between two parties in a controversy

ar·bor \'är-bər\ *n* [ME *erber* plot of grass, arbor, fr. OF *herbier* plot of grass, fr. *herbe* herb, grass] : a shelter formed of or covered with vines or branches

ar·bo·re·al \är-'bōr-ē-əl\ *adj* **1** : of, relating to, or resembling a tree **2** : living in trees ⟨~ monkeys⟩

ar·bo·re·tum \ˌär-bə-'rē-təm\ *n, pl* **-retums** *or* **-re·ta** \-tə\ [L, plantation of trees, fr. *arbor* tree] : a place where trees and plants are grown for scientific and educational purposes

ar·bor·vi·tae \ˌär-bər-'vī-tē\ *n* : any of various evergreen trees and shrubs with scalelike leaves that are related to the cypresses

ar·bour *chiefly Brit var of* ARBOR

ar·bu·tus \är-'byü-təs\ *n* : TRAILING ARBUTUS

¹**arc** \'ärk\ *n* **1** : a sustained luminous discharge of electricity (as between two electrodes) **2** : a continuous portion of a curved line (as part of the circumference of a circle)

²**arc** *vb* **arced** \'ärkt\; **arc·ing** \'är-kiŋ\ : to form an electric arc

ARC *abbr* **1** AIDS-related complex **2** American Red Cross

ar·cade \är-'kād\ *n* **1** : an arched or covered passageway; *esp* : one lined with shops **2** : a row of arches with their supporting columns

ar·cane \är-'kān\ *adj* : SECRET, MYSTERIOUS

¹**arch** \'ärch\ *n* **1** : a curved structure spanning an opening

(as a door) **2** : something resembling an arch **3** : ARCHWAY

²**arch** *vb* **1** : to cover with an arch **2** : to form or bend into an arch

³**arch** *adj* **1** : CHIEF, EMINENT **2** : ROGUISH, MISCHIEVOUS — **arch·ly** *adv* — **arch·ness** *n*

⁴**arch** *abbr* architect; architectural; architecture

ar·chae·ol·o·gy *or* **ar·che·ol·o·gy** \ˌär-kē-'ä-lə-jē\ *n* : the study of past human life as revealed by relics left by ancient peoples — **ar·chae·o·log·i·cal** \-ə-'lä-ji-kəl\ *adj* — **ar·chae·ol·o·gist** \-'ä-lə-jist\ *n*

ar·cha·ic \är-'kā-ik\ *adj* **1** : having the characteristics of the language of the past and surviving chiefly in specialized uses ⟨~ words⟩ **2** : belonging to an earlier time : ANTIQUATED — **ar·cha·i·cal·ly** \-i-k(ə-)lē\ *adv*

arch·an·gel \'är-ˌkān-jəl\ *n* : a chief angel

arch·bish·op \ärch-'bi-shəp\ *n* : a bishop of high rank

arch·bish·op·ric \-ə-(ˌ)prik\ *n* : the jurisdiction or office of an archbishop

arch·con·ser·va·tive \(ˌ)ärch-kən-'sər-və-tiv\ *n* : an extreme conservative — **archconservative** *adj*

arch·dea·con \-'dē-kən\ *n* : a church official who assists a diocesan bishop in ceremonial or administrative functions

arch·di·o·cese \-'dī-ə-səs, -ˌsēz\ *n* : the diocese of an archbishop

arch·duke \-'dük, -'dyük\ *n* **1** : a sovereign prince **2** : a prince of the imperial family of Austria

Ar·che·an \är-'kē-ən\ *adj* : of, relating to, or being the earliest eon of geologic history — **Archean** *n*

arch·en·e·my \ˌärch-'e-nə-mē\ *n, pl* **-mies** : a principal enemy

Ar·cheo·zo·ic \ˌär-kē-ə-'zō-ik\ *adj* : ARCHEAN — **Archeozoic** *n*

ar·chery \'är-chə-rē\ *n* : the art or practice of shooting with bow and arrows — **ar·cher** \'är-chər\ *n*

ar·che·type \'är-ki-ˌtīp\ *n* : the original pattern or model of all things of the same type

arch·fiend \ärch-'fēnd\ *n* : a chief fiend; *esp* : SATAN

ar·chi·epis·co·pal \ˌär-kē-ə-'pis-kə-pəl\ *adj* : of or relating to an archbishop

ar·chi·man·drite \ˌär-kə-'man-ˌdrīt\ *n* : a dignitary in an Eastern church ranking below a bishop

ar·chi·pel·a·go \ˌär-kə-'pe-lə-ˌgō, ˌär-chə-\ *n, pl* **-goes** *or* **-gos** : a group of islands

ar·chi·tect \'är-kə-ˌtekt\ *n* **1** : a person who plans buildings and oversees their construction **2** : a person who designs and guides a plan or undertaking

ar·chi·tec·ture \'är-kə-ˌtek-chər\ *n* **1** : the art or science of planning and building structures **2** : a method or style of building **3** : the manner in which the elements (as of a design) are arranged or organized — **ar·chi·tec·tur·al** \ˌär-kə-'tek-chə-rəl, -'tek-shrəl\ *adj* — **ar·chi·tec·tur·al·ly** *adv*

ar·chi·trave \'är-kə-ˌtrāv\ *n* : the supporting horizontal member just above the columns in a building in the classical style of architecture

ar·chive \'är-ˌkīv\ *n* : a place for keeping public records; *also* : public records — often used in pl.

ar·chi·vist \'är-kə-vist, -ˌkī-\ *n* : a person in charge of archives

ar·chon \'är-ˌkän, -kən\ *n* : a chief magistrate of ancient Athens

arch·way \'ärch-ˌwā\ *n* : a passageway under an arch; *also* : an arch over a passage

arc lamp *n* : a gas-filled electric lamp that produces light when a current arcs between incandescent electrodes

¹**arc·tic** \'ärk-tik, 'är-tik\ *adj* [ME *artik*, fr. L *arcticus*, fr.

\ə\abut \ᵊ\kitten \ər\further \a\ash \ā\ace \ä\mop, mar
\aᵫ\out \ch\chin \e\bet \ē\easy \g\go \i\hit \ī\ice \j\job
\ŋ\sing \ō\go \ȯ\law \ȯi\boy \th\thin \t͟h\the \ü\loot \ u̇\foot
\y\yet \zh\vision *see also* Pronunciation Symbols page

Gk *arktikos,* fr. *arktos* bear, Ursa Major, north] **1** *often cap* : of or relating to the north pole or the region near it **2** : FRIGID

²**arc·tic** \'är-tik, 'ärk-tik\ *n* : a rubber overshoe that reaches to the ankle or above

arctic circle *n, often cap A&C* : the parallel of latitude that is approximately 66½ degrees north of the equator

-ard *also* **-art** *n suffix* : one that is characterized by performing some action, possessing some quality, or being associated with some thing esp. conspicuously or excessively ⟨brag*art*⟩ ⟨dull*ard*⟩

ar·dent \'är-d°nt\ *adj* **1** : characterized by warmth of feeling : PASSIONATE **2** : FIERY, HOT **3** : GLOWING — **ar·dent·ly** *adv*

ar·dor \'är-dər\ *n* **1** : warmth of feeling : ZEAL **2** : sexual excitement

ar·dour *chiefly Brit var of* ARDOR

ar·du·ous \'är-jə-wəs, -dyu-wəs\ *adj* : DIFFICULT, LABORIOUS — **ar·du·ous·ly** *adv* — **ar·du·ous·ness** *n*

¹**are** *pres 2d sing or pres pl of* BE

²**are** \'ar\ *n* — see METRIC SYSTEM table

ar·ea \'ar-ē-ə\ *n* **1** : a flat surface or space **2** : the amount of surface included (as within the lines of a geometric figure) **3** : range or extent of some thing or concept : FIELD **4** : REGION

COMMON AREA FORMULAS

FIGURE	FORMULA	MEANING OF LETTERS
rectangle	$A = ab$	a = base; b = height
square	$A = a^2$	a = a side
triangle	$A = \frac{ab}{2}$	a = base; b = height
trapezoid	$A = \frac{h(a+b)}{2}$	h = height; a = the longer parallel side; b = the shorter side
parallelogram	$A = ab$	a = base; b = height
regular pentagon	$A = 1.720a^2$	a = a side
regular octagon	$A = 4.828a^2$	a = a side
circle	$A = \pi r^2$	r = radius; $\pi = 3.1416$

area code *n* : a 3-digit number that identifies each telephone service area in a country (as the U.S. or Canada)

are·na \ə-'rē-nə\ *n* [L *harena, arena* sand, sandy place] **1** : an enclosed area used for public entertainment **2** : a sphere of activity or competition

Ar·gen·tine \'är-jən-ˌtēn, -ˌtīn\ *or* **Ar·gen·tin·ean** *or* **Ar·gen·tin·i·an** \ˌär-jən-'ti-nē-ən\ *n* : a native or inhabitant of Argentina — **Argentine** *or* **Argentinean** *or* **Argentinian** *adj*

ar·gen·tite \'är-jən-ˌtīt\ *n* : a dark gray mineral that is an important ore of silver

ar·gon \'är-ˌgän\ *n* [Gk, neut. of *argos* idle, lazy, fr. *a*-not + *ergon* work; fr. its relative inertness] : a colorless odorless gaseous chemical element found in the air and used for filling electric lamps — see ELEMENT table

Ar·go·naut \'är-gə-ˌnȯt, -ˌnät\ *n* : one of a band of heroes sailing with Jason in search of the Golden Fleece

ar·go·sy \'är-gə-sē\ *n, pl* **-sies** **1** : a large merchant ship **2** : FLEET

ar·got \'är-gət, -ˌgō\ *n* : the language of a particular group or class

argu·able \'är-gyü-ə-bəl\ *adj* : open to argument, dispute, or question

ar·gu·ably \'är-gyü-(ə-)blē\ *adv* : it can be argued

ar·gue \'är-gyü\ *vb* **ar·gued; ar·gu·ing** **1** : to give reasons for or against something **2** : to contend in words : DISPUTE **3** : DEBATE **4** : to persuade by giving reasons

ar·gu·ment \'är-gyə-mənt\ *n* **1** : a reason offered in proof **2** : discourse intended to persuade **3** : QUARREL

ar·gu·men·ta·tion \ˌär-gyə-mən-'tā-shən\ *n* : the art of formal discussion

ar·gu·men·ta·tive \ˌär-gyə-'men-tə-tiv\ *adj* : inclined to argue

ar·gyle *also* **ar·gyll** \'är-ˌgīl\ *n, often cap* : a geometric knitting pattern of varicolored diamonds on a single background color; *also* : a sock knit in this pattern

aria \'är-ē-ə\ *n* : an accompanied elaborate vocal solo forming part of a larger work

ar·id \'ar-əd\ *adj* : very dry; *esp* : having insufficient rainfall to support agriculture — **arid·i·ty** \ə-'ri-də-tē\ *n*

Ar·i·es \'ar-ˌēz, -ē-ˌēz\ *n* [L, lit., ram] **1** : a zodiacal constellation between Pisces and Taurus pictured as a ram **2** : the 1st sign of the zodiac in astrology; *also* : one born under this sign

aright \ə-'rīt\ *adv* : RIGHT, CORRECTLY

arise \ə-'rīz\ *vb* **arose** \-'rōz\; **aris·en** \-'riz-°n\; **aris·ing** \-'rī-ziŋ\ **1** : to get up **2** : ORIGINATE **3** : ASCEND **syn** rise, derive, spring, issue

ar·is·toc·ra·cy \ˌar-ə-'stä-krə-sē\ *n, pl* **-cies** **1** : government by a noble or privileged class; *also* : a state so governed **2** : the governing class of an aristocracy **3** : UPPER CLASS — **aris·to·crat** \ə-'ris-tə-ˌkrat\ *n* — **aris·to·crat·ic** \ə-ˌris-tə-'kra-tik\ *adj*

arith *abbr* arithmetic; arithmetical

arith·me·tic \ə-'rith-mə-ˌtik\ *n* **1** : a branch of mathematics that deals with computations usu. with nonnegative real numbers **2** : COMPUTATION, CALCULATION — **ar·ith·met·ic** \ˌar-ith-'me-tik\ *or* **ar·ith·met·i·cal** \-ti-kəl\ *adj* — **ar·ith·met·i·cal·ly** \-ti-k(ə-)lē\ *adv* — **arith·me·ti·cian** \ə-ˌrith-mə-'ti-shən\ *n*

arithmetic mean *n* : the sum of a set of numbers divided by the number of numbers in the set

Ariz *abbr* Arizona

ark \'ärk\ *n* **1** : a boat held to resemble that of Noah's at the time of the Flood **2** : the sacred chest in a synagogue representing to Hebrews the presence of God; *also* : the repository for the scrolls of the Torah

Ark *abbr* Arkansas

¹**arm** \'ärm\ *n* **1** : a human upper limb; *also* : a corresponding limb of a lower animal with a backbone **2** : something resembling an arm in shape or position ⟨an ~ of a chair⟩ **3** : POWER, MIGHT ⟨the ~ of the law⟩ — **armed** \'ärmd\ *adj* — **arm·less** *adj*

²**arm** *vb* : to furnish with weapons

³**arm** *n* **1** : WEAPON **2** : a branch of the military forces **3** *pl* : the hereditary heraldic devices of a family

ar·ma·da \är-'mä-də, -'mā-\ *n* : a fleet of warships

ar·ma·dil·lo \ˌär-mə-'di-lō\ *n, pl* **-los** : any of several small burrowing mammals with the head and body protected by an armor of bony plates

armadillo

Ar·ma·ged·don \ˌär-mə-ˈged-ᵊn\ *n* : a final conclusive battle between the forces of good and evil; *also* : the site or time of this

ar·ma·ment \ˈär-mə-mənt\ *n* **1** : military strength **2** : arms and equipment (as of a tank or combat unit) **3** : the process of preparing for war

ar·ma·ture \ˈär-mə-ˌchùr, -chər\ *n* **1** : a protective covering or structure (as the spines of a cactus) **2** : the rotating part of an electric generator or motor; *also* : the movable part in an electromagnetic device (as a loudspeaker)

arm·chair \ˈärm-ˌcher\ *n* : a chair with armrests

armed forces *n pl* : the combined military, naval, and air forces of a nation

Ar·me·nian \är-ˈmē-nē-ən\ *n* : a native or inhabitant of Armenia

arm·ful \ˈärm-ˌfùl\ *n, pl* **armfuls** *or* **arms·ful** \ˈärmz-ˌfùl\ : as much as the arm or arms can hold

arm·hole \ˈärm-ˌhōl\ *n* : an opening for the arm in a garment

ar·mi·stice \ˈär-mə-stəs\ *n* : temporary suspension of hostilities by mutual agreement : TRUCE

arm·let \ˈärm-lət\ *n* : a band worn around the upper arm

ar·mor \ˈär-mər\ *n* **1** : protective covering **2** : armored forces and vehicles — **ar·mored** \-mərd\ *adj*

ar·mor·er \ˈär-mər-ər\ *n* **1** : a person who makes arms and armor **2** : a person who services firearms

ar·mo·ri·al \är-ˈmōr-ē-əl\ *adj* : of or bearing heraldic arms

ar·mory \ˈär-mə-rē\ *n, pl* **ar·mor·ies** **1** : a place where arms are stored **2** : a factory where arms are made

ar·mour, ar·moury *chiefly Brit var of* ARMOR, ARMORY

arm·pit \ˈärm-ˌpit\ *n* : the hollow under the junction of the arm and shoulder

arm·rest \-ˌrest\ *n* : a support for the arm

ar·my \ˈär-mē\ *n, pl* **armies** **1** : a body of men organized for war **2** *often cap* : the complete military organization of a country for land warfare **3** : a great number **4** : a body of persons organized to advance a cause

army ant *n* : any of various nomadic social ants

ar·my·worm \ˈär-mē-ˌwərm\ *n* : any of numerous moths whose larvae move about destroying crops

aro·ma \ə-ˈrō-mə\ *n* : a usu. pleasing odor : FRAGRANCE — **ar·o·mat·ic** \ˌar-ə-ˈma-tik\ *adj*

aro·ma·ther·a·py \ə-ˌrō-mə-ˈther-ə-pē\ *n* : massage with a preparation of fragrant oils extracted from herbs, flowers, and fruits

arose *past of* ARISE

¹**around** \ə-ˈraùnd\ *adv* **1** : in a circle or in circumference ⟨a tree five feet ∼⟩ **2** : in or along a circuit ⟨the road goes ∼ by the lake⟩ **3** : on all sides ⟨nothing for miles ∼⟩ **4** : NEARBY ⟨wait ∼ awhile⟩ **5** : from one place to another ⟨travels ∼ on business⟩ **6** : in an opposite direction ⟨turn ∼⟩

²**around** *prep* **1** : SURROUNDING ⟨trees ∼ the house⟩ **2** : to or on another side of ⟨∼ the corner⟩ **3** : NEAR ⟨stayed right ∼ home⟩ **4** : along the circuit of ⟨go ∼ the world⟩

arouse \ə-ˈraùz\ *vb* **aroused; arous·ing** **1** : to awaken from sleep **2** : to stir up — **arous·al** \-ˈraù-zəl\ *n*

ar·peg·gio \är-ˈpe-jē-ˌō, -ˈpe-jō\ *n, pl* **-gios** [It fr. *arpeggiare* to play on the harp, fr. *arpa* harp] : a chord whose notes are performed in succession and not simultaneously

arr *abbr* **1** arranged **2** arrival; arrive

ar·raign \ə-ˈrān\ *vb* **1** : to call before a court to answer to an indictment **2** : to accuse of wrong or imperfection — **ar·raign·ment** *n*

ar·range \ə-ˈrānj\ *vb* **ar·ranged; ar·rang·ing** **1** : to put in order **2** : to adapt (a musical composition) to voices or instruments other than those for which it was orig. written **3** : to come to an agreement about : SETTLE — **ar·range·ment** *n* — **ar·rang·er** *n*

ar·rant \ˈar-ənt\ *adj* : being notoriously without moderation : EXTREME

ar·ras \ˈar-əs\ *n, pl* **arras** **1** : TAPESTRY **2** : a wall hanging or screen of tapestry

¹**ar·ray** \ə-ˈrā\ *vb* **1** : to dress esp. splendidly **2** : to arrange in order

²**array** *n* **1** : a regular arrangement **2** : rich apparel **3** : an imposing group

ar·rears \ə-ˈrirz\ *n pl* **1** : a state of being behind in the discharge of obligations ⟨in ∼ with the rent⟩ **2** : overdue debts

¹**ar·rest** \ə-ˈrest\ *vb* **1** : STOP, CHECK **2** : to take into legal custody

²**arrest** *n* **1** : the act of stopping; *also* : the state of being stopped **2** : the taking into custody by legal authority

ar·riv·al \ə-ˈrī-vəl\ *n* **1** : the act of arriving **2** : one that arrives

ar·rive \ə-ˈrīv\ *vb* **ar·rived; ar·riv·ing** **1** : to reach a destination **2** : to make an appearance ⟨the guests have *arrived*⟩ **3** : to attain success

ar·ro·gant \ˈar-ə-gənt\ *adj* : offensively exaggerating one's own importance — **ar·ro·gance** \-gəns\ *n* — **ar·ro·gant·ly** *adv*

ar·ro·gate \-ˌgāt\ *vb* **-gat·ed; -gat·ing** : to claim or seize without justification as one's right — **ar·ro·ga·tion** \ˌar-ə-ˈgā-shən\ *n*

ar·row \ˈar-ō\ *n* **1** : a missile shot from a bow and usu. having a slender shaft, a pointed head, and feathers at the butt **2** : a pointed mark used to indicate direction

ar·row·head \ˈar-ō-ˌhed\ *n* : the pointed end of an arrow

ar·row·root \-ˌrüt, -ˌrùt\ *n* : an edible starch from the roots of any of several tropical American plants; *also* : a plant yielding arrowroot

ar·roy·o \ə-ˈròi-ə, -ō\ *n, pl* **-roy·os** [Sp] **1** : a watercourse in a dry region **2** : a water-carved gully or channel

ar·se·nal \ˈärs-nəl, ˈärs-ᵊn-əl\ *n* [ultim. fr. Ar *dārṣinā'ah* house of manufacture] **1** : a place for making and storing arms and military equipment **2** : STORE, REPERTORY

ar·se·nic \ˈärs-nik, ˈärs-ᵊn-ik\ *n* **1** : a solid brittle poisonous chemical element of grayish metallic luster — see ELEMENT table **2** : a very poisonous oxygen compound of arsenic used in making insecticides

ar·son \ˈärs-ᵊn\ *n* : the willful or malicious burning of property — **ar·son·ist** \-ist\ *n*

¹**art** \ˈärt\ *n* **1** : skill acquired by experience or study **2** : a branch of learning; *esp* : one of the humanities **3** : an occupation requiring knowledge or skill **4** : the use of skill and imagination in the production of things of beauty; *also* : works so produced **5** : ARTFULNESS

²**art** *abbr* **1** article **2** artificial **3** artillery

-art — see -ARD

ar·te·fact *chiefly Brit var of* ARTIFACT

ar·te·ri·al \är-ˈtir-ē-əl\ *adj* **1** : of or relating to an artery; *also* : relating to or being the oxygenated blood found in most arteries **2** : of, relating to, or being a route for through traffic

ar·te·ri·ole \är-ˈtir-ē-ˌōl\ *n* : one of the small terminal branches of an artery that ends in capillaries — **ar·te·ri·o·lar** \-ˌtir-ē-ˈō-lər\ *adj*

ar·te·rio·scle·ro·sis \är-ˌtir-ē-ō-sklə-ˈrō- səs\ *n* : a chronic disease in which arterial walls are abnormally thickened and hardened — **ar·te·rio·scle·rot·ic** \-ˈrä-tik\ *adj or n*

ar·tery \ˈär-tə-rē\ *n, pl* **-ter·ies** **1** : one of the tubular vessels that carry blood from the heart **2** : a main channel of transportation or communication

ar·te·sian well \är-ˈtē-zhən-\ *n* : a well from which the

\ə\abut \ᵊ\kitten \ər\further \a\ash \ā\ace \ä\mop, mar \aù\out \ch\chin \e\bet \ē\easy \g\go \i\hit \ī\ice \j\job \ŋ\sing \ō\go \ò\law \òi\boy \th\thin \th̲\the \ü\loot \ù\foot \y\yet \zh\vision *see also* Pronunciation Symbols page water flows to the surface by natural pressure; *also* : a deep well

art·ful \\'ärt-fəl\ *adj* **1** : INGENIOUS **2** : CRAFTY — **art·ful·ly** *adv* — **art·ful·ness** *n*

ar·thri·tis \är-'thrī-təs\ *n, pl* **-thri·ti·des** \-'thri-tə-ˌdēz\ : inflammation of the joints — **ar·thrit·ic** \-'thri-tik\ *adj or n*

ar·thro·pod \'är-thrə-ˌpäd\ *n* : any of a phylum of invertebrate animals comprising those (as insects, spiders, or crabs) with segmented bodies and jointed limbs — **arthropod** *adj*

ar·thros·co·py \är-'thräs-kə-pē\ *n, pl* **-pies** : visual examination of the interior of a joint (as the knee) with a special surgical instrument; *also* : joint surgery using arthroscopy — **ar·thro·scope** \'är-thrə-ˌskōp\ *n* — **ar·thro·scop·ic** \ˌär-thrə-'skä-pik\ *adj*

ar·ti·choke \'är-tə-ˌchōk\ *n* [It dial. *articiocco*, ultim. fr. Ar *al-khurshūf*] : a tall herb related to the daisies; *also* : its edible flower head

artichoke

ar·ti·cle \'är-ti-kəl\ *n* [ME, fr. OF, fr. L *articulus* joint, division, dim. of *artus* joint, limb] **1** : a distinct part of a written document **2** : a nonfictional prose composition forming an independent part of a publication **3** : a word (as *an, the*) used with a noun to limit or give definiteness to its application **4** : a member of a class of things; *esp* : COMMODITY

ar·tic·u·lar \är-'ti-kyə-lər\ *adj* : of or relating to a joint

¹**ar·tic·u·late** \är-'ti-kyə-lət\ *adj* **1** : divided into meaningful parts : INTELLIGIBLE **2** : able to speak; *also* : expressing oneself readily and effectively **3** : JOINTED — **ar·tic·u·late·ly** *adv* — **ar·tic·u·late·ness** *n*

²**ar·tic·u·late** \-ˌlāt\ *vb* **-lat·ed; -lat·ing** **1** : to utter distinctly **2** : to unite by or as if by joints — **ar·tic·u·la·tion** \-ˌti-kyə-'lā-shən\ *n*

ar·ti·fact \'är-tə-ˌfakt\ *n* : something made or modified by humans usu. for a purpose; *esp* : an object remaining from another time or culture ⟨prehistoric ∼s⟩

ar·ti·fice \'är-tə-fəs\ *n* **1** : TRICK; *also* : TRICKERY **2** : an ingenious device; *also* : INGENUITY

ar·ti·fi·cer \är-'ti-fə-sər, 'är-tə-fə-sər\ *n* : a skilled worker

ar·ti·fi·cial \ˌär-tə-'fi-shəl\ *adj* **1** : produced by art rather than nature; *also* : made by humans to imitate nature **2** : not genuine : FEIGNED — **ar·ti·fi·ci·al·i·ty** \-ˌfi-shē-'a-lə-tē\ *n* — **ar·ti·fi·cial·ly** *adv* — **ar·ti·fi·cial·ness** *n*

artificial insemination *n* : introduction of semen into the uterus or oviduct by other than natural means

artificial intelligence *n* : the capability of a machine to imitate intelligent human behavior

artificial respiration *n* : the rhythmic forcing of air into and out of the lungs of a person whose breathing has stopped

ar·til·lery \är-'ti-lə-rē\ *n, pl* **-ler·ies** **1** : crew-served mounted firearms (as guns) **2** : a branch of the army armed with artillery — **ar·til·ler·ist** \-rist\ *n*

ar·ti·san \'är-tə-zən, -sən\ *n* : a skilled manual worker

art·ist \'är-tist\ *n* **1** : one who practices an art; *esp* : one who creates objects of beauty **2** : ARTISTE

ar·tiste \är-'tēst\ *n* : a skilled public performer

ar·tis·tic \är-'tis-tik\ *adj* : showing taste and skill — **ar·tis·ti·cal·ly** \-ti-k(ə-)lē\ *adv*

art·ist·ry \'är-tə-strē\ *n* : artistic quality or ability

art·less \'ärt-ləs\ *adj* **1** : lacking art or skill **2** : free from artificiality : NATURAL **3** : free from guile : SINCERE — **art·less·ly** *adv* — **art·less·ness** *n*

art nou·veau \ˌär-nü-'vō, ˌärt-\ *n, often cap A&N* [F, lit., new art] : a late 19th century design style characterized by sinuous lines and leaf-shaped forms

arty \'är-tē\ *adj* **art·i·er; -est** : showily or pretentiously artistic — **art·i·ly** \'ärt-ᵊl-ē\ *adv* — **art·i·ness** *n*

ar·um \'ar-əm\ *n* : any of a family of plants (as the jack-in-the-pulpit or a skunk cabbage) with flowers in a fleshy enclosed spike

ARV *abbr* American Revised Version

¹**-ary** *n suffix* : thing or person belonging to or connected with ⟨functiona*ry*⟩

²**-ary** *adj suffix* : of, relating to, or connected with ⟨budget*ary*⟩

Ary·an \'ar-ē-ən, 'er-; 'är-yən\ *adj* **1** : INDO-EUROPEAN **2** : NORDIC — **Aryan** *n*

¹**as** \əz, (ˌ)az\ *adv* **1** : to the same degree or amount : EQUALLY ⟨∼ green as grass⟩ **2** : for instance ⟨various trees, ∼ oak or pine⟩ **3** : when considered in a specified relation ⟨my opinion ∼ distinguished from his⟩

²**as** *conj* **1** : in the same amount or degree in which ⟨green ∼ grass⟩ **2** : in the same way that ⟨farmed ∼ his father before him had farmed⟩ **3** : WHILE, WHEN ⟨spoke to me ∼ I was leaving⟩ **4** : THOUGH ⟨improbable ∼ it seems⟩ **5** : SINCE, BECAUSE ⟨∼ I'm not wanted, I'll go⟩ **6** : that the result is ⟨so guilty ∼ to leave no doubt⟩

³**as** *pron* **1** : THAT — used after *same* or *such* ⟨it's the same price ∼ before⟩ **2** : a fact that ⟨he's rich, ∼ you know⟩

⁴**as** *prep* : in the capacity or character of ⟨this will serve ∼ a substitute⟩

As *symbol* arsenic

AS *abbr* **1** American Samoa **2** Anglo-Saxon **3** associate in science

asa·fet·i·da *or* **asa·foe·ti·da** \ˌa-sə-'fi-tə-dē, -'fe-tə-də\ *n* : an ill-smelling plant gum formerly used in medicine

ASAP *abbr* as soon as possible

as·bes·tos \as-'bes-təs, az-\ *n* : a noncombustible grayish mineral that occurs in fibrous form and has been used as a fireproof material

as·cend \ə-'send\ *vb* **1** : to move upward : MOUNT, CLIMB **2** : to succeed to : OCCUPY ⟨he ∼ed the throne⟩

as·cen·dan·cy *also* **as·cen·den·cy** \ə-'sen-dən-sē\ *n* : controlling influence : DOMINATION

¹**as·cen·dant** *also* **as·cen·dent** \ə-'sen-dənt\ *n* : a dominant position

²**ascendant** *also* **ascendent** *adj* **1** : moving upward **2** : DOMINANT

as·cen·sion \ə-'sen-chən\ *n* : the act or process of ascending

Ascension Day *n* : the Thursday 40 days after Easter observed in commemoration of Christ's ascension into heaven

as·cent \ə-'sent\ *n* **1** : the act of mounting upward : CLIMB **2** : degree of upward slope

as·cer·tain \ˌas-ər-'tān\ *vb* : to learn with certainty — **as·cer·tain·able** *adj*

as·cet·ic \ə-'se-tik\ *adj* : practicing self-denial esp. for spiritual reasons : AUSTERE — **ascetic** *n* — **as·cet·i·cism** \-'se-tə-ˌsi-zəm\ *n*

ASCII \'as-kē\ *n* [*American Standard Code for Informa-*

tion *I*nterchange] : a computer code for representing alphanumeric information

ascor·bic acid \ə-ˈskȯr-bik-\ *n* : VITAMIN C

as·cot \ˈas-kət, -ˌkät\ *n* [*Ascot* Heath, racetrack near Ascot, England] : a broad neck scarf that is looped under the chin

as·cribe \ə-ˈskrīb\ *vb* **as·cribed; as·crib·ing** : to refer to a supposed cause, source, or author : ATTRIBUTE — **as·crib·able** *adj* — **as·crip·tion** \-ˈskrip-shən\ *n*

asep·tic \ā-ˈsep-tik\ *adj* : free or freed from disease‐causing germs

asex·u·al \ā-ˈsek-shə-wəl\ *adj* 1 : lacking sex or functional sex organs 2 : occurring or formed without the production and union of two kinds of germ cells ⟨∼ reproduction⟩ — **asex·u·al·ly** *adv*

as for *prep* : with regard to : CONCERNING ⟨*as for* the others, they were late⟩

¹**ash** \ˈash\ *n* 1 : any of a genus of trees related to the olive and having winged seeds and bark with grooves and ridges 2 : the tough elastic wood of an ash

²**ash** *n* 1 : the solid matter left when material is burned 2 : fine mineral particles from a volcano 3 *pl* : the remains of the dead human body after cremation or disintegration

ashamed \ə-ˈshāmd\ *adj* 1 : feeling shame 2 : restrained by anticipation of shame ⟨∼ to say anything⟩ — **asham·ed·ly** \-ˈshā-məd-lē\ *adv*

ash·en \ˈa-shən\ *adj* : resembling ashes (as in color); *esp* : deadly pale

ash·lar \ˈash-lər\ *n* : hewn or squared stone; *also* : masonry of such stone

ashore \ə-ˈshȯr\ *adv* : on or to the shore

as how *conj* : THAT ⟨allowed *as how* she was glad to be here⟩

ash·ram \ˈäsh-rəm\ *n* : a religious retreat esp. of a Hindu sage

ash·tray \ˈash-ˌtrā\ *n* : a receptacle for tobacco ashes

Ash Wednesday *n* : the 1st day of Lent

ashy \ˈa-shē\ *adj* **ash·i·er; -est** : ASHEN

Asian \ˈā-zhən\ *adj* : of, relating to, or characteristic of the continent of Asia or its people — **Asian** *n*

Asi·at·ic \ˌā-zhē-ˈa-tik\ *adj* : ASIAN — sometimes taken to be offensive — **Asiatic** *n*

¹**aside** \ə-ˈsīd\ *adv* 1 : to or toward the side 2 : out of the way : AWAY

²**aside** *n* : an actor's words heard by the audience but supposedly not by other characters on stage

aside from *prep* 1 : BESIDES ⟨*aside from* being pretty, she's intelligent⟩ 2 : with the exception of ⟨*aside from* one D his grades are excellent⟩

as if *conj* 1 : as it would be if ⟨it's *as if* nothing had changed⟩ 2 : as one would if ⟨he acts *as if* he'd never been away⟩ 3 : THAT ⟨it seems *as if* nothing ever happens around here⟩

as·i·nine \ˈas-ᵊn-ˌīn\ *adj* [L *asininus*, fr. *asinus* ass] : STUPID, FOOLISH — **as·i·nin·i·ty** \ˌa-sə-ˈni-nə-tē\ *n*

ask \ˈask\ *vb* **asked** \ˈaskt\ **ask·ing** 1 : to call on for an answer 2 : UTTER ⟨∼ a question⟩ 3 : to make a request of ⟨∼ him for help⟩ 4 : to make a request for ⟨∼ help of her⟩ 5 : to set as a price ⟨∼ed $800 for the car⟩ 6 : INVITE

askance \ə-ˈskans\ *adv* 1 : with a side glance 2 : with distrust

askew \ə-ˈskyü\ *adv or adj* : out of line : AWRY

ASL *abbr* American Sign Language

¹**aslant** \ə-ˈslant\ *adv or adj* : in a slanting direction

²**aslant** *prep* : over or across in a slanting direction

asleep \ə-ˈslēp\ *adv or adj* 1 : in or into a state of sleep 2 : DEAD 3 : NUMB 4 : INACTIVE

as long as *conj* 1 : provided that ⟨do as you like *as long as* you get home on time⟩ 2 : INASMUCH AS, SINCE ⟨*as long as* you're up, turn on the light⟩

aso·cial \(ˌ)ā-ˈsō-shəl\ *adj* : ANTISOCIAL

as of *prep* : AT, DURING, FROM, ON ⟨takes effect *as of* July 1⟩

asp \ˈasp\ *n* : a small poisonous African snake

as·par·a·gus \ə-ˈspar-ə-gəs\ *n* : a tall branching perennial herb related to the lilies; *also* : its edible young stalks

as·par·tame \as-ˈpär-ˌtām\ *n* : a crystalline low‐calorie sweetener

ASPCA *abbr* American Society for the Prevention of Cruelty to Animals

as·pect \ˈas-ˌpekt\ *n* 1 : a position facing a particular direction 2 : APPEARANCE, LOOK 3 : PHASE

as·pen \ˈas-pən\ *n* : any of several poplars with leaves that flutter in the slightest breeze

as per \ˈaz-ˌpər\ *prep* : in accordance with ⟨*as per* instructions⟩

as·per·i·ty \a-ˈsper-ə-tē\ *n, pl* **-ties** 1 : ROUGHNESS 2 : harshness of temper

as·per·sion \ə-ˈspər-zhən\ *n* : a slanderous or defamatory remark

as·phalt \ˈas-ˌfȯlt\ *also* **as·phal·tum** \as-ˈfȯl-təm\ *n* : a dark substance found in natural beds or obtained as a residue in petroleum refining and used esp. in paving streets

asphalt jungle *n* : a big city or a specified part of a big city

as·pho·del \ˈas-fə-ˌdel\ *n* : any of several Old World herbs related to the lilies and bearing flowers in long erect spikes

as·phyx·ia \as-ˈfik-sē-ə\ *n* : a lack of oxygen or excess of carbon dioxide in the body usu. caused by interruption of breathing and causing unconsciousness

as·phyx·i·ate \-sē-ˌāt\ *vb* **-at·ed; -at·ing** : SUFFOCATE — **as·phyx·i·a·tion** \-ˌfik-sē-ˈā-shən\ *n*

as·pic \ˈas-pik\ *n* [F, lit., asp] : a savory meat jelly

as·pi·rant \ˈas-pə-rənt, ə-ˈspī-rənt\ *n* : one who aspires *syn* candidate, applicant, seeker

¹**as·pi·rate** \ˈas-pə-rət\ *n* 1 : an independent sound \h\ or a character (as the letter *h*) representing it 2 : a consonant having aspiration as its final component

²**as·pi·rate** \ˈas-pə-ˌrāt\ *vb* **-rat·ed; -rat·ing** : to draw, remove, or take up or into by suction

as·pi·ra·tion \ˌas-pə-ˈrā-shən\ *n* 1 : the pronunciation or addition of an aspirate; *also* : the aspirate or its symbol 2 : a drawing of something in, out, up, or through by or as if by suction 3 : a strong desire to achieve something noble; *also* : an object of this desire

as·pire \ə-ˈspīr\ *vb* **as·pired; as·pir·ing** 1 : to seek to attain or accomplish a particular goal 2 : to rise aloft

as·pi·rin \ˈas-pə-rən\ *n, pl* **aspirin** *or* **aspirins** 1 : a white crystalline drug used to relieve pain and fever 2 : a tablet of aspirin

as regards *also* **as respects** *prep* : in regard to : with respect to

ass \ˈas\ *n* 1 : any of several long-eared mammals smaller than the related horses; *esp* : one of Africa ancestral to the donkey 2 : a stupid person

as·sail \ə-ˈsāl\ *vb* : to attack violently — **as·sail·able** *adj* — **as·sail·ant** *n*

as·sas·sin \ə-ˈsas-ᵊn\ *n* [ML *assassinus*, fr. Ar *ḥashshāshīn*, pl. of *ḥashshāsh* hashish-user, fr. *ḥashīsh* hashish] : a murderer esp. for hire or fanatical reasons

as·sas·si·nate \ə-ˈsas-ᵊn-ˌāt\ *vb* **-nat·ed; -nat·ing** : to murder by sudden or secret attack — **as·sas·si·na·tion** \-ˌsas-ᵊn-ˈā-shən\ *n*

as·sault \ə-ˈsȯlt\ *n* 1 : a violent attack 2 : an unlawful attempt or threat to do harm to another — **assault** *vb*

assault rifle *n* : a military automatic rifle with a large‐capacity magazine

---

\ə\abut \ᵊ\kitten \ər\further \a\ash \ā\ace \ä\mop, mar
\au̇\out \ch\chin \e\bet \ē\easy \g\go \i\hit \ī\ice \j\job
\ŋ\sing \ō\go \ȯ\law \ȯi\boy \th\thin \t̲h̲\the \ü\loot \u̇\foot
\y\yet \zh\vision *see also* Pronunciation Symbols page

¹**as·say** \\'a-ˌsā, a-ˈsā\\ *n* : analysis to determine the quantity of one or more components present in a sample (as of an ore or drug)

²**as·say** \\a-ˈsā, ˈa-ˌsā\\ *vb* **1** : TRY, ATTEMPT **2** : to subject (as an ore or drug) to an assay **3** : JUDGE 3

as·sem·blage \\ə-ˈsem-blij, *3 & 4 also* ˌas-ˌäm-ˈbläzh\\ *n* **1** : a collection of persons or things : GATHERING **2** : the act of assembling **3** : an artistic composition made from scraps, junk, and odds and ends **4** : the art of making assemblages

as·sem·ble \\ə-ˈsem-bəl\\ *vb* **-bled; -bling 1** : to collect into one place : CONGREGATE **2** : to fit together the parts of **3** : to meet together : CONVENE

as·sem·bly \\ə-ˈsem-blē\\ *n, pl* **-blies 1** : a gathering of persons : MEETING **2** *cap* : a legislative body; *esp* : the lower house of a legislature **3** : a signal for troops to assemble **4** : the fitting together of parts (as of a machine)

assembly language *n* : a computer language consisting of mnemonic codes corresponding to machine-language instructions

assembly line *n* : an arrangement of machines, equipment, and workers in which work passes from operation to operation in a direct line

as·sem·bly·man \\ə-ˈsem-blē-mən\\ *n* : a member of a legislative assembly

as·sem·bly·wom·an \\-ˌwu̇-mən\\ *n* : a woman who is a member of an assembly

as·sent \\ə-ˈsent\\ *vb* : AGREE, CONCUR — **assent** *n*

as·sert \\ə-ˈsərt\\ *vb* **1** : to state positively **2** : to demonstrate the existence of **syn** declare, affirm, protest, avow, claim — **as·ser·tive** \\-ˈsər-tiv\\ *adj* — **as·ser·tive·ness** *n*

as·ser·tion \\ə-ˈsər-shən\\ *n* : a positive statement

as·sess \\ə-ˈses\\ *vb* **1** : to fix the rate or amount of **2** : to impose (as a tax) at a specified rate **3** : to evaluate for taxation — **as·sess·ment** *n* — **as·ses·sor** \\-ˈse-sər\\ *n*

as·set \\'a-ˌset\\ *n* **1** *pl* : the entire property of a person or company that may be used to pay debts **2** : ADVANTAGE, RESOURCE

as·sev·er·ate \\ə-ˈse-və-ˌrāt\\ *vb* **-at·ed; -at·ing** : to assert earnestly — **as·sev·er·a·tion** \\-ˌse-və-ˈrā-shən\\ *n*

as·sid·u·ous \\ə-ˈsi-jə-wəs\\ *adj* : steadily attentive : DILIGENT — **as·si·du·i·ty** \\ˌa-sə-ˈdü-ə-tē, -ˈdyü-\\ *n* — **as·sid·u·ous·ly** *adv* — **as·sid·u·ous·ness** *n*

as·sign \\ə-ˈsīn\\ *vb* **1** : to transfer (property) to another **2** : to appoint to or as a duty ⟨∼ a lesson⟩ **3** : FIX, SPECIFY ⟨∼ a limit⟩ **4** : ASCRIBE ⟨∼ a reason⟩ — **as·sign·able** *adj*

as·sig·na·tion \\ˌa-sig-ˈnā-shən\\ *n* : an appointment for a meeting; *esp* : TRYST

assigned risk *n* : a poor risk (as an accident-prone motorist) that an insurance company is forced to insure by state law

as·sign·ment \\ə-ˈsīn-mənt\\ *n* **1** : the act of assigning **2** : something assigned

as·sim·i·late \\ə-ˈsi-mə-ˌlāt\\ *vb* **-lat·ed; -lat·ing 1** : to take up and absorb as nourishment; *also* : to absorb into a cultural tradition **2** : COMPREHEND **3** : to make or become similar — **as·sim·i·la·tion** \\-ˌsi-mə-ˈlā-shən\\ *n*

¹**as·sist** \\ə-ˈsist\\ *vb* : HELP, AID — **as·sis·tance** \\-ˈsis-təns\\ *n*

²**assist** *n* **1** : an act of assistance **2** : the action of a player who enables a teammate to make a putout (as in baseball) or score a goal (as in hockey)

as·sis·tant \\ə-ˈsis-tənt\\ *n* : a person who assists : HELPER

as·size \\ə-ˈsīz\\ *n* **1** : a judicial inquest **2** *pl* : the former regular sessions of superior courts in English counties

assn *abbr* association

assoc *abbr* associate; associated; association

¹**as·so·ci·ate** \\ə-ˈsō-shē-ˌāt, -sē-\\ *vb* **-at·ed; -at·ing 1** : to join in companionship or partnership **2** : to connect in thought

²**as·so·ciate** \\-shē-ət, -sē-; -shət\\ *n* **1** : a fellow worker

: PARTNER **2** : COMPANION **3** *often cap* : a degree conferred esp. by a junior college ⟨∼ in arts⟩ — **associate** *adj*

as·so·ci·a·tion \\ə-ˌsō-shē-ˈā-shən, -sē-\\ *n* **1** : the act of associating **2** : an organization of persons : SOCIETY

as·so·cia·tive \\ə-ˈsō-shē-ˌā-tiv, -sē-; -shə-tiv\\ *adj* : of, relating to, or involved in association esp. of ideas or images

as·so·nance \\'a-sə-nəns\\ *n* : repetition of vowels esp. as an alternative to rhyme in verse — **as·so·nant** \\-nənt\\ *adj or n*

as soon as *conj* : immediately at or shortly after the time that ⟨we'll start *as soon as* they arrive⟩

as·sort \\ə-ˈsȯrt\\ *vb* **1** : to distribute into like groups : CLASSIFY **2** : HARMONIZE

as·sort·ed \\-ˈsȯr-təd\\ *adj* : consisting of various kinds

as·sort·ment \\-ˈsȯrt-mənt\\ *n* : a collection of assorted things or persons

asst *abbr* assistant

as·suage \\ə-ˈswāj\\ *vb* **as·suaged; as·suag·ing 1** : to make (as pain or grief) less : EASE **2** : SATISFY **syn** alleviate, relieve, lighten, mitigate

as·sume \\ə-ˈsüm\\ *vb* **as·sumed; as·sum·ing 1** : to take upon oneself **2** : to pretend to have or be **3** : to take as granted or true though not proved

as·sump·tion \\ə-ˈsəmp-shən\\ *n* **1** : the taking up of a person into heaven **2** *cap* : August 15 observed in commemoration of the Assumption of the Virgin Mary **3** : a taking upon oneself **4** : PRETENSION **5** : SUPPOSITION

as·sur·ance \\ə-ˈshu̇r-əns\\ *n* **1** : PLEDGE **2** *chiefly Brit* : INSURANCE **3** : SECURITY **4** : SELF-CONFIDENCE; *also* : AUDACITY

as·sure \\ə-ˈshu̇r\\ *vb* **as·sured; as·sur·ing 1** : INSURE **2** : to give confidence to **3** : to state confidently to **4** : to make certain the coming or attainment of

as·sured \\ə-ˈshu̇rd\\ *n, pl* **assured** *or* **assureds** : INSURED

as·ta·tine \\'as-tə-ˌtēn\\ *n* : an unstable radioactive chemical element — see ELEMENT table

as·ter \\'as-tər\\ *n* : any of various mostly fall-blooming leafy-stemmed composite herbs with daisylike purple, white, pink, or yellow flower heads

as·ter·isk \\'as-tə-ˌrisk\\ *n* [L *asteriscus*, fr. Gk *asteriskos*, lit., little star, dim. of *astēr*] : a character * used as a reference mark or as an indication of the omission of letters or words

astern \\ə-ˈstərn\\ *adv or adj* **1** : in, at, or toward the stern **2** : BACKWARD

as·ter·oid \\'as-tə-ˌrȯid\\ *n* : any of the numerous small celestial bodies found esp. between Mars and Jupiter

asth·ma \\'az-mə\\ *n* : an often allergic disorder marked by difficulty in breathing and a cough — **asth·mat·ic** \\az-ˈma-tik\\ *adj or n*

as though *conj* : AS IF

astig·ma·tism \\ə-ˈstig-mə-ˌti-zəm\\ *n* : a defect in a lens or an eye causing improper focusing — **as·tig·mat·ic** \\ˌas-tig-ˈma-tik\\ *adj*

astir \\ə-ˈstər\\ *adj* **1** : being in action : MOVING **2** : being out of bed

as to *prep* **1** : ABOUT, CONCERNING ⟨uncertain *as to* what went on⟩ **2** : ACCORDING TO ⟨graded *as to* size⟩

as·ton·ish \\ə-ˈstä-nish\\ *vb* : to strike with sudden and usu. great wonder : AMAZE — **as·ton·ish·ing·ly** *adv* — **as·ton·ish·ment** *n*

as·tound \\ə-ˈstau̇nd\\ *vb* : to fill with bewilderment or wonder — **as·tound·ing·ly** *adv*

¹**astrad·dle** \\ə-ˈstrad-ᵊl\\ *adv* : on or above and extending onto both sides

²**astraddle** *prep* : ASTRIDE

as·tra·khan \\'as-trə-kən, -ˌkan\\ *n, often cap* **1** : karakul of Russian origin **2** : a cloth with a usu. wool, curled, and looped pile resembling karakul

as·tral \\'as-trəl\\ *adj* : of, relating to, or coming from the stars

astray \ə-'strā\ *adv or adj* **1 :** off the right path or route **2 :** into error

¹astride \ə-'strīd\ *adv* **1 :** with one leg on each side **2 :** with legs apart

²astride *prep* **:** with one leg on each side of

¹as·trin·gent \ə-'strin-jənt\ *adj* **:** able or tending to shrink body tissues — **as·trin·gen·cy** \-jən-sē\ *n*

²astringent *n* **:** an astringent agent or substance

astrol *abbr* astrologer; astrology

as·tro·labe \'as-trə-ˌlāb\ *n* **:** an instrument formerly used for observing the positions of celestial bodies

as·trol·o·gy \ə-'strä-lə-jē\ *n* **:** divination based on the supposed influence of the stars upon human events — **as·trol·o·ger** \-jər\ *n* — **as·tro·log·i·cal** \ˌas-trə-'lä-ji-kəl\ *adj*

astron *abbr* astronomer; astronomy

as·tro·naut \'as-trə-ˌnȯt\ *n* **:** a traveler in a spacecraft

as·tro·nau·tics \ˌas-trə-'nȯ-tiks\ *n* **:** the science of the construction and operation of spacecraft — **as·tro·nau·tic** \-tik\ *or* **as·tro·nau·ti·cal** \-ti-kəl\ *adj*

as·tro·nom·i·cal \ˌas-trə-'nä-mi-kəl\ *also* **as·tro·nom·ic** \-mik\ *adj* **1 :** of or relating to astronomy **2 :** extremely large ⟨an ~ amount of money⟩

astronomical unit *n* **:** a unit of length used in astronomy equal to the mean distance of the earth from the sun or about 93 million miles (150 million kilometers)

as·tron·o·my \ə-'strä-nə-mē\ *n, pl* **-mies :** the science of objects and matter beyond the earth's atmosphere — **as·tron·o·mer** \-mər\ *n*

as·tro·phys·ics \ˌas-trə-'fi-ziks\ *n* **:** astronomy dealing esp. with the physical properties and dynamic processes of celestial objects — **as·tro·phys·i·cal** \-zi-kəl\ *adj* — **as·tro·phys·i·cist** \-'fi-zə-sist\ *n*

as·tute \ə-'stüt, -'styüt, a-\ *adj* [L *astutus*, fr. *astus* craft] **:** shrewdly discerning; *also* **:** WILY — **as·tute·ly** *adv* — **as·tute·ness** *n*

asun·der \ə-'sən-dər\ *adv or adj* **1 :** into separate pieces ⟨torn ~⟩ **2 :** separated in position from each other

ASV *abbr* American Standard Version

¹as well as *conj* **:** and in addition **:** and moreover ⟨brave *as well as* loyal⟩

²as well as *prep* **:** in addition to **:** BESIDES ⟨the coach, *as well as* the team, is ready⟩

asy·lum \ə-'sī-ləm\ *n* [ME, fr. L, fr. Gk *asylon*, neut. of *asylos* inviolable, fr. *a*- not + *sylon* right of seizure] **1 :** a place of refuge **2 :** protection given to esp. political fugitives **3 :** an institution for the care of the needy or sick and esp. of the insane

asym·met·ri·cal \ˌā-sə-'me-tri-kəl\ *or* **asym·met·ric** \-trik\ *adj* **:** not symmetrical — **asym·me·try** \(ˌ)ā-'si-mə-trē\ *n*

as·ymp·tote \'a-səmp-ˌtōt\ *n* **:** a straight line that is associated with a curve and tends to approximate it along an infinite branch — **as·ymp·tot·ic** \ˌa-səmp-'tä-tik\ *adj* — **as·ymp·tot·i·cal·ly** \-ti-k(ə-)lē\ *adv*

¹at \ət, (ˈ)at\ *prep* **1** — used to indicate a point in time or space ⟨be here ~ 3 o'clock⟩ **2** — used to indicate a goal ⟨swung ~ the ball⟩ **3** — used to indicate position or condition ⟨~ rest⟩ **4** — used to indicate means, cause, or manner ⟨sold ~ auction⟩

²at \'ät\ *n, pl* **at** — see *kip* at MONEY table

At *symbol* astatine

AT *abbr* automatic transmission

at all *adv* **:** in any way **:** in any circumstances ⟨not *at all* likely⟩

at·a·vism \'a-tə-ˌvi-zəm\ *n* **:** appearance in an individual of a character typical of an ancestral form; *also* **:** such an individual or character — **at·a·vis·tic** \ˌa-tə-'vis-tik\ *adj*

ate *past of* EAT

¹-ate *n suffix* **1 :** one acted upon (in a specified way) ⟨distill*ate*⟩ **2 :** chemical compound or complex derived from a (specified) compound or element ⟨acet*ate*⟩

²-ate *n suffix* **1 :** office **:** function **:** rank **:** group of persons holding a (specified) office or rank ⟨episcop*ate*⟩ **2 :** state **:** dominion **:** jurisdiction ⟨emir*ate*⟩

³-ate *adj suffix* **1 :** acted on (in a specified way) **:** being in a (specified) state ⟨temper*ate*⟩ ⟨degener*ate*⟩ **2 :** marked by having ⟨vertebr*ate*⟩

⁴-ate *vb suffix* **:** cause to be modified or affected by ⟨pollin*ate*⟩ **:** cause to become ⟨activ*ate*⟩ **:** furnish with ⟨aer*ate*⟩

ate·lier \ˌat-ᵊl-'yā\ *n* **1 :** an artist's or designer's studio **2 :** WORKSHOP

athe·ist \'ā-thē-ist\ *n* **:** one who denies the existence of God — **athe·ism** \-ˌi-zəm\ *n* — **athe·is·tic** \ˌā-thē-'is-tik\ *adj*

ath·e·nae·um *or* **ath·e·ne·um** \ˌa-thə-'nē-əm\ *n* **:** LIBRARY 1

ath·ero·scle·ro·sis \ˌa-thə-rō-sklə-'rō-səs\ *n* **:** arteriosclerosis characterized by the deposition of fatty substances in and the hardening of the inner layer of the arteries — **ath·ero·scle·rot·ic** \-'rä-tik\ *adj*

athirst \ə-'thərst\ *adj* **1** *archaic* **:** THIRSTY **2 :** EAGER, LONGING

ath·lete \'ath-ˌlēt\ *n* [ME, fr. L *athleta*, fr. Gk *athlētēs*, fr. *athlein* to contend for a prize, fr. *athlon* prize, contest] **:** a person who is trained to compete in athletics

athlete's foot *n* **:** ringworm of the feet

ath·let·ic \ath-'le-tik\ *adj* **1 :** of or relating to athletes or athletics **2 :** VIGOROUS, ACTIVE **3 :** STURDY, MUSCULAR

ath·let·ics \ath-'le-tiks\ *n sing or pl* **:** exercises and games requiring physical skill, strength, and endurance

athletic supporter *n* **:** an elastic pouch used to support the male genitals and worn esp. during athletic activity

¹athwart \ə-'thwȯrt\ *prep* **1 :** ACROSS **2 :** in opposition to

²athwart *adv* **:** obliquely across

atilt \ə-'tilt\ *adv or adj* **1 :** in a tilted position **2 :** with lance in hand

-ation *n suffix* **:** action or process ⟨flirt*ation*⟩ **:** something connected with an action or process ⟨discolor*ation*⟩

Atl *abbr* Atlantic

at·las \'at-ləs\ *n* **:** a book of maps

atm *abbr* atmosphere; atmospheric

ATM *abbr* automated teller machine

at·mo·sphere \'at-mə-ˌsfir\ *n* **1 :** the gaseous envelope of a celestial body; *esp* **:** the mass of air surrounding the earth **2 :** a surrounding influence **3 :** a unit of pressure equal to the pressure of air at sea level or about 14.7 pounds per square inch (10 newtons per square centimeter) **4 :** a dominant effect — **at·mo·spher·ic** \ˌat-mə-'sfir-ik, -'sfer-\ *adj* — **at·mo·spher·i·cal·ly** \-i-k(ə-)lē\ *adv*

at·mo·spher·ics \ˌat-mə-'sfir-iks, -'sfer-\ *n pl* **:** radio noise from atmospheric electrical phenomena

atoll \'a-ˌtȯl, -ˌtäl, 'ā-\ *n* **:** a coral island consisting of a reef surrounding a lagoon

atoll

at·om \'a-təm\ *n* [ME, fr. L *atomus*, fr. Gk *atomos*, fr. *atomos* indivisible, fr. *a*- not + *temnein* to cut] **1 :** a

\ə\abut \ᵊ\kitten \ər\further \a\ash \ā\ace \ä\mop, mar \au̇\out \ch\chin \e\bet \ē\easy \g\go \i\hit \ī\ice \j\job \ŋ\sing \ō\go \ȯ\law \ȯi\boy \th\thin \t͟h\the \ü\loot \u̇\foot \y\yet \zh\vision *see also* Pronunciation Symbols page

tiny particle : BIT 2 : the smallest particle of a chemical element that can exist alone or in combination

atom·ic \ə-'tä-mik\ *adj* 1 : of or relating to atoms; *also* : NUCLEAR 2 ⟨~ energy⟩ 2 : extremely small

atomic bomb *n* : a very destructive bomb utilizing the energy released by splitting the atom

atomic clock *n* : a very precise clock regulated by the natural vibration of atoms or molecules (as of cesium)

atomic number *n* : the number of protons in the nucleus of an element

atomic weight *n* : the mass of one atom of an element

at·om·ize \'a-tə-ˌmīz\ *vb* **-ized; -iz·ing** : to reduce to minute particles

at·om·iz·er \'a-tə-ˌmī-zər\ *n* : a device for dispensing a liquid (as perfume) as a mist

atom smasher *n* : ACCELERATOR 3

aton·al \ā-'tōn-ᵊl\ *adj* : marked by avoidance of traditional musical tonality — **ato·nal·i·ty** \ˌā-tō-'na-lə-tē\ *n* — **aton·al·ly** \ā-'tōn-ᵊl-ē\ *adv*

atone \ə-'tōn\ *vb* **atoned; aton·ing** 1 : to make amends 2 : EXPIATE

atone·ment \ə-'tōn-mənt\ *n* 1 : the reconciliation of God and man through the death of Jesus Christ 2 : reparation for an offense : SATISFACTION

¹**atop** \ə-'täp\ *prep* : on top of

²**atop** *adv or adj* : on, to, or at the top

ATP \ˌā-ˌtē-'pē\ *n* [adenosine *tri*phosphate] : a compound that occurs widely in living tissue and supplies energy for many cellular processes by undergoing enzymatic hydrolysis

atri·um \'ā-trē-əm\ *n, pl* **atria** \-trē-ə\ *also* **atri·ums** 1 : the central room of a Roman house; *also* : an open patio or court in the center of a building (as a hotel) 2 : an anatomical cavity or passage; *esp* : one of the chambers of the heart that receives blood from the veins — **atri·al** \-əl\ *adj*

atro·cious \ə-'trō-shəs\ *adj* 1 : savagely brutal, cruel, or wicked 2 : very bad : ABOMINABLE — **atro·cious·ly** *adv* — **atro·cious·ness** *n*

atroc·i·ty \ə-'trä-sə-tē\ *n, pl* **-ties** 1 : ATROCIOUSNESS 2 : an atrocious act or object ⟨the *atrocities* of war⟩

at·ro·phy \'a-trə-fē\ *n, pl* **-phies** : decrease in size or wasting away of a bodily part or tissue — **atrophy** *vb*

at·ro·pine \'a-trə-ˌpēn\ *n* : a drug from belladonna and related plants used esp. to relieve spasms and to dilate the pupil of the eye

att *abbr* 1 attached 2 attention 3 attorney

at·tach \ə-'tach\ *vb* 1 : to seize legally in order to force payment of a debt 2 : to bind by personal ties 3 : FASTEN, CONNECT 4 : to be fastened or connected

at·ta·ché \ˌa-tə-'shā, ˌa-ˌta-, ˌə-ˌta-\ *n* [F] : a technical expert on the diplomatic staff of an ambassador

at·ta·ché case \ə-'ta-shā-, ˌa-tə-'shā-\ *n* : a small thin suitcase used esp. for carrying business papers; *also* : BRIEFCASE

at·tach·ment \ə-'tach-mənt\ *n* 1 : legal seizure of property 2 : connection by ties of affection and regard 3 : a device attached to a machine or implement 4 : a connection by which one thing is attached to another

¹**at·tack** \ə-'tak\ *vb* 1 : to set upon with force or words : ASSAIL, ASSAULT 2 : to set to work on

²**attack** *n* 1 : an offensive action 2 : a fit of sickness

at·tain \ə-'tān\ *vb* 1 : ACHIEVE, ACCOMPLISH 2 : to arrive at : REACH — **at·tain·abil·i·ty** \-ˌtā-nə-'bi-lə-tē\ *n* — **at·tain·able** *adj*

at·tain·der \ə-'tān-dər\ *n* : extinction of the civil rights of a person upon sentence of death or outlawry

at·tain·ment \ə-'tān-mənt\ *n* 1 : the act of attaining 2 : ACCOMPLISHMENT

at·taint \ə-'tānt\ *vb* : to condemn to loss of civil rights

at·tar \'a-tər\ *n* [Per *'aṭir* perfumed, fr. Ar, fr. *'iṭr* perfume] : a fragrant floral oil

at·tempt \ə-'tempt\ *vb* : to make an effort toward : TRY — **attempt** *n*

at·tend \ə-'tend\ *vb* 1 : to look after : TEND 2 : to be present with 3 : to be present at 4 : to apply oneself 5 : to pay attention 6 : to direct one's attention

at·ten·dance \ə-'ten-dəns\ *n* 1 : the act or fact of attending 2 : the number of persons present; *also* : the number of times a person attends

¹**at·ten·dant** \ə-'ten-dənt\ *n* : one that attends another to render a service

²**attendant** *adj* : ACCOMPANYING ⟨~ circumstances⟩

at·ten·tion \ə-'ten-chən\ *n* 1 : the act or state of applying the mind to an object 2 : CONSIDERATION 3 : an act of courtesy 4 : a position of readiness assumed on command by a soldier — **at·ten·tive** \-'ten-tiv\ *adj* — **at·ten·tive·ly** *adv* — **at·ten·tive·ness** *n*

at·ten·u·ate \ə-'ten-yə-ˌwāt\ *vb* **-at·ed; -at·ing** 1 : to make or become thin 2 : WEAKEN — **attenuate** \-wət\ *adj* — **at·ten·u·a·tion** \-ˌten-yə-'wā-shən\ *n*

at·test \ə-'test\ *vb* 1 : to certify as genuine by signing as a witness 2 : MANIFEST 3 : TESTIFY — **at·tes·ta·tion** \ˌa-ˌtes-'tā-shən\ *n*

at·tic \'a-tik\ *n* : the space or room in a building immediately below the roof

¹**at·tire** \ə-'tīr\ *vb* **at·tired; at·tir·ing** : to put garments on : DRESS, ARRAY

²**attire** *n* : DRESS, CLOTHES

at·ti·tude \'a-tə-ˌtüd, -ˌtyüd\ *n* 1 : POSTURE 2 : a mental position or feeling with regard to a fact or state 3 : the position of something in relation to something else

at·ti·tu·di·nize \ˌa-tə-'tüd-ᵊn-ˌīz, -'tyüd-\ *vb* **-nized; -niz·ing** : to assume an affected mental attitude : POSE

attn *abbr* attention

at·tor·ney \ə-'tər-nē\ *n, pl* **-neys** : a legal agent qualified to act for persons in legal proceedings

attorney general *n, pl* **attorneys general** *or* **attorney generals** : the chief legal representative and adviser of a nation or state

at·tract \ə-'trakt\ *vb* 1 : to draw to or toward oneself : cause to approach 2 : to draw by emotional or aesthetic appeal **syn** charm, fascinate, allure, captivate, enchant — **at·trac·tive** \-'trak-tiv\ *adj* — **at·trac·tive·ly** *adv* — **at·trac·tive·ness** *n*

at·trac·tant \ə-'trak-tənt\ *n* : a substance (as a pheromone) used to attract insects or other animals

at·trac·tion \ə-'trak-shən\ *n* 1 : the act or power of attracting; *esp* : personal charm 2 : an attractive quality, object, or feature 3 : a force tending to draw particles together

attrib *abbr* attributive

¹**at·tri·bute** \'a-trə-ˌbyüt\ *n* 1 : an inherent characteristic 2 : a word ascribing a quality; *esp* : ADJECTIVE

²**at·trib·ute** \ə-'tri-ˌbyüt, -byət\ *vb* **-ut·ed; -ut·ing** 1 : to explain as to cause or origin ⟨~ the illness to fatigue⟩ 2 : to regard as a characteristic **syn** ascribe, credit, charge, impute — **at·trib·ut·able** *adj* — **at·tri·bu·tion** \ˌa-trə-'byü-shən\ *n*

at·trib·u·tive \ə-'trib-yə-tiv\ *adj* : joined directly to a modified noun without a linking verb ⟨*red* in *red hair* is an ~ adjective⟩ — **attributive** *n*

at·tri·tion \ə-'tri-shən\ *n* 1 : the act of wearing away by or as if by rubbing 2 : a reduction in numbers as a result of resignation, retirement, or death

at·tune \ə-'tün, -'tyün\ *vb* : to bring into harmony : TUNE — **at·tune·ment** *n*

atty *abbr* attorney

ATV *abbr* all-terrain vehicle

atyp·i·cal \ā-'ti-pi-kəl\ *adj* : not typical : IRREGULAR — **atyp·i·cal·ly** \-k(ə-)lē\ *adv*

Au *symbol* [L *aurum*] gold

au·burn \'ȯ-bərn\ *adj* : reddish brown — **auburn** *n*

au cou·rant \ˌō-kù-'räⁿ\ *adj* [F, lit., in the current] : UP-TO-DATE, STYLISH

¹**auc·tion** \'ȯk-shən\ n [L auction-, auctio, fr. augēre to increase] : public sale of property to the highest bidder

²**auction** vb **auc·tioned; auc·tion·ing** \-shə-niŋ\ : to sell at auction

auc·tion·eer \ˌȯk-shə-'nir\ n : an agent who conducts an auction

aud abbr audit; auditor

au·da·cious \ȯ-'dā-shəs\ adj 1 : DARING, BOLD 2 : INSOLENT — **au·da·cious·ly** adv — **au·da·cious·ness** n — **au·dac·i·ty** \-'da-sə-tē\ n

¹**au·di·ble** \'ȯ-də-bəl\ adj : capable of being heard — **au·di·bil·i·ty** \ˌȯ-də-'bi-lə-tē\ n — **au·di·bly** \'ȯ-də-blē\ adv

²**audible** n : a play called at the line of scrimmage

au·di·ence \'ȯ-dē-əns\ n 1 : a formal interview 2 : an opportunity of being heard 3 : an assembly of listeners or spectators

¹**au·dio** \'ȯ-dē-ˌō\ adj 1 : of or relating to frequencies (as of radio waves) corresponding to those of audible sound waves 2 : of or relating to sound or its reproduction and esp. high-fidelity reproduction 3 : relating to or used in the transmission or reception of sound

²**audio** n 1 : the transmission, reception, or reproduction of sound 2 : the section of television or motion-picture equipment that deals with sound

au·di·ol·o·gy \ˌȯ-dē-'ä-lə-jē\ n : a branch of science dealing with hearing and esp. with the treatment of individuals having trouble with hearing — **au·di·o·log·i·cal** \-ə-'lä-ji-kəl\ adj — **au·di·ol·o·gist** \-'ä-lə-jist\ n

au·dio·phile \'ȯ-dē-ō-ˌfīl\ n : one who is enthusiastic about high-fidelity sound reproduction

au·dio·vi·su·al \ˌȯ-dē-ō-'vi-zhə-wəl\ adj : of, relating to, or making use of both hearing and sight

au·dio·vi·su·als \-wəlz\ n pl : audiovisual teaching materials (as videotapes)

¹**au·dit** \'ȯ-dət\ n : a formal examination and verification of financial accounts

²**audit** vb 1 : to perform an audit on or for 2 : to attend (a course) without expecting formal credit

¹**au·di·tion** \ȯ-'di-shən\ n : HEARING; esp : a trial performance to appraise an entertainer's merits

²**audition** vb **-tioned; -tion·ing** \-'di-shə-niŋ\ : to give an audition to; also : to give a trial performance

au·di·tor \'ȯ-də-tər\ n 1 : LISTENER 2 : a person who audits

au·di·to·ri·um \ˌȯ-də-'tȯr-ē-əm\ n, pl **-riums** or **-ria** \-rē-ə\ 1 : the part of a public building where an audience sits 2 : a hall or building used for public gatherings

au·di·to·ry \'ȯ-də-ˌtȯr-ē\ adj : of or relating to hearing or to the sense or organs of hearing

auditory tube n : EUSTACHIAN TUBE

auf Wie·der·seh·en \ˌauf-'vē-dər-ˌzän\ interj [G] — used to express farewell

Aug abbr August

au·ger \'ȯ-gər\ n : a tool for boring

aught \'ȯt, 'ät\ n 2 : ZERO, CIPHER

aug·ment \ȯg-'ment\ vb : ENLARGE, INCREASE — **aug·men·ta·tion** \ˌȯg-mən-'tā-shən\ n

au gra·tin \ō-'grat-ᵊn, ȯ-, -'grät-\ adj [F, lit., with the burnt scrapings from the pan] : covered with bread crumbs or grated cheese and browned

¹**au·gur** \'ȯ-gər\ n : DIVINER, SOOTHSAYER

²**augur** vb 1 : to foretell esp. from omens 2 : to give promise of : PRESAGE

au·gu·ry \'ȯ-gyə-rē, -gə-\ n, pl **-ries** 1 : divination from omens 2 : OMEN, PORTENT

au·gust \ȯ-'gəst\ adj : marked by majestic dignity or grandeur — **au·gust·ly** adv — **au·gust·ness** n

Au·gust \'ȯ-gəst\ n [ME, fr. OE, fr. L Augustus, fr. Augustus Caesar] : the eighth month of the year having 31 days

au jus \ō-'zhü, -'zhüs, -'jüs; ō-zhᵫ\ adj [F] : served in the juice obtained from roasting

auk \'ȯk\ n : any of several stocky black-and-white diving seabirds that breed in colder parts of the northern hemisphere

auld \'ȯl, 'ȯld, 'äl, 'äld\ adj, chiefly Scot : OLD

aunt \'ant, 'änt\ n 1 : the sister of one's father or mother 2 : the wife of one's uncle

au pair \'ō-'par\ n [F, on even terms] : a usu. young foreign person who does domestic work for a family in return for room and board and to learn the family's language

au·ra \'ȯr-ə\ n 1 : a distinctive atmosphere surrounding a given source 2 : a luminous radiation

au·ral \'ȯr-əl\ adj : of or relating to the ear or to the sense of hearing

aurar pl of EYRIR

au·re·ole \'ȯr-ē-ˌōl\ or **au·re·o·la** \ȯ-'rē-ə-lə\ n : HALO, NIMBUS

au re·voir \ˌō-rə-'vwär\ n [F, lit., till seeing again] : GOOD-BYE

au·ri·cle \'ȯr-i-kəl\ n : an atrium of the heart

au·ric·u·lar \ȯ-'ri-kyə-lər\ adj 1 : told privately ⟨∼ confession⟩ 2 : known or recognized by the sense of hearing

au·ro·ra \ə-'rȯr-ə\ n, pl **auroras** or **au·ro·rae** \-(ˌ)ē\ : a luminous phenomenon of streamers or arches of light appearing in the upper atmosphere esp. of a planet's polar regions — **au·ro·ral** \-əl\ adj

aurora aus·tra·lis \-ȯ-'strā-ləs\ n : an aurora that occurs in earth's southern hemisphere

aurora bo·re·al·is \-ˌbȯr-ē-'a-ləs\ n : an aurora that occurs in earth's northern hemisphere

AUS abbr Army of the United States

aus·pice \'ȯ-spəs\ n, pl **aus·pic·es** \-spə-səz, -ˌsēz\ [L auspicium, fr. auspic-, auspex diviner by birds, fr. avis bird + specere to look, look at] 1 : observation of birds by an augur 2 pl : kindly patronage and protection 3 : a prophetic sign or omen

aus·pi·cious \ȯ-'spi-shəs\ adj 1 : promising success : PROPITIOUS 2 : FORTUNATE, PROSPEROUS — **aus·pi·cious·ly** adv — **aus·pi·cious·ness** n

aus·tere \ȯ-'stir\ adj 1 : STERN, SEVERE, STRICT 2 : ABSTEMIOUS 3 : UNADORNED ⟨∼ style⟩ — **aus·tere·ly** adv — **aus·ter·i·ty** \-'ster-ə-tē\ n

aus·tral \'ȯs-trəl\ adj : SOUTHERN

Aus·tra·lian \ȯ-'strāl-yən\ n : a native or inhabitant of Australia — **Australian** adj

Aus·tri·an \'ȯ-strē-ən\ n : a native or inhabitant of Austria — **Austrian** adj

Aus·tro·ne·sian \ˌȯs-trə-'nē-zhən\ adj : of, relating to, or constituting a family of languages spoken in the area extending from Madagascar eastward through the Malay Peninsula to Hawaii and Easter Island

auth abbr 1 authentic 2 author 3 authorized

au·then·tic \ə-'then-tik, ȯ-\ adj : GENUINE, REAL — **au·then·ti·cal·ly** \-ti-k(ə-)lē\ adv — **au·then·tic·i·ty** \ˌȯ-ˌthen-'ti-sə-tē\ n

au·then·ti·cate \ə-'then-ti-ˌkāt, ȯ-\ vb **-cat·ed; -cat·ing** : to prove genuine — **au·then·ti·ca·tion** \-ˌthen-ti-'kā-shən\ n

au·thor \'ȯ-thər\ n [ME auctour, ultim. fr. L auctor originator, author, fr. augēre to increase] 1 : one that originates or creates 2 : one that writes or composes a literary work

au·thor·ess \'ȯ-thə-rəs\ n : a woman author

au·thor·i·tar·i·an \ə-ˌthär-ə-'ter-ē-ən, ə-, -ˌthȯr-\ adj 1 : characterized by or favoring the principle of blind obedience to authority 2 : characterized by or favoring

---

\ə\abut \ᵊ\kitten \ər\further \a\ash \ā\ace \ä\mop, mar \aù\out \ch\chin \e\bet \ē\easy \g\go \i\hit \ī\ice \j\job \ŋ\sing \ō\go \ȯ\law \ȯi\boy \th\thin \t͟h\the \ü\loot \ù\foot \y\yet \zh\vision see also Pronunciation Symbols page concentration of political power in an authority not responsible to the people — **authoritarian** n

au·thor·i·ta·tive \ə-'thär-ə-ˌtā-tiv, ȯ-, -'thȯr-\ adj : supported by, proceeding from, or being an authority — **au·thor·i·ta·tive·ly** adv — **au·thor·i·ta·tive·ness** n

au·thor·i·ty \ə-'thär-ə-tē, ȯ-, -'thȯr-\ n, pl **-ties 1** : a citation used in support of a statement or in defense of an action; also : the source of such a citation **2** : one appealed to as an expert **3** : power to influence thought or behavior **4** : freedom granted : RIGHT **5** : persons in command; esp : GOVERNMENT **6** : convincing force

au·tho·rize \'ȯ-thə-ˌrīz\ vb **-rized; -riz·ing 1** : SANCTION **2** : to give legal power to — **au·tho·ri·za·tion** \ˌȯ-thə-rə-'zā-shən\ n

au·thor·ship \'ȯ-thər-ˌship\ n **1** : the state of being an author **2** : the source of a piece of writing, music, or art

au·tism \'ȯ-ˌti-zəm\ n **1** : absorption in self-centered mental activity (as delusions and hallucinations) esp. when accompanied by withdrawal from reality **2** : a mental disorder orginating in infancy that is characterized esp. by inability to interact socially, repetitive behavior, and language disorder — **au·tis·tic** \ȯ-'tis-tik\ adj

¹au·to \'ȯ-tō\ n, pl **autos** : AUTOMOBILE

²auto abbr automatic

au·to·bahn \'ȯ-tō-ˌbän, 'au-\ n : a German, Swiss, or Austrian expressway

au·to·bi·og·ra·phy \ˌȯ-tə-bī-'ä-grə-fē\ n : the biography of a person narrated by that person — **au·to·bi·og·ra·pher** \-fər\ n — **au·to·bi·o·graph·i·cal** \-ˌbī-ə-'gra-fi-kəl\ adj — **au·to·bi·o·graph·i·cal·ly** \-k(ə-)lē\ adv

au·toch·tho·nous \ȯ-'täk-thə-nəs\ adj : INDIGENOUS, NATIVE

au·to·clave \'ȯ-tō-ˌklāv\ n : an apparatus (as for sterilizing) using superheated high-pressure steam

au·toc·ra·cy \ȯ-'tä-krə-sē\ n, pl **-cies** : government by one person having unlimited power — **au·to·crat** \'ȯ-tə-ˌkrat\ n — **au·to·crat·ic** \ˌȯ-tə-'kra-tik\ adj — **au·to·crat·i·cal·ly** \-ti-k(ə-)lē\ adv

¹au·to·graph \'ȯ-tə-ˌgraf\ n **1** : an original manuscript **2** : a person's signature written by hand

²autograph vb : to write one's signature on

au·to·im·mune \ˌȯ-tō-i-'myün\ adj : of, relating to, or caused by antibodies or lymphocytes that attack molecules, cells, or tissues of the organism producing them ⟨~ diseases⟩ — **au·to·im·mu·ni·ty** \-i-'myü-nə-tē\ n

au·to·mate \'ȯ-tə-ˌmāt\ vb **-mat·ed; -mat·ing 1** : to operate automatically using mechanical or electronic devices **2** : to convert to automatic operation — **au·to·ma·tion** \ȯ-tə-'mā-shən\ n

automated teller machine n : a computer terminal allowing access to one's own bank accounts

¹au·to·mat·ic \ˌȯ-tə-'ma-tik\ adj **1** : INVOLUNTARY **2** : made so that certain parts act in a desired manner at the proper time : SELF-ACTING — **au·to·mat·i·cal·ly** \-ti-k(ə-)lē\ adv

²automatic n : an automatic device; esp : an automatic firearm

au·tom·a·ton \ȯ-'tä-mə-tən, -ˌtän\ n, pl **-atons** or **-a·ta** \-ə-tə, -ə-ˌtä\ **1** : an automatic machine; esp : ROBOT **2** : an individual who acts mechanically

au·to·mo·bile \'ȯ-tə-mō-ˌbēl, ˌȯ-tə-mə-'bēl\ n : a usu. 4-wheeled automotive vehicle for passenger transportation

au·to·mo·tive \ˌȯ-tə-'mō-tiv\ adj **1** : of or relating to automobiles, trucks, or buses **2** : SELF-PROPELLED

au·to·nom·ic nervous system \ˌȯ-tə-'nä-mik-\ n : a part of the vertebrate nervous system that governs involuntary actions and that consists of the sympathetic nervous system and the parasympathetic nervous system

au·ton·o·mous \ȯ-'tä-nə-məs\ adj : having the right or power of self-government — **au·ton·o·mous·ly** adv — **au·ton·o·my** \-mē\ n

au·top·sy \'ȯ-ˌtäp-sē, 'ȯ-təp-\ n, pl **-sies** [Gk autopsia act of seeing with one's own eyes, fr. autos self + opsis sight] : examination of a dead body usu. with dissection sufficient to determine the cause of death or extent of change produced by disease — **autopsy** vb

au·tumn \'ȯ-təm\ n : the season between summer and winter — **au·tum·nal** \ȯ-'təm-nəl\ adj

aux abbr auxiliary

¹aux·il·ia·ry \ȯg-'zil-yə-rē, -'zi-lə-rē\ adj **1** : providing help **2** : functioning in a subsidiary capacity **3** : accompanying a verb form to express person, number, mood, or tense ⟨~ verbs⟩

²auxiliary n, pl **-ries 1** : an auxiliary person, group, or device **2** : an auxiliary verb

aux·in \'ȯk-sən\ n : a plant hormone that stimulates growth in length

av abbr **1** avenue **2** average **3** avoirdupois

AV abbr **1** ad valorem **2** audiovisual **3** Authorized Version

¹avail \ə-'vāl\ vb : to be of use or advantage : HELP, BENEFIT

²avail n : USE ⟨effort was of no ~⟩

avail·able \ə-'vā-lə-bəl\ adj **1** : USABLE **2** : ACCESSIBLE — **avail·abil·i·ty** \-ˌvā-lə-'bi-lə-tē\ n

av·a·lanche \'a-və-ˌlanch\ n : a mass of snow, ice, earth, or rock sliding down a mountainside

avant–garde \ä-ˌvän-'gärd, -ˌvänt-\ n [F, vanguard] : those esp. in the arts who create or apply new or experimental ideas and techniques — **avant–garde** adj

av·a·rice \'a-və-rəs\ n : excessive desire for wealth : GREED — **av·a·ri·cious** \ˌa-və-'ri-shəs\ adj

avast \ə-'vast\ vb imper — a nautical command to stop or cease

av·a·tar \'a-və-ˌtär\ n [Skt avatāra descent] : INCARNATION

avaunt \ə-'vȯnt\ adv : AWAY, HENCE

avdp abbr avoirdupois

ave abbr avenue

Ave Ma·ria \ˌä-ˌvā-mə-'rē-ə\ n : HAIL MARY

avenge \ə-'venj\ vb **avenged; aveng·ing** : to take vengeance for — **aveng·er** n

av·e·nue \'a-və-ˌnü, -ˌnyü\ n **1** : a way or route to a place or goal : PATH **2** : a broad street

aver \ə-'vər\ vb **averred; aver·ring** : ALLEGE, ASSERT; also : DECLARE

¹av·er·age \'a-və-rij, 'a-vrij\ n [modif. of MF avarie damage to ship or cargo, fr. OIt avaria, fr. Ar 'awārīyah damaged merchandise] **1** : ARITHMETIC MEAN **2** : a ratio of successful tries to total tries esp. in athletics ⟨batting ~ of .303⟩

²average adj **1** : equaling or approximating an arithmetic mean **2** : being about midway between extremes **3** : not out of the ordinary : COMMON

³average vb **av·er·aged; av·er·ag·ing 1** : to be at or come to an average **2** : to be, do, or get usually **3** : to find the average of

averse \ə-'vərs\ adj : having an active feeling of dislike or reluctance ⟨~ to exercise⟩

aver·sion \ə-'vər-zhən\ n **1** : a feeling of repugnance for something with a desire to avoid it **2** : something decidedly disliked

avert \ə-'vərt\ vb **1** : to turn aside or away ⟨~ the eyes⟩ **2** : to ward off

avg abbr average

avi·an \'ā-vē-ən\ adj [L avis bird] : of, relating to, or derived from birds

avi·ary \'ā-vē-ˌer-ē\ n, pl **-ar·ies** : a place for keeping birds confined

avi·a·tion \ˌā-vē-'ā-shən, ˌa-\ n **1** : the operation of heavier-than-air aircraft **2** : aircraft manufacture, development, and design

avi·a·tor \'ā-vē-ˌā-tər, 'a-\ n : an airplane pilot

avi·a·trix \ˌā-vē-ˈā-triks, ˌa-\ *n, pl* **-trix·es** \-trik-səz\ *or* **-tri·ces** \-trə-ˌsēz\ : a woman airplane pilot

av·id \ˈa-vəd\ *adj* **1** : craving eagerly : GREEDY **2** : enthusiastic in pursuit of an interest — **avid·i·ty** \ə-ˈvi-də-tē, a-\ *n* — **av·id·ly** *adv* — **av·id·ness** *n*

avi·on·ics \ˌā-vē-ˈä-niks, ˌa-\ *n pl* : electronics designed for use in aerospace vehicles — **avi·on·ic** \-nik\ *adj*

avo \ˈa-(ˌ)vü\ *n, pl* **avos** — see *pataca* at MONEY table

av·o·ca·do \ˌa-və-ˈkä-dō, ˌä-\ *n, pl* **-dos** *also* **-does** [modif. of Sp *aguacate,* fr. Nahuatl *āhuacatl,* avocado, testicle] : a pulpy green to purple nutty-flavored edible fruit of a tropical American tree; *also* : this tree

av·o·ca·tion \ˌa-və-ˈkā-shən\ *n* : HOBBY

av·o·cet \ˈa-və-ˌset\ *n* : any of several long-legged shorebirds with webbed feet and slender upward-curving bills

avoid \ə-ˈvȯid\ *vb* **1** : to keep away from : SHUN **2** : to prevent the occurrence of **3** : to refrain from — **avoid·able** *adj* — **avoid·ably** *adv* — **avoid·ance** \-ᵊns\ *n*

av·oir·du·pois \ˌa-vər-də-ˈpȯiz\ *n* [ME *avoir de pois* goods sold by weight, fr. OF, lit., goods of weight] **1** : AVOIRDUPOIS WEIGHT **2** : WEIGHT, HEAVINESS; *esp* : personal weight

avoirdupois weight *n* : a system of weights based on a pound of 16 ounces and an ounce of 16 drams (28 grams) — see WEIGHT table

avouch \ə-ˈvau̇ch\ *vb* **1** : to declare positively : AVER **2** : to vouch for

avow \ə-ˈvau̇\ *vb* : to declare openly — **avow·al** \-ˈvau̇(-ə)l\ *n*

avun·cu·lar \ə-ˈvəŋ-kyə-lər\ *adj* : of, relating to, or resembling an uncle

await \ə-ˈwāt\ *vb* : to wait for : EXPECT

¹**awake** \ə-ˈwāk\ *vb* **awoke** \-ˈwōk\ *also* **awaked** \-ˈwākt\; **awo·ken** \-ˈwō-kən\ *or* **awaked** *also* **awoke; awak·ing** : to bring back to consciousness : wake up

²**awake** *adj* : not asleep; *also* : ALERT

awak·en \ə-ˈwā-kən\ *vb* **awak·ened; awak·en·ing** \-ˈwā-kə-niŋ\ : AWAKE

¹**award** \ə-ˈwȯrd\ *vb* **1** : to give by judicial decision ⟨∼ damages⟩ **2** : to give in recognition of merit or achievement

²**award** *n* **1** : a final decision : JUDGMENT **2** : something awarded : PRIZE

aware \ə-ˈwar\ *adj* : having perception or knowledge : CONSCIOUS, INFORMED — **aware·ness** *n*

awash \ə-ˈwȯsh, -ˈwäsh\ *adj* **1** : washed by waves or tide **2** : AFLOAT **3** : FLOODED

¹**away** \ə-ˈwā\ *adv* **1** : from this or that place ⟨go ∼⟩ **2** : out of the way **3** : in another direction ⟨turn ∼⟩ **4** : out of existence ⟨fade ∼⟩ **5** : from one's possession ⟨give ∼⟩ **6** : without interruption ⟨chatter ∼⟩ **7** : at a distance in space or time ⟨far ∼⟩ ⟨∼ back in 1910⟩

²**away** *adj* **1** : ABSENT **2** : distant in space or time ⟨a lake 10 miles ∼⟩

¹**awe** \ˈȯ\ *n* **1** : profound and reverent dread of the supernatural **2** : respectful fear inspired by authority

²**awe** *vb* **awed; aw·ing** : to inspire with awe

aweigh \ə-ˈwā\ *adj* : just clear of the bottom ⟨anchors ∼⟩

awe·some \ˈȯ-səm\ *adj* **1** : expressive of awe **2** : inspiring awe

awe·struck \-ˌstrək\ *also* **awe·strick·en** \-ˌstri-kən\ *adj* : filled with awe

aw·ful \ˈȯ-fəl\ *adj* **1** : inspiring awe **2** : extremely disa-

greeable **3** : very great ⟨an ∼ lot of money⟩ — **aw·ful·ly** *adv*

awhile \ə-ˈhwīl\ *adv* : for a while

awhirl \ə-ˈhwərl\ *adj* : being in a whirl

awk·ward \ˈȯ-kwərd\ *adj* **1** : CLUMSY **2** : UNGRACEFUL **3** : difficult to explain : EMBARRASSING **4** : difficult to deal with — **awk·ward·ly** *adv* — **awk·ward·ness** *n*

awl \ˈȯl\ *n* : a pointed instrument for making small holes

awls

aw·ning \ˈȯ-niŋ\ *n* : a rooflike cover (as of canvas) extended over or in front of a place as a shelter

AWOL \ˈā-ˌwȯl, ˌā-ˌdə-bəl-yü-ˌō-ˈel\ *n* : a person who is absent without leave — **AWOL** *adj or adv*

awry \ə-ˈrī\ *adv or adj* **1** : ASKEW **2** : AMISS

ax *or* **axe** \ˈaks\ *n* : a chopping or cutting tool with an edged head fitted parallel to a handle

ax·i·al \ˈak-sē-əl\ *adj* **1** : of, relating to, or functioning as an axis **2** : situated around, in the direction of, on, or along an axis — **ax·i·al·ly** *adv*

ax·i·om \ˈak-sē-əm\ *n* [L *axioma,* fr. Gk *axiōma,* lit., something worthy, fr. *axioun* to think worthy, fr. *axios* worth, worthy] **1** : a statement generally accepted as true : MAXIM **2** : a proposition regarded as a self-evident truth — **ax·i·om·at·ic** \ˌak-sē-ə-ˈma-tik\ *adj* — **ax·i·om·at·i·cal·ly** \-ti-k(ə-)lē\ *adv*

ax·is \ˈak-səs\ *n, pl* **ax·es** \-ˌsēz\ **1** : a straight line around which a body rotates **2** : a straight line or structure with respect to which a body or figure is symmetrical **3** : one of the reference lines of a system of coordinates **4** : an alliance between major powers

ax·le \ˈak-səl\ *n* : a shaft on which a wheel revolves

ayah \ˈī-ə\ *n* [Hindi *āyā,* fr. Pg *aia,* fr. L *avia* grandmother] : a nurse or maid native to India

aya·tol·lah \ˌī-ə-ˈtō-lə\ *n* [Per., lit., sign of God, fr. Ar *aya* sign, miracle + *allāh* God] : an Islamic religious leader — used as a title of respect

¹**aye** *also* **ay** \ˈā\ *adv* : ALWAYS, EVER

²**aye** *also* **ay** \ˈī\ *adv* : YES

³**aye** *also* **ay** \ˈī\ *n, pl* **ayes** : an affirmative vote

AZ *abbr* Arizona

aza·lea \ə-ˈzāl-yə\ *n* : any of numerous rhododendrons with funnel-shaped blossoms and usu. deciduous leaves

az·i·do·thy·mi·dine \ə-ˌzi-dō-ˈthī-mə-ˌdēn\ *n* : AZT

az·i·muth \ˈa-zə-məth\ *n* : horizontal direction expressed as an angular distance from a fixed point

AZT \ˌā-(ˌ)zē-ˈtē\ *n* : an antiviral drug used to treat AIDS

Az·tec \ˈaz-ˌtek\ *n* : a member of a Nahuatl-speaking people that founded the Mexican empire and were conquered by Hernan Cortes in 1519 — **Az·tec·an** *adj*

azure \ˈa-zhər\ *n* : the blue of the clear sky — **azure** *adj*

\ə\abut \ᵊ\kitten \ər\further \a\ash \ā\ace \ä\mop, mar
\au̇\out \ch\chin \e\bet \ē\easy \g\go \i\hit \ī\ice \j\job
\ŋ\sing \ō\go \ȯ\law \ȯi\boy \th\thin \t͟h\the \ü\loot \u̇\foot
\y\yet \zh\vision *see also* Pronunciation Symbols page

B

¹**b** \'bē\ *n, pl* **b's** *or* **bs** \'bēz\ *often cap* **1** : the 2d letter of the English alphabet **2** : a grade rating a student's work as good

²**b** *abbr, often cap* **1** bachelor **2** bass **3** bishop **4** book **5** born

B *symbol* boron

Ba *symbol* barium

BA *abbr* **1** bachelor of arts **2** batting average

bab·bitt \'ba-bət\ *n* : an alloy used for lining bearings; *esp* : one containing tin, copper, and antimony

bab·ble \'ba-bəl\ *vb* **bab·bled; bab·bling 1** : to talk enthusiastically or excessively **2** : to utter meaningless sounds — **babble** *n* — **bab·bler** \-b(ə-)lər\ *n*

babe \'bāb\ *n* **1** : BABY **2** *slang* : GIRL, WOMAN

ba·bel \'bā-bəl, 'ba-\ *n, often cap* [fr. the Tower of *Babel*, Gen 11:4–9] : a place or scene of noise and confusion; *also* : a confused sound **syn** hubbub, racket, din, uproar, clamor

ba·boon \ba-'bün\ *n* [ME *babewin*, fr. MF *babouin*, fr. *baboue* grimace] : any of several large apes of Asia and Africa with doglike muzzles

ba·bush·ka \bə-'büsh-kə, -'bush-\ *n* [Russ, grandmother, dim. of *baba* old woman] : a kerchief for the head

¹**ba·by** \'bā-bē\ *n, pl* **babies 1** : a very young child : INFANT **2** : the youngest or smallest of a group **3** : a childish person — **baby** *adj* — **ba·by·hood** *n* — **ba·by·ish** *adj*

²**baby** *vb* **ba·bied; ba·by·ing** : to tend or treat often with excessive care

baby's breath *n* : any of a genus of herbs that are related to the pinks and have small delicate flowers

ba·by–sit \'bā-bē-,sit\ *vb* **-sat** \-,sat\; **-sit·ting** : to care for children usu. during a short absence of the parents — **ba·by–sit·ter** *n*

bac·ca·lau·re·ate \,ba-kə-'lòr-ē-ət\ *n* **1** : the degree of bachelor conferred by colleges and universities **2** : a sermon delivered to a graduating class

bac·ca·rat \,bä-kə-'rä, ,ba-\ *n* : a card game played esp. in European casinos

bac·cha·nal \'ba-kən-ºl, ,ba-kə-'nal, ,bä-kə-'näl\ *n* **1** : ORGY **2** : REVELER

bac·cha·na·lia \,ba-kə-'nāl-yə\ *n, pl* **bacchanalia** : a drunken orgy — **bac·cha·na·lian** \-'nāl-yən\ *adj or n*

bach·e·lor \'ba-chə-lər\ *n* **1** : a person who has received the usu. lowest degree conferred by a 4-year college **2** : an unmarried man — **bach·e·lor·hood** *n*

bach·e·lor·ette \,ba-chə-lə-'ret\ *n* : a young unmarried woman

bachelor's button *n* : a European plant related to the daisies and having blue, pink, or white flower heads

ba·cil·lus \bə-'si-ləs\ *n, pl* **-li** \-,lī\ [NL, fr. ML, small staff, dim. of L *baculus* staff] : any of numerous rod=shaped bacteria; *also* : a disease-producing bacterium — **bac·il·lary** \'ba-sə-,ler-ē\ *adj*

¹**back** \'bak\ *n* **1** : the rear or dorsal part of the human body; *also* : the corresponding part of a lower animal **2** : the part or surface opposite the front **3** : a player in the backfield in football — **back·less** \-ləs\ *adj*

²**back** *adv* **1** : to, toward, or at the rear **2** : AGO **3** : so as to be restrained or retarded **4** : to, toward, or in a former place or state **5** : in return or reply

³**back** *adj* **1** : located at or in the back; *also* : REMOTE **2** : OVERDUE **3** : moving or operating backward **4** : not current

⁴**back** *vb* **1** : SUPPORT, UPHOLD **2** : to go or cause to go

backward or in reverse **3** : to furnish with a back : form the back of

back·ache \'ba-,kāk\ *n* : a pain in the lower back

back–bench·er \-'ben-chər\ *n* : a rank-and-file member of a British legislature

back·bite \-,bīt\ *vb* **-bit** \-,bit\; **-bit·ten** \-,bit-ºn\; **-bit·ing** \-,bī-tiŋ\ : to say mean or spiteful things about someone who is absent — **back·bit·er** *n*

back·board \-,bòrd\ *n* : a board placed at or serving as the back of something

back·bone \-,bōn\ *n* **1** : the bony column in the back of a vertebrate that is the chief support of the trunk and consists of a jointed series of vertebrae enclosing and protecting the spinal cord **2** : firm resolute character

back·drop \'bak-,dräp\ *n* : a painted cloth hung across the rear of a stage

back·er \'ba-kər\ *n* : one that supports

back·field \-,fēld\ *n* : the football players whose positions are behind the line

¹**back·fire** \-,fīr\ *n* : a loud noise caused by the improperly timed explosion of fuel in the cylinder of an internal combustion engine

²**backfire** *vb* **1** : to make or undergo a backfire **2** : to have a result opposite to what was intended

back·gam·mon \'bak-,ga-mən\ *n* : a game played with pieces on a double board in which the moves are determined by throwing dice

back·ground \'bak-,graùnd\ *n* **1** : the scenery behind something **2** : the setting within which something takes place; *also* : the sum of a person's experience, training, and understanding

back·hand \'bak-,hand\ *n* : a stroke (as in tennis) made with the back of the hand turned in the direction of movement; *also* : the side on which such a stroke is made — **back·hand** *vb*

backhand

back·hand·ed \'bak-'han-dəd\ *adj* **1** : INDIRECT, DEVIOUS; *esp* : SARCASTIC **2** : using or made with a backhand

back·hoe \-,hō\ *n* : an excavating machine having a bucket that is drawn toward the machine

back·ing \'ba-kiŋ\ *n* **1** : something forming a back **2** : SUPPORT, AID; *also* : a body of supporters

back·lash \'bak-,lash\ *n* **1** : a sudden violent backward movement or reaction **2** : a strong adverse reaction

¹**back·log** \-,lòg, -,läg\ *n* **1** : a large log at the back of a hearth fire **2** : an accumulation of tasks unperformed or materials not processed

²**backlog** *vb* : to accumulate in reserve

back of *prep* : BEHIND

back out *vb* : to withdraw esp. from a commitment or contest

¹**back·pack** \'bak-ˌpak\ *n* : a camping pack supported by an aluminum frame and carried on the back

²**backpack** *vb* : to hike with a backpack — **back·pack·er** *n*

back·ped·al \'bak-ˌped-ᵊl\ *vb* : RETREAT

back·rest \-ˌrest\ *n* : a rest for the back

back·side \-ˌsīd\ *n* : BUTTOCKS

back·slap \-ˌslap\ *vb* : to display excessive cordiality — **back·slap·per** *n*

back·slide \-ˌslīd\ *vb* -slid \-ˌslid\; -slid *or* -slid·den \-ˌslid-ᵊn\; -slid·ing \-ˌslī-diŋ\ : to lapse morally or in religious practice — **back·slid·er** *n*

back·spin \-ˌspin\ *n* : a backward rotary motion of a ball

¹**back·stage** \'bak-ˌstāj\ *adj* 1 : relating to or occurring in the area behind a stage 2 : of or relating to the private lives of theater people 3 : of or relating to the inner working or operation

²**back·stage** \'bak-ˈstāj\ *adv* 1 : in or to a backstage area 2 : SECRETLY

back·stairs \-ˌstarz\ *adj* : SECRET, FURTIVE; *also* : SORDID, SCANDALOUS

¹**back·stop** \-ˌstäp\ *n* : something serving as a stop behind something else; *esp* : a screen or fence to keep a ball from leaving the field of play

²**backstop** *vb* 1 : SUPPORT 2 : to serve as a backstop to

back·stretch \'bak-ˈstrech\ *n* : the side opposite the homestretch on a racecourse

back·stroke \-ˌstrōk\ *n* : a swimming stroke executed on the back

back talk *n* : impudent, insolent, or argumentative replies

back·track \'bak-ˌtrak\ *vb* 1 : to retrace one's course 2 : to reverse a position or stand

back·up \-ˌəp\ *n* : one that serves as a substitute or alternative

¹**back·ward** \'bak-wərd\ *or* **back·wards** \-wərdz\ *adv* 1 : toward the back 2 : with the back foremost 3 : in a reverse or contrary direction or way 4 : toward the past; *also* : toward a worse state

²**backward** *adj* 1 : directed, turned, or done backward 2 : DIFFIDENT, SHY 3 : retarded in development — **back·ward·ly** *adv* — **back·ward·ness** *n*

back·wash \'bak-ˌwȯsh, -ˌwäsh\ *n* : a backward flow or movement (as of water or air) produced by a propelling force (as the motion of oars)

back·wa·ter \-ˌwȯ-tər, -ˌwä-\ *n* 1 : water held or turned back in its course 2 : an isolated or backward place or condition

back·woods \-ˈwu̇dz\ *n pl* 1 : wooded or partly cleared areas far from cities 2 : a remote or isolated place

ba·con \'bā-kən\ *n* : salted and smoked meat from the sides or back of a pig

bacteria *pl of* BACTERIUM

bac·te·ri·cid·al \bak-ˌtir-ə-ˈsīd-ᵊl\ *adj* : destroying bacteria — **bac·te·ri·cide** \-ˈtir-ə-ˌsīd\ *n*

bac·te·ri·ol·o·gy \bak-ˌtir-ē-ˈä-lə-jē\ *n* 1 : a science dealing with bacteria 2 : bacterial life and phenomena — **bac·te·ri·o·log·ic** \-ə-ˈlä-jik\ *or* **bac·te·ri·o·log·i·cal** \-ə-ˈlä-ji-kəl\ *adj* — **bac·te·ri·ol·o·gist** \-ˈä-lə-jist\ *n*

bac·te·rio·phage \bak-ˈtir-ē-ə-ˌfāj\ *n* : any of various viruses that attack specific bacteria

bac·te·ri·um \bak-ˈtir-ē-əm\ *n, pl* -ria \-ē-ə\ [NL, fr. Gk *baktērion* staff] : any of a class of microscopic plants including some that are disease producers and others that are valued esp. for their chemical effects (as fermentation) — **bac·te·ri·al** \-ē-əl\ *adj*

bad \'bad\ *adj* **worse** \'wərs\; **worst** \'wərst\ 1 : below standard : POOR; *also* : UNFAVORABLE ⟨a ~ report⟩ 2 : SPOILED, DECAYED 3 : WICKED; *also* : not well-behaved : NAUGHTY 4 : DISAGREEABLE ⟨a ~ taste⟩; *also*

: HARMFUL 5 : DEFECTIVE, FAULTY ⟨~ wiring⟩; *also* : not valid ⟨a ~ check⟩ 6 : UNWELL, ILL 7 : SORRY, REGRETFUL **syn** evil, wrong, immoral, iniquitous — **bad·ly** *adv* — **bad·ness** *n*

bade *past and past part of* BID

badge \'baj\ *n* : a device or token usu. worn as a sign of status

¹**bad·ger** \'ba-jər\ *n* : any of several sturdy burrowing mammals with long claws on their forefeet

badger

²**badger** *vb* : to harass or annoy persistently

ba·di·nage \ˌbad-ᵊn-ˈäzh\ *n* [F] : playful talk back and forth : BANTER

bad·land \'bad-ˌland\ *n* : a region marked by intricate erosional sculpturing and scanty vegetation — usu. used in pl.

bad·min·ton \'bad-ˌmint-ᵊn\ *n* : a court game played with light rackets and a shuttlecock volleyed over a net

Bae·de·ker \'bā-di-kər, 'be-\ *n* : GUIDEBOOK

¹**baf·fle** \'ba-fəl\ *vb* **baf·fled; baf·fling** \-fə-liŋ\ : FRUSTRATE, THWART, FOIL; *also* : PERPLEX — **baf·fle·ment** *n*

²**baffle** *n* : a device (as a wall or screen) to deflect, check, or regulate flow (as of liquid or sound) — **baf·fled** \'ba-fəld\ *adj*

¹**bag** \'bag\ *n* : a flexible usu. closable container (as for storing or carrying)

²**bag** *vb* **bagged; bag·ging** 1 : DISTEND, BULGE 2 : to put in a bag 3 : to get possession of; *esp* : to take in hunting **syn** trap, snare, catch, capture, collar

ba·gasse \bə-ˈgas\ *n* [F] : plant residue (as of sugarcane) left after a product (as juice) has been extracted

bag·a·telle \ˌba-gə-ˈtel\ *n* [F] : TRIFLE

ba·gel \'bā-gəl\ *n* [Yiddish *beygl*] : a hard glazed doughnut-shaped roll

bag·gage \'ba-gij\ *n* 1 : the traveling bags and personal belongings of a traveler : LUGGAGE 2 : things that get in the way

bag·gy \'ba-gē\ *adj* **bag·gi·er; -est** : puffed out or hanging like a bag — **bag·gi·ly** \-gə-lē\ *adv* — **bag·gi·ness** \-gē-nəs\ *n*

bag·man \'bag-mən\ *n* : a person who collects or distributes illicitly gained money on behalf of another

ba·gnio \'ban-yō\ *n, pl* **bagnios** [It *bagno*, lit., public bath] : BROTHEL

bag of waters : a double-walled fluid-filled sac that encloses and protects the fetus in the womb and that breaks releasing its fluid during the process of birth

bag·pipe \'bag-ˌpīp\ *n* : a musical wind instrument consisting of a bag, a tube with valves, and sounding pipes — often used in pl.

ba·guette \ba-ˈget\ *n* [F, lit., rod] 1 : a gem having the

\ə\abut \ᵊ\kitten \ər\further \a\ash \ā\ace \ä\mop, mar \au̇\out \ch\chin \e\bet \ē\easy \g\go \i\hit \ī\ice \j\job \ŋ\sing \ō\go \ȯ\law \ȯi\boy \th\thin \t̲h̲\the \ü\loot \u̇\foot \y\yet \zh\vision *see also* Pronunciation Symbols page

shape of a narrow rectangle; *also* : the shape itself **2** : a long thin loaf of French bread

Ba·ha·mi·an \bə-ˈhä-mē-ən, -ˈhä-\ *n* : a native or inhabitant of the Bahama Islands

baht \ˈbät\ *n, pl* **baht** *also* **bahts** — see MONEY table

¹bail \ˈbāl\ *n* : a container for ladling water out of a boat

²bail *vb* : to dip and throw out water from a boat — **bail·er** *n*

³bail *n* : security given to guarantee a prisoner's appearance when legally required; *also* : one giving such security or the release secured

⁴bail *vb* : to release under bail; *also* : to procure the release of by giving bail — **bail·able** \ˈbā-lə-bəl\ *adj*

⁵bail *n* : the arched handle (as of a pail or kettle)

bai·liff \ˈbā-ləf\ *n* **1** : an aide of a British sheriff who serves writs and makes arrests; *also* : a minor officer of a U.S. court **2** : an estate or farm manager esp. in Britain : STEWARD

bai·li·wick \ˈbā-li-ˌwik\ *n* : one's special province or domain **syn** territory, field, sphere

bail·out \ˈbā-ˌlau̇t\ *n* : a rescue from financial distress

bairn \ˈbarn\ *n, chiefly Scot* : CHILD

¹bait \ˈbāt\ *vb* **1** : to persecute by continued attacks **2** : to harass with dogs usu. for sport ⟨∼ a bear⟩ **3** : to furnish (as a hook) with bait **4** : ALLURE, ENTICE **5** : to give food and drink to (as an animal) **syn** badger, heckle, hound

²bait *n* **1** : a lure for catching animals (as fish) **2** : LURE, TEMPTATION **syn** snare, trap, decoy, come-on, enticement

bai·za \ˈbī-(ˌ)zä\ *n, pl* **baiza** *or* **baizas** — see *rial* at MONEY table

baize \ˈbāz\ *n* : a coarse feltlike fabric

¹bake \ˈbāk\ *vb* **baked; bak·ing 1** : to cook or become cooked in dry heat esp. in an oven **2** : to dry and harden by heat ⟨∼ bricks⟩ — **bak·er** *n*

²bake *n* : a social gathering featuring baked food

baker's dozen *n* : THIRTEEN

bak·ery \ˈbā-k(ə-)rē\ *n, pl* **-er·ies** : a place for baking or selling baked goods

bake·shop \ˈbāk-ˌshäp\ *n* : BAKERY

baking powder *n* : a powder that consists of a carbonate, an acid, and a starch and that makes the dough rise in baking cakes and biscuits

baking soda *n* : SODIUM BICARBONATE

bak·sheesh \ˈbak-ˌshēsh\ *n* : payment (as a tip or bribe) to expedite service

bal *abbr* balance

bal·a·lai·ka \ˌba-lə-ˈlī-kə\ *n* : a triangular 3-stringed instrument of Russian origin played by plucking or strumming

¹bal·ance \ˈba-ləns\ *n* [ME, fr. OF, fr. LL *bilanc-, bilanx* having two scalepans, fr. L *bi* two + *lanc-, lanx* plate] **1** : a weighing device : SCALE **2** : a weight, force, or influence counteracting the effect of another **3** : an oscillating wheel used to regulate a timepiece **4** : a state of equilibrium **5** : REMAINDER, REST; *esp* : an amount in excess esp. on the credit side of an account — **bal·anced** \-lənst\ *adj*

²balance *vb* **bal·anced; bal·anc·ing 1** : to compute the balance of an account **2** : to arrange so that one set of elements equals another; *also* : to equal or equalize in weight, number, or proportions **3** : WEIGH **4** : to bring or come to a state or position of balance; *also* : to bring into harmony or proportion

bal·boa \bal-ˈbō-ə\ *n* — see MONEY table

bal·brig·gan \bal-ˈbri-gən\ *n* : a knitted cotton fabric used esp. for underwear

bal·co·ny \ˈbal-kə-nē\ *n, pl* **-nies 1** : a platform projecting from the side of a building and enclosed by a railing **2** : a gallery inside a building

bald \ˈbȯld\ *adj* **1** : lacking a natural or usual covering (as of hair) **2** : UNADORNED, PLAIN **syn** bare, barren, naked, nude — **bald·ly** *adv* — **bald·ness** *n*

bal·da·chin \ˈbȯl-də-kən, ˈbal-\ *or* **bal·da·chi·no** \ˌbal-də-ˈkē-nō\ *n, pl* **-chins** *or* **-chinos** : a canopylike structure over an altar

bald cypress *n* : either of two large swamp trees of the southern U.S. with hard red wood

bald eagle *n* : an eagle of No. America that when mature has white head and neck feathers and a white tail

bal·der·dash \ˈbȯl-dər-ˌdash\ *n* : NONSENSE

bald·ing \ˈbȯl-diŋ\ *adj* : getting bald

bal·dric \ˈbȯl-drik\ *n* : a belt worn over the shoulder to carry a sword or bugle

¹bale \ˈbāl\ *n* : a large or closely packed bundle

²bale *vb* **baled; bal·ing** : to pack in a bale — **bal·er** *n*

ba·leen \bə-ˈlēn\ *n* : a horny substance attached in plates to the upper jaw of some large whales (**baleen whales**)

bale·ful \ˈbāl-fəl\ *adj* : DEADLY, HARMFUL; *also* : OMINOUS **syn** sinister, malefic, maleficent, malign

¹balk \ˈbȯk\ *n* **1** : HINDRANCE, CHECK, SETBACK **2** : an illegal motion of the pitcher in baseball while in position

²balk *vb* **1** : BLOCK, THWART **2** : to stop short and refuse to go on **3** : to commit a balk in sports **syn** frustrate, baffle, foil, thwart — **balky** \ˈbȯ-kē\ *adj*

¹ball \ˈbȯl\ *n* **1** : a rounded body or mass (as at the base of the thumb or for use as a missile or in a game) **2** : a game played with a ball **3** : a pitched baseball that misses the strike zone and is not swung at by the batter **4** : a hit or thrown ball in various games ⟨foul ∼⟩ — **on the ball** : COMPETENT, KNOWLEDGEABLE, ALERT

²ball *vb* : to form into a ball

³ball *n* : a large formal dance

bal·lad \ˈba-ləd\ *n* **1** : a narrative poem of strongly marked rhythm suitable for singing **2** : a simple song : AIR **3** : a slow romantic song

bal·lad·eer \ˌba-lə-ˈdir\ *n* : a singer of ballads

¹bal·last \ˈba-ləst\ *n* **1** : heavy material used to stabilize a ship or control a balloon's ascent **2** : crushed stone laid in a railroad bed or used in making concrete

²ballast *vb* : to provide with ballast **syn** balance, stabilize, steady

ball bearing *n* : a bearing in which the revolving part turns upon steel balls that roll easily in a groove; *also* : one of the balls in such a bearing

ball·car·ri·er \ˈbȯl-ˌkar-ē-ər\ *n* : the football player carrying the ball in an offensive play

bal·le·ri·na \ˌba-lə-ˈrē-nə\ *n* : a female ballet dancer

bal·let \ˈba-ˌlā, ba-ˈlā\ *n* **1** : dancing in which fixed poses and steps are combined with light flowing movements often to convey a story; *also* : a theatrical art form using ballet dancing **2** : a company of ballet dancers

bal·let·o·mane \ba-ˈle-tə-ˌmān\ *n* : a devotee of ballet

bal·lis·tic missile \bə-ˈlis-tik-\ *n* : a missile that is guided during ascent and that falls freely during descent

bal·lis·tics \-tiks\ *n sing or pl* **1** : the science of the motion of projectiles (as bullets) in flight **2** : the flight characteristics of a projectile — **ballistic** *adj*

ball of fire : an unusually energetic person

¹bal·loon \bə-ˈlün\ *n* **1** : a bag filled with gas or heated air so as to rise and float in the atmosphere **2** : a toy consisting of an inflatable bag — **bal·loon·ist** *n*

²balloon *vb* **1** : to swell or puff out **2** : to travel in a balloon **3** : to increase rapidly

¹bal·lot \ˈba-lət\ *n* [It *ballotta* small ball used in secret voting, fr. It dial., dim. of *balla* ball] **1** : a piece of paper used to cast a vote **2** : the action or a system of voting; *also* : the right to vote

²ballot *vb* : to decide by ballot : VOTE

¹ball·park \ˈbȯl-ˌpärk\ *n* : a park in which ball games are played

²ballpark *adj* : approximately correct ⟨∼ estimate⟩

ball·point \ˈbȯl-ˌpȯint\ *n* : a pen whose writing point is a small rotating metal ball that inks itself from an inner container

ball·room \ˈbȯl-ˌrüm, -ˌru̇m\ *n* : a large room for dances

bal·ly·hoo \'ba-lē-ˌhü\ *n, pl* **-hoos :** extravagant statements and claims made for publicity — **ballyhoo** *vb*

balm \'bäm, 'bälm\ *n* **1 :** a fragrant healing or soothing lotion or ointment **2 :** any of several spicy fragrant herbs of the mint family **3 :** something that comforts or soothes

balmy \'bä-mē, 'bäl-\ *adj* **balm·i·er; -est 1 :** gently soothing **:** MILD **2 :** FOOLISH, ABSURD **syn** soft, bland, mild, gentle — **balm·i·ness** *n*

ba·lo·ney \bə-'lō-nē\ *n* **:** NONSENSE

bal·sa \'bȯl-sə\ *n* **:** the extremely light strong wood of a tropical American tree; *also* **:** the tree

bal·sam \'bȯl-səm\ *n* **1 :** a fragrant aromatic and usu. resinous substance oozing from various plants; *also* **:** a preparation containing or smelling like balsam **2 :** a balsam-yielding tree (as balsam fir) **3 :** a common garden ornamental plant — **bal·sam·ic** \bȯl-'sa-mik\ *adj*

balsam fir *n* **:** a resinous American evergreen tree that is widely used for pulpwood and as a Christmas tree

Bal·ti·more oriole \'bȯl-tə-ˌmȯr-\ *n* **:** a common American oriole in which the male is brightly colored with orange, black, and white

bal·us·ter \'ba-lə-stər\ *n* [F *balustre*, fr. It *balaustro*, fr. *balaustra* wild pomegranate flower, fr. L *balaustium*; fr. its shape] **:** an upright support for a rail (as of a staircase)

bal·us·trade \'ba-lə-ˌstrād\ *n* **:** a row of balusters topped by a rail

bam·boo \bam-'bü\ *n, pl* **bamboos :** any of various woody mostly tall tropical grasses including some with strong hollow stems used for building, furniture, or utensils

bamboo curtain *n, often cap B&C* **:** a political, military, and ideological barrier in the Orient

bam·boo·zle \bam-'bü-zəl\ *vb* **-boo·zled; -boo·zling :** TRICK, HOODWINK

¹ban \'ban\ *vb* **banned; ban·ning :** PROHIBIT, FORBID

²ban *n* **1 :** CURSE **2 :** a legal or formal prohibiting

³ban \'bän\ *n, pl* **ba·ni** \'bä-nē\ — see *leu* at MONEY table

ba·nal \bə-'näl, -'nal; 'bān-ᵊl\ *adj* [F] **:** COMMONPLACE, TRITE — **ba·nal·i·ty** \bā-'na-lə-tē\ *n*

ba·nana \bə-'na-nə\ *n* **:** a treelike tropical plant bearing thick clusters of yellow or reddish finger-shaped fruit; *also* **:** this fruit

¹band \'band\ *n* **1 :** something that binds, ties, or goes around **2 :** a strip or stripe that can be distinguished (as by color or texture) from nearby matter **3 :** a range of wavelengths (as in radio)

²band *vb* **1 :** to tie up, finish, or enclose with a band **2 :** to gather together or unite esp. for some common end — **band·er** *n*

³band *n* **:** a group of persons, animals, or things; *esp* **:** a group of musicians organized for playing together

¹ban·dage \'ban-dij\ *n* **:** a strip of material used esp. in dressing wounds

²bandage *vb* **ban·daged; ban·dag·ing :** to dress or cover with a bandage

ban·dan·na *or* **ban·dana** \ban-'da-nə\ *n* **:** a large colored figured handkerchief

B and B *abbr* bed-and-breakfast

band·box \'band-ˌbäks\ *n* **:** a usu. cylindrical box for carrying clothing

band·ed \'ban-dəd\ *adj* **:** having or marked with bands

ban·de·role *or* **ban·de·rol** \'ban-də-ˌrōl\ *n* **:** a long narrow forked flag or streamer

ban·dit \'ban-dət\ *n* [It *bandito*, fr. *bandire* to banish] **1** *pl also* **ban·dit·ti** \ban-'di-tē\ **:** an outlaw who lives by plunder; *esp* **:** a member of a band of marauders **2 :** ROBBER — **ban·dit·ry** \'ban-də-trē\ *n*

band·mas·ter \'band-ˌmas-tər\ *n* **:** a conductor of a musical band

ban·do·lier *or* **ban·do·leer** \ˌban-də-'lir\ *n* **:** a belt slung over the shoulder esp. to carry ammunition

band saw *n* **:** a saw in the form of an endless steel belt running over pulleys

band·stand \'band-ˌstand\ *n* **:** a usu. roofed platform on which a band or orchestra performs outdoors

b and w *abbr* black and white

band·wag·on \'band-ˌwa-gən\ *n* **1 :** a wagon carrying musicians in a parade **2 :** a movement that attracts growing support

¹ban·dy \'ban-dē\ *vb* **ban·died; ban·dy·ing 1 :** to exchange (as blows or quips) esp. in rapid succession **2 :** to use in a glib or offhand way

²bandy *adj* **:** curved outward ⟨~ legs⟩

bane \'bān\ *n* **1 :** POISON **2 :** WOE, HARM; *also* **:** a source of this — **bane·ful** *adj*

¹bang \'baŋ\ *vb* **1 :** BUMP ⟨fell and ~ed his knee⟩ **2 :** to strike, thrust, or move usu. with a loud noise

²bang *n* **1 :** a resounding blow **2 :** a sudden loud noise

³bang *adv* **:** DIRECTLY, RIGHT

⁴bang *n* **:** a fringe of hair cut short (as across the forehead) — usu. used in pl.

⁵bang *vb* **:** to cut a bang in

Ban·gla·deshi \ˌbäŋ-glə-'de-shē\ *n* **:** a native or inhabitant of Bangladesh — **Bangladeshi** *adj*

ban·gle \'baŋ-gəl\ *n* **:** BRACELET; *also* **:** a loose-hanging ornament

bang–up \'baŋ-ˌəp\ *adj* **:** FIRST-RATE, EXCELLENT ⟨a ~ job⟩

bani *pl of* ³BAN

ban·ish \'ba-nish\ *vb* **1 :** to require by authority to leave a country **2 :** to drive out **:** EXPEL **syn** exile, ostracize, deport, relegate — **ban·ish·ment** *n*

ban·is·ter \'ba-nə-stər\ *n* **1 :** BALUSTER **2 :** a handrail with its supporting posts **3 :** HANDRAIL

ban·jo \'ban-jō\ *n, pl* **banjos** *also* **banjoes :** a musical instrument with a long neck, a drumlike body, and usu. five strings — **ban·jo·ist** \-ist\ *n*

¹bank \'baŋk\ *n* **1 :** a piled-up mass (as of cloud or earth) **2 :** an undersea elevation **3 :** rising ground bordering a lake, river, or sea **4 :** the sideways slope of a surface along a curve or of a vehicle as it rounds a curve

²bank *vb* **1 :** to form a bank about **2 :** to cover (as a fire) with fuel to keep inactive **3 :** to build (a curve) with the roadbed or track inclined laterally upward from the inside edge **4 :** to pile or heap in a bank; *also* **:** to arrange in a tier **5 :** to incline (an airplane) laterally

³bank *n* [ME, fr. MF or It; MF *banque*, fr. It *banca*, lit., bench] **1 :** an establishment concerned esp. with the custody, loan, exchange, or issue of money, the extension of credit, and the transmission of funds **2 :** a stock of or a place for holding something in reserve ⟨a blood ~⟩

⁴bank *vb* **1 :** to conduct the business of a bank **2 :** to deposit money or have an account in a bank — **bank·er** *n* — **bank·ing** *n*

⁵bank *n* **:** a group of objects arranged close together (as in a row or tier) ⟨a ~ of file drawers⟩

bank·book \'baŋk-ˌbuk\ *n* **:** the depositor's book in which a bank records deposits and withdrawals

bank·card \-ˌkärd\ *n* **:** a credit card issued by a bank

bank·note \-ˌnōt\ *n* **:** a promissory note issued by a bank and circulating as money

bank·roll \-ˌrōl\ *n* **:** supply of money **:** FUNDS

¹bank·rupt \'baŋ-(ˌ)krəpt\ *n* **:** an insolvent person; *esp* **:** one whose property is turned over by court action to a trustee to be handled for the benefit of his creditors — **bankrupt** *vb*

²bankrupt *adj* **1 :** reduced to financial ruin; *esp* **:** legally declared a bankrupt **2 :** wholly lacking in or deprived of

---

\ə\abut \ᵊ\kitten \ər\further \a\ash \ā\ace \ä\mop, mar \au̇\out \ch\chin \e\bet \ē\easy \g\go \i\hit \ī\ice \j\job \ŋ\sing \ō\go \ȯ\law \ȯi\boy \th\thin \t͟h\the \ü\loot \u̇\foot \y\yet \zh\vision *see also* Pronunciation Symbols page

some essential ⟨morally ∼⟩ — **bank·rupt·cy** \'baŋ-(ˌ)krəpt-sē\ *n*

¹ban·ner \'ba-nər\ *n* **1** : a piece of cloth attached to a staff and used by a leader as his standard **2** : FLAG

²banner *adj* : distinguished from all others esp. in excellence ⟨a ∼ year⟩

ban·nock \'ba-nək\ *n* : a flat oatmeal or barley cake usu. cooked on a griddle

banns \'banz\ *n pl* : public announcement esp. in church of a proposed marriage

ban·quet \'baŋ-kwət\ *n* [MF, fr. It *banchetto*, fr. dim. of *banca* bench, bank] : a ceremonial dinner — **banquet** *vb*

ban·quette \baŋ-'ket\ *n* : a long upholstered bench esp. along a wall

ban·shee \'ban-shē\ *n* [Ir *bean sídhe* & ScGael *bean sìth*, lit., woman of fairyland] : a female spirit in Gaelic folklore whose wailing warns a family that one of them will soon die

ban·tam \'ban-təm\ *n* **1** : any of numerous small domestic fowls that are often miniatures of standard breeds **2** : a small but pugnacious person

¹ban·ter \'ban-tər\ *vb* : to speak to in a witty and teasing manner

²banter *n* : good-natured witty joking

Ban·tu \'ban-ˌtü\ *n, pl* **Bantu** *or* **Bantus** **1** : a member of a group of African peoples of central and southern Africa **2** : a group of African languages spoken by the Bantu

Ban·tu·stan \ˌban-tü-'stan, ˌbän-tü-'stän\ *n* : an all-black enclave in the Republic of So. Africa with a limited degree of self-government

ban·yan \'ban-yən\ *n* [earlier *banyan* Hindu merchant, fr. Hindi *baniyā;* fr. a merchant's pagoda erected under a tree of the species in Iran] : a large East Indian tree whose aerial roots grow downward to the ground and form new trunks

banyan

ban·zai \bän-'zī\ *n* : a Japanese cheer or cry of triumph

bao·bab \'baů-ˌbab, 'bä-ə-\ *n* : an Old World tropical tree with short swollen trunk and sour edible gourdlike fruits

bap·tism \'bap-ˌti-zəm\ *n* **1** : a Christian sacrament signifying spiritual rebirth and symbolized by the ritual use of water **2** : an act of baptizing — **bap·tis·mal** \bap-'tiz-məl\ *adj*

baptismal name *n* : GIVEN NAME

Bap·tist \'bap-tist\ *n* : a member of any of several Protestant denominations emphasizing baptism by immersion of believers only

bap·tis·tery *or* **bap·tis·try** \'bap-tə-strē\ *n, pl* **-ter·ies** *or* **-tries** : a place esp. in a church used for baptism

bap·tize \bap-'tīz, 'bap-ˌtīz\ *vb* **bap·tized; bap·tiz·ing** [ME, fr. OF *baptiser*, fr. L *baptizare*, fr. Gk *baptizein* to dip, baptize, fr. *baptein* to dip] **1** : to administer baptism to; *also* : CHRISTEN **2** : to purify esp. by an ordeal

¹bar \'bär\ *n* **1** : a long narrow piece of material (as wood or metal) used esp. for a lever, fastening, or support **2** : BARRIER, OBSTACLE **3** : the railing in a law court at which prisoners are stationed; *also* : the legal profes-

sion or the whole body of lawyers **4** : a stripe, band, or line much longer than wide **5** : a counter at which food or esp. drink is served; *also* : BARROOM **6** : a vertical line across the musical staff

²bar *vb* **barred; bar·ring** **1** : to fasten, confine, or obstruct with or as if with a bar or bars **2** : to mark with bars : STRIPE **3** : to shut or keep out : EXCLUDE **4** : FORBID, PREVENT

³bar *prep* : EXCEPT

⁴bar *abbr* barometer; barometric

Bar *abbr* Baruch

barb \'bärb\ *n* **1** : a sharp projection extending backward (as from the point of an arrow) **2** : a biting critical remark — **barbed** \'bärbd\ *adj*

bar·bar·ian \bär-'ber-ē-ən\ *adj* **1** : of, relating to, or being a land, culture, or people alien to and usu. believed to be inferior to another's **2** : lacking refinement, learning, or artistic or literary culture — **barbarian** *n*

bar·bar·ic \bär-'bar-ik\ *adj* **1** : BARBARIAN **2** : marked by a lack of restraint : WILD **3** : PRIMITIVE, UNSOPHISTICATED

bar·ba·rism \'bär-bə-ˌri-zəm\ *n* **1** : the social condition of barbarians; *also* : the use or display of barbarian or barbarous acts, attitudes, or ideas **2** : a word or expression that offends standards of correctness or purity

bar·ba·rous \'bär-bə-rəs\ *adj* **1** : lacking culture or refinement **2** : using linguistic barbarisms **3** : mercilessly harsh or cruel — **bar·bar·i·ty** \bär-'bar-ə-tē\ *n* — **bar·ba·rous·ly** *adv*

¹bar·be·cue \'bär-bi-ˌkyü\ *n* : a social gathering at which barbecued food is served

²barbecue *vb* **-cued; -cu·ing** **1** : to cook over hot coals or on a revolving spit **2** : to cook in a highly seasoned vinegar sauce

bar·bell \'bär-ˌbel\ *n* : a bar with adjustable weights attached to each end used for exercise and in weight-lifting competition

bar·ber \'bär-bər\ *n* [ME, fr. MF *barbeor*, fr. *barbe* beard, fr. L *barba*] : one whose business is cutting and dressing hair and shaving and trimming beards

bar·ber·ry \'bär-ˌber-ē\ *n* : any of a genus of spiny shrubs bearing yellow flowers and oblong red berries

bar·bi·tu·rate \bär-'bi-chə-rət\ *n* : any of various compounds (as a salt or ester) formed from an organic acid (**bar·bi·tu·ric acid** \ˌbär-bə-'tür-ik-, -'tyür-\; *esp* : one used as a sedative or hypnotic

bar·ca·role *or* **bar·ca·rolle** \'bär-kə-ˌrōl\ *n* : a Venetian boat song characterized by a beat suggesting a rowing rhythm; *also* : a piece of music imitating this

bar chart *n* : BAR GRAPH

bar code *n* : a set of printed and variously spaced bars and sometimes numerals that is designed to be scanned to identify the object it labels

bard \'bärd\ *n* : POET

¹bare \'bar\ *adj* **bar·er; bar·est** **1** : NAKED **2** : UNCONCEALED, EXPOSED **3** : EMPTY **4** : leaving nothing to spare : MERE **5** : PLAIN, UNADORNED **syn** nude, bald — **bareness** *n*

²bare *vb* **bared; bar·ing** : to make or lay bare : UNCOVER

bare·back \-ˌbak\ *or* **bare·backed** \-'bakt\ *adv or adj* : without a saddle

bare·faced \-'fāst\ *adj* **1** : having the face uncovered; *esp* : BEARDLESS **2** : not concealed : OPEN — **bare·faced·ly** \-'fā-səd-lē, -'fāst-lē\ *adv*

bare·foot \-ˌfút\ *or* **bare·foot·ed** \-'fü-təd\ *adv or adj* : with bare feet

bare·hand·ed \-'han-dəd\ *adv or adj* **1** : without gloves **2** : without tools or weapons

bare·head·ed \-'he-dəd\ *adv or adj* : without a hat

bare·ly \'bar-lē\ *adv* **1** : PLAINLY, MEAGERLY **2** : by a narrow margin : only just ⟨∼ enough money⟩

bar·fly \'bär-ˌflī\ *n* : a drinker who frequents bars

¹bar·gain \'bär-gən\ *n* **1** : AGREEMENT **2** : an advantageous purchase **3** : a transaction, situation, or event regarded in the light of its results

²bargain *vb* **1** : to negotiate over the terms of an agreement; *also* : to come to terms **2** : BARTER

bar·gain–base·ment \'bär-gən-'bās-mənt\ *adj* : markedly inexpensive

¹barge \'bärj\ *n* **1** : a broad flat-bottomed boat usu. moved by towing **2** : a motorboat supplied to a flagship (as for an admiral) **3** : a ceremonial boat elegantly furnished — **barge·man** \-mən\ *n*

²barge *vb* **barged; barg·ing** **1** : to carry by barge **2** : to move or thrust oneself clumsily or rudely

bar graph *n* : a graphic technique for comparing amounts by rectangles whose lengths are proportional to the amounts they represent

bari·tone \'bar-ə-ˌtōn\ *n* [F *baryton* or It *baritono*, fr. Gk *barytonos* deep sounding, fr. *barys* heavy + *tonos* tone] : a male voice between bass and tenor; *also* : a man with such a voice

bar·i·um \'bar-ē-əm\ *n* : a silver-white metallic chemical element that occurs only in combination — see ELEMENT table

¹bark \'bärk\ *vb* **1** : to make the short loud cry of a dog **2** : to speak or utter in a curt loud tone : SNAP

²bark *n* : the sound made by a barking dog

³bark *n* : the tough corky outer covering of a woody stem or root

⁴bark *vb* **1** : to strip the bark from **2** : to rub the skin from : ABRADE

⁵bark *n* : a ship of three or more masts with the aft mast fore-and-aft rigged and the others square-rigged

bar·keep \'bär-ˌkēp\ *also* **bar·keep·er** \-ˌkē-pər\ *n* : BARTENDER

bark·er \'bär-kər\ *n* : a person who stands at the entrance esp. to a show and tries to attract customers to it

bar·ley \'bär-lē\ *n* : a cereal grass with seeds used as food and in making malt liquors; *also* : its seed

bar mitz·vah \bär-'mits-və\ *n, often cap B&M* [Heb *bar miṣwāh*, lit., son of the (divine) law] **1** : a Jewish boy who at about 13 years of age assumes religious responsibilities **2** : the ceremony recognizing a boy as a bar mitzvah

barn \'bärn\ *n* [ME *bern*, fr. OE *bereærn*, fr. *bere* barley + *ærn* house, store] : a building used esp. for storing hay and grain and for housing livestock or farm equipment

bar·na·cle \'bär-ni-kəl\ *n* : any of numerous small marine crustaceans free swimming when young but permanently fixed (as to rocks, whales, or ships) when adult

barn·storm \'bärn-ˌstȯrm\ *vb* : to travel through the country making brief stops to entertain (as with shows or flying stunts) or to campaign for political office

barn·yard \-ˌyärd\ *n* : a usu. fenced area adjoining a barn

baro·graph \'bar-ə-ˌgraf\ *n* : a recording barometer

ba·rom·e·ter \bə-'räm-ə-tər\ *n* : an instrument for measuring atmospheric pressure — **baro·met·ric** \ˌbar-ə-'me-trik\ *adj*

bar·on \'bar-ən\ *n* : a member of the lowest grade of the British peerage — **ba·ro·ni·al** \bə-'rō-nē-əl\ *adj* — **bar·ony** \'bar-ə-nē\ *n*

bar·on·age \'bar-ə-nij\ *n* : PEERAGE

bar·on·ess \'bar-ə-nəs\ *n* **1** : the wife or widow of a baron **2** : a woman holding a baronial title in her own right

bar·on·et \'bar-ə-nət\ *n* : a man holding a rank of honor below a baron but above a knight — **bar·on·et·cy** \-sē\ *n*

ba·roque \bə-'rōk, -'räk\ *adj* : marked by the use of complex forms, bold ornamentation, and the juxtapositioning of contrasting elements

ba·rouche \bə-'rüsh\ *n* [G *Barutsche*, fr. It *biroccio*, ul-

tim. fr. LL *birotus* two-wheeled, fr. L *bi* two + *rota* wheel] : a 4-wheeled carriage with a high driver's seat in front and a folding top

bar·racks \'bar-əks\ *n sing or pl* : a building or group of buildings for lodging soldiers

bar·ra·cu·da \ˌbar-ə-'kü-də\ *n, pl* **-da** *or* **-das** : any of several large predaceous sea fishes including some used for food

bar·rage \bə-'räzh, -'räj\ *n* : a heavy concentration of fire (as of artillery)

barred \'bärd\ *adj* : STRIPED

¹bar·rel \'bar-əl\ *n* **1** : a round bulging cask with flat ends of equal diameter **2** : the amount contained in a barrel **3** : a cylindrical or tubular part ⟨gun ∼⟩ — **bar·reled** \-əld\ *adj*

²barrel *vb* **-reled** *or* **-relled; -rel·ing** *or* **-rel·ling** **1** : to pack in a barrel **2** : to travel at high speed

bar·rel·head \-ˌhed\ *n* : the flat end of a barrel — **on the barrelhead** : asking for or granting no credit ⟨paid cash *on the barrelhead*⟩

barrel roll *n* : an airplane maneuver in which a complete revolution about the longitudinal axis is made

¹bar·ren \'bar-ən\ *adj* **1** : STERILE, UNFRUITFUL **2** : unproductive of results ⟨a ∼ scheme⟩ **3** : lacking interest or charm **4** : DULL, STUPID — **bar·ren·ness** \-nəs\ *n*

²barren *n* : a tract of barren land

bar·rette \bä-'ret, bə-\ *n* : a clasp or bar for holding the hair in place

¹bar·ri·cade \'bar-ə-ˌkād, ˌbar-ə-'kād\ *vb* **-cad·ed; -cad·ing** : to block, obstruct, or fortify with a barricade

²barricade *n* [F, fr. MF, fr. *barriquer* to barricade, fr. *barrique* barrel] **1** : a hastily thrown-up obstruction or fortification **2** : BARRIER, OBSTACLE

bar·ri·er \'bar-ē-ər\ *n* : something that separates, demarcates, or serves as a barricade ⟨racial ∼s⟩

barrier island *n* : a long broad sandy island lying parallel to a shore

barrier reef *n* : a coral reef roughly parallel to a shore and separated from it by a lagoon

bar·ring \'bar-iŋ\ *prep* : excluding by exception : EXCEPTING

bar·rio \'bär-ē-ˌō, 'bar-\ *n, pl* **-ri·os** **1** : a district of a city or town in a Spanish-speaking country **2** : a Spanish-speaking quarter in a U.S. city

bar·ris·ter \'bar-ə-stər\ *n* : a British counselor admitted to plead in the higher courts

bar·room \'bär-ˌrüm, -ˌrüm\ *n* : a room or establishment whose main feature is a bar for the sale of liquor

¹bar·row \'bar-ō\ *n* : a large burial mound of earth and stones

²barrow *n* **1** : WHEELBARROW **2** : a cart with a boxlike body and two shafts for pushing it

Bart *abbr* baronet

bar·tend·er \'bär-ˌten-dər\ *n* : one that serves liquor at a bar

bar·ter \'bär-tər\ *vb* : to trade by exchange of goods — **barter** *n* — **bar·ter·er** *n*

Ba·ruch \'bär-ˌük, bə-'rük\ *n* — see BIBLE table

bas·al \'bā-səl\ *adj* **1** : situated at or forming the base **2** : BASIC

basal metabolism *n* : the turnover of energy in a fasting and resting organism using energy solely to maintain vital cellular activity, respiration, and circulation as measured by the rate at which heat is given off

ba·salt \bə-'sȯlt, 'bā-ˌsȯlt\ *n* : a dark fine-grained igneous rock — **ba·sal·tic** \bə-'sȯl-tik\ *adj*

¹base \'bās\ *n, pl* **bas·es** \'bā-səz\ **1** : BOTTOM, FOUNDATION **2** : a side or face on which a geometrical figure stands; *also* : the length of a base **3** : a main ingredient or fundamental part **4** : the point of beginning an act or operation **5** : a place on which a force depends for supplies **6** : a number (as 5 in 5^7) that is raised to a power; *esp* : a number that when raised to a power equal to the logarithm of a number yields the number itself ⟨the logarithm of 100 to $\sim$ 10 is 2 since $10^2 = 100$⟩ **7** : the number of units in a given digit's place of a number system that is required to give the numeral 1 in the next higher place ⟨the decimal system uses a $\sim$ of 10⟩; *also* : such a system using an indicated base ⟨convert from $\sim$ 10 to $\sim$ 2⟩ **8** : any of the four stations at the corners of a baseball diamond **9** : a chemical compound (as lime or ammonia) that reacts with an acid to form a salt, has a bitter taste, and turns litmus blue **syn** basis, ground, groundwork, footing, foundation — **base·man** \ˈbās-mən\ *n*

²**base** *vb* **based; bas·ing 1** : to form or serve as a base for **2** : ESTABLISH

³**base** *adj* **1** : of inferior quality : DEBASED, ALLOYED **2** : CONTEMPTIBLE, IGNOBLE **3** : MENIAL, DEGRADING **4** : of little value **syn** low, vile, despicable, wretched — **base·ly** *adv* — **base·ness** *n*

base·ball \ˈbās-ˌbȯl\ *n* : a game played with a bat and ball by two teams on a field with four bases arranged in a diamond; *also* : the ball used in this game

base·board \-ˌbȯrd\ *n* : a line of boards or molding covering the joint of a wall and the adjoining floor

base·born \-ˈbȯrn\ *adj* **1** : MEAN, IGNOBLE **2** : of humble birth **3** : of illegitimate birth

base exchange *n* : a post exchange at a naval or air force base

base hit *n* : a hit in baseball that enables the batter to reach base safely with no error made and no base runner forced out

base·less \-ləs\ *adj* : having no base or basis : GROUNDLESS

base·line \ˈbās-ˌlīn\ *n* **1** : a line serving as a basis esp. to calculate or locate something **2** : the area within which a baseball player must keep when running between bases

base·ment \-mənt\ *n* **1** : the part of a building that is wholly or partly below ground level **2** : the lowest or fundamental part of something

base on balls : an advance to first base given to a baseball player who receives four balls

base runner *n* : a baseball player who is on base or is attempting to reach a base

¹**bash** \ˈbash\ *vb* **1** : to strike violently : HIT **2** : to smash by a blow **3** : to attack physically or verbally

²**bash** *n* **1** : a heavy blow **2** : a festive social gathering : PARTY

bash·ful \ˈbash-fəl\ *adj* : inclined to shrink from public attention — **bash·ful·ness** *n*

ba·sic \ˈbā-sik\ *adj* **1** : of, relating to, or forming the base or essence : FUNDAMENTAL **2** : of, relating to, or having the character of a chemical base **syn** underlying, basal, primary — **ba·sic·i·ty** \bā-ˈsi-sə-tē\ *n*

BA·SIC \ˈbā-sik\ *n* [Beginner's All-purpose Symbolic Instruction Code] : a simplified language for programming a computer

ba·si·cal·ly \ˈbā-si-k(ə-)lē\ *adv* **1** : at a basic level **2** : for the most part **3** : in a basic manner

ba·sil \ˈbā-zəl, ˈba-, -səl\ *n* : any of several mints with fragrant leaves used in cooking

ba·sil·i·ca \bə-ˈsi-li-kə, -ˈzi-\ *n* [L, fr. Gk *basilikē*, fr. fem. of *basilikos* royal, fr. *basileus* king] **1** : an early Christian church building consisting of nave and aisles with clerestory and apse **2** : a Roman Catholic church given ceremonial privileges

bas·i·lisk \ˈba-sə-ˌlisk, ˈba-zə-\ *n* [ME, fr. L *basiliscus*, fr. Gk *basiliskos*, fr. dim. of *basileus* king] : a legendary reptile with fatal breath and glance

ba·sin \ˈbās-ᵊn\ *n* **1** : an open usu. circular vessel with sloping sides for holding liquid (as water) **2** : a hollow or enclosed place containing water; *also* : the region drained by a river

ba·sis \ˈbā-səs\ *n, pl* **ba·ses** \-ˌsēz\ **1** : FOUNDATION, BASE **2** : a fundamental principle

bask \ˈbask\ *vb* **1** : to expose oneself to comfortable heat **2** : to enjoy something warmly comforting ⟨$\sim$ing in his friends' admiration⟩

bas·ket \ˈbas-kət\ *n* : a container made of woven material (as twigs or grasses); *also* : any of various lightweight usu. wood containers — **bas·ket·ful** *n*

bas·ket·ball \-ˌbȯl\ *n* : a game played on a court by two teams who try to throw an inflated ball through a raised goal; *also* : the ball used in this game

basket case *n* **1** : a person who has all four limbs amputated **2** : one that is totally incapacitated or inoperative

basket weave *n* : a textile weave resembling the checkered pattern of a plaited basket

bas mitz·vah \bäs-ˈmits-və\ *n, often cap B&M* [Heb *bath miṣwāh*, lit., daughter of the (divine) law] **1** : a Jewish girl who at about 13 years of age assumes religious responsibilities **2** : the ceremony recognizing a girl as a bas mitzvah

Basque \ˈbask\ *n* **1** : a member of a people inhabiting a region bordering on the Bay of Biscay in northern Spain and southwestern France **2** : the language of the Basque people — **Basque** *adj*

bas–re·lief \ˌbä-ri-ˈlēf\ *n* [F] : a sculpture in relief with the design raised very slightly from the background

¹**bass** \ˈbas\ *n, pl* **bass** *or* **bass·es** : any of numerous sport and food bony fishes (as a striped bass)

²**bass** \ˈbās\ *adj* : of low pitch

³**bass** \ˈbās\ *n* **1** : a deep sound or tone **2** : the lower half of the musical pitch range **3** : the lowest part in a 4-part chorus; *also* : a singer having this voice or part

bas·set hound \ˈba-sət-\ *n* : any of an old breed of short-legged hunting dogs of French origin having long ears and crooked front legs

bas·si·net \ˌba-sə-ˈnet\ *n* : a baby's bed that resembles a basket and often has a hood over one end

bas·so \ˈba-sō, ˈbä-\ *n, pl* **bassos** *or* **bas·si** \ˈbä-ˌsē\ [It] : a bass singer

bas·soon \bə-ˈsün\ *n* : a musical wind instrument lower in pitch than the oboe

bass·wood \ˈbas-ˌwu̇d\ *n* : any of several New World lindens or their wood

bast \ˈbast\ *n* : BAST FIBER

¹**bas·tard** \ˈbas-tərd\ *n* **1** : an illegitimate child **2** : an offensive or disagreeable person

²**bastard** *adj* **1** : ILLEGITIMATE **2** : of an inferior or nontypical kind, size, or form; *also* : SPURIOUS — **bas·tardy** *n*

bas·tard·ize \ˈbas-tər-ˌdīz\ *vb* **-ized; -iz·ing** : to reduce from a higher to a lower state : DEBASE

¹**baste** \ˈbāst\ *vb* **bast·ed; bast·ing** : to sew with long stitches so as to keep temporarily in place

²**baste** *vb* **bast·ed; bast·ing** : to moisten (as meat) at intervals with liquid while cooking

bast fiber *n* : a strong woody plant fiber obtained chiefly from phloem and used esp. in making ropes

bas·ti·na·do \ˌbas-tə-ˈnā-dō, -ˈnä-\ *or* **bas·ti·nade** \ˌbas-tə-ˈnād, -ˈnäd\ *n, pl* **-na·does** *or* **-nades 1** : a blow or beating esp. with a stick **2** : a punishment consisting of beating the soles of the feet

bas·tion \ˈbas-chən\ *n* : a projecting part of a fortification; *also* : a fortified position

¹**bat** \ˈbat\ *n* **1** : a stout stick : CLUB **2** : a sharp blow **3** : an implement (as of wood) used to hit a ball (as in baseball) **4** : a turn at batting — usu. used with *at*

²**bat** *vb* **bat·ted; bat·ting** : to hit with or as if with a bat

³bat *n* : any of an order of night-flying mammals with forelimbs modified to form wings

⁴bat *vb* **bat·ted; bat·ting** : WINK, BLINK

batch \'bach\ *n* **1** : a quantity (as of bread) baked at one time **2** : a quantity of material for use at one time or produced at one operation

bate \'bāt\ *vb* **bat·ed; bat·ing** : MODERATE, REDUCE

bath \'bath, 'båth\ *n, pl* **baths** \'bathz, 'baths, 'båthz, 'båths\ **1** : a washing of the body **2** : water for washing the body **3** : a liquid in which objects are immersed so that it can act on them **4** : BATHROOM **5** : a financial loss ⟨took a ~ in the market⟩

bathe \'bāth\ *vb* **bathed; bath·ing 1** : to wash in liquid and esp. water; *also* : to apply water or a medicated liquid to ⟨*bathed* her eyes⟩ **2** : to take a bath; *also* : to take a swim **3** : to wash along, over, or against so as to wet **4** : to suffuse with or as if with light — **bath·er** *n*

bath·house \'bath-ˌhaus, 'båth-\ *n* **1** : a building equipped for bathing **2** : a building containing dressing rooms for bathers

bathing suit *n* : SWIMSUIT

ba·thos \'bā-ˌthäs\ *n* [Gk, lit., depth] **1** : the sudden appearance of the commonplace in otherwise elevated matter or style **2** : insincere or overdone pathos — **ba·thet·ic** \bə-'the-tik\ *adj*

bath·robe \'bath-ˌrōb, 'båth-\ *n* : a loose often absorbent robe worn before and after bathing or as a dressing gown

bath·room \-ˌrüm, -ˌrum\ *n* : a room containing a bathtub or shower and usu. a sink and toilet

bath·tub \-ˌtəb\ *n* : a usu. fixed tub for bathing

ba·tik \bə-'tēk, 'ba-tik\ *n* [Javanese *baṭik*] **1** : an Indonesian method of hand-printing textiles by coating with wax the parts not to be dyed; *also* : a design so executed **2** : a fabric printed by batik

ba·tiste \bə-'tēst\ *n* : a fine sheer fabric of plain weave

bat·man \'bat-mən\ *n* : an orderly of a British military officer

ba·ton \bə-'tän\ *n* : STAFF, ROD; *esp* : a stick with which the leader directs an orchestra or band

bats·man \'bats-mən\ *n* : a batter esp. in cricket

bat·tal·ion \bə-'tal-yən\ *n* **1** : a large body of troops organized to act together : ARMY **2** : a military unit composed of a headquarters and two or more units (as companies)

¹bat·ten \'bat-ᵊn\ *vb* **1** : to grow or make fat **2** : THRIVE

²batten *n* : a strip of wood used esp. to seal or strengthen a joint

³batten *vb* : to fasten with battens

¹bat·ter \'ba-tər\ *vb* : to beat or damage with repeated blows

²batter *n* : a soft mixture (as for cake) basically of flour and liquid

³batter *n* : one that bats; *esp* : the player whose turn it is to bat

battering ram *n* **1** : an ancient military machine for battering down walls **2** : a heavy metal bar with handles used to batter down doors

bat·tery \'ba-tə-rē\ *n, pl* **-ter·ies 1** : BEATING; *esp* : unlawful beating or use of force on a person **2** : a grouping of artillery pieces for tactical purposes; *also* : the guns of a warship **3** : a group of electric cells for furnishing electric current; *also* : a single electric cell ⟨a flashlight ~⟩ **4** : a number of similar items grouped or used as a unit ⟨a ~ of tests⟩ **5** : the pitcher and catcher of a baseball team

bat·ting \'ba-tiŋ\ *n* : layers or sheets of cotton or wool (as for lining quilts)

¹bat·tle \'bat-ᵊl\ *n* [ME *batel*, fr. OF *bataille* battle, fortifying tower, battalion, fr. LL *battalia* combat, alter. of *battualia* fencing exercises, fr. L *battuere* to beat] : a general military engagement; *also* : an extended contest or controversy

²battle *vb* **bat·tled; bat·tling** : to engage in battle : CONTEND, FIGHT

bat·tle–ax \'bat-ᵊl-ˌaks\ *n* **1** : a long-handled ax formerly used as a weapon **2** : a quarrelsome domineering woman

battle fatigue *n* : COMBAT FATIGUE

bat·tle·field \'bat-ᵊl-ˌfēld\ *n* : a place where a battle is fought

bat·tle·ment \-mənt\ *n* : a decorative or defensive parapet on top of a wall

bat·tle·ship \-ˌship\ *n* : a warship of the most heavily armed and armored class

bat·tle·wag·on \-ˌwa-gən\ *n* : BATTLESHIP

bat·ty \'ba-tē\ *adj* **bat·ti·er; -est** : CRAZY, FOOLISH

bau·ble \'bò-bəl\ *n* : TRINKET

baud \'bòd, *Brit* 'bōd\ *n, pl* **baud** *also* **bauds** : a unit of data transmission speed

baulk *chiefly Brit var of* BALK

baux·ite \'bòk-ˌsīt\ *n* : a clayey mixture that is the chief ore of aluminum

bawd \'bòd\ *n* **1** : MADAM 2 **2** : PROSTITUTE

bawdy \'bò-dē\ *adj* **bawd·i·er; -est** : OBSCENE, LEWD — **bawd·i·ly** \'bòd-ᵊl-ē\ *adv* — **bawd·i·ness** \-dē-nəs\ *n*

¹bawl \'bòl\ *vb* : to cry or cry out loudly; *also* : to scold harshly

²bawl *n* : a long loud cry : BELLOW

¹bay \'bā\ *adj* : reddish brown

²bay *n* **1** : a bay-colored animal **2** : a reddish brown color

³bay *n* **1** : a section or compartment of a building or vehicle **2** : a compartment projecting outward from the wall of a building and containing a window (**bay window**)

⁴bay *vb* : to bark with deep long tones

⁵bay *n* **1** : the position of one unable to escape and forced to face danger **2** : a baying of dogs

⁶bay *n* : an inlet of a body of water (as the sea) usu. smaller than a gulf

⁷bay *n* : the European laurel; *also* : a shrub or tree resembling this

bay·ber·ry \'bā-ˌber-ē\ *n* : a hardy deciduous shrub of coastal eastern No. America bearing small hard berries coated with a white wax used for candles; *also* : its fruit

bay leaf *n* : the dried leaf of the European laurel used in cooking

¹bay·o·net \'bā-ə-nət, ˌbā-ə-'net\ *n* : a daggerlike weapon made to fit on the muzzle end of a rifle

²bayonet *vb* **-net·ed** *also* **-net·ted; -net·ing** *also* **-net·ting** : to use or stab with a bayonet

bay·ou \'bī-yü, -ō\ *n* [Louisiana French, fr. Choctaw *bayuk*] : a marshy or sluggish body of water

bay rum *n* : a fragrant liquid used esp. as a cologne or after-shave lotion

ba·zaar \bə-'zär\ *n* **1** : a group of shops : MARKETPLACE **2** : a fair for the sale of articles usu. for charity

ba·zoo·ka \bə-'zü-kə\ *n* [*bazooka* (a crude musical instrument made of pipes and a funnel)] : a weapon consisting of a tube and launching an explosive rocket able to pierce armor

¹BB \'bē-(ˌ)bē\ *n* : a small round shot pellet

²BB *abbr* base on balls

BBB *abbr* Better Business Bureau

BBC *abbr* British Broadcasting Corporation

bbl *abbr* barrel; barrels

BC *abbr* **1** before Christ — often printed in small capitals and often punctuated **2** British Columbia

B cell *n* [bone-marrow-derived *cell*] : any of the lymphocytes that secrete antibodies when mature

B complex *n* : VITAMIN B COMPLEX

\ə\abut \ᵊ\kitten \ər\further \a\ash \ā\ace \ä\mop, mar \au\out \ch\chin \e\bet \ē\easy \g\go \i\hit \ī\ice \j\job \ŋ\sing \ō\go \ò\law \òi\boy \th\thin \th\the \ü\loot \u\foot \y\yet \zh\vision *see also* Pronunciation Symbols page

bd *abbr* **1** board **2** bound
bdl *or* **bdle** *abbr* bundle
bdrm *abbr* bedroom
be \'bē\ *vb, past 1st & 3d sing* **was** \'wəz, 'wäz\; *2d sing*
were \'wər\; *pl* **were**; *past subjunctive* **were**; *past part*
been \'bin\; *pres part* **be·ing** \'bē-iŋ\; *pres 1st sing* **am**
\əm, 'am\; *2d sing* **are** \ər, 'är\; *3d sing* **is** \'iz, əz\; *pl*
are; *pres subjunctive* **be 1** : to equal in meaning or symbolically ⟨God *is* love⟩; *also* : to have a specified qualification or relationship ⟨leaves *are* green⟩ ⟨this fish *is* a
trout⟩ **2** : to have objective existence ⟨I think, therefore
I *am*⟩; *also* : to have or occupy a particular place ⟨here
is your pen⟩ **3** : to take place : OCCUR ⟨the meeting *is*
tonight⟩ **4** — used with the past participle of transitive
verbs as a passive voice auxiliary ⟨the door *was*
opened⟩ **5** — used as the auxiliary of the present participle in expressing continuous action ⟨he *is* sleeping⟩
6 — used as an auxiliary with the past participle of
some intransitive verbs to form archaic perfect tenses
7 — used as an auxiliary with *to* and the infinitive to
express futurity, prearrangement, or obligation ⟨you
are to come when called⟩
Be *symbol* beryllium
¹beach \'bēch\ *n* : a sandy or gravelly part of the shore
of an ocean or lake
²beach *vb* : to run or drive ashore
beach buggy *n* : DUNE BUGGY
beach·comb·er \'bēch-ˌkō-mər\ *n* : a person who
searches along a shore for something of use or value
beach·head \'bēch-ˌhed\ *n* : a small area on an enemy≠
held shore occupied in the initial stages of an invasion
bea·con \'bē-kən\ *n* **1** : a signal fire **2** : a guiding or warning signal (as a lighthouse) **3** : a radio transmitter emitting signals for guidance of aircraft
¹bead \'bēd\ *n* [ME *bede* prayer, prayer bead, fr. OE *bed,
gebed* prayer] **1** *pl* : a series of prayers and meditations
made with a rosary **2** : a small piece of material pierced
for threading on a line (as in a rosary) **3** : a small globular body **4** : a narrow projecting rim or band — **bead·
ing** *n* — **beady** *adj*
²bead *vb* : to form into a bead
bea·dle \'bēd-ᵊl\ *n* : a usu. English parish officer whose
duties include keeping order in church
bea·gle \'bē-gəl\ *n* : a small short-legged smooth≠
coated hound

beagle

beak \'bēk\ *n* : the bill of a bird and esp. of a bird of prey;
also : a pointed projecting part — **beaked** \'bēkt\ *adj*
bea·ker \'bē-kər\ *n* **1** : a large widemouthed drinking cup
2 : a widemouthed thin-walled laboratory vessel
¹beam \'bēm\ *n* **1** : a large long piece of timber or metal
2 : the bar of a balance from which the scales hang **3**
: the breadth of a ship at its widest part **4** : a ray or shaft
of light **5** : a collection of nearly parallel rays (as X rays)
or particles (as electrons) **6** : a constant radio signal

transmitted for the guidance of pilots; *also* : the course
indicated by this signal
²beam *vb* **1** : to send out light **2** : to aim (a broadcast) by
directional antennas **3** : to smile with joy
¹bean \'bēn\ *n* : the edible seed borne in pods by some
leguminous plants; *also* : a plant or a pod bearing these
²bean *vb* : to strike on the head with an object
bean·bag \'bēn-ˌbag\ *n* : a cloth bag partially filled typically with dried beans and used as a toy
bean·ball \'bēn-ˌbȯl\ *n* : a pitch thrown at a batter's head
bean curd *n* : TOFU
bean·ie \'bē-nē\ *n* : a small round tight-fitting skullcap
beano \'bē-nō\ *n, pl* **beanos** : BINGO
¹bear \'bar\ *n, pl* **bears 1** *or pl* **bear** : any of a family of
large heavy mammals with shaggy hair and small tails
2 : a gruff or sullen person **3** : one who sells (as
securities) in expectation of a price decline — **bear·
ish** *adj*
²bear *vb* **bore** \'bōr\; **borne** \'bōrn\ *also* **born** \'bȯrn\;
bear·ing 1 : CARRY **2** : to be equipped with **3** : to give
as testimony ⟨∼ witness to the facts of the case⟩ **4** : to
give birth to; *also* : PRODUCE, YIELD ⟨a tree that ∼s reg-
ularly⟩ **5** : ENDURE, SUSTAIN ⟨∼ pain⟩ ⟨*bore* the weight
on piles⟩; *also* : to exert pressure or influence **6** : to go
in an indicated direction ⟨∼ to the right⟩ — **bear·able**
adj — **bear·er** *n*
¹beard \'bird\ *n* **1** : the hair that grows on the face of a
man **2** : a growth of bristly hairs (as on a goat's chin)
— **beard·ed** \'bir-dəd\ *adj* — **beard·less** *adj*
²beard *vb* : to confront boldly
bear·ing \'bar-iŋ\ *n* **1** : manner of carrying oneself : COM-
PORTMENT **2** : a supporting object, purpose, or point **3**
: a machine part in which another part (as an axle or
pin) turns **4** : an emblem in a coat of arms **5** : the position or direction of one point with respect to another
or to the compass; *also* : a determination of position **6**
pl : comprehension of one's situation **7** : connection
with or influence on something; *also* : SIGNIFICANCE
bear·skin \'bar-ˌskin\ *n* : an article made of the skin of
a bear
beast \'bēst\ *n* **1** : ANIMAL 1; *esp* : a 4-footed mammal **2**
: a contemptible person
¹beast·ly \'bēst-lē\ *adj* **beast·li·er; -est 1** : BESTIAL **2**
: ABOMINABLE, DISAGREEABLE — **beast·li·ness** \-nəs\ *n*
²beastly *adv* : VERY
¹beat \'bēt\ *vb* **beat; beat·en** \'bēt-ᵊn\ *or* **beat; beat·ing 1**
: to strike repeatedly **2** : TREAD **3** : to affect or alter by
beating ⟨∼ metal into sheets⟩ **4** : to sound (as an alarm)
on a drum **5** : OVERCOME; *also* : SURPASS **6** : to act or
arrive before ⟨∼ his brother home⟩ **7** : THROB — **beat·
er** *n*
²beat *n* **1** : a single stroke or blow esp. of a series; *also*
: PULSATION **2** : a rhythmic stress in poetry or music or
the rhythmic effect of these **3** : a regularly traversed
course
³beat *adj* **1** : EXHAUSTED **2** : of or relating to beatniks
⁴beat *n* : BEATNIK
be·atif·ic \ˌbē-ə-'ti-fik\ *adj* : giving or indicative of great
joy or bliss
be·at·i·fy \bē-'a-tə-ˌfī\ *vb* **-fied; -fy·ing 1** : to make supremely happy **2** : to declare to have attained the blessedness of heaven and authorize the title "Blessed" for
— **be·at·i·fi·ca·tion** \-ˌa-tə-fə-'kā-shən\ *n*
be·at·i·tude \bē-'a-tə-ˌtüd, -ˌtyüd\ *n* **1** : a state of utmost
bliss **2** : any of the declarations made in the Sermon on
the Mount (Mt 5:3–12) beginning "Blessed are"
beat·nik \'bēt-nik\ *n* : a person who rejects the mores of
established society and indulges in exotic philosophiz-
ing and self-expression
beau \'bō\ *n, pl* **beaux** \'bōz\ *or* **beaus** [F, fr. *beau* beautiful, fr. L *bellus* pretty] **1** : a man of fashion : DANDY
2 : SUITOR, LOVER

BEAUFORT SCALE

BEAUFORT NUMBER	NAME	WIND SPEED		DESCRIPTION
		MPH	KPH	
0	calm	<1	<1	calm; smoke rises vertically
1	light air	1-3	1-5	direction of wind shown by smoke but not by wind vanes
2	light breeze	4-7	6-11	wind felt on face; leaves rustle; wind vane moves
3	gentle breeze	8-12	12-19	leaves and small twigs in constant motion; wind extends light flag
4	moderate breeze	13-18	20-28	wind raises dust and loose paper; small branches move
5	fresh breeze	19-24	29-38	small-leaved trees begin to sway; crested wavelets form on inland waters
6	strong breeze	25-31	39-49	large branches move; overhead wires whistle; umbrellas difficult to control
7	moderate gale	32-38	50-61	whole trees sway; walking against wind is difficult
8	fresh gale or gale	39-46	62-74	twigs break off trees; moving cars veer
9	strong gale	47-54	75-88	slight structural damage occurs; shingles may blow away
10	whole gale or storm	55-63	89-102	trees uprooted; considerable structural damage occurs
11	storm or violent storm	64-72	103-117	widespread damage occurs
12	hurricane*	>72	>117	widespread damage occurs

*The U.S. uses 74 statute mph as the speed criterion for hurricane.

Beau·fort scale \'bō-fərt-\ n : a scale in which the force of the wind is indicated by numbers from 0 to 12
beau geste \bō-'zhest\ n, pl **beaux gestes** or **beau gestes** \bō-'zhest\ : a graceful or magnanimous gesture
beau ide·al \ˌbō-ī-'dē(-ə)l\ n, pl **beau ideals** : the perfect type or model
Beau·jo·lais \ˌbō-zhō-'lā\ n : a French red table wine
beau monde \bo-'mänd, -'mōⁿd\ n, pl **beau mondes** \-'mänz, -'mändz\ or **beaux mondes** \bō-'mōⁿd\ : the world of high society and fashion
beau·te·ous \'byü-tē-əs\ adj : BEAUTIFUL — **beau·te·ous·ly** adv
beau·ti·cian \byü-'ti-shən\ n : COSMETOLOGIST
beau·ti·ful \'byü-ti-fəl\ adj : characterized by beauty : LOVELY **syn** pretty, fair, comely — **beau·ti·ful·ly** \-f(ə-)lē\ adv
beautiful people n pl, often cap B&P : wealthy or famous people whose lifestyle is usu. expensive and well-publicized
beau·ti·fy \'byü-tə-ˌfī\ vb **-fied; -fy·ing** : to make more beautiful — **beau·ti·fi·ca·tion** \ˌbyü-tə-fə-'kā-shən\ n — **beau·ti·fi·er** n
beau·ty \'byü-tē\ n, pl **beauties** : qualities that give pleasure to the senses or exalt the mind : LOVELINESS; also : something having such qualities
beauty shop n : an establishment where hairdressing, facials, and manicures are done
beaux arts \bō-'zär\ n pl [F] : FINE ARTS
bea·ver \'bē-vər\ n, pl **beavers** : a large fur-bearing herbivorous rodent that builds dams and underwater houses of mud and sticks; also : its fur
be·calm \bi-'käm, -'kälm\ vb : to keep (as a ship) motionless by lack of wind

be·cause \bi-'kȯz, -'kəz\ conj : for the reason that
because of prep : by reason of
beck \'bek\ n : a beckoning gesture; also : SUMMONS
beck·on \'be-kən\ vb : to summon or signal esp. by a nod or gesture; also : ATTRACT
be·cloud \bi-'klaůd\ vb : OBSCURE
be·come \bi-'kəm\ vb **-came** \-'kām\; **-come; -com·ing 1** : to come to be ⟨~ tired⟩ **2** : to suit or be suitable to ⟨her dress ~s her⟩
be·com·ing adj : SUITABLE, FIT; also : ATTRACTIVE — **be·com·ing·ly** adv
¹bed \'bed\ n **1** : an article of furniture to sleep on **2** : a plot of ground prepared for plants **3** : FOUNDATION, BOTTOM **4** : LAYER, STRATUM
²bed vb **bed·ded; bed·ding 1** : to put or go to bed **2** : to fix in a foundation : EMBED **3** : to plant in beds **4** : to lay or lie flat or in layers
bed–and–breakfast n : an establishment offering lodging and breakfast
be·daub \bi-'dȯb\ vb : SMEAR
be·daz·zle \bi-'da-zəl\ vb : to confuse by or as if by a strong light; also : FASCINATE — **be·daz·zle·ment** n
bed·bug \'bed-ˌbəg\ n : a wingless bloodsucking bug infesting houses and esp. beds
bed·clothes \'bed-ˌklōthz\ n pl : BEDDING 1
bed·ding \'be-diŋ\ n **1** : materials for making up a bed **2** : FOUNDATION

be·deck \bi-'dek\ *vb* : ADORN

be·dev·il \bi-'de-vəl\ *vb* 1 : HARASS, TORMENT 2 : CONFUSE, MUDDLE

be·dew \bi-'dü, -'dyü\ *vb* : to wet with or as if with dew

bed·fast \'bed-ˌfast\ *adj* : BEDRIDDEN

bed·fel·low \-ˌfe-lō\ *n* 1 : one sharing the bed of another 2 : a close associate : ALLY

be·di·zen \bi-'dīz-ᵊn, -'diz-\ *vb* : to dress or adorn with showy or vulgar finery

bed·lam \'bed-ləm\ *n* [*Bedlam*, popular name for the Hospital of St. Mary of Bethlehem, London, an insane asylum, fr. ME *Bedlem* Bethlehem] 1 : an insane asylum 2 : a scene of uproar and confusion

bed·ou·in *or* **bed·u·in** \'be-də-wən\ *n, pl* **bedouin** *or* **bedouins** *or* **beduin** *or* **beduins** *often cap* [ME *Bedoyne*, fr. MF *bedoïn*, fr. Ar *badawī* desert dweller] : a nomadic Arab of the Arabian, Syrian, or No. African deserts

bed·pan \'bed-ˌpan\ *n* : a shallow vessel used by a bedridden person for urination or defecation

bed·post \-ˌpōst\ *n* : the post of a bed

be·drag·gled \bi-'dra-gəld\ *adj* : soiled and disordered as if by being drenched

bed·rid·den \'bed-ˌrid-ᵊn\ *adj* : kept in bed by illness or weakness

¹bed·rock \-'räk\ *n* : the solid rock underlying surface materials (as soil)

²bedrock *adj* : solidly fundamental, basic, or reliable ⟨traditional ~ values⟩

bed·roll \'bed-ˌrōl\ *n* : bedding rolled up for carrying

bed·room \-ˌrüm, -ˌrům\ *n* : a room containing a bed and used esp. for sleeping

bed·side \-ˌsīd\ *n* : the place beside a bed esp. of a sick or dying person

bed·sore \-ˌsōr\ *n* : an ulceration of tissue deprived of adequate blood supply by prolonged pressure

bed·spread \-ˌspred\ *n* : a usu. ornamental cloth cover for a bed

bed·stead \-ˌsted\ *n* : the framework of a bed

bed·time \-ˌtīm\ *n* : time for going to bed

bed·wet·ting \-ˌwe-tiŋ\ *n* : involuntary discharge of urine esp. in bed during sleep — **bed–wet·ter** *n*

¹bee \'bē\ *n* : HONEYBEE; *also* : any of various related insects

²bee *n* : a gathering of people for a specific purpose ⟨quilting ~⟩

beech \'bēch\ *n, pl* **beech·es** *or* **beech** : any of a genus of deciduous hardwood trees with smooth gray bark and small sweet triangular nuts; *also* : the wood of a beech — **beech·en** \'bē-chən\ *adj*

beech·nut \'bēch-ˌnət\ *n* : the nut of a beech

¹beef \'bēf\ *n, pl* **beefs** \'bēfs\ *or* **beeves** \'bēvz\ 1 : the flesh of a steer, cow, or bull; *also* : the dressed carcass of a beef animal 2 : a steer, cow, or bull esp. when fattened for food 3 : MUSCLE, BRAWN 4 *pl* **beefs** : COMPLAINT

²beef *vb* 1 : STRENGTHEN — usu. used with *up* 2 : COMPLAIN

beef·eat·er \'bē-ˌfē-tər\ *n* : a yeoman of the guard of an English monarch

beef·steak \-ˌstāk\ *n* : a slice of beef suitable for broiling or frying

beefy \'bē-fē\ *adj* **beef·i·er; -est** : THICKSET, BRAWNY

bee·hive \'bē-ˌhīv\ *n* : HIVE 1, 3

bee·keep·er \-ˌkē-pər\ *n* : a person who raises bees — **bee·keep·ing** *n*

bee·line \-ˌlīn\ *n* : a straight direct course

been *past part of* BE

beep·er \'bē-pər\ *n* : a small radio receiver that beeps when signaled to alert the person carrying it

beer \'bir\ *n* : an alcoholic beverage brewed from malt and hops — **beery** *adj*

bees·wax \'bēz-ˌwaks\ *n* : WAX 1

beet \'bēt\ *n* : a garden plant with edible leaves and a thick sweet root used as a vegetable, as a source of sugar, or as forage; *also* : its root

¹bee·tle \'bēt-ᵊl\ *n* : any of an order of insects having four wings of which the stiff outer pair covers the membranous inner pair when not in flight

²beetle *vb* **bee·tled; bee·tling** : to jut out : PROJECT

be·fall \bi-'fòl\ *vb* **-fell** \-'fel\; **-fall·en** \-'fò-lən\ : to happen to : OCCUR

be·fit \bi-'fit\ *vb* : to be suitable to

be·fog \bi-'fòg, -'fäg\ *vb* : OBSCURE; *also* : CONFUSE

¹be·fore \bi-'fōr\ *adv or adj* 1 : in front 2 : EARLIER

²before *prep* 1 : in front of ⟨stood ~ him⟩ 2 : earlier than ⟨got there ~ me⟩ 3 : in a more important category than ⟨put quality ~ quantity⟩

³before *conj* 1 : earlier than the time that ⟨he got here ~ I did⟩ 2 : more willingly than ⟨she'd starve ~ she'd steal⟩

be·fore·hand \bi-'fōr-ˌhand\ *adv or adj* : in advance

be·foul \bi-'faůl\ *vb* : SOIL

be·friend \bi-'frend\ *vb* : to act as friend to

be·fud·dle \bi-'fəd-ᵊl\ *vb* : MUDDLE, CONFUSE

beg \'beg\ *vb* **begged; beg·ging** 1 : to ask as a charity; *also* : ENTREAT 2 : EVADE; *also* : assume as established, settled, or proved ⟨~ the question⟩

be·get \bi-'get\ *vb* **-got** \-'gät\; **-got·ten** \-'gät-ᵊn\ *or* **-got; -get·ting** : to become the father of : SIRE

¹beg·gar \'be-gər\ *n* : one that begs; *esp* : a person who begs as a way of life

²beggar *vb* : IMPOVERISH

beg·gar·ly \'be-gər-lē\ *adj* 1 : contemptibly mean or inadequate 2 : marked by unrelieved poverty ⟨a ~ life⟩

beg·gary \'be-gə-rē\ *n* : extreme poverty

be·gin \bi-'gin\ *vb* **be·gan** \-'gan\; **be·gun** \-'gən\; **be·gin·ning** 1 : to do the first part of an action : COMMENCE 2 : to come into being : ARISE; *also* : FOUND 3 : ORIGINATE, INVENT — **be·gin·ner** *n*

beg off *vb* : to ask to be excused from something

be·gone \bi-'gòn\ *vb* : to go away : DEPART — used esp. in the imperative

be·go·nia \bi-'gōn-yə\ *n* : any of a genus of tropical herbs widely grown for their showy leaves and waxy flowers

be·grime \bi-'grīm\ *vb* **be·grimed; be·grim·ing** : to make dirty

be·grudge \bi-'grəj\ *vb* 1 : to give or concede reluctantly 2 : to be reluctant to grant or allow

be·guile \-'gīl\ *vb* **be·guiled; be·guil·ing** 1 : DECEIVE 2 : to while away 3 : to engage the interest of by guile

be·guine \bi-'gēn\ *n* [AmerF *béguine*, fr. F *béguin* flirtation] : a vigorous popular dance of the islands of Saint Lucia and Martinique

be·gum \'bā-gəm, 'bē-\ *n* : a Muslim woman of high rank

be·half \bi-'haf, -'häf\ *n* : BENEFIT, SUPPORT, DEFENSE

be·have \bi-'hāv\ *vb* **be·haved; be·hav·ing** 1 : to bear, comport, or conduct oneself in a particular and esp. a proper way 2 : to act, function, or react in a particular way

be·hav·ior \bi-'hā-vyər\ *n* : way of behaving; *esp* : personal conduct — **be·hav·ior·al** \-vyə-rəl\ *adj*

be·hav·ior·ism \bi-'hā-vyə-ˌri-zəm\ *n* : a school of psychology concerned with the objective evidence of behavior without reference to conscious experience

be·hav·iour *chiefly Brit var of* BEHAVIOR

be·head \bi-'hed\ *vb* : to cut off the head of

be·he·moth \bi-'hē-məth, 'bē-ə-ˌmäth\ *n* : a huge powerful animal described in Job 40:15–24; *also* : something of monstrous size or power

be·hest \bi-'hest\ *n* 1 : COMMAND 2 : an urgent prompting

¹be·hind \bi-'hīnd\ *adv or adj* 1 : BACK, BACKWARD ⟨look ~⟩ 2 : LATE, SLOW

²**behind** *prep* **1** : in or to a place or situation in back of or to the rear of ⟨look ∼ you⟩ ⟨the staff stayed ∼ the troops⟩ **2** : inferior to (as in rank) : BELOW ⟨three games ∼ the first-place team⟩ **3** : in support of : SUPPORTING ⟨we're ∼ you all the way⟩

be·hind·hand \bi-ˈhīnd-ˌhand\ *adj* : being in arrears **syn** tardy, late, overdue, belated

be·hold \bi-ˈhōld\ *vb* **-held** \-ˈheld\; **-hold·ing 1** : to have in sight : SEE **2** — used imperatively to direct the attention **syn** view, observe, notice, espy — **be·hold·er** *n*

be·hold·en \bi-ˈhōl-dən\ *adj* : OBLIGATED, INDEBTED

be·hoof \bi-ˈhüf\ *n* : ADVANTAGE, PROFIT

be·hoove \bi-ˈhüv\ *vb* **be·hooved; be·hoov·ing** : to be necessary, proper, or advantageous for

beige \ˈbāzh\ *n* : a pale dull yellowish brown — **beige** *adj*

be·ing \ˈbē-iŋ\ *n* **1** : EXISTENCE; *also* : LIFE **2** : the qualities or constitution of an existent thing **3** : a living thing; *esp* : PERSON

be·la·bor \bi-ˈlā-bər\ *vb* : to assail (as with words) tiresomely or at length

be·la·bour *chiefly Brit var of* BELABOR

be·lat·ed \bi-ˈlā-təd\ *adj* : DELAYED, LATE

be·lay \bi-ˈlā\ *vb* **1** : to wind (a rope) around a pin or cleat in order to hold secure **2** : QUIT, STOP — used in the imperative

belch \ˈbelch\ *vb* **1** : to expel (gas) from the stomach through the mouth **2** : to gush forth ⟨a volcano ∼*ing* lava⟩ — **belch** *n*

bel·dam *or* **bel·dame** \ˈbel-dəm\ *n* [ME *beldam* grandmother, fr. MF *bel* beautiful + ME *dam* lady, mother] : an old woman

be·lea·guer \bi-ˈlē-gər\ *vb* **1** : BESIEGE **2** : HARASS ⟨∼*ed* parents⟩

bel·fry \ˈbel-frē\ *n, pl* **belfries** : a tower for a bell (as on a church); *also* : the part of the tower in which the bell hangs

Belg *abbr* Belgian; Belgium

Bel·gian \ˈbel-jən\ *n* : a native or inhabitant of Belgium — **Belgian** *adj*

be·lie \bi-ˈlī\ *vb* **-lied; -ly·ing 1** : MISREPRESENT **2** : to show (something) to be false **3** : to run counter to

be·lief \bə-ˈlēf\ *n* **1** : CONFIDENCE, TRUST **2** : something (as a tenet or creed) believed **syn** conviction, opinion, persuasion, sentiment

be·lieve \bə-ˈlēv\ *vb* **be·lieved; be·liev·ing 1** : to have religious convictions **2** : to have a firm conviction about something : accept as true **3** : to hold as an opinion : SUPPOSE — **be·liev·able** *adj* — **be·liev·er** *n*

be·like \bi-ˈlīk\ *adv, archaic* : PROBABLY

be·lit·tle \bi-ˈlit-ᵊl\ *vb* **-lit·tled; -lit·tling** : to make seem little or less; *also* : DISPARAGE

¹**bell** \ˈbel\ *n* **1** : a hollow metallic device that makes a ringing sound when struck **2** : the sounding or stroke of a bell (as on shipboard to tell the time); *also* : time so indicated **3** : something with the flared form of a typical bell

²**bell** *vb* : to provide with a bell

bel·la·don·na \ˌbe-lə-ˈdä-nə\ *n* [It, lit., beautiful lady; fr. its cosmetic use] : a medicinal extract (as atropine) from a poisonous European herb related to the potato; *also* : this herb

bell–bot·toms \ˈbel-ˈbä-təmz\ *n pl* : pants with wide flaring bottoms — **bell–bottom** *adj*

bell·boy \ˈbel-ˌbói\ *n* : BELLHOP

belle \ˈbel\ *n* : an attractive and popular girl or woman

belles let·tres \bel-ˈletrᵊ\ *n pl* [F] : literature that is an end in itself and not practical or purely informative — **bel·le·tris·tic** \ˌbel-ə-ˈtris-tik\ *adj*

bell·hop \ˈbel-ˌhäp\ *n* : a hotel or club employee who takes guests to rooms, carries luggage, and runs errands

bel·li·cose \ˈbe-li-ˌkōs\ *adj* : WARLIKE, PUGNACIOUS **syn**

belligerent, quarrelsome, combative, contentious — **bel·li·cos·i·ty** \ˌbe-li-ˈkä-sə-tē\ *n*

bel·lig·er·en·cy \bə-ˈli-jə-rən-sē\ *n* **1** : the status of a nation engaged in war **2** : BELLIGERENCE, TRUCULENCE

bel·lig·er·ent \-rənt\ *adj* **1** : waging war **2** : TRUCULENT **syn** bellicose, pugnacious, combative, contentious, warlike — **bel·lig·er·ence** \-rəns\ *n* — **belligerent** *n*

bel·low \ˈbe-lō\ *vb* **1** : to make the deep hollow sound characteristic of a bull **2** : to shout in a deep voice — **bellow** *n*

bel·lows \-lōz, -ləz\ *n sing or pl* : a closed device with sides that can be spread apart and then pressed together to draw in air and expel it through a tube

bellows

bell·weth·er \ˈbel-ˈwe-thər, -ˌwe-\ *n* : one that takes the lead or initiative

¹**bel·ly** \ˈbe-lē\ *n, pl* **bellies** [ME *bely* bellows, belly, fr. OE *belg* bag, skin] **1** : ABDOMEN; *also* : POTBELLY **2** : the underpart of an animal's body

²**belly** *vb* **bel·lied; bel·ly·ing** : BULGE

¹**bel·ly·ache** \ˈbe-lē-ˌāk\ *n* : pain in the abdomen

²**bellyache** *vb* : COMPLAIN

belly button *n* : the human navel

belly dance *n* : a usu. solo dance emphasizing movement of the belly — **belly dance** *vb* — **belly dancer** *n*

belly laugh *n* : a deep hearty laugh

be·long \bi-ˈlóŋ\ *vb* **1** : to be suitable or appropriate; *also* : to be properly situated ⟨shoes ∼ in the closet⟩ **2** : to be the property ⟨this ∼*s* to me⟩; *also* : to be attached (as through birth or membership) ⟨∼ to a club⟩ **3** : to form an attribute or part ⟨this wheel ∼*s* to the cart⟩ **4** : to be classified ⟨whales ∼ among the mammals⟩

be·long·ings \-ˈlóŋ-iŋz\ *n pl* : GOODS, EFFECTS, POSSESSIONS

be·loved \bi-ˈləvd, -ˈlə-vəd\ *adj* : dearly loved — **beloved** *n*

¹**be·low** \bi-ˈlō\ *adv* **1** : in or to a lower place or rank **2** : on earth **3** : in hell

²**below** *prep* **1** : lower than **2** : inferior to (as in rank)

be·low·decks \bi-ˌlō-ˈdeks, -ˈlō-ˌdeks\ *adv* : inside the superstructure of a boat or down to a lower deck

¹**belt** \ˈbelt\ *n* **1** : a strip (as of leather) worn about the waist **2** : a flexible continuous band to communicate motion or convey material **3** : a region marked by some distinctive feature; *esp* : one suited to a particular crop

²**belt** *vb* **1** : to encircle or secure with a belt **2** : to beat with or as if with a belt **3** : to mark with an encircling band **4** : to sing loudly

³**belt** *n* **1** : a jarring blow : WHACK **2** : DRINK ⟨a ∼ of whiskey⟩

belt–tightening *n* : a reduction in spending

belt·way \ˈbelt-ˌwā\ *n* : a highway around a city

be·lu·ga \bə-ˈlü-gə\ *n* [Russ] : a white sturgeon of the Black Sea, Caspian Sea, and their tributaries that is a source of caviar; *also* : caviar from beluga roe

bel·ve·dere \ˈbel-və-ˌdir\ *n* [It, lit., beautiful view] : a structure (as a summerhouse) designed to command a view

be·mire \bi-'mīr\ *vb* : to cover or soil with or sink in mire

be·moan \bi-'mōn\ *vb* : LAMENT, DEPLORE **syn** bewail, grieve, moan, weep

be·muse \bi-'myüz\ *vb* : BEWILDER, CONFUSE

¹bench \'bench\ *n* **1** : a long seat for two or more persons **2** : the seat of a judge in court; *also* : the office or dignity of a judge **3** : COURT; *also* : JUDGES **4** : a table for holding work and tools ⟨a carpenter's ∼⟩

²bench \'bench\ *vb* **1** : to furnish with benches **2** : to seat on a bench **3** : to remove from or keep out of a game

bench mark *n* **1** : a mark on a permanent object serving as an elevation reference in topographical surveys **2** *usu* **bench·mark** : a point of reference for measurement; *also* : STANDARD

bench press *n* : a press in weight lifting performed by a lifter lying on a bench — **bench–press** *vb*

bench warrant *n* : a warrant issued by a presiding judge or by a court against a person guilty of contempt or indicted for a crime

¹bend \'bend\ *vb* **bent** \'bent\; **bend·ing 1** : to draw (as a bow) taut **2** : to curve or cause a change of shape in ⟨∼ a bar⟩ **3** : to make fast : SECURE **4** : DEFLECT **5** : to turn in a certain direction ⟨*bent* his steps toward town⟩ **6** : APPLY ⟨*bent* themselves to the task⟩ **7** : SUBDUE **8** : to curve downward **9** : YIELD, SUBMIT

²bend *n* **1** : an act or process of bending **2** : something bent; *esp* : CURVE **3** *pl* : a painful and sometimes fatal disorder caused by release of gas bubbles in the tissues upon too rapid decrease in air pressure after a stay in a compressed atmosphere

³bend *n* : a knot by which a rope is fastened (as to another rope)

bend·er \'ben-dər\ *n* : SPREE

¹be·neath \bi-'nēth\ *adv* : BELOW **syn** under, underneath

²beneath *prep* **1** : BELOW, UNDER ⟨stood ∼ a tree⟩ **2** : unworthy of ⟨considered such behavior ∼ her⟩ **3** : concealed by

bene·dic·tion \ˌbe-nə-'dik-shən\ *n* : the invocation of a blessing esp. at the close of a public worship service

ben·e·fac·tion \-'fak-shən\ *n* : a charitable donation **syn** contribution, alms, beneficence, offering

ben·e·fac·tor \'ben-ə-ˌfak-tər\ *n* : one that confers a benefit and esp. a benefaction

ben·e·fac·tress \-ˌfak-trəs\ *n* : a woman who is a benefactor

ben·e·fice \'be-nə-fəs\ *n* : an ecclesiastical office to which the revenue from an endowment is attached

be·nef·i·cence \bə-'ne-fə-səns\ *n* **1** : beneficent quality **2** : BENEFACTION

be·nef·i·cent \-sənt\ *adj* : doing or producing good (as by acts of kindness or charity); *also* : BENEFICIAL

ben·e·fi·cial \ˌbe-nə-'fi-shəl\ *adj* : being of benefit or help : HELPFUL **syn** advantageous, profitable, favorable, propitious — **ben·e·fi·cial·ly** *adv*

ben·e·fi·cia·ry \ˌbe-nə-'fi-shē-ˌer-ē, -'fi-shə-rē\ *n, pl* **-ries** : one that receives a benefit (as the income of a trust or the proceeds of an insurance)

¹ben·e·fit \'be-nə-ˌfit\ *n* **1** : ADVANTAGE ⟨the ∼*s* of exercise⟩ **2** : useful aid : HELP; *also* : material aid provided or due (as in sickness or unemployment) as a right **3** : a performance or event to raise funds

²benefit *vb* **-fit·ed** \-ˌfi-təd\ *also* **-fit·ted; -fit·ing** *also* **-fit·ting 1** : to be useful or profitable to **2** : to receive benefit

be·nev·o·lence \bə-'ne-və-ləns\ *n* **1** : charitable nature **2** : an act of kindness : CHARITY — **be·nev·o·lent** \-lənt\ *adj* — **be·nev·o·lent·ly** *adv*

be·night·ed \bi-'nī-təd\ *adj* **1** : overtaken by darkness or night **2** : living in ignorance

be·nign \bi-'nīn\ *adj* [ME *benigne*, fr. MF, fr. L *benig-*

nus] **1** : of a gentle disposition; *also* : showing kindness **2** : of a mild kind; *esp* : not malignant ⟨∼ tumors⟩ **syn** benignant, kind, kindly, good-hearted — **be·nig·ni·ty** \-'nig-nə-tē\ *n*

be·nig·nant \-'nig-nənt\ *adj* : BENIGN 1 **syn** kind, kindly, good-hearted

ben·i·son \'be-nə-sən, -zən\ *n* : BLESSING, BENEDICTION

bent \'bent\ *n* **1** : strong inclination or interest; *also* : TALENT **2** : power of endurance **syn** talent, aptitude, gift, flair, knack, genius

ben·thic \'ben-thik\ *adj* : of, relating to, or occurring at the bottom of a body of water

ben·ton·ite \'bent-ᵊn-ˌīt\ *n* : an absorptive clay used esp. as a filler (in paper)

bent·wood \'bent-ˌwu̇d\ *adj* : made of wood bent into shape ⟨a ∼ rocker⟩

be·numb \bi-'nəm\ *vb* **1** : DULL, DEADEN **2** : to make numb esp. by cold

ben·zene \'ben-ˌzēn\ *n* : a colorless volatile flammable liquid hydrocarbon used in organic synthesis and as a solvent

ben·zine \'ben-ˌzēn\ *n* : any of various flammable petroleum distillates used as solvents or as motor fuels

ben·zo·ate \'ben-zə-ˌwāt\ *n* : a salt or ester of benzoic acid

ben·zo·ic acid \ben-'zō-ik-\ *n* : a white crystalline acid used as a preservative and antiseptic and in synthesizing chemicals

ben·zo·in \'ben-zə-wən, -ˌzȯin\ *n* : a balsamlike resin from trees of southern Asia used esp. in medicine and perfumes

be·queath \bi-'kwēth, -'kwēth\ *vb* [ME *bequethen*, fr. OE *becwethan*, fr. *be-* + *cwethan* to say] **1** : to leave by will **2** : to hand down

be·quest \bi-'kwest\ *n* **1** : the action of bequeathing **2** : something bequeathed : LEGACY

be·rate \-'rāt\ *vb* : to scold harshly

Ber·ber \'bər-bər\ *n* : a member of any of various peoples living in northern Africa west of Tripoli

ber·ceuse \ber-'sœz, -'süz\ *n, pl* **berceuses** *same or* -'sü-zəz\ [F, fr. *bercer* to rock] **1** : LULLABY **2** : a musical composition that resembles a lullaby

¹be·reaved \bi-'rēvd\ *adj* : suffering the death of a loved one — **be·reave·ment** *n*

²bereaved *n, pl* **bereaved** : one who is bereaved

be·reft \-'reft\ *adj* **1** : deprived of or lacking something — usu. used with *of* **2** : BEREAVED

be·ret \bə-'rā\ *n* : a round soft cap with no visor

berg \'bərg\ *n* : ICEBERG

beri·beri \ˌber-ē-'ber-ē\ *n* : a deficiency disease marked by weakness, wasting, and nerve damage and caused by lack of thiamine

berke·li·um \'bər-klē-əm\ *n* : an artificially prepared radioactive chemical element — see ELEMENT table

berm \'bərm\ *n* : a narrow shelf or path at the top or bottom of a slope; *also* : a mound or bank of earth

Ber·mu·das \bər-'myü-dəz\ *n pl* : BERMUDA SHORTS

Bermuda shorts *n pl* : knee-length walking shorts

ber·ry \'ber-ē\ *n, pl* **berries 1** : a small pulpy fruit (as a strawberry) **2** : a simple fruit (as a grape, tomato, or banana) with the wall of the ripened ovary thick and pulpy **3** : the dry seed of some plants (as coffee)

ber·serk \bər-'sərk, -'zərk\ *adj* [ON *berserkr* warrior frenzied in battle, fr. *bjǫrn* bear + *serkr* shirt] : FRENZIED, CRAZED — **berserk** *adv*

¹berth \'bərth\ *n* **1** : adequate distance esp. for a ship to maneuver **2** : the place where a ship is anchored or a vehicle rests **3** : ACCOMMODATIONS **4** : JOB, POSITION **syn** post, situation, office, appointment

²berth *vb* **1** : to bring or come into a berth **2** : to allot a berth to

ber·yl \'ber-əl\ *n* : a hard silicate mineral occurring as green, yellow, pink, or white crystals

be·ryl·li·um \bə-'ri-lē-əm\ *n* : a light strong metallic chemical element used as a hardener in alloys — see ELEMENT table

be·seech \bi-'sēch\ *vb* **-sought** \-'sòt\ *or* **-seeched; -seech·ing** : to beg urgently : ENTREAT **syn** implore, plead, supplicate, importune

be·seem \bi-'sēm\ *vb, archaic* : BEFIT

be·set \-'set\ *vb* **1** : TROUBLE, HARASS **2** : ASSAIL; *also* : SURROUND

be·set·ting *adj* : persistently present

¹be·side \bi-'sīd\ *prep* **1** : by the side of ⟨sit ~ me⟩ **2** : BESIDES **3** : not relevant to

²beside *adv, archaic* : BESIDES

¹be·sides \bi-'sīdz\ *prep* **1** : other than **2** : together with

²besides *adv* **1** : as well : ALSO **2** : MOREOVER

be·siege \bi-'sēj\ *vb* : to lay siege to; *also* : to press with requests — **be·sieg·er** *n*

be·smear \-'smir\ *vb* : SMEAR

be·smirch \-'smərch\ *vb* : SMIRCH, SOIL

be·som \'bē-zəm\ *n* : BROOM

be·sot \bi-'sät\ *vb* **be·sot·ted; be·sot·ting 1** : INFATUATE **2** : to make dull esp. by drinking

be·spat·ter \-'spa-tər\ *vb* : SPATTER

be·speak \bi-'spēk\ *vb* **-spoke** \-'spōk\; **-spo·ken** \-'spō-kən\; **-speak·ing 1** : PREARRANGE **2** : ADDRESS **3** : REQUEST **4** : INDICATE, SIGNIFY **5** : FORETELL

be·sprin·kle \-'sprin-kəl\ *vb* : SPRINKLE

¹best \'best\ *adj, superlative of* GOOD **1** : excelling all others **2** : most productive (as of good or satisfaction) **3** : LARGEST, MOST

²best *adv, superlative of* WELL **1** : in the best way **2** : MOST

³best *n* : something that is best

⁴best *vb* : to get the better of : OUTDO

bes·tial \'bes-chəl\ *adj* **1** : of or relating to beasts **2** : resembling a beast esp. in brutality or lack of intelligence

bes·ti·al·i·ty \ˌbes-chē-'a-lə-tē, ˌbēs-\ *n, pl* **-ties 1** : the condition or status of a lower animal **2** : display or gratification of bestial traits or impulses

bes·ti·ary \'bes-chē-ˌer-ē\ *n, pl* **-ar·ies** : a medieval allegorical or moralizing work on the appearance and habits of animals

be·stir \bi-'stər\ *vb* : to rouse to action

best man *n* : the principal groomsman at a wedding

be·stow \bi-'stō\ *vb* **1** : PUT, PLACE, STOW **2** : to present as a gift — **be·stow·al** *n*

be·stride \bi-'strīd\ *vb* **-strode** \-'strod\; **-strid·den** \-'strid-ᵊn\; **-strid·ing** : to ride, sit, or stand astride

¹bet \'bet\ *n* **1** : something that is wagered, risked, or pledged usu. between two parties on the outcome of a contest; *also* : the making of such a bet **2** : OPTION ⟨the back road is your best ~⟩

²bet *vb* **bet** *also* **bet·ted; bet·ting 1** : to stake on the outcome of an issue or a contest ⟨*bet* $2 on the race⟩ **2** : to make a bet with **3** : to lay a bet

³bet *abbr* between

be·ta \'bā-tə\ *n* : the 2d letter of the Greek alphabet — B or β

beta block·er \-ˌblä-kər\ *n* : any of a group of drugs that tend to decrease heart action and increase coronary blood flow

be·ta–car·o·tene \-'kar-ə-ˌtēn\ *n* : an isomer of carotene found in dark green and dark yellow vegetables and fruits

be·take \bi-'tāk\ *vb* **-took** \-'tùk\; **-tak·en** \-'tā-kən\; **-tak·ing** : to cause (oneself) to go

beta particle *n* : a high-speed electron; *esp* : one emitted by a radioactive nucleus

beta ray *n* **1** : BETA PARTICLE **2** : a stream of beta particles

be·tel \'bēt-ᵊl\ *n* : a climbing pepper whose leaves are chewed together with lime and betel nut as a stimulant esp. by southern Asians

betel nut *n* : the astringent seed of an Asian palm that is chewed with betel leaves

bête noire \ˌbet-'nwär, ˌbät-\ *n, pl* **bêtes noires** *same or* -'nwärz\ [F, lit., black beast] : a person or thing strongly disliked or avoided

beth·el \'be-thəl\ *n* [Heb *bēth'ēl* house of God] : a place of worship esp. for seamen

be·think \bi-'thiŋk\ *vb* **-thought** \-'thòt\; **-think·ing** : REMEMBER; *also* : PONDER

be·tide \bi-'tīd\ *vb* : to happen to

be·times \bi-'tīmz\ *adv* : in good time : EARLY **syn** soon, seasonably, timely

be·to·ken \bi-'tō-kən\ *vb* **1** : PRESAGE **2** : to give evidence of **syn** indicate, attest, bespeak, testify

be·tray \bi-'trā\ *vb* **1** : to lead astray; *esp* : SEDUCE **2** : to deliver to an enemy **3** : ABANDON **4** : to prove unfaithful to **5** : to reveal unintentionally; *also* : SHOW, INDICATE **syn** mislead, delude, deceive, beguile — **be·tray·al** *n* — **be·tray·er** *n*

be·troth \bi-'trōth, -'tròth\ *vb* : to promise to marry — **be·troth·al** *n*

be·trothed *n* : the person to whom one is betrothed

¹bet·ter \'be-tər\ *adj, comparative of* GOOD **1** : greater than half **2** : improved in health **3** : more attractive, favorable, or commendable **4** : more advantageous or effective **5** : improved in accuracy or performance

²better *vb* **1** : to make or become better **2** : SURPASS, EXCEL

³better *adv, comparative of* WELL **1** : in a superior manner **2** : to a higher or greater degree; *also* : MORE

⁴better *n* **1** : something better; *also* : a superior esp. in merit or rank **2** : ADVANTAGE

⁵better *verbal auxiliary* : had better ⟨you ~ hurry⟩

bet·ter·ment \'be-tər-mənt\ *n* : IMPROVEMENT

bet·tor *or* **bet·ter** \'be-tər\ *n* : one that bets

¹be·tween \bi-'twēn\ *prep* **1** : by the common action of ⟨earned $10,000 ~ the two of them⟩ **2** : in the interval separating ⟨an alley ~ two buildings⟩; *also* : in intermediate relation to **3** : in point of comparison of ⟨choose ~ two cars⟩

²between *adv* : in an intervening space or interval

be·twixt \bi-'twikst\ *adv or prep* : BETWEEN

¹bev·el \'be-vəl\ *n* **1** : a device for adjusting the slant of the surfaces of a piece of work **2** : the angle or slant that one surface or line makes with another when not at right angles

²bevel *vb* **-eled** *or* **-elled; -el·ing** *or* **-el·ling 1** : to cut or shape to a bevel **2** : INCLINE, SLANT

bev·er·age \'bev-rij\ *n* : a drinkable liquid

bevy \'be-vē\ *n, pl* **bev·ies 1** : a large group or collection **2** : a group of animals and esp. quail together

be·wail \bi-'wāl\ *vb* : LAMENT **syn** deplore, bemoan, grieve, moan, weep

be·ware \-'war\ *vb* : to be on one's guard : be wary of

be·wil·der \bi-'wil-dər\ *vb* : PERPLEX, CONFUSE **syn** mystify, distract, puzzle — **be·wil·der·ment** *n*

be·witch \-'wich\ *vb* **1** : to affect by witchcraft **2** : CHARM, FASCINATE **syn** enchant, attract, captivate — **be·witch·ment** *n*

bey \'bā\ *n* **1** : a former Turkish provincial governor **2** : the former native ruler of Tunis or Tunisia

¹be·yond \bē-'änd\ *adv* **1** : FARTHER **2** : BESIDES

²beyond *prep* **1** : on or to the farther side of **2** : out of the reach or sphere of **3** : BESIDES

be·zel \'bē-zəl, 'be-\ *n* **1** : a rim that holds a transparent covering (as on a watch) **2** : the faceted part of a cut gem that rises above the setting

bf *abbr* boldface

\ə\abut \ᵊ\kitten \ər\further \a\ash \ā\ace \ä\mop, mar \aù\out \ch\chin \e\bet \ē\easy \g\go \i\hit \ī\ice \j\job \ŋ\sing \ō\go \ò\law \òi\boy \th\thin \th\the \ü\loot \ù\foot \y\yet \zh\vision *see also* Pronunciation Symbols page

BG *or* **B Gen** *abbr* brigadier general

bhang \'baŋ\ *n* [Hindi *bhãng*] : a mildly intoxicating preparation of the leaves and flowering tops of uncultivated hemp

Bi *symbol* bismuth

BIA *abbr* Bureau of Indian Affairs

bi·an·nu·al \(ˌ)bī-'an-yə-wəl\ *adj* : occurring twice a year — **bi·an·nu·al·ly** *adv*

¹bi·as \'bī-əs\ *n* **1** : a line diagonal to the grain of a fabric **2** : PREJUDICE, BENT

²bias *adv* : on the bias : DIAGONALLY

³bias *vb* **bi·ased** *or* **bi·assed; bi·as·ing** *or* **bi·as·sing** : PREJUDICE

bi·ath·lon \bī-'ath-lən, -ˌlän\ *n* : a composite athletic contest consisting of cross-country skiing and target shooting with a rifle

¹bib \'bib\ *n* : a cloth or plastic shield tied under the chin to protect the clothes while eating

²bib *abbr* Bible; biblical

bi·be·lot \'bē-bə-ˌlō\ *n, pl* **bibelots** *same or* -ˌlōz\ : a small household ornament or decorative object

bi·ble \'bī-bəl\ *n* [ME, fr. OF, fr. ML *biblia*, fr. Gk, pl. of *biblion* book, fr. *byblos* papyrus, book, fr. *Byblos*, ancient Phoenician city from which papyrus was exported] **1** *cap* : the sacred scriptures of Christians comprising the Old and New Testaments **2** *cap* : the sacred scriptures of Judaism; *also* : those of some other religion **3** : a publication that is considered authoritative for its subject — **bib·li·cal** \'bi-bli-kəl\ *adj*

bib·li·og·ra·phy \ˌbi-blē-'ä-grə-fē\ *n, pl* **-phies 1** : the history or description of writings or publications **2** : a list of writings (as on a subject or of an author) — **bib·li·og·ra·pher** \-fər\ *n* — **bib·li·o·graph·ic** \-ə-'gra-fik\ *also* **bib·li·o·graph·i·cal** \-fi-kəl\ *adj*

bib·lio·phile \'bi-blē-ə-ˌfīl\ *n* : a lover of books

bib·u·lous \'bi-byə-ləs\ *adj* **1** : highly absorbent **2** : fond of alcoholic beverages

bi·cam·er·al \'bī-'ka-mə-rəl\ *adj* : having or consisting of two legislative branches

bicarb \(ˌ)bī-'kärb, 'bī-ˌ\ *n* : SODIUM BICARBONATE

bi·car·bon·ate \(ˌ)bī-'kär-bə-ˌnāt, -nət\ *n* : an acid carbonate

bicarbonate of soda : SODIUM BICARBONATE

bi·cen·te·na·ry \ˌbī-sen-'te-nə-rē, bī-'sent-ᵊn-ˌer-ē\ *n* : BICENTENNIAL — **bicentenary** *adj*

bi·cen·ten·ni·al \ˌbī-sen-'te-nē-əl\ *n* : a 200th anniversary or its celebration — **bicentennial** *adj*

bi·ceps \'bī-ˌseps\ *n, pl* **biceps** *also* **bicepses** [NL, fr. L, two-headed, fr. *bi-* two + *caput* head] : a muscle (as in the front of the upper arm) having two points of origin

¹bick·er \'bi-kər\ *n* : ALTERCATION

²bicker *vb* : to engage in a petty quarrel

bi·con·cave \ˌbī-(ˌ)kän-'kāv, (ˌ)bī-'kän-ˌkāv\ *adj* : concave on both sides

bi·con·vex \ˌbī-(ˌ)kän-'veks, (ˌ)bī-'kän-ˌveks\ *adj* : convex on both sides

bi·cus·pid \bī-'kəs-pəd\ *n* : PREMOLAR

¹bi·cy·cle \'bī-ˌsi-kəl\ *n* : a light 2-wheeled vehicle with a steering handle, saddle, and pedals

²bicycle *vb* **-cy·cled; -cy·cling** \-ˌsi-k(ə-)liŋ, -ˌsī-\ : to ride a bicycle — **bi·cy·cler** \-k(ə-)lər\ *n* — **bi·cy·clist** \-k(ə-)list\ *n*

¹bid \'bid\ *vb* **bade** \'bad, 'bād\ *or* **bid; bid·den** \'bid-ᵊn\ *or* **bid** *also* **bade; bid·ding 1** : COMMAND, ORDER **2** : INVITE **3** : to give expression to **4** : to make a bid : OFFER — **bid·der** *n*

²bid *n* **1** : the act of one who bids; *also* : an offer for something **2** : INVITATION **3** : an announcement in a card game of what a player proposes to accomplish **4** : an attempt to win or gain ⟨a ~ for mayor⟩

bid·da·ble \'bi-də-bəl\ *adj* **1** : OBEDIENT, DOCILE **2** : capable of being bid

bid·dy \'bi-dē\ *n, pl* **biddies** : HEN; *also* : a young chicken

bide \'bīd\ *vb* **bode** \'bōd\ *or* **bid·ed; bid·ed; bid·ing 1** : to wait for **2** : WAIT, TARRY **3** : DWELL

bi·det \bi-'dā\ *n* : a bathroom fixture used esp. for bathing the external genitals and the posterior parts of the body

bi·di·rec·tion·al \ˌbī-də-'rek-sh(ə-)nəl\ *adj* : involving, moving, or taking place in two usu. opposite directions — **bi·di·rec·tion·al·ly** *adv*

bi·en·ni·al \bī-'e-nē-əl\ *adj* **1** : taking place once in two years **2** : lasting two years **3** : producing leaves the first year and fruiting and dying the second year — **biennial** *n* — **bi·en·ni·al·ly** *adv*

bi·en·ni·um \bī-'e-nē-əm\ *n, pl* **-niums** *or* **-nia** \-ə\ [L, fr. *bi-* two + *annus* year] : a period of two years

bier \'bir\ *n* : a stand bearing a coffin or corpse

bi·fo·cal \'bī-ˌfō-kəl\ *adj* : having two focal lengths

bifocals \-kəlz\ *n pl* : eyeglasses with lenses that have one part that corrects for near vision and one for distant vision

bi·fur·cate \'bī-fər-ˌkāt, bī-'fər-\ *vb* **-cat·ed; -cat·ing :** to divide into two branches or parts — **bi·fur·ca·tion** \ˌbī-fər-'kā-shən\ *n*

big \'big\ *adj* **big·ger; big·gest 1 :** large in size, amount, or scope **2 :** PREGNANT; *also* **:** SWELLING **3 :** IMPORTANT, IMPOSING **4 :** POPULAR — **big·ness** *n*

big·a·my \'bi-gə-mē\ *n* **:** the act of marrying one person while still legally married to another — **big·a·mist** \-mist\ *n* — **big·a·mous** \-məs\ *adj*

big bang theory *n* **:** a theory in astronomy: the universe originated in an explosion (**big bang**) from a single point of nearly infinite energy density

big brother *n* **1 :** an older brother **2 :** a man who befriends a delinquent or friendless boy **3** *cap both Bs* **:** the leader of an authoritarian state or movement

Big Dipper *n* **:** the seven principal stars of Ursa Major in a form resembling a dipper

big·foot \'big-ˌfu̇t\ *n* **:** SASQUATCH

big·horn \'big-ˌhȯrn\ *n, pl* **bighorn** *or* **bighorns :** a wild sheep of mountainous western No. America

bighorn

bight \'bīt\ *n* **1 :** a curve in a coast; *also* **:** the bay formed by such a curve **2 :** a slack part in a rope

big–name \'big-'nām\ *adj* **:** widely popular ⟨a ~ performer⟩ — **big name** *n*

big·ot \'bi-gət\ *n* **:** one intolerantly devoted to his or her own prejudices or opinions **syn** fanatic, enthusiast, zealot — **big·ot·ed** \-gə-təd\ *adj* — **big·ot·ry** \-trē\ *n*

big shot \'big-ˌshät\ *n* **:** an important person

big time \-ˌtīm\ *n* **1 :** a high-paying vaudeville circuit requiring only two performances a day **2 :** the top rank of an activity or enterprise — **big-tim·er** *n*

big top *n* **1 :** the main tent of a circus **2 :** CIRCUS

big·wig \'big-ˌwig\ *n* **:** BIG SHOT

bike \'bīk\ *n* **1 :** BICYCLE **2 :** MOTORCYCLE

bik·er *n* **:** MOTORCYCLIST; *esp* **:** one who is a member of an organized gang

bike·way \'bīk-ˌwā\ *n* **:** a thoroughfare for bicycles

bi·ki·ni \bə-'kē-nē\ *n* **:** a woman's brief 2-piece bathing suit

bi·lat·er·al \bī-'la-tə-rəl\ *adj* **1 :** having or involving two sides **2 :** affecting reciprocally two sides or parties — **bi·lat·er·al·ly** *adv*

bile \'bīl\ *n* **1 :** a bitter greenish fluid secreted by the liver that aids in the digestion of fats **2 :** an ill-humored mood

bilge \'bilj\ *n* **1 :** the part of a ship that lies between the bottom and the point where the sides go straight up **2 :** stale or worthless remarks or ideas

bi·lin·gual \bī-'liŋ-gwəl\ *adj* **:** expressed in, knowing, or using two languages

bil·ious \'bil-yəs\ *adj* **1 :** marked by or suffering from disordered liver function **2 :** IRRITABLE, ILL-TEMPERED — **bil·ious·ness** *n*

bilk \'bilk\ *vb* **:** CHEAT, SWINDLE

¹bill \'bil\ *n* **:** the jaws of a bird together with their horny covering; *also* **:** a mouth structure (as of a turtle) resembling these — **billed** \'bild\ *adj*

²bill *vb* **:** to caress fondly

³bill *n* **1 :** an itemized statement of particulars; *also* **:** INVOICE **2 :** a written document or note **3 :** a printed advertisement (as a poster) announcing an event **4 :** a draft of a law presented to a legislature for enactment **5 :** a written statement of a legal wrong suffered or of some breach of law **6 :** a piece of paper money

⁴bill *vb* **1 :** to enter in or prepare a bill; *also* **:** to submit a bill or account to **2 :** to advertise by bills or posters

bill·board \-ˌbōrd\ *n* **:** a flat surface on which advertising bills are posted

¹bil·let \'bi-lət\ *n* **1 :** an order requiring a person to provide lodging for a soldier; *also* **:** quarters assigned by or as if by such an order **2 :** POSITION, APPOINTMENT

²billet *vb* **:** to assign lodging to by billet

bil·let–doux \ˌbi-lā-'dü\ *n, pl* **billets–doux** *same or* -'düz\ [F *billet doux,* lit., sweet letter] **:** a love letter

bill·fold \'bil-ˌfōld\ *n* **:** WALLET

bil·liards \'bil-yərdz\ *n* **:** any of several games played on an oblong table by driving balls against each other or into pockets with a cue

bil·lings·gate \'bi-liŋz-ˌgāt, *Brit usu* -git\ *n* [*Billingsgate,* old gate and fish market, London, England] **:** coarsely abusive language

bil·lion \'bil-yən\ *n* **1 :** a thousand millions **2** *Brit* **:** a million millions — **billion** *adj* — **bil·lionth** \-yənth\ *adj or n*

bill of health : a usu. favorable report following an examination

bill of sale : a legal document transferring ownership of goods

¹bil·low \'bi-lō\ *n* **1 :** WAVE; *esp* **:** a great wave **2 :** a rolling mass (as of fog or flame) like a great wave — **bil·lowy** \'bi-lə-wē\ *adj*

²billow *vb* **:** to rise and roll in waves; *also* **:** to swell out ⟨~*ing* sails⟩

bil·ly \'bi-lē\ *n, pl* **billies :** BILLY CLUB

billy club *n* **:** a heavy usu. wooden club; *esp* **:** a police officer's club

hil·ly goat \'bi-lē-\ *n* **:** a male goat

bi·met·al \'bī-ˌmet-ᵊl\ *adj* **:** BIMETALLIC — **bimetal** *n*

bi·me·tal·lic \ˌbī-mə-'ta-lik\ *adj* **:** made of two different metals — often used of devices having a bonded expansive part — **bimetallic** *n*

bi·met·al·lism \bī-'met-ᵊl-ˌi-zəm\ *n* **:** the use of two metals at fixed ratios to form a standard of value for a monetary system

¹bi·month·ly \bī-'mənth-lē\ *adj* **1 :** occurring every two months **2 :** occurring twice a month **:** SEMIMONTHLY — **bimonthly** *adv*

²bimonthly *n* **:** a bimonthly publication

bin \'bin\ *n* **:** a box, crib, or enclosure used for storage

bi·na·ry \'bī-nə-rē, -ˌner-ē\ *adj* **1 :** consisting of two things or parts **2 :** relating to, being, or belonging to a system of numbers having 2 as its base ⟨the ~ digits 0 and 1⟩ **3 :** involving a choice between or condition of two alternatives only (as on-off, yes-no) — **binary** *n*

binary star *n* **:** a system of two stars revolving around each other

bin·au·ral \bī-'nȯr-əl\ *adj* **:** of or relating to sound reproduction involving the use of two separated micro-

---

\ə\abut \ᵊ\kitten \ər\further \a\ash \ā\ace \ä\mop, mar
\au̇\out \ch\chin \e\bet \ē\easy \g\go \i\hit \ī\ice \j\job
\ŋ\sing \ō\go \ȯ\law \ȯi\boy \th\thin \t̲h̲\the \ü\loot \u̇\foot
\y\yet \zh\vision *see also* Pronunciation Symbols page

phones and two transmission channels to achieve a stereophonic effect

bind \\'bīnd\\ *vb* **bound** \\'baůnd\\; **bind·ing 1** : TIE; *also* : to restrain as if by tying **2** : to put under an obligation; *also* : to constrain with legal authority **3** : BANDAGE **4** : to unite into a mass **5** : to compel as if by a pledge ⟨a handshake ∼s the deal⟩ **6** : to strengthen or decorate with a band **7** : to fasten together and enclose in a cover ⟨∼ books⟩ **8** : to exert a tying, restraining, or compelling effect — **bind·er** *n*

bind·ing \\'bīn-diŋ\\ *n* : something (as a ski fastening, a cover, or an edging fabric) used to bind

¹binge \\'binj\\ *n* : SPREE

²binge *vb* **binged; binge·ing** *or* **bing·ing** : to go on a binge and esp. an eating binge — **bing·er** *n*

bin·go \\'biŋ-gō\\ *n, pl* **bingos** : a game of chance played with cards having numbered squares corresponding to numbered balls drawn at random and won by covering five squares in a row

bin·na·cle \\'bi-ni-kəl\\ *n* [alter. of ME *bitakle*, fr. Pg or Sp; Pg *bitácola* & Sp *bitácula*, fr. L *habitaculum* dwelling place, fr. *habitare* to inhabit] : a container holding a ship's compass

¹bin·oc·u·lar \\bī-'nä-kyə-lər, bə-\\ *adj* : of, relating to, or adapted to the use of both eyes — **bin·oc·u·lar·ly** *adv*

²bin·oc·u·lar \\bə-'nä-kyə-lər, bī-\\ *n* **1** : a binocular optical instrument (as a microscope) **2** : a hand-held optical instrument composed of two telescopes and a focusing device — usu. used in pl.

bi·no·mi·al \\bī-'nō-mē-əl\\ *n* **1** : a mathematical expression consisting of two terms connected by the sign plus (+) or minus (−) **2** : a biological species name consisting of two terms — **binomial** *adj*

bio·chem·is·try \\ˌbī-ō-'ke-mə-strē\\ *n* : chemistry that deals with the chemical compounds and processes occurring in living things — **bio·chem·i·cal** \\-mi-kəl\\ *adj or n* — **bio·chem·ist** \\-mist\\ *n*

bio·de·grad·able \\-di-'grā-də-bəl\\ *adj* : capable of being broken down esp. into innocuous products by the actions of living things (as microorganisms) ⟨a ∼ detergent⟩ — **bio·de·grad·abil·i·ty** \\-ˌgrā-də-'bi-lə-tē\\ *n* — **bio·deg·ra·da·tion** \\-ˌde-grə-'dā-shən\\ *n* — **bio·de·grade** \\-di-'grād\\ *vb*

bio·di·ver·si·ty \\-də-'vər-sə-tē, -dī-\\ *n* : biological diversity in an environment as indicated by numbers of different species of plants and animals

bio·eth·ics \\-'e-thiks\\ *n* : the ethics of biological research and its applications esp. in medicine — **bio·eth·i·cal** \\-'e-thi-kəl\\ *adj* — **bio·eth·i·cist** \\-'e-thə-sist\\ *n*

bio·feed·back \\-'fēd-ˌbak\\ *n* : the technique of making unconscious or involuntary bodily processes (as heartbeats or brain waves) objectively perceptible to the senses (as by use of an oscilloscope) in order to manipulate them by conscious mental control

biog *abbr* biographer; biographical; biography

bio·ge·og·ra·phy \\ˌbī-ō-jē-'ä-grə-fē\\ *n* : a branch of biology that deals with the distribution of plants and animals — **bio·ge·og·ra·pher** *n*

bi·og·ra·phy \\bī-'ä-grə-fē, bē-\\ *n, pl* **-phies** : a written history of a person's life; *also* : such writings in general — **bi·og·ra·pher** *n* — **bio·graph·i·cal** \\ˌbī-ə-'gra-fi-kəl\\ *also* **bi·o·graph·ic** \\-fik\\ *adj*

biol *abbr* biologic; biological; biologist; biology

bi·o·log·i·cal \\ˌbī-ə-'lä-ji-kəl\\ *also* **bi·o·log·ic** \\-jik\\ *adj* **1** : of, relating to, or produced by biology or life and living processes **2** : related by direct genetic relationship rather than by adoption or marriage ⟨∼ parents⟩ — **bi·o·log·i·cal·ly** \\-ji-k(ə-)lē\\ *adv*

biological clock *n* : an inherent timing mechanism inferred to exist in some living systems (as a cell) in order to explain various cyclic physiological and behavioral responses

biological warfare *n* : warfare in which living organisms (as bacteria) are used as weapons

bi·ol·o·gy \\bī-'ä-lə-jē\\ *n* [G *Biologie*, fr. Gk *bios* mode of life + *logos* word] **1** : a science that deals with living beings and life processes **2** : the life processes of an organism or group — **bi·ol·o·gist** \\bī-'ä-lə-jist\\ *n*

bio·med·i·cal \\ˌbī-ō-'me-di-kəl\\ *adj* : of, relating to, or involving biological, medical, and physical science

bi·on·ic \\bī-'ä-nik\\ *adj* : having normal biological capability or performance enhanced by or as if by electronic or mechanical devices

bio·phys·ics \\ˌbī-ō-'fi-ziks\\ *n* : a branch of science concerned with the application of physical principles and methods to biological problems — **bio·phys·i·cal** \\-zi-kəl\\ *adj* — **bio·phys·i·cist** \\-'fi-zə-sist\\ *n*

bi·op·sy \\'bī-ˌäp-sē\\ *n, pl* **-sies** : the removal of tissue, cells, or fluids from the living body for examination

bio·rhythm \\'bī-ō-ˌri-<u>th</u>əm\\ *n* : an inherent rhythm that appears to control or initiate various biological processes

bio·sphere \\'bī-ə-ˌsfir\\ *n* **1** : the part of the world in which life can exist **2** : living beings together with their environment

bio·tech \\'bī-ō-ˌtek\\ *n* : BIOTECHNOLOGY

bio·tech·nol·ogy \\ˌbī-ō-tek-'nä-lə-jē\\ *n* : biological science when applied esp. in genetic engineering and recombinant DNA technology

bi·ot·ic \\bī-'ä-tik\\ *adj* : of or relating to life; *esp* : caused by living beings

bi·o·tin \\'bī-ə-tən\\ *n* : a vitamin of the vitamin B complex found esp. in yeast, liver, and egg yolk and active in growth promotion

bi·o·tite \\'bī-ə-ˌtīt\\ *n* : a dark mica containing iron, magnesium, potassium, and aluminum

bi·par·ti·san \\bī-'pär-tə-zən\\ *adj* : representing or composed of members of two parties

bi·par·tite \\-'pär-ˌtīt\\ *adj* **1** : being in two parts **2** : shared by two ⟨∼ treaty⟩

bi·ped \\'bī-ˌped\\ *n* : a 2-footed animal — **bi·ped·al** \\(ˌ)bī-'ped-ᵊl\\ *adj*

bi·plane \\'bī-ˌplān\\ *n* : an aircraft with two wings placed one above the other

bi·po·lar \\bī-'pō-lər\\ *adj* : having or involving the use of two poles — **bi·po·lar·i·ty** \\ˌbī-pō-'lar-ə-tē\\ *n*

bi·ra·cial \\bī-'rā-shəl\\ *adj* : of, relating to, or involving members of two races

¹birch \\'bərch\\ *n* **1** : any of a genus of mostly short= lived deciduous shrubs and trees with membranous outer bark and pale close-grained wood; *also* : this wood **2** : a birch rod or bundle of twigs for flogging — **birch** *or* **birch·en** \\'bər-chən\\ *adj*

²birch *vb* : WHIP, FLOG

¹bird \\'bərd\\ *n* : any of a class of warm-blooded egg-laying vertebrates having the body feathered and the forelimbs modified to form wings

²bird *vb* : to observe or identify wild birds in their native habitat — **bird·er** *n*

bird·bath \\'bərd-ˌbath, -ˌbäth\\ *n* : a usu. ornamental basin set up for birds to bathe in

bird·house \\-ˌhaůs\\ *n* : an artificial nesting place for birds; *also* : AVIARY

bird·ie \\'bər-dē\\ *n* : a score of one under par on a hole in golf

bird·lime \\-ˌlīm\\ *n* : a sticky substance smeared on twigs to snare small birds

bird of paradise : any of numerous brilliantly colored plumed birds of the New Guinea area

bird of prey : a carnivorous bird that feeds wholly or chiefly on carrion or on meat taken by hunting

bird·seed \\'bərd-ˌsēd\\ *n* : a mixture of small seeds (as of hemp or millet) used for feeding birds

bird's–eye \\'bərdz-ˌī\\ *adj* **1** : marked with spots resembling birds' eyes ⟨∼ maple⟩ **2** : seen from above as if by a flying bird ⟨∼ view⟩; *also* : CURSORY

bi·ret·ta \bə-'re-tə\ *n* : a square cap with three ridges on top worn esp. by Roman Catholic clergymen

birr \'bir, 'bər\ *n*, *pl* **birr** — see MONEY table

birth \'bərth\ *n* **1** : the act or fact of being born or of bringing forth young **2** : LINEAGE, DESCENT **3** : ORIGIN, BEGINNING

birth canal *n* : the channel formed by the cervix, vagina, and vulva through which the fetus passes during birth

birth control *n* : control of the number of children born esp. by preventing or lessening the frequency of conception

birth·day \'bərth-ˌdā\ *n* : the day or anniversary of one's birth

birth defect *n* : a physical or biochemical defect present at birth and inherited or environmentally induced

birth·mark \'bərth-ˌmärk\ *n* : an unusual mark or blemish on the skin at birth

birth·place \-ˌplās\ *n* : place of birth or origin

birth·rate \-ˌrāt\ *n* : the number of births per number of individuals in a given area or group during a given time

birth·right \-ˌrīt\ *n* : a right, privilege, or possession to which one is entitled by birth **syn** legacy, patrimony, heritage, inheritance

birth·stone \-ˌstōn\ *n* : a gemstone associated symbolically with the month of one's birth

bis·cuit \'bis-kət\ *n* [ME *bisquite*, fr. MF *bescuit*, fr. (*pain*) *bescuit* twice-cooked bread] **1** : a crisp flat cake; *esp, Brit* : CRACKER 2 **2** : a small quick bread made from dough that has been rolled and cut or dropped from a spoon

bi·sect \'bī-ˌsekt\ *vb* : to divide into two usu. equal parts; *also* : CROSS, INTERSECT — **bi·sec·tion** \'bī-ˌsek-shən\ *n* — **bi·sec·tor** \-tər\ *n*

bi·sex·u·al \bī-'sek-shə-wəl\ *adj* **1** : possessing characters of or having sexual desire for both sexes **2** : of, relating to, or involving both sexes — **bisexual** *n* — **bi·sex·u·al·i·ty** \ˌbī-ˌsek-shə-'wal-ə-tē\ *n*

bish·op \'bi-shəp\ *n* [ME *bisshop*, fr. OE *bisceop*, fr. LL *episcopus*, fr. Gk *episkopos*, lit., overseer, fr. *epi-* on, over + *skeptesthai* to look] **1** : a member of the clergy ranking above a priest and typically governing a diocese **2** : any of various Protestant church officials who superintend other clergy **3** : a chess piece that can move diagonally across any number of adjoining unoccupied squares

bish·op·ric \'bi-shə-prik\ *n* **1** : DIOCESE **2** : the office of bishop

bis·muth \'biz-məth\ *n* : a heavy brittle grayish white metallic chemical element used in alloys and medicine — see ELEMENT table

bi·son \'bīs-ᵊn, 'bīz-\ *n*, *pl* **bison** : BUFFALO 2

bisque \'bisk\ *n* : a thick cream soup

bis·tro \'bēs-trō, 'bis-\ *n*, *pl* **bistros** [F] **1** : a small or unpretentious restaurant **2** : BAR; *also* : NIGHTCLUB

¹**bit** \'bit\ *n* **1** : the biting or cutting edge or part of a tool **2** : the part of a bridle that is placed in a horse's mouth

²**bit** *n* **1** : a morsel of food; *also* : a small piece or quantity of something **2** : a small coin; *also* : a unit of value equal to 12½ cents **3** : something small or trivial **4** : an indefinite usu. small degree or extent ⟨a ∼ tired⟩

³**bit** *n* [*binary* dig*it*] : a unit of computer information equivalent to the result of a choice between two alternatives; *also* : its physical representation

¹**bitch** \'bich\ *n* **1** : a female canine; *esp* : a female dog **2** : a malicious, spiteful, and domineering woman

²**bitch** *vb* : COMPLAIN

¹**bite** \'bīt\ *vb* **bit** \'bit\; **bit·ten** \'bit-ᵊn\ *also* **bit**; **bit·ing** \'bī-tiŋ\ **1** : to grip with teeth or jaws; *also* : to wound or sting with or as if with fangs **2** : to cut or pierce with or as if with an edged instrument **3** : to cause to smart or sting **4** : CORRODE **5** : to take bait

²**bite** *n* **1** : the act or manner of biting **2** : FOOD **3** : a wound made by biting; *also* : a penetrating effect

bit·ing \'bī-tiŋ\ *adj* : SHARP, CUTTING

bit·ter \'bi-tər\ *adj* **1** : being or inducing the one of the basic taste sensations that is acrid, astringent, or disagreeable and is suggestive of hops **2** : marked by intensity or severity (as of distress or hatred) **3** : extremely harsh or cruel — **bit·ter·ly** *adv* — **bit·ter·ness** *n*

bit·tern \'bi-tərn\ *n* : any of various small or medium-sized herons

bit·ters \'bi-tərz\ *n sing or pl* : a usu. alcoholic solution of bitter and often aromatic plant products used in mixing drinks and as a mild tonic

¹**bit·ter·sweet** \'bi-tər-ˌswēt\ *n* **1** : a poisonous nightshade with purple flowers and orange-red berries **2** : a woody vine with yellow capsules that open when ripe and disclose scarlet seed coverings

²**bittersweet** *adj* : being at once both bitter and sweet

bi·tu·mi·nous coal \bə-'tü-mə-nəs-, bī-, -'tyü-\ *n* : a coal that when heated yields considerable volatile waste matter

bi·valve \'bī-ˌvalv\ *n* : an animal (as a clam) with a shell composed of two separate parts that open and shut — **bivalve** *adj*

¹**biv·ouac** \'bi-və-ˌwak\ *n* [F, fr. LG *biwacht*, fr. *bi* at + *wacht* guard] : a temporary encampment or shelter

²**bivouac** *vb* **-ouacked**; **-ouack·ing** : to form a bivouac : CAMP

¹**bi·week·ly** \ˌbī-'wē-klē\ *adj* **1** : occurring twice a week **2** : occurring every two weeks : FORTNIGHTLY — **biweekly** *adv*

²**biweekly** *n* : a biweekly publication

bi·year·ly \-'yir-lē\ *adj* **1** : BIANNUAL **2** : BIENNIAL

bi·zarre \bə-'zär\ *adj* : ODD, ECCENTRIC, FANTASTIC — **bi·zarre·ly** *adv*

bk *abbr* **1** bank **2** book

Bk *symbol* berkelium

bkg *abbr* banking

bkgd *abbr* background

bks *abbr* barracks

bkt *abbr* **1** basket **2** bracket

bl *abbr* **1** bale **2** barrel **3** blue

blab \'blab\ *vb* **blabbed**; **blab·bing** : TATTLE, GOSSIP

¹**black** \'blak\ *adj* **1** : of the color black; *also* : very dark **2** : SWARTHY **3** : of or relating to various groups of dark-skinned people **4** : of or relating to the Afro-American people or their culture **5** : SOILED, DIRTY **6** : lacking light ⟨a ∼ night⟩ **7** : WICKED, EVIL ⟨∼ magic⟩ **8** : DISMAL, GLOOMY ⟨a ∼ outlook⟩ **9** : SULLEN ⟨a ∼ mood⟩ — **black·ish** *adj* — **black·ly** *adv* — **black·ness** *n*

²**black** *n* **1** : a black pigment or dye; *also* : something (as clothing) that is black **2** : the characteristic color of soot or coal **3** : a person of a dark-skinned race **4** : AFRO-AMERICAN

³**black** *vb* : BLACKEN

black·a·moor \'bla-kə-ˌmür\ *n* : a dark-skinned person

black–and–blue \ˌbla-kən-'blü\ *adj* : darkly discolored from blood effused by bruising

black·ball \'blak-ˌból\ *vb* **1** : to vote against; *esp* : to exclude from membership by casting a negative vote **2** : OSTRACIZE — **black·ball** *n*

black bass *n* : any of several freshwater sunfishes native to eastern and central No. America

¹**black belt** \'blak-ˌbelt\ *n*, *often cap both Bs* : an area densely populated by blacks

²**black belt** \-'belt\ *n* : one who holds the rating of expert (as in judo or karate); *also* : the rating itself

\ə\abut \ᵊ\kitten \ər\further \a\ash \ā\ace \ä\mop, mar \aů\out \ch\chin \e\bet \ē\easy \g\go \i\hit \ī\ice \j\job \ŋ\sing \ō\go \ó\law \ói\boy \th\thin \th\the \ü\loot \ů\foot \y\yet \zh\vision *see also* Pronunciation Symbols page

black·ber·ry \-₁ber-ē\ *n* : the usu. black or purple juicy but seedy edible fruit of various brambles; *also* : a plant bearing this fruit

black·bird \-₁bərd\ *n* : any of various birds (as the red-winged blackbird) of which the male is largely or wholly black

black·board \-₁bōrd\ *n* : a smooth usu. dark surface used for writing or drawing on with chalk

black·body \-ˈbä-dē\ *n* : a body or surface that completely absorbs incident radiation with no reflection

black box *n* **1** : a usu. complicated electronic device whose components and workings are unknown or mysterious to the user **2** : a device used in aircraft to record cockpit conversations and flight data

black death *n* : an epidemic of bacterial plague and esp. bubonic plague that spread rapidly in Europe and Asia in the 14th century

black·en \ˈbla-kən\ *vb* **black·ened; black·en·ing 1** : to make or become black **2** : DEFAME, SULLY

black·ened *adj* : coated with spices and quickly seared in a very hot skillet ⟨~ swordfish⟩

black eye *n* : a discoloration of the skin around the eye from bruising

black–eyed Su·san \₁blak-₁īd-ˈsüz-ᵊn\ *n* : either of two No. American plants that are related to the daisies and have deep yellow to orange flower heads with dark conical centers

Black·foot \ˈblak-₁fu̇t\ *n, pl* **Black·feet** *or* **Blackfoot** : a member of an American Indian people of Montana, Alberta, and Saskatchewan

black·guard \ˈbla-gərd, -₁gärd\ *n* : SCOUNDREL, RASCAL

black·head \ˈblak-₁hed\ *n* : a small usu. dark oily mass plugging the outlet of a skin gland

black hole *n* : a hypothetical celestial object with a gravitational field so strong that light cannot escape from it

black·ing \ˈbla-kiŋ\ *n* : a substance applied to something to make it black

¹black·jack \ˈblak-₁jak\ *n* **1** : a leather-covered club with a flexible handle **2** : a card game in which the object is to be dealt cards having a higher count than the dealer but not exceeding 21

²blackjack *vb* : to hit with or as if with a blackjack

black light *n* : invisible ultraviolet light

black·list \ˈblak-₁list\ *n* : a list of persons who are disapproved of and are to be punished or boycotted — **blacklist** *vb*

black·mail \ˈblak-₁māl\ *n* : extortion by threats esp. of public exposure; *also* : something so extorted — **black·mail** *vb* — **black·mail·er** *n*

black market *n* : illicit trade in goods; *also* : a place where such trade is carried on

Black Mass *n* : a travesty of the Christian mass ascribed to worshipers of Satan

Black Muslim *n* : a member of a chiefly black group that professes Islamic religious belief

black nationalist *n, often cap B&N* : a member of a group of militant blacks who advocate separatism from whites and the formation of self-governing black communities — **black nationalism** *n, often cap B&N*

black·out \ˈbla-₁kau̇t\ *n* **1** : a period of darkness due to electrical power failure **2** : a transitory loss or dulling of vision or consciousness **3** : the prohibition or restriction of the telecasting of a sports event — **black out** *vb*

black power *n* : the mobilization of the political and economic power of black Americans esp. to compel respect for their rights and improve their condition

black sheep *n* : a discreditable member of an otherwise respectable group

black·smith \ˈblak-₁smith\ *n* : a smith who forges iron — **black·smith·ing** *n*

black·thorn \-₁thȯrn\ *n* : a European thorny plum

black·top \ˈblak-₁täp\ *n* : a dark tarry material (as asphalt) used esp. for surfacing roads — **blacktop** *vb*

black widow *n* : a venomous New World spider having the female black with an hourglass-shaped red mark on the underside of the abdomen

blad·der \ˈbla-dər\ *n* : a sac in which liquid or gas is stored; *esp* : one in a vertebrate into which urine passes from the kidneys

blade \ˈblād\ *n* **1** : a leaf of a plant and esp. of a grass; *also* : the flat part of a leaf as distinguished from its stalk **2** : something (as the flat part of an oar or an arm of a propeller) resembling the blade of a leaf **3** : the cutting part of an instrument or tool **4** : SWORD; *also* : SWORDSMAN **5** : a dashing fellow ⟨a gay ~⟩ **6** : the runner of an ice skate — **blad·ed** \ˈblā-dəd\ *adj*

blain \ˈblān\ *n* : an inflammatory swelling or sore

¹blame \ˈblām\ *vb* **blamed; blam·ing** [ME, fr. OF *blamer*, fr. L *blasphemare* to blaspheme, fr. Gk *blasphēmein*] **1** : to find fault with **2** : to hold responsible or responsible for **syn** censure, denounce, condemn, criticize — **blam·able** *adj*

²blame *n* **1** : CENSURE, REPROOF **2** : responsibility for fault or error **syn** guilt, fault, culpability, onus — **blame·less** *adj* — **blame·less·ly** *adv* — **blame·less·ness** *n*

blame·wor·thy \-₁wər-thē\ *adj* : deserving blame — **blame·wor·thi·ness** *n*

blanch \ˈblanch\ *vb* : to make or become white or pale : BLEACH

blanc·mange \blə-ˈmänj, -ˈmänᶻh\ *n* [ME *blancmanger*, fr. MF *blanc manger*, lit., white food] : a dessert made from gelatin or a starchy substance and milk usu. sweetened and flavored

bland \ˈbland\ *adj* **1** : smooth in manner : SUAVE **2** : gently soothing ⟨a ~ diet⟩; *also* : INSIPID **syn** gentle, mild, soft, balmy — **bland·ly** *adv* — **bland·ness** *n*

blan·dish·ment \ˈblan-dish-mənt\ *n* : flattering or coaxing speech or action : CAJOLERY

¹blank \ˈblaŋk\ *adj* **1** : showing or causing an appearance of dazed dismay; *also* : EXPRESSIONLESS **2** : free from writing or marks; *also* : having spaces to be filled in **3** : DULL, EMPTY ⟨~ moments⟩ **4** : ABSOLUTE, DOWNRIGHT ⟨a ~ refusal⟩ **5** : not shaped in final form — **blank·ly** *adv* — **blank·ness** *n*

²blank *n* **1** : an empty space **2** : a form with spaces for the entry of data **3** : an unfinished form (as of a key) **4** : a cartridge with propellant and a seal but no projectile

³blank *vb* **1** : to cover or close up : OBSCURE **2** : to keep from scoring

blank check *n* **1** : a signed check with the amount unspecified **2** : complete freedom of action

¹blan·ket \ˈblaŋ-kət\ *n* **1** : a heavy woven often woolen covering **2** : a covering layer ⟨a ~ of snow⟩

²blanket *vb* : to cover with a blanket

³blanket *adj* : covering a group or class ⟨~ insurance⟩; *also* : applicable in all instances ⟨~ rules⟩

blank verse *n* : unrhymed iambic pentameter

blare \ˈblar\ *vb* **blared; blar·ing** : to sound loud and harsh; *also* : to proclaim loudly — **blare** *n*

blar·ney \ˈblär-nē\ *n* [*Blarney stone*, a stone in Blarney Castle, near Cork, Ireland, held to bestow skill in flattery on those who kiss it] : skillful flattery : BLANDISHMENT

bla·sé \blä-ˈzā\ *adj* [F] : apathetic to pleasure or excitement as a result of excessive indulgence; *also* : SOPHISTICATED

blas·pheme \blas-ˈfēm, ˈblas-₁\ *vb* **blas·phemed; blas·phem·ing 1** : to speak of or address with irreverence **2** : to utter blasphemy — **blas·phem·er** *n*

blas·phe·my \ˈblas-fə-mē\ *n, pl* **-mies 1** : the act of expressing lack of reverence for God **2** : irreverence toward something considered sacred — **blas·phe·mous** \-məs\ *adj*

¹blast \ˈblast\ *n* **1** : a violent gust of wind; *also* : its effect **2** : sound made by a wind instrument **3** : a current of air forced at high pressure through a hole in a furnace

(blast furnace) 4 : a sudden withering esp. of plants : BLIGHT **5 :** EXPLOSION; *also :* the often destructive shock wave of an explosion

²**blast** *vb :* to shatter by or as if by an explosive

blast off *vb :* TAKE OFF 4 — used esp. of rocket-propelled vehicles — **blast·off** \'blast-ˌȯf\ *n*

bla·tant \'blāt-ᵊnt\ *adj :* offensively obtrusive : vulgarly showy **syn** vociferous, boisterous, clamorous, obstreperous — **bla·tan·cy** \-ᵊn-sē\ *n* — **bla·tant·ly** *adv*

blath·er \'bla-thᵊr\ *vb :* to talk foolishly at length — **blather** *n*

blath·er·skite \'bla-thᵊr-ˌskīt\ *n :* a person who blathers

¹**blaze** \'blāz\ *n* **1 :** FIRE **2 :** intense direct light accompanied by heat **3 :** something (as a dazzling display or sudden outburst) suggesting fire ⟨a ∼ of autumn leaves⟩ **syn** glare, glow, flame

²**blaze** *vb* **blazed; blaz·ing 1 :** to burn brightly; *also :* to flare up **2 :** to be conspicuously bright : GLITTER

³**blaze** *vb* **blazed; blaz·ing :** to make public or conspicuous

⁴**blaze** *n* **1 :** a usu. white stripe on the face of an animal **2 :** a trail marker; *esp :* one made on a tree

⁵**blaze** *vb* **blazed; blaz·ing :** to mark (as a tree or trail) with blazes

blaz·er \'blā-zᵊr\ *n :* a sports jacket often with notched collar and pockets that are stitched on

¹**bla·zon** \'blāz-ᵊn\ *n* **1 :** COAT OF ARMS **2 :** ostentatious display

²**blazon** *vb* **1 :** to publish widely : PROCLAIM **2 :** DECK, ADORN

bldg *abbr* building

bldr *abbr* builder

¹**bleach** \'blēch\ *vb :* WHITEN, BLANCH

²**bleach** *n :* a preparation used in bleaching

bleach·ers \'blē-chᵊrz\ *n sing or pl :* a usu. uncovered stand of tiered seats for spectators

bleak \'blēk\ *adj* **1 :** desolately barren and often windswept **2 :** lacking warm or cheering qualities — **bleak·ish** *adj* — **bleak·ly** *adv* — **bleak·ness** *n*

blear \'blir\ *adj :* dim with water or tears ⟨∼ eyes⟩

bleary \'blir-ē\ *adj* **1 :** dull or dimmed esp. from fatigue or sleep **2 :** poorly outlined or defined

bleat \'blēt\ *n :* the cry of a sheep or goat or a sound like it — **bleat** *vb*

bleed \'blēd\ *vb* **bled** \'bled\; **bleed·ing 1 :** to lose or shed blood **2 :** to be wounded; *also :* to feel pain or distress **3 :** to flow or ooze from a wounded surface; *also :* to draw fluid from ⟨∼ a tire⟩ **4 :** to extort money from

bleed·er \'blē-dᵊr\ *n :* one that bleeds; *esp :* HEMOPHILIAC

bleeding heart *n* **1 :** a garden plant related to the poppies that has usu. deep pink drooping heart-shaped flowers **2 :** a person who shows extreme sympathy esp. for an object of alleged persecution

¹**blem·ish** \'ble-mish\ *vb :* to spoil by a flaw : MAR

²**blemish** *n :* a noticeable flaw

¹**blench** \'blench\ *vb* [ME, to deceive, blench, fr. OE *blencan* to deceive] : FLINCH, QUAIL **syn** shrink, recoil, wince, start

²**blench** *vb :* to grow or make pale

¹**blend** \'blend\ *vb* **blend·ed; blend·ing 1 :** to mix thoroughly **2 :** to prepare (as coffee) by mixing different varieties **3 :** to combine into an integrated whole **4 :** HARMONIZE **syn** fuse, merge, mingle, coalesce — **blend·er** *n*

²**blend** *n :* a product of blending **syn** compound, composite, alloy, mixture

bless \'bles\ *vb* **blessed** \'blest\ *also* **blest** \'blest\; **blessing** [ME, fr. OE *blētsian*, fr. *blōd* blood; fr. the use of blood in consecration] **1 :** to consecrate by religious rite or word **2 :** to sanctify with the sign of the cross **3 :** to invoke divine care for **4 :** PRAISE, GLORIFY **5 :** to confer happiness upon

bless·ed \'ble-sᵊd\ *also* **blest** \'blest\ *adj* **1 :** HOLY **2 :** BEATIFIED **3 :** DELIGHTFUL — **bless·ed·ly** *adv* — **bless·ed·ness** *n*

bless·ing \'ble-siŋ\ *n* **1 :** the act or words of one who blesses; *also :* APPROVAL **2 :** a thing conducive to happiness **3 :** grace said at a meal

blew *past of* BLOW

¹**blight** \'blīt\ *n* **1 :** a plant disease or injury marked by withering; *also :* an organism causing a blight **2 :** an impairing or frustrating influence; *also :* a deteriorated condition ⟨urban ∼⟩

²**blight** *vb :* to affect with or suffer from blight

blimp \'blimp\ *n :* a nonrigid airship

¹**blind** \'blīnd\ *adj* **1 :** lacking or grossly deficient in ability to see; *also :* intended for blind persons **2 :** not based on reason, evidence, or knowledge ⟨∼ faith⟩ **3 :** not intelligently controlled or directed ⟨∼ chance⟩ **4 :** performed solely by using aircraft instruments ⟨a ∼ landing⟩ **5 :** hard to discern or make out : HIDDEN ⟨a ∼ scam⟩ **6 :** lacking an opening or outlet ⟨a ∼ alley⟩ — **blind·ly** *adv* — **blind·ness** \'blīnd-nᵊs\ *n*

²**blind** *vb* **1 :** to make blind **2 :** DAZZLE **3 :** DARKEN; *also :* HIDE

³**blind** *n* **1 :** something (as a shutter) to hinder vision or keep out light **2 :** a place of concealment **3 :** SUBTERFUGE

blind date *n :* a date between persons who have not previously met; *also :* either of these persons

blind·er \'blīn-dᵊr\ *n :* either of two flaps on a horse's bridle to prevent it from seeing to the side

blind·fold \'blīnd-ˌfōld\ *vb :* to cover the eyes of with or as if with a bandage — **blindfold** *n*

¹**blink** \'bliŋk\ *vb* **1 :** WINK **2 :** TWINKLE **3 :** EVADE, IGNORE

²**blink** *n* **1 :** GLIMMER, SPARKLE **2 :** a usu. involuntary shutting and opening of the eye

blink·er \'bliŋ-kᵊr\ *n :* a blinking light used as a signal

blin·tze \'blint-sᵊ\ *or* **blintz** \'blints\ *n* [Yiddish *blintse*] : a thin rolled pancake with a filling usu. of cream cheese

blip \'blip\ *n* **1 :** a spot on a radar screen **2 :** ABERRATION 1

bliss \'blis\ *n :* complete happiness : JOY **syn** beatitude, blessedness — **bliss·ful** \-fᵊl\ *adj* — **bliss·ful·ly** *adv*

¹**blis·ter** \'blis-tᵊr\ *n* **1 :** a raised area of skin containing watery fluid; *also :* an agent that causes blisters **2 :** something (as a raised spot in paint) suggesting a blister **3 :** a disease of plants marked by large swollen patches on the leaves

²**blister** *vb :* to develop a blister; *also :* to cause blisters

blithe \'blīth, 'blīth\ *adj* **blith·er; blith·est :** happily lighthearted **syn** merry, jovial, jolly, jocund — **blithe·ly** *adv* — **blithe·some** \-sᵊm\ *adj*

blitz \'blits\ *n* **1 :** an intensive series of air raids **2 :** a fast intensive campaign **3 :** a rush of the passer by the defensive linebackers in football — **blitz** *vb*

blitz·krieg \-ˌkrēg\ *n* [G, lit., lightning war, fr. *Blitz* lightning + *Krieg* war] : a sudden violent enemy attack

bliz·zard \'bli-zᵊrd\ *n :* a long severe snowstorm

blk *abbr* **1** black **2** block

bloat \'blōt\ *vb :* to swell by or as if by filling with water or air

blob \'bläb\ *n :* a small lump or drop of a thick consistency

bloc \'bläk\ *n* [F, lit., block] : a combination of individuals or groups (as nations) working for a common purpose

¹**block** \'bläk\ *n* **1 :** a solid piece of substantial material (as wood or stone) **2 :** HINDRANCE, OBSTRUCTION; *also :* in-

---

\ᵊ\abut \ᵊ\kitten \ᵊr\further \a\ash \ā\ace \ä\mop, mar \au̇\out \ch\chin \e\bet \ē\easy \g\go \i\hit \ī\ice \j\job \ŋ\sing \ō\go \ȯ\law \ȯi\boy \th\thin \tẖ\the \ü\loot \u̇\foot \y\yet \zh\vision *see also* Pronunciation Symbols page terruption of normal function of body or mind ⟨heart ∼⟩ **3** : a frame enclosing one or more pulleys and having a hook or strap by which it may be attached **4** : a piece of material with a hand-cut design on its surface from which copies are to be made **5** : a large building divided into separate units (as apartments or offices) **6** : a row of houses or shops **7** : a city square; *also* : the distance along one of the sides of such a square **8** : a quantity of things considered as a unit ⟨a ∼ of seats⟩

²**block** *vb* **1** : OBSTRUCT, CHECK **2** : to outline roughly ⟨∼ out a design⟩ **3** : to provide or support with a block ⟨∼ up a wheel⟩ **syn** bar, impede, hinder, obstruct

block·ade \blä-ʼkād\ *n* : the isolation of a place usu. by troops or ships — **blockade** *vb* — **block·ad·er** *n*

block·age \ʼblä-kij\ *n* : an act or instance of obstructing : the state of being blocked

block·bust·er \ʼbläk-ˌbəs-tər\ *n* : one that is very large, successful, or violent ⟨a ∼ of a movie⟩

block·head \ʼbläk-ˌhed\ *n* : DOLT, DUNCE

block·house \-ˌhaüs\ *n* : a small strong building used as a shelter (as from enemy fire) or observation post

¹**blond** *or* **blonde** \ʼbländ\ *adj* : fair in complexion; *also* : of a light or bleached color ⟨∼ mahogany⟩ — **blond·ish** \ʼblän-dish\ *adj*

²**blond** *or* **blonde** *n* : a person having blond hair

blood \ʼbləd\ *n* **1** : a usu. red liquid that circulates in the heart, arteries, and veins of animals **2** : LIFEBLOOD; *also* : LIFE **3** : LINEAGE, STOCK **4** : KINSHIP; *also* : KINDRED **5** : the taking of life **6** : TEMPER, PASSION **7** : DANDY 1 — **blood·less** *adj* — **bloody** *adj*

blood bank *n* : a place where blood or plasma is stored

blood·bath \ʼbləd-ˌbath, -ˌbȧth\ *n* : MASSACRE

blood count *n* : the determination of the number of blood cells in a specific volume of blood; *also* : the number of cells so determined

blood·cur·dling \ʼbləd-kərd-liŋ, -ˌkər-dᵊl-iŋ\ *adj* : arousing fright or horror

blood·ed \ʼblə-dəd\ *adj* **1** : having blood of a specified kind ⟨warm-*blooded* animals⟩ **2** : entirely or largely purebred ⟨∼ horses⟩

blood group *n* : one of the classes into which human beings can be separated by the presence or absence in their blood of specific antigens

blood·hound \ʼbləd-ˌhaünd\ *n* : any of a breed of large powerful hounds with long drooping ears, a wrinkled face, and keen sense of smell

blood·let·ting \-ˌle-tiŋ\ *n* **1** : PHLEBOTOMY **2** : BLOODSHED

blood·line \-ˌlīn\ *n* : a sequence of direct ancestors esp. in a pedigree

blood·mo·bile \-mō-ˌbēl\ *n* : a motor vehicle equipped for collecting blood from donors

blood poisoning *n* : invasion of the bloodstream by virulent microorganisms from a focus of infection accompanied esp. by chills, fever, and prostration

blood pressure *n* : pressure of the blood on the walls of blood vessels and esp. arteries

blood·root \ʼbləd-ˌrüt, -ˌrüt\ *n* : a plant related to the poppy that has a red root and sap, a solitary leaf, and a white flower in early spring

blood·shed \-ˌshed\ *n* : wounding or taking of life : CARNAGE, SLAUGHTER

blood·shot \-ˌshät\ *adj* : inflamed to redness ⟨∼ eyes⟩

blood·stain \-ˌstān\ *n* : a discoloration caused by blood — **blood·stained** \-ˌstānd\ *adj*

blood·stone \-ˌstōn\ *n* : a green quartz sprinkled with red spots

blood·stream \-ˌstrēm\ *n* : the flowing blood in a circulatory system

blood·suck·er \-ˌsə-kər\ *n* : an animal that sucks blood; *esp* : LEECH — **blood·suck·ing** *adj*

blood test *n* : a test of the blood; *esp* : one for syphilis

blood·thirsty \ʼbləd-ˌthər-stē\ *adj* : eager to shed blood

— **blood·thirst·i·ly** \-ˌthər-stə-lē\ *adv* — **blood·thirst·i·ness** \-stē-nəs\ *n*

blood type *n* : BLOOD GROUP — **blood–typ·ing** *n*

blood vessel *n* : a vessel (as a vein or artery) in which blood circulates in the body

Bloody Mary \-ʼmer-ē\ *n, pl* **Bloody Marys** : a drink made essentially of vodka and tomato juice

¹**bloom** \ʼblüm\ *n* **1** : FLOWER 1; *also* : flowers or amount of flowers (as of a plant) **2** : the period or state of flowering **3** : a state or time of beauty and vigor **4** : a powdery coating esp. on fruits and leaves **5** : rosy color; *also* : an appearance of freshness or health — **bloomy** *adj*

²**bloom** *vb* **1** : to produce or yield flowers **2** : MATURE **3** : to glow esp. with healthy color **syn** flower, blossom

bloo·mers \ʼblü-mərz\ *n pl* [Amelia *Bloomer* †1894 Am. reformer] : a woman's garment of short loose trousers gathered at the knee

bloop·er \ʼblü-pər\ *n* **1** : a fly ball hit barely beyond a baseball infield **2** : an embarrassing public blunder

¹**blos·som** \ʼblä-səm\ *n* **1** : the flower of a plant **2** : the period or state of flowering

²**blossom** *vb* : FLOWER, BLOOM

¹**blot** \ʼblät\ *n* **1** : SPOT, STAIN ⟨ink ∼s⟩ **2** : BLEMISH **syn** stigma, brand, slur

²**blot** *vb* **blot·ted; blot·ting** **1** : SPOT, STAIN **2** : OBSCURE, ECLIPSE ⟨∼ out the sun⟩ **3** *obs* : MAR; *esp* : DISGRACE **4** : to dry or remove with or as if with an absorbing material **5** : to make a blot

blotch \ʼbläch\ *n* : a usu. large and irregular spot or mark (as of ink or color) — **blotch** *vb* — **blotchy** *adj*

blot·ter \ʼblä-tər\ *n* **1** : a piece of blotting paper **2** : a book for preliminary records (as of sales or arrests)

blot·ting paper *n* : a spongy paper used to absorb ink

blouse \ʼblaüs, ʼblaüz\ *n* **1** : a loose outer garment like a smock **2** : a usu. loose garment reaching from the neck to about the waist

¹**blow** \ʼblō\ *vb* **blew** \ʼblü\; **blown** \ʼblōn\; **blow·ing** **1** : to move forcibly ⟨the wind *blew*⟩ **2** : to send forth a current of gas (as air) **3** : to act on with a current of gas or vapor; *esp* : to drive with such a current **4** : to sound or cause to sound ⟨∼ a horn⟩ **5** : PANT, GASP; *also* : to expel moist air in breathing ⟨the whale *blew*⟩ **6** : BOAST; *also* : BLUSTER **7** : MELT — used of an electrical fuse **8** : to shape or form by blown or injected air ⟨∼ glass⟩ **9** : to shatter or destroy by or as if by explosion **10** : to make breathless by exertion **11** : to spend recklessly **12** : to foul up hopelessly ⟨*blew* her lines⟩ — **blow·er** *n*

²**blow** *n* **1** : a usu. strong blowing of air : GALE **2** : BOASTING, BRAG **3** : an act or instance of blowing

³**blow** *vb* **blew** \ʼblü\; **blown** \ʼblōn\; **blow·ing** : FLOWER, BLOOM

⁴**blow** *n* **1** : a forcible stroke **2** : COMBAT ⟨come to ∼s⟩ **3** : a severe and usu. unexpected calamity

blow–by–blow *adj* : minutely detailed ⟨∼ account⟩

blow–dry \-ˌdrī\ *vb* : to dry and usu. style hair with a blow-dryer

blow–dryer \-ˌdrī(-ə)r\ *n* : a hand-held hair dryer

blow·fly \ʼblō-ˌflī\ *n* : any of a family of dipteran flies (as a bluebottle) that deposit their eggs or maggots on meat or in wounds

blow·gun \-ˌgən\ *n* : a tube from which an arrow or a dart may be shot by the force of the breath

blow·out \ʼblō-ˌaüt\ *n* : a bursting of something (as a tire) because of pressure of the contents (as air)

blow·sy *also* **blow·zy** \ʼblaü-zē\ *adj* : DISHEVELED, SLOVENLY

blow·torch \ʼblō-ˌtȯrch\ *n* : a small portable burner whose flame is made hotter by a blast of air or oxygen

blow·up \ʼblō-ˌəp\ *n* **1** : EXPLOSION **2** : an outburst of temper **3** : a photographic enlargement

blowy \ʼblō-ē\ *adj* : WINDY

BLT \ˌbē-ˌel-ˈtē\ *n* : a bacon, lettuce, and tomato sandwich

¹**blub·ber** \ˈblə-bər\ *vb* : to cry noisily

²**blubber** *n* 1 : the fat of large sea mammals (as whales) 2 : a noisy crying

¹**blud·geon** \ˈblə-jən\ *n* : a short often loaded club

²**bludgeon** *vb* : to strike with or as if with a bludgeon

¹**blue** \ˈblü\ *adj* **blu·er; blu·est** 1 : of the color blue; *also* : BLUISH 2 : MELANCHOLY; *also* : DEPRESSING 3 : PURITANICAL 4 : INDECENT — **blue·ness** *n*

²**blue** *n* 1 : a color between green and violet in the spectrum : the color of the clear daytime sky 2 : something (as clothing or the sky) that is blue

blue baby *n* : a baby with bluish skin due to faulty circulation caused by a heart defect

blue·bell \-ˌbel\ *n* : any of various plants with blue bell-shaped flowers

blue·ber·ry \ˈblü-ˌber-ē, -bə-rē\ *n* : the edible blue or blackish berry of various shrubs of the heath family; *also* : one of these shrubs

blue·bird \-ˌbərd\ *n* : any of several small No. American thrushes that are blue above and reddish-brown or pale blue below

blue·bon·net \ˈblü-ˌbä-nət\ *n* : either of two low-growing annual lupines of Texas with silky foliage and blue flowers

blue·bot·tle \ˈblü-ˌbät-ᵊl\ *n* : any of several blowflies with iridescent blue bodies or abdomens

blue cheese *n* : cheese having veins of greenish blue mold

blue–col·lar \ˈblü-ˈkä-lər\ *adj* : of, relating to, or being the class of workers whose duties call for work clothes

blue·fish \-ˌfish\ *n* : a marine sport and food fish bluish above and silvery below

blue·grass \-ˌgras\ *n* 1 : KENTUCKY BLUEGRASS 2 : country music played on stringed instruments having free improvisation and close harmonies

blue jay \-ˌjā\ *n* : a crested bright blue No. American jay

blue jeans *n pl* : pants usu. made of blue denim

blue·nose \ˈblü-ˌnōz\ *n* : a person who advocates a rigorous moral code

blue·point \-ˌpȯint\ *n* : a small oyster typically from the south shore of Long Island, New York

blue·print \-ˌprint\ *n* 1 : a photographic print in white on a blue ground used esp. for copying mechanical drawings and architects' plans 2 : a detailed plan of action — **blueprint** *vb*

blues \ˈblüz\ *n pl* 1 : MELANCHOLY 2 : music in a style marked by recurrent minor intervals and melancholy lyrics

blue·stock·ing \ˈblü-ˌstä-kiŋ\ *n* : a woman having intellectual interests

blu·et \ˈblü-ət\ *n* : a low No. American herb with dainty bluish flowers

blue whale *n* : a very large baleen whale that may reach a weight of 150 tons (135 metric tons) and a length of 100 feet (30 meters)

¹**bluff** \ˈbləf\ *adj* 1 : having a broad flattened front 2 : rising steeply with a broad flat front 3 : OUTSPOKEN, FRANK syn abrupt, blunt, brusque, curt, gruff

²**bluff** *n* : a high steep bank : CLIFF

³**bluff** *vb* : to frighten or deceive by pretense or a mere show of strength

⁴**bluff** *n* : an act or instance of bluffing; *also* : one who bluffs

blu·ing *or* **blue·ing** \ˈblü-iŋ\ *n* : a preparation used in laundering to counteract yellowing of white fabrics

blu·ish \ˈblü-ish\ *adj* : somewhat blue

¹**blun·der** \ˈblən-dər\ *vb* 1 : to move clumsily or unsteadily 2 : to make a stupid or needless mistake

²**blunder** *n* : an avoidable and usu. serious mistake

blun·der·buss \ˈblən-dər-ˌbəs\ *n* [obs. D *donderbus*, fr. D *donder* thunder + obs. D *bus* gun] : an obsolete short-barreled firearm with a flaring muzzle

blunderbuss

¹**blunt** \ˈblənt\ *adj* 1 : not sharp : DULL 2 : lacking in tact : BLUFF syn brusque, curt, gruff, abrupt, crusty — **blunt·ly** *adv* — **blunt·ness** *n*

²**blunt** *vb* : to make or become dull

¹**blur** \ˈblər\ *n* 1 : a smear or stain that obscures 2 : something vaguely perceived; *esp* : something moving too quickly to be clearly perceived — **blur·ry** \-ē\ *adj*

²**blur** *vb* **blurred; blur·ring** : DIM, CLOUD, OBSCURE

blurb \ˈblərb\ *n* : a short publicity notice (as on a book jacket)

blurt \ˈblərt\ *vb* : to utter suddenly and impulsively

blush \ˈbləsh\ *n* : a reddening of the face (as from modesty or confusion) : FLUSH — **blush** *vb* — **blush·ful** *adj*

blus·ter \ˈbləs-tər\ *vb* 1 : to blow in stormy noisy gusts 2 : to talk or act with noisy swaggering threats — **bluster** *n* — **blus·tery** \-tə-rē\ *adj*

blvd *abbr* boulevard

B lymphocyte *n* : B CELL

BM *abbr* bowel movement

B movie *n* : a cheaply produced motion picture

BO *abbr* 1 best offer 2 body odor 3 box office 4 branch office

boa \ˈbō-ə\ *n* 1 : a large snake (as the **boa con·stric·tor** \-kən-ˈstrik-tər\ or the related anaconda) that suffocates and kills its prey by constriction 2 : a fluffy scarf usu. of fur or feathers

boar \ˈbōr\ *n* : a male swine; *also* : WILD BOAR

¹**board** \ˈbōrd\ *n* 1 : the side of a ship 2 : a thin flat length of sawed lumber; *also* : material (as cardboard) or a piece of material formed as a thin flat firm sheet 3 *pl* : STAGE 1 4 : a table spread with a meal; *also* : daily meals esp. when furnished for pay 5 : a table at which a council or magistrates sit 6 : a group or association of persons organized for a special responsibility (as the management of a business or institution); *also* : an organized commercial exchange 7 : a sheet of insulating material carrying circuit elements and inserted in an electronic device

²**board** *vb* 1 : to go or put aboard ⟨~ a boat⟩ 2 : to cover with boards 3 : to provide or be provided with meals and often lodging — **board·er** *n*

board·ing·house \ˈbȯr-diŋ-ˌhaus\ *n* : a house at which persons are boarded

board·room \ˈbȯrd-ˌrüm, ˈbȯrd-, -ˌrum\ *n* : a room that is designated for meetings of a board

board·walk \ˈbȯrd-ˌwȯk\ *n* : a promenade (as of planking) along a beach

boast \ˈbōst\ *vb* 1 : to praise oneself 2 : to mention or assert with excessive pride 3 : to prize as a possession; *also* : HAVE ⟨the house ~s a fireplace⟩ — **boast** *n* — **boast·ful** \-fəl\ *adj* — **boast·ful·ly** *adv*

boat \ˈbōt\ *n* : a small vessel for travel on water; *also* : SHIP

boat·er \ˈbō-tər\ *n* 1 : one that travels in a boat 2 : a stiff straw hat

boat·man \ˈbōt-mən\ *n* : a man who operates, works on, or deals in boats

---

\ə\abut \ᵊ\kitten \ər\further \a\ash \ā\ace \ä\mop, mar
\aù\out \ch\chin \e\bet \ē\easy \g\go \i\hit \ī\ice \j\job
\ŋ\sing \ō\go \ȯ\law \ȯi\boy \th\thin \t͟h\the \ü\loot \ù\foot
\y\yet \zh\vision *see also* Pronunciation Symbols page

boat people *n pl* : refugees fleeing by boat
boat·swain \'bōs-ᵊn\ *n* : a subordinate officer of a ship in charge of the hull and related equipment
¹**bob** \'bäb\ *vb* **bobbed; bob·bing 1 :** to move up and down jerkily or repeatedly **2 :** to emerge, arise, or appear suddenly or unexpectedly
²**bob** *n* : a bobbing movement
³**bob** *n* **1 :** a knob, knot, twist, or curl esp. of ribbons, yarn, or hair **2 :** a short haircut of a woman or child **3 :** FLOAT 2 **4 :** a weight hanging from a line
⁴**bob** *vb* **bobbed; bob·bing :** to cut hair in a bob
⁵**bob** *n, pl* **bob** *slang Brit* : SHILLING
bob·bin \'bä-bən\ *n* : a cylinder or spindle for holding or dispensing thread (as in a sewing machine)
bob·ble \'bä-bəl\ *vb* **bob·bled; bob·bling :** FUMBLE — **bobble** *n*
bob·by \'bä-bē\ *n, pl* **bobbies** [*Bobby,* nickname for Sir *Robert* Peel, who organized the London police force] *Brit* : a police officer
bobby pin *n* : a flat wire hairpin with prongs that press close together
bob·cat \'bäb-ˌkat\ *n* : a small usu. rusty-colored No. American lynx
bob·o·link \'bä-bə-ˌliŋk\ *n* : an American migratory songbird related to the meadowlarks
bob·sled \'bäb-ˌsled\ *n* **1 :** a short sled usu. used as one of a joined pair **2 :** a racing sled with two pairs of runners, a steering wheel, and a hand brake — **bobsled** *vb*
bob·white \(ˌ)bäb-'hwīt\ *n* : any of a genus of quail; *esp* : a popular game bird of the eastern and central U.S.
boc·cie *or* **boc·ci** *or* **boc·ce** \'bä-chē\ *n* : Italian lawn bowling played on a long narrow court
bock \'bäk\ *n* : a dark heavy beer usu. sold in early spring
bod \'bäd\ *n* : BODY
¹**bode** \'bōd\ *vb* **bod·ed; bod·ing :** to indicate by signs : PRESAGE
²**bode** *past of* BIDE
bo·de·ga \bō-'dā-gə\ *n* [Sp, fr. L *apotheca* storehouse] : a store specializing in Hispanic groceries
bod·ice \'bä-dəs\ *n* [alter. of *bodies,* pl. of *body*] : the usu. close-fitting part of a dress above the waist
bodi·less \'bä-di-ləs\ *adj* : lacking a body or material form
¹**bodi·ly** \'bäd-ᵊl-ē\ *adj* : of or relating to the body ⟨~ contact⟩
²**bodily** *adv* **1 :** in the flesh **2 :** as a whole ⟨lifted the crate up ~⟩
bod·kin \'bäd-kən\ *n* **1 :** DAGGER **2 :** a pointed implement for punching holes in cloth **3 :** a blunt needle for drawing tape or ribbon through a loop or hem
body \'bä-dē\ *n, pl* **bod·ies 1 :** the physical whole of a living or dead organism; *also* : the trunk or main mass of an organism as distinguished from its appendages **2 :** a human being : PERSON **3 :** the main part of something **4 :** a mass of matter distinct from other masses **5 :** GROUP **6 :** VISCOSITY, FIRMNESS **7 :** richness of flavor — used esp. of wines — **bod·ied** \'bä-dēd\ *adj*
body English *n* : bodily motions made in a usu. unconscious effort to influence the movement of a propelled object (as a ball)
body·guard \'bä-dē-ˌgärd\ *n* : a personal guard; *also* : RETINUE
body stocking *n* : a sheer close-fitting one-piece garment for the torso that often has sleeves and legs
body·work \'bä-dē-ˌwərk\ *n* : the making or repairing of vehicle bodies
Boer \'bōr, 'bùr\ *n* [D, lit., farmer] : a South African of Dutch or Huguenot descent
¹**bog** \'bäg, 'bòg\ *n* : wet, spongy, poorly drained, and usu. acid ground — **bog·gy** *adj*
²**bog** *vb* **bogged; bog·ging :** to sink into or as if into a bog
bo·gey *also* **bo·gie** *or* **bo·gy** \'bù-gē, 'bō- *for 1*; 'bō- *for*

2\ *n, pl* **bogeys** *also* **bogies 1 :** SPECTER, HOBGOBLIN; *also* : a source of fear or annoyance **2 :** a score of one over par on a hole in golf
bo·gey·man \'bù-gē-ˌman, 'bō-, 'bü-\ *n* : an imaginary monster used in threatening children
bog·gle \'bä-gəl\ *vb* **bog·gled; bog·gling :** to overwhelm or be overwhelmed with fright or amazement
bo·gus \'bō-gəs\ *adj* : SPURIOUS, SHAM
Bo·he·mi·an \bō-'hē-mē-ən\ *n* **1 :** a native or inhabitant of Bohemia **2** *often not cap* : VAGABOND, WANDERER **3** *often not cap* : a person (as a writer or artist) living an unconventional life — **bohemian** *adj, often cap*
¹**boil** \'bòil\ *n* : an inflamed swelling on the skin containing pus
²**boil** *vb* **1 :** to heat or become heated to a temperature (**boiling point**) at which vapor is formed and rises in bubbles ⟨water ~s and changes to steam⟩; *also* : to act on or be acted on by a boiling liquid ⟨~ eggs⟩ **2 :** to be in a state of seething agitation
³**boil** *n* : the act or state of boiling
boil·er \'bòi-lər\ *n* **1 :** a container in which something is boiled **2 :** a strong vessel used in making steam **3 :** a tank holding hot water
boil·er·mak·er \'bòi-lər-ˌmā-kər\ *n* : whiskey with a beer chaser
bois·ter·ous \'bòi-st(ə-)rəs\ *adj* : noisily turbulent or exuberant — **bois·ter·ous·ly** *adv*
bok choy \'bäk-'chòi\ *n* : a Chinese vegetable related to the mustards that forms a loose head of green leaves with long thick white stalks
bo·la \'bō-lə\ *or* **bo·las** \-ləs\ *n, pl* **bolas** \-ləz\ *also* **bolas·es** [AmerSp *bolas,* fr. Sp *bola* ball] : a cord with weights attached to the ends for hurling at and entangling an animal

bola

bold \'bōld\ *adj* **1 :** COURAGEOUS, INTREPID **2 :** IMPUDENT **3 :** STEEP **4 :** ADVENTUROUS, FREE ⟨a ~ thinker⟩ **syn** dauntless, brave, valiant — **bold·ly** *adv* — **bold·ness** \'bōld-nəs\ *n*
bold·face \'bōld-ˌfās\ *n* : a heavy-faced type; *also* : printing in boldface — **bold–faced** \-'fāst\ *adj*
bole \'bōl\ *n* : the trunk of a tree
bo·le·ro \bə-'ler-ō\ *n, pl* **-ros 1 :** a Spanish dance or its music **2 :** a short loose jacket open at the front
bo·li·var \bə-'lē-ˌvär, 'bä-lə-vər\ *n, pl* **-va·res** \ˌbä-lə-'vär-ˌās, ˌbō-\ *or* **-vars** — see MONEY table
Bo·liv·i·an \bə-'li-vē-ən\ *n* : a native or inhabitant of Bolivia — **Bolivian** *adj*
bo·li·vi·a·no \bə-ˌli-vē-'ä-(ˌ)nō\ *n, pl* **-nos** — see MONEY table
boll \'bōl\ *n* : a seed pod (as of cotton)

boll weevil *n* : a small grayish weevil that infests the cotton plant both as a larva and as an adult

boll·worm \'bōl-₁wərm\ *n* : any of several moths and esp. the corn earworm whose larvae feed on cotton bolls

bo·lo·gna \bə-'lō-nē\ *n* [short for *Bologna sausage*, fr. *Bologna*, Italy] : a large smoked sausage of beef, veal, and pork

Bol·she·vik \'bōl-shə-₁vik\ *n, pl* **Bolsheviks** *also* **Bol·she·vi·ki** \₁bōl-shə-'vi-kē\ [Russ *bol'shevik*, fr. *bol'shǐǐ* larger] **1** : a member of the party that seized power in Russia in the revolution of November 1917 **2** : COMMUNIST — **Bolshevik** *adj*

bol·she·vism \'bōl-shə-₁vi-zəm\ *n, often cap* : the doctrine or program of the Bolsheviks advocating violent overthrow of capitalism

¹bol·ster \'bōl-stər\ *n* : a long pillow or cushion

²bolster *vb* : to support with or as if with a bolster; *also* : REINFORCE

¹bolt \'bōlt\ *n* **1** : a missile (as an arrow) for a crossbow or catapult **2** : a flash of lightning : THUNDERBOLT **3** : a sliding bar used to fasten a door **4** : a roll of cloth or wallpaper of specified length **5** : a rod with a head at one end and a screw thread at the other used with a nut to fasten objects together **6** : a metal cylinder that drives the cartridge into the chamber of a firearm

²bolt *vb* **1** : to move suddenly (as in fright or hurry) : START, DASH **2** : to break away (as from association) ⟨~ from a political platform⟩ **3** : to produce seed prematurely **4** : to secure or fasten with a bolt **5** : to swallow hastily or without chewing

³bolt *n* : an act of bolting

bo·lus \'bō-ləs\ *n* **1** : a large pill **2** : a soft mass of chewed food

¹bomb \'bäm\ *n* **1** : a fused explosive device designed to detonate under specified conditions (as impact) **2** : an aerosol or foam dispenser (as of insecticide or hair spray) : SPRAY CAN **3** : a long pass in football

²bomb *vb* : to attack with bombs

bom·bard \bäm-'bärd\ *vb* **1** : to attack esp. with artillery or bombers **2** : to assail persistently **3** : to subject to the impact of rapidly moving particles (as electrons) — **bom·bard·ment** *n*

bom·bar·dier \₁bäm-bər-'dir\ *n* : a bomber-crew member who releases the bombs

bom·bast \'bäm-₁bast\ *n* [ME, cotton padding, fr. MF *bombace*, fr. ML *bombax* cotton, alter. of L *bombyx* silkworm, silk, fr. Gk] : pretentious wordy speech or writing — **bom·bas·tic** \bäm-'bas-tik\ *adj* — **bom·bas·ti·cal·ly** \-ti-k(ə-)lē\ *adv*

bom·ba·zine \₁bäm-bə-'zēn\ *n* **1** : a twilled fabric with silk warp and worsted filling **2** : a silk fabric in twill weave dyed black

bomb·er \'bä-mər\ *n* : one that bombs; *esp* : an airplane for dropping bombs

bomb·proof \'bäm-₁prüf\ *adj* : safe against the explosive force of bombs

bomb·shell \'bäm-₁shel\ *n* **1** : BOMB 1 **2** : one that stuns, amazes, or completely upsets

bona fide \'bō-nə-₁fīd, 'bä-; ₁bō-nə-'fī-dē, -də\ *adj* [L, in good faith] **1** : made in good faith ⟨a *bona fide* agreement⟩ **2** : GENUINE, REAL ⟨a *bona fide* bargain⟩

bo·nan·za \bə-'nan-zə\ *n* [Sp, lit., calm sea, fr. ML *bonacia*, alter. of L *malacia*, fr. Gk *malakia*, lit., softness, fr. *malakos* soft] : something yielding a rich return

bon·bon \'bän-₁bän\ *n* : a candy with a creamy center and a soft covering (as of chocolate)

¹bond \'bänd\ *n* **1** : a binding or uniting force or tie ⟨~s of friendship⟩ **3** : an agreement or obligation often made binding by a pledge of money or goods **4** : a person who acts as surety for another **5** : an interest-bearing certificate of public or private indebtedness **6**

: the state of goods subject to supervision pending payment of taxes or duties due

²bond *vb* **1** : to assure payment of duties or taxes on (goods) by giving a bond **2** : to insure against losses caused by the acts of ⟨~ a bank teller⟩ **3** : to make or become firmly united as if by bonds ⟨~ iron to copper⟩

bond·age \'bän-dij\ *n* : SLAVERY, SERVITUDE

bond·hold·er \'bänd-₁hōl-dər\ *n* : one that owns a government or corporation bond

bond·ing *n* **1** : the formation of a close personal relationship esp. through frequent or constant association **2** : the attaching of a material (as porcelain) to a tooth surface esp. for cosmetic purposes

bond·man \'bänd-mən\ *n* : SLAVE, SERF

¹bonds·man \'bändz-mən\ *n* : SURETY 3

²bondsman *n* : BONDMAN

bond·wom·an \'bänd-₁wu̇-mən\ *n* : a female slave or serf

¹bone \'bōn\ *n* **1** : a hard largely calcareous tissue forming most of the skeleton of a vertebrate animal; *also* : one of the pieces of bone making up a vertebrate skeleton **2** : a hard animal substance (as ivory or baleen) similar to true bone **3** : something made of bone — **bone·less** *adj* — **bony** *also* **bon·ey** \'bō-nē\ *adj*

²bone *vb* **boned; bon·ing** : to free from bones ⟨~ a chicken⟩

bone black *n* : the black carbon residue from calcined bones used esp. as a pigment

bone meal *n* : crushed or ground bone used esp. as fertilizer or feed

bon·er \'bō-nər\ *n* : a stupid and ridiculous blunder

bone up *vb* **1** : CRAM **2** : to refresh one's memory ⟨*boned* up on the speech before giving it⟩

bon·fire \'bän-₁fīr\ *n* [ME *bonefire* a fire of bones, fr. *bon* bone + *fire*] : a large fire built in the open air

bon·go \'bäŋ-gō\ *n, pl* **bongos** *also* **bongoes** [AmerSp *bongó*] : one of a pair of small tuned drums played with the hands

bon·ho·mie \₁bä-nə-'mē\ *n* [F *bonhomie*, fr. *bonhomme* good-natured man, fr. *bon* good + *homme* man] : good-natured easy friendliness

bo·ni·to \bə-'nē-tō\ *n, pl* **-tos** *or* **-to** : any of several medium-sized tunas

bon mot \bōⁿ-'mō\ *n, pl* **bons mots** *same*\ *or* **bon mots** *same or* -'mō\ [F, lit., good word] : a clever remark

bon·net \'bä-nət\ *n* : a covering (as a cap) for the head; *esp* : a hat for a woman or infant tied under the chin

bon·ny \'bä-nē\ *adj* **bon·ni·er; -est** *chiefly Brit* : ATTRACTIVE, FAIR; *also* : FINE, EXCELLENT

bon·sai \bōn-'sı\ *n, pl* **bonsai** [Jp] : a potted plant (as a tree) dwarfed by special methods of culture; *also* : the art of growing such a plant

bo·nus \'bō-nəs\ *n* : something in addition to what is expected

bon vi·vant \₁bän-vē-'vänt, ₁bōⁿ-vē-'väⁿ\ *n, pl* **bons vivants** \₁bän-vē-'vänts, ₁bōⁿ-vē-'väⁿ\ *or* **bon vivants** *same*\ [F, lit., good liver] : a person having cultivated, refined, and sociable tastes esp. in food and drink

bon voy·age \₁bōⁿ-₁vȯi-'äzh, ₁bän-; ₁bōⁿ-₁vwä-'yäzh\ *n* : FAREWELL — often used as an interjection

bony fish *n* : any of a very large group of fishes (as a salmon or marlin) with a bony rather than a cartilaginous skeleton

bonze \'bänz\ *n* : a Buddhist monk

boo \'bü\ *n, pl* **boos** : a shout of disapproval or contempt — **boo** *vb*

boo·by \'bü-bē\ *n, pl* **boobies** : an awkward foolish person : DOPE

booby hatch *n* : an insane asylum

\ə\abut \ᵊ\kitten \ər\further \a\ash \ā\ace \ä\mop, mar \au̇\out \ch\chin \e\bet \ē\easy \g\go \i\hit \ī\ice \j\job \ŋ\sing \ō\go \ȯ\law \ȯi\boy \th\thin \t͟h\the \ü\loot \u̇\foot \y\yet \zh\vision *see also* Pronunciation Symbols page

booby prize *n* : an award for the poorest performance in a contest

booby trap *n* : a trap for the unwary; *esp* : a concealed explosive device set to go off when some harmless‑looking object is touched — **booby–trap** *vb*

boo·dle \'büd‑ᵊl\ *n* **1** : bribe money **2** : a large amount of money

¹book \'bùk\ *n* **1** : a set of sheets bound into a volume **2** : a long written or printed narrative or record **3** : a major division of a long literary work **4** *cap* : BIBLE

²book *vb* **1** : to engage, reserve, or schedule by or as if by writing in a book ⟨∼ seats on a plane⟩ **2** : to enter charges against in a police register

book·case \‑ₖās\ *n* : a piece of furniture consisting of shelves to hold books

book·end \‑ₑend\ *n* : a support to hold up a row of books

book·ie \'bù‑kē\ *n* : BOOKMAKER

book·ish \'bù‑kish\ *adj* **1** : fond of books and reading **2** : inclined to rely unduly on book knowledge

book·keep·er \'bùk‑ₖē‑pər\ *n* : one who records the accounts or transactions of a business — **book·keep·ing** *n*

book·let \'bùk‑lət\ *n* : PAMPHLET

book·mak·er \'bùk‑ₘā‑kər\ *n* : one who determines odds and receives and pays off bets — **book·mak·ing** *n*

book·mark \‑ₘärk\ *or* **book·mark·er** \‑ₘär‑kər\ *n* : a marker for finding a place in a book

book·mo·bile \'bùk‑mō‑ₖbēl\ *n* : a truck that serves as a traveling library

book·plate \'bùk‑ₚplāt\ *n* : a label pasted in a book to show who owns it

book·sell·er \'bùk‑ₛse‑lər\ *n* : one who sells books; *esp* : the proprietor of a bookstore

book·shelf \‑ₛhelf \ *n* : a shelf for books

book·worm \'bùk‑ₖwərm\ *n* : a person unusually devoted to reading and study

¹boom \'büm\ *vb* **1** : to make a deep hollow sound : RESOUND **2** : to grow or cause to grow rapidly esp. in value, esteem, or importance

²boom *n* **1** : a booming sound or cry **2** : a rapid expansion or increase esp. of economic activity

³boom *n* **1** : a long spar used to extend the bottom of a sail **2** : a line of floating timbers used to obstruct passage or catch floating objects **3** : a beam projecting from the upright pole of a derrick to support or guide the object lifted

boom box *n* : a large portable radio and often tape player

boo·mer·ang \'bü‑mə‑ₖraŋ\ *n* [Dharuk (an Australian aboriginal language *bumarin*ʸ] : a bent or angular club that can be so thrown as to return near the starting point

¹boon \'bün\ *n* [ME, fr. ON *bōn* petition] : BENEFIT, BLESSING **syn** favor, gift, largess, present

²boon *adj* [ME *bon*, fr. MF, good] : CONVIVIAL ⟨a ∼ companion⟩

boon·docks \'bün‑ₖdäks\ *n pl* [Tagalog (language of the Philippines) *bundok* mountain] **1** : rough country filled with dense brush **2** : a rural area

boon·dog·gle \'bün‑ₖdä‑gəl, ‑ₖdȯ‑\ *n* : a useless or wasteful project or activity

boor \'bùr\ *n* **1** : YOKEL **2** : a rude or insensitive person **syn** churl, lout, clown, clodhopper — **boor·ish** *adj*

boost \'büst\ *vb* **1** : to push up from below **2** : INCREASE, RAISE ⟨∼ prices⟩ **3** : AID, PROMOTE ⟨voted a bonus to ∼ morale⟩ — **boost** *n* — **boost·er** *n*

¹boot \'büt\ *n*, *chiefly dial* : something to equalize a trade — **to boot** : BESIDES

²boot *vb*, *archaic* : AVAIL, PROFIT

³boot *n* **1** : a covering for the foot and leg **2** : a protective sheath (as of a flower) **3** *Brit* : an automobile trunk **4** : KICK; *also* : a discharge from employment **5** : a navy or marine corps trainee

⁴boot *vb* **1** : KICK **2** : to eject or discharge summarily

boot·black \'büt‑ₖblak\ *n* : a person who shines shoes

boo·tee *or* **boo·tie** \'bü‑tē\ *n* : an infant's knitted or crocheted sock

booth \'büth\ *n*, *pl* **booths** \'büthz, 'büths\ **1** : a small enclosed stall (as at a fair) **2** : a small enclosure giving privacy for a person ⟨voting ∼⟩ ⟨telephone ∼⟩ **3** : a restaurant accommodation having a table between backed benches

boot·leg \'büt‑ₖleg\ *vb* : to make, transport, or sell (as liquor) illegally — **boot·leg** *adj or n* — **boot·leg·ger** *n*

boot·less \'büt‑ləs\ *adj* : USELESS **syn** futile, vain, abortive, fruitless — **boot·less·ly** *adv* — **boot·less·ness** *n*

boo·ty \'bü‑tē\ *n*, *pl* **booties** : PLUNDER, SPOIL

¹booze \'büz\ *vb* **boozed; booz·ing** : to drink liquor to excess — **booz·er** *n*

²booze *n* : intoxicating liquor — **boozy** *adj*

bop \'bäp\ *vb* **bopped; bop·ping** : HIT, SOCK — **bop** *n*

BOQ *abbr* bachelor officers' quarters

bor *abbr* borough

bo·rate \'bōr‑ₖāt\ *n* : a salt or ester of boric acid

bo·rax \'bōr‑ₖaks\ *n* : a crystalline borate of sodium that occurs as a mineral and is used as a flux and cleanser

bor·del·lo \bȯr‑'de‑lō\ *n*, *pl* **-los** [It] : BROTHEL

¹bor·der \'bȯr‑dər\ *n* **1** : EDGE, MARGIN **2** : BOUNDARY, FRONTIER **syn** rim, brim, brink, fringe, perimeter

²border *vb* **bor·dered; bor·der·ing 1** : to put a border on **2** : ADJOIN **3** : VERGE

bor·der·land \'bȯr‑dər‑ₖland\ *n* **1** : territory at or near a border **2** : an outlying or intermediate region often not clearly defined

bor·der·line \‑ₖlīn\ *adj* : being in an intermediate position or state; *esp* : not quite up to what is standard or expected ⟨∼ intelligence⟩

¹bore \'bōr\ *vb* **bored; bor·ing 1** : to make a hole in with or as if with a drill **2** : to make (as a well) by boring or digging away material **syn** perforate, drill, prick, puncture — **bor·er** *n*

²bore *n* **1** : a hole made by or as if by boring **2** : a cylindrical cavity **3** : the diameter of a hole or tube; *esp* : the interior diameter of a gun barrel or engine cylinder

³bore *past of* BEAR

⁴bore *n* : a tidal flood with a high abrupt front

⁵bore *n* : one that causes boredom

⁶bore *vb* **bored; bor·ing** : to weary with tedious dullness

bo·re·al \'bōr‑ē‑əl\ *adj* : of, relating to, or located in northern regions

bore·dom \'bōr‑dəm\ *n* : the condition of being bored

bo·ric acid \'bōr‑ik‑\ *n* : a white crystalline weak acid that contains boron and is used esp. as an antiseptic

born \'bȯrn\ *adj* **1** : brought into life by birth **2** : NATIVE ⟨American‑*born*⟩ **3** : having special natural abilities or character from birth ⟨a ∼ leader⟩

born–again *adj* : having experienced a revival of a personal faith or conviction ⟨∼ believer⟩ ⟨∼ liberal⟩

borne *past part of* BEAR

bo·ron \'bōr‑ₖän\ *n* : a chemical element that occurs in nature only in combination (as in borax) — see ELEMENT table

bor·ough \'bər‑ō\ *n* **1** : a British town that sends one or more members to Parliament; *also* : an incorporated British urban area **2** : an incorporated town or village in some U.S. states; *also* : any of the five political divisions of New York City **3** : a civil division of the state of Alaska corresponding to a county in most other states

bor·row \'bär‑ō\ *vb* **1** : to take or receive (something) temporarily and with intent to return **2** : to take into possession or use from another source : DERIVE, APPROPRIATE ⟨∼ a metaphor⟩

borscht \'bȯrsht\ *or* **borsch** \'bȯrsh\ *n* [Yiddish *borsht* & Ukrainian & Russ *borshch*] : a soup made mainly from beets

bosh \'bäsh\ *n* [Turk *boş* empty] : foolish talk or action : NONSENSE

bosky \'bäs-kē\ *adj* : covered with trees or shrubs

¹bos·om \'bu̇-zəm, 'bü-\ *n* **1** : the front of the human chest; *esp* : the female breasts **2** : the seat of secret thoughts and feelings **3** : the part of a garment covering the breast — **bos·omed** \-zəmd\ *adj*

²bosom *adj* : CLOSE, INTIMATE

¹boss \'bäs, 'bȯs\ *n* : a knoblike ornament : STUD

²boss *vb* : to ornament with bosses

³boss \'bȯs\ *n* **1** : one (as a foreman or manager) exercising control or supervision **2** : a politician who controls votes or dictates policies — **bossy** *adj*

⁴boss \'bȯs\ *vb* : to act as a boss : SUPERVISE

bo·sun \'bōs-ᵊn\ *var of* BOATSWAIN

bot *abbr* botanical; botanist; botany

bot·a·ny \'bät-ᵊn-ē, 'bät-nē\ *n, pl* **-nies 1** : a branch of biology dealing with plants and plant life **2** : plant life (as of a given region); *also* : the biology of a plant or plant group — **bo·tan·i·cal** \bə-'ta-ni-kəl\ *adj* — **bot·a·nist** \'bät-ᵊn-ist, 'bät-nist\ *n* — **bot·a·nize** \-ᵊn-ˌīz\ *vb*

botch \'bäch\ *vb* : to foul up hopelessly : BUNGLE — **botch** *n*

¹both \'bōth\ *pron* : both ones : the one as well as the other

²both *conj* — used as a function word to indicate and stress the inclusion of each of two or more things specified by coordinated words, phrases, or clauses ⟨∼ New York and London⟩

³both *adj* : being the two : affecting the one and the other

both·er \'bä-thər\ *vb* : WORRY, PESTER, TROUBLE **syn** vex, annoy, irk, provoke — **bother** *n* — **both·er·some** \-səm\ *adj*

¹bot·tle \'bät-ᵊl\ *n* **1** : a container (as of glass) with a narrow neck and usu. no handles **2** : the quantity held by a bottle **3** : intoxicating liquor

²bottle *vb* **bot·tled; bot·tling 1** : to confine as if in a bottle : RESTRAIN **2** : to put into a bottle

bot·tle·neck \'bät-ᵊl-ˌnek\ *n* **1** : a narrow passage or point of congestion **2** : something that obstructs or impedes

¹bot·tom \'bä-təm\ *n* **1** : an under or supporting surface; *also* : BUTTOCKS **2** : the surface on which a body of water lies **3** : the lowest part or place; *also* : an inferior position ⟨start at the ∼⟩ **4** : BOTTOMLAND — **bottom** *adj* — **bot·tom·less** *adj*

²bottom *vb* **1** : to furnish with a bottom **2** : to reach the bottom **3** : to reach a low point before rebounding — usu. used with *out*

bot·tom·land \'bä-təm-ˌland\ *n* : low land along a river

bottom line *n* **1** : the essential point : CRUX **2** : the final result : OUTCOME

bot·u·lism \'bä-chə-ˌli-zəm\ *n* : an acute paralytic disease caused by a bacterial toxin esp. in food

bou·doir \'bü-ˌdwär, 'bu̇-, ˌbü-ˈ, ˌbu̇-ˈ\ *n* [F, fr. *bouder* to pout] : a woman's dressing room or bedroom

bouf·fant \bü-'fänt, 'bü-ˌfänt\ *adj* [F] : puffed out ⟨∼ hairdos⟩

bough \'bau̇\ *n* : a usu. large or main branch of a tree

bought *past and past part of* BUY

bouil·la·baisse \ˌbü-yə-'bäs\ *n* [F] : a highly seasoned fish stew made with at least two kinds of fish

bouil·lon \'bü-ˌyän; 'bu̇l-ˌyän, -yən\ *n* : a clear soup made usu. from beef

boul·der \'bōl-dər\ *n* : a large detached rounded or worn mass of rock — **boul·dered** \-dərd\ *adj*

bou·le·vard \'bu̇-lə-ˌvärd, 'bü-\ *n* [F, modif. of MD *bolwerc* bulwark] : a broad often landscaped thoroughfare

bounce \'bau̇ns\ *vb* **bounced; bounc·ing 1** : to cause to rebound ⟨∼ a ball⟩ **2** : to rebound after striking — **bounce** *n* — **bouncy** \'bau̇n-sē\ *adj*

bounc·er \'bau̇n-sər\ *n* : a person employed in a public place to remove disorderly persons

¹bound \'bau̇nd\ *adj* : intending to go

²bound *n* : LIMIT, BOUNDARY — **bound·less** *adj* — **bound·less·ness** *n*

³bound *vb* **1** : to set limits to **2** : to form the boundary of **3** : to name the boundaries of

⁴bound *past and past part of* BIND

⁵bound *adj* **1** : constrained by or as if by bonds : CONFINED, OBLIGED **2** : enclosed in a binding or cover **3** : RESOLVED, DETERMINED; *also* : SURE

⁶bound *n* **1** : LEAP, JUMP **2** : REBOUND, BOUNCE

⁷bound *vb* : SPRING, BOUNCE

bound·ary \'bau̇n-drē\ *n, pl* **-aries** : something that marks or fixes a limit (as of territory) **syn** border, frontier, march

bound·en \'bau̇n-dən\ *adj* : BINDING

boun·te·ous \'bau̇n-tē-əs\ *adj* **1** : GENEROUS **2** : ABUNDANT — **boun·te·ous·ly** *adv* — **boun·te·ous·ness** *n*

boun·ti·ful \'bau̇n-ti-fəl\ *adj* **1** : giving freely **2** : PLENTIFUL — **boun·ti·ful·ly** *adv* — **boun·ti·ful·ness** *n*

boun·ty \'bau̇n-tē\ *n, pl* **bounties** [ME *bounte* goodness, fr. OF *bonté*, fr. L *bonitas*, fr. *bonus* good] **1** : GENEROSITY **2** : something given liberally **3** : a reward, premium, or subsidy given usu. for doing something

bou·quet \bō-'kā, bü-\ *n* [F, fr. MF, thicket, fr. OF *bosc* forest] **1** : flowers picked and fastened together in a bunch **2** : a distinctive aroma (as of wine) **syn** scent, fragrance, perfume, redolence

bour·bon \'bər-bən\ *n* : a whiskey distilled from a corn mash

bour·geois \'bu̇rzh-ˌwä, bu̇rzh-'wä\ *n, pl* **bourgeois** *same or* -ˌwäz, -'wäz\ [MF, lit., citizen of a town, fr. *borc* town, borough, fr. L *burgus* fortified place, fr. Gmc origin] : a middle-class person — **bourgeois** *adj*

bour·geoi·sie \ˌbu̇rzh-ˌwä-'zē\ *n* : a social order dominated by bourgeois

bourne *also* **bourn** \'bōrn, 'bu̇rn\ *n* : BOUNDARY; *also* : DESTINATION

bourse \'bu̇rs\ *n* : a European stock exchange

bout \'bau̇t\ *n* **1** : CONTEST, MATCH **2** : OUTBREAK, ATTACK ⟨a ∼ of measles⟩ **3** : SESSION

bou·tique \bü-'tēk\ *n* : a small fashionable specialty shop

bou·ton·niere \ˌbüt-ᵊn-'iər\ *n* : a flower or bouquet worn in a buttonhole

bo·vine \'bō-ˌvīn, -ˌvēn\ *adj* **1** : of or relating to oxen or cows **2** : having qualities (as placidity or dullness) characteristic of oxen or cows — **bovine** *n*

¹bow \'bau̇\ *vb* **1** : SUBMIT, YIELD **2** : to bend the head or body (as in submission, courtesy, or assent)

²bow *n* : an act or posture of bowing

³bow \'bō\ *n* **1** : BEND, ARCH; *esp* : RAINBOW **2** : a weapon for shooting arrows; *also* : ARCHER **3** : a knot formed by doubling a line into two or more loops **4** : a wooden rod strung with horsehairs for playing an instrument of the violin family

⁴bow \'bō\ *vb* **1** : BEND, CURVE **2** : to play (an instrument) with a bow

⁵bow \'bau̇\ *n* : the forward part of a ship — **bow** *adj*

bowd·ler·ize \'bōd-lə-ˌrīz, 'bau̇d-\ *vb* **-ized; -iz·ing** : to expurgate by omitting parts considered vulgar

bow·el \'bau̇(-ə)l\ *n* **1** : INTESTINE; *also* : one of the divisions of the intestine — usu. used in pl. **2** *pl* : the inmost parts ⟨the ∼s of the earth⟩

bow·er \'bau̇(-ə)r\ *n* : a shelter of boughs or vines : ARBOR

¹bowl \'bōl\ *n* **1** : a concave vessel used to hold liquids **2** : a drinking vessel **3** : a bowl-shaped part or structure — **bowl·ful** \-ˌfu̇l\ *n*

²bowl *n* **1** : a ball for rolling on a level surface in bowling **2** : a cast of the ball in bowling

³bowl *vb* **1** : to play a game of bowling; *also* : to roll a ball in bowling **2** : to travel (as in a vehicle) rapidly and smoothly **3** : to strike or knock down with a moving object; *also* : to overwhelm with surprise

bowlder *var of* BOULDER

bow·legged \'bō-ˌle-gəd\ *adj* : having legs that bow outward at or below the knee — **bow·leg** \'bō-ˌleg\ *n*

¹bowl·er \'bō-lər\ *n* : a person who bowls

²bow·ler \'bō-lər\ *n* : DERBY 3

bow·line \'bō-lən, -ˌlīn\ *n* : a knot used to form a loop that neither slips nor jams

bowl·ing \'bō-liŋ\ *n* : any of various games in which balls are rolled on a green or alley at an object or a group of objects; *esp* : TENPINS

bow·man \'bō-mən\ *n* : ARCHER

bow·sprit \'baú-ˌsprit\ *n* : a spar projecting forward from the prow of a ship

bow·string \'bō-ˌstriŋ\ *n* : the cord connecting the two ends of a shooting bow

¹box \'bäks\ *n, pl* **box** *or* **box·es** : an evergreen shrub or small tree used esp. for hedges

²box *n* **1** : a rigid typically rectangular receptacle often with a cover; *also* : the quantity held by a box **2** : a small compartment (as for a group of theater patrons); *also* : a boxlike receptacle or division **3** : any of six spaces on a baseball diamond where the batter, pitcher, coaches, and catcher stand **4** : PREDICAMENT

³box *vb* : to enclose in or as if in a box

⁴box *n* : a punch or slap esp. on the ear

⁵box *vb* **1** : to strike with the hand **2** : to engage in boxing with

box·car \'bäks-ˌkär\ *n* : a roofed freight car usu. with sliding doors in the sides

¹box·er \'bäk-sər\ *n* : a person who engages in boxing

²boxer *n* : a compact short-haired usu. fawn or brindled dog of a breed of German origin

box·ing \'bäk-siŋ\ *n* : the sport of fighting with the fists

box office *n* : an office (as in a theater) where admission tickets are sold

box·wood \'bäks-ˌwúd\ *n* : the tough hard wood of the box; *also* : a box tree or shrub

boy \'bói\ *n* **1** : a male child : YOUTH **2** : SON — **boy·hood** \-ˌhúd\ *n* — **boy·ish** *adj* — **boy·ish·ly** *adv* — **boy·ish·ness** *n*

boy·cott \'bói-ˌkät\ *vb* [Charles C. *Boycott* †1897 Eng. land agent in Ireland who was ostracized for refusing to reduce rents] : to refrain from having any dealings with — **boycott** *n*

boy·friend \'bói-ˌfrend\ *n* **1** : a male friend **2** : a frequent or regular male companion of a girl or woman

Boy Scout *n* : a member of any of various national scouting programs (as the Boy Scouts of America)

boy·sen·ber·ry \'bóiz-ᵊn-ˌber-ē, 'bóis-\ *n* : a large bramble fruit with a raspberry flavor; *also* : the hybrid plant bearing it developed by crossing blackberries and raspberries

bo·zo \'bō-ˌzō\ *n, pl* **bozos** : a foolish or incompetent person

bp *abbr* **1** bishop **2** birthplace

BP *abbr* **1** batting practice **2** blood pressure **3** boiling point

bpl *abbr* birthplace

BPOE *abbr* Benevolent and Protective Order of Elks

br *abbr* **1** branch **2** brass **3** brown

¹Br *abbr* Britain; British

²Br *symbol* bromine

BR *abbr* bedroom

bra \'brä\ *n* : BRASSIERE

¹brace \'brās\ *vb* **braced; brac·ing 1** *archaic* : to make fast : BIND **2** : to tighten preparatory to use; *also* : to get

ready for : prepare oneself **3** : INVIGORATE **4** : to furnish or support with a brace; *also* : STRENGTHEN **5** : to set firmly **6** : to gain courage or confidence

²brace *n, pl* **brac·es 1** *or pl* **brace** : two of a kind ⟨a ∼ of dogs⟩ **2** : a crank-shaped device for turning a bit **3** : something (as a tie, prop, or clamp) that distributes, directs, or resists pressure or weight **4** *pl* : SUSPENDERS **5** : an appliance for supporting a body part (as the shoulders) **6** *pl* : dental appliances used to exert pressure to straighten misaligned teeth **7** : one of two marks { } used to connect words or items to be considered together

brace·let \'brā-slət\ *n* [ME, fr. MF, dim. of *bras* arm, fr. L *bracchium*, fr. Gk *brachiōn*] : an ornamental band or chain worn around the wrist

bra·ce·ro \brä-'ser-ō\ *n, pl* **-ros** : a Mexican laborer admitted to the U.S. esp. for seasonal farm work

brack·en \'bra-kən\ *n* : a large coarse fern; *also* : a growth of such ferns

¹brack·et \'bra-kət\ *n* **1** : a projecting framework or arm designed to support weight; *also* : a shelf on such framework **2** : one of a pair of punctuation marks [ ] used esp. to enclose interpolated matter **3** : a continuous section of a series; *esp* : one of a graded series of income groups

²bracket *vb* **1** : to furnish or fasten with brackets **2** : to place within brackets; *also* : to separate or group with or as if with brackets

brack·ish \'bra-kish\ *adj* : somewhat salty — **brack·ish·ness** *n*

bract \'brakt\ *n* : an often modified leaf on or at the base of a flower stalk

brad \'brad\ *n* : a slender nail with a small head

brae \'brā\ *n, chiefly Scot* : a hillside esp. along a river

brag \'brag\ *vb* **bragged; brag·ging** : to talk or assert boastfully — **brag** *n* — **brag·ger** *n*

brag·ga·do·cio \ˌbra-gə-'dō-shē-ˌō, -sē-, -chē-\ *n, pl* **-cios 1** : BRAGGART, BOASTER **2** : empty boasting **3** : arrogant pretension : COCKINESS

brag·gart \'bra-gərt\ *n* : one who brags

Brah·man *or* **Brah·min** \'brä-mən *for 1*; 'brā-, 'brä-, 'bra- *for 2*\ *n* **1** : a Hindu of the highest caste traditionally assigned to the priesthood **2** : any of a breed of large vigorous humped cattle developed in the southern U.S. from Indian stock **3** *usu* **Brahmin** : a person of high social standing and cultivated intellect and taste

Brah·man·ism \'brä-mə-ˌni-zəm\ *n* : orthodox Hinduism

¹braid \'brād\ *vb* **1** : to form (strands) into a braid : PLAIT; *also* : to make from braids **2** : to ornament with braid

²braid *n* **1** : a length of braided hair **2** : a cord or ribbon of three or more interwoven strands

braille \'brāl\ *n, often cap* : a system of writing for the blind that uses characters made up of raised dots

a	b	c	d	e	f	g	h	i	j
1	2	3	4	5	6	7	8	9	0

k	l	m	n	o	p	q	r	s	t

u	v	w	x	y	z			Capital Sign	Numeral Sign

braille alphabet

¹brain \'brān\ *n* 1 : the part of the vertebrate nervous system that is the organ of thought and nervous coordination, is made up of nerve cells and their fibers, and is enclosed in the skull; *also* : a centralized mass of nerve tissue in an invertebrate 2 : INTELLECT, INTELLIGENCE — often used in pl. — **brained** \'brānd\ *adj* — **brainless** *adj* — **brainy** *adj*

²brain *vb* 1 : to kill by smashing the skull 2 : to hit on the head

brain·child \'brān-ˌchīld\ *n* : a product of one's creative imagination

brain death *n* : final cessation of activity in the central nervous system esp. as indicated by a flat electroencephalogram — **brain–dead** \-ˌded\ *adj*

brain drain *n* : the departure of educated or professional people from one country, sector, or field to another usu. for better pay or living conditions

brain·storm \-ˌstȯrm\ *n* : a sudden inspiration or idea — **brainstorm** *vb*

brain·teas·er \-ˌtē-zər\ *n* : a challenging puzzle

brain·wash·ing \'brān-ˌwȯ-shiŋ, -ˌwä-\ *n* 1 : a forcible indoctrination to induce someone to give up basic political, social, or religious beliefs and attitudes and to accept contrasting regimented ideas 2 : persuasion by propaganda or salesmanship — **brain·wash** *vb*

brain wave *n* 1 : BRAINSTORM 2 : rhythmic fluctuations of voltage between parts of the brain; *also* : a current produced by brain waves

braise \'brāz\ *vb* **braised; brais·ing** : to cook (meat) slowly in fat and little moisture in a closed pot

¹brake \'brāk\ *n* : a common bracken fern

²brake *n* : rough or wet land heavily overgrown (as with thickets or reeds)

³brake *n* : a device for slowing or stopping motion esp. by friction — **brake·less** *adj*

⁴brake *vb* **braked; brak·ing** 1 : to slow or stop by or as if by a brake 2 : to apply a brake

brake·man \'brāk-mən\ *n* : a train crew member who inspects the train and assists the conductor

bram·ble \'bram-bəl\ *n* : any of a large genus of prickly shrubs (as a blackberry) related to the roses; *also* : any rough prickly shrub or vine — **bram·bly** \-b(ə-)lē\ *adj*

bran \'bran\ *n* : the edible broken husks of cereal grain sifted from flour or meal

¹branch \'branch\ *n* [ME, fr. OF *branche*, fr. LL *branca* paw] 1 : a natural subdivision (as a bough or twig) of a plant stem 2 : a division (as of an antler or a river) related to a whole like a plant branch to its stem 3 : a discrete element of a complex system ⟨the executive ∼⟩; *esp* : a division of a family descended from one ancestor — **branched** \'brancht\ *adj*

²branch *vb* 1 : to develop branches 2 : DIVERGE 3 : to extend activities ⟨the business is ∼*ing* out⟩

¹brand \'brand\ *n* 1 : a piece of charred or burning wood 2 : a mark made (as by burning) usu. to identify; *also* : a mark of disgrace : STIGMA 3 : a class of goods identified as the product of a particular firm or producer 4 : a distinctive kind ⟨my own ∼ of humor⟩

²brand *vb* 1 : to mark with a brand 2 : STIGMATIZE

bran·dish \'bran-dish\ *vb* : to shake or wave menacingly **syn** flourish, flash, flaunt

brand–new \'bran-'nü, -'nyü\ *adj* : conspicuously new and unused

bran·dy \'bran-dē\ *n, pl* **brandies** [short for *brandywine*, fr. D *brandewijn*, fr. MD *brantwijn*, fr. *brant* distilled + *wijn* wine] : a liquor distilled from wine or fermented fruit juice — **brandy** *vb*

brash \'brash\ *adj* 1 : IMPETUOUS, AUDACIOUS 2 : aggressively self-assertive

brass \'bras\ *n* 1 : an alloy of copper and zinc; *also* : an object of brass 2 : brazen self-assurance 3 : persons of high rank (as in the military) — **brassy** *adj*

bras·siere \brə-'zir\ *n* : a woman's close-fitting undergarment designed to support the breasts

brat \'brat\ *n* : an ill-behaved child — **brat·ti·ness** *n* — **brat·ty** *adj*

bra·va·do \brə-'vä-dō\ *n, pl* **-does** *or* **-dos** 1 : blustering swaggering conduct 2 : a show of bravery

¹brave \'brāv\ *adj* **brav·er; brav·est** [MF, fr. It & Sp *bravo* courageous, wild, prob. fr. L *barbarus* barbarous] 1 : showing courage 2 : EXCELLENT, SPLENDID **syn** bold, intrepid, courageous, valiant — **brave·ly** *adv*

²brave *vb* **braved; brav·ing** : to face or endure bravely

³brave *n* : an American Indian warrior

brav·ery \'brā-və-rē\ *n, pl* **-er·ies** : COURAGE

bra·vo \'brä-vō\ *n, pl* **bravos** : a shout of approval — often used as an interjection in applauding

bra·vu·ra \brə-'vyür-ə, -'vür-\ *n* 1 : a florid brilliant musical style 2 : self-assured brilliant performance — **bravura** *adj*

brawl \'brȯl\ *n* : a noisy quarrel **syn** fracas, row, rumpus, scrap, fray, melee — **brawl** *vb* — **brawl·er** *n*

brawn \'brȯn\ *n* : strong muscles; *also* : muscular strength — **brawn·i·ness** *n* — **brawny** *adj*

bray \'brā\ *n* : the characteristic harsh cry of a donkey — **bray** *vb*

braze \'brāz\ *vb* **brazed; braz·ing** : to solder with an alloy (as brass) that melts at a lower temperature than the metals being joined — **braz·er** *n*

¹bra·zen \'brāz-ᵊn\ *adj* 1 : made of brass 2 : sounding harsh and loud 3 : of the color of brass 4 : marked by contemptuous boldness — **bra·zen·ly** *adv* — **bra·zen·ness** *n*

²brazen *vb* : to face boldly or defiantly

¹bra·zier \'brā-zhər\ *n* : a worker in brass

²brazier *n* 1 : a vessel holding burning coals (as for heating) 2 : a device on which food is grilled

Bra·zil·ian \brə-'zil-yən\ *n* : a native or inhabitant of Brazil — **Brazilian** *adj*

Bra·zil nut \brə-'zil-\ *n* : a triangular oily edible nut borne in large capsules by a tall So. American tree; *also* : the tree

¹breach \'brēch\ *n* 1 : a breaking of a law, obligation, tie (as of friendship), or standard (as of conduct) 2 : an interruption or opening made by or as if by breaking through **syn** violation, transgression, infringement, trespass

²breach *vb* 1 : to make a breach in 2 : to leap out of water ⟨whales ∼*ing*⟩

¹bread \'bred\ *n* 1 : baked food made basically of flour or meal 2 : FOOD

²bread *vb* : to cover with bread crumbs before cooking

bread·bas·ket \'bred-ˌbas-kət\ *n* : a major cereal–producing region

bread·fruit \-ˌfrüt\ *n* : a round usu. seedless fruit resembling bread in color and texture when baked; *also* : a tall tropical tree related to the mulberry and bearing breadfruit

bread·stuff \-ˌstəf\ *n* : GRAIN, FLOUR

breadth \'bredth, 'bretth\ *n* 1 : WIDTH 2 : comprehensive quality : SCOPE ⟨∼ of knowledge⟩

bread·win·ner \'bred-ˌwi-nər\ *n* : a member of a family whose wages supply its livelihood

¹break \'brāk\ *vb* **broke** \'brōk\; **bro·ken** \'brō-kən\; **break·ing** 1 : to separate into parts usu. suddenly or violently : come or force apart 2 : TRANSGRESS ⟨∼ a law⟩ 3 : to force a way into, out of, or through 4 : to disrupt the order or unity of ⟨∼ ranks⟩ ⟨∼ up a gang⟩; *also* : to bring to submission or helplessness 5 : EXCEED, SURPASS ⟨∼ a record⟩ 6 : RUIN 7 : to make known 8 : HALT,

---

\ə\abut \ᵊ\kitten \ər\further \a\ash \ā\ace \ä\mop, mar \au̇\out \ch\chin \e\bet \ē\easy \g\go \i\hit \ī\ice \j\job \ŋ\sing \ō\go \ȯ\law \ȯi\boy \th\thin \th\the \ü\loot \u̇\foot \y\yet \zh\vision *see also* Pronunciation Symbols page

INTERRUPT; *also* : to act or change abruptly (as a course or activity) **9** : to come esp. suddenly into being or notice ⟨as day ∼s⟩ **10** : to fail under stress **11** : HAPPEN, DEVELOP — **break·able** *adj or n*

²**break** *n* **1** : an act of breaking **2** : a result of breaking; *esp* : an interruption of continuity ⟨coffee ∼⟩ ⟨a ∼ for the commercial⟩ **3** : a stroke of good luck

break·age \'brā-kij\ *n* **1** : the action of breaking **2** : articles or amount broken **3** : loss due to things broken

break·down \'brāk-ˌdaȯn\ *n* **1** : functional failure; *esp* : a physical, mental, or nervous collapse **2** : DISINTEGRATION **3** : DECOMPOSITION **4** : ANALYSIS, CLASSIFICATION — **break down** *vb*

break·er \'brā-kər\ *n* **1** : one that breaks **2** : a wave that breaks into foam (as against the shore)

break·fast \'brek-fəst\ *n* : the first meal of the day — **breakfast** *vb*

break in *vb* **1** : to enter a building by force **2** : INTERRUPT; *also* : INTRUDE **3** : TRAIN — **break–in** \'brāk-ˌin\ *n*

break·neck \'brāk-ˈnek\ *adj* : very fast or dangerous ⟨∼ speed⟩

break out *vb* **1** : to develop or erupt suddenly or with force **2** : to develop a skin rash

break·through \'brāk-ˌthrü\ *n* **1** : an act or instance of breaking through an obstruction or defensive line **2** : a sudden advance in knowledge or technique

break·up \-ˌəp\ *n* **1** : DISSOLUTION **2** : a division into smaller units — **break up** *vb*

break·wa·ter \'brāk-ˌwȯ-tər, -ˌwä-\ *n* : a structure protecting a harbor or beach from the force of waves

bream \'brim, 'brēm\ *n, pl* **bream** *or* **breams** : any of various small freshwater sunfishes

breast \'brest\ *n* **1** : either of the pair of mammary glands extending from the front of the chest esp. in pubescent and adult human females **2** : the front part of the body between the neck and the abdomen **3** : the seat of emotion and thought

breast·bone \'brest-ˌbōn\ *n* : STERNUM

breast–feed \-ˌfēd\ *vb* : to feed (a baby) from a mother's breast rather than from a bottle

breast·plate \-ˌplāt\ *n* : a metal plate of armor for the breast

breast·stroke \-ˌstrōk\ *n* : a swimming stroke executed by extending both arms forward and then sweeping them back with palms out while kicking backward and outward with both legs

breast·work \-ˌwərk\ *n* : a temporary fortification

breath \'breth\ *n* **1** : the act or power of breathing **2** : a slight breeze **3** : air inhaled or exhaled in breathing **4** : spoken sound **5** : SPIRIT — **breath·less** *adj* — **breath·less·ly** *adv* — **breath·less·ness** *n* — **breathy** \'bre-thē\ *adj*

breathe \'brēth\ *vb* **breathed; breath·ing** **1** : to inhale and exhale **2** : LIVE **3** : to halt for rest **4** : to utter softly or secretly — **breath·able** *adj*

breath·er \'brē-thər\ *n* **1** : one that breathes **2** : a short rest

breath·tak·ing \'breth-ˌtā-kiŋ\ *adj* **1** : making one out of breath **2** : EXCITING, THRILLING ⟨∼ beauty⟩ — **breath·tak·ing·ly** *adv*

brec·cia \'bre-chē-ə, -chə\ *n* : a rock consisting of sharp fragments held in fine-grained material

breech \'brēch\ *n* **1** *pl* \usu 'bri-chəz\ : trousers ending near the knee; *also* : PANTS **2** : BUTTOCKS, RUMP **3** : the part of a firearm at the rear of the barrel

¹**breed** \'brēd\ *vb* **bred** \'bred\; **breed·ing** **1** : BEGET; *also* : ORIGINATE **2** : to propagate sexually; *also* : MATE **3** : BRING UP, NURTURE **4** : to produce (fissionable material) from material that is not fissionable **syn** generate, reproduce, procreate, propagate — **breed·er** *n*

²**breed** *n* **1** : a strain of similar and presumably related

plants or animals usu. developed in domestication **2** : KIND, SORT, CLASS

breed·ing *n* **1** : ANCESTRY **2** : training in polite social interaction **3** : sexual propagation of plants or animals

¹**breeze** \'brēz\ *n* **1** : a light wind **2** : CINCH, SNAP — **breeze·less** *adj*

²**breeze** *vb* **breezed; breez·ing** : to progress quickly and easily

breeze·way \'brēz-ˌwā\ *n* : a roofed open passage connecting two buildings (as a house and garage)

breezy \'brē-zē\ *adj* **1** : swept by breezes **2** : briskly informal — **breez·i·ly** \'brē-zə-lē\ *adv* — **breez·i·ness** \-zē-nəs\ *n*

breth·ren \'breth-rən, 'bre-thə-; 'bre-thərn\ *pl of* BROTHER — used esp. in formal or solemn address

Brethren *n pl* : members of one of several Protestant denominations originating chiefly in a German religious movement and stressing personal religious experience

bre·via·ry \'brē-vyə-rē, -vē-ˌer-ē-\ *n, pl* **-ries** *often cap* : a book of prayers, hymns, psalms, and readings used by Roman Catholic priests

brev·i·ty \'bre-və-tē\ *n, pl* **-ties** **1** : shortness or conciseness of expression **2** : shortness of duration

brew \'brü\ *vb* **1** : to prepare (as beer) by steeping, boiling, and fermenting **2** : to prepare (as tea) by steeping in hot water — **brew** *n* — **brew·er** *n* — **brew·ery** \'brü-ə-rē, 'brü(-ə)r-ē\ *n*

¹**bri·ar** \'brī-ər\ *var of* BRIER

²**briar** *n* : a tobacco pipe made from the root or stem of a brier

¹**bribe** \'brīb\ *n* [ME, something stolen, fr. MF, bread given to a beggar] : something (as money or a favor) given or promised to a person to influence conduct

²**bribe** *vb* **bribed; brib·ing** : to influence by offering a bribe — **brib·able** *adj* — **brib·er** *n* — **brib·ery** \'brī-bə-rē\ *n*

bric–a–brac \'bri-kə-ˌbrak\ *n pl* [F] : small ornamental articles

¹**brick** \'brik\ *n* : a block molded from moist clay and hardened by heat used esp. for building

²**brick** *vb* : to close, cover, or pave with bricks

brick·bat \'brik-ˌbat\ *n* **1** : a piece of a hard material (as a brick) esp. when thrown as a missile **2** : an uncomplimentary remark

brick·lay·er \'brik-ˌlā-ər\ *n* : a person who builds or paves with bricks — **brick·lay·ing** *n*

¹**brid·al** \'brīd-ᵊl\ *n* [ME *bridale*, fr. OE *brȳdealu*, fr. *brȳd* bride + *ealu* ale] : MARRIAGE, WEDDING

²**bridal** *adj* : of or relating to a bride or a wedding

bride \'brīd\ *n* : a woman just married or about to be married

bride·groom \'brīd-ˌgrüm, -ˌgrum\ *n* : a man just married or about to be married

brides·maid \'brīdz-ˌmād\ *n* : a woman who attends a bride at her wedding

¹**bridge** \'brij\ *n* **1** : a structure built over a depression or obstacle for use as a passageway **2** : something (as the upper part of the nose) resembling a bridge in form or function **3** : a curved piece raising the strings of a musical instrument **4** : the forward part of a ship's superstructure from which it is navigated **5** : an artificial replacement for missing teeth

²**bridge** *vb* **bridged; bridg·ing** : to build a bridge over — **bridge·able** *adj*

³**bridge** *n* : a card game for four players developed from whist

bridge·head \-ˌhed\ *n* : an advanced position seized in enemy territory

bridge·work \-ˌwərk\ *n* : dental bridges

¹**bri·dle** \'brīd-ᵊl\ *n* **1** : headgear with which a horse is controlled **2** : CURB, RESTRAINT

²**bridle** *vb* **bri·dled; bri·dling** **1** : to put a bridle on; *also*

: to restrain with or as if with a bridle **2** : to show hostility or scorn usu. by tossing the head

Brie \'brē\ *n* : a soft cheese with a whitish rind and a pale yellow interior

¹brief \'brēf\ *adj* **1** : short in duration or extent **2** : CONCISE; *also* : CURT — **brief·ly** *adv* — **brief·ness** *n*

²brief *n* **1** : a concise statement or document; *esp* : one summarizing a law client's case or a legal argument **2** *pl* : short snug underpants

³brief *vb* : to give final instructions or essential information to

brief·case \'brēf-ˌkās\ *n* : a flat flexible case for carrying papers

¹bri·er \'brī(-ə)r\ *n* : a plant (as a bramble or rose) with a thorny or prickly woody stem; *also* : a mass or twig of these — **bri·ery** \'brī(-ə)r-ē\ *adj*

²brier *or* **briar** *n* : a heath of southern Europe whose roots and knotted stems are used for making tobacco pipes

¹brig \'brig\ *n* : a 2-masted square-rigged sailing ship

²brig *n* : the place of confinement for offenders on a naval ship

³brig *abbr* brigade

bri·gade \bri-'gād\ *n* **1** : a military unit composed of a headquarters, one or more units of infantry or armored forces, and supporting units **2** : a group organized for a particular purpose (as fire fighting)

brig·a·dier general \ˌbri-gə-ˌdir-\ *n* : a commissioned officer (as in the army) ranking next below a major general

brig·and \'bri-gənd\ *n* : BANDIT — **brig·and·age** \-gən-dij\ *n*

brig·an·tine \'bri-gən-ˌtēn\ *n* : a 2-masted square-rigged ship with a fore-and-aft mainsail

Brig Gen *abbr* brigadier general

bright \'brīt\ *adj* **1** : SHINING, RADIANT **2** : ILLUSTRIOUS, GLORIOUS **3** : INTELLIGENT, CLEVER; *also* : LIVELY, CHEERFUL **syn** brilliant, lustrous, beaming — **bright** *adv* — **bright·ly** *adv* — **bright·ness** *n*

bright·en \'brīt-ᵊn\ *vb* : to make or become bright or brighter — **bright·en·er** *n*

¹bril·liant \'bril-yənt\ *adj* [F *brillant,* prp. of *briller* to shine, fr. It *brillare*] **1** : very bright **2** : STRIKING, DISTINCTIVE **3** : very intelligent **syn** radiant, lustrous, beaming, lucid, bright, lambent — **bril·liance** \-yəns\ *n* — **bril·lian·cy** \-yən-sē\ *n* — **bril·liant·ly** *adv*

²brilliant *n* : a gem cut in a particular form with many facets

¹brim \'brim\ *n* : EDGE, RIM **syn** brink, border, verge, fringe — **brim·less** *adj*

²brim *vb* **brimmed; brim·ming** : to be or become full often to overflowing

brim·ful \-'fúl\ *adj* : full to the brim

brim·stone \'brim-ˌstōn\ *n* : SULFUR

brin·dled \'brin-dᵊld\ *adj* : having dark streaks or flecks on a gray or tawny ground ⟨a ∼ Great Dane⟩

brine \'brīn\ *n* **1** : water saturated with salt **2** : OCEAN — **brin·i·ness** *n* — **briny** \'brī-nē\ *adj*

bring \'briŋ\ *vb* **brought** \'bròt\; **bring·ing** \'briŋ-iŋ\ **1** : to cause to come with one **2** : INDUCE, PERSUADE, LEAD **3** : PRODUCE, EFFECT **4** : to sell for ⟨∼ a good price⟩ — **bring·er** *n*

bring about *vb* : to cause to take place

bring up *vb* **1** : to give a parent's fostering care to **2** : to come or bring to a sudden halt **3** : to call to notice

brink \'briŋk\ *n* **1** : an edge at the top of a steep place **2** : the point of onset

brio \'brē-ō\ *n* : VIVACITY, SPIRIT

bri·quette *or* **bri·quet** \bri-'ket\ *n* : a compacted often brick-shaped mass of fine material ⟨a charcoal ∼⟩

brisk \'brisk\ *adj* **1** : ALERT, LIVELY **2** : INVIGORATING **syn** agile, spry, nimble — **brisk·ly** *adv* — **brisk·ness** *n*

bris·ket \'bris-kət\ *n* : the breast or lower chest of a quadruped; *also* : a cut of beef from the brisket

bris·ling \'briz-liŋ, 'bris-\ *n* : SPRAT 1

¹bris·tle \'bri-səl\ *n* : a short stiff coarse hair — **bris·tle·like** \'bri-səl-ˌlīk\ *adj* — **bris·tly** *adj*

²bristle *vb* **bris·tled; bris·tling 1** : to stand stiffly erect **2** : to show angry defiance **3** : to appear as if covered with bristles

Brit *abbr* Britain; British

Bri·tan·nic \bri-'ta-nik\ *adj* : BRITISH

britch·es \'bri-chəz\ *n pl* : BREECHES, TROUSERS

Brit·ish \'bri-tish\ *n pl* : the people of Great Britain or the Commonwealth — **British** *adj* — **Brit·ish·ness** *n*

British thermal unit *n* : the quantity of heat needed to raise the temperature of one pound of water one degree Fahrenheit

Brit·on \'brit-ᵊn\ *n* **1** : a member of a people inhabiting Britain before the Anglo-Saxon invasion **2** : a native or inhabitant of Great Britain

brit·tle \'brit-ᵊl\ *adj* **brit·tler; brit·tlest** : easily broken : FRAGILE **syn** crisp, crumbly, friable — **brit·tle·ness** *n*

bro *abbr* brother

¹broach \'brōch\ *n* : a pointed tool

²broach *vb* **1** : to pierce (as a cask) in order to draw the contents **2** : to introduce as a topic of conversation

¹broad \'bròd\ *adj* **1** : WIDE **2** : SPACIOUS **3** : CLEAR, OPEN **4** : OBVIOUS ⟨a ∼ hint⟩ **5** : COARSE, CRUDE ⟨∼ stories⟩ **6** : tolerant in outlook **7** : GENERAL **8** : dealing with essential points — **broad·ly** *adv* — **broad·ness** *n*

²broad *n, slang* : WOMAN

¹broad·cast \'bròd-ˌkast\ *vb* **broadcast** *also* **broad·cast·ed; broad·cast·ing 1** : to scatter or sow broadcast **2** : to make widely known **3** : to transmit a broadcast — **broad·cast·er** *n*

²broadcast *adv* : to or over a wide area

³broadcast *n* **1** : the transmission of sound or images by radio or television **2** : a single radio or television program

broad·cloth \-ˌklòth\ *n* **1** : a smooth dense woolen cloth **2** : a fine soft cloth of cotton, silk, or synthetic fiber

broad·en \'bròd-ᵊn\ *vb* : WIDEN

broad·loom \-ˌlüm\ *adj* : woven on a wide loom esp. in a solid color

broad–mind·ed \-'mīn-dəd\ *adj* : tolerant of varied opinions — **broad–mind·ed·ly** *adv* — **broad–mind·ed·ness** *n*

¹broad·side \-ˌsīd\ *n* **1** : a sheet of paper printed usu. on one side (as an advertisement) **2** : all of the guns on one side of a ship; *also* : their simultaneous firing **3** : a volley of abuse or denunciation

²broadside *adv* **1** : with one side forward : SIDEWAYS **2** : from the side ⟨the car was hit ∼⟩

broad–spectrum *adj* : effective against a wide range of organisms ⟨∼ antibiotics⟩

broad·sword \'bròd-ˌsòrd\ *n* : a broad-bladed sword

broad·tail \-ˌtāl\ *n* : a karakul esp. with flat and wavy fur

bro·cade \brō-'kād\ *n* : a usu. silk fabric with a raised design

broc·co·li \'brä-kə-lē\ *n* [It, pl. of *broccolo* flowering top of a cabbage, dim. of *brocco* small nail, sprout, fr. L *broccus* projecting] : the stems and immature usu. green or purple flower heads of either of two garden vegetable plants closely related to the cabbage; *also* : either of the plants

bro·chette \brō-'shet\ *n* : SKEWER

bro·chure \brō-'shùr\ *n* [F, fr. *brocher* to sew, fr. MF, to prick, fr. OF *brochier,* fr. *broche* pointed tool] : PAMPHLET, BOOKLET

\ə\abut \ᵊ\kitten \ər\further \a\ash \ā\ace \ä\mop, mar
\aú\out \ch\chin \e\bet \ē\easy \g\go \i\hit \ī\ice \j\job
\ŋ\sing \ō\go \ò\law \òi\boy \th\thin \th\the \ü\loot \ú\foot
\y\yet \zh\vision *see also* Pronunciation Symbols page

bro·gan \'brō-gən, brō-'gan\ *n* : a heavy shoe
brogue \'brōg\ *n* : a dialect or regional pronunciation; *esp* : an Irish accent
broil \'brȯil\ *vb* : to cook by exposure to radiant heat : GRILL — **broil** *n*
broil·er \'brȯi-lər\ *n* **1** : a utensil for broiling **2** : a young chicken fit for broiling
¹broke \'brōk\ *past of* BREAK
²broke *adj* : PENNILESS
¹bro·ken \'brō-kən\ *past part of* BREAK
²broken *adj* **1** : SHATTERED **2** : having gaps or breaks : INTERRUPTED, DISRUPTED **3** : SUBDUED, CRUSHED **4** : BANKRUPT **5** : imperfectly spoken ⟨∼ English⟩ — **bro·ken·ly** *adv*
bro·ken·heart·ed \₁brō-kən-'här-təd\ *adj* : overcome by grief or despair
bro·ker \'brō-kər\ *n* : an agent who negotiates contracts of purchase and sale — **broker** *vb*
bro·ker·age \'brō-kə-rij\ *n* **1** : the business of a broker **2** : the fee or commission charged by a broker
bro·mide \'brō-₁mīd\ *n* : a compound of bromine and another element or chemical group including some (as potassium bromide) used as sedatives
bro·mid·ic \brō-'mi-dik\ *adj* : TRITE, UNORIGINAL
bro·mine \'brō-₁mēn\ *n* [F *brome* bromine, fr. Gk *brōmos* stink] : a deep red liquid corrosive chemical element that gives off an irritating vapor — see ELEMENT table
bronc \'bräŋk\ *n* : an unbroken or partly broken range horse of western No. America; *also* : MUSTANG
bron·chi·al \'bräŋ-kē-əl\ *adj* : of, relating to, or affecting the bronchi or their branches
bron·chi·tis \brän-'kī-təs, bräŋ-\ *n* : inflammation of the bronchi and their branches — **bron·chit·ic** \-'ki-tik\ *adj*
bron·chus \'bräŋ-kəs\ *n, pl* **bron·chi** \'bräŋ-₁kī, -₁kē\ : either of the main divisions of the windpipe each leading to a lung
bron·co \'bräŋ-kō\ *n, pl* **broncos** [MexSp, fr. Sp, rough, wild] : BRONC
bron·to·sau·rus \₁brän-tə-'sȯr-əs\ *also* **bron·to·saur** \'brän-tə-₁sȯr\ *n* [NL, fr. Gk *brontē* thunder + *sauros* lizard] : any of a genus of large 4-footed and probably herbivorous sauropod dinosaurs of the Jurassic
Bronx cheer \'bräŋks-\ *n* : RASPBERRY 2
¹bronze \'bränz\ *vb* **bronzed; bronz·ing** : to give the appearance of bronze to
²bronze *n* **1** : an alloy of copper and tin and sometimes other elements; *also* : something made of bronze **2** : a yellowish brown color — **bronzy** \'brän-zē\ *adj*
brooch \'brōch, 'brüch\ *n* : an ornamental clasp or pin
¹brood \'brüd\ *n* : a family of young animals or children and esp. of birds
²brood *adj* : kept for breeding ⟨a ∼ mare⟩
³brood *vb* **1** : to sit on eggs to hatch them; *also* : to shelter (hatched young) with the wings **2** : to think anxiously or gloomily about something — **brood·ing·ly** *adv*
brood·er \'brü-dər\ *n* **1** : one that broods **2** : a heated structure for raising young birds
¹brook \'brük\ *n* : a small natural stream
²brook *vb* : TOLERATE, BEAR
brook·let \'brük-lət\ *n* : a small brook
brook trout *n* : a common speckled cold-water char of No. America
broom \'brüm, 'brum\ *n* **1** : any of several shrubs of the legume family with long slender branches and usu. yellow flowers **2** : an implement with a long handle (**broom·stick** \-₁stik\) used for sweeping
bros *abbr* brothers
broth \'brȯth\ *n, pl* **broths** \'brȯths, 'brȯthz\ **1** : liquid in which meat or sometimes vegetable food has been cooked **2** : a fluid culture medium
broth·el \'brä-thəl, 'brȯ-\ *n* : a house of prostitution
broth·er \'brə-thər\ *n, pl* **brothers** *also* **breth·ren**

\'breth-rən, 'bre-thə-; 'bre-thərn\ **1** : a male having one or both parents in common with another individual **2** : a man who is a religious but not a priest **3** : KINSMAN; *also* : SOUL BROTHER — **broth·er·li·ness** \-lē-nəs\ *n* — **broth·er·ly** *adj*
broth·er·hood \'brə-thər-₁hud\ *n* **1** : the state of being brothers or a brother **2** : ASSOCIATION, FRATERNITY **3** : the whole body of persons in a business or profession
broth·er–in–law \'brə-thə-rən-₁lȯ, 'brə-thərn-₁lȯ\ *n, pl* **brothers–in–law** \'brə-thər-zən-\ : the brother of one's spouse; *also* : the husband of one's sister or of one's spouse's sister
brougham \'brü(-ə)m, 'brō(-ə)m\ *n* : a light closed horse= drawn carriage with the driver outside in front
brought *past and past part of* BRING
brou·ha·ha \'brü-₁hä-₁hä\ *n* : HUBBUB, UPROAR
brow \'brau\ *n* **1** : the eyebrow or the ridge on which it grows; *also* : FOREHEAD **2** : the projecting upper part of a steep place
brow·beat \'brau-₁bēt\ *vb* **-beat; -beat·en** \-'bēt-ᵊn\ *or* **-beat; -beat·ing** : to intimidate by sternness or arrogance
¹brown \'braun\ *adj* : of the color brown; *also* : of dark or tanned complexion
²brown *n* : a color like that of coffee or chocolate that is a blend of red and yellow darkened by black — **brown·ish** *adj*
³brown *vb* : to make or become brown
brown bag·ging \-'ba-giŋ\ *n* : the practice of carrying one's lunch usu. in a brown bag — **brown bag·ger** *n*
brown·ie \'brau-nē\ *n* **1** : a legendary cheerful elf who performs good deeds at night **2** *cap* : a member of a program of the Girl Scouts for girls in the first through third grades
brown·out \'brau-₁naut\ *n* : a period of reduced voltage of electricity caused esp. by high demand and resulting in reduced illumination
brown rice *n* : hulled but unpolished rice that retains most of the bran layers
brown·stone \'braun-₁stōn\ *n* : a dwelling faced with reddish brown sandstone
¹browse \'brauz\ *vb* **browsed; brows·ing 1** : to feed on browse; *also* : GRAZE **2** : to read or look over something in a casual way
²browse *n* : tender shoots, twigs, and leaves fit for food for cattle
bru·in \'brü-ən\ *n* : BEAR
¹bruise \'brüz\ *vb* **bruised; bruis·ing 1** : to inflict a bruise on; *also* : to become bruised **2** : to break down (as leaves or berries) by pounding
²bruise *n* : a surface injury to flesh : CONTUSION
bruis·er \'brü-zər\ *n* : a big husky man
bruit \'brüt\ *vb* : to make widely known by common report
brunch \'brənch\ *n* : a meal that combines a late breakfast and an early lunch
bru·net *or* **bru·nette** \brü-'net\ *adj* [F *brunet,* masc., *brunette,* fem., brownish, fr. OF, fr. *brun* brown] : having brown or black hair and usu. a relatively dark complexion — **brunet** *or* **brunette** *n*
brunt \'brənt\ *n* : the main shock, force, or stress esp. of an attack; *also* : the greater burden
¹brush \'brəsh\ *n* **1** : BRUSHWOOD **2** : scrub vegetation or land covered with it
²brush *n* **1** : a device composed of bristles set in a handle and used esp. for cleaning or painting **2** : a bushy tail (as of a fox) **3** : an electrical conductor that makes contact between a stationary and a moving part (as of a motor) **4** : a quick light touch in passing
³brush *vb* **1** : to treat (as in cleaning or painting) with a brush **2** : to remove with or as if with a brush; *also* : to dismiss in an offhand manner **3** : to touch gently in passing

⁴**brush** *n* : SKIRMISH **syn** encounter, run-in
brush–off \'brəsh-ˌȯf\ *n* : a curt offhand dismissal
brush up *vb* : to renew one's skill
brush·wood \'brəsh-ˌwu̇d\ *n* **1** : small branches of wood esp. when cut **2** : a thicket of shrubs and small trees
brusque \'brəsk\ *adj* [F *brusque*, fr. It *brusco*, fr. ML *bruscus* a plant with stiff twigs used for brooms] : CURT, BLUNT, ABRUPT **syn** gruff, bluff, crusty, short — **brusque·ly** *adv*
brus·sels sprout \'brəs-əlz-\ *n*, *often cap B* : one of the edible small heads borne on the stalk of a plant closely related to the cabbage; *also*, *pl* : this plant
bru·tal \'brüt-ᵊl\ *adj* **1** : befitting a brute : UNFEELING, CRUEL **2** : HARSH, SEVERE ⟨∼ weather⟩ **3** : unpleasantly accurate — **bru·tal·i·ty** \brü-'ta-lə-tē\ *n* — **bru·tal·ly** *adv*
bru·tal·ize \'brüt-ᵊl-ˌīz\ *vb* **-ized; -iz·ing 1** : to make brutal **2** : to treat brutally
¹**brute** \'brüt\ *adj* [ME, fr. MF *brut* rough, fr. L *brutus* brutish, lit., heavy] **1** : of or relating to beasts **2** : BRUTAL **3** : UNREASONING; *also* : purely physical ⟨∼ strength⟩
²**brute** *n* **1** : BEAST 1 **2** : a brutal person
brut·ish \'brü-tish\ *adj* **1** : BRUTE 1 **2** : strongly sensual; *also* : showing little intelligence
BS *abbr* bachelor of science
BSA *abbr* Boy Scouts of America
bskt *abbr* basket
Bt *abbr* baronet
btry *abbr* battery
Btu *abbr* British thermal unit
bu *abbr* bushel
¹**bub·ble** \'bə-bəl\ *n* **1** : a globule of gas in a liquid **2** : a thin film of liquid filled with gas **3** : something lacking firmness or solidity — **bub·bly** *adj*
²**bubble** *vb* **bub·bled; bub·bling** : to form, rise in, or give off bubbles
bu·bo \'bü-bō, 'byü-\ *n*, *pl* **buboes** : an inflammatory swelling of a lymph gland
bu·bon·ic plague \bü-'bä-nik-, byü-\ *n* : plague caused by a bacterium transmitted to human beings by flea bites and marked esp. by chills and fever and by buboes usu. in the groin
buc·ca·neer \ˌbə-kə-'nir\ *n* : PIRATE
¹**buck** \'bək\ *n*, *pl* **bucks 1** *or pl* **buck** : a male animal (as a deer or antelope) **2** : DANDY **3** : DOLLAR
²**buck** *vb* **1** : to spring with an arching leap ⟨a ∼ing horse⟩ **2** : to charge against something; *also* : to strive for advancement sometimes without regard to ethical behavior
buck·board \-ˌbȯrd\ *n* : a 4-wheeled horse-drawn wagon with a floor of long springy boards

buckboard

buck·et \'bə-kət\ *n* **1** : PAIL **2** : an object resembling a bucket in collecting, scooping, or carrying something — **buck·et·ful** *n*
bucket seat *n* : a low separate seat for one person (as in an automobile)
buck·eye \'bə-ˌkī\ *n* : a tree related to the horse chestnut

that occurs chiefly in the central U.S.; *also* : its large nutlike seed
buck fever *n* : nervous excitement of an inexperienced hunter at the sight of game
¹**buck·le** \'bə-kəl\ *n* : a clasp (as on a belt) for two loose ends
²**buckle** *vb* **buck·led; buck·ling 1** : to fasten with a buckle **2** : to apply oneself with vigor **3** : to crumple up : BEND, COLLAPSE
³**buckle** *n* : BEND, FOLD, KINK
buck·ler \'bə-klər\ *n* : SHIELD
buck·ram \'bə-krəm\ *n* : a coarse stiff cloth used esp. for binding books
buck·saw \'bək-ˌsȯ\ *n* : a saw set in a usu. H-shaped frame for sawing wood
buck·shot \'bək-ˌshät\ *n* : lead shot that is from .24 to .33 inch (about 6.1 to 8.4 millimeters) in diameter
buck·skin \-ˌskin\ *n* **1** : the skin of a buck **2** : a soft usu. suede-finished leather — **buckskin** *adj*
buck·tooth \-'tüth\ *n* : a large projecting front tooth — **buck–toothed** \-'tütht\ *adj*
buck·wheat \-ˌhwēt\ *n* : either of two plants grown for their triangular seeds which are used as a cereal grain; *also* : these seeds
bu·col·ic \byü-'kä-lik\ *adj* [L *bucolicus*, fr. Gk *boukolikos*, fr. *boukolos* one who tends cattle, fr. *bous* head of cattle + *-kolos* (akin to L *colere* to cultivate)] : PASTORAL, RURAL
¹**bud** \'bəd\ *n* **1** : an undeveloped plant shoot (as of a leaf or a flower); *also* : a partly opened flower **2** : an asexual reproductive structure that detaches from the parent and forms a new individual **3** : something not yet fully developed ⟨nipped in the ∼⟩
²**bud** *vb* **bud·ded; bud·ding 1** : to form or put forth buds; *also* : to reproduce by asexual buds **2** : to be or develop like a bud **3** : to reproduce a desired variety (as of peach) by inserting a bud in a plant of a different variety
Bud·dhism \'bü-ˌdi-zəm, 'bu̇-\ *n* : a religion of eastern and central Asia growing out of the teachings of Gautama Buddha — **Bud·dhist** \'bü-dist, 'bu̇-\ *n or adj*
bud·dy \'bə-dē\ *n*, *pl* **buddies 1** : COMPANION; *also* : FRIEND **2** : FELLOW
budge \'bəj\ *vb* **budged; budg·ing** : MOVE, SHIFT; *also* : YIELD
bud·ger·i·gar \'bə-jə-rē-ˌgär\ *n* : a small brightly colored Australian parrot often kept as a pet
¹**bud·get** \'bə-jət\ *n* [ME *bowgette*, fr. MF *bougette*, dim. of *bouge* leather bag, fr. L *bulga*] **1** : STOCK, SUPPLY **2** : a financial report containing estimates of income and expenses; *also* : a plan for coordinating income and expenses **3** : the amount of money available for a particular use — **bud·get·ary** \'bə-jə-ˌter-ē\ *adj*
²**budget** *vb* **1** : to allow for in a budget **2** : to draw up a budget
³**budget** *adj* : INEXPENSIVE
bud·gie \'bə-jē\ *n* : BUDGERIGAR
¹**buff** \'bəf\ *n* **1** : a yellow to orange yellow color **2** : FAN, ENTHUSIAST
²**buff** *adj* : of the color buff
³**buff** *vb* : POLISH, SHINE
buf·fa·lo \'bə-fə-ˌlō\ *n*, *pl* **-lo** *or* **-loes** *also* **-los 1** : WATER BUFFALO **2** : a large shaggy-maned No. American wild bovine mammal that has short horns and heavy forequarters with a large muscular hump
¹**buf·fer** \'bə-fər\ *n* : something or someone that protects or shields (as from physical damage or a financial blow)
²**buffer** *n* : one that buffs

\ə\abut \ᵊ\kitten \ər\further \a\ash \ā\ace \ä\mop, mar
\au̇\out \ch\chin \e\bet \ē\easy \g\go \i\hit \ī\ice \j\job
\ŋ\sing \ō\go \ȯ\law \ȯi\boy \th\thin \th̲\the \ü\loot \u̇\foot
\y\yet \zh\vision *see also* Pronunciation Symbols page

¹**buf·fet** \'bə-fət\ *n* : BLOW, SLAP
²**buffet** *vb* **1** : to strike with the hand; *also* : to pound repeatedly **2** : to struggle against or on **syn** beat, batter, drub, pummel, thrash
³**buf·fet** \(ˌ)bə-'fā, bü-\ *n* **1** : SIDEBOARD **2** : a counter for refreshments; *also* : a meal at which people serve themselves informally
buff leather *n* : a strong supple oil-tanned leather
buf·foon \(ˌ)bə-'fün\ *n* [MF *bouffon,* fr. It *buffone*] : CLOWN **2** — **buf·foon·ery** \-'fü-nə-rē\ *n*
¹**bug** \'bəg\ *n* **1** : an insect or other creeping or crawling invertebrate animal; *esp* : an insect pest (as a bedbug) **2** : any of an order of insects with sucking mouthparts and incomplete metamorphosis that includes many plant pests **3** : an unexpected flaw or imperfection ⟨a ～ in a computer program⟩ **4** : a disease-producing germ; *also* : a disease caused by it **5** : a concealed listening device
²**bug** *vb* **bugged; bug·ging 1** : BOTHER, ANNOY **2** : to plant a concealed microphone in
³**bug** *vb* **bugged; bug·ging** *of the eyes* : PROTRUDE, BULGE
bug·a·boo \'bə-gə-ˌbü\ *n, pl* **-boos** : BOGEY 1
bug·bear \'bəg-ˌbar\ *n* : BOGEY 1; *also* : a source of dread
bug·gy \'bə-gē\ *n, pl* **buggies** : a light horse-drawn carriage; *also* : a carriage for a baby
bu·gle \'byü-gəl\ *n* [ME, buffalo, instrument made of buffalo horn, bugle, fr. OF, fr. L *buculus,* dim. of *bos* head of cattle] : a valveless brass instrument resembling a trumpet and used esp. for military calls — **bu·gler** *n*
¹**build** \'bild\ *vb* **built** \'bilt\; **build·ing 1** : to form or have formed by ordering and uniting materials ⟨～ a house⟩; *also* : to bring into being or develop **2** : to produce or create gradually ⟨～ an argument on facts⟩ **3** : INCREASE, ENLARGE; *also* : ENHANCE **4** : to engage in building — **build·er** *n*
²**build** *n* : form or mode of structure; *esp* : PHYSIQUE
build·ing \'bil-diŋ\ *n* **1** : a usu. roofed and walled structure (as a house) for permanent use **2** : the art or business of constructing buildings
build·up \'bil-ˌdəp\ *n* : the act or process of building up; *also* : something produced by this
built–in \'bil-'tin\ *adj* **1** : forming an integral part of a structure **2** : INHERENT
bulb \'bəlb\ *n* **1** : an underground resting stage of a plant (as a lily or an onion) consisting of a short stem base bearing one or more buds enclosed in overlapping leaves; *also* : a fleshy plant structure (as a tuber) resembling a bulb **2** : a plant having or growing from a bulb **3** : a rounded more or less bulb-shaped object or part (as for an electric lamp) — **bul·bous** \'bəl-bəs\ *adj*
Bul·gar·i·an \ˌbəl-'gar-ē-ən, bul-\ *n* : a native or inhabitant of Bulgaria — **Bulgarian** *adj*
¹**bulge** \'bəlj\ *vb* **bulged; bulg·ing** : to become or cause to become protuberant
²**bulge** *n* : a swelling projecting part
bu·li·mia \bü-'lē-mē-ə, byü-, -'li-\ *n* **1** : an abnormal and constant craving for food **2** : a serious eating disorder chiefly of females that is characterized by compulsive overeating usu. followed by self-induced vomiting or laxative or diuretic abuse — **bu·lim·ic** \-'lē-mik, -'li-\ *adj or n*
¹**bulk** \'bəlk\ *n* **1** : MAGNITUDE, VOLUME **2** : material that forms a mass in the intestine; *esp* : FIBER 2 **3** : a large mass **4** : the major portion
²**bulk** *vb* **1** : to cause to swell or bulge **2** : to appear as a factor : LOOM
bulk·head \'bəlk-ˌhed\ *n* **1** : a partition separating compartments **2** : a structure built to cover a shaft or a cellar stairway
bulky \'bəl-kē\ *adj* **bulk·i·er; -est** : having bulk; *esp* : being large and unwieldy

¹**bull** \'bul\ *n* **1** : a male bovine animal; *also* : a usu. adult male of various large animals (as the moose, elephant, or whale) **2** : one who buys securities or commodities in expectation of a price increase — **bull·ish** *adj*
²**bull** *adj* **1** : of, relating to, or suggestive of a bull : MALE **2** : large of its kind
³**bull** *n* [ME *bulle,* fr. ML *bulla,* fr. L, bubble, amulet] **1** : a papal letter **2** : DECREE
⁴**bull** *n, slang* : NONSENSE
⁵**bull** *abbr* bulletin
¹**bull·dog** \'bul-ˌdȯg\ *n* : any of a breed of compact muscular short-haired dogs of English origin

bulldog

²**bulldog** *vb* : to throw (a steer) by seizing the horns and twisting the neck
bull·doze \-ˌdōz\ *vb* **1** : to move, clear, or level with a tractor-driven machine (**bull·doz·er**) having a broad blade for pushing **2** : to force as if by using a bulldozer
bul·let \'bu-lət\ *n* [MF *boulette* small ball & *boulet* missile, dims. of *boule* ball] : a missile to be shot from a firearm — **bul·let·proof** \-ˌprüf\ *adj*
bul·le·tin \'bu-lət-ᵊn\ *n* **1** : a brief public report intended for immediate release on a matter of public interest **2** : a periodical publication (as of a college) — **bulletin** *vb*
bull·fight \'bul-ˌfīt\ *n* : a spectacle in which people ceremonially fight with and usu. kill bulls in an arena — **bull·fight·er** *n*
bull·frog \-ˌfrȯg, -ˌfräg\ *n* : a large deep-voiced frog
bull·head \-ˌhed\ *n* : any of several common freshwater catfishes of the U.S.
bull·head·ed \-'he-dəd\ *adj* : stupidly stubborn : HEADSTRONG
bul·lion \'bul-yən\ *n* : gold or silver esp. in bars or ingots
bul·lock \'bu-lək\ *n* : a young bull; *also* : STEER
bull pen *n* : a place on a baseball field where pitchers warm up; *also* : the relief pitchers of a baseball team
bull session *n* : an informal discussion
bull's–eye \'bul-ˌzī\ *n, pl* **bull's–eyes** : the center of a target; *also* : a shot that hits the bull's-eye
¹**bul·ly** \'bu-lē\ *n, pl* **bullies** : a person habitually cruel to others who are weaker
²**bully** *adj* : EXCELLENT, FIRST-RATE — often used interjectionally
³**bully** *vb* **bul·lied; bul·ly·ing** : to behave as a bully toward : DOMINEER **syn** browbeat, intimidate, hector
bul·rush \'bul-ˌrəsh\ *n* : any of several large rushes or sedges of wetlands
bul·wark \'bul-(ˌ)wərk, -ˌwȯrk; 'bəl-(ˌ)wərk\ *n* **1** : a wall-like defensive structure **2** : a strong support or protection
¹**bum** \'bəm\ *adj* **1** : of poor quality ⟨～ advice⟩ **2** : DISABLED ⟨a ～ knee⟩
²**bum** *vb* **bummed; bum·ming 1** : to spend time unemployed and wandering; *also* : LOAF **2** : to obtain by begging

³**bum** *n* **1 :** LOAFER **2 :** a devotee of a recreational activity ⟨a ski ∼⟩ **3 :** TRAMP

bum·ble·bee \ˈbəm-bəl-ˌbē\ *n* **:** any of numerous large hairy social bees

bum·mer \ˈbə-mər\ *n* **1 :** an unpleasant experience **2 :** FAILURE

¹**bump** \ˈbəmp\ *n* **1 :** a local bulge; *esp* **:** a swelling of tissue **2 :** a sudden forceful blow or impact — **bumpy** *adj*

²**bump** *vb* **1 :** to strike or knock forcibly; *also* **:** to move by or as if by bumping **2 :** to collide with

¹**bum·per** \ˈbəm-pər\ *n* **1 :** a cup or glass filled to the brim **2 :** something unusually large — **bumper** *adj*

²**bump·er** \ˈbəm-pər\ *n* **:** a device for absorbing shock or preventing damage; *esp* **:** a usu. metal bar at either end of an automobile

bump·kin \ˈbəmp-kən\ *n* **:** an awkward and unsophisticated country person

bump·tious \ˈbəmp-shəs\ *adj* **:** obtusely and often noisily self-assertive

bun \ˈbən\ *n* **:** a sweet biscuit or roll

¹**bunch** \ˈbənch\ *n* **1 :** SWELLING **2 :** CLUSTER, GROUP — **bunchy** *adj*

²**bunch** *vb* **:** to form into a group or bunch

bun·co *or* **bun·ko** \ˈbəŋ-kō\ *n, pl* **buncos** *or* **bunkos :** a swindling scheme — **bunco** *vb*

¹**bun·dle** \ˈbən-dᵊl\ *n* **1 :** several items bunched and fastened together; *also* **:** something wrapped for carrying **2 :** a considerable amount **:** LOT **3 :** a small band of mostly parallel nerve or muscle fibers

²**bundle** *vb* **bun·dled; bun·dling :** to gather or tie in a bundle

bun·dling \ˈbənd-(ᵊ-)liŋ\ *n* **:** a former custom of a courting couple's occupying the same bed without undressing

bung \ˈbəŋ\ *n* **:** the stopper in the bunghole of a cask

bun·ga·low \ˈbəŋ-gə-ˌlō\ *n* **:** a one-storied house with a low-pitched roof

bun·gee cord \ˈbən-jē-\ *n* **:** a long elastic cord used esp. in a sport (**bungee jump·ing**) in which it is fastened to a person to arrest a free fall from a high place (as a bridge)

bung·hole \ˈbəŋ-ˌhōl\ *n* **:** a hole for emptying or filling a cask

bun·gle \ˈbəŋ-gəl\ *vb* **bun·gled; bun·gling :** to do badly **:** BOTCH — **bungle** *n* — **bun·gler** *n*

bun·ion \ˈbən-yən\ *n* **:** an inflamed swelling of the first joint of the big toe

¹**bunk** \ˈbəŋk\ *n* **:** BED; *esp* **:** a built-in bed that is often one of a tier

²**bunk** *n* **:** BUNKUM, NONSENSE

bunk bed *n* **:** one of two single beds usu. placed one above the other

bun·ker \ˈbəŋ-kər\ *n* **1 :** a bin or compartment for storage (as for coal on a ship) **2 :** a protective embankment or dugout **3 :** a sand trap or embankment constituting a hazard on a golf course

bun·kum *or* **bun·combe** \ˈbəŋ-kəm\ *n* [*Buncombe* County, N.C.; fr. a remark made by its congressman, who defended an irrelevant speech by claiming that he was speaking to Buncombe] **:** insincere or foolish talk

bun·ny \ˈbə-nē\ *n, pl* **-nies :** RABBIT

Bun·sen burner \ˈbən-sən-\ *n* **:** a gas burner usu. consisting of a straight tube with air holes at the bottom

¹**bunt** \ˈbənt\ *vb* **1 :** ¹BUTT **2 :** to push or tap a baseball lightly without swinging the bat

²**bunt** *n* **:** an act or instance of bunting; *also* **:** a bunted ball

¹**bun·ting** \ˈbən-tiŋ\ *n* **:** any of numerous small stout⹀ billed finches

²**bunting** *n* **:** a thin fabric used esp. for flags; *also* **:** FLAGS

¹**buoy** \ˈbü-ē, ˈbȯi\ *n* **1 :** a floating object anchored in water to mark something (as a channel) **2 :** a float consist-

ing of a ring of buoyant material to support a person who has fallen into the water

²**buoy** *vb* **1 :** to mark by a buoy **2 :** to keep afloat **3 :** to raise the spirits of

buoy·an·cy \ˈbȯi-ən-sē, ˈbü-yən-\ *n* **1 :** the tendency of a body to float or rise when submerged in a fluid **2 :** the power of a fluid to exert an upward force on a body placed in it **3 :** resilience of spirit — **buoy·ant** \-ənt, -yənt\ *adj*

¹**bur** \ˈbər\ *var of* BURR

²**bur** *abbr* bureau

¹**bur·den** \ˈbərd-ᵊn\ *n* **1 :** LOAD; *also* **:** CARE, RESPONSIBILITY **2 :** something oppressive **:** ENCUMBRANCE **3 :** CARGO; *also* **:** capacity for cargo

²**burden** *vb* **:** LOAD, OPPRESS — **bur·den·some** \-səm\ *adj*

³**burden** *n* **1 :** REFRAIN, CHORUS **2 :** a main theme or idea **:** GIST

bur·dock \ˈbər-ˌdäk\ *n* **:** any of a genus of coarse composite herbs with globe-shaped flower heads surrounded by prickly bracts

bu·reau \ˈbyu̇r-ō\ *n, pl* **bureaus** *also* **bu·reaux** \-ōz\ [F, desk, cloth covering for desks, fr. OF *burel* woolen cloth, ultim. fr. L *burra* shaggy cloth] **1 :** a chest of drawers **2 :** an administrative unit (as of a government department) **3 :** a branch of a publication or wire service in an important news center

bu·reau·cra·cy \byu̇-ˈrä-krə-sē\ *n, pl* **-cies 1 :** a body of appointive government officials **2 :** government marked by specialization of functions under fixed rules and a hierarchy of authority; *also* **:** an unwieldy administrative system burdened with excessive complexity and lack of flexibility — **bu·reau·crat** \ˈbyu̇r-ə-ˌkrat\ *n* — **bu·reau·crat·ic** \ˌbyu̇r-ə-ˈkra-tik\ *adj*

bur·geon \ˈbər-jən\ *vb* **:** to put forth fresh growth (as from buds) **:** grow vigorously **:** FLOURISH

burgh \ˈbər-ō\ *n* **:** a Scottish town

bur·gher \ˈbər-gər\ *n* **1 :** TOWNSMAN **2 :** a prosperous solid citizen

bur·glary \ˈbər-glə-rē\ *n, pl* **-glar·ies :** forcible entry into a building esp. at night with the intent to commit a crime (as theft) — **bur·glar** \-glər\ *n* — **bur·glar·ize** \ˈbər-glə-ˌrīz\ *vb*

bur·gle \ˈbər-gəl\ *vb* **bur·gled; bur·gling :** to commit burglary on

bur·go·mas·ter \ˈbər-gə-ˌmas-tər\ *n* **:** the chief magistrate of a town in some European countries

bur·gun·dy \ˈbər-gən dē\ *n, pl* **-dies** *often cap* **1 :** a red or white table wine from the Burgundy region of France **2 :** an American red table wine

buri·al \ˈber-ē-əl\ *n* **:** the act or process of burying

burl \ˈbərl\ *n* **:** a hard woody often flattened hemispherical outgrowth on a tree

bur·lap \ˈbər-ˌlap\ *n* **:** a coarse fabric usu. of jute or hemp used esp. for bags

¹**bur·lesque** \(ˌ)bər-ˈlesk\ *n* [*burlesque,* adj., comic, droll, fr. F, fr. It *burlesco,* fr. *burla* joke, fr. Sp] **1 :** a witty or derisive literary or dramatic imitative work **2 :** broadly **:** humorous theatrical entertainment consisting of several items (as songs, skits, or dances)

²**burlesque** *vb* **bur·lesqued; bur·lesqu·ing :** to make ludicrous by burlesque **syn** caricature, parody, travesty

bur·ly \ˈbər-lē\ *adj* **bur·li·er; -est :** strongly and heavily built **:** HUSKY **syn** muscular, brawny, beefy, hefty

Bur·mese \ˌbər-ˈmēz, -ˈmēs\ *n, pl* **Burmese :** a native or inhabitant of Burma (Myanmar) — **Burmese** *adj*

¹**burn** \ˈbərn\ *vb* **burned** \ˈbərnd, ˈbərnt\ *or* **burnt** \ˈbərnt\; **burn·ing 1 :** to be on fire **2 :** to feel or look as

\ə\abut \ᵊ\kitten \ər\further \a\ash \ā\ace \ä\mop, mar \au̇\out \ch\chin \e\bet \ē\easy \g\go \i\hit \ī\ice \j\job \ŋ\sing \ō\go \ȯ\law \oi\boy \th\thin \t͟h\the \ü\loot \u̇\foot \y\yet \zh\vision *see also* Pronunciation Symbols page if on fire **3** : to alter or become altered by or as if by the action of fire or heat **4** : to use as fuel ⟨∼ coal⟩; *also* : to destroy by fire ⟨∼ trash⟩ **5** : to cause or make by fire ⟨∼ a hole⟩; *also* : to affect as if by heat

²**burn** *n* : an injury or effect produced by or as if by burning

burn·er \'bər-nər\ *n* : the part of a fuel-burning or heat-producing device where the flame or heat is produced

bur·nish \'bər-nish\ *vb* : to make shiny esp. by rubbing : POLISH — **bur·nish·er** *n* — **bur·nish·ing** *adj or n*

bur·noose *or* **bur·nous** \(ˌ)bər-'nüs\ *n* : a hooded cloak worn esp. by Arabs

burn·out \'bər-ˌnau̇t\ *n* **1** : the cessation of operation of a jet or rocket engine **2** : exhaustion of one's physical or emotional strength; *also* : a person suffering from burnout

burp \'bərp\ *n* : an act of belching — **burp** *vb*

burp gun *n* : a small submachine gun

burr \'bər\ *n* **1** *usu* **bur** : a rough or prickly envelope of a fruit; *also* : a plant that bears burs **2** : roughness left in cutting or shaping metal **3** : WHIR — **bur·ry** *adj*

bur·ri·to \bə-'rē-tō\ *n* [AmerSp, fr. Sp, little donkey, dim. of *burro*] : a flour tortilla rolled around a filling and baked

bur·ro \'bər-ō, 'bu̇r-\ *n, pl* **burros** [Sp] : a usu. small donkey

¹**bur·row** \'bər-ō\ *n* : a hole in the ground made by an animal (as a rabbit)

²**burrow** *vb* **1** : to form by tunneling; *also* : to make a burrow **2** : to progress by or as if by digging — **bur·row·er** *n*

bur·sar \'bər-sər\ *n* : a treasurer esp. of a college

bur·si·tis \(ˌ)bər-'sī-təs\ *n* : inflammation of the serous sac (**bur·sa** \'bər-sə\) of a joint (as the elbow or shoulder)

¹**burst** \'bərst\ *vb* **burst** *or* **burst·ed**; **burst·ing** **1** : to fly apart or into pieces **2** : to show one's feelings suddenly; *also* : PLUNGE ⟨∼ into song⟩ **3** : to enter or emerge suddenly : SPRING **4** : to be filled to the breaking point

²**burst** *n* **1** : a sudden outbreak : SPURT **2** : EXPLOSION **3** : result of bursting

Bu·run·di·an \bu̇-'rün-dē-ən\ *n* : a native or inhabitant of Burundi

bury \'ber-ē\ *vb* **bur·ied**; **bury·ing** **1** : to deposit in the earth; *also* : to inter with funeral ceremonies **2** : CONCEAL, HIDE **3** : SUBMERGE, ENGROSS — usu. used with *in*

¹**bus** \'bəs\ *n, pl* **bus·es** *or* **bus·ses** [short for *omnibus*, fr. F, fr. L, for all, dat. pl. of *omnis* all] : a large motor vehicle for carrying passengers

²**bus** *vb* **bused** *or* **bussed**; **bus·ing** *or* **bus·sing** **1** : to travel or transport by bus **2** : to work as a busboy

³**bus** *abbr* business

bus·boy \'bəs-ˌbȯi\ *n* : a waiter's helper

bus·by \'bəz-bē\ *n, pl* **busbies** : a military full-dress fur hat

bush \'bush\ *n* **1** : SHRUB **2** : rough uncleared country **3** : a thick tuft ⟨a ∼ of hair⟩ — **bushy** *adj*

bushed \'busht\ *adj* : TIRED, EXHAUSTED

bush·el \'bu̇-shəl\ *n* — see WEIGHT table

bush·ing \'bu̇-shiŋ\ *n* : a usu. removable cylindrical lining for an opening of a mechanical part to limit the size of the opening, resist wear, or serve as a guide

bush·mas·ter \'bush-ˌmas-tər\ *n* : a large venomous tropical American pit viper

bush·whack \-ˌhwak\ *vb* **1** : AMBUSH **2** : to clear a path through esp. by chopping down bushes and branches — **bush·whack·er** *n*

busi·ly \'bi-zə-lē\ *adv* : in a busy manner

busi·ness \'biz-nəs, -nəz\ *n* **1** : OCCUPATION; *also* : TASK, MISSION **2** : a commercial or industrial enterprise; *also* : TRADE ⟨∼ is good⟩ **3** : AFFAIR, MATTER **4** : personal concern

busi·ness·man \-ˌman\ *n* : a man engaged in business esp. as an executive

busi·ness·per·son \-ˌpərs-ᵊn\ *n* : a businessman or businesswoman

busi·ness·wom·an \-ˌwu̇-mən\ *n* : a woman engaged in business esp. as an executive

bus·kin \'bəs-kən\ *n* **1** : a laced boot reaching halfway to the knee **2** : tragic drama

buss \'bəs\ *n* : KISS — **buss** *vb*

¹**bust** \'bəst\ *n* [F *buste*, fr. It *busto*, fr. L *bustum* tomb] **1** : sculpture representing the upper part of the human figure **2** : the part of the human torso between the neck and the waist; *esp* : the breasts of a woman

²**bust** *vb* **bust·ed** *also* **bust**; **bust·ing** **1** : BREAK, SMASH; *also* : BURST **2** : to ruin financially **3** : TAME **4** : DEMOTE **5** *slang* : ARREST; *also* : RAID

³**bust** *n* **1** : a drinking session **2** : a complete failure : FLOP **3** : a business depression **4** : PUNCH, SOCK **5** *slang* : a police raid; *also* : ARREST

¹**bus·tle** \'bə-səl\ *vb* **bus·tled**; **bus·tling** : to move or work in a brisk busy manner

²**bustle** *n* : briskly energetic activity

³**bustle** *n* : a pad or frame worn to support the fullness at the back of a woman's skirt

¹**busy** \'bi-zē\ *adj* **busi·er**; **-est** **1** : engaged in action : not idle **2** : being in use ⟨∼ telephones⟩ **3** : full of activity ⟨∼ streets⟩ **4** : MEDDLING

²**busy** *vb* **bus·ied**; **busy·ing** : to make or keep busy : OCCUPY

busy·body \'bi-zē-ˌbä-dē\ *n* : MEDDLER

busy·work \-ˌwərk\ *n* : work that appears productive but only keeps one occupied

¹**but** \'bət\ *conj* **1** : except for the fact ⟨would have protested ∼ that he was afraid⟩ **2** : THAT ⟨there's no doubt ∼ he won⟩ **3** : without the certainty that ⟨never rains ∼ it pours⟩ **4** : on the contrary ⟨not one, ∼ two job offers⟩ **5** : YET ⟨poor ∼ proud⟩ **6** : with the exception of ⟨none ∼ the strongest attempt it⟩

²**but** *prep* : other than : EXCEPT ⟨this letter is nothing ∼ an insult⟩; *also* : with the exception of ⟨no one here ∼ me⟩

bu·tane \'byü-ˌtān\ *n* : either of two gaseous hydrocarbons used as a fuel

¹**butch·er** \'bu̇-chər\ *n* [ME *bocher*, fr. OF *bouchier*, fr. *bouc* he-goat] **1** : one who slaughters animals or dresses their flesh; *also* : a dealer in meat **2** : one that kills brutally or needlessly **3** : one that botches — **butch·ery** \-chə-rē\ *n*

²**butcher** *vb* **1** : to slaughter and dress for meat ⟨∼ hogs⟩ **2** : to kill barbarously **3** : BOTCH

but·ler \'bət-lər\ *n* [ME *buteler*, fr. OF *bouteillier* bottle bearer, fr. *bouteille* bottle] : the chief male servant of a household

¹**butt** \'bət\ *vb* : to strike with the head or horns

²**butt** *n* : a blow or thrust with the head or horns

³**butt** *n* : a large cask

⁴**butt** *n* **1** : TARGET **2** : an object of abuse or ridicule

⁵**butt** *n* : a large, thicker, or bottom end of something

⁶**butt** *vb* **1** : ABUT **2** : to place or join edge to edge without overlapping

butte \'byüt\ *n* : an isolated steep hill

¹**but·ter** \'bə-tər\ *n* [ME, fr. OE *butere*, fr. L *butyrum* butter, fr. Gk *boutyron*, fr. *bous* cow + *tyros* cheese] **1** : a solid edible emulsion of fat obtained from cream by churning **2** : a substance resembling butter — **but·tery** *adj*

²**butter** *vb* : to spread with or as if with butter

but·ter–and–eggs \ˌbə-tə-rə-'negz\ *n sing or pl* : a common perennial herb related to the snapdragon that has showy yellow and orange flowers

but·ter·cup \'bə-tər-ˌkəp\ *n* : any of a genus of herbs having usu. yellow flowers with five petals and sepals

but·ter·fat \-ˌfat\ *n* : the natural fat of milk and chief constituent of butter

but·ter·fin·gered \-ˌfiŋ-gərd\ *adj* : likely to let things fall or slip through the fingers — **but·ter·fin·gers** \-gərz\ *n sing or pl*

but·ter·fly \-ˌflī\ *n* : any of a group of slender day‍-flying insects with four broad wings covered with bright-colored scales

but·ter·milk \-ˌmilk\ *n* : the liquid remaining after butter is churned

but·ter·nut \-ˌnət\ *n* : the sweet egg-shaped nut of an American tree related to the walnut; *also* : this tree

but·ter·scotch \-ˌskäch\ *n* : a candy made from brown sugar, corn syrup, and water; *also* : the flavor of such candy

but·tock \ˈbə-tək\ *n* **1** : the back of a hip that forms one of the fleshy parts on which a person sits **2** *pl* : the seat of the body : RUMP

¹but·ton \ˈbət-ᵊn\ *n* **1** : a small knob secured to an article (as of clothing) and used as a fastener by passing it through a buttonhole or loop **2** : something that resembles a button **3** : PUSH BUTTON

²button *vb* : to close or fasten with or as if with buttons

¹but·ton·hole \ˈbət-ᵊn-ˌhōl\ *n* : a slit or loop for a button to pass through

²buttonhole *vb* : to detain in conversation by or as if by holding on to the outer garments of

¹but·tress \ˈbə-trəs\ *n* **1** : a projecting structure to support a wall **2** : PROP, SUPPORT

buttress 1

²buttress *vb* : PROP, SUPPORT

bu·tut \bü-ˈtüt\ *n, pl* **bututs** *or* **butut** — see *dalasi* at MONEY table

bux·om \ˈbək-səm\ *adj* : healthily plump; *esp* : full‍-bosomed

¹buy \ˈbī\ *vb* **bought** \ˈbȯt\; **buy·ing 1** : to obtain for a price : PURCHASE; *also* : BRIBE **2** : to accept as true — **buy·er** *n*

²buy *n* **1** : PURCHASE 1, 2 **2** : an exceptional value : BARGAIN

¹buzz \ˈbəz\ *vb* **1** : to make a buzz **2** : to fly fast and close to

²buzz *n* : a low humming sound

buz·zard \ˈbə-zərd\ *n* : any of various usu. large birds of prey and esp. the turkey vulture

buzz·er \ˈbə-zər\ *n* : a device that signals with a buzzing sound

buzz saw *n* : CIRCULAR SAW

buzz·word \ˈbəz-ˌwərd\ *n* : a voguish word or phrase often from technical jargon

BV *abbr* Blessed Virgin

BWI *abbr* British West Indies

bx *abbr* box

BX *abbr* base exchange

¹by \ˈbī, bə\ *prep* **1** : NEAR ⟨stood ∼ the window⟩ **2** : through or through the medium of : VIA ⟨left ∼ the door⟩ **3** : PAST ⟨drove ∼ the house⟩ **4** : DURING, AT ⟨studied ∼ night⟩ **5** : no later than ⟨get here ∼ 3 p.m.⟩ **6** : through the means or direct agency of ⟨∼ force⟩ **7** : in conformity with; *also* : ACCORDING TO ⟨did it ∼ the book⟩ **8** : with respect to ⟨a vet ∼ profession⟩ **9** : to the amount or extent of ⟨won ∼ a nose⟩ **10** — used to express relationship in multiplication, in division, and in measurements ⟨divide *a* ∼ *b*⟩ ⟨multiply ∼ 6⟩ ⟨15 feet ∼ 20 feet⟩

²by \ˈbī\ *adv* **1** : near at hand; *also* : IN ⟨stop ∼⟩ **2** : PAST **3** : ASIDE, APART

bye \ˈbī\ *n* : a position of a participant in a tournament who advances to the next round without playing

by–elec·tion *also* **bye–election** \ˈbī-ə-ˌlek-shən\ *n* : a special election held between regular elections in order to fill a vacancy

by·gone \ˈbī-ˌgȯn\ *adj* : gone by : PAST — **bygone** *n*

by·law *or* **bye·law** \ˈbī-ˌlȯ\ *n* : a rule adopted by an organization for managing its internal affairs

by–line \ˈbī-ˌlīn\ *n* : a line at the beginning of a news story or magazine article giving the writer's name

BYO *abbr* bring your own

BYOB *abbr* bring your own beer; bring your own booze; bring your own bottle

¹by·pass \ˈbī-ˌpas\ *n* : a passage to one side or around a blocked or congested area; *also* : a surgical procedure establishing this ⟨a coronary ∼⟩

²bypass *vb* : to avoid by means of a bypass

by·path \-ˌpath, -ˌpȧth\ *n* : BYWAY

by·play \ˈbī-ˌplā\ *n* : action engaged in on the side (as of a stage) while the main action proceeds

by–prod·uct \-ˌprä-(ˌ)dəkt\ *n* : a sometimes unexpected product or result produced in addition to the main product or result

by·stand·er \-ˌstan-dər\ *n* : one present but not participating **syn** onlooker, witness, spectator, eyewitness

byte \ˈbīt\ *n* : a group of 8 bits that a computer processes as a unit

by·way \ˈbī-ˌwā\ *n* **1** : a little-traveled side road **2** : a secondary aspect

by·word \-ˌwərd\ *n* **1** : PROVERB **2** : one that is noteworthy or notorious

Byz·an·tine \ˈbiz-ᵊn-ˌtēn, ˈbī-, -ˌtīn; bə-ˈzan-, bī-\ *adj* **1** : of, relating to, or characteristic of the ancient city of Byzantium or the the Byzantine Empire **2** *often not cap* : intricately involved and often devious

C

¹c \'sē\ n, pl c's or cs \'sēz\ often cap 1 : the 3d letter of the English alphabet 2 slang : a sum of $100 3 : a grade rating a student's work as fair

²c abbr, often cap 1 calorie 2 carat 3 Celsius 4 cent 5 centigrade 6 centimeter 7 century 8 chapter 9 circa 10 cocaine 11 copyright

C symbol carbon

ca abbr circa

Ca symbol calcium

CA abbr 1 California 2 chartered accountant 3 chief accountant 4 chronological age

cab \'kab\ n 1 : a light closed horse-drawn carriage 2 : TAXICAB 3 : the covered compartment for the engineer and controls of a locomotive; also : a similar compartment (as on a truck)

CAB abbr Civil Aeronautics Board

ca·bal \kə-'bäl, -'bal\ n [F cabale, fr. ML cabbala cabala, fr. Heb qabbālāh, lit., received (lore)] : a secret group of plotters or political conspirators

ca·ba·la \'ka-bə-lə, kə-'bä-\ n, often cap 1 : a medieval Jewish mysticism marked by belief in creation through emanation and a cipher method of interpreting Scripture 2 : esoteric or mysterious doctrine

ca·bana \kə-'ban-yə, -'ba-nə\ n : a shelter at a beach or swimming pool

cab·a·ret \ˌka-bə-'rā\ n : NIGHTCLUB

cab·bage \'ka-bij\ n [ME caboche, fr. OF, head] : a vegetable related to the mustard with a dense head of leaves

cab·bie or cab·by \'ka-bē\ n, pl cabbies : a driver of a cab

cab·er·net sau·vi·gnon \ˌka-bər-'nā-sō-vē-'nyōⁿ\ n : a dry red wine made from a single variety of black grape

cab·in \'ka-bən\ n 1 : a private room on a ship; also : a compartment below deck on a boat for passengers or crew 2 : an aircraft or spacecraft compartment for passengers, crew, or cargo 3 : a small simple one-story house

cabin boy n : a boy working as servant on a ship

cabin class n : a class of accommodations on a passenger ship superior to tourist class and inferior to first class

cabin cruiser n : CRUISER 3

cab·i·net \'kab-nit\ n 1 : a case or cupboard for holding or displaying articles 2 : the advisory council of a head of state (as a president or sovereign)

cab·i·net·mak·er \-ˌmā-kər\ n : a woodworker who makes fine furniture — cab·i·net·mak·ing n

cab·i·net·work \-ˌwərk\ n : the finished work of a cabinetmaker

¹ca·ble \'kā-bəl\ n 1 : a very strong rope, wire, or chain 2 : a bundle of insulated wires usu. twisted around a central core 3 : CABLEGRAM 4 : CABLE TELEVISION

²cable vb ca·bled; ca·bling : to telegraph by cable

cable car n : a vehicle moved by an endless cable

ca·ble·gram \'kā-bəl-ˌgram\ n : a message sent by a submarine telegraph cable

cable television n : a system of television reception in which signals from distant stations are sent by cable to the receivers of paying subscribers

cab·o·chon \'ka-bə-ˌshän\ n : a gem or bead cut in convex form and highly polished but not given facets; also : this style of cutting — cabochon adv

ca·boose \kə-'büs\ n : a car usu. at the rear of a freight train for the use of the train crew and railroad workers

cab·ri·o·let \ˌka-brē-ə-'lā\ n [F] 1 : a light 2-wheeled one-horse carriage 2 : a convertible coupe

cab·stand \'kab-ˌstand\ n : a place where cabs wait for passengers

ca·cao \kə-'kaù, -'kä-ò\ n, pl cacaos [Sp] : a So. American tree whose seeds (cacao beans) are the source of cocoa and chocolate; also : its dried fatty seeds

cac·cia·to·re \ˌkä-chə-'tór-ē\ adj [It] : cooked with tomatoes and herbs ⟨chicken ∼⟩

cache \'kash\ n [F] : a hiding place esp. for preserving provisions; also : something hidden or stored in a cache — cache vb

ca·chet \ka-'shā\ n [F] 1 : a seal used esp. as a mark of official approval 2 : a feature or quality conferring prestige; also : PRESTIGE 3 : a design, inscription, or advertisement printed or stamped on mail

cack·le \'ka-kəl\ vb cack·led; cack·ling 1 : to make the sharp broken cry characteristic of a hen 2 : to laugh or chatter noisily — cackle n — cack·ler n

ca·coph·o·ny \ka-'kä-fə-nē\ n, pl -nies : harsh or discordant sound — ca·coph·o·nous \-nəs\ adj

cac·tus \'kak-təs\ n, pl cac·ti \-ˌtī\ or cac·tus·es also cactus : any of a large family of drought-resistant flowering plants with succulent stems and with leaves replaced by scales or prickles

cad \'kad\ n : a man who deliberately disregards another's feelings — cad·dish \'ka-dish\ adj — cad·dish·ly adv — cad·dish·ness n

ca·dav·er \kə-'da-vər\ n : a dead body

ca·dav·er·ous \kə-'da-və-rəs\ adj : suggesting a corpse esp. in gauntness or pallor syn wasted, emaciated, gaunt — ca·dav·er·ous·ly adv

cad·die or cad·dy \'ka-dē\ n, pl caddies [F cadet military cadet] : a person who assists a golfer esp. by carrying the clubs — caddie or caddy vb

cad·dy \'ka-dē\ n, pl caddies [Malay kati a unit of weight] : a small box, can, or chest; esp : one to keep tea in

ca·dence \'kād-ᵊns\ n : the measure or beat of a rhythmical flow : RHYTHM — ca·denced \-ᵊnst\ adj

ca·den·za \kə-'den-zə\ n [It] : a brilliant sometimes improvised passage usu. toward the close of a musical composition

ca·det \kə-'det\ n [F, fr. Prov (Gascony) capdet chief, fr. L capitellum, fr. L caput head] 1 : a younger son or brother 2 : a student in a service academy

Ca·dette \kə-'det\ n : a member of a Girl Scout program for girls in sixth through ninth grades

cadge \'kaj\ vb cadged; cadg·ing : SPONGE, BEG — cadg·er n

cad·mi·um \'kad-mē-əm\ n : a bluish white metallic chemical element used esp. in protective platings — see ELEMENT table

cad·re \'ka-ˌdrā, 'kä-, -drē\ n [F] 1 : FRAMEWORK 2 : a central unit esp. of trained personnel able to assume control and train others 3 : a group of indoctrinated leaders active in promoting the interests of a revolutionary party

ca·du·ceus \kə-'dü-sē-əs, -'dyü-, -shəs\ n, pl -cei \-sē-ˌī\ [L] 1 : the staff of a herald; esp : a representation of a staff with two entwined snakes and two wings at the top 2 : an insignia bearing a caduceus and symbolizing a physician

cae·cum var of CECUM

Cae·sar \'sē-zər\ n 1 : any of the Roman emperors succeeding Augustus Caesar — used as a title 2 often not cap : a powerful ruler : AUTOCRAT, DICTATOR; also : the civil or temporal power

caesarean *also* **caesarian** *var of* CESAREAN

cae·si·um *chiefly Brit var of* CESIUM

cae·sura \si-'zhùr-ə\ *n, pl* **-suras** *or* **-su·rae** \-'zhùr-(,)ē\ : a break in the flow of sound usu. in the middle of a line of verse

ca·fé \ka-'fā\ *n* [F, lit., coffee] **1** : RESTAURANT **2** : BARROOM **3** : NIGHTCLUB

ca·fé au lait \(,)ka-,fā-ò-'lā\ *n* : coffee with hot milk in about equal parts

caf·e·te·ria \,ka-fə-'tir-ē-ə\ *n* [AmerSp *cafetería* coffeehouse] : a restaurant in which the customers serve themselves or are served at a counter

caf·feine \ka-'fēn, 'ka-,fēn\ *n* : a stimulating alkaloid found esp. in coffee and tea

caf·tan \kaf-'tan, 'kaf-,tan\ *n* [Russ *kaftan*, fr. Turk. fr. Per *qaftān*] : an ankle-length garment with long sleeves worn in countries of the eastern Mediterranean

¹cage \'kāj\ *n* **1** : an openwork enclosure for confining an animal **2** : something resembling a cage

²cage *vb* **caged; cag·ing** : to put or keep in or as if in a cage

ca·gey *also* **ca·gy** \'kā-jē\ *adj* **ca·gi·er; -est** : wary of being trapped or deceived : SHREWD — **ca·gi·ly** \-jə-lē\ *adv* — **ca·gi·ness** \-jē-nəs\ *n*

CAGS *abbr* Certificate of Advanced Graduate Study

ca·hoot \kə-'hüt\ *n* : PARTNERSHIP, LEAGUE — usu. used in pl. ⟨officials in ∼s with the underworld⟩

cai·man \'kā-mən; kā-'man, kī-\ *n* : any of several Central and So. American reptiles closely related to alligators and crocodiles

cairn \'karn\ *n* : a heap of stones serving as a memorial or a landmark

cais·son \'kā-,sän, 'kās-ⁿn\ *n* **1** : a usu. 2-wheeled vehicle for artillery ammunition **2** : a watertight chamber used in underwater construction work or as a foundation

caisson disease *n* : ²BEND 3

cai·tiff \'kā-təf\ *adj* [ME *caitif*, fr. OF, captive, vile, fr. L *captivus* captive] : being base, cowardly, or despicable — **caitiff** *n*

ca·jole \kə-'jōl\ *vb* **ca·joled; ca·jol·ing** [F *cajoler*] : to persuade or coax esp. with flattery or false promises — **ca·jole·ment** *n* — **ca·jol·ery** \-'jō-lə-rē\ *n*

Ca·jun \'kā-jən\ *n* : a Louisianian descended from French-speaking immigrants from Acadia (Nova Scotia) — **Cajun** *adj*

¹cake \'kāk\ *n* **1** : a baked or fried breadlike food usu. in a small flat shape **2** : a sweet baked food made from batter or dough usu. containing flour, sugar, or shortening, and a leaven (as baking powder) **3** : a hardened or compacted substance ⟨a ∼ of soap⟩

²cake *vb* **caked; cak·ing 1** : ENCRUST **2** : to form or harden into a cake

cake·walk \'kāk-,wòk\ *n* **1** : a stage dance typically involving a high prance with backward tilt **2** : a one= sided contest or an easy task

cal *abbr* **1** calendar **2** caliber

Cal *abbr* **1** California **2** calorie

cal·a·bash \'ka-lə-,bash\ *n* : the fruit of a gourd; *also* : a utensil made from its hard shell

cal·a·boose \'ka-lə-,büs\ *n* [Sp *calabozo* dungeon] : JAIL

ca·la·di·um \kə-'lā-dē-əm\ *n* : any of a genus of tropical American ornamental plants related to the arums

cal·a·mari \,kä-lə-'mär-ē\ *n* [It] : squid used as food

cal·a·mine \'ka-lə-,mīn\ *n* : a lotion of oxides of zinc and iron

ca·lam·i·ty \kə-'la-mə-tē\ *n, pl* **-ties 1** : great distress or misfortune **2** : an event causing great harm or loss and affliction : DISASTER — **ca·lam·i·tous** \-təs\ *adj* — **ca·lam·i·tous·ly** *adv* — **ca·lam·i·tous·ness** *n*

calc *abbr* calculate; calculated

cal·car·e·ous \kal-'kar-ē-əs\ *adj* : resembling calcium carbonate in hardness; *also* : containing calcium or calcium carbonate

cal·cif·er·ous \kal-'si-fə-rəs\ *adj* : producing or containing calcium carbonate

cal·ci·fy \'kal-sə-,fī\ *vb* **-fied; -fy·ing** : to make or become calcareous — **cal·ci·fi·ca·tion** \,kal-sə-fə-'kā-shən\ *n*

cal·ci·mine \'kal-sə-,mīn\ *n* : a thin water paint used esp. on plastered surfaces — **calcimine** *vb*

cal·cine \kal-'sīn\ *vb* **cal·cined; cal·cin·ing** : to heat to a high temperature but without fusing to drive off volatile matter and often to reduce to powder — **cal·ci·na·tion** \,kal-sə-'nā-shən\ *n*

cal·cite \'kal-,sīt\ *n* : a crystalline mineral consisting of calcium carbonate — **cal·cit·ic** \kal-'si-tik\ *adj*

cal·ci·um \'kal-sē-əm\ *n* : a silver-white soft metallic chemical element occurring only in combination — see ELEMENT table

calcium carbonate *n* : a substance found in nature as limestone and marble and in plant ashes, bones, and shells

cal·cu·late \'kal-kyə-,lāt\ *vb* **-lat·ed; -lat·ing** [L *calculare*, fr. *calculus* small stone, pebble used in reckoning] **1** : to determine by mathematical processes : COMPUTE **2** : to reckon by exercise of practical judgment : ESTIMATE **3** : to design or adapt for a purpose **4** : COUNT, RELY — **cal·cu·la·ble** \-lə-bəl\ *adj* — **cal·cu·la·tor** \-,lā-tər\ *n*

cal·cu·lat·ed \-,lā-təd\ *adj* **1** : undertaken after estimating the probability of success or failure ⟨a ∼ risk⟩ **2** : planned purposefully : DELIBERATE

cal·cu·lat·ing \-,lā-tiŋ\ *adj* : marked by shrewd consideration esp. of self-interest — **cal·cu·lat·ing·ly** *adv*

cal·cu·la·tion \,kal-kyə-'lā-shən\ *n* **1** : the process or an act of calculating **2** : the result of an act of calculating **3** : studied care; *also* : cold heartless planning to promote self-interest

cal·cu·lus \'kal-kyə-ləs\ *n, pl* **-li** \-,lī\ *also* **-lus·es** [L, pebble (used in reckoning)] **1** : a method of computation in a special notation (as of logic) **2** : a branch of higher mathematics comprising differential and integral calculus **3** : a concretion usu. of mineral salts esp. in hollow organs or ducts

cal·de·ra \kal-'der-ə, kòl-, -'dir-\ *n* [Sp, lit., caldron] : a large crater usu. formed by the collapse of a volcanic cone

cal·dron *var of* CAULDRON

¹cal·en·dar \'ka-lən-dər\ *n* **1** : an arrangement of time into days, weeks, months, and years; *also* : a sheet or folder containing such an arrangement for a period **2** : an orderly list

²calendar *vb* : to enter in a calendar

¹cal·en·der \'ka-lən-dər\ *vb* : to press (as cloth or paper) between rollers or plates so as to make smooth or glossy or to thin into sheets

²calender *n* : a machine for calendering

ca·lends \'ka-ləndz, 'kā-\ *n sing or pl* : the first day of the ancient Roman month

ca·len·du·la \kə-'len-jə-lə\ *n* : any of a genus of yellow= flowered herbs related to the daisies

¹calf \'kaf, 'kaf\ *n, pl* **calves** \'kavz, 'kàvz\ **1** : the young of the domestic cow; *also* : the young of various large mammals (as the elephant or whale) **2** : CALFSKIN

²calf *n, pl* **calves** \'kavz, 'kàvz\ : the fleshy back of the leg below the knee

calf·skin \'kaf-,skin, 'kàf-\ *n* : leather made of the skin of a calf

cal·i·ber *or* **cal·i·bre** \'ka-lə-bər\ *n* [MF *calibre*, fr. It

\ə\abut \ᵊ\kitten \ər\further \a\ash \ā\ace \ä\mop, mar
\aù\out \ch\chin \e\bet \ē\easy \g\go \i\hit \ī\ice \j\job
\ŋ\sing \ō\go \ò\law \òi\boy \th\thin \t̲h̲\the \ü\loot \ù\foot
\y\yet \zh\vision *see also* Pronunciation Symbols page

calibro, fr. Ar *qālib* shoemaker's last] **1** : degree of mental capacity, excellence, or importance **2** : the diameter of a projectile **3** : the diameter of the bore of a gun

cal·i·brate \'ka-lə-ˌbrāt\ *vb* **-brat·ed; -brat·ing** : to adjust precisely

cal·i·bra·tion \ˌka-lə-'brā-shən\ *n* : a set of graduated marks indicating values or positions — usu. used in pl.

¹**cal·i·co** \'ka-li-ˌkò\ *n, pl* **-coes** *or* **-cos** : printed cotton fabric

²**calico** *adj* **1** : made of calico **2** : having blotched or spotted markings ⟨a ∼ cat⟩

Calif *abbr* California

Cal·i·for·nia poppy \ˌka-lə-'fòr-nyə-\ *n* : a widely cultivated herb with usu. yellow or orange flowers that is related to the poppies

cal·i·for·ni·um \ˌka-lə-'fòr-nē-əm\ *n* : an artificially prepared radioactive chemical element — see ELEMENT table

cal·i·per \'ka-lə-pər\ *n* **1** : any of various instruments having two arms, legs, or jaws used esp. to measure diameter or thickness — usu. used in pl. **2** : a device consisting of two plates lined with a frictional material that press against the sides of a rotating wheel or disk in certain brake systems

ca·liph \'kā-ləf, 'ka-\ *n* : a successor of Muhammad as head of Islam — used as a title — **ca·liph·ate** \-lə-ˌfāt, -fət\ *n*

cal·is·then·ics \ˌka-ləs-'the-niks\ *n sing or pl* [Gk *kalos* beautiful + *sthenos* strength] : bodily exercises usu. done without apparatus — **cal·is·then·ic** *adj*

calk \'kòk\ *var of* CAULK

¹**call** \'kòl\ *vb* **1** : SHOUT, CRY; *also* : to utter a characteristic note or cry **2** : to utter in a loud clear voice **3** : to announce authoritatively **4** : SUMMON **5** : to make a request or demand ⟨∼ for an investigation⟩ **6** : to halt (as a baseball game) because of unsuitable conditions **7** : to demand payment of (a loan); *also* : to demand surrender of (as a bond) for redemption **8** : to get or try to get in communication by telephone **9** : to make a brief visit **10** : to speak of or address by name : give a name to **11** : to estimate or consider for practical purposes ⟨∼ it ten miles⟩ **12** : to temporarily transfer control of computer processing to (as a subroutine or procedure) — **call·er** *n*

²**call** *n* **1** : SHOUT **2** : the cry of an animal (as a bird) **3** : a request or a command to come or assemble : INVITATION, SUMMONS **4** : DEMAND, CLAIM; *also* : REQUEST **5** : a brief usu. formal visit **6** : an act of calling on the telephone **7** : DECISION ⟨a tough ∼⟩ **8** : a temporary transfer of control of computer processing to a particular set of instructions

cal·la lily \'ka-lə-\ *n* : a plant whose flowers form a fleshy yellow spike surrounded by a lilylike usu. white leaf

call·back \'kòl-ˌbak\ *n* a calling back; *esp* : RECALL 5

call–board \-ˌbòrd\ *n* : a board for posting notices (as of rehearsal calls)

call down *vb* : REPRIMAND

call girl *n* : a prostitute with whom appointments are made by phone

cal·lig·ra·phy \kə-'li-grə-fē\ *n* : artistic or elegant handwriting; *also* : the art of producing such writing — **cal·lig·ra·pher** \-fər\ *n*

call–in \'kòl-ˌin\ *adj* : allowing listeners to engage in broadcast telephone conversations ⟨a ∼ show⟩

call in *vb* **1** : to order to return or be returned **2** : to summon to one's aid **3** : to report by telephone

call·ing \'kò-liŋ\ *n* **1** : a strong inner impulse toward a particular course of action **2** : the activity in which one customarily engages as an occupation

cal·li·ope \kə-'lī-ə-(ˌ)pē, 'ka-lē-ˌòp\ *n* [fr. *Calliope,* chief of the Muses, fr. L, fr. Gk *Kalliopē*] : a keyboard mu-

sical instrument similar to an organ and made up of a series of whistles

cal·li·per *chiefly Brit var of* CALIPER

call number *n* : a combination of characters assigned to a library book to indicate its place on a shelf

call off *vb* : CANCEL

cal·los·i·ty \ka-'lä-sə-tē\ *n, pl* **-ties 1** : the quality or state of being callous **2** : CALLUS 1

¹**cal·lous** \'ka-ləs\ *adj* **1** : being thickened and hardened ⟨∼ skin⟩ **2** : feeling no emotion or sympathy — **cal·lous·ly** *adv* — **cal·lous·ness** *n*

²**callous** *vb* : to make callous

cal·low \'ka-lò\ *adj* [ME *calu* bald, fr. OE] : lacking adult sophistication ⟨a ∼ youth⟩ — **cal·low·ness** *n*

call–up \'kò-ˌləp\ *n* : an order to report for active military service

call up *vb* : to summon for active military duty

cal·lus \'ka-ləs\ *n* **1** : a callous area on skin or bark **2** : tissue that is converted into bone in the healing of a bone fracture — **callus** *vb*

¹**calm** \'käm, 'kälm\ *n* **1** : a period or a condition free from storms, high winds, or rough water **2** : complete or almost complete absence of wind **3** : a state of tranquility

²**calm** *vb* : to make or become calm

³**calm** *adj* : marked by calm : STILL, UNRUFFLED — **calm·ly** *adv* — **calm·ness** *n*

cal·o·mel \'ka-lə-məl, -ˌmel\ *n* : a chloride of mercury used esp. as a fungicide

ca·lor·ic \kə-'lò-rik\ *adj* **1** : of or relating to heat **2** : of or relating to calories

cal·o·rie *also* **cal·o·ry** \'ka-lə-rē\ *n, pl* **-ries** : a unit for measuring heat; *esp* : one for measuring the value of foods for producing heat and energy in the human body equivalent to the amount of heat required to raise the temperature of one kilogram of water one degree Celsius

cal·o·rim·e·ter \ˌka-lə-'ri-mə-tər\ *n* : an apparatus for measuring quantities of heat — **cal·o·rim·e·try** \-trē\ *n*

cal·u·met \'kal-yə-ˌmet, -mət\ *n* : an American Indian ceremonial pipe

ca·lum·ni·ate \kə-'ləm-nē-ˌāt\ *vb* **-at·ed; -at·ing** : to make false and malicious statements about syn defame, malign, libel, slander, traduce — **ca·lum·ni·a·tion** \-ˌləm-nē-'ā-shən\ *n* — **ca·lum·ni·a·tor** \-'ləm-nē-ˌā-tər\ *n*

cal·um·ny \'ka-ləm-nē\ *n, pl* **-nies** : false and malicious accusation — **ca·lum·ni·ous** \kə-'ləm-nē-əs\ *adj*

calve \'kav, 'kàv\ *vb* **calved; calv·ing** : to give birth to a calf

calves *pl of* CALF

Cal·vin·ism \'kal-və-ˌni-zəm\ *n* : the theological system of John Calvin and his followers — **Cal·vin·ist** \-nist\ *n or adj* — **Cal·vin·is·tic** \ˌkal-və-'nis-tik\ *adj*

ca·lyp·so \kə-'lip-sò\ *n, pl* **-sos** : a style of music originating in the British West Indies and having lyrics that usu. satirize local personalities and events

ca·lyx \'kā-liks, 'ka-\ *n, pl* **ca·lyx·es** *or* **ca·ly·ces** \'kā-lə-ˌsēz, 'ka-\ : the usu. green or leaflike outer part of a flower consisting of sepals

cam \'kam\ *n* : a rotating or sliding piece in a mechanical linkage by which rotary motion is transformed into linear motion or vice versa

ca·ma·ra·de·rie \ˌkäm-'rä-də-rē, ˌkam-, -'ra-\ *n* [F] : friendly feeling and goodwill among comrades

cam·bi·um \'kam-bē-əm\ *n, pl* **-bi·ums** *or* **-bia** \-bē-ə\ : a thin cellular layer between xylem and phloem of most higher plants from which new tissues develop — **cam·bi·al** \-əl\ *adj*

Cam·bo·di·an \kam-'bò-dē-ən\ *n* : a native or inhabitant of Cambodia — **Cambodian** *adj*

Cam·bri·an \'kam-brē-ən, 'käm-\ *adj* : of, relating to, or being the earliest period of the Paleozoic era — **Cambrian** *n*

cam·bric \'kām-brik\ *n* : a fine thin white linen or cotton fabric

cam·cord·er \'kam-ˌkȯr-dər\ *n* : a small portable video camera and recorder

came *past of* COME

cam·el \'ka-məl\ *n* : either of two large hoofed cud-chewing mammals used esp. in desert regions of Asia and Africa for carrying and riding

camel hair *also* **camel's hair** *n* **1** : the hair of a camel or a substitute for it **2** : cloth made of camel hair or of camel hair and wool

ca·mel·lia \kə-'mēl-yə\ *n* : any of a genus of shrubs and trees related to the tea plant and grown in warm regions and greenhouses for their showy roselike flowers

Cam·em·bert \'ka-məm-ˌber\ *n* : a soft cheese with a grayish rind and yellow interior

cam·eo \'ka-mē-ˌō\ *n, pl* **-eos 1** : a gem carved in relief; *also* : a small medallion with a profiled head in relief **2** : a brief appearance esp. by a well-known actor in a play or movie

cam·era \'kam-rə, 'ka-mər-ə\ *n* : a device with a light-proof chamber fitted with a lens through which the image of an object is projected onto a surface for recording (as on film) or for conversion into electrical signals (as for television broadcast) — **cam·era·man** \-ˌman, -mən\ *n* — **cam·era·wom·an** *n*

Cam·er·oo·ni·an \ˌka-mə-'rü-nē-ən\ *n* : a native or inhabitant of the Republic of Cameroon or the Cameroons region — **Cameroonian** *adj*

cam·i·sole \'ka-mə-ˌsōl\ *n* : a short sleeveless garment for women

camomile *var of* CHAMOMILE

cam·ou·flage \'ka-mə-ˌfläzh, -ˌfläj\ *n* [F] **1** : the disguising of military equipment with paint, nets, or foliage; *also* : the disguise itself **2** : deceptive behavior — **camouflage** *vb*

¹**camp** \'kamp\ *n* **1** : a place where tents or buildings are erected for usu. temporary shelter **2** : a collection of tents or other shelters **3** : a body of persons encamped — **camp·ground** \-ˌgraund\ *n* — **camp·site** \-ˌsīt\ *n*

²**camp** *vb* **1** : to make or occupy a camp **2** : to live in a camp or outdoors

³**camp** *n* **1** : exaggerated effeminate mannerisms **2** : something so outrageous, inappropriate, or theatrical as to be considered amusing — **camp** *adj* — **camp·i·ly** \'kam-pə-lē\ *adv* — **camp·i·ness** \-pē-nəs\ *n* — **campy** \-pē\ *adj*

⁴**camp** *vb* : to engage in camp : exhibit the qualities of camp

cam·paign \kam-'pān\ *n* **1** : a series of military operations forming one distinct stage in a war **2** : a series of activities designed to bring about a particular result (advertising ∼) — **campaign** *vb* — **cam·paign·er** *n*

cam·pa·ni·le \ˌkam-pə-'nē-lē\ *n, pl* **-ni·les** *or* **-ni·li** \-'nē-lē\ : a usu. freestanding bell tower

cam·pa·nol·o·gy \ˌkam-pə-'nä-lə-jē\ *n* : the art of bell ringing — **cam·pa·nol·o·gist** \-jist\ *n*

camp·er \'kam-pər\ *n* **1** : one that camps **2** : a portable dwelling (as a specially equipped vehicle) for use during casual travel and camping

Camp Fire Girl *n* : a member of a national organization of girls from ages 5 to 18

camp follower *n* **1** : a civilian (as a prostitute) who follows a military unit to attend or exploit its personnel **2** : a follower of a group who is not an adherent; *esp* : a politician who joins a movement solely for personal gain

cam·phor \'kam-fər\ *n* : a gummy volatile aromatic compound obtained from an evergreen Asian tree (**camphor tree**) and used esp. in medicine

camp meeting *n* : a series of evangelistic meetings usu. held outdoors

camp·o·ree \ˌkam-pə-'rē\ *n* : a gathering of Boy Scouts or Girl Scouts from a given geographic area

cam·pus \'kam-pəs\ *n* [L, plain] : the grounds and buildings of a college or school; *also* : grounds resembling a campus (hospital ∼)

cam·shaft \'kam-ˌshaft\ *n* : a shaft to which a cam is fastened

¹**can** \kən, 'kan\ *vb, past* **could** \kəd, 'kud\; *pres sing & pl* **can 1** : be able to **2** : may perhaps (∼ he still be alive) **3** : be permitted by conscience or feeling to (you ∼ hardly blame her) **4** : have permission to (you ∼ go now)

²**can** \'kan\ *n* **1** : a usu. cylindrical container or receptacle (garbage ∼) (coffee ∼) **2** : JAIL **3** : TOILET

³**can** \'kan\ *vb* **canned; can·ning 1** : to put in a can : preserve by sealing in airtight cans or jars **2** *slang* : to discharge from employment **3** *slang* : to put a stop or an end to — **can·ner** *n*

Can *or* **Canad** *abbr* Canada; Canadian

Can·a·da goose \'ka-nə-də-\ *n* : a common wild goose of No. America

Ca·na·di·an \kə-'nā-dē-ən\ *n* : a native or inhabitant of Canada — **Canadian** *adj*

ca·naille \kə-'nī, -'näl\ *n* [F, fr. It *canaglia*, fr. *cane* dog] : RABBLE, RIFFRAFF

ca·nal \kə-'nal\ *n* **1** : a tubular passage in the body : DUCT **2** : an artificial waterway (as for boats or irrigation)

can·a·lize \'kan-ᵊl-ˌīz\ *vb* **-lized; -liz·ing 1** : to provide with a canal or make into or like a channel **2** : to provide with an outlet; *esp* : to direct into preferred channels — **ca·nal·i·za·tion** \ˌkan-ᵊl-ə-'zā-shən\ *n*

can·a·pé \'ka-nə-pē, -ˌpā\ *n* [F, lit., sofa, fr. ML *canopeum, canapeum* mosquito net] : a piece of bread or toast or a cracker topped with a savory food

ca·nard \kə-'närd\ *n* : a false or unfounded report or story

ca·nary \kə-'ner-ē\ *n, pl* **ca·nar·ies** [fr. the *Canary* islands] **1** : a usu. sweet wine similar to Madeira **2** : a usu. yellow or greenish finch often kept in a cage as a pet

ca·nas·ta \kə-'nas-tə\ *n* [Sp, lit., basket] : rummy played with two full decks of cards plus four jokers

canc *abbr* canceled

can·can \'kan-ˌkan\ *n* : a woman's dance of French origin characterized by high kicking

¹**can·cel** \'kan-səl\ *vb* **-celed** *or* **-celled; -cel·ing** *or* **-cel·ling** [ME *cancellen*, fr. MF *canceller*, fr. LL *cancellare*, fr. L, to make like a lattice, fr. *cancelli* lattice] **1** : to destroy the force or validity of : ANNUL **2** : to match in force or effect : OFFSET **3** : to cross out : DELETE **4** : to remove (a common divisor) from a numerator and denominator; *also* : to remove (equivalents) on opposite sides of an equation or account **5** : to mark (a postage stamp or check) so that it cannot be reused **6** : to neutralize each other's strength or effect — **can·cel·la·tion** \ˌkan-sə-'lā-shən\ *n* — **can·cel·er** *or* **can·cel·ler** *n*

²**cancel** *n* **1** : CANCELLATION **2** : a deleted part

can·cer \'kan-sər\ *n* [L, lit., crab] **1** *cap* : a zodiacal constellation between Gemini and Leo usu. pictured as a crab **2** *cap* : the 4th sign of the zodiac in astrology; *also* : one born under this sign **3** : a malignant tumor that tends to spread in the body **4** : a malignant evil that spreads destructively — **can·cer·ous** \-sə-rəs\ *adj* — **can·cer·ous·ly** *adv*

\ə\abut \ᵊ\kitten \ər\further \a\ash \ā\ace \ä\mop, mar \au̇\out \ch\chin \e\bet \ē\easy \g\go \i\hit \ī\ice \j\job \ŋ\sing \ō\go \ȯ\law \ȯi\boy \th\thin \t̲h̲\the \ü\loot \u̇\foot \y\yet \zh\vision *see also* Pronunciation Symbols page

can·de·la·bra \ˌkan-də-ˈlä-brə, -ˈla-\ *n* : an ornamental branched candlestick or lamp with several lights

candelabra

can·de·la·brum \-brəm\ *n, pl* **-bra** *also* **-brums** : CANDELABRA

can·did \ˈkan-dəd\ *adj* **1** : FRANK, STRAIGHTFORWARD **2** : relating to photography of subjects acting naturally or spontaneously without being posed — **can·did·ly** *adv* — **can·did·ness** *n*

can·di·da·cy \ˈkan-də-də-sē\ *n, pl* **-cies** : the state of being a candidate

can·di·date \ˈkan-də-ˌdāt, ˈka-nə-, -dət\ *n* [L *candidatus*, fr. *candidatus* clothed in white, fr. *candidus* white; fr. the white toga worn by office seekers in ancient Rome] : one who seeks or is proposed for an office, honor, or membership

can·di·da·ture \ˈkan-də-də-ˌchùr, ˈka-nə-\ *n, chiefly Brit* : CANDIDACY

can·died \ˈkan-dēd\ *adj* : preserved in or encrusted with sugar

¹can·dle \ˈkan-dᵊl\ *n* : a usu. slender mass of tallow or wax molded around a wick that is burned to give light

²candle *vb* **can·dled; can·dling** : to examine (as eggs) by holding between the eye and a light — **can·dler** *n*

can·dle·light \ˈkan-dᵊl-līt\ *n* **1** : the light of a candle; *also* : any soft artificial light **2** : the time when candles are lit : TWILIGHT

can·dle·lit \-ˌlit\ *adj* : illuminated by candlelight ⟨a ~ dinner⟩

Can·dle·mas \ˈkan-dᵊl-məs\ *n* : February 2 observed as a church festival in commemoration of the presentation of Christ in the temple

can·dle·stick \-ˌstik\ *n* : a holder with a socket for a candle

can·dle·wick \-ˌwik\ *n* : a soft cotton yarn; *also* : embroidery made with this yarn usu. in tufts

can·dor \ˈkan-dər\ *n* : FRANKNESS, OUTSPOKENNESS

can·dour *chiefly Brit var of* CANDOR

C and W *abbr* country and western

¹can·dy \ˈkan-dē\ *n, pl* **candies** : a confection made from sugar often with flavoring and filling

²candy *vb* **can·died; can·dy·ing** : to encrust in sugar often by cooking in a syrup

candy strip·er \-ˈstrī-pər\ *n* : a teenage volunteer worker at a hospital

¹cane \ˈkān\ *n* **1** : a slender hollow or pithy stem (as of a reed or bramble) **2** : a tall woody grass or reed (as sugarcane) **3** : a walking stick; *also* : a rod for flogging

²cane *vb* **caned; can·ing** **1** : to beat with a cane **2** : to weave or make with cane — **can·er** *n*

cane·brake \ˈkān-ˌbrāk\ *n* : a thicket of cane

¹ca·nine \ˈkā-ˌnīn\ *n* **1** : a pointed tooth between the outer incisor and the first premolar **2** : a canine mammal (as a domestic dog)

²canine *adj* [L *caninus*, fr. *canis* dog] : of or relating to dogs or to the family to which they belong

can·is·ter \ˈka-nə-stər\ *n* **1** : an often cylindrical container

can·ker \ˈkaŋ-kər\ *n* : a spreading sore that eats into tissue — **can·ker·ous** \-kə-rəs\ *adj*

can·ker·worm \-ˌwərm\ *n* : either of two moths and esp. their larvae that are pests of fruit and shade trees

can·na \ˈka-nə\ *n* : any of a genus of tropical herbs with large leaves and racemes of bright-colored flowers

can·na·bis \ˈka-nə-bəs\ *n* : any of the psychoactive preparations (as marijuana) or chemicals (as THC) derived from hemp; *also* : HEMP

canned \ˈkand\ *adj* : prepared in standardized form for general use or wide distribution

can·nery \ˈka-nə-rē\ *n, pl* **-ner·ies** : a factory for the canning of foods

can·ni·bal \ˈka-nə-bəl\ *n* [NL *Canibalis* a member of a Caribbean Indian people, fr. Sp *Caníbal*] : one that eats the flesh of its own kind — **can·ni·bal·ism** \-bə-ˌli-zəm\ *n* — **can·ni·bal·is·tic** \-bə-ˈlis-tik\ *adj*

can·ni·bal·ize \ˈka-nə-bə-ˌlīz\ *vb* **-ized; -iz·ing** **1** : to take usable parts from (as an inoperative machine) to construct or repair another machine **2** : to practice cannibalism

can·non \ˈka-nən\ *n, pl* **cannons** *or* **cannon** [MF *canon*, fr. It *cannone*, lit., large tube, fr. *canna* reed, tube, fr. L, cane, reed] : a large heavy gun; *esp* : one mounted on a carriage

can·non·ade \ˌka-nə-ˈnād\ *n* : a heavy fire of artillery — **cannonade** *vb*

can·non·ball \ˈka-nən-ˌbȯl\ *n* : a usu. round solid missile for a cannon

can·non·eer \ˌka-nə-ˈnir\ *n* : an artillery gunner

can·not \ˈka-ˌnät; kə-ˈnät\ : can not — **cannot but** : to be unable to do otherwise than

can·nu·la \ˈkan-yə-lə\ *n, pl* **-las** *or* **-lae** \-ˌlē\ : a small tube for insertion into a body cavity or into a duct or vessel

can·ny \ˈka-nē\ *adj* **can·ni·er; -est** : PRUDENT, SHREWD — **can·ni·ly** \ˈkan-ᵊl-ē\ *adv* — **can·ni·ness** \ˈka-nē-nəs\ *n*

ca·noe \kə-ˈnü\ *n* : a light narrow boat with sharp ends and curved sides that is usu. propelled by paddles — **canoe** *vb* — **ca·noe·ist** *n*

canoe

ca·no·la \kə-ˈnȯ-lə\ *n* : a rape plant producing seeds that are low in a toxic acid and yield an edible oil (**canola oil**) high in monounsaturated fatty acids; *also* : this oil

¹can·on \ˈka-nən\ *n* **1** : a regulation decreed by a church council; *also* : a provision of canon law **2** : an official or authoritative list (as of the saints or the books of the Bible) **3** : an accepted principle ⟨the ~s of good taste⟩

²canon *n* : a clergyman on the staff of a cathedral

ca·non·i·cal \kə-ˈnä-ni-kəl\ *adj* **1** : of, relating to, or forming a canon **2** : conforming to a general rule or acceptable procedure : ORTHODOX **3** : of or relating to a clergyman who is a canon — **ca·non·i·cal·ly** \-k(ə-)lē\ *adv*

can·on·ize \ˈka-nə-ˌnīz\ *vb* **can·on·ized** \-ˌnīzd\; **can-**

on·iz·ing 1 : to declare (a deceased person) an officially recognized saint 2 : GLORIFY, EXALT — **can·on·i·za·tion** \ˌka-nə-nə-ˈzā-shən\ n

canon law n : the law governing a church

can·o·py \ˈka-nə-pē\ n, pl **-pies** [ME canope, fr. ML canopeum mosquito net, fr. L conopeum, fr. Gk kōnōpion, fr. kònōps mosquito] 1 : an overhanging cover, shelter, or shade 2 : a transparent cover for an airplane cockpit 3 : the fabric part of a parachute — **canopy** vb

¹**cant** \ˈkant\ vb : to give a slant to

²**cant** n 1 : an oblique or slanting surface 2 : TILT, SLANT

³**cant** vb 1 : to beg in a whining manner 2 : to talk hypocritically

⁴**cant** n 1 : the special idiom of a profession or trade : JARGON 2 : insincere speech; esp : insincerely pious words or statements

Cant abbr Canticle of Canticles

can·ta·bi·le \kän-ˈtä-bə-ˌlā\ adv or adj [It] : in a singing manner — used as a direction in music

can·ta·loupe also **can·te·loupe** \ˈkant-ᵊl-ˌōp\ n : MUSKMELON; esp : one with orange flesh and rough skin

can·tan·ker·ous \kan-ˈtaŋ-kə-rəs\ adj : ILL-NATURED, QUARRELSOME — **can·tan·ker·ous·ly** adv — **can·tan·ker·ous·ness** n

can·ta·ta \kən-ˈtä-tə\ n [It] : a choral composition usu. sung to instrumental accompaniment

can·teen \kan-ˈtēn\ n [F cantine bottle case, canteen (store), fr. It cantina wine cellar] 1 : a flask for carrying liquids 2 : a place of recreation and entertainment for military personnel 3 : a small cafeteria or counter at which snacks are served

can·ter \ˈkan-tər\ n : a horse's 3-beat gait resembling but smoother and slower than a gallop — **canter** vb

Can·ter·bury bell \ˈkant-ər-ˌber-ē-\ n : any of several plants related to the bluebell that are cultivated for their showy flowers

can·ti·cle \ˈkan-ti-kəl\ n : SONG; esp : any of several liturgical songs taken from the Bible

Canticle of Canticles n : SONG OF SONGS

¹**can·ti·le·ver** \ˈkant-ᵊl-ˌē-vər\ n : a projecting beam or structure supported only at one end; also : either of a pair of such structures projecting toward each other so that when joined they form a bridge

²**cantilever** vb 1 : to support by a cantilever ⟨a ~ed shelf⟩ 2 : to build as a cantilever 3 : to project as a cantilever

can·tle \ˈkant-ᵊl\ n : the upwardly projecting rear part of a saddle

can·to \ˈkan-ˌtō\ n, pl **cantos** [It, fr. L cantus song] : one of the major divisions of a long poem

can·ton \ˈkant-ᵊn, ˈkan-ˌtän\ n : a small territorial division of a country; esp : one of the political divisions of Switzerland — **can·ton·al** \ˈkant-ᵊn-əl, kan-ˈtän-ᵊl\ adj

can·ton·ment \kan-ˈtōn-mənt, -ˈtän-\ n : usu. temporary quarters for troops

can·tor \ˈkan-tər\ n 1 : a choir leader 2 : a synagogue official who sings liturgical music and leads the congregation in prayer

can·vas also **can·vass** \ˈkan-vəs\ n 1 : a strong cloth formerly much used for making tents and sails 2 : a set of sails 3 : a group of tents 4 : a piece of cloth prepared as a surface to receive oil paint; also : an oil painting 5 : the canvas-covered floor of a boxing or wrestling ring

can·vas·back \ˈkan-vəs-ˌbak\ n : a No. American wild duck with red head and gray back

¹**can·vass** also **can·vas** \ˈkan-vəs\ vb : to go through (a district) or to (persons) to solicit votes or orders for goods or to determine public opinion or sentiment — **can·vass·er** n

²**canvass** n : an act or instance of canvassing

can·yon \ˈkan-yən\ n : a deep narrow valley with high steep sides

¹**cap** \ˈkap\ n 1 : a covering for the head esp. with a visor and no brim; also : something resembling such a cov-

ering 2 : a container holding an explosive charge 3 : an upper limit (as on expenditures)

²**cap** vb **capped; cap·ping** 1 : to provide or protect with a cap 2 : to form a cap over : CROWN 3 : OUTDO, SURPASS 4 : CLIMAX

³**cap** abbr 1 capacity 2 capital 3 capitalize; capitalized

CAP abbr Civil Air Patrol

ca·pa·ble \ˈkā-pə-bəl\ adj : having ability, capacity, or power to do something : ABLE, COMPETENT — **ca·pa·bil·i·ty** \ˌkā-pə-ˈbi-lə-tē\ n — **ca·pa·bly** adv

ca·pa·cious \kə-ˈpā-shəs\ adj : able to contain much — **ca·pa·cious·ly** adv — **ca·pa·cious·ness** n

ca·pac·i·tance \kə-ˈpa-sə-təns\ n : the property of an electric nonconductor that permits the storage of energy

ca·pac·i·tor \kə-ˈpa-sə-tər\ n : an electronic circuit device for temporary storage of electrical energy

¹**ca·pac·i·ty** \kə-ˈpa-sə-tē\ n, pl **-ties** 1 : legal qualification or fitness 2 : the ability to contain, receive, or accommodate 3 : the maximum amount or number that can be contained — see METRIC SYSTEM table, WEIGHT table 4 : ABILITY 5 : position or character assigned or assumed

²**capacity** adj : equaling maximum capacity ⟨a ~ crowd⟩

cap–a–pie or **cap–à–pie** \ˌka-pə-ˈpē\ adv [MF] : from head to foot : at all points

ca·par·i·son \kə-ˈpar-ə-sən\ n 1 : an ornamental covering for a horse 2 : TRAPPINGS, ADORNMENT — **caparison** vb

¹**cape** \ˈkāp\ n 1 : a point of land jutting out into water 2 often cap : CAPE COD COTTAGE

²**cape** n : a sleeveless garment hanging from the neck over the shoulders

Cape Cod cottage \ˈkāp-ˈkäd-\ n : a compact rectangular dwelling of one or one-and-a-half stories usu. with a steep gable roof

¹**ca·per** \ˈkā-pər\ n : the flower bud or young berry of a Mediterranean shrub pickled for use as a relish; also : this shrub

²**caper** vb **ca·pered; ca·per·ing** : to leap about in a playful manner

³**caper** n 1 : a frolicsome leap 2 : a capricious escapade 3 : an illegal or questionable act

cape·skin \ˈkāp-ˌskin\ n : a light flexible leather made from sheepskins

Cape Verd·ean \-ˈvər-dē-ən\ n : a native or inhabitant of the Republic of Cape Verde

cap·ful \ˈkap-ˌfůl\ n, pl **cap·fuls** also **caps·ful** \ˈkaps-\ : as much as a cap will hold

cap·il·lar·i·ty \ˌka-pə-ˈlar-ə-tē\ n, pl **-ties** : the action by which the surface of a liquid where it is in contact with a solid (as in a slender tube) is raised or lowered depending on the relative attraction of the molecules of the liquid for each other and for those of the solid

¹**cap·il·lary** \ˈka-pə-ˌler-ē\ adj 1 : resembling a hair 2 : having a very small bore ⟨~ tube⟩ 3 : of or relating to capillaries or to capillarity

²**capillary** n, pl **-lar·ies** : any of the tiny thin-walled blood vessels that carry blood between the smallest arteries and their corresponding veins

¹**cap·i·tal** \ˈka-pət-ᵊl\ n : the top part or piece of an architectural column

²**capital** adj 1 : conforming to the series A, B, C rather than a, b, c ⟨~ letters⟩ ⟨~ G⟩ 2 : punishable by death ⟨a ~ crime⟩ 3 : most serious ⟨a ~ error⟩ 4 : first in importance or position : CHIEF; also : being the seat of government ⟨the ~ city⟩ 5 : of or relating to capital ⟨~ expenditures⟩; esp : relating to or being assets that add to the long-term net worth of a corporation 6 : FIRST-RATE, EXCELLENT

---

³**capital** *n* **1** : accumulated wealth esp. as used to produce more wealth **2** : the total face value of shares of stock issued by a company **3** : persons holding capital **4** : ADVANTAGE, GAIN **5** : a letter larger than the ordinary small letter and often different in form **6** : the capital city of a state or country; *also* : a city preeminent in some activity ⟨the fashion ~⟩

capital gain *n* : the increase in value of an asset (as stock or real estate) between the time it is bought and the time it is sold

capital goods *n pl* : machinery, tools, factories, and commodities used in the production of goods

cap·i·tal·ism \'ka-pət-ᵊl-ᵢi-zəm\ *n* : an economic system characterized by private or corporate ownership of capital goods and by prices, production, and distribution of goods that are determined mainly by competition in a free market

¹**cap·i·tal·ist** \-ist\ *n* **1** : a person who has capital esp. invested in business **2** : a person of great wealth : PLUTOCRAT **3** : a believer in capitalism

²**capitalist** *or* **cap·i·tal·is·tic** \ₗka-pət-ᵊl-'is-tik\ *adj* **1** : owning capital **2** : practicing or advocating capitalism **3** : marked by capitalism — **cap·i·tal·is·ti·cal·ly** \-ti-k(ə-)lē\ *adv*

cap·i·tal·iza·tion \ₗka-pət-ᵊl-ə-'zā-shən\ *n* **1** : the act or process of capitalizing **2** : the total amount of money used as capital in a business

cap·i·tal·ize \'ka-pət-ᵊl-ₗīz\ *vb* **-ized; -iz·ing 1** : to write or print with an initial capital or in capitals **2** : to convert into or use as capital **3** : to supply capital for **4** : to gain by turning something to advantage : PROFIT

cap·i·tal·ly \'ka-pət-ᵊl-ē\ *adv* : ADMIRABLY, EXCELLENTLY

cap·i·ta·tion \ₗka-pə-'tā-shən\ *n* : a direct uniform tax levied on each person

cap·i·tol \'ka-pət-ᵊl\ *n* : the building in which a legislature holds its sessions

ca·pit·u·late \kə-'pi-chə-ₗlāt\ *vb* **-lat·ed; -lat·ing 1** : to surrender esp. on conditions agreed upon **2** : to cease resisting : ACQUIESCE **syn** submit, yield, succumb, cave, defer — **ca·pit·u·la·tion** \-ₗpi-chə-'lā-shən\ *n*

ca·pon \'kā-ₗpän, -pən\ *n* : a castrated male chicken

cap·puc·ci·no \ₗka-pə-'chē-nō, ₗkä-\ *n* [It, lit., Capuchin; fr. the likeness of its color to that of a Capuchin's habit] : espresso mixed with foamy hot milk or cream and often flavored with cinnamon

ca·pric·cio \kə-'prē-chē-ₗō, -chò\ *n, pl* **-cios** : an instrumental piece in free form usu. lively in tempo and brilliant in style

ca·price \kə-'prēs\ *n* [F, fr. It *capriccio*] **1** : a sudden whim or fancy **2** : an inclination to do things impulsively **3** : CAPRICCIO — **ca·pri·cious** \-'pri-shəs\ *adj* — **ca·pri·cious·ly** *adv* — **ca·pri·cious·ness** *n*

Cap·ri·corn \'ka-pri-ₗkȯrn\ *n* **1** : a zodiacal constellation between Sagittarius and Aquarius usu. pictured as a goat **2** : the 10th sign of the zodiac in astrology; *also* : one born under this sign

cap·ri·ole \'ka-prē-ₗōl\ *n* : ³CAPER 1; *also* : an upward leap of a horse with a backward kick at the height of the leap — **capriole** *vb*

caps *abbr* **1** capitals **2** capsule

cap·si·cum \'kap-si-kəm\ *n* : PEPPER 2

cap·size \'kap-ₗsīz, kap-'sīz\ *vb* **cap·sized; cap·siz·ing** : UPSET, OVERTURN

cap·stan \'kap-stən, -ₗstan\ *n* **1** : a machine for moving or raising heavy weights that consists of a vertical drum which can be rotated and around which cable is turned **2** : a rotating shaft that drives recorder tape

cap·su·lar \'kap-sə-lər\ *adj* : of, relating to, or resembling a capsule

cap·su·lat·ed \-ₗlā-təd\ *adj* : enclosed in a capsule

¹**cap·sule** \'kap-səl, -sül\ *n* **1** : a membrane or sac enclosing a body part (as of a joint) **2** : a case bearing spores or seeds **3** : a shell usu. of gelatin that is used for packaging something (as a drug); *also* : such a shell together with its contents **4** : a small pressurized compartment or vehicle (as for space flight)

²**capsule** *adj* **1** : very brief **2** : very compact

Capt *abbr* captain

¹**cap·tain** \'kap-tən\ *n* **1** : a commander of a body of troops **2** : a commissioned officer in the army, air force, or marine corps ranking next below a major **3** : an officer in charge of a ship **4** : a commissioned officer in the navy ranking next below a rear admiral or a commodore **5** : a leader of a side or team **6** : a dominant figure — **cap·tain·cy** *n*

²**captain** *vb* : to be captain of : LEAD

cap·tion \'kap-shən\ *n* **1** : a heading esp. of an article or document : TITLE **2** : the explanatory matter accompanying an illustration **3** : a motion-picture subtitle — **cap·tion** *vb*

cap·tious \'kap-shəs\ *adj* : marked by an inclination to find fault — **cap·tious·ly** *adv* — **cap·tious·ness** *n*

cap·ti·vate \'kap-tə-ₗvāt\ *vb* **-vat·ed; -vat·ing** : to attract and hold irresistibly by some special charm or art — **cap·ti·va·tion** \ₗkap-tə-'vā-shən\ *n* — **cap·ti·va·tor** \'kap-tə-ₗvā-tər\ *n*

cap·tive \'kap-tiv\ *adj* **1** : made prisoner esp. in war **2** : kept within bounds : CONFINED **3** : held under control — **captive** *n* — **cap·tiv·i·ty** \kap-'ti-və-tē\ *n*

cap·tor \'kap-tər\ *n* : one that captures

¹**cap·ture** \'kap-chər\ *n* **1** : the act of capturing **2** : one that has been captured

²**capture** *vb* **cap·tured; cap·tur·ing 1** : to take captive : WIN, GAIN **2** : to preserve in a relatively permanent form

Ca·pu·chin \'ka-pyə-shən\ *n* : a member of an austere branch of the order of St. Francis of Assisi engaged in missionary work and preaching

car \'kär\ *n* **1** : a vehicle moving on wheels **2** : the compartment of an elevator **3** : the part of a balloon or airship that carries passengers or equipment

car·a·cole \'kar-ə-ₗkōl\ *n* : a half turn to right or left executed by a mounted horse — **caracole** *vb*

car·a·cul \'kar-ə-ₗkəl\ *n* : the pelt of a karakul lamb after the curl begins to loosen

ca·rafe \kə-'raf, -'räf\ *n* : a bottle with a flaring lip used esp. to hold wine

car·am·bo·la \ₗkar-əm-'bò-lə\ *n* **1** : a five-angled green to yellow edible tropical fruit of star-shaped cross section **2** : a tropical tree widely cultivated for carambolas

car·a·mel \'kar-ə-məl, 'kär-məl\ *n* **1** : an amorphous substance obtained by heating sugar and used for flavoring and coloring **2** : a firm chewy candy

car·a·pace \'kar-ə-ₗpās\ *n* : a protective case or shell on the back of some animals (as turtles or crabs)

¹**carat** *var of* KARAT

²**car·at** \'kar-ət\ *n* : a unit of weight for precious stones equal to 200 milligrams

car·a·van \'kar-ə-ₗvan\ *n* **1** : a group of travelers journeying together through desert or hostile regions **2** : a group of vehicles traveling in a file

car·a·van·sa·ry \ₗkar-ə-'van-sə-rē\ *or* **car·a·van·se·rai** \-sə-ₗrī\ *n, pl* **-ries** *or* **-rais** *or* **-rai** [Per *kārwānsarāī*, fr. *kārwān* caravan + *sarāī* palace, inn] **1** : an inn in eastern countries where caravans rest at night **2** : HOTEL, INN

car·a·vel \'kar-ə-ₗvel\ *n* : a small 15th and 16th century ship with a broad bow, high narrow poop, and usu. three masts

car·a·way \'kar-ə-ₗwā\ *n* : an aromatic herb related to the carrot with fruits (**caraway seed**) used in seasoning and medicine; *also* : its fruit

caravel

car·bide \'kär-ˌbīd\ *n* : a compound of carbon with another element

car·bine \'kär-ˌbēn, -ˌbīn\ *n* : a short-barreled lightweight rifle

car·bo·hy·drate \ˌkär-bō-'hī-ˌdrāt, -drət\ *n* : any of various compounds composed of carbon, hydrogen, and oxygen (as sugars and starches)

car·bol·ic acid \ˌkär-'bä-lik-\ *n* : PHENOL

car·bon \'kär-bən\ *n* **1** : a nonmetallic chemical element occurring in nature esp. as diamond and graphite and as a constituent of coal, petroleum, and limestone — see ELEMENT table **2** : a sheet of carbon paper; *also* : CARBON COPY 1 — **car·bon·less** \-ləs\ *adj*

car·bo·na·ceous \ˌkär-bə-'nā-shəs\ *adj* : relating to, containing, or composed of carbon

¹car·bon·ate \'kär-bə-ˌnāt, -nət\ *n* : a salt or ester of carbonic acid

²car·bon·ate \-ˌnāt\ *vb* **-at·ed; -at·ing** : to combine or impregnate with carbon dioxide ⟨*carbonated* beverages⟩ — **car·bon·ation** \ˌkär-bə-'nā-shən\ *n*

carbon black *n* : any of various black substances consisting chiefly of carbon and used esp. as pigments

carbon copy *n* **1** : a copy made by carbon paper **2** : DUPLICATE

carbon dating *n* : the determination of the age of old material (as an archaeological specimen) by its content of carbon 14

carbon dioxide *n* : a heavy colorless gas that does not support combustion and is formed in animal respiration and in the combustion and decomposition of organic substances

carbon 14 *n* : a heavy radioactive form of carbon used esp. in dating archaeological materials

car·bon·ic acid \ˌkär-'bä-nik-\ *n* : a weak acid that decomposes readily into water and carbon dioxide

car·bon·if·er·ous \ˌkär-bə-'ni-fə-rəs\ *adj* **1** : producing or containing carbon or coal **2** *cap* : of, relating to, or being the period of the Paleozoic era between the Devonian and the Permian — **Carboniferous** *n*

carbon monoxide *n* : a colorless odorless very poisonous gas formed by the incomplete burning of carbon

carbon paper *n* : a thin paper coated with a pigment and used for making copies

carbon tet·ra·chlo·ride \-ˌte-trə-'klȯr-ˌīd\ *n* : a colorless nonflammable toxic liquid used esp. as a solvent

carbon 12 *n* : the most abundant isotope of carbon having a nucleus of 6 protons and 6 neutrons and used as a standard for measurements of atomic weight

car·boy \'kär-ˌbȯi\ *n* [Per *qarāba*, fr. Ar *qarrābah* demijohn] : a large container for liquids

car·bun·cle \'kär-ˌbəŋ-kəl\ *n* : a painful inflammation of the skin and underlying tissue that discharges pus from several openings

car·bu·re·tor \'kär-bə-ˌrā-tər, -byə-\ *n* : an apparatus for supplying an internal combustion engine with an explosive mixture of vaporized fuel and air

car·bu·ret·tor *also* **car·bu·ret·ter** \ˌkär-byə-'re-tər, 'kär-byə-ˌ\ *chiefly Brit var of* CARBURETOR

car·case *Brit var of* CARCASS

car·cass \'kär-kəs\ *n* : a dead body; *esp* : one of an animal dressed for food

car·cin·o·gen \kär-'si-nə-jən\ *n* : an agent causing or inciting cancer — **car·ci·no·gen·ic** \ˌkärs-ᵊn-ō-'je-nik\ *adj* — **car·ci·no·ge·nic·i·ty** \-jə-'ni-sə-tē\ *n*

car·ci·no·ma \ˌkärs-ᵊn-'ō-mə\ *n, pl* **-mas** *or* **-ma·ta** \-tə\ : a malignant tumor of epithelial origin — **car·ci·no·ma·tous** \-təs\ *adj*

¹card \'kärd\ *vb* : to comb with a card : cleanse and untangle before spinning — **card·er** *n*

²card *n* : an instrument for combing fibers (as wool or cotton)

³card *n* **1** : PLAYING CARD **2** *pl* : a game played with playing cards; *also* : card playing **3** : a usu. clownishly amusing person : WAG **4** : a flat stiff usu. small piece of paper, cardboard, or plastic **5** : PROGRAM; *esp* : a sports program

⁴card *vb* **1** : to list or schedule on a card **2** : SCORE

⁵card *abbr* cardinal

car·da·mom \'kär-də-məm\ *n* : the aromatic capsular fruit of an East Indian herb related to the ginger whose seeds are used as a spice or condiment and in medicine; *also* : this plant

card·board \'kärd-ˌbȯrd\ *n* : PAPERBOARD

card–car·ry·ing \'kärd-ˌkar-ē-iŋ\ *adj* : being a regularly enrolled member of an organized group and esp. of the Communist party

card catalog *n* : a catalog (as of books) in which the entries are arranged systematically on cards

car·di·ac \'kär-dē-ˌak\ *adj* **1** : of, relating to, or located near the heart **2** : of, relating to, or affected with heart disease

car·di·gan \'kär-di-gən\ *n* : a sweater or jacket usu. without a collar and with a full-length opening in the front

¹car·di·nal \'kärd-nəl, 'kär-dᵊn-əl\ *n* **1** : an ecclesiastical official of the Roman Catholic Church ranking next below the pope **2** : a crested No. American finch that is nearly completely red in the male

²cardinal *adj* [ME, fr. LL *cardinalis*, fr. L serving as a hinge, fr. *cardo* hinge] : of basic importance : CHIEF, MAIN, PRIMARY — **car·di·nal·ly** *adv*

car·di·nal·ate \'kärd-nə-lət, -'kär-dᵊn-ə-let, -ˌlāt\ *n* : the office, rank, or dignity of a cardinal

cardinal flower *n* : a No. American plant that bears a spike of brilliant red flowers

cardinal number *n* : a number (as 1, 5, 82, 357) that is used in simple counting and answers the question "how many?"

cardinal point *n* : one of the four principal compass points north, south, east, and west

car·di·ol·o·gy \ˌkär-dē-'ä-lə-jē\ *n* : the study of the heart and its action and diseases — **car·di·ol·o·gist** \-jist\ *n*

car·dio·pul·mo·nary resuscitation \ˌkär-dē-ō-'pu̇l-mə-ˌner-ē\ *n* : a procedure to restore normal breathing after cardiac arrest that includes the clearance of air passages to the lungs, mouth-to-mouth method of artificial respiration, and heart massage by the exertion of pressure on the chest

car·dio·vas·cu·lar \-'vas-kyə-lər\ *adj* : of or relating to the heart and blood vessels

card·sharp·er \'kärd-ˌshär-pər\ *or* **card·sharp** \-ˌshärp\ *n* : a cheater at cards

¹care \'ker\ *n* **1** : a disquieted state of uncertainty and responsibility : ANXIETY **2** : watchful attention : HEED **3** : CHARGE, SUPERVISION **4** : a person or thing that is an object of anxiety or solicitude

²care *vb* **cared; car·ing 1** : to feel anxiety **2** : to feel interest **3** : to give care **4** : to have a liking, fondness, taste, or inclination **5** : to be concerned about ⟨∼ what happens⟩

CARE *abbr* Cooperative for American Relief to Everywhere

ca·reen \kə-'rēn\ *vb* **1** : to put (a ship or boat) on a beach esp. in order to clean or repair its hull **2** : to sway from side to side **3** : CAREER

¹ca·reer \kə-'rir\ *n* [MF *carrière*, fr. OProv *carriera* street, fr. ML *carraria* road for vehicles, fr. L *carrus* car] **1** : COURSE, PASSAGE; *also* : speed in a course ⟨ran at full ∼⟩ **2** : an occupation or profession followed as a life's work

²career *vb* : to go at top speed esp. in a headlong manner

care-free \'ker-ˌfrē\ *adj* : free from care or worry

care·ful \-fəl\ *adj* **care·ful·ler; care·ful·lest 1** : using or taking care : VIGILANT **2** : marked by solicitude, caution, or prudence — **care·ful·ly** *adv* — **care·ful·ness** *n*

care·giv·er \-ˌgi-vər\ *n* : a person who provides direct care (as for children, the disabled, or the chronically ill)

care·less \-ləs\ *adj* **1** : free from care : UNTROUBLED **2** : UNCONCERNED, INDIFFERENT **3** : not taking care **4** : not showing or receiving care — **care·less·ly** *adv* — **care·less·ness** *n*

¹ca·ress \kə-'res\ *n* : a tender or loving touch or embrace

²caress *vb* : to touch or stroke tenderly or lovingly — **ca·ress·er** *n*

car·et \'kar-ət\ *n* [L, there is lacking, fr. *carēre* to lack, be without] : a mark ʌ used to indicate the place where something is to be inserted

care·tak·er \'ker-ˌtā-kər\ *n* **1** : one in charge usu. as occupant in place of an absent owner **2** : one temporarily fulfilling the functions of an office

care·worn \-ˌwȯrn\ *adj* : showing the effects of grief or anxiety

car·fare \'kär-ˌfar\ *n* : passenger fare (as on a streetcar or bus)

car·go \'kär-gō\ *n, pl* **cargoes** *or* **cargos** : the goods carried in a ship, airplane, or vehicle : FREIGHT

Ca·rib·be·an \ˌkar-ə-'bē-ən, kə-'ri-bē-ən\ *adj* : of or relating to the eastern and southern West Indies or the Caribbean Sea

car·i·bou \'kar-ə-ˌbü\ *n, pl* **caribou** *or* **caribous** : a large circumpolar gregarious deer of northern taiga and tundra that usu. has palmate antlers in both sexes — used esp. for one of the New World

car·i·ca·ture \'kar-i-kə-ˌchùr\ *n* **1** : distorted representation to produce a ridiculous effect **2** : a representation esp. in literature or art having the qualities of caricature — **caricature** *vb* — **car·i·ca·tur·ist** \-ist\ *n*

car·ies \'kar-ēz\ *n, pl* **caries** : tooth decay

car·il·lon \'kar-ə-ˌlän\ *n* : a set of tuned bells sounded by hammers controlled from a keyboard

car·i·ous \'kar-ē-əs\ *adj* : affected with caries

car·load \'kär-ˌlōd\ *n* : a load that fills a car

car·mi·na·tive \kär-'mi-nə-tiv\ *adj* : expelling gas from the alimentary canal — **carminative** *n*

car·mine \'kär-mən, -ˌmīn\ *n* : a vivid red

car·nage \'kär-nij\ *n* : great destruction of life : SLAUGHTER

car·nal \'kärn-ᵊl\ *adj* [ME, fr. LL *carnalis*, fr. L *carn-, caro* flesh] **1** : of or relating to the body **2** : relating to or given to sensual pleasures and appetites — **car·nal·i·ty** \kär-'na-lə-tē\ *n* — **car·nal·ly** *adv*

car·na·tion \kär-'nā-shən\ *n* : a cultivated pink of any of numerous usu. double-flowered varieties derived from an Old World species

car·nau·ba wax \kär-'nȯ-bə-, -'naù-; ˌkär-nə-'ü-bə-\ *n*

: a brittle yellowish wax from a Brazilian palm that is used esp. in polishes

car·ne·lian \kär-'nēl-yən\ *n* : a hard tough reddish quartz used as a gem

car·ni·val \'kär-nə-vəl\ *n* [It *carnevale*, alter. of *carnelevare*, lit., removal of meat] **1** : a season of merrymaking just before Lent **2** : a boisterous merrymaking **3** : a traveling enterprise offering amusements **4** : an organized program of entertainment

car·ni·vo·ra \kär-'ni-və-rə\ *n pl* : carnivorous mammals

car·ni·vore \'kär-nə-ˌvȯr\ *n* : a flesh-eating animal; *esp* : any of an order of mammals (as dogs, cats, bears, minks, and seals) feeding mostly on animal flesh

car·niv·o·rous \kär-'ni-və-rəs\ *adj* **1** : feeding on animal tissues **2** : of or relating to the carnivores — **car·niv·o·rous·ly** *adv* — **car·niv·o·rous·ness** *n*

car·ny *or* **car·ney** *or* **car·nie** \'kär-nē\ *n, pl* **carnies** *or* **carneys 1** : CARNIVAL **3 2** : one who works with a carnival

car·ol \'kar-əl\ *n* : a song of joy or devotion — **carol** *vb* — **car·ol·er** *or* **car·ol·ler** *n*

car·om \'kar-əm\ *n* **1** : a shot in billiards in which the cue ball strikes two other balls **2** : a rebounding esp. at an angle — **carom** *vb*

car·o·tene \'kar-ə-ˌtēn\ *n* : any of several orange to red pigments (as beta-carotene) formed esp. in plants and used as a source of vitamin A

ca·rot·id \kə-'rä-təd\ *adj* : of, relating to, or being the chief artery or pair of arteries that pass up the neck and supply the head — **carotid** *n*

ca·rous·al \kə-'raù-zəl\ *n* : CAROUSE

ca·rouse \kə-'raùz\ *n* [MF *carrousse*, fr. *carous*, adv., all out (in *boire carous* to empty the cup), fr. G *garaus*] : a drunken revel — **carouse** *vb* — **ca·rous·er** *n*

car·ou·sel \ˌkar-ə-'sel, 'kar-ə-ˌsel\ *n* **1** : MERRY-GO-ROUND **2** : a circular conveyor

¹carp \'kärp\ *vb* : to find fault : CAVIL, COMPLAIN — **carp** *n* — **carp·er** *n*

²carp *n, pl* **carp** *or* **carps** : a large variable Asian freshwater fish of sluggish waters often raised for food

¹car·pal \'kär-pəl\ *adj* : relating to the wrist or the bones of the wrist

²carpal *n* : a carpal element or bone

carpal tunnel syndrome *n* : a condition characterized esp. by weakness, pain, and disturbances of sensation (as numbness) in the hand and caused by compression of a nerve in the wrist

car·pe di·em \'kär-pe-'dē-em, -'dī-\ *n* [L, lit., pluck the day] : enjoyment of the present without concern for the future

car·pel \'kär-pəl\ *n* : one of the highly modified leaves that together form the ovary of a flower of a seed plant

car·pen·ter \'kär-pən-tər\ *n* : one who builds or repairs wooden structures — **carpenter** *vb* — **car·pen·try** \-trē\ *n*

car·pet \'kär-pət\ *n* : a heavy fabric used as a floor covering — **carpet** *vb*

car·pet·bag \-ˌbag\ *n* : a traveling bag common in the 19th century

car·pet·bag·ger \-ˌba-gər\ *n* : a Northerner in the South after the American Civil War usu. seeking private gain under the reconstruction governments

car·pet·ing \'kär-pə-tiŋ\ *n* : material for carpets; *also* : CARPETS

car pool *n* : an arrangement in which a group of people commute together by car; *also* : a group having this arrangement — **car·pool** \-ˌpül\ *vb*

car·port \'kär-ˌpȯrt\ *n* : an open-sided automobile shelter

car·pus \'kär-pəs\ *n* : the wrist or its bones

car·ra·geen·an *or* **car·ra·geen·in** \ˌkar-ə-'gē-nən\ *n* : a colloid extracted esp. from a dark purple branching seaweed and used in foods esp. to stabilize and thicken them

car·rel \'kar-əl\ *n* : a table often partitioned or enclosed for individual study in a library

car·riage \'kar-ij\ *n* **1** : the act of carrying **2** : manner of holding the body **3** : a wheeled vehicle **4** *Brit* : a railway passenger coach **5** : a movable part of a machine for supporting some other moving part ⟨a typewriter ∼⟩

carriage trade *n* : trade from well-to-do or upper= class people

car·ri·er \'kar-ē-ər\ *n* **1** : one that carries **2** : a person or organization in the transportation business **3** : AIRCRAFT CARRIER **4** : one whose system carries germs of a disease but who is immune to the disease **5** : an individual having a gene for a trait or condition that is not expressed bodily **6** : an electromagnetic wave whose amplitude or frequency is varied in order to convey a radio or television signal

carrier pigeon *n* : a pigeon used esp. to carry messages

car·ri·on \'kar-ē-ən\ *n* : dead and decaying flesh

car·rot \'kar-ət\ *n* : the elongated usu. orange root of a common garden plant that is eaten as a vegetable; *also* : this plant

car·rou·sel *var of* CAROUSEL

¹**car·ry** \'kar-ē\ *vb* **car·ried; car·ry·ing 1** : to move while supporting : TRANSPORT, CONVEY, TAKE **2** : to influence by mental or emotional appeal **3** : to get possession or control of : CAPTURE, WIN **4** : to transfer from one place (as a column) to another ⟨∼ a number in adding⟩ **5** : to have or wear on one's person; *also* : to bear within one **6** : INVOLVE, IMPLY **7** : to hold or bear (oneself) in a specified way **8** : to keep in stock for sale **9** : to sustain the weight or burden of : SUPPORT **10** : to prolong in space, time, or degree **11** : to keep on one's books as a debtor **12** : to succeed in (an election) **13** : to win adoption (as in a legislature) **14** : PUBLISH, PRINT **15** : to reach or penetrate to a distance

²**carry** *n* **1** : the range of a gun or projectile or of a struck or thrown ball **2** : PORTAGE **3** : an act or method of carrying ⟨fireman's ∼⟩

car·ry·all \'kar-ē-ˌȯl\ *n* : a capacious bag or case

carry away *vb* : to arouse to a high and often excessive degree of emotion

carrying charge *n* : a charge added to the price of merchandise sold on the installment plan

car·ry–on *n* : a piece of luggage suitable for being carried aboard an airplane by a passenger — **carry–on** *adj*

carry on *vb* **1** : CONDUCT, MANAGE **2** : to behave in a foolish, excited, or improper manner **3** : to continue in spite of hindrance or discouragement

carry out *vb* **1** : to put into execution **2** : to bring to a successful conclusion

car·sick \'kär-ˌsik\ *adj* : affected with motion sickness esp. in an automobile — **car sickness** *n*

¹**cart** \'kärt\ *n* **1** : a heavy 2-wheeled wagon **2** : a small wheeled vehicle

²**cart** *vb* : to convey in or as if in a cart — **cart·er** *n*

cart·age \'kär-tij\ *n* : the act of or rate charged for carting

carte blanche \'kärt-'blänsh\ *n, pl* **cartes blanches** *same or* -'blän-shəz\ [F, lit., blank document] : full discretionary power

car·tel \kär-'tel\ *n* : a combination of independent business enterprises designed to limit competition **syn** pool, syndicate, monopoly, trust

car·ti·lage \'kärt-ᵊl-ij\ *n* : a usu. translucent somewhat elastic tissue that composes most of the skeleton of young vertebrate embryos and later is mostly converted to bone in higher vertebrates — **car·ti·lag·i·nous** \ˌkärt-ᵊl-'a-jə-nəs\ *adj*

cartilaginous fish *n* : any of a class of fishes (as a shark or ray having the skeleton wholly or largely composed of cartilage

car·tog·ra·phy \kär-'tä-grə-fē\ *n* : the making of maps — **car·tog·ra·pher** *n*

car·ton \'kärt-ᵊn\ *n* : a paperboard box or container

car·toon \kär-'tün\ *n* **1** : a preparatory sketch (as for a painting) **2** : a drawing intended as humor, caricature, or satire **3** : COMIC STRIP — **cartoon** *vb* — **car·toon·ist** *n*

car·tridge \'kär-trij\ *n* **1** : a tube containing a complete charge for a firearm **2** : a container of material for insertion into an apparatus **3** : a small case containing a phonograph needle and transducer that is attached to a tonearm **4** : a case containing a magnetic tape or disk **5** : a case for holding integrated circuits containing a computer program

cart·wheel \'kärt-ˌhwēl\ *n* **1** : a large coin (as a silver dollar) **2** : a lateral handspring with arms and legs extended

carve \'kärv\ *vb* **carved; carv·ing 1** : to cut with care or precision : shape by cutting **2** : to cut into pieces or slices **3** : to slice and serve meat at table — **carv·er** *n*

cary·at·id \ˌkar-ē-'a-təd\ *n, pl* **-ids** *or* **-i·des** \-'a-tə-ˌdēz\ : a sculptured draped female figure used as an architectural column

CAS *abbr* certificate of advanced study

ca·sa·ba \kə-'sä-bə\ *n* : any of several muskmelons with a yellow rind and sweet flesh

¹**cas·cade** \kas-'kād\ *n* **1** : a steep usu. small waterfall **2** : something arranged in a series or succession of stages so that each stage derives from or acts upon the product of the preceding

²**cas·cade** *vb* **cas·cad·ed; cas·cad·ing** : to fall, pass, or connect in or as if in a cascade

cas·cara \kas-'kar-ə\ *n* : the dried bark of a small Pacific coastal tree of the U.S. and southern Canada used as a laxative; *also* : this tree

¹**case** \'kās\ *n* [ME *cas*, fr. OF, fr. L *casus* fall, chance, fr. *cadere* to fall] **1** : a particular instance or situation **2** : an inflectional form of a noun, pronoun, or adjective indicating its grammatical relation to other words; *also* : such a relation whether indicated by inflection or not **3** : what actually exists or happens : FACT **4** : a suit or action in law : CAUSE **5** : a convincing argument **6** : an instance of disease or injury; *also* : PATIENT **7** : INSTANCE, EXAMPLE — **in case** : as a precaution — **in case of** : in the event of

²**case** *n* [ME *cas*, fr. OF *casse*, fr. L *capsa*] **1** : a box or container for holding something; *also* : a box with its contents **2** : an outer covering **3** : a divided tray for holding printing type **4** : CASING 2

³**case** *vb* **cased; cas·ing 1** : to enclose in or cover with a case **2** : to inspect esp. with intent to rob

ca·sein \'kā-ˌsēn, kā-'\ *n* : any of several phosphorus= containing proteins occurring in or produced from milk

case·ment \'kās-mənt\ *n* : a window that opens like a door

case·work \-ˌwərk\ *n* : social work that involves the individual person or family — **case·work·er** *n*

¹**cash** \'kash\ *n* [MF or It; MF *casse* money box, fr. It *cassa*, fr. L *capsa* chest, case] **1** : ready money **2** : money or its equivalent paid at the time of purchase or delivery

²**cash** *vb* : to pay or obtain cash for

ca·shew \'ka-shü, kə-'shü\ *n* : an edible kidney= shaped nut of a tropical American tree related to the sumacs; *also* : the tree

¹**ca·shier** \ka-'shir\ *vb* : to dismiss from service; *esp* : to dismiss in disgrace

²**cash·ier** \ka-'shir\ *n* **1** : a bank official responsible for

moneys received and paid out **2** : a person who receives and records payments

cashier's check *n* : a check drawn by a bank upon its own funds and signed by its cashier

cash in *vb* **1** : to convert into cash ⟨*cash in* bonds⟩ **2** : to settle accounts and withdraw from a gambling game or business deal **3** : to obtain financial profit or advantage

cash·mere \'kazh-ˌmir, 'kash-\ *n* : fine wool from the undercoat of an Indian goat (**cashmere goat**) or a yarn spun of this; *also* : a soft twilled fabric orig. woven from this yarn

cash register *n* : a business machine that usu. has a money drawer, indicates each sale, and records the money received

cas·ing \'kā-siŋ\ *n* **1** : something that encases **2** : the frame of a door or window

ca·si·no \kə-'sē-nò\ *n, pl* **-nos** [It, fr. *casa* house] **1** : a building or room for social amusements; *esp* : one used for gambling **2** *also* **cas·si·no** : a card game in which players win cards by matching those on the table

cask \'kask\ *n* : a barrel-shaped container usu. for liquids; *also* : the quantity held by such a container

cas·ket \'kas-kət\ *n* **1** : a small box (as for jewels) **2** : COFFIN

casque \'kask\ *n* : HELMET

cas·sa·va \kə-'sä-və\ *n* : any of several tropical spurges with rootstocks yielding a nutritious starch from which tapioca is prepared; *also* : the rootstock or its starch

cas·se·role \'ka-sə-ˌròl\ *n* **1** : a dish in which food may be baked and served **2** : food cooked and served in a casserole

cas·sette *also* **ca·sette** \kə-'set\ *n* **1** : a lightproof container for photographic plates or film **2** : a plastic case containing magnetic tape

cas·sia \'ka-shə\ *n* **1** : a coarse cinnamon bark **2** : any of a genus of leguminous herbs, shrubs, and trees of warm regions including several which yield senna

cas·sit·er·ite \kə-'si-tə-ˌrīt\ *n* : a dark mineral that is the chief tin ore

cas·sock \'ka-sək\ *n* : an ankle-length garment worn esp. by Roman Catholic and Anglican clergy

cas·so·wary \'ka-sə-ˌwer-ē\ *n, pl* **-war·ies** : any of a genus of large birds closely related to the emu

¹**cast** \'kast\ *vb* **cast; cast·ing 1** : THROW, FLING **2** : DIRECT ⟨~ a glance⟩ **3** : to deposit (a ballot) formally **4** : to throw off, out, or away : DISCARD, SHED **5** : COMPUTE; *esp* : to add up **6** : to assign the parts of (a play) to actors; *also* : to assign to a role or part **7** : to shape (a substance) by pouring in liquid or plastic form into a mold and letting harden without pressure **8** : to make (as a knot or stitch) by looping or catching up

²**cast** *n* **1** : THROW, FLING **2** : a throw of dice **3** : the set of actors in a dramatic production **4** : something formed in or as if in a mold; *also* : a rigid surgical dressing (as for protecting and supporting a fractured bone) **5** : TINGE, HUE **6** : APPEARANCE, LOOK **7** : something thrown out or off, shed, or expelled ⟨worm ~s⟩

cas·ta·net \ˌkas-tə-'net\ *n* [Sp *castañeta*, fr. *castaña* chestnut, fr. L *castanea*] : a rhythm instrument consisting of two small wooden, ivory, or plastic shells held in the hand and clicked together

cast·away \'kas-tə-ˌwā\ *adj* **1** : thrown away : REJECTED **2** : cast adrift or ashore as a survivor of a shipwreck — **castaway** *n*

caste \'kast\ *n* [Port *casta*, lit., race, lineage, fr. fem. of *casto* pure, chaste, fr. L *castus*] **1** : one of the hereditary social classes in Hinduism **2** : a division of a society based on wealth, inherited rank, or occupation **3** : social position : PRESTIGE **4** : a system of rigid social stratification

cas·tel·lat·ed \'kas-tə-ˌlā-təd\ *adj* : having battlements like a castle

cast·er \'kas-tər\ *n* **1** *or* **cas·tor** : a small container to

hold salt or pepper at the table **2** : a small wheel that turns freely and is used to support and move furniture, trucks, and equipment

cas·ti·gate \'kas-tə-ˌgāt\ *vb* **-gat·ed; -gat·ing** : to punish or criticize severely — **cas·ti·ga·tion** \ˌkas-tə-'gā-shən\ *n* — **cas·ti·ga·tor** \'kas-tə-ˌgā-tər\ *n*

cast·ing \'kas-tiŋ\ *n* **1** : CAST 7 **2** : something cast in a mold

casting vote *n* : a deciding vote cast by a presiding officer to break a tie

cast iron *n* : a hard brittle alloy of iron, carbon, and silicon cast in a mold

cas·tle \'ka-səl\ *n* **1** : a large fortified building or set of buildings **2** : a large or imposing house **3** : ³ROOK

castle in the air : an impracticable project

cast–off \'kas-ˌtòf\ *adj* : thrown away or aside — **cast-off** *n*

cas·tor oil \'kas-tər-\ *n* : a thick yellowish oil extracted from the poisonous seeds of an herb (**castor–oil plant**) and used as a lubricant and purgative

cas·trate \'kas-ˌtrāt\ *vb* **cas·trat·ed; cas·trat·ing** : to deprive of sex glands and esp. testes — **cas·tra·tion** \kas-'trā-shən\ *n* — **cas·tra·tor** \-ər\ *n*

ca·su·al \'ka-zhə-wəl\ *adj* **1** : resulting from or occurring by chance **2** : OCCASIONAL, INCIDENTAL **3** : OFFHAND, NONCHALANT **4** : designed for informal use ⟨~ clothing⟩ — **ca·su·al·ly** *adv* — **ca·su·al·ness** *n*

ca·su·al·ty \'ka-zhəl-tē, 'ka-zhə-wəl-\ *n, pl* **-ties 1** : serious or fatal accident **2** : a military person lost through death, injury, sickness, or capture or through being missing in action **3** : a person or thing injured, lost, or destroyed

ca·su·ist·ry \'ka-zhə-wə-strē\ *n, pl* **-ries** : specious argument : RATIONALIZATION — **ca·su·ist** \-wist\ *n* — **ca·su·is·tic** \ˌka-zhə-'wis-tik\ *or* **ca·su·is·ti·cal** \-ti-kəl\ *adj*

ca·sus bel·li \ˌkä-səs-'be-ˌlē, ˌkä-səs-'be-ˌlī\ *n, pl* **ca·sus belli** \ˌkä-ˌsüs-, ˌkä-\ [NL, occasion of war] : a cause or pretext for a declaration of war

¹**cat** \'kat\ *n* **1** : a carnivorous mammal long domesticated as a pet and for catching rats and mice **2** : any of a family of animals (as the lion, lynx, or leopard) including the domestic cat **3** : a spiteful woman **4** : GUY

²**cat** *abbr* catalog

ca·tab·o·lism \kə-'ta-bə-ˌli-zəm\ *n* : destructive metabolism involving the release of energy and resulting in the breakdown of complex materials — **cat·a·bol·ic** \ˌka-tə-'bä-lik\ *adj*

cat·a·clysm \'ka-tə-ˌkli-zəm\ *n* : a violent change or upheaval — **cat·a·clys·mal** \ˌka-tə-'kliz-məl\ *or* **cat·a·clys·mic** \-'kliz-mik\ *adj*

cat·a·comb \'ka-tə-ˌkōm\ *n* : an underground burial place with galleries and recesses for tombs

cat·a·falque \'ka-tə-ˌfalk, -ˌfòlk, -ˌfòk\ *n* : an ornamental structure sometimes used in solemn funerals to hold the body

cat·a·lep·sy \'ka-tə-ˌlep-sē\ *n, pl* **-sies** : a trancelike nervous condition characterized esp. by loss of voluntary motion — **cat·a·lep·tic** \ˌka-tə-'lep-tik\ *adj or n*

¹**cat·a·log** *or* **cat·a·logue** \'kat-ᵊl-ˌòg\ *n* **1** : LIST, REGISTER **2** : a systematic list of items with descriptive details; *also* : a book containing such a list

²**catalog** *or* **catalogue** *vb* **-loged** *or* **-logued; -log·ing** *or* **-logu·ing 1** : to make a catalog of **2** : to enter in a catalog — **cat·a·log·er** *or* **cat·a·logu·er** *n*

ca·tal·pa \kə-'tal-pə\ *n* : a broad-leaved tree with showy flowers and long slim pods

ca·tal·y·sis \kə-'ta-lə-səs\ *n, pl* **-y·ses** \-ˌsēz\ : a change and esp. increase in the rate of a chemical reaction brought about by a substance (**cat·a·lyst** \'kat-ᵊl-ist\) that is itself unchanged at the end of the reaction — **cat·a·lyt·ic** \ˌkat-ᵊl-'i-tik\ *adj* — **cat·a·lyt·i·cal·ly** \-ti-k(ə-)lē\ *adv*

catalytic converter *n* : an automobile exhaust-system

component in which a catalyst changes harmful gases into mostly harmless products

cat·a·lyze \'kat-ᵊl-ˌīz\ *vb* **-lyzed; -lyz·ing** : to bring about the catalysis of (a chemical reaction)

cat·a·ma·ran \ˌka-tə-mə-'ran\ *n* [Tamil (a language of southern India) *kaṭṭumaram*, fr. *kaṭṭu* to tie + *maram* tree] : a boat with twin hulls

cat·a·mount \'ka-tə-ˌmaúnt\ *n* : COUGAR; *also* : LYNX

cat·a·pult \'ka-tə-ˌpəlt, -ˌpúlt\ *n* **1** : an ancient military machine for hurling missiles **2** : a device for launching an airplane (as from an aircraft carrier) — **catapult** *vb*

cat·a·ract \'ka-tə-ˌrakt\ *n* **1** : a cloudiness of the lens of the eye obstructing vision **2** : a large waterfall; *also* : steep rapids in a river

ca·tarrh \kə-'tär\ *n* : inflammation of a mucous membrane esp. of the nose and throat — **ca·tarrh·al** \-əl\ *adj*

ca·tas·tro·phe \kə-'tas-trə-(ˌ)fē\ *n* [Gk *katastrophē*, fr. *katastrephein* to overturn, fr. *kata-* down + *strephein* to turn] **1** : a great disaster or misfortune **2** : utter failure — **cat·a·stroph·ic** \ˌka-tə-'strä-fik\ *adj* — **cat·a·stroph·i·cal·ly** \-fi-k(ə-)lē\ *adv*

cat·a·ton·ic \ˌka-tə-'tä-nik\ *adj* : of, relating to, or marked by schizophrenia characterized esp. by stupor, negativism, rigidity, purposeless excitement, and abnormal posturing — **catatonic** *n*

cat·bird \'kat-ˌbərd\ *n* : an American songbird with a catlike mewing call

cat·boat \'kat-ˌbōt\ *n* : a single-masted sailboat with a single large sail extended by a long boom

cat·call \-ˌkól\ *n* : a loud cry made esp. to express disapproval — **catcall** *vb*

¹catch \'kach, 'kech\ *vb* **caught** \'kót\; **catch·ing 1** : to capture esp. after pursuit **2** : TRAP **3** : to discover unexpectedly ⟨*caught* in the act⟩ **4** : to become suddenly aware of **5** : to take hold of : SNATCH ⟨~ at a straw⟩ **6** : INTERCEPT **7** : to get entangled **8** : to become affected with or by ⟨~ fire⟩ ⟨~ cold⟩ **9** : to seize and hold firmly; *also* : FASTEN **10** : OVERTAKE **11** : to be in time for ⟨~ a train⟩ **12** : to take in and retain **13** : to look at or listen to

²catch *n* **1** : something caught **2** : the act of catching; *also* : a game consisting of throwing and catching a ball **3** : something that catches or checks or holds immovable ⟨a door ~⟩ **4** : one worth catching esp. as a mate **5** : FRAGMENT, SNATCH **6** : a concealed difficulty or complication

catch·all \'ka-ˌchól, 'ke-\ *n* : something to hold a variety of odds and ends

catch–as–catch–can *adj* : using any means available

catch·er \'ka-chər, 'ke-\ *n* : one that catches; *esp* : a player positioned behind home plate in baseball

catch·ing *adj* **1** : INFECTIOUS, CONTAGIOUS **2** : ALLURING, CATCHY

catch·ment \'kach-mənt, 'kech-\ *n* **1** : something that catches water **2** : the action of catching water

catch on *vb* **1** : UNDERSTAND **2** : to become popular

catch·pen·ny \'kach-ˌpe-nē, 'kech-\ *adj* : using sensationalism or cheapness for appeal ⟨a ~ newspaper⟩

catch–22 \-ˌtwen-tē-'tü\ *n, pl* **catch–22's** *or* **catch–22s** *often cap* C [fr. *Catch-22,* a paradoxical rule found in the novel *Catch-22* (1961) by Joseph Heller] : a problematic situation for which the only solution is denied by a circumstance inherent in the problem or by a rule; *also* : the circumstance or rule that denies a solution

catch·up \'ke-chəp, 'ka-\ *var of* KETCHUP

catch up *vb* : to travel or work fast enough to overtake or complete

catch·word \'kach-ˌwərd, 'kech-\ *n* **1** : GUIDE WORD **2** : a word or expression representative of a party, school, or point of view

catchy \'ka-chē, 'ke-\ *adj* **catch·i·er; -est 1** : likely to catch the interest or attention **2** : TRICKY

cat·e·chism \'ka-tə-ˌki-zəm\ *n* : a summary or test (as of religious doctrine) usu. in the form of questions and answers — **cat·e·chist** \-ˌkist\ *n* — **cat·e·chize** \-ˌkīz\ *vb*

cat·e·chu·men \ˌka-tə-'kyü-mən\ *n* : a religious convert receiving training before baptism

cat·e·gor·i·cal \ˌka-tə-'gór-i-kəl\ *adj* **1** : ABSOLUTE, UNQUALIFIED **2** : of, relating to, or constituting a category — **cat·e·gor·i·cal·ly** \-i-k(ə-)lē\ *adv*

cat·e·go·rize \'ka-ti-gə-ˌrīz\ *vb* **-rized; -riz·ing** : to put into a category : CLASSIFY — **cat·e·go·ri·za·tion** \ˌka-ti-gə-rə-'zā-shən\ *n*

cat·e·go·ry \'ka-tə-ˌgór-ē\ *n, pl* **-ries** : a division used in classification; *also* : CLASS, GROUP, KIND

ca·ter \'kā-tər\ *vb* **1** : to provide a supply of food **2** : to supply what is wanted — **ca·ter·er** *n*

cat·er–cor·ner \ˌka-tē-'kór-nər, ˌka-tə-, ˌki-tē-\ *or* **cat·er–cor·nered** *adv or adj* [obs. *cater* four + *corner*] : in a diagonal or oblique position

cat·er·pil·lar \'ka-tər-ˌpi-lər\ *n* [ME *catyrpel,* fr. OF *catepelose,* lit., hairy cat] : a wormlike often hairy insect larva esp. of a butterfly or moth

cat·er·waul \'ka-tər-ˌwól\ *vb* : to make a harsh cry — **caterwaul** *n*

cat·fish \'kat-ˌfish\ *n* : any of an order of chiefly freshwater stout-bodied fishes with slender tactile processes around the mouth

catfish

cat·gut \-ˌgət\ *n* : a tough cord made usu. from sheep intestines

ca·thar·sis \kə-'thär-səs\ *n, pl* **ca·thar·ses** \-ˌsēz\ **1** : an act of purging or purification **2** : elimination of a complex by bringing it to consciousness and affording it expression

¹ca·thar·tic \kə-'thär-tik\ *adj* : of, relating to, or producing catharsis

²cathartic *n* : PURGATIVE

ca·the·dral \kə-'thē-drəl\ *n* : the principal church of a diocese

cath·e·ter \'ka-thə-tər\ *n* : a tube for insertion into a bodily passage or cavity usu. for injecting or drawing off material or for keeping a passage open

cath·ode \'ka-ˌthōd\ *n* **1** : the negative electrode of an electrolytic cell **2** : the positive terminal of a battery **3** : the electron-emitting electrode of an electron tube — **cath·od·al** \'ka-ˌthō-dᵊl\ *adj* — **ca·thod·ic** \ka-'thä-dik\ *adj*

cathode–ray tube *n* : a vacuum tube in which a beam of electrons is projected on a fluorescent screen to produce a luminous spot

cath·o·lic \'kath-lik, 'ka-thə-\ *adj* **1** *cap* : of or relating to Catholics and esp. Roman Catholics **2** : GENERAL, UNIVERSAL

Cath·o·lic \'kath-lik, 'ka-thə-\ *n* : a member of a church claiming historical continuity from the ancient undivided Christian church; *esp* : a member of the Roman Catholic Church — **Ca·thol·i·cism** \kə-'thä-lə-ˌsi-zəm\ *n*

\ə\abut \ᵊ\kitten \ər\further \a\ash \ā\ace \ä\mop, mar \aú\out \ch\chin \e\bet \ē\easy \g\go \i\hit \ī\ice \j\job \ŋ\sing \ō\go \ó\law \ói\boy \th\thin \t̲h̲\the \ü\loot \ú\foot \y\yet \zh\vision *see also* Pronunciation Symbols page

cath·o·lic·i·ty \ˌka-thə-ˈli-sə-tē\ *n, pl* **-ties 1** *cap* : the character of being in conformity with a Catholic church **2** : liberality of sentiments or views **3** : comprehensive range

cat·ion \ˈkat-ˌī-ən\ *n* : the ion in an electrolyte that migrates to the cathode; *also* : a positively charged ion

cat·kin \ˈkat-kən\ *n* : a long flower cluster (as of a willow) bearing crowded flowers and prominent bracts

cat·like \-ˌlīk\ *adj* : resembling a cat or its behavior; *esp* : STEALTHY

cat·nap \-ˌnap\ *n* : a very short light nap — **catnap** *vb*

cat·nip \-ˌnip\ *n* : an aromatic mint that is esp. attractive to cats

cat–o′–nine–tails \ˌka-tə-ˈnīn-ˌtālz\ *n, pl* **cat–o′–nine–tails** : a whip made of usu. nine knotted cords fastened to a handle

CAT scan \ˈkat-\ *n* [*computerized axial tomography*] : an image made by computed tomography

CAT scanner *n* : a medical instrument consisting of integrated X-ray and computing equipment that is used to make CAT scans

cat's cradle *n* : a game played with a string looped on the fingers in such a way as to resemble a small cradle

cat's–eye \ˈkats-ˌī\ *n, pl* **cat's–eyes** : any of various iridescent gems

cat's–paw \-ˌpȯ\ *n, pl* **cat's–paws** : a person used by another as a tool

cat·sup \ˈke-chəp, ˈka-; ˈkat-səp\ *var of* KETCHUP

cat·tail \ˈkat-ˌtāl\ *n* : a tall reedlike marsh plant with furry brown spikes of tiny flowers

cat·tle \ˈkat-ᵊl\ *n pl* : LIVESTOCK; *esp* : domestic bovines (as cows, bulls, or calves) — **cat·tle·man** \-mən, -ˌman\ *n*

cat·ty \ˈka-tē\ *adj* **cat·ti·er, -est** : slyly spiteful — **cat·ti·ly** \ˈka-tᵊl-ē\ *adv* — **cat·ti·ness** *n*

cat·ty–cor·ner *or* **cat·ty–cor·nered** *var of* CATERCORNER

CATV *abbr* community antenna television

cat·walk \ˈkat-ˌwȯk\ *n* : a narrow walk (as along a bridge)

Cau·ca·sian \kȯ-ˈkā-zhən\ *adj* : of or relating to the white race of mankind — **Caucasian** *n* — **Cau·ca·soid** \ˈkȯ-kə-ˌsȯid\ *adj or n*

cau·cus \ˈkȯ-kəs\ *n* : a meeting of a group of persons belonging to the same political party or faction usu. to decide upon policies and candidates — **caucus** *vb*

cau·dal \ˈkȯ-dᵊl\ *adj* : of, relating to, or located near the tail or the hind end of the body — **cau·dal·ly** *adv*

cau·di·llo \kaù-ˈthē-(ˌ)yȯ, -ˈthēl-\ *n, pl* **-llos** : a Spanish or Latin-American military dictator

caught \ˈkȯt\ *past and past part of* CATCH

caul \ˈkȯl\ *n* : the inner fetal membrane of higher vertebrates esp. when covering the head at birth

caul·dron \ˈkȯl-drən\ *n* : a large kettle

cau·li·flow·er \ˈkȯ-li-ˌflaù(-ə)r\ *n* [It *cavolfiore*, fr. *cavolo* cabbage + *fiore* flower] : a garden plant closely related to cabbage and grown for its compact edible head of undeveloped flowers; *also* : this head used as a vegetable

cauliflower ear *n* : an ear deformed from injury and excessive growth of scar tissue

¹**caulk** \ˈkȯk\ *vb* [ME, fr. OF *cauquer* to trample, fr. L *calcare*, fr. *calx* heel] : to stop up and make tight against leakage (as a boat or its seams) — **caulk·er** *n*

²**caulk** *also* **caulk·ing** *n* : material used to caulk

caus·al \ˈkȯ-zəl\ *adj* **1** : expressing or indicating cause **2** : relating to or acting as a cause — **cau·sal·i·ty** \kȯ-ˈza-lə-tē\ *n* — **caus·al·ly** *adv*

cau·sa·tion \kȯ-ˈzā-shən\ *n* **1** : the act or process of causing **2** : the means by which an effect is produced

¹**cause** \ˈkȯz\ *n* **1** : REASON, MOTIVE **2** : something that brings about a result; *esp* : a person or thing that is the agent of bringing something about **3** : a suit or action in court : CASE **4** : a question or matter to be decided **5** : a

principle or movement earnestly supported — **cause·less** *adj*

²**cause** *vb* **caused; caus·ing** : to be the cause or occasion of — **caus·a·tive** \ˈkȯ-zə-tiv\ *adj* — **caus·er** *n*

cause cé·lè·bre \ˌkȯz-sā-ˈlebrᵊ, ˌkȯz-\ *n, pl* **causes cé·lè·bres** *same* \ [F, lit., celebrated case] **1** : a legal case that excites widespread interest **2** : a notorious person, thing, incident, or episode

cau·se·rie \ˌkȯz-ˈrē, ˌkō-zə-\ *n* [F] **1** : an informal conversation : CHAT **2** : a short informal essay

cause·way \ˈkȯz-ˌwā\ *n* : a raised way or road across wet ground or water

¹**caus·tic** \ˈkȯ-stik\ *adj* **1** : CORROSIVE **2** : SHARP, INCISIVE ⟨~ wit⟩

²**caustic** *n* **1** : a substance that burns or destroys organic tissue by chemical action **2** : SODIUM HYDROXIDE

cau·ter·ize \ˈkȯ-tə-ˌrīz\ *vb* **-ized; -iz·ing** : to burn or sear usu. to prevent infection or bleeding — **cau·ter·i·za·tion** \ˌkȯ-tə-rə-ˈzā-shən\ *n*

¹**cau·tion** \ˈkȯ-shən\ *n* **1** : ADMONITION, WARNING **2** : prudent forethought to minimize risk **3** : one that astonishes — **cau·tion·ary** \-shə-ˌner-ē\ *adj*

²**caution** *vb* : to advise caution to

cau·tious \ˈkȯ-shəs\ *adj* : marked by or given to caution : CAREFUL — **cau·tious·ly** *adv* — **cau·tious·ness** *n*

cav *abbr* **1** cavalry **2** cavity

cav·al·cade \ˌka-vəl-ˈkād\ *n* **1** : a procession of riders or carriages; *also* : a procession of vehicles **2** : a dramatic sequence or procession

¹**cav·a·lier** \ˌka-və-ˈlir\ *n* [MF, fr. It *cavaliere*, fr. OProv *cavalier*, fr. LL *caballarius* horseman, fr. L *caballus* horse] **1** : a mounted soldier : KNIGHT **2** *cap* : an adherent of Charles I of England **3** : GALLANT

²**cavalier** *adj* **1** : DEBONAIR **2** : DISDAINFUL, HAUGHTY — **cav·a·lier·ly** *adv*

cav·al·ry \ˈka-vəl-rē\ *n, pl* **-ries** : troops mounted on horseback or moving in motor vehicles — **cav·al·ry·man** \-mən, -ˌman\ *n*

¹**cave** \ˈkāv\ *n* : a natural underground chamber open to the surface

²**cave** *vb* **caved; cav·ing** **1** : to collapse or cause to collapse **2** : to cease to resist : SUBMIT — usu. used with *in*

ca·ve·at \ˈka-vē-ˌät, -ˌat; ˈkä-vē-ˌät\ *n* [L, let him beware] : WARNING

caveat emp·tor \-ˈemp-tər, -ˌtȯr\ *n* [NL, let the buyer beware] : a principle in commerce: without a warranty the buyer takes a risk

cave–in \ˈkā-ˌvin\ *n* **1** : the action of caving in **2** : a place where earth has caved in

cave·man \ˈkāv-ˌman\ *n* **1** : a cave dweller esp. of the Stone Age **2** : a man who acts in a rough or crude manner

cav·ern \ˈka-vərn\ *n* : CAVE; *esp* : one of large or unknown size — **cav·ern·ous** *adj* — **cav·ern·ous·ly** *adv*

cav·i·ar *or* **cav·i·are** \ˈka-vē-ˌär, ˈkä-\ *n* : the salted roe of a large fish (as sturgeon) used as an appetizer

cav·il \ˈka-vəl\ *vb* **-iled** *or* **-illed; -il·ing** *or* **-il·ling** : to make frivolous objections or raise trivial objections to — **cavil** *n* — **cav·il·er** *or* **cav·il·ler** *n*

cav·ing \ˈkā-viŋ\ *n* : the sport of exploring caves : SPELUNKING

cav·i·ta·tion \ˌka-və-ˈtā-shən\ *n* : the formation of partial vacuums in a liquid by a swiftly moving solid body (as a propeller) or by high-intensity sound waves

cav·i·ty \ˈka-və-tē\ *n, pl* **-ties 1** : an unfilled space within a mass : a hollow place **2** : an area of decay in a tooth

ca·vort \kə-ˈvȯrt\ *vb* : PRANCE, CAPER

ca·vy \ˈkā-vē\ *n, pl* **cavies** : GUINEA PIG 1

caw \ˈkȯ\ *vb* : to utter the harsh call of the crow or a similar cry — **caw** *n*

cay \ˈkē, ˈkā\ *n* : ⁴KEY

cay·enne pepper \ˌkī-ˈen-, ˌkā-\ *n* : a condiment consisting of ground dried fruits or seeds of a hot pepper

cay·man *var of* CAIMAN

Ca·yu·ga \kā-'ü-gə, kī-\ *n, pl* **Cayuga** *or* **Cayugas** : a member of an American Indian people of New York

Cay·use \'kī-ˌyüs, kī-'\ *n* **1** *pl* **Cayuse** *or* **Cayuses** : a member of an American Indian people of Oregon and Washington **2** *pl cayuses, not cap, West* : a native range horse

Cb *symbol* columbium

CB \'sē-'bē\ *n* : CITIZENS BAND; *also* : the radio set used for citizens-band communications

CBC *abbr* Canadian Broadcasting Corporation

CBD *abbr* cash before delivery

CBS *abbr* Columbia Broadcasting System

CBW *abbr* chemical and biological warfare

cc *abbr* cubic centimeter

CC *abbr* **1** carbon copy **2** community college **3** country club

CCD \ˌsē-ˌsē-'dē\ *n* : CHARGE-COUPLED DEVICE

CCTV *abbr* closed-circuit television

CCU *abbr* **1** cardiac care unit **2** coronary care unit **3** critical care unit

ccw *abbr* counterclockwise

cd *abbr* cord

Cd *symbol* cadmium

¹CD \ˌsē-'dē\ *n* : COMPACT DISC

²CD *abbr* **1** certificate of deposit **2** Civil Defense

CDR *abbr* commander

CD–ROM \ˌsē-ˌdē-'räm\ *n* : a compact disc containing data that can be read by a computer

CDT *abbr* central daylight (saving) time

Ce *symbol* cerium

CE *abbr* **1** chemical engineer **2** civil engineer **3** Corps of Engineers

cease \'sēs\ *vb* **ceased; ceas·ing** : to come or bring to an end : STOP

cease–fire \'sēs-'fīr\ *n* : a suspension of active hostilities

cease·less \'sēs-ləs\ *adj* : being without pause or stop : CONTINUOUS — **cease·less·ly** *adv* — **cease·less·ness** *n*

ce·cum \'sē-kəm\ *n, pl* **ce·ca** \-kə\ : the blind pouch at the beginning of the large intestine into which the small intestine opens — **ce·cal** \-kəl\ *adj*

ce·dar \'sē-dər\ *n* : any of numerous coniferous trees (as a juniper) noted for their fragrant durable wood; *also* : this wood

cede \'sēd\ *vb* **ced·ed; ced·ing** **1** : to yield or give up esp. by treaty **2** : ASSIGN, TRANSFER — **ced·er** *n*

ce·di \'sā-dē\ *n* — see MONEY table

ce·dil·la \si-'di-lə\ *n* : a mark placed under the letter *c* (as *ç*) to show that the *c* is to be pronounced like *s*

ceil·ing \'sē-liŋ\ *n* **1** : the overhead inside lining of a room **2** : the height above the ground of the base of the lowest layer of clouds when over half of the sky is obscured **3** : the greatest height at which an airplane can operate efficiently **4** : a prescribed upper limit ⟨price ∼⟩

cel·an·dine \'se-lən-ˌdīn, -ˌdēn\ *n* : a yellow-flowered herb related to the poppies

cel·e·brate \'se-lə-ˌbrāt\ *vb* **-brat·ed; -brat·ing** **1** : to perform (as a sacrament) with appropriate rites **2** : to honor (as a holiday) by solemn ceremonies or by refraining from ordinary business **3** : to observe a notable occasion with festivities **4** : EXTOL — **cel·e·brant** \-brənt\ *n* — **cel·e·bra·tion** \ˌse-lə-'brā-shən\ *n* — **cel·e·bra·tor** \'se-lə-brā-tər\ *n* — **cel·e·bra·to·ry** \-brə-ˌtòr-ē, -ˌtòr-; ˌse-lə-'brā-tə-rē\ *adj*

cel·e·brat·ed *adj* : widely known and often referred to **syn** distinguished, renowned, noted, famous, illustrious, notorious

ce·leb·ri·ty \sə-'le-brə-tē\ *n, pl* **-ties** **1** : the state of being celebrated : RENOWN **2** : a celebrated person

ce·ler·i·ty \sə-'ler-ə-tē\ *n* : SPEED, RAPIDITY

cel·ery \'se-lə-rē\ *n, pl* **-er·ies** : a European herb related to the carrot and widely grown for the crisp edible stems of its leaves

celery cabbage *n* : CHINESE CABBAGE 2

ce·les·ta \sə-'les-tə\ *or* **ce·leste** \sə-'lest\ *n* : a keyboard instrument with hammers that strike steel plates

ce·les·tial \sə-'les-chəl\ *adj* **1** : HEAVENLY, DIVINE **2** : of or relating to the sky — **ce·les·tial·ly** *adv*

celestial equator *n* : the great circle on the celestial sphere midway between the celestial poles

celestial navigation *n* : navigation by observation of the positions of stars

celestial pole *n* : either of the two points on the celestial sphere around which the daily rotation of the stars appears to take place

celestial sphere *n* : an imaginary sphere of infinite radius against which the celestial bodies appear to be projected

cel·i·ba·cy \'se-lə-bə-sē\ *n* **1** : the state of being unmarried; *esp* : abstention by vow from marriage **2** : abstention from sexual intercourse

cel·i·bate \'se-lə-bət\ *n* : one who lives in celibacy — **celibate** *adj*

cell \'sel\ *n* **1** : a small room (as in a convent or prison) usu. for one person; *also* : a small compartment, cavity, or bounded space **2** : a tiny mass of protoplasm that usu. contains a nucleus, is enclosed by a membrane, and forms the smallest structural unit of living matter capable of functioning independently **3** : a container holding an electrolyte either for generating electricity or for use in electrolysis **4** : a single unit in a device for converting radiant energy into electrical energy — **celled** \'seld\ *adj*

cel·lar \'se-lər\ *n* **1** : BASEMENT 1 **2** : the lowest position (as in an athletic league) **3** : a stock of wines

cel·lar·ette *or* **cel·lar·et** \ˌse-lə-'ret\ *n* : a case or cabinet for a few bottles of wine or liquor

cel·lo \'che-lō\ *n, pl* **cellos** : a bass member of the violin family tuned an octave below the viola — **cel·list** \-list\ *n*

cel·lo·phane \'se-lə-ˌfān\ *n* : a thin transparent material made from cellulose and used as a wrapping

cel·lu·lar \'sel-yə-lər\ *adj* **1** : of, relating to, or consisting of cells **2** : of, relating to, or being a radiotelephone system in which a geographical area is divided into small sections each served by a transmitter of limited range

cel·lu·lite \'sel-yə-ˌlīt\ *n* : lumpy fat in the thighs, hips, and buttocks of some women

cel·lu·lose \'sel-yə-ˌlōs\ *n* : a complex carbohydrate of the cell walls of plants used esp. in making paper or rayon — **cel·lu·los·ic** \ˌsel-yə-'lō-sik\ *adj or n*

Cel·si·us \'sel-sē-əs\ *adj* : relating to or having a scale for measuring temperature on which the interval between the triple point and the boiling point of water is divided into 99.99 degrees with 0.01° being the triple point and 100.00° the boiling point

Celt \'kelt, 'selt\ *n* : a member of any of a group of peoples (as the Irish or Welsh) of western Europe — **Celt·ic** *adj*

cem·ba·lo \'chem-bə-ˌlò\ *n, pl* **-ba·li** \-ˌlē\ *or* **-balos** [It] : HARPSICHORD

¹ce·ment \si-'ment\ *n* **1** : a powder that is produced from a burned mixture of clay and limestone and that is used in mortar and concrete; *also* : CONCRETE **2** : a binding element or agency **3** : CEMENTUM; *also* : a substance for filling cavities in teeth

²cement *vb* **1** : to unite by or as if by cement **2** : to cover with concrete — **ce·ment·er** *n*

ce·men·tum \si-'men-təm\ *n* : a specialized external bony layer covering the dentin of the part of a tooth normally within the gum

---

\ə\abut \ᵊ\kitten \ər\further \a\ash \ā\ace \ä\mop, mar \aù\out \ch\chin \e\bet \ē\easy \g\go \i\hit \ī\ice \j\job \ŋ\sing \ō\go \ò\law \òi\boy \th\thin \t̷h\the \ü\loot \ù\foot \y\yet \zh\vision *see also* Pronunciation Symbols page

cem·e·tery \'se-mə-ˌter-ē\ *n, pl* **-ter·ies** [ME *cimitery,* fr. MF *cimitere,* fr. LL *coemeterium,* fr. Gk *koimētērion* sleeping chamber, burial place, fr. *koiman* to put to sleep] : a burial ground : GRAVEYARD

cen·o·bite \'se-nə-ˌbīt\ *n* : a member of a religious group living together in a monastic community — **cen·o·bit·ic** \ˌse-nə-'bi-tik\ *adj*

ceno·taph \'se-nə-ˌtaf\ *n* [F *cénotaphe,* fr. L *cenotaphium,* fr. Gk *kenotaphion,* fr. *kenos* empty + *taphos* tomb] : a tomb or a monument erected in honor of a person whose body is elsewhere

Ce·no·zo·ic \ˌsē-nə-'zō-ik, ˌse-\ *adj* : of, relating to, or being the era of geologic history that extends from about 65 million years ago to the present — **Cenozoic** *n*

cen·ser \'sen-sər\ *n* : a vessel for burning incense (as in a religious ritual)

¹**cen·sor** \'sen-sər\ *n* **1** : one of two early Roman magistrates whose duties included taking the census **2** : an official who inspects printed matter or sometimes motion pictures with power to suppress anything objectionable — **cen·so·ri·al** \sen-'sȯr-ē-əl\ *adj*

²**censor** *vb* : to subject to censorship

cen·so·ri·ous \sen-'sȯr-ē-əs\ *adj* : marked by or given to censure : CRITICAL — **cen·so·ri·ous·ly** *adv* — **cen·so·ri·ous·ness** *n*

cen·sor·ship \'sen-sər-ˌship\ *n* **1** : the action of a censor esp. in stopping the transmission or publication of matter considered objectionable **2** : the office of a Roman censor

¹**cen·sure** \'sen-chər\ *n* **1** : the act of blaming or condemning sternly **2** : an official reprimand

²**censure** *vb* **cen·sured; cen·sur·ing** : to find fault with and criticize as blameworthy — **cen·sur·able** *adj* — **cen·sur·er** *n*

cen·sus \'sen-səs\ *n* **1** : a periodic governmental count of population **2** : COUNT, TALLY — **cen·sus** *vb*

¹**cent** \'sent\ *n* [MF, hundred, fr. L *centum*] **1** : a monetary unit equal to ¹⁄₁₀₀ of a basic unit of value — see *birr, dollar, gulden, leone, lilangeni, lira, pound, rand, rupee, shilling* at MONEY table **2** : a coin, token, or note representing one cent

²**cent** *abbr* **1** centigrade **2** central **3** century

cen·taur \'sen-ˌtȯr\ *n* : any of a race of creatures in Greek mythology half man and half horse

¹**cen·ta·vo** \sen-'tä-(ˌ)vō\ *n, pl* **-vos** — see *boliviano, colón, cordoba, lempira, peso, quetzal, sol, sucre* at MONEY table

²**cen·ta·vo** \-'tä-(ˌ)vü, -(ˌ)vō\ *n, pl* **-vos** — see *cruzeiro, escudo, metical* at MONEY table

cen·te·nar·i·an \ˌsent-ᵊn-'er-ē-ən\ *n* : a person who is 100 or more years old

cen·te·na·ry \sen-'te-nə-rē, 'sent-ᵊn-ˌer-ē\ *n, pl* **-ries** : CENTENNIAL — **centenary** *adj*

cen·ten·ni·al \sen-'te-nē-əl\ *n* : a 100th anniversary or its celebration — **centennial** *adj*

¹**cen·ter** \'sen-tər\ *n* **1** : the point that is equally distant from all points on the circumference of a circle or surface of a sphere; *also* : MIDDLE 1 **2** : the point about which an activity concentrates or from which something originates **3** : a region of concentrated population **4** : a middle part **5** *often cap* : political figures holding moderate views esp. between those of conservatives and liberals **6** : a player occupying a middle position (as in football or basketball)

²**center** *vb* **1** : to place or fix at or around a center or central area **2** : to give a central focus or basis : CONCENTRATE **3** : to have a center : FOCUS

cen·ter·board \'sen-tər-ˌbȯrd\ *n* : a retractable keel used esp. in sailboats

cen·ter·piece \-ˌpēs\ *n* **1** : an object in a central position; *esp* : an adornment in the center of a table **2** : one that is of central importance or interest in a larger whole

cen·tes·i·mal \sen-'te-sə-məl\ *adj* : marked by or relating to division into hundredths

¹**cen·tes·i·mo** \chen-'te-zə-ˌmò\ *n, pl* **-mi** \-(ˌ)mē\ — see *lira* at MONEY table

²**cen·tes·i·mo** \sen-'te-sə-ˌmò\ *n, pl* **-mos** — see *balboa, peso* at MONEY table

cen·ti·grade \'sen-tə-ˌgrād, 'sän-\ *adj* : relating to, conforming to, or having a thermometer scale on which the interval between the freezing and boiling points of water is divided into 100 degrees with 0° representing the freezing point and 100° the boiling point ⟨10° $\sim$⟩

cen·ti·gram \-ˌgram\ *n* — see METRIC SYSTEM table

cen·ti·li·ter \'sen-ti-ˌlē-tər\ *n* — see METRIC SYSTEM table

cen·time \'sän-ˌtēm\ *n* — see *dinar, dirham, franc, gourde* at MONEY table

cen·ti·me·ter \'sen-tə-ˌmē-tər, 'sän-\ *n* — see METRIC SYSTEM table

centimeter–gram–second *adj* : of, relating to, or being a system of units based on the centimeter as the unit of length, the gram as the unit of mass, and the second as the unit of time

cen·ti·mo \'sen-tə-ˌmò\ *n, pl* **-mos** — see *bolivar, colón, dobra, guarani, peseta* at MONEY table

cen·ti·pede \'sen-tə-ˌpēd\ *n* [L *centipeda,* fr. *centum* hundred + *pes* foot] : any of a class of long flattened segmented arthropods with one pair of legs on each segment except the first which has a pair of poison fangs

centipede

¹**cen·tral** \'sen-trəl\ *adj* **1** : constituting a center **2** : ESSENTIAL, PRINCIPAL **3** : situated at, in, or near the center **4** : centrally placed and superseding separate units ⟨$\sim$ heating⟩ — **cen·tral·ly** *adv*

²**central** *n* : a central controlling office

cen·tral·ize \'sen-trə-ˌlīz\ *vb* **-ized; -iz·ing** : to bring to a central point or under central control — **cen·tral·i·za·tion** \ˌsen-trə-lə-'zā-shən\ *n* — **cen·tral·iz·er** \'sen-trə-ˌlī-zər\ *n*

central nervous system *n* : the part of the nervous system which integrates nervous function and activity and which in vertebrates consists of the brain and spinal cord

cen·tre *chiefly Brit var of* CENTER

cen·trif·u·gal \sen-'tri-fyə-gəl, -fi-\ *adj* [NL *centrifugus,* fr. *centr-* center + L *fugere* to flee] **1** : proceeding or acting in a direction away from a center or axis **2** : using or acting by centrifugal force

centrifugal force *n* : the force that tends to impel a thing or parts of a thing outward from a center of rotation

cen·tri·fuge \'sen-trə-ˌfyüj\ *n* : a machine using centrifugal force (as for separating substances of different densities or for removing moisture)

cen·trip·e·tal \sen-'tri-pət-ᵊl\ *adj* [NL *centripetus,* fr. *centr-* center + L *petere* seek] : proceeding or acting in a direction toward a center or axis

centripetal force *n* : the force needed to keep an object revolving about a point moving in a circular path

cen·trist \'sen-trist\ *n* **1** *often cap* : a member of a center party **2** : one who holds moderate views

cen·tu·ri·on \sen-'tür-ē-ən, -'tyür-\ *n* : an officer commanding a Roman century

cen·tu·ry \'sen-chə-rē\ *n, pl* **-ries 1** : a subdivision of a Roman legion **2** : a group or sequence of 100 like things **3** : a period of 100 years

century plant *n* : a Mexican agave maturing and flowering only once in many years and then dying

CEO \ˌsē-(ˌ)ē-ˈō\ *n* : the executive with the chief decision-making authority in an organization or business

ce·phal·ic \sə-ˈfa-lik\ *adj* **1** : of or relating to the head **2** : directed toward or situated on or in or near the head

ce·ram·ic \sə-ˈra-mik\ *n* **1** *pl* : the art or process of making articles from a nonmetallic mineral (as clay) by firing **2** : a product produced by ceramics — **ceramic** *adj*

ce·ra·mist \ˈra-mist\ *or* **ce·ram·i·cist** \sə-ˈra-mə-sist\ *n* : one who engages in ceramics

¹ce·re·al \ˈsir-ē-əl\ *adj* [L *cerealis,* fr. *Ceres,* the Roman goddess of agriculture] : relating to grain or to the plants that produce it; *also* : made of grain

²cereal *n* **1** : a grass (as wheat) yielding grain suitable for food; *also* : its grain **2** : a food and esp. a breakfast food prepared from the grain of a cereal

cer·e·bel·lum \ˌser-ə-ˈbe-ləm\ *n, pl* **-bellums** *or* **-bel·la** \-lə\ [ML, fr. L, dim. of *cerebrum*] : a part of the brain that projects over the medulla and is concerned esp. with coordination of muscular action and with bodily balance — **cer·e·bel·lar** \-lər\ *adj*

ce·re·bral \sə-ˈrē-brəl, ˈser-ə-\ *adj* **1** : of or relating to the brain, intellect, or cerebrum **2** : appealing to or involving the intellect — **ce·re·bral·ly** *adv*

cerebral cortex *n* : the surface layer of gray matter of the cerebrum that functions chiefly in coordination of sensory and motor information

cerebral palsy *n* : a disorder caused by brain damage usu. before, during, or shortly after birth and marked esp. by defective muscle control

cer·e·brate \ˈser-ə-ˌbrāt\ *vb* **-brat·ed; -brat·ing** : THINK — **cer·e·bra·tion** \ˌser-ə-ˈbrā-shən\ *n*

ce·re·brum \sə-ˈrē-brəm, ˈser-ə-\ *n, pl* **-brums** *or* **-bra** \-brə\ [L] : the enlarged front and upper part of the brain that contains the higher nervous centers

cere·ment \ˈser-ə-mənt, ˈsir-mənt\ *n* : a shroud for the dead

¹cer·e·mo·ni·al \ˌser-ə-ˈmō-nē-əl\ *adj* : of, relating to, or forming a ceremony; *also* : stressing careful attention to form and detail — **cer·e·mo·ni·al·ly** *adv*

²ceremonial *n* : a ceremonial act or system : RITUAL, FORM

cer·e·mo·ni·ous \ˌser-ə-ˈmō-nē-əs\ *adj* **1** : devoted to forms and ceremony **2** : CEREMONIAL **3** : according to formal usage or procedure **4** : marked by ceremony — **cer·e·mo·ni·ous·ly** *adv* — **cer·e·mo·ni·ous·ness** *n*

cer·e·mo·ny \ˈser-ə-ˌmō-nē\ *n, pl* **-nies 1** : a formal act or series of acts prescribed by law, ritual, or convention **2** : a conventional act of politeness **3** : a mere outward form with no deeper significance **4** : FORMALITY

ce·re·us \ˈsir-ē-əs\ *n* : any of various cacti of the western U.S. and tropical America

ce·rise \sə-ˈrēs\ *n* [F, lit., cherry] : a moderate red color

ce·ri·um \ˈsir-ē-əm\ *n* : a malleable metallic chemical element used esp. in alloys — see ELEMENT table

cer·met \ˈsər-ˌmet\ *n* : a strong alloy of a heat-resistant compound and a metal used esp. for turbine blades

cert *abbr* certificate; certification; certified; certify

¹cer·tain \ˈsərt-ᵊn\ *adj* **1** : FIXED, SETTLED **2** : of a specific but unspecified character ⟨~ people in authority⟩ **3** : DEPENDABLE, RELIABLE **4** : INDISPUTABLE, UNDENIABLE **5** : assured in mind or action — **cer·tain·ly** *adv*

²certain *pron* : certain ones

cer·tain·ty \-tē\ *n, pl* **-ties 1** : something that is certain **2** : the quality or state of being certain

cer·tif·i·cate \sər-ˈti-fi-kət\ *n* **1** : a document testifying to the truth of a fact **2** : a document testifying that one has fulfilled certain requirements (as of a course or school) **3** : a document giving evidence of ownership or debt ⟨~ of deposit⟩

cer·ti·fi·ca·tion \ˌsər-tə-fə-ˈkā-shən\ *n* **1** : the act of cer-

tifying : the state of being certified **2** : a certified statement

certified mail *n* : first class mail for which proof of delivery may be secured but no indemnity value is claimed

certified milk *n* : milk produced in dairies that operate under the rules and regulations of an authorized medical milk commission

certified public accountant *n* : an accountant who has met the requirements of a state law and has been granted a certificate

cer·ti·fy \ˈsər-tə-ˌfī\ *vb* **-fied; -fy·ing 1** : VERIFY, CONFIRM **2** : to endorse officially **3** : to guarantee (a bank check) as good by a statement to that effect stamped on its face **4** : to provide with a usu. professional certificate or license **syn** accredit, approve, sanction, endorse — **cer·ti·fi·able** \-ə-bəl\ *adj* — **cer·ti·fi·ably** \-blē\ *adv* — **cer·ti·fi·er** *n*

cer·ti·tude \ˈsər-tə-ˌtüd, -ˌtyüd\ *n* : the state of being or feeling certain

ce·ru·le·an \sə-ˈrü-lē-ən\ *adj* : AZURE

ce·ru·men \sə-ˈrü-mən\ *n* : EARWAX

cer·vi·cal \ˈsər-vi-kəl\ *adj* : of or relating to a neck or cervix

cervical cap *n* : a contraceptive device in the form of a thimble-shaped molded cap that fits over the uterine cervix and blocks sperm from entering the uterus

cer·vix \ˈsər-viks\ *n, pl* **cer·vi·ces** \-və-ˌsēz\ *or* **cer·vix·es 1** : NECK; *esp* : the back part of the neck **2** : a constricted portion of an organ or part; *esp* : the narrow outer end of the uterus

ce·sar·e·an *also* **ce·sar·i·an** \si-ˈzar-ē-ən, -ˈzer-\ *n* : CESAREAN SECTION — **cesarean** *also* **cesarian** *adj*

cesarean section *also* **cesarian section** *n* [fr. the belief that Julius Caesar was born this way] : surgical incision of the walls of the abdomen and uterus for delivery of offspring

ce·si·um \ˈsē-zē-əm\ *n* : a silver-white soft ductile chemical element — see ELEMENT table

ces·sa·tion \se-ˈsā-shən\ *n* : a temporary or final ceasing (as of action)

ces·sion \ˈse-shən\ *n* : a yielding (as of rights) to another

cess·pool \ˈses-ˌpül\ *n* : an underground pit or tank for receiving household sewage

ce·ta·cean \si-ˈtā-shən\ *n* : any of an order of aquatic mostly marine mammals that includes whales, porpoises, dolphins, and related forms — **cetacean** *adj*

cf *abbr* [L *confer*] compare

Cf *symbol* californium

CF *abbr* cystic fibrosis

CFC *abbr* chlorofluorocarbon

cg *abbr* centigram

CG *abbr* **1** coast guard **2** commanding general

cgs *abbr* centimeter-gram-second

ch *abbr* **1** chain **2** champion **3** chapter **4** church

CH *abbr* **1** clearinghouse **2** courthouse **3** customhouse

Cha·blis \sha-ˈblē, shə-, shä-; ˈsha-ˌblē\ *n, pl* **Cha·blis** \-ˈblēz, -(ˌ)blēz\ **1** : a dry sharp white Burgundy wine **2** : a white California wine

cha–cha \ˈchä-ˌchä\ *n* : a fast rhythmic ballroom dance of Latin American origin

Chad·ian \ˈcha-dē-ən\ *n* : a native or inhabitant of Chad — **Chadian** *adj*

chafe \ˈchāf\ *vb* **chafed; chaf·ing 1** : IRRITATE, VEX **2** : FRET **3** : to warm by rubbing **4** : to rub so as to wear away; *also* : to make sore by rubbing

cha·fer \ˈchā-fər\ *n* : any of various scarab beetles

¹chaff \ˈchaf\ *n* **1** : debris (as husks) separated from grain

---

\ə\abut \ᵊ\kitten \ər\further \a\ash \ā\ace \ä\mop, mar
\au̇\out \ch\chin \e\bet \ē\easy \g\go \i\hit \ī\ice \j\job
\ŋ\sing \ō\go \ȯ\law \ȯi\boy \th\thin \th̲\the \ü\loot \u̇\foot
\y\yet \zh\vision *see also* Pronunciation Symbols page

in threshing **2 :** something comparatively worthless —
chaffy *adj*
²chaff *n* **:** light jesting talk **:** BANTER
³chaff *vb* **:** to tease good-naturedly
chaf·fer \'cha-fər\ *vb* **:** BARGAIN, HAGGLE — **chaf·fer·er** *n*
chaf·finch \'cha-ˌfinch\ *n* **:** a common European finch with a cheerful song
chaf·ing dish \'chā-fiŋ-\ *n* **:** a utensil for cooking food at the table
¹cha·grin \shə-'grin\ *n* **:** mental uneasiness or annoyance caused by failure, disappointment, or humiliation
²chagrin *vb* **cha·grined** \-'grind\; **cha·grin·ing :** to cause to feel chagrin
¹chain \'chān\ *n* [ME *cheyne*, fr. MF *chaeine*, fr. L *catena*] **1 :** a flexible series of connected links **2 :** a chainlike surveying instrument; *also* **:** a unit of length equal to 66 feet (about 20 meters) **3** *pl* **:** BONDS, FETTERS **4 :** a series of things linked together **syn** train, string, sequence, succession, series
²chain *vb* **:** to fasten, bind, or connect with a chain; *also* **:** FETTER
chain gang *n* **:** a gang of convicts chained together
chain letter *n* **:** a letter sent to several persons with a request that each send copies to an equal number of persons
chain mail *n* **:** flexible armor of interlocking metal rings
chain reaction *n* **1 :** a series of events in which each event initiates the succeeding one **2 :** a chemical or nuclear reaction yielding products that cause further reactions of the same kind
chain saw *n* **:** a portable power saw that has teeth linked together to form an endless chain — **chain·saw** \'chān-ˌsò\ *vb*
chain–smoke \'chān-'smòk\ *vb* **:** to smoke esp. cigarettes continuously
chain store *n* **:** any of numerous stores under the same ownership that sell the same lines of goods
¹chair \'cher\ *n* **1 :** a seat with a back for one person **2 :** ELECTRIC CHAIR **3 :** an official seat; *also* **:** an office or position of authority or dignity **4 :** CHAIRMAN
²chair *vb* **:** to act as chairman of
chair·lift \'cher-ˌlift\ *n* **:** a motor-driven conveyor for skiers consisting of seats hung from a moving cable
chair·man \-mən\ *n* **:** the presiding officer of a meeting or of a committee — **chair·man·ship** *n*
chair·wom·an \-ˌwu̇-mən\ *n* **:** a woman who acts as chairman
chaise \'shāz\ *n* **:** a 2-wheeled horse-drawn carriage with a folding top
chaise longue \'shāz-'lòŋ\ *n, pl* **chaise longues** *same or* -'lòŋz\ [F *chaise longue*, lit., long chair] **:** a long reclining chair
chaise lounge \-'laùnj\ *n* **:** CHAISE LONGUE
chal·ced·o·ny \kal-'sed-ᵊn-ē\ *n, pl* **-nies :** a translucent pale blue or gray quartz
chal·co·py·rite \ˌkal-kə-'pī-ˌrīt\ *n* **:** a yellow mineral constituting an important ore of copper
cha·let \sha-'lā\ *n* **1 :** a herdsman's cabin in the Swiss mountains **2 :** a building in the style of a Swiss cottage with a wide roof overhang
chal·ice \'cha-ləs\ *n* **:** a drinking cup; *esp* **:** the eucharistic cup
¹chalk \'chòk\ *n* **1 :** a soft limestone **2 :** chalk or chalky material esp. when used as a crayon — **chalky** *adj*
²chalk *vb* **1 :** to rub or mark with chalk **2 :** to record with or as if with chalk — usu. used with *up*
chalk·board \'chòk-ˌbòrd\ *n* **:** BLACKBOARD
chalk up *vb* **1 :** ASCRIBE, CREDIT **2 :** ATTAIN, ACHIEVE
¹chal·lenge \'cha-lənj\ *vb* **chal·lenged; chal·leng·ing** [ME *chalengen* to accuse, fr. OF *chalengier*, fr. L *calumniari* to accuse falsely, fr. *calumnia* calumny] **1 :** to order to halt and prove identity **2 :** to take exception to **:** DIS-

chalet 2

PUTE **3 :** to issue an invitation to compete against one esp. in single combat **:** DARE, DEFY — **chal·leng·er** *n*
²challenge *n* **1 :** a summons to a duel **2 :** an invitation to compete in a sport **3 :** a calling into question **4 :** an exception taken to a juror **5 :** a sentry's command to halt and prove identity **6 :** a stimulating or interesting task or problem
chal·lis \'sha-lē\ *n, pl* **chal·lises** \-lēz\ **:** a lightweight clothing fabric of wool, cotton, or synthetic yarns
cham·ber \'chām-bər\ *n* **1 :** ROOM; *esp* **:** BEDROOM **2 :** an enclosed space or cavity **3 :** a hall for meetings of a legislative body **4 :** a judge's consultation room — usu. used in pl. **5 :** a legislative or judicial body; *also* **:** a council for a business purpose **6 :** the part of a firearm that holds the cartridge or powder charge during firing — **cham·bered** \-bərd\ *adj*
cham·ber·lain \'chām-bər-lən\ *n* **1 :** a chief officer in the household of a king or nobleman **2 :** TREASURER
cham·ber·maid \-ˌmād\ *n* **:** a maid who takes care of bedrooms
chamber music *n* **:** music intended for performance by a few musicians before a small audience
chamber of commerce : an association of businesspeople for promoting commercial and industrial interests in the community
cham·bray \'sham-ˌbrā\ *n* **:** a lightweight clothing fabric of white and colored threads
cha·me·leon \kə-'mēl-yən\ *n* [ME *camelion*, fr. MF, fr. L *chamaeleon*, fr. Gk *chamaileòn*, fr. *chamai* on the ground + *leòn* lion] **:** a small lizard whose skin changes color esp. according to its surroundings
¹cham·fer \'cham-fər\ *vb* **1 :** to cut a furrow in (as a column) **:** GROOVE **2 :** to make a chamfer on **:** BEVEL
²chamfer *n* **:** a beveled edge
cham·ois \'sha-mē\ *n, pl* **cham·ois** *same or* -mēz\ **1 :** a small goatlike antelope of Europe and the Caucasus region of Russia **2** *also* **cham·my** \'sha-mē\ **:** a soft leather made esp. from the skin of the sheep or goat **3 :** a cotton fabric made in imitation of chamois leather
cham·o·mile \'ka-mə-ˌmīl, -ˌmēl\ *n* **:** any of a genus of strong-scented herbs related to the daisies and having flower heads that yield a bitter substance used esp. in tonics and teas
¹champ \'champ, 'chämp\ *vb* **1 :** to chew noisily **2 :** to show impatience of delay or restraint
²champ \'champ\ *n* **:** CHAMPION
cham·pagne \sham-'pān\ *n* **:** a white effervescent wine
¹cham·pi·on \'cham-pē-ən\ *n* **1 :** a militant advocate or defender **2 :** one that wins first prize or place in a contest **3 :** one that is acknowledged to be better than all others
²champion *vb* **:** to protect or fight for as a champion **syn** back, advocate, uphold, support
cham·pi·on·ship \-ˌship\ *n* **1 :** the position or title of a champion **2 :** the act of championing **:** DEFENSE **3 :** a contest held to determine a champion
¹chance \'chans\ *n* **1 :** something that happens without apparent cause **2 :** the unpredictable element in existence **:** LUCK, FORTUNE **3 :** OPPORTUNITY **4 :** the like-

lihood of a particular outcome in an uncertain situation
: PROBABILITY **5** : RISK **6** : a raffle ticket — **chance** *adj*
— **by chance** : in the haphazard course of events
²**chance** *vb* **chanced; chanc·ing 1** : to take place by
chance : HAPPEN **2** : to come casually and unexpectedly
— used with *upon* **3** : to leave to chance **4** : to accept
the risk of
chan·cel \'chan-səl\ *n* : the part of a church including the
altar and choir
chan·cel·lery *or* **chan·cel·lory** \'chan- sə-lə-rē\ *n, pl*
-ler·ies *or* **-lor·ies 1** : the position or office of a chancellor **2** : the building or room where a chancellor
works **3** : the office or staff of an embassy or consulate
chan·cel·lor \'chan-sə-lər\ *n* **1** : a high state official in
various countries **2** : the head of a university **3** : a judge
in the equity court in various states of the U.S. **4** : the
chief minister of state in some European countries —
chan·cel·lor·ship *n*
chan·cery \'chan-sə-rē\ *n, pl* **-cer·ies 1** : any of various
courts of equity in the U.S. and Britain **2** : a record office for public or diplomatic archives **3** : a chancellor's
court or office **4** : the office of an embassy
chan·cre \'shaŋ-kər\ *n* [F, fr. L *cancer*] : a primary sore
or ulcer at the site of entry of an infective agent (as of
syphilis)
chan·croid \'chaŋ-₁kröid\ *n* : a sexually transmitted disease caused by a bacterium and characterized by chan-
cres that differ from those of syphilis in lacking
hardened margins
chancy \'chan-sē\ *adj* **chanc·i·er; -est 1** *Scot* : AUSPI-
CIOUS **2** : RISKY
chan·de·lier \₁shan-də-'lir\ *n* : a branched lighting fixture suspended from a ceiling
chan·dler \'chand-lər\ *n* [ME *chandeler* a maker or seller of candles, fr. MF *chandelier*, fr. OF, fr. *chandelle*
candle, fr. L *candela*] : a dealer in provisions and supplies of a specified kind ⟨ship's ∼⟩ — **chan·dlery** *n*
¹**change** \'chānj\ *vb* **changed; chang·ing 1** : to make or
become different : ALTER **2** : to replace with another **3**
: to give or receive an equivalent sum in notes or coins
of usu. smaller denominations or of another currency **4**
: to put fresh clothes or covering on ⟨∼ a bed⟩ **5** : to put
on different clothes **6** : EXCHANGE — **change·able** *adj*
— **chang·er** *n*
²**change** *n* **1** : the act, process, or result of changing **2** : a
fresh set of clothes **3** : money given in exchange for other money of higher denomination **4** : money returned
when a payment exceeds the sum due **5** : coins esp. of
small denominations — **change·ful** *adj*
change·ling \'chānj-liŋ\ *n* : a child secretly exchanged
for another in infancy
change of life : MENOPAUSE
change·over \'chānj-₁ō-vər\ *n* : CONVERSION, TRANSI-
TION
change ringing *n* : the art or practice of ringing a set of
tuned bells in continually varying order
¹**chan·nel** \'chan-ᵊl\ *n* **1** : the bed of a stream **2** : the deeper part of a waterway **3** : STRAIT **4** : a means of passage
or transmission **5** : a range of frequencies of sufficient
width for a single radio or television transmission **6** : a
usu. tubular enclosed passage : CONDUIT **7** : a long gutter, groove, or furrow
²**channel** *vb* **-neled** *or* **-nelled; -neling** *or* **-nel·ling 1** : to
make a channel in **2** : to direct into or through a channel
chan·nel·ize \'chan-ᵊl-₁īz\ *vb* **-ized; -iz·ing** : CHANNEL —
chan·nel·iza·tion \₁chan-ᵊl-ə-'zā-shən\ *n*
chan·son \shäⁿ-'sōⁿ\ *n, pl* **chan·sons** *same or* -'sōⁿz\
: SONG; *esp* : a cabaret song
¹**chant** \'chant\ *vb* **1** : SING; *esp* : to sing a chant **2** : to utter
or recite in the manner of a chant **3** : to celebrate or
praise in song — **chant·er** *n*
²**chant** *n* **1** : a repetitive melody in which several words
are sung to one tone : SONG; *esp* : a liturgical melody **2**

: a manner of singing or speaking in musical monotones
chan·teuse \shäⁿ-'tərz, shan-'tüz\ *n, pl* **chan·teuses**
same or -'tər-zəz, -'tü-zəz\ [F] : a woman who is a
concert or nightclub singer
chan·tey *or* **chan·ty** \'shan-tē, 'chan-\ *n, pl* **chanteys** *or*
chanties : a song sung by sailors in rhythm with their
work
chan·ti·cleer \₁chan-tə-'klir, ₁shan-\ *n* : ROOSTER
Cha·nu·kah \'kä-nə-kə, 'hä-\ *var of* HANUKKAH
cha·os \'kā-₁äs\ *n* **1** *often cap* : the confused unorganized
state existing before the creation of distinct forms **2**
: the inherent unpredictability in the behavior of a natural system (as the atmosphere or the beating heart) **3**
: complete disorder syn confusion, jumble, snarl, muddle, disarray — **cha·ot·ic** \kā-'ä-tik\ *adj* — **cha·ot·i·**
cal·ly \-ti-k(ə-)lē\ *adv*
¹**chap** \'chap\ *vb* **chapped; chap·ping** : to dry and crack
open usu. from wind and cold ⟨*chapped* lips⟩
²**chap** *n* : a jaw with its fleshy covering — usu. used in pl.
³**chap** *n* : FELLOW
⁴**chap** *abbr* chapter
chap·ar·ral \₁sha-pə-'ral\ *n* **1** : a dense impenetrable
thicket of shrubs or dwarf trees **2** : an ecological community esp. of southern California composed of shrubby plants
chap·book \'chap-₁búk\ *n* : a small book of ballads,
tales, or tracts
cha·peau \sha-'pō\ *n, pl* **cha·peaus** \-'pōz\ *or* **cha·peaux**
\-'pō, -'pōz\ [MF] : HAT
cha·pel \'cha-pəl\ *n* [ME, fr. OF *chapele*, fr. ML *cappel-*
la, fr. LL *cappa* cloak; fr. the cloak of St. Martin of
Tours preserved as a sacred relic in a chapel built for
that purpose] **1** : a private or subordinate place of worship **2** : an assembly at an educational institution usu.
including devotional exercises **3** : a place of worship
used by a Christian group other than an established
church
¹**chap·er·on** *or* **chap·er·one** \'sha-pə-₁rōn\ *n* [F *chaper-*
on, lit., hood, fr. MF, head covering, fr. *chape* cape, fr.
LL *cappa*] **1** : a person (as a matron) who accompanies
young unmarried women in public for propriety **2** : an
older person who accompanies young people at a social
gathering to ensure proper behavior
²**chaperon** *or* **chaperone** *vb* **-oned; -on·ing 1** : ESCORT,
GUIDE **2** : to act as a chaperon to or for — **chap·er·**
on·age \-₁rō-nij\ *n*
chap·fall·en \'chap-₁fó-lən, 'chap-\ *adj* **1** : having the
lower jaw hanging loosely **2** : DEJECTED, DEPRESSED
chap·lain \'cha-plən\ *n* **1** : a member of the clergy officially attached to a special group (as the army) **2** : a person chosen to conduct religious exercises (as for a club)
— **chap·lain·cy** \-sē\ *n*
chap·let \'cha-plət\ *n* **1** : a wreath for the head **2** : a string
of beads : NECKLACE
chap·man \'chap-mən\ *n, Brit* : an itinerant dealer : PED-
DLER
chaps \'shaps, 'chaps\ *n pl* [MexSp *chaparreras*] : leather leggings resembling trousers without a seat that are
worn esp. by western ranch hands
chap·ter \'chap-tər\ *n* **1** : a main division of a book **2** : a
body of canons (as of a cathedral) **3** : a local branch of
a society or fraternity
¹**char** \'chär\ *n, pl* **char** *or* **chars** : any of a genus of trouts
(as the common brook trout) with small scales
²**char** *vb* **charred; char·ring 1** : to burn or become
burned to charcoal **2** : SCORCH
³**char** *vb* **charred; char·ring** : to work as a cleaning woman

---

\ə\abut \ᵊ\kitten \ər\further \a\ash \ā\ace \ä\mop, mar
\aú\out \ch\chin \e\bet \ē\easy \g\go \i\hit \ī\ice \j\job
\ŋ\sing \ō\go \ó\law \ói\boy \th\thin \t̲h̲\the \ü\loot \ú\foot
\y\yet \zh\vision *see also* Pronunciation Symbols page

char·ac·ter \ˈkar-ik-tər\ *n* [ME *caracter,* fr. MF *caractère,* fr. L *character* mark, distinctive quality, fr. Gk *charaktēr,* fr. *charassein* to scratch, engrave] **1 :** a graphic symbol (as a letter) used in writing or printing **2 :** a symbol that represents information; *also :* a representation of such a character that may be accepted by a computer **3 :** a distinguishing feature : ATTRIBUTE **4 :** the complex of mental and ethical traits marking a person or a group **5 :** a person marked by conspicuous often peculiar traits **6 :** one of the persons in a novel or play **7 :** REPUTATION **8 :** moral excellence

¹**char·ac·ter·is·tic** \ˌkar-ik-tə-ˈris-tik\ *n* : a distinguishing trait, quality, or property

²**characteristic** *adj* : serving to mark individual character **syn** individual, peculiar, distinctive — **char·ac·ter·is·ti·cal·ly** \-ti-k(ə-)lē\ *adv*

char·ac·ter·ize \ˈkar-ik-tə-ˌrīz\ *vb* **-ized; -iz·ing 1 :** to describe the character of **2 :** to be a characteristic of — **char·ac·ter·iza·tion** \ˌkar-ik-tə-rə-ˈzā-shən\ *n*

cha·rades \shə-ˈrādz\ *n sing or pl* : a game in which some of the players try to guess a word or phrase from the actions of another player who may not speak

char·coal \ˈchär-ˌkōl\ *n* **1 :** a porous carbon prepared from vegetable or animal substances **2 :** a piece of fine charcoal used in drawing; *also :* a drawing made with charcoal

chard \ˈchärd\ *n* : SWISS CHARD

char·don·nay \ˌshard-ᵊn-ˈā\ *n, often cap* [F] : a dry white wine made from a single variety of white grape

¹**charge** \ˈchärj\ *n* **1 :** a quantity (as of fuel or ammunition) required to fill something to capacity **2 :** a store or accumulation of force **3 :** an excess or deficiency of electrons in a body **4 :** THRILL, KICK **5 :** a task or duty imposed **6 :** CARE, RESPONSIBILITY **7 :** one given into another's care **8 :** instructions from a judge to a jury **9 :** COST, EXPENSE, PRICE; *also :* a debit to an account **10 :** ACCUSATION, INDICTMENT **11 :** ATTACK, ASSAULT

²**charge** *vb* **charged; charg·ing 1 :** to load or fill to capacity **2 :** to give an electric charge to; *also :* to restore the activity of (a storage battery) by means of an electric current **3 :** to impose a task or responsibility on **4 :** COMMAND, ORDER **5 :** ACCUSE **6 :** to rush against : rush forward in assault **7 :** to make liable for payment; *also :* to record a debt or liability against **8 :** to fix as a price — **charge·able** *adj*

charge–coupled device *n* : a semiconductor device used esp. as an optical sensor

char·gé d'af·faires \shär-ˌzhä-də-ˈfar\ *n, pl* **chargés d'affaires** \-ˌzhä-, -ˌzhäz-\ [F] : a diplomat who substitutes for an ambassador or minister

¹**char·ger** \ˈchär-jər\ *n* : a large platter

²**charg·er** *n* **1 :** a device or a workman that charges something **2 :** WARHORSE

char·i·ot \ˈchar-ē-ət\ *n* : a 2-wheeled horse-drawn vehicle of ancient times used esp. in war and in races — **char·i·o·teer** \ˌchar-ē-ə-ˈtir\ *n*

cha·ris·ma \kə-ˈriz-mə\ *n* : a personal quality of leadership arousing popular loyalty or enthusiasm — **char·is·mat·ic** \ˌkar-əz-ˈma-tik\ *adj*

char·i·ta·ble \ˈchar-ə-tə-bəl\ *adj* **1 :** liberal in giving to needy people **2 :** merciful or lenient in judging others **syn** benevolent, philanthropic, altruistic, humanitarian — **char·i·ta·ble·ness** *n* — **char·i·ta·bly** \-blē\ *adv*

char·i·ty \ˈchar-ə-tē\ *n, pl* **-ties 1 :** goodwill toward or love of humanity **2 :** an act or feeling of generosity **3 :** the giving of aid to the poor; *also :* ALMS **4 :** an institution engaged in relief of the poor **5 :** leniency in judging others **syn** mercy, clemency, lenity

char·la·tan \ˈshär-lə-tən\ *n* : a person making usu. showy pretenses to knowledge or ability : FRAUD, FAKER

Charles·ton \ˈchärl-stən\ *n* : a lively dance in which the

knees are swung in and out and the heels are turned sharply outward on each step

char·ley horse \ˈchär-lē-ˌhȯrs\ *n* : a muscular pain, cramping, or stiffness from a strain or bruise

¹**charm** \ˈchärm\ *n* [ME *charme,* fr. MF, fr. L *carmen* song, fr. *canere* to sing] **1 :** a practice or expression believed to have magic power **2 :** something worn about the person to ward off evil or bring good fortune : AMULET **3 :** a trait that fascinates or allures **4 :** physical grace or attraction **5 :** a small ornament worn on a bracelet or chain

²**charm** *vb* **1 :** to affect by or as if by a magic spell **2 :** to protect by or as if by charms **3 :** FASCINATE, ENCHANT **syn** allure, captivate, bewitch, attract — **charm·er** *n*

charm·ing \ˈchär-miŋ\ *adj* : PLEASING, DELIGHTFUL — **charm·ing·ly** *adv*

char·nel house \ˈchärn-ᵊl-\ *n* : a building or chamber in which bodies or bones are deposited

¹**chart** \ˈchärt\ *n* **1 :** MAP **2 :** a sheet giving information in the form of a table, list, or diagram; *also :* GRAPH

²**chart** *vb* **1 :** to make a chart of **2 :** PLAN

¹**char·ter** \ˈchär-tər\ *n* **1 :** an official document granting rights or privileges (as to a colony, town, or college) from a sovereign or a governing body **2 :** CONSTITUTION **3 :** a written instrument from a society creating a branch **4 :** a mercantile lease of a ship

²**charter** *vb* **1 :** to grant a charter to **2** *Brit* : CERTIFY ⟨~ed engineer⟩ **3 :** to hire, rent, or lease for temporary use — **char·ter·er** *n*

charter member *n* : an original member of an organization

char·treuse \shär-ˈtrüz, -ˈtrüs\ *n* : a brilliant yellow green

char·wom·an \ˈchär-ˌwu̇-mən\ *n* : a cleaning woman esp. in large buildings

chary \ˈchar-ē\ *adj* **chari·er; -est** [ME, sorrowful, dear, fr. OE *cearig* sorrowful, fr. *caru* sorrow] **1 :** CAUTIOUS, CIRCUMSPECT **2 :** SPARING — **char·i·ly** \-ə-lē\ *adv*

¹**chase** \ˈchās\ *n* **1 :** PURSUIT; *also :* HUNTING **2 :** QUARRY **3 :** a tract of unenclosed land used as a game preserve

²**chase** *vb* **chased; chas·ing 1 :** to follow rapidly : PURSUE **2 :** HUNT **3 :** to seek out ⟨*chasing* down clues⟩ **4 :** to cause to depart or flee : drive away **5 :** RUSH, HASTEN

³**chase** *vb* **chased; chas·ing :** to decorate (a metal surface) by embossing or engraving

⁴**chase** *n* : FURROW, GROOVE

chas·er \ˈchā-sər\ *n* **1 :** one that chases **2 :** a mild drink (as beer) taken after hard liquor

chasm \ˈka-zəm\ *n* : GORGE 2

chas·sis \ˈcha-sē, ˈsha-sē\ *n, pl* **chas·sis** \-sēz\ : the supporting frame of a structure (as an automobile or television set)

chaste \ˈchāst\ *adj* **chast·er; chast·est 1 :** innocent of unlawful sexual intercourse : VIRTUOUS, PURE **2 :** CELIBATE **3 :** pure in thought : MODEST **4 :** severe or simple in design — **chaste·ly** *adv* — **chaste·ness** *n*

chas·ten \ˈchās-ᵊn\ *vb* : to correct through punishment or suffering : DISCIPLINE; *also :* PURIFY — **chas·ten·er** *n*

chas·tise \chas-ˈtīz\ *vb* **chas·tised; chas·tis·ing** [ME *chastisen,* alter. of *chasten*] **1 :** to punish esp. bodily **2 :** to censure severely : CASTIGATE — **chas·tise·ment** \-mənt, ˈchas-təz-\ *n*

chas·ti·ty \ˈchas-tə-tē\ *n* : the quality or state of being chaste; *esp :* sexual purity

cha·su·ble \ˈcha-zə-bəl, -sə-\ *n* : the outer vestment of the priest at mass

chat \ˈchat\ *n* : light familiar informal talk — **chat** *vb*

châ·teau \sha-ˈtō\ *n, pl* **châ·teaus** \-ˈtōz\ *or* **châ·teaux** \-ˈtō, -ˈtōz\ [F, fr. L *castellum* castle, dim. of *castra* camp] **1 :** a feudal castle in France **2 :** a large country house **3 :** a French vineyard estate

chat·e·laine \'shat-ᵊl-ˌān\ *n* **1** : the mistress of a chateau **2** : a clasp or hook for a watch, purse, or keys

chat·tel \'chat-ᵊl\ *n* **1** : an item of tangible property other than real estate **2** : SLAVE, BONDMAN

chat·ter \'cha-tər\ *vb* **1** : to utter speechlike but meaningless sounds **2** : to talk idly, incessantly, or fast **3** : to click repeatedly or uncontrollably — **chatter** *n* — **chat·ter·er** *n*

chat·ter·box \'cha-tər-ˌbäks\ *n* : one who talks incessantly

chat·ty \'cha-tē\ *adj* **chat·ti·er; -est** : TALKATIVE — **chat·ti·ly** \-tə-lē\ *adv* — **chat·ti·ness** \-tē-nəs\ *n*

¹chauf·feur \'shō-fər, shō-'fər\ *n* [F, lit., stoker, fr. *chauffer* to heat] : a person employed to drive an automobile

²chauffeur *vb* **chauf·feured; chauf·feur·ing 1** : to do the work of a chauffeur **2** : to transport in the manner of a chauffeur

chaunt \'chȯnt, 'chänt\ *var of* CHANT

chau·vin·ism \'shō-və-ˌni-zəm\ *n* [F *chauvinisme*, fr. Nicolas *Chauvin*, fictional soldier of excessive patriotism and devotion to Napoleon] **1** : excessive or blind patriotism **2** : an attitude of superiority toward members of the opposite sex — **chau·vin·ist** \-nist\ *n or adj* — **chau·vin·is·tic** \ˌshō-və-'nis-tik\ *adj* — **chau·vin·is·ti·cal·ly** \-ti-k(ə-)lē\ *adv*

cheap \'chēp\ *adj* **1** : INEXPENSIVE **2** : costing little effort to obtain **3** : worth little : SHODDY, TAWDRY **4** : worthy of scorn **5** : STINGY — **cheap** *adv* — **cheap·ly** *adv* — **cheap·ness** *n*

cheap·en \'chē-pən\ *vb* **1** : to make or become cheap or cheaper in price or value **2** : to make tawdry

cheap·skate \'chēp-ˌskāt\ *n* : a miserly or stingy person; *esp* : one who tries to avoid paying a fair share of costs

¹cheat \'chēt\ *vb* **1** : to deprive of something through fraud or deceit **2** : to practice fraud or trickery **3** : to violate rules (as of a game) dishonestly — **cheat·er** *n*

²cheat *n* **1** : the act of deceiving : FRAUD, DECEPTION **2** : one that cheats : a dishonest person

¹check \'chek\ *n* **1** : a sudden stoppage of progress **2** : a sudden pause or break **3** : something that stops or restrains **4** : a standard for testing or evaluation **5** : EXAMINATION, INVESTIGATION **6** : the act of testing or verifying **7** : a written order to a bank to pay money **8** : a ticket or token showing ownership or identity **9** : a slip indicating an amount due **10** : a pattern in squares; *also* : a fabric in such a pattern **11** : a mark typically ✔ placed beside an item to show that it has been noted **12** : CRACK, SPLIT

²check *vb* **1** : to slow down or stop : BRAKE **2** : to restrain the action or force of : CURB **3** : to compare with a source, original, or authority : VERIFY **4** : to inspect or test for satisfactory condition **5** : to mark with a check as examined **6** : to consign for shipment for one holding a passenger ticket **7** : to mark into squares **8** : to leave or accept for safekeeping in a checkroom **9** : to prove to be consistent or truthful **10** : CRACK, SPLIT

check·book \'chek-ˌbůk\ *n* : a book containing blank checks

¹check·er \'che-kər\ *n* : a piece in the game of checkers

²checker *vb* **1** : to variegate with different colors or shades **2** : to vary with contrasting elements 〈a ∼ed career〉 **3** : to mark into squares

³checker *n* : one that checks; *esp* : one who checks out purchases in a supermarket

check·er·ber·ry \'che-kər-ˌber-ē\ *n* : WINTERGREEN 1; *also* : the spicy red fruit of this plant

check·er·board \-ˌbȯrd\ *n* : a board of 64 squares of alternate colors used in various games

check·ers \'che-kərz\ *n* : a game for two played on a checkerboard with each player having 12 pieces

check in *vb* : to report one's presence or arrival (as at a hotel)

check·list \'chek-ˌlist\ *n* : a list of things to be checked or done; *also* : a comprehensive list

check·mate \'chek-ˌmāt\ *vb* [ME *chekmaten*, fr. *chekmate*, interj. used to announce checkmate, fr. MF *eschec mat*, fr. Ar *shāh māt*, fr. Per, lit., the king is left unable to escape] **1** : to thwart completely : DEFEAT, FRUSTRATE **2** : to attack (an opponent's king) in chess so that escape is impossible — **checkmate** *n*

check·off \'che-ˌkȯf\ *n* : the deduction of union dues from a worker's paycheck by the employer

check·out \'che-ˌkaůt\ *n* **1** : the action or an instance of checking out **2** : a counter at which checking out is done **3** : the process of examining and testing something as to readiness for intended use

check out *vb* **1** : to settle one's account (as at a hotel) and leave **2** : to total or have totaled the cost of purchases in a store and to make or receive payment for them

check·point \'chek-ˌpȯint\ *n* : a point at which a check is performed

check·room \-ˌrüm, -ˌrům\ *n* : a room at which baggage, parcels, or clothing is checked

check·up \'che-ˌkəp\ *n* : EXAMINATION; *esp* : a general physical examination

ched·dar \'che-dər\ *n, often cap* : a hard mild to sharp white or yellow cheese of smooth texture

cheek \'chēk\ *n* **1** : the fleshy side part of the face **2** : IMPUDENCE, BOLDNESS, AUDACITY **3** : BUTTOCK 1 — **cheeked** \'chēkt\ *adj*

cheek·bone \'chēk-ˌbȯn\ *n* : the bone or bony ridge below the eye

cheeky \'chē-kē\ *adj* **cheek·i·er; -est** : IMPUDENT, SAUCY — **cheek·i·ly** \-kə-lē\ *adv* — **cheek·i·ness** \-kē-nəs\ *n*

cheep \'chēp\ *vb* : to utter faint shrill sounds : PEEP — **cheep** *n*

¹cheer \'chir\ *n* [ME *chere* face, cheer, fr. OF, face, fr. ML *cara*, prob. fr. GK *kara* head, face] **1** : state of mind or heart : SPIRIT **2** : ANIMATION, GAIETY **3** : hospitable entertainment : WELCOME **4** : food and drink for a feast **5** : something that gladdens **6** : a shout of applause or encouragement

²cheer *vb* **1** : to give hope or courage to : COMFORT **2** : to make glad **3** : to urge on esp. by shouts **4** : to applaud with shouts **5** : to grow or be cheerful — usu. used with *up* — **cheer·er** *n*

cheer·ful \'chir-fəl\ *adj* **1** : having or showing good spirits **2** : conducive to good spirits : pleasant and bright — **cheer·ful·ly** *adv* — **cheer·ful·ness** *n*

cheer·lead·er \'chir-ˌlē-dər\ *n* : a person who directs organized cheering esp. at a sports event

cheer·less \'chir-ləs\ *adj* : BLEAK, DISPIRITING — **cheer·less·ly** *adv* — **cheer·less·ness** *n*

cheery \'chir-ē\ *adj* **cheer·i·er; -est** : CHEERFUL — **cheer·i·ly** \-ə-lē\ *adv* — **cheer·i·ness** \-ē-nəs\ *n*

cheese \'chēz\ *n* : the curd of milk usu. pressed into cakes and cured for use as food

cheese·burg·er \-ˌbər-gər\ *n* : a hamburger topped with cheese

cheese·cake \-ˌkāk\ *n* **1** : a dessert consisting of a creamy filling usu. containing cheese baked in a shell **2** : photographs of shapely scantily clad women

cheese·cloth \-ˌklȯth\ *n* : a lightweight coarse cotton gauze

cheese·par·ing \-ˌpar-iŋ\ *n* : miserly economizing — **cheeseparing** *adj*

cheesy \'chē-zē\ *adj* **chees·i·er; -est 1** : resembling, suggesting, or containing cheese **2** *slang* : CHEAP **3**

\ə\abut \ᵊ\kitten \ər\further \a\ash \ā\ace \ä\mop, mar \aů\out \ch\chin \e\bet \ē\easy \g\go \i\hit \ī\ice \j\job \ŋ\sing \ō\go \ȯ\law \ȯi\boy \th\thin \t͟h\the \ü\loot \ů\foot \y\yet \zh\vision *see also* Pronunciation Symbols page

chee·tah \'chē-tə\ *n* [Hindu *cītā* leopard, fr. Skt *citraka*, fr. *citra* bright, variegated] : a large long-legged spotted swift-moving African and formerly Asian cat

cheetah

chef \'shef\ *n* **1** : a cook who manages the kitchen (as of a restaurant) **2** : COOK

chef d'oeu·vre \shā-'dœvrᵊ\ *n, pl* **chefs d'oeuvre** *same*\ : MASTERPIECE

chem *abbr* chemical; chemist; chemistry

¹**chem·i·cal** \'ke-mi-kəl\ *adj* **1** : of, relating to, used in, or produced by chemistry **2** : acting or operated or produced by chemicals — **chem·i·cal·ly** \-k(ə-)lē\ *adv*

²**chemical** *n* : a substance obtained by a chemical process or used for producing a chemical effect

chemical engineering *n* : engineering dealing with the industrial application of chemistry

chemical warfare *n* : warfare using incendiary mixtures, smokes, or irritant, burning, or asphyxiating gases

chemical weapon *n* : a weapon used in chemical warfare

che·mise \shə-'mēz\ *n* **1** : a woman's one-piece undergarment **2** : a loose straight-hanging dress

chem·ist \'ke-mist\ *n* **1** : one trained in chemistry **2** *Brit* : PHARMACIST

chem·is·try \'ke-mə-strē\ *n, pl* **-tries 1** : the science that deals with the composition, structure, and properties of substances and of the changes they undergo **2** : chemical composition or properties ⟨the ∼ of gasoline⟩ **3** : a strong mutual attraction

che·mo·ther·a·py \ˌkē-mō-'ther-ə-pē\ *n* : the use of chemicals in the treatment or control of disease — **che·mo·ther·a·peu·tic** \-ˌther-ə-'pyü-tik\ *adj*

che·nille \shə-'nēl\ *n* [F, lit., caterpillar, fr. L *canicula*, dim. of *canis* dog] : a fabric with a deep fuzzy pile often used for bedspreads and rugs

cheque \'chek\ *chiefly Brit var of* ¹CHECK 7

che·quer *chiefly Brit var of* CHECKER

cher·ish \'cher-ish\ *vb* **1** : to hold dear : treat with care and affection **2** : to keep deeply in mind — **cher·ish·able** *adj* — **cher·ish·er** *n*

Cher·o·kee \'cher-ə-(ˌ)kē\ *n, pl* **Cherokee** *or* **Cherokees** : a member of an American Indian people orig. of Tennessee and No. Carolina; *also* : their language

che·root \shə-'rüt\ *n* : a cigar cut square at both ends

cher·ry \'cher-ē\ *n, pl* **cherries** [ME *chery*, fr. OF *cherise* (taken as a plural), fr. LL *ceresia*, fr. L *cerasus* cherry tree, fr. Gk *kerasos*] **1** : the small fleshy pale yellow to deep blackish red fruit of a tree related to the roses; *also* : the tree or its wood **2** : a moderate red

chert \'chərt, 'chat\ *n* : a rock resembling flint and consisting essentially of fine crystalline quartz and fibrous chalcedony — **cherty** *adj*

cher·ub \'cher-əb\ *n* **1** *pl* **cher·u·bim** \'cher-ə-ˌbim\ : an angel of the 2d highest rank **2** *pl* **cherubs** : a chubby rosy person — **che·ru·bic** \chə-'rü-bik\ *adj*

chess \'ches\ *n* : a game for two played on a chessboard with each player having 16 pieces — **chess·man** \-ˌman, -mən\ *n*

chess·board \'ches-ˌbȯrd\ *n* : a checkerboard used in the game of chess

chest \'chest\ *n* **1** : a box, case, or boxlike receptacle for storage or shipping **2** : the part of the body enclosed by the ribs and sternum — **chest·ed** \'ches-təd\ *adj* — **chest·ful** \'chest-ˌfùl\ *n*

ches·ter·field \'ches-tər-ˌfēld\ *n* : an overcoat with a velvet collar

chest·nut \'ches-(ˌ)nət\ *n* **1** : the edible nut of any of a genus of trees related to the beech and oaks; *also* : this tree **2** : a grayish to reddish brown **3** : an old joke or story

chet·rum \'che-trəm\ *n, pl* **chetrums** *or* **chetrum** — see *ngultrum* at MONEY table

che·val glass \shə-'val-\ *n* : a full-length mirror that may be tilted in a frame

che·va·lier \ˌshe-və-'lir, shə-'val-ˌyā\ *n* : a member of one of various orders of knighthood or of merit

chev·i·ot \'she-vē-ət\ *n, often cap* **1** : a twilled fabric with a rough nap **2** : a sturdy soft-finished cotton fabric

chev·ron \'she-vrən\ *n* : a sleeve badge of one or more V-shaped or inverted V-shaped stripes worn to indicate rank or service (as in the armed forces)

¹**chew** \'chü\ *vb* : to crush or grind with the teeth — **chew·able** *adj* — **chew·er** *n*

²**chew** *n* **1** : an act of chewing **2** : something for chewing

chewy \'chü-ē\ *adj* : requiring much chewing ⟨∼ candy⟩

Chey·enne \shī-'an, -'en\ *n, pl* **Cheyenne** *or* **Cheyennes** [CanF, fr. Dakota *šahíyena*] : a member of an American Indian people of the western plains of the U.S.; *also* : their language

chg *abbr* **1** change **2** charge

chi \'kī\ *n* : the 22d letter of the Greek alphabet — X or χ

Chi·an·ti \kē-'än-tē, -'an-\ *n* : a dry usu. red wine

chiar·oscu·ro \kē-ˌär-ə-'skùr-ȯ, -'skyùr-\ *n, pl* **-ros** [It, fr. *chiaro* clear, light + *oscuro* obscure, dark] **1** : pictorial representation in terms of light and shade without regard to color **2** : the arrangement or treatment of light and dark parts in a pictorial work of art

¹**chic** \'shēk\ *n* : STYLISHNESS

²**chic** *adj* : cleverly stylish : SMART; *also* : currently fashionable

Chi·ca·na \chi-'kä-nə *also* shi-\ *n* : an American woman or girl of Mexican descent — **Chicana** *adj*

chi·cane \shi-'kān\ *n* : CHICANERY

chi·ca·nery \-'ka-nə-rē\ *n, pl* **-ner·ies** : TRICKERY, DECEPTION

Chi·ca·no \chi-'kä-nȯ\ *n, pl* **-nos** : an American of Mexican descent — **Chicano** *adj*

chi·chi \'shē-(ˌ)shē, 'chē-(ˌ)chē\ *adj* [F] **1** : SHOWY, FRILLY **2** : ARTY, PRECIOUS **3** : CHIC — **chichi** *n*

chick \'chik\ *n* **1** : a young chicken; *also* : a young bird **2** *slang* : a young woman

chick·a·dee \'chi-kə-(ˌ)dē\ *n* : any of several small grayish American birds with black or brown caps

Chick·a·saw \'chi-kə-ˌsȯ\ *n, pl* **Chickasaw** *or* **Chickasaws** : a member of an American Indian people of Mississippi and Alabama

¹**chick·en** \'chi-kən\ *n* **1** : a common domestic fowl esp. when young; *also* : its flesh used as food **2** : COWARD

²**chicken** *adj* **1** : COWARDLY **2** *slang* : insistent on petty esp. military discipline

chicken feed *n, slang* : an insignificant sum of money

chick·en·heart·ed \ˌchi-kən-'här-təd\ *adj* : TIMID, COWARDLY

chicken out *vb* : to lose one's courage

chicken pox *n* : an acute contagious virus disease esp. of children characterized by a low fever and vesicles

chicken wire *n* : a light wire netting of hexagonal mesh

chick–pea \'chik-ˌpē\ *n* : an Asian leguminous herb cultivated for its short pods with one or two edible seeds; *also* : its seed

chick·weed \'chik-ˌwēd\ *n* : any of several low-growing small-leaved weeds related to the pinks

chi·cle \'chi-kəl\ *n* : a gum from the latex of a tropical tree used as the chief ingredient of chewing gum

chic·o·ry \'chi-kə-rē\ *n, pl* **-ries** : a usu. blue-flowered herb related to the daisies and grown for its root and for use in salads; *also* : its dried ground root used to flavor or adulterate coffee

chide \'chīd\ *vb* **chid** \'chid\ *or* **chid·ed** \'chī-dəd\; **chid** *or* **chid·den** \'chid-ᵊn\ *or* **chided; chid·ing** : to speak disapprovingly to **syn** reproach, reprove, reprimand, admonish, scold, rebuke

¹**chief** \'chēf\ *adj* **1** : highest in rank **2** : most important **syn** principal, main, leading, major — **chief·ly** *adv*

²**chief** *n* **1** : the leader of a body or organization : HEAD **2** : the principal or most valuable part — **chief·dom** *n*

chief justice *n* : the principal judge of a court of justice

chief master sergeant *n* : a noncommissioned officer of the highest rank in the air force

chief of naval operations : the commanding officer of the navy

chief of staff 1 : the ranking officer of a staff in the armed forces **2** : the ranking office of the army or air force

chief of state : the formal head of a national state as distinguished from the head of the government

chief petty officer *n* : an enlisted man in the navy ranking next below a senior chief petty officer

chief·tain \'chēf-tən\ *n* : a chief esp. of a band, tribe, or clan — **chief·tain·cy** \-sē\ *n* — **chief·tain·ship** *n*

chief warrant officer *n* : a warrant officer of senior rank

chif·fon \shi-'fän, 'shi-\ *n* [F, lit., rag, fr. *chiffe* old rag] : a sheer fabric esp. of silk

chif·fo·nier \ˌshi-fə-'nir\ *n* : a high narrow chest of drawers

chig·ger \'chi-gər\ *n* : a bloodsucking larval mite that causes intense itching

chi·gnon \'shēn-ˌyän\ *n* [F, fr. MF *chignon* chain, collar, nape] : a knot of hair worn at the back of the head

Chi·hua·hua \chə-'wä-ˌwä\ *n* : any of a breed of very small large-eared dogs that originated in Mexico

chil·blain \'chil-ˌblān\ *n* : a sore or inflamed swelling (as on the feet or hands) caused by exposure to cold

child \'chīld\ *n, pl* **chil·dren** \'chil-drən\ **1** : an unborn or recently born person **2** : a young person between the periods of infancy and youth **3** : a male or female offspring : SON, DAUGHTER **4** : one strongly influenced by another or by a place or state of affairs — **child·ish** *adj* — **child·ish·ly** *adv* — **child·ish·ness** *n* — **child·less** *adj* — **child·less·ness** *n* — **child·like** *adj*

child·bear·ing \'chīld-ˌbar-iŋ\ *n* : CHILDBIRTH — **child-bearing** *adj*

child·birth \-ˌbərth\ *n* : the act or process of giving birth to offspring

child·hood \-ˌhüd\ *n* : the state or time of being a child

child·proof \-ˌprüf\ *adj* : made to prevent tampering or opening by children

child's play *n* : a simple task or act

Chil·ean \'chi-lē-ən, chə-'lā-ən\ *n* : a native or inhabitant of Chile — **Chilean** *adj*

chili *or* **chile** *or* **chil·li** \'chi-lē\ *n, pl* **chil·ies** *or* **chil·es** *or* **chil·lies 1** : a pungent pepper related to the tomato **2** : a thick sauce of meat and chilies **3** : CHILI CON CARNE

chili con car·ne \ˌchi-lē-kän-'kär-nē\ *n* [Sp *chile con carne* chili with meat] : a spiced stew of ground beef and chilies or chili powder usu. with beans

chili powder *n* : a seasoning made of ground chilies and other spices

chili sauce *n* : a spiced tomato sauce usu. made with red and green peppers

¹**chill** \'chil\ *n* **1** : a feeling of coldness accompanied by shivering **2** : moderate coldness **3** : a check to enthusiasm or warmth of feeling

²**chill** *adj* **1** : moderately cold **2** : COLD, RAW **3** : DISTANT, FORMAL (a ~ reception) **4** : DEPRESSING, DISPIRITING

³**chill** *vb* **1** : to make or become cold or chilly **2** : to make cool esp. without freezing — **chill·er** *n*

chilly \'chi-lē\ *adj* **chill·i·er; -est 1** : noticeably cold **2**

: unpleasantly affected by cold **3** : lacking warmth of feeling — **chill·i·ness** *n*

¹**chime** \'chīm\ *n* **1** : a set of bells musically tuned **2** : the sound of a set of bells — usu. used in pl. **3** : a musical sound suggesting bells

²**chime** *vb* **chimed; chim·ing 1** : to make bell-like sounds **2** : to indicate (as the time of day) by chiming **3** : to be or act in accord : be in harmony

chime in *vb* : to break into or join in a conversation

chi·me·ra *or* **chi·mae·ra** \kī-'mir-ə, kə-\ *n* [L *chimaera,* fr. Gk *chimaira* she-goat, chimera] **1** : an imaginary monster made up of incongruous parts **2** : an illusion or fabrication of the mind; *esp* : an impossible dream

chi·me·ri·cal \ki-'mer-i-kəl\ *also* **chi·me·ric** \-ik\ *adj* **1** : FANTASTIC, IMAGINARY **2** : inclined to fantastic schemes

chim·ney \'chim-nē\ *n, pl* **chimneys 1** : a vertical structure extending above the roof of a building for carrying off smoke **2** : a glass tube around a lamp flame

chimp \'chimp\ *n* : CHIMPANZEE

chim·pan·zee \ˌchim-ˌpan-'zē, chim-'pan-zē\ *n* : an African ape related to the much larger gorilla

¹**chin** \'chin\ *n* : the part of the face below the lower lip including the prominence of the lower jaw — **chin·less** *adj*

²**chin** *vb* **chinned; chin·ning** : to raise (oneself) while hanging by the hands until the chin is level with the support

chi·na \'chī-nə\ *n* : porcelain ware; *also* : domestic pottery in general

Chi·na·town \-ˌtau̇n\ *n* : the Chinese quarter of a city

chinch bug \'chinch-\ *n* : a small black and white bug destructive to cereal grasses

chin·chil·la \chin-'chi-lə\ *n* **1** : either of two small So. American rodents with soft pearl-gray fur; *also* : this fur **2** : a heavy long-napped woolen cloth

chinchilla 1

chine \'chīn\ *n* : BACKBONE, SPINE, *also* : a cut of meat including all or part of the backbone

Chi·nese \chī-'nēz, -'nēs\ *n, pl* **Chinese 1** : a native or inhabitant of China **2** : any of a group of related languages of China — **Chinese** *adj*

Chinese cabbage *n* **1** : BOK CHOY **2** : an Asian garden plant related to the cabbage and widely grown in the U.S. for its tight elongate cylindrical heads of pale green to cream-colored leaves

Chinese checkers *n* : a game in which each player in turn transfers a set of marbles from a home point to the opposite point of a pitted 6-pointed star

Chinese gooseberry *n* : a subtropical vine that bears kiwifruit; *also* : KIWIFRUIT

Chinese lantern *n* : a collapsible translucent cover for a light

¹**chink** \'chiŋk\ *n* : a small crack or fissure

²**chink** *vb* : to fill the chinks of : stop up

\ə\abut \ᵊ\kitten \ər\further \a\ash \ā\ace \ä\mop, mar
\au̇\out \ch\chin \e\bet \ē\easy \g\go \i\hit \ī\ice \j\job
\ŋ\sing \ō\go \ȯ\law \ȯi\boy \th\thin \t̲h̲\the \ü\loot \u̇\foot
\y\yet \zh\vision *see also* Pronunciation Symbols page

³**chink** *n* : a slight sharp metallic sound
⁴**chink** *vb* : to make a slight sharp metallic sound
chi·no \ˈchē-nò\ *n, pl* **chinos 1** : a usu. khaki cotton twill **2** *pl* : an article of clothing made of chino
Chi·nook \shə-ˈnùk, chə-, -ˈnük\ *n, pl* **Chinook** *or* **Chinooks** : a member of an American Indian people of Oregon
chintz \ˈchints\ *n* : a usu. glazed printed cotton cloth
chintzy \ˈchint-sē\ *adj* **chintz·i·er; -est 1** : decorated with or as if with chintz **2** : GAUDY, CHEAP **3** : STINGY
chin–up \ˈchi-ˌnəp\ *n* : the act of chinning oneself
¹**chip** \ˈchip\ *n* **1** : a small usu. thin and flat piece (as of wood) cut or broken off **2** : a thin crisp morsel of food **3** : a counter used in games (as poker) **4** *pl, slang* : MONEY **5** : a flaw left after a chip is removed **6** : INTEGRATED CIRCUIT **7** : a very small slice of silicon containing electronic circuits
²**chip** *vb* **chipped; chip·ping 1** : to cut or break chips from **2** : to break off in small pieces at the edges **3** : to play a chip shot
chip in *vb* : CONTRIBUTE
chip·munk \ˈchip-ˌməŋk\ *n* : any of a genus of small striped No. American and Asian rodents closely related to the squirrels and marmots
chipped beef \ˈchipt-\ *n* : smoked dried beef sliced thin
¹**chip·per** \ˈchi-pər\ *n* : one that chips
²**chipper** *adj* : LIVELY, CHEERFUL
Chip·pe·wa \ˈchi-pə-ˌwò, -ˌwä, -ˌwā, -wə\ *n, pl* **Chippewa** *or* **Chippewas** : OJIBWA
chip shot *n* : a short usu. low shot to the green in golf
chi·rog·ra·phy \kī-ˈrä-grə-fē\ *n* : HANDWRITING, PENMANSHIP — **chi·ro·graph·ic** \ˌkī-rə-ˈgra-fik\ *adj*
chi·rop·o·dy \kə-ˈrä-pə-dē, shə-\ *n* : PODIATRY — **chi·rop·o·dist** \-dist\ *n*
chi·ro·prac·tic \ˈkī-rə-ˌprak-tik\ *n* : a system of therapy based esp. on manipulation of body structures — **chi·ro·prac·tor** \-tər\ *n*
chirp \ˈchərp\ *n* : a short sharp sound characteristic of a small bird or cricket — **chirp** *vb*
¹**chis·el** \ˈchi-zəl\ *n* : a metal tool with a sharpened edge at one end used to chip, carve, or cut into a solid material (as wood or stone)
²**chisel** *vb* **-eled** *or* **-elled; -el·ing** *or* **-el·ling 1** : to work with or as if with a chisel **2** : to obtain by shrewd often unfair methods; *also* : CHEAT — **chis·el·er** *n*
¹**chit** \ˈchit\ *n* [ME *chitte* kitten, cub] **1** : CHILD **2** : a pert young woman
²**chit** *n* [Hindi *ciṭṭhī* letter, note] : a signed voucher for a small debt
chit·chat \ˈchit-ˌchat\ *n* : casual or trifling conversation — **chitchat** *vb*
chi·tin \ˈkīt-ᵊn\ *n* : a sugar polymer that forms part of the hard outer integument esp. of insects — **chi·tin·ous** *adj*
chit·ter·lings *or* **chit·lins** \ˈchit-lənz\ *n pl* : the intestines of hogs esp. when prepared as food
chi·val·ric \shə-ˈval-rik\ *adj* : relating to chivalry : CHIVALROUS
chiv·al·rous \ˈshi-vəl-rəs\ *adj* **1** : of or relating to chivalry **2** : marked by honor, courtesy, and generosity **3** : marked by especial courtesy to women — **chiv·al·rous·ly** *adv* — **chiv·al·rous·ness** *n*
chiv·al·ry \ˈshi-vəl-rē\ *n, pl* **-ries 1** : mounted men-at-arms **2** : the system or practices of knighthood **3** : the spirit or character of the ideal knight
chive \ˈchīv\ *n* : an herb related to the onion that has leaves used for flavoring
chla·myd·ia \klə-ˈmi-dē-ə\ *n, pl* **-i·ae** \-dē-ˌē\ **1** : any of a genus of bacteria that cause various diseases of the eye and urogenital tract **2** : a disease or infection caused by chlamydiae
chlo·ral hydrate \ˈklòr-əl-\ *n* : a white crystalline compound used as a hypnotic and sedative

chlor·dane \ˈklòr-ˌdān\ *n* : a highly chlorinated persistent insecticide
chlo·ride \ˈklòr-ˌīd\ *n* : a compound of chlorine with another element or group
chlo·ri·nate \ˈklòr-ə-ˌnāt\ *vb* **-nat·ed; -nat·ing** : to treat or combine with chlorine or a chlorine compound — **chlo·ri·na·tion** \ˌklòr-ə-ˈnā-shən\ *n* — **chlo·ri·na·tor** \ˈklòr-ə-ˌnā-tər\ *n*
chlo·rine \ˈklòr-ˌēn\ *n* : a nonmetallic chemical element that is found alone as a strong-smelling greenish yellow irritating gas and is used as a bleach, oxidizing agent, and disinfectant — see ELEMENT table
chlo·rite \ˈklòr-ˌīt\ *n* : a usu. green mineral found with and resembling mica
chlo·ro·flu·o·ro·car·bon \ˌklòr-ə-ˈflòr-ə-ˌkär-bən, -ˈflùr-\ *n* : any of several gaseous compounds that contain carbon, chlorine, fluorine, and sometimes hydrogen and are used esp. as solvents, refrigerants, and aerosol propellants
¹**chlo·ro·form** \ˈklòr-ə-ˌfòrm\ *n* : a colorless heavy fluid with etherlike odor used as a solvent and anesthetic
²**chloroform** *vb* : to treat with chloroform to produce anesthesia or death
chlo·ro·phyll \-ˌfil\ *n* : the green coloring matter of plants that functions in photosynthesis
chm *abbr* chairman
chock \ˈchäk\ *n* : a wedge for steadying something or for blocking the movement of a wheel — **chock** *vb*
chock·a·block \ˈchä-kə-ˌbläk\ *adj* : very full : CROWDED
chock–full \ˈchək-ˈfùl, ˈchäk-\ *adj* : full to the limit : CRAMMED
choc·o·late \ˈchä-k(ə-)lət, ˈchò-\ *n* [Sp, fr. Nahuatl *choc-olātl*] **1** : a food prepared from ground roasted cacao beans; *also* : a drink prepared from this **2** : a candy made of or with a coating of chocolate **3** : a dark brown color
Choc·taw \ˈchäk-ˌtò\ *n, pl* **Choctaw** *or* **Choctaws** : a member of an American Indian people of Mississippi, Alabama, and Louisiana; *also* : their language
¹**choice** \ˈchòis\ *n* **1** : the act of choosing : SELECTION **2** : the power or opportunity of choosing : OPTION **3** : the best part **4** : a person or thing selected **5** : a variety offered for selection
²**choice** *adj* **choic·er; choic·est 1** : worthy of being chosen **2** : selected with care **3** : of high quality
choir \ˈkwī(-ə)r\ *n* **1** : an organized company of singers (as in a church service) **2** : the part of a church occupied by the singers or by the clergy
choir·boy \ˈkwī(-ə)r-ˌbòi\ *n* : a boy member of a church choir
choir·mas·ter \-ˌmas-tər\ *n* : the director of a choir (as in a church)
¹**choke** \ˈchòk\ *vb* **choked; chok·ing 1** : to hinder breathing (as by obstructing the windpipe) : STRANGLE **2** : to check the growth or action of **3** : CLOG, OBSTRUCT **4** : to enrich the fuel mixture of (a motor) by restricting the carburetor air intake **5** : to perform badly in a critical situation
²**choke** *n* **1** : the act of choking **2** : a narrowing in size toward the muzzle in the bore of a gun **3** : a valve for choking a gasoline engine
chok·er \ˈchò-kər\ *n* : something (as a necklace) worn tightly around the neck
cho·ler \ˈkä-lər, ˈkò-\ *n* : a tendency toward anger : IRASCIBILITY
chol·era \ˈkä-lə-rə\ *n* : a disease marked by severe vomiting and dysentery; *esp* : an often fatal epidemic disease (**Asiatic cholera**) chiefly of southeastern Asia caused by a bacillus
cho·ler·ic \ˈkä-lə-rik, kə-ˈler-ik\ *adj* **1** : IRASCIBLE **2** : ANGRY, IRATE
cho·les·ter·ol \kə-ˈles-tə-ˌròl\ *n* : a physiologically important waxy steroid alcohol found in animal tissues

and in high concentrations implicated as a cause of arteriosclerosis

chomp \'chämp, 'chòmp\ *vb* : to chew or bite on something heavily

chon \'chän\ *n, pl* **chon** — see *won* at MONEY table

choose \'chüz\ *vb* **chose** \'chòz\; **cho·sen** \'chòz-ᵊn\; **choos·ing** \'chü-ziŋ\ **1** : to select esp. after consideration **2** : DECIDE **3** : to have a preference for — **choos·er** *n*

choosy *or* **choos·ey** \'chü-zē\ *adj* **choos·i·er; -est** : very particular in making choices

¹chop \'chäp\ *vb* **chopped; chop·ping 1** : to cut by repeated blows **2** : to cut into small pieces : MINCE **3** : to strike (a ball) with a short quick downward stroke

²chop *n* **1** : a sharp downward blow or stroke **2** : a small cut of meat often including part of a rib **3** : a short abrupt motion (as of a wave)

³chop *n* **1** : an official seal or stamp **2** : a mark on goods to indicate quality or kind; *also* : QUALITY, GRADE

chop·house \'chäp-ˌhaùs\ *n* : RESTAURANT

chop·per \'chä-pər\ *n* **1** : one that chops **2** *pl, slang* : TEETH **3** : HELICOPTER

chop·pi·ness \'chä-pē-nəs\ *n* : the quality or state of being choppy

¹chop·py \'chä-pē\ *adj* **chop·pi·er; -est 1** : rough with small waves **2** : JERKY, DISCONNECTED — **chop·pi·ly** \-pə-lē\ *adv*

²choppy *adj* **chop·pi·er; -est** : CHANGEABLE, VARIABLE ⟨a ~ wind⟩

chops \'chäps\ *n pl* : the fleshy covering of the jaws

chop·stick \'chäp-ˌstik\ *n* : one of a pair of sticks used chiefly in oriental countries for lifting food to the mouth

chop su·ey \chäp-'sü-ē\ *n, pl* **chop sueys** : a dish made of vegetables (as bean sprouts, bamboo shoots, water chestnuts, onions, mushrooms) and meat or fish and served with rice

cho·ral \'kòr-əl\ *adj* : of, relating to, or sung by a choir or chorus or in chorus — **cho·ral·ly** *adv*

cho·rale \kə-'ral, -'räl\ *n* **1** : a hymn or psalm sung in church; *also* : a harmonization of a traditional melody **2** : CHORUS, CHOIR

¹chord \'kòrd\ *n* [alter. of ME *cord*, short for *accord*] : three or more musical tones sounded simultaneously

²chord *n* **1** : CORD 2 **2** : a straight line joining two points on a curve

chore \'chòr\ *n* **1** *pl* : the daily light work of a household or farm **2** : a routine task or job **3** : a difficult or disagreeable task

cho·rea \kə-'rē-ə\ *n* : a nervous disorder marked by spasmodic uncontrolled movements

cho·re·og·ra·phy \ˌkòr-ē-'ä-grə-fē\ *n, pl* **-phies** : the art of composing and arranging dances and esp. ballets — **cho·reo·graph** \'kòr-ē-ə-ˌgraf\ *vb* — **cho·re·og·ra·pher** \ˌkòr-ē-'ä-grə-fər\ *n* — **cho·reo·graph·ic** \ˌkòr-ē-ə-'gra-fik\ *adj* — **cho·reo·graph·i·cal·ly** \-fi-k(ə-)lē\ *adv*

cho·ris·ter \'kòr-ə-stər\ *n* : a singer in a choir

chor·tle \'chòrt-ᵊl\ *vb* **chor·tled; chor·tling** : to laugh or chuckle esp. in satisfaction or exultation — **chortle** *n*

¹chorus \'kòr-əs\ *n* **1** : an organized company of singers : CHOIR **2** : a group of dancers and singers (as in a musical comedy) **3** : a part of a song repeated at intervals **4** : a composition to be sung by a chorus; *also* : group singing **5** : sounds uttered by a number of persons or animals together ⟨a ~ of boos⟩

²chorus *vb* : to sing or utter in chorus

chose *past of* CHOOSE

cho·sen \'chòz-ᵊn\ *adj* : selected or marked for special favor or privilege

¹chow \'chaù\ *n* : FOOD

²chow *vb* : EAT — often used with *down*

³chow *n* : CHOW CHOW

chow·chow \'chaù-ˌchaù\ *n* : chopped mixed pickles in mustard sauce

chow chow \'chaù-ˌchaù\ *n* : any of a breed of thick-coated straight-legged muscular dogs of Chinese origin with a blue-black tongue and a short tail curled close to the back

chow·der \'chaù-dər\ *n* : a soup or stew made from seafood or vegetables and containing milk or tomatoes

chow mein \'chaù-'mān\ *n* : a seasoned stew of shredded or diced meat, mushrooms, and vegetables that is usu. served with fried noodles

chrism \'kri-zəm\ *n* : consecrated oil used esp. in baptism, confirmation, and ordination

Christ \'krīst\ *n* [L *Christus*, fr. Gk *Christos*, lit., anointed] : Jesus esp. as the Messiah — **Christ·like** *adj* — **Christ·ly** *adj*

chris·ten \'kris-ᵊn\ *vb* **1** : BAPTIZE **2** : to name at baptism **3** : to name or dedicate (as a ship) by a ceremony suggestive of baptism — **chris·ten·ing** *n*

Chris·ten·dom \'kris-ᵊn-dəm\ *n* **1** : CHRISTIANITY **2** : the part of the world in which Christianity prevails

¹Chris·tian \'kris-chən\ *n* : an adherent of Christianity

²Christian *adj* **1** : of or relating to Christianity **2** : based on or conforming with Christianity **3** : of or relating to a Christian **4** : professing Christianity

chris·ti·a·nia \ˌkris-chē-'a-nē-ə, ˌkris-tē-\ *n* : CHRISTIE

Chris·ti·an·i·ty \ˌkris-chē-'a-nə-tē\ *n* : the religion derived from Jesus Christ, based on the Bible as sacred scripture, and professed by Christians

Chris·tian·ize \'kris-chə-ˌnīz\ *vb* **-ized; -iz·ing** : to make Christian

Christian name *n* : GIVEN NAME

Christian Science *n* : a religion and system of healing founded by Mary Baker Eddy and taught by the Church of Christ, Scientist — **Christian Scientist** *n*

chris·tie *or* **chris·ty** \'kris-tē\ *n, pl* **christies** : a skiing turn made by shifting body weight forward and skidding into a turn with parallel skis

Christ·mas \'kris-məs\ *n* : December 25 celebrated as a church festival in commemoration of the birth of Christ and observed as a legal holiday

Christmas club *n* : a savings account in which regular deposits are made to provide money for Christmas shopping

Christ·mas·tide \'kris-məs-ˌtīd\ *n* : the season of Christmas

chro·mat·ic \krō-'ma-tik\ *adj* **1** : of or relating to color **2** : proceeding by half steps of the musical scale — **chro·mat·i·cism** \tə-ˌsi-zəm\ *n*

chro·mato·graph \krō-'ma-tə-ˌgraf\ *n* : an instrument used in chromatography

chro·ma·tog·ra·phy \ˌkrō-mə-'tä-grə-fē\ *n* : the separation of a complex mixture into its component compounds as a result of the different rates at which the compounds travel through or over a stationary substance due to differing affinities for the substance — **chro·mato·graph·ic** \krō-ˌma-tə-'gra-fik\ *adj* — **chro·mato·graph·i·cal·ly** \-fi-k(ə-)lē\ *adv*

chrome \'krōm\ *n* **1** : CHROMIUM **2** : a chromium pigment **3** : something plated with an alloy of chromium

chro·mi·um \'krō-mē-əm\ *n* : a bluish white metallic element used esp. in alloys and chrome plating — see ELEMENT table

chro·mo·some \'krō-mə-ˌsōm, -ˌzōm\ *n* : any of the linear or sometimes circular DNA-containing bodies of viruses, bacteria, and the nucleus of higher organisms that contain most or all of the individual's genes — **chro·mo·som·al** \ˌkrō-mə-'sō-məl, -ˌzō-\ *adj*

chro·mo·sphere \'krō-mə-ˌsfir\ *n* : the lower part of a star's atmosphere

---

\ə\abut \ᵊ\kitten \ər\further \a\ash \ā\ace \ä\mop, mar \aù\out \ch\chin \e\bet \ē\easy \g\go \i\hit \ī\ice \j\job \ŋ\sing \ō\go \ò\law \òi\boy \th\thin \th̲\the \ü\loot \ù\foot \y\yet \zh\vision *see also* Pronunciation Symbols page

chron *abbr* **1** chronicle **2** chronological; chronology
Chron *abbr* Chronicles
chron·ic \'krä-nik\ *adj* : marked by long duration or frequent recurrence ⟨a ~ disease⟩; *also* : HABITUAL ⟨a ~ grumbler⟩ — **chron·i·cal·ly** \-ni-k(ə-)lē\ *adv*
¹**chron·i·cle** \'krä-ni-kəl\ *n* : HISTORY, NARRATIVE
²**chronicle** *vb* **-cled; -cling** : to record in or as if in a chronicle — **chron·i·cler** *n*
Chronicles *n* — see BIBLE table
chro·no·graph \'krä-nə-ˌgraf\ *n* : an instrument for measuring and recording time intervals with accuracy — **chro·no·graph·ic** \ˌkrä-nə-ˈgra-fik\ *adj* — **chro·nog·ra·phy** \krə-ˈnä-grə-fē\ *n*
chro·nol·o·gy \krə-ˈnä-lə-jē\ *n, pl* **-gies 1** : the science that deals with measuring time and dating events **2** : a chronological list or table **3** : arrangement of events in the order of their occurrence — **chron·o·log·i·cal** \ˌkrän-ᵊl-ˈä-ji-kəl\ *adj* — **chron·o·log·i·cal·ly** \-k(ə-)lē\ *adv* — **chro·nol·o·gist** \krə-ˈnä-lə-jist\ *n*
chro·nom·e·ter \krə-ˈnä-mə-tər\ *n* : a very accurate timepiece
chrys·a·lid \'kri-sə-ləd\ *n* : CHRYSALIS
chrys·a·lis \'kri-sə-ləs\ *n, pl* **chry·sal·i·des** \kri-ˈsa-lə-ˌdēz\ *or* **chrys·a·lis·es** : an insect pupa in a firm case without a cocoon
chry·san·the·mum \kri-ˈsan-thə-məm\ *n* [L, fr. Gk *chrysanthemon*, fr. *chrysos* gold + *anthemon* flower] : any of various plants related to the daisies including some grown for their showy flowers or for medicinal products or insecticides; *also* : a flower of a chrysanthemum
chub \'chəb\ *n, pl* **chub** *or* **chubs** : any of various small freshwater fishes related to the carp
chub·by \'chə-bē\ *adj* **chub·bi·er; -est** : PLUMP — **chub·bi·ness** *n*
¹**chuck** \'chək\ *vb* **1** : to give a pat or tap **2** : TOSS **3** : DISCARD; *also* : EJECT **4** : to have done with
²**chuck** *n* **1** : a light pat under the chin **2** : TOSS
³**chuck** *n* **1** : a cut of beef including most of the neck and the parts around the shoulder blade and the first three ribs **2** : a device for holding work or a tool in a machine (as a lathe)
chuck·hole \'chək-ˌhōl\ *n* : POTHOLE
chuck·le \'chə-kəl\ *vb* **chuck·led; chuck·ling** : to laugh in a quiet hardly audible manner — **chuckle** *n*
chuck wagon *n* : a wagon equipped with a stove and food supplies
¹**chug** \'chəg\ *n* : a dull explosive sound made by or as if by a laboring engine
²**chug** *vb* **chugged; chug·ging** : to move or go with chugs
chuk·ka \'chə-kə\ *n* : a usu. ankle-length leather boot
chuk·ker \'chə-kər\ *also* **chuk·ka** \'chə-kə\ *n* : a playing period of a polo game
¹**chum** \'chəm\ *n* : a close friend
²**chum** *vb* **chummed; chum·ming 1** : to room together **2** : to be a close friend
chum·my \'chə-mē\ *adj* **chum·mi·er; -est** : INTIMATE, SOCIABLE — **chum·mi·ly** \-mə-lē\ *adv* — **chum·mi·ness** \-mē-nəs\ *n*
chump \'chəmp\ *n* : FOOL, BLOCKHEAD
chunk \'chəŋk\ *n* **1** : a short thick piece **2** : a sizable amount
chunky \'chəŋ-kē\ *adj* **chunk·i·er; -est 1** : STOCKY **2** : containing chunks
church \'chərch\ *n* [OE *cirice*, ultim. fr. LGk *kyriakon*, fr. Gk, neut. of *kyriakos* of the lord, fr. *kyrios* lord, master] **1** : a building esp. for Christian public worship **2** : the whole body of Christians **3** : DENOMINATION **4** : CONGREGATION **5** : public divine worship
church·go·er \'chərch-ˌgō-(ə)r\ *n* : one who habitually attends church — **church·go·ing** *adj or n*
church·less \'chərch-ləs\ *adj* : not affiliated with a church

church·man \'chərch-mən\ *n* **1** : CLERGYMAN **2** : a member of a church
church·war·den \'chərch-ˌwȯrd-ᵊn\ *n* : WARDEN 5
church·yard \-ˌyärd\ *n* : a yard that belongs to a church and is often used as a burial ground
churl \'chərl\ *n* **1** : a medieval peasant **2** : RUSTIC **3** : a rude ill-bred person — **churl·ish** *adj* — **churl·ish·ly** *adv* — **churl·ish·ness** *n*
¹**churn** \'chərn\ *n* : a container in which milk or cream is violently stirred in making butter
²**churn** *vb* **1** : to stir in a churn; *also* : to make (butter) by such stirring **2** : to shake around violently
churn out *vb* : to produce mechanically or in large quantity
chute \'shüt\ *n* **1** : an inclined surface, trough, or passage down or through which something may pass ⟨a coal ~⟩ ⟨a mail ~⟩ **2** : PARACHUTE
chut·ney \'chət-nē\ *n, pl* **chutneys** : a thick sauce containing fruits, vinegar, sugar, and spices
chutz·pah \'hùt-spə, 'kùt-, -(ˌ)spä\ *n* : supreme self-confidence
CIA *abbr* Central Intelligence Agency
cía *abbr* [Sp *compañía*] company
ciao \'chaù\ *interj* — used to express greeting or farewell
ci·ca·da \sə-ˈkā-də\ *n* : any of a family of stout-bodied insects related to the aphids and having wide blunt heads and large transparent wings

cicada

ci·ca·trix \'si-kə-ˌtriks\ *n, pl* **ci·ca·tri·ces** \ˌsi-kə-ˈtrī-ˌsēz\ [L] : a scar resulting from formation and contraction of fibrous tissue in a wound
ci·ce·ro·ne \ˌsi-sə-ˈrō-nē, ˌchē-chə-\ *n, pl* **-ni** \-(ˌ)nē\ : a guide who conducts sightseers
CID *abbr* Criminal Investigation Department
ci·der \'sī-dər\ *n* : juice pressed from fruit (as apples) and used as a beverage, vinegar, or flavoring
cie *abbr* [F *compagnie*] company
ci·gar \si-ˈgär\ *n* : a roll of tobacco for smoking
cig·a·rette \ˌsi-gə-ˈret, 'si-gə-ˌret\ *n* [F, dim. of *cigare* cigar] : a slender roll of cut tobacco enclosed in paper for smoking
cig·a·ril·lo \ˌsi-gə-ˈri-lō, -ˈrē-ō\ *n, pl* **-los** [Sp] **1** : a very small cigar **2** : a cigarette wrapped in tobacco rather than paper
ci·lan·tro \si-ˈlän-trō, -ˈlan-\ *n* : leaves of coriander used as a flavoring or garnish; *also* : the coriander plant
cil·i·ate \'si-lē-ˌāt\ *n* : any of a group of protozoans characterized by cilia
cil·i·um \'si-lē-əm\ *n, pl* **-ia** \-lē-ə\ **1** : a minute short hairlike process; *esp* : one of a cell **2** : EYELASH
C in C *abbr* commander in chief
cinch \'sinch\ *n* **1** : a girth for a pack or saddle **2** : a sure or an easy thing — **cinch** *vb*
cin·cho·na \siŋ-ˈkō-nə\ *n* : any of a genus of So. American trees related to the madder; *also* : the bitter quinine-containing bark of a cinchona
cinc·ture \'siŋk-chər\ *n* : BELT, SASH
cin·der \'sin-dər\ *n* **1** : SLAG **2** *pl* : ASHES **3** : a hot piece of partly burned wood or coal **4** : a fragment of lava from an erupting volcano — **cinder** *vb* — **cin·dery** *adj*

cinder block *n* : a building block made of cement and coal cinders

cin·e·ma \'si-nə-mə\ *n* **1** : a motion-picture theater **2** : MOVIES — **cin·e·mat·ic** \ˌsi-nə-'ma-tik\ *adj*

cin·e·ma·theque \ˌsi-nə-mə-'tek\ *n* : a small movie house specializing in avant-garde films

cin·e·ma·tog·ra·phy \ˌsi-nə-mə-'tä-grə-fē\ *n* : motion-picture photography — **cin·e·ma·tog·ra·pher** *n* — **cin·e·mat·o·graph·ic** \-ˌma-tə-'gra-fik\ *adj*

cin·er·ar·i·um \ˌsi-nə-'rer-ē-əm\ *n, pl* **-ia** \-ē-ə\ : a place to receive the ashes of the cremated dead — **cin·er·ary** \'si-nə-ˌrer-ē\ *adj*

cin·na·bar \'si-nə-ˌbär\ *n* : a red mineral that is the only important ore of mercury

cin·na·mon \'si-nə-mən\ *n* : a spice prepared from the highly aromatic bark of any of several trees related to the true laurel; *also* : a tree that yields cinnamon

cinque·foil \'siŋk-ˌfȯil, 'saŋk-\ *n* : any of a genus of plants related to the roses with leaves having five lobes

¹ci·pher \'sī-fər\ *n* [ME, fr. MF *cifre*, fr. ML *cifra*, fr. Ar *ṣifr* empty, zero] **1** : ZERO, NAUGHT **2** : a method of secret writing

²cipher *vb* : to compute arithmetically

cir *or* **circ** *abbr* circular

cir·ca \'sər-kə\ *prep* : ABOUT ⟨~ 1600⟩

cir·ca·di·an \ˌsər-'ka-dē-ən, ˌsər-kə-'dī-ən\ *adj* : being, having, characterized by, or occurring in approximately 24-hour intervals (as of biological activity)

¹cir·cle \'sər-kəl\ *n* **1** : a closed curve every point of which is equally distant from a fixed point within it **2** : something circular **3** : an area of action or influence **4** : CYCLE **5** : a group bound by a common tie

²circle *vb* **cir·cled; cir·cling 1** : to enclose in a circle **2** : to move or revolve around; *also* : to move in a circle

cir·clet \'sər-klət\ *n* : a small circle; *esp* : a circular ornament

cir·cuit \'sər-kət\ *n* **1** : a boundary around an enclosed space **2** : a course around a periphery **3** : a regular tour (as by a judge) around an assigned territory **4** : the complete path of an electric current; *also* : an assemblage of electronic components **5** : LEAGUE; *also* : a chain of theaters — **cir·cuit·al** \-ᵊl\ *adj*

circuit breaker *n* : a switch that automatically interrupts an electric circuit under an abnormal condition

circuit court *n* : a court that sits at two or more places within one judicial district

cir·cu·i·tous \ˌsər-'kyü-ə-təs\ *adj* **1** : having a circular or winding course **2** : not being forthright or direct in language or action

cir·cuit·ry \'sər-kə-trē\ *n, pl* **-ries** : the plan or the components of an electric circuit

cir·cu·ity \ˌsər-'kyü-ə-tē\ *n, pl* **-ities** : INDIRECTION

¹cir·cu·lar \'sər-kyə-lər\ *adj* **1** : having the form of a circle : ROUND **2** : moving in or around a circle **3** : CIRCUITOUS **4** : intended for circulation ⟨a ~ letter⟩ — **cir·cu·lar·i·ty** \ˌsər-kyə-'lar-ə-tē\ *n*

²circular *n* : a paper (as a leaflet) intended for wide distribution

cir·cu·lar·ize \'sər-kyə-lə-ˌrīz\ *vb* **-ized; -iz·ing 1** : to send circulars to **2** : to poll by questionnaire

circular saw *n* : a power saw with a round cutting blade

cir·cu·late \'sər-kyə-ˌlāt\ *vb* **-lat·ed; -lat·ing 1** : to move or cause to move in a circle, circuit, or orbit **2** : to pass from place to place or from person to person — **cir·cu·la·tion** \ˌsər-kyə-'lā-shən\ *n*

cir·cu·la·to·ry \'sər-kyə-lə-ˌtȯr-ē\ *adj* : of or relating to circulation or the circulatory system

circulatory system *n* : the system of blood, blood vessels, lymphatic vessels, and heart concerned with the circulation of the blood and lymph

cir·cum·am·bu·late \ˌsər-kəm-'am-byə-ˌlāt\ *vb* **-lat·ed; -lat·ing** : to circle on foot esp. as part of a ritual

cir·cum·cise \'sər-kəm-ˌsīz\ *vb* **-cised; -cis·ing** : to cut off the foreskin of — **cir·cum·ci·sion** \ˌsər-kəm-'si-zhən\ *n*

cir·cum·fer·ence \sər-'kəm-f(ə-)rəns\ *n* **1** : the perimeter of a circle **2** : the external boundary or surface of a figure or object

cir·cum·flex \'sər-kəm-ˌfleks\ *n* : the mark ˆ over a vowel

cir·cum·lo·cu·tion \ˌsər-kəm-lō-'kyü-shən\ *n* : the use of unnecessary words in expressing an idea

cir·cum·lu·nar \-'lü-nər\ *adj* : revolving about or surrounding the moon

cir·cum·nav·i·gate \-'na-və-ˌgāt\ *vb* : to go completely around (as the earth) esp. by water — **cir·cum·nav·i·ga·tion** \-ˌna-və-'gā-shən\ *n*

cir·cum·po·lar \-'pō-lər\ *adj* **1** : continually visible above the horizon ⟨a ~ star⟩ **2** : surrounding or found near a pole of the earth

cir·cum·scribe \'sər-kəm-ˌskrīb\ *vb* **1** : to constrict the range or activity of **2** : to draw a line around — **cir·cum·scrip·tion** \ˌsər-kəm-'skrip-shən\ *n*

cir·cum·spect \'sər-kəm-ˌspekt\ *adj* : careful to consider all circumstances and consequences : PRUDENT — **cir·cum·spec·tion** \ˌsər-kəm-'spek-shən\ *n*

cir·cum·stance \'sər-kəm-ˌstans\ *n* **1** : a fact or event that must be considered along with another fact or event **2** : surrounding conditions **3** : CHANCE, FATE **4** *pl* : situation with regard to wealth **5** : CEREMONY

cir·cum·stan·tial \ˌsər-kəm-'stan-chəl\ *adj* **1** : consisting of or depending on circumstances **2** : INCIDENTAL **3** : containing full details — **cir·cum·stan·tial·ly** *adv*

cir·cum·vent \ˌsər-kəm-'vent\ *vb* : to check or defeat esp. by stratagem — **cir·cum·ven·tion** \-'vent-shən\ *n*

cir·cus \'sər-kəs\ *n* **1** : a usu. traveling show that features feats of physical skill, wild animal acts, and performances by clowns **2** : a circus performance; *also* : the equipment, livestock, and personnel of a circus

cirque \'sərk\ *n* : a deep steep-walled mountain basin usu. forming the blunt end of a valley

cir·rho·sis \sə-'rō-səs\ *n, pl* **-rho·ses** \-ˌsēz\ [NL, fr. Gk *kirrhos* orange-colored] : fibrosis of the liver — **cir·rhot·ic** \-'rä-tik\ *adj or n*

cir·rus \'sir-əs\ *n, pl* **cir·ri** \'sir-ˌī\ : a wispy white cloud usu. of minute ice crystals at high altitudes

cis·lu·nar \(ˌ)sis-'lü-nər\ *adj* : lying between the earth and the moon or the moon's orbit

cis·tern \'sis-tərn\ *n* : an often underground tank for storing water

cit *abbr* **1** citation; cited **2** citizen

cit·a·del \'si-tə-dəl, -ˌdel\ *n* **1** : a fortress commanding a city **2** : STRONGHOLD

ci·ta·tion \sī-'tā-shən\ *n* **1** : an official summons to appear (as before a court) **2** : QUOTATION **3** : a formal statement of the achievements of a person; *also* : a specific reference in a military dispatch to meritorious performance of duty

cite \'sīt\ *vb* **cit·ed; cit·ing 1** : to summon to appear before a court **2** : QUOTE **3** : to refer to esp. in commendation or praise

cit·i·fied \'si-ti-ˌfīd\ *adj* : of, relating to, or characterized by an urban style of living

cit·i·zen \'si-tə-zən\ *n* **1** : an inhabitant of a city or town **2** : a person who owes allegiance to a government and is entitled to its protection — **cit·i·zen·ship** *n*

cit·i·zen·ry \-rē\ *n, pl* **-ries** : a whole body of citizens

citizens band *n* : a range of radio frequencies set aside for private radio communications

cit·ric acid \'si-trik-\ *n* : a sour organic acid obtained

\ə\abut \ᵊ\kitten \ər\further \a\ash \ā\ace \ä\mop, mar
\au̇\out \ch\chin \e\bet \ē\easy \g\go \i\hit \ī\ice \j\job
\ŋ\sing \ō\go \ȯ\law \ȯi\boy \th\thin \t͟h\the \ü\loot \u̇\foot
\y\yet \zh\vision *see also* Pronunciation Symbols page

from lemon and lime juices or by fermentation of sugars and used as a flavoring

cit·ron \ˈsi-trən\ *n* **1** : the oval lemonlike fruit of an Asian citrus tree; *also* : the tree **2** : a small hard-fleshed watermelon used esp. in pickles and preserves

cit·ro·nel·la \ˌsi-trə-ˈne-lə\ *n* : an oil obtained from a fragrant grass of southern Asia and used in perfumes and as an insect repellent

cit·rus \ˈsi-trəs\ *n, pl* **citrus** *or* **cit·rus·es** : any of a genus of often thorny evergreen trees or shrubs grown in warm regions for their fruits (as the orange, lemon, lime, and grapefruit); *also* : the fruit

city \ˈsi-tē\ *n, pl* **cit·ies** [ME *citie* large or small town, fr. OF *cité*, fr. ML *civitas*, fr. L, citizenship, state, city of Rome, fr. *civis* citizen] **1** : an inhabited place larger or more important than a town **2** : a municipality in the U.S. governed under a charter granted by the state; *also* : an incorporated municipal unit of the highest class in Canada

city manager *n* : an official employed by an elected council to direct the administration of a city government

city–state \ˈsi-tē-ˌstāt\ *n* : an autonomous state consisting of a city and surrounding territory

civ *abbr* **1** civil; civilian **2** civilization

civ·et \ˈsi-vət\ *n* : a yellowish strong-smelling substance obtained from a catlike mammal (**civet cat**) of Africa or Asia and used in making perfumes

civ·ic \ˈsi-vik\ *adj* : of or relating to a city, citizenship, or civil affairs

civ·ics \-viks\ *n* : a social science dealing with the rights and duties of citizens

civ·il \ˈsi-vəl\ *adj* **1** : of or relating to citizens or to the state as a political body **2** : COURTEOUS, POLITE **3** : of or relating to legal proceedings in connection with private rights and obligations ⟨the ~ code⟩ **4** : of or relating to the general population : not military or ecclesiastical

civil defense *n* : protective measures and emergency relief activities conducted by civilians in case of enemy attack or natural disaster

civil disobedience *n* : refusal to obey governmental commands esp. as a nonviolent means of protest

civil engineer *n* : an engineer whose training or occupation is in the design and construction esp. of public works (as roads or harbors) — **civil engineering** *n*

ci·vil·ian \sə-ˈvil-yən\ *n* : a person not on active duty in a military, police, or fire-fighting force

civ·i·li·sa·tion, civ·i·lise *chiefly Brit var of* CIVILIZATION, CIVILIZE

ci·vil·i·ty \sə-ˈvi-lə-tē\ *n, pl* **-ties** **1** : POLITENESS, COURTESY **2** : a polite act or expression

civ·i·li·za·tion \ˌsi-və-lə-ˈzā-shən\ *n* **1** : a relatively high level of cultural and technological development **2** : the culture characteristic of a time or place

civ·i·lize \ˈsi-və-ˌlīz\ *vb* **-lized; -liz·ing** **1** : to raise from a primitive state to an advanced and ordered stage of cultural development **2** : REFINE — **civ·i·lized** *adj*

civil liberty *n* : freedom from arbitrary governmental interference specifically by denial of governmental power — usu. used in pl.

civ·il·ly \ˈsi-vəl-lē\ *adv* **1** : in terms of civil rights, matters, or law ⟨~ dead⟩ **2** : in a civil manner : POLITELY

civil rights *n pl* : the nonpolitical rights of a citizen; *esp* : those guaranteed by the 13th and 14th amendments to the Constitution and by acts of Congress

civil servant *n* : a member of a civil service

civil service *n* : the administrative service of a government

civil war *n* : a war between opposing groups of citizens of the same country

civ·vies \ˈsi-vēz\ *n pl* : civilian clothes as distinguished from a military uniform

CJ *abbr* chief justice

ck *abbr* **1** cask **2** check

cl *abbr* **1** centiliter **2** class

Cl *symbol* chlorine

¹clack \ˈklak\ *vb* **1** : CHATTER, PRATTLE **2** : to make or cause to make a clatter

²clack *n* **1** : rapid continuous talk : CHATTER **2** : a sound of clacking ⟨the ~ of a typewriter⟩

clad \ˈklad\ *adj* **1** : CLOTHED, COVERED **2** : being or consisting of coins made of outer layers of one metal bonded to a core of a different metal

¹claim \ˈklām\ *vb* [ME, fr. MF *clamer*, fr. L *clamare* to cry out, shout] **1** : to ask for as one's own; *also* : to take as the rightful owner **2** : to call for : REQUIRE **3** : to state as a fact : MAINTAIN

²claim *n* **1** : a demand for something due **2** : a right to something usu. in another's possession **3** : an assertion open to challenge **4** : something claimed (as a tract of land)

claim·ant \ˈklā-mənt\ *n* : a person making a claim

clair·voy·ant \klar-ˈvȯi-ənt\ *adj* [F, fr. *clair* clear + *voyant* seeing] **1** : unusually perceptive **2** : having the power of discerning objects not present to the senses — **clair·voy·ance** \-əns\ *n* — **clairvoyant** *n*

clam \ˈklam\ *n* **1** : any of numerous bivalve mollusks including many that are edible **2** : DOLLAR

clam·bake \-ˌbāk\ *n* : a party or gathering (as at the seashore) at which food is cooked usu. on heated rocks covered by seaweed

clam·ber \ˈklam-bər\ *vb* : to climb awkwardly — **clamber·er** *n*

clam·my \ˈkla-mē\ *adj* **clam·mi·er; -est** : being damp, soft, sticky, and usu. cool — **clam·mi·ness** *n*

clam·or \ˈkla-mər\ *n* **1** : a noisy shouting **2** : a loud continuous noise **3** : insistent public expression (as of support or protest) — **clamor** *vb* — **clam·or·ous** *adj*

clam·our *chiefly Brit var of* CLAMOR

¹clamp \ˈklamp\ *n* : a device that holds or presses parts together firmly

²clamp *vb* : to fasten with or as if with a clamp

clamp down *vb* : to impose restrictions : become repressive — **clamp·down** \ˈklamp-ˌdau̇n\ *n*

clam·shell \ˈklam-ˌshel\ *n* : a bucket or grapnel (as on a dredge) having two hinged jaws

clam up *vb* : to become silent

clan \ˈklan\ *n* [ME, fr. ScGael *clann* offspring, clan, fr. Old Irish *cland* plant, offspring, fr. L *planta* plant] : a group (as in the Scottish Highlands) made up of households whose heads claim descent from a common ancestor — **clan·nish** *adj* — **clan·nish·ness** *n*

clan·des·tine \klan-ˈdes-tən\ *adj* : held in or conducted with secrecy

clang \ˈklaŋ\ *n* : a loud metallic ringing sound — **clang** *vb*

clan·gor \ˈklaŋ-ər, -gər\ *n* : a resounding clang or medley of clangs

clan·gour *chiefly Brit var of* CLANGOR

clank \ˈklaŋk\ *n* : a sharp brief metallic ringing sound — **clank** *vb*

¹clap \ˈklap\ *vb* **clapped; clap·ping** **1** : to strike noisily **2** : APPLAUD

²clap *n* **1** : a loud noisy crash **2** : the noise made by clapping the hands

³clap *n* : GONORRHEA

clap·board \ˈkla-bərd, -ˌbȯrd; ˈklap-ˌbȯrd\ *n* : a narrow board thicker at one edge than the other used for siding — **clap·board** *vb*

clap·per \ˈkla-pər\ *n* : one that claps; *esp* : the tongue of a bell

clap·trap \ˈklap-ˌtrap\ *n* : pretentious nonsense

claque \ˈklak\ *n* [F, fr. *claquer* to clap] **1** : a group hired to applaud at a performance **2** : a group of sycophants

clar·et \\'klar-ət\\ *n* [ME, fr. MF (*vin*) *claret* clear wine] : a dry red wine

clar·i·fy \\'klar-ə-ˌfī\\ *vb* **-fied; -fy·ing** : to make or become clear — **clar·i·fi·ca·tion** \ˌklar-ə-fə-'kā-shən\ *n*

clar·i·net \ˌklar-ə-'net\ *n* : a single-reed woodwind instrument in the form of a cylindrical tube with a moderately flaring end — **clar·i·net·ist** *or* **clar·i·net·tist** \-'ne-tist\ *n*

clarinet

clar·i·on \\'klar-ē-ən\\ *adj* : brilliantly clear ⟨a ∼ call⟩

clar·i·ty \\'klar-ə-tē\\ *n* : CLEARNESS

¹**clash** \\'klash\\ *vb* **1** : to make or cause to make a clash **2** : CONFLICT, COLLIDE

²**clash** *n* **1** : a noisy usu. metallic sound of collision **2** : a hostile encounter; *also* : a conflict of opinion

clasp \\'klasp\\ *n* **1** : a device (as a hook) for holding objects or parts together **2** : EMBRACE, GRASP — **clasp** *vb*

¹**class** \\'klas\\ *n* **1** : a group of students meeting regularly in a course; *also* : a group graduating together **2** : a course of instruction; *also* : the period when such a course is taught **3** : social rank; *also* : high quality **4** : a group of the same general status or nature; *esp* : a major category in biological classification that is above the order and below the phylum **5** : a division or rating based on grade or quality — **class·less** *adj*

²**class** *vb* : CLASSIFY

class action *n* : a legal action undertaken in behalf of the plaintiffs and all others having an identical interest in the alleged wrong

¹**clas·sic** \\'kla-sik\\ *adj* **1** : serving as a standard of excellence; *also* : TRADITIONAL **2** : CLASSICAL 2 **3** : notable esp. as the best example **4** : AUTHENTIC

²**classic** *n* **1** : a work of enduring excellence and esp. of ancient Greece or Rome; *also* : its author **2** : a traditional event

clas·si·cal \\'kla-si-kəl\\ *adj* **1** : CLASSIC 2 **2** : of or relating to the ancient Greek and Roman classics **3** : of or relating to a form or system of primary significance before modern times ⟨∼ economics⟩ **4** : concerned with a general study of the arts and sciences — **clas·si·cal·ly** \-k(ə-)lē\ *adv*

clas·si·cism \\'kla-sə-ˌsi-zəm\\ *n* **1** : the principles or style of the literature or art of ancient Greece and Rome **2** : adherence to traditional standards believed to be universally valid — **clas·si·cist** \-sist\ *n*

clas·si·fied \\'kla-sə-ˌfīd\\ *adj* : withheld from general circulation for reasons of national security

clas·si·fy \\'kla-sə-ˌfī\\ *vb* **-fied; -fy·ing** : to arrange in or assign to classes — **clas·si·fi·able** *adj* — **clas·si·fi·ca·tion** \ˌkla-sə-fə-'kā-shən\ *n* — **clas·si·fi·er** *n*

class·mate \\'klas-ˌmāt\\ *n* : a member of the same class (as in a college)

class·room \-ˌrüm-, -ˌrum\\ *n* : a place where classes meet

classy \\'kla-sē\\ *adj* **class·i·er; -est** : ELEGANT, STYLISH — **class·i·ness** *n*

clat·ter \\'kla-tər\\ *n* : a rattling sound ⟨the ∼ of dishes⟩ — **clatter** *vb*

clause \\'klȯz\\ *n* **1** : a group of words having its own subject and predicate but forming only part of a compound or complex sentence **2** : a separate part of an article or document

claus·tro·pho·bia \ˌklȯ-strə-'fō-bē-ə\ *n* : abnormal dread of being in closed or narrow spaces — **claus·tro·pho·bic** \-bik\ *adj*

clav·i·chord \\'kla-və-ˌkȯrd\\ *n* : an early keyboard instrument in use before the piano

clav·i·cle \\'kla-vi-kəl\\ *n* [F *clavicule*, fr. NL *clavicula*, fr. L, dim. of L *clavis* key] : COLLARBONE

cla·vier \klə-'vir; 'klā-vē-ər\ *n* **1** : the keyboard of a musical instrument **2** : an early keyboard instrument

¹**claw** \\'klȯ\\ *n* **1** : a sharp usu. curved nail on the toe of an animal **2** : a sharp curved process (as on the foot of an insect); *also* : a pincerlike organ at the end of a limb of some arthropods (as a lobster) — **clawed** \\'klȯd\\ *adj*

²**claw** *vb* : to rake, seize, or dig with or as if with claws

clay \\'klā\\ *n* **1** : an earthy material that is plastic when moist but hard when fired and is used in making pottery; *also* : finely divided soil consisting largely of such clay **2** : EARTH, MUD **3** : a plastic substance used for modeling **4** : the mortal human body — **clay·ey** \\'klā-ē\\ *adj*

clay·more \\'klā-ˌmȯr\\ *n* : a large 2-edged sword formerly used by Scottish Highlanders

clay pigeon *n* : a saucer-shaped target thrown from a trap in trapshooting

¹**clean** \\'klēn\\ *adj* **1** : free from dirt or disease **2** : PURE; *also* : HONORABLE **3** : THOROUGH ⟨made a ∼ sweep⟩ **4** : TRIM ⟨a ship with ∼ lines⟩; *also* : EVEN **5** : habitually neat — **clean** *adv* — **clean·ly** \\'klēn-lē\\ *adv* — **clean·ness** \\'klēn-nəs\\ *n*

²**clean** *vb* : to make or become clean — **clean·er** *n*

clean–cut \\'klēn-'kət\\ *adj* **1** : cut so that the surface or edge is smooth and even **2** : sharply defined or outlined **3** : giving an effect of wholesomeness

clean·ly \\'klen-lē\\ *adj* **clean·li·er; -est** **1** : careful to keep clean **2** : habitually kept clean — **clean·li·ness** *n*

clean room \\'klēn-ˌrüm, -ˌrum\\ *n* : an uncontaminated room maintained for the manufacture or assembly of objects (as precision parts)

cleanse \\'klenz\\ *vb* **cleansed; cleans·ing** : to make clean — **cleans·er** *n*

¹**clean·up** \\'klē-ˌnəp\\ *n* **1** : an act or instance of cleaning **2** : a very large profit

²**cleanup** *adj* : being 4th in the batting order of a baseball team

clean up *vb* : to make a spectacular business profit

¹**clear** \\'klir\\ *adj* **1** : BRIGHT, LUMINOUS; *also* : UNTROUBLED, SERENE **2** : CLOUDLESS **3** : CLEAN, PURE; *also* : TRANSPARENT **4** : easily heard, seen, or understood **5** : capable of sharp discernment; *also* : free from doubt **6** : INNOCENT **7** : free from restriction, obstruction, or entanglement — **clear** *adv* — **clear·ness** *n*

²**clear** *vb* **1** : to make or become clear **2** : to go away; DISPERSE **3** : to free from accusation or blame; *also* : to certify as trustworthy **4** : EXPLAIN **5** : to get free from obstruction **6** : SETTLE **7** : NET **8** : to get rid of : REMOVE **9** : to jump or go by without touching; *also* : PASS

³**clear** *n* : a clear space or part

clear·ance \\'klir-əns\\ *n* **1** : an act or process of clearing **2** : the distance by which one object clears another **3** : AUTHORIZATION

clear–cut \\'klir-'kət\\ *adj* **1** : sharply outlined **2** : DEFINITE, UNEQUIVOCAL

clear·head·ed \-'he-dəd\ *adj* : having a clear understanding : PERCEPTIVE

clear·ing \\'klir-iŋ\\ *n* **1** : a tract of land cleared of wood and brush **2** : the passage of checks and claims through a clearinghouse

clear·ing·house \-ˌhaús\ *n* : an institution maintained by banks for making an exchange of checks and claims held by each bank against other banks; *also* : an informal channel for information or assistance

clear·ly \\'klir-lē\\ *adv* **1** : in a clear manner **2** : it is clear

cleat \\'klēt\\ *n* : a piece of wood or metal fastened on or

---

\ə\abut \ᵊ\kitten \ər\further \a\ash \ā\ace \ä\mop, mar
\aú\out \ch\chin \e\bet \ē\easy \g\go \i\hit \ī\ice \j\job
\ŋ\sing \ō\go \ò\law \òi\boy \th\thin \th\the \ü\loot \ú\foot
\y\yet \zh\vision *see also* Pronunciation Symbols page

projecting from something to give strength, provide a grip, or prevent slipping

cleav·age \'klē-vij\ *n* **1** : a splitting apart : SPLIT **2** : the depression between a woman's breasts esp. when exposed by a low-cut dress

¹cleave \'klēv\ *vb* **cleaved** \'klēvd\ *or* **clove** \'klōv\; **cleaved; cleav·ing** : ADHERE, CLING

²cleave *vb* **cleaved** \'klēvd\ *also* **cleft** \'kleft\ *or* **clove** \'klōv\; **cleaved** *also* **cleft** *or* **clo·ven** \'klō-vən\; **cleav·ing 1** : to divide by force : split asunder **2** : DIVIDE

cleav·er \'klē-vər\ *n* : a heavy chopping knife for cutting meat

clef \'klef\ *n* : a sign placed on the staff in music to show what pitch is represented by each line and space

cleft \'kleft\ *n* : FISSURE, CRACK

cleft palate *n* : a split in the roof of the mouth that appears as a birth defect

clem·a·tis \'kle-mə-təs; kli-'ma-təs\ *n* : any of a genus of vines or herbs related to the buttercups that have showy usu. white or purple flowers

clem·en·cy \'kle-mən-sē\ *n, pl* **-cies 1** : disposition to be merciful **2** : mildness of weather

clem·ent \'kle-mənt\ *adj* **1** : MERCIFUL, LENIENT **2** : TEMPERATE, MILD

clench \'klench\ *vb* **1** : CLINCH 1 **2** : to hold fast **3** : to set or close tightly

clere·sto·ry \'klir-ˌstōr-ē\ *n* : an outside wall of a room or building that rises above an adjoining roof and contains windows

cler·gy \'klər-jē\ *n* : a body of religious officials authorized to conduct services

cler·gy·man \-mən\ *n* : a member of the clergy

cler·ic \'kler-ik\ *n* : a member of the clergy

cler·i·cal \'kler-i-kəl\ *adj* **1** : of or relating to the clergy **2** : of or relating to a clerk

cler·i·cal·ism \'kler-i-kə-ˌli-zəm\ *n* : a policy of maintaining or increasing the power of a religious hierarchy

clerk \'klərk, *Brit* 'klärk\ *n* **1** : CLERIC **2** : an official responsible for correspondence, records, and accounts; *also* : a person employed to perform general office work **3** : a store salesperson — **clerk** *vb* — **clerk·ship** *n*

clev·er \'kle-vər\ *adj* **1** : showing skill or resourcefulness **2** : marked by wit or ingenuity — **clev·er·ly** *adv* — **clev·er·ness** *n*

clev·is \'kle-vəs\ *n* : a U-shaped shackle used for fastening

¹clew \'klü\ *n* **1** : CLUE **2** : a metal loop on a lower corner of a sail

²clew *vb* : to haul (a sail) up or down by ropes through the clews

cli·ché \klē-'shā\ *n* [F] : a trite phrase or expression — **cli·chéd** \-'shād\ *adj*

¹click \'klik\ *vb* **1** : to make or cause to make a click **2** : to fit or work together smoothly

²click *n* : a slight sharp noise

cli·ent \'klī-ənt\ *n* **1** : DEPENDENT **2** : a person who engages the professional services of another; *also* : PATRON, CUSTOMER

cli·en·tele \ˌklī-ən-'tel, ˌklē-\ *n* : a body of clients and esp. customers

cliff \'klif\ *n* : a high steep face of rock, earth, or ice

cliff–hang·er \-ˌhaŋ-ər\ *n* **1** : an adventure serial or melodrama usu. presented in installments each of which ends in suspense **2** : a contest whose outcome is in doubt up to the very end

cli·mac·ter·ic \klī-'mak-tə-rik\ *n* **1** : a major turning point or critical stage **2** : MENOPAUSE; *also* : a corresponding period in the male

cli·mate \'klī-mət\ *n* [ME *climat*, fr. MF, fr. LL *clima*, fr. Gk *klima* inclination, latitude, climate, fr. *klinein* to lean] **1** : a region having specific climatic conditions **2** : the average weather conditions at a place over a pe-

riod of years **3** : the prevailing set of conditions (as temperature and humidity) indoors **4** : a prevailing atmosphere or environment ⟨the ∼ of opinion⟩ — **cli·mat·ic** \klī-'ma-tik\ *adj* — **cli·mat·i·cal·ly** \-ti-k(ə-)lē\ *adv*

cli·ma·tol·o·gy \ˌklī-mə-'tä-lə-jē\ *n* : the science that deals with climates — **cli·ma·to·log·i·cal** \-mət-ᵊl-'ä-ji-kəl\ *adj* — **cli·ma·to·log·i·cal·ly** \-k(ə-)lē\ *adv* — **cli·ma·tol·o·gist** \-mə-'tä-lə-jist\ *n*

¹cli·max \'klī-ˌmaks\ *n* [L, fr. Gk *klimax* ladder, fr. *klinein* to lean] **1** : a series of ideas or statements so arranged that they increase in force and power from the first to the last; *also* : the last member of such a series **2** : the highest point **3** : ORGASM — **cli·mac·tic** \klī-'mak-tik\ *adj*

²climax *vb* : to come or bring to a climax

¹climb \'klīm\ *vb* **1** : to rise to a higher point **2** : to go up or down esp. by use of hands and feet; *also* : to ascend in growing — **climb·er** *n*

²climb *n* **1** : a place where climbing is necessary **2** : the act of climbing : ascent by climbing

clime \'klīm\ *n* : CLIMATE

¹clinch \'klinch\ *vb* **1** : to turn over or flatten the end of something sticking out ⟨∼ a nail⟩; *also* : to fasten by clinching **2** : to make final : SETTLE **3** : to hold fast or firmly

²clinch *n* **1** : a fastening by means of a clinched nail, rivet, or bolt **2** : an act or instance of clinching in boxing

clinch·er \'klin-chər\ *n* : one that clinches; *esp* : a decisive fact, argument, act, or remark

cling \'kliŋ\ *vb* **clung** \'kləŋ\; **cling·ing 1** : to adhere as if glued; *also* : to hold or hold on tightly **2** : to have a strong emotional attachment

cling·stone \'kliŋ-ˌstōn\ *n* : any of various fruits (as some peaches) whose flesh adheres strongly to the pit

clin·ic \'kli-nik\ *n* **1** : a medical class in which patients are examined and discussed **2** : a group meeting for teaching a certain skill and working on individual problems ⟨a reading ∼⟩ **3** : a facility (as of a hospital) for diagnosis and treatment of outpatients

clin·i·cal \'kli-ni-kəl\ *adj* **1** : of, relating to, or typical of a clinic; *esp* : involving direct observation of the patient **2** : scientifically dispassionate — **clin·i·cal·ly** \-k(ə-)lē\ *adv*

cli·ni·cian \kli-'ni-shən\ *n* : a person qualified in the clinical practice of medicine, psychiatry, or psychology as distinguished from one specializing in laboratory or research techniques or in theory

¹clink \'kliŋk\ *vb* : to make or cause to make a sharp short metallic sound

²clink *n* : a clinking sound

clin·ker \'kliŋ-kər\ *n* : stony matter fused together : SLAG

¹clip \'klip\ *vb* **clipped; clip·ping** : to fasten with a clip

²clip *n* **1** : a device that grips, clasps, or hooks **2** : a cartridge holder for a rifle

³clip *vb* **clipped; clip·ping 1** : to cut or cut off with shears **2** : CURTAIL, DIMINISH **3** : HIT, PUNCH **4** : to illegally block (an opponent) in football

⁴clip *n* **1** : a 2-bladed instrument for cutting esp. the nails **2** : a sharp blow **3** : a rapid pace

clip·board \'klip-ˌbȯrd\ *n* : a small writing board with a spring clip at the top for holding papers

clip joint *n, slang* : an establishment (as a nightclub) that makes a practice of defrauding its customers

clip·per \'kli-pər\ *n* **1** : an implement for clipping esp. the hair or nails — usu. used in pl. **2** : a fast sailing ship

clip·ping \'kli-piŋ\ *n* : a piece clipped from something (as a newspaper)

clique \'klēk, 'klik\ *n* [F] : a small exclusive group of people : COTERIE — **cliqu·ey** \'klē-kē, 'kli-\ *adj* — **cliqu·ish** \-kish\ *adj*

cli·to·ris \'kli-tə-rəs\ *n, pl* **cli·to·ri·des** \kli-'tȯr-ə-ˌdēz\ : a small erectile organ at the anterior or ventral part of the vulva homologous to the penis — **cli·to·ral** \-rəl\ *adj*

clk *abbr* clerk

clo *abbr* clothing

¹cloak \ˈklōk\ *n* **1** : a loose outer garment **2** : something that conceals

²cloak *vb* : to cover or hide with a cloak

cloak–and–dagger *adj* : involving or suggestive of espionage

clob·ber \ˈklä-bər\ *vb* **1** : to pound mercilessly; *also* : to hit with force : SMASH **2** : to defeat overwhelmingly

cloche \ˈklōsh\ *n* [F, lit., bell] : a woman's small close-fitting hat

¹clock \ˈkläk\ *n* : a timepiece not intended to be carried on the person

²clock *vb* **1** : to time (a person or a performance) by a timing device **2** : to register (as speed) on a mechanical recording device — **clock·er** *n*

³clock *n* : an ornamental figure on a stocking or sock

clock·wise \ˈkläk-ˌwīz\ *adv* : in the direction in which the hands of a clock move — **clockwise** *adj*

clock·work \-ˌwərk\ *n* **1** : the machinery that runs a mechanical device (as a clock or toy) **2** : the precision or regularity associated with a clock

clod \ˈkläd\ *n* **1** : a lump esp. of earth or clay **2** : a dull or insensitive person

clod·hop·per \-ˌhä-pər\ *n* **1** : an uncouth rustic **2** : a large heavy shoe

¹clog \ˈkläg\ *n* **1** : a weight so attached as to impede motion **2** : a thick-soled shoe

²clog *vb* **clogged**; **clog·ging 1** : to impede with a clog : HINDER **2** : to obstruct passage through **3** : to become filled with extraneous matter

cloi·son·né \ˌklȯiz-ᵊn-ˈā\ *adj* : a colored decoration made of enamels poured into the divided areas in a design outlined with wire or metal strips

¹clois·ter \ˈklȯi-stər\ *n* [ME *cloistre*, fr. OF, fr. ML *claustrum*, fr. L, bar, bolt, fr. *claudere* to close] **1** : a monastic establishment **2** : a covered usu. colonnaded passage on the side of a court — **clois·tral** \-strəl\ *adj*

²cloister *vb* : to shut away from the world

clone \ˈklōn\ *n* [Gk *klōn* twig, slip] **1** : the offspring produced asexually from an individual (as a plant increased by grafting); *also* : a group of replicas of all or part of a large biological molecule (as DNA) **2** : an individual grown from a single body cell of its parent and genetically identical to the parent **3** : one that appears to be a copy of an original form — **clon·al** \ˈklōn-ᵊl\ *adj* — **clone** *vb*

clop \ˈkläp\ *n* : a sound made by or as if by a hoof or wooden shoe against pavement — **clop** *vb*

¹close \ˈklōz\ *vb* **closed**; **clos·ing 1** : to bar passage through : SHUT **2** : to suspend the operations (as of a school) **3** : END, TERMINATE **4** : to bring together the parts or edges of; *also* : to fill up **5** : GRAPPLE ⟨∼ with the enemy⟩ **6** : to enter into an agreement — **clos·able** *or* **close·able** *adj*

²close \ˈklōz\ *n* : CONCLUSION, END

³close \ˈklōs\ *adj* **clos·er**; **clos·est 1** : having no openings **2** : narrowly restricting or restricted **3** : limited to a privileged class **4** : SECLUDED; *also* : SECRETIVE **5** : RIGOROUS **6** : SULTRY, STUFFY **7** : STINGY **8** : having little space between items or units **9** : fitting tightly; *also* : SHORT ⟨∼ haircut⟩ **10** : NEAR **11** : INTIMATE ⟨∼ friends⟩ **12** : ACCURATE **13** : decided by a narrow margin ⟨a ∼ game⟩ — **close** *adv* — **close·ly** *adv* — **close·ness** *n*

closed–circuit \ˈklōzd-ˈsər-kət\ *adj* : used in, shown on, or being a television installation in which the signal is transmitted by wire to a limited number of receivers

closed shop *n* : an establishment having only members of a labor union on the payroll

close·fist·ed \ˈklōz-ˈfis-təd, ˈklōs-\ *adj* : STINGY

close–knit \ˈklōs-ˈnit\ *adj* : closely bound together by social, cultural, economic, or political ties

close·mouthed \ˈklōz-ˈmau̇thd, ˈklōs-ˈmau̇tht\ *adj* : cautious or reticent in speaking

close·out \ˈklō-ˌzau̇t\ *n* : a sale of a business's entire stock at low prices

close out *vb* **1** : to dispose of by a closeout **2** : to dispose of a business : SELL OUT

¹clos·et \ˈklä-zət, ˈklȯ-\ *n* **1** : a small room for privacy **2** : a small compartment for household utensils or clothing **3** : a state or condition of secrecy ⟨came out of the ∼⟩

²closet *vb* : to take into a private room for an interview

close–up \ˈklō-ˌsəp\ *n* **1** : a photograph or movie shot taken at close range **2** : an intimate view or examination

clo·sure \ˈklō-zhər\ *n* **1** : an act of closing : the condition of being closed **2** : something that closes **3** : CLOTURE

clot \ˈklät\ *n* : a mass formed by a portion of liquid (as blood) thickening and sticking together — **clot** *vb*

cloth \ˈklȯth\ *n, pl* **cloths** \ˈklȯthz, ˈklȯths\ **1** : a pliable fabric made usu. by weaving or knitting natural or synthetic fibers and filaments **2** : TABLECLOTH **3** : distinctive dress of the clergy; *also* : CLERGY

clothe \ˈklȯth\ *vb* **clothed** *or* **clad** \ˈklad\; **cloth·ing 1** : DRESS **2** : to express by suitably significant language

clothes \ˈklȯthz, ˈklȯz\ *n pl* **1** : CLOTHING **2** : BEDDING 1

clothes·horse \-ˌhȯrs\ *n* **1** : a frame on which to hang clothes **2** : a conspicuously dressy person

clothes moth *n* : any of several small pale moths whose larvae eat wool, fur, and feathers

clothes·pin \ˈklȯthz-ˌpin, ˈklȯz-\ *n* : a device for fastening clothes on a line

clothes·press \-ˌpres\ *n* : a receptacle for clothes

cloth·ier \ˈklȯth-yər, ˈklȯ-thē-ər\ *n* : a maker or seller of clothing

cloth·ing \ˈklō-thiŋ\ *n* : garments in general

clo·ture \ˈklō-chər\ *n* : the closing or limitation (as by calling for a vote) of debate in a legislative body

¹cloud \ˈklau̇d\ *n* [ME, rock, cloud, fr. OE *clud*] **1** : a visible mass of particles of condensed vapor (as water or ice) suspended in the atmosphere **2** : a usu. visible mass of minute airborne particles; *also* : a mass of obscuring matter in interstellar space **3** : CROWD, SWARM ⟨a ∼ of mosquitoes⟩ **4** : something having a dark or threatening aspect — **cloud·i·ness** \ˈklau̇-dē-nəs\ *n* — **cloud·less** *adj* — **cloudy** *adj*

²cloud *vb* **1** : to darken or hide with or as if with a cloud **2** : OBSCURE **3** : TAINT, SULLY

cloud·burst \-ˌbərst\ *n* : a sudden heavy rainfall

cloud·let \-lət\ *n* : a small cloud

cloud nine *n* : a feeling of extreme well-being or elation — usu. used with *on*

¹clout \ˈklau̇t\ *n* **1** : a blow esp. with the hand **2** : PULL, INFLUENCE

²clout *vb* : to hit forcefully

¹clove \ˈklōv\ *n* : one of the small bulbs that grows at the base of the scales of a large bulb ⟨a ∼ of garlic⟩

²clove *past of* CLEAVE

³clove *n* [ME *clowe*, fr. OF *clou (de girofle)*, lit., nail of clove, fr. L *clavus* nail] : the dried flower bud of an East Indian tree used esp. as a spice

clo·ven \ˈklō-vən\ *past part of* CLEAVE

cloven foot *n* : CLOVEN HOOF — **cloven–foot·ed** \-ˈfü-təd\ *adj*

cloven hoof *n* : a foot (as of a sheep) with the front part divided into two parts — **cloven–hoofed** \-ˈhu̇ft, -ˈhu̇vd\ *adj*

clo·ver \'klō-vər\ *n* : any of a genus of leguminous herbs with usu. 3-parted leaves and dense flower heads

clo·ver·leaf \-ˌlēf\ *n, pl* **cloverleafs** \-ˌlēfs\ *or* **clo·ver·leaves** \-ˌlēvz\ : an interchange between two major highways that from above resembles a four-leaf clover

¹clown \'klaùn\ *n* **1** : BOOR **2** : a fool or comedian in an entertainment (as a circus) — **clown·ish** *adj* — **clown·ish·ly** *adv* — **clown·ish·ness** *n*

²clown *vb* : to act like a clown

cloy \'klôi\ *vb* : to disgust or nauseate with excess of something orig. pleasing — **cloy·ing·ly** *adv*

clr *abbr* clear

¹club \'kləb\ *n* **1** : a heavy wooden stick or staff used as a weapon; *also* : BAT **2** : any of a suit of playing cards marked with a black figure resembling a clover leaf **3** : a group of persons associated for a common purpose; *also* : the meeting place of such a group

²club *vb* **clubbed; club·bing 1** : to strike with a club **2** : to unite or combine for a common cause

club·foot \'kləb-ˌfùt\ *n* : a misshapen foot twisted out of position from birth; *also* : this deformed condition — **club·foot·ed** \-ˈfù-təd\ *adj*

club·house \'kləb-ˌhaùs\ *n* **1** : a house occupied by a club **2** : locker rooms used by an athletic team

club sandwich *n* : a sandwich of three slices of bread with two layers of meat (as turkey) and lettuce, tomato, and mayonnaise

club soda *n* : SODA WATER

cluck \'klək\ *n* : the call of a hen esp. to her chicks — **cluck** *vb*

¹clue \'klü\ *n* : something that guides through an intricate procedure or maze; *esp* : a piece of evidence leading to the solution of a problem

²clue *vb* **clued; clue·ing** *or* **clu·ing** : to provide with a clue; *also* : to give information to ⟨~ me in⟩

¹clump \'kləmp\ *n* **1** : a group of things clustered together **2** : a heavy tramping sound

²clump *vb* : to tread clumsily and noisily

clum·sy \'kləm-zē\ *adj* **clum·si·er; -est 1** : lacking dexterity, nimbleness, or grace **2** : not tactful or subtle — **clum·si·ly** \-zə-lē\ *adv* — **clum·si·ness** \-zē-nəs\ *n*

clung *past and past part of* CLING

clunk·er \'kləŋ-kər\ *n* **1** : a dilapidated automobile **2** : a notable failure

¹clus·ter \'kləs-tər\ *n* : GROUP, BUNCH

²cluster *vb* : to grow or gather in a cluster

¹clutch \'kləch\ *vb* : to grasp with or as if with the hand

²clutch *n* **1** : the claws or a hand in the act of grasping; *also* : CONTROL, POWER **2** : a device for gripping an object **3** : a coupling used to connect and disconnect a driving and a driven part of a mechanism; *also* : a lever or pedal operating such a coupling **4** : a crucial situation

³clutch *adj* : made, done, or successful in a crucial situation

⁴clutch *n* **1** : a nest or batch of eggs; *also* : a brood of chicks **2** : GROUP, BUNCH

¹clut·ter \'klə-tər\ *vb* : to fill or cover with a disorderly scattering of things

²clutter *n* : a crowded mass

cm *abbr* centimeter

Cm *symbol* curium

CM *abbr* [Commonwealth of the Northern Mariana Islands] Northern Mariana Islands

cmdr *abbr* commander

cml *abbr* commercial

CMSgt *abbr* chief master sergeant

CNO *abbr* chief of naval operations

CNS *abbr* central nervous system

co *abbr* **1** company **2** county

Co *symbol* cobalt

CO *abbr* **1** Colorado **2** commanding officer **3** conscientious objector

c/o *abbr* care of

¹coach \'kōch\ *n* **1** : a large closed 4-wheeled carriage with an elevated outside front seat for the driver **2** : a railroad passenger car esp. for day travel **3** : BUS **4** : a private tutor; *also* : one who instructs or trains a team of performers

coach 1

²coach *vb* : to instruct, direct, or prompt as a coach

coach·man \-mən\ *n* : a man who drives a coach or carriage

co·ad·ju·tor \ˌkō-ə-ˈjü-tər, kō-ˈa-jə-tər\ *n* : ASSISTANT; *esp* : an assistant bishop having the right of succession

co·ag·u·lant \kō-ˈa-gyə-lənt\ *n* : something that produces coagulation

co·ag·u·late \-ˌlāt\ *vb* **-lat·ed; -lat·ing** : CLOT — **co·ag·u·la·tion** \kō-ˌa-gyə-ˈlā-shən\ *n*

¹coal \'kōl\ *n* **1** : EMBER **2** : a black solid combustible mineral used as fuel

²coal *vb* **1** : to supply with coal **2** : to take in coal

co·a·lesce \ˌkō-ə-ˈles\ *vb* **co·a·lesced; co·a·lesc·ing** : to grow together; *also* : FUSE **syn** merge, blend, mingle, mix — **co·a·les·cence** \-ˈns\ *n*

coal·field \'kōl-ˌfēld\ *n* : a region rich in coal deposits

coal gas *n* : gas from coal; *esp* : gas distilled from bituminous coal and used for heating

co·a·li·tion \ˌkō-ə-ˈli-shən\ *n* : UNION; *esp* : a temporary union for a common purpose — **co·a·li·tion·ist** *n*

coal oil *n* : KEROSENE

coal tar *n* : tar distilled from bituminous coal and used in dyes and drugs

co–an·chor \'kō-ˈaŋ-kər\ *n* : a newscaster who shares the duties of head broadcaster

coarse \'kòrs\ *adj* **coars·er; coars·est 1** : of ordinary or inferior quality **2** : composed of large parts or particles ⟨~ sand⟩ **3** : CRUDE ⟨~ manners⟩ **4** : ROUGH, HARSH — **coarse·ly** *adv* — **coarse·ness** *n*

coars·en \'kòrs-ᵊn\ *vb* : to make or become coarse

¹coast \'kōst\ *n* [ME *cost*, fr. MF *coste*, fr. L *costa* rib, side] **1** : SEASHORE **2** : a slide down a slope **3** : the immediate area of view — used in the phrase *the coast is clear* — **coast·al** *adj*

²coast *vb* **1** : to sail along the shore **2** : to move (as downhill on a sled) without effort

coast·er *n* **1** : one that coasts **2** : a shallow container or a plate or mat to protect a surface

coaster brake *n* : a brake in the hub of the rear wheel of a bicycle

coast guard *n* : a military force employed in guarding or patrolling a coast — **coast·guards·man** \'kòst-ˌgärdz-mən\ *n*

coast·line \'kòst-ˌlīn\ *n* : the outline or shape of a coast

¹coat \'kōt\ *n* **1** : an outer garment for the upper part of the body **2** : an external growth (as of fur or feathers) on an animal **3** : a covering layer — **coat·ed** \'kō-təd\ *adj*

²coat *vb* : to cover usu. with a finishing or protective coat

coat·ing \'kō-tiŋ\ *n* : COAT, COVERING

coat of arms : the heraldic bearings (as of a person) usu. depicted on an escutcheon

coat of mail : a garment of metal scales or rings worn as armor

co·au·thor \'kō-'ō-thər\ *n* : a joint or associate author — **coauthor** *vb*

coax \'kōks\ *vb* : WHEEDLE; *also* : to gain by gentle urging or flattery

co·ax·i·al \'kō-'ak-sē-əl\ *adj* : having coincident axes — **co·ax·i·al·ly** *adv*

coaxial cable *n* : a cable that consists of a tube of electrically conducting material surrounding a central conductor

cob \'käb\ *n* **1** : a male swan **2** : CORN-COB **3** : a short-legged stocky horse

co·balt \'kō-₁bȯlt\ *n* [G *Kobalt*, alter. of *Kobold*, lit., goblin; fr. its occurrence in silver ore, believed to be due to goblins] : a tough shiny silver-white magnetic metallic chemical element found with iron and nickel — see ELEMENT table

cob·ble \'kä-bəl\ *vb* **cob·bled; cob·bling** : to make or put together roughly or hastily

cob·bler \'kä-blər\ *n* **1** : a mender or maker of shoes **2** : a deep-dish fruit pie with a thick crust

cob·ble·stone \'kä-bəl-₁stȯn\ *n* : a naturally rounded stone larger than a pebble and smaller than a boulder

co·bra \'kō-brə\ *n* [Pg *cobra (de capello)*, lit., hooded snake] : any of several venomous snakes of Asia and Africa that when excited expand the skin of the neck into a broad hood

cob·web \'käb-₁web\ *n* [ME *coppeweb*, fr. *coppe* spider, fr. OE ātor*coppe*] **1** : SPIDERWEB; *also* : a thread spun by a spider or insect larva **2** : something flimsy or entangling

co·caine \kō-'kān, 'kō-₁kān\ *n* : a drug obtained from the leaves of a So. American shrub (**co·ca** \'kō-kə\) that can result in severe psychological dependence and is sometimes used in medicine as a local anesthetic and illegally to stimulate the central nervous system

coc·cus \'kä-kəs\ *n, pl* **coc·ci** \'käk-₁sī\ : a spherical bacterium

coc·cyx \'käk-siks\ *n, pl* **coc·cy·ges** \'käk-sə-₁jēz\ *also* **coc·cyx·es** \'käk-sik-səz\ : the end of the spinal column beyond the sacrum esp. in humans

co·chi·neal \'kä-chə-₁nēl\ *n* : a red dye made from the dried bodies of females of a tropical American insect (**cochineal insect**)

co·chlea \'kō-klē-ə, 'kä-\ *n, pl* **co·chle·as** *or* **co·chle·ae** \-klē-₁ē, -₁ī\ : the usu. spiral part of the inner ear containing nerve endings which carry information about sound to the brain — **co·chle·ar** \-klē-ər\ *adj*

¹cock \'käk\ *n* **1** : the adult male of a bird and esp. of the common domestic chicken **2** : VALVE, FAUCET **3** : LEADER **4** : the hammer of a firearm; *also* : the position of the hammer when ready for firing

²cock *vb* **1** : to draw back the hammer of a firearm **2** : to set or draw back in readiness for some action ⟨∼ your arm to throw⟩ **3** : to turn or tilt usu. to one side

³cock *n* : a small pile (as of hay)

cock·ade \kä-'kād\ *n* : an ornament worn on the hat as a badge

cock·a·tiel \₁kä-kə-'tēl\ *n* : a small crested parrot often kept as a cage bird

cock·a·too \'kä-kə-₁tü\ *n, pl* **-toos** [D *kaketoe*, fr. Malay *kakatua*] : any of various large noisy Australian crested parrots

cock·a·trice \'kä-kə-trəs, -₁trīs\ *n* : a legendary serpent with a deadly glance

cock·crow \'käk-₁krō\ *n* : DAWN

cocked hat \'käkt-\ *n* : a hat with the brim turned up on two or three sides

cock·er·el \'kä-kə-rəl\ *n* : a young male domestic chicken

cock·er spaniel \'kä-kər-\ *n* [*cocking* woodcock hunting] : any of a breed of small spaniels with long ears, square muzzle, and silky coat

cock·eyed \'kä-'kīd\ *adj* **1** : turned or tilted to one side **2** : slightly crazy : FOOLISH

cock·fight \'käk-₁fīt\ *n* : a contest of gamecocks usu. fitted with metal spurs

¹cock·le \'kä-kəl\ *n* : any of several weedy plants related to the pinks

²cockle *n* : a bivalve mollusk with a heart-shaped shell

cock·le·shell \-₁shel\ *n* **1** : the shell of a cockle **2** : a light flimsy boat

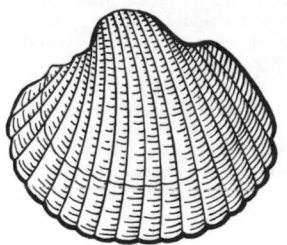

cockleshell 1

cock·ney \'käk-nē\ *n, pl* **cockneys** : a native of London and esp. of the East End of London; *also* : the dialect of a cockney

cock·pit \'käk-₁pit\ *n* **1** : a pit for cockfights **2** : a space or compartment in a vehicle from which it is steered, piloted, or driven

cock·roach \'käk-₁rōch\ *n* [Sp *cucaracha*] : any of an order or suborder of active nocturnal insects including some which infest houses and ships

cock·sure \'käk-'shu̇r\ *adj* **1** : perfectly sure : CERTAIN **2** : COCKY

cock·tail \'käk-₁tāl\ *n* **1** : an iced drink made of liquor and flavoring ingredients **2** : an appetizer (as tomato juice) served as a first course of a meal

cocky \'kä-kē\ *adj* **cock·i·er; -est** : marked by overconfidence : PERT, CONCEITED — **cock·i·ly** \-kə-lē\ *adv* — **cock·i·ness** \-kē-nəs\ *n*

co·coa \'kō-kō\ *n* **1** : CACAO **2** : chocolate deprived of some of its fat and powdered; *also* : a drink made of this heated with water or milk

co·co·nut \'kō-kə-(₁)nət\ *n* : a large edible nut produced by a tall tropical palm (**coconut palm**)

co·coon \kə-'kün\ *n* : a case usu. of silk formed by some insect larvae for protection during the pupal stage

cod \'käd\ *n, pl* **cod** *also* **cods** : a bottom-dwelling bony fish of the No. Atlantic that is an important food fish; *also* : a related fish of the Pacific Ocean

COD *abbr* **1** cash on delivery **2** collect on delivery

co·da \'kō-də\ *n* : a closing section in a musical composition that is formally distinct from the main structure

cod·dle \'käd-ᵊl\ *vb* **cod·dled; cod·dling 1** : to cook slowly in water below the boiling point **2** : PAMPER

¹code \'kōd\ *n* **1** : a systematic statement of a body of law **2** : a system of principles or rules ⟨moral ∼⟩ **3** : a system of signals **4** : a system of symbols (as in secret communication) with special meanings **5** : GENETIC CODE

²code *vb* **cod·ed; cod·ing** : to put into the form or symbols of a code

co·deine \'kō-₁dēn\ *n* : a narcotic drug obtained from opium and used esp. in cough remedies

co·dex \'kō-₁deks\ *n, pl* **co·di·ces** \'kō-də-₁sēz, 'kä-\ : a manuscript book (as of the Scriptures or classics)

cod·fish \'käd-₁fish\ *n* : COD

cod·ger \'kä-jər\ *n* : an odd or cranky and usu. elderly fellow

cod·i·cil \'kä-də-səl, -₁sil\ *n* : a legal instrument modifying an earlier will

cod·i·fy \'kä-də-₁fī, 'kȯ-\ *vb* **-fied; -fy·ing** : to arrange in a systematic form — **cod·i·fi·ca·tion** \₁kä-də-fə-'kā-shən, ₁kȯ-\ *n*

co·ed \'kȯ-₁ed\ *n* : a female student in a coeducational institution — **coed** *adj*

co·ed·u·ca·tion \₁kȯ-₁e-jə-'kā-shən\ *n* : the education of male and female students at the same institution — **co·ed·u·ca·tion·al** \-shə-nəl\ *adj* — **co·ed·u·ca·tion·al·ly** *adv*

co·ef·fi·cient \₁kȯ-ə-'fi-shənt\ *n* **1** : a constant factor as distinguished from a variable in a mathematical term **2** : a number that serves as a measure of some property (as of a substance, device, or process)

coe·len·ter·ate \si-'len-tə-₁rāt, -rət\ *n* : any of a phylum of radially symmetrical invertebrate animals including the corals, sea anemones, and jellyfishes

co·equal \kȯ-'ē-kwəl\ *adj* : equal with another — **co·equal** *n* — **co·equal·i·ty** \₁kȯ-ē-'kwä-lə-tē\ *n* — **co·equal·ly** *adv*

co·erce \kȯ-'ərs\ *vb* **co·erced; co·erc·ing 1** : RESTRAIN, REPRESS **2** : COMPEL **3** : ENFORCE — **co·er·cion** \-'ər-zhən, -shən\ *n* — **co·er·cive** \-'ər-siv\ *adj*

co·e·val \kȯ-'ē-vəl\ *adj* : of the same age — **coeval** *n*

co·ex·ist \₁kȯ-ig-'zist\ *vb* **1** : to exist together or at the same time **2** : to live in peace with each other — **co·ex·is·tence** \-'zis-təns\ *n*

co·ex·ten·sive \₁kȯ-ik-'sten-siv\ *adj* : having the same scope or extent in space or time

C of C *abbr* Chamber of Commerce

cof·fee \'kȯ-fē\ *n* [It & Turk; It *caffè*, fr. Turk *kahve*, fr. Ar *qahwa*] : a drink made from the roasted and ground seeds of a fruit of a tropical shrub or tree; *also* : these seeds (**coffee beans**) or a plant producing them

cof·fee·house \-₁haús\ *n* : a place where refreshments (as coffee) are sold

coffee klatch \-₁klach\ *n* : KAFFEE-KLATSCH

cof·fee·pot \-₁pät\ *n* : a pot for brewing or serving coffee

coffee shop *n* : a small restaurant

coffee table *n* : a low table customarily placed in front of a sofa

cof·fer \'kȯ-fər\ *n* : a chest or box used esp. for valuables

cof·fer·dam \-₁dam\ *n* : a watertight enclosure from which water is pumped to expose the bottom of a body of water and permit construction

cof·fin \'kȯ-fən\ *n* : a box or chest for a corpse to be buried in

C of S *abbr* chief of staff

¹cog \'käg\ *n* : a tooth on the rim of a wheel or gear — **cogged** \'kägd\ *adj*

²cog *abbr* cognate

co·gen·er·a·tion \₁kȯ-₁je-nə-'rā-shən\ *n* : the simultaneous generation of electricity and heat from the same fuel

co·gent \'kȯ-jənt\ *adj* : having power to compel or constrain : CONVINCING — **co·gen·cy** \-jən-sē\ *n*

cog·i·tate \'kä-jə-₁tāt\ *vb* **-tat·ed; -tat·ing** : THINK, PONDER — **cog·i·ta·tion** \₁kä-jə-'tā-shən\ *n* — **cog·i·ta·tive** \'kä-jə-₁tā-tiv\ *adj*

co·gnac \'kȯn-₁yak\ *n* : a French brandy

cog·nate \'käg-₁nāt\ *adj* **1** : of the same or similar nature **2** : RELATED; *esp* : related by descent from the same ancestral language — **cognate** *n*

cog·ni·tive \'käg-nə-tiv\ *adj* : of, relating to, or being conscious mental activity (as thinking, remembering, learning, or using language) — **cog·ni·tion** \käg-'ni-shən\ *n*

cog·ni·zance \'käg-nə-zəns\ *n* **1** : apprehension by the mind : AWARENESS **2** : NOTICE, HEED — **cog·ni·zant** \'käg-nə-zənt\ *adj*

cog·no·men \käg-'nō-mən, 'käg-nə-\ *n, pl* **cognomens** *or* **cog·no·mi·na** \käg-'nä-mə-nə, -'nō-\ : NAME; *esp* : NICKNAME

co·gno·scen·te \₁kän-yə-'shen-tē\ *n, pl* **-scen·ti** \-tē\ [obs. It] : CONNOISSEUR

cog·wheel \'käg-₁hwēl\ *n* : a wheel with cogs or teeth

co·hab·it \kȯ-'ha-bət\ *vb* : to live together as husband and wife — **co·hab·i·ta·tion** \-₁ha-bə-'tā-shən\ *n*

co·here \kȯ-'hir\ *vb* **co·hered; co·her·ing** : to stick together

co·her·ent \kȯ-'hir-ənt\ *adj* **1** : having the quality of cohering **2** : logically consistent — **co·her·ence** \-əns\ *n* — **co·her·ent·ly** *adv*

co·he·sion \kȯ-'hē-zhən\ *n* **1** : a sticking together **2** : molecular attraction by which the particles of a body are united — **co·he·sive** \-siv\ *adj* — **co·he·sive·ly** *adv* — **co·he·sive·ness** *n*

co·ho \'kȯ-₁hȯ\ *n, pl* **cohos** *or* **coho** : a rather small Pacific salmon with light-colored flesh

co·hort \'kȯ-₁hȯrt\ *n* **1** : a group of warriors or followers **2** : COMPANION, ACCOMPLICE

coif \'kȯif; **2** *usu* 'kwäf\ *n* **1** : a close-fitting hat **2** : COIFFURE

coif·feur \kwä-'fər\ *n* [F] : HAIRDRESSER

coif·feuse \kwä-'fərz, -'fəz, -'füz, -'fyüz\ *n* : a female hairdresser

coif·fure \kwä-'fyúr\ *n* : a manner of arranging the hair

¹coil \'kȯil\ *vb* : to wind in a spiral shape

²coil *n* : a series of rings or loops (as of coiled rope, wire, or pipe) : RING, LOOP

¹coin \'kȯin\ *n* [ME, fr. MF, wedge, corner, fr. L *cuneus* wedge] **1** : a piece of metal issued by government authority as money **2** : metal money

²coin *vb* **1** : to make (a coin) esp. by stamping : MINT **2** : CREATE, INVENT ⟨∼ a phrase⟩ — **coin·er** *n*

coin·age \'kȯi-nij\ *n* **1** : the act or process of coining **2** : COINS

co·in·cide \₁kȯ-ən-'sīd, 'kȯ-ən-₁sīd\ *vb* **-cid·ed; -cid·ing 1** : to occupy the same place in space or time **2** : to correspond or agree exactly

co·in·ci·dence \kȯ-'in-sə-dəns\ *n* **1** : exact agreement **2** : occurrence together apparently without reason; *also* : an event that so occurs

co·in·ci·dent \-sə-dənt\ *adj* **1** : of similar nature **2** : occupying the same space or time — **co·in·ci·den·tal** \kȯ-₁in-sə-'dent-ᵊl\ *adj*

co·i·tus \'kȯ-ə-təs\ *n* [L, fr. *coire* to come together] : SEXUAL INTERCOURSE — **co·i·tal** \-ᵊl\ *adj*

¹coke \'kȯk\ *n* : a hard gray porous fuel made by heating soft coal to drive off most of its volatile material

²coke *n* : COCAINE

¹col *abbr* **1** colonial; colony **2** column

²col *or* **coll** *abbr* **1** collect, collected, collection **2** college, collegiate

Col *abbr* **1** colonel **2** Colorado **3** Colossians

COL *abbr* **1** colonel **2** cost of living

co·la \'kȯ-lə\ *n* : a carbonated soft drink usu. containing sugar, caffeine, caramel, and special flavoring

col·an·der \'kə-lən-dər, 'kä-\ *n* : a perforated utensil for draining food

¹cold \'kȯld\ *adj* **1** : having a low or decidedly subnormal temperature **2** : lacking warmth of feeling **3** : suffering or uncomfortable from lack of warmth — **cold·ly** *adv* — **cold·ness** *n* — **in cold blood** : with premeditation : DELIBERATELY

²cold *n* **1** : a condition marked by low temperature; *also* : cold weather **2** : a chilly feeling **3** : a bodily disorder popularly associated with chilling; *esp* : COMMON COLD

³cold *adv* : TOTALLY, FINALLY

cold–blood·ed \'kȯld-'blə-dəd\ *adj* **1** : lacking normal human feelings **2** : having a body temperature not internally regulated but close to that of the environment **3** : sensitive to cold

cold feet *n pl* : doubt or fear that prevents action

cold front *n* : an advancing edge of a cold air mass

cold shoulder *n* : cold or unsympathetic behavior — **cold–shoul·der** *vb*

cold sore *n* : a group of blisters appearing in or about the mouth in the oral form of herpes simplex

cold sweat *n* : concurrent perspiration and chill usu. associated with fear, pain, or shock

¹cold turkey *n* : abrupt complete cessation of the use of an addictive drug

²cold turkey *adv* : without a period of adjustment : all at once

cold war *n* : a conflict characterized by the use of means short of sustained overt military action

cole·slaw \'kōl-ˌslȯ\ *n* [D *koolsla,* fr. *kool* cabbage + *sla* salad] : a salad made of raw cabbage

col·ic \'kä-lik\ *n* : sharp sudden abdominal pain — **col·icky** \'kä-li-kē\ *adj*

col·i·se·um \ˌkä-lə-'sē-əm\ *n* : a large structure esp. for athletic contests

col·lab·o·rate \kə-'la-bə-ˌrāt\ *vb* **-rat·ed; -rat·ing 1** : to work jointly with others (as in writing a book) **2** : to co-operate with an enemy force occupying one's country — **col·lab·o·ra·tion** \-ˌla-bə-'rā-shən\ *n* — **col·lab·o·ra·tor** \-'la-bə-ˌrā-tər\ *n*

col·lage \kə-'läzh\ *n* [F, lit., gluing] : an artistic composition of fragments (as of printed matter) pasted on a surface

¹col·lapse \kə-'laps\ *vb* **col·lapsed; col·laps·ing 1** : to shrink together abruptly **2** : DISINTEGRATE; *also* : to fall in : give way **3** : to break down physically or mentally; *esp* : to fall helpless or unconscious **4** : to fold down compactly — **col·laps·ible** *adj*

²collapse *n* : BREAKDOWN

¹col·lar \'kä-lər\ *n* **1** : a band, strip, or chain worn around the neck or the neckline of a garment **2** : something resembling a collar — **col·lar·less** *adj*

²collar *vb* : to seize by the collar; *also* : ARREST, GRAB

col·lar·bone \-ˌbȯn\ *n* : the bone of the shoulder that joins the breastbone and the shoulder blade

col·lard \'kä-lərd\ *n* : a stalked smooth-leaved kale — usu. used in pl.

col·late \kə-'lāt; 'kä-ˌlāt, 'kȯ-\ *vb* **col·lat·ed; col·lat·ing 1** : to compare (as two texts) carefully and critically **2** : to assemble in proper order

¹col·lat·er·al \kə-'la-tə-rəl\ *adj* **1** : associated but of secondary importance **2** : descended from the same ancestors but not in the same line **3** : PARALLEL **4** : of, relating to, or being collateral used as security; *also* : secured by collateral

²collateral *n* : property (as stocks) used as security for the repayment of a loan

col·la·tion \kä-'lā-shən, kȯ-\ *n* **1** : a light meal **2** : the act, process, or result of collating

col·league \'kä-ˌlēg\ *n* : an associate esp. in a profession

¹col·lect \'kä-likt, -ˌlekt\ *n* : a short prayer comprising an invocation, petition, and conclusion

²col·lect \kə-'lekt\ *vb* **1** : to bring or come together into one body or place : GATHER **2** : to gain control of ⟨∼ his thoughts⟩ **3** : to receive payment of — **col·lect·ible** *or* **col·lect·able** *adj or n* — **col·lec·tor** \-'lek-tər\ *n*

³col·lect \kə-'lekt\ *adv or adj* : to be paid for by the receiver

col·lect·ed \kə-'lek-təd\ *adj* : SELF-POSSESSED, CALM

col·lec·tion \kə-'lek-shən\ *n* **1** : the act or process of collecting ⟨garbage ∼⟩ **2** : something collected ⟨a stamp ∼⟩ **3** : GROUP, AGGREGATE

¹col·lec·tive \kə-'lek-tiv\ *adj* **1** : of, relating to, or denoting a group of individuals considered as a whole **2** : involving all members of a group as distinct from its

individuals **3** : shared or assumed by all members of the group — **col·lec·tive·ly** *adv*

²collective *n* **1** : GROUP **2** : a cooperative unit or organization

collective bargaining *n* : negotiation between an employer and a labor union

col·lec·tiv·ism \kə-'lek-ti-ˌvi-zəm\ *n* : a political or economic theory advocating collective control esp. over production and distribution

col·lec·tiv·ize \-ˌvīz\ *vb* **-ized; -iz·ing** : to organize under collective control — **col·lec·tiv·i·za·tion** \-ˌlek-ti-və-'zā-shən\ *n*

col·leen \kä-'lēn, 'kä-ˌlēn\ *n* : an Irish girl

col·lege \'kä-lij\ *n* [ME, fr. MF, fr. L *collegium* society, fr. *collega* colleague, fr. *com-* with + *legare* to appoint] **1** : a building used for an educational or religious purpose **2** : an institution of higher learning granting a bachelor's degree; *also* : an institution offering instruction esp. in a vocational or technical field ⟨barber ∼⟩ **3** : an organized body of persons having common interests or duties ⟨∼ of cardinals⟩ — **col·le·giate** \kə-'lē-jət\ *adj*

col·le·gi·al·i·ty \kə-ˌlē-jē-'a-lə-tē\ *n* : the relationship of colleagues

col·le·gian \kə-'lē-jən\ *n* : a college student or recent college graduate

col·le·gi·um \kə-'le-gē-əm, -'lā-\ *n, pl* **-gia** \-gē-ə\ *or* **-giums** : a group in which each member has approximately equal power

col·lide \kə-'līd\ *vb* **col·lid·ed; col·lid·ing 1** : to come together with solid impact **2** : to come into conflict : CLASH

col·lid·er \kə-'lī-dər\ *n* : a particle accelerator in which two beams of particles are made to collide

col·lie \'kä-lē\ *n* : a large dog of a breed with rough-coated and smooth-coated varieties developed in Scotland for herding sheep

collie

col·lier \'käl-yər\ *n* **1** : a coal miner **2** : a ship for carrying coal

col·liery \'käl-yə-rē\ *n, pl* **-lier·ies** : a coal mine and its associated buildings

col·li·mate \'kä-lə-ˌmāt\ *vb* **-mat·ed; -mat·ing** : to make (as light rays) parallel

col·li·sion \kə-'li-zhən\ *n* : an act or instance of colliding

col·lo·ca·tion \ˌkä-lə-'kā-shən\ *n* : the act or result of placing or arranging together; *esp* : a noticeable arrangement or conjoining of linguistic elements (as words)

\ə\abut \ᵊ\kitten \ər\further \a\ash \ā\ace \ä\mop, mar \au̇\out \ch\chin \e\bet \ē\easy \g\go \i\hit \ī\ice \j\job \ŋ\sing \ō\go \ȯ\law \ȯi\boy \th\thin \t̲h̲\the \ü\loot \u̇\foot \y\yet \zh\vision *see also* Pronunciation Symbols page

col·loid \'kä-ˌlȯid\ *n* : a substance in the form of submicroscopic particles that when in solution or suspension do not settle out; *also* : such a substance together with the medium in which it is dispersed — **col·loi·dal** \kə-'lȯid-ºl\ *adj*

colloq *abbr* colloquial

col·lo·qui·al \kə-'lō-kwē-əl\ *adj* : of, relating to, or characteristic of conversation and esp. of familiar and informal conversation

col·lo·qui·al·ism \-'lō-kwē-ə-ˌli-zəm\ *n* : a colloquial expression

col·lo·qui·um \kə-'lō-kwē-əm\ *n, pl* **-qui·ums** *or* **-quia** \-ə\ : CONFERENCE, SEMINAR

col·lo·quy \'kä-lə-kwē\ *n, pl* **-quies** : a usu. formal conversation or conference

col·lu·sion \kə-'lü-zhən\ *n* : secret agreement or cooperation for an illegal or deceitful purpose — **col·lu·sive** \-siv\ *adj*

Colo *abbr* Colorado

co·logne \kə-'lōn\ *n* [*Cologne*, Germany] : a perfumed liquid — **co·logned** \-'lōnd\ *adj*

Co·lom·bi·an \kə-'läm-bē-ən\ *n* : a native or inhabitant of Colombia — **Colombian** *adj*

¹co·lon \'kō-lən\ *n, pl* **colons** *or* **co·la** \-lə\ : the part of the large intestine extending from the cecum to the rectum — **co·lon·ic** \kō-'lä-nik\ *adj*

²colon *n, pl* **colons** : a punctuation mark : used esp. to direct attention to following matter (as a list)

co·lón *also* **co·lone** \kə-'lōn\ *n, pl* **co·lo·nes** \-'lō-ˌnäs\ — see MONEY table

col·o·nel \'kərn-ºl\ *n* [alter. of *coronel*, fr. MF, fr. It *colonnello* column of soldiers, colonel, ultim. fr. L *columna*] : a commissioned officer (as in the army) ranking next below a brigadier general

¹co·lo·nial \kə-'lō-nē-əl\ *adj* 1 : of, relating to, or characteristic of a colony; *also* : possessing or composed of colonies 2 *often cap* : of or relating to the original 13 colonies forming the U.S.

²colonial *n* : a member or inhabitant of a colony

co·lo·nial·ism \-ə-ˌli-zəm\ *n* : control by one power over a dependent area or people; *also* : a policy advocating or based on such control — **co·lo·nial·ist** \-list\ *n or adj*

col·o·nist \'kä-lə-nist\ *n* 1 : COLONIAL 2 : one that colonizes or settles in a new country

col·o·nize \'kä-lə-ˌnīz\ *vb* **-nized; -niz·ing** 1 : to establish a colony in or on 2 : SETTLE — **col·o·ni·za·tion** \ˌkä-lə-nə-'zā-shən\ *n* — **col·o·niz·er** *n*

col·on·nade \ˌkä-lə-'nād\ *n* : an evenly spaced row of columns usu. supporting the base of a roof structure

col·o·ny \'kä-lə-nē\ *n, pl* **-nies** 1 : a body of people living in a new territory; *also* : the territory inhabited by these people 2 : a localized population of organisms ⟨a ∼ of bees⟩ 3 : a group with common interests situated in close association ⟨a writers' ∼⟩; *also* : the area occupied by such a group

col·o·phon \'kä-lə-fən, -ˌfän\ *n* 1 : an inscription placed at the end of a book with facts relative to its production 2 : a distinctive symbol used by a printer or publisher

¹col·or \'kə-lər\ *n* 1 : a phenomenon of light (as red or blue) or visual perception that enables one to differentiate otherwise identical objects; *also* : a hue as contrasted with black, white, or gray 2 : APPEARANCE 3 : complexion tint 4 *pl* : FLAG; *also* : military service ⟨a call to the ∼*s*⟩ 5 : VIVIDNESS, INTEREST — **col·or·ful** *adj* — **col·or·less** *adj*

²color *vb* 1 : to give color to; *also* : to change the color of 2 : BLUSH

Col·o·ra·do potato beetle \ˌkä-lə-'ra-dō-, -'rä-\ *n* : a black-and-yellow striped beetle that feeds on the leaves of the potato

col·or·ation \ˌkə-lə-'rā-shən\ *n* : use or arrangement of colors

col·or·a·tu·ra \ˌkə-lə-rə-'tür-ə, -'tyür-\ *n* 1 : elaborate ornamentation in vocal music 2 : a soprano specializing in coloratura

col·or–blind \'kə-lər-ˌblīnd\ *adj* 1 : partially or totally unable to distinguish one or more chromatic colors 2 : not recognizing differences of race — **color blindness** *n*

col·ored \'kə-lərd\ *adj* 1 : having color 2 : SLANTED, BIASED 3 : of a race other than the white; *esp* : BLACK 4 — sometimes taken to be offensive

col·or·fast \'kə-lər-ˌfast\ *adj* : having color that does not fade or run — **col·or·fast·ness** *n*

co·los·sal \kə-'lä-səl\ *adj* : of very great size or degree

Co·los·sians \kə-'lä-shənz\ *n* — see BIBLE table

co·los·sus \kə-'lä-səs\ *n, pl* **co·los·si** \-ˌsī\ [L] : a gigantic statue; *also* : something of great size or scope

col·our *chiefly Brit var of* COLOR

col·por·teur \'käl-ˌpȯr-tər\ *n* [F] : a peddler of religious books

colt \'kōlt\ *n* : FOAL; *also* : a young male horse, ass, or zebra — **colt·ish** *adj*

col·um·bine \'kä-ləm-ˌbīn\ *n* [ME, fr. ML *columbina*, fr. L, fem. of *columbinus* dovelike, fr. *columba* dove] : any of a genus of plants with showy spurred flowers that are related to the buttercups

co·lum·bi·um \kə-'ləm-bē-əm\ *n* : NIOBIUM

Columbus Day \kə-'ləm-bəs-\ *n* : the 2d Monday in October or formerly October 12 observed as a legal holiday in many states in commemoration of the landing of Columbus

col·umn \'kä-ləm\ *n* 1 : one of two or more vertical sections of a printed page; *also* : one in a usu. regular series of articles (as in a newspaper) 2 : a supporting pillar; *esp* : one consisting of a usu. round shaft, a capital, and a base 3 : something resembling a column ⟨∼ of water⟩ 4 : a long row (as of soldiers) — **co·lum·nar** \kə-'ləm-nər\ *adj*

col·um·nist \'kä-ləm-nist\ *n* : a person who writes a newspaper or magazine column

com *abbr* 1 comedy; comic 2 comma

co·ma \'kō-mə\ *n* : a state of deep unconsciousness caused by disease, injury, or poison — **co·ma·tose** \'kō-mə-ˌtōs, 'kä-\ *adj*

Co·man·che \kə-'man-chē\ *n, pl* **Comanche** *or* **Comanches** : a member of an American Indian people ranging from Wyoming and Nebraska south into New Mexico and Texas

¹comb \'kōm\ *n* 1 : a toothed instrument for arranging the hair or for separating and cleaning textile fibers 2 : a fleshy crest on the head of a fowl 3 : HONEYCOMB — **comb** *vb* — **combed** \'kōmd\ *adj*

²comb *abbr* combination; combining

com·bat \kəm-'bat, 'käm-ˌbat\ *vb* **-bat·ed** *or* **-bat·ted; -bat·ing** *or* **-bat·ting** 1 : FIGHT, CONTEND 2 : to struggle against : OPPOSE — **com·bat** \'käm-ˌbat\ *n* — **com·bat·ant** \kəm-'bat-ºnt, 'käm-bə-tənt\ *n* — **com·bat·ive** \kəm-'ba-tiv\ *adj*

combat fatigue *n* : a traumatic neurotic or psychotic reaction occurring under conditions (as wartime combat) that cause intense stress

comb·er \'kō-mər\ *n* 1 : one that combs 2 : a long curling wave of the sea

com·bi·na·tion \ˌkäm-bə-'nā-shən\ *n* 1 : a result or product of combining 2 : a sequence of letters or numbers chosen in setting a lock 3 : the act or process of combining; *also* : the quality or state of being combined

¹com·bine \kəm-'bīn\ *vb* **com·bined; com·bin·ing** : to become one : UNITE

²com·bine \'käm-ˌbīn\ *n* 1 : a combination esp. of business or political interests 2 : a machine that harvests and threshes grain while moving over a field

comb·ings \'kō-miŋz\ *n pl* : loose hairs or fibers removed by a comb

combining form *n* : a linguistic form that occurs only in compounds or derivatives

com·bo \'käm-bò\ *n, pl* **combos** : a small jazz or dance band

com·bus·ti·ble \kəm-'bəs-tə-bəl\ *adj* : capable of being burned — **com·bus·ti·bil·i·ty** \-ˌbəs-tə-'bi-lə-tē\ *n* — **combustible** *n*

com·bus·tion \kəm-'bəs-chən\ *n* 1 : an act or instance of burning 2 : slow oxidation (as in the animal body)

comdg *abbr* commanding

comdr *abbr* commander

comdt *abbr* commandant

come \'kəm\ *vb* **came** \'käm\; **come; com·ing** \'kə-miŋ\ 1 : APPROACH 2 : ARRIVE 3 : to reach the point of being or becoming ⟨∼ to a boil⟩ 4 : AMOUNT ⟨the bill *came* to $10⟩ 5 : to take place 6 : ORIGINATE, ARISE 7 : to be available 8 : REACH, EXTEND — **come clean** : CONFESS — **come into** : ACQUIRE, ACHIEVE — **come to pass** : HAPPEN — **come to terms** : to reach an agreement

come·back \'kəm-ˌbak\ *n* 1 : RETORT 2 : a return to a former position or condition — **come back** *vb*

co·me·di·an \kə-'mē-dē-ən\ *n* 1 : an actor in comedy 2 : a comic person; *esp* : an entertainer specializing in comedy

co·me·di·enne \-ˌmē-dē-'en\ *n* : a woman who is a comedian

come·down \'kəm-ˌdaùn\ *n* : a descent in rank or dignity

com·e·dy \'kä-mə-dē\ *n, pl* **-dies** [ME, fr. MF *comedie*, fr. L *comoedia*, fr. Gk *kōmòidia*, fr. *kòmos* revel + *aeidein* to sing] 1 : a light amusing play with a happy ending 2 : a literary work treating a comic theme or written in a comic style 3 : humorous entertainment

come·ly \'kəm-lē\ *adj* **come·li·er; -est** : ATTRACTIVE, HANDSOME — **come·li·ness** *n*

come off *vb* : SUCCEED

come-on \'kə-ˌmòn, -ˌmän\ *n* : INDUCEMENT, LURE

come out *vb* 1 : to come into public view 2 : to declare oneself 3 : TURN OUT 5 ⟨everything *came* out all right⟩ — **come out with** : SAY 1

com·er \'kə-mər\ *n* 1 : one that comes ⟨all ∼s⟩ 2 : a promising beginner

¹co·mes·ti·ble \kə-'mes-tə-bəl\ *adj* : EDIBLE

²comestible *n* : FOOD — usu. used in pl.

com·et \'kä-mət\ *n* [ME *comete*, fr. OE *cometa*, fr. L, fr. Gk *komētēs*, lit., long-haired, fr. *komē* hair] : a small bright celestial body that develops a long tail when near the sun

come to *vb* : to regain consciousness

come·up·pance \kə-'mə-pəns\ *n* : a deserved rebuke or penalty

com·fit \'kəm-fət\ *n* : a candied fruit or nut

¹com·fort \'kəm-fərt\ *vb* 1 : to give strength and hope to 2 : CONSOLE

²comfort *n* 1 : CONSOLATION 2 : freedom from pain, trouble, or anxiety; *also* : something that gives such freedom

com·fort·able \'kəm-fər-tə-bəl, 'kəmf-tər-\ *adj* 1 : providing comfort or security 2 : feeling at ease — **com·fort·ably** \-blē\ *adv*

com·fort·er \'kəm-fər-tər\ *n* 1 : one that comforts 2 : QUILT

com·fy \'kəm-fē\ *adj* : COMFORTABLE

¹com·ic \'kä-mik\ *adj* 1 : relating to comedy or comic strips 2 : provoking laughter or amusement **syn** laughable, funny, farcical — **com·i·cal** *adj*

²comic *n* 1 : COMEDIAN 2 *pl* : the part of a newspaper devoted to comic strips

comic book *n* : a magazine containing sequences of comic strips

comic strip *n* : a group of cartoons in narrative sequence

coming \'kə-miŋ\ *adj* 1 : APPROACHING, NEXT 2 : gaining importance

co·mi·ty \'kä-mə-tē, 'kò-\ *n, pl* **-ties** : friendly civility : COURTESY

coml *abbr* commercial

comm *abbr* 1 command; commander 2 commerce; commercial 3 commission; commissioner 4 committee 5 common 6 commonwealth

com·ma \'kä-mə\ *n* : a punctuation mark , used esp. as a mark of separation within the sentence

¹com·mand \kə-'mand\ *vb* 1 : to direct authoritatively : ORDER 2 : DOMINATE, CONTROL, GOVERN 3 : to overlook from a strategic position

²command *n* 1 : an order given 2 : ability to control : MASTERY 3 : the act of commanding 4 : a signal that actuates a device (as a computer); *also* : the activation of a device by means of a signal 5 : a body of troops under a commander; *also* : an area or position that one commands 6 : a position of highest authority

com·man·dant \'kä-mən-ˌdant, -ˌdänt\ *n* : an officer in command

com·man·deer \ˌkä-mən-'dir\ *vb* : to take possession of by force

com·mand·er \kə-'man-dər\ *n* 1 : LEADER, CHIEF; *esp* : an officer commanding an army or subdivision of an army 2 : a commissioned officer in the navy ranking next below a captain

commander in chief : the supreme commander of the armed forces

com·mand·ment \kə-'mand-mənt\ *n* : COMMAND, ORDER; *esp* : any of the Ten Commandments

command module *n* : a space vehicle module designed to carry the crew and reentry equipment

com·man·do \kə-'man-dò\ *n, pl* **-dos** *or* **-does** [Afrikaans *kommando*, fr. Dutch *commando* command] : a member of a military unit trained for surprise raids

command sergeant major *n* : a noncommissioned officer in the army ranking above a first sergeant

com·mem·o·rate \kə-'me-mə-ˌrāt\ *vb* **-rat·ed; -rat·ing** 1 : to call or recall to mind 2 : to serve as a memorial of — **com·mem·o·ra·tion** \-ˌme-mə-'rā-shən\ *n*

com·mem·o·ra·tive \kə-'mem-rə-tiv, -'me-mə-ˌrā-tiv\ *adj* : intended to commemorate an event

com·mence \kə-'mens\ *vb* **com·menced; com·menc·ing** : BEGIN, START

com·mence·ment \-mənt\ *n* 1 : the act or time of a beginning 2 : the graduation exercises of a school or college

com·mend \kə-'mend\ *vb* 1 : to commit to one's care 2 : RECOMMEND 3 : PRAISE — **com·mend·able** \-'men-də-bəl\ *adj* — **com·mend·ably** \-blē\ *adv* — **com·men·da·tion** \ˌkä-mən-'dā-shən, -ˌmen-\ *n* — **com·mend·er** *n*

com·men·su·ra·ble \kə-'men-sə-rə-bəl\ *adj* : having a common measure or a common divisor

com·men·su·rate \kə-'men-sə-rət, -'men-chə-\ *adj* : equal in measure or extent; *also* : PROPORTIONAL, CORRESPONDING ⟨a job ∼ with her abilities⟩

com·ment \'kä-ˌment\ *n* 1 : an expression of opinion 2 : an explanatory, illustrative, or critical note or observation : REMARK — **comment** *vb*

com·men·tary \'kä-mən-ˌter-ē\ *n, pl* **-tar·ies** : a systematic series of comments

com·men·ta·tor \-ˌtā-tər\ *n* : one who comments; *esp* : a person who discusses news events on radio or television

com·merce \'kä-(ˌ)mərs\ *n* : the buying and selling of commodities : TRADE

¹com·mer·cial \kə-'mər-shəl\ *adj* : having to do with

\ə\abut \ᵊ\kitten \ər\further \a\ash \ā\ace \ä\mop, mar \aù\out \ch\chin \e\bet \ē\easy \g\go \i\hit \ī\ice \j\job \ŋ\sing \ō\go \ò\law \òi\boy \th\thin \t͟h\the \ü\loot \ù\foot \y\yet \zh\vision *see also* Pronunciation Symbols page

commerce; *also* : designed for profit or for mass appeal — **com·mer·cial·ly** *adv*

²commercial *n* : an advertisement broadcast on radio or television

com·mer·cial·ism \kə-ˈmər-shə-ˌli-zəm\ *n* **1** : a spirit, method, or practice characteristic of business **2** : excessive emphasis on profit

com·mer·cial·ize \-ˌlīz\ *vb* **-ized; -iz·ing 1** : to manage on a business basis for profit **2** : to exploit for profit

com·mi·na·tion \ˌkä-mə-ˈnā-shən\ *n* : DENUNCIATION — **com·mi·na·to·ry** \ˈkä-mə-nə-ˌtȯr-ē\ *adj*

com·min·gle \kə-ˈmiŋ-gəl\ *vb* : MINGLE, BLEND

com·mis·er·ate \kə-ˈmi-zə-ˌrāt\ *vb* **-at·ed; -at·ing** : to feel or express pity : SYMPATHIZE — **com·mis·er·a·tion** \-ˌmi-zə-ˈrā-shən\ *n*

com·mis·sar \ˈkä-mə-ˌsär\ *n* [Russ *komissar*] : a Communist party official

com·mis·sar·i·at \ˌkä-mə-ˈser-ē-ət\ *n* **1** : a system for supplying troops with food **2** : a department headed by a commissar

com·mis·sary \ˈkä-mə-ˌser-ē\ *n, pl* **-sar·ies** : a store for equipment and provisions esp. for military personnel

¹com·mis·sion \kə-ˈmi-shən\ *n* **1** : a warrant granting certain powers and imposing certain duties **2** : a certificate conferring military rank and authority **3** : authority to act as agent for another; *also* : something to be done by an agent **4** : a body of persons charged with performing a duty **5** : the doing of some act; *also* : the thing done **6** : the allowance made to an agent for transacting business for another

²commission *vb* **1** : to give a commission to **2** : to order to be made **3** : to put (a ship) into a state of readiness for service

commissioned officer *n* : an officer of the armed forces holding rank by a commission from the president

com·mis·sion·er \kə-ˈmi-shə-nər\ *n* **1** : a member of a commission **2** : an official in charge of a department of public service **3** : the administrative head of a professional sport — **com·mis·sion·er·ship** *n*

com·mit \kə-ˈmit\ *vb* **com·mit·ted; com·mit·ting 1** : to put into charge or trust : ENTRUST **2** : to put in a prison or mental institution **3** : TRANSFER, CONSIGN **4** : to carry into action : PERPETRATE ⟨∼ a crime⟩ **5** : to pledge or assign to some particular course or use — **com·mit·ment** *n* — **com·mit·tal** *n*

com·mit·tee \kə-ˈmi-tē\ *n* : a body of persons selected to consider and act or report on some matter — **com·mit·tee·man** \-mən\ *n* — **com·mit·tee·wom·an** \-ˌwu̇-mən\ *n*

commo *abbr* commodore

com·mode \kə-ˈmōd\ *n* [F, fr. *commode*, adj., suitable, convenient, fr. L *commodus*, fr. *com-* with + *modus* measure] **1** : a movable washstand with cupboard below **2** : TOILET 3

com·mo·di·ous \kə-ˈmō-dē-əs\ *adj* : comfortably spacious : ROOMY

com·mod·i·ty \kə-ˈmä-də-tē\ *n, pl* **-ties 1** : a product of agriculture or mining **2** : an article of commerce **3** : something useful or valued ⟨that valuable ∼ patience⟩

com·mo·dore \ˈkä-mə-ˌdȯr\ *n* **1** : a commissioned officer in the navy ranking next below a rear admiral **2** : an officer commanding a group of merchant ships **3** : the chief officer of a yacht club

¹com·mon \ˈkä-mən\ *adj* **1** : belonging to or serving the community : PUBLIC **2** : shared by a number in a group **3** : widely or generally known, found, or observed : FAMILIAR ⟨∼ knowledge⟩ **4** : VERNACULAR 3 ⟨∼ names of plants⟩ **5** : not above the average esp. in social status **syn** universal, general, generic — **com·mon·ly** *adv*

²common *n* **1** *pl* : the common people **2** *pl* : a dining hall **3** *pl, cap* : the lower house of the British and Canadian parliaments **4** : a piece of land subject to common use — **in common** : shared together

com·mon·al·ty \ˈkä-mən-ᵊl-tē\ *n, pl* **-ties** : the common people

common cold *n* : a contagious respiratory disease caused by a virus and characterized by a sore, swollen, and inflamed nose and throat, usu. by much mucus, and by coughing and sneezing

common denominator *n* **1** : a common multiple of the denominators of a number of fractions **2** : a common trait or theme

common divisor *n* : a number or expression that divides two or more numbers or expressions without remainder

com·mon·er \ˈkä-mə-nər\ *n* : one of the common people : a person having no rank of nobility

common fraction *n* : a fraction in which the numerator and denominator are both integers and are separated by a horizontal or slanted line

common law *n* : a group of legal practices and traditions based on judges' decisions and social customs and usu. having the same force as laws passed by legislative bodies

common logarithm *n* : a logarithm whose base is 10

common market *n* : an economic association formed to remove trade barriers among members

common multiple *n* : a multiple of each of two or more numbers or expressions

¹com·mon·place \ˈkä-mən-ˌplās\ *n* : something that is ordinary or trite

²commonplace *adj* : ORDINARY

common sense *n* : ordinary good sense and judgment

common stock *n* : stock of a corporation other than preferred stock

com·mon·weal \ˈkä-mən-ˌwēl\ *n* **1** *archaic* : COMMONWEALTH **2** : the general welfare

com·mon·wealth \-ˌwelth\ *n* **1** : the body of people politically organized into a state **2** : STATE; *also* : an association or federation of autonomous states

com·mo·tion \kə-ˈmō-shən\ *n* **1** : DISTURBANCE, UPRISING **2** : AGITATION

com·mu·nal \kə-ˈmyün-ᵊl, ˈkäm-yən-ᵊl\ *adj* **1** : of or relating to a commune or community **2** : marked by collective ownership and use of property **3** : shared or used in common

¹com·mune \kə-ˈmyün\ *vb* **com·muned; com·mun·ing** : to communicate intimately

²com·mune \ˈkäm-ˌyün; kə-ˈmyün\ *n* **1** : the smallest administrative district in some European countries **2** : a community organized on a communal basis

com·mu·ni·ca·ble \kə-ˈmyü-ni-kə-bəl\ *adj* : capable of being communicated ⟨∼ diseases⟩ — **com·mu·ni·ca·bil·i·ty** \-ˌmyü-ni-kə-ˈbi-lə-tē\ *n*

com·mu·ni·cant \-ˈmyü-ni-kənt\ *n* **1** : a church member entitled to receive Communion **2** : one that communicates; *esp* : INFORMANT

com·mu·ni·cate \kə-ˈmyü-nə-ˌkāt\ *vb* **-cat·ed; -cat·ing 1** : to make known **2** : to pass from one to another : TRANSMIT **3** : to receive Communion **4** : to be in communication **5** : JOIN, CONNECT

com·mu·ni·ca·tion \kə-ˌmyü-nə-ˈkā-shən\ *n* **1** : an act of transmitting **2** : MESSAGE **3** : exchange of information or opinions **4** : a means of communicating — **com·mu·ni·ca·tive** \-ˈmyü-nə-ˌkā-tiv, -ni-kə-tiv\ *adj*

com·mu·nion \kə-ˈmyü-nyən\ *n* **1** : a sharing of something with others **2** *cap* : a Christian sacrament in which bread and wine are consumed as the substance or symbols of Christ's body and blood in commemoration of the death of Christ **3** : intimate fellowship or rapport **4** : a body of Christians having a common faith and discipline

com·mu·ni·qué \kə-ˈmyü-nə-ˌkā, -ˌmyü-nə-ˈkā\ *n* : BULLETIN 1

com·mu·nism \ˈkäm-yə-ˌni-zəm\ *n* **1** : social organization in which goods are held in common **2** : a theory of social organization advocating common ownership of means of production and a distribution of products of industry based on need **3** *cap* : a political doctrine based on revolutionary Marxist socialism that was the official ideology of the U.S.S.R. and some other countries; *also* : a system of government in which one party controls state-owned means of production — **com·mu·nist** \-nist\ *n or adj, often cap* — **com·mu·nis·tic** \ˌkäm-yə-'nis-tik\ *adj, often cap*

com·mu·ni·ty \kə-'myü-nə-tē\ *n, pl* **-ties 1** : a body of people living in the same place under the same laws; *also* : a natural population of plants and animals that interact ecologically and live in one place (as a pond) **2** : society at large **3** : joint ownership **4** : SIMILARITY, LIKENESS

community college *n* : a 2-year government-supported college that offers an associate degree

community property *n* : property held jointly by husband and wife

com·mu·ta·tion \ˌkäm-yə-'tā-shən\ *n* : substitution of one form of payment or penalty for another

com·mu·ta·tive \'käm-yə-ˌtā-tiv, kə-'myü-tə-\ *adj* : of, relating to, having, or being the property that a given mathematical operation and set have when the result obtained using any two elements of the set with the operation does not differ with the order in which the numbers are used — **com·mu·ta·tiv·i·ty** \kə-ˌmyü-tə-'ti-və-tē, ˌkäm-yə-tə-\ *n*

com·mu·ta·tor \'käm-yə-ˌtā-tər\ *n* : a device (as on a generator or motor) for changing the direction of electric current

¹com·mute \kə-'myüt\ *vb* **com·mut·ed; com·mut·ing 1** : EXCHANGE **2** : to revoke (a sentence) and impose a milder penalty **3** : to travel back and forth regularly — **com·mut·er** *n*

²commute *n* : a trip made in commuting

comp *abbr* **1** comparative; compare **2** compensation **3** compiled; compiler **4** composition; compositor **5** compound **6** comprehensive **7** comptroller

¹com·pact \kəm-'pakt, 'käm-ˌpakt\ *adj* **1** : SOLID, DENSE **2** : BRIEF, SUCCINCT **3** : occupying a small volume by efficient use of space ⟨~ camera⟩ — **com·pact·ly** *adv* — **com·pact·ness** *n*

²compact *vb* : to pack together : COMPRESS — **com·pac·tor** \kəm-'pak-tər, 'käm-ˌpak-\ *n*

³com·pact \'käm-ˌpakt\ *n* **1** : a small case for cosmetics **2** : a small automobile

⁴com·pact \'käm-ˌpakt\ *n* : AGREEMENT, COVENANT

com·pact disc \'käm-ˌpakt-\ *n* : a small plastic optical disc usu. containing recorded music

¹com·pan·ion \kəm-'pan-yən\ *n* [OF *compagnon*, fr. LL *companion-, companio*, fr. L *com-* together + *panis* bread] **1** : an intimate friend or associate : COMRADE **2** : one that is closely connected with something similar — **com·pan·ion·able** *adj* — **com·pan·ion·ship** *n*

²companion *n* : COMPANIONWAY

com·pan·ion·way \-ˌwā\ *n* : a ship's stairway from one deck to another

com·pa·ny \'kəm-pə-nē\ *n, pl* **-nies 1** : association with others : FELLOWSHIP; *also* : COMPANIONS **2** : GUESTS **3** : a group of persons or things **4** : an infantry unit consisting of two or more platoons and normally commanded by a captain **5** : a group of musical or dramatic performers **6** : the officers and crew of a ship **7** : an association of persons for carrying on a business **syn** party, band, troop, troupe, corps, outfit

com·pa·ra·ble \'käm-pə-rə-bəl, -prə-\ *adj* : capable of being compared **syn** parallel, similar, like, alike, corresponding — **com·pa·ra·bil·i·ty** \ˌkäm-pə-rə-'bi-lə-tē\ *n*

¹com·par·a·tive \kəm-'par-ə-tiv\ *adj* **1** : of, relating to, or constituting the degree of grammatical comparison that denotes increase in quality, quantity, or relation **2** : RELATIVE ⟨a ~ stranger⟩ — **com·par·a·tive·ly** *adv*

²comparative *n* : the comparative degree or form in a language

¹com·pare \kəm-'par\ *vb* **com·pared; com·par·ing 1** : to represent as similar : LIKEN **2** : to examine for likenesses and differences **3** : to inflect or modify (an adjective or adverb) according to the degrees of comparison

²compare *n* : the possibility of comparing ⟨beauty beyond ~⟩

com·par·i·son \kəm-'par-ə-sən\ *n* **1** : the act of comparing **2** : change in the form of an adjective or adverb to show different levels of quality, quantity, or relation

com·part·ment \kəm-'pärt-mənt\ *n* **1** : a separate division **2** : a section of an enclosed space : ROOM

com·part·men·tal·ize \kəm-ˌpärt-'ment-ᵊl-ˌīz\ *vb* **-ized; -iz·ing** : to separate into compartments

¹com·pass \'kəm-pəs, 'käm-\ *vb* [ME, fr. OF *compasser* to measure, fr. (assumed) VL *compassare* to pace off, fr. L *com-* + *passus* pace] **1** : CONTRIVE, PLOT **2** : ENCIRCLE, ENCOMPASS **3** : BRING ABOUT, ACHIEVE

²compass *n* **1** : BOUNDARY, CIRCUMFERENCE **2** : an enclosed space **3** : RANGE, SCOPE **4** : a device for determining direction by means of a magnetic needle swinging freely and pointing to the magnetic north; *also* : a nonmagnetic device that indicates direction **5** : an instrument for drawing circles or transferring measurements consisting of two legs joined by a pivot

com·pas·sion \kəm-'pa-shən\ *n* : sympathetic feeling : PITY, MERCY — **com·pas·sion·ate** \-shə-nət\ *adj* — **com·pas·sion·ate·ly** *adv*

com·pat·i·ble \kəm-'pa-tə-bəl\ *adj* : able to exist or act together harmoniously ⟨~ colors⟩ ⟨~ drugs⟩ **syn** consonant, congenial, sympathetic — **com·pat·i·bil·i·ty** \-ˌpa-tə-'bi-lə-tē\ *n*

com·pa·tri·ot \kəm-'pā-trē-ət, -ˌät\ *n* : a fellow countryman

com·peer \'käm-ˌpir\ *n* : EQUAL, PEER

com·pel \kəm-'pel\ *vb* **com·pelled; com·pel·ling** : to drive or urge with force

com·pen·di·ous \kəm-'pen-dē-əs\ *adj* : concise and comprehensive; *also* : COMPREHENSIVE

com·pen·di·um \kəm-'pen-dē-əm\ *n, pl* **-di·ums** *or* **-dia** \-ə\ **1** : a brief summary of a larger work or of a field of knowledge **2** : COLLECTION

com·pen·sate \'käm-pən-ˌsāt\ *vb* **-sat·ed; -sat·ing 1** : to be equivalent to : make up for **2** : PAY, REMUNERATE **syn** balance, offset, counterbalance, counterpoise — **com·pen·sa·tion** \ˌkäm-pən-'sā-shən\ *n* — **com·pen·sa·to·ry** \kəm-'pen-sə-ˌtȯr-ē\ *adj*

com·pete \kəm-'pēt\ *vb* **com·pet·ed; com·pet·ing** : CONTEND, VIE

com·pe·tence \'käm-pə-təns\ *n* **1** : adequate means for subsistence **2** : FITNESS, ABILITY

com·pe·ten·cy \-tən-sē\ *n, pl* **-cies** : COMPETENCE

com·pe·tent \-tənt\ *adj* : CAPABLE, FIT, QUALIFIED

com·pe·ti·tion \ˌkäm-pə-'ti-shən\ *n* **1** : the act of competing : RIVALRY **2** : CONTEST, MATCH; *also* : one's competitors — **com·pet·i·tive** \-'pe-tə-tiv\ *adj* — **com·pet·i·tive·ly** *adv* — **com·pet·i·tive·ness** *n*

com·pet·i·tor \kəm-'pe-tə-tər\ *n* : one that competes : RIVAL

com·pile \kəm-'pīl\ *vb* **com·piled; com·pil·ing** [ME, fr. MF *compiler*, fr. L *compilare* to plunder] **1** : to compose out of materials from other documents **2** : to collect and edit into a volume **3** : to translate (a computer program) with a compiler **4** : to build up gradually ⟨~ a record of four wins and two losses⟩ — **com·pi·la·tion** \ˌkäm-pə-'lā-shən\ *n*

com·pil·er \kəm-'pī-lər\ *n* **1** : one that compiles **2** : a

---

\ə\abut \ᵊ\kitten \ər\further \a\ash \ā\ace \ä\mop, mar \au̇\out \ch\chin \e\bet \ē\easy \g\go \i\hit \ī\ice \j\job \ŋ\sing \ō\go \ȯ\law \ȯi\boy \th\thin \t͟h\the \ü\loot \u̇\foot \y\yet \zh\vision *see also* Pronunciation Symbols page

computer program that translates any program correctly written in a specific programming language into machine language

com·pla·cence \kəm-ˈplās-ᵊns\ *n* : SATISFACTION; *esp* : SELF-SATISFACTION — **com·pla·cent** \-ᵊnt\ *adj* — **com·pla·cent·ly** *adv*

com·pla·cen·cy \-ᵊn-sē\ *n, pl* **-cies** : COMPLACENCE

com·plain \kəm-ˈplān\ *vb* 1 : to express grief, pain, or discontent 2 : to make a formal accusation — **com·plain·ant** *n* — **com·plain·er** *n*

com·plaint \kəm-ˈplānt\ *n* 1 : expression of grief, pain, or dissatisfaction 2 : a bodily ailment or disease 3 : a formal accusation against a person

com·plai·sance \kəm-ˈplās-ᵊns, ˌkäm-plā-ˈzans\ *n* [F] : disposition to please — **com·plai·sant** \-ᵊnt, -ˈzant\ *adj*

com·pleat \kəm-ˈplēt\ *adj* : PROFICIENT

com·plect·ed \kəm-ˈplek-təd\ *adj* : having a specified facial complexion ⟨dark-*complected*⟩

¹**com·ple·ment** \ˈkäm-plə-mənt\ *n* 1 : something that fills up or completes; *also* : the full quantity, number, or amount that makes a thing complete 2 : an added word by which a predicate is made complete 3 : a group of proteins in blood that combines with antibodies to destroy antigens — **com·ple·men·ta·ry** \ˌkäm-plə-ˈmen-t(ə-)rē\ *adj*

²**com·ple·ment** \-ˌment\ *vb* : to be complementary to : fill out

¹**com·plete** \kəm-ˈplēt\ *adj* **com·plet·er; -est** 1 : having all parts or elements 2 : brought to an end 3 : fully carried out; *also* : ABSOLUTE 2 ⟨~ silence⟩ — **com·plete·ly** *adv* — **com·plete·ness** *n* — **com·ple·tion** \-ˈplē-shən\ *n*

²**complete** *vb* **com·plet·ed; com·plet·ing** 1 : FINISH, CONCLUDE 2 : to make whole or perfect ⟨the hat ~s the outfit⟩

¹**com·plex** \ˈkäm-ˌpleks\ *n* 1 : a whole made up of or involving intricately interrelated elements 2 : a group of repressed desires and memories that exert a dominating influence on one's personality and behavior ⟨a guilt ~⟩

²**com·plex** \käm-ˈpleks, ˈkäm-ˌpleks\ *adj* 1 : composed of two or more parts 2 : consisting of a main clause and one or more subordinate clauses ⟨~ sentence⟩ 3 : hard to separate, analyze, or solve — **com·plex·i·ty** \käm-ˈplek-sə-tē\ *n* — **com·plex·ly** *adv*

complex fraction *n* : a fraction with a fraction or mixed number in the numerator or denominator or both

com·plex·ion \kəm-ˈplek-shən\ *n* 1 : the hue or appearance of the skin esp. of the face 2 : overall appearance — **com·plex·ioned** \-shənd\ *adj*

complex number *n* : a number (as $3 + 4\sqrt{-1}$) formed by adding a real number to the product of a real number and the square root of minus one

com·pli·ance \kəm-ˈplī-əns\ *n* 1 : the act of complying to a demand or proposal 2 : a disposition to yield — **com·pli·ant** \-ənt\ *adj*

com·pli·cate \ˈkäm-plə-ˌkāt\ *vb* **-cat·ed; -cat·ing** : to make or become complex or intricate

com·pli·cat·ed \ˈkäm-plə-ˌkā-təd\ *adj* 1 : consisting of parts intricately combined 2 : difficult to analyze, understand, or explain — **com·pli·cat·ed·ly** *adv*

com·pli·ca·tion \ˌkäm-plə-ˈkā-shən\ *n* 1 : the quality or state of being complicated; *also* : a complex feature 2 : a disease or condition that develops during and affects the course of a primary disease or condition

com·plic·i·ty \kəm-ˈpli-sə-tē\ *n, pl* **-ties** : the state of being an accomplice

¹**com·pli·ment** \ˈkäm-plə-mənt\ *n* 1 : an expression of approval or admiration; *esp* : a flattering remark 2 *pl* : best wishes : REGARDS

²**com·pli·ment** \-ˌment\ *vb* : to pay a compliment to

com·pli·men·ta·ry \ˌkäm-plə-ˈmen-t(ə-)rē\ *adj* 1 : containing or expressing a compliment 2 : given free as a courtesy ⟨~ ticket⟩

com·ply \kəm-ˈplī\ *vb* **com·plied; com·ply·ing** : CONFORM, YIELD

¹**com·po·nent** \kəm-ˈpō-nənt, ˈkäm-ˌpō-\ *n* : a component part **syn** ingredient, element, factor, constituent

²**component** *adj* : serving to form a part of : CONSTITUENT

com·port \kəm-ˈpōrt\ *vb* 1 : AGREE, ACCORD 2 : CONDUCT **syn** behave, acquit, deport — **com·port·ment** *n*

com·pose \kəm-ˈpōz\ *vb* **com·posed; com·pos·ing** 1 : to form by putting together : FASHION 2 : to produce (as pages of type) by composition 3 : ADJUST, ARRANGE 4 : CALM, QUIET 5 : to practice composition ⟨~ music⟩ — **com·pos·er** *n*

¹**com·pos·ite** \käm-ˈpä-zət\ *adj* 1 : made up of distinct parts or elements 2 : of, relating to, or being a large family of flowering plants (as a daisy or aster) that bear many small flowers united into compact heads resembling single flowers

²**composite** *n* 1 : something composite 2 : a plant of the composite family **syn** blend, compound, mixture, amalgamation

com·po·si·tion \ˌkäm-pə-ˈzi-shən\ *n* 1 : the act or process of composing; *esp* : arrangement esp. in artistic form 2 : the arrangement or production of type for printing 3 : general makeup 4 : a product of mixing various elements or ingredients 5 : a literary, musical, or artistic product; *esp* : ESSAY

com·pos·i·tor \kəm-ˈpä-zə-tər\ *n* : one who sets type

com·post \ˈkäm-ˌpōst\ *n* : a fertilizing material consisting largely of decayed organic matter

com·po·sure \kəm-ˈpō-zhər\ *n* : CALMNESS, SELF≠POSSESSION

com·pote \ˈkäm-ˌpōt\ *n* 1 : fruits cooked in syrup 2 : a bowl (as of glass) usu. with a base and stem for serving esp. fruit or compote

¹**com·pound** \käm-ˈpaund, ˈkäm-ˌ\ *vb* [ME *compounen*, fr. MF *compondre*, fr. L *componere*, fr. *com-* together + *ponere* to put] 1 : COMBINE 2 : to form by combining parts ⟨~ a medicine⟩ 3 : SETTLE ⟨~ a dispute⟩; *also* : to refrain from prosecuting (an offense) in return for a consideration 4 : to increase (as interest) by an amount that can itself vary; *also* : to add to

²**com·pound** \ˈkäm-ˌpaund\ *adj* 1 : made up of individual parts 2 : composed of united similar parts esp. of a kind usu. independent ⟨a ~ plant ovary⟩ 3 : formed by the combination of two or more otherwise independent elements ⟨~ sentence⟩

³**com·pound** \ˈkäm-ˌpaund\ *n* 1 : a word consisting of parts that are words 2 : something formed from a union of elements or parts; *esp* : a distinct substance formed by the union of two or more chemical elements **syn** mixture, composite, blend, admixture, alloy

⁴**com·pound** \ˈkäm-ˌpaund\ *n* [by folk etymology fr. Malay *kampung* group of buildings, village] : an enclosure containing buildings

compound interest *n* : interest computed on the sum of an original principal and accrued interest

com·pre·hend \ˌkäm-pri-ˈhend\ *vb* 1 : UNDERSTAND 2 : INCLUDE — **com·pre·hen·si·ble** \-ˈhen-sə-bəl\ *adj* — **com·pre·hen·sion** \-ˈhen-chən\ *n* — **com·pre·hen·sive** \-siv\ *adj*

¹**com·press** \kəm-ˈpres\ *vb* : to squeeze together **syn** constrict, contract, shrink — **com·pres·sion** \-ˈpre-shən\ *n* — **com·pres·sor** \-ˈpre-sər\ *n*

²**com·press** \ˈkäm-ˌpres\ *n* : a folded pad or cloth used to press upon a body part

compressed air *n* : air under pressure greater than that of the atmosphere

com·prise \kəm-ˈprīz\ *vb* **com·prised; com·pris·ing** 1 : INCLUDE, CONTAIN 2 : to be made up of 3 : COMPOSE, CONSTITUTE

¹**com·pro·mise** \'käm-prə-ˌmīz\ *n* : a settlement of differences reached by mutual concessions

²**compromise** *vb* **-mised; -mis·ing** 1 : to settle by compromise 2 : to expose to suspicion or loss of reputation

comp·trol·ler \kən-'trō-lər, 'kämp-ˌtrō-\ *n* : an official who audits and supervises expenditures and accounts

com·pul·sion \kəm-'pəl-shən\ *n* 1 : an act of compelling 2 : a force that compels 3 : an irresistible impulse **syn** constraint, force, violence, duress — **com·pul·sive** \-siv\ *adj* — **com·pul·so·ry** \-sə-rē\ *adj*

com·punc·tion \kəm-'pəŋk-shən\ *n* : anxiety arising from guilt : REMORSE

com·pute \kəm-'pyüt\ *vb* **com·put·ed; com·put·ing** : CALCULATE, RECKON — **com·pu·ta·tion** \ˌkäm-pyü-'tā-shən\ *n* — **com·pu·ta·tion·al** *adj*

computed tomography *n* : radiography in which a three-dimensional image of a body structure is constructed by computer from a series of plane cross-sectional images made along an axis

com·put·er \kəm-'pyü-tər\ *n* : a programmable electronic device that can store, retrieve, and process data

com·put·er·ise *chiefly Brit var of* COMPUTERIZE

com·put·er·ize \kəm-'pyü-tə-ˌrīz\ *vb* **-ized; -iz·ing** 1 : to carry out, control, or produce by means of a computer 2 : to provide with computers 3 : to store in a computer; *also* : put into a form that a computer can use — **com·put·er·iza·tion** \-ˌpyü-tə-rə-'zā-shən\ *n*

computerized axial tomography *n* : COMPUTED TOMOGRAPHY

com·rade \'käm-ˌrad\ *n* [MF *comarade* group sleeping in one room, roommate, companion, fr. Sp *comarada*, fr. *cámara* room, fr. LL *camera*] : COMPANION, ASSOCIATE — **com·rade·ly** *adj* — **com·rade·ship** *n*

¹**con** \'kän\ *vb* **conned; con·ning** 1 : MEMORIZE 2 : STUDY

²**con** *adv* : in opposition : AGAINST

³**con** *n* : an opposing argument, person, or position ⟨pros and ∼s⟩

⁴**con** *vb* **conned; con·ning** 1 : SWINDLE 2 : PERSUADE, CAJOLE

⁵**con** *n* : CONVICT

conc *abbr* concentrated

con·cat·e·nate \kän-'ka-tə-ˌnāt\ *vb* **-nat·ed; -nat·ing** : to link together in a series or chain — **con·cat·e·na·tion** \(ˌ)kän-ˌka-tə-'nā-shən\ *n*

con·cave \kän-'kāv, 'kän-ˌ\ *adj* : curved or rounded inward like the inside of a bowl — **con·cav·i·ty** \kän-'ka-və-tē\ *n*

con·ceal \kən-'sēl\ *vb* : to place out of sight : HIDE — **con·ceal·ment** *n*

con·cede \kən-'sēd\ *vb* **con·ced·ed; con·ced·ing** 1 : to admit to be true 2 : GRANT, YIELD **syn** allow, acknowledge, avow, confess

con·ceit \kən-'sēt\ *n* 1 : excessively high opinion of one's self or ability : VANITY 2 : an elaborate or strained metaphor — **con·ceit·ed** *adj*

con·ceive \kən-'sēv\ *vb* **con·ceived; con·ceiv·ing** 1 : to become pregnant or pregnant with ⟨∼ a child⟩ 2 : to form an idea of : THINK, IMAGINE — **con·ceiv·able** \-'sē-və-bəl\ *adj* — **con·ceiv·ably** \-blē\ *adv*

con·cel·e·brant \kən-'se-lə-brənt\ *n* : one that jointly participates in celebrating the Eucharist

¹**con·cen·trate** \'kän-sən-ˌtrāt\ *vb* **-trat·ed; -trat·ing** 1 : to gather into one body, mass, or force 2 : to make less dilute 3 : to fix one's powers, efforts, or attentions

²**concentrate** *n* : something concentrated

con·cen·tra·tion \ˌkän-sən-'trā-shən\ *n* 1 : the act or process of concentrating : the state of being concentrated; *esp* : direction of attention on a single object 2 : the amount of a component in a given area or volume

concentration camp *n* : a camp where persons (as prisoners of war or political prisoners) are confined

con·cen·tric \kən-'sen-trik\ *adj* 1 : having a common center ⟨∼ circles⟩ 2 : COAXIAL

con·cept \'kän-ˌsept\ *n* : THOUGHT, NOTION, IDEA — **con·cep·tu·al** \kən-'sep-chə-wəl\ *adj*

con·cep·tion \kən-'sep-shən\ *n* 1 : the process of conceiving or being conceived 2 : the power to form or understand ideas or concepts 3 : IDEA, CONCEPT 4 : the originating of something

con·cep·tu·al·ize \-'sep-chə-wə-ˌlīz\ *vb* **-ized; -iz·ing** : to form a conception of

¹**con·cern** \kən-'sərn\ *vb* 1 : to relate to 2 : to be the business of : INVOLVE 3 : ENGAGE, OCCUPY

²**concern** *n* 1 : INTEREST, ANXIETY 2 : AFFAIR, MATTER 3 : a business organization **syn** care, worry, disquiet, unease

con·cerned *adj* 1 : ANXIOUS, UNEASY 2 : INVOLVED

con·cern·ing *prep* : relating to : REGARDING

con·cern·ment \kən-'sərn-mənt\ *n* 1 : something in which one is concerned 2 : IMPORTANCE, CONSEQUENCE

¹**con·cert** \'kän-(ˌ)sərt\ *n* 1 : agreement in a plan or design 2 : a concerted action 3 : a public performance (as of music)

²**con·cert** \kən-'sərt\ *vb* : to plan together

con·cert·ed \kən-'sər-təd\ *adj* : mutually agreed on; *also* : performed in unison

con·cer·ti·na \ˌkän-sər-'tē-nə\ *n* : an instrument of the accordion family

concertina

con·cert·mas·ter \'kän-sərt-ˌmas-tər\ *or* **con·cert·meis·ter** \-ˌmī-stər\ *n* : the leader of the first violins of an orchestra and assistant to the conductor

con·cer·to \kən-'cher-tō\ *n, pl* **-ti** \-(ˌ)tē\ *or* **-tos** [It] : a piece for one or more solo instruments and orchestra in three movements

con·ces·sion \kən-'se-shən\ *n* 1 : an act of conceding or yielding 2 : something yielded 3 : a grant by a government of land or of a right to use it 4 : a grant of a portion of premises for some specific purpose; *also* : the activities or enterprise carried on — **con·ces·sion·ary** \-'se-shə-ˌner-ē\ *adj*

con·ces·sion·aire \kən-ˌse-shə-'nar, -'ner\ *n* : one that owns or operates a concession

conch \'käŋk, 'känch\ *n, pl* **conchs** \'käŋks\ *or* **conch-**

conch

es \ˈkän-chəz\ : a large spiral-shelled marine gastropod mollusk; *also* : its shell

con·cierge \kŏⁿ-ˈsyerzh\ *n, pl* con·cierges *same or* -ˈsyer-zhəz\ [F] **1** : a resident in an apartment building who performs services for the tenants **2** : a usu. multilingual hotel staff member

con·cil·i·ate \kən-ˈsi-lē-ˌāt\ *vb* -at·ed; -at·ing **1** : to bring into agreement : RECONCILE **2** : to gain the goodwill of — con·cil·i·a·tion \-ˌsi-lē-ˈā-shən\ *n* — con·cil·ia·to·ry \-ˈsi-lē-ə-ˌtȯr-ē\ *adj*

con·cise \kən-ˈsīs\ *adj* : expressing much in few words : BRIEF — con·cise·ly *adv* — con·cise·ness *n*

con·clave \ˈkän-ˌklāv\ *n* [ML, fr. L, room that can be locked, fr. *com*- together + *clavis* key] : a private gathering; *also* : CONVENTION

con·clude \kən-ˈklüd\ *vb* con·clud·ed; con·clud·ing **1** : to bring to a close : END **2** : DECIDE, JUDGE **3** : to bring about as a result **syn** close, finish, terminate, complete, halt

con·clu·sion \kən-ˈklü-zhən\ *n* **1** : the logical consequence of a reasoning process **2** : TERMINATION, END **3** : OUTCOME, RESULT — con·clu·sive \-siv\ *adj* — con·clu·sive·ly *adv*

con·coct \kən-ˈkäkt, kän-\ *vb* **1** : to prepare by combining raw materials **2** : DEVISE — con·coc·tion \-ˈkäk-shən\ *n*

con·com·i·tant \-ˈkä-mə-tənt\ *adj* : ACCOMPANYING, ATTENDING — concomitant *n*

con·cord \ˈkän-ˌkȯrd, ˈkäŋ-\ *n* : AGREEMENT, HARMONY

con·cor·dance \kən-ˈkȯr-dᵊns\ *n* **1** : an alphabetical index of words in a book or in an author's works with the passages in which they occur **2** : AGREEMENT, COVENANT

con·cor·dant \-dᵊnt\ *adj* : HARMONIOUS, AGREEING

con·cor·dat \kən-ˈkȯr-ˌdat\ *n* : CONCORDANCE 2

con·course \ˈkän-ˌkȯrs\ *n* **1** : a spontaneous coming together : GATHERING **2** : an open space or hall (as in a bus terminal) where crowds gather

¹con·crete \ˈkän-ˌkrēt, ˈkän-ˌkrēt\ *adj* **1** : naming a real thing or class of things : not abstract **2** : not theoretical : ACTUAL **3** : made of or relating to concrete

²con·crete \ˈkän-ˌkrēt, kän-ˈkrēt\ *vb* con·cret·ed; con·cret·ing **1** : SOLIDIFY **2** : to cover with concrete

³con·crete \ˈkän-ˌkrēt, kän-ˈkrēt\ *n* : a hard building material made by mixing cement, sand, and gravel with water

con·cre·tion \kän-ˈkrē-shən\ *n* : a hard mass esp. when formed abnormally in the body

con·cu·bine \ˈkäŋ-kyu-ˌbīn\ *n* [ME, fr. MF, fr. L *concubina*, fr. *com*- with + *cubare* to lie] : a woman who is not legally a wife but lives with a man and sometimes has a recognized position in his household; *also* : MISTRESS — con·cu·bi·nage \kän-ˈkyü-bə-nij\ *n*

con·cu·pis·cence \kän-ˈkyü-pə-səns\ *n* : ardent sexual desire : LUST

con·cur \kən-ˈkər\ *vb* con·curred; con·cur·ring **1** : to act together **2** : AGREE **3** : COINCIDE **syn** unite, combine, cooperate, band, join

con·cur·rence \-ˈkər-əns\ *n* **1** : agreement in action or opinion **2** : occurrence together : CONJUNCTION

con·cur·rent \-ˈkər-ənt\ *adj* **1** : happening or operating at the same time **2** : joint and equal in authority

con·cus·sion \kən-ˈkə-shən\ *n* **1** : a hard blow or collision; *also* : bodily injury (as to the brain) resulting from a sudden jar **2** : AGITATION, SHAKING

con·demn \kən-ˈdem\ *vb* **1** : to declare to be wrong **2** : to convict of guilt **3** : to sentence judicially **4** : to pronounce unfit for use ⟨∼ a building⟩ **5** : to declare forfeited or taken for public use **syn** denounce, censure, blame, criticize, reprehend — con·dem·na·tion \ˌkän-ˌdem-ˈnā-shən\ *n* — con·dem·na·to·ry \kən-ˈdem-nə-ˌtȯr-ē\ *adj*

con·den·sate \ˈkän-dən-ˌsāt, kən-ˈden-\ *n* : a product of condensation

con·dense \kən-ˈdens\ *vb* con·densed; con·dens·ing **1** : to make or become more compact or dense : CONCENTRATE **2** : to change from vapor to liquid **syn** contract, shrink, compress, constrict — con·den·sa·tion \ˌkän-den-ˈsā-shən\ *n*

con·dens·er \kən-ˈden-sər\ *n* **1** : one that condenses **2** : CAPACITOR

con·de·scend \ˌkän-di-ˈsend\ *vb* : to assume an air of superiority — con·de·scend·ing·ly \-ˈsen-diŋ-lē\ *adv* — con·de·scen·sion \-ˈsen-chən\ *n*

con·dign \kən-ˈdīn, ˈkän-ˌdīn\ *adj* : DESERVED, APPROPRIATE ⟨∼ punishment⟩

con·di·ment \ˈkän-də-mənt\ *n* : something used to make food savory; *esp* : a pungent seasoning (as pepper)

¹con·di·tion \kən-ˈdi-shən\ *n* **1** : something essential to the occurrence of some other thing **2** : state of being **3** : social status **4** *pl* : state of affairs : CIRCUMSTANCES **5** : a bodily state in which something is wrong ⟨a heart ∼⟩ **6** : a state of health, fitness, or working order ⟨in good ∼⟩

²condition *vb* **1** : to put into proper condition for action or use **2** : to adapt, modify, or mold to respond in a particular way **3** : to modify so that an act or response previously associated with one stimulus becomes associated with another

con·di·tion·al \kən-ˈdi-shə-nəl\ *adj* : containing, implying, or depending on a condition — con·di·tion·al·ly *adv*

con·di·tioned *adj* : determined or established by conditioning

con·do \ˈkän-(ˌ)dō\ *n* : CONDOMINIUM 3

con·dole \kən-ˈdōl\ *vb* con·doled; con·dol·ing : to express sympathetic sorrow — con·do·lence \kən-ˈdō-ləns\ *n*

con·dom \ˈkän-dəm, ˈkən-\ *n* : a usu. rubber sheath worn over the penis (as to prevent pregnancy or venereal infection during sexual intercourse)

con·do·min·i·um \ˌkän-də-ˈmi-nē-əm\ *n, pl* -ums **1** : joint sovereignty (as by two or more nations) **2** : a politically dependent territory under condominium **3** : individual ownership of a unit (as an apartment) in a multiunit structure; *also* : a unit so owned

con·done \kən-ˈdōn\ *vb* con·doned; con·don·ing : to overlook or forgive esp. by treating (an offense) as harmless or trivial **syn** excuse, pardon, forgive, remit — con·do·na·tion \ˌkän-də-ˈnā-shən\ *n*

con·dor \ˈkän-dər, -ˌdȯr\ *n* [Sp *cóndor*, fr. Quechua (a So. American Indian language) *kuntur*] : a very large American vulture of the high Andes; *also* : a related nearly extinct vulture of southern California now resident only in captivity

con·duce \kən-ˈdüs, -ˈdyüs\ *vb* con·duced; con·duc·ing : to lead or contribute to a particular result — con·du·cive *adj*

¹con·duct \ˈkän-(ˌ)dəkt\ *n* **1** : MANAGEMENT, DIRECTION **2** : BEHAVIOR

²con·duct \kən-ˈdəkt\ *vb* **1** : GUIDE, ESCORT **2** : MANAGE, DIRECT **3** : to act as a medium for conveying or transmitting **4** : BEHAVE — con·duc·tion \-ˈdək-shən\ *n*

con·duc·tance \kən-ˈdək-təns\ *n* : the readiness with which a conductor transmits an electric current

con·duc·tive \kən-ˈdək-tiv\ *adj* : having the power to conduct (as heat or electricity) — con·duc·tiv·i·ty \ˌkän-ˌdək-ˈti-və-tē\ *n*

con·duc·tor \kən-ˈdək-tər\ *n* **1** : one that conducts; *esp* : a material that permits an electric current to flow easily **2** : a collector of fares in a public conveyance **3** : the leader of a musical ensemble

con·duit \ˈkän-ˌdü-ət, ˌdyü-, -dwət\ *n* **1** : a channel for conveying fluid **2** : a tube or trough for protecting electric wires or cables **3 :** a means of transmitting or distributing

con·dyle \'kän-ˌdīl, -dᵊl\ *n* : an articular prominence of a bone — **con·dy·lar** \-də-lər\ *adj*

cone \'kōn\ *n* **1 :** the scaly fruit of trees of the pine family **2 :** a solid figure formed by rotating a right triangle about one of its legs **3 :** a solid figure that slopes evenly to a point from a usu. circular base **4 :** any of the conical light-sensitive receptor cells of the retina that function in color vision **5 :** something shaped like a cone

Con·es·to·ga wagon \ˌkä-nə-ˈstò-gə-\ *n* : a broad-wheeled covered wagon used esp. for transporting freight across the prairies

co·ney \'kō-nē\ *n, pl* **coneys 1 :** RABBIT; *also* : its fur **2** : PIKA

conf *abbr* **1** conference **2** confidential

con·fab \'kän-ˌfab, kən-ˈfab\ *n* : CONFABULATION 1

con·fab·u·la·tion \kən-ˌfab yə-ˈlā-shən\ *n* **1 :** CHAT; *also* : CONFERENCE **2 :** a filling in of gaps in memory by fabrication

con·fec·tion \kən-ˈfek-shən\ *n* : a fancy dish or sweet; *also* : CANDY

con·fec·tion·er \-sh(ə-)nər\ *n* : a maker of or dealer in confections

con·fec·tion·ery \-shə-ˌner-ē\ *n, pl* **-er·ies 1 :** sweet foods **2 :** a confectioner's place of business

Confed *abbr* Confederate

con·fed·er·a·cy \kən-ˈfe-də-rə-sē\ *n, pl* **-cies 1 :** LEAGUE, ALLIANCE **2** *cap* : the 11 southern states that seceded from the U.S. in 1860 and 1861

¹con·fed·er·ate \kən-ˈfe-də-rət\ *adj* **1 :** united in a league : ALLIED **2** *cap* : of or relating to the Confederacy

²confederate *n* **1 :** ALLY, ACCOMPLICE **2** *cap* : an adherent of the Confederacy

³con·fed·er·ate \-ˈfe-də-ˌrāt\ *vb* **-at·ed; -at·ing :** to unite in a confederacy

con·fed·er·a·tion \kən-ˌfe-də-ˈrā-shən\ *n* **1 :** an act of confederating : ALLIANCE **2 :** LEAGUE

con·fer \kən-ˈfər\ *vb* **con·ferred; con·fer·ring 1 :** GRANT, BESTOW **2 :** to exchange views : CONSULT — **con·fer·ee** \ˌkän-fə-ˈrē\ *n*

con·fer·ence \'kän-f(ə-)rəns\ *n* **1 :** an interchange of views; *also* : a meeting for this purpose **2 :** an association of athletic teams

con·fess \kən-ˈfes\ *vb* **1 :** to acknowledge or disclose one's misdeed, fault, or sin **2 :** to acknowledge one's sins to God or to a priest **3 :** to receive the confession of (a penitent) **syn** admit, own, avow, concede, grant

con·fessed·ly \-ˈfe-səd-lē\ *adv* : by confession : ADMITTEDLY

con·fes·sion \-ˈfe-shən\ *n* **1 :** an act of confessing (as in the sacrament of penance) **2 :** an acknowledgment of guilt **3 :** a formal statement of religious beliefs **4 :** a religious body having a common creed — **con·fes·sion·al** *adj*

con·fes·sion·al \-ˈfe-shə-nəl\ *n* : a place where a priest hears confessions

con·fes·sor \kən-ˈfe-sər\ *n* **1 :** one that confesses **2 :** a priest who hears confessions

con·fet·ti \kən-ˈfe-tē\ *n* [It, pl. of *confetto* sweetmeat, fr. ML *confectum*, fr. L, neut. of *confectus*, pp. of *conficere* to prepare] : bits of colored paper or ribbon for throwing (as at weddings)

con·fi·dant \'kän-fə-ˌdänt, -ˌdant\ *n* : one to whom secrets are confided

con·fi·dante \-ˌdänt, -ˌdant\ *n* : CONFIDANT; *esp* : one who is a woman

con·fide \kən-ˈfīd\ *vb* **con·fid·ed; con·fid·ing 1 :** to have or show faith : TRUST ⟨~ in a friend⟩ **2 :** to tell confidentially ⟨~ a secret⟩ **3 :** ENTRUST

¹con·fi·dence \'kän-fə-dəns\ *n* **1 :** TRUST, RELIANCE **2** : SELF-ASSURANCE, BOLDNESS **3 :** a state of trust or intimacy **4 :** SECRET **2** — **con·fi·dent** \-dənt\ *adj* — **con·fi·dent·ly** *adv*

²confidence *adj* : of or relating to swindling by false promises ⟨a ~ game⟩

con·fi·den·tial \ˌkän-fə-ˈden-chəl\ *adj* **1 :** SECRET, PRIVATE **2 :** entrusted with confidences ⟨~ clerk⟩ — **con·fi·den·tial·ly** *adv*

con·fig·u·ra·tion \kən-ˌfi-gyə-ˈrā-shən\ *n* : structural arrangement of parts : SHAPE

con·fig·ure \kən-ˈfi-gyər\ *vb* **-ured; -ur·ing :** to set up for operation esp. in a particular way

con·fine \kən-ˈfīn\ *vb* **con·fined; con·fin·ing 1 :** to hold within a location; *also* : IMPRISON **2 :** to keep within limits ⟨will ~ my remarks to one subject⟩ — **con·fine·ment** *n* — **con·fin·er** *n*

con·fines \'kän-ˌfīnz\ *n pl* : BOUNDS, BORDERS

con·firm \kən-ˈfərm\ *vb* **1 :** to give approval to : RATIFY **2 :** to make firm or firmer **3 :** to administer the rite of confirmation to **4 :** VERIFY, CORROBORATE — **con·fir·ma·to·ry** \-ˈfər-mə-ˌtòr-ē\ *adj*

con·fir·ma·tion \ˌkän-fər-ˈmā-shən\ *n* **1 :** a religious ceremony admitting a person to full membership in a church or synagogue **2 :** an act of ratifying or corroborating; *also* : PROOF

con·fis·cate \'kän-fə-ˌskāt\ *vb* **-cat·ed; -cat·ing** [L *confiscare,* fr. *com-* with + *fiscus* treasury] : to take possession of by or as if by public authority — **con·fis·ca·tion** \ˌkän-fə-ˈskā-shən\ *n* — **con·fis·ca·to·ry** \kən-ˈfis-kə-ˌtòr-ē\ *adj*

con·fla·gra·tion \ˌkän-flə-ˈgrā-shən\ *n* : FIRE; *esp* : a large disastrous fire

¹con·flict \'kän-ˌflikt\ *n* **1 :** WAR **2 :** a clash between hostile or opposing elements, ideas, or forces

²con·flict \kən-ˈflikt\ *vb* : to show opposition or irreconcilability : CLASH

con·flu·ence \'kän-ˌflü-əns, kən-ˈflü-\ *n* **1 :** a coming together at one point **2 :** the meeting or place of meeting of two or more streams — **con·flu·ent** \-ənt\ *adj*

con·flux \'kän-ˌfləks\ *n* : CONFLUENCE

con·form \kən-ˈfòrm\ *vb* **1 :** to be similar or identical; *also* : AGREE **2 :** to obey customs or standards; *also* : COMPLY — **con·form·able** *adj*

con·for·mance \kən-ˈfòr-məns\ *n* : CONFORMITY

con·for·ma·tion \ˌkän-fòr-ˈmā-shən\ *n* : a forming into a whole by arranging parts

con·for·mi·ty \kən-ˈfòr-mə-tē\ *n, pl* **-ties 1 :** HARMONY, AGREEMENT **2 :** COMPLIANCE, OBEDIENCE

con·found \kən-ˈfaùnd, kän-\ *vb* **1 :** to throw into disorder or confusion **2 :** CONFUSE **2 syn** bewilder, puzzle, perplex, befog

con·fra·ter·ni·ty \ˌkän-frə-ˈtər-nə-tē\ *n* : a society devoted esp. to a religious or charitable cause

con·frere \'kän-ˌfrer, 'kōⁿ-\ *n* : COLLEAGUE, COMRADE

con·front \kən-ˈfrənt\ *vb* **1 :** to face esp. in challenge : OPPOSE; *also* : to deal unflinchingly with ⟨~ed the issue⟩ **2 :** to cause to face or meet — **con·fron·ta·tion** \ˌkän-frən-ˈtā-shən\ *n*

Con·fu·cian \kən-ˈfyü-shən\ *adj* : of or relating to the Chinese philosopher Confucius or his teachings — **Con·fu·cian·ism** \-shə-ˌni-zəm\ *n*

con·fuse \kən-ˈfyüz\ *vb* **con·fused; con·fus·ing 1 :** to make mentally unclear or uncertain; *also* : to disturb the composure of **2 :** to mix up : JUMBLE **syn** muddle, befuddle, addle, fluster — **con·fus·ed·ly** \-ˈfyü-zəd-lē\ *adv*

con·fu·sion \-ˈfyü-zhən\ *n* **1 :** an act or instance of confusing **2 :** the quality or state of being confused

con·fute \kən-ˈfyüt\ *vb* **con·fut·ed; con·fut·ing :** to over-

---

\ə\abut \ᵊ\kitten \ər\further \a\ash \ā\ace \ä\mop, mar
\aù\out \ch\chin \e\bet \ē\easy \g\go \i\hit \ī\ice \j\job
\ŋ\sing \ō\go \ò\law \òi\boy \th\thin \t͟h\the \ü\loot \ù\foot
\y\yet \zh\vision *see also* Pronunciation Symbols page

whelm by argument : REFUTE — **con·fu·ta·tion** \ˌkän-fyü-ˈtā-shən\ *n*

cong *abbr* congress; congressional

con·ga \ˈkäŋ-gə\ *n* : a Cuban dance of African origin performed by a group usu. in single file

con·geal \kən-ˈjēl\ *vb* 1 : FREEZE 2 : to make or become hard or thick

con·ge·ner \ˈkän-jə-nər\ *n* : one related to another; *esp* : a plant or animal of the same taxonomic genus as another — **con·ge·ner·ic** \ˌkän-jə-ˈner-ik\ *adj*

con·ge·nial \kən-ˈjē-nyəl\ *adj* 1 : KINDRED, SYMPATHETIC 2 : suited to one's taste or nature : AGREEABLE — **con·ge·ni·al·i·ty** \-ˌjē-nē-ˈa-lə-tē\ *n* — **con·ge·nial·ly** *adv*

con·gen·i·tal \kən-ˈje-nə-tᵊl\ *adj* : existing at or dating from birth **syn** inborn, innate, natural

con·ger eel \ˈkän-gər-\ *n* : a large edible marine eel of the Atlantic

con·ge·ries \ˈkän-jə-(ˌ)rēz\ *n, pl* **congeries** : AGGREGATION, COLLECTION

con·gest \kən-ˈjest\ *vb* 1 : to cause excessive fullness of the blood vessels of (as a lung) 2 : to obstruct by overcrowding — **con·ges·tion** \-ˈjes-chən\ *n* — **con·ges·tive** \-ˈjes-tiv\ *adj*

congestive heart failure *n* : heart failure in which the heart is unable to keep enough blood circulating in the tissues or is unable to pump out the blood returned to it by the veins

¹**con·glom·er·ate** \kən-ˈglä-mə-rət\ *adj* [L *conglomerare* to roll together, fr. *com-* together + *glomerare* to wind into a ball, fr. *glomer-, glomus* ball] : made up of parts from various sources

²**con·glom·er·ate** \-ˌrāt\ *vb* **-at·ed; -at·ing** : to form into a mass — **con·glom·er·a·tion** \-ˌglä-mə-ˈrā-shən\ *n*

³**con·glom·er·ate** \-rət\ *n* 1 : a mass formed of fragments from various sources; *esp* : a rock composed of fragments varying from pebbles to boulders held together by a cementing material 2 : a widely diversified corporation

Con·go·lese \ˌkäŋ-gə-ˈlēz, -ˈlēs\ *n* : a native or inhabitant of Congo — **Congolese** *adj*

con·grat·u·late \kən-ˈgra-chə-ˌlāt\ *vb* **-lat·ed; -lat·ing** : to express sympathetic pleasure to on account of success or good fortune : FELICITATE — **con·grat·u·la·tion** \-ˌgra-chə-ˈlā-shən\ *n* — **con·grat·u·la·to·ry** \-ˈgra-chə-lə-ˌtȯr-ē\ *adj*

con·gre·gate \ˈkäŋ-gri-ˌgāt\ *vb* **-gat·ed; -gat·ing** [ME, fr. L *congregatus*, pp. of *congregare*, fr. *com-* together + *greg-, grex* flock] : ASSEMBLE

con·gre·ga·tion \ˌkäŋ-gri-ˈgā-shən\ *n* 1 : an assembly of persons met esp. for worship; *also* : a group that habitually so meets 2 : a religious community or order 3 : the act or an instance of congregating

con·gre·ga·tion·al \-shə-nəl\ *adj* 1 : of or relating to a congregation 2 *cap* : observing the faith and practice of certain Protestant churches which recognize the independence of each congregation in church matters — **con·gre·ga·tion·al·ism** \-nə-ˌli-zəm\ *n, often cap* — **con·gre·ga·tion·al·ist** \-list\ *n, often cap*

con·gress \ˈkäŋ-grəs\ *n* 1 : an assembly esp. of delegates for discussion and usu. action on some question 2 : the body of senators and representatives constituting a nation's legislature — **con·gres·sio·nal** \kən-ˈgre-shə-nəl\ *adj*

con·gress·man \ˈkäŋ-grəs-mən\ *n* : a member of a congress

con·gress·wom·an \-ˌwu̇-mən\ *n* : a female member of a congress

con·gru·ence \kən-ˈgrü-əns, ˈkäŋ-grü-\ *n* : the quality of agreeing or coinciding : CONGRUITY — **con·gru·ent** \kən-ˈgrü-ənt, ˈkäŋ-grü-\ *adj*

con·gru·en·cy \-sē\ *n, pl* **-cies** : CONGRUENCE

con·gru·ity \kän-ˈgrü-ə-tē\ *n, pl* **-ities** : correspondence between things — **con·gru·ous** \ˈkäŋ-grü-əs\ *adj*

con·ic \ˈkä-nik\ *adj* 1 : of or relating to a cone 2 : CONICAL

con·i·cal \ˈkä-ni-kəl\ *adj* : resembling a cone esp. in shape

co·ni·fer \ˈkä-nə-fər, ˈkō-\ *n* : any of an order of shrubs or trees (as the pines) that usu. are evergreen and bear cones — **co·nif·er·ous** \kō-ˈni-fə-rəs\ *adj*

conj *abbr* conjunction

con·jec·ture \kən-ˈjek-chər\ *n* : GUESS, SURMISE — **con·jec·tur·al** \-chə-rəl\ *adj* — **conjecture** *vb*

con·join \kən-ˈjȯin\ *vb* : to join together — **con·joint** \-ˈjȯint\ *adj*

con·ju·gal \ˈkän-ji-gəl\ *adj* : of or relating to marriage : MATRIMONIAL

¹**con·ju·gate** \ˈkän-ji-gət, -jə-ˌgāt\ *adj* 1 : united esp. in pairs : COUPLED 2 : of kindred origin and meaning ⟨*sing* and *song* are ∼⟩ — **con·ju·gate·ly** *adv*

²**con·ju·gate** \-jə-ˌgāt\ *vb* **-gat·ed; -gat·ing** 1 : INFLECT ⟨∼ a verb⟩ 2 : to join together : COUPLE

con·ju·ga·tion \ˌkän-jə-ˈgā-shən\ *n* 1 : an arrangement of the inflectional forms of a verb 2 : the act of conjugating : the state of being conjugated

con·junct \kän-ˈjəŋkt\ *adj* : JOINED, UNITED

con·junc·tion \kən-ˈjəŋk-shən\ *n* 1 : COMBINATION 2 : occurrence at the same time 3 : a word that joins together sentences, clauses, phrases, or words

con·junc·ti·va \ˌkän-ˌjəŋk-ˈtī-və\ *n, pl* **-vas** *or* **-vae** \-(ˌ)vē\ : the mucous membrane lining the inner surface of the eyelids and continuing over the forepart of the eyeball

con·junc·tive \kən-ˈjəŋk-tiv\ *adj* 1 : CONNECTIVE 2 : CONJUNCT 3 : being or functioning like a conjunction

con·junc·ti·vi·tis \kən-ˌjəŋk-ti-ˈvī-təs\ *n* : inflammation of the conjunctiva

con·junc·ture \kən-ˈjəŋk-chər\ *n* 1 : CONJUNCTION, UNION 2 : JUNCTURE 3

con·jure \ˈkän-jər, ˈkən- *for 1, 2;* kən-ˈjür *for 3*\ *vb* **con·jured; con·jur·ing** 1 : to implore earnestly or solemnly 2 : to practice magic; *esp* : to summon (as a devil) by sorcery 3 : to practice sleight of hand — **con·ju·ra·tion** \ˌkän-jü-ˈrā-shən, ˌkən-\ *n* — **con·jur·er** *or* **con·ju·ror** \ˈkän-jər-ər, ˈkən-\ *n*

conk \ˈkäŋk\ *vb* : BREAK DOWN; *esp* : STALL ⟨the motor ∼ed out⟩

Conn *abbr* Connecticut

con·nect \kə-ˈnekt\ *vb* 1 : JOIN, LINK 2 : to associate in one's mind — **con·nect·able** *adj* — **con·nec·tor** *n*

con·nec·tion \kə-ˈnek-shən\ *n* 1 : JUNCTION, UNION 2 : logical relationship : COHERENCE; *esp* : relation of a word to other words in a sentence 3 : family relationship 4 : BOND, LINK 5 : a person related by blood or marriage 6 : relationship in social affairs or in business 7 : an association of persons; *esp* : a religious denomination

¹**con·nec·tive** \kə-ˈnek-tiv\ *adj* : serving to connect — **con·nec·tiv·i·ty** \ˌkä-ˌnek-ˈti-və-tē\ *n*

²**connective** *n* : a word (as a conjunction) that connects words or word groups

con·nex·ion *chiefly Brit var of* CONNECTION

con·ning tower \ˈkä-niŋ-\ *n* : a raised structure on the deck of a submarine

con·nip·tion \kə-ˈnip-shən\ *n* : a fit of rage, hysteria, or alarm

con·nive \kə-ˈnīv\ *vb* **con·nived; con·niv·ing** [F or L; F *conniver*, fr. L *conivēre* to close the eyes, connive] 1 : to pretend ignorance of something one ought to oppose as wrong 2 : to cooperate secretly : give secret aid — **con·niv·ance** *n* — **con·niv·er** *n*

con·nois·seur \ˌkä-nə-ˈsər\ *n* : a critical judge in matters of art or taste

con·no·ta·tion \ˌkä-nə-ˈtā-shən\ *n* : a meaning in addition to or apart from the thing explicitly named or described by a word

con·no·ta·tive \'kä-nə-ˌtā-tiv, kə-'nō-tə-\ *adj* **1** : connoting or tending to connote **2** : relating to connotation

con·note \kə-'nōt\ *vb* **con·not·ed; con·not·ing** : to suggest or mean as a connotation

con·nu·bi·al \kə-'nü-bē-əl, -'nyü-\ *adj* : of or relating to marriage : CONJUGAL

con·quer \'käŋ-kər\ *vb* **1** : to gain by force of arms : WIN **2** : to get the better of : OVERCOME **syn** defeat, subjugate, subdue, overthrow, vanquish — **con·quer·or** \-ər\ *n*

con·quest \'kän-ˌkwest, 'käŋ-\ *n* **1** : an act of conquering : VICTORY **2** : something conquered

con·quis·ta·dor \kȯŋ-'kēs-tə-ˌdȯr, kän-'kwis-\ *n, pl* **-do·res** \-ˌkēs-tə-'dȯr-ēz, -ˌkwis-\ *or* **-dors** : CONQUEROR; *esp* : a leader in the Spanish conquest of the Americas in the 16th century

cons *abbr* consonant

con·san·guin·i·ty \ˌkän-ˌsan-'gwi-nə-tē, -ˌsaŋ-\ *n, pl* **-ties** : blood relationship — **con·san·guin·e·ous** \-nē-əs\ *adj*

con·science \'kän-chəns\ *n* : consciousness of the moral right and wrong of one's own acts or motives — **con·science·less** *adj*

con·sci·en·tious \ˌkän-chē-'en-chəs\ *adj* : guided by one's own sense of right and wrong **syn** scrupulous, honorable, honest, upright, just — **con·sci·en·tious·ly** *adv*

conscientious objector *n* : a person who refuses to serve in the armed forces or to bear arms on moral or religious grounds

con·scious \'kän-chəs\ *adj* **1** : AWARE **2** : known or felt by one's inner self **3** : mentally awake or alert : not asleep or unconscious **4** : INTENTIONAL — **con·scious·ly** *adv* — **con·scious·ness** *n*

con·script \kən-'skript\ *vb* : to enroll by compulsion for military or naval service — **conscript** \'kän-ˌskript\ *n* — **con·scrip·tion** \kən-'skrip-shən\ *n*

con·se·crate \'kän-sə-ˌkrāt\ *vb* **-crat·ed; -crat·ing** **1** : to induct (as a bishop) into an office with a religious rite **2** : to make or declare sacred ⟨∼ a church⟩ **3** : to devote solemnly to a purpose — **con·se·cra·tion** \ˌkän-sə-'krā-shən\ *n*

con·sec·u·tive \kən-'se-kyə-tiv\ *adj* : following in regular order : SUCCESSIVE — **con·sec·u·tive·ly** *adv*

con·sen·su·al \kən-'sen-chə-wəl\ *adj* : involving or based on mutual consent

con·sen·sus \kən-'sen-səs\ *n* **1** : agreement in opinion, testimony, or belief **2** : collective opinion

¹con·sent \kən-'sent\ *vb* : to give assent or approval

²consent *n* : approval or acceptance of something done or proposed by another

con·se·quence \'kän-sə-ˌkwens\ *n* **1** : RESULT **2** : IMPORTANCE **syn** effect, outcome, aftermath, upshot

con·se·quent \-kwənt, -ˌkwent\ *adj* : following as a result or effect

con·se·quen·tial \ˌkän-sə-'kwen-chəl\ *adj* **1** : having significant consequences **2** : showing self-importance

con·se·quent·ly \'kän-sə-ˌkwent-lē, -kwənt-\ *adv* : as a result : ACCORDINGLY

con·ser·van·cy \kən-'sər-vən-sē\ *n, pl* **-cies** : an organization or area designated to conserve natural resources

con·ser·va·tion \ˌkän-sər-'vā-shən\ *n* : PRESERVATION; *esp* : planned management of natural resources

con·ser·va·tion·ist \-shə-nist\ *n* : a person who advocates conservation esp. of natural resources

con·ser·va·tism \kən-'sər-və-ˌti-zəm\ *n* : disposition to keep to established ways : opposition to change

¹con·ser·va·tive \kən-'sər-və-tiv\ *adj* **1** : PRESERVATIVE **2** : disposed to maintain existing views, conditions, or institutions **3** : MODERATE, CAUTIOUS — **con·ser·va·tive·ly** *adv*

²conservative *n* : a person who is conservative esp. in politics

con·ser·va·tor \kən-'sər-və-tər, 'kän-sər-ˌvā-\ *n* **1** : PROTECTOR, GUARDIAN **2** : one named by a court to protect the interests of an incompetent (as a child)

con·ser·va·to·ry \kən-'sər-və-ˌtȯr-ē\ *n, pl* **-ries** **1** : GREENHOUSE **2** : a place of instruction in one of the fine arts (as music)

¹con·serve \kən-'sərv\ *vb* **con·served; con·serv·ing** : to keep from losing or wasting : PRESERVE

²con·serve \'kän-ˌsərv\ *n* **1** : CONFECTION; *esp* : a candied fruit **2** : PRESERVE; *esp* : one prepared from a mixture of fruits

con·sid·er \kən-'si-dər\ *vb* [ME, fr. MF *considerer*, fr. L *considerare*, fr. *com-* together + *sider-, sidus* heavenly body] **1** : THINK, PONDER **2** : HEED, REGARD **3** : JUDGE, BELIEVE — **con·sid·ered** *adj*

con·sid·er·able \-'si-dər-ə-bəl, -'si-drə-bəl\ *adj* **1** : IMPORTANT **2** : large in extent, amount, or degree — **con·sid·er·ably** \-blē\ *adv*

con·sid·er·ate \kən-'si-də-rət\ *adj* : observant of the rights and feelings of others **syn** thoughtful, attentive

con·sid·er·ation \kən-ˌsi-də-'rā-shən\ *n* **1** : careful thought : DELIBERATION **2** : a matter taken into account **3** : thoughtful attention **4** : JUDGMENT, OPINION **5** : RECOMPENSE

con·sid·er·ing *prep* : in view of : taking into account

con·sign \kən-'sīn\ *vb* **1** : ENTRUST, COMMIT **2** : to deliver formally **3** : to send (goods) to an agent for sale — **con·sign·ee** \ˌkän-sə-'nē, -ˌsī-; kən-ˌsī-\ *n* — **con·sign·or** \ˌkän-sə-'nȯr, -ˌsī-; kən-ˌsī-\ *n*

con·sign·ment \kən-'sīn-mənt\ *n* : something consigned esp. in a single shipment

con·sist \kən-'sist\ *vb* **1** : to be inherent : LIE — usu. used with *in* **2** : to be composed or made up — usu. used with *of*

con·sis·tence \kən-'sis-təns\ *n* : CONSISTENCY

con·sis·ten·cy \-tən-sē\ *n, pl* **-cies** **1** : COHESIVENESS, FIRMNESS **2** : agreement or harmony in parts or of different things **3** : UNIFORMITY ⟨∼ of behavior⟩ — **con·sis·tent** \-tənt\ *adj* — **con·sis·tent·ly** *adv*

con·sis·to·ry \kən-'sis-tə-rē\ *n, pl* **-ries** : a solemn assembly (as of Roman Catholic cardinals)

consol *abbr* consolidated

¹con·sole \'kän-ˌsōl\ *n* **1** : the desklike part of an organ at which the organist sits **2** : the combination of displays and controls of a device or system **3** : a cabinet for a radio or television set resting directly on the floor **4** : a small storage cabinet between bucket seats in an automobile

²con·sole \kən-'sōl\ *vb* **con·soled; con·sol·ing** : to soothe the grief of : COMFORT, SOLACE — **con·so·la·tion** \ˌkän-sə-'lā-shən\ *n* — **con·so·la·to·ry** \kən-'sō-lə-ˌtȯr-ē, -'sä-\ *adj*

con·sol·i·date \kən-'sä-lə-ˌdāt\ *vb* **-dat·ed; -dat·ing** **1** : to unite or become united into one whole : COMBINE **2** : to make firm or secure **3** : to form into a compact mass — **con·sol·i·da·tion** \-ˌsä-lə-'dā-shən\ *n*

con·som·mé \ˌkän-sə-'mā\ *n* [F] : a clear soup made from well-seasoned stock

con·so·nance \'kän-sə-nəns\ *n* **1** : AGREEMENT, HARMONY **2** : repetition of consonants esp. as an alternative to rhyme in verse

¹con·so·nant \-nənt\ *adj* : having consonance, harmony, or agreement **syn** consistent, compatible, congruous, congenial, sympathetic — **con·so·nant·ly** *adv*

²consonant *n* **1** : a speech sound (as \p\, \g\, \n\, \l\, \s\, \r\) characterized by constriction or closure at one or

\ə\abut \ᵊ\kitten \ər\further \a\ash \ā\ace \ä\mop, mar \aú\out \ch\chin \e\bet \ē\easy \g\go \i\hit \ī\ice \j\job \ŋ\sing \ō\go \ȯ\law \ȯi\boy \th\thin \th\the \ü\loot \ú\foot \y\yet \zh\vision *see also* Pronunciation Symbols page more points in the breath channel **2** : a letter other than *a, e, i, o,* and *u* — **con·so·nan·tal** \ˌkän-sə-ˈnant-ᵊl\ *adj*

¹con·sort \ˈkän-ˌsȯrt\ *n* **1** : a ship accompanying another **2** : SPOUSE, MATE

²con·sort \kən-ˈsȯrt\ *vb* **1** : to keep company **2** : ACCORD, HARMONIZE

con·sor·tium \kən-ˈsȯr-shəm; -shē-əm, -tē-\ *n, pl* **-sor·tia** \-shə-; -shē-ə, -tē-\ [L, fellowship] : an agreement or combination (as of companies) formed to undertake a large enterprise

con·spec·tus \kən-ˈspek-təs\ *n* **1** : a brief survey or summary **2** : SUMMARY

con·spic·u·ous \kən-ˈspi-kyə-wəs\ *adj* : attracting attention : PROMINENT, STRIKING syn noticeable, remarkable, outstanding — **con·spic·u·ous·ly** *adv*

con·spir·a·cy \kən-ˈspir-ə-sē\ *n, pl* **-cies** : an agreement among conspirators : PLOT

con·spire \kən-ˈspīr\ *vb* **conspired; con·spir·ing** [ME, fr. MF *conspirer,* fr. L *conspirare* to be in harmony, conspire, fr. *com-* with + *spirare* to breathe] : to plan secretly an unlawful act : PLOT

con·spir·a·tor \kən-ˈspir-ə-tər\ *n* : one that conspires — **con·spir·a·to·ri·al** \-ˌspir-ə-ˈtȯr-ē-əl\ *adj*

const *abbr* **1** constant **2** constitution; constitutional

con·sta·ble \ˈkän-stə-bəl, ˈkən-\ *n* [ME *conestable,* fr. OF, fr. LL *comes stabuli,* lit., officer of the stable] : a public officer responsible for keeping the peace

con·stab·u·lary \kən-ˈsta-byə-ˌler-ē\ *n, pl* **-lar·ies 1** : the police of a particular district or country **2** : a police force organized like the military

con·stan·cy \ˈkän-stən-sē\ *n, pl* **-cies 1** : firmness of mind **2** : STABILITY

¹con·stant \-stənt\ *adj* **1** : STEADFAST, FAITHFUL **2** : FIXED, UNCHANGING **3** : continually recurring : REGULAR — **con·stant·ly** *adv*

²constant *n* : something unchanging

con·stel·la·tion \ˌkän-stə-ˈlā-shən\ *n* : any of 88 groups of stars forming patterns
☞ For table, see pages 120 and 121.

con·ster·na·tion \ˌkän-stər-ˈnā-shən\ *n* : amazed dismay and confusion

con·sti·pa·tion \ˌkän-stə-ˈpā-shən\ *n* : abnormally difficult or infrequent bowel movements — **con·sti·pate** \ˈkän-stə-ˌpāt\ *vb*

con·stit·u·en·cy \kən-ˈsti-chə-wən-sē\ *n, pl* **-cies** : a body of constituents; *also* : an electoral district

¹con·stit·u·ent \-wənt\ *n* **1** : a person entitled to vote for a representative for a district **2** : a component part

²constituent *adj* **1** : COMPONENT **2** : having power to create a government or frame or amend a constitution

con·sti·tute \ˈkän-stə-ˌtüt, -ˌtyüt\ *vb* **-tut·ed; -tut·ing 1** : to appoint to an office or duty : SET UP, ESTABLISH ⟨∼ a law⟩ **2** : MAKE UP, COMPOSE

con·sti·tu·tion \ˌkän-stə-ˈtü-shən, -ˈtyü-\ *n* **1** : an established law or custom **2** : the physical makeup of the individual **3** : the structure, composition, or makeup of something ⟨∼ of the sun⟩ **4** : the basic law in a politically organized body; *also* : a document containing such law

¹con·sti·tu·tion·al \-shə-nəl\ *adj* **1** : of or relating to the constitution of body or mind **2** : being in accord with the constitution of a state or society; *also* : of or relating to such a constitution — **con·sti·tu·tion·al·ly** *adv*

²constitutional *n* : an exercise (as a walk) taken for one's health

con·sti·tu·tion·al·i·ty \-ˌtü-shə-ˈna-lə-tē, -ˌtyü-\ *n* : the quality or state of being constitutional

con·sti·tu·tive \ˈkän-stə-ˌtü-tiv, -ˌtyü-, kən-ˈsti-chə-tiv\ *adj* **1** : CONSTRUCTIVE **2** : CONSTITUENT, ESSENTIAL

constr *abbr* construction

con·strain \kən-ˈstrān\ *vb* **1** : COMPEL, FORCE **2** : CONFINE **3** : RESTRAIN

con·straint \-ˈstrānt\ *n* **1** : COMPULSION; *also* : RESTRAINT **2** : repression of one's natural feelings

con·strict \kən-ˈstrikt\ *vb* : to draw together : SQUEEZE — **con·stric·tion** \-ˈstrik-shən\ *n* — **con·stric·tive** \-ˈstrik-tiv\ *adj*

con·stric·tor \kən-ˈstrik-tər\ *n* : a snake that kills its prey by crushing it in its coils

con·struct \kən-ˈstrəkt\ *vb* : BUILD, MAKE — **con·struc·tor** \-ˈstrək-tər\ *n*

con·struc·tion \kən-ˈstrək-shən\ *n* **1** : INTERPRETATION **2** : the art, process, or manner of building; *also* : something built, created, or established : STRUCTURE **3** : syntactical arrangement of words in a sentence — **con·struc·tive** \-tiv\ *adj*

con·struc·tion·ist \-shə-nist\ *n* : a person who construes a legal document (as the U.S. Constitution) in a specific way ⟨a strict ∼⟩

con·strue \kən-ˈstrü\ *vb* **con·strued; con·stru·ing 1** : to analyze the mutual relations of words in a sentence; *also* : TRANSLATE **2** : EXPLAIN, INTERPRET — **con·stru·able** *adj*

con·sub·stan·ti·a·tion \ˌkän-səb-ˌstan-chē-ˈā-shən\ *n* : the actual substantial presence and combination of the body and blood of Christ with the eucharistic bread and wine

con·sul \ˈkän-səl\ *n* **1** : a chief magistrate of the Roman republic **2** : an official appointed by a government to reside in a foreign country to care for the commercial interests of the appointing government's citizens — **con·sul·ar** \-sə-lər\ *adj* — **con·sul·ate** \-lət\ *n* — **con·sul·ship** *n*

con·sult \kən-ˈsəlt\ *vb* **1** : to ask the advice or opinion of **2** : CONFER — **con·sul·tant** \-ᵊnt\ *n* — **con·sul·ta·tion** \ˌkän-səl-ˈtā-shən\ *n*

con·sume \kən-ˈsüm\ *vb* **con·sumed; con·sum·ing 1** : DESTROY ⟨*consumed* by fire⟩ **2** : to spend wastefully **3** : to eat up : DEVOUR **4** : to absorb the attention of : ENGROSS — **con·sum·able** *adj* — **con·sum·er** *n*

con·sum·er·ism \kən-ˈsü-mə-ˌri-zəm\ *n* : the promotion of consumers' interests (as against false advertising)

consumer price index *n* : an index measuring the change in the cost of widely purchased goods and services from the cost in some base period

¹con·sum·mate \ˈkän-sə-mət, kən-ˈsə\ *adj* : PERFECT syn finished, accomplished

²con·sum·mate \ˈkän-sə-ˌmāt\ *vb* **-mat·ed; -mat·ing** : to make complete : FINISH, ACHIEVE — **con·sum·ma·tion** \ˌkän-sə-ˈmā-shən\ *n*

con·sump·tion \kən-ˈsəmp-shən\ *n* **1** : progressive bodily wasting away; *also* : TUBERCULOSIS **2** : the act of consuming or using up **3** : the use of economic goods

¹con·sump·tive \-ˈsəmp-tiv\ *adj* **1** : tending to consume **2** : relating to or affected with consumption

²consumptive *n* : a person who has consumption

cont *abbr* **1** containing **2** contents **3** continent; continental **4** continued **5** control

¹con·tact \ˈkän-ˌtakt\ *n* **1** : a touching or meeting of bodies **2** : ASSOCIATION, RELATIONSHIP; *also* : CONNECTION, COMMUNICATION **3** : a person serving as a go-between or source of information **4** : CONTACT LENS

²contact *vb* **1** : to come or bring into contact : TOUCH **2** : to get in communication with

contact lens *n* : a thin lens fitting over the cornea usu. to correct vision

con·ta·gion \kən-ˈtā-jən\ *n* **1** : a contagious disease; *also* : the transmission of such a disease **2** : a disease-producing agent (as a virus) **3** : transmission of an influence on the mind or emotions

con·ta·gious \-jəs\ *adj* **1** : transmitted by contact with an infected person, his or her bodily discharges, or something that has touched either **2** : communicated or transmitted like a contagious disease; *esp* : exciting similar emotion or conduct in others

con·tain \kən-'tān\ *vb* **1** : RESTRAIN **2** : to have within : HOLD **3** : COMPRISE, INCLUDE — **con·tain·ment** *n*

con·tain·er \kən-'tā-nər\ *n* : RECEPTACLE; *esp* : one for shipment of goods

con·tam·i·nant \kən-'ta-mə-nənt\ *n* : something that contaminates

con·tam·i·nate \kən-'ta-mə-ˌnāt\ *vb* **-nat·ed; -nat·ing** : to soil, stain, or infect by contact or association — **con·tam·i·na·tion** \-ˌta-mə-'nā-shən\ *n*

contd *abbr* continued

con·temn \kən-'tem\ *vb* : to view or treat with contempt : DESPISE

con·tem·plate \'kän-təm-ˌplāt\ *vb* **-plat·ed; -plat·ing** [L *contemplari*, fr. *com-* with + *templum* space marked out for observation of auguries] **1** : to view or consider with continued attention **2** : INTEND — **con·tem·pla·tion** \ˌkän-təm-'plā-shən\ *n* — **con·tem·pla·tive** \kən-'tem-plə-tiv, 'kän-təm-ˌplā-\ *adj*

con·tem·po·ra·ne·ous \kən-ˌtem-pə-'rā- nē-əs\ *adj* : CONTEMPORARY 1

con·tem·po·rary \kən-'tem-pə-ˌrer-ē\ *adj* **1** : occurring or existing at the same time **2** : marked by characteristics of the present period — **contemporary** *n*

con·tempt \kən-'tempt\ *n* **1** : the act of despising : the state of mind of one who despises **2** : the state of being despised **3** : disobedience to or open disrespect of a court or legislature

con·tempt·ible \kən-'temp-tə-bəl\ *adj* : deserving contempt : DESPICABLE — **con·tempt·ibly** \-blē\ *adv*

con·temp·tu·ous \-'temp-chə-wəs\ *adj* : feeling or expressing contempt — **con·temp·tu·ous·ly** *adv*

con·tend \kən-'tend\ *vb* **1** : to strive against rivals or difficulties **2** : ARGUE **3** : MAINTAIN, ASSERT — **con·tend·er** *n*

¹con·tent \kən-'tent\ *adj* : SATISFIED

²content *vb* : SATISFY; *esp* : to limit (oneself) in requirements or actions

³content *n* : CONTENTMENT

⁴con·tent \'kän-ˌtent\ *n* **1** : something contained ⟨∼s of a room⟩ **2** : subject matter or topics treated (as in a book) **3** : MEANING, SIGNIFICANCE **4** : the amount of material contained

con·tent·ed \kən-'ten-təd\ *adj* : SATISFIED — **con·tent·ed·ly** *adv* — **con·tent·ed·ness** *n*

con·ten·tion \kən-'ten-chən\ *n* **1** : CONTEST, STRIFE **2** : an idea or point for which a person argues — **con·ten·tious** \-chəs\ *adj* — **con·ten·tious·ly** *adv*

con·tent·ment \kən-'tent-mənt\ *n* : ease of mind : SATISFACTION

con·ter·mi·nous \kän-'tər-mə-nəs\ *adj* : having the same or a common boundary — **con·ter·mi·nous·ly** *adv*

¹con·test \kən-'test\ *vb* **1** : to engage in strife : FIGHT **2** : CHALLENGE, DISPUTE — **con·tes·tant** \-'tes-tənt\ *n*

²con·test \'kän-ˌtest\ *n* : STRUGGLE, COMPETITION

con·text \'kän-ˌtekst\ *n* [L *contextus* connection of words, coherence, fr. *contexere* to weave together] : the parts of a discourse that surround a word or passage and help to explain its meaning; *also* : the circumstances surrounding an act or event — **con·tex·tu·al·ly** *adv*

con·tig·u·ous \kən-'ti-gyə-wəs\ *adj* : being in contact : TOUCHING; *also* : NEXT, ADJOINING — **con·ti·gu·i·ty** \ˌkän-tə-'gyü-ə-tē\ *n*

con·ti·nence \'känt-ᵊn-əns\ *n* **1** : SELF-RESTRAINT; *esp* : a refraining from sexual intercourse **2** : the ability to retain urine or feces voluntarily

¹con·ti·nent \'känt-ᵊn-ənt\ *adj* : exercising continence

²continent *n* **1** : any of the great divisions of land on the globe **2** *cap* : the continent of Europe

¹con·ti·nen·tal \ˌkän-tə-'nent-ᵊl\ *adj* **1** : of or relating to a continent; *esp, often cap* : of or relating to the continent of Europe **2** *often cap* : of or relating to the col-

onies later forming the U.S. **3** : of or relating to cuisine based on classical European cooking

²continental *n* **1** *often cap* : a soldier in the Continental army **2** : EUROPEAN

continental drift *n* : a hypothetical slow movement of the continents over a fluid layer deep within the earth

continental shelf *n* : a shallow submarine plain forming a border to a continent

continental slope *n* : a usu. steep slope from a continental shelf to the ocean floor

con·tin·gen·cy \kən-'tin-jən-sē\ *n, pl* **-cies** : a chance or possible event

¹con·tin·gent \-jənt\ *adj* **1** : liable but not certain to happen : POSSIBLE **2** : happening by chance : not planned **3** : dependent on something that may or may not occur **4** : CONDITIONAL **syn** accidental, casual, incidental, odd

²contingent *n* : a quota (as of troops) supplied from an area or group

con·tin·u·al \kən-'tin-yə-wəl\ *adj* **1** : CONTINUOUS, UNBROKEN **2** : steadily recurring — **con·tin·u·al·ly** *adv*

con·tin·u·ance \-yə-wəns\ *n* **1** : unbroken succession **2** : the extent of continuing : DURATION **3** : adjournment of legal proceedings

con·tin·u·a·tion \kən-ˌtin-yə-'wā-shən\ *n* **1** : extension or prolongation of a state or activity **2** : resumption after an interruption; *also* : something that carries on after a pause or break

con·tin·ue \kən-'tin-yü\ *vb* **-tin·ued; -tinu·ing** **1** : to maintain without interruption **2** : ENDURE, LAST **3** : to remain in a place or condition **4** : to resume (as a story) after an intermission **5** : EXTEND; *also* : to persist in **6** : to allow to remain **7** : to keep (a legal case) on the calendar or undecided

con·ti·nu·i·ty \ˌkän-tə-'nü-ə-tē, -'nyü-\ *n, pl* **-ties** **1** : the state of being continuous **2** : something that has or provides continuity

con·tin·u·ous \kən-'tin-yə-wəs\ *adj* : continuing without interruption — **con·tin·u·ous·ly** *adv*

con·tin·u·um \-yə-wəm\ *n, pl* **-ua** \-yə-wə\ *also* **-u·ums** : something that is the same throughout or consists of a series of variations or of a sequence of things in regular order

con·tort \kən-'tȯrt\ *vb* : to twist out of shape — **con·tor·tion** \-'tȯr-shən\ *n*

con·tor·tion·ist \-'tȯr-shə-nist\ *n* : an acrobat able to twist the body into unusual postures

con·tour \'kän-ˌtu̇r\ *n* [F, fr. It *contorno* fr. *contornare* to round off, sketch in outline, fr. L *com-* together + *tornare* to turn in a lathe, fr. *tornus* lathe] **1** : OUTLINE **2** : SHAPE, FORM — often used in pl. ⟨the ∼s of a statue⟩

contr *abbr* contract; contraction

con·tra·band \'kän-trə-ˌband\ *n* : goods legally prohibited in trade; *also* : smuggled goods

con·tra·cep·tion \ˌkän-trə-'sep-shən\ *n* : intentional prevention of conception and pregnancy — **con·tra·cep·tive** \-'sep-tiv\ *adj or n*

¹con·tract \'kän-ˌtrakt\ *n* **1** : a binding agreement **2** : an undertaking to win a specified number of tricks in bridge — **con·trac·tu·al** \kən-'trak-chə-wəl\ *adj* — **con·trac·tu·al·ly** *adv*

²con·tract \kən-'trakt, *2 usu* 'kän-ˌtrakt\ *vb* **1** : to become affected with ⟨∼ a disease⟩ **2** : to establish or undertake by contract **3** : SHRINK, LESSEN; *esp* : to draw together esp. so as to shorten ⟨∼ a muscle⟩ **4** : to shorten (a word) by omitting letters or sounds in the middle — **con·tract·ible** \kən-'trak-tə-bəl, 'kän-ˌ\ *adj* — **con·trac·tion** \kən-'trak-shən\ *n* — **con·trac·tor** \'kän-ˌtrak-tər, kən-'trak-\ *n*

\ə\abut \ᵊ\kitten \ər\further \a\ash \ā\ace \ä\mop, mar \au̇\out \ch\chin \e\bet \ē\easy \g\go \i\hit \ī\ice \j\job \ŋ\sing \ō\go \ȯ\law \ȯi\boy \th\thin \t͟h\the \ü\loot \u̇\foot \y\yet \zh\vision *see also* Pronunciation Symbols page

120

TABLE OF CONSTELLATIONS

NAME AND MEANING	DECLINATION
[1]Andromeda \an-ˈdräm-əd-ə\ *Andromeda, the Chained Lady*	40° N
Antlia (Antlia Pneumatica) \ˈant-lē-ə-n(y)ü-ˌmat-i-kə\ *Pump (Air Pump)*	35° S
Apus \ˈā-pəs\ *Bird of Paradise*	75° S
[1]Aquarius \ə-ˈkwar-ē-əs\ *Water Carrier*	10° S
[1]Aquila \ə-ˈkwil-ə\ *Eagle*	5° N
[1]Ara \ˈar-ə\ *Altar*	55° S
[1]Aries \ˈar-ˌēz\ *Ram*	20° N
[1]Auriga \ȯ-ˈrī-gə\ *Charioteer*	40° N
[1]Boötes \bō-ˈōt-ēz\ *Herdsman*	30° N
Caelum (Caela Sculptoris) \ˈsē-ləm, ˈsē-lə-ˌskəlp-ˈtōr-əs\ *Graving Tool*	40° S
Camelopardalis \kə-ˌmel-ə-ˈpär-də-ləs, ˌkam-ə-lō-\ *Giraffe*	70° N
[1]Cancer \ˈkan-sər\ *Crab*	20° N
Canes Venatici \ˈkā-ˌnēz-və-ˈnat-ə-ˌsī\ *Hunting Dogs*	40° N
[1]Canis Major \ˈkā-nəs-ˈmā-jər, ˈkan-əs-\ *Larger Dog*	20° S
[1]Canis Minor \ˈkā-nəs-ˈmī-nər, ˈkan-əs-\ *Lesser Dog*	5° N
[1]Capricornis \ˌkap-rə-ˈkȯr-nəs\ *Horned Goat*	20° S
[2]Carina \kə-ˈrī-nə\ *Keel*	60° S
[1]Cassiopeia \ˌkas-ē-ə-ˈpē-ə\ *Cassiopeia, the Lady in the Chair*	60° N
[1]Centaurus \sen-ˈtȯr-əs\ *Centaur*	45° S
[1]Cepheus \ˈsē-ˈfyüs, -fē-əs\ *Cepheus, the Monarch*	70° N
[1]Cetus \ˈsē-təs\ *Whale*	5° S
Chamaeleon \kə-ˈmēl-yən\ *Chameleon*	80° S
Circinus \ˈsərs-ᵊn-əs\ *Pair of Compasses*	65° S
Columba (Columba Noae) \kə-ˈləm-bə-ˈnō-ˌē\ *Dove (Noah's Dove)*	35° S
Coma Berenices \ˈkō-mə-ˌber-ə-ˈnī-(ˌ)sēz\ *Berenice's Hair*	25° N
[1]Corona Australis \kə-ˈrō-nə-ȯ-ˈstrā-ləs\ *Southern Crown*	40° S
[1]Corona Borealis \kə-ˈrō-nə-ˌbōr-ē-ˈal-əs, -ˈā-ləs\ *Northern Crown*	30° N
[1]Corvus \ˈkȯr-vəs\ *Crow*	20° S
[1]Crater \ˈkrāt-ər\ *Cup*	15° S
Crux \ˈkrəks\ *Southern Cross*	60° S
[1]Cygnus \ˈsig-nəs\ *Swan*	40° N
[1]Delphinus \del-ˈfī-nəs\ *Dolphin*	15° N
Dorado \də-ˈrä-(ˌ)dō\ *Dorado [a fish]*	60° S
[1]Draco \ˈdrā-ˌkō\ *Dragon*	65° N
[1]Equuleus \e-ˈkwü-lē-əs\ *Colt*	5° N
[1]Eridanus \ə-ˈrid-ᵊn-əs\ *Eridanus, the River Po*	20° S
Fornax \ˈfȯr-ˌnaks\ *Furnace*	30° S
[1]Gemini \ˈjem-ə-ˌnī\ *Twins*	25° N
Grus \ˈgrəs, ˈgrüs\ *Crane*	45° S
[1]Hercules \ˈhər-kyə-ˌlēz\ *Hercules*	30° N

NAME AND MEANING	DECLINATION
Horologium \ˌhȯr-ə-ˈlō-jē-əm\ *Clock*	50° S
[1]Hydra \ˈhī-drə\ *Water Monster*	10° S
Hydrus \ˈhī-drəs\ *Water Snake*	70° S
Indus \ˈin-dəs\ *Indian*	55° S
Lacerta \lə-ˈsert-ə\ *Lizard*	45° N
[1]Leo \ˈlē-(ˌ)ō\ *Lion*	15° N
Leo Minor \ˈlē-(ˌ)ō-ˈmī-nər\ *Smaller Lion*	25° N
[1]Lepus \ˈlē-pəs, ˈlep-əs\ *Hare*	20° S
[1]Libra \ˈlī-brə, ˈlē-\ *Balance*	15° S
[1]Lupus \ˈlü-pəs\ *Wolf*	40° S
Lynx \ˈliŋks\ *Lynx*	45° N
[1]Lyra \ˈlī-rə\ *Lyre*	35° N
Mensa (Mons Mensae) \ˈmen-sə, ˈmänz-ˈmen-ˌsē\ *Table (Table Mountain)*	75° S
Microscopium \ˌmī-krə-ˈskō-pē-əm\ *Microscope*	35° S
Monoceros \mə-ˈnäs-ə-rəs\ *Unicorn*	5° S
Musca \ˈməs-kə\ *Fly*	70° S
Norma \ˈnȯr-mə\ *Square (and Rule)*	50° S
Octans \ˈäk-ˌtanz\ *Octant*	85° S
[1]Ophiuchus \ˌō-fē-ˈyü-kəs\ *Serpent Holder*	0°
[1]Orion \ȯ-ˈrī-ən\ *Orion, the Hunter*	0°
Pavo \ˈpā-(ˌ)vō, ˈpä-\ *Peacock*	65° S
[1]Pegasus \ˈpeg-ə-səs\ *Pegasus, the Winged Horse*	20° N
[1]Perseus \ˈpər-ˌsüs, -sē-əs\ *Perseus, the Rescuer or Champion*	45° N
Phoenix \ˈfē-niks\ *Phoenix*	50° S
Pictor \ˈpik-tər\ *Painter's Easel*	55° S
[1]Pisces \ˈpī-ˌsēz, ˈpis-ˌēz\ *Fishes*	10° N
[1]Piscis Austrinus \ˈpis-əs-ȯ-ˈstrī-nəs\ *Southern Fish*	30° S
[2]Puppis \ˈpəp-əs\ *Stern*	30° S
[2]Pyxis \ˈpik-səs\ *Mariner's Compass*	30° S
Reticulum \rə-ˈtik-yə-ləm\ *Net*	60° S
[1]Sagitta \sə-ˈjit-ə\ *Arrow*	20° N
[1]Sagittarius \ˌsaj-ə-ˈtar-ē-əs\ *Archer*	30° S
[1]Scorpius \ˈskȯr-pē-əs\ *Scorpion*	30° S
Sculptor \ˈskəlp-tər\ *Sculptor's Workshop*	30° S
Scutum \ˈsk(y)üt-əm\ *Shield*	10° S
[1]Serpens \ˈsər-pənz, -ˌpenz\ *Serpent*	0°
Sextans \ˈsek-ˌstanz\ *Sextant*	5° S
[1]Taurus \ˈtȯr-əs\ *Bull*	20° N
Telescopium \ˌtel-ə-ˈskō-pē-əm\ *Telescope*	50° S
[1]Triangulum \trī-ˈaŋ-gyə-ləm\ *Triangle*	30° N
Triangulum Australe \trī-ˈaŋ-gyə-ləm-ȯ-ˈstrā-(ˌ)lē\ *Southern Triangle*	65° S
Tucana \tü-ˈkan-ə, -ˈkän-\ *Toucan*	65° S
[1]Ursa Major \ˈər-sə-ˈmā-jər\ *Larger Bear*	50° N
[1]Ursa Minor \ˈər-sə-ˈmī-nər\ *Smaller Bear*	80° N
[2]Vela \ˈvē-lə\ *Sails*	45° S
[1]Virgo \ˈvər-ˌgō\ *Virgin*	0°
Volans (Piscis Volans) \ˈpis-əs-ˈvō-ˌlanz\ *Flying Fish*	70° S
Vulpecula \ˌvəl-ˈpek-yə-lə\ *Little Fox*	25° N

[1]One of the 48 constellations of Ptolemy.

[2]One of the subdivisions of the Ptolemaic constellation Argo Navis \ˈär-(ˌ)gō-ˈnā-vəs\ the Ship Argo, which included Carina, Puppis, Pyxis, and Vela.

CONSTELLATIONS AND STARS

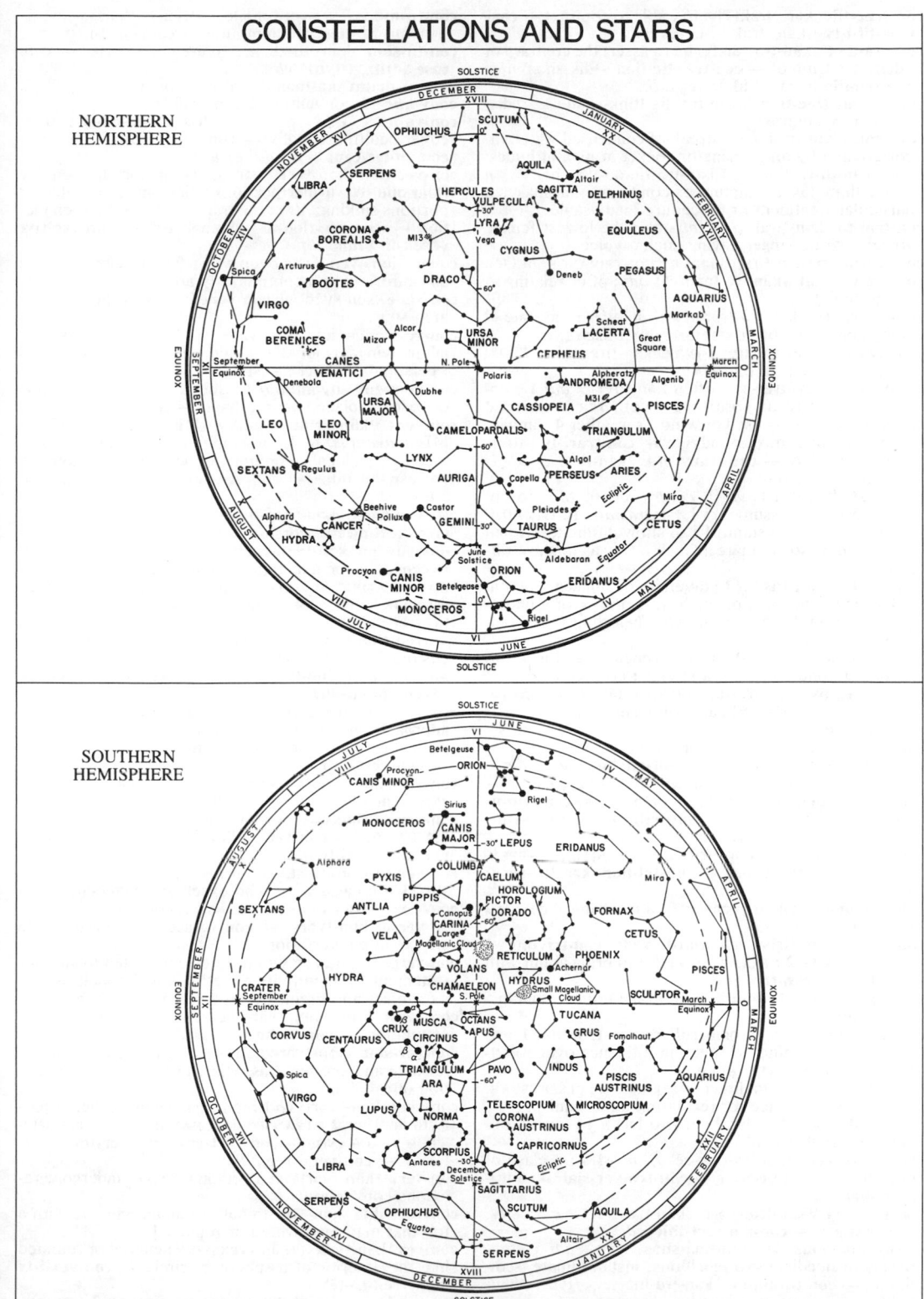

NORTHERN
HEMISPHERE

SOUTHERN
HEMISPHERE

con·trac·tile \kən-ˈtrakt-ᵊl\ *adj* : able to contract — **con·trac·til·i·ty** \ˌkän-ˌtrak-ˈti-lə-tē\ *n*

con·tra·dict \ˌkän-trə-ˈdikt\ *vb* : to assert the contrary of : deny the truth of — **con·tra·dic·tion** \-ˈdik-shən\ *n* — **con·tra·dic·to·ry** \-ˈdik-tə-rē\ *adj*

con·tra·dis·tinc·tion \ˌkän-trə-dis-ˈtiŋk-shən\ *n* : distinction by contrast

con·trail \ˈkän-ˌtrāl\ *n* : a streak of condensed water vapor created by an airplane or rocket at high altitudes

con·tra·in·di·ca·tion \ˌkän-trə-ˌin-də-ˈkā-shən\ *n* : something (as a symptom or condition) that makes a particular treatment or procedure inadvisable

con·tral·to \kən-ˈtral-tō\ *n, pl* **-tos** : the lowest female voice; *also* : a singer having such a voice

con·trap·tion \kən-ˈtrap-shən\ *n* : CONTRIVANCE, DEVICE

con·tra·pun·tal \ˌkän-trə-ˈpənt-ᵊl\ *adj* : of or relating to counterpoint

con·tra·ri·ety \ˌkän-trə-ˈrī-ə-tē\ *n, pl* **-eties** : the state of being contrary : DISAGREEMENT, INCONSISTENCY

con·trari·wise \ˈkän-ˌtrer-ē-ˌwīz, kən-ˈtrer-\ *adv* 1 : on the contrary 2 : VICE VERSA

con·trary \ˈkän-ˌtrer-ē; *4 often* kən-ˈtrer-ē\ *adj* 1 : opposite in nature or position 2 : COUNTER, OPPOSED 3 : UNFAVORABLE — used of wind or weather 4 : unwilling to accept control or advice — **con·trari·ly** \-ˌtrer-ə-lē, -ˈtrer-\ *adv* — **con·trary** *n is* ˈkän-ˌtrer-ē, *adv is like adj*\ *n or adv*

¹**con·trast** \kən-ˈtrast\ *vb* [F *contraster,* fr. MF, to oppose, resist, fr. (assumed) VL *contrastare,* fr. L *contra-* against + *stare* to stand] 1 : to show differences when compared 2 : to compare in such a way as to show differences

²**con·trast** \ˈkän-ˌtrast\ *n* 1 : diversity of adjacent parts in color, emotion, tone, or brightness ⟨the ∼ of a photograph⟩ 2 : unlikeness as shown when things are compared : DIFFERENCE

con·tra·vene \ˌkän-trə-ˈvēn\ *vb* **-vened; -ven·ing** 1 : to go or act contrary to ⟨∼ a law⟩ 2 : CONTRADICT

con·tre·temps \ˈkän-trə-ˌtäⁿ, kòⁿ-trə-ˈtäⁿ\ *n, pl* **con·tre·temps** \-ˌtäⁿ, -ˌtäⁿz\ [F] : an inopportune or embarrassing occurrence

contrib *abbr* contribution; contributor

con·trib·ute \kən-ˈtri-byət\ *vb* **-ut·ed; -ut·ing** : to give along with others (as to a fund); *also* : HELP, ASSIST — **con·tri·bu·tion** \ˌkän-trə-ˈbyü-shən\ *n* — **con·trib·u·tor** \kən-ˈtri-byə-tər\ *n* — **con·trib·u·to·ry** \-byə-ˌtòr-ē\ *adj*

con·trite \ˈkän-ˌtrīt, kən-ˈtrīt\ *adj* : PENITENT, REPENTANT — **con·trite·ly** *adv* — **con·tri·tion** \kən-ˈtri-shən\ *n*

con·triv·ance \kən-ˈtrī-vəns\ *n* 1 : a mechanical device 2 : SCHEME, PLAN

con·trive \kən-ˈtrīv\ *vb* **con·trived; con·triv·ing** 1 : PLAN, DEVISE 2 : FRAME, MAKE 3 : to bring about with difficulty — **con·triv·er** *n*

con·trived \-ˈtrīvd\ *adj* : lacking in natural or spontaneous quality

¹**con·trol** \kən-ˈtrōl\ *vb* **con·trolled; con·trol·ling** 1 : to exercise restraining or directing influence over : REGULATE 2 : DOMINATE, RULE

²**control** *n* 1 : power to direct or regulate 2 : RESERVE, RESTRAINT 3 : a device for regulating a mechanism

con·trol·ler \kən-ˈtrō-lər, ˈkän-ˌtrō-lər\ *n* 1 : COMPTROLLER 2 : one that controls

con·tro·ver·sy \ˈkän-trə-ˌvər-sē\ *n, pl* **-sies** : a clash of opposing views : DISPUTE — **con·tro·ver·sial** \ˌkän-trə-ˌvər-shəl, -sē-əl\ *adj*

con·tro·vert \ˈkän-trə-ˌvərt, ˌkän-trə-ˈvərt\ *vb* : DENY, CONTRADICT — **con·tro·vert·ible** *adj*

con·tu·ma·cious \ˌkän-tü-ˈmā-shəs, -tyü-\ *adj* : stubbornly disobedient **syn** rebellious, insubordinate, seditious — **con·tu·ma·cy** \kən-ˈtü-mə-sē, -ˈtyü-; ˈkän-tyə-\ *n* — **con·tu·ma·cious·ly** *adv*

con·tu·me·ly \kən-ˈtü-mə-lē, -ˈtyü-; ˈkän-tə-ˌmē-lē, -tyə-\ *n, pl* **-lies** : contemptuous treatment : INSULT

con·tu·sion \kən-ˈtü-zhən, -ˈtyü-\ *n* : BRUISE — **con·tuse** \-ˈtüz, -ˈtyüz\ *vb*

co·nun·drum \kə-ˈnən-drəm\ *n* : RIDDLE

conv *abbr* 1 convention 2 convertible

con·va·lesce \ˌkän-və-ˈles\ *vb* **-lesced; -lesc·ing** : to recover health gradually — **con·va·les·cence** \-ᵊns\ *n* — **con·va·les·cent** \-ᵊnt\ *adj or n*

con·vec·tion \kən-ˈvek-shən\ *n* : circulatory motion in a fluid due to warmer portions rising and cooler denser portions sinking; *also* : the transfer of heat by such motion — **con·vec·tion·al** \-shə-nəl\ *adj* — **con·vec·tive** \-ˈvek-tiv\ *adj*

convection oven *n* : an oven with a fan that circulates hot air uniformly and continuously around the food

con·vene \kən-ˈvēn\ *vb* **con·vened; con·ven·ing** : ASSEMBLE, MEET

con·ve·nience \kən-ˈvē-nyəns\ *n* 1 : SUITABLENESS 2 : a laborsaving device 3 : a suitable time ⟨at your ∼⟩ 4 : personal comfort : EASE

con·ve·nient \-nyənt\ *adj* 1 : suited to personal comfort or ease 2 : placed near at hand — **con·ve·nient·ly** *adv*

con·vent \ˈkän-vənt, -ˌvent\ *n* [ME *covent,* fr. OF, fr. ML *conventus,* fr. L, assembly, fr. *convenire* to come together] : a local community or house of a religious order esp. of nuns — **con·ven·tu·al** \kän-ˈven-chə-wəl\ *adj*

con·ven·ti·cle \kən-ˈven-ti-kəl\ *n* : MEETING; *esp* : a secret meeting for worship

con·ven·tion \kən-ˈven-chən\ *n* 1 : an agreement esp. between states on a matter of common concern 2 : MEETING, ASSEMBLY 3 : an assembly of delegates convened for some purpose 4 : generally accepted custom, practice, or belief

con·ven·tion·al \-chə-nəl\ *adj* 1 : sanctioned by general custom 2 : COMMONPLACE, ORDINARY — **con·ven·tion·al·i·ty** \-ˌven-chə-ˈna-lə-tē\ *n* — **con·ven·tion·al·ize** \-ˈven-chə-nə-ˌlīz\ *vb* — **con·ven·tion·al·ly** *adv*

con·verge \kən-ˈvərj\ *vb* **con·verged; con·verg·ing** : to approach one common center or single point — **con·ver·gence** \kən-ˈvər-jəns\ *or* **con·ver·gen·cy** \-jən-sē\ *n* — **con·ver·gent** \-jənt\ *adj*

con·ver·sant \kən-ˈvərs-ᵊnt\ *adj* : having knowledge and experience — used with *with*

con·ver·sa·tion \ˌkän-vər-ˈsā-shən\ *n* : an informal talking together — **con·ver·sa·tion·al** \-shə-nəl\ *adj* — **con·ver·sa·tion·al·ly** *adv*

con·ver·sa·tion·al·ist \-shə-nᵊl-ist\ *n* : a person who converses a great deal or who excels in conversation

¹**con·verse** \ˈkän-ˌvərs\ *n* : CONVERSATION

²**con·verse** \kən-ˈvərs\ *vb* **con·versed; con·vers·ing** : to engage in conversation

³**con·verse** \ˈkän-ˌvərs\ *n* : a statement related to another statement by having its hypothesis and conclusion or its subject and predicate reversed or interchanged

⁴**con·verse** \kən-ˈvərs, ˈkän-ˌvers\ *adj* : reversed in order or relation — **con·verse·ly** *adv*

con·ver·sion \kən-ˈvər-zhən\ *n* 1 : a change in nature or form 2 : an experience associated with a decisive adoption of religion

¹**con·vert** \kən-ˈvərt\ *vb* 1 : to turn from one belief or party to another 2 : TRANSFORM, CHANGE 3 : MISAPPROPRIATE 4 : EXCHANGE — **con·vert·er** *or* **con·ver·tor** \-ˈvər-tər\ *n* — **con·vert·ible** *adj*

²**con·vert** \ˈkän-ˌvərt\ *n* : a person who has undergone religious conversion

con·vert·ible \kən-ˈvər-tə-bəl\ *n* : an automobile with a top that may be lowered or removed

con·vex \kän-ˈveks, ˈkän-ˌveks\ *adj* : curved or rounded like the exterior of a sphere or circle — **con·vex·i·ty** \kän-ˈvek-sə-tē\ *n*

con·vey \kən-ˈvā\ *vb* 1 : CARRY, TRANSPORT 2 : TRANS-

MIT, TRANSFER — **con·vey·or** *also* **con·vey·er** \-ər\ *n*
con·vey·ance \-'vā-əns\ *n* **1** : the act of conveying **2** : a legal paper transferring ownership of property **3** : VEHICLE
¹con·vict \kən-'vikt\ *vb* : to prove or find guilty
²con·vict \'kän-ˌvikt\ *n* : a person serving a prison sentence
con·vic·tion \kən-'vik-shən\ *n* **1** : the act of convicting esp. in a court **2** : the state of being convinced : BELIEF
con·vince \kən-'vins\ *vb* **con·vinced; con·vinc·ing** : to bring (as by argument) to belief or action — **con·vinc·ing** *adj* — **con·vinc·ing·ly** *adv*
con·viv·ial \kən-'vi-vē-əl\ *adj* [LL *convivialis,* fr. L *convivium* banquet, fr. *com-* together + *vivere* to live] : enjoying companionship and the pleasures of feasting and drinking : JOVIAL, FESTIVE — **con·viv·i·al·i·ty** \-ˌvi-vē-'a-lə-tē\ *n* — **con·viv·ial·ly** *adv*
con·vo·ca·tion \ˌkän-və-'kā-shən\ *n* **1** : a ceremonial assembly (as of the clergy) **2** : the act of convoking
con·voke \kən-'vōk\ *vb* **con·voked; con·vok·ing** : to call together to a meeting
con·vo·lut·ed \'kän-və-ˌlü-təd\ *adj* **1** : folded in curved or tortuous windings **2** : INVOLVED, INTRICATE
con·vo·lu·tion \ˌkän-və-'lü-shən\ *n* : a tortuous or sinuous structure; *esp* : one of the ridges of the brain
¹con·voy \'kän-ˌvòi, kən-'vòi\ *vb* : to accompany for protection
²con·voy \'kän-ˌvòi\ *n* **1** : one that convoys; *esp* : a protective escort (as for ships) **2** : the act of convoying **3** : a group of moving vehicles
con·vulse \kən-'vəls\ *vb* **con·vulsed; con·vuls·ing** : to agitate violently
con·vul·sion \kən-'vəl-shən\ *n* **1** : an abnormal and violent involuntary contraction or series of contractions of muscle **2** : a violent disturbance — **con·vul·sive** \-siv\ *adj* — **con·vul·sive·ly** *adv*
cony *var of* CONEY
coo \'kü\ *n* : a soft low sound made by doves or pigeons; *also* : a sound like this — **coo** *vb*
COO *abbr* chief operating officer
¹cook \'kùk\ *n* : a person who prepares food for eating
²cook *vb* **1** : to prepare food for eating **2** : to subject to heat or fire — **cook·er** *n* — **cook·ware** \-ˌwar\ *n*
cook·book \-ˌbùk\ *n* : a book of cooking directions and recipes
cook·ery \'kù-kə-rē\ *n, pl* **-er·ies** : the art or practice of cooking
cook·ie *or* **cooky** \'kù-kē\ *n, pl* **cook·ies** : a small sweet flat cake
cook·out \'kùk-ˌaùt\ *n* : an outing at which a meal is cooked and served in the open
¹cool \'kül\ *adj* **1** : moderately cold **2** : not excited : CALM **3** : not friendly **4** : IMPUDENT **5** : protecting from heat **6** *slang* : very good **syn** unflappable, composed, collected, unruffled, nonchalant — **cool·ly** *adv* — **cool·ness** *n*
²cool *vb* : to make or become cool
³cool *n* **1** : a cool time or place **2** : INDIFFERENCE; *also* : SELF-ASSURANCE, COMPOSURE ⟨kept his ∼⟩
cool·ant \'kü-lənt\ *n* : a usu. fluid cooling agent
cool·er \'kü-lər\ *n* **1** : a container for keeping food or drink cool **2** : JAIL, PRISON **3** : a tall iced drink
coo·lie \'kü-lē\ *n* [Hindi *kulī*] : an unskilled laborer usu. in or from the Far East
coon \'kün\ *n* : RACCOON
coon·hound \-ˌhaùnd\ *n* : a sporting dog trained to hunt raccoons
coon·skin \-ˌskin\ *n* : the pelt of a raccoon; *also* : something (as a cap) made of this
¹coop \'küp, 'kùp\ *n* : a small enclosure or building usu. for poultry
²coop *vb* : to confine in or as if in a coop — usu. used with *up*

co–op \'kō-ˌäp\ *n* : COOPERATIVE
coo·per \'kü-pər, 'kù-\ *n* : one who makes or repairs barrels or casks — **cooper** *vb* — **coo·per·age** \-pə-rij\ *n*
co·op·er·ate \kō-'ä-pə-ˌrāt\ *vb* : to act jointly with another or others — **co·op·er·a·tion** \-ˌä-pə-'rā-shən\ *n* — **co·op·er·a·tor** \-'ä-pə-ˌrā-tər\ *n*
¹co·op·er·a·tive \kō-'ä-prə-tiv, -'ä-pə-ˌrā-\ *adj* **1** : willing to work with others **2** : of or relating to an association formed to enable its members to buy or sell to better advantage by eliminating middlemen's profits
²cooperative *n* : a cooperative association
co–opt \kō-'äpt\ *vb* **1** : to choose or elect as a colleague **2** : ABSORB, ASSIMILATE; *also* : TAKE OVER
¹co·or·di·nate \kō-'òrd-ᵊn-ət\ *adj* **1** : equal in rank or order **2** : of equal rank in a compound sentence ⟨∼ clause⟩ **3** : joining words or word groups of the same rank — **co·or·di·nate·ly** *adv*
²co·or·di·nate \-'òrd-ᵊn-ˌāt\ *vb* **-nat·ed; -nat·ing** **1** : to make or become coordinate **2** : to work or act together harmoniously — **co·or·di·na·tion** \-ˌòrd-ᵊn-'ā-shən\ *n* — **co·or·di·na·tor** \-'òrd-ᵊn-ˌā-tər\ *n*
³co·or·di·nate \-'òrd-ᵊn-ət\ *n* **1** : one of a set of numbers used in specifying the location of a point on a surface or in space **2** *pl* : articles (as of clothing) designed to be used together and to attain their effect through pleasing contrast
coot \'küt\ *n* **1** : a dark-colored ducklike bird related to the rails **2** : any of several No. American sea ducks **3** : a harmless simple person
coo·tie \'kü-tē\ *n* : a body louse
cop \'käp\ *n* : POLICE OFFICER
co–pay·ment \'kō-ˌpā-mənt, ˌkō-'\ *n* : a relatively small fixed fee required of a patient by a health insurer (as an HMO) at the time of each outpatient service or filling of a prescription
¹cope \'kōp\ *n* : a long cloaklike ecclesiastical vestment
²cope *vb* **coped; cop·ing** : to struggle to overcome problems or difficulties
copi·er \'kä-pē-ər\ *n* : one that copies; *esp* : a machine for making copies
co·pi·lot \'kō-ˌpī-lət\ *n* : an assistant pilot of an aircraft or spacecraft
cop·ing \'kō-piŋ\ *n* : the top layer of a wall
co·pi·ous \'kō-pē-əs\ *adj* : LAVISH, ABUNDANT — **co·pi·ous·ly** *adv* — **co·pi·ous·ness** *n*
cop–out \'käp-ˌaùt\ *n* : an excuse for copping out; *also* : an act of copping out
cop out *vb* : to back out (as of an unwanted responsibility)
cop·per \'kä-pər\ *n* **1** : a malleable reddish metallic chemical element that is one of the best conductors of heat and electricity — see ELEMENT table **2** : a coin or token made of copper — **cop·pery** *adj*
cop·per·head \'kä-pər-ˌhed\ *n* : a largely coppery brown pit viper esp. of the eastern and central U.S.
cop·pice \'kä-pəs\ *n* : THICKET
co·pra \'kō-prə\ *n* : dried coconut meat yielding coconut oil
copse \'käps\ *n* : THICKET
cop·ter \'käp-tər\ *n* : HELICOPTER
cop·u·la \'kä-pyə-lə\ *n* : LINKING VERB — **cop·u·la·tive** \-lə-tiv, -ˌlā-\ *adj*
cop·u·late \'kä-pyə-ˌlāt\ *vb* **-lat·ed; -lat·ing** : to engage in sexual intercourse — **cop·u·la·tion** \ˌkä-pyə-'lā-shən\ *n* — **cop·u·la·to·ry** \'kä-pyə-lə-ˌtòr-ē\ *adj*
¹copy \'kä-pē\ *n, pl* **cop·ies** **1** : an imitation or reproduction of an original work **2** : material to be set in type **syn** duplicate, reproduction, facsimile, replica

---

\ə\abut \ᵊ\kitten \ər\further \a\ash \ā\ace \ä\mop, mar
\aù\out \ch\chin \e\bet \ē\easy \g\go \i\hit \ī\ice \j\job
\ŋ\sing \ō\go \ò\law \òi\boy \th\thin \th\the \ü\loot \ù\foot
\y\yet \zh\vision *see also* Pronunciation Symbols page

²**copy** *vb* **cop·ied; copy·ing 1 :** to make a copy of **2 :** IM-ITATE — **copy·ist** *n*
copy·book \'kä-pē-ˌbùk\ *n* **:** a book formerly used to teach handwriting containing examples to be copied
copy·boy \-ˌbòi\ *n* **:** a person who carries copy and runs errands (as in a newspaper office)
copy·cat \-ˌkat\ *n* **:** a slavish imitator
copy·desk \-ˌdesk\ *n* **:** the desk at which newspaper copy is edited
copy editor *n* **:** one who edits newspaper copy and writes headlines; *also* **:** one who reads and corrects manuscript copy in a publishing house
copy·read·er \-ˌrē-dər\ *n* **:** COPY EDITOR
¹**copy·right** \-ˌrīt\ *n* **:** the sole right to reproduce, publish, and sell a literary or artistic work
²**copyright** *vb* **:** to secure a copyright on
copy·writ·er \'kä-pē-ˌrī-tər\ *n* **:** a writer of advertising copy
co·quet *or* **co·quette** \kò-'ket\ *vb* **co·quet·ted; co·quet·ting :** FLIRT — **co·quet·ry** \'kò-kə-trē, kò-'ke-trē\ *n*
co·quette \kò-'ket\ *n* [F, fem. of *coquet*, flirtatious man, dim. of *coq* cock] **:** FLIRT — **co·quett·ish** *adj*
cor *abbr* corner
Cor *abbr* Corinthians
cor·a·cle \'kòr-ə-kəl\ *n* [W *corwgl*] **:** a boat made of a frame covered usu. with hide or tarpaulin
cor·al \'kòr-əl\ *n* **1 :** a stony or horny material that forms the skeleton of colonies of tiny sea polyps and includes a red form used in jewelry; *also* **:** a coral-forming polyp or polyp colony **2 :** a deep pink color — **coral** *adj*
coral snake *n* **:** any of several venomous chiefly tropical New World snakes brilliantly banded in red, black, and yellow or white
cor·bel \'kòr-bəl\ *n* **:** a bracket-shaped architectural member that projects from a wall and supports a weight
¹**cord** \'kòrd\ *n* **1 :** a usu. heavy string consisting of several strands woven or twisted together **2 :** a long slender anatomical structure (as a tendon or nerve) **3 :** a small flexible insulated electrical cable used to connect an appliance with a receptacle **4 :** a cubic measure used esp. for firewood and equal to a stack 4×4×8 feet **5 :** a rib or ridge on cloth
²**cord** *vb* **1 :** to tie or furnish with a cord **2 :** to pile (wood) in cords
cord·age \'kòr-dij\ *n* **:** ROPES, CORDS; *esp* **:** ropes in the rigging of a ship
¹**cor·dial** \'kòr-jəl\ *adj* [ME, fr. ML *cordialis*, fr. L *cord-, cor* heart] **:** warmly receptive or welcoming **:** HEART-FELT, HEARTY — **cor·di·al·i·ty** \ˌkòr-jē-'a-lə-tē, kòr-'ja-\ *n* — **cor·dial·ly** *adv*
²**cordial** *n* **1 :** a stimulating medicine or drink **2 :** LIQUEUR
cor·dil·le·ra \ˌkòr-dəl-'yer-ə, -də-'ler-\ *n* [Sp] **:** a series of parallel mountain ranges
cord·less \'kòrd-ləs\ *adj* **:** having no cord; *esp* **:** powered by a battery
cor·do·ba \'kòr-də-bə, -və\ *n* — see MONEY table
cor·don \'kòrd-ᵊn\ *n* **1 :** an ornamental cord or ribbon **2 :** an encircling line (as of troops or police) — **cordon** *vb*
cor·do·van \'kòr-də-vən\ *n* **:** a soft fine-grained leather
cor·du·roy \'kòr-də-ˌròi\ *n, pl* **-roys :** a heavy ribbed fabric; *also, pl* **:** trousers of this material
cord·wain·er \'kòrd-ˌwā-nər\ *n* **:** SHOEMAKER
¹**core** \'kòr\ *n* **1 :** the central usu. inedible part of some fruits (as the apple); *also* **:** an inmost part of something **2 :** GIST, ESSENCE
²**core** *vb* **cored; cor·ing :** to take out the core of — **cor·er** *n*
CORE \'kòr\ *abbr* Congress of Racial Equality
co·re·spon·dent \ˌkò-ri-'spän-dənt\ *n* **:** a person named as guilty of adultery with the defendant in a divorce suit
co·ri·an·der \'kòr-ē-ˌan-dər\ *n* **:** an herb related to the carrot; *also* **:** its aromatic dried fruit used as a flavoring
Cor·in·thi·ans \kə-'rin-thē-ənz\ *n* — see BIBLE table

¹**cork** \'kòrk\ *n* **1 :** the tough elastic bark of a European oak (**cork oak**) used esp. for stoppers and insulation; *also* **:** a stopper of this **2 :** a tissue of a woody plant making up most of the bark — **corky** *adj*
²**cork** *vb* **:** to furnish with or stop up with cork or a cork
cork·screw \'kòrk-ˌskrü\ *n* **:** a device for drawing corks from bottles
corm \'kòrm\ *n* **:** a solid bulblike underground part of a stem (as of the crocus or gladiolus)
cor·mo·rant \'kòr-mə-rənt, -ˌrant\ *n* [ME *cormeraunt*, fr. MF *cormorant*, fr. OF *cormareng*, fr. *corp* raven + *marenc* of the sea, fr. L *marinus*] **:** any of a family of dark-colored water birds with a long neck, hooked bill, and distensible throat pouch
¹**corn** \'kòrn\ *n* **1 :** the seeds of a cereal grass and esp. of the chief cereal crop of a region (as wheat in Britain and Indian corn in the U.S.); *also* **:** a cereal grass **2 :** sweet corn served as a vegetable
²**corn** *vb* **:** to salt (as beef) in brine and preservatives
³**corn** *n* **:** a local hardening and thickening of skin (as on a toe)
¹**corn·ball** \'kòrn-ˌbòl\ *n* **:** an unsophisticated person; *also* **:** something corny
²**cornball** *adj* **:** CORNY
corn bread *n* **:** bread made with cornmeal
corn·cob \-ˌkäb\ *n* **:** the woody core on which the kernels of Indian corn are arranged
corn·crib \-ˌkrib\ *n* **:** a crib for storing ears of Indian corn
cor·nea \'kòr-nē-ə\ *n* **:** the transparent part of the coat of the eyeball covering the iris and the pupil — **cor·ne·al** *adj*
corn ear·worm \-'ir-ˌwərm\ *n* **:** a moth whose larva is destructive esp. to Indian corn
¹**cor·ner** \'kòr-nər\ *n* [ME, fr. OF *cornere*, fr. *corne* horn, corner, fr. L *cornu* horn, point] **1 :** the point or angle formed by the meeting of lines, edges, or sides **2 :** the place where two streets come together **3 :** a quiet secluded place **4 :** a position from which retreat or escape is impossible **5 :** control of enough of the available supply (as of a commodity) to permit manipulation of the price — **cor·nered** *adj*
²**cor·ner** *vb* **1 :** to drive into a corner **2 :** to get a corner on (~ the wheat market) **3 :** to turn a corner
cor·ner·stone \'kòr-nər-ˌstòn\ *n* **1 :** a stone forming part of a corner in a wall; *esp* **:** such a stone laid at a formal ceremony **2 :** something of basic importance
cor·net \kòr-'net\ *n* **:** a brass band instrument resembling the trumpet
corn flour *n, Brit* **:** CORNSTARCH
corn·flow·er \'kòrn-ˌflaù(-ə)r\ *n* **:** BACHELOR'S BUTTON
cor·nice \'kòr-nəs\ *n* **:** the horizontal projecting part crowning the wall of a building
corn·meal \'kòrn-ˌmēl\ *n* **:** meal ground from corn
corn·row \-ˌrò\ *n* **:** a section of hair braided flat to the scalp in rows — **cornrow** *vb*
corn·stalk \-ˌstòk\ *n* **:** a stalk of Indian corn
corn·starch \-ˌstärch\ *n* **:** a starch made from corn and used in cookery as a thickening agent
corn syrup *n* **:** a sweet syrup obtained from cornstarch
cor·nu·co·pia \ˌkòr-nə-'kò-pē-ə, -nyə-\ *n* [LL, fr. L *cornu copiae* horn of plenty] **:** a horn-shaped container filled with fruits and grain emblematic of abundance
corny \'kòr-nē\ *adj* **corn·i·er; -est :** tiresomely simple or sentimental
co·rol·la \kə-'rä-lə, -'rò-\ *n* **:** the petals of a flower
cor·ol·lary \'kòr-ə-ˌler-ē\ *n, pl* **-lar·ies 1 :** a deduction from a proposition already proved true **2 :** CONSE-QUENCE, RESULT
co·ro·na \kə-'rò-nə\ *n* **1 :** a colored circle often seen around and close to a luminous body (as the sun or moon) **2 :** the outermost part of the atmosphere of a star (as the sun) — **co·ro·nal** \'kòr-ən-ᵊl, kə-'ròn-ᵊl\ *adj*
cor·o·nal \'kòr-ən-ᵊl\ *n* **:** a circlet for the head

cornucopia

¹**cor·o·nary** \'kȯr-ə-ˌner-ē\ *adj* : of or relating to the heart or its blood vessels

²**coronary** *n, pl* **-nar·ies** 1 : a coronary blood vessel 2 : CORONARY THROMBOSIS; *also* : HEART ATTACK

coronary thrombosis *n* : the blocking by a thrombus of one of the arteries supplying the heart tissues

cor·o·na·tion \ˌkȯr-ə-'nā-shən\ *n* : the act or ceremony of crowning a monarch

cor·o·ner \'kȯr-ə-nər\ *n* : a public official who investigates causes of deaths possibly not due to natural causes

cor·o·net \ˌkȯr-ə-'net\ *n* 1 : a small crown 2 : an ornamental band worn around the temples

corp *abbr* 1 corporal 2 corporation

¹**cor·po·ral** \'kȯr-p(ə-)rəl\ *adj* : of or relating to the body ⟨~ punishment⟩

²**corporal** *n* : a noncommissioned officer (as in the army) ranking next below a sergeant

cor·po·rate \'kȯr-p(ə-)rət\ *adj* 1 : INCORPORATED; *also* : belonging to an incorporated body 2 : combined into one body

cor·po·ra·tion \ˌkȯr-pə-'rā-shən\ *n* 1 : the municipal authorities of a town or city 2 : a legal creation authorized to act with the rights and liabilities of a person ⟨a business ~⟩

cor·po·re·al \kȯr-'pȯr-ē-əl\ *adj* 1 : PHYSICAL, MATERIAL 2 *archaic* : BODILY — **cor·po·re·al·i·ty** \kȯr-ˌpȯr-ē-'a-lə-tē\ *n* — **cor·po·re·al·ly** *adv*

corps \'kȯr\ *n, pl* **corps** \'kȯrz\ [F, fr. L *corpus* body] 1 : an organized subdivision of a country's military forces 2 : a group acting under common direction

corpse \'kȯrps\ *n* : a dead body

corps·man \'kȯr-mən, 'kȯrz-\ *n* : an enlisted man trained to give first aid

cor·pu·lence \'kȯr-pyə-ləns\ *n* : excessive fatness : OBESITY

cor·pu·lent \-lənt\ *adj* : OBESE

cor·pus \'kȯr-pəs\ *n, pl* **cor·po·ra** \-pə-rə\ [ME, fr. L] 1 : BODY; *esp* : CORPSE 2 : a body of writings or works

cor·pus·cle \'kȯr-pə-səl, -ˌpə-\ *n* 1 : a minute particle 2 : a living cell (as in blood or cartilage) not aggregated into continuous tissues — **cor·pus·cu·lar** \kȯr-'pəs-kyə-lər\ *adj*

cor·pus de·lic·ti \ˌkȯr-pəs-di-'lik-ˌtī, -tē\ *n, pl* **corpora delicti** [NL, lit., body of the crime] 1 : the substantial fact proving that a crime has been committed 2 : the body of a victim of murder

corr *abbr* 1 correct; corrected; correction 2 correspondence; correspondent; corresponding

cor·ral \kə-'ral\ *n* [Sp] : an enclosure for confining or capturing animals; *also* : an enclosure of wagons for defending a camp — **corral** *vb*

¹**cor·rect** \kə-'rekt\ *vb* 1 : to make right 2 : REPROVE, CHASTISE — **cor·rect·able** \-'rek-tə-bəl\ *adj* — **cor·rec·tion** \-'rek-shən\ *n* — **cor·rec·tion·al** \-'rek-sh(ə-)nəl\ *adj* — **cor·rec·tive** \-'rek-tiv\ *adj*

²**correct** *adj* 1 : conforming to a conventional standard 2 : agreeing with fact or truth — **cor·rect·ly** *adv* — **cor·rect·ness** *n*

cor·re·late \'kȯr-ə-ˌlāt\ *vb* **-lat·ed; -lat·ing** : to connect in a systematic way : establish the mutual relations of — **cor·re·late** \-lət, -ˌlāt\ *n* — **cor·re·la·tion** \ˌkȯr-ə-'lā-shən\ *n*

cor·rel·a·tive \kə-'re-lə-tiv\ *adj* 1 : reciprocally related 2 : regularly used together (as *either* and *or*) — **correlative** *n* — **cor·rel·a·tive·ly** *adv*

cor·re·spond \ˌkȯr-ə-'spänd\ *vb* 1 : to be in agreement : SUIT, MATCH 2 : to communicate by letter — **cor·re·spond·ing·ly** *adv*

cor·re·spon·dence \-'spän-dəns\ *n* 1 : agreement between particular things 2 : communication by letters; *also* : the letters exchanged

¹**cor·re·spon·dent** \-dənt\ *adj* 1 : SIMILAR 2 : FITTING, CONFORMING

²**correspondent** *n* 1 : something that corresponds 2 : a person with whom one communicates by letter 3 : a person employed to contribute news regularly from a place

cor·ri·dor \'kȯr-ə-dər, -ˌdȯr\ *n* 1 : a passageway into which compartments or rooms open (as in a hotel or school) 2 : a narrow strip of land esp. through foreign-held territory 3 : a densely populated strip of land including two or more major cities

cor·ri·gen·dum \ˌkȯr-ə-'jen-dəm\ *n, pl* **-da** \-də\ [L] : an error in a printed work discovered after printing and shown with its correction on a separate sheet

cor·ri·gi·ble \'kȯr-ə-jə-bəl\ *adj* : CORRECTABLE

cor·rob·o·rate \kə-'rä-bə-ˌrāt\ *vb* **-rat·ed; -rat·ing** [L *corroborare*, fr. *robur* strength] : to support with evidence : CONFIRM — **cor·rob·o·ra·tion** \-ˌrä-bə-'rā-shən\ *n* — **cor·rob·o·ra·tive** \-'rä-bə-ˌrā-tiv, -'rä-brə-\ *adj* — **cor·rob·o·ra·to·ry** \-'rä-bə-rə-ˌtȯr-ē\ *adj*

cor·rode \kə-'rōd\ *vb* **cor·rod·ed; cor·rod·ing** : to wear or be worn away gradually (as by chemical action) — **cor·ro·sion** \-'rō-zhən\ *n* — **cor·ro·sive** \-'rō-siv\ *adj or n*

cor·ru·gate \'kȯr-ə-ˌgāt\ *vb* **-gat·ed; -gat·ing** : to form into wrinkles or ridges and grooves — **cor·ru·gat·ed** *adj* — **cor·ru·ga·tion** \ˌkȯr-ə-'gā-shən\ *n*

¹**cor·rupt** \kə-'rəpt\ *vb* 1 : to make evil : DEPRAVE; *esp* : BRIBE 2 : ROT, SPOIL — **cor·rupt·ible** *adj* — **cor·rup·tion** \-'rəp-shən\ *n*

²**corrupt** *adj* : morally degenerate; *also* : characterized by improper conduct ⟨~ officials⟩

cor·sage \kȯr-'säzh, -'säj\ *n* [F, bust, bodice, fr. OF, bust, fr. *cors* body, fr. L *corpus*] 1 : the waist or bodice of a dress 2 : a bouquet to be worn or carried

cor·sair \'kȯr-ˌsar\ *n* : PIRATE

cor·set \'kȯr-sət\ *n* : a stiffened undergarment worn for support or to give shape to the waist and hips

cor·tege *also* **cor·tège** \kȯr-'tezh, 'kȯr-ˌtezh\ *n* [F] : PROCESSION; *esp* : a funeral procession

cor·tex \'kȯr-ˌteks\ *n, pl* **cor·ti·ces** \'kȯr-tə-ˌsēz\ *or* **cor·tex·es** : an outer or covering layer of an organism or one of its parts ⟨the adrenal ~⟩ ⟨~ of a plant stem⟩; *esp* : the outer layer of gray matter of the brain — **cor·ti·cal** \'kȯr-ti-kəl\ *adj*

cor·ti·sone \'kȯr-tə-ˌsōn, -ˌzōn\ *n* : an adrenal hormone used in treating rheumatoid arthritis

co·run·dum \kə-'rən-dəm\ *n* : a very hard aluminum-containing mineral used as an abrasive or as a gem

cor·us·cate \'kȯr-ə-ˌskāt\ *vb* **-cat·ed; -cat·ing** : FLASH, SPARKLE — **cor·us·ca·tion** \ˌkȯr-ə-'skā-shən\ *n*

cor·vette \kȯr-'vet\ *n* 1 : a naval sailing ship smaller than a frigate 2 : an armed escort ship smaller than a destroyer

---

\ə\abut \ᵊ\kitten \ər\further \a\ash \ā\ace \ä\mop, mar
\au̇\out \ch\chin \e\bet \ē\easy \g\go \i\hit \ī\ice \j\job
\ŋ\sing \ō\go \ȯ\law \oi\boy \th\thin \t̲h̲\the \ü\loot \u̇\foot
\y\yet \zh\vision *see also* Pronunciation Symbols page

co·ry·za \kə-'rī-zə\ *n* : an inflammatory disorder of the upper respiratory tract; *esp* : COMMON COLD

COS *abbr* **1** cash on shipment **2** chief of staff

co·sig·na·to·ry \kō-'sig-nə-ˌtȯr-ē\ *n* : a joint signer

co·sign·er \'kō-ˌsī-nər\ *n* : COSIGNATORY; *esp* : a joint signer of a promissory note

¹cos·met·ic \käz-'me-tik\ *adj* [Gk *kosmētikos* skilled in adornment, fr. *kosmein* to arrange, adorn, fr. *kosmos* order, ornament, universe] **1** : intended to beautify the hair or complexion **2** : correcting physical defects esp. to improve appearance ⟨∼ dentistry⟩ **3** : SUPERFICIAL

²cosmetic *n* : a cosmetic preparation

cos·me·tol·o·gist \ˌkäz-mə-'tä-lə-jist\ *n* : one who gives beauty treatments — **cos·me·tol·o·gy** \-jē\ *n*

cos·mic \'käz-mik\ *also* **cos·mi·cal** \-mi-kəl\ *adj* **1** : of or relating to the cosmos **2** : VAST, GRAND — **cos·mi·cal·ly** *adv*

cosmic ray *n* : a stream of very penetrating atomic nuclei that enter the earth's atmosphere from outer space

cos·mog·o·ny \käz-'mä-gə-nē\ *n, pl* **-nies** : the origin or creation of the world or universe

cos·mol·o·gy \-'mä-lə-jē\ *n, pl* **-gies** : a branch of astronomy dealing with the origin and structure of the universe — **cos·mo·log·i·cal** \ˌkäz-mə-'lä-ji-kəl\ *adj* — **cos·mol·o·gist** \käz-'mä-lə-jist\ *n*

cos·mo·naut \'käz-mə-ˌnȯt\ *n* : a Soviet or Russian astronaut

cos·mo·pol·i·tan \ˌkäz-mə-'pä-lət-ᵊn\ *adj* : belonging to all the world : not local **syn** universal, global, catholic — **cosmopolitan** *n*

cos·mos \'käz-məs, **1** *also* -ˌmȯs, -ˌmäs\ *n* **1** : UNIVERSE **2** : a tall garden herb related to the daisies

co·spon·sor \'kō-ˌspän-sər, -'spän-\ *n* : a joint sponsor — **cosponsor** *vb*

cos·sack \'kä-ˌsak, -sək\ *n* [Pol & Ukrainian *kozak*, of Turkic origin] : a member of a group of frontiersmen of southern Russia organized as cavalry in the czarist army

¹cost \'kȯst\ *n* **1** : the amount paid or charged for something : PRICE **2** : the loss or penalty incurred in gaining something **3** *pl* : expenses incurred in a law suit

²cost *vb* **cost; cost·ing 1** : to require a specified amount in payment **2** : to cause to pay, suffer, or lose

co–star \'kō-ˌstär\ *n* : one of two leading players in a motion picture or play — **co–star** *vb*

Cos·ta Ri·can \ˌkäs-tə-'rē-kən\ *n* : a native or inhabitant of Costa Rica — **Costa Rican** *adj*

cos·tive \'käs-tiv\ *adj* : affected with or causing constipation

cost·ly \'kȯst-lē\ *adj* **cost·li·er; -est** : of great cost or value : not cheap **syn** dear, valuable, expensive — **cost·li·ness** *n*

cos·tume \'käs-ˌtüm, -ˌtyüm\ *n* **1** : the style of attire characteristic of a period or country **2** : a special or fancy dress ⟨Halloween ∼s⟩ — **cos·tum·er** \'käs-ˌtü-mər, -ˌtyü-\ *n*

costume jewelry *n* : inexpensive jewelry

co·sy \'kō-zē\ *var of* COZY

¹cot \'kät\ *n* : a small house : COTTAGE

²cot *n* : a small often collapsible bed

cote \'kōt, 'kät\ *n* : a small shed or coop (as for sheep or doves)

co·te·rie \'kō-tə-ˌrē, ˌkō-tə-'rē\ *n* [F] : an intimate often exclusive group of persons with a common interest

co·ter·mi·nous \kō-'tər-mə-nəs\ *adj* : having the same scope or duration

co·til·lion \kō-'til-yən, kə-\ *n* : a formal ball

cot·tage \'kä-tij\ *n* : a small house — **cot·tag·er** *n*

cottage cheese *n* : a soft uncured cheese made from soured skim milk

cot·ter *or* **cot·tar** \'kä-tər\ *n* : a peasant or farm laborer occupying a cottage and often a small holding

cotter pin *n* : a metal strip bent into a pin whose ends

can be spread apart after insertion through a hole or slot

cot·ton \'kät-ᵊn\ *n* [ME *coton*, fr. MF, fr. Ar *quṭun*] **1** : a soft fibrous usu. white substance composed of hairs attached to the seeds of a plant related to the mallow; *also* : this plant **2** : thread or cloth made of cotton — **cot·tony** *adj*

cotton candy *n* : a candy made of spun sugar

cot·ton·mouth \'kät-ᵊn-ˌmaùth\ *n* : WATER MOCCASIN

cot·ton·seed \-ˌsēd\ *n* : the seed of the cotton plant yielding a protein-rich meal and a fatty oil (**cottonseed oil**) used esp. in cooking

cot·ton·tail \-ˌtāl\ *n* : an American rabbit with a white-tufted tail

cot·ton·wood \-ˌwùd\ *n* : a poplar having seeds with cottony hairs

cot·y·le·don \ˌkä-tə-'lēd-ᵊn\ *n* : the first leaf or one of the first pair or whorl of leaves developed by a seed plant

¹couch \'kaùch\ *vb* **1** : to lie or place on a couch **2** : to phrase in a specified manner

²couch *n* : a piece of furniture (as a bed or sofa) that one can sit or lie on

couch·ant \'kaù-chənt\ *adj* : lying down with the head raised ⟨coat of arms with lion ∼⟩

cou·gar \'kü-gər\ *n, pl* **cougars** *also* **cougar** [F *couguar*, fr. NL *cuguacuarana*, modif. of Tupi (a Brazilian Indian language) *siwasuarána*, fr. *siwasú* deer + *-rana* resembling] : a large powerful tawny brown wild American cat

cough \'kȯf\ *vb* : to force air from the lungs with short sharp noises; *also* : to expel by coughing — **cough** *n*

could \kəd, 'kùd\ *past of* CAN — used as an auxiliary in the past or as a polite or less forceful alternative to *can* in the present

cou·lee \'kü-lē\ *n* **1** : a small stream **2** : a dry streambed **3** : GULLY

cou·lomb \'kü-ˌläm, -ˌlȯm\ *n* : a unit of electric charge equal to the electricity transferred by a current of one ampere in one second

coun·cil \'kaùn-səl\ *n* **1** : ASSEMBLY, MEETING **2** : an official body of lawmakers ⟨city ∼⟩ — **coun·cil·lor** *or* **coun·cil·or** \-sə-lər\ *n* — **coun·cil·man** \-səl-mən\ *n* — **coun·cil·wom·an** \-ˌwù-mən\ *n*

¹coun·sel \'kaùn-səl\ *n* **1** : ADVICE **2** : a plan of action **3** : deliberation together **4** *pl* **counsel** : LAWYER

²counsel *vb* **-seled** *or* **-selled; -sel·ing** *or* **-sel·ling 1** : ADVISE **2** : CONSULT

coun·sel·or *or* **coun·sel·lor** \'kaùn-sə-lər\ *n* **1** : ADVISER **2** : LAWYER **3** : one who has supervisory duties at a summer camp

¹count \'kaùnt\ *vb* [ME *counten*, fr. MF *compter*, fr. L *computare*, fr. *com-* with + *putare* to consider] **1** : to name or indicate one by one in order to find the total number **2** : to recite numbers in order **3** : CONSIDER, ACCOUNT **4** : RELY ⟨you can ∼ on me⟩ **5** : to be of value or account — **count·able** *adj*

²count *n* **1** : the act of counting; *also* : the total obtained by counting **2** : a particular charge in an indictment or legal declaration

³count *n* [MF *comte*, fr. LL *comes*, fr. L, companion, one of the imperial court, fr. *com-* with + *ire* to go] : a European nobleman whose rank corresponds to that of a British earl

count·down \'kaùnt-ˌdaùn\ *n* : a backward counting in fixed units (as seconds) to indicate the time remaining before an event (as the launching of a rocket) — **count down** *vb*

¹coun·te·nance \'kaùnt-ᵊn-əns\ *n* **1** : the human face **2** : FAVOR, APPROVAL

²countenance *vb* **-nanced; -nanc·ing** : SANCTION, TOLERATE

¹count·er \'kaùn-tər\ *n* **1** : a piece (as of metal or plastic) used in reckoning or in games **2** : a level surface over which business is transacted, food is served, or work is conducted

²count·er *n* : a device for recording a number or amount

³coun·ter *vb* : to act in opposition to

⁴coun·ter *adv* : in an opposite direction : CONTRARY

⁵coun·ter *n* **1** : OPPOSITE, CONTRARY **2** : an answering or offsetting force or blow

⁶coun·ter *adj* : CONTRARY, OPPOSITE

coun·ter·act \ˌkaùn-tər-ˈakt\ *vb* : to lessen the force of : OFFSET — **coun·ter·ac·tive** \-ˈak-tiv\ *adj*

coun·ter·at·tack \ˈkaùn-tər-ə-ˌtak\ *n* : an attack made to oppose an enemy's attack — **counterattack** *vb*

¹coun·ter·bal·ance \ˈkaùn-tər-ˌba-ləns\ *n* : a weight or influence that balances another

²counterbalance \ˌkaùn-tər-ˈba-ləns\ *vb* : to oppose with equal weight or influence

coun·ter·claim \ˈkaùn-tər-ˌklām\ *n* : an opposing claim esp. in law

coun·ter·clock·wise \ˌkaùn-tər-ˈkläk-ˌwīz\ *adv* : in a direction opposite to that in which the hands of a clock rotate — **counterclockwise** *adj*

coun·ter·cul·ture \ˈkaùn-tər-ˌkəl-chər\ *n* : a culture esp. of the young with values and mores that run counter to those of established society

coun·ter·es·pi·o·nage \ˌkaùn-tər-ˈes-pē-ə-ˌnäzh, -nij\ *n* : activities intended to discover and defeat enemy espionage

¹coun·ter·feit \ˈkaùn-tər-ˌfit\ *adj* : SHAM, SPURIOUS; *also* : FORGED

²counterfeit *vb* **1** : to copy or imitate in order to deceive **2** : PRETEND, FEIGN — **coun·ter·feit·er** *n*

³counterfeit *n* : something counterfeit : FORGERY **syn** fraud, sham, fake, imposture, deceit, deception

coun·ter·in·sur·gen·cy \ˌkaùn-tər-in-ˈsər-jən-sē\ *n* : military activity designed to deal with insurgents

coun·ter·in·tel·li·gence \-in-ˈte-lə-jəns\ *n* : organized activities of an intelligence service designed to counter the activities of an enemy's intelligence service

count·er·man \ˈkaùn-tər-ˌman, -mən\ *n* : one who tends a counter

coun·ter·mand \ˈkaùnt-ər-ˌmand\ *vb* : to withdraw (an order already given) by a contrary order

coun·ter·mea·sure \-ˌme-zhər\ *n* : an action or device designed to counter another

coun·ter·of·fen·sive \-ə-ˌfen-siv\ *n* : a large-scale counterattack

coun·ter·pane \-ˌpān\ *n* : BEDSPREAD

coun·ter·part \-ˌpart\ *n* : a person or thing very closely like or corresponding to another person or thing

coun·ter·point \-ˌpoint\ *n* : music in which one melody is accompanied by one or more other melodies all woven into a harmonious whole

coun·ter·poise \-ˌpóiz\ *n* : COUNTERBALANCE

coun·ter·rev·o·lu·tion \ˌkaùn-tər-ˌre-və-ˈlü-shən\ *n* : a revolution opposed to a current or earlier one — **coun·ter·rev·o·lu·tion·ary** \-shə-ˌner-ē\ *adj or n*

coun·ter·sign \ˈkaùn-tər-ˌsīn\ *n* **1** : a confirmatory signature added to a writing already signed by another person **2** : a military secret signal that must be given by a person who wishes to pass a guard — **countersign** *vb*

coun·ter·sink \-ˌsiŋk\ *vb* **-sunk** \-ˌsəŋk\; **-sink·ing 1** : to form a funnel-shaped enlargement at the outer end of a drilled hole **2** : to set the head of (as a screw) at or below the surface — **countersink** *n*

coun·ter·spy \-ˌspī\ *n* : a spy engaged in counterespionage

coun·ter·ten·or \-ˌte-nər\ *n* : a tenor with an unusually high range

coun·ter·vail \ˌkaùn-tər-ˈvāl\ *vb* : COUNTERACT

coun·ter·weight \ˈkaùn-tər-ˌwāt\ *n* : COUNTERBALANCE

count·ess \ˈkaùn-təs\ *n* **1** : the wife or widow of a count or an earl **2** : a woman holding the rank of a count or an earl in her own right

count·ing·house \ˈkaùn-tiŋ-ˌhaùs\ *n* : a building or office for keeping books and conducting business

count·less \ˈkaùnt-ləs\ *adj* : INNUMERABLE

coun·tri·fied *also* **coun·try·fied** \ˈkən-tri-ˌfīd\ *adj* **1** : RURAL, RUSTIC **2** : UNSOPHISTICATED **3** : played or sung in the manner of country music

¹coun·try \ˈkən-trē\ *n, pl* **countries** [ME *contree*, fr. OF *contrée*, fr. ML *contrata*, fr. L *contra* against, on the opposite side] **1** : REGION, DISTRICT **2** : FATHERLAND **3** : a nation or its territory **4** : rural regions as opposed to towns and cities **5** : COUNTRY MUSIC

²country *adj* **1** : RURAL **2** : of or relating to country music ⟨a ~ singer⟩

country and western *n* : COUNTRY MUSIC

country club *n* : a suburban club for social life and recreation; *esp* : one having a golf course

coun·try–dance \ˈkən-trē-ˌdans\ *n* : an English dance in which partners face each other esp. in rows

coun·try·man \ˈkən-trē-mən, 2 *often* -ˌman\ *n* **1** : an inhabitant of a specified country **2** : COMPATRIOT **3** : one raised or living in the country : RUSTIC

country music *n* : music derived from or imitating the folk style of the southern U.S. or of the Western cowboy

coun·try·side \ˈkən-trē-ˌsīd\ *n* : a rural area or its people

coun·ty \ˈkaùn-tē\ *n, pl* **counties 1** : the domain of a count **2** : a territorial division of a country or state for purposes of local government

coup \ˈkü\ *n, pl* **coups** \ˈküz\ [F, blow, stroke] **1** : a brilliant sudden stroke or stratagem **2** : COUP D'ÉTAT

coup de grace \ˌkü-də-ˈgräs\ *n, pl* **coups de grace** *same*\ [F *coup de grâce*, lit., stroke of mercy] : DEATHBLOW; *also* : a final decisive stroke or event

coup d'état \ˌkü-də-ˈtä\ *n, pl* **coups d'état** *same or* -ˈtäz\ [F, lit., stroke of state] : a sudden violent overthrow of a government by a small group

cou·pé *or* **coupe** \kü-ˈpā, 2 *often* ˈküp\ *n* [F *coupé*, fr. *couper* to cut] **1** : a closed horse-drawn carriage for two persons inside with an outside seat for the driver **2** *usu* **coupe** : a 2-door automobile with an enclosed body

¹cou·ple \ˈkə-pəl\ *n* **1** : two persons closely associated; *esp* : a man and a woman married or otherwise paired **2** : PAIR **3** : BOND, TIE **4** : an indefinite small number : FEW ⟨a ~ of days ago⟩

²couple *vb* **cou·pled**; **cou·pling** : to link together

cou·plet \ˈkə-plət\ *n* : two successive rhyming lines of verse

cou·pling \ˈkə-pliŋ (*usual for 2*), -pə-liŋ\ *n* **1** : CONNECTION **2** : a device for connecting two parts or things

cou·pon \ˈkü-ˌpän, ˈkyü-\ *n* **1** : a statement attached to a bond showing interest due and designed to be cut off and presented for payment **2** : a form surrendered in order to obtain an article, service, or accommodation **3** : a part of an advertisement to be cut off to use as an order blank or inquiry form or to obtain a discount on merchandise

cour·age \ˈkər-ij\ *n* : ability to conquer fear or despair : BRAVERY, VALOR — **cou·ra·geous** \kə-ˈrā-jəs\ *adj* — **cou·ra·geous·ly** *adv*

cou·ri·er \ˈkùr-ē-ər, ˈkər-ē-\ *n* : one who bears messages or information esp. for the diplomatic or military services

¹course \ˈkórs\ *n* **1** : PROGRESS, PASSAGE; *also* : direction of progress **2** : the ground or path over which something moves **3** : method of procedure : CONDUCT, BEHAVIOR **4** : an ordered series of acts or proceedings : sequence of events **5** : a series of instruction periods dealing with a subject **6** : the series of studies leading to graduation from a school or college **7** : the part of a meal served at one time — **of course** : as might be expected

²course *vb* **coursed; cours·ing 1** : to hunt with dogs **2** : to run or go speedily

cours·er \'kȯr-sər\ *n* : a swift or spirited horse

¹court \'kȯrt\ *n* **1** : the residence of a sovereign or similar dignitary **2** : a sovereign's formal assembly of officials and advisers as a governing power **3** : an assembly of the retinue of a sovereign **4** : an open space enclosed by a building or buildings **5** : a space walled or marked off for playing a game (as tennis or basketball) **6** : the place where justice is administered; *also* : a judicial body or a meeting of a judicial body **7** : attention intended to win favor

²court *vb* **1** : to try to gain the favor of **2** : WOO **3** : ATTRACT, TEMPT

cour·te·ous \'kər-tē-əs\ *adj* : marked by respect for others : CIVIL, POLITE — **cour·te·ous·ly** *adv*

cour·te·san \'kȯr-tə-zən, -¡zan\ *n* : PROSTITUTE

cour·te·sy \'kər-tə-sē\ *n, pl* **-sies 1** : courteous behavior : POLITENESS **2** : a favor courteously performed

court·house \'kȯrt-¡haùs\ *n* : a building in which courts of law are held or county offices are located

court·ier \'kȯrt-ē-ər\ *n* : a person in attendance at a royal court

court·ly \'kȯrt-lē\ *adj* **court·li·er; -est** : REFINED, ELEGANT, POLITE **syn** gallant, gracious — **court·li·ness** *n*

court–mar·tial \'kȯrt-¡mär-shəl\ *n, pl* **courts–martial** : a military or naval court for trial of offenses against military or naval law; *also* : a trial by this court — **court–martial** *vb*

court·room \-¡rüm, -¡rùm\ *n* : a room in which a court of law is held

court·ship \-¡ship\ *n* : the act of courting : WOOING

court·yard \-¡yärd\ *n* : an enclosure next to a building

cous·in \'kə-zən\ *n* [ME *cosin,* fr. OF, fr. L *consobrinus,* fr. *com-* with + *sobrinus* second cousin, fr. *soror* sister] : a child of one's uncle or aunt

cou·ture \kü-'tùr, -'tūer\ *n* [F] : the business of designing fashionable custom-made women's clothing; *also* : the designers and establishments engaged in this business

cou·tu·ri·er \kü-'tùr-ē-ər, -ē-¡ā\ *n* [F, dressmaker] : the owner of an establishment engaged in couture

cove \'kōv\ *n* : a small sheltered inlet or bay

co·ven \'kə-vən\ *n* : an assembly or band of witches

cov·e·nant \'kə-və-nənt\ *n* : a formal binding agreement : COMPACT — **cov·e·nant** \-nənt, -¡nant\ *vb*

¹cov·er \'kə-vər\ *vb* **1** : to bring or hold within range of a firearm **2** : PROTECT, SHIELD **3** : HIDE, CONCEAL **4** : to place something over or upon **5** : INCLUDE, COMPRISE **6** : to have as one's field of activity (one salesman ∼*s* the state) **7** : to buy (stocks) in order to have them for delivery on a previous short sale

²cover *n* **1** : something that protects or shelters **2** : LID, TOP **3** : CASE, BINDING **4** : TABLECLOTH **5** : a cloth used on a bed **6** : SCREEN, DISGUISE **7** : an envelope or wrapper for mail

cov·er·age \'kə-və-rij\ *n* **1** : the act or fact of covering **2** : the total group covered : SCOPE

cov·er·all \'kə-vər-¡ȯl\ *n* : a one-piece outer garment worn to protect one's clothes — usu. used in pl.

cover charge *n* : a charge made by a restaurant or nightclub in addition to the charge for food and drink

cover crop *n* : a crop planted to prevent soil erosion and to provide humus

cov·er·let \'kə-vər-lət\ *n* : BEDSPREAD

¹co·vert \'kō-¡vərt, 'kə-vərt\ *adj* **1** : HIDDEN, SECRET **2** : SHELTERED — **co·vert·ly** *adv*

²co·vert \'kə-vərt, 'kō-\ *n* **1** : a secret or sheltered place; *esp* : a thicket sheltering game **2** : a feather covering the bases of the quills of the wings and tail of a bird

cov·er–up \'kə-vər-¡əp\ *n* **1** : a device for masking or

concealing **2** : a usu. concerted effort to keep an illegal or unethical act or situation from being made public

cov·et \'kə-vət\ *vb* : to desire enviously (what belongs to another) — **cov·et·ous** *adj* — **cov·et·ous·ness** *n*

cov·ey \'kə-vē\ *n, pl* **coveys** [ME, fr. MF *covee,* fr. OF, fr. *cover* to sit on, brood over, fr. L *cubare* to lie] **1** : a bird with her brood of young **2** : a small flock (as of quail)

¹cow \'kaù\ *n* **1** : the mature female of cattle or of an animal (as the moose, elephant, or whale) of which the male is called *bull* **2** : any domestic bovine animal irrespective of sex or age

²cow *vb* : INTIMIDATE, DAUNT, OVERAWE

cow·ard \'kaù(-ə)rd\ *n* [ME, fr. OF *coart,* fr. *coe* tail, fr. L *cauda*] : one who lacks courage or shows shameful fear or timidity — **coward** *adj* — **cow·ard·ice** \'kaù-ər-dəs\ *n* — **cow·ard·ly** *adv or adj*

cow·bird \'kaù-¡bərd\ *n* : a small No. American bird that lays its eggs in the nests of other birds

cow·boy \-¡bȯi\ *n* : one (as a mounted ranch hand) who tends cattle or horses

cow·er \'kaù(-ə)r\ *vb* : to shrink or crouch down from fear or cold : QUAIL

cow·girl \'kaù-¡gərl\ *n* : a girl or woman who tends cattle or horses

cow·hand \'kaù-¡hand\ *n* : COWBOY

cow·hide \-¡hīd\ *n* **1** : the hide of a cow; *also* : leather made from it **2** : a coarse whip of braided rawhide

cowl \'kaùl\ *n* : a monk's hood

cow·lick \'kaù-¡lik\ *n* : a turned-up tuft of hair that resists control

cowl·ing \'kaù-liŋ\ *n* : a usu. metal covering for the engine or another part of an airplane

cow·man \'kaù-mən, -¡man\ *n* : COWBOY; *also* : a cattle owner or rancher

co·work·er \'kō-¡wər-kər\ *n* : a fellow worker

cow·poke \'kaù-¡pōk\ *n* : COWBOY

cow pony *n* : a strong and agile horse trained for herding cattle

cow·pox \'kaù-¡päks\ *n* : a mild disease of the cow that when communicated to humans protects against smallpox

cow·punch·er \-¡pən-chər\ *n* : COWBOY

cow·slip \'kaù-¡slip\ *n* **1** : a yellow-flowered European primrose **2** : MARSH MARIGOLD

cox·comb \'käks-¡kōm\ *n* : a conceited foolish person : FOP

cox·swain \'käk-sən, -¡swān\ *n* : the steersman of a ship's boat or a racing shell

coy \'kȯi\ *adj* [ME, quiet, shy, fr. MF *coi* calm, fr. L *quietus* quiet] **1** : BASHFUL, SHY **2** : marked by artful playfulness : COQUETTISH — **coy·ly** *adv* — **coy·ness** *n*

coy·ote \'kī-¡ōt, kī-'ō-tē\ *n, pl* **coyotes** *or* **coyote** : a mammal of No. America smaller than the related wolves

coyote

coy·pu \'kȯi-pü\ *n* : NUTRIA 2

coz·en \'kəz-ᵊn\ *vb* : CHEAT, DEFRAUD — **coz·en·age** \-ij\ *n* — **coz·en·er** *n*

¹**co·zy** \'kō-zē\ *adj* **co·zi·er; -est** : SNUG, COMFORTABLE — **co·zi·ly** \-zə-lē\ *adv* — **co·zi·ness** \-zē-nəs\ *n*

²**cozy** *n, pl* **co·zies** : a padded covering for a vessel (as a teapot) to keep the contents hot

cp *abbr* 1 compare 2 coupon

CP *abbr* 1 cerebral palsy 2 chemically pure 3 command post 4 communist party

CPA *abbr* certified public accountant

CPB *abbr* Corporation for Public Broadcasting

cpd *abbr* compound

CPI *abbr* consumer price index

Cpl *abbr* corporal

CPO *abbr* chief petty officer

CPOM *abbr* master chief petty officer

CPOS *abbr* senior chief petty officer

CPR *abbr* cardiopulmonary resuscitation

CPT *abbr* captain

CQ *abbr* charge of quarters

cr *abbr* credit; creditor

Cr *symbol* chromium

¹**crab** \'krab\ *n* : any of various crustaceans with a short broad shell and small abdomen

²**crab** *n* : an ill-natured person

³**crab** *vb* **crabbed; crab·bing** : COMPLAIN, GROUSE

crab apple *n* : a small often highly colored sour apple; *also* : a tree that produces crab apples

crab·bed \'kra-bəd\ *adj* 1 : MOROSE, PEEVISH 2 : CRAMPED, IRREGULAR

crab·by \'kra-bē\ *adj* **crab·bi·er; -est** : CROSS, ILL-NATURED

crab·grass \'krab-ˌgras\ *n* : a weedy grass with creeping or sprawling stems that root freely at the nodes

crab louse *n* : a louse infesting the pubic region in humans

¹**crack** \'krak\ *vb* 1 : to break with a sharp sudden sound 2 : to break with or without completely separating into parts 3 : to fail in tone or become harsh ⟨her voice ∼*ed*⟩ 4 : to subject (as a petroleum oil) to heat for breaking down into lighter products (as gasoline)

²**crack** *n* 1 : a sudden sharp noise 2 : a witty or sharp remark 3 : a narrow break or opening : FISSURE 4 : a sharp blow 5 : ATTEMPT, TRY 6 : highly purified cocaine in small chips used illicitly usu. for smoking

³**crack** *adj* : extremely proficient

crack·down \'krak-ˌdaȯn\ *n* : an act or instance of taking positive disciplinary action ⟨a ∼ on gambling⟩ — **crack down** *vb*

crack·er \'kra-kər\ *n* 1 : FIRECRACKER 2 : a dry thin crispy baked bread product made of flour and water

crack·er·jack \-ˌjak\ *n* : something very excellent — **crackerjack** *adj*

crack·le \'kra-kəl\ *vb* **crack·led; crack·ling** 1 : to make small sharp snapping noises 2 : to develop fine cracks in a surface — **crackle** *n* — **crack·ly** \-k(ə-)lē\ *adj*

crack·pot \'krak-ˌpät\ *n* : an eccentric person

crack–up \'krak-ˌəp\ *n* : CRASH, WRECK; *also* : BREAK-DOWN

crack up *vb* 1 : PRAISE ⟨isn't all it's *cracked up* to be⟩ 2 : to laugh or cause to laugh out loud 3 : to crash a vehicle

¹**cra·dle** \'krād-ᵊl\ *n* 1 : a baby's bed or cot 2 : a framework or support (as for a telephone receiver) 3 : INFANCY ⟨from ∼ to the grave⟩ 4 : a place of origin

²**cradle** *vb* **cra·dled; cra·dling** 1 : to place in or as if in a cradle 2 : SHELTER, REAR

craft \'kraft\ *n* 1 : ART, SKILL; *also* : an occupation requiring special skill 2 : CUNNING, GUILE 3 *pl usu* **craft** : a boat esp. of small size; *also* : AIRCRAFT, SPACECRAFT

crafts·man \'krafts-mən\ *n* : a skilled artisan — **crafts-man·ship** *n*

crafty \'kraf-tē\ *adj* **craft·i·er; -est** : CUNNING, DECEITFUL, SUBTLE — **craft·i·ly** \-tə-lē\ *adv* — **craft·i·ness** \-tē-nəs\ *n*

crag \'krag\ *n* : a steep rugged cliff or rock — **crag-gy** *adj*

cram \'kram\ *vb* **crammed; cram·ming** 1 : to pack in tight : JAM 2 : to eat greedily 3 : to study rapidly under pressure for an examination

¹**cramp** \'kramp\ *n* 1 : a sudden painful contraction of muscle 2 : sharp abdominal pain — usu. used in pl.

²**cramp** *vb* 1 : to affect with a cramp or cramps 2 : to restrain from free action : HAMPER

cran·ber·ry \'kran-ˌber-ē, -bə-rē\ *n* : the red acid berry of any of several trailing plants related to the heaths; *also* : one of these plants

¹**crane** \'krān\ *n* 1 : any of a family of tall wading birds related to the rails; *also* : any of several herons 2 : a machine for lifting and carrying heavy objects

²**crane** *vb* **craned; cran·ing** : to stretch one's neck to see better

crane fly *n* : any of numerous long-legged slender dipteran flies that resemble large mosquitoes but do not bite

cranial nerve *n* : any of the nerves that arise in pairs from the lower surface of the brain and pass through openings in the skull to the periphery of the body

cra·ni·um \'krā-nē-əm\ *n, pl* **-ni·ums** *or* **-nia** \-ə\ : SKULL; *esp* : the part enclosing the brain — **cra·ni·al** \-əl\ *adj*

¹**crank** \'kraŋk\ *n* 1 : a bent part of an axle or shaft or an arm at right angles to the end of a shaft by which circular motion is imparted to or received from it 2 : an eccentric person 3 : a bad-tempered person : GROUCH

²**crank** *vb* : to start or operate by or as if by turning a crank

crank·case \'kraŋk-ˌkās\ *n* : the housing of a crankshaft

crank out *vb* : to produce in a mechanical manner

crank·shaft \'kraŋk-ˌshaft\ *n* : a shaft turning or driven by a crank

cranky \'kraŋ-kē\ *adj* **crank·i·er; -est** 1 : IRRITABLE 2 : operating uncertainly or imperfectly

cran·ny \'kra-nē\ *n, pl* **crannies** : CREVICE, CHINK

craps \'kraps\ *n* : a gambling game played with two dice

crap·shoot·er \'krap-ˌshü-tər\ *n* : a person who plays craps

¹**crash** \'krash\ *vb* 1 : to break noisily : SMASH 2 : to damage an airplane in landing 3 : to enter or attend without invitation or without paying ⟨∼ a party⟩

²**crash** *n* 1 : a loud sound (as of things smashing) 2 : an instance of crashing ⟨a plane ∼⟩; *also* : COLLISION 3 : a sudden failure (as of a business)

³**crash** *adj* : marked by concerted effort over the shortest possible time

⁴**crash** *n* : coarse linen fabric used for towels and draperies

crash–land \'krash-ˈland\ *vb* : to land an aircraft or spacecraft under emergency conditions usu. with damage to the craft — **crash landing** *n*

crass \'kras\ *adj* : GROSS, INSENSITIVE — **crass·ly** *adv*

crate \'krāt\ *n* : a container often of wooden slats — **crate** *vb*

cra·ter \'krā-tər\ *n* [L, mixing bowl, crater, fr. Gk *kratēr*, fr. *kerannynai* to mix] 1 : the depression around the opening of a volcano 2 : a depression formed by the impact of a meteorite or by the explosion of a bomb or shell

cra·vat \krə-ˈvat\ *n* : NECKTIE

crave \'krāv\ *vb* **craved; crav·ing** 1 : to ask for earnestly : BEG 2 : to long for : DESIRE

\ə\abut \ᵊ\kitten \ər\further \a\ash \ā\ace \ä\mop, mar \aȯ\out \ch\chin \e\bet \ē\easy \g\go \i\hit \ī\ice \j\job \ŋ\sing \ō\go \ȯ\law \ȯi\boy \th\thin \t͟h\the \ü\loot \ȯ\foot \y\yet \zh\vision *see also* Pronunciation Symbols page

cra·ven \'krā-vən\ *adj* : COWARDLY — **craven** *n*
crav·ing \'krā-viŋ\ *n* : an urgent or abnormal desire
craw·fish \'krò-ˌfish\ *n* 1 : CRAYFISH 1 2 : SPINY LOBSTER
¹crawl \'kròl\ *vb* 1 : to move slowly by drawing the body along the ground 2 : to advance feebly, cautiously, or slowly 3 : to be swarming with or feel as if swarming with creeping things ⟨a place ∼*ing* with ants⟩ ⟨her flesh ∼*ed*⟩
²crawl *n* 1 : a very slow pace 2 : a prone speed swimming stroke
cray·fish \'krā-ˌfish\ *n* 1 : any of numerous freshwater crustaceans usu. much smaller than the related lobsters 2 : SPINY LOBSTER

crayfish 1

cray·on \'krā-ˌän, -ən\ *n* : a stick of chalk or wax used for writing, drawing, or coloring; *also* : a drawing made with such material — **crayon** *vb*
¹craze \'krāz\ *vb* **crazed; craz·ing** [ME *crasen* to crush, craze, of Scand origin] : to make or become insane
²craze *n* : FAD, MANIA
cra·zy \'krā-zē\ *adj* **cra·zi·er; -est** 1 : mentally disordered : INSANE 2 : wildly impractical; *also* : ERRATIC — **cra·zi·ly** \-zə-lē\ *adv* — **cra·zi·ness** \-zē-nəs\ *n*
CRC *abbr* Civil Rights Commission
creak \'krēk\ *vb* : to make a prolonged squeaking or grating sound — **creak** *n* — **creaky** *adj*
¹cream \'krēm\ *n* 1 : the yellowish fat-rich part of milk 2 : a thick smooth sauce, confection, or cosmetic 3 : the choicest part 4 : a pale yellow color — **creamy** *adj*
²cream *vb* 1 : to prepare with a cream sauce 2 : to beat or blend into creamy consistency 3 : to defeat decisively
cream cheese *n* : a cheese made from whole milk enriched with cream
cream·ery \'krē-mə-rē\ *n, pl* **-er·ies** : an establishment where butter and cheese are made or milk and cream are prepared for sale
crease \'krēs\ *n* : a mark or line made by or as if by folding — **crease** *vb*
cre·ate \krē-'āt\ *vb* **cre·at·ed; cre·at·ing** : to bring into being : cause to exist : MAKE, PRODUCE — **cre·a·tive** \-'ā-tiv\ *adj* — **cre·a·tiv·i·ty** \ˌkre-(ˌ)ā-'ti-və-tē\ *n*
cre·a·tion \krē-'ā-shən\ *n* 1 : the act of creating or producing ⟨∼ of the world⟩ 2 : something that is created 3 : all created things : WORLD
cre·a·tion·ism \krē-'ā-shə-ˌni-zəm\ *n* : a doctrine or theory holding that matter, the various forms of life, and the world were created by God out of nothing — **cre·a·tion·ist** \-nist\ *n or adj*
cre·a·tor \krē-'ā-tər\ *n* 1 : one that creates : MAKER, AUTHOR 2 *cap* : GOD 1
crea·ture \'krē-chər\ *n* : a lower animal; *also* : a human being
crèche \'kresh\ *n* [F, manger, crib] : a representation of the Nativity scene
cre·dence \'krēd-ᵊns\ *n* : mental acceptance as true or real

cre·den·tial \kri-'den-chəl\ *n* : something that gives a basis for credit or confidence
cre·den·za \kri-'den-zə\ *n* [It, lit., belief, confidence] : a sideboard, buffet, or bookcase usu. without legs
cred·i·ble \'kre-də-bəl\ *adj* : TRUSTWORTHY, BELIEVABLE — **cred·i·bil·i·ty** \ˌkre-də-'bi-lə-tē\ *n*
¹cred·it \'kre-dət\ *vb* 1 : BELIEVE 2 : to give credit to
²credit *n* [MF, fr. It *credito*, fr. L *creditum* something entrusted to another, loan, fr. *credere* to believe, entrust] 1 : the balance (as in a bank) in a person's favor 2 : time given for payment for goods sold on trust 3 : an accounting entry of payment received 4 : BELIEF, FAITH 5 : financial trustworthiness 6 : ESTEEM 7 : a source of honor or distinction 8 : a unit of academic work
cred·it·able \'kre-də-tə-bəl\ *adj* : worthy of esteem or praise — **cred·it·ably** \-blē\ *adv*
credit card *n* : a card authorizing purchases on credit
cred·i·tor \'kre-də-tər\ *n* : a person to whom money is owed
cre·do \'krē-dò, 'krā-\ *n, pl* **credos** [ME, fr. L, I believe] : CREED
cred·u·lous \'kre-jə-ləs\ *adj* : inclined to believe esp. on slight evidence — **cre·du·li·ty** \kri-'dü-lə-tē, -'dyü-\ *n*
Cree \'krē\ *n, pl* **Cree** *or* **Crees** : a member of an American Indian people of Canada
creed \'krēd\ *n* [ME *crede*, fr. OE *crēda*, fr. L *credo* I believe, first word of the Apostles' and Nicene Creeds] : a statement of the essential beliefs of a religious faith
creek \'krēk, 'krik\ *n* 1 *chiefly Brit* : a small inlet 2 : a stream smaller than a river and larger than a brook
Creek \'krēk\ *n* : a member of an American Indian people of Alabama, Georgia, and Florida
creel \'krēl\ *n* : a wicker basket esp. for carrying fish
creep \'krēp\ *vb* **crept** \'krept\; **creep·ing** 1 : CRAWL 2 : to feel as though insects were crawling on the skin 3 : to grow over a surface like ivy — **creep** *n* — **creep·er** *n*
creep·ing \'krē-piŋ\ *adj* : developing or advancing by imperceptible degrees
creepy \'krē-pē\ *adj* **creep·i·er; -est** : having or producing a nervous shivery fear
cre·mate \'krē-ˌmāt\ *vb* **cre·mat·ed; cre·mat·ing** : to reduce (a dead body) to ashes with fire — **cre·ma·tion** \kri-'mā-shən\ *n*
cre·ma·to·ry \'krē-mə-ˌtòr-ē, 'kre-\ *n, pl* **-ries** : a furnace for cremating; *also* : a structure containing such a furnace
crème \'krem, 'krēm\ *n, pl* **crèmes** *same or* 'kremz, 'krēmz\ [F, lit., cream] : a sweet liqueur
cren·el·lat·ed *or* **cren·el·at·ed** \'kren-ᵊl-ˌā-təd\ *adj* : having battlements — **cren·el·la·tion** \ˌkren-ᵊl-'ā-shən\ *n*
Cre·ole \'krē-ˌòl\ *n* 1 : a descendant of early French or Spanish settlers of the U.S. Gulf states preserving their speech and culture; *also* : a person of mixed French or Spanish and black descent speaking a dialect of French or Spanish 2 *not cap* : a language that has evolved from a pidgin but serves as the native language of a speech community
cre·o·sote \'krē-ə-ˌsòt\ *n* : an oily liquid obtained by distillation of coal tar and used in preserving wood
crepe *or* **crêpe** \'krāp\ *n* : a light crinkled fabric of any of various fibers
crêpe su·zette \ˌkrāp-sü-'zet\ *n, pl* **crêpes suzette** *same or* ˌkrāps-\ *or* **crêpe suzettes** \-sü-'zets\ *often cap S* : a thin folded or rolled pancake in a hot orange-butter sauce that is sprinkled with a liqueur and set ablaze for serving
cre·pus·cu·lar \kri-'pəs-kyə-lər\ *adj* 1 : of, relating to, or resembling twilight 2 : active in the twilight ⟨∼ insects⟩
cre·scen·do \krə-'shen-dò\ *adv or adj* [It] : increasing in

loudness — used as a direction in music — **crescendo** *n*

cres·cent \'kres-ᵊnt\ *n* [ME *cressant*, fr. MF *creissant*, fr. *creistre* to grow, increase, fr. L *crescere*] : the moon at any stage between new moon and first quarter and between last quarter and new moon; *also* : something shaped like the figure of the crescent moon with a convex and a concave edge — **cres·cen·tic** \kre-'sen-tik\ *adj*

cress \'kres\ *n* : any of several salad plants related to the mustards

¹**crest** \'krest\ *n* **1** : a tuft or process on the head of an animal (as a bird) **2** : a heraldic device **3** : an upper part, edge, or limit ⟨the ∼ of a hill⟩ — **crest·ed** \'kres-təd\ *adj* — **crest·less** *adj*

²**crest** *vb* **1** : CROWN **2** : to reach the crest of **3** : to rise to a crest

crest·fall·en \'krest-₁fȯ-lən\ *adj* : DISPIRITED, DEJECTED

Cre·ta·ceous \kri-'tā-shəs\ *adj* : of, relating to, or being the latest period of the Mesozoic era marked by great increase in flowering plants, diversification of mammals, and culminating in extinction of the dinosaurs — **Cretaceous** *n*

cre·tin \'krēt-ᵊn\ *n* [F *crétin*, fr. F dial. *cretin*, lit., wretch, innocent victim, fr. L *christianus* Christian] **1** : one affected with cretinism **2** : a stupid person

cre·tin·ism \-₁i-zəm\ *n* : a usu. congenital abnormal condition characterized by physical stunting and mental retardation

cre·tonne \'krē-₁tän\ *n* : a strong unglazed cotton cloth for curtains and upholstery

cre·vasse \kri-'vas\ *n* : a deep fissure esp. in a glacier

crev·ice \'kre-vəs\ *n* : a narrow fissure

¹**crew** \'krü\ *chiefly Brit past of* CROW

²**crew** *n* [ME *crue*, lit., reinforcement, fr. MF *creue* increase, fr. *creistre* to grow, fr. L *crescere*] **1** : a body of people trained to work together for certain purposes **2** : a group of people who operate a ship, train, aircraft, or spacecraft **3** : the rowers and coxswain of a racing shell; *also* : the sport of rowing engaged in by a crew — **crew·man** \-mən\ *n*

crew cut *n* : a very short bristly haircut

crew·el \'krü-əl\ *n* : slackly twisted worsted yarn used for embroidery — **crew·el·work** \-₁wərk\ *n*

¹**crib** \'krib\ *n* **1** : a manger for feeding animals **2** : a child's bedstead with high sides **3** : a building or bin for storage (as of grain) **4** : something used for cheating in an exam

²**crib** *vb* **cribbed; crib·bing 1** : to put in a crib **2** : STEAL, PLAGIARIZE — **crib·ber** *n*

crib·bage \'kri-bij\ *n* : a card game usu. played by two players and scored on a board (**cribbage board**)

crib death *n* : SUDDEN INFANT DEATH SYNDROME

crick \'krik\ *n* : a painful spasm of muscles (as of the neck)

¹**crick·et** \'kri-kət\ *n* : any of a family of leaping insects related to the grasshoppers and noted for the chirping noises of the male

²**cricket** *n* : a game played with a bat and ball by two teams on a field centering upon two wickets each defended by a batsman

cri·er \'krī(-ə)r\ *n* : one who calls out proclamations and announcements

crime \'krīm\ *n* : a serious offense against the public law

¹**crim·i·nal** \'kri-mən-ᵊl\ *adj* **1** : involving or being a crime **2** : relating to crime or its punishment — **crim·i·nal·i·ty** \₁kri-mə-'na-lə-tē\ *n* — **crim·i·nal·ly** *adv*

²**criminal** *n* : one who has committed a crime

crim·i·nol·o·gy \₁kri-mə-'nä-lə-jē\ *n* : the scientific study of crime and criminals — **crim·i·nol·o·gist** \₁kri-mə-'nä-lə-jist\ *n*

¹**crimp** \'krimp\ *vb* : to cause to become crinkled, wavy, or bent

²**crimp** *n* : something (as a curl in hair) produced by or as if by crimping

¹**crim·son** \'krim-zən\ *n* : a deep purplish red color — **crimson** *adj*

²**crimson** *vb* : to make or become crimson

cringe \'krinj\ *vb* **cringed; cring·ing** : to shrink in fear : WINCE, COWER

crin·kle \'kriṇ-kəl\ *vb* **crin·kled; crin·kling** : to form many short bends or curves; *also* : WRINKLE — **crinkle** *n* — **crin·kly** \-kə-lē\ *adj*

crin·o·line \'krin-ᵊl-ən\ *n* **1** : an open-weave cloth used for stiffening and lining **2** : a full stiff skirt or underskirt made of crinoline

¹**crip·ple** \'kri-pəl\ *n* : a lame or disabled person — sometimes taken to be offensive

²**cripple** *vb* **crip·pled; crip·pling 1** : to make lame **2** : to make useless or imperfect

cri·sis \'krī-səs\ *n, pl* **cri·ses** \-₁sēz\ [L, fr. Gk *krisis*, lit., decision, fr. *krinein* to decide] **1** : the turning point for better or worse in an acute disease or fever **2** : a decisive or critical moment

crisp \'krisp\ *adj* **1** : CURLY, WAVY **2** : BRITTLE **3** : FIRM, FRESH ⟨∼ lettuce⟩ **4** : being sharp and clear **5** : LIVELY, SPARKLING **6** : FROSTY, SNAPPY; *also* : INVIGORATING — **crisp** *vb* — **crisp·ly** *adv* — **crisp·ness** *n* — **crispy** *adj*

¹**criss·cross** \'kris-₁krȯs\ *vb* **1** : to mark with crossed lines **2** : to go or pass back and forth

²**crisscross** *adj* : marked or characterized by crisscrossing — **crisscross** *adv*

³**crisscross** *n* : a pattern formed by crossed lines

crit *abbr* critical; criticism

cri·te·ri·on \krī-'tir-ē-ən\ *n, pl* **-ria** \-ē-ə\ : a standard on which a judgment may be based

crit·ic \'kri-tik\ *n* **1** : a person who judges literary or artistic works **2** : one inclined to find fault

crit·i·cal \'kri-ti-kəl\ *adj* **1** : being or relating to a condition or disease involving danger of death **2** : being a crisis **3** : inclined to criticize **4** : relating to criticism or critics **5** : requiring careful judgment **6** : UNCERTAIN — **crit·i·cal·ly** \-k(ə-)lē\ *adv*

crit·i·cism \'kri-tə-₁si-zəm\ *n* **1** : the act of criticizing; *esp* : CENSURE **2** : a judgment or review **3** : the art of judging works of literature or art

crit·i·cize \'kri-tə-₁sīz\ *vb* **-cized; -ciz·ing 1** : to judge as a critic : EVALUATE **2** : to find fault : express criticism **syn** blame, censure, condemn

cri·tique \krə-'tēk\ *n* : a critical estimate or discussion

crit·ter \'kri-tər\ *n* : CREATURE

croak \'krȯk\ *n* : a hoarse harsh cry (as of a frog) — **croak** *vb*

Croat \'krō-₁at\ *n* : CROATIAN

Cro·atian \krō-'ā-shən\ *n* : a native or inhabitant of Croatia — **Croatian** *adj*

cro·chet \krō-'shā\ *n* [F, hook, crochet, fr. MF, dim. of *croche* hook] : needlework done with a single thread and hooked needle — **crochet** *vb*

crock \'kräk\ *n* : a thick earthenware pot or jar

crock·ery \'krä-kə-rē\ *n* : EARTHENWARE

croc·o·dile \'krä-kə-₁dīl\ *n* [ME & L; ME *cocodrille*, fr. OF, fr. ML *cocodrillus*, alter. of L *crocodilus*, fr. Gk *krokodilos* lizard, crocodile, fr. *krokē* shingle, pebble + *drillos* worm] : any of several thick-skinned long-bodied carnivorous reptiles of tropical and subtropical waters

cro·cus \'krō-kəs\ *n, pl* **cro·cus·es** *also* **crocus** *or* **cro·ci** \-₁kī\ : any of a large genus of low herbs related to the irises and having brightly colored flowers borne singly in early spring

---

\ə\abut \ᵊ\kitten \ər\further \a\ash \ā\ace \ä\mop, mar
\au̇\out \ch\chin \e\bet \ē\easy \g\go \i\hit \ī\ice \j\job
\ṇ\sing \ō\go \ȯ\law \ȯi\boy \th\thin \t̲h̲\the \ü\loot \u̇\foot
\y\yet \zh\vision *see also* Pronunciation Symbols page

crois·sant \krȯ-ˈsänt, krwä-ˈsäⁿ\ *n, pl* **croissants** *same or* -ˈsänts, -ˈsäⁿz\ : a rich crescent-shaped roll

Cro–Ma·gnon \krȯ-ˈmag-nən, -ˈman-yən\ *n* : any of a tall erect human race known from skeletal remains found chiefly in southern France and usu. classified as the same species as present-day human beings — **Cro–Magnon** *adj*

crone \ˈkrōn\ *n* : HAG

cro·ny \ˈkrō-nē\ *n, pl* **cronies** : a close friend esp. of long standing

¹**crook** \ˈkru̇k\ *vb* : to curve or bend sharply

²**crook** *n* **1** : a bent or curved implement **2** : a bent or curved part; *also* : BEND, CURVE **3** : SWINDLER, THIEF

crook·ed \ˈkru̇-kəd\ *adj* **1** : having a crook : BENT, CURVED **2** : DISHONEST — **crook·ed·ly** *adv* — **crook·ed·ness** *n*

croon \ˈkrün\ *vb* : to sing or hum in a gentle murmuring voice — **croon·er** *n*

¹**crop** \ˈkräp\ *n* **1** : the handle of a whip; *also* : a short riding whip **2** : a pouch in the throat of many birds and insects where food is received **3** : something that can be harvested; *also* : the yield at harvest

²**crop** *vb* **cropped; crop·ping 1** : to remove the tips of : cut off short; *also* : TRIM **2** : to feed on by cropping **3** : to devote (land) to crops **4** : to appear unexpectedly

crop·land \-ˌland\ *n* : land devoted to the production of plant crops

crop·per \ˈkrä-pər\ *n* : a raiser of crops; *esp* : SHARE-CROPPER

cro·quet \krȯ-ˈkā\ *n* : a game in which mallets are used to drive wooden balls through a series of wickets set out on a lawn

cro·quette \krȯ-ˈket\ *n* [F] : a small often rounded mass of minced meat, fish, or vegetables fried in deep fat

cro·sier \ˈkrō-zhər\ *n* : a staff carried by bishops and abbots

¹**cross** \ˈkrȯs\ *n* **1** : a structure consisting of an upright beam and a crossbar used esp. by the ancient Romans for execution **2** : a figure of the cross on which Christ was crucified used as a Christian symbol **3** : a hybridizing of unlike individuals or strains; *also* : a product of this **4** : a punch delivered with a circular motion over an opponent's lead

²**cross** *vb* **1** : to lie or place across; *also* : INTERSECT **2** : to cancel by marking a cross on or by lining through **3** : THWART, OBSTRUCT **4** : to go or extend across : TRAVERSE **5** : HYBRIDIZE **6** : to meet and pass on the way

³**cross** *adj* **1** : lying across **2** : CONTRARY, OPPOSED **3** : marked by bad temper : HYBRID — **cross·ly** *adv*

cross·bar \ˈkrȯs-ˌbär\ *n* : a transverse bar or piece

cross·bow \-ˌbō\ *n* : a short bow mounted crosswise at the end of a wooden stock that shoots short arrows

crossbow

cross·breed \ˈkrȯs-ˌbrēd, -ˈbrēd\ *vb* **-bred** \-ˈbred\; **-breed·ing** : HYBRIDIZE

cross–coun·try \-ˈkən-trē\ *adj* **1** : extending or moving across a country **2** : proceeding over the countryside (as fields and woods) and not by roads **3** : of or relating to racing or skiing over the countryside instead of over a track or run — **cross–country** *adv*

cross·cur·rent \-ˈkər-ənt\ *n* **1** : a current running counter to another **2** : a conflicting tendency — usu. used in pl.

¹**cross·cut** \-ˌkət\ *vb* : to cut or saw crosswise esp. of the grain of wood

²**crosscut** *adj* **1** : made or used for crosscutting ⟨a ~ saw⟩ **2** : cut across the grain

³**crosscut** *n* : something that cuts through transversely

cross–ex·am·ine \ˌkrȯs-ig-ˈza-mən\ *vb* : to examine with questions to check the answers to previous questions — **cross–ex·am·i·na·tion** \-ˌza-mə-ˈnā-shən\ *n*

cross–eyed \ˈkrȯ-ˌsīd\ *adj* : having one or both eyes turned inward toward the nose

cross–fer·til·i·za·tion \-ˌfərt-ᵊl-ə-ˈzā-shən\ *n* **1** : fertilization between sex cells produced by separate individuals or sometimes by individuals of different kinds; *also* : CROSS-POLLINATION **2** : a broadening or productive interchange (as between cultures) — **cross–fer·til·ize** \-ˈfərt-ᵊl-ˌīz\ *vb*

cross fire *n* **1** : crossing lines of fire in combat **2** : rapid or angry interchange

cross·hair \ˈkrȯs-ˌhar\ *n* : a fine wire or thread in the eyepiece of an optical instrument used as a reference line

cross·hatch \ˈkrȯs-ˌhach\ *vb* : to mark with two series of parallel lines that intersect — **cross–hatch·ing** *n*

cross·ing \ˈkrȯ-siŋ\ *n* **1** : a place or structure for crossing something (as a river) **2** : a point of intersection (as of a street and a railroad track)

cross·over \ˈkrȯs-ˌō-vər\ *n* **1** : CROSSING **2** : a member of a political party who votes in the primary of the other party

cross·piece \ˈkrȯs-ˌpēs\ *n* : a horizontal member

cross–pol·li·na·tion \ˌkrȯs-ˌpä-lə-ˈnā-shən\ *n* : transfer of pollen from one flower to the stigma of another — **cross–pol·li·nate** \ˈkrȯs-ˌpä-lə-ˌnāt\ *vb*

cross–pur·pose \ˈkrȯs-ˈpər-pəs\ *n* : a purpose contrary to another purpose ⟨working at ~s⟩

cross–ques·tion \-ˈkwes-chən\ *vb* : CROSS-EXAMINE — **cross–question** *n*

cross–re·fer \ˌkrȯs-ri-ˈfər\ *vb* : to refer by a notation or direction from one place to another (as in a book or list) — **cross–ref·er·ence** \ˈkrȯs-ˈre-frəns\ *n*

cross·road \ˈkrȯs-ˌrōd\ *n* **1** : a road that crosses a main road or runs between main roads **2** : a place where roads meet — usu. used in pl. **3** : a crucial point where a decision must be made

cross section *n* **1** : a section cut across something; *also* : a representation made by or as if by such cutting **2** : a number of persons or things selected from a group that show the general nature of the whole group — **cross–sec·tion·al** *adj*

cross·walk \ˈkrȯs-ˌwȯk\ *n* : a marked path for pedestrians crossing a street

cross·ways \-ˌwāz\ *adv* : CROSSWISE

cross·wind \-ˌwind\ *n* : a wind not parallel to a course (as of an airplane)

cross·wise \-ˌwīz\ *adv* : so as to cross something : ACROSS — **crosswise** *adj*

cross·word \ˈkrȯs-ˌwərd\ *n* : a puzzle in which words are put into a pattern of numbered squares in answer to clues

crotch \ˈkräch\ *n* : an angle formed by the parting of two legs, branches, or members

crotch·et \ˈkrä-chət\ *n* : an odd notion : WHIM — **crotch·ety** *adj*

crouch \ˈkrau̇ch\ *vb* **1** : to stoop or bend low **2** : CRINGE, COWER — **crouch** *n*

croup \ˈkrüp\ *n* : laryngitis esp. of infants marked by a hoarse ringing cough and difficult breathing — **croupy** *adj*

crou·pi·er \ˈkrü-pē-ər, -pē-ˌā\ *n* [F, lit., rider on the rump of a horse, fr. *croupe* rump] : an employee of a gambling casino who collects and pays bets at a gaming table

crou·ton \'krü-ˌtän\ n [F croûton, dim. of croûte crust] : a small cube of bread toasted or fried crisp

¹crow \'krō\ n 1 : any of various large glossy black birds related to the jays 2 cap : a member of an American Indian people of a region in Montana and Wyoming; also : the language of the Crow people

²crow vb 1 : to make the loud shrill sound characteristic of the cock 2 : to utter a sound expressive of pleasure 3 : EXULT, GLOAT; also : BRAG, BOAST

³crow n : the cry of the cock

crow·bar \'krō-ˌbär\ n : a metal bar usu. wedge-shaped at the end for use as a pry or lever

¹crowd \'kraud\ vb 1 : to press close 2 : to collect in numbers : THRONG 3 : CRAM, STUFF

²crowd n : a large number of people gathered together at random : THRONG

¹crown \'kraun\ n 1 : a mark of victory or honor; esp : the title of a champion in a sport 2 : a royal headdress 3 : the top of the head 4 : the highest part (as of a tree or tooth) 5 often cap : sovereign power; also : MONARCH 6 : a formerly used British silver coin — **crowned** \'kraund\ adj

²crown vb 1 : to place a crown on 2 : HONOR 3 : TOP, SURMOUNT 4 : to fit (a tooth) with an artificial crown

crown vetch n : a European leguminous herb with umbels of pink-and-white flowers and sharp-angled pods

crow's-foot \'krōz-ˌfut\ n, pl **crow's-feet** \-ˌfēt\ : any of the wrinkles around the outer corners of the eyes — usu. used in pl.

crow's nest n : a partly enclosed platform high on a ship's mast for use as a lookout

¹CRT \ˌsē-(ˌ)är-'tē\ n, pl **CRTs** or **CRT's** : CATHODE-RAY TUBE; also : a display device incorporating a cathode-ray tube

²CRT abbr carrier route

cru·cial \'krü-shəl\ adj : DECISIVE; also : IMPORTANT, SIGNIFICANT

cru·ci·ble \'krü-sə-bəl\ n : a heat-resistant container in which material can be subjected to great heat

cru·ci·fix \'krü-sə-ˌfiks\ n : a representation of Christ on the cross

cru·ci·fix·ion \ˌkrü-sə-'fik-shən\ n 1 cap : the crucifying of Christ 2 : the act of crucifying

cru·ci·form \'krü-sə-ˌform\ adj : shaped like a cross

cru·ci·fy \'krü-sə-ˌfī\ vb **-fied; -fy·ing** 1 : to put to death by nailing or binding the hands and feet to a cross 2 : MORTIFY 1 3 : TORTURE, PERSECUTE

¹crude \'krüd\ adj **crud·er; crud·est** 1 : not refined : RAW 〈~ oil〉 〈~ statistics〉 2 : lacking grace, taste, tact, or polish : RUDE — **crude·ly** adv — **cru·di·ty** \'krü-də-tē\ n

²crude n : unrefined petroleum

cru·el \'krü-əl\ adj **cru·el·er** or **cru·el·ler; cru·el·est** or **cru·el·lest** : causing pain and suffering to others : MERCILESS — **cru·el·ly** adv — **cru·el·ty** \-tē\ n

cru·et \'krü-ət\ n : a small usu. glass bottle for vinegar, oil, or sauce

cruise \'krüz\ vb **cruised; cruis·ing** [D kruisen to make a cross, cruise] 1 : to sail about touching at a series of ports 2 : to travel for enjoyment 3 : to travel about the streets at random 4 : to travel at the most efficient operating speed 〈the cruising speed of an airplane〉 — **cruise** n

cruis·er \'krü-zər\ n 1 : SQUAD CAR 2 : a large fast moderately armored and gunned warship 3 : a motorboat equipped for living aboard

crul·ler \'krə-lər\ n 1 : a small sweet cake in the form of a twisted strip fried in deep fat 2 Northern & Midland : an unraised doughnut

¹crumb \'krəm\ n : a small fragment

²crumb vb 1 : to break into crumbs 2 : to cover with crumbs

crum·ble \'krəm-bəl\ vb **crum·bled; crum·bling** : to break into small pieces : DISINTEGRATE — **crum·bly** adj

crum·my also **crumby** \'krə-mē\ adj **crum·mi·er** also **crumb·i·er; -est** 1 : MISERABLE, FILTHY 2 : CHEAP, WORTHLESS

crum·pet \'krəm-pət\ n : a small round unsweetened bread cooked on a griddle

crum·ple \'krəm-pəl\ vb **crum·pled; crum·pling** 1 : to crush together : RUMPLE 2 : COLLAPSE

¹crunch \'krənch\ vb : to chew with a grinding noise; also : to grind or press with a crushing noise

²crunch n 1 : an act of or a sound made by crunching 2 : a tight or critical situation — **crunchy** adj

cru·sade \krü-'sād\ n 1 cap : any of the expeditions in the 11th, 12th, and 13th centuries undertaken by Christian countries to take the Holy Land from the Muslims 2 : a reforming enterprise undertaken with zeal — **crusade** vb — **cru·sad·er** n

cruse \'krüz, 'krüs\ n : a jar for water or oil

¹crush \'krəsh\ vb 1 : to squeeze out of shape 2 : HUG, EMBRACE 3 : to grind or pound to small bits 4 : OVERWHELM, SUPPRESS

²crush n 1 : an act of crushing 2 : a violent crowding 3 : INFATUATION

crust \'krəst\ n 1 : the outside part of bread; also : a piece of old dry bread 2 : the cover of a pie 3 : a hard surface layer — **crust·al** adj

crus·ta·cean \ˌkrəs-'tā-shən\ n : any of a large class of mostly aquatic arthropods (as lobsters or crabs) having a firm crustlike shell — **crustacean** adj

crusty adj **crust·i·er; -est** 1 : having or being a crust 2 : CROSS, GRUMPY

crutch \'krəch\ n : a supporting device; esp : a support fitting under the armpit for use by the disabled in walking

crux \'krəks, 'kruks\ n, pl **crux·es** 1 : a puzzling or difficult problem 2 : a crucial point

cru·zei·ro \krü-'zer-(ˌ)ō, -(ˌ)ü\ n, pl **-ros** — see MONEY table

¹cry \'krī\ vb **cried; cry·ing** 1 : to call out : SHOUT 2 : to proclaim publicly : ADVERTISE 3 : WEEP

²cry n, pl **cries** 1 : a loud outcry 2 : APPEAL, ENTREATY 3 : a fit of weeping 4 : the characteristic sound uttered by an animal 5 : DISTANCE — usu. used in the phrase a far cry

cry·ba·by \'krī-ˌbā-bē\ n : one who cries easily or often

cryo·gen·ic \ˌkrī-ə-'je-nik\ adj : of or relating to the production of very low temperatures; also : involving the use of a very low temperature — **cryo·gen·i·cal·ly** \-ni-k(ə-)lē\ adv

cryo·gen·ics \-niks\ n : a branch of physics that relates to the production and effects of very low temperatures

cryo·lite \'krī-ə-ˌlīt\ n : a usu. white mineral used in making aluminum

crypt \'kript\ n : a chamber wholly or partly underground

cryp·tic \'krip-tik\ adj : meant to be puzzling or mysterious

cryp·to·gram \'krip-tə-ˌgram\ n : a communication in cipher or code

cryp·tog·ra·phy \krip-'tä-grə-fē\ n : the coding and decoding of secret messages — **cryp·tog·ra·pher** \-fər\ n

crys·tal \'krist-ᵊl\ n [ME cristal, fr. OF, fr. L crystallum, fr. Gk krystallos ice, crystal] 1 : transparent quartz 2 : something resembling crystal (as in transparency); esp : a clear glass used for table articles 3 : a body that is formed by solidification of a substance and has a regular repeating arrangement of atoms and often of exter-

---

\ə\abut	\ᵊ\kitten	\ər\further	\a\ash	\ā\ace	\ä\mop, mar
\au\out	\ch\chin	\e\bet	\ē\easy	\g\go	\i\hit
\ī\ice	\j\job	\ŋ\sing	\ō\go	\o\law	\oi\boy
\th\thin	\th\the	\ü\loot	\u\foot		
\y\yet	\zh\vision	see also Pronunciation Symbols page			

nal plane faces ⟨a salt ∼⟩ **4** : the transparent cover of a watch dial

crys·tal·line \'kris-tə-lən\ *adj* **1** : made of or resembling crystal **2** : very clear or sparkling

crys·tal·lize \'kris-tə-ˌlīz\ *vb* **-lized; -liz·ing 1** : to assume or cause to assume a crystalline form **2** : to take or cause to take a definite form — **crys·tal·li·za·tion** \ˌkris-tə-lə-'zā-shən\ *n*

crys·tal·log·ra·phy \ˌkris-tə-'lä-grə-fē\ *n* : the science dealing with the forms and structures of crystals — **crys·tal·log·ra·pher** *n*

cs *abbr* case; cases

Cs *symbol* cesium

CS *abbr* **1** civil service **2** county seat

CSA *abbr* Confederate States of America

CSM *abbr* command sergeant major

CST *abbr* central standard time

ct *abbr* **1** carat **2** cent **3** count **4** county **5** court

CT *abbr* **1** central time **2** Connecticut

ctn *abbr* carton

ctr *abbr* **1** center **2** counter

CT scan \ˌsē-'tē-\ *n* : CAT SCAN

cu *abbr* cubic

Cu *symbol* [L *cuprum*] copper

cub \'kəb\ *n* : a young individual of some animals (as a fox, bear, or lion)

Cu·ban \'kyü-bən\ *n* : a native or inhabitant of Cuba — **Cuban** *adj*

cub·by·hole \'kə-bē-ˌhȯl\ *n* : a snug place (as for storing things)

¹cube \'kyüb\ *n* **1** : a solid having 6 equal square sides **2** : the product obtained by taking a number 3 times as a factor ⟨27 is the ∼ of 3⟩

²cube *vb* **cubed; cub·ing 1** : to raise to the third power **2** : to form into a cube **3** : to cut into cubes

cube root *n* : a number whose cube is a given number

cu·bic \'kyü-bik\ *also* **cu·bi·cal** *adj* **1** : having the form of a cube **2** : being the volume of a cube whose edge is a specified unit **3** : having length, width, and height

cu·bi·cle \'kyü-bi-kəl\ *n* : a small separate space (as for sleeping or studying)

cubic measure *n* : a unit (as cubic inch) for measuring volume — see METRIC SYSTEM table, WEIGHT table

cub·ism \'kyü-ˌbi-zəm\ *n* : a style of art characterized by the abstraction of natural forms into fragmented geometric shapes — **cub·ist** \-bist\ *n or adj*

cu·bit \'kyü-bət\ *n* : an ancient unit of length equal to about 18 inches (46 centimeters)

Cub Scout *n* : a member of the program of the Boy Scouts for boys in the first through fifth grades in school

cuck·old \'kə-kəld, 'kü-\ *n* : a man whose wife is unfaithful — **cuckold** *vb*

¹cuck·oo \'kü-kü, 'kù-\ *n, pl* **cuckoos** : a largely grayish brown European bird that lays its eggs in the nests of other birds for them to hatch

²cuckoo *adj* : SILLY, FOOLISH

cu·cum·ber \'kyü-(ˌ)kəm-bər\ *n* : the long fleshy many‑seeded fruit of a vine of the gourd family that is grown as a garden vegetable; *also* : this vine

cud \'kəd\ *n* : food brought up into the mouth by some animals (as cows) from the rumen to be chewed again

cud·dle \'kəd-ᵊl\ *vb* **cud·dled; cud·dling** : to lie close : SNUGGLE

cud·gel \'kə-jəl\ *n* : a short heavy club — **cudgel** *vb*

¹cue \'kyü\ *n* **1** : a word, phrase, or action in a play serving as a signal for the next actor to speak or act **2** : HINT — **cue** *vb*

²cue *n* : a tapered rod for striking the balls in billiards or pool

cue ball *n* : the ball a player strikes with a cue in billiards or pool

¹cuff \'kəf\ *n* **1** : a part (as of a sleeve or glove) encircling the wrist **2** : the folded hem of a trouser leg

²cuff *vb* : to strike esp. with the open hand : SLAP

³cuff *n* : a blow with the hand esp. when open

cui·sine \kwi-'zēn\ *n* : style of cooking; *also* : the food prepared

cuke \'kyük\ *n* : CUCUMBER

cul–de–sac \ˌkəl-di-'sak, ˌkùl-\ *n, pl* **culs–de–sac** *same or* ˌkəlz-, ˌkùlz-\ *also* **cul–de–sacs** \ˌkəl-də-'saks, ˌkùl-\ [F, lit., bottom of the bag] : a street or passage closed at one end

cu·li·nary \'kə-lə-ˌner-ē, 'kyü-\ *adj* : of or relating to the kitchen or cookery

¹cull \'kəl\ *vb* : to pick out from a group

²cull *n* : something rejected from a group or lot as worthless or inferior

cul·mi·nate \'kəl-mə-ˌnāt\ *vb* **-nat·ed; -nat·ing** : to reach the highest point — **cul·mi·na·tion** \ˌkəl-mə-'nā-shən\ *n*

cu·lotte \'kü-ˌlät, ˌkyü-, kù-ˌlät, kyù-\ *n* [F, breeches, fr. dim. of *cul* backside] : a divided skirt; *also* : a garment having a divided skirt — often used in pl.

cul·pa·ble \'kəl-pə-bəl\ *adj* : deserving blame — **cul·pa·bil·i·ty** \ˌkəl-pə-'bi-lə-tē\ *n*

cul·prit \'kəl-prət\ *n* [Anglo-French (the French of medieval England) *cul.* (abbr. of *culpable* guilty) + *prest, prit* ready (i.e. to prove it), fr. L *praestus*] : one accused or guilty of a crime

cult \'kəlt\ *n* **1** : formal religious veneration **2** : a religious system; *also* : its adherents **3** : faddish devotion; *also* : a group of persons showing such devotion — **cult·ist** *n*

cul·ti·va·ble \'kəl-tə-və-bəl\ *adj* : capable of being cultivated

cul·ti·vate \'kəl-tə-ˌvāt\ *vb* **-vat·ed; -vat·ing 1** : to prepare for the raising of crops **2** : to foster the growth of by tilling or by labor and care ⟨∼ vegetables⟩ **3** : REFINE, IMPROVE **4** : ENCOURAGE, FURTHER — **cul·ti·va·tion** \ˌkəl-tə-'vā-shən\ *n* — **cul·ti·va·tor** \'kəl-tə-ˌvā-tər\ *n*

cul·ture \'kəl-chər\ *n* **1** : TILLAGE, CULTIVATION **2** : the act of developing by education and training **3** : refinement of intellectual and artistic taste **4** : the customary beliefs, social forms, and material traits of a racial, religious, or social group — **cul·tur·al** \'kəl-chə-rəl\ *adj* — **cul·tur·al·ly** *adv* — **cul·tured** \-chərd\ *adj*

cul·vert \'kəl-vərt\ *n* : a drain crossing under a road or railroad

cum *abbr* cumulative

cum·ber \'kəm-bər\ *vb* : to weigh down : BURDEN, HINDER

cum·ber·some \'kəm-bər-səm\ *adj* : hard to handle or manage because of size or weight

cum·brous \'kəm-brəs\ *adj* : CUMBERSOME — **cum·brous·ly** *adv* — **cum·brous·ness** *n*

cum·mer·bund \'kə-mər-ˌbənd, 'kəm-bər-\ *n* [Hindi *kamarband*, fr. Per., fr. *kamar* waist + *band* band] : a broad sash worn as a waistband

cu·mu·la·tive \'kyü-myə-lə-tiv, -ˌlā-\ *adj* : increasing in force or value by successive additions

cu·mu·lo·nim·bus \ˌkyü-myə-lō-'nim- bəs\ *n* : an anvil‑shaped cumulus cloud extending to great heights

cu·mu·lus \'kyü-myə-ləs\ *n, pl* **-li** \-ˌlī, -ˌlē\ : a massive cloud having a flat base and rounded outlines

cu·ne·i·form \kyù-'nē-ə-ˌfȯrm\ *adj* **1** : wedge-shaped **2** : composed of wedge-shaped characters

cun·ni·lin·gus \ˌkə-ni-'liŋ-gəs\ *also* **cun·ni·linc·tus** \-'liŋk-təs\ *n* : oral stimulation of the vulva or clitoris

¹cun·ning \'kə-niŋ\ *adj* **1** : SKILLFUL, DEXTEROUS **2** : marked by wiliness and trickery **3** : CUTE — **cun·ning·ly** *adv*

²cunning *n* **1** : SKILL **2** : SLYNESS

¹cup \'kəp\ *n* **1** : a small bowl-shaped drinking vessel **2**

: the contents of a cup **3** : the consecrated wine of the Communion **4** : something resembling a cup : a small bowl or hollow **5** : a half pint — **cup·ful** *n*

²cup *vb* **cupped; cup·ping** : to curve into the shape of a cup

cup·board \'kə-bərd\ *n* : a small closet with shelves for food or dishes

cup·cake \'kəp-ˌkāk\ *n* : a small cake baked in a cuplike mold

cu·pid \'kyü-pəd\ *n* : a winged naked figure of an infant often with a bow and arrow that represents the god Cupid

cu·pid·i·ty \kyu̇-'pi-də-tē\ *n, pl* **-ties** : excessive desire for money

cu·po·la \'kyü-pə-lə, -ˌlȯ\ *n* : a small structure on top of a roof or building

¹cur \'kər\ *n* : a mongrel dog

²cur *abbr* **1** currency **2** current

cu·rate \'kyu̇r-ət\ *n* **1** : a clergyman in charge of a parish **2** : a member of the clergy who assists a rector or vicar — **cu·ra·cy** \-ə-sē\ *n*

cu·ra·tive \-ə-tiv\ *adj* : relating to or used in the cure of diseases — **curative** *n*

cu·ra·tor \'kyu̇r-ˌā-tər, kyu̇-'rā-\ *n* : CUSTODIAN; *esp* : one in charge of a place of exhibit (as a museum or zoo)

¹curb \'kərb\ *n* **1** : a bit that exerts pressure on a horse's jaws **2** : CHECK, RESTRAINT **3** : a raised edging (as of stone or concrete) along a paved street

²curb *vb* : to hold in or back : RESTRAIN

curb·ing \'kər-biŋ\ *n* **1** : the material for a curb **2** : CURB

curd \'kərd\ *n* : the thick protein-rich part of coagulated milk

cur·dle \'kərd-ᵊl\ *vb* **cur·dled; cur·dling** : to form curds; *also* : SPOIL, SOUR

¹cure \'kyu̇r\ *n* **1** : spiritual care **2** : recovery or relief from disease **3** : a curative agent : REMEDY **4** : a course or period of treatment

²cure *vb* **cured; cur·ing** **1** : to restore to health : HEAL, REMEDY; *also* : to become cured **2** : to process for storage or use ⟨~ bacon⟩ — **cur·able** *adj*

cu·ré \kyu̇-'rā\ *n* [F] : a parish priest

cure–all \'kyu̇r-ˌȯl\ *n* : a remedy for all ills : PANACEA

cu·ret·tage \ˌkyu̇r-ə-'täzh\ *n* : a surgical scraping or cleaning of a body part (as the uterus)

cur·few \'kər-ˌfyü\ *n* [ME, fr. MF *covrefeu*, signal given to bank the hearth fire, curfew, fr. *covrir* to cover + *feu* fire, fr. L *focus* hearth] : a regulation that specified persons (as children) be off the streets at a set hour of the evening; *also* : the sounding of a signal (as a bell) at this hour

cu·ria \'kyu̇r-ē-ə, 'kùr-\ *n, pl* **cu·ri·ae** \'kyu̇r-ē-ˌē, 'kùr-ē-ˌī\ *often cap* : the body of congregations, tribunals, and offices through which the pope governs the Roman Catholic Church

cu·rie \'kyu̇r-ē\ *n* : a unit of radioactivity equal to 37 billion disintegrations per second

cu·rio \'kyu̇r-ē-ˌȯ\ *n, pl* **cu·ri·os** : an object or article valued because it is strange or rare

cu·ri·ous \'kyu̇r-ē-əs\ *adj* **1** : having a desire to investigate and learn **2** : STRANGE, UNUSUAL, ODD — **cu·ri·os·i·ty** \ˌkyu̇r-ē-'ä-sə-tē\ *n* — **cu·ri·ous·ness** *n*

cu·ri·ous·ly *adv* **1** : in a curious manner **2** : as is curious

cu·ri·um \'kyu̇r-ē-əm\ *n* : a metallic radioactive element produced artificially — see ELEMENT table

¹curl \'kərl\ *vb* **1** : to form into ringlets **2** : CURVE, COIL — **curl·er** *n*

²curl *n* **1** : a lock of hair that coils : RINGLET **2** : something having a spiral or twisted form — **curly** *adj*

cur·lew \'kər-lü, 'kərl-yü\ *n, pl* **curlews** *or* **curlew** : any of various long-legged brownish birds that have a down-curved bill and are related to the sandpipers and snipes

curli·cue \'kər-li-ˌkyü\ *n* : a fancifully curved or spiral figure

cur·rant \'kər-ənt\ *n* **1** : a small seedless raisin **2** : the acid berry of a shrub related to the gooseberry; *also* : this plant

cur·ren·cy \'kər-ən-sē\ *n, pl* **-cies** **1** : general use or acceptance **2** : something that is in circulation as a medium of exchange : MONEY

¹cur·rent \'kər-ənt\ *adj* **1** : occurring in or belonging to the present **2** : used as a medium of exchange **3** : generally accepted or practiced

²current *n* **1** : the part of a body of fluid moving continuously in a certain direction; *also* : the swiftest part of a stream **2** : a flow of electric charge; *also* : the rate of such flow

cur·ric·u·lum \kə-'ri-kyə-ləm\ *n, pl* **-la** \-lə\ *also* **-lums** [L, running, course, fr. *currere* to run] : the courses offered by an educational institution

¹cur·ry \'kər-ē\ *vb* **cur·ried; cur·ry·ing** **1** : to clean the coat of (a horse) with a currycomb **2** : to treat (tanned leather) esp. by incorporating oil or grease — **curry favor** : to seek to gain favor by flattery or attention

²cur·ry *n, pl* **cur·ries** : a powder of pungent spices used in cooking; *also* : a food seasoned with curry

cur·ry·comb \-ˌkȯm\ *n* : a comb used esp. to curry horses — **currycomb** *vb*

¹curse \'kərs\ *n* **1** : a prayer for harm to come upon one **2** : something that is cursed **3** : evil or misfortune coming as if in response to a curse

²curse *vb* **cursed; curs·ing** **1** : to call on divine power to send injury upon **2** : BLASPHEME **3** : AFFLICT syn execrate, damn, anathematize, objurgate

cur·sive \'kər-siv\ *adj* : written with the strokes of the letters joined together and the angles rounded

cur·sor \'kər-sər\ *n* : a visual cue (as a pointer) on a computer screen that indicates position (as for data entry)

cur·so·ry \'kər-sə-rē\ *adj* : rapidly and often superficially done : HASTY — **cur·so·ri·ly** \-rə-lē\ *adj*

curt \'kərt\ *adj* : rudely short or abrupt — **curt·ly** *adv* — **curt·ness** *n*

cur·tail \(ˌ)kər-'tāl\ *vb* : to cut off the end of : SHORTEN — **cur·tail·ment** *n*

cur·tain \'kərt-ᵊn\ *n* **1** : a hanging screen that can be drawn back esp. at a window **2** : the screen between the stage and auditorium of a theater — **curtain** *vb*

curt·sy *or* **curt·sey** \'kərt-sē\ *n, pl* **curtsies** *or* **curtseys** : a courteous bow made by women chiefly by bending the knees — **curtsy** *or* **curtsey** *vb*

cur·va·ceous *also* **cur·va·cious** \ˌkər-'vā-shəs\ *adj* : having curves suggestive of a well-proportioned feminine figure

cur·va·ture \'kər-və-ˌchu̇r\ *n* : a measure or amount of curving : BEND

¹curve \'kərv\ *vb* **curved; curv·ing** : to bend from a straight line or course

²curve *n* **1** : a line esp. when curved **2** : something that bends or curves without angles ⟨a ~ in the road⟩ **3** : a baseball pitch thrown so that it swerves esp. downward and to one side

cur·vet \(ˌ)kər-'vet\ *n* : a prancing leap of a horse — **curvet** *vb*

¹cush·ion \'ku̇-shən\ *n* **1** : a soft pillow or pad to rest on or against **2** : the springy pad inside the rim of a billiard table **3** : something soft that prevents discomfort or protects against injury

²cushion *vb* **1** : to provide (as a seat) with a cushion **2** : to soften or lessen the force or shock of

cusp \'kəsp\ *n* : a pointed end or part (as of a tooth)

---

cus·pid \\'kəs-pəd\ *n* : a canine tooth
cus·pi·dor \\'kəs-pə-ˌdȯr\ *n* : SPITTOON
cus·tard \\'kəs-tərd\ *n* : a sweetened cooked mixture of milk and eggs
cus·to·di·al \ˌkəs-'tò-dē-əl\ *adj* : marked by watching and protecting rather than seeking to cure ⟨∼ care⟩
cus·to·di·an \kəs-'tò-dē-ən\ *n* : one who has custody (as of a building)
cus·to·dy \\'kəs-tə-dē\ *n, pl* **-dies** : immediate charge and control
¹**cus·tom** \\'kəs-təm\ *n* **1** : habitual course of action : recognized usage **2** *pl* : taxes levied on imports **3** : business patronage
²**custom** *adj* **1** : made to personal order **2** : doing work only on order
cus·tom·ary \\'kəs-tə-ˌmer-ē\ *adj* **1** : based on or established by custom **2** : commonly practiced or observed : HABITUAL — **cus·tom·ar·i·ly** *adv*
cus·tom–built \\'kəs-təm-'bilt\ *adj* : built to individual order
cus·tom·er \\'kəs-tə-mər\ *n* : BUYER, PURCHASER; *esp* : a regular or frequent buyer
cus·tom·house \\'kəs-təm-ˌhaùs\ *n* : the building where customs are paid
cus·tom·ize \\'kəs-tə-ˌmīz\ *vb* **-ized; -iz·ing** : to build, fit, or alter according to individual specifications
cus·tom–made \\'kəs-təm-'mād\ *adj* : made to individual order
¹**cut** \\'kət\ *vb* **cut; cut·ting** **1** : to penetrate or divide with a sharp edge : CLEAVE, GASH; *also* : to experience the growth of (a tooth) through the gum **2** : to hurt the feelings of **3** : to strike sharply **4** : SHORTEN, REDUCE **5** : to remove by severing or paring **6** : INTERSECT, CROSS **7** : to divide into parts **8** : to go quickly or change direction abruptly **9** : to cause to stop
²**cut** *n* **1** : something made by cutting : GASH, CLEFT **2** : SHARE **3** : a segment or section of a meat carcass **4** : an excavated channel or roadway **5** : BAND 4 **6** : a sharp stroke or blow **7** : REDUCTION ⟨∼ in wages⟩ **8** : the shape or manner in which a thing is cut
cut–and–dried \ˌkət-ᵊn-'drīd\ *also* **cut–and–dry** \-'drī\ *adj* : according to a plan, set procedure, or formula
cu·ta·ne·ous \kyù-'tā-nē-əs\ *adj* : of, relating to, or affecting the skin
cut·back \\'kət-ˌbak\ *n* **1** : something cut back **2** : REDUCTION
cute \\'kyüt\ *adj* **cut·er; cut·est** [short for *acute*] **1** : CLEVER, SHREWD **2** : daintily attractive : PRETTY
cu·ti·cle \\'kyü-ti-kəl\ *n* **1** : an outer layer (as of skin or a leaf) **2** : dead or horny epidermis esp. around a fingernail — **cu·tic·u·lar** \kyù-'ti-kyə-lər\ *adj*
cut in *vb* **1** : to thrust oneself between others **2** : to interrupt a dancing couple and take one as one's partner
cut·lass \\'kət-ləs\ *n* : a short heavy curved sword

cutlass

cut·ler \\'kət-lər\ *n* : one who makes, deals in, or repairs cutlery
cut·lery \\'kət-lə-rē\ *n* : edged or cutting tools; *esp* : implements for cutting and eating food
cut·let \\'kət-lət\ *n* : a slice of meat (as veal) for broiling or frying
cut·off \\'kət-ˌòf\ *n* **1** : the channel formed when a stream cuts through the neck of an oxbow; *also* : SHORTCUT **2** : a device for cutting off **3** *pl* : shorts orig. made from jeans with the legs cut off at the knees or higher

cut·out \\'kət-ˌaùt\ *n* : something cut out or prepared for cutting out from something else ⟨a page of animal ∼s⟩
cut out *vb* **1** : to be all that one can handle ⟨had her work *cut out* for her⟩ **2** : DISCONNECT **3** : to cease operating ⟨the engine *cut out*⟩ **4** : ELIMINATE ⟨*cut out* unnecessary expense⟩
cut–rate \\'kət-'rāt\ *adj* : relating to or dealing in goods sold at reduced rates
cut·ter \\'kə-tər\ *n* **1** : a tool or a machine for cutting **2** : a ship's boat for carrying stores and passengers **3** : a small armed vessel in government service **4** : a light sleigh
¹**cut·throat** \\'kət-ˌthrȯt\ *n* : MURDERER
²**cutthroat** *adj* **1** : MURDEROUS, CRUEL **2** : RUTHLESS ⟨∼ competition⟩
cutthroat trout *n* : a large American trout with a red mark under the jaw
¹**cut·ting** \\'kə-tiŋ\ *n* : a piece of a plant able to grow into a new plant
²**cutting** *adj* **1** : SHARP, EDGED **2** : marked by piercing cold **3** : likely to hurt the feelings : SARCASTIC ⟨a ∼ remark⟩
cut·tle·fish \\'kət-ᵊl-ˌfish\ *n* : a 10-armed mollusk related to the squid with an internal shell (**cut·tle·bone** \-ˌbȯn\) composed of calcium compounds

cuttlefish

cut·up \\'kət-ˌəp\ *n* : a person who clowns or acts boisterously — **cut up** *vb*
cut·worm \-ˌwərm\ *n* : any of various smooth-bodied moth larvae that feed on plants at night
cw *abbr* clockwise
CWO *abbr* **1** cash with order **2** chief warrant officer
cwt *abbr* hundredweight
-cy \sē\ *n suffix* **1** : action : practice ⟨mendican*cy*⟩ **2** : rank : office ⟨chaplain*cy*⟩ **3** : body : class ⟨constituen*cy*⟩ **4** : state : quality ⟨accura*cy*⟩
cy·an \\'sī-ˌan, -ən\ *n* : a greenish blue color
cy·a·nide \\'sī-ə-ˌnīd, -nəd\ *n* : a poisonous compound of carbon and nitrogen with another element (as potassium)
cy·ber·net·ics \ˌsī-bər-'ne-tiks\ *n* : the science of communication and control theory that is concerned esp. with the comparative study of automatic control systems — **cy·ber·net·ic** *adj*
cy·cla·men \\'sī-klə-mən\ *n* : any of a genus of plants related to the primroses and grown for their showy nodding flowers
¹**cy·cle** \\'sī-kəl\ *n* **1** : a period of time occupied by a series of events that repeat themselves regularly and in the same order **2** : a recurring round of operations or events **3** : one complete occurrence of a periodic process (as a vibration or current alternation) **4** : a circular or spiral arrangement **5** : a long period of time : AGE **6** : BICYCLE **7** : MOTORCYCLE — **cy·clic** \\'sī-klik, 'si-\ *or* **cy·cli·cal** \kli-kəl\ *adj* — **cy·cli·cal·ly** \-k(ə-)lē\ *also* **cy·clic·ly** *adv*
²**cy·cle** \\'sī-kəl\ *vb* **cy·cled; cy·cling** : to ride a cycle — **cy·clist** \\'sī-klist, -kə-list\ *n*
cy·clone \\'sī-ˌklōn\ *n* **1** : a storm or system of winds that rotates about a center of low atmospheric pressure and advances at 20 to 30 miles (about 30 to 50 kilometers) an hour **2** : TORNADO — **cy·clon·ic** \sī-'klä-nik\ *adj*

cy·clo·pe·dia or cy·clo·pae·dia \ˌsī-klə-ˈpē-dē-ə\ n : ENCYCLOPEDIA

Cy·clops \ˈsī-ˌkläps\ n, pl Cy·clo·pes \sī-ˈklō-pēz\ : one of a race of giants in Greek legend with a single eye in the middle of the forehead

cy·clo·tron \ˈsī-klə-ˌträn\ n : a device for giving high speed to charged particles by magnetic and electric fields

cy·der Brit var of CIDER

cyg·net \ˈsig-nət\ n : a young swan

cyl abbr cylinder

cyl·in·der \ˈsi-lən-dər\ n : the solid figure formed by turning a rectangle about one side as an axis; also : a body or space of this form ⟨an engine ∼⟩ ⟨a bullet in the ∼ of a revolver⟩ — cy·lin·dri·cal \sə-ˈlin-dri-kəl\ adj

cym·bal \ˈsim-bəl\ n : a concave brass plate that produces a brilliant clashing sound

cyn·ic \ˈsi-nik\ n : one who attributes all actions to selfish motives — cyn·i·cal \-ni-kəl\ adj — cyn·i·cal·ly \-k(ə-)le\ adv — cyn·i·cism \ˈsi-nə-ˌsi-zəm\ n

cy·no·sure \ˈsī-nə-ˌshùr, ˈsi-\ n [MF & L; MF, Ursa Minor, guide, fr. L cynosura Ursa Minor, fr. Gk kynosoura, fr. kynos oura dog's tail] : a center of attraction

CYO abbr Catholic Youth Organization

cy·pher chiefly Brit var of CIPHER

cy·press \ˈsī-prəs\ n 1 : any of a genus of scaly≠leaved evergreen trees and shrubs 2 : BALD CYPRESS 3 : the wood of a cypress

Cyp·ri·ot \ˈsi-prē-ət, -ˌät\ or Cyp·ri·ote \-ˌòt, -ət\ n : a native or inhabitant of Cyprus — Cypriot adj

cyst \ˈsist\ n : an abnormal closed bodily sac usu. containing liquid — cys·tic \ˈsis-tik\ adj

cystic fibrosis n : a common hereditary disease marked esp. by deficiency of pancreatic enzymes, by respiratory symptoms, and by excessive loss of salt in the sweat

cy·tol·o·gy \sī-ˈtä-lə-jē\ n : a branch of biology dealing with cells — cy·to·log·i·cal \ˌsīt-ᵊl-ˈä-ji-kəl\ or cy·to·log·ic \-jik\ adj — cy·tol·o·gist \sī-ˈtä-lə-jist\ n

cy·to·plasm \ˈsī-tə-ˌpla-zəm\ n : the protoplasm of a cell that lies external to the nucleus — cy·to·plas·mic \ˌsī-tə-ˈplaz-mik\ adj

cy·to·sine \ˈsī-tə-ˌsēn\ n : a chemical base that is a pyrimidine coding genetic information in DNA and RNA

CZ abbr Canal Zone

czar \ˈzär, ˈtsär\ n [NL, fr. Russ tsar', ultim. fr. L Caesar Caesar] : the ruler of Russia until 1917; also : one having great authority — czar·ist \-ist\ n or adj

cza·ri·na \zä-ˈrē-nə\ n : the wife of a czar

Czech \ˈchek\ n 1 : a native or inhabitant of Czechoslovakia or the Czech Republic 2 : the language of the Czechs — Czech adj

Czecho·slo·vak \ˌche-kə-ˈslò-ˌväk, -ˌvak\ or Czecho·slo·va·ki·an \-slò-ˈvä-kē-ən, -ˈva-\ adj : of, relating to, or characteristic of Czechoslovakia or its people — Czechoslovak or Czechoslovakian n

D

¹d \ˈdē\ n, pl d's or ds \ˈdēz\ often cap 1 : the 4th letter of the English alphabet 2 : a grade rating a student's work as poor

²d abbr, often cap 1 date 2 daughter 3 day 4 dead 5 deceased 6 degree 7 Democrat 8 [L denarius, denarii] penny; pence 9 depart; departure 10 diameter

D symbol deuterium

DA abbr 1 deposit account 2 district attorney 3 don't answer

¹dab \ˈdab\ n 1 : a sudden blow or thrust : POKE; also : PECK 2 : a gentle touch or stroke : PAT

²dab vb dabbed; dab·bing 1 : to strike or touch gently : PAT 2 : to apply lightly or irregularly : DAUB — dab·ber n

³dab n 1 : DAUB 2 : a small amount

dab·ble \ˈda-bəl\ vb dab·bled; dab·bling 1 : to wet by splashing : SPATTER 2 : to paddle or play in or as if in water 3 : to work or involve oneself without serious effort — dab·bler n

da ca·po \dä-ˈkä-(ˌ)pò\ adv or adj [It] : from the beginning — used as a direction in music to repeat

dace \ˈdās\ n, pl dace : any of various small No. American freshwater fishes related to the carp

da·cha \ˈdä-chə\ n [Russ] : a Russian country house

dachs·hund \ˈdäks-ˌhùnt\ n, pl dachshunds [G, fr.

dachsund

Dachs badger + Hund dog] : a small dog of a breed of German origin with a long body, short legs, and long drooping ears

dac·tyl \ˈdakt-ᵊl\ n [ME dactile, fr. L dactylus, fr. Gk daktylos, lit., finger; fr. the fact that the three syllables have the first one longest like the joints of the finger] : a metrical foot of one accented syllable followed by two unaccented syllables — dac·tyl·ic \dak-ˈti-lik\ adj or n

dad \ˈdad\ n : FATHER 1

Da·da \ˈdä-(ˌ)dä\ n : a movement in art and literature based on deliberate irrationality and negation of traditional artistic values — da·da·ism \-ˌi-zəm\ n, often cap — da·da·ist \-ˌist\ n or adj, often cap

dad·dy \ˈda-dē\ n, pl daddies : FATHER 1

dad·dy long·legs \ˌda-dē-ˈlòŋ-ˌlegz\ n, pl daddy longlegs : any of various arachnids resembling the true spiders but having small rounded bodies and long slender legs

dae·mon var of DEMON

daf·fo·dil \ˈda-fə-ˌdil\ n : any of a genus of bulbous herbs with usu. large flowers having a trumpetlike center

daf·fy \ˈda-fē\ adj daf·fi·er; -est : DAFT

daft \ˈdaft\ adj : FOOLISH; also : INSANE — daft·ness n

dag abbr dekagram

dag·ger \ˈda-gər\ n 1 : a sharp pointed knife for stabbing 2 : a character † used as a reference mark or to indicate a death date

da·guerre·o·type \də-ˈger-(ē-)ə-ˌtīp\ n : an early photograph produced on a silver or a silver-covered copper plate

dahl·ia \ˈdal-yə, ˈdäl-\ n : any of a genus of tuberous herbs related to the daisies and having showy flowers

---

\ə\abut \ᵊ\kitten \ər\further \a\ash \ā\ace \ä\mop, mar \aù\out \ch\chin \e\bet \ē\easy \g\go \i\hit \ī\ice \j\job \ŋ\sing \ō\go \ò\law \òi\boy \th\thin \th̲\the \ü\loot \ù\foot \y\yet \zh\vision see also Pronunciation Symbols page

¹**dai·ly** \'dā-lē\ *adj* **1 :** occurring, done, or used every day or every weekday **2 :** of or relating to every day ⟨∼ visitors⟩ **3 :** computed in terms of one day ⟨∼ wages⟩ **syn** diurnal, quotidian **— dai·li·ness** \-lē-nəs\ *n* **— daily** *adv*

²**daily** *n, pl* **dailies :** a newspaper published every weekday

daily double *n* **:** a system of betting on races in which the bettor must pick the winners of two stipulated races in order to win

¹**dain·ty** \'dān-tē\ *n, pl* **dainties** [ME *deinte*, fr. OF *deintié*, fr. L *dignitas* dignity, worth] **:** something delicious or pleasing to the taste **:** DELICACY

²**dainty** *adj* **dain·ti·er; -est 1 :** pleasing to the taste **2 :** delicately pretty **3 :** having or showing delicate taste; *also* **:** FASTIDIOUS **syn** choice, delicate, exquisite, rare, recherché **— dain·ti·ly** \-ti-lē\ *adv* **— dain·ti·ness** \-tē-nəs\ *n*

dai·qui·ri \'dī-kə-rē, 'da-kə-rē\ *n* [*Daiquirí*, Cuba] **:** a cocktail made of rum, lime juice, and sugar

dairy \'der-ē\ *n, pl* **dair·ies** [ME *deyerie*, fr. *deye* dairymaid, fr. OE *dæge* kneader of bread] **1 :** CREAMERY **2 :** a farm specializing in milk production

dairy·ing \'der-ē-iŋ\ *n* **:** the business of operating a dairy

dairy·maid \-ˌmād\ *n* **:** a woman employed in a dairy

dairy·man \-mən, -ˌman\ *n* **:** a person who operates a dairy farm or works in a dairy

da·is \'dā-əs\ *n* **:** a raised platform usu. above the floor of a hall or large room

dai·sy \'dā-zē\ *n, pl* **daisies** [ME *dayeseye*, fr. OE *dægeseāge*, fr. *dæg* day + *ēage* eye] **:** any of numerous composite plants having flower heads in which the marginal flowers resemble petals

daisy wheel *n* **:** a disk with spokes bearing type that serves as the printing element of an electric typewriter or printer; *also* **:** a printer that uses such a disk

Da·ko·ta \də-'kō-tə\ *n, pl* **Dakotas** *also* **Dakota :** a member of an American Indian people of the northern Mississippi valley; *also* **:** their language

dal *abbr* dekaliter

da·la·si \dä-'lä-sē\ *n, pl* **dalasi** *or* **dalasis — see** MONEY table

dale \'dāl\ *n* **:** VALLEY

dal·ly \'da-lē\ *vb* **dal·lied; dal·ly·ing 1 :** to act playfully; *esp* **:** to play amorously **2 :** to waste time **3 :** LINGER, DAWDLE **syn** flirt, coquet, toy, trifle **— dal·li·ance** \-lē-əns\ *n*

dal·ma·tian \dal-'mā-shən\ *n, often cap* **:** any of a breed of medium-sized dogs having a white short-haired coat with black or brown spots

dalmatian

¹**dam** \'dam\ *n* **:** a female parent — used esp. of a domestic animal

²**dam** *n* **:** a barrier (as across a stream) to stop the flow of water **— dam** *vb*

³**dam** *abbr* dekameter

¹**dam·age** \'da-mij\ *n* **1 :** loss or harm due to injury to persons, property, or reputation **2** *pl* **:** compensation in money imposed by law for loss or injury ⟨bring a suit for ∼s⟩

²**damage** *vb* **dam·aged; dam·ag·ing :** to cause damage to

dam·a·scene \'da-mə-ˌsēn\ *vb* **-scened; -scen·ing :** to ornament (as iron or steel) with wavy patterns or with inlaid work of precious metals

dam·ask \'da-məsk\ *n* **1 :** a firm lustrous reversible figured fabric used for household linen **2 :** a tough steel having decorative wavy lines

dame \'dām\ *n* **1 :** a woman of rank, station, or authority **2 :** an elderly woman **3 :** WOMAN

damn \'dam\ *vb* [ME *dampnen*, fr. OF *dampner*, fr. L *damnare*, fr. *damnum* damage, loss, fine] **1 :** to condemn esp. to hell **2 :** CURSE **— damned** *adj*

dam·na·ble \'dam-nə-bəl\ *adj* **1 :** liable to or deserving punishment **2 :** DETESTABLE ⟨∼ weather⟩ **— dam·na·bly** \-blē\ *adv*

dam·na·tion \dam-'nā-shən\ *n* **1 :** the act of damning **2 :** the state of being damned

¹**damp** \'damp\ *n* **1 :** a noxious gas **2 :** MOISTURE

²**damp** *vb* **:** DAMPEN

³**damp** *adj* **:** MOIST **— damp·ness** *n*

damp·en \'dam-pən\ *vb* **1 :** to check or diminish in activity or vigor **2 :** to make or become damp

damp·er \'dam-pər\ *n* **:** one that damps; *esp* **:** a valve or movable plate (as in the flue of a stove, furnace, or fireplace) to regulate the draft

dam·sel \'dam-zəl\ *n* **:** MAIDEN, GIRL

dam·sel·fly \-ˌflī\ *n* **:** any of a group of insects that are closely related to the dragonflies but fold their wings above the body when at rest

dam·son \'dam-zən\ *n* **:** a plum with acid purple fruit; *also* **:** its fruit

Dan *abbr* Daniel

¹**dance** \'dans\ *vb* **danced; danc·ing 1 :** to glide, step, or move through a set series of movements usu. to music **2 :** to move quickly up and down or about **3 :** to perform or take part in as a dancer **— danc·er** *n*

²**dance** *n* **1 :** an act or instance of dancing **2 :** a social gathering for dancing **3 :** a piece of music (as a waltz) by which dancing may be guided **4 :** the art of dancing

D & C *n* [*d*ilation *and* *c*urettage] **:** a surgical procedure used to test for cancer of the uterus or to perform an abortion that involves stretching the opening of the uterus and scraping the inside walls

dan·de·li·on \'dan-də-ˌlī-ən, -dē-\ *n* [MF *dent de lion*, lit., lion's tooth] **:** any of a genus of common yellow-flowered composite herbs

dan·der \'dan-dər\ *n* **:** ANGER, TEMPER

dan·di·fy \'dan-di-ˌfī\ *vb* **-fied; -fy·ing :** to cause to resemble a dandy

dan·dle \'dand-ᵊl\ *vb* **dan·dled; dan·dling :** to move up and down in one's arms or on one's knee in affectionate play **syn** caress, fondle, love, pet

dan·druff \'dan-drəf\ *n* **:** a whitish scurf on the scalp that comes off in small scales **— dan·druffy** \-drə-fē\ *adj*

¹**dan·dy** \'dan-dē\ *n, pl* **dandies 1 :** a man unduly attentive to personal appearance **2 :** something excellent in its class **syn** fop, coxcomb, popinjay

²**dandy** *adj* **dan·di·er; -est :** very good **:** FIRST-RATE

Dane \'dān\ *n* **1 :** a native or inhabitant of Denmark **2 :** GREAT DANE

dan·ger \'dān-jər\ *n* **1 :** exposure or liability to injury, harm, or evil **2 :** something that may cause injury or harm **syn** peril, hazard, risk, jeopardy

dan·ger·ous \'dān-jə-rəs\ *adj* **1 :** HAZARDOUS, PERILOUS **2 :** able or likely to inflict injury **— dan·ger·ous·ly** *adv*

dan·gle \'daŋ-gəl\ *vb* **dan·gled; dan·gling 1 :** to hang loosely esp. with a swinging motion **:** SWING **2 :** to be a hanger-on or dependent **3 :** to be left without proper grammatical connection in a sentence **4 :** to keep hanging uncertainly **5 :** to offer as an inducement

Dan·iel \'dan-yəl\ *n* — see BIBLE table
Dan·ish \'dā-nish\ *n* : the language of the Danes — **Danish** *adj*
Danish pastry *n* : a pastry made of a rich yeast-raised dough
dank \'daŋk\ *adj* : disagreeably wet or moist : DAMP — **dank·ness** *n*
dan·seuse \dänⁿ-'sərz, -'səz; dän-'süz\ *n* [F] : a female ballet dancer
dap·per \'da-pər\ *adj* 1 : SPRUCE, TRIM 2 : being alert and lively in movement and manners : JAUNTY
dap·ple \'da-pəl\ *vb* **dap·pled; dap·pling** : to mark with different-colored spots
DAR *abbr* Daughters of the American Revolution
¹**dare** \'dar\ *vb* **dared; dar·ing** 1 : to have sufficient courage : be bold enough to 2 : CHALLENGE 3 : to confront boldly
²**dare** *n* : an act or instance of daring : CHALLENGE
dare·dev·il \-ˌde-vəl\ *n* : a recklessly bold person
dar·ing \'dar-iŋ\ *n* : venturesome boldness — **daring** *adj* — **dar·ing·ly** *adv*
¹**dark** \'därk\ *adj* 1 : being without light or without much light 2 : not light in color ⟨a ~ suit⟩ 3 : GLOOMY 4 *often cap* : being a period of stagnation or decline ⟨the *Dark Ages*⟩ 5 : SECRETIVE **syn** dim, dusky, murky, tenebrous — **dark·ly** *adv* — **dark·ness** *n*
²**dark** *n* 1 : absence of light : DARKNESS; *esp* : NIGHT 2 : a dark or deep color — **in the dark** 1 : in secrecy 2 : in ignorance
dark·en \'där-kən\ *vb* 1 : to make or grow dark or darker 2 : DIM 3 : BESMIRCH, TARNISH 4 : to make or become gloomy or forbidding
dark horse *n* : a contestant or a political figure whose abilities and chances as a contender are not known
dark·ling \'där-kliŋ\ *adj* 1 : DARK ⟨a ~ plain⟩ 2 : MYSTERIOUS
dark·room \'därk-ˌrüm, -ˌrùm\ *n* : a lightproof room in which photographic materials are processed
¹**dar·ling** \'där-liŋ\ *n* 1 : a dearly loved person 2 : FAVORITE
²**darling** *adj* 1 : dearly loved : FAVORITE 2 : very pleasing : CHARMING
darn \'därn\ *vb* : to mend with interlacing stitches — **darn·er** *n*
darning needle *n* 1 : a needle for darning 2 : DRAGONFLY
¹**dart** \'därt\ *n* 1 : a small missile with a point on one end and feathers on the other; *also, pl* : a game in which darts are thrown at a target 2 : something causing a sudden pain 3 : a stitched tapering fold in a garment 4 : a quick movement
²**dart** *vb* 1 : to throw with a sudden movement 2 : to thrust or move suddenly or rapidly 3 : to shoot with a dart containing a usu. tranquilizing drug
dart·er \'där-tər\ *n* : any of numerous small American freshwater fishes related to the perches
Dar·win·ism \'där-wə-ˌni-zəm\ *n* : a theory explaining the origin and continued existence of new species of plants and animals by means of natural selection acting on chance variations — **Dar·win·ist** \-nist\ *n or adj*
¹**dash** \'dash\ *vb* 1 : SMASH 2 : to knock, hurl, or thrust violently 3 : SPLASH, SPATTER 4 : RUIN 5 : DEPRESS, SADDEN 6 : to perform or finish hastily 7 : to move with sudden speed
²**dash** *n* 1 : a sudden burst or splash 2 : a stroke of a pen 3 : a punctuation mark — that is used esp. to indicate a break in the thought or structure of a sentence 4 : a small addition ⟨a ~ of salt⟩ 5 : flashy showiness 6 : animation in style and action 7 : a sudden rush or attempt ⟨made a ~ for the door⟩ 8 : a short foot race 9 : DASHBOARD
dash·board \-ˌbȯrd\ *n* : a panel in an automobile or aircraft below the windshield usu. containing dials and controls

dash·er \'da-shər\ *n* : a device (as in a churn) for agitating something
da·shi·ki \də-'shē-kē\ *or* **dai·shi·ki** \dī-\ *n* [modif. of Yoruba (an African language) *dàṣíkí*] : a usu. brightly colored loose-fitting pullover garment
dash·ing \'da-shiŋ\ *adj* 1 : marked by vigorous action 2 : marked by smartness esp. in dress and manners **syn** stylish, chic, fashionable, modish, smart, swank
das·tard \'das-tərd\ *n* 1 : COWARD 2 : a person who acts treacherously — **das·tard·ly** *adj*
dat *abbr* dative
da·ta \'dā-tə, 'da-, 'dä-\ *n sing or pl* [L, pl. of *datum*] : factual information (as measurements or statistics) used as a basis for reasoning, discussion, or calculation
da·ta·base \-ˌbās\ *n* : a usu. large collection of data organized esp. for rapid search and retrieval (as by a computer)
data processing *n* : the action or process of supplying a computer with information and having the computer use it to produce a desired result
¹**date** \'dāt\ *n* [ME, fr. OF, ultim. fr. L *dactylus*, fr. Gk *daktylos*, lit., finger] : the edible fruit of a tall Old World palm; *also* : this palm
²**date** *n* [ME, fr. MF, fr. LL *data*, fr. *data* (as in *data Romae* given at Rome), fem. of L *datus*, pp. of *dare* to give] 1 : the day, month, or year of an event 2 : a statement giving the time of execution or making (as of a coin or check) 3 : the period to which something belongs 4 : APPOINTMENT; *esp* : a social engagement between two persons that often has a romantic character 5 : a person with whom one has a usu. romantic date — **to date** : up to the present moment
³**date** *vb* **dat·ed; dat·ing** 1 : to record the date of or on 2 : to determine, mark, or reveal the date, age, or period of 3 : to make or have a date with 4 : ORIGINATE ⟨~s from ancient times⟩ 5 : EXTEND ⟨*dating* back to childhood⟩ 6 : to show qualities typical of a past period
dat·ed \'dā-təd\ *adj* 1 : provided with a date 2 : OLD-FASHIONED **syn** antiquated, archaic, old hat, outdated, outmoded, passé
date·less \'dāt-ləs\ *adj* 1 : ENDLESS 2 : having no date 3 : too ancient to be dated 4 : TIMELESS
date·line \'dāt-ˌlīn\ *n* : a line in a publication giving the date and place of composition or issue — **dateline** *vb*
da·tive \'dā-tiv\ *adj* : of, relating to, or constituting a grammatical case marking typically the indirect object of a verb — **dative** *n*
da·tum \'dā-təm, 'da-, 'dä-\ *n, pl* **da·ta** \-tə\ *or* **datums** : a single piece of data : FACT
dau *abbr* daughter
¹**daub** \'dȯb\ *vb* 1 : to cover with soft adhesive matter 2 : SMEAR, SMUDGE 3 : to paint crudely — **daub·er** *n*
²**daub** *n* 1 : something daubed on : SMEAR 2 : a crude picture
daugh·ter \'dȯ-tər\ *n* 1 : a female offspring esp. of human beings 2 : a human female having a specified ancestor or belonging to a group of common ancestry — **daughter** *adj*
daugh·ter–in–law \'dȯ-tə-rən-ˌlȯ\ *n, pl* **daugh·ters–in–law** \-tər-zən-\ : the wife of one's son
daunt \'dȯnt\ *vb* [ME, fr. OF *danter*, alter. of *donter*, fr. L *domitare* to tame] : to lessen the courage of : INTIMIDATE, OVERWHELM
daunt·less \-ləs\ *adj* : FEARLESS, UNDAUNTED **syn** brave, bold, courageous, lionhearted — **daunt·less·ly** *adv*
dau·phin \'dȯ-fən\ *n, often cap* : the eldest son of a king of France
DAV *abbr* Disabled American Veterans

\ə\abut \ᵊ\kitten \ər\further \a\ash \ā\ace \ä\mop, mar
\aù\out \ch\chin \e\bet \ē\easy \g\go \i\hit \ī\ice \j\job
\ŋ\sing \ō\go \ò\law \òi\boy \th\thin \t̲h̲\the \ü\loot \ù\foot
\y\yet \zh\vision *see also* Pronunciation Symbols page

dav·en·port \'da-vən-ˌpȯrt\ n : a large upholstered sofa

da·vit \'dā-vət, 'da-\ n : a small crane on a ship used in pairs esp. to raise or lower boats

daw·dle \'dȯd-ᵊl\ vb **daw·dled; daw·dling 1** : to spend time wastefully or idly **2** : LOITER — **daw·dler** n

¹dawn \'dȯn\ vb **1** : to begin to grow light as the sun rises **2** : to begin to appear or develop **3** : to begin to be understood ⟨the solution ∼ed on him⟩

²dawn n **1** : the first appearance of light in the morning **2** : a first appearance : BEGINNING ⟨the ∼ of a new era⟩

day \'dā\ n **1** : the period of light between one night and the next; also : DAYLIGHT **2** : the period of rotation of a planet (as earth) or a moon on its axis **3** : a period of 24 hours beginning at midnight **4** : a specified day or date ⟨wedding ∼⟩ **5** : a specified time or period : AGE ⟨in olden ∼s⟩ **6** : the conflict or contention of the day **7** : the time set apart by usage or law for work ⟨the 8-hour ∼⟩

day·bed \'dā-ˌbed\ n : a couch that can be converted into a bed

day·book \-ˌbu̇k\ n : DIARY, JOURNAL

day·break \-ˌbrāk\ n : DAWN

day care n : supervision of and care for children or disabled adults provided during the day; also : a program offering day care

day·dream \'dā-ˌdrēm\ n : a pleasant reverie — **day·dream** vb

day·light \'dā-ˌlīt\ n **1** : the light of day **2** : DAYTIME **3** : DAWN **4** : understanding of something that has been obscure **5** pl : CONSCIOUSNESS; also : WITS **6** : an opening or opportunity esp. for action

daylight saving time n : time usu. one hour ahead of standard time

Day of Atonement : YOM KIPPUR

day school n : a private school without boarding facilities

day student n : a student who attends regular classes at a college or preparatory school but does not live there

day·time \'dā-ˌtīm\ n : the period of daylight

daze \'dāz\ vb **dazed; daz·ing 1** : to stupefy esp. by a blow **2** : DAZZLE — **daze** n — **da·zed·ly** \'dā-zəd-lē\ adv

daz·zle \'da-zəl\ vb **daz·zled; daz·zling 1** : to overpower with light **2** : to impress greatly or confound with brilliance — **dazzle** n

dB abbr decibel

d/b/a abbr doing business as

dbl or **dble** abbr double

DC abbr **1** [It da capo] from the beginning **2** direct current **3** District of Columbia **4** doctor of chiropractic

DD abbr **1** days after date **2** demand draft **3** dishonorable discharge **4** doctor of divinity

D day n [D, abbr. for day] : a day set for launching an operation (as an invasion)

DDS abbr doctor of dental surgery

DDT \ˌdē-ˌ(ˌ)dē-ˈtē\ n : a persistent insecticide poisonous to many higher animals

DE abbr Delaware

dea·con \'dē-kən\ n [ME dekene, fr. OE dēacon, fr. LL diaconus, fr. Gk diakonos, lit., servant] : a subordinate officer in a Christian church

dea·con·ess \'dē-kə-nəs\ n : a woman chosen to assist in the church ministry

de·ac·ti·vate \dē-ˈak-tə-ˌvāt\ vb : to make inactive or ineffective

¹dead \'ded\ adj **1** : LIFELESS **2** : DEATHLIKE, DEADLY ⟨in a ∼ faint⟩ **3** : NUMB **4** : very tired **5** : UNRESPONSIVE **6** : EXTINGUISHED ⟨∼ coals⟩ **7** : INANIMATE, INERT **8** : no longer active or functioning ⟨a ∼ battery⟩ **9** : lacking power, significance, or effect ⟨a ∼ custom⟩ **10** : OBSOLETE ⟨a ∼ language⟩ **11** : lacking in gaiety or animation ⟨a ∼ party⟩ **12** : QUIET, IDLE, UNPRODUCTIVE ⟨∼ capital⟩ **13** : lacking elasticity ⟨a ∼ tennis ball⟩ **14** : not cir-

culating : STAGNANT ⟨∼ air⟩ **15** : lacking warmth, vigor, or taste ⟨∼ wine⟩ **16** : absolutely uniform ⟨∼ level⟩ **17** : UNERRING, EXACT ⟨a ∼ shot⟩ **18** : ABRUPT ⟨a ∼ stop⟩ **19** : COMPLETE ⟨a ∼ loss⟩

²dead n, pl **dead 1** : one that is dead — usu. used collectively ⟨the living and the ∼⟩ **2** : the time of greatest quiet ⟨the ∼ of the night⟩

³dead adv **1** : UTTERLY ⟨∼ right⟩ **2** : in a sudden and complete manner ⟨stopped ∼⟩ **3** : DIRECTLY ⟨∼ ahead⟩

dead·beat \-ˌbēt\ n : a person who persistently fails to pay personal debts or expenses

dead duck n : GONER

dead·en \'ded-ᵊn\ vb **1** : to impair in vigor or sensation : BLUNT ⟨∼ pain⟩ **2** : to lessen the luster or spirit of **3** : to make (as a wall) soundproof

dead end n **1** : an end (as of a street) without an exit **2** : a position, situation, or course of action that leads to nothing further — **dead-end** \ˌded-ˈend\ adj

dead heat n : a contest in which two or more contestants tie (as by crossing the finish line simultaneously)

dead letter n **1** : something that has lost its force or authority without being formally abolished **2** : a letter that cannot be delivered or returned

dead·line \'ded-ˌlīn\ n : a date or time before which something must be done

dead·lock \'ded-ˌläk\ n : a stoppage of action because neither faction in a struggle will give in — **deadlock** vb

¹dead·ly \'ded-lē\ adj **dead·li·er; -est 1** : likely to cause or capable of causing death **2** : HOSTILE, IMPLACABLE **3** : very accurate : UNERRING **4** : tending to deprive of force or vitality ⟨a ∼ habit⟩ **5** : suggestive of death **6** : very great : EXTREME — **dead·li·ness** n

²deadly adv **1** : suggesting death ⟨∼ pale⟩ **2** : EXTREMELY ⟨∼ dull⟩

deadly sin n : one of seven sins of pride, covetousness, lust, anger, gluttony, envy, and sloth held to be fatal to spiritual progress

¹dead·pan \'ded-ˌpan\ adj : marked by an impassive manner or expression — **deadpan** vb — **deadpan** adv

²deadpan n : a completely expressionless face

dead reckoning n : the determination of the position of a ship or aircraft solely from the record of the direction and distance of its course

dead·weight \'ded-ˈwāt\ n **1** : the unrelieved weight of an inert mass **2** : a ship's load including the weight of cargo, fuel, crew, and passengers

dead·wood \-ˌwu̇d\ n **1** : wood dead on the tree **2** : useless personnel or material

deaf \'def\ adj **1** : unable to hear **2** : unwilling to hear or listen ⟨∼ to all suggestions⟩ — **deaf·ness** n

deaf·en \'de-fən\ vb : to make deaf

deaf-mute \'def-ˌmyüt\ n : a deaf person who has never learned to speak

¹deal \'dēl\ n **1** : a usu. large or indefinite quantity or degree ⟨a great ∼ of support⟩ **2** : the act or right of distributing cards to players in a card game; also : HAND

²deal vb **dealt** \'delt\; **deal·ing 1** : DISTRIBUTE; esp : to distribute playing cards to players in a game **2** : ADMINISTER, DELIVER ⟨dealt him a blow⟩ **3** : to concern itself : TREAT ⟨the book ∼s with crime⟩ **4** : to take action in regard to something ⟨∼ with offenders⟩ **5** : TRADE; also : to sell or distribute something as a business ⟨∼ in used cars⟩ **6** : to reach a state of acceptance ⟨∼ with her child's death⟩ — **deal·er** n

³deal n **1** : BARGAINING, NEGOTIATION; also : TRANSACTION **2** : treatment received ⟨a raw ∼⟩ **3** : an often secret agreement or arrangement for mutual advantage **4** : BARGAIN

⁴deal n : wood or a board of fir or pine

deal·er·ship \'dē-lər-ˌship\ n : an authorized sales agency

deal·ing \'dē-liŋ\ n **1** : a way of acting or of doing business **2** pl : friendly or business transactions

dean \'dēn\ *n* [ME *deen*, fr. MF *deien*, fr. LL *decanus*, lit., chief of ten, fr. Gk *dekanos*, fr. *deka* ten] **1 :** a clergyman who is head of a group of canons or of joint pastors of a church **2 :** the head of a division, faculty, college, or school of a university **3 :** a college or secondary school administrator in charge of counseling and disciplining students **4 :** DOYEN ⟨the ∼ of a diplomatic corps⟩ — **dean·ship** *n*

dean·ery \'dē-nə-rē\ *n, pl* **-er·ies :** the office, jurisdiction, or official residence of a clerical dean

¹dear \'dir\ *adj* **1 :** highly valued : PRECIOUS **2 :** AFFECTIONATE, FOND **3 :** EXPENSIVE **4 :** HEARTFELT — **dear·ly** *adv* — **dear·ness** *n*

²dear *n* **:** a loved one : DARLING

Dear John \-'jän\ *n* **:** a letter (as to a soldier) in which a woman breaks off a marital or romantic relationship

dearth \'dərth\ *n* **:** SCARCITY, FAMINE

death \'deth\ *n* **1 :** the end of life **2 :** the cause of loss of life **3 :** the state of being dead **4 :** DESTRUCTION, EXTINCTION **5 :** SLAUGHTER — **death·like** *adj*

death·bed \-ˌbed\ *n* **1 :** the bed in which a person dies **2 :** the last hours of life

death·blow \-ˌblō\ *n* **:** a destructive or killing stroke or event

death·less \-ləs\ *adj* **:** IMMORTAL, IMPERISHABLE ⟨∼ fame⟩

death·ly \-lē\ *adj* **1 :** FATAL **2 :** of, relating to, or suggestive of death ⟨a ∼ pallor⟩ — **deathly** *adv*

death rattle *n* **:** a sound produced by air passing through mucus in the lungs and air passages of a dying person

death's–head \'deths-ˌhed\ *n* **:** a human skull emblematic of death

death·watch \'deth-ˌwäch\ *n* **:** a vigil kept over the dead or dying

deb \'deb\ *n* **:** DEBUTANTE

de·ba·cle \di-'bä-kəl, -'ba-\ *also* **dé·bâ·cle** *same or* dā-'bäk\ *n* [F *débâcle*] **:** DISASTER, FAILURE, ROUT ⟨stock market ∼⟩

de·bar \di-'bär\ *vb* **:** to bar from having or doing something **:** PRECLUDE

de·bark \di-'bärk\ *vb* **:** DISEMBARK — **de·bar·ka·tion** \ˌdē-ˌbär-'kā-shən\ *n*

de·base \di-'bās\ *vb* **:** to lower in character, quality, or value **syn** degrade, corrupt, deprave — **de·base·ment** *n*

de·bate \di-'bāt\ *vb* **de·bat·ed; de·bat·ing** **1 :** to discuss a question by considering opposed arguments **2 :** to take part in a debate — **de·bat·able** *adj* — **debate** *n* — **de·bat·er** *n*

de·bauch \di-'bóch\ *vb* **:** SEDUCE, CORRUPT **syn** debase, demoralize, deprave, pervert — **de·bauch·ery** \-'bó-chə-rē\ *n*

de·ben·ture \di-'ben-chər\ *n* **:** BOND; *esp* **:** one secured by the general credit of the issuer rather than a lien on particular assets

de·bil·i·tate \di-'bi-lə-ˌtāt\ *vb* **-tat·ed; -tat·ing :** to impair the health or strength of **syn** weaken, disable, enfeeble, undermine

de·bil·i·ty \di-'bi-lə-tē\ *n, pl* **-ties :** an infirm or weakened state

¹deb·it \'de-bət\ *vb* **:** to enter as a debit : charge with or as a debit

²debit *n* **1 :** an entry in an account showing money paid out or owed **2 :** DISADVANTAGE, SHORTCOMING

debit card *n* **:** a card by which money may be withdrawn or the cost of purchases paid directly from the holder's bank account

deb·o·nair \ˌde-bə-'nar\ *adj* [ME *debonere*, fr. OF *debonaire*, fr. *de bon aire* of good family or nature] **:** SUAVE, URBANE; *also* **:** LIGHTHEARTED

de·bouch \di-'baùch, -'büsh\ *vb* [F *déboucher*, fr. *dé-* out of + *bouche* mouth] **:** to come out into an open area **:** EMERGE

de·brief \di-'brēf\ *vb* **:** to question (as a pilot back from a mission) in order to obtain useful information

de·bris \də-'brē, dā-; 'dā-ˌbrē\ *n, pl* **debris** \-'brēz, -ˌbrēz\ **1 :** the remains of something broken down or destroyed **2 :** an accumulation of rock fragments **3 :** RUBBISH

debt \'det\ *n* **1 :** SIN, TRESPASS **2 :** something owed : OBLIGATION **3 :** a condition of owing

debt·or \'de-tər\ *n* **1 :** one guilty of neglect or violation of duty **2 :** one that owes a debt

de·bug \(ˌ)dē-'bəg\ *vb* **:** to eliminate errors in

de·bunk \dē-'bəŋk\ *vb* **:** to expose the sham or falseness of ⟨∼ a legend⟩

¹de·but \'dā-ˌbyü, dā-'byü\ *n* **1 :** a first appearance **2 :** a formal entrance into society

²debut *vb* **:** to make a debut; *also* **:** INTRODUCE

deb·u·tante \'de-byü-ˌtänt\ *n* **:** a young woman making her formal entrance into society

dec *abbr* **1** deceased **2** decrease

Dec *abbr* December

de·cade \'de-ˌkād, de-'kād\ *n* **:** a period of 10 years

dec·a·dence \'de-kə-dəns, di-'kād-ᵊns\ *n* **:** DETERIORATION, DECLINE — **dec·a·dent** \'de-kə-dənt, di-'kād-ᵊnt\ *adj or n*

de·caf \'dē-ˌkaf\ *n* **:** decaffeinated coffee

de·caf·fein·at·ed \(ˌ)dē-'ka-fə-nā-təd\ *adj* **:** having the caffeine removed ⟨∼ coffee⟩

deca·gon \'de-kə-ˌgän\ *n* **:** a plane polygon of 10 angles and 10 sides

de·cal \'dē-ˌkal\ *n* **:** a picture, design, or label made to be transferred (as to glass) from specially prepared paper

de·cal·co·ma·nia \di-ˌkal-kə-'mā-nē-ə\ *n* [F *décalcomanie*, fr. *décalquer* to copy by tracing (fr. *calquer* to trace, fr. It *calcare*, lit., to tread, fr. L) + *manie* mania, fr. LL *mania*] **:** DECAL

Deca·logue \'de-kə-ˌlóg\ *n* **:** TEN COMMANDMENTS

de·camp \di-'kamp\ *vb* **1 :** to break up a camp **2 :** to depart suddenly **syn** escape, abscond, flee

de·cant \di-'kant\ *vb* **:** to pour (as wine) gently from one vessel into another

de·cant·er \di-'kan-tər\ *n* **:** an ornamental glass bottle for serving wine

de·cap·i·tate \di-'ka-pə-ˌtāt\ *vb* **-tat·ed; -tat·ing :** BEHEAD — **de·cap·i·ta·tion** \-ˌka-pə-'tā-shən\ *n* — **de·cap·i·ta·tor** \-'ka-pə-ˌtā-tər\ *n*

deca·syl·lab·ic \ˌde-kə-sə-'la-bik\ *adj* **:** having or composed of verses having 10 syllables — **decasyllabic** *n*

de·cath·lon \di-'kath-lən, -ˌlän\ *n* **:** a 10-event athletic contest

de·cay \di-'kā\ *vb* **1 :** to decline from a sound or prosperous condition **2 :** to cause or undergo decomposition ⟨radium ∼s slowly⟩; *esp* **:** to break down while spoiling **:** ROT — **decay** *n*

decd *abbr* deceased

de·cease \di-'sēs\ *n* **:** DEATH

¹de·ceased \-'sēst\ *adj* **:** no longer living; *esp* **:** recently dead

²deceased *n, pl* **deceased :** a dead person

de·ce·dent \di-'sēd-ᵊnt\ *n* **:** a deceased person

de·ceit \di-'sēt\ *n* **1 :** DECEPTION **2 :** TRICK **3 :** DECEITFULNESS **syn** dissimulation, duplicity, guile

de·ceit·ful \-fəl\ *adj* **1 :** practicing or tending to practice deceit **2 :** MISLEADING, DECEPTIVE ⟨a ∼ answer⟩ — **de·ceit·ful·ly** *adv* — **de·ceit·ful·ness** *n*

de·ceive \di-'sēv\ *vb* **de·ceived; de·ceiv·ing** **1 :** to cause to believe an untruth **2 :** to use or practice deceit **syn** beguile, betray, delude, mislead — **de·ceiv·er** *n*

de·cel·er·ate \dē-'se-lə-ˌrāt\ *vb* **-at·ed; -at·ing :** to slow down

De·cem·ber \di-'sem-bər\ *n* [ME *Decembre*, fr. OF, fr.

L *December* (tenth month), fr. *decem* ten] : the 12th month of the year having 31 days

de·cen·cy \'dēs-ᵊn-sē\ *n, pl* **-cies 1** : PROPRIETY **2** : conformity to standards of taste, propriety, or quality **3** : standard of propriety — usu. used in pl.

de·cen·ni·al \di-'se-nē-əl\ *adj* **1** : consisting of 10 years **2** : happening every 10 years ⟨∼ census⟩

de·cent \'dēs-ᵊnt\ *adj* **1** : conforming to standards of propriety, good taste, or morality **2** : modestly clothed **3** : free from immodesty or obscenity **4** : ADEQUATE ⟨∼ housing⟩ — **de·cent·ly** *adv*

de·cen·tral·i·za·tion \dē-ˌsen-trə-lə-'zā-shən\ *n* **1** : the distribution of powers from a central authority to regional and local authorities **2** : the redistribution of population and industry from urban centers to outlying areas — **de·cen·tral·ize** \-'sen-trə-ˌlīz\ *vb*

de·cep·tion \di-'sep-shən\ *n* **1** : the act of deceiving **2** : the fact or condition of being deceived **3** : FRAUD, TRICK — **de·cep·tive** \-'sep-tiv\ *adj* — **de·cep·tive·ly** *adv* — **de·cep·tive·ness** *n*

deci·bel \'de-sə-ˌbel, -bəl\ *n* : a unit for measuring the relative loudness of sounds

de·cide \di-'sīd\ *vb* **de·cid·ed; de·cid·ing** [ME, fr. MF *decider*, fr. L *decidere*, lit., to cut off, fr. *de-* off + *caedere* to cut] **1** : to arrive at a solution that ends uncertainty or dispute about **2** : to bring to a definitive end ⟨one blow *decided* the fight⟩ **3** : to induce to come to a choice ⟨her pleas *decided* him to help⟩ **4** : to make a choice or judgment

de·cid·ed \di-'sī-dəd\ *adj* **1** : UNQUESTIONABLE **2** : FIRM, DETERMINED — **de·cid·ed·ly** *adv*

de·cid·u·ous \di-'si-jə-wəs\ *adj* **1** : falling off or out usu. at the end of a period of growth or function ⟨∼ leaves⟩ ⟨a ∼ tooth⟩ **2** : having deciduous parts ⟨∼ trees⟩

deci·gram \'de-sə-ˌgram\ *n* — see METRIC SYSTEM table

deci·li·ter \-ˌlē-tər\ *n* — see METRIC SYSTEM table

¹dec·i·mal \'de-sə-məl\ *adj* : based on the number 10 : reckoning by tens

²decimal *n* : any number expressed in base 10; *esp* : DECIMAL FRACTION

decimal fraction *n* : a fraction (as .25 = ²⁵/₁₀₀ or .025 = ²⁵/₁₀₀₀) or mixed number (as 3.025 = 3 ²⁵/₁₀₀₀) in which the denominator is a power of 10 usu. expressed by use of the decimal point

decimal point *n* : a period, centered dot, or in some countries a comma at the left of a decimal fraction (as .678) less than one or between a whole number and a decimal fraction in a mixed number (as 3.678)

dec·i·mate \'de-sə-ˌmāt\ *vb* **-mat·ed; -mat·ing 1** : to take or destroy the 10th part of **2** : to destroy a large part of

dec·i·me·ter \'de-sə-ˌmē-tər\ *n* — see METRIC SYSTEM table

de·ci·pher \di-'sī-fər\ *vb* **1** : DECODE **2** : to make out the meaning of despite indistinctness — **de·ci·pher·able** *adj*

de·ci·sion \di-'si-zhən\ *n* **1** : the act or result of deciding **2** : promptness and firmness in deciding : DETERMINATION

de·ci·sive \-'sī-siv\ *adj* **1** : having the power to decide ⟨the ∼ vote⟩ **2** : RESOLUTE, DETERMINED **3** : CONCLUSIVE ⟨a ∼ victory⟩ — **de·ci·sive·ly** *adv* — **de·ci·sive·ness** *n*

¹deck \'dek\ *n* **1** : a floorlike platform of a ship; *also* : something resembling the deck of a ship **2** : a pack of playing cards

²deck *vb* **1** : ARRAY **2** : DECORATE **3** : to furnish with a deck **4** : KNOCK DOWN, FLOOR

deck·hand \'dek-ˌhand\ *n* : a sailor who performs manual duties

deck·le edge \'dek-əl-\ *n* : the rough untrimmed edge of paper — **deck·le–edged** \-'ejd\ *adj*

de·claim \di-'klām\ *vb* : to speak or deliver in the manner of a formal speech — **dec·la·ma·tion** \ˌde-klə-'mā-

shən\ *n* — **de·clam·a·to·ry** \di-'kla-mə-ˌtȯr-ē\ *adj*

de·clar·a·tive \di-'klar-ə-tiv\ *adj* : making a declaration ⟨∼ sentence⟩

de·clare \di-'klar\ *vb* **de·clared; de·clar·ing 1** : to make known formally, officially, or explicitly : ANNOUNCE ⟨∼ war⟩ **2** : to state emphatically : AFFIRM **3** : to make a full statement of **syn** blazon, broadcast, proclaim, publish — **dec·la·ra·tion** \ˌde-klə-'rā-shən\ *n* — **de·clar·a·to·ry** \di-'klar-ə-ˌtȯr-ē\ *adj* — **de·clar·er** *n*

de·clas·si·fy \dē-'kla-sə-ˌfī\ *vb* : to remove the security classification of — **de·clas·si·fi·ca·tion** \-ˌkla-sə-fə-'kā-shən\ *n*

de·clen·sion \di-'klen-chən\ *n* **1** : the inflectional forms of a noun, pronoun, or adjective **2** : DECLINE, DETERIORATION **3** : DESCENT, SLOPE

dec·li·na·tion \ˌde-klə-'nā-shən\ *n* **1** : angular distance north or south from the celestial equator measured along a great circle passing through the celestial poles **2** : a turning aside or swerving **3** : DETERIORATION **4** : a bending downward **5** : a formal refusal

¹de·cline \di-'klīn\ *vb* **de·clined; de·clin·ing 1** : to slope downward : DESCEND **2** : DROOP **3** : RECEDE **4** : WANE **5** : to withhold consent; *also* : REFUSE, REJECT **6** : INFLECT **2** ⟨∼ a noun⟩ — **de·clin·able** *adj*

²decline *n* **1** : a gradual sinking and wasting away **2** : a change to a lower state or level **3** : the time when something is approaching its end **4** : a descending slope

de·cliv·i·ty \di-'kli-və-tē\ *n, pl* **-ties** : a steep downward slope

de·code \dē-'kȯd\ *vb* : to convert (a coded message) into ordinary language — **de·cod·er** *n*

dé·col·le·té \dā-ˌkäl-'tā\ *adj* [F] **1** : wearing a strapless or low-necked gown **2** : having a low-cut neckline

de·com·mis·sion \ˌdē-kə-'mi-shən\ *vb* : to remove from service

de·com·pose \ˌdē-kəm-'pōz\ *vb* **1** : to separate into constituent parts **2** : to break down in decay : ROT — **de·com·po·si·tion** \dē-ˌkäm-pə-'zi-shən\ *n*

de·com·press \ˌdē-kəm-'pres\ *vb* : to release from pressure or compression — **de·com·pres·sion** \-'pre-shən\ *n*

de·con·ges·tant \ˌdē-kən-'jes-tənt\ *n* : an agent that relieves congestion (as of mucous membranes)

de·con·tam·i·nate \ˌdē-kən-'ta-mə-ˌnāt\ *vb* : to rid of contamination (as radioactive material) — **de·con·tam·i·na·tion** \-ˌta-mə-'nā-shən\ *n*

de·con·trol \ˌdē-kən-'trōl\ *vb* : to end control of ⟨∼ prices⟩ — **decontrol** *n*

de·cor *or* **dé·cor** \dā-'kȯr, 'dā-ˌkȯr\ *n* : DECORATION; *esp* : the style and layout of interior furnishings

dec·o·rate \'de-kə-ˌrāt\ *vb* **-rat·ed; -rat·ing 1** : to furnish with something ornamental ⟨∼ a room⟩ **2** : to award a mark of honor (as a medal) to **syn** adorn, beautify, bedeck, garnish, ornament

dec·o·ra·tion \ˌde-kə-'rā-shən\ *n* **1** : the act or process of decorating **2** : ORNAMENT **3** : a badge of honor

dec·o·ra·tive \'de-kə-rə-tiv\ *adj* : ORNAMENTAL

dec·o·ra·tor \'de-kə-ˌrā-tər\ *n* : one that decorates; *esp* : a person who designs or executes interiors and their furnishings

dec·o·rous \'de-kə-rəs, di-'kȯr-əs\ *adj* : PROPER, SEEMLY, CORRECT

de·co·rum \di-'kȯr-əm\ *n* [L] **1** : conformity to accepted standards of conduct **2** : ORDERLINESS, PROPRIETY

¹de·coy \'dē-ˌkȯi, di-'kȯi\ *n* **1** : something that lures or entices; *esp* : an artificial bird used to attract live birds within shot **2** : something used to draw attention away from another

²de·coy \'dē-ˌkȯi, 'dē-ˌkȯi\ *vb* : to lure by or as if by a decoy : ENTICE

¹de·crease \di-'krēs\ *vb* **de·creased; de·creas·ing** : to grow or cause to grow less : DIMINISH

²**de·crease** \ˈdē-ˌkrēs\ *n* **1** : the process of decreasing **2** : REDUCTION

¹**de·cree** \di-ˈkrē\ *n* **1** : ORDER, EDICT **2** : a judicial decision

²**decree** *vb* **de·creed; de·cree·ing 1** : COMMAND **2** : to determine or order judicially **syn** dictate, ordain, prescribe

dec·re·ment \ˈde-krə-mənt\ *n* **1** : gradual decrease **2** : the quantity lost by diminution or waste

de·crep·it \di-ˈkre-pət\ *adj* : broken down with age : WORN-OUT — **de·crep·i·tude** \-pə-ˌtüd, -ˌtyüd\ *n*

de·cre·scen·do \ˌdā-krə-ˈshen-dò\ *adv or adj* : with a decrease in volume — used as a direction in music

de·crim·i·nal·ize \dē-ˈkri-mən-ᵊl-ˌīz\ *vb* : to remove or reduce the criminal status of

de·cry \di-ˈkrī\ *vb* : to express strong disapproval of

ded·i·cate \ˈde-di-ˌkāt\ *vb* **-cat·ed; -cat·ing 1** : to devote to the worship of a divine being esp. with sacred rites **2** : to set apart for a definite purpose **3** : to inscribe or address as a compliment — **ded·i·ca·tion** \ˌde-di-ˈkā-shən\ *n* — **ded·i·ca·tor** \ˈde-di-ˌkā-tər\ *n* — **ded·i·ca·to·ry** \-kə-ˌtòr-ē\ *adj*

de·duce \di-ˈdüs, -ˈdyüs\ *vb* **de·duced; de·duc·ing 1** : to derive by reasoning : INFER **2** : to trace the course of — **de·duc·ible** *adj*

de·duct \di-ˈdəkt\ *vb* : SUBTRACT — **de·duct·ible** *adj*

de·duc·tion \di-ˈdək-shən\ *n* **1** : SUBTRACTION **2** : something that is or may be subtracted **3** : the deriving of a conclusion by reasoning : the conclusion so reached — **de·duc·tive** \-ˈdək-tiv\ *adj* — **de·duc·tive·ly** *adv*

¹**deed** \ˈdēd\ *n* **1** : something done **2** : FEAT, EXPLOIT **3** : a document containing some legal transfer, bargain, or contract

²**deed** *vb* : to convey or transfer by deed

dee·jay \ˈdē-ˌjā\ *n* : DISC JOCKEY

deem \ˈdēm\ *vb* : THINK, JUDGE **syn** consider, account, reckon, regard, view

de·em·pha·size \dē-ˈem-fə-ˌsīz\ *vb* : to reduce in relative importance; *also* : to attach little importance to — **de·em·pha·sis** \-səs\ *n*

¹**deep** \ˈdēp\ *adj* **1** : extending far down, back, within, or outward **2** : having a specified extension downward or backward **3** : difficult to understand; *also* : MYSTERIOUS, OBSCURE ⟨a ∼ dark secret⟩ **4** : WISE **5** : ENGROSSED, INVOLVED ⟨∼ in thought⟩ **6** : INTENSE, PROFOUND ⟨∼ sleep⟩ **7** : dark and rich in color ⟨a ∼ red⟩ **8** : having a low musical pitch or range ⟨a ∼ voice⟩ **9** : situated well within **10** : covered, enclosed, or filled often to a specified degree — **deep·ly** *adv*

²**deep** *adv* **1** : DEEPLY **2** : far on : LATE ⟨∼ in the night⟩

³**deep** *n* **1** : an extremely deep place or part; *esp* : OCEAN **2** : the middle or most intense part ⟨the ∼ of winter⟩

deep·en \ˈdē-pən\ *vb* : to make or become deep or deeper

deep–freeze \ˈdēp-ˈfrēz\ *vb* **-froze** \-ˈfròz\; **-fro·zen** \-ˈfròz-ᵊn\ : QUICK-FREEZE

deep–fry *vb* : to cook in enough oil to cover the food being fried

deep–root·ed \-ˈrü-təd, -ˈrù-\ *adj* : deeply implanted or established

deep–sea \ˈdēp-ˈsē\ *adj* : of, relating to, or occurring in the deeper parts of the sea ⟨∼ fishing⟩

deep–seat·ed \ˈdēp-ˈsē-təd\ *adj* **1** : situated far below the surface **2** : firmly established ⟨∼ convictions⟩

deer \ˈdir\ *n, pl* **deer** [ME, deer, animal, fr. OE *dēor* beast] : any of numerous ruminant mammals with cloven hoofs and usu. antlers esp. in the males

deer·fly \-ˌflī\ *n* : any of numerous small horseflies

deer·skin \-ˌskin\ *n* : leather made from the skin of a deer; *also* : a garment of such leather

de·es·ca·late \dē-ˈes-kə-ˌlāt\ *vb* : to decrease in extent, volume, or scope : LIMIT — **de·es·ca·la·tion** \-ˌes-kə-ˈlā-shən\ *n*

def *abbr* **1** defendant **2** definite **3** definition

de·face \di-ˈfās\ *vb* : to destroy or mar the face or surface of — **de·face·ment** *n* — **de·fac·er** *n*

de fac·to \di-ˈfak-tò, dā-\ *adj or adv* **1** : actually existing ⟨*de facto* segregation⟩ **2** : actually exercising power ⟨*de facto* government⟩

de·fal·ca·tion \ˌdē-ˌfal-ˈkā-shən, -ˌfòl-; ˌde-fəl-\ *n* : EMBEZZLEMENT

de·fame \di-ˈfām\ *vb* **de·famed; de·fam·ing** : to injure or destroy the reputation of by libel or slander **syn** calumniate, denigrate, libel, malign, slander, vilify — **def·a·ma·tion** \ˌde-fə-ˈmā-shən\ *n* — **de·fam·a·to·ry** \di-ˈfa-mə-ˌtòr-ē\ *adj*

de·fault \di-ˈfòlt\ *n* **1** : failure to do something required by duty or law; *also* : failure to appear for a legal proceeding **2** : failure to compete in or to finish an appointed contest ⟨lose a race by ∼⟩ — **default** *vb* — **de·fault·er** *n*

¹**de·feat** \di-ˈfēt\ *vb* **1** : FRUSTRATE, NULLIFY **2** : to win victory over : BEAT

²**defeat** *n* **1** : FRUSTRATION **2** : an overthrow of an army in battle **3** : loss of a contest

de·feat·ism \-ˈfē-ˌti-zəm\ *n* : acceptance of or resignation to defeat — **de·feat·ist** \-tist\ *n or adj*

def·e·cate \ˈde-fi-ˌkāt\ *vb* **-cat·ed; -cat·ing 1** : to free from impurity or corruption **2** : to discharge feces from the bowels — **def·e·ca·tion** \ˌde-fi-ˈkā-shən\ *n*

¹**de·fect** \ˈdē-ˌfekt, di-ˈfekt\ *n* : BLEMISH, FAULT, IMPERFECTION

²**de·fect** \di-ˈfekt\ *vb* : to desert a cause or party esp. in order to espouse another — **de·fec·tion** \-ˈfek-shən\ *n* — **de·fec·tor** \-ˈfek-tər\ *n*

de·fec·tive \di-ˈfek-tiv\ *adj* : FAULTY, DEFICIENT — **defective** *n*

de·fence *chiefly Brit var of* DEFENSE

de·fend \di-ˈfend\ *vb* [ME, fr. OF *defendre*, fr. L *defendere*, fr. *de-* from + *-fendere* to strike] **1** : to repel danger or attack from **2** : to act as attorney for **3** : to oppose the claim of another in a lawsuit : CONTEST **4** : to maintain against opposition ⟨∼ an idea⟩ — **de·fend·er** *n*

de·fen·dant \di-ˈfen-dənt\ *n* : a person required to make answer in a legal action or suit

de·fense \di-ˈfens\ *n* **1** : the act of defending : resistance against attack **2** : means, method, or capability of defending **3** : an argument in support **4** : the answer made by the defendant in a legal action **5** : a defending party, group, or team — **de·fense·less** *adj* — **de·fen·si·ble** *adj*

defense mechanism *n* : an often unconscious mental process (as repression) that assists in reaching compromise solutions to personal problems

¹**de·fen·sive** \di-ˈfen-siv\ *adj* **1** : serving or intended to defend or protect **2** : of or relating to the attempt to keep an opponent from scoring (as in a game) — **de·fen·sive·ly** *adv* — **de·fen·sive·ness** *n*

²**defensive** *n* : a defensive position

¹**de·fer** \di-ˈfər\ *vb* **de·ferred; de·fer·ring** [ME *deferren*, *differren*, fr. MF *differer*, fr. L *differre* to postpone, be different] : POSTPONE, PUT OFF

²**defer** *vb* **deferred; deferring** [ME *deferren*, *differren*, fr. MF *deferer*, *defferer*, fr. LL *deferre*, fr. L, to bring down, bring, fr. *de-* down + *ferre* to carry] : to submit or yield to the opinion or wishes of another

def·er·ence \ˈde-fər-əns\ *n* : courteous, respectful, or ingratiating regard for another's wishes **syn** honor, homage, obeisance, reverence — **def·er·en·tial** \ˌde-fə-ˈren-chəl\ *adj*

de·fer·ment \di-ˈfər-mənt\ *n* : the act of delaying; *esp* : official postponement of military service

---

\ə\abut \ᵊ\kitten \ər\further \a\ash \ā\ace \ä\mop, mar \aù\out \ch\chin \e\bet \ē\easy \g\go \i\hit \ī\ice \j\job \ŋ\sing \ō\go \ò\law \òi\boy \th\thin \th\the \ü\loot \ù\foot \y\yet \zh\vision *see also* Pronunciation Symbols page

de·fi·ance \di-'fī-əns\ n 1 : CHALLENGE 2 : disposition to resist or contend

de·fi·ant \-ənt\ adj : full of defiance : BOLD — **de·fi·ant·ly** adv

de·fi·bril·la·tor \dē-'fi-brə-ˌlā-tər\ n : an electronic device that applies an electric shock to restore the rhythm of a fibrillating heart — **de·fi·bril·late** \-ˌlāt\ vb — **de·fi·bril·la·tion** \-ˌfi-brə-'lā-shən\ n

deficiency disease n : a disease (as scurvy or beriberi) caused by a lack of essential dietary elements and esp. a vitamin or mineral

de·fi·cient \di-'fi-shənt\ adj : lacking in something necessary; also : not up to a normal standard — **de·fi·cien·cy** \-shən-sē\ n

def·i·cit \'de-fə-sət\ n : a deficiency in amount; esp : an excess of expenditures over revenue

¹**de·file** \di-'fīl\ vb **de·filed; de·fil·ing** 1 : to make filthy 2 : CORRUPT 3 : to violate the chastity of 4 : to violate the sanctity of : DESECRATE 5 : DISHONOR syn contaminate, pollute, soil, taint — **de·file·ment** n

²**de·file** \di-'fīl, 'dē-ˌfīl\ n : a narrow passage or gorge

de·fine \di-'fīn\ vb **de·fined; de·fin·ing** 1 : to set forth the meaning of ⟨~ a word⟩ 2 : to fix or mark the limits of 3 : to clarify in outline or character — **de·fin·able** adj — **de·fin·er** n

def·i·nite \'de-fə-nət\ adj 1 : having distinct limits : FIXED 2 : clear in meaning 3 : typically designating an identified or immediately identifiable person or thing — **def·i·nite·ly** adv — **def·i·nite·ness** n

def·i·ni·tion \ˌde-fə-'ni-shən\ n 1 : an act of determining or settling 2 : a statement of the meaning of a word or word group; also : the action or process of defining 3 : the action or the power of making definite and clear : CLARITY, DISTINCTNESS

de·fin·i·tive \di-'fi-nə-tiv\ adj 1 : DECISIVE, CONCLUSIVE 2 : authoritative and apparently exhaustive 3 : serving to define or specify precisely

de·flate \di-'flāt\ vb **de·flat·ed; de·flat·ing** 1 : to release air or gas from 2 : to reduce in size, importance, or effectiveness; also : to reduce from a state of inflation 3 : to become deflated

de·fla·tion \-'flā-shən\ n 1 : an act or instance of deflating : the state of being deflated 2 : reduction in the volume of available money or credit resulting in a decline of the general price level

de·flect \di-'flekt\ vb : to turn aside — **de·flec·tion** \-'flek-shən\ n

de·flo·ra·tion \ˌde-flə-'rā-shən\ n : rupture of the hymen

de·flow·er \dē-'flaù-(ə)r\ vb : to deprive of virginity

de·fog \dē-'fóg, -'fäg\ vb : to remove fog or condensed moisture from — **de·fog·ger** n

de·fo·li·ant \dē-'fō-lē-ənt\ n : a chemical spray or dust used to defoliate plants

de·fo·li·ate \-ˌāt\ vb : to deprive of leaves esp. prematurely — **de·fo·li·a·tion** \dē-ˌfō-lē-'ā-shən\ n — **de·fo·li·a·tor** \dē-'fō-lē-ˌā-tər\ n

de·for·es·ta·tion \dē-ˌför-ə-'stā-shən\ n : the action or process of clearing an area of forests; also : the state of having been cleared of forests — **de·for·est** \(ˌ)dē-'för-əst, -'fär-\ vb

de·form \di-'förm\ vb 1 : DISFIGURE, DEFACE 2 : to make or become misshapen or changed in shape — **de·for·ma·tion** \ˌdē-för-'mā-shən, ˌde-fər-\ n

de·for·mi·ty \di-'för-mə-tē\ n, pl **-ties** 1 : the state of being deformed 2 : a physical blemish or distortion

de·fraud \di-'fród\ vb : CHEAT

de·fray \di-'frā\ vb : to provide for the payment of : PAY — **de·fray·al** n

de·frock \(ˌ)dē-'fräk\ vb : to deprive (as a priest) of the right to exercise the functions of office

de·frost \di-'fróst\ vb 1 : to thaw out 2 : to free from ice — **de·frost·er** n

deft \'deft\ adj : quick and neat in action — **deft·ly** adv — **deft·ness** n

de·funct \di-'fəŋkt\ adj : DEAD, EXTINCT

de·fuse \dē-'fyüz\ vb 1 : to remove the fuse from (as a bomb) 2 : to make less harmful, potent, or tense

de·fy \di-'fī\ vb **de·fied; de·fy·ing** [ME, to renounce faith in, challenge, fr. OF defier, fr. de- from + fier to entrust, ultim. fr. L fidere to trust] 1 : CHALLENGE, DARE 2 : to refuse boldly to obey or to yield to : DISREGARD ⟨~ the law⟩ 3 : WITHSTAND, BAFFLE ⟨a scene that defies description⟩

deg abbr degree

de·gas \dē-'gas\ vb : to remove gas from

de·gen·er·a·cy \di-'je-nə-rə-sē\ n, pl **-cies** 1 : the state of being degenerate 2 : the process of becoming degenerate 3 : PERVERSION

¹**de·gen·er·ate** \di-'je-nə-rət\ adj : fallen or deteriorated from a former, higher, or normal condition — **de·gen·er·a·tion** \-ˌje-nə-'rā-shən\ n — **de·gen·er·a·tive** \-'je-nə-ˌrā-tiv\ adj

²**de·gen·er·ate** \di-'je-nə-ˌrāt\ vb : to undergo deterioration (as in morality, intelligence, structure, or function)

³**de·gen·er·ate** \-rət\ n : a degenerate person; esp : a sexual pervert

de·grad·able \di-'grā-də-bəl\ adj : capable of being chemically degraded

de·grade \di-'grād\ vb 1 : to reduce from a higher to a lower rank or degree 2 : DEBASE, CORRUPT 3 : DECOMPOSE — **deg·ra·da·tion** \ˌde-grə-'dā-shən\ n

de·gree \di-'grē\ n [ME, fr. OF degré, fr. (assumed) VL degradus, fr. L de- down + gradus step, grade] 1 : a step in a series 2 : a rank or grade of official, ecclesiastical, or social position; also : the civil condition of a person 3 : the extent, intensity, or scope of something esp. as measured by a graded series 4 : one of the forms or sets of forms used in the comparison of an adjective or adverb 5 : a title conferred upon students by a college, university, or professional school on completion of a program of study 6 : a line or space of the musical staff; also : a note or tone of a musical scale 7 : a unit of measure for angles that is equal to an angle with its vertex at the center of a circle and its sides cutting off 1/360 of the circumference; also : a unit of measure of the arc of a circle equal to the amount of arc cut off by an angle of one degree with its vertex at the center of the circle 8 : any of various units for measuring temperature

de·horn \dē-'hórn\ vb : to deprive of horns

de·hu·man·ize \dē-'hyü-mə-ˌnīz\ vb : to deprive of human qualities, personality, or spirit — **de·hu·man·i·za·tion** \ˌdē-ˌhyü-mə-nə-'zā-shən\ n

de·hu·mid·i·fy \ˌdē-hyü-'mi-də-ˌfī\ vb : to remove moisture from (as the air) — **de·hu·mid·i·fi·er** n

de·hy·drate \dē-'hī-ˌdrāt\ vb : to remove water from; also : to lose liquid — **de·hy·dra·tion** \ˌdē-hī-'drā-shən\ n

de·hy·dro·ge·na·tion \ˌdē-(ˌ)hī-ˌdrä-jə-'nā-shən, -drə-\ n : the removal of hydrogen from a chemical compound — **de·hy·dro·ge·nate** \ˌdē-(ˌ)hī-'drä-jə-ˌnāt, dē-'hī-drə-jə-\ vb

de·ice \dē-'īs\ vb : to keep free or rid of ice — **de·ic·er** n

de·i·fy \'dē-ə-ˌfī\ vb **-fied; -fy·ing** 1 : to make a god of 2 : WORSHIP, GLORIFY — **de·i·fi·ca·tion** \ˌdē-ə-fə-'kā-shən\ n

deign \'dān\ vb [ME, fr. OF deignier, fr. L dignare, dignari, fr. dignus worthy] : CONDESCEND

de·ion·ize \dē-'ī-ə-ˌnīz\ vb : to remove ions from

de·ism \'dē-ˌi-zəm\ n, often cap : a system of thought advocating natural religion based on human morality and reason rather than divine revelation — **de·ist** \'dē-ist\ n, often cap — **de·is·tic** \dē-'is-tik\ adj

de·i·ty \\'dē-ə-tē, 'dā-\\ *n, pl* **-ties 1** : DIVINITY **2 2** *cap* : GOD 1 **3** : a god or goddess

dé·jà vu \\dā-ˌzhä-'vü\\ *n* [F, adj., already seen] : the feeling that one has seen or heard something before

de·ject·ed \\di-'jek-təd\\ *adj* : low in spirits : SAD — **de·ject·ed·ly** *adv*

de·jec·tion \\-'jek-shən\\ *n* : lowness of spirits

de ju·re \\dē-'jùr-ē\\ *adv or adj* [ML] : by legal right

deka·gram \\'de-kə-ˌgram\\ *n* — see METRIC SYSTEM table

deka·li·ter \\-ˌlē-tər\\ *n* — see METRIC SYSTEM table

deka·me·ter \\-ˌmē-tər\\ *n* — see METRIC SYSTEM table

del *abbr* delegate; delegation

Del *abbr* Delaware

Del·a·ware \\'de-lə-ˌwar\\ *n, pl* **Delaware** *or* **Delawares** : a member of an American Indian people orig. of the Delaware valley; *also* : their language

¹de·lay \\di-'lā\\ *n* **1** : the act of delaying : the state of being delayed **2** : the time for which something is delayed

²delay *vb* **1** : POSTPONE, PUT OFF **2** : to stop, detain, or hinder for a time **3** : to move or act slowly

de·lec·ta·ble \\di-'lek-tə-bəl\\ *adj* **1** : highly pleasing : DELIGHTFUL **2** : DELICIOUS

de·lec·ta·tion \\ˌdē-ˌlek-'tā-shən\\ *n* : DELIGHT, PLEASURE, DIVERSION

¹del·e·gate \\'de-li-gət, -ˌgāt\\ *n* **1** : DEPUTY, REPRESENTATIVE **2** : a member of the lower house of the legislature of Maryland, Virginia, or West Virginia

²del·e·gate \\-ˌgāt\\ *vb* **-gat·ed; -gat·ing 1** : to entrust to another ⟨∼ authority⟩ **2** : to appoint as one's delegate

del·e·ga·tion \\ˌde-li-'gā-shən\\ *n* **1** : the act of delegating **2** : one or more persons chosen to represent others

de·lete \\di-'lēt\\ *vb* **de·let·ed; de·let·ing** [L *delēre* to wipe out, destroy] : to eliminate esp. by blotting out, cutting out, or erasing — **de·le·tion** \\-'lē-shən\\ *n*

del·e·te·ri·ous \\ˌde-lə-'tir-ē-əs\\ *adj* : HARMFUL, NOXIOUS

delft \\'delft\\ *n* **1** : a Dutch pottery with an opaque white glaze and predominantly blue decoration **2** : glazed pottery esp. when blue and white

delft·ware \\-ˌwar\\ *n* : DELFT

deli \\'de-lē\\ *n, pl* **del·is** : DELICATESSEN

¹de·lib·er·ate \\di-'li-bə-ˌrāt\\ *vb* **-at·ed; -at·ing** : to consider carefully — **de·lib·er·a·tion** \\-ˌli-bə-'rā-shən\\ *n* — **de·lib·er·a·tive** \\-'li-bə-ˌrā-tiv, -brə-tiv\\ *adj* — **de·lib·er·a·tive·ly** *adv*

²de·lib·er·ate \\di-'li-bə-rət, -'li-brət\\ *adj* [L *deliberare* to consider carefully, fr. *libra* scale, pound] **1** : determined after careful thought **2** : done or said intentionally **3** : UNHURRIED, SLOW — **de·lib·er·ate·ly** *adv* — **de·lib·er·ate·ness** *n*

del·i·ca·cy \\'de-li-kə-sē\\ *n, pl* **-cies 1** : something pleasing to eat and considered rare or luxurious **2** : FINENESS, DAINTINESS; *also* : FRAILTY **3** : nicety or expressiveness of touch **4** : precise perception and discrimination : SENSITIVITY **5** : sensibility in feeling or conduct; *also* : SQUEAMISHNESS **6** : the quality or state of requiring delicate handling

del·i·cate \\'de-li-kət\\ *adj* **1** : pleasing to the senses of taste or smell esp. in a mild or subtle way **2** : marked by daintiness or charm : EXQUISITE **3** : FASTIDIOUS, SQUEAMISH, SCRUPULOUS **4** : easily damaged : FRAGILE; *also* : SICKLY **5** : requiring skill or tact **6** : marked by care, skill, or tact **7** : marked by minute precision : very sensitive — **del·i·cate·ly** *adv*

del·i·ca·tes·sen \\ˌde-li-kə-'tes-ᵊn\\ *n pl* [G, pl. of *Delicatesse* delicacy, fr. F *délicatesse*] **1** : ready-to-eat food products (as cooked meats and prepared salads) **2** *sing, pl* **delicatessens** : a store where delicatessen are sold

de·li·cious \\di-'li-shəs\\ *adj* : affording great pleasure : DELIGHTFUL; *esp* : very pleasing to the taste or smell — **de·li·cious·ly** *adv* — **de·li·cious·ness** *n*

¹de·light \\di-'līt\\ *n* **1** : great pleasure or satisfaction : JOY **2** : something that gives great pleasure — **de·light·ful** \\-fəl\\ *adj* — **de·light·ful·ly** *adv*

²delight *vb* **1** : to take great pleasure **2** : to satisfy greatly : PLEASE

de·light·ed *adj* : highly pleased : GRATIFIED — **de·light·ed·ly** *adv*

de·lim·it \\di-'li-mət\\ *vb* : to fix the limits of

de·lin·eate \\di-'li-nē-ˌāt\\ *vb* **-eat·ed; -eat·ing 1** : SKETCH, PORTRAY **2** : to picture in words : DESCRIBE — **de·lin·ea·tion** \\-ˌli-nē-'ā-shən\\ *n*

de·lin·quen·cy \\di-'liŋ-kwən-sē\\ *n, pl* **-cies** : the quality or state of being delinquent

¹de·lin·quent \\-kwənt\\ *n* : a delinquent person

²delinquent *adj* **1** : offending by neglect or violation of duty or of law **2** : being overdue in payment

del·i·quesce \\ˌde-li-'kwes\\ *vb* **-quesced; -quesc·ing** : MELT, DISSOLVE — **del·i·ques·cent** \\-'kwes-ᵊnt\\ *adj*

de·lir·i·um \\di-'lir-ē-əm\\ *n* [L, fr. *delirare* to be crazy, lit., to leave the furrow (in plowing), fr. *de-* from + *lira* furrow] : mental disturbance marked by confusion, disordered speech, and hallucinations; *also* : frenzied excitement — **de·lir·i·ous** \\-ē-əs\\ *adj* — **de·lir·i·ous·ly** *adv*

delirium tre·mens \\-'trē-mənz, -'tre-\\ *n* : a violent delirium with tremors that is induced by excessive and prolonged use of alcoholic liquors

de·liv·er \\di-'li-vər\\ *vb* **-ered; -er·ing 1** : to set free : SAVE **2** : CONVEY, TRANSFER ⟨∼ a letter⟩ **3** : to assist in giving birth or at the birth of; *also* : to give birth to **4** : UTTER, COMMUNICATE **5** : to send to an intended target or destination — **de·liv·er·ance** *n* — **de·liv·er·er** *n*

de·liv·ery \\di-'li-və-rē\\ *n, pl* **-er·ies** : the act of delivering something; *also* : something delivered — **de·liv·ery·man** \\-ˌman\\ *n*

dell \\'del\\ *n* : a small secluded valley

de·louse \\dē-'laùs\\ *vb* : to remove lice from

del·phin·i·um \\del-'fi-nē-əm\\ *n* : any of a genus of mostly perennial herbs related to the buttercups with tall branching spikes of irregular flowers

del·ta \\'del-tə\\ *n* **1** : the 4th letter of the Greek alphabet — Δ or δ **2** : something shaped like a capital Δ; *esp* : the triangular silt-formed land at the mouth of a river — **del·ta·ic** \\del-'tā-ik\\ *adj*

de·lude \\di-'lüd\\ *vb* **de·lud·ed; de·lud·ing** : MISLEAD, DECEIVE, TRICK

¹del·uge \\'del-yüj\\ *n* **1** : a flooding of land by water **2** : a drenching rain **3** : a great amount or number

²deluge *vb* **del·uged; del·ug·ing 1** : INUNDATE, FLOOD **2** : to overwhelm as if with a deluge

de·lu·sion \\di-'lü-zhən\\ *n* : a deluding or being deluded; *esp* : a persistent false psychotic belief — **de·lu·sion·al** \\-'lü-zhə-nəl\\ *adj* — **de·lu·sive** \\-'lü-siv\\ *adj*

de·luxe \\di-'lùks, -'ləks, -'lüks\\ *adj* : notably luxurious or elegant

delve \\'delv\\ *vb* **delved; delv·ing 1** : DIG **2** : to seek laboriously for information

dely *abbr* delivery

Dem *abbr* Democrat; Democratic

de·mag·ne·tize \\dē-'mag-nə-ˌtīz\\ *vb* : to cause to lose magnetic properties — **de·mag·ne·ti·za·tion** \\dē-ˌmag-nə-tə-'zā-shən\\ *n*

dem·a·gogue *or* **dem·a·gog** \\'de-mə-ˌgäg\\ *n* [Gk *dēmagōgos*, fr. *dēmos* people + *agōgos* leading, fr. *agein* to lead] : a person who appeals to the emotions and prejudices of people esp. in order to gain political power — **dem·a·gogu·ery** \\-ˌgä-gə-rē\\ *n* — **dem·a·gogy** \\-ˌgä-gē, -ˌgä-jē\\ *n*

¹de·mand \\di-'mand\\ *n* **1** : an act of demanding; *also*

: something claimed as due or just **2** : the ability and desire to buy goods or services; *also* : the quantity of goods wanted at a stated price **3** : a seeking or being sought after : urgent need **4** : a pressing need or requirement

²demand *vb* **1** : to ask for with authority : claim as due or just **2** : to ask earnestly or in the manner of a command **3** : REQUIRE, NEED

de·mar·cate \di-ˈmär-ˌkāt, ˈdē-ˌmär-\ *vb* **-cat·ed; -cat·ing 1** : DELIMIT **2** : SEPARATE — **de·mar·ca·tion** \ˌdē-ˌmär-ˈkā-shən\ *n*

dé·marche or **de·marche** \dā-ˈmärsh\ *n* : a course of action : MANEUVER

¹de·mean \di-ˈmēn\ *vb* **de·meaned; de·mean·ing** : to behave or conduct (oneself) usu. in a proper manner

²demean *vb* **de·meaned; de·mean·ing** : DEGRADE, DEBASE

de·mean·or \di-ˈmē-nər\ *n* : CONDUCT, BEARING

de·mean·our *Brit var of* DEMEANOR

de·ment·ed \di-ˈmen-təd\ *adj* : MAD, INSANE — **de·ment·ed·ly** *adv*

de·men·tia \di-ˈmen-chə\ *n* **1** : mental deterioration **2** : INSANITY

de·mer·it \di-ˈmer-ət\ *n* **1** : FAULT **2** : a mark placed against a person's record for some fault or offense

de·mesne \di-ˈmān, -ˈmēn\ *n* **1** : REALM **2** : manorial land actually possessed by the lord and not held by free tenants **3** : ESTATE **4** : REGION

demi·god \ˈde-mi-ˌgäd\ *n* : a mythological being with more power than a mortal but less than a god

demi·john \ˈde-mi-ˌjän\ *n* [F *dame-jeanne,* lit., Lady Jane] : a large narrow-necked bottle usu. enclosed in wickerwork

de·mil·i·ta·rize \dē-ˈmi-lə-tə-ˌrīz\ *vb* : to strip of military forces, weapons, or fortifications — **de·mil·i·tar·i·za·tion** \dē-ˌmi-lə-tə-rə-ˈzā-shən\ *n*

demi·mon·daine \ˌde-mi-ˌmän-ˈdān\ *n* : a woman of the demimonde

demi·monde \ˈde-mi-ˌmänd\ *n* [F *demi-monde,* fr. *demi-* half + *monde* world] **1** : a class of women on the fringes of respectable society supported by wealthy lovers **2** : a group engaged in activity of doubtful legality or propriety

de·min·er·al·ize \dē-ˈmi-nə-rə-ˌlīz\ *vb* : to remove the mineral matter from — **de·min·er·al·i·za·tion** \-ˌmi-nə-rə-lə-ˈzā-shən\ *n*

de·mise \di-ˈmīz\ *n* **1** : LEASE **2** : transfer of sovereignty to a successor ⟨~ of the crown⟩ **3** : DEATH **4** : loss of status

demi·tasse \ˈde-mi-ˌtas\ *n* : a small cup of black coffee; *also* : the cup used to serve it

de·mo·bi·lize \di-ˈmō-bə-ˌlīz, dē-\ *vb* **1** : DISBAND **2** : to discharge from military service — **de·mo·bi·li·za·tion** \di-ˌmō-bə-lə-ˈzā-shən, dē-\ *n*

de·moc·ra·cy \di-ˈmä-krə-sē\ *n, pl* **-cies** [MF *democratie,* fr. LL *democratia,* fr. Gk *dēmokratia,* fr. *dēmos* people + *kratos* strength, power] **1** : government by the people; *esp* : rule of the majority **2** : a government in which the supreme power is held by the people **3** : a political unit that has a democratic government **4** *cap* : the principles and policies of the Democratic party in the U.S. **5** : the common people esp. when constituting the source of political authority **6** : the absence of hereditary or arbitrary class distinctions or privileges

dem·o·crat \ˈde-mə-ˌkrat\ *n* **1** : one who believes in or practices democracy **2** *cap* : a member of the Democratic party of the U.S.

dem·o·crat·ic \ˌde-mə-ˈkra-tik\ *adj* **1** : of, relating to, or favoring democracy **2** *often cap* : of or relating to one of the two major political parties in the U.S. associated in modern times with policies of broad social reform and internationalism **3** : relating to or appealing to the

common people ⟨~ art⟩ **4** : not snobbish — **dem·o·crat·i·cal·ly** \-ti-k(ə-)lē\ *adv*

de·moc·ra·tize \di-ˈmä-krə-ˌtīz\ *vb* **-tized; -tiz·ing** : to make democratic

dé·mo·dé \ˌdā-mò-ˈdā\ *adj* [F] : no longer fashionable : OUT-OF-DATE

de·mo·graph·ics \ˌde-mə-ˈgra-fiks, ˌdē-\ *n pl* : the statistical characteristics of human populations

de·mog·ra·phy \di-ˈmä-grə-fē\ *n* : the statistical study of human populations and esp. their size and distribution and the number of births and deaths — **de·mog·ra·pher** \-fər\ *n* — **de·mo·graph·ic** \ˌde-mə-ˈgra-fik, ˌdē-\ *adj* — **de·mo·graph·i·cal·ly** \-fi-k(ə-)lē\ *adv*

dem·oi·selle \ˌdem-wə-ˈzel\ *n* [F] : a young woman

de·mol·ish \di-ˈmä-lish\ *vb* **1** : to destroy by breaking apart : RAZE **2** : SMASH **3** : to put an end to

de·mo·li·tion \ˌde-mə-ˈli-shən, ˌdē-\ *n* : the act of demolishing; *esp* : destruction by means of explosives

de·mon or **dae·mon** \ˈdē-mən\ *n* **1** : an evil spirit : DEVIL **2** *usu daemon* : an attendant power or spirit **3** : one that has unusual drive or effectiveness

de·mon·e·tize \dē-ˈmä-nə-ˌtīz, -ˈmə-\ *vb* : to stop using as money or as a monetary standard ⟨~ silver⟩ — **de·mon·e·ti·za·tion** \dē-ˌmä-nə-tə-ˈzā-shən, -ˌmə-\ *n*

de·mo·ni·ac \di-ˈmō-nē-ˌak\ *also* **de·mo·ni·a·cal** \ˌdē-mə-ˈnī-ə-kəl\ *adj* **1** : possessed or influenced by a demon **2** : DEVILISH, FIENDISH

de·mon·ic \di-ˈmä-nik\ *also* **de·mon·i·cal** \-ni-kəl\ *adj* : DEMONIAC 2

de·mon·ol·o·gy \ˌdē-mə-ˈnä-lə-jē\ *n* **1** : the study of demons **2** : belief in demons

de·mon·stra·ble \di-ˈmän-strə-bəl\ *adj* **1** : capable of being demonstrated **2** : APPARENT, EVIDENT — **de·mon·stra·bly** \-blē\ *adv*

dem·on·strate \ˈde-mən-ˌstrāt\ *vb* **-strat·ed; -strat·ing 1** : to show clearly **2** : to prove or make clear by reasoning or evidence **3** : to explain esp. with many examples **4** : to show publicly ⟨~ a new car⟩ **5** : to make a public display ⟨~ in protest⟩ — **dem·on·stra·tion** \ˌde-mən-ˈstrā-shən\ *n* — **dem·on·stra·tor** \ˈde-mən-ˌstrā-tər\ *n*

¹de·mon·stra·tive \di-ˈmän-strə-tiv\ *adj* **1** : demonstrating as real or true **2** : characterized by demonstration **3** : pointing out the one referred to and distinguishing it from others of the same class ⟨~ pronoun⟩ **4** : marked by display of feeling : EFFUSIVE — **de·mon·stra·tive·ly** *adv* — **de·mon·stra·tive·ness** *n*

²demonstrative *n* : a demonstrative word and esp. a pronoun

de·mor·al·ize \di-ˈmòr-ə-ˌlīz\ *vb* **1** : to corrupt in morals **2** : to weaken in discipline or spirit : DISORGANIZE — **de·mor·al·i·za·tion** \di-ˌmòr-ə-lə-ˈzā-shən\ *n*

de·mote \di-ˈmōt\ *vb* **de·mot·ed; de·mot·ing** : to reduce to a lower grade or rank — **de·mo·tion** \-ˈmō-shən\ *n*

de·mot·ic \di-ˈmä-tik\ *adj* : COMMON, POPULAR

de·mur \di-ˈmər\ *vb* **de·murred; de·mur·ring** [ME *demeoren* to linger, fr. OF *demorer,* fr. L *demorari,* fr. *morari* to linger, fr. *mora* delay] : to take exception : OBJECT — **de·mur** *n*

de·mure \di-ˈmyùr\ *adj* **1** : quietly modest : DECOROUS **2** : affectedly modest, reserved, or serious : PRIM **syn** shy, bashful, coy, difficult, retiring, unassertive — **de·mure·ly** *adv*

de·mur·rer \di-ˈmər-ər\ *n* : a claim by the defendant in a legal action that the plaintiff does not have sufficient grounds to proceed

den \ˈden\ *n* **1** : LAIR **2** : HIDEOUT ⟨a robber's ~⟩; *also* : a place like a hideout or a center of secret activity ⟨opium ~⟩ ⟨a ~ of iniquity⟩ **3** : a cozy private little room

Den *abbr* Denmark

de·na·ture \dē-ˈnā-chər\ *vb* **de·na·tured; de·na·tur·ing** : to remove the natural qualities of; *esp* : to make (alcohol) unfit for drinking

den·drol·o·gy \den-'drä-lə-jē\ *n* : the study of trees — **den·drol·o·gist** \-jist\ *n*

den·gue \'deŋ-gē, -ˌgā\ *n* [Sp] : an acute infectious disease characterized by headache, severe joint pain, and rash

de·ni·al \di-'nī-əl\ *n* **1** : rejection of a request **2** : refusal to admit the truth of a statement or charge; *also* : assertion that something alleged is false **3** : DISAVOWAL **4** : restriction on one's own activity or desires

de·nier \'den-yər\ *n* : a unit of fineness for yarn

den·i·grate \'de-ni-ˌgrāt\ *vb* **-grat·ed; -grat·ing** [L *denigrare*, fr. *nigrare* to blacken, fr. *niger* black] : to cast aspersions on : DEFAME — **den·i·gra·tion** \ˌde-ni-'grā-shən\ *n*

den·im \'de-nəm\ *n* [F *(serge) de Nîmes* serge of Nîmes, France] **1** : a firm durable twilled usu. cotton fabric woven with colored warp and white filling threads **2** *pl* : overalls or trousers of usu. blue denim

den·i·zen \'de-nə-zən\ *n* : INHABITANT

de·nom·i·nate \di-'nä-mə-ˌnāt\ *vb* : to give a name to : DESIGNATE

de·nom·i·na·tion \di-ˌnä-mə-'nā-shən\ *n* **1** : an act of denominating **2** : a value or size of a series of related values (as of money) **3** : NAME, DESIGNATION; *esp* : a general name for a category **4** : a religious organization uniting local congregations in a single body — **de·nom·i·na·tion·al** \-shə-nəl\ *adj*

de·nom·i·na·tor \di-'nä-mə-ˌnā-tər\ *n* : the part of a fraction that is below the line indicating division

de·no·ta·tive \'dē-nō-ˌtā-tiv, di-'nō-tə-tiv\ *adj* **1** : denoting or tending to denote **2** : relating to denotation

de·note \di-'nōt\ *vb* **1** : to mark out plainly : INDICATE **2** : to make known **3** : MEAN, NAME — **de·no·ta·tion** \ˌdē-nō-'tā-shən\ *n*

de·noue·ment \ˌdā-nü-'mäⁿ\ *n* [F *dénouement*, lit., untying] : the final outcome of the dramatic complications in a literary work

de·nounce \di-'naůns\ *vb* **de·nounced; de·nounc·ing** **1** : to pronounce esp. publicly to be blameworthy or evil **2** : to inform against : ACCUSE **3** : to announce formally the termination of (as a treaty) — **de·nounce·ment** *n*

de no·vo \di-'nō-vō\ *adv or adj* [L] : over again : ANEW

dense \'dens\ *adj* **dens·er; dens·est** **1** : marked by compactness or crowding together of parts : THICK ⟨∼ forest⟩ ⟨a ∼ fog⟩ **2** : DULL, STUPID — **dense·ly** *adv* — **dense·ness** *n*

den·si·ty \'den-sə-tē\ *n, pl* **-ties** **1** : the quality or state of being dense **2** : the quantity of something per unit volume, unit area, or unit length

dent \'dent\ *n* **1** : a small depressed place made by a blow or by pressure **2** : an impression or weakening effect made usu. against resistance **3** : initial progress — **dent** *vb*

den·tal \'dent-ᵊl\ *adj* : of or relating to teeth or dentistry — **den·tal·ly** *adv*

dental floss *n* : a thread used to clean between the teeth

dental hygienist *n* : a person licensed to clean and examine teeth

den·tate \'den-ˌtāt\ *adj* : having pointed projections : NOTCHED

den·ti·frice \'den-tə-frəs\ *n* [MF, fr. L *dentifricium*, fr. *dent-, dens* tooth + *fricare* to rub] : a powder, paste, or liquid for cleaning the teeth

den·tin \'dent-ᵊn\ *or* **den·tine** \'den-ˌtēn, den-'tēn\ *n* : a calcareous material like bone but harder and denser that composes the principal mass of a tooth

den·tist \'den-tist\ *n* : a person licensed in the care, treatment, and replacement of teeth — **den·tist·ry** *n*

den·ti·tion \den-'ti-shən\ *n* : the number, kind, and arrangement of teeth (as of a person or animal); *also* : TEETH

den·ture \'den-chər\ *n* : a set of teeth; *esp* : a partial or complete set of false teeth

de·nude \di-'nüd, -'nyüd\ *vb* **de·nud·ed; de·nud·ing** : to strip the covering from — **de·nu·da·tion** \ˌdē-nü-'dā-shən, -nyü-\ *n*

de·nun·ci·a·tion \di-ˌnən-sē-'ā-shən\ *n* : the act of denouncing; *esp* : a public condemnation

de·ny \di-'nī\ *vb* **de·nied; de·ny·ing** **1** : to declare untrue **2** : to refuse to recognize or acknowledge : DISAVOW **3** : to refuse to grant ⟨∼ a request⟩ **4** : to reject as false ⟨∼ a theory⟩

de·o·dar \'dē-ə-ˌdär\ *n* [Hindi *deodār*, fr. Skt *devadāru*, fr. *deva* god + *dāru* wood] : an East Indian cedar

de·odor·ant \dē-'ō-də-rənt\ *n* : a preparation that gets rid of unpleasant odors

de·odor·ize \dē-'ō-də-ˌrīz\ *vb* : to eliminate the offensive odor of

de·ox·i·dize \dē-'äk-sə-ˌdīz\ *vb* : to remove oxygen from

de·oxy·ri·bo·nu·cle·ic acid \dē-ˌäk-si-ˌrī-bō-nü-ˌklē-ik-, -nyü-\ *n* : DNA

de·oxy·ri·bose \dē-ˌäk-si-'rī-ˌbōs\ *n* : a sugar with five carbon and four oxygen atoms in each molecule that is part of DNA

dep *abbr* **1** depart; departure **2** deposit **3** deputy

de·part \di-'pärt\ *vb* **1** : to go away : go away from : LEAVE **2** : DIE **3** : to turn aside : DEVIATE

de·part·ment \di-'pärt-mənt\ *n* **1** : a distinct sphere or category esp. of an activity or attribute **2** : a functional or territorial division (as of a government, business, or college) — **de·part·men·tal** \di-ˌpärt-'ment-ᵊl, ˌdē-\ *adj*

☞ For table, see next page.

department store *n* : a store selling a wide variety of goods arranged in several departments

de·par·ture \di-'pär-chər\ *n* **1** : the act of going away **2** : a starting out (as on a journey) **3** : DIVERGENCE

de·pend \di-'pend\ *vb* **1** : to be determined, based, or contingent ⟨life ∼s on food⟩ **2** : TRUST, RELY ⟨you can ∼ on me⟩ **3** : to be dependent esp. for financial support **4** : to hang down ⟨a vine ∼*ing* from a tree⟩

de·pend·able \di-'pen-də-bəl\ *adj* : TRUSTWORTHY, RELIABLE — **de·pend·abil·i·ty** \-ˌpen-də-'bi-lə-tē\ *n*

de·pen·dence *also* **de·pen·dance** \di-'pen-dəns\ *n* **1** : the quality or state of being dependent; *esp* : the quality or state of being influenced by or subject to another **2** : RELIANCE, TRUST **3** : something on which one relies **4** : drug addiction; *also* : HABITUATION **2**

de·pen·den·cy \-dən-sē\ *n, pl* **-cies** **1** : DEPENDENCE **2** : a territory under the jurisdiction of a nation but not formally annexed by it

¹de·pen·dent \-dənt\ *adj* **1** : hanging down **2** : determined or conditioned by another; *also* : affected with drug dependence **3** : relying on another for support **4** : subject to another's jurisdiction **5** : SUBORDINATE **4**

²dependent *also* **de·pen·dant** \-dənt\ *n* : one that is dependent; *esp* : a person who relies on another for support

de·pict \di-'pikt\ *vb* **1** : to represent by a picture **2** : to describe in words — **de·pic·tion** \-'pik-shən\ *n*

de·pil·a·to·ry \di-'pi-lə-ˌtȯr-ē\ *n, pl* **-ries** : a preparation for removing hair, wool, or bristles

de·plane \dē-'plān\ *vb* : to get out of an airplane

de·plete \di-'plēt\ *vb* **de·plet·ed; de·plet·ing** : to exhaust esp. of strength or resources — **de·ple·tion** \-'plē-shən\ *n*

de·plor·able \di-'plȯr-ə-bəl\ *adj* **1** : LAMENTABLE **2** : WRETCHED — **de·plor·ably** *adv*

de·plore \-'plȯr\ *vb* **de·plored; de·plor·ing** **1** : to feel or express grief for **2** : to regret strongly **3** : to consider unfortunate or deserving of disapproval

---

\ə\abut \ᵊ\kitten \ər\further \a\ash \ā\ace \ä\mop, mar \aů\out \ch\chin \e\bet \ē\easy \g\go \i\hit \ī\ice \j\job \ŋ\sing \ō\go \ȯ\law \ȯi\boy \th\thin \t̲h̲\the \ü\loot \ů\foot \y\yet \zh\vision *see also* Pronunciation Symbols page

EXECUTIVE DEPARTMENTS OF THE UNITED STATES

DEPARTMENT	TITLE OF CHIEF	DATE OF CREATION	FUNCTIONS
Department of State	Secretary of State	July 27, 1789, as Dept. of Foreign Affairs; Sept. 15, 1789, under present name	conduct of foreign relations
Department of the Treasury	Secretary of the Treasury	Sept. 2, 1789	administration of national fiscal policies
*Department of Defense	Secretary of Defense	July 26, 1947, as National Military Establishment; Aug. 10, 1949, under present name	responsibility for national defense and security
Department of Justice	Attorney General (office created Sept. 24, 1789)	June 22, 1870	enforcement of federal laws; provision of legal counsel in federal cases; interpretation of laws for other departments
Department of the Interior	Secretary of the Interior	March 3, 1849	conservation and development of natural resources of U.S. and territories; guardianship of American Indians
Department of Agriculture	Secretary of Agriculture	May 15, 1862; made executive department Feb. 9, 1889	acquisition and diffusion of useful information on agricultural subjects; supervision of national forests; administration of price support programs
Department of Commerce	Secretary of Commerce	Feb. 14, 1903, as the Dept. of Commerce and Labor; reorganized Mar. 4, 1913, under present name	promotion and development of foreign and domestic commerce
Department of Labor	Secretary of Labor	Mar. 4, 1913	administration and enforcement of statutes designed to promote welfare of wage earners
Department of Housing and Urban Development	Secretary of Housing and Urban Development	Sept. 9, 1965	supervision and coordination of federal programs relating to housing and urban renewal
Department of Transportation	Secretary of Transportation	Oct. 15, 1966	administration and coordination of federal agencies and programs dealing with transportation
Department of Energy	Secretary of Energy	August 4, 1977	administration of agencies promoting energy conservation and development
Department of Education	Secretary of Education	October 17, 1979; upon abolition of Dept. of Health, Education, and Welfare (created April 11, 1953), assumed education functions	administration of agencies promoting educational programs and policies
Department of Health and Human Services	Secretary of Health and Human Services	October 17, 1979; upon abolition of Dept. of Health, Education, and Welfare (created April 11, 1953), assumed health and welfare functions	administration of welfare, social security, and health agencies

*The Department of the Army, created Aug. 7, 1789, as the Department of War and the Department of the Navy, created April 30, 1789, lost executive status July 26, 1947, on merger under their present names in the newly created National Military Establishment. The Department of the Air Force was created Sept. 18, 1947, as a third subordinate department of the National Military Establishment.

de·ploy \di-'plȯi\ *vb* : to spread out (as troops or ships) in order for battle — **de·ploy·ment** \-mənt\ *n*

de·po·nent \di-'pō-nənt\ *n* : one who gives evidence

de·pop·u·late \dē-'pä-pyə-ˌlāt\ *vb* : to reduce greatly the population of — **de·pop·u·la·tion** \-ˌpä-pyə-'lā-shən\ *n*

de·port \di-'pȯrt\ *vb* **1** : CONDUCT, BEHAVE **2** : BANISH, EXILE — **de·por·ta·tion** \ˌdē-pȯr-'tā-shən\ *n*

de·port·ment \di-'pȯrt-mənt\ *n* : BEHAVIOR, BEARING

de·pose \di-'pōz\ *vb* **de·posed; de·pos·ing 1** : to remove from high office (as of king) **2** : to testify under oath or by affidavit

¹de·pos·it \di-'pä-zət\ *vb* **de·pos·it·ed** \-zə-təd\; **de·pos·it·ing 1** : to place for safekeeping or as a pledge; *esp* : to put money in a bank **2** : to lay down : PLACE **3** : to let fall or sink ⟨silt ∼ed by a flood⟩ — **de·pos·i·tor** \-zə-tər\ *n*

²deposit *n* **1** : the state of being deposited ⟨money on ∼⟩ **2** : something placed for safekeeping; *esp* : money deposited in a bank **3** : money given as a pledge **4** : an act of depositing **5** : something laid down ⟨a ∼ of silt⟩ **6** : a natural accumulation (as of a mineral)

de·po·si·tion \ˌde-pə-'zi-shən, ˌdē-\ *n* **1** : an act of removing from a position of authority **2** : TESTIMONY **3** : the process of depositing **4** : DEPOSIT

de·pos·i·to·ry \di-'pä-zə-ˌtȯr-ē\ *n, pl* **-ries** : a place where something is deposited esp. for safekeeping

de·pot \ *1, 2 usu* 'de-pō, *3 usu* 'dē-\ *n* **1** : STOREHOUSE **2** : a place where military supplies or replacements are kept or assembled **3** : a building for railroad or bus passengers

depr *abbr* depreciation

de·prave \di-'prāv\ *vb* **de·praved; de·prav·ing** [ME, fr. MF *depraver*, fr. L *depravare* to pervert, fr. *pravus* crooked, bad] **1** : CORRUPT, PERVERT — **de·praved** *adj* — **de·prav·i·ty** \-'pra-və-tē\ *n*

dep·re·cate \'de-pri-ˌkāt\ *vb* **-cat·ed; -cat·ing** [L *deprecari* to avert by prayer, fr. *precari* to pray] **1** : to express disapproval of **2** : BELITTLE — **dep·re·ca·tion** \ˌde-pri-'kā-shən\ *n*

dep·re·ca·to·ry \'de-pri-kə-ˌtȯr-ē\ *adj* **1** : APOLOGETIC **2** : serving to deprecate : DISAPPROVING

de·pre·ci·ate \di-'prē-shē-ˌāt\ *vb* **-at·ed; -at·ing** [LL *depretiare*, fr. L *pretium* price] **1** : BELITTLE, DISPARAGE **2** : to lessen in price or value — **de·pre·ci·a·tion** \-ˌprē-shē-'ā-shən\ *n*

dep·re·da·tion \ˌde-prə-'dā-shən\ *n* : a laying waste or plundering — **dep·re·date** \'de-prə-ˌdāt\ *vb*

de·press \di-'pres\ *vb* **1** : to press down : cause to sink to a lower position **2** : to lessen the activity or force of **3** : SADDEN, DISCOURAGE **4** : to lessen in price or value — **de·pres·sor** \-'pre-sər\ *n*

de·pres·sant \di-'pres-ᵊnt\ *n* : one that depresses; *esp* : a chemical substance (as a drug) that reduces bodily functional activity — **depressant** *adj*

de·pressed *adj* **1** : low in spirits; *also* : affected with psychological depression **2** : suffering from economic depression

de·pres·sion \di-'pre-shən\ *n* **1** : an act of depressing : a state of being depressed **2** : a pressing down : LOWERING **3** : a state of feeling sad **4** : a psychological disorder marked esp. by sadness, inactivity, difficulty in thinking and concentration, and feelings of dejection **5** : a depressed area or part **6** : a period of low general economic activity with widespread unemployment

¹de·pres·sive \di-'pre-siv\ *adj* **1** : tending to depress **2** : characterized or affected by psychological depression

²depressive *n* : a person affected with or prone to psychological depression

de·pres·sur·ize \(ˌ)dē-'pre-shə-ˌrīz\ *vb* : to release pressure from

dep·ri·va·tion \ˌde-prə-'vā-shən\ *n* **1** : an act or instance of depriving : LOSS **2** : PRIVATION

de·prive \di-'prīv\ *vb* **de·prived; de·priv·ing 1** : to take

something away from **2** : to stop from having something

de·prived *adj* : marked by deprivation esp. of the necessities of life

de·pro·gram \(ˌ)dē-'prō-ˌgram, -grəm\ *vb* : to dissuade from convictions usu. of a religious nature often by coercive means

dept *abbr* department

depth \'depth\ *n, pl* **depths** \'depths\ **1** : something that is deep; *esp* : the deep part of a body of water **2** : a part that is far from the outside or surface; *also* : the middle or innermost part **3** : ABYSS **4** : a profound or intense state ⟨the ∼s of reflection⟩; *also* : the worst part ⟨during the ∼s of the depression⟩ **5** : a reprehensibly low condition **6** : the distance from top to bottom or from front to back **7** : the quality of being deep **8** : the degree of intensity

depth charge *n* : an explosive device for use underwater esp. against submarines

dep·u·ta·tion \ˌde-pyə-'tā-shən\ *n* **1** : the act of appointing a deputy **2** : DELEGATION

de·pute \di-'pyüt\ *vb* **de·put·ed; de·put·ing** : DELEGATE

dep·u·tize \'de-pyə-ˌtīz\ *vb* **-tized; -tiz·ing** : to appoint or act as deputy

dep·u·ty \'de-pyə-tē\ *n, pl* **-ties 1** : a person appointed to act for or in place of another **2** : an assistant empowered to act as a substitute in the absence of a superior **3** : a member of a lower house of a legislative assembly

der *or* **deriv** *abbr* derivation; derivative

de·rail \di-'rāl\ *vb* : to leave or cause to leave the rails — **de·rail·ment** *n*

de·rail·leur \di-'rā-lər\ *n* [F *dérailleur*] : a device for shifting gears on a bicycle by moving the chain from one set of exposed gears to another

de·range \di-'rānj\ *vb* **de·ranged; de·rang·ing 1** : DISARRANGE, UPSET **2** : to make insane — **de·range·ment** *n*

der·by \'dər-bē, *Brit* 'där-\ *n, pl* **derbies 1** : a horse race usu. for three-year-olds held annually **2** : a race or contest open to all **3** : a stiff felt hat with dome-shaped crown and narrow brim

derby 3

de·reg·u·la·tion \(ˌ)dē-ˌre-gyu̇-'lā-shən\ *n* : the act of removing restrictions or regulations — **de·reg·u·late** \-'re-gyu̇-ˌlāt\ *vb*

¹der·e·lict \'der-ə-ˌlikt\ *adj* **1** : abandoned by the owner or occupant **2** : NEGLIGENT ⟨∼ in his duty⟩

²derelict *n* **1** : something voluntarily abandoned; *esp* : a ship abandoned on the high seas **2** : a destitute homeless social misfit : VAGRANT, BUM

der·e·lic·tion \ˌder-ə-'lik-shən\ *n* **1** : the act of abandoning : the state of being abandoned **2** : a failure in duty

de·ride \di-'rīd\ *vb* **de·rid·ed; de·rid·ing** [L *deridēre*, fr. *ridēre* to laugh] : to laugh at scornfully : RIDICULE

de ri·gueur \də-rē-'gər\ *adj* [F] : prescribed or required by fashion, etiquette, or custom : PROPER

de·ri·sion \də-'ri-zhən\ *n* : RIDICULE — **de·ri·sive** \-'rī-siv\ *adj* — **de·ri·sive·ly** *adv* — **de·ri·sive·ness** *n* — **de·ri·so·ry** \-'rī-sə-rē\ *adj*

der·i·va·tion \,der-ə-'vā-shən\ *n* **1** : the formation of a word from an earlier word or root; *also* : an act of ascertaining or stating the derivation of a word **2** : ETYMOLOGY **3** : SOURCE, ORIGIN; *also* : DESCENT **4** : an act or process of deriving

de·riv·a·tive \di-'ri-və-tiv\ *n* **1** : a word formed by derivation **2** : something derived — **derivative** *adj*

de·rive \di-'rīv\ *vb* **de·rived; de·riv·ing** [ME, fr. MF *deriver*, fr. L *derivare*, lit., to draw off (water), fr. *de-* from + *rivus* stream] **1** : to receive or obtain from a source **2** : to obtain from a parent substance **3** : INFER, DEDUCE **4** : to trace the derivation of **5** : to come from a certain source

der·mal \'dər-məl\ *adj* : of or relating to the skin : CUTANEOUS

der·ma·ti·tis \,dər-mə-'tī-təs\ *n* : skin inflammation

der·ma·tol·o·gy \-'tä-lə-jē\ *n* : a branch of medical science dealing with the structure, functions, and diseases of the skin — **der·ma·tol·o·gist** \-jist\ *n*

der·mis \'dər-məs\ *n* : the sensitive vascular inner layer of the skin

der·o·gate \'der-ə-,gāt\ *vb* **-gat·ed; -gat·ing 1** : to cause to seem inferior : DISPARAGE **2** : DETRACT — **der·o·ga·tion** \,der-ə-'gā-shən\ *n* — **de·ro·ga·tive** \di-'rä-gə-tiv\ *adj*

de·rog·a·to·ry \di-'rä-gə-,tòr-ē\ *adj* : intended to lower the reputation of a person or thing : DISPARAGING — **de·rog·a·to·ri·ly** \-,rä-gə-'tòr-ə-lē\ *adv*

der·rick \'der-ik\ *n* [obs. *derrick* hangman, gallows, fr. *Derick*, name of 17th cent. Eng. hangman] **1** : a hoisting apparatus : CRANE **2** : a framework over a drill hole (as for oil) for supporting machinery

der·ri·ere *or* **der·ri·ère** \,der-ē-'er\ *n* : BUTTOCKS

der·ring–do \,der-iŋ-'dü\ *n* : DARING

der·rin·ger \'der-ən-jər\ *n* : a short-barreled pocket pistol

der·vish \'dər-vish\ *n* [Turk *derviş*, lit., beggar, fr. Per *darvīsh*] : a member of a Muslim religious order noted for devotional exercises (as bodily movements leading to a trance)

de·sal·i·nate \dē-'sa-lə-,nāt\ *vb* **-nat·ed; -nat·ing** : DESALT — **de·sal·i·na·tion** \-,sa-lə-'nā-shən\ *n*

de·sal·i·nize \dē-'sa-lə-,nīz\ *vb* **-nized; -niz·ing** : DESALT — **de·sal·i·ni·za·tion** \-,sa-lə-nə-'zā-shən\ *n*

de·salt \dē-'sòlt\ *vb* : to remove salt from ⟨∼ seawater⟩ — **de·salt·er** *n*

des·cant \'des-,kant\ *vb* **1** : to sing or play part music : SING **2** : to discourse or write at length

de·scend \di-'send\ *vb* **1** : to pass from a higher to a lower place or level : pass, move, or climb down or down along **2** : DERIVE ⟨∼ed from royalty⟩ **3** : to pass by inheritance or transmission **4** : to incline, lead, or extend downward **5** : to swoop down or appear suddenly (as in an attack)

¹de·scen·dant *or* **de·scen·dent** \di-'sen-dənt\ *adj* **1** : DESCENDING **2** : proceeding from an ancestor or source

²descendant *or* **descendent** *n* **1** : one descended from another or from a common stock **2** : one deriving directly from a precursor or prototype

de·scent \di-'sent\ *n* **1** : ANCESTRY, BIRTH, LINEAGE **2** : the act or process of descending **3** : SLOPE **4** : a descending way (as a downgrade) **5** : a sudden hostile raid or assault **6** : a downward step (as in station or value) : DECLINE

de·scribe \di-'skrīb\ *vb* **de·scribed; de·scrib·ing 1** : to represent or give an account of in words **2** : to trace the outline of — **de·scrib·able** *adj*

de·scrip·tion \di-'skrip-shən\ *n* **1** : an account of something; *esp* : an account that presents a picture to a person who reads or hears it **2** : KIND, SORT — **de·scrip·tive** \-'skrip-tiv\ *adj*

de·scry \di-'skrī\ *vb* **de·scried; de·scry·ing 1** : to catch sight of **2** : to discover by observation or investigation

des·e·crate \'de-si-,krāt\ *vb* **-crat·ed; -crat·ing** : PROFANE — **des·e·cra·tion** \,de-si-'krā-shən\ *n*

de·seg·re·gate \dē-'se-gri-,gāt\ *vb* : to eliminate segregation in; *esp* : to free of any law or practice requiring isolation on the basis of race — **de·seg·re·ga·tion** \-,se-gri-'gā-shən\ *n*

de·sen·si·tize \dē-'sen-sə-,tīz\ *vb* : to make (a sensitized or hypersensitive individual) insensitive or nonreactive to a sensitizing agent — **de·sen·si·ti·za·tion** \-,sen-sə-tə-'zā-shən\ *n*

¹des·ert \'de-zərt\ *n* : dry land with few plants and little rainfall

²des·ert \'de-zərt\ *adj* : of, relating to, or resembling a desert; *esp* : being barren and without life ⟨a ∼ island⟩

³de·sert \di-'zərt\ *n* **1** : deserving of reward or punishment **2** : a just reward or punishment

⁴de·sert \di-'zərt\ *vb* **1** : to withdraw from **2** : ABANDON, FORSAKE — **de·sert·er** *n* — **de·ser·tion** \-'zər-shən\ *n*

de·serve \di-'zərv\ *vb* **de·served; de·serv·ing** : to be worthy of : MERIT — **de·serv·ing** *adj*

de·serv·ed·ly \-'zər-vəd-lē\ *adv* : according to merit : JUSTLY

des·ic·cate \'de-si-,kāt\ *vb* **-cat·ed; -cat·ing** : DRY, DEHYDRATE — **des·ic·ca·tion** \,de-si-'kā-shən\ *n* — **des·ic·ca·tor** \'de-si-,kā-tər\ *n*

de·sid·er·a·tum \di-,si-də-'rä-təm, -,zi-, -'rā-\ *n, pl* **-ta** \-tə\ [L] : something desired as essential

¹de·sign \di-'zīn\ *vb* **1** : to conceive and plan out in the mind **2** : INTEND **3** : to devise for a specific function or end **4** : to make a pattern or sketch of **5** : to conceive and draw the plans for

²design *n* **1** : a particular purpose : deliberate planning **2** : a mental project or scheme : PLAN **3** : a secret project or scheme : PLOT **4** *pl* : aggressive or evil intent — used with *on* or *against* **5** : a preliminary sketch or plan **6** : an underlying scheme that governs functioning, developing, or unfolding : MOTIF **7** : the arrangement of elements or details in a product or a work of art **8** : a decorative pattern **9** : the art of executing designs

¹des·ig·nate \'de-zig-,nāt, -nət\ *adj* : chosen but not yet installed ⟨ambassador ∼⟩

²des·ig·nate \-,nāt\ *vb* **-nat·ed; -nat·ing 1** : to appoint and set apart for a special purpose **2** : to mark or point out : INDICATE; *also* : SPECIFY, STIPULATE **3** : to call by a name or title — **des·ig·na·tion** \,de-zig-'nā-shən\ *n*

designated hitter *n* : a baseball player designated at the start of the game to bat in place of the pitcher without causing the pitcher to be removed from the game

de·sign·er \di-'zī-nər\ *n* **1** : one who creates plans for a project or structure **2** : one who designs and manufactures high-fashion clothing — **designer** *adj*

de·sign·ing \di-'zī-niŋ\ *adj* : CRAFTY, SCHEMING

de·sir·able \di-'zī-rə-bəl\ *adj* **1** : PLEASING, ATTRACTIVE **2** : ADVISABLE ⟨∼ legislation⟩ — **de·sir·abil·i·ty** \-,zī-rə-'bi-lə-tē\ *n* — **de·sir·able·ness** *n*

¹de·sire \di-'zīr\ *vb* **de·sired; de·sir·ing** [ME, fr. OF *desirer*, fr. L *desiderare*, fr. *sider-*, *sidus* heavenly body] **1** : to long or hope for : exhibit or feel desire for **2** : REQUEST

²desire *n* **1** : a strong wish : LONGING, CRAVING **2** : sexual urge or appetite **3** : a usu. formal request for action **4** : something desired

de·sir·ous \di-'zīr-əs\ *adj* : eagerly wishing : DESIRING

de·sist \di-'zist, -'sist\ *vb* : to cease to proceed or act

desk \'desk\ *n* [ME *deske*, fr. ML *desca*, fr. OIt *desco* table, fr. L *discus* dish, disc] **1** : a table, frame, or case esp. for writing and reading **2** : a counter, stand, or booth at which a person performs duties **3** : a specialized division of an organization (as a newspaper) ⟨city ∼⟩

desk·top publishing \'desk-ˌtäp-\ *n* : the production of printed matter by means of a microcomputer

¹**des·o·late** \'de-sə-lət, -zə-\ *adj* 1 : DESERTED, ABANDONED 2 : FORSAKEN, LONELY 3 : DILAPIDATED 4 : BARREN, LIFELESS 5 : CHEERLESS, GLOOMY — **des·o·late·ly** *adv* — **des·o·late·ness** *n*

²**des·o·late** \-ˌlāt\ *vb* **-lat·ed; -lat·ing** : to make desolate : lay waste : make wretched

des·o·la·tion \ˌde-sə-'lā-shən, -zə-\ *n* 1 : the action of desolating 2 : GRIEF, SADNESS 3 : LONELINESS 4 : DEVASTATION, RUIN 5 : barren wasteland

des·oxy·ri·bo·nu·cle·ic acid \de-ˌzäk-sē-'rī-bȯ-nü-ˌklē-ik-, -nyü-\ *n* : DNA

¹**de·spair** \di-'spar\ *vb* : to lose all hope or confidence — **de·spair·ing·ly** *adv*

²**despair** *n* 1 : utter loss of hope 2 : a cause of hopelessness

des·patch \dis-'pach\ *var of* DISPATCH

des·per·a·do \ˌdes-pə-'rä-dȯ, -'rā-\ *n, pl* **-does** *or* **-dos** : a bold or reckless criminal

des·per·ate \'des-pə-rət, -prət\ *adj* 1 : being beyond or almost beyond hope : causing despair 2 : RASH 3 : extremely intense — **des·per·ate·ly** *adv* — **des·per·ate·ness** *n*

des·per·a·tion \ˌdes-pə-'rā-shən\ *n* 1 : a loss of hope and surrender to despair 2 : a state of hopelessness leading to rashness

de·spi·ca·ble \di-'spi-kə-bəl, 'des-pi-\ *adj* : deserving to be despised — **de·spi·ca·bly** \ blō\ *adv*

de·spise \di-'spīz\ *vb* **de·spised; de·spis·ing** 1 : to look down on with contempt or aversion : DISDAIN, DETEST 2 : to regard as negligible, worthless, or distasteful

de·spite \di-'spīt\ *prep* : in spite of

de·spoil \di-'spȯil\ *vb* : to strip of belongings, possessions, or value — **de·spoil·er** *n* — **de·spoil·ment** *n*

de·spo·li·a·tion \di-ˌspȯ-lē-'ā-shən\ *n* : the act of plundering : the state of being despoiled

¹**de·spond** \di-'spänd\ *vb* : to become discouraged or disheartened

²**despond** *n* : DESPONDENCY

de·spon·den·cy \-'spän-dən-sē\ *n* : DEJECTION, HOPELESSNESS — **de·spon·dent** \-dənt\ *adj* — **de·spon·dent·ly** *adv*

des·pot \'des-pət, -ˌpät\ *n* [MF *despote,* fr. Gk *despotēs* master, lord, autocrat] 1 : a ruler with absolute power and authority 2 : a person exercising power tyrannically — **des·pot·ic** \des-'pä-tik\ *adj* — **des·po·tism** \'des-pə-ˌti-zəm\ *n*

des·sert \di-'zərt\ *n* : a course of sweet food, fruit, or cheese served at the close of a meal

des·ti·na·tion \ˌdes-tə-'nā-shən\ *n* 1 : a purpose for which something is destined 2 : an act of appointing, setting aside for a purpose, or predetermining 3 : a place to which one is journeying or to which something is sent

des·tine \'des-tən\ *vb* **des·tined; des·tin·ing** 1 : to settle in advance 2 : to designate, assign, or dedicate in advance 3 : to direct or set apart for a specific purpose or place

des·ti·ny \'des-tə-nē\ *n, pl* **-nies** 1 : something to which a person or thing is destined : FATE, FORTUNE 2 : a predetermined course of events

des·ti·tute \'des-tə-ˌtüt, -ˌtyüt\ *adj* 1 : lacking something needed or desirable 2 : suffering extreme poverty — **des·ti·tu·tion** \ˌdes-tə-'tü-shən, -'tyü-\ *n*

de·stroy \di-'strȯi\ *vb* 1 : to put an end to : RUIN 2 : KILL

de·stroy·er \di-'strȯi-ər\ *n* 1 : one that destroys 2 : a small speedy warship

de·struc·ti·ble \di-'strək-tə-bəl\ *adj* : capable of being destroyed — **de·struc·ti·bil·i·ty** \-ˌstrək-tə-'bi-lə-tē\ *n*

de·struc·tion \di-'strək-shən\ *n* 1 : RUIN 2 : the action or process of destroying something 3 : a destroying agency

de·struc·tive \di-'strək-tiv\ *adj* 1 : causing destruction : RUINOUS 2 : designed or tending to destroy — **de·struc·tive·ly** *adv* — **de·struc·tive·ness** *n*

de·sue·tude \'de-swi-ˌtüd, -ˌtyüd\ *n* : DISUSE

des·ul·to·ry \'de-səl-ˌtȯr-ē\ *adj* : passing aimlessly from one thing or subject to another : DISCONNECTED

det *abbr* 1 detached; detachment 2 detail

de·tach \di-'tach\ *vb* 1 : to separate esp. from a larger mass 2 : DISENGAGE, WITHDRAW — **de·tach·able** *adj*

de·tached \di-'tacht\ *adj* 1 : not joined or connected : SEPARATE 2 : ALOOF, IMPARTIAL ⟨a ∼ attitude⟩

de·tach·ment \di-'tach-mənt\ *n* 1 : SEPARATION 2 : the dispatching of a body of troops or part of a fleet from the main body for special service; *also* : the portion so dispatched 3 : a small permanent military unit of special composition 4 : indifference to worldly concerns : ALOOFNESS 5 : IMPARTIALITY

¹**de·tail** \di-'tāl, 'dē-ˌtāl\ *n* [F *détail,* fr. OF *detail* slice, piece, fr. *detaillier* to cut in pieces, fr. *taillier* to cut] 1 : a dealing with something item by item ⟨go into ∼⟩; *also* : ITEM, PARTICULAR ⟨the ∼*s* of a story⟩ 2 : selection (as of soldiers) for special duty; *also* : the persons thus selected

²**detail** *vb* 1 : to report in particulars : SPECIFY 2 : to assign to a special duty

de·tailed \di-'tāld, 'dē-ˌtāld\ *adj* : marked by abundant detail

de·tain \di-'tān\ *vb* 1 : to hold in or as if in custody 2 : STOP, DELAY

de·tect \di-'tekt\ *vb* : to discover the nature, existence, presence, or fact of — **de·tect·able** *adj* — **de·tec·tion** \-'tek-shən\ *n* — **de·tec·tor** \-'tek-tər\ *n*

¹**de·tec·tive** \di-'tek-tiv\ *adj* 1 : fitted or used for detection 2 : of or relating to detectives

²**detective** *n* : a person employed or engaged in detecting lawbreakers or getting information that is not readily accessible

dé·tente \dā-'tänt\ *n* [F] : a relaxation of strained relations or tensions (as between nations)

de·ten·tion \di-'ten-chən\ *n* 1 : the act or fact of detaining : CONFINEMENT; *esp* : a period of temporary custody prior to disposition by a court 2 : a forced delay

de·ter \di-'tər\ *vb* **de·terred; de·ter·ring** [L *deterrēre,* fr. *terrēre* to frighten] 1 : to turn aside, discourage, or prevent from acting (as by fear) 2 : INHIBIT

de·ter·gent \di-'tər-jənt\ *n* : a cleansing agent; *esp* : a chemical product similar to soap in its cleaning ability

de·te·ri·o·rate \di-'tir-ē-ə-ˌrāt\ *vb* **-rat·ed; -rat·ing** : to make or become worse in quality or condition — **de·te·ri·o·ra·tion** \-ˌtir-ē-ə-'rā-shən\ *n*

de·ter·min·able \-'tər-mə-nə-bəl\ *adj* : capable of being determined; *esp* : ASCERTAINABLE

de·ter·mi·nant \-mə-nənt\ *n* 1 : something that determines or conditions 2 : GENE

de·ter·mi·nate \di-'tər-mə-nət\ *adj* 1 : having fixed limits : DEFINITE 2 : definitely settled — **de·ter·mi·nate·ness** *n*

de·ter·mi·na·tion \di-ˌtər-mə-'nā-shən\ *n* 1 : the act of coming to a decision; *also* : the decision or conclusion reached 2 : a fixing of the extent, position, or character of something 3 : accurate measurement (as of length or volume) 4 : firm or fixed purpose

de·ter·mine \di-'tər-mən\ *vb* **-mined; -min·ing** 1 : to fix conclusively or authoritatively 2 : to come to a decision : SETTLE, RESOLVE 3 : to fix the form or character of beforehand : ORDAIN; *also* : REGULATE 4 : to find out the limits, nature, dimensions, or scope of ⟨∼ a position at sea⟩ 5 : to bring about as a result

---

\ə\abut \ᵊ\kitten \ər\further \a\ash \ā\ace \ä\mop, mar \aů\out \ch\chin \e\bet \ē\easy \g\go \i\hit \ī\ice \j\job \ŋ\sing \ō\go \ȯ\law \ȯi\boy \th\thin \t̲h̲\the \ü\loot \ů\foot \y\yet \zh\vision *see also* Pronunciation Symbols page

de·ter·mined \-ˈtər-mənd\ *adj* **1** : firmly resolved **2** : characterized by or showing determination — **de·ter·mined·ly** \-mənd-lē, -mə-nəd-lē\ *adv* — **de·ter·mined·ness** *n*

de·ter·min·ism \di-ˈtər-mə-ˌni-zəm\ *n* : a doctrine that acts of the will, natural events, or social changes are determined by preceding events or natural causes — **de·ter·min·ist** \-nist\ *n or adj*

de·ter·rence \di-ˈtər-əns\ *n* : the inhibition of criminal behavior by fear esp. of punishment

de·ter·rent \-ənt\ *adj* **1** : serving to deter **2** : relating to deterrence — **deterrent** *n*

de·test \di-ˈtest\ *vb* [L *detestari*, lit., to curse while calling a deity to witness, fr. *de-* from + *testari* to call to witness] : LOATHE, HATE — **de·test·able** *adj* — **de·tes·ta·tion** \ˌdē-ˌtes-ˈtā-shən\ *n*

de·throne \di-ˈthrōn\ *vb* : to remove from a throne : DEPOSE — **de·throne·ment** *n*

det·o·nate \ˈdet-ᵊn-ˌāt\ *vb* **-nat·ed; -nat·ing** : to explode or cause to explode with violence — **det·o·na·tion** \ˌdet-ᵊn-ˈā-shən\ *n*

det·o·na·tor \ˈdet-ᵊn-ˌā-tər\ *n* : a device for detonating an explosive

¹de·tour \ˈdē-ˌtu̇r\ *n* : an indirect way replacing part of a route

²detour *vb* : to go by detour

de·tox \ˈdē-ˌtäks, di-ˈtäks\ *n* : detoxification from a substance (as alcohol) — **detox** *vb*

de·tox·i·fy \dē-ˈtäk-sə-ˌfī\ *vb* **-fied; -fy·ing** **1** : to remove a poison or toxin or the effect of such from **2** : to free (as a drug user) from an intoxicating or addictive substance or from dependence on it — **de·tox·i·fi·ca·tion** \dē-ˌtäk-sə-fə-ˈkā-shən\ *n*

de·tract \di-ˈtrakt\ *vb* **1** : to take away or diminish the value or effect of something **2** : DIVERT — **de·trac·tion** \-ˈtrak-shən\ *n* — **de·trac·tor** \-ˈtrak-tər\ *n*

de·train \dē-ˈtrān\ *vb* : to leave or cause to leave a railroad train

det·ri·ment \ˈde-trə-mənt\ *n* : INJURY, DAMAGE; *also* : a cause of injury or damage — **det·ri·men·tal** \ˌde-trə-ˈment-ᵊl\ *adj* — **det·ri·men·tal·ly** *adv*

de·tri·tus \di-ˈtrī-təs\ *n, pl* **de·tri·tus** : fragments resulting from disintegration (as of rocks) : DEBRIS

deuce \ˈdüs, ˈdyüs\ *n* **1** : a two in cards or dice **2** : a tie in a tennis game with both sides at 40 **3** : DEVIL — used chiefly as a mild oath

Deut *abbr* Deuteronomy

deu·te·ri·um \dü-ˈtir-ē-əm, dyü-\ *n* : an isotope of hydrogen that has twice the mass of ordinary hydrogen

Deu·ter·on·o·my \ˌdü-tə-ˈrä-nə-mē, ˌdyü-\ *n* — see BIBLE table

deut·sche mark \ˈdȯi-chə-ˌmärk\ *n* — see MONEY table

dev *abbr* deviation

de·val·ue \dē-ˈval-yü\ *vb* : to reduce the international exchange value of ⟨∼ a currency⟩ — **de·val·u·a·tion** \-ˌval-yə-ˈwā-shən\ *n*

dev·as·tate \ˈde-və-ˌstāt\ *vb* **-tat·ed; -tat·ing** **1** : to bring to ruin **2** : to reduce to chaos or helplessness — **dev·as·ta·tion** \ˌde-və-ˈstā-shən\ *n*

de·vel·op \di-ˈve-ləp\ *vb* **1** : to unfold gradually or in detail **2** : to place (exposed photographic material) in chemicals to produce a visible image **3** : to bring out the possibilities of **4** : to make more available or usable ⟨∼ land⟩ **5** : to acquire gradually ⟨∼ a taste for olives⟩ **6** : to go through a natural process of growth, differentiation, or evolution **7** : to come into being gradually — **de·vel·op·er** *n* — **de·vel·op·ment** *n* — **de·vel·op·men·tal** \-ˌve-ləp-ˈment-ᵊl\ *adj*

de·vi·ant \ˈdē-vē-ənt\ *adj* : deviating esp. from some accepted norm ⟨∼ behavior⟩ — **de·vi·ance** \-əns\ *n* — **de·vi·an·cy** \-ən-sē\ *n* — **deviant** *n*

de·vi·ate \ˈdē-vē-ˌāt\ *vb* **-at·ed; -at·ing** [LL *deviare*, fr. L *de-* from + *via* way] : to turn aside from a course,

standard, principle, or topic — **de·vi·ate** \-vē-ət, -vē-ˌāt\ *n* — **de·vi·a·tion** \ˌdē-vē-ˈā-shən\ *n*

de·vice \di-ˈvīs\ *n* **1** : SCHEME, STRATAGEM **2** : a piece of equipment or a mechanism for a special purpose **3** : DESIRE, INCLINATION ⟨left to my own ∼s⟩ **4** : an emblematic design

¹dev·il \ˈde-vəl\ *n* [ME *devel*, fr. OE *dēofol*, fr. LL *diabolus*, fr. Gk *diabolos*, lit., slanderer, fr. *diaballein* to throw across, slander, fr. *dia-* across + *ballein* to throw] **1** *often cap* : the personal supreme spirit of evil **2** : DEMON **3** : a wicked person **4** : an energetic, reckless, or dashing person **5** : FELLOW ⟨poor ∼⟩ ⟨lucky ∼⟩

²devil *vb* **-iled** *or* **-illed; -il·ing** *or* **-il·ling** **1** : to season highly ⟨∼ed eggs⟩ **2** : TEASE, ANNOY

dev·il·ish \ˈde-və-lish\ *adj* **1** : befitting a devil : EVIL; *also* : MISCHIEVOUS **2** : EXTREME — **dev·il·ish·ly** *adv* — **dev·il·ish·ness** *n*

dev·il·ment \ˈde-vəl-mənt, -ˌment\ *n* : MISCHIEF

dev·il·ry \-rē\ *or* **dev·il·try** \-trē\ *n, pl* **-il·ries** *or* **-il·tries** **1** : action performed with the help of the devil **2** : MISCHIEF

de·vi·ous \ˈdē-vē-əs\ *adj* **1** : deviating from a straight line : ROUNDABOUT **2** : ERRANT **3 3** : TRICKY, CUNNING

¹de·vise \di-ˈvīz\ *vb* **de·vised; de·vis·ing** **1** : INVENT **2** : PLOT **3** : to give (real estate) by will

²devise *n* **1** : a disposing of real property by will **2** : a will or clause of a will disposing of real property **3** : property given by will

de·vi·tal·ize \dē-ˈvīt-ᵊl-ˌīz\ *vb* : to deprive of life or vitality

de·void \di-ˈvȯid\ *adj* : being without : VOID ⟨a book ∼ of interest⟩

de·voir \də-ˈvwär\ *n* **1** : DUTY **2** : a formal act of civility or respect

de·volve \di-ˈvälv\ *vb* **de·volved; de·volv·ing** : to pass (as rights or responsibility) from one to another usu. by succession or transmission — **dev·o·lu·tion** \ˌde-və-ˈlü-shən, ˌdē-\ *n*

De·vo·ni·an \di-ˈvō-nē-ən\ *adj* : of, relating to, or being the period of the Paleozoic era between the Silurian and the Mississippian — **Devonian** *n*

de·vote \di-ˈvōt\ *vb* **de·vot·ed; de·vot·ing** **1** : to commit to wholly or chiefly **2** : to set apart for a special purpose : DEDICATE

de·vot·ed \-ˈvō-təd\ *adj* : characterized by loyalty and devotion : FAITHFUL

dev·o·tee \ˌde-və-ˈtē, -ˈtā\ *n* : an ardent follower, supporter, or enthusiast

de·vo·tion \di-ˈvō-shən\ *n* **1** : religious fervor **2** : an act of prayer or private worship — usu. used in pl. **3** : a religious exercise for private use **4** : the fact or state of being dedicated and loyal ⟨∼ to music⟩; *also* : the act of devoting — **de·vo·tion·al** \-shə-nəl\ *adj*

de·vour \di-ˈvau̇r\ *vb* **1** : to eat up greedily or ravenously **2** : WASTE, ANNIHILATE **3** : to enjoy avidly ⟨∼ a book⟩ — **de·vour·er** *n*

de·vout \di-ˈvau̇t\ *adj* **1** : devoted to religion : PIOUS **2** : expressing devotion or piety **3** : EARNEST, SERIOUS — **de·vout·ly** *adv* — **de·vout·ness** *n*

dew \ˈdü, ˈdyü\ *n* : moisture that condenses on the surfaces of cool bodies at night — **dewy** *adj*

dew·ber·ry \ˈdü-ˌber-ē, ˈdyü-\ *n* : any of several sweet edible berries related to and resembling blackberries; *also* : a trailing bramble bearing these

dew·claw \-ˌklȯ\ *n* : a digit on the foot of a mammal that does not reach the ground; *also* : its claw or hoof

dew·lap \-ˌlap\ *n* : loose skin hanging under the neck of an animal

dew point *n* : the temperature at which the moisture in the air begins to condense

dex·ter·i·ty \dek-ˈster-ə-tē\ *n, pl* **-ties** **1** : mental skill or quickness **2** : readiness and grace in physical activity; *esp* : skill and ease in using the hands

dex·ter·ous \'dek-strəs\ *adj* **1** : CLEVER **2** : done with skillfulness **3** : skillful and competent with the hands — **dex·ter·ous·ly** *adv*

dex·trose \'dek-ˌstrōs\ *n* : the naturally occurring form of glucose found in plants and blood

DFC *abbr* Distinguished Flying Cross

dg *abbr* decigram

DG *abbr* **1** [LL *Dei gratia*] by the grace of God **2** director general

DH \ˌdē-'āch\ *n* : DESIGNATED HITTER

dhow \'daů\ *n* : an Arab sailing ship usu. having a long overhang forward and a high poop

Dhu'l-Hij·ja \ˌdül-hi-(ˌ)jä, ˌthül-\ *n* [Ar *Dhū-l-hijjah*, lit., the one of pilgrimage] : the 12th month of the Islamic year

Dhu'l-Qa'·dah \ˌdül-'kä-dä, ˌthül-\ *n* [Ar *Dhū-l-qa'dah*, lit., the one of the sitting] : the 11th month of the Islamic year

DI *abbr* drill instructor

dia *abbr* diameter

di·a·be·tes \ˌdī-ə-'bē-tēz, -təs\ *n* : an abnormal state marked by passage of excessive amounts of urine; *esp* : one (**diabetes mel·li·tus** \-'me-lə-təs\) characterized by deficient insulin, by excess sugar in the blood and urine, and by thirst, hunger, and loss of weight — **di·a·bet·ic** \-'be-tik\ *adj or n*

di·a·bol·ic \ˌdī-ə-'bä-lik\ *or* **di·a·bol·i·cal** \-li-kəl\ *adj* : DEVILISH, FIENDISH — **di·a·bol·i·cal·ly** \-k(ə-)lē\ *adv*

di·a·crit·ic \ˌdī-ə-'kri-tik\ *n* : a mark accompanying a letter and indicating a sound value different from that of the same letter when unmarked — **di·a·crit·i·cal** \-ti-kəl\ *adj*

di·a·dem \'dī-ə-ˌdem\ *n* : CROWN; *esp* : a royal headband

di·aer·e·sis \dī-'er-ə-səs\ *n, pl* **-e·ses** \-ˌsēz\ : a mark '' placed over a vowel to show that it is pronounced in a separate syllable (as in *naïve*)

diag *abbr* **1** diagonal **2** diagram

di·ag·no·sis \ˌdī-ig-'nō-səs\ *n, pl* **-no·ses** \-ˌsēz\ : the art or act of identifying a disease from its signs and symptoms; *also* : the decision reached by diagnosis — **di·ag·nose** \'dī-ig-ˌnōs\ *vb* — **di·ag·nos·tic** \ˌdī-ig-'näs-tik\ *adj* — **di·ag·nos·ti·cian** \-ˌnäs-'ti-shən\ *n*

¹di·ag·o·nal \dī-'a-gə-nəl\ *adj* **1** : extending from one corner to the opposite corner in a 4-sided figure **2** : running in a slanting direction ⟨∼ stripes⟩ **3** : having slanting markings or parts ⟨a ∼ weave⟩ — **di·ag·o·nal·ly** *adv*

²diagonal *n* **1** : a diagonal line **2** : a diagonal row, pattern, or direction **3** : a mark / used esp. to mean "or," "and or," or "per"

¹di·a·gram \'dī-ə-ˌgram\ *n* : a design and esp. a drawing that makes something easier to understand — **di·a·gram·ma·ble** \-ˌgra-mə-bəl\ *adj* — **di·a·gram·mat·ic** \ˌdī-ə-grə-'ma-tik\ *adj* — **di·a·gram·mat·i·cal·ly** \-ti-k(ə-)lē\ *adv*

²diagram *vb* **-grammed** *or* **-gramed** \-ˌgramd\; **-gram·ming** *or* **-gram·ing** : to represent by a diagram

¹di·al \'dī(-ə)l\ *n* [ME *dyal*, fr. ML *dialis* clock wheel revolving daily, fr. L *dies* day] **1** : the face of a sundial **2** : the face of a timepiece **3** : a face with a pointer and numbers that indicate something ⟨the ∼ of a gauge⟩ **4** : a device used for making electrical connections or for regulating operation (as of a radio)

²dial *vb* **di·aled** *or* **di·alled**; **di·al·ing** *or* **di·al·ling** **1** : to manipulate a dial so as to operate or select **2** : to make a telephone call or connection

³dial *abbr* dialect

di·a·lect \'dī-ə-ˌlekt\ *n* : a regional variety of a language

di·a·lec·tic \ˌdī-ə-'lek-tik\ *n* : the process or art of reasoning by discussion of conflicting ideas; *also* : the tension between opposing elements

di·a·logue \'dī-ə-ˌlóg\ *n* **1** : a conversation between two or more parties **2** : the parts of a literary or dramatic work that represent conversation

di·al·y·sis \dī-'a-lə-səs\ *n, pl* **-y·ses** \-ˌsēz\ **1** : the separation of substances from solution by means of their unequal diffusion through semipermeable membranes **2** : the medical procedure of removing blood from an artery, purifying it by dialysis, and returning it to a vein

diam *abbr* diameter

di·am·e·ter \dī-'a-mə-tər\ *n* [ME *diametre*, fr. MF, fr. L *diametros*, fr. Gk, fr. *dia-* through + *metron* measure] **1** : a straight line passing through the center of a figure or body; *esp* : one that divides a circle in half **2** : the length of a diameter

di·a·met·ric \ˌdī-ə-'me-trik\ *or* **di·a·met·ri·cal** \-tri-kəl\ *adj* **1** : of, relating to, or constituting a diameter **2** : completely opposed or opposite — **di·a·met·ri·cal·ly** \-k(ə-)lē\ *adv*

di·a·mond \'dī-mənd, 'dī-ə-\ *n* **1** : a hard brilliant mineral that consists of crystalline carbon and is used as a gem **2** : a flat figure having four equal sides, two acute angles, and two obtuse angles **3** : any of a suit of playing cards marked with a red diamond **4** : INFIELD; *also* : the entire playing field in baseball

di·a·mond·back rattlesnake \-ˌbak-\ *n* : a large and deadly rattlesnake of the southern U.S.

di·an·thus \dī-'an-thəs\ *n* : ¹PINK 1

di·a·pa·son \ˌdī-ə-'pāz-ᵊn, -'pās-\ *n* **1** : the organ stop governing the flue pipes that form the primary basis of organ tone **2** : the entire range of musical tones

¹di·a·per \'dī-pər, 'dī-ə-\ *n* **1** : a cotton or linen fabric woven in a simple geometric pattern **2** : a garment for a baby drawn up between the legs and fastened about the waist

²diaper *vb* **1** : to ornament with diaper designs **2** : to put a diaper on

di·aph·a·nous \dī-'a-fə-nəs\ *adj* : of so fine a texture as to be transparent

di·a·pho·ret·ic \ˌdī-ə-fə-'re-tik\ *adj* : having the power to increase perspiration — **diaphoretic** *n*

di·a·phragm \'dī-ə-ˌfram\ *n* **1** : a sheet of muscle between the chest and abdominal cavities of a mammal **2** : a vibrating disk (as in a microphone) **3** : a cup-shaped device usu. of thin rubber fitted over the uterine cervix to act as a mechanical contraceptive barrier — **di·a·phrag·mat·ic** \ˌdī-ə-frəg-'ma-tik, -ˌfrag-\ *adj*

di·a·rist \'dī-ə-rist\ *n* : one who keeps a diary

di·ar·rhea \ˌdī-ə-'rē-ə\ *n* : abnormally frequent and watery bowel movements

di·ar·rhoea *chiefly Brit var of* DIARRHEA

di·a·ry \'dī-ə-rē\ *n, pl* **-ries** : a daily record esp. of personal experiences; *also* : a book used as a diary

di·as·to·le \dī-'as-tə-(ˌ)lē\ *n* : the stretching of the chambers of the heart during which they fill with blood — **di·a·stol·ic** \ˌdī-ə-'stä-lik\ *adj*

dia·ther·my \'dī-ə-ˌthər-mē\ *n* : the generation of heat in tissue by electric currents for medical or surgical purposes

di·a·tom \'dī-ə-ˌtäm\ *n* : any of a class of planktonic one-celled or colonial algae with skeletons of silica

di·atom·ic \ˌdī-ə-'tä-mik\ *adj* : having two atoms in the molecule

di·a·tribe \'dī-ə-ˌtrīb\ *n* : biting or abusive speech or writing

dib·ble \'di-bəl\ *n* : a pointed hand tool for making holes (as for planting bulbs) in the ground — **dibble** *vb*

¹dice \'dīs\ *n, pl* **dice** : DIE 1

²dice *vb* **diced; dic·ing** **1** : to cut into small cubes ⟨∼ carrots⟩ **2** : to play games with dice

di·chot·o·my \dī-'kä-tə-mē\ *n, pl* **-mies** : a division or the process of dividing into two esp. mutually exclusive or contradictory groups — **di·chot·o·mous** \-məs\ *adj*

dick·er \'di-kər\ *vb* : BARGAIN, HAGGLE

dick·ey *or* **dicky** \'di-kē\ *n, pl* **dickeys** *or* **dick·ies** : a small fabric insert worn to fill in the neckline

di·cot·y·le·don \ˌdī-ˌkät-ᵊl-'ēd-ᵊn\ *n* : any of a group of seed plants having an embryo with two cotyledons — **di·cot·y·le·don·ous** *adj*

dict *abbr* dictionary

¹**dic·tate** \'dik-ˌtāt\ *vb* **dic·tat·ed; dic·tat·ing 1** : to speak or read for a person to transcribe or for a machine to record **2** : COMMAND, ORDER — **dic·ta·tion** \dik-'tā-shən\ *n*

²**dic·tate** \'dik-ˌtāt\ *n* : an authoritative rule, prescription, or injunction : COMMAND ⟨the ∼s of conscience⟩

dic·ta·tor \'dik-ˌtā-tər\ *n* **1** : a person ruling absolutely and often brutally and oppressively **2** : one that dictates

dic·ta·to·ri·al \ˌdik-tə-'tor-ē-əl\ *adj* : of, relating to, or characteristic of a dictator or a dictatorship

dic·ta·tor·ship \dik-'tā-tər-ˌship, 'dik-ˌtā-\ *n* **1** : the office of a dictator **2** : autocratic rule, control, or leadership **3** : a government or country in which absolute power is held by a dictator or a small clique

dic·tion \'dik-shən\ *n* **1** : choice of words esp. with regard to correctness, clearness, or effectiveness : WORDING **2** : ENUNCIATION

dic·tio·nary \'dik-shə-ˌner-ē\ *n, pl* **-nar·ies** : a reference book containing words usu. alphabetically arranged along with information about their forms, pronunciations, functions, etymologies, meanings, and syntactical and idiomatic uses

dic·tum \'dik-təm\ *n, pl* **dic·ta** \-tə\ *also* **dictums** : a noteworthy, formal, or authoritative statement or observation

did *past of* DO

di·dac·tic \dī-'dak-tik\ *adj* **1** : intended to instruct, inform, or teach a moral lesson **2** : making moral observations

di·do \'dī-dò\ *n, pl* **didoes** *or* **didos** : a mischievous act : PRANK

¹**die** \'dī\ *vb* **died; dy·ing** \'dī-iŋ\ **1** : to stop living : EXPIRE **2** : to pass out of existence ⟨a *dying* race⟩ **3** : SUBSIDE **4** ⟨the wind *died* down⟩ **4** : to long keenly ⟨*dying* to go⟩ **5** : STOP ⟨the motor *died*⟩

²**die** \'dī\ *n* **1** *pl* **dice** \'dīs\ : a small cube marked on each face with one to six spots and used usu. in pairs in games and gambling **2** *pl* **dies** \'dīz\ : a device used to shape, finish, or impress an object

die·hard \'dī-ˌhärd\ *n* : one who is strongly devoted or determined

die·sel \'dē-zəl, -səl\ *n* **1** : DIESEL ENGINE **2** : a vehicle driven by a diesel engine

diesel engine *n* : an internal combustion engine in whose cylinders air is compressed to a temperature sufficiently high to ignite the fuel

die·sel·ing \'dē-zə-liŋ\ *n* : the continued operation of an internal combustion engine after the ignition has been turned off

¹**di·et** \'dī-ət\ *n* [ME *diete*, fr. OF, fr. L *diaeta*, fr. Gk *diaita*, lit., manner of living, fr. *diaitasthai* to lead one's life] **1** : food and drink regularly consumed : FARE **2** : an allowance of food prescribed for a special reason (as to lose weight) — **di·e·tary** \-ə-ˌter-ē\ *adj or n*

²**diet** *vb* : to eat or cause to eat or drink less or according to a prescribed rule — **di·et·er** *n*

di·e·tet·ics \ˌdī-ə-'te-tiks\ *n sing or pl* : the science or art of applying the principles of nutrition to diet — **di·e·tet·ic** *adj*

di·e·ti·tian *or* **di·e·ti·cian** \ˌdī-ə-'ti-shən\ *n* : a specialist in dietetics

dif *or* **diff** *abbr* difference

dif·fer \'di-fər\ *vb* **dif·fered; dif·fer·ing 1** : to be unlike **2** : VARY **3** : DISAGREE

dif·fer·ence \'di-frəns, 'di-fə-\ *n* **1** : UNLIKENESS ⟨∼ in their looks⟩ **2** : distinction or discrimination in preference **3** : DISAGREEMENT; *also* : an instance or cause of disagreement ⟨unable to settle their ∼s⟩ **4** : the amount by which one number or quantity differs from another

dif·fer·ent \'di-frənt, 'di-fə-\ *adj* **1** : unlike in nature or quality **2** : DISTINCT ⟨∼ age groups⟩; *also* : VARIOUS ⟨∼ members of the club⟩ **3** : ANOTHER ⟨try a ∼ channel⟩ **4** : UNUSUAL, SPECIAL — **dif·fer·ent·ly** *adv*

¹**dif·fer·en·tial** \ˌdi-fə-'ren-chəl\ *adj* : showing, creating, or relating to a difference

²**differential** *n* **1** : the amount or degree by which things differ **2** : DIFFERENTIAL GEAR

differential calculus *n* : a branch of mathematics concerned with the study of the rate of change of functions with respect to their variables

differential gear *n* : an arrangement of gears in an automobile that allows one wheel to turn faster than another (as in rounding curves)

dif·fer·en·ti·ate \ˌdi-fə-'ren-chē-ˌāt\ *vb* **-at·ed; -at·ing 1** : to make or become different **2** : to recognize or state the difference ⟨∼ between them⟩ — **dif·fer·en·ti·a·tion** \-ˌren-chē-'ā-shən\ *n*

dif·fi·cult \'di-fi-(ˌ)kəlt\ *adj* **1** : hard to do or make **2** : hard to understand or deal with ⟨∼ reading⟩ ⟨a ∼ child⟩

dif·fi·cul·ty \-(ˌ)kəl-tē\ *n, pl* **-ties 1** : difficult nature ⟨the ∼ of a task⟩ **2** : DISAGREEMENT ⟨settled their *difficulties*⟩ **3** : OBSTACLE ⟨overcome *difficulties*⟩ **4** : TROUBLE ⟨in financial *difficulties*⟩ **syn** hardship, rigor, vicissitude

dif·fi·dent \'di-fə-dənt\ *adj* **1** : lacking confidence **2** : RESERVED 1 — **dif·fi·dence** \-dəns\ *n* — **dif·fi·dent·ly** *adv*

dif·frac·tion \di-'frak-shən\ *n* : the bending or spreading of waves (as of light) esp. when passing through narrow slits

¹**dif·fuse** \di-'fyüs\ *adj* **1** : VERBOSE, WORDY ⟨∼ writing⟩ **2** : not concentrated or localized ⟨∼ light⟩

²**dif·fuse** \di-'fyüz\ *vb* **dif·fused; dif·fus·ing 1** : to pour out or spread widely **2** : to undergo or cause to undergo diffusion **3** : to break up light by diffusion

dif·fu·sion \di-'fyü-zhən\ *n* **1** : a diffusing or a being diffused **2** : movement of particles (as of a gas) from a region of high to one of lower concentration **3** : the reflection of light from a rough surface or the passage of light through a translucent material

¹**dig** \'dig\ *vb* **dug** \'dəg\; **dig·ging 1** : to turn up the soil (as with a spade) **2** : to hollow out or form by removing earth ⟨∼ a hole⟩ **3** : to uncover or seek by turning up earth ⟨∼ potatoes⟩ **4** : DISCOVER ⟨∼ up information⟩ **5** : POKE, THRUST ⟨∼ a person in the ribs⟩ **6** : to work hard **7** : UNDERSTAND, APPRECIATE; *also* : LIKE, ADMIRE

²**dig** *n* **1** : THRUST, POKE; *also* : a cutting remark : GIBE **2** *pl* : living accommodations

³**dig** *abbr* digest

¹**di·gest** \'dī-ˌjest\ *n* : a summarized or shortened version esp. of a literary work

²**di·gest** \dī-'jest, də-\ *vb* **1** : to think over and arrange in the mind **2** : to convert (food) into simpler forms that can be absorbed by the body **3** : to compress into a short summary — **di·gest·ibil·i·ty** \-ˌjes-tə-'bi-lə-tē\ *n* — **di·gest·ible** *adj* — **di·ges·tion** \-'jes-chən\ *n* — **di·ges·tive** \-'jes-tiv\ *adj*

dig in *vb* **1** : to take a defensive stand esp. by digging trenches **2** : to firmly set to work **3** : to begin eating

dig·it \'di-jət\ *n* [ME, fr. L *digitus* finger, toe] **1** : any of the Arabic numerals 1 to 9 and usu. the symbol 0 **2** : FINGER, TOE

dig·i·tal \'di-jət-ᵊl\ *adj* **1** : of, relating to, or done with a finger or toe **2** : of, relating to, or using calculation directly with digits rather than through measurable physical quantities ⟨a ∼ computer⟩ **3** : providing a readout in numerical digits ⟨a ∼ watch⟩ — **dig·i·tal·ly** *adv*

dig·i·tal·is \ˌdi-jə-'ta-ləs\ *n* : a drug from the common

foxglove that is a powerful heart stimulant; *also* : FOX-
GLOVE

dig·ni·fied \'dig-nə-ˌfīd\ *adj* : showing or expressing
dignity

dig·ni·fy \-ˌfī\ *vb* **-fied; -fy·ing** : to give dignity, distinction, or attention to

dig·ni·tary \'dig-nə-ˌter-ē\ *n, pl* **-tar·ies** : a person of
high position or honor

dig·ni·ty \'dig-nə-tē\ *n, pl* **-ties 1** : the quality or state of
being worthy, honored, or esteemed **2** : high rank, office, or position **3** : formal reserve of manner, language,
or appearance

di·graph \'dī-ˌgraf\ *n* : a group of two successive letters
whose phonetic value is a single sound (as *ea* in *bread*)

di·gress \dī-'gres, də-\ *vb* : to turn aside esp. from the
main subject or argument — **di·gres·sion** \-'gre-shən\ *n*
— **di·gres·sive** \-'gre-siv\ *adj*

dike \'dīk\ *n* : a bank of earth constructed to control water : LEVEE

dil *abbr* dilute

di·lap·i·dat·ed \də-'la-pə-ˌdā-təd\ *adj* : fallen into partial ruin or decay — **di·lap·i·da·tion** \-ˌla-pə-'dā-shən\
n

di·late \dī-'lāt, 'dī-ˌlāt\ *vb* **di·lat·ed; di·lat·ing** : SWELL,
DISTEND, EXPAND — **dil·a·ta·tion** \ˌdi-lə-'tā-shən\ *n* —
di·la·tion \dī-'lā-shən\ *n*

dil·a·to·ry \'di-lə-ˌtȯr-ē\ *adj* **1** : DELAYING **2** : TARDY,
SLOW

di·lem·ma \də-'le-mə\ *n* **1** : a usu. undesirable or unpleasant choice; *also* : a situation involving such a
choice **2** : PREDICAMENT

dil·et·tante \ˌdi-lə-'tänt, -'tant\ *n, pl* **-tantes** *or* **-tan-
ti** \-'tän-tē, -'tan-\ [It, fr. prp. of *dilettare* to delight, fr.
L *dilectare*] : a person having a superficial interest in an
art or a branch of knowledge

dil·i·gent \'di-lə-jənt\ *adj* : characterized by steady, earnest, and energetic effort : PAINSTAKING — **dil·i·gence**
\-jəns\ *n* — **dil·i·gent·ly** *adv*

dill \'dil\ *n* : an herb related to the carrot with aromatic
leaves and seeds used in pickles

dil·ly \'di-lē\ *n, pl* **dil·lies** : one that is remarkable or outstanding

dil·ly·dal·ly \'di-lē-ˌda-lē\ *vb* : to waste time by loitering
or delaying

¹**di·lute** \dī-'lüt, də-\ *vb* **di·lut·ed; di·lut·ing** : to lessen
the consistency or strength of by mixing with some-
thing else — **di·lu·tion** \-'lü-shən\ *n*

²**dilute** *adj* : DILUTED, WEAK

¹**dim** \'dim\ *adj* **dim·mer; dim·mest 1** : LUSTERLESS,
DULL **2** : not bright or distinct : OBSCURE, FAINT **3** : not
seeing or understanding clearly — **dim·ly** *adv* — **dim·
ness** *n*

²**dim** *vb* **dimmed; dim·ming 1** : to make or become dim
or lusterless **2** : to reduce the light from

³**dim** *abbr* **1** dimension **2** diminished **3** diminutive

dime \'dīm\ *n* [ME, tenth part, tithe, fr. MF, fr. L *dec-
ima*, fr. fem. of *decimus* tenth, fr. *decem* ten] : a U.S.
coin worth ¹/₁₀ dollar

di·men·sion \də-'men-chən, dī-\ *n* **1** : the physical property of length, breadth, or thickness; *also* : a measure
of this **2** : EXTENT, SCOPE, PROPORTIONS — usu. used in
pl. — **di·men·sion·al** \-'men-chə-nəl\ *adj* — **di·men·
sion·al·i·ty** \-ˌmen-chə-'na-lə-tē\ *n*

di·min·ish \də-'mi-nish\ *vb* **1** : to make less or cause to
appear less **2** : BELITTLE **3** : DWINDLE **4** : TAPER — **dim·
i·nu·tion** \ˌdi-mə-'nü-shən, -'nyü-\ *n*

di·min·u·en·do \də-ˌmin-yə-'wen-dȯ\ *adv or adj* : DE-
CRESCENDO

¹**di·min·u·tive** \də-'min-yə-tiv\ *n* **1** : a diminutive word or
affix **2** : a diminutive individual

²**diminutive** *adj* **1** : indicating small size and sometimes
the state or quality of being lovable, pitiable, or con-

temptible ⟨the ∼ suffixes *-ette* and *-ling*⟩ **2** : extremely
small : TINY

dim·i·ty \'di-mə-tē\ *n, pl* **-ties** : a thin usu. corded cotton
fabric

dim·mer \'di-mər\ *n* : a device for controlling the
amount of light from an electric lighting unit

di·mor·phic \(ˌ)dī-'mȯr-fik\ *adj* : occurring in two dis-
tinct forms — **di·mor·phism** \-ˌfi-zəm\ *n*

¹**dim·ple** \'dim-pəl\ *n* : a small depression esp. in the
cheek or chin

²**dimple** *vb* **dim·pled; dim·pling** : to form dimples (as in
smiling)

din \'din\ *n* : a loud confused mixture of noises

di·nar \di-'när\ *n* **1** — see MONEY table **2** — see *rial* at
MONEY table

dine \'dīn\ *vb* **dined; din·ing** [ME, fr. OF *diner*, fr.
(assumed) VL *disjejunare* to break one's fast, ultim. fr.
L *jejunus* fasting] **1** : to eat dinner **2** : to give a dinner
to

din·er \'dī-nər\ *n* **1** : one that dines **2** : a railroad dining
car **3** : a restaurant usu. resembling a dining car

di·nette \dī-'net\ *n* : an alcove or small room used for
dining

din·ghy \'diŋ-ē\ *n, pl* **dinghies 1** : a small boat **2** : LIFE
RAFT

din·gle \'diŋ-gəl\ *n* : a small wooded valley

din·go \'diŋ-gȯ\ *n, pl* **dingoes** : a reddish brown wild dog
of Australia

dingo

din·gus \'diŋ-gəs, -əs\ *n* : DOODAD

din·gy \'din-jē\ *adj* **din·gi·er; -est** : DIRTY, DISCOLORED;
also : SHABBY — **din·gi·ness** *n*

din·ky \'diŋ-kē\ *adj* **din·ki·er; -est** : SMALL, INSIGNIFI-
CANT

din·ner \'di-nər\ *n* : the main meal of the day; *also* : a
formal banquet

din·ner·ware \'di-nər-ˌwar\ *n* : tableware other than
flatware

di·no·fla·gel·late \ˌdī-nō-'fla-jə-lət, -ˌlāt\ *n* : any of an
order of planktonic plantlike unicellular flagellates of
which some cause red tide

di·no·saur \'dī-nə-ˌsȯr\ *n* [ultim. fr. Gk *deinos* terrifying
+ *sauros* lizard] : any of a group of extinct long-
tailed Mesozoic reptiles often of huge size

dint \'dint\ *n* **1** : FORCE ⟨by ∼ of sheer grit⟩ **2** : DENT

di·o·cese \'dī-ə-səs, -ˌsēz, -ˌsēs\ *n, pl* **-ces·es** \-sə-səz,
-ˌsē-zəz, -ˌsē-səz\ : the territorial jurisdiction of a bishop — **di·oc·e·san** \dī-'ä-sə-sən, ˌdī-ə-'sēz-ᵊn\ *adj or n*

di·ode \'dī-ˌōd\ *n* **1** : an electronic device with two electrodes or terminals used esp. as a rectifier

di·ox·in \dī-'äk-sən\ *n* : a hydrocarbon that occurs esp.
as a persistent toxic impurity in herbicides (as Agent
Orange)

¹**dip** \'dip\ *vb* **dipped; dip·ping 1** : to plunge temporarily
or partially under the surface (as of a liquid) **2** : to
thrust in a way to suggest immersion **3** : to scoop up or

\ə\abut \ᵊ\kitten \ər\further \a\ash \ā\ace \ä\mop, mar
\au̇\out \ch\chin \e\bet \ē\easy \g\go \i\hit \ī\ice \j\job
\ŋ\sing \ō\go \ȯ\law \ȯi\boy \th\thin \t͟h\the \ü\loot \u̇\foot
\y\yet \zh\vision *see also* Pronunciation Symbols page

out : LADLE **4** : to lower and then raise quickly ⟨~ a flag in salute⟩ **5** : to drop or slope down esp. suddenly ⟨the moon *dipped* below the crest⟩ **6** : to decrease moderately and usu. temporarily ⟨prices *dipped*⟩ **7** : to reach inside or as if inside or below a surface ⟨*dipped* into their savings⟩ **8** : to delve casually into something; *esp* : to read superficially ⟨~ into a book⟩

²dip *n* **1** : an act of dipping; *esp* : a short swim **2** : inclination downward : DROP **3** : something obtained by or used in dipping **4** : a sauce or soft mixture into which food may be dipped **5** : a liquid into which something may be dipped (as for cleansing or coloring)

diph·the·ria \dif-'thir-ē-ə\ *n* : an acute contagious bacterial disease marked by fever and by coating of the air passages with a membrane that interferes with breathing

diph·thong \'dif-ˌthȯŋ\ *n* : two vowel sounds joined in one syllable to form one speech sound (as *ou* in *out*)

dip·loid \'di-ˌplȯid\ *adj* : having the basic chromosome number doubled — **diploid** *n*

di·plo·ma \də-'plō-mə\ *n, pl* **diplomas** : an official record of graduation from or of a degree conferred by a school

di·plo·ma·cy \də-'plō-mə-sē\ *n* **1** : the art and practice of conducting negotiations between nations **2** : TACT

dip·lo·mat \'di-plə-ˌmat\ *n* : one employed or skilled in diplomacy — **dip·lo·mat·ic** \ˌdi-plə-'ma-tik\ *adj*

di·plo·ma·tist \də-'plō-mə-tist\ *n* : DIPLOMAT

dip·per \'di-pər\ *n* **1** : any of a genus of birds that are related to the thrushes and are skilled in diving **2** : something (as a ladle or scoop) that dips or is used for dipping **3** *cap* : BIG DIPPER **4** *cap* : LITTLE DIPPER

dip·so·ma·nia \ˌdip-sə-'mā-nē-ə\ *n* : an uncontrollable craving for alcoholic liquors — **dip·so·ma·ni·ac** \-nē-ˌak\ *n*

dip·stick \'dip-ˌstik\ *n* : a graduated rod for indicating depth

dip·ter·an \'dip-tə-rən\ *adj* : of, relating to, or being a fly (sense 2) — **dipteran** *n* — **dip·ter·ous** \-rəs\ *adj*

dir *abbr* **1** direction **2** director

dire \'dīr\ *adj* **dir·er; dir·est 1** : very horrible : DREADFUL **2** : warning of disaster **3** : EXTREME

¹di·rect \də-'rekt, dī-\ *vb* **1** : ADDRESS ⟨~ a letter⟩; *also* : to impart orally : AIM ⟨~ a remark to the gallery⟩ **2** : to regulate the activities or course of : guide the supervision, organizing, or performance of **3** : to cause to turn, move, or point or to follow a certain course **4** : to point, extend, or project in a specified line or course **5** : to request or instruct with authority **6** : to show or point out the way

²direct *adj* **1** : stemming immediately from a source ⟨~ result⟩ **2** : being or passing in a straight line of descent : LINEAL ⟨~ ancestor⟩ **3** : leading from one point to another in time or space without turn or stop : STRAIGHT **4** : NATURAL, STRAIGHTFORWARD ⟨a ~ manner⟩ **5** : operating without an intervening agency or step ⟨~ action⟩ **6** : effected by the action of the people or the electorate and not by representatives ⟨~ democracy⟩ **7** : consisting of or reproducing the exact words of a speaker or writer — **direct** *adv* — **di·rect·ly** *adv* — **di·rect·ness** *n*

direct current *n* : an electric current flowing in one direction only

di·rec·tion \də-'rek-shən, dī-\ *n* **1** : MANAGEMENT, GUIDANCE **2** : COMMAND, ORDER, INSTRUCTION **3** : the course or line along which something moves, lies, or points **4** : TENDENCY, TREND — **di·rec·tion·al** \-shə-nəl\ *adj*

di·rec·tive \də-'rek-tiv, dī-\ *n* : something that directs and usu. impels toward an action or goal; *esp* : an order issued by a high-level body or official

direct mail *n* : printed matter used for soliciting business or contributions and mailed direct to individuals

di·rec·tor \də-'rek-tər, dī-\ *n* **1** : one that directs : MAN-

AGER, SUPERVISOR, CONDUCTOR **2** : one of a group of persons who direct the affairs of an organized body — **di·rec·to·ri·al** \-ˌrek-'tȯr-ē-əl\ *adj* — **di·rec·tor·ship** *n*

di·rec·tor·ate \-tə-rət\ *n* **1** : the office or position of director **2** : a board of directors; *also* : membership on such a board **3** : an executive staff

di·rec·to·ry \-tə-rē\ *n, pl* **-ries** : an alphabetical or classified list esp. of names and addresses

dire·ful \'dīr-fəl\ *adj* : DREADFUL; *also* : OMINOUS

dirge \'dərj\ *n* : a song of lamentation; *also* : a slow mournful piece of music

dir·ham \'dir-həm\ *n* **1** — see MONEY table **2** — see *dinar, riyal* at MONEY table

di·ri·gi·ble \'dir-ə-jə-bəl, də-'ri-jə-\ *n* : AIRSHIP

dirk \'dərk\ *n* : DAGGER **1**

dirndl \'dərnd-ᵊl\ *n* [short for G *Dirndlkleid*, fr. G dial. *Dirndl* girl + G *Kleid* dress] : a full skirt with a tight waistband

dirt \'dərt\ *n* **1** : a filthy or soiling substance (as mud, dust, or grime) **2** : loose or packed earth : SOIL **3** : moral uncleanness **4** : scandalous gossip **5** : embarrassing or incriminating information

¹dirty \'dər-tē\ *adj* **dirt·i·er; -est 1** : SOILED, FILTHY **2** : INDECENT, SMUTTY ⟨~ jokes⟩ **3** : BASE, UNFAIR ⟨a ~ trick⟩ **4** : STORMY, FOGGY ⟨~ weather⟩ **5** : not clear in color : DULL ⟨a ~ red⟩ — **dirt·i·ness** *n* — **dirty** *adv*

²dirty *vb* **dirt·ied; dirty·ing** : to make or become dirty

dis·able \di-'sā-bəl\ *vb* **dis·abled; dis·abling 1** : to disqualify legally **2** : to make unable to perform by or as if by illness, injury, or malfunction — **dis·abil·i·ty** \ˌdi-sə-'bi-lə-tē\ *n*

dis·abled *adj* : incapacitated by illness, injury, or wounds; *also* : physically or mentally impaired

dis·abuse \ˌdi-sə-'byüz\ *vb* : to free from error, fallacy, or misconception

dis·ad·van·tage \ˌdi-səd-'van-tij\ *n* **1** : loss or damage esp. to reputation or finances **2** : an unfavorable, inferior, or prejudicial condition; *also* : HANDICAP — **dis·ad·van·ta·geous** \di-ˌsad-ˌvan-'tā-jəs, -vən-\ *adj*

dis·ad·van·taged \-tijd\ *adj* : lacking in basic resources or conditions believed necessary for an equal position in society

dis·af·fect \ˌdi-sə-'fekt\ *vb* : to alienate the affection or loyalty of — **dis·af·fec·tion** \-'fek-shən\ *n*

dis·agree \ˌdi-sə-'grē\ *vb* **1** : to fail to agree **2** : to differ in opinion **3** : to cause discomfort or distress ⟨fried foods ~ with her⟩ — **dis·agree·ment** *n*

dis·agree·able \-ə-bəl\ *adj* **1** : causing discomfort : UNPLEASANT, OFFENSIVE **2** : ILL-TEMPERED, PEEVISH — **dis·agree·able·ness** *n* — **dis·agree·ably** \-blē\ *adv*

dis·al·low \ˌdi-sə-'laù\ *vb* : to refuse to admit or recognize : REJECT ⟨~ a claim⟩ — **dis·al·low·ance** *n*

dis·ap·pear \ˌdi-sə-'pir\ *vb* **1** : to pass out of sight **2** : to cease to be : become lost — **dis·ap·pear·ance** *n*

dis·ap·point \ˌdi-sə-'pȯint\ *vb* : to fail to fulfill the expectation or hope of — **dis·ap·point·ment** *n*

dis·ap·pro·ba·tion \di-ˌsa-prə-'bā-shən\ *n* : DISAPPROVAL

dis·ap·prov·al \ˌdi-sə-'prü-vəl\ *n* : adverse judgment : CENSURE

dis·ap·prove \-'prüv\ *vb* **1** : CONDEMN **2** : to feel or express disapproval ⟨~s of smoking⟩ **3** : REJECT

dis·arm \di-'särm\ *vb* **1** : to take arms or weapons from **2** : to reduce the size and strength of the armed forces of a country **3** : to make harmless, peaceable, or friendly : win over ⟨a ~ing smile⟩ — **dis·ar·ma·ment** \-'sär-mə-mənt\ *n*

dis·ar·range \ˌdi-sə-'rānj\ *vb* : to disturb the arrangement or order of — **dis·ar·range·ment** *n*

dis·ar·ray \-'rā\ *n* **1** : DISORDER, CONFUSION **2** : disorderly or careless dress

dis·as·sem·ble \ˌdi-sə-'sem-bəl\ *vb* : to take apart

dis·as·so·ci·ate \-'sȯ-shē-ˌāt, -sē-\ *vb* : to detach from association

di·sas·ter \di-'zas-tər, -'sas-\ *n* [MF *desastre*, fr. It *disastro*, fr. *astro* star, fr. L *astrum*] : a sudden or great misfortune — **di·sas·trous** \-'zas-trəs\ *adj* — **di·sas·trous·ly** *adv*

dis·avow \ˌdi-sə-'vau̇\ *vb* : to deny responsibility for : REPUDIATE — **dis·avow·al** \-'vau̇-əl\ *n*

dis·band \dis-'band\ *vb* : to break up the organization of : DISPERSE

dis·bar \dis-'bär\ *vb* : to expel from the legal profession — **dis·bar·ment** *n*

dis·be·lieve \ˌdis-bə-'lēv\ *vb* 1 : to hold not worthy of belief : not believe 2 : to withhold or reject belief — **dis·be·lief** \-'lēf\ *n* — **dis·be·liev·er** *n*

dis·bur·den \dis-'bərd-ᵊn\ *vb* : to rid of a burden

dis·burse \dis-'bərs\ *vb* **dis·bursed; dis·burs·ing** 1 : to pay out : EXPEND 2 : DISTRIBUTE — **dis·burse·ment** *n*

¹**disc** *var of* DISK

²**disc** *abbr* discount

dis·card \dis-'kärd, 'dis-ˌkärd\ *vb* 1 : to let go a playing card from one's hand; *also* : to play (a card) from a suit other than a trump but different from the one led 2 : to get rid of as unwanted — **dis·card** \'dis-ˌkärd\ *n*

disc brake *n* : a brake that operates by the friction of a pair of plates pressing against the sides of a rotating disc

dis·cern \di-'sərn, -'zərn\ *vb* 1 : to detect with the eyes : DISTINGUISH 2 : DISCRIMINATE 3 : to come to know or recognize mentally — **dis·cern·ible** *adj* — **dis·cern·ment** *n*

dis·cern·ing *adj* : revealing insight and understanding

¹**dis·charge** \dis-'chärj, 'dis-ˌchärj\ *vb* 1 : to relieve of a charge, load, or burden : UNLOAD; *esp* : to remove the electrical energy from ⟨~ a storage battery⟩ 2 : to let or put off ⟨~ passengers⟩ 3 : SHOOT ⟨~ an arrow⟩ 4 : to set free ⟨~ a prisoner⟩ 5 : to dismiss from service or employment ⟨~ a soldier⟩ 6 : to get rid of by paying or doing ⟨~ a debt⟩ 7 : to give forth fluid ⟨the river ~s into the ocean⟩

²**dis·charge** \'dis-ˌchärj, dis-'chärj\ *n* 1 : the act of discharging, unloading, or releasing 2 : something that discharges; *esp* : a certification of release or payment 3 : a firing off (as of a gun) 4 : a flowing out (as of blood from a wound); *also* : something that is emitted ⟨a purulent ~⟩ 5 : release or dismissal esp. from an office or employment; *also* : complete separation from military service 6 : a flow of electricity (as through a gas)

dis·ci·ple \di-'sī-pəl\ *n* 1 : one who accepts and helps to spread the teachings of another; *also* : a convinced adherent 2 *cap* : a member of the Disciples of Christ

dis·ci·pli·nar·i·an \ˌdi-sə-plə-'ner-ē-ən\ *n* : one who enforces order

dis·ci·plin·ary \'di-sə-plə-ˌner-ē\ *adj* : of or relating to discipline; *also* : CORRECTIVE ⟨take ~ action⟩

¹**dis·ci·pline** \'di-sə-plən\ *n* 1 : PUNISHMENT 2 : a field of study : SUBJECT 3 : training that corrects, molds, or perfects 4 : control gained by obedience or training : orderly conduct 5 : a system of rules governing conduct

²**discipline** *vb* **-plined; -plin·ing** 1 : PUNISH 2 : to train or develop by instruction and exercise esp. in self-control 3 : to bring under control ⟨~ troops⟩; *also* : to impose order upon

disc jockey *n* : an announcer of a radio show of popular recorded music

dis·claim \dis-'klām\ *vb* : DENY, DISAVOW — **dis·claim·er** *n*

dis·close \dis-'klōz\ *vb* : to expose to view — **dis·clo·sure** \-'klō-zhər\ *n*

dis·co \'dis-kō\ *n, pl* **discos** 1 : a nightclub for dancing to live or recorded music 2 : popular dance music characterized by hypnotic rhythm, repetitive lyrics, and electronically produced sounds

dis·col·or \dis-'kə-lər\ *vb* : to alter or change in hue or color esp. for the worse — **dis·col·or·ation** \-ˌkə-lə-'rā-shən\ *n*

dis·com·bob·u·late \ˌdis-kəm-'bä-byù-ˌlāt\ *vb* **-lat·ed; -lat·ing** : UPSET, CONFUSE

dis·com·fit \dis-'kəm-fət, *esp Southern* ˌdis-kəm-'fit\ *vb* : UPSET, FRUSTRATE — **dis·com·fi·ture** \dis-'kəm-fə-ˌchu̇r\ *n*

¹**dis·com·fort** \dis-'kəm-fərt\ *vb* : to make uncomfortable or uneasy

²**discomfort** *n* : mental or physical uneasiness

dis·com·mode \ˌdis-kə-'mōd\ *vb* **-mod·ed; -mod·ing** : INCONVENIENCE, TROUBLE

dis·com·pose \-kəm-'pōz\ *vb* 1 : AGITATE 2 : DISARRANGE — **dis·com·po·sure** \-'pō-zhər\ *n*

dis·con·cert \ˌdis-kən-'sərt\ *vb* : CONFUSE, UPSET

dis·con·nect \ˌdis-kə-'nekt\ *vb* : to undo the connection of — **dis·con·nec·tion** \-'nek-shən\ *n*

dis·con·nect·ed *adj* : not connected; *also* : INCOHERENT — **dis·con·nect·ed·ly** *adv*

dis·con·so·late \dis-'kän-sə-lət\ *adj* 1 : CHEERLESS 2 : hopelessly sad — **dis·con·so·late·ly** *adv*

dis·con·tent \ˌdis-kən-'tent\ *n* : uneasiness of mind : DISSATISFACTION — **dis·con·tent·ed** *adj*

dis·con·tin·ue \ˌdis-kən-'tin-yü\ *vb* 1 : to break the continuity of : cease to operate, use, or take 2 : END — **dis·con·tin·u·ance** \-yə-wəns\ *n* — **dis·con·ti·nu·i·ty** \ˌkän-tə-'nü-ə-tē, -'nyü-\ *n* — **dis·con·tin·u·ous** \ˌdis-kən-'tin-yə-wəs\ *adj*

dis·cord \'dis-ˌkȯrd\ *n* 1 : lack of agreement or harmony : DISSENSION, CONFLICT 2 : a harsh combination of musical sounds 3 : a harsh or unpleasant sound — **dis·cor·dant** \dis-'kȯrd-ᵊnt\ *adj* — **dis·cor·dant·ly** *adv*

dis·co·theque \'dis-kə-ˌtek\ *n* : DISCO 1

¹**dis·count** \'dis-ˌkau̇nt\ *n* 1 : a reduction made from a regular or list price 2 : a deduction of interest in advance when lending money

²**dis·count** \'dis-ˌkau̇nt, dis-'kau̇nt\ *vb* 1 : to deduct from the amount of a bill, debt, or charge usu. for cash or prompt payment; *also* : to sell or offer for sale at a discount 2 : to lend money after deducting the discount ⟨~ a note⟩ 3 : DISREGARD; *also* : MINIMIZE 4 : to make allowance for bias or exaggeration 5 : to take into account (as a future event) in present calculations — **dis·count·able** *adj* — **dis·count·er** *n*

³**dis·count** \'dis-ˌkau̇nt\ *adj* : selling goods or services at a discount; *also* : sold at or reflecting a discount

dis·coun·te·nance \dis-'kau̇nt-ᵊn-ənts\ *vb* 1 : EMBARRASS, DISCONCERT 2 : to look with disfavor on

dis·cour·age \dis-'kər-ij\ *vb* **-aged; -ag·ing** 1 : to deprive of courage or confidence : DISHEARTEN 2 : to hinder by disfavoring 3 : to attempt to dissuade — **dis·cour·age·ment** *n* — **dis·cour·ag·ing·ly** *adv*

¹**dis·course** \'dis-ˌkȯrs\ *n* [ME *discours*, fr. ML & LL *discursus*; ML, argument, fr. LL, conversation, fr. L, act of running about, fr. *discurrere* to run about, fr. *currere* to run] 1 : CONVERSATION 2 : formal and usu. extended expression of thought on a subject

²**dis·course** \dis-'kȯrs\ *vb* **dis·coursed; dis·cours·ing** 1 : to express oneself in esp. oral discourse 2 : TALK, CONVERSE

dis·cour·te·ous \(ˌ)dis-'kər-tē-əs\ *adj* : lacking courtesy : UNCIVIL, RUDE — **dis·cour·te·ous·ly** *adv*

dis·cour·te·sy \-'kər-tə-sē\ *n* : RUDENESS; *also* : a rude act

dis·cov·er \dis-'kə-vər\ *vb* 1 : to make known or visible 2 : to obtain sight or knowledge of for the first time; *also* : FIND OUT — **dis·cov·er·er** *n*

\ə\abut \ᵊ\kitten \ər\further \a\ash \ā\ace \ä\mop, mar
\au̇\out \ch\chin \e\bet \ē\easy \g\go \i\hit \ī\ice \j\job
\ŋ\sing \ō\go \ȯ\law \ȯi\boy \th\thin \t͟h\the \ü\loot \u̇\foot
\y\yet \zh\vision *see also* Pronunciation Symbols page

dis·cov·ery \dis-ˈkə-və-rē\ *n, pl* **-er·ies 1** : the act or process of discovering **2** : something discovered **3** : the disclosure usu. before a civil trial of pertinent facts or documents

¹**dis·cred·it** \(ˌ)dis-ˈkre-dət\ *vb* **1** : DISBELIEVE **2** : to cause disbelief in the accuracy or authority of **3** : DISGRACE — **dis·cred·it·able** *adj*

²**discredit** *n* **1** : loss of reputation **2** : lack or loss of belief or confidence

dis·creet \dis-ˈkrēt\ *adj* : showing good judgment; *esp* : capable of observing prudent silence — **dis·creet·ly** *adv*

dis·crep·an·cy \dis-ˈkre-pən-sē\ *n, pl* **-cies 1** : DIFFERENCE, DISAGREEMENT **2** : an instance of being discrepant

dis·crep·ant \-pənt\ *adj* [ME *discrepaunt*, fr. L *discrepans*, prp. of *discrepare* to sound discordantly, fr. *crepare* to rattle, creak] : being at variance : DISAGREEING

dis·crete \dis-ˈkrēt, ˈdis-ˌkrēt\ *adj* **1** : individually distinct **2** : NONCONTINUOUS

dis·cre·tion \dis-ˈkre-shən\ *n* **1** : the quality of being discreet : PRUDENCE **2** : individual choice or judgment **3** : power of free decision or latitude of choice — **dis·cre·tion·ary** *adj*

dis·crim·i·nate \dis-ˈkri-mə-ˌnāt\ *vb* **-nat·ed; -nat·ing 1** : DISTINGUISH, DIFFERENTIATE **2** : to make a difference in treatment on a basis other than individual merit — **dis·crim·i·na·tion** \-ˌkri-mə-ˈnā-shən\ *n*

dis·crim·i·nat·ing *adj* : marked by discrimination; *esp* : DISCERNING, JUDICIOUS

dis·crim·i·na·to·ry \dis-ˈkri-mə-nə-ˌtȯr-ē\ *adj* : marked by esp. unjust discrimination ⟨∼ treatment⟩

dis·cur·sive \dis-ˈkər-siv\ *adj* : passing from one topic to another : RAMBLING — **dis·cur·sive·ly** *adv* — **dis·cur·sive·ness** *n*

dis·cus \ˈdis-kəs\ *n, pl* **dis·cus·es** : a disk that is hurled for distance in a track-and-field contest

dis·cuss \di-ˈskəs\ *vb* [ME, fr. L *discussus*, pp. of *discutere* to disperse, fr. *dis-* apart + *quatere* to shake] **1** : to argue or consider carefully by presenting the various sides **2** : to talk about — **dis·cus·sion** \-ˈskə-shən\ *n*

dis·cus·sant \di-ˈskəs-ᵊnt\ *n* : one who takes part in a formal discussion

¹**dis·dain** \dis-ˈdān\ *n* : CONTEMPT, SCORN — **dis·dain·ful** \-fəl\ *adj* — **dis·dain·ful·ly** *adv*

²**disdain** *vb* **1** : to look on with scorn **2** : to reject or refrain from because of disdain

dis·ease \di-ˈzēz\ *n* : an abnormal bodily condition that impairs functioning and can usu. be recognized by signs and symptoms : SICKNESS — **dis·eased** \-ˈzēzd\ *adj*

dis·em·bark \ˌdi-səm-ˈbärk\ *vb* : to go or put ashore from a ship — **dis·em·bar·ka·tion** \di-ˌsem-ˌbär-ˈkā-shən\ *n*

dis·em·body \ˌdi-səm-ˈbä-dē\ *vb* : to deprive of bodily existence

dis·em·bow·el \-ˈbau̇-əl\ *vb* : EVISCERATE 1 — **dis·em·bow·el·ment** *n*

dis·en·chant \ˌdis-ᵊn-ˈchant\ *vb* : DISILLUSION — **dis·en·chant·ment** *n*

dis·en·chant·ed \-ˈchan-təd\ *adj* : DISAPPOINTED, DISSATISFIED

dis·en·cum·ber \ˌdis-ᵊn-ˈkəm-bər\ *vb* : to free from something that burdens

dis·en·fran·chise \ˌdis-ᵊn-ˈfran-ˌchīz\ *vb* : DISFRANCHISE — **dis·en·fran·chise·ment** *n*

dis·en·gage \ˌdis-ᵊn-ˈgāj\ *vb* : RELEASE, EXTRICATE, DISENTANGLE — **dis·en·gage·ment** *n*

dis·en·tan·gle \ˌdis-ᵊn-ˈtaŋ-gəl\ *vb* : to free from entanglement : UNRAVEL

dis·equi·lib·ri·um \di-ˌsē-kwə-ˈli-brē-əm\ *n* : loss or lack of equilibrium

dis·es·tab·lish \ˌdi-sə-ˈsta-blish\ *vb* : to end the establishment of; *esp* : to deprive of the status of an established church — **dis·es·tab·lish·ment** *n*

dis·es·teem \ˌdi-sə-ˈstēm\ *n* : lack of esteem : DISFAVOR, DISREPUTE

dis·fa·vor \(ˌ)dis-ˈfā-vər\ *n* **1** : DISAPPROVAL, DISLIKE **2** : the state or fact of being no longer favored

dis·fig·ure \dis-ˈfi-gyər\ *vb* : to spoil the appearance of ⟨*disfigured* by a scar⟩ — **dis·fig·ure·ment** *n*

dis·fran·chise \dis-ˈfran-ˌchīz\ *vb* : to deprive of a franchise, a legal right, or a privilege; *esp* : to deprive of the right to vote — **dis·fran·chise·ment** *n*

dis·gorge \-ˈgȯrj\ *vb* : VOMIT; *also* : to discharge forcefully or confusedly

¹**dis·grace** \di-ˈskrās, dis-ˈgrās\ *vb* : to bring reproach or shame to

²**disgrace** *n* **1** : SHAME, DISHONOR; *also* : a cause of shame **2** : the condition of being out of favor : loss of respect — **dis·grace·ful** \-fəl\ *adj* — **dis·grace·ful·ly** *adv*

dis·grun·tle \dis-ˈgrənt-ᵊl\ *vb* **dis·grun·tled; dis·grun·tling** : to put in bad humor

¹**dis·guise** \dis-ˈgīz\ *vb* **dis·guised; dis·guis·ing 1** : to change the appearance of to conceal the identity or to resemble another **2** : HIDE, CONCEAL

²**disguise** *n* **1** : clothing put on to conceal one's identity or counterfeit another's **2** : an outward appearance that hides what something really is

¹**dis·gust** \dis-ˈgəst\ *n* : AVERSION, REPUGNANCE — **dis·gust·ful** \-fəl\ *adj*

²**disgust** *vb* : to provoke to loathing, repugnance, or aversion : be offensive to — **dis·gust·ed·ly** *adv* — **dis·gust·ing·ly** *adv*

¹**dish** \ˈdish\ *n* [ME, fr. OE *disc* plate, fr. L *discus* quoit, disk, dish, fr. Gk *diskos*, fr. *dikein* to throw] **1** : a vessel used for serving food **2** : the food served in a dish ⟨a ∼ of berries⟩ **3** : food prepared in a particular way **4** : something resembling a dish esp. in being shallow and concave

²**dish** *vb* **1** : to put into a dish **2** : to make concave like a dish

dis·ha·bille \ˌdi-sə-ˈbēl\ *n* [F *déshabillé*] : the state of being dressed in a casual or careless manner

dis·har·mo·ny \(ˌ)dis-ˈhär-mə-nē\ *n* : lack of harmony — **dis·har·mo·ni·ous** \ˌdis-(ˌ)här-ˈmȯ-nē-əs\ *adj*

dish·cloth \ˈdish-ˌklȯth\ *n* : a cloth for washing dishes

dis·heart·en \dis-ˈhärt-ᵊn\ *vb* : DISCOURAGE, DEJECT

dished \ˈdisht\ *adj* : CONCAVE

di·shev·el \di-ˈshe-vəl\ *vb* **-shev·eled** *or* **-shev·elled; -shev·el·ing** *or* **-shev·el·ling** [ME *discheveled* with disordered hair, fr. MF *deschevelé*, fr. pp. of *descheveler* to disarrange the hair, fr. *chevel* hair, fr. L *capillus*] : to throw into disorder or disarray — **di·shev·eled** *or* **di·shev·elled** *adj*

dis·hon·est \di-ˈsä-nəst\ *adj* : not honest : UNTRUSTWORTHY, DECEITFUL — **dis·hon·est·ly** *adv* — **dis·hon·es·ty** \-nə-stē\ *n*

¹**dis·hon·or** \di-ˈsä-nər\ *vb* **1** : DISGRACE **2** : to refuse to accept or pay ⟨∼ a check⟩

²**dishonor** *n* **1** : lack or loss of honor **2** : SHAME, DISGRACE **3** : a cause of disgrace **4** : the act of dishonoring a negotiable instrument when presented for payment — **dis·hon·or·able** \di-ˈsä-nə-rə-bəl\ *adj* — **dis·hon·or·ably** \-blē\ *adv*

dish out *vb* : to give freely

dish·rag \ˈdish-ˌrag\ *n* : DISHCLOTH

dish·wash·er \-ˌwȯ-shər, -ˌwä-\ *n* : a person or machine that washes dishes

dish·wa·ter \-ˌwȯ-tər, -ˌwä-\ *n* : water used for washing dishes

dis·il·lu·sion \ˌdi-sə-ˈlü-zhən\ *vb* : to leave without illusion or naive faith and trust — **dis·il·lu·sion·ment** *n*

dis·il·lu·sioned *adj* : DISAPPOINTED, DISSATISFIED

dis·in·cli·na·tion \di-ˌsin-klə-ˈnā-shən\ *n* : a preference for avoiding something : slight aversion

dis·in·cline \ˌdis-ᵊn-ˈklīn\ *vb* : to make unwilling

dis·in·clined *adj* : unwilling because of dislike or disapproval

dis·in·fect \ˌdis-ᵊn-ˈfekt\ *vb* : to cleanse of infection-causing germs — **dis·in·fec·tant** \-ˈfek-tənt\ *n* — **dis·in·fec·tion** \-ˈfek-shən\ *n*

dis·in·for·ma·tion \-ˌin-fər-ˈmā-shən\ *n* : false information deliberately and often covertly spread

dis·in·gen·u·ous \ˌdis-ᵊn-ˈjen-yə-wəs\ *adj* : lacking in candor; *also* : giving a false appearance of simple frankness

dis·in·her·it \ˌdis-ᵊn-ˈher-ət\ *vb* : to deprive of the right to inherit

dis·in·te·grate \di-ˈsin-tə-ˌgrāt\ *vb* **1** : to break or decompose into constituent parts or small particles **2** : to destroy the unity or integrity of — **dis·in·te·gra·tion** \-ˌsin-tə-ˈgrā-shən\ *n*

dis·in·ter \ˌdis-ᵊn-ˈtər\ *vb* **1** : to take from the grave or tomb **2** : UNEARTH

dis·in·ter·est·ed \(ˌ)dis-ˈin-tə-rəs-təd, -ˌres-\ *adj* **1** : not interested **2** : free from selfish motive or interest : UNBIASED — **dis·in·ter·est·ed·ness** *n*

dis·join \(ˌ)dis-ˈjóin\ *vb* : SEPARATE

dis·joint \(ˌ)dis-ˈjóint\ *vb* : to disturb the orderly arrangement of; *also* : to separate at the joints

dis·joint·ed *adj* **1** : DISCONNECTED; *esp* : INCOHERENT **2** : separated at or as if at the joint

disk *or* **disc** \ˈdisk\ *n* **1** : something round and flat; *esp* : a flat rounded anatomical structure (as the central part of the flower head of a composite plant or a pad of cartilage between vertebrae) **2** *usu* **disc** : a phonograph record **3** : a round flat plate coated with a magnetic substance on which data for a computer is stored **4** *usu* **disc** : OPTICAL DISK

dis·kette \ˌdis-ˈket\ *n* : FLOPPY DISK

¹dis·like \(ˌ)dis-ˈlīk\ *n* : a feeling of aversion or disapproval

²dislike *vb* : to regard with dislike : DISAPPROVE

dis·lo·cate \ˈdis-lō-ˌkāt, dis-ˈlō-\ *vb* **1** : to put out of place; *esp* : to displace (a bone or joint) from normal connections ⟨∼ a shoulder⟩ **2** : DISRUPT — **dis·lo·ca·tion** \ˌdis-(ˌ)lō-ˈkā-shən\ *n*

dis·lodge \(ˌ)dis-ˈläj\ *vb* : to force out of a place esp. of rest, hiding, or defense

dis·loy·al \(ˌ)dis-ˈlói-əl\ *adj* : lacking in loyalty — **dis·loy·al·ty** *n*

dis·mal \ˈdiz-məl\ *adj* [ME, fr. *dismal,* n., days marked as unlucky in medieval calendars, fr. AF, fr ML *dies mali,* lit., evil days] **1** : showing or causing gloom or depression **2** : lacking merit — **dis·mal·ly** *adv*

dis·man·tle \(ˌ)dis-ˈmant-ᵊl\ *vb* **-tled; -tling 1** : to take apart **2** : to strip of furniture and equipment — **dis·man·tle·ment** *n*

dis·may \dis-ˈmā\ *vb* : to cause to lose courage or resolution from alarm or fear : DAUNT — **dismay** *n* — **dis·may·ing·ly** *adv*

dis·mem·ber \dis-ˈmem-bər\ *vb* **1** : to cut off or separate the limbs or parts of **2** : to break up or tear into pieces — **dis·mem·ber·ment** *n*

dis·miss \dis-ˈmis\ *vb* **1** : to send away **2** : DISCHARGE **3** : to put aside or out of mind **4** : to put out of judicial consideration ⟨∼ed all charges⟩ — **dis·miss·al** *n*

dis·mount \dis-ˈmaùnt\ *vb* **1** : to get down from something (as a horse or bicycle) **2** : UNHORSE **3** : DISASSEMBLE

dis·obe·di·ence \ˌdis-ə-ˈbē-dē-əns\ *n* : neglect or refusal to obey — **dis·obe·di·ent** \-ənt\ *adj*

dis·obey \ˌdis-ə-ˈbā\ *vb* **1** : to fail to obey : be disobedient

dis·oblige \ˌdis-ə-ˈblīj\ *vb* **1** : to go counter to the wishes of **2** : INCONVENIENCE

¹dis·or·der \di-ˈsór-dər\ *vb* **1** : to disturb the order of **2** : to disturb the regular or normal functions of ⟨a ∼ed digestion⟩

²disorder *n* **1** : lack of order : CONFUSION **2** : breach of the peace or public order : TUMULT **3** : an abnormal state of body or mind : AILMENT

dis·or·der·ly \-lē\ *adj* **1** : offensive to public order **2** : marked by disorder ⟨a ∼ desk⟩ — **dis·or·der·li·ness** *n*

dis·or·ga·nize \di-ˈsór-gə-ˌnīz\ *vb* : to break up the regular system of : throw into disorder — **dis·or·ga·ni·za·tion** \di-ˌsór-gə-nə-ˈzā-shən\ *n*

dis·ori·ent \di-ˈsór-ē-ˌent\ *vb* : to cause to be confused or lost — **dis·ori·en·ta·tion** \di-ˌsór-ē-ən-ˈtā-shən\ *n*

dis·own \di-ˈsón\ *vb* : REPUDIATE, RENOUNCE, DISCLAIM

dis·par·age \di-ˈspar-ij\ *vb* **-aged; -ag·ing** [ME to degrade by marriage below one's class, disparage, fr. MF *desparagier* to marry below one's class, fr. OF, fr. *parage* extraction, lineage, fr. *per* peer] **1** : to lower in rank or reputation : DEGRADE **2** : BELITTLE — **dis·par·age·ment** *n* — **dis·par·ag·ing·ly** *adv*

dis·pa·rate \ˈdis-pə-rət, dis-ˈpar-ət\ *adj* : distinct in quality or character — **dis·par·i·ty** \di-ˈspar-ə-tē\ *n*

dis·pas·sion·ate \(ˌ)dis-ˈpa-shə-nət\ *adj* : not influenced by strong feeling : CALM, IMPARTIAL — **dis·pas·sion** \-ˈpa-shən\ *n* — **dis·pas·sion·ate·ly** *adv*

¹dis·patch \di-ˈspach\ *vb* **1** : to send off or away with promptness or speed esp. on official business **2** : to put to death **3** : to attend to rapidly or efficiently **4** : DEFEAT — **dis·patch·er** *n*

²dis·patch \di-ˈspach, ˈdis-ˌpach\ *n* **1** : MESSAGE **2** : a news item sent in by a correspondent to a newspaper **3** : the act of dispatching; *esp* : SHIPMENT **4** : the act of putting to death **5** : promptness and efficiency in performing a task

dis·pel \di-ˈspel\ *vb* **dis·pelled; dis·pel·ling** : to drive away by scattering : DISSIPATE

dis·pens·able \di-ˈspen-sə-bəl\ *adj* : capable of being dispensed with

dis·pen·sa·ry \di-ˈspen-sə-rē\ *n, pl* **-ries** : a place where medicine or medical or dental aid is dispensed

dis·pen·sa·tion \ˌdis-pən-ˈsā-shən\ *n* **1** : a system of rules for ordering affairs **2** : a particular arrangement or provision esp. of nature **3** : an exemption from a rule or from a vow or oath **4** : the act of dispensing **5** : something dispensed or distributed

dis·pense \di-ˈspens\ *vb* **dis·pensed; dis·pens·ing 1** : to portion out **2** : ADMINISTER ⟨∼ justice⟩ **3** : EXEMPT **4** : to make up and give out (remedies) — **dis·pens·er** *n* — **dispense with 1** : SUSPEND **2** : to do without

dis·perse \di-ˈspərs\ *vb* **dis·persed; dis·pers·ing** : to break up and scatter about : SPREAD — **dis·per·sal** \-ˈspər-səl\ *n* — **dis·per·sion** \-ˈspər-zhən\ *n*

dis·pir·it \dis-ˈpir-ət\ *vb* : DEPRESS, DISCOURAGE, DISHEARTEN

dis·place \dis-ˈplās\ *vb* **1** : to remove from the usual or proper place; *esp* : to expel or force to flee from home or native land ⟨*displaced* persons⟩ **2** : to move out of position ⟨water *displaced* by a floating object⟩ **3** : to take the place of : REPLACE

dis·place·ment \-mənt\ *n* **1** : the act of displacing : the state of being displaced **2** : the volume or weight of a fluid (as water) displaced by a floating body (as a ship) **3** : the difference between the initial position of an object and a later position

¹dis·play \di-ˈsplā\ *vb* : to present to view : make evident

²display *n* **1** : a displaying of something **2** : an electronic device (as a cathode-ray tube) that gives information in visual form; *also* : the visual information

---

\ə\abut \ᵊ\kitten \ər\further \a\ash \ā\ace \ä\mop, mar
\aù\out \ch\chin \e\bet \ē\easy \g\go \i\hit \ī\ice \j\job
\ŋ\sing \ō\go \ó\law \ói\boy \th\thin \t͟h\the \ü\loot \ù\foot
\y\yet \zh\vision *see also* Pronunciation Symbols page

dis·please \(ˌ)dis-ˈplēz\ vb **1** : to arouse the disapproval and dislike of **2** : to be offensive to : give displeasure

dis·plea·sure \-ˈple-zhər\ n : a feeling of dislike and irritation

dis·port \di-ˈspórt\ vb **1** : DIVERT, AMUSE **2** : FROLIC **3** : DISPLAY

dis·pos·able \di-ˈspò-zə-bəl\ adj **1** : remaining after deduction of taxes ⟨∼ income⟩ **2** : designed to be used once and then thrown away ⟨∼ diapers⟩ — **disposable** n

dis·pos·al \di-ˈspò-zəl\ n **1** : CONTROL, COMMAND **2** : an orderly arrangement **3** : a getting rid of **4** : MANAGEMENT, ADMINISTRATION **5** : presenting or bestowing something ⟨∼ of favors⟩ **6** : a device used to reduce waste matter (as by grinding)

dis·pose \di-ˈspóz\ vb **dis·posed; dis·pos·ing 1** : to give a tendency to : INCLINE ⟨disposed to accept⟩ **2** : to put in place : ARRANGE ⟨troops disposed for withdrawal⟩ **3** : SETTLE — **dis·pos·er** n — **dispose of 1** : to transfer to the control of another **2** : to get rid of **3** : to deal with conclusively

dis·po·si·tion \ˌdis-pə-ˈzi-shən\ n **1** : the act or power of disposing : DISPOSAL **2** : RELINQUISHMENT **3** : ARRANGEMENT **4** : TENDENCY, INCLINATION **5** : natural attitude toward things ⟨a cheerful ∼⟩

dis·pos·sess \ˌdis-pə-ˈzes\ vb : to put out of possession or occupancy — **dis·pos·ses·sion** \-ˈze-shən\ n

dis·praise \(ˌ)dis-ˈpráz\ vb : DISPARAGE — **dispraise** n — **dis·prais·er** n

dis·pro·por·tion \ˌdis-prə-ˈpór-shən\ n : lack of proportion, symmetry, or proper relation — **dis·pro·por·tion·ate** \-shə-nət\ adj

dis·prove \(ˌ)dis-ˈprüv\ vb : to prove to be false — **disproof** \-ˈprüf\ n

dis·pu·tant \di-ˈspyüt-ᵊnt, ˈdis-pyə-tənt\ n : one that is engaged in a dispute

dis·pu·ta·tion \ˌdis-pyu̇-ˈtā-shən\ n **1** : DEBATE **2** : an oral defense of an academic thesis

dis·pu·ta·tious \-shəs\ adj : inclined to dispute : ARGUMENTATIVE

¹**dis·pute** \di-ˈspyüt\ vb **dis·put·ed; dis·put·ing 1** : ARGUE, DEBATE **2** : WRANGLE **3** : to deny the truth or rightness of **4** : to struggle against or over : OPPOSE — **disput·able** \di-ˈspyü-tə-bəl, ˈdis-pyə-tə-bəl\ adj — **disput·er** n

²**dis·pute** n **1** : DEBATE **2** : QUARREL

dis·qual·i·fy \(ˌ)dis-ˈkwä-lə-ˌfī\ vb : to make or declare unfit or not qualified — **dis·qual·i·fi·ca·tion** \-ˌkwä-lə-fə-ˈkā-shən\ n

¹**dis·qui·et** \(ˌ)dis-ˈkwī-ət\ vb : to make uneasy or restless : DISTURB

²**disquiet** n : lack of peace or tranquillity : ANXIETY

dis·qui·etude \(ˌ)dis-ˈkwī-ə-ˌtüd, -ˌtyüd\ n : AGITATION, ANXIETY

dis·qui·si·tion \ˌdis-kwə-ˈzi-shən\ n : a formal inquiry or discussion

¹**dis·re·gard** \ˌdis-ri-ˈgärd\ vb : to pay no attention to : treat as unworthy of notice or regard

²**disregard** n : the act of disregarding : the state of being disregarded : NEGLECT — **dis·re·gard·ful** adj

dis·re·pair \ˌdis-ri-ˈpar\ n : the state of being in need of repair

dis·rep·u·ta·ble \dis-ˈre-pyù-tə-bəl\ adj : having a bad reputation

dis·re·pute \ˌdis-ri-ˈpyüt\ n : lack or decline of reputation : low esteem

dis·re·spect \ˌdis-ri-ˈspekt\ n : DISCOURTESY — **dis·re·spect·ful** adj

dis·robe \dis-ˈròb\ vb : UNDRESS

dis·rupt \dis-ˈrəpt\ vb **1** : to break apart **2** : to throw into disorder **3** : INTERRUPT — **dis·rup·tion** \-ˈrəp-shən\ n — **dis·rup·tive** \-ˈrəp-tiv\ adj

dis·sat·is·fac·tion \di-ˌsa-təs-ˈfak-shən\ n : DISCONTENT

dis·sat·is·fy \di-ˈsa-təs-ˌfī\ vb : to fail to satisfy : DISPLEASE

dis·sect \di-ˈsekt\ vb **1** : to divide into parts esp. for examination and study **2** : ANALYZE — **dis·sec·tion** \-ˈsek-shən\ n — **dis·sec·tor** \-ˈsek-tər\ n

dis·sect·ed adj : cut deeply into narrow lobes ⟨a ∼ leaf⟩

dis·sem·ble \di-ˈsem-bəl\ vb **-bled; -bling 1** : to hide under or put on a false appearance : conceal facts, intentions, or feelings under some pretense **2** : SIMULATE — **dis·sem·bler** n

dis·sem·i·nate \di-ˈse-mə-ˌnāt\ vb **-nat·ed; -nat·ing** : to spread abroad as if sowing seed ⟨∼ ideas⟩ — **dis·sem·i·na·tion** \-ˌse-mə-ˈnā-shən\ n

dis·sen·sion \di-ˈsen-chən\ n : disagreement in opinion : DISCORD

¹**dis·sent** \di-ˈsent\ vb **1** : to withhold assent **2** : to differ in opinion

²**dissent** n **1** : difference of opinion; esp : religious nonconformity **2** : a written statement in which a justice disagrees with the opinion of the majority

dis·sent·er \di-ˈsen-tər\ n **1** : one that dissents **2** cap : an English Nonconformist

dis·ser·ta·tion \ˌdi-sər-ˈtā-shən\ n : an extended usu. written treatment of a subject; esp : one submitted for a doctorate

dis·ser·vice \di-ˈsər-vəs\ n : INJURY, HARM, MISCHIEF

dis·sev·er \di-ˈse-vər\ vb : SEPARATE, DISUNITE

dis·si·dent \ˈdi-sə-dənt\ adj [L dissidens, prp. of dissidēre to sit apart, disagree, fr. dis- apart + sedēre to sit] : disagreeing esp. with an established religious or political system, organization, or belief — **dis·si·dence** \-dəns\ n — **dissident** n

dis·sim·i·lar \di-ˈsi-mə-lər\ adj : UNLIKE — **dis·sim·i·lar·i·ty** \di-ˌsi-mə-ˈlar-ə-tē\ n

dis·sim·u·late \di-ˈsi-myə-ˌlāt\ vb : to hide under a false appearance : DISSEMBLE — **dis·sim·u·la·tion** \di-ˌsi-myə-ˈlā-shən\ n

dis·si·pate \ˈdi-sə-ˌpāt\ vb **-pat·ed; -pat·ing 1** : to break up and drive off : DISPERSE, SCATTER ⟨the breeze dissipated the fog⟩ **2** : SQUANDER **3** : to break up and vanish **4** : to be dissolute; esp : to drink alcoholic beverages to excess — **dis·si·pat·ed** adj — **dis·si·pa·tion** \ˌdi-sə-ˈpā-shən\ n

dis·so·ci·ate \di-ˈsò-shē-ˌāt\ vb **-at·ed; -at·ing** : DISCONNECT, DISUNITE — **dis·so·ci·a·tion** \di-ˌso-shē-ˈā-shən\ n

dis·so·lute \ˈdi-sə-ˌlüt\ adj : loose in morals or conduct — **dis·so·lute·ly** adv — **dis·so·lute·ness** n

dis·so·lu·tion \ˌdi-sə-ˈlü-shən\ n **1** : the action or process of dissolving **2** : separation of a thing into its parts **3** : DECAY; also : DEATH **4** : the termination or breaking up of (as an assembly)

dis·solve \di-ˈzälv\ vb **1** : to separate into component parts **2** : to pass or cause to pass into solution ⟨sugar ∼s in water⟩ **3** : TERMINATE, DISPERSE ⟨∼ parliament⟩ **4** : to waste or fade away ⟨his courage dissolved⟩ **5** : to be overcome emotionally ⟨∼ in tears⟩ **6** : to resolve itself as if by dissolution

dis·so·nance \ˈdi-sə-nəns\ n : DISCORD — **dis·so·nant** \-nənt\ adj

dis·suade \di-ˈswād\ vb **dis·suad·ed; dis·suad·ing** : to advise against a course of action : persuade or try to persuade not to do something — **dis·sua·sion** \-ˈswā-zhən\ n — **dis·sua·sive** \-ˈswā-siv\ adj

dist abbr **1** distance **2** district

¹**dis·taff** \ˈdis-ˌtaf\ n, pl **distaffs** \-ˌtafs, -ˌtavz\ **1** : a staff for holding the flax, tow, or wool in spinning **2** : a woman's work or domain **3** : the female branch or side of a family

²**distaff** adj : MATERNAL, FEMALE

dis·tal \ˈdist-ᵊl\ adj **1** : away from the point of attachment or origin esp. on the body **2** : of, relating to, or being the surface of a tooth that is farthest from the middle of the front of the jaw — **dis·tal·ly** *adv*

1dis·tance \'dis-təns\ *n* **1** : measure of separation in space or time **2** : EXPANSE **3** : the full length ⟨go the ∼⟩ **4** : spatial remoteness **5** : COLDNESS, RESERVE **6** : DIFFERENCE, DISPARITY **7** : a distant point

2distance *vb* **dis·tanced; dis·tanc·ing** : to leave far behind : OUTSTRIP

dis·tant \'dis-tənt\ *adj* **1** : separate in space : AWAY **2** : FAR-OFF **3** : far apart or behind **4** : not close in relationship ⟨a ∼ cousin⟩ **5** : different in kind **6** : RESERVED, ALOOF, COLD ⟨∼ politeness⟩ **7** : going a long distance — **dis·tant·ly** *adv* — **dis·tant·ness** *n*

dis·taste \(ˌ)dis-'tāst\ *n* : DISINCLINATION, DISLIKE — **dis·taste·ful** *adj*

dis·tem·per \(ˌ)dis-'tem-pər\ *n* : a bodily disorder usu. of a domestic animal; *esp* : a contagious often fatal virus disease of dogs

dis·tend \di-'stend\ *vb* : EXPAND, SWELL — **dis·ten·si·ble** \-'sten-sə-bəl\ *adj* — **dis·ten·sion** *or* **dis·ten·tion** \-chən\ *n*

dis·tich \'dis-(ˌ)tik\ *n* : a unit of two lines of poetry

dis·till *also* **dis·til** \di-'stil\ *vb* **dis·tilled; dis·till·ing 1** : to fall or let fall in drops **2** : to obtain or purify by distillation — **dis·till·er** *n* — **dis·till·ery** \-'sti-lə-rē\ *n*

dis·til·late \'dis-tə-ˌlāt, -lət\ *n* : a liquid product condensed from vapor during distillation

dis·til·la·tion \ˌdis-tə-'lā-shən\ *n* : the process of purifying a liquid by successive evaporation and condensation

dis·tinct \di-'stiŋkt\ *adj* **1** : SEPARATE, INDIVIDUAL **2** : presenting a clear unmistakable impression — **dis·tinct·ly** *adv* — **dis·tinct·ness** *n*

dis·tinc·tion \di-'stiŋk-shən\ *n* **1** : the distinguishing of a difference; *also* : the difference distinguished **2** : something that distinguishes **3** : special honor or recognition

dis·tinc·tive \di-'stiŋk-tiv\ *adj* **1** : serving to distinguish **2** : having or giving style or distinction — **dis·tinc·tive·ly** *adv* — **dis·tinc·tive·ness** *n*

dis·tin·guish \di-'stiŋ-gwish\ *vb* [MF *distinguer*, fr. L *distinguere*, lit., to separate by pricking] **1** : to recognize by some mark or characteristic **2** : to hear or see clearly : DISCERN **3** : to make distinctions ⟨∼ between right and wrong⟩ **4** : to give prominence or distinction to; *also* : to take special notice of — **dis·tin·guish·able** *adj*

dis·tin·guished \-gwisht\ *adj* **1** : marked by eminence or excellence **2** : befitting an eminent person

dis·tort \di-'stort\ *vb* **1** : to twist out of the true meaning **2** : to twist out of a natural, normal, or original shape or condition **3** : to cause to be perceived unnaturally — **dis·tor·tion** \-'stor-shən\ *n*

distr *abbr* distribute; distribution

dis·tract \di-'strakt\ *vb* **1** : to draw (the attention or mind) to a different object : DIVERT **2** : to stir up or confuse with conflicting emotions or motives — **dis·trac·tion** \-'strak-shən\ *n*

dis·trait \di-'strā\ *adj* : DISTRAUGHT 1

dis·traught \di-'strot\ *adj* **1** : agitated with doubt or mental conflict **2** : INSANE

1dis·tress \di-'stres\ *n* **1** : suffering of body or mind : PAIN, ANGUISH **2** : TROUBLE, MISFORTUNE **3** : a condition of danger or desperate need — **dis·tress·ful** *adj*

2distress *vb* **1** : to subject to great strain or difficulties **2** : UPSET

dis·trib·ute \di-'stri-byüt\ *vb* **-ut·ed; -ut·ing 1** : to divide among several or many **2** : to spread out : SCATTER; *also* : DELIVER **3** : CLASSIFY — **dis·tri·bu·tion** \ˌdis-trə-'byü-shən\ *n*

dis·trib·u·tive \di-'stri-byù-tiv\ *adj* **1** : of or relating to distribution **2** : being or concerned with a mathematical operation (as multiplication in $a(b + c) = ab + ac$) that produces the same result when operating on a whole mathematical expression as when operating on each part and collecting the results — **dis·trib·u·tive·ly** *adv*

dis·trib·u·tor \di-'stri-byù-tər\ *n* **1** : one that distributes **2** : one that markets goods **3** : a device for directing current to the spark plugs of an engine

dis·trict \'dis-(ˌ)trikt\ *n* **1** : a fixed territorial division (as for administrative or electoral purposes) **2** : an area, region, or section with a distinguishing character

district attorney *n* : the prosecuting attorney of a judicial district

1dis·trust \dis-'trəst\ *n* : a lack or absence of trust — **dis·trust·ful** \-fəl\ *adj* — **dis·trust·ful·ly** *adv*

2distrust *vb* : to have no trust or confidence in

dis·turb \di-'stərb\ *vb* **1** : to interfere with : INTERRUPT **2** : to alter the position or arrangement of; *also* : to upset the natural and esp. the ecological balance of **3** : to destroy the tranquillity or composure of : make uneasy **4** : to throw into disorder **5** : INCONVENIENCE — **dis·tur·bance** \-'stər-bəns\ *n* — **dis·turb·er** *n*

dis·turbed \-'stərbd\ *adj* : showing symptoms of emotional illness

dis·unite \ˌdis-yü-'nīt\ *vb* : DIVIDE, SEPARATE

dis·uni·ty \dis-'yü-nə-tē\ *n* : lack of unity; *esp* : DISSENSION

dis·use \-'yüs\ *n* : a cessation of use or practice

1ditch \'dich\ *n* : a long narrow channel or trench dug in the earth

2ditch *vb* **1** : to enclose with a ditch; *also* : to dig a ditch in **2** : to get rid of : DISCARD **3** : to make a forced landing of an airplane on water

dith·er \'di-thər\ *n* : a highly nervous, excited, or agitated state

dit·sy *or* **dit·zy** \'dit-sē\ *adj* **dits·i·er** *or* **ditz·i·er; -est** : eccentrically silly, giddy, or inane

dit·to \'di-tò\ *n, pl* **dittos** [It *ditto, detto,* pp. of *dire* to say, fr. L *dicere*] **1** : a thing mentioned previously or above — used to avoid repeating a word **2** : a mark " or " used as a symbol for the word *ditto*

dit·ty \'di-tē\ *n, pl* **ditties** : a short simple song

di·uret·ic \ˌdī-yə-'re-tik\ *adj* : tending to increase urine flow — **diuretic** *n*

di·ur·nal \dī-'ərn-ᵊl\ *adj* **1** : DAILY **2** : of, relating to, occurring, or active in the daytime

div *abbr* **1** divided **2** dividend **3** division **4** divorced

di·va \'dē-və\ *n, pl* **divas** *or* **di·ve** \-ˌvā\ [It, lit., goddess, fr. L, fem. of *divus* divine, god] : PRIMA DONNA

di·va·gate \'dī-və-ˌgāt\ *vb* **-gat·ed; -gat·ing** : to wander or stray from a course or subject : DIVERGE — **di·va·ga·tion** \ˌdī-və-'gā-shən\ *n*

di·van \'dī-ˌvan, di-'van\ *n* : COUCH, SOFA

1dive \'dīv\ *vb* **dived** \'dīvd\ *or* **dove** \'dōv\; **dived; div·ing 1** : to plunge into water headfirst **2** : SUBMERGE **3** : to come or drop down precipitously **4** : to descend in an airplane at a steep angle **5** : to plunge into some matter or activity **6** : DART, LUNGE — **div·er** *n*

2dive *n* **1** : the act or an instance of diving **2** : a sharp decline **3** : a disreputable bar or place of amusement

di·verge \də-'vərj, dī-\ *vb* **di·verged; di·verg·ing 1** : to move or extend in different directions from a common point : draw apart **2** : to differ in character, form, or opinion **3** : DEVIATE **4** : DEFLECT — **di·ver·gence** \-'vər-jəns\ *n* — **di·ver·gent** \-jənt\ *adj*

di·vers \'dī-vərz\ *adj* : VARIOUS

di·verse \dī-'vərs, də-, 'dī-ˌvərs\ *adj* **1** : UNLIKE **2** : composed of distinct forms or qualities — **di·verse·ly** *adv*

di·ver·si·fy \də-'vər-sə-ˌfī, dī-\ *vb* **-fied; -fy·ing** : to

\ə\abut \ᵊ\kitten \ər\further \a\ash \ā\ace \ä\mop, mar \au̇\out \ch\chin \e\bet \ē\easy \g\go \i\hit \ī\ice \j\job \ŋ\sing \ō\go \ȯ\law \ȯi\boy \th\thin \th̲\the \ü\loot \u̇\foot \y\yet \zh\vision *see also* Pronunciation Symbols page

make different or various in form or quality — **di·ver·si·fi·ca·tion** \-₁vər-sə-fə-ˈkā-shən\ *n*

di·ver·sion \də-ˈvər-zhən, dī-\ *n* **1** : a turning aside from a course, activity, or use : DEVIATION **2** : something that diverts or amuses : PASTIME

di·ver·si·ty \də-ˈvər-sə-tē, dī-\ *n, pl* **-ties 1** : the condition of being diverse : VARIETY **2** : an instance of being diverse

di·vert \də-ˈvərt, dī-\ *vb* **1** : to turn from a course or purpose : DEFLECT **2** : DISTRACT **3** : ENTERTAIN, AMUSE

di·vest \dī-ˈvest, də-\ *vb* **1** : to deprive or dispossess esp. of property, authority, or rights **2** : to strip esp. of clothing, ornament, or equipment

¹di·vide \də-ˈvīd\ *vb* **di·vid·ed; di·vid·ing 1** : SEPARATE; *also* : CLASSIFY **2** : CLEAVE, PART **3** : DISTRIBUTE, APPORTION **4** : to possess or make use of in common : share in **5** : to cause to be separate, distinct, or apart from one another **6** : to separate into opposing sides or parties **7** : to mark divisions on **8** : to subject to or use in mathematical division; *also* : to be used as a divisor with respect to **9** : to branch out

²divide *n* : WATERSHED 1

div·i·dend \ˈdi-və-₁dend\ *n* **1** : an individual share of something distributed **2** : BONUS **3** : a number to be divided **4** : a sum or fund to be divided or distributed

di·vid·er \də-ˈvī-dər\ *n* **1** : one that divides (as a partition) (room ∼) **2** *pl* : COMPASS 5

div·i·na·tion \₁di-və-ˈnā-shən\ *n* **1** : the art or practice of using omens or magic powers to foretell the future **2** : unusual insight or intuitive perception

¹di·vine \də-ˈvīn\ *adj* **di·vin·er; -est 1** : of, relating to, or being God or a god **2** : supremely good : SUPERB; *also* : HEAVENLY — **di·vine·ly** *adv*

²divine *n* **1** : CLERGYMAN **2** : THEOLOGIAN

³divine *vb* **di·vined; di·vin·ing 1** : INFER, CONJECTURE **2** : PROPHESY **3** : DOWSE — **di·vin·er** *n*

divining rod *n* : a forked rod believed to reveal the presence of water or minerals by dipping downward when held over a vein

di·vin·i·ty \də-ˈvi-nə-tē\ *n, pl* **-ties 1** : THEOLOGY **2** : the quality or state of being divine **3** : a divine being; *esp* : GOD 1

di·vis·i·ble \də-ˈvi-zə-bəl\ *adj* : capable of being divided — **di·vis·i·bil·i·ty** \-₁vi-zə-ˈbi-lə-tē\ *n*

di·vi·sion \də-ˈvi-zhən\ *n* **1** : DISTRIBUTION, SEPARATION **2** : one of the parts or groupings into which a whole is divided **3** : DISAGREEMENT, DISUNITY **4** : something that divides or separates **5** : the mathematical operation of finding how many times one number is contained in another **6** : a large self-contained military unit **7** : an administrative or operating unit of a governmental, business, or educational organization — **di·vi·sion·al** \-ˈvi-zhə-nəl\ *adj*

di·vi·sive \də-ˈvī-siv, -ˈvi-ziv\ *adj* : creating disunity or dissension — **di·vi·sive·ly** *adv* — **di·vi·sive·ness** *n*

di·vi·sor \də-ˈvī-zər\ *n* : the number by which a dividend is divided

di·vorce \də-ˈvȯrs\ *n* **1** : an act or instance of legally dissolving a marriage **2** : SEPARATION, SEVERANCE — **divorce** *vb* — **di·vorce·ment** *n*

di·vor·cé \də-₁vȯr-ˈsā\ *n* [F] : a divorced man

di·vor·cée \də-₁vȯr-ˈsā, -ˈsē\ *n* : a divorced woman

div·ot \ˈdi-vət\ *n* : a piece of turf dug from a golf fairway in making a stroke

di·vulge \də-ˈvəlj, dī-\ *vb* **di·vulged; di·vulg·ing** : REVEAL, DISCLOSE

Dix·ie·land \ˈdik-sē-₁land\ *n* : jazz music in duple time played in a style developed in New Orleans

diz·zy \ˈdi-zē\ *adj* **diz·zi·er; -est** [ME *disy*, fr. OE *dysig* stupid] **1** : FOOLISH, SILLY **2** : having a sensation of whirling : GIDDY **3** : causing or caused by giddiness — **diz·zi·ly** \-zə-lē\ *adv* — **diz·zi·ness** \-zē-nəs\ *n*

DJ *n, often not cap* : DISC JOCKEY

dk *abbr* **1** dark **2** deck **3** dock

dl *abbr* deciliter

DLitt *or* **DLit** *abbr* [NL *doctor litterarum*] doctor of letters; doctor of literature

DLO *abbr* dead letter office

dm *abbr* decimeter

DMD *abbr* [NL *dentariae medicinae doctor*] doctor of dental medicine

DMZ *abbr* demilitarized zone

dn *abbr* down

DNA \₁dē-(₁)en-ˈā\ *n* : any of various nucleic acids that are usu. the molecular basis of heredity and are localized esp. in cell nuclei

¹do \ˈdü\ *vb* **did** \ˈdid\; **done** \ˈdən\; **do·ing; does** \ˈdəz\ **1** : to bring to pass : ACCOMPLISH **2** : ACT, BEHAVE ⟨∼ as I say⟩ **3** : to be active or busy ⟨up and ∼*ing*⟩ **4** : HAPPEN ⟨what's ∼*ing*?⟩ **5** : to be engaged in the study or practice of : work at ⟨he *does* tailoring⟩ **6** : COOK ⟨steak *done* rare⟩ **7** : to put in order (as by cleaning or arranging) ⟨∼ the dishes⟩ **8** : DECORATE ⟨*did* the hall in blue⟩ **9** : GET ALONG ⟨∼ well in school⟩ **10** : CARRY ON, MANAGE **11** : RENDER ⟨sleep will ∼ you good⟩ **12** : FINISH ⟨when he had *done*⟩ **13** : EXERT ⟨*did* my best⟩ **14** : PRODUCE ⟨*did* a poem⟩ **15** : to play the part of **16** : CHEAT ⟨*did* him out of his share⟩ **17** : TRAVERSE, TOUR **18** : TRAVEL **19** : to spend or serve out a period of time ⟨*did* ten years in prison⟩ **20** : SUFFICE, SUIT **21** : to be fitting or proper **22** : USE ⟨doesn't ∼ drugs⟩ **23** — used as an auxiliary verb (1) before the subject in an interrogative sentence ⟨*does* he work?⟩ and after some adverbs ⟨never *did* she say so⟩, (2) in a negative statement ⟨I *don't* know⟩, (3) for emphasis ⟨you ∼ know⟩, and (4) as a substitute for a preceding predicate ⟨he works harder than I ∼⟩ — **do·able** \ˈdü-ə-bəl\ *adj* — **do away with 1** : to put an end to **2** : DESTROY, KILL — **do by** : to deal with : TREAT ⟨*did* right *by* her⟩ — **do for** : to bring about the death or ruin of — **do the trick** : to produce a desired result

²do *n* **1** : AFFAIR, PARTY **2** : a command or entreaty to do something ⟨list of ∼*s* and don'ts⟩ **3** : HAIRDO

³do *abbr* ditto

DOA *abbr* dead on arrival

DOB *abbr* date of birth

dob·bin \ˈdä-bən\ *n* [*Dobbin*, nickname for *Robert*] **1** : a farm horse **2** : a quiet plodding horse

Do·ber·man pin·scher \ˈdō-bər-mən- ˈpin-chər\ *n* : a short-haired medium-sized dog of a breed of German origin

do·bra \ˈdō-brə\ *n* — see MONEY table

¹doc \ˈdäk\ *n* : DOCTOR

²doc *abbr* document

do·cent \ˈdōs-ᵊnt, dȯt-ˈsent\ *n* [obs. G (now *Dozent*), fr. L *docens*, prp. of *docēre* to teach] : TEACHER, LECTURER; *also* : a person who leads a guided tour

doc·ile \ˈdä-səl\ *adj* [L *docilis*, fr. *docēre* to teach] : easily taught, led, or managed : TRACTABLE — **do·cil·i·ty** \dä-ˈsi-lə-tē\ *n*

¹dock \ˈdäk\ *n* : any of a genus of coarse weedy herbs related to buckwheat

²dock *vb* **1** : to cut off the end of : cut short **2** : to take away a part of : deduct from ⟨∼ a worker's wages⟩

³dock *n* **1** : an artificial basin to receive ships **2** : ²SLIP 2 **3** : a wharf or platform for loading or unloading materials

⁴dock *vb* **1** : to bring or come into dock **2** : to join (as two spacecraft) mechanically in space

⁵dock *n* : the place in a court where a prisoner stands or sits during trial

dock·age \ˈdä-kij\ *n* : docking facilities

dock·et \ˈdä-kət\ *n* **1** : a formal abridged record of the proceedings in a legal action; *also* : a register of such records **2** : a list of legal causes to be tried **3** : a calendar of matters to be acted on : AGENDA **4** : a label attached

to a document containing identification or directions —
docket *vb*
dock·hand \'däk-ˌhand\ *n* : LONGSHOREMAN
dock·work·er \-ˌwər-kər\ *n* : LONGSHOREMAN
dock·yard \-ˌyärd\ *n* : SHIPYARD
¹**doc·tor** \'däk-tər\ *n* [ME *doctour* teacher, doctor, fr. MF & ML; MF, fr. ML *doctor*, fr. L, teacher, fr. *docēre* to teach] **1** : a person holding one of the highest academic degrees (as a PhD) conferred by a university **2** : one skilled in healing arts; *esp* : an academically and legally qualified physician, surgeon, dentist, or veterinarian **3** : a person who restores or repairs things — **doc·tor·al** \-tə-rəl\ *adj*
²**doctor** *vb* **1** : to give medical treatment to **2** : to practice medicine **3** : REPAIR **4** : to adapt or modify for a desired end **5** : to alter deceptively
doc·tor·ate \'däk-tə-rət\ *n* : the degree, title, or rank of a doctor
doc·tri·naire \ˌdäk-trə-'nar\ *n* [F] : one who attempts to put an abstract theory into effect without regard to practical difficulties — **doctrinaire** *adj*
doc·trine \'däk-trən\ *n* **1** : something that is taught **2** : DOGMA, TENET — **doc·tri·nal** \-trən-ᵊl\ *adj*
docu·dra·ma \'dä-kyə-ˌdrä-mə, -ˌdra-\ *n* : a drama for television, motion pictures, or theater that deals freely with historical events
doc·u·ment \'dä-kyə-mənt\ *n* : a paper that furnishes information, proof, or support of something else — **doc·u·ment** \-ˌment\ *vb* — **doc·u·men·ta·tion** \ˌdä-kyə-mən-'tä-shən\ *n* — **doc·u·ment·er** *n*
doc·u·men·ta·ry \ˌdä-kyə-'men-tə-rē\ *adj* **1** : consisting of documents; *also* : being in writing ⟨~ proof⟩ **2** : giving a factual presentation in artistic form ⟨a ~ movie⟩ — **documentary** *n*
DOD *abbr* Department of Defense
¹**dod·der** \'dä-dər\ *n* : any of a genus of leafless elongated wiry parasitic herbs deficient in chlorophyll
²**dodder** *vb* **dod·dered; dod·der·ing 1** : to tremble or shake usu. from age **2** : to progress feebly and unsteadily
¹**dodge** \'däj\ *n* **1** : an act of evading by sudden bodily movement **2** : an artful device to evade, deceive, or trick **3** : EXPEDIENT
²**dodge** *vb* **dodged; dodg·ing 1** : to evade usu. by trickery **2** : to move suddenly aside; *also* : to avoid or evade by so doing — **dodg·er** *n*
do·do \'dō dō\ *n, pl* **dodoes** *or* **dodos** [Pg *doudo*, fr. *doudo* silly, stupid] **1** : an extinct heavy flightless bird of the island of Mauritius related to the pigeons and larger than a turkey **2** : one hopelessly behind the times; *also* : a stupid person

dodo 1

doe \'dō\ *n, pl* **does** *or* **doe** : an adult female of various mammals (as a deer, rabbit, or kangaroo) of which the male is called *buck*

DOE *abbr* Department of Energy
do·er \'dü-ər\ *n* : one that does
does *pres 3d sing of* DO, *pl of* DOE
doff \'däf\ *vb* [ME, fr. *don* to do + *of* off] **1** : to take off (the hat) in greeting or as a sign of respect **2** : to rid oneself of
¹**dog** \'dȯg\ *n* **1** : a flesh-eating domestic mammal related to the wolves; *esp* : a male of this animal **2** : a worthless person **3** : FELLOW, CHAP ⟨you lucky ~⟩ **4** : a mechanical device for holding something **5** : uncharacteristic or affected stylishness or dignity ⟨put on the ~⟩ **6** *pl* : RUIN ⟨gone to the ~s⟩
²**dog** *vb* **dogged; dog·ging 1** : to hunt or track like a hound **2** : to worry as if by pursuit with dogs : PLAGUE
dog·bane \'dȯg-ˌbān\ *n* : any of a genus of mostly poisonous herbs with milky juice and often showy flowers
dog·cart \-ˌkärt\ *n* : a light one-horse carriage with two seats back to back
dog·catch·er \-ˌka-chər, -ˌke-\ *n* : a community official assigned to catch and dispose of stray dogs
dog–ear \'dȯ-ˌgir\ *n* : the turned-down corner of a leaf of a book — **dog–ear** *vb* — **dog–eared** \-ˌgird\ *adj*
dog·fight \'dȯg-ˌfīt\ *n* : a fight between fighter planes at close range
dog·fish \-ˌfish\ *n* : any of various small sharks
dog·ged \'dȯ-gəd\ *adj* : stubbornly determined : TENACIOUS — **dog·ged·ly** *adv* — **dog·ged·ness** *n*
dog·ger·el \'dȯ-gə-rəl\ *n* : verse that is loosely styled and irregular in measure esp. for comic effect
dog·gie bag *or* **doggy bag** \'dȯ-gē-\ *n* : a container for carrying home leftover food from a restaurant meal
¹**dog·gy** *or* **dog·gie** \'dȯ-gē\ *n, pl* **doggies** : a small dog
²**dog·gy** *adj* **dog·gi·er; -est** : of or resembling a dog ⟨a ~ odor⟩
dog·house \'dȯg-ˌhaus\ *n* : a shelter for a dog — **in the doghouse** : in a state of disfavor
do·gie \'dȯ-gē\ *n, chiefly West* : a motherless calf in a range herd
dog·leg \'dȯg-ˌleg\ *n* : a sharp bend or angle (as in a road) — **dogleg** *vb*
dog·ma \'dȯg-mə\ *n, pl* **dogmas** *also* **dog·ma·ta** \-mə-tə\ **1** : a tenet or code of tenets **2** : a doctrine or body of doctrines formally proclaimed by a church
dog·ma·tism \'dȯg-mə-ˌti-zəm\ *n* : positiveness in stating matters of opinion esp. when unwarranted or arrogant — **dog·mat·ic** \dȯg-'ma-tik\ *adj* — **dog·mat·i·cal·ly** \-ti-k(ə-)lē\ *adv*
do–good·er \'dü-ˌgù-dər\ *n* : an earnest often naive humanitarian or reformer
dog·tooth violet \'dȯg-ˌtüth-\ *n* : any of a genus of wild spring-flowering bulbous herbs related to the lilies
dog·trot \'dȯg-ˌträt\ *n* : a gentle trot — **dogtrot** *vb*
dog·wood \'dȯg-ˌwůd\ *n* : any of a genus of trees and shrubs having heads of small flowers often with showy white, pink, or red bracts

dogwood

doi·ly \'dȯi-lē\ *n, pl* **doilies** : a small often decorative mat
do in *vb* **1** : RUIN **2** : KILL **3** : TIRE, EXHAUST **4** : CHEAT
do·ings \'dü-iŋz\ *n pl* : GOINGS-ON
do–it–yourself *n* : the activity of doing or making something without professional training or help — **do–it–your·self·er** *n*
dol *abbr* dollar
dol·drums \'dōl-drəmz, 'däl-\ *n pl* **1** : a spell of listlessness or despondency **2** *often cap* : a part of the ocean near the equator known for calms **3** : a state or period of inactivity, stagnation, or slump
¹dole \'dōl\ *n* **1** : a distribution esp. of food, money, or clothing to the needy; *also* : something so distributed **2** : a grant of government funds to the unemployed
²dole *vb* **doled; dol·ing** : to give or distribute as a charity — usu. used with *out*
dole·ful \'dōl-fəl\ *adj* : full of grief : SAD — **dole·ful·ly** *adv*
dole out *vb* **1** : to give or deliver in small portions **2** : DISH OUT
doll \'däl, 'dȯl\ *n* **1** : a small figure of a human being used esp. as a child's plaything **2** : a pretty woman **3** : an attractive person — **doll·ish** \'dä-lish, 'dȯ-\ *adj*
dol·lar \'dä-lər\ *n* [Dutch or LG *daler*, fr. G *Taler*, short for *Joachimstaler*, fr. Sankt *Joachimsthal*, Bohemia, where talers were first made] **1** : any of various basic monetary units (as in the U.S. and Canada) — see MONEY table **2** : a coin, note, or token representing one dollar **3** : RINGGIT
dol·lop \'dä-ləp\ *n* **1** : LUMP, GLOB **2** : PORTION 1 — **dol·lop** *vb*
doll up *vb* **1** : to dress elegantly or extravagantly **2** : to make more attractive **3** : to get dolled up
dol·ly \'dä-lē\ *n, pl* **dollies** : a small cart or wheeled platform (as for a television or movie camera)
dol·men \'dōl-mən, 'däl-\ *n* : a prehistoric monument consisting of two or more upright stones supporting a horizontal stone slab
do·lo·mite \'dō-lə-ˌmīt, 'dä-\ *n* : a mineral found in broad layers as a compact limestone
do·lor \'dō-lər, 'dä-\ *n* : mental suffering or anguish : SORROW — **do·lor·ous** *adj* — **do·lor·ous·ly** *adv*
dol·phin \'däl-fən\ *n* **1** : any of various small toothed whales with the snout more or less elongated into a beak **2** : either of two active food fishes of tropical and temperate seas
dolt \'dōlt\ *n* : a stupid person — **dolt·ish** \'dōl-tish\ *adj* — **dolt·ish·ness** *n*
dom *abbr* **1** domestic **2** dominant **3** dominion
-dom *n suffix* **1** : dignity : office ⟨duke*dom*⟩ **2** : realm : jurisdiction ⟨king*dom*⟩ **3** : state or fact of being ⟨free*dom*⟩ **4** : those having a (specified) office, occupation, interest, or character ⟨official*dom*⟩
do·main \dō-'mān\ *n* **1** : complete and absolute ownership of land **2** : land completely owned **3** : a territory over which dominion is exercised **4** : a sphere of knowledge, influence, or activity ⟨the ∼ of science⟩
dome \'dōm\ *n* **1** : a large hemispherical roof or ceiling **2** : a structure or natural formation that resembles the dome of a building **3** : a roofed sports stadium — **dome** *vb*
¹do·mes·tic \də-'mes-tik\ *adj* **1** : living near or about human habitations **2** : TAME, DOMESTICATED **3** : relating and limited to one's own country or the country under consideration **4** : of or relating to the household or the family **5** : devoted to home duties and pleasures **6** : INDIGENOUS — **do·mes·ti·cal·ly** \-ti-k(ə-)lē\ *adv*
²domestic *n* : a household servant
do·mes·ti·cate \də-'mes-ti-ˌkāt\ *vb* **-cat·ed; -cat·ing** : to adapt to life in association with and to the use of humans — **do·mes·ti·ca·tion** \-ˌmes-ti-'kā-shən\ *n*
do·mes·tic·i·ty \ˌdō-ˌmes-'ti-sə-tē, də-\ *n, pl* **-ties 1** : the

quality or state of being domestic or domesticated **2** : domestic activities or life
do·mi·cile \'dä-mə-ˌsīl, 'dō-; 'dä-mə-səl\ *n* : a dwelling place : HOME — **domicile** *vb* — **dom·i·cil·i·ary** \ˌdä-mə-'si-lē-ˌer-ē, ˌdō-\ *adj*
dom·i·nance \'dä-mə-nəns\ *n* **1** : AUTHORITY, CONTROL **2** : the property of a genetic dominant that prevents expression of a genetic recessive
¹dom·i·nant \-nənt\ *adj* **1** : controlling or prevailing over all others **2** : overlooking from a high position **3** : producing or being a bodily characteristic that is expressed when a contrasting recessive gene or trait is present
²dominant *n* : a dominant gene or trait
dom·i·nate \'dä-mə-ˌnāt\ *vb* **-nat·ed; -nat·ing 1** : RULE, CONTROL **2** : to have a commanding position or controlling power over **3** : to rise high above in a position suggesting power to dominate — **dom·i·na·tor** \-ˌnā-tər\ *n*
dom·i·na·tion \ˌdä-mə-'nā-shən\ *n* **1** : supremacy or preeminence over another **2** : exercise of mastery, ruling power, or preponderant influence
do·mi·na·trix \ˌdä-mə-'nā-triks\ *n, pl* **-trices** \-'nā-trə-ˌsēz, -nə-'trī-sēz\ : a woman who dominates and abuses her sexual partner; *also* : a dominating woman
dom·i·neer \ˌdä-mə-'nir\ *vb* **1** : to rule in an arrogant manner **2** : to be overbearing
Do·min·i·can \də-'mi-ni-kən\ *n* : a native or inhabitant of the Dominican Republic — **Dominican** *adj*
do·mi·nie *1* *usu* 'dä-mə-nē, *2* *usu* 'dō-\ *n* **1** *chiefly Scot* : SCHOOLMASTER **2** : CLERGYMAN
do·min·ion \də-'min-yən\ *n* **1** : DOMAIN **2** : supreme authority : SOVEREIGNTY **3** *often cap* : a self-governing nation of the Commonwealth
dom·i·no \'dä-mə-ˌnō\ *n, pl* **-noes** *or* **-nos 1** : a long loose hooded cloak usu. worn with a half mask as a masquerade costume **2** : a flat rectangular block used as a piece in a game (**dominoes**)
¹don \'dän\ *vb* **donned; don·ning** [ME, fr. *don* to do + *on*] : to put on (as clothes)
²don *n* [Sp, fr. L *dominus* lord, master] **1** : a Spanish nobleman or gentleman — used as a title prefixed to the Christian name **2** : a head, tutor, or fellow in an English university
do·ña \'dō-nyə\ *n* : a Spanish woman of rank — used as a title prefixed to the Christian name
do·nate \'dō-ˌnāt\ *vb* **do·nat·ed; do·nat·ing 1** : to make a gift of : CONTRIBUTE **2** : to make a donation
do·na·tion \dō-'nā-shən\ *n* **1** : the making of a gift esp. to a charity **2** : a free contribution : GIFT
¹done \'dən\ *past part of* DO
²done *adj* **1** : doomed to failure, defeat, or death **2** : gone by : OVER ⟨when day is ∼⟩ **3** : cooked sufficiently **4** : conformable to social convention
dong \'dȯŋ, 'däŋ\ *n* — see MONEY table
don·key \'däŋ-kē, 'dəŋ-\ *n, pl* **donkeys 1** : a sturdy and patient domestic mammal classified with the asses **2** : a stupid or obstinate person
don·ny·brook \'dä-nē-ˌbrük\ *n, often cap* [*Donnybrook Fair*, annual Irish event once known for its brawls] : an uproarious brawl
do·nor \'dō-nər\ *n* : one that gives, donates, or presents
donut *var of* DOUGHNUT
doo·dad \'dü-ˌdad\ *n* : an often small article whose common name is unknown or forgotten
doo·dle \'düd-ᵊl\ *vb* **doo·dled; doo·dling** : to draw or scribble aimlessly while occupied with something else — **doodle** *n* — **doo·dler** *n*
doom \'düm\ *n* **1** : JUDGMENT; *esp* : a judicial condemnation or sentence **2** : DESTINY **3** : RUIN, DEATH — **doom** *vb*
dooms·day \'dümz-ˌdā\ *n* : JUDGMENT DAY
door \'dȯr\ *n* **1** : a barrier by which an entry is closed and opened; *also* : a similar part of a piece of furniture

2 : DOORWAY 3 : a means of access or participation : OP-
PORTUNITY
door·keep·er \-ˌkē-pər\ *n* : a person who tends a door
door·knob \-ˌnäb\ *n* : a knob that when turned releases
a door latch
door·man \-ˌman, -mən\ *n* : a usu. uniformed attendant
at the door of a building (as a hotel)
door·mat \-ˌmat\ *n* : a mat placed before or inside a door
for wiping dirt from the shoes
door·plate \-ˌplāt\ *n* : a nameplate on a door
door·step \-ˌstep\ *n* : a step or series of steps before an
outer door
door·way \-ˌwā\ *n* **1** : the opening that a door closes **2**
: DOOR 3
do·pa \ˈdō-pə\ *n* : a form of an amino acid that is used
esp. in the treatment of Parkinson's disease
¹dope \ˈdōp\ *n* **1** : a preparation for giving a desired quality **2** : a drug esp. when narcotic or addictive and used
illegally **3** : a stupid person **4** : INFORMATION
²dope *vb* **doped; dop·ing 1** : to treat with dope; *esp* : to
give a narcotic to **2** : FIGURE OUT — usu. used with *out*
3 : to take dope — **dop·er** *n*
dop·ey *also* **dopy** \ˈdō-pē\ *adj* **dop·i·er; -est 1** : dulled by
alcohol or a narcotic **2** : SLUGGISH **3** : STUPID — **dop-
i·ness** *n*
Dopp·ler effect \ˈdä-plər-\ *n* : a change in the frequency
at which waves (as of sound) reach an observer from a
source in motion with respect to the observer
dork \ˈdork\ *n, slang* : NERD; *also* : JERK 2
dorm \ˈdorm\ *n* : DORMITORY
dor·mant \ˈdor-mənt\ *adj* : INACTIVE; *esp* : not actively
growing or functioning ⟨∼ buds⟩ — **dor·man·cy** \-mən-
sē\ *n*
dor·mer \ˈdor-mər\ *n* [MF *dormeor* dormitory, fr. L *dor-
mitorium*, fr. *dormire* to sleep] : a window built upright
in a sloping roof; *also* : the roofed structure containing
such a window
dor·mi·to·ry \ˈdor-mə-ˌtor-ē\ *n, pl* **-ries 1** : a room for
sleeping; *esp* : a large room containing a number of
beds **2** : a residence hall providing sleeping rooms
dor·mouse \ˈdor-ˌmau̇s\ *n* : any of numerous Old World
squirrellike rodents
dor·sal \ˈdor-səl\ *adj* : of, relating to, or located near or
on the surface of the body that in humans is the back
but in most other animals is the upper surface — **dor-
sal·ly** *adv*
do·ry \ˈdor-ē\ *n, pl* **dories** : a flat-bottomed boat with
high flaring sides and a sharp bow
DOS *abbr* disk operating system
¹dose \ˈdōs\ *n* [ME, fr. MF, fr. LL *dosis*, fr. Gk, lit., act
of giving, fr. *didonai* to give] **1** : a measured quantity (as
of medicine) to be taken or administered at one time **2**
: the quantity of radiation administered or absorbed —
dos·age \ˈdō-sij\ *n*
²dose *vb* **dosed; dos·ing 1** : to give in doses **2** : to give
medicine to
do·sim·e·ter \dō-ˈsi-mə-tər\ *n* : a device for measuring
doses of X rays or of radioactivity — **do·sim·e·try**
\-mə-trē\ *n*
dos·sier \ˈdos-ˌyā, ˈdo-sē-ˌā\ *n* [F, bundle of documents
labeled on the back, dossier, fr. *dos* back, fr. L *dorsum*]
: a file containing detailed records on a particular person or subject
¹dot \ˈdät\ *n* **1** : a small spot : SPECK **2** : a small round mark
3 : a precise point esp. in time ⟨be here on the ∼⟩
²dot *vb* **dot·ted; dot·ting 1** : to mark with a dot ⟨∼ an *i*⟩
2 : to cover with or as if with dots — **dot·ter** *n*
DOT *abbr* Department of Transportation
dot·age \ˈdō-tij\ *n* : feebleness of mind esp. in old age
: SENILITY
dot·ard \-tərd\ *n* : a person in dotage
dote \ˈdōt\ *vb* **dot·ed; dot·ing 1** : to be feebleminded esp.
from old age **2** : to be lavish or excessive in one's at-

tention, affection, or fondness ⟨*doted* on her niece⟩
dot matrix *n* : a rectangular arrangement of dots from
which alphanumeric characters can be formed (as by a
computer printer)
Dou·ay Version \dü-ˈā-\ *n* : an English translation of the
Vulgate used by Roman Catholics
¹dou·ble \ˈdə-bəl\ *adj* **1** : TWOFOLD, DUAL **2** : consisting
of two members or parts **3** : being twice as great or as
many **4** : folded in two **5** : having more than one whorl
of petals ⟨∼ roses⟩
²double *vb* **dou·bled; dou·bling 1** : to make, be, or become twice as great or as many **2** : to make a call in
bridge that increases the trick values and penalties of
(an opponent's bid) **3** : FOLD **4** : CLENCH **5** : to be or
cause to be bent over **6** : to take the place of another
7 : to hit a double **8** : to turn sharply and suddenly; *esp*
: to turn back on one's course
³double *adv* **1** : DOUBLY **2** : two together
⁴double *n* **1** : something twice another in size, strength,
speed, quantity, or value **2** : a base hit that enables the
batter to reach second base **3** : COUNTERPART, DUPLI-
CATE; *esp* : a person who closely resembles another **4**
: UNDERSTUDY, SUBSTITUTE **5** : a sharp turn : REVERSAL
6 : FOLD **7** : a combined bet placed on two different contests **8** *pl* : a game between two pairs of players **9** : an
act of doubling in a card game
double bond *n* : a chemical bond in which two atoms in
a molecule share two pairs of electrons
double cross *n* : an act of betraying or cheating esp. an
associate — **dou·ble-cross** \ˌdə-bəl-ˈkrȯs\ *vb* — **dou-
ble-cross·er** *n*
dou·ble-deal·ing \ˌdə-bəl-ˈdē-liŋ\ *n* : DUPLICITY — **dou-
ble-deal·er** \-ˈdē-lər\ *n* — **double-dealing** *adj*
dou·ble-deck·er \-ˈde-kər\ *n* : something having two
decks, levels, or layers — **dou·ble-deck** \-ˌdek\ *or* **dou-
ble-decked** \-ˌdekt\ *adj*
dou·ble-dig·it \ˌdə-bəl-ˈdi-jət\ *adj* : amounting to 10 percent or more
dou·ble en·ten·dre \ˌdüb-əl-än-ˈtänd, ˌdə-bəl-, -ˈtänd-rⁿ\
n, pl **double entendres** *same or* -ˈtän-drəz\ [obs. F,
lit., double meaning] : a word or expression capable of
two interpretations with one usu. risqué
dou·ble-head·er \ˌdə-bəl-ˈhe-dər\ *n* : two games played
consecutively on the same day
double helix *n* : a helix or spiral consisting of two
strands (as of DNA) in the surface of a cylinder which
coil around its axis
dou·ble-hung \ˌdə-bəl-ˈhəŋ\ *adj, of a window* : having
an upper and a lower sash that can slide past each other
dou·ble-joint·ed \-ˈjȯin-təd\ *adj* : having a joint that permits an exceptional degree of freedom of motion of the
parts joined ⟨a ∼ finger⟩
double play *n* : a play in baseball by which two players
are put out
dou·blet \ˈdə-blət\ *n* **1** : a man's close-fitting jacket worn
in Europe esp. in the 16th century **2** : one of two similar
or identical things
dou·ble take \ˈdə-bəl-ˌtāk\ *n* : a delayed reaction to a
surprising or significant situation after an initial failure
to notice anything unusual
dou·ble-talk \-ˌtȯk\ *n* : language that appears to be
meaningful but in fact is a mixture of sense and nonsense
double up *vb* : to share accommodations designed for
one
double whammy *n* : a combination of two usu. adverse
forces, circumstances, or effects

\ə\abut \ᵊ\kitten \ər\further \a\ash \ā\ace \ä\mop, mar
\au̇\out \ch\chin \e\bet \ē\easy \g\go \i\hit \ī\ice \j\job
\ŋ\sing \ō\go \ȯ\law \ȯi\boy \th\thin \t͟h\the \ü\loot \u̇\foot
\y\yet \zh\vision *see also* Pronunciation Symbols page

dou·bloon \də-'blün\ n : a former gold coin of Spain and Spanish America

dou·bly \'də-blē\ adv 1 : in a twofold manner 2 : to twice the degree

¹**doubt** \'daut\ vb 1 : to be uncertain about 2 : to lack confidence in : DISTRUST 3 : to consider unlikely — **doubt·able** adj — **doubt·er** n

²**doubt** n 1 : uncertainty of belief or opinion 2 : a condition causing uncertainty, hesitation, or suspense ⟨the outcome was in ∼⟩ 3 : DISTRUST 4 : an inclination not to believe or accept

doubt·ful \'daut-fəl\ adj 1 : QUESTIONABLE 2 : UNDECIDED — **doubt·ful·ly** adv — **doubt·ful·ness** n

¹**doubt·less** \'daut-ləs\ adv 1 : without doubt 2 : PROBABLY

²**doubtless** adj : free from doubt : CERTAIN — **doubt·less·ly** adv

douche \'düsh\ n [F] 1 : a jet of fluid (as water) directed against a part or into a cavity of the body; also : a cleansing with a douche 2 : a device for giving douches — **douche** vb

dough \'dō\ n 1 : a mixture that consists of flour or meal and a liquid (as milk or water) and is stiff enough to knead or roll 2 : something resembling dough esp. in consistency 3 : MONEY — **doughy** \'dō-ē\ adj

dough·boy \-ˌbòi\ n : an American infantryman esp. in World War I

dough·nut \-(ˌ)nət\ n : a small usu. ring-shaped cake fried in fat

dough·ty \'daù-tē\ adj **dough·ti·er; -est** : ABLE, STRONG, VALIANT

Doug·las fir \'də-gləs-\ n : a tall evergreen timber tree of the western U.S.

do up vb 1 : to prepare (as by cleaning) for use 2 : to wrap up 3 : CLOTHE, DECORATE

dour \'daùr, 'dùr\ adj [ME, fr. L durus hard] 1 : STERN, HARSH 2 : OBSTINATE 3 : SULLEN — **dour·ly** adv

douse \'daùs, 'daùz\ vb **doused; dous·ing** 1 : to plunge into water 2 : DRENCH 3 : EXTINGUISH

¹**dove** \'dəv\ n 1 : any of numerous pigeons; esp : a small wild pigeon 2 : an advocate of peace or of a peaceful policy — **dov·ish** \'də-vish\ adj

²**dove** \'dōv\ past of DIVE

¹**dove·tail** \'dəv-ˌtāl\ n : something that resembles a dove's tail; esp : a flaring tenon and a mortise into which it fits tightly

²**dovetail** vb 1 : to join by means of dovetails 2 : to fit skillfully together to form a whole ⟨our plans ∼ nicely⟩

dow·a·ger \'daù-i-jər\ n 1 : a widow owning property or a title from her deceased husband 2 : a dignified elderly woman

dowdy \'daù-dē\ adj **dowd·i·er; -est** : lacking neatness and charm : SHABBY, UNTIDY; also : lacking smartness

dow·el \'daù-əl\ n 1 : a pin used for fastening together two pieces of wood 2 : a round rod (as of wood) — **dowel** vb

¹**dow·er** \'daù-ər\ n 1 : the part of a deceased husband's real estate which the law gives for life to his widow 2 : DOWRY

²**dower** vb : to supply with a dower or dowry : ENDOW

dow·itch·er \'daù-i-chər\ n : any of several long-billed wading birds related to the sandpipers

¹**down** \'daùn\ adv 1 : toward or in a lower physical position 2 : to a lying or sitting position 3 : toward or to the ground, floor, or bottom 4 : as a down payment ⟨paid $5 ∼⟩ 5 : on paper ⟨put ∼ what he says⟩ 6 : in a direction that is the opposite of up 7 : SOUTH 8 : to or in a lower or worse condition or status 9 : from a past time 10 : to or in a state of less activity 11 : into defeat ⟨voted the motion ∼⟩

²**down** prep : down in, on, along, or through : toward the bottom of

³**down** vb 1 : to go or cause to go or come down 2 : DEFEAT 3 : to cause (a football) to be out of play

⁴**down** adj 1 : occupying a low position; esp : lying on the ground 2 : directed or going downward 3 : being in a state of reduced or low activity 4 : DEPRESSED, DEJECTED 5 : SICK ⟨∼ with a cold⟩ 6 : FINISHED, DONE

⁵**down** n 1 : a low or falling period (as in activity, emotional life, or fortunes) 2 : one of a series of attempts to advance a football

⁶**down** n : a rolling usu. treeless upland with sparse soil — usu. used in pl.

⁷**down** n 1 : a covering of soft fluffy feathers; also : such feathers 2 : a downlike covering or material

down·beat \'daùn-ˌbēt\ n : the downward stroke of a conductor indicating the principally accented note of a measure of music

down·burst \-ˌbərst\ n : a powerful downdraft usu. associated with a thunderstorm that is a hazard for low-flying aircraft; also : MICROBURST

down·cast \-ˌkast\ adj 1 : DEJECTED 2 : directed down ⟨a ∼ glance⟩

down·draft \-ˌdraft\ n : a downward current of gas (as air)

down·er \'daù-nər\ n 1 : a depressant drug; esp : BARBITURATE 2 : someone or something depressing

down·fall \'daùn-ˌfól\ n 1 : a sudden fall (as from high rank) 2 : something that causes a downfall — **down·fall·en** \-ˌfó-lən\ adj

¹**down·grade** \'daùn-ˌgrād\ n 1 : a downward slope (as of a road) 2 : a decline toward a worse condition

²**downgrade** vb : to lower in quality, value, extent, or status

down·heart·ed \-'här-təd\ adj : DEJECTED

down·hill \'daùn-'hil\ adv : toward the bottom of a hill — **downhill** \-ˌhil\ adj

down·load \-ˌlōd\ vb : to transfer (data) from a computer to another device — **down·load·able** \-ˌlō-də-bəl\ adj

down payment n : a part of the full price paid at the time of purchase or delivery with the balance to be paid later

down·pour \'daùn-ˌpòr\ n : a heavy rain

down·range \-ˌrānj\ adv : away from a launching site

¹**down·right** \-ˌrīt\ adv : THOROUGHLY

²**downright** adj 1 : ABSOLUTE, UTTER ⟨a ∼ lie⟩ 2 : PLAIN, BLUNT ⟨a ∼ man⟩

down·shift \-ˌshift\ vb : to shift an automotive vehicle into a lower gear

down·size \-ˌsīz\ vb : to reduce or undergo reduction in size or numbers

down·spout \-ˌspaùt\ n : a vertical pipe used to drain rainwater from a roof

Down's syndrome \'daùnz-\ or **Down syndrome** \'daùn-\ n : a birth defect characterized by mental retardation, slanting eyes, a broad short skull, broad hands with short fingers, and the presence of an extra chromosome

down·stage \'daùn-'stāj\ adv or adj : toward or at the front of a theatrical stage

down·stairs \-'starz\ adv : on or to a lower floor and esp. the main or ground floor — **down·stairs** \-ˌstarz\ adj or n

down·stream \-'strēm\ adv or adj : in the direction of flow of a stream

down·stroke \-ˌstrōk\ n : a downward stroke

down·swing \-ˌswiŋ\ n 1 : a swing downward 2 : DOWNTURN

down-to-earth adj : PRACTICAL, REALISTIC

down·town \'daùn-ˌtaùn\ n : the main business district of a town or city — **downtown** \'daùn-'taùn\ adj or adv

down·trod·den \'daùn-'träd-ᵊn\ adj : suffering oppression

down·turn \-ˌtərn\ n : a downward turn esp. in business activity

¹**down·ward** \'daùn-wərd\ or **down·wards** \-wərdz\ adv 1 : from a higher to a lower place or condition 2 : from an earlier time 3 : from an ancestor or predecessor

²**downward** *adj* : directed toward or situated in a lower place or condition

down·wind \'daùn-'wind\ *adv or adj* : in the direction that the wind is blowing

downy \'daù-nē\ *adj* **down·i·er; -est** : resembling or covered with down

downy mildew *n* : any of various parasitic fungi producing whitish masses esp. on the underside of plant leaves; *also* : a plant disease caused by downy mildew

downy woodpecker *n* : a small black-and-white woodpecker of No. America

dow·ry \'daùr-ē\ *n, pl* **dowries** : the property that a woman brings to her husband in marriage

dowse \'daùz\ *vb* **dowsed; dows·ing** : to use a divining rod esp. to find water — **dows·er** *n*

dox·ol·o·gy \däk-'sä-lə-jē\ *n, pl* **-gies** : a usu. short hymn of praise to God

doy·en \'dòi-ən, 'dwä-ˌyaᵐ\ *n* : the senior or most experienced person in a group

doy·enne \dòi-'yen, dwä-'yen\ *n* : a woman who is a doyen

doy·ley *chiefly Brit var of* DOILY

doz *abbr* dozen

doze \'dòz\ *vb* **dozed; doz·ing** : to sleep lightly — **doze** *n*

doz·en \'dəz-ᵊn\ *n, pl* **dozens or dozen** [ME *dozeine*, fr. OF *dozaine*, fr. *doze* twelve, fr. L *duodecim*, fr. *duo* two + *deçem* ten] : a group of twelve — **doz·enth** \-ᵊnth\ *adj*

¹**DP** \ˌdē-'pē\ *n, pl* **DP's or DPs** : a displaced person

²**DP** *abbr* **1** data processing **2** double play

dpt *abbr* department

DPT *abbr* diphtheria-pertussis-tetanus (vaccines)

dr *abbr* **1** debtor **2** dram **3** drive **4** drum

Dr *abbr* doctor

DR *abbr* **1** dead reckoning **2** dining room

drab \'drab\ *adj* **drab·ber; drab·best 1** : being of a light olive-brown color **2** : DULL, MONOTONOUS, CHEERLESS — **drab·ly** *adv* — **drab·ness** *n*

drach·ma \'drak-mə\ *n, pl* **drach·mas or drach·mai** \-ˌmī\ *or* **drach·mae** \-(ˌ)mē\ — see MONEY table

dra·co·ni·an \drā-'kō-nē-ən, drə-\ *adj, often cap* : CRUEL; *also* : SEVERE

¹**draft** \'draft, 'dråft\ *n* **1** : the act of drawing or hauling **2** : the act or an instance of drinking or inhaling; *also* : the portion drunk or inhaled in one such act **3** : DOSE, POTION **4** : DELINEATION, PLAN, DESIGN; *also* : a preliminary sketch, outline, or version ⟨a rough ∼ of a speech⟩ **5** : the act of drawing (as from a cask); *also* : a portion of liquid so drawn **6** : the depth of water a ship draws esp. when loaded **7** : a system for or act of selecting persons esp. for compulsory military service; *also* : the persons so selected **8** : an order for the payment of money drawn by one person or bank on another **9** : a heavy demand : STRAIN **10** : a current of air; *also* : a device to regulate air supply (as in a stove) — **on draft** : ready to be drawn from a receptacle ⟨beer *on draft*⟩

²**draft** *adj* **1** : used or adapted for drawing loads ⟨∼ horses⟩ **2** : being or having been on draft ⟨∼ beer⟩

³**draft** *vb* **1** : to select usu. on a compulsory basis; *esp* : to conscript for military service **2** : to draw the preliminary sketch, version, or plan of **3** : COMPOSE, PREPARE **4** : to draw off or away — **draft·ee** \draf-'tē, dråf-\ *n*

drafts·man \'draft-smən, 'dråft-\ *n* : a person who draws plans (as for buildings or machinery)

drafty \'draf-tē, 'dråf-\ *adj* **draft·i·er; -est** : exposed to or abounding in drafts of air

¹**drag** \'drag\ *n* **1** : a device pulled along under water for detecting or gathering **2** : something (as a harrow or sledge) that is dragged along over a surface **3** : the act or an instance of dragging **4** : something that hinders progress; *also* : something boring **5** : STREET ⟨the main ∼⟩ **6** : clothing typical of one sex worn by a member of the opposite sex

²**drag** *vb* **dragged; drag·ging 1** : HAUL **2** : to move with painful or undue slowness or difficulty **3** : to force into or out of some situation, condition, or course of action **4** : PROTRACT ⟨∼ a story out⟩ **5** : to hang or lag behind **6** : to explore, search, or fish with a drag **7** : to trail along on the ground **8** : DRAW, PUFF ⟨∼ on a cigarette⟩ — **drag·ger** *n*

drag·net \-ˌnet\ *n* **1** : NET, TRAWL **2** : a network of planned actions for pursuing and catching ⟨a police ∼⟩

drag·o·man \'dra-gə-mən\ *n, pl* **-mans or -men** \-mən\ : an interpreter employed esp. in the Near East

drag·on \'dra-gən\ *n* [ME, fr. OF, fr. L *dracon-, draco* serpent, dragon, fr. Gk *drakòn* serpent] : a fabulous animal usu. represented as a huge winged scaly serpent with a crested head and large claws

drag·on·fly \-ˌflī\ *n* : any of a group of large harmless 4-winged insects that hold the wings horizontal and unfolded in repose

dragonfly

¹**dra·goon** \drə-'gün, dra-\ *n* [F *dragon* dragon, dragoon, fr. MF] : a heavily armed mounted soldier

²**dragoon** *vb* : to force or attempt to force into submission : COERCE

drag race *n* : an acceleration contest between vehicles

drag strip *n* : a site for drag races

¹**drain** \'drān\ *vb* **1** : to draw off or flow off gradually or completely **2** : to exhaust physically or emotionally **3** : to make or become gradually dry or empty **4** : to carry away the surface water of : discharge surface or surplus water **5** : EMPTY, EXHAUST — **drain·er** *n*

²**drain** *n* **1** : a means (as a channel or sewer) of draining **2** : the act of draining **3** : a gradual outflow; *also* : something causing an outflow ⟨a ∼ on our savings⟩

drain·age \'drā-nij\ *n* **1** : the act or process of draining; *also* : something that is drained off **2** : a means for draining : DRAIN, SEWER **3** : an area drained

drain·pipe \'drān-ˌpīp\ *n* : a pipe for drainage

drake \'drāk\ *n* : a male duck

dram \'dram\ *n* **1** — see WEIGHT table **2** : FLUID DRAM **3** : a small drink

dra·ma \'drä-mə, 'dra-\ *n* [LL, fr. Gk, deed, drama, fr. *dran* to do, act] **1** : a literary composition designed for theatrical presentation **2** : dramatic art, literature, or affairs **3** : a series of events involving conflicting forces — **dra·mat·ic** \drə-'ma-tik\ *adj* — **dra·mat·i·cal·ly** \-ti-k(ə-)lē\ *adv* — **dra·ma·tist** \'dra-mə-tist, 'drä-\ *n*

dra·ma·tize \'dra-mə-ˌtīz, 'drä-\ *vb* **-tized; -tiz·ing 1** : to adapt for or be suitable for theatrical presentation **2** : to present or represent in a dramatic manner — **dra·ma·ti·za·tion** \ˌdra-mə-tə-'zā-shən, ˌdrä-\ *n*

drank *past and past part of* DRINK

¹**drape** \'drāp\ *vb* **draped; drap·ing 1** : to cover or adorn with or as if with folds of cloth **2** : to cause to hang or

---

\ə\abut \ᵊ\kitten \ər\further \a\ash \ā\ace \ä\mop, mar
\aù\out \ch\chin \e\bet \ē\easy \g\go \i\hit \ī\ice \j\job
\ŋ\sing \ō\go \ò\law \òi\boy \th\thin \th̲\the \ü\loot \ù\foot
\y\yet \zh\vision *see also* Pronunciation Symbols page

stretch out loosely or carelessly **3** : to arrange or become arranged in flowing lines or folds
²**drape** *n* **1** : CURTAIN **2** : arrangement in or of folds **3** : the cut or hang of clothing
drap·er \'drā-pər\ *n, chiefly Brit* : a dealer in cloth and sometimes in clothing and dry goods
drap·ery \'drā-pə-rē\ *n, pl* **-er·ies 1** *Brit* : DRY GOODS **2** : a decorative fabric esp. when hung loosely and in folds; *also* : hangings of heavy fabric used as a curtain
dras·tic \'dras-tik\ *adj* : HARSH, RIGOROUS, SEVERE ⟨∼ punishment⟩ — **dras·ti·cal·ly** \-ti-k(ə-)lē\ *adv*
draught \'drȧft\, **draughty** \'drȧf-tē\ *chiefly Brit var of* DRAFT, DRAFTY
draughts \'drȧfts\ *n, Brit* : CHECKERS
draughts·man *chiefly Brit var of* DRAFTSMAN
¹**draw** \'drȯ\ *vb* **drew** \'drü\; **drawn** \'drȯn\; **draw·ing 1** : to cause to move toward a force exerted **2** : to cause to go in a certain direction ⟨*drew* him aside⟩ **3** : to move or go steadily or gradually ⟨night ∼s near⟩ **4** : ATTRACT, ENTICE **5** : PROVOKE, ROUSE ⟨*drew* enemy fire⟩ **6** : INHALE ⟨∼ a deep breath⟩ **7** : to bring or pull out ⟨*drew* a gun⟩ **8** : to cause to come out of a container ⟨∼ water for a bath⟩ **9** : EVISCERATE **10** : to require ⟨a specified depth⟩ to float in **11** : ACCUMULATE, GAIN ⟨∼*ing* interest⟩ **12** : to take money from a place of deposit : WITHDRAW **13** : to receive regularly ⟨∼ a salary⟩ **14** : to take ⟨cards⟩ from a stack or the dealer **15** : to receive or take at random ⟨∼ a winning number⟩ **16** : to bend ⟨a bow⟩ by pulling back the string **17** : WRINKLE, SHRINK **18** : to change shape by or as if by pulling or stretching ⟨a face *drawn* with sorrow⟩ **19** : to leave ⟨a contest⟩ undecided : TIE **20** : DELINEATE, SKETCH **21** : to write out in due form : DRAFT ⟨∼ up a will⟩ **22** : FORMULATE ⟨∼ comparisons⟩ **23** : INFER ⟨∼ a conclusion⟩ **24** : to spread or elongate ⟨metal⟩ by hammering or by pulling through dies **25** : to produce or allow a draft or current of air ⟨the chimney ∼s well⟩ **26** : to swell out in a wind ⟨all sails ∼*ing*⟩
²**draw** *n* **1** : the act, process, or result of drawing **2** : a lot or chance drawn at random **3** : a contest left undecided or deadlocked : TIE **4** : one that draws attention or patronage
draw·back \'drȯ-ˌbak\ *n* : DISADVANTAGE 2
draw·bridge \-ˌbrij\ *n* : a bridge made to be raised, lowered, or turned to permit or deny passage
draw·er \'drȯr, 'drȯ-ər\ *n* **1** : one that draws **2** *pl* : an undergarment for the lower part of the body **3** : a sliding boxlike compartment ⟨as in a table or desk⟩
draw·ing \'drȯ-iŋ\ *n* **1** : an act or instance of drawing; *esp* : an occasion when something is decided by drawing lots ⟨tonight's lottery ∼⟩ **2** : the act or art of making a figure, plan, or sketch by means of lines **3** : a representation made by drawing : SKETCH
drawing card *n* : DRAW 4
drawing room *n* : a formal reception room
drawl \'drȯl\ *vb* : to speak or utter slowly with vowels greatly prolonged — **drawl** *n*
draw on *vb* : APPROACH ⟨night *draws on*⟩
draw out *vb* **1** : PROLONG **2** : to cause to speak freely
draw·string \'drȯ-ˌstriŋ\ *n* : a string, cord, or tape for use in closing a bag or controlling fullness in garments or curtains
draw up *vb* **1** : to prepare a draft or version of **2** : to pull oneself erect **3** : to bring or come to a stop
dray \'drā\ *n* : a strong low cart for carrying heavy loads
¹**dread** \'dred\ *vb* **1** : to fear greatly **2** : to feel extreme reluctance to meet or face
²**dread** *n* : great fear esp. of some harm to come
³**dread** *adj* **1** : causing great fear or anxiety **2** : inspiring awe
dread·ful \'dred-fəl\ *adj* **1** : inspiring dread or awe : FRIGHTENING **2** : extremely distasteful, unpleasant, or shocking — **dread·ful·ly** *adv*

dread·locks \'dred-ˌläks\ *n pl* : long braids of hair over the entire head
dread·nought \'dred-ˌnȯt\ *n* : BATTLESHIP
¹**dream** \'drēm\ *n* [ME *dreem*, fr. OE *drēam* noise, joy, and ON *draumr* dream] **1** : a series of thoughts, images, or emotions occurring during sleep **2** : a dreamlike vision : DAYDREAM, REVERIE **3** : something notable for its beauty, excellence, or enjoyable quality **4** : IDEAL — **dreamy** *adj*
²**dream** *vb* **dreamed** \'dremt, 'drēmd\ *or* **dreamt** \'dremt\; **dream·ing 1** : to have a dream of **2** : to indulge in daydreams or fantasies : pass ⟨time⟩ in reverie or inaction **3** : IMAGINE — **dream·er** *n*
dream·land \'drēm-ˌland\ *n* : an unreal delightful country that exists in imagination or in dreams
dream up *vb* : INVENT, CONCOCT
dream·world \-ˌwərld\ *n* : a world of illusion or fantasy
drear \'drir\ *adj* : DREARY
drea·ry \'drir-ē\ *adj* **drea·ri·er; -est** [ME *drery*, fr. OE *drēorig* sad, bloody, fr. *drēor* gore] **1** : DOLEFUL, SAD **2** : DISMAL, GLOOMY — **drea·ri·ly** \-ə-lē\ *adv*
¹**dredge** \'drej\ *vb* **dredged; dredg·ing** : to gather or search with or as if with a dredge — **dredg·er** *n*
²**dredge** *n* : a machine or barge for removing earth or silt
³**dredge** *vb* **dredged; dredg·ing** : to coat ⟨food⟩ by sprinkling ⟨as with flour⟩
dregs \'dregz\ *n pl* **1** : SEDIMENT 1 **2** : the most undesirable part ⟨the ∼ of humanity⟩
drench \'drench\ *vb* : to wet thoroughly
¹**dress** \'dres\ *vb* **1** : to make or set straight : ALIGN **2** : to prepare for use; *esp* : BUTCHER **3** : TRIM, EMBELLISH ⟨∼ a store window⟩ **4** : to put clothes on : CLOTHE; *also* : to put on or wear formal or fancy clothes **5** : to apply dressings or medicine to **6** : to arrange ⟨the hair⟩ by combing, brushing, or curling **7** : to apply fertilizer to **8** : SMOOTH, FINISH ⟨∼ leather⟩
²**dress** *n* **1** : APPAREL, CLOTHING **2** : a garment usu. consisting of a one-piece bodice and skirt — **dress·mak·er** \-ˌmā-kər\ *n* — **dress·mak·ing** \-ˌmā-kiŋ\ *n*
³**dress** *adj* : suitable for a formal occasion; *also* : requiring formal dress
dres·sage \drə-'säzh\ *n* [F] : the execution by a trained horse of complex movements in response to barely perceptible signals from its rider
dress down *vb* : to scold severely
¹**dress·er** \'dre-sər\ *n* : a chest of drawers or bureau with a mirror
²**dresser** *n* : one that dresses
dress·ing \'dre-siŋ\ *n* **1** : the act or process of one who dresses **2** : a sauce for adding to a dish ⟨as a salad⟩ **3** : a seasoned mixture usu. used as stuffing **4** : material used to cover an injury
dressing gown *n* : a loose robe worn esp. while dressing or resting
dressy \'dre-sē\ *adj* **dress·i·er; -est 1** : showy in dress **2** : STYLISH, SMART
drew *past of* DRAW
¹**drib·ble** \'dri-bəl\ *vb* **drib·bled; drib·bling 1** : to fall or flow in drops : TRICKLE **2** : DROOL **3** : to propel by successive slight taps or bounces
²**dribble** *n* **1** : a small trickling stream or flow **2** : a drizzling shower **3** : the dribbling of a ball or puck
drib·let \'dri-blət\ *n* **1** : a trifling amount **2** : a drop of liquid
dri·er *or* **dry·er** \'drī-ər\ *n* **1** : a substance that speeds drying ⟨as of paint or ink⟩ **2** *usu dryer* : a device for drying
¹**drift** \'drift\ *n* **1** : the motion or course of something drifting **2** : a mass of matter ⟨as snow or sand⟩ piled up esp. by wind **3** : earth, gravel, and rock deposited by a glacier **4** : a general underlying design or tendency : MEANING
²**drift** *vb* **1** : to float or be driven along by or as if by a

current of water or air **2** : to become piled up by wind or water

drift·er \\'drif-tər\ *n* : a person without aim, ambition, or initiative

drift net *n* : a fishing net often miles in extent arranged to drift with the tide or current

drift·wood \\'drift-ˌwùd\ *n* : wood drifted or floated by water

¹drill \\'dril\ *n* **1** : a tool for boring holes **2** : the training of soldiers in marching and the handling of arms **3** : a regularly practiced exercise

²drill *vb* **1** : to instruct and exercise by repetition **2** : to train in or practice military drill **3** : to bore with a drill — **drill·er** *n*

³drill *n* **1** : a shallow furrow or trench in which seed is sown **2** : an agricultural implement for making furrows and dropping seed into them

⁴drill *n* : a firm cotton twilled fabric

drill·mas·ter \\'dril-ˌmas-tər\ *n* : an instructor in military drill

drill press *n* : an upright drilling machine in which the drill is pressed to the work usu. by a hand lever

drily *var of* DRYLY

¹drink \\'driŋk\ *vb* **drank** \\'draŋk\; **drunk** \\'drəŋk\ *or* **drank**; **drink·ing** **1** : to swallow liquid : IMBIBE **2** : AB-SORB **3** : to take in through the senses ⟨∼ in the beautiful scenery⟩ **4** : to give or join in a toast **5** : to drink alcoholic beverages esp. to excess — **drink·able** *adj* — **drink·er** *n*

²drink *n* **1** : BEVERAGE; *also* : an alcoholic beverage **2** : a draft or portion of liquid **3** : excessive consumption of alcoholic beverages

¹drip \\'drip\ *vb* **dripped; drip·ping** **1** : to fall or let fall in drops **2** : to let fall drops of moisture or liquid ⟨a *dripping* faucet⟩ **3** : to overflow with or as if with moisture

²drip *n* **1** : a falling in drops **2** : liquid that falls, overflows, or is extruded in drops **3** : the sound made by or as if by falling drops

¹drive \\'drīv\ *vb* **drove** \\'drōv\; **driv·en** \\'dri-vən\; **driv·ing** **1** : to urge, push, or force onward **2** : to carry through strongly ⟨∼ a bargain⟩ **3** : to set or keep in motion or operation **4** : to direct the movement or course of **5** : to convey in a vehicle **6** : to bring into a specified condition ⟨the noise ∼s me crazy⟩ **7** : FORCE, COMPEL ⟨*driven* by hunger to steal⟩ **8** : to project, inject, or impress forcefully ⟨*drove* the lesson home⟩ **9** : to produce by opening a way ⟨∼ a well⟩ **10** : to progress with strong momentum ⟨a *driving* rain⟩ **11** : to propel an object of play (as a golf ball) by a hard blow — **driv·er** *n*

²drive *n* **1** : a trip in a carriage or automobile **2** : a driving or collecting of animals ⟨a cattle ∼⟩ **3** : the guiding of logs downstream to a mill **4** : the act of driving a ball; *also* : the flight of a ball **5** : DRIVEWAY **6** : a public road for driving (as in a park) **7** : the state of being hurried and under pressure **8** : an intensive campaign ⟨membership ∼⟩ **9** : the apparatus by which motion is imparted to a machine **10** : an offensive or aggressive move : a military attack **11** : NEED, LONGING **12** : dynamic quality **13** : a device for reading and writing on magnetic media (as magnetic tape or disks)

drive–in \\'drī-ˌvin\ *adj* : accommodating patrons while they remain in their automobiles — **drive–in** *n*

¹driv·el \\'dri-vəl\ *vb* **-eled** *or* **-elled; -el·ing** *or* **-el·ling** **1** : DROOL, SLAVER **2** : to talk or utter stupidly, carelessly, or in an infantile way — **driv·el·er** *n*

²drivel *n* : NONSENSE

drive·shaft \\'drīv-ˌshaft\ *n* : a shaft that transmits mechanical power

drive·way \-ˌwā\ *n* : a short private road leading from the street to a house, garage, or parking lot

¹driz·zle \\'dri-zəl\ *n* : a fine misty rain

²drizzle *vb* **driz·zled; driz·zling** : to rain in very small drops

drogue \\'drōg\ *n* : a small parachute for slowing down or stabilizing something (as a space capsule)

droll \\'drōl\ *adj* [F *drôle*, fr. *drôle* scamp, fr. MF *drolle*, fr. MD, imp] : having a humorous, whimsical, or odd quality ⟨a ∼ expression⟩ — **droll·ery** \\'drō-lə-rē\ *n* — **drol·ly** *adv*

drom·e·dary \\'drä-mə-ˌder-ē\ *n, pl* **-dar·ies** [ME *dromedarie*, fr. MF *dromedaire*, fr. LL *dromedarius*, fr. L *dromad-, dromas*, fr. Gk, running] : CAMEL; *esp* : a domesticated one-humped camel of western Asia and northern Africa

¹drone \\'drōn\ *n* **1** : a male honeybee **2** : one that lives on the labors of others : PARASITE **3** : an unmanned aircraft or ship guided by remote control

²drone *vb* **droned; dron·ing** : to sound with a low dull monotonous murmuring sound : speak monotonously

³drone *n* : a deep monotonous sound

drool \\'drül\ *vb* **1** : to let liquid flow from the mouth **2** : to talk foolishly

droop \\'drüp\ *vb* **1** : to hang or incline downward **2** : to sink gradually **3** : LANGUISH — **droop** *n* — **droopy** *adj*

¹drop \\'dräp\ *n* **1** : the quantity of fluid that falls in one spherical mass **2** *pl* : a dose of medicine measured by drops **3** : a small quantity of drink **4** : the smallest practical unit of liquid measure **5** : something (as a pendant or a small round candy) that resembles a liquid drop **6** : FALL **7** : a decline in quantity or quality **8** : a descent by parachute **9** : the distance through which something drops **10** : a slot into which something is to be dropped **11** : something that drops or has dropped

²drop *vb* **dropped; drop·ping** **1** : to fall or let fall in drops **2** : to let fall : LOWER ⟨∼ a glove⟩ ⟨*dropped* his voice⟩ **3** : SEND ⟨∼ me a note⟩ **4** : to let go : DISMISS ⟨∼ the subject⟩ **5** : to knock down : cause to fall **6** : to go lower : become less ⟨prices *dropped*⟩ **7** : to come or go unexpectedly or informally ⟨∼ in to call⟩ **8** : to pass from one state into a less active one ⟨∼ off to sleep⟩ **9** : to move downward or with a current **10** : QUIT ⟨*dropped* out of the race⟩ — **drop back** : to move toward the rear — **drop behind** : to fail to keep up

drop·kick \-ˈkik\ *n* : a kick made by dropping a ball to the ground and kicking it at the moment it starts to rebound — **drop–kick** *vb*

drop·let \\'drä-plət\ *n* : a tiny drop

drop–off \\'dräp-ˌȯf\ *n* **1** : a steep or perpendicular descent **2** : a marked decline ⟨a ∼ in attendance⟩

drop off *vb* : to fall asleep

drop out *vb* : to withdraw from participation or membership; *esp* : to leave school before graduation — **drop·out** \\'dräp-ˌaùt\ *n*

drop·per \\'drä-pər\ *n* **1** : one that drops **2** : a short glass tube with a rubber bulb used to measure out liquids by drops

drop·pings *n pl* : MANURE, DUNG

drop·sy \\'dräp-sē\ *n* [ME *dropesie*, short for *ydropesie*, fr. OF, fr. L *hydropisis*, fr. Gk *hydrōps*, fr. *hydōr* water] : EDEMA — **drop·si·cal** \-si-kəl\ *adj*

dross \\'dräs\ *n* **1** : the scum that forms on the surface of a molten metal **2** : waste matter : REFUSE

drought \\'draùt\ *also* **drouth** \\'draùth\ *n* : a long spell of dry weather

¹drove \\'drōv\ *n* **1** : a group of animals driven or moving in a body **2** : a large number : CROWD — usu. used in pl. ⟨tourists arriving in ∼s⟩

²drove *past of* DRIVE

drov·er \\'drō-vər\ *n* : one that drives domestic animals usu. to market

drown \\'draùn\ *vb* **drowned** \\'draùnd\; **drown·ing** **1** : to suffocate by submersion esp. in water **2** : to become drowned **3** : to cover with water **4** : to cause to be muted (as a sound) by a loud noise **5** : OVERPOWER, OVERWHELM

drowse \'draùz\ *vb* **drowsed; drows·ing** : DOZE — **drowse** *n*

drowsy \'draù-zē\ *adj* **drows·i·er; -est 1** : ready to fall asleep **2** : making one sleepy — **drows·i·ly** \-zə-lē\ *adv* — **drows·i·ness** \-zē-nəs\ *n*

drub \'drəb\ *vb* **drubbed; drub·bing 1** : to beat severely **2** : to defeat decisively

drudge \'drəj\ *vb* **drudged; drudg·ing** : to do hard, menial, or monotonous work — **drudge** *n* — **drudg·ery** \'drə-jə-rē\ *n*

¹**drug** \'drəg\ *n* **1** : a substance used as or in medicine **2** : a substance (as heroin or marijuana) that can cause addiction, a marked change in mental status, or psychological dependency

²**drug** *vb* **drugged; drug·ging** : to affect with or as if with drugs; *esp* : to stupefy with a narcotic

drug·gist \'drə-gist\ *n* : a dealer in drugs and medicines; *also* : PHARMACIST

drug·store \'drəg-ˌstòr\ *n* : a retail shop where medicines and miscellaneous articles are sold

dru·id \'drü-əd\ *n, often cap* : one of an ancient Celtic priesthood appearing in Irish, Welsh, and Christian legends as magicians and wizards

¹**drum** \'drəm\ *n* **1** : a percussion instrument usu. consisting of a hollow cylinder with a skin or plastic head stretched over one or both ends that is beaten with the hands or with a stick **2** : the sound of a drum; *also* : a similar sound **3** : a drum-shaped object

²**drum** *vb* **drummed; drum·ming 1** : to beat a drum **2** : to sound rhythmically : THROB, BEAT **3** : to summon or enlist by or as if by beating a drum ⟨*drummed* into service⟩ **4** : EXPEL — usu. used with *out* **5** : to drive or force by steady effort ⟨~ the facts into memory⟩ **6** : to strike or tap repeatedly so as to produce rhythmic sounds

drum·beat \'drəm-ˌbēt\ *n* : a stroke on a drum or its sound

drum major *n* : the leader of a marching band

drum ma·jor·ette \-ˌmā-jə-ˈrət\ *n* : a girl or woman who leads a marching band; *also* : a baton twirler who accompanies a marching band

drum·mer \'drə-mər\ *n* **1** : one that plays a drum **2** : a traveling salesman

drum·stick \'drəm-ˌstik\ *n* **1** : a stick for beating a drum **2** : the lower segment of a fowl's leg

drum up *vb* **1** : to bring about by persistent effort ⟨*drum up* business⟩ **2** : INVENT, ORIGINATE

¹**drunk** *past part of* DRINK

²**drunk** \'drəŋk\ *adj* **1** : having the faculties impaired by alcohol ⟨~ drivers⟩ **2** : dominated by an intense feeling ⟨~ with power⟩ **3** : of, relating to, or caused by intoxication

³**drunk** *n* **1** : a period of excessive drinking **2** : a drunken person

drunk·ard \'drəŋ-kərd\ *n* : one who is habitually drunk

drunk·en \'drəŋ-kən\ *adj* **1** : DRUNK **2** : given to habitual excessive use of alcohol **3** : of, relating to, or resulting from intoxication **4** : unsteady or lurching as if from intoxication — **drunk·en·ly** *adv* — **drunk·en·ness** *n*

drupe \'drüp\ *n* : a partly fleshy one-seeded fruit (as a plum or cherry) that remains closed at maturity

¹**dry** \'drī\ *adj* **dri·er** \'drī-ər\; **dri·est** \-əst\ **1** : free or freed from water or liquid ⟨~ fruits⟩; *also* : not being in or under water **2** : characterized by lack of water or moisture ⟨~ climate⟩ **3** : lacking freshness : STALE **4** : devoid of natural moisture; *also* : THIRSTY **5** : no longer liquid or sticky ⟨the ink is ~⟩ **6** : not giving milk ⟨a ~ cow⟩ **7** : marked by the absence of alcoholic beverages **8** : prohibiting the making or distributing of alco-

holic beverages **9** : not sweet ⟨~ wine⟩ **10** : solid as opposed to liquid ⟨~ groceries⟩ **11** : containing or employing no liquid **12** : SEVERE; *also* : UNINTERESTING, WEARISOME **13** : not productive **14** : marked by a matter-of-fact, ironic, or terse manner of expression ⟨~ humor⟩ — **dry·ly** *adv* — **dry·ness** *n*

²**dry** *vb* **dried; dry·ing** : to make or become dry

³**dry** *n, pl* **drys** : PROHIBITIONIST

dry·ad \'drī-əd, -ˌad\ *n* : WOOD NYMPH

dry cell *n* : a battery whose contents are not spillable

dry–clean \'drī-ˌklēn\ *vb* : to clean (fabrics) chiefly with solvents other than water — **dry cleaning** *n*

dry dock \'drī-ˌdäk\ *n* : a dock that can be kept dry during ship construction or repair

dry·er *var of* DRIER

dry farm·ing *n* : farming without irrigation in areas of limited rainfall — **dry–farm** *vb* — **dry farm·er** *n*

dry goods \'drī-ˌgúdz\ *n pl* : cloth goods (as fabrics, ribbon, and ready-to-wear clothing

dry ice *n* : solid carbon dioxide

dry measure *n* : a series of units of capacity for dry commodities — see METRIC SYSTEM table, WEIGHT table

dry run *n* : REHEARSAL, TRIAL

dry·wall \'drī-ˌwòl\ *n* : PLASTERBOARD

DSC *abbr* **1** Distinguished Service Cross **2** doctor of surgical chiropody

DSM *abbr* Distinguished Service Medal

DST *abbr* daylight saving time

DTP *abbr* diphtheria, tetanus, pertussis (vaccines)

d.t.'s \ˌdē-ˈtēz\ *n pl, often cap D&T* : DELIRIUM TREMENS

du·al \'dü-əl, 'dyü-\ *adj* **1** : TWOFOLD, DOUBLE **2** : having a double character or nature — **du·al·ism** \-ə-ˌli-zəm\ *n* — **du·al·i·ty** \dü-ˈa-lə-tē, dyü-\ *n*

¹**dub** \'dəb\ *vb* **dubbed; dub·bing 1** : to confer knighthood upon **2** : NAME, NICKNAME

²**dub** *n* : a clumsy person : DUFFER

³**dub** *vb* **dubbed; dub·bing** : to add (sound effects) to a motion picture or to a radio or television production

du·bi·ety \dü-ˈbī-ə-tē, dyü-\ *n, pl* **-eties 1** : UNCERTAINTY **2** : a matter of doubt

du·bi·ous \'dü-bē-əs, 'dyü-\ *adj* **1** : UNCERTAIN **2** : QUESTIONABLE **3** : feeling doubt : UNDECIDED — **du·bi·ous·ly** *adv* — **du·bi·ous·ness** *n*

du·cal \'dü-kəl, 'dyü-\ *adj* : of or relating to a duke or dukedom

duc·at \'də-kət\ *n* : a gold coin formerly used in various European countries

duch·ess \'də-chəs\ *n* **1** : the wife or widow of a duke **2** : a woman holding the rank of duke in her own right

duchy \'də-chē\ *n, pl* **duch·ies** : the territory of a duke or duchess : DUKEDOM

¹**duck** \'dək\ *n, pl* **ducks** : any of various swimming birds related to but smaller than geese and swans

²**duck** *vb* **1** : to thrust or plunge under water **2** : to lower the head or body suddenly : BOW; *also* : DODGE **3** : to evade a duty, question, or responsibility ⟨~ the issue⟩

³**duck** *n* **1** : a durable closely woven usu. cotton fabric **2** *pl* : light clothes made of duck

duck·bill \'dək-ˌbil\ *n* : PLATYPUS

duck·ling \-liŋ\ *n* : a young duck

duck·pin \-ˌpin\ *n* **1** : a small bowling pin shorter and wider in the middle than a tenpin **2** *pl but sing in constr* : a bowling game using duckpins

duct \'dəkt\ *n* **1** : a tube or canal for conveying a bodily fluid **2** : a pipe or tube through which a fluid (as air) flows — **duct·less** *adj*

duc·tile \'dək-t³l\ *adj* **1** : capable of being drawn out (as into wire) or hammered thin **2** : easily led : DOCILE — **duc·til·i·ty** \ˌdək-ˈti-lə-tē\ *n*

ductless gland *n* : an endocrine gland

dud \'dəd\ *n* **1** *pl* : CLOTHING **2** : one that fails completely; *also* : a bomb or missile that fails to explode

dude \'düd, 'dyüd\ *n* **1** : DANDY 1 **2** : a city dweller; *esp* : an Easterner in the West **3** : FELLOW, GUY

dude ranch *n* : a vacation resort offering activities (as horseback riding) typical of western ranches

dud·geon \'də-jən\ *n* : a fit or state of indignation ⟨in high ∼⟩

¹**due** \'dü, 'dyü\ *adj* [ME, fr. MF *deu,* pp. of *devoir* to owe, fr. L *debēre*] **1** : owed or owing as a debt **2** : owed or owing as a right **3** : APPROPRIATE, FITTING **4** : SUFFICIENT, ADEQUATE **5** : REGULAR, LAWFUL ⟨∼ process of law⟩ **6** : ATTRIBUTABLE, ASCRIBABLE ⟨∼ to negligence⟩ **7** : PAYABLE ⟨a bill ∼ today⟩ **8** : SCHEDULED ⟨∼ to arrive soon⟩

²**due** *n* **1** : something that rightfully belongs to one ⟨give everyone their ∼⟩ **2** : DEBT **3** *pl* : FEES, CHARGES

³**due** *adv* : DIRECTLY, EXACTLY ⟨∼ north⟩

du·el \'dü-əl, 'dyü-\ *n* : a combat between two persons; *esp* : one fought with weapons in the presence of witnesses — **duel** *vb* — **du·el·ist** \-ə-list\ *n*

du·en·de \dü-'en-dā\ *n* [Sp dial., charm, fr. Sp, ghost, goblin, fr. *duen de casa,* prob. fr. *dueño de casa* owner of a house] : the power to attract through personal magnetism and charm

du·en·na \dü-'e-nə, dyü-\ *n* **1** : an elderly woman in charge of the younger ladies in a Spanish or Portuguese family **2** : CHAPERON

du·et \dü-'et, dyü-\ *n* : a musical composition for two performers

due to *prep* : BECAUSE OF

duf·fel bag \'də-fəl-\ *n* : a large cylindrical bag for personal belongings

duf·fer \'də-fər\ *n* : an incompetent or clumsy person

dug *past and past part of* DIG

dug·out \'dəg-ˌaüt\ *n* **1** : a boat made by hollowing out a log **2** : a shelter dug in the ground **3** : a low shelter facing a baseball diamond that contains the players' bench

DUI *abbr* driving under the influence

duke \'dük, 'dyük\ *n* **1** : a sovereign ruler of a continental European duchy **2** : a nobleman of the highest rank; *esp* : a member of the highest grade of the British peerage **3** *slang* : FIST 1 ⟨put up your ∼s⟩ — **duke·dom** *n*

dul·cet \'dəl-sət\ *adj* **1** : pleasing to the ear **2** : AGREEABLE, SOOTHING

dul·ci·mer \'dəl-sə-mər\ *n* **1** : a stringed instrument of trapezoidal shape played with light hammers held in the hands *or* **dul·ci·more** \-ˌmȯr\ : an American folk instrument with three or four strings that is held on the lap and played by plucking or strumming

¹**dull** \'dəl\ *adj* **1** : mentally slow : STUPID **2** : slow in perception or sensibility **3** : LISTLESS **4** : slow in action : SLUGGISH ⟨a ∼ market⟩ **5** : lacking intensity; *also* : not resonant or ringing **6** : BLUNT **7** : lacking brilliance or luster **8** : low in saturation and lightness ⟨∼ color⟩ **9** : CLOUDY, OVERCAST **10** : TEDIOUS, UNINTERESTING — **dull·ness** *or* **dul·ness** *n* — **dul·ly** *adv*

²**dull** *vb* : to make or become dull

dull·ard \'də-lərd\ *n* : a stupid person

du·ly \'dü-lē, 'dyü-\ *adv* : in a due manner or time

dumb \'dəm\ *adj* **1** : lacking the power of speech **2** : SILENT **3** : STUPID — **dumb·ly** *adv*

dumb·bell \'dəm-ˌbel\ *n* **1** : a bar with weights at the end used for exercise **2** : one who is stupid

dumb·found *or* **dum·found** \ˌdəm-'faünd\ *vb* : ASTONISH, AMAZE

dumb·wait·er \'dəm-ˌwā-tər\ *n* : a small elevator for conveying food and dishes from one floor to another

dum·my \'də-mē\ *n, pl* **dummies 1** : a person who cannot speak; *also* : a stupid person **2** : the exposed hand in bridge played by the declarer in addition to that player's own hand; *also* : a bridge player whose hand is a dummy **3** : an imitative substitute for something; *also* : MANNEQUIN **4** : one seeming to act alone but really

acting for another **5** : a mock-up of matter to be reproduced esp. by printing

¹**dump** \'dəmp\ *vb* : to let fall in a pile; *also* : to get rid of carelessly

²**dump** *n* **1** : a place for dumping something (as refuse) **2** : a reserve supply; *also* : a place where such supplies are kept ⟨an ammunition ∼⟩ **3** : a messy or objectionable place

dump·ing \'dəm-piŋ\ *n* : the selling of goods in quantity at below market price

dump·ling \'dəm-pliŋ\ *n* **1** : a small mass of boiled or steamed dough **2** : a dessert of fruit baked in biscuit dough

dumps \'dəmps\ *n pl* : a gloomy state of mind : low spirits ⟨in the ∼⟩

dump truck *n* : a truck for transporting and dumping bulk material

dumpy \'dəm-pē\ *adj* **dump·i·er; -est 1** : short and thick in build **2** : SHABBY

¹**dun** \'dən\ *n* : a brownish dark gray

²**dun** *vb* **dunned; dun·ning 1** : to make persistent demands for payment **2** : PLAGUE, PESTER — **dun** *n*

dunce \'dəns\ *n* [John *Duns* Scotus, whose once accepted writings were ridiculed in the 16th cent.] : a slow stupid person

dun·der·head \'dən-dər-ˌhed\ *n* : DUNCE, BLOCKHEAD

dune \'dün, 'dyün\ *n* : a hill or ridge of sand piled up by the wind

dune buggy *n* : a motor vehicle with oversize tires for use on sand

¹**dung** \'dəŋ\ *n* : MANURE

²**dung** *vb* : to dress (land) with dung

dun·ga·ree \ˌdəŋ-gə-'rē\ *n* **1** : a heavy coarse cotton twill; *esp* : blue denim **2** *pl* : clothes made of blue denim

dun·geon \'dən-jən\ *n* [ME *donjon,* fr. MF, fr. (assumed) VL *domnion-, domnio* keep, mastery, fr. L *dominus* lord] : a dark prison commonly underground

dung·hill \'dəŋ-ˌhil\ *n* : a manure pile

dunk \'dəŋk\ *vb* **1** : to dip or submerge temporarily in liquid **2** : to submerge oneself in water **3** : to shoot a basketball into the basket from above the rim

duo \'dü-(ˌ)ȯ, 'dyü-\ *n, pl* **du·os 1** : DUET 2 **3** : PAIR 3

duo·dec·i·mal \ˌdü-ə-'de-sə-məl, ˌdyü-\ *adj* : of, relating to, or being a system of numbers with a base of 12

du·o·de·num \ˌdü-ə-'dē-nəm, ˌdyü-, dù-'äd-ᵊn-əm, dyü-\ *n, pl* **-de·na** \-'dē-nə, -ᵊn-ə\ *or* **-denums** : the first part of the small intestine extending from the stomach to the jejunum — **du·o·de·nal** \-'dēn-ᵊl, -ᵊn-əl\ *adj*

dup *abbr* **1** duplex **2** duplicate

¹**dupe** \'düp, 'dyüp\ *n* : one who is easily deceived or cheated : FOOL

²**dupe** *vb* **duped; dup·ing** : to make a dupe of : DECEIVE, FOOL

du·ple \'dü-pəl, 'dyü-\ *adj* : having two beats or a multiple of two beats to the measure ⟨∼ time⟩

¹**du·plex** \'dü-ˌpleks, 'dyü-\ *adj* : DOUBLE

²**duplex** *n* : something duplex; *esp* : a 2-family house

¹**du·pli·cate** \'dü-pli-kət, 'dyü-\ *adj* **1** : consisting of or existing in two corresponding or identical parts or examples **2** : being the same as another

²**du·pli·cate** \'dü-pli-ˌkāt, 'dyü-\ *vb* **-cat·ed; -cat·ing 1** : to make double or twofold **2** : to make a copy of — **du·pli·ca·tion** \ˌdü-pli-'kā-shən, ˌdyü-\ *n*

³**du·pli·cate** \-kət\ *n* : a thing that exactly resembles another in appearance, pattern, or content : COPY

du·pli·ca·tor \'dü-pli-ˌkā-tər, 'dyü-\ *n* : COPIER

du·plic·i·ty \dü-'pli-sə-tē, dyü-\ *n, pl* **-ties** : the disguising of true intentions by deceptive words or action

\ə\abut \ᵊ\kitten \ər\further \a\ash \ā\ace \ä\mop, mar \aü\out \ch\chin \e\bet \ē\easy \g\go \i\hit \ī\ice \j\job \ŋ\sing \ō\go \ȯ\law \ȯi\boy \th\thin \t͟h\the \ü\loot \ù\foot \y\yet \zh\vision *see also* Pronunciation Symbols page

du·ra·ble \'dùr-ə-bəl, 'dyùr-\ *adj* : able to exist for a long time without significant deterioration ⟨∼ goods⟩ — **du·ra·bil·i·ty** \ˌdùr-ə-'bi-lə-tē, ˌdyùr-\ *n*
du·rance \'dùr-əns, 'dyùr-\ *n* : restraint by or as if by physical force ⟨held in ∼ vile⟩
du·ra·tion \dù-'rā-shən, dyù-\ *n* : the time during which something exists or lasts
du·ress \dù-'res, dyù-\ *n* : compulsion by threat ⟨confession made under ∼⟩
dur·ing \'dùr-iŋ, 'dyùr-\ *prep* **1** : THROUGHOUT ⟨swims every day ∼ the summer⟩ **2** : at some point in ⟨broke in ∼ the night⟩
dusk \'dəsk\ *n* **1** : the darker part of twilight esp. at night **2** : partial darkness
dusky \'dəs-kē\ *adj* **dusk·i·er; -est 1** : somewhat dark in color **2** : SHADOWY — **dusk·i·ness** *n*
¹dust \'dəst\ *n* **1** : fine particles of matter **2** : the particles into which something disintegrates **3** : something worthless **4** : the surface of the ground — **dust·less** *adj* — **dusty** *adj*
²dust *vb* **1** : to make free of or remove dust **2** : to sprinkle with fine particles **3** : to sprinkle in the form of dust
dust bowl *n* : a region suffering from long droughts and dust storms
dust devil *n* : a small whirlwind containing sand or dust
dust·er \'dəs-tər\ *n* **1** : one that removes dust **2** : a dress-length housecoat **3** : one that scatters fine particles; *esp* : a device for applying insecticides to crops
dust·pan \'dəst-ˌpan\ *n* : a flat-ended pan for sweepings
dust storm *n* : a violent wind carrying dust across a dry region
dutch \'dəch\ *adv, often cap* : with each person paying his or her own way ⟨go ∼⟩
Dutch \'dəch\ *n* **1 Dutch** *pl* : the people of the Netherlands **2** : the language of the Netherlands — **Dutch** *adj* — **Dutch·man** \-mən\ *n*
Dutch elm disease *n* : a fungous disease of elms characterized by yellowing of the foliage, defoliation, and death
dutch treat *n, often cap D* : an entertainment (as a meal) for which each person pays his or her own way — **dutch treat** *adv, often cap D*
du·te·ous \'dü-tē-əs, 'dyü-\ *adj* : DUTIFUL, OBEDIENT
du·ti·able \'dü-tē-ə-bəl, 'dyü-\ *adj* : subject to a duty ⟨∼ imports⟩
du·ti·ful \'dü-ti-fəl, 'dyü-\ *adj* **1** : motivated by a sense of duty ⟨a ∼ son⟩ **2** : coming from or showing a sense of duty ⟨∼ affection⟩ — **du·ti·ful·ly** *adv* — **du·ti·ful·ness** *n*
du·ty \'dü-tē, 'dyü-\ *n, pl* **duties 1** : conduct or action required by one's occupation or position **2** : assigned service or business; *esp* : active military service **3** : a moral or legal obligation **4** : TAX **5** : the service required (as of a machine) : USE ⟨a heavy-*duty* tire⟩
DV *abbr* **1** [L *Deo volente*] God willing **2** Douay Version
DVM *abbr* doctor of veterinary medicine
¹dwarf \'dwòrf\ *n, pl* **dwarfs** \'dwòrfs\ *or* **dwarves**

\'dwòrvz\ : one that is much below normal size — **dwarf·ish** *adj*
²dwarf *vb* **1** : to restrict the growth or development of : STUNT **2** : to cause to appear smaller ⟨*dwarfed* by comparison⟩
dwell \'dwel\ *vb* **dwelt** \'dwelt\ *or* **dwelled** \'dweld, 'dwelt\; **dwell·ing** [ME, fr. OE *dwellan* to go astray, hinder] **1** : ABIDE, REMAIN **2** : RESIDE, EXIST **3** : to keep the attention directed **4** : to write or speak insistently — used with *on* or *upon* — **dwell·er** *n*
dwell·ing \'dwe-liŋ\ *n* : RESIDENCE
DWI *abbr* driving while intoxicated
dwin·dle \'dwind-ᵊl\ *vb* **dwin·dled; dwin·dling** : to make or become steadily less : DIMINISH
dwt *abbr* pennyweight
Dy *symbol* dysprosium
dyb·buk \'di-bək\ *n, pl* **dyb·bu·kim** \ˌdi-bù-'kēm\ *also* **dybbuks** : a wandering soul believed in Jewish folklore to enter and possess a person
¹dye \'dī\ *n* **1** : color produced by dyeing **2** : material used for coloring or staining
²dye *vb* **dyed; dye·ing 1** : to impart a new color to esp. by impregnating with a dye **2** : to take up or impart color in dyeing
dye·stuff \'dī-ˌstəf\ *n* : DYE 2
dying *pres part of* DIE
dyke *chiefly Brit var of* DIKE
dy·nam·ic \dī-'na-mik\ *also* **dy·nam·i·cal** \-mi-kəl\ *adj* : of or relating to physical force producing motion : ENERGETIC, FORCEFUL
¹dy·na·mite \'dī-nə-ˌmīt\ *n* : an explosive made of nitroglycerin absorbed in a porous material; *also* : an explosive made without nitroglycerin
²dynamite *vb* **-mit·ed; -mit·ing** : to blow up with dynamite
dy·na·mo \'dī-nə-ˌmò\ *n, pl* **-mos** : an electrical generator
dy·na·mom·e·ter \ˌdī-nə-'mä-mə-tər\ *n* : an instrument for measuring mechanical power (as of an engine)
dy·nas·ty \'dī-nəs-tē, -ˌnas-\ *n, pl* **-ties 1** : a succession of rulers of the same family **2** : a powerful group or family that maintains its position for a long time — **dy·nas·tic** \dī-'nas-tik\ *adj*
dys·en·tery \'dis-ᵊn-ˌter-ē\ *n, pl* **-ter·ies** : a disease marked by diarrhea with blood and mucus in the feces; *also* : DIARRHEA
dys·lex·ia \dis-'lek-sē-ə\ *n* : a disturbance of the ability to read or use language — **dys·lex·ic** \-sik\ *adj or n*
dys·pep·sia \dis-'pep-shə, -sē-ə\ *n* : INDIGESTION — **dys·pep·tic** \-'pep-tik\ *adj or n*
dys·pro·si·um \dis-'prò-zē-əm\ *n* : a metallic chemical element that forms highly magnetic compounds — see ELEMENT table
dys·tro·phy \'dis-trə-fē\ *n, pl* **-phies** : a disorder involving atrophy of muscular tissue; *esp* : MUSCULAR DYSTROPHY
dz *abbr* dozen

E

¹e \'ē\ *n, pl* **e's** *or* **es** \'ēz\ *often cap* **1** : the 5th letter of the English alphabet **2** : the base of the system of natural logarithms having the approximate value 2.71828 **3** : a grade rating a student's work as poor or failing
²e *abbr, often cap* **1** east; eastern **2** error **3** excellent
ea *abbr* each
¹each \'ēch\ *adj* : being one of the class named ⟨∼ man⟩
²each *pron* : every individual one

³each *adv* : APIECE ⟨cost five cents ∼⟩
each other *pron* : each of two or more in reciprocal action or relation ⟨looked at *each other*⟩
ea·ger \'ē-gər\ *adj* : marked by urgent or enthusiastic desire or interest ⟨∼ to learn⟩ **syn** avid, anxious, ardent, keen — **ea·ger·ly** *adv* — **ea·ger·ness** *n*
ea·gle \'ē-gəl\ *n* **1** : a large bird of prey related to the hawks **2** : a score of two under par on a hole in golf

ea·glet \'ē-glət\ *n* : a young eagle

-ean — see -AN

E and OE *abbr* errors and omissions excepted

¹ear \'ir\ *n* **1** : the organ of hearing; *also* : the outer part of this in a vertebrate **2** : something resembling a mammal's ear in shape, position, or function **3** : an ability to understand and appreciate something heard ⟨a good ∼ for music⟩ **4** : sympathetic attention

²ear *n* : the fruiting spike of a cereal (as wheat)

ear·ache \-ˌāk\ *n* : an ache or pain in the ear

ear·drum \-ˌdrəm\ *n* : a thin membrane that receives and transmits sound waves in the ear

eared \'ird\ *adj* : having ears esp. of a specified kind or number ⟨a long-*eared* dog⟩

ear·ful \'ir-ˌfül\ *n* : a verbal outpouring (as of news, gossip, anger, or complaint)

earl \'ərl\ *n* [ME *erl,* fr. OE *eorl* warrior, nobleman] : a member of the British peerage ranking below a marquess and above a viscount — **earl·dom** \-dəm\ *n*

ear·lobe \'ir-ˌlōb\ *n* : the pendent part of the ear

¹ear·ly \'ər-lē\ *adv* **ear·li·er; -est** : at an early time (as in a period or series)

²early *adj* **ear·li·er; -est 1** : of, relating to, or occurring near the beginning **2** : ANCIENT, PRIMITIVE **3** : occurring before the usual time ⟨an ∼ breakfast⟩; *also* : occurring in the near future

¹ear·mark \'ir-ˌmärk\ *n* : an identification mark (as on the ear of an animal); *also* : a distinguishing mark ⟨∼s of poverty⟩

²earmark *vb* **1** : to mark with an earmark **2** : to designate for a specific purpose

ear·muff \-ˌməf\ *n* : one of a pair of ear coverings worn to protect against cold

earn \'ərn\ *vb* **1** : to receive as a return for service **2** : DESERVE, MERIT **syn** gain, secure, get, obtain, acquire, win

¹ear·nest \'ər-nəst\ *n* : an intensely serious state of mind ⟨spoke in ∼⟩

²earnest *adj* **1** : seriously intent and sober ⟨an ∼ face⟩ ⟨an ∼ attempt⟩ **2** : GRAVE, IMPORTANT **syn** solemn, sedate, staid — **ear·nest·ly** *adv* — **ear·nest·ness** *n*

³earnest *n* **1** : something of value given by a buyer to a seller to bind a bargain **2** : PLEDGE

earn·ings \'ər-niŋz\ *n pl* **1** : something (as wages) earned **2** : the balance of revenue after deduction of costs and expenses

ear·phone \'ir-ˌfōn\ *n* : a device that reproduces sound and is worn over or in the ear

ear·plug \-ˌpləg\ *n* : a protective device for insertion into the opening of the ear

ear·ring \-ˌriŋ\ *n* : an ornament for the earlobe

ear·shot \-ˌshät\ *n* : range of hearing

ear·split·ting \-ˌspli-tiŋ\ *adj* : intolerably loud or shrill

earth \'ərth\ *n* **1** : SOIL, DIRT **2** : LAND, GROUND **3** *often cap* : the planet on which we live that is 3d in order from the sun — see PLANET table

earth·en \'ər-thən\ *adj* : made of earth or baked clay

earth·en·ware \-ˌwar\ *n* : slightly porous opaque pottery fired at low heat

earth·ling \'ərth-liŋ\ *n* : an inhabitant of the earth

earth·ly \'ərth-lē\ *adj* : having to do with the earth esp. as distinguished from heaven — **earth·li·ness** *n*

earth·quake \-ˌkwāk\ *n* : a shaking or trembling of a portion of the earth

earth science *n* : any of the sciences (as geology or meteorology) that deal with the earth or one of its parts

earth·shak·ing \'ərth-ˌshā-kiŋ\ *adj* : of great importance : MOMENTOUS

earth·ward \-wərd\ *also* **earth·wards** \-wərdz\ *adv* : toward the earth

earth·work \'ərth-ˌwərk\ *n* : an embankment or fortification of earth

earth·worm \-ˌwərm\ *n* : a long segmented worm found in damp soil

earthy \'ər-thē\ *adj* **earth·i·er; -est 1** : of, relating to, or consisting of earth; *also* : suggesting earth ⟨∼ flavors⟩ **2** : PRACTICAL **3** : COARSE, GROSS — **earth·i·ness** *n*

ear·wax \'ir-ˌwaks\ *n* : the yellow waxy secretion from the ear

ear·wig \-ˌwig\ *n* : any of numerous insects with slender many-jointed antennae and a pair of appendages resembling forceps at the end of the body

¹ease \'ēz\ *n* **1** : comfort of body or mind **2** : naturalness of manner **3** : freedom from difficulty or effort **syn** relaxation, rest, repose, leisure

²ease *vb* **eased; eas·ing 1** : to relieve from distress **2** : to lessen the pressure or tension of **3** : to make or become less difficult ⟨∼ credit⟩

ea·sel \'ē-zəl\ *n* [Dutch *ezel,* lit., ass] : a frame for supporting something (as an artist's canvas)

¹east \'ēst\ *adv* : to or toward the east

²east *adj* **1** : situated toward or at the east **2** : coming from the east

³east *n* **1** : the general direction of sunrise **2** : the compass point directly opposite to west **3** *cap* : regions or countries east of a specified or implied point — **east·er·ly** \'ē-stər-lē\ *adv or adj* — **east·ward** *adv or adj* — **east·wards** *adv*

Eas·ter \'ē-stər\ *n* : a church feast observed on a Sunday in March or April in commemoration of Christ's resurrection

EASTER DATES

YEAR	ASH WEDNESDAY		EASTER	
1995	March	1	April	16
1996	February	21	April	7
1997	February	12	March	30
1998	February	25	April	12
1999	February	17	April	4
2000	March	8	April	23
2001	February	28	April	15
2002	February	13	March	31
2003	March	5	April	20
2004	February	25	April	11
2005	February	9	March	27
2006	March	1	April	16
2007	February	21	April	8
2008	February	6	March	23
2009	February	25	April	12
2010	February	17	April	4
2011	March	9	April	24
2012	February	22	April	8
2013	February	13	March	31
2014	March	5	April	20

east·ern \'ē-stərn\ *adj* **1** *often cap* : of, relating to, or characteristic of a region designated East **2** *cap* : of, relating to, or being the Christian churches originating in the Church of the Eastern Roman Empire **3** : lying toward or coming from the east — **East·ern·er** *n*

easy \'ē-zē\ *adj* **eas·i·er; -est 1** : marked by ease ⟨an ∼ life⟩; *esp* : not causing distress or difficulty ⟨∼ tasks⟩ **2** : MILD, LENIENT ⟨be ∼ on him⟩ **3** : GRADUAL ⟨an ∼ slope⟩ **4** : free from pain, trouble, or worry ⟨rest ∼⟩ **5** : LEISURELY ⟨an ∼ pace⟩ **6** : NATURAL ⟨an ∼ manner⟩ **7** : COMFORTABLE ⟨an ∼ chair⟩ — **eas·i·ly** \'ē-zə-lē\ *adv* — **eas·i·ness** \-zē-nəs\ *n*

\ə\abut \ᵊ\kitten \ər\further \a\ash \ā\ace \ä\mop, mar \au̇\out \ch\chin \e\bet \ē\easy \g\go \i\hit \ī\ice \j\job \ŋ\sing \ō\go \ȯ\law \ȯi\boy \th\thin \t̲h̲\the \ü\loot \u̇\foot \y\yet \zh\vision *see also* Pronunciation Symbols page

easy·go·ing \ē-zē-'gō-iŋ\ *adj* : relaxed and casual in style or manner

eat \'ēt\ *vb* **ate** \'āt\; **eat·en** \'ēt-ᵊn\; **eat·ing 1** : to take in as food : take food **2** : to use up : DEVOUR **3** : CORRODE — **eat·able** *adj or n* — **eat·er** *n*

eat·ery \'ē-tə-rē\ *n, pl* **-er·ies** : LUNCHEONETTE, RESTAURANT

eaves \'ēvz\ *n pl* : the overhanging lower edge of a roof

eaves·drop \'ēvz-ˌdräp\ *vb* : to listen secretly — **eaves·drop·per** *n*

¹**ebb** \'eb\ *n* **1** : the flowing back from shore of water brought in by the tide **2** : a point or state of decline

²**ebb** *vb* **1** : to recede from the flood **2** : DECLINE ⟨his fortunes ∼ed⟩

EBCDIC \'eb-sə-ˌdik\ *n* [extended *b*inary *c*oded *d*ecimal *i*nterchange *c*ode] : a computer code for representing alphanumeric information

¹**eb·o·ny** \'e-bə-nē\ *n, pl* **-nies** : a hard heavy wood of Old World tropical trees related to the persimmon

²**ebony** *adj* **1** : made of or resembling ebony **2** : BLACK, DARK

ebul·lient \i-'bul-yənt, -'bəl-\ *adj* **1** : BOILING, AGITATED **2** : EXUBERANT — **ebul·lience** \-yəns\ *n*

EC *abbr* European Community

ec·cen·tric \ik-'sen-trik\ *adj* **1** : deviating from a usual or accepted pattern **2** : deviating from a circular path ⟨∼ orbits⟩ **3** : set with axis or support off center ⟨an ∼ cam⟩; *also* : being off center **syn** erratic, queer, singular, curious, odd — **eccentric** *n* — **ec·cen·tri·cal·ly** \-tri-k(ə-)lē\ *adv* — **ec·cen·tric·i·ty** \ek-ˌsen-'tri-sə-tē\ *n*

Eccles *abbr* Ecclesiastes

Ec·cle·si·as·tes \i-ˌklē-zē-'as-tēz\ *n* — see BIBLE table

ec·cle·si·as·tic \i-ˌklē-zē-'as-tik\ *n* : CLERGYMAN

ec·cle·si·as·ti·cal \-ti-kəl\ *or* **ec·cle·si·as·tic** \-tik\ *adj* : of or relating to a church esp. as an institution ⟨∼ art⟩ — **ec·cle·si·as·ti·cal·ly** \-ti-k(ə-)lē\ *adv*

Ec·cle·si·as·ti·cus \i-ˌklē-zē-'as-ti-kəs\ *n* — see BIBLE table

Ecclus *abbr* Ecclesiasticus

ECG *abbr* electrocardiogram

ech·e·lon \'e-shə-ˌlän\ *n* [F *échelon,* lit., rung of a ladder] **1** : a steplike arrangement (as of troops or airplanes) **2** : a level (as of authority or responsibility) within an organization

echi·no·derm \i-'kī-nə-ˌdərm\ *n* : any of a phylum of marine animals (as starfishes and sea urchins) having similar body parts (as the arms of a starfish) arranged around a central axis and often having a calcium-containing outer skeleton

echo \'e-kō\ *n, pl* **ech·oes** *also* **ech·os** : repetition of a sound caused by a reflection of the sound waves; *also* : the reflection of a radar signal by an object — **echo** *vb* — **echo·ic** \e-'kō-ik\ *adj*

echo·lo·ca·tion \ˌe-kō-lō-'kā-shən\ *n* : a process for locating distant or invisible objects by means of sound waves reflected back to the sender (as a bat) by the objects

éclair \ā-'klar\ *n* [F, lit., lightning] : an oblong shell of light pastry with whipped cream or custard filling

éclat \ā-'klä\ *n* [F] **1** : a dazzling effect or success **2** : ACCLAIM

eclec·tic \e-'klek-tik\ *adj* : selecting or made up of what seems best of varied sources — **eclectic** *n*

¹**eclipse** \i-'klips\ *n* **1** : the total or partial obscuring of one heavenly body by another; *also* : a passing into the shadow of a heavenly body **2** : a falling into obscurity or decline

²**eclipse** *vb* **eclipsed; eclips·ing** : to cause an eclipse of; *also* : SURPASS

eclip·tic \i-'klip-tik\ *n* : the great circle of the celestial sphere that is the apparent path of the sun

ec·logue \'ek-ˌlóg, -ˌläg\ *n* : a pastoral poem

ECM *abbr* European Common Market

ecol *abbr* ecological; ecology

ecol·o·gy \i-'kä-lə-jē, e-\ *n, pl* **-gies** [G *Ökologie,* fr. Gk *oikos* house + *logos* word] **1** : a branch of science concerned with the relationships between organisms and their environment **2** : the pattern of relations between one or more organisms and the environment — **ecolog·i·cal** \ˌē-kə-'lä-ji-kəl, ˌe-\ *also* **eco·log·ic** \-jik\ *adj* — **eco·log·i·cal·ly** \-ji-k(ə-)lē\ *adv* — **ecol·o·gist** \i-'kä-lə-jist, e-\ *n*

econ *abbr* economics; economist; economy

eco·nom·ic \ˌe-kə-'nä-mik, ˌē-\ *adj* : of or relating to the production, distribution, and consumption of goods and services

eco·nom·i·cal \-'nä-mi-kəl\ *adj* **1** : THRIFTY **2** : operating with little waste or at a saving **syn** frugal, sparing, provident — **ec·o·nom·i·cal·ly** \-k(ə-)lē\ *adv*

eco·nom·ics \ˌe-kə-'nä-miks, ˌē-\ *n* : a social science dealing with the production, distribution, and consumption of goods and services — **econ·o·mist** \i-'kä-nə-mist\ *n*

econ·o·mize \i-'kä-nə-ˌmīz\ *vb* **-mized; -miz·ing** : to practice economy : be frugal — **econ·o·miz·er** *n*

¹**econ·o·my** \i-'kä-nə-mē\ *n, pl* **-mies** [MF *yconomie,* fr. ML *oeconomia,* fr. Gk *oikonomia,* fr. *oikonomos* household manager, fr. *oikos* house + *nemein* to manage] **1** : thrifty and efficient use of resources; *also* : an instance of this **2** : manner of arrangement or functioning : ORGANIZATION **3** : an economic system ⟨a money ∼⟩

²**economy** *adj* : ECONOMICAL ⟨∼ cars⟩

eco·sys·tem \'ē-kō-ˌsis-təm, 'e-\ *n* : the complex of an ecological community and its environment functioning as a unit in nature

ecru \'e-krü, 'ā-\ *n* [F *écru,* lit., unbleached] : BEIGE — **ecru** *adj*

ec·sta·sy \'ek-stə-sē\ *n, pl* **-sies** : extreme and usu. rapturous emotional excitement — **ec·stat·ic** \ek-'sta-tik, ik-\ *adj* — **ec·stat·i·cal·ly** \-ti-k(ə-)lē\ *adv*

Ecua *abbr* Ecuador

Ec·ua·dor·an \ˌe-kwə-'dòr-ən\ *or* **Ec·ua·dor·ean** *or* **Ec·ua·dor·ian** \-ē-ən\ *n* : a native or inhabitant of Ecuador — **Ecuadorean** *or* **Ecuadorian** *adj*

ec·u·men·i·cal \ˌe-kyù-'me-ni-kəl\ *adj* : general in extent or influence; *esp* : promoting or tending toward worldwide Christian unity — **ec·u·men·i·cal·ly** \-k(ə-)lē\ *adv*

ec·ze·ma \ig-'zē-mə, 'eg-zə-mə, 'ek-sə-\ *n* : an itching skin inflammation with oozing and then crusted lesions — **ec·zem·a·tous** \ig-'ze-mə-təs\ *adj*

ed *abbr* **1** edited; edition; editor **2** education

¹**-ed** \d *after a vowel or* b, g, j, l, m, n, ŋ, r, th, v, z, zh; əd, id *after* d, t; t *after other sounds*\ *vb suffix or adj suffix* **1** — used to form the past participle of regular weak verbs ⟨ended⟩ ⟨faded⟩ ⟨tried⟩ ⟨patted⟩ **2** : having : characterized by ⟨cultured⟩ ⟨2-legged⟩; *also* : having the characteristics of ⟨bigoted⟩

²**-ed** *vb suffix* — used to form the past tense of regular weak verbs ⟨judged⟩ ⟨denied⟩ ⟨dropped⟩

Edam \'ē-dəm, -ˌdam\ *n* : a yellow Dutch pressed cheese made in balls

ed·dy \'e-dē\ *n, pl* **eddies** : WHIRLPOOL — **eddy** *vb*

edel·weiss \'ād-ᵊl-ˌwīs, -ˌvīs\ *n* [G, fr. *edel* noble + *weiss* white] : a small perennial woolly composite herb that grows high in the Alps

ede·ma \i-'dē-mə\ *n* : abnormal accumulation of watery fluid in connective tissue or in a serous cavity — **edem·a·tous** \-'de-mə-təs\ *adj*

Eden \'ēd-ᵊn\ *n* : PARADISE 2

¹**edge** \'ej\ *n* **1** : the cutting side of a blade **2** : SHARPNESS; *also* : FORCE, EFFECTIVENESS **3** : the line where something begins or ends; *also* : the area adjoining such an edge **4** : a line segment that is the intersection of two plane faces of a solid **5** : ADVANTAGE — **edged** \'ejd\ *adj*

²**edge** *vb* **edged; edg·ing 1 :** to give or form an edge **2 :** to move or force gradually ⟨∼ into a crowd⟩ **3 :** to defeat by a small margin ⟨*edged* out her opponent⟩ — **edg·er** *n*

edge·wise \'ej-ˌwīz\ *adv* : SIDEWAYS

edg·ing \'e-jiŋ\ *n* : something that forms an edge or border ⟨a lace ∼⟩

edgy \'e-jē\ *adj* **edg·i·er; -est 1 :** SHARP ⟨an ∼ tone⟩ **2 :** TENSE, NERVOUS — **edg·i·ness** *n*

ed·i·ble \'e-də-bəl\ *adj* : fit or safe to be eaten — **ed·i·bil·i·ty** \ˌe-də-'bi-lə-tē\ *n* — **edible** *n*

edict \'ē-ˌdikt\ *n* : ORDER, DECREE

ed·i·fi·ca·tion \ˌe-də-fə-'kā-shən\ *n* : instruction and improvement esp. in morality — **ed·i·fy** \'e-də-ˌfī\ *vb*

ed·i·fice \'e-də-fəs\ *n* : a usu. large building

ed·it \'e-dət\ *vb* **1 :** to revise, assemble, or prepare for publication or release (as a motion picture) **2 :** to direct the publication and policies of (as a newspaper) **3 :** DELETE — **ed·i·tor** \'e-də-tər\ *n* — **ed·i·tor·ship** *n* — **ed·i·tress** \-trəs\ *n*

edi·tion \i-'di-shən\ *n* **1 :** the form in which a text is published **2 :** the total number of copies (as of a book) published at one time **3 :** VERSION

¹**ed·i·to·ri·al** \ˌe-də-'tōr-ē-əl\ *adj* **1 :** of or relating to an editor or editing **2 :** being or resembling an editorial — **ed·i·to·ri·al·ly** *adv*

²**editorial** *n* : an article (as in a newspaper) giving the views of the editors or publishers; *also* : an expression of opinion resembling an editorial ⟨a television ∼⟩

ed·i·to·ri·al·ize \ˌe-də-'tōr-ē-ə-ˌlīz\ *vb* **-ized; -iz·ing 1 :** to express an opinion in an editorial **2 :** to introduce opinions into factual reporting **3 :** to express an opinion — **ed·i·to·ri·al·i·za·tion** \-ˌtōr-ē-ə-lə-'zā-shən\ *n* — **ed·i·to·ri·al·iz·er** *n*

EDP *abbr* electronic data processing

EDT *abbr* Eastern daylight (saving) time

educ *abbr* education; educational

ed·u·ca·ble \'e-jə-kə-bəl\ *adj* : capable of being educated

ed·u·cate \'e-jə-ˌkāt\ *vb* **-cat·ed; -cat·ing 1 :** to provide with schooling **2 :** to develop mentally and morally; *also* : to provide with information **syn** train, discipline, school, instruct, teach — **ed·u·ca·tor** \-ˌkā-tər\ *n*

ed·u·ca·tion \ˌe-jə-'kā-shən\ *n* **1 :** the action or process of educating or being educated **2 :** a field of study dealing with methods of teaching and learning — **ed·u·ca·tion·al** \-shə-nəl\ *adj*

educational television *n* : PUBLIC TELEVISION

educe \i-'düs, -'dyüs\ *vb* **educed; educ·ing 1 :** ELICIT, EVOKE **2 :** DEDUCE **syn** extract, evince, extort

¹**-ee** \'ē, (ˌ)ē\ *n suffix* **1 :** one that receives or benefits from (a specified action or thing) ⟨grant*ee*⟩ ⟨patent*ee*⟩ **2 :** a person who does (a specified action) ⟨escap*ee*⟩

²**-ee** *n suffix* **1 :** a particular esp. small kind of ⟨boot*ee*⟩ **2 :** one resembling or suggestive of ⟨goat*ee*⟩

EE *abbr* electrical engineer

EEC *abbr* European Economic Community

EEG *abbr* **1** electroencephalogram **2** electroencephalograph

eel \'ēl\ *n* : any of numerous snakelike bony fishes with a smooth slimy skin

eel

EEO *abbr* equal employment opportunity

ee·rie *also* **ee·ry** \'ir-ē\ *adj* **ee·ri·er; -est :** WEIRD, UNCANNY — **ee·ri·ly** \'ir-ə-lē\ *adv*

eff *abbr* efficiency

ef·face \i-'fās, e-\ *vb* **ef·faced; ef·fac·ing :** to obliterate or obscure by or as if by rubbing out **syn** erase, delete, annul, cancel, expunge — **ef·face·able** *adj* — **ef·face·ment** *n*

¹**ef·fect** \i-'fekt\ *n* **1 :** MEANING, INTENT **2 :** RESULT **3 :** APPEARANCE **4 :** INFLUENCE **5** *pl* : GOODS, POSSESSIONS **6** : the quality or state of being operative : OPERATION **syn** consequence, outcome, upshot, aftermath, issue

²**effect** *vb* : to cause to happen ⟨∼ repairs⟩ ⟨∼ changes⟩

ef·fec·tive \i-'fek-tiv\ *adj* **1 :** producing a decisive or desired effect **2 :** IMPRESSIVE, STRIKING **3 :** ready for service or action **4 :** being in effect — **ef·fec·tive·ly** *adv* — **ef·fec·tive·ness** *n*

ef·fec·tu·al \i-'fek-chə-wəl\ *adj* : producing an intended effect : ADEQUATE — **ef·fec·tu·al·ly** *adv*

ef·fec·tu·ate \i-'fek-chə-ˌwāt\ *vb* **-at·ed; -at·ing :** BRING ABOUT, EFFECT

ef·fem·i·nate \ə-'fe-mə-nət\ *adj* : marked by qualities more typical of women than men — **ef·fem·i·na·cy** \-nə-sē\ *n*

ef·fen·di \e-'fen-dē\ *n* [Turk *efendi* master, fr. NGk *aphentēs*, alter. of Gk *authentēs*] : a man of property, authority, or education in an eastern Mediterranean country

ef·fer·ent \'e-fə-rənt\ *adj* : bearing or conducting outward from a more central part ⟨∼ nerves⟩

ef·fer·vesce \ˌe-fər-'ves\ *vb* **-vesced; -vesc·ing :** to bubble and hiss as gas escapes; *also* : to be exhilarated — **ef·fer·ves·cence** \-'ves-ᵊns\ *n* — **ef·fer·ves·cent** \-ᵊnt\ *adj* — **ef·fer·ves·cent·ly** *adv*

ef·fete \e-'fēt\ *adj* **1 :** having lost character, vitality, or strength; *also* : DECADENT **2 :** EFFEMINATE

ef·fi·ca·cious \ˌe-fə-'kā-shəs\ *adj* : producing an intended effect ⟨∼ remedies⟩ **syn** effectual, effective, efficient — **ef·fi·ca·cy** \'e-fi-kə-sē\ *n*

ef·fi·cient \i-'fi-shənt\ *adj* : productive of desired effects esp. without waste — **ef·fi·cien·cy** \-shən-sē\ *n* — **ef·fi·cient·ly** *adv*

ef·fi·gy \'e-fə-jē\ *n, pl* **-gies :** IMAGE; *esp* : a crude figure of a hated person

ef·flo·res·cence \ˌe-flə-'res-ᵊns\ *n* **1 :** the period or state of flowering **2 :** the action or process of developing **3** : fullness of development — **ef·flo·res·cent** *adj*

ef·flu·ence \'e-ˌflü-əns\ *n* : something that flows out

ef·flu·ent \'e-ˌflü-ənt\ *n* : something that flows out; *esp* : a fluid (as sewage) discharged as waste — **effluent** *adj*

ef·flu·vi·um \e-'flü-vē-əm\ *n, pl* **-via** \-vē-ə\ *or* **-vi·ums** [L, *outflow*] **1 :** a usu. unpleasant emanation **2 :** a by-product usu. in the form of waste

ef·fort \'e-fərt\ *n* **1 :** EXERTION, ENDEAVOR; *also* : a product of effort **2 :** active or applied force — **ef·fort·less** *adj* — **ef·fort·less·ly** *adv*

ef·fron·tery \i-'frən-tə-rē\ *n, pl* **-ter·ies :** shameless boldness : IMPUDENCE **syn** temerity, audacity, brass, gall, nerve, chutzpah

ef·ful·gence \i-'ful-jəns, -'fəl-\ *n* : radiant splendor : BRILLIANCE — **ef·ful·gent** \-jənt\ *adj*

ef·fu·sion \i-'fyü-zhən, e-\ *n* : a gushing forth; *also* : unrestrained utterance — **ef·fuse** \-'fyüz, e-\ *vb* — **ef·fu·sive** \i-'fyü-siv, e-\ *adj* — **ef·fu·sive·ly** *adv*

eft \'eft\ *n* : NEWT

EFT *or* **EFTS** *abbr* electronic funds transfer (system)

e.g. *abbr* [L *exempli gratia*] for example

Eg *abbr* Egypt; Egyptian

egal·i·tar·i·an·ism \i-ˌga-lə-'ter-ē-ə-ˌni-zəm\ *n* : a belief in human equality esp. in social, political, and economic affairs — **egal·i·tar·i·an** *adj or n*

¹**egg** \'eg\ *vb* [ME, fr. ON *eggja;* akin to OE *ecg* edge] : to urge to action — usu. used with *on*

²**egg** *n* [ME *egge,* fr. ON *egg;* akin to OE *ǣg* egg, L *ovum*] **1** : a rounded usu. hard-shelled reproductive body esp. of birds and reptiles from which the young hatches; *also* : the egg of the common domestic chicken as an article of food **2** : a germ cell produced by a female

egg·beat·er \'eg-ˌbē-tər\ *n* : a hand-operated kitchen utensil for beating, stirring, or whipping

egg cell *n* : EGG 2

egg·head \-ˌhed\ *n* : INTELLECTUAL, HIGHBROW

egg·nog \-ˌnäg\ *n* : a drink consisting of eggs beaten with sugar, milk or cream, and often alcoholic liquor

egg·plant \-ˌplant\ *n* : the edible usu. large and purplish fruit of a plant related to the potato; *also* : the plant

egg roll *n* : a thin egg-dough casing filled with minced vegetables and often bits of meat and usu. deep-fried

egg·shell \'eg-ˌshel\ *n* : the hard exterior covering of an egg

egis \'ē-jəs\ *var of* AEGIS

eg·lan·tine \'e-glən-ˌtīn, -ˌtēn\ *n* : SWEETBRIER

ego \'ē-gō\ *n, pl* **egos** [L, I] **1** : the self as distinguished from others **2** : the one of the three divisions of the psyche in psychoanalytic theory that is the organized conscious mediator between the person and reality

ego·cen·tric \ˌē-gō-'sen-trik\ *adj* : concerned or overly concerned with the self; *esp* : SELF-CENTERED

ego·ism \'ē-gō-ˌi-zəm\ *n* **1** : a doctrine holding self-interest to be the motive or the valid end of action **2** : excessive concern for oneself with or without exaggerated feelings of self-importance — **ego·ist** \-ist\ *n* — **ego·is·tic** \ˌē-gō-'is-tik\ *adj* — **ego·is·ti·cal·ly** *adv*

ego·tism \'ē-gə-ˌti-zəm\ *n* **1** : the practice of talking about oneself too much **2** : an exaggerated sense of self-importance : CONCEIT — **ego·tist** \-tist\ *n* — **ego·tis·tic** \ˌē-gə-'tis-tik\ *or* **ego·tis·ti·cal** \-ti-kəl\ *adj* — **ego·tis·ti·cal·ly** *adv*

ego trip *n* : an act that enhances and satisfies one's ego

egre·gious \i-'grē-jəs\ *adj* [L *egregius* outstanding, fr. *ex, e* out of + *greg-, grex* flock, herd] : notably bad : FLAGRANT — **egre·gious·ly** *adv* — **egre·gious·ness** *n*

egress \'ē-ˌgres\ *n* : a way out : EXIT

egret \'ē-grət, i-'gret\ *n* : any of various herons that bear long plumes during the breeding season

Egyp·tian \i-'jip-shən\ *n* **1** : a native or inhabitant of Egypt **2** : the language of the ancient Egyptians from earliest times to about the 3d century A.D. — **Egyptian** *adj*

ei·der \'ī-dər\ *n* : any of several northern sea ducks that yield a soft down

ei·der·down \-ˌdaùn\ *n* **1** : the down of the eider **2** : a quilt filled with eiderdown

ei·do·lon \ī-'dō-lən\ *n, pl* **-lons** *or* **-la** \-lə\ **1** : PHANTOM **2** : IDEAL

eight \'āt\ *n* **1** : one more than seven **2** : the 8th in a set or series **3** : something having eight units — **eight** *adj or pron* — **eighth** \'ātth\ *adj or adv or n*

eight ball *n* : a black pool ball numbered 8 — **behind the eight ball** : in a highly disadvantageous position

eigh·teen \'āt-'tēn\ *n* : one more than 17 — **eighteen** *adj or pron* — **eigh·teenth** \-'tēnth\ *adj or n*

eighty \'ā-tē\ *n, pl* **eight·ies** : eight times 10 — **eight·i·eth** \'ā-tē-əth\ *adj or n* — **eighty** *adj or pron*

ein·stei·ni·um \īn-'stī-nē-əm\ *n* : an artificially produced radioactive element — see ELEMENT table

¹**ei·ther** \'ē-thər, 'ī-\ *adj* **1** : being the one and the other of two : EACH ⟨trees on ~ side⟩ **2** : being the one or the other of two ⟨take ~ road⟩

²**either** *pron* : the one or the other

³**either** *conj* — used as a function word before the first of two or more words or word groups of which the last is preceded by *or* to indicate that they represent alternatives ⟨a statement is ~ true or false⟩

ejac·u·late \i-'ja-kyə-ˌlāt\ *vb* **-lat·ed; -lat·ing 1** : to eject a fluid (as semen) **2** : to utter suddenly : EXCLAIM — **ejac·u·la·tion** \-ˌja-kyə-'lā-shən\ *n* — **ejac·u·la·to·ry** \-'ja-kyə-lə-ˌtōr-ē\ *adj*

eject \i-'jekt\ *vb* : to drive or throw out or off **syn** expel, oust, evict, dismiss — **ejec·tion** \-'jek-shən\ *n*

eke \'ēk\ *vb* **eked; ek·ing** : to gain, supplement, or extend usu. with effort — usu. used with *out* ⟨~ out a living⟩

EKG *abbr* [G *Elektrokardiogramm*] electrocardiogram; electrocardiograph

el *abbr* elevation

¹**elab·o·rate** \i-'la-bə-rət, -'la-brət\ *adj* **1** : planned or carried out with great care **2** : being complex and usu. ornate — **elab·o·rate·ly** *adv* — **elab·o·rate·ness** *n*

²**elab·o·rate** \i-'la-bə-ˌrāt\ *vb* **-rat·ed; -rat·ing 1** : to build up from simpler ingredients **2** : to work out in detail : develop fully — **elab·o·ra·tion** \-ˌla-bə-'rā-shən\ *n*

élan \ā-'läⁿ\ *n* [F] : ARDOR, SPIRIT

eland \'ē-lənd, -ˌland\ *n, pl* **eland** *also* **elands** [Afrikaans] : either of two large African antelopes with spirally twisted horns in both sexes

elapse \i-'laps\ *vb* **elapsed; elaps·ing** : to slip by : PASS

¹**elas·tic** \i-'las-tik\ *adj* **1** : SPRINGY **2** : FLEXIBLE, PLIABLE **3** : ADAPTABLE **syn** resilient, supple, stretch — **elas·tic·i·ty** \-ˌlas-'ti-sə-tē, ˌē-ˌlas-\ *n*

²**elastic** *n* **1** : elastic material **2** : a rubber band

elate \i-'lāt\ *vb* **elat·ed; elat·ing** : to fill with joy — **ela·tion** \-'lā-shən\ *n*

¹**el·bow** \'el-ˌbō\ *n* **1** : the joint of the arm; *also* : the outer curve of the bent arm **2** : a bend or joint resembling an elbow in shape

²**elbow** *vb* : to push aside with the elbow; *also* : to make one's way by elbowing

el·bow·room \'el-bō-ˌrüm, -ˌrùm\ *n* : enough space for work or operation

¹**el·der** \'el-dər\ *n* : ELDERBERRY 2

²**elder** *adj* **1** : OLDER **2** : EARLIER, FORMER **3** : of higher rank : SENIOR

³**elder** *n* **1** : an older individual : SENIOR **2** : one having authority by reason of age and experience **3** : a church officer

el·der·ber·ry \'el-dər-ˌber-ē\ *n* **1** : the edible black or red fruit of a shrub or tree related to the honeysuckle and bearing flat clusters of small white or pink flowers **2** : a tree or shrub bearing elderberries

el·der·ly \'el-dər-lē\ *adj* **1** : rather old; *esp* : past middle age **2** : of, relating to, or characteristic of later life

el·dest \'el-dəst\ *adj* : of the greatest age

El Do·ra·do \ˌel-də-'rä-dō, -'rä-\ *n* [Sp, lit., the gilded one] : a place of vast riches, abundance, or opportunity

elec *abbr* electric; electrical; electricity

¹**elect** \i-'lekt\ *adj* **1** : CHOSEN, SELECT **2** : elected but not yet installed in office ⟨the president-*elect*⟩

²**elect** *n, pl* **elect 1** : a selected person **2** *pl* : a select or exclusive group

³**elect** *vb* **1** : to select by vote (as for office or membership) **2** : CHOOSE, PICK

elec·tion \i-'lek-shən\ *n* **1** : an act or process of electing **2** : the fact of being elected

elec·tion·eer \i-ˌlek-shə-'nir\ *vb* : to work for the election of a candidate or party

¹**elec·tive** \i-'lek-tiv\ *adj* **1** : chosen or filled by election : permitting a choice : OPTIONAL

²**elective** *n* : an elective course or subject of study

elec·tor \i-'lek-tər\ *n* **1** : one qualified to vote in an election **2** : one elected to an electoral college — **elec·tor·al** \i-'lek-tə-rəl\ *adj*

electoral college *n* : a body of electors who elect the president and vice president of the U.S.

elec·tor·ate \i-ˈlek-tə-rət\ *n* : a body of persons entitled to vote

elec·tric \i-ˈlek-trik\ *adj* [NL *electricus* produced from amber by friction, electric, fr. ML, of amber, fr. L *electrum* amber, fr. Gk *ēlektron*] **1** *or* **elec·tri·cal** \-tri-kəl\ : of, relating to, operated by, or produced by electricity **2** : ELECTRIFYING, THRILLING — **elec·tri·cal·ly** *adv*

electrical storm *n* : THUNDERSTORM

electric chair *n* : a chair used to carry out the death penalty by electrocution

electric eye *n* : PHOTOELECTRIC CELL

elec·tri·cian \i-ˌlek-ˈtri-shən\ *n* : a person who installs, operates, or repairs electrical equipment

elec·tric·i·ty \i-ˌlek-ˈtri-sə-tē\ *n, pl* **-ties 1** : a form of energy that occurs in nature and is observable in natural phenomena (as lightning) and that can be produced by friction, chemical reaction, or mechanical effort **2** : electric current

elec·tri·fy \i-ˈlek-trə-ˌfī\ *vb* **-fied; -fy·ing 1** : to charge with electricity **2** : to equip for use of electric power **3** : THRILL — **elec·tri·fi·ca·tion** \i-ˌlek-trə-fə-ˈkā-shən\ *n*

elec·tro·car·dio·gram \i-ˌlek-trō-ˈkär-dē-ə-ˌgram\ *n* : the tracing made by an electrocardiograph

elec·tro·car·dio·graph \-ˌgraf\ *n* : a device for recording the changes of electrical potential occurring during the heartbeat — **elec·tro·car·dio·graph·ic** \-ˌkär-dē-ə-ˈgra-fik\ *adj* — **elec·tro·car·di·og·ra·phy** \-dē-ˈä-grə-fē\ *n*

elec·tro·chem·is·try \-ˈke-mə-strē\ *n* : a branch of chemistry that deals with the relation of electricity to chemical changes — **elec·tro·chem·i·cal** \-ˈke-mi-kəl\ *adj*

elec·tro·cute \i-ˈlek-trə-ˌkyüt\ *vb* **-cut·ed; -cut·ing** : to kill by an electric shock; *esp* : to kill (a criminal) in this way — **elec·tro·cu·tion** \-ˌlek-trə-ˈkyü-shən\ *n*

elec·trode \i-ˈlek-ˌtrōd\ *n* : a conductor used to establish electrical contact with a nonmetallic part of a circuit

elec·tro·en·ceph·a·lo·gram \i-ˌlek-trō-in-ˈse-fə-lə-ˌgram\ *n* : the tracing made by an electroencephalograph

elec·tro·en·ceph·a·lo·graph \-ˌgraf\ *n* : an apparatus for detecting and recording brain waves — **elec·tro·en·ceph·a·lo·graph·ic** \-ˌse-fə-lə-ˈgra-fik\ *adj* — **elec·tro·en·ceph·a·log·ra·phy** \-ˈlä-grə-fē\ *n*

elec·trol·o·gist \i-ˌlek-ˈträ-lə-jist\ *n* : one that uses electrical means to remove hair, warts, moles, and birthmarks from the body

elec·trol·y·sis \i-ˌlek-ˈträ-lə-səs\ *n* **1** : the production of chemical changes by passage of an electric current through an electrolyte **2** : the destruction of hair roots with an electric current — **elec·tro·lyt·ic** \-trə-ˈli-tik\ *adj*

elec·tro·lyte \i-ˈlek-trə-ˌlīt\ *n* : a nonmetallic electric conductor in which current is carried by the movement of ions; *also* : a substance whose solution or molten form is such a conductor

elec·tro·mag·net \i-ˌlek-trō-ˈmag-nət\ *n* : a core of magnetic material surrounded by a coil of wire through which an electric current is passed to magnetize the core

elec·tro·mag·net·ic \-mag-ˈne-tik\ *adj* : of, relating to, or produced by electromagnetism — **elec·tro·mag·net·i·cal·ly** *adv*

electromagnetic radiation *n* : a series of electromagnetic waves

electromagnetic wave *n* : a wave (as a radio wave, an X ray, or a wave of visible light) that consists of associated electric and magnetic effects and that travels at the speed of light

elec·tro·mag·ne·tism \i-ˌlek-trō-ˈmag-nə-ˌti-zəm\ *n* **1** : magnetism developed by a current of electricity **2** : a natural force responsible for interactions between charged particles which result from their charge

elec·tro·mo·tive force \i-ˌlek-trə-ˈmō-tiv-\ *n* : the poten-

tial difference derived from an electrical source per unit quantity of electricity passing through the source

elec·tron \i-ˈlek-ˌträn\ *n* : a negatively charged elementary particle

elec·tron·ic \i-ˌlek-ˈträ-nik\ *adj* : of or relating to electrons or electronics — **elec·tron·i·cal·ly** \-ni-k(ə-)lē\ *adv*

electronic mail *n* : messages sent and received electronically

elec·tron·ics \i-ˌlek-ˈträ-niks\ *n* **1** : the physics of electrons and electronic devices **2** : electronic devices or equipment

electron microscope *n* : an instrument in which a focused beam of electrons is used to produce an enlarged image of a minute object

electron tube *n* : a device in which electrical conduction by electrons takes place within a sealed container and which is used for the controlled flow of electrons

elec·tro·pho·re·sis \i-ˌlek-trə-fə-ˈrē-səs\ *n* : the movement of suspended particles through a fluid by an electromotive force — **elec·tro·pho·ret·ic** \-ˈre-tik\ *adj*

elec·tro·plate \i-ˈlek-trə-ˌplāt\ *vb* : to coat (as with metal) by electrolysis

elec·tro·shock therapy \i-ˈlek-trō-ˌshäk-\ *n* : the treatment of mental disorder by the induction of coma with an electric current

elec·tro·stat·ics \i-ˌlek-trə-ˈsta-tiks\ *n* : physics dealing with the interactions of stationary electric charges

el·ee·mos·y·nary \e-li-ˈmäs-ᵊn-ˌer-ē\ *adj* : CHARITABLE

el·e·gance \ˈe-li-gəns\ *n* **1** : refined gracefulness; *also* : tasteful richness (as of design) **2** : something marked by elegance — **el·e·gant** \-gənt\ *adj* — **el·e·gant·ly** *adv*

ele·giac \ˌe-lə-ˈjī-ək, -ˌak\ *adj* : of or relating to an elegy

el·e·gy \ˈe-lə-jē\ *n, pl* **-gies** : a song, poem, or speech expressing grief for one who is dead; *also* : a reflective poem usu. melancholy in tone

elem *abbr* elementary

el·e·ment \ˈe-lə-mənt\ *n* **1** *pl* : weather conditions; *esp* : severe weather ⟨boards exposed to the ∼s⟩ **2** : natural environment ⟨in her ∼⟩ **3** : a constituent part **4** *pl* : the simplest principles (as of an art or science) : RUDIMENTS **5** : a member of a mathematical set **6** : any of more than 100 fundamental substances that consist of atoms of only one kind **syn** component, ingredient, constituent — **el·e·men·tal** \ˌe-lə-ˈment-ᵊl\ *adj*

CHEMICAL ELEMENTS

ELEMENT	SYMBOL	ATOMIC NUMBER	ATOMIC WEIGHT (C = 12)
actinium	Ac	89	227.0278
aluminum	Al	13	26.98154
americium	Am	95	
antimony	Sb	51	121.75
argon	Ar	18	39.948
arsenic	As	33	74.9216
astatine	At	85	
barium	Ba	56	137.33
berkelium	Bk	97	
beryllium	Be	4	9.01218
bismuth	Bi	83	208.9804
boron	B	5	10.81
bromine	Br	35	79.904
cadmium	Cd	48	112.41
calcium	Ca	20	40.08
californium	Cf	98	
carbon	C	6	12.011

ELEMENT	SYMBOL	ATOMIC NUMBER	ATOMIC WEIGHT (C = 12)
cerium	Ce	58	140.12
cesium	Cs	55	132.9054
chlorine	Cl	17	35.453
chromium	Cr	24	51.996
cobalt	Co	27	58.9332
copper	Cu	29	63.546
curium	Cm	96	
dysprosium	Dy	66	162.50
einsteinium	Es	99	
erbium	Er	68	167.26
europium	Eu	63	151.96
fermium	Fm	100	
fluorine	F	9	18.998403
francium	Fr	87	
gadolinium	Gd	64	157.25
gallium	Ga	31	69.72
germanium	Ge	32	72.59
gold	Au	79	196.9665
hafnium	Hf	72	178.49
helium	He	2	4.00260
holmium	Ho	67	164.9304
hydrogen	H	1	1.0079
indium	In	49	114.82
iodine	I	53	126.9045
iridium	Ir	77	192.22
iron	Fe	26	55.847
krypton	Kr	36	83.80
lanthanum	La	57	138.9055
lawrencium	Lr	103	
lead	Pb	82	207.2
lithium	Li	3	6.941
lutetium	Lu	71	174.967
magnesium	Mg	12	24.305
manganese	Mn	25	54.9380
mendelevium	Md	101	
mercury	Hg	80	200.59
molybdenum	Mo	42	95.94
neodymium	Nd	60	144.24
neon	Ne	10	20.179
neptunium	Np	93	237.0482
nickel	Ni	28	58.69
niobium	Nb	41	92.9064
nitrogen	N	7	14.0067
nobelium	No	102	
osmium	Os	76	190.2
oxygen	O	8	15.9994
palladium	Pd	46	106.42
phosphorus	P	15	30.97376
platinum	Pt	78	195.08
plutonium	Pu	94	
polonium	Po	84	
potassium	K	19	39.0983
praseodymium	Pr	59	140.9077
promethium	Pm	61	
protactinium	Pa	91	231.0359
radium	Ra	88	226.0254
radon	Rn	86	
rhenium	Re	75	186.207
rhodium	Rh	45	102.9055
rubidium	Rb	37	85.4678
ruthenium	Ru	44	101.07
samarium	Sm	62	150.36
scandium	Sc	21	44.9559
selenium	Se	34	78.96
silicon	Si	14	28.0855
silver	Ag	47	107.868
sodium	Na	11	22.98977
strontium	Sr	38	87.62
sulfur	S	16	32.06
tantalum	Ta	73	180.9479
technetium	Tc	43	
tellurium	Te	52	127.60
terbium	Tb	65	158.9254

ELEMENT	SYMBOL	ATOMIC NUMBER	ATOMIC WEIGHT (C = 12)
thallium	Tl	81	204.383
thorium	Th	90	232.0381
thulium	Tm	69	168.9342
tin	Sn	50	118.69
titanium	Ti	22	47.88
tungsten	W	74	183.85
unnilhexium	Unh	106	
unnilpentium	Unp	105	
unnilquadium	Unq	104	
uranium	U	92	238.0289
vanadium	V	23	50.9415
xenon	Xe	54	131.29
ytterbium	Yb	70	173.04
yttrium	Y	39	88.9059
zinc	Zn	30	65.38
zirconium	Zr	40	91.22

el·e·men·ta·ry \ˌe-lə-ˈmen-trē, -tə-rē\ *adj* : SIMPLE, RUDIMENTARY; *also* : of, relating to, or teaching the basic subjects of education

elementary particle *n* : a subatomic particle of matter and energy that does not appear to be made up of other smaller particles

elementary school *n* : a school usu. including the first six or the first eight grades

el·e·phant \ˈe-lə-fənt\ *n, pl* **elephants** *also* **elephant** : any of a family of huge thickset nearly hairless mammals that have the snout lengthened into a trunk and two long curving pointed ivory tusks

elephant

el·e·phan·ti·a·sis \ˌe-lə-fən-ˈtī-ə-səs\ *n, pl* **-a·ses** \-ˌsēz\ : enlargement and thickening of tissues in response esp. to infection by minute parasitic worms

el·e·phan·tine \ˌe-lə-ˈfan-ˌtēn, -ˌtīn, ˈe-lə-fən-\ *adj* **1** : of great size or strength **2** : CLUMSY, PONDEROUS

elev *abbr* elevation

el·e·vate \ˈe-lə-ˌvāt\ *vb* **-vat·ed; -vat·ing 1** : to lift up : RAISE **2** : EXALT, ENNOBLE **3** : ELATE

el·e·va·tion \ˌe-lə-ˈvā-shən\ *n* **1** : the height to which something is raised (as above sea level) **2** : a lifting up **3** : something (as a hill or swelling) that is elevated

el·e·va·tor \ˈe-lə-ˌvā-tər\ *n* **1** : a cage or platform for conveying people or things from one level to another **2** : a building for storing and discharging grain **3** : a movable surface on an airplane to produce motion up or down

elev·en \i-ˈle-vən\ *n* **1** : one more than 10 **2** : the 11th in a set or series **3** : something having 11 units; *esp* : a football team — **eleven** *adj or pron* — **elev·enth** \-vənth\ *adj or n*

elf \ˈelf\ *n, pl* **elves** \ˈelvz\ : a mischievous fairy — **elf·ish** \ˈel-fish\ *adj*

ELF *abbr* extremely low frequency

elf·in \ˈel-fən\ *adj* : of, relating to, or resembling an elf

elic·it \i-ˈli-sət\ *vb* : to draw out or forth **syn** evoke, educe, extract, extort

elide \i-ˈlīd\ *vb* **elid·ed; elid·ing** : to suppress or alter by elision

el·i·gi·ble \'e-lə-jə-bəl\ *adj* : qualified to participate or to be chosen — **el·i·gi·bil·i·ty** \ˌe-lə-jə-'bi-lə-tē\ *n* — **eligible** *n*

elim·i·nate \i-'li-mə-ˌnāt\ *vb* **-nat·ed; -nat·ing** [L *eliminatus,* pp. of *eliminare,* fr. *limen* threshold] **1** : REMOVE, ERADICATE **2** : to pass (wastes) from the body **3** : to leave out : IGNORE — **elim·i·na·tion** \-ˌli-mə-'nā-shən\ *n*

eli·sion \i-'li-zhən\ *n* : the omission of a final or initial sound or a word; *esp* : the omission of an unstressed vowel or syllable in a verse to achieve a uniform rhythm

elite \ā-'lēt, ē-\ *n* [F *élite*] **1** : the choice part; *also* : a superior group **2** : a typewriter type providing 12 characters to the inch — **elite** *adj*

elit·ism \-'lē-ˌti-zəm\ *n* : leadership or rule by an elite; *also* : advocacy of such elitism

elix·ir \i-'lik-sər\ *n* [ME, fr. ML, fr. Ar *al-iksīr* the elixir, fr. *al* the + *iksīr* elixir] **1** : a substance held capable of prolonging life indefinitely; *also* : PANACEA **2** : a sweetened alcoholic medicinal solution

Eliz·a·be·than \i-ˌli-zə-'bē-thən\ *adj* : of, relating to, or characteristic of Elizabeth I of England or her times

elk \'elk\ *n, pl* **elk** *or* **elks 1** : MOOSE — used for one of the Old World **2** : a large gregarious deer of No. America, Europe, Asia, and northwestern Africa with curved antlers having many branches

¹**ell** \'el\ *n* : a former English cloth measure of 45 inches

²**ell** *n* : an extension at right angles to a building

el·lipse \i-'lips, e-\ *n* : a closed curve of oval shape

el·lip·sis \i-'lip-səs, e-\ *n, pl* **el·lip·ses** \-ˌsēz\ **1** : omission from an expression of a word clearly implied **2** : marks (as . . .) to show omission

el·lip·soid \i-'lip-ˌsȯid, e-\ *n* : a surface all plane sections of which are circles or ellipses — **el·lip·soi·dal** \-ˌlip-'sȯid-ᵊl\ *also* **ellipsoid** *adj*

el·lip·ti·cal \i-'lip-ti-kəl, e-\ *or* **el·lip·tic** \-tik\ *adj* **1** : of, relating to, or shaped like an ellipse **2** : of, relating to, or marked by ellipsis — **el·lip·ti·cal·ly** \-ti-k(ə-)lē\ *adv*

elm \'elm\ *n* : any of a genus of large trees that have toothed leaves and nearly circular one-seeded winged fruits and are often grown as shade trees; *also* : the wood of an elm

el·o·cu·tion \ˌe-lə-'kyü-shən\ *n* : the art of effective public speaking — **el·o·cu·tion·ist** \-shə-nist\ *n*

elon·gate \i-'lȯṅ-ˌgāt\ *vb* **-gat·ed; -gat·ing** : to make or grow longer *syn* extend, lengthen, prolong, protract — **elon·ga·tion** \(ˌ)ē-ˌlȯṅ-'gā-shən\ *n*

elope \i-'lōp\ *vb* **eloped; elop·ing** : to run away esp. to be married — **elope·ment** *n* — **elop·er** *n*

el·o·quent \'e-lə-kwənt\ *adj* **1** : having or showing clear and forceful expression **2** : clearly showing some feeling or meaning — **el·o·quence** \-kwəns\ *n* — **el·o·quent·ly** *adv*

¹**else** \'els\ *adv* **1** : in a different or additional manner or place or at a different or additional time ⟨where ~ can we meet⟩ **2** : OTHERWISE ⟨obey or ~ you'll be sorry⟩

²**else** *adj* : OTHER; *esp* : being in addition ⟨what ~ do you want⟩

else·where \-ˌhwer\ *adv* : in or to another place

elu·ci·date \i-'lü-sə-ˌdāt\ *vb* **-dat·ed; -dat·ing** : to make clear usu. by explanation *syn* clarify, explain, illuminate — **elu·ci·da·tion** \-ˌlü-sə-'dā-shən\ *n*

elude \ē-'lüd\ *vb* **elud·ed; elud·ing 1** : EVADE **2** : to escape the notice of

Elul \e-'lül\ *n* [Heb *Elūl*] : the 12th month of the civil year or the 6th month of the ecclesiastical year in the Jewish calendar

elu·sive \ē-'lü-siv\ *adj* : tending to elude : EVASIVE — **elu·sive·ly** *adv* — **elu·sive·ness** *n*

el·ver \'el-vər\ *n* [alter. of *eelfare* migration of eels] : a young eel

elves *pl of* ELF

Ely·si·um \i-'li-zhē-əm, -zē-\ *n, pl* **-si·ums** *or* **-sia** \-zhē-ə, -zē-\ : PARADISE 2 — **Ely·sian** \-'li-zhən\ *adj*

em \'em\ *n* : a length approximately the width of the letter *M*

EM *abbr* **1** electromagnetic **2** electron microscope **3** enlisted man

ema·ci·ate \i-'mā-shē-ˌāt\ *vb* **-at·ed; -at·ing** : to become or cause to become very thin — **ema·ci·a·tion** \-ˌmā-shē-'ā-shən, -sē-\ *n*

E–mail \'ē-ˌmāl\ *n* : ELECTRONIC MAIL

emalangeni *pl of* LILANGENI

em·a·nate \'e-mə-ˌnāt\ *vb* **-nat·ed; -nat·ing** : to come out from a source *syn* proceed, spring, rise, arise, originate — **em·a·na·tion** \ˌe-mə-'nā-shən\ *n*

eman·ci·pate \i-'man-sə-ˌpāt\ *vb* **-pat·ed; -pat·ing** : to set free *syn* liberate, release, deliver, discharge — **eman·ci·pa·tion** \-ˌman-sə-'pā-shən\ *n* — **eman·ci·pa·tor** \-'man-sə-ˌpā-tər\ *n*

emas·cu·late \i-'mas-kyü-ˌlāt\ *vb* **-lat·ed; -lat·ing** : CASTRATE, GELD; *also* : WEAKEN — **emas·cu·la·tion** \-ˌmas-kyü-'lā-shən\ *n*

em·balm \im-'bäm, -'bälm\ *vb* : to treat (a corpse) so as to protect from decay — **em·balm·er** *n*

em·bank·ment \im-'baṅk-mənt\ *n* : a raised structure (as of earth) to hold back water or carry a roadway

em·bar·go \im-'bär-gō\ *n, pl* **-goes** [Sp, fr. *embargar* to bar] : a prohibition on commerce — **embargo** *vb*

em·bark \im-'bärk\ *vb* **1** : to put on or go on board a ship or airplane **2** : to make a start — **em·bar·ka·tion** \ˌem-ˌbär-'kā-shən\ *n*

em·bar·rass \im-'bar-əs\ *vb* **1** : CONFUSE, DISCONCERT **2** : to involve in financial difficulties **3** : to cause to experience self-conscious distress **4** : HINDER, IMPEDE — **em·bar·rass·ing·ly** *adv* — **em·bar·rass·ment** *n*

em·bas·sy \'em-bə-sē\ *n, pl* **-sies 1** : a group of representatives headed by an ambassador **2** : the function, position, or mission of an ambassador **3** : the official residence and offices of an ambassador

em·bat·tle \im-'bat-ᵊl\ *vb* : to arrange in order for battle; *also* : FORTIFY

em·bat·tled *adj* **1** : engaged in battle, conflict, or controversy **2** : being a site of battle, conflict, or controversy **3** : characterized by conflict or controversy

em·bed \im-'bed\ *vb* **em·bed·ded; em·bed·ding 1** : to enclose closely in a surrounding mass **2** : to make something an integral part of

em·bel·lish \im-'be-lish\ *vb* **1** : ADORN, DECORATE **2** : to add ornamental details to *syn* beautify, deck, bedeck, garnish, ornament, dress — **em·bel·lish·ment** *n*

em·ber \'em-bər\ *n* **1** : a glowing or smoldering fragment from a fire **2** *pl* : the smoldering remains of a fire

em·bez·zle \im-'be-zəl\ *vb* **-zled; -zling** : to steal (as money) by falsifying records — **em·bez·zle·ment** *n* — **em·bez·zler** *n*

em·bit·ter \im-'bi-tər\ *vb* **1** : to arouse bitter feelings in **2** : to make bitter

em·bla·zon \-'blāz-ᵊn\ *vb* **1** : to adorn with heraldic devices **2** : to display conspicuously

em·blem \'em-bləm\ *n* : something (as an object or picture) suggesting another object or an idea : SYMBOL — **em·blem·at·ic** \ˌem-blə-'ma-tik\ *also* **em·blem·at·i·cal** \-ti-kəl\ *adj*

em·body \im-'bä-dē\ *vb* **em·bod·ied; em·body·ing 1** : INCARNATE **2** : to express in definite form **3** : to incorporate into a system or body **4** : PERSONIFY *syn* combine, integrate — **em·bodi·ment** \-di-mənt\ *n*

\ə\abut \ᵊ\kitten \ər\further \a\ash \ā\ace \ä\mop, mar
\au̇\out \ch\chin \e\bet \ē\easy \g\go \i\hit \ī\ice \j\job
\ṅ\sing \ō\go \ȯ\law \ȯi\boy \th\thin \t̲h̲\the \ü\loot \u̇\foot
\y\yet \zh\vision *see also* Pronunciation Symbols page

em·bold·en \im-'bōl-dən\ *vb* : to inspire with courage

em·bo·lism \'em-bə-ˌli-zəm\ *n* : the obstruction of a blood vessel by a foreign or abnormal particle

em·bon·point \äⁿ-bōⁿ-'pwaⁿ\ *n* [F] : plumpness of person : STOUTNESS

em·boss \im-'bäs, -'bòs\ *vb* : to ornament with raised work

em·bou·chure \'äm-bù-ˌshùr, ˌäm-bù-'shùr\ *n* [F, ultim. fr. *bouche* mouth] : the position and use of the lips, tongue, and teeth in playing a wind instrument

em·bow·er \im-'baù-ər\ *vb* : to shelter or enclose in a bower

¹**em·brace** \im-'brās\ *vb* **em·braced; em·brac·ing 1** : to clasp in the arms; *also* : CHERISH, LOVE **2** : ENCIRCLE **3** : TAKE UP, ADOPT; *also* : WELCOME **4** : INCLUDE **5** : to participate in an embrace **syn** comprehend, involve, encompass, embody

²**embrace** *n* : an encircling with the arms

em·bra·sure \im-'brā-zhər\ *n* **1** : an opening in a wall through which a cannon is fired **2** : a recess of a door or window

em·bro·ca·tion \ˌem-brə-'kā-shən\ *n* : LINIMENT

em·broi·der \im-'bròi-dər\ *vb* **1** : to ornament with or do needlework **2** : to elaborate with exaggerated detail

em·broi·dery \im-'bròi-də-rē\ *n, pl* **-der·ies 1** : the forming of decorative designs with needlework **2** : something embroidered

em·broil \im-'bròil\ *vb* **1** : to throw into confusion or disorder **2** : to involve in conflict or difficulties — **em·broil·ment** *n*

em·bryo \'em-brē-ˌō\ *n, pl* **embryos** : a living thing in its earliest stages of development — **em·bry·on·ic** \ˌem-brē-'ä-nik\ *adj*

em·bry·ol·o·gy \ˌem-brē-'ä-lə-jē\ *n* : a branch of biology dealing with embryos and their development — **em·bry·o·log·i·cal** \-brē-ə-'lä-ji-kəl\ *adj* — **em·bry·ol·o·gist** \-brē-'ä-lə-jist\ *n*

em·cee \ˌem-'sē\ *n* : MASTER OF CEREMONIES — **emcee** *vb*

emend \ē-'mend\ *vb* : to correct usu. by altering the text of **syn** rectify, revise, amend — **emen·da·tion** \ˌē-ˌmen-'dā-shən\ *n*

emer *abbr* emeritus

¹**em·er·ald** \'em-rəld, 'e-mə-\ *n* : a green beryl prized as a gem

²**emerald** *adj* : brightly or richly green

emerge \i-'mərj\ *vb* **emerged; emerg·ing** : to rise, come forth, or come out into view — **emer·gence** \-'mər-jəns\ *n* — **emer·gent** \-jənt\ *adj*

emer·gen·cy \i-'mər-jən-sē\ *n, pl* **-cies** : an unforeseen event or condition requiring prompt action **syn** exigency, contingency, crisis, juncture

emergency room *n* : a hospital room for receiving and treating persons needing immediate medical care

emer·i·ta \i-'mer-ə-tə\ *adj* : EMERITUS — used of a woman

emer·i·tus \i-'mer-ə-təs\ *adj* [L] : retired from active duty ⟨professor ∼⟩

em·ery \'e-mə-rē\ *n, pl* **em·er·ies** : a dark granular corundum used esp. for grinding and polishing

emet·ic \i-'me-tik\ *n* : an agent that induces vomiting — **emetic** *adj*

emf *n* [electromotive *force*] : POTENTIAL DIFFERENCE

em·i·grate \'e-mə-ˌgrāt\ *vb* **-grat·ed; -grat·ing** : to leave a place (as a country) to settle elsewhere — **em·i·grant** \-mi-grənt\ *n* — **em·i·gra·tion** \ˌe-mə-'grā-shən\ *n*

émi·gré *also* **emi·gré** \'e-mi-ˌgrā, ˌe-mi-'grā\ *n* [F] : a person who emigrates esp. because of political conditions

em·i·nence \'e-mə-nəns\ *n* **1** : high rank or position; *also* : a person of high rank or attainments **2** : a lofty place

em·i·nent \'e-mə-nənt\ *adj* **1** : CONSPICUOUS, EVIDENT **2** : DISTINGUISHED, PROMINENT — **em·i·nent·ly** *adv*

eminent domain *n* : a right of a government to take private property for public use

emir \i-'mir, ā-\ *n* [Ar *amīr* commander] : a ruler, chief, or commander in Islamic countries — **emir·ate** \'e-mər-ət\ *n*

em·is·sary \'e-mə-ˌser-ē\ *n, pl* **-sar·ies** : AGENT; *esp* : a secret agent

emis·sion \ē-'mi-shən\ *n* : something emitted; *esp* : substances discharged into the air

emit \ē-'mit\ *vb* **emit·ted; emit·ting 1** : to give off or out ⟨∼ light⟩; *also* : EJECT **2** : EXPRESS, UTTER — **emit·ter** *n*

emol·lient \i-'mäl-yənt\ *adj* : making soft or supple; *also* : soothing esp. to the skin or mucous membrane — **emol·lient** *n*

emol·u·ment \i-'mäl-yə-mənt\ *n* [ME, fr. L *emolumentum* advantage, fr. *emolere* to produce by grinding] : the product (as salary or fees) of an employment

emote \i-'mōt\ *vb* **emot·ed; emot·ing** : to give expression to emotion in or as if in a play

emo·tion \i-'mō-shən\ *n* : a usu. intense feeling (as of love, hate, or despair) — **emo·tion·al** \-shə-nəl\ *adj* — **emo·tion·al·ly** *adv*

emp *abbr* emperor; empress

em·pa·thy \'em-pə-thē\ *n* : the experiencing as one's own of the feelings of another; *also* : the capacity for this — **em·path·ic** \em-'pa-thik\ *adj*

em·pen·nage \ˌäm-pə-'näzh, ˌem-\ *n* [F] : the tail assembly of an airplane

em·per·or \'em-pər-ər\ *n* : the sovereign male ruler of an empire

em·pha·sis \'em-fə-səs\ *n, pl* **-pha·ses** \-ˌsēz\ : particular prominence given (as to a syllable in speaking or to a phase of action)

em·pha·size \-ˌsīz\ *vb* **-sized; -siz·ing** : to place emphasis on : STRESS

em·phat·ic \im-'fa-tik, em-\ *adj* : uttered with emphasis : STRESSED — **em·phat·i·cal·ly** \-'ti-k(ə-)lē\ *adv*

em·phy·se·ma \ˌem-fə-'zē-mə, -'sē-\ *n* : a condition marked esp. by abnormal expansion of the air spaces of the lungs and often by impairment of heart action

em·pire \'em-ˌpīər\ *n* **1** : a large state or a group of states under a single sovereign who is usu. an emperor; *also* : something resembling a political empire **2** : imperial sovereignty or dominion

em·pir·i·cal \im-'pir-i-kəl\ *also* **em·pir·ic** \-ik\ *adj* : based on observation; *also* : subject to verification by observation or experiment ⟨∼ laws⟩ — **em·pir·i·cal·ly** \-i-k(ə-)lē\ *adv*

em·pir·i·cism \im-'pir-ə-ˌsi-zəm, em-\ *n* : the practice of relying on observation and experiment esp. in the natural sciences — **em·pir·i·cist** \-sist\ *n*

em·place·ment \im-'plās-mənt\ *n* **1** : a prepared position for weapons or military equipment **2** : PLACEMENT

¹**em·ploy** \im-'plòi\ *vb* **1** : to make use of **2** : to use the services of **3** : OCCUPY, DEVOTE — **em·ploy·er** *n*

²**em·ploy** \im-'plòi; 'im-ˌplòi, 'em-\ *n* : EMPLOYMENT

em·ploy·ee *or* **em·ploye** \im-ˌplòi-'ē, ˌem-; im-'plòi-ˌē, em-\ *n* : a person who works for another

em·ploy·ment \im-'plòi-mənt\ *n* **1** : OCCUPATION, ACTIVITY **2** : the act of employing : the condition of being employed

em·po·ri·um \im-'pōr-ē-əm, em-\ *n, pl* **-ri·ums** *also* **-ria** \-ē-ə\ [L, fr. Gk *emporion*, fr. *emporos* traveler, trader] : a commercial center; *esp* : a store carrying varied articles

em·pow·er \im-'paù-ər\ *vb* : to give authority or power to; *also* : ENABLE — **em·pow·er·ment** \-mənt\ *n*

em·press \'em-prəs\ *n* **1** : the wife or widow of an emperor **2** : a sovereign female ruler of an empire

¹**emp·ty** \'emp-tē\ *adj* **emp·ti·er; -est 1** : containing nothing **2** : UNOCCUPIED, UNINHABITED **3** : lacking value,

force, sense, or purpose **syn** vacant, blank, void, stark, vacuous — **emp·ti·ness** *n*

²**empty** *vb* **emp·tied; emp·ty·ing 1** : to make or become empty **2** : to discharge contents; *also* : to remove from what holds or encloses

³**empty** *n, pl* **empties** : an empty container or vehicle

emp·ty–hand·ed \₁emp-tē-ʰhan-dəd\ *adj* **1** : having or bringing nothing **2** : having acquired or gained nothing

em·py·re·an \₁em-₁pī-ʰrē-ən, -pə-\ *n* **1** : the highest heaven; *also* : FIRMAMENT **2** : an ideal place or state

EMT \₁ē-(₁)em-ʰtē\ *n* [*emergency medical technician*] : a specially trained medical technician licensed to provide basic medical services before and during transportation to a hospital

¹**emu** \ʰē-myü, -mü\ *n* : a swift-running flightless Australian bird smaller than the related ostrich

²**emu** *abbr* electromagnetic unit

em·u·late \ʰem-yù-₁lāt\ *vb* **-lat·ed; -lat·ing** : to strive to equal or excel : IMITATE — **em·u·la·tion** \₁em-yù-ʰlā-shən\ *n* — **em·u·lous** \ʰem-yù-ləs\ *adj*

emul·si·fi·er \i-ʰməl-sə-₁fī-ər\ *n* : a substance (as a soap) that helps to form and stabilize an emulsion

emul·si·fy \-₁fī\ *vb* **-fied; -fy·ing** : to disperse (as an oil) in an emulsion — **emul·si·fi·ca·tion** \i-₁məl-sə-fə-ʰkā-shən\ *n*

emul·sion \i-ʰməl-shən\ *n* **1** : a mixture of mutually insoluble liquids in which one is dispersed in droplets throughout the other (an ∼ of oil in water) **2** : a light-sensitive coating on photographic film or paper

en \ʰen\ *n* : a length approximately half the width of the letter *M*

¹**-en** *also* **-n** *adj suffix* : made of : consisting of ⟨earth*en*⟩

²**-en** *vb suffix* **1** : become or cause to be ⟨sharp*en*⟩ **2** : cause or come to have ⟨length*en*⟩

en·able \i-ʰnā-bəl\ *vb* **en·abled; en·abling 1** : to make able or feasible **2** : to give legal power, capacity, or sanction to

en·act \i-ʰnakt\ *vb* **1** : to make into law **2** : to act out — **en·act·ment** *n*

enam·el \i-ʰna-məl\ *n* **1** : a glasslike substance used to coat the surface of metal or pottery **2** : the hard outer layer of a tooth **3** : a usu. glossy paint that forms a hard coat — **enamel** *vb*

enam·el·ware \-₁war\ *n* : metal utensils coated with enamel

en·am·or \i-ʰna-mər\ *vb* : to inflame with love

en·am·our *chiefly Brit var of* ENAMOR

en bloc \än-ʰbläk\ *adv or adj* : as a whole : in a mass

enc *or* **encl** *abbr* enclosure

en·camp \in-ʰkamp\ *vb* : to make camp — **en·camp·ment** *n*

en·cap·su·late \in-ʰkap-sə-₁lāt\ *vb* **-lat·ed; -lat·ing 1** : to encase or become encased in a capsule **2** : SUMMARIZE — **en·cap·su·la·tion** \-₁kap-sə-ʰlā-shən\ *n*

en·case \in-ʰkās\ *vb* : to enclose in or as if in a case

-ence *n suffix* **1** : action or process ⟨emerg*ence*⟩ : instance of an action or process ⟨refer*ence*⟩ **2** : quality or state ⟨depend*ence*⟩

en·ceinte \änⁿ-ʰsant\ *adj* : PREGNANT

en·ceph·a·li·tis \in-₁se-fə-ʰlī-təs\ *n, pl* **-lit·i·des** \-ʰli-tə-₁dēz\ : inflammation of the brain — **en·ceph·a·lit·ic** \-ʰli-tik\ *adj*

en·chain \in-ʰchān\ *vb* : FETTER, CHAIN

en·chant \in-ʰchant\ *vb* **1** : BEWITCH **2** : ENRAPTURE, FASCINATE — **en·chant·er** *n* — **en·chant·ing·ly** *adv* — **en·chant·ment** *n* — **en·chant·ress** \-ʰchan-trəs\ *n*

en·chi·la·da \₁en-chə-ʰlä-də\ *n* : a rolled filled tortilla covered with chili sauce and usu. baked

en·ci·pher \in-ʰsī-fər, en-\ *vb* : ENCODE

en·cir·cle \in-ʰsər-kəl\ *vb* : to pass completely around : SURROUND — **en·cir·cle·ment** *n*

en·clave \ʰen-₁klāv; ʰän-₁kläv\ *n* : a distinct territorial, cultural, or social unit enclosed within or as if within foreign territory

en·close \in-ʰklōz\ *vb* **1** : to shut up or in; *esp* : to surround with a fence **2** : to include along with something else in a parcel or envelope ⟨∼ a check⟩ — **en·clo·sure** \-ʰklō-zhər\ *n*

en·code \in-ʰkōd, en-\ *vb* : to convert (a message) into code

en·co·mi·um \en-ʰkō-mē-əm\ *n, pl* **-mi·ums** *or* **-mia** \-mē-ə\ : high or glowing praise

en·com·pass \in-ʰkəm-pəs\ *vb* **1** : ENCIRCLE **2** : ENVELOP, INCLUDE

¹**en·core** \ʰän-₁kōr\ *n* : a demand for repetition or reappearance; *also* : a further performance (as of a singer) in response to such a demand

²**encore** *vb* **en·cored; en·cor·ing** : to request an encore from

¹**en·coun·ter** \in-ʰkaun-tər\ *vb* **1** : to meet as an enemy : FIGHT **2** : to meet usu. unexpectedly

²**encounter** *n* **1** : a hostile meeting; *esp* : COMBAT **2** : a chance meeting

en·cour·age \in-ʰkər-ij\ *vb* **-aged; -ag·ing 1** : to inspire with courage and hope **2** : STIMULATE, INCITE **3** : FOSTER — **en·cour·age·ment** *n* — **en·cour·ag·ing·ly** *adv*

en·croach \in-ʰkrōch\ *vb* [ME *encrochen* to seize, fr. MF *encrochier*, fr. OF, fr. *croche* hook] : to enter gradually or stealthily upon another's property or rights — **en·croach·ment** *n*

en·crust \in-ʰkrəst\ *vb* : to provide with or form a crust

en·crus·ta·tion \(₁)in-₁krəs-ʰtā-shən, ₁en-\ *var of* INCRUSTATION

en·cum·ber \in-ʰkəm-bər\ *vb* **1** : to weigh down : BURDEN **2** : to hinder the function or activity of — **en·cum·brance** \-brəns\ *n*

ency *or* **encyc** *abbr* encyclopedia

-en·cy *n suffix* : quality or state ⟨despond*ency*⟩

¹**en·cyc·li·cal** \in-ʰsi-kli-kəl, en-\ *adj* : addressed to all the individuals of a group

²**encyclical** *n* : an encyclical letter; *esp* : a papal letter to the bishops of the church

en·cy·clo·pe·dia *also* **en·cy·clo·pae·dia** \in-₁sī-klə-ʰpē-dē-ə\ *n* [ML *encyclopaedia* course of general education, fr. Gk *enkyklios paideia* general education] : a work treating the various branches of learning — **en·cy·clo·pe·dic** \-ʰpē-dik\ *adj*

en·cyst \in-ʰsist, en-\ *vb* : to form or become enclosed in a cyst — **en·cyst·ment** *n*

¹**end** \ʰend\ *n* **1** : the part of an area that lies at the boundary; *also* : a point which marks the extent or limit of something or at which something ceases to exist **2** : a ceasing of a course (as of action or activity); *also* : DEATH **3** : the ultimate state; *also* : RESULT, ISSUE **4** : REMNANT **5** : PURPOSE, OBJECTIVE **6** : a player stationed at the extremity of a line (as in football) **7** : a share, operation, or aspect of an undertaking

²**end** *vb* **1** : to bring or come to an end **2** : DESTROY; *also* : DIE **3** : to form or be at the end of **syn** close, conclude, terminate, finish, complete

en·dan·ger \in-ʰdān-jər\ *vb* : to bring into danger; *also* : to create danger

en·dan·gered *adj* : being or relating to an endangered species

endangered species *n* : a species threatened with extinction

en·dear \in-ʰdir\ *vb* : to cause to become beloved or admired

en·dear·ment \-mənt\ *n* : a sign of affection : CARESS

\ə\abut \ᵊ\kitten \ər\further \a\ash \ā\ace \ä\mop, mar
\aù\out \ch\chin \e\bet \ē\easy \g\go \i\hit \ī\ice \j\job
\ŋ\sing \ō\go \ò\law \òi\boy \th\thin \th̲\the \ü\loot \ù\foot
\y\yet \zh\vision *see also* Pronunciation Symbols page

en·deav·or \in-ˈde-vər\ *vb* : TRY, ATTEMPT — **endeavor** *n*

en·deav·our *chiefly Brit var of* ENDEAVOR

en·dem·ic \en-ˈde-mik, in-\ *adj* : restricted to a particular place ⟨∼ plants⟩ ⟨an ∼ disease⟩ — **endemic** *n*

end·ing \ˈen-diŋ\ *n* : something that forms an end; *esp* : SUFFIX

en·dive \ˈen-ˌdīv\ *n* **1** : an herb related to chicory and grown as a salad plant **2** : the blanched shoot of chicory

end·less \ˈend-ləs\ *adj* **1** : having or seeming to have no end : ETERNAL **2** : united at the ends : CONTINUOUS ⟨an ∼ belt⟩ **syn** interminable, everlasting, unceasing, ceaseless, unending — **end·less·ly** *adv*

end·most \-ˌmōst\ *adj* : situated at the very end

end·note \-ˌnōt\ *n* : a note placed at the end of a text

en·do·crine \ˈen-də-krən, -ˌkrīn, -ˌkrēn\ *adj* : producing secretions that are distributed by way of the bloodstream ⟨∼ glands⟩ — **endocrine** *n* — **en·do·cri·nol·o·gist** \-kri-ˈnä-lə-jist\ *n* — **en·do·cri·nol·o·gy** \-jē\ *n*

en·dog·e·nous \en-ˈdä-jə-nəs\ *adj* : caused or produced by factors inside the organism or system ⟨∼ psychic depression⟩ — **en·dog·e·nous·ly** *adv*

en·dorse \in-ˈdȯrs\ *vb* **en·dorsed; en·dors·ing** **1** : to sign one's name on the back of (as a check) **2** : APPROVE, SANCTION — **en·dorse·ment** *n*

en·do·scope \ˈen-də-ˌskōp\ *n* : an instrument with which the interior of a hollow organ (as the rectum) may be visualized — **en·do·scop·ic** \ˌen-də-ˈskä-pik\ *adj* — **en·dos·co·py** \en-ˈdäs-kə-pē\ *n*

en·do·ther·mic \ˌen-də-ˈthər-mik\ *adj* : characterized by or formed with absorption of heat

en·dow \in-ˈdau̇\ *vb* **1** : to furnish with funds for support ⟨∼ a school⟩ **2** : to furnish with something freely or naturally — **en·dow·ment** *n*

en·due \in-ˈdü, -ˈdyü\ *vb* **en·dued; en·du·ing** : PROVIDE, ENDOW

en·dur·ance \in-ˈdu̇r-əns, -ˈdyu̇r-\ *n* **1** : DURATION **2** : the ability to withstand hardship or stress : FORTITUDE

en·dure \in-ˈdu̇r, -ˈdyu̇r\ *vb* **en·dured; en·dur·ing** **1** : LAST, PERSIST **2** : to suffer firmly or patiently : BEAR **3** : TOLERATE — **en·dur·able** *adj*

end·ways \ˈend-ˌwāz\ *adv or adj* **1** : LENGTHWISE **2** : with the end forward **3** : on end

end·wise \-ˌwīz\ *adv or adj* : ENDWAYS

ENE *abbr* east-northeast

en·e·ma \ˈe-nə-mə\ *n, pl* **enemas** *also* **ene·ma·ta** \ˌe-nə-ˈmä-tə, ˈe-nə-mə-tə\ : injection of liquid into the rectum; *also* : material so injected

en·e·my \ˈe-nə-mē\ *n, pl* **-mies** : one that attacks or tries to harm another : FOE; *esp* : a military opponent

en·er·get·ic \ˌe-nər-ˈje-tik\ *adj* : marked by energy : ACTIVE, VIGOROUS **syn** strenuous, lusty, dynamic, vital — **en·er·get·i·cal·ly** \-ti-k(ə-)lē\ *adv*

en·er·gize \ˈe-nər-ˌjīz\ *vb* **-gized; -giz·ing** : to give energy to

en·er·gy \ˈe-nər-jē\ *n, pl* **-gies** **1** : vigorous action : EFFORT **2** : capacity for action **3** : capacity for performing work **4** : usable power (as heat or electricity); *also* : the resources for producing such power

energy level *n* : one of the stable states of constant energy that may be assumed by a physical system (as the electrons in an atom)

en·er·vate \ˈe-nər-ˌvāt\ *vb* **-vat·ed; -vat·ing** : to lessen the strength or vigor of : weaken in mind or body — **en·er·va·tion** \ˌe-nər-ˈvā-shən\ *n*

en·fee·ble \in-ˈfē-bəl\ *vb* **-bled; -bling** : to make feeble **syn** weaken, debilitate, sap, undermine, cripple — **en·fee·ble·ment** *n*

en·fi·lade \ˈen-fə-ˌlād, -ˌläd\ *n* : gunfire directed along the length of an enemy battle line — **enfilade** *vb*

en·fold \in-ˈfōld\ *vb* **1** : ENVELOP **2** : EMBRACE

en·force \in-ˈfōrs\ *vb* **1** : COMPEL ⟨∼ obedience by

threats⟩ **2** : to execute effectively ⟨∼ the law⟩ — **en·force·able** *adj* — **en·force·ment** *n*

en·forc·er \in-ˈfȯr-sər\ *n* : one that enforces; *esp* : an aggressive player (as in ice hockey) known for rough play

en·fran·chise \in-ˈfran-ˌchīz\ *vb* **-chised; -chis·ing** **1** : to set free (as from slavery) **2** : to admit to citizenship; *also* : to grant the vote to — **en·fran·chise·ment** \-ˌchīz-mənt, -chəz-\ *n*

eng *abbr* engine; engineer; engineering

Eng *abbr* England; English

en·gage \in-ˈgāj\ *vb* **en·gaged; en·gag·ing** **1** : PLEDGE; *esp* : to bind by a pledge to marry **2** : EMPLOY, HIRE **3** : to attract and hold esp. by interesting; *also* : to cause to participate **4** : to commence or take part in a venture **5** : to bring or enter into conflict **6** : to connect or interlock with : MESH; *also* : to cause to mesh

en·gage·ment \in-ˈgāj-mənt\ *n* **1** : APPOINTMENT **2** : EMPLOYMENT **3** : a mutual promise to marry **4** : a hostile encounter

en·gag·ing *adj* : ATTRACTIVE — **en·gag·ing·ly** *adv*

en·gen·der \in-ˈjen-dər\ *vb* **1** : BEGET **2** : BRING ABOUT, CREATE **syn** generate, breed, occasion, produce

en·gine \ˈen-jən\ *n* [ME *engin*, fr. OF, fr. L *ingenium* natural disposition, talent] **1** : a mechanical device **2** : a machine for converting energy into mechanical motion **3** : LOCOMOTIVE

¹en·gi·neer \ˌen-jə-ˈnir\ *n* **1** : a member of a military unit specializing in engineering work **2** : a designer or builder of engines **3** : one trained in engineering **4** : one that operates an engine

²engineer *vb* **1** : to lay out or manage as an engineer **2** : to guide the course of **syn** pilot, lead, steer

en·gi·neer·ing *n* : the practical applications of scientific and mathematical principles

En·glish \ˈiŋ-glish\ *n* **1** : the language of England, the U.S., and many areas now or formerly under British rule **2 English** *pl* : the people of England **3** : spin imparted to a ball that is driven or rolled — **English** *adj* — **En·glish·man** \-mən\ *n* — **En·glish·wom·an** \-ˌwu̇-mən\ *n*

English horn *n* : a woodwind instrument longer than and having a range lower than the oboe

English setter *n* : any of a breed of bird dogs with a flat silky coat of white or white with color

English sparrow *n* : HOUSE SPARROW

English system *n* : a system of weights and measures in which the foot is the principal unit of length and the pound is the principal unit of weight

engr *abbr* **1** engineer **2** engraved

en·gram \ˈen-ˌgram\ *n* : a hypothetical change in neural tissue postulated in order to account for persistence of memory

en·grave \in-ˈgrāv\ *vb* **en·graved; en·grav·ing** **1** : to produce (as letters or lines) by incising a surface **2** : to cut figures, letters, or designs on for printing; *also* : to print from an engraved plate **3** : PHOTOENGRAVE — **en·grav·er** *n*

en·grav·ing \in-ˈgrā-viŋ\ *n* **1** : the art of one who engraves **2** : an engraved plate; *also* : a print made from it

en·gross \in-ˈgrōs\ *vb* : to take up the whole interest or attention of **syn** monopolize, absorb, consume

en·gulf \in-ˈgəlf\ *vb* : to flow over and enclose

en·hance \in-ˈhans\ *vb* **en·hanced; en·hanc·ing** : to increase or improve (as in value or desirability) **syn** heighten, intensify, magnify — **en·hance·ment** *n*

enig·ma \i-ˈnig-mə\ *n* [L *aenigma*, fr. Gk *ainigma*, fr. *ainissesthai* to speak in riddles, fr. *ainos* fable] : something obscure or hard to understand

enig·mat·ic \ˌen-ig-ˈma-tik\ *adj* : resembling an enigma **syn** obscure, cryptic, mystifying — **en·ig·mat·i·cal·ly** \-ti-k(ə-)lē\ *adv*

en·join \in-ʲjȯin\ *vb* 1 : COMMAND, ORDER 2 : FORBID **syn** direct, bid, charge, command, instruct

en·joy \in-ʲjȯi\ *vb* 1 : to have for one's benefit or use ⟨~ good health⟩ 2 : to take pleasure or satisfaction in ⟨~ed the concert⟩ — **en·joy·able** *adj* — **en·joy·ment** *n*

enl *abbr* 1 enlarged 2 enlisted

en·large \in-ʲlärj\ *vb* **en·larged; en·larg·ing** 1 : to make or grow larger 2 : ELABORATE **syn** increase, augment, multiply, expand — **en·large·ment** *n*

en·light·en \in-ʲlīt-ᵊn\ *vb* 1 : INSTRUCT, INFORM 2 : to give spiritual insight to — **en·light·en·ment** *n*

en·list \in-ʲlist\ *vb* 1 : to secure the aid or support of 2 : to engage for service in the armed forces — **en·list·ee** \-ₗlis-ʲtē\ *n* — **en·list·ment** \-ʲlist-mənt\ *n*

en·list·ed \in-ʲlis-təd\ *adj* : of, relating to, or forming the part of a military force below commissioned or warrant officers

enlisted man *n* : a man or woman in the armed forces ranking below a commissioned or warrant officer

en·liv·en \in-ʲlī-vən\ *vb* : to give life, action, or spirit to : ANIMATE

en masse \äⁿ-ʲmas\ *adv* [F] : in a body : as a whole

en·mesh \in-ʲmesh\ *vb* : to catch or entangle in or as if in meshes

en·mi·ty \ʲen-mə-tē\ *n, pl* **-ties** : ILL WILL; *esp* : mutual hatred **syn** hostility, antipathy, animosity, rancor, antagonism

en·no·ble \i-ʲnō-bəl\ *vb* **-bled; -bling** : EXALT, ELEVATE; *esp* : to raise to noble rank — **en·no·ble·ment** *n*

en·nui \ₐän-ʲwē\ *n* [F] : BOREDOM

enor·mi·ty \i-ʲnȯr-mə-tē\ *n, pl* **-ties** 1 : an outrageous, vicious, or immoral act 2 : great wickedness 3 : IMMENSITY

enor·mous \i-ʲnȯr-məs\ *adj* [L *enormis,* fr. *e, ex* out of + *norma* rule] 1 : exceedingly wicked 2 : great in size, number, or degree : HUGE **syn** immense, vast, gigantic, colossal, mammoth, elephantine

¹**enough** \i-ʲnəf\ *adj* : SUFFICIENT

²**enough** *adv* 1 : SUFFICIENTLY 2 : FULLY, QUITE 3 : TOLERABLY

³**enough** *pron* : a sufficient number, quantity, or amount

en·quire \in-ʲkwīr\, **en·qui·ry** \ʲin-ₖkwīr-ē, in-ʲkwīr-; ʲin-kwə-rē, ʲiŋ-\ *var of* INQUIRE, INQUIRY

en·rage \in-ʲrāj\ *vb* : to fill with rage

en·rap·ture \in-ʲrap-chər\ *vb* **en·rap·tured; en·rap·tur·ing** : DELIGHT

en·rich \in-ʲrich\ *vb* 1 : to make rich or richer 2 : ORNAMENT, ADORN — **en·rich·ment** *n*

en·roll *or* **en·rol** \in-ʲrōl\ *vb* **en·rolled; en·roll·ing** 1 : to enter or register on a roll or list 2 : to offer (oneself) for enrolling — **en·roll·ment** *n*

en route \än-ʲrüt, en-\ *adv or adj* : on or along the way

ENS *abbr* ensign

en·sconce \in-ʲskäns\ *vb* **en·sconced; en·sconc·ing** 1 : SHELTER, CONCEAL 2 : to settle snugly or securely **syn** secrete, hide, cache, stash

en·sem·ble \än-ʲsäm-bəl\ *n* [F, fr. *ensemble* together, fr. L *insimul* at the same time] : a group (as of singers, dancers, or players) or a set (as of clothes) producing a single effect

en·sheathe \in-ʲshēth\ *vb* : to cover with or as if with a sheath

en·shrine \in-ʲshrīn\ *vb* 1 : to enclose in or as if in a shrine 2 : to cherish as sacred

en·shroud \in-ʲshraüd\ *vb* : SHROUD, OBSCURE

en·sign \ʲen-sən, *1 also* ʲen-ₛsīn\ *n* 1 : FLAG; *also* : BADGE, EMBLEM 2 : a commissioned officer in the navy ranking next below a lieutenant junior grade

en·slave \in-ʲslāv\ *vb* : to make a slave of — **en·slave·ment** *n*

en·snare \in-ʲsnar\ *vb* : SNARE, TRAP **syn** entrap, bag, catch, capture

en·sue \in-ʲsü\ *vb* **en·sued; en·su·ing** : to follow in time or as a result

en·sure \in-ʲshur\ *vb* **en·sured; en·sur·ing** : INSURE, GUARANTEE

en·tail \in-ʲtāl\ *vb* 1 : to limit the inheritance of (property) to the owner's lineal descendants or to a class thereof 2 : to include or involve as a necessary step or result — **en·tail·ment** *n*

en·tan·gle \in-ʲtaŋ-gəl\ *vb* : TANGLE, CONFUSE — **en·tan·gle·ment** *n*

en·tente \än-ʲtänt\ *n* [F understanding, agreement] : an understanding providing for joint action; *also* : parties linked by such an entente

en·ter \ʲen-tər\ *vb* 1 : to go or come in or into 2 : to become a member of : JOIN ⟨~ the ministry⟩ 3 : BEGIN 4 : to take part in : CONTRIBUTE 5 : to go into or upon and take possession 6 : to set down (as in a list) : REGISTER 7 : to place (a complaint) before a court; *also* : to put on record ⟨~ a complaint⟩

en·ter·i·tis \ₐen-tə-ʲrī-təs\ *n* : intestinal inflammation; *also* : a disease marked by this

en·ter·prise \ʲen-tər-ₚprīz\ *n* 1 : UNDERTAKING, PROJECT 2 : readiness for daring action : INITIATIVE 3 : a business organization

en·ter·pris·ing \-ₚprī-ziŋ\ *adj* : bold and vigorous in action : ENERGETIC

en·ter·tain \ₐen-tər-ʲtān\ *vb* 1 : to treat or receive as a guest 2 : AMUSE, DIVERT 3 : to hold in mind **syn** harbor, shelter, lodge, house, billet — **en·ter·tain·er** *n* — **en·ter·tain·ment** *n*

en·thrall *or* **en·thral** \in-ʲthrȯl\ *vb* **en·thralled; en·thrall·ing** 1 : ENSLAVE 2 : to hold spellbound

en·throne \in-ʲthrōn\ *vb* 1 : to seat on or as if on a throne 2 : EXALT

en·thuse \in-ʲthüz, -ʲthyüz\ *vb* **en·thused; en·thus·ing** 1 : to make enthusiastic 2 : to show enthusiasm

en·thu·si·asm \in-ʲthü-zē-ₐa-zəm, -ʲthyü-\ *n* [Gk *enthousiasmos,* fr. *enthousiazein* to be inspired, irreg. fr. *entheos* inspired, fr. *theos* god] 1 : strong warmth of feeling : keen interest : FERVOR 2 : a cause of fervor — **en·thu·si·ast** \-ₐast, -əst\ *n* — **en·thu·si·as·tic** \in-ₐthü-zē-ʲas-tik, -ₐthyü-\ *adj* — **en·thu·si·as·ti·cal·ly** \-ti-k(ə-)lē\ *adv*

en·tice \in-ʲtīs\ *vb* **en·ticed; en·tic·ing** : ALLURE, TEMPT — **en·tice·ment** *n*

en·tire \in-ʲtīr\ *adj* : COMPLETE, WHOLE **syn** sound, perfect, intact, undamaged — **en·tire·ly** *adv*

en·tire·ty \in-ʲtī-rə-tē, -ʲtīr-tē\ *n, pl* **-ties** 1 : COMPLETENESS 2 : WHOLE, TOTALITY

en·ti·tle \in-ʲtīt-ᵊl\ *vb* **en·ti·tled; en·ti·tling** 1 : NAME, DESIGNATE 2 : to give a right or claim to

en·ti·tle·ment \in-ʲtīt-ᵊl-mənt\ *n* : a government program providing benefits to members of a specified group

en·ti·ty \ʲen-tə-tē\ *n, pl* **-ties** 1 : EXISTENCE, BEING 2 : something with separate and real existence

en·tomb \in-ʲtüm\ *vb* : to place in a tomb : BURY — **en·tomb·ment** *n*

en·to·mol·o·gy \ₐen-tə-ʲmä-lə-jē\ *n* : a branch of zoology that deals with insects — **en·to·mo·log·i·cal** \-mə-ʲläji-kəl\ *adj* — **en·to·mol·o·gist** \-jist\ *n*

en·tou·rage \än-tü-ʲräzh\ *n* [F] : RETINUE

en·tr'acte \ʲäⁿ-ₜtrakt\ *n* [F] 1 : something (as a dance) performed between two acts of a play 2 : the interval between two acts of a play

en·trails \ʲen-ₜtrālz\ *n pl* : VISCERA; *esp* : INTESTINES

¹**en·trance** \ʲen-trəns\ *n* 1 : permission or right to enter 2 : the act of entering 3 : a means or place of entry

²**en·trance** \in-ˈtrans\ *vb* **en·tranced; en·tranc·ing**
: CHARM, DELIGHT

en·trant \ˈen-trənt\ *n* : one that enters esp. as a competitor

en·trap \in-ˈtrap\ *vb* : ENSNARE, TRAP — **en·trap·ment** *n*

en·treat \in-ˈtrēt\ *vb* : to ask urgently : BESEECH **syn** beg, implore, plead, supplicate — **en·treaty** \-ˈtrē-tē\ *n*

en·trée *or* **en·tree** \ˈän-ˌtrā\ *n* [F *entrée*] **1** : freedom of entry or access **2** : the main course of a meal in the U.S. **syn** admission, admittance, entrance

en·trench \in-ˈtrench\ *vb* **1** : to place within or surround with a trench esp. for defense; *also* : to establish solidly ⟨∼ed customs⟩ **2** : ENCROACH, TRESPASS — **en·trench·ment** *n*

en·tre·pre·neur \ˌän-trə-prə-ˈnər, -ˈnùr, -ˈnyùr\ *n* [F, fr. OF, fr. *entreprendre* to undertake] : one who organizes and assumes the risk of a business or enterprise — **en·tre·pre·neur·ial** \-ˈnùr-ē-əl, -ˈnyùr-\ *adj*

en·tro·py \ˈen-trə-pē\ *n, pl* **-pies 1** : the degree of disorder in a system **2** : an ultimate state of inert uniformity

en·trust \in-ˈtrəst\ *vb* **1** : to commit something to as a trust **2** : to commit to another with confidence **syn** confide, consign, relegate, commend

en·try \ˈen-trē\ *n, pl* **entries 1** : ENTRANCE 2, 3; *also* : VESTIBULE 2 **2** : an entering in a record; *also* : an item so entered **3** : a headword with its definition or identification; *also* : VOCABULARY ENTRY **4** : one entered in a contest

en·twine \in-ˈtwīn\ *vb* : to twine together or around

enu·mer·ate \i-ˈnü-mə-ˌrāt, -ˈnyü-\ *vb* **-at·ed; -at·ing 1** : to determine the number of : COUNT **2** : LIST — **enu·mer·a·tion** \-ˌnü-mə-ˈrā-shən, -ˌnyü-\ *n*

enun·ci·ate \ē-ˈnən-sē-ˌāt\ *vb* **-at·ed; -at·ing 1** : to state definitely; *also* : ANNOUNCE, PROCLAIM **2** : PRONOUNCE, ARTICULATE — **enun·ci·a·tion** \-ˌnən-sē-ˈā-shən\ *n*

en·ure·sis \ˌen-yù-ˈrē-səs\ *n* : involuntary discharge of urine : BED-WETTING

env *abbr* envelope

en·vel·op \in-ˈve-ləp\ *vb* : to enclose completely with or as if with a covering — **en·vel·op·ment** *n*

en·ve·lope \ˈen-və-ˌlōp, ˈän-\ *n* **1** : a usu. paper container for a letter **2** : WRAPPER, COVERING

en·ven·om \in-ˈve-nəm\ *vb* **1** : to make poisonous **2** : EMBITTER

en·vi·able \ˈen-vē-ə-bəl\ *adj* : highly desirable — **en·vi·ably** \-blē\ *adv*

en·vi·ous \ˈen-vē-əs\ *adj* : feeling or showing envy — **en·vi·ous·ly** *adv* — **en·vi·ous·ness** *n*

en·vi·ron·ment \in-ˈvī-rən-mənt, -ˈvīrn-\ *n* **1** : SURROUNDINGS **2** : the whole complex of factors (as soil, climate, and living things) that influence the form and the ability to survive of a plant or animal or ecological community — **en·vi·ron·men·tal** \-ˌvī-rən-ˈment-ᵊl, -ˌvīrn-\ *adj*

en·vi·ron·men·tal·ist \-ˌvī-rən-ˈment-ᵊl-ist, -ˌvīrn-\ *n* : a person concerned about environmental quality esp. with respect to control of pollution

en·vi·rons \in-ˈvī-rənz\ *n pl* **1** : SUBURBS **2** : SURROUNDINGS; *also* : VICINITY

en·vis·age \in-ˈvi-zij\ *vb* **-aged; -ag·ing** : to have a mental picture of

en·vi·sion \in-ˈvi-zhən, en-\ *vb* : to picture to oneself ⟨∼s world peace⟩

en·voy \ˈen-ˌvói, ˈän-\ *n* **1** : a diplomatic agent **2** : REPRESENTATIVE, MESSENGER

¹**en·vy** \ˈen-vē\ *n, pl* **envies** [ME *envie*, fr. OF, fr. L *invidia*, fr. *invidus* envious, fr. *invidēre* to look askance at, envy, fr. *vidēre* to see] : painful or resentful awareness of another's advantages; *also* : an object of envy

²**envy** *vb* **en·vied; en·vy·ing** : to feel envy toward or on account of

en·zyme \ˈen-ˌzīm\ *n* : any of various complex proteins produced by living cells that catalyze specific biochemical reactions at body temperatures — **en·zy·mat·ic** \ˌen-zə-ˈma-tik\ *adj*

Eo·cene \ˈē-ə-ˌsēn\ *adj* : of, relating to, or being the epoch of the Tertiary between the Paleocene and the Oligocene — **Eocene** *n*

EOE *abbr* equal opportunity employer

eo·lian \ē-ˈō-lē-ən\ *adj* : borne, deposited, or produced by the wind

EOM *abbr* end of month

eon \ˈē-ən, ˈē-ˌän\ *var of* AEON

EP *abbr* European plan

EPA *abbr* Environmental Protection Agency

ep·au·let *also* **ep·au·lette** \ˌe-pə-ˈlet\ *n* [F *épaulette*, dim. of *épaule* shoulder] : a shoulder ornament esp. on a coat or military uniform

épée \ˈe-ˌpā, ā-ˈpā\ *n* [F] : a fencing or dueling sword

épée

Eph *or* **Ephes** *abbr* Ephesians

ephed·rine \i-ˈfe-drən\ *n* : a drug used in relieving hay fever, asthma, and nasal congestion

ephem·era \i-ˈfe-mər-ə\ *n pl* : collectibles (as posters or tickets) not intended to have lasting value

ephem·er·al \i-ˈfe-mə-rəl\ *adj* [Gk *ephēmeros* lasting a day, daily, fr. *epi*-on *hēmera* day] : SHORT-LIVED, TRANSITORY **syn** passing, fleeting, transient, evanescent

Ephe·sians \i-ˈfē-zhənz\ *n* — see BIBLE table

ep·ic \ˈe-pik\ *n* : a long poem in elevated style narrating the deeds of a hero — **epic** *adj*

epi·cen·ter \ˈe-pi-ˌsen-tər\ *n* : the point on the earth's surface directly above the point of origin of an earthquake

ep·i·cure \ˈe-pi-ˌkyùr\ *n* : a person with sensitive and discriminating tastes esp. in food and wine

ep·i·cu·re·an \ˌe-pi-kyù-ˈrē-ən, -ˈkyùr-ē-\ *n* : EPICURE — **epicurean** *adj*

¹**ep·i·dem·ic** \ˌe-pə-ˈde-mik\ *adj* : affecting many persons at one time ⟨∼ disease⟩; *also* : excessively prevalent

²**epidemic** *n* : an epidemic outbreak esp. of disease

epi·der·mis \ˌe-pə-ˈdər-məs\ *n* : an outer layer esp. of skin — **epi·der·mal** \-məl\ *adj*

epi·glot·tis \ˌe-pə-ˈglä-təs\ *n* : a thin plate of flexible tissue protecting the tracheal opening during swallowing

ep·i·gram \ˈe-pə-ˌgram\ *n* : a short witty poem or saying — **ep·i·gram·mat·ic** \ˌe-pə-grə-ˈma-tik\ *adj*

ep·i·lep·sy \ˈe-pə-ˌlep-sē\ *n, pl* **-sies** : a disorder typically marked by disturbed electrical rhythms of the central nervous system, by attacks of convulsions, and by loss of consciousness — **ep·i·lep·tic** \ˌe-pə-ˈlep-tik\ *adj or n*

ep·i·logue *also* **ep·i·log** \ˈe-pə-ˌlóg, -ˌläg\ *n* : a speech addressed to the spectators by an actor at the end of a play

epi·neph·rine *also* **epi·neph·rin** \ˌe-pə-ˈne-frən\ *n* : an adrenal hormone used medicinally esp. as a heart stimulant, a muscle relaxant, and a vasoconstrictor

epiph·a·ny \i-ˈpi-fə-nē\ *n, pl* **-nies 1** *cap* : January 6 observed as a church festival in commemoration of the coming of the Magi to Jesus at Bethlehem **2** : a sudden striking understanding of something

epis·co·pa·cy \i-ˈpis-kə-pə-sē\ *n, pl* **-cies 1** : government of a church by bishops **2** : EPISCOPATE

epis·co·pal \i-ˈpis-kə-pəl\ *adj* **1** : of or relating to a bishop or episcopacy **2** *cap* : of or relating to the Protestant Episcopal Church

Epis·co·pa·lian \i-ˌpis-kə-ˈpāl-yən\ *n* : a member of the Protestant Episcopal Church

epis·co·pate \i-ˈpis-kə-pət, -ˌpāt\ *n* **1** : the rank, office, or term of a bishop **2** : a body of bishops

ep·i·sode \ˈe-pə-ˌsōd\ *n* [Gk *epeisodios* coming in besides, fr. *epeisodios*, fr. *epeisodion*, fr. *eisodios* coming in, fr. *eis* into + *hodos* road, journey] **1** : a unit of action in a dramatic or literary work **2** : an incident in a course of events : OCCURRENCE ⟨a feverish ∼⟩ — **ep·i·sod·ic** \ˌe-pə-ˈsä-dik\ *adj*

epis·tle \i-ˈpi-səl\ *n* **1** *cap* : one of the letters of the New Testament **2** : LETTER — **epis·to·lary** \i-ˈpis-tə-ˌler-ē\ *adj*

ep·i·taph \ˈe-pə-ˌtaf\ *n* : an inscription in memory of a dead person

ep·i·tha·la·mi·um \ˌe-pə-thə-ˈlā-mē-əm\ *or* **ep·i·tha·la·mi·on** \-mē-ən\ *n pl* **-mi·ums** *or* **-mia** \-mē-ə\ : a song or poem in honor of a bride and bridegroom

ep·i·the·li·um \ˌe-pə-ˈthē-lē-əm\ *n, pl* **-lia** \-lē-ə\ : a cellular membrane covering a bodily surface or lining a cavity — **ep·i·the·li·al** \-lē-əl\ *adj*

ep·i·thet \ˈe-pə-ˌthet, -thət\ *n* : a characterizing and often abusive word or phrase

epit·o·me \i-ˈpi-tə-mē\ *n* **1** : ABSTRACT, SUMMARY **2** : EMBODIMENT — **epit·o·mize** \-ˌmīz\ *vb*

ep·och \ˈe-pək, -ˌpäk\ *n* **1** : a usu. extended period : ERA, AGE **2** : any of the shorter divisions of geologic time into which a period may be divided — **ep·och·al** \-pə-kəl, -ˌpä-\ *adj*

ep·oxy \i-ˈpäk-sē\ *vb* **ep·ox·ied** *or* **ep·oxyed; ep·oxy·ing** : to glue with epoxy resin

epoxy resin *n* : a synthetic resin used in coatings and adhesives

ep·si·lon \ˈep-sə-län, -lən\ *n* : the 5th letter of the Greek alphabet — E or ε

Ep·som salts \ˈep-səm-\ *n* : a bitter colorless or white magnesium salt with cathartic properties

eq *abbr* **1** equal **2** equation

equa·ble \ˈe-kwə-bəl, ˈē-\ *adj* : UNIFORM, EVEN; *esp* : free from unpleasant extremes — **eq·ua·bil·i·ty** \ˌe-kwə-ˈbi-lə-tē, ˌē-\ *n* — **eq·ua·bly** \ˈe-kwə-blē, ˈē-\ *adv*

¹**equal** \ˈē-kwəl\ *adj* **1** : of the same measure, quantity, value, quality, number, degree, or status as another **2** : IMPARTIAL **3** : free from extremes **4** : able to cope with a situation or task — **equal·i·ty** \i-ˈkwä-lə-tē\ *n* — **equal·ly** *adv*

²**equal** *vb* **equaled** *or* **equalled; equal·ing** *or* **equal·ling** : to be or become equal to; *also* : to be identical in value to

³**equal** *n* : one that is equal

equal·ize \ˈē-kwə-ˌlīz\ *vb* **-ized; -iz·ing** : to make equal, uniform, or constant — **equal·i·za·tion** \ˌē-kwə-lə-ˈzā-shən\ *n* — **equal·iz·er** *n*

equals sign *or* **equal sign** *n* : a sign = indicating equivalence

equa·nim·i·ty \ˌē-kwə-ˈni-mə-tē, ˌe-\ *n, pl* **-ties** : COMPOSURE

equate \i-ˈkwāt\ *vb* **equat·ed; equat·ing** : to make, treat, or regard as equal or comparable

equa·tion \i-ˈkwā-zhən\ *n* **1** : an act of equating : the state of being equated **2** : a usu. formal statement of equivalence esp. of mathematical expressions

equa·tor \i-ˈkwā-tər, ˈē-ˌ\ *n* : an imaginary circle around the earth that is everywhere equally distant from the two poles — **equa·to·ri·al** \ˌē-kwə-ˈtōr-ē-əl, ˌe-\ *adj*

equer·ry \ˈe-kwə-rē, i-ˈkwer-ē\ *n, pl* **-ries 1** : an officer in charge of the horses of a prince or noble **2** : a personal attendant of a member of the British royal family

¹**eques·tri·an** \i-ˈkwes-trē-ən\ *adj* : of or relating to horseback riding; *also* : representing a person on horseback ⟨an ∼ statue⟩

²**equestrian** *n* : one who rides a horse

eques·tri·enne \i-ˌkwes-trē-ˈen\ *n* : a female rider on horseback

equi·dis·tant \ˌē-kwə-ˈdis-tənt\ *adj* : equally distant

equi·lat·er·al \ˌē-kwə-ˈla-tə-rəl\ *adj* : having all sides or faces equal ⟨∼ triangles⟩

equi·lib·ri·um \ˌē-kwə-ˈli-brē-əm, ˌe-\ *n, pl* **-ri·ums** *or* **-ria** \-brē-ə\ : a state of intellectual or emotional balance; *also* : a state of balance between opposing forces or actions **syn** poise, balance, equipoise

equine \ˈē-ˌkwīn, ˈe-\ *adj* [L *equinus*, fr. *equus* horse] : of or relating to the horse — **equine** *n*

equi·noc·tial \ˌē-kwə-ˈnäk-shəl, ˌe-\ *adj* : relating to an equinox

equi·nox \ˈē-kwə-ˌnäks, ˈe-\ *n* : either of the two times each year when the sun appears directly overhead at the equator and day and night are everywhere of equal length

equip \i-ˈkwip\ *vb* **equipped; equip·ping** : to supply with needed resources

eq·ui·page \ˈe-kwə-pij\ *n* : a horse-drawn carriage usu. with its servants

equip·ment \i-ˈkwip-mənt\ *n* **1** : things used in equipping : SUPPLIES, OUTFIT **2** : the equipping of a person or thing : the state of being equipped

equi·poise \ˈe-kwə-ˌpȯiz, ˈē-\ *n* **1** : BALANCE, EQUILIBRIUM **2** : COUNTERBALANCE

eq·ui·ta·ble \ˈe-kwə-tə-bəl\ *adj* : JUST, FAIR — **eq·ui·ta·bly** \-blē\ *adv*

eq·ui·ta·tion \ˌe-kwə-ˈtā-shən\ *n* : the act or art of riding on horseback

eq·ui·ty \ˈe-kwə-tē\ *n, pl* **-ties 1** : JUSTNESS, IMPARTIALITY **2** : value of a property or of an interest in it in excess of claims against it

equiv *abbr* equivalent

equiv·a·lent \i-ˈkwi-və-lənt\ *adj* : EQUAL; *also* : virtually identical — **equiv·a·lence** \-ləns\ *n* — **equivalent** *n*

equiv·o·cal \i-ˈkwi-və-kəl\ *adj* **1** : AMBIGUOUS **2** : UNCERTAIN, UNDECIDED **3** : SUSPICIOUS, DUBIOUS ⟨∼ behavior⟩ **syn** obscure, dark, vague, enigmatic — **equiv·o·cal·ly** *adv*

equiv·o·cate \i-ˈkwi-və-ˌkāt\ *vb* **-cat·ed; -cat·ing 1** : to use misleading language **2** : to avoid giving a definite answer — **equiv·o·ca·tion** \-ˌkwi-və-ˈkā-shən\ *n*

¹**-er** \ər\ *adj suffix or adv suffix* — used to form the comparative degree of adjectives and adverbs of one or two syllables ⟨hotter⟩ ⟨drier⟩ ⟨sillier⟩ and sometimes of longer ones

²**-er** \ər\ *also* **-ier** \ē-ər, yər\ *or* **-yer** \yər\ *n suffix* **1** : a person occupationally connected with ⟨hatter⟩ ⟨lawyer⟩ **2** : a person or thing belonging to or associated with ⟨old-timer⟩ **3** : a native of : resident of ⟨New Zealander⟩ **4** : one that has ⟨double-decker⟩ **5** : one that produces or yields ⟨porker⟩ **6** : one that does or performs (a specified action) ⟨reporter⟩ **7** : one that is a suitable object of (a specified action) ⟨broiler⟩ **8** : one that is ⟨foreigner⟩

Er *symbol* erbium

ER *abbr* emergency room

era \ˈir-ə, ˈer-ə, ˈē-rə\ *n* [LL *aera*, fr. L, counters, pl. of *aes* copper, money] **1** : a chronological order or system of notation reckoned from a given date as basis **2** : a period identified by some special feature **3** : a large division of geologic time usu. shorter than an eon **syn** age, epoch, period, time

ERA *abbr* Equal Rights Amendment

erad·i·cate \i-ˈra-də-ˌkāt\ *vb* **-cat·ed; -cat·ing** [L *eradicatus*, pp. of *eradicare*, fr. *e-* out + *radix* root] : UPROOT, ELIMINATE **syn** exterminate, annihilate, abolish, extinguish — **erad·i·ca·ble** \-di-kə-bəl\ *adj*

erase \i-ˈrās\ *vb* **erased; eras·ing** : to rub or scratch out (as written words); *also* : OBLITERATE **syn** cancel, ef-

\ə\abut \ᵊ\kitten \ər\further \a\ash \ā\ace \ä\mop, mar \au̇\out \ch\chin \e\bet \ē\easy \g\go \i\hit \ī\ice \j\job \ŋ\sing \ō\go \ȯ\law \ȯi\boy \th\thin \t͟h\the \ü\loot \u̇\foot \y\yet \zh\vision *see also* Pronunciation Symbols page

face, delete, expunge — **eras·er** *n* — **era·sure** \i-ˈrā-shər\ *n*

er·bi·um \ˈər-bē-əm\ *n* : a rare metallic element found with yttrium — see ELEMENT table

¹ere \ˈer\ *prep* : BEFORE

²ere *conj* : BEFORE

¹erect \i-ˈrekt\ *adj* **1** : not leaning or lying down : UPRIGHT **2** : being in a state of physiological erection

²erect *vb* **1** : BUILD **2** : to fix or set in an upright position **3** : SET UP; *also* : ESTABLISH, DEVELOP

erec·tile \i-ˈrekt-ᵊl, -ˈrek-ˌtīl\ *adj* : capable of becoming erect ⟨∼ tissue⟩ ⟨∼ feathers of a bird⟩

erec·tion \i-ˈrek-shən\ *n* **1** : the turgid state of a previously flaccid bodily part when it becomes dilated with blood **2** : CONSTRUCTION

ere·long \er-ˈlȯŋ\ *adv* : before long

er·e·mite \ˈer-ə-ˌmīt\ *n* : HERMIT

er·go \ˈer-gō, ˈər-\ *adv* [L] : THEREFORE

er·got \ˈȯr-gət, -ˌgät\ *n* **1** : a disease of rye and other cereals caused by a fungus; *also* : this fungus **2** : a medicinal compound or preparation derived from an ergot fungus

Er·i·tre·an \er-ə-ˈtrē-ən, -ˈtrā-\ *n* : a native or inhabitant of Eritrea — **Eritrean** *adj*

er·mine \ˈər-mən\ *n, pl* **ermines** **1** : any of several weasels with winter fur mostly white; *also* : the white fur of an ermine **2** : a rank or office whose official robe is ornamented with ermine

erode \i-ˈrōd\ *vb* **erod·ed; erod·ing** : to diminish or destroy by degrees; *esp* : to gradually eat into or wear away ⟨soil *eroded* by wind and water⟩ — **erod·ible** \-ˈrō-də-bəl\ *adj*

erog·e·nous \i-ˈrä-jə-nəs\ *adj* **1** : sexually sensitive ⟨∼ zones⟩ **2** : of, relating to, or arousing sexual feelings

ero·sion \i-ˈrō-zhən\ *n* : the process or state of being eroded — **ero·sion·al** \-ˈrō-zhə-nəl\ *adj* — **ero·sion·al·ly** *adv*

ero·sive \i-ˈrō-siv\ *adj* : tending to erode — **ero·sive·ness** *n*

erot·ic \i-ˈrä-tik\ *adj* : relating to or dealing with sexual love : AMATORY — **erot·i·cal·ly** \-ti-k(ə-)lē\ *adv* — **erot·i·cism** \-tə-ˌsi-zəm\ *n*

err \ˈər, ˈer\ *vb* : to be or do wrong

er·rand \ˈer-ənd\ *n* : a short trip taken to do something; *also* : the object or purpose of such a trip

er·rant \ˈer-ənt\ *adj* **1** : WANDERING ⟨an ∼ knight⟩ **2** : straying outside proper bounds **3** : deviating from an accepted pattern or standard

er·ra·ta \e-ˈrä-tə\ *n* : a list of corrigenda

er·rat·ic \i-ˈra-tik\ *adj* **1** : having no fixed course **2** : INCONSISTENT; *also* : ECCENTRIC — **er·rat·i·cal·ly** \-ti-k(ə-)lē\ *adv*

er·ra·tum \e-ˈrä-təm\ *n, pl* **-ta** \-tə\ : CORRIGENDUM

er·ro·ne·ous \i-ˈrō-nē-əs, e-ˈrō-\ *adj* : INCORRECT — **er·ro·ne·ous·ly** *adv*

er·ror \ˈer-ər\ *n* **1** : a usu. ignorant or unintentional deviating from accuracy or truth ⟨made an ∼ in adding⟩ **2** : a defensive misplay in baseball **3** : the state of one that errs ⟨to be in ∼⟩ **4** : a product of mistake ⟨a typographical ∼⟩ — **er·ror·less** *adj*

er·satz \ˈer-ˌzäts\ *adj* [G *ersatz-*, fr. *Ersatz*, n., substitute] : being usu. an artificial and inferior substitute

erst \ˈərst\ *adv, archaic* : ERSTWHILE

¹erst·while \-ˌhwīl\ *adv* : in the past : FORMERLY

²erstwhile *adj* : FORMER, PREVIOUS

er·u·di·tion \ˌer-ə-ˈdi-shən, ˌer-yə-\ *n* : SCHOLARSHIP, LEARNING — **er·u·dite** \ˈer-ə-ˌdīt, ˈer-yə-\ *adj*

erupt \i-ˈrəpt\ *vb* **1** : to burst forth or cause to burst forth : EXPLODE **2** : to break through a surface ⟨teeth ∼*ing* through the gum⟩ **3** : to break out with or as if with a skin rash — **erup·tion** \-ˈrəp-shən\ *n* — **erup·tive** \-tiv\ *adj*

-ery *n suffix* **1** : qualities collectively : character : -NESS ⟨snobb*ery*⟩ **2** : art : practice ⟨cook*ery*⟩ **3** : place of doing, keeping, producing, or selling (the thing specified) ⟨fish*ery*⟩ ⟨bak*ery*⟩ **4** : collection : aggregate ⟨fin*ery*⟩ **5** : state or condition ⟨slav*ery*⟩

ery·sip·e·las \ˌer-ə-ˈsi-pə-ləs, ˌir-\ *n* : an acute bacterial disease marked by fever and severe skin inflammation

er·y·the·ma \ˌer-ə-ˈthē-mə\ *n* : abnormal redness of the skin due to capillary congestion (as in inflammation)

eryth·ro·cyte \i-ˈri-thrə-ˌsīt\ *n* : RED BLOOD CELL

Es *symbol* einsteinium

¹-es \əz, iz *after* s, z, sh, ch; z *after* v *or a vowel*\ *n pl suffix* — used to form the plural of most nouns that end in s ⟨glass*es*⟩, z ⟨fuzz*es*⟩, sh ⟨bush*es*⟩, ch ⟨peach*es*⟩, or a final y that changes to i ⟨lad*ies*⟩ and of some nouns ending in f that changes to v ⟨loav*es*⟩

²-es *vb suffix* — used to form the third person singular present of most verbs that end in s ⟨bless*es*⟩, z ⟨fizz*es*⟩, sh ⟨hush*es*⟩, ch ⟨catch*es*⟩, or a final y that changes to i ⟨defi*es*⟩

es·ca·late \ˈes-kə-ˌlāt\ *vb* **-lat·ed; -lat·ing** : to increase in extent, volume, number, intensity, or scope — **es·ca·la·tion** \ˌes-kə-ˈlā-shən\ *n*

es·ca·la·tor \ˈes-kə-ˌlā-tər\ *n* : a moving set of stairs

es·cal·lop \is-ˈkä-ləp, -ˈka-\ *var of* SCALLOP

es·ca·pade \ˈes-kə-ˌpād\ *n* [F, action of escaping] : a mischievous adventure

¹es·cape \is-ˈkāp\ *vb* **es·caped; es·cap·ing** [ME, fr. OF *escaper*, fr. (assumed) VL *excappare*, fr. L *ex-* out + LL *cappa* head covering, cloak] **1** : to get free or away **2** : to avoid a threatening evil **3** : AVOID 2 ⟨∼ injury⟩ **4** : ELUDE ⟨his name ∼*s* me⟩ **5** : to be produced or uttered involuntarily ⟨let a sob ∼ him⟩

²escape *n* **1** : flight from or avoidance of something unpleasant **2** : LEAKAGE **3** : a means of escape

³escape *adj* : providing a means or way of escape

es·cap·ee \is-ˌkā-ˈpē, ˌes-(ˌ)kā-\ *n* : one that has escaped esp. from prison

escape velocity *n* : the minimum velocity needed by a body (as a rocket) to escape from the gravitational field of a celestial body (as the earth)

es·cap·ism \is-ˈkā-ˌpi-zəm\ *n* : diversion of the mind to imaginative activity as an escape from routine — **es·cap·ist** \-pist\ *adj or n*

es·ca·role \ˈes-kə-ˌrōl\ *n* : ENDIVE 1

es·carp·ment \es-ˈkärp-mənt\ *n* **1** : a steep slope in front of a fortification **2** : a long cliff

es·chew \is-ˈchü\ *vb* : SHUN, AVOID

¹es·cort \ˈes-ˌkȯrt\ *n* : one (as a person or warship) accompanying another esp. as a protection or courtesy

²es·cort \is-ˈkȯrt, es-\ *vb* : to accompany as an escort

es·crow \ˈes-ˌkrō\ *n* : something (as a deed or a sum of money) delivered by one person to another to be delivered to a third party only upon the fulfillment of a condition; *also* : a fund or deposit serving as an escrow

es·cu·do \is-ˈkü-dō\ *n, pl* **-dos** **1** — see MONEY table **2** : the peso of Guinea-Bissau

es·cutch·eon \is-ˈkə-chən\ *n* : the usu. shield-shaped surface on which a coat of arms is shown

Esd *abbr* Esdras

Es·dras \ˈez-drəs\ *n* — see BIBLE table

ESE *abbr* east-southeast

Es·ki·mo \ˈes-kə-ˌmō\ *n* **1** : a member of a group of peoples of northern Canada, Greenland, Alaska, and eastern Siberia **2** : any of the languages of the Eskimo peoples

Eskimo dog *n* : a sled dog of American origin

ESL *abbr* English as a second language

esoph·a·gus \i-ˈsä-fə-gəs\ *n, pl* **-gi** \-ˌgī, -ˌjī\ : a muscular tube that leads from the cavity behind the mouth to the stomach — **esoph·a·geal** \-ˌsä-fə-ˈjē-əl\ *adj*

es·o·ter·ic \ˌe-sə-ˈter-ik\ *adj* **1** : designed for or understood only by the specially initiated **2** : PRIVATE, SECRET

esp *abbr* especially

ESP \ˌē-ˌ(ˌ)es-ˈpē\ *n* : EXTRASENSORY PERCEPTION

es·pa·drille \ˈes-pə-ˌdril\ *n* [F] : a flat sandal usu. having a fabric upper and a flexible sole

es·pal·ier \is-ˈpal-yər, -ˌyā\ *n* : a plant (as a fruit tree) trained to grow flat against a support — **espalier** *vb*

es·pe·cial \is-ˈpe-shəl\ *adj* : SPECIAL, PARTICULAR — **es·pe·cial·ly** *adv*

Es·pe·ran·to \ˌes-pə-ˈran-tō, -ˈrän-\ *n* : an artificial international language based esp. on words common to the chief European languages

es·pi·o·nage \ˈes-pē-ə-ˌnäzh, -nij\ *n* [F *espionnage*] : the practice of spying

es·pla·nade \ˈes-plə-ˌnäd\ *n* : a level open stretch or area; *esp* : one for walking or driving along a shore

es·pous·al \i-ˈspaů-zəl\ *n* **1** : BETROTHAL; *also* : WEDDING **2** : a taking up (as of a cause) as a supporter — **espouse** \-ˈspaůz\ *vb*

espres·so \e-ˈspre-sō\ *n, pl* **-sos** [It (*caffè*) *espresso*, lit., pressed out coffee] : coffee brewed by forcing steam through finely ground darkly roasted coffee beans

es·prit \i-ˈsprē\ *n* : sprightly wit

es·prit de corps \i-ˌsprē-də-ˈkȯr\ *n* [F] : the common spirit existing in the members of a group

es·py \i-ˈspī\ *vb* **es·pied; es·py·ing** : to catch sight of **syn** behold, see, view, descry

Esq *or* **Esqr** *abbr* esquire

es·quire \ˈes-ˌkwīr\ *n* [ME, fr. MF *esquier* squire, fr. LL *scutarius*, fr. L *scutum* shield] **1** : a man of the English gentry ranking next below a knight **2** : a candidate for knighthood serving as attendant to a knight **3** — used as a title of courtesy

-ess \əs, ˌes\ *n suffix* : female ⟨author*ess*⟩

¹es·say \e-ˈsā, ˈe-ˌsā\ *vb* : ATTEMPT, TRY

²es·say *n* **1** \ˈe-ˌsā, e-ˈsā\ : ATTEMPT **2** \ˈe-ˌsā\ : a literary composition usu. dealing with a subject from a limited or personal point of view — **es·say·ist** \ˈe-ˌsā-ist\ *n*

es·sence \ˈes-ᵊns\ *n* **1** : fundamental nature or quality **2** : a substance distilled or extracted from another substance (as a plant or drug) and having the special qualities of the original substance **3** : PERFUME

¹es·sen·tial \i-ˈsen-chəl\ *adj* **1** : of, relating to, or constituting an essence ⟨voting is an ∼ right of citizenship⟩ ⟨∼ oils⟩ **2** : of the utmost importance : INDISPENSABLE **syn** imperative, necessary, necessitous — **es·sen·tial·ly** *adv*

²essential *n* : something essential

est *abbr* **1** established **2** estimate; estimated

EST *abbr* eastern standard time

¹-est \əst, ist\ *adj suffix or adv suffix* — used to form the superlative degree of adjectives and adverbs of one or two syllables ⟨fatt*est*⟩ ⟨lat*est*⟩ ⟨lucki*est*⟩ ⟨often*est*⟩ and less often of longer ones

²-est \əst, ist\ *or* **-st** \st\ *vb suffix* — used to form the archaic second person singular of English verbs (with *thou*) ⟨did*st*⟩

es·tab·lish \i-ˈsta-blish\ *vb* **1** : to institute permanently ⟨∼ a law⟩ **2** : FOUND ⟨∼ a settlement⟩; *also* : EFFECT **3** : to make firm or stable **4** : to put on a firm basis : SET UP ⟨∼ a son in business⟩ **5** : to gain acceptance or recognition of ⟨the movie ∼ed her as a star⟩; *also* : PROVE

es·tab·lish·ment \-mənt\ *n* **1** : something established **2** : a place of residence or business with its furnishings and staff **3** : an established ruling or controlling group ⟨the literary ∼⟩ **4** : the act or state of establishing or being established

es·tate \i-ˈstāt\ *n* **1** : STATE, CONDITION; *also* : social standing : STATUS **2** : a social or political class ⟨the three ∼s of nobility, clergy, and commons⟩ **3** : a person's possessions : FORTUNE **4** : a landed property

¹es·teem \i-ˈstēm\ *n* : high regard

²esteem *vb* **1** : REGARD **2** : to set a high value on **syn** respect, admire, revere

es·ter \ˈes-tər\ *n* : an often fragrant organic compound formed by the reaction of an acid and an alcohol

Esth *abbr* Esther

Es·ther \ˈes-tər\ *n* — see BIBLE table

esthete, esthetic, esthetics *var of* AESTHETE, AESTHETIC, AESTHETICS

es·ti·ma·ble \ˈes-tə-mə-bəl\ *adj* : worthy of esteem

¹es·ti·mate \ˈes-tə-ˌmāt\ *vb* **-mat·ed; -mat·ing 1** : to give or form an approximation (as of value, size, or cost) **2** : JUDGE, CONCLUDE **syn** evaluate, value, rate, appraise, assay, assess — **es·ti·ma·tor** \-ˌmā-tər\ *n*

²es·ti·mate \ˈes-tə-mət\ *n* **1** : OPINION, JUDGMENT **2** : a rough or approximate calculation **3** : a statement of the cost of work to be done

es·ti·ma·tion \ˌes-tə-ˈmā-shən\ *n* **1** : JUDGMENT, OPINION **2** : ESTIMATE **3** : ESTEEM, HONOR

es·ti·vate \ˈes-tə-ˌvāt\ *vb* **-vat·ed; -vat·ing** : to pass the summer in an inactive or resting state — **es·ti·va·tion** \ˌes-tə-ˈvā-shən\ *n*

Es·to·nian \e-ˈstō-nē-ən\ *n* : a native or inhabitant of Estonia — **Estonian** *adj*

es·trange \i-ˈstrānj\ *vb* **es·tranged; es·trang·ing** : to alienate the affections or confidence of — **es·trange·ment** *n*

es·tro·gen \ˈes-trə-jən\ *n* : a substance (as a sex hormone) that tends to cause estrus and the development of female secondary sex characteristics — **es·tro·gen·ic** \ˌes-trə-ˈje-nik\ *adj*

estrous cycle *n* : the cycle of changes in the endocrine and reproductive systems of a female mammal from the beginning of one period of estrus to the beginning of the next

es·trus \ˈes-trəs\ *n* : a periodic state of sexual excitability during which the female of most mammals is willing to mate with the male and is capable of becoming pregnant : HEAT — **es·trous** \-trəs\ *adj*

es·tu·ary \ˈes-chù-ˌwer-ē\ *n, pl* **-ar·ies** : an arm of the sea at the mouth of a river

ET *abbr* eastern time

eta \ˈā-tə\ *n* : the 7th letter of the Greek alphabet — H or η

ETA *abbr* estimated time of arrival

et al \et-ˈal\ *abbr* [L *et alii* (masc.), *et aliae* (fem.), or *et alia* (neut.)] and others

etc *abbr* et cetera

et cet·era \et-ˈse-tə-rə, -ˈse-trə\ [L] and others esp. of the same kind

etch \ˈech\ *vb* [D *etsen*, fr. G *ätzen* to etch, corrode, fr. OHG *azzen* to feed] **1** : to produce (as a design) on a hard material by corroding its surface (as by acid) **2** : to delineate clearly — **etch·er** *n*

etch·ing *n* **1** : the action, process, or art of etching **2** : a design produced on or print made from an etched plate

ETD *abbr* estimated time of departure

eter·nal \i-ˈtərn-ᵊl\ *adj* : EVERLASTING, PERPETUAL — **eter·nal·ly** *adv*

eter·ni·ty \i-ˈtər-nə-tē\ *n, pl* **-ties 1** : infinite duration **2** : IMMORTALITY

¹-eth \əth, ith\ *or* **-th** \th\ *vb suffix* — used to form the archaic third person singular present of verbs ⟨do*th*⟩

²-eth — see ²-TH

eth·ane \ˈe-ˌthān\ *n* : a colorless odorless gaseous hydrocarbon found in natural gas and used esp. as a fuel

eth·a·nol \ˈe-thə-ˌnȯl\ *n* : ALCOHOL 1

ether \ˈē-thər\ *n* **1** : the upper regions of space; *also* : the gaseous element formerly held to fill these regions **2** : a light flammable liquid used as an anesthetic and solvent

ethe·re·al \i-ˈthir-ē-əl\ *adj* **1** : CELESTIAL, HEAVENLY **2**

\ə\abut \ᵊ\kitten \ər\further \a\ash \ā\ace \ä\mop, mar \aů\out \ch\chin \e\bet \ē\easy \g\go \i\hit \ī\ice \j\job \ŋ\sing \ō\go \ȯ\law \ȯi\boy \th\thin \t̲h̲\the \ü\loot \ů\foot \y\yet \zh\vision *see also* Pronunciation Symbols page

: exceptionally delicate : AIRY, DAINTY — **ethe·re·al·ly** *adv* — **ethe·re·al·ness** *n*

eth·i·cal \'e-thi-kəl\ *adj* **1** : of or relating to ethics **2** : conforming to accepted and esp. professional standards of conduct **syn** virtuous, moral, principled — **eth·i·cal·ly** *adv*

eth·ics \'e-thiks\ *n sing or pl* **1** : a discipline dealing with good and evil and with moral duty **2** : moral principles or practice

Ethi·o·pi·an \ˌē-thē-'ō-pē-ən\ *n* : a native or inhabitant of Ethiopia — **Ethiopian** *adj*

¹**eth·nic** \'eth-nik\ *adj* [ME, heathen, fr. LL *ethnicus*, fr. Gk *ethnikos* national, gentile, fr. *ethnos* nation, people] : of or relating to races or large groups of people classed according to common traits and customs — **eth·ni·cal·ly** *adv*

²**ethnic** *n* : a member of a minority ethnic group who retains its customs, language, or social views

eth·nol·o·gy \eth-'nä-lə-jē\ *n* : a science dealing with the races of human beings, their origin, distribution, characteristics, and relations — **eth·no·log·i·cal** \ˌeth-nə-'lä-ji-kəl\ *adj* — **eth·nol·o·gist** \eth-'nä-lə-jist\ *n*

ethol·o·gy \ē-'thä-lə-jē\ *n* : the scientific and objective study of animal behavior — **etho·log·i·cal** \ˌē-thə-'lä-ji-kəl, ˌe-\ *adj* — **ethol·o·gist** \ē-'thä-lə-jist\ *n*

ethos \'ē-ˌthäs\ *n* : the distinguishing character, sentiment, moral nature, or guiding beliefs of a person, group, or institution

ethyl alcohol *n* : ALCOHOL 1

eth·yl·ene \'e-thə-ˌlēn\ *n* : a colorless flammable gas found in coal gas or obtained from petroleum

eti·ol·o·gy \ˌē-tē-'ä-lə-jē\ *n* : the causes of a disease or abnormal condition; *also* : a branch of medicine concerned with the causes and origins of diseases — **eti·o·log·ic** \ˌē-tē-ə-'lä-jik\ *or* **eti·o·log·i·cal** \-ji-kəl\ *adj*

et·i·quette \'e-ti-kət, -ˌket\ *n* [F *étiquette*, lit., ticket] : the forms prescribed by custom or authority to be observed in social, official, or professional life **syn** propriety, decorum, decency, dignity

Etrus·can \i-'trəs-kən\ *n* **1** : the language of the Etruscans **2** : an inhabitant of ancient Etruria — **Etruscan** *adj*

et seq *abbr* [L *et sequens*] and the following one; [L *et sequentes* (masc. & fem. pl.) or *et sequentia* (neut. pl.)] and the following ones

-ette \'et, ˌet, ət, it\ *n suffix* **1** : little one ⟨din*ette*⟩ **2** : female ⟨usher*ette*⟩

étude \'ā-ˌtüd, -ˌtyüd\ *n* [F, lit., study] : a musical composition for practice to develop technical skill

et·y·mol·o·gy \ˌe-tə-'mä-lə-jē\ *n, pl* **-gies 1** : the history of a linguistic form (as a word) shown by tracing its development and relationships **2** : a branch of linguistics dealing with etymologies — **et·y·mo·log·i·cal** \-mə-'lä-ji-kəl\ *adj* — **et·y·mol·o·gist** \-'mä-lə-jist\ *n*

Eu *symbol* europium

eu·ca·lyp·tus \ˌyü-kə-'lip-təs\ *n, pl* **-ti** \-ˌtī\ *or* **-tus·es** : any of a genus of mostly Australian evergreen trees widely grown for shade or their wood, oils, resins, and gums

Eu·cha·rist \'yü-kə-rəst\ *n* : COMMUNION 2 — **eu·cha·ris·tic** \ˌyü-kə-'ris-tik\ *adj, often cap*

¹**eu·chre** \'yü-kər\ *n* : a card game in which the side naming the trump must take three of five tricks to win

²**euchre** *vb* **eu·chred; eu·chring** : CHEAT, TRICK

eu·clid·e·an *also* **eu·clid·i·an** \yü-'kli-dē-ən\ *adj, often cap* : of or relating to the geometry of Euclid or a geometry based on similar axioms

eu·gen·ics \yù-'je-niks\ *n* : a science dealing with the improvement (as by selective breeding) of hereditary qualities esp. of human beings — **eu·gen·ic** \-nik\ *adj*

eu·lo·gy \'yü-lə-jē\ *n, pl* **-gies 1** : a speech in praise of some person or thing **2** : high praise — **eu·lo·gis·tic** \ˌyü-lə-'jis-tik\ *adj* — **eu·lo·gize** \'yü-lə-ˌjīz\ *vb*

eu·nuch \'yü-nək\ *n* : a castrated man

eu·phe·mism \'yü-fə-ˌmi-zəm\ *n* [Gk *euphēmismos*, fr. *euphēmos* auspicious, sounding good, fr. *eu-* good + *phēmē* speech] : the substitution of a mild or pleasant expression for one offensive or unpleasant; *also* : the expression substituted — **eu·phe·mis·tic** \ˌyü-fə-'mis-tik\ *adj*

eu·pho·ni·ous \yù-'fō-nē-əs\ *adj* : pleasing to the ear — **eu·pho·ni·ous·ly** *adv*

eu·pho·ny \'yü-fə-nē\ *n, pl* **-nies** : the effect produced by words so combined as to please the ear

eu·pho·ria \yù-'fōr-ē-ə\ *n* : a marked feeling of well-being or elation — **eu·phor·ic** \-'fòr-ik\ *adj*

Eur *abbr* Europe; European

Eur·asian \yù-'rā-zhən, -shən\ *adj* **1** : of mixed European and Asian origin **2** : of or relating to Europe and Asia — **Eurasian** *n*

eu·re·ka \yù-'rē-kə\ *interj* [Gk *heurēka* I have found, fr. *heuriskein* to find; fr. the exclamation attributed to Archimedes on discovering a method for determining the purity of gold] — used to express triumph on a discovery

Eu·ro·bond \'yùr-ō-ˌbänd\ *n* : a bond of a U.S. corporation that is sold outside the U.S. but that is valued and paid for in dollars and yields interest in dollars

Eu·ro·cur·ren·cy \ˌyùr-ō-'kər-ən-sē\ *n* : moneys (as of the U.S. and Japan) held outside their countries of origin and used in the money markets of Europe

Eu·ro·dol·lar \'yùr-ō-ˌdä-lər\ *n* : a U.S. dollar held as Eurocurrency

Eu·ro·pe·an \ˌyùr-ə-'pē-ən\ *n* **1** : a native or inhabitant of Europe **2** : a person of European descent — **European** *adj*

European plan *n* : a hotel plan whereby the daily rates cover only the cost of the room

eu·ro·pi·um \yù-'rō-pē-əm\ *n* : a rare metallic chemical element — see ELEMENT table

eu·sta·chian tube \yù-'stā-shən-\ *n, often cap E* : a tube connecting the inner cavity of the ear with the throat and equalizing air pressure on both sides of the eardrum

eu·tha·na·sia \ˌyü-thə-'nā-zhə\ *n* [Gk, easy death, fr. *eu-* good + *thanatos* death] : MERCY KILLING

EVA *abbr* extravehicular activity

evac·u·ate \i-'va-kyə-ˌwāt\ *vb* **-at·ed; -at·ing 1** : EMPTY **2** : to discharge wastes from the body **3** : to remove or withdraw from : VACATE — **evac·u·a·tion** \-ˌva-kyə-'wā-shən\ *n*

evac·u·ee \i-ˌva-kyə-'wē\ *n* : a person removed from a dangerous place

evade \i-'vād\ *vb* **evad·ed; evad·ing** : to manage to avoid esp. by dexterity or slyness : ELUDE, ESCAPE

eval·u·ate \i-'val-yù-ˌwāt\ *vb* **-at·ed; -at·ing** : APPRAISE, VALUE — **eval·u·a·tion** \-ˌval-yù-'wā-shən\ *n*

ev·a·nes·cent \ˌe-və-'nes-ᵊnt\ *adj* : tending to vanish like vapor **syn** passing, transient, transitory, momentary — **ev·a·nes·cence** \-ᵊns\ *n*

evan·gel·i·cal \ˌē-ˌvan-'je-li-kəl, ˌe-vən-\ *adj* [LL *evangelium* gospel, fr. Gk *evangelion*, fr. *eu-* good + *angelos* messenger] **1** : of or relating to the Christian gospel esp. as presented in the four Gospels **2** : of or relating to certain Protestant churches emphasizing the authority of Scripture and the importance of preaching as contrasted with ritual **3** : ZEALOUS ⟨∼ fervor⟩ — **Evangelical** *n* — **Evan·gel·i·cal·ism** \-kə-ˌli-zəm\ *n* — **evan·gel·i·cal·ly** *adv*

evan·ge·lism \i-'van-jə-ˌli-zəm\ *n* **1** : the winning or revival of personal commitments to Christ **2** : militant or crusading zeal — **evan·ge·lis·tic** \-ˌvan-jə-'lis-tik\ *adj* — **evan·ge·lis·ti·cal·ly** *adv*

evan·ge·list \i-'van-jə-list\ *n* **1** *often cap* : the writer of any of the four Gospels **2** : a person who evangelizes;

esp : a Protestant minister or layman who preaches at special services

evan·ge·lize \i-'van-jə-ˌlīz\ *vb* **-lized; -liz·ing 1** : to preach the gospel **2** : to convert to Christianity

evap *abbr* evaporate

evap·o·rate \i-'va-pə-ˌrāt\ *vb* **-rat·ed; -rat·ing 1** : to pass off or cause to pass off in vapor **2** : to disappear quickly **3** : to drive out the moisture from (as by heat) — **evap·o·ra·tion** \-ˌva-pə-'rā-shən\ *n* — **evap·o·ra·tor** \-ˌrā-tər\ *n*

evap·o·rite \i-'va-pə-ˌrīt\ *n* : a sedimentary rock that originates by the evaporation of seawater in an enclosed basin

eva·sion \i-'vā-zhən\ *n* **1** : a means of evading **2** : an act or instance of evading — **eva·sive** \i-'vā-siv\ *adj* — **eva·sive·ness** *n*

eve \'ēv\ *n* **1** : EVENING **2** : the period just before some important event

¹even \'ē-vən\ *adj* **1** : LEVEL, FLAT **2** : REGULAR, SMOOTH **3** : EQUAL, FAIR **4** : BALANCED; *also* : fully revenged **5** : divisible by two **6** : EXACT — **even·ly** *adv* — **even·ness** *n*

²even *adv* **1** : EXACTLY, PRECISELY **2** : FULLY, QUITE **3** : at the very time **4** — used as an intensive to stress identity ⟨∼ I know that⟩ **5** — used as an intensive to emphasize something extreme or highly unlikely ⟨so simple ∼ a child can do it⟩ **6** — used as an intensive to stress the comparative degree ⟨did ∼ better⟩ **7** — used as an intensive to indicate a small or minimum degree ⟨didn't ∼ try⟩

³even *vb* : to make or become even

even·hand·ed \ˌē-vən-'han-dəd\ *adj* : FAIR, IMPARTIAL — **even·hand·ed·ly** *adv*

eve·ning \'ēv-niŋ\ *n* **1** : the end of the day and early part of the night **2** *chiefly Southern & Midland* : AFTERNOON

evening primrose *n* : a coarse biennial herb with yellow flowers that open in the evening

evening star *n* : a bright planet (as Venus) seen esp. in the western sky at or after sunset

even·song \'ē-vən-ˌsȯŋ\ *n, often cap* **1** : VESPERS **2** : evening prayer esp. when sung

event \i-'vent\ *n* [MF or L; MF, fr. L *eventus*, fr. *evenire* to happen, fr. *venire* to come] **1** : OCCURRENCE **2** : a noteworthy happening **3** : CONTINGENCY ⟨in the ∼ of rain⟩ **4** : a contest in a program of sports — **event·ful** *adj*

even·tide \'ē-vən-ˌtīd\ *n* : EVENING

even·tu·al \i-'ven-chü-wəl\ *adj* : coming at some later time : ULTIMATE — **even·tu·al·ly** *adv*

even·tu·al·i·ty \i-ˌven-chü-'wa-lə-tē\ *n, pl* **-ties** : a possible event or outcome

even·tu·ate \i-'ven-chü-ˌwāt\ *vb* **-at·ed; -at·ing** : to result finally

ev·er \'e-vər\ *adv* **1** : ALWAYS **2** : at any time **3** : in any way : AT ALL

ev·er·glade \'e-vər-ˌglād\ *n* : a low-lying tract of swampy or marshy land

ev·er·green \-ˌgrēn\ *adj* : having foliage that remains green ⟨most coniferous trees are ∼⟩ — **evergreen** *n*

¹ev·er·last·ing \ˌe-vər-'las-tiŋ\ *adj* **1** : enduring forever : ETERNAL **2** : having or being flowers or foliage that retain form or color for a long time when dried — **ev·er·last·ing·ly** *adv*

²everlasting *n* **1** : ETERNITY ⟨from ∼⟩ **2** : a plant with everlasting flowers; *also* : its flower

ev·er·more \ˌe-vər-'mōr\ *adv* : FOREVER

ev·ery \'ev-rē\ *adj* **1** : being each one of a group **2** : all possible ⟨given ∼ chance⟩; *also* : COMPLETE ⟨have ∼ confidence⟩

ev·ery·body \'ev-ri-ˌbä-dē, -bə-\ *pron* : every person

ev·ery·day \'ev-rē-ˌdā\ *adj* : encountered or used routinely : ORDINARY

ev·ery·one \-(ˌ)wən\ *pron* : EVERYBODY

ev·ery·thing \'ev-rē-ˌthiŋ\ *pron* **1** : all that exists **2** : all that is relevant

ev·ery·where \'ev-rē-ˌhwer\ *adv* : in every place or part

evg *abbr* evening

evict \i-'vikt\ *vb* **1** : to put (a person) out from a property by legal process **2** : EXPEL *syn* eject, oust, dismiss — **evic·tion** \-'vik-shən\ *n*

ev·i·dence \'e-və-dəns\ *n* **1** : an outward sign **2** : PROOF, TESTIMONY; *esp* : matter submitted in court to determine the truth of alleged facts

ev·i·dent \-dənt\ *adj* : clear to the vision and understanding *syn* manifest, distinct, obvious, apparent, plain

ev·i·dent·ly \'e-və-dənt-lē, ˌe-və-'dent-\ *adv* **1** : in an evident manner **2** : on the basis of available evidence

¹evil \'ē-vəl\ *adj* **evil·er** *or* **evil·ler; evil·est** *or* **evil·lest 1** : WICKED **2** : causing or threatening distress or harm : PERNICIOUS — **evil·ly** *adv*

²evil *n* **1** : the fact of suffering, misfortune, and wrongdoing **2** : a source of sorrow or distress

evil·do·er \ˌē-vəl-'dü-ər\ *n* : one who does evil

evil–mind·ed \-'mīn-dəd\ *adj* : having an evil disposition or evil thoughts — **evil–mind·ed·ly** *adv*

evince \i-'vins\ *vb* **evinced; evinc·ing** : SHOW, REVEAL

evis·cer·ate \i-'vi-sə-ˌrāt\ *vb* **-at·ed; -at·ing 1** : to remove the entrails of **2** : to deprive of vital content or force — **evis·cer·a·tion** \-ˌvi-sə-'rā-shən\ *n*

evoke \i-'vōk\ *vb* **evoked; evok·ing** : to call forth or up — **evo·ca·tion** \ˌē-vō-'kā-shən, ˌe-və-\ *n* — **evoc·a·tive** \i-'vä-kə-tiv\ *adj*

evo·lu·tion \ˌe-və-'lü-shən\ *n* **1** : one of a set of prescribed movements (as in a dance) **2** : a process of change in a particular direction **3** : a theory that the various kinds of plants and animals are descended from other kinds that lived in earlier times and that the differences are due to inherited changes that occurred over many generations — **evo·lu·tion·ary** \-shə-ˌner-ē\ *adj* — **evo·lu·tion·ist** \-shə-nist\ *n*

evolve \i-'välv\ *vb* **evolved; evolv·ing** [L *evolvere* to unroll] : to develop or change by or as if by evolution

EW *abbr* enlisted woman

ewe \'yü\ *n* : a female sheep

ew·er \'yü-ər\ *n* : a water pitcher

¹ex \'eks\ *prep* [L] : out of : FROM

²ex *n* : a former spouse

³ex *abbr* **1** example **2** express **3** extra

Ex *abbr* Exodus

ex- lc. also occurs in this prefix where only i is shown below (as in "express") and ks sometimes occurs where only gz is shown (as in "exact")\ prefix **1** : out of : outside **2** : former ⟨ex-president⟩

ex·ac·er·bate \ig-'za-sər-ˌbāt\ *vb* **-bat·ed; -bat·ing** : to make more violent, bitter, or severe — **ex·ac·er·ba·tion** \-ˌza-sər-'bā-shən\ *n*

¹ex·act \ig-'zakt\ *vb* **1** : to compel to furnish **2** : to call for as suitable or necessary — **ex·ac·tion** \-'zak-shən\ *n*

²exact *adj* : precisely accurate or correct — **ex·act·ly** *adv* — **ex·act·ness** *n*

ex·act·ing \ig-'zak-tiŋ\ *adj* **1** : greatly demanding ⟨an ∼ taskmaster⟩ **2** : requiring close attention and precision

ex·ac·ti·tude \ig-'zak-tə-ˌtüd, -ˌtyüd\ *n* : the quality or state of being exact

ex·ag·ger·ate \ig-'za-jə-ˌrāt\ *vb* **-at·ed; -at·ing** [L *exaggeratus*, pp. of *exaggerare*, lit., to heap up, fr. *agger* heap] : to enlarge (as a statement) beyond normal : OVERSTATE — **ex·ag·ger·at·ed·ly** *adv* — **ex·ag·ger·a·tion** \-ˌza-jə-'rā-shən\ *n* — **ex·ag·ger·a·tor** \-'za-jə-ˌrā-tər\ *n*

ex·alt \ig-'zȯlt\ *vb* **1** : to raise up esp. in rank, power, or

\ə\abut \ᵊ\kitten \ər\further \a\ash \ā\ace \ä\mop, mar \au\out \ch\chin \e\bet \ē\easy \g\go \i\hit \ī\ice \j\job \ŋ\sing \ō\go \ȯ\law \ȯi\boy \th\thin \t͟h\the \ü\loot \u̇\foot \y\yet \zh\vision *see also* Pronunciation Symbols page dignity **2** : GLORIFY — **ex·al·ta·tion** \ˌeg-ˌzȯl-ˈtā-shən, ˌek-ˌsȯl-\ *n*

ex·am \ig-ˈzam\ *n* : EXAMINATION

ex·am·ine \ig-ˈza-mən\ *vb* **ex·am·ined; ex·am·in·ing 1** : to inspect closely **2** : QUESTION; *esp* : to test by questioning **syn** interrogate, query, quiz, catechize — **ex·am·i·na·tion** \-ˌza-mə-ˈnā-shən\ *n*

ex·am·ple \ig-ˈzam-pəl\ *n* **1** : something forming a model to be followed or avoided **2** : a representative sample **3** : a problem to be solved in order to show the application of some rule

ex·as·per·ate \ig-ˈzas-pə-ˌrāt\ *vb* **-at·ed; -at·ing** : VEX, IRRITATE — **ex·as·per·a·tion** \ig-ˌzas-pə-ˈrā-shən\ *n*

exc *abbr* **1** excellent **2** except

ex·ca·vate \ˈek-skə-ˌvāt\ *vb* **-vat·ed; -vat·ing 1** : to hollow out; *also* : to form by hollowing out **2** : to dig out and remove (as earth) **3** : to reveal to view by digging away a covering — **ex·ca·va·tion** \ˌek-skə-ˈvā-shən\ *n* — **ex·ca·va·tor** \ˈek-skə-ˌvā-tər\ *n*

ex·ceed \ik-ˈsēd\ *vb* **1** : to go or be beyond the limit of **2** : SURPASS

ex·ceed·ing·ly \-ˈsē-diŋ-lē\ *also* **ex·ceed·ing** *adv* : EXTREMELY, VERY

ex·cel \ik-ˈsel\ *vb* **ex·celled; ex·cel·ling** : SURPASS, OUTDO

ex·cel·lence \ˈek-sə-ləns\ *n* **1** : the quality of being excellent **2** : an excellent or valuable quality : VIRTUE **3** : EXCELLENCY **2**

ex·cel·len·cy \-lən-sē\ *n, pl* **-cies 1** : EXCELLENCE **2** — used as a title of honor

ex·cel·lent \-lənt\ *adj* : very good of its kind : FIRST-CLASS — **ex·cel·lent·ly** *adv*

ex·cel·si·or \ik-ˈsel-sē-ər\ *n* : fine curled wood shavings used esp. for packing fragile items

¹ex·cept \ik-ˈsept\ *also* **ex·cept·ing** *prep* : with the exclusion or exception of ⟨daily ∼ Sundays⟩

²except *vb* **1** : to take or leave out **2** : OBJECT

³except *also* **excepting** *conj* **1** : UNLESS ⟨∼ you repent⟩ **2** : ONLY ⟨I'd go, ∼ it's too far⟩

ex·cep·tion \ik-ˈsep-shən\ *n* **1** : the act of excepting **2** : something excepted **3** : OBJECTION

ex·cep·tion·able \ik-ˈsep-shə-nə-bəl\ *adj* : OBJECTIONABLE

ex·cep·tion·al \ik-ˈsep-shə-nəl\ *adj* **1** : UNUSUAL **2** : SUPERIOR — **ex·cep·tion·al·ly** *adv*

ex·cerpt \ˈek-ˌsərpt, ˈeg-ˌzərpt\ *n* : a passage selected or copied : EXTRACT — **excerpt** \ek-ˈsərpt, eg-ˈzərpt; ˈek-ˌsərpt, ˈeg-ˌzərpt\ *vb*

ex·cess \ik-ˈses, ˈek-ˌses\ *n* **1** : SUPERFLUITY, SURPLUS **2** : the amount by which one quantity exceeds another **3** : INTEMPERANCE; *also* : an instance of intemperance — **excess** *adj* — **ex·ces·sive** \ik-ˈse-siv\ *adj* — **ex·ces·sive·ly** *adv*

exch *abbr* exchange; exchanged

¹ex·change \iks-ˈchānj\ *n* **1** : the giving or taking of one thing in return for another : TRADE **2** : a substituting of one thing for another **3** : interchange of valuables and esp. of bills of exchange or money of different countries **4** : a place where things and services are exchanged; *esp* : a marketplace for securities **5** : a central office in which telephone lines are connected for communication

²exchange *vb* **ex·changed; ex·chang·ing** : to transfer in return for some equivalent : BARTER, SWAP — **ex·change·able** \iks-ˈchān-jə-bəl\ *adj*

ex·che·quer \ˈeks-ˌche-kər\ *n* [ME *escheker,* fr. OF *eschequier* chessboard, counting table] : TREASURY; *esp* : a national treasury

ex·cise \ˈek-ˌsīz\ *n* : a tax on the manufacture, sale, or consumption of a commodity

ex·ci·sion \ik-ˈsi-zhən\ *n* : removal by or as if by cutting out esp. by surgical means — **ex·cise** \ik-ˈsīz\ *vb*

ex·cit·able \ik-ˈsī-tə-bəl\ *adj* : easily excited — **ex·cit·abil·i·ty** \-ˌsī-tə-ˈbi-lə-tē\ *n*

ex·cite \ik-ˈsīt\ *vb* **ex·cit·ed; ex·cit·ing 1** : to stir up the emotions of : ROUSE **2** : to increase the activity of : STIMULATE **syn** provoke, pique, quicken — **ex·ci·ta·tion** \ˌek-ˌsī-ˈtā-shən, ˌek-sə-\ *n* — **ex·cit·ed·ly** *adv* — **ex·cit·ing·ly** *adv*

ex·cite·ment \ik-ˈsīt-mənt\ *n* : AGITATION, STIR

ex·claim \iks-ˈklām\ *vb* : to cry out, speak, or utter sharply or vehemently — **ex·cla·ma·tion** \ˌeks-klə-ˈmā-shən\ *n* — **ex·clam·a·to·ry** \iks-ˈkla-mə-ˌtōr-ē\ *adj*

exclamation point *n* : a punctuation mark ! used esp. after an interjection or exclamation

ex·clude \iks-ˈklüd\ *vb* **ex·clud·ed; ex·clud·ing 1** : to prevent from using or participating : BAR **2** : to put out : EXPEL — **ex·clu·sion** \-ˈklü-zhən\ *n*

ex·clu·sive \iks-ˈklü-siv\ *adj* **1** : reserved for particular persons **2** : snobbishly aloof; *also* : STYLISH **3** : SOLE ⟨∼ rights⟩; *also* : UNDIVIDED **syn** chic, modish, smart, swank, fashionable — **exclusive** *n* — **ex·clu·sive·ly** *adv* — **ex·clu·sive·ness** *n* — **ex·clu·siv·i·ty** \ˌeks-ˌklü-si-və-tē, iks-, -zi-\ *n*

exclusive of *prep* : not taking into account

ex·cog·i·tate \ek-ˈskä-jə-ˌtāt\ *vb* : to think out : DEVISE

ex·com·mu·ni·cate \ˌek-skə-ˈmyü-nə-ˌkāt\ *vb* : to cut off officially from the rites of the church — **ex·com·mu·ni·ca·tion** \-ˌmyü-nə-ˈkā-shən\ *n*

ex·co·ri·ate \ek-ˈskōr-ē-ˌāt\ *vb* **-at·ed; -at·ing** : to criticize severely — **ex·co·ri·a·tion** \(ˌ)ek-ˌskōr-ē-ˈā-shən\ *n*

ex·cre·ment \ˈek-skrə-mənt\ *n* : waste discharged from the body and esp. from the alimentary canal — **ex·cre·men·tal** \ˌek-skrə-ˈment-ᵊl\ *adj*

ex·cres·cence \ik-ˈskres-ᵊns\ *n* : OUTGROWTH; *esp* : an abnormal outgrowth (as a wart)

ex·cre·ta \ik-ˈskrē-tə\ *n pl* : waste matter separated or eliminated from an organism

ex·crete \ik-ˈskrēt\ *vb* **ex·cret·ed; ex·cret·ing** : to separate and eliminate wastes from the body esp. in urine or sweat — **ex·cre·tion** \-ˈskrē-shən\ *n* — **ex·cre·to·ry** \ˈek-skrə-ˌtōr-ē\ *adj*

ex·cru·ci·at·ing \ik-ˈskrü-shē-ˌā-tiŋ\ *adj* [L *excruciare,* fr. *cruciare* to crucify, fr. *crux* cross] : intensely painful or distressing **syn** agonizing, harrowing, torturous — **ex·cru·ci·at·ing·ly** *adv*

ex·cul·pate \ˈek-(ˌ)skəl-ˌpāt\ *vb* **-pat·ed; -pat·ing** : to clear from alleged fault or guilt **syn** absolve, exonerate, acquit, vindicate, clear

ex·cur·sion \ik-ˈskər-zhən\ *n* **1** : EXPEDITION; *esp* : a pleasure trip **2** : DIGRESSION — **ex·cur·sion·ist** \-zhə-nist\ *n*

ex·cur·sive \-ˈskər-siv\ *adj* : constituting or characterized by digression

¹ex·cuse \ik-ˈskyüz\ *vb* **ex·cused; ex·cus·ing** [ME, fr. OF *excuser,* fr. L *excusare,* fr. *causa* cause, explanation] **1** : to make apology for **2** : PARDON **3** : to release from an obligation **4** : JUSTIFY — **ex·cus·able** *adj*

²excuse \ik-ˈskyüs\ *n* **1** : an act of excusing **2** : something that excuses or is a reason for excusing : JUSTIFICATION

exec *n* : EXECUTIVE

ex·e·cra·ble \ˈek-si-krə-bəl\ *adj* **1** : DETESTABLE **2** : very bad ⟨∼ spelling⟩

ex·e·crate \ˈek-sə-ˌkrāt\ *vb* **-crat·ed; -crat·ing** [L *exsecratus,* pp. of *exsecrari* to put under a curse, fr. *ex-* out of + *sacer* sacred] : to denounce as evil or detestable; *also* : DETEST — **ex·e·cra·tion** \ˌek-sə-ˈkrā-shən\ *n*

ex·e·cute \ˈek-si-ˌkyüt\ *vb* **-cut·ed; -cut·ing 1** : to carry out fully : put completely into effect **2** : to do what is called for by (as a law) **3** : to put to death in accordance with a legal sentence **4** : to produce by carrying out a design **5** : to do what is needed to give validity to ⟨∼ a deed⟩ — **ex·e·cu·tion** \ˌek-si-ˈkyü-shən\ *n* — **ex·e·cu·tion·er** *n*

¹ex·ec·u·tive \ig-'ze-kyə-tiv\ *adj* **1** : of or relating to the enforcement of laws and the conduct of affairs **2** : designed for or related to carrying out plans or purposes

²executive *n* **1** : the branch of government with executive duties **2** : one having administrative or managerial responsibility

ex·ec·u·tor \ig-'ze-kyə-tər\ *n* : the person named in a will to execute it

ex·ec·u·trix \ig-'ze-kyə-ˌtriks\ *n, pl* **ex·ec·u·tri·ces** \-ˌze-kyə-'trī-ˌsēz\ *or* **ex·ec·u·trix·es** \-'ze-kyə-ˌtrik-səz\ : a woman who is an executor

ex·e·ge·sis \ˌek-sə-'jē-səs\ *n, pl* **-ge·ses** \-'jē-ˌsēz\ : explanation or critical interpretation of a text

ex·e·gete \'ek-sə-ˌjēt\ *n* : one who practices exegesis — **ex·e·get·i·cal** \ˌek-sə-'je-ti-kəl\ *adj*

ex·em·plar \ig-'zem-ˌplär, -plər\ *n* **1** : one that serves as a model or example; *esp* : an ideal model **2** : a typical instance or example

ex·em·pla·ry \ig-'zem-plə-rē\ *adj* : serving as a pattern; *also* : COMMENDABLE

ex·em·pli·fy \ig-'zem-plə-ˌfī\ *vb* **-fied; -fy·ing** : to illustrate by example : serve as an example of — **ex·em·pli·fi·ca·tion** \-ˌzem-plə-fə-'kā-shən\ *n*

¹ex·empt \ig-'zempt\ *adj* : free from some liability to which others are subject

²exempt *vb* : to make exempt : EXCUSE — **ex·emp·tion** \ig-'zemp-shən\ *n*

¹ex·er·cise \'ek-sər-ˌsīz\ *n* **1** : EMPLOYMENT, USE ⟨∼ of authority⟩ **2** : exertion made for the sake of training or physical fitness **3** : a task or problem done to develop skill **4** *pl* : a public exhibition or ceremony

²exercise *vb* **-cised; -cis·ing** **1** : EXERT ⟨∼ control⟩ **2** : to train by or engage in exercise **3** : WORRY, DISTRESS — **ex·er·cis·er** *n*

ex·ert \ig-'zərt\ *vb* : to bring or put into action ⟨∼ influence⟩ ⟨∼*ed* himself⟩ — **ex·er·tion** \-'zər-shən\ *n*

ex·hale \eks-'hāl\ *vb* **ex·haled; ex·hal·ing** **1** : to breathe out **2** : to give or pass off in the form of vapor — **ex·ha·la·tion** \ˌeks-hə-'lā-shən\ *n*

¹ex·haust \ig-'zȯst\ *vb* **1** : to use up wholly **2** : to tire or wear out **3** : to draw off or let out completely; *also* : EMPTY **4** : to develop (a subject) completely

²exhaust *n* **1** : the escape of used vapor or gas from an engine; *also* : the gas that escapes **2** : a system of pipes through which exhaust escapes

ex·haus·tion \ig-'zȯs-chən\ *n* : extreme weariness : FATIGUE

ex·haus·tive \ig-'zȯ-stiv\ *adj* : covering all possibilities : THOROUGH — **ex·haus·tive·ly** *adv*

¹ex·hib·it \ig-'zi-bət\ *vb* **1** : to display esp. publicly **2** : to present to a court in legal form **syn** display, show, parade, flaunt — **ex·hi·bi·tion** \ˌek-sə-'bi-shən\ *n* — **ex·hib·i·tor** \ig-'zi-bə-tər\ *n*

²exhibit *n* **1** : an act or instance of exhibiting; *also* : something exhibited **2** : something produced and identified in court for use as evidence

ex·hi·bi·tion·ism \ˌek-sə-'bi-shə-ˌni-zəm\ *n* **1** : a perversion marked by a tendency to indecent exposure **2** : the act or practice of behaving so as to attract attention to oneself — **ex·hi·bi·tion·ist** \-nist\ *n or adj*

ex·hil·a·rate \ig-'zi-lə-ˌrāt\ *vb* **-rat·ed; -rat·ing** : ENLIVEN, STIMULATE — **ex·hil·a·ra·tion** \-ˌzi-lə-'rā-shən\ *n*

ex·hort \ig-'zȯrt\ *vb* : to urge, advise, or warn earnestly — **ex·hor·ta·tion** \ˌek-sȯr-tā-shən, ˌeg-ˌzȯr-, -zər-\ *n*

ex·hume \ig-'züm, iks-'hyüm\ *vb* **ex·humed; ex·hum·ing** [F or ML; F *exhumer*, fr. ML *exhumare*, fr. L *ex* out of + *humus* earth] : DISINTER — **ex·hu·ma·tion** \ˌeks-hyü-'mā-shən, ˌeg-zü-\ *n*

ex·i·gen·cy \'ek-sə-jən-sē, ig-'zi-jən-\ *n, pl* **-cies** **1** *pl* : REQUIREMENTS **2** : urgent need — **ex·i·gent** \'ek-sə-jənt\ *adj*

ex·ig·u·ous \ig-'zi-gyə-wəs\ *adj* : scanty in amount — **ex·i·gu·i·ty** \ˌeg-zi-'gyü-ə-tē\ *n*

¹ex·ile \'eg-ˌzīl, 'ek-ˌsīl\ *n* **1** : BANISHMENT; *also* : voluntary absence from one's country or home **2** : a person driven from his or her native place

²exile *vb* **ex·iled; ex·il·ing** : BANISH, EXPEL **syn** expatriate, deport, ostracize

ex·ist \ig-'zist\ *vb* **1** : to have being **2** : to continue to be : LIVE

ex·is·tence \ig-'zis-təns\ *n* **1** : continuance in living **2** : actual occurrence **3** : something existing — **ex·is·tent** \-tənt\ *adj*

ex·is·ten·tial \ˌeg-zis-'ten-chəl, ˌek-sis-\ *adj* **1** : of or relating to existence **2** : EMPIRICAL **3** : having being in time and space **4** : of or relating to existentialism or existentialists

ex·is·ten·tial·ism \ˌeg-zis-'ten-chə-ˌli-zəm\ *n* : a philosophy centered on individual existence and personal responsibility for acts of free will in the absence of certain knowledge of what is right or wrong — **ex·is·ten·tial·ist** \-list\ *adj or n*

ex·it \'eg-zət, 'ek-sət\ *n* **1** : a departure from a stage **2** : a going out or away; *also* : DEATH **3** : a way out of an enclosed space **4** : a point of departure from an expressway — **exit** *vb*

exo·bi·ol·o·gy \ˌek-sō-bī-'ä-lə-jē\ *n* : biology concerned with life originating or existing outside the earth or its atmosphere — **exo·bi·ol·o·gist** \-jist\ *n*

exo·crine gland \'ek-sə-krən-, -ˌkrīn-, -ˌkrēn-\ *n* : a gland (as a salivary gland) that releases a secretion externally by means of a canal or duct

Exod *abbr* Exodus

ex·o·dus \'ek-sə-dəs\ *n* **1** *cap* — see BIBLE table **2** : a mass departure : EMIGRATION

ex of·fi·cio \ˌek-sə-'fi-shē-ˌō\ *adv or adj* : by virtue of or because of an office ⟨*ex officio* chairman⟩

ex·og·e·nous \ek-'sä-jə-nəs\ *adj* : caused or produced by factors outside the organism or system — **ex·og·e·nous·ly** *adv*

ex·on·er·ate \ig-'zä-nə-ˌrāt\ *vb* **-at·ed; -at·ing** [ME, fr. L *exoneratus*, pp. of *exonerare* to unburden, fr. *ex-* out + *onus* load] : to free from blame **syn** acquit, absolve, exculpate, vindicate — **ex·on·er·a·tion** \-ˌzä-nə-'rā-shən\ *n*

ex·or·bi·tant \ig-'zȯr-bə-tənt\ *adj* : exceeding what is usual or proper

ex·or·cise \'ek-ˌsȯr-ˌsīz, -sər-\ *vb* **-cised; -cis·ing** **1** : to get rid of by or as if by solemn command **2** : to free of an evil spirit — **ex·or·cism** \-ˌsi-zəm\ *n* — **ex·or·cist** \-ˌsist\ *n*

exo·sphere \'ek-sō-ˌsfir\ *n* : the outermost region of the atmosphere

exo·ther·mic \ˌek-sō-'thər-mik\ *adj* : characterized by or formed with evolution of heat

ex·ot·ic \ig-'zä-tik\ *adj* **1** : introduced from another country **2** : strikingly, excitingly, or mysteriously different or unusual — **exotic** *n* — **ex·ot·i·cal·ly** \-ti-k(ə-)lē\ *adv* — **ex·ot·i·cism** \-tə-ˌsi-zəm\ *n*

exp *abbr* **1** expense **2** experiment **3** export **4** express

ex·pand \ik-'spand\ *vb* **1** : to open up : UNFOLD **2** : ENLARGE **3** : to develop in detail **syn** amplify, swell, distend, inflate, dilate — **ex·pand·er** *n*

ex·panse \ik-'spans\ *n* : a broad extent (as of land or sea)

ex·pan·sion \ik-'span-chən\ *n* **1** : the act or process of expanding **2** : the quality or state of being expanded **3** : an expanded part or thing

ex·pan·sive \ik-'span-siv\ *adj* **1** : tending to expand or to cause expansion **2** : warmly benevolent, generous, or ready to talk **3** : of large extent or scope — **ex·pan·sive·ly** *adv* — **ex·pan·sive·ness** *n*

\ə\abut \ᵊ\kitten \ər\further \a\ash \ā\ace \ä\mop, mar \au̇\out \ch\chin \e\bet \ē\easy \g\go \i\hit \ī\ice \j\job \ŋ\sing \ō\go \ȯ\law \ȯi\boy \th\thin \t̲h̲\the \ü\loot \u̇\foot \y\yet \zh\vision *see also* Pronunciation Symbols page

ex par·te \eks-ˈpär-tē\ *adv or adj* [ML] : from a one-sided point of view

ex·pa·ti·ate \ek-ˈspā-shē-ˌāt\ *vb* **-at·ed; -at·ing** : to talk or write at length — **ex·pa·ti·a·tion** \ek-ˌspā-shē-ˈā-shən\ *n*

¹**ex·pa·tri·ate** \ek-ˈspā-trē-ˌāt\ *vb* **-at·ed; -at·ing** : EXILE — **ex·pa·tri·a·tion** \ek-ˌspā-trē-ˈā-shon\ *n*

²**ex·pa·tri·ate** \ek-ˈspā-trē-ˌāt, -trē-ət\ *adj* : living in a foreign country — **expatriate** *n*

ex·pect \ik-ˈspekt\ *vb* **1** : SUPPOSE, THINK **2** : to look forward to : ANTICIPATE **3** : to consider reasonable, due, or necessary **4** : to consider to be obliged

ex·pec·tan·cy \-ˈspek-tən-sē\ *n, pl* **-cies 1** : EXPECTATION **2** : the expected amount (as of years of life)

ex·pec·tant \-tənt\ *adj* : marked by expectation; *esp* : expecting the birth of a child — **ex·pec·tant·ly** *adv*

ex·pec·ta·tion \ek-ˌspek-ˈtā-shən\ *n* **1** : the act or state of expecting **2** : prospect of good or bad fortune — usu. used in pl. **3** : something expected

ex·pec·to·rant \ik-ˈspek-tə-rənt\ *n* : an agent that promotes the discharge or expulsion of mucus from the respiratory tract — **expectorant** *adj*

ex·pec·to·rate \-ˌrāt\ *vb* **-rat·ed; -rat·ing** : SPIT — **ex·pec·to·ra·tion** \-ˌspek-tə-ˈrā-shən\ *n*

ex·pe·di·ence \ik-ˈspē-dē-əns\ *n* : EXPEDIENCY

ex·pe·di·en·cy \-ən-sē\ *n, pl* **-cies 1** : fitness to some end **2** : use of expedient means and methods; *also* : something expedient

¹**ex·pe·di·ent** \-ənt\ *adj* [ME, fr. MF or L; MF, fr. L *expediens*, prp. of *expedire* to extricate, prepare, be useful, fr. *ex-* out + *ped-, pes* foot] **1** : adapted for achieving a particular end **2** : marked by concern with what is advantageous; *esp* : governed by self-interest

²**expedient** *n* : something expedient; *esp* : a temporary means to an end

ex·pe·dite \ˈek-spə-ˌdīt\ *vb* **-dit·ed; -dit·ing** : to carry out promptly; *also* : to speed up

ex·pe·dit·er \-ˌdī-tər\ *n* : one that expedites; *esp* : one employed to ensure efficient movement of goods or supplies in a business

ex·pe·di·tion \ek-spə-ˈdi-shən\ *n* **1** : a journey for a particular purpose; *also* : the persons making it **2** : efficient promptness

ex·pe·di·tion·ary \-ˈdi-shə-ˌner-ē\ *adj* : of, relating to, or constituting an expedition; *also* : sent on military service abroad

ex·pe·di·tious \-ˈdi-shəs\ *adj* : marked by or acting with prompt efficiency **syn** swift, fast, rapid, speedy

ex·pel \ik-ˈspel\ *vb* **ex·pelled; ex·pel·ling** : to drive or force out : EJECT

ex·pend \ik-ˈspend\ *vb* **1** : to pay out : SPEND **2** : UTILIZE; *also* : USE UP — **ex·pend·able** *adj*

ex·pen·di·ture \ik-ˈspen-di-chər, -ˌchür\ *n* : the act or process of expending **2** : something expended

ex·pense \ik-ˈspens\ *n* **1** : EXPENDITURE **2** : COST **3** : a cause of expenditure **4** : SACRIFICE

ex·pen·sive \ik-ˈspen-siv\ *adj* : COSTLY, DEAR — **ex·pen·sive·ly** *adv*

¹**ex·pe·ri·ence** \ik-ˈspir-ē-əns\ *n* **1** : observation of or participation in events resulting in or tending toward knowledge **2** : knowledge, practice, or skill derived from observation or participation in events; *also* : the length of such participation **3** : something encountered, undergone, or lived through (as by a person or community)

²**experience** *vb* **-enced; -enc·ing 1** : FIND OUT, DISCOVER **2** : to have experience of : UNDERGO

ex·pe·ri·enced *adj* : made capable through experience

¹**ex·per·i·ment** \ik-ˈsper-ə-mənt\ *n* : a controlled procedure carried out to discover, test, or demonstrate something; *also* : the process of testing — **ex·per·i·men·tal** \-ˌsper-ə-ˈment-ᵊl\ *adj*

²**ex·per·i·ment** \-ˌment\ *vb* : to make experiments — **ex·per·i·men·ta·tion** \ik-ˌsper-ə-mən-ˈtā-shən\ *n* — **ex·per·i·men·ter** *n*

¹**ex·pert** \ˈek-spərt\ *adj* : showing special skill or knowledge — **ex·pert·ly** *adv* — **ex·pert·ness** *n*

²**ex·pert** \ˈek-spərt\ *n* : an expert person : SPECIALIST

ex·per·tise \ek-(ˌ)spər-ˈtēz\ *n* : the skill of an expert

expert system *n* : computer software that attempts to mimic the reasoning of a human specialist

ex·pi·ate \ˈek-spē-ˌāt\ *vb* **-at·ed; -at·ing** : to give satisfaction for : ATONE — **ex·pi·a·tion** \ek-spē-ˈā-shən\ *n*

ex·pi·a·to·ry \ˈek-spē-ə-ˌtōr-ē\ *adj* : serving to expiate

ex·pire \ik-ˈspīr, ek-\ *vb* **ex·pired; ex·pir·ing 1** : to breathe one's last breath : DIE **2** : to come to an end **3** : to breathe out from or as if from the lungs — **ex·pi·ra·tion** \ek-spə-ˈrā-shən\ *n*

ex·plain \ik-ˈsplān\ *vb* [ME *explanen*, fr. L *explanare*, lit., to make level, fr. *planus* level, flat] **1** : to make clear **2** : to give the reason for — **ex·pla·na·tion** \ek-splə-ˈnā-shən\ *n* — **ex·plan·a·to·ry** \ik-ˈspla-nə-ˌtōr-ē\ *adj*

ex·ple·tive \ˈek-splə-tiv\ *n* : a usu. profane exclamation

ex·pli·ca·ble \ek-ˈspli-kə-bəl, ˈek- (ˌ)spli-\ *adj* : capable of being explained

ex·pli·cate \ˈek-splə-ˌkāt\ *vb* **-cat·ed; -cat·ing** : to give a detailed explanation of — **ex·pli·ca·tion** \ek-splə-ˈkā-shən\ *n*

ex·plic·it \ik-ˈspli-sət\ *adj* : clearly and precisely expressed — **ex·plic·it·ly** *adv* — **ex·plic·it·ness** *n*

ex·plode \ik-ˈsplōd\ *vb* **ex·plod·ed; ex·plod·ing** [L *explodere* to drive off the stage by clapping, fr. *ex-* out + *plaudere* to clap] **1** : DISCREDIT ⟨∼ a belief⟩ **2** : to burst or cause to burst violently and noisily ⟨∼ a bomb⟩ ⟨the boiler *exploded*⟩ **3** : to undergo a rapid chemical or nuclear reaction with production of heat and violent expansion of gas ⟨dynamite ∼s⟩ **4** : to give forth a sudden strong and noisy outburst of emotion **5** : to increase rapidly

ex·plod·ed *adj* : showing the parts separated but in correct relationship to each other ⟨an ∼ view of a carburetor⟩

¹**ex·ploit** \ˈek-ˌsplȯit\ *n* : DEED; *esp* : a notable or heroic act

²**ex·ploit** \ik-ˈsplȯit\ *vb* **1** : to make productive use of : UTILIZE **2** : to use unfairly for one's own advantage — **ex·ploi·ta·tion** \ek-ˌsplȯi-ˈtā-shən\ *n*

ex·plore \ik-ˈsplȯr\ *vb* **ex·plored; ex·plor·ing 1** : to look into or travel over thoroughly **2** : to examine carefully ⟨∼ a wound⟩ — **ex·plo·ra·tion** \ek-splə-ˈrā-shən\ *n* — **ex·plor·ato·ry** \ik-ˈsplȯr-ə-ˌtōr-ē\ *adj* — **ex·plor·er** *n*

ex·plo·sion \ik-ˈsplō-zhən\ *n* : the act or an instance of exploding

ex·plo·sive \ik-ˈsplō-siv\ *adj* **1** : relating to or able to cause explosion **2** : tending to explode — **explosive** *n* — **ex·plo·sive·ly** *adv*

ex·po \ˈek-spō\ *n, pl* **expos** : EXPOSITION 2

ex·po·nent \ik-ˈspō-nənt, ˈek-ˌspō-\ *n* **1** : a symbol written above and to the right of a mathematical expression (as ^{3} in a^3) to signify how many times it is to be used as a factor **2** : INTERPRETER, EXPOUNDER **3** : ADVOCATE, CHAMPION — **ex·po·nen·tial** \ek-spə-ˈnen-chəl\ *adj* — **ex·po·nen·tial·ly** *adv*

ex·po·nen·ti·a·tion \ek-spə-ˌnen-chē-ˈā-shen\ *n* : the mathematical operation of raising a quantity to a power

¹**ex·port** \ek-ˈspȯrt, ˈek-ˌspȯrt\ *vb* : to send (as merchandise) to foreign countries — **ex·por·ta·tion** \ek-ˌspȯr-ˈtā-shən, -spər-\ *n* — **ex·port·er** *n*

²**ex·port** \ˈek-ˌspȯrt\ *n* **1** : something exported esp. for trade **2** : the act of exporting

ex·pose \ik-ˈspōz\ *vb* **ex·posed; ex·pos·ing 1** : to deprive of shelter or protection **2** : to submit or subject to an action or influence; *esp* : to subject (as photographic film) to radiant energy (as light) **3** : to bring to light : DISCLOSE **4** : to cause to be open to view

ex·po·sé *or* **ex·po·se** \ˌek-spō-ˈzā\ *n* : an exposure of something discreditable

ex·po·si·tion \ˌek-spə-ˈzi-shən\ *n* **1** : a setting forth of the meaning or purpose (as of a writing); *also* : discourse designed to convey information **2** : a public exhibition

ex·pos·i·tor \ik-ˈspä-zə-tər\ *n* : one who explains : COMMENTATOR

ex post fac·to \ˌeks-ˈpōst-ˌfak-tō\ *adv or adj* : after the fact

ex·pos·tu·late \ik-ˈspäs-chə-ˌlāt\ *vb* : to reason earnestly with a person esp. in dissuading : REMONSTRATE — **ex·pos·tu·la·tion** \-ˌspäs-chə-ˈlā-shən\ *n*

ex·po·sure \ik-ˈspō-zhər\ *n* **1** : the fact or condition of being exposed **2** : the act or an instance of exposing **3** : the length of time for which a film is exposed **4** : a section of a photographic film for one picture

ex·pound \ik-ˈspaůnd\ *vb* **1** : STATE **2** : INTERPRET, EXPLAIN — **ex·pound·er** *n*

¹ex·press \ik-ˈspres\ *adj* **1** : EXPLICIT; *also* : EXACT, PRECISE **2** : SPECIFIC ⟨this ∼ purpose⟩ **3** : traveling at high speed and esp. with few stops ⟨an ∼ train⟩; *also* : adapted to high speed use ⟨∼ roads⟩ — **ex·press·ly** *adv*

²express *adv* : by express ⟨ship it ∼⟩

³express *n* **1** : a system for the prompt transportation of goods; *also* : a company operating such a service or the shipments so transported **2** : an express vehicle

⁴express *vb* **1** : to make known : SHOW, STATE ⟨∼ regret⟩; *also* : SYMBOLIZE **2** : to squeeze out : extract by pressing **3** : to send by express

ex·pres·sion \ik-ˈspre-shən\ *n* **1** : UTTERANCE **2** : something that represents or symbolizes : SIGN; *esp* : a mathematical symbol or combination of signs and symbols representing a quantity or operation **3** : a significant word or phrase; *also* : manner of expressing (as in writing or music) **4** : facial aspect or vocal intonation indicative of feeling — **ex·pres·sion·less** *adj*

ex·pres·sion·ism \ik-ˈspre-shə-ˌni-zəm\ *n* : a theory or practice in art of seeking to depict the artist's subjective responses to objects and events — **ex·pres·sion·ist** \-nist\ *n or adj* — **ex·pres·sion·is·tic** \-ˌspre-shə-ˈnis-tik\ *adj*

ex·pres·sive \ik-ˈspre-siv\ *adj* **1** : of or relating to expression **2** : serving to express — **ex·pres·sive·ly** *adv* — **ex·pres·sive·ness** *n*

ex·press·way \ik-ˈspres-ˌwā\ *n* : a divided superhighway with limited access

ex·pro·pri·ate \ek-ˈsprō-prē-ˌāt\ *vb* **-at·ed; -at·ing** : to deprive of possession or the right to own — **ex·pro·pri·a·tion** \(ˌ)ek-ˌsprō-prē-ˈā-shən\ *n*

expt *abbr* experiment

ex·pul·sion \ik-ˈspəl-shən\ *n* : an expelling or being expelled : EJECTION

ex·punge \ik-ˈspənj\ *vb* **ex·punged; ex·pung·ing** [L *expungere* to mark for deletion by dots, fr. *ex-* out + *pungere* to prick] : OBLITERATE, ERASE

ex·pur·gate \ˈek-spər-ˌgāt\ *vb* **-gat·ed; -gat·ing** : to clear (as a book) of objectionable passages — **ex·pur·ga·tion** \ˌek-spər-ˈgā-shən\ *n*

ex·qui·site \ek-ˈskwi-zət, ˈek-(ˌ)skwi-\ *adj* [ME *exquisit,* fr. L *exquisitus,* pp. of *exquirere* to search out, fr. *ex* out *quaerere* to seek] **1** : marked by flawless form or workmanship **2** : keenly appreciative or sensitive **3** : pleasingly beautiful or delicate **4** : INTENSE

ext *abbr* **1** extension **2** exterior **3** external **4** extra **5** extract

ex·tant \ˈek-stənt; ek-ˈstant\ *adj* : EXISTENT; *esp* : not lost or destroyed

ex·tem·po·ra·ne·ous \ek-ˌstem-pə-ˈrā-nē-əs\ *adj* : not planned beforehand : IMPROMPTU — **ex·tem·po·ra·ne·ous·ly** *adv*

ex·tem·po·rary \ik-ˈstem-pə-ˌrer-ē\ *adj* : EXTEMPORANEOUS

ex·tem·po·re \ik-ˈstem-pə-(ˌ)rē\ *adv* : EXTEMPORANEOUSLY

ex·tem·po·rize \ik-ˈstem-pə-ˌrīz\ *vb* **-rized; -riz·ing** : to do something extemporaneously

ex·tend \ik-ˈstend\ *vb* **1** : to spread or stretch forth or out (as in reaching) **2** : to exert or cause to exert to full capacity **3** : PROFFER ⟨∼ credit⟩ **4** : PROLONG ⟨∼ a note⟩ **5** : to make greater or broader ⟨∼ knowledge⟩ ⟨∼ a business⟩ **6** : to stretch out or reach across a distance, space, or time **syn** lengthen, elongate, protract — **ex·tend·able** *also* **ex·tend·ible** \-ˈsten-də-bəl\ *adj*

ex·ten·sion \ik-ˈsten-chən\ *n* **1** : an extending or being extended **2** : a program that geographically extends the educational resources of an institution **3** : an additional part; *also* : an extra telephone connected to a line

ex·ten·sive \ik-ˈsten-siv\ *adj* : of considerable extent : FAR-REACHING, BROAD — **ex·ten·sive·ly** *adv*

ex·tent \ik-ˈstent\ *n* **1** : the range or space over which something extends ⟨a property of large ∼⟩ **2** : the point or degree to which something extends ⟨to the fullest ∼ of the law⟩

ex·ten·u·ate \ik-ˈsten-yü-ˌwāt\ *vb* **-at·ed; -at·ing** : to lessen the seriousness of — **ex·ten·u·a·tion** \-ˌsten-yü-ˈwā-shən\ *n*

¹ex·te·ri·or \ek-ˈstir-ē-ər\ *adj* **1** : EXTERNAL **2** : suitable for use on an outside surface ⟨∼ paint⟩

²exterior *n* : an exterior part or surface

ex·ter·mi·nate \ik-ˈstər-mə-ˌnāt\ *vb* **-nat·ed; -nat·ing** : to get rid of completely usu. by killing off **syn** extirpate, eradicate, abolish, annihilate — **ex·ter·mi·na·tion** \-ˌstər-mə-ˈnā-shən\ *n* — **ex·ter·mi·na·tor** \-ˈstər-mə-ˌnā-tər\ *n*

¹ex·ter·nal \ek-ˈstərn-ᵊl\ *adj* **1** : outwardly perceivable; *also* : SUPERFICIAL **2** : of, relating to, or located on the outside or an outer part **3** : arising or acting from without; *also* : FOREIGN ⟨∼ affairs⟩ — **ex·ter·nal·ly** *adv*

²external *n* : an external feature

ex·tinct \ik-ˈstiŋkt\ *adj* **1** : EXTINGUISHED; *also* : no longer active ⟨an ∼ volcano⟩ **2** : no longer existing or in use ⟨dinosaurs are ∼⟩ ⟨∼ languages⟩ — **ex·tinc·tion** \ik-ˈstiŋk-shən\ *n*

ex·tin·guish \ik-ˈstiŋ-gwish\ *vb* : to cause to stop burning; *also* : to bring to an end (as by destroying) — **ex·tin·guish·able** *adj* — **ex·tin·guish·er** *n*

ex·tir·pate \ˈek-stər-ˌpāt\ *vb* **-pat·ed; -pat·ing** [L *exstirpatus,* pp. of *exstirpare,* fr. *ex-* out + *stirps* trunk, root] **1** : to destroy completely **2** : UPROOT **syn** exterminate, eradicate, abolish, annihilate — **ex·tir·pa·tion** \ˌek-stər-ˈpā-shən\ *n*

ex·tol *also* **ex·toll** \ik-ˈstōl\ *vb* **ex·tolled; ex·tol·ling** : to praise highly : GLORIFY

ex·tort \ik-ˈstȯrt\ *vb* [L *extortus,* pp. of *extorquēre* to wrench out, extort, fr. *ex-* out + *torquēre* to twist] : to obtain by force or improper pressure ⟨∼ a bribe⟩ — **ex·tor·tion** \-ˈstȯr-shən\ *n* — **ex·tor·tion·er** *n* — **ex·tor·tion·ist** *n*

ex·tor·tion·ate \ik-ˈstȯr-shə-nət\ *adj* : EXCESSIVE, EXORBITANT — **ex·tor·tion·ate·ly** *adv*

¹ex·tra \ˈek-strə\ *adj* **1** : ADDITIONAL **2** : SUPERIOR

²extra *n* **1** : a special edition of a newspaper **2** : an added charge **3** : an additional worker or performer (as in a motion picture)

\ə\abut \ᵊ\kitten \ər\further \a\ash \ā\ace \ä\mop, mar \aů\out \ch\chin \e\bet \ē\easy \g\go \i\hit \ī\ice \j\job \ŋ\sing \ō\go \ȯ\law \ȯi\boy \th\thin \ṯẖ\the \ü\loot \ů\foot \y\yet \zh\vision **see also** Pronunciation Symbols page

³**extra** *adv* : beyond what is usual
¹**ex·tract** \ik-ˈstrakt, *esp for 3* ˈek-ˌstrakt\ *vb* **1** : to draw out; *esp* : to pull out forcibly ⟨~ a tooth⟩ **2** : to withdraw (as a juice or a constituent) by a physical or chemical process **3** : to select for citation : QUOTE — **ex·tract·able** *adj* — **ex·trac·tion** \ik-ˈstrak-shən\ *n* — **ex·trac·tor** \-tər\ *n*
²**ex·tract** \ˈek-ˌstrakt\ *n* **1** : EXCERPT, CITATION **2** : a product (as a juice or concentrate) obtained by extracting
ex·tra·cur·ric·u·lar \ˌek-strə-kə-ˈri-kyə-lər\ *adj* : lying outside the regular curriculum; *esp* : of or relating to school-connected activities (as sports) usu. carrying no academic credit
ex·tra·dite \ˈek-strə-ˌdīt\ *vb* **-dit·ed; -dit·ing** : to obtain by or deliver up to extradition
ex·tra·di·tion \ˌek-strə-ˈdi-shən\ *n* : the surrender of an alleged criminal to a different jurisdiction for trial
ex·tra·mar·i·tal \ˌek-strə-ˈmar-ət-ᵊl\ *adj* : of or relating to sexual intercourse by a married person with someone other than his or her spouse
ex·tra·mu·ral \-ˈmyür-əl\ *adj* : existing or functioning beyond the bounds of an organized unit
ex·tra·ne·ous \ek-ˈstrā-nē-əs\ *adj* **1** : coming from without **2** : not forming a vital part; *also* : IRRELEVANT — **ex·tra·ne·ous·ly** *adv*
ex·traor·di·nary \ik-ˈstrȯrd-ᵊn-ˌer-ē, ˌek-strə-ˈȯrd-\ *adj* **1** : notably unusual or exceptional **2** : employed on special service — **ex·traor·di·nari·ly** \-ˌstrȯrd-ᵊn-ˈer-ə-lē, ˌek-strə-ˌȯrd-\ *adv*
ex·trap·o·late \ik-ˈstra-pə-ˌlāt\ *vb* **-lat·ed; -lat·ing** : to infer (unknown data) from known data — **ex·trap·o·la·tion** \-ˌstra-pə-ˈlā-shən\ *n*
ex·tra·sen·so·ry \ˌek-strə-ˈsen-sə-rē\ *adj* : not acting or occurring through the known senses
extrasensory perception *n* : perception (as in telepathy) of events external to the self not gained through the senses and not deducible from previous experience
ex·tra·ter·res·tri·al \-tə-ˈres-trē-əl\ *adj* : originating or existing outside the earth or its atmosphere ⟨~ life⟩ — **extraterrestrial** *n*
ex·tra·ter·ri·to·ri·al \-ˌter-ə-ˈtōr-ē-əl\ *adj* : existing or taking place outside the territorial limits of a jurisdiction
ex·tra·ter·ri·to·ri·al·i·ty \-ˌtōr-ē-ˈa-lə-tē\ *n* : exemption from the application or jurisdiction of local law or tribunals ⟨diplomats enjoy ~⟩
ex·trav·a·gant \ik-ˈstra-vi-gənt\ *adj* **1** : EXCESSIVE ⟨~ claims⟩ **2** : unduly lavish : WASTEFUL **3** : too costly **syn** immoderate, exorbitant, extreme, inordinate, undue — **ex·trav·a·gance** \-gəns\ *n* — **ex·trav·a·gant·ly** *adv*
ex·trav·a·gan·za \ik-ˌstra-və-ˈgan-zə\ *n* **1** : a literary or musical work marked by extreme freedom of style and structure **2** : a spectacular show
ex·tra·ve·hic·u·lar \ˌek-strə-vē-ˈhi-kyə-lər\ *adj* : taking place outside a vehicle (as a spacecraft) ⟨~ activity⟩
¹**ex·treme** \ik-ˈstrēm\ *adj* **1** : very great or intense ⟨~ cold⟩ **2** : very severe or radical ⟨~ measures⟩ **3** : going to great lengths or beyond normal limits ⟨politically ~⟩ **4** : most remote ⟨the ~ end⟩ **5** : UTMOST; *also* : MAXIMUM — **ex·treme·ly** *adv*
²**extreme** *n* **1** : something located at one end or the other of a range or series **2** : EXTREMITY 4
extremely low frequency *n* : a radio frequency in the lowest range of the radio spectrum
ex·trem·ism \ik-ˈstrē-ˌmi-zəm\ *n* : the quality or state of being extreme; *esp* : advocacy of extreme political measures — **ex·trem·ist** \-mist\ *n or adj*
ex·trem·i·ty \ik-ˈstre-mə-tē\ *n, pl* **-ties 1** : the most remote part or point **2** : a limb of the body; *esp* : a human

hand or foot **3** : the greatest need or danger **4** : the utmost degree; *also* : a drastic or desperate measure
ex·tri·cate \ˈek-strə-ˌkāt\ *vb* **-cat·ed; -cat·ing** [L *extricatus*, pp. of *extricare*, fr. *ex-* out + *tricae* trifles, perplexities] : to free from an entanglement or difficulty **syn** disentangle, untangle, disencumber — **ex·tri·ca·ble** \ik-ˈstri-kə-bəl, ek-; ˈek-(ˌ)stri-\ *adj* — **ex·tri·ca·tion** \ˌek-strə-ˈkā-shən\ *n*
ex·trin·sic \ek-ˈstrin-zik, -sik\ *adj* **1** : not forming part of or belonging to a thing **2** : EXTERNAL — **ex·trin·si·cal·ly** \-zi-k(ə-)lē, -si-\ *adv*
ex·tro·vert *also* **ex·tra·vert** \ˈek-strə-ˌvərt\ *n* : a gregarious and unreserved person — **ex·tro·ver·sion** *or* **ex·tra·ver·sion** \ˌek-strə-ˈvər-zhən\ *n* — **ex·tro·vert·ed** *also* **ex·tra·vert·ed** *adj*
ex·trude \ik-ˈstrüd\ *vb* **ex·trud·ed; ex·trud·ing 1** : to force, press, or push out **2** : to shape (as plastic) by forcing through a die — **ex·tru·sion** \-ˈstrü-zhən\ *n* — **ex·trud·er** *n*
ex·u·ber·ant \ig-ˈzü-bə-rənt\ *adj* **1** : unrestrained in enthusiasm or style **2** : PROFUSE — **ex·u·ber·ance** \-rəns\ *n* — **ex·u·ber·ant·ly** *adv*
ex·ude \ig-ˈzüd\ *vb* **ex·ud·ed; ex·ud·ing** [L *exsudare*, fr. *ex-* out + *sudare* to sweat] **1** : to discharge slowly through pores or cuts : OOZE **2** : to display conspicuously or abundantly ⟨~s charm⟩ — **ex·u·date** \ˈek-sù-ˌdāt, -syù-\ *n* — **ex·u·da·tion** \ˌek-sù-ˈdā-shən, -syù-\ *n*
ex·ult \ig-ˈzəlt\ *vb* : REJOICE, GLORY — **ex·ul·tant** \-ˈzəlt-ᵊnt\ *adj* — **ex·ul·tant·ly** *adv* — **ex·ul·ta·tion** \ˌek-(ˌ)səl-ˈtā-shən, ˌeg-(ˌ)zəl-\ *n*
ex·urb \ˈek-ˌsərb, ˈeg-ˌzərb\ *n* : a region outside a city and its suburbs inhabited chiefly by well-to-do families
ex·ur·ban·ite \ek-ˈsər-bə-ˌnīt; eg-ˈzər-\ *n* : one who lives in an exurb
ex·ur·bia \ek-ˈsər-bē-ə, eg-ˈzer-\ *n* : the generalized region of exurbs
-ey — see -Y
¹**eye** \ˈī\ *n* **1** : an organ of sight typically consisting in vertebrates of a globular structure that is located in a socket of the skull, is lined with a sensitive retina, and is normally paired **2** : VISION, PERCEPTION; *also* : faculty of discrimination ⟨an ~ for bargains⟩ **3** : POINT OF VIEW, JUDGMENT — often used in pl. ⟨in the ~s of the law⟩ **4** : something suggesting an eye ⟨the ~ of a needle⟩; *esp* : an undeveloped bud (as on a potato) **5** : the calm center of a cyclone — **eyed** \ˈīd\ *adj*
²**eye** *vb* **eyed; eye·ing** *or* **ey·ing** : to look at : WATCH
eye·ball \ˈī-ˌbȯl\ *n* : the globular capsule of the vertebrate eye
eye·brow \-ˌbraù\ *n* : the ridge over the eye or the hair growing on it
eye·drop·per \-ˌdrä-pər\ *n* : DROPPER 2
eye·glass \-ˌglas\ *n* : a lens worn to aid vision; *also, pl* : GLASSES
eye·lash \-ˌlash\ *n* **1** : the fringe of hair edging the eyelid — usu. used in pl. **2** : a single hair of the eyelashes
eye·let \-lət\ *n* **1** : a small hole intended for ornament or for passage of a cord or lace **2** : a typically metal ring for reinforcing an eyelet : GROMMET
eye·lid \-ˌlid\ *n* : either of the movable folds of skin and muscle that can be closed over the eyeball
eye·lin·er \-ˌlī-nər\ *n* : makeup used to emphasize the contour of the eyes
eye–open·er \-ˌō-pə-nər\ *n* : something startling or surprising — **eye–open·ing** *adj*
eye·piece \-ˌpēs\ *n* : the lens or combination of lenses at the eye end of an optical instrument
eye shadow *n* : a colored cosmetic applied to the eyelids to accent the eyes
eye·sight \-ˌsīt\ *n* : SIGHT, VISION
eye·sore \-ˌsōr\ *n* : something offensive to view

eye·strain \-₁strān\ *n* : weariness or a strained state of the eye

eye·tooth \-'tüth\ *n* : a canine tooth of the upper jaw

eye·wash \-₁wȯsh, -₁wäsh\ *n* 1 : an eye lotion 2 : misleading or deceptive statements, actions, or procedures

eye·wit·ness \-'wit-nəs\ *n* : a person who actually sees something happen

ey·rie \'īr-ē, *or like* AERIE\ *var of* AERIE

ey·rir \'ā-₁rir\ *n, pl* **au·rar** \'au̇-₁rär\ — see *krona* at MONEY table

Ez *or* **Ezr** *abbr* Ezra

Ezech *abbr* Ezechiel

Eze·chiel \i-'zē-kyəl\ *n* — see BIBLE table

Ezek *abbr* Ezekiel

Eze·kiel \i-'zē-kyəl\ *n* — see BIBLE table

Ez·ra \'ez-rə\ *n* — see BIBLE table

F

¹f \'ef\ *n, pl* **f's** *or* **fs** \'efs\ *often cap* 1 : the 6th letter of the English alphabet 2 : a grade rating a student's work as failing

²f *abbr, often cap* 1 Fahrenheit 2 false 3 family 4 farad 5 female 6 feminine 7 forte 8 French 9 frequency 10 Friday

³f *symbol* focal length

F *symbol* fluorine

FAA *abbr* Federal Aviation Administration

Fa·bi·an \'fā-bē-ən\ *adj* : of, relating to, or being a society of socialists organized in England in 1884 to spread socialist principles gradually — **Fabian** *n* — **Fa·bi·an·ism** *n*

fa·ble \'fā-bəl\ *n* 1 : a legendary story of supernatural happenings 2 : a narration intended to teach a lesson; *esp* : one in which animals speak and act like people 3 : FALSEHOOD

fa·bled \'fā-bəld\ *adj* 1 : FICTITIOUS 2 : told or celebrated in fable

fab·ric \'fa-brik\ *n* [MF *fabrique*, fr. L *fabrica* workshop, structure] 1 : STRUCTURE, FRAMEWORK ⟨the ~ of society⟩ 2 : CLOTH; *also* : a material that resembles cloth

fab·ri·cate \'fa-bri-₁kāt\ *vb* **-cat·ed; -cat·ing** 1 : INVENT, CREATE 2 : to make up for the sake of deception 3 : CONSTRUCT, MANUFACTURE — **fab·ri·ca·tion** \₁fa-bri-'kā-shən\ *n*

fab·u·lous \'fa-byə-ləs\ *adj* 1 : resembling a fable; *also* : INCREDIBLE, MARVELOUS 2 : told in or based on fable — **fab·u·lous·ly** *adv*

fac *abbr* 1 facsimile 2 faculty

fa·cade *also* **fa·çade** \fə-'säd\ *n* [F *façade*, fr. It *facciata*, fr. *faccia* face] 1 : the principal face or front of a building 2 : a false, superficial, or artificial appearance ⟨a ~ of composure⟩ **syn** mask, disguise, front, guise, pretense, veneer

¹face \'fās\ *n* 1 : the front part of the head 2 : PRESENCE ⟨in the ~ of danger⟩ 3 : facial expression : LOOK ⟨put a sad ~ on⟩ 4 : GRIMACE ⟨made a ~⟩ 5 : outward appearance ⟨looks easy on the ~ of it⟩ 6 : CONFIDENCE; *also* : BOLDNESS 7 : DIGNITY, PRESTIGE ⟨afraid to lose ~⟩ 8 : SURFACE; *esp* : a front, principal, or bounding surface ⟨~ of a cliff⟩ ⟨the ~s of a cube⟩ — **faced** \'fāst, 'fā-səd\ *adj*

²face *vb* **faced; fac·ing** 1 : to confront brazenly 2 : to line near the edge esp. with a different material; *also* : to cover the front or surface of ⟨~ a building with marble⟩ 3 : to meet or bring in direct contact or confrontation ⟨*faced* the problem⟩ 4 : to stand or sit with the face toward ⟨~ the sun⟩ 5 : to have the front oriented toward ⟨a house *facing* the park⟩ 6 : to have as or be a prospect ⟨~ a grim future⟩ 7 : to turn the face or body in a specified direction — **face the music** : to meet the unpleasant consequences of one's actions

face·down \₁fās-'daun\ *adv* : with the face downward

face·less \-ləs\ *n* 1 : lacking a face 2 : lacking character or individuality

face–lift \'fās-₁lift\ *n* 1 : a cosmetic surgical operation for removal of facial defects (as wrinkles) typical of aging 2 : MODERNIZATION — **face–lift** *vb*

face–off \'fās-₁ȯf\ *n* 1 : a method of beginning play by dropping a puck (as in ice hockey) between two opposing players each of whom attempts to control it 2 : CONFRONTATION

fac·et \'fa-sət\ *n* [F *facette*, dim. of *face*] 1 : a small plane surface of a cut gem 2 : ASPECT, PHASE

fa·ce·tious \fə-'sē-shəs\ *adj* 1 : joking often inappropriately 2 : JOCULAR, JOCOSE **syn** witty, humorous — **fa·ce·tious·ly** *adv* — **fa·ce·tious·ness** *n*

¹fa·cial \'fā-shəl\ *adj* 1 : of or relating to the face 2 : used to improve the appearance of the face

²facial *n* : a facial treatment

fac·ile \'fa-səl\ *adj* 1 : easily accomplished, handled, or attained 2 : SUPERFICIAL 3 : readily manifested and often insincere ⟨~ prose⟩ 4 : READY, FLUENT ⟨a ~ writer⟩

fa·cil·i·tate \fə-'si-lə-₁tāt\ *vb* **-tat·ed; -tat·ing** : to make easier

fa·cil·i·ty \fə-'si-lə-tē\ *n, pl* **-ties** 1 : the quality of being easily performed 2 : ease in performance : APTITUDE 3 : PLIANCY 4 : something that makes easier an action, operation, or course of conduct; *also* : REST ROOM — often used in pl. 5 : something (as a hospital) built or installed for a particular purpose

fac·ing \'fā-siŋ\ *n* 1 : a lining at the edge esp. of a garment 2 *pl* : the collar, cuffs, and trimmings of a uniform coat 3 : an ornamental or protective layer 4 : material for facing

fac·sim·i·le \fak-'si-mə-lē\ *n* [L *fac simile* make similar] 1 : an exact copy 2 : a system of transmitting and reproducing printed matter or pictures by means of signals sent over telephone lines

fact \'fakt\ *n* 1 : DEED; *esp* : CRIME ⟨accessory after the ~⟩ 2 : the quality of being actual 3 : something that exists or occurs 4 : a piece of information

fac·tion \'fak-shən\ *n* : a group or combination (as in a government) acting together within and usu. against a larger body : CLIQUE — **fac·tion·al·ism** \-shə-nə-₁li-zəm\ *n*

fac·ti·tious \fak-'ti-shəs\ *adj* : ARTIFICIAL, SHAM ⟨a ~ display of grief⟩

¹fac·tor \'fak-tər\ *n* 1 : AGENT 2 : something that actively contributes to a result 3 : GENE 4 : any of the numbers or symbols in mathematics that when multiplied together form a product; *esp* : any of the integers that divide a given integer without a remainder

²factor *vb* 1 : to work as a factor 2 : to find the mathematical factors of and esp. the prime mathematical factors of

---

\ə\abut \ᵊ\kitten \ər\further \a\ash \ā\ace \ä\mop, mar \au̇\out \ch\chin \e\bet \ē\easy \g\go \i\hit \ī\ice \j\job \ŋ\sing \ō\go \ȯ\law \ȯi\boy \th\thin \th\the \ü\loot \u̇\foot \y\yet \zh\vision *see also* Pronunciation Symbols page

¹**fac·to·ri·al** \fak-ˈtōr-ē-əl\ *adj* : of, relating to, or being a factor

²**factorial** *n* : the product of all the positive integers from 1 to a given integer *n*

fac·to·ry \ˈfak-trē, -tə-rē\ *n, pl* **-ries 1** : a trading post where resident brokers trade **2** : a building or group of buildings used for manufacturing

fac·to·tum \fak-ˈtō-təm\ *n* [NL, lit., do everything, fr. L *fac* do + *totum* everything] : a person (as a servant) having numerous or varied duties

facts of life : the physiological processes and behavior involved in sex and reproduction

fac·tu·al \ˈfak-chə-wəl\ *adj* : of or relating to facts; *also* : based on fact — **fac·tu·al·ly** *adv*

fac·ul·ty \ˈfa-kəl-tē\ *n, pl* **-ties 1** : ability to act or do : POWER; *also* : natural aptitude **2** : one of the powers of the mind or body ⟨the ∼ of hearing⟩ **3** : the teachers in a school or college or one of its divisions

fad \ˈfad\ *n* : a practice or interest followed for a time with exaggerated zeal : CRAZE — **fad·dish** *adj* — **fad·dist** *n*

fade \ˈfād\ *vb* **fad·ed; fad·ing 1** : WITHER **2** : to lose or cause to lose freshness or brilliance of color **3** : VANISH **4** : to grow dim or faint

FADM *abbr* fleet admiral

fae·cal, fae·ces *var of* FECAL, FECES

fa·er·ie *also* **fa·ery** \ˈfā-rē, ˈfar-ē\ *n, pl* **fa·er·ies 1** : FAIRY-LAND **2** : FAIRY

¹**fag** \ˈfag\ *vb* **fagged; fag·ging 1** : DRUDGE **2** : to act as a fag **3** : TIRE, EXHAUST

²**fag** *n* **1** : an English public-school boy who acts as servant to another **2** : MENIAL, DRUDGE

³**fag** *n* : CIGARETTE

fag end *n* **1** : REMNANT **2** : the extreme end **3** : the last part or coarser end of a web of cloth **4** : the untwisted end of a rope

fag·ot *or* **fag·got** \ˈfa-gət\ *n* : a bundle of sticks or twigs

fag·ot·ing *or* **fag·got·ing** *n* : an embroidery produced by tying threads in hourglass-shaped clusters

Fah *or* **Fahr** *abbr* Fahrenheit

Fahr·en·heit \ˈfar-ən-ˌhīt\ *adj* : relating to, conforming to, or having a thermometer scale with the boiling point of water at 212 degrees and the freezing point at 32 degrees above zero

fa·ience *or* **fa·ïence** \fā-ˈäns\ *n* [F] : earthenware decorated with opaque colored glazes

¹**fail** \ˈfāl\ *vb* **1** : to become feeble; *esp* : to decline in health **2** : to die away **3** : to stop functioning **4** : to fall short ⟨∼ed in his duty⟩ **5** : to be or become absent or inadequate **6** : to be unsuccessful **7** : to become bankrupt **8** : DISAPPOINT **9** : NEGLECT

²**fail** *n* : FAILURE ⟨without ∼⟩

¹**fail·ing** \ˈfā-liŋ\ *n* : WEAKNESS, SHORTCOMING

²**failing** *prep* : in the absence or lack of

faille \ˈfīl\ *n* : a somewhat shiny closely woven ribbed fabric (as silk)

fail–safe \ˈfāl-ˌsāf\ *adj* **1** : incorporating a counteractive feature for a possible source of failure **2** : having no chance of failure

fail·ure \ˈfāl-yər\ *n* **1** : a failing to do or perform **2** : a state of inability to perform a normal function adequately ⟨heart ∼⟩ **3** : a fracturing or giving way under stress **4** : a lack of success **5** : BANKRUPTCY **6** : DEFICIENCY **7** : DETERIORATION, DECAY **8** : one that has failed

¹**fain** \ˈfān\ *adj* **1** *archaic* : GLAD; *also* : INCLINED **2** : being obliged or compelled

²**fain** *adv* **1** : with pleasure **2** : by preference

¹**faint** \ˈfānt\ *adj* [ME *faint, feint,* fr. OF, fr. *faindre, feindre* to feign, shirk] **1** : COWARDLY, SPIRITLESS **2** : weak, dizzy, and likely to faint **3** : lacking vigor or strength : FEEBLE ⟨∼ praise⟩ **4** : INDISTINCT, DIM — **faint·ly** *adv* — **faint·ness** *n*

²**faint** *vb* : to lose consciousness

³**faint** *n* : the action of fainting; *also* : the resulting condition

faint–heart·ed \ˌfānt-ˈhär-təd\ *adj* : lacking courage : TIMID

¹**fair** \ˈfar\ *adj* **1** : pleasing in appearance : BEAUTIFUL **2** : superficially pleasing : SPECIOUS **3** : CLEAN, PURE **4** : CLEAR, LEGIBLE **5** : not stormy or cloudy **6** : JUST **7** : conforming with the rules : ALLOWED; *also* : being within the foul lines ⟨∼ ball⟩ **8** : open to legitimate pursuit or attack ⟨∼ game⟩ **9** : PROMISING, LIKELY ⟨a ∼ chance of winning⟩ **10** : favorable to a ship's course ⟨a ∼ wind⟩ **11** : light in complexion : BLOND **12** : ADEQUATE — **fair·ness** *n*

²**fair** *adv, chiefly Brit* : FAIRLY 4

³**fair** *n* **1** : a gathering of buyers and sellers at a stated time and place for trade **2** : a competitive exhibition (as of farm products) **3** : a sale of assorted articles usu. for a charitable purpose

fair·ground \-ˌgraund\ *n* : an area where outdoor fairs, circuses, or exhibitions are held

fair·ing \ˈfar-iŋ\ *n* : a structure for producing a smooth outline and reducing drag (as on an airplane)

fair·ly \ˈfar-lē\ *adv* **1** : HANDSOMELY **2** : in a manner of speaking ⟨∼ bursting with pride⟩ **3** : without bias **4** : to a full degree or extent : PLAINLY, DISTINCTLY **5** : SOMEWHAT, RATHER ⟨a ∼ easy job⟩

fair–spo·ken \ˈfar-ˈspō-kən\ *adj* : pleasant and courteous in speech

fair–trade \-ˈtrād\ *adj* : of, relating to, or being an agreement between a producer and a seller that branded merchandise will be sold at or above a specified price — **fair–trade** *vb*

fair·way \-ˌwā\ *n* : the mowed part of a golf course between tee and green

fairy \ˈfar-ē\ *n, pl* **fair·ies** [ME *fairie* fairyland, fairy people, fr. OF *faerie*, fr. *feie, fee* fairy, fr. L *Fata*, goddess of fate, fr. *fatum* fate] : an imaginary being of folklore and romance usu. having diminutive human form and magic powers — **fairy** *adj*

fairy·land \-ˌland\ *n* **1** : the land of fairies **2** : a beautiful or charming place

fairy tale *n* **1** : a children's story about fairies **2** : FIB

fait ac·com·pli \ˈfāt-ˌa-kōⁿ-ˈplē\ *n, pl* **faits accomplis** *same or* -ˈplēz\ [F, accomplished fact] : a thing accomplished and presumably irreversible

faith \ˈfāth\ *n, pl* **faiths** \ˈfāths, ˈfā<u>th</u>z\ [ME *feith,* fr. OF *feid, foi,* fr. L *fides*] **1** : allegiance to duty or a person : LOYALTY **2** : belief and trust in God **3** : complete trust **4** : a system of religious beliefs — **faith·ful** \-fəl\ *adj* — **faith·ful·ly** *adv* — **faith·ful·ness** *n*

faith·less \ˈfāth-ləs\ *adj* **1** : DISLOYAL **2** : not to be relied on **syn** false, traitorous, treacherous, unfaithful — **faith·less·ly** *adv* — **faith·less·ness** *n*

fa·ji·ta \fə-ˈhē-tə\ *n* : a marinated strip usu. of beef or chicken grilled or broiled and served usu. with a flour tortilla and savory fillings — usu. used in pl.

¹**fake** \ˈfāk\ *adj* : COUNTERFEIT, SHAM

²**fake** *n* **1** : IMITATION, FRAUD; *also* : IMPOSTOR **2** : a simulated move in sports (as a pretended pass)

³**fake** *vb* **faked; fak·ing 1** : to treat so as to falsify **2** : COUNTERFEIT **3** : to deceive (an opponent) in a sports contest by making a fake — **fak·er** *n*

fa·kir \fə-ˈkir\ *n* [Ar *faqīr*, lit., poor man] **1** : a Muslim mendicant : DERVISH **2** : a wandering Hindu ascetic

fal·con \ˈfal-kən, ˈfȯl-\ *n* **1** : a hawk trained for use in falconry **2** : any of various swift long-winged long-tailed hawks having a notched beak and usu. inhabiting open areas

fal·con·ry \ˈfal-kən-rē, ˈfȯl-\ *n* **1** : the art of training hawks to hunt in cooperation with a person **2** : the sport of hunting with hawks — **fal·con·er** *n*

¹**fall** \ˈfȯl\ *vb* **fell** \ˈfel\; **fall·en** \ˈfȯ-lən\; **fall·ing 1** : to de-

scend freely by the force of gravity **2** : to hang freely **3** : to come or go as if by falling ⟨darkness *fell*⟩ **4** : to become uttered **5** : to lower or become lowered : DROP ⟨her eyes *fell*⟩ **6** : to leave an erect position suddenly and involuntarily **7** : STUMBLE, STRAY **8** : to drop down wounded or dead esp. in battle **9** : to become captured ⟨the city *fell* to the enemy⟩ **10** : to suffer ruin, defeat, or failure **11** : to commit an immoral act **12** : to move or extend in a downward direction **13** : SUBSIDE, ABATE **14** : to decline in quality, activity, quantity, or value **15** : to assume a look of shame or dejection ⟨her face *fell*⟩ **16** : to occur at a certain time **17** : to come by chance **18** : DEVOLVE ⟨the duties *fell* to him⟩ **19** : to have the proper place or station ⟨the accent ∼s on the first syllable⟩ **20** : to come within the scope of something **21** : to pass from one condition to another ⟨*fell* ill⟩ **22** : to set about heartily or actively ⟨∼ to work⟩ — **fall flat** : to produce no response or result — **fall for 1** : to fall in love with **2** : to become a victim of — **fall foul** : to have a quarrel : CLASH — **fall from grace** : BACKSLIDE — **fall into line** : to comply with a certain course of action — **fall over oneself** *or* **fall over backward** : to display excessive eagerness — **fall short 1** : to be deficient **2** : to fail to attain

²fall *n* **1** : the act of falling **2** : a falling out, off, or away : DROPPING **3** : AUTUMN **4** : a thing or quantity that falls ⟨a light ∼ of snow⟩ **5** : COLLAPSE, DOWNFALL **6** : the surrender or capture of a besieged place **7** : departure from virtue or goodness **8** : SLOPE **9** : WATERFALL — usu. used in pl. **10** : a decrease in size, quantity, degree, or value ⟨a ∼ in price⟩ **11** : the distance which something falls **12** : an act of forcing a wrestler's shoulders to the mat; *also* : a bout of wrestling

fal·la·cious \fə-ˈlā-shəs\ *adj* **1** : embodying a fallacy ⟨a ∼ argument⟩ **2** : MISLEADING, DECEPTIVE

fal·la·cy \ˈfa-lə-sē\ *n, pl* **-cies 1** : a false or mistaken idea **2** : an often plausible argument using false or illogical reasoning

fall back *vb* : RETREAT, RECEDE

fall guy *n* **1** : one that is easily duped **2** : SCAPEGOAT

fal·li·ble \ˈfa-lə-bəl\ *adj* **1** : liable to be erroneous **2** : capable of making a mistake — **fal·li·bly** \-blē\ *adv*

fall·ing-out \ˌfȯ-liŋ-ˈau̇t\ *n, pl* **fallings-out** *or* **falling-outs** : QUARREL

falling star *n* : METEOR

fal·lo·pi·an tube \fə-ˈlō-pē-ən-\ *n, often cap F* : either of the pair of anatomical tubes that carry the eggs from the ovary to the uterus

fall·out \ˈfȯ-ˌlau̇t\ *n* **1** : the often radioactive particles that result from a nuclear explosion and descend through the air **2** : a secondary and often lingering effect or result

fall out *vb* : QUARREL

¹fal·low \ˈfa-(ˌ)lō\ *n* : fallow land; *also* : the state or period of being fallow — **fallow** *vb*

²fallow *adj* **1** : left without tilling or sowing after plowing **2** : DORMANT, INACTIVE ⟨a writer's ∼ period⟩

false \ˈfȯls\ *adj* **fals·er; fals·est 1** : not genuine : ARTIFICIAL **2** : intentionally untrue **3** : adjusted or made so as to deceive ⟨∼ scales⟩ **4** : tending to mislead : DECEPTIVE ⟨∼ promises⟩ **5** : not true ⟨∼ concepts⟩ **6** : not faithful or loyal : TREACHEROUS **7** : not essential or permanent ⟨∼ front⟩ **8** : inaccurate in pitch **9** : based on mistaken ideas — **false·ly** *adv* — **false·ness** *n* — **fal·si·ty** \ˈfȯl-sə-tē\ *n*

false·hood \ˈfȯls-ˌhu̇d\ *n* **1** : LIE **2** : absence of truth or accuracy **3** : the practice of lying

fal·set·to \fȯl-ˈse-tō\ *n, pl* **-tos** [It, fr. dim. of *falso* false] : an artificially high voice; *esp* : an artificial singing voice that overlaps and extends above the range of the full voice esp. of a tenor

fal·si·fy \ˈfȯl-sə-ˌfī\ *vb* **-fied; -fy·ing 1** : to prove to be false **2** : to alter so as to deceive **3** : LIE; *also* : MISREPRESENT — **fal·si·fi·ca·tion** \ˌfȯl-sə-fə-ˈkā-shən\ *n*

fal·ter \ˈfȯl-tər\ *vb* **1** : to move unsteadily : STUMBLE, TOTTER **2** : to hesitate in speech : STAMMER **3** : to hesitate in purpose or action : WAVER, FLINCH — **fal·ter·ing·ly** *adv*

fam *abbr* **1** familiar **2** family

fame \ˈfām\ *n* : public reputation : RENOWN — **famed** \ˈfāmd\ *adj*

fa·mil·ial \fə-ˈmil-yəl\ *adj* **1** : of, relating to, or suggestive of a family **2** : tending to occur in more members of a family than expected by chance alone ⟨a ∼ disorder⟩

¹fa·mil·iar \fə-ˈmil-yər\ *n* **1** : COMPANION **2** : a spirit held to attend and serve or guard a person **3** : one who frequents a place

²familiar *adj* **1** : closely acquainted : INTIMATE **2** : of or relating to a family **3** : INFORMAL **4** : FORWARD, PRESUMPTUOUS **5** : frequently seen or experienced **6** : of everyday occurrence — **fa·mil·iar·ly** *adv*

fa·mil·iar·i·ty \fə-ˌmil-ˈyar-ə-tē, -ˌmi-lē-ˈar-\ *n, pl* **-ties 1** : close friendship : INTIMACY **2** : INFORMALITY **3** : an unduly bold or forward act or expression : IMPROPRIETY **4** : close acquaintance with something

fa·mil·iar·ize \fə-ˈmil-yə-ˌrīz\ *vb* **-ized; -iz·ing 1** : to make known or familiar **2** : to make thoroughly acquainted

fam·i·ly \ˈfam-lē, ˈfa-mə-\ *n, pl* **-lies** [ME *familie*, fr. L *familia* household, fr. *famulus* servant] **1** : a group of individuals living under one roof and under one head : HOUSEHOLD **2** : a group of persons of common ancestry : CLAN **3** : a group of things having common characteristics; *esp* : a group of related plants or animals ranking in biological classification above a genus and below an order **4** : a social unit usu. consisting of one or two parents and their children

family planning *n* : planning intended to determine the number and spacing of one's children by using birth control

family tree *n* : GENEALOGY; *also* : a genealogical diagram

fam·ine \ˈfa-mən\ *n* **1** : an extreme scarcity of food **2** : a great shortage

fam·ish \ˈfa-mish\ *vb* **1** : STARVE **2** : to suffer for lack of something necessary

fa·mous \ˈfā-məs\ *adj* **1** : widely known **2** : honored for achievement **3** : EXCELLENT, FIRST-RATE **syn** renowned, celebrated, noted, notorious, distinguished, eminent, illustrious

fa·mous·ly *adv* : SPLENDIDLY, EXCELLENTLY

¹fan \ˈfan\ *n* : a device (as a hand-waved triangular piece or a mechanism with blades) for producing a current of air

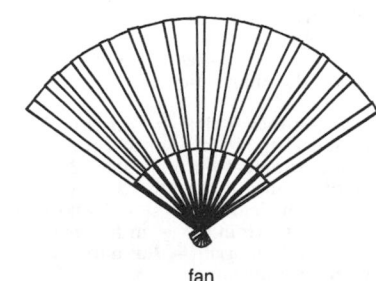

fan

²**fan** *vb* **fanned; fan·ning 1 :** to drive away the chaff from grain by winnowing **2 :** to move (air) with or as if with a fan **3 :** to direct a current of air upon ⟨~ a fire⟩ **4 :** to stir up to activity **:** STIMULATE **5 :** to spread like a fan **6 :** to strike out in baseball

³**fan** *n* **:** an enthusiastic follower or admirer

fa·nat·ic \fə-'na-tik\ *or* **fa·nat·i·cal** \-ti-kəl\ *adj* [L *fanaticus* inspired by a deity, frenzied, fr. *fanum* temple] **:** marked by excessive enthusiasm and often intense uncritical devotion — **fanatic** *n* — **fa·nat·i·cism** \-tə-ˌsi-zəm\ *n*

fan·ci·er \'fan-sē-ər\ *n* **1 :** one that has a special liking or interest **2 :** a person who breeds or grows some kind of animal or plant for points of excellence

fan·ci·ful \'fan-si-fəl\ *adj* **1 :** marked by, existing in, or given to unrestrained imagination or whim rather than reason **2 :** curiously made or shaped — **fan·ci·ful·ly** *adv*

¹**fan·cy** \'fan-sē\ *vb* **fan·cied; fan·cy·ing 1 :** LIKE **2 :** IMAGINE **3 :** to believe without evidence or certainty **4 :** to visualize or interpret as

²**fancy** *n, pl* **fancies** [ME *fantasie, fantsy* fantasy, fancy, fr. MF *fantasie*, fr. L *phantasia*, fr. Gk, appearance, imagination] **1 :** LIKING, INCLINATION; *also* **:** LOVE **2 :** WHIM, NOTION, IDEA ⟨a passing ~⟩ **3 :** IMAGINATION **4 :** TASTE, JUDGMENT **syn** caprice, crotchet, vagary

³**fancy** *adj* **fan·ci·er; -est 1 :** WHIMSICAL **2 :** not plain **:** ORNAMENTAL, POSH **3 :** of particular excellence **4 :** bred esp. for a showy appearance **5 :** EXCESSIVE **6 :** executed with technical skill and style — **fan·ci·ly** \'fan-sə-lē\ *adv*

fancy dress *n* **:** a costume (as for a masquerade) chosen to suit a fancy

fan·cy–free \ˌfan-sē-'frē\ *adj* **:** free from amorous attachment; *also* **:** free to imagine

fan·cy·work \'fan-sē-ˌwərk\ *n* **:** ornamental needlework (as embroidery)

fan·dan·go \fan-'daŋ-gō\ *n, pl* **-gos 1 :** a lively Spanish or Spanish-American dance **2 :** TOMFOOLERY

fane \'fān\ *n* **1 :** TEMPLE **2 :** CHURCH

fan·fare \'fan-ˌfar\ *n* **1 :** a flourish of trumpets **2 :** a showy display

fang \'faŋ\ *n* **:** a long sharp tooth; *esp* **:** a grooved or hollow tooth of a venomous snake — **fanged** \'faŋd\ *adj*

fan·light \'fan-ˌlīt\ *n* **:** a semicircular window with radiating bars like a fan that is set over a door or window

fan·tail \'fan-ˌtāl\ *n* **1 :** a fan-shaped tail or end **2 :** an overhang at the stern of a ship

fan·ta·sia \fan-'tā-zhə, -zhē-ə, -zē-ə; ˌfan-tə-'zē-ə\ *n* **:** a musical composition free and fanciful in form

fan·ta·size \'fan-tə-ˌsīz\ *vb* **-sized; -siz·ing :** IMAGINE, DAYDREAM

fan·tas·tic \fan-'tas-tik\ *also* **fan·tas·ti·cal** \-ti-kəl\ *adj* **1 :** IMAGINARY, UNREAL **2 :** conceived by unrestrained fancy **3 :** exceedingly or unbelievably great **4 :** ECCENTRIC **syn** chimerical, fanciful, imaginary — **fan·tas·ti·cal·ly** \-ti-k(ə-)lē\ *adv*

fan·ta·sy \'fan-tə-sē\ *n, pl* **-sies 1 :** IMAGINATION, FANCY **2 :** a product of the imagination **:** ILLUSION **3 :** FANTASIA — **fantasy** *vb*

¹**far** \'fär\ *adv* **far·ther** \-thər\ *or* **fur·ther** \'fər-\; **far·thest** *or* **fur·thest** \-thəst\ **1 :** at or to a considerable distance in space or time ⟨~ from home⟩ **2 :** by a broad interval **:** WIDELY, MUCH ⟨~ better⟩ **3 :** to or at a definite distance, point, or degree ⟨as ~ as I know⟩ **4 :** to an advanced point or extent ⟨go ~ in his field⟩ — **by far :** by a considerable margin — **far and away :** DECIDEDLY — **so far :** until now

²**far** *adj* **farther** *or* **further; farthest** *or* **furthest 1 :** remote in space or time **2 :** DIFFERENT **3 :** LONG ⟨a ~ journey⟩ **4 :** being the more distant of two ⟨on the ~ side of the lake⟩

far·ad \'far-ˌad, -əd\ *n* **:** a unit of capacitance equal to the capacitance of a capacitor having a potential difference of one volt between its plates when it is charged with one coulomb of electricity

far·away \'fär-ə-ˌwä\ *adj* **1 :** DISTANT, REMOTE **2 :** DREAMY

farce \'färs\ *n* **1 :** a broadly satirical comedy with an improbable plot **2 :** the humor characteristic of farce or pretense **3 :** a ridiculous or empty display — **far·ci·cal** \'fär-si-kəl\ *adj*

¹**fare** \'far\ *vb* **fared; far·ing 1 :** GO, TRAVEL **2 :** GET ALONG, SUCCEED **3 :** EAT, DINE

²**fare** *n* **1 :** range of food **:** DIET; *also* **:** material provided for use, consumption, or enjoyment **2 :** the price charged to transport a person **:** a person paying a fare **:** PASSENGER

¹**fare·well** \far-'wel\ *vb imper* **:** get along well — used interjectionally to or by one departing

²**farewell** *n* **1 :** a wish of well-being at parting **:** GOOD-BYE **2 :** LEAVE-TAKING

³**fare·well** \'far-ˌwel\ *adj* **:** PARTING, FINAL ⟨a ~ concert⟩

far–fetched \'fär-'fecht\ *adj* **:** not easily or naturally deduced or introduced **:** IMPROBABLE ⟨~ story⟩

far–flung \-'fləŋ\ *adj* **:** widely spread or distributed

fa·ri·na \fə-'rē-nə\ *n* [L, meal, flour] **:** a fine meal (as of wheat) used in puddings or as a breakfast cereal

far·i·na·ceous \ˌfar-ə-'nā-shəs\ *adj* **1 :** having a mealy texture or surface **2 :** containing or rich in starch

¹**farm** \'färm\ *n* [ME *ferme* rent, lease, fr. OF, lease, fr. *fermer* to fix, make a contract, fr. L *firmare* to make firm, fr. *firmus* firm] **1 :** a tract of land used for raising crops or livestock **2 :** a minor-league subsidiary of a major-league baseball team

²**farm** *vb* **:** to use (land) as a farm ⟨~ed 200 acres⟩; *also* **:** to raise crops or livestock — **farm·er** *n*

farm·hand \'färm-ˌhand\ *n* **:** a farm laborer

farm·house \-ˌhaùs\ *n* **:** a dwelling on a farm

farm·ing \'fär-miŋ\ *n* **:** the occupation or business of a person who farms

farm·land \'färm-ˌland\ *n* **:** land used or suitable for farming

farm out *vb* **:** to turn over (as a task) to another

farm·stead \'färm-ˌsted\ *n* **:** a farm with its buildings

farm·yard \-ˌyärd\ *n* **:** land around or enclosed by farm buildings

far–off \'fär-'òf\ *adj* **:** remote in time or space **:** DISTANT

fa·rouche \fə-'rüsh\ *adj* [F] **1 :** WILD **2 :** marked by shyness and lack of polish

far–out \'fär-'aùt\ *adj* **:** very unconventional ⟨~ clothes⟩

far·ra·go \fə-'rä-gō, -'rā-\ *n, pl* **-goes** [L, mixed fodder, mixture] **:** a confused collection **:** MIXTURE

far–reach·ing \'fär-'rē-chiŋ\ *adj* **:** having a wide range or effect

far·ri·er \'far-ē-ər\ *n* **:** a person who shoes horses

¹**far·row** \'far-ō\ *vb* **:** to give birth to a litter of pigs

²**farrow** *n* **:** a litter of pigs

far·see·ing \'fär-ˌsē-iŋ\ *adj* **:** FARSIGHTED 1, 2

far·sight·ed \'fär-ˌsī-təd\ *adj* **1 :** seeing or able to see to a great distance **2 :** JUDICIOUS, WISE, SHREWD **3 :** affected with an eye condition in which vision is better for distant than near objects — **far·sight·ed·ness** *n*

¹**far·ther** \'fär-thər\ *adv* **1 :** at or to a greater distance or more advanced point **2 :** to a greater degree or extent

²**farther** *adj* **1 :** more distant **2 :** ADDITIONAL

far·ther·most \-ˌmōst\ *adj* **:** FARTHEST

¹**far·thest** \'fär-thəst\ *adj* **:** most distant

²**farthest** *adv* **1 :** to or at the greatest distance **:** REMOTEST **2 :** to the most advanced point **3 :** by the greatest degree or extent **:** MOST

far·thing \'fär-thiŋ\ *n* **1 :** a former British monetary unit equal to ¼ of a penny; *also* **:** a coin representing this unit **2 :** something of small value

fas·ci·cle \'fa-si-kəl\ *n* **1 :** a small or slender bundle (as of pine needles or nerve fiber) **2 :** one of the divisions of a book published in parts — **fas·ci·cled** \-kəld\ *adj*

fas·ci·nate \'fas-ᵊn-ˌāt\ *vb* **-nat·ed; -nat·ing** [L *fascinare*, fr. *fascinum* evil spell] **1 :** to transfix and hold spellbound by an irresistible power **2 :** ALLURE **3 :** to be irresistibly attractive — **fas·ci·na·tion** \ˌfas-ᵊn-'ā-shən\ *n*

fas·cism \'fa-ˌshi-zəm\ *n, often cap* **:** a political philosophy, movement, or regime that exalts nation and often race and stands for a centralized autocratic often militaristic government — **fas·cist** \-shist\ *n or adj, often cap* — **fas·cis·tic** \fa-'shis-tik\ *adj, often cap*

¹fash·ion \'fa-shən\ *n* **1 :** the make or form of something **2 :** MANNER, WAY **3 :** a prevailing custom, usage, or style **4 :** the prevailing style (as in dress) **syn** mode, vogue, rage, trend

²fashion *vb* **1 :** MOLD, CONSTRUCT **2 :** FIT, ADAPT

fash·ion·able \'fa-shə-nə-bəl\ *adj* **1 :** dressing or behaving according to fashion **:** STYLISH **2 :** of or relating to the world of fashion 〈∼ resorts〉 **syn** chic, modish, smart, swank — **fash·ion·ably** \-blē\ *adv*

¹fast \'fast\ *adj* **1 :** firmly fixed **2 :** tightly shut **3 :** adhering firmly **4 :** STUCK **5 :** STAUNCH 〈∼ friends〉 **6 :** characterized by quick motion, operation, or effect 〈a ∼ trip〉 〈a ∼ track〉 **7 :** indicating ahead of the correct time 〈the clock is ∼〉 **8 :** not easily disturbed **:** SOUND 〈a ∼ sleep〉 **9 :** permanently dyed; *also* **:** being proof against fading 〈colors ∼ to sunlight〉 **10 :** DISSIPATED, WILD **11 :** sexually promiscuous **syn** rapid, swift, fleet, quick, speedy, hasty

²fast *adv* **1 :** in a firm or fixed manner 〈stuck ∼ in the mud〉 **2 :** SOUNDLY, DEEPLY 〈∼ asleep〉 **3 :** SWIFTLY **4 :** RECKLESSLY

³fast *vb* **1 :** to abstain from food **2 :** to eat sparingly or abstain from some foods

⁴fast *n* **1 :** the act or practice of fasting **2 :** a time of fasting

fast·back \'fast-ˌbak\ *n* **:** an automobile having a roof with a long slope to the rear

fast·ball \-ˌbȯl\ *n* **:** a baseball pitch thrown at full speed

fas·ten \'fas-ᵊn\ *vb* **1 :** to attach or join by or as if by pinning, tying, or nailing **2 :** to make fast **:** fix securely **3 :** to become fixed or joined **4 :** to focus attention 〈∼ed onto the newest trends〉 — **fas·ten·er** *n*

fas·ten·ing *n* **:** something that fastens **:** FASTENER

fast–food \ˌfast–'füd\ *adj* **:** specializing in food that is prepared and served quickly 〈a ∼ restaurant〉

fast–for·ward \-'fȯr-wərd\ *n* **1 :** a function of a tape player that advances tape rapidly **2 :** a state of rapid advancement — **fast–forward** *vb*

fas·tid·i·ous \fa-'sti-dē-əs\ *adj* **1 :** overly difficult to please **2 :** showing a meticulous or demanding attitude 〈∼ workmanship〉 **syn** nice, finicky, fussy, particular, persnickety, squeamish — **fas·tid·i·ous·ly** *adv* — **fas·tid·i·ous·ness** *n*

fast·ness \'fast-nəs\ *n* **1 :** the quality or state of being fast **2 :** a fortified or secure place **:** STRONGHOLD

fast–talk \'fast-ˌtȯk\ *vb* **:** to influence by persuasive and usu. deceptive talk

fast–track \'fast-ˌtrak\ *vb* **:** to speed up the processing or production of

fast track *n* **:** a course leading to rapid advancement or success

¹fat \'fat\ *adj* **fat·ter; fat·test** **1 :** PLUMP, FLESHY **2 :** OILY, GREASY **3 :** well filled out **:** BIG **4 :** well stocked **:** ABUNDANT **5 :** richly rewarding — **fat·ness** *n*

²fat *n* **1 :** animal tissue rich in greasy or oily matter **2 :** any of numerous energy-rich esters that occur naturally in animal fats and in plants and are soluble in organic solvents (as ether) but not in water **3 :** the best or richest portion 〈lived on the ∼ of the land〉 **4 :** OBESITY **5 :** excess matter

fa·tal \'fāt-ᵊl\ *adj* **1 :** FATEFUL 〈that ∼ day〉 **2 :** causing death or ruin 〈a ∼ mistake〉 — **fa·tal·ly** *adv*

fa·tal·ism \-ˌi-zəm\ *n* **:** the belief that events are deter-

mined by fate — **fa·tal·ist** \-ist\ *n* — **fa·tal·is·tic** \ˌfāt-ᵊl-'is-tik\ *adj* — **fa·tal·is·ti·cal·ly** \-ti-k(ə-)lē\ *adv*

fa·tal·i·ty \fā-'ta-lə-tē, fə-\ *n, pl* **-ties** **1 :** DEADLINESS **2 :** FATE **3 :** death resulting from a disaster or accident; *also* **:** one who suffers such a death

fat·back \'fat-ˌbak\ *n* **:** a fatty strip from the back of the hog usu. cured by salting and drying

fat cat *n* **1 :** a wealthy contributor to a political campaign **2 :** a wealthy privileged person

fate \'fāt\ *n* [ME, fr. MF or L; MF, fr. L *fatum*, lit., what has been spoken, fr. *fari* to speak] **1 :** the cause or will that is held to determine events **:** DESTINY **2 :** LOT, FORTUNE **3 :** DISASTER; *esp* **:** DEATH **4 :** END, OUTCOME **5** *cap, pl* **:** the three goddesses of classical mythology who determine the course of human life

fat·ed \'fā-təd\ *adj* **:** decreed, controlled, or marked by fate

fate·ful \'fāt-fəl\ *adj* **1 :** OMINOUS, PROPHETIC **2 :** IMPORTANT, DECISIVE **3 :** DEADLY, DESTRUCTIVE **4 :** determined by fate — **fate·ful·ly** *adv*

fath *abbr* fathom

fat·head \'fat-ˌhed\ *n* **:** a stupid person — **fat·head·ed** \-'he-dəd\ *adj*

¹fa·ther \'fä-thər\ *n* **1 :** a male parent **2** *cap* **:** God esp. as the first person of the Trinity **3 :** FOREFATHER **4 :** one deserving the respect and love given to a father **5** *often cap* **:** an early Christian writer accepted by the church as an authoritative witness to its teaching and practice **6 :** ORIGINATOR 〈the ∼ of modern radio〉; *also* **:** SOURCE **7 :** PRIEST — used esp. as a title **8 :** one of the leading men 〈city ∼s〉 — **fa·ther·hood** \-ˌhu̇d\ *n* — **fa·ther·less** *adj* — **fa·ther·ly** *adj*

²father *vb* **1 :** BEGET **2 :** to be the founder, producer, or author of **3 :** to treat or care for as a father

father–in–law \'fä-thə-rən-ˌlȯ\ *n, pl* **fa·thers–in–law** \-thər-zən-\ **:** the father of one's husband or wife

fa·ther·land \'fä-thər-ˌland\ *n* **1 :** the native land of one's ancestors **2 :** one's native land

¹fath·om \'fa-thəm\ *n* [ME *fadme*, fr. OE *fæthm* outstretched arms, fathom] **:** a unit of length equal to 6 feet (about 1.8 meters) used esp. for measuring the depth of water

²fathom *vb* **1 :** to measure by a sounding line **2 :** PROBE **3 :** to penetrate and come to understand — **fath·om·able** \'fa-thə-mə-bəl\ *adj*

fath·om·less \'fa-thəm-ləs\ *adj* **:** incapable of being fathomed

¹fa·tigue \fə-'tēg\ *n* [F] **1 :** manual or menial work performed by military personnel **2** *pl* **:** the uniform or work clothing worn on fatigue and in the field **3 :** weariness from labor or stress **4 :** the tendency of a material to break under repeated stress

²fatigue *vb* **fa·tigued; fa·tigu·ing** **:** WEARY, TIRE

fat·ten \'fat-ᵊn\ *vb* **:** to make or grow fat

¹fat·ty \'fa-tē\ *adj* **fat·ti·er; -est** **1 :** containing fat esp. in unusual amounts **2 :** GREASY

²fatty *n, pl* **fat·ties** **:** a fat person

fatty acid *n* **:** any of numerous acids that contain only carbon, hydrogen, and oxygen and that occur naturally in fats and various oils

fa·tu·ity \fə-'tü-ə-tē, -'tyü-\ *n, pl* **-ities** **:** FOOLISHNESS, STUPIDITY

fat·u·ous \'fa-chu̇-wəs\ *adj* **:** FOOLISH, INANE, SILLY — **fat·u·ous·ly** *adv*

fau·bourg \fō-'bu̇r\ *n* **1 :** a suburb esp. of a French city **2 :** a city quarter

fau·ces \'fȯ-ˌsēz\ *n pl* [L, throat] **:** the narrow passage

\ə\abut \ᵊ\kitten \ər\further \a\ash \ā\ace \ä\mop, mar
\au̇\out \ch\chin \e\bet \ē\easy \g\go \i\hit \ī\ice \j\job
\ŋ\sing \ō\go \ȯ\law \ȯi\boy \th\thin \th\the \ü\loot \u̇\foot
\y\yet \zh\vision *see also* Pronunciation Symbols page

located between the soft palate and the base of the tongue that joins the mouth to the pharynx

fau·cet \'fȯ-sət, 'fä-\ *n* : a fixture for drawing off a liquid (as from a pipe)

¹fault \'fȯlt\ *n* **1** : a weakness in character : FAILING **2** : IMPERFECTION, IMPAIRMENT, DEFECT **3** : an error esp. in service in a net or racket game **4** : MISDEMEANOR; *also* : MISTAKE **5** : responsibility for something wrong **6** : a fracture in the earth's crust accompanied by a displacement of one side relative to the other — **fault·i·ly** \'fȯl-tə-lē\ *adv* — **fault·less** *adj* — **fault·less·ly** *adv* — **faulty** *adj*

²fault *vb* **1** : to commit a fault : ERR **2** : to fracture so as to produce a geologic fault **3** : to find a fault in

fault·find·er \'fȯlt-ˌfīn-dər\ *n* : a person who tends to find fault or complain **syn** critic, carper, caviler, complainer — **fault·find·ing** *n or adj*

faun \'fȯn\ *n* : a Roman god similar to but gentler than a satyr

fau·na \'fȯ-nə\ *n, pl* **faunas** *also* **fau·nae** \-ˌnē, -ˌnī\ [NL, fr. L *Fauna*, sister of Faunus (the Roman god of animals)] : animals or animal life esp. of a region, period, or environment — **fau·nal** \-nəl\ *adj*

fau·vism \'fō-ˌvi-zəm\ *n, often cap* : a movement in painting characterized by vivid colors, free treatment of form, and a vibrant and decorative effect — **fau·vist** \-vist\ *n, often cap*

faux pas \'fō-ˌpä, fo-'\ *n, pl* **faux pas** *same or* -ˌpäz, -'päz\ [F, lit., false step] : BLUNDER; *esp* : a social blunder

¹fa·vor \'fā-vər\ *n* **1** : friendly regard shown toward another esp. by a superior **2** : APPROVAL **3** : PARTIALITY **4** : POPULARITY **5** : gracious kindness; *also* : an act of such kindness **6** *pl* : effort in one's behalf : ATTENTION **7** : a token of love (as a ribbon) usu. worn conspicuously **8** : a small gift or decorative item given out at a party **9** : a special privilege **10** : sexual privileges — usu. used in pl. **11** *archaic* : LETTER **12** : BEHALF, INTEREST

²favor *vb* **1** : to regard or treat with favor **2** : OBLIGE **3** : ENDOW ⟨∼ed by nature⟩ **4** : to treat gently or carefully : SPARE ⟨∼ a lame leg⟩ **5** : PREFER **6** : SUPPORT, SUSTAIN **7** : FACILITATE ⟨darkness ∼s attack⟩ **8** : RESEMBLE ⟨he ∼s his father⟩

fa·vor·able \'fā-və-rə-bəl\ *adj* **1** : APPROVING **2** : HELPFUL, PROMISING, ADVANTAGEOUS ⟨∼ weather⟩ — **fa·vor·ably** \-blē\ *adv*

fa·vor·ite \'fā-və-rət, -vrət\ *n* **1** : a person or a thing that is favored above others **2** : a competitor regarded as most likely to win — **favorite** *adj*

favorite son *n* : a candidate supported by the delegates of his state at a presidential nominating convention

fa·vor·it·ism \'fā-və-rə-ˌti-zəm\ *n* : PARTIALITY, BIAS

fa·vour *chiefly Brit var of* FAVOR

¹fawn \'fȯn, 'fän\ *vb* **1** : to show affection ⟨a dog ∼ing on its master⟩ **2** : to court favor by a cringing or flattering manner **syn** grovel, kowtow, toady, truckle

²fawn *n* **1** : a young deer **2** : a light grayish brown

fax \'faks\ *n* **1** : FACSIMILE 2 **2** : a device used to send or receive facsimile communications; *also* : such a communication — **fax** *vb*

fay \'fā\ *n* : FAIRY, ELF — **fay** *adj*

faze \'fāz\ *vb* **fazed; faz·ing** : to disturb the composure or courage of : DAUNT

FBI *abbr* Federal Bureau of Investigation

FCC *abbr* Federal Communications Commission

FD *abbr* fire department

FDA *abbr* Food and Drug Administration

FDIC *abbr* Federal Deposit Insurance Corporation

Fe *symbol* [L *ferrum*] iron

fe·al·ty \'fēl-tē\ *n, pl* **-ties** : LOYALTY, ALLEGIANCE **syn** fidelity, devotion, faithfulness, piety

¹fear \'fir\ *vb* **1** : to have a reverent awe of ⟨∼ God⟩ **2** : to be afraid of : have fear **3** : to be apprehensive

²fear *n* **1** : an unpleasant often strong emotion caused by expectation or awareness of danger; *also* : an instance of or a state marked by this emotion **2** : anxious concern : SOLICITUDE **3** : profound reverence esp. toward God **syn** dread, fright, alarm, panic, terror, trepidation

fear·ful \-fəl\ *adj* **1** : causing fear **2** : filled with fear **3** : showing or caused by fear **4** : extremely bad, intense, or large — **fear·ful·ly** *adv*

fear·less \-ləs\ *adj* : free from fear : BRAVE — **fear·less·ly** *adv* — **fear·less·ness** *n*

fear·some \-səm\ *adj* **1** : causing fear **2** : TIMID

fea·si·ble \'fē-zə-bəl\ *adj* **1** : capable of being done or carried out ⟨a ∼ plan⟩ **2** : SUITABLE **3** : REASONABLE, LIKELY **syn** possible, practicable, viable, workable — **fea·si·bil·i·ty** \ˌfē-zə-'bi-lə-tē\ *n* — **fea·si·bly** \'fē-zə-blē\ *adv*

¹feast \'fēst\ *n* **1** : an elaborate meal : BANQUET **2** : FESTIVAL 1

²feast *vb* **1** : to take part in a feast; *also* : to give a feast for **2** : to enjoy some unusual pleasure or delight **3** : DELIGHT, GRATIFY

feat \'fēt\ *n* : DEED, EXPLOIT, ACHIEVEMENT; *esp* : an act notable for courage, skill, endurance, or ingenuity

¹feath·er \'fe-thər\ *n* **1** : any of the light horny outgrowths that form the external covering of the body of a bird **2** : PLUME **3** : PLUMAGE **4** : KIND, NATURE ⟨birds of a ∼⟩ **5** : ATTIRE, DRESS ⟨in full ∼⟩ **6** : CONDITION, MOOD ⟨in fine ∼⟩ — **feath·ered** \-thərd\ *adj* — **feath·er·less** *adj* — **feath·ery** *adj* — **a feather in one's cap** : a mark of distinction : HONOR

²feather *vb* **1** : to furnish with a feather ⟨∼ an arrow⟩ **2** : to cover, clothe, line, or adorn with or as if with feathers — **feather one's nest** : to provide for oneself esp. while in a position of trust

feath·er·bed·ding \'fe-thər-ˌbe-diŋ\ *n* : the requiring of an employer usu. under a union rule or safety statute to employ more workers than are needed

feath·er·edge \-ˌej\ *n* : a very thin sharp edge

feath·er·weight \-ˌwāt\ *n* : one that is very light in weight; *esp* : a boxer weighing more than 118 but not over 126 pounds

¹fea·ture \'fē-chər\ *n* **1** : the shape or appearance of the face or its parts **2** : a part of the face : LINEAMENT **3** : a prominent part or characteristic **4** : a special attraction (as in a newspaper) **5** : something offered to the public or advertised as particularly attractive — **fea·ture·less** *adj*

²feature *vb* **1** : to picture in the mind : IMAGINE **2** : to give special prominence to ⟨∼ a story in a newspaper⟩ **3** : to play an important part

feaze \'fēz, 'fāz\ *var of* FAZE

Feb *abbr* February

fe·brile \'fe-ˌbrīl\ *adj* : FEVERISH

Feb·ru·ary \'fe-b(y)ə-ˌwer-ē, 'fe-brə-\ *n* [ME *Februarie*, fr. L *Februarius*, fr. *Februa*, pl., feast of purification] : the second month of the year having 28 and in leap years 29 days

fe·ces \'fē-ˌsēz\ *n pl* : bodily waste discharged from the intestine — **fe·cal** \-kəl\ *adj*

feck·less \'fek-ləs\ *adj* **1** : WEAK, INEFFECTIVE **2** : WORTHLESS, IRRESPONSIBLE

fe·cund \'fe-kənd, 'fē-\ *adj* : FRUITFUL, PROLIFIC — **fe·cun·di·ty** \fi-'kən-də-tē, fe-\ *n*

fe·cun·date \'fe-kən-ˌdāt, 'fē-\ *vb* **-dat·ed; -dat·ing 1** : to make fecund **2** : IMPREGNATE — **fe·cun·da·tion** \ˌfe-kən-'dā-shən, ˌfē-\ *n*

fed *abbr* federal; federation

fed·er·al \'fe-də-rəl, -drəl\ *adj* **1** : formed by a compact between political units that surrender individual sovereignty to a central authority but retain certain limited powers **2** : of or constituting a form of government in which power is distributed between a central authority and constituent territorial units **3** : of or relating to the central government of a federation **4** *cap* : FEDERALIST **5** *often cap* : of, relating to, or loyal to the federal government or the Union armies of the U.S. in the American Civil War — **fed·er·al·ly** *adv*

Federal *n* : a supporter of the U.S. government in the Civil War; *esp* : a soldier in the federal armies

federal district *n* : a district (as the District of Columbia) set apart as the seat of the central government of a federation

fed·er·al·ism \'fe-də-rə-li-zəm, -drə-\ *n* **1** *often cap* : the distribution of power in an organization (as a government) between a central authority and the constituent units **2** : support or advocacy of federalism **3** *cap* : the principles of the Federalists

fed·er·al·ist \-list\ *n* **1** : an advocate of federalism **2** *often cap* : an advocate of a federal union between the American colonies after the Revolution and of adoption of the U.S. Constitution **3** *cap* : a member of a major political party in the early years of the U.S. favoring a strong centralized national government — **federalist** *adj, often cap*

fed·er·al·ize \'fe-də-rə-ˌlīz, -drə-\ *vb* **-ized; -iz·ing 1** : to unite in or under a federal system **2** : to bring under the jurisdiction of a federal government

fed·er·ate \'fe-də-ˌrāt\ *vb* **-at·ed; -at·ing** : to join in a federation

fed·er·a·tion \ˌfe-də-'rā-shən\ *n* **1** : the act of federating; *esp* : the forming of a federal union **2** : a federal government **3** : a union of organizations

fedn *abbr* federation

fe·do·ra \fi-'dōr-ə\ *n* : a low soft felt hat with the crown creased lengthwise

fed up *adj* : satiated, tired, or disgusted beyond endurance

fee \'fē\ *n* **1** : an estate in land held from a feudal lord **2** : an inherited or heritable estate in land **3** : a fixed charge; *also* : a charge for a service

fee·ble \'fē-bəl\ *adj* **fee·bler** \-bə-lər\; **fee·blest** \-bə-ləst\ [ME *feble*, fr. OF, fr. L *flebilis* lamentable, wretched, fr. *flēre* to weep] **1** : DECREPIT, FRAIL **2** : INEFFECTIVE, INADEQUATE ⟨a ~ protest⟩ — **fee·ble·ness** *n* — **fee·bly** \-blē\ *adv*

fee·ble·mind·ed \ˌfē-bəl-'mīn-dəd\ *adj* : lacking normal intelligence — **fee·ble·mind·ed·ness** *n*

¹feed \'fēd\ *vb* **fed** \'fed\; **feed·ing 1** : to give food to; *also* : to give as food **2** : EAT 1; *also* : PREY **3** : to furnish what is necessary to the growth or function of — **feed·er** *n*

²feed *n* **1** : a usu. large meal **2** : food for livestock **3** : a mechanism for feeding material to a machine

feed·back \'fēd-ˌbak\ *n* **1** : the return to the input of a part of the output of a machine, system, or process **2** : response esp. to one in authority about an activity or policy

feed·lot \'fēd-ˌlät\ *n* : land on which cattle are fattened for market

feed·stuff \-ˌstəf\ *n* : FEED 2

¹feel \'fēl\ *vb* **felt** \'felt\; **feel·ing 1** : to perceive or examine through physical contact : TOUCH, HANDLE **2** : EXPERIENCE; *also* : to suffer from **3** : to ascertain by cautious trial ⟨~ out public sentiment⟩ **4** : to be aware of **5** : to be conscious of an inward impression, state of mind, or physical condition **6** : BELIEVE, THINK **7** : to search for something with the fingers : GROPE **8** : SEEM ⟨it ~s like spring⟩ **9** : to have sympathy or pity

²feel *n* **1** : the sense of touch **2** : SENSATION, FEELING **3** : the quality of a thing as imparted through touch

feel·er \'fē-lər\ *n* **1** : one that feels; *esp* : a tactile organ (as on the head of an insect) **2** : a proposal or remark made to find out the views of other people

¹feel·ing \'fē-liŋ\ *n* **1** : the sense of touch; *also* : a sensation perceived by this **2** : a state of mind ⟨a ~ of lone-

liness⟩ **3** *pl* : general emotional condition : SENSIBILITIES ⟨hurt their ~s⟩ **4** : OPINION, BELIEF **5** : capacity to respond emotionally

²feeling *adj* **1** : SENSITIVE; *esp* : easily moved emotionally **2** : expressing emotion or sensitivity — **feel·ing·ly** *adv*

feet *pl of* FOOT

feign \'fān\ *vb* **1** : to give a false appearance of : SHAM ⟨~ illness⟩ **2** : to assert as if true : PRETEND

feint \'fānt\ *n* : something feigned; *esp* : a mock blow or attack intended to distract attention from the real point of attack — **feint** *vb*

feld·spar \'feld-ˌspär\ *n* : any of a group of crystalline minerals consisting of silicates of aluminum with another element (as potassium or sodium)

fe·lic·i·tate \fi-'li-sə-ˌtāt\ *vb* **-tat·ed; -tat·ing** : CONGRATULATE — **fe·lic·i·ta·tion** \-ˌli-sə-'tā-shən\ *n*

fe·lic·i·tous \fi-'li-sə-təs\ *adj* **1** : suitably expressed : APT **2** : PLEASANT, DELIGHTFUL — **fe·lic·i·tous·ly** *adv*

fe·lic·i·ty \fi-'li-sə-tē\ *n, pl* **-ties 1** : the quality or state of being happy; *esp* : great happiness **2** : something that causes happiness **3** : a pleasing manner or quality esp. in art or language **4** : an apt expression

fe·line \'fē-ˌlīn\ *adj* [L *felinus*, fr. *felis* cat] **1** : of or relating to cats or their kin **2** : SLY, TREACHEROUS **3** : STEALTHY — **feline** *n*

¹fell \'fel\ *n* : SKIN, HIDE, PELT

²fell *vb* **1** : to cut, beat, or knock down; *also* : KILL **2** : to sew (a seam) by folding one raw edge under the other

³fell *past of* FALL

⁴fell *adj* : CRUEL, FIERCE; *also* : DEADLY

fel·lah \'fe-lə, fə-'lä\ *n, pl* **fel·la·hin** *or* **fel·la·heen** \ˌfe-lə-'hēn\ : a peasant or agricultural laborer in Arab countries (as Egypt or Syria)

fel·la·tio \fə-'lā-shē-ˌō\ *also* **fel·la·tion** \-shən\ *n* : oral stimulation of the penis

fel·low \'fe-lō\ *n* [ME *felawe*, fr. OE *fēolaga*, fr. ON *fēlagi*, fr. *fēlag* partnership, fr. *fē* cattle, money + *lag* act of laying] **1** : COMRADE, ASSOCIATE **2** : EQUAL, PEER **3** : one of a pair : MATE **4** : a member of an incorporated literary or scientific society **5** : MAN, BOY **6** : BOYFRIEND **7** : a person granted a stipend for advanced study

fel·low·man \ˌfe-lō-'man\ *n* : a kindred human being

fel·low·ship \'fe-lō-ˌship\ *n* **1** : the condition of friendly relationship existing among persons : COMRADESHIP **2** : a community of interest or feeling **3** : a group with similar interests **4** : the position of a fellow (as of a university) **5** : the stipend granted a fellow

fellow traveler *n* : a person who sympathizes with and often furthers the ideals and program of an organized group (as the Communist party) without joining it

fel·on \'fe-lən\ *n* **1** : one who has committed a felony **2** : WHITLOW

fel·o·ny \'fe-lə-nē\ *n, pl* **-nies** : a serious crime punishable by a heavy sentence — **fe·lo·ni·ous** \fə-'lō-nē-əs\ *adj*

¹felt \'felt\ *n* **1** : a cloth made of wool and fur often mixed with natural or synthetic fibers **2** : a material resembling felt

²felt *past and past part of* FEEL

fem *abbr* **1** female **2** feminine

fe·male \'fē-ˌmāl\ *adj* [ME, alter. of *femel*, fr. MF *femelle*, fr. ML *femella*, fr. L, girl, dim. of *femina* woman] : of, relating to, or being the sex that bears young; *also* : PISTILLATE **syn** feminine, womanly, womanlike, womanish, effeminate — **female** *n*

¹fem·i·nine \'fe-mə-nən\ *adj* **1** : of the female sex; *also* : characteristic of or appropriate or peculiar to women **2** : of, relating to, or constituting the gender that includes most words or grammatical forms referring to females — **fem·i·nin·i·ty** \\,fe-mə-'ni-nə-tē\\ *n*

²**feminine** *n* : a noun, pronoun, adjective, or inflectional form or class of the feminine gender; *also* : the feminine gender

fem·i·nism \\'fe-mə-‚ni-zəm\\ *n* **1** : the theory of the political, economic, and social equality of the sexes **2** : organized activity on behalf of women's rights and interests — **fem·i·nist** \\-nist\\ *n or adj*

femme fa·tale \\,fem-fə-'tal\\ *n, pl* **femmes fa·tales** *same or* -'talz\\ [F, lit., disastrous woman] : a seductive woman

fe·mur \\'fē-mər\\ *n, pl* **fe·murs** *or* **fem·o·ra** \\'fe-mə-rə\\ : the long leg bone extending from the hip to the knee — **fem·o·ral** \\'fe-mə-rəl\\ *adj*

¹**fen** \\'fen\\ *n* : low swampy land

²**fen** \\'fən\\ *n, pl* **fen** — see *yuan* at MONEY table

¹**fence** \\'fens\\ *n* [ME *fens*, short for *defens* defense] **1** : a barrier (as of wood or wire) to prevent escape or entry or to mark a boundary **2** : a person who receives stolen goods; *also* : a place where stolen goods are disposed of — **on the fence** : in a position of neutrality or indecision

²**fence** *vb* **fenced; fenc·ing 1** : to enclose with a fence **2** : to keep in or out with a fence **3** : to practice fencing **4** : to use tactics of attack and defense esp. in debate — **fenc·er** *n*

fenc·ing *n* **1** : the art or practice of attack and defense with the foil, épée, or saber **2** : the fences of a property or region **3** : material used for building fences

fend \\'fend\\ *vb* **1** : to keep or ward off : REPEL **2** : SHIFT ⟨~ for yourself⟩

fend·er \\'fen-dər\\ *n* : a protective device (as a guard over the wheel of an automobile)

fen·es·tra·tion \\,fe-nə-'strā-shən\\ *n* : the arrangement and design of windows and doors in a building

Fe·ni·an \\'fē-nē-ən\\ *n* : a member of a secret 19th century Irish and Irish-American organization dedicated to overthrowing British rule in Ireland

fen·nel \\'fen-ᵊl\\ *n* : a garden plant related to the carrot and grown for its aromatic foliage and seeds

FEPC *abbr* Fair Employment Practices Commission

fe·ral \\'fir-əl, 'fer-\\ *adj* **1** : SAVAGE **2** : WILD 1 **3** : having escaped from domestication and become wild

fer–de–lance \\'fer-də-'lans\\ *n, pl* **fer–de–lance** [F, lit., lance iron, spearhead] : a large venomous pit viper of Central and So. America

¹**fer·ment** \\fər-'ment\\ *vb* **1** : to cause or undergo fermentation **2** : to be or cause to be in a state of agitation or intense activity

²**fer·ment** \\'fər-‚ment\\ *n* **1** : a living organism (as a yeast) causing fermentation by its enzymes; *also* : ENZYME **2** : AGITATION, TUMULT

fer·men·ta·tion \\,fər-mən-'tā-shən, -‚men-\\ *n* **1** : chemical decomposition of an organic substance (as in the souring of milk or the formation of alcohol from sugar) by enzymatic action in the absence of oxygen often with formation of gas **2** : FERMENT 2

fer·mi·um \\'fer-mē-əm, 'fər-\\ *n* : an artificially produced radioactive metallic chemical element — see ELEMENT table

fern \\'fərn\\ *n* : any of an order of vascular plants resembling seed plants in having roots, stems, and leaflike fronds but reproducing by spores instead of by flowers and seeds

fern·ery \\'fər-nə-rē\\ *n, pl* **-er·ies 1** : a place for growing ferns **2** : a collection of growing ferns

fe·ro·cious \\fə-'rō-shəs\\ *adj* **1** : FIERCE, SAVAGE **2** : extremely intense — **fe·ro·cious·ly** *adv* — **fe·ro·cious·ness** *n*

fe·roc·i·ty \\fə-'rä-sə-tē\\ *n* : the quality or state of being ferocious

¹**fer·ret** \\'fer-ət\\ *n* : a partially domesticated usu. white European mammal related to the weasels

²**ferret** *vb* **1** : to hunt game with ferrets **2** : to drive out of a hiding place **3** : to find and bring to light by searching ⟨~ out the truth⟩

fer·ric \\'fer-ik\\ *adj* : of, relating to, or containing iron

ferric oxide *n* : an oxide of iron found in nature as hematite and as rust and used as a pigment and for polishing

Fer·ris wheel \\'fer-əs-\\ *n* : an amusement device consisting of a large upright power-driven wheel with seats that remain horizontal around its rim

fer·ro·mag·net·ic \\,fer-ō-mag-'ne-tik\\ *adj* : of or relating to substances that are easily magnetized

fer·rous \\'fer-əs\\ *adj* : of, relating to, or containing iron

fer·rule \\'fer-əl\\ *n* : a metal ring or cap around a slender wooden shaft to prevent splitting

¹**fer·ry** \\'fer-ē\\ *vb* **fer·ried; fer·ry·ing** [ME *ferien*, fr. OE *ferian* to carry, convey] **1** : to carry by boat across a body of water **2** : to cross by a ferry **3** : to convey from one place to another

²**ferry** *n, pl* **ferries 1** : a place where persons or things are ferried **2** : FERRYBOAT

fer·ry·boat \\'fer-ē-‚bōt\\ *n* : a boat used in ferrying

fer·tile \\'fərt-ᵊl\\ *adj* **1** : producing plentifully : PRODUCTIVE ⟨~ soils⟩ ⟨a ~ mind⟩ **2** : capable of developing or reproducing ⟨~ seed⟩ ⟨a ~ bull⟩ **syn** fruitful, prolific, fecund, productive — **fer·til·i·ty** \\(‚)fər-'ti-lə-tē\\ *n*

fer·til·ize \\'fərt-ᵊl-‚īz\\ *vb* **-ized; -iz·ing 1** : to unite with in the process of fertilization ⟨a sperm ~s an egg⟩ **2** : to apply fertilizer to — **fer·til·iza·tion** \\,fərt-ᵊl-ə-'zā-shən\\ *n*

fer·til·iz·er \\-‚ī-zər\\ *n* : material (as manure or a chemical mixture) for enriching land

fer·ule \\'fer-əl\\ *n* : a rod or ruler used to punish children

fer·ven·cy \\'fər-vən-sē\\ *n, pl* **-cies** : FERVOR

fer·vent \\'fər-vənt\\ *adj* **1** : very hot : GLOWING **2** : marked by great intensity of feeling **syn** impassioned, ardent, fervid, fiery, passionate — **fer·vent·ly** *adv*

fer·vid \\-vəd\\ *adj* **1** : very hot **2** : ARDENT, ZEALOUS — **fer·vid·ly** *adv*

fer·vor \\'fər-vər\\ *n* **1** : intense heat **2** : intensity of feeling or expression

fer·vour *chiefly Brit var of* FERVOR

fes·tal \\'fest-ᵊl\\ *adj* : FESTIVE

fester \\'fes-tər\\ *vb* **1** : to form pus **2** : PUTREFY, ROT **3** : RANKLE

fes·ti·val \\'fes-tə-vəl\\ *n* **1** : a time of celebration marked by special observances; *esp* : an occasion marked with religious ceremonies **2** : a periodic season or program of cultural events or entertainment ⟨a dance ~⟩

fes·tive \\'fes-tiv\\ *adj* **1** : of, relating to, or suitable for a feast or festival **2** : JOYFUL, GAY — **fes·tive·ly** *adv*

fes·tiv·i·ty \\fes-'ti-və-tē\\ *n, pl* **-ties 1** : FESTIVAL 1 **2** : the quality or state of being festive **3** : festive activity

¹**fes·toon** \\fes-'tün\\ *n* [F *feston*, fr. It *festone*, fr. *festa* festival] **1** : a decorative chain or strip hanging between two points **2** : a carved, molded, or painted ornament representing a decorative chain

²**festoon** *vb* **1** : to hang or form festoons on **2** : to shape into festoons

fe·tal \\'fēt-ᵊl\\ *adj* : of, relating to, or being a fetus

fetch \\'fech\\ *vb* **1** : to go or come after and bring or take back ⟨teach a dog to ~ a stick⟩ **2** : to bring in (as a price) **3** : to cause to come : bring out ⟨~ed tears from the eyes⟩ **4** : to give by striking ⟨~ him a blow⟩

fetch·ing *adj* : ATTRACTIVE, PLEASING — **fetch·ing·ly** *adv*

¹**fete** *or* **fête** \\'fāt, 'fet\\ *n* [F *fête*, fr. OF *feste*] **1** : FESTIVAL **2** : a large elaborate entertainment or party

²**fete** *or* **fête** *vb* **fet·ed** *or* **fêt·ed; fet·ing** *or* **fêt·ing 1** : to honor or commemorate with a fete **2** : to pay high honor to

fet·id \'fe-təd\ *adj* : having an offensive smell : STINKING

fe·tish *also* **fe·tich** \'fe-tish\ *n* [F & Pg; F *fétiche*, fr. Pg *feitiço*, fr. *feitiço* artificial, false, fr. L *facticius* factitious] **1** : an object (as an idol or image) believed to have magical powers (as in curing disease) **2** : an object of unreasoning devotion or concern **3** : an object whose real or fantasied presence is psychologically necessary for sexual gratification

fe·tish·ism \-ti-ₒshi-zəm\ *n* **1** : belief in or devotion to fetishes **2** : the pathological transfer of sexual interest and gratification to a fetish — **fe·tish·ist** \-shist\ *n* — **fe·tish·is·tic** \ₒfe-ti-'shis-tik\ *adj*

fet·lock \'fet-ₒläk\ *n* : a projection on the back of a horse's leg above the hoof; *also* : a tuft of hair on this

fet·ter \'fe-tər\ *n* **1** : a chain or shackle for the feet **2** : something that confines : RESTRAINT — **fetter** *vb*

fet·tle \'fet-ᵊl\ *n* : a state of fitness or order : CONDITION ⟨in fine ∼⟩

fe·tus \'fē-təs\ *n* : an unborn or unhatched vertebrate esp. after its basic structure is laid down; *esp* : a developing human being in the uterus from usu. three months after pregnancy occurs to birth

feud \'fyüd\ *n* : a prolonged quarrel; *esp* : a lasting conflict between families or clans marked by violent attacks made for revenge — **feud** *vb*

feu·dal \'fyüd-ᵊl\ *adj* **1** : of, relating to, or having the characteristics of a medieval fee **2** : of, relating to, or characteristic of feudalism

feu·dal·ism \'fyüd-ᵊl-ₒi-zəm\ *n* : a system of political organization prevailing in medieval Europe in which a vassal renders service to a lord and receives protection and land in return; *also* : a similar political or social system — **feu·dal·is·tic** \ₒfyüd-ᵊl-'is-tik\ *adj*

¹feu·da·to·ry \'fyü-də-ₒtōr-ē\ *adj* : owing feudal allegiance

²feudatory *n, pl* **-ries 1** : FIEF **2** : a person who holds lands by feudal law or usage

fe·ver \'fē-vər\ *n* **1** : a rise in body temperature above the normal; *also* : a disease of which this is a chief symptom **2** : a state of heightened emotion or activity **3** : CRAZE — **fe·ver·ish** *adj* — **fe·ver·ish·ly** *adv*

¹few \'fyü\ *pron* : not many : a small number

²few *adj* **1** : consisting of or amounting to a small number **2** : not many but some ⟨caught a ∼ fish⟩ — **few·ness** *n* — **few and far between** : RARE **3**

³few *n* **1** : a small number of units or individuals ⟨a ∼ of them⟩ **2** : a special limited number ⟨among the ∼⟩

few·er \'fyü-ər\ *pron* : a smaller number of persons or things

fey \'fā\ *adj* **1** *chiefly Scot* : fated to die; *also* : marked by a foreboding of death or calamity **2** : able to see into the future : VISIONARY **3** : marked by an otherworldly air or attitude **4** : CRAZY, TOUCHED

fez \'fez\ *n, pl* **fez·zes** *also* **fez·es** : a round red felt hat that has a flat top and a tassel but no brim

fez

ff *abbr* **1** folios **2** [*following*] and the following ones **3** fortissimo

FHA *abbr* Federal Housing Administration

fi·an·cé \ₒfē-ₒän-'sā\ *n* [F, fr. MF, fr. pp. of *fiancer* to promise, betroth, fr. OF *fiancier*, fr. *fiance* promise, trust, fr. *fier* to trust, ultim. fr. L *fidere*] : a man engaged to be married

fi·an·cée \ₒfē-ₒän-'sā\ *n* : a woman engaged to be married

fi·as·co \fē-'as-kō\ *n, pl* **-coes** [F] : a complete failure

fi·at \'fē-ət, -ₒat, -ₒät; 'fī-ət, -ₒat\ *n* [L, let it be done] : an authoritative and often arbitrary order or decree

¹fib \'fib\ *n* : a trivial or childish lie

²fib *vb* **fibbed; fib·bing** : to tell a fib — **fib·ber** *n*

fi·ber *or* **fi·bre** \'fī-bər\ *n* **1** : a threadlike substance or structure (as a muscle cell or fine root); *esp* : a natural (as wool or flax) or artificial (as rayon) filament capable of being spun or woven **2** : indigestible material in human food that stimulates the intestine to move its contents along **3** : an element that gives texture or substance **4** : basic toughness : STRENGTH — **fi·brous** \-brəs\ *adj*

fi·ber·board \'fī-bər-ₒbōrd\ *n* : a material made by compressing fibers (as of wood) into stiff sheets

fi·ber·fill \-ₒfil\ *n* : synthetic fibers used as a filling material (as for cushions)

fi·ber·glass \-ₒglas\ *n* : glass in fibrous form used in making various products (as insulation)

fiber optics *n* **1** *pl* : thin transparent fibers of glass or plastic that are enclosed by a less refractive material and that transmit light by internal reflection; *also* : a bundle of such fibers used in an instrument **2** : the technique of the use of fiber optics — **fiber-optic** *adj*

fi·bril \'fī-brəl, 'fi-\ *n* : a small fiber

fi·bril·la·tion \ₒfi-brə-'lā-shən, ₒfī-\ *n* : rapid irregular contractions of the heart muscle fibers resulting in a lack of synchronism between heartbeat and pulse — **fib·ril·late** \'fi-brə-ₒlāt, 'fī-\ *vb*

fi·brin \'fī-brən\ *n* : a white insoluble fibrous protein formed in the clotting of blood

fi·broid \'fī-ₒbroid, 'fi-\ *adj* : resembling, forming, or consisting of fibrous tissue ⟨∼ tumors⟩

fi·bro·sis \fī-'brō-səs\ *n* : a condition marked by abnormal increase of fiber-containing tissue

fib·u·la \'fi-byə-lə\ *n, pl* **-lae** \-lē, -ₒlī\ *or* **-las** : the outer and usu. the smaller of the two bones between the knee and ankle — **fib·u·lar** \-lər\ *adj*

FICA *abbr* Federal Insurance Contributions Act

-fication *n comb form* : making : production ⟨simplification⟩

fiche \'fēsh\ *n, pl* **fiche** : MICROFICHE

fi·chu \'fi-shü\ *n* [F] : a woman's light triangular scarf draped over the shoulders and fastened in front

fick·le \'fi-kəl\ *adj* : not firm or steadfast in disposition or character : INCONSTANT — **fick·le·ness** *n*

fic·tion \'fik-shən\ *n* **1** : something (as a story) invented by the imagination **2** : fictitious literature (as novels) — **fic·tion·al** \-shə-nəl\ *adj* — **fic·tion·al·ly** *adv*

fic·ti·tious \fik-'ti-shəs\ *adj* **1** : of, relating to, or characteristic of fiction : IMAGINARY **2** : FEIGNED **syn** chimerical, fanciful, fantastic, unreal

¹fid·dle \'fid-ᵊl\ *n* : VIOLIN

²fiddle *vb* **fid·dled; fid·dling 1** : to play on a fiddle **2** : to move the hands or fingers restlessly **3** : PUTTER **4** : MEDDLE, TAMPER — **fid·dler** *n*

fiddler crab *n* : any of a genus of burrowing crabs with one claw much enlarged in the male

fid·dle·stick \'fid-ᵊl-ₒstik\ *n* **1** *archaic* : a violin bow **2** *pl* : NONSENSE — used as an interjection

fi·del·i·ty \fə-ˈde-lə-tē, fī-\ *n, pl* **-ties 1** : the quality or state of being faithful **2** : ACCURACY ⟨~ in sound reproduction⟩ **syn** allegiance, loyalty, devotion, fealty
¹**fidg·et** \ˈfi-jət\ *n* **1** *pl* : uneasiness or restlessness as shown by nervous movements **2** : one that fidgets — **fidg·ety** *adj*
²**fidget** *vb* : to move or cause to move or act restlessly or nervously
fi·du·cia·ry \fə-ˈdü-shē-ˌer-ē, -ˈdyü-, -shə-rē\ *adj* **1** : involving a confidence or trust **2** : held or holding in trust for another ⟨~ accounts⟩ — **fiduciary** *n*
fie \ˈfī\ *interj* — used to express disgust or disapproval
fief \ˈfēf\ *n* : a feudal estate : FEE
¹**field** \ˈfēld\ *n* **1** : open country **2** : a piece of cleared land for cultivation or pasture **3** : a piece of land yielding some special product **4** : the place where a battle is fought; *also* : BATTLE **5** : an area, division, or sphere of activity ⟨the ~ of science⟩ ⟨salesmen in the ~⟩ **6** : an area for military exercises **7** : an area for sports **8** : a background on which something is drawn or projected ⟨a flag with white stars on a ~ of blue⟩ **9** : a region or space in which a given effect (as magnetism) exists — **field** *adj*
²**field** *vb* **1** : to handle a batted or thrown baseball while on defense **2** : to put into the field **3** : to answer satisfactorily ⟨~ a tough question⟩ — **field·er** *n*
field day *n* **1** : a day devoted to outdoor sports and athletic competition **2** : a time of extraordinary pleasure or opportunity
field event *n* : a track-and-field event (as weight-throwing) other than a race
field glass *n* : a hand-held binocular telescope — usu. used in pl.
field hockey *n* : a field game played between two teams of 11 players each whose object is to knock a ball into the opponent's goal with a curved stick
field marshal *n* : an officer (as in the British army) of the highest rank
field–test \-ˌtest\ *vb* : to test (as a new product) in a natural environment — **field test** *n*
fiend \ˈfēnd\ *n* **1** : DEVIL 1 **2** : DEMON **3** : an extremely wicked or cruel person **4** : a person excessively devoted to a pursuit **5** : ADDICT ⟨dope ~⟩ — **fiend·ish** *adj* — **fiend·ish·ly** *adv*
fierce \ˈfirs\ *adj* **fierc·er; fierc·est 1** : violently hostile or aggressive in temperament **2** : PUGNACIOUS **3** : INTENSE **4** : furiously active or determined **5** : wild or menacing in appearance **syn** ferocious, barbarous, savage, cruel — **fierce·ly** *adv* — **fierce·ness** *n*
fi·ery \ˈfī-ə-rē\ *adj* **fi·er·i·er; -est 1** : consisting of fire **2** : BURNING, BLAZING **3** : FLAMMABLE **4** : hot like a fire : INFLAMED, FEVERISH **5** : RED **6** : full of emotion or spirit **7** : IRRITABLE — **fi·eri·ness** \-rē-nəs\ *n*
fi·es·ta \fē-ˈes-tə\ *n* [Sp] : FESTIVAL
fife \ˈfīf\ *n* [G *Pfeife* pipe, fife] : a small flute
FIFO *abbr* first in, first out
fif·teen \fif-ˈtēn\ *n* : one more than 14 — **fifteen** *adj or pron* — **fif·teenth** \-ˈtēnth\ *adj or n*
fifth \ˈfifth\ *n* **1** : one that is number five in a countable series **2** : one of five equal parts of something **3** : a unit of measure for liquor equal to ⅕ U.S. gallon (0.757 liter) — **fifth** *adj or adv*
fifth column *n* : a group of secret supporters of a nation's enemy that engage in espionage or sabotage within the country — **fifth columnist** *n*
fifth wheel *n* : one that is unnecessary and often burdensome
fif·ty \ˈfif-tē\ *n, pl* **fifties** : five times 10 — **fif·ti·eth** \-tē-əth\ *adj or n* — **fifty** *adj or pron*
fif·ty–fif·ty \ˌfif-tē-ˈfif-tē\ *adj* **1** : shared equally ⟨a ~ proposition⟩ **2** : half favorable and half unfavorable
¹**fig** \ˈfig\ *n* : a usu. pear-shaped edible fruit of warm re-

gions; *also* : a tree related to the mulberry that bears this fruit

fig: leaves and fruit

²**fig** *abbr* **1** figurative; figuratively **2** figure
¹**fight** \ˈfīt\ *vb* **fought** \ˈfȯt\; **fight·ing 1** : to contend against another in battle or physical combat **2** : BOX **3** : to put forth a determined effort **4** : STRUGGLE, CONTEND **5** : to attempt to prevent the success or effectiveness of **6** : WAGE **7** : to gain by struggle
²**fight** *n* **1** : a hostile encounter : BATTLE **2** : a boxing match **3** : a verbal disagreement **4** : a struggle for a goal or an objective **5** : strength or disposition for fighting ⟨full of ~⟩
fight·er \ˈfī-tər\ *n* **1** : one that fights; *esp* : WARRIOR **2** : BOXER **3** : a fast maneuverable warplane for destroying enemy aircraft
fig·ment \ˈfig-mənt\ *n* : something imagined or made up
fig·u·ra·tion \ˌfi-gyə-ˈrā-shən, -gə-\ *n* **1** : FORM, OUTLINE **2** : an act or instance of representation in figures and shapes
fig·u·ra·tive \ˈfi-gyə-rə-tiv, -gə-\ *adj* **1** : EMBLEMATIC **2** : SYMBOLIC, METAPHORICAL ⟨~ language⟩ — **fig·u·ra·tive·ly** *adv*
¹**fig·ure** \ˈfi-gyər, -gər\ *n* **1** : NUMERAL **2** *pl* : arithmetical calculations **3** : a written or printed character **4** : PRICE, SUM **5** : a combination of points, lines, or surfaces in geometry ⟨a circle is a closed plane ~⟩ **6** : SHAPE, FORM, OUTLINE **7** : the graphic representation of a form esp. of a person **8** : a diagram or pictorial illustration of textual matter **9** : PATTERN, DESIGN **10** : appearance made or impression produced ⟨they cut quite a ~⟩ **11** : a series of movements (as in a dance) **12** : PERSONAGE
²**figure** *vb* **fig·ured; fig·ur·ing 1** : to represent by or as if by a figure or outline **2** : to decorate with a pattern **3** : to indicate or represent by numerals **4** : REGARD, CONSIDER **5** : to be or appear important or conspicuous **6** : COMPUTE, CALCULATE
fig·ure·head \ˈfi-gyər-ˌhed, -gər-\ *n* **1** : a figure on the bow of a ship **2** : a head or chief in name only
figure of speech : a form of expression (as a simile or metaphor) that often compares or identifies one thing with another to convey meaning or heighten effect
figure out *vb* **1** : FIND OUT, DISCOVER **2** : SOLVE
fig·u·rine \ˌfi-gyə-ˈrēn, -gə-\ *n* : a small carved or molded figure
Fi·ji·an \ˈfē-jē-ən, fi-ˈjē-ən\ *n* : a native or inhabitant of the Pacific island country of Fiji — **Fijian** *adj*
fil·a·ment \ˈfi-lə-mənt\ *n* : a fine thread or threadlike object, part, or process — **fil·a·men·tous** \ˌfi-lə-ˈmen-təs\ *adj*
fil·bert \ˈfil-bərt\ *n* : the sweet thick-shelled nut of either of two European hazels; *also* : a shrub or small tree bearing filberts
filch \ˈfilch\ *vb* : to steal furtively
¹**file** \ˈfīl\ *n* : a usu. steel tool with a ridged or toothed surface used esp. for smoothing a hard substance

²file *vb* **filed; fil·ing** : to rub, smooth, or cut away with a file

³file *vb* **filed; fil·ing** [ME, fr. MF *filer* to string documents on a string or wire, fr. *fil* thread, fr. L *filum*] **1** : to arrange in order **2** : to enter or record officially or as prescribed by law ⟨~ a lawsuit⟩ **3** : to send (copy) to a newspaper

⁴file *n* **1** : a device (as a folder or cabinet) by means of which papers may be kept in order **2** : a collection of papers or publications usu. arranged or classified **3** : a collection of data (as text) treated by a computer as a unit

⁵file *n* : a row of persons, animals, or things arranged one behind the other

⁶file *vb* **filed; fil·ing** : to march or proceed in file

fi·let mi·gnon \fi-(ˌ)lā-mēn-ˈyōⁿ, fi-lā-\ *n, pl* **filets mignons** \-(ˌ)lā-mēn-ˈyōⁿz, -ˌlā-\ [F, lit., dainty fillet] : a thick slice of beef cut from the narrow end of a beef tenderloin

fil·ial \ˈfi-lē-əl, ˈfil-yəl\ *adj* : of, relating to, or befitting a son or daughter

fil·i·bus·ter \ˈfi-lə-ˌbəs-tər\ *n* [Sp *filibustero*, lit., freebooter] **1** : a military adventurer; *esp* : an American engaged in fomenting 19th century Latin American uprisings **2** : the use of delaying tactics (as extremely long speeches) esp. in a legislative assembly; *also* : an instance of this practice — **filibuster** *vb* — **fil·i·bus·ter·er** *n*

fil·i·gree \ˈfi-lə-ˌgrē\ *n* [F *filigrane*] : ornamental openwork (as of fine wire) — **fil·i·greed** \-ˌgrēd\ *adj*

fil·ing \ˈfī-liŋ\ *n* **1** : the act or instance of using a file **2** : a small piece scraped off by a file ⟨iron ~s⟩

Fil·i·pi·no \ˌfi-lə-ˈpē-nō\ *n, pl* **Filipinos** : a native or inhabitant of the Philippines — **Filipino** *adj*

¹fill \ˈfil\ *vb* **1** : to make or become full **2** : to stop up : PLUG ⟨~ a cavity⟩ **3** : FEED, SATIATE **4** : SATISFY, FULFILL ⟨~ all requirements⟩ **5** : to occupy fully **6** : to spread through ⟨laughter ~ed the room⟩ **7** : OCCUPY ⟨~ the office of president⟩ **8** : to put a person in ⟨~ a vacancy⟩ **9** : to supply as directed ⟨~ a prescription⟩

²fill *n* **1** : a full supply; *esp* : a quantity that satisfies or satiates **2** : material used esp. for filling a low place

¹fill·er \ˈfi-lər\ *n* **1** : one that fills **2** : a substance added to another substance (as to increase bulk or weight) **3** : a material used for filling cracks and pores in wood before painting

²fil·ler \ˈfi-ˌler\ *n, pl* **fillers** *or* **filler** — see *forint* at MONEY table

¹fil·let \ˈfi-lət, *in sense 2* fi-ˈlā, ˈfi-(ˌ)lā\ *also* **fi·let** \fi-ˈlā, ˈfi-(ˌ)lā\ *n* [ME *filet*, fr. MF, dim. of *fil* thread] **1** : a narrow band, strip, or ribbon **2** : a piece or slice of boneless meat or fish; *esp* : the tenderloin of beef

²fil·let \ˈfi-lət, *in sense 2 also* fi-ˈlā, ˈfi-(ˌ)lā\ *vb* **1** : to bind or adorn with or as if with a fillet **2** : to cut into fillets

fill in *vb* **1** : to provide necessary or recent information **2** : to serve as a temporary substitute

fill·ing \ˈfi-liŋ\ *n* **1** : material used to fill something ⟨a ~ for a tooth⟩ **2** : the yarn interlacing the warp in a fabric **3** : a food mixture used to fill pastry or sandwiches

filling station *n* : SERVICE STATION

fil·lip \ˈfi-ləp\ *n* **1** : a blow or gesture made by a flick or snap of the finger across the thumb **2** : something that serves to arouse or excite — **fillip** *vb*

fill-up \ˈfil-ˌəp\ *n* : an act or instance of filling something

fil·ly \ˈfi-lē\ *n, pl* **fillies** : a young female horse usu. less than four years old

¹film \ˈfilm\ *n* **1** : a thin skin or membrane **2** : a thin coating or layer **3** : a flexible strip of chemically treated material used in taking pictures **4** : MOTION PICTURE — **filmy** *adj*

²film *vb* **1** : to cover with a film **2** : to make a motion picture of

film·dom \ˈfilm-dəm\ *n* : the motion-picture industry

film·og·ra·phy \fil-ˈmä-grə-fē\ *n, pl* **-phies** : a list of motion pictures featuring the work of a film figure or a particular topic

film·strip \ˈfilm-ˌstrip\ *n* : a strip of film bearing a sequence of images for projection as still pictures

fils \ˈfils\ *n, pl* **fils** — see *dinar, dirham, rial* at MONEY table

¹fil·ter \ˈfil-tər\ *n* **1** : a porous material through which a fluid is passed to separate out matter in suspension; *also* : a device containing such material **2** : a device for suppressing waves of certain frequencies; *esp* : one (as for a camera) that absorbs light of certain colors

²filter *vb* **1** : to remove by means of a filter **2** : to pass through a filter — **fil·ter·able** *also* **fil·tra·ble** \-tə-rə-bəl, -trə-\ *adj* — **fil·tra·tion** \fil-ˈtrā-shən\ *n*

filth \ˈfilth\ *n* [ME, fr. OE *fȳlth*, fr. *fūl* foul] **1** : foul matter; *esp* : loathsome dirt or refuse **2** : moral corruption **3** : OBSCENITY — **filth·i·ness** *n* — **filthy** \ˈfil-thē\ *adj*

fil·trate \ˈfil-ˌtrāt\ *n* : fluid that has passed through a filter

¹fin \ˈfin\ *n* **1** : one of the thin external processes by which an aquatic animal (as a fish) moves through water **2** : a fin-shaped part (as on an airplane) **3** : FLIPPER 2 — **finned** \ˈfind\ *adj*

²fin *abbr* **1** finance; financial **2** finish

fi·na·gle \fə-ˈnā-gəl\ *vb* **-gled; -gling** **1** : to obtain by indirect or dishonest means : WANGLE **2** : to use devious dishonest methods to achieve one's ends — **fi·na·gler** *n*

¹fi·nal \ˈfīn-ᵊl\ *adj* **1** : not to be altered or undone **2** : ULTIMATE **3** : relating to or occurring at the end or conclusion — **fi·nal·i·ty** \fī-ˈna-lə-tē, fə-\ *n* — **fi·nal·ly** *adv*

²final *n* **1** : a deciding match or game — usu. used in pl. **2** : the last examination in a course — often used in pl.

fi·na·le \fə-ˈna-lē, fi-ˈnä-\ *n* : the close or end of something; *esp* : the last section of a musical composition

fi·nal·ist \ˈfīn-ᵊl-əst\ *n* : a contestant in the finals of a competition

fi·nal·ize \ˈfīn-ᵊl-ˌīz\ *vb* **-ized; -iz·ing** : to put in final or finished form

¹fi·nance \fə-ˈnans, ˈfī-ˌnans\ *n* [ME, payment, ransom, fr. MF, fr. *finer* to end, pay, fr. *fin* end, fr. L *finis* boundary, end] **1** *pl* : money resources available esp. to a government or business **2** : management of money affairs

²finance *vb* **fi·nanced; fi·nanc·ing** **1** : to raise or provide funds for **2** : to furnish with necessary funds **3** : to sell or supply on credit

finance company *n* : a company that makes usu. small short-term loans usu. to individuals

fi·nan·cial \fə-ˈnan-chəl, fī-\ *adj* : relating to finance or financiers — **fi·nan·cial·ly** *adv*

fi·nan·cier \ˌfi-nən-ˈsir, ˌfī-nan-\ *n* **1** : a person skilled in managing public moneys **2** : a person who deals with large-scale finance and investment

finch \ˈfinch\ *n* : any of numerous songbirds with strong conical bills

¹find \ˈfīnd\ *vb* **found** \ˈfau̇nd\; **find·ing** **1** : to meet with either by chance or by searching or study : ENCOUNTER, DISCOVER **2** : to obtain by effort or management ⟨~ time to read⟩ **3** : to arrive at : REACH ⟨the bullet *found* its mark⟩ **4** : EXPERIENCE, FEEL ⟨*found* happiness⟩ **5** : to gain or regain the use of ⟨*found* his voice again⟩ **6** : to determine and make a statement about ⟨~ a verdict⟩

²find *n* **1** : an act or instance of finding **2** : something found; *esp* : a valuable item of discovery

find·er \ˈfīn-dər\ *n* : one that finds; *esp* : VIEWFINDER

fin de siè·cle \ˌfaⁿ-də-sē-ˈekl\ *adj* [F, end of century]

\ə\abut \ᵊ\kitten \ər\further \a\ash \ā\ace \ä\mop, mar \au̇\out \ch\chin \e\bet \ē\easy \g\go \i\hit \ī\ice \j\job \ŋ\sing \ō\go \o\law \oi\boy \th\thin \t̲h̲\the \ü\loot \u̇\foot \y\yet \zh\vision *see also* Pronunciation Symbols page

: of, relating to, or characteristic of the close of the 19th century

find·ing \'fīn-diŋ\ *n* **1** : the act of finding **2** : FIND **2 3** : the result of a judicial proceeding or inquiry

find out *vb* : to learn by study, observation, or search : DISCOVER

¹fine \'fīn\ *n* : money exacted as a penalty for an offense

²fine *vb* **fined; fin·ing** : to impose a fine on : punish by a fine

³fine *adj* **fin·er; fin·est 1** : free from impurity **2** : very thin in gauge or texture **3** : not coarse **4** : SUBTLE, SENSITIVE ⟨a ∼ distinction⟩ **5** : superior in quality or appearance **6** : ELEGANT, REFINED — **fine·ly** *adv* — **fine·ness** *n*

⁴fine *adv* : FINELY

fine art *n* : art (as painting, sculpture, or music) concerned primarily with the creation of beautiful objects — usu. used in pl.

fin·ery \'fī-nə-rē\ *n, pl* **-er·ies** : ORNAMENT, DECORATION; *esp* : showy clothing and jewels

fine·spun \'fīn-'spən\ *adj* : developed with extremely or excessively fine delicacy or detail

fi·nesse \fə-'nes\ *n* **1** : refinement or delicacy of workmanship, structure, or texture **2** : CUNNING, SUBTLETY — **finesse** *vb*

fine–tune \'fīn-'tün\ *vb* : to adjust so as to bring to the highest level of performance or effectiveness

fin·fish \'fin-ˌfish\ *n* : FISH 2

¹fin·ger \'fiŋ-gər\ *n* **1** : any of the five divisions at the end of the hand; *esp* : one other than the thumb **2** : something that resembles or does the work of a finger **3** : a part of a glove into which a finger is inserted

²finger *vb* **fin·gered; fin·ger·ing 1** : to touch or feel with the fingers : HANDLE **2** : to perform with the fingers or with a certain fingering **3** : to mark the notes of a piece of music as a guide in playing **4** : to point out

fin·ger·board \'fiŋ-gər-ˌbōrd\ *n* : the part of a stringed instrument against which the fingers press the strings to vary the pitch

finger bowl *n* : a small water bowl for rinsing the fingers at the table

fin·ger·ing \'fiŋ-gə-riŋ\ *n* **1** : handling or touching with the fingers **2** : the act or method of using the fingers in playing an instrument **3** : the marking of the method of fingering

fin·ger·ling \'fiŋ-gər-liŋ\ *n* : a small fish

fin·ger·nail \'fiŋ-gər-ˌnāl\ *n* : the nail of a finger

fin·ger·print \-ˌprint\ *n* : the pattern of marks made by pressing the tip of a finger or thumb on a surface; *esp* : an ink impression of such a pattern taken for the purpose of identification — **fingerprint** *vb*

fin·ger·tip \-ˌtip\ *n* : the tip of a finger

fin·i·al \'fi-nē-əl\ *n* : an ornamental projection or end (as on a spire)

fin·ick·ing \'fi-ni-kiŋ\ *adj* : FINICKY

fin·icky \'fi-ni-kē\ *adj* : excessively particular in taste or standards

fi·nis \'fi-nəs\ *n* : END, CONCLUSION

¹fin·ish \'fi-nish\ *vb* **1** : TERMINATE **2** : to use or dispose of entirely **3** : to bring to completion : ACCOMPLISH **4** : to put a final coat or surface on **5** : to come to the end of a course or undertaking — **fin·ish·er** *n*

²finish *n* **1** : END, CONCLUSION **2** : something that completes or perfects **3** : the final treatment or coating of a surface

fi·nite \'fī-ˌnīt\ *adj* **1** : having definite or definable limits; *also* : having a limited nature or existence **2** : being less than some positive integer in number or measure and greater than its negative **3** : showing distinction of grammatical person and number ⟨a ∼ verb⟩

fink \'fiŋk\ *n* **1** : a contemptible person **2** : STRIKEBREAKER **3** : INFORMER

Finn \'fin\ *n* : a native or inhabitant of Finland

fin·nan had·die \ˌfi-nən-'ha-dē\ *n* : smoked haddock

¹Finn·ish \'fi-nish\ *adj* : of or relating to Finland, the Finns, or Finnish

²Finnish *n* : the language of Finland

fin·ny \'fi-nē\ *adj* **1** : having or characterized by fins **2** : relating to or being fish

fiord *var of* FJORD

fir \'fər\ *n* : any of a genus of erect evergreen trees related to the pines; *also* : the light soft wood of a fir

¹fire \'fīr\ *n* **1** : the light or heat and esp. the flame of something burning **2** : ENTHUSIASM, ZEAL **3** : fuel that is burning (as in a stove or fireplace) **4** : destructive burning (as of a house) **5** : the firing of weapons — **fireless** *adj*

²fire *vb* **fired; fir·ing 1** : KINDLE, IGNITE ⟨∼ a house⟩ **2** : STIR, ENLIVEN ⟨∼ the imagination⟩ **3** : to dismiss from employment **4** : SHOOT ⟨∼ a gun⟩ ⟨∼ an arrow⟩ **5** : BAKE ⟨*firing* pottery in a kiln⟩ **6** : to apply fire or fuel to something ⟨∼ a furnace⟩

fire ant *n* : either of two small fiercely stinging South American ants that are pests in the southeastern U.S. esp. in fields used to grow crops

fire·arm \'fīr-ˌärm\ *n* : a weapon (as a pistol) from which a shot is discharged by gunpowder

fire·ball \-ˌbȯl\ *n* **1** : a ball of fire **2** : a very bright meteor **3** : the highly luminous cloud of vapor and dust created by a nuclear explosion **4** : a highly energetic person

fire·boat \-ˌbōt\ *n* : a boat equipped for fighting fires

fire·bomb \-ˌbäm\ *n* : an incendiary bomb — **firebomb** *vb*

fire·box \-ˌbäks\ *n* **1** : a chamber (as of a furnace) that contains a fire **2** : a box containing a fire alarm

fire·brand \-ˌbrand\ *n* **1** : a piece of burning wood **2** : a person who creates unrest or strife : AGITATOR

fire·break \-ˌbrāk\ *n* : a barrier of cleared or plowed land intended to check a forest or grass fire

fire·bug \-ˌbəg\ *n* : a person who deliberately sets destructive fires

fire·crack·er \-ˌkra-kər\ *n* : a paper tube containing an explosive and a fuse and set off to make a noise

fire department *n* : an organization for preventing or extinguishing fires; *also* : its members

fire engine *n* : a motor vehicle with equipment for extinguishing fires

fire escape *n* : a stairway or ladder for escape from a burning building

fire·fight·er \'fīr-ˌfī-tər\ *n* : a person who fights fires; *esp* : a member of a fire department

fire·fly \-ˌflī\ *n* : any of various small night-flying beetles that produce flashes of light for courtship purposes

fire·house \-ˌhaus\ *n* : FIRE STATION

fire irons *n pl* : tools for tending a fire esp. in a fireplace

fire·man \'fīr-mən\ *n* **1** : STOKER **2** : FIREFIGHTER

fire off *vb* : to write and send

fire·place \-ˌplās\ *n* **1** : a framed opening made in a chimney to hold an open fire **2** : an outdoor structure of brick or stone for an open fire

fire·plug \-ˌpləg\ *n* : HYDRANT

fire·pow·er \-ˌpau̇-ər\ *n* : the ability to deliver gunfire or warheads on a target

¹fire·proof \-'prüf\ *adj* : resistant to fire

²fireproof *vb* : to make fireproof

fire screen *n* : a protective screen before a fireplace

¹fire·side \'fīr-ˌsīd\ *n* **1** : a place near the fire or hearth **2** : HOME

²fireside *adj* : having an informal or intimate quality

fire station *n* : a building housing fire engines and usu. firefighters

fire·storm \'fīr-ˌstȯrm\ *n* **1** : a large destructive very hot fire **2** : a sudden or violent outburst ⟨∼ of criticism⟩

fire tower *n* : a tower (as in a forest) from which a watch for fires is kept

fire·trap \'fīr-ˌtrap\ *n* : a building or place apt to catch on fire or difficult to escape from in case of fire

fire truck *n* : FIRE ENGINE
fire·wa·ter \'fīr-ˌwȯ-tər, -ˌwä-\ *n* : intoxicating liquor
fire·wood \-ˌwùd\ *n* : wood used for fuel
fire·work \-ˌwərk\ *n* : a device designed to produce a display of light, noise, and smoke by the burning of explosive or flammable materials
firing line *n* 1 : a line from which fire is delivered against a target 2 : the forefront of an activity
¹**firm** \'fərm\ *adj* 1 : securely fixed in place 2 : SOLID, VIGOROUS ⟨a ∼ handshake⟩ 3 : having a solid or compact texture 4 : not subject to change or fluctuation : STEADY ⟨∼ prices⟩ 5 : STEADFAST 6 : indicating firmness or resolution — **firm·ly** *adv* — **firm·ness** *n*
²**firm** *vb* : to make or become firm
³**firm** *n* [G *Firma*, fr. It, signature, ultim. fr. L *firmare* to make firm, confirm] 1 : the name under which a company transacts business 2 : a business partnership of two or more persons 3 : a business enterprise
fir·ma·ment \'fər-mə-mənt\ *n* : the arch of the sky : HEAVENS
firm·ware \'firm-ˌwar\ *n* : computer programs contained permanently in a hardware device
¹**first** \'fərst\ *adj* : preceding all others as in time, order, or importance
²**first** *adv* 1 : before any other 2 : for the first time 3 : in preference to something else
³**first** *n* 1 : number one in a countable series 2 : something that is first 3 : the lowest forward gear in an automotive vehicle 4 : the winning or highest place in a competition or examination
first aid *n* : emergency care or treatment given an injured or ill person
first·born \'fərst-'bȯrn\ *adj* : ELDEST — **firstborn** *n*
first class *n* : the best or highest group in a classification — **first–class** *adj or adv*
first·hand \'fərst-'hand\ *adj* : coming from direct personal observation or experience — **firsthand** *adv*
first lady *n, often cap F&L* : the wife or hostess of the chief executive of a political unit (as a country)
first lieutenant *n* : a commissioned officer (as in the army) ranking next below a captain
first·ling \'fərst-liŋ\ *n* : one that comes or is produced first
first·ly \-lē\ *adv* : in the first place : FIRST
¹**first–rate** \-'rāt\ *adj* : of the first order of size, importance, or quality
²**first–rate** *adv* : very well
first sergeant *n* 1 : a noncommissioned officer serving as the chief assistant to the commander of a military unit 2 : a rank in the army below a command sergeant major and in the marine corps below a sergeant major
first strike *n* : a preemptive nuclear attack
first–string \'fərst-'striŋ\ *adj* : being a regular as distinguished from a substitute
firth \'fərth\ *n* [ME, fr. ON *fjǫrthr*] : ESTUARY
fis·cal \'fis-kəl\ *adj* [L *fiscalis*, fr. *fiscus* basket, treasury] 1 : of or relating to taxation, public revenues, or public debt 2 : of or relating to financial matters — **fis·cal·ly** *adv*
¹**fish** \'fish\ *n, pl* **fish** *or* **fish·es** 1 : a water-dwelling animal — usu. used in combination ⟨star*fish*⟩ ⟨shell*fish*⟩ 2 : any of numerous cold-blooded water-breathing vertebrates with fins, gills, and usu. scales that include the bony fishes and usu. the cartilaginous and jawless fishes 3 : the flesh of fish used as food
²**fish** *vb* 1 : to attempt to catch fish 2 : to seek something by roundabout means ⟨∼ for praise⟩ 3 : to search for something underwater 4 : to engage in a search by groping 5 : to draw forth
fish–and–chips *n pl* : fried fish and french fried potatoes
fish·bowl \'fish-ˌbōl\ *n* 1 : a bowl for the keeping of live fish 2 : a place or condition that affords no privacy
fish·er \'fi-shər\ *n* 1 : one that fishes 2 : a large dark

brown No. American arboreal carnivorous mammal related to the weasels
fish·er·man \-mən\ *n* : a person engaged in fishing; *also* : a fishing boat
fish·ery \'fi-shə-rē\ *n, pl* **-er·ies** : the business of catching fish; *also* : a place for catching fish
fish·hook \'fish-ˌhùk\ *n* : a usu. barbed hook for catching fish
fish ladder *n* : an arrangement of pools in steps by which fish can pass over a dam
fish·net \'fish-ˌnet\ *n* : netting for catching fish 2 : a coarse open-mesh fabric
fish·tail \-ˌtāl\ *vb* : to have the rear end slide from side to side out of control while moving forward
fish·wife \-ˌwīf\ *n* 1 : a woman who sells fish 2 : a vulgar abusive woman
fishy \'fi-shē\ *adj* **fish·i·er; -est** 1 : of or resembling fish 2 : QUESTIONABLE
fis·sion \'fi-shən, -zhən\ *n* [L *fissio*, fr. *findere* to split] 1 : a cleaving into parts 2 : a method of reproduction in which a living cell or body divides into two or more parts each of which grows into a whole new individual 3 : the splitting of an atomic nucleus resulting in the release of large amounts of energy — **fis·sion·able** \'fi-shə-nə-bəl, -zhə-\ *adj*
fis·sure \'fi-shər\ *n* : a narrow opening or crack
fist \'fist\ *n* 1 : the hand with fingers folded into the palm 2 : INDEX 6
fist·ful \'fist-ˌfùl\ *n* : HANDFUL
fist·i·cuffs \'fis-ti-ˌkəfs\ *n pl* : a fight with usu. bare fists
fis·tu·la \'fis-chə-lə\ *n, pl* **-las** *or* **-lae** : an abnormal passage leading from an abscess or hollow organ — **fis·tu·lous** \-ləs\ *adj*
¹**fit** \'fit\ *adj* **fit·ter; fit·test** 1 : adapted to a purpose : APPROPRIATE 2 : PROPER, RIGHT 3 : PREPARED, READY 4 : physically and mentally sound — **fit·ly** *adv* — **fit·ness** *n*
²**fit** *n* 1 : a sudden violent attack (as of bodily disorder) 2 : a sudden outburst
³**fit** *vb* **fit·ted** *also* **fit; fit·ting** 1 : to be suitable for or to 2 : to be correctly adjusted to or shaped for 3 : to insert or adjust until correctly in place 4 : to make a place or room for 5 : to be in agreement or accord with 6 : PREPARE 7 : ADJUST 8 : SUPPLY, EQUIP ⟨*fitted* out with gear⟩ 9 : BELONG — **fit·ter** *n*
⁴**fit** *n* : the fact, condition, or manner of fitting or being fitted
fit·ful \'fit-fəl\ *adj* : not regular : INTERMITTENT ⟨∼ sleep⟩ — **fit·ful·ly** *adv*
¹**fit·ting** \'fi-tiŋ\ *adj* : APPROPRIATE, SUITABLE — **fit·ting·ly** *adv*
²**fitting** *n* 1 : the action or act of one that fits; *esp* : a trying on of clothes being made or altered 2 : a small often standardized part ⟨a plumbing ∼⟩
five \'fīv\ *n* 1 : one more than four 2 : the 5th in a set or series 3 : something having five units; *esp* : a basketball team 4 : a 5-dollar bill — **five** *adj or pron*
¹**fix** \'fiks\ *vb* 1 : to make firm, stable, or fast 2 : to give a permanent or final form to 3 : AFFIX, ATTACH 4 : to hold or direct steadily ⟨∼*es* his eyes on the horizon⟩ 5 : ESTABLISH, SET 6 : ASSIGN ⟨∼ the blame⟩ 7 : to set in order 8 : ADJUST 9 : PREPARE 9 : to make whole or sound again 10 : to get even with 11 : to influence by improper or illegal methods ⟨∼ a race⟩ — **fix·er** *n*
²**fix** *n* 1 : PREDICAMENT 2 : a determination of position (as of a ship) 3 : an accurate determination or understanding 4 : an act of improper influence 5 : a supply or dose

\ə\abut \ᵊ\kitten \ər\further \a\ash \ā\ace \ä\mop, mar
\aù\out \ch\chin \e\bet \ē\easy \g\go \i\hit \ī\ice \j\job
\ŋ\sing \ō\go \ȯ\law \ȯi\boy \th\thin \t͟h\the \ü\loot \ù\foot
\y\yet \zh\vision *see also* Pronunciation Symbols page

of something (as an addictive drug) strongly desired or craved **6** : something that fixes or restores

fix·a·tion \fik-ˈsā-shən\ *n* : an obsessive or unhealthy preoccupation or attachment — **fix·ate** \ˈfik-ˌsāt\ *vb*

fix·a·tive \ˈfik-sə-tiv\ *n* : something that stabilizes or sets

fixed \ˈfikst\ *adj* **1** : securely placed or fastened : STATIONARY **2** : not volatile **3** : SETTLED, FINAL **4** : INTENT, CONCENTRATED ⟨a ~ stare⟩ **5** : supplied with a definite amount of something needed (as money) — **fixed·ly** \ˈfik-səd-lē\ *adv* — **fixed·ness** \ˈfik-səd-nəs\ *n*

fix·i·ty \ˈfik-sə-tē\ *n, pl* **-ties** : the quality or state of being fixed or stable

fix·ture \ˈfiks-chər\ *n* **1** : something firmly attached as a permanent part of some other thing **2** : a familiar feature in a particular setting; *esp* : a person associated with a place or activity

¹**fizz** \ˈfiz\ *vb* : to make a hissing or sputtering sound

²**fizz** *n* : an effervescent beverage

¹**fiz·zle** \ˈfi-zəl\ *vb* **fiz·zled; fiz·zling 1** : FIZZ **2** : to fail after a good start — often used with *out*

²**fizzle** *n* : FAILURE

fjord \fē-ˈȯrd\ *n* [Norw] : a narrow inlet of the sea between cliffs or steep slopes

fjord

fl *abbr* **1** [L *floruit*] flourished **2** fluid

FL *or* **Fla** *abbr* Florida

flab \ˈflab\ *n* : soft flabby body tissue

flab·ber·gast \ˈfla-bər-ˌgast\ *vb* : ASTOUND

flab·by \ˈfla-bē\ *adj* **flab·bi·er; -est** : lacking firmness : FLACCID ⟨~ muscles⟩ — **flab·bi·ness** \-bē-nəs\ *n*

flac·cid \ˈflak-səd\ *adj* : deficient in firmness ⟨~ plant stems⟩

¹**flag** \ˈflag\ *n* : any of various irises; *esp* : a wild iris

²**flag** *n* **1** : a usu. rectangular piece of fabric of distinctive design that is used as a symbol (as of a nation) or as a signaling device **2** : something used like a flag to signal or attract attention **3** : one of the cross strokes of a musical note less than a quarter note in value

³**flag** *vb* **flagged; flag·ging 1** : to signal with or as if with a flag; *esp* : to signal to stop ⟨~ a taxi⟩ **2** : to put a flag on **3** : to call a penalty on

⁴**flag** *vb* **flagged; flag·ging 1** : to hang loose or limp **2** : to become unsteady, feeble, or spiritless **3** : to decline in interest or attraction ⟨the topic *flagged*⟩

⁵**flag** *n* : a hard flat stone suitable for paving

flag·el·late \ˈfla-jə-ˌlāt\ *vb* **-lat·ed; -lat·ing** : to punish by whipping — **flag·el·la·tion** \ˌfla-jə-ˈlā-shən\ *n*

fla·gel·lum \flə-ˈje-ləm\ *n, pl* **-la** \-lə\ *also* **-lums** : a long whiplike process that is the primary organ of motion of many microorganisms — **fla·gel·lar** \-lər\ *adj*

fla·geo·let \ˌfla-jə-ˈlet, -ˈlā\ *n* [F] : a small woodwind instrument belonging to the flute class

fla·gi·tious \flə-ˈji-shəs\ *adj* : grossly wicked : VILLAINOUS

flag·on \ˈfla-gən\ *n* : a container for liquids usu. with a handle, spout, and lid

flag·pole \ˈflag-ˌpōl\ *n* : a pole on which to raise a flag

fla·grant \ˈflā-grənt\ *adj* [L *flagrans*, prp. of *flagrare* to burn] : conspicuously bad — **fla·grant·ly** *adv*

fla·gran·te de·lic·to \flə-ˌgran-tē-di-ˈlik-tō\ *adv or adj* [ML, lit., while the crime is blazing] : in the very act of committing a misdeed; *also* : in the midst of sexual activity

flag·ship \ˈflag-ˌship\ *n* **1** : the ship that carries the commander of a fleet or subdivision thereof and flies his flag **2** : the most important one of a group

flag·staff \-ˌstaf\ *n* : FLAGPOLE

flag·stone \-ˌstōn\ *n* : ⁵FLAG

¹**flail** \ˈflāl\ *n* : a tool for threshing grain by hand

²**flail** *vb* : to strike or swing with or as if with a flail

flair \ˈflar\ *n* [F, lit., sense of smell, fr. OF, odor, fr. *flairier* to give off an odor, fr. (assumed) VL *flagrare*, fr. L *fragrare*] **1** : ability to appreciate or make good use of something : BENT, TALENT **2** : a unique style

flak \ˈflak\ *n, pl* **flak** [G, fr. *Fliegerabwehrkanonen*, fr. *Flieger* flyer + *Abwehr* defense + *Kanonen* cannons] **1** : antiaircraft guns or bursting shells fired from them **2** : CRITICISM, OPPOSITION

¹**flake** \ˈflāk\ *n* **1** : a small loose mass or bit **2** : a thin flattened piece or layer : CHIP — **flaky** *adj*

²**flake** *vb* **flaked; flak·ing** : to form or separate into flakes

³**flake** *n* : a markedly eccentric person : ODDBALL — **flak·i·ness** \ˈflā-kē-nəs\ *n* — **flaky** *adj*

flam·beau \ˈflam-ˌbō\ *n, pl* **flambeaux** \-ˌbōz\ *or* **flambeaus** [F, fr. MF, fr. *flambe* flame] : a flaming torch

flam·boy·ant \flam-ˈbȯi-ənt\ *adj* : marked by or given to strikingly elaborate or colorful display or behavior — **flam·boy·ance** \-əns\ *n* — **flam·boy·an·cy** \-ən-sē\ *n* — **flam·boy·ant·ly** *adv*

flame \ˈflām\ *n* **1** : the glowing gaseous part of a fire **2** : a state of blazing combustion **3** : a flamelike condition **4** : burning zeal or passion **5** : BRILLIANCE **6** : SWEETHEART — **flame** *vb*

fla·men·co \flə-ˈmeŋ-kō\ *n, pl* **-cos** [Sp, fr. *flamenco* of the Gypsies, lit., Flemish, fr. MD *Vlaminc* Fleming] : a vigorous rhythmic dance style of the Spanish Gypsies

flame·throw·er \ˈflām-ˌthrō-ər\ *n* : a device that expels from a nozzle a burning stream of liquid or semiliquid fuel under pressure

fla·min·go \flə-ˈmiŋ-gō\ *n, pl* **-gos** *also* **-goes** : any of several long-legged long-necked tropical water birds with scarlet wings and a broad bill bent downward

flam·ma·ble \ˈfla-mə-bəl\ *adj* : easily ignited and quick= burning — **flam·ma·bil·i·ty** \ˌfla-mə-ˈbi-lə-tē\ *n* — **flammable** *n*

flange \ˈflanj\ *n* : a rim used for strengthening or guiding something or for attachment to another object

¹**flank** \ˈflaŋk\ *n* **1** : the fleshy part of the side between the ribs and the hip; *also* : the side of a quadruped **2** : SIDE **3** : the right or left of a formation

²**flank** *vb* **1** : to attack or threaten the flank of **2** : to be situated on the side of : BORDER

flank·er \ˈflaŋ-kər\ *n* : a football player stationed wide of the formation slightly behind the line of scrimmage as a pass receiver

flan·nel \ˈflan-ᵊl\ *n* **1** : a soft twilled wool or worsted fabric with a napped surface **2** : a stout cotton fabric napped on one side **3** *pl* : flannel underwear or trousers

¹**flap** \ˈflap\ *n* **1** : a stroke with something broad : SLAP **2** : something broad, limber, or flat and usu. thin that hangs loose **3** : the motion or sound of something broad and limber as it swings to and fro **4** : a state of excitement or confusion

²**flap** *vb* **flapped; flap·ping 1** : to beat with something broad and flat **2** : FLING **3** : to move (as wings) with a beating motion **4** : to sway loosely usu. with a noise of striking

flap·jack \'flap-ˌjak\ *n* : PANCAKE
flap·per \'fla-pər\ *n* **1** : one that flaps **2** : a young woman of the 1920s who showed freedom from conventions (as in conduct)
¹flare \'flar\ *vb* **flared; flar·ing 1** : to flame with a sudden unsteady light **2** : to become suddenly excited or angry ⟨~ up⟩ **3** : to spread outward
²flare *n* **1** : an unsteady glaring light **2** : a blaze of light used esp. to signal or illuminate; *also* : a device for producing such a blaze
flare–up \-ˌəp\ *n* : a sudden outburst or intensification
¹flash \'flash\ *vb* **1** : to break forth in or like a sudden flame **2** : to appear or pass suddenly or with great speed **3** : to send out in or as if in flashes ⟨~ a message⟩ **4** : to make a sudden display (as of brilliance or feeling) **5** : to gleam or glow intermittently **6** : to fill by a sudden rush of water **7** : to expose to view very briefly ⟨~ a badge⟩
syn glance, glint, sparkle, twinkle — **flash·er** *n*
²flash *n* **1** : a sudden burst of light **2** : a movement of a flag or light in signaling **3** : a sudden and brilliant burst (as of wit) **4** : a brief time **5** : SHOW, DISPLAY; *esp* : ostentatious display **6** : one that attracts notice; *esp* : an outstanding athlete **7** : GLIMPSE, LOOK **8** : a first brief news report **9** : FLASHLIGHT **10** : a device for producing a brief and very bright flash of light for taking photographs **11** : a quick-spreading flame or momentary intense outburst of radiant heat
³flash *adj* **1** : of sudden origin and short duration **2** : involving brief exposure to an intense agent (as heat or cold)
flash·back \'flash-ˌbak\ *n* **1** : interruption of the chronological sequence (as of a film or literary work) by an event of earlier occurrence **2** : a past event remembered vividly
flash back *vb* **1** : to vividly remember a past incident **2** : to employ a flashback
flash·bulb \-ˌbəlb\ *n* : an electric bulb that can be used only once to produce a brief and very bright flash of light for taking photographs
flash card *n* : a card bearing words, numbers, or pictures briefly displayed usu. as a learning aid
flash·cube \'flash-ˌkyüb\ *n* : a cubical device incorporating four flashbulbs
flash·gun \-ˌgən\ *n* : a device for producing a bright flash of light for photography
flash·ing \'fla-shiŋ\ *n* : sheet metal used in waterproofing (as at the angle between a chimney and a roof)
flash·light \'flash-ˌlīt\ *n* : a battery-operated portable electric light
flashy \'fla-shē\ *adj* **flash·i·er; -est 1** : momentarily dazzling **2** : superficially attractive or impressive : SHOWY — **flash·i·ly** \-shə-lē\ *adv* — **flash·i·ness** \-shē-nəs\ *n*
flask \'flask\ *n* : a flattened bottle-shaped container ⟨a whiskey ~⟩
¹flat \'flat\ *adj* **flat·ter; flat·test 1** : spread out along a surface; *also* : being or characterized by a horizontal line **2** : having a smooth, level, or even surface **3** : having a broad smooth surface and little thickness **4** : DOWNRIGHT, POSITIVE ⟨a ~ refusal⟩ **5** : FIXED, UNCHANGING ⟨charge a ~ rate⟩ **6** : EXACT, PRECISE ⟨in four minutes ~⟩ **7** : DULL, UNINTERESTING; *also* : INSIPID **8** : DEFLATED **9** : lower than the true pitch; *also* : lower by a half step **10** : free from gloss **11** : lacking depth of characterization — **flat·ly** *adv* — **flat·ness** *n*
²flat *n* **1** : a level surface of land : PLAIN **2** : a flat part or surface **3** : a character ♭ that indicates that a specified note is to be lowered by a half step; *also* : the resulting note **4** : something flat **5** : an apartment on one floor **6** : a deflated tire
³flat *adv* **1** : FLATLY **2** : COMPLETELY ⟨~ broke⟩ **3** : below the true musical pitch
⁴flat *vb* **flat·ted; flat·ting 1** : FLATTEN **2** : to lower in pitch esp. by a half step

flat·bed \'flat-ˌbed\ *n* : a truck or trailer with a body in the form of a platform or shallow box
flat·boat \-ˌbōt\ *n* : a flat-bottomed boat used esp. for carrying bulky freight
flat·car \-ˌkär\ *n* : a railroad freight car without sides or roof
flat·fish \-ˌfish\ *n* : any of an order of flattened marine bony fishes with both eyes on the upper side
flat·foot \-ˌfut, -ˈfut\ *n, pl* **flat·feet** \-ˌfēt, -ˈfēt\ : a condition in which the arch of the foot is flattened so that the entire sole rests upon the ground — **flat–foot·ed** \-ˈfu-təd\ *adj*
Flat·head \-ˌhed\ *n, pl* **Flatheads** *or* **Flathead** : a member of an American Indian people of Montana
flat·iron \-ˌīrn\ *n* : IRON 3
flat·land \-ˌland\ *n* : land lacking significant variation in elevation
flat–out \'flat-ˌaut\ *adj* **1** : being or going at maximum effort or speed **2** : OUT-AND-OUT, DOWNRIGHT ⟨it was a ~ lie⟩
flat out *adv* **1** : BLUNTLY, DIRECTLY **2** : at top speed **3** *usu* **flat–out** : to the greatest degree : COMPLETELY ⟨is just *flat-out* confusing⟩
flat·ten \'flat-ᵊn\ *vb* : to make or become flat
flat·ter \'fla-tər\ *vb* [ME *flateren,* fr. OF *flater* to lick, flatter] **1** : to praise too much or without sincerity **2** : to represent too favorably **3** : to display to advantage **4** : to judge (oneself) favorably or too favorably — **flat·ter·er** *n*
flat·tery \'fla-tə-rē\ *n, pl* **-ter·ies** : flattering speech or attentions : insincere or excessive praise
flat·top \'flat-ˌtäp\ *n* **1** : AIRCRAFT CARRIER **2** : CREW CUT
flat·u·lent \'fla-chə-lənt\ *adj* **1** : full of gas ⟨a ~ stomach⟩ **2** : INFLATED, POMPOUS — **flat·u·lence** \-ləns\ *n*
fla·tus \'flā-təs\ *n* : gas formed in the intestine or stomach
flat·ware \'flat-ˌwar\ *n* : eating and serving utensils
flat·worm \-ˌwürm\ *n* : any of a phylum of flattened mostly parasitic segmented worms (as trematodes and tapeworms)
flaunt \'flont\ *vb* **1** : to display oneself to public notice **2** : to wave or flutter showily **3** : to display ostentatiously or impudently : PARADE — **flaunt** *n*
flau·tist \'flo-tist, 'flaù-\ *n* [It *flautista*] : FLUTIST
¹fla·vor \'flā-vər\ *n* **1** : the quality of something that affects the sense of taste or of taste and smell **2** : a substance that adds flavor **3** : characteristic or predominant quality — **fla·vored** \-vərd\ *adj* — **fla·vor·ful** *adj* — **fla·vor·less** *adj* — **fla·vor·some** *adj*
²flavor *vb* : to give or add flavor to
fla·vor·ing *n* : FLAVOR 2
fla·vour *chiefly Brit var of* FLAVOR
flaw \'flo\ *n* : a small often hidden defect — **flaw·less** *adj* — **flaw·less·ly** *adv* — **flaw·less·ness** *n*
flax \'flaks\ *n* : a fiber that is the source of linen; *also* : a blue-flowered plant grown for this fiber and its oily seeds
flax·en \'flak-sən\ *adj* **1** : made of flax **2** : resembling flax esp. in pale soft straw color
flay \'flā\ *vb* **1** : to strip off the skin or surface of **2** : to criticize harshly
fl dr *abbr* fluid dram
flea \'flē\ *n* : any of an order of small wingless leaping bloodsucking insects
flea·bane \'flē-ˌbān\ *n* : any of various plants of the daisy family once believed to drive away fleas
flea–bit·ten \-ˌbit-ᵊn\ *adj* : bitten by or infested with fleas

flea market *n* : a usu. open-air market for secondhand articles and antiques

¹**fleck** \'flek\ *vb* : STREAK, SPOT

²**fleck** *n* 1 : SPOT, MARK 2 : FLAKE, PARTICLE

fledge \'flej\ *vb* **fledged; fledg·ing** : to develop the feathers necessary for flying

fledg·ling \'flej-liŋ\ *n* 1 : a young bird with flight feathers newly developed 2 : an immature or inexperienced person

flee \'flē\ *vb* **fled** \'fled\; **flee·ing** 1 : to run away often from danger or evil 2 : VANISH 3 : to run away from : SHUN

¹**fleece** \'flēs\ *n* 1 : the woolly coat of an animal and esp. a sheep 2 : a soft or woolly covering — **fleecy** *adj*

²**fleece** *vb* **fleeced; fleec·ing** 1 : to strip of money or property by fraud or extortion 2 : SHEAR

¹**fleet** \'flēt\ *vb* : to pass rapidly

²**fleet** *n* [ME *flete*, fr. OE *flēot* ship, fr. *flēotan* to float] 1 : a group of warships under one command 2 : a group (as of ships, planes, or trucks) under one management

³**fleet** *adj* 1 : SWIFT, NIMBLE 2 : not enduring : FLEETING — **fleet·ness** *n*

fleet admiral *n* : an admiral of the highest rank in the navy

fleet·ing \'flē-tiŋ\ *adj* : passing swiftly

Flem·ing \'fle-miŋ\ *n* : a member of a Germanic people inhabiting chiefly northern Belgium

Flem·ish \'fle-mish\ *n* 1 : the Dutch language as spoken by the Flemings 2 **Flemish** *pl* : FLEMINGS — **Flemish** *adj*

flesh \'flesh\ *n* 1 : the soft parts of an animal's body; *esp* : muscular tissue 2 : MEAT 3 : the physical nature of humans as distinguished from the soul 4 : human beings; *also* : living beings 5 : STOCK, KINDRED 6 : fleshy plant tissue (as fruit pulp) — **fleshed** \'flesht\ *adj*

flesh fly *n* : a dipteran fly whose maggots feed on flesh

flesh·ly \'flesh-lē\ *adj* 1 : CORPOREAL, BODILY 2 : not spiritual : WORLDLY 3 : CARNAL, SENSUAL

flesh out *vb* : to make fuller or more nearly complete

flesh·pot \'flesh-ˌpät\ *n* 1 *pl* : bodily comfort : LUXURY 2 : a place of lascivious entertainment — usu. used in pl.

fleshy \'fle-shē\ *adj* **flesh·i·er; -est** 1 : consisting of or resembling animal flesh 2 : PLUMP, FAT

flew *past of* ¹FLY

flex \'fleks\ *vb* : to bend esp. repeatedly — **flex** *n*

flex·i·ble \'flek-sə-bəl\ *adj* 1 : capable of being flexed : PLIANT 2 : yielding to influence : TRACTABLE 3 : readily changed or changing : ADAPTABLE **syn** elastic, supple, resilient, springy — **flex·i·bil·i·ty** \ˌflek-sə-'bi-lə-tē\ *n*

flex·ure \'flek-shər\ *n* : TURN, FOLD

flib·ber·ti·gib·bet \ˌfli-bər-tē-'ji-bət\ *n* : a silly flighty person

¹**flick** \'flik\ *n* 1 : a light sharp jerky stroke or movement 2 : a sound produced by a flick 3 : ²FLICKER 4 : MOVIE — often used in pl.

²**flick** *vb* 1 : to strike lightly with a quick sharp motion 2 : FLUTTER, FLIT

¹**flick·er** \'fli-kər\ *vb* 1 : to move irregularly or unsteadily : FLUTTER 2 : to burn fitfully or with a fluctuating light — **flick·er·ing·ly** *adv*

²**flicker** *n* 1 : an act of flickering 2 : a sudden brief movement ⟨a ~ of an eyelid⟩ 3 : a momentary stirring ⟨a ~ of interest⟩ 4 : a slight indication : HINT 5 : a wavering light

³**flicker** *n* : a large barred and spotted No. American woodpecker with a brown back that occurs as an eastern form with yellow on the underside of the wings and tail and a western form with red in these areas

flied *past and past part of* ³FLY

fli·er \'flī-ər\ *n* 1 : one that flies; *esp* : PILOT 2 : a reckless or speculative undertaking 3 *usu* **fly·er** : an advertising circular

¹**flight** \'flīt\ *n* 1 : an act or instance of flying 2 : the ability to fly 3 : a passing through air or space 4 : the distance covered in a flight 5 : swift movement 6 : a trip made by or in an airplane or spacecraft 7 : a group of similar individuals (as birds or airplanes) flying as a unit 8 : a passing (as of the imagination) beyond ordinary limits 9 : a series of stairs from one landing to another — **flight·less** *adj*

²**flight** *n* : an act or instance of running away

flight bag *n* 1 : a lightweight traveling bag with zippered outside pockets 2 : a small canvas satchel

flight line *n* : a parking and servicing area for airplanes

flighty \'flī-tē\ *adj* **flight·i·er; -est** 1 : easily upset : VOLATILE 2 : easily excited : SKITTISH 3 : CAPRICIOUS, SILLY — **flight·i·ness** \-tē-nəs\ *n*

flim·flam \'flim-ˌflam\ *n* : DECEPTION, FRAUD — **flim·flam·mery** \-ˌfla-mə-re\ *n*

flim·sy \'flim-zē\ *adj* **flim·si·er; -est** 1 : lacking strength or substance 2 : of inferior materials and workmanship 3 : having little worth or plausibility ⟨a ~ excuse⟩ — **flim·si·ly** \-zə-lē\ *adv* — **flim·si·ness** \-zē-nəs\ *n*

flinch \'flinch\ *vb* [MF *flenchir* to bend] : to shrink from or as if from pain : WINCE — **flinch** *n*

¹**fling** \'fliŋ\ *vb* **flung** \'fləŋ\; **fling·ing** 1 : to move hastily, brusquely, or violently ⟨*flung* out of the room⟩ 2 : to kick or plunge vigorously 3 : to throw with force or recklessness; *also* : to cast as if by throwing 4 : to put suddenly into a state or condition

²**fling** *n* 1 : an act or instance of flinging 2 : a casual try : ATTEMPT 3 : a period of self-indulgence

flint \'flint\ *n* 1 : a hard quartz that produces a spark when struck by steel 2 : an alloy used for producing a spark in lighters — **flinty** *adj*

flint glass *n* : heavy glass containing an oxide of lead and used in lenses and prisms

flint·lock \'flint-ˌläk\ *n* 1 : a lock for a gun using a flint to ignite the charge 2 : a firearm fitted with a flintlock

¹**flip** \'flip\ *vb* **flipped; flip·ping** 1 : to turn by tossing ⟨~ a coin⟩ 2 : to turn over; *also* : to leaf through 3 : FLICK, JERK ⟨~ a light switch⟩ 4 : to lose self-control — **flip** *n*

²**flip** *adj* : FLIPPANT, IMPERTINENT

flip·pant \'fli-pənt\ *adj* : lacking proper respect or seriousness — **flip·pan·cy** \'fli-pən-sē\ *n*

flip·per \'fli-pər\ *n* 1 : a broad flat limb (as of a seal) adapted for swimming 2 : a paddlelike shoe used in skin diving

flip side *n* : the reverse and usu. less popular side of a phonograph record

¹**flirt** \'flərt\ *vb* 1 : to move erratically : FLIT 2 : to behave amorously without serious intent 3 : to show casual interest ⟨~ed with the idea⟩; *also* : to come close to ⟨~ with danger⟩ — **flir·ta·tion** \ˌflər-'tā-shən\ *n* — **flir·ta·tious** \-shəs\ *adj*

²**flirt** *n* 1 : an act or instance of flirting 2 : a person who flirts

flit \'flit\ *vb* **flit·ted; flit·ting** : to pass or move quickly or abruptly from place to place : DART — **flit** *n*

flitch \'flich\ *n* : a side of cured meat; *esp* : a side of bacon

fliv·ver \'fli-vər\ *n* : a small cheap usu. old automobile

¹**float** \'flōt\ *n* 1 : something (as a raft) that floats 2 : a cork buoying up the baited end of a fishing line 3 : a hollow ball that floats at the end of a lever in a cistern or tank and regulates the liquid level 4 : a vehicle with a platform to carry an exhibit 5 : a soft drink with ice cream floating in it

²**float** *vb* 1 : to rest on the surface of or be suspended in a fluid 2 : to move gently on or through a fluid 3 : to cause to float 4 : WANDER 5 : to offer (securities) in order to finance an enterprise 6 : to finance by floating an

issue of stocks or bonds **7** : to arrange for ⟨∼ a loan⟩ — **float·er** *n*

¹flock \'fläk\ *n* **1** : a group of birds or mammals assembled or herded together **2** : a group of people under the guidance of a leader; *esp* : CONGREGATION **3** : a large number

²flock *vb* : to gather or move in a flock

floe \'flō\ *n* : a flat mass of floating ice

flog \'fläg\ *vb* **flogged; flog·ging 1** : to beat with or as if with a rod or whip **2** : SELL ⟨∼ encyclopedias⟩ — **flog·ger** *n*

¹flood \'fləd\ *n* **1** : a great flow of water over the land; *also, cap* : a flood described in the Bible as covering the earth in the time of Noah **2** : the flowing in of the tide **3** : an overwhelming volume

²flood *vb* **1** : to cover or become filled with a flood **2** : to fill abundantly or excessively; *esp* : to supply (a carburetor) with too much fuel **3** : to pour forth in a flood — **flood·er** *n*

flood·gate \'fləd-ˌgāt\ *n* : a gate for controlling a body of water : SLUICE

flood·light \-ˌlīt\ *n* : a lamp that throws a broad beam of light; *also* : the beam itself — **floodlight** *vb*

flood·plain \-ˌplān\ *n* : a plain along a river or stream subject to periodic flooding

flood tide *n* **1** : a rising tide **2** : an overwhelming quantity **3** : a high point

flood·wa·ter \'fləd-ˌwȯ-tər, -ˌwä-\ *n* : the water of a flood

¹floor \'flōr\ *n* **1** : the bottom of a room on which one stands **2** : a ground surface **3** : a story of a building **4** : a main level space (as in a legislative chamber) distinguished from a platform or gallery **5** : AUDIENCE **6** : the right to address an assembly **7** : a lower limit ⟨put a ∼ under wheat prices⟩ — **floor·ing** *n*

²floor *vb* **1** : to furnish with a floor **2** : to knock down **3** : AMAZE, DUMBFOUND **4** : to press (a vehicle's accelerator) to the floorboard esp. rapidly

floor·board \-ˌbōrd\ *n* **1** : a board in a floor **2** : the floor of an automobile

floor leader *n* : a member of a legislative body who has charge of a party's organization and strategy on the floor

floor show *n* : a series of acts presented in a nightclub

floor·walk·er \'flōr-ˌwȯ-kər\ *n* : a person employed in a retail store to oversee the sales force and aid customers

floo·zy *or* **floo·zie** \'flü-zē\ *n, pl* **floozies** : a usu. young woman of loose morals

flop \'fläp\ *vb* **flopped; flop·ping 1** : FLAP **2** : to throw oneself down heavily, clumsily, or in a relaxed manner ⟨*flopped* into a chair⟩ **3** : FAIL — **flop** *n* — **flop** *adv* — **flop·per** *n*

flop·house \'fläp-ˌhaùs\ *n* : a cheap hotel

¹flop·py \'flä-pē\ *adj* **flop·pi·er; -est** : tending to flop; *esp* : soft and flexible — **flop·pi·ly** \-pə-lē\ *adv*

²floppy *n, pl* **flop·pies** : FLOPPY DISK

floppy disk *n* : a small flexible disk with a magnetic coating on which computer data can be stored

flo·ra \'flōr-ə\ *n, pl* **floras** *also* **flo·rae** \-ˌē, -ˌī\ [L *Flora,* Roman goddess of flowers] : plants or plant life esp. of a region or period

flo·ral \'flōr-əl\ *adj* : of or relating to flowers or a flora

flo·res·cence \flȯ-'res-ᵊns, flə-\ *n* : a state or period of being in bloom or flourishing — **flo·res·cent** \-ᵊnt\ *adj*

flor·id \'flȯr-əd\ *adj* **1** : very flowery in style : ORNATE ⟨∼ prose⟩ **2** : tinged with red : RUDDY **3** : marked by emotional or sexual fervor

flo·rin \'flȯr-ən\ *n* **1** : an old gold coin first struck at Florence, Italy, in 1252 **2** : a gold coin of a European country patterned after the florin of Florence **3** : any of several modern silver coins issued in Commonwealth countries **4** : GULDEN

flo·rist \'flȯr-ist\ *n* : a person who sells flowers or ornamental plants

¹floss \'fläs\ *n* **1** : soft thread of silk or mercerized cotton for embroidery **2** : DENTAL FLOSS **3** : fluffy fibrous material

²floss *vb* : to use dental floss on (one's teeth) : use dental floss

flossy \'flä-sē\ *adj* **floss·i·er; -est 1** : of, relating to, or having the characteristics of floss **2** : STYLISH, GLAMOROUS — **floss·i·ly** \-sə-lē\ *adv*

flo·ta·tion \flō-'tā-shən\ *n* : the process or an instance of floating

flo·til·la \flō-'ti-lə\ *n* [Sp, dim. of *flota* fleet] : a fleet esp. of small ships

flot·sam \'flät-səm\ *n* : floating wreckage of a ship or its cargo

¹flounce \'flaùns\ *vb* **flounced; flounc·ing 1** : to move with exaggerated jerky or bouncy motions **2** : to go with sudden determination

²flounce *n* : an act or instance of flouncing — **flouncy** \'flaùn-sē\ *adj*

³flounce *n* : a strip of fabric attached by one edge; *also* : a wide ruffle

¹floun·der \'flaùn-dər\ *n, pl* **flounder** *or* **flounders** : FLATFISH; *esp* : any of various important marine food fishes

²flounder *vb* **1** : to struggle to move or obtain footing **2** : to proceed clumsily ⟨∼ed through the speech⟩

flour \'flaùr\ *n* : finely ground and sifted meal of a grain (as wheat); *also* : a fine soft powder — **floury** *adj*

²flour *vb* : to coat with or as if with flour

¹flour·ish \'flər-ish\ *vb* **1** : THRIVE, PROSPER **2** : to be in a state of activity or production ⟨∼ed about 1850⟩ **3** : to reach a height of development or influence **4** : to make bold and sweeping gestures **5** : BRANDISH

²flourish *n* **1** : a florid bit of speech or writing; *also* : an ornamental touch or decorative detail **2** : FANFARE **3** : WAVE ⟨with a ∼ of his cane⟩ **4** : showiness in doing something

¹flout \'flaùt\ *vb* : to treat with contemptuous disregard ⟨∼ the law⟩ — **flout·er** *n*

²flout *n* : TAUNT

¹flow \'flō\ *vb* **1** : to issue or move in a stream **2** : RISE ⟨the tide ebbs and ∼s⟩ **3** : ABOUND **4** : to proceed smoothly and readily **5** : to have a smooth continuity **6** : to hang loose and billowing **7** : COME, ARISE **8** : MENSTRUATE

²flow *n* **1** : an act of flowing **2** : FLOOD 1, 2 **3** : a smooth uninterrupted movement **4** : STREAM, *also* : a mass of material that has flowed when molten **5** : the quantity that flows in a certain time **6** : MENSTRUATION **7** : a continuous transfer of energy — **flow·age** \'flō-ij\ *n*

flow·chart \'flō-ˌchärt\ *n* : a symbolic diagram showing step-by-step progression through a procedure

flow diagram *n* : FLOWCHART

¹flow·er \'flaù(-ə)r\ *n* **1** : a plant shoot modified for reproduction and bearing leaves specialized into floral organs; *esp* : one of a seed plant consisting of a calyx, corolla, stamens, and carpels **2** : a plant cultivated for its blossoms **3** : the best part or example **4** : the finest most vigorous period **5** : a state of blooming or flourishing — **flow·ered** \'flaù(-ə)rd\ *adj* — **flow·er·less** *adj*

²flower *vb* : DEVELOP; *also* : FLOURISH **2** : to produce flowers : BLOOM

flower girl *n* : a little girl who carries flowers at a wedding

flower head *n* : a compact cluster of small flowers without stems suggesting a single flower

flowering plant *n* : any of a major group of vascular plants (as magnolias, grasses, or roses) that produce

\ə\abut \ᵊ\kitten \ər\further \a\ash \ā\ace \ä\mop, mar
\aù\out \ch\chin \e\bet \ē\easy \g\go \i\hit \ī\ice \j\job
\ŋ\sing \ō\go \ȯ\law \ȯi\boy \th\thin \t̲h̲\the \ü\loot \ù\foot
\y\yet \zh\vision   *see also* Pronunciation Symbols page

flowers and fruit and have the seeds enclosed in an ovary

flow·er·pot \'flaù(-ə)r-ˌpät\ *n* : a pot in which to grow plants

flow·ery \'flaù(-ə)r-ē\ *adj* **1** : of, relating to, or resembling flowers **2** : full of fine words or phrases — **flow·er·i·ly** \-ə-lē\ *adv* — **flow·er·i·ness** \-ē-nəs\ *n*

flown \'flōn\ *past part of* ¹FLY

fl oz *abbr* fluid ounce

flu \'flü\ *n* **1** : INFLUENZA **2** : any of several virus diseases marked esp. by respiratory symptoms

flub \'fləb\ *vb* **flubbed; flub·bing** : BOTCH, BLUNDER — **flub** *n*

fluc·tu·ate \'flək-chə-ˌwāt\ *vb* **-at·ed; -at·ing 1** : WAVER **2** : to move up and down or back and forth — **fluc·tu·a·tion** \ˌflək-chə-'wā-shən\ *n*

flue \'flü\ *n* : a passage (as in a chimney) for directing a current (as of smoke or gases)

flu·ent \'flü-ənt\ *adj* **1** : capable of flowing : FLUID **2** : ready or facile in speech ⟨∼ in French⟩ **3** : effortlessly smooth and rapid ⟨∼ speech⟩ — **flu·en·cy** \-ən-sē\ *n* — **flu·ent·ly** *adv*

flue pipe *n* : an organ pipe whose tone is produced by an air current striking the beveled opening of the pipe

¹**fluff** \'fləf\ *n* **1** : ⁷DOWN 1 ⟨∼ from a pillow⟩ **2** : something fluffy **3** : something inconsequential **4** : BLUNDER; *esp* : an actor's lapse of memory

²**fluff** *vb* **1** : to make or become fluffy ⟨∼ up a pillow⟩ **2** : to make a mistake

fluffy \'flə-fē\ *adj* **fluff·i·er; -est 1** : covered with or resembling fluff **2** : being light and soft or airy ⟨a ∼ omelet⟩ **3** : lacking in meaning or substance — **fluff·i·ly** \-fə-lē\ *adv*

¹**flu·id** \'flü-əd\ *adj* **1** : capable of flowing **2** : subject to change or movement **3** : showing a smooth easy style ⟨∼ movements⟩ **4** : available for a different use; *esp* : LIQUID **5** ⟨∼ assets⟩ — **flu·id·i·ty** \flü-'i-də-tē\ *n* — **flu·id·ly** *adv*

²**fluid** *n* : a substance (as a liquid or gas) tending to flow or take the shape of its container

fluid dram *or* **flu·i·dram** \ˌflü-ə-'dram\ *n* — see WEIGHT table

fluid ounce *n* — see WEIGHT table

¹**fluke** \'flük\ *n* : any of various trematode flatworms

²**fluke** *n* **1** : the part of an anchor that fastens in the ground **2** : a lobe of a whale's tail

³**fluke** *n* : a stroke of luck — **fluky** *also* **fluk·ey** \'flü-kē\ *adj*

flume \'flüm\ *n* **1** : an inclined channel for carrying water **2** : a ravine or gorge with a stream running through it

flung *past and past part of* FLING

flunk \'fləŋk\ *vb* : to fail esp. in an examination or course — **flunk** *n*

flun·ky *or* **flun·key** \'flən-kē\ *n, pl* **flunkies** *or* **flunkeys 1** : a liveried servant; *also* : one performing menial or miscellaneous duties **2** : YES-MAN

fluo·res·cence \flò-'res-ᵊns\ *n* : luminescence caused by radiation absorption that ceases almost immediately after the incident radiation has stopped; *also* : the emitted radiation — **fluo·resce** \-'res\ *vb* — **fluo·res·cent** \-'res-ᵊnt\ *adj*

fluorescent lamp *n* : a tubular electric lamp in which light is produced by the action of ultraviolet light on a fluorescent material that coats the inner surface of the lamp

fluo·ri·date \'flòr-ə-ˌdāt\ *vb* **-dat·ed; -dat·ing** : to add a fluoride to (as drinking water) to reduce tooth decay — **fluo·ri·da·tion** \ˌflòr-ə-'dā-shən\ *n*

fluo·ride \'flòr-ˌīd\ *n* : a compound of fluorine

fluo·ri·nate \'flòr-ə-ˌnāt\ *vb* **-nat·ed; -nat·ing** : to treat or cause to combine with fluorine or a compound of fluorine — **fluo·ri·na·tion** \ˌflòr-ə-'nā-shən\ *n*

fluo·rine \'flòr-ˌēn, -ən\ *n* : a pale yellowish flammable irritating toxic gaseous chemical element — see ELEMENT table

fluo·rite \'flòr-ˌīt\ *n* : a mineral that consists of the fluoride of calcium used as a flux and in making glass

fluo·ro·car·bon \ˌflòr-ō-'kär-bən\ *n* : a compound containing fluorine and carbon used chiefly as a lubricant, refrigerant, or nonstick coating; *also* : CHLOROFLUOROCARBON

fluo·ro·scope \'flòr-ə-ˌskōp\ *n* : an instrument for observing the internal structure of an opaque object (as the living body) by means of X rays — **fluo·ro·scop·ic** \ˌflòr-ə-'skä-pik\ *adj* — **fluo·ros·co·py** \-'ä-skə-pē\ *n*

fluo·ro·sis \ˌflü-'rō-səs, ˌflò-\ *n* : an abnormal condition (as spotting of the teeth) caused by fluorine or its compounds

flur·ry \'flər-ē\ *n, pl* **flurries 1** : a gust of wind **2** : a brief light snowfall **3** : COMMOTION, BUSTLE **4** : a brief outburst of activity ⟨a ∼ of trading⟩ — **flurry** *vb*

¹**flush** \'fləsh\ *vb* : to cause (a bird) to take wing suddenly

²**flush** *n* : a hand of cards all of the same suit

³**flush** *n* **1** : a sudden flow (as of water) **2** : a surge esp. of emotion ⟨a ∼ of triumph⟩ **3** : a tinge of red : BLUSH **4** : a fresh and vigorous state ⟨in the ∼ of youth⟩ **5** : a passing sensation of extreme heat

⁴**flush** *vb* **1** : to flow and spread suddenly and freely **2** : to glow brightly **3** : BLUSH **4** : to wash out with a rush of fluid **5** : INFLAME, EXCITE **6** : to cause to blush

⁵**flush** *adj* **1** : of a ruddy healthy color **2** : full of life and vigor **3** : filled to overflowing : AFFLUENT **5** : readily available : ABUNDANT **6** : having an unbroken or even surface **7** : directly abutting : immediately adjacent **8** : set even with an edge of a type page or column — **flush·ness** *n*

⁶**flush** *adv* **1** : in a flush manner **2** : SQUARELY ⟨a blow ∼ on the chin⟩

⁷**flush** *vb* : to make flush

flus·ter \'fləs-tər\ *vb* : to put into a state of agitated confusion — **fluster** *n*

flute \'flüt\ *n* **1** : a hollow pipelike musical instrument **2** : a grooved pleat **3** : GROOVE — **flute** *vb* — **flut·ed** *adj*

flute 1

flut·ing *n* : fluted decoration

flut·ist \'flü-tist\ *n* : a flute player

¹**flut·ter** \'flə-tər\ *vb* [ME *floteren* to float, flutter, fr. OE *floterian*, fr. *flotian* to float] **1** : to flap the wings rapidly **2** : to move with quick wavering or flapping motions **3** : to vibrate in irregular spasms **4** : to move about or behave in an agitated aimless manner — **flut·tery** \-tə-rē\ *adj*

²**flutter** *n* **1** : an act of fluttering **2** : a state of nervous confusion **3** : FLURRY

¹**flux** \'fləks\ *n* **1** : an act of flowing **2** : a state of continuous change **3** : a substance used to aid in fusing metals

²**flux** *vb* : ¹FUSE

¹**fly** \'flī\ *vb* **flew** \'flü\; **flown** \'flōn\; **fly·ing 1** : to move in or pass through the air with wings **2** : to move through the air or before the wind **3** : to float or cause

to float, wave, or soar in the air **4** : FLEE **5** : to fade and disappear : VANISH **6** : to move or pass swiftly **7** : to become expended or dissipated rapidly **8** : to operate or travel in an aircraft or spacecraft **9** : to journey over by flying **10** : AVOID, SHUN **11** : to transport by flying

²fly *n, pl* **flies 1** : the action or process of flying : FLIGHT **2** *pl* : the space over a theater stage **3** : a garment closing concealed by a fold of cloth **4** : the length of an extended flag from its staff or support **5** : a baseball hit high into the air **6** : the outer canvas of a tent with a double top — **on the fly** : while still in the air

³fly *vb* **flied; fly·ing** : to hit a fly in baseball

⁴fly *n, pl* **flies 1** : a winged insect — usu. used in combination ⟨butter*fly*⟩ **2** : any of a large order of insects mostly with one pair of functional wings and another pair that if present are reduced to balancing organs and often with larvae without a head, eyes, or legs; *esp* : one (as a housefly) that is large and stout-bodied **3** : a fishhook dressed to suggest an insect

fly·able \'flī-ə-bəl\ *adj* : suitable for flying or being flown

fly ball *n* : ²FLY 5

fly·blown \'flī-ˌblōn\ *adj* : not pure : TAINTED, CORRUPT

fly·by \-ˌbī\ *n, pl* **flybys 1** : a usu. low-altitude flight by an aircraft over a public gathering **2** : a flight of a spacecraft past a heavenly body (as Jupiter) close enough to obtain scientific data

fly–by–night \-bī-ˌnīt\ *adj* **1** : seeking a quick profit usu. by shady acts **2** : TRANSITORY, PASSING

fly casting *n* : the casting of artificial flies in flyfishing or as a competitive sport

fly·catch·er \-ˌka-chər, -ˌke-\ *n* : any of various passerine birds that feed on insects caught in flight

fly·er *var of* FLIER

fly–fish·ing \'flī-ˌfi-shiŋ\ *n* : a method of fishing in which an artificial fly is used for bait

flying boat *n* : a seaplane with a hull designed for floating

flying buttress *n* : a projecting arched structure to support a wall or building

flying fish *n* : any of numerous sea fishes capable of long gliding flights out of water by spreading their large fins like wings

flying saucer *n* : an unidentified flying object reported to be saucer-shaped or disk-shaped

flying squirrel *n* : any of several No. American squirrels with folds of skin connecting the forelegs and hind legs that enable them to make long gliding leaps

fly·leaf \'flī-ˌlēf\ *n, pl* **fly·leaves** \-ˌlēvz\ : a blank leaf at the beginning or end of a book

fly·pa·per \-ˌpā-pər\ *n* : paper poisoned or coated with a sticky substance for killing or catching flies

fly·speck \-ˌspek\ *n* **1** : a speck of fly dung **2** : something small and insignificant — **flyspeck** *vb*

fly·way \-ˌwā\ *n* : an established air route of migratory birds

fly·wheel \-ˌhwēl\ *n* : a heavy wheel for regulating the speed of machinery

fm *abbr* fathom

Fm *symbol* fermium

FM \'ef-ˌem\ *n* : a broadcasting system using frequency modulation; *also* : a radio receiver of such a system

fn *abbr* footnote

fo *or* **fol** *abbr* folio

FO *abbr* foreign office

foal \'fōl\ *n* : a young horse or related animal; *esp* : one under one year — **foal** *vb*

¹foam \'fōm\ *n* **1** : a mass of bubbles formed on the surface of a liquid : FROTH, SPUME **2** : material (as rubber) in a lightweight cellular form — **foamy** *adj*

²foam *vb* : to form foam : FROTH

fob \'fäb\ *n* **1** : a short strap, ribbon, or chain attached esp. to a pocket watch **2** : a small ornament worn on a fob

FOB *abbr* free on board

fob off *vb* **1** : to put off with a trick, excuse, or inferior substitute **2** : to pass or offer as genuine **3** : to put aside

FOC *abbr* free of charge

focal length *n* : the distance of a focus from a lens or curved mirror

fo'·c'sle *var of* FORECASTLE

¹fo·cus \'fō-kəs\ *n, pl* **fo·ci** \-ˌsī\ *also* **fo·cus·es** [NL, fr. L, hearth] **1** : a point at which rays (as of light, heat, or sound) meet or diverge or appear to diverge; *esp* : the point at which an image is formed by a mirror, lens, or optical system **2** : FOCAL LENGTH **3** : adjustment (as of eyes or eyeglasses) that gives clear vision **4** : central point : CENTER — **fo·cal** \'fō-kəl\ *adj* — **fo·cal·ly** *adv*

²focus *vb* **-cused** *also* **-cussed; -cus·ing** *also* **-cus·sing 1** : to bring or come to a focus ⟨~ rays of light⟩ **2** : CENTER ⟨~ attention on a problem⟩ **3** : to adjust the focus of

fod·der \'fä-dər\ *n* : coarse dry food (as cornstalks) for livestock

foe \'fō\ *n* [ME *fo,* fr. OE *fāh,* fr. *fāh* hostile] : ENEMY

FOE *abbr* Fraternal Order of Eagles

foehn *or* **föhn** \'farn, 'fœn, 'fān\ *n* [G *Föhn*] : a warm dry wind blowing down a mountainside

foe·man \'fō-mən\ *n* : FOE

foe·tal, foe·tus *chiefly Brit var of* FETAL, FETUS

¹fog \'fòg, 'fäg\ *n* **1** : fine particles of water suspended in the lower atmosphere **2** : mental confusion — **fog·gy** *adj*

²fog *vb* **fogged; fog·ging** : to obscure or be obscured with or as if with fog

fog·horn \'fòg-ˌhòrn, 'fäg-\ *n* : a horn sounded in a fog to give warning

fo·gy *also* **fo·gey** \'fō-gē\ *n, pl* **fogies** *also* **fogeys** : a person with old-fashioned ideas ⟨an old ~⟩

foi·ble \'fòi-bəl\ *n* : a minor failing or weakness in character or behavior

¹foil \'fòil\ *vb* [ME, to trample, full cloth, fr. MF *fouler*] **1** : to prevent from attaining an end : DEFEAT **2** : to bring to naught : THWART

²foil *n* : a light fencing sword with a flexible blade tapering to a blunt point

³foil *n* [ME, leaf, fr. MF *foille, foil,* fr. L *folium*] **1** : a very thin sheet of metal ⟨aluminum ~⟩ **2** : one that serves as a contrast to another

foist \'fòist\ *vb* : to pass off (something false or worthless) as genuine

¹fold \'fōld\ *n* **1** : an enclosure for sheep **2** : a group of people with a common faith, belief, or interest

²fold *vb* : to house (sheep) in a fold

³fold *vb* **1** : to lay one part over or against another part **2** : to clasp together **3** : EMBRACE **4** : to bend (as a layer of rock) into folds **5** : to incorporate into a mixture by overturning repeatedly without stirring or beating **6** : to become doubled or pleated **7** : FAIL, COLLAPSE

⁴fold *n* **1** : a doubling or folding over **2** : a part doubled or laid over another part

fold·away \'fōl-də-ˌwā\ *adj* : designed to fold out of the way or out of sight

fold·er \'fōl-dər\ *n* **1** : one that folds **2** : a folded printed circular **3** : a folded cover or large envelope for loose papers

fol·de·rol \'fäl-də-ˌräl\ *n* **1** : a useless trifle **2** : NONSENSE

fold·out \'fōl-ˌdaùt\ *n* : a folded leaf (as in a magazine) larger in some dimension than the page

fo·liage \'fō-lē-ij\ *n* : a mass of leaves (as of a plant or forest)

fo·li·at·ed \'fō-lē-ˌā-təd\ *adj* : composed of or separable into layers

---

\ə\abut \ᵊ\kitten \ər\further \a\ash \ā\ace \ä\mop, mar
\au\out \ch\chin \e\bet \ē\easy \g\go \i\hit \ī\ice \j\job
\ŋ\sing \ō\go \ò\law \òi\boy \th\thin \t̷h\the \ü\loot \ù\foot
\y\yet \zh\vision *see also* Pronunciation Symbols page

fo·lic acid \ˌfō-lik-\ *n* : a vitamin of the vitamin B complex used esp. to treat nutritional anemias

fo·lio \ˈfō-lē-ˌō\ *n, pl* **fo·li·os 1** : a leaf of a book; *also* : a page number **2** : the size of a piece of paper cut two from a sheet **3** : a book printed on folio pages

¹folk \ˈfōk\ *n, pl* **folk** *or* **folks 1** : a group of people forming a tribe or nation; *also* : the largest number or most characteristic part of such a group **2** *pl* : PEOPLE, PERSONS ⟨country ∼⟩ ⟨old ∼s⟩ **3** *folks pl* : the persons of one's own family

²folk *adj* : of, relating to, or originating among the common people ⟨∼ music⟩

folk·lore \ˈfōk-ˌlōr\ *n* : customs, beliefs, stories, and sayings of a people handed down from generation to generation — **folk·lor·ist** \-ist\ *n*

folk mass *n* : a mass in which traditional liturgical music is replaced by folk music

folk·sing·er \ˈfōk-ˌsiŋ-ər\ *n* : a singer of folk songs — **folk·sing·ing** *n*

folksy \ˈfōk-sē\ *adj* **folks·i·er; -est 1** : SOCIABLE, FRIENDLY **2** : informal, casual, or familiar in manner or style

folk·way \ˈfōk-ˌwā\ *n* : a way of thinking, feeling, or acting common to a given group of people; *esp* : a traditional social custom

fol·li·cle \ˈfä-li-kəl\ *n* **1** : a small anatomical cavity or gland ⟨a hair ∼⟩ **2** : a small fluid-filled cavity in the ovary of a mammal enclosing a developing egg

fol·low \ˈfä-lō\ *vb* **1** : to go or come after **2** : to proceed along **3** : to engage in as a way of life ⟨∼ the sea⟩ ⟨∼ a profession⟩ **4** : OBEY **5** : PURSUE **6** : to come after in order or rank or natural sequence **7** : to keep one's attention fixed on **8** : to result from **syn** succeed, ensue, supervene — **fol·low·er** *n* — **follow suit 1** : to play a card of the same suit as the card led **2** : to follow an example set

¹fol·low·ing \ˈfä-lə-wiŋ\ *adj* **1** : next after : SUCCEEDING **2** : that immediately follows

²following *n* : a group of followers, adherents, or partisans

³following *prep* : subsequent to : AFTER

follow–up \ˈfä-lə-ˌwəp\ *n* : a system or instance of pursuing an initial effort by supplementary action

fol·ly \ˈfä-lē\ *n, pl* **follies** [ME *folie*, fr. OF, fr. *fol* fool] **1** : lack of good sense **2** : a foolish act or idea : FOOLISHNESS **3** : an excessively costly or unprofitable undertaking

fo·ment \fō-ˈment\ *vb* : INCITE

fo·men·ta·tion \ˌfō-mən-ˈtā-shən, -ˌmen-\ *n* **1** : a hot moist material (as a damp cloth) applied to the body to ease pain **2** : the act of fomenting : INSTIGATION

fond \ˈfänd\ *adj* [ME, fr. *fonne* fool] **1** : FOOLISH, SILLY ⟨∼ pride⟩ **2** : prizing highly : DESIROUS ⟨∼ of praise⟩ **3** : strongly attracted or predisposed ⟨∼ of music⟩ **4** : foolishly tender : INDULGENT; *also* : LOVING, AFFECTIONATE **5** : CHERISHED, DEAR ⟨his ∼est hopes⟩ — **fond·ly** *adv* — **fond·ness** *n*

fon·dant \ˈfän-dənt\ *n* : a creamy preparation of sugar used as a basis for candies or icings

fon·dle \ˈfänd-ᵊl\ *vb* **fon·dled; fon·dling** : to touch or handle lovingly : CARESS

fon·due *also* **fon·du** \fän-ˈdü, -ˈdyü\ *n* [F] : a preparation of melted cheese often flavored with white wine

¹font \ˈfänt\ *n* **1** : a receptacle for baptismal or holy water **2** : FOUNTAIN, SOURCE

²font *n* : an assortment of printing type of one size and style

food \ˈfüd\ *n* **1** : material taken into an organism and used for growth, repair, and vital processes and as a source of energy; *also* : organic material produced by green plants and used by them as food **2** : nourishment in solid form **3** : something that nourishes, sustains, or supplies ⟨∼ for thought⟩

food chain *n* : a hierarchical arrangement of organisms in an ecological community such that each uses the next usu. lower member as a food source

food poisoning *n* : a digestive illness caused by bacteria or by chemicals in food

food·stuff \ˈfüd-ˌstəf\ *n* : a substance with food value; *esp* : a specific nutrient (as fat or protein)

¹fool \ˈfül\ *n* [ME, fr. OF *fol*, fr. LL *follis*, fr. L, bellows, bag] **1** : a person who lacks sense or judgment **2** : JESTER **3** : DUPE **4** : IDIOT

²fool *vb* **1** : to spend time idly or aimlessly **2** : to meddle or tamper thoughtlessly or ignorantly **3** : JOKE **4** : DECEIVE **5** : FRITTER ⟨∼ed away his time⟩

fool·ery \ˈfü-lə-rē\ *n, pl* **-er·ies 1** : a foolish act, utterance, or belief **2** : foolish behavior

fool·har·dy \ˈfül-ˌhär-dē\ *adj* : foolishly daring : RASH — **fool·har·di·ness** \-dē-nəs\ *n*

fool·ish \ˈfü-lish\ *adj* **1** : showing or arising from folly or lack of judgment **2** : ABSURD, RIDICULOUS **3** : ABASHED — **fool·ish·ly** *adv* — **fool·ish·ness** *n*

fool·proof \ˈfül-ˌprüf\ *adj* : so simple or reliable as to leave no opportunity for error, misuse, or failure ⟨a ∼ plan⟩

fools·cap \ˈfül-ˌskap\ *n* [fr. the watermark of a fool's cap formerly applied to such paper] : a size of paper typically 16×13 inches

fool's gold *n* : PYRITE

¹foot \ˈfüt\ *n, pl* **feet** \ˈfēt\ *also* **foot 1** : the end part of a leg below the ankle of a vertebrate animal **2** — see WEIGHT table **3** : a group of syllables forming the basic unit of verse meter **4** : something resembling an animal's foot in position or use **5** : the lowest part : BOTTOM **6** : the part at the opposite end from the head **7** : the part (as of a stocking) that covers the foot

²foot *vb* **1** : DANCE **2** : to go on foot **3** : to add up **4** : to pay or provide for paying

foot·age \ˈfu-tij\ *n* : length expressed in feet

foot·ball \ˈfut-ˌbȯl\ *n* **1** : any of several games played by two teams on a rectangular field with goalposts at each end in which the object is to get the ball over the goal line or between goalposts by running, passing, or kicking **2** : the ball used in football

foot·board \-ˌbōrd\ *n* **1** : a narrow platform on which to stand or brace the feet **2** : a board forming the foot of a bed

foot·bridge \-ˌbrij\ *n* : a bridge for pedestrians

foot·ed \ˈfu-təd\ *adj* : having a foot or feet of a specified kind or number ⟨flat-*footed*⟩ ⟨four-*footed*⟩

-foot·er \ˈfu-tər\ *comb form* : one that is a specified number of feet in height, length, or breadth ⟨a six=*footer*⟩

foot·fall \ˈfut-ˌfȯl\ *n* : the sound of a footstep

foot·hill \-ˌhil\ *n* : a hill at the foot of higher hills or mountains

foot·hold \-ˌhōld\ *n* **1** : a hold for the feet : FOOTING **2** : a position usable as a base for further advance

foot·ing *n* **1** : the placing of one's feet in a stable position **2** : the act of moving on foot **3** : a place or space for standing : FOOTHOLD **4** : position with respect to one another : STATUS **5** : BASIS

foot·less \ˈfut-ləs\ *adj* **1** : having no feet **2** : INEPT

foot·lights \-ˌlīts\ *n pl* **1** : a row of lights along the front of a stage floor **2** : the stage as a profession

foo·tling \ˈfut-liŋ\ *adj* **1** : INEPT **2** : TRIVIAL

foot·lock·er \ˈfut-ˌlä-kər\ *n* : a small trunk designed to be placed at the foot of a bed (as in a barracks)

foot·loose \-ˌlüs\ *adj* : having no ties : FREE, UNTRAMMELED

foot·man \-mən\ *n* : a male servant who attends a carriage, waits on table, admits visitors, and runs errands

foot·note \-ˌnōt\ *n* **1** : a note of reference, explanation, or comment placed usu. at the bottom of a page **2** : COMMENTARY

foot·pad \-ˌpad\ *n* : a round somewhat flat foot on the leg of a spacecraft for distributing weight to minimize sinking into a surface

foot·path \-ˌpath, -ˌpȧth\ *n* : a narrow path for pedestrians

foot·print \-ˌprint\ *n* **1** : an impression of the foot **2** : the area on a surface covered by something

foot·race \-ˌrās\ *n* : a race run on foot

foot·rest \-ˌrest\ *n* : a support for the feet

foot·sore \-ˌsōr\ *adj* : having sore or tender feet (as from much walking)

foot·step \-ˌstep\ *n* **1** : the mark of the foot : TRACK **2** : TREAD **3** : distance covered by a step : PACE **4** : a step on which to ascend or descend **5** : a way of life, conduct, or action

foot·stool \-ˌstül\ *n* : a low stool to support the feet

foot·wear \-ˌwar\ *n* : apparel (as shoes or boots) for the feet

foot·work \-ˌwərk\ *n* : the management of the feet (as in boxing)

fop \ˈfäp\ *n* : DANDY 1 — **fop·pery** \ˈfä-pə-rē\ *n* — **foppish** *adj*

¹for \fər, ˈfȯr\ *prep* **1** : as a preparation toward (dress ∼ dinner) **2** : toward the purpose or goal of (need time ∼ study) (money ∼ a trip) **3** : so as to reach or attain (run ∼ cover) **4** : as being (took him ∼ a fool) **5** : because of (cry ∼ joy) **6** — used to indicate a recipient (a letter ∼ you) **7** : in support of (fought ∼ his country) **8** : directed at : AFFECTING (a cure ∼ what ails you) **9** — used with a noun or pronoun followed by an infinitive to form the equivalent of a noun clause (∼ you to go would be silly) **10** : in exchange as equal to : so as to return the value of (a lot of trouble ∼ nothing) (pay $10 ∼ a hat) **11** : CONCERNING (a stickler ∼ detail) **12** : CONSIDERING (tall ∼ her age) **13** : through the period of (served ∼ three years) **14** : in honor of

²for *conj* : BECAUSE

³for *abbr* **1** foreign **2** forestry

fora *pl of* FORUM

¹for·age \ˈfȯr-ij\ *n* **1** : food for animals esp. when taken by browsing or grazing **2** : a search for food or supplies

²forage *vb* **for·aged; for·ag·ing 1** : to collect forage from **2** : to search for food or supplies **3** : to get by foraging **4** : to make a search : RUMMAGE

for·ay \ˈfȯr-ˌā, fȯ-ˈrā\ *vb* : to raid esp. in search of plunder — **foray** *n*

¹for·bear \fȯr-ˈbar\ *vb* **-bore** \-ˈbōr\; **-borne** \-ˈbōrn\; **-bear·ing 1** : to refrain from : ABSTAIN **2** : to be patient — **for·bear·ance** \-ˈbar-əns\ *n*

²forbear *var of* FOREBEAR

for·bid \fər-ˈbid\ *vb* **-bade** \-ˈbad, -ˈbād\ *or* **-bad** \-ˈbad\; **-bid·den** \-ˈbid-ᵊn\; **-bid·ding 1** : to command against : PROHIBIT **2** : HINDER, PREVENT **syn** enjoin, interdict, inhibit, ban

for·bid·ding *adj* : DISAGREEABLE, REPELLENT

forbode *var of* FOREBODE

¹force \ˈfōrs\ *n* **1** : strength or energy esp. of an exceptional degree : active power **2** : capacity to persuade or convince **3** : military strength; *also, pl* : the whole military strength (as of a nation) **4** : a body (as of persons or ships) available for a particular purpose **5** : VIOLENCE, COMPULSION **6** : an influence (as a push or pull) that causes motion or a change of motion — **force·ful** \-fəl\ *adj* — **force·ful·ly** *adv* — **in force 1** : in great numbers **2** : VALID, OPERATIVE

²force *vb* **forced; forc·ing 1** : COMPEL, COERCE **2** : to cause through necessity (*forced* to admit defeat) **3** : to press, attain to, or effect against resistance or inertia (∼ your way through) **4** : to raise or accelerate to the utmost (∼ the pace) **5** : to produce with unnatural or unwilling effort (*forced* a smile) **6** : to hasten (as in growth) by artificial means

for·ceps \ˈfȯr-səps\ *n, pl* **forceps** [L] : a hand-held instru-

ment for grasping, holding, or pulling objects esp. for delicate operations (as by a surgeon)

forceps

forc·i·ble \ˈfȯr-sə-bəl\ *adj* **1** : obtained or done by force **2** : showing force or energy : POWERFUL — **forc·i·bly** \-blē\ *adv*

¹ford \ˈfōrd\ *n* : a place where a stream may be crossed by wading

²ford *vb* : to cross (a body of water) by wading

¹fore \ˈfōr\ *adv* : in, toward, or adjacent to the front : FORWARD

²fore *adj* : being or coming before in time, order, or space

³fore *n* : something that occupies a front position

⁴fore *interj* — used by a golfer to warn anyone within range of the probable line of flight of the ball

fore–and–aft \ˌfōr-ə-ˈnaft\ *adj* : lying, running, or acting along the length of a structure (as a ship)

¹fore·arm \(ˌ)fōr-ˈärm\ *vb* : to arm in advance : PREPARE

²fore·arm \ˈfōr-ˌärm\ *n* : the part of the arm between the elbow and the wrist

fore·bear \-ˌbar\ *n* : ANCESTOR, FOREFATHER

fore·bode \fȯr-ˈbōd\ *vb* **1** : to have a premonition esp. of misfortune **2** : FORETELL, PREDICT **syn** augur, bode, foreshadow, portend, promise — **fore·bod·ing** *n*

fore·cast \ˈfōr-ˌkast\ *vb* **-cast** *also* **-cast·ed; -cast·ing 1** : PREDICT, CALCULATE (∼ weather conditions) **2** : to indicate as likely to occur — **forecast** *n* — **fore·cast·er** *n*

fore·cas·tle \ˈfōk-səl\ *n* **1** : the forward part of the upper deck of a ship **2** : the crew's quarters usu. in a ship's bow

fore·close \fōr-ˈklōz\ *vb* **1** : to shut out : PRECLUDE **2** : to take legal measures to terminate a mortgage and take possession of the mortgaged property

fore·clo·sure \-ˈklō-zhər\ *n* : the act of foreclosing; *esp* : the legal procedure of foreclosing a mortgage

fore·doom \fōr-ˈdüm\ *vb* : to doom beforehand

fore·fa·ther \ˈfōr-ˌfä-<u>th</u>ər\ *n* **1** : ANCESTOR **2** : a person of an earlier period and common heritage

forefend *var of* FORFEND

fore·fin·ger \-ˌfiŋ-gər\ *n* : the finger next to the thumb

fore·foot \-ˌfut\ *n* : either of the front feet of a quadruped; *also* : the front part of the human foot

fore·front \-ˌfrənt\ *n* : the foremost part or place

fore·gath·er *var of* FORGATHER

¹fore·go \fōr-ˈgō\ *vb* **-went** \-ˈwent\; **-gone** \-ˈgȯn\; **-go·ing** : PRECEDE

²forego *var of* FORGO

fore·go·ing *adj* : PRECEDING

fore·gone \ˈfōr-ˌgȯn\ *adj* : determined in advance (a ∼ conclusion)

fore·ground \-ˌgraund\ *n* **1** : the part of a scene or representation that appears nearest to and in front of the spectator **2** : a position of prominence

fore·hand \-ˌhand\ *n* : a stroke (as in tennis) made with the palm of the hand turned in the direction in which the hand is moving; *also* : the side on which such a stroke is made — **forehand** *adj*

forehand

fore·hand·ed \(ˌ)fōr-ʹhan-dəd\ *adj* : mindful of the future : PRUDENT
fore·head \ʹfȯr-əd, ʹfōr-ˌhed\ *n* : the part of the face above the eyes
for·eign \ʹfȯr-ən\ *adj* [ME *forein*, fr. OF, fr. LL *foranus* on the outside, fr. L *foris* outside] **1** : situated outside a place or country and esp. one's own country **2** : born in, belonging to, or characteristic of some place or country other than the one under consideration ⟨∼ language⟩ **3** : not connected, pertinent, or characteristically present **4** : related to or dealing with other nations ⟨∼ affairs⟩ **5** : occurring in an abnormal situation in the living body ⟨a ∼ body in the eye⟩
for·eign·er \ʹfȯr-ə-nər\ *n* : a person belonging to or owing allegiance to a foreign country
foreign minister *n* : a governmental minister for foreign affairs
fore·know \fōr-ʹnō\ *vb* **-knew** \-ʹnü, -ʹnyü\; **-known** \-ʹnōn\; **-know·ing** : to have previous knowledge of — **fore·knowl·edge** \ʹfōr-ˌnä-lij, fōr-ʹnä-\ *n*
fore·la·dy \ʹfōr-ˌlā-dē\ *n* : FOREWOMAN
fore·leg \-ˌleg\ *n* : a front leg
fore·limb \-ˌlim\ *n* : either of an anterior pair of limbs (as wings, arms, or fins)
fore·lock \-ˌläk\ *n* : a lock of hair growing from the front part of the head
fore·man \-mən\ *n* **1** : a spokesperson of a jury **2** : a person in charge of a group of workers
fore·mast \-ˌmast\ *n* : the mast nearest the bow of a ship
fore·most \-ˌmōst\ *adj* : first in time, place, or order : most important : PREEMINENT — **foremost** *adv*
fore·name \-ˌnām\ *n* : a first name
fore·named \-ˌnāmd\ *adj* : previously named : AFORESAID
fore·noon \-ˌnün\ *n* : MORNING
¹fo·ren·sic \fə-ʹren-sik\ *adj* [L *forensis* public, forensic, fr. *forum* forum] **1** : belonging to, used in, or suitable to courts of law or to public speaking or debate **2** : relating to the application of scientific knowledge to legal problems ⟨∼ medicine⟩
²forensic *n* **1** : an argumentative exercise **2** *pl* : the art or study of argumentative discourse
fore·or·dain \ˌfōr-ȯr-ʹdān\ *vb* : to ordain or decree beforehand : PREDESTINE
fore·part \ʹfōr-ˌpärt\ *n* **1** : the anterior part of something **2** : the earlier part of a period of time
fore·quar·ter \-ˌkwȯr-tər\ *n* : the front half of a lateral half of the body or carcass of a quadruped ⟨a ∼ of beef⟩
fore·run·ner \-ˌrə-nər\ *n* **1** : one that goes before to give notice of the approach of others : HARBINGER **2** : PREDECESSOR, ANCESTOR **syn** precursor, herald
fore·sail \-ˌsāl, -səl\ *n* **1** : the lowest sail on the foremast of a square-rigged ship or schooner **2** : the principal sail forward of the foremast (as of a sloop)

fore·see \fōr-ʹsē\ *vb* **-saw** \-ʹsȯ\; **-seen** \-ʹsēn\; **-see·ing** : to see or realize beforehand : EXPECT **syn** foreknow, divine, apprehend, anticipate — **fore·see·able** *adj*
fore·shad·ow \-ʹsha-dō\ *vb* : to give a hint or suggestion of beforehand
fore·short·en \fōr-ʹshȯrt-ᵊn\ *vb* : to shorten (a detail) in a drawing or painting so that it appears to have depth
fore·sight \ʹfōr-ˌsīt\ *n* **1** : the act or power of foreseeing **2** : care or provision for the future : PRUDENCE **3** : an act of looking forward; *also* : a view forward — **fore·sight·ed** \-ˌsī-təd\ *adj* — **fore·sight·ed·ness** *n*
fore·skin \-ˌskin\ *n* : a fold of skin enclosing the end of the penis
for·est \ʹfȯr-əst\ *n* [ME, fr. OF, fr. LL *forestis* (*silva*) unenclosed (woodland), fr. L *foris* outside] : a large thick growth of trees and underbrush — **for·est·ed** \ʹfȯr-ə-stəd\ *adj* — **for·est·land** \ʹfȯr-əst-ˌland\ *n*
fore·stall \fȯr-ʹstȯl, fōr-\ *vb* **1** : to keep out, hinder, or prevent by measures taken in advance **2** : ANTICIPATE
forest ranger *n* : a person in charge of the management and protection of a portion of a forest
for·est·ry \ʹfȯr-ə-strē\ *n* : the science of growing and caring for forests — **for·est·er** \ʹfȯr-ə-stər\ *n*
foreswear *var of* FORSWEAR
¹fore·taste \ʹfōr-ˌtāst\ *n* : an advance indication, warning, or notion
²fore·taste \fōr-ʹtāst\ *vb* : to taste beforehand : ANTICIPATE
fore·tell \fōr-ʹtel\ *vb* **-told** \-ʹtōld\; **-tell·ing** : to tell of beforehand : PREDICT **syn** forecast, prophesy, prognosticate
fore·thought \ʹfōr-ˌthȯt\ *n* **1** : PREMEDITATION **2** : consideration for the future
fore·to·ken \fōr-ʹtō-kən\ *vb* : to indicate in advance
fore·top \ʹfōr-ˌtäp\ *n* : a platform near the top of a ship's foremast
for·ev·er \fȯr-ʹe-vər\ *adv* **1** : for a limitless time **2** : at all times : ALWAYS
for·ev·er·more \-ˌe-vər-ʹmōr\ *adv* : FOREVER
fore·warn \fȯr-ʹwȯrn\ *vb* : to warn beforehand
forewent *past of* FOREGO
fore·wing \ʹfōr-ˌwiŋ\ *n* : either of the anterior wings of a 4-winged insect
fore·wom·an \ʹfōr-ˌwu̇-mən\ *n* : a woman having the responsibilities of a foreman
fore·word \-ˌwərd\ *n* : PREFACE
¹for·feit \ʹfȯr-fət\ *n* **1** : something forfeited : PENALTY, FINE **2** : FORFEITURE **3** : something deposited and then redeemed on payment of a fine **4** *pl* : a game in which forfeits are exacted
²forfeit *vb* : to lose or lose the right to by some error, offense, or crime
for·fei·ture \ʹfȯr-fə-ˌchu̇r\ *n* **1** : the act of forfeiting **2** : something forfeited : PENALTY
for·fend \fȯr-ʹfend\ *vb* **1** : PREVENT **2** : PROTECT, PRESERVE
for·gath·er \fȯr-ʹga-thər\ *vb* **1** : to come together : ASSEMBLE **2** : to meet someone usu. by chance
¹forge \ʹfōrj\ *n* [ME, fr. OF, fr. L *fabrica*, fr. *faber* smith] : a furnace or shop with its furnace where metal is heated and worked
²forge *vb* **forged**; **forg·ing** **1** : to form (metal) by heating and hammering **2** : FASHION, SHAPE ⟨∼ an agreement⟩ **3** : to make or imitate falsely esp. with intent to defraud ⟨∼ a signature⟩ — **forg·er** *n* — **forg·ery** \ʹfōr-jə-rē\ *n*
³forge *vb* **forged**; **forg·ing** : to move ahead steadily but gradually
for·get \fər-ʹget\ *vb* **for·got** \-ʹgät\; **for·got·ten** \-ʹgät-ᵊn\ *or* **for·got**; **for·get·ting** **1** : to be unable to think of or recall **2** : to fail to become mindful of at the proper time **3** : NEGLECT, DISREGARD — **for·get·ful** \-ʹget-fəl\ *adj* — **for·get·ful·ly** *adv*

for·get–me–not \fər-'get-mē-ˌnät\ *n* : any of a genus of small herbs with bright blue or white flowers

forg·ing *n* : a piece of forged work

for·give \fər-'giv\ *vb* **for·gave** \-'gāv\; **for·giv·en** \-'gi-vən\; **for·giv·ing** **1** : to give up resentment of **2** : PARDON, ABSOLVE **3** : to grant relief from payment of — **for·giv·able** *adj* — **for·give·ness** *n*

for·giv·ing *adj* **1** : willing or able to forgive **2** : allowing room for error or weakness

for·go \fōr-'gō\ *vb* **for·went** \-'went\; **for·gone** \-'gòn\; **for·go·ing** : to give up the enjoyment or advantage of : do without

fo·rint \'fòr-int\ *n, pl* **forints** *also* **forint** — see MONEY table

¹fork \'fòrk\ *n* **1** : an implement with two or more prongs for taking up (as in eating), pitching, or digging **2** : a forked part, tool, or piece of equipment **3** : a dividing into branches or a place where something branches; *also* : a branch of such a fork

²fork *vb* **1** : to divide into two or more branches **2** : to give the form of a fork to ⟨~*ing* her fingers⟩ **3** : to raise or pitch with a fork ⟨~ hay⟩ **4** : PAY, CONTRIBUTE — used with *over, out,* or *up*

forked \'fòrkt, 'fòr-kəd\ *adj* : having a fork : shaped like a fork ⟨~ lightning⟩

fork·lift \'fòrk-ˌlift\ *n* : a machine for lifting heavy objects by means of steel fingers inserted under the load

for·lorn \fər-'lòrn, fòr-\ *adj* **1** : sad and lonely because of isolation or desertion **2** : WRETCHED **3** : nearly hopeless — **for·lorn·ly** *adv* — **for·lorn·ness** *n*

¹form \'fòrm\ *n* **1** : SHAPE, STRUCTURE **2** : a body esp. of a person : FIGURE **3** : the essential nature of a thing **4** : established manner of doing or saying something **5** : FORMULA **6** : a document with blank spaces for insertion of information ⟨tax ~⟩ **7** : CEREMONY **8** : manner of performing according to recognized standards **9** : a long seat : BENCH **10** : a model of the human figure used for displaying clothes **11** : MOLD ⟨a ~ for concrete⟩ **12** : type or plates in a frame ready for printing **13** : MODE, KIND, VARIETY ⟨coal is a ~ of carbon⟩ **14** : orderly method of arrangement; *also* : a particular kind or instance of such arrangement ⟨the sonnet ~ in poetry⟩ **15** : the structural element, plan, or design of a work of art **16** : a bounded surface or volume **17** : a grade in a British school or in some American private schools **18** : RACING FORM **19** : known ability to perform; *also* : condition (as of an athlete) suitable for performing **20** : one of the ways in which a word is changed to show difference in use ⟨the plural ~ of a noun⟩ — **form·less** *adj*

²form *vb* **1** : to give form or shape to : FASHION, MAKE **2** : TRAIN, INSTRUCT **3** : CONSTITUTE, COMPOSE **4** : DEVELOP, ACQUIRE ⟨~ a habit⟩ **5** : to arrange in order ⟨~ a battle line⟩ **6** : to take form : ARISE ⟨clouds are ~*ing*⟩ **7** : to take a definite form, shape, or arrangement

¹for·mal \'fòr-məl\ *adj* **1** : according with conventional forms and rules ⟨a ~ dinner party⟩ **2** : done in due or lawful form ⟨a ~ contract⟩ **3** : CEREMONIOUS, PRIM ⟨a ~ manner⟩ **4** : NOMINAL — **for·mal·ly** *adv*

²formal *n* : something (as a social event) formal in character

form·al·de·hyde \fòr-'mal-də-ˌhīd\ *n* : a colorless pungent gas used in water solution as a preservative and disinfectant

for·mal·ism \'fòr-mə-ˌli-zəm\ *n* : strict adherence to set forms

for·mal·i·ty \fòr-'ma-lə-tē\ *n, pl* **-ties** **1** : compliance with formal or conventional rules **2** : the quality or state of being formal **3** : an established form that is required or conventional

for·mal·ize \'fòr-mə-ˌlīz\ *vb* **-ized; -iz·ing** **1** : to give a certain or definite form to **2** : to make formal; *also* : to give formal status or approval to

¹for·mat \'fòr-ˌmat\ *n* **1** : the general composition or style of a publication **2** : the general plan or arrangement of something

²format *vb* **for·mat·ted; for·mat·ting** : to arrange (as material to be printed) in a particular format — **for·mat·ter** *n*

for·ma·tion \fòr-'mā-shən\ *n* **1** : a giving form to something : DEVELOPMENT **2** : something that is formed **3** : STRUCTURE, SHAPE **4** : an arrangement of persons or things in a prescribed manner or for a certain purpose

for·ma·tive \'fòr-mə-tiv\ *adj* **1** : giving or capable of giving form : CONSTRUCTIVE **2** : of, relating to, or characterized by important growth or formation ⟨a child's ~ years⟩

for·mer \'fòr-mər\ *adj* **1** : PREVIOUS, EARLIER **2** : FOREGOING **3** : being first mentioned or in order of two or more things

for·mer·ly \-lē\ *adv* : in time past : PREVIOUSLY

form–fit·ting \'fòrm-ˌfi-tiŋ\ *adj* : conforming to the outline of the body

for·mi·da·ble \'fòr-mə-də-bəl, fòr-'mi-\ *adj* **1** : exciting fear, dread, or awe **2** : imposing serious difficulties — **for·mi·da·bly** \-blē\ *adv*

form letter *n* **1** : a letter on a frequently recurring topic that can be sent to different people at different times **2** : a letter for mass circulation sent out in many printed copies

for·mu·la \'fòr-myə-lə\ *n, pl* **-las** *or* **-lae** \-ˌlē, -ˌlī\ **1** : a set form of words for ceremonial use **2** : RECIPE, PRESCRIPTION **3** : a milk mixture or substitute for a baby **4** : a group of symbols or figures joined to express information concisely **5** : a customary or set form or method

for·mu·late \-ˌlāt\ *vb* **-lat·ed; -lat·ing** **1** : to express in a formula **2** : DESIGN, DEVISE ⟨~ a policy⟩ **3** : to prepare according to a formula — **for·mu·la·tion** \ˌfòr-myə-'lā-shən\ *n*

for·ni·ca·tion \ˌfòr-nə-'kā-shən\ *n* : consensual sexual intercourse between two persons not married to each other — **for·ni·cate** \'fòr-nə-ˌkāt\ *vb* — **for·ni·ca·tor** \-ˌkā-tər\ *n*

for·sake \fər-'sāk, fòr-\ *vb* **for·sook** \-'sùk\; **for·sak·en** \-'sā-kən\; **for·sak·ing** [ME, fr. OE *forsacan,* fr. *sacan* to dispute] : to renounce or turn away from entirely

for·sooth \fər-'süth\ *adv* : in truth : INDEED

for·swear \fòr-'swar\ *vb* **for·swore** \-'swōr\; **for·sworn** \-'swōrn\; **for·swear·ing** **1** : to swear falsely : commit perjury **2** : to renounce earnestly or under oath **3** : to deny under oath

for·syth·ia \fər-'si-thē-ə\ *n* : any of a genus of shrubs related to the olive and having yellow bell-shaped flowers appearing before the leaves in early spring

fort \'fòrt\ *n* [ME *forte,* fr. MF *fort,* fr. *fort* strong, fr. L *fortis*] **1** : a fortified place **2** : a permanent army post

¹forte \'fòrt, 'fòr-ˌtā\ *n* [F *fort,* fr. *fort,* adj., strong] : one's strong point

²for·te \'fòr-ˌtā\ *adv or adj* [It, fr. *forte* strong] : LOUD — used as a direction in music

forth \'fōrth\ *adv* **1** : FORWARD, ONWARD ⟨from that day ~⟩ **2** : out into view ⟨put ~ leaves⟩

forth·com·ing \fōrth-'kə-miŋ\ *adj* **1** : coming or available soon ⟨the ~ holidays⟩ **2** : marked by openness and candor : OUTGOING

forth·right \'fōrth-ˌrīt\ *adj* : free from ambiguity or evasiveness : going straight to the point ⟨a ~ answer⟩ — **forth·right·ly** *adv* — **forth·right·ness** *n*

forth·with \fōrth-'with\ *adv* : IMMEDIATELY

for·ti·fy \'fòr-tə-ˌfī\ *vb* **-fied; -fy·ing** **1** : to strengthen by military defenses **2** : to give physical strength or endur-

---

\ə\abut　\ᵊ\kitten　\ər\further　\a\ash　\ā\ace　\ä\mop, mar
\au̇\out　\ch\chin　\e\bet　\ē\easy　\g\go　\i\hit　\ī\ice　\j\job
\ŋ\sing　\ō\go　\ȯ\law　\ȯi\boy　\th\thin　\th̲\the　\ü\loot　\u̇\foot
\y\yet　\zh\vision　*see also* Pronunciation Symbols page

ance to **3** : ENCOURAGE **4** : to strengthen or enrich with a material ⟨∼ bread with vitamins⟩ — **for·ti·fi·ca·tion** \ˌfȯr-tə-fə-ˈkā-shən\ n

for·tis·si·mo \fȯr-ˈti-sə-ˌmō\ adv or adj : very loud — used as a direction in music

for·ti·tude \ˈfȯr-tə-ˌtüd, -ˌtyüd\ n : strength of mind that enables one to meet danger or bear pain or adversity with courage **syn** grit, backbone, pluck, guts

fort·night \ˈfȯrt-ˌnīt\ n [ME fourtenight, alter. of fourtene night fourteen nights] : two weeks — **fort·night·ly** \-lē\ adj or adv

for·tress \ˈfȯr-trəs\ n : FORT 1

for·tu·itous \fȯr-ˈtü-ə-təs, -ˈtyü-\ adj **1** : happening by chance **2** : FORTUNATE

for·tu·ity \-ə-tē\ n, pl **-ities 1** : the quality or state of being fortuitous **2** : a chance event or occurrence

for·tu·nate \ˈfȯr-chə-nət\ adj **1** : bringing some good thing not foreseen **2** : LUCKY

for·tu·nate·ly \-lē\ adv **1** : in a fortunate manner **2** : it is fortunate that

for·tune \ˈfȯr-chən\ n **1** : prosperity attained partly through luck; also : CHANCE, LUCK **2** : what happens to a person : good or bad luck **3** : FATE, DESTINY **4** : RICHES, WEALTH

fortune hunter n : a person who seeks wealth esp. by marriage

for·tune–tell·er \-ˌte-lər\ n : a person who professes to tell future events — **for·tune–tell·ing** n or adj

for·ty \ˈfȯr-tē\ n, pl **forties** : four times 10 — **for·ti·eth** \ˈfȯr-tē-əth\ adj or n — **forty** adj or pron

for·ty–five \ˌfȯr-tē-ˈfīv\ n **1** : a .45 caliber handgun — usu. written .45 **2** : a phonograph record designed to be played at 45 revolutions per minute

for·ty–nin·er \-ˈnī-nər\ n : a person in the rush to California for gold in 1849

forty winks n sing or pl : a short sleep

fo·rum \ˈfȯr-əm\ n, pl **forums** also **fo·ra** \-ə\ [L] **1** : the marketplace or central meeting place of an ancient Roman city **2** : a medium (as a publication) of open discussion **3** : COURT **4** : a public assembly, lecture, or program involving audience or panel discussion

¹**for·ward** \ˈfȯr-wərd\ adj **1** : being near or at or belonging to the front **2** : EAGER, READY **3** : BRASH, BOLD **4** : notably advanced or developed : PRECOCIOUS **5** : moving, tending, or leading toward a position in front **6** : EXTREME, RADICAL **7** : of, relating to, or getting ready for the future — **for·ward·ness** n

²**forward** adv : to or toward what is ahead or in front

³**forward** vb **1** : to help onward : ADVANCE **2** : to send forward : TRANSMIT **3** : to send or ship onward

⁴**forward** n : a player who plays at the front of a team's offensive formation near the opponent's goal

for·ward·er \-wər-dər\ n : one that forwards; esp : an agent who forwards goods — **for·ward·ing** n

for·wards \ˈfȯr-wərdz\ adv : FORWARD

¹**fos·sil** \ˈfä-səl\ adj [L fossilis obtained by digging, fr. fodere to dig] **1** : preserved from a past geologic age ⟨∼ plants⟩ **2** : of or relating to fossil fuels

²**fossil** n **1** : a trace or impression or the remains of a plant or animal of a past geologic age preserved in the earth's crust **2** : a person whose ideas are out-of-date — **fos·sil·ize** \ˈfä-sə-ˌlīz\ vb

fossil fuel n : a fuel (as coal or oil) that is formed in the earth from plant or animal remains

¹**fos·ter** \ˈfȯs-tər\ adj [ME, fr. OE fōstor-, fr. fōstor food, feeding] : affording, receiving, or sharing nourishment or parental care though not related by blood or legal ties ⟨∼ parent⟩ ⟨∼ child⟩

²**foster** vb **1** : to give parental care to : NURTURE **2** : to promote the growth or development of : ENCOURAGE

foster home n : a household in which an orphaned, neglected, or delinquent child is placed for care

fos·ter·ling \-tər-liŋ\ n : a foster child

Fou·cault pendulum \ˌfü-ˈkō-\ n : a device that consists of a heavy weight hung by a long wire and that swings in a constant direction which appears to change showing that the earth rotates

fought past and past part of FIGHT

¹**foul** \ˈfaul\ adj **1** : offensive to the senses : LOATHSOME; also : clogged with dirt **2** : ODIOUS, DETESTABLE **3** : OBSCENE, ABUSIVE **4** : DISAGREEABLE, STORMY ⟨∼ weather⟩ **5** : TREACHEROUS, DISHONORABLE, UNFAIR **6** : marking the bounds of a playing field ⟨∼ lines⟩; also : being outside the foul line ⟨∼ ball⟩ ⟨∼ territory⟩ **7** : containing marked-up corrections **8** : ENTANGLED — **foul·ly** adv — **foul·ness** n

²**foul** n **1** : an entanglement or collision in fishing or sailing **2** : an infraction of the rules in a game or sport; also : a baseball hit outside the foul line

³**foul** vb **1** : to make or become foul or filthy **2** : to entangle or become entangled **3** : OBSTRUCT, BLOCK **4** : to collide with **5** : to make or hit a foul

⁴**foul** adv : in a foul manner

fou·lard \fu-ˈlärd\ n : a lightweight silk of plain or twill weave usu. decorated with a printed pattern

foul-mouthed \ˈfaul-ˈmau̇thd, -ˈmau̇tht\ adj : given to the use of obscene, profane, or abusive language

foul play n : VIOLENCE; esp : MURDER

foul–up \ˈfaul-ˌəp\ n **1** : a state of being fouled up **2** : a mechanical difficulty

foul up vb **1** : to spoil by mistakes or poor judgment **2** : to cause a foul-up : BUNGLE

¹**found** \ˈfaund\ past and past part of FIND

²**found** vb **1** : to take the first steps in building **2** : to set or ground on something solid : BASE **3** : to establish (as an institution) often with provision for future maintenance — **found·er** n

foun·da·tion \faun-ˈdā-shən\ n **1** : the act of founding **2** : a basis upon which something stands or is supported ⟨suspicions without ∼⟩ **3** : funds given for the permanent support of an institution : ENDOWMENT; also : an institution so endowed **4** : supporting structure : BASE **5** : CORSET — **foun·da·tion·al** \-shə-nəl\ adj

foun·der \ˈfaun-dər\ vb **1** : to make or become lame ⟨the horse ∼ed⟩ **2** : COLLAPSE **3** : SINK ⟨a ∼ing ship⟩ **4** : FAIL

found·ling \ˈfaund-liŋ\ n : an infant found after its unknown parents have abandoned it

found·ry \ˈfaun-drē\ n, pl **foundries** : a building or works where metal is cast

fount \ˈfaunt\ n : SOURCE, FOUNTAIN

foun·tain \ˈfaunt-ᵊn\ n **1** : a spring of water **2** : SOURCE **3** : an artificial jet of water **4** : a container for liquid that can be drawn off as needed

foun·tain·head \-ˌhed\ n : SOURCE

fountain pen n : a pen with a reservoir that feeds the writing point with ink

four \ˈfȯr\ n **1** : one more than three **2** : the 4th in a set or series **3** : something having four units — **four** adj or pron

four–flush \-ˌfləsh\ vb : to make a false claim : BLUFF — **four–flush·er** n

four·fold \-ˌfōld, -ˈfōld\ adj **1** : being four times as great or as many **2** : having four units or members — **fourfold** \-ˈfōld\ adv

4–H \ˈfȯr-ˈāch\ adj [fr. the fourfold aim of improving the head, heart, hands, and health] : of or relating to a program set up by the U.S. Department of Agriculture to help young people become productive citizens — **4–H'·er** n

Four Hundred or **400** n : the exclusive social set of a community — used with the

four–in–hand \ˈfȯr-ən-ˌhand\ n **1** : a team of four horses driven by one person; also : a vehicle drawn by such a team **2** : a necktie tied in a slipknot with long ends overlapping vertically in front

four–o'clock \ˈfȯr-ə-ˌkläk\ n : a garden plant with fragrant yellow, red, or white flowers without petals that open late in the afternoon

four-post-er \ˌfȯr-ˈpō-stər\ *n* : a bed with tall corner posts orig. designed to support curtains or a canopy

four-score \ˈfȯr-ˈskȯr\ *adj* : being four times twenty : EIGHTY

four-some \ˈfȯr-səm\ *n* **1** : a group of four persons or things **2** : a golf match between two pairs of partners

four-square \-ˈskwar\ *adj* **1** : SQUARE **2** : marked by boldness and conviction : FORTHRIGHT — **foursquare** *adv*

four-teen \fȯr-ˈtēn\ *n* : one more than 13 — **fourteen** *adj or pron* — **four-teenth** \-ˈtēnth\ *adj or n*

fourth \ˈfȯrth\ *n* **1** : one that is number four in a countable series **2** : one of four equal parts of something — **fourth** *adj or adv*

fourth estate *n, often cap F&E* : the public press

4WD *abbr* four-wheel drive

four-wheel \ˈfȯr-ˌhwēl\ *or* **four-wheeled** \-ˌhwēld\ *adj* : acting on or by means of four wheels of a motor vehicle

¹**fowl** \ˈfau̇l\ *n, pl* **fowl** *or* **fowls 1** : BIRD **2** : a cock or hen of the domestic chicken; *also* : the flesh of these used as food

²**fowl** *vb* : to hunt wildfowl

¹**fox** \ˈfäks\ *n, pl* **fox-es** *also* **fox 1** : any of various flesh-eating mammals related to the wolves but smaller and with shorter legs and a more pointed muzzle; *also* : the fur of a fox **2** : a clever crafty person **3** *cap* : a member of an American Indian people formerly living in Wisconsin

²**fox** *vb* : TRICK, OUTWIT

fox-glove \ˈfäks-ˌgləv\ *n* : a common plant related to the snapdragons that is grown for its showy spikes of dotted white or purple tubular flowers and as a source of digitalis

fox-hole \-ˌhōl\ *n* : a pit dug for protection against enemy fire

fox-hound \-ˌhau̇nd\ *n* : any of various large swift powerful hounds used in hunting foxes

fox terrier *n* : a small lively terrier that occurs in varieties with smooth dense coats or with harsh wiry coats

fox-trot \ˈfäks-ˌträt\ *n* **1** : a short broken slow trotting gait **2** : a ballroom dance in duple time

foxy \ˈfäk-sē\ *adj* **fox-i-er; -est 1** : resembling or suggestive of a fox **2** : WILY **3** : physically attractive

foy-er \ˈfȯi-ər, ˈfȯi-ˌyā\ *n* [F, lit., fireplace, fr. (assumed) VL *focarium*, fr. L *focus* hearth] : LOBBY; *also* : an entrance hallway

fpm *abbr* feet per minute

FPO *abbr* fleet post office

fps *abbr* feet per second

fr *abbr* **1** father **2** franc **3** friar **4** from

¹**Fr** *abbr* **1** France; French **2** Friday

²**Fr** *symbol* francium

fra-cas \ˈfrā-kəs, ˈfra-\ *n, pl* **fra-cas-es** \-kə-səz\ [F, din, row, fr. It *fracasso*, fr. *fracassare* to shatter] : BRAWL

frac-tal \ˈfrak-tᵊl\ *n* : an irregular curve or shape that repeats itself at any scale on which it is examined — **fractal** *adj*

frac-tion \ˈfrak-shən\ *n* **1** : a numerical representation (as ½, ¾, or 3.323) indicating the quotient of two numbers **2** : FRAGMENT **3** : PORTION — **frac-tion-al** \-shə-nəl\ *adj* — **frac-tion-al-ly** *adv*

frac-tious \ˈfrak-shəs\ *adj* **1** : tending to be troublesome : hard to handle or control **2** : QUARRELSOME, IRRITABLE

frac-ture \ˈfrak-chər\ *n* **1** : a breaking of something and esp. a bone **2** : CRACK, CLEFT — **fracture** *vb*

frag-ile \ˈfra-jəl, -ˌjīl\ *adj* : easily broken : DELICATE — **fra-gil-i-ty** \frə-ˈji-lə-tē\ *n*

¹**frag-ment** \ˈfrag-mənt\ *n* : a part broken off, detached, or incomplete

²**frag-ment** \-ˌment\ *vb* : to break into fragments — **frag-men-ta-tion** \ˌfrag-mən-ˈtā-shən, -ˌmən-\ *n*

frag-men-tary \ˈfrag-mən-ˌter-ē\ *adj* : made up of fragments : INCOMPLETE

fra-grant \ˈfrā-grənt\ *adj* : sweet or agreeable in smell — **fra-grance** \-grəns\ *n* — **fra-grant-ly** *adv*

frail \ˈfrāl\ *adj* **1** : morally or physically weak **2** : FRAGILE, DELICATE

frail-ty \ˈfrāl-tē\ *n, pl* **frailties 1** : the quality or state of being frail **2** : a fault due to weakness

¹**frame** \ˈfrām\ *vb* **framed; fram-ing 1** : PLAN, CONTRIVE **2** : SHAPE, CONSTRUCT **3** : FORMULATE **4** : DRAW UP ⟨∼ a constitution⟩ **5** : to make appear guilty **6** : to fit or adjust for a purpose : ARRANGE **7** : to provide with or enclose in a frame — **fram-er** *n*

²**frame** *n* **1** : something made of parts fitted and joined together **2** : the physical makeup of the body **3** : an arrangement of structural parts that gives form or support **4** : a supporting or enclosing border or open case (as for a window or picture) **5** : one picture of a series (as on a length of film) **6** : FRAME-UP

³**frame** *adj* : having a wood frame

frame of mind *n* : mental attitude or outlook : MOOD

frame-up \ˈfrā-ˌməp\ *n* **1** : an act or series of actions in which someone is framed **2** : an action that is planned, contrived, or formulated

frame-work \ˈfrām-ˌwərk\ *n* : a basic supporting part or structure

franc \ˈfraŋk\ *n* — see MONEY table

fran-chise \ˈfran-ˌchīz\ *n* [ME, fr. MF, fr. *franchir* to free, fr. OF *franc* free] **1** : a special privilege granted to an individual or group ⟨a ∼ to operate a ferry⟩ **2** : a constitutional or statutory right or privilege; *esp* : the right to vote

fran-chi-see \ˌfran-ˌchī-ˈzē, -chə-\ *n* : one granted a franchise

fran-chis-er \ˈfran-ˌchī-zər\ *n* **1** : FRANCHISEE **2** : FRANCHISOR

fran-chi-sor \ˌfran-ˌchī-ˈzȯr, -chə-\ *n* : one that grants a franchise

fran-ci-um \ˈfran-sē-əm\ *n* : a radioactive metallic chemical element — see ELEMENT table

Fran-co-Amer-i-can \ˌfraŋ-kō-ə-ˈmer-ə-kən\ *n* : an American of French or esp. French-Canadian descent — **Franco-American** *adj*

fran-gi-ble \ˈfran-jə-bəl\ *adj* : BREAKABLE — **fran-gi-bil-i-ty** \ˌfran-jə-ˈbi-lə-tē\ *n*

¹**frank** \ˈfraŋk\ *adj* : marked by free, forthright, and sincere expression — **frank-ness** *n*

²**frank** *vb* : to mark (a piece of mail) with an official sign so that it can be mailed free; *also* : to mail free

³**frank** *n* **1** : the signature or mark on a piece of mail indicating free or paid postage **2** : the privilege of sending mail free

Frank \ˈfraŋk\ *n* : a member of a West Germanic people entering the Roman provinces in A.D. 253 and establishing themselves in the Netherlands, in Gaul, and along the Rhine — **Frank-ish** *adj*

Fran-ken-stein \ˈfraŋ-kən-ˌstīn\ *n* **1** : a monstrous creation that usu. ruins its originator **2** : a monster in the shape of a man

frank-furt-er \ˈfraŋk-fər-tər, -ˌfər-\ *or* **frank-furt** \-fərt\ *n* : a seasoned sausage (as of beef or beef and pork)

frank-in-cense \ˈfraŋ-kən-ˌsens\ *n* : a fragrant resin burned as incense

frank-ly \ˈfraŋ-klē\ *adv* **1** : in a frank manner **2** : in truth : INDEED

fran-tic \ˈfran-tik\ *adj* : marked by uncontrolled emotion

\ə\abut \ᵊ\kitten \ər\further \a\ash \ā\ace \ä\mop, mar \au̇\out \ch\chin \e\bet \ē\easy \g\go \i\hit \ī\ice \j\job \ŋ\sing \ō\go \ȯ\law \ȯi\boy \th\thin \t͟h\the \ü\loot \u̇\foot \y\yet \zh\vision *see also* Pronunciation Symbols page

or disordered anxious activity — **fran·ti·cal·ly** \-ti-k(ə-)lē\ adv

frap·pé \fra-'pā\ or **frappe** \same or 'frap\ [F frappé, fr. pp. of frapper to strike, chill] n **1** : an iced or frozen drink **2** : a thick milk shake — **frap·pé** \fra-'pā\ adj

fra·ter·nal \frə-'tərn-ᵊl\ adj **1** : of, relating to, or involving brothers **2** : of, relating to, or being a fraternity or society **3** : FRIENDLY, BROTHERLY — **fra·ter·nal·ly** adv

fra·ter·ni·ty \frə-'tər-nə-tē\ n, pl **-ties 1** : a social, honorary, or professional group; esp : a men's student organization **2** : BROTHERLINESS, BROTHERHOOD **3** : persons of the same class, profession, or tastes

frat·er·nize \'fra-tər-ˌnīz\ vb **-nized; -niz·ing 1** : to mingle as friends **2** : to associate on close terms with members of a hostile group — **frat·er·ni·za·tion** \ˌfra-tər-nə-'zā-shən\ n

frat·ri·cide \'fra-trə-ˌsīd\ n **1** : one that kills a sibling or countryman **2** : the act of a fratricide — **frat·ri·cid·al** \ˌfra-trə-'sīd-ᵊl\ adj

fraud \'frȯd\ n **1** : DECEIT, TRICKERY **2** : TRICK **3** : IMPOSTOR, CHEAT

fraud·u·lent \'frȯ-jə-lənt\ adj : characterized by, based on, or done by fraud : DECEITFUL — **fraud·u·lent·ly** adv

fraught \'frȯt\ adj : full of or accompanied by something specified ⟨∼ with danger⟩

¹fray \'frā\ n : FIGHT, STRUGGLE; also : QUARREL, DISPUTE

²fray vb **1** : to wear (as an edge of cloth) by rubbing **2** : to separate the threads at the edge of **3** : STRAIN, IRRITATE ⟨∼ed nerves⟩

fraz·zle \'fra-zəl\ vb **fraz·zled; fraz·zling 1** : FRAY **2** : to put in a state of extreme physical or nervous fatigue — **frazzle** n

¹freak \'frēk\ n **1** : WHIM, CAPRICE **2** : a strange, abnormal, or unusual person or thing **3** slang : a person who uses an illicit drug **4** : an ardent enthusiast — **freak·ish** adj

²freak vb **1** : to experience the effects (as hallucinations) of taking illicit drugs — often used with out **2** : to distress or become distressed — often used with out — **freak–out** \'frē-ˌkaut\ n

freck·le \'fre-kəl\ n : a brownish spot on the skin — **freckle** vb

¹free \'frē\ adj **fre·er; fre·est 1** : having liberty **2** : enjoying political or personal independence; also : not subject to or allowing slavery **3** : made or done voluntarily : SPONTANEOUS **4** : relieved from or lacking something unpleasant **5** : not subject to a duty, tax, or charge **6** : not obstructed : CLEAR **7** : not being used or occupied **8** : not fastened **9** : LAVISH **10** : OPEN, FRANK **11** : given without charge **12** : not literal or exact **13** : not restricted by conventional forms — **free·ly** adv

²free vb **freed; free·ing 1** : to set free **2** : RELIEVE, RID **3** : DISENTANGLE, CLEAR **syn** release, liberate, discharge, emancipate, loose

³free adv **1** : FREELY **2** : without charge

free·base \'frē-ˌbās\ n : purified cocaine smoked as crack or heated to produce vapors for inhalation — **freebase** vb

free·bie or **free·bee** \'frē-bē\ n : something given without charge

free·board \'frē-ˌbȯrd\ n : the vertical distance between the waterline and the upper edge of the side of a boat

free·boo·ter \-ˌbü-tər\ n [D vrijbuiter, fr. vrijbuit plunder, fr. vrij free + buit booty] : PLUNDERER, PIRATE

free·born \-'bȯrn\ adj **1** : not born in vassalage or slavery **2** : of, relating to, or befitting one that is freeborn

freed·man \'frēd-mən, -ˌman\ n : a man freed from slavery

free·dom \'frē-dəm\ n **1** : the quality or state of being free : INDEPENDENCE **2** : EXEMPTION, RELEASE **3** : EASE, FACILITY **4** : FRANKNESS **5** : unrestricted use **6** : a political right; also : FRANCHISE, PRIVILEGE

free enterprise n : freedom of private business to operate with little regulation by the government

free–for–all \'frē-fə-ˌrȯl\ n : a competition or fight open to all comers and usu. with no rules : BRAWL — **free-for–all** adj

free·hand \-ˌhand\ adj : done without mechanical aids or devices

free·hold \'frē-ˌhōld\ n : ownership of an estate for life usu. with the right to bequeath it to one's heirs; also : an estate thus owned — **free·hold·er** n

free·lance \-ˌlans\ n : one who pursues a profession (as writing) without a long-term commitment to any one employer — **free·lance** adj or vb

free–living \'frē-'li-viŋ\ adj **1** : unrestricted in pursuing personal pleasures **2** : being neither parasitic nor symbiotic ⟨∼ organisms⟩

free·load \'frē-ˌlōd\ vb : to impose upon another's hospitality — **free·load·er** n

free love n : the practice of living openly with one of the opposite sex without marriage

free·man \'frē-mən, -ˌman\ n **1** : one who has civil or political liberty **2** : one having the full rights of a citizen

Free·ma·son \-ˌmās-ᵊn\ n : a member of a secret fraternal society called Free and Accepted Masons — **Free·ma·son·ry** \-rē\ n

free·stand·ing \'frē-'stan-diŋ\ adj : standing alone or on its own foundation free of support

free·stone \'frē-ˌstōn\ n **1** : a stone that may be cut freely without splitting **2** : a fruit stone to which the flesh does not cling; also : a fruit (as a peach or cherry) having such a stone

free·think·er \-'thiŋ-kər\ n : one who forms opinions on the basis of reason independently of authority; esp : one who doubts or denies religious dogma — **free·think·ing** n or adj

free trade n : trade between nations without restrictions (as high taxes on imports)

free verse n : verse whose meter is irregular or whose rhythm is not metrical

free·way \'frē-ˌwā\ n : an expressway without tolls

free·wheel \-'hwēl\ vb : to move, live, or play freely or irresponsibly

free·will \'frē-ˌwil\ adj : VOLUNTARY

free will n : voluntary choice or decision

¹freeze \'frēz\ vb **froze** \'frōz\; **fro·zen** \'frōz-ᵊn\; **freez·ing 1** : to harden or cause to harden into a solid (as ice) by loss of heat **2** : to withstand freezing **3** : to chill or become chilled with cold **4** : to damage by frost **5** : to adhere solidly by or as if by freezing **6** : to become fixed, motionless, or incapable of speech **7** : to cause to grip tightly **8** : to become clogged with ice **9** : to fix at a certain stage or level

²freeze n **1** : an act or instance of freezing **2** : the state of being frozen **3** : a state of weather marked by low temperature

freeze–dry \'frēz-'drī\ vb : to dry in a frozen state under vacuum esp. for preservation — **freeze–dried** adj

freez·er \'frē-zər\ n : a compartment, device, or room for freezing food or keeping it frozen

¹freight \'frāt\ n **1** : payment for carrying goods **2** : CARGO **3** : BURDEN **4** : the carrying of goods by a common carrier **5** : a train that carries freight

²freight vb **1** : to load with goods for transportation **2** : BURDEN, CHARGE **3** : to ship or transport by freight

freight·er \'frā-tər\ n : a ship or airplane used chiefly to carry freight

French \'french\ n **1** : the language of France **2 French** pl : the people of France **3** : strong language — **French** adj — **French·man** \-mən\ n — **French·wom·an** \-ˌwu-mən\ n

French door n : a door with small panes of glass extending the full length

French dressing n **1** : a thin salad dressing usu. made of vinegar and oil with spices **2** : a creamy salad dressing flavored with tomatoes

french fry *vb, often cap 1st F* : to fry (as strips of potato) in deep fat until brown — **french fry** *n, often cap 1st F*

French horn *n* : a curved brass instrument with a funnel=shaped mouthpiece and a flaring bell

French toast *n* : bread dipped in a mixture of eggs and milk and fried at a low heat

fre·net·ic \fri-'ne-tik\ *adj* : FRANTIC — **fre·net·i·cal·ly** \-ti-k(ə-)lē\ *adv*

fren·zy \'fren-zē\ *n, pl* **frenzies 1** : temporary madness or a violently agitated state **2** : intense often disordered activity — **fren·zied** \-zēd\ *adj*

freq *abbr* frequency; frequent; frequently

fre·quen·cy \'frē-kwən-sē\ *n, pl* **-cies 1** : the fact or condition of occurring frequently **2** : rate of occurrence **3** : the number of cycles per second of an alternating current **4** : the number of waves (as of sound or electromagnetic energy) that pass a fixed point each second

frequency modulation *n* : variation of the frequency of a carrier wave according to another signal; *also* : FM

¹**fre·quent** \frē-'kwent, 'frē-kwənt\ *vb* : to associate with, be in, or resort to habitually — **fre·quent·er** *n*

²**fre·quent** \'frē-kwənt\ *adj* **1** : happening often or at short intervals **2** : HABITUAL — **fre·quent·ly** *adv*

fres·co \'fres-kō\ *n, pl* **frescoes** [It. fr. *fresco* fresh] : the art of painting on fresh plaster; *also* : a painting done by this method

fresh \'fresh\ *adj* **1** : VIGOROUS, REFRESHED **2** : not containing salt **3** : not altered by processing (as freezing or canning) **4** : free from taint : PURE **5** : fairly strong : BRISK ⟨∼ breeze⟩ **6** : not stale, sour, or decayed ⟨∼ bread⟩ **7** : not faded **8** : not worn or rumpled **9** : experienced, made, or received newly or anew **10** : ADDITIONAL, ANOTHER ⟨made a ∼ start⟩ **11** : ORIGINAL, VIVID **12** : INEXPERIENCED **13** : newly come or arrived ⟨∼ from school⟩ **14** : IMPUDENT — **fresh·ly** *adv* — **fresh·ness** *n*

fresh·en \'fre-shən\ *vb* : to make, grow, or become fresh

fresh·et \'fre-shət\ *n* : an overflowing of a stream (as by heavy rains)

fresh·man \'fresh-mən\ *n* **1** : a 1st-year student **2** : BEGINNER, NEWCOMER

fresh·wa·ter \-ˌwȯ-tər, -ˌwä-\ *n* : water that is not salty — **freshwater** *adj*

¹**fret** \'fret\ *vb* **fret·ted; fret·ting** [ME, to devour, fret, fr. OE *fretan* to devour] **1** : WEAR, CORRODE; *also* : FRAY **2** : RUB, CHAFE **3** : to make by wearing away **4** : to become irritated : WORRY, VEX **5** : GRATE; *also* : AGITATE

²**fret** *n* : an irritated or worried state ⟨in a ∼ about the interview⟩

³**fret** *n* : ornamental work esp. of straight lines in symmetrical patterns

⁴**fret** *n* : one of a series of ridges across the fingerboard of a stringed musical instrument — **fret·ted** *adj*

fret·ful \'fret-fəl\ *adj* : IRRITABLE — **fret·ful·ly** *adv* — **fret·ful·ness** *n*

fret·saw \-ˌsȯ\ *n* : a narrow-bladed saw used for cutting curved outlines

fret·work \-ˌwərk\ *n* **1** : decoration consisting of frets **2** : ornamental openwork or work in relief

Fri *abbr* Friday

fri·a·ble \'frī-ə-bəl\ *adj* : easily crumbled or pulverized ⟨∼ soil⟩

fri·ar \'frī-ər\ *n* [ME *frere, fryer*, fr. OF *frere*, lit., brother, fr. L *frater*] : a member of a religious order that orig. lived by alms

fri·ary \'frī-ər-ē\ *n, pl* **-ar·ies** : a monastery of friars

¹**fric·as·see** \'fri-kə-ˌsē, ˌfri-kə-'sē\ *n* : a dish made of meat (as chicken) cut into pieces, stewed in stock, and served in sauce

²**fricassee** *vb* **-seed; -see·ing** : to cook as a fricassee

fric·tion \'frik-shən\ *n* **1** : the rubbing of one body against another **2** : the force that resists motion between bodies in contact **3** : clash in opinions between persons or groups : DISAGREEMENT — **fric·tion·al** *adj*

friction tape *n* : a usu. cloth adhesive tape impregnated with insulating material and used esp. to protect and insulate electrical conductors

Fri·day \'frī-dē, -(ˌ)dā\ *n* : the sixth day of the week

fridge \'frij\ *n* : REFRIGERATOR

fried·cake \'frīd-ˌkāk\ *n* : DOUGHNUT, CRULLER

friend \'frend\ *n* **1** : one attached to another by respect or affection **2** : ACQUAINTANCE **3** : one who is not hostile **4** : one who supports or favors something ⟨a ∼ of art⟩ **5** *cap* : a member of the Society of Friends : QUAKER — **friend·less** *adj* — **friend·li·ness** \-lē-nəs\ *n* — **friend·ly** *adj* — **friend·ship** \-ˌship\ *n*

frieze \'frēz\ *n* : an ornamental often sculptured band extending around something (as a building or room)

frig·ate \'fri-gət\ *n* **1** : a square-rigged warship **2** : a warship smaller than a destroyer

fright \'frīt\ *n* **1** : sudden terror : ALARM **2** : something that is ugly or shocking

fright·en \'frīt-ᵊn\ *vb* **1** : to make afraid **2** : to drive away or out by frightening **3** : to become frightened — **fright·en·ing·ly** *adv*

fright·ful \'frīt-fəl\ *adj* **1** : TERRIFYING **2** : STARTLING **3** : EXTREME ⟨∼ thirst⟩ — **fright·ful·ly** *adv* — **fright·ful·ness** *n*

frig·id \'fri-jəd\ *adj* **1** : intensely cold **2** : lacking warmth or ardor : INDIFFERENT **3** : abnormally averse to or unable to achieve orgasm during sexual intercourse — used esp. of women — **fri·gid·i·ty** \fri-'ji-də-tē\ *n*

frigid zone *n* : the area or region between the arctic circle and the north pole or between the antarctic circle and the south pole

frill \'fril\ *n* **1** : a gathered, pleated, or ruffled edging **2** : something unessential — **frilly** *adj*

fringe \'frinj\ *n* **1** : an ornamental border consisting of short threads or strips hanging from an edge or band **2** : something that resembles a fringe : EDGE **3** : something that is additional or secondary to an activity, process, or subject — **fringe** *vb*

fringe benefit *n* **1** : an employment benefit paid for by an employer without affecting basic wage rates **2** : any additional benefit

frip·pery \'fri-pə-rē\ *n, pl* **-per·ies** [MF *friperie*] **1** : FINERY **2** : pretentious display

frisk \'frisk\ *vb* **1** : to leap, skip, or dance in a lively or playful way : GAMBOL **2** : to search (a person) esp. for concealed weapons by running the hand rapidly over the clothing

frisky \'fris-kē\ *adj* **frisk·i·er; -est** : PLAYFUL — **frisk·i·ly** \-kə-lē\ *adv* — **frisk·i·ness** \-kē-nəs\ *n*

¹**frit·ter** \'fri-tər\ *n* : a small lump of fried batter often containing fruit or meat

²**fritter** *vb* **1** : to reduce or waste piecemeal **2** : to break into small fragments

fritz \'frits\ *n* : a state of disorder or disrepair ⟨the car is on the ∼⟩

friv·o·lous \'fri-və-ləs\ *adj* **1** : of little importance : TRIVIAL **2** : lacking in seriousness — **fri·vol·i·ty** \fri-'vä-lə-tē\ *n* — **friv·o·lous·ly** *adv*

frizz \'friz\ *vb* : to form into small tight curls — **frizz** *n* — **frizzy** *adj*

¹**friz·zle** \'fri-zəl\ *vb* **friz·zled; friz·zling** : FRIZZ, CURL — **frizzle** *n*

²**frizzle** *vb* **friz·zled; friz·zling** **1** : to fry until crisp and curled **2** : to cook with a sizzling noise

---

\ə\abut \ᵊ\kitten \ər\further \a\ash \ā\ace \ä\mop, mar
\aù\out \ch\chin \e\bet \ē\easy \g\go \i\hit \ī\ice \j\job
\ŋ\sing \ō\go \ȯ\law \ȯi\boy \th\thin \t͟h\the \ü\loot \ù\foot
\y\yet \zh\vision   *see also* Pronunciation Symbols page

fro \\'frō\\ *adv* : BACK, AWAY — used in the phrase *to and fro*

frock \\'fräk\\ *n* 1 : an outer garment worn by monks and friars 2 : an outer garment worn esp. by men 3 : a woman's or girl's dress

frock coat *n* : a man's usu. double-breasted coat with knee-length skirts

frog \\'frȯg, 'fräg\\ *n* 1 : any of various largely aquatic smooth-skinned tailless leaping amphibians 2 : an ornamental braiding for fastening the front of a garment by a loop through which a button passes 3 : a condition in the throat causing hoarseness 4 : a small holder (as of metal, glass, or plastic) with perforations or spikes that is placed in a bowl or vase to keep cut flowers in position

frog·man \\'frȯg-ˌman, 'fräg-, -mən\\ *n* : a swimmer equipped to work underwater for long periods of time

¹frol·ic \\'frä-lik\\ *vb* **frol·icked; frol·ick·ing** 1 : to make merry 2 : to play about happily : ROMP

²frolic *n* 1 : a playful or mischievous action 2 : FUN, MERRIMENT — **frol·ic·some** \\-səm\\ *adj*

from \\'frəm, 'främ\\ *prep* 1 — used to show a starting point ⟨a letter ∼ home⟩ 2 — used to show removal or separation ⟨subtract 3 ∼ 9⟩ 3 — used to show a material, source, or cause ⟨suffering ∼ a cold⟩

frond \\'fränd\\ *n* : a usu. large divided leaf esp. of a fern or palm tree

¹front \\'frənt\\ *n* 1 : FOREHEAD; *also* : the whole face 2 : external and often feigned appearance 3 : a region of active fighting; *also* : a sphere of activity 4 : a political coalition 5 : the side of a building containing the main entrance 6 : the forward part or surface 7 : FRONTAGE 8 : a boundary between two dissimilar air masses 9 : a position directly before or ahead of something else 10 : a person, group, or thing used to mask the identity of the actual controlling agent

²front *vb* 1 : to have the principal side adjacent to something 2 : to serve as a front 3 : CONFRONT

front·age \\'frən-tij\\ *n* 1 : a piece of land lying adjacent (as to a street or the ocean) 2 : the length of a frontage 3 : the front side of a building

front·al \\'frənt-ᵊl\\ *adj* 1 : of, relating to, or next to the forehead 2 : of, relating to, or directed at the front ⟨a ∼ attack⟩ — **fron·tal·ly** *adv*

fron·tier \\ˌfrən-'tir\\ *n* 1 : a border between two countries 2 : a region that forms the margin of settled territory 3 : the outer limits of knowledge or achievement ⟨the ∼s of science⟩ — **fron·tiers·man** \\-'tirz-mən\\ *n*

fron·tis·piece \\'frən-tə-ˌspēs\\ *n* : an illustration preceding and usu. facing the title page of a book

front man *n* : a person serving as a front or figurehead

front·ward \\'frənt-wərd\\ *or* **front·wards** \\-wərdz\\ *adv or adj* : toward the front

¹frost \\'frȯst\\ *n* 1 : freezing temperature 2 : a covering of tiny ice crystals on a cold surface — **frosty** *adj*

²frost *vb* 1 : to cover with frost 2 : to put icing on (as a cake) 3 : to produce a slightly roughened surface on (as glass) 4 : to injure or kill by frost

¹frost·bite \\'frȯst-ˌbīt\\ *vb* **-bit** \\-ˌbit\\; **-bit·ten** \\-ˌbit-ᵊn\\; **-bit·ing** : to injure by frost or frostbite

²frostbite *n* : the freezing or the local effect of a partial freezing of some part of the body

frost heave *n* : an upthrust of pavement caused by freezing of moist soil

frost·ing \\'frȯ-stiŋ\\ *n* 1 : ICING 2 : dull finish on metal or glass

froth \\'frȯth\\ *n, pl* **froths** \\'frȯths, 'frȯthz\\ 1 : bubbles formed in or on a liquid 2 : something light or worthless — **frothy** *adj*

frou-frou \\'frü-ˌfrü\\ *n* [F] 1 : a rustling esp. of a woman's skirts 2 : showy or frilly ornamentation

fro·ward \\'frō-wərd\\ *adj* : DISOBEDIENT, WILLFUL

frown \\'fraun\\ *vb* 1 : to wrinkle the forehead (as in dis-

pleasure or thought) 2 : to look with disapproval 3 : to express with a frown — **frown** *n*

frow·sy *or* **frow·zy** \\'frau-zē\\ *adj* **frow·si·er** *or* **frow·zi·er; -est** : having a slovenly or uncared-for appearance

froze *past of* FREEZE

fro·zen \\'frōz-ᵊn\\ *adj* 1 : treated, affected, or crusted over by freezing 2 : subject to long and severe cold 3 : incapable of being changed, moved, or undone : FIXED ⟨∼ wages⟩ 4 : not available for present use ⟨∼ capital⟩ 5 : expressing or characterized by cold unfriendliness

FRS *abbr* Federal Reserve System

frt *abbr* freight

fruc·ti·fy \\'frək-tə-ˌfī, 'frük-\\ *vb* **-fied; -fy·ing** 1 : to bear fruit 2 : to make fruitful or productive

fru·gal \\'frü-gəl\\ *adj* : ECONOMICAL, THRIFTY — **fru·gal·i·ty** \\frü-'ga-lə-tē\\ *n* — **fru·gal·ly** *adv*

¹fruit \\'früt\\ *n* [ME, fr. OF, fr. L *fructus* fruit, use, fr. *frui* to enjoy, have the use of] 1 : a product of plant growth; *esp* : a usu. edible and sweet reproductive body (as a strawberry or apple) of a seed plant 2 : a product of fertilization in a plant; *esp* : the ripe ovary of a seed plant with its contents and appendages 3 : CONSEQUENCE, RESULT — **fruit·ed** \\'frü-təd\\ *adj*

²fruit *vb* : to bear or cause to bear fruit

fruit·cake \\'früt-ˌkāk\\ *n* : a rich cake containing nuts, dried or candied fruits, and spices

fruit fly *n* : any of various small dipteran flies whose larvae feed on fruit or decaying vegetable matter

fruit·ful \\'früt-fəl\\ *adj* 1 : yielding or producing fruit 2 : very productive ⟨a ∼ soil⟩; *also* : bringing results ⟨a ∼ idea⟩ — **fruit·ful·ly** *adv* — **fruit·ful·ness** *n*

fru·ition \\frü-'i-shən\\ *n* 1 : ENJOYMENT 2 : the state of bearing fruit 3 : REALIZATION, ACCOMPLISHMENT

fruit·less \\'früt-ləs\\ *adj* 1 : not bearing fruit 2 : UNSUCCESSFUL ⟨a ∼ attempt⟩ — **fruit·less·ly** *adv*

fruity \\'frü-tē\\ *adj* **fruit·i·er; -est** : resembling a fruit esp. in flavor

frumpy \\'frəm-pē\\ *adj* **frump·i·er; -est** : DOWDY, DRAB

frus·trate \\'frəs-ˌtrāt\\ *vb* **frus·trat·ed; frus·trat·ing** 1 : to balk or defeat in an endeavor 2 : to induce feelings of insecurity, discouragement, or dissatisfaction in 3 : to bring to nothing — **frus·trat·ing·ly** *adv* — **frus·tra·tion** \\ˌfrəs-'trā-shən\\ *n*

frus·tum \\'frəs-təm\\ *n, pl* **frustums** *or* **frus·ta** \\-tə\\ : the part of a cone or pyramid formed by cutting off the top by a plane parallel to the base

frwy *abbr* freeway

¹fry \\'frī\\ *vb* **fried; fry·ing** 1 : to cook in a pan or on a griddle over heat esp. with the use of fat 2 : to undergo frying

²fry *n, pl* **fries** 1 : a social gathering where fried food is eaten 2 : a dish of something fried; *esp, pl* : FRENCH FRIES

³fry *n, pl* **fry** 1 : recently hatched fishes; *also* : very small adult fishes 2 : members of a group or class ⟨small ∼⟩

fry·er \\'frī-ər\\ *n* 1 : something (as a young chicken) suitable for frying 2 : a deep utensil for frying foods

FSLIC *abbr* Federal Savings and Loan Insurance Corporation

ft *abbr* 1 feet; foot 2 fort

FTC *abbr* Federal Trade Commission

fuch·sia \\'fyü-shə\\ *n* 1 : any of a genus of shrubs related to the evening primrose and grown for their showy nodding often red or purple flowers 2 : a vivid reddish purple color

fud·dle \\'fəd-ᵊl\\ *vb* **fud·dled; fud·dling** : MUDDLE, CONFUSE

fud·dy–dud·dy \\'fə-dē-ˌdə-dē\\ *n, pl* **-dies** : one that is old-fashioned, unimaginative, or conservative

¹fudge \\'fəj\\ *vb* **fudged; fudg·ing** 1 : to exceed the proper bounds of something 2 : CHEAT; *also* : FALSIFY 3 : to fail to come to grips with

²**fudge** *n* **1** : NONSENSE **2** : a soft candy of milk, sugar, butter, and flavoring

¹**fu·el** \ˈfyü-əl, ˈfyül\ *n* : a material used to produce heat or power by burning; *also* : a material from which nuclear energy can be liberated

²**fuel** *vb* **-eled** *or* **-elled; -el·ing** *or* **-el·ling** : to provide with or take in fuel

fuel cell *n* : a device that continuously changes the chemical energy of a fuel directly into electrical energy

¹**fu·gi·tive** \ˈfyü-jə-tiv\ *n* **1** : one who flees or tries to escape **2** : something elusive or hard to find

²**fugitive** *adj* **1** : running away or trying to escape **2** : likely to vanish suddenly : not fixed or lasting

fugue \ˈfyüg\ *n* **1** : a musical composition in which different parts successively repeat the theme **2** : a disturbed state of consciousness characterized by acts that are not recalled upon recovery

füh·rer *or* **fueh·rer** \ˈfyùr-ər, ˈfir-\ *n* : LEADER; *esp* : TYRANT

¹**-ful** \fəl\ *adj suffix, sometimes* **-ful·ler;** *sometimes* **-fullest** **1** : full of ⟨pride*ful*⟩ **2** : characterized by ⟨peace*ful*⟩ **3** : having the qualities of ⟨master*ful*⟩ **4** : tending, given, or liable to ⟨help*ful*⟩

²**-ful** \ˌfùl\ *n suffix* : number or quantity that fills or would fill ⟨room*ful*⟩

ful·crum \ˈfùl-krəm, ˈfəl-\ *n, pl* **ful·crums** *or* **ful·cra** \-krə\ [LL, fr. L, bedpost] : the support on which a lever turns

F fulcrum

ful·fill *or* **ful·fil** \fùl-ˈfil\ *vb* **ful·filled; ful·fill·ing** **1** : to put into effect **2** : to bring to an end **3** : SATISFY — **ful·fill·ment** *n*

¹**full** \ˈfùl\ *adj* **1** : FILLED **2** : complete esp. in detail, number, or duration **3** : having all the distinguishing characteristics ⟨a ∼ member⟩ **4** : MAXIMUM **5** : rounded in outline ⟨a ∼ figure⟩ **6** : possessing or containing an abundance ⟨∼ of wrinkles⟩ **7** : having an abundance of material ⟨a ∼ skirt⟩ **8** : satisfied esp. with food or drink **9** : having volume or depth of sound **10** : completely occupied with a thought or plan — **full·ness** *also* **ful·ness** *n*

²**full** *adv* **1** : VERY, EXTREMELY **2** : ENTIRELY **3** : STRAIGHT, SQUARELY ⟨hit him ∼ in the face⟩

³**full** *n* **1** : the highest or fullest state or degree **2** : the utmost extent **3** : the requisite or complete amount

⁴**full** *vb* : to shrink and thicken (woolen cloth) by moistening, heating, and pressing — **full·er** *n*

full·back \ˈfùl-ˌbak\ *n* : a football back stationed between the halfbacks

full–blood·ed \ˈfùl-ˈblə-dəd\ *adj* : of unmixed ancestry : PUREBRED

full–blown \-ˈblōn\ *adj* **1** : being at the height of bloom **2** : fully mature or developed

full–bod·ied \-ˈbä-dēd\ *adj* : marked by richness and fullness

full dress *n* : the style of dress worn for ceremonial or formal occasions

full–fledged \ˈfùl-ˈflejd\ *adj* **1** : fully developed **2** : having attained complete status ⟨a ∼ lawyer⟩

full house *n* : a poker hand containing three of a kind and a pair

full moon *n* : the moon with its whole disk illuminated

full–scale \ˈfùl-ˈskāl\ *adj* **1** : identical to an original in proportion and size ⟨∼ drawing⟩ **2** : involving full use of available resources ⟨a ∼ revolt⟩

full tilt *adv* : at high speed

full–time \ˈfùl-ˈtīm\ *adj or adv* : involving or working a normal or standard schedule

ful·ly \ˈfù-lē\ *adv* **1** : in a full manner or degree : COMPLETELY **2** : at least

ful·mi·nate \ˈfùl-mə-ˌnāt, ˈfəl-\ *vb* **-nat·ed; -nat·ing** [ME, fr. ML *fulminare*, fr. L, to strike (of lightning), fr. *fulmen* lightning] : to utter or send out censure or invective : condemn severely — **ful·mi·na·tion** \ˌfùl-mə-ˈnā-shən, ˌfəl-\ *n*

ful·some \ˈfùl-səm\ *adj* **1** : COPIOUS, ABUNDANT ⟨∼ detail⟩ **2** : generous in amount or extent ⟨a ∼ victory⟩ **3** : excessively flattering ⟨∼ praise⟩

fu·ma·role \ˈfyü-mə-ˌrōl\ *n* : a hole in a volcanic region from which hot gases issue

fum·ble \ˈfəm-bəl\ *vb* **fum·bled; fum·bling** **1** : to grope about clumsily **2** : to fail to hold, catch, or handle properly — **fumble** *n*

¹**fume** \ˈfyüm\ *n* : a usu. irritating smoke, vapor, or gas

²**fume** *vb* **fumed; fum·ing** **1** : to treat with fumes **2** : to give off fumes **3** : to express anger or annoyance

fu·mi·gant \ˈfyü-mi-gənt\ *n* : a substance used for fumigation

fu·mi·gate \ˈfyü-mə-ˌgāt\ *vb* **-gat·ed; -gat·ing** : to treat with fumes to disinfect or destroy pests — **fu·mi·ga·tion** \ˌfyü-mə-ˈgā-shən\ *n* — **fu·mi·ga·tor** \ˈfyü-mə-ˌgā-tər\ *n*

¹**fun** \ˈfən\ *n* [E dial. *fun* to hoax] **1** : something that provides amusement or enjoyment **2** : ENJOYMENT

²**fun** *adj* : full of fun ⟨a ∼ person⟩ ⟨had a ∼ time⟩

¹**func·tion** \ˈfəŋk-shən\ *n* **1** : OCCUPATION **2** : special purpose **3** : the particular purpose for which a person or thing is specially fitted or used or for which a thing exists ⟨the ∼ of a hammer⟩; *also* : the natural or proper action of a bodily part in a living thing ⟨the ∼ of the heart⟩ **4** : a formal ceremony or social affair **5** : a mathematical relationship that assigns to each element of a set one and only one element of the same or another set **6** : a variable (as a quality, trait, or measurement) that depends on and varies with another ⟨height is a ∼ of age in children⟩ — **func·tion·al** \-shə-nəl\ *adj* — **func·tion·al·ly** *adv*

²**function** *vb* : to have or carry on a function

func·tion·ary \ˈfəŋk-shə-ˌner-ē\ *n, pl* **-ar·ies** : one who performs a certain function; *esp* : OFFICIAL

function word *n* : a word (as a preposition, auxiliary verb, or conjunction) expressing the grammatical relationship between other words

¹**fund** \ˈfənd\ *n* [L *fundus* bottom, country estate] **1** : a sum of money or resources intended for a special purpose **2** : STORE, SUPPLY **3** *pl* : available money **4** : an organization administering a special fund

²**fund** *vb* **1** : to provide funds for **2** : to convert (a short-term obligation) into a long-term interest-bearing debt

fun·da·men·tal \ˌfən-də-ˈment-ᵊl\ *adj* **1** : serving as an origin : PRIMARY **2** : BASIC, ESSENTIAL **3** : RADICAL ⟨∼ change⟩ **4** : of central importance : PRINCIPAL — **fundamental** *n* — **fun·da·men·tal·ly** *adv*

fun·da·men·tal·ism \-ˌi-zəm\ *n,* **1** *often cap* : a Protestant religious movement emphasizing the literal infallibility of the Bible **2** : a movement or attitude stressing

---

strict adherence to a set of basic principles — **fun·da·men·tal·ist** \-ist\ *adj or n*

¹fu·ner·al \'fyü-nə-rəl\ *adj* **1** : of, relating to, or constituting a funeral **2** : FUNEREAL 2

²funeral *n* : the ceremonies held for a dead person usu. before burial

fu·ner·ary \'fyü-nə-ˌrer-ē\ *adj* : of, used for, or associated with burial

fu·ne·re·al \fyù-'nir-ē-əl\ *adj* **1** : of or relating to a funeral **2** : suggesting a funeral

fun·gi·cide \'fən-jə-ˌsīd, 'fəŋ-gə-\ *n* : an agent that kills or checks the growth of fungi — **fun·gi·cid·al** \ˌfən-jə-'sīd-ᵊl, ˌfən-gə-\ *adj*

fun·gus \'fəŋ-gəs\ *n, pl* **fun·gi** \'fən-ˌjī, 'fəŋ-ˌgī\ *also* **fun·gus·es** \'fəŋ-gə-səz\ : any of a major group of organisms (as molds, mildews, and mushrooms) that lack chlorophyll and are usu. classified as plants — **fun·gal** \-gəl\ *adj* — **fun·gous** \-gəs\ *adj*

fu·nic·u·lar \fyù-'ni-kyə-lər, fə-\ *n* : a cable railway ascending a mountain

funk \'fəŋk\ *n* : a depressed state of mind

funky \'fəŋ-kē\ *adj* **funk·i·er; -est 1** : having an earthy unsophisticated style and feeling; *esp* : having the style and feeling of older black American music **2** : odd or quaint in appearance or style

¹fun·nel \'fən-ᵊl\ *n* **1** : a cone-shaped utensil with a tube used for catching and directing a downward flow (as of liquid) **2** : FLUE, SMOKESTACK

²funnel *vb* **-neled** *also* **-nelled; -nel·ing** *also* **-nel·ling 1** : to pass through or as if through a funnel **2** : to move to a central point or into a central channel

¹fun·ny \'fə-nē\ *adj* **fun·ni·er; -est 1** : AMUSING **2** : FACETIOUS **3** : PECULIAR **3 4** : UNDERHANDED — **funny** *adv*

²funny *n, pl* **funnies** : a comic strip or a comic section (as of a newspaper)

funny bone *n* : a place at the back of the elbow where a blow easily compresses a nerve and causes a painful tingling sensation

¹fur \'fər\ *n* **1** : an article of clothing made of or with fur **2** : the hairy coat of a mammal esp. when fine, soft, and thick; *also* : this coat dressed for use — **fur** *adj* — **furred** \'fərd\ *adj*

²fur *abbr* furlong

fur·be·low \'fər-bə-ˌlō\ *n* **1** : FLOUNCE, RUFFLE **2** : showy trimming

fur·bish \'fər-bish\ *vb* **1** : to make lustrous : POLISH **2** : to give a new look to : RENOVATE

fu·ri·ous \'fyùr-ē-əs\ *adj* **1** : FIERCE, ANGRY, VIOLENT **2** : BOISTEROUS **3** : INTENSE — **fu·ri·ous·ly** *adv*

furl \'fərl\ *vb* **1** : to wrap or roll (as a sail or a flag) close to or around something **2** : to curl in furls — **furl** *n*

fur·long \'fər-ˌlòŋ\ *n* [ME, fr. OE *furlang*, fr. *furh* furrow + *lang* long] : a unit of distance equal to 220 yards (about 201 meters)

fur·lough \'fər-lō\ *n* [D *verlof*, lit., permission] : a leave of absence from duty granted esp. to a soldier — **furlough** *vb*

fur·nace \'fər-nəs\ *n* : an enclosed structure in which heat is produced

fur·nish \'fər-nish\ *vb* **1** : to provide with what is needed : EQUIP **2** : SUPPLY, GIVE

fur·nish·ings \-ni-shiŋz\ *n pl* **1** : articles or accessories of dress **2** : FURNITURE

fur·ni·ture \'fər-ni-chər\ *n* : equipment that is necessary or desirable; *esp* : movable articles (as chairs or beds) for a room

fu·ror \'fyùr-ˌòr\ *n* **1** : ANGER, RAGE **2** : a contagious excitement; *esp* : a fashionable craze **3** : UPROAR

fu·rore \-ˌòr\ *n* [It] : FUROR 2, 3

fur·ri·er \'fər-ē-ər\ *n* : one who prepares or deals in fur

fur·ring \'fər-iŋ\ *n* : wood or metal strips applied to a wall or ceiling to form a level surface or an air space

fur·row \'fər-ō\ *n* **1** : a trench in the earth made by a plow **2** : a narrow groove or wrinkle — **furrow** *vb*

fur·ry \'fər-ē\ *adj* **fur·ri·er; -est 1** : resembling or consisting of fur **2** : covered with fur

¹fur·ther \'fər-thər\ *adv* **1** : FARTHER 1 **2** : in addition : MOREOVER **3** : to a greater extent or degree

²further *vb* : to help forward — **fur·ther·ance** \'fər-thə-rəns\ *n*

³further *adj* **1** : FARTHER 1 **2** : ADDITIONAL

fur·ther·more \'fər-thər-ˌmōr\ *adv* : in addition to what precedes : BESIDES

fur·ther·most \-ˌmōst\ *adj* : most distant : FARTHEST

fur·thest \'fər-thəst\ *adv or adj* : FARTHEST

fur·tive \'fər-tiv\ *adj* [F or L; F *furtif*, fr. L *furtivus*, fr. *furtum* theft, fr. *fur* thief] : done by stealth : SLY — **fur·tive·ly** *adv* — **fur·tive·ness** *n*

fu·ry \'fyùr-ē\ *n, pl* **furies 1** : intense and often destructive rage **2** : extreme fierceness or violence **3** : FRENZY

furze \'fərz\ *n* : GORSE

¹fuse \'fyüz\ *vb* **fused; fus·ing 1** : MELT **2** : to unite by or as if by melting together — **fus·ible** *adj*

²fuse *n* : an electrical safety device having a metal wire or strip that melts and interrupts the circuit when the current becomes too strong

³fuse *n* **1** : a cord or cable that is set afire to ignite an explosive charge **2** *usu* **fuze** : a mechanical or electrical device for setting off the explosive charge of a projectile, bomb, or torpedo

⁴fuse *or* **fuze** \'fyüz\ *vb* **fused** *or* **fuzed; fus·ing** *or* **fuz·ing** : to equip with a fuse

fu·se·lage \'fyü-sə-ˌläzh, -zə-\ *n* : the central body portion of an aircraft

fu·sil·lade \'fyü-sə-ˌläd, -ˌlād\ *n* : a number of shots fired simultaneously or in rapid succession

fu·sion \'fyü-zhən\ *n* **1** : the act or process of melting or making plastic by heat **2** : union by or as if by melting **3** : the union of light atomic nuclei to form heavier nuclei with the release of huge quantities of energy

¹fuss \'fəs\ *n* **1** : needless bustle or excitement : COMMOTION **2** : effusive praise **3** : a state of agitation **4** : OBJECTION, PROTEST **5** : DISPUTE

²fuss *vb* : to make a fuss

fuss·bud·get \'fəs-ˌbə-jət\ *n* : one who fusses or is fussy about trifles

fussy \'fə-sē\ *adj* **fuss·i·er; -est 1** : IRRITABLE **2** : overly decorated **3** : requiring or giving close attention or concern to details or niceties — **fuss·i·ly** \-sə-lē\ *adv* — **fuss·i·ness** \-sē-nəs\ *n*

fus·tian \'fəs-chən\ *n* **1** : a strong usu. cotton fabric **2** : pretentious writing or speech — **fustian** *adj*

fus·ty \'fəs-tē\ *adj* **fus·ti·er; -est** [ME, fr. *fust* wine cask, fr. MF, club, cask, fr. L *fustis*] **1** : MUSTY **2** : OLD-FASHIONED

fut *abbr* future

fu·tile \'fyüt-ᵊl, 'fyü-ˌtīl\ *adj* **1** : USELESS, VAIN **2** : FRIVOLOUS, TRIVIAL — **fu·til·i·ty** \fyü-'ti-lə-tē\ *n*

¹fu·ture \'fyü-chər\ *adj* **1** : of, relating to, or constituting a verb tense that expresses time yet to come **2** : coming after the present

²future *n* **1** : time that is to come **2** : what is going to happen **3** : an expectation of advancement or progressive development **4** : the future tense; *also* : a verb form in it

fu·tur·ism \'fyü-chə-ˌri-zəm\ *n* : a modern movement in art, music, and literature that tries esp. to express the energy and activity of mechanical processes — **fu·tur·ist** \'fyü-chə-rist\ *n*

fu·tur·is·tic \ˌfyü-chə-'ris-tik\ *adj* : of or relating to the future or to futurism; *also* : very modern

fu·tu·ri·ty \fyü-'tùr-ə-tē, -'tyùr-\ *n, pl* **-ties 1** : FUTURE **2** : the quality or state of being future **3** *pl* : future events or prospects

fuze *var of* FUSE

fuzz \\'fəz\\ *n* : fine light particles or fibers (as of down or fluff)

fuzzy \\'fə-zē\\ *adj* **fuzz·i·er; -est 1** : having or resembling fuzz **2** : INDISTINCT — **fuzz·i·ness** \\-zē-nəs\\ *n*

fwd *abbr* forward

FWD *abbr* front-wheel drive

FY *abbr* fiscal year

-fy *vb suffix* : make : form into ⟨dandi*fy*⟩

FYI *abbr* for your information

G

¹**g** \\'jē\\ *n, pl* **g's** *or* **gs** \\'jēz\\ *often cap* **1** : the 7th letter of the English alphabet **2** : a unit of force equal to the force exerted by gravity on a body at rest and used to indicate the force to which a body is subjected when accelerated **3** *slang* : a sum of $1000

²**g** *abbr, often cap* **1** game **2** gauge **3** good **4** gram **5** gravity

ga *abbr* gauge

¹**Ga** *abbr* Georgia

²**Ga** *symbol* gallium

GA *abbr* **1** general assembly **2** general average **3** general of the army **4** Georgia

gab \\'gab\\ *vb* **gabbed; gab·bing** : to talk in a rapid or thoughtless manner ; CHATTER — **gab** *n*

gab·ar·dine \\'ga-bər-ˌdēn\\ *n* **1** : GABERDINE 1 **2** : a firm durable twilled fabric having diagonal ribs and made of various fibers; *also* : a garment of gabardine

gab·ble \\'ga-bəl\\ *vb* **gab·bled; gab·bling** : JABBER, BAB-BLE

gab·by \\'ga-bē\\ *adj* **gab·bi·er; -est** : TALKATIVE, GARRU-LOUS

gab·er·dine \\'ga-bər-ˌdēn\\ *n* **1** : a long loose outer garment worn in medieval times and associated esp. with Jews **2** : GABARDINE 2

gab·fest \\'gab-ˌfest\\ *n* **1** : an informal gathering for general talk **2** : an extended conversation

ga·ble \\'ga-bəl\\ *n* : the vertical triangular end of a building formed by the sides of the roof sloping from the ridge down to the eaves — **ga·bled** \\-bəld\\ *adj*

Gab·o·nese \\ˌga-bə-'nēz, -'nēs\\ *n* : a native or inhabitant of Gabon — **Gabonese** *adj*

gad \\'gad\\ *vb* **gad·ded; gad·ding** : to be constantly active without specific purpose — usu. used with *about* — **gad·der** *n*

gad·about \\'ga-də-ˌbaut\\ *n* : a person who flits about in social activity

gad·fly \\'gad-ˌflī\\ *n* **1** : a fly that bites or harasses livestock **2** : a person who annoys esp. by persistent criticism

gad·get \\'ga-jət\\ *n* : DEVICE, CONTRIVANCE — **gad·get·ry** \\'ga-jə-trē\\ *n*

gad·o·lin·i·um \\ˌgad-ᵊl-'i-nē-əm\\ *n* : a magnetic metallic chemical element — see ELEMENT table

¹**Gael** \\'gāl\\ *n* : a Celtic inhabitant of Ireland or Scotland

²**Gael** *abbr* Gaelic

Gael·ic \\'gā-lik\\ *adj* : of or relating to the Gaels or their languages — **Gaelic** *n*

gaff \\'gaf\\ *n* **1** : a spear used in taking fish or turtles; *also* : a metal hook for holding or lifting heavy fish **2** : the spar supporting the top of a fore-and-aft sail **3** : rough treatment — ABUSE — **gaff** *vb*

gaffe \\'gaf\\ *n* : a social blunder

gaf·fer \\'ga-fər\\ *n* **1** : an old man **2** : a lighting electrician on a motion-picture or television set

¹**gag** \\'gag\\ *vb* **gagged; gag·ging 1** : to restrict use of the mouth with a gag **2** : to prevent from speaking freely **3** : to retch or cause to retch **4** : OBSTRUCT, CHOKE **5** : BALK **6** : to make quips — **gag·ger** *n*

²**gag** *n* **1** : something thrust into the mouth esp. to prevent speech or outcry **2** : an official check or restraint on

free speech **3** : a laugh-provoking remark or act **4** : PRANK, TRICK

¹**gage** \\'gāj\\ *n* **1** : a token of defiance; *esp* : a glove or cap cast on the ground as a pledge of combat **2** : SECURITY

²**gage** *var of* GAUGE

gag·gle \\'ga-gəl\\ *n* [ME *gagyll*, fr. *gagelen* to cackle] **1** : a flock of geese **2** : GROUP, CLUSTER

gai·ety \\'gā-ə-tē\\ *n, pl* **-eties 1** : festive activity : MERRY-MAKING **2** : MERRIMENT **3** : FINERY **syn** mirth, festivity, glee, hilarity, jollity

gai·ly \\'gā-lē\\ *adv* : in a gay manner

¹**gain** \\'gān\\ *n* **1** : PROFIT **2** : ACQUISITION, ACCUMULATION **3** : INCREASE

²**gain** *vb* **1** : to get possession of : EARN **2** : WIN ⟨∼ a victory⟩ **3** : to increase in ⟨∼ momentum⟩ **4** : PERSUADE **5** : to arrive at **6** : ACHIEVE ⟨∼ strength⟩ **7** : to run fast ⟨the watch ∼s a minute a day⟩ **8** : PROFIT **9** : INCREASE **10** : to improve in health **syn** accomplish, attain, realize — **gain·er** *n*

gain·ful \\'gān-fəl\\ *adj* : PROFITABLE — **gain·ful·ly** *adv*

gain·say \\gān-'sā\\ *vb* **-said** \\-'sād, -'sed\\; **-say·ing; -says** \\-'sāz, -'sez\\ [ME *gainsayen*, fr. *gain-* against + *-sayen* to say] **1** : DENY, DISPUTE **2** : to speak against **syn** contradict, contravene, impugn, negate — **gain·say·er** *n*

gait \\'gāt\\ *n* : manner of moving on foot; *also* : a particular pattern or style of such moving — **gait·ed** *adj*

gai·ter \\'gā-tər\\ *n* **1** : a leg covering reaching from the instep to ankle, mid-calf, or knee **2** : an overshoe with a fabric upper **3** : an ankle-high shoe with elastic gores in the sides

¹**gal** \\'gal\\ *n* : GIRL

²**gal** *abbr* gallon

Gal *abbr* Galatians

ga·la \\'gā-lə, 'ga-, 'gä-\\ *n* : a gay celebration : FESTIVITY — **gala** *adj*

ga·lac·tic \\gə-'lak-tik\\ *adj* : of or relating to a galaxy

Ga·la·tians \\gə-'lā-shənz\\ *n* — see BIBLE table

gal·axy \\'ga-lək-sē\\ *n, pl* **-ax·ies** [ME *galaxie, galaxias*, fr. LL *galaxias*, fr. Gk, fr. *galakt-, gala* milk] **1** *often cap* : MILKY WAY GALAXY — used with *the* **2** : a very large group of stars **3** : an assemblage of brilliant or famous persons or things

gale \\'gāl\\ *n* **1** : a strong wind **2** : an emotional outburst ⟨∼s of laughter⟩

ga·le·na \\gə-'lē-nə\\ *n* : a lustrous bluish gray mineral that consists of the sulfide of lead and is the chief ore of lead

¹**gall** \\'gol\\ *n* **1** : BILE **2** : something bitter to endure **3** : RANCOR **4** : IMPUDENCE **syn** effrontery, brass, cheek, chutzpah, audacity, presumption

²**gall** *n* : a skin sore caused by chafing

³**gall** *vb* **1** : CHAFE; *esp* : to become sore or worn by rubbing **2** : VEX, HARASS

⁴**gall** *n* : a swelling of plant tissue caused by parasites

¹**gal·lant** \\gə-'lant, -'länt; 'ga-lənt\\ *n* **1** : a young man of

\\ə\\abut \\ᵊ\\kitten \\ər\\further \\a\\ash \\ā\\ace \\ä\\mop, mar \\aù\\out \\ch\\chin \\e\\bet \\ē\\easy \\g\\go \\i\\hit \\ī\\ice \\j\\job \\ŋ\\sing \\ō\\go \\ò\\law \\òi\\boy \\th\\thin \\t͟h\\the \\ü\\loot \\ù\\foot \\y\\yet \\zh\\vision *see also* Pronunciation Symbols page fashion **2** : a man who shows a marked fondness for the company of women and who is esp. attentive to them **3** : SUITOR

²**gal·lant** \'ga-lənt (*usual for 2, 3, 4*); gə-'lant, -'länt (*usual for 5*)\ *adj* **1** : showy in dress or bearing : SMART **2** : SPLENDID, STATELY **3** : SPIRITED, BRAVE **4** : CHIVALROUS, NOBLE **5** : polite and attentive to women — **gal·lant·ly** *adv*

gal·lant·ry \'ga-lən-trē\ *n, pl* **-ries 1** *archaic* : gallant appearance **2** : an act of marked courtesy **3** : courteous attention to a woman **4** : conspicuous bravery **syn** heroism, valor, prowess

gall·blad·der \'gȯl-ˌbla-dər\ *n* : a membranous muscular sac attached to the liver and serving to store bile

gal·le·on \'ga-lē-ən\ *n* : a large square-rigged sailing ship formerly used esp. by the Spanish

galleon

gal·le·ria \ˌga-lə-'rē-ə\ *n* [It] : a roofed and usu. glass= enclosed promenade or court

gal·lery \'ga-lə-rē\ *n, pl* **-ler·ies 1** : an outdoor balcony; *also* : PORCH, VERANDA **2** : a long narrow passage, apartment, or hall **3** : a narrow passage (as one made underground by a miner or through wood by an insect) **4** : a room where works of art are exhibited; *also* : an organization dealing in works of art **5** : a balcony in a theater, auditorium, or church; *esp* : the highest one in a theater **6** : the spectators at a tennis or golf match **7** : a photographer's studio — **gal·ler·ied** \-rēd\ *adj*

gal·ley \'ga-lē\ *n, pl* **galleys 1** : a long low ship propelled esp. by oars and formerly used esp. in the Mediterranean Sea **2** : the kitchen esp. of a ship or airplane **3** : a proof of typeset matter esp. in a single column

Gal·lic \'ga-lik\ *adj* : of or relating to Gaul or France

gal·li·mau·fry \ˌga-lə-'mȯ-frē\ *n, pl* **-fries** [MF *galimafree* stew] : HODGEPODGE

gal·li·nule \'ga-lə-ˌnül, -ˌnyül\ *n* : any of several aquatic birds related to the rails

gal·li·um \'ga-lē-əm\ *n* : a rare bluish white metallic chemical element — see ELEMENT table

gal·li·vant \'ga-lə-ˌvant\ *vb* : to travel, roam, or move about for pleasure

gal·lon \'ga-lən\ *n* — see WEIGHT table

¹**gal·lop** \'ga-ləp\ *vb* **1** : to go or cause to go at a gallop **2** : to run fast — **gal·lop·er** *n*

²**gallop** *n* **1** : a bounding gait of a quadruped; *esp* : a fast 3-beat gait of a horse **2** : a ride or run at a gallop

gal·lows \'ga-lōz\ *n, pl* **gallows** or **gal·lows·es** : a frame usu. of two upright posts and a crosspiece from which criminals are hanged; *also* : the punishment of hanging

gall·stone \'gȯl-ˌstōn\ *n* : an abnormal concretion occurring in the gallbladder or bile passages

gal·lus·es \'ga-lə-səz\ *n pl* : SUSPENDERS

ga·lore \gə-'lȯr\ *adj* [Ir *go leor* enough] : ABUNDANT, PLENTIFUL

ga·losh \gə-'läsh\ *n* : a high overshoe

galv *abbr* galvanized

gal·va·nise *Brit var of* GALVANIZE

gal·va·nize \'gal-və-ˌnīz\ *vb* **-nized; -niz·ing 1** : to stim-

ulate as if by an electric shock **2** : to coat (iron or steel) with zinc — **gal·va·ni·za·tion** \ˌgal-və-nə-'zā-shən\ *n* — **gal·va·niz·er** *n*

gal·va·nom·e·ter \ˌgal-və-'nä-mə-tər\ *n* : an instrument for detecting or measuring a small electric current

Gam·bi·an \'gam-bē-ən\ *n* : a native or inhabitant of Gambia — **Gambian** *adj*

gam·bit \'gam-bət\ *n* [It *gambetto*, lit., act of tripping someone, fr. *gamba* leg] **1** : a chess opening in which a player risks one or more minor pieces to gain an advantage in position **2** : a calculated move : STRATAGEM **syn** trick, artifice, gimmick, maneuver, play, ruse

¹**gam·ble** \'gam-bəl\ *vb* **gam·bled; gam·bling 1** : to play a game for money or property **2** : BET, WAGER **3** : VENTURE, HAZARD — **gam·bler** *n*

²**gamble** *n* : a risky undertaking

gam·bol \'gam-bəl\ *vb* **-boled** or **-bolled; -bol·ing** or **-bol·ling** : to skip about in play : FRISK — **gambol** *n*

gam·brel roof \'gam-brəl-\ *n* : a roof with a lower steeper slope and an upper flatter one on each side

¹**game** \'gām\ *n* **1** : AMUSEMENT, DIVERSION **2** : SPORT, FUN **3** : SCHEME, PROJECT **4** : a line of work : PROFESSION **5** : CONTEST **6** : animals hunted for sport or food; *also* : the flesh of a game animal

²**game** *vb* **gamed; gam·ing** : to play for a stake : GAMBLE

³**game** *adj* : PLUCKY — **game·ly** *adv* — **game·ness** *n*

⁴**game** *adj* : LAME ⟨a ∼ leg⟩

game·cock \'gām-ˌkäk\ *n* : a rooster trained for fighting

game fish *n* : SPORT FISH

game·keep·er \'gām-ˌkē-pər\ *n* : a person in charge of the breeding and protection of game animals or birds in a private preserve

game·some \'gām-səm\ *adj* : MERRY **syn** playful, frolicsome, sportive, antic

game·ster \'gām-stər\ *n* : GAMBLER

gam·ete \'ga-ˌmēt\ *n* : a mature germ cell — **ga·met·ic** \gə-'me-tik\ *adj*

game theory *n* : the analysis of a situation involving conflicting interests (as in business) in terms of gains and losses among opposing players

gam·in \'ga-mən\ *n* [F] **1** : a boy who hangs around on the streets **2** : GAMINE 2

ga·mine \ga-'mēn\ *n* **1** : a girl who hangs around on the streets **2** : a small playfully mischievous girl

gam·ma \'ga-mə\ *n* : the 3d letter of the Greek alphabet — Γ or γ

gamma globulin *n* : a blood protein fraction rich in antibodies; *also* : a solution of this from human blood donors that is given to provide immunity against some infectious diseases (as measles)

gamma ray *n* : a photon emitted by a radioactive substance; *also* : a high-energy photon — usu. used in pl.

gam·mer \'ga-mər\ *n, archaic* : an old woman

gam·mon \'ga-mən\ *n, chiefly Brit* : a cured ham or side of bacon

gam·ut \'ga-mət\ *n* : an entire range or series **syn** scale, spectrum

gamy or **gam·ey** \'gā-mē\ *adj* **gam·i·er; -est 1** : GAME, PLUCKY **2** : having the flavor of game esp. when near tainting **3** : SCANDALOUS; *also* : DISREPUTABLE — **gam·i·ness** \-mē-nəs\ *n*

¹**gan·der** \'gan-dər\ *n* : a male goose

²**gander** *n* : LOOK, GLANCE

¹**gang** \'gaŋ\ *n* **1** : a set of implements or devices arranged to operate together **2** : a group of persons working or associated together; *esp* : a group of criminals or young delinquents

²**gang** *vb* **1** : to attack in a gang — usu. used with *up* **2** : to form into or move or act as a gang

gang·land \'gaŋ-ˌland\ *n* : the world of organized crime

gan·gling \'gaŋ-gliŋ\ *adj* : loosely and awkwardly built : LANKY

gan·gli·on \'gaŋ-glē-ən\ *n, pl* **-glia** \-ə\ also **-gli·ons** : a mass of nerve cells outside the central nervous system; *also* : NUCLEUS 3 — **gan·gli·on·ic** \ˌgaŋ-glē-ˈä-nik\ *adj*

gan·gly \ˈgaŋ-glē\ *adj* : GANGLING

gang·plank \ˈgaŋ-ˌplaŋk\ *n* : a movable bridge from a ship to the shore

gang·plow \-ˌplaú\ *n* : a plow that turns two or more furrows at one time

gan·grene \ˈgaŋ-ˌgrēn, gaŋ-ˈgrēn\ *n* : the death of soft tissues in a local area of the body due to loss of the blood supply — **gangrene** *vb* — **gan·gre·nous** \ˈgaŋ-grə-nəs\ *adj*

gang·ster \ˈgaŋ-stər\ *n* : a member of a gang of criminals : RACKETEER

gang·way \ˈgaŋ-ˌwā\ *n* 1 : PASSAGEWAY; *also* : GANG-PLANK 2 : clear passage through a crowd

gan·net \ˈga-nət\ *n, pl* **gannets** *also* **gannet** : any of several large fish-eating usu. white and black marine birds that breed on offshore islands

gant·let \ˈgónt-lət\ *var of* GAUNTLET

gan·try \ˈgan-trē\ *n, pl* **gantries** : a frame structure on side supports over or around something

GAO *abbr* General Accounting Office

gaol \ˈjāl\, **gaol·er** \ˈjā-lər\ *chiefly Brit var of* JAIL, JAILER

gap \ˈgap\ *n* 1 : BREACH, CLEFT 2 : a mountain pass 3 : a blank space; *also* : an incomplete or deficient area 4 : a wide difference in character or attitude 5 : a problem caused by a disparity ⟨credibility ∼⟩

gape \ˈgāp\ *vb* **gaped; gap·ing** 1 : to open the mouth wide 2 : to open or part widely 3 : to stare with mouth open 4 : YAWN — **gape** *n*

¹**gar** \ˈgär\ *n* : any of several fishes that have a long body resembling that of a pike and long narrow jaws

²**gar** *abbr* garage

GAR *abbr* Grand Army of the Republic

¹**ga·rage** \gə-ˈräzh, -ˈräj\ *n* [F] : a shelter or repair shop for automobiles

²**garage** *vb* **ga·raged; ga·rag·ing** : to keep or put in a garage

garage sale *n* : a sale of used household or personal articles held on the seller's own premises

garb \ˈgärb\ *n* 1 : style of dress 2 : outward form : APPEARANCE — **garb** *vb*

gar·bage \ˈgär-bij\ *n* 1 : food waste 2 : unwanted or useless material — **gar·bage·man** \-ˌman\ *n*

gar·ble \ˈgär-bəl\ *vb* **gar·bled; gar·bling** [ME *garbelen,* fr. It *garbellare* to sift, fr. Ar *gharbala*] : to distort the meaning of ⟨∼ a story⟩

gar·çon \gär-ˈsōⁿ\ *n, pl* **garçons** *same or* -ˈsoⁿz\ [F, boy, servant] : WAITER

¹**gar·den** \ˈgärd-ᵊn\ *n* 1 : a plot for growing fruits, flowers, or vegetables 2 : a public recreation area; *esp* : one for displaying plants or animals

²**garden** *vb* : to lay out or work in a garden — **gar·den·er** *n*

gar·de·nia \gär-ˈdē-nyə\ *n* [NL, genus name, fr. Alexander *Garden* †1791 Scot. naturalist] : the fragrant white or yellow flower of any of a genus of trees or shrubs related to the madder; *also* : one of these trees

garden–variety *adj* : COMMONPLACE, ORDINARY

gar·fish \ˈgär-ˌfish\ *n* : GAR

gar·gan·tuan \gär-ˈgan-chə-wən\ *adj, often cap* : of tremendous size or volume **syn** huge, colossal, gigantic, mammoth, monstrous, titanic

gar·gle \ˈgär-gəl\ *vb* **gar·gled; gar·gling** : to rinse the throat with liquid agitated by air forced through it from the lungs — **gargle** *n*

gar·goyle \ˈgär-ˌgóil\ *n* 1 : a waterspout in the form of a grotesque human or animal figure projecting from the roof or eaves of a building 2 : a grotesquely carved figure

gar·ish \ˈgar-ish\ *adj* : FLASHY, GLARING, SHOWY, GAUDY

¹**gar·land** \ˈgär-lənd\ *n* : WREATH, CHAPLET

²**garland** *vb* : to form into or deck with a garland

gar·lic \ˈgär-lik\ *n* [ME *garlek,* fr. OE *gārlēac,* fr. *gār* spear + *lēac* leek] : an herb related to the lilies and grown for its pungent bulbs used in cooking; *also* : its bulb — **gar·licky** \-li-kē\ *adj*

gar·ment \ˈgär-mənt\ *n* : an article of clothing

gar·ner \ˈgär-nər\ *vb* 1 : to gather into storage 2 : to acquire by effort 3 : ACCUMULATE, COLLECT

gar·net \ˈgär-nət\ *n* [ME *grenat,* fr. MF, fr. *grenat,* adj., red like a pomegranate, fr. *(pomme) grenate* pomegranate] : a transparent deep red mineral sometimes used as a gem

gar·nish \ˈgär-nish\ *vb* 1 : DECORATE, EMBELLISH 2 : to add decorative or savory touches to (food) 3 : GARNISH-EE — **garnish** *n*

gar·nish·ee \ˌgär-nə-ˈshē\ *vb* **-eed; -ee·ing** 1 : to serve with a garnishment 2 : to take (as a debtor's wages) by legal authority

gar·nish·ment \ˈgär-nish-mənt\ *n* 1 : GARNISH 2 : a legal warning concerning the attachment of property to satisfy a debt; *also* : the attachment of such property

gar·ni·ture \-ni-chər, -ˌchúr\ *n* : EMBELLISHMENT, TRIMMING

gar·ret \ˈgar-ət\ *n* [ME *garette* watchtower, fr. MF *garite*] : the part of a house just under the roof : ATTIC

gar·ri·son \ˈgar-ə-sən\ *n* 1 : a military post; *esp* : a permanent military installation 2 : the troops stationed at a garrison — **garrison** *vb*

garrison state *n* : a state organized on a primarily military basis

gar·rote *or* **ga·rotte** \gə-ˈrät, -ˈrōt\ *n* [Sp *garrote*] 1 : a method of execution by strangulation; *also* : the apparatus used 2 : an implement (as a wire with handles) for strangulation — **garrote** *or* **garotte** *vb*

gar·ru·lous \ˈgar-ə-ləs\ *adj* : TALKATIVE, WORDY — **gar·ru·li·ty** \gə-ˈrü-lə-tē\ *n* — **gar·ru·lous·ly** *adv* — **gar·ru·lous·ness** *n*

gar·ter \ˈgär-tər\ *n* : a band or strap worn to hold up a stocking or sock

garter snake *n* : any of numerous harmless American snakes with longitudinal stripes on the back

¹**gas** \ˈgas\ *n, pl* **gas·es** *also* **gas·ses** [NL, alter. of L *chaos* space, chaos] 1 : a fluid (as hydrogen or air) that tends to expand indefinitely 2 : a gas or mixture of gases used as a fuel or anesthetic 3 : a substance that can be used to produce a poisonous, asphyxiating, or irritant atmosphere 4 : GASOLINE — **gas·eous** \ˈga-sē-əs, -shəs\ *adj*

²**gas** *vb* **gassed; gas·sing** 1 : to treat with gas; *also* : to poison with gas 2 : to fill with gasoline ⟨∼ up the car⟩

gash \ˈgash\ *n* : a deep long cut — **gash** *vb*

gas·ket \ˈgas-kət\ *n* : material (as rubber) or a part used to seal a joint

gas·light \ˈgas-ˌlīt\ *n* 1 : light made by burning illuminating gas 2 : a gas flame; *also* : a gas lighting fixture

gas mask *n* : a mask with a chemical air filter used to protect the face and lungs against poison gas

gas·o·line \ˈga-sə-ˌlēn, ˌga-sə-ˈlēn\ *n* : a flammable liquid mixture made from petroleum and used esp. as a motor fuel

gasp \ˈgasp\ *vb* 1 : to catch the breath audibly (as with shock) 2 : to breathe laboriously : PANT 3 : to utter in a gasping manner — **gasp** *n*

gas·tric \ˈgas-trik\ *adj* : of or relating to the stomach

gastric juice *n* : the acid digestive secretion of the stomach

gas·tri·tis \gas-ˈtrī-təs\ *n* : inflammation of the lining of the stomach

gas·tro·en·ter·ol·o·gy \ˌgas-trō-ˌen-tə-ˈrä-lə-jē\ *n* : a

\ə\abut \ᵊ\kitten \ər\further \a\ash \ā\ace \ä\mop, mar
\aú\out \ch\chin \e\bet \ē\easy \g\go \i\hit \ī\ice \j\job
\ŋ\sing \ō\go \ó\law \ói\boy \th\thin \ṯh\the \ü\loot \ú\foot
\y\yet \zh\vision *see also* Pronunciation Symbols page

branch of medicine concerned with the structure, functions, and diseases of the stomach and intestines — **gas·tro·en·ter·ol·o·gist** \-jist\ n

gas·tro·in·tes·ti·nal \ˌgas-trō-in-'tes-tən-ᵊl\ adj : of, relating to, affecting, or including both the stomach and intestine ⟨∼ tract⟩ ⟨∼ distress⟩

gas·tron·o·my \gas-'trä-nə-mē\ n [F gastronomie, fr. Gk Gastronomia, title of a 4th cent. B.C. poem, fr. gastēr belly + -nomia system of laws] : the art of good eating — **gas·tro·nom·ic** \ˌgas-trə-'nä-mik\ also **gas·tro·nom·i·cal** \-mi-kəl\ adj

gas·tro·pod \'gas-trə-ˌpäd\ n : any of a large class of mollusks (as snails and slugs) with a muscular foot and a spiral shell or none — **gastropod** adj

gas·works \'gas-ˌwərks\ n sing or pl : a plant for manufacturing gas

gate \'gāt\ n 1 : an opening for passage in a wall or fence 2 : a city or castle entrance often with defensive structures 3 : the frame or door that closes a gate 4 : a device (as a valve) for controlling the passage of a fluid or signal 5 : the total admission receipts or the number of people at an event

-gate \ˌgāt\ n comb form [Watergate, scandal that resulted in the resignation of President Richard Nixon in 1974] : usu. political scandal often involving the concealment of wrongdoing

gate–crash·er \'gāt-ˌkra-shər\ n : a person who enters without paying admission or attends without invitation

gate·keep·er \-ˌkē-pər\ n : a person who tends or guards a gate

gate·post \-ˌpōst\ n : the post to which a gate is hung or the one against which it closes

gate·way \-ˌwā\ n 1 : an opening for a gate 2 : a means of entrance or exit

¹**gath·er** \'ga-thər\ vb 1 : to bring together : COLLECT 2 : PICK, HARVEST 3 : to pick up little by little 4 : to gain or win by gradual increase : ACCUMULATE ⟨∼ speed⟩ 5 : to summon up ⟨∼ courage to dive⟩ 6 : to draw about or close to something 7 : to pull (fabric) along a line of stitching into puckers 8 : GUESS, DEDUCE, INFER 9 : ASSEMBLE 10 : to swell out and fill with pus 11 : GROW, INCREASE syn congregate, forgather — **gath·er·er** n

²**gather** n : a puckering in cloth made by gathering

GATT \'gat\ abbr General Agreement on Tariffs and Trade

gauche \'gōsh\ adj [F, lit., left] 1 : lacking social experience or grace; also : not tactful 2 : crudely made or done syn clumsy, heavy-handed, inept, maladroit

gau·che·rie \ˌgō-shə-'rē\ n : a tactless or awkward action

gau·cho \'gaů-chō\ n, pl **gauchos** : a cowboy of the So. American pampas

gaud \'gȯd\ n : ORNAMENT, TRINKET

gaudy \'gȯ-dē\ adj **gaud·i·er; -est** 1 : ostentatiously or tastelessly ornamented 2 : marked by showiness or extravagance syn garish, flashy, glaring, tawdry — **gaud·i·ly** \-də-lē\ adv — **gaud·i·ness** \-dē-nəs\ n

¹**gauge** or **gage** \'gāj\ n 1 : measurement according to some standard or system 2 : DIMENSIONS, SIZE 3 usu gage : an instrument for measuring, testing, or registering

²**gauge** or **gage** vb **gauged** or **gaged; gaug·ing** or **gag·ing** 1 : MEASURE 2 : to determine the capacity or contents of 3 : ESTIMATE, JUDGE

gaunt \'gȯnt\ adj 1 : being thin and angular 2 : BARREN, DESOLATE syn bony, lank, lanky, lean, rawboned, skinny — **gaunt·ness** n

¹**gaunt·let** \'gȯnt-lət\ n 1 : a protective glove 2 : an open challenge (as to combat) 3 : a dress glove extending above the wrist

²**gauntlet** n 1 : ORDEAL 2 : a double file of men armed with weapons (as clubs) with which to strike at an individual who is made to run between them

gauze \'gȯz\ n : a very thin often transparent fabric used esp. for draperies and surgical dressings — **gauzy** adj

gave past of GIVE

gav·el \'ga-vəl\ n : the mallet of a presiding officer or auctioneer

ga·votte \gə-'vät\ n : a dance of French peasant origin marked by the raising rather than sliding of the feet

gawk \'gȯk\ vb : to gape or stare stupidly

gawky \'gȯ-kē\ adj **gawk·i·er; -est** : AWKWARD, CLUMSY — **gawk·i·ly** \-kə-lē\ adv

gay \'gā\ adj 1 : MERRY 2 : BRIGHT, LIVELY 3 : brilliant in color 4 : given to social pleasures; also : LICENTIOUS 5 : HOMOSEXUAL; also : of, relating to, or used by homosexuals

gay·ety, gay·ly var of GAIETY, GAILY

gaz abbr gazette

gaze \'gāz\ vb **gazed; gaz·ing** : to fix the eyes in a steady intent look syn gape, gawk, glare, goggle, peer, stare — **gaze** n — **gaz·er** n

ga·ze·bo \gə-'zē-bō\ n, pl **-bos** 1 : BELVEDERE 2 : a freestanding roofed structure usu. open on the sides

ga·zelle \gə-'zel\ n, pl **gazelles** also **gazelle** : any of numerous small swift graceful antelopes

gazelle

ga·zette \gə-'zet\ n 1 : NEWSPAPER 2 : an official journal

gaz·et·teer \ˌga-zə-'tir\ n : a geographical dictionary

gaz·pa·cho \gəz-'pä-(ˌ)chō, gä-'spä-\ n, pl **-chos** [Sp] : a spicy soup usu. made from raw vegetables and served cold

GB abbr Great Britain

GCA abbr ground-controlled approach

gd abbr good

Gd symbol gadolinium

GDR abbr German Democratic Republic

Ge symbol germanium

gear \'gir\ n 1 : CLOTHING 2 : movable property : GOODS 3 : EQUIPMENT ⟨fishing ∼⟩ 4 : a mechanism that performs a specific function ⟨steering ∼⟩ 5 : a toothed wheel 6 : working adjustment of gears ⟨in ∼⟩ 7 : an adjustment of transmission gears (as of an automobile or bicycle) that determines speed and direction of travel — **gear** vb

gear·box \'gir-ˌbäks\ n : TRANSMISSION 3

gear·shift \-ˌshift\ n : a mechanism by which transmission gears are shifted

gear·wheel \-ˌhwēl\ n : GEAR 5

GED abbr 1 General Educational Development (tests) 2 general equivalency diploma

geek \'gēk\ n : a person often of an intellectual bent who is disapproved of — **geeky** adj

geese pl of GOOSE

gee·zer \'gē-zər\ n : an odd or eccentric person

Gei·ger counter \'gī-gər-\ n : an electronic instrument for detecting the presence of cosmic rays or radioactive substances

gei·sha \'gā-shə, 'gē-\ *n, pl* **geisha** *or* **geishas** [Jp, fr. *gei* art + *-sha* person] : a Japanese girl or woman who is trained to provide entertaining company for men

gel \'jel\ *n* : a solid jellylike colloid (as gelatin dessert) — **gel** *vb*

gel·a·tin *also* **gel·a·tine** \'je-lət-ᵊn\ *n* : glutinous material and esp. protein obtained from animal tissues by boiling and used as a food, in dyeing, and in photography; *also* : an edible jelly formed with gelatin — **ge·lat·i·nous** \jə-'lat-ᵊn-əs\ *adj*

geld \'geld\ *vb* : CASTRATE

geld·ing *n* : a castrated male horse

gel·id \'je-ləd\ *adj* : extremely cold

gem \'jem\ *n* **1** : JEWEL **2** : a usu. valuable stone cut and polished for ornament **3** : something valued for beauty or perfection

Gem·i·ni \'je-mə-(ˌ)nē, -ˌnī; 'ge-mə-ˌnē\ *n* **1** : a zodiacal constellation between Taurus and Cancer usu. pictured as twins sitting together **2** : the 3d sign of the zodiac in astrology; *also* : one born under this sign

gem·ol·o·gy *or* **gem·mol·o·gy** \je-'mä-lə-jē, jə-\ *n* : the science of gems — **gem·olog·i·cal** \ˌje-mə-'lä-ji-kəl\ *adj* — **gem·ol·o·gist** *or* **gem·mol·o·gist** \-'jist\ *n*

gem·stone \'jem-ˌstōn\ *n* : a mineral or petrified material that when cut and polished can be used in jewelry

gen *abbr* **1** general **2** genitive

Gen *abbr* Genesis

Gen AF *abbr* general of the air force

gen·darme \'zhän-ˌdärm, 'jän-\ *n* [F, intended as sing. of *gensdarmes*, pl. of *gent d'armes*, lit., armed people] : a member of a body of soldiers esp. in France serving as an armed police force

gen·der \'jen-dər\ *n* **1** : any of two or more divisions within a grammatical class that determine agreement with and selection of other words or grammatical forms **2** : SEX 1

gene \'jēn\ *n* : a part of DNA or RNA that contains chemical information needed to make a particular protein (as an enzyme) controlling or influencing an inherited bodily trait or activity (as eye color) or that influences or controls the activity of another gene or genes — **gen·ic** \'jē-nik, 'je-\ *adj*

ge·ne·al·o·gy \ˌjē-nē-'ä lə jē, ˌje-, -'a-\ *n, pl* **-gies** : PEDIGREE, LINEAGE; *also* : the study of family pedigrees — **ge·ne·a·log·i·cal** \ˌjē-nē-ə-'lä-ji-kəl, ˌje-\ *adj* — **ge·ne·a·log·i·cal·ly** \-k(ə-)lē\ *adv* — **ge·ne·al·o·gist** \ˌjē-nē-'ä-lə-jist, ˌje-; -'a-\ *n*

genera *pl of* GENUS

¹gen·er·al \'je-nə-rəl, 'jen-rəl\ *adj* **1** : of or relating to the whole **2** : taken as a whole **3** : relating to or covering all instances **4** : not special or specialized **5** : common to many ⟨a ~ custom⟩ **6** : not limited in meaning : not specific **7** : holding superior rank ⟨inspector ~⟩ **syn** generic, universal

²general *n* **1** : something that involves or is applicable to the whole **2** : a commissioned officer ranking next below a general of the army or a general of the air force **3** : a commissioned officer of the highest rank in the marine corps — **in general** : for the most part

general assembly *n* **1** : a legislative assembly; *esp* : a U.S. state legislature **2** *cap* G&A : the supreme deliberative body of the United Nations

gen·er·a·lis·si·mo \ˌje-nə-rə-'li-sə-ˌmō\ *n, pl* **-mos** [It, fr. *generale* general] : the chief commander of an army

gen·er·al·i·ty \ˌje-nə-'ra-lə-tē\ *n, pl* **-ties** **1** : the quality or state of being general **2** : GENERALIZATION **2 3** : a vague or inadequate statement **4** : the greatest part : BULK

gen·er·al·i·za·tion \ˌje-nə-rə-lə-'zā- shən, ˌjen-rə-\ *n* **1** : the act or process of generalizing **2** : a general statement, law, principle, or proposition

gen·er·al·ize \'je-nə-rə-ˌlīz, 'jen-rə-\ *vb* **-ized; -iz·ing 1** : to make general **2** : to draw general conclusions from **3** : to reach a general conclusion esp. on the basis of particular instances **4** : to extend throughout the body

gen·er·al·ly \'jen-rə-lē, 'jē-nə-\ *adv* **1** : in a general manner **2** : as a rule

general of the air force : a commissioned officer of the highest rank in the air force

general of the army : a commissioned officer of the highest rank in the army

general practitioner *n* : a physician or veterinarian whose practice is not limited to a specialty

gen·er·al·ship \'je-nə-rəl-ˌship, 'jen-rəl-\ *n* **1** : office or tenure of office of a general **2** : LEADERSHIP **3** : military skill as a high commander

general store *n* : a retail store that carries a wide variety of goods but is not divided into departments

gen·er·ate \'je-nə-ˌrāt\ *vb* **-at·ed; -at·ing** : to bring into existence : PRODUCE **syn** create, originate, procreate, spawn

gen·er·a·tion \ˌje-nə-'rā-shən\ *n* **1** : a body of living beings constituting a single step in the line of descent from an ancestor; *also* : the average period between generations **2** : PRODUCTION

gen·er·a·tive \'je-nə-rə-tiv, -ˌrā-tiv\ *adj* : having the power or function of generating, originating, producing, or reproducing ⟨~ organs⟩

gen·er·a·tor \'je-nə-ˌrā-tər\ *n* : one that generates; *esp* : a machine by which mechanical energy is changed into electrical energy

ge·ner·ic \jə-'ner-ik\ *adj* **1** : not specific : GENERAL **2** : not protected by a trademark ⟨a ~ drug⟩ **3** : of or relating to a biological genus — **generic** *n* — **ge·ner·i·cal·ly** \-i-k(ə-)lē\ *adv*

gen·er·ous \'je-nə-rəs\ *adj* **1** : free in giving or sharing **2** : HIGH-MINDED, NOBLE **3** : ABUNDANT, AMPLE, COPIOUS **syn** liberal, bountiful, munificent, openhanded — **gen·er·os·i·ty** \ˌje-nə-'rä-sə-tē\ *n* — **gen·er·ous·ly** \'je-nə-rəs-lē\ *adv* — **gen·er·ous·ness** *n*

gen·e·sis \'je-nə-səs\ *n, pl* **-e·ses** \-ˌsēz\ : the origin or coming into existence of something

Genesis *n* — see BIBLE table

gene–splic·ing \-ˌsplī-siŋ\ *n* : the technique by which recombinant DNA is produced and made to function in an organism

gene therapy *n* : the insertion of normal or altered genes into cells usu. to replace defective genes esp. in the treatment of genetic disorders

ge·net·ic \jə-'ne-tik\ *adj* : of or relating to the origin, development, or causes of something; *also* : of or relating to genetics — **ge·net·i·cal·ly** \-ti-k(ə-)lē\ *adv*

genetic code *n* : the chemical code that is the basis of genetic inheritance and consists of triplets of three linked chemical groups in DNA and RNA which specify particular amino acids used to make proteins or which start or stop the process of making proteins

genetic engineering *n* : the directed alteration of genetic material by intervention in genetic processes; *esp* : GENE-SPLICING — **genetically engineered** *adj*

ge·net·ics \jə-'ne-tiks\ *n* : a branch of biology dealing with heredity and variation — **ge·net·i·cist** \-tə-sist\ *n*

ge·nial \'jē-nyəl, 'jē-nē-əl\ *adj* **1** : favorable to growth or comfort ⟨~ sunshine⟩ **2** : CHEERFUL, KINDLY ⟨a ~ host⟩ **syn** affable, congenial, cordial, gracious, sociable — **ge·nial·i·ty** \ˌjē-nē-'a-lə-tē, jēn-'ya-\ *n* — **ge·nial·ly** *adv*

-gen·ic \'je-nik\ *adj comb form* **1** : producing : forming **2** : produced by : formed from **3** : suitable for production or reproduction by (such) a medium

---

ge·nie \'jē-nē\ *n, pl* **ge·nies** *also* **ge·nii** \-nē-ˌī\ [F *génie,* fr. Ar *jinnīy*] : a supernatural spirit that often takes human form usu. serving the person who calls on it

gen·i·tal \'je-nət-ᵊl\ *adj* 1 : concerned with reproduction ⟨∼ organs⟩ 2 : of, relating to, or characterized by the stage of psychosexual development in psychoanalytic theory in which oral and anal impulses are subordinated to adaptive interpersonal mechanisms — **gen·i·tal·ly** *adv*

gen·i·ta·lia \ˌje-nə-'tāl-yə\ *n pl* : reproductive organs; *esp* : the external genital organs — **gen·i·ta·lic** \-'ta-lik, -'tā-\ *adj*

gen·i·tals \'je-nət-ᵊlz\ *n pl* : GENITALIA

gen·i·tive \'je-nə-tiv\ *adj* : of, relating to, or constituting a grammatical case marking typically a relationship of possessor or source — **genitive** *n*

gen·i·to·uri·nary \ˌje-nə-tō-'yùr-ə-ˌner-ē\ *adj* : of or relating to the genital and urinary organs or functions

ge·nius \'jē-nyəs\ *n, pl* **ge·nius·es** *or* **ge·nii** \-nē-ˌī\ [L, tutelary spirit, natural inclinations, fr. *gignere* to beget] 1 *pl genii* : an attendant spirit of a person or place; *also* : a person who influences another for good or evil 2 : a strong leaning or inclination 3 : a peculiar or distinctive character or spirit (as of a nation or a language) 4 *pl usu genii* : SPIRIT, GENIE 5 *pl usu geniuses* : a single strongly marked capacity or aptitude 6 : extraordinary intellectual power; *also* : a person having such power **syn** gift, faculty, flair, knack, talent

genl *abbr* general

geno·cide \'je-nə-ˌsīd\ *n* : the deliberate and systematic destruction of a racial, political, or cultural group

-genous \jə-nəs\ *adj comb form* 1 : producing : yielding ⟨erog*enous*⟩ 2 : having (such) an origin ⟨endo*genous*⟩

genre \'zhän-rə, 'zhän-; 'zhänʳ; 'jän-rə\ *n* 1 : a distinctive type or category esp. of literary composition 2 : a style of painting in which everyday subjects are treated realistically

gens \'jenz, 'gens\ *n, pl* **gen·tes** \'jen-ˌtēz, 'gen-ˌtās\ : a Roman clan embracing the families of the same stock in the male line

gent *n* : GENTLEMAN

gen·teel \jen-'tēl\ *adj* 1 : ARISTOCRATIC 2 : ELEGANT, STYLISH 3 : POLITE, REFINED 4 : maintaining the appearance of superior social status 5 : marked by false delicacy, prudery, or affectation — **gen·teel·ly** *adv* — **gen·teel·ness** *n*

gen·tian \'jen-chən\ *n* : any of numerous herbs with opposite leaves and showy usu. blue flowers in the fall

gen·tile \'jen-ˌtīl\ *n* [LL *gentilis* heathen, pagan, fr. L *gent-, gens* clan, nation] 1 *often cap* : a person who is not Jewish; *esp* : a Christian as distinguished from a Jew 2 : HEATHEN, PAGAN — **gentile** *adj, often cap*

gen·til·i·ty \jen-'ti-lə-tē\ *n, pl* **-ties** 1 : good birth and family 2 : the qualities characteristic of a well-bred person 3 : good manners 4 : superior social status shown in manners or mode of life

¹**gen·tle** \'jent-ᵊl\ *adj* **gen·tler** \'jent-lər, -ᵊl-ər\; **gen·tlest** \'jent-ləst, -ᵊl-əst\ 1 : belonging to a family of high social station 2 : of, relating to, or characteristic of a gentleman 3 : KIND, AMIABLE 4 : TRACTABLE, DOCILE 5 : not harsh, stern, or violent 6 : SOFT, DELICATE 7 : MODERATE — **gen·tle·ness** *n* — **gen·tly** *adv*

²**gentle** *vb* **gen·tled; gen·tling** 1 : to make or become mild, docile, soft, or moderate 2 : MOLLIFY, PLACATE

gen·tle·folk \'jent-ᵊl-ˌfōk\ *also* **gen·tle·folks** \-ˌfōks\ *n* : persons of good family and breeding

gen·tle·man \-mən\ *n* 1 : a man of good family 2 : a well≠ bred man 3 : MAN — used in pl. as a form of address — **gen·tle·man·ly** *adj*

gen·tle·wom·an \-ˌwù-mən\ *n* 1 : a woman of good family 2 : a woman attending a lady of rank 3 : a woman with very good manners : LADY

gen·tri·fi·ca·tion \ˌjen-trə-fə-'kā-shən\ *n* : the process of renewal accompanying the influx of middle-class people into deteriorating areas that often displaces earlier usu. poorer residents — **gen·tri·fy** \'jen-trə-fī\ *vb*

gen·try \'jen-trē\ *n, pl* **gentries** 1 : people of good birth, breeding, and education : ARISTOCRACY 2 : the class of English people between the nobility and the yeomanry 3 : persons of a designated class

gen·u·flect \'jen-yü-ˌflekt\ *vb* : to bend the knee esp. in worship — **gen·u·flec·tion** \ˌjen-yü-'flek-shən\ *n*

gen·u·ine \'jen-yə-wən\ *adj* 1 : AUTHENTIC, REAL 2 : SINCERE, HONEST **syn** bona fide, true, veritable — **gen·u·ine·ly** *adv* — **gen·u·ine·ness** *n*

ge·nus \'jē-nəs\ *n, pl* **gen·era** \'je-nə-rə\ [L, birth, race, kind] : a category of biological classification that ranks between the family and the species and contains related species

geo·cen·tric \ˌjē-ō-'sen-trik\ *adj* 1 : relating to or measured from the earth's center 2 : having or relating to the earth as a center

geo·chem·is·try \-'ke-mə-strē\ *n* : a branch of geology that deals with the chemical composition of and chemical changes in the earth — **geo·chem·i·cal** \-mi-kəl\ *adj* — **geo·chem·ist** \-mist\ *n*

ge·ode \'jē-ˌōd\ *n* : a nodule of stone having a cavity lined with mineral matter

¹**geo·de·sic** \ˌjē-ə-'de-sik\ *adj* : made of light straight structural elements ⟨a ∼ dome⟩

²**geodesic** *n* : the shortest line between two points on a surface

geo·det·ic \ˌjē-ə-'de-tik\ *adj* : of, relating to, or being precise measurement of the earth and its features ⟨a ∼ survey⟩

geog *abbr* geographic; geographical; geography

ge·og·ra·phy \jē-'ä-grə-fē\ *n, pl* **-phies** 1 : a science that deals with the natural features of the earth and the climate, products, and inhabitants 2 : the natural features of a region — **ge·og·ra·pher** \-fər\ *n* — **geo·graph·ic** \ˌjē-ə-'gra-fik\ *or* **geo·graph·i·cal** \-fi-kəl\ *adj* — **geo·graph·i·cal·ly** \-fi-k(ə-)lē\ *adv*

geol *abbr* geologic; geological; geology

geologic time *n* : the period of time of the earth's geologic history

☞ For table, see next page.

ge·ol·o·gy \jē-'ä-lə-jē\ *n, pl* **-gies** 1 : a science that deals with the history of the earth and its life esp. as recorded in rocks; *also* : a study of the features of a celestial body (as the moon) 2 : the geologic features of an area — **ge·o·log·ic** \ˌjē-ə-'lä-jik\ *or* **ge·o·log·i·cal** \-ji-kəl\ *adj* — **geo·log·i·cal·ly** \-ji-k(ə-)lē\ *adv* — **ge·ol·o·gist** \jē-'ä-lə-jist\ *n*

geom *abbr* geometric; geometrical; geometry

geo·mag·net·ic \ˌjē-ō-mag-'ne-tik\ *adj* : of or relating to the magnetism of the earth — **geo·mag·ne·tism** \-'mag-nə-ˌti-zəm\ *n*

geometric mean *n* : the *n*th root of the product of *n* numbers; *esp* : a number that is the second term of three consecutive terms of a geometric progression ⟨the *geometric mean* of 9 and 4 is 6⟩

geometric progression *n* : a progression (as 1, ½, ¼) in which the ratio of a term to its predecessor is always the same

ge·om·e·try \jē-'ä-mə-trē\ *n, pl* **-tries** [ultim. fr. Gk *geōmetria,* fr. *geōmetrein* to measure the earth, fr. *gē* earth + *metron* measure] : a branch of mathematics dealing with the relations, properties, and measurements of solids, surfaces, lines, points, and angles — **ge·om·e·ter** \-tər\ *n* — **ge·o·met·ric** \ˌjē-ə-'me-trik\ *or* **ge·o·met·ri·cal** \-tri-kəl\ *adj*

geo·phys·ics \ˌjē-ō-'fi-ziks\ *n* : the physics of the earth — **geo·phys·i·cal** \-zi-kəl\ *adj* — **geo·phys·i·cist** \-zə-sist\ *n*

geo·pol·i·tics \-'pä-lə-ˌtiks\ *n* : a combination of political and geographic factors relating to a state

GEOLOGIC TIME

EON	ERA	PERIOD	EPOCH	BEGINNING OF INTERVAL*	BIOLOGICAL FORMS
Phanerozoic	Cenozoic	Quaternary	Holocene	0.01	
			Pleistocene	1.6	Earliest humans
		Tertiary	Pliocene	5	
			Miocene	24	Earliest hominids
			Oligocene	37	
			Eocene	58	Earliest grasses
			Paleocene	65	Earliest large mammals
		Cretaceous-Tertiary boundary (65 million years ago): extinction of dinosaurs			
	Mesozoic	Cretaceous	Upper	98	
			Lower	144	Earliest flowering plants; dinosaurs in ascendancy
		Jurassic		208	Earliest birds & mammals
		Triassic		245	Age of Dinosaurs begins
	Paleozoic	Permian		286	
		Carboniferous			
		Pennsylvanian		320	Earliest reptiles
		Mississippian		360	Earliest winged insects
		Devonian		408	Earliest vascular plants (as ferns & mosses) & amphibians
		Silurian		438	Earliest land plants & insects
		Ordovician		505	Earliest corals
		Cambrian		570	Earliest fish
Proterozoic	Precambrian			2500	Earliest colonial algae & soft-bodied invertebrates
Archean				4000	Life appears: earliest algae & primitive bacteria

*In millions of years before the present

Geor·gian \'jȯr-jən\ *n* : a native or inhabitant of the Republic of Georgia — **Georgian** *adj*

geo·ther·mal \ˌjē-ō-'thər-məl\ *adj* : of, relating to, or using the heat of the earth's interior

ger *abbr* gerund

Ger *abbr* German; Germany

ge·ra·ni·um \jə-'rā-nē-əm\ *n* [L, fr. Gk *geranion,* fr. *geranos* crane] **1** : any of a genus of herbs with usu. deeply cut leaves and pink, purple, or white flowers followed by long slender dry fruits **2** : any of a genus of herbs of the same family as the geraniums that have clusters of scarlet, pink, or white flowers with the sepals joined at the base into a hollow tube closed at one end

ger·bil *also* **ger·bile** \'jər-bəl\ *n* : any of numerous Old World burrowing desert rodents with long hind legs

ge·ri·at·ric \ˌjer-ē-'a-trik\ *adj* **1** : of or relating to geriatrics or the process of aging **2** : of, relating to, or appropriate for elderly people **3** : OLD

ge·ri·at·rics \-triks\ *n* : a branch of medicine dealing with the problems and diseases of old age and aging

germ \'jərm\ *n* **1** : a bit of living matter capable of growth and development (as into an organism) **2** : SOURCE, RUDIMENTS **3** : MICROORGANISM; *esp* : one causing disease

Ger·man \'jər-mən\ *n* **1** : a native or inhabitant of Germany **2** : the language of Germany, Austria, and parts of Switzerland — **German** *adj* — **Ger·man·ic** \jər-'manik\ *adj*

ger·mane \jər-'mān\ *adj* [ME *germain,* lit., having the same parents, fr. MF, fr. L *germanus,* fr. *germen* sprout, bud] : RELEVANT, APPROPRIATE **syn** applicable, material, pertinent

ger·ma·ni·um \jər-'mā-nē-əm\ *n* : a grayish white hard chemical element used as a semiconductor — see ELEMENT table

German measles *n sing or pl* : an acute contagious virus disease milder than typical measles but damaging to the fetus when occurring early in pregnancy

German shepherd *n* : any of a breed of intelligent responsive working dogs of German origin often used in police work and as guide dogs for the blind

germ cell *n* : an egg or sperm or one of their antecedent cells

\ə\abut \ᵊ\kitten \ər\further \a\ash \ā\ace \ä\mop, mar
\au̇\out \ch\chin \e\bet \ē\easy \g\go \i\hit \ī\ice \j\job
\ŋ\sing \ō\go \ȯ\law \ȯi\boy \th\thin \t̲h̲\the \ü\loot \u̇\foot
\y\yet \zh\vision *see also* Pronunciation Symbols page

ger·mi·cide \'jər-mə-₁sīd\ *n* : an agent that destroys germs — **ger·mi·cid·al** \₁jər-mə-'sīd-ᵊl\ *adj*

ger·mi·nal \'jər-mə-nəl\ *adj* : of or relating to a germ or germ cell; *also* : EMBRYONIC

ger·mi·nate \'jər-mə-₁nāt\ *vb* **-nat·ed; -nat·ing 1** : to cause to develop : begin to develop : SPROUT **2** : to come into being : EVOLVE — **ger·mi·na·tion** \₁jər-mə-'nā-shən\ *n*

ger·on·tol·o·gy \₁jer-ən-'tä-lə-jē\ *n* : a scientific study of aging and the problems of the aged — **ge·ron·to·log·i·cal** \jə-₁ränt-ᵊl-'ä-ji-kəl\ *adj* — **ger·on·tol·o·gist** \₁jer-ən-'tä-lə-jist\ *n*

ger·ry·man·der \'jer-ē-₁man-dər\ *vb* : to divide into election districts so as to give one political party an advantage — **gerrymander** *n*

ger·und \'jer-ənd\ *n* : a word having the characteristics of both verb and noun

ge·sta·po \gə-'stä-pō\ *n, pl* **-pos** [G, fr. *Geheime Staatspolizei*, lit., secret state police] : a usu. terrorist secret-police organization operating against persons suspected of disloyalty

ges·ta·tion \je-'stā-shən\ *n* : PREGNANCY, INCUBATION — **ges·tate** \'jes-₁tāt\ *vb*

ges·tic·u·late \je-'sti-kyə-₁lāt\ *vb* **-lat·ed; -lat·ing** : to make gestures esp. when speaking — **ges·tic·u·la·tion** \-₁sti-kyə-'lā-shən\ *n*

ges·ture \'jes-chər\ *n* **1** : a movement usu. of the body or limbs that expresses or emphasizes an idea, sentiment, or attitude **2** : something said or done by way of formality or courtesy, as a symbol or token, or for its effect on the attitudes of others — **ges·tur·al** \-chə-rəl\ *adj* — **gesture** *vb*

ge·sund·heit \gə-'zûnt-₁hīt\ *interj* [G, lit., health] — used to wish good health esp. to one who has just sneezed

¹**get** \'get\ *vb* **got** \'gät\; **got** *or* **got·ten** \'gät-ᵊn\; **get·ting 1** : to gain possession of (as by receiving, acquiring, earning, buying, or winning) : PROCURE, OBTAIN, FETCH **2** : to succeed in coming or going ⟨*got* away to the lake⟩ **3** : to cause to come or go ⟨*got* the car to the station⟩ **4** : BEGET **5** : to cause to be in a certain condition or position ⟨don't ∼ wet⟩ **6** : BECOME ⟨∼ sick⟩ **7** : PREPARE **8** : SEIZE **9** : to move emotionally; *also* : IRRITATE **10** : BAFFLE, PUZZLE **11** : KILL **12** : HIT **13** : to be subjected to ⟨∼ the measles⟩ **14** : to receive as punishment **15** : to find out by calculation **16** : HEAR; *also* : UNDERSTAND **17** : PERSUADE, INDUCE **18** : HAVE ⟨he's *got* no money⟩ **19** : to have as an obligation or necessity ⟨you have *got* to come⟩ **20** : to establish communication with **21** : to be able ⟨finally *got* to go to med school⟩ **22** : to come to be ⟨*got* talking about old times⟩ **23** : to leave at once

²**get** \'get\ *n* : OFFSPRING, PROGENY

get along *vb* **1** : GET BY **2** : to be on friendly terms

get·away \'ge-tə-₁wā\ *n* **1** : ESCAPE **2** : START

get by *vb* : to meet one's needs

get–to·geth·er \'get-tə-₁ge-thər\ *n* : an informal social gathering

get·up \'get-₁əp\ *n* **1** : OUTFIT, COSTUME **2** : general composition or structure

gew·gaw \'gü-₁gò, 'gyü-\ *n* : a showy trifle : BAUBLE, TRINKET

gey·ser \'gī-zər\ *n* [Icelandic *Geysir*, hot spring in Iceland] : a spring that intermittently shoots up hot water and steam

Gha·na·ian \gä-'nä-ən\ *n* : a native or inhabitant of Ghana — **Ghanaian** *adj*

ghast·ly \'gast-lē\ *adj* **ghast·li·er; -est 1** : HORRIBLE, SHOCKING **2** : resembling a ghost : DEATHLIKE, PALE **syn** gruesome, grim, lurid, grisly, macabre

ghat \'gót\ *n* [Hindi] : a broad flight of steps on an Indian riverbank that provides access to the water

gher·kin \'gər-kən\ *n* **1** : a small prickly fruit of a vine

related to the cucumber used to make pickles **2** : an immature cucumber

ghet·to \'ge-tō\ *n, pl* **ghettos** *or* **ghettoes** : a quarter of a city in which members of a minority group live because of social, legal, or economic pressure

¹**ghost** \'gōst\ *n* **1** : the seat of life : SOUL **2** : a disembodied soul; *esp* : the soul of a dead person believed to be an inhabitant of the unseen world or to appear in bodily form to living people **3** : SPIRIT, DEMON **4** : a faint trace ⟨a ∼ of a smile⟩ **5** : a false image in a photographic negative or on a television screen — **ghost·ly** *adv*

²**ghost** *vb* : GHOSTWRITE

ghost·write \-₁rīt\ *vb* **-wrote** \-₁rōt\; **-writ·ten** \-₁rit-ᵊn\ : to write for and in the name of another — **ghost·writ·er** *n*

ghoul \'gül\ *n* [Ar *ghūl*] : a legendary evil being that robs graves and feeds on corpses — **ghoul·ish** *adj*

GHQ *abbr* general headquarters

gi *abbr* gill

¹**GI** \₁jē-'ī\ *adj* [galvanized *i*ron; fr. abbr. used in listing such articles as garbage cans, but taken as abbr. for *government issue*] **1** : provided by an official U.S. military supply department ⟨∼ shoes⟩ **2** : of, relating to, or characteristic of U.S. military personnel **3** : conforming to military regulations or customs ⟨a ∼ haircut⟩

²**GI** *n, pl* **GI's** *or* **GIs** \-'īz\ : a member or former member of the U.S. armed forces; *esp* : an enlisted man

³**GI** *abbr* **1** galvanized iron **2** gastrointestinal **3** general issue **4** government issue

gi·ant \'jī-ənt\ *n* **1** : a legendary humanlike being of great size and strength **2** : a living being or thing of extraordinary size or powers — **giant** *adj*

gi·ant·ess \'jī-ən-təs\ *n* : a female giant

gib·ber \'ji-bər\ *vb* : to speak rapidly, inarticulately, and often foolishly

gib·ber·ish \'ji-bə-rish\ *n* : unintelligible or confused speech or language

¹**gib·bet** \'ji-bət\ *n* : GALLOWS

²**gibbet** *vb* **1** : to hang on a gibbet **2** : to expose to public scorn **3** : to execute by hanging

gib·bon \'gi-bən\ *n* : any of several tailless apes of southeastern Asia

gib·bous \'ji-bəs, 'gi-\ *adj* **1** : rounded like the exterior of a sphere or circle **2** : seen with more than half but not all of the apparent disk illuminated ⟨∼ moon⟩ **3** : having a hump : HUMPBACKED

gibe \'jīb\ *vb* **gibed; gib·ing** : to utter taunting words : SNEER — **gibe** *n*

gib·lets \'jib-ləts\ *n pl* : the edible viscera of a fowl

Gib·son girl \'gib-sən-\ *adj* : of or relating to a style in women's clothing characterized by high necks, full sleeves, and slender waistlines

gid·dy \'gi-dē\ *adj* **gid·di·er; -est 1** : DIZZY **2** : causing dizziness **3** : not serious : FRIVOLOUS, SILLY — **gid·di·ness** \-dē-nəs\ *n*

gift \'gift\ *n* **1** : a special ability : TALENT **2** : something given : PRESENT **3** : the act or power of giving

gift·ed \'gif-təd\ *adj* : TALENTED

¹**gig** \'gig\ *n* **1** : a long light ship's boat **2** : a light 2-wheeled one-horse carriage

²**gig** *n* : a pronged spear for catching fish — **gig** *vb*

³**gig** *n* : a job for a specified time; *esp* : an entertainer's engagement

⁴**gig** *n* : a military demerit — **gig** *vb*

giga·byte \'ji-gə-₁bīt, 'gi-\ *n* : a unit of computer storage capacity approximately equal to one billion bytes

gi·gan·tic \jī-'gan-tik\ *adj* : exceeding the usual (as in size or force)

gig·gle \'gi-gəl\ *vb* **gig·gled; gig·gling** : to laugh with repeated short catches of the breath — **giggle** *n* — **gig·gly** \-gə-lē\ *adj*

GIGO *abbr* garbage in, garbage out

gig·o·lo \'ji-gə-₁lō\ *n, pl* **-los 1** : a man supported by a woman usu. in return for his attentions **2** : a profession-al dancing partner or male escort

Gi·la monster \'hē-lə-\ *n* : a large orange and black ven-omous lizard of the southwestern U.S.

¹**gild** \'gild\ *vb* **gild·ed** *or* **gilt** \'gilt\; **gild·ing 1** : to overlay with or as if with a thin covering of gold **2** : to give an attractive but often deceptive appearance to

²**gild** *var of* GUILD

¹**gill** \'jil\ *n* — see WEIGHT table

²**gill** \'gil\ *n* : an organ (as of a fish) for obtaining oxygen from water

¹**gilt** \'gilt\ *adj* : of the color of gold

²**gilt** *n* : gold or a substance resembling gold laid on the surface of an object

³**gilt** *n* : a young female swine

gim·crack \'jim-,krak\ *n* : a showy object of little use or value

gim·let \'gim-lət\ *n* : a small tool with screw point and cross handle for boring holes

gim·mick \'gi-mik\ *n* **1** : CONTRIVANCE, GADGET **2** : an important feature that is not immediately apparent : CATCH **3** : a new and ingenious scheme — **gim·micky** \-mi-kē\ *adj*

gim·mick·ry \'gi-mi-krē\ *n, pl* **-ries** : an array of or the use of gimmicks

gimpy \'gim-pē\ *adj* : CRIPPLED, LAME

¹**gin** \'jin\ *n* [ME *gin*, modif. of OF *engin*] **1** : TRAP, SNARE **2** : a machine to separate seeds from cotton — **gin** *vb*

²**gin** *n* [by shortening & alter. fr. *geneva*, kind of gin] : a liquor distilled from a grain mash and flavored with ju-niper berries

gin·ger \'jin-jər\ *n* : the pungent aromatic rootstock of a tropical plant used esp. as a spice and in medicine; *also* : the spice or the plant

ginger ale *n* : a carbonated soft drink flavored with gin-ger

gin·ger·bread \'jin-jər-,bred\ *n* **1** : a cake made with mo-lasses and flavored with ginger **2** : lavish or superfluous ornament

gin·ger·ly \'jin-jər-lē\ *adj* : very cautious or careful — **gingerly** *adv*

gin·ger·snap \-,snap\ *n* : a thin brittle molasses cookie flavored with ginger

ging·ham \'giŋ-əm\ *n* : a clothing fabric usu. of yarn=dyed cotton in plain weave

gin·gi·vi·tis \,jin-jə-'vī-təs\ *n* : inflammation of the gums

gink·go *also* **ging·ko** \'giŋ-(,)kō\ *n, pl* **ginkgoes** *or* **ginkgos** : a tree of eastern China with fan-shaped leaves of-ten grown as a shade tree

gin·seng \'jin-,seŋ\ *n* : an aromatic root of a Chinese or No. American herb used esp. in Oriental medicine; *also* : one of these herbs

gi·raffe \jə-'raf\ *n, pl* **giraffes** [It *giraffa,* fr. Ar *zirāfah*] : an African ruminant mammal with a very long neck and a short coat with dark blotches

gird \'gərd\ *vb* **gird·ed** *or* **girt** \'gərt\; **gird·ing 1** : to en-circle or fasten with or as if with a belt ⟨~ on a sword⟩ **2** : to invest esp. with power or authority **3** : PREPARE, BRACE

gird·er \'gər-dər\ *n* : a horizontal main supporting beam

gir·dle \'gərd-³l\ *n* **1** : something (as a belt or sash) that encircles or confines **2** : a woman's supporting under-garment that extends from the waist to below the hips — **girdle** *vb*

girl \'gərl\ *n* **1** : a female child **2** : a young woman **3** : SWEETHEART — **girl·hood** \-,hud\ *n* — **girl·ish** *adj*

girl Friday *n* : a female assistant (as in an office) entrust-ed with a wide variety of tasks

girl·friend \'gərl-,frend\ *n* **1** : a female friend **2** : a fre-quent or regular female companion of a boy or man

Girl Scout *n* : a member of any of the scouting programs of the Girl Scouts of the United States of America

girth \'gərth\ *n* **1** : a band around an animal by which

something (as a saddle) may be fastened on its back **2** : a measure around something

gist \'jist\ *n* [MF, it lies, fr. *gesir* to lie, ultim. fr. L *jac-ēre*] : the main point or part

¹**give** \'giv\ *vb* **gave** \'gāv\; **giv·en** \'gi-vən\; **giv·ing 1** : to make a present of **2** : to bestow by formal action **3** : to accord or yield to another **4** : to yield to force, strain, or pressure **5** : to put into the possession or keeping of another **6** : PROFFER **7** : DELIVER ⟨*gave* away the bride⟩ **8** : to present in public performance or to view **9** : PRO-VIDE ⟨~ a party⟩ **10** : ATTRIBUTE **11** : to make, form, or yield as a product or result ⟨cows ~ milk⟩ **12** : PAY **13** : to deliver by some bodily action ⟨*gave* me a push⟩ **14** : to offer as a pledge ⟨I ~ you my word⟩ **15** : DEVOTE **16** : to cause to have or receive

²**give** *n* **1** : capacity or tendency to yield to force or strain **2** : the quality or state of being springy

give–and–take \,giv-ən-'tāk\ *n* **1** : COMPROMISE **2** : a usu. good-natured exchange (as of remarks or ideas)

give·away \'gi-və-,wā\ *n* **1** : an unintentional revelation or betrayal **2** : something given away free; *esp* : PRE-MIUM

give in *vb* : SUBMIT, SURRENDER

¹**giv·en** \'gi-vən\ *adj* **1** : DISPOSED, INCLINED ⟨~ to swear-ing⟩ **2** : SPECIFIED, PARTICULAR ⟨at a ~ time⟩

²**given** *prep* : CONSIDERING

given name *n* : a name that precedes one's surname

give out *vb* **1** : EMIT **2** : BREAK DOWN **3** : to become ex-hausted : COLLAPSE

give up *vb* **1** : SURRENDER **2** : to abandon (oneself) to a feeling, influence, or activity **3** : QUIT

giz·mo *also* **gis·mo** \'giz-mō\ *n, pl* **gizmos** *also* **gismos** : GADGET

giz·zard \'gi-zərd\ *n* : the muscular usu. horny-lined en-largement of the alimentary canal of a bird used for churning and grinding up food

gla·cial \'glā-shəl\ *adj* **1** : extremely cold **2** : of or relating to glaciers **3** : being or relating to a past period of time when a large part of the earth was covered by glaciers **4** *cap* : PLEISTOCENE **5** : very slow ⟨a ~ pace⟩ — **gla-cial·ly** *adv*

gla·ci·ate \'glā-shē-,āt\ *vb* **-at·ed; -at·ing 1** : to subject to glacial action **2** : to produce glacial effects in or on — **gla·ci·a·tion** \,glā-shē-'ā-shən, -sē-\ *n*

gla·cier \'glā-shər\ *n* : a large body of ice moving slowly down a slope or spreading outward on a land surface

¹**glad** \'glad\ *adj* **glad·der; glad·dest 1** : experiencing pleasure, joy, or delight **2** : PLEASED **3** : very willing **4** : PLEASANT, JOYFUL **5** : CHEERFUL — **glad·ly** *adv* — **glad·ness** *n*

²**glad** *n* : GLADIOLUS

glad·den \'glad-³n\ *vb* : to make glad

glade \'glād\ *n* : a grassy open space surrounded by woods

glad·i·a·tor \'gla-dē-,ā-tər\ *n* **1** : a person engaged in a fight to the death for public entertainment in ancient Rome **2** : a person engaging in a public fight or contro-versy; *also* : PRIZEFIGHTER — **glad·i·a·to·ri·al** \,gla-dē-ə-'tōr-ē-əl\ *adj*

glad·i·o·lus \,gla-dē-'ō-ləs\ *n, pl* **-li** \-(,)lē, -,lī\ [L, fr. dim. of *gladius* sword] : any of a genus of chiefly Af-rican plants related to the irises and having erect sword=shaped leaves and stalks of bright colored flowers

glad·some \'glad-səm\ *adj* : giving or showing joy : CHEERFUL

glad·stone \'glad-,stōn\ *n, often cap* : a suitcase with flexible sides on a rigid frame that opens flat into two compartments

---

\ə\abut \³\kitten \ər\further \a\ash \ā\ace \ä\mop, mar \au̇\out \ch\chin \e\bet \ē\easy \g\go \i\hit \ī\ice \j\job \ŋ\sing \ō\go \ȯ\law \oi̇\boy \th\thin \th\the \ü\loot \u̇\foot \y\yet \zh\vision *see also* Pronunciation Symbols page

glam·or·ize also **glam·our·ize** \'gla-mə-ˌrīz\ vb **-ized; -iz·ing** : to make or look upon as glamorous

glam·our or **glam·or** \'gla-mər\ n [Sc glamour magic spell, alter. of E grammar; fr. the popular association of erudition with occult practices] : an exciting and often illusory and romantic attractiveness; esp : alluring personal attraction — **glam·or·ous** also **glam·our·ous** \-mə-rəs\ adj

¹**glance** \'glans\ vb **glanced; glanc·ing** 1 : to strike and fly off to one side 2 : GLEAM 3 : to give a quick look

²**glance** n 1 : a quick intermittent flash or gleam 2 : a deflected impact or blow 3 : a quick look

gland \'gland\ n : a cell or group of cells that prepares and secretes a substance (as saliva or sweat) for further use in or discharge from the body

glan·du·lar \'glan-jə-lər\ adj : of, relating to, or involving glands

glans \'glanz\ n, pl **glan·des** \'glan-ˌdēz\ [L, lit., acorn] : a conical vascular body forming the extremity of the penis or clitoris

¹**glare** \'glar\ vb **glared; glar·ing** 1 : to shine with a harsh dazzling light 2 : to stare fiercely or angrily

²**glare** n 1 : a harsh dazzling light 2 : an angry or fierce stare

glar·ing \'glar-iŋ\ adj : painfully obvious ⟨a ∼ error⟩ — **glar·ing·ly** adv

glass \'glas\ n 1 : a hard brittle amorphous usu. transparent or translucent material consisting esp. of silica 2 : something made of glass; esp : TUMBLER 2 3 pl : a pair of lenses used to correct defects of vision : SPECTACLES 4 : the quantity held by a glass container — **glass** adj — **glass·ful** \-ˌfūl\ n — **glassy** adj

glass·blow·ing \-ˌblō-iŋ\ n : the art of shaping a mass of glass that has been softened by heat by blowing air into it through a tube — **glass·blow·er** n

glass·ware \-ˌwar\ n : articles made of glass

glau·co·ma \glaù-'kō-mə, glò-\ n : a disease of the eye marked by increased pressure within the eyeball resulting in damage to the retina and gradual loss of vision

¹**glaze** \'glāz\ vb **glazed; glaz·ing** 1 : to furnish (as a window frame) with glass 2 : to apply glaze to

²**glaze** n : a glassy coating or surface

gla·zier \'glā-zhər\ n : a person who sets glass in window frames

¹**gleam** \'glēm\ n 1 : a transient subdued or partly obscured light 2 : GLINT 3 : a faint trace ⟨a ∼ of hope⟩

²**gleam** vb 1 : to shine with subdued light or moderate brightness 2 : to appear briefly or faintly **syn** flash, glimmer, glisten, glitter, shimmer, sparkle

glean \'glēn\ vb 1 : to gather grain left by reapers 2 : to collect little by little or with patient effort — **glean·able** adj — **glean·er** n

glean·ings \-niŋz\ n pl : things acquired by gleaning

glee \'glē\ n [ME, fr. OE glēo entertainment, music] 1 : JOY, HILARITY 2 : a part-song for three usu. male voices — **glee·ful** adj

glee club n : a chorus organized for singing usu. short choral pieces

glen \'glen\ n : a narrow hidden valley

glen·gar·ry \glen-'gar-ē\ n, pl **-ries** often cap : a woolen cap of Scottish origin

glib \'glib\ adj **glib·ber; glib·best** : speaking or spoken with careless ease — **glib·ly** adv

glide \'glīd\ vb **glid·ed; glid·ing** 1 : to move smoothly and effortlessly 2 : to descend gradually without engine power ⟨∼ in an airplane⟩ — **glide** n

glid·er \'glī-dər\ n 1 : one that glides 2 : an aircraft resembling an airplane but having no engine 3 : a porch seat suspended from an upright frame

¹**glim·mer** \'gli-mər\ vb : to shine faintly or unsteadily

²**glimmer** n 1 : a faint unsteady light 2 : INKLING 3 : a small amount : HINT

¹**glimpse** \'glimps\ vb **glimpsed; glimps·ing** : to take a brief look : see momentarily or incompletely

²**glimpse** n 1 : a faint idea : GLIMMER 2 : a short hurried look

glint \'glint\ vb 1 : to shine by reflection : SPARKLE, GLITTER, GLEAM 2 : to appear briefly or faintly — **glint** n

glis·san·do \gli-'sän-(ˌ)dō\ n, pl **-di** \-(ˌ)dē\ or **-dos** : a rapid sliding up or down the musical scale

¹**glis·ten** \'glis-ᵊn\ vb : to shine by reflection with a soft luster or sparkle

²**glisten** n : GLITTER, SPARKLE

glis·ter \'glis-tər\ vb : GLITTER

glitch \'glich\ n : MALFUNCTION; also : SNAG 2

¹**glit·ter** \'gli-tər\ vb 1 : to shine with brilliant or metallic luster : SPARKLE 2 : to shine with strong emotion : FLASH ⟨eyes ∼ing in anger⟩ 3 : to be brilliantly attractive esp. in a superficial way

²**glitter** n 1 : sparkling brilliancy, showiness, or attractiveness 2 : small glittering objects used for ornamentation — **glit·tery** \'gli-tə-rē\ adj

gloam·ing \'glō-miŋ\ n : TWILIGHT, DUSK

gloat \'glōt\ vb : to think about something with triumphant and often malicious delight

glob \'gläb\ n 1 : a small drop 2 : a large rounded mass

glob·al \'glō-bəl\ adj 1 : WORLDWIDE 2 : COMPREHENSIVE, GENERAL — **glob·al·ly** adv

globe \'glōb\ n 1 : BALL, SPHERE 2 : EARTH; also : a spherical representation of the earth

globe–trot·ter \'glōb-ˌträ-tər\ n : a person who travels widely — **globe–trot·ting** n or adj

glob·u·lar \'glä-byə-lər\ adj : having the shape of a globe or globule

glob·ule \'glä-(ˌ)byül\ n : a tiny globe or ball esp. of a liquid

glob·u·lin \'glä-byə-lən\ n : any of a class of simple proteins insoluble in pure water but soluble in dilute salt solutions that occur widely in plant and animal tissues

glock·en·spiel \'glä-kən-ˌshpēl, -ˌspēl\ n [G, fr. Glocke bell + Spiel play] : a percussion musical instrument consisting of a series of metal bars played with two hammers

gloom \'glüm\ n 1 : partial or total darkness 2 : lowness of spirits : DEJECTION 3 : an atmosphere of despondency — **gloom·i·ly** \'glü-mə-lē\ adv — **gloom·i·ness** \-mē-nəs\ n — **gloomy** \'glü-mē\ adj

glop \'gläp\ n : a messy mass or mixture

glo·ri·fy \'glōr-ə-ˌfī\ vb **-fied; -fy·ing** 1 : to raise to heavenly glory 2 : to light up brilliantly 3 : EXTOL 4 : to give glory to (as in worship) — **glo·ri·fi·ca·tion** \ˌglōr-ə-fə-'kā-shən\ n

glo·ri·ous \'glōr-ē-əs\ adj 1 : possessing or deserving glory : PRAISEWORTHY 2 : conferring glory 3 : RESPLENDENT, MAGNIFICENT 4 : DELIGHTFUL, WONDERFUL — **glo·ri·ous·ly** adv

¹**glo·ry** \'glōr-ē\ n, pl **glories** 1 : RENOWN 2 : honor and praise rendered in worship 3 : something that secures praise or renown 4 : a distinguishing quality or asset 5 : RESPLENDENCE, MAGNIFICENCE 6 : heavenly bliss 7 : a height of prosperity or achievement

²**glory** vb **glo·ried; glo·ry·ing** : to rejoice proudly : EXULT

¹**gloss** \'gläs, 'glòs\ n 1 : LUSTER, SHEEN, BRIGHTNESS 2 : outward show

²**gloss** vb 1 : to give a false appearance of acceptableness to ⟨∼ over inadequacies⟩ 2 : to deal with too lightly or not at all

³**gloss** n [alter. of gloze, fr. ME glose, fr. MF, fr. ML glosa, glossa, fr. Gk glōssa, glōtta tongue, language, unusual word] 1 : an explanatory note (as in the margin of a text) 2 : GLOSSARY 3 : an interlinear translation 4 : a continuous commentary accompanying a text

⁴**gloss** vb : to furnish glosses for

glos·sa·ry \'glä-sə-rē, 'glò-\ n, pl **-ries** : a collection of

difficult or specialized terms with their meanings —
glos·sar·i·al \glä-ˈsar-ē-əl, glò-\ *adj*
glos·so·la·lia \ˌglä-sə-ˈlä-lē-ə, ˌglò-\ *n* [Gk *glōssa* tongue, language + *lalia* chatter] : TONGUE 6
¹**glossy** \ˈglä-sē, ˈglò-\ *adj* **gloss·i·er; -est** : having a surface luster or brightness — **gloss·i·ly** \-sə-lē\ *adv* — **gloss·i·ness** \-sē-nəs\ *n*
²**glossy** *n, pl* **gloss·ies** : a photograph printed on smooth shiny paper
glot·tis \ˈglä-təs\ *n, pl* **glot·tis·es** *or* **glot·ti·des** \-tə-ˌdēz\ : the slitlike opening between the vocal cords in the larynx — **glot·tal** \ˈglät-ᵊl\ *adj*
glove \ˈgləv\ *n* **1** : a covering for the hand having separate sections for each finger **2** : a padded leather covering for the hand for use in a sport
¹**glow** \ˈglō\ *vb* **1** : to shine with or as if with intense heat **2** : to have a rich warm usu. ruddy color : FLUSH, BLUSH **3** : to feel hot **4** : to show exuberance or elation ⟨∼ with pride⟩
²**glow** *n* **1** : brightness or warmth of color; *esp* : REDNESS **2** : warmth of feeling or emotion **3** : a sensation of warmth **4** : light such as is emitted from a heated substance
glow·er \ˈglaù-ər\ *vb* : to stare angrily : SCOWL — **glower** *n*
glow·worm \ˈglō-ˌwərm\ *n* : any of various insect larvae or adults that give off light
glox·in·ia \gläk-ˈsi-nē-ə\ *n* : any of a genus of Brazilian herbs related to the African violets; *esp* : one with showy bell-shaped or slipper-shaped flowers
gloze \ˈglōz\ *vb* **glozed; gloz·ing** : to make appear right or acceptable : GLOSS
glu·cose \ˈglü-ˌkōs\ *n* **1** : a sugar known in two different forms; *esp* : DEXTROSE **2** : a sweet light-colored syrup made from cornstarch
glue \ˈglü\ *n* : a jellylike protein substance made from animal materials and used for sticking things together; *also* : any of various other strong adhesives — **glue** *vb* — **glu·ey** \ˈglü-ē\ *adj*
glum \ˈgləm\ *adj* **glum·mer; glum·mest 1** : broodingly morose : SULLEN **2** : DREARY, GLOOMY **syn** crabbed, dour, saturnine, sulky
¹**glut** \ˈglət\ *vb* **glut·ted; glut·ting 1** : OVERSUPPLY **2** : to fill esp. with food to satiety : SATIATE
²**glut** *n* : an excessive supply
glu·ten \ˈglüt-ᵊn\ *n* : a gluey protein substance that causes dough to be sticky
glu·ti·nous \ˈglüt-ᵊn-əs\ *adj* : STICKY
glut·ton \ˈglət-ᵊn\ *n* : one that eats to excess — **glut·ton·ous** \ˈglət-ᵊn-əs\ *adj* — **glut·tony** \ˈglət-ᵊn-ē\ *n*
glyc·er·in *or* **glyc·er·ine** \ˈgli-sə-rən\ *n* : GLYCEROL
glyc·er·ol \ˈgli-sə-ˌról, -ˌról\ *n* : a sweet syrupy alcohol usu. obtained from fats and used esp. as a solvent
gly·co·gen \ˈglī-kə-jən\ *n* : a white tasteless substance that is the chief storage carbohydrate of animals
gm *abbr* gram
GM *abbr* **1** general manager **2** guided missile
G–man \ˈjē-ˌman\ *n* : a special agent of the Federal Bureau of Investigation
GMT *abbr* Greenwich mean time
gnarled \ˈnärld\ *adj* **1** : KNOTTY **2** : GLOOMY, SULLEN
gnash \ˈnash\ *vb* : to grind (as teeth) together
gnat \ˈnat\ *n* : any of various small usu. biting dipteran flies
gnaw \ˈnò\ *vb* **1** : to consume, wear away, or make by persistent biting or nibbling **2** : to affect as if by gnawing — **gnaw·er** *n*
gneiss \ˈnīs\ *n* : a layered rock similar in composition to granite
gnome \ˈnōm\ *n* : a dwarf of folklore who lives inside the earth and guards precious ore or treasure — **gnom·ish** *adj*
GNP *abbr* gross national product

gnu \ˈnü\ *n, pl* **gnu** *or* **gnus** : either of two large African antelopes with an oxlike head and horns and a horselike mane and tail

gnu

¹**go** \ˈgō\ *vb* **went** \ˈwent\; **gone** \ˈgòn, ˈgän\; **go·ing; goes** \ˈgōz\ **1** : to move on a course : PROCEED ⟨∼ slow⟩ **2** : LEAVE, DEPART **3** : to take a certain course or follow a certain procedure ⟨reports ∼ through department channels⟩ **4** : EXTEND, RUN ⟨his land ∼es to the river⟩; *also* : LEAD ⟨that door ∼es to the cellar⟩ **5** : to be habitually in a certain state ⟨∼es armed after dark⟩ **6** : to become lost, consumed, or spent; *also* : DIE **7** : ELAPSE, PASS **8** : to pass by sale ⟨*went* for a good price⟩ **9** : to become impaired or weakened **10** : to give way under force or pressure : BREAK **11** : to move along in a specified manner ⟨it *went* well⟩ **12** : to be in general or on an average ⟨cheap, as yachts ∼⟩ **13** : to become esp. as the result of a contest ⟨the decision *went* against him⟩ **14** : to put or subject oneself ⟨∼ to great expense⟩ **15** : RESORT ⟨*went* to court to recover damages⟩ **16** : to begin or maintain an action or motion ⟨here ∼es⟩ **17** : to function properly ⟨the clock doesn't ∼⟩ **18** : to be known ⟨∼es by an alias⟩ **19** : to be or act in accordance ⟨a good rule to ∼ by⟩ **20** : to come to be applied **21** : to pass by award, assignment, or lot **22** : to contribute to a result ⟨qualities that ∼ to make a hero⟩ **23** : to be about, intending, or expecting something ⟨is ∼ing to leave town⟩ **24** : to arrive at a certain state or condition ⟨∼ to sleep⟩ **25** : to come to be ⟨the tire *went* flat⟩ **26** : to be capable of being sung or played ⟨the tune ∼es like this⟩ **27** : to be suitable or becoming : HARMONIZE **28** : to be capable of passing, extending, or being contained or inserted ⟨this coat will ∼ in the trunk⟩ **29** : to have a usual or proper place or position : BELONG ⟨these books ∼ on the top shelf⟩ **30** : to be capable of being divided ⟨3 ∼es into 6 twice⟩ **31** : to have a tendency ⟨that ∼es to show that he is honest⟩ **32** : to be acceptable, satisfactory, or adequate **33** : to empty the bladder or bowels **34** : to proceed along or according to : FOLLOW **35** : TRAVERSE **36** : BET, BID ⟨willing to ∼ $50⟩ **37** : to assume the function or obligation of ⟨∼ bail for a friend⟩ **38** : to participate to the extent of ⟨∼ halves⟩ **39** : WEIGH **40** : ENDURE, TOLERATE **41** : AFFORD ⟨can't ∼ the price⟩ **42** : SAY — used chiefly in oral narration of speech **43** : to engage in ⟨don't ∼ telling everyone⟩ — **go at 1** : ATTACK, ATTEMPT **2** : UNDERTAKE — **go back on 1** : ABANDON **2** : BETRAY **3** : FAIL — **go by the board** : to be discarded — **go down the line** : to give wholehearted support — **go for 1** : to pass for or serve as **2** : to try to secure **3** : FAVOR — **go one better** : OUTDO, SURPASS — **go over 1** : EXAMINE **2** : REPEAT **3**

\ə\abut \ᵊ\kitten \ər\further \a\ash \ā\ace \ä\mop, mar \aù\out \ch\chin \e\bet \ē\easy \g\go \i\hit \ī\ice \j\job \ŋ\sing \ō\go \ò\law \òi\boy \th\thin \t̲h̲\the \ü\loot \ù\foot \y\yet \zh\vision *see also* Pronunciation Symbols page

: STUDY, REVIEW — **go places** : to be on the way to success — **go steady** : to date one person exclusively — **go to bat for** : DEFEND, CHAMPION — **go to town 1** : to work or act efficiently **2** : to be very successful

²**go** *n, pl* **goes 1** : the act or manner of going **2** : the height of fashion ⟨boots are all the ∼⟩ **3** : a turn of affairs : OCCURRENCE **4** : ENERGY, VIGOR **5** : ATTEMPT, TRY **6** : a spell of activity — **no go** : USELESS, HOPELESS — **on the go** : constantly active

³**go** *adj* : functioning properly

goad \'gōd\ *n* [ME *gode*, fr. OE *gād* spear, goad] **1** : a pointed rod used to urge on an animal **2** : something that urges **syn** stimulus, impetus, incentive, spur, stimulant — **goad** *vb*

go–ahead \'gō-ə-ˌhed\ *n* : authority to proceed

goal \'gōl\ *n* **1** : the mark set as limit to a race; *also* : an area to be reached safely in children's games **2** : AIM, PURPOSE **3** : an area or object toward which play is directed to score; *also* : a successful attempt to score

goal·ie \'gō-lē\ *n* : GOALKEEPER

goal·keep·er \'gōl-ˌkē-pər\ *n* : a player who defends the goal in various games

goal·post \-ˌpōst\ *n* : one of the two vertical posts with a crossbar that constitute the goal in various games

goat \'gōt\ *n, pl* **goats** *or* **goat** : any of various hollow-horned ruminant mammals related to the sheep that have backward-curving horns, a short tail, and usu. straight hair

goa·tee \gō-'tē\ *n* : a small trim pointed or tufted beard on a man's chin

goat·herd \'gōt-ˌhərd\ *n* : a person who tends goats

goat·skin \-ˌskin\ *n* : the skin of a goat or a leather made from it

¹**gob** \'gäb\ *n* : LUMP, MASS

²**gob** *n* : SAILOR

gob·bet \'gä-bət\ *n* : LUMP, MASS

¹**gob·ble** \'gä-bəl\ *vb* **gob·bled; gob·bling 1** : to swallow or eat greedily **2** : to take eagerly : GRAB

²**gobble** *vb* **gob·bled; gob·bling** : to make the natural guttural noise of a male turkey

gob·ble·dy·gook *also* **gob·ble·de·gook** \'gä-bəl-dē-ˌgùk, -ˌgük\ *n* : generally unintelligible jargon

gob·bler \'gä-blər\ *n* : a male turkey

go–be·tween \'gō-bə-ˌtwēn\ *n* : an intermediate agent : BROKER

gob·let \'gä-blət\ *n* : a drinking glass with a foot and stem

gob·lin \'gä-blən\ *n* : an ugly or grotesque sprite that is mischievous and sometimes evil and malicious

god \'gäd, 'gòd\ *n* **1** *cap* : the supreme reality; *esp* : the Being worshiped as the creator and ruler of the universe **2** : a being or object believed to have supernatural attributes and powers and to require worship **3** : a person or thing of supreme value

god·child \'gäd-ˌchīld, 'gòd-\ *n* : a person for whom another person stands as sponsor at baptism

god·daugh·ter \-ˌdò-tər\ *n* : a female godchild

god·dess \'gä-dəs, 'gò-\ *n* **1** : a female god **2** : a woman whose charm or beauty arouses adoration

god·fa·ther \'gäd-ˌfä-thər, 'gòd-\ *n* **1** : a man who sponsors a person at baptism **2** : the leader of an organized crime syndicate

god·head \-ˌhed\ *n* **1** : divine nature or essence **2** *cap* : GOD 1; *also* : the nature of God esp. as existing in three persons

god·hood \-ˌhùd\ *n* : DIVINITY

god·less \-ləs\ *adj* : not acknowledging a deity or divine law — **god·less·ness** *n*

god·like \-ˌlīk\ *adj* : resembling or having the qualities of God or a god

god·ly \-lē\ *adj* **god·li·er; -est 1** : DIVINE **2** : PIOUS, DEVOUT — **god·li·ness** *n*

god·moth·er \-ˌmə-thər\ *n* : a woman who sponsors a person at baptism

god·par·ent \-ˌpar-ənt\ *n* : a sponsor at baptism

god·send \-ˌsend\ *n* : a desirable or needed thing or event that comes unexpectedly

god·son \-ˌsən\ *n* : a male godchild

God·speed \-'spēd\ *n* : a prosperous journey : SUCCESS ⟨bade him ∼⟩

go·fer \'gō-fər\ *n* [alter. of *go for*] : an employee whose duties include running errands

go–get·ter \'gō-ˌge-tər\ *n* : an aggressively enterprising person — **go–get·ting** *adj or n*

gog·gle \'gä-gəl\ *vb* **gog·gled; gog·gling** : to stare with wide or protuberant eyes

gog·gles \'gä-gəlz\ *n pl* : protective glasses set in a flexible frame that fits snugly against the face

go–go \'gō-ˌgō\ *adj* **1** : related to, being, or employed to entertain in a disco ⟨∼ dancers⟩ **2** : aggressively enterprising and energetic

go·ings–on \ˌgō-iŋ-'zòn, -'zän\ *n pl* : ACTIONS, EVENTS

goi·ter \'gòi-tər\ *n* : an abnormally enlarged thyroid gland visible as a swelling at the base of the neck — **goi·trous** \-trəs, -tə-rəs\ *adj*

goi·tre *chiefly Brit var of* GOITER

gold \'gōld\ *n* **1** : a malleable yellow metallic chemical element used esp. for coins and jewelry — see ELEMENT table **2** : gold coins; *also* : MONEY **3** : a yellow color

gold·brick \'gōld-ˌbrik\ *n* : a person who shirks assigned work — **goldbrick** *vb*

gold coast *n, often cap G&C* : an exclusive residential district

gold digger *n* : a person who uses charm to extract money or gifts from others

gold·en \'gōl-dən\ *adj* **1** : made of or relating to gold **2** : having the color of gold; *also* : BLOND **3** : SHINING, LUSTROUS **4** : SUPERB **5** : FLOURISHING, PROSPEROUS **6** : radiantly youthful and vigorous **7** : FAVORABLE, ADVANTAGEOUS ⟨a ∼ opportunity⟩ **8** : MELLOW, RESONANT

gold·en·ag·er \'gōl-dən-'ā-jər\ *n* : an elderly and often retired person usu. engaging in club activities

Golden Fleece *n* : a treasure in the form of a fleece of gold placed in a grove guarded by dragons and sought and recovered by Jason and the Argonauts

golden hamster *n* : a small tawny hamster often kept as a pet

gold·en·rod \'gōl-dən-ˌräd\ *n* : any of numerous plants related to the daisies but having tall slender stalks with many tiny usu. yellow flower heads

gold·finch \-ˌfinch\ *n* **1** : a small largely red, black, and yellow Old World finch often kept in a cage **2** : any of three small American finches of which the males usu. become bright yellow and black in summer

gold·fish \-ˌfish\ *n* : a small usu. yellow or golden carp often kept as an aquarium or pond fish

gold·smith \-ˌsmith\ *n* : a person who makes or deals in articles of gold

golf \'gälf, 'gòlf\ *n* : a game played with a small ball and various clubs on a course having 9 or 18 holes — **golf** *vb* — **golf·er** *n*

-gon \ˌgän\ *n comb form* : figure having (so many) angles ⟨hexa*gon*⟩

go·nad \'gō-ˌnad\ *n* : a sperm- or egg-producing gland : OVARY, TESTIS — **go·nad·al** \gō-'nad-ᵊl\ *adj*

go·nad·o·trop·ic \gō-ˌna-də-'trä-pik\ *also* **go·nad·o·tro·phic** \-'trä-fik, -'trä-\ *adj* : acting on or stimulating the gonads ⟨∼ hormones⟩

go·nad·o·tro·pin \-'trō-pən\ *also* **go·nad·o·tro·phin** \-fən\ *n* : a gonadotropic hormone

gon·do·la \'gän-də-lə (*usual for 1*), gän-'dō-\ *n* **1** : a long narrow boat used on the canals of Venice **2** : a railroad car used for hauling loose freight (as coal) **3** : an enclosure beneath an airship or balloon **4** : an enclosed car suspended from a cable and used esp. for transporting skiers

gondola 1

gon·do·lier \ˌgän-də-ˈlir\ *n* : a person who propels a gondola

¹gone \ˈgȯn\ *past part of* GO

²gone *adj* **1** : DEAD **2** : LOST, RUINED **3** : SINKING, WEAK **4** : INVOLVED, ABSORBED **5** : INFATUATED **6** : PREGNANT **7** : PAST

gon·er \ˈgȯ-nər\ *n* : one whose case is hopeless

gong \ˈgäŋ, ˈgȯŋ\ *n* : a metallic disk that produces a resounding tone when struck

gono·coc·cus \ˌgä-nə-ˈkä-kəs\ *n, pl* **-coc·ci** \-ˈkäk-ˌsī, -(ˌ)sē, -ˈkä-ˌkī, -(ˌ)kē\ : a pus-producing bacterium causing gonorrhea — **gono·coc·cal** \-ˈkä-kəl\ *adj*

gon·or·rhea \ˌgä-nə-ˈrē-ə\ *n* : a contagious sexually transmitted inflammation of the genital tract caused by a bacterium — **gon·or·rhe·al** \-ˈrē-əl\ *adj*

goo \ˈgü\ *n* **1** : a viscid or sticky substance **2** : sentimental tripe — **goo·ey** \-ē\ *adj*

goo·ber \ˈgü-bər, ˈgü-\ *n, Southern & Midland* : PEANUT

¹good \ˈgu̇d\ *adj* **bet·ter** \ˈbe-tər\; **best** \ˈbest\ **1** : of a favorable character or tendency **2** : BOUNTIFUL, FERTILE **3** : COMELY, ATTRACTIVE **4** : SUITABLE, FIT **5** : SOUND, WHOLE **6** : AGREEABLE, PLEASANT **7** : SALUTARY, WHOLESOME **8** : CONSIDERABLE, AMPLE **9** : FULL **10** : WELL-FOUNDED **11** : TRUE ⟨holds ∼ for everybody⟩ **12** : legally valid or effectual **13** : ADEQUATE, SATISFACTORY **14** : conforming to a standard **15** : DISCRIMINATING **16** : COMMENDABLE, VIRTUOUS **17** : KIND **18** : UPPER-CLASS **19** : COMPETENT **20** : LOYAL, CLOSE — **good–heart·ed** \-ˈhär-təd\ *adj* — **good·ish** *adj* — **good–look·ing** \-ˈlu̇-kiŋ\ *adj* — **good–tem·pered** \-ˈtem-pərd\ *adj*

²good *n* **1** : something good **2** : GOODNESS **3** : BENEFIT, WELFARE ⟨for the ∼ of mankind⟩ **4** : something that has economic utility **5** *pl* : personal property **6** *pl* : CLOTH **7** *pl* : WARES, MERCHANDISE **8** : good persons ⟨the ∼ die young⟩ **9** *pl* : proof of wrongdoing — **for good** : FOREVER, PERMANENTLY — **to the good** : in a position of net gain or profit ($10 *to the good*)

³good *adv* : WELL

good–bye *or* **good–by** \gu̇d-ˈbī, gə-\ *n* : a concluding remark at parting

good–for–noth·ing \ˈgu̇d-fər-ˌnə-thiŋ\ *n* : an idle worthless person

Good Friday *n* : the Friday before Easter observed as the anniversary of the crucifixion of Christ

good·ly \ˈgu̇d-lē\ *adj* **good·li·er; -est 1** : of pleasing appearance **2** : LARGE, CONSIDERABLE

good·man \ˈgu̇d-mən\ *n, archaic* : MR.

good–na·tured \ˈgu̇d-ˈnā-chərd\ *adj* : of a cheerful disposition — **good–na·tured·ly** \-chərd-lē\ *adv*

good·ness \-nəs\ *n* : EXCELLENCE, VIRTUE

good·wife \-ˌwīf\ *n, archaic* : MRS.

good·will \-ˈwil\ *n* **1** : BENEVOLENCE **2** : the value of the trade a business has built up over time **3** : cheerful consent **4** : willing effort

goody \ˈgu̇-dē\ *n, pl* **good·ies** : something that is good esp. to eat

goody–goody \ˌgu̇-dē-ˈgu̇-dē\ *adj* : affectedly good — **goody–goody** *n*

goof \ˈgüf\ *vb* **1** : to spend time idly or foolishly **2** : BLUNDER — often used with *off* — **goof** *n*

goof·ball \ˈgüf-ˌbȯl\ *n* **1** *slang* : a barbiturate sleeping pill **2** : a goofy person

go off *vb* **1** : EXPLODE **2** : to follow a course ⟨the party *went off* well⟩

goof–off \ˈgü-ˌfȯf\ *n* : one who evades work or responsibility

goofy \ˈgü-fē\ *adj* **goof·i·er; -est** : CRAZY, SILLY — **goof·i·ness** \-fē-nəs\ *n*

goon \ˈgün\ *n* : a man hired to terrorize or kill opponents

go on *vb* **1** : to continue in a course of action **2** : to take place : HAPPEN

goose \ˈgüs\ *n, pl* **geese** \ˈgēs\ **1** : any of numerous long-necked web-footed birds related to the swans and ducks; *esp* : a female goose as distinguished from a gander **2** : a foolish person **3** *pl* **goos·es** : a tailor's smoothing iron

goose·ber·ry \ˈgüs-ˌber-ē, ˈgüz-, -bə-rē\ *n* : the acid berry of any of several shrubs related to the currant and used esp. in jams and pies

goose bumps *n pl* : roughening of the skin caused usu. by cold, fear, or a sudden feeling of excitement

goose·flesh \-ˌflesh\ *n* : GOOSE BUMPS

goose pimples *n pl* : GOOSE BUMPS

go out *vb* **1** : to become extinguished **2** : to become a candidate ⟨*went out* for the football team⟩

go over *vb* : SUCCEED

GOP *abbr* Grand Old Party (Republican)

go·pher \ˈgō-fər\ *n* **1** : a burrowing American land tortoise **2** : any of a family of No. American burrowing rodents with large cheek pouches opening beside the mouth **3** : any of several small ground squirrels of the prairie region of No. America

¹gore \ˈgȯr\ *n* : BLOOD

²gore *n* : a tapering or triangular piece (as of cloth in a skirt)

³gore *vb* **gored; gor·ing** : to pierce or wound with something pointed

¹gorge \ˈgȯrj\ *n* **1** : THROAT **2** : a narrow ravine **3** : a mass of matter that chokes up a passage

²gorge *vb* **gorged; gorg·ing** : to eat greedily : stuff to capacity : GLUT

gor·geous \ˈgȯr-jəs\ *adj* : resplendently beautiful

Gor·gon·zo·la \ˌgȯr-gən-ˈzō-lə\ *n* : a blue cheese of Italian origin

go·ril·la \gə-ˈri-lə\ *n* [NL, fr. Gk *Gorillai*, a tribe of hairy women in an account of a voyage around Africa] : an African anthropoid ape related to but much larger than the chimpanzee

gor·man·dize \ˈgȯr-mən-ˌdīz\ *vb* **-dized; -diz·ing** : to eat ravenously — **gor·man·diz·er** *n*

gorp \ˈgȯrp\ *n* : a snack consisting of high-calorie food (as raisins and nuts)

gorse \ˈgȯrs\ *n* : a spiny yellow-flowered Old World evergreen shrub of the legume family

gory \ˈgōr-ē\ *adj* **gor·i·er; -est 1** : BLOODSTAINED **2** : HORRIBLE, SENSATIONAL

gos·hawk \ˈgäs-ˌhȯk\ *n* : any of several long-tailed hawks with short rounded wings

gos·ling \ˈgäz-liŋ, ˈgȯz-\ *n* : a young goose

¹gos·pel \ˈgäs-pəl\ *n* [ME, fr. OE *gōdspel*, fr. *gōd* good + *spell* message, news] **1** : the teachings of Christ and the apostles **2** *cap* : any of the first four books of the New Testament **3** : something accepted as infallible truth

²gospel *adj* **1** : of, relating to, or emphasizing the gospel **2** : relating to or being American religious songs associated with evangelism

gos·sa·mer \ˈgä-sə-mər\ *n* [ME *gossomer*, fr. *gos* goose + *somer* summer] **1** : a film of cobwebs floating in the air **2** : something light, delicate, or tenuous

¹gos·sip \ˈgä-səp\ *n* **1** : a person who habitually reveals

\ə\abut \ᵊ\kitten \ər\further \a\ash \ā\ace \ä\mop, mar \au̇\out \ch\chin \e\bet \ē\easy \g\go \i\hit \ī\ice \j\job \ŋ\sing \ō\go \ȯ\law \ȯi\boy \th\thin \th̶\the \ü\loot \u̇\foot \y\yet \zh\vision *see also* Pronunciation Symbols page personal or sensational facts **2** : rumor or report of an intimate nature **3** : an informal conversation — **gossipy** *adj*

²**gossip** *vb* : to spread gossip

got *past and past part of* GET

Goth \'gäth\ *n* : a member of a Germanic people that early in the Christian era overran the Roman Empire

¹**Goth·ic** \'gä-thik\ *adj* **1** : of or relating to the Goths **2** : of or relating to a style of architecture prevalent in western Europe from the middle 12th to the early 16th century

²**Gothic** *n* **1** : the Germanic language of the Goths **2** : the Gothic architectural style or decoration

gotten *past part of* GET

Gou·da \'gü-də\ *n* : a mild Dutch milk cheese shaped in balls

¹**gouge** \'gaůj\ *n* **1** : a rounded troughlike chisel **2** : a hole or groove made with or as if with a gouge

²**gouge** *vb* **gouged; goug·ing 1** : to cut holes or grooves in with or as if with a gouge **2** : DEFRAUD, CHEAT

gou·lash \'gü-₁läsh, -₁lash\ *n* [Hungarian *gulyás*] : a stew made with meat, assorted vegetables, and paprika

go under *vb* : to be overwhelmed, defeated, or destroyed : FAIL

gourd \'gōrd, 'gůrd\ *n* **1** : any of a family of tendril-bearing vines including the cucumber, squash, and melon **2** : the fruit of a gourd; *esp* : any of various inedible hard-shelled fruits used esp. for ornament or implements

gourde \'gůrd\ *n* — see MONEY table

gour·mand \'gůr-₁mänd\ *n* **1** : one who is excessively fond of eating and drinking **2** : GOURMET

gour·met \'gůr-₁mā, gůr-'mā\ *n* [F, fr. MF, alter. of *gromet* boy servant, vintner's assistant] : a connoisseur of food and drink

gout \'gaůt\ *n* : a metabolic disease marked by painful inflammation and swelling of the joints — **gouty** *adj*

gov *abbr* **1** government **2** governor

gov·ern \'gə-vərn\ *vb* **1** : to control and direct the making and administration of policy in : RULE **2** : CONTROL, DIRECT, INFLUENCE **3** : DETERMINE, REGULATE **4** : RESTRAIN — **gov·er·nance** \-vər-nəns\ *n*

gov·ern·ess \'gə-vər-nəs\ *n* : a woman who teaches and trains a child esp. in a private home

gov·ern·ment \'gə-vərn-mənt\ *n* **1** : authoritative direction or control : RULE **2** : the making of policy **3** : the organization or agency through which a political unit exercises authority **4** : the complex of institutions, laws, and customs through which a political unit is governed **5** : the governing body — **gov·ern·men·tal** \₁gə-vərn-'ment-ᵊl\ *adj*

gov·er·nor \'gə-vər-nər\ *n* **1** : one that governs; *esp* : a ruler, chief executive, or head of a political unit (as a state) **2** : an attachment to a machine for automatic control of speed — **gov·er·nor·ship** *n*

govt *abbr* government

gown \'gaůn\ *n* **1** : a loose flowing outer garment **2** : an official robe worn esp. by a judge, clergyman, or teacher **3** : a woman's dress ⟨evening ~s⟩ **4** : a loose robe — **gown** *vb*

gp *abbr* group

GP *abbr* general practitioner

GPO *abbr* **1** general post office **2** Government Printing Office

GQ *abbr* general quarters

gr *abbr* **1** grade **2** grain **3** gram **4** gravity **5** gross

grab \'grab\ *vb* **grabbed; grab·bing** : to take hastily : SNATCH — **grab** *n*

¹**grace** \'grās\ *n* **1** : unmerited help given to people by God (as in overcoming temptation) **2** : freedom from sin through divine grace **3** : a virtue coming from God **4** — used as a title for a duke, a duchess, or an archbishop **5** : a short prayer at a meal **6** : a temporary respite (as

from the payment of a debt) **7** : APPROVAL, ACCEPTANCE ⟨in his good ~s⟩ **8** : CHARM **9** : ATTRACTIVENESS, BEAUTY **10** : fitness or proportion of line or expression **11** : ease of movement **12** : a musical trill or ornament — **grace·ful** \-fəl\ *adj* — **grace·ful·ly** *adv* — **grace·ful·ness** *n* — **grace·less** *adj*

²**grace** *vb* **graced; grac·ing 1** : HONOR **2** : ADORN, EMBELLISH

gra·cious \'grā-shəs\ *adj* **1** : marked by kindness and courtesy **2** : GRACEFUL **3** : characterized by charm and good taste **4** : MERCIFUL — **gra·cious·ly** *adv* — **gra·cious·ness** *n*

grack·le \'gra-kəl\ *n* : any of several American blackbirds with glossy iridescent plumage

grad *abbr* graduate; graduated

gra·da·tion \grā-'dā-shən, grə-\ *n* **1** : a series forming successive stages **2** : a step, degree, or stage in a series **3** : an advance by regular degrees **4** : the act or process of grading

¹**grade** \'grād\ *vb* **grad·ed; grad·ing 1** : to arrange in grades : SORT **2** : to make level or evenly sloping ⟨~ a highway⟩ **3** : to give a grade to ⟨~ a pupil in history⟩ **4** : to assign to a grade

²**grade** *n* **1** : a degree or stage in a series, order, or ranking **2** : a position in a scale of rank, quality, or order **3** : a class of persons or things of the same rank or quality **4** : a division of the school course representing one year's work; *also* : the pupils in such a division **5** *pl* : the elementary school system **6** : a mark or rating esp. of accomplishment in school **7** : the degree of slope (as of a road); *also* : SLOPE

grad·er \'grā-dər\ *n* : a machine for leveling earth

grade school *n* : ELEMENTARY SCHOOL

gra·di·ent \'grā-dē-ənt\ *n* : SLOPE, GRADE

grad·u·al \'gra-jə-wəl\ *adj* : proceeding or changing by steps or degrees — **grad·u·al·ly** *adv*

grad·u·al·ism \-wə-₁li-zəm\ *n* : the policy of approaching a desired end gradually

¹**grad·u·ate** \'gra-jə-wət\ *n* **1** : a holder of an academic degree or diploma **2** : a graduated container for measuring contents

²**graduate** *adj* **1** : holding an academic degree or diploma **2** : of or relating to studies beyond the first or bachelor's degree ⟨~ school⟩

³**grad·u·ate** \'gra-jə-₁wāt\ *vb* **-at·ed; -at·ing 1** : to grant or receive an academic degree or diploma **2** : to divide into grades, classes, or intervals **3** : to admit to a particular standing or grade

grad·u·a·tion \₁gra-jə-'wā-shən\ *n* **1** : a mark that graduates something **2** : an act or process of graduating **3** : COMMENCEMENT **2**

graf·fi·to \grə-'fē-tō, gra-\ *n, pl* **-ti** \-(₁)tē\ : an inscription or drawing made on a public surface (as a wall)

¹**graft** \'graft\ *n* **1** : a grafted plant; *also* : the point of union in this **2** : material (as skin) used in grafting **3** : the getting of money or advantage dishonestly; *also* : the money or advantage so gained

graft 1

²**graft** *vb* **1** : to insert a shoot from one plant into another so that they join and grow; *also* : to join one thing to another as in plant grafting ⟨~ skin over a burn⟩ **2** : to get (as money) dishonestly — **graft·er** *n*

gra·ham cracker \\'grā-əm-, 'gram-\\ *n* : a slightly sweet cracker made chiefly of whole wheat flour

Grail \\'grāl\\ *n* : the cup or platter used according to medieval legend by Christ at the Last Supper and thereafter the object of knightly quests

grain \\'grān\\ *n* **1** : a seed or fruit of a cereal grass **2** : seeds or fruits of various food plants and esp. cereal grasses; *also* : a plant (as wheat) producing grain **3** : a small hard particle **4** : a unit of weight based on the weight of a grain of wheat — see WEIGHT table **5** : TEXTURE; *also* : the arrangement of fibers in wood **6** : natural disposition — **grained** \\'grānd\\ *adj*

grain alcohol *n* : ALCOHOL 1

grainy \\'grā-nē\\ *adj* **grain·i·er; -est 1** : resembling or having some characteristic of grain : not smooth or fine **2** *of a photograph* : appearing to be composed of grain=like particles

¹**gram** \\'gram\\ *n* [F *gramme*, fr. LL *gramma*, a small weight, fr. Gk *gramma* letter, writing, a small weight, fr. *graphein* to write] : a metric unit of mass and weight equal to ¹⁄₁₀₀₀ kilogram — see METRIC SYSTEM table

²**gram** *abbr* grammar; grammatical

-gram \\ˌgram\\ *n comb form* : drawing : writing : record ⟨tele*gram*⟩

gram·mar \\'gra-mər\\ *n* **1** : the study of the classes of words, their inflections, and their functions and relations in the sentence **2** : a study of what is to be preferred and what avoided in inflection and syntax **3** : speech or writing evaluated according to its conformity to grammatical rules — **gram·mar·i·an** \\grə-'mer-ē-ən, -'mar-\\ *n* — **gram·mat·i·cal** \\-'ma-ti-kəl\\ *adj* — **gram·mat·i·cal·ly** \\-k(ə-)lē\\ *adv*

grammar school *n* **1** : a secondary school emphasizing Latin and Greek in preparation for college; *also* : a British college preparatory school **2** : a school intermediate between the primary grades and high school **3** : ELEMENTARY SCHOOL

gramme \\'gram\\ *chiefly Brit var of* GRAM

gram·o·phone \\'gra-mə-ˌfōn\\ *n* : PHONOGRAPH

gra·na·ry \\'grā-nə-rē, 'gra-\\ *n, pl* **-ries 1** : a storehouse for grain **2** : a region producing grain in abundance

¹**grand** \\'grand\\ *adj* **1** : higher in rank or importance : FOREMOST, CHIEF **2** : great in size **3** : INCLUSIVE, COMPLETE ⟨a ∼ total⟩ **4** : MAGNIFICENT, SPLENDID **5** : showing wealth or high social standing **6** : IMPRESSIVE, STATELY **7** : very good : FINE — **grand·ly** *adv* — **grand·ness** *n*

²**grand** *n, slang* : a thousand dollars

gran·dam \\'gran-ˌdam, -dəm\\ *or* **gran·dame** \\-ˌdam, -dəm\\ *n* : an old woman

grand·child \\'grand-ˌchīld\\ *n* : a child of one's son or daughter

grand·daugh·ter \\'gran-ˌdȯ-tər\\ *n* : a daughter of one's son or daughter

grande dame \\'grän-'däm\\ *n, pl* **grandes dames** : a usu. elderly woman of great prestige or ability

gran·dee \\gran-'dē\\ *n* : a high-ranking Spanish or Portuguese nobleman

gran·deur \\'gran-jər\\ *n* **1** : the quality or state of being grand : MAGNIFICENCE **2** : something that is grand

grand·fa·ther \\'grand-ˌfä-thər\\ *n* : the father of one's father or mother; *also* : ANCESTOR

grandfather clock *n* : a tall clock that stands on the floor

gran·dil·o·quence \\gran-'di-lə-kwəns\\ *n* : pompous eloquence — **gran·dil·o·quent** \\-kwənt\\ *adj*

gran·di·ose \\'gran-dē-ˌōs, ˌgran-dē-'ōs\\ *adj* : IMPRESSIVE, IMPOSING; *also* : affectedly splendid — **gran·di·ose·ly** *adv* — **gran·di·os·i·ty** \\ˌgran-dē-'ä-sə-tē\\ *n*

grand jury *n* : a jury that examines accusations of crime against persons and makes formal charges on which the persons are later tried

grand mal \\'grän-ˌmäl; 'grand-ˌmal\\ *n* [F, lit., great illness] : severe epilepsy

grand·moth·er \\'grand-ˌmə-thər\\ *n* : the mother of one's father or mother; *also* : a female ancestor

grand·par·ent \\-ˌpar-ənt\\ *n* : a parent of one's father or mother

grand piano *n* : a piano with horizontal frame and strings

grand prix \\'grän-'prē\\ *n, pl* **grand prix** *same or* -'prēz\\ *often cap G&P* : a long-distance auto race over a road course

grand slam *n* **1** : a total victory or success **2** : a home run hit with three runners on base

grand·son \\'grand-ˌsən\\ *n* : a son of one's son or daughter

grand·stand \\-ˌstand\\ *n* : a usu. roofed stand for spectators at a racecourse or stadium

grange \\'grānj\\ *n* **1** : a farm or farmhouse with its various buildings **2** *cap* : one of the lodges of a national association originally made up of farmers; *also* : the association itself — **grang·er** \\'grān-jər\\ *n*

gran·ite \\'gra-nət\\ *n* : a hard granular igneous rock used esp. for building — **gra·nit·ic** \\grə-'ni-tik\\ *adj*

gran·ite·ware \\'gra-nət-ˌwar\\ *n* : ironware with mottled enamel

gra·no·la \\grə-'nō-lə\\ *n* : a cereal made of rolled oats and usu. raisins and nuts

¹**grant** \\'grant\\ *vb* **1** : to consent to : ALLOW, PERMIT **2** : GIVE, BESTOW **3** : to admit as true — **grant·er** *n* — **grant·or** \\'gran-tər, -ˌtȯr\\ *n*

²**grant** *n* **1** : the act of granting **2** : something granted; *esp* : a gift for a particular purpose ⟨a ∼ for study abroad⟩ **3** : a transfer of property by deed or writing; *also* : the instrument by which such a transfer is made **4** : the property transferred by grant — **grant·ee** \\gran-'tē\\ *n*

gran·u·lar \\'gra-nyə-lər\\ *adj* : consisting of or appearing to consist of granules — **gran·u·lar·i·ty** \\ˌgra-nyə-'lar-ə-tē\\ *n*

gran·u·late \\'gra-nyə-ˌlāt\\ *vb* **-lat·ed; -lat·ing** : to form into grains or crystals — **gran·u·la·tion** \\ˌgra-nyə-'lā-shən\\ *n*

gran·ule \\'gra-nyül\\ *n* : a small grain or particle

grape \\'grāp\\ *n* [ME, fr. OF *crape, grape* hook, grape stalk, bunch of grapes, grape] **1** : a smooth-skinned juicy edible greenish white, deep red, or purple berry that is the chief source of wine **2** : any of numerous woody vines widely grown for their bunches of grapes

grape·fruit \\'grāp-ˌfrüt\\ *n* **1** *pl* **grapefruit** *or* **grapefruits** : a large edible yellow-skinned citrus fruit **2** : a tree bearing grapefruit

grape hyacinth *n* : any of several small bulbous spring-flowering herbs with clusters of usu. blue flowers that are related to the lilies

grape·shot \\'grāp-ˌshät\\ *n* : a cluster of small iron balls formerly fired at people from short range by a cannon

grape·vine \\-ˌvīn\\ *n* **1** : GRAPE 2 **2** : RUMOR; *also* : an informal means of circulating information or gossip

graph \\'graf\\ *n* : a diagram that usu. by means of dots and lines shows change in one variable factor in comparison with one or more other factors — **graph** *vb*

-graph \\ˌgraf\\ *n comb form* **1** : something written ⟨auto*graph*⟩ **2** : instrument for making or transmitting records ⟨seismo*graph*⟩

¹**graph·ic** \\'gra-fik\\ *also* **graph·i·cal** \\-fi-kəl\\ *adj* **1** : being written, drawn, or engraved **2** : vividly described **3** : of or relating to the arts (**graphic arts**) of representation, decoration, and printing on flat surfaces — **graph·i·cal·ly** \\-fi-k(ə-)lē\\ *adv*

²**graphic** *n* **1** : a picture, map, or graph used for illustra-

tion **2** *pl* : a display (as of pictures or graphs) generated by a computer on a screen, printer, or plotter

graph·ics tablet \-fiks-\ *n* : a computer input device for entering pictorial information by drawing or tracing

graph·ite \'gra-ˌfīt\ *n* [G *Graphit,* fr. Gk *graphein* to write] : a soft black form of carbon used esp. for lead pencils and lubricants

grap·nel \'grap-nəl\ *n* : a small anchor with usu. four claws used esp. in dragging or grappling operations

¹**grap·ple** \'gra-pəl\ *n* [MF *grappelle,* dim. of *grape* hook] : the act of grappling

²**grapple** *vb* **grap·pled; grap·pling 1** : to seize or hold with or as if with a hooked implement **2** : to come to grips with : WRESTLE

¹**grasp** \'grasp\ *vb* **1** : to make the motion of seizing **2** : to take or seize firmly **3** : to enclose and hold with the fingers or arms **4** : COMPREHEND

²**grasp** *n* **1** : HANDLE **2** : EMBRACE **3** : HOLD, CONTROL **4** : the reach of the arms **5** : the power of seizing and holding **6** : COMPREHENSION

grasp·ing *adj* : GREEDY, AVARICIOUS

grass \'gras\ *n* **1** : herbage for grazing animals **2** : any of a large family of plants (as wheat, bamboo, or sugarcane) with jointed stems and narrow leaves **3** : grass-covered land **4** : MARIJUANA — **grassy** *adj*

grass·hop·per \-ˌhä-pər\ *n* : any of numerous leaping plant-eating insects

grass·land \-ˌland\ *n* : land covered naturally or under cultivation with grasses and low-growing herbs

grass roots *n pl* : society at the local level as distinguished from the centers of political leadership

¹**grate** \'grāt\ *vb* **grat·ed; grat·ing 1** : to pulverize by rubbing against something rough **2** : to grind or rub against with a rasping noise **3** : IRRITATE — **grat·er** *n* — **grat·ing·ly** *adv*

²**grate** *n* **1** : GRATING **2** : a frame of iron bars for holding fuel while it burns

grate·ful \'grāt-fəl\ *adj* **1** : THANKFUL, APPRECIATIVE; *also* : expressing gratitude **2** : PLEASING — **grate·ful·ly** *adv* — **grate·ful·ness** *n*

grat·i·fy \'gra-tə-ˌfī\ *vb* **-fied; -fy·ing** : to afford pleasure to — **grat·i·fi·ca·tion** \ˌgra-tə-fə-'kā-shən\ *n*

grat·ing \'grā-tiŋ\ *n* : a framework with parallel bars or crossbars

gra·tis \'gra-təs, 'grä-\ *adv or adj* : without charge or recompense : FREE

grat·i·tude \'gra-tə-ˌtüd, -ˌtyüd\ *n* : THANKFULNESS

gra·tu·itous \grə-'tü-ə-təs, -'tyü-\ *adj* **1** : done or provided without recompense : FREE **2** : UNWARRANTED

gra·tu·ity \-ə-tē\ *n, pl* **-ities** : ¹⁰TIP

gra·va·men \grə-'vä-mən\ *n, pl* **-va·mens** *or* **-vam·i·na** \-'va-mə-nə\ [LL, burden] : the basic or significant part of a grievance or complaint

¹**grave** \'grāv\ *vb* **graved; grav·en** \'grā-vən\ *or* **graved; grav·ing** : SCULPTURE, ENGRAVE

²**grave** *n* : an excavation in the earth as a place of burial; *also* : TOMB

³**grave** \'grāv; *5 also* 'gräv\ *adj* **1** : IMPORTANT **2** : threatening great harm or danger **3** : DIGNIFIED, SOLEMN **4** : drab in color : SOMBER **5** : of, marked by, or being an accent mark having the form ` — **grave·ly** *adv* — **grave·ness** *n*

grav·el \'gra-vəl\ *n* : pebbles and small pieces of rock larger than grains of sand — **grav·el·ly** *adj*

grave·stone \'grāv-ˌstōn\ *n* : a burial monument

grave·yard \-ˌyärd\ *n* : CEMETERY

grav·id \'gra-vəd\ *adj* [L *gravidus,* fr. *gravis* heavy] : PREGNANT

gra·vi·me·ter \gra-'vi-mə-tər, 'gra-və-ˌmē-\ *n* : a device for measuring variations in a gravitational field

grav·i·tate \'gra-və-ˌtāt\ *vb* **-tat·ed; -tat·ing** : to move or tend to move toward something

grav·i·ta·tion \ˌgra-və-'tā-shən\ *n* **1** : a natural force of

attraction that tends to draw bodies together and that occurs because of the mass of the bodies **2** : the action or process of gravitating — **grav·i·ta·tion·al** \-shə-nəl\ *adj* — **grav·i·ta·tion·al·ly** *adv*

grav·i·ty \'gra-və-tē\ *n, pl* **-ties 1** : IMPORTANCE; *esp* : SERIOUSNESS **2** : ²MASS 5 **3** : the gravitational attraction of the mass of a celestial object (as earth) for bodies close to it; *also* : GRAVITATION 1

gra·vure \grə-'vyùr\ *n* [F] : PHOTOGRAVURE

gra·vy \'grā-vē\ *n, pl* **gravies 1** : a sauce made from the thickened and seasoned juices of cooked meat **2** : unearned or illicit gain : GRAFT

¹**gray** \'grā\ *adj* **1** : of the color gray; *also* : dull in color **2** : having gray hair **3** : CHEERLESS, DISMAL **4** : intermediate in position or character — **gray·ish** *adj* — **gray·ness** *n*

²**gray** *n* **1** : something of a gray color **2** : a neutral color ranging between black and white

³**gray** *vb* : to make or become gray

gray·beard \'grā-ˌbird\ *n* : an old man

gray·ling \'grā-liŋ\ *n, pl* **grayling** *also* **graylings** : any of several slender freshwater food and sport fishes related to the trouts

gray matter *n* **1** : the grayish part of nervous tissue consisting mostly of nerve cell bodies **2** : INTELLIGENCE

gray wolf *n* : a large wolf of northern No. America and Asia that is usu. gray

¹**graze** \'grāz\ *vb* **grazed; graz·ing 1** : to feed on herbage or pasture **2** : to feed (livestock) on grass or pasture — **graz·er** *n*

²**graze** *vb* **grazed; graz·ing 1** : to touch lightly in passing **2** : SCRATCH, ABRADE

¹**grease** \'grēs\ *n* **1** : rendered animal fat **2** : oily material **3** : a thick lubricant — **greasy** \'grē-sē, -zē\ *adj*

²**grease** \'grēs, 'grēz\ *vb* **greased; greas·ing** : to smear or lubricate with grease

grease·paint \'grēs-ˌpānt\ *n* : theater makeup

great \'grāt\ *adj* **1** : large in size : BIG **2** : ELABORATE, AMPLE **3** : large in number : NUMEROUS **4** : being beyond the average : MIGHTY, INTENSE ⟨a ～ weight⟩ ⟨in ～ pain⟩ **5** : EMINENT, GRAND **6** : long continued ⟨a ～ while⟩ **7** : MAIN, PRINCIPAL **8** : more distant in a family relationship by one generation ⟨a *great*-grandfather⟩ **9** : markedly superior in character, quality, or skill ⟨～ at bridge⟩ **10** : EXCELLENT, FINE ⟨had a ～ time⟩ — **great·ly** *adv* — **great·ness** *n*

great circle *n* : a circle on the surface of a sphere that has the same center as the sphere; *esp* : one on the surface of the earth an arc of which is the shortest travel distance between two points

great·coat \'grāt-ˌkōt\ *n* : a heavy overcoat

Great Dane *n* : any of a breed of tall massive powerful smooth-coated dogs

great·heart·ed \'grāt-'här-təd\ *adj* **1** : COURAGEOUS **2** : MAGNANIMOUS

great power *n, often cap G&P* : one of the nations that figure most decisively in international affairs

great white shark *n* : a large and dangerous shark of warm seas that is light colored below and darker above becoming dirty white in older and larger specimens

grebe \'grēb\ *n* : any of a family of lobe-toed diving birds related to the loons

Gre·cian \'grē-shən\ *adj* : GREEK

greed \'grēd\ *n* : acquisitive or selfish desire beyond reason — **greed·i·ly** \'grē-də-lē\ *adv* — **greed·i·ness** \-dē-nəs\ *n* — **greedy** \'grē-dē\ *adj*

¹**Greek** \'grēk\ *n* **1** : a native or inhabitant of Greece **2** : the ancient or modern language of Greece
☞ For table, see next page.

²**Greek** *adj* **1** : of, relating to, or characteristic of Greece, the Greeks, or Greek **2** : ORTHODOX 3

¹**green** \'grēn\ *adj* **1** : of the color green **2** : covered with verdure; *also* : consisting of green plants or of the leafy

GREEK ALPHABET

NAME	CAPITAL	LOWERCASE
alpha	A	α
beta	B	β
gamma	Γ	γ
delta	Δ	δ
epsilon	E	ε
zeta	Z	ζ
eta	H	η
theta	Θ	θ
iota	I	ι
kappa	K	κ
lambda	Λ	λ
mu	M	μ
nu	N	ν
xi	Ξ	ξ
omicron	O	ο
pi	Π	π
rho	P	ρ
sigma	Σ	σ or ς
tau	T	τ
upsilon	Υ	υ
phi	Φ	φ
chi	X	χ
psi	Ψ	ψ
omega	Ω	ω

parts of plants ⟨a ∼ salad⟩ **3** : UNRIPE; *also* : IMMATURE **4** : having a sickly appearance **5** : not fully processed or treated ⟨∼ liquor⟩ ⟨∼ hides⟩ **6** : INEXPERIENCED; *also* : NAIVE **7** : concerned with or supporting environmentalism — **green·ish** *adj* — **green·ness** *n*
²**green** *vb* : to make or become green
³**green** *n* **1** : a color between blue and yellow in the spectrum : the color of growing fresh grass or of the emerald **2** : something of a green color **3** : green vegetation; *esp, pl* : leafy herbs or leafy parts of a vegetable ⟨collard ∼s⟩ ⟨beet ∼s⟩ **4** : a grassy plot; *esp* : a smooth grassy area around the hole into which the ball must be played in golf
green·back \'grēn-ˌbak\ *n* : a U.S. legal-tender note
green bean *n* : a kidney bean that is used as a snap bean when the pods are colored green
green·belt \'grēn-ˌbelt\ *n* : a belt of parks or farmlands around a community
green·ery \'grē-nə-rē\ *n, pl* **-er·ies** : green foliage or plants
green—eyed \'grē-'nīd\ *adj* : JEALOUS
green·gro·cer \'grēn-ˌgrō-sər\ *n* : a retailer of fresh vegetables and fruit
green·horn \-ˌhòrn\ *n* : an inexperienced person; *also* : NEWCOMER
green·house \-ˌhaùs\ *n* : a glass structure for the growing of tender plants
greenhouse effect *n* : warming of a planet's atmosphere that occurs when the sun's radiation passes through the atmosphere, is absorbed by the planet, and is reradiated as radiation of longer wavelength that can be absorbed by atmospheric gases
green manure *n* : an herbaceous crop (as clover) plowed under when green to enrich the soil
green onion *n* : a young onion pulled before the bulb has enlarged and used esp. in salads; *also* : SCALLION

green pepper *n* : a sweet pepper before it turns red at maturity
green·room \'grēn-ˌrüm, -ˌrùm\ *n* : a room in a theater or concert hall where actors or musicians relax before, between, or after appearances
green·sward \-ˌswòrd\ *n* : turf that is green with growing grass
green thumb *n* : an unusual ability to make plants grow
Green·wich mean time \'gri-nij-, 'gre-, -nich-\ *n* [*Greenwich*, England] : the time of the meridian of Greenwich used as the basis of worldwide standard time
Greenwich time *n* : GREENWICH MEAN TIME
green·wood \'grēn-ˌwùd\ *n* : a forest green with foliage
greet \'grēt\ *vb* **1** : to address with expressions of kind wishes **2** : to meet or react to in a specified manner **3** : to be perceived by — **greet·er** *n*
greet·ing *n* **1** : a salutation on meeting **2** *pl* : best wishes : REGARDS
greeting card *n* : a card that bears a message usu. sent on a special occasion
gre·gar·i·ous \gri-'gar-ē-əs\ *adj* [L *gregarius* of a flock or herd, fr. *greg-, grex* flock, herd] **1** : SOCIAL, COMPANIONABLE **2** : tending to flock together — **gre·gar·i·ous·ly** *adv* — **gre·gar·i·ous·ness** *n*
Gre·gor·i·an calendar \gri-'gōr-ē-ən-\ *n* : a calendar introduced by Pope Gregory XIII in 1582 and adopted in Great Britain and the American colonies in 1752
grem·lin \'grem-lən\ *n* : a cause of error or equipment malfunction conceived of as a small gnome
gre·nade \grə-'nād\ *n* [MF, pomegranate, fr. LL *granuta*, fr. L, fem. of *granatus* seedy, fr. *granum* grain] : a small bomb that is thrown by hand or launched (as by a rifle)
gren·a·dier \ˌgre-nə-'dir\ *n* : a member of a European regiment formerly armed with grenades
gren·a·dine \ˌgre-nə-'dēn, 'gre-nə-ˌdēn\ *n* : a syrup flavored with pomegranates and used in mixed drinks
grew *past of* GROW
grey *var of* GRAY
grey·hound \'grā-ˌhaùnd\ *n* : any of a breed of tall slender dogs noted for speed and keen sight

greyhound

grid \'grid\ *n* **1** : GRATING **2** : a network of conductors for distributing electric power **3** : a network of horizontal and perpendicular lines (as for locating points on a map) **4** : GRIDIRON 2; *also* : FOOTBALL
grid·dle \'grid-ᵊl\ *n* : a flat usu. metal surface for cooking food

\ə\abut \ᵊ\kitten \ər\further \a\ash \ā\ace \ä\mop, mar
\aù\out \ch\chin \e\bet \ē\easy \g\go \i\hit \ī\ice \j\job
\ŋ\sing \ō\go \ò\law \òi\boy \th\thin \th̲\the \ü\loot \ù\foot
\y\yet \zh\vision *see also* Pronunciation Symbols page

griddle cake *n* : PANCAKE
grid·iron \'grid-ˌīrn, -ˌī-ərn\ *n* 1 : a grate for broiling food 2 : a football field
grid·lock \-ˌläk\ *n* : a traffic jam in which an intersection is so blocked that vehicles cannot move
grief \'grēf\ *n* 1 : emotional distress caused by or as if by bereavement; *also* : a cause of such distress 2 : MISHAP 3 : DISASTER
griev·ance \'grē-vəns\ *n* 1 : a cause of distress affording reason for complaint or resistance 2 : COMPLAINT
grieve \'grēv\ *vb* **grieved; griev·ing** [ME *greven*, fr. OF *grever*, fr. L *gravare* to burden, fr. *gravis* heavy, grave] 1 : to cause grief or sorrow to : DISTRESS 2 : to feel grief : SORROW
griev·ous \'grē-vəs\ *adj* 1 : causing suffering, grief, or sorrow : SEVERE ⟨a ~ wound⟩ 2 : OPPRESSIVE, ONEROUS 3 : SERIOUS, GRAVE — **griev·ous·ly** *adv*
¹**grill** \'gril\ *vb* 1 : to broil on a grill; *also* : to fry or toast on a griddle 2 : to question intensely
²**grill** *n* 1 : a cooking utensil of parallel bars on which food is grilled 2 : an informal restaurant
grille *or* **grill** \'gril\ *n* : a grating that forms a barrier or screen
grill·work \'gril-ˌwərk\ *n* : work constituting or resembling a grille
grim \'grim\ *adj* **grim·mer; grim·mest** 1 : CRUEL, FIERCE 2 : harsh and forbidding in appearance 3 : ghastly or repellent in character 4 : RELENTLESS — **grim·ly** *adv* — **grim·ness** *n*
gri·mace \'gri-məs, gri-ˈmās\ *n* : a facial expression usu. of disgust or disapproval — **grimace** *vb*
grime \'grīm\ *n* : soot, smut, or dirt adhering to or embedded in a surface; *also* : accumulated dirtiness and disorder — **grimy** *adj*
grin \'grin\ *vb* **grinned; grin·ning** : to draw back the lips so as to show the teeth esp. in amusement — **grin** *n*
¹**grind** \'grīnd\ *vb* **ground** \'graund\; **grind·ing** 1 : to reduce to small particles 2 : to wear down, polish, or sharpen by friction 3 : OPPRESS 4 : to press with a grating noise : GRIT ⟨~ the teeth⟩ 5 : to operate or produce by turning a crank 6 : DRUDGE; *esp* : to study hard 7 : to move with difficulty or friction ⟨gears ~ing⟩
²**grind** *n* 1 : dreary monotonous labor, routine, or study 2 : one who works or studies excessively
grind·er \'grīn-dər\ *n* 1 : MOLAR 2 *pl* : TEETH 3 : one that grinds 4 : SUBMARINE 2
grind·stone \'grīnd-ˌstōn\ *n* : a flat circular stone of natural sandstone that revolves on an axle and is used for grinding, shaping, or smoothing
¹**grip** \'grip\ *vb* **gripped; grip·ping** 1 : to seize or hold firmly 2 : to hold the interest of strongly
²**grip** *n* 1 : GRASP; *also* : strength in gripping 2 : a firm tenacious hold 3 : UNDERSTANDING 4 : a device for gripping 5 : TRAVELING BAG
gripe \'grīp\ *vb* **griped; grip·ing** 1 : IRRITATE, VEX 2 : to cause or experience spasmodic pains in the bowels 3 : COMPLAIN — **gripe** *n*
grippe \'grip\ *n* : INFLUENZA
gris–gris \'grē-ˌgrē\ *n, pl* **gris–gris** \-ˌgrēz\ [F] : an amulet or incantation used chiefly by people of black African ancestry
gris·ly \'griz-lē\ *adj* **gris·li·er; -est** : HORRIBLE, GRUESOME
grist \'grist\ *n* : grain to be ground or already ground
gris·tle \'gri-səl\ *n* : CARTILAGE — **gris·tly** \'gris-lē\ *adj*
grist·mill \'grist-ˌmil\ *n* : a mill for grinding grain
¹**grit** \'grit\ *n* 1 : a hard sharp granule (as of sand); *also* : material composed of such granules 2 : unyielding courage — **grit·ty** *adj*
²**grit** *vb* **grit·ted; grit·ting** : GRIND, GRATE
grits \'grits\ *n pl* : coarsely ground hulled grain ⟨hominy ~⟩
griz·zled \'gri-zəld\ *adj* : streaked or mixed with gray

griz·zly \'griz-lē\ *adj* **griz·zli·er; -est´** : GRIZZLED
grizzly bear *n* : a large pale-coated bear of western No. America
gro *abbr* gross
groan \'grōn\ *vb* 1 : MOAN 2 : to make a harsh sound under sudden or prolonged strain ⟨the chair ~ed under his weight⟩ — **groan** *n*
groat \'grōt\ *n* : an old British coin worth four pennies
gro·cer \'grō-sər\ *n* [ME, fr. MF *grossier* wholesaler, fr. *gros* coarse, wholesale, fr. L *grossus* coarse] : a dealer esp. in staple foodstuffs — **gro·cery** \'grōs-rē, 'grōsh-, 'grō-sə-\ *n*
grog \'gräg\ *n* [*Old Grog*, nickname of Edward Vernon †1757 Eng. admiral responsible for diluting the sailors' rum] : alcoholic liquor; *esp* : liquor (as rum) mixed with water
grog·gy \'grä-gē\ *adj* **grog·gi·er; -est** : weak and unsteady on the feet or in action — **grog·gi·ly** \-gə-lē\ *adv* — **grog·gi·ness** \-gē-nəs\ *n*
groin \'groin\ *n* 1 : the juncture of the lower abdomen and inner part of the thigh; *also* : the region of this juncture 2 : the curved line or rib on a ceiling along which two vaults meet
grom·met \'grä-mət, 'grə-\ *n* 1 : a ring of rope 2 : an eyelet of firm material to strengthen or protect an opening
¹**groom** \'grüm, 'grum\ *n* 1 : a person responsible for the care of horses 2 : BRIDEGROOM
²**groom** *vb* 1 : to clean and care for (an animal) 2 : to make neat or attractive 3 : PREPARE
grooms·man \'grümz-mən, 'grumz-\ *n* : a male friend who attends a bridegroom at his wedding
groove \'grüv\ *n* 1 : a long narrow channel 2 : a fixed routine — **groove** *vb*
groovy \'grü-vē\ *adj* **groov·i·er; -est** 1 : EXCELLENT 2 : HIP
grope \'grōp\ *vb* **groped; grop·ing** 1 : to feel about or search for blindly or uncertainly ⟨~ for the right word⟩ 2 : to feel one's way by groping
gros·beak \'grōs-ˌbēk\ *n* : any of several finches of Europe or America with large stout conical bills
gro·schen \'grō-shən\ *n, pl* **groschen** — see *schilling* at MONEY table
gros·grain \'grō-ˌgrān\ *n* [F *gros grain* coarse texture] : a silk or rayon fabric with crosswise cotton ribs
¹**gross** \'grōs\ *adj* 1 : glaringly noticeable 2 : OUT-AND-OUT, UTTER 3 : BIG, BULKY; *esp* : excessively fat 4 : GENERAL, BROAD 5 : consisting of an overall total exclusive of deductions ⟨~ earnings⟩ 6 : CARNAL, EARTHY ⟨~ pleasures⟩ 7 : UNREFINED; *also* : crudely vulgar 8 : lacking knowledge — **gross·ly** *adv* — **gross·ness** *n*
²**gross** *n* : an overall total exclusive of deductions — **gross** *vb*
³**gross** *n, pl* **gross** : a total of 12 dozen things ⟨a ~ of pencils⟩
gross national product *n* : the total value of the goods and services produced in a nation during a year
gro·szy \'grō-shē\ *n, pl* **groszy** — see *zloty* at MONEY table
grot \'grät\ *n* : GROTTO
gro·tesque \grō-ˈtesk\ *adj* 1 : FANCIFUL, BIZARRE 2 : absurdly incongruous 3 : ECCENTRIC — **gro·tesque·ly** *adv*
grot·to \'grä-tō\ *n, pl* **grottoes** *also* **grottos** 1 : CAVE 2 : an artificial cavelike structure
grouch \'grauch\ *n* 1 : a fit of bad temper 2 : an habitually irritable or complaining person — **grouch** *vb* — **grouchy** *adj*
¹**ground** \'graund\ *n* 1 : the bottom of a body of water 2 *pl* : sediment at the bottom of a liquid 3 : a basis for belief, action, or argument 4 : BACKGROUND 5 : the surface of the earth; *also* : SOIL 6 : an area with a particular use ⟨fishing ~s⟩ 7 *pl* : the area about and belonging to a building 8 : a conductor that makes electrical connection with the earth — **ground·less** *adj*

²**ground** *vb* **1** : to bring to or place on the ground **2** : to run or cause to run aground **3** : to provide a reason or justification for **4** : to furnish with a foundation of knowledge **5** : to connect electrically with a ground **6** : to restrict to the ground; *also* : prohibit from some activity

³**ground** *past and past part of* GRIND

ground ball *n* : a batted baseball that rolls or bounces along the ground

ground cover *n* : low plants that grow over and cover the soil; *also* : a plant suitable for use as ground cover

ground·er \'graùn-dər\ *n* : GROUND BALL

ground·hog \'graùnd-ˌhȯg, -ˌhäg\ *n* : WOODCHUCK

ground·ling \'graùnd-liŋ\ *n* : a spectator in the pit of an Elizabethan theater

ground rule *n* **1** : a sports rule adopted to modify play on a particular field, court, or course **2** : a rule of procedure

ground squirrel *n* : any of various burrowing rodents of No. America and Eurasia that are related to the squirrels and live in colonies in open areas

ground swell *n* **1** : a broad deep ocean swell caused by an often distant gale or earthquake **2** *usu* **ground·swell** : a rapid spontaneous growth (as of political opinion)

ground·wa·ter \'graùnd-ˌwȯ-tər, -ˌwä-\ *n* : water within the earth that supplies wells and springs

ground·work \-ˌwərk\ *n* : FOUNDATION, BASIS

ground zero *n* : the point above, below, or at which a nuclear explosion occurs

¹**group** \'grüp\ *n* **1** : a number of individuals related by a common factor (as physical association, community of interests, or blood) **2** : a combination of atoms commonly found together in a molecule ⟨a methyl ∼⟩

²**group** *vb* : to associate in groups : CLUSTER, AGGREGATE

grou·per \'grü-pər\ *n, pl* **groupers** *also* **grouper** : any of numerous large solitary bottom fishes of warm seas

group·ie \'grü-pē\ *n* : a fan of a rock group who usu. follows the group around on concert tours; *also* : ENTHUSIAST, FAN

group therapy *n* : therapy in the presence of a therapist in which several patients discuss their personal problems

¹**grouse** \'graùs\ *n, pl* **grouse** *or* **grouses** : any of numerous ground-dwelling game birds that have feathered legs and are usu. of reddish brown or other protective color

²**grouse** *vb* **groused; grous·ing** : COMPLAIN, GRUMBLE

grout \'graùt\ *n* : material (as mortar) used for filling spaces — **grout** *vb*

grove \'grōv\ *n* : a small wood usu. without underbrush

grov·el \'grä-vəl, 'grə-\ *vb* **-eled** *or* **-elled; -el·ing** *or* **-el·ling 1** : to creep or lie with the body prostrate in fear or humility **2** : to abase oneself

grow \'grō\ *vb* **grew** \'grü\; **grown** \'grōn\; **grow·ing 1** : to spring up and develop to maturity **2** : to be able to grow : THRIVE **3** : to take on some relation through or as if through growth ⟨tree limbs *grown* together⟩ **4** : INCREASE, EXPAND **5** : to develop from a parent source **6** : BECOME **7** : to have an increasing influence **8** : to cause to grow — **grow·er** *n*

growl \'graùl\ *vb* **1** : RUMBLE **2** : to utter a deep throaty sound **3** : GRUMBLE — **growl** *n*

grown–up \'grō-ˌnəp\ *adj* : not childish : ADULT — **grown–up** *n*

growth \'grōth\ *n* **1** : stage or condition attained in growing **2** : a process of growing esp. through progressive development or increase **3** : a result or product of growing ⟨a fine ∼ of hair⟩; *also* : an abnormal mass of tissue (as a tumor)

¹**grub** \'grəb\ *vb* **grubbed; grub·bing 1** : to clear or root out by digging **2** : to dig in the ground usu. for a hidden object **3** : to search about

²**grub** *n* **1** : a soft thick wormlike insect larva ⟨beetle ∼s⟩ **2** : DRUDGE; *also* : a slovenly person **3** : FOOD

grub·by \'grə-bē\ *adj* **grub·bi·er; -est** : DIRTY, SLOVENLY — **grub·bi·ness** \-bē-nəs\ *n*

grub·stake \'grəb-ˌstāk\ *n* : supplies or funds furnished a mining prospector in return for a share in his finds

¹**grudge** \'grəj\ *vb* **grudged; grudg·ing** : to be reluctant to give : BEGRUDGE

²**grudge** *n* : a feeling of deep-seated resentment or ill will

gru·el \'grü-əl\ *n* : a thin porridge

gru·el·ing *or* **gru·el·ling** \'grü-liŋ, 'grü-ə-\ *adj* : requiring extreme effort : EXHAUSTING

grue·some \'grü-səm\ *adj* [fr. earlier *growsome*, fr. E dial. *grow, grue* to shiver] : inspiring horror or repulsion

gruff \'grəf\ *adj* **1** : rough in speech or manner **2** : being deep and harsh : HOARSE — **gruff·ly** *adv*

grum·ble \'grəm-bəl\ *vb* **grum·bled; grum·bling 1** : to mutter in discontent **2** : GROWL, RUMBLE — **grum·bler** *n*

grumpy \'grəm-pē\ *adj* **grump·i·er; -est** : moodily cross : SURLY — **grump·i·ly** \-pə-lē\ *adv* — **grump·i·ness** \-pē-nəs\ *n*

grun·gy \'grən-jē\ *adj* **grun·gi·er; -est** : shabby or dirty in character or condition

grun·ion \'grən-yən\ *n* : a fish of the California coast which comes inshore to spawn at nearly full moon

grunt \'grənt\ *n* : a deep throaty sound (as that of a hog) — **grunt** *vb*

GSA *abbr* **1** General Services Administration **2** Girl Scouts of America

G suit *n* [*gravity suit*] : a suit for a pilot or astronaut designed to counteract the physiological effects of acceleration

GSUSA *abbr* Girl Scouts of the United States of America

gt *abbr* great

Gt Brit *abbr* Great Britain

gtd *abbr* guaranteed

GU *abbr* Guam

gua·ca·mo·le \ˌgwä-kə-'mō-lē\ *n* [MexSp] : mashed and seasoned avocado

gua·nine \'gwä-ˌnēn\ *n* : a purine base that codes genetic information in the molecular chain of DNA and RNA

gua·no \'gwä-nō\ *n* [Sp, fr. Quechua (a South American Indian language) *wanu* fertilizer, dung] : a substance composed chiefly of the excrement of seabirds and used as a fertilizer

gua·ra·ni \ˌgwär-ə-'nē\ *n, pl* **guaranies** *also* **guaranis** — see MONEY table

¹**guar·an·tee** \ˌgar-ən-'tē\ *n* **1** : GUARANTOR **2** : GUARANTY **1 3** : an agreement by which one person undertakes to secure another in the possession or enjoyment of something **4** : an assurance of the quality of or of the length of use to be expected from a product offered for sale **5** : GUARANTY **4**

²**guarantee** *vb* **-teed; -tee·ing 1** : to undertake to answer for the debt, failure to perform, or faulty performance of (another) **2** : to undertake an obligation to establish, perform, or continue **3** : to give security to

guar·an·tor \ˌgar-ən-'tȯr\ *n* : one who gives a guarantee

¹**guar·an·ty** \'gar-ən-tē\ *n, pl* **-ties 1** : an undertaking to answer for another's failure to pay a debt or perform a duty **2** : GUARANTEE **3 3** : GUARANTOR **4** : PLEDGE, SECURITY

²**guaranty** *vb* **-tied; -ty·ing** : GUARANTEE

¹**guard** \'gärd\ *n* **1** : a person or a body of persons on sentinel duty **2** *pl* : troops assigned to protect a sovereign

\ə\abut \ᵊ\kitten \ər\further \a\ash \ā\ace \ä\mop, mar
\aù\out \ch\chin \e\bet \ē\easy \g\go \i\hit \ī\ice \j\job
\ŋ\sing \ō\go \ȯ\law \ȯi\boy \th\thin \th\the \ü\loot \ù\foot
\y\yet \zh\vision *see also* Pronunciation Symbols page

3 : a defensive position (as in boxing) **4** : the act or duty of protecting or defending **5** : PROTECTION **6** : a protective or safety device **7** : a football lineman playing between center and tackle; *also* : a basketball player stationed toward the rear — **on guard** : WATCHFUL, ALERT

²**guard** *vb* **1** : PROTECT, DEFEND **2** : to watch over **3** : to be on guard

guard·house \\'gärd-ˌhaus\ *n* **1** : a building occupied by a guard or used as a headquarters by soldiers on guard duty **2** : a military jail

guard·ian \\'gär-dē-ən\ *n* **1** : CUSTODIAN **2** : one who has the care of the person or property of another — **guardian·ship** *n*

guard·room \\'gärd-ˌrüm\ *n* **1** : a room used by a military guard while on duty **2** : a room where military prisoners are confined

guards·man \\'gärdz-mən\ *n* : a member of a military body called *guard* or *guards*

Gua·te·ma·lan \ˌgwä-tə-'mä-lən\ *n* : a native or inhabitant of Guatemala — **Guatemalan** *adj*

gua·va \\'gwä-və\ *n* : the sweet yellow or pink acid fruit of a shrubby tropical American tree used esp. for making jam and jelly; *also* : the tree

gu·ber·na·to·ri·al \ˌgü-bər-nə-'tōr-ē-əl\ *adj* : of or relating to a governor

guer·don \\'gərd-ᵊn\ *n* : REWARD, RECOMPENSE

Guern·sey \\'gərn-zē\ *n, pl* **Guernseys** : any of a breed of fawn and white dairy cattle that produce rich yellowish milk

guer·ril·la *or* **gue·ril·la** \gə-'ri-lə\ *n* [Sp *guerrilla*, fr. dim. of *guerra* war, of Gmc origin] : one who engages in irregular warfare esp. as a member of an independent unit

guess \\'ges\ *vb* **1** : to form an opinion from little or no evidence **2** : BELIEVE, SUPPOSE **3** : to conjecture correctly about : DISCOVER — **guess** *n*

guest \\'gest\ *n* **1** : a person to whom hospitality (as of a house or a club) is extended **2** : a patron of a commercial establishment (as a hotel) **3** : a person not a regular member of a cast who appears on a program

guf·faw \(ˌ)gə-'fȯ\ *n* : a loud burst of laughter — **guffaw** *vb*

guid·ance \\'gīd-ᵊns\ *n* **1** : the act or process of guiding **2** : ADVICE, DIRECTION

¹**guide** \\'gīd\ *n* **1** : one who leads or directs another's course **2** : one who shows and explains points of interest **3** : something that provides guiding information; *also* : SIGNPOST **4** : a device to direct the motion of something

²**guide** *vb* **guid·ed; guid·ing 1** : to act as a guide to **2** : MANAGE, DIRECT **3** : to superintend the training of — **guid·able** \\'gī-də-bəl\ *adj*

guide·book \\'gīd-ˌbuk\ *n* : a book of information for travelers

guided missile *n* : a missile whose course may be altered during flight

guide dog *n* : a dog trained to lead the blind

guide·line \\'gīd-ˌlīn\ *n* : an indication or outline of policy or conduct

guide word *n* : a term at the head of a page of an alphabetical reference work that indicates the alphabetically first and last words on that page

gui·don \\'gī-ˌdän, 'gīd-ᵊn\ *n* : a small flag (as of a military unit)

guild \\'gild\ *n* : an association of people with common aims and interests; *esp* : a medieval association of merchants or craftsmen — **guild·hall** \-ˌhȯl\ *n*

guil·der \\'gil-dər\ *n* : GULDEN

guile \\'gīl\ *n* : deceitful cunning : DUPLICITY — **guileful** *adj* — **guile·less·ness** *n*

guil·lo·tine \\'gi-lə-ˌtēn, ˌgē-ə-'tēn\ *n* [F, fr. Joseph *Guil-*

lotin †1814 Fr. physician] : a machine for beheading persons — **guillotine** *vb*

guilt \\'gilt\ *n* **1** : the fact of having committed an offense esp. against the law **2** : BLAMEWORTHINESS **3** : a feeling of responsibility for wrongdoing — **guilt·less** *adj*

guilty \\'gil-tē\ *adj* **guilt·i·er; -est 1** : having committed a breach of conduct or a crime **2** : suggesting or involving guilt **3** : aware of or suffering from guilt — **guilt·i·ly** \-tə-lē\ *adv* — **guilt·i·ness** \-tē-nəs\ *n*

guin·ea \\'gi-nē\ *n* **1** : a British gold coin no longer issued worth 21 shillings **2** : a unit of value equal to 21 shillings

guinea fowl *n* : a gray and white spotted West African bird related to the pheasants and widely raised for food; *also* : any of several related birds

guinea hen *n* : a female guinea fowl; *also* : GUINEA FOWL

Guin·ean \\'gi-nē-ən\ *n* : a native or inhabitant of Guinea — **Guinean** *adj*

guinea pig *n* **1** : a small stocky short-eared and nearly tailless So. American rodent often kept as a pet or used in lab research **2** : a subject of research or testing

guise \\'gīz\ *n* **1** : a form or style of dress : COSTUME **2** : external appearance : SEMBLANCE

gui·tar \gi-'tär\ *n* : a musical instrument with usu. six strings plucked with a pick or with the fingers

gulch \\'gəlch\ *n* : RAVINE

gul·den \\'gul-dən, 'gul-\ *n, pl* **guldens** *or* **gulden** — see MONEY table

gulf \\'gəlf\ *n* [ME *goulf*, fr. MF *golfe*, fr. It *golfo*, fr. LL *colpus*, fr. Gk *kolpos* bosom, gulf] **1** : a part of an ocean or sea partly or mostly surrounded by land **2** : ABYSS, CHASM **3** : a wide separation

¹**gull** \\'gəl\ *n* : any of numerous mostly white or gray long-winged web-footed seabirds

²**gull** *vb* : to make a dupe of : DECEIVE — **gull·ible** \\'gə-lə-bəl\ *adj*

³**gull** *n* : DUPE

gul·let \\'gə-lət\ *n* : ESOPHAGUS; *also* : THROAT

gul·ly \\'gə-lē\ *n, pl* **gullies** : a trench worn in the earth by and often filled with running water after rains

gulp \\'gəlp\ *vb* **1** : to swallow hurriedly or greedily **2** : SUPPRESS ⟨~ down a sob⟩ **3** : to catch the breath as if in taking a long drink — **gulp** *n*

¹**gum** \\'gəm\ *n* : the oral tissue that surrounds the necks of the teeth

²**gum** *n* **1** : a sticky plant exudate; *esp* : one that hardens on drying **2** : a sticky substance **3** : a preparation usu. of a plant gum sweetened and flavored and used for chewing — **gum·my** *adj*

gum arabic *n* : a water-soluble gum obtained from several acacias and used esp. in making inks, adhesives, confections, and pharmaceuticals

gum·bo \\'gəm-bō\ *n* [AmerF *gombo*, of Bantu origin] : a rich thick soup usu. thickened with okra

gum·drop \\'gəm-ˌdräp\ *n* : a candy made usu. from corn syrup with gelatin and coated with sugar crystals

gump·tion \\'gəmp-shən\ *n* **1** : shrewd common sense **2** : ENTERPRISE, INITIATIVE

gum·shoe \\'gəm-ˌshü\ *n* : DETECTIVE — **gumshoe** *vb*

¹**gun** \\'gən\ *n* **1** : CANNON **2** : a portable firearm **3** : a discharge of a gun **4** : something suggesting a gun in shape or function **5** : THROTTLE — **gunned** \\'gənd\ *adj*

²**gun** *vb* **gunned; gun·ning 1** : to hunt with a gun **2** : SHOOT **3** : to open up the throttle of so as to increase speed

gun·boat \\'gən-ˌbōt\ *n* : a small lightly armed ship for use in shallow waters

gun·fight \-ˌfīt\ *n* : a duel with guns — **gun·fight·er** *n*

gun·fire \-ˌfīr\ *n* : the firing of guns

gung ho \\'gəŋ-'hō\ *adj* [*Gung ho!*, motto (taken to mean "work together") adopted by certain U.S. marines in World War II, fr. Chin *gōnghé*, short for *Zhōngguó Gōngyè Hézuò Shè* Chinese Industrial Cooperatives Society] : extremely zealous or enthusiastic

gun·man \-mən\ *n* : a man armed with a gun; *esp* : a professional killer

gun·ner \'gə-nər\ *n* **1** : a soldier or airman who operates or aims a gun **2** : one who hunts with a gun

gun·nery \'gə-nə-rē\ *n* : the use of guns; *esp* : the science of the flight of projectiles and effective use of guns

gunnery sergeant *n* : a noncommissioned officer in the marine corps ranking next below a first sergeant

gun·ny·sack \'gə-nē-ˌsak\ *n* : a sack made of a coarse heavy fabric (as burlap)

gun·point \'gən-ˌpȯint\ *n* : the muzzle of a gun — **at gunpoint** : under a threat of death by being shot

gun·pow·der \-ˌpau̇-dər\ *n* : an explosive powder used in guns and blasting

gun·shot \-ˌshät\ *n* **1** : shot fired from a gun **2** : the range of a gun ⟨within ∼⟩

gun–shy \-ˌshī\ *adj* **1** : afraid of a loud noise **2** : markedly distrustful

gun·sling·er \-ˌsliŋ-ər\ *n* : a skilled gunman esp. in the old West

gun·smith \-ˌsmith\ *n* : one who designs, makes, or repairs firearms

gun·wale *also* **gun·nel** \'gən-ᵊl\ *n* : the upper edge of a ship's or boat's side

gup·py \'gə-pē\ *n, pl* **guppies** [R.J.L. *Guppy* †1916 Trinidadian naturalist] : a small brightly colored tropical fish

gur·gle \'gər-gəl\ *vb* **gur·gled; gur·gling** : to make a sound like that of an irregularly flowing or gently splashing liquid — **gurgle** *n*

Gur·kha \'gu̇r-kə, 'gər-\ *n* : a soldier from Nepal in the British or Indian army

gur·ney \'gər-nē\ *n, pl* **gurneys** : a wheeled cot or stretcher

gu·ru \'gu̇r-ü\ *n, pl* **gurus** [Hindi *gurū*, fr. Sanskrit *guru*, fr. *guru*, adj., heavy, venerable] **1** : a personal religious and spiritual teacher in Hinduism **2** : a teacher in matters of fundamental concern **3** : EXPERT ⟨a fitness ∼⟩

gush \'gəsh\ *vb* **1** : to issue or pour forth copiously or violently : SPOUT **2** : to make an effusive display of affection or enthusiasm

gush·er \'gə-shər\ *n* : one that gushes; *esp* : an oil well with a large natural flow

gushy \'gə-shē\ *adj* **gush·i·er; -est** : marked by effusive sentimentality

gus·set \'gə-sət\ *n* : a triangular insert (as in a seam of a sleeve) to give width or strength — **gusset** *vb*

gus·sy up \'gə-sē-\ *vb* : to dress up

¹**gust** \'gəst\ *n* **1** : a sudden brief rush of wind **2** : a sudden outburst : SURGE — **gusty** *adj*

²**gust** *vb* : to blow in gusts

gus·ta·to·ry \'gəs-tə-ˌtōr-ē\ *adj* : relating to or associated with the sense of taste

gus·to \'gəs-tō\ *n, pl* **gustoes** : enthusiastic enjoyment; *also* : VITALITY 4

¹**gut** \'gət\ *n* **1** *pl* : BOWELS, ENTRAILS **2** : the alimentary canal or a part of it (as the intestine); *also* : BELLY, ABDOMEN **3** *pl* : the inner essential parts **4** *pl* : COURAGE, PLUCK

²**gut** *vb* **gut·ted; gut·ting 1** : EVISCERATE **2** : to destroy the inside of

gutsy \'gət-sē\ *adj* **guts·i·er; -est** : marked by courage and determination

gut·ter \'gə-tər\ *n* : a groove or channel for carrying off esp. rainwater

gut·ter·snipe \-ˌsnīp\ *n* : a street urchin

gut·tur·al \'gə-tə-rəl\ *adj* **1** : sounded in the throat **2** : being or marked by an utterance that is strange, unpleasant, or disagreeable — **guttural** *n*

gut·ty \'gə-tē\ *adj* **gut·ti·er; -est 1** : GUTSY **2** : having a vigorous challenging quality

gut–wrench·ing \'gət-ˌren-chiŋ\ *adj* : causing emotional anguish

¹**guy** \'gī\ *n* : a rope, chain, or rod attached to something as a brace or guide

²**guy** *vb* : to steady or reinforce with a guy

³**guy** *n* : MAN, FELLOW; *also, pl* : PERSONS ⟨all the ∼s came⟩

⁴**guy** *vb* : to make fun of : RIDICULE

Guy·a·nese \ˌgī-ə-'nēz\ *n, pl* **Guyanese** : a native or inhabitant of Guyana — **Guyanese** *adj*

guz·zle \'gə-zəl\ *vb* **guz·zled; guz·zling** : to drink greedily

gym \'jim\ *n* : GYMNASIUM

gym·kha·na \jim-'kä-nə\ *n* : a meet featuring sports contests; *esp* : a contest of automobile-driving skill

gym·na·si·um *for 1* jim-'nä-zē-əm, -zhəm, *for 2* gim-'nä-zē-əm\ *n, pl* **-na·si·ums** *or* **-na·sia** \-'nä-zē-ə, -'nä-zhə; -'nä-zē-ə\ [L, exercise ground, school, fr. Gk *gymnasion*, fr. *gymnazein* to exercise naked, fr. *gymnos* naked] **1** : a room or building for indoor sports **2** : a European secondary school that prepares students for the university

gym·nas·tics \jim-'nas-tiks\ *n* : a competitive sport developed from physical exercises designed to demonstrate strength, balance, and body control — **gym·nast** \'jim-ˌnast\ *n* — **gym·nas·tic** *adj*

gym·no·sperm \'jim-nə-ˌspərm\ *n* : any of a class or subdivision of woody vascular seed plants (as conifers) that produce naked seeds not enclosed in an ovary

gyn *or* **gynecol** *abbr* gynecology

gy·nae·col·o·gy *chiefly Brit var of* GYNECOLOGY

gy·ne·col·o·gy \ˌgī-nə-'kä-lə-jē\ *n* : a branch of medicine dealing with the diseases and hygiene of women — **gy·ne·co·log·ic** \-ni-kə-'lä-jik\ *or* **gy·ne·co·log·i·cal** \-ji-kəl\ *adj* — **gy·ne·col·o·gist** \-nə-'kä-lə-jist\ *n*

gyp \'jip\ *n* **1** : CHEAT, SWINDLER **2** : FRAUD, SWINDLE — **gyp** *vb*

gyp·sum \'jip-səm\ *n* : a calcium-containing mineral used in making plaster of paris

Gyp·sy \'jip-sē\ *n, pl* **Gypsies** [by shortening & alter. fr. *Egyptian*] : a member of a traditionally traveling people coming orig. from India and living chiefly in Europe, Asia, and No. America; *also* : the language of the Gypsies

gypsy moth *n* : an Old World moth that was introduced into the U.S. where its caterpillar is a destructive defoliator of many trees

gy·rate \'jī-ˌrāt\ *vb* **gy·rat·ed; gy·rat·ing 1** : to revolve around a point or axis **2** : to oscillate with or as if with a circular or spiral motion — **gy·ra·tion** \jī-'rā-shən\ *n*

gyr·fal·con \'jər-ˌfal-kən, -ˌfȯl-\ *n* : an arctic falcon with several color forms that is the largest of all falcons

gy·ro \'jī-rō\ *n, pl* **gyros** : GYROSCOPE

gy·ro·scope \'jī-rō-ˌskōp\ *n* : a wheel or disk mounted to spin rapidly about an axis that is free to turn in various directions

Gy Sgt *abbr* gunnery sergeant

gyve \'jīv, 'gīv\ *n* : FETTER — **gyve** *vb*

H

¹**h** \ˈāch\ *n, pl* **h's** *or* **hs** \ˈā-chəz\ *often cap* : the 8th letter of the English alphabet

²**h** *abbr, often cap* **1** hard; hardness **2** heroin **3** hit **4** husband

H *symbol* hydrogen

¹**ha** \ˈhä\ *interj* — used esp. to express surprise or joy

²**ha** *abbr* hectare

Hab *abbr* Habacuc; Habakkuk

Ha·ba·cuc \ˈha-bə-ˌkək, hə-ˈba-kək\ *n* : HABAKKUK

Ha·bak·kuk \ˈha-bə-ˌkək, hə-ˈba-kək\ *n* — see BIBLE table

ha·ba·ne·ra \ˌhä-bə-ˈner-ə\ *n* [Sp *(danza) habanera*, lit., dance of Havana] : a Cuban dance in slow time; *also* : the music for this dance

ha·be·as cor·pus \ˈhä-bē-əs-ˈkȯr-pəs\ *n* [ME, fr. ML, lit., you should have the body (the opening words of the writ)] : a writ issued to bring a party before a court

hab·er·dash·er \ˈha-bər-ˌda-shər\ *n* : a dealer in men's clothing and accessories

hab·er·dash·ery \-ˌda-shə-rē\ *n, pl* **-er·ies 1** : goods sold by a haberdasher **2** : a haberdasher's shop

ha·bil·i·ment \hə-ˈbi-lə-mənt\ *n* **1** *pl* : TRAPPINGS, EQUIPMENT **2** : DRESS; *esp* : the dress characteristic of an occupation or occasion — usu. used in pl.

hab·it \ˈha-bət\ *n* **1** : DRESS, GARB **2** : BEARING, CONDUCT **3** : PHYSIQUE **4** : mental makeup **5** : a usual manner of behavior : CUSTOM **6** : a behavior pattern acquired by frequent repetition **7** : ADDICTION **8** : mode of growth or occurrence ⟨trees with a spreading ∼⟩

hab·it·able \ˈha-bə-tə-bəl\ *adj* : capable of being lived in — **hab·it·abil·i·ty** \ˌha-bə-tə-ˈbi-lə-tē\ *n*

hab·i·tat \ˈha-bə-ˌtat\ *n* [L, it inhabits] : the place or environment where a plant or animal naturally occurs

hab·i·ta·tion \ˌha-bə-ˈtā-shən\ *n* **1** : OCCUPANCY **2** : a dwelling place : RESIDENCE **3** : SETTLEMENT

hab·it-form·ing \ˈha-bət-ˌfȯr-miŋ\ *adj* : causing addiction : ADDICTIVE

ha·bit·u·al \hə-ˈbi-chə-wəl\ *adj* **1** : CUSTOMARY **2** : doing, practicing, or acting by force of habit **3** : inherent in an individual — **ha·bit·u·al·ly** *adv* — **ha·bit·u·al·ness** *n*

ha·bit·u·ate \hə-ˈbi-chə-ˌwāt\ *vb* **-at·ed; -at·ing 1** : ACCUSTOM **2** : to cause or undergo habituation

ha·bit·u·a·tion \hə-ˌbi-chə-ˈwā-shən\ *n* **1** : the process of making habitual **2** : psychological dependence on a drug after a period of use

ha·bi·tué *also* **ha·bi·tue** \hə-ˈbi-chə-ˌwā\ *n* [F] : one who may be regularly found in or at (as a place of entertainment)

ha·ci·en·da \ˌhä-sē-ˈen-də\ *n* **1** : a large estate in a Spanish-speaking country **2** : the main building of a farm or ranch

¹**hack** \ˈhak\ *vb* **1** : to cut or sever with repeated irregular blows **2** : to cough in a short dry manner **3** : to manage successfully; *also* : TOLERATE

²**hack** *n* **1** : an implement for hacking **2** : a short dry cough **3** : a hacking blow

³**hack** *n* **1** : a horse hired or used for varied work **2** : a horse worn out in service **3** : a light easy often 3-gaited saddle horse **4** : HACKNEY, TAXICAB **5** : a person who works solely for mercenary reasons; *esp* : a writer working solely for commercial success — **hack** *adj*

⁴**hack** *vb* : to operate a taxicab

hack·er \ˈha-kər\ *n* **1** : one that hacks; *also* : a person unskilled at something **2** : an expert at using a computer **3** : a person who illegally gains access to and sometimes tampers with information in a computer system

hack·ie \ˈha-kē\ *n* : a taxicab driver

hack·le \ˈha-kəl\ *n* **1** : one of the long feathers on the neck or back of a bird **2** *pl* : hairs (as on a dog's neck) that can be erected **3** *pl* : TEMPER, DANDER

hack·man \ˈhak-mən\ *n* : HACKIE

¹**hack·ney** \ˈhak-nē\ *n, pl* **hackneys 1** : a horse for riding or driving **2** : a carriage or automobile kept for hire

²**hackney** *vb* : to make trite

hack·neyed \ˈhak-nēd\ *adj* : lacking in freshness or originality

hack·saw \ˈhak-ˌsȯ\ *n* : a fine-tooth saw in a frame for cutting metal

hack·work \-ˌwərk\ *n* : work done on order usu. according to a formula

had *past and past part of* HAVE

had·dock \ˈha-dək\ *n, pl* **haddock** *also* **haddocks** : an Atlantic food fish usu. smaller than the related cod

Ha·des \ˈhā-(ˌ)dēz\ *n* **1** : the abode of the dead in Greek mythology **2** *often not cap* : HELL

haf·ni·um \ˈhaf-nē-əm\ *n* : a gray metallic chemical element — see ELEMENT table

haft \ˈhaft\ *n* : the handle of a weapon or tool

hag \ˈhag\ *n* **1** : an ugly or evil-looking old woman **2** : WITCH 1

Hag *abbr* Haggai

Hag·gai \ˈha-gē-ˌī, ˈha-ˌgī\ *n* — see BIBLE table

hag·gard \ˈha-gərd\ *adj* : having a worn or emaciated appearance **syn** careworn, wasted, drawn — **hag·gard·ly** *adv* — **hag·gard·ness** *n*

hag·gis \ˈha-gəs\ *n* : a traditionally Scottish dish made of the heart, liver, and lungs of a sheep or a calf minced with suet, onions, oatmeal, and seasonings

hag·gle \ˈha-gəl\ *vb* **hag·gled; hag·gling** : to argue in bargaining — **hag·gler** *n*

Ha·gi·og·ra·pha \ˌha-gē-ˈä-grə-fə, ˌhā-jē-\ *n pl* — see BIBLE table

ha·gi·og·ra·phy \ˌha-gē-ˈä-grə-fē, ˌhā-jē-\ *n* **1** : biography of saints or venerated persons **2** : idealizing or idolizing biography — **ha·gi·og·ra·pher** \-fər\ *n*

hai·ku \ˈhī-(ˌ)kü\ *n, pl* **haiku** : an unrhymed Japanese verse form of three lines containing usu. 5, 7, and 5 syllables respectively; *also* : a poem in this form

¹**hail** \ˈhāl\ *n* **1** : precipitation in the form of small lumps of ice **2** : something that gives the effect of falling hail

²**hail** *vb* **1** : to precipitate hail **2** : to pour down and strike like hail

³**hail** *interj* [ME, fr. ON *heill*, fr. *heill* healthy] — used to express acclamation

⁴**hail** *vb* **1** : SALUTE, GREET **2** : SUMMON

⁵**hail** *n* **1** : an expression of greeting, approval, or praise **2** : hearing distance

Hail Mary *n* : a salutation and prayer to the Virgin Mary

hail·stone \ˈhāl-ˌstōn\ *n* : a pellet of hail

hail·storm \-ˌstȯrm\ *n* : a storm accompanied by hail

hair \ˈhar\ *n* : a threadlike outgrowth esp. from the skin of a mammal; *also* : a covering or growth of hairs of an animal or a body part — **haired** \ˈhard\ *adj* — **hairless** *adj*

hair·breadth \ˈhar-ˌbredth\ *or* **hairs·breadth** \ˈharz-\ : a very small distance or margin

hair·brush \-ˌbrəsh\ *n* : a brush for the hair

hair·cloth \-ˌklȯth\ *n* : a stiff wiry fabric used esp. for upholstery

hair·cut \-ˌkət\ *n* : the act, process, or style of cutting and shaping the hair

hair·do \-ˌdü\ *n, pl* **hairdos** : a way of wearing the hair

hair·dress·er \-ˌdre-sər\ *n* : one who dresses or cuts hair — **hair·dress·ing** *n*

hair·line \-ˌlīn\ *n* 1 : a very thin line 2 : the outline of the hair on the head

hair·piece \-ˌpēs\ *n* 1 : supplementary hair (as a switch) used in some women's hairdos 2 : TOUPEE

hair·pin \-ˌpin\ *n* 1 : a U-shaped pin to hold the hair in place 2 : a sharp U-shaped turn in a road — **hairpin** *adj*

hair–rais·ing \ˈhar-ˌrā-ziŋ\ *adj* : causing terror or astonishment

hair·split·ter \-ˌspli-tər\ *n* : a person who makes excessively fine distinctions in reasoning — **hair·split·ting** \-ˌspli-tiŋ\ *adj or n*

hair·style \-ˌstīl\ *n* : HAIRDO —**hair·styl·ing** *n*

hair·styl·ist \-ˌstī-list\ *n* : HAIRDRESSER

hair–trigger *adj* : immediately responsive to the slightest stimulus

hairy \ˈhar-ē\ *adj* **hair·i·er; -est** 1 : covered with or as if with hair 2 : tending to cause nervous tension ⟨a few ∼ moments⟩ — **hair·i·ness** \-ē-nəs\ *n*

hairy woodpecker *n* : a common No. American woodpecker with a white back that is larger than the similarly marked downy woodpecker

Hai·tian \ˈhā-shən\ *n* : a native or inhabitant of Haiti — **Haitian** *adj*

hajj \ˈhaj\ *n* : the Islamic religious pilgrimage to Mecca

hajji \ˈha-jē\ *n* : one who has made a pilgrimage to Mecca — often used as a title

hake \ˈhāk\ *n* : any of several marine food fishes related to the cod

ha·la·la \hə-ˈlä-lə\ *n, pl* **halala** *or* **halalas** — see *riyal* at MONEY table

hal·berd \ˈhal-bərd, ˈhȯl-\ *also* **hal·bert** \-bərt\ *n* : a weapon esp. of the 15th and 16th centuries consisting of a battle-ax and pike on a long handle

hal·cy·on \ˈhal-sē-ən\ *adj* [Gk *halkyōn*, a mythical bird believed to nest at sea and to calm the waves] : CALM, PEACEFUL

¹**hale** \ˈhāl\ *adj* : free from defect, disease, or infirmity **syn** healthy, sound, robust, well

²**hale** *vb* **haled; hal·ing** 1 : HAUL, PULL 2 : to compel to go

ha·ler \ˈhä-lər\ *n, pl* **ha·le·ru** \ˈhä-lə-ˌrü\ — see *koruna* at MONEY table

¹**half** \ˈhaf, ˈhȧf\ *n, pl* **halves** \ˈhavz, ˈhȧvz\ 1 : either of two equal parts into which something is divisible 2 : one of a pair

²**half** *adj* 1 : being one of two equal parts 2 : amounting to nearly half 3 : PARTIAL, INCOMPLETE — **half** *adv*

half–and–half \ˌhaf-ən-ˈhaf, ˌhȧf-ən-ˈhȧf\ *n* : something that is half one thing and half another

half·back \ˈhaf-ˌbak, ˈhȧf-\ *n* 1 : a football back stationed on or near the flank 2 : a player stationed immediately behind the forward line

half–baked \-ˈbākt\ *adj* 1 : not thoroughly baked 2 : poorly planned; *also* : lacking common sense

half–breed \-ˌbrēd\ *n* : one of mixed racial descent — often used disparagingly — **half–breed** *adj*

half brother *n* : a brother related through one parent only

half–caste \ˈhaf-ˌkast, ˈhȧf-\ *n* : HALF-BREED — **half–caste** *adj*

half–dol·lar \-ˈdä-lər\ *n* 1 : a coin representing one half of a dollar 2 : the sum of fifty cents

half–heart·ed \-ˈhär-təd\ *adj* : lacking spirit or interest — **half·heart·ed·ly** *adv* — **half·heart·ed·ness** *n*

half–life \-ˌlīf\ *n* : the time required for half of something (as atoms or a drug) to undergo a process

half–mast \-ˈmast\ *n* : a point about halfway down from the top of a mast or staff

half note *n* : a musical note equal in time to one half of a whole note

half·pen·ny \ˈhāp-nē\ *n, pl* **half·pence** \ˈhā-pəns\ *or*

halfpennies : a formerly used British coin representing one half of a penny

half–pint \ˈhaf-ˌpīnt, ˈhȧf-\ *adj* : of less than average size — **half–pint** *n*

half sister *n* : a sister related through one parent only

half sole *n* : a shoe sole extending from the shank forward — **half–sole** *vb*

half–staff \ˈhaf-ˈstaf, ˈhȧf-\ *n* : HALF-MAST

half step *n* : a musical interval equivalent to one twelfth of an octave

half·time \ˈhaf-ˌtīm, ˈhȧf-\ *n* : an intermission between halves of a game

half–track \-ˌtrak\ *n* : a motor vehicle propelled by an endless chain-track drive system; *esp* : such a vehicle lightly armored for military use

half–truth \-ˌtrüth\ *n* : a statement that is only partially true; *esp* : one that deliberately mixes truth and falsehood

half·way \-ˈwā\ *adj* 1 : midway between two points 2 : PARTIAL 1 — **halfway** *adv*

half–wit \-ˌwit\ *n* : a foolish or imbecilic person — **half·wit·ted** \-ˈwi-təd\ *adj* — **half–wit·ted·ness** *n*

hal·i·but \ˈha-lə-bət\ *n, pl* **halibut** *also* **halibuts** [ME *halybutte*, fr. *haly, holy* holy + *butte* flatfish; fr. its being eaten on holy days] : a large edible marine flatfish

ha·lite \ˈha-ˌlīt, ˈhā-\ *n* : ROCK SALT

hal·i·to·sis \ˌha-lə-ˈtō-səs\ *n* : the condition of having fetid breath

hall \ˈhȯl\ *n* 1 : the residence of a medieval king or noble; *also* : the house of a landed proprietor 2 : a large public building 3 : a college or university building; *also* : DORMITORY 4 : LOBBY; *also* : CORRIDOR 5 : AUDITORIUM

hal·le·lu·jah \ˌha-lə-ˈlü-yə\ *interj* [Heb *hallĕlūyāh* praise (ye) the Lord] — used to express praise, joy, or thanks

hall·mark \ˈhȯl-ˌmärk\ *n* 1 : a mark put on an article to indicate origin, purity, or genuineness 2 : a distinguishing characteristic

hal·low \ˈha-lō\ *vb* 1 : CONSECRATE 2 : REVERE — **hallowed** \-lōd, -lə-wəd\ *adj*

Hal·low·een *also* **Hal·low·e'en** \ˌha-lə-ˈwēn, ˌhä-\ *n* : the evening of October 31 observed esp. by children in merrymaking and masquerading

hal·lu·ci·nate \hə-ˈlüs-ᵊn-ˌāt\ *vb* **-nat·ed; -nat·ing** : to have hallucinations or experience as a hallucination

hal·lu·ci·na·tion \hə-ˌlüs-ᵊn-ˈā-shən\ *n* : perception of objects with no reality due usu. to use of drugs or to disorder of the nervous system; *also* : something so perceived **syn** delusion, illusion, mirage — **hal·lu·ci·na·to·ry** \-ᵊn-ə-ˌtōr-ē\ *adj*

hal·lu·ci·no·gen \hə-ˈlüs-ᵊn-ə-jən\ *n* : a substance that induces hallucinations — **hal·lu·ci·no·gen·ic** \-ˌlüs-ᵊn-ə-ˈje-nik\ *adj or n*

hall·way \ˈhȯl-ˌwā\ *n* 1 : an entrance hall 2 : CORRIDOR

ha·lo \ˈhā-lō\ *n, pl* **halos** *or* **haloes** [L *halos,* fr. Gk *halōs* threshing floor, disk, halo] 1 : a circle of light appearing to surround a shining body (as the sun) 2 : the aura of glory surrounding an idealized person or thing

hal·o·gen \ˈha-lə-jən\ *n* : any of the five elements fluorine, chlorine, bromine, iodine, and astatine

¹**halt** \ˈhȯlt\ *adj* : LAME

²**halt** *n* : STOP

³**halt** *vb* 1 : to stop marching or traveling 2 : DISCONTINUE, END

¹**hal·ter** \ˈhȯl-tər\ *n* 1 : a rope or strap for leading or tying an animal; *also* : HEADSTALL 2 : NOOSE 3 : a brief blouse held in place by straps around the neck and across the back

²**halter** *vb* **hal·tered; hal·ter·ing** 1 : to catch with or as if

\ə\abut \ᵊ\kitten \ər\further \a\ash \ā\ace \ä\mop, mar \au̇\out \ch\chin \e\bet \ē\easy \g\go \i\hit \ī\ice \j\job \ŋ\sing \ō\go \ȯ\law \ȯi\boy \th\thin \th̲\the \ü\loot \u̇\foot \y\yet \zh\vision *see also* Pronunciation Symbols page with a halter; *also* : to put a halter on (as a horse) **2** : HANG **3** : IMPEDE, RESTRAIN

halt·ing \'hȯl-tiŋ\ *adj* : UNCERTAIN, FALTERING — **halt·ing·ly** *adv*

halve \'hav, 'hȧv\ *vb* **halved; halv·ing 1** : to divide into two equal parts **2** : to reduce to one half

halv·ers \'ha-vərz, 'hȧ-\ *n pl* : half shares : HALVES

halves *pl of* HALF

hal·yard \'hal-yərd\ *n* : a rope or tackle for hoisting and lowering (as sails)

¹ham \'ham\ *n* **1** : a buttock with its associated thigh — usu. used in pl. **2** : a cut of meat and esp. pork from the thigh **3** : a showy performer **4** : an operator of an amateur radio station — **ham** *adj*

²ham *vb* **hammed; ham·ming** : to overplay a part : OVERACT

ham·burg·er \'ham-,bər-gər\ *or* **ham·burg** \-,bərg\ *n* [G *Hamburger* of Hamburg, Germany] **1** : ground beef **2** : a sandwich consisting of a ground-beef patty in a round roll

ham·let \'ham-lət\ *n* : a small village

¹ham·mer \'ha-mər\ *n* **1** : a hand tool used for pounding; *also* : something resembling a hammer in form or function **2** : the part of a gun whose striking action causes explosion of the charge **3** : a metal sphere hurled for distance in a track-and-field event (**hammer throw**) **4** : ACCELERATOR 2

²hammer *vb* **1** : to beat, drive, or shape with repeated blows of a hammer : POUND **2** : to produce or bring about as if by repeated blows — usu. used with *out*

ham·mer·head \'ha-mər-,hed\ *n* **1** : the striking part of a hammer **2** : any of a family of medium-sized sharks with eyes at the ends of lateral extensions of the flattened head

hammerhead 2

ham·mer·lock \-,läk\ *n* : a wrestling hold in which an opponent's arm is held bent behind the back

ham·mer·toe \-,tō\ *n* : a toe deformed by having one or more joints permanently flexed

¹ham·mock \'ha-mək\ *n* [Sp *hamaca,* of AmerInd origin] : a swinging couch hung by cords at each end

²hammock *n* : a fertile elevated area of the southern U.S. and esp. Florida with hardwood vegetation and soil rich in humus

¹ham·per \'ham-pər\ *vb* : IMPEDE; *also* : RESTRAIN **syn** trammel, clog, fetter, shackle

²hamper *n* : a large basket

ham·ster \'ham-stər\ *n* [G, fr. OHG *hamustro,* of Slavic origin] : any of a subfamily of small Old World rodents with large cheek pouches

¹ham·string \'ham-,striŋ\ *n* : any of several muscles at the back of the thigh or tendons at the back of the knee

²hamstring *vb* **-strung** \-,strəŋ\; **-string·ing 1** : to cripple by cutting the leg tendons **2** : to make ineffective or powerless

¹hand \'hand\ *n* **1** : the end of a front limb when modified (as in humans) for grasping **2** : an indicator or pointer on a dial **3** : personal possession — usu. used in pl.; *also* : CONTROL **4** : SIDE 5 **5** : a pledge esp. of betrothal **6** : HANDWRITING **7** : SKILL, ABILITY; *also* : a significant part **8** : ASSISTANCE; *also* : PARTICIPATION **9** : an outburst of applause **10** : a single round in a card game;

also : the cards held by a player after a deal **11** : WORKER, EMPLOYEE; *also* : a member of a ship's crew — **hand·less** *adj* — **at hand** : near in time or place — **on hand** : in present possession or readily available

²hand *vb* **1** : to lead, guide, or assist with the hand **2** : to give, pass, or transmit with the hand

hand·bag \'hand-,bag\ *n* : a bag for carrying small personal articles and money

hand·ball \-,bȯl\ *n* : a game played by striking a small rubber ball against a wall with the hand

hand·bill \-,bil\ *n* : a small printed sheet for distribution by hand

hand·book \-,bu̇k\ *n* : a concise reference book : MANUAL

hand·car \-,kär\ *n* : a small 4-wheeled railroad car propelled by hand or by a small motor

hand·clasp \-,klasp\ *n* : HANDSHAKE

hand·craft \-,kraft\ *vb* : to fashion by manual skill

¹hand·cuff \-,kəf\ *n* : a metal fastening that can be locked around a wrist and is usu. connected with another such fastening — usu. used in pl.

²handcuff *vb* : MANACLE

hand·ful \,hand-,fu̇l\ *n, pl* **hand·fuls** \-,fu̇lz\ *also* **hands·ful** \'handz-,fu̇l\ **1** : as much or as many as the hand will grasp **2** : a small number **3** : as much as one can manage

hand·gun \-,gən\ *n* : a firearm held and fired with one hand

¹hand·i·cap \'han-di-,kap\ *n* [obs. E *handicap,* a game in which forfeits were held in a cap, fr. *hand in cap*] **1** : a contest in which an artificial advantage is given or disadvantage imposed on a contestant to equalize chances of winning; *also* : the advantage given or disadvantage imposed **2** : a disadvantage that makes achievement difficult

²handicap *vb* **-capped; -cap·ping 1** : to give a handicap to **2** : to put at a disadvantage

hand·i·capped *adj* : having a physical or mental disability that limits activity

hand·i·cap·per \-,ka-pər\ *n* : a person who predicts the winners in a horse race usu. for a publication

hand·i·craft \'han-di-,kraft\ *n* **1** : manual skill **2** : an occupation requiring manual skill **3** : the articles fashioned by those engaged in handicraft — **hand·i·craft·er** \-,kraf-tər\ *n* — **hand·i·crafts·man** \-,krafts-mən\ *n*

hand in glove *or* **hand and glove** *adv* : in an extremely close relationship

hand·i·work \'han-di-,wərk\ *n* : work done personally or by the hands

hand·ker·chief \'haŋ-kər-chəf, -,chēf \ *n, pl* **-chiefs** \-chəfs, -,chēfs\ *also* **-chieves** \-,chēvz\ : a small piece of cloth used for various personal purposes (as the wiping of the face)

¹han·dle \'hand-ᵊl\ *n* : a part (as of a tool) designed to be grasped by the hand — **han·dled** \-ᵊld\ *adj* — **off the handle** : into a state of sudden and violent anger — usu. used with *fly*

²handle *vb* **han·dled; han·dling 1** : to touch, hold, or manage with the hands **2** : to have responsibility for **3** : to deal or trade in **4** : to behave in a certain way when managed or directed (a car that ~s well) — **han·dler** *n*

han·dle·bar \'hand-ᵊl-,bär\ *n* : a usu. bent bar with a grip at each end (as for steering a bicycle) — usu. used in pl.

hand·made \'hand-'mād\ *adj* : made by hand or by a hand process

hand·maid·en \-,mād-ᵊn\ *also* **hand·maid** \-,mād\ *n* : a female attendant

hand–me–down \-me-,dau̇n\ *adj* : used by one person after having been used by another — **hand–me–down** *n*

hand·out \'han-,dau̇t\ *n* **1** : a portion (as of food) given to a beggar **2** : a piece of printed information for free distribution; *also* : a prepared statement released to the press

hand·pick \'hand-ˌpik\ *vb* : to select personally ⟨a ~ed candidate⟩

hand·rail \-ˌrāl\ *n* : a narrow rail for grasping as a support

hand·saw \-ˌsò\ *n* : a saw designed to be used with one hand

hands down *adv* **1** : with little effort **2** : without question

hand·sel \'han-səl\ *n* **1** : a gift made as a token of good luck **2** : a first installment : earnest money

hand·set \'hand-ˌset\ *n* : a combined telephone transmitter and receiver mounted on a handle

hand·shake \-ˌshāk\ *n* : a clasping usu. of right hands by two people

hands–off \'handz-'òf\ *adj* : characterized by noninterference

hand·some \'han-səm\ *adj* **hand·som·er; -est** [ME *handsom* easy to manipulate] **1** : SIZABLE, AMPLE **2** : GENEROUS, LIBERAL **3** : pleasing and usu. impressive in appearance **syn** beautiful, lovely, pretty, comely, fair — **hand·some·ly** *adv* — **hand·some·ness** *n*

hands–on \'handz-'òn, -'än\ *adj* **1** : being or providing direct practical experience in the operation of something **2** : characterized by active personal involvement ⟨~ management⟩

hand·spring \'hand-ˌspriŋ\ *n* : an acrobatic feat in which the body turns in a full circle from a standing position and lands first on the hands and then on the feet

hand·stand \-ˌstand\ *n* : an act of supporting the body on the hands with the trunk and legs balanced in the air

hand–to–hand *adj* : involving physical contact or very close range ⟨~ fighting⟩ — **hand to hand** *adv*

hand–to–mouth *adj* : having or providing nothing to spare

hand·wo·ven \'hand-ˌwō-vən\ *adj* : produced on a hand-operated loom

hand·writ·ing \-ˌrī-tiŋ\ *n* : writing done by hand; *also* : the form of writing peculiar to a person — **hand·writ·ten** \-ˌrit-ᵊn\ *adj*

handy \'han-dē\ *adj* **hand·i·er; -est 1** : conveniently near **2** : easily used **3** : DEXTEROUS — **hand·i·ly** \-də-lē\ *adv* — **hand·i·ness** \-dē-nəs\ *n*

handy·man \-ˌman\ *n* **1** : one who does odd jobs **2** : one competent in a variety of small skills or repair work

¹hang \'haŋ\ *vb* **hung** \'həŋ\ *also* **hanged; hang·ing 1** : to fasten or remain fastened to an elevated point without support from below; *also* : to fasten or be fastened so as to allow free motion on the point of suspension ⟨~ a door⟩ **2** : to suspend by the neck until dead; *also* : to die by hanging **3** : DROOP ⟨*hung* his head in shame⟩ **4** : to fasten to a wall ⟨~ wallpaper⟩ **5** : to prevent (a jury) from coming to a decision **6** : to display (pictures) in a gallery **7** : to remain stationary in the air **8** : to be imminent **9** : DEPEND **10** : to take hold for support **11** : to be burdensome **12** : to undergo delay **13** : to incline downward; *also* : to fit or fall from the figure in easy lines **14** : to be raptly attentive **15** : LINGER, LOITER — **hang·er** *n*

²hang *n* **1** : the manner in which a thing hangs **2** : an understanding of something

han·gar \'haŋ-ər\ *n* [F] : a covered and usu. enclosed area for housing and repairing aircraft

hang·dog \'haŋ-ˌdòg\ *adj* **1** : ASHAMED, GUILTY **2** : ABJECT, COWED

hang·er–on \'haŋ-ər-'òn, -'än\ *n, pl* **hangers–on** : one who hangs around a person or place esp. for personal gain

hang in *vb* : to persist tenaciously

hang·ing *n* **1** : an execution by strangling or snapping the neck by a suspended noose **2** : something hung

hang·man \-mən\ *n* : a public executioner

hang·nail \-ˌnāl\ *n* : a bit of skin hanging loose at the edge of a fingernail

hang on *vb* **1** : HANG IN **2** : to keep a telephone connection open

hang·out \'haŋ-ˌaùt\ *n* : a favorite place for spending time

hang·over \-ˌō-vər\ *n* **1** : something that remains from what is past **2** : disagreeable physical effects following heavy drinking

hang–up \'haŋ-ˌəp\ *n* : a source of mental or emotional difficulty

hang up *vb* **1** : to place on a hook or hanger **2** : to end a telephone conversation by replacing the receiver on the cradle **3** : to keep delayed or suspended

hank \'haŋk\ *n* : COIL, LOOP

han·ker \'haŋ-kər\ *vb* : to desire strongly or persistently — **han·ker·ing** *n*

han·kie *or* **han·ky** \'haŋ-kē\ *n, pl* **hankies** : HANDKERCHIEF

han·ky–pan·ky \ˌhaŋ-kē-'paŋ-kē\ *n* **1** : questionable or underhanded activity **2** : sexual dalliance

han·sel *var of* HANDSEL

han·som \'han-səm\ *n* : a 2-wheeled covered carriage with the driver's seat elevated at the rear

Ha·nuk·kah \'kä-nə-kə, 'hä-\ *n* [Heb *ḥănukkāh* dedication] : an 8-day Jewish holiday commemorating the rededication of the Temple of Jerusalem after its defilement by Antiochus of Syria

hap \'hap\ *n* **1** : HAPPENING **2** : CHANCE, FORTUNE

¹hap·haz·ard \hap-'ha-zərd\ *n* : CHANCE

²haphazard *adj* : marked by lack of plan or order — **hap·haz·ard·ly** *adv* — **hap·haz·ard·ness** *n*

hap·less \'hap-ləs\ *adj* : UNFORTUNATE — **hap·less·ly** *adv* — **hap·less·ness** *n*

hap·loid \'hap-ˌlòid\ *adj* : having the number of chromosomes characteristic of gametic cells — **haploid** *n*

hap·ly \'hap-lē\ *adv* : by chance

hap·pen \'ha-pən\ *vb* **1** : to occur by chance **2** : to take place **3** : CHANCE 2

hap·pen·ing *n* **1** : OCCURRENCE **2** : an event that is especially interesting, entertaining, or important

hap·pi·ly \'ha-pə-lē\ *adv* **1** : LUCKILY **2** : in a happy manner or state ⟨lived ~ ever after⟩ **3** : APTLY, SUCCESSFULLY

hap·pi·ness \'ha-pē-nəs\ *n* **1** : a state of well-being and contentment; *also* : a pleasurable satisfaction **2** : APTNESS

hap·py \'ha-pē\ *adj* **hap·pi·er; -est 1** : FORTUNATE **2** : APT, FELICITOUS **3** : enjoying well-being and contentment **4** : PLEASANT; *also* : PLEASED, GRATIFIED **syn** glad, cheerful, lighthearted, joyful, joyous

hap·py–go–lucky \ˌha-pē-gō-'lə-kē\ *adj* : CAREFREE

happy hour *n* : a period of time when the price of drinks at a bar is reduced

hara–kiri \ˌhar-i-'kir-ē, -'kar-ē\ *n* [Jp *harakiri*, fr. *hara* belly + *kiri* cutting] : ritual suicide by disembowelment

ha·rangue \hə-'raŋ\ *n* **1** : a ranting speech or writing **2** : LECTURE — **harangue** *vb* — **ha·rangu·er** *n*

ha·rass \hə-'ras, 'har-əs\ *vb* [F *harasser*, fr. MF, fr. *harer* to set a dog on, fr. OF *hare*, interj. used to incite dogs, of Gmc origin] **1** : EXHAUST, FATIGUE **2** : to worry and impede by repeated raids **3** : to annoy continually **syn** harry, plague, pester, tease, bedevil — **ha·rass·ment** *n*

har·bin·ger \'här-bən-jər\ *n* : one that announces or foreshadows what is coming : PRECURSOR; *also* : PORTENT

¹har·bor \'här-bər\ *n* **1** : a place of security and comfort **2** : a part of a body of water protected and deep enough to furnish anchorage : PORT

\ə\abut \ᵊ\kitten \ər\further \a\ash \ā\ace \ä\mop, mar \aù\out \ch\chin \e\bet \ē\easy \g\go \i\hit \ī\ice \j\job \ŋ\sing \ō\go \ò\law \òi\boy \th\thin \t̲h̲\the \ü\loot \ù\foot \y\yet \zh\vision *see also* Pronunciation Symbols page

²**harbor** *vb* **1** : to give or take refuge : SHELTER **2** : to be the home or habitat of; *also* : LIVE **3** : to hold a thought or feeling ⟨∼ a grudge⟩

har·bor·age \'här-bə-rij\ *n* : HARBOR

har·bour *chiefly Brit var of* HARBOR

hard \'härd\ *adj* **1** : not easily penetrated : not easily yielding to pressure **2** : high in alcoholic content **3** : containing salts that prevent lathering with soap ⟨∼ water⟩ **4** : stable in value ⟨∼ currency⟩ **5** : physically fit **6** : FIRM, DEFINITE ⟨∼ agreement⟩; *also* : based on clear fact ⟨∼ evidence⟩ **7** : CLOSE, SEARCHING ⟨∼ look⟩ **8** : REALISTIC ⟨good ∼ sense⟩ **9** : OBDURATE, UNFEELING ⟨∼ heart⟩ **10** : difficult to bear ⟨∼ times⟩; *also* : HARSH, SEVERE **11** : RESENTFUL ⟨∼ feelings⟩ **12** : STRICT, UNRELENTING ⟨∼ bargain⟩ **13** : INCLEMENT ⟨∼ winter⟩ **14** : intense in force or manner ⟨∼ blow⟩ **15** : ARDUOUS, STRENUOUS ⟨∼ work⟩ **16** : sounding as in *arcing* and *geese* respectively — used of *c* and *g* **17** : TROUBLESOME ⟨∼ problem⟩ **18** : having difficulty in doing something ⟨∼ of hearing⟩ **19** : addictive and gravely detrimental to health ⟨∼ drugs⟩ **20** : of or relating to the natural sciences and esp. the physical sciences — **hard** *adv* — **hard·ness** *n*

hard–and–fast *adj* : rigidly binding : STRICT ⟨a ∼ rule⟩

hard·back \'härd-ˌbak\ *n* : a hardcover book

hard·ball \-ˌból\ *n* **1** : BASEBALL **2** : forceful uncompromising methods

hard–bit·ten \-ˈbit-ᵊn\ *adj* : SEASONED, TOUGH ⟨∼ campaigners⟩

hard·board \-ˌbórd\ *n* : a very dense fiberboard

hard–boiled \-ˈbóild\ *adj* **1** *of an egg* : boiled until both white and yolk have solidified **2** : lacking sentiment : TOUGH; *also* : HARDHEADED 2

hard·bound \-ˌbaùnd\ *adj* : HARDCOVER

hard copy *n* : copy of textual or graphic information (as from computer storage) produced on paper

hard–core \'härd-ˈkór\ *adj* **1** : extremely resistant to solution or improvement **2** : being the most determined or dedicated members of a specified group **3** : containing explicit depictions of sex acts — **hard core** *n*

hard·cov·er \-ˈkə-vər\ *adj* : having rigid boards on the sides covered in cloth or paper ⟨∼ books⟩

hard disk *n* : a sealed rigid metal disk used as a computer storage device

hard·en \'härd-ᵊn\ *vb* **1** : to make or become hard or harder **2** : to confirm or become confirmed in disposition or action — **hard·en·er** *n*

hard·hack \'härd-ˌhak\ *n* : an American spirea with dense clusters of pink or white flowers and leaves having a hairy rusty yellow underside

hard hat *n* **1** : a protective hat worn esp. by construction workers **2** : a construction worker

hard·head·ed \'härd-ˈhe-dəd\ *adj* **1** : STUBBORN, WILLFUL **2** : SOBER, REALISTIC — **hard·head·ed·ly** *adv* — **hard·head·ed·ness** *n*

hard·heart·ed \-ˈhär-təd\ *adj* : PITILESS, CRUEL — **hard·heart·ed·ly** *adv* — **hard·heart·ed·ness** *n*

har·di·hood \'här-dē-ˌhùd\ *n* **1** : resolute courage and fortitude **2** : VIGOR, ROBUSTNESS

hard–line \'härd-ˈlīn\ *adj* : advocating or involving a rigidly uncompromising course of action — **hard–lin·er** \-ˈlī-nər\ *n*

hard·ly \'härd-lē\ *adv* **1** : with force **2** : SEVERELY **3** : with difficulty **4** : only just : BARELY **5** : certainly not

hard–nosed \'härd-ˈnózd\ *adj* : TOUGH, UNCOMPROMISING; *also* : HARDHEADED 2

hard palate *n* : the bony anterior part of the palate forming the roof of the mouth

hard·pan \'härd-ˌpan\ *n* : a compact layer in soil that is impenetrable by roots

hard–pressed \-ˈprest\ *adj* : HARD PUT; *esp* : being under financial strain

hard put *adj* **1** : barely able **2** : faced with difficulty or perplexity

hard rock *n* : rock music marked by a heavy beat, high amplification, and usu. frenzied performances

hard–shell \'härd-ˌshel\ *adj* : HIDEBOUND, UNCOMPROMISING ⟨a ∼ conservative⟩

hard·ship \-ˌship\ *n* **1** : SUFFERING, PRIVATION **2** : something that causes suffering or privation

hard·tack \-ˌtak\ *n* : a saltless hard biscuit, bread, or cracker

hard·top \-ˌtäp\ *n* : an automobile having a permanent rigid top

hard·ware \-ˌwar\ *n* **1** : ware (as cutlery or tools) made of metal **2** : the physical components (as electronic devices) of a vehicle (as a spacecraft) or an apparatus (as a computer)

hard·wood \-ˌwùd\ *n* : the wood of a broad-leaved usu. deciduous tree as distinguished from that of a conifer; *also* : such a tree — **hardwood** *adj*

hard·work·ing \-ˈwər-kiŋ\ *adj* : INDUSTRIOUS

har·dy \'här-dē\ *adj* **har·di·er; -est** **1** : BOLD, BRAVE **2** : AUDACIOUS, BRAZEN **3** : ROBUST; *also* : able to withstand adverse conditions (as of weather) ⟨∼ shrubs⟩ — **har·di·ly** \-də-lē\ *adv* — **har·di·ness** \-dē-nəs\ *n*

hare \'har\ *n, pl* **hare** *or* **hares** : any of various swift timid long-eared mammals like the related rabbits but born with open eyes and fur

hare·bell \'har-ˌbel\ *n* : a slender herb with bright blue bell-shaped flowers

hare·brained \-ˈbrānd\ *adj* : FOOLISH

hare·lip \-ˈlip\ *n* : a birth defect in which the upper lip is vertically split — **hare·lipped** \-ˈlipt\ *adj*

ha·rem \'har-əm\ *n* [Ar *ḥarīm*, lit., something forbidden & *ḥaram*, lit., sanctuary] **1** : a house or part of a house allotted to women in a Muslim household **2** : the women and servants occupying a harem **3** : a group of females associated with one male

hark \'härk\ *vb* : LISTEN

harken *var of* HEARKEN

har·le·quin \'här-li-kən, -kwən\ *n* **1** *cap* : a character (as in comedy) with a shaved head, masked face, variegated tights, and wooden sword **2** : CLOWN 2

har·lot \'här-lət\ *n* : PROSTITUTE

¹**harm** \'härm\ *n* **1** : physical or mental damage : INJURY **2** : MISCHIEF, HURT — **harm·ful** \-fəl\ *adj* — **harm·ful·ly** *adv* — **harm·ful·ness** *n* — **harm·less** *adj* — **harm·less·ly** *adv* — **harm·less·ness** *n*

²**harm** *vb* : to cause harm to : INJURE

¹**har·mon·ic** \här-ˈmä-nik\ *adj* **1** : of or relating to musical harmony or harmonics **2** : pleasing to the ear — **har·mon·i·cal·ly** \-ni-k(ə-)lē\ *adv*

²**harmonic** *n* : a musical overtone

har·mon·i·ca \här-ˈmä-ni-kə\ *n* : a small wind instrument in which the sound is produced by metal reeds

har·mo·ni·ous \här-ˈmō-nē-əs\ *adj* **1** : musically concordant **2** : CONGRUOUS **3** : marked by accord in sentiment or action — **har·mo·ni·ous·ly** *adv* — **har·mo·ni·ous·ness** *n*

har·mo·ni·um \här-ˈmō-nē-əm\ *n* : a keyboard wind instrument in which the wind acts on a set of metal reeds

har·mo·nize \'här-mə-ˌnīz\ *vb* **-nized; -niz·ing** **1** : to play or sing in harmony **2** : to be in harmony **3** : to bring into consonance or accord — **har·mo·ni·za·tion** \ˌhär-mə-nə-ˈzā-shən\ *n*

har·mo·ny \'här-mə-nē\ *n, pl* **-nies** **1** : musical agreement of sounds; *esp* : the combination of tones into chords and progressions of chords **2** : a pleasing arrangement of parts; *also* : ACCORD **3** : internal calm

¹**har·ness** \'här-nəs\ *n* **1** : the gear other than a yoke of a draft animal **2** : something that resembles a harness

²**harness** *vb* **1** : to put a harness on; *also* : YOKE **2** : UTILIZE

¹**harp** \'härp\ *n* : a musical instrument consisting of a tri-

angular frame set with strings plucked by the fingers —
harp·ist \\'här-pist\ *n*

²**harp** *vb* **1** : to play on a harp **2** : to dwell on a subject tiresomely — **harp·er** *n*

har·poon \här-'pün\ *n* : a barbed spear used esp. in hunting whales — **harpoon** *vb* — **har·poon·er** *n*

harp·si·chord \\'härp-si-ˌkȯrd\ *n* : a keyboard instrument producing tones by the plucking of its strings with quills or with leather or plastic points

har·py \\'här-pē\ *n, pl* **harpies** [L *Harpyia*, a mythical predatory monster having a woman's head and a bird's body, fr. Gk] **1** : a predatory person : LEECH **2** : a shrewish woman

har·ri·dan \\'har-əd-ᵊn\ *n* : SHREW 2

¹**har·ri·er** \\'har-ē-ər\ *n* **1** : any of a breed of medium-sized foxhounds **2** : a runner on a cross-country team

²**harrier** *n* : a slender long-legged hawk

¹**har·row** \\'har-ō\ *n* : a cultivating tool that has spikes, spring teeth, or disks and is used esp. to pulverize and smooth the soil

²**harrow** *vb* **1** : to cultivate with a harrow **2** : TORMENT, VEX

har·ry \\'har-ē\ *vb* **har·ried; har·ry·ing 1** : RAID, PILLAGE **2** : to torment by or as if by constant attack **syn** worry, annoy, plague, pester

harsh \\'härsh\ *adj* **1** : disagreeably rough **2** : causing discomfort or pain **3** : unduly exacting : SEVERE — **harsh·ly** *adv* — **harsh·ness** *n*

hart \\'härt\ *n, chiefly Brit* : STAG

har·um–scar·um \ˌhar-əm-'skar-əm\ *adj* : RECKLESS, IRRESPONSIBLE

¹**har·vest** \\'här-vəst\ *n* **1** : the season for gathering in crops; *also* : the act of gathering in a crop **2** : a mature crop **3** : the product or reward of effort

²**harvest** *vb* **1** : to gather in a crop : REAP **2** : to gather, hunt, or kill (as deer) for human use or population control — **har·vest·er** *n*

has *pres 3d sing of* HAVE

has–been \\'haz-ˌbin\ *n* : one that has passed the peak of ability, power, effectiveness, or popularity

¹**hash** \\'hash\ *vb* [F *hacher*, fr. OF *hachier*, fr. *hache* battle-ax, fr. of Gmc origin] **1** : to chop into small pieces **2** : to talk about

²**hash** *n* **1** : chopped meat mixed with potatoes and browned **2** : HODGEPODGE, JUMBLE

³**hash** *n* : HASHISH

hash browns *n pl* : boiled potatoes that have been diced, mixed with chopped onions and shortening, and fried

hash·ish \\'ha-ˌshēsh, ha-'shēsh\ [Ar *ḥashīsh*] *n* : the concentrated resin from the flowering tops of the female hemp plant

hasp \\'hasp\ *n* : a fastener (as for a door) consisting of a hinged metal strap that fits over a staple and is secured by a pin or padlock

hasp

has·sle \\'ha-səl\ *n* **1** : WRANGLE; *also* : FIGHT **2** : an annoying or troublesome concern — **hassle** *vb*

has·sock \\'ha-sək\ *n* **1** : a cushion that serves as a seat or leg rest; *also* : a cushion to kneel on in prayer

haste \\'hāst\ *n* **1** : rapidity of motion or action : SPEED **2** : rash or headlong action **3** : excessive eagerness —

hast·i·ly \\'hā-stə-lē\ *adv* — **hast·i·ness** \-stē-nəs\ *n* — **hasty** \\'hā-stē\ *adj*

has·ten \\'hās-ᵊn\ *vb* **1** : to urge on **2** : to move or act quickly : HURRY **syn** speed, accelerate, quicken

hat \\'hat\ *n* : a covering for the head usu. having a shaped crown and brim

hat·box \\'hat-ˌbäks\ *n* : a round piece of luggage esp. for carrying hats

¹**hatch** \\'hach\ *n* **1** : a small door or opening **2** : a door or cover for access down into a compartment of a ship

²**hatch** *vb* **1** : to produce by incubation; *also* : INCUBATE **2** : to emerge from an egg or pupa; *also* : to give forth young **3** : ORIGINATE — **hatch·ery** \\'ha-chə-rē\ *n*

hatch·back \\'hach-ˌbak\ *n* : an automobile with a rear hatch that opens upward

hatch·et \\'ha-chət\ *n* **1** : a short-handled ax with a hammerlike part opposite the blade **2** : TOMAHAWK

hatchet man *n* : a person hired for murder, coercion, or unscrupulous attack

hatch·ing \\'ha-chiŋ\ *n* : the engraving or drawing of closely spaced fine lines chiefly to give an effect of shading; *also* : the pattern so created

hatch·way \\'hach-ˌwā\ *n* : a hatch giving access usu. by a ladder or stairs

¹**hate** \\'hāt\ *n* **1** : intense hostility and aversion **2** : an object of hatred — **hate·ful** \-fəl\ *adj* — **hate·ful·ly** *adv* — **hate·ful·ness** *n*

²**hate** *vb* **hat·ed; hat·ing 1** : to express or feel extreme enmity **2** : to find distasteful **syn** detest, abhor, abominate, loathe — **hat·er** *n*

ha·tred \\'hā-trəd\ *n* : HATE; *also* : prejudiced hostility or animosity

hat·ter \\'ha-tər\ *n* : one that makes, sells, or cleans and repairs hats

hau·berk \\'hȯ-bərk\ *n* : a coat of mail

haugh·ty \\'hȯ-tē\ *adj* **haugh·ti·er; -est** [obs. *haught*, fr. ME *haute*, fr. MF *haut*, lit., high, fr. L *altus*] : disdainfully proud **syn** insolent, lordly, overbearing, arrogant — **haugh·ti·ly** \-tə-lē\ *adv* — **haugh·ti·ness** \-tē-nəs\ *n*

¹**haul** \\'hȯl\ *vb* **1** : to exert traction on : DRAW, PULL **2** : to furnish transportation : CART — **haul·er** *n*

²**haul** *n* **1** : PULL, TUG **2** : the result of an effort to obtain, collect, or win **3** : the length or course of a transportation route; *also* : LOAD

haul·age \\'hȯ-lij\ *n* **1** : the act or process of hauling **2** : a charge for hauling

haunch \\'hȯnch\ *n* **1** : ²HIP 1 **2** : HINDQUARTER **2** — usu. used in pl. **3** : HINDQUARTER 1

¹**haunt** \\'hȯnt\ *vb* **1** : to visit often : FREQUENT **2** : to recur constantly and spontaneously to; *also* : to reappear continually in **3** : to visit or inhabit as a ghost — **haunt·er** *n* — **haunt·ing·ly** *adv*

²**haunt** \\'hȯnt, 2 is usu 'hant\ *n* **1** : a place habitually frequented **2** *chiefly dial* : GHOST

haute cou·ture \ˌōt-kù-'tùr\ *n* [F] : the establishments or designers that create exclusive and often trend-setting fashions for women; *also* : the fashions created

haute cui·sine \-kwi-'zēn\ *n* : artful or elaborate cuisine

hau·teur \hȯ-'tər, ō-, hō-\ *n* : ARROGANCE, HAUGHTINESS

¹**have** \\'hav, həv, v; *in sense 2 before* "to" *usu* 'haf\ *vb* **had** \\'had, həd\; **hav·ing; has** \\'haz, həz, *in sense 2 before* "to" *usu* 'has\ **1** : to hold in possession; *also* : to hold in one's use, service, or regard **2** : to be compelled or forced ⟨~ to go now⟩ **3** : to stand in relationship to ⟨*has* many enemies⟩ **4** : OBTAIN; *also* : RECEIVE, ACCEPT **5** : to be marked by **6** : SHOW; *also* : USE, EXERCISE **7** : EXPERIENCE; *also* : TAKE ⟨~ a look⟩ **8** : to entertain in the mind ⟨~ an idea⟩ **9** : to cause to **10** : ALLOW **11** : to

be competent in **12 :** to hold in a disadvantageous position; *also* : TRICK **13 :** BEGET **14 :** to partake of **15** — used as an auxiliary with the past participle to form the present perfect, past perfect, or future perfect — **have at** : ATTACK — **have coming** : DESERVE — **have done with** : to be finished with — **have had it** : to have endured all one will permit or can stand — **have to do with** : to have in the way of relation with or effect on

²have \'hav\ *n* : one that has material wealth

ha·ven \'hā-vən\ *n* **1** : HARBOR, PORT **2 :** a place of safety **3 :** a place offering favorable conditions ⟨a tourist's ∼⟩

have–not \'hav-ˌnät, -ˈnät\ *n* : one that is poor in material wealth

hav·er·sack \'ha-vər-ˌsak\ *n* [F *havresac*, fr. G *Habersack* bag for oats] : a bag similar to a knapsack but worn over one shoulder

hav·oc \'ha-vək\ *n* **1 :** wide and general destruction **2** : great confusion and disorder

haw \'hȯ\ *n* : a hawthorn berry; *also* : HAWTHORN

Ha·wai·ian \hə-ˈwä-yən\ *n* : the Polynesian language of Hawaii

¹hawk \'hȯk\ *n* **1 :** any of numerous mostly small or medium-sized day-flying birds of prey (as a falcon or kite) **2 :** a supporter of a war or a warlike policy — **hawk·ish** *adj*

²hawk *vb* : to offer goods for sale by calling out in the street — **hawk·er** *n*

³hawk *vb* : to make a harsh coughing sound in or as if in clearing the throat; *also* : to raise by hawking

hawk·weed \'hȯk-ˌwēd\ *n* : any of several plants related to the daisies usu. having red or orange flower heads

haw·ser \'hȯ-zər\ *n* : a large rope for towing, mooring, or securing a ship

haw·thorn \'hȯ-ˌthȯrn\ *n* : any of a genus of spiny spring=flowering shrubs or trees related to the apple

¹hay \'hā\ *n* **1 :** herbage (as grass) mowed and cured for fodder **2 :** REWARD **3** *slang* : BED ⟨hit the ∼⟩ **4 :** a small amount of money

²hay *vb* : to cut, cure, and store for hay

hay·cock \'hā-ˌkäk\ *n* : a small conical pile of hay

hay fever *n* : an acute allergic reaction esp. to plant pollen that resembles a cold

hay·loft \'hā-ˌlȯft\ *n* : a loft for hay

hay·mow \-ˌmaú\ *n* : a mow of or for hay

hay·rick \-ˌrik\ *n* : a large sometimes thatched outdoor stack of hay

hay·seed \-ˌsēd\ *n, pl* **hayseed** *or* **hayseeds 1 :** clinging bits of straw or chaff from hay **2 :** BUMPKIN, YOKEL

hay·stack \-ˌstak\ *n* : a stack of hay

hay·wire \-ˌwīr\ *adj* : being out of order or control : CRAZY

¹haz·ard \'ha-zərd\ *n* [ME, a dice game, fr. MF *hasard*, fr. Ar *az-zahr* the die] **1 :** a source of danger **2 :** CHANCE; *also* : ACCIDENT **3 :** an obstacle on a golf course — **haz·ard·ous** *adj*

²hazard *vb* : VENTURE, RISK

¹haze \'hāz\ *n* **1 :** fine dust, smoke, or light vapor causing lack of transparency in the air **2 :** vagueness of mind or perception

²haze *vb* **hazed; haz·ing :** to harass by abusive and humiliating tricks usu. by way of initiation

ha·zel \'hā-zəl\ *n* **1 :** any of a genus of shrubs or small trees related to the birches and bearing edible nuts (**ha·zel·nuts** \-ˌnəts\) **2 :** a light brown color

hazy \'hā-zē\ *adj* **haz·i·er; -est 1 :** obscured or darkened by haze **2 :** VAGUE, INDEFINITE — **haz·i·ly** \-zə-lē\ *adv* — **haz·i·ness** \-zē-nəs\ *n*

Hb *abbr* hemoglobin

HBM *abbr* Her Britannic Majesty; His Britannic Majesty

H–bomb \'āch-ˌbäm\ *n* : HYDROGEN BOMB

HC *abbr* **1** Holy Communion **2** House of Commons

hd *abbr* head

HD *abbr* heavy-duty

hdbk *abbr* handbook

hdkf *abbr* handkerchief

HDL \ˌāch-(ˌ)dē-ˈel\ *n* [*high-density lipoprotein*] **:** a cholesterol-poor protein-rich lipoprotein of blood plasma correlated with reduced risk of atherosclerosis

hdwe *abbr* hardware

he \'hē\ *pron* **1 :** that male one **2 :** a person : the person ⟨∼ who hesitates is lost⟩

He *symbol* helium

HE *abbr* **1** Her Excellency **2** His Eminence **3** His Excellency

¹head \'hed\ *n* **1 :** the front or upper part of the body containing the brain, the chief sense organs, and the mouth **2 :** MIND; *also* : natural aptitude **3 :** POISE **4 :** the obverse of a coin **5 :** INDIVIDUAL; *also, pl* **head :** one of a number (as of cattle) **6 :** the end that is upper or higher or opposite the foot; *also* : either end of something (as a drum) whose two ends need not be distinguished **7 :** the source of a stream **8 :** DIRECTOR, LEADER; *also* : a leading element (as of a procession) **9 :** a projecting part; *also* : the striking part of a weapon **10 :** the place of leadership or honor **11 :** a separate part or topic **12 :** the foam on a fermenting or effervescing liquid **13 :** CRISIS — **head·ed** \'he-dəd\ *adj* — **head·less** *adj*

²head *adj* : PRINCIPAL, CHIEF

³head *vb* **1 :** to provide with or form a head; *also* : to form the head of **2 :** LEAD, CONDUCT **3 :** to get in front of esp. so as to stop; *also* : SURPASS **4 :** to put or stand at the head **5 :** to point or proceed in a certain direction

head·ache \'he-ˌdāk\ *n* **1 :** pain in the head **2 :** a baffling situation or problem

head·band \'hed-ˌband\ *n* : a band worn on or around the head

head·board \-ˌbōrd\ *n* : a board forming the head (as of a bed)

head cold *n* : a common cold centered in the nasal passages and adjacent mucous tissues

head·dress \'hed-ˌdres\ *n* : an often elaborate covering for the head

head·first \-ˈfərst\ *adv* : HEADLONG 1 — **headfirst** *adj*

head·gear \-ˌgir\ *n* : a covering or protective device for the head

head–hunt·ing \-ˌhən-tiŋ\ *n* : the practice of seeking out and decapitating enemies and preserving their heads as trophies — **head·hunt·er** \-tər\ *n*

head·ing \'he-diŋ\ *n* **1 :** the compass direction in which the longitudinal axis of a ship or airplane points **2** : something that forms or serves as a head

head·land \'hed-lənd, -ˌland\ *n* : PROMONTORY

head·light \-ˌlīt\ *n* : a light mounted on the front of a vehicle to illuminate the road ahead

head·line \-ˌlīn\ *n* : a head of a newspaper story or article usu. printed in large type

head·lock \-ˌläk\ *n* : a wrestling hold in which one encircles the opponent's head with one arm

¹head·long \-ˈlȯŋ\ *adv* **1 :** with the head foremost **2** : RECKLESSLY **3** : without delay

²head·long \-ˌlȯŋ\ *adj* **1 :** PRECIPITATE, RASH **2 :** plunging with the head foremost

head·man \'hed-ˈman, -ˌman\ *n* : one who is a leader : CHIEF

head·mas·ter \-ˌmas-tər\ *n* : a man who is head of a private school

head·mis·tress \-ˌmis-trəs\ *n* : a woman who is head of a private school

head–on \'hed-ˈȯn, -ˈän\ *adj* : having the front facing in the direction of initial contact or line of sight ⟨∼ collision⟩ — **head–on** *adv*

head·phone \-ˌfōn\ *n* : an earphone held on by a band over the head

head·piece \-ˌpēs\ *n* : a covering for the head

head·pin \-ˌpin\ *n* : a bowling pin that stands foremost in the arrangement of pins

head·quar·ters \-ˌkwȯr-tərz\ *n sing or pl* 1 : a place from which a commander exercises command 2 : the administrative center of an enterprise

head·rest \-ˌrest\ *n* 1 : a support for the head 2 : a pad at the top of the back of an automobile seat

head·room \-ˌrüm, -ˌrum\ *n* : vertical space in which to stand, sit, or move

head·set \-ˌset\ *n* : a pair of headphones

head·ship \-ˌship\ *n* : the position, office, or dignity of a head

heads·man \ˈhedz-mən\ *n* : EXECUTIONER

head·stall \ˈhed-ˌstȯl\ *n* : a part of a bridle or halter that encircles the head

head·stone \-ˌstōn\ *n* : a memorial stone at the head of a grave

head·strong \-ˌstrȯŋ\ *adj* 1 : not easily restrained 2 : directed by ungovernable will **syn** unruly, intractable, willful, pertinacious, refractory, stubborn

head·wait·er \-ˈwā-tər\ *n* : the head of the dining-room staff of a restaurant or hotel

head·wa·ter \-ˌwȯ-tər, -ˌwä-\ *n* : the source of a stream — usu. used in pl.

head·way \-ˌwā\ *n* : forward motion; *also* : PROGRESS

head wind *n* : a wind blowing in a direction opposite to a course esp. of a ship or aircraft

head·word \ˈhed-ˌwərd\ *n* 1 : a word or term placed at the beginning 2 : a word qualified by a modifier

head·work \-ˌwərk\ *n* : mental work or effort : THINKING

heady \ˈhe-dē\ *adj* **head·i·er; -est** 1 : WILLFUL, RASH; *also* : IMPETUOUS 2 : INTOXICATING 3 : SHREWD

heal \ˈhēl\ *vb* 1 : to make or become healthy, sound, or whole 2 : CURE, REMEDY — **heal·er** *n*

health \ˈhelth\ *n* 1 : sound physical or mental condition; *also* : overall condition of the body ⟨in poor ∼⟩ 2 : WELL-BEING 3 : a toast to someone's health or prosperity

health·ful \ˈhelth-fəl\ *adj* 1 : beneficial to health 2 : HEALTHY — **health·ful·ly** *adv* — **health·ful·ness** *n*

health maintenance organization *n* : HMO

healthy \ˈhel-thē\ *adj* **health·i·er; -est** 1 : enjoying or typical of good health : WELL 2 : evincing or conducive to health 3 : PROSPEROUS; *also* : CONSIDERABLE — **health·i·ly** \-thə-lē\ *adv* — **health·i·ness** \-thē-nəs\ *n*

¹heap \ˈhēp\ *n* : PILE; *also* : LOT

²heap *vb* 1 : to throw or lay in a heap 2 : to give in large quantities; *also* : to load heavily

hear \ˈhir\ *vb* **heard** \ˈhərd\; **hear·ing** 1 : to perceive by the ear 2 : to gain knowledge of by hearing : LEARN 3 : HEED; *also* : ATTEND 4 : to give a legal hearing to or take testimony from — **hear·er** *n*

hear·ing *n* 1 : the process, function, or power of perceiving sound; *esp* : the special sense by which noises and tones are received as stimuli 2 : EARSHOT 3 : opportunity to be heard 4 : a listening to arguments (as in a court); *also* : a session of (as of a legislative committee) in which testimony is taken from witnesses

hear·ken \ˈhär-kən\ *vb* : to give attention : LISTEN **syn** hear, hark, heed

hear·say \ˈhir-ˌsā\ *n* : RUMOR

hearse \ˈhərs\ *n* : a vehicle for carrying the dead to the grave

heart \ˈhärt\ *n* 1 : a hollow muscular organ that by rhythmic contraction keeps up the circulation of the blood in the body; *also* : something resembling a heart in shape 2 : any of a suit of playing cards marked with a red figure of a heart; *also, pl* : a card game in which the object is to avoid taking tricks containing hearts 3 : the whole personality; *also* : the emotional or moral as distinguished from the intellectual nature 4 : COURAGE 5 : one's innermost being 6 : CENTER; *also* : the essential part 7 : the younger central part of a compact leafy

cluster (as of lettuce) — **heart·ed** \ˈhär-təd\ *adj* — **by heart** : by rote or from memory

heart·ache \-ˌāk\ *n* : anguish of mind

heart attack *n* : an acute episode of heart disease due to insufficient blood supply to the heart muscle

heart·beat \ˈhärt-ˌbēt\ *n* : one complete pulsation of the heart

heart·break \-ˌbrāk\ *n* : crushing grief

heart·break·ing \-ˌbrā-kiŋ\ *adj* : causing extreme sorrow or distress — **heart·break·er** \-ˌbrā-kər\ *n*

heart·bro·ken \-ˌbrō-kən\ *adj* : overcome by sorrow

heart·burn \-ˌbərn\ *n* : a burning distress in the area of the heart usu. due to spasms of the esophagus or upper stomach

heart disease *n* : an abnormal organic condition of the heart or of the heart and circulation

heart·en \ˈhärt-ᵊn\ *vb* : ENCOURAGE, CHEER

heart·felt \ˈhärt-ˌfelt\ *adj* : deeply felt : SINCERE

hearth \ˈhärth\ *n* 1 : an area (as of brick) in front of a fireplace; *also* : the floor of a fireplace 2 : HOME

hearth·stone \ˈhärth-ˌstōn\ *n* 1 : stone forming a hearth 2 : HOME

heart·less \ˈhärt-ləs\ *adj* : CRUEL

heart·rend·ing \-ˌren-diŋ\ *adj* : HEARTBREAKING

heart·sick \-ˌsik\ *adj* : very despondent — **heart·sick·ness** *n*

heart·strings \-ˌstriŋz\ *n pl* : the deepest emotions or affections

heart·throb \-ˌthräb\ *n* 1 : the throb of a heart 2 : sentimental emotion 3 : SWEETHEART

heart–to–heart *adj* : SINCERE, FRANK

heart·warm·ing \ˈhärt-ˌwȯr-miŋ\ *adj* : inspiring sympathetic feeling

heart·wood \-ˌwud\ *n* : the older harder nonliving and usu. darker wood of the central part of a tree trunk

¹hearty \ˈhär-tē\ *adj* **heart·i·er; -est** 1 : giving full support; *also* : JOVIAL 2 : vigorously healthy 3 : ABUNDANT; *also* : NOURISHING **syn** sincere, wholehearted, unfeigned, heartfelt — **heart·i·ly** \-tə-lē\ *adv* — **heart·i·ness** \-tē-nəs\ *n*

²hearty *n, pl* **heart·ies** : an enthusiastic jovial fellow; *also* : SAILOR

¹heat \ˈhēt\ *vb* 1 : to make or become warm or hot 2 : EXCITE — **heat·ed·ly** *adv* — **heat·er** *n*

²heat *n* 1 : a condition of being hot : WARMTH 2 : a form of energy that when added to a body causes the body to rise in temperature, to fuse, to evaporate, or to expand 3 : high temperature 4 : intensity of feeling; *also* : sexual excitement esp. in a female mammal 5 : a preliminary race for narrowing the competition 6 : pungency of flavor 7 *slang* : POLICE 8 : PRESSURE, COERCION; *also* : ABUSE, CRITICISM

heat exchanger *n* : a device (as an automobile radiator) for transferring heat from one fluid to another without allowing them to mix

heat exhaustion *n* : a condition marked by weakness, nausea, dizziness, and profuse sweating resulting from physical exertion in a hot environment

heath \ˈhēth\ *n* 1 : any of a large family of often evergreen shrubby plants (as a blueberry or heather) of wet acid soils 2 : a tract of wasteland — **heathy** *adj*

hea·then \ˈhē-thən\ *n, pl* **heathens** *or* **heathen** 1 : an unconverted member of a people or nation that does not acknowledge the God of the Bible 2 : an uncivilized or irreligious person — **heathen** *adj* — **hea·then·dom** *n* — **hea·then·ish** *adj* — **hea·then·ism** *n*

heath·er \ˈhe-thər\ *n* : a northern and alpine evergreen heath with usu. lavender flowers — **heath·ery** *adj*

\ə\abut \ᵊ\kitten \ər\further \a\ash \ā\ace \ä\mop, mar
\au̇\out \ch\chin \e\bet \ē\easy \g\go \i\hit \ī\ice \j\job
\ŋ\sing \ō\go \ȯ\law \ȯi\boy \th\thin \th\the \ü\loot \u̇\foot
\y\yet \zh\vision *see also* Pronunciation Symbols page

heat lightning *n* : flashes of light without thunder ascribed to distant lightning reflected by high clouds
heat·stroke \'hēt-ˌstrōk\ *n* : a disorder marked esp. by high body temperature without sweating and by collapse that follows prolonged exposure to excessive heat
¹**heave** \'hēv\ *vb* **heaved** *or* **hove** \'hōv\; **heav·ing 1** : to rise or lift upward **2** : THROW **3** : to rise and fall rhythmically; *also* : PANT **4** : RETCH **5** : PULL, PUSH — **heav·er** *n*
²**heave** *n* **1** : an effort to lift or raise **2** : THROW, CAST **3** : an upward motion **4** *pl* : a chronic lung disease of horses marked by difficult breathing and persistent cough
heav·en \'he-vən\ *n* **1** : FIRMAMENT — usu. used in pl. **2** *often cap* : the abode of the Deity and of the blessed dead; *also* : a spiritual state of everlasting communion with God **3** *cap* : GOD 1 **4** : a place of supreme happiness — **heav·en·ly** *adj* — **heav·en·ward** *adv or adj*
¹**heavy** \'he-vē\ *adj* **heavi·er; -est 1** : having great weight **2** : hard to bear **3** : SERIOUS **4** : DEEP, PROFOUND **5** : burdened with something oppressive; *also* : PREGNANT **6** : SLUGGISH **7** : DRAB; *also* : DOLEFUL **8** : DROWSY **9** : greater than the average of its kind or class **10** : very rich and hard to digest; *also* : not properly raised or leavened **11** : producing goods (as steel) used in the production of other goods — **heavi·ly** \-və-lē\ *adv* — **heavi·ness** \-vē-nəs\ *n*
²**heavy** *n, pl* **heav·ies** : a theatrical role representing a dignified or imposing person; *also* : a villain esp. in a story
heavy–du·ty \ˌhe-vē-'dü-tē, -'dyü-\ *adj* : able to withstand unusual strain
heavy–hand·ed \-'han-dəd\ *adj* **1** : CLUMSY **2** : OPPRESSIVE, HARSH
heavy–heart·ed \-'här-təd\ *adj* : SADDENED, DESPONDENT
heavy metal *n* : energetic and highly amplified electronic rock music
heavy·set \ˌhe-vē-'set\ *adj* : stocky and compact in build
heavy water *n* : water enriched in deuterium
heavy·weight \'he-vē-ˌwāt\ *n* : one above average in weight; *esp* : a boxer weighing over 175 pounds
Heb *abbr* Hebrews
He·bra·ism \'hē-brā-ˌi-zəm\ *n* : the thought, spirit, or practice characteristic of the Hebrews — **He·bra·ic** \hi-'brā-ik\ *adj*
He·bra·ist \'hē-brā-ist\ *n* : a specialist in Hebrew and Hebraic studies
He·brew \'hē-brü\ *n* **1** : the language of the Hebrews **2** : a member of or descendant from a group of Semitic peoples; *esp* : ISRAELITE — **Hebrew** *adj*
He·brews \'hē-(ˌ)brüz\ *n* — see BIBLE table
hec·a·tomb \'he-kə-ˌtōm\ *n* : an ancient Greek and Roman sacrifice of 100 oxen or cattle
heck·le \'he-kəl\ *vb* **heck·led; heck·ling** : to harass with questions or gibes : BADGER — **heck·ler** *n*
hect·are \'hek-ˌtar\ *n* — see METRIC SYSTEM table
hec·tic \'hek-tik\ *adj* **1** : being hot and flushed **2** : filled with excitement, activity, or confusion — **hec·ti·cal·ly** \-ti-k(ə)lē\ *adv*
hec·to·gram \'hek-tə-ˌgram\ *n* — see METRIC SYSTEM table
hec·to·li·ter \'hek-tə-ˌlē-tər\ *n* — see METRIC SYSTEM table
hec·to·me·ter \'hek-tə-ˌmē-tər, hek-'tä-mə-tər\ *n* — see METRIC SYSTEM table
hec·tor \'hek-tər\ *vb* [*hector* bully, fr. *Hector,* champion of Troy in Greek legend] **1** : SWAGGER **2** : to intimidate by bluster or personal pressure
¹**hedge** \'hej\ *n* **1** : a fence or boundary formed of shrubs or small trees **2** : BARRIER **3** : a means of protection (as against financial loss)
²**hedge** *vb* **hedged; hedg·ing 1** : ENCIRCLE **2** : HINDER **3** : to protect oneself financially by a counterbalancing action **4** : to evade the risk of commitment — **hedg·er** *n*

hedge·hog \'hej-ˌhȯg, -ˌhäg\ *n* : a small Old World insect-eating mammal covered with spines; *also* : PORCUPINE

hedgehog

hedge·hop \-ˌhäp\ *vb* : to fly an airplane very close to the ground
hedge·row \-ˌrō\ *n* : a row of shrubs or trees bounding or separating fields
he·do·nism \'hēd-ᵊn-ˌi-zəm\ *n* [Gk *hēdonē* pleasure] : the doctrine that pleasure is the chief good in life; *also* : a way of life based on this — **he·do·nist** \-ist\ *n* — **he·do·nis·tic** \ˌhēd-ᵊn-'i-stik\ *adj*
¹**heed** \'hēd\ *vb* : to pay attention
²**heed** *n* : ATTENTION, NOTICE — **heed·ful** \-fəl\ *adj* — **heed·ful·ly** *adv* — **heed·ful·ness** *n* — **heed·less** *adj* — **heed·less·ly** *adv* — **heed·less·ness** *n*
¹**heel** \'hēl\ *n* **1** : the hind part of the foot **2** : one of the crusty ends of a loaf of bread **3** : a solid attachment forming the back of the sole of a shoe **4** : a rear, low, or bottom part **5** : a contemptible person
²**heel** *vb* : to tilt to one side : LIST
¹**heft** \'heft\ *n* : WEIGHT, HEAVINESS
²**heft** *vb* : to test the weight of by lifting
hefty \'hef-tē\ *adj* **heft·i·er; -est 1** : marked by bigness, bulk, and usu. strength **2** : impressively large
he·ge·mo·ny \hi-'je-mə-nē\ *n* : preponderant influence or authority over others : DOMINATION
he·gi·ra \hi-'jī-rə\ *n* [the *Hegira,* flight of Muhammad from Mecca in A.D. 622, fr. ML, fr. Ar *hijrah,* lit., flight] : a journey esp. when undertaken to escape a dangerous or undesirable environment
heif·er \'he-fər\ *n* : a young cow; *esp* : one that has not had a calf
height \'hīt\ *n* **1** : the highest part or point **2** : the distance from the bottom to the top of something standing upright **3** : ALTITUDE
height·en \'hīt-ᵊn\ *vb* **1** : to increase in amount or degree **2** : to make or become high or higher **syn** enhance, intensify, aggravate, magnify
Heim·lich maneuver \'hīm-lik-\ *n* [Henry J. *Heimlich* b1920 Am. surgeon] : the manual application of sudden upward pressure on the upper abdomen of a choking victim to force a foreign object from the windpipe
hei·nous \'hā-nəs\ *adj* [ME, fr. MF *haineus,* fr. *haine* hate, fr. *hair* to hate] : hatefully or shockingly evil — **hei·nous·ly** *adv* — **hei·nous·ness** *n*
heir \'ar\ *n* : one who inherits or is entitled to inherit property, rank, title, or office — **heir·ship** *n*
heir apparent *n, pl* **heirs apparent** : an heir whose right to succeed (as to a title) cannot be taken away if he or she survives the present holder
heir·ess \'ar-əs\ *n* : a female heir esp. to great wealth
heir·loom \'ar-ˌlüm\ *n* **1** : a piece of personal property that descends by inheritance **2** : something handed on from one generation to another
heir presumptive *n, pl* **heirs presumptive** : an heir whose present right to inherit could be lost through the birth of a nearer relative

heist \'hīst\ *vb, slang* : to commit armed robbery on; *also* : STEAL — **heist** *n, slang*
held *past and past part of* HOLD
he·li·cal \'he-li-kəl, 'hē-\ *adj* : SPIRAL
he·li·cop·ter \'he-lə-ˌkäp-tər, 'hē-\ *n* [F *hélicoptère*, fr. Gk *helix* spiral + *pteron* wing] : an aircraft that is supported in the air by one or more rotors revolving on substantially vertical axes
he·lio·cen·tric \ˌhē-lē-ō-'sen-trik\ *adj* : having or relating to the sun as center
he·lio·trope \'hē-lē-ə-ˌtrōp\ *n* [L *heliotropium*, fr. Gk *hēliotropion*, fr. *hēlios* sun + *tropos* turn; fr. its flowers' turning toward the sun] : any of a genus of herbs or shrubs related to the forget-me-not that have small white or purple flowers
he·li·port \'he-lə-ˌpōrt\ *n* : a landing and takeoff place for a helicopter
he·li·um \'hē-lē-əm\ *n* [NL, fr. Gk *hēlios* sun] : a very light nonflammable gaseous chemical element occurring in various natural gases — see ELEMENT table
he·lix \'hē-liks\ *n, pl* **he·li·ces** \'he-lə-ˌsēz, 'hē-\ *also* **he·lix·es** \'hē-lik-səz\ : something spiral in form
hell \'hel\ *n* 1 : a nether world in which the dead continue to exist 2 : the realm of the devil in which the damned suffer everlasting punishment 3 : a place or state of torment or destruction — **hell·ish** *adj*
hell–bent \'hel-'bent\ *adj* : stubbornly determined
hell·cat \-ˌkat\ *n* 1 : WITCH 2 2 : a violently temperamental person; *esp* : an ill-tempered woman
hel·le·bore \'he-lə-ˌbōr\ *n* 1 : any of a genus of poisonous herbs related to the buttercups; *also* : the dried root of a hellebore 2 : a poisonous plant related to the lilies; *also* : its dried roots used in medicine and insecticides
Hel·lene \'he-ˌlēn\ *n* : GREEK
Hel·le·nism \'he-lə-ˌni-zəm\ *n* : a body of humanistic and classical ideals associated with ancient Greece — **Hel·len·ic** \he-'le-nik\ *adj* — **Hel·le·nist** \'he-lə-nist\ *n*
Hel·le·nis·tic \ˌhe-lə-'nis-tik\ *adj* : of or relating to Greek history, culture, or art after Alexander the Great
hell–for–leather *adv* : at full speed
hell·gram·mite \'hel-grə-ˌmīt\ *n* : an aquatic insect larva that is used as bait in fishing
hell·hole \'hel-ˌhōl\ *n* : a place of extreme misery or squalor
hel·lion \'hel-yən\ *n* : a troublesome or mischievous person
hel·lo \hə-'lō, he-\ *n, pl* **hellos** : an expression of greeting — used interjectionally
helm \'helm\ *n* 1 : a lever or wheel for steering a ship 2 : a position of control
hel·met \'hel-mət\ *n* : a protective covering for the head
helms·man \'helmz-mən\ *n* : the person at the helm : STEERSMAN
hel·ot \'he-lət\ *n* : SLAVE, SERF
¹help \'help\ *vb* 1 : AID, ASSIST 2 : IMPROVE, RELIEVE 3 : to be of use; *also* : PROMOTE 4 : to change for the better 5 : to refrain from; *also* : PREVENT 6 : to serve with food or drink ⟨∼ yourself⟩ — **help·er** *n*
²help *n* 1 : AID, ASSISTANCE; *also* : a source of aid 2 : REMEDY, RELIEF 3 : one who assists another 4 : EMPLOYEE — **help·ful** \-fəl\ *adj* — **help·ful·ly** *adv* — **help·ful·ness** *n* — **help·less** *adj* — **help·less·ly** *adv* — **help·less·ness** *n*
helper T cell *n* : a T cell of the immune system that has a protein on its surface to which HIV attaches and that is reduced to 20 percent or less of normal numbers in AIDS
help·ing *n* : a portion of food
help·mate \'help-ˌmāt\ *n* 1 : HELPER 2 : WIFE
help·meet \-ˌmēt\ *n* : HELPMATE
hel·ter–skel·ter \ˌhel-tər-'skel-tər\ *adv* 1 : in undue haste or disorder 2 : HAPHAZARDLY
helve \'helv\ *n* : a handle of a tool or weapon

Hel·ve·tian \hel-'vē-shən\ *adj* : SWISS — **Helvetian** *n*
¹hem \'hem\ *n* 1 : a border of an article (as of cloth) doubled back and stitched down 2 : RIM, MARGIN
²hem *vb* **hemmed; hem·ming** 1 : to make a hem in sewing; *also* : BORDER, EDGE 2 : to surround restrictively
he–man \'hē-ˌman\ *n* : a strong virile man
he·ma·tite \'hē-mə-ˌtīt\ *n* : a mineral that consists of an oxide of iron and that constitutes an important iron ore
he·ma·tol·o·gy \ˌhē-mə-'tä-lə-jē\ *n* : a branch of biology that deals with the blood and blood-forming organs — **he·ma·to·log·ic** \-tə-'lä-jik\ *also* **he·ma·to·log·i·cal** \-ji-kəl\ *adj* — **he·ma·tol·o·gist** \-'tä-lə-jist\ *n*
heme \'hēm\ *n* : the deep red iron-containing part of hemoglobin
hemi·sphere \'he-mə-ˌsfir\ *n* 1 : one of the halves of the earth as divided by the equator into northern and southern parts (**northern hemisphere, southern hemisphere**) or by a meridian into two parts so that one half (**eastern hemisphere**) to the east of the Atlantic ocean includes Europe, Asia, and Africa and the half (**western hemisphere**) to the west includes No. and So. America and surrounding waters 2 : either of two half spheres formed by a plane through the sphere's center — **hemi·spher·ic** \ˌhe-mə-'sfir-ik, -'sfer-\ *or* **hemi·spher·i·cal** \-'sfir-i-kəl, -'sfer-\ *adj*
hem·line \'hem-ˌlīn\ *n* : the line formed by the lower edge of a garment
hem·lock \'hem-ˌläk\ *n* 1 : any of several poisonous herbs related to the carrot 2 : an evergreen tree related to the pines; *also* : its soft light wood
he·mo·glo·bin \'hē-mə-ˌglō-bən\ *n* : an iron-containing compound found in red blood cells that carries oxygen from the lungs to the body tissues
he·mo·phil·ia \ˌhē-mə-'fi-lē-ə\ *n* : a hereditary blood defect usu. of males that slows blood clotting with resulting difficulty in stopping bleeding — **he·mo·phil·i·ac** \-lē-ˌak\ *adj or n*
hem·or·rhage \'hem-rij, 'he-mə-\ *n* : a large discharge of blood from the blood vessels — **hemorrhage** *vb* — **hem·or·rhag·ic** \ˌhe-mə-'ra-jik\ *adj*
hem·or·rhoid \'hem-ˌroid, 'he-mə-\ *n* : a swollen mass of dilated veins at or just within the anus — usu. used in pl.
hemp \'hemp\ *n* : a tall widely grown Asian herb related to the mulberry that is the source of a tough fiber used in rope and of marijuana and hashish from its flowers and leaves; *also* : the fiber — **hemp·en** \'hem-pən\ *adj*
hem·stitch \'hem-ˌstich\ *vb* : to embroider (fabric) by drawing out parallel threads and stitching the exposed threads in groups to form designs
hen \'hen\ *n* : a female chicken esp. over a year old; *also* : a female bird
hence \'hens\ *adv* 1 : AWAY 2 : from this time 3 : CONSEQUENTLY 4 : from this source or origin
hence·forth \hens-ˌfōrth\ *adv* : from this point on
hence·for·ward \-'fōr-wərd\ *adv* : HENCEFORTH
hench·man \'hench-mən\ *n* [ME *hengestman* groom, fr. *hengest* stallion] : a trusted follower or supporter
hen·na \'he-nə\ *n* 1 : an Old World tropical shrub with fragrant white flowers; *also* : a reddish brown dye obtained from its leaves and used esp. on hair 2 : the color of henna dye
hen·peck \'hen-ˌpek\ *vb* : to nag and boss one's husband
hep \'hep\ *adj* : HIP
hep·a·rin \'he-pə-rən\ *n* : a compound found esp. in liver that slows the clotting of blood and is used medically
he·pat·ic \hi-'pa-tik\ *adj* : of, relating to, or associated with the liver

---

\ə\abut \ᵊ\kitten \ər\further \a\ash \ā\ace \ä\mop, mar
\au̇\out \ch\chin \e\bet \ē\easy \g\go \i\hit \ī\ice \j\job
\ŋ\sing \ō\go \ȯ\law \ȯi\boy \th\thin \t̲h̲\the \ü\loot \u̇\foot
\y\yet \zh\vision *see also* Pronunciation Symbols page

he·pat·i·ca \hi-'pa-ti-kə\ *n* : any of a genus of herbs related to the buttercups that have lobed leaves and delicate white, pink, or bluish flowers

hep·a·ti·tis \,he-pə-'tī-təs\ *n, pl* **-tit·i·des** \-'ti-tə-,dēz\ : inflammation of the liver; *also* : a virus disease of which this is a feature

hep·tam·e·ter \hep-'ta-mə-tər\ *n* : a line of verse containing seven metrical feet

¹**her** \'hər\ *adj* : of or relating to her or herself

²**her** *pron, objective case of* SHE

¹**her·ald** \'her-əld\ *n* **1** : an official crier or messenger **2** : HARBINGER **3** : ANNOUNCER **4** : ADVOCATE

²**herald** *vb* **1** : to give notice of **2** : HAIL, GREET; *also* : PUBLICIZE

he·ral·dic \he-'ral-dik, hə-\ *adj* : of or relating to heralds or heraldry

her·ald·ry \'her-əl-drē\ *n, pl* **-ries 1** : the practice of devising and granting armorial insignia and of tracing genealogies **2** : INSIGNIA **3** : PAGEANTRY

herb \'ərb, 'hərb\ *n* **1** : a seed plant that lacks woody tissue and dies to the ground at the end of a growing season **2** : a plant or plant part valued for medicinal or savory qualities — **her·ba·ceous** \,ər-'bā-shəs, ,hər-\ *adj*

herb·age \'ər-bij, 'hər-\ *n* : green plants esp. when used or fit for grazing

herb·al·ist \'ər-bə-list, 'hər-\ *n* **1** : one who practices healing by the use of herbs **2** : one who collects or grows herbs

her·bar·i·um \,ər-'bar-ē-əm, ,hər-\ *n, pl* **-ia** \-ē-ə\ **1** : a collection of dried plant specimens **2** : a place that houses an herbarium

her·bi·cide \'ər-bə-,sīd, 'hər-\ *n* : an agent used to destroy or inhibit plant growth — **her·bi·cid·al** \,ər-bə-'sīd-ᵊl, ,hər-\ *adj*

her·biv·o·rous \,ər-'bi-və-rəs, ,hər-\ *adj* : feeding on plants — **her·bi·vore** \'ər-bə-,vōr, 'hər-\ *n*

her·cu·le·an \,hər-kyə-'lē-ən, ,hər-'kyü-lē-\ *adj, often cap* [*Hercules*], hero of Greek myth renowned for his strength] : of extraordinary power, size, or difficulty

¹**herd** \'hərd\ *n* **1** : a group of animals of one kind kept or living together **2** : a group of people with a common bond **3** : MOB

²**herd** *vb* : to assemble or move in a herd — **herd·er** *n*

herds·man \'hərdz-mən\ *n* : one who manages, breeds, or tends livestock

¹**here** \'hir\ *adv* **1** : in or at this place; *also* : NOW **2** : at or in this point, particular, or case **3** : in the present life or state **4** : to this place

²**here** *n* : this place ⟨get away from ∼⟩

here·abouts \'hir-ə-,baùts\ *or* **here·about** \-,baùt\ *adv* : in this vicinity

¹**here·af·ter** \hir-'af-tər\ *adv* **1** : after this in sequence or in time **2** : in some future time or state

²**hereafter** *n, often cap* **1** : FUTURE **2** : an existence beyond earthly life

here·by \hir-'bī\ *adv* : by means of this

he·red·i·tary \hə-'re-də-,ter-ē\ *adj* **1** : genetically passed or passable from parent to offspring **2** : passing by inheritance; *also* : having title or possession through inheritance **3** : of a kind established by tradition

he·red·i·ty \-də-tē\ *n* : the qualities and potentialities genetically derived from one's ancestors; *also* : the passing of these from ancestor to descendant

Her·e·ford \'hər-fərd\ *n* : any of a breed of red⸗ coated beef cattle with white faces and markings

here·in \hir-'in\ *adv* : in this

here·of \-'əv, -'äv\ *adv* : of this

here·on \-'òn, -'än\ *adv* : on this

her·e·sy \'her-ə-sē\ *n, pl* **-sies** [ME *heresie*, fr. OF, fr. LL *haeresis*, fr. LGk *hairesis*, fr. Gk, action of taking, choice, sect, fr. *hairein* to take] **1** : adherence to a religious opinion contrary to church dogma **2** : an opinion

or doctrine contrary to church dogma **3** : dissent from a dominant theory, opinion, or practice — **her·e·tic** \-,tik\ *n* — **he·ret·i·cal** \hə-'re-ti-kəl\ *adj*

here·to \hir-'tü\ *adv* : to this document

here·to·fore \'hir-tə-,fōr\ *adv* : up to this time

here·un·der \hir-'ən-dər\ *adv* : under this or according to this writing

here·un·to \hir-'ən-tü\ *adv* : to this

here·upon \'hir-ə-,pòn, -,pän\ *adv* : on this or immediately after this

here·with \hir-'with, -'with\ *adv* **1** : with this **2** : HEREBY

her·i·ta·ble \'her-ə-tə-bəl\ *adj* : capable of being inherited

her·i·tage \'her-ə-tij\ *n* **1** : property that descends to an heir **2** : LEGACY **3** : BIRTHRIGHT

her·maph·ro·dite \(,)hər-'ma-frə-,dīt\ *n* : an animal or plant having both male and female reproductive organs — **hermaphrodite** *adj* — **her·maph·ro·dit·ic** \(,)hər-,ma-frə-'di-tik\ *adj*

her·met·ic \hər-'me-tik\ *also* **her·met·i·cal** \-ti-kəl\ *adj* : AIRTIGHT — **her·met·i·cal·ly** \-ti-k(ə-)lē\ *adv*

her·mit \'hər-mət\ *n* [ME *eremite*, fr. OF, fr. LL *eremita*, fr. LGk *erēmitēs*, fr. Gk, adj., living in the desert, fr. *erēmia* desert, fr. *erēmos* desolate] : one who lives in solitude esp. for religious reasons

her·mit·age \-mə-tij\ *n* **1** : the dwelling of a hermit **2** : a secluded dwelling

her·nia \'hər-nē-ə\ *n, pl* **-ni·as** *or* **-ni·ae** \-nē-,ē, -nē-,ī\ : a protrusion of a bodily part (as a loop of intestine) into a pouch of the weakened wall of a cavity in which it is normally enclosed — **her·ni·ate** \-nē-,āt\ *vb* — **her·ni·a·tion** \,hər-nē-'ā-shən\ *n*

he·ro \'hē-rō\ *n, pl* **heroes 1** : a mythological or legendary figure of great strength or ability **2** : a man admired for his achievements and qualities **3** : the chief male character in a literary or dramatic work **4** *pl usu* **heros** : SUBMARINE **2** — **he·ro·ic** \hi-'rō-ik\ *adj* — **he·ro·i·cal·ly** \-i-k(ə-)lē\ *adv*

heroic couplet *n* : a rhyming couplet in iambic pentameter

he·ro·ics \hi-'rō-iks\ *n pl* : heroic or showy behavior

her·o·in \'her-ə-wən\ *n* : an illicit addictive narcotic drug made from morphine

her·o·ine \'her-ə-wən\ *n* **1** : a woman admired for her achievements and qualities **2** : the chief female character in a literary or dramatic work

her·o·ism \'her-ə-,wi-zəm\ *n* **1** : heroic conduct **2** : the qualities of a hero **syn** valor, prowess, gallantry

her·on \'her-ən\ *n, pl* **herons** *also* **heron** : any of various long-legged long-billed wading birds with soft plumage

her·pes \'hər-pēz\ *n* : any of several virus diseases characterized by the formation of blisters on the skin or mucous membranes

herpes sim·plex \-'sim-,pleks\ *n* : either of two virus diseases marked in one by watery blisters above the waist (as on the mouth and lips) and in the other on the sex organs

herpes zos·ter \-'zäs-tər\ *n* : SHINGLES

her·pe·tol·o·gy \,hər-pə-'tä-lə-jē\ *n* : a branch of zoology dealing with reptiles and amphibians — **her·pe·tol·o·gist** \,hər-pə-'tä-lə-jist\ *n*

her·ring \'her-iŋ\ *n, pl* **herring** *or* **herrings** : a valuable narrow-bodied food fish of the north Atlantic; *also* : a related fish of the north Pacific harvested esp. for its roe

her·ring·bone \'her-iŋ-,bōn\ *n* : a pattern made up of rows of parallel lines with adjacent rows slanting in reverse directions; *also* : a twilled fabric with this pattern

hers \'hərz\ *pron* : one or the ones belonging to her

her·self \hər-'self\ *pron* : SHE, HER — used reflexively, for emphasis, or in absolute constructions

hertz \'hərts, 'herts\ *n, pl* **hertz** : a unit of frequency equal to one cycle per second

Hesh·van \ˈkesh-vən\ *n* [Heb Ḥeshwān] : the 2d month of the civil year or the 8th month of the ecclesiastical year in the Jewish calendar

hes·i·tant \ˈhe-zə-tənt\ *adj* : tending to hesitate — **hes·i·tance** \-təns\ *n* — **hes·i·tan·cy** \-tən-sē\ *n* — **hes·i·tant·ly** *adv*

hes·i·tate \ˈhe-zə-ˌtāt\ *vb* **-tat·ed; -tat·ing** 1 : to hold back (as in doubt) 2 : PAUSE syn waver, vacillate, falter, shilly-shally — **hes·i·ta·tion** \ˌhe-zə-ˈtā-shən\ *n*

het·ero·dox \ˈhe-tə-rə-ˌdäks\ *adj* 1 : differing from an acknowledged standard 2 : holding unorthodox opinions — **het·er·o·doxy** \-ˌdäk-sē\ *n*

het·er·o·ge·neous \ˌhe-tə-rə-ˈjē-nē-əs, -nyəs\ *adj* : consisting of dissimilar ingredients or constituents : MIXED — **het·er·o·ge·ne·ity** \-jə-ˈnē-ə-tē\ *n* — **het·er·o·ge·neous·ly** *adv*

het·ero·sex·u·al \ˌhe-tə-rō-ˈsek-shə-wəl\ *adj* 1 : of, relating to, or marked by sexual interest in the opposite sex; *also* : of, relating to, or involving sexual intercourse between members of opposite sex 2 : of or relating to different sexes — **heterosexual** *n* — **het·ero·sex·u·al·i·ty** \-ˌsek-shə-ˈwa-lə-tē\ *n*

hew \ˈhyü\ *vb* **hewed; hewed** *or* **hewn** \ˈhyün\; **hew·ing** 1 : to cut or fell with blows (as of an ax) 2 : to give shape to with or as if with an ax 3 : to conform strictly — **hew·er** *n*

HEW *abbr* Department of Health, Education, and Welfare

¹**hex** \ˈheks\ *vb* 1 : to practice witchcraft 2 : JINX

²**hex** *n* : SPELL, JINX

³**hex** *adj* : HEXAGONAL

⁴**hex** *abbr* hexagon

hexa·gon \ˈhek-sə-ˌgän\ *n* : a polygon having six angles and six sides — **hex·ag·o·nal** \hek-ˈsa-gən-ᵊl\ *adj*

hex·am·e·ter \hek-ˈsa-mə-tər\ *n* : a line of verse containing six metrical feet

hey·day \ˈhā-ˌdā\ *n* : a period of greatest strength, vigor, or prosperity

hf *abbr* half

Hf *symbol* hafnium

HF *abbr* high frequency

hg *abbr* hectogram

Hg *symbol* [NL *hydrargyrum*, lit., water silver] mercury

hgt *abbr* height

hgwy *abbr* highway

HH *abbr* 1 Her Highness 2 His Highness 3 His Holiness

HHS *abbr* Department of Health and Human Services

HI *abbr* 1 Hawaii 2 humidity index

hi·a·tus \hī-ˈā-təs\ *n* [L, fr. *hiare* to yawn] 1 : a break in an object : GAP 2 : a lapse in continuity

hi·ba·chi \hi-ˈbä-chē\ *n* [Jp] : a charcoal brazier

hi·ber·nate \ˈhī-bər-ˌnāt\ *vb* **-nat·ed; -nat·ing** : to pass the winter in a torpid or resting state — **hi·ber·na·tion** \ˌhī-bər-ˈnā-shən\ *n* — **hi·ber·na·tor** \ˈhī-bər-ˌnā-tər\ *n*

hi·bis·cus \hī-ˈbis-kəs, hə-\ *n* : any of a genus of herbs, shrubs, and trees related to the mallows and noted for large showy flowers

hic·cup *also* **hic·cough** \ˈhi-(ˌ)kəp\ *n* : a spasmodic breathing movement checked by sudden closing of the glottis accompanied by a peculiar sound; *also, pl* : an attack of hiccuping — **hiccup** *vb*

hick \ˈhik\ *n* [*Hick*, nickname for *Richard*] : an awkward provincial person — **hick** *adj*

hick·o·ry \ˈhi-kə-rē\ *n, pl* **-ries** : any of a genus of No. American hardwood trees related to the walnuts; *also* : the wood of a hickory — **hickory** *adj*

hi·dal·go \hi-ˈdal-gō\ *n, pl* **-gos** *often cap* [Sp, fr. earlier *fijo dalgo*, lit., son of something] : a member of the lower nobility of Spain

hidden tax *n* 1 : a tax ultimately paid by someone other than the person on whom it is formally levied 2 : an economic injustice that reduces one's income or buying power

¹**hide** \ˈhīd\ *vb* **hid** \ˈhid\; **hid·den** \ˈhid-ᵊn\ *or* **hid; hid·ing** 1 : to put or remain out of sight 2 : to conceal for shelter or protection; *also* : to seek protection 3 : to keep secret 4 : to turn away in shame or anger — **hid·er** *n*

²**hide** *n* : the skin of an animal

hide–and–seek \ˌhīd-ᵊn-ˈsēk\ *n* : a children's game in which everyone hides from one player who tries to find them

hide·away \ˈhī-də-ˌwā\ *n* : HIDEOUT

hide·bound \ˈhīd-ˌbaund\ *adj* : being inflexible or conservative

hid·eous \ˈhi-dē-əs\ *adj* [ME *hidous*, fr. OF, fr. *hisde, hide* terror] 1 : offensive to one of the senses : UGLY 2 : morally offensive : SHOCKING syn ghastly, grisly, gruesome, horrible, lurid, macabre — **hid·eous·ly** *adv* — **hid·eous·ness** *n*

hide·out \ˈhī-ˌdaut\ *n* : a place of refuge or concealment

hie \ˈhī\ *vb* **hied; hy·ing** *or* **hie·ing** : HASTEN

hi·er·ar·chy \ˈhī-ə-ˌrär-kē\ *n, pl* **-chies** 1 : a ruling body of clergy organized into ranks 2 : persons or things arranged in a graded series — **hi·er·ar·chi·cal** \ˌhī-ə-ˈrär-ki-kəl\ *adj* — **hi·er·ar·chi·cal·ly** \-k(ə-)lē\ *adv*

hi·er·o·glyph·ic \ˌhī-ə-rə-ˈgli-fik\ *n* [MF *hieroglyphique*, adj., ultim. fr. Gk *hieroglyphikos*, fr. *hieros* sacred + *glyphein* to carve] 1 : a character in a system of picture writing (as of the ancient Egyptians) 2 : a symbol or sign difficult to decipher

hieroglyphic 1

hi–fi \ˈhī-ˈfī\ *n* 1 : HIGH FIDELITY 2 : equipment for reproduction of sound with high fidelity

hig·gle·dy–pig·gle·dy \ˌhi-gəl-dē-ˈpi-gəl-dē\ *adv* : in confusion

¹**high** \ˈhī\ *adj* 1 : ELEVATED; *also* : TALL 2 : advanced toward fullness or culmination; *also* : slightly tainted 3 : advanced esp. in complexity ⟨∼er mathematics⟩ 4 : long past 5 : SHRILL, SHARP 6 : far from the equator ⟨∼ latitudes⟩ 7 : exalted in character 8 : of greater degree, size, or amount than average ⟨∼ in cholesterol⟩ 9 : of relatively great importance 10 : FORCIBLE, STRONG ⟨∼ winds⟩ 11 : showing elation or excitement 12 : INTOXICATED; *also* : excited or stupefied by or as if by a drug — **high·ly** *adv*

²**high** *adv* 1 : at or to a high place or degree 2 : LUXURIOUSLY ⟨living ∼⟩

³**high** *n* 1 : an elevated place 2 : a region of high barometric pressure 3 : a high point or level 4 : the gear of a vehicle giving the highest speed 5 : an excited or stupefied state produced by or as if by a drug

high·ball \ˈhī-ˌbȯl\ *n* : a usu. tall drink of liquor mixed with water or a carbonated beverage

high beam *n* : the long-range focus of a vehicle headlight

high·born \ˈhī-ˈbȯrn\ *adj* : of noble birth

high·boy \-ˌbȯi\ *n* : a high chest of drawers mounted on a base with legs

high·bred \-ˈbred\ *adj* : coming from superior stock

high·brow \-ˌbrau\ *n* : a person of superior learning or culture — **highbrow** *adj* — **high·brow·ism** \-ˌbrau-ˌi-zəm\ *n*

high–density li·po·pro·tein \-ˌlī-pō-ˈprō-tēn, -ˌli-\ *n* : HDL

\ə\abut \ᵊ\kitten \ər\further \a\ash \ā\ace \ä\mop, mar
\au̇\out \ch\chin \e\bet \ē\easy \g\go \i\hit \ī\ice \j\job
\ŋ\sing \ō\go \ȯ\law \ȯi\boy \th\thin \t͟h\the \ü\loot \u̇\foot
\y\yet \zh\vision *see also* Pronunciation Symbols page

high·er–up \ˌhī-ər-'əp\ *n* : a superior officer or official
high·fa·lu·tin \ˌhī-fə-'lüt-ᵊn\ *adj* : PRETENTIOUS, POMPOUS
high fashion *n* **1** : HIGH STYLE **2** : HAUTE COUTURE
high fidelity *n* : the reproduction of sound or image with a high degree of faithfulness to the original
high five *n* : a slapping of upraised right hands by two people (as in celebration) — **high–five** *vb*
high–flown \'hī-'flōn\ *adj* **1** : EXALTED **2** : BOMBASTIC
high frequency *n* : a radio frequency between 3 and 30 megahertz
high gear *n* **1** : HIGH 4 **2** : a state of intense or maximum activity
high–hand·ed \'hī-'han-dəd\ *adj* : OVERBEARING — **high–hand·ed·ly** *adv* — **high–hand·ed·ness** *n*
high–hat \-'hat\ *adj* : SUPERCILIOUS, SNOBBISH — **high–hat** *vb*
high·land \'hī-lənd\ *n* : elevated or mountainous land
high·land·er \-lən-dər\ *n* **1** : an inhabitant of a highland **2** *cap* : an inhabitant of the Scottish Highlands
¹high·light \-ˌlīt\ *n* : an event or detail of major importance
²highlight *vb* **1** : EMPHASIZE **2** : to constitute a highlight of
high–mind·ed \-'mīn-dəd\ *adj* : marked by elevated principles and feelings — **high–mind·ed·ness** *n*
high·ness \'hī-nəs\ *n* **1** : the quality or state of being high **2** — used as a title (as for kings)
high–pres·sure \-'pre-shər\ *adj* : using or involving aggressive and insistent sales techniques
high–rise \-'rīz\ *adj* : having several stories and being equipped with elevators ⟨∼ apartments⟩; *also* : of or relating to high-rise buildings
high road *n* : HIGHWAY
high school *n* : a school usu. including grades 9 to 12 or 10 to 12
high sea *n* : the open sea outside territorial waters — usu. used in pl.
high–sound·ing \'hī-'saun-diŋ\ *adj* : POMPOUS, IMPOSING
high–spir·it·ed \-'spir-ə-təd\ *adj* : characterized by a bold or energetic spirit
high–strung \-'strəŋ\ *adj* : having an extremely nervous or sensitive temperament
high style *n* : the newest in fashion or design
high·tail \'hī-ˌtāl\ *vb* : to retreat at full speed
high tech \-'tek\ *n* : HIGH TECHNOLOGY
high technology *n* : technology involving the use of advanced devices
high–ten·sion \'hī-'ten-chən\ *adj* : having or using a high voltage
high–test \-'test\ *adj* : having a high octane number
high–toned \-'tōnd\ *adj* **1** : high in social, moral, or intellectual quality **2** : PRETENTIOUS, POMPOUS
high·way \'hī-ˌwā\ *n* : a main direct road
high·way·man \'hī-ˌwā-mən\ *n* : a person who robs travelers on a road
hi·jack *also* **high·jack** \'hī-ˌjak\ *vb* : to steal esp. by stopping a vehicle on the highway; *also* : to commandeer a flying airplane — **hijack** *n* — **hi·jack·er** *n*
¹hike \'hīk\ *vb* **hiked; hik·ing 1** : to move or raise with a sudden motion **2** : to take a long walk — **hik·er** *n*
²hike *n* **1** : a long walk **2** : RISE, INCREASE
hi·lar·i·ous \hi-'lar-ē-əs, hī-\ *adj* : marked by or providing boisterous merriment — **hi·lar·i·ous·ly** *adv* — **hi·lar·i·ty** \-ə-tē\ *n*
hill \'hil\ *n* **1** : a usu. rounded elevation of land **2** : a little heap or mound (as of earth) — **hilly** *adj*
hill·bil·ly \'hil-ˌbi-lē\ *n, pl* **-lies** : a person from a backwoods area
hill·ock \'hi-lək\ *n* : a small hill
hill·side \'hil-ˌsīd\ *n* : the part of a hill between the summit and the foot
hill·top \-ˌtäp\ *n* : the top of a hill

hilt \'hilt\ *n* : a handle esp. of a sword or dagger
him \'him\ *pron, objective case of* HE
Hi·ma·la·yan \ˌhi-mə-'lā-ən, hi-'mäl-yən\ *adj* : of, relating to, or characteristic of the Himalaya mountains or the people living there
him·self \him-'self\ *pron* : HE, HIM — used reflexively, for emphasis, or in absolute constructions
¹hind \'hīnd\ *n, pl* **hinds** *also* **hind** : a female of a common Eurasian deer
²hind *adj* : REAR
¹hin·der \'hin-dər\ *vb* **1** : to impede the progress of **2** : to hold back **syn** obstruct, block, bar, impede
²hind·er \'hīn-dər\ *adj* : HIND
Hin·di \'hin-dē\ *n* : a literary and official language of northern India
hind·most \'hīnd-ˌmōst\ *adj* : farthest to the rear
hind·quar·ter \-ˌkwȯr-tər\ *n* **1** : one side of the back half of the carcass of a quadruped **2** *pl* : the part of the body of a quadruped behind the junction of hind limbs and trunk
hin·drance \'hin-drəns\ *n* **1** : the state of being hindered; *also* : the action of hindering **2** : IMPEDIMENT 1
hind·sight \'hīnd-ˌsīt\ *n* : understanding of an event after it has happened
Hindu–Arabic *adj* : relating to, being, or composed of Arabic numerals
Hin·du·ism \'hin-dü-ˌi-zəm\ *n* : a body of religious beliefs and practices native to India — **Hin·du** *n or adj*
hind wing *n* : either of the posterior wings of a 4-winged insect
¹hinge \'hinj\ *n* : a jointed device on which a swinging part (as a door, gate, or lid) turns
²hinge *vb* **hinged; hing·ing 1** : to attach by or furnish with hinges **2** : to be contingent on a single consideration
hint \'hint\ *n* **1** : an indirect or summary suggestion **2** : CLUE **3** : a very small amount **syn** dash, soupçon, suspicion, tincture, touch — **hint** *vb*
hin·ter·land \'hin-tər-ˌland\ *n* **1** : a region behind a coast **2** : a region remote from cities
¹hip \'hip\ *n* : the fruit of a rose
²hip *n* **1** : the part of the body on either side below the waist consisting of the side of the pelvis and the upper thigh **2** : HIP JOINT
³hip *adj* **hip·per; hip·pest** : keenly aware of or interested in the newest developments or styles — **hip·ness** *n*
⁴hip *vb* **hipped; hip·ping** : TELL, INFORM
hip·bone \'hip-'bōn, -ˌbōn\ *n* : the large flaring bone that makes a lateral half of the pelvis in mammals
hip joint *n* : the articulation between the femur and the hipbone
hipped \'hipt\ *adj* : having hips esp. of a specified kind ⟨broad-*hipped*⟩
hip·pie *or* **hip·py** \'hi-pē\ *n, pl* **hippies** : a usu. young person who rejects established mores, advocates nonviolence, and often uses psychedelic drugs or marijuana; *also* : a long-haired unconventionally dressed young person
hip·po·drome \'hi-pə-ˌdrōm\ *n* : an arena for equestrian performances
hip·po·pot·a·mus \ˌhi-pə-'pä-tə-məs\ *n, pl* **-mus·es** *or* **-mi** \-ˌmī\ [L, fr. Gk *hippopotamos*, alter. of *hippos potamios*, lit., river horse] : a large thick-skinned river mammal of sub-Saharan Africa that is related to the swine
¹hire \'hīr\ *n* **1** : payment for labor or personal services : WAGES **2** : EMPLOYMENT **3** : one who is hired
²hire *vb* **hired; hir·ing 1** : to employ for pay **2** : to engage the temporary use of for pay **3** : to take employment
hire·ling \'hīr-liŋ\ *n* : a hired person; *esp* : one with mercenary motives
hir·sute \'hər-ˌsüt, 'hir-\ *adj* : HAIRY
¹his \'hiz\ *adj* : of or relating to him or himself
²his *pron* : one or the ones belonging to him

His·pan·ic \hi-ˈspa-nik\ *adj* : of, relating to, or being a person of Latin-American descent living in the U.S. — **Hispanic** *n*

hiss \ˈhis\ *vb* : to make a sharp sibilant sound; *also* : to express disapproval of by hissing — **hiss** *n*

hist *abbr* historian; historical; history

his·ta·mine \ˈhis-tə-ˌmēn, -mən\ *n* : a compound widespread in animal tissues that plays a major role in allergic reactions (as hay fever)

his·to·gram \ˈhis-tə-ˌgram\ *n* : a representation of statistical data by rectangles whose widths represent class intervals and whose heights usu. represent corresponding frequencies

his·to·ri·an \hi-ˈstōr-ē-ən\ *n* : a student or writer of history

his·to·ric·i·ty \ˌhis-tə-ˈri-sə-tē\ *n* : historical actuality

his·to·ri·og·ra·pher \hi-ˌstōr-ē-ˈä-grə-fər\ *n* : HISTORIAN

his·to·ry \ˈhis-tə-rē\ *n, pl* **-ries** [L *historia*, fr. Gk, inquiry, history, fr. *histōr, istōr* knowing, learned] **1** : a chronological record of significant events often with an explanation of their causes **2** : a branch of knowledge that records and explains past events **3** : events that form the subject matter of history **4** : an established record ⟨a convict's ∼ of violence⟩ — **his·tor·ic** \hi-ˈstōr-ik\ *adj* — **his·tor·i·cal** \-i-kəl\ *adj* — **his·tor·i·cal·ly** \-k(ə-)lē\ *adv*

his·tri·on·ic \ˌhis-trē-ˈä-nik\ *adj* [LL *histrionicus*, fr. L *histrio* actor] **1** : deliberately affected **2** : of or relating to actors, acting, or the theater — **his·tri·on·i·cal·ly** \-ni-k(ə-)lē\ *adv*

his·tri·on·ics \-niks\ *n pl* **1** : theatrical performances **2** : deliberate display of emotion for effect

¹hit \ˈhit\ *vb* **hit; hit·ting 1** : to reach with a blow : STRIKE; *also* : to arrive with a force like a blow ⟨the storm ∼⟩ **2** : to make or bring into contact : COLLIDE **3** : to affect detrimentally ⟨was ∼ by the flu⟩ **4** : to make a request of **5** : to come upon **6** : to accord with : SUIT **7** : REACH, ATTAIN **8** : to indulge in often to excess — **hit·ter** *n*

²hit *n* **1** : an act or instance of hitting or being hit **2** : a great success **3** : BASE HIT **4** : a dose of an illegal drug **5** : a murder committed by a gangster

¹hitch \ˈhich\ *vb* **1** : to move by jerks **2** : to catch or fasten esp. by a hook or knot **3** : HITCHHIKE

²hitch *n* **1** : JERK, PULL **2** : a sudden halt **3** : a connection between something towed and its mover **4** : KNOT

hitch·hike \ˈhich-ˌhīk\ *vb* : to travel by securing free rides from passing vehicles — **hitch·hik·er** *n*

¹hith·er \ˈhi-thər\ *adv* : to this place

²hither *adj* : being on the near or adjacent side

hith·er·to \-ˌtü\ *adv* : up to this time

HIV \ˌāch-(ˌ)ī-ˈvē\ *n* [*h*uman *i*mmunodeficiency *v*irus] : any of several retroviruses that infect and destroy helper T cells causing the great reduction in their numbers diagnostic of AIDS

hive \ˈhīv\ *n* **1** : a container for housing honeybees **2** : a colony of bees **3** : a place swarming with busy occupants — **hive** *vb*

hives \ˈhīvz\ *n sing or pl* : an allergic disorder marked by raised itching patches on the skin or mucous membranes

hl *abbr* hectoliter

HL *abbr* House of Lords

hm *abbr* hectometer

HM *abbr* **1** Her Majesty; Her Majesty's **2** His Majesty; His Majesty's

HMO \ˌāch-(ˌ)em-ˈō\ *n* [*h*ealth *m*aintenance *o*rganization] : a comprehensive health-care organization financed by periodic fixed payments by voluntarily enrolled individuals and families

HMS *abbr* **1** Her Majesty's ship **2** His Majesty's ship

Ho *symbol* holmium

hoa·gie *also* **hoa·gy** \ˈhō-gē\ *n, pl* **hoagies** : SUBMARINE 2

hoard \ˈhōrd\ *n* : a hidden accumulation — **hoard** *vb* — **hoard·er** *n*

hoar·frost \ˈhōr-ˌfròst\ *n* : FROST 2

hoarse \ˈhōrs\ *adj* **hoars·er; hoars·est 1** : rough and harsh in sound **2** : having a grating voice — **hoarse·ly** *adv* — **hoarse·ness** *n*

hoary \ˈhōr-ē\ *adj* **hoar·i·er; -est 1** : gray or white with or as if with age **2** : ANCIENT — **hoar·i·ness** \ˈhōr-ē-nəs\ *n*

hoax \ˈhōks\ *n* : an act intended to trick or dupe; *also* : something accepted or established by fraud — **hoax** *vb* — **hoax·er** *n*

hob \ˈhäb\ *n* : MISCHIEF, TROUBLE

¹hob·ble \ˈhä-bəl\ *vb* **hob·bled; hob·bling 1** : to limp along; *also* : to make lame **2** : FETTER

²hobble *n* **1** : a hobbling movement **2** : something used to hobble an animal

hob·by \ˈhä-bē\ *n, pl* **hobbies** : a pursuit or interest engaged in for relaxation — **hob·by·ist** \-ist\ *n*

hob·by·horse \ˈhä-bē-ˌhòrs\ *n* **1** : a stick with a horse's head on which children pretend to ride **2** : a toy horse mounted on rockers **3** : a topic to which one constantly reverts

hob·gob·lin \ˈhäb-ˌgäb-lən\ *n* **1** : a mischievous goblin **2** : BOGEY 1

hob·nail \-ˌnāl\ *n* : a short large-headed nail for studding shoe soles — **hob·nailed** \-ˌnāld\ *adj*

hob·nob \-ˌnäb\ *vb* **hob·nobbed; hob·nob·bing** : to associate familiarly

ho·bo \ˈhō-bō\ *n, pl* **hoboes** *also* **hobos** : TRAMP 2

¹hock \ˈhäk\ *n* : a joint or region in the hind limb of a quadruped just above the foot and corresponding to the human ankle

²hock *n* [D *hok* pen, prison] : PAWN; *also* : DEBT 3 — **hock** *vb*

hock·ey \ˈhä-kē\ *n* **1** : FIELD HOCKEY **2** : ICE HOCKEY

ho·cus-po·cus \ˌhō-kəs-ˈpō-kəs\ *n* **1** : SLEIGHT OF HAND **2** : nonsense or sham used to conceal deception

hod \ˈhäd\ *n* : a long-handled carrier for mortar or bricks

hodge·podge \ˈhäj-ˌpäj\ *n* : a heterogeneous mixture : JUMBLE

hoe \ˈhō\ *n* : a long-handled implement with a thin flat blade used esp. for cultivating, weeding, or loosening the earth around plants — **hoe** *vb*

hoe·cake \ˈhō-ˌkāk\ *n* : a small cornmeal cake

hoe·down \-ˌdaůn\ *n* **1** : SQUARE DANCE **2** : a gathering featuring hoedowns

¹hog \ˈhóg, ˈhäg\ *n, pl* **hogs** *also* **hog 1** : a domestic swine esp. when grown **2** : a selfish, gluttonous, or filthy person — **hog·gish** *adj*

²hog *vb* **hogged; hog·ging** : to take or hold selfishly

ho·gan \ˈhō-gän\ *n* : a Navajo Indian dwelling usu. made of logs and mud

hogan

hog·back \'hòg-,bak, 'häg-\ n : a ridge with a sharp summit and steep sides

hog·nose snake \'hòg-,nōz-, 'häg-\ or hog·nosed snake \-,nōzd-\ n : any of a genus of rather small harmless stout-bodied No. American snakes that seldom bite but hiss wildly and often play dead when disturbed

hogs·head \'hògz-,hed, 'hägz-\ n 1 : a large cask or barrel 2 : a liquid measure equal to 63 U.S. gallons

hog–tie \'hòg-,tī, 'häg-\ vb 1 : to tie together the feet of ⟨~ a calf⟩ 2 : to make helpless

hog·wash \-,wòsh, -,wäsh\ n 1 : SWILL, SLOP 2 : NONSENSE, BALONEY

hog–wild \-'wīld\ adj : lacking in restraint

hoi pol·loi \,hòi-pə-'lòi\ n pl [Gk, the many] : the general populace

¹hoist \'hòist\ vb : RAISE, LIFT

²hoist n 1 : LIFT 2 : an apparatus for hoisting

hoke \'hōk\ vb hoked; hok·ing : FAKE — usu. used with up

hok·ey \'hō-kē\ adj hok·i·er; -est : CORNY; also : PHONY

ho·kum \'hō-kəm\ n : NONSENSE

¹hold \'hōld\ vb held \'held\; hold·ing 1 : POSSESS; also : KEEP 2 : RESTRAIN 3 : to have a grasp on 4 : to support, remain, or keep in a particular situation or position 5 : SUSTAIN; also : RESERVE 6 : BEAR, COMPORT 7 : to maintain in being or action : PERSIST 8 : CONTAIN, ACCOMMODATE 9 : HARBOR, ENTERTAIN; also : CONSIDER, REGARD 10 : to carry on by concerted action; also : CONVOKE 11 : to occupy esp. by appointment or election 12 : to be valid 13 : HALT, PAUSE — hold·er n — hold forth : to speak at length — hold to : to adhere to : MAINTAIN — hold with : to agree with or approve of

²hold n 1 : STRONGHOLD 2 : CONFINEMENT; also : PRISON 3 : the act or manner of holding : GRIP 4 : a restraining, dominating, or controlling influence 5 : something that may be grasped as a support 6 : an order or indication that something is to be reserved or delayed — on hold : in a temporary state of waiting (as during a phone call); also : in a state of postponement ⟨plans on hold⟩

³hold n 1 : the interior of a ship below decks; esp : a ship's cargo deck 2 : an airplane's cargo compartment

hold·ing n 1 : land or other property owned 2 : a ruling of a court esp. on an issue of law

holding pattern n : a course flown by an aircraft waiting to land

hold out vb 1 : to continue to fight or work 2 : to refuse to come to an agreement — hold·out \'hōl-,daut\ n

hold·over \'hōl-,dō-vər\ n : one that is held over

hold·up \'hōl-,dəp\ n 1 : DELAY 2 : robbery at the point of a gun

hole \'hōl\ n 1 : an opening into or through something 2 : a hollow place (as a pit or cave) 3 : DEN, BURROW 4 : a wretched or dingy place 5 : a unit of play from tee to cup in golf 6 : an awkward position — hole vb

hol·i·day \'hä-lə-,dā\ n [ME, fr. OE hāligdæg, fr. hālig holy + dæg day] 1 : a day set aside for special religious observance 2 : a day of freedom from work; esp : one in commemoration of an event 3 : VACATION — holiday vb

ho·li·ness \'hō-lē-nəs\ n : the quality or state of being holy — used as a title for various high religious officials

ho·lis·tic \hō-'lis-tik\ adj : relating to or concerned with integrated wholes or complete systems rather than with the analysis or treatment of separate parts ⟨~ medicine⟩ ⟨~ ecology⟩

hol·ler \'hä-lər\ vb : to cry out : SHOUT — holler n

¹hol·low \'hä-lō\ n 1 : CAVITY, HOLE 2 : a surface depression

²hollow adj hol·low·er \'hä-lə-wər\; hol·low·est \-lə-wəst\ 1 : CONCAVE, SUNKEN 2 : having a cavity within 3 : lacking in real value, sincerity, or substance; also : FALSE 4 : MUFFLED ⟨a ~ sound⟩ — hol·low·ness n

³hollow vb : to make or become hollow

hol·low·ware or hol·lo·ware \'hä-lō-,war\ n : vessels (as bowls or cups) with a significant depth and volume

hol·ly \'hä-lē\ n, pl hollies : either of two trees or shrubs with branches of usu. evergreen glossy spiny-margined leaves and red berries

hol·ly·hock \'hä-lē-,häk, -,hòk\ n [ME holihoc, fr. holi holy + hoc mallow] : a perennial Chinese herb related to the mallows that is widely grown for its tall stalks of showy flowers

hol·mi·um \'hōl-mē-əm\ n : a metallic chemical element — see ELEMENT table

ho·lo·caust \'hä-lə-,kòst, 'hō-\ n 1 : a thorough destruction esp. by fire 2 often cap : the killing of European Jews by the Nazis during World War II; also : GENOCIDE

Ho·lo·cene \'hō-lə-,sēn\ adj : of, relating to, or being the present geologic epoch — Holocene n

ho·lo·gram \'hō-lə-,gram, 'hä-\ n : a three-dimensional image produced by an interference pattern of light (as laser light)

ho·lo·graph \'hō-lə-,graf, 'hä-\ n : a document wholly in the handwriting of its author

ho·log·ra·phy \hō-'lä-grə-fē\ n : the process of making a hologram — ho·lo·graph·ic \,hō-lə-'gra-fik, ,hä-\ adj

Hol·stein \'hōl-,stēn, -,stīn\ n : any of a breed of large black-and-white dairy cattle that produce large quantities of comparatively low-fat milk

Hol·stein–Frie·sian \-'frē-zhən\ n : HOLSTEIN

hol·ster \'hōl-stər\ n [D] : a usu. leather case for a firearm

ho·ly \'hō-lē\ adj ho·li·er; -est 1 : worthy of absolute devotion 2 : SACRED 3 : having a divine quality syn hallowed, blessed, sanctified, consecrated — ho·li·ly \-lə-lē\ adv

Holy Grail n : GRAIL

Holy Spirit n : the third person of the Christian Trinity

ho·ly·stone \'hō-lē-,stōn\ n : a soft sandstone used to scrub a ship's decks — holystone vb

hom·age \'ä-mij, 'hä-\ n [ME, fr. OF hommage, fr. homme man, vassal, fr. L homo human being] : expression of high regard; also : TRIBUTE 3

hom·bre \'äm-brē, 'əm-, -,brā\ n : GUY, FELLOW

hom·burg \'häm-,bərg\ n [Homburg, Germany] : a man's felt hat with a stiff curled brim and a high crown creased lengthwise

¹home \'hōm\ n 1 : one's residence; also : HOUSE 2 : the social unit formed by a family living together 3 : a congenial environment; also : HABITAT 4 : a place of origin 5 : the objective in various games

²home vb homed; hom·ing 1 : to go or return home 2 : to proceed to or toward a source of radiated energy used as a guide

home·body \'hōm-,bä-dē\ n : one whose life centers in the home

home·boy \-,bòi\ n 1 : a boy or man from one's neighborhood, hometown, or region 2 : a fellow member of a youth gang

home·bred \-'bred\ adj : produced at home : INDIGENOUS

home·com·ing \-,kə-miŋ\ n 1 : a return home 2 : the return of a group of people esp. on a special occasion to a place formerly frequented

home computer n : a small inexpensive microcomputer

home economics n : the theory and practice of homemaking

home·grown \'hōm-'grōn\ adj 1 : grown domestically 2 : LOCAL, INDIGENOUS

home·land \-,land\ n 1 : native land 2 : an area set aside to be a state for a people of a particular national, cultural, or racial origin

¹home·less \-ləs\ adj : having no home or permanent residence

²**homeless** *n, pl* : persons esp. in urban areas that have no home

home·ly \'hōm-lē\ *adj* **home·li·er; -est 1** : FAMILIAR **2** : unaffectedly natural **3** : lacking beauty or proportion — **home·li·ness** \-lē-nəs\ *n*

home·made \'hōm-₁mād\ *adj* : made in the home, on the premises, or by one's own efforts

home·mak·er \-₁mā-kər\ *n* : one who manages a household esp. as a wife and mother — **home·mak·ing** \-kiŋ\ *n*

ho·me·op·a·thy \₁hō-mē-'ä-pə-thē\ *n* : a system of medical practice that treats disease esp. with minute doses of a remedy that would in healthy persons produce symptoms similar to those of the disease treated — **ho·meo·path** \'hō-mē-ə-₁path\ *n* — **ho·meo·path·ic** \₁hō-mē-ə-'pa-thik\ *adj*

ho·meo·sta·sis \₁hō-mē-ō-'stā-səs\ *n* : the maintence of a relatively stable state of equilibrium between interrelated physiological, psychological, or social factors characteristic of an individual or group — **ho·meo·stat·ic** \-'sta-tik\ *adj*

home plate *n* : a slab at the apex of a baseball diamond that a base runner must touch in order to score

hom·er \'hō-mər\ *n* : HOME RUN — **homer** *vb*

home·room \'hōm-₁rüm, -₁rüm\ *n* : a classroom where pupils report at the beginning of each school day

home run *n* : a hit in baseball that enables the batter to go around all the bases and score a run

home·sick \'hōm-₁sik\ *adj* : longing for home and family while absent from them — **home·sick·ness** *n*

home·spun \-₁spən\ *adj* **1** : spun or made at home; *also* : made of a loosely woven usu. woolen or linen fabric **2** : SIMPLE, HOMELY

¹**home·stead** \-₁sted\ *n* : the home and land occupied by a family

²**homestead** *vb* : to acquire or settle on public land — **home·stead·er** *n*

home·stretch \-'strech\ *n* **1** : the part of a racecourse between the last curve and the winning post **2** : a final stage (as of a project)

¹**home·ward** \-wərd\ *or* **home·wards** \-wərdz\ *adv* : toward home

²**homeward** *adj* : being or going toward home

home·work \-₁wərk\ *n* **1** : an assignment given a student to be completed outside the classroom **2** : preparatory reading or research

hom·ey \'hō-mē\ *adj* **hom·i·er; -est** : characteristic of home

ho·mi·cide \'hä-mə-₁sīd, 'hō-\ *n* [L *homicida* murderer & *homicidium* manslaughter; both fr. *homo* human being + *caedere* to cut, kill] **1** : a person who kills another **2** : a killing of one human being by another — **hom·i·cid·al** \₁hä-mə-'sīd-ᵊl\ *adj*

hom·i·ly \'hä-mə-lē\ *n, pl* **-lies** : SERMON — **hom·i·let·ic** \₁hä-mə-'le-tik\ *adj*

homing pigeon *n* : a racing pigeon trained to return home

hom·i·nid \'hä-mə-nəd, -₁nid\ *n* : any of a family of primate mammals that comprise all living humans and extinct ancestral and related forms — **hominid** *adj*

hom·i·ny \'hä-mə-nē\ *n* : hulled corn with the germ removed

ho·mo·ge·neous \₁hō-mə-'jē-nē-əs, -nyəs\ *adj* : of the same or a similar kind; *also* : of uniform structure — **ho·mo·ge·ne·i·ty** \-jə-'nē-ə-tē\ *n* — **ho·mo·ge·neous·ly** *adv*

ho·mog·e·nize \hō-'mä-jə-₁nīz, hə-\ *vb* **-nized; -niz·ing 1** : to make homogeneous **2** : to reduce the particles in (as milk) to uniform size and distribute them evenly throughout the liquid — **ho·mog·e·ni·za·tion** \-₁mä-jə-nə-'zā-shən\ *n* — **ho·mog·e·niz·er** *n*

ho·mo·graph \'hä-mə-₁graf, 'hō-\ *n* : one of two or more words spelled alike but different in origin, meaning, or

pronunciation (as the *bow* of a ship, a *bow* and arrow)

ho·mol·o·gy \hō-'mä-lə-jē, hə-\ *n, pl* **-gies 1** : structural likeness between corresponding parts of different plants or animals due to evolution from a common ancestor **2** : structural likeness between different parts of the same individual — **ho·mol·o·gous** \-'mä-lə-gəs\ *adj*

hom·onym \'hä-mə-₁nim, 'hō-\ *n* **1** : HOMOPHONE, HOMOGRAPH **2** : one of two or more words spelled and pronounced alike but different in meaning (as *pool* of water and *pool* the game)

ho·mo·phone \'hä-mə-₁fōn, 'hō-\ *n* : one of two or more words (as *to, too, two*) pronounced alike but different in meaning or derivation or spelling

Ho·mo sa·pi·ens \₁hō-mō-'sā-pē-ənz, -'sa-\ *n* : HUMANKIND

ho·mo·sex·u·al \₁hō-mō-'sek-shə-wəl\ *adj* : of, relating to, or marked by sexual interst in the same sex as oneself; *also* : of, relating to, or involving sexual intercourse between members of the same sex — **homosexual** *n* — **ho·mo·sex·u·al·i·ty** \-₁sek-shə-'wa-lə-tē\ *n*

hon *abbr* honor; honorable; honorary

Hon·du·ran \hän-'dür-ən\ *or* **Hon·du·ra·ne·an** *or* **Hon·du·ra·ni·an** \₁han-dü-'rä-nē-ən, -dyü-\ *n* : a native or inhabitant of Honduras — **Honduran** *or* **Honduranean** *or* **Honduranian** *adj*

hone \'hōn\ *n* : WHETSTONE — **hone** *vb* — **hon·er** *n*

hone in *vb* : to move toward or direct attention to an objective

¹**hon·est** \'ä-nəst\ *adj* **1** : free from deception : TRUTHFUL; *also* : GENUINE, REAL **2** : REPUTABLE **3** : CREDITABLE **4** : marked by integrity **5** : FRANK **syn** upright, just, conscientious, honorable — **hon·est·ly** *adv* — **hon·es·ty** \-nə-stē\ *n*

²**honest** *adv* : HONESTLY; *also* : with all sincerity ⟨I didn't do it, ~⟩

hon·ey \'hə-nē\ *n, pl* **honeys** : a sweet sticky substance made by honeybees from the nectar of flowers

hon·ey·bee \'hə-nē-₁bē\ *n* : a social and colonial 4-winged insect often kept in hives for the honey it produces

¹**hon·ey·comb** \-₁kōm\ *n* : a mass of 6-sided wax cells built by honeybees; *also* : something of similar structure or appearance

²**honeycomb** *vb* : to make or become full of cavities like a honeycomb

hon·ey·dew \-₁dü, -₁dyü\ *n* : a sweetish deposit secreted on plants by aphids, scale insects, or fungi

honeydew melon *n* : a smooth-skinned muskmelon with sweet green flesh

honey locust *n* : a tall usu. spiny No. American leguminous tree with hard durable wood and long twisted pods

hon·ey·moon \'hə-nē-₁mün\ *n* **1** : a period of harmony esp. just after marriage **2** : a holiday taken by a newly married couple — **honeymoon** *vb*

hon·ey·suck·le \'hə-nē-₁sə-kəl\ *n* : any of a genus of shrubs or vines with tube-shaped flowers rich in nectar

honk \'häŋk, 'hôŋk\ *n* : the cry of a goose; *also* : a similar sound (as of a horn) — **honk** *vb* — **honk·er** *n*

hon·ky–tonk \'häŋ-kē-₁täŋk, 'hôŋ-kē-₁tôŋk\ *n* : a tawdry nightclub or dance hall — **honky–tonk** *adj*

¹**hon·or** \'ä-nər\ *n* **1** : REPUTATION; *also* : outward respect **2** : PRIVILEGE **3** : a person of superior standing — used esp. as a title **4** : one who brings respect or fame **5** : an evidence or symbol of distinction **6** : CHASTITY, PURITY **7** : INTEGRITY **syn** homage, reverence, deference, obeisance

---

\ə\abut \ᵊ\kitten \ər\further \a\ash \ā\ace \ä\mop, mar \aú\out \ch\chin \e\bet \ē\easy \g\go \i\hit \ī\ice \j\job \ŋ\sing \ō\go \ò\law \òi\boy \th\thin \t͟h\the \ü\loot \ù\foot \y\yet \zh\vision *see also* Pronunciation Symbols page

²**honor** *vb* **1** : to regard or treat with honor **2** : to confer honor on **3** : to fulfill the terms of; *also* : to accept as payment — **hon·or·ee** \ä-nə-ˈrē\ *n* — **hon·or·er** *n*

hon·or·able \ˈä-nə-rə-bəl\ *adj* **1** : deserving of honor **2** : of great renown **3** : accompanied with marks of honor **4** : doing credit to the possessor **5** : characterized by integrity — **hon·or·able·ness** *n* — **hon·or·ably** \-blē\ *adv*

hon·o·rar·i·um \ä-nə-ˈrer-ē-əm\ *n, pl* **-ia** \-ē-ə\ *also* **-i·ums** : a reward usu. for services on which custom or propriety forbids a price to be set

hon·or·ary \ˈä-nə-ˌrer-ē\ *adj* **1** : having or conferring distinction **2** : conferred in recognition of achievement without the usual prerequisites ⟨∼ degree⟩ **3** : UNPAID, VOLUNTARY — **hon·or·ari·ly** \ä-nə-ˈrer-ə-lē\ *adv*

hon·or·if·ic \ä-nə-ˈri-fik\ *adj* : conferring or conveying honor ⟨∼ titles⟩

hon·our, hon·our·able *chiefly Brit var of* HONOR, HONORABLE

¹**hood** \ˈhud\ *n* **1** : a covering for the head and neck and sometimes the face **2** : an ornamental fold (as at the back of an ecclesiastical vestment) **3** : a cover for parts of mechanisms; *esp* : the covering over an automobile engine — **hood·ed** \ˈhu-dəd\ *adj*

²**hood** \ˈhud, ˈhüd\ *n* : HOODLUM

³**hood** \ˈhud\ *n* : NEIGHBORHOOD 4

-hood \ˌhud\ *n suffix* **1** : state : condition : quality : character ⟨boy*hood*⟩ ⟨hardi*hood*⟩ **2** : instance of a (specified) state or quality ⟨false*hood*⟩ **3** : individuals sharing a (specified) state or character ⟨brother*hood*⟩

hood·lum \ˈhud-ləm, ˈhud-\ *n* **1** : THUG **2** : a young ruffian

hoo·doo \ˈhü-dü\ *n, pl* **hoodoos** **1** : a body of magical practices traditional esp. among blacks in the southern U.S. **2** : something that brings bad luck — **hoodoo** *vb*

hood·wink \ˈhud-ˌwiŋk\ *vb* : to deceive by false appearance

hoo·ey \ˈhü-ē\ *n* : NONSENSE

hoof \ˈhuf, ˈhüf\ *n, pl* **hooves** \ˈhuvz, ˈhüvz\ *or* **hoofs** : a horny covering that protects the ends of the toes of ungulate mammals (as horses or cattle); *also* : a hoofed foot — **hoofed** \ˈhuft, ˈhüft\ *adj*

¹**hook** \ˈhuk\ *n* **1** : a curved or bent device for catching, holding, or pulling **2** : something curved or bent like a hook **3** : a flight of a ball (as in golf) that curves in a direction opposite to the dominant hand of the player propelling it **4** : a short punch delivered with a circular motion and with the elbow bent and rigid

²**hook** *vb* **1** : CURVE, CROOK **2** : to seize or make fast with a hook **3** : STEAL **4** : to work as a prostitute

hoo·kah \ˈhu-kə, ˈhü-\ *n* [Ar *huqqah* bottle of a water pipe] : WATER PIPE

hook·er \ˈhu-kər\ *n* **1** : one that hooks **2** : PROSTITUTE

hook·up \ˈhu-ˌkəp\ *n* : an assemblage (as of apparatus or circuits) used for a specific purpose (as in radio)

hook·worm \ˈhuk-ˌwərm\ *n* : any of several parasitic intestinal nematode worms having hooks or plates around the mouth; *also* : infestation with or disease caused by hookworms

hoo·li·gan \ˈhü-li-gən\ *n* : RUFFIAN, HOODLUM

hoop \ˈhup, ˈhüp\ *n* **1** : a circular strip used esp. for holding together the staves of a barrel **2** : a circular figure or object : RING **3** : a circle of flexible material for expanding a woman's skirt **4** : BASKETBALL — usu. used in pl.

hoop·la \ˈhup-ˌlä, ˈhup-\ *n* [F *houp-là*, interj.] : TO-DO; *also* : BALLYHOO

hoose·gow \ˈhüs-ˌgau\ *n* [Sp *juzgado* panel of judges, courtroom] : JAIL

¹**hoot** \ˈhüt\ *vb* **1** : to shout or laugh usu. in contempt **2** : to make the natural throat noise of an owl — **hoot·er** *n*

²**hoot** *n* **1** : a sound of hooting **2** : the least bit ⟨don't give

a ∼⟩ **3** : something or someone amusing ⟨the play is a real ∼⟩

¹**hop** \ˈhäp\ *vb* **hopped; hop·ping** **1** : to move by quick springy leaps **2** : to make a quick trip **3** : to ride on esp. surreptitiously and without authorization

²**hop** *n* **1** : a short brisk leap esp. on one leg **2** : DANCE **3** : a short trip by air

³**hop** *n* : a vine related to the mulberry whose ripe dried pistillate catkins are used esp. in flavoring malt liquors; *also, pl* : its pistillate catkins

¹**hope** \ˈhōp\ *vb* **hoped; hop·ing** : to desire with expectation of fulfillment

²**hope** *n* **1** : TRUST, RELIANCE **2** : desire accompanied by expectation of fulfillment; *also* : something hoped for **3** : one that gives promise for the future — **hope·ful** \-fəl\ *adj* — **hope·ful·ness** *n* — **hope·less** *adj* — **hope·less·ly** *adv* — **hope·less·ness** *n*

HOPE *abbr* Health Opportunity for People Everywhere

hope·ful·ly \ˈhōp-fə-lē\ *adv* **1** : in a hopeful manner **2** : it is hoped

Ho·pi \ˈhō-pē\ *n, pl* **Hopi** *also* **Hopis** : a member of an American Indian people of Arizona; *also* : the language of the Hopi people

hopped-up \ˈhäpt-ˈəp\ *adj* **1** : being under the influence of a narcotic; *also* : full of enthusiasm or excitement **2** : having more power than usual ⟨a ∼ engine⟩

hop·per \ˈhä-pər\ *n* **1** : a usu. immature hopping insect (as a grasshopper) **2** : a usu. funnel-shaped container for delivering material (as grain) **3** : a freight car with hinged doors in a sloping bottom **4** : a box into which a bill to be considered by a legislative body is dropped **5** : a tank holding a liquid and having a device for releasing its contents through a pipe

hop·scotch \ˈhäp-ˌskäch\ *n* : a child's game in which a player tosses an object (as a stone) into areas of a figure drawn on the ground and hops through the figure to pick up the object

hor *abbr* horizontal

horde \ˈhōrd\ *n* : THRONG, SWARM

ho·ri·zon \hə-ˈrīz-ᵊn\ *n* [Gk *horizont-, horizōn,* fr. prp. of *horizein* to bound, fr. *horos* limit, boundary] **1** : the apparent junction of earth and sky **2** : range of outlook or experience

hor·i·zon·tal \ˌhor-ə-ˈzänt-ᵊl\ *adj* : parallel to the horizon : LEVEL — **horizontal** *n* — **hor·i·zon·tal·ly** *adv*

hor·mon·al \hor-ˈmōn-ᵊl\ *adj* : of, relating to, or effected by hormones

hor·mone \ˈhor-ˌmōn\ *n* [Gk *hormōn,* prp. of *horman* to stir up, fr. *hormē* impulse, assault] : a product of living cells that circulates in body fluids and has a specific effect on the activity of cells remote from its point of origin

horn \ˈhorn\ *n* **1** : one of the hard projections of bone or keratin on the head of many hoofed mammals **2** : something resembling or suggesting a horn **3** : a brass wind instrument **4** : a usu. electrical device that makes a noise ⟨automobile ∼⟩ — **horned** \ˈhornd\ *adj* — **horn·less** *adj*

horn·book \ˈhorn-ˌbuk\ *n* **1** : a child's primer consisting of a sheet of parchment or paper protected by a sheet of transparent horn **2** : a rudimentary treatise

horned toad *n* : any of several small harmless insect-eating lizards with spines on the head resembling horns and spiny scales on the body

hor·net \ˈhor-nət\ *n* : any of the larger social wasps

horn in *vb* : to participate without invitation : INTRUDE

horn·pipe \ˈhorn-ˌpīp\ *n* : a lively folk dance of the British Isles

horny \ˈhor-nē\ *adj* **horn·i·er; -est** **1** : of or made of horn; *also* : HARD, CALLOUS **2** : having horns **3** : desiring sexual gratification; *also* : excited sexually

ho·rol·o·gy \hə-ˈrä-lə-jē\ *n* : the science of measuring time or constructing time-indicating instruments —

hor·o·log·ic \ˌhȯr-ə-ˈlä-jik\ *adj* — ho·rol·o·gist \hə-ˈrä-lə-jist\ *n*

horo·scope \ˈhȯr-ə-ˌskōp\ *n* [ME *oruscope,* fr. MF *horoscope,* fr. L *horoscopus,* fr. Gk *hōroskopos,* fr. *hōra* hour + *skopos* watcher] 1 : a diagram of the relative positions of planets and signs of the zodiac at a particular time for use by astrologers to foretell events of a person's life 2 : an astrological forecast

hor·ren·dous \hȯ-ˈren-dəs\ *adj* : DREADFUL, HORRIBLE

hor·ri·ble \ˈhȯr-ə-bəl\ *adj* 1 : marked by or conducive to horror 2 : highly disagreeable — hor·ri·ble·ness *n* — hor·ri·bly \-blē\ *adv*

hor·rid \ˈhȯr-əd\ *adj* 1 : HIDEOUS 2 : REPULSIVE — hor·rid·ly *adv*

hor·ri·fy \ˈhȯr-ə-ˌfī\ *vb* -fied; -fy·ing : to cause to feel horror syn appall, daunt, dismay

hor·ror \ˈhȯr-ər\ *n* 1 : painful and intense fear, dread, or dismay 2 : intense repugnance 3 : something that horrifies

hors de com·bat \ˌȯr-də-kōⁿ-ˈbä\ *adv or adj* : in a disabled condition

hors d'oeuvre \ȯr-ˈdərv\ *n, pl* hors d'oeuvres *same or* -ˈdərvz\ *also* hors d'oeuvre [F *hors-d'oeuvre,* lit., outside of the work] : any of various savory foods usu. served as appetizers

horse \ˈhȯrs\ *n, pl* hors·es *also* horse 1 : a large solid-hoofed herbivorous mammal domesticated as a draft and saddle animal 2 : a supporting framework usu. with legs — horse·less *adj*

¹horse·back \ˈhȯrs-ˌbak\ *n* : the back of a horse

²horseback *adv* : on horseback

horse chestnut *n* : a large Asian tree with palmate leaves, erect conical clusters of showy flowers, and large glossy brown seeds enclosed in a prickly bur; *also* : its seed

horse·flesh \ˈhȯrs-ˌflesh\ *n* : horses for riding, driving, or racing

horse·fly \-ˌflī\ *n* : any of a family of large dipteran flies with bloodsucking females

horse·hair \-ˌhar\ *n* 1 : the hair of a horse esp. from the mane or tail 2 : cloth made from horsehair

horse·hide \-ˌhīd\ *n* 1 : the dressed or raw hide of a horse 2 : the ball used in baseball

horse latitudes *n pl* : either of two calm regions near 30°N and 30°S latitude

horse·laugh \ˈhȯrs-ˌlaf, -ˌläf\ *n* : a loud boisterous laugh

horse·man \-mən\ *n* 1 : one who rides horseback; *also* : one skilled in managing horses 2 : a breeder or raiser of horses — horse·man·ship *n*

horse·play \-ˌplā\ *n* : rough boisterous play

horse·play·er \-ər\ *n* : a bettor on horse races

horse·pow·er \ˈhȯrs-ˌpau̇-ər\ *n* : a unit of power equal in the U.S. to 746 watts

horse·rad·ish \-ˌra-dish\ *n* : a tall white-flowered herb related to the mustards whose pungent root is used as a condiment; *also* : the pungent condiment

horse·shoe \ˈhȯrs-ˌshü\ *n* 1 : a usu. U-shaped protective metal plate fitted to the rim of a horse's hoof 2 *pl* : a game in which horseshoes are pitched at a fixed object — horse·shoe *vb* — horse·sho·er *n*

horseshoe crab *n* : any of several marine arthropods with a broad crescent-shaped combined head and thorax

horse·tail \ˈhȯrs-ˌtāl\ *n* : any of a genus of primitive spore-producing plants with hollow jointed stems and leaves reduced to sheaths about the joints

horse·whip \-ˌhwip\ *vb* : to flog with a whip made to be used on a horse

horse·wom·an \-ˌwu̇-mən\ *n* : a woman skilled in riding horseback or in caring for or managing horses; *also* : a woman who breeds or raises horses

hors·ey *or* horsy \ˈhȯr-sē\ *adj* hors·i·er; -est 1 : of, re-

lating to, or suggesting a horse 2 : having to do with horses or horse racing

hort *abbr* horticultural; horticulture

hor·ta·tive \ˈhȯr-tə-tiv\ *adj* : giving exhortation

hor·ta·to·ry \ˈhȯr-tə-ˌtōr-ē\ *adj* : HORTATIVE

hor·ti·cul·ture \ˈhȯr-tə-ˌkəl-chər\ *n* : the science and art of growing fruits, vegetables, flowers, and ornamental plants — hor·ti·cul·tur·al \ˌhȯr-tə-ˈkəl-chə-rəl\ *adj* — hor·ti·cul·tur·ist \-rist\ *n*

Hos *abbr* Hosea

ho·san·na \hō-ˈza-nə, -ˈzä-\ *interj* [Gk *hōsanna,* fr. Heb *hōshī'āh-nnā* pray, save (us)!] — used as a cry of acclamation and adoration — hosanna *n*

¹hose \ˈhōz\ *n, pl* hose *or* hos·es 1 *pl* hose : STOCKING, SOCK; *also* : a close-fitting garment covering the legs and waist 2 : a flexible tube for conveying fluids (as from a faucet)

²hose *vb* hosed; hos·ing : to spray, water, or wash with a hose

Ho·sea \hō-ˈzā-ə, -ˈzē-\ *n* — see BIBLE table

ho·siery \ˈhō-zhə-rē, -zə-\ *n* : STOCKINGS, SOCKS

hosp *abbr* hospital

hos·pice \ˈhäs-pəs\ *n* 1 : a lodging for travelers or for young persons or the underprivileged 2 : a facility or program for caring for dying persons

hos·pi·ta·ble \hä-ˈspi-tə-bəl, ˈhäs-(ˌ)pi-\ *adj* 1 : given to generous and cordial reception of guests 2 : readily receptive — hos·pi·ta·bly \-blē\ *adv*

hos·pi·tal \ˈhäs-ˌpit-ᵊl\ *n* [ME, fr. OF, fr. ML *hospitale* hospice, guest house, fr neut. of L *hospitalis* of a guest, fr. *hospit-, hospes* guest, host] : an institution where the sick or injured receive medical or surgical care

hos·pi·tal·i·ty \ˌhäs-pə-ˈta-lə-tē\ *n, pl* -ties : hospitable treatment, reception, or disposition

hos·pi·tal·ize \ˈhäs-ˌpit-ᵊl-ˌīz\ *vb* -ized; -iz·ing : to place in a hospital as a patient — hos·pi·tal·i·za·tion \ˌhäs-ˌpit-ᵊl-ə-ˈzā-shən\ *n*

¹host \ˈhōst\ *n* [ME, fr. OF, fr. LL *hostis,* fr. L, stranger, enemy] 1 : ARMY 2 : MULTITUDE

²host *n* [ME *hoste* host, guest, fr. OF, fr. L *hospit-, hospes*] 1 : one who receives or entertains guests 2 : an animal or plant on or in which a parasite lives — host *vb*

³host *n, often cap* [ultim. fr. L *hostia* sacrifice] : the eucharistic bread

hos·tage \ˈhäs-tij\ *n* 1 : a person kept as a pledge pending the fulfillment of an agreement 2 : a person taken by force to secure the taker's demands

hos·tel \ˈhäst-ᵊl\ *n* [ME, fr. OF, fr. ML *hospitale* hospice] 1 : INN 2 : a supervised lodging for youth — hos·tel·er *n*

hos·tel·ry \-rē\ *n, pl* -ries : INN, HOTEL

host·ess \ˈhō-stəs\ *n* : a woman who acts as host

hos·tile \ˈhäst-ᵊl, ˈhäs-ˌtīl\ *adj* : marked by usu. overt antagonism : UNFRIENDLY — hostile *n* — hos·tile·ly *adv*

hos·til·i·ty \hä-ˈsti-lə-tē\ *n, pl* -ties 1 : an unfriendly state or action 2 *pl* : overt acts of war

hos·tler \ˈhäs-lər, ˈäs-\ *n* : one who takes care of horses or mules

hot \ˈhät\ *adj* hot·ter; hot·test 1 : marked by a high temperature or an uncomfortable degree of body heat 2 : giving a sensation of heat or of burning 3 : ARDENT, FIERY 4 : sexually excited 5 : EAGER 6 : newly made or received 7 : PUNGENT 8 : unusually lucky or favorable ⟨∼ dice⟩ 9 : recently and illegally obtained ⟨∼ jewels⟩ — hot *adv* — hot·ly *adv* — hot·ness *n*

hot·bed \-ˌbed\ *n* 1 : a glass-covered bed of soil heated (as by fermenting manure) and used esp. for raising

---

\ə\abut \ᵊ\kitten \ər\further \a\ash \ā\ace \ä\mop, mar \au̇\out \ch\chin \e\bet \ē\easy \g\go \i\hit \ī\ice \j\job \ŋ\sing \ō\go \ȯ\law \ȯi\boy \th\thin \th\the \ü\loot \u̇\foot \y\yet \zh\vision *see also* Pronunciation Symbols page

seedlings **2 :** an environment that favors rapid growth or development

hot-blood·ed \-ˈblə-dəd\ *adj* **:** easily roused or excited

hot·box \-ˌbäks\ *n* **:** a bearing (as of a railroad car) overheated by friction

hot·cake \-ˌkāk\ *n* **:** PANCAKE

hot dog *n* **:** a cooked frankfurter usu. served in a long split roll

ho·tel \hō-ˈtel\ *n* [F *hôtel,* fr. OF *hostel,* fr. ML *hospitale* hospice] **:** a building where lodging and usu. meals, entertainment, and various personal services are provided for the public

hot flash *n* **:** a sudden brief flushing and sensation of heat usu. associated with menopausal endocrine imbalance

hot·head·ed \ˈhät-ˈhe-dəd\ *adj* **:** FIERY, IMPETUOUS — **hot·head** \-ˌhed\ *n* — **hot·head·ed·ly** *adv* — **hot·head·ed·ness** *n*

hot·house \-ˌhaús\ *n* **:** a heated greenhouse esp. for raising tropical plants

hot line *n* **:** a telephone line for emergency use (as between governments or to a counseling service)

hot plate *n* **:** a simple portable appliance for heating or for cooking

hot potato *n* **:** an embarrassing or controversial issue

hot rod *n* **:** an automobile modified for high speed and fast acceleration — **hot-rod·der** \-ˈrä-dər\ *n*

hots \ˈhäts\ *n pl* **:** strong sexual desire — usu. used with *the*

hot seat *n* **:** a position of anxiety or embarrassment

hot·shot \ˈhät-ˌshät\ *n* **:** a showily skillful person

hot tub *n* **:** a large wooden tub of hot water in which bathers soak and usu. socialize

hot water *n* **:** TROUBLE, DIFFICULTY

hot–wire \ˈhät-ˌwīr\ *vb* **:** to start (an automobile) by short-circuiting the ignition system

¹hound \ˈhaúnd\ *n* **1 : :** any of various long-eared hunting dogs that track prey by scent **2 :** FAN, ADDICT

²hound *vb* **:** to pursue relentlessly

hour \ˈaúr\ *n* **1 :** the 24th part of a day **:** 60 minutes **2 :** the time of day **3 :** a particular or customary time **4 :** a class session — **hour·ly** *adv or adj*

hour·glass \ˈaúr-ˌglas\ *n* **:** a glass vessel for measuring time in which sand runs from an upper compartment to a lower compartment in an hour

hou·ri \ˈhùr-ē\ *n* [F, fr. Per *hūri,* fr. Ar *ḥūrīyah*] **:** one of the beautiful maidens of the Muslim paradise

¹house \ˈhaús\ *n, pl* **hous·es** \ˈhaú-zəz\ **1 :** a building for human habitation **2 :** an animal shelter (as a den or nest) **3 :** a building in which something is stored **4 :** HOUSEHOLD; *also* **:** FAMILY **5 :** a residence for a religious community or for students; *also* **:** those in residence **6 :** a legislative body **7 :** a place of business or entertainment **8 :** a business organization **9 :** the audience in a theater or concert hall — **house·ful** *n*

²house \ˈhaúz\ *vb* **housed; hous·ing 1 :** to provide with or take shelter **:** LODGE **2 :** STORE

house·boat \ˈhaús-ˌbōt\ *n* **:** a pleasure boat fitted for use as a dwelling or for leisurely cruising

house·boy \-ˌbói\ *n* **:** a boy or man hired to act as a household servant

house·break \-ˌbrāk\ *vb* **house·broke; house·bro·ken; house·break·ing :** to train in excretory habits acceptable in indoor living

house·break·ing \-ˌbrā-kiŋ\ *n* **:** the act of breaking into a dwelling with the intent of committing a felony

house·clean \-ˌklēn\ *vb* **:** to clean a house and its furniture — **house·clean·ing** *n*

house·coat \-ˌkōt\ *n* **:** a woman's often long-skirted informal garment for wear around the house

house·fly \-ˌflī\ *n* **:** a dipteran fly that is common about human habitations

¹house·hold \-ˌhōld\ *n* **:** those who dwell as a family under the same roof — **house·hold·er** *n*

²household *adj* **1 :** DOMESTIC **2 :** FAMILIAR, COMMON ⟨a ∼ name⟩

house·keep·er \-ˌkē-pər\ *n* **:** a woman employed to take care of a house

house·keep·ing \-ˌkē-piŋ\ *n* **:** the care and management of a house or institutional property

house·lights \-ˌlīts\ *n pl* **:** the lights that illuminate the auditorium of a theater

house·maid \-ˌmād\ *n* **:** a female servant employed to do housework

house·moth·er \-ˌmə-t͟hər\ *n* **:** a woman acting as hostess, chaperon, and often housekeeper in a group residence

house·plant \-ˌplant\ *n* **:** a plant grown or kept indoors

house sparrow *n* **:** a Eurasian sparrow widely introduced in urban and agricultural areas

house·top \ˈhaús-ˌtäp\ *n* **:** ROOF

house·wares \-ˌwarz\ *n pl* **:** small articles of household equipment

house·warm·ing \-ˌwȯr-miŋ\ *n* **:** a party to celebrate the taking possession of a house or premises

house·wife \-ˌwīf\ *n* **:** a married woman in charge of a household — **house·wife·ly** *adj* — **house·wif·ery** \-ˌwī-fə-rē\ *n*

house·work \-ˌwərk\ *n* **:** the work of housekeeping

¹hous·ing \ˈhaú-ziŋ\ *n* **1 :** SHELTER; *also* **:** dwellings provided for people **2 :** something that covers or protects

²housing *n* **:** CAPARISON 1

HOV *abbr* high-occupancy vehicle

hove *past and past part of* HEAVE

hov·el \ˈhə-vəl, ˈhä-\ *n* **:** a small, wretched, and often dirty house **:** HUT

hov·er \ˈhə-vər, ˈhä-\ *vb* **hov·ered; hov·er·ing 1 :** FLUTTER; *also* **:** to move to and fro **2 :** to be in an uncertain state

hov·er·craft \-ˌkraft\ *n* **:** a vehicle that rides on a cushion of air over a surface

¹how \ˈhaú\ *adv* **1 :** in what way or manner ⟨∼ was it done⟩ **2 :** with what meaning ⟨∼ do we interpret such behavior⟩ **3 :** for what reason ⟨∼ could you have done such a thing⟩ **4 :** to what extent or degree ⟨∼ deep is it⟩ **5 :** in what state or condition ⟨∼ are you⟩ — **how about :** what do you say to or think of ⟨*how about* coming with me⟩ — **how come :** why is it that

²how *conj* **1 :** in the way or manner in which ⟨remember ∼ they fought⟩ **2 :** HOWEVER ⟨do it ∼ you like⟩

¹how·be·it \haú-ˈbē-ət\ *conj* **:** ALTHOUGH

²howbeit *adv* **:** NEVERTHELESS

how·dah \ˈhaú-də\ *n* [Hindi *hauda*] **:** a seat or covered pavilion on the back of an elephant or camel

¹how·ev·er \haú-ˈe-vər\ *conj* **:** in whatever manner that

²however *adv* **1 :** to whatever degree; *also* **:** in whatever manner **2 :** in spite of that

how·it·zer \ˈhaú-ət-sər\ *n* **:** a short cannon that shoots shells at a high angle

howl \ˈhaúl\ *vb* **1 :** to emit a loud long doleful sound characteristic of dogs **2 :** to cry loudly — **howl** *n*

howl·er \ˈhaú-lər\ *n* **1 :** one that howls **2 :** a humorous and ridiculous blunder

howl·ing *adj* **1 :** DESOLATE, WILD **2 :** very great ⟨a ∼ success⟩

how·so·ev·er \ˌhaú-sə-ˈwe-vər\ *adv* **:** HOWEVER 1

hoy·den \ˈhói-d⁷n\ *n* **:** a girl or woman of saucy, boisterous, or carefree behavior — **hoy·den·ish** *adj*

hp *abbr* horsepower

HP *abbr* high pressure

HPF *abbr* highest possible frequency

HQ *abbr* headquarters

hr *abbr* **1** here **2** hour

HR *abbr* House of Representatives

HRH *abbr* **1** Her Royal Highness **2** His Royal Highness

hrzn *abbr* horizon

HS *abbr* high school

HST *abbr* Hawaiian standard time

ht *abbr* height

HT *abbr* **1** Hawaii time **2** high-tension

hua·ra·che \wə-ˈrä-chē\ *n* [MexSp] : a sandal with an upper made of interwoven leather strips

hub \ˈhəb\ *n* **1** : the central part of a circular object (as a wheel) **2** : a center of activity; *esp* : an airport or city with heavy air traffic

hub·bub \ˈhə-bəb\ *n* : UPROAR; *also* : TURMOIL

hub·cap \ˈhəb-ˌkap\ *n* : a removable metal cap over the end of an axle

hu·bris \ˈhyü-brəs\ *n* : exaggerated pride or self-confidence

huck·le·ber·ry \ˈhə-kəl-ˌber-ē\ *n* **1** : an American shrub related to the blueberry; *also* : its edible dark blue berry **2** : BLUEBERRY

huck·ster \ˈhək-stər\ *n* : PEDDLER, HAWKER — **huckster** *vb*

HUD *abbr* Department of Housing and Urban Development

¹**hud·dle** \ˈhəd-ᵊl\ *vb* **hud·dled; hud·dling 1** : to crowd together **2** : CONFER

²**huddle** *n* **1** : a closely packed group **2** : MEETING, CONFERENCE

hue \ˈhyü\ *n* **1** : COLOR; *also* : gradation of color **2** : the attribute of colors that permits them to be classed as red, yellow, green, blue, or an intermediate color — **hued** \ˈhyüd\ *adj*

hue and cry *n* : a clamor of pursuit or protest

huff \ˈhəf\ *n* : a fit of anger or pique — **huff** *vb* — **huffy** *adj*

hug \ˈhəg\ *vb* **hugged; hug·ging 1** : EMBRACE **2** : to stay close to — **hug** *n*

huge \ˈhyüj\ *adj* **hug·er; hug·est** : very large or extensive — **huge·ly** *adv* — **huge·ness** *n*

hug·ger–mug·ger \ˈhə-gər-ˌmə-gər\ *n* **1** : SECRECY **2** : CONFUSION, MUDDLE

Hu·gue·not \ˈhyü-gə-ˌnät\ *n* : a French Protestant of the 16th and 17th centuries

hu·la \ˈhü-lə\ *n* : a sinuous Polynesian dance usu. accompanied by chants

hulk \ˈhəlk\ *n* **1** : a heavy clumsy ship **2** : an old ship unfit for service **3** : a bulky or unwieldy person or thing

hulk·ing \ˈhəl-kiŋ\ *adj* : BURLY, MASSIVE

¹**hull** \ˈhəl\ *n* **1** : the outer covering of a fruit or seed **2** : the frame or body esp. of a ship or boat

²**hull** *vb* : to remove the hulls of — **hull·er** *n*

hul·la·ba·loo \ˈhə-lə-bə-ˌlü\ *n, pl* **-loos** : a confused noise : UPROAR

hul·lo \ˌhə-ˈlō\ *chiefly Brit var of* HELLO

hum \ˈhəm\ *vb* **hummed; hum·ming 1** : to utter a sound like that of the speech sound \m\ prolonged **2** : DRONE **3** : to be busily active **4** : to run smoothly **5** : to sing with closed lips — **hum** *n* — **hum·mer** *n*

¹**hu·man** \ˈhyü-mən, ˈyü-\ *adj* **1** : of, relating to, being, or characteristic of humans **2** : having human form or attributes — **hu·man·ly** *adv* — **hu·man·ness** *n*

²**human** *n* : any of a species of primate mammals comprising all living persons and their recent ancestors; *also* : HOMINID

hu·mane \hyü-ˈmān, yü-\ *adj* **1** : marked by compassion, sympathy, or consideration for others **2** : HUMANISTIC — **hu·mane·ly** *adv* — **hu·mane·ness** *n*

human immunodeficiency virus *n* : HIV

hu·man·ism \ˈhyü-mə-ˌni-zəm, ˈyü-\ *n* **1** : devotion to the humanities; *also* : the revival of classical letters characteristic of the Renaissance **2** : a doctrine or way of life centered on human interests or values — **hu·man·ist** \-nist\ *n or adj* — **hu·man·is·tic** \ˌhyü-mə-ˈnis-tik, ˌyü-\ *adj*

hu·man·i·tar·i·an \hyü-ˌma-nə-ˈter-ē-ən, yü-\ *n* : one who practices philanthropy — **humanitarian** *adj* — **hu·man·i·tar·i·an·ism** *n*

hu·man·i·ty \hyü-ˈma-nə-tē, yü-\ *n, pl* **-ties 1** : the quality or state of being human or humane **2** *pl* : the branches of learning dealing with human concerns (as philosophy) as opposed to natural processes (as physics) **3** : the human race

hu·man·ize \ˈhyü-mə-ˌnīz, ˈyü-\ *vb* **-ized; -iz·ing** : to make human or humane — **hu·man·iza·tion** \ˌhyü-mə-nə-ˈzā-shən, ˌyü-\ *n* — **hu·man·iz·er** *n*

hu·man·kind \ˈhyü-mən-ˌkīnd, ˈyü-\ *n* : the human race

hu·man·oid \ˈhyü-mə-ˌnȯid, ˈyü-\ *adj* : having human form or characteristics — **humanoid** *n*

¹**hum·ble** \ˈhəm-bəl\ *adj* **hum·bler** \-bə-lər\; **hum·blest** \-bə-ləst\ [ME, fr. OF, fr. L *humilis* low, humble, fr. *humus* earth] **1** : not proud or haughty **2** : not pretentious : UNASSUMING **3** : INSIGNIFICANT **syn** meek, modest, lowly — **hum·ble·ness** *n* — **hum·bly** *adv*

²**humble** *vb* **hum·bled; hum·bling 1** : to make humble **2** : to destroy the power or prestige of — **hum·bler** *n*

¹**hum·bug** \ˈhəm-ˌbəg\ *n* **1** : HOAX, FRAUD **2** : NONSENSE

²**humbug** *vb* **hum·bugged; hum·bug·ging** : DECEIVE

hum·ding·er \ˈhəm-ˈdiŋ-ər\ *n* : a person or thing of striking excellence

hum·drum \ˈhəm-ˌdrəm\ *adj* : MONOTONOUS, DULL — **humdrum** *n*

hu·mer·us \ˈhyü-mə-rəs\ *n, pl* **hu·meri** \ˈhyü-mə-ˌrī, -ˌrē\ : the long bone extending from shoulder to elbow

hu·mid \ˈhyü-məd, ˈyü-\ *adj* : containing or characterized by perceptible moisture : DAMP — **hu·mid·ly** *adv*

hu·mid·i·fy \hyü-ˈmi-də-ˌfī\ *vb* **-fied; -fy·ing** : to make humid — **hu·mid·i·fi·ca·tion** \-ˌmi-də-fə-ˈkā-shən\ *n* — **hu·mid·i·fi·er** \-ˈmi-də-ˌfī-ər\ *n*

hu·mid·i·ty \hyü-ˈmi-də-tē, yü-\ *n, pl* **-ties** : the amount of atmospheric moisture

hu·mi·dor \ˈhyü-mə-ˌdȯr, ˈyü-\ *n* : a case (as for storing cigars) in which the air is kept properly humidified

hu·mil·i·ate \hyü-ˈmi-lē-ˌāt, yü-\ *vb* **-at·ed; -at·ing** : to injure the self-respect of : MORTIFY — **hu·mil·i·at·ing·ly** *adv* — **hu·mil·i·a·tion** \-ˌmi-lē-ˈā-shən\ *n*

hu·mil·i·ty \hyü-ˈmi-lə-tē, yü-\ *n* : the quality or state of being humble

hum·ming·bird \ˈhə-miŋ-ˌbərd\ *n* : any of a family of tiny American birds related to the swifts

hum·mock \ˈhə-mək\ *n* : a rounded mound : KNOLL — **hum·mocky** \-mə-kē\ *adj*

hu·mon·gous \hyü-ˈməŋ-gəs, -ˈmäŋ-\ *adj* [perh. alter. of *huge* + *monstrous*] : extremely large

¹**hu·mor** \ˈhyü-mər, ˈyü-\ *n* **1** : TEMPERAMENT **2** : MOOD **3** : WHIM **4** : a quality that appeals to a sense of the ludicrous or incongruous; *also* : a keen perception of the ludicrous or incongruous **5** : comical or amusing entertainment — **hu·mor·ist** \ˈhyü-mə-rist, ˈyü-\ *n* — **hu·mor·less** \ˈhyü-mər-ləs, ˈyü-\ *adj* — **hu·mor·less·ly** *adv* — **hu·mor·less·ness** *n* — **hu·mor·ous** \ˈhyü-mə-rəs, ˈyü-\ *adj* — **hu·mor·ous·ly** *adv* — **hu·mor·ous·ness** *n*

²**humor** *vb* : to comply with the wishes or mood of

hu·mour *chiefly Brit var of* HUMOR

hump \ˈhəmp\ *n* **1** : a rounded protuberance (as on the back of a camel) **2** : a difficult phase or obstacle ⟨over the ∼⟩ — **humped** *adj*

hump·back \ˈhəmp-ˌbak; *1 also* -ˈbak\ *n* **1** : HUNCHBACK **2** : HUMPBACK WHALE — **hump·backed** *adj*

humpback whale *n* : a large baleen whale having very long flippers

hu·mus \ˈhyü-məs, ˈyü-\ *n* : the dark organic part of soil formed from decaying matter

Hun \ˈhən\ *n* : a member of an Asian people that invaded Europe about A.D. 450

¹**hunch** \ˈhənch\ *vb* **1** : to thrust oneself forward **2** : to as-

\ə\abut \ᵊ\kitten \ər\further \a\ash \ā\ace \ä\mop, mar \au̇\out \ch\chin \e\bet \ē\easy \g\go \i\hit \ī\ice \j\job \ŋ\sing \ō\go \ȯ\law \ȯi\boy \th\thin \t̲h̲\the \ü\loot \u̇\foot \y\yet \zh\vision *see also* Pronunciation Symbols page

sume or cause to assume a bent or crooked posture

²**hunch** n **1** : PUSH **2** : a strong intuitive feeling about what will happen

hunch·back \'hənch-ˌbak\ n : a person with a crooked back; *also* : a back with a hump — **hunch·backed** *adj*

hun·dred \'hən-drəd\ n, pl **hundreds** or **hundred** : 10 times 10 — **hundred** *adj* — **hun·dredth** \-drədth\ *adj or n*

hun·dred·weight \-ˌwāt\ n, pl **hundredweight** or **hundredweights** — see WEIGHT table

¹**hung** *past and past part of* HANG

²**hung** *adj* : unable to reach a decision or verdict ⟨a ∼ jury⟩

Hung *abbr* Hungarian; Hungary

Hun·gar·i·an \ˌhəŋ-'ger-ē-ən\ n **1** : a native or inhabitant of Hungary **2** : the language of the Hungarians — **Hungarian** *adj*

hun·ger \'həŋ-gər\ n **1** : a craving or urgent need for food **2** : a strong desire — **hunger** *vb* — **hun·gri·ly** *adv* — **hun·gry** *adj*

hung·over \'həŋ-'ō-vər\ *adj* : having a hangover

hung up *adj* **1** : DELAYED **2** : ENTHUSIASTIC; *also* : PREOCCUPIED

hunk \'həŋk\ n **1** : a large piece **2** : an attractive well-built man — **hunky** *adj*

hun·ker \'həŋ-kər\ *vb* **1** : CROUCH, SQUAT — usu. used with *down* **2** : to settle in for a sustained period — used with *down*

hun·ky–do·ry \ˌhəŋ-kē-'dōr-ē\ *adj* : quite satisfactory : FINE

¹**hunt** \'hənt\ *vb* **1** : to pursue for food or in sport; *also* : to take part in a hunt **2** : to try to find : SEEK **3** : to drive or chase esp. by harrying **4** : to traverse in search of prey — **hunt·er** n

²**hunt** n : an act, practice, or instance of hunting

hunt·ress \'hən-trəs\ n : a woman who hunts game

hunts·man \'hənts-mən\ n **1** : HUNTER **2** : a person who manages a hunt and looks after the hounds

hur·dle \'hərd-ᵊl\ n **1** : a barrier to leap over in a race **2** : OBSTACLE — **hurdle** *vb* — **hur·dler** n

hur·dy–gur·dy \ˌhər-dē-'gər-dē, 'hər-dē-ˌgər-dē\ n, pl **-gur·dies** : a musical instrument in which the sound is produced by turning a crank

hurl \'hərl\ *vb* **1** : to move or cause to move vigorously **2** : to throw down with violence **3** : FLING; *also* : PITCH — **hurl** n — **hurl·er** n

hur·ly–bur·ly \ˌhər-lē-'bər-lē\ n : UPROAR, TUMULT

Hu·ron \'hyùr-ən, 'hyùr-ˌän\ n, pl **Hurons** or **Huron** : a member of a confederacy of American Indian peoples formerly living between Georgian Bay and Lake Ontario

hur·rah \hù-'rò, -'rä\ *also* **hur·ray** \hù-'rā\ *interj* — used to express joy, approval, or encouragement

hur·ri·cane \'hər-ə-ˌkān\ n [Sp *huracán*, of AmerInd origin] : a tropical cyclone with winds of 74 miles (118 kilometers) per hour or greater that is usu. accompanied by rain, thunder, and lightning

¹**hur·ry** \'hər-ē\ *vb* **hur·ried; hur·ry·ing 1** : to carry or cause to go with haste **2** : to impel to a greater speed **3** : to move or act with haste — **hur·ried·ly** *adv* — **hur·ried·ness** n

²**hurry** n : extreme haste or eagerness

¹**hurt** \'hərt\ *vb* **hurt; hurt·ing 1** : to feel or cause to feel physical or emotional pain **2** : to do harm to : DAMAGE **3** : OFFEND **4** : HAMPER **5** : to be in need — usu. used with *for* — **hurt** *adj*

²**hurt** n **1** : a bodily injury or wound **2** : SUFFERING **3** : HARM, WRONG — **hurt·ful** *adj* — **hurt·ful·ness** n

hur·tle \'hərt-ᵊl\ *vb* **hur·tled; hur·tling 1** : to move rapidly or forcefully **2** : FLING, FLING

¹**hus·band** \'həz-bənd\ n [ME *husbonde*, fr. OE *hūsbonda* master of a house, fr. ON *hūsbōndi*, fr. *hūs* house + *bōndi* householder] : a male partner in a marriage

²**husband** *vb* : to manage prudently

hus·band·man \'həz-bənd-mən\ n : FARMER

hus·band·ry \'həz-bən-drē\ n **1** : the control or judicious use of resources **2** : AGRICULTURE

¹**hush** \'həsh\ *vb* **1** : to make or become quiet or calm **2** : SUPPRESS

²**hush** n : SILENCE, QUIET

hush–hush \'həsh-ˌhəsh\ *adj* : SECRET, CONFIDENTIAL

¹**husk** \'həsk\ n **1** : a usu. thin dry outer covering of a seed or fruit **2** : an outer layer : SHELL

²**husk** *vb* : to strip the husk from — **husk·er** n

¹**hus·ky** \'həs-kē\ *adj* **hus·ki·er; -est** : HOARSE — **hus·ki·ly** \-kə-lē\ *adv* — **hus·ki·ness** \-kē-nəs\ n

²**husky** *adj* **1** : BURLY, ROBUST **2** : LARGE

³**husky** n, pl **huskies** : a heavy-coated working dog of the New World arctic

hus·sar \(ˌ)hə-'zär\ n [Hung *huszár*] : a member of any of various European cavalry units

hus·sy \'hə-zē, -sē\ n, pl **hussies** [alter. of *housewife*] : a lewd or brazen woman **2** : a pert or mischievous girl

hus·tings \'həs-tiŋz\ n pl : a place where political campaign speeches are made; *also* : the proceedings in an election campaign

hus·tle \'hə-səl\ *vb* **hus·tled; hus·tling 1** : JOSTLE, SHOVE **2** : HASTEN, HURRY **3** : to work energetically — **hustle** n — **hus·tler** \'həs-lər\ n

hut \'hət\ n : a small and often temporary dwelling : SHACK

hutch \'həch\ n **1** : a chest or compartment for storage **2** : a cupboard usu. surmounted with open shelves **3** : a pen or coop for an animal **4** : HUT

huz·zah or **huz·za** \(ˌ)hə-'zä\ n : a shout of acclaim — often used interjectionally to express joy or approbation

HV *abbr* **1** high velocity **2** high voltage

HVAC *abbr* heating, ventilating and air-conditioning

hvy *abbr* heavy

HW *abbr* hot water

hwy *abbr* highway

hy·a·cinth \'hī-ə-(ˌ)sinth\ n : a bulbous Mediterranean herb related to the lilies that is widely grown for its spikes of fragrant bell-shaped flowers

hy·ae·na *var of* HYENA

hy·brid \'hī-brəd\ n **1** : an offspring of genetically differing parents (as members of different breeds or species) **2** : one of mixed origin or composition — **hybrid** *adj* — **hy·brid·i·za·tion** \ˌhī-brə-də-'zā-shən\ n — **hy·brid·ize** \'hī-brə-ˌdīz\ *vb* — **hy·brid·iz·er** n

hy·dra \'hī-drə\ n : any of numerous small tubular freshwater coelenterates that are polyps having at one end a mouth surrounded by tentacles

hy·dran·gea \hī-'drān-jə\ n : any of a genus of shrubs related to the currants and grown for their showy clusters of white or tinted flowers

hy·drant \'hī-drənt\ n : a pipe with a valve and spout at which water may be drawn from a main pipe

hy·drate \'hī-ˌdrāt\ n : a compound formed by union of water with some other substance — **hydrate** *vb*

hy·drau·lic \hī-'drò-lik\ *adj* **1** : operated, moved, or effected by means of water **2** : of or relating to hydraulics **3** : operated by the resistance offered or the pressure transmitted when a quantity of liquid is forced through a small orifice or through a tube **4** : hardening or setting under water

hy·drau·lics \-liks\ n : a science that deals with practical applications of liquid (as water) in motion

hydro \'hī-drō\ n : HYDROPOWER

hy·dro·car·bon \ˌhī-drō-ˌkär-bən\ n : an organic compound containing only carbon and hydrogen

hy·dro·ceph·a·lus \ˌhī-drō-'se-fə-ləs\ n : abnormal increase in the amount of fluid in the cranial cavity accompanied by enlargement of the skull and atrophy of the brain

hy·dro·chlo·ric acid \ˌhī-drə-ˈklōr-ik-\ *n* : a sharp-smelling corrosive acid used in the laboratory and in industry and present in dilute form in gastric juice

hy·dro·dy·nam·ics \ˌhī-drō-dī-ˈna-miks\ *n* : a science that deals with the motion of fluids and the forces acting on moving bodies immersed in fluids — **hy·dro·dy·nam·ic** *adj*

hy·dro·elec·tric \ˌhī-drō-i-ˈlek-trik\ *adj* : of or relating to production of electricity by waterpower — **hy·dro·elec·tric·i·ty** \-ˌlek-ˈtri-sə-tē\ *n*

hy·dro·foil \ˈhī-drə-ˌfȯil\ *n* : a boat that has fins attached to the bottom by struts for lifting the hull clear of the water to allow faster speeds

hy·dro·gen \ˈhī-drə-jən\ *n* [F *hydrogène*, fr. Gk *hydōr* water + *-genēs* born; fr. the fact that water is generated by its combustion] : a gaseous colorless odorless highly flammable chemical element that is the lightest of the elements — **hy·drog·e·nous** \hī-ˈdrä-jə-nəs\ *adj* — see ELEMENT table

hy·dro·ge·nate \hī-ˈdrä-jə-ˌnāt, ˈhī-drə-\ *vb* **-nat·ed; -nat·ing** : to combine or treat with hydrogen; *esp* : to add hydrogen to the molecule of — **hy·dro·ge·na·tion** \hī-ˌdrä-jə-ˈnā-shən, ˌhī-drə-\ *n*

hydrogen bomb *n* : a bomb whose violent explosive power is due to the sudden release of atomic energy resulting from the fusion of light nuclei (as of hydrogen atoms)

hydrogen peroxide *n* : an unstable compound of hydrogen and oxygen used esp. as an oxidizing and bleaching agent, an antiseptic, and a propellant

hy·dro·graph·ic \ˌhī-drə-ˈgra-fik\ *adj* : of or relating to the description and study of bodies of water — **hy·drog·ra·pher** *n* — **hy·drog·ra·phy** \hī-ˈdrä-grə-fē\ *n*

hy·drol·o·gy \hī-ˈdrä-lə-jē\ *n* : a science dealing with the properties, distribution, and circulation of water — **hy·dro·log·ic** \ˌhī-drə-ˈlä-jik\ *or* **hy·dro·log·i·cal** \-ji-kəl\ *adj* — **hy·drol·o·gist** \hī-ˈdrä-lə-jist\ *n*

hy·dro·ly·sis \hī-ˈdrä-lə-səs\ *n* : a chemical decomposition involving the addition of the elements of water

hy·drom·e·ter \hī-ˈdrä-mə-tər\ *n* : a floating instrument for determining specific gravities of liquids and hence the strength (as of alcoholic liquors)

hy·dro·pho·bia \ˌhī-drə-ˈfō-bē-ə\ *n* [LL, fr. Gk, fr. *hydōr* water + *phobos* fear] : RABIES

hy·dro·phone \ˈhī-drə-ˌfōn\ *n* : an underwater listening device

¹**hy·dro·plane** \ˈhī-drə-ˌplān\ *n* **1** : a powerboat designed for racing that skims the surface of the water **2** : SEAPLANE

²**hydroplane** *vb* : to skid on a wet road due to loss of contact between the tires and road

hy·dro·pon·ics \ˌhī-drə-ˈpä-niks\ *n* : the growing of plants in nutrient solutions — **hy·dro·pon·ic** *adj*

hy·dro·pow·er \ˈhī-drə-ˌpau̇-ər\ *n* : hydroelectric power

hy·dro·sphere \ˈhī-drə-ˌsfir\ *n* : the water (as vapor or lakes) of the earth

hy·dro·stat·ic \ˌhī-drə-ˈsta-tik\ *adj* : of or relating to fluids at rest or to the pressures they exert or transmit

hy·dro·ther·a·py \ˌhī-drə-ˈther-ə-pē\ *n* : the use of water esp. externally in the treatment of disease or disability

hy·dro·ther·mal \ˌhī-drə-ˈthər-məl\ *adj* : of or relating to hot water

hy·drous \ˈhī-drəs\ *adj* : containing water

hy·drox·ide \hī-ˈdräk-ˌsīd\ *n* **1** : a negatively charged ion consisting of one atom of oxygen and one atom of hydrogen **2** : a compound of hydroxide with an element or group

hy·e·na \hī-ˈē-nə\ *n* [L *hyaena*, fr. Gk *hyaina*, fr. *hys* hog] : any of several large nocturnal carnivorous mammals of Asia and Africa

hy·giene \ˈhī-ˌjēn\ *n* **1** : a science concerned with establishing and maintaining good health **2** : conditions or practices conducive to health — **hy·gien·ic** \hī-ˈje-nik,

-ˈjē-\ *adj* — **hy·gien·i·cal·ly** \-ni-k(ə-)lē\ *adv* — **hy·gien·ist** \hī-ˈjē-nist, ˈhī-ˌjē-, hī-ˈje-\ *n*

hy·grom·e·ter \hī-ˈgrä-mə-tər\ *n* : any of several instruments for measuring the humidity of the atmosphere

hy·gro·scop·ic \ˌhī-grə-ˈskä-pik\ *adj* : readily taking up and retaining moisture

hying *pres part of* HIE

hy·men \ˈhī-mən\ *n* : a fold of mucous membrane partly closing the orifice of the vagina

hy·me·ne·al \ˌhī-mə-ˈnē-əl\ *adj* : NUPTIAL

hymn \ˈhim\ *n* : a song of praise esp. to God — **hymn** *vb*

hym·nal \ˈhim-nəl\ *n* : a book of hymns

hyp *abbr* hypothesis; hypothetical

¹**hype** \ˈhīp\ *vb* **hyped; hyp·ing 1** : STIMULATE — usu. used with *up* **2** : INCREASE — **hyped–up** *adj*

²**hype** *vb* **hyped; hyping 1** : DECEIVE **2** : PUBLICIZE

³**hype** *n* **1** : DECEPTION, PUT-ON **2** : PUBLICITY

hy·per \ˈhī-pər\ *adj* **1** : HIGH-STRUNG, EXCITABLE **2** : extremely active

hy·per·acid·i·ty \ˌhī-pər-ə-ˈsi-də-tē\ *n* : the condition of containing excessive acid esp. in the stomach — **hy·per·ac·id** \-ˈa-səd\ *adj*

hy·per·ac·tive \-ˈak-tiv\ *adj* : excessively or pathologically active — **hy·per·ac·tiv·i·ty** \-ˌak-ˈti-və-tē\ *n*

hy·per·bar·ic \ˌhī-pər-ˈbar-ik\ *adj* : of, relating to, or utilizing greater than normal pressure (as of oxygen)

hy·per·bo·la \hī-ˈpər-bə-lə\ *n, pl* **-las** *or* **-lae** \-(ˌ)lē\ : a curve formed by the intersection of a double right circular cone with a plane that cuts both halves of the cone — **hy·per·bol·ic** \ˌhī-pər-ˈbä-lik\ *adj*

hy·per·bo·le \hī-ˈpər-bə-(ˌ)lē\ *n* : extravagant exaggeration used as a figure of speech

hy·per·crit·i·cal \ˌhī-pər-ˈkri-ti-kəl\ *adj* : excessively critical — **hy·per·crit·i·cal·ly** \-k(ə-)lē\ *adv*

hy·per·opia \ˌhī-pə-ˈrō-pē-ə\ *n* : a condition in which visual images come to focus behind the retina resulting esp. in defective vision for near objects — **hy·per·opic** \-ˈrō-pik, -ˈrä-\ *adj*

hy·per·sen·si·tive \-ˈsen-sə-tiv\ *adj* **1** : excessively or abnormally sensitive **2** : abnormally susceptible physiologically to a specific agent (as a drug) — **hy·per·sen·si·tive·ness** *n* — **hy·per·sen·si·tiv·i·ty** \-ˌsen-sə-ˈti-və-tē\ *n*

hy·per·ten·sion \ˈhī-pər-ˌten-chən\ *n* : high blood pressure — **hy·per·ten·sive** \ˌhī-pər-ˈten-siv\ *adj or n*

hy·per·thy·roid·ism \ˌhī-pər-ˈthī-ˌrȯi-ˌdi-zəm\ *n* : excessive activity of the thyroid gland; *also* : the resulting bodily condition — **hy·per·thy·roid** \-ˈthī-ˌrȯid\ *adj*

hy·per·tro·phy \hī-ˈpər-trə-fē\ *n, pl* **-phies** : excessive development of a body part — **hy·per·tro·phic** \ˌhī-pər-ˈtrō-fik\ *adj* — **hypertrophy** *vb*

hy·per·ven·ti·late \ˌhī-pər-ˈven-tə-ˌlāt\ *vb* : to breathe rapidly and deeply esp. to the point of losing an abnormal amount of carbon dioxide from the blood — **hy·per·ven·ti·la·tion** \-ˌven-tə-ˈlā-shən\ *n*

hy·phen \ˈhī-fən\ *n* : a punctuation mark - used esp. to divide or to compound words or word parts — **hyphen** *vb*

hy·phen·ate \ˈhī-fə-ˌnāt\ *vb* **-at·ed; -at·ing** : to connect or divide with a hyphen — **hy·phen·ation** \ˌhī-fə-ˈnā-shən\ *n*

hyp·no·sis \hip-ˈnō-səs\ *n, pl* **-no·ses** \-ˌsēz\ : an induced state that resembles sleep and in which the subject is responsive to suggestions of the inducer (**hyp·no·tist** \ˈhip-nə-tist\) — **hyp·no·tism** \ˈhip-nə-ˌti-zəm\ *n* — **hyp·no·tiz·able** \ˈhip-nə-ˌtī-zə-bəl\ *adj* — **hyp·no·tize** \-ˌtīz\ *vb*

\ə\abut \ᵊ\kitten \ər\further \a\ash \ā\ace \ä\mop, mar
\au̇\out \ch\chin \e\bet \ē\easy \g\go \i\hit \ī\ice \j\job
\ŋ\sing \ō\go \ȯ\law \ȯi\boy \th\thin \t͟h\the \ü\loot \u̇\foot
\y\yet \zh\vision *see also* Pronunciation Symbols page

¹**hyp·not·ic** \hip-'nä-tik\ *adj* **1** : inducing sleep : SOPORIFIC **2** : of or relating to hypnosis or hypnotism **3** : readily holding the attention — **hyp·not·i·cal·ly** \-ti-k(ə-)lē\ *adv*

²**hypnotic** *n* : a sleep-inducing drug

hy·po \'hī-pō\ *n, pl* **hypos** : SODIUM THIOSULFATE

hy·po·cen·ter \'hī-pə-ˌsen-tər\ *n* : the point of origin of an earthquake

hy·po·chon·dria \ˌhī-pə-'kän-drē-ə\ *n* [NL, fr. LL, pl., upper abdomen (formerly regarded as the seat of hypochondria), fr. Gk, lit., the parts under the cartilage (of the breastbone), fr. *hypo-* under + *chondros* cartilage] : depression of mind often centered on imaginary physical ailments — **hy·po·chon·dri·ac** \-drē-ˌak\ *adj or n*

hy·poc·ri·sy \hi-'pä-krə-sē\ *n, pl* **-sies** : a feigning to be what one is not or to believe what one does not; *esp* : the false assumption of an appearance of virtue or religion — **hyp·o·crite** \'hi-pə-ˌkrit\ *n* — **hyp·o·crit·i·cal** \ˌhi-pə-'kri-ti-kəl\ *adj* — **hyp·o·crit·i·cal·ly** \-k(ə-)lē\ *adv*

¹**hy·po·der·mic** \ˌhī-pə-'dər-mik\ *adj* : administered by or used in making an injection beneath the skin

²**hypodermic** *n* : HYPODERMIC SYRINGE; *also* : an injection made with this

hypodermic needle *n* : NEEDLE 3; *also* : HYPODERMIC SYRINGE

hypodermic syringe *n* : a small syringe with a hollow needle for injecting material into or through the skin

hy·po·gly·ce·mia \ˌhī-pō-glī-'sē-mē-ə\ *n* : abnormal decrease of sugar in the blood — **hy·po·gly·ce·mic** \-mik\ *adj*

hy·pot·e·nuse \hī-'pät-ᵊn-ˌüs, -ˌyüs, -ˌüz, -ˌyüz\ *n* : the side of a triangle having a right angle that is opposite the right angle; *also* : its length

hy·poth·e·sis \hī-'pä-thə-səs\ *n, pl* **-e·ses** \-ˌsēz\ : an assumption made esp. in order to test its logical or empirical consequences — **hy·po·thet·i·cal** \ˌhī-pə-'the-ti-kəl\ *adj* — **hy·po·thet·i·cal·ly** \-k(ə-)lē\ *adv*

hy·poth·e·size \-ˌsīz\ *vb* **-sized; -siz·ing** : to adopt as a hypothesis

hy·po·thy·roid·ism \ˌhī-pō-'thī-ˌroi-ˌdi-zəm\ *n* : deficient activity of the thyroid gland; *also* : a resultant lowered metabolic rate and general loss of vigor — **hy·po·thy·roid** *adj*

hys·sop \'hi-səp\ *n* : a European mint sometimes used as a potherb

hys·ter·ec·to·my \ˌhis-tə-'rek-tə-mē\ *n, pl* **-mies** : surgical removal of the uterus

hys·te·ria \hi-'ster-ē-ə, -'stir-\ *n* [NL, fr. E *hysteric*, adj., fr. L *hystericus*, fr. Gk *hysterikos*, fr. *hystera* womb; fr. the Greek notion that hysteria was peculiar to women and caused by disturbances in the uterus] **1** : a nervous disorder marked esp. by defective emotional control **2** : unmanageable fear or outburst of emotion — **hys·ter·ic** \-'ster-ik\ *n* — **hys·ter·i·cal** \-'ster-i-kəl\ *also* **hysteric** *adj* — **hys·ter·i·cal·ly** \-k(ə-)lē\ *adv*

hys·ter·ics \-'ster-iks\ *n pl* : a fit of uncontrollable laughter or crying

Hz *abbr* hertz

I

¹**i** \'ī\ *n, pl* **i's** *or* **is** \'īz\ *often cap* : the 9th letter of the English alphabet

²**i** *abbr, often cap* island; isle

¹**I** \'ī, ə\ *pron* : the one speaking or writing

²**I** *abbr* interstate

³**I** *symbol* iodine

Ia *or* **IA** *abbr* Iowa

-ial *adj suffix* : '-AL ⟨manor*ial*⟩

iamb \'ī-ˌam\ *or* **iam·bus** \ī-'am-bəs\ *n, pl* **iambs** \'ī-ˌamz\ *or* **iam·bus·es** : a metrical foot of one unaccented syllable followed by one accented syllable — **iam·bic** \ī-'am-bik\ *adj or n*

-ian — see -AN

-i·at·ric \ē-'a-trik\ *also* **-i·at·ri·cal** \-tri-kəl\ *adj comb form* : of or relating to (such) medical treatment or healing ⟨pedi*atric*⟩

-i·at·rics \ē-'a-triks\ *n pl comb form* : medical treatment ⟨pedi*atrics*⟩

ib *or* **ibid** *abbr* ibidem

ibex \'ī-ˌbeks\ *n, pl* **ibex** *or* **ibex·es** [L] : any of several Old World wild goats with large curved horns

ibi·dem \'i-bə-ˌdem, i-'bī-dəm\ *adv* [L] : in the same place

-ibility — see -ABILITY

ibis \'ī-bəs\ *n, pl* **ibis** *or* **ibis·es** [L, fr. Gk, fr. Egypt *hb*] : any of various wading birds related to the herons but having a downwardly curved bill

-ible — see -ABLE

ibu·pro·fen \ˌī-byù-'prō-fən\ *n* : a nonsteroidal anti‑inflammatory drug used to relieve pain and fever

IC \ˌī-'sē\ *n* : INTEGRATED CIRCUIT

¹**-ic** \ik\ *adj suffix* **1** : of, relating to, or having the form of : being ⟨panoram*ic*⟩ **2** : related to, derived from, or containing ⟨alcohol*ic*⟩ **3** : in the manner of : like that of : characteristic of **4** : associated or dealing with : utilizing ⟨electron*ic*⟩ **5** : characterized by : exhibiting ⟨nostalg*ic*⟩ : affected with ⟨allerg*ic*⟩ **6** : caused by **7** : tending to produce ⟨analges*ic*⟩

²**-ic** *n suffix* : one having the character or nature of : one belonging to or associated with : one exhibiting or affected by : one that produces

-i·cal \i-kəl\ *adj suffix* : -IC ⟨symmetr*ical*⟩ ⟨geolog*ical*⟩ — **-i·cal·ly** \i-kə-lē, -klē\ *adv suffix*

ICBM \ˌī-ˌsē-(ˌ)bē-'em\ *n, pl* **ICBM's** *or* **ICBMs** \-'emz\ : an intercontinental ballistic missile

ICC *abbr* Interstate Commerce Commission

¹**ice** \'īs\ *n* **1** : frozen water **2** : a substance resembling ice **3** : a state of coldness (as from formality or reserve) **4** : a flavored frozen dessert; *esp* : one containing no milk or cream

²**ice** *vb* **iced; ic·ing 1** : FREEZE **2** : CHILL **3** : to cover with or as if with icing

ice age *n* : a time of widespread glaciation

ice bag *n* : a waterproof bag to hold ice for local application of cold to the body

ice·berg \'īs-ˌbərg\ *n* : a large floating mass of ice broken off from a glacier

iceberg lettuce *n* : any of various crisp light green lettuces that form a compact head like a cabbage

ice·boat \'īs-ˌbōt\ *n* : a boatlike frame on runners propelled on ice by sails

ice·bound \-ˌbaùnd\ *adj* : surrounded, obstructed, or covered by ice

ice·box \-ˌbäks\ *n* : REFRIGERATOR

ice·break·er \-ˌbrā-kər\ *n* : a ship equipped to make a channel through ice

ice cap *n* : a glacier forming on relatively level land and flowing outward from its center

ice cream *n* : a frozen food containing sweetened or flavored cream or butterfat

ice hockey *n* : a game in which two teams of ice-skating players try to shoot a puck into the opponent's goal

ice·house \'īs-ₜhaüs\ *n* : a building in which ice is made or stored

Ice·land·er \-ₜlan-dər, -lən-\ *n* : a native or inhabitant of Iceland

¹**Ice·lan·dic** \īs-'lan-dik\ *adj* : of, relating to, or characteristic of Iceland, the Icelanders, or their language

²**Icelandic** *n* : the language of Iceland

ice·man \'īs-ₜman\ *n* : one who sells or delivers ice

ice milk *n* : a sweetened frozen food made of skim milk

ice pick *n* : a hand tool ending in a spike for chipping ice

ice–skate \'īs-ₜskāt\ *vb* : to skate on ice — **ice–skater** *n*

ice storm *n* : a storm in which falling rain freezes on contact

ice water *n* : chilled or iced water esp. for drinking

ich·thy·ol·o·gy \ik-thē-'ä-lə-jē\ *n* : a branch of zoology dealing with fishes — **ich·thy·ol·o·gist** \-jist\ *n*

ici·cle \'ī-ₜsi-kəl\ *n* : a hanging mass of ice formed by the freezing of dripping water

ic·ing \'ī-siŋ\ *n* : a sweet usu. creamy mixture used to coat baked goods

ICJ *abbr* International Court of Justice

icky \'i-kē\ *adj* **ick·i·er; -est** : OFFENSIVE, DISTASTEFUL — **ick·i·ness** *n*

icon \'ī-ₜkän\ *n* 1 : IMAGE; *esp* : a religious image painted on a wood panel 2 : a small picture on a computer display that suggests the purpose of an available function

icon·o·clasm \ī-'kä-nə-ₜkla-zəm\ *n* : the doctrine, practice, or attitude of an iconoclast

icon·o·clast \-ₜklast\ *n* [ML *iconoclastes,* fr. MGk *eikonoklastēs,* lit., image destroyer, fr. Gk *eikōn* image + *klan* to break] 1 : one who destroys religious images or opposes their veneration 2 : one who attacks cherished beliefs or institutions

-ics \iks\ *n sing or pl suffix* 1 : study : knowledge : skill : practice 〈linguist*ics*〉 〈electron*ics*〉 2 : characteristic actions or activities 〈acrobat*ics*〉 3 : characteristic qualities, operations, or phenomena 〈mechan*ics*〉

ic·tus \'ik-təs\ *n* : the recurring stress or beat in a rhythmic or metrical series of sounds

ICU *abbr* intensive care unit

icy \'ī-sē\ *adj* **ic·i·er; -est** 1 : covered with, abounding in, or consisting of ice 2 : intensely cold 3 : being cold and unfriendly — **ic·i·ly** \'ī-sə-lē\ *adv* — **ic·i·ness** \-sē-nəs\ *n*

¹**id** \'id\ *n* [L, it] : the part of the psyche in psychoanalytic theory that is completely unconscious and concerned with instinctual needs and drives

²**id** *abbr* idem

ID *abbr* 1 Idaho 2 identification

idea \ī-'dē-ə\ *n* 1 : a plan for action : DESIGN 2 : something imagined or pictured in the mind 3 : a central meaning or purpose **syn** concept, conception, notion, impression

¹**ide·al** \ī-'dēl\ *adj* 1 : existing only in the mind : IMAGINARY; *also* : lacking practicality 2 : of or relating to an ideal or to perfection : PERFECT

²**ideal** *n* 1 : a standard of excellence 2 : one regarded as a model worthy of imitation 3 : GOAL **syn** archetype, example, exemplar, paradigm, pattern

ide·al·ism \ī-'dē-ə-ₜli-zəm\ *n* : the practice of forming ideals or living under their influence; *also* : an idealized representation — **ide·al·ist** \-list\ *n* — **ide·al·is·tic** \ī-ₜdē-ə-'lis-tik\ *adj* — **ide·al·is·ti·cal·ly** \-ti-k(ə-)lē\ *adv*

ide·al·ize \ī-'dē-ə-ₜlīz\ *vb* **-ized; -iz·ing** : to think of or represent as ideal — **ide·al·i·za·tion** \-ₜdē-ə-lə-'zā-shən\ *n*

ide·al·ly \ī-'dē-lē, -'dē-ə-lē\ *adv* 1 : in idea or imagination : MENTALLY 2 : in agreement with an ideal : PERFECTLY

ide·a·tion \ₜī-dē-'ā-shən\ *n* : the forming of ideas — **ide-**ate \'ī-dē-ₜāt\ *vb* — **ide·a·tion·al** \ₜī-dē-'ā-shə-nəl\ *adj*

idem \'ī-ₜdem, 'ē-, 'i-\ *pron* [L, same] : something previously mentioned

iden·ti·cal \ī-'den-ti-kəl\ *adj* 1 : being the same 2 : essentially alike **syn** equivalent, equal, tantamount

iden·ti·fi·ca·tion \ī-ₜden-tə-fə-'kā-shən\ *n* 1 : an act of identifying : the state of being identified 2 : evidence of identity 3 : an unconscious psychological process by which an individual models thoughts, feelings, and actions after another person or an object

iden·ti·fy \ī-'den-tə-ₜfī\ *vb* **-fied; -fy·ing** 1 : to regard as identical 2 : ASSOCIATE 3 : to establish the identity of 4 : to practice psychological identification — **iden·ti·fi·able** \-ₜden-tə-'fī-ə-bəl\ *adj* — **iden·ti·fi·ably** \-blē\ *adv* — **iden·ti·fi·er** \-ₜfī-(-ə)r\ *n*

iden·ti·ty \ī-'den-tə-tē\ *n, pl* **-ties** 1 : sameness of essential character 2 : INDIVIDUALITY 3 : the fact of being the same person or thing as claimed

identity crisis *n* : psychological conflict esp. in adolescence involving confusion about one's social role and one's personality

ideo·gram \'ī-dē-ə-ₜgram, 'i-\ *n* 1 : a picture or symbol used in a system of writing to represent a thing or an idea 2 : a character or symbol used in a system of writing to represent an entire word

ide·ol·o·gy \ₜī-dē-'ä-lə-jē, ₜi-\ *also* **ide·al·o·gy** \-'ä-lə-jē, -'a-\ *n, pl* **-gies** 1 : the body of ideas characteristic of a particular individual, group, or culture 2 : the assertions, theories, and aims that constitute a political, social, and economic program — **ide·o·log·i·cal** \ₜī-dē-ə-'lä-ji-kəl, ₜi-\ *adj* — **ide·ol·o·gist** \-'dē-'ä-lə-jist\ *n*

ides \'īdz\ *n sing or pl* : the 15th day of March, May, July, or October or the 13th day of any other month in the ancient Roman calendar

id·i·o·cy \'i-dē-ə-sē\ *n, pl* **-cies** 1 : extreme mental retardation 2 : something notably stupid or foolish

id·i·om \'i-dē-əm\ *n* 1 : the language peculiar to a person or group 2 : the characteristic form or structure of a language 3 : an expression that cannot be understood from the meanings of its separate words (as *give way*) — **id·i·o·mat·ic** \ₜi-dē-ə-'ma-tik\ *adj* — **id·i·o·mat·i·cal·ly** \-ti-k(ə-)lē\ *adv*

id·i·o·path·ic \ₜi-dē-ə-'pa-thik\ *adj* : arising spontaneously or from an obscure or unknown cause 〈an ~ disease〉

id·i·o·syn·cra·sy \ₜi-dē-ə-'siŋ-krə-sē\ *n, pl* **-sies** : personal peculiarity — **id·i·o·syn·crat·ic** \ₜi-dē-ō-sin-'kra-tik\ *adj* — **id·i·o·syn·crat·i·cal·ly** \-'kra ti k(ə)lē\ *adv*

id·i·ot \'i-dē-ət\ *n* [ME, fr. L *idiota* ignorant person, fr. Gk *idiōtēs* one in a private station, ignorant person, fr. *idios* one's own, private] 1 : a mentally retarded person requiring complete custodial care 2 : a foolish or stupid person — **id·i·ot·ic** \ₜi-dē-'ä-tik\ *adj* — **id·i·ot·i·cal·ly** \-ti-k(ə-)lē\ *adv*

¹**idle** \'īd-ᵊl\ *adj* **idler** \'ī-də-lər\; **idlest** \'ī-də-ləst\ 1 : GROUNDLESS, WORTHLESS, USELESS 〈~ talk〉 2 : not occupied or employed : INACTIVE 3 : LAZY — **idle·ness** *n* — **idly** \'īd-lē\ *adv*

²**idle** *vb* **idled; idling** 1 : to spend time doing nothing 2 : to make idle 3 : to run without being connected so that power is not used for useful work — **idler** *n*

idol \'īd-ᵊl\ *n* 1 : an image worshiped as a god; *also* : a false god 2 : an object of passionate devotion

idol·a·ter *or* **idol·a·tor** \ī-'dä-lə-tər\ *n* : a worshiper of idols

idol·a·try \-trē\ *n, pl* **-tries** 1 : the worship of a physical object as a god 2 : excessive devotion — **idol·a·trous** \-trəs\ *adj*

---

idol·ize \ˈīd-ᵊl-ˌīz\ *vb* **-ized; -iz·ing** : to make an idol of — **idol·i·za·tion** \ˌīd-ᵊl-ə-ˈzā-shən\ *n*
idyll \ˈīd-ᵊl\ *n* **1** : a simple work of writing or poetry that describes country life or suggests a peaceful setting **2** : a fit subject for an idyll — **idyl·lic** \ī-ˈdi-lik\ *adj*
i.e. \ˈī-ˈē\ *abbr* [L *id est*] that is
IE *abbr* industrial engineer
-ier — see -ER
if \ˈif\ *conj* **1** : in the event that ⟨∼ he stays, I leave⟩ **2** : WHETHER ⟨ask ∼ he left⟩ **3** — used as a function word to introduce an exclamation expressing a wish ⟨∼ it would only rain⟩ **4** : even though ⟨an interesting ∼ untenable argument⟩
IF *abbr* intermediate frequency
if·fy \ˈi-fē\ *adj* : full of contingencies or unknown conditions
-i·fy \ə-ˌfī\ *vb suffix* : -FY
IG *abbr* inspector general
ig·loo \ˈi-glü\ *n, pl* **igloos** [Inuit (an Eskimo language) *iglu* house] : an Eskimo house or hut often made of snow blocks and in the shape of a dome
ig·ne·ous \ˈig-nē-əs\ *adj* **1** : FIERY **2** : formed by solidification of molten rock
ig·nite \ig-ˈnīt\ *vb* **ig·nit·ed; ig·nit·ing** : to set afire or catch fire — **ig·nit·able** \-ˈnī-tə-bəl\ *adj*
ig·ni·tion \ig-ˈni-shən\ *n* **1** : a setting on fire **2** : the process or means (as an electric spark) of igniting the fuel mixture in an engine
ig·no·ble \ig-ˈnō-bəl\ *adj* **1** : of common birth **2** : not honorable : BASE, MEAN **syn** despicable, scurvy, sordid, vile, wretched — **ig·no·bly** *adv*
ig·no·min·i·ous \ˌig-nə-ˈmi-nē-əs\ *adj* **1** : DISHONORABLE **2** : DESPICABLE **3** : HUMILIATING, DEGRADING **syn** disreputable, discreditable, disgraceful, inglorious — **ig·no·min·i·ous·ly** *adv* — **ig·no·mi·ny** \ˈig-nə-ˌmi-nē, ig-ˈnä-mə-nē\ *n*
ig·no·ra·mus \ˌig-nə-ˈrā-məs\ *n* [*Ignoramus,* ignorant lawyer in *Ignoramus* (1615), play by George Ruggle] : an utterly ignorant person
ig·no·rance \ˈig-nə-rəns\ *n* : the state of being ignorant
ig·no·rant \ˈig-nə-rənt\ *adj* **1** : lacking knowledge **2** : resulting from or showing lack of knowledge or intelligence **3** : UNAWARE, UNINFORMED **syn** benighted, illiterate, uneducated, unlettered, untutored — **ig·no·rant·ly** *adv*
ig·nore \ig-ˈnōr\ *vb* **ig·nored; ig·nor·ing** : to refuse to take notice of **syn** overlook, slight, neglect
igua·na \i-ˈgwä-nə\ *n* : any of various large tropical American lizards

iguana

ihp *abbr* indicated horsepower
IHS \ˌī-ˌäch-ˈes\ [LL, part transliteration of Gk IHΣ, abbreviation for IHΣOYΣ *Iēsous* Jesus] — used as a Christian symbol and monogram for *Jesus*
ikon *var of* ICON
IL *abbr* Illinois
il·e·itis \ˌi-lē-ˈī-təs\ *n* : inflammation of the ileum
il·e·um \ˈi-lē-əm\ *n, pl* **il·ea** \-lē-ə\ : the part of the small intestine between the jejunum and the large intestine
il·i·ac \ˈi-lē-ˌak\ *adj* : of, relating to, or located near the ilium

il·i·um \ˈi-lē-əm\ *n* : the uppermost and largest of the three bones making up either side of the pelvis
ilk \ˈilk\ *n* : SORT, KIND
¹ill \ˈil\ *adj* **worse** \ˈwərs\; **worst** \ˈwərst\ **1** : attended or caused by an evil intent ⟨∼ deeds⟩ **2** : not normal or sound ⟨∼ health⟩; *also* : not in good health : SICK **3** : BAD, UNLUCKY ⟨∼ omen⟩ **4** : not right or proper ⟨∼ manners⟩ **5** : UNFRIENDLY, HOSTILE ⟨∼ feeling⟩
²ill *adv* **worse; worst 1** : with displeasure **2** : in a harsh manner **3** : HARDLY, SCARCELY ⟨can ∼ afford it⟩ **4** : BADLY, UNLUCKILY **5** : in a faulty way
³ill *n* **1** : EVIL **2** : MISFORTUNE, DISTRESS **3** : AILMENT, SICKNESS; *also* : TROUBLE
⁴ill *abbr* illustrated; illustration; illustrator
Ill *abbr* Illinois
ill—ad·vised \ˌil-əd-ˈvīzd\ *adj* : not well counseled ⟨∼ efforts⟩ — **ill—ad·vis·ed·ly** \-ˈvī-zəd-lē\ *adv*
ill—bred \-ˈbred\ *adj* : badly brought up : IMPOLITE
il·le·gal \il-ˈlē-gəl\ *adj* : not lawful; *also* : not sanctioned by official rules **syn** unlawful, criminal, illegitimate, illicit, wrongful — **il·le·gal·i·ty** \ˌi-li-ˈga-lə-tē\ *n* — **il·le·gal·ly** *adv*
il·leg·i·ble \il-ˈle-jə-bəl\ *adj* : not legible — **il·leg·i·bil·i·ty** \il-ˌle-jə-ˈbi-lə-tē\ *n* — **il·leg·i·bly** \il-ˈle-jə-blē\ *adv*
il·le·git·i·mate \ˌi-li-ˈji-tə-mət\ *adj* **1** : born of unmarried parents **2** : ILLOGICAL **3** : ILLEGAL — **il·le·git·i·ma·cy** \-ˈji-tə-mə-sē\ *n* — **il·le·git·i·mate·ly** *adv*
ill—fat·ed \ˈil-ˈfā-təd\ *adj* : UNFORTUNATE
ill—fa·vored \-ˈfā-vərd\ *adj* : UGLY, UNATTRACTIVE
ill—got·ten \-ˈgät-ᵊn\ *adj* : acquired by improper means ⟨∼ gains⟩
ill—hu·mored \-ˈhyü-mərd, -ˈyü-\ *adj* : SURLY, IRRITABLE
il·lib·er·al \il-ˈli-bə-rəl\ *adj* : not liberal : NARROW, BIGOTED
il·lic·it \il-ˈli-sət\ *adj* : not permitted : UNLAWFUL — **il·lic·it·ly** *adv*
il·lim·it·able \il-ˈli-mə-tə-bəl\ *adj* : BOUNDLESS, MEASURELESS — **il·lim·it·ably** \-blē\ *adv*
Il·li·nois \ˌi-lə-ˈnȯi *also* -ˈnȯiz\ *n, pl* **Illinois** : a member of an American Indian people of Illinois, Iowa, and Wisconsin
il·lit·er·ate \il-ˈli-tə-rət\ *adj* **1** : having little or no education; *esp* : unable to read or write **2** : showing a lack of familiarity with the fundamentals of a particular field of knowledge — **il·lit·er·a·cy** \-ˈli-tə-rə-sē\ *n* — **illiterate** *n*
ill—man·nered \ˈil-ˈma-nərd\ *adj* : marked by bad manners : RUDE
ill—na·tured \-ˈnā-chərd\ *adj* : CROSS, SURLY — **ill—na·tured·ly** *adv*
ill·ness \ˈil-nəs\ *n* : SICKNESS
il·log·i·cal \il-ˈlä-ji-kəl\ *adj* : lacking sound reasoning; *also* : SENSELESS — **il·log·i·cal·ly** \-ji-k(ə-)lē\ *adv*
ill—starred \ˈil-ˈstärd\ *adj* : UNLUCKY 1
ill—tem·pered \-ˈtem-pərd\ *adj* : CROSS
ill—treat \-ˈtrēt\ *vb* : to treat cruelly or improperly : MALTREAT — **ill—treat·ment** *n*
il·lu·mi·nate \i-ˈlü-mə-ˌnāt\ *vb* **-nat·ed; -nat·ing 1** : to supply or brighten with light : light up **2** : to make clear : ELUCIDATE **3** : to decorate (as a manuscript) with designs or pictures in gold or colors — **il·lu·mi·nat·ing·ly** *adv* — **il·lu·mi·na·tion** \-ˌlü-mə-ˈnā-shən\ *n* — **il·lu·mi·na·tor** \-ˈlü-mə-ˌnā-tər\ *n*
il·lu·mine \i-ˈlü-mən\ *vb* **-mined; -min·ing** : ILLUMINATE
ill—us·age \ˈil-ˈyü-sij\ *n* : harsh, unkind, or abusive treatment
ill—use \-ˈyüz\ *vb* : MALTREAT, ABUSE
il·lu·sion \i-ˈlü-zhən\ *n* [ME, fr. MF, fr. LL *illusio,* fr. L, action of mocking, fr. *illudere* to mock at, fr. *ludere* to play, mock] **1** : a mistaken idea : MISCONCEPTION **2** : a misleading visual image; *also* : HALLUCINATION
il·lu·sion·ist \i-ˈlü-zhə-nist\ *n* : one that produces illusions; *esp* : a sleight-of-hand performer

il·lu·sive \i-ˈlü-siv\ *adj* : DECEPTIVE
il·lu·so·ry \i-ˈlü-sə-rē, -zə-\ *adj* : DECEPTIVE
illust *or* **illus** *abbr* illustrated; illustration
il·lus·trate \ˈi-ləs-ˌtrāt\ *vb* **-trat·ed; -trat·ing** [L *illustrare*, fr. *lustrare* to purify, make bright] **1** : to explain by use of examples : CLARIFY; *also* : DEMONSTRATE **2** : to provide with pictures or figures that explain or decorate **3** : to serve to explain or decorate — **il·lus·tra·tor** \ˈi-lə-ˌstrā-tər\ *n*
il·lus·tra·tion \ˌi-lə-ˈstrā-shən\ *n* **1** : the act of illustrating : the condition of being illustrated **2** : an example or instance that helps make something clear **3** : a picture or diagram that explains or decorates
il·lus·tra·tive \i-ˈləs-trə-tiv, ˈi-lə-ˌstrā-\ *adj* : serving, tending, or designed to illustrate — **il·lus·tra·tive·ly** *adv*
il·lus·tri·ous \i-ˈləs-trē-əs\ *adj* : notably outstanding because of rank or achievement **syn** distinguished, eminent, famous, great, notable, prominent — **il·lus·tri·ous·ness** *n*
ill will *n* : unfriendly feeling
ILS *abbr* instrument landing system
¹im·age \ˈi-mij\ *n* **1** : a likeness or imitation of a person or thing; *esp* : STATUE **2** : a picture of an object formed by a device (as a mirror or lens) **3** : a person strikingly like another person ⟨he is the ∼ of his father⟩ **4** : a mental picture or conception : IMPRESSION, IDEA, CONCEPT **5** : a vivid representation or description
²image *vb* **im·aged; im·ag·ing 1** : to call up a mental picture of **2** : to describe or portray in words **3** : to create a representation of **4** : REFLECT, MIRROR **5** : to make appear : PROJECT
im·ag·ery \ˈi-mij-rē\ *n* **1** : IMAGES; *also* : the art of making images **2** : figurative language **3** : mental images; *esp* : the products of imagination
imag·in·able \i-ˈma-jə-nə-bəl\ *adj* : capable of being imagined : CONCEIVABLE — **imag·in·ably** *adv*
imag·i·nary \i-ˈma-jə-ˌner-ē\ *adj* **1** : existing only in the imagination **2** : containing or relating to a quantity (**imaginary unit**) that is the positive square root of minus 1 ($\sqrt{-1}$)
imaginary number *n* : a complex number (as $2 + 3i$) with a nonzero term (**imaginary part**) containing the imaginary unit as a factor
imag·i·na·tion \i-ˌma-jə-ˈnā-shən\ *n* **1** : the act or power of forming a mental image of something not present to the senses or not previously known or experienced **2** : creative ability **3** : RESOURCEFULNESS **4** : a mental image : a creation of the mind — **imag·i·na·tive** \i-ˈma-jə-nə-tiv, -ˌnā-\ *adj* — **imag·i·na·tive·ly** *adv*
imag·ine \i-ˈma-jən\ *vb* **imag·ined; imag·in·ing 1** : to form a mental picture of something not present **2** : THINK, GUESS ⟨I ∼ it will rain⟩
im·ag·ism \ˈi-mi-ˌji-zəm\ *n, often cap* : a movement in poetry advocating free verse and the expression of ideas and emotions through clear precise images — **im·ag·ist** \-jist\ *n*
ima·go \i-ˈmā-gō, -ˈmä-\ *n, pl* **imagoes** *or* **ima·gi·nes** \-ˈmā-gə-ˌnēz, -ˈmä-\ [NL, fr. L, image] : an insect in its final adult stage — **ima·gi·nal** \i-ˈmā-gən-ᵊl, -ˈmä-\ *adj*
im·bal·ance \ˈim-ˈba-ləns\ *n* : lack of balance : the state of being out of equilibrium or out of proportion
im·be·cile \ˈim-bə-səl, -ˌsil\ *n* **1** : a mentally retarded person who needs help in routine personal care **2** : FOOL, IDIOT — **imbecile** *or* **im·be·cil·ic** \ˌim-bə-ˈsi-lik\ *adj* — **im·be·cil·i·ty** \ˌim-bə-ˈsi-lə-tē\ *n*
imbed *var of* EMBED
im·bibe \im-ˈbīb\ *vb* **im·bibed; im·bib·ing 1** : to receive and retain in the mind **2** : DRINK **3** : to take in or up : ABSORB — **im·bib·er** *n*
im·bri·ca·tion \ˌim-brə-ˈkā-shən\ *n* **1** : an overlapping of edges (as of tiles) **2** : a pattern showing imbrication — **im·bri·cate** \ˈim-bri-kət\ *adj*

im·bro·glio \im-ˈbrōl-yō\ *n, pl* **-glios** [It, fr. *imbrogliare* to entangle] **1** : a confused mass **2** : a complicated situation; *also* : a serious or embarrassing misunderstanding
im·brue \im-ˈbrü\ *vb* **im·brued; im·bru·ing** : STAIN ⟨hands *imbrued* with blood⟩
im·bue \-ˈbyü\ *vb* **im·bued; im·bu·ing 1** : to permeate or influence as if by dyeing **2** : to tinge or dye deeply
IMF *abbr* International Monetary Fund
imit *abbr* imitative
im·i·ta·ble \ˈi-mə-tə-bəl\ *adj* : capable or worthy of being imitated or copied
im·i·tate \ˈi-mə-ˌtāt\ *vb* **-tat·ed; -tat·ing 1** : to follow as a model : COPY **2** : RESEMBLE **3** : REPRODUCE **4** : MIMIC, COUNTERFEIT — **im·i·ta·tor** \-ˌtā-tər\ *n*
im·i·ta·tion \ˌi-mə-ˈtā-shən\ *n* **1** : an act of imitating **2** : COPY, COUNTERFEIT **3** : a literary work that reproduces the style of another author — **imitation** *adj*
im·i·ta·tive \ˈi-mə-ˌtā-tiv\ *adj* **1** : marked by imitation **2** : inclined to imitate **3** : COUNTERFEIT
im·mac·u·late \i-ˈma-kyə-lət\ *adj* **1** : being without stain or blemish : PURE **2** : spotlessly clean ⟨∼ linen⟩ — **im·mac·u·late·ly** *adv*
im·ma·nent \ˈi-mə-nənt\ *adj* : having existence only in the mind — **im·ma·nence** \-nəns\ *n* — **im·ma·nen·cy** \-nən-sē\ *n*
im·ma·te·ri·al \ˌi-mə-ˈtir-ē-əl\ *adj* **1** : not consisting of matter : SPIRITUAL **2** : UNIMPORTANT, TRIFLING **syn** bodiless, disembodied, incorporeal, insubstantial, nonphysical — **im·ma·te·ri·al·i·ty** \-ˌtir-ē-ˈa-lə-tē\ *n*
im·ma·ture \ˌi-mə-ˈtùr, -ˈtyùr\ *adj* : lacking complete development : not yet mature — **im·ma·tu·ri·ty** \-ˈtùr-ə-tē, -ˈtyùr-\ *n*
im·mea·sur·able \(ˌ)i-ˈme-zhə-rə-bəl\ *adj* : not capable of being measured : indefinitely extensive : ILLIMITABLE — **im·mea·sur·ably** \-blē\ *adv*
im·me·di·a·cy \i-ˈmē-dē-ə-sē\ *n, pl* **-cies 1** : the quality or state of being immediate **2** : something that is of immediate importance
im·me·di·ate \i-ˈmē-dē-ət\ *adj* **1** : acting directly and alone : DIRECT ⟨the ∼ cause of death⟩ **2** : being next in line or relation ⟨members of the ∼ family⟩ **3** : not distant : CLOSE **4** : made or done at once ⟨an ∼ response⟩ **5** : near to or related to the present time ⟨the ∼ future⟩ — **im·me·di·ate·ly** *adv*
im·me·mo·ri·al \ˌi-mə-ˈmōr-ē-əl\ *adj* : extending beyond the reach of memory, record, or tradition
im·mense \i-ˈmens\ *adj* [MF, fr. L *immensus* immeasurable, fr. *mensus*, pp. of *metiri* to measure] **1** : very great in size or degree : VAST, HUGE **2** : EXCELLENT — **im·mense·ly** *adv* — **im·men·si·ty** \-ˈmen-sə-tē\ *n*
im·merse \i-ˈmərs\ *vb* **im·mersed; im·mers·ing 1** : to plunge or dip into a fluid **2** : ENGROSS, ABSORB **3** : to baptize by immersing — **im·mer·sion** \-ˈmər-zhən\ *n*
im·mi·grant \ˈi-mi-grənt\ *n* **1** : a person who immigrates **2** : a plant or animal that becomes established where it did not previously occur
im·mi·grate \ˈi-mə-ˌgrāt\ *vb* **-grat·ed; -grat·ing** : to come into a foreign country and take up residence — **im·mi·gra·tion** \ˌi-mə-ˈgrā-shən\ *n*
im·mi·nent \ˈi-mə-nənt\ *adj* : ready to take place; *esp* : hanging threateningly over one's head — **im·mi·nence** \-nəns\ *n* — **im·mi·nent·ly** *adv*
im·mis·ci·ble \(ˌ)i-ˈmi-sə-bəl\ *adj* : incapable of mixing — **im·mis·ci·bil·i·ty** \-ˌmi-sə-ˈbi-lə-tē\ *n*
im·mo·bile \(ˌ)i-ˈmō-bəl\ *adj* : incapable of being moved : IMMOVABLE, FIXED — **im·mo·bil·i·ty** \ˌi-mō-ˈbi-lə-tē\ *n*

\ə\abut \ᵊ\kitten \ər\further \a\ash \ā\ace \ä\mop, mar
\aù\out \ch\chin \e\bet \ē\easy \g\go \i\hit \ī\ice \j\job
\ŋ\sing \ō\go \ò\law \òi\boy \th\thin \t̲h̲\the \ü\loot \ù\foot
\y\yet \zh\vision *see also* Pronunciation Symbols page

im·mo·bi·lize \i-'mō-bə-ˌlīz\ *vb* : to make immobile — im·mo·bi·li·za·tion \i-ˌmō-bə-lə-'zā-shən\ *n*

im·mod·er·ate \(ˌ)i-'mä-də-rət\ *adj* : lacking in moderation : EXCESSIVE — im·mod·er·a·cy \-rə-sē\ *n* — im·mod·er·ate·ly *adv*

im·mod·est \(ˌ)i-'mä-dəst\ *adj* : not modest : BRAZEN, INDECENT ⟨an ∼ dress⟩ ⟨∼ conduct⟩ — im·mod·est·ly *adv* — im·mod·es·ty \-də-stē\ *n*

im·mo·late \'i-mə-ˌlāt\ *vb* -lat·ed; -lat·ing [L *immolare*, fr. *mola* grits; fr. the custom of sprinkling victims with sacrificial meal] : to offer in sacrifice; *esp* : to kill as a sacrificial victim — im·mo·la·tion \ˌi-mə-'lā-shən\ *n*

im·mor·al \(ˌ)i-'mȯr-əl\ *adj* : not moral — im·mor·al·ly *adv*

im·mo·ral·i·ty \ˌi-mȯ-'ra-lə-tē, ˌi-mə-\ *n* 1 : WICKEDNESS; *esp* : UNCHASTITY 2 : an immoral act or practice

¹im·mor·tal \(ˌ)i-'mȯrt-ᵊl\ *adj* 1 : not mortal : exempt from death ⟨∼ gods⟩ 2 : destined to be remembered forever ⟨those ∼ words⟩ — im·mor·tal·ly *adv*

²immortal *n* 1 : one exempt from death 2 *pl, often cap* : the gods in Greek and Roman mythology 3 : a person whose fame is lasting ⟨an ∼ of baseball⟩

im·mor·tal·i·ty \ˌi-mȯr-'ta-lə-tē\ *n* : the quality or state of being immortal; *esp* : unending existence

im·mor·tal·ize \i-'mȯrt-ᵊl-ˌīz\ *vb* -ized; -iz·ing : to make immortal

im·mov·able \(ˌ)i-'mü-və-bəl\ *adj* 1 : firmly fixed, settled, or fastened : FAST, STATIONARY ⟨∼ mountains⟩ 2 : STEADFAST, UNYIELDING 3 : IMPASSIVE — im·mov·abil·i·ty \ˌmü-və-'bi-lə-tē\ *n* — im·mov·ably \-blē\ *adv*

im·mune \i-'myün\ *adj* 1 : EXEMPT 2 : having a special capacity for resistance (as to a disease) 3 : containing or producing antibodies — im·mu·ni·ty \-'myü-nə-tē\ *n*

immune response *n* : a response of the body to an antigen resulting in the formation of antibodies and cells designed to react with the antigen and render it harmless

immune system *n* : the bodily system that protects the body from foreign substances, cells, and tissues by producing the immune response and that includes esp. the thymus, spleen, lymph nodes, and lymphocytes

im·mu·nize \'i-myə-ˌnīz\ *vb* -nized; -niz·ing : to make immune — im·mu·ni·za·tion \ˌi-myə-nə-'zā-shən\ *n*

im·mu·no·de·fi·cien·cy \ˌi-myə-nō-di-'fi-shən-sē\ *n* : inability to produce the normal number of antibodies or immunologically sensitized cells esp. in response to specific antigens — im·mu·no·de·fi·cient \-'fi-shənt\ *adj*

im·mu·no·glob·u·lin \ˌi-myə-nō-'glä-byə-lən\ *n* : ANTIBODY

im·mu·nol·o·gy \ˌi-myə-'nä-lə-jē\ *n* : a science that deals with the immune system, immunity, and the immune response — im·mu·no·log·ic \-nə-'lä-jik\ *or* im·mu·no·log·i·cal \-ji-kəl\ *adj* — im·mu·no·log·i·cal·ly \-ji-k(ə-)lē\ *adv* — im·mu·nol·o·gist \-'nä-lə-jist\ *n*

im·mu·no·sup·pres·sion \ˌi-myə-nō-sə-'pre-shən\ *n* : suppression (as by drugs) of natural immune responses — im·mu·no·sup·press \-'pres\ *vb* — im·mu·no·sup·pres·sive \-'pre-siv\ *adj*

im·mu·no·ther·a·py \-'ther-ə-pē\ *n* : treatment or prevention of disease by attempting to induce immunity

im·mure \i-'myu̇r\ *vb* im·mured; im·mur·ing 1 : to enclose within or as if within walls 2 : to build into a wall; *esp* : to entomb in a wall

im·mu·ta·ble \(ˌ)i-'myü-tə-bəl\ *adj* : UNCHANGEABLE, UNCHANGING — im·mu·ta·bil·i·ty \ˌmyü-tə-'bi-lə-tē\ *n* — im·mu·ta·bly \-'myü-tə-blē\ *adv*

¹imp \'imp\ *n* 1 : a small demon : FIEND 2 : a mischievous child

²imp *abbr* 1 imperative 2 imperfect 3 imperial 4 import; imported

¹im·pact \im-'pakt\ *vb* 1 : to press together 2 : to have an impact on

²im·pact \'im-ˌpakt\ *n* 1 : a forceful contact, collision, or onset; *also* : the impetus communicated in or as if in a collision 2 : EFFECT

im·pact·ed \im-'pak-təd\ *adj* 1 : packed or wedged in 2 : wedged between the jawbone and another tooth

im·pair \im-'par\ *vb* : to diminish in quantity, value, excellence, or strength : DAMAGE, LESSEN — im·pair·ment *n*

im·paired \-'pard\ *adj* : being in a less than perfect or whole condition; *esp* : handicapped or functionally defective — often used in combination ⟨hearing-*impaired*⟩

im·pa·la \im-'pa-lə\ *n, pl* impalas *or* impala : a large brownish African antelope that in the male has slender curving horns

im·pale \im-'pāl\ *vb* im·paled; im·pal·ing : to pierce with or as if with something pointed — im·pale·ment *n*

im·pal·pa·ble \(ˌ)im-'pal-pə-bəl\ *adj* 1 : unable to be felt by touch : INTANGIBLE 2 : not easily seen or understood — im·pal·pa·bly \-blē\ *adv*

im·pan·el \im-'pan-ᵊl\ *vb* : to enter in or on a panel : ENROLL ⟨∼ a jury⟩

im·part \im-'pärt\ *vb* 1 : to give from one's store or abundance ⟨the sun ∼s warmth⟩ 2 : to make known

im·par·tial \(ˌ)im-'pär-shəl\ *adj* : not partial : UNBIASED, JUST — im·par·tial·i·ty \-ˌpär-shē-'a-lə-tē\ *n* — im·par·tial·ly *adv*

im·pass·able \(ˌ)im-'pa-sə-bəl\ *adj* : incapable of being passed, traversed, or crossed ⟨∼ roads⟩ — im·pass·ably \-blē\ *adv*

im·passe \'im-ˌpas\ *n* 1 : an impassable road or way 2 : a predicament from which there is no obvious escape

im·pas·si·ble \(ˌ)im-'pa-sə-bəl\ *adj* : incapable of feeling : IMPASSIVE

im·pas·sioned \im-'pa-shənd\ *adj* : filled with passion or zeal : showing great warmth or intensity of feeling **syn** passionate, ardent, fervent, fervid

im·pas·sive \(ˌ)im-'pa-siv\ *adj* : showing no signs of feeling, emotion, or interest : EXPRESSIONLESS, INDIFFERENT **syn** stoic, phlegmatic, apathetic, stolid — im·pas·sive·ly *adv* — im·pas·siv·i·ty \ˌim-ˌpa-'si-və-tē\ *n*

im·pas·to \im-'pas-tō, -'päs-\ *n* : the thick application of a pigment to a canvas or panel in painting; *also* : the body of pigment so applied

im·pa·tiens \im-'pā-shənz, -shəns\ *n* : any of a genus of annual herbs with usu. spurred flowers and seed capsules that readily split open

im·pa·tient \(ˌ)im-'pā-shənt\ *adj* 1 : not patient : restless or short of temper esp. under irritation, delay, or opposition 2 : INTOLERANT ⟨∼ of poverty⟩ 3 : prompted or marked by impatience 4 : ANXIOUS — im·pa·tience \-shəns\ *n* — im·pa·tient·ly *adv*

im·peach \im-'pēch\ *vb* [ME *empechen* to accuse, fr. MF *empeechier* to hinder, fr. LL *impedicare* to fetter, fr. L *pedica* fetter, fr. *ped-, pes* foot] 1 : to charge (a public official) before an authorized tribunal with misconduct in office 2 : to challenge the credibility or validity of 3 : to remove from public office for misconduct — im·peach·ment *n*

im·pec·ca·ble \(ˌ)im-'pe-kə-bəl\ *adj* 1 : not capable of sinning or wrongdoing 2 : FAULTLESS, IRREPROACHABLE ⟨a man of ∼ character⟩ — im·pec·ca·bil·i·ty \-ˌpe-kə-'bi-lə-tē\ *n* — im·pec·ca·bly \-'pe-kə-blē\ *adv*

im·pe·cu·nious \ˌim-pi-'kyü-nyəs, -nē-əs\ *adj* : having little or no money — im·pe·cu·nious·ness *n*

im·ped·ance \im-'pēd-ᵊns\ *n* : the opposition in an electrical circuit to the flow of an alternating current

im·pede \im-'pēd\ *vb* im·ped·ed; im·ped·ing [L *impedire*, fr. *ped-, pes* foot] : to interfere with the progress of

im·ped·i·ment \im-'pe-də-mənt\ *n* 1 : something that impedes, hinders, or obstructs 2 : a speech defect

im·ped·i·men·ta \im-ˌpe-də-ˈmen-tə\ *n pl* : things that impede

im·pel \im-ˈpel\ *vb* **im·pelled; im·pel·ling** : to urge or drive forward or on : FORCE; *also* : PROPEL

im·pel·ler *also* **im·pel·lor** \im-ˈpe-lər\ *n* : a rotor esp. in a pump

im·pend \im-ˈpend\ *vb* **1** : to hover or hang over threateningly : MENACE **2** : to be about to occur

im·pen·e·tra·ble \(ˌ)im-ˈpe-nə-trə-bəl\ *adj* **1** : incapable of being penetrated or pierced ⟨an ∼ jungle⟩ **2** : incapable of being comprehended : INSCRUTABLE ⟨an ∼ mystery⟩ — **im·pen·e·tra·bil·i·ty** \-ˌpe-nə-trə-ˈbi-lə-tē\ *n* — **im·pen·e·tra·bly** \-ˈpe-nə-trə-blē\ *adv*

im·pen·i·tent \(ˌ)im-ˈpe-nə-tənt\ *adj* : not penitent : not repenting of sin — **im·pen·i·tence** \-təns\ *n*

im·per·a·tive \im-ˈper-ə-tiv\ *adj* **1** : expressing a command, request, or encouragement ⟨∼ sentence⟩ **2** : having power to restrain, control, or direct **3** : NECESSARY — **imperative** *n* — **im·per·a·tive·ly** *adv*

im·per·cep·ti·ble \ˌim-pər-ˈsep-tə-bəl\ *adj* : not perceptible; *esp* : too slight to be perceived ⟨∼ changes⟩ — **im·per·cep·ti·bly** \-blē\ *adv*

im·per·cep·tive \ˌim-pər-ˈsep-tiv\ *adj* : not perceptive

imperf *abbr* imperfect

¹**im·per·fect** \(ˌ)im-ˈpər-fikt\ *adj* **1** : not perfect : DEFECTIVE, INCOMPLETE **2** : of, relating to, or being a verb tense used to designate a continuing state or an incomplete action esp. in the past — **im·per·fect·ly** *adv*

²**imperfect** *n* : the imperfect tense; *also* : a verb form in it

im·per·fec·tion \ˌim-pər-ˈfek-shən\ *n* : the quality or state of being imperfect; *also* : FAULT, BLEMISH

im·pe·ri·al \im-ˈpir-ē-əl\ *adj* **1** : of, relating to, or befitting an empire or an emperor; *also* : of or relating to the United Kingdom or to the Commonwealth or British Empire **2** : ROYAL, SOVEREIGN; *also* : REGAL, IMPERIOUS **3** : of unusual size or excellence

im·pe·ri·al·ism \im-ˈpir-ē-ə-ˌli-zəm\ *n* : the policy of seeking to extend the power, dominion, or territories of a nation — **im·pe·ri·al·ist** \-list\ *n or adj* — **im·pe·ri·al·is·tic** \-ˌpir-ē-ə-ˈlis-tik\ *adj* — **im·pe·ri·al·is·ti·cal·ly** \-ti-k(ə-)lē\ *adv*

im·per·il \im-ˈper-əl\ *vb* **-iled** *or* **-illed; -il·ing** *or* **-il·ling** : ENDANGER

im·pe·ri·ous \im-ˈpir-ē-əs\ *adj* **1** : COMMANDING, LORDLY **2** : ARROGANT, DOMINEERING **3** : IMPERATIVE, URGENT — **im·pe·ri·ous·ly** *adv*

im·per·ish·able \(ˌ)im-ˈper-i-shə-bəl\ *adj* : not perishable or subject to decay

im·per·ma·nent \(ˌ)im-ˈpər-mə-nənt\ *adj* : not permanent : TRANSIENT — **im·per·ma·nent·ly** *adv*

im·per·me·able \(ˌ)im-ˈpər-mē-ə-bəl\ *adj* : not permitting passage (as of a fluid) through its substance

im·per·mis·si·ble \ˌim-pər-ˈmi-sə-bəl\ *adj* : not permissible

im·per·son·al \(ˌ)im-ˈpər-sə-nəl\ *adj* **1** : not referring to any particular person or thing **2** : not involving human emotions — **im·per·son·al·i·ty** \-ˌpər-sə-ˈna-lə-tē\ *n* — **im·per·son·al·ly** *adv*

im·per·son·ate \im-ˈpər-sə-ˌnāt\ *vb* **-at·ed; -at·ing** : to assume or act the character of — **im·per·son·ation** \-ˌpər-sə-ˈnā-shən\ *n* — **im·per·son·ator** \-ˈpər-sə-ˌnā-tər\ *n*

im·per·ti·nent \(ˌ)im-ˈpərt-ᵊn-ənt\ *adj* **1** : IRRELEVANT **2** : not restrained within due or proper bounds : RUDE, INSOLENT, SAUCY — **im·per·ti·nence** \-əns\ *n* — **im·per·ti·nent·ly** *adv*

im·per·turb·able \ˌim-pər-ˈtər-bə-bəl\ *adj* : marked by extreme calm, impassivity, and steadiness : SERENE

im·per·vi·ous \(ˌ)im-ˈpər-vē-əs\ *adj* **1** : incapable of being penetrated (as by moisture) **2** : not capable of being affected or disturbed ⟨∼ to criticism⟩

im·pe·ti·go \ˌim-pə-ˈtē-gō, -ˈtī-\ *n* : a contagious skin disease characterized by vesicles, pustules, and yellowish crusts

im·pet·u·ous \im-ˈpe-chə-wəs\ *adj* **1** : marked by impulsive vehemence ⟨∼ temper⟩ **2** : marked by force and violence ⟨with ∼ speed⟩ — **im·pet·u·os·i·ty** \(ˌ)im-ˌpe-chə-ˈwä-sə-tē\ *n* — **im·pet·u·ous·ly** *adv*

im·pe·tus \ˈim-pə-təs\ *n* [L, assault, impetus, fr. *impetere* to attack, fr. *petere* to go to, seek] **1** : a driving force : IMPULSE; *also* : INCENTIVE **2** : MOMENTUM

im·pi·e·ty \(ˌ)im-ˈpī-ə-tē\ *n, pl* **-ties 1** : the quality or state of being impious **2** : an impious act

im·pinge \im-ˈpinj\ *vb* **im·pinged; im·ping·ing 1** : to strike or dash esp. with a sharp collision **2** : ENCROACH, INFRINGE — **im·pinge·ment** *n*

im·pi·ous \ˈim-pē-əs, (ˌ)im-ˈpī-\ *adj* : not pious : IRREVERENT, PROFANE

imp·ish \ˈim-pish\ *adj* : of, relating to, or befitting an imp; *esp* : MISCHIEVOUS — **imp·ish·ly** *adv* — **imp·ish·ness** *n*

im·pla·ca·ble \(ˌ)im-ˈpla-kə-bəl, -ˈplā-\ *adj* : not capable of being appeased, pacified, mitigated, or changed ⟨an ∼ enemy⟩ — **im·pla·ca·bil·i·ty** \-ˌpla-kə-ˈbi-lə-tē, -ˌplā-\ *n* — **im·pla·ca·bly** \-ˈpla-kə-blē\ *adv*

im·plant \im-ˈplant\ *vb* **1** : to set firmly or deeply **2** : to fix in the mind or spirit **3** : to insert in a living site for growth or absorption — **im·plant** \ˈim-ˌplant\ *n* — **im·plan·ta·tion** \ˌim-ˌplan-ˈtā-shən\ *n*

im·plau·si·ble \(ˌ)im-ˈplȯ-zə-bəl\ *adj* : not plausible — **im·plau·si·bil·i·ty** \-ˌplȯ-zə-ˈbi-lə-tē\ *n* — **im·plau·si·bly** \-ˈplȯ-zə-blē\ *adv*

¹**im·ple·ment** \ˈim-plə-mənt\ *n* [ME, fr. LL *implementum* action of filling up, fr. L *implēre* to fill up] : TOOL, UTENSIL, INSTRUMENT

²**im·ple·ment** \-ˌment\ *vb* **1** : CARRY OUT; *esp* : to put into practice **2** : to provide implements for — **im·ple·men·ta·tion** \ˌim-plə-mən-ˈtā-shən\ *n*

im·pli·cate \ˈim-plə-ˌkāt\ *vb* **-cat·ed; -cat·ing 1** : IMPLY **2** : INVOLVE — **im·pli·ca·tion** \ˌim-plə-ˈkā-shən\ *n*

im·plic·it \im-ˈpli-sət\ *adj* **1** : understood though not directly stated or expressed : IMPLIED; *also* : POTENTIAL **2** : COMPLETE, UNQUESTIONING, ABSOLUTE ⟨∼ faith⟩ — **im·plic·it·ly** *adv*

im·plode \im-ˈplōd\ *vb* **im·plod·ed; im·plod·ing** : to burst or collapse inward — **im·plo·sion** \-ˈplō-zhən\ *n* — **im·plo·sive** \-siv\ *adj*

im·plore \im-ˈplȯr\ *vb* **im·plored; im·plor·ing** : BESEECH, ENTREAT **syn** supplicate, beg, importune, plead

im·ply \im-ˈplī\ *vb* **im·plied; im·ply·ing 1** : to involve or indicate by inference, association, or necessary consequence rather than by direct statement ⟨war *implies* fighting⟩ **2** : to express indirectly : hint at : SUGGEST

im·po·lite \ˌim-pə-ˈlīt\ *adj* : not polite : RUDE, DISCOURTEOUS

im·pol·i·tic \(ˌ)im-ˈpä-lə-ˌtik\ *adj* : not politic : RASH

im·pon·der·a·ble \(ˌ)im-ˈpän-də-rə-bəl\ *adj* : incapable of being weighed or evaluated with exactness — **imponderable** *n*

¹**im·port** \im-ˈpōrt\ *vb* **1** : MEAN, SIGNIFY **2** : to bring (as merchandise) into a place or country from a foreign or external source — **im·port·er** *n*

²**im·port** \ˈim-ˌpōrt\ *n* **1** : IMPORTANCE, SIGNIFICANCE **2** : MEANING, SIGNIFICATION **3** : something (as merchandise) brought in from another country

im·por·tance \im-ˈpȯrt-ᵊns\ *n* : the quality or state of being important : MOMENT, SIGNIFICANCE **syn** consequence, import, weight

im·por·tant \im-ˈpȯrt-ᵊnt\ *adj* **1** : marked by importance

---

\ə\abut \ᵊ\kitten \ər\further \a\ash \ā\ace \ä\mop, mar
\au̇\out \ch\chin \e\bet \ē\easy \g\go \i\hit \ī\ice \j\job
\ŋ\sing \ō\go \ȯ\law \ȯi\boy \th\thin \t͟h\the \ü\loot \u̇\foot
\y\yet \zh\vision *see also* Pronunciation Symbols page

: SIGNIFICANT **2** : giving an impression of importance — **im·por·tant·ly** *adv*

im·por·ta·tion \ˌim-ˌpŏr-ˈtā-shən, -pər-\ *n* **1** : the act or practice of importing **2** : something imported

im·por·tu·nate \im-ˈpȯr-chə-nət\ *adj* **1** : troublesomely urgent or persistent **2** : BURDENSOME, TROUBLESOME

im·por·tune \ˌim-pər-ˈtün, -ˈtyün; im-ˈpȯr-chən\ *vb* **-tuned; -tun·ing** : to urge or beg with troublesome persistence — **im·por·tu·ni·ty** \-pər-ˈtü-nə-tē, -ˈtyü-\ *n*

im·pose \im-ˈpōz\ *vb* **im·posed; im·pos·ing 1** : to establish or apply by authority ⟨∼ a tax⟩; *also* : to establish by force ⟨*imposed* a government⟩ **2** : OBTRUDE ⟨*imposed* herself on others⟩ **3** : to take unwarranted advantage of something ⟨∼ on her good nature⟩ — **im·po·si·tion** \ˌim-pə-ˈzi-shən\ *n*

im·pos·ing *adj* : impressive because of size, bearing, dignity, or grandeur — **im·pos·ing·ly** *adv*

im·pos·si·ble \(ˌ)im-ˈpä-sə-bəl\ *adj* **1** : incapable of being or of occurring **2** : enormously difficult **3** : extremely undesirable : UNACCEPTABLE — **im·pos·si·bil·i·ty** \-ˌpä-sə-ˈbi-lə-tē\ *n* — **im·pos·si·bly** \-ˈpä-sə-blē\ *adv*

¹**im·post** \ˈim-ˌpōst\ *n* : TAX, DUTY

²**impost** *n* : a block, capital, or molding from which an arch springs

im·pos·tor *or* **im·pos·ter** \im-ˈpäs-tər\ *n* : one that assumes an identity or title not one's own in order to deceive

im·pos·ture \im-ˈpäs-chər\ *n* : DECEPTION; *esp* : fraudulent impersonation

im·po·tent \ˈim-pə-tənt\ *adj* **1** : lacking in power or strength : HELPLESS **2** : unable to copulate; *also* : STERILE — **im·po·tence** \-təns\ *n* — **im·po·ten·cy** \-tən-sē\ *n* — **im·po·tent·ly** *adv*

im·pound \im-ˈpaund\ *vb* **1** : CONFINE, ENCLOSE ⟨∼ stray dogs⟩ **2** : to seize and hold in legal custody **3** : to collect in a reservoir ⟨∼ water⟩ — **im·pound·ment** *n*

im·pov·er·ish \im-ˈpä-və-rish\ *vb* : to make poor; *also* : to deprive of strength, richness, or fertility — **im·pov·er·ish·ment** *n*

im·prac·ti·ca·ble \(ˌ)im-ˈprak-ti-kə-bəl\ *adj* : not practicable : incapable of being put into practice or use

im·prac·ti·cal \(ˌ)im-ˈprak-ti-kəl\ *adj* **1** : not practical **2** : IMPRACTICABLE

im·pre·cate \ˈim-pri-ˌkāt\ *vb* **-cat·ed; -cat·ing** : CURSE — **im·pre·ca·tion** \ˌim-pri-ˈkā-shən\ *n*

im·pre·cise \ˌim-pri-ˈsīs\ *adj* : not precise — **im·pre·cise·ly** *adv* — **im·pre·cise·ness** *n* — **im·pre·ci·sion** \-ˈsi-zhən\ *n*

im·preg·na·ble \im-ˈpreg-nə-bəl\ *adj* : incapable of being taken by assault : UNCONQUERABLE, UNASSAILABLE — **im·preg·na·bil·i·ty** \(ˌ)im-ˌpreg-nə-ˈbi-lə-tē\ *n*

im·preg·nate \im-ˈpreg-ˌnāt\ *vb* **-nat·ed; -nat·ing 1** : to fertilize or make pregnant **2** : to cause to be filled, permeated, or saturated — **im·preg·na·tion** \ˌim-ˌpreg-ˈnā-shən\ *n*

im·pre·sa·rio \ˌim-prə-ˈsär-ē-ˌō\ *n, pl* **-ri·os** [It, fr. *impresa* undertaking, fr. *imprendere* to undertake] **1** : the manager or conductor of an opera or concert company **2** : one who puts on an entertainment **3** : MANAGER, PRODUCER

¹**im·press** \im-ˈpres\ *vb* **1** : to apply with or produce (as a mark) by pressure : IMPRINT **2** : to press, stamp, or print in or upon **3** : to produce a vivid impression of **4** : to affect esp. forcibly or deeply — **im·press·ible** *adj*

²**im·press** \ˈim-ˌpres\ *n* **1** : a characteristic or distinctive mark **2** : IMPRESSION, EFFECT **3** : IMPRESSION 2 **4** : an image of something formed by or as if by pressure; *esp* : SEAL **5** : a product of pressure or influence

³**im·press** \im-ˈpres\ *vb* **1** : to force into naval service **2** : to get the aid or services of by forcible argument or persuasion — **im·press·ment** *n*

im·pres·sion \im-ˈpre-shən\ *n* **1** : a characteristic trait or feature resulting from influence : IMPRESS **2** : a stamp,

form, or figure made by impressing : IMPRINT **3** : an esp. marked influence or effect on feeling, sense, or mind **4** : a single print or copy (as from type or from an engraved plate or book) **5** : all the copies of a publication (as a book) printed for one issue : PRINTING **6** : a usu. vague notion or remembrance **7** : an imitation in caricature of a noted personality as a form of entertainment

im·pres·sion·able \im-ˈpre-shə-nə-bəl\ *adj* : capable of being easily impressed : easily molded or influenced

im·pres·sion·ism \im-ˈpre-shə-ˌni-zəm\ *n, often cap* : a theory or practice in modern art of depicting the natural appearances of objects by dabs or strokes of primary unmixed colors in order to simulate actual reflected light — **im·pres·sion·is·tic** \-ˌpre-shə-ˈnis-tik\ *adj*

im·pres·sion·ist \im-ˈpre-shə-nist\ *n* **1** *often cap* : a painter who practices impressionism **2** : an entertainer who does impressions

im·pres·sive \im-ˈpre-siv\ *adj* : making or tending to make a marked impression ⟨an ∼ speech⟩ — **im·pres·sive·ly** *adv* — **im·pres·sive·ness** *n*

im·pri·ma·tur \ˌim-prə-ˈmä-ˌtùr\ *n* [NL, let it be printed] **1** : a license to print or publish; *also* : official approval of a publication by a censor **2** : SANCTION, APPROVAL

¹**im·print** \im-ˈprint, ˈim-ˌprint\ *vb* **1** : to stamp or mark by or as if by pressure : IMPRESS **2** : to fix firmly (as on the memory)

²**im·print** \ˈim-ˌprint\ *n* **1** : something imprinted or printed **2** : a publisher's name printed at the foot of a title page **3** : an indelible distinguishing effect or influence

im·pris·on \im-ˈpriz-ᵊn\ *vb* : to put in or as if in prison : CONFINE — **im·pris·on·ment** *n*

im·prob·a·ble \(ˌ)im-ˈprä-bə-bəl\ *adj* : unlikely to be true or to occur — **im·prob·a·bil·i·ty** \-ˌprä-bə-ˈbi-lə-tē\ *n* — **im·prob·a·bly** \-ˈprä-bə-blē\ *adv*

im·promp·tu \im-ˈprämp-tü, -tyü\ *adj* [F, fr. *impromptu* extemporaneously, fr. L *in promptu* in readiness] **1** : made or done on or as if on the spur of the moment **2** : EXTEMPORANEOUS, UNREHEARSED — **impromptu** *adv or n*

im·prop·er \(ˌ)im-ˈprä-pər\ *adj* **1** : not proper, fit, or suitable **2** : INCORRECT, INACCURATE **3** : not in accord with propriety, modesty, or good manners — **im·prop·er·ly** *adv*

improper fraction *n* : a fraction whose numerator is equal to or larger than the denominator

im·pro·pri·e·ty \ˌim-prə-ˈprī-ə-tē\ *n, pl* **-ties 1** : an improper act or remark; *esp* : an unacceptable use of a word or of language **2** : the quality or state of being improper

im·prove \im-ˈprüv\ *vb* **im·proved; im·prov·ing 1** : to enhance or increase in value or quality **2** : to grow or become better ⟨your work is *improving*⟩ **3** : to make good use of ⟨∼ the time by reading⟩ — **im·prov·able** \-ˈprü-və-bəl\ *adj*

im·prove·ment \im-ˈprüv-mənt\ *n* **1** : the act or process of improving **2** : increased value or excellence of something **3** : something that adds to the value or appearance of a thing

im·prov·i·dent \(ˌ)im-ˈprä-və-dənt\ *adj* : not providing for the future — **im·prov·i·dence** \-dəns\ *n*

im·pro·vise \ˈim-prə-ˌvīz\ *vb* **-vised; -vis·ing** [F *improviser*, fr. It *improvvisare*, fr. *improvviso* sudden, fr. L *improvisus*, lit., unforeseen] **1** : to compose, recite, play, or sing on the spur of the moment : EXTEMPORIZE ⟨∼ on the piano⟩ **2** : to make, invent, or arrange offhand ⟨∼ a sail out of shirts⟩ — **im·pro·vi·sa·tion** \im-ˌprä-və-ˈzā-shən, ˌim-prə-və-\ *n* — **im·pro·vis·er** *or* **im·pro·vi·sor** \ˌim-prə-ˈvī-zər, ˈim-prə-ˌvī-\ *n*

im·pru·dent \(ˌ)im-ˈprüd-ᵊnt\ *adj* : not prudent : lacking discretion — **im·pru·dence** \-ᵊns\ *n*

im·pu·dent \ˈim-pyù-dənt\ *adj* : marked by contemptuous boldness or disregard of others — **im·pu·dence** \-dəns\ *n* — **im·pu·dent·ly** *adv*

im·pugn \im-'pyün\ *vb* [ME, to assail, ultim. fr. L *in-pugnare,* fr. *pugnare* to fight] : to attack by words or arguments : oppose or attack as false or as lacking integrity

im·puis·sance \im-'pwis-°ns, -'pyü-ə-səns\ *n* [ME, fr. MF] : the quality or state of being powerless : WEAKNESS

im·pulse \'im-ˌpəls\ *n* **1** : a force that starts a body into motion; *also* : the motion produced by such a force **2** : an arousing of the mind and spirit to some usu. unpremeditated action **3** : NERVE IMPULSE

im·pul·sion \im-'pəl-shən\ *n* **1** : the act of impelling : the state of being impelled **2** : a force that impels **3** : IMPULSE 2; *also* : COMPULSION 3

im·pul·sive \im-'pəl-siv\ *adj* **1** : having the power of or actually driving or impelling **2** : acting or prone to act on impulse ⟨∼ buying⟩ — **im·pul·sive·ly** *adv* — **im·pul·sive·ness** *n*

im·pu·ni·ty \im-'pyü-nə-tē\ *n* [MF or L; MF *impunité,* fr. L *impunitas,* fr. *impune* without punishment, fr. *poena* penalty, punishment] : exemption from punishment, harm, or loss

im·pure \(ˌ)im-'pyur\ *adj* **1** : not pure : UNCHASTE, OBSCENE **2** : DIRTY, FOUL **3** : ADULTERATED, MIXED — **im·pu·ri·ty** \-'pyur-ə-tē\ *n*

im·pute \im-'pyüt\ *vb* **im·put·ed; im·put·ing 1** : to lay the responsibility or blame for often falsely or unjustly **2** : to credit to a person or a cause : ATTRIBUTE — **im·put·able** \-'pyü-tə-bəl\ *adj* — **im·pu·ta·tion** \ˌim-pyü-'tā-shən\ *n*

¹in \'in\ *prep* **1** — used to indicate physical surroundings ⟨swim ∼ the lake⟩ **2** : INTO 1 ⟨ran ∼ the house⟩ **3** : DURING ⟨∼ the summer⟩ **4** : WITH ⟨written ∼ pencil⟩ **5** — used to indicate one's situation or state of being ⟨∼ luck⟩ ⟨∼ love⟩ **6** — used to indicate manner or purpose ⟨∼ a hurry⟩ ⟨said ∼ reply⟩ **7** : INTO 2 ⟨broke ∼ pieces⟩

²in *adv* **1** : to or toward the inside ⟨come ∼⟩; *also* : to or toward some destination or place ⟨flew ∼ from the South⟩ **2** : at close quarters : NEAR ⟨the enemy closed ∼⟩ **3** : into the midst of something ⟨mix ∼ the flour⟩ **4** : to or at its proper place ⟨fit a piece ∼⟩ **5** : WITHIN ⟨locked ∼⟩ **6** : in vogue or season **7** : in one's presence, possession, or control ⟨the results are ∼⟩

³in *adj* **1** : located inside or within **2** : that is in position, operation, or power ⟨the ∼ party⟩ **3** : directed inward : INCOMING ⟨the ∼ train⟩ **4** : keenly aware of and responsive to what is new and smart ⟨the ∼ crowd⟩; *also* : extremely fashionable ⟨the ∼ thing to do⟩

⁴in *n* **1** : one who is in office or power or on the inside **2** : INFLUENCE, PULL ⟨he has an ∼ with the owner⟩

⁵in *abbr* **1** inch **2** inlet

In *symbol* indium

IN *abbr* Indiana

in- \(ˌ)in\ *prefix* : not : absence of : NON-, UN-

inaccessibility	inarguable
inaccessible	inartistic
inaccuracy	inattentive
inaccurate	inaudible
inaction	inaudibly
inactive	inauspicious
inactivity	inauthentic
inadmissibility	incautious
inadmissible	incombustible
inadvisability	incomprehension
inadvisable	inconclusive
inapparent	incongruent
inapplicable	inconsistency
inapposite	inconsistent
inapproachable	incoordination
inappropriate	incurious
inaptitude	indecipherable

indemonstrable	inexpedient
indestructible	inexpensive
indeterminable	inexpressive
indiscernible	inextinguishable
indistinguishable	infeasible
inedible	inharmonious
ineducable	inhospitable
ineffaceable	injudicious
inefficacious	inoffensive
inefficacy	insanitary
inelastic	insensitive
inelasticity	insensitivity
inequitable	insignificance
inequity	insignificant
ineradicable	insolvable
inerrant	insusceptible

in·abil·i·ty \ˌi-nə-'bi-lə-tē\ *n* : the quality or state of being unable

in ab·sen·tia \ˌin-ab-'sen-chə, -chē-ə\ *adv* : in one's absence

in·ac·ti·vate \(ˌ)i-'nak-tə-ˌvāt\ *vb* : to make inactive — **in·ac·ti·va·tion** \(ˌ)i-ˌnak-tə-'vā-shən\ *n*

in·ad·e·quate \(ˌ)i-'na-di-kwət\ *adj* : not adequate : INSUFFICIENT — **in·ad·e·qua·cy** \-kwə-sē\ *n* — **in·ad·e·quate·ly** *adv* — **in·ad·e·quate·ness** *n*

in·ad·ver·tent \ˌi-nəd-'vərt-°nt\ *adj* **1** : HEEDLESS, INATTENTIVE **2** : UNINTENTIONAL — **in·ad·ver·tence** \-°ns\ *n* — **in·ad·ver·ten·cy** \-°n-sē\ *n* — **in·ad·ver·tent·ly** *adv*

in·alien·able \(ˌ)i-'nāl-yə-nə-bəl, -'nā-lē-ə-\ *adj* : incapable of being alienated, surrendered, or transferred ⟨∼ rights⟩ — **in·alien·abil·i·ty** \(ˌ)i-ˌnāl-yə-nə-'bi-lə-tē, -ˌnā-lē-ə-\ *n* — **in·alien·ably** *adv*

in·amo·ra·ta \i-ˌnä-mə-'rä-tə\ *n* : a woman with whom one is in love

inane \i-'nān\ *adj* **inan·er; -est** : EMPTY, INSUBSTANTIAL; *also* : SHALLOW, SILLY — **inan·i·ty** \i-'na-nə-tē\ *n*

in·an·i·mate \(ˌ)i-'na-nə-mət\ *adj* : not animate or animated : lacking the qualities of living things — **in·an·i·mate·ly** *adv* — **in·an·i·mate·ness** *n*

in·ap·pre·cia·ble \ˌi-nə-'prē-shə-bəl\ *adj* : too small to be perceived — **in·ap·pre·cia·bly** \-blē\ *adv*

in·apt \(ˌ)i-'napt\ *adj* **1** : not suitable **2** : INEPT — **in·apt·ly** *adv* — **in·apt·ness** *n*

in·ar·tic·u·late \ˌi-när-'ti-kyə-lət\ *adj* **1** : not understandable as spoken words **2** : MUTE **3** : incapable of being expressed by speech; *also* : UNSPOKEN **4** : not having the power of distinct utterance or effective expression — **in·ar·tic·u·late·ly** *adv*

in·as·much as \ˌi-nəz-'məch-\ *conj* : seeing that : SINCE

in·at·ten·tion \ˌi-nə-'ten-chən\ *n* : failure to pay attention : DISREGARD

¹in·au·gu·ral \i-'nȯ-gyə-rəl, -gə-\ *adj* **1** : of or relating to an inauguration **2** : marking a beginning

²inaugural *n* **1** : an inaugural address **2** : INAUGURATION

in·au·gu·rate \i-'nȯ-gyə-ˌrāt, -gə-\ *vb* **-rat·ed; -rat·ing 1** : to introduce into an office with suitable ceremonies : INSTALL **2** : to dedicate ceremoniously **3** : BEGIN, INITIATE — **in·au·gu·ra·tion** \-ˌnȯ-gyə-'rā-shən, -gə-\ *n*

in·board \'in-ˌbōrd\ *adv* **1** : inside the hull of a ship **2** : close or closest to the center line of a vehicle or craft — **inboard** *adj*

in·born \'in-'bȯrn\ *adj* **1** : present from or as if from birth **2** : HEREDITARY, INHERITED **syn** innate, congenital, native

in·bound \'in-ˌbaund\ *adj* : inward bound ⟨∼ traffic⟩

in·bred \'in-'bred\ *adj* **1** : ingrained in one's nature as deeply as if by heredity **2** : subjected to or produced by inbreeding

---

\ə\abut \ˀ\kitten \ər\further \a\ash \ā\ace \ä\mop, mar \au\out \ch\chin \e\bet \ē\easy \g\go \i\hit \ī\ice \j\job \ŋ\sing \ō\go \ȯ\law \ȯi\boy \th\thin \th\the \ü\loot \u̇\foot \y\yet \zh\vision *see also* Pronunciation Symbols page

in·breed·ing \'in-ˌbrē-diŋ\ *n* **1** : the interbreeding of closely related individuals esp. to preserve and fix desirable characters of and to eliminate unfavorable characters from a stock **2** : confinement to a narrow range or a local or limited field of choice — **in·breed** \-ˈbrēd\ *vb*

inc *abbr* **1** incomplete **2** incorporated **3** increase

In·ca \'iŋ-kə\ *n* [Sp, fr. Quechua (a So. American Indian language) *inka* ruler of the Inca empire] **1** : a noble or a member of the ruling family of an Indian empire of Peru, Bolivia, and Ecuador until the Spanish conquest **2** : a member of any people under Inca influence

in·cal·cu·la·ble \(ˌ)in-ˈkal-kyə-lə-bəl\ *adj* : not capable of being calculated; *esp* : too large or numerous to be calculated — **in·cal·cu·la·bly** \-blē\ *adv*

in·can·des·cent \ˌin-kən-ˈdes-ᵊnt\ *adj* **1** : glowing with heat **2** : SHINING, BRILLIANT — **in·can·des·cence** \-ᵊns\ *n*

incandescent lamp *n* : a lamp in which an electrically heated filament emits light

in·can·ta·tion \ˌin-ˌkan-ˈtā-shən\ *n* : a use of spells or verbal charms spoken or sung as a part of a ritual of magic; *also* : a formula of words used in or as if in such a ritual

in·ca·pa·ble \(ˌ)in-ˈkā-pə-bəl\ *adj* : lacking ability or qualification for a particular purpose; *also* : UNQUALIFIED — **in·ca·pa·bil·i·ty** \-ˌkā-pə-ˈbi-lə-tē\ *n*

in·ca·pac·i·tate \ˌin-kə-ˈpa-sə-ˌtāt\ *vb* **-tat·ed; -tat·ing** : to make incapable or unfit : DISQUALIFY, DISABLE

in·ca·pac·i·ty \ˌin-kə-ˈpa-sə-tē\ *n, pl* **-ties** : the quality or state of being incapable

in·car·cer·ate \in-ˈkär-sə-ˌrāt\ *vb* **-at·ed; -at·ing** : IMPRISON, CONFINE — **in·car·cer·a·tion** \(ˌ)in-ˌkär-sə-ˈrā-shən\ *n*

in·car·na·dine \in-ˈkär-nə-ˌdīn, -ˌdēn\ *vb* **-dined; -din·ing** : REDDEN

in·car·nate \in-ˈkär-nət, -ˌnāt\ *adj* **1** : having bodily and esp. human form and substance **2** : PERSONIFIED — **in·car·nate** \-ˌnāt\ *vb*

in·car·na·tion \ˌin-ˌkär-ˈnā-shən\ *n* **1** : the embodiment of a deity or spirit in an earthly form **2** *cap* : the union of divine and human natures in Jesus Christ **3** : a person showing a trait or typical character to a marked degree **4** : the act of incarnating : the state of being incarnate

incase *var of* ENCASE

in·cen·di·ary \in-ˈsen-dē-ˌer-ē\ *adj* **1** : of or relating to a deliberate burning of property **2** : tending to excite or inflame **3** : designed to start fires ⟨an ~ bomb⟩ — **incendiary** *n*

¹in·cense \'in-ˌsens\ *n* **1** : material used to produce a fragrant odor when burned **2** : the perfume or smoke from some spices and gums when burned

²in·cense \in-ˈsens\ *vb* **in·censed; in·cens·ing** : to make extremely angry

in·cen·tive \in-ˈsen-tiv\ *n* [ME, fr. LL *incentivum*, fr. *incentivus* stimulating, fr. L, setting the tune, fr. *incinere* to set the tune, fr. *canere* to sing] : something that incites or is likely to incite to determination or action

in·cep·tion \in-ˈsep-shən\ *n* : BEGINNING, COMMENCEMENT

in·cer·ti·tude \(ˌ)in-ˈsər-tə-ˌtüd, -ˌtyüd\ *n* **1** : UNCERTAINTY, DOUBT, INDECISION **2** : INSECURITY, INSTABILITY

in·ces·sant \(ˌ)in-ˈses-ᵊnt\ *adj* : continuing or flowing without interruption ⟨~ rains⟩ — **in·ces·sant·ly** *adv*

in·cest \'in-ˌsest\ *n* [ME, fr. L *incestus* sexual impurity, fr. *incestus* impure, fr. *castus* pure] : sexual intercourse between persons so closely related that marriage is illegal — **in·ces·tu·ous** \in-ˈses-chù-wəs\ *adj*

¹inch \'inch\ *n* [ME, fr. OE *ynce*, fr. L *uncia* twelfth part, inch, ounce] — see WEIGHT table

²inch *vb* : to move by small degrees

in·cho·ate \in-ˈkō-ət, 'in-kə-ˌwāt\ *adj* : being only partly in existence or operation : INCOMPLETE, INCIPIENT

inch·worm \'inch-ˌwərm\ *n* : LOOPER

in·ci·dence \'in-sə-dəns\ *n* : rate of occurrence or effect

¹in·ci·dent \-dənt\ *n* **1** : OCCURRENCE, HAPPENING **2** : an action likely to lead to grave consequences esp. in diplomatic matters

²incident *adj* **1** : occurring or likely to occur esp. in connection with some other happening **2** : falling or striking on something ⟨~ light rays⟩

¹in·ci·den·tal \ˌin-sə-ˈdent-ᵊl\ *adj* **1** : subordinate, nonessential, or attendant in position or significance ⟨~ expenses⟩ **2** : CASUAL, CHANCE

²incidental *n* **1** *pl* : minor items (as of expense) that are not individually accounted for **2** : something incidental

in·ci·den·tal·ly \ˌin-sə-ˈden-tə-lē, -ˈdent-lē\ *adv* **1** : in an incidental manner **2** : by the way

in·cin·er·ate \in-ˈsi-nə-ˌrāt\ *vb* **-at·ed; -at·ing** : to burn to ashes

in·cin·er·a·tor \in-ˈsi-nə-ˌrā-tər\ *n* : a furnace for burning waste

in·cip·i·ent \in-ˈsi-pē-ənt\ *adj* : beginning to be or become apparent

in·cise \in-ˈsīz\ *vb* **in·cised; in·cis·ing** **1** : to cut into **2** : CARVE, ENGRAVE

in·ci·sion \in-ˈsi-zhən\ *n* : CUT, GASH; *esp* : a surgical cut

in·ci·sive \in-ˈsī-siv\ *adj* : impressively direct and decisive — **in·ci·sive·ly** *adv*

in·ci·sor \in-ˈsī-zər\ *n* : a front tooth typically adapted for cutting

in·cite \in-ˈsīt\ *vb* **in·cit·ed; in·cit·ing** : to arouse to action : stir up — **in·cite·ment** *n* — **in·cit·er** *n*

in·ci·vil·i·ty \ˌin-sə-ˈvi-lə-tē\ *n* **1** : RUDENESS, DISCOURTESY **2** : a rude or discourteous act

incl *abbr* include; included; including; inclusive

in·clem·ent \(ˌ)in-ˈkle-mənt\ *adj* : SEVERE, STORMY ⟨~ weather⟩ — **in·clem·en·cy** \-mən-sē\ *n*

in·cli·na·tion \ˌin-klə-ˈnā-shən\ *n* **1** : PROPENSITY, BENT; *esp* : LIKING **2** : BOW, NOD ⟨an ~ of the head⟩ **3** : a tilting of something **4** : SLANT, SLOPE

¹in·cline \in-ˈklīn\ *vb* **in·clined; in·clin·ing** **1** : BOW, BEND **2** : to be drawn toward an opinion or course of action **3** : to deviate from the vertical or horizontal : SLOPE **4** : INFLUENCE, PERSUADE — **in·clin·er** *n*

²in·cline \'in-ˌklīn\ *n* : SLOPE

inclose, inclosure *var of* ENCLOSE, ENCLOSURE

in·clude \in-ˈklüd\ *vb* **in·clud·ed; in·clud·ing** : to take in or comprise as a part of a whole ⟨the price ~s tax⟩ — **in·clu·sion** \in-ˈklü-zhən\ *n* — **in·clu·sive** \-ˈklü-siv\ *adj*

incog *abbr* incognito

¹in·cog·ni·to \ˌin-ˌkäg-ˈnē-tō, in-ˈkäg-nə-ˌtō\ *n, pl* **-tos 1** : one appearing or living incognito **2** : the state or disguise of an incognito

²incognito *adv or adj* [It, fr. L *incognitus* unknown, fr. *cognoscere* to know] : with one's identity concealed

in·co·her·ent \ˌin-kō-ˈhir-ənt, -ˈher-\ *adj* **1** : not sticking closely or compactly together : LOOSE **2** : not clearly or logically connected : RAMBLING — **in·co·her·ence** \-əns\ *n* — **in·co·her·ent·ly** *adv*

in·come \'in-ˌkəm\ *n* : a gain usu. measured in money that derives from labor, business, or property

income tax *n* : a tax on the net income of an individual or business concern

in·com·ing \'in-ˌkə-miŋ\ *adj* : coming in ⟨the ~ tide⟩ ⟨~ freshmen⟩

in·com·men·su·rate \ˌin-kə-ˈmen-sə-rət, -ˈmen-chə-\ *adj* : not commensurate; *esp* : INADEQUATE

in·com·mode \ˌin-kə-ˈmōd\ *vb* **-mod·ed; -mod·ing** : INCONVENIENCE, DISTURB

in·com·mu·ni·ca·ble \ˌin-kə-ˈmyü-ni-kə-bəl\ *adj* : not communicable : not capable of being communicated or imparted; *also* : UNCOMMUNICATIVE

in·com·mu·ni·ca·do \ˌin-kə-ˌmyü-nə-ˈkä-dō\ *adv or adj*

: without means of communication; *also* : in solitary confinement ⟨a prisoner held ∼⟩

in·com·pa·ra·ble \(ˌ)in-ˈkäm-pə-rə-bəl, -prə-\ *adj* **1** : eminent beyond comparison : MATCHLESS **2** : not suitable for comparison — **in·com·pa·ra·bly** \-blē\ *adv*

in·com·pat·i·ble \ˌin-kəm-ˈpa-tə-bəl\ *adj* : incapable of or unsuitable for association or use together ⟨∼ colors⟩ ⟨temperamentally ∼⟩ — **in·com·pat·i·bil·i·ty** \ˌin-kəm-ˌpa-tə-ˈbi-lə-tē\ *n*

in·com·pe·tent \(ˌ)in-ˈkäm-pə-tənt\ *adj* **1** : not legally qualified **2** : not competent : lacking sufficient knowledge, skill, or ability — **in·com·pe·tence** \-təns\ *n* — **in·com·pe·ten·cy** \-tən-sē\ *n* — **incompetent** *n*

in·com·plete \ˌin-kəm-ˈplēt\ *adj* : lacking a part or parts : UNFINISHED, IMPERFECT — **in·com·plete·ly** *adv* — **in·com·plete·ness** *n*

in·com·pre·hen·si·ble \ˌin-ˌkäm-prē-ˈhen-sə-bəl\ *adj* : impossible to comprehend : UNINTELLIGIBLE

in·con·ceiv·able \ˌin-kən-ˈsē-və-bəl\ *adj* **1** : impossible to comprehend **2** : UNBELIEVABLE

in·con·gru·ous \(ˌ)in-ˈkäŋ-grü-wəs\ *adj* : not consistent with or suitable to the surroundings or associations — **in·con·gru·i·ty** \ˌin-kən-ˈgrü-ə-tē, -ˌkän-\ *n* — **in·con·gru·ous·ly** *adv*

in·con·se·quen·tial \ˌin-ˌkän-sə-ˈkwen-chəl\ *adj* **1** : ILLOGICAL; *also* : IRRELEVANT **2** : of no significance : UNIMPORTANT — **in·con·se·quence** \(ˌ)in-ˈkän-sə-ˌkwens\ *n* — **in·con·se·quen·tial·ly** *adv*

in·con·sid·er·able \ˌin-kən-ˈsi-də-rə-bəl\ *adj* : SLIGHT, TRIVIAL

in·con·sid·er·ate \ˌin-kən-ˈsi-də-rət\ *adj* : HEEDLESS, THOUGHTLESS; *esp* : not respecting the rights or feelings of others — **in·con·sid·er·ate·ly** *adv* — **in·con·sid·er·ate·ness** *n*

in·con·sol·able \ˌin-kən-ˈsō-lə-bəl\ *adj* : incapable of being consoled — **in·con·sol·ably** \-blē\ *adv*

in·con·spic·u·ous \ˌin-kən-ˈspi-kyə-wəs\ *adj* : not readily noticeable — **in·con·spic·u·ous·ly** *adv*

in·con·stant \(ˌ)in-ˈkän-stənt\ *adj* : not constant : CHANGEABLE **syn** fickle, capricious, mercurial, unstable, volatile — **in·con·stan·cy** \-stən-sē\ *n* — **in·con·stant·ly** *adv*

in·con·test·able \ˌin-kən-ˈtes-tə-bəl\ *adj* : not contestable : INDISPUTABLE — **in·con·test·ably** \-ˈtes-tə-blē\ *adv*

in·con·ti·nent \(ˌ)in-ˈkänt-ᵊn-ənt\ *adj* **1** : lacking self-restraint **2** : unable to retain a bodily discharge (as of urine) voluntarily — **in·con·ti·nence** \-əns\ *n*

in·con·tro·vert·ible \ˌin-ˌkän-trə-ˈvər-tə-bəl\ *adj* : not open to question : INDISPUTABLE ⟨∼ evidence⟩ — **in·con·tro·vert·ibly** \-blē\ *adv*

¹in·con·ve·nience \ˌin-kən-ˈvē-nyəns\ *n* **1** : something that is inconvenient **2** : the quality or state of being inconvenient

²inconvenience *vb* : to subject to inconvenience

in·con·ve·nient \ˌin-kən-ˈvē-nyənt\ *adj* : not convenient : causing trouble or annoyance : INOPPORTUNE — **in·con·ve·nient·ly** *adv*

in·cor·po·rate \in-ˈkȯr-pə-ˌrāt\ *vb* **-rat·ed; -rat·ing 1** : to unite closely or so as to form one body : BLEND **2** : to form, form into, or become a corporation **3** : to give material form to : EMBODY — **in·cor·po·ra·tion** \-ˌkȯr-pə-ˈrā-shən\ *n*

in·cor·po·re·al \ˌin-kȯr-ˈpōr-ē-əl\ *adj* : having no material body or form

in·cor·rect \ˌin-kə-ˈrekt\ *adj* **1** : INACCURATE, FAULTY **2** : not true : WRONG **3** : UNBECOMING, IMPROPER — **in·cor·rect·ly** *adv* — **in·cor·rect·ness** *n*

in·cor·ri·gi·ble \(ˌ)in-ˈkȯr-ə-jə-bəl\ *adj* : incapable of being corrected, amended, or reformed — **in·cor·ri·gi·bil·i·ty** \(ˌ)in-ˌkȯr-ə-jə-ˈbi-lə-tē\ *n* — **in·cor·ri·gi·bly** \-ˈkȯr-ə-jə-blē\ *adv*

in·cor·rupt·ible \ˌin-kə-ˈrəp-tə-bəl\ *adj* **1** : not subject to decay or dissolution **2** : incapable of being bribed or

morally corrupted — **in·cor·rupt·ibil·i·ty** \-ˌrəp-tə-ˈbi-lə-tē\ *n* — **in·cor·rupt·ibly** \-ˈrəp-tə-blē\ *adv*

incr *abbr* increase; increased

¹in·crease \in-ˈkrēs, ˈin-ˌkrēs\ *vb* **in·creased; in·creas·ing 1** : to become greater : GROW **2** : to multiply by the production of young ⟨rabbits ∼ rapidly⟩ **3** : to make greater — **in·creas·ing·ly** \-ˈkrē-siŋ-lē\ *adv*

²in·crease \ˈin-ˌkrēs, in-ˈkrēs\ *n* **1** : addition or enlargement in size, extent, or quantity : GROWTH **2** : something that is added to an original stock or amount (as by growth)

in·cred·i·ble \(ˌ)in-ˈkre-də-bəl\ *adj* : too extraordinary and improbable to be believed; *also* : hard to believe — **in·cred·ibil·i·ty** \(ˌ)in-ˌkre-də-ˈbi-lə-tē\ *n* — **in·cred·i·bly** \-ˈkre-də-blē\ *adv*

in·cred·u·lous \-ˈkre-jə-ləs\ *adj* **1** : SKEPTICAL **2** : expressing disbelief — **in·cre·du·li·ty** \ˌin-kri-ˈdü-lə-tē, -ˈdyü-\ *n* — **in·cred·u·lous·ly** *adv*

in·cre·ment \ˈiŋ-krə-mənt, ˈin-\ *n* **1** : the action or process of increasing esp. in quantity or value : ENLARGEMENT; *also* : QUANTITY **2** : something gained or added; *esp* : one of a series of regular consecutive additions — **in·cre·men·tal** \ˌiŋ-krə-ˈment-ᵊl, ˌin-\ *adj* — **in·cre·men·tal·ly** *adv*

in·crim·i·nate \in-ˈkri-mə-ˌnāt\ *vb* **-nat·ed; -nat·ing** : to charge with or prove involvement in a crime or fault : ACCUSE — **in·crim·i·na·tion** \-ˌkri-mə-ˈnā-shən\ *n* — **in·crim·i·na·to·ry** \-ˈkri-mə-nə-ˌtȯr-ē\ *adj*

incrust *var of* ENCRUST

in·crus·ta·tion \ˌin-ˌkrəs-ˈtā-shən\ *n* **1** : CRUST; *also* : something resembling a crust ⟨∼ of habits⟩ **2** : the act of encrusting : the state of being encrusted

in·cu·bate \ˈiŋ-kyù-ˌbāt, ˈin-\ *vb* **-bat·ed; -bat·ing** : to sit on (eggs) to hatch by the warmth of the body; *also* : to keep (as an embryo) under conditions favorable for development — **in·cu·ba·tion** \ˌiŋ-kyù-ˈbā-shən, ˌin-\ *n*

incubation period *n* : the period of brooding or incubating required to bring an egg to hatching

in·cu·ba·tor \ˈiŋ-kyù-ˌbāt-ər, ˈin-\ *n* : one that incubates; *esp* : an apparatus providing suitable conditions (as of warmth and moisture) for incubating something (as a premature baby)

in·cu·bus \ˈiŋ-kyə-bəs, ˈin-\ *n, pl* **-bi** \-ˌbī, -ˌbē\ *also* **-bus·es** [ME, fr. LL, fr. L *incubare* to lie on] **1** : a spirit supposed to work evil on persons in their sleep **2** : NIGHTMARE **1 3** : one that oppresses like a nightmare

in·cul·cate \in-ˈkəl-ˌkāt, ˈin-(ˌ)kəl-\ *vb* **-cat·ed; -cat·ing** [L *inculcare*, lit., to tread on, tr. *calcare* to trample, fr. *calx* heel] : to teach and impress by frequent repetitions or admonitions — **in·cul·ca·tion** \ˌin-(ˌ)kəl-ˈkā-shən\ *n*

in·cul·pa·ble \(ˌ)in-ˈkəl-pə-bəl\ *adj* : free from guilt : INNOCENT

in·cul·pate \in-ˈkəl-ˌpāt, ˈin-(ˌ)kəl-\ *vb* **-pat·ed; -pat·ing** : INCRIMINATE

in·cum·ben·cy \in-ˈkəm-bən-sē\ *n, pl* **-cies 1** : something that is incumbent **2** : the quality or state of being incumbent **3** : the office or period of office of an incumbent

¹in·cum·bent \in-ˈkəm-bənt\ *n* : the holder of an office or position

²incumbent *adj* **1** : imposed as a duty **2** : occupying a specified office **3** : lying or resting on something else

in·cu·nab·u·lum \ˌin-kyə-ˈna-byə-ləm, iŋ-\ *n, pl* **-la** \-lə\ [NL, fr. L *incunabula*, pl., bands holding the baby in a cradle, fr. *cunae* cradle] : a book printed before 1501

in·cur \in-ˈkər\ *vb* **in·curred; in·cur·ring** : to become liable or subject to : bring down upon oneself

in·cur·able \(ˌ)in-ˈkyùr-ə-bəl\ *adj* **1** : not subject to cure

\ə\abut \ᵊ\kitten \ər\further \a\ash \ā\ace \ä\mop, mar
\aù\out \ch\chin \e\bet \ē\easy \g\go \i\hit \ī\ice \j\job
\ŋ\sing \ō\go \ȯ\law \ȯi\boy \th\thin \th\the \ü\loot \ù\foot
\y\yet \zh\vision *see also* Pronunciation Symbols page

2 : not likely to be changed — **incurable** *n* — **in·cur·ably** \(ˌ)in-ˈkyůr-ə-blē\ *adv*

in·cur·sion \in-ˈkər-zhən\ *n* **1** : a sudden hostile invasion : RAID **2** : an entering in or into (as an activity)

in·cus \ˈiŋ-kəs\ *n, pl* **in·cu·des** \iŋ-ˈkyü-(ˌ)dēz\ [NL, fr. L, anvil] : the middle bone of a chain of three small bones in the ear of a mammal

ind *abbr* **1** independent **2** index **3** industrial; industry

Ind *abbr* **1** Indian **2** Indiana

in·debt·ed \in-ˈde-təd\ *adj* **1** : owing gratitude or recognition to another **2** : owing money — **in·debt·ed·ness** *n*

in·de·cent \(ˌ)in-ˈdēs-ᵊnt\ *adj* : not decent; *esp* : morally offensive — **in·de·cen·cy** \-ᵊn-sē\ *n* — **in·de·cent·ly** *adv*

in·de·ci·sion \ˌin-di-ˈsi-zhən\ *n* : a wavering between two or more possible courses of action : IRRESOLUTION

in·de·ci·sive \ˌin-di-ˈsī-siv\ *adj* **1** : INCONCLUSIVE **2** : marked by or prone to indecision **3** : INDEFINITE — **in·de·ci·sive·ly** *adv* — **in·de·ci·sive·ness** *n*

in·de·co·rous \(ˌ)in-ˈde-kə-rəs; ˌin-di-ˈkōr-əs\ *adj* : not decorous **syn** improper, unseemly, indecent, unbecoming, indelicate — **in·de·co·rous·ly** *adv* — **in·de·co·rous·ness** *n*

in·deed \in-ˈdēd\ *adv* **1** : without any question : TRULY — often used interjectionally to express irony, disbelief, or surprise **2** : in reality **3** : all things considered

indef *abbr* indefinite

in·de·fat·i·ga·ble \ˌin-di-ˈfa-ti-gə-bəl\ *adj* : UNTIRING — **in·de·fat·i·ga·bly** \-blē\ *adv*

in·de·fea·si·ble \-ˈfē-zə-bəl\ *adj* : not capable of being annulled or voided — **in·de·fea·si·bly** \-blē\ *adv*

in·de·fen·si·ble \-ˈfen-sə-bəl\ *adj* **1** : incapable of being maintained as right or valid **2** : INEXCUSABLE **3** : incapable of being protected against physical attack

in·de·fin·able \-ˈfī-nə-bəl\ *adj* : incapable of being precisely described or analyzed — **in·de·fin·ably** \-blē\ *adv*

in·def·i·nite \(ˌ)in-ˈde-fə-nət\ *adj* **1** : not defining or identifying ⟨*an* is an ~ article⟩ **2** : not precise : VAGUE **3** : having no fixed limit — **in·def·i·nite·ly** *adv* — **in·def·i·nite·ness** *n*

in·del·i·ble \in-ˈde-lə-bəl\ *adj* [ME, fr. ML *indelibilis,* alter. of L *indelebilis,* fr. *delēre* to delete, destroy] **1** : not capable of being removed or erased **2** : making marks that cannot be erased **3** : LASTING, UNFORGETTABLE — **in·del·i·bly** \in-ˈde-lə-blē\ *adv*

in·del·i·cate \(ˌ)in-ˈde-li-kət\ *adj* : not delicate; *esp* : IMPROPER, COARSE, TACTLESS **syn** indecent, unseemly, indecorous, unbecoming — **in·del·i·ca·cy** \in-ˈde-lə-kə-sē\ *n*

in·dem·ni·fy \in-ˈdem-nə-ˌfī\ *vb* **-fied; -fy·ing** [L *indemnis* unharmed, fr. *in-* not + *damnum* damage] **1** : to secure against hurt, loss, or damage **2** : to make compensation to for hurt, loss, or damage — **in·dem·ni·fi·ca·tion** \-ˌdem-nə-fə-ˈkā-shən\ *n*

in·dem·ni·ty \in-ˈdem-nə-tē\ *n, pl* **-ties** **1** : security against hurt, loss, or damage; *also* : exemption from incurred penalties or liabilities **2** : something that indemnifies

¹in·dent \in-ˈdent\ *vb* [ME, fr. MF *endenter,* fr. OF, fr. *dent* tooth, fr. L *dent-, dens*] **1** : to notch the edge of **2** : INDENTURE **3** : to set (as a line of a paragraph) in from the margin

²indent *vb* **1** : to force inward so as to form a depression **2** : to form a dent in

in·den·ta·tion \ˌin-ˌden-ˈtā-shən\ *n* **1** : NOTCH; also: a usu. deep recess (as in a coastline) **2** : the action of indenting : the condition of being indented **3** : DENT **4** : INDENTION 2

in·den·tion \in-ˈden-chən\ *n* **1** : INDENTATION 2 **2** : the blank space produced by indenting

¹in·den·ture \in-ˈden-chər\ *n* **1** : a written certificate or agreement; *esp* : a contract binding one person (as an apprentice) to work for another for a given period of time — usu. used in pl. **2** : INDENTATION 1 **3** : DENT

²indenture *vb* **in·den·tured; in·den·tur·ing** : to bind (as an apprentice) by indentures

in·de·pen·dence \ˌin-də-ˈpen-dəns\ *n* : the quality or state of being independent : FREEDOM

Independence Day *n* : July 4 observed as a legal holiday in commemoration of the adoption of the Declaration of Independence in 1776

in·de·pen·dent \ˌin-də-ˈpen-dənt\ *adj* **1** : SELF-GOVERNING; *also* : not affiliated with a larger controlling unit **2** : not requiring or relying on something else or somebody else ⟨an ~ conclusion⟩ ⟨~ of her parents⟩ **3** : not easily influenced : showing self-reliance and personal freedom ⟨an ~ mind⟩ **4** : not committed to a political party ⟨an ~ voter⟩ **5** : MAIN ⟨an ~ clause⟩ — **independent** *n* — **in·de·pen·dent·ly** *adv*

in·de·scrib·able \ˌin-di-ˈskrī-bə-bəl\ *adj* **1** : that cannot be described **2** : being too intense or great for description — **in·de·scrib·ably** \-blē\ *adv*

in·de·ter·mi·nate \ˌin-di-ˈtər-mə-nət\ *adj* **1** : VAGUE; *also* : not known in advance **2** : not limited in advance; *also* : not leading to a definite end or result — **in·de·ter·mi·na·cy** \-nə-sē\ *n* — **in·de·ter·mi·nate·ly** *adv*

¹in·dex \ˈin-ˌdeks\ *n, pl* **in·dex·es** *or* **in·di·ces** \-də-ˌsēz\ **1** : POINTER **2** : SIGN, INDICATION ⟨an ~ of character⟩ **3** : a guide for facilitating references; *esp* : an alphabetical list of items treated in a printed work with the page number where each item may be found **4** : a list of restricted or prohibited material **5** *pl usu* **indices** : a number or symbol or expression (as an exponent) associated with another to indicate a mathematical operation or use or position in an arrangement or expansion **6** : a character ☞ used to direct attention (as to a note) **7** : INDEX NUMBER

²index *vb* **1** : to provide with or put into an index **2** : to serve as an index of **3** : to regulate by indexation

in·dex·ation \ˌin-ˌdek-ˈsā-shən\ *n* : a system of economic control in which a body of variables (as wages and interest) rise or fall at the same rate as an index of the cost of living

index finger *n* : FOREFINGER

in·dex·ing *n* : INDEXATION

index number *n* : a number used to indicate change in magnitude (as of cost) as compared with the magnitude at some specified time usu. taken as 100

index of refraction : the ratio of the speed of radiation in one medium to that in another medium

in·dia ink \ˈin-dē-ə-\ *n, often cap 1st I* **1** : a solid black pigment used in drawing **2** : a fluid made from india ink

In·di·an \ˈin-dē-ən\ *n* **1** : a native or inhabitant of the subcontinent of India **2** : a person of Indian descent **3** : AMERICAN INDIAN — **Indian** *adj*

Indian corn *n* : a tall widely grown American cereal grass bearing seeds on long ears; *also* : its ears or seeds

Indian meal *n* : CORNMEAL

Indian paintbrush *n* : any of a genus of herbaceous plants related to the snapdragon that have brightly colored bracts

Indian pipe *n* : a waxy white leafless saprophytic herb of Asia and the U.S.

Indian summer *n* : a period of mild weather in late autumn or early winter

In·dia paper \ˈin-dē-ə-\ *n* **1** : a thin absorbent paper used esp. for taking impressions (as of steel engravings) **2** : a thin tough opaque printing paper

indic *abbr* indicative

in·di·cate \ˈin-də-ˌkāt\ *vb* **-cat·ed; -cat·ing** **1** : to point out or to **2** : to show indirectly **3** : to state briefly — **in·di·ca·tion** \ˌin-də-ˈkā-shən\ *n* — **in·di·ca·tor** \ˈin-də-ˌkā-tər\ *n*

¹in·dic·a·tive \in-ˈdi-kə-tiv\ *adj* **1** : of, relating to, or being a verb form that represents an act or state as a fact

⟨∼ mood⟩ **2** : serving to indicate ⟨actions ∼ of fear⟩

²**indicative** *n* **1** : the indicative mood of a language **2** : a form in the indicative mood

in·di·cia \in-ˈdi-shə, -shē-ə\ *n pl* **1** : distinctive marks **2** : postal markings often imprinted on mail or mailing labels

in·dict \in-ˈdīt\ *vb* [alter. of earlier *indite*, fr. ME, fr. OF *enditer*, lit., to write down] **1** : to charge with a fault or offense **2** : to charge with a crime by the finding of a jury — **in·dict·able** *adj* — **in·dict·ment** *n*

in·dif·fer·ent \in-ˈdi-frənt, -fə-rənt\ *adj* **1** : UNBIASED, UNPREJUDICED **2** : of no importance one way or the other **3** : marked by no special liking for or dislike of something **4** : being neither excessive nor inadequate **5** : PASSABLE, MEDIOCRE **6** : being neither right nor wrong — **in·dif·fer·ence** \-frəns, -fə-rəns\ *n* — **in·dif·fer·ent·ly** *adv*

in·dig·e·nous \in-ˈdi-jə-nəs\ *adj* : produced, growing, or living naturally in a particular region

in·di·gent \ˈin-di-jənt\ *adj* : IMPOVERISHED, NEEDY — **in·di·gence** \-jəns\ *n*

in·di·gest·ible \ˌin-dī-ˈjes-tə-bəl, -də-\ *adj* : not readily digested

in·di·ges·tion \-ˈjes-chən\ *n* : inadequate or difficult digestion : DYSPEPSIA

in·dig·nant \in-ˈdig-nənt\ *adj* : filled with or marked by indignation — **in·dig·nant·ly** *adv*

in·dig·na·tion \ˌin-dig-ˈnā-shən\ *n* : anger aroused by something unjust, unworthy, or mean

in·dig·ni·ty \in-ˈdig-nə-tē\ *n, pl* **-ties** : an offense against personal dignity or self-respect; *also* : humiliating treatment

in·di·go \ˈin-di-ˌgō\ *n, pl* **-gos** *or* **-goes** [It dial., fr. L *indicum*, fr. Gk *indikon*, fr. *indikos* Indic, fr. *Indos* India] **1** : a blue dye obtained from plants or synthesized **2** : a deep reddish blue color

in·di·rect \ˌin-də-ˈrekt, -dī-\ *adj* **1** : not straight ⟨an ∼ route⟩ **2** : not straightforward and open ⟨∼ methods⟩ **3** : not having a plainly seen connection ⟨an ∼ cause⟩ **4** : not directly to the point ⟨an ∼ answer⟩ — **in·di·rec·tion** \-ˈrek-shən\ *n* — **in·di·rect·ly** *adv* — **in·di·rect·ness** *n*

in·dis·creet \ˌin-di-ˈskrēt\ *adj* : not discreet : IMPRUDENT — **in·dis·creet·ly** *adv*

in·dis·cre·tion \ˌin-di-ˈskre-shən\ *n* **1** : IMPUDENCE **2** : something marked by lack of discretion; *esp* : an act deviating from accepted morality

in·dis·crim·i·nate \ˌin-di-ˈskri-mə-nət\ *adj* **1** : not marked by discrimination or careful distinction **2** : HAPHAZARD, RANDOM **3** : UNRESTRAINED **4** : MOTLEY — **in·dis·crim·i·nate·ly** *adv*

in·dis·pens·able \ˌin-di-ˈspen-sə-bəl\ *adj* : absolutely essential : REQUISITE — **in·dis·pens·abil·i·ty** \-ˌspen-sə-ˈbi-lə-tē\ *n* — **indispensable** *n* — **in·dis·pens·ably** \-ˈspen-sə-blē\ *adv*

in·dis·posed \-ˈspōzd\ *adj* **1** : slightly ill **2** : AVERSE — **in·dis·po·si·tion** \(ˌ)in-ˌdis-pə-ˈzi-shən\ *n*

in·dis·put·able \ˌin-di-ˈspyü-tə-bəl, (ˌ)in-ˈdis-pyə-\ *adj* : not disputable : UNQUESTIONABLE ⟨∼ proof⟩ — **in·dis·put·ably** \-blē\ *adv*

in·dis·sol·u·ble \ˌin-di-ˈsäl-yə-bəl\ *adj* : not capable of being dissolved, undone, or broken : PERMANENT

in·dis·tinct \ˌin-di-ˈstiŋkt\ *adj* **1** : not sharply outlined or separable : BLURRED, FAINT, DIM **2** : not readily distinguishable : UNCERTAIN — **in·dis·tinct·ly** *adv* — **in·dis·tinct·ness** *n*

in·dite \in-ˈdīt\ *vb* **in·dit·ed; in·dit·ing** : COMPOSE ⟨∼ a poem⟩; *also* : to put in writing ⟨∼ a letter⟩

in·di·um \ˈin-dē-əm\ *n* : a malleable silvery metallic chemical element — see ELEMENT table

indiv *abbr* individual

¹**in·di·vid·u·al** \ˌin-də-ˈvi-jə-wəl\ *adj* **1** : of, relating to, or associated with an individual ⟨∼ traits⟩ **2** : being an individual : existing as an indivisible whole **3** : intended for one person **4** : SEPARATE ⟨∼ copies⟩ **5** : having marked individuality ⟨an ∼ style⟩ — **in·di·vid·u·al·ly** *adv*

²**individual** *n* **1** : a single member of a category : a particular person, animal, or thing **2** : PERSON ⟨a disagreeable ∼⟩

in·di·vid·u·al·ism \ˌin-də-ˈvi-jə-wə-ˌli-zəm\ *n* **1** : a doctrine that the interests of the individual are primary **2** : a doctrine holding that the individual has political or economic rights with which the state must not interfere **3** : INDIVIDUALITY

in·di·vid·u·al·ist \-list\ *n* **1** : one that pursues a markedly independent course in thought or action **2** : one that advocates or practices individualism — **individualist** *or* **in·di·vid·u·al·is·tic** \-ˌvi-jə-wə-ˈlis-tik\ *adj*

in·di·vid·u·al·i·ty \-ˌvi-jə-ˈwa-lə-tē\ *n, pl* **-ties** **1** : the sum of qualities that characterize and distinguish an individual from all others; *also* : PERSONALITY **2** : separate or distinct existence **3** : INDIVIDUAL, PERSON

in·di·vid·u·al·ize \-ˈvi-jə-wə-ˌlīz\ *vb* **-ized; -iz·ing** **1** : to make individual in character **2** : to treat or notice individually : PARTICULARIZE **3** : to adapt to the needs of an individual

individual retirement account *n* : IRA

in·di·vid·u·ate \ˌin-də-ˈvi-jə-ˌwāt\ *vb* **-at·ed; -at·ing** : to give individuality to : form into an individual — **in·di·vid·u·a·tion** \-ˌvi-jə-ˈwā-shən\ *n*

in·di·vis·i·ble \ˌin-də-ˈvi-zə-bəl\ *adj* : impossible to divide or separate — **in·di·vis·i·bil·i·ty** \-ˌvi-zə-ˈbi-lə-tē\ *n* — **in·di·vis·i·bly** *adv*

in·doc·tri·nate \in-ˈdäk-trə-ˌnāt\ *vb* **-nat·ed; -nat·ing** **1** : to instruct esp. in fundamentals or rudiments : TEACH **2** : to teach the beliefs and doctrines of a particular group — **in·doc·tri·na·tion** \(ˌ)in-ˌdäk-trə-ˈnā-shən\ *n* — **in·doc·tri·na·tor** *n*

In·do–Eu·ro·pe·an \ˌin-dō-ˌyùr-ə-ˈpē-ən\ *adj* : of, relating to, or constituting a family of languages comprising those spoken in most of Europe and in the parts of the world colonized by Europeans since 1500 and also in Persia, the subcontinent of India, and some other parts of Asia

in·do·lent \ˈin-də-lənt\ *adj* [LL *indolens* insensitive to pain, fr. L *dolēre* to feel pain] **1** : slow to develop or heal ⟨∼ ulcers⟩ **2** : LAZY — **in·do·lence** \-ləns\ *n* — **in·do·lent·ly** *adv*

in·dom·i·ta·ble \in-ˈdä-mə-tə-bəl\ *adj* : UNCONQUERABLE ⟨∼ courage⟩ — **in·dom·i·ta·bly** \-blē\ *adv*

In·do·ne·sian \ˌin-də-ˈnē-zhən\ *n* : a native or inhabitant of the Republic of Indonesia — **Indonesian** *adj*

in·door \ˈin-ˌdōr\ *adj* **1** : of or relating to the inside of a building **2** : living, located, or carried on within a building

in·doors \in-ˈdōrz\ *adv* : in or into a building

indorse *var of* ENDORSE

in·du·bi·ta·ble \(ˌ)in-ˈdü-bə-tə-bəl, -ˈdyü-\ *adj* : UNQUESTIONABLE — **in·du·bi·ta·bly** \-blē\ *adv*

in·duce \in-ˈdüs, -ˈdyüs\ *vb* **in·duced; in·duc·ing** **1** : PERSUADE, INFLUENCE **2** : BRING ABOUT **3** : to produce (as an electric current) by induction **4** : to determine by induction; *esp* : to infer from particulars — **in·duc·er** *n*

in·duce·ment \-mənt\ *n* **1** : something that induces : MOTIVE **2** : the act or process of inducing

in·duct \in-ˈdəkt\ *vb* **1** : to place in office **2** : to admit as a member **3** : to enroll for military training or service — **in·duct·ee** \-ˌdək-ˈtē\ *n*

in·duc·tance \in-ˈdək-təns\ *n* : a property of an electric

\ə\abut \ᵊ\kitten \ər\further \a\ash \ā\ace \ä\mop, mar
\aù\out \ch\chin \e\bet \ē\easy \g\go \i\hit \ī\ice \j\job
\ŋ\sing \ō\go \ò\law \òi\boy \th\thin \th̷\the \ü\loot \ù\foot
\y\yet \zh\vision *see also* Pronunciation Symbols page

circuit by which a varying current produces an electromotive force in that circuit or in a nearby circuit; *also* : the measure of this property

in·duc·tion \in-'dək-shən\ *n* **1** : the act or process of inducting; *also* : INITIATION **2** : the formality by which a civilian is inducted into military service **3** : inference of a generalized conclusion from particular instances; *also* : a conclusion so reached **4** : the act of causing or bringing on or about **5** : the process by which an electric current, an electric charge, or magnetism is produced in a body by the proximity of an electric or magnetic field

in·duc·tive \in-'dək-tiv\ *adj* : of, relating to, or employing induction

in·duc·tor \in-'dək-tər\ *n* : an electrical component that acts upon another or is itself acted upon by induction

in·dulge \in-'dəlj\ *vb* **in·dulged; in·dulg·ing 1** : to give free rein to : GRATIFY **2** : HUMOR **3** : to gratify one's taste or desire for ⟨∼ in alcohol⟩

in·dul·gence \in-'dəl-jəns\ *n* **1** : remission of temporal punishment due in Roman Catholic doctrine for sins whose eternal punishment has been remitted by reception of the sacrifice of penance **2** : the act of indulging : the state of being indulgent **3** : an indulgent act **4** : the thing indulged in **5** : SELF-INDULGENCE — **in·dul·gent** \-jənt\ *adj* — **in·dul·gent·ly** *adv*

in·du·rated \'in-dyu̇-ˌrā-təd, -du̇-\ *adj* : physically or emotionally hardened — **in·du·ra·tion** \ˌin-dyu̇-'rā-shən, -du̇-\ *n*

in·dus·tri·al \in-'dəs-trē-əl\ *adj* **1** : of or relating to industry; *also* : HEAVY-DUTY **2** : characterized by highly developed industries — **in·dus·tri·al·ly** *adv*

in·dus·tri·al·ist \-ə-list\ *n* : a person owning or engaged in the management of an industry

in·dus·tri·al·ize \in-'dəs-trē-ə-ˌlīz\ *vb* **-ized; -iz·ing** : to make or become industrial — **in·dus·tri·al·i·za·tion** \-ˌdəs-trē-ə-lə-'zā-shən\ *n*

in·dus·tri·ous \in-'dəs-trē-əs\ *adj* : DILIGENT, BUSY — **in·dus·tri·ous·ly** *adv* — **in·dus·tri·ous·ness** *n*

in·dus·try \'in-(ˌ)dəs-trē\ *n, pl* **-tries 1** : DILIGENCE **2** : a department or branch of a craft, art, business, or manufacture; *esp* : one that employs a large personnel and capital **3** : a distinct group of productive enterprises **4** : manufacturing activity as a whole

in·dwell \(ˌ)in-'dwel\ *vb* : to exist within as an activating spirit or force

¹ine·bri·ate \i-'nē-brē-ˌāt\ *vb* **-at·ed; -at·ing** : to make drunk : INTOXICATE — **ine·bri·a·tion** \-ˌnē-brē-'ā-shən\ *n*

²ine·bri·ate \-ət\ *n* : one that is drunk; *esp* : DRUNKARD

in·ef·fa·ble \(ˌ)in-'e-fə-bəl\ *adj* **1** : incapable of being expressed in words : INDESCRIBABLE ⟨∼ joy⟩ **2** : UNSPEAKABLE ⟨∼ disgust⟩ **3** : not to be uttered : TABOO — **in·ef·fa·bly** \-blē\ *adv*

in·ef·fec·tive \ˌi-nə-'fek-tiv\ *adj* **1** : INEFFECTUAL **2** : not able to perform efficiently or as expected : INCAPABLE — **in·ef·fec·tive·ly** *adv* — **in·ef·fec·tive·ness** *n*

in·ef·fec·tu·al \-'fek-chə-wəl\ *adj* **1** : not producing the proper or usual effect **2** : INEFFECTIVE **2** — **in·ef·fec·tu·al·ly** *adv*

in·ef·fi·cient \ˌi-nə-'fi-shənt\ *adj* **1** : not producing the desired effect **2** : wasteful of time or energy **3** : INCAPABLE, INCOMPETENT — **in·ef·fi·cien·cy** \-'fi-shən-sē\ *n* — **in·ef·fi·cient·ly** *adv*

in·el·e·gant \(ˌ)i-'ne-li-gənt\ *adj* : lacking in refinement, grace, or good taste — **in·el·e·gance** \-gəns\ *n* — **in·el·e·gant·ly** *adv*

in·el·i·gi·ble \(ˌ)i-'ne-lə-jə-bəl\ *adj* : not qualified for an office or position — **in·el·i·gi·bil·i·ty** \(ˌ)i-ˌne-lə-jə-'bi-lə-tē\ *n*

in·eluc·ta·ble \ˌi-ni-'lək-tə-bəl\ *adj* : not to be avoided, changed, or resisted — **in·eluc·ta·bly** \-blē\ *adv*

in·ept \i-'nept\ *adj* **1** : lacking in fitness or aptitude : UN-

FIT **2** : FOOLISH **3** : being out of place : INAPPROPRIATE **4** : generally incompetent : BUNGLING — **in·ept·ly** *adv* — **in·ept·ness** *n*

in·ep·ti·tude \(ˌ)i-'nep-ti-ˌtüd, -ˌtyüd\ *n* : the quality or state of being inept; *esp* : INCOMPETENCE

in·equal·i·ty \ˌi-ni-'kwä-lə-tē\ *n* **1** : the quality of being unequal or uneven; *esp* : UNEVENNESS, DISPARITY **2** : an instance of being unequal

in·ert \i-'nərt\ *adj* [L *inert-, iners* unskilled, idle, fr. *art-, ars* skill] **1** : powerless to move **2** : SLUGGISH **3** : lacking in active properties ⟨chemically ∼⟩ — **in·ert·ly** *adv* — **in·ert·ness** *n*

in·er·tia \i-'nər-shə, -shē-ə\ *n* **1** : a property of matter whereby it remains at rest or continues in uniform motion unless acted upon by some outside force **2** : INERTNESS, SLUGGISHNESS — **in·er·tial** \-shəl\ *adj*

in·es·cap·able \ˌi-nə-'skā-pə-bəl\ *adj* : incapable of being escaped : INEVITABLE — **in·es·cap·ably** \-blē\ *adv*

in·es·ti·ma·ble \(ˌ)i-'nes-tə-mə-bəl\ *adj* **1** : incapable of being estimated or computed ⟨∼ errors⟩ **2** : too valuable or excellent to be fully appreciated — **in·es·ti·ma·bly** \-blē\ *adv*

in·ev·i·ta·ble \i-'ne-və-tə-bəl\ *adj* : incapable of being avoided or evaded : bound to happen — **in·ev·i·ta·bil·i·ty** \(ˌ)i-ˌne-və-tə-'bi-lə-tē\ *n*

in·ev·i·ta·bly \-blē\ *adv* **1** : in an inevitable way **2** : as is to be expected

in·ex·act \ˌi-nig-'zakt\ *adj* **1** : not precisely correct or true : INACCURATE **2** : not rigorous and careful — **in·ex·act·ly** *adv* — **in·ex·act·ness** *n*

in·ex·cus·able \ˌi-nik-'skyü-zə-bəl\ *adj* : being without excuse or justification — **in·ex·cus·ably** \-blē\ *adv*

in·ex·haust·ible \ˌi-nig-'zȯ-stə-bəl\ *adj* **1** : incapable of being used up ⟨an ∼ supply⟩ **2** : UNTIRING — **in·ex·haust·ibly** \-blē\ *adv*

in·ex·o·ra·ble \(ˌ)i-'nek-sə-rə-bəl\ *adj* : not to be moved by entreaty : RELENTLESS — **in·ex·o·ra·bly** *adv*

in·ex·pe·ri·ence \ˌi-nik-'spir-ē-əns\ *n* : lack of experience or of knowledge gained by experience — **in·ex·pe·ri·enced** \-ənst\ *adj*

in·ex·pert \(ˌ)i-'nek-ˌspərt\ *adj* : not expert : UNSKILLED — **in·ex·pert·ly** *adv*

in·ex·pi·a·ble \(ˌ)i-'nek-spē-ə-bəl\ *adj* : not capable of being atoned for

in·ex·pli·ca·ble \ˌi-nik-'spli-kə-bəl, (ˌ)i-'nek-(ˌ)spli-\ *adj* : incapable of being explained or accounted for — **in·ex·pli·ca·bly** \-blē\ *adv*

in·ex·press·ible \-'spre-sə-bəl\ *adj* : not capable of being expressed — **in·ex·press·ibly** \-blē\ *adv*

in ex·tre·mis \ˌin-ik-'strā-məs, -'strē-\ *adv* : in extreme circumstances; *esp* : at the point of death

in·ex·tri·ca·ble \ˌi-nik-'stri-kə-bəl, (ˌ)i-'nek-(ˌ)stri-\ *adj* **1** : forming a maze or tangle from which it is impossible to get free **2** : incapable of being disentangled or untied — **in·ex·tri·ca·bly** \-blē\ *adv*

inf *abbr* **1** infantry **2** infinitive

in·fal·li·ble \(ˌ)in-'fa-lə-bəl\ *adj* **1** : incapable of error : UNERRING **2** : SURE, CERTAIN ⟨an ∼ remedy⟩ — **in·fal·li·bil·i·ty** \(ˌ)in-ˌfa-lə-'bi-lə-tē\ *n* — **in·fal·li·bly** \(ˌ)in-'fa-lə-blē\ *adv*

in·fa·mous \'in-fə-məs\ *adj* **1** : having a reputation of the worst kind : DISGRACEFUL — **in·fa·mous·ly** *adv*

in·fa·my \-mē\ *n, pl* **-mies 1** : evil reputation brought about by something grossly criminal, shocking, or brutal **2** : an extreme and publicly known criminal or evil act **3** : the state of being infamous

in·fan·cy \'in-fən-sē\ *n, pl* **-cies 1** : early childhood **2** : a beginning or early period of existence

in·fant \'in-fənt\ *n* [ME *enfaunt*, fr. MF *enfant*, fr. L *infant-, infans*, adj., incapable of speech, young, fr. *fant-, fans*, prp. of *fari* to speak] : BABY; *also* : a person who is a legal minor

in·fan·ti·cide \in-'fan-tə-ˌsīd\ *n* : the killing of an infant

in·fan·tile \'in-fən-ˌtīl, -tˀl, -ˌtēl\ *adj* : of or relating to infants; *also* : CHILDISH

infantile paralysis *n* : POLIOMYELITIS

in·fan·try \'in-fən-trē\ *n, pl* **-tries** [MF & It; MF *infanterie*, fr. It *infanteria*, fr. *infante* boy, foot soldier] : soldiers trained, armed, and equipped to fight on foot — **in·fan·try·man** \-mən\ *n*

in·farct \'in-ˌfärkt\ *n* [L *infarctus*, pp. of *infarcire* to stuff] : an area of dead tissue (as of the heart wall) caused by blocking of local blood circulation — **in·farc·tion** \in-'färk-shən\ *n*

in·fat·u·ate \in-'fa-chə-ˌwāt\ *vb* **-at·ed; -at·ing** : to inspire with a foolish or extravagant love or admiration — **in·fat·u·a·tion** \-ˌfa-chə-'wā-shən\ *n*

in·fect \in-'fekt\ *vb* **1** : to contaminate with disease-producing matter **2** : to communicate a germ or disease to **3** : to cause to share one's feelings

in·fec·tion \in-'fek-shən\ *n* **1** : a disease or condition caused by a germ or parasite; *also* : such a germ or parasite **2** : an act or process of infecting — **in·fec·tious** \-shəs\ *adj* — **in·fec·tive** \-'fek-tiv\ *adj*

infectious mononucleosis *n* : an acute infectious disease characterized by fever, swelling of lymph glands, and increased numbers of lymph cells in the blood

in·fe·lic·i·tous \ˌin-fi-'li-sə-təs\ *adj* : not appropriate in application or expression — **in·fe·lic·i·ty** \-sə-tē\ *n*

in·fer \in-'fər\ *vb* **in·ferred; in·fer·ring 1** : to derive as a conclusion from facts or premises **2** : GUESS, SURMISE **3** : to lead to as a conclusion or consequence **4** : HINT, SUGGEST **syn** deduce, conclude, judge, gather — **in·fer·ence** \'in-frəns, -fə-rəns\ *n* — **in·fer·en·tial** \ˌin-fə-'ren-chəl\ *adj*

¹**in·fe·ri·or** \in-'fir-ē-ər\ *adj* **1** : situated lower down **2** : of low or lower degree or rank **3** : of lesser quality **4** : of little or less importance, value, or merit — **inferior** *n* — **in·fe·ri·or·i·ty** \(ˌ)in-ˌfir-ē-'ór-ə-tē\ *n*

²**inferior** *n* : SUBSCRIPT

in·fer·nal \in-'fərn-ˀl\ *adj* **1** : of or relating to hell **2** : HELLISH, FIENDISH ⟨∼ schemes⟩ **3** : DAMNABLE ⟨an ∼ pest⟩ — **in·fer·nal·ly** *adv*

in·fer·no \in-'fər-nō\ *n, pl* **-nos** [It, hell, fr. LL *infernus* hell, fr. L, lower] : a place or a state that resembles or suggests hell; *also* : intense heat

in·fer·tile \(ˌ)in-'fərt-ˀl\ *adj* : not fertile or productive : BARREN — **in·fer·til·i·ty** \ˌin-fər-'ti-lə-tē\ *n*

in·fest \in-'fest\ *vb* : to trouble by spreading or swarming in or over; *also* : to live in or on as a parasite — **in·fes·ta·tion** \ˌin-ˌfes-'tā-shən\ *n*

in·fi·del \'in-fəd-ˀl, -fə-ˌdel\ *n* **1** : one who is not a Christian or opposes Christianity **2** : an unbeliever esp. with respect to a particular religion

in·fi·del·i·ty \ˌin-fə-'de-lə-tē, -fī-\ *n, pl* **-ties 1** : lack of belief in a religion **2** : UNFAITHFULNESS, DISLOYALTY **3** : marital unfaithfulness or an instance of it

in·field \'in-ˌfēld\ *n* : the part of a baseball field inside the baselines — **in·field·er** *n*

in·fight·ing \'in-ˌfī-tiŋ\ *n* **1** : fighting at close quarters **2** : dissension or rivalry among members of a group

in·fil·trate \in-'fil-ˌtrāt, 'in-(ˌ)fil-\ *vb* **-trat·ed; -trat·ing 1** : to enter or filter into or through something **2** : to pass into or through by or as if by filtering or permeating — **in·fil·tra·tion** \ˌin-(ˌ)fil-'trā-shən\ *n* — **in·fil·tra·tor** *n*

in·fi·nite \'in-fə-nət\ *adj* **1** : LIMITLESS, BOUNDLESS, ENDLESS ⟨∼ space⟩ ⟨∼ patience⟩ **2** : VAST, IMMENSE; *also* : INEXHAUSTIBLE ⟨∼ wealth⟩ **3** : greater than any preassigned finite value however large ⟨∼ number of positive integers⟩; *also* : extending to infinity ⟨∼ plane surface⟩ — **infinite** *n* — **in·fi·nite·ly** *adv*

in·fin·i·tes·i·mal \(ˌ)in-ˌfi-nə-'te-sə-məl\ *adj* : immeasurably or incalculably small — **in·fin·i·tes·i·mal·ly** *adv*

in·fin·i·tive \in-'fi-nə-tiv\ *n* : a verb form having the

characteristics of both verb and noun and in English usu. being used with *to*

in·fi·ni·tude \in-'fi-nə-ˌtüd, -ˌtyüd\ *n* **1** : the quality or state of being infinite **2** : something that is infinite esp. in extent

in·fin·i·ty \in-'fi-nə-tē\ *n, pl* **-ties 1** : the quality of being infinite **2** : unlimited extent of time, space, or quantity : BOUNDLESSNESS **3** : an indefinitely great number or amount

in·firm \in-'fərm\ *adj* **1** : deficient in vitality; *esp* : feeble from age **2** : weak of mind, will, or character : IRRESOLUTE **3** : not solid or stable : INSECURE

in·fir·ma·ry \in-'fər-mə-rē\ *n, pl* **-ries** : a place for the care of the infirm or sick

in·fir·mi·ty \in-'fər-mə-tē\ *n, pl* **-ties 1** : FEEBLENESS **2** : DISEASE, AILMENT **3** : a personal failing : FOIBLE

infl *abbr* influenced

in·flame \in-'flām\ *vb* **in·flamed; in·flam·ing 1** : KINDLE **2** : to excite to excessive or uncontrollable action or feeling; *also* : INTENSIFY **3** : to affect or become affected with inflammation

in·flam·ma·ble \in-'fla-mə-bəl\ *adj* **1** : FLAMMABLE **2** : easily inflamed, excited, or angered : IRASCIBLE

in·flam·ma·tion \ˌin-flə-'mā-shən\ *n* : a bodily response to injury in which an affected area becomes red, hot, and painful and congested with blood

in·flam·ma·to·ry \in-'fla-mə-ˌtōr-ē\ *adj* **1** : tending to excite the senses or to arouse anger, disorder, or tumult : SEDITIOUS **2** : causing or accompanied by inflammation ⟨an ∼ disease⟩

in·flate \in-'flāt\ *vb* **in·flat·ed; in·flat·ing 1** : to swell with air or gas ⟨∼ a balloon⟩ **2** : to puff up : ELATE **3** : to expand or increase abnormally ⟨∼ prices⟩ — **in·flat·able** *adj*

in·fla·tion \in-'flā-shən\ *n* **1** : an act of inflating : the state of being inflated **2** : empty pretentiousness : POMPOSITY **3** : an increase in the volume of money and credit resulting in a continuing rise in the general price level

in·fla·tion·ary \-shə-ˌner-ē\ *adj* : of, characterized by, or productive of inflation

in·flect \in-'flekt\ *vb* **1** : to turn from a direct line or course : CURVE **2** : to vary a word by inflection **3** : to change or vary the pitch of the voice

in·flec·tion \in-'flek-shən\ *n* **1** : the act or result of curving or bending **2** : a change in pitch or loudness of the voice **3** : the change of form that words undergo to mark case, gender, number, tense, person, mood, or voice — **in·flec·tion·al** \-shə-nəl\ *adj*

in·flex·i·ble \(ˌ)in-'flek-sə-bəl\ *adj* **1** : UNYIELDING **2** : RIGID **3** : incapable of change — **in·flex·i·bil·i·ty** \-ˌflek-sə-'bi-lə-tē\ *n* — **in·flex·i·bly** \-'flek-sə-blē\ *adv*

in·flex·ion \in-'flek-shən\ *chiefly Brit var of* INFLECTION

in·flict \in-'flikt\ *vb* : AFFLICT; *also* : to give by or as if by striking — **in·flic·tion** \-'flik-shən\ *n*

in·flo·res·cence \ˌin-flə-'res-ˀns\ *n* : the manner of development and arrangement of flowers on a stem; *also* : a flowering stem with its appendages : a flower cluster

in·flow \'in-ˌflō\ *n* : a flowing in

¹**in·flu·ence** \'in-ˌflü-əns\ *n* **1** : the act or power of producing an effect without apparent force or direct authority **2** : the power or capacity of causing an effect in indirect or intangible ways ⟨under the ∼ of liquor⟩ **3** : a person or thing that exerts influence — **in·flu·en·tial** \ˌin-flü-'en-chəl\ *adj*

²**influence** *vb* **-enced; -enc·ing 1** : to affect or alter by influence : SWAY **2** : to have an effect on the condition or development of : MODIFY

in·flu·en·za \ˌin-flü-'en-zə\ *n* [It, lit., influence, fr. ML

\ə\abut \ˀ\kitten \ər\further \a\ash \ā\ace \ä\mop, mar
\au̇\out \ch\chin \e\bet \ē\easy \g\go \i\hit \ī\ice \j\job
\ŋ\sing \ō\go \ȯ\law \ȯi\boy \th\thin \t͟h\the \ü\loot \u̇\foot
\y\yet \zh\vision *see also* Pronunciation Symbols page

influentia; fr. the belief that epidemics were due to the influence of the stars] : an acute and very contagious virus disease marked by fever, prostration, aches and pains, and respiratory inflammation; *also* : any of various feverish usu. virus diseases typically with respiratory symptoms

in·flux \'in-₁fləks\ *n* : a coming in

in·fo \'in-(₁)fō\ *n* : INFORMATION

in·fold \in-'fōld\ *vb* 1 : ENFOLD 2 : to fold inward or toward one another

in·fo·mer·cial \'in-fō-₁mər-shəl\ *n* : a television program that is an extended advertisement often including a discussion or demonstration

in·form \in-'fȯrm\ *vb* 1 : to communicate knowledge to : TELL 2 : to give information or knowledge 3 : to act as an informer **syn** acquaint, apprise, advise, notify

in·for·mal \(₁)in-'fȯr-məl\ *adj* 1 : conducted or carried out without formality or ceremony ⟨an ∼ party⟩ 2 : characteristic of or appropriate to ordinary, casual, or familiar use ⟨∼ clothes⟩ — **in·for·mal·i·ty** \in-fȯr-'ma-lə-tē, -fər-\ *n* — **in·for·mal·ly** \(₁)in-'fȯr-mə-lē\ *adv*

in·for·mant \in-'fȯr-mənt\ *n* : a person who gives information : INFORMER

in·for·ma·tion \₁in-fər-'mā-shən\ *n* 1 : the communication or reception of knowledge or intelligence 2 : knowledge obtained from investigation, study, or instruction : FACTS, DATA — **in·for·ma·tion·al** \-shə-nəl\ *adj*

in·for·ma·tive \in-'fȯr-mə-tiv\ *adj* : imparting knowledge : INSTRUCTIVE

in·formed \in-'fȯrmd\ *adj* 1 : having or based on information 2 : EDUCATED, KNOWLEDGEABLE

informed consent *n* : consent to a medical procedure by someone who understands what is involved

in·form·er \-'fȯr-mər\ *n* : one that informs; *esp* : a person who informs against others for illegalities esp. for financial gain

in·fo·tain·ment \₁in-fō-'tān-mənt\ *n* : a television program that presents information (as news) in a manner intended to be entertaining

in·frac·tion \in-'frak-shən\ *n* [ME, fr. ML *infractio,* fr. L, subduing, fr. *infringere* to break, crush] : the act of infringing : VIOLATION

in·fra dig \₁in-frə-'dig\ *adj* [short for L *infra dignitatem*] : being beneath one's dignity

in·fra·red \₁in-frə-'red\ *adj* : being, relating to, or using radiation having wavelengths longer than those of red light — **infrared** *n*

in·fra·struc·ture \'in-frə-₁strək-chər\ *n* 1 : the underlying foundation or basic framework (as of a system or organization) 2 : the system of public works of a country, state, or region; *also* : the resources (as buildings or equipment) required for an activity

in·fre·quent \(₁)in-'frē-kwənt\ *adj* 1 : seldom happening : RARE 2 : placed or occurring at wide intervals in space or time **syn** uncommon, scarce, sporadic — **in·fre·quent·ly** *adv*

in·fringe \in-'frinj\ *vb* **in·fringed; in·fring·ing** 1 : VIOLATE, TRANSGRESS ⟨∼ a patent⟩ 2 : ENCROACH, TRESPASS — **in·fringe·ment** *n*

in·fu·ri·ate \in-'fyu̇r-ē-₁āt\ *vb* **-at·ed; -at·ing** : to make furious : ENRAGE — **in·fu·ri·at·ing·ly** *adv*

in·fuse \in-'fyüz\ *vb* **in·fused; in·fus·ing** 1 : to instill a principle or quality in : INTRODUCE 2 : INSPIRE, ANIMATE 3 : to steep (as tea) without boiling — **in·fu·sion** \-'fyü-zhən\ *n*

¹-ing \iŋ\ *n suffix* 1 : action or process ⟨sleep*ing*⟩ : instance of an action or process ⟨a meet*ing*⟩ 2 : product or result of an action or process ⟨an engrav*ing*⟩ ⟨earn*ings*⟩ 3 : something used in an action or process ⟨a bed cover*ing*⟩ 4 : something connected with, consisting of, or used in making (a specified thing) ⟨scaffold*ing*⟩ 5 : something related to (a specified concept) ⟨off*ing*⟩

²-ing *n suffix* : one of a (specified) kind

³-ing *vb suffix or adj suffix* — used to form the present participle ⟨sail*ing*⟩ and sometimes to form an adjective resembling a present participle but not derived from a verb ⟨swashbuckl*ing*⟩

in·ga·ther \'in-₁ga-thər\ *vb* : to gather in : ASSEMBLE

in·ge·nious \in-'jēn-yəs\ *adj* 1 : marked by special aptitude at discovering, inventing, or contriving 2 : marked by originality, resourcefulness, and cleverness in conception or execution — **in·ge·nious·ly** *adv* — **in·ge·nious·ness** *n*

in·ge·nue *or* **in·gé·nue** \'an-jə-₁nü, 'än-; 'aⁿ-zhə-, 'äⁿ-\ *n* : a naive girl or young woman; *esp* : an actress portraying such a person

in·ge·nu·ity \₁in-jə-'nü-ə-tē, -'nyü-\ *n, pl* **-ties** : skill or cleverness in planning or inventing : INVENTIVENESS

in·gen·u·ous \in-'jen-yə-wəs\ *adj* [L *ingenuus* native, freeborn, fr. *gignere* to beget] 1 : STRAIGHTFORWARD, FRANK 2 : NAIVE — **in·gen·u·ous·ly** *adv* — **in·gen·u·ous·ness** *n*

in·gest \in-'jest\ *vb* : to take in for or as if for digestion — **in·ges·tion** \-'jes-chən\ *n*

in·gle·nook \'iŋ-gəl-₁nu̇k\ *n* : a nook by a large open fireplace; *also* : a bench occupying this nook

in·glo·ri·ous \(₁)in-'glōr-ē-əs\ *adj* 1 : SHAMEFUL 2 : not glorious : lacking fame or honor — **in·glo·ri·ous·ly** *adv*

in·got \'iŋ-gət\ *n* : a mass of metal cast in a form convenient for storage or transportation

¹in·grain \(₁)in-'grān\ *vb* : to work indelibly into the natural texture or mental or moral constitution — **ingrained** *adj*

²in·grain \'in-₁grān\ *adj* 1 : made of fiber that is dyed before being spun into yarn 2 : made of yarn that is dyed before being woven or knitted 3 : INNATE — **in·grain** *n*

in·grate \'in-₁grāt\ *n* : an ungrateful person

in·gra·ti·ate \in-'grā-shē-₁āt\ *vb* **-at·ed; -at·ing** : to gain favor by deliberate effort

in·gra·ti·at·ing *adj* 1 : capable of winning favor : PLEASING ⟨an ∼ smile⟩ 2 : FLATTERING ⟨an ∼ manner⟩

in·grat·i·tude \(₁)in-'gra-tə-₁tüd, -₁tyüd\ *n* : lack of gratitude : UNGRATEFULNESS

in·gre·di·ent \in-'grē-dē-ənt\ *n* : one of the substances that make up a mixture or compound : CONSTITUENT

in·gress \'in-₁gres\ *n* : ENTRANCE, ACCESS — **in·gres·sion** \in-'gre-shən\ *n*

in·grow·ing \'in-₁grō-iŋ\ *adj* : growing or tending inward

in·grown \-₁grōn\ *adj* : grown in; *esp* : having the free tip or edge embedded in the flesh ⟨∼ toenail⟩

in·gui·nal \'iŋ-gwən-ᵊl\ *adj* : of, relating to, or situated in or near the region of the groin

in·hab·it \in-'ha-bət\ *vb* : to live or dwell in — **in·hab·it·able** *adj*

in·hab·i·tant \in-'ha-bə-tənt\ *n* : a permanent resident in a place

in·hal·ant \in-'hā-lənt\ *n* : something (as a medicine) that is inhaled

in·ha·la·tor \'in-hə-₁lā-tər\ *n* : a device that provides a mixture of carbon dioxide and oxygen for breathing

in·hale \in-'hāl\ *vb* **in·haled; in·hal·ing** : to breathe in — **in·ha·la·tion** \₁in-hə-'lā-shən\ *n*

in·hal·er \in-'hā-lər\ *n* : a device by means of which medicinal material is inhaled

in·here \in-'hir\ *vb* **in·hered; in·her·ing** : to be inherent

in·her·ent \in-'hir-ənt, -'her-\ *adj* : established as an essential part of something : INTRINSIC — **in·her·ent·ly** *adv*

in·her·it \in-'her-ət\ *vb* : to receive esp. from one's ancestors — **in·her·it·able** \-ə-tə-bəl\ *adj* — **in·her·i·tance** \-ə-təns\ *n* — **in·her·i·tor** \-ə-tər\ *n*

in·hib·it \in-'hi-bət\ *vb* 1 : PROHIBIT, FORBID 2 : to hold in check : RESTRAIN

in·hi·bi·tion \₁in-hə-'bi-shən\ *n* 1 : PROHIBITION, RE-

STRAINT **2** : a usu. inner check on free activity, expression, or functioning

in–house \'in-₁haùs, -₁haùs\ *adj* : existing, originating, or carried on within a group or organization

in·hu·man \(₁)in-'hyü-mən, -'yü-\ *adj* **1** : lacking pity, kindness, or mercy : SAVAGE **2** : COLD, IMPERSONAL **3** : not worthy of or conforming to the needs of human beings **4** : of or suggesting a nonhuman class of beings — **in·hu·man·ly** *adv* — **in·hu·man·ness** *n*

in·hu·mane \₁in-hyü-'mān, -yü-\ *adj* : not humane : INHUMAN 1

in·hu·man·i·ty \-'ma-nə-tē\ *n, pl* **-ities 1** : the quality or state of being cruel or barbarous **2** : a cruel or barbarous act

in·im·i·cal \i-'ni-mi-kəl\ *adj* **1** : being adverse often by reason of hostility **2** : HOSTILE, UNFRIENDLY — **in·im·i·cal·ly** *adv*

in·im·i·ta·ble \(₁)i-'ni-mə-tə-bəl\ *adj* : not capable of being imitated

in·iq·ui·ty \i-'ni-kwə-tē\ *n, pl* **-ties** [ME *iniquite,* fr. MF *iniquité,* fr. L *iniquitas,* fr. *iniquus* uneven, fr. *aequus* equal] **1** : WICKEDNESS **2** : a wicked act — **in·iq·ui·tous** \-təs\ *adj*

¹**ini·tial** \i-'ni-shəl\ *adj* **1** : of or relating to the beginning : INCIPIENT **2** : FIRST — **ini·tial·ly** *adv*

²**initial** *n* : the first letter of a word or name

³**initial** *vb* **-tialed** *or* **-tialled; -tial·ing** *or* **-tial·ling** : to affix an initial to

¹**ini·ti·ate** \i-'ni-shē-₁āt\ *vb* **-at·ed; -at·ing 1** : START, BEGIN **2** : to induct into membership by or as if by special ceremonies **3** : to instruct in the rudiments or principles of something — **ini·ti·a·tion** \-₁ni-shē-'ā-shən\ *n*

²**ini·tiate** \i-'ni-shē-ət\ *n* **1** : a person who is undergoing or has passed an initiation **2** : a person who is instructed or adept in some special field

ini·tia·tive \i-'ni-shə-tiv\ *n* **1** : an introductory step **2** : self-reliant enterprise ⟨showed great ∼⟩ **3** : a process by which laws may be introduced or enacted directly by vote of the people

ini·tia·to·ry \i-'ni-shē-ə-₁tōr-ē\ *adj* **1** : INTRODUCTORY **2** : tending or serving to initiate ⟨∼ rites⟩

in·ject \in-'jekt\ *vb* **1** : to force into something ⟨∼ serum with a needle⟩ **2** : to introduce as an element into some situation or subject ⟨∼ a note of suspicion⟩ — **in·jec·tion** \-'jek-shən\ *n*

in·junc·tion \in-'jəŋk-shən\ *n* **1** : ORDER, ADMONITION **2** : a court writ whereby one is required to do or to refrain from doing a specified act

in·jure \'in-jər\ *vb* **in·jured; in·jur·ing** : WRONG, DAMAGE, HURT **syn** harm, impair, mar, spoil

in·ju·ry \'in-jə-rē\ *n, pl* **-ries 1** : an act that damages or hurts : WRONG **2** : hurt, damage, or loss sustained — **in·ju·ri·ous** \in-'jùr-ē-əs\ *adj*

in·jus·tice \(₁)in-'jəs-təs\ *n* **1** : violation of a person's rights : UNFAIRNESS **2** : an unjust act or deed : WRONG

¹**ink** \'iŋk\ *n* [ME *enke,* fr. OF, fr. LL *encaustum,* fr. L *encaustus* burned in, fr. Gk *enkaustos,* fr. *enkaiein* to burn in] : a usu. liquid and colored material for writing and printing — **inky** *adj*

²**ink** *vb* : to put ink on; *esp* : SIGN

ink·blot test \'iŋk-₁blät-\ *n* : any of several psychological tests based on the interpretation of irregular figures

ink·horn \-₁hòrn\ *n* : a small bottle (as of horn) for holding ink

in–kind \'in-'kīnd\ *adj* : consisting of something (as goods) other than money

in·kling \'iŋ-kliŋ\ *n* **1** : HINT, INTIMATION **2** : a vague idea

ink·stand \'iŋk-₁stand\ *n* : INKWELL; *also* : a pen and ink stand

ink·well \-₁wel\ *n* : a container for ink

in·laid \'in-'lād\ *adj* : decorated with material set into a surface

¹**in·land** \'in-₁land, -lənd\ *adj* **1** *chiefly Brit* : not foreign

: DOMESTIC ⟨∼ revenue⟩ **2** : of or relating to the interior of a country

²**inland** *n* : the interior of a country

³**inland** *adv* : into or toward the interior

in–law \'in-₁lò\ *n* : a relative by marriage

¹**in·lay** \(₁)in-'lā, 'in-₁lā\ *vb* **in·laid** \-'lād\; **in·lay·ing** : to set (a material) into a surface or ground material esp. for decoration

²**in·lay** \'in-₁lā\ *n* **1** : inlaid work **2** : a shaped filling cemented into a tooth

in·let \'in-₁let, -lət\ *n* **1** : a small or narrow bay **2** : an opening for intake esp. of a fluid

in·mate \'in-₁māt\ *n* : any of a group occupying a single place of residence; *esp* : a person confined (as in a hospital or prison)

in me·di·as res \in-₁mā-dē-əs-'rās\ *adv* [L, lit., into the midst of things] : in or into the middle of a narrative or plot

in me·mo·ri·am \₁in-mə-'mōr-ē-əm\ *prep* [L] : in memory of

in·most \'in-₁mōst\ *adj* : deepest within : INNERMOST

inn \'in\ *n* : HOTEL, TAVERN

in·nards \'i-nərdz\ *n pl* **1** : the internal organs of a human being or animal; *esp* : VISCERA **2** : the internal parts of a structure or mechanism

in·nate \i-'nāt\ *adj* **1** : existing in, belonging to, or determined by factors present in an individual from birth : NATIVE **2** : INHERENT, INTRINSIC — **in·nate·ly** *adv*

in·ner \'i-nər\ *adj* **1** : situated farther in ⟨the ∼ bark⟩ **2** : near a center esp. of influence ⟨the ∼ circle⟩ **3** : of or relating to the mind or spirit

inner city *n* : the usu. older, poorer, and more densely populated section of a city — **inner–city** *adj*

in·ner–di·rect·ed \₁i-nər-də-'rek-təd, -(₁)dī-\ *adj* : directed in thought and action by one's own scale of values as opposed to external norms

inner ear *n* : the part of the ear that is most important for hearing, is located in a cavity in the temporal bone, and contains sense organs of hearing and of awareness of position in space

in·ner·most \'i-nər-₁mōst\ *adj* : farthest inward : INMOST

in·ner·sole \'i-nər-'sōl\ *n* : INSOLE

in·ner·spring \'i-nər-'spriŋ\ *adj* : having coil springs inside a padded casing

inner tube *n* : an airtight rubber tube inside a tire to hold air under pressure

in·ning \'i-niŋ\ *n* **1** *sing or pl* : a division of a cricket match **2** : a baseball team's turn at bat, *also* : a division of a baseball game consisting of a turn at bat for each team

inn·keep·er \'in-₁kē-pər\ *n* **1** : a proprietor of an inn **2** : a hotel manager

in·no·cence \'i-nə-səns\ *n* **1** : BLAMELESSNESS; *also* : freedom from legal guilt **2** : GUILELESSNESS, SIMPLICITY; *also* : IGNORANCE

in·no·cent \-sənt\ *adj* [ME, fr. MF, fr. L *innocens,* fr. *nocens* wicked, fr. *nocēre* to harm] **1** : free from guilt or sin : BLAMELESS **2** : harmless in effect or intention; *also* : CANDID **3** : free from legal guilt or fault : LAWFUL **4** : INGENUOUS **5** : UNAWARE — **innocent** *n* — **in·no·cent·ly** *adv*

in·noc·u·ous \i-'nä-kyə-wəs\ *adj* **1** : HARMLESS **2** : not offensive; *also* : INSIPID

in·nom·i·nate \i-'nä-mə-nət\ *adj* : having no name; *also* : ANONYMOUS

in·no·vate \'i-nə-₁vāt\ *vb* **-vat·ed; -vat·ing** : to introduce as or as if new : make changes — **in·no·va·tive** \-₁vā-tiv\ *adj* — **in·no·va·tor** \-₁vā-tər\ *n*

\ə\abut \ᵊ\kitten \ər\further \a\ash \ā\ace \ä\mop, mar
\aù\out \ch\chin \e\bet \ē\easy \g\go \i\hit \ī\ice \j\job
\ŋ\sing \ō\go \ò\law \òi\boy \th\thin \th\the \ü\loot \ù\foot
\y\yet \zh\vision *see also* Pronunciation Symbols page

in·no·va·tion \ˌi-nə-ˈvā-shən\ n **1** : the introduction of something new **2** : a new idea, method, or device

in·nu·en·do \ˌin-yə-ˈwen-dō\ n, pl **-dos** or **-does** [L, by hinting, fr. *innuere* to hint, fr. *nuere* to nod] : HINT, INSINUATION; esp : a veiled reflection on character or reputation

in·nu·mer·a·ble \i-ˈnü-mə-rə-bəl, -ˈnyü-\ adj : too many to be numbered

in·oc·u·late \i-ˈnä-kyə-ˌlāt\ vb **-lat·ed; -lat·ing** [ME, to insert a bud in a plant, fr. L *inoculare*, fr. *oculus* eye, bud] : to introduce something into; esp : to introduce a serum or antibody into (an organism) to treat or prevent a disease — **in·oc·u·la·tion** \-ˌnä-kyə-ˈlā-shən\ n

in·op·er·a·ble \(ˌ)i-ˈnä-pə-rə-bəl\ adj **1** : not suitable for surgery **2** : not operable

in·op·er·a·tive \-ˈnä-pə-rə-tiv, -ˈnä-pə-ˌrā-\ adj : not functioning

in·op·por·tune \(ˌ)i-ˌnä-pər-ˈtün, -ˈtyün\ adj : INCONVENIENT, INAPPROPRIATE — **in·op·por·tune·ly** adv

in·or·di·nate \i-ˈnȯrd-ᵊn-ət\ adj : exceeding reasonable limits : IMMODERATE ⟨an ∼ curiosity⟩ — **in·or·di·nate·ly** adv

in·or·gan·ic \ˌi-ˌnȯr-ˈga-nik\ adj : being or composed of matter of other than plant or animal origin : MINERAL

in·pa·tient \ˈin-ˌpā-shənt\ n : a hospital patient who receives lodging and food as well as treatment

in·put \ˈin-ˌpu̇t\ n **1** : something put in **2** : power or energy put into a machine or system **3** : information fed into a computer or data processing system **4** : ADVICE, OPINION — **input** vb

in·quest \ˈin-ˌkwest\ n **1** : an official inquiry or examination esp. before a jury **2** : INQUIRY, INVESTIGATION

in·qui·etude \(ˌ)in-ˈkwī-ə-ˌtüd, -ˌtyüd\ n : UNEASINESS, RESTLESSNESS

in·quire \in-ˈkwīr\ vb **in·quired; in·quir·ing 1** : to ask about : ASK **2** : INVESTIGATE, EXAMINE — **in·quir·er** n — **in·quir·ing·ly** adv

in·qui·ry \ˈin-ˌkwīr-ē, in-ˈkwīr-ē; ˈin-kwə-rē, ˈiŋ-\ n, pl **-ries 1** : a request for information; also : RESEARCH **2** : a systematic investigation of a matter of public interest

in·qui·si·tion \ˌin-kwə-ˈzi-shən, ˌiŋ-\ n **1** : a judicial or official inquiry usu. before a jury **2** cap : a former Roman Catholic tribunal for the discovery and punishment of heresy **3** : a severe questioning — **in·quis·i·tor** \in-ˈkwi-zə-tər\ n — **in·quis·i·to·ri·al** \-ˌkwi-zə-ˈtōr-ē-əl\ adj

in·quis·i·tive \in-ˈkwi-zə-tiv\ adj **1** : given to examination or investigation ⟨an ∼ mind⟩ **2** : unduly curious — **in·quis·i·tive·ly** adv — **in·quis·i·tive·ness** n

in re \in-ˈrā, -ˈrē\ prep : in the matter of

INRI abbr [L *Iesus Nazarenus Rex Iudaeorum*] Jesus of Nazareth, King of the Jews

in·road \ˈin-ˌrōd\ n **1** : INVASION, RAID **2** : ENCROACHMENT

in·rush \ˈin-ˌrəsh\ n : a crowding or flooding in

ins abbr **1** inches **2** insurance

INS abbr Immigration and Naturalization Service

in·sa·lu·bri·ous \ˌin-sə-ˈlü-brē-əs\ adj : UNWHOLESOME, NOXIOUS

ins and outs n pl **1** : characteristic peculiarities **2** : RAMIFICATIONS

in·sane \(ˌ)in-ˈsān\ adj **1** : exhibiting serious and debilitating mental disorder; also : used by or for the insane **2** : ABSURD — **in·sane·ly** adv — **in·san·i·ty** \in-ˈsa-nə-tē\ n

in·sa·tia·ble \(ˌ)in-ˈsā-shə-bəl\ adj : incapable of being satisfied — **in·sa·tia·bil·i·ty** \(ˌ)in-ˌsā-shə-ˈbi-lə-tē\ n — **in·sa·tia·bly** adv

in·sa·tiate \(ˌ)in-ˈsā-shē-ət, -shət\ adj : INSATIABLE — **in·sa·tiate·ly** adv

in·scribe \in-ˈskrīb\ vb **1** : to write, engrave, or print as a lasting record **2** : ENROLL **3** : to write, engrave, or print characters upon **4** : to dedicate to someone **5** : to draw within a figure so as to touch in as many places as possible — **in·scrip·tion** \-ˈskrip-shən\ n

in·scru·ta·ble \in-ˈskrü-tə-bəl\ adj : not readily comprehensible : MYSTERIOUS — **in·scru·ta·bly** \-blē\ adv

in·seam \ˈin-ˌsēm\ n : the seam on the inside of the leg of a pair of pants; also : the length of this seam

in·sect \ˈin-ˌsekt\ n [L *insectum*, fr. *insectus*, pp. of *insecare* to cut into, fr. *secare* to cut] : any of a class of small usu. winged arthropod animals (as flies, bees, beetles, and moths) with usu. three pairs of legs as adults

in·sec·ti·cide \in-ˈsek-tə-ˌsīd\ n : a preparation for destroying insects — **in·sec·ti·cid·al** \(ˌ)in-ˌsek-tə-ˈsīd-ᵊl\ adj

in·sec·tiv·o·rous \ˌin-ˌsek-ˈti-və-rəs\ adj : depending on insects as food

in·se·cure \ˌin-si-ˈkyu̇r\ adj **1** : UNCERTAIN **2** : not protected : UNSAFE **3** : LOOSE, SHAKY **4** : not highly stable; also : lacking assurance : ANXIOUS, FEARFUL — **in·se·cure·ly** adv — **in·se·cu·ri·ty** \-ˈkyu̇r-ə-tē\ n

in·sem·i·nate \in-ˈse-mə-ˌnāt\ vb **-nat·ed; -nat·ing** : to introduce semen into the genital tract of (a female) — **in·sem·i·na·tion** \-ˌse-mə-ˈnā-shən\ n

in·sen·sate \(ˌ)in-ˈsen-ˌsāt, -sət\ adj **1** : lacking sense or understanding; also : FOOLISH **2** : INANIMATE **3** : BRUTAL, INHUMAN ⟨∼ rage⟩

in·sen·si·ble \(ˌ)in-ˈsen-sə-bəl\ adj **1** : IMPERCEPTIBLE; also : SLIGHT, GRADUAL **2** : INANIMATE **3** : UNCONSCIOUS **4** : lacking sensory perception or ability to react ⟨∼ to pain⟩ **5** : APATHETIC, INDIFFERENT; also : UNAWARE ⟨∼ of their danger⟩ **6** : MEANINGLESS **7** : lacking delicacy or refinement — **in·sen·si·bil·i·ty** \-ˌsen-sə-ˈbi-lə-tē\ n — **in·sen·si·bly** \-ˈsen-sə-blē\ adv

in·sen·tient \(ˌ)in-ˈsen-chē-ənt\ adj : lacking perception, consciousness, or animation — **in·sen·tience** \-chē-əns\ n

in·sep·a·ra·ble \(ˌ)in-ˈse-prə-bəl, -pə-rə-\ adj : incapable of being separated or disjoined — **in·sep·a·ra·bil·i·ty** \-ˌse-prə-bəl-ə-tē, -pə-rə-\ n — **inseparable** n — **in·sep·a·ra·bly** \-ˈse-prə-blē, -pə-rə-\ adv

¹**in·sert** \in-ˈsərt\ vb **1** : to put or thrust in ⟨∼ a key in a lock⟩ ⟨∼ a comma⟩ **2** : INTERPOLATE **3** : to set in (as a piece of fabric) and make fast

²**in·sert** \ˈin-ˌsərt\ n : something that is inserted or is for insertion; esp : written or printed material inserted (as between the leaves of a book)

in·ser·tion \in-ˈsər-shən\ n **1** : something that is inserted **2** : the act or process of inserting

in·set \ˈin-ˌset\ vb **inset** or **in·set·ted; in·set·ting** : to set in : INSERT — **inset** n

¹**in·shore** \ˈin-ˈshȯr\ adj **1** : situated, living, or carried on near shore **2** : moving toward shore

²**inshore** adv : to or toward shore

¹**in·side** \in-ˈsīd, ˈin-ˌsīd\ n **1** : an inner side or surface : INTERIOR **2** : inward nature, thoughts, or feeling **3** pl : VISCERA, ENTRAILS **4** : a position of power, trust, or familiarity — **inside** adj

²**inside** adv **1** : on the inner side **2** : in or into the interior

³**inside** prep **1** : in or into the inside of **2** : WITHIN ⟨∼ an hour⟩

inside of prep : INSIDE

in·sid·er \in-ˈsī-dər\ n : a person who is in a position of power or has access to confidential information

in·sid·i·ous \in-ˈsi-dē-əs\ adj [L *insidiosus*, fr. *insidiae* ambush, fr. *insidēre* to sit in, sit on, fr. *sedēre* to sit] **1** : SLY, TREACHEROUS **2** : SEDUCTIVE **3** : having a gradual and cumulative effect : SUBTLE — **in·sid·i·ous·ly** adv — **in·sid·i·ous·ness** n

in·sight \ˈin-ˌsīt\ n : the power, act, or result of seeing into a situation : UNDERSTANDING, PENETRATION — **in·sight·ful** \ˈin-ˌsīt-fəl, in-ˈsīt-\ adj

in·sig·nia \in-ˈsig-nē-ə\ or **in·sig·ne** \-(ˌ)nē\ n, pl **-nia** or

-ni·as : a distinguishing mark esp. of authority or honor : BADGE

in·sin·cere \,in-sin-'sir\ adj : not sincere : HYPOCRITICAL — **in·sin·cere·ly** adv — **in·sin·cer·i·ty** \-'ser-ə-tē\ n

in·sin·u·ate \in-'sin-yə-,wāt\ vb **-at·ed; -at·ing** [L insinuare, fr. sinuare to bend, curve, fr. sinus curve] **1** : to introduce gradually or in a subtle, indirect, or artful way **2** : to imply in a subtle or devious way — **in·sin·u·a·tion** \(,)in-,sin-yə-'wā-shən\ n

in·sin·u·at·ing adj **1** : winning favor and confidence by imperceptible degrees **2** : tending gradually to cause doubt, distrust, or change of outlook

in·sip·id \in-'si-pəd\ adj **1** : lacking taste or savor **2** : DULL, FLAT — **in·si·pid·i·ty** \,in-sə-'pi-də-tē\ n

in·sist \in-'sist\ vb [MF or L; MF insister, fr. L insistere to stand upon, persist, fr. sistere to take a stand] : to take a resolute stand

in·sis·tence \in-'sis-təns\ n : the act of insisting; also : an insistent attitude or quality : URGENCY

in·sis·tent \in-'sis-tənt\ adj : disposed to insist — **in·sis·tent·ly** adv

in si·tu \in-'sī-tü, -'sē-\ adv or adj [L, in position] : in the natural or original position

in·so·far as \,in-sə-'fär\ conj : to the extent or degree that

insol abbr insoluble

in·so·la·tion \,in-(,)sō-'lā-shən\ n : solar radiation that has been received

in·sole \'in-,sōl\ n **1** : an inside sole of a shoe **2** : a loose thin strip placed inside a shoe for warmth or comfort

in·so·lent \'in-sə-lənt\ adj : contemptuous, rude, disrespectful, or bold in behavior or language — **in·so·lence** \-ləns\ n

in·sol·u·ble \(,)in-'säl-yə-bəl\ adj **1** : having or admitting of no solution or explanation **2** : difficult or impossible to dissolve — **in·sol·u·bil·i·ty** \-,säl-yə-'bi-lə-tē\ n

in·sol·vent \(,)in-'säl-vənt\ adj **1** : unable or insufficient to pay all debts ⟨an ~ estate⟩ **2** : IMPOVERISHED, DEFICIENT — **in·sol·ven·cy** \-vən-sē\ n

in·som·nia \in-'säm-nē-ə\ n : prolonged and usu. abnormal sleeplessness

in·so·much as \,in-sə-'məch-\ conj : INASMUCH AS

insomuch that conj : to such a degree that : so

in·sou·ci·ance \in-'sü-sē-əns, aⁿ-süs-'yäⁿs\ n [F] : lighthearted unconcern — **in·sou·ci·ant** \in-'sü-sē-ənt, aⁿ-süs-'yäⁿ\ adj

insp abbr inspector

in·spect \in-'spekt\ vb : to view closely and critically : EXAMINE — **in·spec·tion** \-'spek-shən\ n — **in·spec·tor** \-tər\ n

inspector general n : the head of a system of inspection (as of an army)

in·spi·ra·tion \,in-spə-'rā-shən\ n **1** : the act or power of moving the intellect or emotions **2** : INHALATION **3** : the quality or state of being inspired; also : something that is inspired **4** : an inspiring agent or influence — **in·spi·ra·tion·al** \-shə-nəl\ adj

in·spire \in-'spīr\ vb **in·spired; in·spir·ing** **1** : to influence, move, or guide by divine or supernatural inspiration **2** : exert an animating, enlivening, or exalting influence upon; also : AFFECT **3** : to communicate to an agent supernaturally; also : bring out or about **4** : INHALE **5** : INCITE **6** : to spread by indirect means — **in·spir·er** n

in·spir·it \in-'spir-ət\ vb : ENCOURAGE, HEARTEN

inst abbr **1** instant **2** institute; institution; institutional

in·sta·bil·i·ty \,in-stə-'bi-lə-tē\ n : lack of steadiness; esp : lack of emotional or mental stability

in·stall or **in·stal** \in-'stȯl\ vb **in·stalled; in·stall·ing** **1** : to place formally in office : induct into an office, rank, or order **2** : to establish in an indicated place, condition, or status **3** : to set up for use or service — **in·stal·la·tion** \,in-stə-'lā-shən\ n

¹in·stall·ment also **in·stal·ment** \in-'stȯl-mənt\ n : INSTALLATION

²installment also **instalment** n **1** : one of the parts into which a debt or sum is divided for payment **2** : one of several parts presented at intervals

¹in·stance \'in-stəns\ n **1** : INSTIGATION, REQUEST **2** : EXAMPLE ⟨for ~⟩ **3** : an event or step that is part of a process or series **syn** case, illustration, sample, specimen

²instance vb **in·stanced; in·stanc·ing** : to mention as a case or example

¹in·stant \'in-stənt\ n **1** : MOMENT ⟨the ~ we met⟩ **2** : the present or current month

²instant adj **1** : URGENT **2** : PRESENT, CURRENT **3** : IMMEDIATE ⟨~ relief⟩ **4** : premixed or precooked for easy final preparation ⟨~ cake mix⟩; also : immediately soluble in water ⟨~ coffee⟩

in·stan·ta·neous \,in-stən-'tā-nē-əs\ adj : done or occurring in an instant or without delay — **in·stan·ta·neous·ly** adv

in·stan·ter \in-'stan-tər\ adv : at once

in·stan·ti·ate \in-'stan-chē-,āt\ vb **-at·ed; -at·ing** : to represent (an abstraction) by a concrete example — **in·stan·ti·a·tion** \-,stan-chē-'ā-shən\ n

in·stant·ly \'in-stənt-lē\ adv : at once : IMMEDIATELY

in·state \in-'stāt\ vb : to establish in a rank or office : INSTALL

in·stead \in-'sted\ adv **1** : as a substitute or equivalent **2** : as an alternative : RATHER

instead of prep : as a substitute for or alternative to

in·step \'in-,step\ n : the arched part of the human foot in front of the ankle joint; esp : its upper surface

instep

in·sti·gate \'in-stə-,gāt\ vb **-gat·ed; -gat·ing** : to goad or urge forward : PROVOKE, INCITE ⟨~ a revolt⟩ — **in·sti·ga·tion** \,in-stə-'gā-shən\ n — **in·sti·ga·tor** \'in-stə-,gā-tər\ n

in·still also **in·stil** \in-'stil\ vb **in·stilled; in·still·ing** **1** : to cause to enter drop by drop **2** : to impart gradually

¹in·stinct \'in-,stiŋkt\ n **1** : a natural aptitude **2** : a largely inheritable and unalterable tendency of an organism to make a complex and specific response to environmental stimuli without involving reason; also : behavior originating below the conscious level — **in·stinc·tive** \in-'stiŋk-tiv\ adj — **in·stinc·tive·ly** adv

²in·stinct \in-'stiŋkt, 'in-,stiŋkt\ adj : IMBUED, INFUSED

in·stinc·tu·al \in-'stiŋk-chə-wəl\ adj : of, relating to, or based on instinct

¹in·sti·tute \'in-stə-,tüt, -,tyüt\ vb **-tut·ed; -tut·ing** **1** : to establish in a position or office **2** : ORGANIZE **3** : INAUGURATE, INITIATE

²institute n **1** : an elementary principle recognized as authoritative; also, pl : a collection of such principles and precepts **2** : an organization for the promotion of a cause : ASSOCIATION **3** : an educational institution **4** : a brief course of instruction on a particular field

in·sti·tu·tion \ˌin-stə-ˈtü-shən, -ˈtyü-\ *n* **1** : an act of originating, setting up, or founding **2** : an established practice, law, or custom **3** : a society or corporation esp. of a public character ⟨a charitable ∼⟩; *also* : ASYLUM **3** — **in·sti·tu·tion·al** \-ˈtü-shə-nəl, -ˈtyü-\ *adj* — **in·sti·tu·tion·al·ize** \-nə-ˌlīz\ *vb* — **in·sti·tu·tion·al·ly** *adv*

instr *abbr* **1** instructor **2** instrument; instrumental

in·struct \in-ˈstrəkt\ *vb* [ME, fr. L *instructus,* pp. of *instruere,* fr. *struere* to build] **1** : TEACH **2** : INFORM **3** : to give an order or a command to

in·struc·tion \in-ˈstrək-shən\ *n* **1** : LESSON, PRECEPT **2** : COMMAND, ORDER **3** *pl* : DIRECTIONS **4** : the action, practice, or profession of a teacher — **in·struc·tion·al** \-shə-nəl\ *adj*

in·struc·tive \in-ˈstrək-tiv\ *adj* : carrying a lesson : ENLIGHTENING

in·struc·tor \in-ˈstrək-tər\ *n* : one that instructs; *esp* : a college teacher below professorial rank — **in·struc·tor·ship** *n*

in·stru·ment \ˈin-strə-mənt\ *n* **1** : a device used to produce music **2** : a means by which something is done **3** : a device for doing work and esp. precision work **4** : a legal document (as a deed) **5** : a device used in navigating an airplane — **in·stru·ment** \-ˌment\ *vb*

in·stru·men·tal \ˌin-strə-ˈment-ᵊl\ *adj* **1** : acting as an agent or means **2** : of, relating to, or done with an instrument **3** : relating to, composed for, or performed on a musical instrument

in·stru·men·tal·ist \-ˈmen-tə-list\ *n* : a player on a musical instrument

in·stru·men·tal·i·ty \ˌin-strə-mən-ˈta-lə-tē, -ˌmen-\ *n, pl* **-ties 1** : the quality or state of being instrumental **2** : MEANS, AGENCY

in·stru·men·ta·tion \ˌin-strə-mən-ˈtā-shən, -ˌmen-\ *n* **1** : ORCHESTRATION **2** : instruments for a particular purpose

instrument panel *n* : DASHBOARD

in·sub·or·di·nate \ˌin-sə-ˈbȯrd-ᵊn-ət\ *adj* : disobedient to authority — **in·sub·or·di·na·tion** \-ˌbȯrd-ᵊn-ˈā-shən\ *n*

in·sub·stan·tial \ˌin-səb-ˈstan-chəl\ *adj* **1** : lacking substance or reality **2** : lacking firmness or solidity

in·suf·fer·able \(ˌ)in-ˈsə-fə-rə-bəl\ *adj* : not to be endured : INTOLERABLE ⟨an ∼ bore⟩ — **in·suf·fer·ably** \-blē\ *adv*

in·suf·fi·cient \ˌin-sə-ˈfi-shənt\ *adj* : not sufficient; *also* : INCOMPETENT — **in·suf·fi·cien·cy** \-shən-sē\ *n* — **in·suf·fi·cient·ly** *adv*

in·su·lar \ˈin-sə-lər, -syə-\ *adj* **1** : of, relating to, or forming an island **2** : dwelling or situated on an island **3** : NARROW-MINDED — **in·su·lar·i·ty** \ˌin-sə-ˈlar-ə-tē, -syə-\ *n*

in·su·late \ˈin-sə-ˌlāt\ *vb* **-lat·ed; -lat·ing** [L *insula* island] : ISOLATE; *esp* : to separate a conductor of electricity, heat, or sound from other conducting bodies by means of a nonconductor — **in·su·la·tion** \ˌin-sə-ˈlā-shən\ *n* — **in·su·la·tor** \ˈin-sə-ˌlā-tər\ *n*

in·su·lin \ˈin-sə-lən\ *n* : a pancreatic hormone essential esp. for the metabolism of carbohydrates and used in the control of diabetes mellitus

¹in·sult \in-ˈsəlt\ *vb* [MF or L; MF *insulter,* fr. L *insultare,* lit., to spring upon, fr. *saltare* to leap] : to treat with insolence or contempt : AFFRONT — **in·sult·ing·ly** *adv*

²in·sult \ˈin-ˌsəlt\ *n* : a gross indignity

in·su·per·a·ble \(ˌ)in-ˈsü-pə-rə-bəl\ *adj* : incapable of being surmounted, overcome, passed over, or solved — **in·su·per·a·bly** \-blē\ *adv*

in·sup·port·able \ˌin-sə-ˈpōr-tə-bəl\ *adj* **1** : UNENDURABLE **2** : UNJUSTIFIABLE

in·sur·able \in-ˈshu̇-rə-bəl\ *adj* : capable of being or proper to be insured

in·sur·ance \in-ˈshu̇r-əns\ *n* **1** : the business of insuring persons or property **2** : coverage by contract whereby one party agrees to guarantee another against a specified loss **3** : the sum for which something is insured **4** : a means of guaranteeing protection or safety

in·sure \in-ˈshu̇r\ *vb* **in·sured; in·sur·ing 1** : to provide or obtain insurance on or for : UNDERWRITE **2** : to make certain : ENSURE

in·sured \in-ˈshu̇rd\ *n* : a person whose life or property is insured

in·sur·er \in-ˈshu̇r-ər\ *n* : one that insures; *esp* : an insurance company

in·sur·gent \in-ˈsər-jənt\ *n* **1** : a person who revolts against civil authority or an established government : REBEL **2** : a member of a political party who rebels against it — **in·sur·gence** \-jəns\ *n* — **in·sur·gen·cy** \-jən-sē\ *n* — **in·sur·gent** *adj*

in·sur·mount·able \ˌin-sər-ˈmau̇n-tə-bəl\ *adj* : INSUPERABLE — **in·sur·mount·ably** \-blē\ *adv*

in·sur·rec·tion \ˌin-sə-ˈrek-shən\ *n* : an act or instance of revolting against civil authority or an established government — **in·sur·rec·tion·ist** \-shə-nist\ *n*

int *abbr* **1** interest **2** interior **3** intermediate **4** internal **5** international **6** intransitive

in·tact \in-ˈtakt\ *adj* : untouched esp. by anything that harms or diminishes

in·ta·glio \in-ˈtal-yō\ *n, pl* **-glios** [It] : an engraving cut deeply into the surface of a hard material (as stone)

in·take \ˈin-ˌtāk\ *n* **1** : an opening through which fluid enters **2** : the act of taking in **3** : something taken in

in·tan·gi·ble \(ˌ)in-ˈtan-jə-bəl\ *adj* : incapable of being touched : IMPALPABLE — **intangible** *n* — **in·tan·gi·bly** \-blē\ *adv*

in·te·ger \ˈin-ti-jər\ *n* [L, adj., whole, entire] : a number (as 1, 2, 3, 12, 432) that is not a fraction and does not include a fraction, is the negative of such a number, or is 0

in·te·gral \ˈin-ti-grəl\ *adj* **1** : essential to completeness **2** : formed as a unit with another part **3** : composed of parts that make up a whole **4** : ENTIRE

integral calculus *n* : calculus concerned esp. with advanced methods of finding lengths, areas, and volumes

in·te·grate \ˈin-tə-ˌgrāt\ *vb* **-grat·ed; -grat·ing 1** : to form, coordinate, or blend into a functioning whole : UNITE **2** : to incorporate into a larger unit **3** : to end the segregation of and bring into equal membership in society or an organization; *also* : DESEGREGATE — **in·te·gra·tion** \ˌin-tə-ˈgrā-shən\ *n*

integrated circuit *n* : a group of tiny electronic components and their connections that is produced in or on a small slice of material (as silicon)

in·teg·ri·ty \in-ˈte-grə-tē\ *n* **1** : adherence to a code of values : INCORRUPTIBILITY **2** : SOUNDNESS **3** : COMPLETENESS

in·teg·u·ment \in-ˈte-gyə-mənt\ *n* : a covering layer (as a skin or cuticle) of an organism

in·tel·lect \ˈint-ᵊl-ˌekt\ *n* **1** : the power of knowing : the capacity for knowledge **2** : the capacity for rational or intelligent thought esp. when highly developed **3** : a person with great intellectual powers

in·tel·lec·tu·al \ˌint-ᵊl-ˈek-chə-wəl\ *adj* **1** : of, relating to, or performed by the intellect : RATIONAL **2** : given to study, reflection, and speculation **3** : engaged in activity requiring the creative use of the intellect — **intellectual** *n* — **in·tel·lec·tu·al·ly** *adv*

in·tel·lec·tu·al·ism \-chə-wə-ˌli-zəm\ *n* : devotion to the exercise of intellect or to intellectual pursuits

in·tel·li·gence \in-ˈte-lə-jəns\ *n* **1** : ability to learn and understand or to deal with new or trying situations **2** : mental acuteness **3** : INFORMATION, NEWS **4** : an agency engaged in obtaining information esp. concerning an enemy or possible enemy; *also* : the information so gained

intelligence quotient *n* : a number often used as a measure of a person's intelligence

in·tel·li·gent \in-'te-lə-jənt\ *adj* [L *intelligens*, fr. *intelligere* to understand, fr. *inter* between + *legere* to select] : having or showing intelligence or intellect — **in·tel·li·gent·ly** *adv*

in·tel·li·gen·tsia \in-te-lə-'jent-sē-ə, -'gent-\ *n* [Russ *intelligentsiya*, fr. L *intelligentia* intelligence] : intellectuals forming a vanguard or elite

in·tel·li·gi·ble \in-'te-lə-jə-bəl\ *adj* : capable of being understood or comprehended — **in·tel·li·gi·bil·i·ty** \-te-lə-jə-'bi-lə-tē\ *n* — **in·tel·li·gi·bly** \-'te-lə-blē\ *adv*

in·tem·per·ance \(,)in-'tem-pə-rəns\ *n* : lack of moderation; *esp* : habitual or excessive drinking of intoxicants — **in·tem·per·ate** \-pə-rət\ *adj* — **in·tem·per·ate·ness** *n*

in·tend \in-'tend\ *vb* [ME *entenden, intenden*, fr. MF *entendre* to purpose, fr. L *intendere* to stretch out, aim at, fr. *tendere* to stretch] **1** : to have in mind as a purpose or aim **2** : to design for a specified use or future

in·ten·dant \in-'ten-dənt\ *n* : an official (as a governor) esp. under the French, Spanish, or Portuguese monarchies

¹in·tend·ed *adj* **1** : expected to be such in the future; *esp* : BETROTHED **2** : INTENTIONAL

²intended *n* : an engaged person

in·tense \in-'tens\ *adj* **1** : existing in an extreme degree **2** : marked by great zeal, energy, or eagerness **3** : showing strong feeling; *also* : deeply felt — **in·tense·ly** *adv*

in·ten·si·fy \in-'ten-sə-fī\ *vb* **-fied; -fy·ing 1** : to make or become intense or more intensive **2** : to make more acute : SHARPEN **syn** aggravate, heighten, enhance, magnify — **in·ten·si·fi·ca·tion** \-ten-sə-fə-'kā-shən\ *n*

in·ten·si·ty \in-'ten-sə-tē\ *n, pl* **-ties 1** : the quality or state of being intense; *esp* : degree of strength, energy, or force

¹in·ten·sive \in-'ten-siv\ *adj* **1** : highly concentrated **2** : serving to give emphasis — **in·ten·sive·ly** *adv*

²intensive *n* : an intensive word, particle, or prefix

intensive care *n* : special medical equipment and services for taking care of seriously ill patients ⟨an *intensive care* unit⟩

¹in·tent \in-'tent\ *n* **1** : the state of mind with which an act is done : VOLITION **2** : PURPOSE, AIM **3** : MEANING, SIGNIFICANCE

²intent *adj* **1** : directed with keen attention ⟨an ~ gaze⟩ **2** : ENGROSSED; *also* : DETERMINED — **in·tent·ly** *adv* — **in·tent·ness** *n*

in·ten·tion \in-'ten-chən\ *n* **1** : a determination to act in a certain way **2** : PURPOSE, AIM, END **syn** intent, design, object, objective, goal

in·ten·tion·al \in-'ten-chə-nəl\ *adj* : done by intention or design : INTENDED — **in·ten·tion·al·ly** *adv*

in·ter \in-'tər\ *vb* **in·terred; in·ter·ring** : BURY

in·ter·ac·tion \in-tər-'ak-shən\ *n* : mutual or reciprocal action or influence — **in·ter·act** \-'akt\ *vb*

in·ter·ac·tive \-'ak-tiv\ *adj* **1** : mutually or reciprocally active **2** : allowing two-way electronic communications (as between a person and a computer) — **in·ter·ac·tive·ly** *adv*

in·ter alia \in-tər-'ä-lē-ə, -'ä-\ *adv* : among other things

in·ter·atom·ic \in-tər-ə-'tä-mik\ *adj* : existing or acting between atoms

in·ter·breed \-'brēd\ *vb* **-bred** \-'bred\; **-breed·ing** : to breed together

in·ter·ca·la·ry \in-'tər-kə-ler-ē\ *adj* **1** : INTERCALATED ⟨February 29 is an ~ day⟩ **2** : INTERPOLATED

in·ter·ca·late \-lāt\ *vb* **-lat·ed; -lat·ing 1** : to insert (as a day) in a calendar **2** : to insert between or among existing elements or layers — **in·ter·ca·la·tion** \-tər-kə-'lā-shən\ *n*

in·ter·cede \in-tər-'sēd\ *vb* **-ced·ed; -ced·ing** : to act between parties with a view to reconciling differences

¹in·ter·cept \in-tər-'sept\ *vb* **1** : to stop or interrupt the progress or course of **2** : to include (as part of a curve or solid) between two points, curves, or surfaces **3** : to gain possession of (an opponent's pass in football) — **in·ter·cep·tion** \-'sep-shən\ *n*

²in·ter·cept \'in-tər-sept\ *n* : INTERCEPTION; *esp* : the interception of a target by an interceptor or missile

in·ter·cep·tor \in-tər-'sep-tər\ *n* : a fighter plane designed for defense against attacking bombers

in·ter·ces·sion \in-tər-'se-shən\ *n* **1** : MEDIATION **2** : prayer or petition in favor of another — **in·ter·ces·sor** \-'se-sər\ *n* — **in·ter·ces·so·ry** \-'se-sə-rē\ *adj*

¹in·ter·change \in-tər-'chānj\ *vb* **1** : to put each in the place of the other **2** : EXCHANGE **3** : to change places mutually — **in·ter·change·able** \-'chān-jə-bəl\ *adj* — **in·ter·change·ably** \-blē\ *adv*

²in·ter·change \'in-tər-chānj\ *n* **1** : EXCHANGE **2** : a highway junction that by separated levels permits passage between highways without crossing traffic streams

in·ter·col·le·giate \in-tər-kə-'lē-jət\ *adj* : existing or carried on between colleges

in·ter·com \'in-tər-käm\ *n* : a two-way system for localized communication

in·ter·con·ti·nen·tal \-känt-ªn-'ent-ªl\ *adj* **1** : extending among or carried on between continents ⟨~ trade⟩ **2** : capable of traveling between continents ⟨~ ballistic missiles⟩

in·ter·course \'in-tər-kōrs\ *n* **1** : connection or dealings between persons or nations **2** : physical sexual contact between individuals that involves the genitalia of at least one person ⟨oral ~⟩; *esp* : SEXUAL INTERCOURSE

in·ter·de·nom·i·na·tion·al \in-tər-di-nä-mə-'nä-shə-nəl\ *adj* : involving different denominations

in·ter·de·part·men·tal \in-tər-di-pärt-'ment-ªl, -dē-\ *adj* : carried on between or involving different departments (as of a college)

in·ter·de·pen·dent \in-tər-di-'pen-dənt\ *adj* : dependent upon one another — **in·ter·de·pen·dence** \-dəns\ *n*

in·ter·dict \in-tər-'dikt\ *vb* **1** : to prohibit by decree **2** : to destroy, cut off, or damage (as an enemy line of supply) — **in·ter·dic·tion** \-'dik-shən\ *n*

in·ter·dis·ci·plin·ary \-'di-sə-plə-ner-ē\ *adj* : involving two or more academic, scientific, or artistic disciplines

¹in·ter·est \'in-trəst; 'in-tə-rəst, -rest\ *n* **1** : right, title, or legal share in something **2** : a charge for borrowed money that is generally a percentage of the amount borrowed, *also* : the return received by capital on its investment **3** : WELFARE, BENEFIT; *also* : SELF-INTEREST **4** : CURIOSITY, CONCERN **5** : readiness to be concerned with or moved by an object or class of objects **6** : a quality in a thing that arouses interest

²interest *vb* **1** : to persuade to participate or engage **2** : to engage the attention of

in·ter·est·ing *adj* : holding the attention — **in·ter·est·ing·ly** *adv*

¹in·ter·face \'in-tər-fās\ *n* **1** : a surface forming a common boundary of two bodies, spaces, or phases ⟨an oil-water ~⟩ **2** : the place at which two independent systems meet and act on or communicate with each other ⟨the man-machine ~⟩ **3** : the means by which interaction or communication is achieved at an interface — **in·ter·fa·cial** \in-tər-'fā-shəl\ *adj*

²interface *vb* **-faced; -fac·ing 1** : to connect by means of an interface **2** : to serve as an interface

in·ter·faith \in-tər-'fāth\ *adj* : involving persons of different religious faiths

---

\ə\abut \ª\kitten \ər\further \a\ash \ā\ace \ä\mop, mar
\aů\out \ch\chin \e\bet \ē\easy \g\go \i\hit \ī\ice \j\job
\ŋ\sing \ō\go \ò\law \òi\boy \th\thin \th̲\the \ü\loot \ů\foot
\y\yet \zh\vision *see also* Pronunciation Symbols page

in·ter·fere \ˌin-tər-ˈfir\ vb **-fered; -fer·ing** [MF (s') entreferir to strike one another, fr. OF, fr. entre between, among + ferir to strike, fr. L ferire] 1 : to come in collision or be in opposition : CLASH 2 : to enter into the affairs of others 3 : to affect one another

in·ter·fer·ence \-ˈfir-əns\ n 1 : the act or process of interfering 2 : something that interferes : OBSTRUCTION 3 : the mutual effect on meeting of two waves resulting in areas of increased and decreased amplitude 4 : the blocking of an opponent in football to make way for the ballcarrier 5 : the illegal hindering of an opponent in sports

in·ter·fer·om·e·ter \ˌin-tər-fə-ˈrä-mə-tər\ n : a device that uses the interference of waves (as of light) for making precise measurements — **in·ter·fer·om·e·try** \-fə-ˈrä-mə-trē\ n

in·ter·fer·on \ˌin-tər-ˈfir-ˌän\ n : any of a group of antiviral proteins of low molecular weight produced usu. by animal cells in response to a virus, a parasite in the cell, or a chemical

in·ter·ga·lac·tic \ˌin-tər-gə-ˈlak-tik\ adj : relating to or situated in the spaces between galaxies

in·ter·gla·cial \-ˈglā-shəl\ n : a warm period between successive glaciations

in·ter·gov·ern·men·tal \-ˌgə-vərn-ˈment-əl\ adj : existing or occurring between two governments or levels of government

in·ter·im \ˈin-tə-rəm\ n [L, adv., meanwhile, fr. inter between] : a time intervening : INTERVAL — **interim** adj

¹**in·te·ri·or** \in-ˈtir-ē-ər\ adj 1 : lying, occurring, or functioning within the limiting boundaries : INSIDE, INNER 2 : remote from the surface, border, or shore : INLAND

²**interior** n 1 : the inland part (as of a country) 2 : INSIDE 3 : the internal affairs of a state or nation 4 : a scene or view of the interior of a building

interior decoration n : INTERIOR DESIGN — **interior decorator** n

interior design n : the art or practice of planning and supervising the design and execution of architectural interiors and their furnishings — **interior designer** n

interj abbr interjection

in·ter·ject \ˌin-tər-ˈjekt\ vb : to throw in between or among other things

in·ter·jec·tion \ˌin-tər-ˈjek-shən\ n : an exclamatory word (as ouch) — **in·ter·jec·tion·al·ly** \-shə-nə-lē\ adv

in·ter·lace \ˌin-tər-ˈlās\ vb 1 : to unite by or as if by lacing together : INTERWEAVE 2 : INTERSPERSE

in·ter·lard \ˌin-tər-ˈlärd\ vb : to vary by inserting or interjecting something

in·ter·leave \ˌin-tər-ˈlēv\ vb **-leaved; -leav·ing** : to arrange in alternate layers

in·ter·leu·kin \ˌin-tər-ˈlü-kən\ n : any of several proteins of low molecular weight that are produced by cells of the body and regulate the immune system and immune responses

¹**in·ter·line** \ˌin-tər-ˈlīn\ vb : to insert between lines already written or printed

²**interline** vb : to provide (as a coat) with an interlining

in·ter·lin·ear \ˌin-tər-ˈli-nē-ər\ adj : inserted between lines already written or printed ⟨an ～ translation of a text⟩

in·ter·lin·ing \ˈin-tər-ˌlī-niŋ\ n : a lining (as of a coat) between the ordinary lining and the outside fabric

in·ter·link \ˌin-tər-ˈliŋk\ vb : to link together

in·ter·lock \ˌin-tər-ˈläk\ vb 1 : to engage or interlace together : lock together : UNITE 2 : to connect so that action of one part affects action of another part — **in·ter·lock** \ˈin-tər-ˌläk\ n

in·ter·loc·u·tor \ˌin-tər-ˈlä-kyə-tər\ n : one who takes part in dialogue or conversation

in·ter·loc·u·to·ry \-ˌtōr-ē\ adj : pronounced during the progress of a legal action and having only provisional force ⟨an ～ decree⟩

in·ter·lope \ˌin-tər-ˈlōp\ vb **-loped; -lop·ing** 1 : to encroach on the rights (as in trade) of others 2 : INTRUDE, INTERFERE — **in·ter·lop·er** n

in·ter·lude \ˈin-tər-ˌlüd\ n 1 : a usu. short simple play or dramatic entertainment 2 : an intervening period, space, or event 3 : a piece of music inserted between the parts of a longer composition or a religious service

in·ter·mar·riage \ˌin-tər-ˈmar-ij\ n 1 : marriage within one's own group as required by custom 2 : marriage between members of different groups

in·ter·mar·ry \-ˈmar-ē\ vb 1 : to marry each other 2 : to marry within a group 3 : to become connected by intermarriage

¹**in·ter·me·di·ary** \ˌin-tər-ˈmē-dē-ˌer-ē\ adj 1 : INTERMEDIATE 2 : acting as a mediator

²**intermediary** n, pl **-ar·ies** : MEDIATOR, GO-BETWEEN

¹**in·ter·me·di·ate** \ˌin-tər-ˈmē-dē-ət\ adj : being or occurring at the middle place or degree or between extremes

²**intermediate** n 1 : one that is intermediate 2 : INTERMEDIARY

intermediate school n 1 : JUNIOR HIGH SCHOOL 2 : a school usu. comprising grades 4 – 6

in·ter·ment \in-ˈtər-mənt\ n : BURIAL

in·ter·mez·zo \ˌin-tər-ˈmet-sō, -ˈmed-zō\ n, pl **-zi** \-sē, -zē\ or **-zos** [It, ultim. fr. L intermedius intermediate] : a short movement connecting major sections of an extended musical work (as a symphony); also : a short independent instrumental composition

in·ter·mi·na·ble \(ˌ)in-ˈtər-mə-nə-bəl\ adj : ENDLESS; esp : wearisomely protracted — **in·ter·mi·na·bly** \-blē\ adv

in·ter·min·gle \ˌin-tər-ˈmiŋ-gəl\ vb : to mingle or mix together

in·ter·mis·sion \ˌin-tər-ˈmi-shən\ n 1 : INTERRUPTION, BREAK 2 : a temporary halt esp. in a public performance

in·ter·mit \-ˈmit\ vb **-mit·ted; -mit·ting** : DISCONTINUE; also : to be intermittent

in·ter·mit·tent \-ˈmit-ənt\ adj : coming and going at intervals **syn** recurrent, periodic, alternate — **in·ter·mit·tent·ly** adv

in·ter·mix \ˌin-tər-ˈmiks\ vb : to mix together : INTERMINGLE — **in·ter·mix·ture** \-ˈmiks-chər\ n

in·ter·mo·lec·u·lar \-mə-ˈle-kyə-lər\ adj : existing or acting between molecules

in·ter·mon·tane \ˌin-tər-ˈmän-ˌtān\ adj : situated between mountains

¹**in·tern** \ˈin-ˌtərn, in-ˈtərn\ vb : to confine or impound esp. during a war — **in·tern·ee** \(ˌ)in-ˌtər-ˈnē\ n — **in·tern·ment** \in-ˈtərn-mənt\ n

²**in·tern** or **in·terne** \ˈin-ˌtərn\ n : an advanced student or recent graduate (as in medicine) gaining supervised practical experience — **in·tern·ship** n

³**in·tern** \ˈin-ˌtərn\ vb : to act as an intern

in·ter·nal \in-ˈtərn-əl\ adj 1 : INWARD, INTERIOR 2 : relating to or located in the inside of the body ⟨～ pain⟩ 3 : of, relating to, or occurring within the confines of an organized structure ⟨～ affairs⟩ 4 : of, relating to, or existing within the mind 5 : INTRINSIC, INHERENT — **in·ter·nal·ly** adv

internal combustion engine n : an engine in which the fuel is ignited within the engine cylinder

internal medicine n : a branch of medicine that deals with the diagnosis and treatment of diseases not requiring surgery

¹**in·ter·na·tion·al** \ˌin-tər-ˈna-shə-nəl\ adj 1 : common to or affecting two or more nations ⟨～ trade⟩ 2 : of, relating to, or constituting a group having members in two or more nations — **in·ter·na·tion·al·ly** adv

²**international** n : one that is international; esp : an organization of international scope

in·ter·na·tion·al·ise Brit var of INTERNATIONALIZE

in·ter·na·tion·al·ism \-ˈna-shə-nə-ˌli-zəm\ n : a policy of cooperation among nations; also : an attitude favoring such a policy

in·ter·na·tion·al·ize \-ʹna-shə-nə-ˌlīz\ *vb* : to make international; *esp* : to place under international control

in·ter·ne·cine \ˌin-tər-ʹne-ˌsēn, -ʹnē-ˌsīn\ *adj* [L *internecinus*, fr. *internecare* to destroy, kill, fr. *necare* to kill, fr. *nec-, nex* violent death] **1** : DEADLY; *esp* : mutually destructive **2** : of, relating to, or involving conflict within a group ⟨∼ feuds⟩

in·ter·nist \ʹin-ˌtər-nist\ *n* : a physician who specializes in internal medicine

in·ter·nun·cio \ˌin-tər-ʹnən-sē-ˌō, -ʹnün-\ *n* [It *internunzio*] : a papal legate of lower rank than a nuncio

in·ter·of·fice \-ʹȯ-fəs\ *adj* : functioning or communicating between the offices of an organization

in·ter·per·son·al \-ʹpərs-ᵊn-əl\ *adj* : being, relating to, or involving relations between persons — **in·ter·per·son·al·ly** *adv*

in·ter·plan·e·tary \ˌin-tər-ʹpla-nə-ˌter-ē\ *adj* : existing, carried on, or operating between planets ⟨∼ space⟩

in·ter·play \ʹin-tər-ˌplā\ *n* : INTERACTION

in·ter·po·late \in-ʹtər-pə-ˌlāt\ *vb* **-lat·ed; -lat·ing 1** : to change (as a text) by inserting new or foreign matter **2** : to insert (as words) into a text or into a conversation **3** : to estimate values of (a function) between two known values — **in·ter·po·la·tion** \-ˌtər-pə-ʹlā-shən\ *n*

in·ter·pose \ˌin-tər-ʹpōz\ *vb* **-posed; -pos·ing 1** : to place between **2** : to thrust in : INTRUDE, INTERRUPT **3** : to inject between parts of a conversation or argument **4** : to come or be between **syn** interfere, intercede, intermediate, intervene — **in·ter·po·si·tion** \-pə-ʹzi-shən\ *n*

in·ter·pret \in-ʹtər-prət\ *vb* **1** : to explain the meaning of; *also* : to act as an interpreter : TRANSLATE **2** : to understand according to individual belief, judgment, or interest **3** : to represent artistically — **in·ter·pret·er** *n* — **in·ter·pre·tive** \-ʹtər-prə-tiv\ *adj*

in·ter·pre·ta·tion \in-ˌtər-prə-ʹtā-shən\ *n* **1** : EXPLANATION **2** : an instance of artistic interpretation in performance or adaptation — **in·ter·pre·ta·tive** \-ʹtər-prə-ˌtā-tiv\ *adj*

in·ter·ra·cial \-ʹrā-shəl\ *adj* : of, involving, or designed for members of different races

in·ter·reg·num \ˌin-tə-ʹreg-nəm\ *n, pl* **-nums** *or* **-na** \-nə\ **1** : the time during which a throne is vacant between two successive reigns or regimes **2** : a pause in a continuous series

in·ter·re·late \ˌin-tər-ri-ʹlāt\ *vb* : to bring into or have a mutual relationship — **in·ter·re·lat·ed·ness** \-ʹlā-təd-nəs\ *n* — **in·ter·re·la·tion** \-ʹlā-shən\ *n* — **in·ter·re·la·tion·ship** *n*

interrog *abbr* interrogative

in·ter·ro·gate \in-ʹter-ə-ˌgāt\ *vb* **-gat·ed; -gat·ing** : to question esp. formally and systematically : ASK — **in·ter·ro·ga·tion** \-ˌter-ə-ʹgā-shən\ *n* — **in·ter·ro·ga·tor** \-ʹter-ə-ˌgā-tər\ *n*

in·ter·rog·a·tive \ˌin-tə-ʹrä-gə-tiv\ *adj* : asking a question ⟨∼ sentence⟩ — **interrogative** *n* — **in·ter·rog·a·tive·ly** *adv*

in·ter·rog·a·to·ry \ˌin-tə-ʹrä-gə-ˌtōr-ē\ *adj* : INTERROGATIVE

in·ter·rupt \ˌin-tə-ʹrəpt\ *vb* **1** : to stop or hinder by breaking in **2** : to break the uniformity or continuity of **3** : to break in by speaking while another is speaking — **in·ter·rupt·er** *n* — **in·ter·rup·tion** \-ʹrəp-shən\ *n* — **in·ter·rup·tive** \-ʹrəp-tiv\ *adv*

in·ter·scho·las·tic \ˌin-tər-skə-ʹlas-tik\ *adj* : existing or carried on between schools

in·ter·sect \ˌin-tər-ʹsekt\ *vb* **1** : to divide by passing through or across **2** : to meet and cross (as at a point); *also* : OVERLAP — **in·ter·sec·tion** \-ʹsek-shən\ *n*

in·ter·sperse \ˌin-tər-ʹspərs\ *vb* **-spersed; -spers·ing 1** : to place something at intervals in or among **2** : to insert at intervals among other things — **in·ter·sper·sion** \-ʹspər-zhən\ *n*

¹in·ter·state \ˌin-tər-ʹstāt\ *adj* : relating to, including, or connecting two or more states esp. of the U.S.

²in·ter·state \ʹin-tər-ˌstāt\ *n* : an interstate highway

in·ter·stel·lar \ˌin-tər-ʹste-lər\ *adj* : located or taking place among the stars

in·ter·stice \in-ʹtər-stəs\ *n, pl* **-stic·es** \-stə-ˌsēz, -stə-səz\ : a space that intervenes between things : CHINK — **in·ter·sti·tial** \ˌin-tər-ʹsti-shəl\ *adj*

in·ter·tid·al \ˌin-tər-ʹtīd-ᵊl\ *adj* : of, relating to, or being the area that is above low-tide mark but exposed to tidal flooding ⟨life in the ∼ mud⟩

in·ter·twine \-ʹtwīn\ *vb* : to twine or cause to twine about one another : INTERLACE — **in·ter·twine·ment** *n*

in·ter·twist \-ʹtwist\ *vb* : INTERTWINE

in·ter·ur·ban \-ʹər-bən\ *adj* : connecting cities or towns

in·ter·val \ʹin-tər-vəl\ *n* [ME *intervalle*, fr. MF, fr. L *intervallum* space between ramparts, interval, fr. *inter-* between + *vallum* rampart] **1** : a space of time between events or states : PAUSE **2** : a space between objects, units, or states **3** : the difference in pitch between two tones

in·ter·vene \ˌin-tər-ʹvēn\ *vb* **-vened; -ven·ing 1** : to occur, fall, or come between points of time or between events **2** : to enter or appear as an unrelated feature or circumstance ⟨rain *intervened* and we postponed the trip⟩ **3** : to come in or between in order to stop, settle, or modify ⟨∼ in a quarrel⟩ **4** : to occur or lie between two things — **in·ter·ven·tion** \-ʹven-chən\ *n*

in·ter·ven·tion·ism \-ʹven-chə-ˌni-zəm\ *n* : interference by one country in the political affairs of another — **in·ter·ven·tion·ist** \-ʹven-chə-nist\ *n or adj*

in·ter·view \ʹin-tər-ˌvyü\ *n* **1** : a formal consultation usu. to evaluate qualifications **2** : a meeting at which a writer or reporter obtains information from a person; *also* : the recorded or written account of such a meeting — **interview** *vb* — **in·ter·view·ee** \ˌin-tər-(ˌ)vyü-ʹē\ *n* — **in·ter·view·er** *n*

in·ter·vo·cal·ic \ˌin-tər-vō-ʹka-lik\ *adj* : immediately preceded and immediately followed by a vowel

in·ter·weave \ˌin-tər-ʹwēv\ *vb* **-wove** \-ʹwōv\ *also* **-weaved; -wo·ven** \-ʹwō-vən\ *also* **-weaved; -weav·ing** : to weave or blend together : INTERTWINE, INTERMINGLE — **interwoven** *adj*

in·tes·tate \in-ʹtes-ˌtāt, -tət\ *adj* **1** : having made no valid will ⟨died ∼⟩ **2** : not disposed of by will ⟨∼ estate⟩

in·tes·tine \in-ʹtes-tən\ *n* : the tubular part of the alimentary canal that extends from stomach to anus and consists of a long narrow upper part (**small intestine**) followed by a broader shorter lower part (**large intestine**) — **in·tes·ti·nal** \-tən-ᵊl\ *adj*

¹in·ti·mate \ʹin-tə-ˌmāt\ *vb* **-mat·ed; -mat·ing 1** : ANNOUNCE, NOTIFY **2** : to communicate indirectly : HINT — **in·ti·ma·tion** \ˌin-tə-mā-shən\ *n*

²in·ti·mate \ʹin-tə-mət\ *adj* **1** : INTRINSIC; *also* : INNERMOST **2** : marked by very close association, contact, or familiarity **3** : marked by a warm friendship **4** : suggesting informal warmth or privacy **5** : of a very personal or private nature — **in·ti·ma·cy** \ʹin-tə-mə-sē\ *n* — **in·ti·mate·ly** *adv*

³in·ti·mate \ʹin-tə-mət\ *n* : an intimate friend, associate, or confidant

in·tim·i·date \in-ʹti-mə-ˌdāt\ *vb* **-dat·ed; -dat·ing** : to make timid or fearful : FRIGHTEN; *esp* : to compel or deter by or as if by threats **syn** cow, bulldoze, bully, browbeat — **in·tim·i·dat·ing·ly** *adv* — **in·tim·i·da·tion** \-ˌti-mə-ʹdā-shən\ *n*

intl *or* **intnl** *abbr* international

in·to \ʹin-tü\ *prep* **1** : to the inside of ⟨ran ∼ the house⟩

\ə\abut \ᵊ\kitten \ər\further \a\ash \ā\ace \ä\mop, mar
\aů\out \ch\chin \e\bet \ē\easy \g\go \i\hit \ī\ice \j\job
\ŋ\sing \ō\go \ȯ\law \ȯi\boy \th\thin \th̲\the \ü\loot \ů\foot
\y\yet \zh\vision *see also* Pronunciation Symbols page

2 : to the state, condition, or form of ⟨got ∼ trouble⟩ **3** : AGAINST ⟨ran ∼ a wall⟩

in·tol·er·a·ble \(ˌ)in-ˈtä-lə-rə-bəl\ *adj* **1** : UNBEARABLE **2** : EXCESSIVE — **in·tol·er·a·bly** \-blē\ *adv*

in·tol·er·ant \(ˌ)in-ˈtä-lə-rənt\ *adj* **1** : unable or unwilling to endure **2** : unwilling to grant equality, freedom, or other social rights : BIGOTED — **in·tol·er·ance** \-rəns\ *n*

in·to·na·tion \ˌin-tō-ˈnā-shən\ *n* **1** : the act of intoning and esp. of chanting **2** : something that is intoned **3** : the manner of singing, playing, or uttering tones **4** : the rise and fall in pitch of the voice in speech

in·tone \in-ˈtōn\ *vb* **in·toned; in·ton·ing** : to utter in musical or prolonged tones : CHANT

in to·to \in-ˈtō-tō\ *adv* [L, on the whole] : TOTALLY, ENTIRELY

in·tox·i·cant \in-ˈtäk-si-kənt\ *n* : something that intoxicates; *esp* : an alcoholic drink — **intoxicant** *adj*

in·tox·i·cate \-sə-ˌkāt\ *vb* **-cat·ed; -cat·ing** **1** : to affect by a drug (as alcohol or cocaine) esp. to the point of physical or mental impairment **2** : to excite to enthusiasm or frenzy — **in·tox·i·ca·tion** \-ˌtäk-sə-ˈkā-shən\ *n*

in·trac·ta·ble \(ˌ)in-ˈtrak-tə-bəl\ *adj* : not easily controlled : OBSTINATE

in·tra·mu·ral \-ˈmyùr-əl\ *adj* : being or occurring within the walls or limits (as of a city or college) ⟨∼ sports⟩

in·tra·mus·cu·lar \-ˈməs-kyə-lər\ *adj* : situated within, occurring in, or administered by entering a muscle — **in·tra·mus·cu·lar·ly** *adv*

intrans *abbr* intransitive

in·tran·si·gent \-jənt\ *adj* : UNCOMPROMISING; *also* : IRRECONCILABLE — **in·tran·si·gence** \-jəns\ *n* — **intransigent** *n*

in·tran·si·tive \(ˌ)in-ˈtran-sə-tiv, -zə-\ *adj* : not transitive; *esp* : not having or containing an object ⟨an ∼ verb⟩ — **in·tran·si·tive·ly** *adv* — **in·tran·si·tive·ness** *n*

in·tra·state \ˌin-trə-ˈstāt\ *adj* : existing or occurring within a state

in·tra·uter·ine device \-ˈyü-tə-rən-, -ˌrīn-\ *n* : a device (as a spiral of plastic) inserted and left in the uterus to prevent pregnancy

in·tra·ve·nous \ˌin-trə-ˈvē-nəs\ *adj* : being within or entering by way of the veins; *also* : used in or using intravenous procedures — **in·tra·ve·nous·ly** *adv*

intrench *var of* ENTRENCH

in·trep·id \in-ˈtre-pəd\ *adj* : characterized by resolute fearlessness, fortitude, and endurance — **in·tre·pid·i·ty** \ˌin-trə-ˈpi-də-tē\ *n*

in·tri·cate \ˈin-tri-kət\ *adj* [ME, fr. L *intricatus,* pp. of *intricare* to entangle, fr. *tricae* trifles, complications] **1** : having many complexly interrelated parts : COMPLICATED **2** : difficult to follow, understand, or solve — **in·tri·ca·cy** \-tri-kə-sē\ *n* — **in·tri·cate·ly** *adv*

¹in·trigue \in-ˈtrēg\ *vb* **in·trigued; in·trigu·ing** **1** : to accomplish by intrigue **2** : to carry on an intrigue; *esp* : PLOT, SCHEME **3** : to arouse the interest, desire, or curiosity of — **in·trigu·ing·ly** *adv*

²in·trigue \ˈin-ˌtrēg, in-ˈtrēg\ *n* **1** : a secret scheme : MACHINATION **2** : a clandestine love affair

in·trin·sic \in-ˈtrin-zik, -sik\ *adj* : belonging to the essential nature or constitution of a thing — **in·trin·si·cal·ly** \-zi-k(ə-)lē, -si-\ *adv*

introd *abbr* introduction

in·tro·duce \ˌin-trə-ˈdüs, -ˈdyüs\ *vb* **-duced; -duc·ing** **1** : to lead or bring in esp. for the first time **2** : to bring into practice or use **3** : to cause to be acquainted **4** : to present for discussion **5** : PLACE, INSERT **syn** insinuate, interpolate, interpose, interject — **in·tro·duc·tion** \-ˈdək-shən\ *n* — **in·tro·duc·to·ry** \-ˈdək-tə-rē\ *adj*

in·troit \ˈin-ˌtróit, -ˌtrō-ət\ *n* **1** *often cap* : the first part of the traditional proper of the Mass **2** : a piece of music sung or played at the beginning of a worship service

in·tro·spec·tion \-ˈspek-shən\ *n* : a reflective looking inward : an examination of one's own thoughts or feelings — **in·tro·spect** \ˌin-trə-ˈspekt\ *vb* — **in·tro·spec·tive** \-ˈspek-tiv\ *adj* — **in·tro·spec·tive·ly** *adv*

in·tro·vert \ˈin-trə-ˌvərt\ *n* : a reserved or shy person — **in·tro·ver·sion** \ˌin-trə-ˈvər-zhən\ *n* — **introvert** *adj* — **in·tro·vert·ed** \ˈin-trə-ˌvər-təd\ *adj*

in·trude \in-ˈtrüd\ *vb* **in·trud·ed; in·trud·ing** **1** : to thrust, enter, or force in or upon **2** : ENCROACH, TRESPASS — **in·trud·er** *n* — **in·tru·sion** \-ˈtrü-zhən\ *n* — **in·tru·sive** \-ˈtrü-siv\ *adj* — **in·tru·sive·ness** *n*

intrust *var of* ENTRUST

in·tu·it \in-ˈtü-ət, -ˈtyü-\ *vb* : to apprehend by intuition

in·tu·ition \ˌin-tü-ˈwi-shən, -tyù-\ *n* **1** : quick and ready insight **2** : the power or faculty of knowing things without conscious reasoning — **in·tu·i·tive** \in-ˈtü-ə-tiv, -ˈtyü-\ *adj* — **in·tu·i·tive·ly** *adv*

In·u·it \ˈi-nù-wət, ˈin-yù-\ *n* [Inuit *inuit,* pl. of *inuk* person] **1** : a member of the Eskimo people of No. America and Greenland **2** : the language of the Inuit people

in·un·date \ˈi-nən-ˌdāt\ *vb* **-dat·ed; -dat·ing** : to cover with or as if with a flood : OVERFLOW — **in·un·da·tion** \ˌi-nən-ˈdā-shən\ *n*

in·ure \i-ˈnùr, -ˈnyùr\ *vb* **in·ured; in·ur·ing** [ME *enuren,* fr. *en-* in + *ure,* n., use, custom, fr. MF *uevre* work, practice, fr. L *opera* work] **1** : to accustom to accept something undesirable **2** : to become of advantage

inv *abbr* **1** inventor **2** invoice

in vac·uo \in-ˈva-kyù-ˌwō\ *adv* [L] : in a vacuum

in·vade \in-ˈvād\ *vb* **in·vad·ed; in·vad·ing** **1** : to enter for conquest or plunder **2** : to encroach upon **3** : to spread through and usu. harm ⟨germs ∼ the tissues⟩ — **in·vad·er** *n*

¹in·val·id \(ˌ)in-ˈva-ləd\ *adj* : being without foundation or force in fact, reason, or law — **in·va·lid·i·ty** \ˌin-və-ˈli-də-tē\ *n* — **in·val·id·ly** *adv*

²in·va·lid \ˈin-və-ləd\ *adj* : being in ill health : SICKLY

³invalid \ˈin-və-ləd\ *n* : a person in usu. chronic ill health — **in·va·lid·ism** \-lə-ˌdi-zəm\ *n*

⁴in·va·lid \ˈin-və-ləd, -ˌlid\ *vb* **1** : to remove from active duty by reason of sickness or disability **2** : to make sickly or disabled

in·val·i·date \(ˌ)in-ˈva-lə-ˌdāt\ *vb* : to make invalid; *esp* : to weaken or make valueless — **in·val·i·da·tion** \in-ˌva-lə-ˈdā-shən\ *n*

in·valu·able \-ˈval-yə-bəl, -yə-wə-bəl\ *adj* : valuable beyond estimation

in·vari·able \-ˈver-ē-ə-bəl\ *adj* : not changing or capable of change : CONSTANT — **in·vari·ably** \-blē\ *adv*

in·va·sion \in-ˈvā-zhən\ *n* : an act or instance of invading; *esp* : entry of an army into a country for conquest

in·va·sive \in-ˈvā-siv, -ziv\ *adj* **1** : tending to spread ⟨∼ cancer cells⟩ **2** : involving entry into the living body (as by surgery) ⟨∼ therapy⟩

in·vec·tive \in-ˈvek-tiv\ *n* **1** : an abusive expression or speech **2** : abusive language — **invective** *adj*

in·veigh \in-ˈvā\ *vb* : to protest or complain bitterly or vehemently : RAIL

in·vei·gle \in-ˈvā-gəl, -ˈvē-\ *vb* **in·vei·gled; in·vei·gling** [modif. of MF *aveugler* to blind, hoodwink] **1** : to win over by flattery : ENTICE **2** : to acquire by ingenuity or flattery

in·vent \in-ˈvent\ *vb* **1** : to think up **2** : to create or produce for the first time — **in·ven·tor** \-ˈven-tər\ *n*

in·ven·tion \in-ˈven-chən\ *n* **1** : INVENTIVENESS **2** : a creation of the imagination; *esp* : a false conception **3** : a device, contrivance, or process originated after study and experiment **4** : the act or process of inventing

in·ven·tive \in-ˈven-tiv\ *adj* **1** : CREATIVE, INGENIOUS ⟨an ∼ composer⟩ **2** : characterized by invention ⟨an ∼ turn of mind⟩ — **in·ven·tive·ness** *n*

in·ven·to·ry \ˈin-vən-ˌtōr-ē\ *n, pl* **-ries** **1** : an itemized list of current goods or assets **2** : SURVEY, SUMMARY **3** : STOCK, SUPPLY **4** : the act or process of taking an inventory — **inventory** *vb*

¹in·verse \(ˌ)in-ˈvərs, ˈin-ˌvərs\ *adj* : opposite in order, nature, or effect : REVERSED — in·verse·ly *adv*

²inverse *n* : something inverse or resulting in or from inversion : OPPOSITE

in·ver·sion \in-ˈvər-zhən\ *n* 1 : a reversal of position, order, or relationship; *esp* : an increase of temperature with altitude through a layer of air 2 : the act or process of inverting

in·vert \in-ˈvərt\ *vb* 1 : to reverse in position, order, or relationship 2 : to turn upside down or inside out 3 : to turn inward

¹in·ver·te·brate \(ˌ)in-ˈvər-tə-brət, -ˌbrāt\ *adj* : lacking a backbone; *also* : of or relating to invertebrates

²invertebrate *n* : an invertebrate animal (as a jellyfish, insect, or worm)

¹in·vest \in-ˈvest\ *vb* 1 : to install formally in an office or honor 2 : to furnish with power or authority : VEST 3 : to cover completely : ENVELOP 4 : CLOTHE, ADORN 5 : BESIEGE 6 : to endow with a quality or characteristic

²invest *vb* 1 : to commit (money) in order to earn a financial return 2 : to expend for future benefits or advantages 3 : to make an investment — in·ves·tor \-ˈves-tər\ *n*

in·ves·ti·gate \in-ˈves-tə-ˌgāt\ *vb* -gat·ed; -gat·ing [L *investigare* to track, investigate, fr. *vestigium* footprint, track] : to study by close examination and systematic inquiry — in·ves·ti·ga·tion \-ˌves-tə-ˈgā-shən\ *n* — in·ves·ti·ga·tive \-ˈves-tə-ˌgā-tiv\ *adj* — in·ves·ti·ga·tor \-ˌgā-tər\ *n*

in·ves·ti·ture \in-ˈves-tə-ˌchùr, -chər\ *n* 1 : the act of ratifying or establishing in office 2 : something that covers or adorns

¹in·vest·ment \in-ˈvest-mənt\ *n* 1 : an outer layer : ENVELOPE 2 : INVESTITURE 1 3 : BLOCKADE, SIEGE

²investment *n* : the outlay of money for income or profit; *also* : the sum invested or the property purchased

in·vet·er·ate \in-ˈve-tə-rət\ *adj* 1 : firmly established by age or long persistence 2 : confirmed in a habit

in·vi·a·ble \(ˌ)in-ˈvī-ə-bəl\ *adj* : incapable of surviving

in·vid·i·ous \in-ˈvi-dē-əs\ *adj* 1 : tending to cause discontent, animosity, or envy 2 : ENVIOUS 3 : OBNOXIOUS — in·vid·i·ous·ly *adv*

in·vig·o·rate \in-ˈvi-gə-ˌrāt\ *vb* -rat·ed; -rat·ing : to give life and energy to : ANIMATE — in·vig·o·ra·tion \-ˌvi-gə-ˈrā-shən\ *n*

in·vin·ci·ble \(ˌ)in-ˈvin-sə-bəl\ *adj* : incapable of being conquered, overcome, or subdued — in·vin·ci·bil·i·ty \-ˌvin-sə-ˈbi-lə-tē\ *n* — in·vin·ci·bly \-ˈvin-sə-blē\ *adv*

in·vi·o·la·ble \-ˈvī-ə-lə-bəl\ *adj* 1 : safe from violation or profanation 2 : UNASSAILABLE — in·vi·o·la·bil·i·ty \-ˌvī-ə-lə-ˈbi-lə-tē\ *n*

in·vi·o·late \-ˈvī-ə-lət\ *adj* : not violated or profaned : PURE

in·vis·i·ble \-ˈvi-zə-bəl\ *adj* 1 : incapable of being seen (⟨∼ to the naked eye⟩) 2 : HIDDEN 3 : IMPERCEPTIBLE, INCONSPICUOUS — in·vis·i·bil·i·ty \-ˌvi-zə-ˈbi-lə-tē\ *n* — in·vis·i·bly \-ˈvi-zə-blē\ *adv*

in·vi·ta·tion·al \ˌin-və-ˈtā-shə-nəl\ *adj* : limited to invited participants (⟨an ∼ tournament⟩) — invitational *n*

in·vite \in-ˈvīt\ *vb* in·vit·ed; in·vit·ing 1 : ENTICE, TEMPT 2 : to increase the likelihood of 3 : to request the presence or participation of : ASK 4 : to request formally 5 : ENCOURAGE — in·vi·ta·tion \ˌin-və-ˈtā-shən\ *n*

in·vit·ing *adj* : ATTRACTIVE, TEMPTING

in vi·tro \in-ˈvē-trō, -ˈvī-, -ˈvi-\ *adv or adj* [NL, lit., in glass] : outside the living body and in an artificial environment ⟨in vitro fertilization⟩

in·vo·ca·tion \ˌin-və-ˈkā-shən\ *n* 1 : SUPPLICATION; *esp* : a prayer at the beginning of a service 2 : a formula for conjuring : INCANTATION

¹in·voice \ˈin-ˌvòis\ *n* [modif. of MF *envois*, pl. of *envoi* message] : an itemized list of goods shipped usu. specifying the price and the terms of sale : BILL

²invoice *vb* in·voiced; in·voic·ing : to send an invoice to or for : BILL

in·voke \in-ˈvōk\ *vb* in·voked; in·vok·ing 1 : to petition for help or support 2 : to appeal to or cite as authority ⟨∼ a law⟩ 3 : to call forth by incantation : CONJURE ⟨∼ spirits⟩ 4 : to make an earnest request for : SOLICIT 5 : to put into effect or operation 6 : to bring about : CAUSE

in·vol·un·tary \(ˌ)in-ˈvä-lən-ˌter-ē\ *adj* 1 : done contrary to or without choice 2 : COMPULSORY 3 : not controlled by the will : REFLEX ⟨∼ contractions⟩ — in·vol·un·tari·ly \-ˌvä-lən-ˈter-ə-lē\ *adv*

in·vo·lute \ˈin-və-ˌlüt\ *adj* : INVOLVED, INTRICATE

in·vo·lu·tion \ˌin-və-ˈlü-shən\ *n* 1 : the act or an instance of enfolding or entangling 2 : COMPLEXITY, INTRICACY

in·volve \in-ˈvälv\ *vb* in·volved; in·volv·ing 1 : to draw in as a participant 2 : ENVELOP 3 : to occupy (as oneself) absorbingly; *esp* : to commit oneself emotionally 4 : to relate closely : CONNECT 5 : to have as part of itself : INCLUDE 6 : ENTAIL, IMPLY 7 : to have an effect on — in·volve·ment *n*

in·volved \-ˈvälvd\ *adj* : INTRICATE, COMPLEX ⟨an ∼ plot⟩

in·vul·ner·a·ble \(ˌ)in-ˈvəl-nə-rə-bəl\ *adj* 1 : incapable of being wounded, injured, or damaged 2 : immune to or proof against attack — in·vul·ner·a·bil·i·ty \-ˌvəl-nə-rə-ˈbi-lə-tē\ *n* — in·vul·ner·a·bly \-ˈvəl-nə-rə-blē\ *adv*

¹in·ward \ˈin-wərd\ *adj* 1 : situated on the inside 2 : MENTAL; *also* : SPIRITUAL 3 : directed toward the interior

²inward *or* in·wards \-wərdz\ *adv* 1 : toward the inside, center, or interior 2 : toward the inner being

in·ward·ly \ˈin-wərd-lē\ *adv* 1 : MENTALLY, SPIRITUALLY 2 : INTERNALLY ⟨bled ∼⟩ 3 : to oneself ⟨cursed ∼⟩

IOC *abbr* International Olympic Committee

io·dide \ˈī-ə-ˌdīd\ *n* : a compound of iodine with another element or group

io·dine \ˈī-ə-ˌdīn, -əd-ᵊn\ *n* 1 : a nonmetallic chemical element used esp. in medicine and photography — see ELEMENT table 2 : a solution of iodine used as a local antiseptic

io·dize \ˈī-ə-ˌdīz\ *vb* io·dized; io·diz·ing : to treat with iodine or an iodide

ion \ˈī-ən, ˈī-ˌän\ *n* [Gk, neut. of *iōn*, prp. of *ienai* to go; so called because in electrolysis it goes to one of the two poles] : an electrically charged particle, atom, or group of atoms — ion·ic \ī-ˈä-nik\ *adj*

-ion *n suffix* : act, process, state, or condition ⟨validation⟩

ion·ize \ˈī-ə-ˌnīz\ *vb* ion·ized; ion·iz·ing 1 : to convert wholly or partly into ions 2 : to become ionized — ion·iz·able \ˌī-ə-ˈnī-zə-bəl\ *adj* — ion·iza·tion \ˌī-ə-nə-ˈzā-shən\ *n* — ion·iz·er \ˈī-ə-ˌnī-zər\ *n*

ion·o·sphere \ī-ˈä-nə-ˌsfir\ *n* : the part of the earth's atmosphere extending from about 30 miles (50 kilometers) to the exosphere that contains ionized atmospheric gases — ion·o·spher·ic \ī-ˌä-nə-ˈsfir-ik, -ˈsfer-\ *adj*

IOOF *abbr* Independent Order of Odd Fellows

io·ta \ī-ˈō-tə\ *n* [L, fr. Gk *iōta*] 1 : the 9th letter of the Greek alphabet — I or ι 2 : a very small quantity : JOT

IOU \ˌī-(ˌ)ō-ˈyü\ *n* : an acknowledgment of a debt

IP *abbr* innings pitched

ip·e·cac \ˈi-pi-ˌkak\ *n* [Pg *ipecacuanha*] : an emetic and expectorant drug used esp. as a syrup in treating accidental poisoning; *also* : either of two So. American plants or their rhizomes and roots used to make ipecac

ip·so fac·to \ˌip-sō-ˈfak-tō\ *adv* [NL, lit., by the fact itself] : by the very nature of the case

---

\ə\abut \ᵊ\kitten \ər\further \a\ash \ā\ace \ä\mop, mar
\aù\out \ch\chin \e\bet \ē\easy \g\go \i\hit \ī\ice \j\job
\ŋ\sing \ō\go \ò\law \òi\boy \th\thin \th\the \ü\loot \ù\foot
\y\yet \zh\vision *see also* Pronunciation Symbols page

iq *abbr* [L *idem quod*] the same as

IQ \'ī-'kyü\ *n* : INTELLIGENCE QUOTIENT

¹Ir *abbr* Irish

²Ir *symbol* iridium

IR *abbr* infrared

¹IRA \ī-(ˌ)är-'ā; 'ī-rə\ *n* [*individual retirement account*] : a savings account in which a person may make tax deductible deposits up to a stipulated amount each year with deposits and interest taxable after the person's retirement

²IRA *abbr* Irish Republican Army

Ira·ni·an \i-'rā-nē-ən *also* -'rä-\ *n* : a native or inhabitant of Iran — **Iranian** *adj*

Iraqi \i-'rä-kē, -'ra-\ *n* : a native or inhabitant of Iraq — **Iraqi** *adj*

iras·ci·ble \i-'ra-sə-bəl\ *adj* : marked by hot temper and easily provoked anger **syn** choleric, testy, touchy, cranky, cross — **iras·ci·bil·i·ty** \-ˌra-sə-'bi-lə-tē\ *n*

irate \ī-'rāt\ *adj* **1** : roused to ire **2** : arising from anger — **irate·ly** *adv*

ire \'īr\ *n* : ANGER, WRATH — **ire·ful** *adj*

Ire *abbr* Ireland

ire·nic \ī-'re-nik\ *adj* : favoring, conducive to, or operating toward peace or conciliation

ir·i·des·cence \ir-ə-'des-ᵊns\ *n* : a rainbowlike play of colors — **ir·i·des·cent** \-ᵊnt\ *adj*

irid·i·um \ir-'i-dē-əm\ *n* : a hard brittle heavy metallic chemical element — see ELEMENT table

iris \'ī-rəs\ *n, pl* **iris·es** *or* **iri·des** \'ī-rə-ˌdēz, 'ir-ə-\ [ME, fr. L *iris* rainbow, iris plant, fr. Gk, rainbow, iris plant, iris of the eye] **1** : the colored part around the pupil of the eye **2** : any of a large genus of plants with linear basal leaves and large showy flowers

Irish \'ī-rish\ *n* **1 Irish** *pl* : the people of Ireland **2** : the Celtic language of Ireland — **Irish** *adj* — **Irish·man** \-mən\ *n* — **Irish·wom·an** \-ˌwu̇-mən\ *n*

Irish bull *n* : an incongruous statement (as "it was hereditary in his family to have no children")

Irish coffee *n* : hot sugared coffee with Irish whiskey and whipped cream

Irish moss *n* : the dried and bleached plants of two red algae; *also* : either of these red algae

Irish setter *n* : any of a breed of bird dogs with a mahogany-red coat

irk \'ərk\ *vb* : to make weary, irritated, or bored : ANNOY

irk·some \'ərk-səm\ *adj* : tending to irk : ANNOYING — **irk·some·ly** *adv*

¹iron \'īrn, 'ī-ərn\ *n* **1** : a heavy malleable magnetic metallic chemical element that rusts easily and is vital to biological processes — see ELEMENT table **2** : something made of metal and peg iron; *also* : something (as handcuffs) used to bind or restrain ⟨put them in ∼s⟩ **3** : a household device with a flat base that is heated and used for pressing cloth **4** : STRENGTH, HARDNESS

²iron *vb* **1** : to press or smooth with or as if with a heated iron **2** : to remove (as wrinkles) by ironing — **iron·er** *n*

¹iron·clad \-'klad\ *adj* **1** : sheathed in iron armor **2** : so firm or secure as to be unbreakable

²iron·clad \-ˌklad\ *n* : an armored naval vessel esp. of the 19th century

iron curtain *n* : a political, military, and ideological barrier that isolates an area; *esp, often cap* : one isolating an area under Soviet control

iron·ic \ī-'rä-nik\ *or* **iron·i·cal** \-ni-kəl\ *adj* **1** : of, relating to, or marked by irony **2** : given to irony

iron·i·cal·ly \-ni-k(ə-)lē\ *adv* **1** : in an ironic manner **2** : it is ironic

iron·ing *n* : clothes ironed or to be ironed

iron lung *n* : a device for artificial respiration that encloses the chest in a chamber in which changes of pressure force air into and out of the lungs

iron out *vb* : to remove or lessen difficulties in or extremes of

iron oxide *n* : FERRIC OXIDE

iron·stone \'īrn-ˌstōn, 'ī-ərn-\ *n* **1** : a hard iron-rich sedimentary rock **2** : a hard heavy durable pottery developed in England in the 19th century

iron·ware \-ˌwar\ *n* : articles made of iron

iron·weed \-ˌwēd\ *n* : any of several mostly weedy American plants related to the asters that have terminal heads of red or purple flowers

iron·wood \-ˌwu̇d\ *n* : any of numerous trees or shrubs with exceptionally hard wood; *also* : the wood

iron·work \-ˌwərk\ *n* **1** : work in iron **2** *pl* : a mill or building where iron or steel is smelted or heavy iron or steel products are made — **iron·work·er** *n*

iro·ny \'ī-rə-nē\ *n, pl* **-nies** [L *ironia,* fr. Gk *eirōnia,* fr. *eirōn* dissembler] **1** : the use of words to express the opposite of what one really means **2** : incongruity between the actual result of a sequence of events and the expected result

Ir·o·quois \'ir-ə-ˌkwȯi\ *n, pl* **Iroquois** *same or* -ˌkwȯiz\ **1** *pl* : an American Indian confederacy of New York that consisted of the Cayuga, Mohawk, Oneida, Onondaga, and Seneca and later included the Tuscarora **2** : a member of any of the Iroquois peoples

ir·ra·di·ate \i-'rā-dē-ˌāt\ *vb* **-at·ed; -at·ing 1** : ILLUMINATE **2** : ENLIGHTEN **3** : to treat by exposure to radiation **4** : RADIATE — **ir·ra·di·a·tion** \-ˌrā-dē-'ā-shən\ *n*

¹ir·ra·tio·nal \(ˌ)i-'ra-shə-nəl\ *adj* **1** : incapable of reasoning ⟨∼ beasts⟩; *also* : defective in mental power ⟨∼ with fever⟩ **2** : not based on reason ⟨∼ fears⟩ **3** : being or numerically equal to an irrational number — **ir·ra·tio·nal·i·ty** \(ˌ)i-ˌra-shə-'na-lə-tē\ *n* — **ir·ra·tio·nal·ly** *adv*

²irrational *n* : IRRATIONAL NUMBER

irrational number *n* : a real number that cannot be expressed as the quotient of two integers

ir·rec·on·cil·able \(ˌ)i-ˌre-kən-'sī-lə-bəl, -'re-kən-ˌsī-\ *adj* : impossible to reconcile, adjust, or harmonize — **ir·rec·on·cil·abil·i·ty** \(ˌ)i-ˌre-kən-ˌsī-lə-'bi-lə-tē\ *n*

ir·re·cov·er·able \ir-i-'kə-və-rə-bəl\ *adj* : not capable of being recovered or rectified : IRREPARABLE — **ir·re·cov·er·ably** \-blē\ *adv*

ir·re·deem·able \ir-i-'dē-mə-bəl\ *adj* **1** : not redeemable; *esp* : not terminable by payment of the principal ⟨an ∼ bond⟩ **2** : not convertible into gold or silver at the will of the holder **3** : being beyond remedy : HOPELESS

ir·re·den·tism \-'den-ˌti-zəm\ *n* : a principle or policy directed toward the incorporation of a territory historically or ethnically part of another into that other — **ir·re·den·tist** \-tist\ *n or adj*

ir·re·duc·ible \ir-i-'dü-sə-bəl, -'dyü-\ *adj* : not reducible — **ir·re·duc·ibly** \-blē\ *adv*

ir·re·fut·able \ir-i-'fyü-tə-bəl, (ˌ)i-'re-fyət-\ *adj* : impossible to refute

irreg *abbr* irregular

ir·reg·u·lar \(ˌ)i-'re-gyə-lər\ *adj* **1** : not regular : not natural or uniform **2** : not conforming to the normal or usual manner of inflection ⟨∼ verbs⟩ **3** : not belonging to a regular or organized army ⟨∼ troops⟩ — **irregular** *n* — **ir·reg·u·lar·ly** *adv*

ir·reg·u·lar·i·ty \i-ˌre-gyə-'lar-ə-tē\ *n, pl* **-ties 1** : something that is irregular **2** : the quality or state of being irregular **3** : occasional constipation

ir·rel·e·vant \(ˌ)i-'re-lə-vənt\ *adj* : not relevant — **ir·rel·e·vance** \-vəns\ *n*

ir·re·li·gious \ir-i-'li-jəs\ *adj* : lacking religious emotions, doctrines, or practices

ir·re·me·di·a·ble \ir-i-'mē-dē-ə-bəl\ *adj* : impossible to remedy or correct

ir·re·mov·able \-'mü-və-bəl\ *adj* : not removable

ir·rep·a·ra·ble \(ˌ)i-'re-pə-rə-bəl\ *adj* : impossible to make good, undo, repair, or remedy ⟨∼ damage⟩

ir·re·place·able \,ir-i-'plā-sə-bəl\ *adj* : not replaceable
ir·re·press·ible \-'pre-sə-bəl\ *adj* : impossible to repress or control
ir·re·proach·able \-'prō-chə-bəl\ *adj* : not reproachable : BLAMELESS
ir·re·sist·ible \,ir-i-'zis-tə-bəl\ *adj* : impossible to successfully resist — **ir·re·sist·ibly** \-blē\ *adv*
ir·res·o·lute \(,)i-'re-zə-,lüt\ *adj* : uncertain how to act or proceed : VACILLATING — **ir·res·o·lute·ly** \-,lüt-lē; (,)i-,re-zə-'lüt-\ *adv* — **ir·res·o·lu·tion** \(,)i-,re-zə-'lü-shən\ *n*
ir·re·spec·tive of \,ir-i-'spek-tiv-\ *prep* : without regard to
ir·re·spon·si·ble \-'spän-sə-bəl\ *adj* : not responsible — **ir·re·spon·si·bil·i·ty** \-,spän-sə-'bi-lə-tē\ *n* — **ir·re·spon·si·bly** \-'spän-sə-blē\ *adv*
ir·re·triev·able \,ir-i-'trē-və-bəl\ *adj* : not retrievable : IRRECOVERABLE
ir·rev·er·ence \(,)i-'re-və-rəns\ *n* **1** : lack of reverence **2** : an irreverent act or utterance — **ir·rev·er·ent** \-rənt\ *adj*
ir·re·vers·ible \,ir-i-'vər-sə-bəl\ *adj* : incapable of being reversed
ir·rev·o·ca·ble \(,)i-'re-və-kə-bəl\ *adj* : incapable of being revoked or recalled — **ir·rev·o·ca·bly** \-blē\ *adv*
ir·ri·gate \'ir-ə-,gāt\ *vb* **-gat·ed; -gat·ing** : to supply (as land) with water by artificial means; *also* : to flush with liquid — **ir·ri·ga·tion** \,ir-ə-'gā-shən\ *n*
ir·ri·ta·bil·i·ty \,ir·ə-tə-'hi-lə-tē\ *n* **1** : the property of living things and of protoplasm that enables reaction to stimuli **2** : the quality or state of being irritable; *esp* : readiness to become annoyed or angry
ir·ri·ta·ble \'ir-ə-tə-bəl\ *adj* : capable of being irritated; *esp* : readily or easily irritated — **ir·ri·ta·bly** \-blē\ *adv*
ir·ri·tate \'ir-ə-,tāt\ *vb* **-tat·ed; -tat·ing** **1** : to excite to anger : EXASPERATE **2** : to make sore or inflamed — **ir·ri·tant** \'ir-ə-tənt\ *adj or n* — **ir·ri·tat·ing·ly** *adv* — **ir·ri·ta·tion** \,ir-ə-'tā-shən\ *n*
ir·rupt \(,)i-'rəpt\ *vb* **1** : to rush in forcibly or violently **2** : to increase suddenly in numbers ⟨rabbits ∼ in cycles⟩ — **ir·rup·tion** \-'rəp-shən\ *n*
IRS *abbr* Internal Revenue Service
is *pres 3d sing of* BE
Isa *or* **Is** *abbr* Isaiah
Isa·iah \ī-'zā-ə\ *n* — see BIBLE table
Isa·ias \ī-'zā-əs\ *n* : ISAIAH
ISBN *abbr* International Standard Book Number
-ish \ish\ *adj suffix* **1** : of, relating to, or being ⟨Finn*ish*⟩ **2** : characteristic of ⟨boy*ish*⟩ ⟨mul*ish*⟩ **3** : inclined or liable to ⟨book*ish*⟩ **4** : having a touch or trace of : somewhat ⟨purpl*ish*⟩ **5** : having the approximate age of ⟨forty*ish*⟩
isin·glass \'īz-ᵊn-,glas, 'ī-ziŋ-\ *n* **1** : a gelatin obtained from various fish **2** : mica esp. in thin sheets
isl *abbr* island
Is·lam \is-'läm, iz-, -'lam, 'is-,, 'iz-,\ *n* [Ar *islām* submission (to the will of God)] : the religious faith of Muslims; *also* : the civilization built on this faith — **Is·lam·ic** \is-'lä-mik, iz-, -'la-\ *adj*
Islamic calendar *n* : a calendar measured by the moon's revolution, reckoned from the Hegira in A.D. 622, and organized in cycles of 30 years
is·land \'ī-lənd\ *n* **1** : a body of land smaller than a continent surrounded by water **2** : something resembling an island in its isolation
is·land·er \'ī-lən-dər\ *n* : a native or inhabitant of an island
isle \'īl\ *n* : ISLAND; *esp* : a small island
is·let \'ī-lət\ *n* : a small island
ism \'i-zəm\ *n* : a distinctive doctrine, cause, or theory
-ism \,i-zəm\ *n suffix* **1** : act : practice : process ⟨criti*cism*⟩ **2** : manner of action or behavior characteristic of a (specified) person or thing ⟨fanatic*ism*⟩ **3** : state : con-

dition : property ⟨dual*ism*⟩ **4** : abnormal state or condition ⟨alcohol*ism*⟩ **5** : doctrine : theory : cult ⟨Buddh*ism*⟩ **6** : adherence to a set of principles ⟨stoi*cism*⟩ **7** : prejudice or discrimination on the basis of a (specified) attribute ⟨rac*ism*⟩ ⟨sex*ism*⟩ **8** : characteristic or peculiar feature or trait ⟨colloquial*ism*⟩
iso·bar \'ī-sə-,bär\ *n* : a line on a map connecting places of equal barometric pressure — **iso·bar·ic** \,ī-sə-'bär-ik, -'bar-\ *adj*
iso·late \'ī-sə-,lāt\ *vb* **-lat·ed; -lat·ing** [fr. *isolated* set apart, fr. F *isolé*, fr. It *isolato*, fr. *isola* island, fr. L *insula*] : to place or keep by itself : separate from others — **iso·la·tion** \,ī-sə-'lā-shən\ *n*
iso·lat·ed *adj* **1** : occurring alone or once : UNIQUE **2** : SPORADIC
iso·la·tion·ism \,ī-sə-'lā-shə-,ni-zəm\ *n* : a policy of national isolation by abstention from international political and economic relations — **iso·la·tion·ist** \-shə-nist\ *n or adj*
iso·mer \'ī-sə-mər\ *n* : any of two or more chemical compounds that contain the same numbers of atoms of the same elements but differ in structural arrangement and properties — **iso·mer·ic** \,ī-sə-'mer-ik\ *adj* — **isom·er·ism** \ī-'sä-mə-,ri-zəm\ *n*
iso·met·rics \,ī-sə-'me-triks\ *n sing or pl* : exercise involving a series of brief and intense contractions of muscles against each other or against an immovable resistance — **iso·met·ric** *adj*
iso·prene \'ī-sə-,prēn\ *n* : a hydrocarbon used esp. in making synthetic rubber
isos·ce·les \ī-'sä-sə-,lēz\ *adj* : having two equal sides ⟨an ∼ triangle⟩
iso·therm \'ī-sə-,thərm\ *n* : a line on a map connecting points having the same temperature
iso·ther·mal \,ī-sə-'thər-məl\ *adj* : of, relating to, or marked by equality of temperature
iso·tope \'ī-sə-,tōp\ *n* [Gk *isos* equal + *topos* place] : any of the forms of a chemical element that differ chiefly in the number of neutrons in an atom — **iso·to·pic** \,ī-sə-'tä-pik, -'tō-\ *adj* — **iso·to·pi·cal·ly** \-'tä-pi-k(ə-)lē, -'tō-\ *adv*
Isr *abbr* Israel; Israeli
Is·rae·li \iz-'rā-lē\ *n, pl* **Israelis** *also* **Israeli** : a native or inhabitant of Israel — **Israeli** *adj*
Is·ra·el·ite \'iz-rē-ə-,līt\ *n* : a member of the Hebrew people descended from Jacob
is·su·ance \'i-shü-wəns\ *n* : the act of issuing or giving out esp. officially
¹is·sue \'i-shü\ *n* **1** : the action of going, coming, or flowing out : EGRESS, EMERGENCE **2** : EXIT, OUTLET, VENT **3** : OFFSPRING, PROGENY **4** : OUTCOME, RESULT **5** : a point of debate or controversy; *also* : the point at which an unsettled matter is ready for a decision **6** : a discharge (as of blood) from the body **7** : something coming forth from a specified source **8** : the act of officially giving out or printing : PUBLICATION; *also* : the quantity of things given out at one time
²issue *vb* **is·sued; is·su·ing** **1** : to go, come, or flow out **2** : to come forth or cause to come forth : EMERGE, DISCHARGE, EMIT **3** : ACCRUE **4** : to descend from a specified parent or ancestor **5** : to result in **6** : to put forth or distribute officially **7** : PUBLISH **8** : EMANATE, RESULT — **is·su·er** *n*
¹-ist \ist\ *n suffix* **1** : one that performs a (specified) action ⟨cycl*ist*⟩ : one that makes or produces ⟨novel*ist*⟩ **2** : one that plays a (specified) musical instrument ⟨harp*ist*⟩ **3** : one that operates a (specified) mechanical instrument or contrivance ⟨machin*ist*⟩ **4** : one that specializes in a

---

\ə\abut \ᵊ\kitten \ər\further \a\ash \ā\ace \ä\mop, mar
\au̇\out \ch\chin \e\bet \ē\easy \g\go \i\hit \ī\ice \j\job
\ŋ\sing \ō\go \ȯ\law \ȯi\boy \th\thin \t̲h̲\the \ü\loot \u̇\foot
\y\yet \zh\vision *see also* Pronunciation Symbols page

(specified) art or science or skill ⟨geolog*ist*⟩ **5** : one that adheres to or advocates a (specified) doctrine or system or code of behavior ⟨social*ist*⟩ or that of a (specified) individual ⟨Darwin*ist*⟩

²-ist *adj suffix* : -ISTIC

isth·mi·an \'is-mē-ən\ *adj* : of, relating to, or situated in or near an isthmus

isth·mus \'is-məs\ *n* : a narrow strip of land connecting two larger portions of land

-is·tic \'is-tik\ *or* **-is·ti·cal** \'is-ti-kəl\ *adj suffix* : of, relating to, or characteristic of ⟨altru*istic*⟩

¹it \'it\ *pron* **1** : that one — used of a lifeless thing, a plant, a person or animal, or an abstract entity ⟨~'s a big building⟩ ⟨~'s a shade tree⟩ ⟨who is ~⟩ ⟨beauty is everywhere and ~ is a source of joy⟩ **2** — used as a subject of an impersonal verb that expresses a condition or action without reference to an agent ⟨~ is raining⟩ **3** — used as an anticipatory subject or object ⟨~'s good to see you⟩

²it \'it\ *n* : the player in a game who performs the principal action of the game (as trying to find others in hide=and-seek)

It *abbr* Italian; Italy

ital *abbr* italic; italicized

Ital *abbr* Italian

Ital·ian \i-'tal-yən\ *n* **1** : a native or inhabitant of Italy **2** : the language of Italy — **Italian** *adj*

ital·ic \i-'ta-lik, ī-\ *adj* : relating to type in which the letters slope up toward the right (as in *"italic"*) — **italic** *n*

ital·i·cize \i-'ta-lə-ˌsīz, ī-\ *vb* **-cized; -ciz·ing** : to print in italics

itch \'ich\ *n* **1** : an uneasy irritating skin sensation prob. related to sensing pain **2** : a skin disorder accompanied by an itch **3** : a persistent desire — **itch** *vb* — **itchy** *adj*

-ite \ˌīt\ *n suffix* **1** : native : resident ⟨suburban*ite*⟩ **2** : adherent : follower ⟨Lenin*ite*⟩ **3** : product ⟨metabol*ite*⟩ **4** : mineral : rock ⟨quartz*ite*⟩

item \'ī-təm\ *n* [L, likewise, also] **1** : a separate particular in a list, account, or series : ARTICLE **2** : a separate piece of news (as in a newspaper)

item·ize \'ī-tə-ˌmīz\ *vb* **-ized; -iz·ing** : to set down in detail : LIST — **item·i·za·tion** \ˌī-tə-mə-'zā-shən\ *n*

it·er·ate \'i-tə-ˌrāt\ *vb* **-at·ed; -at·ing** : REITERATE, REPEAT

it·er·a·tion \ˌi-tə-'rā-shən\ *n* **1** : REPETITION; *esp* : a computational process in which a series of operations is repeated until a condition is met **2** : one repetition of the series of operations in iteration

itin·er·ant \ī-'ti-nə-rənt, ə-\ *adj* : traveling from place to place; *esp* : covering a circuit ⟨an ~ preacher⟩

itin·er·ary \ī-'ti-nə-ˌrer-ē, ə-\ *n, pl* **-ar·ies 1** : the route of a journey or the proposed outline of one **2** : a travel diary **3** : GUIDEBOOK

its \'its\ *adj* : of or relating to it or itself

it·self \it-'self\ *pron* : that identical one — used reflexively, for emphasis, or in absolute constructions

-ity \ə-tē\ *n suffix* : quality : state : degree ⟨alkalin*ity*⟩

IUD \ˌī-(ˌ)yü-'dē\ *n* : INTRAUTERINE DEVICE

IV \ˌī-'vē\ *n* [intravenous] : an apparatus used to give an intravenous injection or feeding; *also* : such an injection or feeding

-ive \iv\ *adj suffix* : that performs or tends toward an (indicated) action ⟨correct*ive*⟩

ivo·ry \'ī-vrē, -və-rē\ *n, pl* **-ries** [ME *ivorie*, fr. OF *ivoire*, fr. L *eboreus* of ivory, fr. *ebur* ivory] **1** : the hard creamy-white material composing the tusks of an elephant or walrus **2** : a pale yellow color **3** : something made of ivory or of a similar substance

ivory tower *n* **1** : an impractical lack of concern with urgent problems **2** : a place of learning

ivy \'ī-vē\ *n, pl* **ivies** : a trailing woody evergreen vine with small black berries that is related to ginseng

IWW *abbr* Industrial Workers of the World

Iyar \'ē-ˌyär\ *n* [Heb *Iyyār*] : the 8th month of the civil year or the 2d month of the ecclesiastical year in the Jewish calendar

-ize \ˌīz\ *vb suffix* **1** : cause to be or conform to or resemble ⟨American*ize*⟩ : cause to be formed into ⟨union*ize*⟩ **2** : subject to a (specified) action ⟨satir*ize*⟩ **3** : saturate, treat, or combine with ⟨macadam*ize*⟩ **4** : treat like ⟨idol*ize*⟩ **5** : become : become like ⟨crystal*lize*⟩ **6** : be productive in or of : engage in a (specified) activity ⟨philosoph*ize*⟩ **7** : adopt or spread the manner of activity or the teaching of ⟨Christian*ize*⟩

J

¹j \'jā\ *n, pl* **j's** *or* **js** \'jāz\ *often cap* : the 10th letter of the English alphabet

²j *abbr, often cap* **1** jack **2** journal **3** judge **4** justice

¹jab \'jab\ *vb* **jabbed; jab·bing** : to thrust quickly or abruptly : POKE

²jab *n* : a usu. short straight punch

jab·ber \'ja-bər\ *vb* : to talk rapidly, indistinctly, or unintelligibly : CHATTER — **jabber** *n* — **jab·ber·er** *n*

jab·ber·wocky \'ja-bər-ˌwä-kē\ *n* : meaningless speech or writing

ja·bot \zha-'bō, 'ja-ˌbō\ *n* : a ruffle worn down the front of a dress or shirt

jac·a·ran·da \ˌja-kə-'ran-də\ *n* : any of a genus of pinnate-leaved tropical American trees with clusters of showy blue flowers

¹jack \'jak\ *n* **1** : a mechanical device; *esp* : one used to raise a heavy body a short distance **2** : a male donkey **3** : a small target ball in lawn bowling **4** : a small national flag flown by a ship **5** : a small 6-pointed metal object used in a game (**jacks**) **6** : a playing card bearing the figure of a soldier or servant **7** : a socket into which a plug is inserted for connecting electric circuits

²jack *vb* **1** : to raise by means of a jack **2** : INCREASE ⟨~ up prices⟩

jack·al \'ja-kəl\ *n* [Turk *çakal*, fr. Per *shagāl*] : any of several mammals of Asia and Africa related to the wolves

jack·a·napes \'ja-kə-ˌnāps\ *n* **1** : MONKEY, APE **2** : an impudent or conceited person

jack·ass \'jak-ˌas\ *n* **1** : DONKEY; *esp* : a male donkey **2** : a stupid person : FOOL

jack·boot \-ˌbüt\ *n* **1** : a heavy military boot of glossy black leather extending above the knee **2** : a laceless military boot reaching to the calf

jack·daw \'jak-ˌdò\ *n* : a black and gray Old World crowlike bird

jack·et \'ja-kət\ *n* [ME *jaket*, fr. MF *jaquet*, dim. of *jaque* short jacket, fr. *jacque* peasant, fr. the name *Jacques* James] **1** : a garment for the upper body usu. having a front opening, collar, and sleeves **2** : an outer covering or casing ⟨a book ~⟩

Jack Frost *n* : frost or frosty weather personified

jack·ham·mer \'jak-ˌha-mər\ *n* : a pneumatic percussion tool for drilling rock or breaking pavement

jack–in–the–box *n, pl* **jack–in–the–boxes** *or* **jacks–in–the–box** : a toy consisting of a small box out of which a figure springs when the lid is raised

jack–in–the–pulpit *n, pl* **jack–in–the–pulpits** *or* **jacks–in–the–pulpit** : an American spring-flowering woodland herb having an upright club-shaped spadix arched over by a green and purple spathe

¹**jack·knife** \'jak-ˌnīf\ *n* **1** : a large pocketknife **2** : a dive in which the diver bends from the waist and touches the ankles before straightening out

²**jackknife** *vb* : to fold like a jackknife ⟨the trailer truck *jackknifed*⟩

jack·leg \'jak-ˌleg\ *adj* **1** : lacking skill or training **2** : MAKESHIFT

jack–of–all–trades *n, pl* **jacks–of–all–trades** : one who is able to do passable work at various tasks

jack–o'–lan·tern \'ja-kə-ˌlan-tərn\ *n* : a lantern made of a pumpkin cut to look like a human face

jack·pot \'jak-ˌpät\ *n* **1** : a large sum of money formed by the accumulation of stakes from previous play (as in poker) **2** : an impressive and often unexpected success or reward

jack·rab·bit \-ˌra-bət\ *n* : any of several large hares of western No. America with very long ears and hind legs

jack·straw \-ˌstrȯ\ *n* **1** *pl* : a game in which straws or thin sticks are let fall in a heap and each player in turn tries to remove them one at a time without disturbing the rest **2** : one of the straws or sticks in jackstraws

jack·tar \-'tär\ *n, often cap* : SAILOR

Ja·cob's ladder \'jā-kəbz-\ *n* : any of several perennial herbs related to phlox that have pinnate leaves and blue or white bell-shaped flowers

jac·quard \'ja-ˌkärd\ *n, often cap* : a fabric of intricate variegated weave or pattern

¹**jade** \'jād\ *n* **1** : a broken-down, vicious, or worthless horse **2** : a disreputable woman

²**jade** *vb* **jad·ed; jad·ing 1** : to wear out by overwork or abuse **2** : to become weary **syn** exhaust, fatigue, tire

³**jade** *n* [F, fr. obs. Sp (*piedra de la*) *ijada*, lit., loin stone; fr. the belief that jade cures renal colic] : a usu. green gemstone that takes a high polish

jad·ed *adj* : dulled by a surfeit or excess

¹**jag** \'jag\ *n* : a sharp projecting part

²**jag** *n* : SPREE

jag·ged \'ja-gəd\ *adj* : sharply notched

jag·uar \'ja-ˌgwär\ *n* : a black-spotted tropical American cat that is larger and stockier than the Old World leopard

jaguar

jai alai \'hī-ˌlī\ *n* [Sp, fr. Basque, fr. *jai* festival + *alai* merry] : a court game played by usu. two or four players with a ball and a curved wicker basket strapped to the wrist

jail \'jāl\ *n* [ME *jaiole*, fr. OF, fr. LL *caveola*, dim. of L *cavea* cage] : PRISON; *esp* : one for persons held in lawful custody — **jail** *vb*

jail·bird \-ˌbərd\ *n* : an habitual criminal

jail·break \-ˌbrāk\ *n* : a forcible escape from jail

jail·er *or* **jail·or** \'jā-lər\ *n* : a keeper of a jail

jal·ap \'ja-ləp, 'jä-\ *n* : a powdered purgative drug from the root of a Mexican plant related to the morning glory; *also* : this root or plant

ja·la·pe·ño \ˌhä-lə-'pān-(ˌ)yō\ *n* : a Mexican hot pepper

ja·lopy \jə-'lä-pē\ *n, pl* **ja·lop·ies** : a dilapidated vehicle (as an automobile)

jal·ou·sie \'ja-lə-sē\ *n* [F, lit., jealousy] : a blind, window, or door with adjustable horizontal slats or louvers

¹**jam** \'jam\ *vb* **jammed; jam·ming 1** : to press into a close or tight position **2** : to cause to become wedged so as to be unworkable; *also* : to make or become unworkable through the jamming of a movable part **3** : to push forcibly ⟨∼ on the brakes⟩ **4** : CRUSH, BRUISE **5** : to make unintelligible by sending out interfering signals or messages **6** : to take part in a jam session — **jam·mer** *n*

²**jam** *n* **1** : a crowded mass that impedes or blocks ⟨traffic ∼⟩ **2** : a difficult state of affairs

³**jam** *n* : a food made by boiling fruit and sugar to a thick consistency

Jam *abbr* Jamaica

Ja·mai·can \jə-'mā-kən\ *n* : a native or inhabitant of Jamaica — **Jamaican** *adj*

jamb \'jam\ *n* [ME *jambe*, fr. MF, lit., leg] : an upright piece forming the side of an opening (as of a door)

jam·ba·laya \ˌjəm-bə-'lī-ə\ *n* [LaF] : rice cooked with ham, sausage, chicken, shrimp, or oysters and seasoned with herbs

jam·bo·ree \ˌjam-bə-'rē\ *n* : a large festive gathering

James \'jāmz\ *n* — see BIBLE table

jam–pack \'jam-'pak\ *vb* : to pack tightly or to excess

jam session *n* : an impromptu performance esp. by jazz musicians

Jan *abbr* January

jan·gle \'jaŋ-gəl\ *vb* **jan·gled; jan·gling** : to make a harsh or discordant sound — **jangle** *n*

jan·i·tor \'ja-nə-tər\ *n* [L, fr. *janua* door] : a person who has the care of a building — **jan·i·to·ri·al** \ˌja-nə-'tōr-ē-əl\ *adj*

Jan·u·ary \'ja-nyə-ˌwer-ē\ *n* [ME *Januarie*, fr. L *Januarius*, first month of the ancient Roman year, fr. *Janus*, two-faced god of gates and beginnings] : the 1st month of the year having 31 days

¹**ja·pan** \jə-'pan\ *n* : a varnish giving a hard brilliant finish

²**japan** *vb* **ja·panned; ja·pan·ning** : to cover with a coat of japan

Jap·a·nese \ˌja-pə-'nēz, -'nēs\ *n, pl* **Japanese 1** : a native or inhabitant of Japan **2** : the language of Japan — **Japanese** *adj*

Japanese beetle *n* : a small metallic green and brown scarab beetle introduced from Japan that is a pest on the roots of grasses as a grub and on foliage and fruits as an adult

¹**jape** \'jāp\ *vb* **japed; jap·ing 1** : JOKE **2** : MOCK

²**jape** *n* : JEST, GIBE

¹**jar** \'jär\ *vb* **jarred; jar·ring 1** : to make a harsh or discordant sound **2** : to have a harsh or disagreeable effect **3** : VIBRATE, SHAKE

²**jar** *n* **1** : a state of conflict **2** : a harsh discordant sound **3** : JOLT **4** : a painful effect : SHOCK

³**jar** *n* : a widemouthed container usu. of glass or earthenware

jar·di·niere \ˌjärd-ᵊn-'ir\ *n* : an ornamental stand for plants or flowers

jar·gon \'jär-gən\ *n* **1** : confused unintelligible language **2** : the special vocabulary of a particular group or activity **3** : obscure and often pretentious language

Jas *abbr* James

\ə\abut \ᵊ\kitten \ər\further \a\ash \ā\ace \ä\mop, mar
\aú\out \ch\chin \e\bet \ē\easy \g\go \i\hit \ī\ice \j\job
\ŋ\sing \ō\go \ȯ\law \ȯi\boy \th\thin \t̲h̲\the \ü\loot \ú\foot
\y\yet \zh\vision *see also* Pronunciation Symbols page

jas·mine \'jaz-mən\ *n* [F *jasmin,* fr. Ar *yāsamīn*] : any of various climbing shrubs with fragrant flowers

jas·per \'jas-pər\ *n* : a usu. red, yellow, or brown opaque quartz

jaun·dice \'jȯn-dəs\ *n* : yellowish discoloration of skin, tissues, and body fluids by bile pigments; *also* : an abnormal condition marked by jaundice

jaun·diced \-dəst\ *adj* **1** : affected with or as if with jaundice **2** : exhibiting envy, distaste, or hostility

jaunt \'jȯnt\ *n* : a short trip usu. for pleasure

jaun·ty \'jȯn-tē\ *adj* **jaun·ti·er; -est** : sprightly in manner or appearance : LIVELY — **jaun·ti·ly** \-tə-lē\ *adv* — **jaun·ti·ness** \-tē-nəs\ *n*

Ja·va·nese \ˌja-və-'nēz, ˌjä-, -'nēs\ *n* : a native or inhabitant of the Indonesian island of Java

jav·e·lin \'ja-və-lən\ *n* **1** : a light spear **2** : a slender shaft thrown for distance in a track-and-field contest

¹jaw \'jȯ\ *n* **1** : either of the bony or cartilaginous structures that support the soft tissues enclosing the mouth and that usu. bear teeth **2** : the parts forming the walls of the mouth and serving to open and close it — usu. used in pl. **3** : one of a pair of movable parts for holding or crushing something — **jawed** \'jȯd\ *adj*

²jaw *vb* : to talk abusively, indignantly, or at length

jaw·bone \-ˌbōn\ *n* : JAW 1

jaw·break·er \-ˌbrā-kər\ *n* **1** : a word difficult to pronounce **2** : a round hard candy

jay \'jā\ *n* : any of various noisy brightly colored often largely blue birds smaller than the related crows

jay·bird \'jā-ˌbərd\ *n* : JAY

jay·vee \ˌjā-'vē\ *n* **1** : JUNIOR VARSITY **2** : a member of a junior varsity team

jay·walk \'jā-ˌwȯk\ *vb* : to cross a street carelessly without regard for traffic regulations — **jay·walk·er** *n*

¹jazz \'jaz\ *n* **1** : American music characterized by improvisation, syncopated rhythms, and contrapuntal ensemble playing **2** : empty talk **3** : similar but unspecified things : STUFF

²jazz *vb* : ENLIVEN ⟨∼ things up⟩

jazzy \'ja-zē\ *adj* **jazz·i·er; -est 1** : having the characteristics of jazz **2** : marked by unrestraint, animation, or flashiness

JCS *abbr* joint chiefs of staff

jct *abbr* junction

JD *abbr* **1** [L *juris doctor*] doctor of jurisprudence; doctor of law **2** [L *jurum doctor*] doctor of laws **3** justice department **4** juvenile delinquent

jeal·ous \'je-ləs\ *adj* **1** : demanding complete devotion **2** : suspicious of a rival or of one believed to enjoy an advantage **3** : VIGILANT — **jeal·ous·ly** *adv* — **jeal·ou·sy** \-lə-sē\ *n*

jeans \'jēnz\ *n pl* [pl. of *jean* twilled cloth, short for *jean fustian,* fr. ME *Gene* Genoa, Italy] : pants made of durable twilled cotton cloth

jeep \'jēp\ *n* [prob. fr. *g.p.* (abbr. of *general purpose*)] : a small four-wheel drive general-purpose motor vehicle used in World War II

¹jeer \'jir\ *vb* : to speak or cry out in derision : MOCK

²jeer *n* : TAUNT

Je·ho·vah \ji-'hō-və\ *n* : GOD 1

je·hu \'jē-hü, -hyü\ *n* : a driver of a coach or cab

je·june \ji-'jün\ *adj* [L *jejunus* empty of food, hungry, meager] : lacking interest or significance : DULL

je·ju·num \ji-'jü-nəm\ *n* [L] : the section of the small intestine between the duodenum and the ileum — **je·ju·nal** \-'jün-ᵊl\ *adj*

jell \'jel\ *vb* **1** : to come to the consistency of jelly **2** : to take shape

jel·ly \'je-lē\ *n, pl* **jellies 1** : a food with a soft elastic consistency due usu. to the presence of gelatin or pectin; *esp* : a fruit product made by boiling sugar and the juice of a fruit **2** : a substance resembling jelly — **jelly** *vb*

jelly bean *n* : a bean-shaped candy

jel·ly·fish \'je-lē-ˌfish\ *n* : a coelenterate with a saucer-shaped jellylike body

jen·net \'je-nət\ *n* **1** : a small Spanish horse **2** : a female donkey

jen·ny \'je-nē\ *n, pl* **jennies** : a female bird or donkey

jeop·ar·dy \'je-pər-dē\ *n* [ME *jeopardie,* fr. OF *jeu parti* alternative, lit., divided game] : exposure to death, loss, or injury **syn** peril, hazard, risk, danger — **jeop·ar·dize** \-ˌdīz\ *vb*

Jer *abbr* Jeremiah; Jeremias

jer·e·mi·ad \ˌjer-ə-'mī-əd, -ˌad\ *n* : a prolonged lamentation or complaint; *also* : a cautionary or angry harangue

Jer·e·mi·ah \ˌjer-ə-'mī-ə\ *n* — see BIBLE table

Jer·e·mi·as \ˌjer-ə-'mī-əs\ *n* : JEREMIAH

¹jerk \'jərk\ *n* **1** : a short quick pull or twist : TWITCH **2** : an annoyingly stupid or foolish person — **jerk·i·ly** \'jər-kə-lē\ *adv* — **jerky** \'jər-kē\ *adj*

²jerk *vb* **1** : to give a sharp quick push, pull, or twist **2** : to move in short abrupt motions

jer·kin \'jər-kən\ *n* : a close-fitting usu. sleeveless jacket

jerk·wa·ter \'jərk-ˌwȯ-tər, -ˌwä-\ *adj* [fr. *jerkwater* rural train] : of minor importance : INSIGNIFICANT ⟨∼ towns⟩

jer·ry–built \'jer-ē-ˌbilt\ *adj* : built cheaply and flimsily

jer·sey \'jər-zē\ *n, pl* **jerseys** [*Jersey,* one of the Channel islands] **1** : a plain weft-knitted fabric **2** : a close-fitting knitted shirt **3** *often cap* : any of a breed of small usu. fawn-colored dairy cattle

jess \'jes\ *n* : a leg strap by which a captive bird of prey may be controlled

jes·sa·mine \'je-sə-mən\ *var of* JASMINE

jest \'jest\ *n* **1** : an act intended to provoke laughter **2** : a witty remark **3** : a frivolous mood ⟨said in ∼⟩ — **jest** *vb*

jest·er \'jes-tər\ *n* : a retainer formerly kept to provide casual entertainment

¹jet \'jet\ *n* : a velvet-black coal that takes a good polish and is often used for jewelry

²jet *vb* **jet·ted; jet·ting** : to spout or emit in a stream

³jet *n* **1** : a forceful rush (as of liquid or gas) through a narrow opening; *also* : a nozzle for a jet of fluid **2** : a jet-propelled airplane

⁴jet *vb* **jet·ted; jet·ting** : to travel by jet

jet lag *n* : a condition that is marked esp. by fatigue and irritability and occurs following a long flight through several time zones — **jet–lagged** *adj*

jet·lin·er \'jet-ˌlī-nər\ *n* : a jet-propelled airliner

jet·port \-ˌpȯrt\ *n* : an airport designed to handle jets

jet–propelled \ˌjet-prə-'peld\ *adj* : driven by an engine (**jet engine**) that produces propulsion (**jet propulsion**) by the rearward discharge of a jet of fluid (as heated air and exhaust gases)

jet·sam \'jet-səm\ *n* : jettisoned goods; *esp* : such goods washed ashore

jet set *n* : an international group of wealthy people who frequent fashionable resorts

jet stream *n* : a long narrow high-altitude current of high-speed winds blowing generally from the west

jet·ti·son \'je-tə-sən\ *vb* **1** : to throw (goods) overboard to lighten a ship or aircraft in distress **2** : DISCARD — **jettison** *n*

jet·ty \'je-tē\ *n, pl* **jetties 1** : a pier built to influence the current or to protect a harbor **2** : a landing wharf

jeu d'es·prit \zhœ-des-'prē\ *n, pl* **jeux d'esprit** *same*\ [F, lit., play of the mind] : a witty comment or composition

Jew \'jü\ *n* **1** : ISRAELITE **2** : one whose religion is Judaism — **Jew·ish** *adj*

¹jew·el \'jü-əl\ *n* [ME *juel,* fr. OF, prob. dim. of *jeu* game, play, fr. L *jocus* game, joke] **1** : an ornament of precious metal **2** : GEMSTONE, GEM

²jewel *vb* **-eled** *or* **-elled; -el·ing** *or* **-el·ling** : to adorn or equip with jewels

jew·el·er *or* **jew·el·ler** \'jü-ə-lər\ *n* : a person who makes or deals in jewelry and related articles

jew·el·lery *chiefly Brit var of* JEWELRY

jew·el·ry \'jü-əl-rē\ *n* : JEWELS; *esp* : objects of precious metal set with gems and worn for personal adornment

Jewish calendar *n* : a calendar in use among Jewish people that is reckoned from the year 3761 B.C. and dates in its present form from about A.D. 360

JEWISH YEARS 5754–5773

JEWISH YEAR		A.D.
5754	begins	Sept. 16, 1993
5755	begins	Sept. 6, 1994
5756	begins	Sept. 25, 1995
5757	begins	Sept. 14, 1996
5758	begins	Oct. 2, 1997
5759	begins	Sept. 21, 1998
5760	begins	Sept. 11, 1999
5761	begins	Sept. 30, 2000
5762	begins	Sept. 18, 2001
5763	begins	Sept. 7, 2002
5764	begins	Sept. 27, 2003
5765	begins	Sept. 16, 2004
5766	begins	Oct. 4, 2005
5767	begins	Sept. 23, 2006
5768	begins	Sept. 13, 2007
5769	begins	Sept. 30, 2008
5770	begins	Sept. 19, 2009
5771	begins	Sept. 9, 2010
5772	begins	Sept. 29, 2011
5773	begins	Sept. 17, 2012

Jew·ry \'jùr-ē, 'jü-ər-ē, 'jü-rē\ *n* : the Jewish people

jg *abbr* junior grade

¹jib \'jib\ *n* : a triangular sail set on a line running from the bow to the mast

²jib *vb* **jibbed; jib·bing** : to refuse to proceed further

jibe \'jib\ *vb* **jibed; jib·ing** : to be in accord : AGREE

jif·fy \'ji-fē\ *n, pl* **jiffies** : MOMENT, INSTANT ⟨I'll be ready in a ∼⟩

¹jig \'jig\ *n* **1** : a lively dance in triple rhythm **2** : TRICK, GAME ⟨the ∼ is up⟩ **3** : a device used to hold work during manufacture or assembly

²jig *vb* **jigged; jig·ging** : to dance a jig

jig·ger \'ji-gər\ *n* : a measure usu. holding 1 to 2 ounces (30 to 60 milliliters) used in mixing drinks

jig·gle \'ji-gol\ *vb* **jig·gled; jig·gling** : to move with quick little jerks — **jiggle** *n*

jig·saw \'jig-₁sò\ *n* : a machine saw with a narrow vertically reciprocating blade for cutting curved lines

jigsaw puzzle *n* : a puzzle consisting of small irregularly cut pieces to be fitted together to form a picture

ji·had \ji-'häd, -'had\ *n* **1** : a Muslim holy war **2** : CRUSADE 2

¹jilt \'jilt\ *vb* : to drop (a lover) capriciously or unfeelingly

²jilt *n* : one who jilts a lover

jim crow \'jim-'krō\ *n, often cap J&C* : discrimination against blacks esp. by legal enforcement or traditional sanctions — **jim crow** *adj, often cap J&C* — **jim crow·ism** \-'krō-₁i-zəm\ *n, often cap J&C*

jim–dan·dy \'jim-'dan-dē\ *n* : something excellent of its kind

jim·mies \'ji-mēz\ *n pl* : tiny rod-shaped bits of usu. chocolate-flavored candy often sprinkled on ice cream

¹jim·my \'ji-mē\ *n, pl* **jimmies** : a small crowbar

²jimmy *vb* **jim·mied; jim·my·ing** : to force open with a jimmy

jim·son·weed \'jim-sən-₁wēd\ *n, often cap* : a coarse poisonous weed related to the tomato that has large trumpet-shaped white or violet flowers

¹jin·gle \'jiŋ-gəl\ *vb* **jin·gled; jin·gling** : to make a light clinking or tinkling sound

²jingle *n* **1** : a light clinking or tinkling sound **2** : a short verse or song with catchy repetition

jin·go·ism \'jiŋ-gō-₁i-zəm\ *n* : extreme chauvinism or nationalism marked esp. by a belligerent foreign policy — **jin·go·ist** \-ist\ *n* — **jin·go·is·tic** \₁jiŋ-gō-'is-tik\ *adj*

jin·rik·sha \jin-'rik-₁shò\ *n* : RICKSHA

¹jinx \'jiŋks\ *n* : one that brings bad luck

²jinx *vb* : to foredoom to failure or misfortune

jit·ney \'jit-nē\ *n, pl* **jitneys** : a small bus that serves a regular route on a flexible schedule

jit·ter·bug \'ji-tər-₁bəg\ *n* : a dance in which couples two-step, balance, and twirl vigorously in standardized patterns — **jitterbug** *vb*

jit·ters \'ji-tərz\ *n pl* : extreme nervousness — **jit·tery** \-tə-rē\ *adj*

¹jive \'jīv\ *n* **1** : swing music or dancing performed to it **2** : glib, deceptive, or foolish talk **3** : the jargon of jazz enthusiasts

²jive *vb* **jived; jiv·ing 1** : KID, TEASE **2** : to dance to or play jive

Jn *or* **Jno** *abbr* John

Jo *abbr* Joel

¹job \'jäb\ *n* **1** : a piece of work **2** : something that has to be done : TASK **3** : a regular remunerative position — **job·less** *adj*

²job *vb* **jobbed; job·bing 1** : to do occasional pieces of work for hire **2** : to hire or let by the job

Job \'jōb\ *n* — see BIBLE table

job action *n* : a protest action by workers to force compliance with demands

job·ber \'jä-bər\ *n* **1** : a person who buys goods and then sells them to other dealers : MIDDLEMAN **2** : a person who does work by the job

job·hold·er \'jäb-₁hōl-dər\ *n* : one having a regular job

jock \'jäk\ *n* [*jockstrap*] : ATHLETE; *esp* : a college athlete

¹jock·ey \'jä-kē\ *n, pl* **jockeys** : one who rides a horse esp. as a professional in a race

²jockey *vb* **jock·eyed; jock·ey·ing** : to maneuver or manipulate by adroit or devious means

jock·strap \'jäk-₁strap\ *n* [E slang *jock* penis] : ATHLETIC SUPPORTER

jo·cose \jō-'kōs\ *adj* : MERRY, HUMOROUS **syn** jocular, facetious, witty

joc·u·lar \'jä-kyə-lər\ *adj* : marked by jesting : PLAYFUL — **joc·u·lar·i·ty** \₁jäk-yə-'lar-ə-tē\ *n* — **joc·u·lar·ly** *adv*

jo·cund \'jä-kənd\ *adj* : marked by mirth or cheerfulness

jodh·pur \'jäd-pər\ *n* **1** *pl* : riding breeches loose above the knee and tight-fitting below **2** : an ankle-high boot fastened with a strap

Jo·el \'jō-əl\ *n* — see BIBLE table

¹jog \'jäg\ *vb* **jogged; jog·ging 1** : to give a slight shake or push to **2** : to go at a slow monotonous pace **3** : to run or ride at a slow trot — **jog·ger** *n*

²jog *n* **1** : a slight shake **2** : a jogging movement or pace

³jog *n* **1** : a projecting or retreating part of a line or surface **2** : a brief abrupt change in direction

jog·gle \'jä-gəl\ *vb* **jog·gled; jog·gling** : to shake slightly — **joggle** *n*

john \'jän\ *n* **1** : TOILET **2** : a prostitute's client

John \'jän\ *n* — see BIBLE table

john·ny \'jä-nē\ *n, pl* **johnnies** : a short-sleeved gown opening in the back that is worn by hospital patients

John·ny–jump–up \₁jä-nē-'jəmp-₁əp\ *n* : any of various small-flowered cultivated pansies

\ə\abut \ᵊ\kitten \ər\further \a\ash \ā\ace \ä\mop, mar \aù\out \ch\chin \e\bet \ē\easy \g\go \i\hit \ī\ice \j\job \ŋ\sing \ō\go \ò\law \òi\boy \th\thin \t̲h̲\the \ü\loot \ù\foot \y\yet \zh\vision *see also* Pronunciation Symbols page

joie de vi·vre \‚zhwä-də-'vēvrᵃ\ *n* [F] : keen enjoyment of life

join \'jȯin\ *vb* **1** : to come or bring together so as to form a unit **2** : to come or bring into close association **3** : to become a member of **4** : ADJOIN **5** : to take part in a collective activity

join·er \'jȯi-nər\ *n* **1** : a worker who constructs articles by joining pieces of wood **2** : a gregarious person who joins many organizations

¹**joint** \'jȯint\ *n* **1** : the point of contact between bones of an animal skeleton with the parts that surround and support it **2** : a cut of meat suitable for roasting **3** : a place where two things or parts are connected **4** : ESTABLISHMENT; *esp* : a shabby or disreputable establishment **5** : a marijuana cigarette — **joint·ed** *adj*

²**joint** *adj* **1** : UNITED **2** : common to two or more — **joint·ly** *adv*

³**joint** *vb* **1** : to unite by or provide with a joint **2** : to separate the joints of

joist \'jȯist\ *n* : any of the small beams ranged parallel from wall to wall in a building to support a floor or ceiling

¹**joke** \'jōk\ *n* : something said or done to provoke laughter; *esp* : a brief narrative with a humorous climax

²**joke** *vb* **joked; jok·ing** : to make jokes — **jok·ing·ly** *adv*

jok·er \'jō-kər\ *n* **1** : a person who jokes **2** : an extra card used in some card games **3** : a misleading part of an agreement that works to one party's disadvantage

jol·li·fi·ca·tion \‚jä-li-fə-'kā-shən\ *n* : a festive celebration

jol·li·ty \'jä-lə-tē\ *n, pl* **-ties** : GAIETY, MERRIMENT

jol·ly \'jä-lē\ *adj* **jol·li·er; -est** : full of high spirits : MERRY

¹**jolt** \'jōlt\ *vb* **1** : to give a quick hard knock or blow to **2** : to move with a sudden jerky motion — **jolt·er** *n*

²**jolt** *n* **1** : an abrupt jerky blow or movement **2** : a sudden shock

Jon *abbr* Jonah; Jonas

Jo·nah \'jō-nə\ *n* — see BIBLE table

Jo·nas \'jō-nəs\ *n* : JONAH

jon·gleur \zhōⁿ-'glər\ *n* : an itinerant medieval minstrel

jon·quil \'jän-kwəl\ *n* [F *jonquille,* fr. Sp *junquillo,* dim. of *junco* reed, fr. L *juncus*] : a narcissus with fragrant clustered white or yellow flowers

Jor·da·ni·an \jȯr-'dā-nē-ən\ *n* : a native or inhabitant of Jordan — **Jordanian** *adj*

josh \'jäsh\ *vb* : TEASE, JOKE

Josh *abbr* Joshua

Josh·ua \'jä-shů-ə\ *n* — see BIBLE table

Joshua tree *n* : a tall branched yucca of the southwestern U.S.

jos·tle \'jä-səl\ *vb* **jos·tled; jos·tling 1** : to come in contact or into collision **2** : to make one's way by pushing and shoving

Jos·ue \'jä-shů-ē\ *n* : JOSHUA

¹**jot** \'jät\ *n* : the least bit : IOTA

²**jot** *vb* **jot·ted; jot·ting** : to write briefly and hurriedly

jot·ting \'jä-tiŋ\ *n* : a brief note

joule \'jül\ *n* : a unit of work or energy equal to the work done by a force of one newton acting through a distance of one meter

jounce \'jaůns\ *vb* **jounced; jounc·ing** : JOLT — **jounce** *n*

jour *abbr* **1** journal **2** journeyman

jour·nal \'jərn-ᵊl\ *n* [ME, service book containing the day hours, fr. MF, fr. *journal* daily, fr. L *diurnalis,* fr. *dies* day] **1** : a brief account of daily events **2** : a record of proceedings (as of a legislative body) **3** : a periodical (as a newspaper) dealing esp. with current events **4** : the part of a rotating axle or spindle that turns in a bearing

jour·nal·ese \‚jər-nə-'lēz, -'lēs\ *n* : a style of writing held to be characteristic of newspapers

jour·nal·ism \'jər-nə-‚li-zəm\ *n* **1** : the business of writing for, editing, or publishing periodicals (as newspapers) **2** : writing designed for or characteristic of newspapers — **jour·nal·ist** \-list\ *n* — **jour·nal·is·tic** \‚jər-nə-'lis-tik\ *adj*

¹**jour·ney** \'jər-nē\ *n, pl* **journeys** [ME, fr. OF *journee* day's journey, fr. *jour* day] : a traveling from one place to another

²**journey** *vb* **jour·neyed; jour·ney·ing** : to go on a journey : TRAVEL

jour·ney·man \-mən\ *n* **1** : a worker who has learned a trade and works for another person **2** : an experienced reliable worker

¹**joust** \'jaůst\ *vb* : to engage in a joust

²**joust** *n* : a combat on horseback between two knights with lances esp. as part of a tournament

jo·vial \'jō-vē-əl\ *adj* : marked by good humor — **jo·vi·al·i·ty** \‚jō-vē-'a-lə-tē\ *n* — **jo·vi·al·ly** *adv*

¹**jowl** \'jaůl\ *n* : loose flesh about the lower jaw or throat

²**jowl** *n* **1** : the lower jaw **2** : CHEEK

¹**joy** \'jȯi\ *n* [ME, fr. OF *joie,* fr. L *gaudia*] **1** : a feeling of happiness that comes from success, good fortune, or a sense of well-being **2** : a source of happiness **syn** bliss, delight, enjoyment, pleasure — **joy·less** *adj*

²**joy** *vb* : REJOICE

joy·ful \-fəl\ *adj* : experiencing, causing, or showing joy — **joy·ful·ly** *adv*

joy·ous \'jȯi-əs\ *adj* : JOYFUL — **joy·ous·ly** *adv* — **joy·ous·ness** *n*

joy·ride \'jȯi-‚rīd\ *n* : a ride for pleasure often marked by reckless driving — **joyride** *vb* — **joy·rid·er** *n* — **joy·rid·ing** *n*

joy·stick \-‚stik\ *n* : a control device (as for a computer display) consisting of a lever capable of motion in two or more directions

JP *abbr* **1** jet propulsion **2** justice of the peace

Jr *abbr* junior

jt *or* **jnt** *abbr* joint

ju·bi·lant \'jü-bə-lənt\ *adj* [L *jubilans,* prp. of *jubilare* to rejoice] : EXULTANT — **ju·bi·lant·ly** *adv*

ju·bi·la·tion \‚jü-bə-'lā-shən\ *n* : EXULTATION

ju·bi·lee \'jü-bə-‚lē, ‚jü-bə-'lē\ *n* [ME, fr. MF & LL; MF *jubilé,* fr. LL *jubilaeus,* fr. LGk *iōbēlaios,* fr. Heb *yōbhēl* ram's horn, trumpet, jubilee] **1** : a 50th anniversary **2** : a season or occasion of celebration

Jud *abbr* Judith

Ju·da·ic \jü-'dā-ik\ *also* **Ju·da·ical** \-'dā-ə-kəl\ *adj* : of, relating to, or characteristic of Jews or Judaism

Ju·da·ism \'jü-də-‚i-zəm, -dä-, -dē-\ *n* : a religion developed among the ancient Hebrews and marked by belief in one God and by the moral and ceremonial laws of the Old Testament and the rabbinic tradition

Jude \'jüd\ *n* — see BIBLE table

Judg *abbr* Judges

¹**judge** \'jəj\ *vb* **judged; judg·ing 1** : to form an authoritative opinion **2** : to decide as a judge : TRY **3** : to form an estimate or evaluation about something : THINK **syn** conclude, deduce, gather, infer

²**judge** *n* **1** : a public official authorized to decide questions brought before a court **2** : UMPIRE **3** : one who gives an authoritative opinion : CRITIC — **judge·ship** *n*

Judges *n* — see BIBLE table

judg·ment *or* **judge·ment** \'jəj-mənt\ *n* **1** : a decision or opinion given after judging; *esp* : a formal decision given by a court **2** *cap* : the final judging of mankind by God **3** : the process of forming an opinion by discerning and comparing **4** : the capacity for judging : DISCERNMENT

judg·men·tal \‚jəj-'men-təl\ *adj* **1** : of, relating to, or involving judgment **2** : characterized by a tendency to judge harshly — **judg·men·tal·ly** *adv*

Judgment Day *n* : the day of the final judging of all human beings by God

ju·di·ca·ture \'jü-di-kə-ˌchùr\ *n* **1** : the administration of justice **2** : JUDICIARY 1

ju·di·cial \jù-'di-shəl\ *adj* **1** : of or relating to the administration of justice or the judiciary **2** : ordered or enforced by a court **3** : CRITICAL — **ju·di·cial·ly** *adv*

ju·di·cia·ry \jù-'di-shē-ˌer-ē, -shə-rē\ *n* **1** : a system of courts of law; *also* : the judges of these courts **2** : a branch of government in which judicial power is vested — **judiciary** *adj*

ju·di·cious \jù-'di-shəs\ *adj* : having, exercising, or characterized by sound judgment **syn** prudent, sage, sane, sensible, wise — **ju·di·cious·ly** *adv*

Ju·dith \'jü-dəth\ *n* — see BIBLE table

ju·do \'jü-dō\ *n* [Jp, fr. *jū* weakness + *dō* art] : a sport derived from jujitsu that emphasizes the use of quick movement and leverage to throw an opponent — **ju·do·ist** \-ist\ *n*

¹jug \'jəg\ *n* **1** : a large deep container with a narrow mouth and a handle **2** : JAIL, PRISON

²jug *vb* **jugged; jug·ging** : JAIL, IMPRISON

jug·ger·naut \'jə-gər-ˌnot\ *n* [Hindi *Jagannāth*, title of Vishnu (a Hindu god), lit., lord of the world] : a massive inexorable force or object that crushes everything in its path

jug·gle \'jə-gəl\ *vb* **jug·gled; jug·gling** **1** : to keep several objects in motion in the air at the same time **2** : to manipulate esp. in order to achieve a desired and often fraudulent end — **jug·gler** \'jə-glər\ *n*

jug·u·lar \'jə-gyə-lər\ *adj* : of, relating to, or situated in or on the throat or neck ⟨the ~ veins⟩

juice \'jüs\ *n* **1** : the extractable fluid contents of cells or tissues **2** *pl* : the natural fluids of an animal body **3** : something that supplies power; *esp* : ELECTRICITY **2**

juic·er \'jü-sər\ *n* : an appliance for extracting juice (as from fruit)

juice up *vb* : to give life, energy, or spirit to

juicy \'jü-sē\ *adj* **juic·i·er; -est** **1** : SUCCULENT **2** : rich in interest; *also* : RACY — **juic·i·ly** \-sə-lē\ *adv* — **juic·i·ness** \-sē-nəs\ *n*

ju·jit·su *or* **ju·jut·su** \jü-'jit-sü\ *n* [Jp *jūjutsu*, fr. *jū* weakness + *jutsu* art, skill] : an art of fighting employing holds, throws, and paralyzing blows

ju·jube \'jü-ˌjüb, 'jü-jü-ˌbē\ *n* : a fruit-flavored gumdrop or lozenge

juke·box \'jük-ˌbäks\ *n* : a coin-operated machine that automatically plays selected recordings

Jul *abbr* July

ju·lep \'jü-ləp\ *n* [ME, sweetened water, fr. MF, fr. Ar *julāb*, fr. Per *gulāb*, fr. *gul* rose + *āb* water] : a drink made of bourbon, sugar, and mint served over crushed ice

Ju·ly \jù-'lī\ *n* [ME *Julie*, fr. OE *Julius*, fr. L, fr. Gaius *Julius* Caesar] : the 7th month of the year having 31 days

Ju·ma·da \jù-'ma-də\ *n* [Ar *Jumāda*] **1** : the 5th month of the Islamic year **2** : the 6th month of the Islamic year

¹jum·ble \'jəm-bəl\ *vb* **jum·bled; jum·bling** : to mix in a confused mass

²jumble *n* : a disorderly mass or pile

jum·bo \'jəm-bō\ *n, pl* **jumbos** [*Jumbo*, a huge elephant exhibited by P.T. Barnum] : a very large specimen of its kind — **jumbo** *adj*

¹jump \'jəmp\ *vb* **1** : to spring into the air : leap over **2** : to give a start **3** : to rise or increase suddenly or sharply **4** : to make a sudden attack **5** : ANTICIPATE ⟨~ the gun⟩ **6** : to leave hurriedly and often furtively ⟨~ town⟩ **7** : to act or move before (as a signal) — **jump bail** : to abscond after being released from custody on bail — **jump ship** **1** : to leave the company of a ship without authority **2** : to desert a cause

²jump *n* **1** : a spring into the air; *esp* : one made for height or distance in a track meet **2** : a sharp sudden increase **3** : an initial advantage

¹jump·er \'jəm-pər\ *n* : one that jumps

²jumper *n* **1** : a loose blouse **2** : a sleeveless one-piece dress worn usu. with a blouse **3** *pl* : a child's sleeveless coverall

jumping bean *n* : a seed of any of several Mexican shrubs that tumbles about because of the movements of a small moth larva inside it

jumping-off place *n* **1** : a remote or isolated place **2** : a place from which an enterprise is launched

jump–start \'jəmp-ˌstärt\ *vb* : to start (an engine or vehicle) by connection to an external power source

jump·suit \'jəmp-ˌsüt\ *n* **1** : a coverall worn by parachutists in jumping **2** : a one-piece garment consisting of a blouse or shirt with attached trousers or shorts

jumpy \'jəm-pē\ *adj* **jump·i·er; -est** : NERVOUS, JITTERY

jun *abbr* junior

Jun *abbr* June

junc *abbr* junction

jun·co \'jəŋ-kō\ *n, pl* **juncos** *or* **juncoes** : any of a genus of small common pink-billed American finches that are largely gray with conspicuous white feathers in the tail

junc·tion \'jəŋk-shən\ *n* **1** : an act of joining **2** : a place or point of meeting

junc·ture \'jeŋk-chər\ *n* **1** : JOINT, CONNECTION **2** : UNION **3** : a critical time or state of affairs

June \'jün\ *n* [ME, fr. L *Junius*] : the 6th month of the year having 30 days

jun·gle \'jəŋ-gəl\ *n* **1** : a thick tangled mass of tropical vegetation; *also* : a tract overgrown with vegetation **2** : a place of ruthless struggle for survival

¹ju·nior \'jü-nyər\ *adj* **1** : YOUNGER **2** : lower in rank **3** : of or relating to juniors

²junior *n* **1** : a person who is younger or of lower rank than another **2** : a student in the next-to-last year before graduating

junior college *n* : a school that offers studies corresponding to those of the 1st two years of college

junior high school *n* : a school usu. including grades 7–9

junior varsity *n* : a team whose members lack the experience or qualifications required for the varsity

ju·ni·per \'jü-nə-pər\ *n* : any of numerous coniferous shrubs or trees with leaves like needles or scales and female cones like berries

¹junk \'jəŋk\ *n* **1** : old iron, glass, paper, or waste; *also* : discarded articles **2** : a shoddy product **3** *slang* : NARCOTICS; *esp* : HEROIN — **junky** *adj*

²junk *vb* : DISCARD, SCRAP

³junk *n* : a ship of eastern Asia with a high stern and 4-cornered sails

junk

junk·er \'jəŋ-kər\ *n* : something (as an old automobile) ready for scrapping

Jun·ker \'yüŋ-kər\ *n* [G] : a member of the Prussian landed aristocracy

jun·ket \'jəŋ-kət\ *n* 1 : a pudding of sweetened flavored milk set by rennet 2 : a trip made by an official at public expense

junk food *n* : food that is high in calories but low in nutritional content

junk·ie *also* **junky** \'jəŋ-kē\ *n, pl* **junkies** 1 *slang* : a narcotics peddler or addict 2 : one that derives inordinate pleasure from or is dependent on something ⟨sugar ∼⟩

jun·ta \'hün-tə, 'jən-, 'hən-\ *n* [Sp, fr. *junto* joined, fr. L *junctus*, pp. of *jungere* to join] : a group of persons controlling a government esp. after a revolutionary seizure of power

Ju·pi·ter \'jü-pə-tər\ *n* : the largest of the planets and the one 5th in order of distance from the sun — see PLANET table

Ju·ras·sic \ju̇-'ra-sik\ *adj* : of, relating to, or being the period of the Mesozoic era between the Triassic and the Cretaceous that is marked esp. by the presence of dinosaurs — **Jurassic** *n*

ju·rid·i·cal \ju̇-'ri-di-kəl\ *or* **ju·rid·ic** \-dik\ *adj* 1 : of or relating to the administration of justice 2 : LEGAL — **ju·rid·i·cal·ly** \-di-k(ə-)lē\ *adv*

ju·ris·dic·tion \ju̇r-əs-'dik-shən\ *n* 1 : the power, right, or authority to interpret and apply the law 2 : the authority of a sovereign power 3 : the limits or territory within which authority may be exercised — **ju·ris·dic·tion·al** \-shə-nəl\ *adj*

ju·ris·pru·dence \-'prüd-ᵊns\ *n* 1 : a system of laws 2 : the science or philosophy of law

ju·rist \'ju̇r-ist\ *n* : one having a thorough knowledge of law; *esp* : JUDGE

ju·ris·tic \ju̇-'ris-tik\ *adj* 1 : of or relating to a jurist or jurisprudence 2 : of, relating to, or recognized in law

ju·ror \'ju̇r-ər, -ˌȯr\ *n* : a member of a jury

¹ju·ry \'ju̇r-ē\ *n, pl* **juries** 1 : a body of persons sworn to inquire into a matter submitted to them and to give their verdict 2 : a committee for judging and awarding prizes

²jury *adj* : improvised for temporary use esp. in an emergency ⟨a ∼ mast⟩

jury–rig \'ju̇r-ē-ˌrig\ *vb* : to construct or arrange in a makeshift fashion

¹just \'jəst\ *adj* 1 : having a basis in or conforming to fact or reason : REASONABLE ⟨∼ comment⟩ 2 : CORRECT, PROPER ⟨∼ proportions⟩ 3 : morally or legally right ⟨a ∼ title⟩ 4 : DESERVED, MERITED ⟨∼ punishment⟩ **syn** upright, honorable, conscientious, honest — **just·ly** *adv* — **just·ness** *n*

²just \'jəst, 'jist\ *adv* 1 : EXACTLY ⟨∼ right⟩ 2 : very recently ⟨has ∼ left⟩ 3 : BARELY ⟨∼ too late⟩ 4 : DIRECTLY ⟨∼ west of here⟩ 5 : ONLY ⟨∼ last year⟩ 6 : QUITE ⟨∼ wonderful⟩ 7 : POSSIBLY ⟨it ∼ might work⟩

jus·tice \'jəs-təs\ *n* 1 : the administration of what is just (as by assigning merited rewards or punishments) 2 : JUDGE 3 : the administration of law 4 : FAIRNESS; *also* : RIGHTEOUSNESS

justice of the peace : a local magistrate empowered chiefly to try minor cases, to administer oaths, and to perform marriages

jus·ti·fy \'jəs-tə-ˌfī\ *vb* **-fied; -fy·ing** 1 : to prove to be just, right, or reasonable 2 : to pronounce free from guilt or blame 3 : to adjust spaces in a line of printed text so the margins are even — **jus·ti·fi·able** *adj* — **jus·ti·fi·ca·tion** \ˌjəs-tə-fə-'kā-shən\ *n*

jut \'jət\ *vb* **jut·ted; jut·ting** : PROJECT, PROTRUDE

jute \'jüt\ *n* : a strong glossy fiber from either of two tropical plants used esp. for making sacks and twine

juv *abbr* juvenile

¹ju·ve·nile \'jü-və-ˌnīl, -nəl\ *adj* 1 : showing incomplete development 2 : of, relating to, or characteristic of children or young people

²juvenile *n* 1 : a young person; *esp* : one below the legally established age of adulthood 2 : a young animal (as a fish or a bird) or plant 3 : an actor or actress who plays youthful parts

juvenile delinquency *n* : violation of the law or antisocial behavior by a juvenile — **juvenile delinquent** *n*

jux·ta·pose \'jək-stə-ˌpōz\ *vb* **-posed; -pos·ing** : to place side by side — **jux·ta·po·si·tion** \ˌjək-stə-pə-'zi-shən\ *n*

JV *abbr* junior varsity

K

¹k \'kā\ *n, pl* **k's** *or* **ks** \'kāz\ 1 *often cap* : the 11th letter of the English alphabet 2 *cap* : STRIKEOUT

²k *abbr* 1 karat 2 kitchen 3 knit 4 kosher — often enclosed in a circle

¹K *abbr* Kelvin

²K *symbol* [NL *kalium*] potassium

ka·bob \kə-'bäb, 'kā-ˌbäb\ *n* : cubes of meat cooked with vegetables usu. on a skewer

Ka·bu·ki \kə-'bü-kē\ *n* : traditional Japanese popular drama with highly stylized singing and dancing

kad·dish \'kä-dish\ *n, often cap* : a Jewish prayer recited in the daily synagogue ritual and by mourners at public services after the death of a close relative

kaf·fee·klatsch \'kȯ-fē-ˌklach, 'kä-\ *n, often cap* [G] : an informal social gathering for coffee and conversation

kai·ser \'kī-zər\ *n* : EMPEROR; *esp* : the ruler of Germany from 1871 to 1918

kale \'kāl\ *n* : a hardy cabbage with curled leaves that do not form a head

ka·lei·do·scope \kə-'lī-də-ˌskōp\ *n* : a tube containing loose bits of colored material (as glass) and two mirrors at one end that shows many different patterns as it is turned — **ka·lei·do·scop·ic** \-ˌlī-də-'skä-pik\ *adj* — **ka·lei·do·scop·i·cal·ly** \-pi-k(ə-)lē\ *adv*

ka·ma·ai·na \ˌkä-mə-'ī-nə\ *n* [Hawaiian *kama'āina*, fr. *kama* child + *'āina* land] : one who has lived in Hawaii for a long time

kame \'kām\ *n* [Sc, lit., comb] : a short ridge or mound of material deposited by water from a melting glacier

ka·mi·ka·ze \ˌkä-mi-'kä-zē\ *n* [Jp, lit., divine wind] : a member of a corps of Japanese pilots assigned to make a suicidal crash on a target; *also* : an airplane flown in such an attack

Kan *or* **Kans** *abbr* Kansas

kan·ga·roo \ˌkaŋ-gə-'rü\ *n, pl* **-roos** : any of various large leaping marsupial mammals of Australia and adjacent islands with powerful hind legs and a long thick tail

kangaroo court *n* : a court or an illegal self-appointed tribunal characterized by irresponsible, perverted, or irregular procedures

ka·o·lin \'kā-ə-lən\ *n* : a fine usu. white clay used in ceramics and refractories and for the treatment of diarrhea

ka·pok \\'kā-ˌpäk\ *n* : silky fiber from the seeds of a tropical tree used esp. as a filling (as for life preservers)

Kap·o·si's sar·co·ma \\'ka-pə-sēz-sär-'kō-mə\ *n* : a neoplastic disease associated esp. with AIDS that affects esp. the skin and mucous membranes and is characterized usu. by the formation of pink to reddish-brown or bluish plaques

kap·pa \\'ka-pə\ *n* : the 10th letter of the Greek alphabet — K or κ

ka·put *also* **ka·putt** \kä-'pùt, kə-, -'püt\ *adj* [G, fr. F *capot* not having made a trick at piquet] **1** : utterly defeated or destroyed **2** : unable to function : USELESS

kar·a·kul \\'kar-ə-kəl\ *n* : the dark tightly curled pelt of the newborn lamb of a hardy Asian breed of sheep

kar·at \\'kar-ət\ *n* : a unit for expressing proportion of gold in an alloy equal to ¹⁄₂₄ part of pure gold

ka·ra·te \kə-'rä-tē\ *n* [Jp, lit., empty hand] : an art of self=defense in which an attacker is disabled by crippling kicks and punches

kar·ma \\'kär-mə\ *n, often cap* [Skt] : the force generated by a person's actions held in Hinduism and Buddhism to perpetuate reincarnation and to determine the nature of the person's next existence — **kar·mic** \-mik\ *adj*

karst \\'kärst\ *n* [G] : an irregular limestone region with sinks, underground streams, and caverns

ka·ty·did \\'kä-tē-ˌdid\ *n* : any of several large green tree=dwelling American grasshoppers with long antennae

kay·ak \\'kī-ˌak\ *n* : an Eskimo canoe made of a skin=covered frame with a small opening and propelled by a double-bladed paddle; *also* : a similar portable boat

kayo \(ˌ)kā-'o, 'ka-o\ *n* : KNOCKOUT — **kayo** *vb*

ka·zoo \kə-'zü\ *n, pl* **kazoos** : a toy musical instrument consisting of a tube with a membrane sealing one end and a side hole to sing or hum into

KB *abbr* kilobyte

kc *abbr* kilocycle

KC *abbr* **1** Kansas City **2** King's Counsel **3** Knights of Columbus

kc/s *abbr* kilocycles per second

KD *abbr* knocked down

ke·bab *or* **ke·bob** \kə-'bäb\ *var of* KABOB

kedge \\'kej\ *n* : a small anchor

¹keel \\'kēl\ *n* **1** : the chief structural member of a ship running lengthwise along the center of its bottom **2** : something (as a bird's breastbone) like a ship's keel in form or use — **keeled** \\'kēld\ *adj*

²keel *vb* : FAINT, SWOON — usu. used with *over*

keel·boat \\'kēl-ˌbōt\ *n* : a shallow covered keeled riverboat for freight that is usu. rowed, poled, or towed

keel·haul \-ˌhȯl\ *vb* : to haul under the keel of a ship as punishment

¹keen \\'kēn\ *adj* **1** : SHARP ⟨a ∼ knife⟩ **2** : SEVERE ⟨a ∼ wind⟩ **3** : ENTHUSIASTIC ⟨∼ about swimming⟩ **4** : mentally alert ⟨a ∼ mind⟩ **5** : STRONG, ACUTE ⟨∼ eyesight⟩ **6** : WONDERFUL, EXCELLENT — **keen·ly** *adv* — **keen·ness** *n*

²keen *n* : a lamentation for the dead uttered in a loud wailing voice or in a wordless cry — **keen** *vb*

¹keep \\'kēp\ *vb* **kept** \\'kept\; **keep·ing** **1** : FULFILL, OBSERVE ⟨∼ a promise⟩ ⟨∼ a holiday⟩ **2** : GUARD ⟨∼ us from harm⟩; *also* : to take care of ⟨∼ a neighbor's children⟩ **3** : MAINTAIN ⟨∼ silence⟩ **4** : to have in one's service or at one's disposal ⟨∼ a horse⟩ **5** : to preserve a record in ⟨∼ a diary⟩ **6** : to have in stock for sale **7** : to retain in one's possession ⟨∼ what you find⟩ **8** : to carry on (as a business) : CONDUCT **9** : HOLD, DETAIN ⟨∼ him in jail⟩ **10** : to refrain from revealing ⟨∼ a secret⟩ **11** : to continue in good condition ⟨meat will ∼ in a freezer⟩ **12** : ABSTAIN, REFRAIN — **keep·er** *n*

²keep *n* **1** : FORTRESS **2** : the means or provisions by which one is kept — **for keeps** **1** : with the provision that one keep what one has won ⟨play marbles *for keeps*⟩ **2** : PERMANENTLY

keep·ing *n* : CONFORMITY ⟨in ∼ with good taste⟩

keep·sake \\'kēp-ˌsāk\ *n* : MEMENTO

keep up *vb* **1** : to persevere in **2** : MAINTAIN, SUSTAIN **3** : to keep informed **4** : to continue without interruption

keg \\'keg\ *n* : a small cask or barrel

keg·ler \\'ke-glər\ *n* : ¹BOWLER

kelp \\'kelp\ *n* : any of various coarse brown seaweeds; *also* : a mass of these or their ashes often used as fertilizer

Kelt \\'kelt\ *var of* CELT

kel·vin \\'kel-vən\ *n* : a unit of temperature equal to ¹⁄₂₇₃.₁₆ of the Kelvin scale temperature of the triple point of water and equal to the Celsius degree

Kelvin *adj* : relating to, conforming to, or being a temperature scale according to which absolute zero is 0 K, the equivalent of −273.15°C

ken \\'ken\ *n* **1** : range of vision : SIGHT **2** : range of understanding

ken·nel \\'ken-ᵊl\ *n* : a shelter for a dog or cat; *also* : an establishment for the breeding or boarding of dogs or cats — **kennel** *vb*

ke·no \\'kē-nō\ *n* : a game resembling bingo

Ken·tucky bluegrass \kən-'tə-kē-\ *n* : a valuable pasture and meadow grass of both Europe and America

Ke·nyan \\'ke-nyən, 'kē-\ *n* : a native or inhabitant of Kenya — **Kenyan** *adj*

Ke·ogh plan \\'kē-(ˌ)ō-\ *n* [Eugene James *Keogh* †1989 Am. politician] : an individual retirement account for the self-employed

ke·pi \\'kā-pē, 'ke-\ *n* [F] : a military cap with a round flat top and a visor

ker·a·tin \\'ker-ət-ᵊn\ *n* : any of various sulfur-containing proteins that make up hair and horny tissues

kerb \\'kərb\ *n, Brit* : CURB 3

ker·chief \\'kər-chəf, -ˌchēf\ *n, pl* **kerchiefs** \-chəfs, -ˌchēfs\ *also* **kerchieves** \-ˌchēvz\ [ME *courchef*, fr. OF *cuevrechief*, fr. *covrir* to cover + *chief* head] **1** : a square of cloth worn by women esp. as a head covering **2** : HANDKERCHIEF

kerf \\'kərf\ *n* : a slit or notch made by a saw or cutting torch

ker·nel \\'kərn-ᵊl\ *n* **1** : the inner softer part of a seed, fruit stone, or nut **2** : a whole seed of a cereal ⟨a ∼ of corn⟩ **3** : a central or essential part : CORE

ker·o·sene *or* **ker·o·sine** \\'ker-ə-ˌsēn, ˌker-ə-'sēn\ *n* : a flammable oil produced from petroleum and used for a fuel and as a solvent

ketch \\'kech\ *n* : a large fore-and-aft rigged boat with two masts

ketch·up \\'ke-chəp, 'ka-\ *n* : a seasoned tomato puree

ket·tle \\'ket-ᵊl\ *n* : a metallic vessel for boiling liquids

ket·tle·drum \-ˌdrəm\ *n* : a brass, copper, or fiberglass drum with calfskin or plastic stretched across the top

¹key \\'kē\ *n* **1** : a usu. metal instrument by which the bolt of a lock is turned; *also* : a device having the form or function of a key **2** : a means of gaining or preventing entrance, possession, or control **3** : EXPLANATION, SOLUTION **4** : one of the levers pressed by a finger in operating or playing an instrument **5** : a leading individual or principle **6** : a system of seven tones based on their relationship to a tonic; *also* : the tone or pitch of a voice **7** : a small switch for opening or closing an electric circuit ⟨a telegraph ∼⟩

²key *vb* **1** : SECURE, FASTEN **2** : to regulate the musical pitch of **3** : to bring into harmony or conformity **4** : to make nervous — usu. used with *up*

³key *adj* : BASIC, CENTRAL ⟨∼ issues⟩

\ə\abut \ᵊ\kitten \ər\further \a\ash \ā\ace \ä\mop, mar \aù\out \ch\chin \e\bet \ē\easy \g\go \i\hit \ī\ice \j\job \ŋ\sing \ō\go \ȯ\law \ȯi\boy \th\thin \t͟h\the \ü\loot \ù\foot \y\yet \zh\vision *see also* Pronunciation Symbols page

⁴key *n* : a low island or reef (as off the southern coast of Florida)

⁵key *n, slang* : a kilogram esp. of marijuana or heroin

key·board \-₁bōrd\ *n* **1** : a row of keys (as on a piano) **2** : an assemblage of keys for operating a machine

key club *n* : a private club serving liquor and providing entertainment

key·hole \'kē-₁hōl\ *n* : a hole for receiving a key

¹key·note \-₁nōt\ *n* **1** : the first and harmonically fundamental tone of a scale **2** : the central fact, idea, or mood

²keynote *vb* **1** : to set the keynote of **2** : to deliver the major address (as at a convention) — **key·not·er** *n*

key·punch \'kē-₁pənch\ *n* : a machine with a keyboard used to cut holes or notches in punch cards — **key·punch** *vb* — **key·punch·er** *n*

key·stone \-₁stōn\ *n* : the wedge-shaped piece at the crown of an arch that locks the other pieces in place

key·stroke \-₁strōk\ *n* : an act or instance of depressing a key on a keyboard

key word *n* : a word that is a key; *esp, usu* **key·word** : a significant word used as an indication of the content of or in searching (as a document or database)

kg *abbr* kilogram

KGB *abbr* [Russ *Komitet gosudarstvennoĭ bezopasnosti*] (Soviet) State Security Committee

kha·ki \'ka-kē, 'kä-\ *n* [Hindi *khaki* dust-colored, fr. *khāk* dust, fr. Per] **1** : a light yellowish brown color **2** : a khaki-colored cloth; *also* : a military uniform of this cloth

khan \'kän, 'kan\ *n* : a Mongol leader; *esp* : a successor of Genghis Khan

khe·dive \kə-'dēv\ *n* : a ruler of Egypt from 1867 to 1914 governing as a viceroy of the sultan of Turkey

khoum \'küm\ *n* — see *ouguiya* at MONEY table

kHz *abbr* kilohertz

KIA *abbr* killed in action

kib·ble \'ki-bəl\ *vb* **kib·bled; kib·bling** : to grind coarsely — **kibble** *n*

kib·butz \ki-'buts, -'büts\ *n, pl* **kib·but·zim** \-₁but-'sēm, -₁büt-\ [NHeb *qibbūṣ*] : a communal farm or settlement in Israel

ki·bitz·er \'ki-bət-sər, kə-'bit-\ *n* : one who looks on and usu. offers unwanted advice esp. at a card game — **kib·itz** \'ki-bəts\ *vb*

ki·bosh \'kī-₁bäsh\ *n* : something that serves as a check or stop ⟨put the ∼ on his plan⟩

¹kick \'kik\ *vb* **1** : to strike out or hit with the foot; *also* : to score by kicking a ball **2** : to object strongly **3** : to recoil when fired — **kick·er** *n*

²kick *n* **1** : a blow or thrust with the foot; *esp* : a propelling of a ball with the foot **2** : the recoil of a gun **3** : a feeling or expression of objection **4** : stimulating effect esp. of pleasure

kick·back \'kik-₁bak\ *n* **1** : a sharp violent reaction **2** : a secret return of a part of a sum received

kick in *vb* **1** : CONTRIBUTE **2** *slang* : DIE

kick·off \'kik-₁òf\ *n* **1** : a kick that puts the ball in play (as in football) **2** : COMMENCEMENT

kick off *vb* **1** : to start or resume play with a placekick **2** : to begin proceedings **3** *slang* : DIE

kick over *vb* : to begin or cause to begin to fire — used of an internal combustion engine

kick·shaw \'kik-₁shò\ *n* [modif. of F *quelque chose* something] **1** : DELICACY **2** : TRINKET

kick·stand \'kik-₁stand\ *n* : a swiveling metal bar attached to a 2-wheeled vehicle for holding it up when not in use

kicky \'ki-kē\ *adj* : providing a kick or thrill : EXCITING

¹kid \'kid\ *n* **1** : a young goat **2** : the flesh, fur, or skin of a young goat; *also* : something made of kid **3** : CHILD, YOUNGSTER — **kid·dish** *adj*

²kid *vb* **kid·ded; kid·ding 1** : FOOL **2** : TEASE — **kid·der** *n* — **kid·ding·ly** *adv*

kid·nap \'kid-₁nap\ *vb* **kid·napped** *or* **kid·naped** \-₁napt\; **kid·nap·ping** *or* **kid·nap·ing** \-₁na-piŋ\ : to hold or carry a person away by unlawful force or by fraud and against one's will — **kid·nap·per** *or* **kid·nap·er** \-₁na-pər\ *n*

kid·ney \'kid-nē\ *n, pl* **kidneys** : either of a pair of organs lying near the backbone that excrete waste products of the body in the form of urine

kidney bean *n* **1** : an edible seed of the common cultivated bean; *esp* : one that is large and dark red **2** : a plant bearing kidney beans

kid·skin \'kid-₁skin\ *n* : the skin of a young goat used for leather

kiel·ba·sa \kēl-'bä-sə, kil-\ *n, pl* **-basas** *also* **-ba·sy** \-'bä-sē\ [Pol *kiełbasa*] : a smoked sausage of Polish origin

¹kill \'kil\ *vb* **1** : to deprive of life **2** : to put an end to ⟨∼ competition⟩; *also* : DEFEAT ⟨∼ a proposed amendment⟩ **3** : USE UP ⟨∼ time⟩ **4** : to mark for omission **syn** slay, murder, assassinate, execute — **kill·er** *n*

²kill *n* **1** : an act of killing **2** : an animal or animals killed (as in a hunt); *also* : an aircraft, ship, or vehicle destroyed by military action

kill·deer \'kil-₁dir\ *n, pl* **killdeers** *or* **killdeer** [imit.] : an American plover with a plaintive penetrating cry

killdeer

killer bee *n* : AFRICANIZED BEE

killer whale *n* : a small gregarious black and white flesh-eating whale with a white oval patch behind each eye

kill·ing *n* : a sudden notable gain or profit

kill·joy \'kil-₁jòi\ *n* : one who spoils the pleasures of others

kiln \'kil, 'kiln\ *n* : a heated enclosure (as an oven) for processing a substance by burning, firing, or drying — **kiln** *vb*

ki·lo \'kē-lō\ *n, pl* **kilos** : KILOGRAM

ki·lo·byte \'ki-lə-₁bīt, 'kē-\ *n* : 1024 bytes

kilo·cy·cle \'ki-lə-₁sī-kəl\ *n* : KILOHERTZ

ki·lo·gram \'kē-lə-₁gram, 'ki-\ *n* **1** : the basic metric unit of mass that is nearly equal to the mass of 1000 cubic centimeters of water at its maximum density — see METRIC SYSTEM table **2** : the weight of a kilogram mass under earth's gravity

ki·lo·hertz \'ki-lə-₁hərts, 'kē-, -₁herts\ *n* : 1000 hertz

kilo·li·ter \'ki-lə-₁lē-tər\ *n* — see METRIC SYSTEM table

ki·lo·me·ter \ki-'lä-mə-tər, 'ki-lə-₁mē-\ *n* — see METRIC SYSTEM table

ki·lo·ton \'ki-lə-₁tən, 'kē-lō-\ *n* **1** : 1000 tons **2** : an explosive force equivalent to that of 1000 tons of TNT

ki·lo·volt \-₁vōlt\ *n* : 1000 volts

kilo·watt \'ki-lə-₁wät\ *n* : 1000 watts

kilowatt–hour *n* : a unit of energy equal to that expended by one kilowatt in one hour

kilt \'kilt\ *n* : a knee-length pleated skirt usu. of tartan worn by men in Scotland

kil·ter \'kil-tər\ *n* : proper condition ⟨out of ∼⟩

ki·mo·no \kə-'mō-nə\ *n, pl* **-nos 1** : a loose robe with wide sleeves traditionally worn with a wide sash as an outer garment by the Japanese **2** : a loose dressing gown or jacket

kin \'kin\ *n* **1** : an individual's relatives **2** : KINSMAN

ki·na \'kē-nə\ *n* — see MONEY table

¹kind \'kīnd\ *n* **1** : essential quality or character **2** : a group united by common traits or interests : CATEGORY; *also* : VARIETY **3** : goods or commodities as distinguished from money

²kind *adj* **1** : of a sympathetic, forbearing, or pleasant nature **2** : arising from sympathy or forbearance ⟨∼ deeds⟩ **syn** benevolent, benign, benignant, kindly — **kind·ness** *n*

kin·der·gar·ten \'kin-dər-₁gärt-°n\ *n* [Ger, lit., children's garden] : a school or class for children usu. from four to six years old

kin·der·gart·ner \-₁gärt-nər\ *n* **1** : a kindergarten pupil **2** : a kindergarten teacher

kind·heart·ed \₁kīnd-'här-təd\ *adj* : marked by a sympathetic nature

kin·dle \'kind-°l\ *vb* **kin·dled; kin·dling 1** : to set on fire : start burning **2** : to stir up : AROUSE **3** : ILLUMINATE, GLOW

kin·dling \'kind-liŋ, 'kin-lən\ *n* : easily combustible material for starting a fire

¹kind·ly \'kīnd-lē\ *adj* **kind·li·er; -est 1** : of an agreeable or beneficial nature **2** : of a sympathetic or generous nature — **kind·li·ness** *n*

²kindly *adv* **1** : READILY ⟨does not take ∼ to criticism⟩ **2** : SYMPATHETICALLY **3** : COURTEOUSLY, OBLIGINGLY

kind of *adv* : to a moderate degree ⟨it's *kind of* late to begin⟩

¹kin·dred \'kin-drəd\ *n* **1** : a group of related individuals **2** : one's relatives

²kindred *adj* : of a like nature or character

kine \'kīn\ *archaic pl of* COW

kin·e·ma \'ki-nə-mə\ *Brit var of* CINEMA

ki·ne·mat·ics \₁ki-nə-'ma-tiks\ *n* : a science that deals with motion apart from considerations of mass and force — **ki·ne·mat·ic** \-tik\ *or* **ki·ne·mat·i·cal** \-ti-kəl\ *adj*

kin·es·the·sia \₁ki-nəs-'thē-zhə, -zhē-ə\ *or* **kin·es·the·sis** \-'thē-səs\ *n, pl* **-the·sias** *or* **-the·ses** \-₁sēz\ : a sense that perceives bodily movement, position, and weight and is mediated by nervous elements in tendons, muscles, and joints; *also* : sensory experience derived from this sense — **kin·es·thet·ic** \-'the-tik\ *adj*

ki·net·ic \kə-'ne-tik\ *adj* : of or relating to the motion of material bodies and the forces and energy (**kinetic energy**) associated with them

ki·net·ics \-tiks\ *n sing or pl* : a science that deals with the effects of forces upon the motions of material bodies or with changes in a physical or chemical system

kin·folk \'kin-₁fōk\ *or* **kinfolks** *n pl* : RELATIVES

king \'kiŋ\ *n* **1** : a male sovereign **2** : a chief among competitors ⟨home-run ∼⟩ **3** : the principal piece in the game of chess **4** : a playing card bearing the figure of a king **5** : a checker that has been crowned — **king·less** *adj* — **king·ly** *adj* — **king·ship** *n*

king crab *n* **1** : HORSESHOE CRAB **2** : a large crab of the north Pacific caught commercially for food

king·dom \'kiŋ-dəm\ *n* **1** : a country whose head is a king or queen **2** : a realm or region in which something or someone is dominant ⟨a cattle ∼⟩ **3** : one of the three primary divisions of lifeless material, plants, and animals into which natural objects are grouped; *also* : a biological category that ranks above the phylum

king·fish·er \-₁fi-shər\ *n* : any of numerous usu. brightcolored crested birds that feed chiefly on fish

king·pin \'kiŋ-₁pin\ *n* **1** : HEADPIN **2** : the leader in a group or undertaking

Kings *n* — see BIBLE table

king–size \'kiŋ-₁sīz\ *or* **king–sized** \-₁sīzd\ *adj* **1** : longer than the regular or standard size **2** : unusually large **3** : having dimensions of about 76 by 80 inches (1.9 by 2.0 meters) ⟨a ∼ bed⟩; *also* : of a size that fits a king-size bed

kink \'kiŋk\ *n* **1** : a short tight twist or curl **2** : a mental peculiarity : QUIRK **3** : CRAMP ⟨a ∼ in the back⟩ **4** : an imperfection likely to cause difficulties in operation — **kinky** *adj*

kin·ship \'kin-₁ship\ *n* : RELATIONSHIP

kins·man \'kinz-mən\ *n* : RELATIVE; *esp* : a male relative

kins·wom·an \-₁wu̇-mən\ *n* : a female relative

ki·osk \'kē-₁äsk\ *n* : a small structure with one or more open sides

Ki·o·wa \'kī-ə-₁wȯ, -₁wä, -₁wā\ *n, pl* **Kiowa** *or* **Kiowas** : a member of an American Indian people of Colorado, Kansas, New Mexico, Oklahoma, and Texas

kip \'kip, 'gip\ *n, pl* **kip** *or* **kips** — see MONEY table

kip·per \'ki-pər\ *n* : a fish (as a herring) preserved by salting and drying or smoking — **kipper** *vb*

kirk \'kərk, 'kirk\ *n, chiefly Scot* : CHURCH

kir·tle \'kərt-°l\ *n* : a long gown or dress worn by women

Kis·lev \'kis-ləf\ *n* [Heb *Kislēw*] : the 3d month of the civil year or the 9th month of the ecclesiastical year in the Jewish calendar

kis·met \'kiz-₁met, -mət\ *n, often cap* [Turk, fr. Ar *qismah* portion, lot] : FATE

¹kiss \'kis\ *vb* **1** : to touch or caress with the lips as a mark of affection or greeting **2** : to touch gently or lightly

²kiss *n* **1** : a caress with the lips **2** : a gentle touch or contact **3** : a bite-size candy

kiss·er \'ki-sər\ *n* **1** : one that kisses **2** *slang* : MOUTH **3** *slang* : FACE

kit \'kit\ *n* **1** : a set of articles for personal use; *also* : a set of tools or implements or of parts to be assembled **2** : a container (as a case) for a kit

kitch·en \'ki-chən\ *n* **1** : a room with cooking facilities **2** : the personnel that prepares, cooks, and serves food

kitch·en·ette \₁ki-chə-'net\ *n* : a small kitchen or an alcove containing cooking facilities

kitchen police *n* **1** : KP **2** : the work of KPs

kitch·en·ware \'ki-chən-₁war\ *n* : utensils and appliances for kitchen use

kite \'kīt\ *n* **1** : any of various long-winged hawks often with deeply forked tails **2** : a light frame covered with paper or cloth and designed to be flown in the air at the end of a long string

kith \'kith\ *n* [ME, fr. OE *cȳthth*, fr. *cūth* known] : familiar friends, neighbors, or relatives ⟨∼ and kin⟩

kitsch \'kich\ *n* [G] : shoddy or cheap artistic or literary material — **kitschy** *adj*

kit·ten \'kit-°n\ *n* : a young cat — **kit·ten·ish** *adj*

¹kit·ty \'ki-tē\ *n, pl* **kitties** : CAT; *esp* : KITTEN

²kitty *n, pl* **kitties** : a fund in a poker game made up of contributions from each pot; *also* : POOL

kit·ty–cor·ner *or* **kit·ty–cor·nered** *var of* CATERCORNER

ki·wi \'kē-(₁)wē\ *n* : any of a small genus of flightless New Zealand birds

☞ For illustration, see next page.

ki·wi·fruit \-₁früt\ *n* : a brownish hairy egg-shaped fruit of a subtropical vine that has sweet bright green flesh and small edible black seeds

KJV *abbr* King James Version

KKK *abbr* Ku Klux Klan

kl *abbr* kiloliter

klatch *or* **klatsch** \'klach\ *n* [G *Klatsch* gossip] : a gathering marked by informal conversation

\ə\abut \ᵊ\kitten \ər\further \a\ash \ā\ace \ä\mop, mar \au̇\out \ch\chin \e\bet \ē\easy \g\go \i\hit \ī\ice \j\job \ŋ\sing \ō\go \ȯ\law \ȯi\boy \th\thin \th̲\the \ü\loot \u̇\foot \y\yet \zh\vision *see also* Pronunciation Symbols page

kiwi

klep·to·ma·nia \ˌklep-tə-ˈmä-nē-ə\ *n* : a persistent neurotic impulse to steal esp. without economic motive — **klep·to·ma·ni·ac** \-nē-ˌak\ *n*

klieg light *or* **kleig light** \ˈklēg-\ *n* : a very bright lamp used in making motion pictures

klutz \ˈkləts\ *n* [Yiddish *klots*, lit., wooden beam] : a clumsy person — **klutzy** *adj*

km *abbr* kilometer

kn *abbr* knot

knack \ˈnak\ *n* 1 : a clever way of doing something 2 : natural aptitude

knap·sack \ˈnap-ˌsak\ *n* : a bag (as of canvas) strapped on the back and used esp. for carrying supplies

knave \ˈnāv\ *n* 1 : ROGUE 2 : JACK 6 — **knav·ery** \ˈnā-və-rē\ *n* — **knav·ish** \ˈnā-vish\ *adj*

knead \ˈnēd\ *vb* : to work and press into a mass with the hands; *also* : MASSAGE — **knead·er** *n*

knee \ˈnē\ *n* : the joint in the middle part of the leg — **kneed** \ˈnēd\ *adj*

knee·cap \ˈnē-ˌkap\ *n* : a thick flat movable bone forming the front of the knee

knee·hole \-ˌhōl\ *n* : a space (as under a desk) for the knees

kneel \ˈnēl\ *vb* **knelt** \ˈnelt\ *or* **kneeled; kneel·ing** : to bend the knee : fall or rest on the knees

¹knell \ˈnel\ *vb* 1 : to ring esp. for a death or disaster 2 : to summon, announce, or proclaim by a knell

²knell *n* 1 : a stroke of a bell esp. when tolled (as for a funeral) 2 : an indication of the end or failure of something

knew *past of* KNOW

knick·ers \ˈni-kərz\ *n pl* : loose-fitting short pants gathered at the knee

knick·knack \ˈnik-ˌnak\ *n* : a small trivial article intended for ornament

¹knife \ˈnīf\ *n, pl* **knives** \ˈnīvz\ 1 : a cutting instrument consisting of a sharp blade fastened to a handle 2 : a sharp cutting tool in a machine

²knife *vb* **knifed; knif·ing** : to stab, slash, or wound with a knife

¹knight \ˈnīt\ *n* 1 : a mounted warrior of feudal times serving a king 2 : a man honored by a sovereign for merit and in Great Britain ranking below a baronet 3 : a man devoted to the service of a lady 4 : a member of an order or society 5 : a chess piece having an L-shaped move — **knight·ly** *adj*

²knight *vb* : to make a knight of

knight·hood \ˈnīt-ˌhùd\ *n* 1 : the rank, dignity, or profession of a knight 2 : CHIVALRY 3 : knights as a class or body

knish \kə-ˈnish\ *n* [Yiddish] : a small round or square of dough stuffed with a filling (as of meat or fruit) and baked or fried

¹knit \ˈnit\ *vb* **knit** *or* **knit·ted; knit·ting** 1 : to link firmly or closely 2 : WRINKLE ⟨~ her brows⟩ 3 : to form a fabric by interlacing yarn or thread in connected loops with needles 4 : to grow together — **knit·ter** *n*

²knit *n* 1 : a basic knitting stitch 2 : a knitted garment or fabric

knit·wear \-ˌwar\ *n* : knitted clothing

knob \ˈnäb\ *n* 1 : a rounded protuberance; *also* : a small rounded ornament or handle 2 : a rounded usu. isolated hill — **knobbed** \ˈnäbd\ *adj* — **knob·by** \ˈnä-bē\ *adj*

¹knock \ˈnäk\ *vb* 1 : to strike with a sharp blow 2 : BUMP, COLLIDE 3 : to make a pounding noise; *esp* : to have engine knock 4 : to find fault with

²knock *n* 1 : a sharp blow 2 : a pounding noise; *esp* : one caused by abnormal ignition in an automobile engine

knock·down \ˈnäk-ˌdaùn\ *n* 1 : the action of knocking down 2 : something (as a blow) that knocks down 3 : something that can be easily assembled or disassembled

knock down *vb* 1 : to strike to the ground with or as if with as sharp blow 2 : to take apart : DISASSEMBLE 3 : to receive as income or salary : EARN 4 : to make a reduction in

knock·er \ˈnä-kər\ *n* : one that knocks; *esp* : a device hinged to a door for use in knocking

knock–knee \ˈnäk-ˌnē\ *n* : a condition in which the legs curve inward at the knees — **knock–kneed** \-ˌnēd\ *adj*

knock·off \ˈnäk-ˌòf\ *n* : a copy or imitation of someone or something popular

knock off *vb* 1 : to stop doing something 2 : to do quickly, carelessly, or routinely 3 : to deduct from a price 4 : KILL 5 : ROB 6 : COPY, IMITATE

knock·out \ˈnäk-ˌaùt\ *n* 1 : a blow that fells and immobilizes an opponent (as in boxing) 2 : something sensationally striking or attractive

knock out *vb* 1 : to defeat by a knockout 2 : to make unconscious or inoperative 3 : to tire out : EXHAUST

knock·wurst *or* **knack·wurst** \ˈnäk-ˌwərst, -ˌvùrst\ *n* : a short thick heavily seasoned sausage

knoll \ˈnōl\ *n* : a small round hill

¹knot \ˈnät\ *n* 1 : an interlacing (as of string) forming a lump or knob and often used for fastening or tying together 2 : PROBLEM 3 : a bond of union; *esp* : the marriage bond 4 : a protuberant lump or swelling in tissue 5 : a rounded cross-grained area in lumber that is a section through the junction of a tree branch with the trunk; *also* : the woody tissue forming this junction in a tree 6 : GROUP, CLUSTER 7 : an ornamental bow of ribbon 8 : one nautical mile per hour; *also* : one nautical mile — **knot·ty** *adj*

²knot *vb* **knot·ted; knot·ting** 1 : to tie in or with a knot 2 : ENTANGLE

knot·hole \-ˌhōl\ *n* : a hole in a board or tree trunk where a knot has come out

knout \ˈnaùt, ˈnüt\ *n* : a whip used for flogging

know \ˈnō\ *vb* **knew** \ˈnü, ˈnyü\; **known** \ˈnōn\; **know·ing** 1 : to perceive directly : have understanding or direct cognition of; *also* : to recognize the nature of 2 : to be acquainted or familiar with 3 : to be aware of the truth of 4 : to have a practical understanding of — **know·able** *adj* — **know·er** *n* — **in the know** : possessing confidential information

know–how \ˈnō-ˌhaù\ *n* : knowledge of how to do something smoothly and efficiently

know·ing *adj* 1 : having or reflecting knowledge, intelligence, or information 2 : shrewdly and keenly alert 3 : DELIBERATE, INTENTIONAL **syn** clever, bright, smart — **know·ing·ly** *adv*

knowl·edge \ˈnä-lij\ *n* 1 : understanding gained by actual experience ⟨a ~ of carpentry⟩ 2 : range of information ⟨to the best of my ~⟩ 3 : clear perception of truth 4 : something learned and kept in the mind

knowl·edge·able \ˈnä-li-jə-bəl\ *adj* : having or showing knowledge or intelligence

knuck·le \ˈnə-kəl\ *n* : the rounded knob at a joint and esp. at a finger joint

knuckle down *vb* : to apply oneself earnestly

knuckle under *vb* : SUBMIT, SURRENDER

knurl \ˈnərl\ *n* 1 : KNOB 2 : one of a series of small ridges on a metal surface to aid in gripping — **knurled** \\'nərld\ *adj* — **knurly** *adj*

¹KO \\(ˌ)kā-'ō, 'kā-ˌō\ *n* : KNOCKOUT

²KO *vb* **KO'd; KO'·ing** : to knock out in boxing

ko·ala \kō-'ä-lə\ *n* : a gray furry Australian marsupial with large hairy ears that feeds on eucalyptus leaves

ko·bo \'kō-(ˌ)bō\ *n, pl* **kobo** : see *naira* at MONEY table

K of C *abbr* Knights of Columbus

kohl·ra·bi \kōl-'rä-bē\ *n, pl* **-bies** [G, fr. It *cavolo rapa*, lit., cabbage turnip] : a cabbage that forms no head but has a swollen fleshy edible stem

ko·lin·sky \kə-'lin-skē\ *n, pl* **-skies** : the fur of various Asian minks

kook \'kük\ *n* : SCREWBALL 2

kooky *also* **kook·ie** \'kü-kē\ *adj* **kook·i·er; -est** : having the characteristics of a kook : CRAZY, ECCENTRIC — **kook·i·ness** *n*

ko·peck *or* **ko·pek** \'kō-ˌpek\ *n* [Russ *kopeĭka*] — see *ru·ble* at MONEY table

Ko·ran \kə-'ran, -'rän\ *n* [Ar *qur'ān*] : a sacred book of Islam that contains revelations made to Muhammad by Allah

Ko·re·an \kə-'rē-ən\ *n* : a native or inhabitant of Korea — **Korean** *adj*

ko·ru·na \'kȯr-ə-ˌnä\ *n, pl* **ko·ru·ny** \-ə-nē\ *or* **korunas** *or* **ko·rum** \'kȯr-əm\ — see MONEY table

ko·sher \'kō-shər\ *adj* [Yiddish, fr. Heb *kāshēr* fit, proper] **1** : ritually fit for use according to Jewish law **2** : selling or serving kosher food

kow·tow \kaù-'taù, 'kaù-ˌtaù\ *vb* [Chin *kòutóu*, fr. *kòu* to knock + *tóu* head] **1** : to show obsequious deference **2** : to kneel and touch the forehead to the ground as a sign of homage or deep respect

KP \ˌkā-'pē\ *n* **1** : an enlisted man detailed to help the cooks in a military mess **2** : the work of KPs

kph *abbr* kilometers per hour

Kr *symbol* krypton

kraal \'kräl, 'krȯl\ *n* **1** : a native village in southern Africa **2** : an enclosure for domestic animals in southern Africa

kraut \'kraùt\ *n* : SAUERKRAUT

Krem·lin \'krem-lən\ *n* : the Russian or Soviet government

Krem·lin·ol·o·gist \ˌkrem-lə-'nä-lə-jist\ *n* : a specialist in the policies and practices of the Soviet government

¹kro·na \'krō-nə\ *n, pl* **kro·nor** \-ˌnȯr\ [Sw] — see MONEY table

²kro·na \'krō-nə\ *n, pl* **kro·nur** \-nər\ [Icel] — see MONEY table

kro·ne \'krō-nə\ *n, pl* **kro·ner** \-nər\ — see MONEY table

Kru·ger·rand \'krü-gər-ˌrand, -ˌränd\ *n* : a 1-ounce gold coin of the Republic of South Africa

kryp·ton \'krip-ˌtän\ *n* : a gaseous chemical element used esp. in electric lamps — see ELEMENT table

KS *abbr* Kansas

kt *abbr* **1** karat **2** knight

ku·do \'kü-dō, 'kyü-\ *n, pl* **kudos** [fr. *kudos* (taken as pl.)] **1** : AWARD, HONOR **2** : COMPLIMENT, PRAISE

ku·dos \'kü-ˌdäs, 'kyü-\ *n* : fame and renown resulting from achievement

kud·zu \'kùd-zü, 'kəd-\ *n* [Jp *kuzu*] : a creeping leguminous vine used for hay, forage, and erosion control

ku·lak \kü-'lak, kyü-, -'läk\ *n* [Russ, lit., fist] **1** : a wealthy peasant farmer in 19th century Russia **2** : a farmer characterized by Communists as too wealthy

kum·quat \'kəm-ˌkwät\ *n* : any of several small citrus fruits with sweet spongy rind and acid pulp

kung fu \ˌkəŋ-'fü, ˌkùŋ-\ *n* : a Chinese art of self= defense resembling karate

ku·rus \kə-'rüsh\ *n, pl* **kurus** — see *lira* at MONEY table

Ku·waiti \kù-'wä-tē\ *n* : a native or inhabitant of Kuwait — **Kuwaiti** *adj*

kV *abbr* kilovolt

kvetch \'kvech, 'kfech\ *vb* : to complain habitually — **kvetch** *n*

kW *abbr* kilowatt

kwa·cha \'kwä-chə\ *n, pl* **kwacha** — see MONEY table

kwan·za \'kwän-zə\ *n, pl* **kwanzas** *or* **kwanza** — see MONEY table

kwash·i·or·kor \ˌkwä-shē-'ȯr-kȯr, -ȯr-'kȯr\ *n* : a disease of young children caused by deficient intake of protein

kWh *abbr* kilowatt-hour

Ky *or* **KY** *abbr* Kentucky

kyat \'chät\ *n* — see MONEY table

L

¹l \'el\ *n, pl* **l's** *or* **ls** \'elz\ *often cap* : the 12th letter of the English alphabet

²l *abbr, often cap* **1** lake **2** large **3** left **4** [L *libra*] pound **5** line **6** liter

¹La *abbr* Louisiana

²La *symbol* lanthanum

LA *abbr* **1** law agent **2** Los Angeles **3** Louisiana

lab \'lab\ *n* : LABORATORY

Lab *n* : LABRADOR RETRIEVER

¹la·bel \'lā-bəl\ *n* **1** : a slip attached to something for identification or description **2** : a descriptive or identifying word or phrase **3** : BRAND 3

²label *vb* **-beled** *or* **-belled; -bel·ing** *or* **-bel·ling** **1** : to affix a label to **2** : to describe or name with a label

la·bi·al \'lā-bē-əl\ *adj* : of or relating to the lips or labia

la·bia ma·jo·ra \'lā-bē-ə-mə-'jȯr-ə\ *n pl* : the outer fatty folds of the vulva

labia mi·no·ra \-mə-'nȯr-ə\ *n pl* : the inner highly vascular folds of the vulva

la·bile \'lā-ˌbīl, -bəl\ *adj* **1** : UNSTABLE **2** : ADAPTABLE

la·bi·um \'lā-bē-əm\ *n, pl* **la·bia** \-ə\ [NL, fr. L, lip] : any of the folds at the margin of the vulva

¹la·bor \'lā-bər\ *n* **1** : physical or mental effort; *also* : human activity that provides the goods or services in an economy **2** : the physical efforts of giving birth; *also* : the period of such labor **3** : TASK **4** : those who do manual labor or work for wages; *also* : labor unions or their officials

²labor *vb* **1** : WORK **2** : to move with great effort **3** : to be in the labor of giving birth **4** : to suffer from some disadvantage or distress ⟨~ under a delusion⟩ **5** : to treat or work out laboriously — **la·bor·er** *n*

lab·o·ra·to·ry \'la-brə-ˌtōr-ē, -bə-rə-\ *n, pl* **-ries** : a place equipped for making scientific experiments or tests

Labor Day *n* : the 1st Monday in September observed as a legal holiday in recognition of the working people

la·bored \'lā-bərd\ *adj* : not freely or easily done ⟨~ breathing⟩

la·bo·ri·ous \lə-'bȯr-ē-əs\ *adj* **1** : INDUSTRIOUS **2** : requiring great effort — **la·bo·ri·ous·ly** *adv*

\ə\abut \ᵊ\kitten \ər\further \a\ash \ā\ace \ä\mop, mar
\aù\out \ch\chin \e\bet \ē\easy \g\go \i\hit \ī\ice \j\job
\ŋ\sing \ō\go \ȯ\law \ȯi\boy \th\thin \th\the \ü\loot \ù\foot
\y\yet \zh\vision *see also* Pronunciation Symbols page

la·bor·sav·ing \\'lā-bər-ˌsā-viŋ\\ *adj* : designed to replace or decrease labor

labor union *n* : an organization of workers formed to advance its members' interest in respect to wages and working conditions

la·bour *chiefly Brit var of* LABOR

lab·ra·dor·ite \\'la-brə-ˌdor-ˌīt\\ *n* : an iridescent feldspar used in jewelry

Lab·ra·dor retriever \\'la-brə-ˌdor-\\ *n* : a strongly built retriever having a short dense black, yellow, or chocolate coat

la·bur·num \\lə-'bər-nəm\\ *n* : a leguminous shrub or tree with hanging clusters of yellow flowers

lab·y·rinth \\'la-bə-ˌrinth\\ *n* : a place constructed of or filled with confusing intricate passageways — MAZE

lab·y·rin·thine \\ˌla-bə-'rin-thən, -ˌthīn, -ˌthēn\\ *adj* : INTRICATE, INVOLVED

lac \\'lak\\ *n* : a resinous substance secreted by a scale insect and used chiefly in the form of shellac

¹lace \\'lās\\ *vb* **laced; lac·ing 1** : TIE **2** : to adorn with lace **3** : INTERTWINE **4** : BEAT, LASH **5** : to add to something to impart zest or savor to

²lace *n* [ME, fr. OF *laz*, fr. L *laqueus* snare, noose] **1** : a cord or string used for drawing together two edges **2** : an ornamental braid **3** : a fine openwork usu. figured fabric made of thread — **lacy** \\'lā-sē\\ *adj*

lac·er·ate \\'la-sə-ˌrāt\\ *vb* **-at·ed; -at·ing** : to tear roughly — **lac·er·a·tion** \\ˌla-sə-'rā-shən\\ *n*

lace·wing \\'lās-ˌwiŋ\\ *n* : any of various insects with delicate wing veins, long antennae, and often brilliant eyes

lach·ry·mal *or* **lac·ri·mal** \\'la-krə-məl\\ *adj* **1** *usu lacrimal* : of, relating to, or being glands that produce tears **2** : of, relating to, or marked by tears

lach·ry·mose \\'la-krə-ˌmōs\\ *adj* **1** : TEARFUL **2** : MOURNFUL

¹lack \\'lak\\ *vb* **1** : to be wanting or missing **2** : to be deficient in

²lack *n* : the fact or state of being wanting or deficient : NEED

lack·a·dai·si·cal \\ˌla-kə-'dā-zi-kəl\\ *adj* : lacking life, spirit, or zest — **lack·a·dai·si·cal·ly** \\-k(ə-)lē\\ *adv*

lack·ey \\'la-kē\\ *n, pl* **lackeys 1** : FOOTMAN, SERVANT **2** : TOADY

lack·lus·ter \\'lak-ˌləs-tər\\ *adj* : DULL

la·con·ic \\lə-'kä-nik\\ *adj* [L *laconicus* Spartan, fr. Gk *lakōnikos*; fr. the Spartan reputation for terseness of speech] : sparing of words : TERSE **syn** concise, curt, short, succinct, brusque — **la·con·i·cal·ly** \\-ni-k(ə-)lē\\ *adv*

lac·quer \\'la-kər\\ *n* : a clear or colored usu. glossy and quick-drying surface coating — **lacquer** *vb*

lac·ri·ma·tion \\ˌla-krə-'mā-shən\\ *n* : secretion of tears

la·crosse \\lə-'kros\\ *n* [CanF *la crosse*, lit., the crosier] : a goal game in which players use a long-handled triangular-headed stick having a mesh pouch for catching, carrying, and throwing the ball

lac·tate \\'lak-ˌtāt\\ *vb* **lac·tat·ed; lac·tat·ing** : to secrete milk — **lac·ta·tion** \\lak-'tā-shən\\ *n*

lac·tic \\'lak-tik\\ *adj* **1** : of or relating to milk **2** : obtained from sour milk or whey

lactic acid *n* : a syrupy acid present in blood and muscle tissue and used in food and medicine

lac·tose \\'lak-ˌtōs\\ *n* : a sugar present in milk

la·cu·na \\lə-'kü-nə, -'kyü-\\ *n, pl* **la·cu·nae** \\-nē\\ *or* **la·cu·nas** [L, pool, pit, gap, fr. *lacus* lake] : a blank space or missing part : GAP

lad \\'lad\\ *n* : YOUTH; *also* : FELLOW

lad·der \\'la-dər\\ *n* : a structure for climbing that consists of two parallel sidepieces joined at intervals by crosspieces

lad·die \\'la-dē\\ *n* : a young lad

lad·en \\'lād-ᵊn\\ *adj* : LOADED, BURDENED

lad·ing \\'lā-diŋ\\ *n* : CARGO, FREIGHT

la·dle \\'lād-ᵊl\\ *n* : a deep-bowled long-handled spoon used in taking up and conveying liquids — **ladle** *vb*

la·dy \\'lā-dē\\ *n, pl* **ladies** [ME, fr. OE *hlǣfdīge*, fr. *hlāf* bread + *-dīge* (akin to *dǣge* kneader of bread)] **1** : a woman of property, rank, or authority; *also* : a woman of superior social position or of refinement **2** : WOMAN **3** : WIFE

lady beetle *n* : LADYBUG

la·dy·bird \\'lā-dē-ˌbərd\\ *n* : LADYBUG

la·dy·bug \\-ˌbəg\\ *n* : any of various small nearly hemispherical and usu. brightly colored beetles that feed mostly on other insects

la·dy·fin·ger \\-ˌfiŋ-gər\\ *n* : a small finger-shaped sponge cake

lady–in–waiting *n, pl* **ladies–in–waiting** : a lady appointed to attend or wait on a queen or princess

la·dy·like \\'lā-dē-ˌlīk\\ *adj* : WELL-BRED

la·dy·ship \\-ˌship\\ *n* : the condition of being a lady : rank of lady

lady's slipper *or* **lady slipper** *n* : any of several No. American orchids with slipper-shaped flowers

¹lag \\'lag\\ *n* **1** : a slowing up or falling behind; *also* : the amount by which one lags **2** : INTERVAL

²lag *vb* **lagged; lag·ging 1** : to fail to keep up : stay behind **2** : to slacken gradually **syn** dawdle, dally, tarry, loiter

la·ger \\'lä-gər\\ *n* : a light-colored usu. dry beer

lag·gard \\'la-gərd\\ *adj* : tending to lag — **laggard** *n* — **lag·gard·ly** *adv or adj* — **lag·gard·ness** *n*

la·gniappe \\'lan-ˌyap\\ *n* : something given free esp. with a purchase

la·goon \\lə-'gün\\ *n* : a shallow sound, channel, or pond near or connected to a larger body of water

laid *past and past part of* LAY

laid–back \\'lād-'bak\\ *adj* : having a relaxed style or character ⟨∼ music⟩

lain *past part of* ¹LIE

lair \\'lar\\ *n* : the resting or living place of a wild animal : DEN

laird \\'lard\\ *n, Scot* : a landed proprietor

lais·ser–faire *chiefly Brit var of* LAISSEZ-FAIRE

lais·sez–faire \\ˌle-ˌsā-'far, ˌlā-, -ˌzā-\\ *n* [F *laissez faire* let do] : a doctrine opposing governmental control of economic affairs beyond that necessary to maintain peace and property rights

la·ity \\'lā-ə-tē\\ *n* **1** : the people of a religious faith as distinct from its clergy **2** : the mass of people as distinct from those of a particular field

lake \\'lāk\\ *n* : an inland body of standing water of considerable size; *also* : a pool of liquid (as lava or pitch)

¹lam \\'lam\\ *vb* **lammed; lam·ming** : to flee hastily — **lam** *n*

²lam *abbr* laminated

Lam *abbr* Lamentations

la·ma \\'lä-mə\\ *n* : a Buddhist monk of Tibet or Mongolia

la·ma·sery \\'lä-mə-ˌser-ē\\ *n, pl* **-ser·ies** : a monastery for lamas

¹lamb \\'lam\\ *n* **1** : a young sheep; *also* : its flesh used as food **2** : an innocent or gentle person

²lamb *vb* : to bring forth a lamb

lam·baste *or* **lam·bast** \\lam-'bāst, -'bast\\ *vb* **1** : BEAT **2** : EXCORIATE **syn** castigate, flay, lash

lamb·da \\'lam-də\\ *n* : the 11th letter of the Greek alphabet — Λ or λ

lam·bent \\'lam-bənt\\ *adj* [L *lambens*, prp. of *lambere* to lick] **1** : FLICKERING **2** : softly radiant ⟨∼ eyes⟩ **3** : marked by lightness or brilliance ⟨∼ humor⟩ **syn** effulgent, incandescent, lucent, luminous — **lam·ben·cy** \\-bən-sē\\ *n* — **lam·bent·ly** *adv*

lamb·skin \\'lam-ˌskin\\ *n* : a lamb's skin or a small fine-grade sheepskin or the leather made from either

¹lame \\'lām\\ *adj* **lam·er; lam·est 1** : having a body part and esp. a limb so disabled as to impair freedom of movement; *also* : marked by stiffness and soreness **2**

: lacking substance : WEAK — **lame·ly** *adv* — **lame-ness** *n*

²lame *vb* **lamed; lam·ing** : to make lame : CRIPPLE, DISABLE

la·mé \lä-'mā, la-\ *n* [F] : a brocaded clothing fabric with tinsel filling threads (as of gold or silver)

lame·brain \'lām-₁brān\ *n* : DOLT

lame duck *n* : an elected official continuing to hold office between an election and the inauguration of a successor — **lame–duck** *adj*

¹la·ment \lə-'ment\ *vb* **1** : to mourn aloud : WAIL **2** : to express sorrow or regret for : BEWAIL — **lam·en·ta·ble** \'la-mən-tə-bəl, lə-'men-tə-\ *adj* — **lam·en·ta·bly** \-blē\ *adv* — **lam·en·ta·tion** \₁la-mən-'tā-shən\ *n*

²lament *n* **1** : a crying out in grief : WAIL **2** : DIRGE, ELEGY **3** : COMPLAINT

Lamentations *n* — see BIBLE table

la·mia \'lā-mē-ə\ *n* : a female demon

lam·i·na \'la-mə-nə\ *n, pl* **-nae** \-₁nē\ *or* **-nas** : a thin plate or scale

¹lam·i·nate \'la-mə-₁nāt\ *vb* **-nat·ed; -nat·ing** : to make by uniting layers of one or more materials — **lam·i·na·tion** \₁la-mə-'nā-shən\ *n*

²lam·i·nate \-nət\ *n* : a product manufactured by laminating

lamp \'lamp\ *n* **1** : a vessel with a wick for burning a flammable liquid (as oil) to produce light **2** : a device for producing light or heat

lamp·black \-₁blak\ *n* : black soot used esp. as a pigment

lamp·light·er \-₁lī-tər\ : one that lights a lamp

lam·poon \lam-'pün\ *n* : SATIRE; *esp* : a harsh satiric directed against an individual — **lampoon** *vb*

lam·prey \'lam-prē\ *n, pl* **lampreys** : any of a family of eel-shaped jawless fishes that have well-developed eyes and a large disk-shaped sucking mouth armed with horny teeth

la·nai \lə-'nī\ *n* [Hawaiian *lānai*] : PORCH, VERANDA

¹lance \'lans\ *n* **1** : a spear carried by mounted soldiers **2** : any of various sharp-pointed implements; *esp* : LANCET

²lance *vb* **lanced; lanc·ing** : to pierce or open with a lance ⟨~ a boil⟩

lance corporal *n* : an enlisted man in the marine corps ranking above a private first class and below a corporal

lanc·er \'lan-sər\ *n* : a cavalryman of a unit formerly armed with lances

lan·cet \'lan-sət\ *n* : a sharp-pointed and usu. 2-edged surgical instrument

¹land \'land\ *n* **1** : the solid part of the surface of the earth; *also* : a part of the earth's surface ⟨fenced ~⟩ ⟨marshy ~⟩ **2** : NATION **3** : REALM, DOMAIN — **landless** *adj*

²land *vb* **1** : DISEMBARK; *also* : to touch at a place on shore **2** : to alight or cause to alight on a surface **3** : to bring to or arrive at a destination **4** : to catch and bring in ⟨~ a fish⟩; *also* : GAIN, SECURE ⟨~ a job⟩

lan·dau \'lan-₁daù\ *n* : a 4-wheeled carriage with a top divided into two sections that can be lowered, thrown back, or removed

land·ed *adj* : having an estate in land ⟨~ gentry⟩

land·er \'lan-dər\ *n* : a space vehicle designed to land on a celestial body

land·fall \'land-₁fòl\ *n* : a sighting or making of land (as after a voyage); *also* : the land first sighted

land·fill \-₁fil\ *n* : a low-lying area on which refuse is buried between layers of earth

land·form \-₁fòrm\ *n* : a natural feature of a land surface

land·hold·er \-₁hōl-dər\ *n* : a holder or owner of land — **land·hold·ing** \-diŋ\ *adj or n*

land·ing \'lan-diŋ\ *n* **1** : the action of one that lands **2** : a place for discharging or taking on passengers and cargo **3** : a level part of a staircase

landing gear *n* : the part that supports the weight of an aircraft when it is on the ground

land·la·dy \'land-₁lā-dē\ *n* : a woman who is a landlord

land·locked \-₁läkt\ *adj* **1** : enclosed or nearly enclosed by land ⟨a ~ country⟩ **2** : confined to fresh water by some barrier ⟨~ salmon⟩

land·lord \-₁lòrd\ *n* **1** : the owner of property leased or rented to another **2** : a person who rents lodgings : INNKEEPER

land·lub·ber \-₁lə-bər\ *n* : one who knows little of the sea or seamanship

land·mark \-₁märk\ *n* **1** : an object that marks a course or boundary or serves as a guide **2** : an event that marks a turning point **3** : a structure of unusual historical and usu. aesthetic interest

land·mass \-₁mas\ *n* : a large area of land

land mine *n* **1** : a mine placed on or just below the surface of the ground and designed to be exploded by the weight of someone or something passing over it **2** : a trap for the unwary

land·own·er \-₁ō-nər\ *n* : an owner of land

¹land·scape \-₁skāp\ *n* **1** : a picture of natural inland scenery **2** : a portion of land that can be seen in one glance

²landscape *vb* **land·scaped; land·scap·ing** : to modify (a natural landscape) by grading, clearing, or decorative planting

land·slide \-₁slīd\ *n* **1** : the slipping down of a mass of rocks or earth on a steep slope; *also* : the mass of material that slides **2** : an overwhelming victory esp. in a political contest

lands·man \'landz-mən\ *n* : a person who lives on land; *esp* : LANDLUBBER

land·ward \'land-wərd\ *adv or adj* : to or toward the land

lane \'lān\ *n* **1** : a narrow passageway (as between fences) **2** : a relatively narrow way or track ⟨traffic ~⟩

lang *abbr* language

lan·guage \'laŋ-gwij\ *n* [ME, fr. OF, fr. *langue* tongue, language, fr. L *lingua*] **1** : the words, their pronunciation, and the methods of combining them used and understood by a community **2** : form or style of verbal expression **3** : a system of signs and symbols and rules for using them that is used to carry information

lan·guid \'laŋ-gwəd\ *adj* **1** : WEAK **2** : sluggish in character or disposition : LISTLESS **3** : SLOW — **lan·guid·ly** *adv* — **lan·guid·ness** *n*

lan·guish \'laŋ-gwish\ *vb* **1** : to become languid **2** : to become dispirited : PINE **3** : to appeal for sympathy by assuming an expression of grief

lan·guor \'laŋ-gər\ *n* **1** : a languid feeling **2** : listless indolence or inertia **syn** lethargy, lassitude, torpidity, torpor — **lan·guor·ous** *adj* — **lan·guor·ous·ly** *adv*

lank \'laŋk\ *adj* **1** : not well filled out **2** : hanging straight and limp

lanky \'laŋ-kē\ *adj* **lank·i·er; -est** : ungracefully tall and thin

lan·o·lin \'lan-ᵊl-ən\ *n* : the fatty coating of sheep's wool esp. when refined for use in ointments and cosmetics

lan·ta·na \lan-'tä-nə\ *n* : any of a genus of tropical shrubs related to the vervains with showy heads of small bright flowers

lan·tern \'lan-tərn\ *n* **1** : a usu. portable light with a protective covering **2** : the chamber in a lighthouse containing the light **3** : a projector for slides

lan·tha·nide series \'lan-thə-₁nīd-\ *n* : the series of chemical elements in the periodic table that begins with lanthanum or cerium and ends with lutetium

---

\ə\abut \ᵊ\kitten \ər\further \a\ash \ā\ace \ä\mop, mar
\aù\out \ch\chin \e\bet \ē\easy \g\go \i\hit \ī\ice \j\job
\ŋ\sing \ō\go \ò\law \òi\boy \th\thin \th̲\the \ü\loot \ù\foot
\y\yet \zh\vision *see also* Pronunciation Symbols page

lan·tha·num \'lan-thə-nəm\ n : a soft malleable metallic chemical element — see ELEMENT table

lan·yard \'lan-yərd\ n : a piece of rope for fastening something in ships; also : any of various cords

Lao·tian \lā-'ō-shən, 'laü-shən\ n : a native or inhabitant of Laos — **Laotian** adj

¹**lap** \'lap\ n 1 : a loose panel of a garment 2 : the clothing that lies on the knees, thighs, and lower part of the trunk when one sits; also : the front part of the lower trunk and thighs of a seated person 3 : an environment of nurture ⟨the ~ of luxury⟩ 4 : CHARGE, CONTROL ⟨in the ~ of the gods⟩

²**lap** vb **lapped; lap·ping** 1 : FOLD 2 : WRAP 3 : to lay over or near so as to partly cover

³**lap** n 1 : the amount by which an object overlaps another; also : the part of an object that overlaps another 2 : an act or instance of going over a course (as a track or swimming pool)

⁴**lap** vb **lapped; lap·ping** 1 : to scoop up food or drink with the tip of the tongue; also : DEVOUR — usu. used with up 2 : to splash gently ⟨lapping waves⟩

⁵**lap** n 1 : an act or instance of lapping 2 : a gentle splashing sound

lap·dog \'lap-ˌdȯg\ n : a small dog that may be held in the lap

la·pel \lə-'pel\ n : the fold of the front of a coat that is usu. a continuation of the collar

¹**lap·i·dary** \'la-pə-ˌder-ē\ n, pl **-dar·ies** : a person who cuts, polishes, or engraves precious stones

²**lapidary** adj 1 : of, relating to, or suitable for engraved inscriptions 2 : of or relating to precious stones or the art of cutting them

lap·in \'la-pən\ n : rabbit fur usu. sheared and dyed

la·pis la·zu·li \ˌla-pəs-'la-zə-lē, -zhə-\ n : a usu. blue semiprecious stone often having sparkling bits of pyrite

Lapp \'lap\ n : a member of a people of northern Scandinavia, Finland, and the Kola peninsula of Russia

lap·pet \'la-pət\ n : a fold or flap on a garment

¹**lapse** \'laps\ n [L lapsus, fr. labi to slip] 1 : a slight error 2 : a fall from a higher to a lower state 3 : the termination of a right or privilege through failure to meet requirements 4 : INTERRUPTION 5 : APOSTASY 6 : a passage of time; also : INTERVAL **syn** blooper, blunder, boner, goof, mistake, slip

²**lapse** vb **lapsed; laps·ing** 1 : to commit apostasy 2 : to sink or slip gradually : SUBSIDE 3 : CEASE

lap·top \'lap-ˌtäp\ adj : of a size that can be used conveniently on one's lap ⟨a ~ computer⟩ — **laptop** n

lap·wing \'lap-ˌwiŋ\ n : an Old World crested plover

lar·board \'lär-bərd\ n : ⁵PORT

lar·ce·ny \'lär-sə-nē\ n, pl **-nies** [ME, fr. MF larcin theft, fr. L latrocinium robbery, fr. latro mercenary soldier] : THEFT — **lar·ce·nous** \-nəs\ adj

larch \'lärch\ n : any of a genus of trees related to the pines that shed their needles in the fall

¹**lard** \'lärd\ vb 1 : to insert strips of usu. pork fat into (meat) before cooking; also : GREASE 2 obs : ENRICH

²**lard** n : a soft white fat obtained by rendering fatty tissue of the hog

lar·der \'lär-dər\ n : a place where foods (as meat) are kept

lar·es and pe·na·tes \'lar-ēz . . . pə-'nä-tēz\ n pl 1 : household gods 2 : personal or household effects

large \'lärj\ adj **larg·er; larg·est** 1 : having more than usual power, capacity, or scope 2 : exceeding most other things of like kind in quantity or size **syn** big, great, oversize — **large·ness** n — **at large** 1 : UNCONFINED 2 : as a whole

large·ly \'lärj-lē\ adv : to a large extent

lar·gesse or **lar·gess** \lär-'zhes, -'jes\ n 1 : liberal giving 2 : a generous gift

¹**lar·go** \'lär-gō\ adv or adj [It, slow, broad, fr. L largus

abundant] : at a very slow tempo — used as a direction in music

²**largo** n, pl **largos** : a largo movement

lar·i·at \'lar-ē-ət\ n [AmerSp la reata the lasso, fr. Sp la the + AmerSp reata lasso, fr. Sp reatar to tie again] : a long rope used to catch or tether livestock : LASSO

¹**lark** \'lärk\ n : any of a family of small songbirds; esp : SKYLARK

²**lark** n : something done solely for fun or adventure

³**lark** vb : to engage in harmless fun or mischief — often used with about

lark·spur \'lärk-ˌspər\ n : DELPHINIUM; esp : any of the cultivated annual delphiniums

lar·va \'lär-və\ n, pl **lar·vae** \-(ˌ)vē\ also **larvas** [L, specter, mask] : the wingless often wormlike form in which insects hatch from the egg; also : any young animal (as a tadpole) that is fundamentally unlike its parent — **lar·val** \-vəl\ adj

lar·yn·gi·tis \ˌlar-ən-'jī-təs\ n : inflammation of the larynx

lar·ynx \'lar-iŋks\ n, pl **la·ryn·ges** \lə-'rin-ˌjēz\ or **lar·ynx·es** : the upper part of the trachea containing the vocal cords — **la·ryn·ge·al** \lə-'rin-jəl\ adj

la·sa·gna \lə-'zän-yə\ n [It] : boiled broad flat noodles baked with a sauce usu. of tomatoes, cheese, and meat

las·car \'las-kər\ n : an Indian sailor

las·civ·i·ous \lə-'si-vē-əs\ adj : LUSTFUL, LEWD **syn** licentious, lecherous, libidinous, salacious — **las·civ·i·ous·ness** n

la·ser \'lā-zər\ n [light amplification by stimulated emission of radiation] : a device that produces an intense monochromatic beam of light

¹**lash** \'lash\ vb 1 : to move violently or suddenly 2 : WHIP 3 : to attack verbally

²**lash** n 1 : a stroke esp. with a whip; also : WHIP 2 : a stinging rebuke 3 : EYELASH

³**lash** vb : to bind with or as if with a line

lass \'las\ n : GIRL

lass·ie \'la-sē\ n : LASS

las·si·tude \'la-sə-ˌtüd, -ˌtyüd\ n 1 : WEARINESS, FATIGUE 2 : LANGUOR

las·so \'la-sō, la-'sü\ n, pl **lassos** or **lassoes** [Sp lazo] : a rope or long leather thong with a noose used for catching livestock — **lasso** vb

¹**last** \'last\ vb 1 : to continue in existence or operation 2 : to remain fresh or unimpaired : ENDURE 3 : to manage to continue 4 : to be enough for the needs of

²**last** n : a foot-shaped form on which a shoe is shaped or repaired

³**last** vb : to shape with a last

⁴**last** adv 1 : at the end 2 : most recently 3 : in conclusion

⁵**last** adj 1 : following all the rest : FINAL 2 : next before the present 3 : most up-to-date 4 : farthest from a specified quality, attitude, or likelihood ⟨the ~ thing we want⟩ 4 : CONCLUSIVE; also : SUPREME — **last·ly** adv

⁶**last** n : something that is last — **at last** : FINALLY

Last Supper n : the supper eaten by Jesus and his disciples on the night of his betrayal

lat abbr latitude

Lat abbr Latin

¹**latch** \'lach\ vb : to catch or get hold

²**latch** n : a catch that holds a door or gate closed

³**latch** vb : to make fast with a latch

latch·et \'la-chət\ n : a strap, thong, or lace for fastening a shoe or sandal

latch·key \'lach-ˌkē\ n : a key for opening a door latch esp. from the outside

latch·string \-ˌstriŋ\ n : a string on a latch that may be left hanging outside the door for raising the latch

¹**late** \'lāt\ adj **lat·er; lat·est** 1 : coming or remaining after the due, usual, or proper time 2 : far advanced toward the close or end 3 : recently deceased 4 : made, appear-

ing, or happening just previous to the present : RECENT — **late·ly** *adv* — **late·ness** *n*

²late *adv* **lat·er; lat·est 1** : after the usual or proper time; *also* : at or to an advanced point in time **2** : RECENTLY

late·com·er \'lāt-ˌkə-mər\ *n* : one who arrives late

la·teen \lə-'tēn\ *adj* : relating to or being a triangular sail extended by a long spar slung to a low mast

la·tent \'lāt-ᵊnt\ *adj* : present but not visible or active **syn** dormant, quiescent, potential — **la·ten·cy** \-ᵊn-sē\ *n*

¹lat·er·al \'la-tə-rəl\ *adj* : situated on, directed toward, or coming from the side — **lat·er·al·ly** *adv*

²lateral *n* **1** : a branch from the main part **2** : a football pass thrown parallel to the line of scrimmage or away from the opponent's goal

la·tex \'lā-ˌteks\ *n, pl* **la·ti·ces** \'lā-tə-ˌsēz, 'la-\ *or* **la·tex·es 1** : a milky juice produced by various plant cells (as of milkweeds, poppies, and the rubber tree) **2** : a water emulsion of a synthetic rubber or plastic used esp. in paint

lath \'lath, 'la̲t̲h̲\ *n, pl* **laths** *or* **lath** : a thin narrow strip of wood used esp. as a base for plaster; *also* : a building material in sheets used for the same purpose — **lath** *vb*

lathe \'lā̲t̲h̲\ *n* : a machine in which a piece of material is held and turned while being shaped by a tool

¹lath·er \'la-t̲h̲ər\ *n* **1** : a foam or froth formed when a detergent is agitated in water; *also* : foam from profuse sweating (as by a horse) **2** : DITHER

²lather *vb* : to spread lather over; *also* : to form a lather

Lat·in \'lat-ᵊn\ *n* **1** : the language of ancient Rome **2** : a member of any of the peoples whose languages derive from Latin — **Latin** *adj*

Latin American *n* : a native or inhabitant of any of the countries of No., Central, or So. America whose official language is Spanish or Portuguese — **Latin–American** *adj*

La·ti·no \lə-'tē-nō\ *n, pl* **-nos** : a native or inhabitant of Latin America; *also* : a person of Latin-American origin living in the U.S. — **Latino** *adj*

lat·i·tude \'la-tə-ˌtüd, -ˌtyüd\ *n* **1** : angular distance north or south from the earth's equator measured in degrees **2** : a region marked by its latitude **3** : freedom of action or choice

lat·i·tu·di·nar·i·an \ˌla-tə-ˌtü-də-'ner-ē-ən, -ˌtyü-\ *n* : a person who is liberal in religious belief and conduct

la·trine \lə-'trēn\ *n* **:** TOILET

lat·ter \'la-tər\ *adj* **1** : more recent; *also* : FINAL **2** : of, relating to, or being the second of two things referred to

lat·ter–day *adj* **1** : of present or recent times **2** : of a later or subsequent time

Latter–day Saint *n* : a member of a religious body founded by Joseph Smith in 1830 and accepting the Book of Mormon as divine revelation — MORMON

lat·ter·ly \'la-tər-lē\ *adv* **1** : LATER **2** : of late : RECENTLY

lat·tice \'la-təs\ *n* **1** : a framework of crossed wood or metal strips; *also* : a window, door, or gate having a lattice **2** : a regular geometrical arrangement

lat·tice·work \-ˌwərk\ *n* **:** LATTICE; *also* : work made of lattices

Lat·vi·an \'lat-vē-ən\ *n* : a native or inhabitant of Latvia — **Latvian** *adj*

¹laud \'lȯd\ *n* **:** PRAISE, ACCLAIM

²laud *vb* **:** PRAISE, EXTOL **syn** celebrate, eulogize, glorify, magnify — **laud·able** *adj* — **laud·ably** *adv*

lau·da·num \'lȯd-ᵊn-əm\ *n* : a tincture of opium

lau·da·to·ry \'lȯ-də-ˌtȯr-ē\ *adj* : of, relating to, or expressive of praise

¹laugh \'laf, 'läf\ *vb* : to show mirth, joy, or scorn with a smile and chuckle or explosive sound; *also* : to become amused or derisive — **laugh·able** *adj* — **laugh·ing·ly** *adv*

²laugh *n* **1** : the act of laughing **2** : JOKE; *also* : JEER **3** *pl* : SPORT **1**

laugh·ing·stock \'la-fiŋ-ˌstäk, 'lä-\ *n* : an object of ridicule

laugh·ter \'laf-tər, 'läf-\ *n* : the action or sound of laughing

¹launch \'lȯnch\ *vb* [ME, fr. OF *lancher*, fr. LL *lanceare* to wield a lance] **1** : THROW, HURL; *also* : to send off ⟨∼ a rocket⟩ **2** : to set afloat **3** : to set in operation : START — **launch·er** *n*

²launch *n* : an act or instance of launching

³launch *n* : a small open or half-decked motorboat

launch·pad \'lȯnch-ˌpad\ *n* : a platform from which a rocket is launched

laun·der \'lȯn-dər\ *vb* **1** : to wash or wash and iron clothing and household linens **2** : to transfer (as money of an illegal origin) through an outside party to conceal the true source — **laun·der·er** *n*

laun·dress \'lȯn-drəs\ *n* : a woman who is a laundry worker

laun·dry \'lȯn-drē\ *n, pl* **laundries** [fr. obs. *launder* launderer, fr. MF *lavandier*, fr. ML *lavandarius*, fr. L *lavandus* needing to be washed, fr. *lavare* to wash] **1** : a place where laundering is done **2** : clothes or linens that have been or are to be laundered — **laun·dry·man** \-mən\ *n*

lau·re·ate \'lȯr-ē-ət\ *n* : the recipient of honor for achievement in an art or science — **lau·re·ate·ship** *n*

lau·rel \'lȯ-rəl\ *n* **1** : any of a genus of evergreen trees related to the sassafras and cinnamon; *esp* : a small tree of southern Europe **2** : MOUNTAIN LAUREL **3** : a crown of laurel : HONOR — usu. used in pl.

lav *abbr* lavatory

la·va \'lä-və, 'la-\ *n* [It] : melted rock coming from a volcano; *also* : such rock that has cooled and hardened

la·vage \lə-'väzh\ *n* [F] : WASHING; *esp* : the washing out (as of an organ) esp. for medicinal reasons

lav·a·to·ry \'la-və-ˌtȯr-ē\ *n, pl* **-ries 1** : a fixed washbowl with running water and drainpipe **2** : BATHROOM

lave \'lāv\ *vb* **laved; lav·ing** : WASH

lav·en·der \'la-vən-dər\ *n* **1** : a Mediterranean mint or its dried leaves and flowers used to perfume clothing and bed linen **2** : a pale purple color

¹lav·ish \'la-vish\ *adj* [ME *lavas* abundance, fr. MF *lavasse* downpour, fr. *laver* to wash] **1** : expending or bestowing profusely **2** : expended or produced in abundance **3** : marked by excess — **lav·ish·ly** *adv* — **lav·ish·ness** *n*

²lavish *vb* : to expend or give freely

law \'lȯ\ *n* **1** : a rule of conduct or action established by custom or laid down and enforced by a governing authority; *also* : the whole body of such rules **2** : the control brought about by enforcing rules **3** *cap* : the revelation of the divine will set forth in the Old Testament; *also* : the first part of the Jewish scriptures — see BIBLE table **4** : a rule or principle of construction or procedure **5** : the science that deals with laws and their interpretation and application **6** : the profession of a lawyer **7** : a rule or principle stating something that always works in the same way under the same conditions

law·break·er \'lȯ-ˌbrā-kər\ *n* : one who violates the law

law·ful \'lȯ-fəl\ *adj* **1** : permitted by law **2** : RIGHTFUL — **law·ful·ly** *adv*

law·giv·er \-ˌgi-vər\ *n* **:** LEGISLATOR

law·less \'lȯ-ləs\ *adj* **1** : having no laws **2** : UNRULY, DISORDERLY ⟨a ∼ mob⟩ — **law·less·ly** *adv* — **law·less·ness** *n*

law·mak·er \-ˌmā-kər\ *n* **:** LEGISLATOR

\ə\abut \ᵊ\kitten \ər\further \a\ash \ā\ace \ä\mop, mar \au̇\out \ch\chin \e\bet \ē\easy \g\go \i\hit \ī\ice \j\job \ŋ\sing \ō\go \ȯ\law \ȯi\boy \th\thin \t̲h̲\the \ü\loot \u̇\foot \y\yet \zh\vision *see also* Pronunciation Symbols page

law·man \'lȯ-mən\ *n* : a law enforcement official (as a sheriff or marshal)

¹lawn \'lȯn\ *n* : ground (as around a house) covered with mowed grass

²lawn *n* : a fine sheer linen or cotton fabric

lawn bowling *n* : a bowling game played on a green with wooden balls which are rolled at a jack

law·ren·ci·um \lȯ-'ren-sē-əm\ *n* : a short-lived radioactive element — see ELEMENT table

law·suit \'lȯ-ˌsüt\ *n* : a suit in law

law·yer \'lȯ-yər\ *n* : one who conducts lawsuits for clients or advises as to legal rights and obligations in other matters — **law·yer·ly** *adj*

lax \'laks\ *adj* **1** : not strict ⟨∼ discipline⟩ **2** : not tense or rigid *syn* remiss, negligent, neglectful, delinquent, derelict — **lax·i·ty** \'lak-sə-tē\ *n* — **lax·ly** *adv* — **lax·ness** *n*

¹lax·a·tive \'lak-sə-tiv\ *adj* : relieving constipation

²laxative *n* : a usu. mild laxative drug

¹lay \'lā\ *vb* **laid** \'lād\; **lay·ing 1** : to beat or strike down **2** : to put on or set down : PLACE **3** : to produce and deposit eggs **4** : SETTLE; *also* : ALLAY **5** : SPREAD **6** : PREPARE, CONTRIVE **7** : WAGER **8** : to impose esp. as a duty or burden **9** : to set in order or position **10** : to bring to a specified condition **11** : to put forward : SUBMIT

²lay *n* : the way in which something lies or is laid in relation to something else

³lay *past of* ¹LIE

⁴lay *n* **1** : a simple narrative poem **2** : SONG

⁵lay *adj* **1** : of or relating to the laity **2** : not of a particular profession; *also* : lacking extensive knowledge of a particular subject

lay·away \'lā-ə-ˌwā\ *n* : a purchasing agreement by which a retailer agrees to hold merchandise secured by a deposit until the price is paid in full

lay·er \'lā-ər\ *n* **1** : one that lays **2** : one thickness, course, or fold laid or lying over or under another

lay·ette \lā-'et\ *n* [F, fr. MF, dim. of *laye* box] : an outfit of clothing and equipment for a newborn infant

lay·man \'lā-mən\ *n* : a person who is a member of the laity

lay·off \'lā-ˌȯf\ *n* **1** : a period of inactivity **2** : the act of dismissing an employee usu. temporarily

lay·out \'lā-ˌaút\ *n* : the final arrangement, plan, or design of something

lay·over \-ˌō-vər\ *n* : STOPOVER

lay·per·son \-ˌpər-sən\ *n* : a member of the laity

lay·wom·an \'lā-ˌwú-mən\ *n* : a woman who is a member of the laity

la·zar \'la-zər, 'lā-\ *n* : LEPER

laze \'lāz\ *vb* **lazed; laz·ing** : to pass time in idleness or relaxation

la·zy \'lā-zē\ *adj* **la·zi·er; -est 1** : disliking activity or exertion **2** : encouraging idleness **3** : SLUGGISH **4** : DROOPY, LAX **5** : not rigorous or strict — **la·zi·ly** \-zə-lē\ *adv* — **la·zi·ness** \-zē-nəs\ *n*

la·zy·bones \-ˌbōnz\ *n sing or pl* : a lazy person

lazy Su·san \ˌlā-zē-'süz-ᵊn\ *n* : a revolving tray used for serving food

lb *abbr* [L *libra*] pound

lc *abbr* lowercase

LC *abbr* Library of Congress

¹LCD \ˌel-(ˌ)sē-'dē\ *n* [*liquid crystal display*] : a display (as of the time in a watch) that consists of segments of a liquid crystal whose reflectivity varies with the voltage applied to them

²LCD *abbr* least common denominator; lowest common denominator

LCDR *abbr* lieutenant commander

LCM *abbr* least common multiple; lowest common multiple

LCpl *abbr* lance corporal

LCS *abbr* League Championship Series

ld *abbr* **1** load **2** lord

LD *abbr* learning disabled; learning disability

LDC *abbr* less developed country

ldg *abbr* **1** landing **2** loading

LDL \ˌel-(ˌ)dē-'el\ *n* [*low-density lipoprotein*] : a cholesterol-rich protein-poor lipoprotein of blood plasma correlated with increased risk of atherosclerosis

L-do·pa \'el-'dō-pə\ *n* : an isomer of dopa used esp. in the treatment of Parkinson's disease

LDS *abbr* Latter-day Saints

lea \'lē, 'lā\ *n* : PASTURE, MEADOW

leach \'lēch\ *vb* : to pass a liquid (as water) through to carry off the soluble components; *also* : to dissolve out by such means ⟨∼ alkali from ashes⟩

¹lead \'lēd\ *vb* **led** \'led\; **lead·ing 1** : to guide on a way **2** : LIVE ⟨∼ a quiet life⟩ **3** : to direct the operations, activity, or performance of ⟨∼ an orchestra⟩ **4** : to go at the head of : be first ⟨∼ a parade⟩ **5** : to begin play with; *also* : BEGIN, OPEN **6** : to tend toward a definite result ⟨study ∼ing to a degree⟩ — **lead·er** *n* — **lead·er·less** *adj* — **lead·er·ship** *n*

²lead \'lēd\ *n* **1** : a position at the front; *also* : a margin by which one leads **2** : the privilege of leading in cards; *also* : the card or suit led **3** : EXAMPLE **4** : one that leads **5** : a principal role (as in a play); *also* : one who plays such a role **6** : INDICATION, CLUE **7** : an insulated electrical conductor

³lead \'led\ *n* **1** : a heavy malleable bluish white chemical element —see ELEMENT table **2** : an article made of lead; *esp* : a weight for sounding at sea **3** : a thin strip of metal used to separate lines of type in printing **4** : a thin stick of marking substance in or for a pencil

⁴lead \'led\ *vb* **1** : to cover, line, or weight with lead **2** : to fix (glass) in position with lead **3** : to treat or mix with lead or a lead compound

lead·en \'led-ᵊn\ *adj* **1** : made of lead; *also* : of the color of lead **2** : SLUGGISH, DULL

lead off *vb* : OPEN, BEGIN; *esp* : to bat first in an inning — **lead·off** \'lēd-ˌȯf\ *n or adj*

¹leaf \'lēf\ *n, pl* **leaves** \'lēvz\ **1** : a usu. flat and green outgrowth of a plant stem that is a unit of foliage and functions esp. in photosynthesis; *also* : FOLIAGE **2** : something that is suggestive of a leaf — **leaf·less** *adj* — **leafy** *adj*

²leaf *vb* **1** : to produce leaves **2** : to turn the pages of a book

leaf·age \'lē-fij\ *n* : FOLIAGE

leafed \'lēft\ *adj* : LEAVED

leaf·hop·per \'lēf-ˌhä-pər\ *n* : any of a family of small leaping insects related to the cicadas that suck the juices of plants

leaf·let \'lē-flət\ *n* **1** : a division of a compound leaf **2** : PAMPHLET, FOLDER

leaf mold *n* : a compost or layer composed chiefly of decayed vegetable matter

leaf·stalk \'lēf-ˌstȯk\ *n* : PETIOLE

¹league \'lēg\ *n* : a unit of distance equal to about three miles (five kilometers)

²league *n* **1** : an association or alliance for a common purpose **2** : CLASS, CATEGORY — **league** *vb* — **leagu·er** \'lē-gər\ *n*

¹leak \'lēk\ *vb* **1** : to enter or escape through a leak **2** : to let a substance in or out through an opening **3** : to become or make known

²leak *n* **1** : a crack or hole that accidentally admits a fluid or light or lets it escape; *also* : something that secretly or accidentally permits the admission or escape of something else **2** : LEAKAGE — **leaky** *adj*

leak·age \'lē-kij\ *n* **1** : the act of leaking **2** : the thing or amount that leaks

¹lean \'lēn\ *vb* **1** : to bend from a vertical position : INCLINE **2** : to cast one's weight to one side for support **3**

: to rely on for support **4** : to incline in opinion, taste, or desire — **lean** *n*

²**lean** *adj* **1** : lacking or deficient in flesh and esp. in fat **2** : lacking richness or productiveness **3** : low in fuel content — **lean·ness** *n*

leant \'lent\ *chiefly Brit past of* LEAN

lean–to \'lēn-ˌtü\ *n, pl* **lean–tos** \-ˌtüz\ : a wing or extension of a building having a roof of only one slope; *also* : a rough shed or shelter with a similar roof

¹**leap** \'lēp\ *vb* **leapt** \'lept, 'lept\ *or* **leaped; leap·ing** : to spring free from a surface or over an obstacle : JUMP

²**leap** *n* : JUMP

leap·frog \'lēp-ˌfròg, -ˌfräg\ *n* : a game in which a player bends down and is vaulted over by another — **leapfrog** *vb*

leap year *n* : a year containing 366 days with February 29 as the extra day

learn \'lərn\ *vb* **learned** \'lərnd, 'lərnt\; **learn·ing 1** : to gain knowledge, understanding, or skill by study or experience; *also* : MEMORIZE **2** : to find out : ASCERTAIN — **learn·er** *n*

learn·ed \'lər-nəd\ *adj* : SCHOLARLY, ERUDITE — **learn·ed·ly** *adv* — **learn·ed·ness** *n*

learn·ing \'lər-niŋ\ *n* : KNOWLEDGE, ERUDITION

learning disabled *adj* : having difficulty in learning a basic scholastic skill because of a disorder (as dyslexia) that interferes with the learning process — **learning disability** *n*

learnt \'lərnt\ *chiefly Brit past and past part of* LEARN

¹**lease** \'lēs\ *n* : a contract transferring real estate for a term of years or at will usu. for a specified rent

²**lease** *vb* **leased; leas·ing 1** : to grant by lease **2** : to hold under a lease **syn** let, charter, hire, rent

lease·hold \'lēs-ˌhōld\ *n* **1** : a tenure by lease **2** : land held by lease — **lease·hold·er** *n*

leash \'lēsh\ *n* [ME *lees, leshe,* fr. OF *laisse,* fr. *laissier* to let go, fr. L *laxare* to loosen, fr. *laxus* slack] : a line for leading or restraining an animal — **leash** *vb*

¹**least** \'lēst\ *adj* **1** : lowest in importance or position **2** : smallest in size or degree **3** : SLIGHTEST

²**least** *n* : one that is least

³**least** *adv* : in the smallest or lowest degree

least common denominator *n* : the least common multiple of two or more denominators

least common multiple *n* : the smallest common multiple of two or more numbers

least·wise \'lēst-ˌwīz\ *adv* : at least

leath·er \'le-thər\ *n* : animal skin dressed for use — **leath·ern** \-thərn\ *adj* — **leath·ery** *adj*

leath·er·neck \-ˌnek\ *n* : MARINE

¹**leave** \'lēv\ *vb* **left** \'left\; **leav·ing 1** : to allow or cause to remain behind **2** : to have as a remainder **3** : BEQUEATH **4** : to let stay without interference **5** : to go away : depart from **6** : GIVE UP, ABANDON

²**leave** *n* **1** : PERMISSION; *also* : authorized absence from duty **2** : DEPARTURE

³**leave** *vb* **leaved; leav·ing** : LEAF

leaved \'lēvd\ *adj* : having leaves

¹**leav·en** \'le-vən\ *n* **1** : a substance (as yeast) used to produce fermentation (as in dough) **2** : something that modifies or lightens

²**leaven** *vb* : to raise (dough) with a leaven; *also* : to permeate with a modifying or vivifying element

leav·en·ing *n* : LEAVEN

leaves *pl of* LEAF

leave-tak·ing \'lēv-ˌtā-kiŋ\ *n* : DEPARTURE, FAREWELL

leav·ings \'lē-viŋz\ *n pl* : REMNANT, RESIDUE

Leb·a·nese \ˌle-bə-'nēz, -'nēs\ *n* : a native or inhabitant of Lebanon — **Lebanese** *adj*

lech·ery \'le-chə-rē\ *n* : inordinate indulgence in sexual activity — **lech·er** \'le-chər\ *n* — **lech·er·ous** \'le-chə-rəs\ *adj* — **lech·er·ous·ly** *adv* — **lech·er·ous·ness** *n*

lec·i·thin \'le-sə-thən\ *n* : any of several waxy phosphorus-containing substances that are common in animals and plants, form colloidal solutions in water, and have emulsifying and wetting properties

lect *abbr* lecture; lecturer

lec·tern \'lek-tərn\ *n* : a stand to support a book for a standing reader

lec·tor \-tər\ *n* : one whose chief duty is to read the lessons in a church service

lec·ture \'lek-chər\ *n* **1** : a discourse given before an audience esp. for instruction **2** : REPRIMAND — **lec·ture** *vb* — **lec·tur·er** *n* — **lec·ture·ship** *n*

led *past and past part of* LEAD

LED \ˌel-(ˌ)ē-'dē\ *n* [*light-emitting diode*] : a semiconductor diode that emits light when a voltage is applied to it and is used esp. for electronic displays

le·der·ho·sen \'lā-dər-ˌhōz-ᵊn\ *n pl* : leather shorts often with suspenders worn esp. in Bavaria

ledge \'lej\ *n* [ME *legge* bar of a gate] **1** : a shelflike projection from a top or an edge **2** : REEF

led·ger \'le-jər\ *n* : a book containing accounts to which debits and credits are transferred in final form

lee \'lē\ *n* **1** : a protecting shelter **2** : the side (as of a ship) that is sheltered from the wind — **lee** *adj*

leech \'lēch\ *n* **1** : any of various segmented usu. freshwater worms that are related to the earthworms and have a sucker at each end **2** : a hanger-on who seeks gain

leek \'lēk\ *n* : an onionlike herb grown for its mildly pungent leaves and stalk

leer \'lir\ *n* : a suggestive, knowing, or malicious look — **leer** *vb*

leery \'lir-ē\ *adj* : SUSPICIOUS, WARY

lees \'lēz\ *n pl* : DREGS

¹**lee·ward** \'lē-wərd, 'lü-ərd\ *n* : the lee side

²**leeward** *adj* : situated away from the wind

lee·way \'lē-ˌwā\ *n* **1** : lateral movement of a ship when under way **2** : an allowable margin of freedom or variation

¹**left** \'left\ *adj* [ME, fr. OE, weak; fr. the left hand's being the weaker in most individuals] **1** : of, relating to, or being the side of the body in which the heart is mostly located; *also* : located nearer to this side than to the right **2** *often cap* : of, adhering to, or constituted by the political Left — **left** *adv*

²**left** *n* **1** : the left hand; *also* : the side or part that is on or toward the left side **2** *cap* : those professing political views marked by desire to reform the established order and usu. to give greater freedom to the common man

³**left** *past and past part of* LEAVE

left–hand *adj* **1** : situated on the left **2** : LEFT-HANDED

left–hand·ed \'left-'han-dəd\ *adj* **1** : using the left hand habitually or more easily than the right **2** : designed for or done with the left hand **3** : INSINCERE, BACKHANDED ⟨a ~ compliment⟩ **4** : COUNTERCLOCKWISE — **left–handed** *adv*

left·ism \'lef-ˌti-zəm\ *n* **1** : the principles and views of the Left **2** : advocacy of the doctrines of the Left — **left·ist** \-tist\ *n or adj*

left·over \'left-ˌō-vər\ *n* : something that remains unused or unconsumed

¹**leg** \'leg\ *n* **1** : a limb of an animal used esp. for supporting the body and in walking; *also* : the part of the vertebrate leg between knee and foot **2** : something resembling or analogous to an animal leg ⟨table ~⟩ **3** : the part of an article of clothing that covers the leg **4** : a portion of a trip — **legged** \'legd, 'le-gəd\ *adj* — **legless** *adj*

\ə\abut \ᵊ\kitten \ər\further \a\ash \ā\ace \ä\mop, mar \aü\out \ch\chin \e\bet \ē\easy \g\go \i\hit \ī\ice \j\job \ŋ\sing \ō\go \ò\law \òi\boy \th\thin \t̲h̲\the \ü\loot \u̇\foot \y\yet \zh\vision *see also* Pronunciation Symbols page

²**leg** *vb* **legged; leg·ging** : to use the legs in walking or esp. in running

³**leg** *abbr* **1** legal **2** legislative; legislature

leg·a·cy \'le-gə-sē\ *n, pl* **-cies** : INHERITANCE; *also* : something that has come from a predecessor or the past

le·gal \'lē-gəl\ *adj* **1** : of or relating to law or lawyers **2** : LAWFUL; *also* : STATUTORY **3** : enforced in courts of law — **le·gal·i·ty** \li-'ga-lə-tē\ *n* — **le·gal·ize** \'lē-gə-ˌlīz\ *vb* — **le·gal·ly** *adv*

le·gal·ism \'lē-gə-ˌli-zəm\ *n* **1** : strict, literal, or excessive conformity to the law or to a religious or moral code **2** : a legal term — **le·gal·is·tic** \ˌlē-gə-'lis-tik\ *adj*

leg·ate \'le-gət\ *n* : an official representative

leg·a·tee \ˌle-gə-'tē\ *n* : a person to whom a legacy is bequeathed

le·ga·tion \li-'gā-shən\ *n* **1** : a diplomatic mission headed by a minister **2** : the official residence and office of a minister in a foreign country

le·ga·to \li-'gä-tō\ *adv or adj* [It, lit., tied] : in a smooth and connected manner (as of music)

leg·end \'le-jənd\ *n* [ME *legende*, fr. MF & ML; MF *legende*, fr. ML *legenda*, fr. L *legere* to read] **1** : a story coming down from the past; *esp* : one popularly accepted as historical though not verifiable **2** : an inscription on an object; *also* : CAPTION **3** : an explanatory list of the symbols on a map or chart

leg·end·ary \'le-jən-ˌder-ē\ *adj* **1** : of, relating to, or characteristic of a legend **2** : FAMOUS — **leg·en·dari·ly** \-ˌder-ə-lē\ *adv*

leg·er·de·main \ˌle-jər-də-'mān\ *n* [ME, fr. MF *leger de main* light of hand] : SLEIGHT OF HAND

leg·ging *or* **leg·gin** \'le-gən, -giŋ\ *n* : a covering for the leg; *also* : TIGHTS

leg·gy \'le-gē\ *adj* **leg·gi·er; -est 1** : having unusually long legs **2** : having long and attractive legs **3** : SPINDLY — used of a plant

leg·horn \'leg-ˌhȯrn, 'le-gərn\ *n* **1** : a fine plaited straw; *also* : a hat made of this straw **2** : any of a Mediterranean breed of small hardy fowls

leg·i·ble \'le-jə-bəl\ *adj* : capable of being read : CLEAR — **leg·i·bil·i·ty** \ˌle-jə-'bi-lə-tē\ *n* — **leg·i·bly** \'le-jə-blē\ *adv*

¹**le·gion** \'lē-jən\ *n* **1** : a unit of the Roman army comprising 3000 to 6000 soldiers **2** : MULTITUDE **3** : an association of ex-servicemen — **le·gion·ary** \-jə-ˌner-ē\ *n* — **le·gion·naire** \ˌlē-jə-'nar\ *n*

²**legion** *adj* : MANY, NUMEROUS

legis *abbr* legislation; legislative; legislature

leg·is·late \'le-jəs-ˌlāt\ *vb* **-lat·ed; -lat·ing** : to make or enact laws; *also* : to bring about by legislation — **leg·is·la·tor** \-ˌlā-tər\ *n*

leg·is·la·tion \ˌle-jəs-'lā-shən\ *n* **1** : the action of legislating **2** : laws made by a legislative body

leg·is·la·tive \'le-jəs-ˌlā-tiv\ *adj* **1** : having the power of legislating **2** : of or relating to a legislature or legislation

leg·is·la·ture \'le-jəs-ˌlā-chər\ *n* : an organized body of persons having the authority to make laws

le·git \li-'jit\ *adj, slang* : LEGITIMATE

¹**le·git·i·mate** \li-'ji-tə-mət\ *adj* **1** : lawfully begotten **2** : GENUINE **3** : LAWFUL **4** : conforming to recognized principles or accepted rules or standards — **le·git·i·ma·cy** \-mə-sē\ *n* — **le·git·i·mate·ly** *adv*

²**le·git·i·mate** \-ˌmāt\ *vb* : to make legitimate

le·git·i·mize \li-'ji-tə-ˌmīz\ *vb* **-mized; -miz·ing** : LEGITIMATE

leg·man \'leg-ˌman\ *n* **1** : a reporter assigned usu. to gather information **2** : an assistant who gathers information and runs errands

le·gume \'le-ˌgyüm, li-'gyüm\ *n* [F] **1** : any of a large family of plants having fruits that are dry pods and split when ripe and including important food and forage plants (as beans and clover); *also* : the part (as seeds or pods) of a legume used as food **2** : the pod of a legume — **le·gu·mi·nous** \li-'gyü-mə-nəs\ *adj*

¹**lei** \'lā, 'lā-ē\ *n* : a wreath or necklace usu. of flowers

²**lei** \'lā\ *pl of* LEU

lei·sure \'lē-zhər, 'le-, 'lā-\ *n* **1** : time free from work or duties **2** : EASE; *also* : CONVENIENCE **syn** relaxation, rest, repose — **lei·sure·ly** *adj or adv*

leit·mo·tiv *or* **leit·mo·tif** \'līt-mō-ˌtēf\ *n* [G *Leitmotiv*, fr. *leiten* to lead + *Motiv* motive] : a dominant recurring theme

lek \'lek\ *n, pl* **leks** *or* **le·ke** *also* **lek** *or* **le·ku** — see MONEY table

lem·ming \'le-miŋ\ *n* [Norw] : any of various short-tailed northern rodents; *esp* : one of Europe noted for recurrent mass migrations

lem·on \'le-mən\ *n* **1** : an acid yellow usu. nearly oblong citrus fruit; *also* : a citrus tree that bears lemons **2** : something (as an automobile) unsatisfactory or defective — **lem·ony** *adj*

lem·on·ade \ˌle-mə-'nād\ *n* : a beverage of lemon juice, sugar, and water

lem·pi·ra \lem-'pir-ə\ *n* — see MONEY table

le·mur \'lē-mər\ *n* : any of various arboreal mammals largely of Madagascar that are related to the monkeys and have large eyes, very soft woolly fur, and a long furry tail

lemur

lend \'lend\ *vb* **lent** \'lent\; **lend·ing 1** : to give for temporary use on condition that the same or its equivalent be returned **2** : AFFORD, FURNISH **3** : ACCOMMODATE — **lend·er** *n*

lend–lease \-'lēs\ *n* : the transfer of goods and services to an ally to aid in a common cause with payment made by a return of the items or their use in the cause or by a similar transfer of other goods and services

length \'leŋth\ *n* **1** : the longer or longest dimension of an object; *also* : a measured distance **2** : duration or extent in time or space **3** : the length of something taken as a unit of measure **4** : a single piece of a series of pieces that may be joined together ⟨a ∼ of pipe⟩ — **at length 1** : in full **2** : FINALLY

length·en \'leŋ-thən\ *vb* : to make or become longer **syn** extend, elongate, prolong, protract

length·wise \'leŋth-ˌwīz\ *adv* : in the direction of the length — **lengthwise** *adj*

lengthy \'leŋ-thē\ *adj* **length·i·er; -est 1** : protracted excessively **2** : EXTENDED, LONG

le·nient \'lē-nē-ənt, -nyənt\ *adj* : of mild and tolerant disposition or effect **syn** indulgent, forbearing, merciful, tolerant — **le·ni·en·cy** \'lē-nē-ən-sē, -nyən-sē\ *n* — **le·ni·ent·ly** *adv*

len·i·tive \'le-nə-tiv\ *adj* : alleviating pain or harshness

len·i·ty \'le-nə-tē\ *n* : LENIENCY

lens \'lenz\ *n* [L *lent-, lens* lentil; so called fr. the shape of a convex lens] **1** : a curved piece of glass or plastic used singly or combined in an optical instrument for forming an image; *also* : a device for focusing radiation other than light **2** : a transparent body in the eye that focuses light rays on receptors at the back of the eye

Lent \'lent\ *n* : a 40-day period of penitence and fasting observed from Ash Wednesday to Easter by many churches — **Lent·en** \-ᵊn\ *adj*

len·til \'lent-ᵊl\ *n* : a Eurasian annual legume grown for its flat edible seeds and for fodder; *also* : its seed

Leo \'lē-ō\ *n* [L, lit., lion] **1** : a zodiacal constellation between Cancer and Virgo usu. pictured as a lion **2** : the 5th sign of the zodiac in astrology; *also* : one born under this sign

le·one \lē-'ōn\ *n, pl* **leones** *or* **leone** — see MONEY table

le·o·nine \'lē-ə-ˌnīn\ *adj* : of, relating to, or resembling a lion

leop·ard \'le-pərd\ *n* : a large usu. tawny and black-spotted cat of southern Asia and Africa

le·o·tard \'lē-ə-ˌtärd\ *n* : a close-fitting garment worn esp. by dancers and for exercise

lep·er \'le-pər\ *n* **1** : a person affected with leprosy **2** : OUTCAST

lep·re·chaun \'le-prə-ˌkän\ *n* : a mischievous elf of Irish folklore

lep·ro·sy \'le-prə-sē\ *n* : a chronic bacterial disease marked esp. if not treated by slow-growing swellings with deformity and loss of sensation of affected parts — **lep·rous** \-prəs\ *adj*

lep·ton \lep-'tän\ *n, pl* **lep·ta** \-'tä\ — see *drachma* at MONEY table

les·bi·an \'lez-bē-ən\ *n, often cap* [fr. the reputed homosexual group associated with the poet Sappho of Lesbos] : a female homosexual — **lesbian** *adj, often cap* — **les·bi·an·ism** \-ə-ˌni-zəm\ *n*

lèse ma·jes·té *or* **lese maj·es·ty** \'lāz-'ma-jə-stē, 'lez-, 'lēz-\ *n* [MF *lese majesté*, fr. L *laesa majestas*, lit., injured majesty] : an offense violating the dignity of a sovereign

le·sion \'lē-zhən\ *n* : an abnormal structural change in the body due to injury or disease; *esp* : one clearly marked off from healthy tissue around it

¹less \'les\ *adj, comparative of* ¹LITTLE **1** : FEWER ⟨∼ than six⟩ **2** : of lower rank, degree, or importance **3** : SMALLER; *also* : more limited in quantity

²less *adv, comparative of* ²LITTLE : to a lesser extent or degree

³less *n, pl* **less** **1** : a smaller portion **2** : something of less importance

⁴less *prep* : diminished by : MINUS

-less \ləs\ *adj suffix* **1** : destitute of : not having ⟨childless⟩ **2** : unable to be acted on or to act (in a specified way) ⟨daunt*less*⟩

les·see \le-'sē\ *n* : a tenant under a lease

less·en \'les-ᵊn\ *vb* : to make or become less **syn** decrease, diminish, dwindle, abate

less·er \'le-sər\ *adj, comparative of* ¹LITTLE : of less size, quality, or significance

les·son \'les-ᵊn\ *n* **1** : a passage from sacred writings read in a service of worship **2** : a reading or exercise to be studied by a pupil; *also* : something learned **3** : a period of instruction **4** : an instructive example

les·sor \'le-ˌsȯr, le-'sȯr\ *n* : one who conveys property by a lease

lest \ˌlest\ *conj* : for fear that

¹let \'let\ *n* [ME *lette*, fr. *letten* to delay, hinder, fr. OE *lettan*] **1** : HINDRANCE, OBSTACLE **2** : a shot or point in racket games that does not count

²let *vb* **let; let·ting** [ME *leten*, fr. OE *lǣtan*] **1** : to cause to : MAKE ⟨∼ it be known⟩ **2** : RENT, LEASE; *also* : to

assign esp. after bids **3** : ALLOW, PERMIT ⟨∼ me go⟩

-let \lət\ *n suffix* **1** : small one ⟨book*let*⟩ **2** : article worn on ⟨wrist*let*⟩

let·down \'let-ˌdaůn\ *n* **1** : DISAPPOINTMENT **2** : a slackening of effort

le·thal \'lē-thəl\ *adj* : DEADLY, FATAL — **le·thal·ly** *adv*

leth·ar·gy \'le-thər-jē\ *n* **1** : abnormal drowsiness **2** : the quality or state of being lazy or indifferent **syn** languor, lassitude, torpor — **le·thar·gic** \li-'thär-jik\ *adj*

let on *vb* **1** : REVEAL 1 **2** : PRETEND

¹let·ter \'le-tər\ *n* **1** : a symbol that stands for a speech sound and constitutes a unit of an alphabet **2** : a written or printed communication **3** *pl* : LITERATURE; *also* : LEARNING **4** : the literal meaning ⟨the ∼ of the law⟩ **5** : a single piece of type

²letter *vb* : to mark with letters : INSCRIBE — **let·ter·er** *n*

let·ter·head \'le-tər-ˌhed\ *n* : stationery with a printed or engraved heading; *also* : the heading itself

let·ter–per·fect \ˌle-tər-'pər-fikt\ *adj* : correct to the smallest detail

let·ter·press \'le-tər-ˌpres\ *n* : printing done directly by impressing the paper on an inked raised surface

letters of marque \-'märk\ : a license granted to a private person by a government to fit out an armed ship to capture enemy shipping

letters patent *n pl* : a written grant from a government to a person in a form readily open for inspection by all

let·tuce \'le-təs\ *n* [ME *letuse*, fr. MF *laitues*, pl. of *laitue*, fr. L *lactuca*, fr. *lac* milk; fr. its milky juice] : a garden composite plant with crisp leaves used esp. in salads

let·up \'let-ˌəp\ *n* : a lessening of effort

leu \'leů\ *n, pl* **lei** \'lā\ — see MONEY table

leu·kae·mia *chiefly Brit var of* LEUKEMIA

leu·ke·mia \lü-'kē-mē-ə\ *n* : a disease in which white blood cells increase greatly — **leu·ke·mic** \-mik\ *adj or n*

leu·ko·cyte \'lü-kə-ˌsīt\ *n* : any of the white or colorless cells with a nucleus found in bodily tissues and esp. blood

lev \'lef\ *n, pl* **le·va** \'le-və\ — see MONEY table

Lev *or* **Levit** *abbr* Leviticus

¹le·vee \'le-vē; lə-'vē, -'vā\ *n* [F *lever* act of arising] : a reception held by or for a person of distinction

²lev·ee \'le-vē\ *n* : an embankment to prevent or confine flooding; *also* : a river landing place

¹lev·el \'le-vəl\ *n* **1** : a device for establishing a horizontal line or plane **2** : horizontal condition **3** : a horizontal position, line, or surface often taken as an index of altitude; *also* : a flat area of ground **4** : height, position, rank, or size in a scale

²level *vb* **-eled** *or* **-elled; -el·ing** *or* **-el·ling** **1** : to make flat or level; *also* : to come to a level **2** : AIM, DIRECT **3** : EQUALIZE **4** : RAZE — **lev·el·er** *n*

³level *adj* **1** : having a flat even surface **2** : HORIZONTAL **3** : of the same height or rank; *also* : UNIFORM **4** : steady and cool in judgment — **lev·el·ly** *adv* — **lev·el·ness** *n*

lev·el·head·ed \ˌle-vəl-'he-dəd\ *adj* : having sound judgment : SENSIBLE

le·ver \'le-vər, 'lē-\ *n* **1** : a bar used for prying or dislodging something; *also* : a means for achieving one's purpose **2** : a rigid piece turning about an axis and used for transmitting and changing force and motion

le·ver·age \'le-vrij, 'lē-, -və-rij\ *n* : the action or mechanical effect of a lever

le·vi·a·than \li-'vī-ə-thən\ *n* **1** : a large sea animal **2** : something large or formidable

---

\ə\abut \ᵊ\kitten \ər\further \a\ash \ā\ace \ä\mop, mar
\aů\out \ch\chin \e\bet \ē\easy \g\go \i\hit \ī\ice \j\job
\ŋ\sing \ō\go \ȯ\law \ȯi\boy \th\thin \th\the \ü\loot \ů\foot
\y\yet \zh\vision *see also* Pronunciation Symbols

lev·i·tate \'le-və-ˌtāt\ *vb* **-tat·ed; -tat·ing** : to rise or cause to rise in the air in seeming defiance of gravitation — **lev·i·ta·tion** \ˌle-və-'tā-shən\ *n*

Le·vit·i·cus \li-'vi-tə-kəs\ *n* — see BIBLE table

lev·i·ty \'le-və-tē\ *n* : lack of seriousness **syn** lightness, flippancy, frivolity

¹**levy** \'le-vē\ *n, pl* **lev·ies** **1** : the imposition or collection of an assessment; *also* : an amount levied **2** : the enlistment or conscription of men for military service; *also* : troops raised by levy

²**levy** *vb* **lev·ied; levy·ing** **1** : to impose or collect by legal authority **2** : to enlist for military service **3** : WAGE ⟨∼ war⟩ **4** : to seize property

lewd \'lüd\ *adj* [ME *lewed* vulgar, fr. OE *lǣwede* lay, ignorant] **1** : sexually unchaste **2** : OBSCENE, VULGAR — **lewd·ly** *adv* — **lewd·ness** *n*

lex·i·cog·ra·phy \ˌlek-sə-'kä-grə-fē\ *n* **1** : the editing or making of a dictionary **2** : the principles and practices of dictionary making — **lex·i·cog·ra·pher** \-fər\ *n* — **lex·i·co·graph·i·cal** \-kō-'gra-fi-kəl\ *or* **lex·i·co·graph·ic** \-fik\ *adj*

lex·i·con \'lek-sə-ˌkän\ *n, pl* **lex·i·ca** \-si-kə\ *or* **lexicons** **1** : DICTIONARY **2** : the vocabulary of a language, speaker, or subject

lg *abbr* **1** large **2** long

LH *abbr* **1** left hand **2** lower half

li *abbr* link

Li *symbol* lithium

LI *abbr* Long Island

li·a·bil·i·ty \ˌlī-ə-'bi-lə-tē\ *n, pl* **-ties 1** : the quality or state of being liable **2** *pl* : DEBTS **3** : DISADVANTAGE

li·a·ble \'lī-ə-bəl\ *adj* **1** : legally obligated : RESPONSIBLE **2** : LIKELY, APT ⟨∼ to fall⟩ **3** : SUSCEPTIBLE

li·ai·son \'lē-ə-ˌzän, lē-'ā-\ *n* [F] **1** : a close bond : INTERRELATIONSHIP **2** : an illicit sexual relationship **3** : communication for mutual understanding (as between parts of an armed force); *also* : one that carries on a liaison

li·ar \'lī-ər\ *n* : a person who lies

¹**lib** \'lib\ *n* : LIBERATION

²**lib** *abbr* **1** liberal **2** librarian; library

li·ba·tion \lī-'bā-shən\ *n* **1** : an act of pouring a liquid as a sacrifice (as to a god); *also* : the liquid poured **2** : DRINK

¹**li·bel** \'lī-bəl\ *n* [ME, written declaration, fr. MF, fr. L *libellus,* dim. of *liber* book] **1** : a spoken or written statement or a representation that gives an unjustly unfavorable impression of a person or thing **2** : the action or crime of publishing a libel — **li·bel·ous** *or* **li·bel·lous** \-bə-ləs\ *adj*

²**libel** *vb* **-beled** *or* **-belled; -bel·ing** *or* **-bel·ling** : to make or publish a libel — **li·bel·er** *n* — **li·bel·ist** *n*

¹**lib·er·al** \'li-brəl, -bə-rəl\ *adj* [ME, fr. MF, fr. L *liberalis* suitable for a freeman, generous, fr. *liber* free] **1** : of, relating to, or based on the liberal arts **2** : GENEROUS, BOUNTIFUL **3** : not literal **4** : not narrow in opinion or judgment : TOLERANT; *also* : not orthodox **5** : not conservative — **lib·er·al·i·ty** \ˌli-bə-'ra-lə-tē\ *n* — **lib·er·al·ize** \'li-brə-ˌlīz, -bə-rə-\ *vb* — **lib·er·al·ly** *adv*

²**liberal** *n* : a person who holds liberal views

liberal arts *n pl* : the studies (as language, philosophy, history, literature, or abstract science) in a college or university intended to provide chiefly general knowledge and to develop the general intellectual capacities

lib·er·al·ism \'li-brə-ˌli-zəm, -bə-rə-\ *n* : liberal principles and theories

lib·er·ate \'li-bə-ˌrāt\ *vb* **-at·ed; -at·ing 1** : to free from bondage or restraint; *also* : to raise to equal rights and status **2** : to free (as a gas) from combination — **lib·er·a·tion** \ˌli-bə-'rā-shən\ *n* — **lib·er·a·tor** \'li-bə-ˌrā-tər\ *n*

lib·er·at·ed *adj* : freed from or opposed to traditional social and sexual attitudes or roles ⟨a ∼ marriage⟩

Li·be·ri·an \lī-'bir-ē-ən\ *n* : a native or inhabitant of Liberia — **Liberian** *adj*

lib·er·tar·i·an \ˌli-bər-'ter-ē-ən\ *n* **1** : an advocate of the doctrine of free will **2** : one who upholds the principles of unrestricted liberty

lib·er·tine \'li-bər-ˌtēn\ *n* : a person who leads a dissolute life

lib·er·ty \'li-bər-tē\ *n, pl* **-ties 1** : FREEDOM **2** : an action going beyond normal limits; *esp* : FAMILIARITY **3** : a short leave from naval duty

li·bid·i·nous \lə-'bid-ᵊn-əs\ *adj* **1** : LASCIVIOUS **2** : LIBIDINAL

li·bi·do \lə-'bē-dō, -'bī-\ *n, pl* **-dos** [NL, fr. L, desire, lust] **1** : psychic energy derived from basic biological urges **2** : sexual drive — **li·bid·i·nal** \lə-'bid-ᵊn-əl\ *adj*

Li·bra \'lē-brə\ *n* [L, lit., scales] **1** : a zodiacal constellation between Virgo and Scorpio usu. pictured as a balance scale **2** : the 7th sign of the zodiac in astrology; *also* : one born under this sign

li·brar·i·an \lī-'brer-ē-ən\ *n* : a specialist in the management of a library

li·brary \'lī-ˌbrer-ē\ *n, pl* **-brar·ies 1** : a place in which books and related materials are kept for use but not for sale **2** : a collection of books

li·bret·to \lə-'bre-tō\ *n, pl* **-tos** *or* **-ti** \-tē\ [It, dim. of *libro* book, fr. L *liber*] : the text esp. of an opera — **li·bret·tist** \-tist\ *n*

Lib·y·an \'li-bē-ən\ *n* : a native or inhabitant of Libya — **Libyan** *adj*

lice *pl of* LOUSE

li·cense *or* **li·cence** \'līs-ᵊns\ *n* **1** : permission to act **2** : a permission granted by authority to engage in an activity **3** : a document, plate, or tag providing proof of a license **4** : freedom used irresponsibly — **license** *vb*

licensed practical nurse *n* : a specially trained person who is licensed (as by a state) to provide routine care for the sick

licensed vocational nurse *n* : a licensed practical nurse licensed to practice in the states of California and Texas

li·cens·ee \ˌlīs-ᵊn-'sē\ *n* : a licensed person

licente *pl of* SENTE

li·cen·ti·ate \lī-'sen-chē-ət\ *n* : one licensed to practice a profession

li·cen·tious \lī-'sen-chəs\ *adj* : LEWD, LASCIVIOUS — **li·cen·tious·ly** *adv* — **li·cen·tious·ness** *n*

li·chee *var of* LITCHI

li·chen \'lī-kən\ *n* : any of various complex lower plants made up of an alga and a fungus growing as a unit on a solid surface — **li·chen·ous** *adj*

lic·it \'li-sət\ *adj* : LAWFUL

¹**lick** \'lik\ *vb* **1** : to draw the tongue over; *also* : to flicker over like a tongue **2** : THRASH; *also* : DEFEAT

²**lick** *n* **1** : a stroke of the tongue **2** : a small amount **3** : a hasty careless effort **4** : BLOW **5** : a natural deposit of salt that animals lick

lick·e·ty–split \ˌli-kə-tē-'split\ *adv* : at great speed

lick·spit·tle \'lik-ˌspit-ᵊl\ *n* : a fawning subordinate : TOADY

lic·o·rice \'li-kə-rish, -rəs\ *n* [ME *licorice,* fr. OF, fr. LL *liquiritia,* alter. of L *glycyrrhiza,* fr. Gk *glykyrrhiza,* fr. *glykys* sweet + *rhiza* root] **1** : the dried root of a European leguminous plant; *also* : an extract from it used esp. as a flavoring and in medicine **2** : a candy flavored with licorice **3** : a plant yielding licorice

lid \'lid\ *n* **1** : a movable cover **2** : EYELID **3** : something that confines or suppresses — **lid·ded** \'li-dəd\ *adj*

li·do \'lē-dō\ *n, pl* **lidos** : a fashionable beach resort

¹**lie** \'lī\ *vb* **lay** \'lā\; **lain** \'lān\; **ly·ing** \'lī-iŋ\ **1** : to be in, stay at rest in, or assume a horizontal position; *also* : to be in a helpless or defenseless state **2** : EXTEND **3** : to occupy a certain relative position **4** : to have an effect esp. through mere presence

²**lie** *n* : the position in which something lies

³lie *vb* lied; ly·ing \'lī-iŋ\ : to tell a lie
⁴lie *n* : an untrue statement made with intent to deceive
lied \'lēt\ *n, pl* lie·der \'lē-dər\ [G] : a German song esp. of the 19th century
lie detector *n* : an instrument for detecting physiological evidence of the tension that accompanies lying
lief \'lēv, 'lēf\ *adv* : GLADLY, WILLINGLY
¹liege \'lēj\ *adj* : LOYAL, FAITHFUL
²liege *n* 1 : VASSAL 2 : a feudal superior
lien \'lēn, 'lē-ən\ *n* : a legal claim on the property of another for the satisfaction of a debt or duty
lieu \'lü\ *n, archaic* : PLACE, STEAD — in lieu of : in the place of
lieut *abbr* lieutenant
lieu·ten·ant \lü-'te-nənt\ *n* [ME, fr. MF, fr. *lieu* place + *tenant* holding, fr. *tenir* to hold, fr. L *tenēre*] 1 : a representative of another in the performance of duty 2 : FIRST LIEUTENANT; *also* : SECOND LIEUTENANT 3 : a commissioned officer in the navy ranking next below a lieutenant commander — lieu·ten·an·cy \-nən-sē\ *n*
lieutenant colonel *n* : a commissioned officer (as in the army) ranking next below a colonel
lieutenant commander *n* : a commissioned officer in the navy ranking next below a commander
lieutenant general *n* : a commissioned officer (as in the army) ranking next below a general
lieutenant governor *n* : a deputy or subordinate governor
lieutenant junior grade *n, pl* lieutenants junior grade : a commissioned officer in the navy ranking next below a lieutenant
life \'līf\ *n, pl* lives \'līvz\ 1 : the quality that distinguishes a vital and functional being from a dead body or inanimate matter; *also* : a state of an organism characterized esp. by capacity for metabolism, growth, reaction to stimuli, and reproduction 2 : the physical and mental experiences of an individual 3 : BIOGRAPHY 4 : a specific phase or period ⟨adult ∼⟩ 5 : the period from birth to death; *also* : a sentence of imprisonment for the remainder of a person's life 6 : a way of living 7 : PERSON 8 : ANIMATION, SPIRIT; *also* : LIVELINESS 9 : living beings ⟨forest ∼⟩ 10 : animate activity ⟨signs of ∼⟩ 11 : one providing interest and vigor ⟨∼ of the party⟩ — life·less *adj* — life·like *adj*
life·blood \'līf-ˌbləd\ *n* : a basic source of strength and vitality
life·boat \-ˌbōt\ *n* : a sturdy boat designed for use in saving lives at sea
life·guard \-ˌgärd\ *n* : a usu. expert swimmer employed to safeguard bathers
life·line \-ˌlīn\ *n* 1 : a line to which persons may cling for safety 2 : something considered vital for survival
life·long \-ˌlȯŋ\ *adj* : continuing through life
life preserver *n* : a buoyant device designed to save a person from drowning
lif·er \'lī-fər\ *n* 1 : a person sentenced to life imprisonment 2 : a person who makes a career in the armed forces
life raft *n* : a raft for use by people forced into the water
life·sav·ing \'līf-ˌsā-viŋ\ *n* : the skill or practice of saving or protecting lives esp. of drowning persons — life·sav·er \-ˌsā-vər\ *n*
life science *n* : a branch of science (as biology, medicine, anthropology, or sociology) that deals with living organisms and life processes — usu. used in pl. — life scientist *n*
life·style \'līf-stīl\ *n* : a way of living
life·time \-ˌtīm\ *n* : the duration of an individual's existence
life·work \-'wərk\ *n* : the entire or principal work of one's lifetime; *also* : a work extending over a lifetime
LIFO *abbr* last in, first out
¹lift \'lift\ *vb* 1 : RAISE, ELEVATE; *also* : RISE, ASCEND 2 : to put an end to : STOP 3 : to pay off ⟨∼ a mortgage⟩ — lift·er *n*
²lift *n* 1 : LOAD 2 : the action or an instance of lifting 3 : HELP; *also* : a ride along one's way 4 : RISE, ADVANCE 5 *chiefly Brit* : ELEVATOR 6 : an elevation of the spirits 7 : the upward force that is developed by a moving airfoil and that opposes the pull of gravity
lift·off \'lif-ˌtȯf\ *n* : a vertical takeoff (as by a rocket)
lift truck *n* : a small truck for lifting and transporting loads
lig·a·ment \'li-gə-mənt\ *n* : a band of tough tissue that holds bones together or supports an organ in place
li·gate \'lī-ˌgāt\ *vb* li·gat·ed; li·gat·ing : to tie with a ligature — li·ga·tion \lī-'gā-shən\ *n*
lig·a·ture \'li-gə-ˌchu̇r, -chər\ *n* 1 : something that binds or ties; *also* : a thread used in surgery esp. for tying blood vessels 2 : a printed or written character consisting of two or more letters or characters (as æ) united
¹light \'līt\ *n* 1 : something that makes vision possible : electromagnetic radiation visible to the human eye; *also* : the sensation aroused by stimulation of the visual sense organs 2 : DAYLIGHT 3 : a source of light (as a candle) 4 : ENLIGHTENMENT; *also* : TRUTH 5 : public knowledge ⟨facts brought to ∼⟩ 6 : a particular aspect presented to view ⟨saw the matter in a different ∼⟩ 7 : WINDOW 8 *pl* : STANDARDS ⟨according to his ∼s⟩ 9 : CELEBRITY 10 : LIGHTHOUSE, BEACON; *also* : TRAFFIC LIGHT 11 : a flame for lighting something
²light *adj* 1 : having light : BRIGHT 2 : PALE 2 ⟨∼ blue⟩ — light·ness *n*
³light *vb* lit \'lit\ *or* light·ed; light·ing 1 : to make or become light 2 : to cause to burn : BURN 3 : to conduct with a light 4 : ILLUMINATE
⁴light *adj* 1 : not heavy 2 : not serious ⟨∼ reading⟩ 3 : SCANTY ⟨∼ rain⟩ 4 : easily disturbed ⟨a ∼ sleeper⟩ 5 : GENTLE ⟨a ∼ blow⟩ 6 : easily endurable ⟨a ∼ cold⟩; *also* : requiring little effort ⟨∼ exercise⟩ 7 : SWIFT, NIMBLE 8 : FRIVOLOUS 9 : DIZZY 10 : made with lower calorie content or less of some ingredient than usual ⟨∼ salad dressing⟩ 11 : producing goods for direct consumption by the consumer ⟨∼ industry⟩ — light·ly *adv* — light·ness *n*
⁵light *adv* 1 : LIGHTLY 2 : with little baggage ⟨travel ∼⟩
⁶light *vb* lit \'lit\ *or* light·ed; light·ing 1 : SETTLE, ALIGHT 2 : to fall unexpectedly 3 : HAPPEN
light–emitting diode *n* : LED
¹light·en \'lī-tᵊn\ *vb* 1 : ILLUMINATE, BRIGHTEN 2 : to give out flashes of lightning
²lighten *vb* 1 : to relieve of a burden 2 : GLADDEN 3 : to become lighter
lighten up *vb* : to take things less seriously
¹ligh·ter \'lī-tər\ *n* : a barge used esp. in loading or unloading ships
²light·er \'lī-tər\ *n* : one that lights; *esp* : a device for lighting
light·face \'līt-ˌfās\ *n* : a type having light thin lines — light·faced \-ˌfāst\ *adj*
light–head·ed \'līt-ˌhe-dəd\ *adj* 1 : feeling confused or dizzy 2 : lacking maturity or seriousness
light·heart·ed \-ˌhär-təd\ *adj* : free from worry — light·heart·ed·ly *adv* — light·heart·ed·ness *n*
light·house \-ˌhau̇s\ *n* : a structure with a powerful light for guiding sailors
light meter *n* : a usu. hand-held device for indicating correct photographic exposure
¹light·ning \'līt-niŋ\ *n* : the flashing of light produced by a discharge of atmospheric electricity; *also* : the discharge itself

²**lightning** *adj* : extremely fast
lightning bug *n* : FIREFLY
lightning rod *n* : a grounded metallic rod set up on a structure to protect it from lightning
light out *vb* : to leave in a hurry
light·proof \'līt-ˌprüf\ *adj* : impenetrable by light
lights \'līts\ *n pl* : the lungs esp. of a slaughtered animal
light·ship \'līt-ˌship\ *n* : a ship with a powerful light moored at a place dangerous to navigation
light show *n* : a kaleidoscopic display (as of colored lights)
light·some \'līt-səm\ *adj* **1** : free from care **2** : NIMBLE
¹**light·weight** \'līt-ˌwāt\ *n* : one of less than average weight; *esp* : a boxer weighing more than 126 but not over 135 pounds
²**lightweight** *adj* **1** : INCONSEQUENTIAL **2** : of less than average weight
light–year \'līt-ˌyir\ *n* **1** : an astronomical unit of distance equal to the distance that light travels in one year in a vacuum or about 5.88 trillion miles (9.46 trillion kilometers) **2** : an extremely large measure of comparison ⟨saw it ∼s ago⟩
lig·nin \'lig-nən\ *n* : a substance related to cellulose that occurs in the woody cell walls of plants and in the cementing material between them
lig·nite \'lig-ˌnīt\ *n* : brownish black soft coal
¹**like** \'līk\ *vb* **liked; lik·ing 1** : ENJOY ⟨∼s baseball⟩ **2** : WANT **3** : CHOOSE ⟨does as she ∼s⟩ — **lik·able** *or* **like·able** \'lī-kə-bəl\ *adj*
²**like** *n* : PREFERENCE
³**like** *adj* : SIMILAR *syn* alike, analogous, comparable, parallel, uniform
⁴**like** *prep* **1** : similar or similarly to ⟨it's ∼ when we were kids⟩ **2** : typical of **3** : comparable to **4** : as though there would be ⟨looks ∼ rain⟩ **5** : such as ⟨a subject ∼ physics⟩
⁵**like** *n* **1** : COUNTERPART **2** : one that is similar to another — **and the like** : ET CETERA
⁶**like** *conj* : in the same way that
-like \ˌlīk\ *adj comb form* : resembling or characteristic of ⟨lady*like*⟩ ⟨life*like*⟩
like·li·hood \'lī-klē-ˌhùd\ *n* : PROBABILITY
¹**like·ly** \'lī-klē\ *adj* **like·li·er; -est 1** : very probable **2** : BELIEVABLE **3** : PROMISING ⟨a ∼ place to fish⟩
²**likely** *adv* : in all probability
lik·en \'lī-kən\ *vb* : COMPARE
like·ness \'līk-nəs\ *n* **1** : COPY, PORTRAIT **2** : SEMBLANCE **3** : RESEMBLANCE
like·wise \-ˌwīz\ *adv* **1** : in like manner **2** : in addition : ALSO
lik·ing \'lī-kiŋ\ *n* : favorable regard; *also* : TASTE
li·ku·ta \li-'kü-tə\ *n, pl* **ma·ku·ta** \mä-\ — see *zaire* at MONEY table
li·lac \'lī-lək, -ˌlak, -ˌläk\ *n* [obs. F (now *lilas*), fr. Ar *līlak*, fr. Per *nīlak* bluish, fr. *nīl* blue, fr. Skt *nīla* dark blue] **1** : a shrub related to the olive that produces large clusters of fragrant grayish pink, purple, or white flowers **2** : a moderate purple color
lil·an·ge·ni \ˌli-lən-'ge-nē\ *n, pl* **em·a·lan·ge·ni** \ˌe-mə-lən-'ge-nē\ — see MONEY table
lil·li·pu·tian \ˌli-lə-'pyü-shən\ *adj, often cap* **1** : SMALL, MINIATURE **2** : PETTY
lilt \'lilt\ *n* **1** : a cheerful lively song or tune **2** : a rhythmical swing or flow
lily \'li-lē\ *n, pl* **lil·ies** : any of a genus of tall bulbous herbs with leafy stems and usu. funnel-shaped flowers; *also* : any of various related plants
lily of the valley : a low perennial herb related to the lilies that produces a raceme of fragrant nodding bell-shaped white flowers
li·ma bean \'lī-mə-\ *n* : a bushy or tall-growing bean widely cultivated for its flat edible usu. pale green or whitish seeds; *also* : the seed

limb \'lim\ *n* **1** : one of the projecting paired appendages (as legs, arms, or wings) used by an animal esp. in moving or grasping **2** : a large branch of a tree : BOUGH — **limb·less** *adj*
¹**lim·ber** \'lim-bər\ *adj* **1** : FLEXIBLE, SUPPLE **2** : LITHE, NIMBLE
²**limber** *vb* : to make or become limber
¹**lim·bo** \'lim-bō\ *n, pl* **limbos** [ME, fr. ML, abl. of *limbus* limbo, fr. L, border] **1** *often cap* : an abode of souls barred from heaven through no fault of their own **2** : a place or state of confinement, oblivion, or uncertainty
²**limbo** *n, pl* **limbos** : a West Indian acrobatic dance orig. for men
Lim·burg·er \'lim-ˌbər-gər\ *n* : a pungent semisoft surface-ripened cheese
¹**lime** \'līm\ *n* : a caustic powdery white solid that consists of calcium and oxygen, is obtained from limestone or shells, and is used in making cement and in fertilizer — **lime** *vb* — **limy** \'lī-mē\ *adj*
²**lime** *n* : a small yellowish green citrus fruit with juicy acid pulp
lime·ade \ˌlīm-'ād, 'lī-ˌmād\ *n* : a beverage of lime juice, sugar, and water
lime·light \'līm-ˌlīt\ *n* **1** : a device in which flame is directed against a cylinder of lime formerly used in the theater to cast a strong white light on the stage **2** : the center of public attention
lim·er·ick \'li-mə-rik\ *n* : a light or humorous poem of 5 lines
lime·stone \'līm-ˌstōn\ *n* : a rock that is formed by accumulation of organic remains (as shells), is used in building, and yields lime when burned
¹**lim·it** \'li-mət\ *n* **1** : something that restrains or confines; *also* : the utmost extent **2** : BOUNDARY; *also, pl* : BOUNDS **3** : a prescribed maximum or minimum — **lim·it·less** *adj* — **lim·it·less·ness** *n*
²**limit** *vb* **1** : to set limits to **2** : to reduce in quantity or extent — **lim·i·ta·tion** \ˌli-mə-'tā-shən\ *n*
lim·it·ed *adj* **1** : confined within limits **2** : offering faster service esp. by making fewer stops
limn \'lim\ *vb* **limned; limn·ing** \'li-miŋ, 'lim-niŋ\ **1** : DRAW; *also* : PAINT **2** : DELINEATE **3** : DESCRIBE
limo \'li-(ˌ)mō\ *n, pl* **limos** : LIMOUSINE
li·mo·nite \'lī-mə-ˌnīt\ *n* : a ferric oxide that is a major ore of iron — **li·mo·nit·ic** \ˌlī-mə-'ni-tik\ *adj*
lim·ou·sine \'li-mə-ˌzēn, ˌli-mə-'zēn\ *n* [F] **1** : a large luxurious often chauffeur-driven sedan **2** : a large vehicle for transporting passengers to and from an airport
¹**limp** \'limp\ *vb* : to walk lamely; *also* : to proceed with difficulty
²**limp** *n* : a limping movement or gait
³**limp** *adj* **1** : having no defined shape; *also* : not stiff or rigid **2** : lacking in strength or firmness — **limp·ly** *adv* — **limp·ness** *n*
lim·pet \'lim-pət\ *n* : any of numerous gastropod sea mollusks with a conical shell that clings to rocks or timbers
lim·pid \'lim-pəd\ *adj* : CLEAR, TRANSPARENT
lin *abbr* **1** lineal **2** linear
lin·age \'lī-nij\ *n* : the number of lines of written or printed matter
linch·pin \'linch-ˌpin\ *n* : a locking pin inserted crosswise (as through the end of an axle)
lin·den \'lin-dən\ *n* : any of a genus of trees with large heart-shaped leaves and clustered yellowish flowers rich in nectar
¹**line** \'līn\ *n* **1** : CORD, ROPE, WIRE; *also* : a length of material used in measuring and leveling **2** : pipes for conveying a fluid ⟨a gas ∼⟩ **3** : a horizontal row of written or printed characters; *also* : VERSE **4** : NOTE **5** : the words making up a part in a drama — usu. used in pl. **6** : something distinct, long, and narrow; *also* : ROUTE **7** : a state of agreement **8** : a course of conduct, action,

or thought; *also* : OCCUPATION **9** : LIMIT **10** : an arrangement of persons or objects of one kind in an orderly series ⟨waiting in ∼⟩ **11** : a transportation system **12** : the football players who are stationed on the line of scrimmage **13** : a long narrow mark; *also* : EQUATOR **14** : a geometric element that is the path of a moving point **15** : CONTOUR **16** : a general plan **17** : an indication based on insight or investigation

²**line** *vb* **lined; lin·ing** **1** : to mark with a line **2** : to place or form a line along **3** : ALIGN

³**line** *vb* **lined; lin·ing** : to cover the inner surface of

lin·eage \ˈli-nē-ij\ *n* : lineal descent from a common progenitor; *also* : FAMILY

lin·eal \ˈli-nē-əl\ *adj* **1** : LINEAR **2** : consisting of or being in a direct line of ancestry; *also* : HEREDITARY

lin·ea·ment \ˈli-nē-ə-mənt\ *n* : an outline, feature, or contour of a body and esp. of a face — usu. used in pl.

lin·ear \ˈli-nē-ər\ *adj* **1** : of, relating to, resembling, or having a graph that is a line and esp. a straight line : STRAIGHT **2** : composed of simply drawn lines with little attempt at pictorial representation ⟨∼ script⟩ **3** : being long and uniformly narrow

line·back·er \ˈlīn-ˌba-kər\ *n* : a defensive football player who lines up just behind the line of scrimmage

line drive *n* : a batted baseball hit in a flatter path than a fly ball

line·man \ˈlīn-mən\ *n* **1** : a person who sets up or repairs communication or power lines **2** : a player in the line in football

lin·en \ˈli-nən\ *n* **1** : cloth made of flax; *also* : thread or yarn spun from flax **2** : clothing or household articles made of linen cloth or similar fabric

line of scrimmage : an imaginary line in football parallel to the goal lines and tangent to the nose of the ball laid on the ground before a play

¹**lin·er** \ˈlī-nər\ *n* : a ship or airplane of a regular transportation line

²**liner** *n* : one that lines or is used as a lining — **lin·er·less** *adj*

line score *n* : a score of a baseball game giving the runs, hits, and errors made by each team

lines·man \ˈlīnz-mən\ *n* **1** : LINEMAN 1 **2** : an official who assists a referee

line·up \ˈlī-ˌnəp\ *n* **1** : a list of players taking part in a game (as of baseball) **2** : a line of persons arranged esp. for identification by police

ling \ˈliŋ\ *n* : any of various fishes related to the cod

-**ling** \liŋ\ *n suffix* **1** : one associated with ⟨nestling⟩ **2** : young, small, or minor one ⟨duckling⟩

lin·ger \ˈliŋ-gər\ *vb* : TARRY; *also* : PROCRASTINATE — **lin·ger·er** *n*

lin·ge·rie \ˌlän-jə-ˈrā, ˌlaⁿ-zhə-, -ˈrē\ *n* [F, fr. MF, fr. *linge* linen, fr. L *lineus* made of linen, fr. *linum* flax, linen] : women's intimate apparel

lin·go \ˈliŋ-gō\ *n, pl* **lingoes** : a usu. strange or incomprehensible language

lin·gua fran·ca \ˌliŋ-gwə-ˈfraŋ-kə\ *n, pl* **lingua francas** *or* **lin·guae fran·cae** \-gwē-ˈfraŋ-ˌkē\ [It] **1** *often cap* : a common language consisting of Italian mixed with French, Spanish, Greek, and Arabic that was formerly spoken in Mediterranean ports **2** : a common or commercial tongue among speakers of different languages

lin·gual \ˈliŋ-gwəl\ *adj* : of, relating to, or produced by the tongue

lin·guist \ˈliŋ-gwist\ *n* **1** : a person skilled in languages **2** : a person who specializes in linguistics

lin·guis·tics \liŋ-ˈgwis-tiks\ *n* : the study of human speech including the units, nature, structure, and modification of language — **lin·guis·tic** \-tik\ *adj*

lin·i·ment \ˈli-nə-mənt\ *n* : a liquid preparation rubbed on the skin esp. to relieve pain

lin·ing \ˈlī-niŋ\ *n* : material used to line esp. an inner surface

link \ˈliŋk\ *n* **1** : a connecting structure; *esp* : a single ring of a chain **2** : BOND, TIE — **link** *vb* — **link·er** *n*

link·age \ˈliŋ-kij\ *n* **1** : the manner or style of being united **2** : the quality or state of being linked **3** : a system of links

linking verb *n* : a word or expression (as a form of *be*, *become*, *feel*, or *seem*) that links a subject with its predicate

links \ˈliŋks\ *n pl* : a golf course

link·up \ˈliŋ-ˌkəp\ *n* **1** : MEETING **2** : something that serves as a linking device or factor

lin·net \ˈli-nət\ *n* : an Old World finch

li·no·leum \lə-ˈnō-lē-əm\ *n* [L *linum* flax + *oleum* oil] : a floor covering with a canvas back and a surface of hardened linseed oil and a filler

lin·seed \ˈlin-ˌsēd\ *n* : the seeds of flax yielding a yellowish oil (**linseed oil**) used esp. in paints and linoleum

lin·sey–wool·sey \ˌlin-zē-ˈwùl-zē\ *n* : a coarse sturdy fabric of wool and linen or cotton

lint \ˈlint\ *n* **1** : linen made into a soft fleecy substance **2** : fine ravels and short fibers of yarn or fabric **3** : the fibers that surround cotton seeds and form the cotton staple

lin·tel \ˈlint-əl\ *n* : a horizontal piece across the top of an opening (as of a door) that carries the weight of the structure above it

li·on \ˈlī-ən\ *n, pl* **lions** : a large heavily-built cat of Africa and southern Asia with a shaggy mane in the male

li·on·ess \ˈlī-ə-nəs\ *n* : a female lion

li·on·heart·ed \ˌlī-ən-ˈhär-təd\ *adj* : COURAGEOUS, BRAVE

li·on·ize \ˈlī-ə-ˌnīz\ *vb* -**ized; -iz·ing** : to treat as an object of great interest or importance — **li·on·i·za·tion** \ˌlī-ə-nə-ˈzā-shən\ *n*

lip \ˈlip\ *n* **1** : either of the two fleshy folds that surround the mouth; *also* : the margin of the human lip **2** : a part or projection suggesting a lip **3** : the edge of a hollow vessel or cavity — **lipped** \ˈlipt\ *adj*

lip·id \ˈli-pəd\ *n* : any of various substances (as fats and waxes) that with proteins and carbohydrates make up the principal structural parts of living cells

li·po·pro·tein \ˌli-pō-ˈprō-ˌtēn, ˌli-\ *n* : a protein that is a complex of protein and lipid

li·po·suc·tion \ˈli-pə-ˌsək-shən, ˈlī-\ *n* : surgical removal of local fat deposits (as in the thighs) esp. for cosmetic purposes

lip·read·ing \ˈlip-ˌrē-diŋ\ *n* : the interpreting of a speaker's words by watching lip and facial movements without hearing the voice

lip service *n* : an avowal of allegiance that is only verbal

lip·stick \ˈlip-ˌstik\ *n* : a waxy solid colored cosmetic in stick form for the lips — **lip·sticked** \-ˌstikt\ *adj*

liq *abbr* **1** liquid **2** liquor

liq·ue·fy *also* **liq·ui·fy** \ˈli-kwə-ˌfī\ *vb* -**fied; -fy·ing** : to make or become liquid — **liq·ue·fi·er** \-ˌfī-ər\ *n*

li·queur \li-ˈkər\ *n* [F] : a distilled alcoholic liquor flavored with aromatic substances and usu. sweetened

¹**liq·uid** \ˈli-kwəd\ *adj* **1** : flowing freely like water **2** : neither solid nor gaseous **3** : shining and clear ⟨large ∼ eyes⟩ **4** : smooth and musical in tone; *also* : smooth and unconstrained in movement **5** : consisting of or capable of ready conversion into cash ⟨∼ assets⟩ — **li·quid·i·ty** \li-ˈkwi-də-tē\ *n*

²**liquid** *n* : a liquid substance

liq·ui·date \ˈli-kwə-ˌdāt\ *vb* -**dat·ed; -dat·ing** **1** : to settle the accounts and distribute the assets of (as a business) **2** : to pay off ⟨∼ a debt⟩ **3** : to get rid of; *esp* : KILL — **liq·ui·da·tion** \ˌli-kwə-ˈdā-shən\ *n*

\ə\abut \ᵊ\kitten \ər\further \a\ash \ā\ace \ä\mop, mar \aù\out \ch\chin \e\bet \ē\easy \g\go \i\hit \ī\ice \j\job \ŋ\sing \ō\go \ò\law \òi\boy \th\thin \th\the \ü\loot \ù\foot \y\yet \zh\vision *see also* Pronunciation Symbols page

liquid crystal *n* : an organic liquid that resembles a crystal in having ordered molecular arrays

liquid crystal display *n* : LCD

liquid measure *n* : a unit or series of units for measuring liquid capacity — see METRIC SYSTEM table, WEIGHT table

li·quor \'li-kər\ *n* : a liquid substance; *esp* : a distilled alcoholic beverage

li·quo·rice *chiefly Brit var of* LICORICE

li·ra \'lir-ə, 'lē-rə\ *n* — see MONEY table

lisente *pl of* SENTE

lisle \'līl\ *n* : a smooth tightly twisted thread usu. made of long-staple cotton

lisp \'lisp\ *vb* : to pronounce \s\ and \z\ imperfectly esp. by turning them into \th\ and \th\; *also* : to speak childishly — **lisp** *n* — **lisp·er** *n*

lis·some *also* **lis·som** \'li-səm\ *adj* 1 : easily flexed 2 : LITHE 2 3 : NIMBLE — **lis·some·ly** *adv*

¹**list** \'list\ *vb, archaic* : PLEASE; *also* : WISH

²**list** *vb, archaic* : LISTEN

³**list** *n* 1 : a simple series of words or numerals; *also* : an official roster 2 : CATALOG, CHECKLIST

⁴**list** *vb* : to make a list of; *also* : to include on a list — **list·ee** \li-'stē\ *n*

⁵**list** *vb* : TILT

⁶**list** *n* : a leaning to one side : TILT

lis·ten \'lis-ᵊn\ *vb* 1 : to pay attention in order to hear 2 : HEED — **lis·ten·er** *n*

lis·ten·er·ship \'lis-ᵊn-ər-ˌship\ *n* : the audience for a radio program or recording

list·ing \'lis-tiŋ\ *n* 1 : an act or instance of making or including in a list 2 : something that is listed

list·less \'list-ləs\ *adj* : SPIRITLESS, LANGUID — **list·less·ly** *adv* — **list·less·ness** *n*

list price *n* : the price of an item as published in a catalog, price list, or advertisement before being discounted

lists \'lists\ *n pl* : an arena for combat (as jousting)

¹**lit** \'lit\ *past and past part of* LIGHT

²**lit** *abbr* 1 liter 2 literal; literally 3 literary 4 literature

lit·a·ny \'lit-ᵊn-ē\ *n, pl* **-nies** [ME *letanie,* fr. OF, fr. LL *litania,* fr. LGk *litaneia,* fr. Gk, entreaty, fr. *litanos* suppliant] 1 : a prayer consisting of a series of supplications and responses said alternately by a leader and a group 2 : a lengthy recitation ⟨a ∼ of complaints⟩

li·tchi \'lē-chē, 'lī-\ *n* [Chin (Beijing dialect) *lìzhī*] 1 : an oval fruit with a hard scaly outer covering, a small hard seed, and edible flesh 2 : an Asian tree bearing litchis

lite *var of* ³LIGHT 10

li·ter \'lē-tər\ *n* — see METRIC SYSTEM table

lit·er·al \'li-tə-rəl\ *adj* 1 : adhering to fact or to the ordinary or usual meaning (as of a word) 2 : UNADORNED; *also* : PROSAIC 3 : VERBATIM

lit·er·al·ism \-rə-ˌli-zəm\ *n* 1 : adherence to the explicit substance (as of an idea) 2 : fidelity to observable fact — **lit·er·al·ist** \-list\ *n* — **lit·er·al·is·tic** \ˌli-tə-rə-'lis-tik\ *adj*

lit·er·al·ly \'li-tə-rə-lē, 'li-trə-\ *adv* 1 : ACTUALLY ⟨was ∼ insane⟩ 2 : VIRTUALLY ⟨∼ poured out new ideas⟩

lit·er·ary \'li-tə-ˌrer-ē\ *adj* 1 : of or relating to literature 2 : WELL-READ

lit·er·ate \'li-trət, -tə-rət\ *adj* 1 : EDUCATED; *also* : able to read and write 2 : LITERARY; *also* : POLISHED, LUCID — **lit·er·a·cy** \'li-trə-sē, -tə-rə-\ *n* — **literate** *n*

li·te·ra·ti \ˌli-tə-'rä-tē\ *n pl* 1 : the educated class 2 : persons interested in literature or the arts

lit·er·a·ture \'li-trə-ˌchur, -tə-rə-, -chər\ *n* 1 : the production of written works having excellence of form or expression and dealing with ideas of permanent interest 2 : the written works produced in a particular language, country, or age

lithe \'līth, 'līth\ *adj* 1 : SUPPLE 2 : characterized by effortless grace; *also* : athletically slim

lithe·some \'līth-səm, 'līth-\ *adj* : LISSOME

lith·i·um \'li-thē-əm\ *n* : a light silver-white metallic chemical element — see ELEMENT table

li·thog·ra·phy \li-'thä-grə-fē\ *n* : the process of printing from a plane surface (as a smooth stone or metal plate) on which the image to be printed is ink-receptive and the blank area ink-repellent — **lith·o·graph** \'li-thə-ˌgraf\ *vb* — **lithograph** *n* — **li·thog·ra·pher** \li-'thä-grə-fər, 'li-thə-ˌgra-fər\ *n* — **lith·o·graph·ic** \ˌli-thə-'gra-fik\ *adj* — **lith·o·graph·i·cal·ly** \-fi-k(ə-)lē\ *adv*

li·thol·o·gy \li-'thä-lə-jē\ *n, pl* **-gies** : the study of rocks — **lith·o·log·ic** \ˌli-thə-'lä-jik\ *or* **lith·o·log·i·cal** \-ji-kəl\ *adj*

lith·o·sphere \'li-thə-ˌsfir\ *n* : the outer part of the solid earth

Lith·u·a·nian \ˌli-thù-'wā-nē-ən, -thyù-\ *n* 1 : a native or inhabitant of Lithuania 2 : the language of the Lithuanians — **Lithuanian** *adj*

lit·i·gant \'li-ti-gənt\ *n* : a party to a lawsuit — **litigant** *adj*

lit·i·gate \-ˌgāt\ *vb* **-gat·ed; -gat·ing** : to carry on a legal contest by judicial process; *also* : to contest at law — **lit·i·ga·tion** \ˌli-tə-'gā-shən\ *n*

li·ti·gious \lə-'ti-jəs\ *adj* 1 : CONTENTIOUS 2 : prone to engage in lawsuits 3 : of or relating to litigation — **li·ti·gious·ly** *adv* — **li·ti·gious·ness** *n*

lit·mus \'lit-məs\ *n* : a coloring matter from lichens that turns red in acid solutions and blue in alkaline

litmus test *n* : a test in which a single factor (as an attitude) is decisive

Litt D *or* **Lit D** *abbr* [ML *litterarum doctor*] : doctor of letters; doctor of literature

¹**lit·ter** \'li-tər\ *n* [ME, fr. OF *litiere,* fr. *lit* bed, fr. L *lectus*] 1 : a covered and curtained couch with shafts that is used to carry a single passenger; *also* : a device (as a stretcher) for carrying a sick or injured person 2 : material used as bedding for animals; *also* : material used to absorb the urine and feces of animals 3 : the offspring of an animal at one birth 4 : RUBBISH

litter 1

²**litter** *vb* 1 : to give birth to young 2 : to strew or mark with scattered objects

lit·ter·bug \'li-tər-ˌbəg\ *n* : one who litters a public area

¹**lit·tle** \'lit-ᵊl\ *adj* **lit·tler** \'lit-ᵊl-ər\ *or* **less** \'les\ *or* **less·er** \'le-sər\; **lit·tlest** \'lit-ᵊl-əst\ *or* **least** \'lēst\ 1 : not big; *also* : YOUNG 2 : not important 3 : PETTY 3 4 : not much — **lit·tle·ness** *n*

²**little** *adv* **less** \'les\; **least** \'lēst\ 1 : SLIGHTLY; *also* : not at all 2 : INFREQUENTLY

³**little** *n* 1 : a small amount or quantity 2 : a short time or distance

Little Dipper *n* : the seven bright stars of Ursa Minor arranged in a form resembling a dipper

little theater *n* : a small theater for low-cost dramatic productions designed for a limited audience

lit·to·ral \'li-tə-rəl, ˌli-tə-'ral\ *adj* : of, relating to, or growing on or near a shore esp. of the sea — **littoral** *n*

lit·ur·gy \'li-tər-jē\ *n, pl* **-gies** : a rite or body of rites prescribed for public worship — **li·tur·gi·cal** \lə-'tər-ji-kəl\ *adj* — **li·tur·gi·cal·ly** \-k(ə-)lē\ *adv* — **lit·ur·gist** \'li-tər-jist\ *n*

liv·able *also* **live·able** \'li-və-bəl\ *adj* **1** : suitable for living in or with **2** : ENDURABLE — **liv·a·bil·i·ty** \,li-və-'bi-lə-tē\ *n*

¹live \'liv\ *vb* **lived; liv·ing** **1** : to be or continue alive **2** : SUBSIST **3** : RESIDE **4** : to conduct one's life **5** : to remain in human memory or record

²live \'līv\ *adj* **1** : having life **2** : BURNING, GLOWING ⟨a ∼ cigar⟩ **3** : connected to electric power ⟨a ∼ wire⟩ **4** : UNEXPLODED ⟨a ∼ bomb⟩ **5** : of continuing interest ⟨a ∼ issue⟩ **6** : of or involving the actual presence of real people ⟨∼ audience⟩; *also* : broadcast directly at the time of production ⟨a ∼ radio program⟩ **7** : being in play ⟨a ∼ ball⟩

lived–in \'livd-,in\ *adj* : of or suggesting long-term human habitation or use

live down *vb* : to live so as to wipe out the memory or effects of

live in *vb* : to live in one's place of employment — used of a servant — **live–in** \'liv-,in\ *adj*

live·li·hood \'līv-lē-,hùd\ *n* : means of support or subsistence

live·long \'liv-,lòŋ\ *adj* [ME *lef long*, fr. *lef* dear + *long* long] : WHOLE, ENTIRE ⟨the ∼ day⟩

live·ly \'līv-lē\ *adj* **live·li·er; -est** **1** : ANIMATED ⟨∼ debate⟩ **2** : KEEN, VIVID ⟨∼ interest⟩ **3** : showing activity or vigor ⟨a ∼ manner⟩ **4** : quick to rebound ⟨a ∼ ball⟩ **5** : full of life **syn** vivacious, sprightly, gay, spirited — **live·li·ness** *n* — **live·ly** *adv*

liv·en \'lī-vən\ *vb* : ENLIVEN

¹liv·er \'li-vər\ *n* **1** : a large glandular organ of vertebrates that secretes bile and is a center of metabolic activity **2** : the liver of an animal (as a calf or chicken) eaten as food

²liver *n* : one that lives esp. in a specified way ⟨a fast ∼⟩

liv·er·ish \'li-və-rish\ *adj* **1** : resembling liver esp. in color **2** : BILIOUS **3** : PEEVISH — **liv·er·ish·ness** *adj*

liv·er·wort \'li-vər-,wərt\ *n* : any of a class of flowerless plants resembling the related mosses

liv·er·wurst \-,wərst, -,wùrst\ *n* [part trans. of G *Leberwurst*, fr. *Leber* liver + *Wurst* sausage] : a sausage consisting chiefly of liver

livery \'li-ve-rē\ *n, pl* **-er·ies** **1** : a servant's uniform; *also* : distinctive dress **2** : the feeding, care, and stabling of horses for pay; *also* : an establishment (as a stable or business) keeping horses or vehicles for hire — **liv·er·ied** \-rēd\ *adj*

liv·ery·man \-mən\ *n* : the keeper of a livery

lives *pl of* LIFE

live·stock \'līv-,stäk\ *n* : farm animals kept for use and profit

live wire *n* : an alert, active, or aggressive person

liv·id \'li-vəd\ *adj* [F *livide*, fr. L *lividus*, fr. *livēre* to be blue] **1** : discolored by bruising **2** : ASHEN, PALLID **3** : REDDISH **4** : ENRAGED — **li·vid·i·ty** \li-'vi-də-tē\ *n*

¹liv·ing \'li-viŋ\ *adj* **1** : having life **2** : NATURAL **3** : full of life and vigor; *also* : VIVID

²living *n* **1** : the condition of being alive **2** : LIVELIHOOD **3** : manner of life

living room *n* : a room in a residence used for the common social activities of the occupants

living wage *n* : a wage sufficient to provide an acceptable standard of living

living will *n* : a document requesting that the signer not be kept alive by artificial means unless there is a reasonable expectation of recovery

livre \'lēvrᵊ\ *n* : the pound of Lebanon

liz·ard \'li-zərd\ *n* : any of a group of 4-legged reptiles with long tapering tails

Lk *abbr* Luke

ll *abbr* lines

lla·ma \'lä-mə\ *n* [Sp] : any of a genus of wild or domesticated So. American mammals related to the camels but smaller and without a hump

lla·no \'lä-nō\ *n, pl* **llanos** : an open grassy plain esp. of Latin America

LLD *abbr* [NL *legum doctor*] doctor of laws

LNG *abbr* liquefied natural gas

¹load \'lōd\ *n* **1** : PACK; *also* : CARGO **2** : a mass of weight supported by something **3** : something that burdens the mind or spirits **4** : a large quantity — usu. used in pl. **5** : a standard, expected, or authorized burden

²load *vb* **1** : to put a load in or on; *also* : to receive a load **2** : to encumber with an obligation or something heavy or dishearterning **3** : to increase the weight of by adding something **4** : to supply abundantly **5** : to put a charge in (as a firearm)

load·ed *adj* **1** *slang* : HIGH **12** **2** : having a large amount of money

load·stone *var of* LODESTONE

¹loaf \'lōf\ *n, pl* **loaves** \'lōvz\ : a shaped or molded mass esp. of bread

²loaf *vb* : to spend time in idleness : LOUNGE — **loaf·er** *n*

loam \'lōm, 'lüm\ *n* : SOIL; *esp* : a loose soil of mixed clay, sand, and silt — **loamy** *adj*

¹loan \'lōn\ *n* **1** : money lent at interest; *also* : something lent for the borrower's temporary use **2** : the grant of temporary use

²loan *vb* : LEND

loan shark *n* : a person who lends money at excessive rates of interest — **loan·shark·ing** \'lōn-,shär-kiŋ\ *n*

loan·word \'lōn-,wərd\ *n* : a word taken from another language and at least partly naturalized

loath \'lōth, 'lòth\ *also* **loathe** \lōth, lòth\ *adj* : RELUCTANT

loathe \'lōth\ *vb* **loathed; loath·ing** : to dislike greatly **syn** abominate, abhor, detest, hate

loath·ing \'lō-thiŋ\ *n* : extreme disgust

loath·some \'lōth-səm, 'lòth-\ *adj* : exciting loathing : REPULSIVE

lob \'läb\ *vb* **lobbed; lob·bing** : to throw, hit, or propel something in a high arc — **lob** *n*

¹lob·by \'lä-bē\ *n, pl* **lobbies** **1** : a corridor used esp. as a passageway or waiting room **2** : a group of persons engaged in lobbying

²lobby *vb* **lob·bied; lob·by·ing** : to try to influence public officials and esp. legislators — **lob·by·ist** *n*

lobe \'lōb\ *n* : a curved or rounded part esp. of a bodily organ — **lo·bar** \'lō-bər\ *adj* — **lobed** \'lōbd\ *adj*

lo·bot·o·my \lō-'bä-tə-mē\ *n, pl* **-mies** : surgical severance of certain nerve fibers in the brain for the relief of some mental disorders

lob·ster \'läb-stər\ *n* [ME, fr. OE *loppestre*, fr. *loppe* spi-

lobster

der] : any of a family of edible marine crustaceans with two large pincerlike claws and four other pairs of legs; *also* : SPINY LOBSTER

¹lo·cal \'lō-kəl\ *adj* 1 : of, relating to, or occupying a particular place 2 : serving a particular limited district; *also* : making all stops ⟨a ~ train⟩ 3 : affecting a small part of the body ⟨~ infection⟩ — lo·cal·ly *adv*

²local *n* : one that is local

lo·cale \lō-'kal\ *n* : a place that is the setting for a particular event

lo·cal·i·ty \lō-'ka-lə-tē\ *n*, *pl* -ties : a particular spot, situation, or location

lo·cal·ize \'lō-kə-,līz\ *vb* -ized; -iz·ing : to fix in or confine to a definite place or locality — lo·cal·i·za·tion \,lō-kə- lə-'zā-shən\ *n*

lo·cate \'lō-,kāt, lō-'kāt\ *vb* lo·cat·ed; lo·cat·ing 1 : STATION, SETTLE 2 : to determine the site of 3 : to find or fix the place of in a sequence

lo·ca·tion \lō-'kā-shən\ *n* 1 : SITUATION, PLACE 2 : the process of locating 3 : a place outside a studio where a motion picture is filmed

loc cit *abbr* [L *loco citato*] in the place cited

loch \'läk, 'läk\ *n*, *Scot* : LAKE; *also* : a bay or arm of the sea esp. when nearly landlocked

¹lock \'läk\ *n* : a tuft, strand, or ringlet of hair; *also* : a cohering bunch (as of wool or flax)

²lock *n* 1 : a fastening in which a bolt is operated 2 : the mechanism of a firearm by which the charge is exploded 3 : an enclosure (as in a canal) used in raising or lowering boats from level to level 4 : AIR LOCK 5 : a wrestling hold

³lock *vb* 1 : to fasten the lock of; *also* : to make fast with a lock 2 : to confine or exclude by means of a lock 3 : INTERLOCK 4 : to make or become motionless by the interlocking of parts

lock·er \'lä-kər\ *n* 1 : a drawer, cupboard, or compartment for individual storage use 2 : an insulated compartment for storing frozen food

lock·et \'lä-kət\ *n* : a small usu. metal case for a memento worn suspended from a chain or necklace

lock·jaw \'läk-,jö\ *n* : a symptom of tetanus marked by spasms of the jaw muscles and inability to open the jaws; *also* : TETANUS

lock·nut \-,nət\ *n* 1 : a nut screwed tight on another to prevent it from slacking back 2 : a nut designed to lock itself when screwed tight

lock·out \-,aút\ *n* : the suspension of work by an employer during a labor dispute in order to make employees accept the terms being offered

lock·smith \-,smith\ *n* : one who makes or repairs locks

lock·step \-,step\ *n* : a mode of marching in step by a body of men moving in a very close single file

lock·up \-,əp\ *n* : JAIL

lo·co \'lō-kō\ *adj* [Sp] *slang* : CRAZY, FRENZIED

lo·co·mo·tion \,lō-kə-'mō-shən\ *n* 1 : the act or power of moving from place to place 2 : TRAVEL

¹lo·co·mo·tive \,lō-kə-'mō-tiv\ *adj* : of or relating to locomotion or a locomotive

²locomotive *n* : a self-propelled vehicle used to move railroad cars

lo·co·mo·tor \,lō-kə-'mō-tər\ *adj* : of or relating to locomotion or organs used in locomotion

lo·co·weed \'lō-kō-,wēd\ *n* : any of several leguminous plants of western No. America that are poisonous to livestock

lo·cus \'lō-kəs\ *n*, *pl* lo·ci \'lō-,sī\ [L] 1 : PLACE, LOCALITY 2 : the set of all points whose location is determined by stated conditions

lo·cust \'lō-kəst\ *n* 1 : a usu. destructive migratory grasshopper 2 : CICADA 3 : any of various leguminous trees; *also* : the wood of a locust

lo·cu·tion \lō-'kyü-shən\ *n* : a particular form of expression; *also* : PHRASEOLOGY

lode \'lōd\ *n* : an ore deposit

lode·stone \-,stōn\ *n* : an iron-containing rock with magnetic properties

¹lodge \'läj\ *vb* lodged; lodg·ing 1 : to provide quarters for; *also* : to settle in a place 2 : CONTAIN 3 : to come to a rest and remain 4 : to deposit for safekeeping 5 : to vest (as authority) in an agent 6 : FILE ⟨~ a complaint⟩

²lodge *n* 1 : a house set apart for residence in a special season or by an employee on an estate; *also* : INN 2 : a den or lair esp. of gregarious animals 3 : the meeting place of a branch of a fraternal organization; *also* : the members of such a branch

lodg·er \'lä-jər\ *n* : a person who occupies a rented room in another's house

lodg·ing \'lä-jiŋ\ *n* 1 : DWELLING 2 : a room or suite of rooms in another's house rented as a dwelling place — usu. used in pl.

lodg·ment *or* lodge·ment \'läj-mənt\ *n* 1 : a lodging place 2 : the act or manner of lodging 3 : DEPOSIT

loess \'les, 'ləs\ *n* : a usu. yellowish brown loamy deposit believed to be chiefly deposited by the wind

¹loft \'löft\ *n* [ME, fr. OE, air, sky, fr. ON *lopt*] 1 : ATTIC 2 : GALLERY ⟨organ ~⟩ 3 : an upper floor (as in a warehouse or barn) esp. when not partitioned 4 : the thickness of a fabric or insulated material (as of a sleeping bag)

²loft *vb* : to strike or throw a ball so that it rises high in the air

lofty \'löf-tē\ *adj* loft·i·er; -est 1 : NOBLE; *also* : SUPERIOR 2 : extremely proud 3 : HIGH, TALL — loft·i·ly \'löf-tə-lē\ *adv* — loft·i·ness \-tē-nəs\ *n*

¹log \'lög, 'läg\ *n* 1 : a bulky piece of unshaped timber 2 : an apparatus for measuring a ship's speed 3 : the daily record of a ship's progress; *also* : a regularly kept record of performance (as of an airplane)

²log *vb* logged; log·ging 1 : to cut (trees) for lumber; *also* : to clear (land) of trees in lumbering 2 : to enter in a log 3 : to sail a ship or fly an airplane for (an indicated distance or period of time) 4 : to have (an indicated record) to one's credit : ACHIEVE — log·ger \'lö-gər, 'lä-\ *n*

³log *n* : LOGARITHM

lo·gan·ber·ry \'lō-gən-,ber-ē\ *n* : a red-fruited upright≈ growing dewberry; *also* : its fruit

log·a·rithm \'lö-gə-,ri-thəm, 'lä-\ *n* : the exponent that indicates the power to which a base is raised to produce a given number ⟨the ~ of 100 to base 10 is 2 since 10^2 = 100⟩ — log·a·rith·mic \,lö-gə-'rith-mik, ,lä-\ *adj*

loge \'lōzh\ *n* 1 : a small compartment; *also* : a box in a theater 2 : a small partitioned area; *also* : the forward section of a theater mezzanine

log·ger·head \'lö-gər-,hed, 'lä-\ *n* : a large sea turtle of subtropical and temperate waters — at loggerheads : in a state of quarrelsome disagreement

log·gia \'lō-jē-ə, 'lö-jä\ *n*, *pl* loggias \'lō-jē-əz, 'lö-jäz\ : a roofed open gallery

log·ic \'lä-jik\ *n* 1 : a science that deals with the rules and tests of sound thinking and proof by reasoning 2 : sound reasoning 3 : the arrangement of circuit elements for arithmetical computation in a computer — log·i·cal \-ji-kəl\ *adj* — log·i·cal·ly \-jik(ə-)lē\ *adv* — lo·gi·cian \lō-'ji-shən\ *n*

lo·gis·tics \lō-'jis-tiks\ *n sing or pl* : the procurement, maintenance, and transportation of matériel, facilities, and personnel — lo·gis·tic \-tik\ *adj*

log·jam \'lög-,jam, 'läg-\ *n* 1 : a deadlocked jumble of logs in a watercourse 2 : DEADLOCK

logo \'lō-gō\ *n*, *pl* log·os \-gōz\ : an identifying symbol (as for advertising)

logo·type \'lö-gə-,tīp, 'lä-\ *n* : LOGO

log·roll·ing \-,rō-liŋ\ *n* : the trading of votes by legislators to secure favorable action on projects of individual interest

lo·gy \'lō-gē\ *also* **log·gy** \'lȯ-gē, 'lä-\ *adj* **lo·gi·er; -est** : deficient in vitality : SLUGGISH

loin \'lȯin\ *n* **1** : the part of the body on each side of the spinal column and between the hip and the lower ribs; *also* : a cut of meat from this part of an animal **2** *pl* : the pubic region; *also* : the organs of reproduction

loin·cloth \-ˌklȯth\ *n* : a cloth worn about the loins often as the sole article of clothing in warm climates

loi·ter \'lȯi-tər\ *vb* **1** : LINGER **2** : to hang around idly **syn** dawdle, dally, procrastinate, lag, tarry — **loi·ter·er** *n*

loll \'läl\ *vb* **1** : DROOP, DANGLE **2** : LOUNGE

lol·li·pop *or* **lol·ly·pop** \'lä-li-ˌpäp\ *n* : a lump of hard candy on a stick

lol·ly·gag \'lä-lē-ˌgag\ *vb* **-gagged; -gag·ging** : DAWDLE

Lond *abbr* London

lone \'lōn\ *adj* **1** : SOLITARY ⟨a ~ sentinel⟩ **2** : SOLE, ONLY ⟨the ~ theater in town⟩ **3** : ISOLATED ⟨a ~ tree⟩

lone·ly \'lōn-lē\ *adj* **lone·li·er; -est 1** : being without company **2** : UNFREQUENTED ⟨a ~ spot⟩ **3** : LONESOME — **lone·li·ness** *n*

lon·er \'lō-nər\ *n* : one that avoids others

lone·some \'lōn-səm\ *adj* **1** : sad from lack of companionship **2** : REMOTE; *also* : SOLITARY — **lone·some·ly** *adv* — **lone·some·ness** *n*

¹long \'lȯŋ\ *adj* **lon·ger** \'lȯŋ-gər\; **lon·gest** \'lȯŋ-gəst\ **1** : extending for a considerable distance; *also* : TALL, ELONGATED **2** : having a specified length **3** : extending over a considerable time; *also* : TEDIOUS **4** : containing many items in a series **5** : being a syllable or speech sound of relatively great duration **6** : extending far into the future **7** : well furnished with something — used with *on*

²long *adv* : for or during a long time

³long *n* : a long period of time

⁴long *vb* **longed; long·ing** \'lȯŋ-iŋ\ : to feel a strong desire or wish **syn** yearn, hanker, pine, hunger, thirst

⁵long *abbr* longitude

long·boat \'lȯŋ-ˌbōt\ *n* : a large boat usu. carried by a merchant sailing ship

long·bow \-ˌbō\ *n* : a wooden bow drawn by hand and used esp. by medieval English archers

lon·gev·i·ty \län-'je-və-tē\ *n* [LL *longaevitas*, fr. L *longaevus* long-lived, fr. *longus* long + *aevum* age] : a long duration of individual life; *also* : length of life

long·hair \'lȯŋ-ˌhar\ *n* **1** : a lover of classical music **2** : HIPPIE **3** : a domestic cat having long outer fur — **long·haired** \-ˌhard\ *or* **long·hair** *adj*

long·hand \-ˌhand\ *n* : HANDWRITING

long·horn \-ˌhȯrn\ *n* : any of the cattle with long horns formerly common in the southwestern U.S.

long hundredweight *n, Brit* — see WEIGHT table

long·ing \'lȯŋ-iŋ\ *n* : a strong desire esp. for something unattainable — **long·ing·ly** *adv*

lon·gi·tude \'län-jə-ˌtüd, -ˌtyüd\ *n* : angular distance expressed usu. in degrees east or west from the prime meridian through Greenwich, England

lon·gi·tu·di·nal \ˌlän-jə-'tüd-ᵊn-əl, -'tyüd-\ *adj* **1** : extending lengthwise **2** : of or relating to length — **lon·gi·tu·di·nal·ly** *adv*

long·shore·man \'lȯŋ-ˌshȯr-mən\ *n* : a laborer at a wharf who loads and unloads cargo

long·suf·fer·ing \-'sə-friŋ, -fə-riŋ\ *n* : long and patient endurance of offense

long–term \'lȯŋ-'tərm\ *adj* **1** : extending over or involving a long period of time **2** : constituting a financial obligation based on a term usu. of more than 10 years ⟨~ bonds⟩

long·time \'lȯŋ-'tīm\ *adj* : of long duration ⟨~ friends⟩

long ton *n* — see WEIGHT table

lon·gueur \lōⁿ-'gœr\ *n, pl* **longueurs** *same or* -'gœrz\ [F, lit., length] : a dull tedious passage or section

long–wind·ed \ˌlȯŋ-'win-dəd\ *adj* : tediously long in speaking or writing

loo·fah \'lü-fə\ *n* : a sponge consisting of the fibrous skeleton of a gourd

¹look \'lu̇k\ *vb* **1** : to exercise the power of vision : SEE **2** : EXPECT **3** : to have an appearance that befits ⟨~s the part⟩ **4** : SEEM ⟨~s thin⟩ **5** : to direct one's attention : HEED **6** : POINT, FACE **7** : to show a tendency — **look after** : to take care of — **look for** : EXPECT

²look *n* **1** : the action of looking : GLANCE **2** : EXPRESSION; *also* : physical appearance **3** : ASPECT

look down *vb* : to regard with contempt — used with *on* or *upon*

looking glass *n* : MIRROR

look·out \'lu̇k-ˌau̇t\ *n* **1** : a person assigned to watch (as on a ship) **2** : a careful watch **3** : VIEW **4** : a matter of concern

look up *vb* **1** : IMPROVE ⟨business is *looking up*⟩ **2** : to search for in or as if in a reference work **3** : to seek out esp. for a brief visit

¹loom \'lüm\ *n* : a frame or machine for weaving together threads or yarns into cloth

²loom *vb* **1** : to come into sight in an unnaturally large, indistinct, or distorted form **2** : to appear in an impressively exaggerated form

loon \'lün\ *n* : any of several web-footed black-and-white fish-eating diving birds

loo·ny *or* **loo·ney** \'lü-nē\ *adj* **loo·ni·er; -est** : CRAZY, FOOLISH

loony bin *n* : an insane asylum

loop \'lüp\ *n* **1** : a fold or doubling of a line through which another line or hook can be passed; *also* : a loop-shaped figure or course ⟨a ~ in a river⟩ **2** : a circular airplane maneuver executed in the vertical plane **3** : a piece of film or magnetic tape whose ends are spliced together to project or play continuously — **loop** *vb*

loop·er \'lü-pər\ *n* : any of numerous rather small hairless moth caterpillars that move with a looping movement

loop·hole \'lüp-ˌhōl\ *n* **1** : a small opening in a wall through which firearms may be discharged **2** : a means of escape; *esp* : an ambiguity or omission that allows one to evade the intent of a law or contract

¹loose \'lüs\ *adj* **loos·er; loos·est 1** : not rigidly fastened **2** : free from restraint or obligation **3** : not dense or compact in structure **4** : not chaste : LEWD **5** : SLACK **6** : not precise or exact — **loose·ly** *adv* — **loose·ness** *n*

²loose *vb* **loosed; loos·ing 1** : RELEASE **2** : UNTIE **3** : DETACH **4** : DISCHARGE **5** : RELAX, SLACKEN

³loose *adv* : LOOSELY

loos·en \'lüs-ᵊn\ *vb* **1** : FREE **2** : to make or become loose **3** : to relax the severity of

loot \'lüt\ *n* [Hindi *lūṭ*; akin to Skt *luṇṭati* he plunders] : goods taken in war or by robbery : PLUNDER — **loot** *vb* — **loot·er** *n*

¹lop \'läp\ *vb* **lopped; lop·ping** : to cut branches or twigs from : TRIM; *also* : to cut off

²lop *vb* **lopped; lop·ping** : to hang downward; *also* : to flop or sway loosely

lope \'lōp\ *n* : an easy bounding gait — **lope** *vb*

lop·sid·ed \'läp-'sī-dəd\ *adj* **1** : leaning to one side **2** : UNSYMMETRICAL — **lop·sid·ed·ly** *adv* — **lop·sid·ed·ness** *n*

lo·qua·cious \lō-'kwā-shəs\ *adj* : excessively talkative — **lo·quac·i·ty** \-'kwa-sə-tē\ *n*

¹lord \'lȯrd\ *n* [ME *loverd, lord*, fr. OE *hlāford*, fr. *hlāf* loaf + *weard* keeper] **1** : one having power and authority over others; *esp* : a person from whom a feudal fee or estate is held **2** : a man of rank or high position; *esp* : a British nobleman **3** *pl, cap* : the upper house of the

---

British parliament **4** : a person of great power in some field

²lord *vb* : to act like a lord; *esp* : to put on airs — usu. used with *it*

lord chancellor *n, pl* **lords chancellor** : a British officer of state who presides over the House of Lords, serves as head of the British judiciary, and is usu. a leading member of the cabinet

lord·ly \-lē\ *adj* **lord·li·er; -est 1** : DIGNIFIED; *also* : NOBLE **2** : HAUGHTY

lord·ship \-ˌship\ *n* **1** : the rank or dignity of a lord — used as a title **2** : the authority or territory of a lord

Lord's Supper *n* : COMMUNION

lore \ˈlȯr\ *n* : KNOWLEDGE; *esp* : traditional knowledge or belief

lor·gnette \lȯrn-ˈyet\ *n* [F, fr. *lorgner* to take a sidelong look at, fr. MF, fr. *lorgne* squinting] : a pair of eyeglasses or opera glasses with a handle

lorn \ˈlȯrn\ *adj* : FORSAKEN, DESOLATE

lor·ry \ˈlȯr-ē\ *n, pl* **lorries** *chiefly Brit* : MOTORTRUCK

lose \ˈlüz\ *vb* **lost** \ˈlȯst\; **los·ing** \ˈlü-ziŋ\ **1** : DESTROY **2** : to miss from a customary place : MISLAY **3** : to suffer deprivation of **4** : to fail to use : WASTE **5** : to fail to win or obtain ⟨~ the game⟩ **6** : to fail to keep or maintain ⟨~ his balance⟩ **7** : to wander from ⟨~ her way⟩ **8** : to get rid of — **los·er** *n*

loss \ˈlȯs\ *n* **1** : RUIN **2** : the harm resulting from losing **3** : something that is lost **4** *pl* : killed, wounded, or captured soldiers **5** : failure to win **6** : an amount by which the cost exceeds the selling price **7** : decrease in amount or degree

loss leader *n* : an article sold at a loss in order to draw customers

lost \ˈlȯst\ *adj* **1** : not used, won, or claimed **2** : no longer possessed or known **3** : ruined or destroyed physically or morally **4** : DENIED; *also* : HARDENED **5** : unable to find the way; *also* : HELPLESS **6** : ABSORBED, RAPT **7** : not appreciated or understood ⟨his jokes were ~ on me⟩

lot \ˈlät\ *n* **1** : an object used in deciding something by chance; *also* : the use of lots to decide something **2** : SHARE, PORTION; *also* : FORTUNE, FATE **3** : a plot of land **4** : a group of individuals : SET **5** : a considerable quantity

loth \ˈlōth, ˈlōth\ *var of* LOATH

lo·ti \ˈlō-tē\ *n, pl* **ma·lo·ti** \mə-ˈlō-tē\ — see MONEY table

lo·tion \ˈlō-shən\ *n* : a liquid preparation for cosmetic and external medicinal use

lot·tery \ˈlä-tə-rē\ *n, pl* **-ter·ies 1** : a drawing of lots in which prizes are given to the winning names or numbers **2** : a matter determined by chance

lo·tus \ˈlō-təs\ *n* **1** : a fruit held in Greek legend to cause dreamy contentment and forgetfulness **2** : any of various water lilies represented esp. in ancient Egyptian and Hindu art **3** : any of several leguminous forage plants

loud \ˈlau̇d\ *adj* **1** : marked by intensity or volume of sound **2** : CLAMOROUS, NOISY **3** : obtrusive or offensive in color or pattern ⟨a ~ suit⟩ — **loud** *adv* — **loud·ly** *adv* — **loud·ness** *n*

loud-mouthed \-ˌmau̇tht, -ˌmau̇thd\ *adj* : given to loud offensive talk

loud·speak·er \-ˌspē-kər\ *n* : a device that changes electrical signals into sound

¹lounge \ˈlau̇nj\ *vb* **lounged; loung·ing** : to act or move lazily or listlessly

²lounge *n* **1** : a room with comfortable furniture; *also* : a room (as in a theater) with lounging, smoking, and toilet facilities **2** : a long couch

lour \ˈlau̇r\, **loury** \ˈlau̇r-ē\ *var of* LOWER, LOWERY

louse \ˈlau̇s\ *n, pl* **lice** \ˈlīs\ **1** : any of various small wingless usu. flattened insects parasitic on warm-blooded animals **2** : a plant pest (as an aphid) **3** : a contemptible person

lousy \ˈlau̇-zē\ *adj* **lous·i·er; -est 1** : infested with lice **2** : POOR, INFERIOR **3** : amply supplied ⟨~ with money⟩ — **lous·i·ly** \-zə-lē\ *adv* — **lous·i·ness** \-zē-nəs\ *n*

lout \ˈlau̇t\ *n* : a stupid awkward fellow — **lout·ish** *adj* — **lout·ish·ly** *adv*

lou·ver *or* **lou·vre** \ˈlü-vər\ *n* **1** : an opening having parallel slanted slats to allow flow of air but to exclude rain or sun or to provide privacy; *also* : a slat in such an opening **2** : a device with movable slats for controlling the flow of air or light

¹love \ˈləv\ *n* **1** : strong affection **2** : warm attachment ⟨~ of the sea⟩ **3** : attraction based on sexual desire **4** : a beloved person **5** : unselfish loyal and benevolent concern for others **6** : a score of zero in tennis — **love·less** *adj*

²love *vb* **loved; lov·ing 1** : CHERISH **2** : to feel a passion, devotion, or tenderness for **3** : CARESS **4** : to take pleasure in ⟨~s to play bridge⟩ — **lov·able** \ˈlə-və-bəl\ *adj* — **lov·er** *n*

love·bird \ˈləv-ˌbərd\ *n* : any of various small usu. gray or green parrots that seem to show caring behavior for their mates

love·lorn \-ˌlȯrn\ *adj* : deprived of love or of a lover

love·ly \ˈləv-lē\ *adj* **love·li·er; -est** : BEAUTIFUL — **love·li·ly** \ˈləv-lə-lē\ *adv* — **love·li·ness** *n* — **lovely** *adv*

love·mak·ing \-ˌmā-kiŋ\ *n* **1** : COURTSHIP **2** : sexual activity; *esp* : COPULATION

love·sick \-ˌsik\ *adj* **1** : YEARNING **2** : expressing a lover's longing — **love·sick·ness** *n*

lov·ing \ˈlə-viŋ\ *adj* **1** : AFFECTIONATE **2** : PAINSTAKING — **lov·ing·ly** *adv*

¹low \ˈlō\ *vb* : MOO

²low *n* : MOO

³low *adj* **low·er** \ˈlō-ər\; **low·est** \ˈlō-əst\ **1** : not high or tall ⟨~ wall⟩; *also* : DÉCOLLETÉ **2** : situated or passing below the normal level or surface ⟨~ ground⟩; *also* : marking a nadir **3** : not loud ⟨~ voice⟩ **4** : being near the equator **5** : humble in status **6** : WEAK; *also* : DEPRESSED **7** : STRICKEN, PROSTRATE **8** : less than usual in number, amount, or value; *also* : of lesser degree than average **9** : falling short of a standard **10** : UNFAVORABLE — **low** *adv* — **low·ness** *n*

⁴low *n* **1** : something that is low **2** : a region of low barometric pressure **3** : the arrangement of gears in an automobile transmission that gives the slowest speed and greatest power

low beam *n* : the short-range focus of a vehicle headlight

low blow *n* : an unprincipled attack

low·brow \ˈlō-ˌbrau̇\ *n* : a person with little taste or intellectual interest

low–density lipoprotein *n* : LDL

low–down \-ˌdau̇n\ *n* : pertinent and esp. guarded information

low–down \-ˌdau̇n\ *adj* **1** : MEAN, CONTEMPTIBLE **2** : deeply emotional

low–end \-ˌend\ *adj* : of, relating to, or being the lowest-priced merchandise in a manufacturer's line

¹low·er \ˈlau̇-ər\ *vb* **1** : FROWN **2** : to become dark, gloomy, and threatening

²low·er \ˈlō-ər\ *adj* **1** : relatively low (as in rank) **2** : situated beneath the earth's surface **3** *cap* : being an earlier part or formation of a specific geologic period **4** : constituting the popular and more representative branch of a bicameral legislative body

³low·er \ˈlō-ər\ *vb* **1** : DROP; *also* : DIMINISH **2** : to let descend by its own weight; *also* : to reduce the height of **3** : to reduce in value, number, or amount **4** : DEGRADE; *also* : HUMBLE

low·er·case \ˌlō-ər-ˈkās\ *adj* : being a letter that belongs to or conforms to the series a, b, c, etc., rather than A, B, C, etc. — **lowercase** *n*

lower class *n* : a social class occupying a position below the middle class and having the lowest status in a society — **lower–class** \-ˈklas\ *adj*

low·er·most \ˈlō-ər-ˌmōst\ *adj* : LOWEST

low·ery \ˈlaù-ə-rē\ *adj* : GLOOMY, LOWERING

lowest common denominator *n* **1** : LEAST COMMON DENOMINATOR **2** : something designed to appeal to a lowbrow audience; *also* : such an audience

lowest common multiple *n* : LEAST COMMON MULTIPLE

low–key \ˈlō-ˈkē\ *also* **low–keyed** \-ˈkēd\ *adj* : of low intensity : RESTRAINED

low·land \ˈlō-lənd, -ˌland\ *n* : low and usu. level country

low·life \ˈlō-ˌlīf\ *n*, *pl* **low·lifes** \-ˌlīfs\ *also* **low–lives** \-ˌlīvz\ : a person of low social status or moral character

low·ly \ˈlō-lē\ *adj* **low·li·er; -est 1** : HUMBLE, MEEK **2** : ranking low in some hierarchy — **low·li·ness** *n*

low–rise \ˈlō-ˈrīz\ *adj* **1** : having few stories and not equipped with elevators ⟨a ∼ building⟩ **2** : of, relating to, or characterized by low-rise buildings

low–tech \ˈlō-ˈtek\ *adj* : technologically simple or unsophisticated

¹lox \ˈläks\ *n* : liquid oxygen

²lox *n*, *pl* **lox** *or* **lox·es** : smoked salmon

loy·al \ˈlòi-əl\ *adj* [MF, fr. OF *leial, leel*, fr. L *legalis* legal] **1** : faithful in allegiance to one's government **2** : faithful esp. to a cause or ideal : CONSTANT — **loy·al·ly** \ˈlòi-ə-lē\ *adv* — **loy·al·ty** \ˈlòi-əl-tē\ *n*

loy·al·ist \ˈlòi-ə-list\ *n* : one who is or remains loyal to a political party, government, or sovereign

loz·enge \ˈlä-zənj\ *n* **1** : a diamond-shaped figure • **2** : a small flat often medicated candy

LP *abbr* low pressure

LPG *abbr* liquefied petroleum gas

LPGA *abbr* Ladies Professional Golf Association

LPN \ˈel-ˌpē-ˈen\ *n* : LICENSED PRACTICAL NURSE

Lr *symbol* Lawrencium

LSD \ˌel-(ˌ)es-ˈdē\ *n* [G *Lysergsäure-Di*äthylamid lysergic acid diethylamide] : an illicit drug that causes psychotic symptoms similar to those of schizophrenia

lt *abbr* light

Lt *abbr* lieutenant

LT *abbr* long ton

LTC *or* **Lt Col** *abbr* lieutenant colonel

Lt Comdr *abbr* lieutenant commander

ltd *abbr* limited

LTG *or* **Lt Gen** *abbr* lieutenant general

LTJG *abbr* lieutenant, junior grade

ltr *abbr* letter

Lu *symbol* lutetium

lu·au \ˈlü-ˌaù\ *n* : a Hawaiian feast

lub *abbr* lubricant; lubricating

lub·ber \ˈlə-bər\ *n* **1** : LOUT **2** : an unskilled seaman — **lub·ber·ly** *adj*

lube \ˈlüb\ *n* : LUBRICANT; *also* : an application of a lubricant

lu·bri·cant \ˈlü-bri-kənt\ *n* : a material capable of reducing friction when applied between moving parts

lu·bri·cate \ˈlü-brə-ˌkāt\ *vb* **-cat·ed; -cat·ing** : to apply a lubricant to — **lu·bri·ca·tion** \ˌlü-brə-ˈkā-shən\ *n* — **lu·bri·ca·tor** \ˈlü-brə-ˌkā-tər\ *n*

lu·bri·cious \lü-ˈbri-shəs\ *or* **lu·bri·cous** \ˈlü-bri-kəs\ *adj* **1** : SMOOTH, SLIPPERY **2** : LECHEROUS; *also* : SALACIOUS — **lu·bric·i·ty** \lü-ˈbri-sə-tē\ *n*

lu·cent \ˈlüs-ᵊnt\ *adj* **1** : LUMINOUS **2** : CLEAR, LUCID — **lu·cent·ly** *adv*

lu·cerne \lü-ˈsərn\ *n*, *chiefly Brit* : ALFALFA

lu·cid \ˈlü-səd\ *adj* **1** : SHINING **2** : mentally sound **3** : easily understood — **lu·cid·i·ty** \lü-ˈsi-də-tē\ *n* — **lu·cid·ly** *adv* — **lu·cid·ness** *n*

Lu·ci·fer \ˈlü-sə-fər\ *n* [ME, the morning star, a fallen rebel archangel, the Devil, fr. OE, fr. L, the morning star, fr. *lucifer* light-bearing] : DEVIL, SATAN

¹luck \ˈlək\ *n* **1** : CHANCE, FORTUNE **2** : good fortune — **luck·less** *adj*

²luck *vb* **1** : to prosper or succeed esp. through chance or good fortune — usu. used with *out* **2** : to come upon something desirable by chance — usu. used with *out, on, onto*, or *into*

luck·i·ly \ˈlə-kə-lē\ *adv* **1** : in a lucky manner **2** : FORTUNATELY **2**

lucky \ˈlə-kē\ *adj* **luck·i·er; -est 1** : favored by luck : FORTUNATE **2** : FORTUITOUS **3** : seeming to bring good luck — **luck·i·ness** *n*

lu·cra·tive \ˈlü-krə-tiv\ *adj* : PROFITABLE — **lu·cra·tive·ly** *adv* — **lu·cra·tive·ness** *n*

lu·cre \ˈlü-kər\ *n* [ME, fr. L *lucrum*] : PROFIT; *also* : MONEY

lu·cu·bra·tion \ˌlü-kyə-ˈbrā-shən, -kə-\ *n* : laborious study : MEDITATION

lu·di·crous \ˈlü-də-krəs\ *adj* : LAUGHABLE, RIDICULOUS — **lu·di·crous·ly** *adv* — **lu·di·crous·ness** *n*

luff \ˈləf\ *vb* : to turn the head of a ship toward the wind

¹lug \ˈləg\ *vb* **lugged; lug·ging 1** : DRAG, PULL **2** : to carry laboriously

²lug *n* **1** : a projecting piece (as for fastening, support, or traction) **2** : a nut securing a wheel on an automobile

lug·gage \ˈlə-gij\ *n* : containers (as suitcases) for carrying personal belongings : BAGGAGE

lu·gu·bri·ous \lù-ˈgü-brē-əs\ *adj* : mournful often to an exaggerated degree — **lu·gu·bri·ous·ly** *adv* — **lu·gu·bri·ous·ness** *n*

Luke \ˈlük\ *n* — see BIBLE table

luke·warm \ˈlük-ˈwórm\ *adj* **1** : moderately warm : TEPID **2** : not enthusiastic — **luke·warm·ly** *adv*

¹lull \ˈləl\ *vb* **1** : SOOTHE, CALM **2** : to cause to relax vigilance

²lull *n* **1** : a temporary calm (as during a storm) **2** : a temporary drop in activity

lul·la·by \ˈlə-lə-ˌbī\ *n*, *pl* **-bies** : a song to lull children to sleep

lum·ba·go \ˌləm-ˈbā-gō\ *n* : rheumatic pain in the lower back and loins

lum·bar \ˈləm-bər, -ˌbär\ *adj* : of, relating to, or constituting the loins or the vertebrae between the thoracic vertebrae and sacrum ⟨∼ region⟩

¹lum·ber \ˈləm-bər\ *vb* : to move heavily or clumsily

²lumber *n* **1** : surplus or disused articles that are stored away **2** : timber or logs esp. when dressed for use

³lumber *vb* : to cut logs; *also* : to saw logs into lumber — **lum·ber·man** \-mən\ *n*

lum·ber·jack \-ˌjak\ *n* : LOGGER

lum·ber·yard \-ˌyärd\ *n* : a place where lumber is kept for sale

lu·mi·nary \ˈlü-mə-ˌner-ē\ *n*, *pl* **-nar·ies 1** : a very famous person **2** : a source of light; *esp* : a celestial body

lu·mi·nes·cence \ˌlü-mə-ˈnes-ᵊns\ *n* : the low-temperature emission of light (as by a chemical or physiological process); *also* : such light — **lu·mi·nes·cent** \-ᵊnt\ *adj*

lu·mi·nous \ˈlü-mə-nəs\ *adj* **1** : emitting light; *also* : LIGHTED **2** : CLEAR, INTELLIGIBLE — **lu·mi·nance** \-nəns\ *n* — **lu·mi·nos·i·ty** \ˌlü-mə-ˈnä-sə-tē\ *n* — **lu·mi·nous·ly** *adv*

lum·mox \ˈlə-məks\ *n* : a clumsy person

¹lump \ˈləmp\ *n* **1** : a piece or mass of indefinite size and shape **2** : AGGREGATE, TOTALITY **3** : a usu. abnormal swelling — **lump·ish** *adj* — **lumpy** *adj*

²lump *vb* **1** : to heap together in a lump **2** : to form into lumps

³lump *adj* : not divided into parts ⟨a ∼ sum⟩

\ə\abut \ᵊ\kitten \ər\further \a\ash \ā\ace \ä\mop, mar
\aù\out \ch\chin \e\bet \ē\easy \g\go \i\hit \ī\ice \j\job
\ŋ\sing \ō\go \ò\law \òi\boy \th\thin \t̲h̲\the \ü\loot \ù\foot
\y\yet \zh\vision *see also* Pronunciation Symbols page

lu·na·cy \'lü-nə-sē\ *n, pl* **-cies** **1** : INSANITY **2** : extreme folly

lu·nar \'lü-nər\ *adj* : of or relating to the moon

lu·na·tic \'lü-nə-ˌtik\ *adj* [ME *lunatik*, fr. LL *lunaticus*, fr. L *luna* moon; fr. the belief that lunacy fluctuated with the phases of the moon] **1** : INSANE; *also* : used for insane persons **2** : extremely foolish — **lunatic** *n*

¹lunch \'lənch\ *n* **1** : a light meal usu. eaten in the middle of the day **2** : the food prepared for a lunch

²lunch *vb* : to eat lunch

lun·cheon \'lən-chən\ *n* : a usu. formal lunch

lun·cheon·ette \ˌlən-chə-'net\ *n* : a small restaurant serving light lunches

lunch·room \'lənch-ˌrüm, -ˌrùm\ *n* **1** : LUNCHEONETTE **2** : a room (as in a school) where lunches are sold and eaten or lunches brought from home may be eaten

lu·nette \lü-'net\ *n* : something shaped like a crescent

lung \'ləŋ\ *n* **1** : one of the usu. paired baglike breathing organs in the chest of an air-breathing vertebrate **2** : a mechanical device to promote breathing and make it easier — **lunged** \'ləŋd\ *adj*

lunge \'lənj\ *n* **1** : a sudden thrust or pass (as with a sword) **2** : a sudden forward stride or leap — **lunge** *vb*

lu·pine \'lü-pən\ *n* : any of a genus of leguminous plants with long upright clusters of pealike flowers

lu·pus \'lü-pəs\ *n* [ML, fr. L, wolf] : any of several diseases characterized by skin lesions; *esp* : SYSTEMIC LUPUS ERYTHEMATOSUS

lurch \'lərch\ *n* : a sudden swaying or tipping movement — **lurch** *vb*

¹lure \'lùr\ *n* **1** : ENTICEMENT; *also* : APPEAL **2** : an artificial bait for catching fish

²lure *vb* **lured; lur·ing** : to draw on with a promise of pleasure or gain

lu·rid \'lùr-əd\ *adj* **1** : wan and ghostly pale in appearance **2** : shining with the red glow of fire seen through smoke or cloud **3** : GRUESOME; *also* : SENSATIONAL **syn** ghastly, grisly, grim, horrible, macabre — **lu·rid·ly** *adv*

lurk \'lərk\ *vb* **1** : to move furtively : SNEAK **2** : to lie concealed

lus·cious \'lə-shəs\ *adj* **1** : having a pleasingly sweet taste or smell **2** : sensually appealing — **lus·cious·ly** *adv* — **lus·cious·ness** *n*

¹lush \'ləsh\ *adj* : having or covered with abundant growth ⟨~ pastures⟩

²lush *n* : an habitual heavy drinker

lust \'ləst\ *n* **1** : usu. intense or unbridled sexual desire : LASCIVIOUSNESS **2** : an intense longing — **lust** *vb* — **lust·ful** *adj*

lus·ter *or* **lus·tre** \'ləs-tər\ *n* **1** : a shine or sheen esp. from reflected light **2** : BRIGHTNESS, GLITTER **3** : GLORY, SPLENDOR — **lus·ter·less** *adj* — **lus·trous** \-trəs\ *adj*

lus·tral \'ləs-trəl\ *adj* : PURIFICATORY

lusty \'ləs-tē\ *adj* **lust·i·er; -est** : full of vitality : ROBUST — **lust·i·ly** \'ləs-tə-lē\ *adv* — **lust·i·ness** \-tē-nəs\ *n*

lute \'lüt\ *n* : a stringed musical instrument with a large pear-shaped body and a fretted fingerboard — **lu·te·nist** *or* **lu·ta·nist** \'lüt-ᵊn-ist\ *n*

lu·te·tium *also* **lu·te·cium** \lü-'tē-shē-əm, -shəm\ *n* : a metallic chemical element — see ELEMENT table

Lu·ther·an \'lü-thə-rən\ *n* : a member of a Protestant denomination adhering to the doctrines of Martin Luther — **Lu·ther·an·ism** \-rə-ˌni-zəm\ *n*

lux·u·ri·ant \ˌləg-'zhùr-ē-ənt, ˌlək-'shùr-\ *adj* **1** : yielding or growing abundantly : LUSH, PRODUCTIVE **2** : abundantly rich and varied; *also* : FLORID **syn** exuberant, lavish, opulent, prodigal, profuse, riotous — **lux·u·ri·ance** \-ē-əns\ *n* — **lux·u·ri·ant·ly** *adv*

lux·u·ri·ate \-ē-ˌāt\ *vb* **-at·ed; -at·ing** **1** : to grow profusely **2** : REVEL

lux·u·ry \'lək-shə-rē, 'ləg-zhə-\ *n, pl* **-ries** **1** : great ease and comfort **2** : something adding to pleasure or comfort but not absolutely necessary — **lux·u·ri·ous** \ˌləg-'zhùr-ē-əs, ˌlək-'shùr-\ *adj* — **lux·u·ri·ous·ly** *adv*

lv *abbr* leave

LVN *n* : LICENSED VOCATIONAL NURSE

lwei \lə-'wā\ *n, pl* **lwei** — see *kwanza* at MONEY table

LWV *abbr* League of Women Voters

¹-ly \lē\ *adj suffix* **1** : like in appearance, manner, or nature ⟨queen*ly*⟩ **2** : characterized by regular recurrence in (specified) units of time : every ⟨hour*ly*⟩

²-ly *adv suffix* **1** : in a (specified) manner ⟨slow*ly*⟩ **2** : from a (specified) point of view ⟨grammatical*ly*⟩

ly·ce·um \lī-'sē-əm, 'lī-sē-\ *n* **1** : a hall for public lectures **2** : an association providing public lectures, concerts, and entertainments

lye \'lī\ *n* : a corrosive alkaline substance used esp. in making soap

ly·ing \'lī-iŋ\ *adj* : UNTRUTHFUL, FALSE

ly·ing–in \ˌlī-iŋ-'in\ *n, pl* **lyings–in** *or* **lying–ins** : the state during and consequent to childbirth : CONFINEMENT

Lyme disease \'līm-\ *n* [*Lyme*, Connecticut, where it was first reported] : an acute inflammatory disease that is caused by a spirochete transmitted by ticks, is characterized esp. by chills and fever, and if left untreated may result in joint pain, arthritis, and cardiac and neurological disorders

lymph \'limf\ *n* : a pale liquid consisting chiefly of blood plasma and white blood cells, circulating in thin-walled tubes (**lymphatic vessels**), and bathing the body tissues — **lym·phat·ic** \lim-'fa-tik\ *adj*

lymph·ade·nop·a·thy \ˌlim-ˌfad-ᵊn-'ä-pə-thē\ *n, pl* **-thies** : abnormal enlargement of the lymph nodes

lymph node *n* : any of the rounded masses of lymphoid tissue surrounded by a capsule

lym·pho·cyte \'lim-fə-ˌsīt\ *n* : any of the weakly motile leukocytes produced in lymphoid tissue that are the typical cells in lymph and include the cellular mediators (as a B cell or a T cell) of immunity

lym·phoid \'lim-ˌfòid\ *adj* **1** : of, relating to, or being tissue (as of the lymph nodes) containing lymphocytes **2** : of, relating to, or resembling lymph

lym·pho·ma \lim-'fō-mə\ *n, pl* **-mas** *or* **-ma·ta** \-mə-tə\ : a tumor of lymphoid tissue

lynch \'linch\ *vb* : to put to death by mob action without legal sanction or due process of law — **lynch·er** *n*

lynx \'liŋks\ *n, pl* **lynx** *or* **lynx·es** : any of several wildcats with a short tail, long legs, and usu. tufted ears

lynx

lyre \'līr\ *n* : a stringed musical instrument of the harp class used by the ancient Greeks

¹lyr·ic \'lir-ik\ *n* **1** : a lyric poem **2** *pl* : the words of a popular song — **lyr·i·cal** \-i-kəl\ *adj*

²lyric *adj* **1** : suitable for singing : MELODIC **2** : expressing direct and usu. intense personal emotion

ly·ser·gic acid di·eth·yl·am·ide \lə-ˌsər-jik . . . ˌdī-ˌe-thə-'la-ˌmīd, lī-, -'la-məd\ *n* : LSD

LZ *abbr* landing zone

M

¹**m** \ˈem\ *n, pl* **m's** *or* **ms** \ˈemz\ *often cap* : the 13th letter of the English alphabet

²**m** *abbr, often cap* 1 Mach 2 male 3 married 4 masculine 5 medium 6 [L *meridies*] noon 7 meter 8 mile 9 [L *mille*] thousand 10 minute 11 month 12 moon

ma \ˈmä, ˈmȯ\ *n* : MOTHER

MA *abbr* 1 [ML *magister artium*] master of arts 2 Massachusetts 3 mental age

ma'am \ˈmam, *after* "yes" *often* əm\ *n* : MADAM

Mac *abbr* Machabees

Mac *or* **Macc** *abbr* Maccabees

ma·ca·bre \mə-ˈkäb; ˈkä-brə, -bər\ *adj* [F] 1 : having death as a subject 2 : GRUESOME 3 : HORRIBLE

mac·ad·am \mə-ˈka-dəm\ *n* : a roadway or pavement of small closely packed broken stone — **mac·ad·am·ize** \-də-ˌmīz\ *vb*

ma·caque \mə-ˈkak, -ˈkäk\ *n* : any of a genus of short-tailed chiefly Asian monkeys

mac·a·ro·ni \ˌma-kə-ˈrō-nē\ *n* 1 : pasta made chiefly of wheat flour and shaped in the form of slender tubes 2 *pl* **-nis** *or* **-nies** : FOP, DANDY

mac·a·roon \ˌma-kə-ˈrün\ *n* : a small cookie made chiefly of egg whites, sugar, and ground almonds or coconut

ma·caw \mə-ˈkȯ\ *n* : any of numerous parrots of Central and So. America

Mac·ca·bees \ˈma-kə-ˌbēz\ *n* — see BIBLE table

¹**mace** \ˈmās\ *n* : a spice made from the fibrous coating of the nutmeg

²**mace** *n* 1 : a heavy often spiked club used as a weapon esp. in the Middle Ages 2 : an ornamental staff carried as a symbol of authority

mace 1

Mac·e·do·nian \ˌma-sə-ˈdō-nyən, -nē-ən\ *n* : a native or inhabitant of Macedonia — **Macedonian** *adj*

mac·er·ate \ˈma-sə-ˌrāt\ *vb* **-at·ed; -at·ing** 1 : to cause to waste away 2 : to soften by steeping or soaking so as to separate the parts — **mac·er·a·tion** \ˌma-sə-ˈrā-shən\ *n*

mach *abbr* machine; machinery; machinist

Mach \ˈmäk\ *n* : a speed expressed by a Mach number

Mach·a·bees \ˈma-kə-ˌbēz\ *n* : MACCABEES

ma·chete \mə-ˈshe-tē\ *n* : a large heavy knife used for cutting sugarcane and underbrush and as a weapon

Ma·chi·a·vel·lian \ˌma-kē-ə-ˈve-lē-ən\ *adj* [Niccolò *Machiavelli*, †1527 Ital. political philosopher] : characterized by cunning, duplicity, and bad faith — **Ma·chi·a·vel·lian·ism** *n*

mach·i·na·tion \ˌma-kə-ˈnā-shən, ˌma-shə-\ *n* : an act of planning esp. to do harm; *esp* : PLOT — **mach·i·nate** \ˈma-kə-ˌnāt, ˈma-shə-\ *vb*

¹**ma·chine** \mə-ˈshēn\ *n* 1 : CONVEYANCE, VEHICLE; *esp* : AUTOMOBILE 2 : a combination of mechanical parts that transmit forces, motion, and energy one to another 3 : an instrument (as a lever) for transmitting or mod-

ifying force or motion 4 : an electrical, electronic, or mechanical device for performing a task ⟨a sewing ∼⟩ 5 : a highly organized political group under the leadership of a boss or small clique

²**machine** *vb* **ma·chined; ma·chin·ing** : to shape or finish by machine-operated tools — **ma·chin·able** \-ˈshē-nə-bəl\ *adj*

machine gun *n* : an automatic gun capable of rapid continuous firing — **machine–gun** *vb* — **machine gunner** *n*

machine language *n* : the set of symbolic instruction codes used to represent operations and data in a machine (as a computer)

machine–readable *adj* : directly usable by a computer

ma·chin·ery \mə-ˈshē-nə-rē\ *n, pl* **-er·ies** 1 : MACHINES; *also* : the working parts of a machine 2 : the means by which something is done

ma·chin·ist \mə-ˈshē-nist\ *n* : a person who makes or works on machines

ma·chis·mo \mä-ˈchēz-(ˌ)mō, -ˈchiz-\ *n* : a strong or exaggerated pride in one's masculinity

Mach number \ˈmäk-\ *n* : a number representing the ratio of the speed of a body to the speed of sound in the surrounding atmosphere

ma·cho \ˈmä-chō\ *adj* [Sp, lit., male, fr. L *masculus*] : characterized by machismo

mack·er·el \ˈma-kə-rəl\ *n, pl* **mackerel** *or* **mackerels** : a No. Atlantic food fish greenish above and silvery below

mack·i·naw \ˈma-kə-ˌnȯ\ *n* : a short heavy plaid coat

mack·in·tosh *also* **mac·in·tosh** \ˈma-kən-ˌtäsh\ *n* 1 *chiefly Brit* : RAINCOAT 2 : a lightweight waterproof fabric

mac·ra·mé *also* **mac·ra·me** \ˈma-krə-ˌmā\ *n* [ultim. fr. Ar *miqramah* coverlet] : a coarse lace or fringe made by knotting threads or cords in a geometrical pattern

mac·ro \ˈma-(ˌ)krō\ *adj* : very large; *also* : involving large quantities or being on a large scale

mac·ro·bi·ot·ic \ˌma-krō-bī-ˈä-tik, -bē-\ *adj* : relating to or being a very restricted diet (as one containing chiefly whole grains)

mac·ro·cosm \ˈma-krə-ˌkä-zəm\ *n* : the great world : UNIVERSE

ma·cron \ˈmā-ˌkrän, ˈma-\ *n* : a mark ⁻ placed over a vowel (as in \māk\) to show that the vowel is long

mac·ro·scop·ic \ˌma-krə-ˈskä-pik\ *adj* : visible to the naked eye — **mac·ro·scop·i·cal·ly** \-pi-k(ə-)lē\ *adv*

mad \ˈmad\ *adj* **mad·der; mad·dest** 1 : disordered in mind : INSANE 2 : being rash and foolish 3 : FURIOUS, ENRAGED 4 : carried away by enthusiasm 5 : RABID 6 : marked by wild gaiety and merriment 7 : FRANTIC — **mad·ly** *adv* — **mad·ness** *n*

Mad·a·gas·can \ˌma-də-ˈgas-kən\ *n* : a native or inhabitant of Madagascar

mad·am \ˈma-dəm\ *n* 1 *pl* **mes·dames** \mā-ˈdäm\ — used as a form of polite address to a woman 2 *pl* **madams** : the female head of a house of prostitution

ma·dame \mə-ˈdam, *before a surname also* ˈma-dəm\ *n, pl* **mes·dames** \mā-ˈdäm\ : MISTRESS — used as a title equivalent to *Mrs.* for a married woman not of English-speaking nationality

\ə\abut \ᵊ\kitten \ər\further \a\ash \ā\ace \ä\mop, mar \au̇\out \ch\chin \e\bet \ē\easy \g\go \i\hit \ī\ice \j\job \ŋ\sing \ō\go \ȯ\law \ȯi\boy \th\thin \t̲h̲\the \ü\loot \u̇\foot \y\yet \zh\vision *see also* Pronunciation Symbols page

mad·cap \'mad-ˌkap\ adj : WILD, RECKLESS — **madcap** n

mad·den \'mad-ᵊn\ vb : to make mad — **mad·den·ing·ly** adv

mad·der \'ma-dər\ n : a Eurasian herb with yellow flowers and fleshy red roots; also : its root or a dye prepared from it

made past and past part of MAKE

Ma·dei·ra \mə-ˈdir-ə\ n : an amber-colored dessert wine

ma·de·moi·selle \ˌma-də-mə-ˈzel, -mwə-, mam-ˈzel\ n, pl **ma·de·moi·selles** \-ˈzelz\ or **mes·de·moi·selles** \ˌmā-də-me-ˈzel, -mwe-\ : an unmarried girl or woman — used as a title for an unmarried woman not of English-speaking nationality

made–up \'mā-ˈdəp\ adj 1 : fancifully conceived or falsely devised 2 : marked by the use of makeup

mad·house \'mad-ˌhaus\ n 1 : a place for the detention and care of the insane 2 : a place of great uproar

mad·man \'mad-ˌman, -mən\ n : LUNATIC

Ma·don·na \mə-ˈdä-nə\ n : a representation (as a picture or statue) of the Virgin Mary

ma·dras \'ma-drəs; ˌmə-ˈdras, -ˈdräs\ n [Madras, India] : a fine usu. cotton fabric with various designs (as plaid)

mad·ri·gal \'ma-dri-gəl\ n [It madrigale] 1 : a short lyrical poem in a strict poetic form 2 : an elaborate part-song esp. of the 16th and 17th centuries

mad·wom·an \'mad-ˌwu̇-mən\ n : a woman who is insane

mael·strom \'māl-strəm\ n 1 : a violent whirlpool 2 : TUMULT

mae·stro \'mī-strō\ n, pl **maestros** or **mae·stri** \-ˌstrē\ [It] : a master in an art; esp : an eminent composer, conductor, or teacher of music

Ma·fia \'mä-fē-ə\ n [It] : a secret criminal society of Sicily or Italy; also : a similar organization elsewhere

ma·fi·o·so \ˌmä-fē-ˈō-(ˌ)sō\ n, pl **-si** \-(ˌ)sē\ : a member of the Mafia

¹**mag** \'mag\ n : MAGAZINE

²**mag** abbr 1 magnetism 2 magneto 3 magnitude

mag·a·zine \'ma-gə-ˌzēn\ n 1 : a storehouse esp. for military supplies 2 : a place for keeping gunpowder in a fort or ship 3 : a publication usu. containing stories, articles, or poems and issued periodically 4 : a container in a gun for holding cartridges; also : a chamber (as on a camera) for film

ma·gen·ta \mə-ˈjen-tə\ n : a deep purplish red color

mag·got \'ma-gət\ n : the legless wormlike larva of a dipteran fly — **mag·goty** adj

ma·gi \'mā-ˌjī\ n pl, often cap : the three wise men from the East who paid homage to the infant Jesus

mag·ic \'ma-jik\ n 1 : the use of means (as charms or spells) believed to have supernatural power over natural forces 2 : an extraordinary power or influence seemingly from a supernatural force 3 : SLEIGHT OF HAND — **magic** adj — **mag·i·cal** \-ji-kəl\ adj — **mag·i·cal·ly** \-ji-k(ə-)lē\ adv

ma·gi·cian \mə-ˈji-shən\ n : one skilled in magic

mag·is·te·ri·al \ˌma-jə-ˈstir-ē-əl\ adj 1 : AUTHORITATIVE 2 : of or relating to a magistrate or a magistrate's office or duties

ma·gis·tral \'ma-jə-strəl\ adj : AUTHORITATIVE

mag·is·trate \'ma-jə-ˌstrāt\ n : an official entrusted with administration of the laws — **mag·is·tra·cy** \-strə-sē\ n

mag·ma \'mag-mə\ n : molten rock material within the earth — **mag·mat·ic** \mag-ˈma-tik\ adj

mag·nan·i·mous \mag-ˈna-nə-məs\ adj 1 : showing or suggesting a lofty and courageous spirit 2 : NOBLE, GENEROUS — **mag·na·nim·i·ty** \ˌmag-nə-ˈni-mə-tē\ n — **mag·nan·i·mous·ly** adv — **mag·nan·i·mous·ness** n

mag·nate \'mag-ˌnāt\ n : a person of rank, influence, or distinction

mag·ne·sia \mag-ˈnē-shə, -zhə\ n [NL, fr. magnes car-neus, a white earth, lit., flesh magnet] : a light white oxide of magnesium used as a laxative

mag·ne·sium \mag-ˈnē-zē-əm, -zhəm\ n : a silver-white light malleable metallic chemical element — see ELEMENT table

mag·net \'mag-nət\ n 1 : LODESTONE 2 : a body that is able to attract iron 3 : something that attracts

mag·net·ic \mag-ˈne-tik\ adj 1 : having an unusual ability to attract ⟨a ∼ leader⟩ 2 : of or relating to a magnet or magnetism 3 : magnetized or capable of being magnetized — **mag·net·i·cal·ly** \-ti-k(ə-)lē\ adv

magnetic disk n : DISK 3

magnetic north n : the northerly direction in the earth's magnetic field indicated by the north-seeking pole of a compass needle

magnetic resonance imaging n : a noninvasive diagnostic technique that produces computerized images of internal body tissues based on electromagnetically induced activity of atoms within the body

magnetic tape n : a ribbon coated with a magnetic material on which information (as sound) may be stored

mag·ne·tism \'mag-nə-ˌti-zəm\ n 1 : the power (as of a magnet) to attract iron 2 : the science that deals with magnetic phenomena 3 : an ability to attract

mag·ne·tise Brit var of MAGNETIZE

mag·ne·tite \'mag-nə-ˌtīt\ n : a black mineral that is an important iron ore

mag·ne·tize \'mag-nə-ˌtīz\ vb **-tized; -tiz·ing** 1 : to induce magnetic properties in 2 : to attract like a magnet : CHARM — **mag·ne·tiz·able** adj — **mag·ne·ti·za·tion** \ˌmag-nə-tə-ˈzā-shən\ n — **mag·ne·tiz·er** n

mag·ne·to \mag-ˈnē-tō\ n, pl **-tos** : a generator used to produce sparks in an internal combustion engine

mag·ne·tom·e·ter \ˌmag-nə-ˈtä-mə-tər\ n : an instrument for measuring the strength of a magnetic field

mag·ne·to·sphere \mag-ˈnē-tə-ˌsfir, -ˈne-\ n : a region around a celestial object (as the earth) in which charged particles are trapped by its magnetic field — **mag·ne·to·spher·ic** \-ˌnē-tə-ˈsfir-ik, -ˈsfer-\ adj

mag·ni·fi·ca·tion \ˌmag-nə-fə-ˈkā-shən\ n 1 : the act of magnifying 2 : the amount by which an optical lens or instrument magnifies

mag·nif·i·cent \mag-ˈni-fə-sənt\ adj 1 : characterized by grandeur or beauty : SPLENDID 2 : EXALTED, NOBLE syn imposing, stately, grand, majestic — **mag·nif·i·cence** \-səns\ n — **mag·nif·i·cent·ly** adv

mag·nif·i·co \mag-ˈni-fi-ˌkō\ n, pl **-coes** or **-cos** 1 : a nobleman of Venice 2 : a person of high position

mag·ni·fy \'mag-nə-ˌfī\ vb **-fied; -fy·ing** 1 : EXTOL, LAUD; also : to cause to be held in greater esteem 2 : INTENSIFY; also : EXAGGERATE 3 : to enlarge in fact or in appearance ⟨a microscope magnifies an object⟩ — **mag·ni·fi·er** \'mag-nə-ˌfī-ər\ n

mag·nil·o·quent \mag-ˈni-lə-kwənt\ adj : characterized by an exalted and often bombastic style or manner — **mag·nil·o·quence** \-kwəns\ n

mag·ni·tude \'mag-nə-ˌtüd, -ˌtyüd\ n 1 : greatness of size or extent 2 : SIZE 3 : QUANTITY 4 : a number representing the brightness of a celestial body

mag·no·lia \mag-ˈnōl-yə\ n : any of a genus of usu. spring-flowering shrubs and trees with large often fragrant flowers

mag·num opus \'mag-nəm-ˈō-pəs\ n [L] : the greatest achievement of an artist or writer

mag·pie \'mag-ˌpī\ n : any of various long-tailed often black-and-white birds related to the jays

Mag·yar \'mag-ˌyär, 'mäg-; 'mä-ˌjär\ n : a member of the dominant people of Hungary — **Magyar** adj

ma·ha·ra·ja or **ma·ha·ra·jah** \ˌmä-hə-ˈrä-jə\ n : a Hindu prince ranking above a raja

ma·ha·ra·ni or **ma·ha·ra·nee** \-ˈrä-nē\ n 1 : the wife of a maharaja 2 : a Hindu princess ranking above a rani

ma·ha·ri·shi \\mä-hə-'rē-shē\ *n* : a Hindu teacher of mystical knowledge

ma·hat·ma \mə-'hät-mə, -'hat-\ *n* [Skt *mahātman,* fr. *mahātman* great-souled, fr. *mahat* great + *ātman* soul] : a person revered for high-mindedness, wisdom, and selflessness

Ma·hi·can \mə-'hē-kən\ *n, pl* **Mahican** *or* **Mahicans** : a member of an American Indian people of the upper Hudson River valley

ma·hog·a·ny \mə-'hä-gə-nē\ *n, pl* **-nies** : the reddish wood of any of various chiefly tropical trees that is used in furniture; *also* : a tree yielding this wood

ma·hout \mə-'haút\ *n* [Hindi *mahāut*] : a keeper and driver of an elephant

maid \'mād\ *n* **1** : an unmarried girl or young woman **2** : MAIDSERVANT

¹maid·en \'mād-ᵊn\ *n* : MAID 1 — **maid·en·ly** *adj*

²maiden *adj* **1** : UNMARRIED; *also* : VIRGIN **2** : of, relating to, or befitting a maiden **3** : FIRST ⟨~ voyage⟩

maid·en·hair fern \-ˌhar-\ *n* : any of a genus of ferns with delicate feathery fronds

maid·en·head \'mād-ᵊn-ˌhed\ *n* **1** : VIRGINITY **2** : HYMEN

maid·en·hood \-ˌhùd\ *n* : the condition or time of being a maiden

maid–in–waiting *n, pl* **maids–in–waiting** : a young woman appointed to attend a queen or princess

maid of honor : a bride's principal unmarried wedding attendant

maid·ser·vant \'mād-ˌsər-vənt\ *n* : a girl or woman who is a servant

¹mail \'māl\ *n* [ME *male* bag, fr. OF] **1** : something sent or carried in the postal system **2** : a nation's postal system — often used in pl.

²mail *vb* : to send by mail

³mail *n* [ME *maille,* fr. MF, fr. L *macula* spot, mesh] : armor made of metal links or plates

mail·box \'māl-ˌbäks\ *n* **1** : a public box for the collection of mail **2** : a private box for the delivery of mail

mail·man \-ˌman\ *n* : a man who delivers mail

maim \'mām\ *vb* : to mutilate, disfigure, or wound seriously : CRIPPLE

¹main \'mān\ *n* **1** : FORCE ⟨with might and ~⟩ **2** : MAINLAND; *also* : HIGH SEA **3** : the chief part **4** : a principal pipe, duct, or circuit of a utility system

²main *adj* **1** : CHIEF, PRINCIPAL **2** : fully exerted ⟨~ force⟩ **3** : expressing the chief predication in a complex sentence ⟨the ~ clause⟩ — **main·ly** *adv*

main·frame \'mān-ˌfrām\ *n* : a large fast computer

main·land \-ˌland, -lənd\ *n* : a continuous body of land constituting the chief part of a country or continent

main·line \-ˌlīn\ *vb, slang* : to inject a narcotic drug into a vein

main line *n* : a principal highway or railroad line

main·mast \'mān-ˌmast, -məst\ *n* : the principal mast on a sailing ship

main·sail \-ˌsāl, -səl\ *n* : the largest sail on the mainmast

main·spring \-ˌspriŋ\ *n* **1** : the chief spring in a mechanism (as of a watch) **2** : the chief motive, agent, or cause

main·stay \-ˌstā\ *n* **1** : a stay running from the head of the mainmast to the foot of the foremast **2** : a chief support

main·stream \-ˌstrēm\ *n* : a prevailing current or direction of activity or influence — **mainstream** *adj*

main·tain \mān-'tān\ *vb* [ME *mainteinen,* fr. OF *maintenir,* fr. ML *manutenēre,* fr. L *manu tenēre* to hold in the hand] **1** : to keep in an existing state (as of repair) **2** : to sustain against opposition or danger **3** : to continue in : CARRY ON **4** : to provide for : SUPPORT **5** : ASSERT — **main·tain·abil·i·ty** \-ˌtā-nə-'bi-lə-tē\ *n* — **main·tain·able** \-'tā-nə-bəl\ *adj* — **main·te·nance** \'mānt-ᵊn-əns\ *n*

main·top \'mān-ˌtäp\ *n* : a platform at the head of the mainmast of a square-rigged ship

mai·son·ette \ˌmāz-ᵊn-'et\ *n* **1** : a small house **2** : an apartment often on two floors

maî·tre d' *or* **mai·tre d'** \ˌmā-trə-'dē, ˌme-\ *n, pl* **maître d's** *or* **maitre d's** \-'dēz\ : MAÎTRE D'HÔTEL

maî·tre d'hô·tel \ˌmā-trə-dō-'tel, ˌme-\ *n, pl* **maîtres d'hôtel** *same*\ [F, lit., master of house] **1** : MAJORDOMO **2** : HEADWAITER

maize \'māz\ *n* : INDIAN CORN

Maj *abbr* major

maj·es·ty \'ma-jə-stē\ *n, pl* **-ties 1** : sovereign power, authority, or dignity; *also* : the person of a sovereign — used as a title **2** : GRANDEUR, SPLENDOR — **ma·jes·tic** \mə-'jes-tik\ *adj* — **ma·jes·ti·cal·ly** \-ti-k(ə-)lē\ *adv*

Maj Gen *abbr* Major General

ma·jol·i·ca \mə-'jä-li-kə\ *also* **ma·iol·i·ca** \-'yä-\ *n* : any of several faiences; *esp* : an Italian tin-glazed pottery

¹ma·jor \'mā-jər\ *adj* **1** : greater in number, extent, or importance ⟨a ~ poet⟩ **2** : notable or conspicuous in effect or scope ⟨a ~ improvement⟩ **3** : SERIOUS ⟨a ~ illness⟩ **4** : having half steps between the 3d and 4th and the 7th and 8th degrees ⟨~ scale⟩; *also* : based on a major scale ⟨~ key⟩ ⟨~ chord⟩

²major *n* **1** : a commissioned officer (as in the army) ranking next below a lieutenant colonel **2** : an academic subject chosen as a field of specialization; *also* : a student specializing in such a field

³major *vb* : to pursue an academic major

ma·jor·do·mo \ˌmā-jər-'dō-mō\ *n, pl* **-mos** [Sp *mayordomo* or obs. It *maiordomo,* fr. ML *major domus,* lit., chief of the house] **1** : a head steward **2** : BUTLER

ma·jor·ette \ˌmā-jə-'ret\ *n* : DRUM MAJORETTE

major general *n* : a commissioned officer (as in the army) ranking next below a lieutenant general

ma·jor·i·ty \mə-'jòr-ə-tē\ *n, pl* **-ties 1** : the age at which full civil rights are accorded; *also* : the status of one who has attained this age **2** : a number greater than half of a total; *also* : the excess of this greater number over the remainder **3** : the rank of a major

ma·jus·cule \'ma-jəs-ˌkyül, mə-'jəs-\ *n* : a large letter (as a capital)

¹make \'māk\ *vb* **made** \'mād\; **mak·ing 1** : to cause to exist, occur, or appear; *also* : DESTINE ⟨was *made* to be an actor⟩ **2** : FASHION ⟨~ a dress⟩; *also* : COMPOSE **3** : to formulate in the mind ⟨~ plans⟩ **4** : CONSTITUTE ⟨house *made* of stone⟩ **5** : to compute to be **6** : to set in order : PREPARE ⟨~ a bed⟩ **7** : to cause to be or become; *also* : APPOINT **8** : ENACT; *also* : EXECUTE ⟨~ a will⟩ **9** : CONCLUDE ⟨didn't know what to ~ of it⟩ **10** : CARRY OUT, PERFORM ⟨~ a gesture⟩ **11** : COMPEL **12** : to assure the success of ⟨will ~ us or break us⟩ **13** : to amount to in significance ⟨~s no difference⟩ **14** : to be capable of developing or being fashioned into **15** : REACH, ATTAIN; *also* : GAIN **16** : to start out : GO **17** : to have weight or effect ⟨courtesy ~s for safer driving⟩ **syn** form, shape, fabricate, manufacture — **mak·er** *n* — **make believe** : PRETEND — **make do** : to manage with the means at hand — **make fun of** : RIDICULE, MOCK — **make good 1** : INDEMNIFY ⟨*make good* the loss⟩; *also* : to carry out successfully ⟨*make good* his promise⟩ **2** : SUCCEED — **make way 1** : to give room for passing, entering, or occupying **2** : to make progress

²make *n* **1** : the manner or style of construction; *also* : BRAND **3 2** : MAKEUP **3** : the action of manufacturing — **on the make** : in search of wealth, social status, or sexual adventure

¹make–be·lieve \'māk-bə-ˌlēv\ *n* : a pretending to believe : PRETENSE

²make–believe *adj* : IMAGINED, PRETENDED

\ə\abut \ᵊ\kitten \ər\further \a\ash \ā\ace \ä\mop, mar \aú\out \ch\chin \e\bet \ē\easy \g\go \i\hit \ī\ice \j\job \ŋ\sing \ō\go \ò\law \ói\boy \th\thin \t̲h̲\the \ü\loot \ú\foot \y\yet \zh\vision *see also* Pronunciation Symbols page

make–do \-ˌdü\ *adj* : MAKESHIFT
make out *vb* **1** : to draw up in writing ⟨*make out* a list⟩ **2** : to find or grasp the meaning of ⟨can you *make* that *out*⟩ **3** : to represent as being **4** : to pretend to be true **5** : DISCERN ⟨*make out* a ship in the fog⟩ **6** : GET ALONG, FARE ⟨*make out* well in life⟩ **7** : to engage in amorous kissing and caressing
make over *vb* : REMAKE, REMODEL — **make·over** \ˈmā-ˌkō-vər\ *n*
make·shift \ˈmāk-ˌshift\ *n* : a temporary expedient — **makeshift** *adj*
make·up \ˈmā-ˌkəp\ *n* **1** : the way in which something is put together; *also* : physical, mental, and moral constitution **2** : cosmetics esp. for the face; *also* : materials (as wigs and cosmetics) used in making up
make up *vb* **1** : FORM, COMPOSE **2** : to compensate for a deficiency **3** : SETTLE ⟨*made up* my mind⟩ **4** : INVENT, IMPROVISE **5** : to become reconciled **6** : to put on make-up (as for a play)
make–work \ˈmāk-ˌwərk\ *n* : BUSYWORK
mak·ings \ˈmā-kiŋz\ *n pl* : the material from which something is made
makuta *pl of* LIKUTA
Mal *abbr* Malachi
Mal·a·chi \ˈma-lə-ˌkī\ *n* — see BIBLE table
Mal·a·chi·as \ˌma-lə-ˈkī-əs\ *n* : MALACHI
mal·a·chite \ˈma-lə-ˌkīt\ *n* : a mineral that is a green carbonate of copper used for making ornamental objects
mal·adapt·ed \ˌma-lə-ˈdap-təd\ *adj* : poorly suited to a particular use, purpose, or situation
mal·ad·just·ed \ˌma-lə-ˈjəs-təd\ *adj* : poorly or inadequately adjusted (as to one's environment) — **mal·ad·just·ment** \-ˈjəst-mənt\ *n*
mal·adroit \ˌma-lə-ˈdroit\ *adj* : not adroit : INEPT
mal·a·dy \ˈma-lə-dē\ *n, pl* **-dies** : a disease or disorder of body or mind
mal·aise \mə-ˈlāz, ma-\ *n* [F] : a hazy feeling of not being well
mal·a·mute \ˈma-lə-ˌmyüt\ *n* : a dog often used to draw sleds esp. in northern No. America
mal·a·prop·ism \ˈma-lə-ˌprä-ˌpi-zəm\ *n* : a usu. humorous misuse of a word
mal·ap·ro·pos \ˌma-ˌla-prə-ˈpō, ma-ˈla-prə-ˌpō\ *adv* : in an inappropriate or inopportune way — **malapropos** *adj*
ma·lar·ia \mə-ˈler-ē-ə\ *n* [It, fr. *mala aria* bad air] : a disease marked by recurring chills and fever and caused by a protozoan parasite of the blood that is transmitted by anopheles mosquitoes — **ma·lar·i·al** \-əl\ *adj*
ma·lar·key \mə-ˈlär-kē\ *n* : insincere or foolish talk
mal·a·thi·on \ˌma-lə-ˈthī-ən, -ˌän\ *n* : an insecticide with a relatively low toxicity for mammals
Ma·la·wi·an \mə-ˈlä-wē-ən\ *n* : a native or inhabitant of Malawi — **Malawian** *adj*
Ma·lay \mə-ˈlā, ˈmā-ˌlā\ *n* **1** : a member of a people of the Malay Peninsula and Archipelago **2** : the language of the Malays — **Malay** *adj* — **Ma·lay·an** \mə-ˈlā-ən, ˈmā-ˌlā-\ *n or adj*
Ma·lay·sian \mə-ˈlā-zhən, -shən\ *n* : a native or inhabitant of Malaysia — **Malaysian** *adj*
mal·con·tent \ˌmal-kən-ˈtent\ *adj* : marked by a dissatisfaction with the existing state of affairs : DISCONTENTED — **malcontent** *n*
mal de mer \ˌmal-də-ˈmer\ *n* [F] : SEASICKNESS
¹male \ˈmāl\ *adj* **1** : of, relating to, or being the sex that produces germ cells which fertilize the eggs of a female; *also* : STAMINATE **2** : MASCULINE — **male·ness** *n*
²male *n* : a male individual
male·dic·tion \ˌma-lə-ˈdik-shən\ *n* : CURSE, EXECRATION
male·fac·tor \ˈma-lə-ˌfak-tər\ *n* : EVILDOER; *esp* : one who commits an offense against the law — **mal·e·fac·tion** \ˌma-lə-ˈfak-shən\ *n*
ma·lef·ic \mə-ˈle-fik\ *adj* **1** : BALEFUL **2** : MALICIOUS

ma·lef·i·cent \-fə-sənt\ *adj* : working or productive of harm or evil
ma·lev·o·lent \mə-ˈle-və-lənt\ *adj* : having, showing, or arising from ill will, spite, or hatred **syn** malignant, malign, malicious, spiteful — **ma·lev·o·lence** \-ləns\ *n*
mal·fea·sance \mal-ˈfēz-²ns\ *n* : wrongful conduct esp. by a public official
mal·for·ma·tion \ˌmal-fȯr-ˈmā-shən\ *n* : irregular or faulty formation or structure; *also* : an instance of this — **mal·formed** \mal-ˈfȯrmd\ *adj*
mal·func·tion \mal-ˈfəŋk-shən\ *vb* : to fail to operate normally — **malfunction** *n*
Ma·li·an \ˈmä-lē-ən\ *n* : a native or inhabitant of Mali — **Malian** *adj*
mal·ice \ˈma-ləs\ *n* : desire to cause injury or distress to another — **ma·li·cious** \mə-ˈli-shəs\ *adj* — **ma·li·cious·ly** *adv*
¹ma·lign \mə-ˈlīn\ *adj* **1** : evil in nature, influence, or effect; *also* : MALIGNANT **2** **2** : moved by ill will
²malign *vb* : to speak evil of : DEFAME
ma·lig·nant \mə-ˈlig-nənt\ *adj* **1** : INJURIOUS, MALIGN **2** : tending to produce death or deterioration ⟨a ∼ tumor⟩ — **ma·lig·nan·cy** \-nən-sē\ *n* — **ma·lig·nant·ly** *adv* — **ma·lig·ni·ty** \-nə-tē\ *n*
ma·lin·ger \mə-ˈliŋ-gər\ *vb* [F *malingre* sickly] : to pretend illness so as to avoid duty — **ma·lin·ger·er** *n*
mal·i·son \ˈma-lə-sən, -zən\ *n* : CURSE
mall \ˈmȯl, ˈmal\ *n* **1** : a shaded walk : PROMENADE **2** : an urban shopping area featuring a variety of shops surrounding a concourse **3** : a usu. large enclosed suburban shopping area containing various shops
mal·lard \ˈma-lərd\ *n, pl* **mallard** *or* **mallards** : a common wild duck that is the source of domestic ducks

mallard

mal·lea·ble \ˈma-lē-ə-bəl\ *adj* **1** : capable of being extended or shaped by beating with a hammer or by the pressure of rollers **2** : ADAPTABLE, PLIABLE **syn** plastic, pliant, ductile, supple — **mal·le·a·bil·i·ty** \ˌma-lē-ə-ˈbi-lə-tē\ *n*
mal·let \ˈma-lət\ *n* **1** : a tool with a large head for driving another tool or for striking a surface without marring it **2** : a long-handled hammerlike implement for striking a ball (as in croquet)
mal·le·us \ˈma-lē-əs\ *n, pl* **mal·lei** \-lē-ˌī, -lē-ˌē\ [NL, fr. L, hammer] : the outermost of the three small bones of the mammalian middle ear
mal·low \ˈma-lō\ *n* : any of a genus of herbs with lobed leaves, usu. showy flowers, and a disk-shaped fruit
malm·sey \ˈmälm-zē\ *n, often cap* : the sweetest variety of Madeira
mal·nour·ished \mal-ˈnər-isht\ *adj* : UNDERNOURISHED
mal·nu·tri·tion \ˌmal-nü-ˈtri-shən, -nyü-\ *n* : faulty and esp. inadequate nutrition
mal·oc·clu·sion \ˌma-lə-ˈklü-zhən\ *n* : faulty coming together of teeth in biting
mal·odor·ous \ma-ˈlō-də-rəs\ *adj* : ill-smelling — **mal·odor·ous·ly** *adv* — **mal·odor·ous·ness** *n*
ma·lo·ti \mä-ˈlō-tē\ *pl of* LOTI
mal·prac·tice \mal-ˈprak-təs\ *n* : a dereliction of professional duty or a failure of professional skill that results in injury, loss, or damage

malt \'mȯlt\ *n* **1** : grain and esp. barley steeped in water until it has sprouted and used in brewing and distilling **2** : liquor made with malt — **malty** *adj*
malted milk \'mȯl-təd-\ *n* : a powder prepared from dried milk and an extract from malt; *also* : a beverage of this powder in milk or other liquid
Mal·thu·sian \mal-'thü-zhən, -'thyü-\ *adj* : of or relating to a theory that population unless checked (as by war) tends to increase faster than its means of subsistence — **Malthusian** *n* — **Mal·thu·sian·ism** \-zhə-ˌni-zəm\ *n*
malt·ose \'mȯl-ˌtōs\ *n* : a sugar formed esp. from starch by the action of enzymes
mal·treat \mal-'trēt\ *vb* : to treat cruelly or roughly : ABUSE — **mal·treat·ment** *n*
ma·ma *or* **mam·ma** \'mä-mə\ *n* : MOTHER
mam·bo \'mäm-bō\ *n, pl* **mambos** : a dance of Cuban origin related to the rumba — **mambo** *vb*
mam·mal \'ma-məl\ *n* : any of a class of warm-blooded vertebrates that includes humans and all other animals which nourish their young with milk and have the skin more or less covered with hair — **mam·ma·li·an** \mə-'mā-lē-ən, ma-\ *adj or n*
mam·ma·ry \'ma-mə-rē\ *adj* : of, relating to, or being the glands (**mammary glands**) that in female mammals secrete milk
mam·mo·gram \'ma-mə-ˌgram\ *n* : an X-ray photograph of the breasts
mam·mog·ra·phy \ma-'mä-grə-fē\ *n* : X-ray examination of the breasts (as for early detection of cancer)
mam·mon \'ma-mən\ *n, often cap* : material wealth having a debasing influence
¹mam·moth \'ma-məth\ *n* : any of a genus of large hairy extinct elephants
²mammoth *adj* : of very great size : GIGANTIC **syn** colossal, enormous, immense, vast, elephantine
¹man \'man\ *n, pl* **men** \'men\ **1** : a human being; *esp* : an adult male **2** : the human race : MANKIND **3** : one possessing in high degree the qualities considered distinctive of manhood **4** : an adult male servant or employee **5** : the individual who can fulfill one's requirements ⟨he's your ∼⟩ **6** : one of the pieces with which various games (as chess) are played; *also* : one of the players on a team **7** *often cap* : white society or people
²man *vb* **manned; man·ning 1** : to supply with men ⟨∼ a fleet⟩ **2** : FORTIFY, BRACE
³man *abbr* manual
Man *abbr* Manitoba
man–about–town *n, pl* **men–about–town** : a worldly and socially active man
man·a·cle \'ma-ni-kəl\ *n* **1** : a shackle for the hand or wrist **2** : something used as a restraint
man·age \'ma-nij\ *vb* **man·aged; man·ag·ing 1** : HANDLE, CONTROL; *also* : to direct or carry on business or affairs **2** : to make and keep compliant **3** : to treat with care : HUSBAND **4** : to achieve one's purpose : CONTRIVE — **man·age·abil·i·ty** \ˌma-ni-jə-'bi-lə-tē\ *n* — **man·age·able** \'ma-ni-jə-bəl\ *adj* — **man·age·able·ness** *n* — **man·age·ably** \-blē\ *adv*
man·age·ment \'ma-nij-mənt\ *n* **1** : the act or art of managing : CONTROL **2** : judicious use of means to accomplish an end **3** : the group of those who manage or direct an enterprise
man·ag·er \'ma-ni-jər\ *n* : one that manages — **man·a·ge·ri·al** \ˌma-nə-'jir-ē-əl\ *adj*
ma·ña·na \mən-'yä-nə\ \[Sp, lit., tomorrow\] *n* : an indefinite time in the future
man–at–arms *n, pl* **men–at–arms** : SOLDIER; *esp* : one who is heavily armed and mounted
man·a·tee \'ma-nə-ˌtē\ *n* : any of a genus of chiefly tropical plant-eating aquatic mammals having a broad rounded tail
Man·chu·ri·an \man-'chu̇r-ē-ən\ *n* : a native or inhabitant of Manchuria, China — **Manchurian** *adj*

man·ci·ple \'man-sə-pəl\ *n* : a steward or purveyor esp. for a college or monastery
man·da·mus \man-'dā-məs\ *n* \[L, we enjoin\] : a writ issued by a superior court commanding that an official act or duty be performed
man·da·rin \'man-də-rən\ *n* **1** : a public official of high rank under the Chinese Empire **2** *cap* : the chief dialect group of China **3** : a yellow to reddish orange loose-skinned citrus fruit; *also* : a tree that bears mandarins
man·date \'man-ˌdāt\ *n* **1** : an authoritative command **2** : an authorization to act given to a representative **3** : a commission granted by the League of Nations to a member nation for governing conquered territory; *also* : a territory so governed
man·da·to·ry \'man-də-ˌtȯr-ē\ *adj* **1** : containing or constituting a command : OBLIGATORY **2** : of or relating to a League of Nations mandate
man·di·ble \'man-də-bəl\ *n* **1** : JAW; *esp* : a lower jaw **2** : either segment of a bird's bill — **man·dib·u·lar** \man-'di-byə-lər\ *adj*
man·do·lin \ˌman-də-'lin, 'mand-ᵊl-ən\ *n* : a stringed musical instrument with a pear-shaped body and a fretted neck
man·drake \'man-ˌdrāk\ *n* **1** : an Old World herb of the nightshade family or its large forked root superstitiously credited with human and medicinal attributes **2** : MAYAPPLE
man·drel *also* **man·dril** \'man-drəl\ *n* **1** : an axle or spindle inserted into a hole in a piece of work to support it during machining **2** : a metal bar used as a core around which material may be cast, shaped, or molded
man·drill \'man-drəl\ *n* : a large baboon of western central Africa
mane \'mān\ *n* : long heavy hair growing about the neck of some mammals (as a horse) — **maned** \'mānd\ *adj*
man·eat·er \'man-ˌē-tər\ *n* : one (as a shark or cannibal) that has or is thought to have an appetite for human flesh — **man·eat·ing** *adj*
ma·nège \ma-'nezh, mə-\ *n* : the art of horsemanship or of training horses
ma·nes \'mä-ˌnās, 'mā-ˌnēz\ *n pl, often cap* : the spirits of the dead and gods of the lower world in ancient Roman belief
ma·neu·ver \mə-'nü-vər, -'nyü-\ *n* \[F *manœuvre*, fr. OF *maneuvre* work done by hand, fr. ML *manuopera*, fr. L *manu operare* to work by hand\] **1** : a military or naval movement; *also* : an armed forces training exercise — often used in pl. **2** : a procedure involving expert physical movement **3** : an evasive movement or shift of tactics; *also* : an action taken to gain a tactical end — **maneuver** *vb* — **ma·neu·ver·abil·i·ty** \-ˌnü-və-rə-'bi-lə-tē, -ˌnyü-\ *n* — **ma·neu·ver·able** \-'nü-və-rə-bəl, -'nyü-\ *adj*
man Friday *n* : an efficient and devoted aide or employee
man·ful \'man-fəl\ *adj* : having or showing courage and resolution — **man·ful·ly** *adv*
man·ga·nese \'maŋ-gə-ˌnēz, -ˌnēs\ *n* : a metallic chemical element resembling iron but not magnetic — see ELEMENT table
mange \'mānj\ *n* : any of several contagious itchy skin diseases esp. of domestic animals — **mangy** \'mān-jē\ *adj*
man·ger \'mān-jər\ *n* : a trough or open box for livestock feed or fodder
¹man·gle \'maŋ-gəl\ *vb* **man·gled; man·gling 1** : to cut, bruise, or hack with repeated blows **2** : to spoil or injure esp. through ineptitude — **man·gler** *n*

\ə\abut \ᵊ\kitten \ər\further \a\ash \ā\ace \ä\mop, mar
\au̇\out \ch\chin \e\bet \ē\easy \g\go \i\hit \ī\ice \j\job
\ŋ\sing \ō\go \ȯ\law \ȯi\boy \th\thin \th̲\the \ü\loot \u̇\foot
\y\yet \zh\vision   *see also* Pronunciation Symbols page

²**mangle** n : a machine with heated rollers for ironing laundry

man·go \\'maŋ-gō\\ n, pl **mangoes** also **mangos** [Pg manga] : a usu. yellowish red slightly acid juicy tropical fruit borne by an evergreen tree related to the sumacs; also : this tree

man·grove \\'man-ıgrōv\\ n : any of a genus of tropical maritime trees that send out many prop roots and form dense thickets important in coastal land building

man·han·dle \\'man-ıhand-ᵊl\\ vb : to handle roughly

man·hat·tan \man-'hat-ᵊn\\ n, often cap : a cocktail made of whiskey and vermouth

man·hole \\'man-ıhōl\\ n : a hole through which a person may go esp. to gain access to an underground or enclosed structure

man·hood \-ıhud\\ n 1 : the condition of being an adult male 2 : manly qualities : COURAGE 3 : MEN ⟨the nation's ∼⟩

man–hour \-'aur\\ n : a unit of one hour's work by one person

man·hunt \-ıhənt\\ n : an organized hunt for a person and esp. for one charged with a crime

ma·nia \\'mā-nē-ə, -nyə\\ n 1 : excitement of psychotic proportions accompanied by disorganized behavior and elevated mood 2 : excessive enthusiasm

ma·ni·ac \\'mā-nē-ıak\\ n : LUNATIC, MADMAN

ma·ni·a·cal \mə-'nī-ə-kəl\\ also **ma·ni·ac** \\'mā-nē-ak\\ adj 1 : affected with or suggestive of madness 2 : FRANTIC

man·ic \\'ma-nik\\ adj : affected with, relating to, or resembling mania — **manic** n — **man·i·cal·ly** \-ni-k(ə-)lē\\ adv

man·ic–de·pres·sive \ıma-nik-di-'pre-siv\\ adj : characterized by mania or by psychotic depression or by alternating mania and depression — **manic–depressive** n

¹**man·i·cure** \\'ma-nə-ıkyur\\ n 1 : MANICURIST 2 : a treatment for the care of the hands and nails

²**manicure** vb **-cured; -cur·ing** 1 : to do manicure work on 2 : to trim closely and evenly

man·i·cur·ist \-ıkyur-ist\\ n : a person who gives manicure treatments

¹**man·i·fest** \\'ma-nə-ıfest\\ adj [ME, fr. MF or L; MF manifeste, fr. L manifestus, caught in the act, flagrant, perh. fr. manus hand + -festus (akin to L infestus hostile)] 1 : readily perceived by the senses and esp. by the sight 2 : easily understood : OBVIOUS — **man·i·fest·ly** adv

²**manifest** vb : to make evident or certain by showing or displaying syn evince, demonstrate, exhibit

³**manifest** n : a list of passengers or an invoice of cargo for a ship or plane

man·i·fes·ta·tion \ıma-nə-fə-'stā-shən\\ n : DISPLAY, DEMONSTRATION

man·i·fes·to \ıma-nə-'fes-tō\\ n, pl **-tos** or **-toes** : a public declaration of intentions, motives, or views

¹**man·i·fold** \\'ma-nə-ıfōld\\ adj 1 : marked by diversity or variety 2 : consisting of or operating many of one kind combined

²**manifold** n : a pipe fitting with several lateral outlets for connecting it with other pipes

³**manifold** vb 1 : MULTIPLY 2 : to make a number of copies of (as a letter)

man·i·kin or **man·ni·kin** \\'ma-ni-kən\\ n 1 : MANNEQUIN 2 : a little man : DWARF

Ma·nila hemp \mə-'ni-lə-\\ n : a tough fiber from a Philippine plant related to the banana that is used for cordage

manila paper n, often cap M : a tough brownish paper made orig. from Manila hemp

man·i·oc \\'ma-nē-ıäk\\ n : CASSAVA

ma·nip·u·late \mə-'ni-pyə-ılāt\\ vb **-lat·ed; -lat·ing** 1 : to treat or operate manually or mechanically esp. with skill 2 : to manage or use skillfully 3 : to influence esp.

with intent to deceive — **ma·nip·u·la·tion** \mə-ni-pyə-'lā-shən\\ n — **ma·nip·u·la·tive** \-'ni-pyə-ılā-tiv\\ adj — **ma·nip·u·la·tor** \-ılā-tər\\ n

man·kind n 1 \\'man-'kīnd\\ : the human race 2 \-ıkīnd\\ : men as distinguished from women

¹**man·ly** \\'man-lē\\ adj **man·li·er; -est** : having qualities appropriate to or generally associated with a man : BOLD, RESOLUTE — **man·li·ness** n

²**manly** adv : in a manly manner

man–made \\'man-'mād\\ adj : made by humans rather than nature ⟨∼ systems⟩; esp : SYNTHETIC ⟨∼ fibers⟩

man·na \\'ma-nə\\ n 1 : food miraculously supplied to the Israelites in the wilderness 2 : something of value that comes unexpectedly : WINDFALL

manned \\'mand\\ adj : carrying or performed by a person ⟨∼ spaceflight⟩

man·ne·quin \\'ma-ni-kən\\ n 1 : a form representing the human figure used esp. for displaying clothes 2 : a person employed to model clothing

man·ner \\'ma-nər\\ n 1 : KIND, SORT 2 : a way of acting or proceeding ⟨worked in a brisk ∼⟩; also : normal behavior ⟨spoke bluntly as was his ∼⟩ 3 : a method of artistic execution 4 pl : social conduct; also : BEARING 5 pl : BEHAVIOR ⟨taught the child good ∼s⟩

man·nered \\'ma-nərd\\ adj 1 : having manners of a specified kind ⟨well-mannered⟩ 2 : having an artificial character ⟨a highly ∼ style⟩

man·ner·ism \\'ma-nə-ıri-zəm\\ n 1 : ARTIFICIALITY, PRECIOSITY 2 : a peculiarity of action, bearing, or treatment syn pose, air, affectation

man·ner·ly \\'ma-nər-lē\\ adj : showing good manners : POLITE — **man·ner·li·ness** n — **mannerly** adv

man·nish \\'ma-nish\\ adj 1 : resembling or suggesting a man rather than a woman 2 : generally associated with or characteristic of a man — **man·nish·ly** adv — **man·nish·ness** n

ma·noeu·vre \mə-'nü-vər, -'nyü-\\ chiefly Brit var of MANEUVER

man–of–war \ıman-əv-'wor\\ n, pl **men–of–war** \ımen-\\ : WARSHIP

ma·nom·e·ter \mə-'nä-mə-tər\\ n : an instrument for measuring the pressure of gases and vapors — **mano·met·ric** \ıma-nə-'me-trik\\ adj

man·or \\'ma-nər\\ n 1 : the house or hall of an estate; also : a landed estate 2 : an English estate of a feudal lord — **ma·no·ri·al** \mə-'nor-ē-əl\\ adj — **ma·no·ri·al·ism** \-ə-ıli-zəm\\ n

man power n 1 : power available from or supplied by the physical effort of human beings 2 usu **man·pow·er** : the total supply of persons available and fitted for service

man·qué \män-'kā\\ adj [F, fr. pp. of manquer to lack, fail] : short of or frustrated in the fulfillment of one's aspirations or talents ⟨a poet ∼⟩

man·sard \\'man-ısärd, -sərd\\ n : a roof having two slopes on all sides with the lower slope steeper than the upper one

manse \\'mans\\ n : the residence esp. of a Presbyterian minister

man·ser·vant \\'man-ısər-vənt\\ n, pl **men·ser·vants** \\'men-ısər-vənts\\ : a male servant

man·sion \\'man-chən\\ n : a large imposing residence; also : a separate apartment in a large structure

man–size \\'man-ısīz\\ or **man–sized** \-ısīzd\\ adj : suitable for or requiring a man

man·slaugh·ter \-ıslo-tər\\ n : the unlawful killing of a human being without express or implied malice

man·ta \\'man-tə\\ n : a square piece of cloth or blanket used in southwestern U.S. and Latin America as a cloak or shawl

man·teau \man-'tō\\ n : a loose cloak, coat, or robe

man·tel \\'mant-ᵊl\\ n : a beam, stone, or arch serving as a lintel to support the masonry above a fireplace; also : a shelf above a fireplace

man·tel·piece \'mant-ᵊl-ˌpēs\ *n* : the shelf of a mantel

man·til·la \man-'tē-yə, -'ti-lə\ *n* : a light scarf worn over the head and shoulders esp. by Spanish and Latin= American women

man·tis \'man-təs\ *n, pl* **man·tis·es** *or* **man·tes** \-ˌtēz\ [NL, fr. Gk, lit., diviner, prophet] : any of a group of large usu. green insect-eating insects that hold their prey in forelimbs folded as if in prayer

man·tis·sa \man-'ti-sə\ *n* : the part of a logarithm to the right of the decimal point

¹man·tle \'mant-ᵊl\ *n* **1** : a loose sleeveless garment worn over other clothes **2** : something that covers, enfolds, or envelopes **3** : a lacy sheath that gives light by incandescence when placed over a flame **4** : the portion of the earth lying between the crust and the core **5** : MANTEL

²mantle *vb* **man·tled; man·tling 1** : to cover with a mantle **2** : BLUSH

man·tra \'man-trə\ *n* : a mystical formula of invocation or incantation (as in Hinduism)

¹man·u·al \'man-yə-wəl\ *adj* **1** : of, relating to, or involving the hands; *also* : worked by hand ⟨a ∼ pump⟩ **2** : requiring or using physical skill and energy — **man·u·al·ly** *adv*

²manual *n* **1** : a small book; *esp* : HANDBOOK **2** : the prescribed movements in the handling of a military item and esp. a weapon during a drill or ceremony ⟨the ∼ of arms⟩ **3** : a keyboard esp. of an organ

man·u·fac·to·ry \ˌman-yə-'fak-tə-rē\ *n* : FACTORY

¹man·u·fac·ture \ˌman-yə-'fak-chər\ *n* [MF, fr. ML *manufactura*, L *manu factus* made by hand] **1** : something made from raw materials **2** : the process of making wares by hand or by machinery; *also* : a productive industry using machinery

²manufacture *vb* **-tured; -tur·ing 1** : to make from raw materials by hand or by machinery; *also* : to engage in manufacture **2** : INVENT, FABRICATE; *also* : CREATE — **man·u·fac·tur·er** *n*

man·u·mit \ˌman-yə-'mit\ *vb* **-mit·ted; -mit·ting** : to free from slavery — **man·u·mis·sion** \-'mi-shən\ *n*

¹ma·nure \mə-'nùr, -nyùr\ *vb* **ma·nured; ma·nur·ing** : to fertilize land with manure

²manure *n* : FERTILIZER; *esp* : refuse from stables and barnyards — **ma·nu·ri·al** \-'nùr-ē-əl, -'nyùr-\ *adj*

man·u·script \'man-yə-ˌskript\ *n* [L *manu scriptus* written by hand] **1** : a written or typewritten composition or document; *also* : a document submitted for publication **2** : writing as opposed to print

Manx \'maŋks\ *n pl* : the people of the Isle of Man — **Manx** *adj*

¹many \'me-nē\ *adj* **more** \'mōr\; **most** \'mōst\ : consisting of or amounting to a large but indefinite number ⟨∼ years ago⟩

²many *pron* : a large number ⟨∼ are called⟩

³many *n* : a large but indefinite number ⟨a good ∼ of them⟩

many·fold \ˌme-nē-'fōld\ *adv* : by many times

many–sid·ed \-'sī-dəd\ *adj* **1** : having many sides or aspects **2** : VERSATILE

Mao·ism \'maù-ˌi-zəm\ *n* : the theory and practice of Communism developed in China chiefly by Mao Tse=tung — **Mao·ist** \'maù-ist\ *n or adj*

Mao·ri \'maùr-ē\ *n, pl* **Maori** *or* **Maoris** : a member of a Polynesian people native to New Zealand

¹map \'map\ *n* [ML *mappa*, fr. L, napkin, towel] **1** : a representation usu. on a flat surface of the whole or part of an area **2** : a representation of the celestial sphere or part of it

²map *vb* **mapped; map·ping 1** : to make a map of **2** : to plan in detail ⟨∼ out a program⟩ — **map·pa·ble** \'ma-pə-bəl\ *adj* — **map·per** *n*

MAP *abbr* modified American plan

ma·ple \'mā-pəl\ *n* : any of a genus of trees or shrubs with 2-winged dry fruit and opposite leaves; *also* : the hard light-colored wood of a maple used esp. for floors and furniture

maple sugar *n* : sugar made by boiling maple syrup

maple syrup *n* : syrup made by concentrating the sap of maple trees and esp. the sugar maple

mar \'mär\ *vb* **marred; mar·ring** : to detract from the wholeness or perfection of : SPOIL **syn** injure, hurt, harm, damage, impair, blemish

Mar *abbr* March

ma·ra·ca \mə-'rä-kə, -'ra-\ *n* [Pg *maracá*] : a rattle usu. made from a gourd and used as a percussion instrument

mar·a·schi·no cherry \ˌmar-ə-'skē-nō-, -'shē-\ *n, often cap M* : a cherry preserved in a sweet liqueur made from the juice of a bitter wild cherry

mar·a·thon \'mar-ə-ˌthän\ *n* [*Marathon*, Greece, site of a victory of Greeks over Persians in 490 B.C. the news of which was carried to Athens by a long-distance runner] **1** : a long-distance race esp. on foot **2** : an endurance contest

mar·a·thon·er \'mar-ə-ˌthä-nər\ *n* : a person who takes part in a marathon — **mar·a·thon·ing** *n*

ma·raud \mə-'rȯd\ *vb* : to roam about and raid in search of plunder — **ma·raud·er** *n*

mar·ble \'mär-bəl\ *n* **1** : a limestone that can be polished and used in fine building work **2** : something resembling marble (as in coldness) **3** : a small ball (as of glass) used in various games; *also, pl* : a children's game played with these small balls — **marble** *adj*

mar·bling \-bə-liŋ, -bliŋ\ *n* : an intermixture of fat through the lean of a cut of meat

mar·cel \mär-'sel\ *n* : a deep soft wave made in the hair by the use of a heated curling iron — **marcel** *vb*

¹march \'märch\ *n* : a border region : FRONTIER

²march *vb* **1** : to move along in or as if in military formation **2** : to walk in a direct purposeful manner; *also* : PROGRESS, ADVANCE **3** : TRAVERSE ⟨∼ed 10 miles⟩ — **march·er** *n*

³march *n* **1** : the action of marching; *also* : the distance covered (as by a military unit) in a march **2** : a regular measured stride or rhythmic step used in marching **3** : forward movement **4** : a piece of music with marked rhythm suitable for marching to

March *n* [ME, fr. OF, fr. L *martius*, fr. *martius* of Mars fr. *Mart-, Mars*, Roman god of war] : the third month of the year having 31 days

mar·chio·ness \'mär-shə-nəs\ *n* **1** : the wife or widow of a marquess **2** : a woman holding the rank of a marquess in her own right

Mar·di Gras \'mär-dē-ˌgrä\ *n* [F, lit., fat Tuesday] : the Tuesday before Ash Wednesday often observed with parades and merrymaking

¹mare \'mar\ *n* : an adult female of the horse or a related mammal

²ma·re \'mär-(ˌ)ā\ *n, pl* **ma·ria** \'mär-ē-ə\ : any of several large dark areas on the surface of the moon or Mars

mar·ga·rine \'mär-jə-rən\ *n* : a food product made usu. from vegetable oils churned with skimmed milk and used as a substitute for butter

mar·gin \'mär-jən\ *n* **1** : the part of a page outside the main body of printed or written matter **2** : EDGE **3** : a spare amount, measure, or degree allowed for use if needed **4** : measure or degree of difference ⟨a one=vote ∼⟩

mar·gin·al \-jə-nəl\ *adj* **1** : written or printed in the margin **2** : of, relating to, or situated at a margin or border **3** : close to the lower limit of quality or acceptability **4**

\ə\abut \ᵊ\kitten \ər\further \a\ash \ā\ace \ä\mop, mar
\aù\out \ch\chin \e\bet \ē\easy \g\go \i\hit \ī\ice \j\job
\ŋ\sing \ō\go \ò\law \òi\boy \th\thin \t͟h\the \ü\loot \ù\foot
\y\yet \zh\vision *see also* Pronunciation Symbols page

: excluded from or existing outside the mainstream of society or a group — **mar·gin·al·ly** *adv*

mar·gi·na·lia \ˌmär-jə-ˈnā-lē-ə\ *n pl* : marginal notes

mar·grave \ˈmär-ˌgrāv\ *n* : the military governor esp. of a medieval German border province

ma·ri·a·chi \ˌmär-ē-ˈä-chē, ˌmar-\ *n* : a Mexican street band; *also* : a member of or the music of such a band

mari·gold \ˈmar-ə-ˌgōld, ˈmer-\ *n* : any of a genus of tropical American herbs related to the daisies that are grown for their double yellow, orange, or reddish flower heads

mar·i·jua·na *also* **mar·i·hua·na** \ˌmar-ə-ˈwä-nə, -ˈhwä-\ *n* [MexSp *marihuana*] : the dried leaves and flowering tops of the female hemp plant smoked usu. illegally for their intoxicating effect; *also* : HEMP

ma·rim·ba \mə-ˈrim-bə\ *n* : a xylophone of southern Africa and Central America; *also* : a modern version of it

ma·ri·na \mə-ˈrē-nə\ *n* : a dock or basin providing secure moorings for pleasure boats

mar·i·na·ra \ˌmar-ə-ˈnar-ə\ *adj* [It (*alla*) *marinara*, lit., in sailor style] : made with tomatoes, onions, garlic, and spices; *also* : served with marinara sauce

mar·i·nate \ˈmar-ə-ˌnāt\ *vb* **-nat·ed; -nat·ing** : to steep (as meat or fish) in a brine or pickle

¹**ma·rine** \mə-ˈrēn\ *adj* **1** : of or relating to the sea or its navigation or commerce **2** : of or relating to marines

²**marine** *n* **1** : the mercantile and naval shipping of a country **2** : any of a class of soldiers serving on shipboard or with a naval force

mar·i·ner \ˈmar-ə-nər\ *n* : SAILOR

mar·i·o·nette \ˌmar-ē-ə-ˈnet, ˌmer-\ *n* : a puppet moved by strings or by hand

mar·i·tal \ˈmar-ət-ᵊl\ *adj* : of or relating to marriage : CONJUGAL **syn** matrimonial, connubial, nuptial

mar·i·time \ˈmar-ə-ˌtīm\ *adj* **1** : of, relating to, or bordering on the sea **2** : of or relating to navigation or commerce of the sea

mar·jo·ram \ˈmär-jə-rəm\ *n* : any of various fragrant mints often used in cookery

¹**mark** \ˈmärk\ *n* **1** : something (as a line or fixed object) designed to record position; *also* : the starting line or position in a track event **2** : TARGET; *also* : GOAL, OBJECT **3** : an object of abuse or ridicule **4** : the question under discussion **5** : NORM ⟨not up to the ∼⟩ **6** : a visible sign : INDICATION; *also* : CHARACTERISTIC **7** : a written or printed symbol **8** : GRADE ⟨a ∼ of B+⟩ **9** : IMPORTANCE, DISTINCTION **10** : a lasting impression ⟨made his ∼ in the world⟩; *also* : a damaging impression left on a surface

²**mark** *vb* **1** : to set apart by a line or boundary **2** : to designate by a mark or make a mark on **3** : CHARACTERIZE ⟨the vehemence that ∼s his speeches⟩; *also* : SIGNALIZE ⟨this year ∼s our 50th anniversary⟩ **4** : to take notice of : OBSERVE — **mark·er** *n*

³**mark** *n* — see MONEY table

Mark \ˈmärk\ *n* — see BIBLE table

mark·down \ˈmärk-ˌdaún\ *n* **1** : a lowering of price **2** : the amount by which an original price is reduced

mark down *vb* : to put a lower price on

marked \ˈmärkt\ *adj* : NOTICEABLE — **mark·ed·ly** \ˈmär-kəd-lē\ *adv*

¹**mar·ket** \ˈmär-kət\ *n* **1** : a meeting together of people for trade by purchase and sale; *also* : a public place where such a meeting is held **2** : the rate or price offered for a commodity or security **3** : a geographical area of demand for commodities; *also* : extent of demand **4** : a retail establishment usu. of a specific kind

²**market** *vb* : to go to a market to buy or sell; *also* : SELL — **mar·ket·able** *adj*

mar·ket·place \ˈmär-kət-ˌplās\ *n* **1** : an open square in a town where markets are held **2** : the world of trade or economic activity

mark·ka \ˈmär-ˌkä\ *n, pl* **mark·kaa** \ˈmär-ˌkä\ *or* **mark·kas** \-ˌkäz\ — see MONEY table

marks·man \ˈmärks-mən\ *n* : a person skillful at hitting a target — **marks·man·ship** *n*

mark·up \ˈmär-ˌkəp\ *n* **1** : a raising of price **2** : an amount added to the cost price of an article to determine the selling price

mark up *vb* : to put a higher price on

marl \ˈmärl\ *n* : an earthy deposit rich in lime used esp. as fertilizer — **marly** \ˈmär-lē\ *adj*

mar·lin \ˈmär-lən\ *n* : any of several large oceanic sport fishes related to sailfishes

mar·line·spike *also* **mar·lin·spike** \ˈmär-lən-ˌspīk\ *n* : a pointed iron tool used to separate strands of rope or wire (as in splicing)

mar·ma·lade \ˈmär-mə-ˌlād\ *n* : a clear jelly holding in suspension pieces of fruit and fruit rind

mar·mo·re·al \mär-ˈmōr-ē-əl\ *adj* : of, relating to, or suggestive of marble

mar·mo·set \ˈmär-mə-ˌset\ *n* : any of numerous small bushy-tailed tropical American monkeys

mar·mot \ˈmär-mət\ *n* : any of a genus of stout short-legged burrowing No. American rodents

marmot

¹**ma·roon** \mə-ˈrün\ *vb* **1** : to put ashore (as on a desolate island) and leave to one's fate **2** : to leave in isolation and without hope of escape

²**maroon** *n* : a dark red color

mar·quee \mär-ˈkē\ *n* [modif. of F *marquise*, lit., marchioness] **1** : a large tent set up (as for an outdoor party) **2** : a usu. metal and glass canopy over an entrance (as of a theater)

mar·quess \ˈmär-kwəs\ *n* **1** : a nobleman of hereditary rank in Europe and Japan **2** : a member of the British peerage ranking below a duke and above an earl

mar·que·try \ˈmär-kə-trē\ *n* : inlaid work of wood, shell, or ivory (as on a table or cabinet)

mar·quis \ˈmär-kwəs, mär-ˈkē\ *n* : MARQUESS

mar·quise \mär-ˈkēz\ *n, pl* **mar·quises** *same or* -ˈkē-zəz\ : MARCHIONESS

mar·riage \ˈmar-ij\ *n* **1** : the state of being married **2** : a wedding ceremony and attendant festivities **3** : a close union — **mar·riage·able** *adj*

mar·row \ˈmar-ō\ *n* : a soft vascular tissue that fills the cavities of most bones

mar·row·bone \ˈmar-ə-ˌbōn, ˈmar-ō-\ *n* : a bone (as a shinbone) rich in marrow

mar·ry \ˈmar-ē\ *vb* **mar·ried; mar·ry·ing** **1** : to join as husband and wife according to law or custom **2** : to take as husband or wife : WED **3** : to enter into a close union — **mar·ried** *adj or n*

Mars \ˈmärz\ *n* : the planet 4th from the sun and conspicuous for its red color — see PLANET table

marsh \ˈmärsh\ *n* : a tract of soft wet land — **marshy** *adj*

¹**mar·shal** \ˈmär-shəl\ *n* **1** : a high official in a medieval

household; *also* : a person in charge of the ceremonial aspects of a gathering **2** : a general officer of the highest military rank **3** : an administrative officer (as of a U.S. judicial district) having duties similar to a sheriff's **4** : the administrative head of a city police or fire department

²**marshal** *vb* **mar·shaled** *or* **mar·shalled; mar·shal·ing** *or* **mar·shal·ling 1** : to arrange in order, rank, or position **2** : to bring together **3** : to lead with ceremony : USHER

marsh gas *n* : METHANE

marsh·mal·low \'märsh-ˌme-lō, -ˌma-\ *n* : a light creamy confection made from corn syrup, sugar, albumen, and gelatin

marsh marigold *n* : a swamp herb related to the buttercups that has bright yellow flowers

mar·su·pi·al \mär-'sü-pē-əl\ *n* : any of an order of primitive mammals (as opossums, kangaroos, or wombats) that bear very immature young which are nourished in a pouch on the abdomen of the female — **marsupial** *adj*

mart \'märt\ *n* : MARKET

mar·ten \'märt-ᵊn\ *n, pl* **marten** *or* **martens** : a slender weasel-like mammal with fine gray or brown fur; *also* : this fur

mar·tial \'mär-shəl\ *adj* [L *martialis* of Mars, fr. *Mart-, Mars* Mars, Roman god of war] **1** : of, relating to, or suited for war or a warrior ⟨~ music⟩ **2** : of or relating to an army or military life **3** : WARLIKE

martial law *n* **1** : the law applied in occupied territory by the occupying military forces **2** : the established law of a country administered by military forces in an emergency when civilian law enforcement agencies are unable to maintain public order and safety

mar·tian \'mär-shən\ *adj, often cap* : of or relating to the planet Mars or its hypothetical inhabitants — **martian** *n, often cap*

mar·tin \'märt-ᵊn\ *n* : any of several small swallows and flycatchers

mar·ti·net \ˌmärt-ᵊn-'et\ *n* : a strict disciplinarian

mar·tin·gale \'märt-ᵊn-ˌgāl\ *n* : a strap connecting a horse's girth to the bit or reins so as to hold down its head

mar·ti·ni \mär-'tē-nē\ *n* : a cocktail made of gin or vodka and dry vermouth

¹**mar·tyr** \'mär-tər\ *n* [ME, fr. OE, fr. LL, fr. Gk *martyr-, martys*, lit., witness] **1** : a person who dies rather than renounce a religion; *also* : a person who makes a great sacrifice for the sake of principle **2** : a great or constant sufferer

²**martyr** *vb* **1** : to put to death for adhering to a belief **2** : TORTURE

mar·tyr·dom \'mär-tər-dəm\ *n* **1** : the suffering and death of a martyr **2** : TORTURE

¹**mar·vel** \'mär-vəl\ *n* **1** : something that causes wonder or astonishment **2** : intense surprise or interest

²**marvel** *vb* **mar·veled** *or* **mar·velled; mar·vel·ing** *or* **mar·vel·ling** : to feel surprise, wonder, or amazed curiosity

mar·vel·ous *or* **mar·vel·lous** \'mär-və-ləs\ *adj* **1** : causing wonder **2** : of the highest kind or quality — **mar·vel·ous·ly** *adv* — **mar·vel·ous·ness** *n*

Marx·ism \'märk-ˌsi-zəm\ *n* : the political, economic, and social principles and policies advocated by Karl Marx — **Marx·ist** \-sist\ *n or adj*

mar·zi·pan \'märt-sə-ˌpän, -ˌpan; 'mär-zə-ˌpan\ *n* [G] : a confection of almond paste, sugar, and egg whites

masc *abbr* masculine

mas·cara \mas-'kar-ə\ *n* : a cosmetic esp. for coloring the eyelashes

mas·cot \'mas-ˌkät, -kət\ *n* [F *mascotte*, fr. Provençal *mascoto*, fr. *masco* witch, fr. ML *masca*] : a person, animal, or object believed to bring good luck

¹**mas·cu·line** \'mas-kyə-lən\ *adj* **1** : MALE; *also* : MANLY **2** : of, relating to, or constituting the gender that includes most words or grammatical forms referring to males — **mas·cu·lin·i·ty** \ˌmas-kyə-'li-nə-tē\ *n*

²**masculine** *n* : a noun, pronoun, adjective, or inflectional form or class of the masculine gender; *also* : the masculine gender

¹**mash** \'mash\ *n* **1** : a mixture of ground feeds for livestock **2** : crushed malt or grain steeped in hot water to make wort **3** : a soft pulpy mass

²**mash** *vb* **1** : to reduce to a soft pulpy state **2** : CRUSH, SMASH ⟨~ a finger⟩ — **mash·er** *n*

MASH *abbr* mobile army surgical hospital

¹**mask** \'mask\ *n* **1** : a cover for the face usu. for disguise or protection **2** : MASQUE **3** : a figure of a head worn on the stage in antiquity **4** : a copy of a face made by means of a mold ⟨death ~⟩ **5** : something that conceals or disguises **6** : the face of an animal

²**mask** *vb* **1** : to conceal from view : DISGUISE **2** : to cover for protection

mask·er \'mas-kər\ *n* : a participant in a masquerade

mas·och·ism \'ma-sə-ˌki-zəm, 'ma-zə-\ *n* **1** : a sexual perversion characterized by pleasure in being subjected to pain or humiliation **2** : pleasure in being abused or dominated — **mas·och·ist** \-kist\ *n* — **mas·och·is·tic** \ˌma-sə-'kis-tik, ˌma-zə-\ *adj*

ma·son \'mās-ᵊn\ *n* **1** : a skilled worker who builds with stone, brick, or concrete **2** *cap* : FREEMASON

Ma·son·ic \mə-'sä-nik\ *adj* : of or relating to Freemasons or Freemasonry

ma·son·ry \'mās-ᵊn-rē\ *n, pl* **-ries 1** : something constructed of materials used by masons **2** : the art, trade, or work of a mason **3** *cap* : FREEMASONRY

masque \'mask\ *n* **1** : MASQUERADE **2** : a short allegorical dramatic performance (as of the 17th century)

¹**mas·quer·ade** \ˌmas-kə-'rād\ *n* **1** : a social gathering of persons wearing masks; *also* : a costume for wear at such a gathering **2** : DISGUISE

²**masquerade** *vb* **-ad·ed; -ad·ing 1** : to disguise oneself : POSE **2** : to take part in a masquerade — **mas·quer·ad·er** *n*

¹**mass** \'mas\ *n* **1** *cap* : a sequence of prayers and ceremonies forming the eucharistic service of the Roman Catholic Church **2** *often cap* : a celebration of the Eucharist **3** : a musical setting for parts of the Mass

²**mass** *n* **1** : a quantity or aggregate of matter usu. of considerable size **2** : EXPANSE, BULK; *also* : MASSIVENESS **3** : the principal part **4** : AGGREGATE, WHOLE **5** : the quantity of matter that a body possesses as measured by its inertia **6** : a large quantity, amount, or number **7** : the great body of people — usu. used in pl. — **massy** *adj*

³**mass** *vb* : to form or collect into a mass

Mass *abbr* Massachusetts

mas·sa·cre \'ma-si-kər\ *n* **1** : the killing of many persons under cruel or atrocious circumstances **2** : a wholesale slaughter — **massacre** *vb*

¹**mas·sage** \mə-'säzh, -'säj\ *n* : manipulation of tissues (as by rubbing and kneading) esp. for therapeutic purposes

²**massage** *vb* **mas·saged; mas·sag·ing 1** : to subject to massage **2** : to treat flatteringly; *also* : MANIPULATE, DOCTOR ⟨~ data⟩

mas·seur \ma-'sər\ *n* : a man who practices massage

mas·seuse \-'sərz, -'süz\ *n* : a woman who practices massage

mas·sif \ma-'sēf\ *n* : a principal mountain mass

mas·sive \'ma-siv\ *adj* **1** : forming or consisting of a large mass **2** : large in structure, scope, or degree — **mas·sive·ly** *adv* — **mas·sive·ness** *n*

mass·less \'mas-ləs\ *adj* : having no mass ⟨~ particles⟩

\ə\abut \ᵊ\kitten \ər\further \a\ash \ā\ace \ä\mop, mar
\aů\out \ch\chin \e\bet \ē\easy \g\go \i\hit \ī\ice \j\job
\ŋ\sing \ō\go \ȯ\law \ȯi\boy \th\thin \t͟h\the \ü\loot \u̇\foot
\y\yet \zh\vision *see also* Pronunciation Symbols page

mass medium *n, pl* **mass media** : a medium of communication (as the newspapers or television) that is designed to reach the mass of the people

mass–pro·duce \,mas-prə-'düs, -'dyüs\ *vb* : to produce in quantity usu. by machinery — **mass production** *n*

¹**mast** \'mast\ *n* 1 : a long pole or spar rising from the keel or deck of a ship and supporting the yards, booms, and rigging 2 : a slender vertical structure — **mast·ed** \'mas-təd\ *adj*

²**mast** *n* : nuts (as acorns) accumulated on the forest floor and often serving as food for animals (as hogs)

mas·tec·to·my \ma-'stek-tə-mē\ *n, pl* **-mies** : surgical removal of the breast

¹**mas·ter** \'mas-tər\ *n* 1 : a male teacher; *also* : a person holding an academic degree higher than a bachelor's but lower than a doctor's 2 : one highly skilled (as in an art or profession) 3 : one having authority or control 4 : VICTOR, SUPERIOR 5 : the commander of a merchant ship 6 : a youth or boy too young to be called *mister* — used as a title 7 : an original from which copies are made

²**master** *vb* 1 : to become master of : OVERCOME 2 : to become skilled or proficient in 3 : to produce a master recording of (as a musical performance)

master chief petty officer *n* : a petty officer of the highest rank in the navy

master chief petty officer of the coast guard : a master chief petty officer chosen to serve as the senior enlisted advisor to the commandant

master chief petty officer of the navy : a master chief petty officer chosen to serve as the senior enlisted advisor to the chief of naval operations

mas·ter·ful \'mas-tər-fəl\ *adj* 1 : inclined and usu. competent to act as a master 2 : having or reflecting the skill of a master — **mas·ter·ful·ly** *adv* — **mas·ter·ful·ness** *n*

master gunnery sergeant *n* : a noncommissioned officer in the marine corps ranking above a master sergeant

master key *n* : a key designed to open several different locks

mas·ter·ly \'mas-tər-lē\ *adj* : indicating thorough knowledge or superior skill ⟨∼ performance⟩ — **mas·ter·ly** *adv*

mas·ter·mind \-,mīnd\ *n* : a person who provides the directing or creative intelligence for a project — **mastermind** *vb*

master of ceremonies : a person who acts as host at a formal event or a program of entertainment

mas·ter·piece \'mas-tər-,pēs\ *n* : a work done with extraordinary skill

master plan *n* : an overall plan

mas·ter's \'mas-tərz\ *n* : a master's degree

master sergeant *n* 1 : a noncommissioned officer in the army ranking next below a sergeant major 2 : a noncommissioned officer in the air force ranking next below a senior master sergeant 3 : a noncommissioned officer in the marine corps ranking next below a master gunnery sergeant

mas·ter·stroke \'mas-tər-,strōk\ *n* : a masterly performance or move

mas·ter·work \-,wərk\ *n* : MASTERPIECE

mas·tery \'mas-tə-rē\ *n* 1 : DOMINION; *also* : SUPERIORITY 2 : possession or display of great skill or knowledge

mast·head \'mast-,hed\ *n* 1 : the top of a mast 2 : the printed matter in a newspaper or periodical giving the title and details of ownership and rates of subscription or advertising

mas·tic \'mas-tik\ *n* : a pasty material used as a coating or cement

mas·ti·cate \'mas-tə-,kāt\ *vb* **-cat·ed; -cat·ing** : CHEW — **mas·ti·ca·tion** \,mas-tə-'kā-shən\ *n*

mas·tiff \'mas-təf\ *n* : any of a breed of large smooth-coated dogs used esp. as guard dogs

mast·odon \'mas-tə-,dän\ *n* [NL, fr. Gk *mastos* breast

+ *odōn, odous* tooth] : any of numerous huge extinct mammals related to the mammoths

mas·toid \'mas-,tȯid\ *n* : a bony prominence behind the ear — **mastoid** *adj*

mas·tur·ba·tion \,mas-tər-'bā-shən\ *n* : stimulation of the genital organs apart from sexual intercourse, usu. to orgasm, and esp. by use of one's own hand — **mas·tur·bate** \'mas-tər-,bāt\ *vb* — **mas·tur·ba·to·ry** \'mas-tər-bə-,tōr-ē\ *adj*

¹**mat** \'mat\ *n* 1 : a piece of coarse woven or plaited fabric 2 : something made up of many intertwined strands 3 : a large thick pad used as a surface for wrestling and gymnastics

²**mat** *vb* **mat·ted; mat·ting** 1 : to provide with a mat 2 : to form into a tangled mass

³**mat** *vb* **mat·ted; mat·ting** 1 : to make (as a color) matte 2 : to provide (a picture) with a mat

⁴**mat** *var of* ²MATTE

⁵**mat** *or* **matt** *or* **matte** *n* : a border going around a picture between picture and frame or serving as the frame

mat·a·dor \'ma-tə-,dȯr\ *n* [Sp, fr. *matar* to kill] : a bullfighter whose role is to kill the bull in a bullfight

¹**match** \'mach\ *n* 1 : a person or thing equal or similar to another; *also* : one able to cope with another : RIVAL 2 : a suitable pairing of persons or objects 3 : a contest or game between two or more individuals 4 : a marriage union; *also* : a prospective marriage partner — **match·less** *adj*

²**match** *vb* 1 : to meet as an antagonist; *also* : PIT 2 : to provide with a worthy competitor; *also* : to set in comparison with 3 : MARRY 4 : to combine suitably or congenially; *also* : ADAPT, SUIT 5 : to provide with a counterpart

³**match** *n* : a short slender piece of flammable material (as wood) tipped with a combustible mixture that ignites through friction

match·book \'mach-,bûk\ *n* : a small folder containing rows of paper matches

match·lock \-,läk\ *n* : a musket with a slow-burning cord lowered over a hole in the breech to ignite the charge

match·mak·er \-,mā-kər\ *n* : one who arranges a match and esp. a marriage

match·wood \-,wûd\ *n* : small pieces of wood

¹**mate** \'māt\ *vb* **mat·ed; mat·ing** : CHECKMATE — **mate** *n*

²**mate** *n* 1 : ASSOCIATE, COMPANION; *also* : HELPER 2 : a deck officer on a merchant ship ranking below the captain 3 : one of a pair; *esp* : either member of a married couple or a breeding pair of animals

³**mate** *vb* **mat·ed; mat·ing** 1 : to join or fit together 2 : to come or bring together as mates 3 : COPULATE

¹**ma·te·ri·al** \mə-'tir-ē-əl\ *adj* 1 : PHYSICAL ⟨∼ world⟩; *also* : BODILY ⟨∼ needs⟩ 2 : of or relating to matter rather than form ⟨∼ cause⟩; *also* : EMPIRICAL ⟨∼ knowledge⟩ 3 : highly important : SIGNIFICANT 4 : of a physical or worldly nature ⟨∼ progress⟩ — **ma·te·ri·al·ly** *adv*

²**material** *n* 1 : the elements or substance of which something is composed or made 2 : apparatus necessary for doing or making something

ma·te·ri·al·ise *Brit var of* MATERIALIZE

ma·te·ri·al·ism \mə-'tir-ē-ə-,li-zəm\ *n* 1 : a theory that everything can be explained as being or coming from matter 2 : a preoccupation with material rather than intellectual or spiritual things — **ma·te·ri·al·ist** \-list\ *n or adj* — **ma·te·ri·al·is·tic** \-,tir-ē-ə-'lis-tik\ *adj* — **ma·te·ri·al·is·ti·cal·ly** \-ti-k(ə-)lē\ *adv*

ma·te·ri·al·ize \mə-'tir-ē-ə-,līz\ *vb* **-ized; -iz·ing** 1 : to give material form to; *also* : to assume bodily form 2 : to make an often unexpected appearance — **ma·te·ri·al·i·za·tion** \mə-,tir-ē-ə-lə-'zā-shən\ *n*

ma·té·ri·el *or* **ma·te·ri·el** \mə-,tir-ē-'el\ *n* [F *matériel*]

: equipment, apparatus, and supplies used by an organization

ma·ter·nal \mə-'tərn-ᵊl\ adj **1** : MOTHERLY **2** : related through or inherited or derived from a female parent — **ma·ter·nal·ly** adv

¹ma·ter·ni·ty \mə-'tər-nə-tē\ n, pl **-ties 1** : the quality or state of being a mother; also : MOTHERLINESS **2** : a hospital facility for the care of women before and during childbirth and for newborn babies

²maternity adj **1** : designed for wear during pregnancy ⟨a ∼ dress⟩ **2** : effective for the period close to and including childbirth ⟨∼ leave⟩

¹math \'math\ n : MATHEMATICS

²math abbr mathematical; mathematician

math·e·mat·ics \ma-thə-'ma-tiks\ n : the science of numbers and their properties, operations, and relations and with shapes in space and their structure and measurement — **math·e·mat·i·cal** \-'ma-ti-kəl\ adj — **math·e·mat·i·cal·ly** \-ti-k(ə-)lē\ adv — **math·e·ma·ti·cian** \ma-thə-mə-'ti-shən\ n

mat·i·nee or **mat·i·née** \mat-ᵊn-'ā\ n [F matinée, lit., morning, fr. OF, fr. matin morning, fr. L matutinum, fr. neut. of matutinus of the morning, fr. Matuta, goddess of morning] : a musical or dramatic performance in the daytime and esp. the afternoon

mat·ins \'mat-ᵊnz\ n pl, often cap **1** : special prayers said between midnight and 4 a.m. **2** : a morning service of liturgical prayer in Anglican churches

ma·tri·arch \'mā-trē-ärk\ n : a female who rules or dominates a family, group, or state — **ma·tri·ar·chal** \mā-trē-'är-kəl\ adj — **ma·tri·ar·chy** \'mā-trē-är-kē\ n

ma·tri·cide \'ma-trə-sīd, 'mā-\ n : the murder of a mother by her child — **ma·tri·cid·al** \ma-trə-'sīd-ᵊl, mā-\ adj

ma·tric·u·late \mə-'tri-kyə-lāt\ vb **-lat·ed; -lat·ing** : to enroll as a member of a body and esp. of a college or university — **ma·tric·u·la·tion** \-tri-kyə-'lā-shən\ n

mat·ri·mo·ny \'ma-trə-mō-nē\ n [ME, fr. MF matremoine, fr. L matrimonium, fr. mater mother, matron] : MARRIAGE — **mat·ri·mo·nial** \ma-trə-'mō-nē-əl\ adj — **mat·ri·mo·nial·ly** adv

ma·trix \'mā-triks\ n, pl **ma·tri·ces** \'mā-trə-sēz, 'ma-\ or **ma·trix·es** \'mā-trik-səz\ **1** : something within or from which something else originates, develops, or takes form **2** : a mold from which a relief surface (as a piece of type) is made

ma·tron \'mā-trən\ n **1** : a married woman usu. of dignified maturity or social distinction **2** : a woman supervisor (as in a school or police station) — **ma·tron·ly** adj

Matt abbr Matthew

¹matte or **matt** \'mat\ var of ³MAT

²matte also **matt** \'mat\ adj : not shiny : DULL

¹mat·ter \'ma-tər\ n **1** : a subject of interest or concern **2** pl : events or circumstances of a particular situation **3** : the subject of a discourse or writing **4** : TROUBLE, DIFFICULTY ⟨what's the ∼⟩ **5** : the substance of which a physical object is composed **6** : PUS **7** : an indefinite amount or quantity ⟨a ∼ of a few days⟩ **8** : something written or printed **9** : MAIL

²matter vb : to be of importance

mat·ter-of-fact \ma-tə-rəv-'fakt\ adj : adhering to fact; also : being plain, straightforward, or unemotional — **mat·ter-of-fact·ly** adv — **mat·ter-of-fact·ness** n

Mat·thew \'ma-thyü\ n — see BIBLE table

mat·tins often cap, chiefly Brit var of MATINS

mat·tock \'ma-tək\ n : a digging and grubbing tool with features of an adze and an ax or pick

mat·tress \'ma-trəs\ n **1** : a fabric case filled with resilient material used as or for a bed **2** : an inflatable airtight sack for use as a mattress

mat·u·rate \'ma-chə-rāt\ vb **-rat·ed; -rat·ing** : MATURE

mat·u·ra·tion \ma-chə-'rā-shən\ n **1** : the process of becoming mature **2** : the emergence of personal and behavioral characteristics through growth processes — **mat·u·ra·tion·al** \-shə-nəl\ adj

¹ma·ture \mə-'tùr, -'tyùr\ adj **ma·tur·er; -est 1** : based on slow careful consideration **2** : having attained a final or desired state **3** : of or relating to a condition of full development **4** : due for payment — **ma·ture·ly** adv

²mature vb **ma·tured; ma·tur·ing** : to reach or bring to maturity or completion

ma·tu·ri·ty \mə-'tùr-ə-tē, -'tyùr-\ n **1** : the quality or state of being mature; esp : full development **2** : the date when a note becomes due for payment

ma·tu·ti·nal \ma-chù-'tīn-ᵊl; mə-'tüt-ᵊn-əl, -'tyüt-\ adj : of, relating to, or occurring in the morning : EARLY

mat·zo \'mät-sə\ n, pl **mat·zoth** \-sōt, -sōth, -sōs\ or **mat·zos** [Yiddish matse, fr. Heb maṣṣāh] : unleavened bread eaten esp. at the Passover

maud·lin \'mod-lən\ adj [alter. of Mary Magdalene; fr. her depiction as a weeping, penitent sinner] **1** : drunk enough to be silly **2** : weakly and effusively sentimental

¹maul \'mol\ n : a heavy hammer often with a wooden head used esp. for driving wedges

²maul vb **1** : BEAT, BRUISE; also : MANGLE **2** : to handle roughly

maun·der \'mon-dər\ vb **1** : to wander slowly and idly **2** : to speak indistinctly or disconnectedly

mau·so·le·um \mo-sə-'lē-əm, mo-zə-\ n, pl **-leums** or **-lea** \-'lē-ə\ [L, fr. Gk mausōleion, fr. Mausōlos Mausolus † ab 353 B.C. ruler of Caria whose tomb was one of the seven wonders of the ancient world] : a large tomb; esp : a usu. stone building for entombment of the dead above ground

mauve \'mōv, 'mòv\ n : a moderate purple, violet, or lilac color

ma·ven or **ma·vin** \'mā-vən\ n [Yiddish meyvn, fr. LHeb mēbhīn] : EXPERT

mav·er·ick \'ma-vrik, -və-rik\ n [perh. fr. Samuel A. Maverick † 1870 Am. pioneer who did not brand his calves] **1** : an unbranded range animal **2** : NONCONFORMIST

maw \'mò\ n **1** : STOMACH; also : the crop of a bird **2** : the throat, gullet, or jaws esp. of a voracious animal

mawk·ish \'mò-kish\ adj : sickly sentimental — **mawk·ish·ly** adv — **mawk·ish·ness** n

max abbr maximum

maxi \'mak-sē\ n, pl **max·is** : a long skirt, dress, or coat

maxi- comb form **1** : extra long ⟨maxi-kilt⟩ **2** : extra large ⟨maxi-problems⟩

max·il·la \mak-'si-lə\ n, pl **max·il·lae** \-'si-(ˌ)lē\ or **max·illas** : JAW 1; esp : an upper jaw — **max·il·lary** \'mak-sə-ler-ē\ adj

max·im \'mak-səm\ n : a proverbial saying

max·i·mal \'mak-sə-məl\ adj : MAXIMUM — **max·i·mal·ly** adv

max·i·mise Brit var of MAXIMIZE

max·i·mize \'mak-sə-mīz\ vb **-mized; -miz·ing 1** : to increase to a maximum **2** : to make the most of — **max·i·mi·za·tion** \mak-sə-mə-'zā-shən\ n

max·i·mum \'mak-sə-məm\ n, pl **-ma** \-mə\ or **-mums 1** : the greatest quantity, value, or degree **2** : an upper limit allowed by authority **3** : the largest of a set of numbers — **maximum** adj

may \'mā\ verbal auxiliary, past **might** \'mīt\; pres sing & pl **may 1** : have permission or liberty to ⟨you ∼ go now⟩ **2** : be in some degree likely to ⟨you ∼ be right⟩ **3** — used as an auxiliary to express a wish, purpose, contingency, or concession

May \'mā\ n [ME, fr. OF mai, fr. L Maius, fr. Maia, Ro-

\ə\abut \ᵊ\kitten \ər\further \a\ash \ā\ace \ä\mop, mar \au̇\out \ch\chin \e\bet \ē\easy \g\go \i\hit \ī\ice \j\job \ŋ\sing \ō\go \ò\law \òi\boy \th\thin \th̲\the \ü\loot \u̇\foot \y\yet \zh\vision   see also Pronunciation Symbols page man goddess] : the fifth month of the year having 31 days

Ma·ya \'mī-ə\ *n, pl* **Maya** *or* **Mayas** : a member of a group of peoples of Yucatán, Guatemala, and adjacent areas — **Ma·yan** \'mī-ən\ *n or adj*

may·ap·ple \'mā-ˌa-pəl\ *n* : a No. American woodland herb related to the barberry that has a poisonous root, one or two large leaves, and an edible but insipid yellow fruit

may·be \'mā-bē, 'me-\ *adv* : PERHAPS

May Day \'mā-ˌdā\ *n* : May 1 celebrated as a springtime festival and in some countries as Labor Day

may·flow·er \'mā-ˌflaù-ər\ *n* : any of several spring blooming herbs (as the trailing arbutus or an anemone)

may·fly \'mā-flī\ *n* : any of an order of insects with an aquatic nymph and a short-lived fragile adult having membranous wings

may·hem \'mā-ˌhem, 'mā-əm\ *n* **1** : willful and permanent crippling, mutilation, or disfigurement of a person **2** : needless or willful damage

may·on·naise \'mā-ə-ˌnāz\ *n* [F] : a dressing made of egg yolks, vegetable oil, and vinegar or lemon juice

may·or \'mā-ər\ *n* : an official elected to act as chief executive or nominal head of a city or borough — **may·or·al** \-əl\ *adj* — **may·or·al·ty** \-əl-tē\ *n*

may·pole \'mā-ˌpōl\ *n, often cap* : a tall flower-wreathed pole forming a center for May Day sports and dances

maze \'māz\ *n* : a confusing intricate network of passages — **mazy** *adj*

ma·zur·ka \mə-'zər-kə\ *n* : a Polish dance in moderate triple measure

MB *abbr* Manitoba

MBA *abbr* master of business administration

mc *abbr* megacycle

¹**MC** *n* : MASTER OF CEREMONIES

²**MC** *abbr* member of Congress

Mc·Coy \mə-'kòi\ *n* : something that is neither imitation nor substitute ⟨the real ∼⟩

MCPO *abbr* master chief petty officer

¹**Md** *abbr* Maryland

²**Md** *symbol* mendelevium

MD *abbr* **1** [NL *medicinae doctor*] doctor of medicine **2** Maryland **3** muscular dystrophy

mdnt *abbr* midnight

mdse *abbr* merchandise

MDT *abbr* mountain daylight (saving) time

me \'mē\ *pron, objective case of* I

Me *abbr* Maine

ME *abbr* **1** Maine **2** mechanical engineer **3** medical examiner

¹**mead** \'mēd\ *n* : an alcoholic beverage brewed from water and honey, malt, and yeast

²**mead** *n, archaic* : MEADOW

mead·ow \'me-dō\ *n* : land in or mainly in grass; *esp* : a tract of moist low-lying usu. level grassland — **mead·ow·land** \-ˌland\ *n* — **mead·owy** \'me-də-wē\ *adj*

mead·ow·lark \'me-dō-ˌlärk\ *n* : any of several No. American songbirds related to the orioles that are streaked brown above and in northernmost forms have a yellow breast marked with a black crescent

mead·ow·sweet \-ˌswēt\ *n* : a No. American native or naturalized spirea

mea·ger *or* **mea·gre** \'mē-gər\ *adj* **1** : THIN **2** : lacking richness, fertility, or strength; *also* : POOR **syn** scanty, scant, spare, sparse — **mea·ger·ly** *adv* — **mea·ger·ness** *n*

¹**meal** \'mēl\ *n* **1** : an act or the time of eating a portion of food **2** : the portion of food eaten at a meal

²**meal** *n* **1** : usu. coarsely ground seeds of a cereal **2** : a product resembling seed meal — **mealy** *adj*

meal·time \'mēl-ˌtīm\ *n* : the usual time at which a meal is served

mealy·bug \'mē-lē-ˌbəg\ *n* : any of a family of scale insects with a white powdery covering that are destructive pests esp. of fruit trees

mealy·mouthed \'mē-lē-ˌmaúthd, -ˌmaútht\ *adj* : not plain and straightforward : DEVIOUS

¹**mean** \'mēn\ *vb* **meant** \'ment\; **mean·ing** **1** : to have in the mind as a purpose **2** : to serve to convey, show, or indicate : SIGNIFY **3** : to have importance to the degree of **4** : to direct to a particular individual

²**mean** *adj* **1** : HUMBLE **2** : lacking acumen : DULL **3** : SHABBY, CONTEMPTIBLE **4** : IGNOBLE, BASE **5** : STINGY **6** : pettily selfish or malicious **7** : VEXATIOUS **8** : EXCELLENT — **mean·ly** *adv* — **mean·ness** *n*

³**mean** *adj* **1** : occupying a middle position (as in space, order, or time) **2** : being a mean : AVERAGE ⟨a ∼ value⟩

⁴**mean** *n* **1** : a middle point between extremes **2** *pl* : something helpful in achieving a desired end **3** *pl* : material resources affording a secure life **4** : ARITHMETIC MEAN

¹**me·an·der** \mē-'an-dər\ *n* [L *maeander*, fr. Gk *maiandros*, fr. *Maiandros* (now *Menderes*), river in Asia Minor] **1** : a winding course **2** : a winding of a stream — **me·an·drous** \-drəs\ *adj*

²**meander** *vb* **1** : to follow a winding course **2** : to wander aimlessly or casually

mean·ing *n* **1** : the thing one intends to convey esp. by language; *also* : the thing that is thus conveyed **2** : AIM **3** : SIGNIFICANCE; *esp* : implication of a hidden significance **4** : CONNOTATION; *also* : DENOTATION — **mean·ing·ful** \-fəl\ *adj* — **mean·ing·ful·ly** *adv* — **mean·ing·less** *adj*

¹**mean·time** \'mēn-ˌtīm\ *n* : the intervening time

²**meantime** *adv* : MEANWHILE

¹**mean·while** \-ˌhwīl\ *n* : MEANTIME

²**meanwhile** *adv* **1** : during the intervening time **2** : at the same time

meas *abbr* measure

mea·sles \'mē-zəlz\ *n pl* : an acute virus disease marked by fever and an eruption of distinct circular red spots

mea·sly \'mēz-lē, -zə-lē\ *adj* **mea·sli·er**; **-est** : contemptibly small or insignificant

¹**mea·sure** \'me-zhər, 'mā-\ *n* **1** : an adequate or moderate portion; *also* : a suitable limit **2** : the dimensions, capacity, or amount of something ascertained by measuring; *also* : an instrument for measuring **3** : a unit of measurement; *also* : a system of such units **4** : the act or process of measuring **5** : rhythmic structure or movement **6** : the part of a musical staff between two bars **7** : CRITERION **8** : a means to an end **9** : a legislative bill — **mea·sure·less** *adj*

²**measure** *vb* **mea·sured**; **mea·sur·ing** **1** : to mark or fix in multiples of a specific unit ⟨∼ off five centimeters⟩ **2** : to find out the size, extent, or amount of **3** : to bring into comparison or competition **4** : to serve as a means of measuring **5** : to have a specified measurement — **mea·sur·able** \'me-zhə-rə-bəl, 'mā-\ *adj* — **mea·sur·ably** \-blē\ *adv* — **mea·sur·er** *n*

mea·sure·ment \'me-zhər-mənt, 'mā-\ *n* **1** : the act or process of measuring **2** : a figure, extent, or amount obtained by measuring

measure up *vb* **1** : to have necessary or fitting qualifications **2** : to equal esp. in ability

meat \'mēt\ *n* **1** : FOOD; *esp* : solid food as distinguished from drink **2** : animal and esp. mammal flesh considered as food **3** : the edible part inside a covering (as a shell or rind) — **meaty** *adj*

meat·ball \-ˌbòl\ *n* : a small ball of chopped or ground meat

meat loaf *n* : a dish of ground meat seasoned and baked in the form of a loaf

mec·ca \'me-kə\ *n, often cap* [*Mecca*, Saudi Arabia, a destination of pilgrims in the Islamic world] : a center of activity sought as a goal by people sharing a common interest

mech *abbr* mechanical; mechanics

¹me·chan·ic \mi-'ka-nik\ *adj* : of or relating to manual work or skill

²mechanic *n* 1 : a manual worker 2 : MACHINIST; *esp* : one who repairs cars

me·chan·i·cal \mi-'ka-ni-kəl\ *adj* 1 : of or relating to machinery, to manual operations, or to mechanics 2 : done as if by a machine : AUTOMATIC **syn** instinctive, impulsive, spontaneous — **me·chan·i·cal·ly** \-k(ə-)lē\ *adv*

mechanical drawing *n* : drawing done with the aid of instruments

me·chan·ics \mi-'ka-niks\ *n sing or pl* 1 : a branch of physics that deals with energy and forces and their effect on bodies 2 : the practical application of mechanics (as to the operation of machines) 3 : mechanical or functional details

mech·a·nism \'me-kə-ˌni-zəm\ *n* 1 : a piece of machinery; *also* : a process or technique for achieving a result 2 : mechanical operation or action 3 : the fundamental processes involved in or responsible for a natural phenomenon (the visual ∼)

mech·a·nis·tic \ˌme-kə-'nis-tik\ *adj* 1 : mechanically determined ⟨∼ universe⟩ 2 : MECHANICAL — **mech·a·nis·ti·cal·ly** \-ti-k(ə-)lē\ *adv*

mech·a·nize \'me-kə-ˌnīz\ *vb* **-nized; -niz·ing** 1 : to make mechanical 2 : to equip with machinery esp. in order to replace human or animal labor 3 : to equip with armed and armored motor vehicles — **mech·a·ni·za·tion** \ˌme-kə-nə-'zā-shən\ *n* — **mech·a·niz·er** *n*

med *abbr* 1 medical; medicine 2 medieval 3 medium

MEd *abbr* master of education

med·al \'med-ᵊl\ *n* [MF *medaille*, fr. OIt *medaglia* coin worth half a denarius, medal, fr. (assumed) VL *medalis* half, alter. of LL *medialis* middle, fr. L *medius*] 1 : a small usu. metal object bearing a religious emblem or picture 2 : a piece of metal issued to commemorate a person or event or to award excellence or achievement

med·al·ist *or* **med·al·list** \'med-ᵊl-ist\ *n* 1 : a designer or maker of medals 2 : a recipient of a medal as an award

me·dal·lion \mə-'dal-yən\ *n* 1 : a large medal 2 : a tablet or panel bearing a portrait or an ornament

med·dle \'med-ᵊl\ *vb* **med·dled; med·dling** : to interfere without right or propriety — **med·dler** \'med-ᵊl-ər\ *n*

med·dle·some \'med-ᵊl-səm\ *adj* : inclined to meddle

me·dia \'mē-dē-ə\ *n, pl* **me·di·as** : MEDIUM 4

me·di·al \'mē-dē-əl\ *adj* : occurring in or extending toward the middle

¹me·di·an \'mē-dē-ən\ *n* 1 : a value in an ordered set of values below and above which there are an equal number of values 2 : MEDIAN STRIP

²median *adj* 1 : being in the middle or in an intermediate position 2 : relating to or constituting a statistical median

median strip *n* : a strip dividing a highway into lanes according to the direction of travel

me·di·ate \'mē-dē-ˌāt\ *vb* **-at·ed; -at·ing** 1 : to act as an intermediary; *esp* : to work with opposing sides in order to resolve (as a dispute) or bring about (as a settlement) 2 : to bring about, influence, or transmit (as a physical process or effect) by acting as an intermediate or controlling agent or mechanism **syn** intercede, intervene, interpose, interfere — **me·di·a·tion** \ˌmē-dē-'ā-shən\ *n* — **me·di·a·tor** \'mē-dē-ˌā-tər\ *n*

med·ic \'me-dik\ *n* : one engaged in medical work; *esp* : CORPSMAN

med·i·ca·ble \'me-di-kə-bəl\ *adj* : CURABLE

med·ic·aid \'me-di-ˌkād\ *n, often cap* : a program of financial assistance for medical care designed for those unable to afford regular medical service and financed jointly by the state and federal governments

med·i·cal \'me-di-kəl\ *adj* : of or relating to the science or practice of medicine or the treatment of disease — **med·i·cal·ly** \-k(ə-)lē\ *adv*

medical examiner *n* : a public officer who performs autopsies on bodies to find the cause of death

me·di·ca·ment \mi-'di-kə-mənt, 'me-di-kə-\ *n* : a substance used in therapy

medi·care \'me-di-ˌker\ *n, often cap* : a government program of financial assistance for medical care esp. for the aged

med·i·cate \'me-də-ˌkāt\ *vb* **-cat·ed; -cat·ing** : to treat with medicine

med·i·ca·tion \ˌme-də-'kā-shən\ *n* 1 : the act or process of medicating 2 : MEDICINE 1

me·dic·i·nal \mə-'dis-ᵊn-əl\ *adj* : tending or used to cure disease or relieve pain — **me·dic·i·nal·ly** *adv*

med·i·cine \'me-də-sən\ *n* 1 : a substance or preparation used in treating disease 2 : a science and art dealing with the prevention and cure of disease

medicine ball *n* : a heavy stuffed leather ball used for conditioning exercises

medicine man *n* : a priestly healer or sorcerer esp. among the American Indians : SHAMAN

med·i·co \'me-di-ˌkō\ *n, pl* **-cos** : a medical practitioner or student

me·di·eval *or* **me·di·ae·val** \ˌmē-dē-'ē-vəl, ˌme-, mē-'dē-vəl\ *adj* 1 : of, relating to, or characteristic of the Middle Ages 2 : extremely outmoded or antiquated — **me·di·e·val·ism** \-və-ˌli-zəm\ *n* — **me·di·e·val·ist** \-list\ *n*

me·di·o·cre \ˌmē-dē-'ō-kər\ *adj* [ME, fr. MF, fr. L *mediocris*, fr. *medius* middle + *ocris* stony mountain] : of moderate or low quality : ORDINARY — **me·di·oc·ri·ty** \-'ä-krə-tē\ *n*

med·i·tate \'me-də-ˌtāt\ *vb* **-tat·ed; -tat·ing** 1 : to muse over : CONTEMPLATE, PONDER 2 : INTEND, PLAN — **med·i·ta·tion** \ˌme-də-'tā-shən\ *n* — **med·i·ta·tive** \'me-də-ˌtā-tiv\ *adj* — **med·i·ta·tive·ly** *adv*

Med·i·ter·ra·nean \ˌme-də-tə-'rā-nē-ən, -'rā-nyən\ *adj* : of or relating to the Mediterranean Sea or to the lands or people around it

¹me·di·um \'mē-dē-əm\ *n, pl* **mediums** *or* **me·dia** \-dē-ə\ [L] 1 : something in a middle position; *also* : a middle position or degree 2 : a means of effecting or conveying something 3 : a surrounding or enveloping substance 4 : a channel or system of communication, information, or entertainment 5 : a mode of artistic expression 6 : an individual held to be a channel of communication between the earthly world and a world of spirits 7 : a condition or environment in which something may function or flourish

²medium *adj* : intermediate in amount, quality, position, or degree

me·di·um·is·tic \ˌmē-dē-ə-'mis-tik\ *adj* : of, relating to, or being a spiritualistic medium

med·ley \'med-lē\ *n, pl* **medleys** 1 : HODGEPODGE 2 : a musical composition made up esp. of a series of songs

me·dul·la \mə-'də-lə\ *n, pl* **-las** *or* **-lae** \-(ˌ)lē, -ˌlī\ : an inner or deep anatomical part; *also* : the posterior part (**medulla ob·lon·ga·ta** \-ˌä-ˌblȯŋ-'gä-tə\) of the vertebrate brain that is continuous with the spinal cord

meed \'mēd\ *n* : a fitting return

meek \'mēk\ *adj* 1 : characterized by patience and long-suffering 2 : deficient in spirit and courage 3 : MODERATE — **meek·ly** *adv* — **meek·ness** *n*

meer·schaum \'mir-shəm, -ˌshȯm\ *n* [G, fr. *Meer* sea + *Schaum* foam] : a tobacco pipe made of a light white clayey mineral

¹meet \'mēt\ *vb* **met** \'met\; **meet·ing** 1 : to come upon : FIND 2 : JOIN, INTERSECT 3 : to appear to the perception of 4 : OPPOSE, FIGHT 5 : to join in conversation or

---

\ə\abut \ᵊ\kitten \ər\further \a\ash \ā\ace \ä\mop, mar \au̇\out \ch\chin \e\bet \ē\easy \g\go \i\hit \ī\ice \j\job \ŋ\sing \ō\go \ȯ\law \ȯi\boy \th\thin \t̲h̲\the \ü\loot \u̇\foot \y\yet \zh\vision *see also* Pronunciation Symbols page

discussion; *also* : ASSEMBLE **6** : to conform to **7** : to pay fully **8** : to cope with **9** : to provide for **10** : to be introduced to

²**meet** *n* : an assembling esp. for a hunt or for competitive sports

³**meet** *adj* : SUITABLE, PROPER

meet·ing \'mē-tiŋ\ *n* **1** : an act of coming together : ASSEMBLY **2** : JUNCTION, INTERSECTION

meet·ing·house \-ˌhaus\ *n* : a building for public assembly and esp. for Protestant worship

mega- *or* **meg-** *comb form* **1** : great : large ⟨*mega*hit⟩ **2** : million : multiplied by one million ⟨*mega*hertz⟩

mega·byte \'me-gə-ˌbīt\ *n* : a unit of computer storage capacity equal to 1,048,576 bytes

mega·cy·cle \-ˌsī-kəl\ *n* : MEGAHERTZ

mega·death \-ˌdeth\ *n* : one million deaths — used as a unit in reference to nuclear warfare

mega·hertz \'me-gə-ˌhərts, -ˌherts\ *n* : a unit of frequency equal to one million hertz

mega·lith \'me-gə-ˌlith\ *n* : a large stone used in prehistoric monuments — **mega·lith·ic** \ˌme-gə-'li-thik\ *adj*

meg·a·lo·ma·nia \ˌme-gə-lō-'mā-nē-ə, -nyə\ *n* : a mental disorder marked by feelings of personal omnipotence and grandeur — **meg·a·lo·ma·ni·ac** \-'mā-nē-ˌak\ *adj or n*

meg·a·lop·o·lis \ˌme-gə-'lä-pə-ləs\ *n* : a very large urban unit

mega·phone \'me-gə-ˌfōn\ *n* : a cone-shaped device used to intensify or direct the voice — **megaphone** *vb*

mega·ton \-ˌtən\ *n* : an explosive force equivalent to that of one million tons of TNT

mega·vi·ta·min \-ˌvī-tə-mən\ *adj* : relating to or consisting of very large doses of vitamins — **mega·vi·ta·mins** *n pl*

mei·o·sis \mī-'ō-səs\ *n* : a process of cell division in gamete-producing cells in which the number of chromosomes is reduced to one half — **mei·ot·ic** \mī-'ä-tik\ *adj*

mel·an·cho·lia \ˌme-lən-'kō-lē-ə\ *n* : a mental disorder marked by extreme depression often with delusions

mel·an·chol·ic \ˌme-lən-'kä-lik\ *adj* **1** : DEPRESSED **2** : of or relating to melancholia

mel·an·choly \'me-lən-ˌkä-lē\ *n, pl* **-chol·ies** [ME *malencolie*, fr. MF *melancolie*, fr. LL *melancholia*, fr. Gk, fr. *melan-, melas* black + *cholē* bile; so called fr. the former belief that it was caused by an excess of black bile, a substance supposedly secreted by the kidneys or spleen] : depression of spirits : DEJECTION — **melancholy** *adj*

Mel·a·ne·sian \ˌme-lə-'nē-zhən\ *n* : a member of the dominant native group of the Pacific island grouping of Melanesia — **Melanesian** *adj*

mé·lange \mā-'länzh, -'länj\ *n* : a mixture esp. of incongruous elements

mel·a·nin \'me-lə-nən\ *n* : a dark brown or black animal or plant pigment

mel·a·nism \'me-lə-ˌni-zəm\ *n* : an increased amount of black or nearly black pigmentation

mel·a·no·ma \ˌme-lə-'nō-mə\ *n, pl* **-mas** *also* **-ma·ta** \-mə-tə\ : a usu. malignant tumor containing dark pigment

¹**meld** \'meld\ *vb* : to show or announce for a score in a card game

²**meld** *n* : a card or combination of cards that is or can be melded

me·lee \'mā-ˌlā, mā-'lā\ *n* [F *mêlée*] : a confused struggle **syn** fracas, row, brawl, donnybrook

me·lio·rate \'mēl-yə-ˌrāt, 'mē-lē-ə-\ *vb* **-rat·ed; -rat·ing** : AMELIORATE — **me·lio·ra·tion** \ˌmēl-yə-'rā-shən, ˌmē-lē-ə-\ *n* — **me·lio·ra·tive** \'mēl-yə-ˌrā-tiv, 'mē-lē-ə-\ *adj*

mel·lif·lu·ous \me-'li-flə-wəs, mə-\ *adj* [LL *mellifluus*,

fr. L *mel* honey + *fluere* to flow] : sweetly flowing — **mel·lif·lu·ous·ly** *adv* — **mel·lif·lu·ous·ness** *n*

¹**mel·low** \'me-lō\ *adj* **1** : soft and sweet because of ripeness; *also* : well aged and pleasingly mild ⟨~ wine⟩ **2** : made gentle by age or experience **3** : being rich and full but not garish or strident ⟨~ colors⟩ **4** : of soft loamy consistency ⟨~ soil⟩ — **mel·low·ness** *n*

²**mellow** *vb* : to make or become mellow

me·lo·di·ous \mə-'lō-dē-əs\ *adj* : pleasing to the ear — **me·lo·di·ous·ly** *adv* — **me·lo·di·ous·ness** *n*

melo·dra·ma \'me-lə-ˌdrä-mə, -ˌdra-\ *n* : an extravagantly theatrical play in which action and plot predominate over characterization — **melo·dra·mat·ic** \ˌme-lə-drə-'ma-tik\ *adj* — **melo·dra·mat·i·cal·ly** \-ti-k(ə-)lē\ *adv* — **melo·dra·ma·tist** \ˌme-lə-'drä-mə-tist, -'drä-\ *n*

mel·o·dy \'me-lə-dē\ *n, pl* **-dies 1** : sweet or agreeable sound **2** : a particular succession of notes : TUNE, AIR — **me·lod·ic** \mə-'lä-dik\ *adj* — **me·lod·i·cal·ly** \-di-k(ə-)lē\ *adv*

mel·on \'me-lən\ *n* : any of various fruits (as a muskmelon or watermelon) of the gourd family usu. eaten raw

¹**melt** \'melt\ *vb* **1** : to change from a solid to a liquid state usu. by heat **2** : DISSOLVE, DISINTEGRATE; *also* : to cause to disperse or disappear **3** : to make or become tender or gentle

²**melt** *n* : a melted substance

melt·down \'melt-ˌdaun\ *n* : the melting of the core of a nuclear reactor

melt·wa·ter \-ˌwö-tər, -ˌwä-\ *n* : water derived from the melting of ice and snow

mem *abbr* **1** member **2** memoir **3** memorial

mem·ber \'mem-bər\ *n* **1** : a part (as an arm, leg, leaf, or branch) of an animal or plant **2** : one of the individuals composing a group **3** : a constituent part of a whole

mem·ber·ship \-ˌship\ *n* **1** : the state or status of being a member **2** : the body of members

mem·brane \'mem-ˌbrān\ *n* : a thin pliable layer esp. of animal or plant origin — **mem·bra·nous** \-brə-nəs\ *adj*

me·men·to \mə-'men-tō\ *n, pl* **-tos** *or* **-toes** [ME, fr. L, remember] : something that serves to warn or remind; *also* : SOUVENIR

memo \'me-mō\ *n, pl* **mem·os** : MEMORANDUM

mem·oir \'mem-ˌwär\ *n* **1** : MEMORANDUM **2** : AUTOBIOGRAPHY — usu. used in pl. **3** : an account of something noteworthy; *also, pl* : the record of the proceedings of a learned society

mem·o·ra·bil·ia \ˌme-mə-rə-'bi-lē-ə, -'bil-yə\ *n pl* [L] : things worthy of remembrance; *also* : MEMENTOS

mem·o·ra·ble \'me-mə-rə-bəl\ *adj* : worth remembering : NOTABLE — **mem·o·ra·bil·i·ty** \ˌme-mə-rə-'bi-lə-tē\ *n* — **mem·o·ra·ble·ness** *n* — **mem·o·ra·bly** \-blē\ *adv*

mem·o·ran·dum \ˌme-mə-'ran-dəm\ *n, pl* **-dums** *or* **-da** \-də\ **1** : an informal record; *also* : a written reminder **2** : an informal written note

¹**me·mo·ri·al** \mə-'mōr-ē-əl\ *adj* : serving to preserve remembrance

²**memorial** *n* **1** : something designed to keep remembrance alive; *esp* : MONUMENT **2** : a statement of facts often accompanied with a petition — **me·mo·ri·al·ize** *vb*

Memorial Day *n* : the last Monday in May or formerly May 30 observed as a legal holiday in honor of those who died in war

mem·o·rize \'me-mə-ˌrīz\ *vb* **-rized; -riz·ing** : to learn by heart — **mem·o·ri·za·tion** \ˌme-mə-rə-'zā-shən\ *n* — **mem·o·riz·er** *n*

mem·o·ry \'me-mə-rē\ *n, pl* **-ries 1** : the power or process of remembering **2** : the store of things remembered **3** : COMMEMORATION **4** : something remembered **5** : the time within which past events are remembered **6** : a device (as in a computer) in which information can be stored **syn** remembrance, recollection, reminiscence

men *pl of* MAN

¹men·ace \'me-nəs\ *n* **1** : THREAT **2** : DANGER; *also* : NUISANCE

²menace *vb* **men·aced; men·ac·ing 1** : THREATEN **2** : ENDANGER — **men·ac·ing·ly** *adv*

mé·nage \mā-'näzh\ *n* [F] : HOUSEHOLD

me·nag·er·ie \mə-'na-jə-rē\ *n* : a collection of wild animals esp. for exhibition

¹mend \'mend\ *vb* **1** : to improve in manners or morals **2** : to put into good shape : REPAIR **3** : to improve in or restore to health : HEAL — **mend·er** *n*

²mend *n* **1** : an act of mending **2** : a mended place

men·da·cious \men-'dā-shəs\ *adj* : given to deception or falsehood : UNTRUTHFUL **syn** dishonest, deceitful — **men·da·cious·ly** *adv* — **men·dac·i·ty** \-'da-sə-tē\ *n*

men·de·le·vi·um \ˌmen-də-'lē-vē-əm, -'lā-\ *n* : a radioactive chemical element artificially produced — see ELEMENT table

men·di·cant \'men-di-kənt\ *n* **1** : BEGGAR **2** *often cap* : FRIAR — **men·di·can·cy** \-kən-sē\ *n* — **mendicant** *adj*

men·folk \'men-ˌfōk\ *or* **men·folks** \-ˌfōks\ *n pl* **1** : men in general **2** : the men of a family or community

men·ha·den \men-'hād-ᵊn, mən-\ *n, pl* **-den** *also* **-dens** : a marine fish related to the herring that is abundant along the Atlantic coast of the U.S.

¹me·nial \'mē-nē-əl, -nyəl\ *adj* **1** : of or relating to servants **2** : HUMBLE; *also* : SERVILE — **me·ni·al·ly** *adv*

²menial *n* : a domestic servant

men·in·gi·tis \ˌme-nən-'jī-təs\ *n, pl* **-git·i·des** \-'ji-tə-ˌdēz\ : inflammation of the membranes enclosing the brain and spinal cord; *also* : a usu. bacterial disease marked by this

me·ninx \'mē-niŋks, 'me-\ *n, pl* **me·nin·ges** \mə-'nin-(ˌ)jēz\ : any of the three membranes that envelop the brain and spinal cord — **men·in·ge·al** \ˌme-nən-'jē-əl\ *adj*

me·nis·cus \mə-'nis-kəs\ *n, pl* **me·nis·ci** \-'nis-ˌkī, -ˌkē\ *also* **me·nis·cus·es 1** : CRESCENT **2** : the curved upper surface of a column of liquid

meno·pause \'me-nə-ˌpoz\ *n* : the period of life when menstruation stops naturally — **meno·paus·al** \ˌme-nə-'po-zəl\ *adj*

me·no·rah \mə-'nōr-ə\ *n* [Heb *mĕnōrāh* candlestick] : a candelabrum that is used in Jewish worship

men·ses \'men-ˌsēz\ *n pl* : the menstrual flow

men·stru·a·tion \ˌmen-strə-'wā-shən, men-'strā-\ *n* : a discharging of bloody matter at approximately monthly intervals from the uterus of breeding-age nonpregnant primate females; *also* : PERIOD 6 — **men·stru·al** \'men-strə-wəl\ *adj* — **men·stru·ate** \'men-strə-ˌwāt, -ˌstrāt\ *vb*

men·su·ra·ble \'men-sə-rə-bəl, '-chə-\ *adj* : MEASURABLE

men·su·ra·tion \ˌmen-sə-'rā-shən, ˌmen-chə-\ *n* : MEASUREMENT

-ment \mənt\ *n suffix* **1** : concrete result, object, or agent of a (specified) action ⟨embank*ment*⟩ ⟨entangle*ment*⟩ **2** : concrete means or instrument of a (specified) action ⟨entertain*ment*⟩ **3** : action : process ⟨encircle*ment*⟩ ⟨develop*ment*⟩ **4** : place of a (specified) action ⟨encamp*ment*⟩ **5** : state : condition ⟨amaze*ment*⟩

men·tal \'ment-ᵊl\ *adj* **1** : of or relating to the mind **2** : of, relating to, or affected with a disorder of the mind ⟨∼ illness⟩ — **men·tal·ly** *adv*

mental age *n* : a measure of a child's mental development in terms of the number of years it takes an average child to reach the same level

mental deficiency *n* : MENTAL RETARDATION

men·tal·i·ty \men-'ta-lə-tē\ *n, pl* **-ties 1** : mental power or capacity **2** : mode or way of thought

mental retardation *n* : subaverage intellectual ability present from infancy that is characterized by an IQ of 70 or less and problems in development, learning, and social adjustment

men·thol \'men-ˌthol, -ˌthōl\ *n* : an alcohol occurring esp. in mint oils that has the odor and cooling properties of peppermint — **men·tho·lat·ed** \-thə-ˌlā-təd\ *adj*

¹men·tion \'men-chən\ *n* **1** : a brief or casual reference **2** : a formal citation for outstanding achievement

²mention *vb* **1** : to refer to : CITE **2** : to cite for superior achievement — **not to mention** : to say nothing of

men·tor \'men-ˌtor, -tər\ *n* : a trusted counselor or guide; *also* : TUTOR, COACH

menu \'men-yü, 'mān-\ *n, pl* **menus** [F, fr. *menu* small, detailed, fr. L *minutus* minute (adj.)] **1** : a list of the dishes available (as in a restaurant) for a meal; *also* : the dishes served **2** : a list of offerings or options

me·ow \mē-'au\ *vb* : to make the characteristic cry of a cat — **meow** *n*

mer *abbr* meridian

mer·can·tile \'mər-kən-ˌtēl, -ˌtīl\ *adj* : of or relating to merchants or trading

¹mer·ce·nary \'mərs-ᵊn-ˌer-ē\ *n, pl* **-nar·ies** : a person who serves merely for wages; *esp* : a soldier hired into foreign service

²mercenary *adj* **1** : serving merely for pay or gain **2** : hired for service in a foreign army

mer·cer \'mər-sər\ *n, Brit* : a dealer in usu. expensive fabrics

mer·cer·ize \'mər-sə-ˌrīz\ *vb* **-ized; -iz·ing** : to treat cotton yarn or cloth with alkali so that it looks silky or takes a better dye

¹mer·chan·dise \'mər-chən-ˌdīz, -ˌdīs\ *n* : the commodities or goods that are bought and sold in business

²mer·chan·dise \-ˌdīz\ *vb* **-dised; -dis·ing** : to buy and sell in business : TRADE — **mer·chan·dis·er** *n*

mer·chant \'mər-chənt\ *n* **1** : a buyer and seller of commodities for profit **2** : STOREKEEPER

mer·chant·able \'mər-chən-tə-bəl\ *adj* : acceptable to buyers : MARKETABLE

mer·chant·man \'mər-chənt-mən\ *n* : a ship used in commerce

merchant marine *n* : the commercial ships of a nation

merchant ship *n* : MERCHANTMAN

mer·ci·ful·ly \'mər-si-fə-lē\ *adv* **1** : in a merciful manner **2** : FORTUNATELY 2

mer·cu·ri·al \ˌmər-'kyur-ē-əl\ *adj* **1** : unpredictably changeable **2** : MERCURIC — **mer·cu·ri·al·ly** *adv* — **mer·cu·ri·al·ness** *n*

mer·cu·ric \ˌmər-'kyur-ik\ *adj* : of, relating to, or containing mercury

mercuric chloride *n* : a poisonous compound of mercury and chlorine used as an antiseptic and fungicide

mer·cu·ry \'mər-kyə-rē\ *n, pl* **-ries 1** : a heavy silver-white liquid metallic chemical element used esp. in scientific instruments — see ELEMENT table **2** *cap* : the planet nearest the sun — see PLANET table

mer·cy \'mər-sē\ *n, pl* **mercies** [ME, fr. OF *merci*, fr. ML *merced-, merces*, fr. L, price paid, wages, fr. *merc-, merx* merchandise] **1** : compassion shown to an offender; *also* : imprisonment rather than death for first-degree murder **2** : a blessing resulting from divine favor or compassion; *also* : a fortunate circumstance **3** : compassion shown to victims of misfortune — **mer·ci·ful** \-si-fəl\ *adj* — **mer·ci·less** \-si-ləs\ *adj* — **mer·ci·less·ly** *adv* — **mercy** *adj*

mercy killing *n* : the act or practice of killing or permitting the death of hopelessly sick or injured persons or animals with as little pain as possible for reasons of mercy

¹mere \'mir\ *n* : LAKE, POOL

²mere *adj, superlative* **mer·est 1** : being nothing more than ⟨a ∼ child⟩ **2** : not diluted : PURE — **mere·ly** *adv*

\ə\abut \ᵊ\kitten \ər\further \a\ash \ā\ace \ä\mop, mar \au\out \ch\chin \e\bet \ē\easy \g\go \i\hit \ī\ice \j\job \ŋ\sing \ō\go \o\law \oi\boy \th\thin \t̲h̲\the \ü\loot \u̇\foot \y\yet \zh\vision *see also* Pronunciation Symbols page

mer·e·tri·cious \ˌmer-ə-ˈtri-shəs\ adj [L meretricius, fr. meretrix prostitute, fr. merēre to earn] : tawdrily attractive; also : SPECIOUS — **mer·e·tri·cious·ly** adv — **mer·e·tri·cious·ness** n

mer·gan·ser \(ˌ)mər-ˈgan-sər\ n : any of various fish-eating wild ducks with a usu. crested head and a slender bill hooked at the end and serrated along the margins

merge \ˈmərj\ vb **merged; merg·ing** 1 : to blend gradually 2 : to combine, unite, or coalesce into one syn mingle, amalgamate, fuse, interfuse, intermingle

merg·er \ˈmər-jər\ n 1 : the act or process of merging 2 : absorption by a corporation of one or more others

me·rid·i·an \mə-ˈri-dē-ən\ n [ME, fr. MF meridien, fr. meridien of noon, fr. L meridianus, fr. meridies noon, south, irreg. fr. medius mid + dies day] 1 : the highest point : CULMINATION 2 : any of the imaginary circles on the earth's surface passing through the north and south poles — **meridian** adj

me·ringue \mə-ˈraŋ\ n [F] : a baked dessert topping of stiffly beaten egg whites and powdered sugar

me·ri·no \mə-ˈrē-nō\ n, pl **-nos** [Sp] 1 : any of a breed of sheep noted for fine soft wool 2 : a fine soft fabric or yarn of wool or wool and cotton

¹**mer·it** \ˈmer-ət\ n 1 : laudable or blameworthy traits or actions 2 : a praiseworthy quality; also : character or conduct deserving reward or honor 3 pl : the intrinsic nature of a legal case; also : legal significance

²**merit** vb : EARN, DESERVE

mer·i·toc·ra·cy \ˌmer-ə-ˈtä-krə-sē\ n, pl **-cies** : a system in which the talented are chosen and moved ahead based on their achievement; also : leadership by the talented

mer·i·to·ri·ous \ˌmer-ə-ˈtōr-ē-əs\ adj : deserving honor or esteem — **mer·i·to·ri·ous·ly** adv — **mer·i·to·ri·ous·ness** n

mer·maid \ˈmər-ˌmād\ n : a legendary sea creature with a woman's upper body and a fish's tail

mer·man \-ˌman, -mən\ n : a legendary sea creature with a man's upper body and a fish's tail

mer·ri·ment \ˈmer-i-mənt\ n 1 : HILARITY 2 : FESTIVITY

mer·ry \ˈmer-ē\ adj **mer·ri·er; -est** 1 : full of gaiety or high spirits 2 : marked by festivity 3 : BRISK ⟨a ∼ pace⟩ syn blithe, jocund, jovial, jolly, mirthful — **mer·ri·ly** \ˈmer-ə-lē\ adv

merry–go–round \ˈmer-ē-gō-ˌraund\ n 1 : a circular revolving platform with benches and figures of animals on which people sit for a ride 2 : a busy round of activities

mer·ry·mak·ing \ˈmer-ē-ˌmā-kiŋ\ n 1 : jovial or festive activity 2 : a festive occasion — **mer·ry·mak·er** \-ˌmā-kər\ n

me·sa \ˈmā-sə\ n [Sp, lit., table, fr. L mensa] : a flat-topped hill with steep sides

mes·cal \me-ˈskal, mə-\ n 1 : a small cactus that is the source of a stimulant used esp. by Mexican Indians 2 : a usu. colorless liquor distilled from the leaves of an agave; also : this agave

mes·ca·line \ˈmes-kə-lən, -ˌlēn\ n : a hallucinatory alkaloid from the mescal cactus

mesdames pl of MADAM or of MADAME or of MRS.

mesdemoiselles pl of MADEMOISELLE

¹**mesh** \ˈmesh\ n 1 : one of the openings between the threads or cords of a net; also : one of the similar spaces in a network 2 : the fabric of a net 3 : NETWORK 4 : working contact (as of the teeth of gears) ⟨in ∼⟩ — **meshed** \ˈmesht\ adj

²**mesh** vb 1 : to catch in or as if in a mesh 2 : to be in or come into mesh : ENGAGE 3 : to fit together properly

mesh·work \ˈmesh-ˌwərk\ n : NETWORK

me·si·al \ˈmē-zē-əl, -sē-\ adj : of, relating to, or being the surface of a tooth that is closest to the middle of the front of the jaw

mes·mer·ize \ˈmez-mə-ˌrīz\ vb **-ized; -iz·ing** : HYPNOTIZE — **mes·mer·ic** \mez-ˈmer-ik\ adj — **mes·mer·ism** \ˈmez-mə-ˌri-zəm\ n

Me·so·lith·ic \ˌme-zə-ˈli-thik\ adj : of, relating to, or being a transitional period of the Stone Age between the Paleolithic and the Neolithic periods

me·so·sphere \ˈme-zə-ˌsfir\ n : a layer of the atmosphere between the stratosphere and the thermosphere

Me·so·zo·ic \ˌme-zə-ˈzō-ik, ˌmē-\ adj : of, relating to, or being the era of geologic history between the Paleozoic and the Cenozoic and extending from about 245 million years ago to about 65 million years ago — **Mesozoic** n

mes·quite \mə-ˈskēt, me-\ n : any of several spiny leguminous trees and shrubs chiefly of the southwestern U.S. with sugar-rich pods important as fodder; also : mesquite wood used esp. in grilling food

¹**mess** \ˈmes\ n 1 : a quantity of food; also : enough food of a specified kind for a dish or meal ⟨a ∼ of beans⟩ 2 : a group of persons who regularly eat together; also : a meal eaten by such a group 3 : a place where meals are regularly served to a group 4 : a confused, dirty, or offensive state — **messy** adj

²**mess** vb 1 : to supply with meals; also : to take meals with a mess 2 : to make dirty or untidy; also : BUNGLE 3 : INTERFERE, MEDDLE 4 : PUTTER, TRIFLE

mes·sage \ˈme-sij\ n : a communication sent by one person to another

messeigneurs pl of MONSEIGNEUR

mes·sen·ger \ˈmes-ᵊn-jər\ n : one who carries a message or does an errand

messenger RNA n : an RNA that carries the code for a particular protein from DNA in the nucleus to a ribosome in the cytoplasm and acts as a template for the formation of that protein

Mes·si·ah \mə-ˈsī-ə\ n 1 : the expected king and deliverer of the Jews 2 : Jesus 3 not cap : a professed or accepted leader of a cause — **mes·si·an·ic** \ˌme-sē-ˈa-nik\ adj

messieurs pl of MONSIEUR

mess·mate \ˈmes-ˌmāt\ n : a member of a group who eat regularly together

Messrs. \ˈme-sərz\ pl of MR.

mes·ti·zo \me-ˈstē-zō\ n, pl **-zos** [Sp, fr. mestizo mixed, fr. LL mixticius, fr. L mixtus, pp. of miscēre to mix] : a person of mixed blood

¹**met** past and past part of MEET

²**met** abbr metropolitan

me·tab·o·lism \mə-ˈta-bə-ˌli-zəm\ n : the processes by which the substance of plants and animals incidental to life is built up and broken down; also : the processes by which a substance is handled in the body ⟨∼ of sugar⟩ — **met·a·bol·ic** \ˌme-tə-ˈbä-lik\ adj — **me·tab·o·lize** \mə-ˈta-bə-ˌlīz\ vb

me·tab·o·lite \-ˌlīt\ n 1 : a product of metabolism 2 : a substance essential to the metabolism of a particular organism or to a metabolic process

meta·car·pal \ˌme-tə-ˈkär-pəl\ n : any of usu. five more or less elongated bones of the part of the hand or forefoot between the wrist and the bones of the digits — **metacarpal** adj

meta·car·pus \-ˈkär-pəs\ n : the part of the hand or forefoot that contains the metacarpals

met·al \ˈmet-ᵊl\ n 1 : any of various opaque, fusible, ductile, and typically lustrous substances that are good conductors of electricity and heat 2 : METTLE; also : the material out of which a person or thing is made — **me·tal·lic** \mə-ˈta-lik\ adj

met·al·lur·gy \ˈmet-ᵊl-ˌər-jē\ n : the science and technology of metals — **met·al·lur·gi·cal** \ˌmet-ᵊl-ˈər-ji-kəl\ adj — **met·al·lur·gist** \ˈmet-ᵊl-ˌər-jist\ n

met·al·ware \ˈmet-ᵊl-ˌwar\ n : metal utensils for household use

met·al·work \-ˌwərk\ n : work and esp. artistic work

made of metal — **met·al·work·er** \-ₐwər-kər\ *n* — **met·al·work·ing** *n*

meta·mor·phism \ₐme-tə-'mȯr-fi-zəm\ *n* : a change in the structure of rock; *esp* : a change to a more compact and more highly crystalline form produced by pressure, heat, and water — **meta·mor·phic** \-'mȯr-fik\ *adj*

meta·mor·pho·sis \ₐme-tə-'mȯr-fə-səs\ *n, pl* **-pho·ses** \-ₐsēz\ **1** : a change of physical form, structure, or substance esp. by supernatural means; *also* : a striking alteration (as in appearance or character) **2** : a fundamental change in form and often habits of an animal accompanying the transformation of a larva into an adult — **meta·mor·phose** \-ₐfōz, -ₐfōs\ *vb*

met·a·phor \'me-tə-ₐfȯr\ *n* : a figure of speech in which a word for one idea or thing is used in place of another to suggest a likeness between them (as in "the ship plows the sea") — **met·a·phor·i·cal** \ₐme-tə-'fȯr-i-kəl\ *adj*

meta·phys·ics \ₐme-tə-'fi-ziks\ *n* [ML *Metaphysica*, title of Aristotle's treatise on the subject, fr. Gk (*ta*) *meta* (*ta*) *physika*, lit., the (works) after the physical (works); fr. its position in his collected works] : the philosophical study of the ultimate causes and underlying nature of things — **meta·phys·i·cal** \-'fi-zi-kəl\ *adj* — **meta·phy·si·cian** \-fə-'zi-shən\ *n*

me·tas·ta·sis \mə-'tas-tə-səs\ *n, pl* **-ta·ses** \-ₐsēz\ : transfer of a health-impairing agency (as cancer cells) to a new site in the body; *also* : a secondary growth of a malignant tumor — **me·tas·ta·size** \-tə-ₐsīz\ *vb* — **met·a·stat·ic** \ₐme-tə-'sta-tik\ *adj*

meta·tar·sal \ₐme-tə-'tär-səl\ *n* : any of the bones of the foot between the tarsus and the bones of the digits that in humans include five more or less elongated bones — **metatarsal** *adj*

meta·tar·sus \-'tär-səs\ *n* : the part of the human foot or the hind foot in quadrupeds that contains the metatarsals

¹mete \'mēt\ *vb* **met·ed; met·ing 1** *archaic* : MEASURE **2** : ALLOT

²mete *n* : BOUNDARY ⟨∼s and bounds⟩

me·te·or \'mē-tē-ər, -ₐȯr\ *n* **1** : a small particle of matter in the solar system directly observable only by its glow from frictional heating on falling into the earth's atmosphere **2** : the streak of light produced by a meteor

me·te·or·ic \ₐmē-tē-'ȯr-ik\ *adj* **1** : of, relating to, or resembling a meteor **2** : transiently brilliant ⟨a ∼ career⟩ — **me·te·or·i·cal·ly** \-i-k(ə-)lē\ *adv*

me·te·or·ite \'mē-tē-ə-ₐrīt\ *n* : a meteor that reaches the surface of the earth

me·te·or·oid \'mē-tē-ə-ₐrȯid\ *n* : a small particle of matter in the solar system

me·te·o·rol·o·gy \ₐmē-tē-ə-'rä-lə-jē\ *n* : a science that deals with the atmosphere and its phenomena and esp. with weather forecasting — **me·te·o·ro·log·ic** \ₐmē-tē-ₐȯr-ə-'lä-jik\ *or* **me·te·o·ro·log·i·cal** \-'lä-ji-kəl\ *adj* — **me·te·o·rol·o·gist** \ₐmē-tē-ə-'rä-lə-jist\ *n*

¹me·ter \'mē-tər\ *n* : rhythm in verse or music

²met·er \'mē-tər\ *n* : the basic metric unit of length — see METRIC SYSTEM table

³me·ter \'mē-tər\ *n* : a measuring and sometimes recording instrument

⁴me·ter *vb* **1** : to measure by means of a meter **2** : to print postal indicia on by means of a postage meter ⟨∼ed mail⟩

meter–kilogram–second *adj* : of, relating to, or being a system of units based on the meter, the kilogram, and the second

meter maid *n* : a policewoman assigned to write tickets for parking violations

meth·a·done \'me-thə-ₐdōn\ *also* **meth·a·don** \-ₐdän\ *n* : a synthetic addictive narcotic drug used esp. as a substitute narcotic in the treatment of heroin addiction

meth·am·phet·amine \ₐme-tham-'fe-tə-ₐmēn, -thəm-,

-mən\ *n* : a drug used medically in the form of its hydrochloride in the treatment of obesity and often illicitly as a stimulant

meth·ane \'me-ₐthān\ *n* : a colorless odorless flammable gas produced by decomposition of organic matter or from coal and used esp. as a fuel

meth·a·nol \'me-thə-ₐnȯl, -ₐnōl\ *n* : a volatile flammable poisonous liquid alcohol used esp. as a solvent and as an antifreeze

meth·aqua·lone \me-'tha-kwə-ₐlōn\ *n* : a sedative and hypnotic habit-forming drug that is not a barbiturate

meth·od \'me-thəd\ *n* [MF *methode*, fr. L *methodus*, fr. Gk *methodos*, fr. *meta* with + *hodos* way] **1** : a procedure or process for achieving an end **2** : orderly arrangement : PLAN **syn** mode, manner, way, fashion, system — **me·thod·i·cal** \mə-'thä-di-kəl\ *adj* — **me·thod·i·cal·ly** \-k(ə-)lē\ *adv* — **me·thod·i·cal·ness** *n*

Meth·od·ist \'me-thə-dist\ *n* : a member of a Protestant denomination adhering to the doctrines of John Wesley — **Meth·od·ism** \-ₐdi-zəm\ *n*

meth·od·ize \'me-thə-ₐdīz\ *vb* **-ized; -iz·ing** : SYSTEMATIZE

meth·od·ol·o·gy \ₐme-thə-'dä-lə-jē\ *n, pl* **-gies 1** : a body of methods and rules followed in a science or discipline **2** : the study of the principles or procedures of inquiry in a particular field

meth·yl \'me-thəl\ *n* : a chemical group consisting of carbon and hydrogen

methyl alcohol *n* : METHANOL

meth·yl·mer·cury \ₐme-thəl-'mər-kyə-rē\ *n* : any of various toxic compounds of mercury that often occur as pollutants which accumulate in animals esp. at the top of a food chain

met·i·cal \'me-ti-kəl\ *n* — see MONEY table

me·tic·u·lous \mə-'ti-kyə-ləs\ *adj* [L *meticulosus* fearful, fr. *metus* fear] : extremely careful in attending to details — **me·tic·u·lous·ly** *adv* — **me·tic·u·lous·ness** *n*

mé·tier \'me-ₐtyā, me-'tyā\ *n* : an area of activity in which one is expert or successful

me·tre \'mē-tər\ *chiefly Brit var of* METER

met·ric \'me-trik\ *adj* **1** : of or relating to measurement; *esp* : of or relating to the metric system **2** : METRICAL 1

met·ri·cal \'me-tri-kəl\ *adj* **1** : of, relating to, or composed in meter **2** : METRIC 1 — **met·ri·cal·ly** \-k(ə-)lē\ *adv*

met·ri·ca·tion \ₐme-tri-'kā-shən\ *n* : the act or process of converting into or expressing in the metric system

met·ri·cize \'me-trə-ₐsīz\ *vb* **-cized; -ciz·ing** : to change into or express in the metric system

metric system *n* : a decimal system of weights and measures based on the meter and on the kilogram ☞ For table, see next page.

metric ton *n* — see METRIC SYSTEM table

¹met·ro \'me-trō\ *n, pl* **metros** : SUBWAY

²metro *adj* : of, relating to, or characteristic of a metropolis and sometimes including its suburbs

met·ro·nome \'me-trə-ₐnōm\ *n* : an instrument for marking exact time by a regularly repeated tick

me·trop·o·lis \mə-'trä-pə-ləs\ *n* [ME, fr. LL, fr. Gk *mētropolis*, fr. *mētēr* mother + *polis* city] : the chief or capital city of a country, state, or region — **met·ro·pol·i·tan** \ₐme-trə-'pä-lət-ᵊn\ *adj*

met·tle \'met-ᵊl\ *n* **1** : SPIRIT, COURAGE **2** : quality of temperament

met·tle·some \'met-ᵊl-səm\ *adj* : full of mettle : COURAGEOUS

MeV *abbr* million electron volts

METRIC SYSTEM[1]

LENGTH

unit	abbreviation	number of meters	approximate U.S. equivalent
kilometer	km	1,000	0.62 mile
hectometer	hm	100	328.08 feet
dekameter	dam	10	32.81 feet
meter	m	1	39.37 inches
decimeter	dm	0.1	3.94 inches
centimeter	cm	0.01	0.39 inch
millimeter	mm	0.001	0.039 inch

AREA

unit	abbreviation	number of square meters	approximate U.S. equivalent
square kilometer	sq km *or* km²	1,000,000	0.3861 square mile
hectare	ha	10,000	2.47 acres
are	a	100	119.60 square yards
square centimeter	sq cm *or* cm²	0.0001	0.155 square inch

VOLUME

unit	abbreviation	number of cubic meters	approximate U.S. equivalent
cubic meter	m³	1	1.307 cubic yards
cubic decimeter	dm³	0.001	61.023 cubic inches
cubic centimeter	cu cm *or* cm³ *also* cc	0.000001	0.061 cubic inch

CAPACITY

unit	abbreviation	number of liters	approximate U.S. equivalent cubic	dry	liquid
kiloliter	kl	1,000	1.31 cubic yards		
hectoliter	hl	100	3.53 cubic feet	2.84 bushels	
dekaliter	dal	10	0.35 cubic foot	1.14 pecks	2.64 gallons
liter	l	1	61.02 cubic inches	0.908 quart	1.057 quarts
deciliter	dl	0.1	6.1 cubic inches	0.18 pint	0.21 pint
centiliter	cl	0.01	0.61 cubic inch		0.338 fluid ounce
milliliter	ml	0.001	0.061 cubic inch		0.27 fluid dram

MASS AND WEIGHT

unit	abbreviation	number of grams	approximate U.S. equivalent
metric ton	t	1,000,000	1.102 short tons
kilogram	kg	1,000	2.2046 pounds
hectogram	hg	100	3.527 ounces
dekagram	dag	10	0.353 ounce
gram	g	1	0.035 ounce
decigram	dg	0.1	1.543 grains
centigram	cg	0.01	0.154 grain
milligram	mg	0.001	0.015 grain

[1]For metric equivalents of U.S. units see Weights and Measures table

---

¹mew \ˈmyü\ *vb* : MEOW — **mew** *n*

²mew *vb* : CONFINE

mews \ˈmyüz\ *n pl, chiefly Brit* : stables usu. with living quarters built around a court; *also* : a narrow street with dwellings converted from stables

Mex *abbr* Mexican; Mexico

Mex·i·can \ˈmek-si-kən\ *n* : a native or inhabitant of Mexico — **Mexican** *adj*

mez·za·nine \ˈmez-ᵊn-ˌēn, ˌmez-ᵊn-ˈēn\ *n* **1** : a low-ceilinged story between two main stories of a building **2** : the lowest balcony in a theater; *also* : the first few rows of such a balcony

mez·zo for·te \ˌmet-(ˌ)sō-ˈför-ˌtā, ˌmed- (ˌ)zō-, -tē\ *adj or adv* [It] : moderately loud — used as a direction in music

mez·zo pia·no \-pē-ˈä-(ˌ)nō\ *adj or adv* [It] : moderately soft — used as a direction in music

mez·zo–so·pra·no \-sə-ˈpra-nō, -ˈprä-\ *n* : a woman's voice having a range between that of the soprano and contralto; *also* : a singer having such a voice

MFA *abbr* master of fine arts

mfr *abbr* manufacture; manufacturer

mg *abbr* milligram

Mg *symbol* magnesium

MG *abbr* **1** machine gun **2** major general **3** military government

mgr *abbr* **1** manager **2** monseigneur **3** monsignor

mgt *or* **mgmt** *abbr* management

MGy Sgt *abbr* master gunnery sergeant

MHz *abbr* megahertz

mi *abbr* **1** mile; mileage **2** mill

MI *abbr* **1** Michigan **2** military intelligence

MIA \ˌem-(ˌ)ī-ˈā\ *n* [*missing in action*] : a member of the armed forces whose whereabouts following a combat mission are unknown

Mi·ami \mī-ˈa-mē, -mə\ *n, pl* **Mi·ami** *or* **Mi·am·is** : a member of an American Indian people orig. of Wisconsin and Indiana

mi·as·ma \mī-ˈaz-mə, mē-\ *n, pl* **-mas** *also* **-ma·ta** \-mə-tə\ **1** : a vapor from a swamp formerly believed to cause disease **2** : a harmful influence or atmosphere — **mi·as·mal** \-məl\ *adj* — **mi·as·mic** \-mik\ *adj*

Mic *abbr* Micah

mi·ca \'mī-kə\ *n* [NL, fr. L, grain, crumb] : any of various mineral silicates readily separable into thin transparent sheets

Mi·cah \'mī-kə\ *n* — see BIBLE table

mice *pl of* MOUSE

Mich *abbr* Michigan

Mi·che·as \'mī-kē-əs, mī-'kē-əs\ *n* : MICAH

Mic·mac \'mik-₁mak\ *n, pl* **Micmac** *or* **Micmacs** : a member of an American Indian people of eastern Canada

micr- *or* **micro-** *comb form* **1** : small : minute ⟨*micro*capsule⟩ **2** : one millionth part of a specified unit ⟨*micro*second⟩

¹**mi·cro** \'mī-krō\ *adj* **1** : very small; *esp* : MICROSCOPIC **2** : involving minute quantities or variations

²**micro** *n* : MICROCOMPUTER

mi·crobe \'mī-₁krōb\ *n* : MICROORGANISM; *esp* : one causing disease — **mi·cro·bi·al** \mī-'krō-bē-əl\ *adj*

mi·cro·bi·ol·o·gy \₁mī-krō-bī-'ä-lə-jē\ *n* : a branch of biology dealing esp. with microscopic forms of life — **mi·cro·bi·o·log·i·cal** \-₁bī-ə-'lä-ji-kəl\ *adj* — **mi·cro·bi·ol·o·gist** \-bī-'ä-lə-jist\ *n*

mi·cro·burst \'mī-krō-₁bərst\ *n* : a violent short-lived localized downdraft that creates extreme wind shears at low altitudes

mi·cro·cap·sule \'mī-krō-₁kap-səl, -₁sül\ *n* : a tiny capsule containing material (as a medicine) released when the capsule is broken, melted, or dissolved

mi·cro·chip \-₁chip\ *n* : INTEGRATED CIRCUIT

mi·cro·cir·cuit \-₁sər-kət\ *n* : a compact electronic circuit

mi·cro·com·put·er \-kəm-₁pyü-tər\ *n* : a very small computer that uses a microprocessor

mi·cro·cosm \'mī-krə-₁kä-zəm\ *n* : an individual or community thought of as a miniature world or universe

mi·cro·elec·tron·ics \'mī-krō-i-₁lek-'trä-niks\ *n* : a branch of electronics that deals with the miniaturization of electronic circuits and components — **mi·cro·elec·tron·ic** \-nik\ *adj*

mi·cro·en·cap·su·late \₁mī-krō-in-'kap-sə-₁lāt\ *vb* : to enclose (as a drug) in a microcapsule — **mi·cro·en·cap·su·la·tion** \-in-₁kap-sə-'lā-shən\ *n*

mi·cro·fiche \'mī-krō-₁fēsh\ *n, pl* **fiche** *or* **fiches** *same or* -₁fē-shəz, -₁fi-\ : a sheet of microfilm containing rows of images of pages of printed matter

mi·cro·film \-₁film\ *n* : a film bearing a photographic record (as of print) on a reduced scale — **microfilm** *vb*

mi·cro·graph \'mī-krə-₁graf\ *n* : a graphic reproduction of the image of an object formed by a microscope

mi·cro·me·te·or·ite \₁mī-krō-'mē-tē-ə-₁rīt\ *n* : a very small particle in interplanetary space

mi·crom·e·ter \mī-'krä-mə-tər\ *n* : an instrument used with a telescope or microscope for measuring minute distances

mi·cro·min·ia·tur·iza·tion \₁mī-krō-₁mi-nē-ə-₁chùr-ə-'zā-shən, -₁mi-ni-₁chùr-, -chər-\ *n* : the process of producing things in a very small size and esp. in a size smaller than one considered miniature — **mi·cro·min·ia·tur·ized** \-'mi-nē-ə-chə-₁rīzd, -'mi-ni-chə-\ *adj*

mi·cron \'mī-₁krän\ *n,* : one millionth of a meter

mi·cro·or·gan·ism \₁mī-krō-'òr-gə-₁ni-zəm\ *n* : an organism (as a bacterium) too tiny to be seen by the unaided eye

mi·cro·phone \'mī-krə-₁fōn\ *n* : an instrument for converting sound waves into variations of an electric current for transmitting or recording sound

mi·cro·pho·to·graph \₁mī-krə-'fō-tə-₁graf\ *n* : PHOTOMICROGRAPH

mi·cro·pro·ces·sor \₁mī-krō-'prä-₁se-sər\ *n* : a computer processor contained on a microchip

mi·cro·scope \'mī-krə-₁skōp\ *n* : an instrument for making magnified images of minute objects usu. using light — **mi·cros·co·py** \mī-'kräs-kə-pē\ *n*

mi·cro·scop·ic \₁mī-krə-'skä-pik\ *also* **mi·cro·scop·i·cal** \-pi-kəl\ *adj* **1** : of, relating to, or involving the use of the microscope **2** : too tiny to be seen without the use of a microscope : very small — **mi·cro·scop·i·cal·ly** \-pi-k(ə-)lē\ *adv*

mi·cro·sec·ond \'mī-krō-₁se-kənd\ *n* : one millionth of a second

mi·cro·sur·gery \₁mī-krō-'sər-jə-rē\ *n* : minute dissection or manipulation (as by a laser beam) of living structures or tissue — **mi·cro·sur·gi·cal** \-'sər-ji-kəl\ *adj*

¹**mi·cro·wave** \'mī-krə-₁wāv\ *n* **1** : a radio wave between one millimeter and one meter in wavelength **2** : MICROWAVE OVEN

²**microwave** *vb* : to heat or cook in a microwave oven — **mi·cro·wav·able** *or* **mi·cro·wave·able** \₁mī-krə-'wā-və-bəl\ *adj*

microwave oven *n* : an oven in which food is cooked by the absorption of microwave energy by water molecules in the food

¹**mid** \'mid\ *adj* : MIDDLE

²**mid** *abbr* middle

mid·air \'mid-'ar\ *n* : a point or region in the air well above the ground

mid·day \'mid-₁dā, -'dā\ *n* : NOON

mid·den \'mid-ᵊn\ *n* : a refuse heap

¹**mid·dle** \'mid-ᵊl\ *adj* **1** : equally distant from the extremes : MEDIAL, CENTRAL **2** : being at neither extreme : INTERMEDIATE **3** *cap* : constituting an intermediate period

²**middle** *n* **1** : a middle part, point, or position **2** : WAIST

middle age *n* : the period of life from about 40 to about 60 — **mid·dle–aged** \₁mid-ᵊl-'ājd\ *adj*

Middle Ages *n pl* : the period of European history from about A.D. 500 to about 1500

mid·dle·brow \'mid-ᵊl-₁braú\ *n* : a person who is moderately but not highly cultivated — **middlebrow** *adj*

middle class *n* : a social class holding a position between the upper class and the lower class — **middle–class** *adj*

middle ear *n* : a small membrane-lined cavity of the ear through which sound waves are transmitted by a chain of tiny bones

middle finger *n* : the midmost of the five digits of the hand

mid·dle·man \'mid-ᵊl-₁man\ *n* : INTERMEDIARY; *esp* : one intermediate between the producer of goods and the retailer or consumer

middle–of–the–road *adj* : standing for or following a course of action midway between extremes; *esp* : being neither liberal nor conservative in politics — **mid·dle–of–the–road·er** \-'rō-dər\ *n* — **mid·dle–of–the–road·ism** \-'rō-₁di-zəm\ *n*

middle school *n* : a school usu. including grades 5 to 8 or 6 to 8

mid·dle·weight \'mid-ᵊl-₁wāt\ *n* : one of average weight; *esp* : a boxer weighing more than 147 but not over 160 pounds

mid·dling \'mid-liŋ, -lən\ *adj* **1** : of middle, medium, or moderate size, degree, or quality **2** : MEDIOCRE

mid·dy \'mi-dē\ *n, pl* **middies** : MIDSHIPMAN

midge \'mij\ *n* : a very small fly : GNAT

midg·et \'mi-jət\ *n* **1** : a very small person **2** : something (as an animal) very small for its kind

midi \'mi-dē\ *n* : a calf-length dress, coat, or skirt

\ə\abut \ᵊ\kitten \ər\further \a\ash \ā\ace \ä\mop, mar
\aú\out \ch\chin \e\bet \ē\easy \g\go \i\hit \ī\ice \j\job
\ŋ\sing \ō\go \ò\law \òi\boy \th\thin \th\the \ü\loot \ù\foot
\y\yet \zh\vision *see also* Pronunciation Symbols page

mid·land \'mid-lənd, -ˌland\ *n* : the interior or central region of a country

mid·life \'mid-ˈlīf\ *n* : MIDDLE AGE

midlife crisis *n* : a period of emotional turmoil in middle age characterized esp. by a strong desire for change

mid·most \-ˌmōst\ *adj* : being in or near the exact middle — **midmost** *adv*

mid·night \-ˌnīt\ *n* : 12 o'clock at night

mid·point \'mid-ˌpȯint, -ˈpȯint\ *n* : a point at or near the center or middle

mid·riff \'mi-ˌdrif\ *n* [ME *midrif*, fr. OE *midhrif*, fr. *midde* mid + *hrif* belly] **1** : DIAPHRAGM 1 **2** : the mid= region of the human torso

mid·sec·tion \-ˌsek-shən\ *n* : a section midway between the extremes; *esp* : MIDRIFF 2

mid·ship·man \'mid-ˌship-mən, (ˌ)mid-ˈship-\ *n* : a student in a naval academy

mid·ships \-ˌships\ *adv* : AMIDSHIPS

midst \'midst\ *n* **1** : the interior or central part or point **2** : a position of proximity to the members of a group ⟨in our ∼⟩ **3** : the condition of being surrounded or beset — **midst** *prep*

mid·stream \'mid-ˈstrēm, -ˌstrēm\ *n* : the middle of a stream

mid·sum·mer \-ˈsə-mər, -ˌsə-\ *n* **1** : the middle of summer **2** : the summer solstice

mid·town \'mid-ˌtaun, -ˈtaun\ *n* : a central section of a city; *esp* : one situated between sections called *downtown* and *uptown* — **midtown** *adj*

¹mid·way \'mid-ˌwā, -ˈwā\ *adv* : in the middle of the way or distance

²mid·way \-ˌwā\ *n* : an avenue (as at a carnival) for concessions and amusements

mid·week \-ˌwēk\ *n* : the middle of the week — **mid·week·ly** \-ˌwē-klē, -ˈwē-\ *adj or adv*

mid·wife \'mid-ˌwīf\ *n* : a person who helps women in childbirth — **mid·wife·ry** \-ˌwī-fə-rē\ *n*

mid·win·ter \'mid-ˈwin-tər, -ˌwin-\ *n* **1** : the winter solstice **2** : the middle of winter

mid·year \-ˌyir\ *n* **1** : the middle of a year **2** : a midyear examination — **midyear** *adj*

mien \'mēn\ *n* **1** : air or bearing esp. as expressive of mood or personality : DEMEANOR **2** : APPEARANCE, ASPECT

miff \'mif\ *vb* : to put into an ill humor

¹might \'mīt\ *past of* MAY — used as an auxiliary to express permission or possibility in the past, a present condition contrary to fact, less probability or possibility than *may*, or as a polite alternative to *may, ought*, or *should*

²might *n* : the power, authority, or resources of an individual or a group

mighty \'mī-tē\ *adj* **might·i·er; -est 1** : very strong : POWERFUL **2** : GREAT, NOTABLE — **might·i·ly** \'mī-tə-lē\ *adv* — **might·i·ness** \-tē-nəs\ *n* — **mighty** *adv*

mi·gnon·ette \ˌmin-yə-ˈnet\ *n* : an annual garden herb with spikes of tiny fragrant flowers

mi·graine \'mī-ˌgrān\ *n* [F, fr. LL *hemicrania* pain in one side of the head, fr. Gk *hēmikrania*, fr. *hēmi-* half + *kranion* cranium] : a condition marked by recurrent severe headache and often nausea; *also* : an attack of migraine

mi·grant \'mī-grənt\ *n* : one that migrates; *esp* : a person who moves in order to find work (as picking crops) — **migrant** *adj*

mi·grate \'mī-ˌgrāt\ *vb* **mi·grat·ed; mi·grat·ing 1** : to move from one country or place to another **2** : to pass usu. periodically from one region or climate to another for feeding or breeding — **mi·gra·tion** \mī-ˈgrā-shən\ *n* — **mi·gra·to·ry** \'mī-grə-ˌtōr-ē\ *adj*

mi·ka·do \mə-ˈkä-dō\ *n, pl* **-dos** : an emperor of Japan

mike \'mīk\ *n* : MICROPHONE

¹mil \'mil\ *n* : a unit of length equal to ¹⁄₁₀₀₀ inch

²mil *abbr* military

milch \'milk, ˈmilch\ *adj* : giving milk ⟨∼ cow⟩

mild \'mīld\ *adj* **1** : gentle in nature or behavior **2** : moderate in action or effect **3** : TEMPERATE **syn** easy, complaisant, amiable, lenient — **mild·ly** *adv* — **mild·ness** *n*

mil·dew \'mil-ˌdü, -ˌdyü\ *n* : a superficial usu. whitish growth produced on organic matter and on plants by a fungus; *also* : a fungus producing this growth — **mildew** *vb*

mile \'mīl\ *n* [ME, fr. OE *mīl*, fr. L *milia* miles, fr. *milia passuum*, lit., thousands of paces] **1** — see WEIGHT table **2** : NAUTICAL MILE

mile·age \'mī-lij\ *n* **1** : an allowance for traveling expenses at a certain rate per mile **2** : distance in miles traveled (as in a day) **3** : the amount of service yielded (as by a tire) expressed in terms of miles of travel **4** : the average number of miles a car will travel on a gallon of gasoline

mile·post \'mīl-ˌpōst\ *n* : a post indicating the distance in miles from a given point

mile·stone \-ˌstōn\ *n* **1** : a stone serving as a milepost **2** : a significant point in development

mi·lieu \mēl-ˈyər, -ˈyü, -ˈyœ̄\ *n, pl* **mi·lieus** *or* **mi·lieux** *same or* -ˈyərz, -ˈyüz, -ˈyœ̄z\ [F] : ENVIRONMENT, SETTING

mil·i·tant \'mi-lə-tənt\ *adj* **1** : engaged in warfare **2** : aggressively active esp. in a cause — **mil·i·tance** \-təns\ *n* — **mil·i·tan·cy** \-tən-sē\ *n* — **militant** *n* — **mil·i·tant·ly** *adv*

mil·i·ta·rism \'mi-lə-tə-ˌri-zəm\ *n* **1** : predominance of the military class or its ideals **2** : a policy of aggressive military preparedness — **mil·i·ta·rist** \-rist\ *n* — **mil·i·ta·ris·tic** \ˌmi-lə-tə-ˈris-tik\ *adj*

mil·i·ta·rize \'mi-lə-tə-ˌrīz\ *vb* **-rized; -riz·ing 1** : to equip with military forces and defenses **2** : to give a military character to

¹mil·i·tary \'mi-lə-ˌter-ē\ *adj* **1** : of or relating to soldiers, arms, war, or the army **2** : performed by armed forces; *also* : supported by armed force **syn** martial, warlike — **mil·i·tar·i·ly** \ˌmi-lə-ˈter-ə-lē\ *adv*

²military *n, pl* **military** *also* **mil·i·tar·ies 1** : the military, naval, and air forces of a nation **2** : military persons

mil·i·tate \'mi-lə-ˌtāt\ *vb* **-tat·ed; -tat·ing** : to have weight or effect

mi·li·tia \mə-ˈli-shə\ *n* : a part of the organized armed forces of a country liable to call only in emergency — **mi·li·tia·man** \-mən\ *n*

¹milk \'milk\ *n* **1** : a nutritive usu. whitish fluid secreted by female mammals for feeding their young **2** : a milklike liquid (as a plant juice) — **milk·i·ness** \'mil-kē-nəs\ *n* — **milky** *adj*

²milk *vb* **1** : to draw off the milk of ⟨∼ a cow⟩ **2** : to draw something from as if by milking

milk·maid \'milk-ˌmād\ *n* : DAIRYMAID

milk·man \-ˌman, -mən\ *n* : a person who sells or delivers milk

milk of magnesia : a milk-white mixture of hydroxide of magnesium and water used as an antacid and laxative

milk shake *n* : a thoroughly blended drink made of milk, a flavoring syrup, and often ice cream

milk·sop \'milk-ˌsäp\ *n* : an unmanly man

milk·weed \-ˌwēd\ *n* : any of a genus of herbs with milky juice and clustered flowers

Milky Way *n* **1** : a broad irregular band of light that stretches across the sky and is caused by the light of a very great number of faint stars **2** : MILKY WAY GALAXY

Milky Way galaxy *n* : the galaxy of which the sun is a member and which includes the stars that comprise the Milky Way

¹mill \'mil\ *n* **1** : a building with machinery for grinding grain into flour **2** : a machine used in processing (as by

grinding, stamping, cutting, or finishing) raw material **3** : FACTORY
²**mill** *vb* **1** : to process in a mill **2** : to move in a circle or in an eddying mass
³**mill** *n* : one tenth of a cent
mill·age \\'mi-lij\ *n* : a rate (as of taxation) expressed in mills
mil·len·ni·um \mə-'le-nē-əm\ *n, pl* **-nia** \-nē-ə\ *or* **-niums** **1** : a period of 1000 years; *also* : a 1000th anniversary or its celebration **2** : the 1000 years mentioned in Revelation 20 when holiness is to prevail and Christ is to reign on earth **3** : a period of great happiness or perfect government
mill·er \\'mi-lər\ *n* **1** : one that operates a mill and esp. a flour mill **2** : any of various moths having powdery wings
mil·let \\'mi-lət\ *n* : any of several small-seeded cereal and forage grasses cultivated for grain or hay; *also* : the grain of a millet
mil·li·am·pere \,mi-lē-'am-,pir\ *n* : one thousandth of an ampere
mil·liard \\'mil-,yärd, 'mi-lē-,ärd\ *n, Brit* : a thousand millions
mil·li·bar \\'mi-lə-,bär\ *n* : a unit of atmospheric pressure
mil·li·gram \-,gram\ *n* — see METRIC SYSTEM table
mil·li·li·ter \-,lē-tər\ *n* — see METRIC SYSTEM table
mil·lime \mə-'lēm\ *n* — see *dinar* at MONEY table
mil·li·me·ter \\'mi-lə-,mē-tər\ *n* — see METRIC SYSTEM table
mil·li·ner \\'mi-lə-nər\ *n* [irreg. fr. *Milan*, Italy; fr. the importation of women's finery from Italy in the 16th century] : a person who designs, makes, trims, or sells women's hats
mil·li·nery \\'mi-lə-,ner-ē\ *n* **1** : women's apparel for the head **2** : the business or work of a milliner
mill·ing \\'mi-liŋ\ *n* : a corrugated edge on a coin
mil·lion \\'mil-yən\ *n, pl* **millions** *or* **million** : a thousand thousands — **million** *adj* — **mil·lionth** \-yənth\ *adj or n*
mil·lion·aire \,mil-yə-'ner, 'mil-yə-,ner\ *n* : one whose wealth is estimated at a million or more (as of dollars or pounds)
mil·li·pede \\'mi-lə-,pēd\ *n* : any of a class of arthropods related to the centipedes and having a long segmented body with a hard covering, two pairs of legs on most segments, and no poison fangs
mil·li·sec·ond \-,se-kənd\ *n* : one thousandth of a second
mil·li·volt \-,vōlt\ *n* : one thousandth of a volt
mill·pond \\'mil-,pänd\ *n* : a pond made by damming a stream to produce a fall of water for operating a mill
mill·race \-,rās\ *n* : a canal in which water flows to and from a mill wheel
mill·stone \-,stōn\ *n* : either of two round flat stones used for grinding grain
mill·stream \-,strēm\ *n* : a stream whose flow is used to run a mill; *also* : the stream in a millrace
mill wheel *n* : a waterwheel that drives a mill
mill·wright \\'mil-,rīt\ *n* : a person who builds mills or sets up or maintains their machinery
milt \\'milt\ *n* : the sperm-containing fluid of a male fish
mime \\'mīm\ *n* **1** : MIMIC **2** : PANTOMIME — **mime** *vb*
mim·eo·graph \\'mi-mē-ə-,graf\ *n* : a machine for making many copies by means of a stencil through which ink is pressed — **mimeograph** *vb*
mi·me·sis \mə-'mē-səs, mī-\ *n* : IMITATION, MIMICRY
mi·met·ic \-'me-tik\ *adj* **1** : IMITATIVE **2** : relating to, characterized by, or exhibiting mimicry
¹**mim·ic** \\'mi-mik\ *n* : one that mimics
²**mimic** *vb* **mim·icked** \-mikt\; **mim·ick·ing** **1** : to imitate closely **2** : to ridicule by imitation **3** : to resemble by biological mimicry
mim·ic·ry \\'mi-mi-krē\ *n, pl* **-ries** **1** : an instance of mim-

icking **2** : a superficial resemblance of one organism to another or to natural objects among which it lives that gives it an advantage (as protection from predation)
mi·mo·sa \mə-'mō-sə, mī-, -zə\ *n* : any of a genus of leguminous trees, shrubs, and herbs of warm regions with ball-shaped heads of small white or pink flowers
min *abbr* **1** minim **2** minimum **3** mining **4** minister **5** minor **6** minute
min·a·ret \,mi-nə-'ret\ *n* [F, fr. Turk *minare*, fr. Ar *manārah* lighthouse] : a tall slender tower of a mosque from which a muezzin calls the faithful to prayer

1 minaret

mi·na·to·ry \\'mi-nə-,tōr-ē, 'mī-\ *adj* : THREATENING, MENACING
mince \\'mins\ *vb* **minced**; **minc·ing** **1** : to cut into very small pieces **2** : to restrain (words) within the bounds of decorum **3** : to walk in a prim affected manner
mince·meat \\'mins-,mēt\ *n* : a finely chopped mixture esp. of raisins, apples, spices, and often meat used as a filling for a pie
¹**mind** \\'mīnd\ *n* **1** : MEMORY **2** : the part of an individual that feels, perceives, thinks, wills, and esp. reasons **3** : INTENTION, DESIRE **4** : normal mental condition **5** : OPINION, VIEW **6** : MOOD **7** : mental qualities of a person or group **8** : intellectual ability
²**mind** *vb* **1** *chiefly dial* : REMEMBER **2** : to attend to closely **3** : HEED, OBEY **4** : to be concerned about; *also* : DISLIKE **5** : to be careful or cautious **6** : to take charge of **7** : to regard with attention
mind–bend·ing \\'mīnd-,ben-diŋ\ *adj* : MIND-BLOWING
mind–blow·ing \-,blō-iŋ\ *adj* : PSYCHEDELIC 1; *also* : MIND-BOGGLING
mind–bog·gling \-,bä-gə-liŋ\ *adj* : mentally or emotionally exciting or overwhelming
mind·ed \\'mīn-dəd\ *adj* **1** : INCLINED, DISPOSED **2** : having a mind of a specified kind or concerned with a specific thing — usu. used in combination ⟨narrow-*minded*⟩
mind·ful \\'mīnd-fəl\ *adj* : bearing in mind : AWARE — **mind·ful·ly** *adv* — **mind·ful·ness** *n*
mind·less \-ləs\ *adj* **1** : marked by a lack of mind or consciousness; *esp* : marked by no use of the intellect **2** : not mindful : HEEDLESS — **mind·less·ly** *adv* — **mind·less·ness** *n*
¹**mine** \\'mīn\ *pron* : that which belongs to me
²**mine** *n* **1** : an excavation in the earth from which minerals are taken; *also* : an ore deposit **2** : an underground passage beneath an enemy position **3** : an explosive device for destroying enemy personnel, vehicles, or ships **4** : a rich source of supply

---

\ə\abut \ᵊ\kitten \ər\further \a\ash \ā\ace \ä\mop, mar
\au̇\out \ch\chin \e\bet \ē\easy \g\go \i\hit \ī\ice \j\job
\ŋ\sing \ō\go \ȯ\law \ȯi\boy \th\thin \t̲h̲\the \ü\loot \u̇\foot
\y\yet \zh\vision *see also* Pronunciation Symbols page

³**mine** *vb* **mined; min·ing 1 :** to dig a mine **2 :** UNDERMINE **3 :** to get ore from the earth **4 :** to place military mines in — **min·er** *n*

mine·field \'mīn-ˌfēld\ *n* **1 :** an area set with mines **2 :** something resembling a minefield esp. in having many dangers

mine·lay·er \-ˌlā-ər\ *n* **:** a naval vessel for laying underwater mines

min·er·al \'mi-nə-rəl\ *n* **1 :** a crystalline substance (as diamond or quartz) of inorganic origin **2 :** a naturally occurring substance (as coal, salt, or water) obtained usu. from the ground — **mineral** *adj*

min·er·al·ize \'mi-nə-rə-ˌlīz\ *vb* **-ized; -iz·ing 1 :** to impregnate or supply with minerals **2 :** to change into mineral form — **min·er·al·i·za·tion** \-rə-lə-'zā-shən\ *n*

min·er·al·o·gy \ˌmi-nə-'rä-lə-jē, -'ra-\ *n* **:** a science dealing with minerals — **min·er·al·og·i·cal** \ˌmi-nə-rə-'lä-ji-kəl\ *adj* — **min·er·al·o·gist** \ˌmi-nə-'rä-lə-jist, -'ra-\ *n*

mineral oil *n* **:** an oil of mineral origin; *esp* **:** a refined petroleum oil used as a laxative

mineral water *n* **:** water infused with mineral salts or gases

min·e·stro·ne \ˌmi-nə-'strō-nē, -'strōn\ *n* [It, fr. *minestra,* fr. *minestrare* to serve, dish up, fr. L *ministrare,* fr. *minister* servant] **:** a rich thick vegetable soup

mine·sweep·er \'mīn-ˌswē-pər\ *n* **:** a warship designed for removing or neutralizing underwater mines

min·gle \'miŋ-gəl\ *vb* **min·gled; min·gling 1 :** to bring or combine together **:** MIX **2 :** ASSOCIATE; *also* **:** to move about (as in a group)

ming tree \'miŋ-\ *n* **:** a dwarfed usu. evergreen tree grown as bonsai; *also* **:** an artificial plant resembling this

mini \'mi-nē\ *n, pl* **min·is :** something small of its kind — **mini** *adj*

mini- *comb form* **:** smaller or briefer than usual, normal, or standard

min·ia·ture \'mi-nē-ə-ˌchur, 'mi-ni-ˌchur, -chər\ *n* [It *miniatura* art of illuminating a manuscript, fr. ML, fr. L *miniare* to color with red lead, fr. *minium* red lead] **1 :** a copy on a much reduced scale; *also* **:** something small of its kind **2 :** a small painting (as on ivory or metal) — **miniature** *adj* — **min·ia·tur·ist** \-ˌchur-ist, -chər-\ *n*

min·ia·tur·ize \'mi-nē-ə-ˌchə-ˌrīz, 'mi-ni-\ *vb* **-ized; -iz·ing :** to design or construct in small size — **min·ia·tur·i·za·tion** \ˌmi-nē-ə-ˌchur-ə-'zā-shən, ˌmi-ni-, -chər-\ *n*

mini·bike \'mi-nē-ˌbīk\ *n* **:** a small one-passenger motorcycle

mini·bus \-ˌbəs\ *n* **:** a small bus or van

mini·com·put·er \-kəm-ˌpyü-tər\ *n* **:** a computer between a mainframe and a microcomputer in size and speed

min·im \'mi-nəm\ *n* — see WEIGHT table

min·i·mal \'mi-nə-məl\ *adj* **1 :** relating to or being a minimum **:** LEAST **2 :** of or relating to minimalism or minimal art — **min·i·mal·ly** *adv*

minimal art *n* **:** abstract art consisting primarily of simple geometric forms executed in an impersonal style — **minimal artist** *n*

min·i·mal·ism \'mi-nə-mə-ˌli-zəm\ *n* **:** MINIMAL ART; *also* **:** a style (as in music or literature) marked by extreme spareness or simplicity — **min·i·mal·ist** \-list\ *n*

min·i·mize \'mi-nə-ˌmīz\ *vb* **-mized; -miz·ing 1 :** to reduce or keep to a minimum **2 :** to underestimate intentionally; *also* **:** BELITTLE **syn** depreciate, decry, disparage

min·i·mum \'mi-nə-məm\ *n, pl* **-ma** \-mə\ *or* **-mums 1 :** the least quantity assignable, admissible, or possible **2 :** the least of a set of numbers **3 :** the lowest degree or amount of variation (as of temperature) reached or recorded — **minimum** *adj*

min·ion \'min-yən\ *n* [MF *mignon* darling] **1 :** a servile dependent, follower, or underling **2 :** one highly favored **3 :** a subordinate official

min·is·cule \'mi-nəs-ˌkyül\ *var of* MINUSCULE

mini·se·ries \'mi-nē-ˌsir-ēz\ *n* **:** a television story presented in sequential episodes

mini·skirt \-ˌskərt\ *n* **:** a skirt with the hemline several inches above the knee

¹**min·is·ter** \'mi-nə-stər\ *n* **1 :** AGENT **2 :** a member of the clergy esp. of a Protestant communion **3 :** a high officer of state who heads a division of governmental activities **4 :** a diplomatic representative to a foreign state — **min·is·te·ri·al** \ˌmi-nə-'stir-ē-əl\ *adj*

²**minister** *vb* **1 :** to perform the functions of a minister of religion **2 :** to give aid or service — **min·is·tra·tion** \ˌmi-nə-'strā-shən\ *n*

¹**min·is·trant** \'mi-nə-strənt\ *adj, archaic* **:** performing service as a minister

²**ministrant** *n* **:** one that ministers

min·is·try \'mi-nə-strē\ *n, pl* **-tries 1 :** MINISTRATION **2 :** the office, duties, or functions of a minister; *also* **:** the period of service or office **3 :** CLERGY **4 :** AGENCY **5** *often cap* **:** the body of ministers governing a nation or state; *also* **:** a government department headed by a minister

mini·van \'mi-nē-ˌvan\ *n* **:** a small van

mink \'miŋk\ *n, pl* **mink** *or* **minks :** either of two slender mammals resembling the related weasels; *also* **:** the soft lustrous typically dark brown fur of a mink

mink

Minn *abbr* Minnesota

min·ne·sing·er \'mi-ni-ˌsiŋ-ər, -ˌziŋ-\ *n* [G, fr. Middle High German, fr. *minne* love + *singer* singer] **:** any of a class of German lyric poets and musicians of the 12th to the 14th centuries

min·now \'mi-nō\ *n, pl* **minnows** *also* **minnow :** any of numerous small freshwater fishes

¹**mi·nor** \'mī-nər\ *adj* **1 :** inferior in importance, size, or degree **2 :** not having reached majority **3 :** having the third, sixth, and sometimes the seventh degrees lowered by a half step ⟨∼ scale⟩; *also* **:** based on a minor scale ⟨∼ key⟩ **4 :** not serious ⟨∼ illness⟩

²**minor** *n* **1 :** a person who has not attained majority **2 :** a subject of academic study chosen as a secondary field of specialization

³**minor** *vb* **:** to pursue an academic minor

mi·nor·i·ty \mə-'nȯr-ə-tē, mī-\ *n, pl* **-ties 1 :** the period or state of being a minor **2 :** the smaller in number of two groups; *esp* **:** a group having less than the number of votes necessary for control **3 :** a part of a population differing from others (as in race); *also* **:** a member of a minority

mi·nox·i·dil \mə-'näk-sə-ˌdil\ *n* **:** a drug used orally to treat hypertension and topically in solution to promote hair regrowth in some forms of baldness

min·ster \'min-stər\ *n* **:** a large or important church

min·strel \'min-strəl\ *n* **1 :** a medieval singer of verses; *also* **:** MUSICIAN, POET **2 :** any of a group of performers usu. with blackened faces in a program of black American songs, jokes, and impersonations ⟨a ∼ show⟩

min·strel·sy \-sē\ *n* **:** the singing and playing of a minstrel; *also* **:** a body of minstrels

¹**mint** \'mint\ *n* **1** : any of a large family of square=stemmed herbs and shrubs; *esp* : one (as spearmint) that is fragrant and is the source of a flavoring oil **2** : a mint-flavored piece of candy — **minty** *adj*

²**mint** *n* **1** : a place where coins are made **2** : a vast sum — **mint** *vb* — **mint·age** \-ij\ *n* — **mint·er** *n*

³**mint** *adj* : unmarred as if fresh from a mint ⟨in ~ condition⟩

min·u·end \'min-yə-ˌwend\ *n* : a number from which another is to be subtracted

min·u·et \ˌmin-yə-'wet\ *n* : a slow graceful dance

¹**mi·nus** \'mī-nəs\ *prep* **1** : diminished by : LESS ⟨7 ~ 3 equals 4⟩ **2** : LACKING, WITHOUT ⟨~ his hat⟩

²**minus** *n* : a negative quantity or quality

³**minus** *adj* **1** : algebraically negative ⟨~ quantity⟩ **2** : having negative qualities

¹**mi·nus·cule** \'mi-nəs-ˌkyül\ *n* : a lowercase letter

²**minuscule** *adj* : very small

minus sign *n* : a sign – used in mathematics to indicate subtraction or a negative quantity

¹**min·ute** \'mi-nət\ *n* **1** : a 60th part of an hour or of a degree : 60 seconds **2** : a short space of time **3** *pl* : the official record of the proceedings of a meeting

²**mi·nute** \mī-'nüt, mə-, -'nyüt\ *adj* **mi·nut·er; -est 1** : very small **2** : of little importance : TRIFLING **3** : marked by close attention to details **syn** diminutive, tiny, miniature, wee — **mi·nute·ly** *adv* — **mi·nute·ness** *n*

min·ute·man \'mi-nət-ˌman\ *n* : a member of a group of armed men pledged to take the field at a minute's notice during and immediately before the American Revolution

mi·nu·tia \mə-'nü-shə, -'nyü-, -shē-ə\ *n, pl* **-ti·ae** \-shē-ˌē\ [L] : a minute or minor detail — usu. used in pl.

minx \'miŋks\ *n* : a pert girl

Mio·cene \'mī-ə-ˌsēn\ *adj* : of, relating to, or being the epoch of the Tertiary between the Oligocene and the Pliocene — **Miocene** *n*

mir·a·cle \'mir-i-kəl\ *n* **1** : an extraordinary event manifesting divine intervention in human affairs **2** : an unusual event, thing, or accomplishment : WONDER, MARVEL — **mi·rac·u·lous** \mə-'ra-kyə-ləs\ *adj* — **mi·rac·u·lous·ly** *adv*

miracle drug *n* : a usu. newly discovered drug that elicits a dramatic response in a patient's condition

mi·rage \mə-'räzh\ *n* **1** : an illusion that often appears as a pool of water or a mirror in which distant objects are seen inverted, is sometimes seen at sea, in the desert, or over a hot pavement, and results from atmospheric conditions **2** : something illusory and unattainable

¹**mire** \'mīr\ *n* : heavy and often deep mud or slush — **miry** *adj*

²**mire** *vb* **mired; mir·ing** : to stick or sink in or as if in mire

¹**mir·ror** \'mir-ər\ *n* **1** : a polished or smooth surface (as of glass) that forms images by reflection **2** : a true representation

²**mirror** *vb* : to reflect in or as if in a mirror

mirth \'mərth\ *n* : gladness or gaiety accompanied with laughter **syn** glee, jollity, hilarity, merriment — **mirth·ful** \-fəl\ *adj* — **mirth·ful·ly** *adv* — **mirth·ful·ness** *n* — **mirth·less** *adj*

MIRV \'mərv\ *n* [multiple independently targeted reentry vehicle] : an ICBM with multiple warheads that have different targets — **MIRV** *vb*

mis·ad·ven·ture \ˌmi-səd-'ven-chər\ *n* : MISFORTUNE, MISHAP

mis·aligned \ˌmi-sə-'līnd\ *adj* : not properly aligned — **mis·align·ment** \-'līn-mənt\ *n*

mis·al·li·ance \ˌmi-sə-'lī-əns\ *n* : an improper or unsuitable marriage

mis·al·lo·ca·tion \ˌmi-ˌsa-lə-'kā-shən\ *n* : faulty or improper allocation

mis·an·thrope \'mis-ᵊn-ˌthrōp\ *n* : one who hates mankind — **mis·an·throp·ic** \ˌmis-ᵊn-'thrä-pik\ *adj* — **mis·an·throp·i·cal·ly** \-pi-k(ə-)lē\ *adv* — **mis·an·thro·py** \mi-'san-thrə-pē\ *n*

mis·ap·ply \ˌmi-sə-'plī\ *vb* : to apply wrongly — **mis·ap·pli·ca·tion** \ˌmi-ˌsa-plə-'kā-shən\ *n*

mis·ap·pre·hend \ˌmi-ˌsa-pri-'hend\ *vb* : MISUNDERSTAND — **mis·ap·pre·hen·sion** \-'hen-chən\ *n*

mis·ap·pro·pri·ate \ˌmi-sə-'prō-prē-ˌāt\ *vb* : to appropriate wrongly (as by embezzlement) — **mis·ap·pro·pri·a·tion** \-ˌprō-prē-'ā-shən\ *n*

mis·be·got·ten \-bi-'gät-ᵊn\ *adj* : ILLEGITIMATE; *also* : ill-conceived

mis·be·have \ˌmis-bi-'hāv\ *vb* : to behave improperly — **mis·be·hav·er** *n* — **mis·be·hav·ior** \-'hā-vyər\ *n*

mis·be·liev·er \ˌmis-bə-'lē-vər\ *n* : one who holds a false or unorthodox belief

mis·brand \mis-'brand\ *vb* : to brand falsely or in a misleading manner

misc *abbr* miscellaneous

mis·cal·cu·late \mis-'kal-kyə-ˌlāt\ *vb* : to calculate wrongly — **mis·cal·cu·la·tion** \ˌmis-ˌkal-kyə-'lā-shən\ *n*

mis·call \mis-'kȯl\ *vb* : MISNAME

mis·car·riage \-'kar-ij\ *n* **1** : failure in the administration of justice **2** : spontaneous expulsion of a fetus before it is capable of independent life

mis·car·ry \-'kar-ē\ *vb* **1** : to have a miscarriage of a fetus **2** : to go wrong; *also* : to be unsuccessful

mis·ce·ge·na·tion \ˌmi-se-jə-'nā-shən, ˌmi-si-jə-'nā-\ *n* [L *miscēre* to mix + *genus* race] : marriage or cohabitation between persons of different races

mis·cel·la·neous \ˌmi-sə-'lā-nē-əs\ *adj* **1** : consisting of diverse things or members **2** : having various traits; *also* : dealing with or interested in diverse subjects — **mis·cel·la·neous·ly** *adv* — **mis·cel·la·neous·ness** *n*

mis·cel·la·ny \'mi-sə-ˌlā-nē\ *n, pl* **-nies 1** : a collection of writings on various subjects **2** : HODGEPODGE

mis·chance \mis-'chans\ *n* : bad luck; *also* : MISHAP

mis·chief \'mis-chəf\ *n* **1** : injury caused by a particular agent **2** : a source of harm or irritation **3** : action that annoys; *also* : MISCHIEVOUSNESS

mis·chie·vous \'mis-chə-vəs\ *adj* **1** : HARMFUL, INJURIOUS **2** : causing annoyance or minor injury **3** : irresponsibly playful — **mis·chie·vous·ly** *adv* — **mis·chie·vous·ness** *n*

mis·ci·ble \'mi-sə-bəl\ *adj* : capable of being mixed

mis·com·mu·ni·ca·tion \ˌmis-kə-ˌmyü-nə-'ka-shən\ *n* : failure to communicate clearly

mis·con·ceive \ˌmis-kən-'sēv\ *vb* : to interpret incorrectly — **mis·con·cep·tion** \-'sep-shən\ *n*

mis·con·duct \mis-'kän-(ˌ)dəkt\ *n* **1** : MISMANAGEMENT **2** : intentional wrongdoing **3** : improper behavior

mis·con·strue \ˌmis-kən-'strü\ *vb* : MISINTERPRET — **mis·con·struc·tion** \-'strək-shən\ *n*

mis·count \mis-'kaȯnt\ *vb* : to count incorrectly : MISCALCULATE

mis·cre·ant \'mis-krē-ənt\ *n* : one who behaves criminally or viciously — **miscreant** *adj*

mis·cue \mis-'kyü\ *n* : MISTAKE, ERROR — **miscue** *vb*

mis·deed \mis-'dēd\ *n* : a wrong deed

mis·de·mean·or \ˌmis-di-'mē-nər\ *n* **1** : a crime less serious than a felony **2** : MISDEED

mis·di·rect \ˌmis-də-'rekt, -dī-\ *vb* : to give a wrong direction to — **mis·di·rec·tion** \-'rek-shən\ *n*

mis·do·ing \mis-'dü-iŋ\ *n* : WRONGDOING — **mis·do** \-'dü\ *vb* — **mis·do·er** \-'dü-ər\ *n*

mise–en–scène \ˌmē-ˌzäⁿ-'sen, -'säⁿ\ *n, pl* **mise–en–**

scènes \same or -ˈsenz, -ˈsänz\ [F] **1** : the arrangement of the scenery, property, and actors on a stage **2** : SET-TING; also : ENVIRONMENT

mi·ser \ˈmī-zər\ n [L miser miserable] : a person who hoards and is stingy with money — **mi·ser·li·ness** \-lē-nəs\ n — **mi·ser·ly** adj

mis·er·a·ble \ˈmi-zə-rə-bəl, ˈmiz-rə-\ adj **1** : wretchedly deficient; also : causing extreme discomfort **2** : being in a state of distress **3** : SHAMEFUL — **mis·er·a·ble·ness** n — **mis·er·a·bly** \-blē\ adv

mis·ery \ˈmi-zə-rē\ n, pl **-er·ies 1** : suffering and want caused by poverty or affliction **2** : a cause of suffering or discomfort **3** : emotional distress

mis·fea·sance \mis-ˈfēz-ᵊns\ n : the performance of a lawful action in an illegal or improper manner

mis·file \-ˈfīl\ vb : to file in the wrong place

mis·fire \-ˈfīr\ vb **1** : to fail to fire **2** : to miss an intended effect — **misfire** n

mis·fit \ˈmis-ˌfit, sense 1 also mis-ˈfit\ n **1** : something that fits badly **2** : one who is poorly adjusted to a situation or environment

mis·for·tune \mis-ˈfȯr-chən\ n **1** : bad luck **2** : an unfortunate condition or event

mis·giv·ing \-ˈgi-viŋ\ n : a feeling of doubt or suspicion esp. concerning a future event

mis·gov·ern \-ˈgə-vərn\ vb : to govern badly — **mis·gov·ern·ment** n

mis·guid·ance \mis-ˈgīd-ᵊns\ n : faulty guidance — **mis·guide** \-ˈgīd\ vb

mis·guid·ed \-ˈgī-dəd\ adj : led or prompted by wrong or inappropriate motives or ideals — **mis·guid·ed·ly** adv

mis·han·dle \-ˈhand-ᵊl\ vb **1** : MALTREAT **2** : to manage wrongly

mis·hap \ˈmis-ˌhap\ n : an unfortunate accident

mish·mash \ˈmish-ˌmash, -ˌmäsh\ n : HODGEPODGE, JUMBLE

mis·in·form \ˌmis-ᵊn-ˈfȯrm\ vb : to give false or misleading information to — **mis·in·for·ma·tion** \ˌmi-ˌsin-fər-ˈmā-shən\ n

mis·in·ter·pret \ˌmis-ᵊn-ˈtər-prət\ vb : to understand or explain wrongly — **mis·in·ter·pre·ta·tion** \-ˌtər-prə-ˈtā- shən\ n

mis·judge \mis-ˈjəj\ vb **1** : to estimate wrongly **2** : to have an unjust opinion of — **mis·judg·ment** \mis-ˈjəj-mənt\ n

mis·la·bel \-ˈlā-bəl\ vb : to label incorrectly or falsely

mis·lay \mis-ˈlā\ vb **-laid** \-ˈlād\; **-lay·ing** : MISPLACE, LOSE

mis·lead \mis-ˈlēd\ vb **-led** \-ˈled\; **-lead·ing** : to lead in a wrong direction or into a mistaken action or belief — **mis·lead·ing·ly** adv

mis·like \-ˈlīk\ vb : DISLIKE — **mis·like** n

mis·man·age \-ˈma-nij\ vb : to manage badly — **mis·man·age·ment** n

mis·match \-ˈmach\ vb : to match unsuitably or badly — **mis·match** \mis-ˈmach, ˈmis-ˌmach\ n

mis·name \-ˈnām\ vb : to name incorrectly : MISCALL

mis·no·mer \mis-ˈnō-mər\ n : a wrong name or designation

mi·sog·y·ny \mə-ˈsä-jə-nē\ n [Gk misogynia, fr. misein to hate + gynē woman] : a hatred of women — **mi·sog·y·nist** \-nist\ n or adj — **mi·sog·y·nis·tic** \mə-ˌsä-jə-ˈnis-tik\ adj

mis·ori·ent \mi-ˈsȯr-ē-ˌent\ vb : to orient improperly or incorrectly — **mis·ori·en·ta·tion** \mi-ˌsȯr-ē-ən-ˈtā-shən\ n

mis·place \mis-ˈplās\ vb **1** : to put in a wrong or unremembered place **2** : to set on a wrong object ⟨∼ trust⟩

mis·play \-ˈplā\ n : a wrong or unskillful play — **mis·play** \mis-ˈplā, ˈmis-ˌplā\ vb

mis·print \ˈmis-ˌprint\ n : a mistake in printed matter — **mis·print** \mis-ˈprint\ vb

mis·pro·nounce \ˌmis-prə-ˈnaüns\ vb : to pronounce in-

correctly — **mis·pro·nun·ci·a·tion** \-prə-ˌnən-sē-ˈā-shən\ n

mis·quote \mis-ˈkwōt\ vb : to quote incorrectly — **mis·quo·ta·tion** \ˌmis-kwō-ˈtā-shən\ n

mis·read \-ˈrēd\ vb **-read** \-ˈred\; **-read·ing** \-ˈrē-diŋ\ : to read or interpret incorrectly

mis·rep·re·sent \ˌmis-ˌre-pri-ˈzent\ vb : to represent falsely or unfairly — **mis·rep·re·sen·ta·tion** \-ˌzen-ˈtā-shən\ n

¹mis·rule \mis-ˈrül\ vb : MISGOVERN

²misrule n **1** : MISGOVERNMENT **2** : DISORDER

¹miss \ˈmis\ vb **1** : to fail to hit, reach, or contact **2** : to feel the absence of **3** : to fail to obtain **4** : AVOID ⟨just ∼ed hitting the other car⟩ **5** : OMIT **6** : to fail to understand **7** : to fail to perform or attend; also : MISFIRE

²miss n **1** : a failure to hit or to attain a result **2** : MISFIRE

³miss n **1** cap — used as a title prefixed to the name of an unmarried woman or girl **2** : a young unmarried woman or girl

Miss abbr Mississippi

mis·sal \ˈmi-səl\ n : a book containing all that is said or sung at mass during the entire year

mis·send \mis-ˈsend\ vb : to send incorrectly ⟨missent mail⟩

mis·shap·en \-ˈshā-pən\ adj : badly shaped : having an ugly shape

mis·sile \ˈmi-səl\ n [L, fr. neut. of missilis capable of being thrown, fr. mittere to let go, send] : an object (as a stone, bullet, or rocket) thrown or projected usu. so as to strike a target

miss·ing \ˈmi-siŋ\ adj : ABSENT; also : LOST ⟨∼ in action⟩

mis·sion \ˈmi-shən\ n **1** : a group of missionaries; also : a place where missionaries work **2** : a group of envoys to a foreign country; also : a team of specialists or cultural leaders sent to a foreign country **3** : TASK

¹mis·sion·ary \ˈmi-shə-ˌner-ē\ adj : of, relating to, or engaged in missions

²missionary n, pl **-ar·ies** : a person commissioned by a church to spread its faith or carry on humanitarian work

mis·sion·er \ˈmi-shə-nər\ n : MISSIONARY

Mis·sis·sip·pi·an \ˌmi-sə-ˈsi-pē-ən\ adj : of, relating to, or being the period of the Paleozoic era between the Devonian and the Pennsylvanian — **Mississippian** n

mis·sive \ˈmi-siv\ n : LETTER

mis·speak \mis-ˈspēk\ vb : to say imperfectly or incorrectly

mis·spell \-ˈspel\ vb : to spell incorrectly — **mis·spell·ing** n

mis·spend \-ˈspend\ vb **-spent** \-ˈspent\; **-spend·ing** : WASTE, SQUANDER ⟨my misspent youth⟩

mis·state \mis-ˈstāt\ vb : to state incorrectly — **mis·state·ment** n

mis·step \-ˈstep\ n **1** : a wrong step **2** : MISTAKE, BLUNDER

mist \ˈmist\ n **1** : water in the form of particles suspended or falling in the air **2** : something that obscures understanding — **mist** vb

mis·tak·able \mə-ˈstā-kə-bəl\ adj : capable of being misunderstood or mistaken

¹mis·take \mi-ˈstāk\ vb **-took** \-ˈstùk\; **-tak·en** \-ˈstā-kən\; **-tak·ing 1** : to blunder in the choice of **2** : MISINTERPRET **3** : to make a wrong judgment of the character or ability of **4** : to confuse with another — **mis·tak·en·ly** adv — **mis·tak·er** n

²mistake n **1** : a wrong judgment : MISUNDERSTANDING **2** : a wrong action or statement : ERROR

¹mis·ter \ˈmis-tər\ n **1** cap — used sometimes instead of Mr. **2** : SIR — used without a name in addressing a man

²mister \ˈmis-tər\ n : a device for spraying mist

mis·tle·toe \ˈmi-səl-ˌtō\ n : a European parasitic green shrub with yellowish flowers and waxy white berries that grows on trees

mis·tral \'mis-trəl, mi-'sträl\ *n* [F, fr. Provençal, fr. *mistral* masterful, fr. LL *magistralis* of a teacher, fr. L *magister* master] : a strong cold dry northerly wind of southern France

mis·treat \mis-'trēt\ *vb* : to treat badly : ABUSE — **mis·treat·ment** *n*

mis·tress \'mis-trəs\ *n* 1 : a woman who has power, authority, or ownership ⟨∼ of the house⟩ 2 : something personified as female that rules or dominates ⟨when Rome was ∼ of the world⟩ 3 : a woman other than his wife with whom a married man has sexual relations; *also, archaic* : SWEETHEART 4 — used archaically as a title prefixed to the name of a married or unmarried woman

mis·tri·al \'mis-ˌtrīl\ *n* : a trial that has no legal effect

¹**mis·trust** \mis-'trəst\ *n* : a lack of confidence : DISTRUST — **mis·trust·ful** \-fəl\ *adj* — **mis·trust·ful·ly** *adv* — **mis·trust·ful·ness** *n*

²**mistrust** *vb* : to have no trust or confidence in : SUSPECT

misty \'mis-tē\ *adj* **mist·i·er; -est** 1 : obscured by or as if by mist : INDISTINCT 2 : TEARFUL — **mist·i·ly** \-tə-lē\ *adv* — **mist·i·ness** \-tē-nəs\ *n*

mis·un·der·stand \ˌmi-sən-dər-'stand\ *vb* **-stood** \-'stüd\; **-stand·ing** 1 : to fail to understand 2 : to interpret incorrectly

mis·un·der·stand·ing \-'stan-diŋ\ *n* 1 : MISINTERPRETATION 2 : DISAGREEMENT, QUARREL

mis·us·age \mis-'yü-sij\ *n* 1 : bad treatment : ABUSE 2 : wrong or improper use

mis·use \mis-'yüz\ *vb* 1 : to use incorrectly 2 : ABUSE, MISTREAT — **mis·use** \-'yüs\ *n*

mite \'mīt\ *n* 1 : any of numerous tiny arthropod animals related to the spiders that often live and feed on animals or plants 2 : a small coin or sum of money 3 : a small amount : BIT

¹**mi·ter** *or* **mi·tre** \'mī-tər\ *n* [ME *mitre*, fr. MF, fr. L *mitra* headband, turban, fr. Gk] 1 : a headdress worn by bishops and abbots 2 : MITER JOINT

²**miter** *or* **mitre** *vb* **mi·tered** *or* **mi·tred; mi·ter·ing** *or* **mi·tring** \'mī-tə-riŋ\ 1 : to match or fit together in a miter joint 2 : to bevel the ends of for making a miter joint

miter joint *n* : a joint made by fitting together two parts with the ends cut at an angle

mit·i·gate \'mi-tə-ˌgāt\ *vb* **-gat·ed; -gat·ing** 1 : to make less harsh or hostile 2 : to make less severe or painful — **mit·i·ga·tion** \ˌmi-tə-'gā-shən\ *n* — **mit·i·ga·tive** \'mi-tə-ˌgā-tiv\ *adj*

mi·to·sis \mī-'tō-səs\ *n, pl* **-to·ses** \-ˌsēz\ : a process that takes place in the nucleus of a dividing cell and results in the formation of two new nuclei each of which has the same number of chromosomes as the parent nucleus; *also* : cell division in which mitosis occurs — **mi·tot·ic** \-'tä-tik\ *adj*

mitt \'mit\ *n* 1 : a baseball catcher's or first baseman's glove 2 *slang* : HAND

mit·ten \'mit-ᵊn\ *n* : a covering for the hand having a separate section for the thumb only

¹**mix** \'miks\ *vb* 1 : to combine into one mass 2 : ASSOCIATE 3 : to form by mingling components 4 : to produce (a recording) by electronically combining sounds from different sources 5 : HYBRIDIZE 6 : CONFUSE ⟨∼es up the facts⟩ 7 : to become involved **syn** blend, merge, coalesce, amalgamate, fuse — **mix·able** *adj* — **mix·er** *n*

²**mix** *n* : a product of mixing; *esp* : a commercially prepared mixture of food ingredients

mixed number *n* : a number (as 5⅔) composed of an integer and a fraction

mixed–up \'mikst-'əp\ *adj* : CONFUSED

mixt *abbr* mixture

mix·ture \'miks-chər\ *n* 1 : the act or process of mixing; *also* : the state of being mixed 2 : a product of mixing

mix–up \'miks-ˌəp\ *n* 1 : an instance of confusion 2 : CONFLICT, FIGHT

miz·zen *also* **miz·en** \'miz-ᵊn\ *n* 1 : a fore-and-aft sail set on the mizzenmast 2 : MIZZENMAST — **mizzen** *also* **mizen** *adj*

miz·zen·mast \-ˌmast, -məst\ *n* : the mast aft or next aft of the mainmast

mk *abbr* 1 mark 2 markka

Mk *abbr* Mark

mks *abbr* meter-kilogram-second

mkt *abbr* market

mktg *abbr* marketing

ml *abbr* milliliter

Mlle *abbr* [F] mademoiselle

Mlles *abbr* [F] mesdemoiselles

mm *abbr* millimeter

MM *abbr* [F] messieurs

Mme *abbr* [F] madame

Mmes *abbr* mesdames

Mn *symbol* manganese

MN *abbr* Minnesota

mne·mon·ic \nə-'mä-nik\ *adj* : assisting or designed to assist memory; *also* : of or relating to memory

mo *abbr* month

¹**Mo** *abbr* 1 Missouri 2 Monday

²**Mo** *symbol* molybdenum

MO *abbr* 1 mail order 2 medical officer 3 Missouri 4 modus operandi 5 money order

moan \'mōn\ *n* : a low prolonged sound indicative of pain or grief — **moan** *vb*

moat \'mōt\ *n* : a deep wide usu. water-filled trench around a castle

¹**mob** \'mäb\ *n* [L *mobile vulgus* vacillating crowd] 1 : MASSES, RABBLE 2 : a disorderly crowd 3 : a criminal gang

²**mob** *vb* **mobbed; mob·bing** 1 : to crowd about and attack or annoy 2 : to crowd into or around ⟨shoppers *mobbed* the stores⟩

¹**mo·bile** \'mō-bəl, -ˌbīl, -ˌbēl\ *adj* 1 : capable of moving or being moved 2 : changeable in appearance, mood, or purpose; *also* : ADAPTABLE 3 : having the opportunity for or undergoing a shift in social status 4 : using vehicles for transportation ⟨∼ warfare⟩ — **mo·bil·i·ty** \mō-'bi-lə-tē\ *n*

²**mo·bile** \'mō-ˌbēl\ *n* : a construction or sculpture (as of wire and sheet metal) with parts that can be set in motion by air currents; *also* : a similar structure suspended so that it is moved by a current of air

mobile home *n* : a trailer used as a permanent dwelling

mo·bi·lize \'mō-bə-ˌlīz\ *vb* **-lized; -liz·ing** 1 : to put into movement or circulation 2 : to assemble and make ready for action ⟨∼ army reserves⟩ — **mo·bi·li·za·tion** \ˌmō-bə-lə-'zā-shən\ *n* — **mo·bi·liz·er** \'mō-bə-ˌlī-zər\ *n*

mob·ster \'mäb-stər\ *n* : a member of a criminal gang

moc·ca·sin \'mä-kə-sən\ *n* 1 : a soft leather heelless shoe 2 : WATER MOCCASIN

mo·cha \'mō-kə\ *n* [*Mocha*, port in Yemen] 1 : choice coffee grown in Arabia 2 : a mixture of coffee and chocolate or cocoa 3 : a dark chocolate-brown color

¹**mock** \'mäk, 'mȯk\ *vb* 1 : to treat with contempt or ridicule 2 : DELUDE 3 : DEFY 4 : to mimic in sport or derision — **mock·er** *n* — **mock·ery** \'mä-kə-rē, 'mȯ-\ *n* — **mock·ing·ly** *adv*

²**mock** *adj* : SHAM, PSEUDO

mock–he·ro·ic \ˌmäk-hi-'rō-ik, ˌmȯk-\ *adj* : ridiculing or burlesquing heroic style, character, or action ⟨a ∼ poem⟩

---

mock·ing·bird \\'mä-kiŋ-ˌbərd, 'mò-\\ *n* : a grayish No. American songbird related to the catbirds and thrashers that mimics the calls of other birds

mock–up \\'mä-ˌkəp, 'mò-\\ *n* : a full-sized structural model built for study, testing, or display ⟨a ∼ of a car⟩

¹mod \\'mäd\\ *adj* 1 : of, relating to, or being the style of the 1960s British youth culture 2 : HIP, TRENDY

²mod *abbr* 1 moderate 2 modern 3 modification; modified

mode \\'mōd\\ *n* 1 : a particular form or variety of something; *also* : STYLE 2 : a manner of doing something 3 : the most frequent value of a set of data — **mod·al** \\'mōd-°l\\ *adj*

¹mod·el \\'mäd-°l\\ *n* 1 : structural design 2 : a miniature representation; *also* : a pattern of something to be made 3 : an example for imitation or emulation 4 : one who poses for an artist; *also* : MANNEQUIN 5 : TYPE, DESIGN

²model *vb* **mod·eled** *or* **mod·elled; mod·el·ing** *or* **mod·el·ling** 1 : SHAPE, FASHION, CONSTRUCT 2 : to work as a fashion model

³model *adj* 1 : serving as or worthy of being a pattern ⟨a ∼ student⟩ 2 : being a miniature representation of something ⟨a ∼ airplane⟩

mo·dem \\'mō-dəm, -ˌdem\\ *n* : a device that converts signals from one device (as a computer) to a form compatible with another (as a telephone)

¹mod·er·ate \\'mä-də-rət\\ *adj* 1 : avoiding extremes; *also* : TEMPERATE 2 : AVERAGE; *also* : MEDIOCRE 3 : limited in scope or effect 4 : not expensive — **moderate** *n* — **mod·er·ate·ly** *adv* — **mod·er·ate·ness** *n*

²mod·er·ate \\'mä-də-ˌrāt\\ *vb* **-at·ed; -at·ing** 1 : to lessen the intensity of : TEMPER 2 : to act as a moderator — **mod·er·a·tion** \\ˌmä-də-'rā-shən\\ *n*

mod·er·a·tor \\'mä-də-ˌrā-tər\\ *n* 1 : MEDIATOR 2 : one who presides over an assembly, meeting, or discussion

mod·ern \\'mä-dərn\\ *adj* [LL *modernus*, fr. L *modo* just now, fr. *modus* measure] : of, relating to, or characteristic of the present or the immediate past : CONTEMPORARY — **modern** *n* — **mo·der·ni·ty** \\mə-'dər-nə-tē\\ *n* — **mod·ern·ly** *adv* — **mod·ern·ness** *n*

mod·ern·ism \\'mä-dər-ˌni-zəm\\ *n* : a practice, movement, or belief peculiar to modern times

mod·ern·ize \\'mä-dər-ˌnīz\\ *vb* **-ized; -iz·ing** : to make or become modern — **mod·ern·i·za·tion** \\ˌmä-dər-nə-'zā-shən\\ *n* — **mod·ern·iz·er** *n*

mod·est \\'mä-dəst\\ *adj* 1 : having a moderate estimate of oneself; *also* : DIFFIDENT 2 : observing the proprieties of dress and behavior 3 : limited in size, amount, or scope — **mod·est·ly** *adv* — **mod·es·ty** \\-də-stē\\ *n*

mod·i·cum \\'mä-di-kəm\\ *n* : a small amount

modif *abbr* modification

mod·i·fy \\'mä-də-ˌfī\\ *vb* **-fied; -fy·ing** 1 : MODERATE 2 : to limit the meaning of esp. in a grammatical construction 3 : CHANGE, ALTER — **mod·i·fi·ca·tion** \\ˌmä-də-fə-'kā-shən\\ *n* — **mod·i·fi·er** \\'mä-də-ˌfī-ər\\ *n*

mod·ish \\'mō-dish\\ *adj* : FASHIONABLE, STYLISH — **mod·ish·ly** *adv* — **mod·ish·ness** *n*

mo·diste \\mō-'dēst\\ *n* : a maker of fashionable dresses and hats

mod·u·lar \\'mä-jə-lər\\ *adj* : constructed with standardized units

mod·u·lar·ized \\'mä-jə-lə-ˌrīzd\\ *adj* : containing or consisting of modules

mod·u·late \\'mä-jə-ˌlāt\\ *vb* **-lat·ed; -lat·ing** 1 : to tune to a key or pitch 2 : to keep in proper measure or proportion : TEMPER 3 : to vary the amplitude or frequency of a carrier wave for the transmission of intelligence (as in radio or television) — **mod·u·la·tion** \\ˌmä-jə-'lā-shən\\ *n* — **mod·u·la·tor** \\'mä-jə-ˌlā-tər\\ *n* — **mod·u·la·to·ry** \\-lə-ˌtōr-ē\\ *adj*

mod·ule \\'mä-jül\\ *n* 1 : any in a series of standardized units for use together 2 : an assembly of wired electronic parts for use with other such assemblies 3 : an independent unit that constitutes a part of the total structure of a space vehicle ⟨a propulsion ∼⟩

mo·dus ope·ran·di \\ˌmō-dəs-ˌä-pə-'ran-dē, -ˌdī\\ *n, pl* **mo·di operandi** \\'mō-ˌdē-ˌäp-, 'mō-ˌdī-\\ [NL] : a method of procedure

¹mo·gul \\'mō-gəl, mō-'gəl\\ *n* [fr. *Mogul*, member of a Muslim dynasty ruling northern India] : an important person : MAGNATE

²mogul \\'mō-gəl\\ *n* : a bump in a ski run

mo·hair \\'mō-ˌhar\\ *n* [modif. of obs. It *mocaiarro*, fr. Ar *mukhayyar*, lit., choice] : a fabric or yarn made wholly or in part from the long silky hair of the Angora goat; *also* : this goat hair

Mo·ham·med·an *var of* MUHAMMADAN

Mo·hawk \\'mō-ˌhòk\\ *n, pl* **Mohawk** *or* **Mohawks** : a member of an American Indian people of the Mohawk River valley, New York; *also* : the language of the Mohawk people

Mo·he·gan \\mō-'hē-gən, mə-\\ *or* **Mo·hi·can** \\-'hē-kən\\ *n, pl* **Mohegan** *or* **Mohegans** *or* **Mohican** *or* **Mohicans** : a member of an American Indian people of southeastern Connecticut

Mo·hi·can \\mō-'hē-kən, mə-\\ *var of* MAHICAN

moi·e·ty \\'mòi-ə-tē\\ *n, pl* **-ties** : one of two equal or approximately equal parts

moil \\'mòil\\ *vb* : to work hard : DRUDGE — **moil** *n* — **moil·er** *n*

moi·ré \\mò-'rā, mwä-\\ *or* **moire** *same or* 'mòir, 'mwär\\ *n* : a fabric (as silk) having a watered appearance

moist \\'mòist\\ *adj* : slightly or moderately wet — **moist·ly** *adv* — **moist·ness** *n*

moist·en \\'mòis-°n\\ *vb* : to make or become moist — **moist·en·er** *n*

mois·ture \\'mòis-chər\\ *n* : the small amount of liquid that causes dampness

mois·tur·ize \\'mòis-chə-ˌrīz\\ *vb* **-ized; -iz·ing** : to add moisture to — **mois·tur·iz·er** *n*

mol *abbr* molecular; molecule

mo·lar \\'mō-lər\\ *n* [ME *molares*, pl., fr. L *molaris*, fr. *molaris* of a mill, fr. *mola* millstone] : any of the broad teeth adapted to grinding food and located in the back of the jaw — **molar** *adj*

mo·las·ses \\mə-'la-səz\\ *n* : the thick brown syrup that is separated from raw sugar in sugar manufacture

¹mold \\'mōld\\ *n* : crumbly soil rich in organic matter

²mold *n* 1 : distinctive nature or character 2 : the frame on or around which something is constructed 3 : a cavity in which something is shaped; *also* : an object so shaped 4 : MOLDING

³mold *vb* 1 : to shape in or as if in a mold 2 : to ornament with molding — **mold·er** *n*

⁴mold *n* : a surface growth of fungus esp. on damp or decaying matter; *also* : a fungus that forms molds — **mold·i·ness** \\'mōl-dē-nəs\\ *n* — **moldy** *adj*

⁵mold *vb* : to become moldy

mold·board \\'mōld-ˌbòrd\\ *n* : a curved iron plate attached above the plowshare to lift and turn the soil

mold·er \\'mōl-dər\\ *vb* : to crumble into small pieces

mold·ing \\'mōl-diŋ\\ *n* 1 : an act or process of shaping in a mold; *also* : an object so shaped 2 : a decorative surface, plane, or curved strip

¹mole \\'mōl\\ *n* : a small often pigmented spot or protuberance on the skin

²mole *n* : any of numerous small burrowing insect-eating mammals related to the shrews and hedgehogs

³mole *n* : a massive breakwater or jetty

molecular biology *n* : a branch of biology dealing with the ultimate physical and chemical organization of living matter and esp. with the molecular basis of inheritance and protein synthesis — **molecular biologist** *n*

molecular weight *n* : the mass of a molecule that is equal to the sum of the masses of all atoms contained in the molecule's formula

mol·e·cule \'mä-li-ˌkyül\ *n* : the smallest particle of matter that is the same chemically as the whole mass — **mo·lec·u·lar** \mə-'le-kyə-lər\ *adj*

mole·hill \'mōl-ˌhil\ *n* : a little ridge of earth thrown up by a mole

mole·skin \-ˌskin\ *n* **1** : the skin of the mole used as fur **2** : a heavy durable cotton fabric

mo·lest \mə-'lest\ *vb* **1** : ANNOY, DISTURB **2** : to make annoying sexual advances to; *esp* : to force physical and usu. sexual contact on — **mo·les·ta·tion** \ˌmō-ˌles-'tā-shən\ *n* — **mo·lest·er** *n*

moll \'mäl\ *n* : a gangster's girlfriend

mol·li·fy \'mä-lə-ˌfī\ *vb* **-fied; -fy·ing 1** : to soothe in temper : APPEASE **2** : SOFTEN **3** : to reduce in intensity : ASSUAGE — **mol·li·fi·ca·tion** \ˌmä-lə-fə-'kā-shən\ *n*

mol·lusk *or* **mol·lusc** \'mä-ləsk\ *n* : any of a large phylum of usu. shelled and aquatic invertebrate animals (as snails, clams, and squids) — **mol·lus·can** *also* **mol·lus·kan** \mə-'ləs-kən\ *adj*

¹mol·ly·cod·dle \'mä-lē-ˌkäd-ᵊl\ *n* : a pampered man or boy

²mollycoddle *vb* **mol·ly·cod·dled; mol·ly·cod·dling** : PAMPER

Mo·lo·tov cocktail \'mä-lə-ˌtȯf-, 'mȯ-\ *n* [Vyacheslav M. *Molotov* †1986 Soviet foreign minister] : a crude bomb made of a bottle filled usu. with gasoline and fitted with a wick (as a saturated rag) that is ignited just prior to hurling

¹molt \'mōlt\ *vb* : to shed hair, feathers, outer skin, or horns periodically with the cast-off parts being replaced by new growth — **molt·er** *n*

²molt *n* : the act or process of molting

mol·ten \'mōlt-ᵊn\ *adj* **1** : fused or liquefied by heat **2** : GLOWING

mo·ly \'mō-lē\ *n* : a mythical herb with black root, white flowers, and magic powers

mo·lyb·de·num \mə-'lib-də-nəm\ *n* : a metallic chemical element used in strengthening and hardening steel — see ELEMENT table

mom \'mäm, 'məm\ *n* : MOTHER

mom–and–pop *adj* : being a small owner-operated business

mo·ment \'mō-mənt\ *n* **1** : a minute portion of time : INSTANT **2** : a time of excellence (he has his ~) **3** : IMPORTANCE syn consequence, significance, weight, import

mo·men·tari·ly \ˌmō-mən-'ter-ə-lē\ *adv* **1** : for a moment **2** *archaic* : INSTANTLY **3** : at any moment : SOON

mo·men·tary \'mō-mən-ˌter-ē\ *adj* **1** : continuing only a moment; *also* : EPHEMERAL **2** : recurring at every moment — **mo·men·tar·i·ness** \-ˌter-ē-nəs\ *n*

mo·men·tous \mō-'men-təs\ *adj* : very important — **mo·men·tous·ly** *adv* — **mo·men·tous·ness** *n*

mo·men·tum \mō-'men-təm\ *n, pl* **mo·men·ta** \-'men-tə\ *or* **momentums** : a property that a moving body has due to its mass and motion; *also* : IMPETUS

mom·my \'mä-mē, 'mə-\ *n, pl* **mom·mies** : MOTHER

Mon *abbr* Monday

mon·arch \'mä-nərk, -ˌnärk\ *n* **1** : a person who reigns over a kingdom or an empire **2** : one holding preeminent position or power **3** : MONARCH BUTTERFLY — **mo·nar·chi·cal** \mə-'när-ki-kəl\ *also* **mo·nar·chic** \-'när-kik\ *adj*

monarch butterfly *n* : a large orange and black migratory American butterfly whose larva feeds on milkweed

mon·ar·chist \'mä-nər-kist\ *n* : a believer in monarchical government — **mon·ar·chism** \-ˌki-zəm\ *n*

mon·ar·chy \'mä-nər-kē\ *n, pl* **-chies** : a nation or state governed by a monarch

monarch butterfly

mon·as·tery \'mä-nə-ˌster-ē\ *n, pl* **-ter·ies** : a house for persons under religious vows (as monks)

mo·nas·tic \mə-'nas-tik\ *adj* : of or relating to monasteries or to monks or nuns — **monastic** *n* — **mo·nas·ti·cal·ly** \-ti-k(ə-)lē\ *adv* — **mo·nas·ti·cism** \-tə-ˌsi-zəm\ *n*

mon·au·ral \mä-'nȯr-əl\ *adj* : MONOPHONIC — **mon·au·ral·ly** *adv*

Mon·day \'mən-dē, -ˌdā\ *n* : the second day of the week

mon·e·tary \'mä-nə-ˌter-ē, 'mə-\ *adj* : of or relating to money or to the mechanisms by which it is supplied and circulated in the economy

mon·ey \'mə-nē\ *n, pl* **moneys** *or* **mon·ies** \'mə-nez\ **1** : something (as metal currency) accepted as a medium of exchange **2** : wealth reckoned in monetary terms **3** : the 1st, 2d, and 3d places in a horse or dog race

MONEY

NAME	SUBDIVISIONS	COUNTRY
afghani	100 puls	Afghanistan
baht *or* tical	100 satang	Thailand
balboa	100 centesimos	Panama
birr	100 cents	Ethiopia
bolivar	100 centimos	Venezuela
boliviano	100 centavos	Bolivia
cedi	100 pesewas	Ghana
colón	100 centimos	Costa Rica
colón	100 centavos	El Salvador
cordoba	100 centavos	Nicaragua
cruzeiro	100 centavos	Brazil
dalasi	100 bututs	Gambia
deutsche mark	100 pfennig	Germany
dinar	100 centimes	Algeria
dinar	1000 fils	Bahrain
dinar	1000 fils	Iraq
dinar	1000 fils	Jordan
dinar	1000 fils	Kuwait
dinar	1000 dirhams	Libya
dinar	1000 millimes	Tunisia
dinar¹	1000 fils	Yemen
dinar	100 paras	Yugoslavia
dirham	100 centimes	Morocco
dirham	100 fils	United Arab Emirates
dobra	100 centimos	Sao Tome and Principe
dollar²	100 cents	Antigua and Barbuda, Dominica, Grenada, St. Kitts-Nevis, St. Lucia, St. Vincent and the Grenadines
dollar	100 cents	Australia
dollar	100 cents	Bahamas
dollar	100 cents	Barbados

NAME	SUBDIVISIONS	COUNTRY	NAME	SUBDIVISIONS	COUNTRY
dollar	100 cents	Belize	lira	100 kurus	Turkey
dollar	100 cents	Bermuda	livre—see POUND, below		
dollar	100 sen *or* cents	Brunei	loti (*pl*	100 licente	Lesotho
dollar	100 cents	Canada	maloti)	*or* lisente	
dollar *or* yuan	100 cents	China (Taiwan)		(*sing* sente)	
dollar	100 cents	Fiji	mark—see DEUTSCHE MARK, above		
dollar	100 cents	Guyana	markka	100 pennia	Finland
dollar	100 cents	Hong Kong	metical	100 centavos	Mozambique
dollar	100 cents	Jamaica	naira	100 kobo	Nigeria
dollar	100 cents	Liberia	ngultrum	100 chetrums	Bhutan
dollar	100 cents	New Zealand	ouguiya	5 khoums	Mauritania
dollar	100 cents	Singapore	pa'anga	100 seniti	Tonga
dollar	100 cents	Trinidad and Tobago	pataca	100 avos	Macao
dollar	100 cents	United States	peseta	100 centimos	Spain
dollar	100 cents	Zimbabwe	peso		Argentina
dollar—see RINGGIT, below			peso	100 centavos	Chile
dong	100 xu	Vietnam	peso	100 centavos	Colombia
drachma	100 lepta	Greece	peso	100 centavos	Cuba
escudo	100 centavos	Cape Verde	peso	100 centavos	Dominican Republic
escudo	100 centavos	Portugal	peso *or*	100 centavos	Guinea-Bissau
escudo—see PESO, below			escudo		
florin—see GULDEN, below			peso	100 centavos	Mexico
forint	100 filler	Hungary	peso *or*	100 sentimos	Philippines
franc	100 centimes	Belgium	piso	*or* centavos	
franc[3]	100 centimes	Benin, Burkina Faso,	peso	100 centesimos	Uruguay
		Cameroon, Central	pound	100 cents	Cyprus
		African Republic,	pound	100 piastres	Egypt
		Chad, Congo,	pound	100 pence	Ireland
		Equatorial Guinea,	pound	100 piastres	Lebanon
		Gabon, Ivory Coast,	*or* livre		
		Mali, Niger, Senegal,	pound	100 piastres	Sudan
		Togo	pound	100 piastres	Syria
franc	100 centimes	Burundi	pound	100 pence	United Kingdom
franc	100 centimes	Djibouti	pound—see LIRA, above		
franc	100 centimes	France	pula	100 thebe	Botswana
franc	100 centimes	Guinea	quetzal	100 centavos	Guatemala
franc	100 centimes	Luxembourg	rand	100 cents	South Africa
franc	100 centimes	Madagascar	rial	100 dinars	Iran
franc	100 centimes	Rwanda	rial	1000 baiza	Oman
franc	100 centimes	Switzerland	rial[1]	100 fils	Yemen
	or rappen		riel	100 sen	Cambodia
gourde	100 centimes	Haiti	ringgit *or*	100 sen	Malaysia
guarani	100 centimos	Paraguay	dollar		
gulden *or*	100 cents	Netherlands	riyal	100 dirhams	Qatar
guilder *or*			riyal	100 halala	Saudi Arabia
florin			ruble	100 kopecks	Russia
gulden *or*	100 cents	Suriname	rupee	100 paise	India
guilder *or*			rupee	100 cents	Mauritius
florin			rupee	100 paisa	Nepal
kina	100 toea	Papua New Guinea	rupee	100 paisa	Pakistan
kip	100 at	Laos	rupee	100 cents	Seychelles
koruna	100 haleru	Czech Republic	rupee	100 cents	Sri Lanka
krona	100 aurar	Iceland	rupiah	100 sen	Indonesia
	(*sing* eyrir)		schilling	100 groschen	Austria
krona	100 ore	Sweden	shekel *or*	100 agorot	Israel
krone	100 ore	Denmark	sheqel		
krone	100 ore	Norway	shilling	100 cents	Kenya
kwacha	100 tambala	Malawi	shilling	100 cents	Somalia
kwacha	100 ngwee	Zambia	shilling	100 cents	Tanzania
kwanza	100 lwei	Angola	shilling	100 cents	Uganda
kyat	100 pyas	Myanmar	sol	100 centavos	Peru
lek	100 qindarka	Albania	sucre	100 centavos	Ecuador
lempira	100 centavos	Honduras	taka	100 paisa	Bangladesh
leone	100 cents	Sierra Leone		*or* poisha	
leu	100 bani	Romania	tala	100 sene	Western Samoa
lev	100 stotinki	Bulgaria	tical—see BAHT, above		
lilangeni (*pl*	100 cents	Swaziland	tugrik	100 mongo	Mongolia
emalangeni)			won	100 chon	North Korea
lira	100 centesimi[4]	Italy	won	100 chon	South Korea
lira *or* pound	100 cents	Malta	yen	100 sen[4]	Japan

NAME	SUBDIVISIONS	COUNTRY
yuan	100 fen	China (mainland)
yuan—see DOLLAR, above		
zaire	100 makuta (*sing* likuta)	Zaire
zloty	100 groszy	Poland

¹ The currencies of the formerly separate countries of Southern Yemen and the Yemen Arab Republic are both legal in unified Yemen.
² Dollars issued by the Eastern Caribbean Central Bank, established to promote economic cooperation among the member nations.
³ Francs issued by the African Financial Community, established to promote economic cooperation among the member nations.
⁴ No longer minted; a subdivision in name only.

mon·eyed \'mə-nēd\ *adj* **1** : having money : WEALTHY **2** : consisting in or derived from money

mon·ey·lend·er \'mə-nē-₁len-dər\ *n* : one (as a bank or pawnbroker) whose business is lending money

money market *n* : the trade in short-term negotiable financial instruments

money of account : a denominator of value or basis of exchange used in keeping accounts

money order *n* : an order purchased at a post office, bank, or telegraph office directing another office to pay a sum of money to a party named on it

mon·ger \'məŋ-gər, 'mäŋ-\ *n* **1** : DEALER **2** : one who tries to stir up or spread something

mon·go \'mäŋ-₍₎gō\ *n, pl* mongo — see *tugrik* at MONEY table

Mon·gol \'mäŋ-gəl, 'män-₁gōl\ *n* : a member of any of several traditionally pastoral peoples of Mongolia — **Mongol** *adj*

Mon·go·lian \män-'gōl-yən, mäŋ-, -'gō-lē-ən\ *n* **1** : a native or inhabitant of Mongolia **2** : a member of the Mongoloid racial stock — **Mongolian** *adj*

mon·gol·ism \'mäŋ-gə-₁li-zəm\ *n* : DOWN'S SYNDROME

Mon·gol·oid \'mäŋ-gə-₁lȯid\ *adj* **1** : of or relating to a major racial stock native to Asia that includes peoples of northern and eastern Asia, Malaysians, Eskimos, and often American Indians **2** *often not cap* : of, relating to, or affected with Down's syndrome — **Mongoloid** *n*

mon·goose \'män-₁güs, 'mäŋ-\ *n, pl* **mon·goos·es** *also* **mon·geese** \-₁gēs\ : any of a group of small agile Old World mammals that are related to the civet cats and feed on small animals and fruits

mon·grel \'mäŋ-grəl, 'məŋ-\ *n* : an offspring of parents of different breeds; *esp* : one of uncertain ancestry

mo·nism \'mō-₁ni-zəm, 'mä-\ *n* : a view that reality is basically one unitary organic whole — **mo·nist** \'mō-nist, 'mä-\ *n*

mo·ni·tion \mō-'ni-shən, mə-\ *n* : WARNING, CAUTION

¹mon·i·tor \'mä-nə-tər\ *n* **1** : a student appointed to assist a teacher **2** : one that monitors; *esp* : a video display screen (as for a computer)

²monitor *vb* : to watch, check, or observe for a special purpose

mon·i·to·ry \'mä-nə-₁tōr-ē\ *adj* : giving admonition : WARNING

¹monk \'məŋk\ *n* [ME, fr. OE *munuc*, fr. LL *monachus*, fr. LGk *monachos*, fr. Gk, adj., single, fr. *monos* single, alone] : a man belonging to a religious order and living in a monastery — **monk·ish** *adj*

²monk *n* : MONKEY

¹mon·key \'məŋ-kē\ *n, pl* **monkeys** : a nonhuman primate mammal; *esp* : one of the smaller, longer-tailed, and usu. more arboreal primates as contrasted with the apes

²monkey *vb* **mon·keyed; mon·key·ing 1** : FOOL, TRIFLE **2** : TAMPER

monkey bars *n pl* : a framework of bars on which children can play

mon·key·shine \'mən-kē-₁shīn\ *n* : PRANK — usu. used in pl.

monkey wrench *n* : a wrench with one fixed and one adjustable jaw at right angles to a handle

monks·hood \'məŋks-₁hùd\ *n* : any of a genus of poisonous plants related to the buttercups; *esp* : a tall Old World plant with usu. purplish flowers

¹mono \'mä-nō\ *adj* : MONOPHONIC

²mono *n* : INFECTIOUS MONONUCLEOSIS

mono·chro·mat·ic \₁mä-nə-krō-'ma-tik\ *adj* **1** : having or consisting of one color **2** : consisting of radiation (as light) of a single wavelength

mono·chrome \'mä-nə-₁krōm\ *adj* : involving or producing visual images in a single color or in varying tones of a single color ⟨∼ television⟩

mon·o·cle \'mä-ni-kəl\ *n* : an eyeglass for one eye

mono·clo·nal \₁mä-nə-'klō-nəl\ *adj* : produced by, being, or composed of cells derived from a single cell ⟨∼ antibodies⟩

mono·cot·y·le·don \₁mä-nə-₁kät-ᵊl-'ēd-ᵊn\ *n* : any of a class or subclass of chiefly herbaceous seed plants having an embryo with a single cotyledon and usu. parallel-veined leaves

mon·o·dy \'mä-nə-dē\ *n, pl* **-dies** : ELEGY, DIRGE — **mo·nod·ic** \mə-'nä-dik\ *or* **mo·nod·i·cal** \-di-kəl\ *adj* — **mon·o·dist** \'mä-nə-dist\ *n*

mo·nog·a·my \mə-'nä-gə-mē\ *n* **1** : marriage with but one person at a time **2** : the practice of having a single mate during a period of time — **mo·nog·a·mist** \-mist\ *n* — **mo·nog·a·mous** \-məs\ *adj*

mono·gram \'mä-nə-₁gram\ *n* : a sign of identity composed of the combined initials of a name — **monogram** *vb*

mono·graph \'mä-nə-₁graf\ *n* : a learned treatise on a small area of learning

mono·lin·gual \₁mä-nə-'liŋ-gwəl\ *adj* : knowing or using only one language

mono·lith \'män-ᵊl-₁ith\ *n* **1** : a single great stone often in the form of a monument or column **2** : something large and powerful that acts as a single unified force — **mono·lith·ic** \₁män-ᵊl-'i-thik\ *adj*

mono·logue *also* **mono·log** \'män-ᵊl-₁ȯg\ *n* **1** : a dramatic soliloquy; *also* : a long speech monopolizing conversation **2** : the routine of a stand-up comic — **mono·logu·ist** \-₁ȯg-ist\ *or* **mo·no·lo·gist** \mə-'nä-lə-jist; 'män-ᵊl-₁ȯ-gist\ *n*

mono·ma·nia \₁mä-nə-'mā-nē-ə, -nyə\ *n* **1** : mental disorder limited in expression to one area of thought **2** : excessive concentration on a single object or idea — **mono·ma·ni·ac** \-nē-₁ak\ *n or adj*

mono·mer \'mä-nə-mər\ *n* : a simple chemical compound that can be polymerized

mono·nu·cle·o·sis \₁mä-nō-₁nü-klē-'ō-səs, -₁nyü-\ *n* : INFECTIOUS MONONUCLEOSIS

mono·phon·ic \₁mä-nə-'fä-nik\ *adj* : of or relating to sound recording or reproduction involving a single transmission path

mono·plane \'mä-nə-₁plān\ *n* : an airplane with only one set of wings

mo·nop·o·ly \mə-'nä-pə-lē\ *n, pl* **-lies** [L *monopolium*, fr. Gk *monopōlion*, fr. *monos* alone, single + *pōlein* to sell] **1** : exclusive ownership (as through command of supply) **2** : a commodity controlled by one party **3** : one that has a monopoly — **mo·nop·o·list** \-list\ *n* — **mo-**

\ə\abut \ᵊ\kitten \ər\further \a\ash \ā\ace \ä\mop, mar
\au̇\out \ch\chin \e\bet \ē\easy \g\go \i\hit \ī\ice \j\job
\ŋ\sing \ō\go \ȯ\law \ȯi\boy \th\thin \t͟h\the \ü\loot \u̇\foot
\y\yet \zh\vision *see also* Pronunciation Symbols page

nop·o·lis·tic \mə-ˌnä-pə-ˈlis-tik\ *adj* — **mo·nop·o·li·za·tion** \-lə-ˈzā-shən\ *n* — **mo·nop·o·lize** \mə-ˈnä-pə-ˌlīz\ *vb*

mono·rail \ˈmä-nə-ˌrāl\ *n* : a single rail serving as a track for a vehicle; *also* : a vehicle traveling on such a track

mono·so·di·um glu·ta·mate \ˌmä-nə-ˌsō-dē-əm-ˈglü-tə-ˌmāt\ *n* : a crystalline salt used to enhance the flavor of food

mono·syl·la·ble \ˈmä-nə-ˌsi-lə-bəl\ *n* : a word of one syllable — **mono·syl·lab·ic** \ˌmä-nə-sə-ˈla-bik\ *adj* — **mono·syl·lab·i·cal·ly** \-bi-k(ə-)lē\ *adv*

mono·the·ism \ˈmä-nə-(ˌ)thē-ˌi-zəm\ *n* : a doctrine or belief that there is only one deity — **mono·the·ist** \-ˌthē-ist\ *n* — **mono·the·is·tic** \-thē-ˈis-tik\ *adj*

mono·tone \ˈmä-nə-ˌtōn\ *n* : a succession of syllables, words, or sentences in one unvaried key or pitch

mo·not·o·nous \mə-ˈnät-ᵊn-əs\ *adj* **1** : uttered or sounded in one unvarying tone **2** : tediously uniform — **mo·not·o·nous·ly** *adv* — **mo·not·o·nous·ness** *n*

mo·not·o·ny \mə-ˈnät-ᵊn-ē\ *n* : tedious sameness or uniformity

mono·un·sat·u·rat·ed \ˌmä-nō-ˌən-ˈsa-chə-ˌrā-təd\ *adj* : containing one double or triple bond per molecule — used esp. of an oil or fatty acid

mon·ox·ide \mə-ˈnäk-ˌsīd\ *n* : an oxide containing one atom of oxygen in a molecule

mon·sei·gneur \ˌmōⁿ-ˌsān-ˈyər\ *n, pl* **mes·sei·gneurs** \ˌmā-sān-ˈyər, -ˈyərz\ : a French dignitary — used as a title

mon·sieur \məs-ˈyər, mə-ˈshər, *Fr* mə-ˈsyœ̄\ *n, pl* **messieurs** *same or* -ˈyərz, -ˈshərz\ : a Frenchman of high rank or station — used as a title equivalent to *Mister*

mon·si·gnor \män-ˈsē-nyər\ *n, pl* **monsignors** *or* **mon·si·gno·ri** \ˌmän-ˌsēn-ˈyōr-ē\ [It *monsignore*] : a Roman Catholic prelate — used as a title

mon·soon \män-ˈsün\ *n* [obs. Dutch *monssoen*, fr. Pg *monção*, fr. Ar *mawsim* time, season] **1** : a periodic wind esp. in the Indian Ocean and southern Asia **2** : the season of the southwest monsoon esp. in India **3** : rainfall associated with the monsoon

¹**mon·ster** \ˈmän-stər\ *n* **1** : an abnormally developed plant or animal **2** : an animal of strange or terrifying shape; *also* : one unusually large of its kind **3** : an extremely ugly, wicked, or cruel person — **mon·stros·i·ty** \män-ˈsträ-sə-tē\ *n* — **mon·strous** \ˈmän-strəs\ *adj* — **mon·strous·ly** *adv*

²**monster** *adj* : very large : ENORMOUS

mon·strance \ˈmän-strəns\ *n* : a vessel in which the consecrated Host is exposed for the adoration of the faithful

Mont *abbr* Montana

mon·tage \män-ˈtäzh\ *n* [F] **1** : a composite photograph made by combining several separate pictures **2** : an artistic composition made up of several different kinds of elements **3** : a varied mixture : JUMBLE

month \ˈmənth\ *n, pl* **months** \ˈməns, ˈmənths\ : one of the 12 parts into which the year is divided — **month·ly** *adv or adj or n*

☞ For table, see next page.

month·long \ˈmənth-ˈloŋ\ *adj* : lasting a month

mon·u·ment \ˈmän-yə-mənt\ *n* **1** : a lasting reminder; *esp* : a structure erected in remembrance of a person or event **2** : NATIONAL MONUMENT

mon·u·men·tal \ˌmän-yə-ˈment-ᵊl\ *adj* **1** : of or relating to a monument **2** : MASSIVE; *also* : OUTSTANDING **3** : very great — **mon·u·men·tal·ly** *adv*

moo \ˈmü\ *vb* : to make the natural throat noise of a cow — **moo** *n*

¹**mood** \ˈmüd\ *n* **1** : a conscious state of mind or predominant emotion : FEELING **2** : a prevailing attitude : DISPOSITION **3** : a distinctive atmosphere

²**mood** *n* : distinction of form of a verb to express whether its action or state is conceived as fact or in some other manner (as wish)

moody \ˈmü-dē\ *adj* **mood·i·er; -est 1** : GLOOMY **2** : subject to moods : TEMPERAMENTAL — **mood·i·ly** \-də-lē\ *adv* — **mood·i·ness** \-dē-nəs\ *n*

¹**moon** \ˈmün\ *n* **1** : the earth's natural satellite **2** : SATELLITE 2

²**moon** *vb* : to engage in idle reverie

moon·beam \ˈmün-ˌbēm\ *n* : a ray of light from the moon

¹**moon·light** \-ˌlīt\ *n* : the light of the moon — **moon·lit** \-ˌlit\ *adj*

²**moonlight** *vb* **moon·light·ed; moon·light·ing** : to hold a second job in addition to a regular one — **moon·light·er** *n*

moon·scape \-ˌskāp\ *n* : the surface of the moon as seen or as pictured

moon·shine \-ˌshīn\ *n* **1** : MOONLIGHT **2** : empty talk **3** : intoxicating liquor usu. illegally distilled

moon·stone \-ˌstōn\ *n* : a transparent or translucent feldspar of pearly luster used as a gem

moon·struck \-ˌstrək\ *adj* **1** : mentally unbalanced **2** : romantically sentimental **3** : lost in fantasy

¹**moor** \ˈmur\ *n* **1** *chiefly Brit* : an expanse of open rolling infertile land **2** : a boggy area; *esp* : one that is peaty and dominated by grasses and sedges

²**moor** *vb* : to make fast with or as if with cables, lines, or anchors

Moor \ˈmur\ *n* : one of the Arab and Berber conquerors of Spain — **Moor·ish** *adj*

moor·ing \ˈmur-iŋ\ *n* **1** : a place where or an object to which a craft can be made fast **2** : an established practice or stabilizing influence — usu. used in pl.

moor·land \-lənd, -ˌland\ *n* : land consisting of moors

moose \ˈmüs\ *n, pl* **moose** : a large heavy-antlered ruminant mammal of the deer family with humped shoulders and long legs that inhabits northern New and Old World forested areas

¹**moot** \ˈmüt\ *vb* : to bring up for discussion; *also* : DEBATE

²**moot** *adj* **1** : open to question; *also* : DISPUTED **2** : having no practical significance

¹**mop** \ˈmäp\ *n* : an implement made of absorbent material fastened to a handle and used esp. for cleaning floors

²**mop** *vb* **mopped; mop·ping** : to use a mop on : clean with a mop

mope \ˈmōp\ *vb* **moped; mop·ing 1** : to become dull, dejected, or listless **2** : DAWDLE

mo·ped \ˈmō-ˌped\ *n* : a light low-powered motorbike that can be pedaled

mop·pet \ˈmä-pət\ *n* [obs. E *mop* fool, child] : CHILD

mo·raine \mə-ˈrān\ *n* : an accumulation of earth and stones left by a glacier

¹**mor·al** \ˈmòr-əl\ *adj* **1** : of or relating to principles of right and wrong **2** : conforming to a standard of right behavior; *also* : capable of right and wrong action **3** : probable but not proved ⟨a ∼ certainty⟩ **4** : having the effects of such on the mind, confidence, or will ⟨a ∼ victory⟩ **syn** virtuous, righteous, noble, ethical, principled — **mor·al·ly** *adv*

²**moral** *n* **1** : the practical meaning (as of a story) **2** *pl* : moral practices or teachings

mo·rale \mə-ˈral\ *n* **1** : MORALITY **2** : the mental and emotional attitudes of an individual to the tasks at hand; *also* : ESPRIT DE CORPS

mor·al·ist \ˈmòr-ə-list\ *n* **1** : one who leads a moral life **2** : a thinker or writer concerned with morals **3** : one concerned with regulating the morals of others — **mor·al·is·tic** \ˌmòr-ə-ˈlis-tik\ *adj* — **mor·al·is·ti·cal·ly** \-ti-k(ə-)lē\ *adv*

mo·ral·i·ty \mə-ˈra-lə-tē\ *n, pl* **-ties** : moral conduct : VIRTUE

MONTHS OF THE PRINCIPAL CALENDARS

GREGORIAN[1]		JEWISH		ISLAMIC	
Name	*Days*	*Name*	*Days*	*Name*	*Days*
January begins 10 days after the winter solstice	31	Tishri in year 5755 began Sept. 6, 1994	30	Muharram[4] in A.H. 1415 began June 10, 1994	30
February	28	Heshvan	29 *or* 30	Safar	29
in leap years	29	Kislev	29 *or* 30	Rabi I	30
March	31	Tebet	29	Rabi II	29
April	30	Shebat	30	Jumada I	30
May	31	Adar[2]	29 *or* 30	Jumada II	29
June	30	Nisan[3]	30	Rajab	30
July	31	Iyar	29	Sha'ban	29
August	31	Sivan	30	Ramadan	30
September	30	Tammuz	29	Shawwal	29
October	31	Ab	30	Dhu'l-Qa'dah	30
November	30	Elul	29	Dhu'l-Hijja	29
December	31			in leap years	30

[1] The equinoxes occur about March 21 and September 23, the solstices about June 22 and December 22.

[2] In leap years an intercalary month of 30 days takes the place of Adar, and is sometimes called Adar I. Adar then becomes the 29-day Veadar or Adar Sheni (sometimes called Adar II), and retains the usual festivals and holidays of Adar.

[3] The first month of the ecclesiastical year; anciently called Abib.

[4] Retrogresses through the seasons; the Islamic year is lunar and each month begins at the approximate new moon; the year 1 A.H. began on Friday, July 16, A.D. 622.

mor·al·ize \'mȯr-ə-ˌlīz\ *vb* **-ized; -iz·ing** : to make moral reflections — **mor·al·i·za·tion** \ˌmȯr-ə-lə-'zā-shən\ *n* — **mor·al·iz·er** \'mȯr-ə-ˌlī-zər\ *n*

mo·rass \mə-'ras\ *n* : SWAMP; *also* : something that entangles, impedes, or confuses

mor·a·to·ri·um \ˌmȯr-ə-'tōr-ē-əm\ *n, pl* **-ri·ums** *or* **-ria** \-ē-ə\ [ultim. fr. L *mora* delay] : a suspension of activity

mo·ray \mə-'rā, 'mȯr-ˌā\ *n* : any of numerous often brightly colored biting eels of warm seas

mor·bid \'mȯr-bəd\ *adj* **1** : of, relating to, or typical of disease; *also* : DISEASED, SICKLY **2** : characterized by gloomy or unwholesome ideas or feelings **3** : GRISLY, GRUESOME ⟨∼ details⟩ — **mor·bid·i·ty** \mȯr-'bi-də-tē\ *n* — **mor·bid·ly** *adv* — **mor·bid·ness** *n*

mor·dant \'mȯrd-ᵊnt\ *adj* **1** : biting or caustic in manner or style **2** : BURNING, PUNGENT — **mor·dant·ly** *adv*

¹**more** \'mȯr\ *adj* **1** : GREATER **2** : ADDITIONAL

²**more** *adv* **1** : in addition **2** : to a greater or higher degree

³**more** *n* **1** : a greater quantity, number, or amount ⟨the ∼ the merrier⟩ **2** : an additional amount ⟨costs a little ∼⟩

⁴**more** *pron* : additional persons or things or a greater amount

mo·rel \mə-'rel\ *n* : any of several pitted edible fungi

more·over \mȯr-'ō-vər\ *adv* : in addition : FURTHER

mo·res \'mȯr-ˌāz\ *n pl* [L, pl. of *mor-, mos* custom] **1** : the fixed morally binding customs of a group **2** : HABITS, MANNERS

Mor·gan \'mȯr-gən\ *n* : any of an American breed of lightly built horses

morgue \'mȯrg\ *n* : a place where the bodies of dead persons are kept until released for burial

mor·i·bund \'mȯr-ə-(ˌ)bənd\ *adj* : being in a dying condition

Mor·mon \'mȯr-mən\ *n* : a member of the Church of Jesus Christ of Latter-day Saints — **Mor·mon·ism** \-mə-ˌni-zəm\ *n*

morn \'mȯrn\ *n* : MORNING

morn·ing \'mȯr-niŋ\ *n* **1** : the early part of the day; *esp* : the time from the sunrise to noon **2** : BEGINNING

morning glory *n* : any of various twining plants related to the sweet potato that have often showy bell-shaped or funnel-shaped flowers

morning sickness *n* : nausea and vomiting that occur in the morning esp. during early pregnancy

morning star *n* : a bright planet (as Venus) seen in the eastern sky before or at sunrise

Mo·roc·can \mə-'rä-kən\ *n* : a native or inhabitant of Morocco

mo·roc·co \mə-'rä-kō\ *n* : a fine leather made of goatskins tanned with sumac

mo·ron \'mȯr-ˌän\ *n* **1** : a mentally retarded person having a potential mental age of between 8 and 12 years and capable of doing routine work under supervision **2** : a very stupid person — **mo·ron·ic** \mə-'rä-nik\ *adj* — **mo·ron·i·cal·ly** \-ni-k(ə-)lē\ *adv*

mo·rose \mə-'rōs\ *adj* [L *morosus* hard to please, exacting, fr. *mor-, mos* custom, disposition] : having a sullen disposition; *also* : GLOOMY — **mo·rose·ly** *adv* — **mo·rose·ness** *n*

mor·pheme \'mȯr-ˌfēm\ *n* : a meaningful linguistic unit that contains no smaller meaningful parts — **mor·phe·mic** \mȯr-'fē-mik\ *adj*

mor·phia \'mȯr-fē-ə\ *n* : MORPHINE

mor·phine \'mȯr-ˌfēn\ *n* [F, fr. Gk *Morpheus*, Greek god of dreams] : an addictive drug obtained from opium and used to ease pain or induce sleep

mor·phol·o·gy \mȯr-'fä-lə-jē\ *n* **1** : a branch of biology dealing with the form and structure of organisms **2** : a study and description of word formation in a language

\ə\abut \ᵊ\kitten \ər\further \a\ash \ā\ace \ä\mop, mar
\au̇\out \ch\chin \e\bet \ē\easy \g\go \i\hit \ī\ice \j\job
\ŋ\sing \ō\go \ȯ\law \ȯi\boy \th\thin \t͟h\the \ü\loot \u̇\foot
\y\yet \zh\vision *see also* Pronunciation Symbols page

— **mor·pho·log·i·cal** \ˌmȯr-fə-ˈlä-ji-kəl\ *adj* — **mor·phol·o·gist** \mȯr-ˈfä-lə-jist\ *n*
mor·ris \ˈmȯr-əs\ *n* : a vigorous English dance traditionally performed by men wearing costumes and bells
mor·row \ˈmär-ō\ *n* : the next day
Morse code \ˈmȯrs-\ *n* : either of two codes consisting of dots and dashes or long and short sounds used for transmitting messages
mor·sel \ˈmȯr-səl\ *n* [ME, fr. OF, dim. of *mors* bite, fr. L *morsus*, fr. *mordēre* to bite] **1** : a small piece or quantity **2** : a tasty dish
mor·tal \ˈmȯrt-ᵊl\ *adj* **1** : causing death : FATAL; *also* : leading to eternal punishment ⟨~ sin⟩ **2** : subject to death ⟨~ man⟩ **3** : implacably hostile ⟨~ foe⟩ **4** : very great : EXTREME ⟨~ fear⟩ **5** : HUMAN ⟨~ limitations⟩ — **mortal** *n* — **mor·tal·i·ty** \mȯr-ˈta-lə-tē\ *n* — **mor·tal·ly** \ˈmȯrt-ᵊl-ē\ *adv*
¹mor·tar \ˈmȯr-tər\ *n* **1** : a strong bowl in which substances are pounded or crushed with a pestle **2** : a short-barreled cannon used to fire shells at high angles
²mortar *n* : a building material (as a mixture of lime and cement with sand and water) that is spread between bricks or stones to bind them together as it hardens — **mortar** *vb*
mor·tar·board \ˈmȯr-tər-ˌbȯrd\ *n* **1** : a square board for holding mortar **2** : an academic cap with a flat square top
mort·gage \ˈmȯr-gij\ *n* [ME *morgage*, fr. MF, fr. OF, fr. *mort* dead + *gage* gage] : a transfer of rights to a piece of property usu. as security for the payment of a loan or debt that becomes void when the debt is paid — **mortgage** *vb* — **mort·gag·ee** \ˌmȯr-gi-ˈjē\ *n* — **mort·gag·or** \ˌmȯr-gi-ˈjȯr\ *n*
mor·ti·cian \mȯr-ˈti-shən\ *n* [L *mort-, mors* death + E *-ician* (as in *physician*)] : UNDERTAKER
mor·ti·fy \ˈmȯr-tə-ˌfī\ *vb* **-fied; -fy·ing 1** : to subdue (as the body) esp. by abstinence or self-inflicted pain **2** : HUMILIATE **3** : to become necrotic or gangrenous — **mor·ti·fi·ca·tion** \ˌmȯr-tə-fə-ˈkā-shən\ *n*
mor·tise *also* **mor·tice** \ˈmȯr-təs\ *n* : a hole cut in a piece of wood into which another piece fits to form a joint
mor·tu·ary \ˈmȯr-chə-ˌwer-ē\ *n, pl* **-ar·ies** : a place in which dead bodies are kept until burial
mos *abbr* months
mo·sa·ic \mō-ˈzā-ik\ *n* : a surface decoration made by inlaying small pieces (as of colored glass or stone) to form figures or patterns; *also* : a design made in mosaic — **mosaic** *adj*
mo·sey \ˈmō-zē\ *vb* **mo·seyed; mo·sey·ing** : SAUNTER
Mos·lem \ˈmäz-ləm\ *var of* MUSLIM
mosque \ˈmäsk\ *n* : a building used for public worship by Muslims
mos·qui·to \mə-ˈskē-tō\ *n, pl* **-toes** *also* **-tos** : any of a family of dipteran flies the female of which sucks the blood of animals
mosquito net *n* : a net or screen for keeping out mosquitoes
moss \ˈmȯs\ *n* : any of a class of green plants that lack flowers but have small leafy stems and often grow in clumps — **mossy** *adj*
moss·back \ˈmȯs-ˌbak\ *n* : an extremely conservative person : FOGY
¹most \ˈmōst\ *adj* **1** : GREATEST ⟨the ~ ability⟩ **2** : the majority of ⟨~ people⟩
²most *adv* **1** : to the greatest or highest degree ⟨~ beautiful⟩ **2** : to a very great degree ⟨a ~ careful driver⟩
³most *n* : the greatest amount ⟨the ~ I can do⟩
⁴most *pron* : the greatest number or part ⟨~ became discouraged⟩
-most \ˌmōst\ *adj suffix* : most ⟨inner*most*⟩ : most toward ⟨end*most*⟩
most·ly \ˈmōst-lē\ *adv* : MAINLY

mot \ˈmō\ *n, pl* **mots** *same or* ˈmōz\ [F, word, saying, fr. LL *muttum* grunt] : a witty saying
mote \ˈmōt\ *n* : a small particle
mo·tel \mō-ˈtel\ *n* [blend of *motor* and *hotel*] : a hotel in which the rooms are accessible from the parking area
mo·tet \mō-ˈtet\ *n* : a choral work on a sacred text for several voices usu. without instrumental accompaniment
moth \ˈmȯth\ *n, pl* **moths** \ˈmȯthz, ˈmȯths\ : any of various insects belonging to the same order as the butterflies but usu. night-flying and with a stouter body and smaller wings
moth·ball \ˈmȯth-ˌbȯl\ *n* **1** : a ball (as of naphthalene) used to keep moths out of clothing **2** *pl* : protective storage
¹moth·er \ˈmə-thər\ *n* **1** : a female parent **2** : the superior of a religious community of women **3** : SOURCE, ORIGIN — **moth·er·hood** \-ˌhu̇d\ *n* — **moth·er·less** *adj* — **moth·er·li·ness** \-lē-nəs\ *n* — **moth·er·ly** *adj*
²mother *vb* **1** : to give birth to; *also* : PRODUCE **2** : to care for or protect like a mother
moth·er·board \ˈmə-thər-ˌbȯrd\ *n* : the main circuit board esp. of a microcomputer
moth·er–in–law \ˈmə-thər-ən-ˌlȯ\ *n, pl* **mothers–in–law** \ˈmə-thərz-\ : the mother of one's spouse
moth·er·land \ˈmə-thər-ˌland\ *n* **1** : the land of origin of something **2** : the native land of one's ancestors
moth·er–of–pearl \ˌmə-thər-əv-ˈpərl\ *n* : the hard pearly matter forming the inner layer of a mollusk shell
mo·tif \mō-ˈtēf\ *n* [F, motive, motif] : a dominant idea or central theme (as in a work of art)
mo·tile \ˈmōt-ᵊl, ˈmō-ˌtīl\ *adj* : capable of spontaneous movement — **mo·til·i·ty** \mō-ˈti-lə-tē\ *n*
¹mo·tion \ˈmō-shən\ *n* **1** : an act, process, or instance of moving **2** : a proposal for action (as by a deliberative body) **3** *pl* : ACTIVITIES, MOVEMENTS — **mo·tion·less** *adj* — **mo·tion·less·ly** *adv* — **mo·tion·less·ness** *n*
²motion *vb* : to direct or signal by a movement
motion picture *n* : a series of pictures projected on a screen so rapidly that they produce a continuous picture in which persons and objects seem to move
motion sickness *n* : sickness induced by motion and characterized by nausea
mo·ti·vate \ˈmō-tə-ˌvāt\ *vb* **-vat·ed; -vat·ing** : to provide with a motive : IMPEL — **mo·ti·va·tion** \ˌmō-tə-ˈvā-shən\ *n* — **mo·ti·va·tion·al** \-shə-nəl\ *adj* — **mo·ti·va·tor** \ˈmō-tə-ˌvā-tər\ *n*
¹mo·tive \ˈmō-tiv, 2 also mō-ˈtēv\ *n* **1** : something (as a need or desire) that causes a person to act **2** : a recurrent theme in a musical composition **3** : MOTIF — **mo·tive·less** *adj*
²mo·tive \ˈmō-tiv\ *adj* **1** : moving to action **2** : of or relating to motion
mot·ley \ˈmät-lē\ *adj* **1** : variegated in color **2** : made up of diverse often incongruous elements **syn** heterogeneous, miscellaneous, assorted, mixed, varied
¹mo·tor \ˈmō-tər\ *n* **1** : one that imparts motion **2** : a machine that produces motion or power for doing work **3** : AUTOMOBILE
²motor *vb* : to travel or transport by automobile : DRIVE — **mo·tor·ist** *n*
mo·tor·bike \ˈmō-tər-ˌbīk\ *n* : a small lightweight motorcycle
mo·tor·boat \-ˌbōt\ *n* : a boat propelled by a motor
mo·tor·cade \-ˌkād\ *n* : a procession of motor vehicles
mo·tor·car \-ˌkär\ *n* : AUTOMOBILE
mo·tor·cy·cle \ˈmō-tər-ˌsī-kəl\ *n* : a 2-wheeled automotive vehicle — **mo·tor·cy·clist** \-k(ə-)list\ *n*
motor home *n* : a large motor vehicle equipped as living quarters
motor inn *n* : MOTEL
mo·tor·ize \ˈmō-tə-ˌrīz\ *vb* **-ized; -iz·ing 1** : to equip with a motor **2** : to equip with automobiles

mo·tor·man \\'mō-tər-mən\ *n* : an operator of a motor-driven vehicle (as a streetcar or subway train)

motor scooter *n* : a low 2- or 3-wheeled automotive vehicle resembling a child's scooter but having a seat

mo·tor·truck \\'mō-tər-₁trək\ *n* : an automotive truck

motor vehicle *n* : an automotive vehicle (as an automobile) not operated on rails

mot·tle \\'mät-ᵊl\ *vb* **mot·tled; mot·tling** : to mark with spots of different color : BLOTCH

mot·to \\'mä-tō\ *n, pl* **mottoes** *also* **mottos** [It, fr. LL *muttum* grunt, fr. L *muttire* to mutter] **1** : a sentence, phrase, or word inscribed on something to indicate its character or use **2** : a short expression of a guiding rule of conduct

moue \\'mü\ *n* : a little grimace

mould \\'mōld\ *var of* MOLD

moult \\'mōlt\ *var of* MOLT

mound \\'maund\ *n* **1** : an artificial bank or hill of earth or stones **2** : KNOLL **3** : HEAP, PILE

¹mount \\'maunt\ *n* : a high hill

²mount *vb* **1** : to increase in amount or extent; *also* : RISE, ASCEND **2** : to get up on something; *esp* : to seat oneself on (as a horse) for riding **3** : to put in position ⟨∼ artillery⟩ **4** : to set on something that elevates **5** : to attach to a support **6** : to prepare esp. for examination or display — **mount·able** *adj* — **mount·er** *n*

³mount *n* **1** : FRAME, SUPPORT **2** : a means of conveyance; *esp* : SADDLE HORSE

moun·tain \\'maunt-ᵊn\ *n* : a landmass higher than a hill — **moun·tain·ous** \-ᵊn-əs\ *adj* — **moun·talny** \-ᵊn-ē\ *adj*

mountain ash *n* : any of various trees related to the roses that have pinnate leaves and red or orange-red fruits

moun·tain·eer \₁maunt-ᵊn-'ir\ *n* **1** : a native or inhabitant of a mountainous region **2** : one who climbs mountains for sport

mountain goat *n* : a ruminant mammal of mountainous northwestern No. America that resembles a goat

mountain goat

mountain laurel *n* : a No. American evergreen shrub or small tree of the heath family with glossy leaves and clusters of rose-colored or white flowers

mountain lion *n* : COUGAR

moun·tain·side \\'maunt-ᵊn-₁sīd\ *n* : the side of a mountain

moun·tain·top \-₁täp\ *n* : the summit of a mountain

moun·te·bank \\'maun-ti-₁baŋk\ *n* [It *montimbanco*, fr. *montare* to mount + *in* in, on + *banco, banca* bench] : QUACK, CHARLATAN

Mount·ie \\'maun-tē\ *n* : a member of the Royal Canadian Mounted Police

mount·ing \\'maun-tiŋ\ *n* : something that serves as a frame or support

mourn \\'mōrn\ *vb* : to feel or express grief or sorrow — **mourn·er** *n*

mourn·ful \-fəl\ *adj* : expressing, feeling, or causing sorrow — **mourn·ful·ly** *adv* — **mourn·ful·ness** *n*

mourn·ing \\'mōr-niŋ\ *n* **1** : an outward sign (as black clothes) of grief for a person's death **2** : a period of time during which signs of grief are shown

mouse \\'maus\ *n, pl* **mice** \\'mīs\ **1** : any of numerous small rodents with pointed snout, long body, and slender tail **2** : a small manual device that controls cursor movement on a computer display

mous·er \\'mau-sər\ *n* : a cat proficient at catching mice

mouse·trap \\'maus-₁trap\ *n* **1** : a trap for catching mice **2** : a stratagem that lures one to defeat or destruction — **mousetrap** *vb*

mousse \\'müs\ *n* [F, lit., froth] **1** : a molded chilled dessert made with sweetened and flavored whipped cream or egg whites and gelatin **2** : a foamy preparation used in styling hair — **mousse** *vb*

mous·tache \\'məs-₁tash, (₁)məs-'tash\ *var of* MUSTACHE

mousy *or* **mous·ey** \\'mau-sē, -zē\ *adj* **mous·i·er; -est** **1** : QUIET, STEALTHY **2** : TIMID **3** : grayish brown — **mous·i·ness** \\'mau-sē-nəs, -zē-\ *n*

¹mouth \\'mauth\ *n, pl* **mouths** \\'mauᵺz, 'mauths\ **1** : the opening through which an animal takes in food; *also* : the cavity that encloses the tongue, lips, and teeth in the typical vertebrate **2** : something resembling a mouth (as in affording entrance) — **mouthed** \\'mauᵺd, 'mautht\ *adj* — **mouth·ful** *n*

²mouth \\'mauᵺ\ *vb* **1** : SPEAK; *also* : DECLAIM **2** : to repeat without comprehension or sincerity **3** : to form soundlessly with the lips

mouth·part \\'mauth-₁pärt\ *n* : a structure or appendage near the mouth (as of an insect) esp. when adapted for eating

mouth·piece \-₁pēs\ *n* **1** : a part (as of a musical instrument) that goes in the mouth or to which the mouth is applied **2** : SPOKESMAN

mouth·wash \-₁wȯsh, -₁wäsh\ *n* : a usu. antiseptic liquid preparation for cleaning the mouth and teeth

mou·ton \\'mü-₁tän\ *n* : processed sheepskin that has been sheared or dyed to resemble beaver or seal

¹move \\'müv\ *vb* **moved; mov·ing** **1** : to change or cause to change position or posture **2** : to go or cause to go from one point to another; *also* : DEPART **3** : to take or cause to take action **4** : to show marked activity **5** : to stir the emotions **6** : to make a formal request, application, or appeal **7** : to change one's residence **8** : EVACUATE 2 — **mov·able** *or* **move·able** \\'mü-və-bəl\ *adj*

²move *n* **1** : an act of moving **2** : a calculated step taken to gain an objective **3** : a change of location **4** : an agile action esp. in sports

move·ment \\'müv-mənt\ *n* **1** : the act or process of moving : MOVE **2** : a series of organized activities working toward an objective **3** : the moving parts of a mechanism (as of a watch) **4** : RHYTHM **5** : a section of an extended musical composition **6** : an act of voiding the bowels; *also* : STOOL 4

mov·er \\'mü-vər\ *n* : one that moves; *esp* : one that moves the belongings of others from one location to another

mov·ie \\'mü-vē\ *n* **1** : MOTION PICTURE **2** *pl* : a showing of a motion picture **3** *pl* : the motion-picture industry

¹mow \\'mau\ *n* : the part of a barn where hay or straw is stored

²mow \\'mō\ *vb* **mowed; mowed** *or* **mown** \\'mōn\; **mow·ing** **1** : to cut (as grass) with a scythe or machine **2** : to cut the standing herbage of ⟨∼ the lawn⟩ — **mow·er** *n*

\ə\abut \ᵊ\kitten \ər\further \a\ash \ā\ace \ä\mop, mar \au\out \ch\chin \e\bet \ē\easy \g\go \i\hit \ī\ice \j\job \ŋ\sing \ō\go \ȯ\law \ȯi\boy \th\thin \ᵺ\the \ü\loot \u̇\foot \y\yet \zh\vision *see also* Pronunciation Symbols page

Mo·zam·bi·can \ˌmō-zəm-ˈbē-kən\ *n* : a native or inhabitant of Mozambique

moz·za·rel·la \ˌmät-sə-ˈre-lə\ *n* [It] : a moist white unsalted unripened mild cheese of a smooth rubbery texture

MP *abbr* 1 melting point 2 member of parliament 3 metropolitan police 4 military police; military policeman

mpg *abbr* miles per gallon

mph *abbr* miles per hour

Mr. \ˈmis-tər\ *n, pl* **Messrs.** \ˈme-sərz\ — used as a conventional title of courtesy before a man's surname or his title of office

MRI *abbr* magnetic resonance imaging

Mrs. \ˈmi-səz, -səs, *esp Southern* ˈmi-zəz, -zəs\ *n, pl* **Mes·dames** \mā-ˈdäm, -ˈdam\ — used as a conventional title of courtesy before a married woman's surname

Ms. \ˈmiz\ *n, pl* **Mss.** *or* **Mses.** \ˈmi-zez\ — used instead of *Miss* or *Mrs.*

MS *abbr* 1 manuscript 2 master of science 3 military science 4 Mississippi 5 motor ship 6 multiple sclerosis

msec *abbr* millisecond

msg *abbr* message

MSG *abbr* 1 master sergeant 2 monosodium glutamate

msgr *abbr* 1 monseigneur 2 monsignor

MSgt *abbr* master sergeant

MSS *abbr* manuscripts

MST *abbr* mountain standard time

mt *abbr* mount; mountain

Mt *abbr* Matthew

MT *abbr* 1 metric ton 2 Montana 3 mountain time

mtg *abbr* 1 meeting 2 mortgage

mtge *abbr* mortgage

mu \ˈmyü, ˈmü\ *n* : the 12th letter of the Greek alphabet — M or μ

¹much \ˈməch\ *adj* **more** \ˈmōr\; **most** \ˈmōst\ : great in quantity, amount, extent, or degree ⟨∼ money⟩

²much *adv* **more; most** 1 : to a great degree or extent ⟨∼ happier⟩ 2 : ALMOST, NEARLY ⟨looks ∼ as he did before⟩

³much *n* 1 : a great quantity, amount, extent, or degree 2 : something considerable or impressive

mu·ci·lage \ˈmyü-sə-lij\ *n* : a watery sticky solution (as of a gum) used esp. as an adhesive — **mu·ci·lag·i·nous** \ˌmyü-sə-ˈla-jə-nəs\ *adj*

muck \ˈmək\ *n* 1 : soft moist barnyard manure 2 : FILTH, DIRT 3 : a dark richly organic soil; *also* : MUD, MIRE — **mucky** *adj*

muck·rake \-ˌrāk\ *vb* : to expose publicly real or apparent misconduct of a prominent individual or business — **muck·rak·er** *n*

mu·cus \ˈmyü-kəs\ *n* : a slimy slippery protective secretion of membranes (**mucous membranes**) lining some body cavities — **mu·cous** \-kəs\ *adj*

mud \ˈməd\ *n* : soft wet earth : MIRE — **mud·di·ly** \ˈmə-də-lē\ *adv* — **mud·di·ness** \-dē-nəs\ *n* — **mud·dy** \ˈmə-dē\ *adj or vb*

mud·dle \ˈməd-ᵊl\ *vb* **mud·dled; mud·dling** 1 : to make muddy 2 : to confuse esp. with liquor 3 : to mix up or make a mess of 4 : to think or act in a confused way

mud·dle·head·ed \ˌməd-ᵊl-ˈhe-dəd\ *adj* 1 : mentally confused 2 : INEPT

mud·flat \ˈməd-ˌflat\ *n* : a level tract alternately covered and left bare by the tide

mud·guard \ˈməd-ˌgärd\ *n* : a guard over or a flap behind a wheel of a vehicle to catch or deflect mud

mud·room \-ˌrüm, -ˌrüm\ *n* : a room in a house for removing dirty or wet footwear and clothing

mud·sling·er \-ˌsliŋ-ər\ *n* : one who uses invective esp. against a political opponent — **mud·sling·ing** \-ˌsliŋ-iŋ\ *n*

Muen·ster \ˈmən-stər, ˈmün-, ˈmùn-\ *n* : a semisoft bland cheese

mu·ez·zin \mü-ˈez-ᵊn, myü-\ *n* : a Muslim crier who calls the hour of daily prayer

¹muff \ˈməf\ *n* : a warm tubular covering for the hands

²muff *n* : a bungling performance; *esp* : a failure to hold a ball in attempting a catch — **muff** *vb*

muf·fin \ˈmə-fən\ *n* : a small soft cake baked in a cup-shaped container

muf·fle \ˈmə-fəl\ *vb* **muf·fled; muf·fling** 1 : to wrap up so as to conceal or protect 2 : to wrap or pad with something to dull the sound of 3 : to keep down : SUPPRESS

muf·fler \ˈmə-flər\ *n* 1 : a scarf worn around the neck 2 : a device (as on a car's exhaust) to deaden noise

muf·ti \ˈməf-tē\ *n* : civilian clothes

¹mug \ˈməg\ *n* : a usu. metal or earthenware cylindrical drinking cup

²mug *vb* **mugged; mug·ging** 1 : to pose or make faces esp. to attract attention or for a camera 2 : PHOTOGRAPH

³mug *vb* **mugged; mug·ging** : to assault usu. with intent to rob — **mug·ger** *n*

mug·gy \ˈmə-gē\ *adj* **mug·gi·er; -est** : being warm and humid — **mug·gi·ness** \-gē-nəs\ *n*

mug·wump \ˈməg-ˌwəmp\ *n* [obs. slang *mugwump* kingpin, fr. Massachuset (a No. American Indian language) *mugquomp* war leader] : an independent in politics

Mu·ham·mad·an \mō-ˈha-mə-dən, -ˈhä-\ *n* : MUSLIM — **Mu·ham·mad·an·ism** \-də-ˌni-zəm\ *n*

Mu·har·ram \mü-ˈhar-əm\ *n* [Ar *Muḥarram*] : the 1st month of the Islamic year

mu·ja·hid·een *or* **mu·ja·hed·in** \mü-ˌja-hi-ˈdēn, -ˌjä-\ *n pl* [Ar *mujāhidīn*, pl. of *mujāhid*, lit., person who wages jihad] : Islamic guerrilla fighters esp. in the Middle East

muk·luk \ˈmək-ˌlək\ *n* 1 : an Eskimo boot of sealskin or reindeer skin 2 : a boot with a soft leather sole worn over several pairs of socks

mu·lat·to \mù-ˈla-tō, myü-, -ˈlä-\ *n, pl* **-toes** *or* **-tos** [Sp *mulato*, fr. *mulo* mule, fr. L *mulus*] : a first-generation offspring of a black person and a white person; *also* : a person of mixed white and black ancestry

mul·ber·ry \ˈməl-ˌber-ē\ *n* : any of a genus of trees with edible berrylike fruit and leaves used as food for silkworms; *also* : the fruit

mulch \ˈməlch\ *n* : a protective covering (as of straw or leaves) spread on the ground esp. to reduce evaporation or control weeds — **mulch** *vb*

¹mulct \ˈməlkt\ *n* : FINE, PENALTY

²mulct *vb* 1 : FINE 2 : CHEAT, DEFRAUD

¹mule \ˈmyül\ *n* 1 : a hybrid offspring of a male donkey and a female horse 2 : a very stubborn person — **mul·ish** \ˈmyü-lish\ *adj* — **mul·ish·ly** *adv* — **mu·lish·ness** *n*

²mule *n* : a slipper whose upper does not extend around the heel of the foot

mule deer *n* : a long-eared deer of western No. America

mu·le·teer \ˌmyü-lə-ˈtir\ *n* : one who drives mules

¹mull \ˈməl\ *vb* : PONDER, MEDITATE

²mull *vb* : to heat, sweeten, and flavor (as wine) with spices

mul·lein \ˈmə-lən\ *n* : a tall herb related to the snapdragons that has coarse woolly leaves and flowers in spikes

mul·let \ˈmə-lət\ *n, pl* **mullet** *or* **mullets** : any of a family of largely gray chiefly marine bony fishes including valuable food fishes

mul·li·gan stew \ˈmə-li-gən-\ *n* : a stew made from whatever ingredients are available

mul·li·ga·taw·ny \ˌmə-li-gə-ˈto-nē\ *n* : a soup usu. of chicken stock seasoned with curry

mul·lion \ˈməl-yən\ *n* : a vertical strip separating windowpanes

multi- *comb form* 1 : many : multiple ⟨*multi*unit⟩ 2 : many times over ⟨*multi*millionaire⟩

mul·ti·col·ored \ˌməl-ti-ˈkə-lərd\ *adj* : having many colors

mul·ti·cul·tur·al \ˌməl-tē-ˈkəl-chə-rəl, -ˌtī-\ *adj* : of, relating to, reflecting, or adapted to diverse cultures ⟨a ∼ society⟩

mul·ti·di·men·sion·al \-ti-də-'men-chə-nəl, -ˌtī-, -dī-\ *adj* : of, relating to, or having many facets or dimensions ⟨a ∼ problem⟩ ⟨∼ space⟩

mul·ti·fac·et·ed \-'fa-sə-təd\ *adj* : having several distinct facets

mul·ti·fam·i·ly \-'fam-lē, -'fa-mə-\ *adj* : designed for use by several families

mul·ti·far·i·ous \ˌməl-tə-'far-ē-əs\ *adj* : having great variety : DIVERSE — **mul·ti·far·i·ous·ness** *n*

mul·ti·form \'məl-ti-ˌfȯrm\ *adj* : having many forms or appearances — **mul·ti·for·mi·ty** \ˌməl-ti-'fȯr-mə-tē\ *n*

mul·ti·lat·er·al \ˌməl-ti-'la-tə-rəl, -ˌtī-, -'la-trəl\ *adj* : having many sides or participants ⟨∼ treaty⟩ — **mul·ti·lat·er·al·ism** \-'la-tə-rə-ˌli-zəm\ *n*

mul·ti·lev·el \-'le-vəl\ *adj* : having several levels

mul·ti·lin·gual \-'liŋ-gwəl\ *adj* : knowing or using several languages — **mul·ti·lin·gual·ism** \-gwə-ˌli-zəm\ *n*

mul·ti·me·dia \-'mē-dē-ə\ *adj* : using, involving, or encompassing several media ⟨a ∼ advertising campaign⟩

mul·ti·mil·lion·aire \ˌməl-ti-ˌmil-yə-'nar, -ˌtī-, -'mil-yə-ˌnar\ *n* : a person worth several million dollars

mul·ti·na·tion·al \-'na-shə-nəl\ *adj* **1** : of or relating to several nationalities **2** : relating to or involving several nations **3** : having divisions in several countries ⟨a ∼ corporation⟩ — **multinational** *n*

¹mul·ti·ple \'məl-tə-pəl\ *adj* **1** : more than one; *also* : MANY **2** : VARIOUS

²multiple *n* : the product of a quantity by an integer ⟨35 is a ∼ of 7⟩

multiple–choice *adj* : having several answers given from which the correct one is to be chosen ⟨a ∼ question⟩

multiple personality *n* : a mental and emotional disorder which is a neurosis and in which the personality becomes separated into two or more parts each of which controls behavior part of the time

multiple sclerosis *n* : a disease marked by patches of hardened tissue in the brain or spinal cord and associated esp. with partial or complete paralysis and muscular tremor

mul·ti·pli·cand \ˌməl-tə-pli-'kand\ *n* : the number that is to be multiplied by another

mul·ti·pli·ca·tion \ˌməl-tə-plə-'kā-shən\ *n* **1** : INCREASE **2** : a short method of finding the result of adding a figure the number of times indicated by another figure

multiplication sign *n* **1** : TIMES SIGN **2** : a centered dot indicating multiplication

mul·ti·plic·i·ty \ˌməl-tə-'pli-sə-tē\ *n, pl* **-ties** : a great number or variety

mul·ti·pli·er \'məl-tə-ˌplī-ər\ *n* : one that multiplies; *esp* : a number by which another number is multiplied

mul·ti·ply \'məl-tə-ˌplī\ *vb* **-plied; -ply·ing** **1** : to increase in number (as by breeding) **2** : to find the product of by multiplication; *also* : to perform multiplication

mul·ti·pur·pose \ˌməl-ti-'pər-pəs, -ˌtī-\ *adj* : having or serving several purposes

mul·ti·ra·cial \-'rā-shəl\ *adj* : composed of, involving, or representing various races

mul·ti·sense \-ˌsens\ *adj* : having several meanings ⟨∼ words⟩

mul·ti·sto·ry \-ˌstȯr-ē\ *adj* : having several stories ⟨∼ buildings⟩

mul·ti·tude \'məl-tə-ˌtüd, -ˌtyüd\ *n* : a great number — **mul·ti·tu·di·nous** \ˌməl-tə-'tüd-ᵊn-əs, -'tyüd-\ *adj*

mul·ti·unit \ˌməl-ti-'yü-nət, -ˌtī-\ *adj* : having several units

mul·ti·vi·ta·min \-'vī-tə-mən\ *adj* : containing several vitamins and esp. all known to be essential to health

¹mum \'məm\ *adj* : SILENT

²mum *n* : CHRYSANTHEMUM

³mum *chiefly Brit var of* MOM

mum·ble \'məm-bəl\ *vb* **mum·bled; mum·bling** : to speak in a low indistinct manner — **mumble** *n* — **mum·bler** *n* — **mum·bly** *adj*

mum·ble·ty–peg \'məm-bəl-tē-ˌpeg\ *also* **mum·ble–the–peg** \'məm-bəl-thə-\ *n* : a game in which the players try to flip a knife from various positions so that the blade will stick into the ground

mum·bo jum·bo \ˌməm-bō-'jəm-bō\ *n* **1** : a complicated ritual with elaborate trappings **2** : GIBBERISH, NONSENSE

mum·mer \'mə-mər\ *n* **1** : an actor esp. in a pantomime **2** : a person who goes merrymaking in disguise during festivals — **mum·mery** *n*

mum·my \'mə-mē\ *n, pl* **mummies** [ME *mummie* powdered parts of a mummified body used as a drug, fr. MF *momie*, fr. ML *mumia*, fr. Ar *mūmiyah* bitumen, mummy, fr. Per *mūm* wax] : a body embalmed for burial in the manner of the ancient Egyptians — **mum·mi·fi·ca·tion** \ˌmə-mi-fə-'kā-shən\ *n* — **mum·mi·fy** \'mə-mi-ˌfī\ *vb*

mumps \'məmps\ *n sing or pl* [fr. pl. of obs. *mump* grimace] : a virus disease marked by fever and swelling esp. of the salivary glands

mun *or* **munic** *abbr* municipal

munch \'mənch\ *vb* : to eat with a chewing action; *also* : to snack on

munch·ies \'mən-chēz\ *n pl* **1** : hunger pangs **2** : light snack foods

mun·dane \ˌmən-'dān, 'mən-ˌdān\ *adj* **1** : of or relating to the world **2** : concerned with the practical details of everyday life — **mun·dane·ly** *adv*

mu·nic·i·pal \myu̇-'ni-sə-pəl\ *adj* **1** : of, relating to, or characteristic of a municipality **2** : restricted to one locality — **mu·nic·i·pal·ly** *adv*

mu·nic·i·pal·i·ty \myu̇-ˌni-sə-'pa-lə-tē\ *n, pl* **-ties** : an urban political unit with corporate status and usu. powers of self-government

mu·nif·i·cent \myu̇-'ni-fə-sənt\ *adj* : liberal in giving : GENEROUS — **mu·nif·i·cence** \-səns\ *n*

mu·ni·tion \myu̇-'ni-shən\ *n* : ARMAMENT, AMMUNITION

¹mu·ral \'myu̇r-əl\ *adj* **1** : of or relating to a wall **2** : applied to and made part of a wall or ceiling surface

²mural *n* : a mural painting — **mu·ral·ist** *n*

¹mur·der \'mər-dər\ *n* **1** : the crime of unlawfully killing a person esp. with malice aforethought **2** : something unusually difficult or dangerous

²murder *vb* **1** : to commit a murder; *also* : to kill brutally **2** : to put an end to **3** : to spoil by performing poorly ⟨∼ a song⟩ — **mur·der·er** *n*

mur·der·ess \'mər-də-rəs\ *n* : a woman who murders

mur·der·ous \'mər-də-rəs\ *adj* **1** : having or appearing to have the purpose of murder **2** : marked by or causing murder or bloodshed ⟨∼ gunfire⟩ — **mur·der·ous·ly** *adv*

murk \'mərk\ *n* : DARKNESS, GLOOM — **murk·i·ly** \'mər-kə-lē\ *adv* — **murk·i·ness** \-kē-nəs\ *n* — **murky** *adj*

mur·mur \'mər-mər\ *n* **1** : a muttered complaint **2** : a low indistinct often continuous sound — **murmur** *vb* — **mur·mur·er** *n* — **mur·mur·ous** *adj*

mus *abbr* **1** museum **2** music; musical; musician

mus·ca·tel \ˌməs-kə-'tel\ *n* : a sweet fortified wine

¹mus·cle \'mə-səl\ *n* [ME, fr. MF, fr. L *musculus*, fr. dim. of *mus* mouse] **1** : a body tissue consisting of long cells that contract when stimulated and produce motion; *also* : an organ consisting of this tissue and functioning in moving a body part **2** : STRENGTH, BRAWN — **mus·cled** \'mə-səld\ *adj* — **mus·cu·lar** \'məs-kyə-lər\ *adj* — **mus·cu·lar·i·ty** \ˌməs-kyə-'lar-ə-tē\ *n*

²muscle *vb* **mus·cled; mus·cling** : to force one's way

mus·cle–bound \'mə-səl-ˌbau̇nd\ *adj* : having some of the muscles abnormally enlarged and lacking in elasticity (as from excessive exercise)

Mus·co·vy duck \'məs-ˌkō-vē-\ *n* : a large dark crested duck of Central and So. America that is widely kept in domestication

muscular dystrophy *n* : any of a group of diseases characterized by progressive wasting of muscles

mus·cu·la·ture \'məs-kyə-lə-ˌchùr\ *n* : the muscles of the body or its parts

¹muse \'myüz\ *vb* **mused; mus·ing** [ME, fr. MF *muser* to gape, idle, muse, fr. *muse* mouth of an animal, fr. ML *musus*] : to become absorbed in thought — **mus·ing·ly** *adv*

²muse *n* [fr. *Muse* any of the nine sister goddesses of learning and the arts in Greek myth, fr. ME, fr. MF, fr. L *Musa*, fr. Gk *Mousa*] : a source of inspiration

mu·se·um \myù-'zē-əm\ *n* : an institution devoted to the procurement, care, and display of objects of lasting interest or value

¹mush \'məsh\ *n* **1** : cornmeal boiled in water **2** : sentimental drivel

²mush *vb* : to travel esp. over snow with a sled drawn by dogs

¹mush·room \'məsh-ˌrüm, -ˌrùm\ *n* : the fleshy usu. caplike spore-bearing organ of various fungi esp. when edible; *also* : such a fungus

²mushroom *vb* **1** : to collect wild mushrooms **2** : to spread out : EXPAND **3** : to grow rapidly

mushy \'mə-shē\ *adj* **mush·i·er; -est 1** : soft like mush **2** : excessively sentimental

mu·sic \'myü-zik\ *n* **1** : the science or art of combining tones into a composition having structure and continuity; *also* : vocal or instrumental sounds having rhythm, melody, or harmony **2** : an agreeable sound

¹mu·si·cal \'myü-zi-kəl\ *adj* **1** : of or relating to music or musicians **2** : having the pleasing tonal qualities of music **3** : fond of or gifted in music — **mu·si·cal·ly** \-k(ə-)lē\ *adv*

²musical *n* : a film or theatrical production consisting of musical numbers and dialogue based on a unifying plot

mu·si·cale \ˌmyü-zi-'kal\ *n* : a usu. private social gathering featuring music

mu·si·cian \myù-'zi-shən\ *n* : a composer, conductor, or performer of music — **mu·si·cian·ly** *adj* — **mu·si·cian·ship** *n*

mu·si·col·o·gy \ˌmyü-zi-'kä-lə-jē\ *n* : the study of music as a field of knowledge or research — **mu·si·co·log·i·cal** \-kə-'lä-ji-kəl\ *adj* — **mu·si·col·o·gist** \-'kä-lə-jist\ *n*

musk \'məsk\ *n* : a substance obtained esp. from a small Asian deer **(musk deer)** and used as a perfume fixative — **musk·i·ness** \'məs-kē-nəs\ *n* — **musky** *adj*

mus·keg \'məs-ˌkeg\ *n* : BOG; *esp* : a mossy bog in northern No. America

mus·kel·lunge \'məs-kə-ˌlənj\ *n, pl* **muskellunge** : a large No. American pike that is a valuable sport fish

mus·ket \'məs-kət\ *n* [MF *mousquet*, fr. It *moschetto* arrow for a crossbow, musket, fr. dim. of *mosca* fly, fr. L *musca*] : a heavy large-caliber muzzle-loading shoulder firearm — **mus·ke·teer** \ˌməs-kə-'tir\ *n*

mus·ket·ry \'məs-kə-trē\ *n* **1** : MUSKETS **2** : MUSKETEERS **3** : musket fire

musk·mel·on \'məsk-ˌme-lən\ *n* : a small round to oval melon that has usu. a sweet edible green or orange flesh

musk ox *n* : a heavyset shaggy-coated wild ox of Greenland and the arctic tundra of northern No. America

musk·rat \'məs-ˌkrat\ *n, pl* **muskrat** *or* **muskrats** : a large No. American aquatic rodent with webbed feet and dark brown fur; *also* : its fur

Mus·lim \'məz-ləm\ *n* : an adherent of Islam — **Muslim** *adj*

mus·lin \'məz-lən\ *n* : a plain-woven sheer to coarse cotton fabric

¹muss \'məs\ *n* : a state of disorder — **muss·i·ly** \'mə-sə-lē\ *adv* — **muss·i·ness** \-sē-nəs\ *n* — **mussy** *adj*

²muss *vb* : to make untidy : DISARRANGE

mus·sel \'mə-səl\ *n* **1** : a dark edible saltwater bivalve mollusk **2** : any of various freshwater bivalve mollusks of the central U.S. having shells with a pearly lining

¹must \'məst\ *vb* — used as an auxiliary esp. to express a command, requirement, obligation, or necessity

²must *n* **1** : an imperative duty **2** : an indispensable item

mus·tache \'məs-ˌtash, (ˌ)məs-'tash\ *n* : the hair growing on the human upper lip — **mus·tached** \-ˌtasht, -'tasht\ *adj*

mus·tang \'məs-ˌtaŋ\ *n* [MexSp *mestengo*, fr. Sp, stray, fr. *mesteño* strayed, fr. *mesta* annual roundup of cattle that disposed of strays, fr. ML *(animalia) mixta* mixed animals] : a small hardy naturalized horse of the western plains of America; *also* : BRONC

mus·tard \'məs-tərd\ *n* **1** : a pungent yellow powder of the seeds of an herb related to the cabbage and used as a condiment or in medicine **2** : a plant that yields mustard; *also* : a closely related plant — **mustardy** *adj*

mustard gas *n* : a poison gas used in warfare that has violent irritating and blistering effects

¹mus·ter \'məs-tər\ *n* **1** : an act of assembling (as for military inspection); *also* : critical examination **2** : an assembled group

²muster *vb* [ME *mustren* to show, muster, fr. OF *monstrer*, fr. L *monstrare* to show, fr. *monstrum* evil omen, monster] **1** : CONVENE, ASSEMBLE; *also* : to call the roll of **2** : ACCUMULATE **3** : to call forth : ROUSE **4** : to amount to : COMPRISE

muster out *vb* : to discharge from military service

musty \'məs-tē\ *adj* **mus·ti·er; -est** : MOLDY, STALE; *also* : tasting or smelling of damp or decay — **must·i·ly** \-tə-lē\ *adv* — **must·i·ness** \-tē-nəs\ *n*

mu·ta·ble \'myü-tə-bəl\ *adj* **1** : prone to change : FICKLE **2** : capable of or subject to mutation : VARIABLE — **mu·ta·bil·i·ty** \ˌmyü-tə-'bi-lə-tē\ *n*

mu·tant \'myüt-ᵊnt\ *adj* : of, relating to, or produced by mutation — **mu·tant** *n*

mu·tate \'myü-ˌtāt\ *vb* **mu·tat·ed; mu·tat·ing** : to undergo or cause to undergo mutation — **mu·ta·tive** \'myü-ˌtā-tiv, -tə-tiv\ *adj*

mu·ta·tion \myü-'tā-shən\ *n* **1** : CHANGE **2** : an inherited physical or biochemical change in genetic material; *also* : the process of producing a mutation **3** : an individual, strain, or trait resulting from mutation — **mu·ta·tion·al** *adj*

¹mute \'myüt\ *adj* **mut·er; mut·est 1** : unable to speak : DUMB **2** : SILENT — **mute·ly** *adv* — **mute·ness** *n*

²mute *n* **1** : a person who cannot or does not speak **2** : a device on a musical instrument that reduces, softens, or muffles the tone

³mute *vb* **mut·ed; mut·ing** : to muffle, reduce, or eliminate the sound of

mu·ti·late \'myüt-ᵊl-ˌāt\ *vb* **-lat·ed; -lat·ing 1** : to cut up or alter radically so as to make imperfect **2** : MAIM, CRIPPLE — **mu·ti·la·tion** \ˌmyüt-ᵊl-'ā-shən\ *n* — **mu·ti·la·tor** \'myüt-ᵊl-ˌā-tər\ *n*

mu·ti·ny \'myü-tə-nē\ *n, pl* **-nies** : willful refusal to obey constituted authority; *esp* : revolt against a superior officer — **mu·ti·neer** \ˌmyüt-ᵊn-'ir\ *n* — **mu·ti·nous** \'myüt-ᵊn-əs\ *adj* — **mu·ti·nous·ly** *adv* — **mutiny** *vb*

mutt \'mət\ *n* : MONGREL, CUR

mut·ter \'mə-tər\ *vb* **1** : to speak indistinctly or with a low voice and lips partly closed **2** : GRUMBLE — **mutter** *n*

mut·ton \'mət-ᵊn\ *n* [ME *motoun*, fr. OF *moton* ram] : the flesh of a mature sheep used for food — **mut·tony** *adj*

mut·ton·chops \'mət-ᵊn-ˌchäps\ *n pl* : whiskers on the side of the face that are narrow at the temple and broad and round by the lower jaws

mu·tu·al \'myü-chə-wəl\ *adj* **1** : given and received in equal amount ⟨~ trust⟩ **2** : having the same feelings one

for the other ⟨~ enemies⟩ **3** : COMMON, JOINT ⟨a ~ friend⟩ — **mu·tu·al·ly** *adv*
mutual fund *n* : an investment company that invests money of its shareholders in a usu. diversified group of securities of other corporations
muu·muu \'mü-ˌmü\ *n* : a loose dress of Hawaiian origin
¹muz·zle \'mə-zəl\ *n* **1** : the nose and jaws of an animal; *also* : a covering for the muzzle to prevent biting or eating **2** : the mouth of a gun

muzzle 1

²muzzle *vb* **muz·zled; muz·zling 1** : to put a muzzle on **2** : to restrain from expression : GAG
mV *abbr* millivolt
MV *abbr* motor vessel
MVP *abbr* most valuable player
MW *abbr* megawatt
my \'mī\ *adj* **1** : of or relating to me or myself **2** — used interjectionally esp. to express surprise
my·col·o·gy \mī-'kä-lə-jē\ *n* : a branch of biology dealing with fungi — **my·co·log·i·cal** \ˌmī-kə-'lä-ji-kəl\ *adj* — **my·col·o·gist** \mī-'kä-lə-jist\ *n*
my·elo·ma \ˌmī-ə-'lō-mə\ *n, pl* **-mas** *or* **-ma·ta** \-mə-tə\ : a primary tumor of the bone marrow
my·nah *or* **my·na** \'mī-nə\ *n* : any of several Asian starlings; *esp* : a dark brown slightly crested bird sometimes taught to mimic speech
my·o·pia \mī-'ō-pē-ə\ *n* : a condition in which visual images come to a focus in front of the retina resulting esp. in defective vision of distant objects — **my·o·pic** \-'ō-pik, -'ä-\ *adj* — **my·o·pi·cal·ly** \-pi-k(ə-)lē\ *adv*
¹myr·i·ad \'mir-ē-əd\ *n* [Gk *myriad-, myrias*, fr. *myrioi*

countless, ten thousand] : an indefinitely large number
²myriad *adj* : consisting of a very great but indefinite number
myr·mi·don \'mər-mə-ˌdän\ *n* : a loyal follower; *esp* : one who executes orders without protest or pity
myrrh \'mər\ *n* : a fragrant aromatic plant gum used in perfumes and formerly for incense
myr·tle \'mərt-ᵊl\ *n* : an evergreen shrub of southern Europe with shiny leaves, fragrant flowers, and black berries; *also* : PERIWINKLE
my·self \mī-'self, mə-\ *pron* : I, ME — used reflexively, for emphasis, or in absolute constructions ⟨I hurt ~⟩ ⟨I ~ did it⟩ ⟨~ busy, I sent him instead⟩
mys·tery \'mis-tə-rē\ *n, pl* **-ter·ies 1** : a religious truth known by revelation alone **2** : something not understood or beyond understanding **3** : enigmatic quality or character **4** : a work of fiction dealing with the solution of a mysterious crime — **mys·te·ri·ous** \mis-'tir-ē-əs\ *adj* — **mys·te·ri·ous·ly** *adv* — **mys·te·ri·ous·ness** *n*
¹mys·tic \'mis-tik\ *adj* **1** : of or relating to mystics or mysticism **2** : MYSTERIOUS; *also* : MYSTIFYING
²mystic *n* : a person who follows, advocates, or experiences mysticism
mys·ti·cal \'mis-ti-kəl\ *adj* **1** : SPIRITUAL, SYMBOLIC **2** : of or relating to an intimate knowledge of or direct communion with God (as through contemplation or visions)
mys·ti·cism \'mis-tə-ˌsi-zəm\ *n* : the belief that direct knowledge of God or ultimate reality is attainable through immediate intuition or insight
mys·ti·fy \'mis-tə-ˌfī\ *vb* **-fied; -fy·ing 1** : to perplex the mind of **2** : to make mysterious — **mys·ti·fi·ca·tion** \ˌmis-tə-fə-'kā-shən\ *n*
mys·tique \mi-'stēk\ *n* [F] **1** : an air or attitude of mystery and reverence developing around something or someone **2** : the special esoteric skill essential in a calling or activity
myth \'mith\ *n* **1** : a usu. legendary narrative that presents part of the beliefs of a people or explains a practice or natural phenomenon **2** : an imaginary or unverifiable person or thing — **myth·i·cal** \'mi-thi-kəl\ *adj*
my·thol·o·gy \mi-'thä-lə-jē\ *n, pl* **-gies** : a body of myths and esp. of those dealing with the gods and heroes of a people — **myth·o·log·i·cal** \ˌmi-thə-'lä-ji-kəl\ *adj* — **my·thol·o·gist** \mi-'thä-lə-jist\ *n*

N

¹n \'en\ *n, pl* **n's** *or* **ns** \'enz\ *often cap* **1** : the 14th letter of the English alphabet **2** : an unspecified quantity
²n *abbr, often cap* **1** net **2** neuter **3** noon **4** normal **5** north; northern **6** note **7** noun **8** number
N *symbol* nitrogen
-n — see -EN
Na *symbol* [NL *natrium*] sodium
NA *abbr* **1** no account **2** North America **3** not applicable **4** not available
NAACP \ˌen-ˌdə-bəl-ˌā-ˌsē-'pē, ˌen-ˌā-ˌā-ˌsē-\ *abbr* National Association for the Advancement of Colored People
nab \'nab\ *vb* **nabbed; nab·bing** : SEIZE; *esp* : ARREST
NAB *abbr* New American Bible
na·bob \'nā-ˌbäb\ *n* [Urdu *nawwāb*, provincial governor (in the Mogul empire), fr. Ar *nuwwāb*, pl. of *nā'ib* governor] : a man of great wealth or prominence
na·celle \nə-'sel\ *n* : an enclosure (as for an engine) on an aircraft

na·cre \'nā-kər\ *n* : MOTHER-OF-PEARL
na·dir \'nā-ˌdir, -dər\ *n* [ME, fr. MF, fr. Ar *naẓīr* opposite] **1** : the point of the celestial sphere that is directly opposite the zenith and directly beneath the observer **2** : the lowest point
¹nag \'nag\ *n* : HORSE; *esp* : an old or decrepit horse
²nag *vb* **nagged; nag·ging 1** : to find fault incessantly : COMPLAIN **2** : to irritate by constant scolding or urging **3** : to be a continuing source of annoyance ⟨a *nagging* backache⟩
³nag *n* : one who nags habitually
Nah *abbr* Nahum
Na·huatl \'nä-ˌwät-ᵊl\ *n* : a group of American Indian languages of central and southern Mexico

Na·hum \'nā-həm, -əm\ *n* — see BIBLE table
NAIA *abbr* National Association of Intercollegiate Athletes
na·iad \'nā-əd, 'nī-, -ˌad\ *n, pl* **naiads** *or* **na·ia·des** \-ə-ˌdēz\ **1** : one of the nymphs in ancient mythology living in lakes, rivers, springs, and fountains **2** : an aquatic young of some insects (as a dragonfly)
¹na·if *or* **na·if** \nä-'ēf\ *adj* : NAIVE
²naïf *or* **naif** *n* : a naive person
¹nail \'nāl\ *n* **1** : a horny sheath protecting the end of each finger and toe in humans and related primates **2** : a slender pointed fastener with a head designed to be pounded in
²nail *vb* : to fasten with or as if with a nail — **nail·er** *n*
nail down *vb* : to settle or establish clearly and unmistakably
nain·sook \'nān-ˌsuk\ *n* [Hindi *nainsukh,* fr. *nain* eye + *sukh* delight] : a soft lightweight muslin
nai·ra \'nī-rə\ *n* — see MONEY table
na·ive *or* **na·ïve** \nä-'ēv\ *adj* **na·iv·er; -est** [F *naïve,* fem. of *naïf,* fr. OF, inborn, natural, fr. L *nativus* native] **1** : marked by unaffected simplicity : ARTLESS, INGENUOUS **2** : CREDULOUS **syn** natural, innocent, simple, unaffected, unsophisticated, unstudied — **na·ive·ly** *adv* — **na·ive·ness** *n*
na·ive·té *also* **na·ive·té** *or* **na·ive·te** \ˌnä-ē-və-'tā, nä-'ē-və-ˌtā\ *n* **1** : a naive remark or action **2** : the quality or state of being naive
na·ive·ty *also* **na·ïve·ty** \nä-'ē-və-tē\ *n, pl* **-ties** : NAÏVETÉ
na·ked \'nā-kəd\ *adj* **1** : having no clothes on : NUDE **2** : UNSHEATHED ⟨a ~ sword⟩ **3** : lacking a usual or natural covering (as of foliage or feathers) **4** : PLAIN, UNADORNED ⟨the ~ truth⟩ **5** : not aided by artificial means ⟨seen by the ~ eye⟩ — **na·ked·ly** *adv* — **na·ked·ness** *n*
nam·by–pam·by \ˌnam-bē-'pam-bē\ *adj* **1** : INSIPID **2** : WEAK, INDECISIVE **syn** bland, flat, inane, jejune, vapid, wishy-washy
¹name \'nām\ *n* **1** : a word or words by which a person or thing is known **2** : a disparaging epithet ⟨call him ~s⟩ **3** : REPUTATION; *esp* : distinguished reputation ⟨made a ~ for herself⟩ **4** : FAMILY, CLAN ⟨was a disgrace to their ~⟩ **5** : appearance as opposed to reality ⟨a friend in ~ only⟩
²name *vb* **named; nam·ing 1** : to give a name to : CALL **2** : to mention or identify by name **3** : NOMINATE, APPOINT **4** : to decide on : CHOOSE **5** : to mention explicitly : SPECIFY ⟨~ a price⟩ — **name·able** *adj*
³name *adj* **1** : of, relating to, or bearing a name ⟨~ tag⟩ **2** : having an established reputation ⟨~ brands⟩
name day *n* : the church feast day of the saint after whom one is named
name·less \'nām-ləs\ *adj* **1** : having no name **2** : not marked with a name ⟨a ~ grave⟩ **3** : not known by name ⟨a ~ hero⟩ **4** : too distressing to be described ⟨~ fears⟩ — **name·less·ly** *adv*
name·ly \-lē\ *adv* : that is to say : AS ⟨the cat family, ~, lions, tigers, and similar animals⟩
name·plate \-ˌplāt\ *n* : a plate or plaque bearing a name (as of a resident)
name·sake \-ˌsāk\ *n* : one that has the same name as another; *esp* : one named after another
Na·mib·ian \nə-'mi-bē-ən, -byən\ *n* : a native or inhabitant of Namibia — **Namibian** *adj*
nan·keen \nan-'kēn\ *n* : a durable brownish yellow cotton fabric orig. woven by hand in China
nan·ny goat \'na-nē-\ *n* : a female domestic goat
nano·me·ter \'na-nə-ˌmē-tər\ *n* : one billionth of a meter
nano·sec·ond \-ˌse-kənd\ *n* : one billionth of a second
¹nap \'nap\ *vb* **napped; nap·ping 1** : to sleep briefly esp. during the day : DOZE **2** : to be off guard ⟨was caught *napping*⟩

²nap *n* : a short sleep esp. during the day
³nap *n* : a soft downy fibrous surface (as on yarn and cloth) — **nap·less** *adj* — **napped** \'napt\ *adj*
na·palm \'nā-ˌpälm, -ˌpäm\ *n* [*naphthalene* + *palmitate,* salt of a fatty acid] **1** : a thickener used in jelling gasoline (as for incendiary bombs) **2** : fuel jelled with napalm
nape \'nāp, 'nap\ *n* : the back of the neck
na·pery \'nā-pə-rē\ *n* : household linen esp. for the table
naph·tha \'naf-thə, 'nap-\ *n* : any of various liquid hydrocarbon mixtures used chiefly as solvents
naph·tha·lene \-ˌlēn\ *n* : a crystalline substance used esp. in organic synthesis and as a moth repellent
nap·kin \'nap-kən\ *n* **1** : a piece of material (as cloth) used at table to wipe the lips or fingers and protect the clothes **2** : a small cloth or towel
na·po·leon \nə-'pōl-yən, -'pō-lē-ən\ *n* : an oblong pastry with a filling of cream, custard, or jelly
Na·po·le·on·ic \nə-ˌpō-lē-'ä-nik\ *adj* : of, relating to, or characteristic of Napoleon I or his family
narc *also* **nark** \'närk\ *n, slang* : a person (as a government agent) who investigates narcotics violations
nar·cis·sism \'när-sə-ˌsi-zəm\ *n* [G *Narzissismus,* fr. *Narziss* Narcissus, beautiful youth of Greek mythology who fell in love with his own image] **1** : undue dwelling on one's own self or attainments **2** : love of or sexual desire for one's own body — **nar·cis·sist** \-sist\ *n or adj* — **nar·cis·sis·tic** \ˌnär-sə-'sis-tik\ *adj*
nar·cis·sus \när-'si-səs\ *n, pl* **-cis·sus** *or* **-cis·sus·es** *or* **-cis·si** \-ˌsī, -ˌsē\ : DAFFODIL; *esp* : one with short-tubed flowers usu. borne separately
nar·co·sis \när-'kō-səs\ *n, pl* **-co·ses** \-ˌsēz\ : a state of stupor, unconsciousness, or arrested activity produced by the influence of chemicals (as narcotics)
nar·cot·ic \när-'kä-tik\ *n* [ME *narkotik,* fr. MF *narcotique,* fr. *narcotique,* adj., fr. ML *narcoticus,* fr. Gk *narkōtikos,* fr. *narkoun* to benumb, fr. *narkē* numbness] : a drug (as opium) that dulls the senses and induces sleep — **narcotic** *adj*
nar·co·tize \'när-kə-ˌtīz\ *vb* **-tized; -tiz·ing 1** : to treat with or subject to a narcotic; *also* : to put into a state of narcosis **2** : to soothe to unconsciousness or unawareness
nard \'närd\ *n* : a fragrant ointment of the ancients
na·res \'nar-(ˌ)ēz\ *n pl* [L] : the pair of openings of the nose
Nar·ra·gan·set \ˌnar-ə-'gan-sət\ *n, pl* **Narraganset** *or* **Narragansets** : a member of an American Indian people of Rhode Island
nar·rate \'nar-ˌāt\ *vb* **nar·rat·ed; nar·rat·ing** : to recite the details of (as a story) : RELATE, TELL — **nar·ra·tion** \na-'rā-shən\ *n* — **nar·ra·tor** \'nar-ˌā-tər\ *n*
nar·ra·tive \'nar-ə-tiv\ *n* **1** : something that is narrated : STORY **2** : the art or practice of narrating
¹nar·row \'nar-ō\ *adj* **1** : of slender or less than standard width **2** : limited in size or scope : RESTRICTED **3** : not liberal in views : PREJUDICED **4** : interpreted or interpreting strictly **5** : CLOSE ⟨won by a ~ margin⟩; *also* : barely successful ⟨a ~ escape⟩ — **nar·row·ly** *adv* — **nar·row·ness** *n*
²narrow *n* : a narrow passage : STRAIT — usu. used in pl.
³narrow *vb* : to lessen in width or extent
nar·row–mind·ed \ˌnar-ō-'mīn-dəd\ *adj* : not liberal or broad-minded **syn** illiberal, bigoted, hidebound, intolerant
nar·whal \'när-ˌhwäl, 'när-wəl\ *n* : an arctic sea mammal about 20 feet (6 meters) long that is related to the dolphins and in the male has a long twisted ivory tusk
NAS *abbr* naval air station
NASA \'na-sə\ *abbr* National Aeronautics and Space Administration
¹na·sal \'nā-zəl\ *n* **1** : a nasal part **2** : a nasal consonant or vowel

narwhal

²**nasal** *adj* **1** : of or relating to the nose **2** : uttered through the nose — **na·sal·ly** *adv*

na·sal·ize \ˈnā-zə-ˌlīz\ *vb* **-ized; -iz·ing** : to make nasal or pronounce as a nasal sound — **na·sal·i·za·tion** \ˌnā-zə-lə-ˈzā-shən\ *n*

na·scent \ˈnas-ᵊnt, ˈnās-\ *adj* : coming into existence : beginning to grow or develop — **na·scence** \-ᵊns\ *n*

nas·tur·tium \nə-ˈstər-shəm, na-\ *n* : either of two widely cultivated watery-stemmed herbs with showy spurred flowers and pungent seeds

nas·ty \ˈnas-tē\ *adj* **nas·ti·er; -est 1** : FILTHY **2** : INDECENT, OBSCENE **3** : HARMFUL, DANGEROUS ⟨took a ~ fall⟩ **4** : DISAGREEABLE ⟨~ weather⟩ **5** : MEAN, ILL≈NATURED ⟨a ~ temper⟩ **6** : DIFFICULT, VEXATIOUS ⟨a ~ problem⟩ **7** : UNFAIR, DIRTY ⟨a ~ trick⟩ — **nas·ti·ly** \ˈnas-tə-lē\ *adv* — **nas·ti·ness** \-tē-nəs\ *n*

nat *abbr* **1** national **2** native **3** natural

na·tal \ˈnāt-ᵊl\ *adj* **1** : NATIVE **2** : of, relating to, or present at birth

na·ta·to·ri·um \ˌnā-tə-ˈtōr-ē-əm, ˌna-\ *n* : a swimming pool esp. indoors

na·tion \ˈnā-shən\ *n* [ME *nacioun*, fr. MF *nation*, fr. L *nation-, natio* birth, race, nation, fr. *nasci* to be born] **1** : NATIONALITY 5; *also* : a politically organized nationality **2** : a community of people composed of one or more nationalities with its own territory and government **3** : the territory of a nation **4** : a federation of tribes (as of American Indians) — **na·tion·hood** *n*

¹**na·tion·al** \ˈna-shə-nəl\ *adj* **1** : of or relating to a nation **2** : comprising or characteristic of a nationality **3** : FEDERAL **3** — **na·tion·al·ly** *adv*

²**national** *n* **1** : one who owes allegiance to a nation **2** : a competition that is national in scope — usu. used in pl.

National Guard *n* **1** : a militia force recruited by each state of the U.S., equipped by the federal government, and jointly maintained subject to the call of either **2** *often not cap* : a military force serving as a national constabulary and defense force

na·tion·al·ism \ˈna-shə-nə-ˌli-zəm\ *n* : devotion to national interests, unity, and independence

na·tion·al·ist \-list\ *n* **1** : an advocate of or believer in nationalism **2** *cap* : a member of a political party or group advocating national independence or strong national government — **nationalist** *adj, often cap* — **na·tion·al·is·tic** \ˌna-shə-nə-ˈlis-tik\ *adj*

na·tion·al·i·ty \ˌna-shə-ˈna-lə-tē\ *n, pl* **-ties 1** : national character **2** : a legal relationship involving allegiance of an individual and protection on the part of the state **3** : membership in a particular nation **4** : political independence or existence as a separate nation **5** : a people having a common origin, tradition, and language and capable of forming a state **6** : an ethnic group within a larger unit (as a nation)

na·tion·al·ize \ˈna-shə-nə-ˌlīz\ *vb* **-ized; -iz·ing 1** : to make national : make a nation of **2** : to remove from private ownership and place under government control — **na·tion·al·i·za·tion** \ˌna-shə-nə-lə-ˈzā-shən\ *n*

national monument *n* : a place of historic, scenic, or scientific interest set aside for preservation usu. by presidential proclamation

national park *n* : an area of special scenic, historical, or scientific importance set aside and maintained by a national government esp. for recreation or study

national seashore *n* : a recreational area adjacent to a seacoast and maintained by the federal government

na·tion·wide \ˌnā-shən-ˈwīd\ *adj* : extending throughout a nation

¹**na·tive** \ˈnā-tiv\ *adj* **1** : INBORN, NATURAL **2** : born in a particular place or country **3** : belonging to a person because of the place or circumstances of birth ⟨her ~ language⟩ **4** : grown, produced, or originating in a particular place : INDIGENOUS **syn** aboriginal, autochthonous, endemic

²**native** *n* : one that is native; *esp* : a person who belongs to a particular country by birth

Native American *n* : AMERICAN INDIAN

na·tiv·ism \ˈnā-ti-ˌvi-zəm\ *n* **1** : a policy of favoring native inhabitants over immigrants **2** : the revival or perpetuation of a native culture esp. in opposition to acculturation

na·tiv·i·ty \nə-ˈti-və-tē, nā-\ *n, pl* **-ties 1** : the process or circumstances of being born : BIRTH **2** *cap* : the birth of Christ

natl *abbr* national

NATO \ˈnā-(ˌ)tō\ *abbr* North Atlantic Treaty Organization

nat·ty \ˈna-tē\ *adj* **nat·ti·er; -est** : trimly neat and tidy : SMART — **nat·ti·ly** \-tə-lē\ *adv* — **nat·ti·ness** \-tē-nəs\ *n*

¹**nat·u·ral** \ˈna-chə-rəl\ *adj* **1** : determined by nature : INBORN, INNATE ⟨~ ability⟩ **2** : BORN ⟨a ~ fool⟩ **3** : ILLEGITIMATE **4** : HUMAN **5** : of or relating to nature **6** : not artificial **7** : being simple and sincere : not affected **8** : LIFELIKE **9** : being neither sharp nor flat **syn** ingenuous, naive, unsophisticated, artless, guileless — **nat·u·ral·ness** *n*

²**natural** *n* **1** : IDIOT **2** : a character placed on a line or space of the musical staff to nullify the effect of a preceding sharp or flat **3** : one obviously suitable for a purpose **4** : AFRO

natural childbirth *n* : a system of managing childbirth in which the mother prepares to remain conscious and assist in delivery with little or no use of drugs

natural gas *n* : a combustible gaseous mixture of hydrocarbons coming from the earth's crust and used chiefly as a fuel and raw material

natural history *n* **1** : a treatise on some aspect of nature **2** : the study of natural objects esp. from an amateur or popular point of view

nat·u·ral·ism \ˈna-chə-rə-ˌli-zəm\ *n* **1** : action or thought based only on natural desires and instincts **2** : a doctrine that denies a supernatural explanation of the origin or development of the universe and holds that scientific laws account for all of nature **3** : realism in art and literature — **nat·u·ral·is·tic** \ˌna-chə-rə-ˈlis-tik\ *adj*

nat·u·ral·ist \-list\ *n* **1** : one that advocates or practices naturalism **2** : a student of animals or plants esp. in the field

nat·u·ral·ize \-ˌlīz\ *vb* **-ized; -iz·ing 1** : to become or cause to become established as if native ⟨~ new forage crops⟩ **2** : to confer the rights of a citizen on — **nat·u·ral·iza·tion** \ˌna-chə-rə-lə-ˈzā-shən\ *n*

nat·u·ral·ly \ˈna-chə-rə-lē, ˈnach-rə-\ *adv* **1** : by nature : by natural character or ability **2** : as might be expected **3** : without artificial aid; *also* : without affectation **4** : REALISTICALLY

natural science *n* : a science (as physics, chemistry, or biology) that deals with matter, energy, and their interrelations and transformations or with objectively measurable phenomena — **natural scientist** *n*

natural selection *n* : the natural process that results in the survival of individuals or groups best adjusted to their environment

na·ture \'nā-chər\ *n* [ME, fr. MF, fr. L *natura*, fr. *natus*, pp. of *nasci* to be born] 1 : the inherent quality or basic constitution of a person or thing 2 : KIND, SORT 3 : DISPOSITION, TEMPERAMENT 4 : the physical universe 5 : one's natural instincts or way of life ⟨quirks of human ∼⟩; *also* : primitive state ⟨a return to ∼⟩ 6 : natural scenery or environment ⟨beauties of ∼⟩

naught \'nȯt, 'nät\ *n* 1 : NOTHING 2 : the arithmetical symbol 0 : ZERO

naugh·ty \'nȯ-tē, 'nä-\ *adj* **naugh·ti·er; -est** 1 : guilty of disobedience or misbehavior 2 : lacking in taste or propriety — **naugh·ti·ly** \-tə-lē\ *adv* — **naugh·ti·ness** \-tē-nəs\ *n*

nau·sea \'nȯ-zē-ə, -sē-; 'nȯ-zhə, -shə\ *n* [L, seasickness, nausea, fr. Gk *nautia, nausia*, fr. *nautēs* sailor] 1 : sickness of the stomach with a desire to vomit 2 : extreme disgust

nau·se·ate \'nȯ-zē-ˌāt, -sē-, -zhē-, -shē-\ *vb* **-at·ed; -at·ing** : to affect or become affected with nausea — **nau·se·at·ing·ly** *adv*

nau·seous \'nȯ-shəs, -zē-əs\ *adj* 1 : causing nausea or disgust 2 : affected with nausea or disgust

naut *abbr* nautical

nau·ti·cal \'nȯ-ti-kəl\ *adj* : of or relating to sailors, navigation, or ships — **nau·ti·cal·ly** \-k(ə-)lē\ *adv*

nautical mile *n* : a unit of distance equal to about 6080 feet (1852 meters)

nau·ti·lus \'nȯt-ᵊl-əs\ *n, pl* **-lus·es** *or* **-li** \-ᵊl-ˌī, -ˌē\ : any of a genus of sea mollusks related to the octopuses but having a spiral chambered shell

nav *abbr* 1 naval 2 navigable; navigation

Na·va·jo *also* **Na·va·ho** \'na-və-ˌhō, 'nä-\ *n, pl* **-jo** *or* **-jos** *also* **-ho** *or* **-hos** : a member of an American Indian people of northern New Mexico and Arizona; *also* : their language

na·val \'nā-vəl\ *adj* : of, relating to, or possessing a navy

naval stores *n pl* : products (as pitch, turpentine, or rosin) obtained from resinous conifers (as pines)

nave \'nāv\ *n* [ML *navis*, fr. L, ship] : the central part of a church running lengthwise

na·vel \'nā-vəl\ *n* : a depression in the middle of the abdomen that marks the point of attachment of fetus and mother

navel orange *n* : a seedless orange having a pit at the blossom end where the fruit encloses a small secondary fruit

nav·i·ga·ble \'na-vi-gə-bəl\ *adj* 1 : capable of being navigated ⟨a ∼ river⟩ 2 : capable of being steered — **nav·i·ga·bil·i·ty** \ˌna-vi-gə-'bi-lə-tē\ *n*

nav·i·gate \'na-və-ˌgāt\ *vb* **-gat·ed; -gat·ing** 1 : to sail on or through ⟨∼ the Atlantic Ocean⟩ 2 : to steer or direct the course of a ship or aircraft 3 : MOVE; *esp* : WALK ⟨could hardly ∼⟩ — **nav·i·ga·tion** \ˌna-və-'gā-shən\ *n* — **nav·i·ga·tor** \'na-və-ˌgā-tər\ *n*

na·vy \'nā-vē\ *n, pl* **navies** 1 : FLEET; *also* : the warships belonging to a nation 2 *often cap* : a nation's organization for naval warfare

navy yard *n* : a yard where naval vessels are built or repaired

¹**nay** \'nā\ *adv* 1 : NO

²**nay** *n* : a negative vote; *also* : a person casting such a vote

³**nay** *conj* : not merely this but also : not only so but ⟨he was happy, ∼, ecstatic⟩

nay·say·er \'nā-ˌsā-ər\ *n* : one who denies, refuses, or opposes something

Na·zi \'nät-sē, 'nat-\ *n* [G, fr. *Nationalsozialist*, lit., national socialist] : a member of a German fascist party controlling Germany from 1933 to 1945 under Adolf Hitler — **Nazi** *adj* — **Na·zism** \'nät-ˌsi-zəm, 'nat-\ *or* **Na·zi·ism** \-sē-ˌi-zəm\ *n*

Nb *symbol* niobium

NB *abbr* 1 New Brunswick 2 nota bene

NBA *abbr* 1 National Basketball Association 2 National Boxing Association

NBC *abbr* National Broadcasting Company

NBS *abbr* National Bureau of Standards

NC *abbr* 1 no charge 2 North Carolina

NCAA *abbr* National Collegiate Athletic Association

NCE *abbr* New Catholic Edition

NCO \ˌen-ˌsē-'ō\ *n* : NONCOMMISSIONED OFFICER

nd *abbr* no date

Nd *symbol* neodymium

ND *abbr* North Dakota

N Dak *abbr* North Dakota

Ne *symbol* neon

NE *abbr* 1 Nebraska 2 New England 3 northeast

Ne·an·der·thal \nē-'an-dər-ˌthȯl, nä-'än-dər-ˌtäl\ *adj* : of, relating to, or being an extinct Old World human; *also* : suggestive of a caveman — **Neanderthal** *n*

neap tide \'nēp-\ *n* : a tide of minimum range occurring at the first and third quarters of the moon

¹**near** \'nir\ *adv* 1 : at, within, or to a short distance or time 2 : ALMOST

²**near** *prep* : close to

³**near** *adj* 1 : closely related or associated; *also* : INTIMATE 2 : not far away; *also* : being the closer or left-hand member of a pair 3 : barely avoided ⟨a ∼ accident⟩ 4 : DIRECT, SHORT ⟨by the ∼*est* route⟩ 5 : STINGY 6 : not real but very like ⟨∼ silk⟩ — **near·ly** *adv* — **near·ness** *n*

⁴**near** *vb* : APPROACH

near beer *n* : any of various malt liquors low in alcohol

near·by \nir-'bī, 'nir-ˌbī\ *adv or adj* : close at hand

near·sight·ed \'nir-'sī-təd\ *adj* : able to see near things more clearly than distant ones : MYOPIC — **near·sight·ed·ly** *adv* — **near·sight·ed·ness** *n*

neat \'nēt\ *adj* [MF *net*, fr. L *nitidus* bright, neat, fr. *nitēre* to shine] 1 : being orderly and clean 2 : not mixed or diluted ⟨∼ brandy⟩ 3 : marked by tasteful simplicity 4 : PRECISE, SYSTEMATIC 5 : SKILLFUL, ADROIT 6 : FINE, ADMIRABLE **syn** shipshape, tidy, trig, trim — **neat** *adv* — **neat·ly** *adv* — **neat·ness** *n*

neath \'nēth\ *prep, dial* : BENEATH

neat's-foot oil \'nēts-ˌfüt-\ *n* [*neat* ox or cow] : a pale yellow fatty oil made esp. from the bones of cattle and used chiefly as a leather dressing

neb \'neb\ *n* 1 : the beak of a bird or tortoise; *also* : NOSE, SNOUT 2 : NIB

Neb *or* **Nebr** *abbr* Nebraska

NEB *abbr* New English Bible

neb·u·la \'ne-byə-lə\ *n, pl* **-lae** \-ˌlē, -ˌlī\ *also* **-las** [NL, fr. L, mist, cloud] 1 : any of numerous clouds of gas or dust in interstellar space 2 : GALAXY — **neb·u·lar** \-lər\ *adj*

neb·u·liz·er \'ne-byə-ˌlī-zər\ *n* : ATOMIZER

neb·u·lous \'ne-byə-ləs\ *adj* 1 : of or relating to a nebula 2 : HAZY, INDISTINCT

¹**nec·es·sary** \'ne-sə-ˌser-ē\ *n, pl* **-saries** : an indispensable item

²**necessary** *adj* 1 : INEVITABLE, INESCAPABLE; *also* : CERTAIN 2 : PREDETERMINED 3 : COMPULSORY 4 : positively needed : INDISPENSABLE **syn** imperative, necessitous, essential — **nec·es·sar·i·ly** \ˌne-sə-'ser-ə-lē\ *adv*

ne·ces·si·tate \ni-'se-sə-ˌtāt\ *vb* **-tat·ed; -tat·ing** : to make necessary

ne·ces·si·tous \ni-'se-sə-təs\ *adj* 1 : NEEDY, IMPOVERISHED 2 : URGENT 3 : NECESSARY

ne·ces·si·ty \ni-'se-sə-tē\ *n, pl* **-ties** 1 : conditions that cannot be changed 2 : WANT, POVERTY 3 : something that is necessary 4 : very great need

¹**neck** \'nek\ *n* 1 : the part of the body connecting the head and the trunk 2 : the part of a garment covering or near to the neck 3 : a relatively narrow part sugges-

tive of a neck ⟨∼ of a bottle⟩ ⟨∼ of land⟩ **4** : a narrow margin esp. of victory ⟨won by a ∼⟩ — **necked** \'nekt\ *adj*

²**neck** *vb* : to kiss and caress amorously

neck and neck *adv or adj* : very close (as in a race)

neck·er·chief \'ne-kər-chəf, -ˌchēf\ *n, pl* **-chiefs** \-chəfs, -ˌchēfs\ *also* **-chieves** \-ˌchēvz\ : a square of cloth worn folded about the neck like a scarf

neck·lace \'ne-kləs\ *n* : an ornament worn around the neck

neck·line \'nek-ˌlīn\ *n* : the outline of the neck opening of a garment

neck·tie \-ˌtī\ *n* : a strip of cloth worn around the neck and tied in front

ne·crol·o·gy \nə-'krä-lə-jē\ *n, pl* **-gies 1** : OBITUARY **2** : a list of the recently dead

nec·ro·man·cy \'ne-krə-ˌman-sē\ *n* **1** : the art or practice of conjuring up the spirits of the dead for purposes of magically revealing the future **2** : MAGIC, SORCERY — **nec·ro·man·cer** \-sər\ *n*

ne·crop·o·lis \nə-'krä-pə-ləs, ne-\ *n, pl* **-lis·es** *or* **-les** \-ˌlēz\ *or* **-leis** \-ˌlās\ *or* **-li** \-ˌlī, -ˌlē\ : CEMETERY; *esp* : a large elaborate cemetery of an ancient city

ne·cro·sis \nə-'krō-səs, ne-\ *n, pl* **ne·cro·ses** \-ˌsēz\ : usu. local death of body tissue — **ne·crot·ic** \-'krä-tik\ *adj*

nec·tar \'nek-tər\ *n* **1** : the drink of the Greek and Roman gods; *also* : any delicious drink **2** : a sweet plant secretion that is the raw material of honey

nec·tar·ine \ˌnek-tə-'rēn\ *n* : a smooth-skinned peach

née *or* **nee** \'nā\ *adj* [F, lit., born] — used to identify a woman by her maiden family name

¹**need** \'nēd\ *n* **1** : OBLIGATION ⟨no ∼ to hurry⟩ **2** : a lack of something requisite, desirable, or useful **3** : a condition requiring supply or relief ⟨when the ∼ arises⟩ **4** : POVERTY **syn** necessity, exigency

²**need** *vb* **1** : to be in want **2** : to have cause or occasion for : REQUIRE ⟨he ∼s advice⟩ **3** : to be under obligation or necessity ⟨we ∼ to know the truth⟩

need·ful \'nēd-fəl\ *adj* : NECESSARY, REQUISITE

¹**nee·dle** \'nēd-ᵊl\ *n* **1** : a slender pointed usu. steel implement used in sewing **2** : a slender rod (as for knitting, controlling a small opening, or transmitting vibrations to or from a recording) ⟨a phonograph ∼⟩ **3** : a slender hollow instrument by which material is introduced into or withdrawn from the body **4** : a slender indicator on a dial **5** : a needle-shaped leaf (as of a pine)

²**needle** *vb* **nee·dled; nee·dling** : PROD, GOAD; *esp* : to incite to action by repeated gibes

nee·dle·point \'nēd-ᵊl-ˌpóint\ *n* **1** : lace worked with a needle over a paper pattern **2** : embroidery done on canvas across counted threads — **needlepoint** *adj*

need·less \'nēd-ləs\ *adj* : UNNECESSARY — **need·less·ly** *adv* — **need·less·ness** *n*

nee·dle·wom·an \'nēd-ᵊl-ˌwu̇-mən\ *n* : a woman who does needlework; *esp* : SEAMSTRESS

nee·dle·work \-ˌwərk\ *n* : work done with a needle; *esp* : work (as embroidery) other than plain sewing

needs \'nēdz\ *adv* : of necessity : NECESSARILY ⟨must ∼ be recognized⟩

needy \'nē-dē\ *adj* **need·i·er; -est** : being in want : POVERTY-STRICKEN

ne'er \'ner\ *adv* : NEVER

ne'er–do–well \'ner-dú-ˌwel\ *n* : an idle worthless person — **ne'er–do–well** *adj*

ne·far·i·ous \ni-'far-ē-əs\ *adj* [L *nefarius*, fr. *nefas* crime, fr. *ne-* not + *fas* right, divine law] : very wicked : EVIL **syn** bad, immoral, iniquitous, sinful, vicious — **ne·far·i·ous·ly** *adv*

neg *abbr* negative

ne·gate \ni-'gāt\ *vb* **ne·gat·ed; ne·gat·ing 1** : to deny the existence or truth of **2** : to cause to be ineffective or invalid : NULLIFY

ne·ga·tion \ni-'gā-shən\ *n* **1** : the action or operation of negating or making negative **2** : a negative doctrine or statement

¹**neg·a·tive** \'ne-gə-tiv\ *adj* **1** : marked by denial, prohibition, or refusal ⟨a ∼ reply⟩ **2** : not positive or constructive; *esp* : not affirming the presence of what is sought or suspected to be present ⟨test results were ∼⟩ **3** : less than zero ⟨a ∼ number⟩ **4** : being, relating to, or charged with electricity of which the electron is the elementary unit **5** : having the light and dark parts opposite to what they were in the original photographic subject — **neg·a·tive·ly** *adv* — **neg·a·tive·ness** *n* — **neg·a·tiv·i·ty** \ˌne-gə-'ti-və-tē\ *n*

²**negative** *n* **1** : a negative word or statement **2** : a negative vote or reply; *also* : REFUSAL **3** : something that is the opposite or negation of something else **4** : the side that votes or argues for the opposition (as in a debate) **5** : a negative number **6** : a negative photographic image on transparent material

³**negative** *vb* **-tived; -tiv·ing 1** : to refuse to accept or approve **2** : to vote against **3** : DISPROVE

negative income tax *n* : a system of federal subsidy payments to families with incomes below a stipulated level

neg·a·tiv·ism \'ne-gə-ti-ˌvi-zəm\ *n* : an attitude of skepticism and denial of nearly everything affirmed or suggested by others

¹**ne·glect** \ni-'glekt\ *vb* [L *neglegere, neclegere,* fr. *nec-* not + *legere* to gather] **1** : DISREGARD **2** : to leave undone or unattended to esp. through carelessness **syn** omit, ignore, over-look, slight, forget, miss

²**neglect** *n* **1** : an act or instance of neglecting something **2** : the condition of being neglected — **ne·glect·ful** *adj*

neg·li·gee *also* **neg·li·gé** \ˌne-glə-'zhā\ *n* : a woman's long flowing dressing gown

neg·li·gent \'ne-gli-jənt\ *adj* : marked by neglect **syn** neglectful, remiss, delinquent, derelict — **neg·li·gence** \-jəns\ *n* — **neg·li·gent·ly** *adv*

neg·li·gi·ble \'ne-gli-jə-bəl\ *adj* : so small as to be neglected or disregarded

ne·go·tiant \ni-'gō-shē-ənt\ *n* : NEGOTIATOR

ne·go·ti·ate \ni-'gō-shē-ˌāt\ *vb* **-at·ed; -at·ing** [L *negotiari* to carry on business, fr. *negotium* business, fr. *neg-* not + *otium* leisure] **1** : to confer with another so as to arrive at the settlement of some matter; *also* : to arrange for or bring about by such conferences ⟨∼ a treaty⟩ **2** : to transfer to another by delivery or endorsement in return for equivalent value ⟨∼ a check⟩ **3** : to get through, around, or over successfully ⟨∼ a turn⟩ — **ne·go·tia·ble** \-shə-bəl, -shē-ə-\ *adj* — **ne·go·ti·a·tion** \ni-ˌgō-sē-'ā-shən, -shē-\ *n* — **ne·go·ti·a·tor** \-'gō-shē-ˌā-tər\ *n*

ne·gri·tude \'ne-grə-ˌtüd, -ˌtyüd, 'nē-\ *n* : a consciousness of and pride in one's African heritage

Ne·gro \'nē-grō\ *n, pl* **Negroes** [Sp *or* Pg, fr. *negro* black] : a member of the black race — **Negro** *adj* — **Ne·groid** \'nē-ˌgróid\ *n or adj, often not cap*

Neh *abbr* Nehemiah

Ne·he·mi·ah \ˌnē-ə-'mī-ə\ *n* — see BIBLE table

neigh \'nā\ *n* : a loud prolonged cry of a horse — **neigh** *vb*

¹**neigh·bor** \'nā-bər\ *n* **1** : one living or located near another **2** : FELLOWMAN

²**neighbor** *vb* : to be next to or near to : border on

neigh·bor·hood \'nā-bər-ˌhu̇d\ *n* **1** : NEARNESS **2** : a place or region near : VICINITY; *also* : a number or amount near ⟨costs in the ∼ of $10⟩ **3** : the people living near one another **4** : a section lived in by neighbors and usu. having distinguishing characteristics

neigh·bor·ly \-lē\ *adj* : befitting congenial neighbors; *esp* : FRIENDLY — **neigh·bor·li·ness** *n*

neigh·bour *chiefly Brit var of* NEIGHBOR

¹nei·ther \'nē-thər, 'nī-\ *pron* : neither one : not the one and not the other ⟨∼ of the two⟩

²neither *conj* **1** : not either ⟨∼ good nor bad⟩ **2** : NOR ⟨∼ did I⟩

³neither *adj* : not either ⟨∼ hand⟩

nel·son \'nel-sən\ *n* : a wrestling hold in which one applies leverage against an opponent's arm, neck, and head

nem·a·tode \'ne-mə-ˌtōd\ *n* : any of a phylum of elongated cylindrical worms parasitic in animals or plants or free-living in soil or water

nem·e·sis \'ne-mə-səs\ *n, pl* **-e·ses** \-ˌsēz\ [L *Nemesis,* goddess of divine retribution, fr. Gk] **1** : one that inflicts retribution or vengeance **2** : a formidable and usu. victorious rival **3** : an act or effect of retribution; *also* : CURSE

neo·clas·sic \ˌnē-ō-'kla-sik\ *or* **neo·clas·si·cal** \-si-kəl\ *adj* : of or relating to a revival or adaptation of the classical style esp. in literature, art, or music

neo·co·lo·nial·ism \ˌnē-ō-kə-'lō-nē-ə-ˌli-zəm\ *n* : the economic and political policies by which a nation indirectly maintains or extends its influence over other areas or peoples — **neo·co·lo·nial** *adj* — **neo·co·lo·nial·ist** \-list\ *n or adj*

neo·con·ser·va·tive \-kən-'sər-və-tiv\ *n* : a former liberal espousing political conservatism — **neo·con·ser·va·tism** \-və-ˌti-zəm\ *n* — **neoconservative** *adj*

neo·dym·i·um \ˌnē-ō-'di-mē-əm\ *n* : a yellow metallic chemical element — see ELEMENT table

neo–im·pres·sion·ism \ˌnē-ō-im-'pre-shə-ˌni-zəm\ *n, often cap N&I* : a late 19th century French art movement that attempted to make impressionism more precise and to use a pointillist painting technique

Neo·lith·ic \ˌnē-ə-'li-thik\ *adj* : of or relating to the latest period of the Stone Age characterized by polished stone implements

ne·ol·o·gism \nē-'ä-lə-ˌji-zəm\ *n* : a new word or expression

ne·on \'nē-ˌän\ *n* [Gk, neut. of *neos* new] **1** : a gaseous colorless chemical element used in electric lamps — see ELEMENT table **2** : a lamp in which a discharge through neon gives a reddish glow — **neon** *adj*

neo·na·tal \ˌnē-ō-'nāt-ᵊl\ *adj* : of, relating to, or affecting the newborn — **neo·na·tal·ly** *adv*

ne·o·nate \'nē-ə-ˌnāt\ *n* : a newborn child

neo·phyte \'nē-ə-ˌfīt\ *n* **1** : a new convert : PROSELYTE **2** : NOVICE **3** : BEGINNER syn apprentice, freshman, newcomer, rookie, tenderfoot, tyro

neo·plasm \'nē-ə-ˌpla-zəm\ *n* : a new growth of tissue serving no useful purpose in the body : TUMOR — **neo·plas·tic** \ˌnē-ə-'plas-tik\ *adj*

neo·prene \'nē-ə-ˌprēn\ *n* : a synthetic rubber used esp. for special-purpose clothing (as wet suits)

Ne·pali \nə-'pò-lē, -'pä-\ *n, pl* **Nepali** : a native or inhabitant of Nepal — **Nepali** *adj*

ne·pen·the \nə-'pen-thē\ *n* **1** : a potion used by the ancients to dull pain and sorrow **2** : something capable of making one forget grief or suffering

neph·ew \'ne-fyü, *chiefly Brit* -vyü\ *n* : a son of one's brother, sister, brother-in-law, or sister-in-law

ne·phrit·ic \ni-'fri-tik\ *adj* **1** : RENAL **2** : of, relating to, or affected with nephritis

ne·phri·tis \ni-'frī-təs\ *n, pl* **ne·phrit·i·des** \-'fri-tə-ˌdēz\ : kidney inflammation

ne plus ul·tra \ˌnē-ˌpləs-'əl-trə\ *n* [NL, (go) no more beyond] : the highest point capable of being attained

nep·o·tism \'ne-pə-ˌti-zəm\ *n* [F *népotisme,* fr. It *nepotismo,* fr. *nepote* nephew, fr. L *nepot-, nepos* grandson, nephew] : favoritism shown to a relative (as in the granting of jobs)

Nep·tune \'nep-ˌtün, -ˌtyün\ *n* : the planet 8th in order from the sun — see PLANET table — **Nep·tu·ni·an** \nep-'tü-nē-ən, -'tyü-\ *adj*

nep·tu·ni·um \nep-'tü-nē-əm, -'tyü-\ *n* : a short-lived radioactive element — see ELEMENT table

nerd \'nərd\ *n* : an unstylish or socially inept person; *esp* : one slavishly devoted to intellectual pursuits — **nerdy** *adj*

Ne·re·id \'nir-ē-əd\ *n* : a sea nymph in Greek mythology

¹nerve \'nərv\ *n* **1** : SINEW, TENDON ⟨strain every ∼⟩ **2** : any of the strands of nervous tissue that carry nerve impulses between the brain and spinal cord and every part of the body **3** : power of endurance or control : FORTITUDE; *also* : BOLDNESS, DARING **4** *pl* : NERVOUSNESS **5** : a vein of a leaf or insect wing — **nerved** \'nərvd\ *adj* — **nerve·less** *adj*

²nerve *vb* **nerved; nerv·ing** : to give strength or courage to

nerve cell *n* : NEURON; *also* : the nucleus-containing central part of a neuron exclusive of its processes

nerve gas *n* : a chemical weapon damaging esp. to the nervous and respiratory systems

nerve impulse *n* : a physical and chemical change that moves along a process of a neuron after stimulation and carries a record of sensation or an instruction to act

nerve–rack·ing *or* **nerve–wrack·ing** \'nərv-ˌra-kiŋ\ *adj* : extremely trying on the nerves

ner·vous \'nər-vəs\ *adj* **1** : FORCIBLE, SPIRITED **2** : of, relating to, or made up of nerve cells or nerves **3** : easily excited or annoyed : JUMPY **4** : TIMID, APPREHENSIVE ⟨a ∼ smile⟩ **5** : UNEASY, UNSTEADY — **ner·vous·ly** *adv* — **ner·vous·ness** *n*

nervous breakdown *n* : an attack of mental or emotional disorder of sufficient severity to be incapacitating esp. when requiring hospitalization

nervous system *n* : a bodily system that in vertebrates is made up of the brain and spinal cord, nerves, ganglia, and parts of the sense organs and that receives and interprets stimuli and transmits nerve impulses

nervy \'nər-vē\ *adj* **nerv·i·er; -est** **1** : showing calm courage **2** : marked by impudence or presumption ⟨a ∼ salesperson⟩ **3** : EXCITABLE, NERVOUS syn bold, cheeky, forward, fresh, impudent, saucy

-ness \nəs\ *n suffix* : state : condition : quality : degree ⟨good*ness*⟩

¹nest \'nest\ *n* **1** : the shelter prepared by a bird for its eggs and young **2** : a place where eggs (as of insects or fish) are laid and hatched **3** : a place of rest, retreat, or lodging **4** : DEN, HANGOUT ⟨a ∼ of thieves⟩ **5** : the occupants of a nest **6** : a series of objects (as bowls or tables) fitting inside or under one another

²nest *vb* **1** : to build or occupy a nest **2** : to fit compactly together or within one another

nest egg *n* : a fund of money accumulated as a reserve

nes·tle \'ne-səl\ *vb* **nes·tled; nes·tling** **1** : to settle snugly or comfortably **2** : to press closely and affectionately : CUDDLE **3** : to settle, shelter, or house as if in a nest

nest·ling \'nest-liŋ\ *n* : a bird too young to leave its nest

¹net \'net\ *n* **1** : a meshed fabric twisted, knotted, or woven together at regular intervals **2** : a device made all or partly of net and used esp. to catch birds, fish, or insects **3** : something made of net used esp. for protecting, confining, carrying, or dividing ⟨a tennis ∼⟩ **4** : SNARE, TRAP

²net *vb* **net·ted; net·ting** **1** : to cover or enclose with or as if with a net **2** : to catch in or as if in a net

³net *adj* : free from all charges or deductions ⟨∼ profit⟩ ⟨∼ weight⟩

⁴net *vb* **net·ted; net·ting** : to gain or produce as profit : CLEAR, YIELD ⟨his business *netted* $50,000 a year⟩

⁵net *n* : a net amount, profit, weight, or price

Neth *abbr* Netherlands

neth·er \\'ne-thər\ *adj* : situated down or below ⟨the ∼ regions of the earth⟩

Neth·er·land·er \\'ne-thər-ˌlan-dər\ *n* : a native or inhabitant of the Netherlands

neth·er·most \-ˌmōst\ *adj* : LOWEST

neth·er·world \-ˌwərld\ *n* **1** : the world of the dead **2** : UNDERWORLD

nett *Brit var of* NET

net·ting *n* **1** : NETWORK **2** : the act or process of making a net or network

¹net·tle \\'net-ᵊl\ *n* : any of a genus of coarse herbs with stinging hairs

²nettle *vb* **net·tled; net·tling** : PROVOKE, VEX, IRRITATE

net·tle·some \\'net-ᵊl-səm\ *adj* : causing vexation : IRRITATING

net·work \\'net-ˌwərk\ *n* **1** : NET **2** : a system of elements (as lines or channels) that cross in the manner of the threads in a net **3** : a group or system of related or connected parts; *esp* : a chain of radio or television stations

net·work·ing \\'net-ˌwər-kiŋ\ *n* : the exchange of information or services among individuals, groups, or institutions

neu·ral \\'nùr-əl, 'nyùr-\ *adj* : of, relating to, or involving a nerve or the nervous system

neu·ral·gia \nù-'ral-jə, nyù-\ *n* : acute pain that follows the course of a nerve — **neu·ral·gic** \-jik\ *adj*

neur·as·then·ic \ˌnùr-əs-'the-nik, ˌnyùr-, -thē-\ *adj* : affected with or suggestive of mental disorder characterized esp. by fatiguing easily, lack of motivation, feelings of inadequacy, and psychosomatic symptoms — **neur·as·then·ia** \-'thē-nē-ə\ *n* — **neurasthenic** *n*

neu·ri·tis \-'rī-təs\ *n, pl* **-rit·i·des** \-'ri-tə-ˌdēz\ *or* **-ri·tis·es** : inflammation of a nerve — **neu·rit·ic** \-'ri-tik\ *adj or n*

neu·rol·o·gy \nù-'rä-lə-jē, nyù-\ *n* : the scientific study of the nervous system — **neu·ro·log·i·cal** \ˌnùr-ə-'lä-ji-kəl, ˌnyùr-\ *or* **neu·ro·log·ic** \-jik\ *adj* — **neu·ro·log·i·cal·ly** \-ji-k(ə-)lē\ *adv* — **neu·rol·o·gist** \nù-'rä-lə-jist, nyù-\ *n*

neu·ron \\'nù-ˌrän, 'nyù-\ *also* **neu·rone** \-ˌrōn\ *n* : a cell with specialized processes that is the fundamental functional unit of nervous tissue

neu·ro·sci·ence \ˌnùr-ō-'sī-əns, ˌnyùr-\ *n* : a branch of the life sciences that deals with the anatomy, physiology, biochemistry, or molecular biology of nerves and nervous tissue and with their relation to behavior and learning — **neu·ro·sci·en·tist** \-ən-tist\ *n*

neu·ro·sis \nù-'rō-səs, nyù-\ *n, pl* **-ro·ses** \-ˌsēz\ : a mental and emotional disorder that is less serious than a psychosis, is not characterized by disturbance of the use of language, and is accompanied by various bodily and mental disturbances (as visceral symptoms, anxieties, or phobias)

neu·ro·sur·gery \-'sər-jə-rē\ *n* : surgery of nervous structures (as nerves, the brain, or the spinal cord) — **neu·ro·sur·geon** \-'sər-jən\ *n*

¹neu·rot·ic \nù-'rä-tik, nyù-\ *adj* : of, relating to, being, or affected with a neurosis; *also* : NERVOUS — **neu·rot·i·cal·ly** \-ti-k(ə-)lē\ *adv*

²neurotic *n* : an emotionally unstable or neurotic person

neu·ro·trans·mit·ter \ˌnùr-ō-trans-'mi-tər, ˌnyùr-, -tranz-\ *n* : a substance (as acetylcholine) that transmits nerve impulses across the gap between neurons

neut *abbr* neuter

¹neu·ter \\'nü-tər, 'nyü-\ *adj* [ME *neutre*, fr. MF & L; MF *neutre*, fr. L *neuter*, lit., neither, fr. *ne-* not + *uter* which of two] **1** : of, relating to, or constituting the gender that includes most words or grammatical forms referring to things classed as neither masculine nor feminine **2** : having imperfectly developed or no sex organs

²neuter *n* **1** : a noun, pronoun, adjective, or inflectional form or class of the neuter gender; *also* : the neuter gender **2** : WORKER 2; *also* : a spayed or castrated animal

³neuter *vb* : CASTRATE, SPAY

¹neu·tral \\'nü-trəl, 'nyü-\ *n* **1** : one that is neutral **2** : a neutral color **3** : a position of disengagement (as of gears)

²neutral *adj* **1** : not favoring either side in a quarrel, contest, or war **2** : of or relating to a neutral state or power **3** : MIDDLING, INDIFFERENT **4** : having no hue : GRAY; *also* : not decided in color **5** : neither acid nor basic ⟨a ∼ solution⟩ **6** : not electrically charged

neu·tral·ism \\'nü-trə-ˌli-zəm, 'nyü-\ *n* : a policy or the advocacy of neutrality esp. in international affairs

neu·tral·i·ty \nü-'tra-lə-tē, nyü-\ *n* : the quality or state of being neutral; *esp* : refusal to take part in a war between other powers

neu·tral·ize \\'nü-trə-ˌlīz, 'nyü-\ *vb* **-ized; -iz·ing** : to make neutral; *esp* : COUNTERACT — **neu·tral·i·za·tion** \ˌnü-trə-lə-'zā-shən, ˌnyü-\ *n*

neu·tri·no \nü-'trē-nō, nyü-\ *n, pl* **-nos** : an uncharged elementary particle held to be massless or very light

neu·tron \\'nü-ˌträn, 'nyü-\ *n* : an uncharged atomic particle that is nearly equal in mass to the proton

neutron bomb *n* : a nuclear bomb designed to produce lethal neutrons but less blast and fire damage than other nuclear bombs

neutron star *n* : a hypothetical dense celestial object that results from the collapse of a large star

Nev *abbr* Nevada

nev·er \\'ne-vər\ *adv* **1** : not ever **2** : not in any degree, way, or condition

nev·er·more \ˌne-vər-'mōr\ *adv* : never again

nev·er–nev·er land \ˌne-vər-'ne-vər-\ *n* : an ideal or imaginary place

nev·er·the·less \ˌne-vər-thə-'les\ *adv* : in spite of that : HOWEVER

ne·vus \\'nē-vəs\ *n, pl* **ne·vi** \-ˌvī\ : a usu. pigmented birthmark

¹new \\'nü, 'nyü\ *adj* **1** : not old : RECENT, MODERN **2** : recently discovered, recognized, or learned about ⟨∼ drugs⟩ **3** : UNFAMILIAR **4** : different from the former **5** : not accustomed ⟨∼ to the work⟩ **6** : beginning as a repetition of a previous act or thing ⟨a ∼ year⟩ **7** : REFRESHED, REGENERATED ⟨rest made a ∼ man of him⟩ **8** : being in a position or place for the first time ⟨a ∼ member⟩ **9** *cap* : having been in use after medieval times : MODERN ⟨*New* Latin⟩ **syn** novel, newfangled, fresh — **new·ish** *adj* — **new·ness** *n*

²new *adv* : NEWLY ⟨*new*-mown hay⟩

New Age *adj* **1** : of, relating to, or being a late 20th century social movement incorporating various untraditional concepts and practices relating esp. to spiritual, emotional, and physical well-being **2** : of, relating to, or being a soft soothing form of instrumental music

¹new·born \-'bòrn\ *adj* **1** : recently born **2** : born anew ⟨∼ hope⟩

²newborn *n, pl* **newborn** *or* **newborns** : a newborn individual

new·com·er \-ˌkə-mər\ *n* **1** : one recently arrived **2** : BEGINNER

New Deal *n* : the legislative and administrative program of President F. D. Roosevelt to promote economic recovery and social reform during the 1930s — **New Dealer** *n*

new·el \\'nü-əl, 'nyü-\ *n* : a post about which the steps of a circular staircase wind; *also* : a post at the foot of a stairway or one at a landing

---

\ə\abut \ᵊ\kitten \ər\further \a\ash \ā\ace \ä\mop, mar
\aù\out \ch\chin \e\bet \ē\easy \g\go \i\hit \ī\ice \j\job
\ŋ\sing \ō\go \ò\law \òi\boy \th\thin \t͟h\the \ü\loot \ù\foot
\y\yet \zh\vision *see also* Pronunciation Symbols page

new·fan·gled \'nü-'faŋ-gəld, 'nyü-\ *adj* **1** : attracted to novelty **2** : of the newest style : NOVEL

new–fash·ioned \-'fa-shənd\ *adj* **1** : made in a new fashion or form **2** : UP-TO-DATE

new·found \-'faùnd\ *adj* : newly found

New Left *n* : a radical political movement originating in the 1960s

new·ly \'nü-lē, 'nyü-\ *adv* **1** : LATELY, RECENTLY **2** : ANEW, AFRESH

new·ly·wed \-'wed\ *n* : one recently married

new moon *n* : the phase of the moon with its dark side toward the earth; *also* : the thin crescent moon seen for a few days after the new moon phase

news \'nüz, 'nyüz\ *n* **1** : a report of recent events : TIDINGS **2** : material reported in a newspaper or news periodical or on a newscast

news·boy \'nüz-ˌbòi, 'nyüz-\ *n* : one who delivers or sells newspapers

news·cast \-ˌkast\ *n* : a radio or television broadcast of news — **news·cast·er** \-ˌkas-tər\ *n*

news·let·ter \-ˌle-tər\ *n* : a small newspaper containing news or information of interest chiefly to a special group

news·mag·a·zine \-ˌma-gə-ˌzēn\ *n* : a usu. weekly magazine devoted chiefly to summarizing and analyzing news

news·man \-mən, -ˌman\ *n* : one who gathers, reports, or comments on the news : REPORTER

news·pa·per \-ˌpā-pər\ *n* : a paper that is published at regular intervals and contains news, articles of opinion, features, and advertising

news·pa·per·man \-ˌpā-pər-ˌman\ *n* : one who owns or is employed by a newspaper

news·print \-ˌprint\ *n* : paper made chiefly from wood pulp and used mostly for newspapers

news·reel \-ˌrēl\ *n* : a short motion picture portraying current events

news·stand \-ˌstand\ *n* : a place where newspapers and periodicals are sold

news·week·ly \-ˌwēk-lē\ *n* : a weekly newspaper or newsmagazine

news·wom·an \-ˌwù-mən\ *n* : a woman who gathers, reports, or comments on the news : REPORTER

news·wor·thy \-ˌwər-thē\ *adj* : sufficiently interesting to the general public to warrant reporting (as in a newspaper)

newsy \'nü-zē, 'nyü-\ *adj* **news·i·er; -est** : filled with news; *esp* : TALKATIVE

newt \'nüt, 'nyüt\ *n* : any of various small chiefly aquatic salamanders

New Testament *n* : the second of the two chief divisions of the Bible — see BIBLE table

new·ton \'nüt-ᵊn, 'nyüt-\ *n* : the unit of force in the metric system equal to the force required to impart an acceleration of one meter per second per second to a mass of one kilogram

new wave *n, often cap N&W* : the latest and esp. the most outrageous style — **new–wave** *adj*

New World *n* : the western hemisphere; *esp* : the continental landmass of No. and So. America

New Year *n* **1** : NEW YEAR'S DAY; *also* : the first days of the year **2** : ROSH HASHANAH

New Year's Day *n* : January 1 observed as a legal holiday

New Zea·land·er \nü-'zē-lən-dər, nyü-\ *n* : a native or inhabitant of New Zealand

¹**next** \'nekst\ *adj* : immediately preceding or following : NEAREST

²**next** *prep* : nearest or adjacent to

³**next** *adv* **1** : in the time, place, or order nearest or immediately succeeding **2** : on the first occasion to come

nex·us \'nek-səs\ *n, pl* **nex·us·es** \-sə-səz\ *or* **nex·us** \-səs, -ˌsüs\ : CONNECTION, LINK

Nez Percé \'nez-'pərs, *F* nā-per-sā\ *n* : a member of an American Indian people of Idaho, Washington, and Oregon; *also* : the language of the Nez Percé

NF *abbr* Newfoundland

NFC *abbr* National Football Conference

NFL *abbr* National Football League

Nfld *abbr* Newfoundland

NG *abbr* **1** National Guard **2** no good

ngul·trum \eŋ-'gùl-trəm\ *n* — see MONEY table

ngwee \eŋ-'gwē\ *n, pl* **ngwee** — see *kwacha* at MONEY table

NH *abbr* New Hampshire

NHL *abbr* National Hockey League

Ni *symbol* nickel

ni·a·cin \'nī-ə-sən\ *n* : NICOTINIC ACID

nib \'nib\ *n* : POINT; *esp* : a pen point

¹**nib·ble** \'ni-bəl\ *vb* **nib·bled; nib·bling** : to bite gently or bit by bit

²**nibble** *n* : a small or cautious bite

Nic·a·ra·guan \ˌni-kə-'rä-gwən\ *n* : a native or inhabitant of Nicaragua — **Nicaraguan** *adj*

nice \'nīs\ *adj* **nic·er; nic·est** [ME, foolish, wanton, fr. OF, fr. L *nescius* ignorant, fr. *nescire* to not know] **1** : FASTIDIOUS, DISCRIMINATING **2** : marked by delicate discrimination or treatment **3** : PLEASING, AGREEABLE; *also* : well-executed **4** : WELL-BRED ⟨~ people⟩ **5** : VIRTUOUS, RESPECTABLE **syn** choosy, finicky, particular, persnickety, picky — **nice·ly** *adv* — **nice·ness** *n*

nice–nel·ly \'nīs-'ne-lē\ *adj, often cap 2d N* **1** : marked by euphemism **2** : PRUDISH — **nice nelly** *n, often cap 2d N* — **nice–nel·ly·ism** \-ˌi-zəm\ *n, often cap 2d N*

nice·ty \'nī-sə-tē\ *n, pl* **-ties 1** : a dainty, delicate, or elegant thing ⟨enjoy the *niceties* of life⟩ **2** : a fine point or distinction ⟨*niceties* of workmanship⟩ **3** : EXACTNESS, PRECISION, ACCURACY

niche \'nich\ *n* [F] **1** : a recess in a wall esp. for a statue **2** : a place, employment, or activity for which a person or thing is best fitted **3** : the living space or role of an organism in an ecological community esp. with regard to food consumption

¹**nick** \'nik\ *n* **1** : a small notch or groove **2** : the final critical moment ⟨in the ~ of time⟩

²**nick** *vb* : NOTCH, CHIP

nick·el \'ni-kəl\ *n* **1** : a hard silver-white metallic chemical element capable of a high polish and used in alloys — see ELEMENT table **2** : the U.S. 5-cent piece made of copper and nickel; *also* : the Canadian 5-cent piece

nick·el·ode·on \ˌni-kə-'lō-dē-ən\ *n* **1** : an early movie theater to which admission cost five cents **2** : JUKEBOX

nick·er \'ni-kər\ *vb* : NEIGH, WHINNY — **nicker** *n*

nick·name \'nik-ˌnām\ *n* [ME *nekename* additional name, alter. (from misdivision of *an ekename*) of *ekename*, fr. *eke* also + *name*] **1** : a usu. descriptive name given instead of or in addition to the one belonging to a person, place, or thing **2** : a familiar form of a proper name — **nickname** *vb*

nic·o·tine \'ni-kə-ˌtēn\ *n* : a poisonous and addictive substance in tobacco that is used as an insecticide

nic·o·tin·ic acid \ˌni-kə-'tē-nik-, -'ti-\ *n* : an organic acid of the vitamin B complex found in plants and animals and used against pellagra

niece \'nēs\ *n* : a daughter of one's brother, sister, brother-in-law, or sister-in-law

nif·ty \'nif-tē\ *adj* **nif·ti·er; -est** : very good : very attractive

Ni·ge·ri·an \nī-'jir-ē-ən\ *n* : a native or inhabitant of Nigeria — **Nigerian** *adj*

nig·gard \'ni-gərd\ *n* : a stingy person : MISER — **nig·gard·li·ness** \-lē-nəs\ *n* — **nig·gard·ly** *adj or adv*

nig·gling \'ni-gə-liŋ\ *adj* **1** : PETTY **2** : bothersome in a petty way **syn** inconsequential, measly, picayune, piddling, trifling, trivial

¹nigh \'nī\ *adv* **1** : near in place, time, or relationship **2** : NEARLY, ALMOST

²nigh *adj* : CLOSE, NEAR

³nigh *prep* : NEAR

night \'nīt\ *n* **1** : the period between dusk and dawn **2** : the darkness of night **3** : a period of misery or unhappiness **4** : NIGHTFALL — **night** *adj*

night blindness *n* : reduced visual capacity in faint light (as at night)

night·cap \'nīt-ˌkap\ *n* **1** : a cloth cap worn with nightclothes **2** : a usu. alcoholic drink taken at bedtime

night·clothes \-ˌklō͟t͟hz, -ˌklōz\ *n pl* : garments worn in bed

night·club \-ˌkləb\ *n* : a place of entertainment open at night usu. serving food and liquor and providing music for dancing

night crawl·er \-ˌkrȯ-lər\ *n* : EARTHWORM; *esp* : a large earthworm found on the soil surface at night

night·dress \'nīt-ˌdres\ *n* : NIGHTGOWN

night·fall \-ˌfȯl\ *n* : the coming of night

night·gown \-ˌgau̇n\ *n* : a loose garment for wear in bed

night·hawk \-ˌhȯk\ *n* : any of a genus of American birds related to and resembling the whippoorwill

night·in·gale \'nīt-ᵊn-ˌgāl, 'nī-tiŋ-\ *n* [ME, fr. OE *nihtegale*, fr. *niht* night + *galan* to sing] : any of several Old World thrushes noted for the sweet usu. nocturnal song of the male

night·life \'nīt-ˌlīf\ *n* : the activity of pleasure-seekers at night

night·ly \'nīt-lē\ *adj* **1** : happening, done, or produced by night or every night **2** : of or relating to the night or every night — **nightly** *adv*

night·mare \'nīt-ˌmar\ *n* **1** : a frightening dream **2** : a frightening or horrible experience — **nightmare** *adj* — **night·mar·ish** *adj*

night rider *n* : a member of a secret band who ride masked at night doing violence to punish or terrorize

night·shade \'nīt-ˌshād\ *n* : any of a large genus of herbs, shrubs, and trees that include poisonous forms (as belladonna) and important food plants (as the potato, tomato, and eggplant)

night·shirt \-ˌshərt\ *n* : a nightgown resembling a shirt

night soil *n* : human excrement used esp. for fertilizing the soil

night·stick \'nīt-ˌstik\ *n* : a police officer's club

night·time \-ˌtīm\ *n* : the time from dusk to dawn

night·walk·er \-ˌwȯ-kər\ *n* : a person who roves about at night esp. with criminal or immoral intent

ni·hil·ism \'nī-ə-ˌli-zəm, 'nē-hə-\ *n* **1** : a viewpoint that traditional values and beliefs are unfounded and that existence is senseless and useless **2** : ANARCHISM **3** : TERRORISM — **ni·hil·ist** \-list\ *n or adj* — **ni·hil·is·tic** \ˌnī-ə-'lis-tik, ˌnē-hə-\ *adj*

nil \'nil\ *n* : ZERO, NOTHING

nim·ble \'nim-bəl\ *adj* **nim·bler; nim·blest** [ME *nimel*, fr. OE *numol* holding much, fr. *niman* to take] **1** : quick and light in motion : AGILE ⟨a ~ dancer⟩ **2** : quick in understanding and learning : CLEVER ⟨a ~ mind⟩ **syn** active, brisk, sprightly, spry, zippy — **nim·ble·ness** *n* — **nim·bly** \-blē\ *adv*

nim·bus \'nim-bəs\ *n, pl* **nim·bi** \-ˌbī, -bē\ *or* **nim·bus·es 1** : a figure (as a disk) in an art work suggesting radiant light about the head of a divinity, saint, or sovereign **2** : a rain cloud; *also* : THUNDERHEAD

NIMBY \'nim-bē\ *abbr* not in my backyard

nim·rod \'nim-ˌräd\ *n* : HUNTER

nin·com·poop \'nin-kəm-ˌpüp\ *n* : FOOL, SIMPLETON

nine \'nīn\ *n* **1** : one more than eight **2** : the 9th in a set or series **3** : something having nine units; *esp* : a baseball team — **nine** *adj or pron* — **ninth** \'nīnth\ *adj or adv or n*

nine days' wonder *n* : something that creates a short-lived sensation

nine·pins \'nīn-ˌpinz\ *n* : tenpins played without the headpin

nine·teen \'nīn-'tēn\ *n* : one more than 18 — **nineteen** *adj or pron* — **nine·teenth** \-'tēnth\ *adj or n*

nine·ty \'nīn-tē\ *n, pl* **nineties** : nine times 10 — **nine·ti·eth** \-tē-əth\ *adj or n* — **ninety** *adj or pron*

nin·ja \'nin-jə, -(ˌ)jä\ *n, pl* **ninja** *or* **ninjas** [Jp] : a person trained in ancient Japanese martial arts and employed esp. for espionage and assassinations

nin·ny \'ni-nē\ *n, pl* **ninnies** : FOOL

ni·o·bi·um \nī-'ō-bē-əm\ *n* : a gray metallic chemical element used in alloys — see ELEMENT table

¹nip \'nip\ *vb* **nipped; nip·ping 1** : to catch hold of and squeeze tightly between two surfaces, edges, or points **2** : ³CLIP **3** : to destroy the growth, progress, or fulfillment of ⟨nipped in the bud⟩ **4** : to injure or make numb with cold : CHILL **5** : SNATCH, STEAL

²nip *n* **1** : a sharp stinging cold **2** : a biting or pungent flavor **3** : PINCH, BITE **4** : a small portion : BIT

³nip *n* : a small quantity of liquor : SIP

⁴nip *vb* **nipped; nip·ping** : to take liquor in nips : TIPPLE

nip and tuck *adj or adv* : so close that the lead shifts rapidly from one contestant to another

nip·per \'ni-pər\ *n* **1** : one that nips **2** *pl* : PINCERS **3** : CHILD; *esp* : a small boy

nip·ple \'ni-pəl\ *n* : the protuberance of a mammary gland through which milk is drawn off : TEAT; *also* : something resembling a nipple

nip·py \'ni-pē\ *adj* **nip·pi·er; -est 1** : PUNGENT, SHARP **2** : CHILLY

nir·va·na \nir-'vä-nə\ *n, often cap* [Skt *nirvāṇa*, lit., act of extinguishing, fr. *nis-* out + *vāti* it blows] **1** : the final freeing of a soul from all that enslaves it; *esp* : the supreme happiness that according to Buddhism comes when all passion, hatred, and delusion die out and the soul is released from the necessity of further purification **2** : OBLIVION; *also* : PARADISE

Ni·san \'ni-sən, nē-'sän\ *n* [Heb *Nīsān*] : the 7th month of the civil year or the 1st month of the ecclesiastical year in the Jewish calendar

ni·sei \nē-'sā, 'nē-ˌsā\ *n, pl* **nisei** *also* **niseis** : a son or daughter of immigrant Japanese parents who is born and educated in America

ni·si \'nī-ˌsī\ *adj* [L, unless, fr. *ne-* not + *si* if] : taking effect at a specified time unless previously modified or voided ⟨a divorce decree ~⟩

nit \'nit\ *n* : the egg of a parasitic insect (as a louse); *also* : the young insect

nite *var of* NIGHT

ni·ter \'nī-tər\ *n* : POTASSIUM NITRATE

nit–pick·ing \'nit-ˌpi-kiŋ\ *n* : minute and usu. unjustified criticism — **nit·pick·er** *n*

¹ni·trate \'nī-ˌtrāt, -trət\ *n* **1** : a salt or ester of nitric acid **2** : sodium nitrate or potassium nitrate used as a fertilizer

²ni·trate \-ˌtrāt\ *vb* **ni·trat·ed; ni·trat·ing** : to treat or combine with nitric acid or a nitrate — **ni·tra·tion** \nī-'trā-shən\ *n*

ni·tre *chiefly Brit var of* NITER

nitric acid \'nī-trik-\ *n* : a corrosive liquid acid used esp. in making dyes, explosives, and fertilizers

ni·tri·fi·ca·tion \ˌnī-trə-fə-'kā-shən\ *n* : the oxidation (as by bacteria) of ammonium salts to nitrites and then to nitrates — **ni·tri·fy·ing** \'nī-trə-ˌfī-iŋ\ *adj*

ni·trite \'nī-ˌtrīt\ *n* : a salt of nitrous acid

ni·tro \'nī-trō\ *n, pl* **nitros** : any of various nitrated products; *esp* : NITROGLYCERIN

ni·tro·gen \'nī-trə-jən\ *n* : a tasteless odorless gaseous

\ə\abut \ᵊ\kitten \ər\further \a\ash \ā\ace \ä\mop, mar \au̇\out \ch\chin \e\bet \ē\easy \g\go \i\hit \ī\ice \j\job \ŋ\sing \ō\go \ȯ\law \ȯi\boy \t͟h\thin \t͟h\the \ü\loot \u̇\foot \y\yet \zh\vision *see also* Pronunciation Symbols page chemical element constituting 78 percent of the atmosphere by volume — see ELEMENT table — **ni·trog·e·nous** \nī-'trä-jə-nəs\ adj

nitrogen narcosis n : a state of euphoria and exhilaration caused by nitrogen forced into a diver's bloodstream from atmospheric air under pressure

ni·tro·glyc·er·in or **ni·tro·glyc·er·ine** \ˌnī-trə-'gli-sə-rən\ n : a heavy oily explosive liquid used to make dynamite and in medicine to dilate blood vessels

ni·trous acid \'nī-trəs-\ n : an unstable nitrogen-containing acid known only in solution or in the form of its salts

nitrous oxide n : a colorless gas used esp. as an anesthetic in dentistry

nit·ty-grit·ty \ˌni-tē-'gri-tē, ˌni-tē-'gri-tē\ n : what is essential and basic : specific practical details

nit·wit \'nit-ˌwit\ n : a scatterbrained or stupid person

¹**nix** \'niks\ n : NOTHING

²**nix** vb : VETO, REJECT

³**nix** adv : NO

NJ abbr New Jersey

NL abbr National League

NLRB abbr National Labor Relations Board

NM abbr 1 nautical mile 2 New Mexico

N Mex abbr New Mexico

NMI abbr no middle initial

NNE abbr north-northeast

NNW abbr north-northwest

¹**no** \'nō\ adv 1 — used to express the negative of an alternative ⟨shall we continue or ∼⟩ 2 : in no respect or degree ⟨he is ∼ better than the others⟩ 3 : not so ⟨∼, I'm not ready⟩ 4 — used with an adjective to imply a meaning opposite to the positive statement ⟨in ∼ uncertain terms⟩ 5 — used to introduce a more emphatic or explicit statement ⟨has the right, ∼, the duty to continue⟩ 6 — used as an interjection to express surprise or doubt ⟨∼—you don't say⟩ 7 — used in combination with a verb to form a compound adjective ⟨no-bake pie⟩

²**no** adj 1 : not any; also : hardly any 2 : not a ⟨she's ∼ expert⟩

³**no** \'nō\ n, pl **noes** or **nos** \'nōz\ 1 : REFUSAL, DENIAL 2 : a negative vote or decision; also, pl : persons voting in the negative

⁴**no** abbr 1 north; northern 2 [L numero, abl. of numerus] number

¹**No** or **Noh** \'nō\ n, pl **No** or **Noh** : classic Japanese dance-drama having a heroic theme, a chorus, and highly stylized action, costuming, and scenery

²**No** symbol nobelium

No·bel·ist \nō-'be-list\ n : a winner of a Nobel prize

no·bel·i·um \nō-'be-lē-əm\ n : a radioactive chemical element produced artificially — see ELEMENT table

No·bel prize \nō-'bel-, 'nō-ˌbel-\ n : any of various annual prizes (as in peace, literature, or medicine) established by the will of Alfred Nobel for the encouragement of persons who work for the interests of humanity

no·bil·i·ty \nō-'bi-lə-tē\ n 1 : the quality or state of being noble 2 : nobles considered as forming a class

¹**no·ble** \'nō-bəl\ adj **no·bler; no·blest** [ME, fr. OF, fr. L nobilis well known, noble, fr. noscere to come to know] 1 : ILLUSTRIOUS; also : FAMOUS, NOTABLE 2 : of high birth, rank, or station : ARISTOCRATIC 3 : EXCELLENT 4 : STATELY, IMPOSING ⟨a ∼ edifice⟩ 5 : of a superior nature syn august, baronial, grand, grandiose, magnificent, majestic — **no·ble·ness** n — **no·bly** \-blē\ adv

²**no·ble** n : a person of noble rank or birth

noble gas n : any of a group of rare gases that exhibit great stability and extremely low reaction rates

no·ble·man \'nō-bəl-mən\ n : a member of the nobility : PEER

no·blesse oblige \nō-ˌbles-ə-'blēzh\ n [F, lit., nobility obligates] : the obligation of honorable, generous, and

responsible behavior associated with high rank or birth

no·ble·wom·an \'nō-bəl-ˌwu̇-mən\ n : a woman of noble rank : PEERESS

¹**no·body** \'nō-ˌbä-dē, -bə-\ pron : no person

²**nobody** n, pl **no·bod·ies** : a person of no influence or importance

noc·tur·nal \näk-'tərn-əl\ adj 1 : of, relating to, or occurring in the night 2 : active at night ⟨a ∼ bird⟩

noc·turne \'näk-ˌtərn\ n : a work of art dealing with night; esp : a dreamy pensive composition for the piano

noc·u·ous \'nä-kyə-wəs\ adj : HARMFUL — **noc·u·ous·ly** adv

nod \'näd\ vb **nod·ded; nod·ding** 1 : to bend the head downward or forward (as in bowing, going to sleep, or giving assent) 2 : to move up and down ⟨tulips nodding in the breeze⟩ 3 : to show by a nod of the head ⟨∼ agreement⟩ 4 : to make a slip or error in a moment of abstraction — **nod** n

nod·dle \'näd-əl\ n : HEAD

nod·dy \'nä-dē\ n, pl **noddies** 1 : FOOL 2 : a stout-bodied tropical tern

node \'nōd\ n : a thickened, swollen, or differentiated area (as of tissue); esp : the part of a stem from which a leaf arises — **nod·al** \-əl\ adj

nod·ule \'nä-jül\ n : a small lump or swelling — **nod·u·lar** \'nä-jə-lər\ adj

no·el \nō-'el\ n [F noël Christmas, carol, fr. L natalis birthday] 1 : a Christmas carol 2 cap : the Christmas season

noes pl of NO

no–fault \'nō-'fȯlt\ adj 1 : of, relating to, or being a motor vehicle insurance plan under which someone involved in an accident is compensated usu. up to a stipulated limit for actual losses by that person's own insurance company regardless of who is responsible 2 : of, relating to, or being a divorce law under which neither party is held responsible for the breakup of the marriage

nog·gin \'nä-gən\ n 1 : a small mug or cup; also : a small quantity of drink 2 : a person's head

no–good \'nō-'gu̇d\ adj : having no worth, virtue, use, or chance of success — **no–good** \'nō-ˌgu̇d\ n

Noh var of NO

no–hit·ter \(ˌ)nō-'hi-tər\ n : a baseball game or part of a game in which a pitcher allows no base hits

no·how \'nō-ˌhau̇\ adv : in no manner

¹**noise** \'nȯiz\ n [ME, fr. OF, strife, quarrel, noise, fr. L nausea nausea] 1 : loud, confused, or senseless shouting or outcry 2 : SOUND; esp : one that lacks agreeable musical quality or is noticeably unpleasant 3 : unwanted electronic signal or disturbance — **noise·less** adj — **noise·less·ly** adv

²**noise** vb **noised; nois·ing** : to spread by rumor or report ⟨the story was noised abroad⟩

noise·mak·er \'nȯiz-ˌmā-kər\ n : one that makes noise; esp : a device used to make noise at parties

noise pollution n : annoying or harmful noise in an environment

noi·some \'nȯi-səm\ adj 1 : HARMFUL, UNWHOLESOME 2 : offensive to the senses (as smell) : DISGUSTING syn insalubrious, noxious, sickly, unhealthful, unhealthy

noisy \'nȯi-zē\ adj **nois·i·er; -est** 1 : making loud noises 2 : full of noises : LOUD — **nois·i·ly** \-zə-lē\ adv — **nois·i·ness** \-zē-nəs\ n

nol·le pro·se·qui \ˌnä-lē-'prä-sə-ˌkwī\ n [L, to be unwilling to pursue] : an entry on the record of a legal action that the prosecutor or plaintiff will proceed no further in an action or suit or in some aspect of it

no·lo con·ten·de·re \ˌnō-lō-kən-'ten-də-rē\ n [L, I do not wish to contend] : a plea in a criminal prosecution that subjects the defendant to conviction but does not admit guilt or preclude denying the charges in another proceeding

nol–pros \'näl-'präs\ *vb* **nol–prossed; nol–pros·sing** : to discontinue by entering a nolle prosequi

nom *abbr* nominative

no·mad \'nō-,mad\ *n* **1** : a member of a people who have no fixed residence but move from place to place **2** : an individual who roams about aimlessly — **nomad** *adj* — **no·mad·ic** \nō-'ma-dik\ *adj*

no–man's–land \'nō-,manz-,land\ *n* **1** : an area of unowned, unclaimed, or uninhabited land **2** : an unoccupied area between opposing troops

nom de guerre \,näm-di-'ger\ *n, pl* **noms de guerre** *same or* ,nämz-\ [F, lit., war name] : PSEUDONYM

nom de plume \-'plüm\ *n, pl* **noms de plume** *same or* ,nämz-\ [F, pen name; prob. coined in E] : PEN NAME

no·men·cla·ture \'nō-mən-,klā-chər\ *n* **1** : NAME, DESIGNATION **2** : a system of terms used in a science or art

nom·i·nal \'nä-mən-ᵊl\ *adj* **1** : being something in name or form only ⟨∼ head of a party⟩ **2** : TRIFLING ⟨a ∼ price⟩ — **nom·i·nal·ly** *adv*

nom·i·nate \'nä-mə-,nāt\ *vb* **-nat·ed; -nat·ing** : to choose as a candidate for election, appointment, or honor **syn** appoint, designate, name, tap — **nom·i·na·tion** \,nä-mə-'nā-shən\ *n*

nom·i·na·tive \'nä-mə-nə-tiv\ *adj* : of, relating to, or constituting a grammatical case marking typically the subject of a verb — **nominative** *n*

nom·i·nee \,nä-mə-'nē\ *n* : a person nominated for an office, duty, or position

non- \(')nän *or* ,nän *before stressed syllables;* ,nän *elsewhere*\ *prefix* **1** : not : reverse of : absence of **2** : having no importance

nonabrasive	noncritical
nonabsorbent	noncrystalline
nonacademic	nondeductible
nonacceptance	nondelivery
nonacid	nondemocratic
nonactivated	nondenominational
nonadaptive	nondepartmental
nonaddictive	nondestructive
nonadhesive	nondevelopment
nonadjacent	nondiscrimination
nonadjustable	nondiscriminatory
nonaggression	nondistinctive
nonalcoholic	nondurable
nonappearance	noneconomic
nonaromatic	noneducational
nonathletic	nonelastic
nonattendance	nonelection
nonbeliever	nonelective
nonbelligerent	nonelectric
nonbreakable	nonelectrical
noncancerous	nonemotional
noncandidate	nonenforcement
noncellular	nonessential
nonclerical	nonethical
noncoital	non-euclidean
noncombat	nonexclusive
noncombustible	nonexempt
noncommercial	nonexistence
noncommunist	nonexistent
noncompeting	nonexplosive
noncompetitive	nonfarm
noncompliance	nonfatal
noncomplying	nonfattening
nonconducting	nonfederated
nonconflicting	nonferrous
nonconformance	nonfiction
nonconforming	nonfictional
nonconstructive	nonfilamentous
noncontagious	nonfilterable
noncontinuous	nonflammable
noncorroding	nonflowering
noncorrosive	nonfood

nonfreezing	nonprotein
nonfulfillment	nonradioactive
nonfunctional	nonrandom
nongraded	nonreactive
nonhereditary	nonreciprocal
nonhomogeneous	nonrecognition
nonhomologous	nonrecurrent
nonhuman	nonrecurring
nonidentical	nonrefillable
nonimportation	nonreligious
nonindustrial	nonrenewable
noninfectious	nonresidential
noninflammable	nonrestricted
nonintellectual	nonreturnable
nonintercourse	nonreversible
noninterference	nonruminant
nonintoxicant	nonsalable
nonintoxicating	nonscientific
noninvasive	nonscientist
nonionizing	nonseasonal
nonirritating	nonsectarian
nonlegal	nonsegregated
nonlethal	nonselective
nonlife	non-self-governing
nonlinear	nonsexist
nonliterary	nonsexual
nonliving	nonshrinkable
nonlogical	nonsinkable
nonmagnetic	nonsmoker
nonmalignant	nonsmoking
nonmaterial	nonsocial
nonmember	nonspeaking
nonmembership	nonspecialist
nonmigratory	nonspecific
nonmilitary	nonsteroidal
nonmoral	nonsuccess
nonmotile	nonsurgical
nonmoving	nontaxable
nonnegotiable	nonteaching
nonobservance	nontechnical
nonoccurrence	nontemporal
nonofficial	nontenured
nonoily	nontheistic
nonorthodox	nonthreatening
nonparallel	nontoxic
nonparasitic	nontraditional
nonparticipant	nontransferable
nonparticipating	nontypical
nonpathogenic	nonuniform
nonpaying	nonuser
nonpayment	nonvascular
nonperformance	nonvenomous
nonperishable	nonviable
nonphysical	nonvisual
nonpoisonous	nonvocal
nonpolar	nonvolatile
nonpolitical	nonvoter
nonporous	nonvoting
nonpregnant	nonworker
nonproductive	nonworking
nonprofessional	nonzero

non·age \'nä-nij, 'nō-\ *n* **1** : legal minority **2** : a period of youth **3** : IMMATURITY

no·na·ge·nar·i·an \,nō-nə-jə-'ner-ē-ən, ,nä-\ *n* : a person whose age is in the nineties

non·aligned \,nän-ə-'līnd\ *adj* : not allied with other nations

non·book \'nän-,bůk\ *n* : a book of little literary merit

\ə\abut \ᵊ\kitten \ər\further \a\ash \ā\ace \ä\mop, mar
\aů\out \ch\chin \e\bet \ē\easy \g\go \i\hit \ī\ice \j\job
\ŋ\sing \ō\go \ȯ\law \ȯi\boy \th\thin \t̲h̲\the \ü\loot \ů\foot
\y\yet \zh\vision *see also* Pronunciation Symbols page

that is often a compilation (as of pictures or speeches)

¹nonce \'näns\ *n* : the one, particular, or present occasion or purpose ⟨for the ∼⟩

²nonce *adj* : occurring, used, or made only once or for a special occasion ⟨a ∼ word⟩

non·cha·lant \ˌnän-shə-'länt\ *adj* [F, fr. OF, fr. prp. of *nonchaloir* to disregard, fr. *non-* not + *chaloir* to concern, fr. L *calēre* to be warm] : giving an effect of unconcern or indifference **syn** collected, composed, cool, imperturbable, unflappable, unruffled — **non·cha·lance** \-'läns\ *n* — **non·cha·lant·ly** *adv*

non·com \'nän-ˌkäm\ *n* : NONCOMMISSIONED OFFICER

non·com·ba·tant \ˌnän-kəm-'bat-ᵊnt, nän-'käm-bə-tənt\ *n* : a member (as a chaplain) of the armed forces whose duties do not include fighting; *also* : CIVILIAN — **noncombatant** *adj*

non·com·mis·sioned officer \ˌnän-kə-'mi-shənd-\ *n* : a subordinate officer in the armed forces appointed from enlisted personnel

non·com·mit·tal \ˌnän-kə-'mit-ᵊl\ *adj* : indicating neither consent nor dissent

non com·pos men·tis \ˌnän-ˌkäm-pəs-'men-təs\ *adj* : not of sound mind

non·con·duc·tor \ˌnän-kən-'dək-tər\ *n* : a substance that is a very poor conductor of heat, electricity, or sound

non·con·form·ist \-kən-'för-mist\ *n* **1** *often cap* : a person who does not conform to an established church and esp. the Church of England **2** : a person who does not conform to a generally accepted pattern of thought or action **syn** dissenter, dissident, heretic, schismatic, sectary, separatist — **non·con·for·mi·ty** \-'för-mə-tē\ *n*

non·co·op·er·a·tion \ˌnän-kō-ˌä-pə-'rā-shən\ *n* : failure or refusal to cooperate; *esp* : refusal through civil disobedience of a people to cooperate with the government of a country

non·cred·it \(ˌ)nän-'kre-dət\ *adj* : not offering credit toward a degree

non·cus·to·di·al \ˌnän-kə-'stō-dē-əl\ *adj* : of or being a parent who does not have legal custody of a child

non·dairy \'nän-'der-ē\ *adj* : containing no milk or milk products

non·de·script \ˌnän-di-'skript\ *adj* **1** : not belonging to any particular class or kind **2** : lacking distinctive qualities

non·drink·er \-'driŋ-kər\ *n* : a person who abstains from alcohol

¹none \'nən\ *pron* **1** : not any ⟨∼ of them went⟩ **2** : not one ⟨∼ of the family⟩ **3** : not any such thing or person ⟨half a loaf is better than ∼⟩

²none *adj, archaic* : not any : NO

³none *adv* : by no means : not at all ⟨he got there ∼ too soon⟩

non·en·ti·ty \ˌnän-'en-tə-tē\ *n* **1** : something that does not exist or exists only in the imagination **2** : one of no consequence or significance **syn** nobody, nothing, whippersnapper

nones \'nōnz\ *n sing or pl* : the 7th day of March, May, July, or October or the 5th day of any other month in the ancient Roman calendar

none·such \'nən-ˌsəch\ *n* : one without an equal — **nonesuch** *adj*

none·the·less \ˌnən-thə-'les\ *adv* : NEVERTHELESS

non·event \'nän-i-ˌvent\ *n* **1** : an event that fails to take place or to satisfy expectations **2** : a highly promoted event of little intrinsic interest

non·fat \-'fat\ *adj* : lacking fat solids : having fat solids removed ⟨∼ milk⟩

non·gono·coc·cal \ˌnän-ˌgä-nə-'kä-kəl\ *adj* : not caused by a gonococcus

non·he·ro \'nän-'hē-rō\ *n* : ANTIHERO

non·in·ter·ven·tion \ˌnän-ˌin-tər-'ven-chən\ *n* : refusal or failure to intervene (as in the affairs of other countries)

non·met·al \'nän-'met-ᵊl\ *n* : a chemical element (as carbon) that lacks the characteristics of a metal — **non·me·tal·lic** \ˌnän-mə-'ta-lik\ *adj*

non·neg·a·tive \-'ne-gə-tiv\ *adj* : not negative : being either positive or zero

non·nu·cle·ar \'nän-'nü-klē-ər\ *adj* **1** : not nuclear **2** : not having, using, or involving nuclear weapons

non·ob·jec·tive \ˌnän-əb-'jek-tiv\ *adj* **1** : not objective **2** : representing no natural or actual object, figure, or scene ⟨∼ art⟩

¹non·pa·reil \ˌnän-pə-'rel\ *adj* : having no equal : PEERLESS

²nonpareil *n* **1** : an individual of unequaled excellence : PARAGON **2** : a small flat disk of chocolate covered with white sugar pellets

non·par·ti·san \'nän-'pär-tə-zən\ *adj* : not partisan; *esp* : not influenced by political party·spirit or interests

non·per·son \-'pərs-ᵊn\ *n* **1** : UNPERSON **2** : a person having no social or legal status

non·plus \'nän-'pləs\ *vb* **-plussed** *also* **-plused** \-'pləst\; **-plus·sing** *also* **-plus·ing** : PUZZLE, PERPLEX

non·pre·scrip·tion \ˌnän-pri-'skrip-shən\ *adj* : available for sale legally without a doctor's prescription

non·prof·it \'nän-'prä-fət\ *adj* : not conducted or maintained for the purpose of making a profit ⟨a ∼ organization⟩

non·pro·lif·er·a·tion \ˌnän-prə-ˌli-fə-'rā-shən\ *adj* : providing for the stoppage of proliferation (as of nuclear arms) ⟨a ∼ treaty⟩

non·read·er \'nän-'rē-dər\ *n* : one who does not read

non·rep·re·sen·ta·tion·al \ˌnän-ˌre-pri-ˌzen-'tā-shə-nəl\ *adj* : NONOBJECTIVE 2

non·res·i·dent \'nän-'re-zə-dənt\ *adj* : not living in a particular place — **non·res·i·dence** \-dəns\ *n* — **nonresident** *n*

non·re·sis·tance \ˌnän-ri-'zis-təns\ *n* : the principles or practice of passive submission to authority even when unjust or oppressive

non·re·stric·tive \-ri-'strik-tiv\ *adj* **1** : not serving or tending to restrict **2** : not limiting the reference of the word or phrase modified ⟨a ∼ clause⟩

non·rig·id \nän-'ri-jəd\ *adj* : maintaining form by pressure of contained gas ⟨a ∼ airship⟩

non·sched·uled \'nän-'ske-jüld\ *adj* : licensed to carry passengers or freight by air without a regular schedule

non·sense \'nän-ˌsens, -səns\ *n* **1** : foolish or meaningless words or actions **2** : things of no importance or value — **non·sen·si·cal** \nän-'sen-si-kəl\ *adj* — **non·sen·si·cal·ly** \-k(ə-)lē\ *adv*

non se·qui·tur \nän-'se-kwə-tər\ *n* [L, it does not follow] : an inference that does not follow from the premises

non·sked \'nän-'sked\ *n* : a nonscheduled transport plane or airline

non·skid \'nän-'skid\ *adj* : designed to prevent skidding

non·slip \-'slip\ *adj* : designed to prevent slipping

non·stan·dard \ˌnän-'stan-dərd\ *adj* **1** : not standard **2** : not conforming to the usage characteristic of educated native speakers of a language

non·start·er \'nän-'stär-tər\ *n* **1** : one that does not start **2** : one that is not productive or effective

non·stick \-'stik\ *adj* : allowing easy removal of cooked food particles

non·stop \-'stäp\ *adj* : done or made without a stop — **nonstop** *adv*

non·sup·port \ˌnän-sə-'pōrt\ *n* : failure to support; *esp* : failure on the part of one under obligation to provide maintenance

non–U \'nän-'yü\ *adj* : not characteristic of the upper classes

non·union \-'yü-nyən\ *adj* **1** : not belonging to a trade union ⟨∼ carpenters⟩ **2** : not recognizing or favoring trade unions or their members ⟨∼ employers⟩

non·us·er \-'yü-zər\ *n* : one who does not make use of something (as drugs)

non·vi·o·lence \'nän-'vī-ə-ləns\ *n* **1** : abstention from violence as a matter of principle **2** : avoidance of violence **3** : nonviolent political demonstrations — **non·vi·o·lent** \-lənt\ *adj*

non·white \,nän-'hwīt, -'wīt\ *n* : a person whose features and esp. skin color are different from those of peoples of northwestern Europe — **nonwhite** *adj*

non·wo·ven \'nän-'wō-vən\ *adj* : made of fibers held together by interlocking or bonding (as by chemical or thermal means) — **nonwoven** *n*

noo·dle \'nüd-ᵊl\ *n* [G *Nudel*] : a food paste made with egg and shaped typically in ribbon form

nook \'nük\ *n* **1** : an interior angle or corner formed usu. by two walls ⟨a chimney ∼⟩ **2** : a sheltered or hidden place ⟨searched every ∼ and cranny⟩

noon \'nün\ *n* : the middle of the day : 12 o'clock in the daytime — **noon** *adj*

noon·day \'nün-,dā\ *n* : NOON, MIDDAY

no one *pron* : NOBODY

noon·tide \'nün-,tīd\ *n* : NOON

noon·time \-,tīm\ *n* : NOON

noose \'nüs\ *n* : a loop with a running knot (as in a lasso) that binds closer the more it is drawn

nope \'nōp\ *adv* : NO

nor \'nȯr\ *conj* : and not ⟨not for you ∼ for me⟩ — used esp. to introduce and negate the second member and each later member of a series of items preceded by *neither* ⟨neither here ∼ there⟩

Nor *abbr* Norway; Norwegian

Nor·dic \'nȯr-dik\ *adj* **1** : of or relating to the Germanic peoples of northern Europe and esp. of Scandinavia **2** : of or relating to competitive ski events involving cross=country racing, ski jumping, or biathlon — **Nordic** *n*

nor·epi·neph·rine \'nȯr-,e-pə-'ne-frən\ *n* : a nitrogen=containing neurotransmitter in parts of the sympathetic and central nervous systems

norm \'nȯrm\ *n* [L *norma*, lit., carpenter's square] **1** : an authoritative standard or model; *esp* : a set standard of development or achievement usu. derived from the average or median achievement of a large group **2** : a typical or widespread practice, procedure, or custom **syn** average, mean, median, par

¹nor·mal \'nȯr-məl\ *adj* **1** : REGULAR, STANDARD, NATURAL **2** : of average intelligence; *also* : sound in mind and body — **nor·mal·cy** \-sē\ *n* — **nor·mal·i·ty** \nȯr-'ma-lə-tē\ *n* — **nor·mal·ly** *adv*

²normal *n* **1** : one that is normal **2** : the usual condition, level, or quantity

nor·mal·ize \'nȯr-mə-,līz\ *vb* **-ized; -iz·ing** : to make or restore to normal — **nor·mal·i·za·tion** \,nȯr-mə-lə-'zā-shən\ *n*

Nor·man \'nȯr-mən\ *n* **1** : a native or inhabitant of Normandy **2** : one of the 10th century Scandinavian conquerors of Normandy **3** : one of the Norman-French conquerors of England in 1066 — **Norman** *adj*

nor·ma·tive \'nȯr-mə-tiv\ *adj* : of, relating to, or determining norms — **nor·ma·tive·ly** *adv* — **nor·ma·tive·ness** *n*

Norse \'nȯrs\ *n, pl* **Norse 1** : NORWEGIAN; *also* : any of the western Scandinavian dialects or languages **2** *pl* : SCANDINAVIANS; *also* : NORWEGIANS

Norse·man \-mən\ *n* : any of the ancient Scandinavians

¹north \'nȯrth\ *adv* : to, toward, or in the north

²north *adj* **1** : situated toward or at the north **2** : coming from the north

³north *n* **1** : the direction to the left of one facing east **2** : the compass point directly opposite to south **3** *cap* : regions or countries north of a specified or implied point — **north·er·ly** \'nȯr-thər-lē\ *adv or adj* — **north·ern** \-thərn\ *adj* — **North·ern·er** \-thər-nər\ *n* — **north-**

ern·most \-thərn-,mōst\ *adj* — **north·ward** \'nȯrth-wərd\ *adv or adj* — **north·wards** \-wərdz\ *adv*

north·east \nȯr-'thēst\ *n* **1** : the general direction between north and east **2** : the compass point midway between north and east **3** *cap* : regions or countries northeast of a specified or implied point — **northeast** *adj or adv* — **north·east·er·ly** \-'thē-stər-lē\ *adv or adj* — **north·east·ern** \-stərn\ *adj*

north·east·er \-'thēs-tər\ *n* **1** : a strong northeast wind **2** : a storm with northeast winds

north·er \'nȯr-thər\ *n* **1** : a strong north wind **2** : a storm with north winds

northern lights *n pl* : AURORA BOREALIS

north pole *n, often cap N&P* : the northernmost point of the earth

North Star *n* : the star toward which the northern end of the earth's axis points

north·west \nȯrth-'west\ *n* **1** : the general direction between north and west **2** : the compass point midway between north and west **3** *cap* : regions or countries northwest of a specified or implied point — **northwest** *adj or adv* — **north·west·er·ly** \-'we-stər-lē\ *adv or adj* — **north·west·ern** \-'we-stərn\ *adj*

Norw *abbr* Norway; Norwegian

Nor·we·gian \nȯr-'wē-jən\ *n* **1** : a native or inhabitant of Norway **2** : the language of Norway — **Norwegian** *adj*

nos *abbr* numbers

¹nose \'nōz\ *n* **1** : the part of the face or head containing the nostrils and covering the front of the nasal cavity **2** : the sense of smell **3** : something (as a point, edge, or projecting front part) that resembles a nose ⟨the ∼ of a plane⟩ — **nosed** \'nōzd\ *adj*

²nose *vb* **nosed; nos·ing 1** : to detect by or as if by smell : SCENT **2** : to push or move with the nose **3** : to touch or rub with the nose : NUZZLE **4** : PRY **5** : to move ahead slowly ⟨the ship *nosed* into her berth⟩

nose·bleed \'nōz-,blēd\ *n* : a bleeding from the nose

nose cone *n* : a protective cone constituting the forward end of an aerospace vehicle

nose dive *n* **1** : a downward nose-first plunge (as of an airplane) **2** : a sudden extreme drop (as in prices)

nose·gay \'nōz-,gā\ *n* : a small bunch of flowers : POSY

nose out *vb* **1** : to discover often by prying **2** : to defeat by a narrow margin

nose·piece \-,pēs\ *n* **1** : a fitting at the lower end of a microscope tube to which the objectives are attached **2** : the bridge of a pair of eyeglasses

no–show \'nō-,shō\ *n* : a person who reserves space (as on an airplane or at a concert) but neither uses nor cancels the reservation

nos·tal·gia \nä-'stal-jə\ *n* [NL, fr. Gk *nostos* return home + *algos* pain, grief] **1** : HOMESICKNESS **2** : a wistful yearning for something past or irrecoverable — **nos·tal·gic** \-jik\ *adj*

nos·tril \'näs-trəl\ *n* [ME *nosethirl*, fr. OE *nosthyrl*, fr. *nosu* nose + *thyrel* hole] **1** : either of the nares usu. with the adjoining nasal wall and passage **2** : either fleshy lateral wall of the nose

nos·trum \'näs-trəm\ *n* [L, neut. of *noster* our, ours, fr. *nos* we] : a questionable medicine or remedy

nosy *or* **nos·ey** \'nō-zē\ *adj* **nos·i·er; -est** : INQUISITIVE, PRYING

not \'nät\ *adv* **1** — used to make negative a group of words or a word ⟨the boys are ∼ here⟩ **2** — used to stand for the negative of a preceding group of words ⟨sometimes hard to see and sometimes ∼⟩

no·ta be·ne \,nō-tə-'bē-nē, -'be-\ [L, mark well] — used to call attention to something important

---

\ə\abut \ᵊ\kitten \ər\further \a\ash \ā\ace \ä\mop, mar
\au̇\out \ch\chin \e\bet \ē\easy \g\go \i\hit \ī\ice \j\job
\ŋ\sing \ō\go \ȯ\law \ȯi\boy \th\thin \t͟h\the \ü\loot \u̇\foot
\y\yet \zh\vision *see also* Pronunciation Symbols page

no·ta·bil·i·ty \ˌnō-tə-ˈbi-lə-tē\ *n, pl* **-ties 1** : the quality or state of being notable **2** : NOTABLE
¹**no·ta·ble** \ˈnō-tə-bəl\ *adj* **1** : NOTEWORTHY, REMARKABLE ⟨a ~ achievement⟩ **2** : DISTINGUISHED, PROMINENT ⟨two ~ politicians made speeches⟩
²**notable** *n* : a person of note **syn** bigwig, eminence, nabob, personage, somebody, VIP
no·ta·bly \ˈnō-tə-blē\ *adv* **1** : in a notable manner **2** : ESPECIALLY, PARTICULARLY
no·tar·i·al \nō-ˈter-ē-əl\ *adj* : of, relating to, or done by a notary public
no·ta·rize \ˈnō-tə-ˌrīz\ *vb* **-rized; -riz·ing** : to acknowledge or make legally authentic as a notary public
no·ta·ry public \ˈnō-tə-rē-\ *n, pl* **notaries public** *or* **notary publics** : a public official who attests or certifies writings (as deeds) to make them legally authentic
no·ta·tion \nō-ˈtā-shən\ *n* **1** : ANNOTATION, NOTE **2** : the act, process, or method of representing data by marks, signs, figures, or characters; *also* : a system of symbols (as letters, numerals, or musical notes) used in such notation
¹**notch** \ˈnäch\ *n* **1** : a V-shaped hollow in an edge or surface **2** : a narrow pass between two mountains
²**notch** *vb* **1** : to cut or make notches in **2** : to score or record by or as if by cutting a series of notches ⟨~ed 20 points for the team⟩
notch·back \ˈnäch-ˌbak\ *n* : an automobile with a trunk whose lid forms a distinct deck
¹**note** \ˈnōt\ *vb* **not·ed; not·ing 1** : to notice or observe with care; *also* : to record or preserve in writing **2** : to make special mention of : REMARK
²**note** *n* **1** : a musical sound **2** : a cry, call, or sound esp. of a bird **3** : a special tone in a person's words or voice ⟨a ~ of fear⟩ **4** : a character in music used to indicate duration of a tone by its shape and pitch by its position on the staff **5** : a characteristic feature : MOOD, QUALITY ⟨a ~ of optimism⟩ **6** : MEMORANDUM **7** : a brief and informal record; *also* : a written or printed comment or explanation **8** : a written promise to pay a debt **9** : a piece of paper money **10** : a short informal letter **11** : a formal diplomatic or official communication **12** : DISTINCTION, REPUTATION ⟨an artist of ~⟩ **13** : OBSERVATION, NOTICE, HEED ⟨take ~ of the time⟩
note·book \ˈnōt-ˌbu̇k\ *n* : a book for notes or memoranda
not·ed \ˈnō-təd\ *adj* : well known by reputation : EMINENT, CELEBRATED
note·wor·thy \ˈnōt-ˌwər-thē\ *adj* : worthy of note : REMARKABLE
¹**noth·ing** \ˈnə-thiŋ\ *pron* **1** : no thing ⟨leaves ~ to the imagination⟩ **2** : no part **3** : one of no interest, value, or importance ⟨she's ~ to me⟩
²**nothing** *adv* : not at all : in no degree
³**nothing** *n* **1** : something that does not exist **2** : ZERO **3** : a person or thing of little or no value or importance
⁴**nothing** *adj* : of no account : worthless
noth·ing·ness \ˈnə-thiŋ-nəs\ *n* **1** : the quality or state of being nothing **2** : NONEXISTENCE; *also* : utter insignificance **3** : something insignificant or valueless
¹**no·tice** \ˈnō-təs\ *n* **1** : WARNING, ANNOUNCEMENT **2** : notification of the termination of an agreement or contract at a specified time **3** : ATTENTION, HEED ⟨bring the matter to my ~⟩ **4** : a written or printed announcement **5** : a short critical account or examination (as of a play) : REVIEW
²**notice** *vb* **no·ticed; no·tic·ing 1** : to make mention of : remark on : NOTE **2** : to take notice of : OBSERVE, MARK
no·tice·able \ˈnō-tə-sə-bəl\ *adj* **1** : worthy of notice **2** : capable of being or likely to be noticed — **no·tice·ably** \-blē\ *adv*
no·ti·fy \ˈnō-tə-ˌfī\ *vb* **-fied; -fy·ing 1** : to give notice of : report the occurrence of **2** : to give notice to — **no·ti·fi·ca·tion** \ˌnō-tə-fə-ˈkā-shən\ *n*

no·tion \ˈnō-shən\ *n* **1** : IDEA, CONCEPTION ⟨have a ~ of what he means⟩ **2** : a belief held : OPINION, VIEW **3** : WHIM, FANCY ⟨a sudden ~ to go⟩ **4** *pl* : small useful articles (as pins, needles, or thread)
no·tion·al \ˈnō-shə-nəl\ *adj* **1** : existing in the mind only : IMAGINARY, UNREAL **2** : given to foolish or fanciful moods or ideas : WHIMSICAL
no·to·ri·ous \nō-ˈtȯr-ē-əs\ *adj* : generally known and talked of; *esp* : widely and unfavorably known — **no·to·ri·ety** \ˌnō-tə-ˈrī-ə-tē\ *n* — **no·to·ri·ous·ly** \nō-ˈtȯr-ē-əs-lē\ *adv*
¹**not·with·stand·ing** \ˌnät-with-ˈstan-diŋ, -ˌwith-\ *prep* : in spite of
²**notwithstanding** *adv* : NEVERTHELESS
³**notwithstanding** *conj* : ALTHOUGH
nou·gat \ˈnü-gət\ *n* [F, fr. Provençal, fr. Old Provençal *nogat*, fr. *noga* nut, ultim. fr. L *nuc-, nux*] : a confection of nuts or fruit pieces in a sugar paste
nought \ˈnȯt, ˈnät\ *var of* NAUGHT
noun \ˈnau̇n\ *n* : a word that is the name of a subject of discourse (as a person or place)
nour·ish \ˈnər-ish\ *vb* : to promote the growth or development of
nour·ish·ing *adj* : giving nourishment
nour·ish·ment \ˈnər-ish-mənt\ *n* **1** : FOOD, NUTRIENT **2** : the action or process of nourishing
nou·veau riche \ˌnü-ˌvō-ˈrēsh\ *n, pl* **nou·veaux riches** *same*\ [F] : a person newly rich : PARVENU
Nov *abbr* November
no·va \ˈnō-və\ *n, pl* **novas** *or* **no·vae** \-(ˌ)vē, -ˌvī\ [NL, fem. of L *novus* new] : a star that suddenly increases greatly in brightness and then within a few months or years grows dim again
¹**nov·el** \ˈnä-vəl\ *adj* **1** : having no precedent : NEW **2** : STRANGE, UNUSUAL
²**novel** *n* : a long invented prose narrative dealing with human experience through a connected sequence of events — **nov·el·ist** \-və-list\ *n*
nov·el·ette \ˌnä-və-ˈlet\ *n* : a brief novel or long short story
nov·el·ize \ˈnä-və-ˌlīz\ *vb* **-ized; -iz·ing** : to convert into the form of a novel — **nov·el·i·za·tion** \ˌnä-və-lə-ˈzā-shən\ *n*
no·vel·la \nō-ˈve-lə\ *n, pl* **novellas** *or* **no·vel·le** \-ˈve-lē\ : NOVELETTE
nov·el·ty \ˈnä-vəl-tē\ *n, pl* **-ties 1** : something new or unusual **2** : NEWNESS **3** : a small manufactured article intended mainly for personal or household adornment — usu. used in pl.
No·vem·ber \nō-ˈvem-bər\ *n* [ME *Novembre*, fr. OF, fr. L *November* (ninth month), fr. *novem* nine] : the 11th month of the year having 30 days
no·ve·na \nō-ˈvē-nə\ *n* : a Roman Catholic nine-day period of prayer
nov·ice \ˈnä-vəs\ *n* **1** : a new member of a religious order who is preparing to take the vows of religion **2** : one who is inexperienced or untrained
no·vi·tiate \nō-ˈvi-shət\ *n* **1** : the period or state of being a novice **2** : a house where novices are trained **3** : NOVICE
¹**now** \ˈnau̇\ *adv* **1** : at the present time or moment **2** : in the time immediately before the present **3** : IMMEDIATELY, FORTHWITH **4** — used with the sense of present time weakened or lost (as to express command, introduce an important point, or indicate a transition) ⟨~ hear this⟩ **5** : SOMETIMES ⟨~ one and ~ another⟩ **6** : under the present circumstances **7** : at the time referred to
²**now** *conj* : in view of the fact ⟨~ that you're here, we'll start⟩
³**now** *n* : the present time or moment : PRESENT
⁴**now** *adj* **1** : of or relating to the present time ⟨the ~ president⟩ **2** : excitingly new ⟨~ clothes⟩; *also* : constantly aware of what is new ⟨~ people⟩

NOW *abbr* **1** National Organization for Women **2** negotiable order of withdrawal

now·a·days \'naù-ə-ˌdāz\ *adv* : at the present time

no·way \'nō-ˌwā\ *or* **no·ways** \-ˌwāz\ *adv* : NOWISE

no·where \-ˌhwer\ *adv* : not anywhere — **nowhere** *n*

nowhere near *adv* : not nearly

no·wise \'nō-ˌwīz\ *adv* : in no way

nox·ious \'näk-shəs\ *adj* : harmful esp. to health or morals

noz·zle \'nä-zəl\ *n* : a short tube constricted in the middle or at one end and used (as on a hose) to speed up or direct a flow of fluid

np *abbr* **1** no pagination **2** no place (of publication)

Np *symbol* neptunium

NP *abbr* notary public

NR *abbr* not rated

NRA *abbr* National Rifle Association

NS *abbr* **1** not specified **2** Nova Scotia

NSA *abbr* National Security Agency

NSC *abbr* National Security Council

NSF *abbr* **1** National Science Foundation **2** not sufficient funds

NSW *abbr* New South Wales

NT *abbr* **1** New Testament **2** Northern Territory **3** Northwest Territories

nth \'enth\ *adj* **1** : numbered with an unspecified or indefinitely large ordinal number ⟨for the ∼ time⟩ **2** : EXTREME, UTMOST ⟨to the ∼ degree⟩

NTP *abbr* normal temperature and pressure

nt wt *or* **n wt** *abbr* net weight

nu \'nü, 'nyü\ *n* : the 13th letter of the Greek alphabet— N or ν

NU *abbr* name unknown

nu·ance \'nü-ˌäns, 'nyü-, nù-'äns, nyù-\ *n* [F] : a shade of difference : a delicate variation (as in tone or meaning)

nub \'nəb\ *n* **1** : KNOB, LUMP **2** : GIST, POINT ⟨the ∼ of the story⟩

nub·bin \'nə-bən\ *n* **1** : something (as an ear of Indian corn) that is small for its kind, stunted, undeveloped, or imperfect **2** : a small projecting bit

nu·bile \'nü-ˌbīl, 'nyü-, -bəl\ *adj* **1** : of marriageable condition or age **2** : sexually attractive ⟨∼ young women⟩

nu·cle·ar \'nü-klē-ər, 'nyü-\ *adj* **1** : of, relating to, or constituting a nucleus **2** : of, relating to, or using the atomic nucleus or energy derived from it **3** : of, relating to, or being a weapon whose destructive power results from an uncontrolled nuclear reaction

nu·cle·ate \'nü-klē-ˌāt, 'nyü-\ *vb* **-at·ed; -at·ing** : to form, act as, or have a nucleus — **nu·cle·ation** \ˌnü-klē-'ā-shən, ˌnyü-\ *n*

nu·cle·ic acid \nù-'klē-ik-, nyù-, -'klā-\ *n* : any of various complex organic acids (as DNA) found esp. in cell nuclei

nu·cle·us \'nü-klē-əs, 'nyü-\ *n, pl* **nu·clei** \-klē-ˌī\ *also* **nu·cle·us·es** [NL, fr. L, kernel, dim. of *nuc-, nux* nut] **1** : a central mass or part about which matter gathers or is collected : CORE **2** : a cell part that is characteristic of all living things except viruses, bacteria, and certain algae, that is necessary for heredity and for making proteins, that contains the chromosomes with their genes, and that is enclosed in a membrane **3** : a mass of gray matter or group of nerve cells in the central nervous system **4** : the central part of an atom that comprises nearly all of the atomic mass

¹**nude** \'nüd, 'nyüd\ *adj* **nud·er; nud·est** : BARE, NAKED, UNCLOTHED — **nu·di·ty** \'nü-də-tē, 'nyü-\ *n*

²**nude** *n* **1** : a nude human figure esp. as depicted in art **2** : the condition of being nude ⟨in the ∼⟩

nudge \'nəj\ *vb* **nudged; nudg·ing** : to touch or push gently (as with the elbow) usu. in order to seek attention — **nudge** *n*

nud·ism \'nü-ˌdi-zəm, 'nyü-\ *n* : the practice of going

nude esp. in mixed groups at specially secluded places — **nud·ist** \-dist\ *n*

nu·ga·to·ry \-gə-ˌtōr-ē\ *adj* **1** : INCONSEQUENTIAL, WORTHLESS **2** : having no force : INEFFECTUAL

nug·get \'nə-gət\ *n* : a lump of precious metal (as gold)

nui·sance \'nüs-ᵊns, 'nyüs-\ *n* : an annoying or troublesome person or thing

nuisance tax *n* : an excise tax collected in small amounts directly from the consumer

¹**nuke** \'nük, 'nyük\ *n* **1** : a nuclear weapon **2** : a nuclear power plant

²**nuke** *vb* **nuked; nuk·ing 1** : to attack with nuclear weapons **2** : MICROWAVE

null \'nəl\ *adj* **1** : having no legal or binding force : INVALID, VOID **2** : amounting to nothing **2** : INSIGNIFICANT — **nul·li·ty** \'nə-lə-tē\ *n*

null and void *adj* : having no force, binding power, or validity

nul·li·fy \'nə-lə-ˌfī\ *vb* **-fied; -fy·ing** : to make null or valueless; *also* : ANNUL — **nul·li·fi·ca·tion** \ˌnə-lə-fə-'kā-shən\ *n*

num *abbr* numeral

Num *or* **Numb** *abbr* Numbers

numb \'nəm\ *adj* : lacking sensation or emotion : BENUMBED — **numb** *vb* — **numb·ly** *adv* — **numb·ness** *n*

¹**num·ber** \'nəm-bər\ *n* **1** : the total of individuals or units taken together **2** : an indefinite total ⟨a small ∼ of tickets remain unsold⟩ **3** : an ascertainable total ⟨the sands of the desert are without ∼⟩ **4** : a distinction of word form to denote reference to one or more than one **5** : a unit belonging to a mathematical system and subject to its laws; *also, pl* : ARITHMETIC **6** : a symbol used to represent a mathematical number; *also* : such a number used to identify or designate ⟨a phone ∼⟩ **7** : one in a series ⟨the best ∼ on the program⟩
☞ For table, see next page.

²**number** *vb* **1** : COUNT, ENUMERATE **2** : to include with or be one of a group **3** : to restrict to a small or definite number **4** : to assign a number to **5** : to comprise in number : TOTAL

num·ber·less \-ləs\ *adj* : INNUMERABLE, COUNTLESS

Numbers *n* — see BIBLE table

nu·mer·al \'nü-mə-rəl, 'nyü-\ *n* : conventional symbol representing a number — **numeral** *adj*

nu·mer·ate \'nü-mə-ˌrāt, 'nyü-\ *vb* **-at·ed; -at·ing** : ENUMERATE

nu·mer·a·tor \-ˌrā-tər\ *n* : the part of a fraction above the line

nu·mer·ic \nù-'mer-ik, nyù-\ *adj* : NUMERICAL; *esp* : denoting a number or a system of numbers

nu·mer·i·cal \-'mer-i-kəl\ *adj* **1** : of or relating to numbers **2** : expressed in or involving numbers — **nu·mer·i·cal·ly** \-k(ə-)lē\ *adv*

nu·mer·ol·o·gy \ˌnü-mə-'rä-lə-jē, ˌnyü-\ *n* : the study of the occult significance of numbers — **nu·mer·ol·o·gist** \-jist\ *n*

nu·mer·ous \'nü-mə-rəs, 'nyü-\ *adj* : consisting of, including, or relating to a great number : MANY

nu·mis·mat·ics \ˌnü-məz-'ma-tiks, ˌnyü-\ *n* : the study or collection of monetary objects — **nu·mis·mat·ic** \-tik\ *adj* — **nu·mis·ma·tist** \nü-'miz-mə-tist, nyü-\ *n*

num·skull \'nəm-ˌskəl\ *n* : a stupid person : DUNCE

nun \'nən\ *n* : a woman belonging to a religious order; *esp* : one under solemn vows of poverty, chastity, and obedience

nun·cio \'nən-sē-ˌō, 'nùn-\ *n, pl* **-ci·os** [It, fr. L *nuntius* messenger] : a permanent high-ranking papal representative to a civil government

TABLE OF NUMBERS

CARDINAL NUMBERS[1]			ORDINAL NUMBERS[4]	
NAME[2]	SYMBOL		NAME[5]	SYMBOL
	Hindu-Arabic	*Roman[3]*		
zero *or* naught *or* cipher	0		first	1st
one	1	I	second	2d *or* 2nd
two	2	II	third	3d *or* 3rd
three	3	III	fourth	4th
four	4	IV	fifth	5th
five	5	V	sixth	6th
six	6	VI	seventh	7th
seven	7	VII	eighth	8th
eight	8	VIII	ninth	9th
nine	9	IX	tenth	10th
ten	10	X	eleventh	11th
eleven	11	XI	twelfth	12th
twelve	12	XII	thirteenth	13th
thirteen	13	XIII	fourteenth	14th
fourteen	14	XIV	fifteenth	15th
fifteen	15	XV	sixteenth	16th
sixteen	16	XVI	seventeenth	17th
seventeen	17	XVII	eighteenth	18th
eighteen	18	XVIII	nineteenth	19th
nineteen	19	XIX	twentieth	20th
twenty	20	XX	twenty-first	21st
twenty-one	21	XXI	twenty-second	22d *or* 22nd
twenty-two	22	XXII	twenty-third	23d *or* 23rd
twenty-three	23	XXIII	twenty-fourth	24th
twenty-four	24	XXIV	twenty-fifth	25th
twenty-five	25	XXV	twenty-sixth	26th
twenty-six	26	XXVI	twenty-seventh	27th
twenty-seven	27	XXVII	twenty-eighth	28th
twenty-eight	28	XXVIII	twenty-ninth	29th
twenty-nine	29	XXIX	thirtieth	30th
thirty	30	XXX	thirty-first *etc*	31st
thirty-one *etc*	31	XXXI	fortieth	40th
forty	40	XL	fiftieth	50th
fifty	50	L	sixtieth	60th
sixty	60	LX	seventieth	70th
seventy	70	LXX	eightieth	80th
eighty	80	LXXX	ninetieth	90th
ninety	90	XC	hundredth *or*	100th
one hundred	100	C	one hundredth	
one hundred one *or*	101	CI	hundred and first *or*	101st
one hundred and one *etc*			one hundred and first *etc*	
two hundred	200	CC	two hundredth	200th
three hundred	300	CCC	three hundredth	300th
four hundred	400	CD	four hundredth	400th
five hundred	500	D	five hundredth	500th
six hundred	600	DC	six hundredth	600th
seven hundred	700	DCC	seven hundredth	700th
eight hundred	800	DCCC	eight hundredth	800th
nine hundred	900	CM	nine hundredth	900th
one thousand *or* ten	1,000	M	thousandth *or* one thousandth	1,000th
hundred *etc*			two thousandth *etc*	2,000th
two thousand *etc*	2,000	MM	five thousandth	5,000th
five thousand	5,000	$\overline{\text{V}}$	ten thousandth	10,000th
ten thousand	10,000	$\overline{\text{X}}$	hundred thousandth *or*	100,000th
one hundred thousand	100,000	$\overline{\text{C}}$	one hundred thousandth	
one million	1,000,000	$\overline{\text{M}}$	millionth *or* one millionth	1,000,000th

[1]The cardinal numbers are used in simple counting or in answer to "how many?" The words for these numbers may be used as nouns (I counted to *ten*), as pronouns (*ten* were found), or as adjectives (*ten* cows).

[2]In formal writing the numbers one to one hundred and in less formal writing the numbers one to nine are commonly written out, while larger numbers are given in numerals. A number occurring at the beginning of a sentence is usually written out. Except in very formal writing numerals are used for dates. Hindu-Arabic numerals from 1,000 to 9,999 are often written without commas (1000; 9999). Year numbers are always written without commas (1783).

[3]The Roman numerals are written either in capitals or in lowercase letters.

[4]The ordinal numbers are used to show the order in which such items as names, objects, and periods of time are considered (the *twelfth* month; the *fourth* row of seats; the *18th* century).

[5]Each of the names of the ordinal numbers except *first* and *second* is used for one of the equal parts into which a whole may be divided (a *fourth*; a *sixth*; a *tenth*) and also as the denominator in fractions (*one fourth*; *three fifths*). Fractions used as nouns are usually written as two words, but fractions used as adjectives are usually hyphenated (a *two-thirds* majority). When a two-word ordinal number is used as a noun to name a denominator, a hyphen is usually used to make sure that there is only one meaning (*six hundred ten-thousandths* means only 600/10,000 and not 610/1000). When fractions are written in numerals, the cardinal symbols are used (¼, ⅗, ⅘).

nun·nery \'nə-nə-rē\ *n, pl* **-ner·ies** : a convent of nuns
¹**nup·tial** \'nəp-shəl\ *adj* : of or relating to marriage or a wedding
²**nuptial** *n* : MARRIAGE, WEDDING — usu. used in pl.
¹**nurse** \'nərs\ *n* [ME, fr. OF *nurice*, fr. LL *nutricia*, fr. L, fem. of *nutricius* nourishing] **1** : a girl or woman employed to take care of children **2** : a person trained to care for sick people
²**nurse** *vb* **nursed; nurs·ing 1** : SUCKLE **2** : to take charge of and watch over **3** : TEND ⟨~ an invalid⟩ **4** : to treat with special care ⟨~ a headache⟩ **5** : to hold in one's mind or consideration ⟨~ a grudge⟩ **6** : to act or serve as a nurse
nurse·maid \'nərs-ˌmād\ *n* : NURSE 1
nurse–prac·ti·tion·er \-prak-'ti-shə-nər\ *n* : a registered nurse who is qualified to assume some of the duties formerly assumed only by a physician
nurs·ery \'nər-sə-rē\ *n, pl* **-er·ies 1** : a room for children **2** : a place where children are temporarily cared for in their parents' absence **3** : a place where young plants are grown usu. for transplanting
nurs·ery·man \-mən\ *n* : a man who keeps or works in a plant nursery
nursery school *n* : a school for children under kindergarten age
nursing home *n* : a private establishment providing care for persons (as the aged or the chronically ill) who are unable to care for themselves
nurs·ling \'nərs-liŋ\ *n* **1** : one that is solicitously cared for **2** : a nursing child
¹**nur·ture** \'nər-chər\ *n* **1** : TRAINING, UPBRINGING; *also* : the influences that modify the expression of an individual's heredity **2** : FOOD, NOURISHMENT
²**nurture** *vb* **nur·tured; nur·tur·ing 1** : to care for : FEED, NOURISH **2** : EDUCATE, TRAIN **3** : FOSTER
nut \'nət\ *n* **1** : a dry fruit or seed with a hard shell and a firm inner kernel; *also* : its kernel **2** : a metal block with a hole through it that is fastened to a bolt or screw by means of a screw thread within the hole **3** : the ridge on the upper end of the fingerboard in a stringed musical instrument over which the strings pass **4** : a foolish, eccentric, or crazy person **5** : ENTHUSIAST
nut·crack·er \'nət-ˌkra-kər\ *n* : an instrument for cracking nuts

nut·hatch \-ˌhach\ *n* : any of various small tree-climbing chiefly insect-eating birds
nut·meg \-ˌmeg, -ˌmāg\ *n* [ME *notemuge*, ultim. fr. Old Provençal *noz muscada*, lit., musky nut] : a spice made by grinding the nutlike aromatic seed of a tropical tree; *also* : the seed or tree
nu·tria \'nü-trē-ə, 'nyü-\ *n* [Sp] **1** : the durable usu. light brown fur of a nutria **2** : a So. American aquatic rodent with webbed hind feet
¹**nu·tri·ent** \'nü-trē-ənt, 'nyü-\ *adj* : NOURISHING
²**nutrient** *n* : a nutritive substance or ingredient
nu·tri·ment \-trə-mənt\ *n* : NUTRIENT
nu·tri·tion \nu̇-'tri-shən, nyu̇-\ *n* : the act or process of nourishing; *esp* : the processes by which an individual takes in and utilizes food material — **nu·tri·tion·al** \-shə-nəl\ *adj* — **nu·tri·tious** \-shəs\ *adj* — **nu·tri·tive** \'nü-trə-tiv, 'nyü-\ *adj*
nuts \'nəts\ *adj* **1** : ENTHUSIASTIC, KEEN **2** : CRAZY, DEMENTED
nut·shell \'nət-ˌshel\ *n* : the shell of a nut — **in a nutshell** : in a few words ⟨that's the story *in a nutshell*⟩
nut·ty \'nə-tē\ *adj* **nut·ti·er; -est 1** : containing or suggesting nuts ⟨a ~ flavor⟩ **2** : mentally unbalanced
nuz·zle \'nə-zəl\ *vb* **nuz·zled; nuz·zling 1** : to root around, push, or touch with or as if with the nose **2** : NESTLE, SNUGGLE
NV *abbr* Nevada
NW *abbr* northwest
NWT *abbr* Northwest Territories
NY *abbr* New York
NYC *abbr* New York City
ny·lon \'nī-ˌlän\ *n* **1** : any of numerous strong tough elastic synthetic materials used esp. in textiles and plastics **2** *pl* : stockings made of nylon
nymph \'nimf\ *n* **1** : any of the lesser goddesses in ancient mythology represented as maidens living in the mountains, forests, meadows, and waters **2** : GIRL **3** : an immature insect resembling the adult but smaller, less differentiated, and usu. lacking wings
nym·pho·ma·nia \ˌnim-fə-'mā-nē-ə, -nyə\ *n* : excessive sexual desire by a female — **nym·pho·ma·ni·ac** \-nē-ˌak\ *n or adj*
NZ *abbr* New Zealand

O

¹**o** \'ō\ *n, pl* **o's** *or* **os** \'ōz\ *often cap* **1** : the 15th letter of the English alphabet **2** : ZERO
²**o** *abbr, often cap* **1** ocean **2** Ohio **3** ohm
¹**O** \'ō\ *var of* OH
²**O** *symbol* oxygen
o/a *abbr* on or about
oaf \'ōf\ *n* : a stupid or awkward person — **oaf·ish** *adj*
oak \'ōk\ *n, pl* **oaks** *or* **oak** : any of a genus of trees or shrubs related to the beech and chestnut and bearing a rounded thin-shelled nut surrounded at the base by a hardened cup; *also* : the usu. tough hard durable wood of an oak — **oak·en** \'ō-kən\ *adj*
oa·kum \'ō-kəm\ *n* : loosely twisted hemp or jute fiber impregnated with tar and used esp. in caulking ships
oar \'ōr\ *n* : a long pole with a broad blade at one end used for propelling or steering a boat
oar·lock \'ōr-ˌläk\ *n* : a U-shaped device for holding an oar in place
oars·man \'ōrz-mən\ *n* : one who rows esp. in a racing crew
OAS *abbr* Organization of American States

oa·sis \ō-'ā-səs\ *n, pl* **oa·ses** \-ˌsēz\ : a fertile or green area in an arid region
oat \'ōt\ *n* : a cereal grass widely grown for its edible seed; *also* : this seed — **oat·en** \-ᵊn\ *adj*
oat·cake \'ōt-ˌkāk\ *n* : a thin flat oatmeal cake
oath \'ōth\ *n, pl* **oaths** \'ōthz, 'ōths\ **1** : a solemn appeal to God to witness to the truth of a statement or the sacredness of a promise **2** : an irreverent or careless use of a sacred name
oat·meal \'ōt-ˌmēl\ *n* **1** : ground or rolled oats **2** : porridge made from ground or rolled oats
Ob *or* **Obad** *abbr* Obadiah
Oba·di·ah \ˌō-bə-'dī-ə\ *n* — see BIBLE table
ob·bli·ga·to \ˌä-blə-'gä-tō\ *n, pl* **-tos** *also* **-ti** \-'gä-tē\ [It] : an accompanying part usu. played by a solo instrument

---

\ə\abut \ᵊ\kitten \ər\further \a\ash \ā\ace \ä\mop, mar
\au̇\out \ch\chin \e\bet \ē\easy \g\go \i\hit \ī\ice \j\job
\ŋ\sing \ō\go \ȯ\law \ȯi\boy \th\thin \t͟h\the \ü\loot \u̇\foot
\y\yet \zh\vision *see also* Pronunciation Symbols page

ob·du·rate \'äb-də-rət, -dyə-\ *adj* : stubbornly resistant : UNYIELDING **syn** inflexible, adamant, rigid, uncompromising — **ob·du·ra·cy** \-rə-sē\ *n*

obe·di·ent \ō-'bē-dē-ənt\ *adj* : submissive to the restraint or command of authority **syn** docile, tractable, amenable, biddable — **obe·di·ence** \-əns\ *n* — **obe·di·ent·ly** *adv*

obei·sance \ō-'bē-səns, -'bā-\ *n* : a bow made to show respect or submission; *also* : DEFERENCE, HOMAGE

obe·lisk \'ä-bə-ˌlisk\ *n* [MF *obelisque*, fr. L *obeliscus*, fr. Gk *obeliskos*, fr. dim. of *obelos* spit, pointed pillar] : a 4-sided pillar that tapers toward the top and ends in a pyramid

obese \ō-'bēs\ *adj* [L *obesus*, fr. *ob-* against + *esus*, pp. of *edere* to eat] : excessively fat **syn** corpulent, fleshy, gross, overweight, portly, stout — **obe·si·ty** \-'bē-sə-tē\ *n*

obey \ō-'bā\ *vb* **obeyed; obey·ing** 1 : to follow the commands or guidance of : behave obediently 2 : to comply with (∼ orders) **syn** conform, keep, mind, observe

ob·fus·cate \'äb-fə-ˌskāt\ *vb* **-cat·ed; -cat·ing** 1 : to make dark or obscure 2 : CONFUSE — **ob·fus·ca·tion** \ˌäb-fəs-'kā-shən\ *n*

OB–GYN *abbr* obstetrician gynecologist; obstetrics gynecology

obi \'ō-bē\ *n* [Jp] : a broad sash worn esp. with a Japanese kimono

obit \ō-'bit, 'ō-bət\ *n* : OBITUARY

obi·ter dic·tum \ˌō-bə-tər-'dik-təm\ *n, pl* **obiter dic·ta** \-tə\ [LL, lit., something said in passing] : an incidental remark or observation

obit·u·ary \ə-'bi-chə-ˌwer-ē\ *n, pl* **-ar·ies** : a notice of a person's death usu. with a short biographical account

obj *abbr* object; objective

¹**ob·ject** \'äb-jikt\ *n* 1 : something that may be seen or felt; *also* : something that may be perceived or examined mentally 2 : something that arouses an emotional response (as of affection or pity) 3 : AIM, PURPOSE 4 : a word or word group denoting that on or toward which the action of a verb is directed; *also* : a noun or noun equivalent in a prepositional phrase

²**ob·ject** \əb-'jekt\ *vb* 1 : to offer in opposition 2 : to oppose something; *also* : DISAPPROVE **syn** protest, remonstrate, expostulate — **ob·jec·tor** \-'jek-tər\ *n*

ob·jec·ti·fy \əb-'jek-tə-ˌfī\ *vb* **-fied; -fy·ing** : to make objective

ob·jec·tion \əb-'jek-shən\ *n* 1 : the act of objecting 2 : a reason for or a feeling of disapproval

ob·jec·tion·able \əb-'jek-shə-nə-bəl\ *adj* : UNDESIRABLE, OFFENSIVE — **ob·jec·tion·ably** \-blē\ *adv*

¹**ob·jec·tive** \əb-'jek-tiv\ *adj* 1 : of or relating to an object or end 2 : existing outside and independent of the mind 3 : of, relating to, or constituting a grammatical case marking typically the object of a verb or preposition 4 : treating or dealing with facts without distortion by personal feelings or prejudices — **ob·jec·tive·ly** *adv* — **ob·jec·tive·ness** *n* — **ob·jec·tiv·i·ty** \ˌäb-ˌjek-'ti-və-tē\ *n*

²**objective** *n* 1 : the lens (as in a microscope) nearest the object and forming an image of it 2 : an aim, goal, or end of action

ob·jet d'art \ˌòb-ˌzhā-'där\ *n, pl* **ob·jets d'art** *same*\ [F] : an article of artistic worth; *also* : CURIO **syn** knick-knack, bauble, bibelot, gewgaw, novelty, trinket

ob·jet trou·vé \ˌòb-ˌzhā-trü-'vā\ *n, pl* **objets trouvés** *same*\ [F, lit., found object] : a found natural object (as a piece of driftwood) held to have aesthetic value; *also* : an artifact not orig. intended as art but displayed as a work of art

ob·jur·ga·tion \ˌäb-jər-'gā-shən\ *n* : a harsh rebuke — **ob·jur·gate** \'äb-jər-ˌgāt\ *vb*

obl *abbr* 1 oblique 2 oblong

ob·late \ä-'blāt\ *adj* : flattened or depressed at the poles ⟨an ∼ spheroid⟩

ob·la·tion \ə-'blā-shən\ *n* : a religious offering

ob·li·gate \'ä-blə-ˌgāt\ *vb* **-gat·ed; -gat·ing** : to bind legally or morally

ob·li·ga·tion \ˌä-blə-'gā-shən\ *n* 1 : an act of obligating oneself to a course of action 2 : something (as a promise or a contract) that binds one to a course of action 3 : INDEBTEDNESS; *also* : LIABILITY 4 : DUTY — **oblig·a·to·ry** \ə-'bli-gə-ˌtōr-ē\ *adj*

oblige \ə-'blīj\ *vb* **obliged; oblig·ing** [ME, fr. OF *obliger*, fr. L *obligare*, lit., to bind to, fr. *ob-* toward + *ligare* to bind] 1 : FORCE, COMPEL 2 : to bind by a favor; *also* : to do a favor for or do something as a favor

oblig·ing *adj* : willing to do favors — **oblig·ing·ly** *adv*

oblique \ō-'blēk\ *adj* 1 : neither perpendicular nor parallel : SLANTING 2 : not straightforward : INDIRECT — **oblique·ly** *adv* — **oblique·ness** *n* — **obliq·ui·ty** \-'bli-kwə-tē\ *n*

oblit·er·ate \ə-'bli-tə-ˌrāt\ *vb* **-at·ed; -at·ing** [L *oblitterare*, fr. *ob* in the way of + *littera* letter] 1 : to make undecipherable by wiping out or covering over 2 : to remove from recognition or memory 3 : CANCEL — **oblit·er·a·tion** \-ˌbli-tə-'rā-shən\ *n*

obliv·i·on \ə-'bli-vē-ən\ *n* 1 : the condition of being oblivious 2 : the condition or state of being forgotten

obliv·i·ous \ə-'bli-ve-əs\ *adj* 1 : lacking memory or mindful attention 2 : UNAWARE — **obliv·i·ous·ly** *adv* — **obliv·i·ous·ness** *n*

ob·long \'ä-ˌblȯŋ\ *adj* : deviating from a square, circular, or spherical form by elongation in one dimension — **oblong** *n*

ob·lo·quy \'ä-blə-kwē\ *n, pl* **-quies** 1 : strongly condemnatory utterance or language 2 : bad repute : DISGRACE **syn** dishonor, shame, infamy, disrepute, ignominy

ob·nox·ious \äb-'näk-shəs\ *adj* : REPUGNANT, OFFENSIVE — **ob·nox·ious·ly** *adv* — **ob·nox·ious·ness** *n*

oboe \'ō-bō\ *n* [It, fr. F *hautbois*, fr. *haut* high + *bois* wood] : a woodwind instrument with a slender conical tube and a double reed mouthpiece — **obo·ist** \'ō-ˌbō-ist\ *n*

oboe

ob·scene \äb-'sēn\ *adj* 1 : REPULSIVE 2 : deeply offensive to morality or decency; *esp* : designed to incite to lust or depravity **syn** gross, vulgar, coarse, crude, indecent — **ob·scene·ly** *adv* — **ob·scen·i·ty** \-'se-nə-tē\ *n*

ob·scu·ran·tism \äb-'skyùr-ən-ˌti-zəm, ˌäb-skyù-'ran-\ *n* 1 : opposition to the spread of knowledge 2 : deliberate vagueness or abstruseness — **ob·scu·ran·tist** \-tist\ *n or adj*

¹**ob·scure** \äb-'skyùr\ *adj* 1 : DIM, GLOOMY 2 : not readily understood : VAGUE 3 : REMOTE; *also* : HUMBLE **syn** dark, dusky, murky, tenebrous — **ob·scure·ly** *adv* — **ob·scu·ri·ty** \-'skyùr-ə-tē\ *n*

²**obscure** *vb* **ob·scured; ob·scur·ing** 1 : to make dark, dim, or indistinct 2 : to conceal or hide by or as if by covering

ob·se·qui·ous \əb-'sē-kwē-əs\ *adj* : humbly or excessively attentive (as to a person in authority) : FAWNING, SYCOPHANTIC **syn** menial, servile, slavish, subservient — **ob·se·qui·ous·ly** *adv* — **ob·se·qui·ous·ness** *n*

ob·se·quy \ˈäb-sə-kwē\ *n, pl* **-quies** : a funeral or burial rite — usu. used in pl.

ob·serv·able \əb-ˈzər-və-bəl\ *adj* **1** : NOTEWORTHY **2** : capable of being observed — **ob·serv·abil·ity** \-ˈbi-lə-tē\ *n*

ob·ser·vance \əb-ˈzər-vəns\ *n* **1** : a customary practice or ceremony **2** : an act or instance of following a custom, rule, or law **3** : OBSERVATION

ob·ser·vant \-vənt\ *adj* **1** : WATCHFUL ⟨∼ spectators⟩ **2** : KEEN, PERCEPTIVE **3** : MINDFUL ⟨∼ of the amenities⟩

ob·ser·va·tion \ˌäb-sər-ˈvā-shən, -zər-\ *n* **1** : an act or instance of observing **2** : the gathering of information (as for scientific studies) by noting facts or occurrences **3** : a conclusion drawn from observing; *also* : REMARK, STATEMENT **4** : the fact of being observed

ob·ser·va·to·ry \əb-ˈzər-və-ˌtōr-ē\ *n, pl* **-ries** : a place or institution equipped for observation of natural phenomena (as in astronomy)

ob·serve \əb-ˈzərv\ *vb* **ob·served; ob·serv·ing** **1** : to conform one's action or practice to **2** : CELEBRATE **3** : to make a scientific observation of **4** : to see or sense esp. through careful attention **5** : to come to realize esp. through consideration of noted facts **6** : REMARK — **ob·serv·er** *n*

ob·sess \əb-ˈses\ *vb* : to preoccupy intensely or abnormally

ob·ses·sion \äb-ˈse-shən\ *n* : a persistent disturbing preoccupation with an idea or feeling; *also* : an emotion or idea causing such a preoccupation — **ob·ses·sive** \-ˈse-siv\ *adj or n* — **ob·ses·sive·ly** *adv*

ob·sid·i·an \əb-ˈsi-dē-ən\ *n* : a dark natural glass formed by the cooling of molten lava

ob·so·les·cent \ˌäb-sə-ˈles-ᵊnt\ *adj* : going out of use : becoming obsolete — **ob·so·les·cence** \-ᵊns\ *n*

ob·so·lete \ˌäb-sə-ˈlēt, ˈäb-sə-ˌlēt\ *adj* : no longer in use; *also* : OLD-FASHIONED **syn** extinct, outworn, passé, superseded

ob·sta·cle \ˈäb-sti-kəl\ *n* : something that stands in the way or opposes

ob·stet·rics \əb-ˈste-triks\ *n sing or pl* : a branch of medicine that deals with birth and with its antecedents and sequels — **ob·stet·ric** \-trik\ *or* **ob·stet·ri·cal** \-tri-kəl\ *adj* — **ob·ste·tri·cian** \ˌäb-stə-ˈtri-shən\ *n*

ob·sti·nate \ˈäb-stə-nət\ *adj* : fixed and unyielding (as in an opinion or course) despite reason or persuasion : STUBBORN — **ob·sti·na·cy** \-nə-sē\ *n* — **ob·sti·nate·ly** *adv*

ob·strep·er·ous \əb-ˈstre-pə-rəs\ *adj* **1** : uncontrollably noisy **2** : stubbornly resistant to control : UNRULY — **ob·strep·er·ous·ness** *n*

ob·struct \əb-ˈstrəkt\ *vb* **1** : to block by an obstacle **2** : to impede the passage, action, or operation of **3** : to cut off from sight — **ob·struc·tive** \-ˈstrək-tiv\ *adj* — **ob·struc·tor** \-tər\ *n*

ob·struc·tion \əb-ˈstrək-shən\ *n* **1** : an act of obstructing : the state of being obstructed **2** : something that obstructs : HINDRANCE

ob·struc·tion·ist \-shə-nist\ *n* : a person who hinders progress or business esp. in a legislative body — **ob·struc·tion·ism** \-shə-ˌni-zəm\ *n*

ob·tain \əb-ˈtān\ *vb* **1** : to gain or attain usu. by planning or effort **2** : to be generally recognized or established **syn** procure, secure, win, earn, acquire — **ob·tain·able** *adj*

ob·trude \əb-ˈtrüd\ *vb* **ob·trud·ed; ob·trud·ing** **1** : to thrust out **2** : to thrust forward without warrant or request **3** : INTRUDE — **ob·tru·sion** \-ˈtrü-zhən\ *n* — **ob·tru·sive** \-ˈtrü-siv\ *adj* — **ob·tru·sive·ly** *adv* — **ob·tru·sive·ness** *n*

ob·tuse \äb-ˈtüs, -ˈtyüs\ *adj* **ob·tus·er; -est** **1** : exceeding 90 degrees but less than 180 degrees ⟨∼ angle⟩ **2** : not pointed or acute : BLUNT **3** : not sharp or quick of wit — **ob·tuse·ly** *adv* — **ob·tuse·ness** *n*

obv *abbr* obverse

¹ob·verse \äb-ˈvərs, ˈäb-ˌvərs\ *adj* **1** : facing the observer or opponent **2** : being a counterpart or complement — **ob·verse·ly** *adv*

²ob·verse \ˈäb-ˌvərs, äb-ˈvərs\ *n* **1** : the side (as of a coin) bearing the principal design and lettering **2** : a front or principal surface **3** : a counterpart having the opposite orientation or force

ob·vi·ate \ˈäb-vē-ˌāt\ *vb* **-at·ed; -at·ing** : to anticipate and prevent (as a situation) or make unnecessary (as an action) **syn** prevent, avert, forestall, forfend, preclude — **ob·vi·a·tion** \ˌäb-vē-ˈā-shən\ *n*

ob·vi·ous \ˈäb-vē-əs\ *adj* [L *obvius,* fr. *obviam* in the way, fr. *ob* in the way of + *viam,* acc. of *via* way] : easily found, seen, or understood : PLAIN **syn** evident, manifest, patent, clear — **ob·vi·ous·ly** *adv* — **ob·vi·ous·ness** *n*

OC *abbr* officer candidate

oc·a·ri·na \ˌä-kə-ˈrē-nə\ *n* [It] : a wind instrument typically having an oval body with finger holes and a projecting mouthpiece

occas *abbr* occasionally

¹oc·ca·sion \ə-ˈkā-zhən\ *n* **1** : a favorable opportunity **2** : a direct or indirect cause **3** : the time of an event **4** : EXIGENCY **5** *pl* : AFFAIRS, BUSINESS **6** : a special event : CELEBRATION

²occasion *vb* : BRING ABOUT, CAUSE

oc·ca·sion·al \ə-ˈkā-zhə-nəl\ *adj* **1** : happening or met with now and then ⟨∼ visits⟩ **2** : used or designed for a special occasion ⟨∼ verse⟩ **syn** infrequent, rare, sporadic — **oc·ca·sion·al·ly** *adv*

oc·ci·den·tal \ˌäk-sə-ˈdent-ᵊl\ *adj, often cap* [fr. *Occident* West, fr. ME, fr. L *occident-, occidens,* fr. prp. of *occidere* to fall, set (of the sun)] : WESTERN — **Occidental** *n*

oc·clude \ə-ˈklüd\ *vb* **oc·clud·ed; oc·clud·ing** **1** : OBSTRUCT ⟨an *occluded* artery⟩ **2** : to come together with opposing surfaces in contact — used of teeth — **oc·clu·sion** \-ˈklü-zhən\ *n* — **oc·clu·sive** \-ˈklü-siv\ *adj*

¹oc·cult \ə-ˈkəlt\ *adj* **1** : not revealed : SECRET **2** : ABSTRUSE, MYSTERIOUS **3** : of or relating to supernatural agencies, their effects, or knowledge of them — **oc·cult·ism** \-ˈkəl-ˌti-zəm\ *n* — **oc·cult·ist** \-tist\ *n*

²occult *n* : occult matters — used with *the*

oc·cu·pan·cy \ˈä-kyə-pən-sē\ *n, pl* **-cies** **1** : the act of occupying : the state of being occupied **2** : an occupied building or part of a building

oc·cu·pant \-pənt\ *n* : one who occupies something; *esp* : RESIDENT

oc·cu·pa·tion \ˌä-kyə-ˈpā-shən\ *n* **1** : an activity in which one engages; *esp* : VOCATION **2** : the taking possession of property; *also* : the taking possession of an area by a foreign military force — **oc·cu·pa·tion·al** \-shə-nəl\ *adj* — **oc·cu·pa·tion·al·ly** *adv*

occupational therapy *n* : therapy by means of activity; *esp* : creative activity prescribed for its effect in promoting recovery or rehabilitation — **occupational therapist** *n*

oc·cu·py \ˈä-kyə-ˌpī\ *vb* **-pied; -py·ing** **1** : to engage the attention or energies of **2** : to fill up (an extent in space or time) **3** : to take or hold possession of **4** : to reside in as owner or tenant — **oc·cu·pi·er** *n*

oc·cur \ə-ˈkər\ *vb* **oc·curred; oc·cur·ring** [L *occurrere,* fr. *ob-* in the way + *currere* to run] **1** : to be found or met with : APPEAR **2** : HAPPEN **3** : to come to mind

oc·cur·rence \ə-ˈkər-əns\ *n* **1** : something that takes place **2** : the action or process of occurring

ocean \ˈō-shən\ *n* **1** : the whole body of salt water that

---

\ə\abut \ᵊ\kitten \ər\further \a\ash \ā\ace \ä\mop, mar \au̇\out \ch\chin \e\bet \ē\easy \g\go \i\hit \ī\ice \j\job \ŋ\sing \ō\go \ȯ\law \ȯi\boy \th\thin \th\the \ü\loot \u̇\foot \y\yet \zh\vision *see also* Pronunciation Symbols page covers nearly three fourths of the surface of the earth **2** : any of the large bodies of water into which the great ocean is divided — **oce·an·ic** \ˌō-shē-ˈa-nik\ adj

ocean·ar·i·um \ˌō-shə-ˈnar-ē-əm\ n, pl **-iums** or **-ia** \-ē-ə\ : a large marine aquarium

ocean·front \ˈō-shən-ˌfrənt\ n : a shore area on the ocean

ocean·go·ing \-ˌgō-iŋ\ adj : of, relating to, or suitable for travel on the ocean

ocean·og·ra·phy \ˌō-shə-ˈnä-grə-fē\ n : a science dealing with the ocean and its phenomena — **ocean·og·ra·pher** \-fər\ n — **ocean·o·graph·ic** \-nə-ˈgra-fik\ adj

oce·lot \ˈä-sə-ˌlät, ˈō-\ n : a medium-sized American wildcat ranging southward from Texas to northern Argentina and having a tawny yellow or gray coat with black markings

ocher or **ochre** \ˈō-kər\ n : an earthy usu. red or yellow iron ore used as a pigment; also : the color esp. of yellow ocher

o'·clock \ə-ˈkläk\ adv : according to the clock

OCR abbr optical character reader; optical character recognition

OCS abbr officer candidate school

oct abbr octavo

Oct abbr October

oc·ta·gon \ˈäk-tə-ˌgän\ n : a polygon of eight angles and eight sides — **oc·tag·o·nal** \äk-ˈta-gən-ᵊl\ adj

oc·tane \ˈäk-ˌtān\ n : OCTANE NUMBER

octane number n : a number used to measure the antiknock properties of gasoline that increases as the likelihood of knocking decreases

oc·tant \ˈäk-tənt\ n : an instrument for observing altitudes of a celestial body from a moving ship or aircraft

oc·tave \ˈäk-tiv\ n **1** : a musical interval embracing eight degrees; also : a tone or note at this interval or the whole series of notes, tones, or keys within this interval **2** : a group of eight

oc·ta·vo \äk-ˈtä-vō, -ˈtä-\ n, pl **-vos 1** : the size of a piece of paper cut eight from a sheet **2** : a book printed on octavo pages

oc·tet \äk-ˈtet\ n **1** : a musical composition for eight voices or eight instruments; also : the performers of such a composition **2** : a group or set of eight

Oc·to·ber \äk-ˈtō-bər\ n [ME Octobre, fr. OF, fr. L October (eighth month), fr. octo eight] : the 10th month of the year having 31 days

oc·to·ge·nar·i·an \ˌäk-tə-jə-ˈner-ē-ən\ n : a person whose age is in the eighties

oc·to·pus \ˈäk-tə-pəs\ n, pl **-pus·es** or **-pi** \-ˌpī\ : any of various sea mollusks with eight long arms furnished with suckers

octopus

oc·to·syl·lab·ic \ˌäk-tə-sə-ˈla-bik\ adj : composed of verses having eight syllables — **octosyllabic** n

¹**oc·u·lar** \ˈä-kyə-lər\ adj **1** : VISUAL **2** : of or relating to the eye or the eyesight

²**ocular** n : EYEPIECE

oc·u·list \ˈä-kyə-list\ n **1** : OPHTHALMOLOGIST **2** : OPTOMETRIST

¹**OD** \ˌō-ˈdē\ n : an overdose of a drug and esp. a narcotic

²**OD** vb **OD'd** or **ODed; OD'ing** : to become ill or die from an OD

³**OD** abbr **1** doctor of optometry **2** [L oculus dexter] right eye **3** officer of the day **4** olive drab **5** overdraft **6** overdrawn

odd \ˈäd\ adj [ME odde, fr. ON oddi point of land, triangle, odd number] **1** : being only one of a pair or set ⟨an ∼ shoe⟩ **2** : somewhat more than the number mentioned ⟨forty ∼ years ago⟩ **3** : being an integer (as 1, 3, or 5) not divisible by two without leaving a remainder **4** : additional to what is usual ⟨∼ jobs⟩ **5** : STRANGE ⟨an ∼ way of behaving⟩ — **odd·ness** n

odd·ball \ˈäd-ˌbȯl\ n : one that is eccentric — **oddball** adj

odd·i·ty \ˈä-də-tē\ n, pl **-ties 1** : one that is odd **2** : the quality or state of being odd

odd·ly \ˈäd-lē\ adv **1** : in an odd manner **2** : it is odd that

odd·ment \ˈäd-mənt\ n : something left over : REMNANT

odds \ˈädz\ n pl **1** : a difference by which one thing is favored over another **2** : DISAGREEMENT — usu. used with at **3** : the ratio between the amount to be paid for a winning bet and the amount of the bet ⟨the horse went off at ∼ of 6–1⟩

odds and ends n pl : miscellaneous things or matters

odds–on \ˈädz-ˈȯn, -ˈän\ adj : having a better than even chance to win

ode \ˈōd\ n : a lyric poem that expresses a noble feeling with dignity

odi·ous \ˈō-dē-əs\ adj : causing or deserving hatred or repugnance — **odi·ous·ly** adv — **odi·ous·ness** n

odi·um \ˈō-dē-əm\ n **1** : merited loathing : HATRED **2** : DISGRACE

odom·e·ter \ō-ˈdä-mə-tər\ n [F odomètre, fr. Gk hodometron, fr. hodos way, road + metron measure] : an instrument for measuring distance traveled (as by a vehicle)

odor \ˈō-dər\ n **1** : the quality of something that stimulates the sense of smell; also : a sensation resulting from such stimulation **2** : REPUTE, ESTIMATION — **odored** \ˈō-dərd\ adj — **odor·less** adj — **odor·ous** adj

odour chiefly Brit var of ODOR

od·ys·sey \ˈä-də-sē\ n, pl **-seys** [the Odyssey, epic poem attributed to Homer recounting the long wanderings of Odysseus] : a long wandering marked usu. by many changes of fortune

oe·cu·men·i·cal \esp Brit ˌē-\ var of ECUMENICAL

OED abbr Oxford English Dictionary

oe·de·ma chiefly Brit var of EDEMA

oe·di·pal \ˈe-də-pəl, ˈē-\ adj, often cap : of, relating to, or resulting from the Oedipus complex

Oe·di·pus complex \-pəs-\ n : the positive sexual feelings of a child toward the parent of the opposite sex and hostile or jealous feelings toward the parent of the same sex that may be a source of adult personality disorder when unresolved

OEO abbr Office of Economic Opportunity

o'er \ˈȯr\ adv or prep : OVER

OES abbr Order of the Eastern Star

oe·soph·a·gus chiefly Brit var of ESOPHAGUS

oeu·vre \œvrᵊ\ n, pl **oeuvres** \same\ : a substantial body of work constituting the lifework of a writer, an artist, or a composer

of \ˈəv, ˈäv\ prep **1** : FROM ⟨a man ∼ the West⟩ **2** : having as a significant background or character element ⟨a man ∼ noble birth⟩ ⟨a woman ∼ ability⟩ **3** : owing to ⟨died ∼ flu⟩ **4** : BY ⟨the plays ∼ Shakespeare⟩ **5** : having as component parts or material, contents, or members ⟨a house ∼ brick⟩ ⟨a glass ∼ water⟩ ⟨a pack ∼ fools⟩ **6** : belonging to or included by ⟨the front ∼ the house⟩ ⟨a time ∼ life⟩ ⟨one ∼ you⟩ ⟨the best ∼ its kind⟩ ⟨the son ∼ a doctor⟩ **7** : ABOUT ⟨tales ∼ the West⟩ **8** : connected with : OVER ⟨the queen ∼ England⟩ **9** : that is : signified as ⟨the city ∼ Rome⟩ **10** — used to indicate apposition of the words it joins 〈that fool ~ a husband〉 **11** : as concerns : FOR 〈love ~ nature〉 **12** — used to indicate the application of an adjective 〈fond ~ candy〉 **13** : BEFORE 〈quarter ~ ten〉

OF *abbr* outfield

¹off \'òf\ *adv* **1** : from a place or position 〈drove ~ in a new car〉; *also* : ASIDE 〈turned ~ into a side road〉 **2** : at a distance in time or space 〈stood ~ a few yards〉 〈several years ~〉 **3** : so as to be unattached or removed 〈the lid blew ~〉 **4** : to a state of discontinuance, exhaustion, or completion 〈shut the radio ~〉 **5** : away from regular work 〈took time ~ for lunch〉

²off *prep* **1** : away from 〈just ~ the highway〉 〈take it ~ the table〉 **2** : to seaward of 〈two miles ~ the coast〉 **3** : FROM 〈borrowed a dollar ~ me〉 **4** : at the expense of 〈lives ~ his parents〉 **5** : not now engaged in 〈~ duty〉 **6** : abstaining from 〈~ liquor〉 **7** : below the usual level of 〈~ his game〉

³off *adj* **1** : more removed or distant **2** : started on the way **3** : not operating **4** : not correct **5** : REMOTE, SLIGHT **6** : INFERIOR **7** : provided for 〈well ~〉

⁴off *abbr* office; officer; official

of·fal \'ò-fəl\ *n* : the waste or by-product of a process; *esp* : the viscera and trimmings of a butchered animal removed in dressing

off and on *adv* : INTERMITTENTLY

¹off·beat \'òf-ˌbēt\ *n* : the unaccented part of a musical measure

²offbeat *adj* : ECCENTRIC, UNCONVENTIONAL

off–col·or \'òf-'kə-lər\ *or* **off–col·ored** \-lərd\ *adj* : not having the right or standard color **2** : of doubtful propriety : verging on indecency 〈~ stories〉

of·fend \ə-'fend\ *vb* **1** : SIN, TRANSGRESS **2** : to cause discomfort or pain : HURT **3** : to cause dislike or vexation : ANNOY **syn** affront, insult, outrage — **of·fend·er** *n*

of·fense *or* **of·fence** \ə-'fens, *esp for 2 & 3* 'ä-ˌfens\ *n* **1** : something that outrages the senses **2** : ATTACK, ASSAULT **3** : the offensive team or members of a team playing offensive positions **4** : DISPLEASURE **5** : SIN, MISDEED **6** : an infraction of law : CRIME

¹of·fen·sive \ə-'fen-siv *esp for 1 & 2* 'ä-ˌfen-\ *adj* **1** : AGGRESSIVE **2** : of or relating to an attempt to score in a game; *also* : of or relating to a team in possession of the ball or puck **3** : OBNOXIOUS **4** : INSULTING — **of·fen·sive·ly** *adv* — **of·fen·sive·ness** *n*

²offensive *n* : ATTACK

¹of·fer \'ò-fər\ *vb* **of·fered; of·fer·ing** **1** : SACRIFICE **2** : to present for acceptance : TENDER; *also* : to propose as payment **3** : PROPOSE, SUGGEST; *also* : to declare one's readiness **4** : to try or begin to exert 〈~ resistance〉 **5** : to place on sale — **of·fer·ing** *n*

²offer *n* **1** : PROPOSAL **2** : BID **3** : TRY

of·fer·to·ry \'ò-fər-ˌtòr-ē\ *n, pl* **-ries** : the presentation of offerings at a church service; *also* : the musical accompaniment during it

off·hand \'òf-'hand\ *adv or adj* : without previous thought or preparation

off–hour \-ˌaú(-ə)r\ *n* : a period of time other than a rush hour; *also* : a period of time other than business hours

of·fice \'ò-fəs\ *n* **1** : a special duty or position; *esp* : a position of authority in government 〈run for ~〉 **2** : a prescribed form or service of worship; *also* : RITE **3** : an assigned or assumed duty or role **4** : a place where a business is transacted or a service is supplied

of·fice·hold·er \'ò-fəs-ˌhōl-dər\ *n* : one holding a public office

of·fi·cer \'ò-fə-sər\ *n* **1** : one charged with the enforcement of law **2** : one who holds an office of trust or authority **3** : a person who holds a position of authority or command in the armed forces; *esp* : COMMISSIONED OFFICER

¹of·fi·cial \ə-'fi-shəl\ *n* : OFFICER 2

²official *adj* **1** : of or relating to an office or to officers **2**

: AUTHORIZED, AUTHORITATIVE **3** : befitting or characteristic of a person in office — **of·fi·cial·ly** *adv*

of·fi·cial·dom \ə-'fi-shəl-dəm\ *n* : officials as a class

of·fi·cial·ism \ə-'fi-shə-ˌli-zəm\ *n* : lack of flexibility and initiative combined with excessive adherence to regulations

of·fi·ci·ant \ə-'fi-shē-ənt\ *n* : one (as a priest) who officiates at a religious rite

of·fi·ci·ate \ə-'fi-shē-ˌāt\ *vb* **-at·ed; -at·ing** **1** : to perform a ceremony, function, or duty **2** : to act in an official capacity

of·fi·cious \ə-'fi-shəs\ *adj* : volunteering one's services where they are neither asked for nor needed — **of·fi·cious·ly** *adv* — **of·fi·cious·ness** *n*

off·ing \'ò-fiŋ\ *n* : the near or foreseeable future

off–line \'òf-'līn\ *adj or adv* : not connected to or controlled directly by a computer

off of *prep* : OFF

off·print \'òf-ˌprint\ *n* : a separately printed excerpt (as from a magazine)

off–road \-'rōd\ *adj* : of, relating to, or being a vehicle designed for use away from public roads

off–sea·son \-ˌsēz-ᵊn\ *n* : a time of suspended or reduced activity

¹off·set \-ˌset\ *n* **1** : a sharp bend (as in a pipe) by which one part is turned aside out of line **2** : a printing process in which an inked impression is first made on a rubber-blanketed cylinder and then transferred to the paper

²off·set *vb* **off·set; off·set·ting** **1** : to place over against : BALANCE **2** : to compensate for **3** : to form an offset in 〈as a wall〉

off·shoot \'òf-ˌshüt\ *n* **1** : a collateral or derived branch, descendant, or member **2** : a branch of a main stem (as of a plant)

¹off·shore \'òf-'shòr\ *adv* **1** : at a distance from the shore **2** : outside the country : ABROAD

²off·shore \'òf-ˌshòr\ *adj* **1** : moving away from the shore **2** : situated off the shore but within waters under a country's control

off·side \-'sīd\ *adv or adj* : illegally in advance of the ball or puck

off·spring \-ˌspriŋ\ *n, pl* **offspring** *also* **offsprings** : PROGENY, YOUNG

off·stage \'òf-'stāj, -ˌstāj\ *adv or adj* **1** : off or away from the stage **2** : out of the public view 〈deals made ~〉

off–the–record *adj* : given or made in confidence and not for publication

off–the–shelf *adj* : available as a stock item : not specially designed or made

off–the–wall *adj* : highly unusual : BIZARRE

off·track \'òf-'trak\ *adv or adj* : away from a racetrack

off–white \'òf-'hwīt\ *n* : a yellowish or grayish white

off year *n* **1** : a year in which no major election is held **2** : a year of diminished activity or production

oft \'òft\ *adv* : OFTEN

of·ten \'ò-fən\ *adv* : many times : FREQUENTLY

of·ten·times \-ˌtīmz\ *or* **oft·times** \'òf-ˌtīmz, 'òft-\ *adv* : OFTEN

ogle \'ō-gəl\ *vb* **ogled; ogling** : to look at in a flirtatious way — **ogle** *n* — **ogler** *n*

ogre \'ō-gər\ *n* **1** : a monster of fairy tales and folklore that eats people **2** : a dreaded person or object

ogress \'ō-grəs\ *n* : a female ogre

oh \'ō\ *interj* **1** — used to express an emotion or in response to physical stimuli **2** — used in direct address

OH *abbr* Ohio

ohm \'ōm\ *n* : a unit of electrical resistance equal to the resistance of a circuit in which a potential difference of

---

\ə\abut \ᵊ\kitten \ər\further \a\ash \ā\ace \ä\mop, mar
\au̇\out \ch\chin \e\bet \ē\easy \g\go \i\hit \ī\ice \j\job
\ŋ\sing \ō\go \ȯ\law \ȯi\boy \th\thin \t͟h\the \ü\loot \u̇\foot
\y\yet \zh\vision   *see also* Pronunciation Symbols page

one volt produces a current of one ampere — **ohm-ic** \ˈō-mik\ *adj*

ohm·me·ter \ˈōm-ˌmē-tər\ *n* : an instrument for indicating resistance in ohms directly

¹**oil** \ˈȯil\ *n* [ME *oile*, fr. OF, fr. L *oleum* olive oil, fr. Gk *elaion*, fr. *elaia* olive] **1** : any of numerous fatty or greasy liquid substances obtained from plants, animals, or minerals and used for fuel, food, medicines, and manufacturing **2** : PETROLEUM **3** : artists' colors made with oil; *also* : a painting in such colors — **oil·i·ness** \ˈȯi-lē-nəs\ *n* — **oily** \ˈȯi-lē\ *adj*

²**oil** *vb* : to put oil in or on — **oil·er** *n*

oil·cloth \ˈȯil-ˌklȯth\ *n* : cloth treated with oil or paint and used for table and shelf coverings

oil pan *n* : the lower section of a crankcase used as an oil reservoir

oil shale *n* : a rock (as shale) from which oil can be recovered

oil·skin \ˈȯil-ˌskin\ *n* **1** : an oiled waterproof cloth **2** : an oilskin raincoat **3** *pl* : an oilskin coat and trousers

oink \ˈȯiŋk\ *n* : the natural noise of a hog — **oink** *vb*

oint·ment \ˈȯint-mənt\ *n* : a salve for use on the skin

OJ *abbr* orange juice

Ojib·wa or **Ojib·way** \ō-ˈjib-ˌwä\ *n, pl* **Ojibwa** or **Ojibwas** or **Ojibway** or **Ojibways** : a member of an American Indian people of the region around Lake Superior and westward

OJT *abbr* on-the-job training

¹**OK** or **okay** \ō-ˈkā\ *adv or adj* : all right

²**OK** or **okay** *vb* **OK'd** or **okayed**; **OK'·ing** or **okay-ing** : APPROVE, AUTHORIZE — **OK** or **okay** *n*

³**OK** *abbr* Oklahoma

Okla *abbr* Oklahoma

okra \ˈō-krə\ *n* : a tall annual plant related to the hollyhocks that has edible green pods; *also* : these pods

¹**old** \ˈōld\ *adj* **1** : ANCIENT; *also* : of long standing **2** *cap* : belonging to an early period ⟨*Old* Irish⟩ **3** : having existed for a specified period of time **4** : of or relating to a past era **5** : advanced in years **6** : showing the effects of age or use **7** : no longer in use — **old·ish** \ˈōl-dish\ *adj*

²**old** *n* : old or earlier time ⟨days of ∼⟩

old·en \ˈōl-dən\ *adj* : of or relating to a bygone era

¹**old–fash·ioned** \ˈōld-ˈfa-shənd\ *adj* **1** : OUT-OF-DATE, ANTIQUATED **2** : CONSERVATIVE

²**old–fashioned** *n* : a cocktail usu. made with whiskey, bitters, sugar, a twist of lemon peel, and water or soda water

old guard *n, often cap O&G* : the conservative members of an organization

old hat *adj* **1** : OLD-FASHIONED **2** : STALE, TRITE

old·ie \ˈōl-dē\ *n* : something old; *esp* : a popular song from the past

old–line \ˈōld-ˈlīn\ *adj* **1** : ORIGINAL, ESTABLISHED ⟨an ∼ business⟩ **2** : adhering to old policies or practices

old maid *n* **1** : SPINSTER **2** : a prim fussy person — **old–maid·ish** \ˈōld-ˈmā-dish\ *adj*

old man *n* **1** : HUSBAND **2** : FATHER

old·ster \ˈōld-stər\ *n* : an old or elderly person

Old Testament *n* : the first of the two chief divisions of the Bible — see BIBLE table

old–time \ˈōld-ˈtīm\ *adj* **1** : of, relating to, or characteristic of an earlier period **2** : of long standing

old–tim·er \-ˈtī-mər\ *n* VETERAN; *also* : OLDSTER

old–world \-ˈwərld\ *adj* : having old-fashioned charm

Old World *n* : the eastern hemisphere exclusive of Australia; *esp* : continental Europe

ole·ag·i·nous \ˌō-lē-ˈa-jə-nəs\ *adj* : OILY

ole·an·der \ˈō-lē-ˌan-dər\ *n* : a poisonous evergreen shrub often grown for its fragrant white to red flowers

oleo \ˈō-lē-ˌō\ *n, pl* **oleos** : MARGARINE

oleo·mar·ga·rine \ˌō-lē-ō-ˈmär-jə-rən\ *n* : MARGARINE

ol·fac·to·ry \äl-ˈfak-tə-rē, ōl-\ *adj* : of or relating to the sense of smell

oli·gar·chy \ˈä-lə-ˌgär-kē, ˈō-\ *n, pl* **-chies 1** : a government in which power is in the hands of a few **2** : a state having an oligarchy; *also* : the group holding power in such a state — **oli·garch** \-ˌgärk\ *n* — **oli·gar·chic** \ˌä-lə-ˈgär-kik, ˌō-\ *or* **oli·gar·chi·cal** \-ki-kəl\ *adj*

Oli·go·cene \ˈä-li-gō-ˌsēn, ə-ˈli-gə-ˌsēn\ *adj* : of, relating to, or being the epoch of the Tertiary between the Eocene and the Miocene — **Oligocene** *n*

olio \ˈō-lē-ˌō\ *n, pl* **oli·os** : HODGEPODGE, MEDLEY

ol·ive \ˈä-liv\ *n* **1** : an Old World evergreen tree grown in warm regions for its fruit that is a food and the source of an edible oil (**olive oil**) **2** : a dull yellow to yellowish green color

olive drab *n* **1** : a grayish olive color **2** : an olive drab wool or cotton fabric; *also* : a uniform of this fabric

ol·iv·ine \ˈä-lə-ˌvēn\ *n* : a usu. greenish mineral that is a complex silicate of magnesium and iron

Olym·pic Games \ō-ˈlim-pik-\ *n pl* : a modified revival of an ancient Greek festival consisting of international athletic contests that are held at separate winter and summer gatherings at four-year intervals

om \ˈōm\ *n* : a mantra consisting of the sound "om" used in contemplating ultimate reality

Oma·ha \ˈō-mə-ˌhä, -ˌhȯ\ *n, pl* **Omaha** or **Omahas** : a member of an American Indian people of northeastern Nebraska

om·buds·man \ˈäm-ˌbu̇dz-mən, äm-ˈbu̇dz-\ *n, pl* **-men** \-mən\ **1** : a government official appointed to investigate complaints made by individuals against abuses or capricious acts of public officials **2** : one that investigates reported complaints (as from students or consumers)

ome·ga \ō-ˈmā-gə\ *n* : the 24th and last letter of the Greek alphabet — Ω or ω

om·elet *or* **om·elette** \ˈäm-lət, ˈä-mə-\ *n* [F *omelette*, alter. of MF *alumelle*, lit., knife blade, modif. of L *lamella*, dim. of *lamina* thin plate] : eggs beaten with milk or water, cooked without stirring until set, and folded over

omen \ˈō-mən\ *n* : an event or phenomenon believed to be a sign or warning of a future occurrence

om·i·cron \ˈä-mə-ˌkrän, ˈō-\ *n* : the 15th letter of the Greek alphabet — O or ο

om·i·nous \ˈä-mə-nəs\ *adj* : foretelling evil : THREATENING — **om·i·nous·ly** *adv* — **om·i·nous·ness** *n*

omis·si·ble \ō-ˈmi-sə-bəl\ *adj* : that may be omitted

omis·sion \ō-ˈmi-shən\ *n* **1** : something neglected or left undone **2** : the act of omitting : the state of being omitted

omit \ō-ˈmit\ *vb* **omit·ted; omit·ting 1** : to leave out or leave unmentioned **2** : to fail to perform : NEGLECT

¹**om·ni·bus** \ˈäm-ni-(ˌ)bəs\ *n* : BUS

²**omnibus** *adj* : of, relating to, or providing for many things at once ⟨an ∼ bill⟩

om·nip·o·tent \äm-ˈni-pə-tənt\ *adj* : having unlimited authority or influence — ALMIGHTY — **om·nip·o·tence** \-əns\ *n* — **om·nip·o·tent·ly** *adv*

om·ni·pres·ent \ˌäm-ni-ˈprez-ᵊnt\ *adj* : present in all places at all times — **om·ni·pres·ence** \-ᵊns\ *n*

om·ni·scient \äm-ˈni-shənt\ *adj* : having infinite awareness, understanding, and insight — **om·ni·science** \-shəns\ *n* — **om·ni·scient·ly** *adv*

om·ni·um–gath·er·um \ˌäm-nē-əm-ˈga-thə-rəm\ *n, pl* **omnium–gatherums** : a miscellaneous collection

om·niv·o·rous \äm-ˈni-və-rəs\ *adj* : feeding on both animal and vegetable substances; *also* : AVID ⟨an ∼ reader⟩ — **om·niv·o·rous·ly** *adv*

¹**on** \ˈȯn, ˈän\ *prep* **1** : in or to a position over and in contact with ⟨jumped ∼ his horse⟩ **2** : touching the surface of ⟨shadows ∼ the wall⟩ **3** : AT, TO ⟨∼ the right were the mountains⟩ **4** : IN, ABOARD ⟨went ∼ the train⟩ **5**

: during or at the time of ⟨came ~ Monday⟩ ⟨every hour ~ the hour⟩ **6** : through the agency of ⟨was cut ~ a tin can⟩ **7** : in a state or process of ⟨~ fire⟩ ⟨~ the wane⟩ **8** : connected with as a member or participant ⟨~ a committee⟩ ⟨~ tour⟩ **9** — used to indicate a basis, source, or standard of computation ⟨has it ~ good authority⟩ ⟨10 cents ~ the dollar⟩ **10** : with regard to ⟨a monopoly ~ wheat⟩ **11** : at or toward as an object ⟨crept up ~ her⟩ **12** : ABOUT, CONCERNING ⟨a book ~ minerals⟩

²on *adv* **1** : in or into a position of contact with or attachment to a surface **2** : FORWARD **3** : into operation

³on *adj* : being in operation or in progress

ON *abbr* Ontario

¹once \'wəns\ *adv* **1** : one time only **2** : at any one time **3** : FORMERLY **4** : by one degree of relationship

²once *n* : one single time — **at once 1** : at the same time **2** : IMMEDIATELY

³once *adj* : FORMER

⁴once *conj* : AS SOON AS

once–over \'wəns-ₒō-vər\ *n* : a swift examination or survey

on·com·ing \'ȯn-ₒkə-miŋ, 'än-\ *adj* : APPROACHING ⟨~ traffic⟩

¹one \'wən\ *adj* **1** : being a single unit or thing ⟨~ person went⟩ **2** : being one in particular ⟨early ~ morning⟩ **3** : being the same in kind or quality ⟨members of ~ race⟩; *also* : UNITED **4** : being not specified or fixed ⟨~ day soon⟩

²one *n* **1** : the number denoting unity **2** : the 1st in a set or series **3** : a single person or thing — **one·ness** \'wən-nəs\ *n*

³one *pron* **1** : a certain indefinitely indicated person or thing ⟨saw ~ of his friends⟩ **2** : a person in general ⟨~ never knows⟩ **3** — used in place of a first-person pronoun

Onei·da \ō-'nī-də\ *n, pl* **Oneida** *or* **Oneidas** : a member of an American Indian people orig. of New York

oner·ous \'ä-nə-rəs, 'ō-\ *adj* : imposing or constituting a burden : TROUBLESOME **syn** oppressive, exacting, burdensome, weighty

one·self \(ₒ)wən-'self\ *also* **one's self** *pron* : one's own self — usu. used reflexively or for emphasis

one–sid·ed \'wən-'sī-dəd\ *adj* **1** : having or occurring on one side only; *also* : having one side prominent or more developed **2** : PARTIAL ⟨a ~ interpretation⟩

one–time \-ₒtīm\ *adj* : FORMER

one–to–one \ₒwən-tə-'wən\ *adj* : pairing each element of a set uniquely with an element of another set

one up *adj* : being in a position of advantage ⟨was *one up* on the others⟩

one–way *adj* : moving, allowing movement, or functioning in only one direction ⟨~ streets⟩

on·go·ing \'ȯn-ₒgō-iŋ, 'än-\ *adj* : continuously moving forward

on·ion \'ən-yən\ *n* : the pungent edible bulb of a cultivated plant related to the lilies; *also* : this plant

on·ion·skin \-ₒskin\ *n* : a thin strong translucent paper of very light weight

on–line *adj or adv* : connected to or controlled directly by a computer

on·look·er \'ȯn-ₒlu̇-kər, 'än-\ *n* : SPECTATOR

¹on·ly \'ȯn-lē\ *adj* **1** : unquestionably the best **2** : SOLE

²only *adv* **1** : MERELY, JUST ⟨~ $2⟩ **2** : SOLELY ⟨known ~ to me⟩ **3** : at the very least ⟨was ~ too true⟩ **4** : as a final result ⟨will ~ make you sick⟩

³only *conj* : except that

on·o·mato·poe·ia \ₒä-nə-ₒmä-tə-'pē-ə\ *n* **1** : formation of words in imitation of natural sounds (as *buzz* or *hiss*) **2** : the use of words whose sound suggests the sense — **on·o·mato·poe·ic** \-'pē-ik\ *or* **on·o·mato·po·et·ic** \-ₒpō-'e-tik\ *adj* — **on·o·mato·poe·i·cal·ly** \-'pē-ə-k(ə-)lē\ *or* **on·o·mato·po·et·i·cal·ly** \-ₒpō-'e-ti-k(ə-)lē\ *adv*

On·on·da·ga \ₒä-nən-'dȯ-gə, -'dä-, -'dä-\ *n, pl* **-ga** *or* **-gas** : a member of an American Indian people of New York and Canada

on·rush \'ȯn-ₒrəsh, 'än-\ *n* : a rushing onward — **on·rush·ing** *adj*

on·set \-ₒset\ *n* **1** : ATTACK **2** : BEGINNING

on·shore \-ₒshōr\ *adj* **1** : moving toward the shore **2** : situated on or near the shore — **on·shore** \-'shōr\ *adv*

on·slaught \'ȯn-ₒslȯt, 'än-\ *n* : a fierce attack; *also* : something resembling such an attack ⟨an ~ of questions⟩

Ont *abbr* Ontario

on·to \'ȯn-tü, 'än-\ *prep* : to a position or point on

onus \'ō-nəs\ *n* **1** : BURDEN **2** : OBLIGATION **3** : BLAME

¹on·ward \'ȯn-wərd, 'än-\ *also* **on·wards** \-wərdz\ *adv* : FORWARD

²onward *adj* : directed or moving onward : FORWARD

on·yx \'ä-niks\ *n* [ME *onix*, fr. MF & L; MF, fr. L *onyx*, fr. Gk, lit., claw, nail] : a translucent chalcedony in parallel layers of different colors

oo·dles \'üd-ᵊlz\ *n pl* : a great quantity

oo·lite \'ō-ə-ₒlīt\ *n* : a rock consisting of small round grains cemented together — **oo·lit·ic** \ₒō-ə-'li-tik\ *adj*

¹ooze \'üz\ *n* **1** : a soft deposit (as of mud) on the bottom of a body of water **2** : soft wet ground : MUD — **oozy** \'ü-zē\ *adj*

²ooze *vb* **oozed; ooz·ing 1** : to flow or leak out slowly or imperceptibly **2** : EXUDE

³ooze *n* : something that oozes

op *abbr* **1** operation; operative; operator **2** opportunity **3** opus

OP *abbr* **1** observation post **2** out of print

opac·i·ty \ō-'pa-sə-tē\ *n, pl* **-ties 1** : the quality or state of being opaque **2** : obscurity of meaning **3** : mental dullness **4** : an opaque spot in a normally transparent structure

opal \'ō-pəl\ *n* : a mineral with iridescent colors that is used as a gem

opal·es·cent \ₒō-pə-'les-ᵊnt\ *adj* : IRIDESCENT — **opal·es·cence** \-ᵊns\ *n*

opaque \ō-'pāk\ *adj* **1** : blocking the passage of radiant energy and esp. light **2** : not easily understood **3** : OBTUSE — **opaque·ly** *adv* — **opaque·ness** *n*

op art \'äp-\ *n* : OPTICAL ART — **op artist** *n*

op cit *abbr* [L *opere citato*] in the work cited

ope \'ōp\ *vb* **oped; op·ing** *archaic* : OPEN

OPEC *abbr* Organization of Petroleum Exporting Countries

¹open \'ō-pən\ *adj* **open·er; open·est 1** : not shut or shut up ⟨an ~ door⟩ **2** : not secret or hidden; *also* : FRANK **3** : not enclosed or covered ⟨an ~ fire⟩; *also* : not protected **4** : free to be entered or used ⟨an ~ tournament⟩ **5** : easy to get through or see ⟨~ country⟩ **6** : spread out : EXTENDED **7** : not decided ⟨an ~ question⟩ **8** : readily accessible and cooperative; *also* : GENEROUS **9** : having components separated by a space in writing and printing ⟨the name *Spanish moss* is an ~ compound⟩ **10** : having openings, interruptions, or spaces ⟨an ~ mesh⟩ **11** : ready to operate ⟨stores are ~⟩ **12** : free from restraints or controls ⟨~ season⟩ — **open·ly** *adv* — **open·ness** *n*

²open \'ō-pən\ *vb* **opened; open·ing 1** : to change or move from a shut position; *also* : to make open by clearing away obstacles **2** : to make accessible **3** : to make openings in **4** : to make or become functional ⟨~ a store⟩ **5** : REVEAL; *also* : ENLIGHTEN **6** : BEGIN — **open·er** *n*

³open *n* **1** : OUTDOORS **2** : a contest or tournament open to all

---

\ə\abut \ᵊ\kitten \ər\further \a\ash \ā\ace \ä\mop, mar \au̇\out \ch\chin \e\bet \ē\easy \g\go \i\hit \ī\ice \j\job \ŋ\sing \ō\go \ȯ\law \ȯi\boy \th\thin \t̲h̲\the \ü\loot \u̇\foot \y\yet \zh\vision *see also* Pronunciation Symbols page

open–air *adj* : OUTDOOR ⟨∼ theaters⟩

open–hand·ed \ˌō-pən-ˈhan-dəd\ *adj* : GENEROUS — **open·hand·ed·ly** *adv*

open–heart *adj* : of, relating to, or performed on a heart temporarily relieved of circulatory function and laid open for inspection and treatment

open–hearth *adj* : of, relating to, or being a process of making steel in a furnace that reflects the heat from the roof onto the material

open·ing *n* 1 : an act or instance of making or becoming open 2 : BEGINNING 3 : something that is open 4 : OCCASION; *also* : an opportunity for employment

open–mind·ed \ˌō-pən-ˈmīn-dəd\ *adj* : free from rigidly fixed preconceptions

open sentence *n* : a statement (as in mathematics) containing at least one blank or unknown so that when the blank is filled or a quantity substituted for the unknown the statement becomes a complete statement that is either true or false

open shop *n* : an establishment having members and nonmembers of a labor union on the payroll

open·work \ˈō-pən-ˌwərk\ *n* : work so made as to show openings through its substance ⟨a railing of wrought≈ iron ∼⟩ — **open–worked** \-ˌwərkt\ *adj*

¹opera *pl of* OPUS

²op·era \ˈä-prə, -pə-rə\ *n* : a drama set to music — **op·er·at·ic** \ˌä-pə-ˈra-tik\ *adj*

op·er·a·ble \ˈä-pə-rə-bəl\ *adj* 1 : fit, possible, or desirable to use 2 : likely to result in a favorable outcome upon surgical treatment

opera glasses *n pl* : small binoculars for use in a theater

op·er·ate \ˈä-pə-ˌrāt\ *vb* **-at·ed; -at·ing** 1 : to perform work : FUNCTION 2 : to produce an effect 3 : to put or keep in operation 4 : to perform or subject to an operation — **op·er·a·tor** \-ˌrā-tər\ *n*

operating system *n* : software that controls the operation of a computer

op·er·a·tion \ˌä-pə-ˈrā-shən\ *n* 1 : a doing or performing of a practical work 2 : an exertion of power or influence; *also* : method or manner of functioning 3 : a surgical procedure 4 : a process of deriving one mathematical expression from others according to a rule 5 : a military action or mission — **op·er·a·tion·al** \-shə-nəl\ *adj*

¹op·er·a·tive \ˈä-pə-rə-tiv, -ˌrā-\ *adj* 1 : producing an appropriate effect 2 : OPERATING ⟨an ∼ force⟩ 3 : having to do with physical operations; *also* : WORKING ⟨an ∼ craftsman⟩ 4 : based on or consisting of an operation ⟨∼ dentistry⟩

²operative *n* : OPERATOR; *esp* : a secret agent

op·er·et·ta \ˌä-pə-ˈre-tə\ *n* [It, dim. of *opera* opera] : a light musical-dramatic work with a romantic plot, spoken dialogue, and dancing scenes

oph·thal·mic \äf-ˈthal-mik, äp-\ *adj* [Gk *ophthalmikos*, fr. *ophthalmos* eye] : of, relating to, or located near the eye

oph·thal·mol·o·gy \ˌäf-ˌthal-ˈmä-lə-jē, ˌäp-\ *n* : a branch of medicine dealing with the structure, functions, and diseases of the eye — **oph·thal·mol·o·gist** \-jist\ *n*

oph·thal·mo·scope \äf-ˈthal-mə-ˌskōp, äp-\ *n* : an instrument for use in viewing the interior of the eye and esp. the retina

opi·ate \ˈō-pē-ət, -pē-ˌāt\ *n* : a preparation or derivative of opium; *also* : a narcotic or a substance with similar activity — **opiate** *adj*

opine \ō-ˈpīn\ *vb* **opined; opin·ing** : to express an opinion : STATE

opin·ion \ə-ˈpin-yən\ *n* 1 : a belief stronger than impression and less strong than positive knowledge 2 : JUDGMENT 3 : a formal statement by an expert after careful study

opin·ion·at·ed \ə-ˈpin-yə-ˌnā-təd\ *adj* : obstinately adhering to personal opinions

opi·um \ˈō-pē-əm\ *n* [ME, fr. L, fr. Gk *opion*, fr. dim. of *opos* sap] : an addictive narcotic drug that is the dried juice of a poppy

opos·sum \ə-ˈpä-səm\ *n, pl* **opossums** *also* **opossum** : a common omnivorous tree-dwelling marsupial mammal of the eastern U.S. that is active esp. at night

opp *abbr* opposite

op·po·nent \ə-ˈpō-nənt\ *n* : one that opposes : ADVERSARY

op·por·tune \ˌä-pər-ˈtün, -ˈtyün\ *adj* [ME, fr. MF *opportun*, fr. L *opportunus*, fr. *ob-* toward + *portus* port, harbor] : SUITABLE — **op·por·tune·ly** *adv*

op·por·tun·ism \ˌä-pər-ˈtü-ni-zəm, -ˈtyü-\ *n* : a taking advantage of opportunities or circumstances esp. with little regard for principles or ultimate consequences — **op·por·tun·ist** \-nist\ *n* — **op·por·tu·nis·tic** \-tü-ˈnis-tik, -tyü-\ *adj*

op·por·tu·ni·ty \ˌä-pər-ˈtü-nə-tē, -ˈtyü-\ *n, pl* **-ties** 1 : a favorable combination of circumstances, time, and place 2 : a chance for advancement

op·pose \ə-ˈpōz\ *vb* **op·posed; op·pos·ing** 1 : to place opposite or against something (as to provide resistance or contrast) 2 : to strive against : RESIST — **op·po·si·tion** \ˌä-pə-ˈzi-shən\ *n*

¹op·po·site \ˈä-pə-zət\ *adj* 1 : set over against something that is at the other end or side 2 : OPPOSED, HOSTILE; *also* : CONTRARY 3 : contrarily turned or moving — **op·po·site·ly** *adv* — **op·po·site·ness** *n*

²opposite *n* : one that is opposed or contrary

³opposite *adv* : on or to an opposite side

⁴opposite *prep* : across from and usu. facing ⟨the house ∼ ours⟩

op·press \ə-ˈpres\ *vb* 1 : to crush by abuse of power or authority 2 : to weigh down : BURDEN **syn** aggrieve, wrong, persecute — **op·pres·sive** \-ˈpre-siv\ *adj* — **op·pres·sive·ly** *adv* — **op·pres·sor** \-ˈpre-sər\ *n*

op·pres·sion \ə-ˈpre-shən\ *n* 1 : unjust or cruel exercise of power or authority 2 : DEPRESSION — **op·pres·sive** \-ˈpre-siv\ *adj*

op·pro·bri·ous \ə-ˈprō-brē-əs\ *adj* : expressing or deserving opprobrium — **op·pro·bri·ous·ly** *adv*

op·pro·bri·um \-brē-əm\ *n* 1 : something that brings disgrace 2 : INFAMY

¹opt \ˈäpt\ *vb* : to make a choice; *esp* : to decide in favor of something

²opt *abbr* 1 optical; optician; optics 2 option; optional

op·tic \ˈäp-tik\ *adj* : of or relating to vision or the eye

op·ti·cal \ˈäp-ti-kəl\ *adj* 1 : relating to optics 2 : OPTIC 3 : of, relating to, or using light

optical art *n* : nonobjective art characterized by the use of geometric patterns often for an illusory effect

optical disk *n* : a disk on which information has been recorded digitally and which is read using a laser

optical fiber *n* : a single fiber-optic strand

op·ti·cian \äp-ˈti-shən\ *n* 1 : a maker of or dealer in optical items and instruments 2 : a person who makes or orders eyeglass and contact lenses to prescription and sells glasses

op·tics \ˈäp-tiks\ *n pl* : a science that deals with the nature and properties of light

op·ti·mal \ˈäp-tə-məl\ *adj* : most desirable or satisfactory — **op·ti·mal·ly** *adv*

op·ti·mism \ˈäp-tə-ˌmi-zəm\ *n* [F *optimisme*, fr. L *optimum*, n., best, fr. neut. of *optimus* best] 1 : a doctrine that this world is the best possible world 2 : an inclination to anticipate the best possible outcome of actions or events — **op·ti·mist** \-mist\ *n* — **op·ti·mis·tic** \ˌäp-tə-ˈmis-tik\ *adj* — **op·ti·mis·ti·cal·ly** \-ti-k(ə-)lē\ *adv*

op·ti·mum \ˈäp-tə-məm\ *n, pl* **-ma** \-mə\ *also* **-mums** [L] : the amount or degree of something most favorable to an end; *also* : greatest degree attained under implied or specified conditions

op·tion \\'äp-shən\ *n* **1** : the power or right to choose **2** : a right to buy or sell something at a specified price during a specified period **3** : something offered for choice — **op·tion·al** \-shə-nəl\ *adj*

op·tom·e·try \äp-'tä-mə-trē\ *n* : the art or profession of examining the eyes for defects of vision and of prescribing corrective lenses or exercises — **op·tom·e·trist** \-trist\ *n*

opt out *vb* : to choose not to participate

op·u·lence \'ä-pyə-ləns\ *n* **1** : WEALTH **2** : ABUNDANCE

op·u·lent \'ä-pyə-lənt\ *adj* **1** : WEALTHY **2** : richly abundant — **op·u·lent·ly** *adv*

opus \'ō-pəs\ *n, pl* **opera** \'ō-pə-rə, 'ä-\ *also* **opus·es** \'ō-pə-səz\ : WORK; *esp* : a musical composition

or \'òr\ *conj* — used as a function word to indicate an alternative ⟨sink ∼ swim⟩

OR *abbr* **1** operating room **2** Oregon

-or \ər\ *n suffix* : one that does a (specified) thing ⟨calculator⟩

or·a·cle \'òr-ə-kəl\ *n* **1** : one held to give divinely inspired answers or revelations **2** : an authoritative or wise utterance; *also* : a person of great authority or wisdom — **orac·u·lar** \ò-'ra-kyə-lər\ *adj*

¹oral \'òr-əl\ *adj* **1** : SPOKEN **2** : of or relating to the mouth **3** : of, relating to, or characterized by the first stage of psychosexual development in psychoanalytic theory in which libidinal gratification is derived from intake (as of food), by sucking, and later by biting **4** : relating to or characterized by personality traits of passive dependency and aggressiveness — **oral·ly** *adv*

²oral *n* : an oral examination — usu. used in pl.

orang \ə-'raŋ\ *n* : ORANGUTAN

or·ange \'òr-inj\ *n* **1** : a juicy citrus fruit with reddish yellow rind; *also* : an evergreen tree with fragrant white flowers that bears this fruit **2** : a color between red and yellow

or·ange·ade \ˌòr-in-'jād\ *n* : a beverage of orange juice, sugar, and water

orange hawkweed *n* : a weedy herb related to the daisies with bright orange-red flower heads

or·ange·ry \'òr-inj-rē\ *n, pl* **-ries** : a protected place (as a greenhouse) for raising oranges in cool climates

orang·utan \ə-'raŋ-ə-ˌtaŋ, -ˌtan\ *n* [Bazaar Malay (Malay-based pidgin), fr. Malay *orang* man + *hutan* forest] : a large reddish brown tree-living anthropoid ape of Borneo and Sumatra

orate \ò-'rāt\ *vb* **orat·ed; orat·ing** : to speak in a declamatory manner

ora·tion \ə-'rā-shən\ *n* : an elaborate discourse delivered in a formal and dignified manner

or·a·tor \'òr-ə-tər\ *n* : one noted for skill and power as a public speaker

or·a·tor·i·cal \ˌòr-ə-'tòr-i-kəl\ *adj* : of, relating to, or characteristic of an orator or oratory — **or·a·tor·i·cal·ly** \-'tòr-i-k(ə-)lē\ *adv*

or·a·to·rio \ˌòr-ə-'tòr-ē-ˌō\ *n, pl* **-rios** : a lengthy choral work usu. on a scriptural subject

¹or·a·to·ry \'òr-ə-ˌtòr-ē\ *n, pl* **-ries** : a private or institutional chapel

²oratory *n* : the art of speaking eloquently and effectively in public **syn** rhetoric, elocution

orb \'òrb\ *n* : a spherical body; *also* : EYE

¹or·bit \'òr-bət\ *n* [L *orbita*, lit., path, rut] **1** : a path described by one body in its revolution about another **2** : range or sphere of activity — **or·bit·al** \-ᵊl\ *adj*

²orbit *vb* **1** : CIRCLE **2** : to send up and make revolve in an orbit ⟨∼ a satellite⟩ — **or·bit·er** *n*

orch *abbr* orchestra

or·chard \'òr-chərd\ *n* [ME, fr. OE *ortgeard*, fr. *ort-* (fr. L *hortus* garden) + *geard* yard] : a place where fruit trees, sugar maples, or nut trees are grown; *also* : the trees of such a place — **or·chard·ist** \-chər-dist\ *n*

or·ches·tra \'òr-kə-strə\ *n* **1** : the front section of seats on the main floor of a theater **2** : a group of instrumentalists organized to perform ensemble music — **or·ches·tral** \òr-'kes-trəl\ *adj* — **or·ches·tral·ly** *adv*

or·ches·trate \'òr-kə-ˌstrāt\ *vb* **-trat·ed; -trat·ing 1** : to compose or arrange for an orchestra **2** : to arrange so as to achieve a desired effect — **or·ches·tra·tion** \ˌòr-kə-'strā-shən\ *n*

or·chid \'òr-kəd\ *n* : any of a large family of plants having often showy flowers with three petals of which the middle one is enlarged into a lip; *also* : a flower of an orchid

ord *abbr* **1** order **2** ordnance

or·dain \òr-'dān\ *vb* **1** : to admit to the ministry or priesthood by the ritual of a church **2** : DECREE, ENACT; *also* : DESTINE — **or·dain·ment** *n*

or·deal \òr-'dēl, 'òr-ˌdēl\ *n* : a severe trial or experience

¹or·der \'òr-dər\ *vb* **1** : ARRANGE, REGULATE **2** : COMMAND **3** : to place an order

²order *n* **1** : a group of people formally united; *also* : a badge or medal of such a group **2** : any of the several grades of the Christian ministry; *also, pl* : ORDINATION **3** : a rank, class, or special group of persons or things **4** : a category of biological classification ranking above the family and below the class **5** : ARRANGEMENT, SEQUENCE; *also* : the prevailing state of things **6** : a customary mode of procedure; *also* : the rule of law or proper authority **7** : a specific rule, regulation, or authoritative direction **8** : a style of building; *also* : an architectural column forming the unit of a style **9** : condition esp. with regard to repair **10** : a written direction to pay money or to buy or sell goods; *also* : goods bought or sold

¹or·der·ly \'òr-dər-lē\ *adj* **1** : arranged according to some order; *also* : NEAT, TIDY **2** : well behaved ⟨an ∼ crowd⟩ **syn** methodical, systematic, regular — **or·der·li·ness** *n*

²orderly *n, pl* **-lies 1** : a soldier who attends a superior officer **2** : a hospital attendant who does general work

¹or·di·nal \'òrd-ᵊn-əl\ *n* : an ordinal number

²ordinal *adj* : indicating order or rank (as sixth) in a series

or·di·nance \'òrd-ᵊn-əns\ *n* : an authoritative decree or law; *esp* : a municipal regulation

or·di·nary \'òrd-ᵊn-ˌer-ē\ *adj* **1** : to be expected : USUAL **2** : of common quality, rank, or ability; *also* : POOR, INFERIOR **syn** customary, routine, normal, everyday — **or·di·nar·i·ly** \ˌòrd-ᵊn-'er-ə-lē\ *adv* — **or·di·nar·i·ness** \'òrd-ᵊn-ˌer-ē-nəs\ *n*

or·di·nate \'òrd-ᵊn-ət, -ˌāt\ *n* : the coordinate of a point in a plane coordinate system that is the distance of the point from the horizontal axis found by measuring along a line parallel to the vertical axis

or·di·na·tion \ˌòrd-ᵊn-'ā-shən\ *n* : the act or ceremony by which a person is ordained

ord·nance \'òrd-nəns\ *n* **1** : military supplies **2** : CANNON, ARTILLERY

Or·do·vi·cian \ˌòr-də-'vi-shən\ *adj* : of, relating to, or being the period of the Paleozoic era between the Cambrian and the Silurian — **Ordovician** *n*

or·dure \'òr-jər\ *n* : EXCREMENT

¹ore \'òr\ *n* : a mineral mined to obtain a substance that it contains

²ore \'ər-ə\ *n, pl* **ore** — see krona, krone at MONEY table

Ore *or* **Oreg** *abbr* Oregon

oreg·a·no \ə-'re-gə-ˌnō\ *n* : a bushy perennial mint used as a seasoning and a source of oil

org *abbr* organization; organized

or·gan \'òr-gən\ *n* **1** : a musical instrument having sets of pipes sounded by compressed air and controlled by keyboards; *also* : an instrument in which the sounds of

---

\ə\abut \ᵊ\kitten \ər\further \a\ash \ā\ace \ä\mop, mar \au̇\out \ch\chin \e\bet \ē\easy \g\go \i\hit \ī\ice \j\job \ŋ\sing \ō\go \ȯ\law \ȯi\boy \th\thin \t̲h̲\the \ü\loot \u̇\foot \y\yet \zh\vision *see also* Pronunciation Symbols page

the pipe organ are approximated by electronic devices **2** : a differentiated animal or plant structure (as a heart or a leaf) made up of cells and tissues and performing some bodily function **3** : a group that performs a specialized function ⟨the various ~s of government⟩ **4** : PERIODICAL

or·gan·dy also **or·gan·die** \'ȯr-gən-dē\ n, pl **-dies** [F organdi] : a fine transparent muslin with a stiff finish

or·gan·elle \ˌȯr-gə-'nel\ n : a specialized cell part that resembles an organ in having a special function

or·gan·ic \ȯr-'ga-nik\ adj **1** : of, relating to, or arising in a bodily organ **2** : of, relating to, or derived from living things **3** : of, relating to, or containing carbon compounds **4** : of or relating to a branch of chemistry dealing with carbon compounds **5** : involving, producing, or dealing in foods produced without the use of laboratory-made fertilizers, growth substances, antibiotics, or pesticides **6** : ORGANIZED ⟨an ~ whole⟩ — **or·gan·i·cal·ly** \-ni-k(ə-)lē\ adv

or·gan·ism \'ȯr-gə-ˌni-zəm\ n : an individual living thing (as a person, animal, or plant) — **or·gan·is·mic** \ˌȯr-gə-'niz-mik\ adj

or·gan·ist \'ȯr-gə-nist\ n : a person who plays an organ

or·ga·ni·za·tion \ˌȯr-gə-nə-'zā-shən\ n **1** : the act or process of organizing or of being organized; also : the condition or manner of being organized **2** : ASSOCIATION, SOCIETY **3** : an administrative structure (as a business or a political party) — **or·ga·ni·za·tion·al** \-shə-nəl\ adj

or·ga·nize \'ȯr-gə-ˌnīz\ vb **-nized; -niz·ing 1** : to develop an organic structure **2** : to form into a complete and functioning whole **3** : to set up an administrative structure for **4** : to arrange by systematic planning and united effort **5** : to join in a union; also : UNIONIZE **syn** institute, found, establish, constitute — **or·ga·niz·er** n

or·gano·chlo·rine \ȯr-ˌga-nə-'klȯr-ˌēn\ adj : of or relating to the chlorinated hydrocarbon pesticides (as DDT) — **organochlorine** n

or·gano·phos·phate \-'fäs-ˌfāt\ n : an organophosphorus pesticide — **organophosphate** adj

or·gano·phos·pho·rus \-'fäs-fə-rəs\ also **or·gano·phos·pho·rous** \-fäs-'fōr-əs\ adj : of, relating to, or being a phosphorus-containing organic pesticide (as malathion)

or·gan·za \ȯr-'gan-zə\ n : a sheer dress fabric resembling organdy and usu. made of silk, rayon, or nylon

or·gasm \'ȯr-ˌga-zəm\ n : the climax of sexual excitement — **or·gas·mic** \ȯr-'gaz-mik\ adj

or·gi·as·tic \ˌȯr-jē-'as-tik\ adj : of, relating to, or marked by orgies

or·gu·lous \'ȯr-gyə-ləs, -gə-\ adj : PROUD

or·gy \'ȯr-jē\ n, pl **orgies** : a gathering marked by unrestrained indulgence (as in sexual activity, alcohol, or drugs)

ori·el \'ōr-ē-əl\ n : a window built out from a wall and usu. supported by a bracket

ori·ent \'ōr-ē-ˌent\ vb **1** : to set in a definite position esp. in relation to the points of the compass **2** : to acquaint with an existing situation or environment **3** : to direct toward the interests of a particular group — **ori·en·ta·tion** \ˌōr-ē-ən-'tā-shən\ n

Orient n : EAST **3**; esp : the countries of eastern Asia

ori·en·tal \ˌōr-ē-'ent-əl\ adj [fr. Orient East, fr. ME, fr. MF, fr. L orient-, oriens, fr. prp. of oriri to rise] often cap : of or situated in the Orient — **Oriental** n

ori·en·tate \'ōr-ē-ən-ˌtāt\ vb **-tat·ed; -tat·ing 1** : ORIENT **2** : to face east

or·i·fice \'ȯr-ə-fəs\ n : OPENING, MOUTH

ori·flamme \'ȯr-ə-ˌflam\ n : a brightly colored banner used as a standard or ensign in battle

orig abbr original; originally

ori·ga·mi \ˌȯr-ə-'gä-mē\ n : the art or process of Japanese paper folding

or·i·gin \'ȯr-ə-jən\ n **1** : ANCESTRY **2** : rise, beginning, or

derivation from a source; also : CAUSE **3** : the intersection of coordinate axes

¹orig·i·nal \ə-'ri-jə-nəl\ n : something from which a copy, reproduction, or translation is made : PROTOTYPE

²original adj **1** : FIRST, INITIAL **2** : not copied from something else : FRESH **3** : INVENTIVE — **orig·i·nal·i·ty** \-ˌri-jə-'na-lə-tē\ n — **orig·i·nal·ly** \-'ri-jən-əl-ē\ adv

orig·i·nate \ə-'ri-jə-ˌnāt\ vb **-nat·ed; -nat·ing 1** : to give rise to : INITIATE **2** : to come into existence : BEGIN — **orig·i·na·tor** \-ˌnā-tər\ n

ori·ole \'ōr-ē-ˌōl\ n : any of various New World birds of which the males are usu. black and yellow or black and orange

or·i·son \'ȯr-ə-sən\ n : PRAYER

or·mo·lu \'ȯr-mə-ˌlü\ n : a golden or gilded brass used for decorative purposes

¹or·na·ment \'ȯr-nə-mənt\ n : something that lends grace or beauty — **or·na·men·tal** \ˌȯr-nə-'ment-əl\ adj

²or·na·ment \-ˌment\ vb : to provide with ornament : ADORN — **or·na·men·ta·tion** \ˌȯr-nə-mən-'tā-shən\ n

or·nate \ȯr-'nāt\ adj : elaborately decorated — **or·nate·ly** adv — **or·nate·ness** n

or·nery \'ȯr-nə-rē, 'ä-nə-\ adj : having an irritable disposition

or·ni·thol·o·gy \ˌȯr-nə-'thä-lə-jē\ n, pl **-gies** : a branch of zoology dealing with birds — **or·ni·tho·log·i·cal** \-thə-'lä-ji-kəl\ adj — **or·ni·thol·o·gist** \-'thä-lə-jist\ n

oro·tund \'ȯr-ə-ˌtənd\ adj **1** : SONOROUS **2** : POMPOUS — **oro·tun·di·ty** \ȯr-ə-'tən-di-tē\ n

or·phan \'ȯr-fən\ n : a child deprived by death of one or usu. both parents — **orphan** vb

or·phan·age \'ȯr-fə-nij\ n : an institution for the care of orphans

or·tho·don·tia \ˌȯr-thə-'dän-chə, -chē-ə\ n : ORTHODONTICS

or·tho·don·tics \ˌȯr-thə-'dän-tiks\ n : a branch of dentistry concerned with the correction of faults in the arrangement and placing of the teeth — **or·tho·don·tist** \-'dän-tist\ n

or·tho·dox \'ȯr-thə-ˌdäks\ adj [MF or LL; MF orthodoxe, fr. LL orthodoxus, fr. LGk orthodoxos, fr. Gk orthos right + doxa opinion] **1** : conforming to established doctrine esp. in religion **2** : CONVENTIONAL **3** cap : of or relating to a Christian church originating in the church of the Eastern Roman Empire — **or·tho·doxy** \-ˌdäk-sē\ n

or·thog·ra·phy \ȯr-'thä-grə-fē\ n : SPELLING — **or·tho·graph·ic** \ˌȯr-thə-'gra-fik\ adj

or·tho·pe·dics \ˌȯr-thə-'pē-diks\ n sing or pl : a branch of medicine concerned with the correction or prevention of skeletal deformities — **or·tho·pe·dic** \-dik\ adj — **or·tho·pe·dist** \-dist\ n

-ory \ˌōr-ē, ə-rē\ adj suffix **1** : of, relating to, or characterized by ⟨anticipatory⟩ **2** : serving for, producing, or maintaining ⟨illusory⟩

Os symbol osmium

OS abbr **1** [L oculus sinister] left eye **2** ordinary seaman **3** out of stock

Osage \ō-'sāj\ n, pl **Osag·es** or **Osage** : a member of an American Indian people orig. of Missouri

os·cil·late \'ä-sə-ˌlāt\ vb **-lat·ed; -lat·ing 1** : to swing backward and forward like a pendulum **2** : to move or travel back and forth between two points **3** : VARY, FLUCTUATE — **os·cil·la·tion** \ˌä-sə-'lā-shən\ n — **os·cil·la·tor** \'ä-sə-ˌlā-tər\ n — **os·cil·la·to·ry** \'ä-sə-lə-ˌtōr-ē\ adj

os·cil·lo·scope \ä-'si-lə-ˌskōp\ n : an instrument in which variations in current or voltage appear as a visible wave form on a fluorescent screen

os·cu·late \'äs-kyə-ˌlāt\ vb **-lat·ed; -lat·ing** : KISS — **os·cu·la·tion** \ˌäs-kyə-'lā-shən\ n — **os·cu·la·to·ry** \'äs-kyə-lə-ˌtōr-ē\ adj

Osee \'ō-ˌzē, ō-'zā-ə\ n : HOSEA

OSHA \ˈō-shə\ *abbr* Occupational Safety and Health Administration

osier \ˈō-zhər\ *n* : any of various willows with pliable twigs used esp. in making baskets and furniture; *also* : a twig from an osier

os·mi·um \ˈäz-mē-əm\ *n* : a heavy hard brittle metallic chemical element used esp. as a catalyst and in alloys — see ELEMENT table

os·mo·sis \äz-ˈmō-səs, äs-\ *n* : movement of a solvent through a semipermeable membrane into a solution of higher concentration that tends to equalize the concentrations of the solutions on either side of the membrane — **os·mot·ic** \-ˈmä-tik\ *adj*

os·prey \ˈäs-prē, -ˌprā\ *n, pl* **ospreys** : a large brown and white fish-eating hawk

os·si·fy \ˈä-sə-ˌfī\ *vb* **-fied; -fy·ing** : to make or become hardened or set in one's ways — **os·si·fi·ca·tion** \ˌä-sə-fə-ˈkā-shən\ *n*

os·su·ary \ˈä-shə-ˌwer-ē, -syə-\ *n, pl* **-ar·ies** : a depository for the bones of the dead

os·ten·si·ble \ä-ˈsten-sə-bəl\ *adj* : shown outwardly : PROFESSED, APPARENT — **os·ten·si·bly** \-blē\ *adv*

os·ten·ta·tion \ˌäs-tən-ˈtā-shən\ *n* : pretentious or excessive display — **os·ten·ta·tious** \-shəs\ *adj* — **os·ten·ta·tious·ly** *adv*

os·teo·path \ˈäs-tē-ə-ˌpath\ *n* : a practitioner of osteopathy

os·te·op·a·thy \ˌäs-tē-ˈä-pə-thē\ *n* : a system of treating diseases emphasizing manipulation (as of joints) but not excluding other agencies (as the use of medicine and surgery) — **os·teo·path·ic** \ˌäs-tē-ə-ˈpa-thik\ *adj*

os·teo·po·ro·sis \ˌäs-tē-ō-pə-ˈrō-səs\ *n, pl* **-ro·ses** \-ˌsēz\ : a condition affecting esp. older women and characterized by fragile and porous bones

ost·mark \ˈōst-ˌmärk, ˈôst-\ *n* : the former East German mark

os·tra·cize \ˈäs-trə-ˌsīz\ *vb* **-cized; -ciz·ing** [Gk *ostrakizein* to banish by voting with potsherds, fr. *ostrakon* shell, potsherd] : to exclude from a group by common consent — **os·tra·cism** \-ˌsi-zəm\ *n*

os·trich \ˈäs-trich, ˈôs-\ *n* : a very large swift-footed flightless bird of Africa and Arabia

Os·we·go tea \ä-ˈswē-gō-\ *n* : a No. American mint with showy scarlet flowers

OT *abbr* **1** occupational therapy **2** Old Testament **3** overtime

¹**oth·er** \ˈə-thər\ *adj* **1** : being the one left; *also* : being the ones distinct from those first mentioned **2** : ALTERNATE ⟨every ~ day⟩ **3** : DIFFERENT **4** : ADDITIONAL **5** : recently past ⟨the ~ night⟩

²**other** *pron* **1** : remaining one or ones **2** : a different or additional one ⟨something or ~⟩

oth·er·wise \ˈə-thər-ˌwīz\ *adv* **1** : in a different way **2** : in different circumstances **3** : in other respects **4** : if not **5** : NOT — **otherwise** *adj*

oth·er·world \-ˌwərld\ *n* : a world beyond death or beyond present reality

oth·er·world·ly \ˌə-thər-ˈwərld-lē\ *adj* : not worldly : concerned with spiritual, intellectual, or imaginative matters

oti·ose \ˈō-shē-ˌōs, ˈō-tē-\ *adj* **1** : FUTILE **2** : IDLE **3** : USELESS

oto·lar·yn·gol·o·gy \ˌō-tō-ˌlar-ən-ˈgä-lə-jē\ *n* : a medical specialty concerned esp. with the ear, nose, and throat — **oto·lar·yn·gol·o·gist** \-jist\ *n*

oto·rhi·no·lar·yn·gol·o·gy \ˌō-tō-ˌrī-nō-ˌlar-ən-ˈgä-lə-jē\ *n* : OTOLARYNGOLOGY — **oto·rhi·no·lar·yn·gol·o·gist** \-jist\ *n*

OTS *abbr* officers' training school

Ot·ta·wa \ˈä-tə-wə, -ˌwä, -ˌwȯ\ *n, pl* **Ottawas** *or* **Ottawa** : a member of an American Indian people of Michigan and southern Ontario

ot·ter \ˈä-tər\ *n, pl* **otters** *also* **otter** : any of various web-footed fish-eating mammals with dark brown fur that are related to the weasels; *also* : the fur

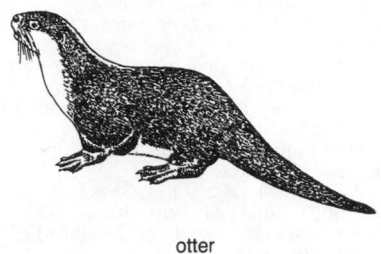

otter

ot·to·man \ˈä-tə-mən\ *n* : an upholstered seat or couch usu. without a back; *also* : an overstuffed footstool

ou·bli·ette \ˌü-blē-ˈet\ *n* [F, fr. MF, fr. *oublier* to forget, ultim. fr. L *oblivisci*] : a dungeon with an opening at the top

ought \ˈȯt\ *verbal auxiliary* — used to express moral obligation, advisability, natural expectation, or logical consequence

ou·gui·ya \ü-ˈgwē-ə, -ˈgē\ *n, pl* **ouguiya** — see MONEY table

ounce \ˈaȯns\ *n* [ME, fr. MF *unce*, fr. L *uncia* twelfth part, ounce, fr. *unus* one] **1** : a unit of avoirdupois, troy, and apothecaries' weight — see WEIGHT table **2** : FLUID OUNCE

our \är, ˈaȯr\ *adj* : of or relating to us or ourselves

ours \ˈaȯrz, ˈärz\ *pron* : that which belongs to us

our·selves \är-ˈselvz, aȯr-\ *pron* : our own selves — used reflexively, for emphasis, or in absolute constructions ⟨we pleased ~⟩ ⟨we'll do it ~⟩ ⟨we were tourists ~⟩

-ous \əs\ *adj suffix* : full of : abounding in : having : possessing the qualities of ⟨clamor*ous*⟩ ⟨poison*ous*⟩

oust \ˈaȯst\ *vb* : to eject from or deprive of property or position : EXPEL **syn** evict, dismiss, banish, deport

oust·er \ˈaȯs-tər\ *n* : EXPULSION

¹**out** \ˈaȯt\ *adv* **1** : in a direction away from the inside or center **2** : beyond control **3** : to extinction, exhaustion, or completion **4** : in or into the open **5** : so as to retire a batter or base runner; *also* : so as to be retired

²**out** *vb* : to become known ⟨the truth will ~⟩

³**out** *prep* **1** : out through ⟨looked ~ the window⟩ **2** : outward on or along ⟨drive ~ the river road⟩

⁴**out** *adj* **1** : situated outside or at a distance **2** : not in : ABSENT; *also* : not being in power **3** : not successful in reaching base **4** : not being in vogue or fashion : not up-to-date

⁵**out** *n* **1** : one who is out of office **2** : the retiring of a batter or base runner

out·age \ˈaȯ-tij\ *n* : a period or instance of interruption esp. of electricity

out–and–out *adj* : COMPLETE, THOROUGHGOING ⟨an ~ fraud⟩

out·bid \ˌaȯt-ˈbid\ *vb* : to make a higher bid than

¹**out·board** \ˈaȯt-ˌbȯrd\ *adj* **1** : situated outboard **2** : having or using an outboard motor

²**outboard** *adv* **1** : outside a ship's hull : away from the long axis of a ship **2** : in a position closer to the wing tip of an airplane

outboard motor *n* : a small internal combustion engine with propeller attached for mounting at the stern of a small boat

out·bound \ˈaȯt-ˌbaȯnd\ *adj* : outward bound ⟨~ traffic⟩

\ə\abut \ᵊ\kitten \ər\further \a\ash \ā\ace \ä\mop, mar
\aȯ\out \ch\chin \e\bet \ē\easy \g\go \i\hit \ī\ice \j\job
\ŋ\sing \ō\go \ȯ\law \ȯi\boy \th\thin \th\the \ü\loot \u̇\foot
\y\yet \zh\vision *see also* Pronunciation Symbols page

out·break \-ıbrāk\ *n* **1** : a sudden increase in activity, incidence, or numbers **2** : INSURRECTION, REVOLT

out·build·ing \-ıbil-diŋ\ *n* : a building separate from but accessory to a main house

out·burst \-ıbərst\ *n* : ERUPTION; *esp* : a violent expression of feeling

out·cast \-ıkast\ *n* : one that is cast out by society

out·class \aüt-'klas\ *vb* : SURPASS

out·come \'aüt-ıkəm\ *n* : a final consequence : RESULT

out·crop \-ıkräp\ *n* : a coming out of bedrock to the surface of the ground; *also* : the part of a rock formation that thus appears — **outcrop** *vb*

out·cry \-ıkrī\ *n* : a loud cry : CLAMOR

out·dat·ed \-ıdā-təd\ *adj* : OUTMODED

out·dis·tance \-'dis-təns\ *vb* : to go far ahead of (as in a race) : OUTSTRIP

out·do \-'dü\ *vb* **-did** \-'did\; **-done** \-'dən\; **-do·ing; -does** \-'dəz\ : to go beyond in action or performance

out·door \'aüt-ıdōr, -'dōr\ *also* **out·doors** \-ıdōrz, -'dōrz\ *adj* **1** : of or relating to the outdoors **2** : performed outdoors **3** : not enclosed (as by a roof)

¹out·doors \'aüt-ıdōrz, -'dōrz\ *adv* : in or into the open air

²outdoors *n* **1** : the open air **2** : the world away from human habitation

out·draw \aüt-'drȯ\ *vb* **-drew** \-'drü\; **-drawn** \-'drȯn\; **-draw·ing 1** : to attract a larger audience than **2** : to draw a handgun more quickly than

out·er \'aü-tər\ *adj* **1** : EXTERNAL **2** : situated farther out; *also* : being away from a center

out·er·most \-ımōst\ *adj* : farthest out

outer space *n* : SPACE 5

out·face \aüt-'fās\ *vb* **1** : to cause to waver or submit **2** : DEFY

out·field \'aüt-ıfēld\ *n* : the part of a baseball field beyond the infield and within the foul lines; *also* : players in the outfield — **out·field·er** \-ıfēl-dər\ *n*

out·fight \aüt-'fīt\ *vb* : to surpass in fighting : DEFEAT

¹out·fit \'aüt-ıfit\ *n* **1** : the equipment or apparel for a special purpose or occasion **2** : GROUP

²outfit *vb* **out·fit·ted; out·fit·ting** : EQUIP — **out·fit·ter** *n*

out·flank \aüt-'flaŋk\ *vb* : to get around the flank of (an opposing force)

out·flow \'aüt-ıflō\ *n* **1** : a flowing out **2** : something that flows out

out·fox \aüt-'fäks\ *vb* : OUTWIT

out·go \'aüt-ıgō\ *n, pl* **outgoes** : EXPENDITURES, OUTLAY

out·go·ing \-ıgō-iŋ\ *adj* **1** : going out (∼ tide) **2** : retiring from a place or position **3** : FRIENDLY

out·grow \aüt-'grō\ *vb* **-grew** \-'grü\; **-grown** \-'grōn\; **-grow·ing 1** : to grow faster than **2** : to grow too large for

out·growth \'aüt-ıgrōth\ *n* : a product of growing out : OFFSHOOT; *also* : CONSEQUENCE, RESULT

out·guess \aüt-'ges\ *vb* : OUTWIT

out·gun \-'gən\ *vb* : to surpass in firepower

out·house \'aüt-ıhaüs\ *n* : OUTBUILDING; *esp* : an outdoor toilet

out·ing \'aü-tiŋ\ *n* : a brief stay or trip in the open

out·land·ish \aüt-'lan-dish\ *adj* **1** : of foreign appearance or manner; *also* : BIZARRE **2** : remote from civilization — **out·land·ish·ly** *adv*

out·last \-'last\ *vb* : to last longer than

¹out·law \'aüt-ılȯ\ *n* **1** : a person excluded from the protection of the law **2** : a lawless person

²outlaw *vb* **1** : to deprive of the protection of the law **2** : to make illegal — **out·law·ry** \'aüt-ılȯr-ē\ *n*

out·lay \'aüt-ılā\ *n* **1** : the act of spending **2** : EXPENDITURE

out·let \'aüt-ılet, -lət\ *n* **1** : EXIT, VENT **2** : a means of release (as for an emotion) **3** : a market for a commodity **4** : a receptacle for the plug of an electrical device

¹out·line \'aüt-ılīn\ *n* **1** : a line marking the outer limits of an object or figure **2** : a drawing in which only contours are marked **3** : SUMMARY, SYNOPSIS **4** : PLAN

²outline *vb* **1** : to draw the outline of **2** : to indicate the chief features or parts of

out·live \aüt-'liv\ *vb* : to live longer than **syn** outlast, survive

out·look \'aüt-ılük\ *n* **1** : a place offering a view; *also* : VIEW **2** : STANDPOINT **3** : the prospect for the future

out·ly·ing \-ılī-iŋ\ *adj* : distant from a center or main body

out·ma·neu·ver \ıaüt-mə-'nü-vər, -'nyü-\ *vb* : to defeat by more skillful maneuvering

out·mod·ed \aüt-'mō-dəd\ *adj* **1** : no longer in style **2** : no longer acceptable or current

out·num·ber \-'nəm-bər\ *vb* : to exceed in number

out of *prep* **1** : out from within or behind (walk *out of* the room) (look *out of* the window) **2** : from a state of (wake up *out of* a deep sleep) **3** : beyond the limits of (*out of* sight) **4** : BECAUSE OF (came *out of* curiosity) **5** : FROM, WITH (built it *out of* scrap) **6** : in or into a state of loss or not having (cheated him *out of* $5000) (we're *out of* matches) **7** : from among (one *out of* four) — **out of it** : SQUARE, OLD-FASHIONED

out–of–bounds *adv or adj* : outside the prescribed boundaries or limits

out–of–date *adj* : no longer in fashion or in use : OUTMODED

out–of–door *or* **out–of–doors** *adj* : OUTDOOR

out–of–the–way *adj* **1** : UNUSUAL **2** : being off the beaten track

out·pa·tient \'aüt-ıpā-shənt\ *n* : a patient who visits a hospital or clinic for diagnosis or treatment without staying overnight

out·per·form \ıaüt-pər-'fȯrm\ *vb* : to perform better than

out·play \aüt-'plā\ *vb* : to play more skillfully than

out·point \-'pȯint\ *vb* : to win more points than

out·post \'aüt-ıpōst\ *n* **1** : a security detachment dispatched by a main body of troops to protect it from enemy surprise; *also* : a military base established (as by treaty) in a foreign country **2** : an outlying or frontier settlement

out·pour·ing \-ıpōr-iŋ\ *n* : something that pours out or is poured out

out·pull \aüt-'pül\ *vb* : OUTDRAW 1

¹out·put \'aüt-ıpüt\ *n* **1** : the amount produced (as by a machine or factory) : PRODUCTION **2** : the information produced by a computer

²output *vb* **out·put·ted** *or* **output; out·put·ting** : to produce as output

¹out·rage \'aüt-ırāj\ *n* [ME, fr. MF, excess, outrage, fr. *outre* beyond, in excess, fr. L *ultra*] **1** : a violent or shameful act **2** : INJURY, INSULT **3** : the anger or resentment aroused by an outrage

²outrage *vb* **out·raged; out·rag·ing 1** : RAPE **2** : to subject to violent injury or gross insult **3** : to arouse to extreme resentment

out·ra·geous \aüt-'rā-jəs\ *adj* : extremely offensive, insulting, or shameful : SHOCKING — **out·ra·geous·ly** *adv*

out·rank \-'raŋk\ *vb* : to rank higher than

ou·tré \ü-'trā\ *adj* [F] : violating convention or propriety : BIZARRE

¹out·reach \aüt-'rēch\ *vb* **1** : to surpass in reach **2** : to get the better of by trickery

²out·reach \'aüt-ırēch\ *n* **1** : the act of reaching out **2** : the extent of reach **3** : the extending of services beyond usual limits

out·rid·er \-ırī-dər\ *n* : a mounted attendant

out·rig·ger \-ıri-gər\ *n* **1** : a frame that extends from the side of a canoe or boat to prevent upsetting **2** : a craft equipped with an outrigger

¹out·right \aüt-'rīt\ *adv* **1** : COMPLETELY **2** : INSTANTANEOUSLY

²**out·right** \'aut-ˌrīt\ adj **1** : being exactly what is stated ⟨an ~ lie⟩ **2** : given or made without reservation or encumbrance ⟨~ sale⟩

out·run \aut-'rən\ vb **-ran** \-'ran\; **-run; -run·ning** : to run faster than; also : EXCEED

out·sell \-'sel\ vb **-sold** \-'sōld\; **-sell·ing** : to exceed in sales

out·set \'aut-ˌset\ n : BEGINNING, START

out·shine \aut-'shīn\ vb **-shone** \-'shōn\ or **-shined**; **-shin·ing 1** : to shine brighter than **2** : SURPASS

¹**out·side** \aut-ˌsīd, 'aut-ˌsīd\ n **1** : a place or region beyond an enclosure or boundary **2** : EXTERIOR **3** : the utmost limit or extent

²**outside** adj **1** : OUTER **2** : coming from without ⟨~ influences⟩ **3** : being apart from one's regular duties ⟨~ activities⟩ **4** : REMOTE ⟨an ~ chance⟩

³**outside** adv : on or to the outside

⁴**outside** prep **1** : on or to the outside of **2** : beyond the limits of **3** : EXCEPT

outside of prep **1** : OUTSIDE **2** : BESIDES

out·sid·er \aut-'sī-dər\ n : a person who does not belong to a group

out·size \'aut-ˌsīz\ also **out·sized** \-ˌsīzd\ adj : unusually large : extravagant in size or degree

out·skirts \-ˌskərts\ n pl : the outlying parts (as of a city) : BORDERS

out·smart \aut-'smärt\ vb : OUTWIT

out·sourc·ing \'aut-ˌsōr-siŋ\ n : the subcontracting of manufacturing work to outside and esp. foreign and nonunion companies

out·spend \-'spend\ vb **1** : to exceed the limits of in spending ⟨~s his income⟩ **2** : to spend more than

out·spo·ken \aut-'spō-kən\ adj : direct and open in speech or expression — **out·spo·ken·ly** adv — **out·spo·ken·ness** n

out·spread \-'spred\ vb **-spread; -spread·ing** : to spread out

out·stand·ing \-'stan-diŋ\ adj **1** : PROJECTING **2** : UNPAID; also : UNRESOLVED **3** : publicly issued and sold **4** : CONSPICUOUS; also : DISTINGUISHED — **out·stand·ing·ly** adv

out·stay \-'stā\ vb **1** : OVERSTAY **2** : to surpass in endurance

out·stretched \-'strecht\ adj : stretched out : EXTENDED

out·strip \-'strip\ vb **1** : to go faster than **2** : EXCEL, SURPASS

out·take \'aut-ˌtāk\ n : something taken out; esp : a take that is not used in an edited version of a film or videotape

out·vote \-'vōt\ vb : to defeat by a majority of votes

¹**out·ward** \'aut-wərd\ adj **1** : moving or directed toward the outside **2** : showing outwardly

²**outward** or **out·wards** \-wərdz\ adv : toward the outside

out·ward·ly \-wərd-lē\ adv : on the outside : EXTERNALLY

out·wear \aut-'war\ vb **-wore** \-'wōr\; **-worn** \-'wōrn\; **-wear·ing** : to wear longer than : OUTLAST

out·weigh \-'wā\ vb : to exceed in weight, value, or importance

out·wit \-'wit\ vb : to get the better of by superior cleverness

¹**out·work** \-'wərk\ vb : to outdo in working

²**out·work** \'aut-ˌwərk\ n : a minor defensive position outside a fortified area

out·worn \aut-'wōrn\ adj : OUTMODED

ou·zo \'ü-(ˌ)zō\ n : a colorless anise-flavored unsweetened Greek liqueur

ova pl of OVUM

oval \'ō-vəl\ adj [ML ovalis, fr. LL, of an egg, fr. L ovum] : egg-shaped; also : broadly elliptical — **oval** n

ova·ry \'ō-və-rē\ n, pl **-ries 1** : one of the usu. paired female reproductive organs producing eggs and in vertebrates sex hormones **2** : the part of a flower in which

seeds are produced — **ovar·i·an** \ō-'var-ē-ən, -'ver-\ adj

ovate \'ō-ˌvāt\ adj : egg-shaped

ova·tion \ō-'vā-shən\ n [L ovation-, ovatio, fr. ovare to exult] : an enthusiastic popular tribute

ov·en \'ə-vən\ n : a chamber (as in a stove) for baking, heating, or drying

oven·bird \-ˌbərd\ n : a large olive-green American warbler that builds its dome-shaped nest on the ground

¹**over** \'ō-vər\ adv **1** : across a barrier or intervening space **2** : across the brim ⟨boil ~⟩ **3** : so as to bring the underside up **4** : out of a vertical position **5** : beyond some quantity, limit, or norm **6** : ABOVE **7** : at an end **8** : THROUGH; also : THOROUGHLY **9** : AGAIN ⟨do it ~⟩

²**over** prep **1** : above in position, authority, or scope ⟨towered ~ her⟩ ⟨obeyed those ~ him⟩ **2** : more than ⟨cost ~ $100⟩ **3** : ON, UPON ⟨a cape ~ her shoulders⟩ **4** : along the length of ⟨~ the road⟩ **5** : through the medium of : ON ⟨spoke ~ TV⟩ **6** : all through ⟨showed me ~ the house⟩ **7** : on or to the other side or beyond ⟨jump ~ a ditch⟩ **8** : DURING ⟨~ the past 25 years⟩ **9** : on account of ⟨trouble ~ money⟩

³**over** adj **1** : UPPER, HIGHER **2** : REMAINING **3** : ENDED

over- prefix **1** : so as to exceed or surpass **2** : excessive; excessively

overabundance	overgeneralization
overabundant	overgeneralize
overactive	overgenerous
overaggressive	overgraze
overambitious	overhasty
overanxious	overheat
overbid	overindulge
overbold	overindulgence
overbuild	overindulgent
overburden	overlarge
overbuy	overlearn
overcapacity	overload
overcapitalize	overlong
overcareful	overmodest
overcautious	overnice
overcompensation	overoptimism
overconfidence	overoptimistic
overconfident	overpay
overconscientious	overpraise
overcook	overproduce
overcritical	overproduction
overcrowd	overprotect
overdecorated	overprotective
overdependence	overrate
overdetermined	overreact
overdevelop	overreaction
overdress	overrefinement
overeager	overrepresented
overeat	overripe
overeducated	oversensitive
overemphasis	oversensitiveness
overemphasize	oversimple
overenthusiastic	oversimplification
overestimate	oversimplify
overexcite	overspecialization
overexcited	overspecialize
overexert	overspend
overexertion	overstimulation
overextend	overstock
overfatigued	oversubtle
overfeed	oversupply
overfill	overtax

\ə\abut \ə\kitten \ər\further \a\ash \ā\ace \ä\mop, mar \au\out \ch\chin \e\bet \ē\easy \g\go \i\hit \ī\ice \j\job \ŋ\sing \ō\go \o\law \oi\boy \th\thin \th\the \ü\loot \u\foot \y\yet \zh\vision   see also Pronunciation Symbols page

overtired
overtrain
overuse

overvalue
overzealous

over·act \ō-vər-'akt\ *vb* : to exaggerate in acting

[1]**over·age** \ō-vər-'āj\ *adj* **1** : too old to be useful **2** : older than is normal for one's position, function, or grade

[2]**over·age** \'ō-və-rij\ *n* : SURPLUS

over·all \ō-vər-'ol\ *adj* : including everything 〈∼ expenses〉

over·alls \'ō-vər-olz\ *n pl* : trousers of strong material usu. with a piece extending up to cover the chest

over·arm \-ärm\ *adj* : done with the arm raised above the shoulder

over·awe \ō-vər-'o\ *vb* : to restrain or subdue by awe

over·bal·ance \-'ba-ləns\ *vb* **1** : OUTWEIGH **2** : to cause to lose balance

over·bear·ing \-'bar-iŋ\ *adj* : ARROGANT, DOMINEERING

over·blown \-'blōn\ *adj* **1** : PORTLY **2** : INFLATED, PRETENTIOUS

over·board \'ō-vər-bord\ *adv* **1** : over the side of a ship into the water **2** : to extremes of enthusiasm

[1]**over·cast** \'ō-vər-kast\ *adj* : clouded over : GLOOMY

[2]**overcast** *n* : COVERING; *esp* : a covering of clouds

over·charge \ō-vər-'chärj\ *vb* **1** : to charge too much **2** : to fill or load too full — **over·charge** \'ō-vər-chärj\ *n*

over·coat \'ō-vər-kōt\ *n* : a warm coat worn over indoor clothing

over·come \ō-vər-'kəm\ *vb* **-came** \-'kām\; **-come; -com·ing** **1** : CONQUER **2** : to make helpless or exhausted

over·do \ō-vər-'dü\ *vb* **-did** \-'did\; **-done** \-'dən\; **-do·ing; -does** \-'dəz\ **1** : to do too much; *also* : to tire oneself **2** : EXAGGERATE **3** : to cook too long

over·dose \'ō-vər-dōs\ *n* : too great a dose (as of medicine); *also* : a lethal or toxic amount (as of a drug) — **over·dose** \ō-vər-'dōs\ *vb*

over·draft \'ō-vər-draft, -dräft\ *n* : an overdrawing of a bank account; *also* : the sum overdrawn

over·draw \ō-vər-'dro\ *vb* **-drew** \-'drü\; **-drawn** \-'dron\; **-draw·ing** **1** : to draw checks on a bank account for more than the balance **2** : EXAGGERATE

over·drive \'ō-vər-drīv\ *n* : an automotive transmission gear that transmits to the driveshaft a speed greater than the engine speed

over·dub \ō-vər-'dəb\ *vb* : to transfer (recorded sound) onto an earlier recording for a combined effect — **over·dub** \'ō-vər-dəb\ *n*

over·due \-'dü, -'dyü\ *adj* **1** : unpaid when due; *also* : not appearing or presented on time **2** : more than ready

over·ex·pose \ō-vər-ik-'spōz\ *vb* : to expose (as film) for more time than is needed — **over·ex·po·sure** \-'spō-zhər\ *n*

[1]**over·flow** \-'flō\ *vb* **1** : INUNDATE; *also* : to pour forth in a flood **2** : to flow over the brim or top of

[2]**over·flow** \'ō-vər-flō\ *n* **1** : FLOOD; *also* : SURPLUS **2** : an outlet for surplus liquid

over·fly \ō-vər-'flī\ *vb* **-flew** \-'flü\; **-flown** \-'flōn\; **-fly·ing** : to fly over in an airplane or spacecraft — **over·flight** \'ō-vər-flīt\ *n*

over·grow \ō-vər-'grō\ *vb* **-grew** \-'grü\; **-grown** \-'grōn\; **-grow·ing** **1** : to grow over so as to cover **2** : OUTGROW **3** : to grow excessively

over·hand \'ō-vər-hand\ *adj* : made with the hand brought down from above — **overhand** *adv* — **over·hand·ed** \-han-dəd\ *adv or adj*

[1]**over·hang** \'ō-vər-haŋ, ō-vər-'haŋ\ *vb* **-hung** \-həŋ, -'həŋ\; **-hang·ing** **1** : to project over : jut out **2** : to hang over threateningly

[2]**over·hang** \'ō-vər-haŋ\ *n* : a part (as of a roof) that overhangs

over·haul \ō-vər-'hol\ *vb* **1** : to examine thoroughly and make necessary repairs and adjustments **2** : OVERTAKE

[1]**over·head** \ō-vər-'hed\ *adv* : ALOFT

[2]**over·head** \'ō-vər-hed\ *adj* : operating or lying above 〈∼ door〉

[3]**over·head** \'ō-vər-hed\ *n* : business expenses not chargeable to a particular part of the work

over·hear \ō-vər-'hir\ *vb* **-heard** \-'hərd\; **-hear·ing** : to hear without the speaker's knowledge or intention

over·joyed \ō-vər-'joid\ *adj* : filled with great joy

over·kill \'ō-vər-kil\ *n* **1** : destructive capacity greatly exceeding that required for a target **2** : a large excess

over·land \'ō-vər-land, -lənd\ *adv or adj* : by, on, or across land

over·lap \ō-vər-'lap\ *vb* **1** : to lap over **2** : to have something in common — **over·lap** \'ō-vər-lap\ *n*

over·lay \ō-vər-'lā\ *vb* **-laid** \-'lād\; **-lay·ing** : to lay or spread over or across — **over·lay** \'ō-vər-lā\ *n*

over·leap \ō-vər-'lēp\ *vb* **-leaped** *or* **-leapt** \-'lēpt, -'lept\; **-leap·ing** **1** : to leap over or across **2** : to defeat (oneself) by going too far

over·lie \ō-vər-'lī\ *vb* **-lay** \-'lā\; **-lain** \-'lān\; **-ly·ing** : to lie over or upon

[1]**over·look** \ō-vər-'luk\ *vb* **1** : INSPECT **2** : to look down on from above **3** : to fail to see **4** : IGNORE; *also* : EXCUSE **5** : SUPERINTEND

[2]**over·look** \'ō-vər-luk\ *n* : a place from which to look upon a scene below

over·lord \-lord\ *n* : a lord who has supremacy over other lords

over·ly \'ō-vər-lē\ *adv* : EXCESSIVELY

over·match \ō-vər-'mach\ *vb* : to be more than a match for : DEFEAT

over·much \-'məch\ *adj or adv* : too much

[1]**over·night** \-'nīt\ *adv* **1** : on or during the night **2** : SUDDENLY 〈became famous ∼〉

[2]**overnight** *adj* : of, lasting, or staying the night 〈∼ guests〉

over·pass \'ō-vər-pas\ *n* **1** : a crossing (as of two highways) at different levels by means of a bridge **2** : the upper level of an overpass

over·play \ō-vər-'plā\ *vb* **1** : EXAGGERATE; *also* : OVEREMPHASIZE **2** : to rely too much on the strength of

over·pop·u·la·tion \ō-vər-pä-pyə-'lā-shən\ *n* : the condition of having a population so dense as to cause a decline in population or in living conditions — **over·pop·u·la·ted** \-'pä-pyə-lā-təd\ *adj*

over·pow·er \-'pau-ər\ *vb* : to overcome by superior force

over·price \ō-vər-'prīs\ *vb* : to price too high

over·print \-'print\ *vb* : to print over with something additional — **over·print** \'ō-vər-print\ *n*

over·qual·i·fied \-'kwä-lə-fīd\ *adj* : having more education, training, or experience than a job calls for

over·reach \ō-vər-'rēch\ *vb* : to defeat (oneself) by too great an effort

over·ride \-'rīd\ *vb* **-rode** \-'rōd\; **-rid·den** \-'rid-ən\; **-rid·ing** **1** : to ride over or across **2** : to prevail over; *also* : to set aside 〈∼ a veto〉

over·rule \-'rül\ *vb* **1** : to prevail over **2** : to rule against **3** : to set aside

[1]**over·run** \-'rən\ *vb* **-ran** \-'ran\; **-run·ning** **1** : to defeat and occupy the positions of **2** : OVERSPREAD; *also* : INFEST **3** : to go beyond **4** : to flow over

[2]**over·run** \'ō-vər-rən\ *n* **1** : an act or instance of overrunning; *esp* : an exceeding of estimated costs **2** : the amount by which something overruns

over·sea \ō-vər-'sē, 'ō-vər-sē\ *adj or adv* : OVERSEAS

over·seas \ō-vər-'sēz, -sēz\ *adv or adj* : beyond or across the sea : ABROAD

over·see \ō-vər-'sē\ *vb* **-saw** \-'so\; **-seen** \-'sēn\; **-see·ing** **1** : OVERLOOK **2** : INSPECT; *also* : SUPERVISE — **over·seer** \'ō-vər-sir\ *n*

over·sell \ō-vər-'sel\ *vb* **-sold; -sel·ling** : to sell too much to or too much of

over·sexed \ˌō-vər-'sekst\ *adj* : exhibiting excessive sexual drive or interest

over·shad·ow \-'sha-dō\ *vb* **1** : to cast a shadow over **2** : to exceed in importance

over·shoe \'ō-vər-ˌshü\ *n* : a protective outer shoe; *esp* : GALOSH

over·shoot \ˌō-vər-'shüt\ *vb* **-shot** \-'shät\; **-shoot·ing 1** : to pass swiftly beyond **2** : to shoot over or beyond

over·sight \'ō-vər-ˌsīt\ *n* **1** : SUPERVISION **2** : an inadvertent omission or error

over·size \ˌō-vər-'sīz\ *or* **over·sized** \-'sīzd\ *adj* : of more than ordinary size

over·sleep \ˌō-vər-'slēp\ *vb* **-slept** \-'slept\; **-sleep·ing** : to sleep beyond the time for waking

over·spread \-'spred\ *vb* **-spread; -spread·ing** : to spread over or above

over·state \-'stāt\ *vb* : EXAGGERATE — **over·state·ment** *n*

over·stay \-'stā\ *vb* : to stay beyond the time or limits of

over·step \-'step\ *vb* : EXCEED

over·sub·scribe \-səb-'skrīb\ *vb* : to subscribe for more of than is available, asked for, or offered for sale

overt \ō-'vərt, 'ō-ˌvərt\ *adj* [ME, fr. MF *ouvert, overt,* fr. pp. of *ouvrir* to open] : not secret — **overt·ly** *adv*

over·take \ˌō-vər-'tāk\ *vb* **-took** \-'tùk\; **-tak·en** \-'tā-kən\; **-tak·ing** : to catch up with; *also* : to catch up with and pass by

over–the–counter *adj* : sold lawfully without a prescription 〈~ drugs〉

over·throw \ˌō-vər-'thrō\ *vb* **-threw** \-'thrü\; **-thrown** \-'thrōn\; **-throw·ing 1** : UPSET **2** : to bring down : DEFEAT 〈~ a government〉 **3** : to throw over or past — **over·throw** \'ō-vər-ˌthrō\ *n*

over·time \'ō-vər-ˌtīm\ *n* : time beyond a set limit; *esp* : working time in excess of a standard day or week — **overtime** *adv*

over·tone \-ˌtōn\ *n* **1** : one of the higher tones in a complex musical tone **2** : IMPLICATION, SUGGESTION

over·trick \'ō-vər-ˌtrik\ *n* : a card trick won in excess of the number bid

over·ture \'ō-vər-ˌchùr, -chər\ *n* [ME, lit., opening, fr. MF, fr. (assumed) VL *opertura,* alter. of L *apertura*] **1** : an opening offer **2** : an orchestral introduction to a musical dramatic work

over·turn \ˌō-vər-'tərn\ *vb* **1** : to turn over : UPSET **2** : INVALIDATE

over·view \'ō-vər-ˌvyü\ *n* : a general survey : SUMMARY

over·ween·ing \ˌō-vər-'wē-niŋ\ *adj* **1** : ARROGANT **2** : IMMODERATE

over·weight \'ō-vər-ˌwāt\ *n* **1** : weight above what is required or allowed **2** : bodily weight greater than normal — **overweight** *adj*

over·whelm \ˌō-vər-'hwelm\ *vb* **1** : OVERTHROW **2** : SUBMERGE **3** : to overcome completely

over·whelm·ing *adj* : EXTREME, GREAT 〈~ joy〉 — **over·whelm·ing·ly** *adv*

over·win·ter \-'win-tər\ *vb* : to survive the winter

over·work \-'wərk\ *vb* **1** : to work or cause to work too hard or long **2** : to use too much — **overwork** *n*

over·wrought \ˌō-vər-'rót\ *adj* **1** : extremely excited **2** : elaborated to excess

ovi·duct \'ō-və-ˌdəkt\ *n* : a tube that serves for the passage of eggs from an ovary

ovip·a·rous \ō-'vi-pə-rəs\ *adj* : reproducing by eggs that hatch outside the parent's body

ovoid \'ō-ˌvóid\ *or* **ovoi·dal** \ō-'vóid-ᵊl\ *adj* : egg-shaped : OVAL

ovu·la·tion \ˌäv-yə-'lā-shən, ˌōv-\ *n* : the discharge of a mature egg from the ovary — **ovu·late** \'äv-yə-ˌlāt, 'ōv-\ *vb*

ovule \'äv-yül, 'ōv-\ *n* : any of the bodies in a plant ovary that after fertilization become seeds

ovum \'ō-vəm\ *n, pl* **ova** \-və\ : EGG 2

ow \'aù\ *interj* — used esp. to express sudden pain

owe \'ō\ *vb* **owed; ow·ing 1** : to be under obligation to pay or render **2** : to be indebted to or for; *also* : to be in debt

owing to *prep* : BECAUSE OF

owl \'aùl\ *n* : any of an order of chiefly nocturnal birds of prey with a large head and eyes and strong talons — **owl·ish** *adj* — **owl·ish·ly** *adv*

owl·et \'aù-lət\ *n* : a young or small owl

¹own \'ōn\ *adj* : belonging to oneself — used as an intensive after a possessive adjective 〈her ~ car〉

²own *vb* **1** : to have or hold as property **2** : ACKNOWLEDGE; *also* : CONFESS — **own·er** *n* — **own·er·ship** *n*

³own *pron* : one or ones belonging to oneself

ox \'äks\ *n, pl* **ox·en** \'äk-sən\ *also* **ox** : any of the common large domestic cattle kept for milk, draft, and meat; *esp* : an adult castrated male ox

ox·blood \'äks-ˌbləd\ *n* : a moderate reddish brown

ox·bow \-ˌbō\ *n* **1** : a U-shaped collar worn by a draft ox **2** : a U-shaped bend in a river — **oxbow** *adj*

ox·ford \'äks-fərd\ *n* : a low shoe laced or tied over the instep

ox·i·dant \'äk-sə-dənt\ *n* : OXIDIZING AGENT — **oxidant** *adj*

ox·i·da·tion \ˌäk-sə-'dā-shən\ *n* : the act or process of oxidizing; *also* : the condition of being oxidized — **ox·i·da·tive** \'äk-sə-ˌdā-tiv\ *adj*

ox·ide \'äk-ˌsīd\ *n* : a compound of oxygen with another element or group

ox·i·dize \'äk-sə-ˌdīz\ *vb* **-dized; -diz·ing** : to combine with oxygen 〈iron rusts because it is *oxidized* by exposure to the air〉 — **ox·i·diz·er** *n*

oxidizing agent *n* : a substance (as oxygen or nitric acid) that oxidizes by taking up electrons

ox·y·gen \'äk-si-jən\ *n* [F *oxygène,* fr. Gk *oxys* acidic, lit., sharp + *-genēs* giving rise to; so called because it was once thought to be an essential element of all acids] : a colorless odorless gaseous chemical element that is found in the air, is essential to life, and is involved in combustion — see ELEMENT table

ox·y·gen·ate \'äk-si-jə-ˌnāt\ *vb* **-at·ed; -at·ing** : to impregnate, combine, or supply with oxygen — **ox·y·gen·a·tion** \ˌäk-si-jə-'nā-shən\ *n*

oxygen mask *n* : a device worn over the nose and mouth through which oxygen is supplied

oxygen tent *n* : a canopy which can be placed over a bedridden person and within which a flow of oxygen can be maintained

ox·y·mo·ron \ˌäk-sē-'mōr-ˌän\ *n* : a combination of contradictory words (as *cruel kindness*)

oys·ter \'ói-stər\ *n* : any of various marine mollusks with an irregular 2-valved shell that include commercially important edible shellfish and pearl producers — **oys·ter·ing** *n* — **oys·ter·man** \'ói-stər-mən\ *n*

oz *abbr* [obs. It *onza* (now *oncia*)] ounce; ounces

ozone \'ō-ˌzōn\ *n* **1** : a bluish gaseous reactive form of oxygen that is formed naturally in the atmosphere and is used for disinfecting, deodorizing, and bleaching **2** : pure and refreshing air

ozone layer *n* : an atmospheric layer at heights of about 25 miles (40 kilometers) with high ozone content which blocks most solar ultraviolet radiation

---

\ə\abut \ᵊ\kitten \ər\further \a\ash \ā\ace \ä\mop, mar \aù\out \ch\chin \e\bet \ē\easy \g\go \i\hit \ī\ice \j\job \ŋ\sing \ō\go \ò\law \òi\boy \th\thin \t͟h\the \ü\loot \ù\foot \y\yet \zh\vision *see also* Pronunciation Symbols page

P

¹p \\'pē\ *n*, *pl* **p's** *or* **ps** \\'pēz\ *often cap* : the 16th letter of the English alphabet

²p *abbr, often cap* **1** page **2** participle **3** past **4** pawn **5** pence; penny **6** per **7** petite **8** pint **9** pressure **10** purl

P *symbol* phosphorus

pa \\'pä, 'pȯ\ *n* : FATHER

¹Pa *abbr* **1** pascal **2** Pennsylvania

²Pa *symbol* protactinium

¹PA \\(ˌ)pē-'ā\ *n* : PHYSICIAN'S ASSISTANT

²PA *abbr* **1** Pennsylvania **2** per annum **3** power of attorney **4** press agent **5** private account **6** professional association **7** public address **8** purchasing agent

pa·'an·ga \pä-'äŋ-gə\ *n* — see MONEY table

pab·u·lum \\'pa-byə-ləm\ *n* [L, food, fodder] : usu. soft digestible food

Pac *abbr* Pacific

PAC *abbr* political action committee

¹pace \\'pās\ *n* **1** : rate of movement or progress (as in walking or working) **2** : a step in walking; *also* : a measure of length based on such a step **3** : GAIT; *esp* : a horse's gait in which the legs on the same side move together

²pace *vb* **paced; pac·ing** **1** : to go or cover at a pace or with slow steps **2** : to measure off by paces **3** : to set or regulate the pace of

³pace \\'pā-sē; 'pä-ˌkā, -ˌchā\ *prep* : contrary to the opinion of

pace·mak·er \\'pās-ˌmā-kər\ *n* **1** : one that sets the pace for another **2** : a body part (as of the heart) that serves to establish and maintain a rhythmic activity **3** : an electrical device for stimulating or steadying the heartbeat

pac·er \\'pā-sər\ *n* **1** : a horse that paces **2** : PACEMAKER

pachy·derm \\'pa-ki-ˌdərm\ *n* [F *pachyderme*, fr. Gk *pachydermos* thick-skinned, fr. *pachys* thick + *derma* skin] : any of various thick-skinned hoofed mammals (as an elephant)

pach·ys·an·dra \ˌpa-ki-'san-drə\ *n* : any of a genus of low shrubby evergreen plants used as a ground cover

pa·cif·ic \pə-'si-fik\ *adj* **1** : tending to lessen conflict **2** : CALM, PEACEFUL

pac·i·fi·er \\'pa-sə-ˌfī-ər\ *n* : one that pacifies; *esp* : a device for a baby to chew or suck on

pac·i·fism \\'pa-sə-ˌfi-zəm\ *n* : opposition to war or violence as a means of settling disputes — **pac·i·fist** \-fist\ *n or adj* — **pac·i·fis·tic** \ˌpa-sə-'fis-tik\ *adj*

pac·i·fy \\'pa-sə-ˌfī\ *vb* **-fied; -fy·ing** **1** : to allay anger or agitation in : SOOTHE **2** : SETTLE; *also* : SUBDUE — **pac·i·fi·ca·tion** \ˌpa-sə-fə-'kā-shən\ *n*

¹pack \\'pak\ *n* **1** : a compact bundle; *also* : a flexible container for carrying a bundle esp. on the back **2** : a large amount : HEAP **3** : a set of playing cards **4** : a group or band of people or animals **5** : wet absorbent material for application to the body

²pack *vb* **1** : to stow goods in for transportation **2** : to fill in or surround so as to prevent passage of air, steam, or water **3** : to put into a protective container **4** : to load with a pack ⟨∼ a mule⟩ **5** : to crowd in **6** : to make into a pack **7** : to cause to go without ceremony ⟨∼ them off to school⟩ **8** : WEAR, CARRY ⟨∼ a gun⟩

³pack *vb* : to make up fraudulently so as to secure a desired result ⟨∼ a jury⟩

¹pack·age \\'pa-kij\ *n* **1** : BUNDLE, PARCEL **2** : a group of related things offered as a whole

²package *vb* **pack·aged; pack·ag·ing** : to make into or enclose in a package

package deal *n* : an offer containing several items all or none of which must be accepted

package store *n* : a store that sells alcoholic beverages in sealed containers for consumption off the premises

pack·er \\'pa-kər\ *n* : one that packs; *esp* : a wholesale food dealer

pack·et \\'pa-kət\ *n* **1** : a small bundle or package **2** : a passenger boat carrying mail and cargo on a regular schedule

pack·horse \\'pak-ˌhȯrs\ *n* : a horse used to carry goods or supplies

pack·ing \\'pa-kiŋ\ *n* : material used to pack something

pack·ing·house \-ˌhau̇s\ *n* : an establishment for processing and packing food and esp. meat and its byproducts

pack rat *n* : a bushy-tailed rodent of the Rocky Mountain area that hoards food and miscellaneous objects

pack·sad·dle \\'pak-ˌsad-ᵊl\ *n* : a saddle for supporting loads on the back of an animal

pack·thread \-ˌthred\ *n* : strong thread for tying

pact \\'pakt\ *n* : AGREEMENT, TREATY

¹pad \\'pad\ *n* **1** : a cushioning part or thing : CUSHION **2** : the cushioned underside of the foot or toes of some mammals **3** : the floating leaf of a water plant **4** : a writing tablet **5** : LAUNCHPAD **6** : living quarters; *also* : BED

²pad *vb* **pad·ded; pad·ding** **1** : to furnish with a pad or padding **2** : to expand with needless or fraudulent matter

pad·ding *n* : the material with which something is padded

¹pad·dle \\'pad-ᵊl\ *vb* **pad·dled; pad·dling** : to move the hands and feet about in shallow water

²paddle *n* **1** : an implement with a flat blade used in propelling and steering a small craft (as a canoe) **2** : an implement used for stirring, mixing, or beating **3** : a broad board on the outer rim of a waterwheel or a paddle wheel

³paddle *vb* **pad·dled; pad·dling** **1** : to move on or through water by or as if by using a paddle **2** : to beat or stir with a paddle

paddle wheel *n* : a wheel with paddles around its outer edge used to move a boat

paddle wheeler *n* : a steam-driven vessel propelled by a paddle wheel

pad·dock \\'pa-dək\ *n* **1** : a usu. enclosed area for pasturing or exercising animals; *esp* : one where racehorses are saddled and paraded before a race **2** : an area at a racecourse where racing cars are parked

pad·dy \\'pa-dē\ *n*, *pl* **paddies** : wet land where rice is grown

paddy wagon *n* : an enclosed motortruck for carrying prisoners

pad·lock \\'pad-ˌläk\ *n* : a removable lock with a curved piece that snaps into a catch — **padlock** *vb*

pa·dre \\'pä-drā\ *n* [Sp or It or Pg, lit., father, fr. L *pater*] **1** : PRIEST **2** : a military chaplain

pae·an \\'pē-ən\ *n* : an exultant song of praise or thanksgiving

pae·di·at·ric, pae·di·a·tri·cian, pae·di·at·rics *chiefly Brit var of* PEDIATRIC, PEDIATRICIAN, PEDIATRICS

pa·gan \\'pā-gən\ *n* [ME, fr. LL *paganus*, fr. L, country dweller, fr. *pagus* country district] : HEATHEN — **pagan** *adj* — **pa·gan·ism** \-gə-ˌni-zəm\ *n*

¹page \\'pāj\ *n* : ATTENDANT; *esp* : one employed to deliver messages

²**page** *vb* **paged; pag·ing** : to summon by repeatedly calling out the name of

³**page** *n* : a single leaf (as of a book); *also* : a single side of such a leaf

⁴**page** *vb* **paged; pag·ing** : to mark or number the pages of

pag·eant \'pa-jənt\ *n* [ME *pagyn, padgeant*, lit., scene of a play, fr. ML *pagina*, perh. fr. L, page] : an elaborate spectacle, show, or procession esp. with tableaux or floats — **pag·eant·ry** \-jən-trē\ *n*

page·boy \'pāj-ˌbòi\ *n* [¹*page*] : an often shoulder-length hairdo with the ends of the hair turned smoothly under

pag·er \'pā-jər\ *n* : one that pages; *esp* : BEEPER

pag·i·nate \'pa-jə-ˌnāt\ *vb* **-nat·ed; -nat·ing** : ⁴PAGE

pag·i·na·tion \ˌpa-jə-'nā-shən\ *n* 1 : the paging of written or printed matter 2 : the number and arrangement of pages (as of a book)

pa·go·da \pə-'gō-də\ *n* : a tower with roofs curving upward at the division of each of several stories

paid *past and past part of* PAY

pail \'pāl\ *n* : a usu. cylindrical vessel with a handle — **pail·ful** \-ˌfúl\ *n*

¹**pain** \'pān\ *n* 1 : PUNISHMENT, PENALTY 2 : suffering or distress of body or mind; *also* : a basic bodily sensation marked by discomfort (as throbbing or aching) 3 *pl* : great care — **pain·ful** \-fəl\ *adj* — **pain·ful·ly** *adv* — **pain·less** *adj* — **pain·less·ly** *adv*

²**pain** *vb* : to cause or experience pain

pain·kill·er \'pān-ˌki-lər\ *n* : something (as a drug) that relieves pain — **pain·kill·ing** *adj*

pains·tak·ing \-ˌstā-kiŋ\ *adj* : taking pains : showing care — **pains·taking** *n* — **pains·tak·ing·ly** *adv*

¹**paint** \'pānt\ *vb* 1 : to apply color, pigment, or paint to 2 : to produce or portray in lines or colors on a surface; *also* : to practice the art of painting 3 : to decorate with colors 4 : to use cosmetics 5 : to describe vividly 6 : SWAB — **paint·er** *n*

²**paint** *n* 1 : something produced by painting 2 : MAKEUP 3 : a mixture of a pigment and a liquid that forms a thin adherent coating when spread on a surface; *also* : the dry pigment used in making this mixture 4 : an applied coating of paint

paint·brush \'pānt-ˌbrəsh\ *n* : a brush for applying paint

painting *n* 1 : a work (as a picture) produced by painting 2 : the art or occupation of painting

¹**pair** \'par\ *n*, *pl* **pairs** *also* **pair** [ME *paire*, fr. OF, fr. L *paria* equal things, fr. neut. pl. of *par* equal] 1 : two things of a kind designed for use together 2 : something made up of two corresponding pieces ⟨a ∼ of trousers⟩ 3 : a set of two people or animals

²**pair** *vb* 1 : to arrange in pairs 2 : to form a pair : MATCH 3 : to become associated with another

pai·sa \pī-'sä\ *n*, *pl* **paisa** *or* **pai·se** \-'sā\ — see *rupee, taka* at MONEY table

pais·ley \'pāz-lē\ *adj*, *often cap* : decorated with colorful curved abstract figures ⟨a ∼ shawl⟩

Pai·ute \'pī-ˌüt, -ˌyüt\ *n* : a member of an American Indian people orig. of Utah, Arizona, Nevada, and California

pa·ja·mas \pə-'jä-məz, -'ja-\ *n pl* : a loose suit for sleeping or lounging

Pak·i·stani \ˌpa-ki-'sta-nē, ˌpä-ki-'stä-nē\ *n* : a native or inhabitant of Pakistan — **Pak·i·stani** *adj*

pal \'pal\ *n* : a close friend

pal·ace \'pa-ləs\ *n* [ME *palais*, fr. OF, fr. L *palatium*, fr. *Palatium*, the Palatine Hill in Rome where the emperors' residences were built] 1 : the official residence of a chief of state 2 : MANSION

pal·a·din \'pa-lə-dən\ *n* 1 : a trusted military leader (as for a medieval prince) 2 : a leading champion of a cause

pa·laes·tra \pə-'les-trə\ *n*, *pl* **-trae** \-ˌ(ˌ)trē\ : a school in ancient Greece or Rome for sports (as wrestling)

pa·lan·quin \ˌpa-lən-'kēn\ *n* : an enclosed couch for one person borne on the shoulders of men by means of poles

pal·at·able \'pa-lə-tə-bəl\ *adj* : agreeable to the taste **syn** appetizing, savory, tasty, toothsome

pal·a·tal \'pa-lət-ᵊl\ *adj* 1 : of or relating to the palate 2 : pronounced with some part of the tongue near or touching the hard palate ⟨the \y\ in *yeast* and the \sh\ in *she* are ∼ sounds⟩

pal·a·tal·ize \'pa-lət-ᵊl-ˌīz\ *vb* **-ized; -iz·ing** : to pronounce as or change into a palatal sound — **pal·a·tal·i·za·tion** \ˌpa-lət-ᵊl-ə-'zā-shən\ *n*

pal·ate \'pa-lət\ *n* 1 : the roof of the mouth separating the mouth from the nasal cavity 2 : TASTE

pa·la·tial \pə-'lā-shəl\ *adj* 1 : of, relating to, or being a palace 2 : MAGNIFICENT

pa·lat·i·nate \pə-'lat-ᵊn-ət\ *n* : the territory of a palatine

¹**pal·a·tine** \'pa-lə-ˌtīn\ *adj* 1 : possessing royal privileges; *also* : of or relating to a palatine or a palatinate 2 : of or relating to a palace : PALATIAL

²**palatine** *n* 1 : a feudal lord having sovereign power within his domains 2 : a high officer of an imperial palace

pa·la·ver \pə-'la-vər, -'lä-\ *n* [Pg *palavra* word, speech, fr. LL *parabola* parable, speech] 1 : a long parley 2 : idle talk — **palaver** *vb*

¹**pale** \'pāl\ *n* 1 : a stake or picket of a fence 2 : an enclosed place; *also* : a district or territory within certain bounds or under a particular jurisdiction 3 : LIMITS, BOUNDS ⟨conduct beyond the ∼⟩

²**pale** *vb* **paled; pal·ing** : to enclose with or as if with pales : FENCE

³**pale** *adj* **pal·er; pal·est** 1 : deficient in color or intensity : WAN ⟨∼ face⟩ 2 : lacking in brightness : DIM ⟨∼ star⟩ 3 : not dark or intense in hue ⟨∼ blue⟩ — **pale·ness** *n*

⁴**pale** *vb* **paled; pal·ing** : to make or become pale

pale·face \'pāl-ˌfās\ *n* : a white person

Pa·leo·cene \'pā-lē-ə-ˌsēn\ *adj* : of, relating to, or being the earliest epoch of the Tertiary — **Paleocene** *n*

pa·le·og·ra·phy \ˌpā-lē-'ä-grə-fē\ *n* [NL *palaeographia*, fr. Gk *palaios* ancient + *graphein* to write] : the study of ancient writings and inscriptions — **pa·le·og·ra·pher** *n*

Pa·leo·lith·ic \ˌpā-lē-ə-'li-thik\ *adj* : of or relating to the earliest period of the Stone Age characterized by rough or chipped stone implements

pa·le·on·tol·o·gy \ˌpā-lē-ˌän-'tä-lə-jē\ *n* : a science dealing with the life of past geologic periods as known from fossil remains — **pa·le·on·tol·o·gist** \-ˌän-'tä-lə-jist, -ən-\ *n*

Pa·leo·zo·ic \ˌpā-lē-ə-'zō-ik\ *adj* : of, relating to, or being the era of geologic history extending from about 570 million years ago to about 245 million years ago — **Paleozoic** *n*

pal·ette \'pa-lət\ *n* : a thin often oval board that a painter holds and mixes colors on; *also* : the colors on a palette

pal·frey \'pòl-frē\ *n*, *pl* **palfreys** *archaic* : a saddle horse that is not a warhorse; *esp* : one suitable for a woman

pa·limp·sest \'pa-ləmp-ˌsest\ *n* [L *palimpsestus*, fr. Gk *palimpsēstos* scraped again] : writing material (as a parchment) used after the erasure of earlier writing

pal·in·drome \'pa-lən-ˌdrōm\ *n* : a word, verse, or sentence (as "Able was I ere I saw Elba") or a number (as 1881) that reads the same backward or forward

pal·ing \'pā-liŋ\ *n* 1 : a fence of pales 2 : material for pales 3 : PALE, PICKET

pal·i·sade \ˌpa-lə-'sād\ *n* 1 : a high fence of stakes esp. for defense 2 : a line of steep cliffs

---

\ə\abut \ᵊ\kitten \ər\further \a\ash \ā\ace \ä\mop, mar
\au̇\out \ch\chin \e\bet \ē\easy \g\go \i\hit \ī\ice \j\job
\ŋ\sing \ō\go \ò\law \òi\boy \th\thin \t̲h̲\the \ü\loot \ú\foot
\y\yet \zh\vision *see also* Pronunciation Symbols page

¹pall \'pȯl\ *vb* **1** : to lose in interest or attraction **2** : SA-TIATE, CLOY

²pall *n* **1** : a heavy cloth draped over a coffin **2** : something that produces a gloomy atmosphere

pal·la·di·um \pə-'lā-dē-əm\ *n* : a silver-white metallic chemical element used esp. as a catalyst and in alloys — see ELEMENT table

pall·bear·er \'pȯl-ˌbar-ər\ *n* : a person who attends the coffin at a funeral

¹pal·let \'pa-lət\ *n* : a small, hard, or makeshift bed

²pallet *n* : a portable platform for transporting and storing materials

pal·li·ate \'pa-lē-ˌāt\ *vb* **-at·ed; -at·ing 1** : to ease (as a disease) without curing **2** : to cover by excuses and apologies — **pal·li·a·tion** \ˌpa-lē-'ā-shən\ *n* — **pal·li·a·tive** \'pa-lē-ˌā-tiv\ *adj or n*

pal·lid \'pa-ləd\ *adj* : PALE, WAN

pal·lor \'pa-lər\ *n* : PALENESS

¹palm \'päm, 'pälm\ *n* [ME, fr. OE, fr. L *palma* palm of the hand, palm tree; fr. the resemblance of the tree's leaves to the outstretched hand] **1** : any of a family of mostly tropical trees, shrubs, or vines usu. with a tall unbranched stem topped by a crown of large leaves **2** : a symbol of victory; *also* : VICTORY

²palm *n* : the underpart of the hand between the fingers and the wrist

³palm *vb* **1** : to conceal in or with the hand ⟨∼ a card⟩ **2** : to impose by fraud

pal·mate \'pal-ˌmāt, 'päl-\ *also* **pal·mat·ed** \-ˌmā-təd\ *adj* : resembling a hand with the fingers spread

pal·met·to \pal-'me-tō\ *n, pl* **-tos** *or* **-toes** : any of several usu. small palms with fan-shaped leaves

palm·ist·ry \'pä-mə-strē, 'päl-\ *n* : the practice of reading a person's character or future from the markings on the palms — **palm·ist** \'pä-mist, 'päl-\ *n*

Palm Sunday *n* : the Sunday preceding Easter and commemorating Christ's triumphal entry into Jerusalem

palmy \'pä-mē, 'päl-\ *adj* **palm·i·er; -est 1** : abounding in or bearing palms **2** : FLOURISHING, PROSPEROUS

pal·o·mi·no \ˌpa-lə-'mē-nō\ *n, pl* **-nos** [AmerSp, fr. Sp, like a dove, fr. L *palumbinus*, fr. *palumbes*, a species of dove] : a horse with a pale cream to golden coat and cream or white mane and tail

pal·pa·ble \'pal-pə-bəl\ *adj* **1** : capable of being touched or felt : TANGIBLE **2** : OBVIOUS, PLAIN **syn** perceptible, sensible, appreciable, tangible, detectable — **pal·pa·bly** \-blē\ *adv*

pal·pate \'pal-ˌpāt\ *vb* **pal·pat·ed; pal·pat·ing** : to examine by touch esp. medically — **pal·pa·tion** \pal-'pā-shən\ *n*

pal·pi·tate \'pal-pə-ˌtāt\ *vb* **-tat·ed; -tat·ing** : to beat rapidly and strongly : THROB — **pal·pi·ta·tion** \ˌpal-pə-'tā-shən\ *n*

pal·sy \'pȯl-zē\ *n, pl* **palsies 1** : PARALYSIS **2** : a condition marked by tremor — **pal·sied** \-zēd\ *adj*

pal·ter \'pȯl-tər\ *vb* **pal·tered; pal·ter·ing 1** : to act insincerely : EQUIVOCATE **2** : HAGGLE

pal·try \'pȯl-trē\ *adj* **pal·tri·er; -est 1** : TRASHY ⟨a ∼ pamphlet⟩ **2** : MEAN, DESPICABLE ⟨a ∼ trick⟩ **3** : TRIVIAL ⟨∼ excuses⟩ **4** : MEAGER, MEASLY ⟨a ∼ sum⟩

pam *abbr* pamphlet

pam·pas \'pam-pəz, 'päm-, -pəs\ *n pl* : wide grassy So. American plains

pam·per \'pam-pər\ *vb* : to treat with excessive attention : INDULGE **syn** coddle, humor, baby, spoil

pam·phlet \'pam-flət\ *n* [ME *pamflet* unbound booklet, fr. *Pamphilus seu De Amore* Pamphilus or On Love, popular Latin love poem of the 12th cent.] : an unbound printed publication

pam·phlet·eer \ˌpam-flə-'tir\ *n* : a writer of pamphlets attacking something or urging a cause

¹pan \'pan\ *n* **1** : a usu. broad, shallow, and open container for domestic use; *also* : something resembling such

a container **2** : a basin or depression in land **3** : HARD-PAN

²pan *vb* **panned; pan·ning 1** : to wash earth or gravel in a pan in searching for gold **2** : to criticize severely

Pan *abbr* Panama

pan·a·cea \ˌpa-nə-'sē-ə\ *n* : a remedy for all ills or difficulties : CURE-ALL

pa·nache \pə-'nash, -'näsh\ *n* [MF *pennache*, ultim. fr. LL *pinnaculum* small wing] **1** : an ornamental tuft (as of feathers) esp. on a helmet **2** : dash or flamboyance in style and action

pan·a·ma \'pa-nə-ˌmä, -ˌmȯ\ *n, often cap* : a handmade hat braided from strips of the leaves from a tropical American tree

Pan·a·ma·ni·an \ˌpa-nə-'mä-nē-ən\ *n* : a native or inhabitant of Panama — **Panamanian** *adj*

pan·a·te·la \ˌpa-nə-'te-lə\ *n* [Sp, fr. AmerSp, a long thin biscuit, ultim. fr. L *panis* bread] : a long slender cigar with straight sides

pan·cake \'pan-ˌkāk\ *n* : a flat cake made of thin batter and fried on both sides

pan·chro·mat·ic \ˌpan-krō-'ma-tik\ *adj* : sensitive to all colors of visible light ⟨∼ film⟩

pan·cre·as \'paŋ-krē-əs, 'pan-\ *n* : a large compound gland of vertebrates that produces insulin and discharges enzymes into the intestine — **pan·cre·at·ic** \ˌpaŋ-krē-'a-tik, ˌpan-\ *adj*

pan·da \'pan-də\ *n* **1** : a long-tailed Himalayan mammal related to and resembling the racoon **2** : a large black and-white mammal of western China usu. classified with the bears

panda: *A* panda 1, *B* panda 2

pan·dem·ic \pan-'de-mik\ *n* : a widespread outbreak of disease — **pandemic** *adj*

pan·de·mo·ni·um \ˌpan-də-'mō-nē-əm\ *n* : a wild uproar : TUMULT

¹pan·der \'pan-dər\ *n* **1** : a go-between in love intrigues **2** : PIMP **3** : someone who caters to or exploits others' desires or weaknesses

²pander *vb* : to act as a pander

P & I *abbr* principal and interest

P & L *abbr* profit and loss

pan·dow·dy \pan-'daủ-dē\ *n, pl* **-dies** : a deep-dish apple dessert spiced, sweetened, and covered with a crust

pane \'pān\ *n* : a sheet of glass (as in a door or window)

pan·e·gy·ric \ˌpa-nə-'jir-ik\ *n* : a eulogistic oration or writing — **pan·e·gyr·ist** \-'jir-ist\ *n*

¹pan·el \'pan-ᵊl\ *n* **1** : a list of persons appointed for special duty ⟨a jury ∼⟩; *also* : a group of people taking part in a discussion or quiz program **2** : a section of something (as a wall or door) often sunk below the level of the frame; *also* : a flat piece of construction material **3** : a flat piece of wood on which a picture is painted **4** : a mount for controls or dials

²**panel** *vb* **-eled** *or* **-elled; -el·ing** *or* **-el·ling** : to decorate with panels

paneling *n* : decorative panels

pan·el·ist \'pan-ᵊl-ist\ *n* : a member of a discussion or quiz panel

panel truck *n* : a small motortruck with a fully enclosed body

pang \'paŋ\ *n* : a sudden sharp spasm (as of pain) or attack (as of remorse)

¹**pan·han·dle** \'pan-₁hand-ᵊl\ *n* : a narrow projection of a larger territory (as a state) ⟨the Texas ∼⟩

²**panhandle** *vb* **-dled; -dling** : to ask for money on the street — **pan·han·dler** *n*

¹**pan·ic** \'pa-nik\ *n* : a sudden overpowering fright **syn** terror, consternation, dismay, alarm, dread, fear — **pan·icky** \-ni-kē\ *adj*

²**panic** *vb* **pan·icked** \-nikt\; **pan·ick·ing** : to affect or be affected with panic

pan·i·cle \'pa-ni-kəl\ *n* : a branched flower cluster (as of a lilac) in which each branch from the main stem has one or more flowers

pan·jan·drum \pan-'jan-drəm\ *n, pl* **-drums** *also* **-dra** \-drə\ : a powerful personage or pretentious official

pan·nier *also* **pan·ier** \'pan-yər\ *n* : a large basket esp. for bearing on the back

pan·o·ply \'pa-nə-plē\ *n, pl* **-plies 1** : a full suit of armor **2** : a protective covering **3** : an impressive array

pan·ora·ma \₁pa-nə-'ra-mə, -'rä-\ *n* **1** : a picture unrolled before one's eyes **2** : a complete view in every direction — **pan·oram·ic** \-'ra-mik\ *adj*

pan out *vb* : TURN OUT; *esp* : SUCCEED

pan·sy \'pan-zē\ *n, pl* **pansies** [ME *pensee*, fr. MF *pensée*, fr. *pensée* thought, fr. *penser* to think, fr. L *pensare* to ponder] : a low-growing garden herb related to the violet; *also* : its showy flower

¹**pant** \'pant\ *vb* [ME, fr. MF *pantaisier*, fr. (assumed) VL *phantasiare* to have hallucinations, fr. Gk *phantasioun*, fr. *phantasia* appearance, imagination] **1** : to breathe in a labored manner **2** : YEARN **3** : THROB

²**pant** *n* : a panting breath or sound

³**pant** *n* **1** : an outer garment covering each leg separately and usu. extending from the waist to the ankle — usu. used in pl. **2** *pl* : PANTIE

pan·ta·loons \₁pan-tə-'lünz\ *n pl* **1** : close-fitting trousers of the 19th century usu. having straps passing under the instep **2** : loose-fitting usu. shorter than ankle-length trousers

pan·the·ism \'pan-thē-₁i-zəm\ *n* : a doctrine that equates God with the forces and laws of the universe — **pan·the·ist** \-ist\ *n* — **pan·the·is·tic** \₁pan-thē-'is-tik\ *adj*

pan·the·on \'pan-thē-₁än, -ᵊn\ *n* **1** : a temple dedicated to all the gods; *also* : the gods of a people **2** : a group of illustrious people

pan·ther \'pan-thər\ *n, pl* **panthers** *also* **panther 1** : LEOPARD; *esp* : a black one **2** : COUGAR **3** : JAGUAR

pant·ie *or* **panty** \'pan-tē\ *n, pl* **pant·ies** : a woman's or child's short underpants — usu. used in pl.

pan·to·mime \'pan-tə-₁mīm\ *n* **1** : a play in which the actors use no words **2** : expression of something by bodily or facial movements only — **pantomime** *vb* — **pan·to·mim·ic** \₁pan-tə-'mi-mik\ *adj*

pan·try \'pan-trē\ *n, pl* **pantries** : a storage room for food or dishes

pant·suit \'pant-₁süt\ *n* : a woman's outfit consisting usu. of a long jacket and pants of the same material

panty hose *n pl* : a one-piece undergarment for women consisting of hosiery combined with a pantie

panty·waist \'pan-tē-₁wāst\ *n* : SISSY

pap \'pap\ *n* : soft food for infants or invalids

pa·pa \'pä-pə\ *n* : FATHER

pa·pa·cy \'pā-pə-sē\ *n, pl* **-cies 1** : the office of pope **2** : a succession of popes **3** : the term of a pope's reign **4** *cap* : the system of government of the Roman Catholic Church

pa·pa·in \pə-'pī-ən, -'pī-ən\ *n* : an enzyme in papaya juice used esp. as a meat tenderizer and in medicine

pa·pal \'pā-pəl\ *adj* : of or relating to the pope or to the Roman Catholic Church

pa·paw *n* **1** \pə-'pȯ\ : PAPAYA **2** \'pä-₁pȯ\ : a No. American tree with yellow edible fruit; *also* : its fruit

pa·pa·ya \pə-'pī-ə\ *n* : a tropical American tree with large yellow black-seeded edible fruit; *also* : its fruit

pa·per \'pā-pər\ *n* [ME *papir*, fr. MF *papier*, fr. L *papyrus* papyrus, paper, fr. Gk *papyros* papyrus] **1** : a pliable substance made usu. of vegetable matter and used to write or print on, to wrap things in, or to cover walls; *also* : a single sheet of this substance **2** : a printed or written document **3** : NEWSPAPER **4** : WALLPAPER — **paper** *adj or vb* — **pa·pery** \'pā-pə-rē\ *adj*

pa·per·back \-₁bak\ *n* : a paper-covered book

pa·per·board \-₁bȯrd\ *n* : a material made from cellulose fiber (as wood pulp) like paper but usu. thicker

pa·per·hang·er \'pā-pər-₁haŋ-ər\ *n* : one that applies wallpaper — **pa·per·hang·ing** *n*

pa·per·weight \-₁wāt\ *n* : an object used to hold down loose papers by its weight

pa·pier–mâ·ché \₁pā-pər-mə-'shā, ₁pa-₁pyä-mə-, -ma-\ *n* [F, lit., chewed paper] : a molding material of wastepaper and additives (as glue) — **papier–mâché** *adj*

pa·pil·la \pə-'pi-lə\ *n, pl* **-lae** \-(₁)lē, -₁lī\ [L, nipple] : a small projecting bodily part (as one of the nubs on the surface of the tongue) that resembles a tiny nipple in form — **pap·il·lary** \'pa-pə-₁ler-ē, pə-'pi-lə-rē\ *adj*

pa·poose \pa-'püs, pə-\ *n* : a young child of No. American Indian parents

pa·pri·ka \pə-'prē-kə, pa-\ *n* [Hung] : a mild red spice made from the fruit of various cultivated sweet peppers

Pap smear \'pap-\ *n* : a method for the early detection of cancer esp. of the uterine cervix

Pap test *n* : PAP SMEAR

pap·ule \'pa-pyül\ *n* : a small solid usu. conical lesion of the skin — **pap·u·lar** \-pyə-lər\ *adj*

pa·py·rus \pə-'pī-rəs\ *n, pl* **-rus·es** *or* **-ri** \-(₁)rē, -₁rī\ **1** : a tall grassy sedge of the Nile valley **2** : paper made from papyrus pith

¹**par** \'pär\ *n* **1** : a stated value (as of a security) **2** : a common level : EQUALITY **3** : an accepted standard or normal condition **4** : the score standard set for each hole of a golf course — **par** *adj*

²**par** *abbr* **1** paragraph **2** parallel **3** parish

pa·ra \'pär-ə\ *n, pl* **paras** *or* **para** — see *dinar* at MONEY table

par·a·ble \'par-ə-bəl\ *n* : a simple story told to illustrate a moral truth

pa·rab·o·la \pə-'ra-bə-lə\ *n* : a plane curve formed by the intersection of a cone with a plane parallel to a straight line in its surface — **par·a·bol·ic** \₁par-ə-'bä-lik\ *adj*

para·chute \'par-ə-₁shüt\ *n* [F, fr. *para-* (as in *parasol*) + *chute* fall] : a device for slowing the descent of a person or object through the air that consists of a usu. hemispherical canopy beneath which the person or object is suspended — **parachute** *vb* — **par·a·chut·ist** \-'shü-tist\ *n*

¹**pa·rade** \pə-'rād\ *n* **1** : a pompous display : EXHIBITION **2** : MARCH, PROCESSION; *esp* : a ceremonial formation and march **3** : a place for strolling

²**parade** *vb* **pa·rad·ed; pa·rad·ing 1** : to march in a pa-

---

\ə\abut \ᵊ\kitten \ər\further \a\ash \ā\ace \ä\mop, mar
\au̇\out \ch\chin \e\bet \ē\easy \g\go \i\hit \ī\ice \j\job
\ŋ\sing \ō\go \ȯ\law \ȯi\boy \th\thin \t̲h̲\the \ü\loot \u̇\foot
\y\yet \zh\vision *see also* Pronunciation Symbols page

rade **2** : PROMENADE **3** : SHOW OFF **4** : MASQUERADE

par·a·digm \'par-ə-ˌdīm, -ˌdim\ *n* **1** : MODEL, PATTERN **2** : a systematic inflection of a verb or noun showing a complete conjugation or declension — **par·a·dig·mat·ic** \ˌpar-ə-dig-'ma-tik\ *adj*

par·a·dise \'par-ə-ˌdīs, -ˌdīz\ *n* [ME *paradis*, fr. OF, fr. LL *paradisus*, fr. Gk *paradeisos*, lit., enclosed park, of Iranian origin] **1** : HEAVEN **2** : a place or state of bliss **par·a·di·si·a·cal** \ˌpar-ə-də-'sī-ə-kəl\ *or* **par·a·dis·i·ac** \-'di-zē-ˌak, -sē-\ *adj* : of, relating to, or resembling paradise

par·a·dox \'par-ə-ˌdäks\ *n* : a statement that seems contrary to common sense and yet is perhaps true — **par·a·dox·i·cal** \ˌpar-ə-'däk-si-kəl\ *adj* — **par·a·dox·i·cal·ly** \-k(ə-)lē\ *adv*

par·af·fin \'par-ə-fən\ *n* : a waxy substance used esp. for making candles and sealing foods

par·a·gon \'par-ə-ˌgän, -gən\ *n* : a model of perfection : PATTERN

¹**para·graph** \'par-ə-ˌgraf\ *n* : a subdivision of a written composition that deals with one point or gives the words of one speaker; *also* : a character (as ¶) marking the beginning of a paragraph

²**paragraph** *vb* : to divide into paragraphs

Par·a·guay·an \ˌpar-ə-'gwī-ən, -'gwä-\ *n* : a native or inhabitant of Paraguay — **Paraguayan** *adj*

par·a·keet \'par-ə-ˌkēt\ *n* : any of numerous usu. small slender parrots with a long graduated tail

para·le·gal \ˌpar-ə-'lē-gəl\ *adj* : of, relating to, or being a paraprofessional who assists a lawyer — **paralegal** *n*

Par·a·li·pom·e·non \ˌpar-ə-lə-'pä-mə-ˌnän\ *n* : CHRONICLES

par·al·lax \'par-ə-ˌlaks\ *n* : the difference in apparent direction of an object as seen from two different points

¹**par·al·lel** \'par-ə-ˌlel\ *adj* [L *parallelus*, fr. Gk *parallēlos*, fr. *para* beside + *allēlōn*, of one another, fr. *allos* ... *allos* one ... another, fr. *allos* other] **1** : lying or moving in the same direction but always the same distance apart **2** : similar in essential parts — **par·al·lel·ism** \-ˌle-ˌli-zəm\ *n*

²**parallel** *n* **1** : a parallel line, curve, or surface **2** : one of the imaginary circles on the earth's surface that parallel the equator and mark the latitude **3** : something essentially similar to another **4** : SIMILARITY, LIKENESS

³**parallel** *vb* **1** : COMPARE **2** : to correspond to **3** : to extend in a parallel direction with

par·al·lel·o·gram \ˌpar-ə-'le-lə-ˌgram\ *n* : a 4-sided geometric figure with opposite sides equal and parallel

parallelogram

par·a·lyse *Brit var of* PARALYZE

pa·ral·y·sis \pə-'ra-lə-səs\ *n, pl* **-y·ses** \-ˌsēz\ : loss of function and esp. of feeling or the power of voluntary motion — **par·a·lyt·ic** \ˌpar-ə-'li-tik\ *adj or n*

par·a·lyze \'par-ə-ˌlīz\ *vb* **-lyzed; -lyz·ing 1** : to affect with paralysis **2** : to make powerless or inactive — **par·a·lyz·ing·ly** *adv*

par·a·me·cium \ˌpar-ə-'mē-shəm, -shē-əm, -sē-əm\ *n, pl* **-cia** \-shə, -shē-ə, -sē-ə\ *also* **-ci·ums** : any of a genus of slipper-shaped protozoans that move by cilia

para·med·ic \ˌpar-ə-'me-dik\ *also* **para·med·i·cal** \-di-**

kəl\ *n* **1** : a person who assists a physician in a paramedical capacity **2** : a specially trained medical technician licensed to provide a wide range of emergency services before or during transportation to a hospital

para·med·i·cal \ˌpar-ə-'me-di-kəl\ *also* **para·med·ic** \-'me-dik\ *adj* : concerned with supplementing the work of trained medical professionals

pa·ram·e·ter \pə-'ra-mə-tər\ *n* **1** : a quantity whose value characterizes a statistical population or a member of a system (as a family of curves) **2** : a physical property whose value determines the characteristics or behavior of a system **3** : a characteristic element : FACTOR — **para·met·ric** \ˌpar-ə-'me-trik\ *adj*

para·mil·i·tary \ˌpar-ə-'mi-lə-ˌter-ē\ *adj* : formed on a military pattern esp. as an auxiliary military force

par·a·mount \'par-ə-ˌmaůnt\ *adj* : superior to all others : SUPREME **syn** preponderant, predominant, dominant, chief, sovereign

par·amour \'par-ə-ˌmùr\ *n* : an illicit lover

para·noia \ˌpar-ə-'nȯi-ə\ *n* : a psychosis marked by delusions and irrational suspicion usu. without hallucinations — **par·a·noid** \'par-ə-ˌnȯid\ *adj or n*

par·a·pet \'par-ə-pət, -ˌpet\ *n* **1** : a protecting rampart **2** : a low wall or railing (as at the edge of a bridge)

par·a·pher·na·lia \ˌpar-ə-fə-'nāl-yə, -fər-\ *n sing or pl* **1** : personal belongings **2** : EQUIPMENT, APPARATUS

para·phrase \'par-ə-ˌfrāz\ *n* : a restatement of a text giving the meaning in different words — **paraphrase** *vb*

para·ple·gia \ˌpar-ə-'plē-jə, -jē-ə\ *n* : paralysis of the lower trunk and legs — **para·ple·gic** \-jik\ *adj or n*

para·pro·fes·sion·al \-prə-'fe-shə-nəl\ *n* : a trained aide who assists a professional — **paraprofessional** *adj*

para·psy·chol·o·gy \ˌpar-ə-sī-'kä-lə-jē\ *n* : a field of study concerned with investigating telepathy and related subjects — **para·psy·chol·o·gist** \-jist\ *n*

par·a·site \'par-ə-ˌsīt\ *n* [MF, fr. L *parasitus*, fr. Gk *parasitos*, fr. *para-* beside + *sitos* grain, food] **1** : a plant or animal living in, with, or on another organism usu. to its harm **2** : one depending on another and not making adequate return — **par·a·sit·ic** \ˌpar-ə-'si-tik\ *adj* — **par·a·sit·ism** \'par-ə-sə-ˌti-zəm, -ˌsī-ˌti-\ *n* — **par·a·sit·ize** \-sə-ˌtīz\ *vb*

par·a·si·tol·o·gy \ˌpar-ə-sə-'tä-lə-jē\ *n* : a branch of biology dealing with parasites and parasitism esp. among animals — **par·a·si·tol·o·gist** \-jist\ *n*

para·sol \'par-ə-ˌsȯl\ *n* [F, fr. It *parasole*, fr. *parare* to shield + *sole* sun, fr. L *sol*] : a lightweight umbrella used as a shield against the sun

para·sym·pa·thet·ic nervous system \ˌpar-ə-ˌsim-pə-'the-tik-\ *n* : the part of the autonomic nervous system that tends to induce secretion, to increase the tone and contractility of smooth muscle, and to slow heart rate

para·thi·on \ˌpar-ə-'thī-ən, -ˌän\ *n* : an extremely toxic insecticide

para·thy·roid \-'thī-ˌrȯid\ *n* : PARATHYROID GLAND — **parathyroid** *adj*

parathyroid gland *n* : any of usu. four small endocrine glands adjacent to or embedded in the thyroid gland that produce a hormone (**parathyroid hormone**) concerned with calcium and phosphorus metabolism

para·troop·er \'par-ə-ˌtrü-pər\ *n* : a member of the paratroops

para·troops \-ˌtrüps\ *n pl* : troops trained to parachute from an airplane

para·ty·phoid \ˌpar-ə-'tī-ˌfȯid\ *n* : a bacterial food poisoning resembling typhoid fever

par·boil \'pär-ˌbȯil\ *vb* : to boil briefly

¹**par·cel** \'pär-səl\ *n* **1** : a tract or plot of land **2** : COLLECTION, LOT **3** : a wrapped bundle : PACKAGE

²**parcel** *vb* **-celed** *or* **-celled; -cel·ing** *or* **-cel·ling** : to divide into portions

parcel post *n* **1** : a mail service handling parcels **2** : packages handled by parcel post

parch \\'pärch\\ *vb* **1** : to toast under dry heat **2** : to shrivel with heat

parch·ment \\'pärch-mənt\\ *n* : the skin of an animal prepared for writing on; *also* : a writing on such material

pard \\'pärd\\ *n* : LEOPARD

¹par·don \\'pärd-ᵊn\\ *n* : excuse of an offense without penalty; *esp* : an official release from legal punishment

²pardon *vb* : to free from penalty : EXCUSE, FORGIVE — **par·don·able** \\'pärd-ᵊn-ə-bəl\\ *adj*

par·don·er \\'pärd-ᵊn-ər\\ *n* **1** : a medieval preacher delegated to raise money for religious works by soliciting offerings and granting indulgences **2** : one that pardons

pare \\'par\\ *vb* **pared; par·ing 1** : to trim off an outside part (as the skin or rind) of **2** : to reduce as if by paring ⟨∼ expenses⟩ — **par·er** *n*

par·e·gor·ic \\par-ə-'gȯr-ik\\ *n* : an alcoholic preparation of opium and camphor used esp. to relieve pain

par·ent \\'par-ənt\\ *n* **1** : one that begets or brings forth offspring; *esp* : FATHER, MOTHER **2** : one who brings up and cares for another **3** : SOURCE, ORIGIN — **par·ent·age** \\-ən-tij\\ *n* — **pa·ren·tal** \\pə-'rent-ᵊl\\ *adj* — **par·ent·hood** *n*

pa·ren·the·sis \\pə-'ren-thə-səs\\ *n, pl* **-the·ses** \\-ₐsēz\\ **1** : a word, phrase, or sentence inserted in a passage to explain or modify the thought **2** : one of a pair of punctuation marks ( ) used esp. to enclose parenthetic matter — **par·en·thet·ic** \\par-ən-'the-tik\\ *or* **par·en·thet·i·cal** \\-ti-kəl\\ *adj* — **par·en·thet·i·cal·ly** \\-k(ə-)lē\\ *adv*

pa·ren·the·size \\pə-'ren-thə-ₐsīz\\ *vb* **-sized; -siz·ing** : to make a parenthesis of

par·ent·ing \\'par-ən-tiŋ, 'per-\\ *n* : the raising of a child by its parents

pa·re·sis \\pə-'rē-səs, 'par-ə-\\ *n, pl* **pa·re·ses** \\-ₐsēz\\ : a usu. incomplete paralysis; *also* : insanity caused by syphilitic alteration of the brain that leads to dementia and paralysis

par ex·cel·lence \\par-ₐek-sə-'lä⁽n⁾s\\ *adj* [F, lit., by excellence] : being the best of a kind : PREEMINENT

par·fait \\pär-'fā\\ *n* [F, lit., something perfect] : a cold dessert made of layers of fruit, syrup, ice cream, and whipped cream

pa·ri·ah \\pə-'rī-ə\\ *n* : OUTCAST

pa·ri·etal \\pə-'rī-ət-ᵊl\\ *adj* **1** : of, relating to, or forming the walls of an anatomical structure **2** : of or relating to college living or its regulation

pari–mu·tu·el \\par-i-'myü-chə-wəl\\ *n* : a betting system in which winners share the total stakes minus a percentage for the management

par·ing \\'par-iŋ\\ *n* : a pared-off piece

pa·ri pas·su \\par-i-'pa-sü\\ *adv or adj* [L, with equal step] : at an equal rate or pace

par·ish \\'par-ish\\ *n* **1** : a church district in the care of one pastor; *also* : the residents of such an area **2** : a local church community **3** : a civil division of the state of Louisiana : COUNTY

pa·rish·io·ner \\pə-'ri-shə-nər\\ *n* : a member or resident of a parish

par·i·ty \\'par-ə-tē\\ *n, pl* **-ties** : EQUALITY, EQUIVALENCE

¹park \\'pärk\\ *n* **1** : a tract of ground kept as a game preserve or recreation area **2** : a place where vehicles (as automobiles) are parked **3** : an enclosed stadium used esp. for ball games

²park *vb* **1** : to leave a vehicle temporarily (as in a parking lot or garage) **2** : to set and leave temporarily

par·ka \\'pär-kə\\ *n* : a very warm jacket with a hood

Par·kin·son's disease \\'pär-kən-sənz-\\ *n* : a chronic progressive nervous disease chiefly of later life marked by tremor and weakness of resting muscles and by a shuffling gait

Parkinson's law *n* : an observation in office organization: work expands so as to fill the time available for its completion

park·way \\'pärk-ₐwā\\ *n* : a broad landscaped thoroughfare

par·lance \\'pär-ləns\\ *n* **1** : SPEECH **2** : manner of speaking ⟨military ∼⟩

¹par·lay \\'pär-ₐlā, -lē\\ *vb* : to increase or change into something of much greater value

²parlay *n* : a series of bets in which the original stake plus its winnings are risked on successive wagers

par·ley \\'pär-lē\\ *n, pl* **parleys** : a conference usu. over matters in dispute : DISCUSSION — **parley** *vb*

par·lia·ment \\'pär-lə-mənt\\ *n* [ME, fr. OF *parlement*, fr. *parler* to speak, fr. ML *parabolare*, fr. LL *parabola* speech, parable] **1** : a formal governmental conference **2** *cap* : an assembly that constitutes the supreme legislative body of a country (as the United Kingdom) — **par·lia·men·ta·ry** \\ₐpär-lə-'men-tə-rē\\ *adj*

par·lia·men·tar·i·an \\ₐpär-lə-ₐmen-'ter-ē-ən\\ *n* **1** *often cap* : an adherent of the parliament during the English Civil War **2** : an expert in parliamentary procedure

par·lor \\'pär-lər\\ *n* **1** : a room for conversation or the reception of guests **2** : a place of business ⟨beauty ∼⟩

par·lour \\'pär-lər\\ *chiefly Brit var of* PARLOR

par·lous \\'pär-ləs\\ *adj* : full of danger or risk : PRECARIOUS — **par·lous·ly** *adv*

Par·me·san \\'pär-mə-ₐzän, -ₐzhän, -ₐzan\\ *n* : a hard dry cheese with a sharp flavor

par·mi·gia·na \\ₐpär-mi-'jä-nə, ₐpär-mi-'zhän\\ *or* **par·mi·gia·no** \\-'jä-(ₐ)nō\\ *adj* : made or covered with Parmesan cheese ⟨veal ∼⟩

pa·ro·chi·al \\pə-'rō-kē-əl\\ *adj* **1** : of or relating to a church parish **2** : limited in scope : NARROW, PROVINCIAL — **pa·ro·chi·al·ism** \\-ə-ₐli-zəm\\ *n*

parochial school *n* : a school maintained by a religious body

par·o·dy \\'par-ə-dē\\ *n, pl* **-dies** [L *parodia*, fr. Gk *parōidia*, fr. *para-* beside + *aidein* to sing] : a humorous or satirical imitation — **parody** *vb*

pa·role \\pə-'rōl\\ *n* : a conditional release of a prisoner whose sentence has not expired — **parole** *vb* — **pa·rol·ee** \\-ₐrō-'lē, -'rō-ₐlē\\ *n*

par·ox·ysm \\'par-ək-ₐsi-zəm, pə-'räk-\\ *n* : a sudden sharp attack (as of pain or coughing) : CONVULSION — **par·ox·ys·mal** \\ₐpar-ək-'siz-məl, pə-ₐräk-\\ *adj*

par·quet \\'pär-ₐkā, pär-'kā\\ *n* [F] **1** : a flooring of parquetry **2** : the lower floor of a theater; *esp* : the forward part of the orchestra

par·que·try \\'pär-kə-trē\\ *n, pl* **-tries** : fine woodwork inlaid in patterns

par·ra·keet *var of* PARAKEET

par·ri·cide \\'par-ə-ₐsīd\\ *n* **1** : one that murders a parent or a close relative **2** : the act of a parricide

par·rot \\'par-ət\\ *n* : any of numerous bright-colored tropical birds that have a stout hooked bill

parrot fever *n* : an infectious disease of birds marked by diarrhea and wasting and transmissible to humans

par·ry \\'par-ē\\ *vb* **par·ried; par·ry·ing 1** : to ward off a weapon or blow **2** : to evade esp. by an adroit answer — **parry** *n*

parse \\'pärs *also* 'pärz\\ *vb* **parsed; pars·ing** : to give a grammatical description of a word or a group of words

par·sec \\'pär-ₐsek\\ *n* : a unit of measure for interstellar space equal to 3.26 light-years

par·si·mo·ny \\'pär-sə-ₐmō-nē\\ *n* : extreme or excessive frugality — **par·si·mo·ni·ous** \\ₐpär-sə-'mō-nē-əs\\ *adj* — **par·si·mo·ni·ous·ly** *adv*

pars·ley \\'pär-slē\\ *n* : a garden plant related to the carrot that has finely divided leaves used as a seasoning or garnish

---

pars·nip \'pär-snəp\ *n* : a garden plant related to the carrot that has a long edible usu. whitish root; *also* : this root

par·son \'pärs-ᵊn\ *n* [ME *persone,* fr. OF, fr. ML *persona,* lit., person, fr. L] : MINISTER 2, PASTOR

par·son·age \'pärs-ᵊn-ij\ *n* : a house provided by a church for its pastor

¹**part** \'pärt\ *n* 1 : a division or portion of a whole 2 : the melody or score for a particular voice or instrument 3 : a spare piece for a machine 4 : DUTY, FUNCTION 5 : one of the sides in a dispute 6 : ROLE; *also* : an actor's lines in a play 7 *pl* : TALENTS, ABILITY 8 : the line where one's hair divides (as in combing)

²**part** *vb* 1 : to take leave of someone 2 : to divide or break into parts : SEPARATE 3 : to go away : DEPART; *also* : DIE 4 : to give up possession ⟨∼ed with her jewels⟩ 5 : APPORTION, SHARE

³**part** *abbr* 1 participial; participle 2 particular

par·take \pär-'tāk\ *vb* **-took** \-'tůk\; **-tak·en** \-'tā-kən\; **-tak·ing** 1 : to have a share or part 2 : to take a portion (as of food) — **par·tak·er** *n*

par·terre \pär-'ter\ *n* [F, fr. MF, fr. *par terre* on the ground] 1 : an ornamental garden with paths between the flower beds 2 : the part of a theater floor behind the orchestra

par·the·no·gen·e·sis \ˌpär-thə-nō-'je-nə-səs\ *n* [NL, fr. Gk *parthenos* virgin + L *genesis* genesis] : development of a new individual from an unfertilized usu. female sex cell — **par·the·no·ge·net·ic** \-jə-'ne-tik\ *adj*

par·tial \'pär-shəl\ *adj* 1 : not total or general : affecting a part only 2 : favoring one party over the other : BIASED 3 : markedly fond — used with *to* — **par·tial·i·ty** \ˌpär-shē-'a-lə-tē\ *n* — **par·tial·ly** *adv*

par·tic·i·pate \pär-'ti-sə-ˌpāt\ *vb* **-pat·ed; -pat·ing** 1 : to take part in something ⟨∼ in a game⟩ 2 : SHARE — **par·tic·i·pant** \-pənt\ *adj or n* — **par·tic·i·pa·tion** \-ˌti-sə-'pā-shən\ *n* — **par·tic·i·pa·tor** \-'ti-sə-ˌpā-tər\ *n* — **par·tic·i·pa·to·ry** \-'ti-sə-pə-ˌtȯr-ē\ *adj*

par·ti·ci·ple \'pär-tə-ˌsi-pəl\ *n* : a word having the characteristics of both verb and adjective — **par·ti·cip·i·al** \ˌpär-tə-'si-pē-əl\ *adj*

par·ti·cle \'pär-ti-kəl\ *n* 1 : a very small bit of matter 2 : a unit of speech (as an article, preposition, or conjunction) expressing some general aspect of meaning or some connective or limiting relation

par·ti·cle·board \-ˌbȯrd\ *n* : a board made of very small pieces of wood bonded together

par·ti–col·or \ˌpär-tē-ˈkə-lər\ *or* **par·ti–col·ored** \-lərd\ *adj* : showing different colors or tints; *esp* : having one main color broken by patches of one or more other colors

¹**par·tic·u·lar** \pər-'ti-kyə-lər\ *adj* 1 : of or relating to a specific person or thing ⟨the laws of a ∼ state⟩ 2 : DISTINCTIVE, SPECIAL ⟨the ∼ point of his talk⟩ 3 : SEPARATE, INDIVIDUAL ⟨each ∼ hair⟩ 4 : attentive to details : PRECISE 5 : hard to please : EXACTING — **par·tic·u·lar·i·ty** \-ˌti-kyə-'lar-ə-tē\ *n* — **par·tic·u·lar·ly** *adv*

²**particular** *n* : an individual fact or detail

par·tic·u·lar·ize \pər-'ti-kyə-lə-ˌrīz\ *vb* **-ized; -iz·ing** 1 : to state in detail : SPECIFY 2 : to go into details

par·tic·u·late \pər-'ti-kyə-lət, pär-, -ˌlāt\ *adj* : relating to or existing as minute separate particles — **particulate** *n*

¹**part·ing** *n* : a place or point of separation or divergence

²**parting** *adj* : given, taken, or performed at parting ⟨a ∼ kiss⟩

par·ti·san *also* **par·ti·zan** \'pär-tə-zən, -sən\ *n* 1 : one that takes the part of another : ADHERENT 2 : GUERRILLA — **partisan** *adj* — **par·ti·san·ship** *n*

par·tite \'pär-ˌtīt\ *adj* : divided into a usu. specified number of parts

par·ti·tion \pär-'ti-shən\ *n* 1 : DIVISION 2 : something that divides or separates; *esp* : an interior dividing wall — **partition** *vb*

par·ti·tive \'pär-tə-tiv\ *adj* : of, relating to, or denoting a part

part·ly \'pärt-lē\ *adv* : in part : in some measure or degree

part·ner \'pärt-nər\ *n* 1 : ASSOCIATE, COLLEAGUE 2 : either of two persons who dance together 3 : one who plays on the same team with another 4 : SPOUSE 5 : one of two or more persons contractually associated as joint principals in a business — **part·ner·ship** *n*

part of speech : a class of words (as nouns or verbs) distinguished according to the kind of idea denoted and the function performed in a sentence

par·tridge \'pär-trij\ *n, pl* **partridge** *or* **par·tridg·es** : any of various stout-bodied game birds

part–song \'pärt-ˌsȯŋ\ *n* : a song with two or more voice parts

part–time \-'tīm\ *adj or adv* : involving or working less than a full or regular schedule — **part–tim·er** \-ˌtī-mər\ *n*

par·tu·ri·tion \ˌpär-tə-'ri-shən, ˌpär-chə-, ˌpär-tyů-\ *n* : CHILDBIRTH

part·way \'pärt-'wā\ *adv* : to some extent : PARTLY

par·ty \'pär-tē\ *n, pl* **parties** 1 : a person or group taking one side of a question; *esp* : a group of persons organized for the purpose of directing the policies of a government 2 : a person or group concerned in an action or affair : PARTICIPANT 3 : a group of persons detailed for a common task 4 : a social gathering

par·ve·nu \'pär-və-ˌnü, -ˌnyü\ *n* [F, fr. pp. of *parvenir* to arrive, fr. L *pervenire,* fr. *per* through + *venire* to come] : one who has recently or suddenly risen to wealth or power but has not yet secured the social position associated with it

pas \'pä\ *n, pl* **pas** *same or* '**päz\ : a dance step or combination of steps

pas·cal \pas-'kal\ *n* : a unit of pressure in the metric system equal to one newton per square meter

pas·chal \'pas-kəl\ *adj* : of, relating to, appropriate for, or used during Passover or Easter ceremonies

pa·sha \'pä-shə, 'pa-; pə-'shä\ *n* : a man (as formerly a governor in Turkey) of high rank

¹**pass** \'pas\ *vb* 1 : MOVE, PROCEED 2 : to go away; *also* : DIE 3 : to move past, beyond, or over 4 : to allow to elapse : SPEND 5 : to go or make way through 6 : to go or allow to go unchallenged 7 : to undergo transfer 8 : to render a legal judgment 9 : OCCUR 10 : to secure the approval of (as a legislature) 11 : to go or cause to go through an inspection, test, or course of study successfully 12 : to be regarded 13 : CIRCULATE 14 : VOID 2 15 : to transfer the ball or puck to another player 16 : to decline to bid or bet on one's hand in a card game 17 : to give a base on balls to — **pass·er** *n*

²**pass** *n* : a gap in a mountain range

³**pass** *n* 1 : the act or an instance of passing 2 : REALIZATION, ACCOMPLISHMENT 3 : a state of affairs 4 : a written authorization to leave, enter, or move about freely 5 : a transfer of a ball or puck from one player to another 6 : BASE ON BALLS 7 : EFFORT, TRY 8 : a sexually inviting gesture or approach

⁴**pass** *abbr* 1 passenger 2 passive

pass·able \'pa-sə-bəl\ *adj* 1 : capable of being passed or traveled on 2 : just good enough : TOLERABLE — **pass·ably** \-blē\ *adv*

pas·sage \'pa-sij\ *n* 1 : a means (as a road or corridor) of passing 2 : the action or process of passing 3 : a voyage esp. by sea or air 4 : a right or permission to pass 5 : ENACTMENT 6 : a usu. brief portion or section (as of a book)

pas·sage·way \-ˌwā\ *n* : a way that allows passage

pass·book \'pas-ˌbůk\ *n* : BANKBOOK

pas·sé \pa-'sā\ *adj* **1** : past one's prime **2** : not up=to-date : OUTMODED

pas·sel \'pa-səl\ *n* : a large number

pas·sen·ger \'pas-ᵊn-jər\ *n* : a traveler in a public or private conveyance

pass·er·by \'pa-sər-ˌbī\ *n, pl* **pass·ers·by** : one who passes by

pas·ser·ine \'pa-sə-ˌrīn\ *adj* : of or relating to the large order of birds comprising singing birds that perch

pas·sim \'pa-səm\ *adv* [L, fr. *passus* scattered, fr. pp. of *pandere* to spread] : here and there : THROUGHOUT

pass·ing *n* : the act of one that passes or causes to pass; *esp* : DEATH

pas·sion \'pa-shən\ *n* **1** *often cap* : the sufferings of Christ between the night of the Last Supper and his death **2** : strong feeling; *also, pl* : the emotions as distinguished from reason **3** : RAGE, ANGER **4** : LOVE; *also* : an object of affection or enthusiasm **5** : sexual desire — **pas·sion·ate** \'pa-shə-nət\ *adj* — **pas·sion·ate·ly** *adv* — **pas·sion·less** *adj*

pas·sion·flow·er \'pa-shən-ˌflaù-ər\ *n* [fr. the fancied resemblance of parts of the flower to the instruments of Christ's crucifixion] : any of a genus of chiefly tropical woody climbing vines or erect herbs with showy flowers and pulpy often edible berries (**passion fruit**)

pas·sive \'pa-siv\ *adj* **1** : not active : acted upon **2** : asserting that the grammatical subject is subjected to or affected by the action represented by the verb ⟨~ voice⟩ **3** : making use of the sun's heat usu. without the aid of mechanical devices **4** : SUBMISSIVE, PATIENT — **passive** *n* — **pas·sive·ly** *adv* — **pas·siv·i·ty** \pa-'si-və-tē\ *n*

pass·key \'pas-ˌkē\ *n* : a key for opening two or more locks

pass out *vb* : to lose consciousness

Pass·over \'pas-ˌō-vər\ *n* [fr. the exemption of the Israelites from the slaughter of the firstborn in Egypt (Exod 12:23–27)] : a Jewish holiday celebrated in March or April in commemoration of the Hebrews' liberation from slavery in Egypt

pass·port \'pas-ˌpōrt\ *n* : an official document issued by a country upon request to a citizen requesting protection during travel abroad

pass up *vb* : DECLINE, REJECT

pass·word \'pas-ˌwərd\ *n* **1** : a word or phrase that must be spoken by a person before being allowed to pass a guard **2** : a sequence of characters required for access to a computer system

¹past \'past\ *adj* **1** : AGO ⟨10 years ~⟩ **2** : just gone or elapsed ⟨the ~ month⟩ **3** : having existed or taken place in a period before the present : BYGONE **4** : of, relating to, or constituting a verb tense that expresses time gone by

²past *prep or adv* : BEYOND

³past *n* **1** : time gone by **2** : something that happened or was done in a former time **3** : the past tense; *also* : a verb form in it **4** : a secret past life

pas·ta \'päs-tə\ *n* [It] **1** : a paste in processed form (as spaghetti) or in the form of fresh dough (as ravioli) **2** : a dish of cooked pasta

¹paste \'pāst\ *n* **1** : DOUGH **2** : a smooth food product made by evaporation or grinding ⟨tomato ~⟩ **3** : a shaped dough (as spaghetti or ravioli) **4** : a preparation (as of flour and water) for sticking things together **5** : a brilliant glass used for artificial gems

²paste *vb* **past·ed; past·ing** : to cause to adhere by paste : STICK

paste·board \'pāst-ˌbōrd\ *n* : PAPERBOARD

¹pas·tel \'pas-'tel\ *n* **1** : a paste made of powdered pigment; *also* : a crayon of such paste **2** : a drawing in pastel **3** : a pale or light color

²pastel *adj* **1** : of or relating to a pastel **2** : pale in color

pas·tern \'pas-tərn\ *n* : the part of a horse's foot extending from the fetlock to the top of the hoof

pas·teur·i·za·tion \ˌpas-chə-rə-'zā-shən, ˌpas-tə-\ *n* : partial sterilization of a substance (as milk) by heat or radiation — **pas·teur·ize** \'pas-chə-ˌrīz, 'pas-tə-\ *vb* — **pas·teur·iz·er** *n*

pas·tiche \pas-'tēsh\ *n* : a composition (as in literature or music) made up of selections from different works

pas·tille \pas-'tēl\ *n* : an aromatic or medicated lozenge

pas·time \'pas-ˌtīm\ *n* : DIVERSION; *esp* : something that serves to make time pass agreeably

pas·tor \'pas-tər\ *n* [ME *pastour*, fr. OF, fr. L *pastor*, herdsman, fr. *pascere* to feed, pasture, nurture] : a minister or priest serving a local church or parish — **pas·tor·ate** \-tə-rət\ *n*

¹pas·to·ral \'pas-tə-rəl\ *adj* **1** : of or relating to shepherds or to rural life **2** : of or relating to spiritual guidance esp. of a congregation **3** : of or relating to the pastor of a church

²pastoral *n* : a literary work dealing with shepherds or rural life

pas·to·rale \ˌpas-tə-'räl, -'ral\ *n* [It] : a musical composition having a pastoral theme

past participle *n* : a participle that typically expresses completed action, that is one of the principal parts of the verb, and that is used in the formation of perfect tenses in the active voice and of all tenses in the passive voice

pas·tra·mi \pə-'strä-mē\ *n* [Yiddish *pastrame*] : a highly seasoned smoked beef prepared esp. from shoulder cuts

pas·try \'pā-strē\ *n, pl* **pastries** : sweet baked goods made of dough or with a crust made of enriched dough

pas·tur·age \'pas-chə-rij\ *n* : PASTURE

¹pas·ture \'pas-chər\ *n* **1** : plants (as grass) for the feeding esp. of grazing livestock **2** : land or a plot of land used for grazing

²pasture *vb* **pas·tured; pas·tur·ing 1** : GRAZE **2** : to use as pasture

pasty \'pā-stē\ *adj* **past·i·er; -est** : resembling paste; *esp* : pallid and unhealthy in appearance

¹pat \'pat\ *n* **1** : a light tap esp. with the hand or a flat instrument; *also* : the sound made by it **2** : something (as butter) shaped into a small flat usu. square individual portion

²pat *adv* : in a pat manner : PERFECTLY

³pat *vb* **pat·ted; pat·ting 1** : to strike lightly with a flat instrument **2** : to flatten, smooth, or put into place or shape with a pat **3** : to tap gently or lovingly with the hand

⁴pat *adj* **1** : exactly suited to the occasion : APT **2** : memorized exactly **3** : UNYIELDING

PAT *abbr* point after touchdown

pa·ta·ca \pə-'tä-kə\ *n* — see MONEY table

¹patch \'pach\ *n* **1** : a piece used to cover a torn or worn place; *also* : one worn on a garment as an ornament or insignia **2** : a small area distinct from that about it **3** : a shield worn over the socket of an injured or missing eye

²patch *vb* **1** : to mend or cover with a patch **2** : to make of fragments **3** : to repair usu. in hasty fashion

patch test *n* : a test for allergic sensitivity made by applying to the unbroken skin small pads soaked with the allergen to be tested

patch·work \'pach-ˌwərk\ *n* : something made of pieces of different materials, shapes, or colors

patchy \'pa-chē\ *adj* **patch·i·er; -est** : marked by or consisting of patches; *also* : irregular in appearance or quality — **patch·i·ness** \-chē-nəs\ *n*

\ə\abut \ᵊ\kitten \ər\further \a\ash \ā\ace \ä\mop, mar
\aù\out \ch\chin \e\bet \ē\easy \g\go \i\hit \ī\ice \j\job
\ŋ\sing \ō\go \ò\law \òi\boy \th\thin \t̲h̲\the \ü\loot \ù\foot
\y\yet \zh\vision *see also* Pronunciation Symbols page

pate \\'pāt\ *n* : HEAD; *esp* : the crown of the head

pâ·té *also* **pate** \pä-'tā\ *n* [F] **1** : a meat or fish pie or patty **2** : a spread of finely chopped or pureed seasoned meat

pa·tel·la \pə-'te-lə\ *n, pl* **-lae** \-'te-(,)lē, -,lī\ *or* **-las** [L] : KNEECAP

pat·en \\'pat-ᵊn\ *n* **1** : PLATE; *esp* : one of precious metal for the eucharistic bread **2** : a thin disk

¹pa·tent \/ *& 4 are* 'pat-ᵊnt, *Brit also* 'pāt-, *2 & 3 are* 'pat-ᵊnt, 'pāt-\ *adj* **1** : open to public inspection — used chiefly in the phrase *letters patent* **2** : free from obstruction **3** : EVIDENT, OBVIOUS **4** : protected by a patent **syn** manifest, distinct, apparent, palpable, plain, clear — **pat·ent·ly** *adv*

²pat·ent \\'pat-ᵊnt, *Brit also* 'pāt-\ *n* **1** : an official document conferring a right or privilege **2** : a document securing to an inventor for a term of years exclusive right to his or her invention **3** : something patented

³pat·ent *vb* : to secure by patent

pat·en·tee \,pat-ᵊn-'tē, *Brit also* ,pāt-\ *n* : one to whom a grant is made or a privilege secured by patent

pat·ent medicine \\'pat-ᵊnt-\ *n* : a packaged nonprescription drug protected by a trademark; *also* : any proprietary drug

pa·ter·fa·mil·i·as \,pā-tər-fə-'mi-lē-əs\ *n, pl* **pa·tres·fa·mil·i·as** \,pā-,trēz-\ [L] : the father of a family : the male head of a household

pa·ter·nal \pə-'tərn-ᵊl\ *adj* **1** : FATHERLY **2** : related through or inherited or derived from a father — **pa·ter·nal·ly** *adv*

pa·ter·nal·ism \-,i-zəm\ *n* : a system under which an authority treats those under its control paternally (as by regulating their conduct and supplying their needs)

pa·ter·ni·ty \pə-'tər-nə-tē\ *n* **1** : FATHERHOOD **2** : descent from a father

¹path \\'path, 'pàth\ *n, pl* **paths** \\'pathz, 'paths, 'pàthz, 'pàths\ **1** : a trodden way **2** : ROUTE, COURSE — **path·less** *adj*

²path *or* **pathol** *abbr* pathology

path·break·ing \\'path-,brā-kiŋ\ *adj* : TRAILBLAZING

pa·thet·ic \pə-'the-tik\ *adj* : evoking tenderness, pity, or sorrow **syn** pitiful, piteous, pitiable, poor — **pa·thet·i·cal·ly** \-ti-k(ə-)lē\ *adv*

path·find·er \\'path-,fīn-dər, 'pàth-\ *n* : one that discovers a way; *esp* : one that explores untraveled regions to mark out a new route

patho·gen \\'pa-thə-jən\ *n* : a specific agent (as a bacterium) causing disease — **patho·gen·ic** \,pa-thə-'je-nik\ *adj* — **patho·ge·nic·i·ty** \-jə-'ni-sə-tē\ *n*

pa·thol·o·gy \pə-'thä-lə-jē\ *n, pl* **-gies 1** : the study of the essential nature of disease **2** : the abnormality of structure and function characteristic of a disease — **path·o·log·i·cal** \,pa-thə-'lä-ji-kəl\ *adj* — **pa·thol·o·gist** \pə-'thä-lə-jist\ *n*

pa·thos \\'pā-,thäs, -,thōs\ *n* : an element in experience or artistic representation evoking pity or compassion

path·way \\'path-,wā, 'pàth-\ *n* : PATH

pa·tience \\'pā-shəns\ *n* **1** : the capacity, habit, or fact of being patient **2** *chiefly Brit* : SOLITAIRE 2

¹pa·tient \\'pā-shənt\ *adj* **1** : bearing pain or trials without complaint **2** : showing self-control : CALM **3** : STEADFAST, PERSEVERING — **pa·tient·ly** *adv*

²patient *n* : one under medical care

pa·ti·na \\'pa-tə-nə, pə-'tē-\ *n, pl* **pa·ti·nas** \-nəz\ *or* **pa·ti·nae** \\'pa-tə-,nē, -,nī\ **1** : a green film formed on copper and bronze by exposure to moist air **2** : a superficial covering or exterior

pa·tio \\'pa-tē-,ō, 'pä-\ *n, pl* **pa·ti·os 1** : COURTYARD **2** : an often paved area near a dwelling used esp. for outdoor dining

pa·tois \\'pa-,twä\ *n, pl* **pa·tois** \-,twäz\ [F] **1** : a dialect other than the standard dialect; *esp* : uneducated or provincial speech **2** : JARGON 2

pa·tri·arch \\'pā-trē-,ärk\ *n* **1** : a man revered as father or founder (as of a tribe) **2** : a venerable old man **3** : an ecclesiastical dignitary (as the bishop of an Eastern Orthodox see) — **pa·tri·ar·chal** \,pā-trē-'är-kəl\ *adj* — **pa·tri·arch·ate** \\'pā-trē-,är-kət, -,kät\ *n* — **pa·tri·ar·chy** \-,är-kē\ *n*

pa·tri·cian \pə-'tri-shən\ *n* : a person of high birth : ARISTOCRAT — **patrician** *adj*

pat·ri·cide \\'pa-trə-,sīd\ *n* **1** : one who murders his or her own father **2** : the murder of one's own father

pat·ri·mo·ny \\'pa-trə-,mō-nē\ *n* : something (as an estate) inherited or derived esp. from one's father : HERITAGE — **pat·ri·mo·ni·al** \,pa-trə-'mō-nē-əl\ *adj*

pa·tri·ot \\'pā-trē-ət, -,ät\ *n* [MF *patriote* compatriot, fr. LL *patriota*, fr. Gk *patriōtēs*, fr. *patria* lineage, fr. *patr-, patēr* father] : one who loves his or her country — **pa·tri·ot·ic** \,pā-trē-'ä-tik\ *adj* — **pa·tri·ot·i·cal·ly** \-ti-k(ə-)lē\ *adv* — **pa·tri·o·tism** \\'pā-trē-ə-,ti-zəm\ *n*

pa·tris·tic \pə-'tris-tik\ *adj* : of or relating to the church fathers or their writings

¹pa·trol \pə-'trōl\ *n* : the action of going the rounds (as of an area) for observation or the maintenance of security; *also* : a person or group performing such an action

²patrol *vb* **pa·trolled; pa·trol·ling** : to carry out a patrol

patrol car *n* : SQUAD CAR

pa·trol·man \pə-'trōl-mən\ *n* : a police officer assigned to a beat

patrol wagon *n* : PADDY WAGON

pa·tron \\'pā-trən\ *n* [ME, fr. MF, fr. ML & L; ML *patronus* patron saint, patron of a benefice, pattern, fr. L, defender, fr. *patr-, pater* father] **1** : a person chosen or named as special protector ⟨~ of poets⟩; *also* : BENEFACTOR **3** : a regular client or customer

pa·tron·age \\'pa-trə-nij, 'pā-\ *n* **1** : the support or influence of a patron **2** : the trade of customers **3** : control of appointment to government jobs

pa·tron·ess \\'pā-trə-nəs\ *n* : a woman who is a patron

pa·tron·ize \\'pā-trə-,nīz, 'pa-\ *vb* **-ized; -iz·ing 1** : to be a customer of **2** : to treat condescendingly, haughtily, or coolly

pat·ro·nym·ic \,pa-trə-'ni-mik\ *n* : a name derived from the name of one's father or a paternal ancestor usu. by the addition of an affix

pa·troon \pə-'trün\ *n* : the proprietor of a manorial estate esp. in New York under Dutch rule

pat·sy \\'pat-sē\ *n, pl* **pat·sies** : a person who is easily duped or victimized

¹pat·ter \\'pa-tər\ *vb* : to talk glibly or mechanically **syn** chatter, prate, chat, prattle, babble

²patter *n* **1** : a specialized lingo **2** : extremely rapid talk ⟨a comedian's ~⟩

³patter *vb* : to strike, pat, or tap rapidly

⁴patter *n* : a quick succession of taps or pats ⟨the ~ of rain⟩

¹pat·tern \\'pa-tərn\ *n* [ME *patron*, fr. MF, fr. ML *patronus*, fr. L, defender, fr. *patr-, pater* father] **1** : an ideal model **2** : something used as a model for making things ⟨a dressmaker's ~⟩ **3** : SAMPLE **4** : an artistic design **5** : CONFIGURATION

²pattern *vb* : to form according to a pattern

pat·ty *also* **pat·tie** \\'pa-tē\ *n, pl* **patties 1** : a little pie **2** : a small flat cake esp. of chopped food

pau·ci·ty \\'pò-sə-tē\ *n* : smallness of number or quantity

paunch \\'pònch\ *n* : a usu. large belly : POTBELLY — **paunchy** *adj*

pau·per \\'pò-pər\ *n* : a person without means of support except from charity — **pau·per·ism** \-pə-,ri-zəm\ *n* — **pau·per·ize** \-pə-,rīz\ *vb*

¹pause \\'pòz\ *n* **1** : a temporary stop; *also* : a period of inaction **2** : a brief suspension of the voice **3** : a sign ⌒ or ⌣ above or below a musical note or rest to show it is to be prolonged **4** : a reason for pausing

²**pause** *vb* **paused; paus·ing** : to stop, rest, or linger for a time

pave \'pāv\ *vb* **paved; pav·ing** : to cover (as a road) with hard material in order to smooth or firm the surface

pave·ment \'pāv-mənt\ *n* **1** : a paved surface **2** : the material with which something is paved

pa·vil·ion \pə-'vil-yən\ *n* [ME *pavilon*, fr. OF *paveillon*, fr. L *papilion-, papilio* butterfly] **1** : a large tent **2** : a light structure (as in a park) used for entertainment or shelter

pav·ing \'pā-viŋ\ *n* : PAVEMENT

¹**paw** \'pȯ\ *n* : the foot of a quadruped (as a dog or lion) having claws

²**paw** *vb* **1** : to touch or strike with a paw; *also* : to scrape with a hoof **2** : to feel or handle clumsily or rudely **3** : to flail about or grab for with the hands

pawl \'pȯl\ *n* : a pivoted tongue or sliding bolt designed to fall into notches on another machine part to permit motion in one direction only

¹**pawn** \'pȯn\ *n* [ME *pown*, fr. MF *poon*, fr. ML *pedon-, pedo* foot soldier, fr. LL, one with broad feet, fr. L *ped-, pes* foot] : a chess piece of the least value

²**pawn** *n* **1** : something deposited as security for a loan; *also* : HOSTAGE **2** : the state of being pledged

³**pawn** *vb* : to deposit as a pledge

pawn·bro·ker \'pȯn-ˌbrō-kər\ *n* : one who lends money on goods pledged

Paw·nee \pȯ-'nē\ *n, pl* **Pawnee** *or* **Pawnees** : a member of an American Indian people orig. of Kansas and Nebraska

pawn·shop \'pȯn-ˌshän\ *n* : a pawnbroker's place of business

paw·paw *var of* PAPAW

¹**pay** \'pā\ *vb* **paid** \'pād\ *also in sense 7* **payed; pay·ing** [ME, fr. OF *paier*, fr. L *pacare* to pacify, fr. *pac-, pax* peace] **1** : to make due return to for goods or services **2** : to discharge indebtedness for : SETTLE ⟨~ a bill⟩ **3** : to give in forfeit ⟨~ the penalty⟩ **4** : REQUITE **5** : to give, offer, or make freely or as fitting ⟨~ attention⟩ **6** : to be profitable to : RETURN **7** : to make slack and allow to run out ⟨~ out a rope⟩ — **pay·able** *adj* — **pay·ee** \pā-'ē\ *n* — **pay·er** *n*

²**pay** *n* **1** : something paid; *esp* : WAGES **2** : the status of being paid by an employer : EMPLOY

³**pay** *adj* **1** : containing something valuable (as gold) ⟨~ dirt⟩ **2** : equipped to receive a fee for use ⟨~ telephone⟩ **3** : requiring payment

pay·check \'pā-ˌchek\ *n* **1** : a check in payment of wages or salary **2** : WAGES, SALARY

pay·load \-ˌlōd\ *n* : the load carried by a vehicle in addition to what is necessary for its operation; *also* : the weight of such a load

pay·mas·ter \-ˌmas-tər\ *n* : one who distributes the payroll

pay·ment \'pā-mənt\ *n* **1** : the act of paying **2** : something paid

pay·off \-ˌȯf\ *n* **1** : PROFIT, REWARD; *also* : RETRIBUTION **2** : the climax of an incident or enterprise ⟨the ~ of a story⟩

pay–per–view *n* : a cable television service by which customers can order access to a single airing of a TV feature

pay·roll \-ˌrōl\ *n* : a list of persons entitled to receive pay; *also* : the money to pay those on such a list

payt *abbr* payment

pay up *vb* : to pay what is due; *also* : to pay in full

Pb *symbol* [L *plumbum*] lead

PBS *abbr* Public Broadcasting Service

PBX \ˌpē-ˌ(ˌ)bē-'eks\ *n* [*private branch exchange*] : a private telephone switchboard

¹**PC** \ˌpē-'sē\ *n, pl* **PCs** *or* **PC's** **1** : PERSONAL COMPUTER **2** : MICROCOMPUTER

²**PC** *abbr* **1** Peace Corps **2** percent; percentage **3** politi-

cally correct **4** postcard **5** [L *post cibum*] after meals **6** professional corporation

PCB \ˌpē-sē-'bē\ *n* : POLYCHLORINATED BIPHENYL

PCP \ˌpē-sē-'pē\ *n* : PHENCYCLIDINE

pct *abbr* percent; percentage

pd *abbr* paid

Pd *symbol* palladium

PD *abbr* **1** per diem **2** police department **3** potential difference

PDQ \ˌpē-dē-'kyü\ *adv, often not cap* [abbr. of *pretty damned quick*] : IMMEDIATELY

PDT *abbr* Pacific daylight (saving) time

PE *abbr* **1** physical education **2** printer's error **3** professional engineer

pea \'pē\ *n, pl* **peas** *also* **pease** \'pēz\ **1** : the round edible protein-rich seed borne in the pod of a widely grown leguminous vine; *also* : this vine **2** : any of various plants resembling or related to the pea

peace \'pēs\ *n* **1** : a state of calm and quiet; *esp* : public security under law **2** : freedom from disturbing thoughts or emotions **3** : a state of concord (as between persons or governments); *also* : an agreement to end hostilities — **peace·able** \'pē-sə-bəl\ *adj* — **peace·ably** \-blē\ *adv* — **peace·ful** *adj* — **peace·ful·ly** *adv*

peace·keep·ing \'pēs-ˌkē-piŋ\ *n* : the preserving of peace; *esp* : international enforcement and supervision of a truce — **peace·keep·er** *n*

peace·mak·er \-ˌmā-kər\ *n* : one who settles an argument or stops a fight

peace·time \-ˌtīm\ *n* : a time when a nation is not at war

peach \'pēch\ *n* [ME *peche*, fr. MF, fr. LL *persica*, fr. L *(malum) Persicum*, lit., Persian fruit] : a sweet juicy fruit of a low tree with pink blossoms related to the cherry and plums; *also* : this tree

pea·cock \'pē-ˌkäk\ *n* [ME *pecok*, fr. *pe-* (fr. OE *pēa* peafowl, fr. L *pavo* peacock) + *cok* cock] : the male peafowl that can spread its long tail feathers to make a colorful display

pea·fowl \-ˌfau̇l\ *n* : either of two large domesticated Asian pheasants

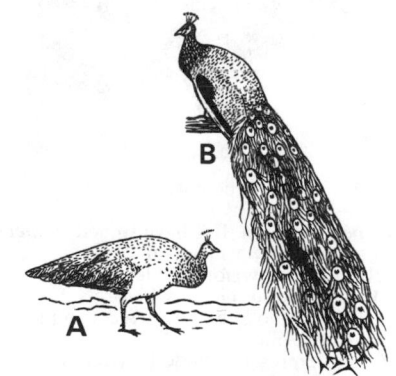

peafowl: *A* female, *B* male

pea·hen \-ˌhen\ *n* : the female peafowl

¹**peak** \'pēk\ *n* **1** : a pointed or projecting part **2** : the top of a hill or mountain; *also* : MOUNTAIN **3** : the front projecting part of a cap **4** : the narrow part of a ship's bow or stern **5** : the highest level or greatest degree — **peak** *adj*

²**peak** *vb* : to bring to or reach a maximum

peak·ed \'pē-kəd\ *adj* : THIN, SICKLY

¹**peal** \'pēl\ *n* **1** : the loud ringing of bells **2** : a set of tuned bells **3** : a loud sound or succession of sounds

²**peal** *vb* : to give out peals : RESOUND

pea·nut \'pē-(₁)nət\ *n* **1** : an annual herb related to the pea but having pods that ripen underground; *also* : this pod or one of the edible seeds it bears **2** *pl* : a very small amount

pear \'par\ *n* : the fleshy fruit of a tree related to the apple; *also* : this tree

pearl \'pərl\ *n* **1** : a small hard often lustrous body formed within the shell of some mollusks and used as a gem **2** : one that is choice or precious ⟨∼s of wisdom⟩ **3** : a slightly bluish medium gray — **pearly** \'pər-lē\ *adj*

peas·ant \'pez-³nt\ *n* **1** : any of a class of small landowners or laborers tilling the soil **2** : a usu. uneducated person of low social status — **peas·ant·ry** \-³n-trē\ *n*

pea·shoot·er \'pē-₁shü-tər\ *n* : a toy blowgun for shooting peas

peat \'pēt\ *n* : a dark substance formed by partial decay of plants (as mosses) in water — **peaty** *adj*

peat moss *n* : SPHAGNUM

¹**peb·ble** \'pe-bəl\ *n* : a small usu. round stone — **peb·bly** \-b(ə-)lē\ *adj*

²**pebble** *vb* **peb·bled; peb·bling** : to produce a rough surface texture in ⟨∼ leather⟩

pec \'pek\ *n* : PECTORAL MUSCLE

pe·can \pi-'kän, -'kan; 'pē-₁kan\ *n* : the smooth-shelled edible nut of a large American hickory; *also* : this tree

pec·ca·dil·lo \₁pe-kə-'di-lō\ *n, pl* **-loes** *or* **-los** : a slight offense

pec·ca·ry \'pe-kə-rē\ *n, pl* **-ries** : any of several American chiefly tropical mammals resembling but smaller than the related pigs

peccary

pec·ca·vi \pe-'kä-₁vē\ *n* [L, I have sinned, fr. *peccare* to sin] : an acknowledgment of sin

¹**peck** \'pek\ *n* — see WEIGHT table

²**peck** *vb* **1** : to strike or pierce with or as if with the bill **2** : to make (as a hole) by pecking **3** : to pick up with or as if with the bill

³**peck** *n* **1** : an impression made by pecking **2** : a quick sharp stroke

pecking order *also* **peck order** *n* : a basic pattern of social organization within a flock of poultry in which each bird pecks another lower in the scale without being pecked in return and submits to pecking by one of higher rank; *also* : a social hierarchy

pec·tin \'pek-tən\ *n* : any of various water-soluble plant substances that cause fruit jellies to set — **pec·tic** \-tik\ *adj*

pec·to·ral \'pek-tə-rəl\ *adj* : of or relating to the breast or chest

pectoral muscle *n* : either of two muscles on each side of the body which connect the front walls of the chest with the bones of the upper arm and shoulder

pe·cu·liar \pi-'kyül-yər\ *adj* [ME *peculier*, fr. L *peculiaris* of private property, special, fr. *peculium* private property, fr. *pecus* cattle] **1** : belonging exclusively to one person or group **2** : CHARACTERISTIC, DISTINCTIVE **3** : QUEER, ODD **syn** idiosyncratic, eccentric, singular, strange, weird — **pe·cu·liar·i·ty** \-₁kyül-'yar-ə-tē, -₁kyü-lē-'ar-\ *n* — **pe·cu·liar·ly** *adv*

pe·cu·ni·ary \pi-'kyü-nē-₁er-ē\ *adj* : of or relating to money : MONETARY

ped·a·gogue *also* **ped·a·gog** \'pe-də-₁gäg\ *n* : TEACHER, SCHOOLMASTER

ped·a·go·gy \'pe-də-₁gō-jē, -₁gä-\ *n* : the art or profession of teaching; *esp* : EDUCATION **2** — **ped·a·gog·ic** \₁pe-də-'gä-jik, -'gō-\ *or* **ped·a·gog·i·cal** \-ji-kəl\ *adj*

¹**pedal** \'ped-³l\ *n* : a lever worked by the foot

²**ped·al** *adj* : of or relating to the foot

³**ped·al** \'ped-³l\ *vb* **ped·aled** *also* **ped·alled; ped·al·ing** *also* **ped·al·ling** **1** : to use or work a pedal (as of a piano or bicycle) **2** : to ride a bicycle

ped·ant \'ped-³nt\ *n* **1** : a person who makes a display of his learning **2** : a formal uninspired teacher — **pe·dan·tic** \pi-'dan-tik\ *adj* — **ped·ant·ry** \'ped-³n-trē\ *n*

ped·dle \'ped-³l\ *vb* **ped·dled; ped·dling** : to sell or offer for sale from place to place — **ped·dler** *also* **ped·lar** \'ped-lər\ *n*

ped·er·ast \'pe-də-₁rast\ *n* [Gk *paiderastēs*, lit., lover of boys] : one that practices anal intercourse esp. with a boy — **ped·er·as·ty** \'pe-də-₁ras-tē\ *n*

ped·es·tal \'pe-dəst-³l\ *n* **1** : the support or foot of something (as a column, statue, or vase) that is upright **2** : a position of high regard

¹**pe·des·tri·an** \pə-'des-trē-ən\ *adj* **1** : COMMONPLACE **2** : going on foot

²**pedestrian** *n* : WALKER

pe·di·at·rics \₁pē-dē-'a-triks\ *n* : a branch of medicine dealing with the development, care, and diseases of children — **pe·di·at·ric** \-trik\ *adj* — **pe·di·a·tri·cian** \₁pē-dē-ə-'tri-shən\ *n*

pedi·cab \'pe-di-₁kab\ *n* : a pedal-driven tricycle with seats for a driver and two passengers

ped·i·cure \'pe-di-₁kyùr\ *n* : care of the feet, toes, and nails; *also* : a single treatment of these parts — **ped·i·cur·ist** \-₁kyùr-ist\ *n*

ped·i·gree \'pe-də-₁grē\ *n* [ME *pedegru*, fr. MF *pie de grue* crane's foot; fr. the shape made by the lines of a genealogical chart] **1** : a record of a line of ancestors **2** : an ancestral line — **ped·i·greed** \-grēd\ *adj*

ped·i·ment \'pe-də-mənt\ *n* : a low triangular gablelike decoration (as over a door or window) on a building

pe·dom·e·ter \pi-'dä-mə-tər\ *n* : an instrument that measures the distance one walks

pe·dun·cle \'pē-₁dəŋ-kəl\ *n* : a narrow supporting stalk

peek \'pēk\ *vb* **1** : to look furtively **2** : to peer from a place of concealment **3** : GLANCE — **peek** *n*

¹**peel** \'pēl\ *vb* [ME *pelen*, fr. MF *peler*, fr. L *pilare* to remove the hair from, fr. *pilus* hair] **1** : to strip the skin, bark, or rind from **2** : to strip off (as a coat); *also* : to come off **3** : to lose the skin, bark, or rind

²**peel** *n* : a skin or rind esp. of a fruit

peel·ing \'pē-liŋ\ *n* : a peeled-off piece or strip (as of skin or rind)

peen \'pēn\ *n* : the usu. hemispherical or wedge-shaped end of the head of a hammer opposite the face

¹**peep** \'pēp\ *vb* : to utter a feeble shrill sound or the slightest sound

²**peep** *n* : a feeble shrill sound

³**peep** *vb* **1** : to look slyly esp. through an aperture : PEEK **2** : to begin to emerge — **peep·er** *n*

⁴**peep** *n* **1** : a first faint appearance **2** : a brief or furtive look

peep·hole \'pēp-₁hōl\ *n* : a hole to peep through

¹**peer** \'pir\ *n* **1** : one of equal standing with another : EQUAL **2** : NOBLE — **peer·age** \-ij\ *n*

²**peer** \vb\ **1** : to look intently or curiously **2** : to come slightly into view
peer·ess \'pir-əs\ n : a woman who is a peer
peer·less \'pir-ləs\ adj : having no equal : MATCHLESS **syn** supreme, unequalled, unparalleled, incomparable
¹**peeve** \'pēv\ vb **peeved; peev·ing** : to make resentful : ANNOY
²**peeve** n **1** : a feeling or mood of resentment **2** : a particular grievance
pee·vish \'pē-vish\ adj : querulous in temperament : FRETFUL **syn** irritable, petulant, huffy — **pee·vish·ly** adv — **pee·vish·ness** n
pee·wee \'pē-(ˌ)wē\ n : one that is diminutive or tiny
¹**peg** \'peg\ n **1** : a small pointed piece (as of wood) used to pin down or fasten things or to fit into holes **2** : a projecting piece used as a support or boundary marker **3** : SUPPORT, PRETEXT **4** : STEP, DEGREE **5** : THROW
²**peg** vb **pegged; peg·ging 1** : to put a peg into : fasten, pin down, or attach with or as if with pegs **2** : to work hard and steadily : PLUG **3** : HUSTLE **4** : to mark by pegs **5** : to hold (as prices) at a set level or rate **6** : IDENTIFY **7** : THROW
PEI abbr Prince Edward Island
pei·gnoir \pān-'wär, pen-\ n [F, lit., garment worn while combing the hair, fr. MF, fr. peigner to comb the hair, fr. L pectinare, fr. pectin-, pecten comb] : NEGLIGEE
¹**pe·jo·ra·tive** \pi-'jòr-ə-tiv\ n : a pejorative word or phrase
²**pejorative** adj : having negative connotations : DISPARAGING — **pe·jo·ra·tive·ly** adv
peke \'pēk\ n, often cap : PEKINGESE
Pe·king·ese or **Pe·kin·ese** \ˌpē-kə-'nēz, -'nēs; -kiŋ-'ēz, -'ēs\ n, pl **Pekingese** or **Pekinese** : any of a breed of Chinese origin of small short-legged long-haired dogs
pe·koe \'pē-(ˌ)kō\ n : a black tea made from young tea leaves
pel·age \'pe-lij\ n : the hairy covering of a mammal
pe·lag·ic \pə-'la-jik\ adj : OCEANIC
pelf \'pelf\ n : MONEY, RICHES
pel·i·can \'pe-li-kən\ n : any of a genus of large web-footed birds having a pouched lower bill used to scoop in fish
pel·la·gra \pə-'la-grə, -'lä-\ n : a disease caused by a diet with too little nicotinic acid and protein and marked by a skin rash, disease of the digestive system, and nervous symptoms
pel·let \'pe-lət\ n **1** : a little ball (as of medicine) **2** : BULLET — **pel·let·al** \-lə-təl\ adj — **pel·let·ize** \-ˌtīz\ vb
pell–mell \ˌpel-'mel\ adv **1** : in mingled confusion **2** : HEADLONG
pel·lu·cid \pə-'lü-səd\ adj : extremely clear : LIMPID, TRANSPARENT **syn** translucent, lucid, lucent
¹**pelt** \'pelt\ n : a skin esp. of a fur-bearing animal
²**pelt** vb : to strike with a succession of blows or missiles
pel·vis \'pel-vəs\ n, pl **pel·vis·es** \-və-səz\ or **pel·ves** \-ˌvēz\ : a basin-shaped part of the vertebrate skeleton consisting of the large bone of each hip and the nearby bones of the spine — **pel·vic** \-vik\ adj
pem·mi·can also **pem·i·can** \'pe-mi-kən\ n : dried meat pounded fine and mixed with melted fat
¹**pen** \'pen\ vb **penned; pen·ning** : to shut in or as if in a pen
²**pen** n **1** : a small enclosure for animals **2** : a small place of confinement or storage
³**pen** n **1** : an implement for writing or drawing with ink or a similar fluid **2** : a writing instrument regarded as a means of expression
⁴**pen** vb **penned; pen·ning** : WRITE
⁵**pen** n : PENITENTIARY
⁶**pen** abbr peninsula
PEN abbr International Association of Poets, Playwrights, Editors, Essayists and Novelists
pe·nal \'pēn-ᵊl\ adj : of or relating to punishment

pe·nal·ize \'pēn-ᵊl-ˌīz, 'pen-\ vb **-ized; -iz·ing** : to put a penalty on
pen·al·ty \'pen-ᵊl-tē\ n, pl **-ties 1** : punishment for crime or offense **2** : something forfeited when a person fails to do something agreed to **3** : disadvantage, loss, or hardship due to some action
pen·ance \'pe-nəns\ n **1** : an act performed to show sorrow or repentance for sin **2** : a sacrament (as in the Roman Catholic Church) consisting of confession, absolution, and a penance directed by the confessor
pence \'pens\ pl of PENNY
pen·chant \'pen-chənt\ n [F, fr. prp. of pencher to incline, fr. (assumed) VL pendicare, fr. L pendere to weigh] : a strong inclination : LIKING **syn** leaning, propensity, predilection, predisposition
¹**pen·cil** \'pen-səl\ n : a writing or drawing tool consisting of or containing a slender cylinder of a solid marking substance
²**pencil** vb **-ciled** or **-cilled; -cil·ing** or **-cil·ling** : to draw or write with a pencil
pen·dant also **pen·dent** \'pen-dənt\ n : a hanging ornament (as an earring)
pen·dent or **pen·dant** \'pen-dənt\ adj : SUSPENDED, OVERHANGING
¹**pend·ing** \'pen-diŋ\ prep **1** : DURING **2** : while awaiting
²**pending** adj **1** : not yet decided **2** : IMMINENT
pen·du·lous \'pen-jə-ləs, -də-\ adj : hanging loosely : DROOPING
pen·du·lum \-ləm\ n : a body that swings freely from a fixed point
pe·ne·plain also **pe·ne·plane** \'pē-ni-ˌplān\ n : a large almost flat land surface shaped by erosion
pen·e·trate \'pe-nə-ˌtrāt\ vb **-trat·ed; -trat·ing 1** : to enter into : PIERCE **2** : PERMEATE **3** : to see into : UNDERSTAND **4** : to affect deeply — **pen·e·tra·ble** \-trə-bəl\ adj — **pen·e·tra·tion** \ˌpe-nə-'trā-shən\ n — **pen·e·tra·tive** \'pe-nə-ˌtrā-tiv\ adj
pen·e·trat·ing adj **1** : having the power of entering, piercing, or pervading ⟨a ~ shriek⟩ ⟨a ~ odor⟩ **2** : ACUTE, DISCERNING ⟨a ~ look⟩
pen·guin \'pen-gwən, 'peŋ-\ n : any of various erect short-legged flightless seabirds of the southern hemisphere
pen·i·cil·lin \ˌpe-nə-'si-lən\ n : any of several antibiotics produced by molds or synthetically and used against various bacteria
pen·in·su·la \pə-'ni-nsə-lə\ n [L paeninsula, fr. paene almost + insula island] : a long narrow portion of land extending out into the water — **pen·in·su·lar** \-lər\ adj
pe·nis \'pē-nəs\ n, pl **pe·nes** \-ˌnēz\ or **pe·nis·es** : a male organ of copulation that in the human male also functions as the channel by which urine leaves the body
¹**pen·i·tent** \'pe-nə-tənt\ adj : feeling sorrow for sins or offenses : REPENTANT — **pen·i·tence** \-təns\ n — **pen·i·ten·tial** \ˌpe-nə-'ten-chəl\ adj
²**penitent** n : a penitent person
¹**pen·i·ten·tia·ry** \ˌpe-nə-'ten-chə-rē\ n, pl **-ries** : a state or federal prison
²**penitentiary** adj : of, relating to, or incurring confinement in a penitentiary
pen·knife \'pen-ˌnīf\ n : a small pocketknife
pen·light or **pen·lite** \-ˌlīt\ n : a small flashlight resembling a fountain pen in size or shape
pen·man \'pen-mən\ n **1** : COPYIST **2** : one skilled in penmanship **3** : AUTHOR
pen·man·ship \-ˌship\ n : the art or practice of writing with the pen
Penn or **Penna** abbr Pennsylvania

\ə\abut \ᵊ\kitten \ər\further \a\ash \ā\ace \ä\mop, mar
\au̇\out \ch\chin \e\bet \ē\easy \g\go \i\hit \ī\ice \j\job
\ŋ\sing \ō\go \ȯ\law \ȯi\boy \th\thin \t̲h̲\the \ü\loot \u̇\foot
\y\yet \zh\vision *see also* Pronunciation Symbols page

pen name *n* : an author's pseudonym

pen·nant \'pe-nənt\ *n* **1** : a tapering flag used esp. for signaling **2** : a flag symbolic of championship

pen·ni \'pe-nē\ *n, pl* **pen·nia** \-nē-ə\ *or* **pen·nis** \-nēz\ — see *markka* at MONEY table

pen·non \'pe-nən\ *n* **1** : a long narrow ribbonlike flag borne on a lance **2** : WING

Penn·syl·va·nian \ˌpen-səl-'vā-nyən\ *adj* : of, relating to, or being the period of the Paleozoic era between the Mississippian and the Permian — **Pennsylvanian** *n*

pen·ny \'pe-nē\ *n, pl* **pennies** \-nēz\ *or* **pence** \'pens\ **1** : a British monetary unit formerly equal to ¹/₁₂ shilling but now equal to ¹/₁₀₀ pound; *also* : a coin of this value — see *pound* at MONEY table **2** *pl* **pennies** : a cent of the U.S. or Canada — **pen·ni·less** \'pe-ni-ləs\ *adj*

pen·ny–pinch·ing \'pe-nē-ˌpin-chiŋ\ *n* : PARSIMONY — **pen·ny–pinch·er** *n* — **penny–pinching** *adj*

pen·ny·weight \-ˌwāt\ *n* — see WEIGHT table

pen·ny–wise \-ˌwīz\ *adj* : wise or prudent only in small matters

pe·nol·o·gy \pi-'nä-lə-jē\ *n* : a branch of criminology dealing with prisons and the treatment of offenders

¹pen·sion \'pen-chən\ *n* : a fixed sum paid regularly esp. to a person retired from service

²pension *vb* : to pay a pension to — **pen·sion·er** *n*

pen·sive \'pen-siv\ *adj* : musingly, dreamily, or sadly thoughtful **syn** reflective, speculative, contemplative, meditative — **pen·sive·ly** *adv*

pen·stock \'pen-ˌstäk\ *n* **1** : a sluice or gate for regulating a flow **2** : a pipe for carrying water

pent \'pent\ *adj* : shut up : CONFINED

pen·ta·gon \'pen-tə-ˌgän\ *n* : a polygon of five angles and five sides — **pen·tag·o·nal** \pen-'ta-gən-ᵊl\ *adj*

pen·tam·e·ter \pen-'ta-mə-tər\ *n* : a line of verse containing five metrical feet

Pen·te·cost \'pen-ti-ˌkȯst\ *n* : the 7th Sunday after Easter observed as a church festival commemorating the descent of the Holy Spirit on the apostles — **Pen·te·cos·tal** \ˌpen-ti-'käst-ᵊl\ *adj*

Pentecostal *n* : a member of a Christian religious body that stresses expressive worship, evangelism, and spiritual gifts — **Pen·te·cos·tal·ism** \ˌpen-ti-'käst-ᵊl-ˌi-zəm\ *n*

pent·house \'pent-ˌhaus\ *n* [alter. of ME *pentis,* fr. MF *appentiz,* fr. *apent,* pp. of *apendre* to attach, hang against] **1** : a shed or sloping roof attached to a wall or building **2** : an apartment built on the roof of a building

pen·ul·ti·mate \pi-'nəl-tə-mət\ *adj* : next to the last ⟨∼ syllable⟩

pen·um·bra \pə-'nəm-brə\ *n, pl* **-brae** \-(ˌ)brē\ *or* **-bras** : the partial shadow surrounding a complete shadow (as in an eclipse)

pe·nu·ri·ous \pə-'nur-ē-əs, -'nyur-\ *adj* **1** : marked by penury **2** : MISERLY **syn** stingy, close, tightfisted, parsimonious

pen·u·ry \'pe-nyə-rē\ *n* **1** : extreme poverty **2** : extreme frugality

pe·on \'pē-ˌän, -ən\ *n, pl* **peons** *or* **pe·o·nes** \pā-'ō-nēz\ **1** : a member of the landless laboring class in Spanish America **2** : one bound to service for payment of a debt — **pe·on·age** \-ə-nij\ *n*

pe·o·ny \'pē-ə-nē\ *n, pl* **-nies** : any of a genus of chiefly Eurasian plants with large often double red, pink, or white flowers; *also* : the flower

¹peo·ple \'pē-pəl\ *n, pl* **people** [ME *peple,* fr. OF *peuple,* fr. L *populus*] **1** *pl* : human beings making up a group or linked by a common characteristic or interest **2** *pl* : human beings — often used in compounds instead of *persons* ⟨sales*people*⟩ **3** *pl* : the mass of persons in a community : POPULACE; *also* : ELECTORATE ⟨the ∼'s choice⟩ **4** *pl* **peoples** : a body of persons (as a tribe, nation, or race) united by a common culture, sense of kinship, or political organization

²people *vb* **peo·pled; peo·pling** : to supply or fill with or as if with people

¹pep \'pep\ *n* : brisk energy or initiative — **pep·py** *adj*

²pep *vb* **pepped; pep·ping** : to put pep into : STIMULATE

¹pep·per \'pe-pər\ *n* **1** : either of two pungent condiments from the berry (**pep·per·corn** \-ˌkȯrn\) of an East Indian climbing plant; *also* : this plant **2** : a plant related to the tomato and widely grown for its hot or mild sweet fruit; *also* : this fruit

²pepper *vb* **pep·pered; pep·per·ing** **1** : to sprinkle or season with or as if with pepper **2** : to shower with missiles or rapid blows

pep·per·mint \-ˌmint, -mənt\ *n* : a pungent aromatic mint; *also* : candy flavored with its oil

pep·per·o·ni \ˌpe-pə-'rō-nē\ *n* : a highly seasoned beef and pork sausage

pep·pery \'pe-pə-rē\ *adj* **1** : having the qualities of pepper : PUNGENT, HOT **2** : having a hot temper **3** : FIERY

pep·sin \'pep-sən\ *n* : an enzyme of the stomach that promotes digestion by breaking down proteins; *also* : a preparation of this used medicinally

pep·tic \'pep-tik\ *adj* **1** : relating to or promoting digestion **2** : caused by digestive juices ⟨a ∼ ulcer⟩

Pe·quot \'pē-ˌkwät\ *n* : a member of an American Indian people of eastern Connecticut

¹per \'pər\ *prep* **1** : by means of **2** : to or for each **3** : ACCORDING TO

²per *adv* : for each : APIECE

³per *abbr* **1** period **2** person

¹per·ad·ven·ture \'pər-əd-ˌven-chər\ *adv, archaic* : PERHAPS

²peradventure *n* **1** : DOUBT **2** : CHANCE 4

per·am·bu·late \pə-'ram-byə-ˌlāt\ *vb* **-lat·ed; -lat·ing** : to travel over esp. on foot — **per·am·bu·la·tion** \-ˌram-byə-'lā-shən\ *n*

per·am·bu·la·tor \pə-'ram-byə-ˌlā-tər\ *n, chiefly Brit* : a baby carriage

per an·num \(ˌ)pər-'a-nəm\ *adv* [ML] : in or for each year : ANNUALLY

per·cale \(ˌ)pər-'kāl, 'pər-ˌ; (ˌ)pər-'kal\ *n* : a fine woven cotton cloth

per cap·i·ta \(ˌ)pər-'ka-pə-tə\ *adv or adj* [ML, by heads] : by or for each person

per·ceive \pər-'sēv\ *vb* **per·ceived; per·ceiv·ing** **1** : to attain awareness : REALIZE **2** : to become aware of through the senses — **per·ceiv·able** *adj*

¹per·cent \pər-'sent\ *adv* [*per* + L *centum* hundred] : in each hundred

²percent *n, pl* **percent** *or* **percents** **1** : one part in a hundred : HUNDREDTH **2** : PERCENTAGE

per·cent·age \pər-'sen-tij\ *n* **1** : a part of a whole expressed in hundredths **2** : the result obtained by multiplying a number by a percent **3** : ADVANTAGE, PROFIT **4** : PROBABILITY; *also* : favorable odds

per·cen·tile \pər-'sen-ˌtīl\ *n* : a value on a scale of one hundred indicating the standing of a score or grade in terms of the percentage of scores or grades falling with or below it

per·cept \'pər-ˌsept\ *n* : an impression of an object obtained by use of the senses

per·cep·ti·ble \pər-'sep-tə-bəl\ *adj* : capable of being perceived — **per·cep·ti·bly** \-blē\ *adv*

per·cep·tion \pər-'sep-shən\ *n* **1** : an act or result of perceiving **2** : awareness of one's environment through physical sensation **3** : ability to understand : INSIGHT, COMPREHENSION **syn** penetration, discernment, discrimination

per·cep·tive \pər-'sep-tiv\ *adj* : capable of or exhibiting keen perception : OBSERVANT — **per·cep·tive·ly** *adv*

per·cep·tu·al \pər-'sep-chə-wəl\ *adj* : of, relating to, or involving sensory stimulus as opposed to abstract concept — **per·cep·tu·al·ly** *adv*

¹**perch** \'pərch\ *n* **1** : a roost for a bird **2** : a high station or vantage point

²**perch** *vb* : ROOST

³**perch** *n*, *pl* **perch** *or* **perch·es** : either of two small freshwater bony fishes used for food; *also* : any of various fishes resembling or related to these

per·chance \pər-'chans\ *adv* : PERHAPS

per·cip·i·ent \pər-'si-pē-ənt\ *adj* : capable of or characterized by perception — **per·cip·i·ence** \-əns\ *n*

per·co·late \'pər-kə-ˌlāt\ *vb* **-lat·ed; -lat·ing 1** : to trickle or filter through a permeable substance **2** : to filter hot water through or to extract the essence ⟨~ coffee⟩ — **per·co·la·tor** \-ˌlā-tər\ *n*

per con·tra \(ˌ)pər-'kän-trə\ *adv* [It, by the opposite side (of the ledger)] **1** : on the contrary **2** : by way of contrast

per·cus·sion \pər-'kə-shən\ *n* **1** : a sharp blow : IMPACT; *esp* : a blow upon a cap (**percussion cap**) designed to explode the charge in a firearm **2** : the beating or striking of a musical instrument; *also* : instruments sounded by striking, shaking, or scraping

per di·em \pər-'dē-əm, -'dī-\ *adv* [ML] : by the day — **per diem** *adj or n*

per·di·tion \pər-'di-shən\ *n* **1** : eternal damnation **2** : HELL

per·du·ra·ble \(ˌ)pər-'dùr-ə-bəl, -'dyùr-\ *adj* : very durable — **per·du·ra·bil·i·ty** \-ˌdùr-ə-'bi-lə-tē, -ˌdyùr-\ *n*

per·e·gri·na·tion \ˌper-ə-grə-'nā-shən\ *n* : a traveling about esp. on foot

per·e·grine \'per-ə-grən, -ˌgrēn\ *n* : a swift nearly cosmopolitan falcon that often nests in cities and is used in falconry

pe·remp·to·ry \pə-'remp-tə-rē\ *adj* **1** : barring a right of action or delay **2** : expressive of urgency or command : IMPERATIVE **3** : marked by arrogant self-assurance **syn** imperious, masterful, domineering, magisterial — **pe·remp·to·ri·ly** \-tə-rə-lē\ *adv*

¹**pe·ren·ni·al** \pə-'re-nē-əl\ *adj* **1** : present at all seasons of the year ⟨~ streams⟩ **2** : continuing to live from year to year ⟨~ plants⟩ **3** : recurring regularly : PERMANENT ⟨~ problems⟩ **syn** lasting, perpetual, enduring, everlasting — **pe·ren·ni·al·ly** *adv*

²**perennial** *n* : a perennial plant

perf *abbr* **1** perfect **2** perforated

¹**per·fect** \'pər-fikt\ *adj* **1** : being without fault or defect **2** : EXACT, PRECISE **3** : COMPLETE **4** : relating to or being a verb tense that expresses an action or state completed at the time of speaking or at a time spoken of — **per·fect·ly** *adv* — **per·fect·ness** *n*

²**per·fect** \pər-'fekt\ *vb* : to make perfect

³**per·fect** \'pər-fikt\ *n* : the perfect tense; *also* : a verb form in it

per·fect·ible \pər-'fek-tə-bəl, 'pər-fik-\ *adj* : capable of improvement or perfection — **per·fect·ibil·i·ty** \pər-ˌfek-tə-'bi-lə-tē, ˌpər-fik-\ *n*

per·fec·tion \pər-'fek-shən\ *n* **1** : the quality or state of being perfect **2** : the highest degree of excellence **3** : the act or process of perfecting

per·fec·tion·ist \-shə-nist\ *n* : a person who will not accept or be content with anything less than perfection

per·fec·to \pər-'fek-tō\ *n*, *pl* **-tos** : a cigar that is thick in the middle and tapers almost to a point at each end

per·fi·dy \'pər-fə-dē\ *n*, *pl* **-dies** [L *perfidia*, fr. *perfidus* faithless, fr. *per-* detrimental to + *fides* faith] : violation of faith or loyalty : TREACHERY — **per·fid·i·ous** \pər-'fi-dē-əs\ *adj* — **per·fid·i·ous·ly** *adv*

per·fo·rate \'pər-fə-ˌrāt\ *vb* **-rat·ed; -rat·ing** : to bore through : PIERCE; *esp* : to make a line of holes in to facilitate separation — **per·fo·ra·tion** \ˌpər-fə-'rā-shən\ *n*

per·force \pər-'fōrs\ *adv* : of necessity

per·form \pər-'fórm\ *vb* **1** : FULFILL **2** : CARRY OUT, DO **3** : FUNCTION **4** : to do in a set manner **5** : to give a performance — **per·form·er** *n*

per·for·mance \pər-'fòr-ˌməns\ *n* **1** : the act or process

of performing **2** : DEED, FEAT **3** : a public presentation

¹**per·fume** \pər-'fyüm, 'pər-ˌfyüm\ *n* **1** : a usu. pleasant odor : FRAGRANCE **2** : a preparation used for scenting

²**per·fume** \pər-'fyüm, 'pər-ˌfyüm\ *vb* **per·fumed; per·fum·ing** : SCENT

per·fum·ery \ˌpər-'fyü-mə-rē\ *n* : PERFUMES

per·func·to·ry \pər-'fəŋk-tə-rē\ *adj* : done merely as a duty — **per·func·to·ri·ly** *adv*

per·go·la \'pər-gə-lə\ *n* [It] : a structure consisting of posts supporting an open roof in the form of a trellis

perh *abbr* perhaps

per·haps \pər-'haps\ *adv* : possibly but not certainly

per·i·gee \'per-ə-ˌjē\ *n* [MF, fr. NL *perigeum*, fr. Gk *perigeion*, fr. *peri* around, near + *gē* earth] : the point at which an orbiting object is nearest the body (as the earth) being orbited

peri·he·lion \ˌper-ə-'hēl-yən\ *n*, *pl* **-he·lia** \-'hēl-yə\ : the point in the path of a celestial body (as a planet) that is nearest to the sun

per·il \'per-əl\ *n* : DANGER; *also* : a source of danger : RISK — **per·il·ous** *adj* — **per·il·ous·ly** *adv*

pe·rim·e·ter \pə-'ri-mə-tər\ *n* **1** : the boundary of a closed plane figure; *also* : its length **2** : a line bounding or protecting an area

¹**pe·ri·od** \'pir-ē-əd\ *n* **1** : SENTENCE; *also* : the full pause closing the utterance of a sentence **2** : END, STOP **3** : a punctuation mark . used esp. to mark the end of a declarative sentence or an abbreviation **4** : an extent of time; *esp* : one regarded as a stage or division in a process or development **5** : a portion of time in which a recurring phenomenon completes one cycle and is ready to begin again **6** : a single cyclic occurrence of menstruation **7** : any of the divisions of geologic time into which an era may be divided

²**period** *adj* : of or relating to a particular historical period ⟨~ furniture⟩

pe·ri·od·ic \ˌpir-ē-'ä-dik\ *adj* **1** : occurring at regular intervals of time **2** : happening repeatedly **3** : of or relating to a sentence that has no trailing elements following full grammatical statement of the essential idea

¹**pe·ri·od·i·cal** \ˌpir-ē-'ä-di-kəl\ *adj* **1** : PERIODIC **2** : published at regular intervals **3** : of or relating to a periodical — **pe·ri·od·i·cal·ly** \-k(ə-)lē\ *adv*

²**periodical** *n* : a periodical publication

periodic table *n* : an arrangement of chemical elements based on their atomic structure and on their properties ☞ For table, see next page.

peri·odon·tal \ˌper-ē-ō-'dänt-ᵊl\ *adj* **1** : surrounding a tooth **2** : of or affecting periodontal tissues or regions ⟨~ disease⟩

per·i·pa·tet·ic \ˌper-ə-pə-'te-tik\ *adj* : performed or performing while moving about : ITINERANT

pe·riph·er·al \pə-'ri-fər-əl\ *n* : a device connected to a computer to provide communication or auxiliary functions

peripheral nervous system *n* : the part of the nervous system that is outside the central nervous system and comprises the spinal nerves, the cranial nerves except the one supplying the retina, and the autonomic nervous system

pe·riph·ery \pə-'ri-fə-rē\ *n*, *pl* **-er·ies 1** : the boundary of a rounded figure **2** : outward bounds : border area — **pe·riph·er·al** \-fə-rəl\ *adj*

pe·riph·ra·sis \pə-'ri-frə-səs\ *n*, *pl* **-ra·ses** \-ˌsēz\ : CIRCUMLOCUTION

peri·scope \'per-ə-ˌskōp\ *n* : a tubular optical instrument enabling an observer to see an otherwise blocked field of view

\ə\abut \ᵊ\kitten \ər\further \a\ash \ā\ace \ä\mop, mar \aù\out \ch\chin \e\bet \ē\easy \g\go \i\hit \ī\ice \j\job \ŋ\sing \ō\go \ò\law \òi\boy \th\thin \t͟h\the \ü\loot \ù\foot \y\yet \zh\vision *see also* Pronunciation Symbols page

PERIODIC TABLE

This is a common long form of the table. Roman numerals and letters heading the vertical columns indicate the groups (there are differences of opinion regarding the letter designations, those given here being probably the most generally used). The horizontal rows represent the periods, with two series removed from the two very long periods and represented below the main table. Atomic numbers are given above the symbols for the elements. Compare ELEMENT table.

IA[1]																VIIA[3]	Zero[4]
1 H	IIA[2]															1 H	2 He
3 Li	4 Be											IIIA	IVA	VA	VIA	5 B	6 C	7 N	8 O	9 F	10 Ne
11 Na	12 Mg	IIIB	IVB	VB	VIB	VIIB	VIII			IB	IIB	13 Al	14 Si	15 P	16 S	17 Cl	18 Ar
19 K	20 Ca	21 Sc	22 Ti	23 V	24 Cr	25 Mn	26 Fe	27 Co	28 Ni	29 Cu	30 Zn	31 Ga	32 Ge	33 As	34 Se	35 Br	36 Kr
37 Rb	38 Sr	39 Y	40 Zr	41 Nb	42 Mo	43 Tc	44 Ru	45 Rh	46 Pd	47 Ag	48 Cd	49 In	50 Sn	51 Sb	52 Te	53 I	54 Xe
55 Cs	56 Ba	57 *La	72 Hf	73 Ta	74 W	75 Re	76 Os	77 Ir	78 Pt	79 Au	80 Hg	81 Tl	82 Pb	83 Bi	84 Po	85 At	86 Rn
87 Fr	88 Ra	89 #Ac	104 Unq	105 Unp	106 Unh												

*LANTHANIDE SERIES	58 Ce	59 Pr	60 Nd	61 Pm	62 Sm	63 Eu	64 Gd	65 Tb	66 Dy	67 Ho	68 Er	69 Tm	70 Yb	71 Lu
#ACTINIDE SERIES	90 Th	91 Pa	92 U	93 Np	94 Pu	95 Am	96 Cm	97 Bk	98 Cf	99 Es	100 Fm	101 Md	102 No	103 Lr

[1]Group IA (excluding hydrogen) comprises the alkali metals.
[2]Group IIA comprises the alkaline-earth metals.
[3]Group VIIA (excluding hydrogen) comprises the halogens.
[4]Group Zero comprises the noble gases.

---

per·ish \'per-ish\ vb : to become destroyed or ruined : DIE

per·ish·able \'per-i-shə-bəl\ adj : easily spoiled ⟨∼ foods⟩ — **perishable** n

peri·stal·sis \,per-ə-'stȯl-səs, -'stal-\ n, pl **-stal·ses** : waves of contraction passing along the walls of a hollow muscular organ and esp. the intestine and forcing its contents onward — **per·i·stal·tic** \-'stȯl-tik, -'stal-\ adj

peri·style \'per-ə-,stīl\ n : a row of columns surrounding a building or court

peri·to·ne·um \,per-ə-tə-'nē-əm\ n, pl **-ne·ums** or **-nea** : the smooth transparent serous membrane that lines the cavity of the abdomen — **peri·to·ne·al** \-'nē-əl\ adj

peri·to·ni·tis \,per-ə-tə-'nī-təs\ n : inflammation of the peritoneum

peri·wig \'per-i-,wig\ n : WIG

¹**per·i·win·kle** \'per-i-,wiŋ-kəl\ n : a usu. blue-flowered creeping plant cultivated as a ground cover

²**periwinkle** n : any of various small edible seashore snails

per·ju·ry \'pər-jə-rē\ n : the voluntary violation of an oath to tell the truth : lying under oath — **per·jure** \'pər-jər\ vb — **per·jur·er** n

¹**perk** \'pərk\ vb **1** : to thrust (as the head) up impudently or jauntily **2** : to regain vigor or spirit **3** : to make trim or brisk : FRESHEN — **perky** adj

²**perk** vb : PERCOLATE

³**perk** n : PERQUISITE — usu. used in pl.

per·lite \'pər-,līt\ n : volcanic glass that when expanded by heat forms a lightweight material used esp. in concrete and plaster and for potting plants

¹**perm** \'pərm\ n : PERMANENT

²**perm** vb : to give (hair) a permanent

³**perm** abbr permanent

per·ma·frost \'pər-mə-,frȯst\ n : a permanently frozen layer below the surface in frigid regions of a planet

¹**per·ma·nent** \'pər-mə-nənt\ adj : LASTING, STABLE —

per·ma·nence \-nəns\ n — **per·ma·nen·cy** \-nən-sē\ n — **per·ma·nent·ly** adv

²**permanent** n : a long-lasting hair wave or straightening

permanent press n : the process of treating fabrics with chemicals (as resin) and heat for setting the shape and for aiding wrinkle resistance

per·me·able \'pər-mē-ə-bəl\ adj : having small openings that permit liquids or gases to seep through — **per·me·a·bil·i·ty** \,pər-mē-ə-'bi-lə-tē\ n

per·me·ate \'pər-mē-,āt\ vb **-at·ed; -at·ing 1** : PERVADE **2** : to seep through the pores of : PENETRATE — **per·me·ation** \,pər-mē-'ā-shən\ n

Perm·ian \'pər-mē-ən\ adj : of, relating to, or being the latest period of the Paleozoic era — **Permian** n

per·mis·si·ble \pər-'mi-sə-bəl\ adj : that may be permitted : ALLOWABLE

per·mis·sion \pər-'mi-shən\ n : formal consent : AUTHORIZATION

per·mis·sive \pər-'mi-siv\ adj : granting permission; esp : INDULGENT — **per·mis·sive·ly** adv — **per·mis·sive·ness** n

¹**per·mit** \pər-'mit\ vb **per·mit·ted; per·mit·ting 1** : to consent to : ALLOW **2** : to make possible

²**per·mit** \'pər-,mit, pər-'mit\ n : a written permission : LICENSE

per·mu·ta·tion \,pər-myu-'tā-shən\ n **1** : a major or fundamental change **2** : the act or process of changing the order of an ordered set of objects **syn** innovation, mutation, vicissitude

per·ni·cious \pər-'ni-shəs\ adj [ME, fr. MF pernicieus, fr. L perniciosus, fr. pernicies destruction, fr. per- through + nec-, nex violent death] : very destructive or injurious — **per·ni·cious·ly** adv

per·ora·tion \'per-ə-,rā-shən, 'pər-\ n : the concluding part of a speech

¹**per·ox·ide** \pə-'räk-,sīd\ n : an oxide containing a large proportion of oxygen; esp : HYDROGEN PEROXIDE

²**per·ox·ide** *vb* **-id·ed; -id·ing** : to bleach with hydrogen peroxide

perp *abbr* **1** perpendicular **2** perpetrator

per·pen·dic·u·lar \ˌpər-pən-'di-kyə-lər\ *adj* **1** : standing at right angles to the plane of the horizon **2** : forming a right angle with each other or with a given line or plane — **perpendicular** *n* — **per·pen·dic·u·lar·i·ty** \-ˌdi-kyə-'lar-ə-tē\ *n* — **per·pen·dic·u·lar·ly** *adv*

per·pe·trate \'pər-pə-ˌtrāt\ *vb* **-trat·ed; -trat·ing** : to be guilty of : COMMIT — **per·pe·tra·tion** \ˌpər-pə-'trā-shən\ *n* — **per·pe·tra·tor** \'pər-pə-ˌtrā-tər\ *n*

per·pet·u·al \pər-'pe-chə-wəl\ *adj* **1** : continuing forever : EVERLASTING **2** : occurring continually : CONSTANT ⟨~ annoyance⟩ **syn** ceaseless, unceasing, continual, continuous, incessant, unremitting — **per·pet·u·al·ly** *adv*

perpetual calendar *n* : a table for finding the day of the week for any one of a large range of dates ☞ For table, see next page.

per·pet·u·ate \pər-'pe-chə-ˌwāt\ *vb* **-at·ed; -at·ing** : to make perpetual : cause to last indefinitely — **per·pet·u·a·tion** \-ˌpe-chə-'wā-shən\ *n*

per·pe·tu·i·ty \ˌpər-pə-'tü-ə-tē, -'tyü-\ *n, pl* **-ties 1** : ETERNITY 1 **2** : the quality or state of being perpetual

per·plex \pər-'pleks\ *vb* : to disturb mentally; *esp* : CONFUSE — **per·plex·i·ty** \-'plek-sə-tē\ *n*

per·plexed \-'plekst\ *adj* **1** : filled with uncertainty : PUZZLED **2** : full of difficulty : COMPLICATED — **per·plexed·ly** \-'plek-səd-lē\ *adv*

per·qui·site \'pər-kwə-zət\ *n* : a privilege or profit beyond regular pay

pers *abbr* person; personal

per se \(ˌ)pər-'sā\ *adv* [L] : by, of, or in itself : as such

per·se·cute \'pər-si-ˌkyüt\ *vb* **-cut·ed; -cut·ing** : to pursue in such a way as to injure or afflict : HARASS; *esp* : to cause to suffer because of belief — **per·se·cu·tion** \ˌpər-si-'kyü-shən\ *n* — **per·se·cu·tor** \'pər-si-ˌkyü-tər\ *n*

per·se·vere \ˌpər-sə-'vir\ *vb* **-vered; -ver·ing** : to persist (as in an undertaking) in spite of difficulties — **per·se·ver·ance** \-'vir-əns\ *n*

Per·sian \'pər-zhən\ *n* **1** : a native or inhabitant of ancient Persia **2** : a member of one of the peoples of modern Iran **3** : the language of the Persians

Persian cat *n* : any of a breed of stocky round-headed domestic cats that have a long silky coat

Persian lamb *n* : a pelt that is obtained from lambs that are older than those yielding broadtail and that has very silky tightly curled fur

per·si·flage \'pər-si-ˌfläzh, 'per-\ *n* [F, fr. *persifler* to banter, fr. *per-* thoroughly + *siffler* to whistle, hiss, boo, ultim. fr. L *sibilare*] : lightly jesting or mocking talk

per·sim·mon \pər-'si-mən\ *n* : either of two trees related to the ebony; *also* : the edible orange-red plumlike fruit of a persimmon

per·sist \pər-'sist, -'zist\ *vb* **1** : to go on resolutely or stubbornly in spite of difficulties **2** : to continue to exist — **per·sis·tence** \-'sis-təns, -'zis-\ *n* — **per·sis·ten·cy** \-tən-sē\ *n* — **per·sis·tent** \-tənt\ *adj* — **per·sis·tent·ly** *adv*

per·snick·e·ty \pər-'sni-kə-tē\ *adj* : fussy about small details

per·son \'pər-sən\ *n* [ME, fr. OF *persone*, fr. L *persona* actor's mask, character in a play, person, prob. fr. Etruscan *phersu* mask, fr. Gk *prosōpa*, pl. of *prosōpon* face, mask] **1** : a human being : INDIVIDUAL — used in combination esp. by those who prefer to avoid *man* in compounds applicable to both sexes ⟨chair*person*⟩ **2** : one of the three modes of being in the Godhead as understood by Trinitarians **3** : the body of a human being **4** : the individual personality of a human being : SELF **5** : reference of a segment of discourse to the speaker, to one spoken to, or to one spoken of esp. as indicated by certain pronouns

per·son·able \'pər-sə-nə-bəl\ *adj* : pleasant in person : ATTRACTIVE

per·son·age \'pər-sə-nij\ *n* : a person of rank, note, or distinction

¹**per·son·al** \'pər-sə-nəl\ *adj* **1** : of, relating to, or affecting a person : PRIVATE ⟨~ correspondence⟩ **2** : done in person ⟨a ~ inquiry⟩ **3** : relating to the person or body ⟨~ injuries⟩ **4** : relating to an individual esp. in an offensive way ⟨resented such ~ remarks⟩ **5** : of or relating to temporary or movable property as distinguished from real estate **6** : denoting grammatical person

²**personal** *n* **1** : a short newspaper paragraph relating to a person or group or to personal matters **2** : a short personal or private communication in the classified ads section of a newspaper

personal computer *n* : MICROCOMPUTER

per·son·al·i·ty \ˌpər-sə-'na-lə-tē\ *n, pl* **-ties 1** : an offensively personal remark ⟨indulges in *personalities*⟩ **2** : the collection of emotional and behavioral traits that characterize a person **3** : distinction of personal and social traits **4** : a well-known person ⟨a TV ~⟩ **syn** individuality, temperament, disposition, makeup

per·son·al·ize \'pər-sə-nə-ˌlīz\ *vb* **-ized; -iz·ing** : to make personal or individual; *esp* : to mark as belonging to a particular person

per·son·al·ly \-nə-lē\ *adv* **1** : in person **2** : as a person **3** : as far as oneself is concerned

per·son·al·ty \'pər-sə-nəl-tē\ *n, pl* **-ties** : personal property

per·so·na non gra·ta \pər-'sō-nə-ˌnän-'gra-tə, -'grä-\ *adj* [L] : being personally unacceptable or unwelcome

per·son·ate \'pər-sə-ˌnāt\ *vb* **-at·ed; -at·ing** : IMPERSONATE, REPRESENT

per·son·i·fy \pər-'sä-nə-ˌfī\ *vb* **-fied; -fy·ing 1** : to think of or represent as a person **2** : to be the embodiment of : INCARNATE ⟨~ the law⟩ — **per·son·i·fi·ca·tion** \-ˌsä-nə-fə-'kā-shən\ *n*

per·son·nel \ˌpər-sə-'nel\ *n* : a body of persons employed

per·spec·tive \pər-'spek-tiv\ *n* **1** : the science of painting and drawing so that objects represented have apparent depth and distance **2** : the aspect in which a subject or its parts are mentally viewed; *esp* : a view of things (as objects or events) in their true relationship or relative importance

per·spi·ca·cious \ˌpər-spə-'kā-shəs\ *adj* : having or showing keen understanding or discernment — **per·spi·cac·i·ty** \-'ka-sə-tē\ *n*

per·spic·u·ous \pər-'spi-kyə-wəs\ *adj* : plain to the understanding — **per·spi·cu·i·ty** \ˌpər-spə-'kyü-ə-tē\ *n*

per·spire \pər-'spīr\ *vb* **per·spired; per·spir·ing** : SWEAT — **per·spi·ra·tion** \ˌpər-spə-'rā-shən\ *n*

per·suade \pər-'swād\ *vb* **per·suad·ed; per·suad·ing** : to win over to a belief or course of action by argument or entreaty — **per·sua·sive** \-'swā-siv, -ziv\ *adj* — **per·sua·sive·ly** *adv* — **per·sua·sive·ness** *n*

per·sua·sion \pər-'swā-zhən\ *n* **1** : the act or process of persuading **2** : a system of religious beliefs; *also* : a group holding such beliefs

¹**pert** \'pərt\ *adj* [ME, open, bold, pert, modif. of OF *apert*, fr. L *apertus* open, fr. pp. of *aperire* to open] **1** : saucily free and forward : IMPUDENT **2** : stylishly trim : JAUNTY **3** : LIVELY

²**pert** *abbr* pertaining

per·tain \pər-'tān\ *vb* **1** : to belong to as a part, quality, or function ⟨duties ~*ing* to the office⟩ **2** : to have reference : RELATE ⟨books ~*ing* to birds⟩

per·ti·na·cious \ˌpər-tə-'nā-shəs\ *adj* **1** : holding reso-

\ə\abut \ᵊ\kitten \ər\further \a\ash \ā\ace \ä\mop, mar \aü\out \ch\chin \e\bet \ē\easy \g\go \i\hit \ī\ice \j\job \ŋ\sing \ō\go \o\law \oi\boy \th\thin \th̲\the \ü\loot \u̇\foot \y\yet \zh\vision *see also* Pronunciation Symbols page

PERPETUAL CALENDAR (1753–2050)

DAY OF THE MONTH					Jan. Oct.	Apr. July *Jan.	Sept. Dec.	June	Feb. Mar. Nov.	Aug. *Feb.	May	DAY OF THE WEEK
1	8	15	22	29	a	b	c	d	e	f	g	Monday
2	9	16	23	30	g	a	b	c	d	e	f	Tuesday
3	10	17	24	31	f	g	a	b	c	d	e	Wednesday
4	11	18	25		e	f	g	a	b	c	d	Thursday
5	12	19	26		d	e	f	g	a	b	c	Friday
6	13	20	27		c	d	e	f	g	a	b	Saturday
7	14	21	28		b	c	d	e	f	g	a	Sunday

Jan. Oct.	Apr. July *Jan.	Sept. Dec.	June	Feb. Mar. Nov.	Aug. *Feb.	May
1753	1754	1755	1761	1756	1757	1758
1759	1765	1760	1767	1762	1763	1769
1764	1771	1766	1772	1773	1768	1775
1770	1776	1777	1778	1779	1774	1780
1781	1782	1783	1789	1784	1785	1786
1787	1793	1788	1795	1790	1791	1797
1792	1799	1794	1801	1802	1796	1809
1798	1805	1800	1807	1813	1803	1815
1804	1811	1806	1812	1819	1808	1820
1810	1816	1817	1818	1824	1814	1826
1821	1822	1823	1829	1830	1825	1837
1827	1833	1828	1835	1841	1831	1843
1832	1839	1834	1840	1847	1836	1848
1838	1844	1845	1846	1852	1842	1854
1849	1850	1851	1857	1858	1853	1865
1855	1861	1856	1863	1869	1859	1871
1860	1867	1862	1868	1875	1864	1876
1866	1872	1873	1874	1880	1870	1882
1877	1878	1879	1885	1886	1881	1893
1883	1889	1884	1891	1897	1887	1899
1888	1895	1890	1896	1909	1892	1905
1894	1901	1902	1903	1915	1898	1911
1900	1907	1913	1908	1920	1904	1916
1906	1912	1919	1914	1926	1910	1922
1917	1918	1924	1925	1937	1921	1933
1923	1929	1930	1931	1943	1927	1939
1928	1935	1941	1936	1948	1932	1944
1934	1940	1947	1942	1954	1938	1950
1945	1946	1952	1953	1965	1949	1961
1951	1957	1958	1959	1971	1955	1967
1956	1963	1969	1964	1976	1960	1972
1962	1968	1975	1970	1982	1966	1978
1973	1974	1980	1981	1993	1977	1989
1979	1985	1986	1987	1999	1983	1995
1984	1991	1997	1992	2004	1988	2000
1990	1996	2003	1998	2010	1994	2006
2001	2002	2008	2009	2021	2005	2017
2007	2013	2014	2015	2027	2011	2023
2012	2019	2025	2020	2032	2016	2028
2018	2024	2031	2026	2038	2022	2034
2029	2030	2036	2037	2049	2033	2045
2035	2041	2042	2043		2039	
2040	2047		2048		2044	
2046					2050	

To find the day of the week corresponding to any date:

1. Find the small letter directly under the name of the month* and opposite the number of the day of the month.
2. Next, find the year in the year columns and follow the column up to where that same letter appears.
3. Follow the row out to the right to find the day of the week that the date occurred in that year.

For example, to find the day of the week on which July 20, 1969 fell, find the row in which number 20 appears and the column in which July appears. Follow the row across and the column down to find that they converge on the letter d. Next, find the year 1969 in the third year column and follow the column up to where the letter d appears. Follow that row out to the right to find that July 20, 1969 was a Sunday.

*Leap years are shown in *italics*. For dates occurring in January or February of a leap year, use *italic* names of months, above.

lutely to an opinion or purpose **2** : obstinately persistent ⟨a ~ bill collector⟩ **syn** dogged, mulish, headstrong, perverse — **per·ti·nac·i·ty** \-'na-sə-tē\ *n*

per·ti·nent \'pərt-ᵊn-ənt\ *adj* : relating to the matter under consideration **syn** relevant, germane, applicable, apropos — **per·ti·nence** \-əns\ *n*

per·turb \pər-'tərb\ *vb* : to disturb greatly esp. in mind : UPSET — **per·tur·ba·tion** \ˌpər-tər-'bā-shən\ *n*

per·tus·sis \pər-'tə-səs\ *n* : WHOOPING COUGH

pe·ruke \pə-'rük\ *n* : WIG

pe·ruse \pə-'rüz\ *vb* **pe·rused; pe·rus·ing** : READ; *esp* : to read over attentively or leisurely — **pe·rus·al** \-'rü-zəl\ *n*

Pe·ru·vi·an \pə-'rü-vē-ən\ *n* : a native or inhabitant of Peru

per·vade \pər-'vād\ *vb* **per·vad·ed; per·vad·ing** : to spread through every part of : PERMEATE, PENETRATE — **per·va·sive** \-ˌvā-siv, -ziv\ *adj*

per·verse \pər-'vərs\ *adj* **1** : turned away from what is right or good : CORRUPT **2** : obstinate in opposing what is reasonable or accepted — **per·verse·ly** *adv* — **per·verse·ness** *n* — **per·ver·si·ty** \-'vər-sə-tē\ *n*

per·ver·sion \pər-'vər-zhən\ *n* **1** : the action of perverting : the condition of being perverted **2** : a perverted form of something; *esp* : aberrant sexual behavior

¹**per·vert** \pər-'vərt\ *vb* **1** : to lead astray : CORRUPT ⟨~ the young⟩ **2** : to divert to a wrong purpose : MISAPPLY ⟨~ evidence⟩ **syn** deprave, debase, debauch, demoralize — **per·ver·ter** *n*

²**per·vert** \'pər-ˌvərt\ *n* : one that is perverted; *esp* : one given to sexual perversion

pe·se·ta \pə-'sā-tə\ *n* — see MONEY table

pe·se·wa \pə-'sā-wə\ *n* — see *cedi* at MONEY table

pes·ky \'pes-kē\ *adj* **pes·ki·er; -est** : causing annoyance : TROUBLESOME

pe·so \'pā-sō\ *n, pl* **pesos** — see MONEY table

pes·si·mism \'pe-sə-ˌmi-zəm\ *n* [F *pessimisme*, fr. L *pessimus* worst] : an inclination to take the least favorable view (as of events) or to expect the worst — **pes·si·mist** \-mist\ *n* — **pes·si·mis·tic** \ˌpe-sə-'mis-tik\ *adj*

pest \'pest\ *n* **1** : a destructive epidemic disease : PLAGUE **2** : a plant or animal detrimental to humans **3** : one that pesters : NUISANCE — **pesty** *adj*

pes·ter \'pes-tər\ *vb* : to harass with petty irritations : ANNOY

pes·ti·cide \'pes-tə-ˌsīd\ *n* : an agent used to destroy pests

pes·tif·er·ous \pes-'ti-fə-rəs\ *adj* **1** : PESTILENT **2** : ANNOYING

pes·ti·lence \'pes-tə-ləns\ *n* : a destructive infectious swiftly spreading disease; *esp* : BUBONIC PLAGUE

pes·ti·lent \-lənt\ *adj* **1** : dangerous to life : DEADLY **2** : PERNICIOUS, HARMFUL **3** : TROUBLESOME **4** : INFECTIOUS, CONTAGIOUS

pes·ti·len·tial \ˌpes-tə-'len-chəl\ *adj* **1** : causing or tending to cause pestilence : DEADLY **2** : morally harmful

pes·tle \'pes-əl, 'pest-ᵊl\ *n* : an implement for grinding substances in a mortar — **pestle** *vb*

¹**pet** \'pet\ *n* **1** : FAVORITE, DARLING **2** : a domesticated animal kept for pleasure rather than utility

²**pet** *adj* **1** : kept or treated as a pet ⟨~ dog⟩ **2** : expressing fondness ⟨~ name⟩ **3** : particularly liked or favored

³**pet** *vb* **pet·ted; pet·ting 1** : to stroke gently or lovingly **2** : to make a pet of : PAMPER **3** : to engage in amorous kissing and caressing

⁴**pet** *n* : a fit of peevishness, sulkiness, or anger — **pet·tish** *adj*

Pet *abbr* Peter

pet·al \'pet-ᵊl\ *n* : one of the modified leaves of a flower's corolla

pe·tard \pə-'tärd, -'tär\ *n* : a case containing an explosive to break down a door or gate or breach a wall

pe·ter \'pē-tər\ *vb* : to diminish gradually and come to an end ⟨his energy ~ed out⟩

Pe·ter \'pē-tər\ *n* — see BIBLE table

pet·i·ole \'pe-tē-ˌōl\ *n* : a slender stem that supports a leaf

pe·tite \pə-'tēt\ *adj* [F] : small and trim of figure ⟨a ~ woman⟩ — **petite** *n*

pe·tit four \ˌpe-tē-'för\ *n, pl* **petits fours** *or* **petit fours** \-'förz\ [F, lit., small oven] : a small cake cut from pound or sponge cake and frosted

¹**pe·ti·tion** \pə-'ti-shən\ *n* : an earnest request : ENTREATY; *esp* : a formal written request made to an authority

²**petition** *vb* : to make a request to or for — **pe·ti·tion·er** *n*

pe·trel \'pe-trəl\ *n* : any of numerous seabirds that fly far from land

pet·ri·fy \'pe-trə-ˌfī\ *vb* **-fied; -fy·ing 1** : to convert (organic matter) into stone or stony material **2** : to make rigid or inactive (as from fear or awe) — **pet·ri·fac·tion** \ˌpe-trə-'fak-shən\ *n*

pet·ro·chem·i·cal \ˌpe-trō-'ke-mi-kəl\ *n* : a chemical isolated or derived from petroleum or natural gas — **pet·ro·chem·is·try** \-'ke-mə-strē\ *n*

pet·rol \'pe-trəl\ *n, Brit* : GASOLINE

pet·ro·la·tum \ˌpe-trə-'lā-təm\ *n* : PETROLEUM JELLY

pe·tro·leum \pə-'trō-lē-əm\ *n* [ML, fr. Gk *petra* rock + L *oleum* oil] : an oily flammable liquid obtained from wells drilled in the ground and refined into gasoline, fuel oils, and other products

petroleum jelly *n* : a tasteless, odorless, and oily or greasy substance from petroleum that is used esp. in ointments and dressings

¹**pet·ti·coat** \'pe-tē-ˌkōt\ *n* **1** : a skirt worn under a dress **2** : an outer skirt

²**petticoat** *adj* : of, relating to, or exercised by women : FEMALE

pet·ti·fog \'pe-tē-ˌfòg, -ˌfäg\ *vb* **-fogged; -fog·ging 1** : to engage in legal trickery **2** : to quibble over insignificant details — **pet·ti·fog·ger** *n*

pet·ty \'pe-tē\ *adj* **pet·ti·er; -est** [ME *pety* small, minor, alter. of *petit*, fr. MF, small] **1** : having secondary rank : MINOR ⟨~ prince⟩ **2** : of little importance : TRIFLING ⟨~ faults⟩ **3** : marked by narrowness or meanness — **pet·ti·ly** \'pe-tə-lē\ *adv* — **pet·ti·ness** \-tē-nəs\ *n*

petty officer *n* : a subordinate officer in the navy or coast guard appointed from among the enlisted men

petty officer first class *n* : a petty officer ranking below a chief petty officer

petty officer second class *n* : a petty officer ranking below a petty officer first class

petty officer third class *n* : a petty officer ranking below a petty officer second class

pet·u·lant \'pe-chə-lənt\ *adj* : marked by capricious ill humor **syn** irritable, peevish, fretful, fractious, querulous — **pet·u·lance** \-ləns\ *n* — **pet·u·lant·ly** *adv*

pe·tu·nia \pi-'tün-yə, -'tyün-\ *n* : any of a genus of tropical American herbs related to the potato and having bright funnel-shaped flowers

pew \'pyü\ *n* [ME *pewe*, fr. MF *puie* balustrade, fr. L *podia*, pl. of *podium* parapet, podium, fr. Gk *podion* base, dim. of *pod-, pous* foot] : any of the benches with backs fixed in rows in a church

pe·wee \'pē-(ˌ)wē\ *n* : any of various small flycatchers

pew·ter \'pyü-tər\ *n* **1** : an alloy of tin used esp. for household utensils **2** : a bluish gray — **pewter** *adj* — **pew·ter·er** *n*

pey·o·te \pā-'ō-tē\ *also* **pey·otl** \-'ōt-ᵊl\ *n* : a stimulant

---

\ə\abut \ᵊ\kitten \ər\further \a\ash \ā\ace \ä\mop, mar
\au̇\out \ch\chin \e\bet \ē\easy \g\go \i\hit \ī\ice \j\job
\ŋ\sing \ō\go \ȯ\law \ȯi\boy \th\thin \th̲\the \ü\loot \u̇\foot
\y\yet \zh\vision *see also* Pronunciation Symbols page

drug derived from an American cactus; *also* : this cactus

pf *abbr* **1** pfennig **2** preferred

PFC *or* **Pfc** *abbr* private first class

pfd *abbr* preferred

pfen·nig \'fe-nig\ *n, pl* **pfennig** *also* **pfennigs** *or* **pfen·ni·ge** \'fe-ni-gə\ — see *deutsche mark* at MONEY table

pg *abbr* page

PG *abbr* postgraduate

PGA *abbr* Professional Golfers' Association

pH \(ˌ)pē-'āch\ *n* : a value used to express acidity and alkalinity; *also* : the condition represented by such a value

PH *abbr* **1** pinch hit **2** public health

pha·eton \'fā-ət-ᵊn\ *n* [F *phaéton*, fr. Gk *Phaethōn*, son of the sun god who persuaded his father to let him drive the chariot of the sun but who lost control of the horses with disastrous consequences] **1** : a light 4-wheeled horse-drawn vehicle **2** : an open automobile with two cross seats

phaeton 1

phage \'fāj\ *n* : BACTERIOPHAGE

pha·lanx \'fā-ˌlaŋks\ *n, pl* **pha·lanx·es** *or* **pha·lan·ges** \fə-'lan-ˌjēz\ **1** : a group or body (as of troops) in compact formation **2** *pl* **phalanges** : one of the digital bones of the hand or foot of a vertebrate

phal·a·rope \'fa-lə-ˌrōp\ *n, pl* **-ropes** *also* **-rope** : any of a genus of small shorebirds related to sandpipers

phal·lic \'fa-lik\ *adj* **1** : of, relating to, or resembling a phallus **2** : relating to or being the stage of psychosexual development in psychoanalytic theory during which children become interested in their own sexual organs

phal·lus \'fa-ləs\ *n, pl* **phal·li** \'fa-ˌlī\ *or* **phal·lus·es** : PENIS; *also* : a symbolic representation of the penis

Phan·er·o·zo·ic \ˌfa-nə-rə-'zō-ik\ *adj* : of, relating to, or being an eon of geologic history comprising the Paleozoic, Mesozoic, and Cenozoic

phan·tasm \'fan-ˌta-zəm\ *n* : a product of the imagination : ILLUSION — **phan·tas·mal** \fan-'taz-məl\ *adj*

phan·tas·ma·go·ria \fan-ˌtaz-mə-'gōr-ē-ə\ *n* : a constantly shifting complex succession of things seen or imagined; *also* : a scene that constantly changes or fluctuates

phantasy *var of* FANTASY

phan·tom \'fan-təm\ *n* **1** : something (as a specter) that is apparent to sense but has no substantial existence **2** : a mere show : SHADOW — **phantom** *adj*

pha·raoh \'fer-ō, 'fā-rō\ *n, often cap* : a ruler of ancient Egypt

phar·i·sa·ical \ˌfar-ə-'sā-ə-kəl\ *adj* : hypocritically self-righteous

phar·i·see \'far-ə-ˌsē\ *n* **1** *cap* : a member of an ancient Jewish sect noted for strict observance of rites and ceremonies of the traditional law **2** : a self-righteous or hypocritical person — **phar·i·sa·ic** \ˌfar-ə-'sā-ik\ *adj*

pharm *abbr* pharmaceutical; pharmacist; pharmacy

phar·ma·ceu·ti·cal \ˌfär-mə-'sü-ti-kəl\ *adj* : of, relating to, or engaged in pharmacy or the manufacture and sale of medicinal drugs — **pharmaceutical** *n*

phar·ma·col·o·gy \ˌfär-mə-'kä-lə-jē\ *n* **1** : the science of drugs esp. as related to medicinal uses **2** : the reactions and properties of one or more drugs — **phar·ma·co·log·i·cal** \-ji-kəl\ *also* **phar·ma·co·log·ic** \-kə-'lä-jik\ *adj* — **phar·ma·col·o·gist** \-'kä-lə-jist\ *n*

phar·ma·co·poe·ia *also* **phar·ma·co·pe·ia** \-kə-'pē-ə\ *n* **1** : a book describing drugs and medicinal preparations **2** : a stock of drugs

phar·ma·cy \'fär-mə-sē\ *n, pl* **-cies** **1** : the art, practice, or profession of preparing and dispensing medical drugs **2** : DRUGSTORE — **phar·ma·cist** \-sist\ *n*

phar·ynx \'far-iŋks\ *n, pl* **pha·ryn·ges** \fə-'rin-ˌjēz\ *also* **phar·ynx·es** : the space just back of the mouth into which the nostrils, esophagus, and trachea open — **pha·ryn·ge·al** \fə-'rin-jəl, ˌfar-ən-'jē-əl\ *adj*

phase \'fāz\ *n* **1** : a particular appearance in a recurring series of changes ⟨∼s of the moon⟩ **2** : a stage or interval in a process or cycle ⟨first ∼ of an experiment⟩ **3** : an aspect or part under consideration — **pha·sic** \'fā-zik\ *adj*

phase in *vb* : to introduce in stages

phase·out \'fā-ˌzaút\ *n* : a gradual stopping of operations or production

phase out *vb* : to stop production or use of in stages

PhD *abbr* [L *philosophiae doctor*] doctor of philosophy

pheas·ant \'fez-ᵊnt\ *n, pl* **pheasant** *or* **pheasants** : any of numerous long-tailed brilliantly colored game birds related to the domestic chicken

pheasant

phen·cy·cli·dine \ˌfen-'sī-klə-ˌdēn\ *n* : a drug used esp. as a veterinary anesthetic and sometimes illicitly to induce vivid mental imagery

phe·no·bar·bi·tal \ˌfē-nō-'bär-bə-ˌtöl\ *n* : a crystalline drug used as a hypnotic and sedative

phe·nol \'fē-ˌnöl\ *n* : a corrosive poisonous acidic compound present in coal and wood tars and used in solution as a disinfectant

phe·nom·e·non \fi-'nä-mə-ˌnän, -nən\ *n, pl* **-na** \-nə\ *or* **-nons** [LL *phaenomenon*, fr. Gk *phainomenon*, fr. neut. of *phainomenos*, prp. of *phainesthai* to appear] **1** *pl* **-na** : an observable fact or event **2** : an outward sign of the working of a law of nature **3** *pl* **-nons** : an extraordinary person or thing : PRODIGY — **phe·nom·e·nal** \-'nä-mən-ᵊl\ *adj* — **phe·nom·e·non·al·ly** *adv*

pher·o·mone \'fer-ə-ˌmōn\ *n* : a chemical substance that is produced by an animal and serves to stimulate a behavioral response in other individuals of the same species — **pher·o·mon·al** \ˌfer-ə-'mōn-ᵊl\ *adj*

phi \'fī\ *n* : the 21st letter of the Greek alphabet — Φ or φ

phi·al \'fī-əl\ *n* : VIAL

Phil *abbr* Philippians

phi·lan·der \fə-'lan-dər\ *vb* **1** : to make love without serious intent **2** : to have many love affairs — **phi·lan·der·er** *n*

phi·lan·thro·py \fə-'lan-thrə-pē\ *n, pl* **-pies** **1** : goodwill toward all people; *esp* : effort to promote human wel-

fare **2** : a charitable act or gift; *also* : an organization that distributes or is supported by donated funds —
phil·an·throp·ic \ˌfi-lən-ˈthrä-pik\ *adj* — **phi·lan·throp·i·cal·ly** \-pi-k(ə-)lē\ *adv* — **phi·lan·thro·pist** \fə-ˈlan-thrə-pist\ *n*
phi·lat·e·ly \fə-ˈlat-ᵊl-ē\ *n* : the collection and study of postage and imprinted stamps — **phi·lat·e·lic** \ˌfi-lə-ˈte-lik\ *adj* — **phi·lat·e·list** \-ᵊl-ist\ *n*
Phi·le·mon \fə-ˈlē-mən, fī-\ *n* — see BIBLE table
Phi·lip·pi·ans \fə-ˈli-pē-ənz\ *n* — see BIBLE table
phi·lip·pic \fə-ˈli-pik\ *n* : TIRADE
Phil·lips \ˈfi-ləps\ *adj* : of, relating to, or being a screw having a head with a cross slot or its corresponding screwdriver
phi·lis·tine \ˈfi-lə-ˌstēn; fə-ˈlis-tən\ *n, often cap* [*Philistine,* inhabitant of ancient Philistia (Palestine)] : a person who is smugly insensitive or indifferent to intellectual or artistic values — **philistine** *adj, often cap*
philo·den·dron \ˌfi-lə-ˈden-drən\ *n, pl* **-drons** *or* **-dra** \-drə\ [NL, fr. Gk, neut. of *philodendros* loving trees, fr. *philos* dear, friendly + *dendron* tree] : any of various plants of the arum family grown for their showy foliage
phi·lol·o·gy \fə-ˈlä-lə-je\ *n* **1** : the study of literature and relevant fields **2** : LINGUISTICS; *esp* : historical and comparative linguistics — **phil·o·log·i·cal** \ˌfi-lə-ˈlä-ji-kəl\ *adj* — **phi·lol·o·gist** \fə-ˈlä-lə-jist\ *n*
philos *abbr* philosopher; philosophy
phi·los·o·pher \fə-ˈlä-sə-fər\ *n* **1** : a reflective thinker : SCHOLAR **2** : a student of or specialist in philosophy **3** : a person whose philosophical perspective makes it possible to meet trouble calmly
phi·los·o·phize \fə-ˈlä-sə-ˌfīz\ *vb* **-phized; -phiz·ing 1** : to reason like a philosopher : THEORIZE **2** : to expound a philosophy esp. superficially
phi·los·o·phy \fə-ˈlä-sə-fē\ *n, pl* **-phies 1** : sciences and liberal arts exclusive of medicine, law, and theology ⟨doctor of ∼⟩ **2** : a critical study of fundamental beliefs and the grounds for them **3** : a system of philosophical concepts ⟨Aristotelian ∼⟩ **4** : a basic theory concerning a particular subject or sphere of activity **5** : the sum of the ideas and convictions of an individual or group ⟨her ∼ of life⟩ **6** : calmness of temper and judgment — **phil·o·soph·ic** \ˌfi-lə-ˈsä-fik\ *or* **phil·o·soph·i·cal** \-fi-kəl\ *adj* — **phil·o·soph·i·cal·ly** \-k(ə-)lē\ *adv*
phil·ter *or* **phil·tre** \ˈfil-tər\ *n* **1** : a potion, drug, or charm held to arouse sexual passion **2** : a magic potion
phle·bi·tis \fli-ˈbī-təs\ *n* : inflammation of a vein
phle·bot·o·my \fli-ˈbä-tə-mē\ *n, pl* **-mies** : the opening of a vein esp. for removing or releasing blood
phlegm \ˈflem\ *n* : thick mucus secreted in abnormal quantity esp. in the nose and throat
phleg·mat·ic \fleg-ˈma-tik\ *adj* : having or showing a slow and stolid temperament **syn** impassive, apathetic, stoic
phlo·em \ˈflō-ˌem\ *n* : a vascular plant tissue external to the xylem that carries dissolved food material and functions in support and storage
phlox \ˈfläks\ *n, pl* **phlox** *or* **phlox·es** : any of a genus of American herbs that have tall stalks with showy spreading terminal clusters of flowers
pho·bia \ˈfō-bē-ə\ *n* : an irrational persistent fear or dread
phoe·be \ˈfē-(ˌ)bē\ *n* : a flycatcher of the eastern U.S. that has a slight crest and is grayish brown above and yellowish white below
phoe·nix \ˈfē-niks\ *n* : a legendary bird held to live for centuries and then to burn itself to death and rise fresh and young from its ashes
phon *abbr* phonetics
¹phone \ˈfōn\ *n* **1** : TELEPHONE **2** : EARPHONE
²phone *vb* **phoned; phon·ing** : TELEPHONE

pho·neme \ˈfō-ˌnēm\ *n* : one of the elementary units of speech that distinguish one utterance from another — **pho·ne·mic** \fō-ˈnē-mik\ *adj*
pho·net·ics \fə-ˈne-tiks\ *n* : the study and systematic classification of the sounds made in spoken utterance — **pho·net·ic** \-tik\ *adj* — **pho·ne·ti·cian** \ˌfō-nə-ˈti-shən\ *n*
pho·nic \ˈfä-nik\ *adj* **1** : of, relating to, or producing sound **2** : of or relating to the sounds of speech or to phonics — **pho·ni·cal·ly** \-ni-k(ə-)lē\ *adv*
pho·nics \ˈfä-niks\ *n* : a method of teaching people to read and pronounce words by learning the phonetic value of letters, letter groups, and esp. syllables
pho·no·graph \ˈfō-nə-ˌgraf\ *n* : an instrument for reproducing sounds by means of the vibration of a needle following a spiral groove on a revolving disc
pho·nol·o·gy \fə-ˈnä-lə-jē\ *n* : a study and description of the sound changes in a language — **pho·no·log·i·cal** \ˌfō-nə-ˈlä-ji-kəl\ *adj* — **pho·nol·o·gist** \fə-ˈnä-lə-jist\ *n*
pho·ny *or* **pho·ney** \ˈfō-nē\ *adj* **pho·ni·er; -est** : marked by empty pretension : FAKE — **phony** *n*
phos·phate \ˈfäs-ˌfāt\ *n* : a salt of a phosphoric acid — **phos·phat·ic** \fäs-ˈfa-tik\ *adj*
phos·phor \ˈfäs-fər\ *n* : a phosphorescent substance
phos·pho·res·cence \ˌfäs-fə-ˈres-ᵊns\ *n* **1** : luminescence caused by radiation absorption followed by emission that continues after the incident radiation stops **2** : an enduring luminescence without sensible heat — **phos·pho·res·cent** \-ᵊnt\ *adj* — **phos·pho·res·cent·ly** *adv*
phosphoric acid \fäs-ˈfȯr-ik-, -ˈfär-\ *n* : any of several oxygen-containing acids of phosphorus
phos·pho·rus \ˈfäs-fə-rəs\ *n* [NL, fr. Gk *phōsphoros* light-bearing, fr. *phōs* light + *pherein* to carry, bring] : a nonmetallic chemical element that has characteristics similar to nitrogen and occurs widely esp. as phosphates — see ELEMENT table — **phos·phor·ic** \fäs-ˈfȯr-ik, -ˈfär-\ *adj* — **phos·pho·rous** \ˈfäs-fə-rəs; fäs-ˈfōr-əs, -ˈfȯr-\ *adj*
phot- *or* **photo-** *comb form* **1** : light ⟨*photo*graphy⟩ **2** : photograph : photographic ⟨*photo*engraving⟩ **3** : photoelectric ⟨*photo*cell⟩
pho·to \ˈfō-tō\ *n, pl* **photos** : PHOTOGRAPH — **photo** *vb or adj*
pho·to·cell \ˈfō-tə-ˌsel\ *n* : PHOTOELECTRIC CELL
pho·to·chem·i·cal \ˌfō-tō-ˈke-mi-kəl\ *adj* : of, relating to, or resulting from the chemical action of radiant energy
pho·to·com·pose \-kəm-ˈpōz\ *vb* : to compose reading matter for reproduction by means of characters photographed on film — **pho·to·com·po·si·tion** \-ˌkäm-pə-ˈzi-shən\ *n*
pho·to·copy \ˈfō-tə-ˌkä-pē\ *n* : a photographic reproduction of graphic matter — **photocopy** *vb*
pho·to·elec·tric \ˌfō-tō-i-ˈlek-trik\ *adj* : relating to an electrical effect due to the interaction of light with matter — **pho·to·elec·tri·cal·ly** \-tri-k(ə-)lē\ *adv*
photoelectric cell *n* : a device whose electrical properties are modified by the action of light
pho·to·en·grave \ˌfō-tō-in-ˈgrāv\ *vb* : to make a photoengraving of
pho·to·en·grav·ing *n* : a process by which an etched printing plate is made from a photograph or drawing; *also* : a print made from such a plate
photo finish *n* : a race finish so close that a photograph of the finish is used to determine the winner
¹pho·tog \fə-ˈtäg\ *n* : PHOTOGRAPHER
²photog *abbr* photographic; photography

\ə\abut \ᵊ\kitten \ər\further \a\ash \ā\ace \ä\mop, mar \au̇\out \ch\chin \e\bet \ē\easy \g\go \i\hit \ī\ice \j\job \ŋ\sing \ō\go \ȯ\law \ȯi\boy \th\thin \t̲h̲\the \ü\loot \u̇\foot \y\yet \zh\vision *see also* Pronunciation Symbols page

pho·to·ge·nic \ˌfō-tə-ˈje-nik\ *adj* : eminently suitable esp. aesthetically for being photographed

pho·to·graph \ˈfō-tə-ˌgraf\ *n* : a picture taken by photography — **photograph** *vb* — **pho·tog·ra·pher** \fə-ˈtä-grə-fər\ *n*

pho·tog·ra·phy \fə-ˈtä-grə-fē\ *n* : the art or process of producing images on a sensitized surface (as film in a camera) by the action of light — **pho·to·graph·ic** \ˌfō-tə-ˈgra-fik\ *adj* — **pho·to·graph·i·cal·ly** \-fi-k(ə-)lē\ *adv*

pho·to·gra·vure \ˌfō-tə-grə-ˈvyūr\ *n* : a process for making prints from an intaglio plate prepared by photographic methods

pho·to·li·thog·ra·phy \ˌfō-tō-li-ˈthä-grə-fē\ *n* : the process of photographically transferring a pattern to a surface for etching (as in making an integrated circuit)

pho·tom·e·ter \fō-ˈtä-mə-tər\ *n* : an instrument for measuring the intensity of light — **pho·to·met·ric** \ˌfō-tə-ˈme-trik\ *adj* — **pho·tom·e·try** \fō-ˈtä-mə-trē\ *n*

pho·to·mi·cro·graph \ˌfō-tə-ˈmī-krə-ˌgraf\ *n* : a photograph of a microscope image — **pho·to·mi·crog·ra·phy** \-mī-ˈkrä-grə-fē\ *n*

pho·ton \ˈfō-ˌtän\ *n* : a quantum of electromagnetic radiation

pho·to·play \ˈfō-tō-ˌplā\ *n* : MOTION PICTURE

pho·to·sen·si·tive \ˌfō-tə-ˈsen-sə-tiv\ *adj* : sensitive or sensitized to the action of radiant energy

pho·to·sphere \ˈfō-tə-ˌsfir\ *n* : the luminous surface of a star — **pho·to·spher·ic** \ˌfō-tə-ˈsfir-ik, -ˈsfer-\ *adj*

pho·to·syn·the·sis \ˌfō-tō-ˈsin-thə-səs\ *n* : the process by which chlorophyll-containing plants make carbohydrates from water and from carbon dioxide in the air in the presence of light — **pho·to·syn·the·size** \-ˌsīz\ *vb* — **pho·to·syn·thet·ic** \-sin-ˈthe-tik\ *adj*

phr *abbr* phrase

¹**phrase** \ˈfrāz\ *n* **1** : a brief expression **2** : a group of two or more grammatically related words that form a sense unit expressing a thought

²**phrase** *vb* **phrased; phras·ing** : to express in words

phrase·ol·o·gy \ˌfrā-zē-ˈä-lə-jē\ *n, pl* **-gies** : a manner of phrasing : STYLE

phras·ing *n* : style of expression

phre·net·ic \fri-ˈne-tik\ *adj* : FRENETIC

phren·ic \ˈfre-nik\ *adj* : of or relating to the diaphragm ⟨~ nerves⟩

phre·nol·o·gy \fri-ˈnä-lə-jē\ *n* : the study of the conformation of the skull based on the belief that it indicates mental faculties and character traits

phy·lac·tery \fə-ˈlak-tə-rē\ *n, pl* **-ter·ies 1** : one of two small square leather boxes containing slips inscribed with scripture passages and traditionally worn on the left arm and forehead by Jewish men during morning weekday prayers **2** : AMULET

phy·lum \ˈfī-ləm\ *n, pl* **phy·la** \-lə\ [NL, fr. Gk *phylon* tribe, race] : a major division of the animal and in some classifications the plant kingdom; *also* : a group (as of people) apparently of common origin

phys *abbr* **1** physical **2** physics

¹**phys·ic** \ˈfi-zik\ *n* **1** : the profession of medicine **2** : MEDICINE; *esp* : PURGATIVE

²**physic** *vb* **phys·icked; phys·ick·ing** : PURGE 2

¹**phys·i·cal** \ˈfi-zi-kəl\ *adj* **1** : of or relating to nature or the laws of nature **2** : material as opposed to mental or spiritual **3** : of, relating to, or produced by the forces and operations of physics **4** : of or relating to the body — **phys·i·cal·ly** \-k(ə-)lē\ *adv*

²**physical** *n* : PHYSICAL EXAMINATION

physical education *n* : instruction in the development and care of the body ranging from simple calisthenics to training in hygiene, gymnastics, and the performance and management of athletic games

physical examination *n* : an examination of the bodily functions and condition of an individual

physical science *n* : any of the sciences (as physics and astronomy) that deal primarily with nonliving materials — **physical scientist** *n*

physical therapy *n* : the treatment of disease by physical and mechanical means (as massage, exercise, water, or heat) — **physical therapist** *n*

phy·si·cian \fə-ˈzi-shən\ *n* : a doctor of medicine

physician's assistant *n* : a person certified to provide basic medical care usu. under a licensed physician's supervision

phys·i·cist \ˈfi-zə-sist\ *n* : a scientist who specializes in physics

phys·ics \ˈfi-ziks\ *n* [L *physica*, pl., natural sciences, fr. Gk *physika*, fr. *physis* growth, nature, fr. *phyein* to bring forth] **1** : the science of matter and energy and their interactions **2** : the physical properties and composition of something

phys·i·og·no·my \ˌfi-zē-ˈäg-nə-mē\ *n, pl* **-mies** : facial appearance esp. as a reflection of inner character

phys·i·og·ra·phy \ˌfi-zē-ˈä-grə-fē\ *n* : geography dealing with physical features of the earth — **phys·io·graph·ic** \ˌfi-zē-ō-ˈgra-fik\ *adj*

phys·i·ol·o·gy \ˌfi-zē-ˈä-lə-jē\ *n* **1** : a branch of biology dealing with the functions and functioning of living matter and organisms **2** : functional processes in an organism or any of its parts — **phys·i·o·log·i·cal** \-zē-ə-ˈlä-ji-kəl\ *or* **phys·i·o·log·ic** \-jik\ *adj* — **phys·i·o·log·i·cal·ly** \-ji-k(ə-)lē\ *adv* — **phys·i·ol·o·gist** \-zē-ˈä-lə-jist\ *n*

phys·io·ther·a·py \ˌfi-zē-ō-ˈther-ə-pē\ *n* : PHYSICAL THERAPY — **phys·io·ther·a·pist** \-pist\ *n*

phy·sique \fə-ˈzēk\ *n* : the build of a person's body : bodily constitution

phy·to·plank·ton \ˈfī-tō-ˌplaŋk-tən\ *n* : plant life of the plankton

pi \ˈpī\ *n, pl* **pis** \ˈpīz\ **1** : the 16th letter of the Greek alphabet — Π or π **2** : the symbol π denoting the ratio of the circumference of a circle to its diameter; *also* : the ratio itself equal to approximately 3.1416

PI *abbr* private investigator

pi·a·nis·si·mo \ˌpē-ə-ˈni-sə-ˌmō\ *adv or adj* : very softly — used as a direction in music

pi·a·nist \pē-ˈa-nist, ˈpē-ə-\ *n* : one who plays the piano

¹**pi·a·no** \pē-ˈä-nō\ *adv or adj* : SOFTLY — used as a direction in music

²**piano** \pē-ˈa-nō\ *n, pl* **pianos** [It, short for *pianoforte*, fr. *gravicembalo col piano e forte*, lit., harpsichord with soft and loud; fr. the fact that its tones could be varied in loudness] : a musical instrument having steel strings sounded by felt-covered hammers operated from a keyboard

pi·ano·forte \pē-ˌa-nō-ˈfȯr-ˌtā, -tē; pē-ˈa-nə-ˌfȯrt\ *n* : PIANO

pi·as·tre *also* **pi·as·ter** \pē-ˈas-tər\ *n* — see *pound* at MONEY table

pi·az·za \pē-ˈa-zə, *esp for 1* -ˈat-sə\ *n, pl* **piazzas** *or* **pi·az·ze** \-ˈat-(ˌ)sā, -ˈät-\ [It, fr. L *platea* broad street] **1** : an open square esp. in an Italian town **2** : a long hall with an arched roof *dial* : VERANDA, PORCH

pi·broch \ˈpē-ˌbräk\ *n* : a set of variations for the bagpipe

pic \ˈpik\ *n, pl* **pics** *or* **pix** \ˈpiks\ **1** : PHOTOGRAPH **2** : MOTION PICTURE

pi·ca \ˈpī-kə\ *n* : a typewriter type with 10 characters to the inch

pi·ca·resque \ˌpi-kə-ˈresk, ˌpē-\ *adj* : of or relating to rogues ⟨~ fiction⟩

pic·a·yune \ˌpi-kē-ˈyün\ *adj* : of little value : TRIVIAL; *also* : PETTY

pic·ca·lil·li \ˌpi-kə-ˈli-lē\ *n* : a relish of chopped vegetables and spices

pic·co·lo \ˈpi-kə-ˌlō\ *n, pl* **-los** [It, short for *piccolo flauto* small flute] : a small shrill flute pitched an octave higher than the ordinary flute

pice \ˈpīs\ *n, pl* **pice** : PAISA

¹**pick** \'pik\ *vb* **1** : to pierce or break up with a pointed instrument **2** : to remove bit by bit; *also* : to remove covering matter from **3** : to gather by plucking ⟨~ apples⟩ **4** : CULL, SELECT **5** : ROB ⟨~ a pocket⟩ **6** : PROVOKE ⟨~ a quarrel⟩ **7** : to dig into or pull lightly at **8** : to pluck with fingers or a pick **9** : to loosen or pull apart with a sharp point ⟨~ wool⟩ **10** : to unlock with a wire **11** : to eat sparingly — **pick·er** *n*

²**pick** *n* **1** : the act or privilege of choosing **2** : the best or choicest one **3** : the part of a crop gathered at one time

³**pick** *n* **1** : a heavy wooden-handled tool pointed at one or both ends **2** : a pointed implement used for picking **3** : a small thin piece (as of plastic) used to pluck the strings of a stringed instrument

pick·a·back \'pi-gē-ˌbak, 'pi-kə-\ *var of* PIGGYBACK

pick·ax \'pik-ˌaks\ *n* : ³PICK 1

pick·er·el \'pi-kə-rəl\ *n, pl* **pickerel** *or* **pickerels** : either of two bony fishes related to the pikes; *also* : WALLEYE 2

pickerel

pick·er·el·weed \-ˌwēd\ *n* : an American shallow-water herb that bears spikes of blue flowers

¹**pick·et** \'pi-kət\ *n* **1** : a pointed stake (as for a fence) **2** : a detached body of soldiers on outpost duty; *also* : SENTINEL **3** : a person posted by a labor union where workers are on strike; *also* : a person posted for a protest

²**picket** *vb* **1** : to guard with pickets **2** : TETHER **3** : to post pickets at ⟨~ a factory⟩ **4** : to serve as a picket

pick·ings \'pi-kiŋz, -kənz\ *n pl* **1** : gleanable or eatable fragments : SCRAPS **2** : yield for effort expended : RETURN

pick·le \'pi-kəl\ *n* **1** : a brine or vinegar solution for preserving foods; *also* : a food (as a cucumber) preserved in a pickle **2** : a difficult situation : PLIGHT — **pickle** *vb*

pick·lock \'pik-ˌläk\ *n* **1** : BURGLAR, THIEF **2** : a tool for picking locks

pick·pock·et \'pik-ˌpä-kət\ *n* : one who steals from pockets

pick·up \'pik-ˌəp\ *n* **1** : a hitchhiker who is given a ride **2** : a temporary chance acquaintance **3** : a picking up **4** : revival of business activity **5** : ACCELERATION **6** : the conversion of mechanical movements into electrical impulses in the reproduction of sound; *also* : a device for making such conversion **7** : a light truck having an enclosed cab and an open body with low sides and a tailgate

pick up *vb* **1** : to take hold of and lift **2** : IMPROVE **3** : to put in order

picky \'pi-kē\ *adj* **pick·i·er; -est** : FUSSY, FINICKY

¹**pic·nic** \'pik-ˌnik\ *n* : an outing with food usu. provided by members of the group and eaten in the open

²**picnic** *vb* **pic·nicked; pic·nick·ing** : to go on a picnic : eat in picnic fashion

pi·cot \'pē-ˌkō\ *n* : one of a series of small loops forming an edging on ribbon or lace

pic·to·ri·al \pik-'tōr-ē-əl\ *adj* : of, relating to, or consisting of pictures

¹**pic·ture** \'pik-chər\ *n* **1** : a representation made by painting, drawing, or photography **2** : a vivid description in words **3** : IMAGE, COPY **4** : a transitory visual image (as on a TV screen) **5** : MOTION PICTURE **6** : SITUATION

²**picture** *vb* **pic·tured; pic·tur·ing 1** : to paint or draw a

picture of **2** : to describe vividly in words **3** : to form a mental image of

pic·tur·esque \ˌpik-chə-'resk\ *adj* **1** : resembling a picture ⟨a ~ landscape⟩ **2** : CHARMING, QUAINT ⟨a ~ character⟩ **3** : GRAPHIC, VIVID ⟨a ~ account⟩ — **pic·tur·esque·ness** *n*

picture tube *n* : a cathode-ray tube on which the picture in a television set appears

pid·dle \'pid-ᵊl\ *vb* **pid·dled; pid·dling** : to act or work idly : DAWDLE

pid·dling \'pid-ᵊl-in, -iŋ\ *adj* : TRIVIAL, PALTRY

pid·gin \'pi-jən\ *n* [fr. *pidgin English*, fr. Chinese Pidgin English *pidgin* business] : a simplified speech used for communication between people with different languages

pie \'pī\ *n* : a dish consisting of a pastry crust and a filling (as of fruit or meat)

¹**pie·bald** \'pī-ˌbȯld\ *adj* : of different colors; *esp* : blotched with white and black ⟨a ~ horse⟩

²**piebald** *n* : a piebald animal

¹**piece** \'pēs\ *n* **1** : a part of a whole : FRAGMENT **2** : one of a group, set, or mass ⟨chess ~⟩; *also* : a single item ⟨a ~ of news⟩ **3** : a length, weight, or size in which something is made or sold **4** : a product (as an essay) of creative work **5** : FIREARM **6** : COIN

²**piece** *vb* **pieced; piec·ing 1** : to repair or complete by adding pieces : PATCH **2** : to join into a whole

pièce de ré·sis·tance \pē-ˌes-də-rā-ˌzē-'stäns\ *n, pl* **pièces de ré·sis·tance** *same*\ [F] **1** : the chief dish of a meal **2** : an outstanding item

piece·meal \'pēs-ˌmēl\ *adv or adj* : one piece at a time : GRADUALLY

piece·work \-ˌwərk\ *n* : work done and paid for by the piece — **piece·work·er** *n*

pie chart *n* : a circular chart that shows quantities or frequencies by parts of a circle shaped like pieces of pie

pied \'pīd\ *adj* : of two or more colors in blotches : VARIEGATED

pied–à–terre \pē-ˌā-də-'ter\ *n, pl* **pieds–à–terre** *same*\ [F, lit., foot to the ground] : a temporary or second lodging

pier \'pir\ *n* **1** : a support for a bridge span **2** : a structure built out into the water for use as a landing place or a promenade or to protect or form a harbor **3** : an upright supporting part (as a pillar) of a building or structure

pierce \'pirs\ *vb* **pierced; pierc·ing 1** : to enter or thrust into sharply or painfully : STAB **2** : to make a hole in or through : PERFORATE **3** : to force or make a way into or through : PENETRATE **4** : to see through : DISCERN

pies *pl of* PI *or of* PIE

pi·ety \'pī-ə-tē\ *n, pl* **pi·et·ies 1** : fidelity to natural obligations (as to parents) **2** : dutifulness in religion : DEVOUTNESS **3** : a pious act

pif·fle \'pi-fəl\ *n* : trifling talk or action

pig \'pig\ *n* **1** : SWINE; *esp* : a young swine **2** : PORK **3** : one that resembles a pig (as in dirtiness or greed) **4** : a crude casting of metal (as iron)

pi·geon \'pi-jən\ *n* : any of numerous stout-bodied short-legged birds with smooth thick plumage

¹**pi·geon·hole** \'pi-jən-ˌhōl\ *n* : a small open compartment (as in a desk) for keeping letters or documents

²**pigeonhole** *vb* **1** : to place in or as if in a pigeonhole : FILE **2** : to lay aside **3** : CLASSIFY

pi·geon–toed \-ˌtōd\ *adj* : having the toes turned in

pig·gish \'pi-gish\ *adj* **1** : GREEDY **2** : STUBBORN

pig·gy·back \'pi-gē-ˌbak\ *adv or adj* **1** : up on the back and shoulders **2** : on a railroad flatcar

pig·head·ed \'pig-'he-dəd\ *adj* : OBSTINATE, STUBBORN

\ə\abut \ᵊ\kitten \ər\further \a\ash \ā\ace \ä\mop, mar
\au̇\out \ch\chin \e\bet \ē\easy \g\go \i\hit \ī\ice \j\job
\ŋ\sing \ō\go \o\law \oi\boy \th\thin \ṯẖ\the \ü\loot \u̇\foot
\y\yet \zh\vision *see also* Pronunciation Symbols page

pig latin *n, often cap L* : a jargon that is made by systematic alteration of English

pig·let \'pi-glət\ *n* : a small usu. young swine

pig·ment \'pig-mənt\ *n* **1** : coloring matter **2** : a powder mixed with a liquid to give color (as in paints)

pig·men·ta·tion \ˌpig-mən-'tā-shən\ *n* : coloration with or deposition of pigment; *esp* : an excessive deposition of bodily pigment

pig·my *var of* PYGMY

pig·nut \'pig-ˌnət\ *n* : the bitter nut of any of several hickory trees; *also* : any of these trees

pig·pen \-ˌpen\ *n* **1** : a pen for pigs **2** : a dirty place

pig·skin \-ˌskin\ *n* **1** : the skin of a swine or leather made of it **2** : FOOTBALL 2

pig·sty \-ˌstī\ *n* : PIGPEN

pig·tail \-ˌtāl\ *n* : a tight braid of hair

pi·ka \'pī-kə\ *n* : any of various small short-eared mammals related to the rabbits and occurring in rocky uplands of Asia and western No. America

¹pike \'pīk\ *n* : a sharp point or spike

²pike *n, pl* **pike** *or* **pikes** : a large slender long-snouted freshwater bony fish valued for food; *also* : any of various related fishes

³pike *n* : a long wooden shaft with a pointed steel head formerly used as a foot soldier's weapon

⁴pike *n* : TURNPIKE

pik·er \'pī-kər\ *n* **1** : one who does things in a small way or on a small scale **2** : TIGHTWAD, CHEAPSKATE

pike·staff \'pīk-ˌstaf\ *n* : the staff of a foot soldier's pike

pi·laf *or* **pi·laff** \pi-'läf, 'pē-ˌläf\ *or* **pi·lau** \pi-'lȯ, -'lȯ, 'pē-lō, -lȯ\ *n* : a dish made of seasoned rice often with meat

pi·las·ter \pi-'las-tər, 'pī-ˌlas-tər\ *n* : an architectural support that looks like a rectangular column and projects slightly from a wall

pil·chard \'pil-chərd\ *n* : any of several fishes related to the herrings and often packed as sardines

¹pile \'pīl\ *n* : a long slender column (as of wood or steel) driven into the ground to support a vertical load

²pile *n* **1** : a quantity of things heaped together **2** : PYRE **3** : a great number or quantity : LOT

³pile *vb* **piled; pil·ing 1** : to lay in a pile : STACK **2** : to heap up : ACCUMULATE **3** : to press forward in a mass : CROWD

⁴pile *n* : a velvety surface of fine short hairs or threads (as on cloth) — **piled** \'pīld\ *adj* — **pile·less** *adj*

piles \'pīlz\ *n pl* : HEMORRHOIDS

pil·fer \'pil-fər\ *vb* : to steal in small quantities

pil·grim \'pil-grəm\ *n* [ME, fr. OF *peligrin*, fr. LL *pelegrinus*, alter. of L *peregrinus* foreigner, fr. *peregrinus* foreign, fr. *peregri* abroad, fr. *per* through + *ager* land] **1** : one who journeys in foreign lands : WAYFARER **2** : one who travels to a shrine or holy place as an act of devotion **3** *cap* : one of the English settlers founding Plymouth colony in 1620

pil·grim·age \-grə-mij\ *n* : a journey of a pilgrim esp. to a shrine or holy place

pil·ing \'pī-liŋ\ *n* : a structure of piles

pill \'pil\ *n* **1** : a medicine in a small rounded mass to be swallowed whole **2** : a disagreeable or tiresome person **3** *often cap* : an oral contraceptive — usu. used with *the*

pil·lage \'pi-lij\ *vb* **pil·laged; pil·lag·ing** : to take booty : LOOT, PLUNDER — **pillage** *n* — **pil·lag·er** *n*

pil·lar \'pi-lər\ *n* **1** : a strong upright support (as for a roof) **2** : a column or shaft standing alone esp. as a monument — **pil·lared** \-lərd\ *adj*

pill·box \'pil-ˌbäks\ *n* **1** : a shallow round box for pills **2** : a low concrete emplacement esp. for machine guns

pil·lion \'pil-yən\ *n* **1** : a pad or cushion placed behind a saddle for an extra rider **2** *chiefly Brit* : a motorcycle or bicycle saddle for a passenger

¹pil·lo·ry \'pi-lə-rē\ *n, pl* **-ries** : a wooden frame for public

punishment having holes in which the head and hands can be locked

²pillory *vb* **-ried; -ry·ing 1** : to set in a pillory **2** : to expose to public scorn

¹pil·low \'pi-lō\ *n* : a case filled with springy material (as feathers) and used to support the head of a resting person

²pillow *vb* : to rest or place on or as if on a pillow; *also* : to serve as a pillow for

pil·low·case \-ˌkās\ *n* : a removable covering for a pillow

¹pi·lot \'pī-lət\ *n* **1** : HELMSMAN, STEERSMAN **2** : a person qualified and licensed to take ships into and out of a port **3** : GUIDE, LEADER **4** : one that flies an aircraft or spacecraft **5** : a television show filmed or taped as a sample of a proposed series — **pi·lot·less** *adj*

²pilot *vb* : CONDUCT, GUIDE; *esp* : to act as pilot of

³pilot *adj* : serving as a guiding ŏr activating device or as a testing or trial unit ⟨a ~ light⟩ ⟨a ~ factory⟩

pi·lot·house \'pī-lət-ˌhaus\ *n* : a shelter on the upper deck of a ship for the steering gear and the helmsman

pil·sner *also* **pil·sen·er** \'pilz-nər, 'pil-zə-\ *n* [G, lit., fr. Pilsen (Plzeň), city in the Czech Republic] **1** : a light beer with a strong flavor of hops **2** : a tall slender footed glass for beer

pi·men·to \pə-'men-tō\ *n, pl* **pimentos** *or* **pimento** [Sp *pimienta* allspice, pepper, fr. LL *pigmenta*, pl. of *pigmentum* plant juice, fr. L, pigment] **1** : ALLSPICE **2** : PIMIENTO

pi·mien·to \pə-'men-tō\ *n, pl* **-tos** : any of various mild red sweet pepper fruits used esp. to stuff olives and to make paprika

pimp \'pimp\ *n* : a man who solicits clients for a prostitute — **pimp** *vb*

pim·per·nel \'pim-pər-ˌnel, -nəl\ *n* : any of a genus of herbs related to the primroses

pim·ple \'pim-pəl\ *n* : a small inflamed swelling on the skin often containing pus — **pim·ply** \-p(ə-)lē\ *adj*

¹pin \'pin\ *n* **1** : a piece of wood or metal used esp. for fastening articles together or as a support by which one article may be suspended from another; *esp* : a small pointed piece of wire with a head used for fastening clothes or attaching papers **2** : an ornament or emblem fastened to clothing with a pin **3** : one of the wooden pieces constituting the target (as in bowling); *also* : the staff of the flag marking a hole on a golf course **4** : LEG

²pin *vb* **pinned; pin·ning 1** : to fasten, join, or secure with a pin **2** : to hold fast or immobile **3** : ATTACH, HANG ⟨*pinned* their hopes on one man⟩ **4** : to assign the blame for ⟨~ a crime on someone⟩ **5** : to define clearly : ESTABLISH ⟨~ down an idea⟩

PIN *abbr* personal identification number

pi·ña co·la·da \ˌpēn-yə-kō-'lä-də, ˌpē-nə-\ *n* [Sp, lit., strained pineapple] : a tall drink made of rum, cream of coconut, and pineapple juice mixed with ice

pin·afore \'pi-nə-ˌfȯr\ *n* : a sleeveless dress or apron fastened at the back

pince–nez \paⁿs-'nā\ *n, pl* **pince–nez** *same or* -'nāz\ [F, lit., pinch-nose] : eyeglasses clipped to the nose by a spring

pin·cer \'pin-sər\ *n* **1** *pl* : a gripping instrument with two handles and two grasping jaws **2** : a claw (as of a lobster) resembling pincers

¹pinch \'pinch\ *vb* **1** : to squeeze between the finger and thumb or between the jaws of an instrument **2** : to compress painfully **3** : CONTRACT, SHRIVEL **4** : to be miserly; *also* : to subject to strict economy **5** : to confine or limit narrowly **6** : STEAL **7** : ARREST

²pinch *n* **1** : a critical point : EMERGENCY **2** : painful effect **3** : an act of pinching **4** : a very small quantity **5** : ARREST

³pinch *adj* : SUBSTITUTE ⟨a ~ runner⟩

pinch–hit \ˌpinch-'hit\ *vb* **1** : to bat in the place of another player esp. when a hit is particularly needed **2** : to act or serve in place of another — **pinch hit** *n* — **pinch hitter** *n*

pin curl *n* : a curl made usu. by dampening a strand of hair, coiling it, and securing it by a hairpin or clip

pin·cush·ion \'pin-ˌku̇-shən\ *n* : a cushion for pins not in use

¹**pine** \'pīn\ *n* : any of a genus of evergreen cone‑bearing trees; *also* : the light durable resinous wood of a pine

²**pine** *vb* **pined; pin·ing 1** : to lose vigor or health through distress **2** : to long for something intensely

pi·ne·al \'pī-nē-əl, pī-'nē-əl\ *n* : PINEAL GLAND — **pineal** *adj*

pineal gland *n* : a small usu. conical appendage of the brain of all vertebrates with a cranium that functions primarily as an endocrine organ

pine·ap·ple \'pīn-ˌa-pəl\ *n* : a tropical plant bearing an edible juicy fruit; *also* : its fruit

pin·feath·er \'pin-ˌfe-thər\ *n* : a new feather just coming through the skin

ping \'piŋ\ *n* **1** : a sharp sound like that of a bullet striking **2** : engine knock

pin·hole \'pin-ˌhōl\ *n* : a small hole made by, for, or as if by a pin

¹**pin·ion** \'pin-yən\ *n* : the end section of a bird's wing; *also* : WING

²**pinion** *vb* : to restrain by binding the arms; *also* : SHACKLE

³**pinion** *n* : a gear with a small number of teeth designed to mesh with a larger wheel or rack

¹**pink** \'piŋk\ *n* **1** : any of a genus of plants with narrow leaves often grown for their showy flowers **2** : the highest degree : HEIGHT ⟨the ∼ of condition⟩

²**pink** *n* : a light tint of red

³**pink** *adj* **1** : of the color pink **2** : holding socialistic views — **pink·ish** *adj*

⁴**pink** *vb* **1** : to perforate in an ornamental pattern **2** : PIERCE, STAB **3** : to cut a saw-toothed edge on

pink elephants *n pl* : hallucinations arising esp. from heavy drinking or use of narcotics

pink·eye \'piŋk-ˌī\ *n* : an acute contagious eye inflammation

pin·kie *or* **pin·ky** \'piŋ-kē\ *n, pl* **pinkies** : the smallest finger of the hand

pin·nace \'pi-nəs\ *n* **1** : a light sailing ship **2** : a ship's boat

pin·na·cle \'pi-ni-kəl\ *n* [ME *pinacle*, fr. MF, fr. LL *pinnaculum* small wing, gable, fr. L *pinna* wing, battlement] **1** : a turret ending in a small spire **2** : a lofty peak **3** : ACME

pin·nate \'pi-ˌnāt\ *adj* : resembling a feather esp. in having similar parts arranged on each side of an axis ⟨a ∼ leaf⟩ — **pin·nate·ly** *adv*

pi·noch·le \'pē-ˌnə-kəl\ *n* : a card game played with a 48‑card deck

pi·ñon *or* **pin·yon** \'pin-ˌyōn, -ˌyän\ *n, pl* **pi·ñons** *or* **pin·yons** *or* **pi·ño·nes** \pin-'yō-nēz\ [AmerSp *piñón*] : any of various low-growing pines of western No. America with edible seeds; *also* : the edible seed of a piñon

pin·point \'pin-ˌpȯint\ *vb* : to locate, hit, or aim with great precision

pin·prick \-ˌprik\ *n* **1** : a small puncture made by or as if by a pin **2** : a petty irritation or annoyance

pins and needles *n pl* : a pricking tingling sensation in a limb growing numb or recovering from numbness — **on pins and needles** : in a nervous or jumpy state of anticipation

pin·stripe \'pin-ˌstrīp\ *n* : a narrow stripe on a fabric; *also* : a suit with such stripes — **pin–striped** \-ˌstrīpt\ *adj*

pint \'pīnt\ *n* — see WEIGHT table

pin·to \'pin-ˌtō\ *n, pl* **pintos** *also* **pintoes** : a spotted horse or pony

pinto bean *n* : a spotted seed produced by a kind of kidney bean and used for food

pin·up \'pin-ˌəp\ *adj* : suitable or designed for hanging on a wall; *also* : suited (as by beauty) to be the subject of a pinup photograph

pin·wheel \-ˌhwēl, -ˌwēl\ *n* **1** : a fireworks device in the form of a revolving wheel of colored fire **2** : a toy consisting of lightweight vanes that revolve at the end of a stick

pin·worm \-ˌwərm\ *n* : a nematode worm parasitic in the human intestine

pin·yin \'pin-'yin\ *n, often cap* : a system for writing Chinese ideograms by using Roman letters to represent the sounds

¹**pi·o·neer** \ˌpī-ə-'nir\ *n* **1** : one that originates or helps open up a new line of thought or activity **2** : an early settler in a territory

²**pioneer** *vb* **1** : to act as a pioneer **2** : to open or prepare for others to follow; *also* : SETTLE

pi·ous \'pī-əs\ *adj* **1** : marked by reverence for deity : DEVOUT **2** : excessively or affectedly religious **3** : SACRED, DEVOTIONAL **4** : showing loyal reverence for a person or thing : DUTIFUL **5** : marked by sham or hypocrisy — **pi·ous·ly** *adv*

¹**pip** \'pip\ *n* : one of the dots used on dice and dominoes to indicate numerical value

²**pip** *n* : a small fruit seed (as of an apple)

¹**pipe** \'pīp\ *n* **1** : a tubular musical instrument played by forcing air through it **2** : BAGPIPE **3** : a tube designed to conduct something (as water, steam, or oil) **4** : a device for smoking having a tube with a bowl at one end and a mouthpiece at the other

²**pipe** *vb* **piped; pip·ing 1** : to play on a pipe **2** : to speak in a high or shrill voice **3** : to convey by or as if by pipes — **pip·er** *n*

pipe down *vb* : to stop talking or making noise

pipe dream *n* : an illusory or fantastic hope

pipe·line \'pīp-ˌlīn\ *n* **1** : a line of pipe with pumps, valves, and control devices for conveying fluids **2** : a channel for information

pi·pette *or* **pi·pet** \pī-'pet\ *n* : a device for measuring and transferring small volumes of liquid

pipe up *vb* : to speak loudly and distinctly; *also* : to express an opinion freely

pip·ing \'pī-piŋ\ *n* **1** : the music of pipes **2** : a narrow fold of material used to decorate edges or seams

piping hot *adj* : very hot

pip·pin \'pi-pən\ *n* : any of several yellowish apples

pip–squeak \'pip-ˌskwēk\ *n* : one that is small or insignificant

pi·quant \'pē-kənt\ *adj* **1** : pleasantly savory : PUNGENT **2** : engagingly provocative; *also* : having a lively charm — **pi·quan·cy** \-kən-sē\ *n*

¹**pique** \'pēk\ *n* [F] : a passing feeling of wounded vanity : RESENTMENT

²**pique** *vb* **piqued; piqu·ing 1** : IRRITATE 1 **2** : to arouse by a provocation or challenge : GOAD

pi·qué *or* **pi·que** \pi-'kā\ *n* : a durable ribbed clothing fabric

pi·quet \pi-'kā\ *n* : a 2-handed card game played with 32 cards

pi·ra·cy \'pī-rə-sē\ *n, pl* **-cies 1** : robbery on the high seas; *also* : an act resembling such robbery **2** : the unauthorized use of another's production or invention

pi·ra·nha \pə-'rä-nə, -'rän-yə\ *n* [Pg, fr. Tupi (So. American Indian language) *pirãya*, fr. *pira* fish + *áya* tooth] : any of various usu. small So. American fishes with

---

sharp teeth that include some known to attack humans and large animals

pi·rate \'pī-rət\ n [ME, fr. MF or L; MF, fr. L *pirata*, fr. Gk *peiratēs*, fr. *peiran* to attempt, test] : one who commits piracy — **pirate** vb — **pi·rat·i·cal** \pə-'ra-ti-kəl, pī-\ adj

pir·ou·ette \ˌpir-ə-'wet\ n [F] : a rapid whirling about of the body; *esp* : a full turn on the toe or ball of one foot in ballet — **pirouette** vb

pis pl of PI

pis·ca·to·ri·al \ˌpis-kə-'tōr-ē-əl\ adj : of or relating to fishing

Pi·sces \'pī-sēz\ n [ME, fr. L, lit., fishes] 1 : a zodiacal constellation between Aquarius and Aries usu. pictured as a fish 2 : the 12th sign of the zodiac in astrology; *also* : one born under this sign

pis·mire \'pis-ˌmīr\ n : ANT

pi·so \'pē-(ˌ)sō\ n : the peso of the Philippines

pis·ta·chio \pə-'sta-shē-ˌō, -'stä-\ n, pl **-chios** : the greenish edible seed of a small Asian tree related to the sumacs; *also* : the tree

pis·til \'pist-ᵊl\ n : the female reproductive organ in a flower — **pis·til·late** \'pis-tə-ˌlāt\ adj

pis·tol \'pist-ᵊl\ n : a handgun whose chamber is integral with the barrel

pis·tol–whip \-ˌhwip\ vb : to beat with a pistol

pis·ton \'pis-tən\ n : a sliding piece that receives and transmits motion and that usu. consists of a short cylinder inside a large cylinder

¹pit \'pit\ n 1 : a hole, shaft, or cavity in the ground 2 : an often sunken area designed for a particular use; *also* : an enclosed place (as for cockfights) 3 : HELL; *also, pl* : WORST ⟨it's the ∼s⟩ 4 : a natural hollow or indentation in a surface 5 : a small indented mark or scar (as from disease or corrosion) 6 : an area beside a racecourse where cars are fueled and repaired during a race

²pit vb **pit·ted; pit·ting** 1 : to form pits in or become marred with pits 2 : to match for fighting

³pit n : the stony seed of some fruits (as the cherry, peach, and date)

⁴pit vb **pit·ted; pit·ting** : to remove the pit from

pi·ta \'pē-tə\ n [NGk] : a thin flat bread

pit–a–pat \ˌpi-ti-'pat\ n : PITTER-PATTER — **pit–a–pat** adv or adj

pit bull n : a powerful compact short-haired dog developed for fighting

¹pitch \'pich\ n 1 : a dark sticky substance left over esp. from distilling tar or petroleum 2 : resin from various conifers — **pitchy** adj

²pitch vb 1 : to erect and fix firmly in place ⟨∼ a tent⟩ 2 : THROW, FLING 3 : to deliver a baseball to a batter 4 : to toss (as coins) toward a mark 5 : to set at a particular level ⟨∼ the voice low⟩ 6 : to fall headlong 7 : to have the front end (as of a ship) alternately plunge and rise 8 : to incline downward : SLOPE

³pitch n 1 : the action or a manner of pitching 2 : degree of slope ⟨∼ of a roof⟩ 3 : the relative level of some quality or state ⟨a high ∼ of excitement⟩ 4 : highness or lowness of sound; *also* : a standard frequency for tuning instruments 5 : an often high-pressure sales talk 6 : the delivery of a baseball to a batter; *also* : the baseball delivered

pitch·blende \'pich-ˌblend\ n : a dark mineral that is the chief source of uranium

¹pitch·er \'pi-chər\ n : a container for liquids that usu. has a lip and a handle

²pitcher n : one that pitches esp. in a baseball game

pitcher plant n : any of various plants with leaves modified to resemble pitchers in which insects are trapped and digested

pitch·fork \'pich-ˌfork\ n : a long-handled fork used esp. in pitching hay

pitch in vb 1 : to begin to work 2 : to contribute to a common effort

pitch·man \'pich-mən\ n : SALESMAN; *esp* : one who sells merchandise on the streets or from a concession

pit·e·ous \'pi-tē-əs\ adj : arousing pity : PITIFUL — **pit·e·ous·ly** adv

pit·fall \'pit-ˌfol\ n 1 : TRAP, SNARE; *esp* : a covered pit used for capturing animals 2 : a hidden danger or difficulty

pith \'pith\ n 1 : loose spongy tissue esp. in the center of the stem of vascular plants 2 : the essential part : CORE

pithy \'pi-thē\ adj **pith·i·er; -est** 1 : consisting of or filled with pith 2 : having substance and point : CONCISE

piti·able \'pi-tē-ə-bəl\ adj : PITIFUL

piti·ful \'pi-ti-fəl\ adj 1 : arousing or deserving pity ⟨a ∼ sight⟩ 2 : MEAN, MEAGER — **piti·ful·ly** adv

piti·less \'pi-ti-ləs\ adj : devoid of pity : MERCILESS — **pit·i·less·ly** adv

pi·ton \'pē-ˌtän\ n [F] : a spike, wedge, or peg that can be driven into a rock or ice surface as a support

pit·tance \'pit-ᵊns\ n : a small portion, amount, or allowance

pit·ted \'pi-təd\ adj : marked with pits

pit·ter–pat·ter \'pi-tər-ˌpa-tər, 'pi-tē-\ n : a rapid succession of light taps or sounds — **pitter–patter** \ˌpi-tər-'pa-tər, ˌpi-tē-\ adv or adj — **pitter–patter** \same as adv\ vb

pi·tu·itary \pə-'tü-ə-ˌter-ē, -'tyü-\ n, pl **-itar·ies** : PITUITARY GLAND — **pituitary** adj

pituitary gland n : a small oval endocrine gland attached to the brain which produces various hormones that affect most basic bodily functions

pit viper n : any of various mostly New World venomous snakes with a sensory pit on each side of the head and hollow perforated fangs

¹pity \'pi-tē\ n, pl **pit·ies** [ME *pite*, fr. OF *pité*, fr. L *pietas* piety, pity, fr. *pius* pious] 1 : sympathetic sorrow : COMPASSION 2 : something to be regretted

²pity vb **pit·ied; pity·ing** : to feel pity for

¹piv·ot \'pi-vət\ n : a fixed pin on which something turns — **pivot** adj — **piv·ot·al** \'pi-vət-ᵊl\ adj

²pivot vb : to turn on or as if on a pivot

pix pl of PIC

pix·el \'pik-səl, -ˌsel\ n : any of the small elements that together make up an image (as on a television screen)

pix·ie or **pixy** \'pik-sē\ n, pl **pix·ies** : FAIRY; *esp* : a mischievous sprite

piz·za \'pēt-sə\ n [It] : an open pie made of rolled bread dough spread with a spiced mixture (as of tomatoes, cheese, and ground meat) and baked

piz·zazz or **pi·zazz** \pə-'zaz\ n 1 : GLAMOUR 2 : VITALITY

piz·ze·ria \ˌpēt-sə-'rē-ə\ n : an establishment where pizzas are made and sold

piz·zi·ca·to \ˌpit-si-'kä-tō\ adv or adj [It] : by means of plucking instead of bowing — used as a direction in music

pj's \'pē-ˌjāz\ n pl : PAJAMAS

pk abbr 1 park 2 peak 3 peck 4 pike

pkg abbr package

pkt abbr 1 packet 2 pocket

pkwy abbr parkway

pl abbr 1 place 2 plate 3 plural

¹plac·ard \'pla-kərd, -ˌkärd\ n : a notice posted in a public place : POSTER

²plac·ard \-ˌkärd, -kərd\ vb 1 : to cover with or as if with placards 2 : to announce by or as if by posting

pla·cate \'plā-ˌkāt, 'pla-\ vb **pla·cat·ed; pla·cat·ing** : to soothe esp. by concessions : APPEASE — **pla·ca·ble** \'pla-kə-bəl, 'plā-\ adj

¹place \'plās\ n [ME, fr. OF, open space, fr. L *platea* broad street, fr. Gk *plateia* (*hodos*), fr. fem. of *platys* broad, flat] 1 : SPACE, ROOM 2 : an indefinite region : AR-

EA **3** : a building or locality used for a special purpose **4** : a center of population **5** : a particular part of a surface : SPOT **6** : relative position in a scale or sequence; *also* : position at the end of a competition ⟨last ∼⟩ **7** : ACCOMMODATION; *esp* : SEAT **8** : the position of a figure within a numeral ⟨12 is a two ∼ number⟩ **9** : JOB; *esp* : public office **10** : a public square **11** : 2d place at the finish (as of a horse race)

²**place** *vb* **placed; plac·ing 1** : to put in a particular place : SET **2** : to distribute in an orderly manner : ARRANGE **3** : IDENTIFY **4** : to give an order for ⟨∼ a bet⟩ **5** : to earn a given spot in a competition; *esp* : to come in 2d

pla·ce·bo \plə-¹sē-bō\ *n, pl* **-bos** [L, I shall please] : an inert medication used for its psychological effect or for purposes of comparison in an experiment

place·hold·er \¹plās-ˌhōl-dər\ *n* : a symbol in a mathematical or logical expression that may be replaced by the name of any element of a set

place·kick \-ˌkik\ *n* : the kicking of a ball placed or held on the ground — **placekick** *vb* — **place·kick·er** *n*

place·ment \¹plās-mənt\ *n* : an act or instance of placing

pla·cen·ta \plə-¹sen-tə\ *n, pl* **-tas** *or* **-tae** \-(ˌ)tē\ [NL, fr. L, flat cake] : the organ in most mammals by which the fetus is joined to the maternal uterus and is nourished — **pla·cen·tal** \-¹sent-ᵊl\ *adj*

plac·er \¹pla-sər\ *n* : a deposit of sand or gravel containing particles of valuable mineral (as gold)

plac·id \¹pla-səd\ *adj* : UNDISTURBED, PEACEFUL **syn** tranquil, serene, calm — **pla·cid·i·ty** \pla-¹si-də-tē\ *n* — **plac·id·ly** *adv*

plack·et \¹pla-kət\ *n* : a slit in a garment

pla·gia·rize \¹plā-jə-ˌrīz\ *vb* **-rized; -riz·ing** : to present the ideas or words of another as one's own — **pla·gia·rism** \-ˌri-zəm\ *n* — **pla·gia·rist** \-rist\ *n*

¹**plague** \¹plāg\ *n* **1** : a disastrous evil or influx; *also* : NUISANCE **2** : PESTILENCE; *esp* : a destructive contagious bacterial disease (as bubonic plague)

²**plague** *vb* **plagued; plagu·ing 1** : to afflict with or as if with disease or disaster **2** : TEASE, TORMENT, HARASS

plaid \¹plad\ *n* **1** : a rectangular length of tartan worn esp. over the left shoulder as part of the Scottish national costume **2** : a twilled woolen fabric with a tartan pattern **3** : a pattern of unevenly spaced repeated stripes crossing at right angles — **plaid** *adj*

¹**plain** \¹plān\ *n* : an extensive area of level or rolling treeless country

²**plain** *adj* **1** : lacking ornament ⟨a ∼ dress⟩ **2** : free of extraneous matter **3** : OPEN, UNOBSTRUCTED ⟨∼ view⟩ **4** : EVIDENT, OBVIOUS **5** : easily understood : CLEAR **6** : CANDID, BLUNT **7** : SIMPLE, UNCOMPLICATED ⟨∼ cooking⟩ **8** : lacking beauty or ugliness — **plain·ly** *adv* — **plain·ness** *n*

plain·clothes·man \¹plān-¹klōthz-mən, -¹klōz-, -ˌman\ *n* : a police officer who wears civilian clothes instead of a uniform while on duty : DETECTIVE

plain·spo·ken \-¹spō-kən\ *adj* : FRANK

plaint \¹plānt\ *n* **1** : LAMENTATION, WAIL **2** : PROTEST, COMPLAINT

plain·tiff \¹plān-təf\ *n* : the complaining party in a lawsuit

plain·tive \¹plān-tiv\ *adj* : expressive of suffering or woe : MELANCHOLY — **plain·tive·ly** *adv*

plait \¹plāt, ¹plat\ *n* **1** : PLEAT **2** : a braid esp. of hair or straw — **plait** *vb*

¹**plan** \¹plan\ *n* **1** : a drawing or diagram showing the parts or details of something **2** : a method for accomplishing an objective; *also* : GOAL, AIM

²**plan** *vb* **planned; plan·ning 1** : to form a plan of ⟨∼ a new city⟩ **2** : INTEND ⟨*planned* to go⟩ — **plan·ner** *n*

¹**plane** \¹plān\ *vb* **planed; plan·ing** : to smooth or level off with or as if with a plane — **plan·er** *n*

²**plane** *n* : PLANE TREE

³**plane** *n* : a tool for smoothing or shaping a wood surface

⁴**plane** *n* **1** : a level or flat surface **2** : a level of existence, consciousness, or development **3** : AIRPLANE

⁵**plane** *adj* **1** : FLAT, LEVEL **2** : dealing with flat surfaces or figures ⟨∼ geometry⟩

plane·load \¹plān-ˌlōd\ *n* : a load that fills an airplane

plan·et \¹pla-nət\ *n* [ME *planete*, fr. OF, fr. LL *planeta*, modif. of Gk *planēt-, planēs*, lit., wanderer, fr. *planasthai* to wander] : any of the large bodies in the solar system that revolve around the sun — **plan·e·tary** \-nə-ˌter-ē\ *adj*

☞ For table, see next page.

plan·e·tar·i·um \ˌpla-nə-¹ter-ē-əm\ *n, pl* **-i·ums** *or* **-ia** \-ē-ə\ : a building or room housing a device to project images of celestial bodies

plan·e·tes·i·mal \ˌpla-nə-¹tes-ə-məl\ *n* : any of numerous small solid celestial bodies which may have existed during the formation of the solar system

plan·e·toid \¹pla-nə-ˌtöid\ *n* : a body resembling a planet; *esp* : ASTEROID

plane tree *n* : any of a genus of trees (as a sycamore) with large lobed leaves and globe-shaped fruit

plan·gent \¹plan-jənt\ *adj* **1** : having a loud reverberating sound **2** : having an expressive esp. plaintive quality — **plan·gen·cy** \-jən-sē\ *n*

¹**plank** \¹plaŋk\ *n* **1** : a heavy thick board **2** : an article in the platform of a political party

²**plank** *vb* **1** : to cover with planks **2** : to set or lay down forcibly **3** : to cook and serve on a board

plank·ing \¹plaŋ-kiŋ\ *n* : a quantity or covering of planks

plank·ton \¹plaŋk-tən\ *n* [G, fr. Gk, neut. of *planktos* drifting] : the passively floating or weakly swimming animal and plant life of a body of water — **plank·ton·ic** \plaŋk-¹tä-nik\ *adj*

¹**plant** \¹plant\ *vb* **1** : to set in the ground to grow **2** : ESTABLISH, SETTLE **3** : to stock or provide with something **4** : to place firmly or forcibly **5** : to hide or arrange with intent to deceive

²**plant** *n* **1** : any of a kingdom of living things that usu. have no locomotor ability or obvious sense organs and have cellulose cell walls and usu. capacity for indefinite growth **2** : the land, buildings, and machinery used in carrying on a trade or business

¹**plan·tain** \¹plant-ᵊn\ *n* [ME, fr. OF, fr. L *plantagin-, plantago*, fr. *planta* sole of the foot; fr. its broad leaves] : any of a genus of short-stemmed weedy herbs with spikes of tiny greenish flowers

²**plantain** *n* [Sp *plántano, plátano* plane tree, banana tree, fr. ML *plantanus* plane tree, alter. of L *platanus*] : a banana plant with starchy greenish fruit that are eaten cooked; *also* : its fruit

plan·tar \¹plan-tər, -ˌtär\ *adj* : of or relating to the sole of the foot

plan·ta·tion \plan-¹tā-shən\ *n* **1** : a large group of plants and esp. trees under cultivation **2** : an agricultural estate usu. worked by resident laborers

plant·er \¹plan-tər\ *n* **1** : one that plants or sows; *esp* : owner or operator of a plantation **2** : a container for plants

plant louse *n* : APHID

plaque \¹plak\ *n* [F] **1** : an ornamental brooch **2** : a flat thin piece (as of metal) used for decoration; *also* : a commemorative tablet **3** : a bacteria-containing film on a tooth

plash \¹plash\ *n* : SPLASH — **plash** *vb*

plas·ma \¹plaz-mə\ *n* **1** : the fluid part of blood, lymph, or milk **2** : a gas composed of ionized particles — **plas·mat·ic** \plaz-¹ma-tik\ *adj*

¹**plas·ter** \¹plas-tər\ *n* **1** : a dressing consisting of a back-

---

\ə\abut \ᵊ\kitten \ər\further \a\ash \ā\ace \ä\mop, mar
\aú\out \ch\chin \e\bet \ē\easy \g\go \i\hit \ī\ice \j\job
\ŋ\sing \ō\go \ó\law \ói\boy \th\thin \th\the \ü\loot \ú\foot
\y\yet \zh\vision *see also* Pronunciation Symbols page

PLANETS

NAME	SYMBOL	MEAN DISTANCE FROM THE SUN		PERIOD OF REVOLUTION IN DAYS OR YEARS	EQUATORIAL DIAMETER IN MILES
		astronomical units	million miles		
Mercury	☿	0.387	36.0	87.97 d.	3,032
Venus	♀	0.723	67.2	224.70 d.	7,523
Earth	⊕	1.000	92.9	365.26 d.	7,928
Mars	♂	1.524	141.5	686.98 d.	4,218
Jupiter	♃	5.203	483.4	11.86 y.	88,900
Saturn	♄	9.522	884.6	29.46 y.	74,900
Uranus	♅	19.201	1783.8	84.01 y.	31,800
Neptune	♆	30.074	2793.9	164.79 y.	30,800
Pluto	♇	39.725	3690.5	247.69 y.	1,400

ing spread with an often medicated substance that clings to the skin ⟨adhesive ∼⟩ **2** : a paste that hardens as it dries and is used for coating walls and ceilings

²plaster *vb* : to cover with or as if with plaster — **plas·ter·er** *n*

plas·ter·board \'plas-tər-ˌbōrd\ *n* : a wallboard consisting of fiberboard, paper, or felt over a plaster core

plaster of par·is \-ˈpar-əs\ *often cap 2d P* : a white powder made from gypsum and used as a quick-setting paste with water for casts and molds

¹plas·tic \ˈplas-tik\ *adj* [L *plasticus* of molding, fr. Gk *plastikos*, fr. *plassein* to mold, form] **1** : capable of being molded ⟨∼ clay⟩ **2** : characterized by or using modeling ⟨∼ arts⟩ **3** : made or consisting of a plastic **syn** pliable, pliant, ductile, malleable, adaptable — **plas·tic·i·ty** \plas-ˈti-sə-tē\ *n*

²plastic *n* : a plastic substance; *esp* : a synthetic or processed material that can be formed into rigid objects or into films or filaments

plastic surgery *n* : surgery to repair, restore, or improve lost, injured, defective, or misshapen body parts — **plastic surgeon** *n*

¹plat \ˈplat\ *n* **1** : a small plot of ground **2** : a plan of a piece of land with actual or proposed features (as lots)

²plat *vb* **plat·ted**; **plat·ting** : to make a plat of

¹plate \ˈplāt\ *n* **1** : a flat thin piece of material **2** : domestic hollowware made of or plated with gold, silver, or base metals **3** : DISH **4** : HOME PLATE **5** : the molded metal or plastic cast of a page of type to be printed from **6** : a sheet of glass coated with a chemical sensitive to light and used in photography **7** : the part of a denture that fits to the mouth; *also* : DENTURE **8** : something printed from an engraving **9** : a huge mobile segment of the earth's crust

²plate *vb* **plat·ed**; **plat·ing** **1** : to overlay with metal (as gold or silver) **2** : to make a printing plate of

pla·teau \pla-ˈtō\ *n*, *pl* **plateaus** *or* **pla·teaux** \-ˈtōz\ [F] : a large level area of high land

plate glass *n* : rolled, ground, and polished sheet glass

plat·en \ˈplat-ᵊn\ *n* **1** : a flat plate; *esp* : one that exerts or receives pressure (as in a printing press) **2** : the roller of a typewriter or printer

plate tectonics *n* : a theory in geology that the lithosphere is divided into plates at the boundaries of which much of earth's seismic activity occurs

plat·form \ˈplat-ˌförm\ *n* **1** : a raised flooring or stage for speakers, performers, or workers **2** : a declaration of the principles on which a group of persons (as a political party) stands

plat·ing \ˈplā-tiŋ\ *n* : a coating of metal plates or plate ⟨the ∼ of a ship⟩

plat·i·num \ˈplat-ᵊn-əm\ *n* : a heavy grayish white metallic chemical element — see ELEMENT table

plat·i·tude \ˈplat-ə-ˌtüd, -ˌtyüd\ *n* : a flat or trite remark — **plat·i·tu·di·nous** \-ˈtüd-ᵊn-əs, -ˈtyüd-\ *adj*

pla·ton·ic love \plə-ˈtä-nik-, plā-\ *n*, *often cap P* : a close relationship between two persons without sexual desire

pla·toon \plə-ˈtün\ *n* [F *peloton* small detachment, lit., ball, fr. *pelote* little ball] **1** : a subdivision of a company-size military unit usu. consisting of two or more squads or sections **2** : a group of football players trained either for offense or for defense and sent into the game as a body

platoon sergeant *n* : a noncommissioned officer in the army ranking below a first sergeant

plat·ter \ˈpla-tər\ *n* **1** : a large serving plate **2** : a phonograph record

platy \ˈpla-tē\ *n*, *pl* **platy** *or* **plat·ys** *or* **plat·ies** : either of two small stocky often brilliantly colored bony fishes that are popular for tropical aquariums

platy·pus \ˈpla-ti-pəs\ *n*, *pl* **platy·pus·es** *also* **platy·pi** \-ˌpī\ [NL, fr. Gk *platypous* flat-footed, fr. *platys* broad, flat + *pous* foot] : a small aquatic egg-laying marsupial mammal of Australia with webbed feet and a fleshy bill like a duck's

platypus

plau·dit \ˈplö-dət\ *n* : an act of applause

plau·si·ble \ˈplö-zə-bəl\ *adj* [L *plausibilis* worthy of applause, fr. *plausus*, pp. of *plaudere* to applaud] : seemingly worthy of belief — **plau·si·bil·i·ty** \ˌplö-zə-ˈbi-lə-tē\ *n* — **plau·si·bly** \ˈplö-zə-blē\ *adv*

¹play \ˈplā\ *n* **1** : brisk handling of something (as a weapon) **2** : the course of a game; *also* : a particular act or maneuver in a game **3** : recreational activity; *esp* : the spontaneous activity of children **4** : JEST ⟨said in ∼⟩ **5** : the act or an instance of punning **6** : GAMBLING **7** : OPERATION ⟨bring extra force into ∼⟩ **8** : a brisk or light movement **9** : free motion (as of part of a machine) **10** : scope for action **11** : PUBLICITY **12** : an effort to arouse liking ⟨made a ∼ for her⟩ **13** : a stage representation of a drama; *also* : a dramatic composition — **play·ful** \-fəl\ *adj* — **play·ful·ly** *adv* — **play·ful·ness** *n* — **in play** : in condition or position to be played

²**play** *vb* **1 :** to engage in recreation : FROLIC **2 :** to handle or behave lightly or absentmindedly **3 :** to make a pun ⟨~ on words⟩ **4 :** to take advantage ⟨~ on fears⟩ **5 :** to move or operate in a brisk or irregular manner ⟨a flashlight ~*ed* over the wall⟩ **6 :** to perform music ⟨~ on a violin⟩; *also* : to perform (music) on an instrument ⟨~ a waltz⟩ **7 :** to perform music upon ⟨~ the piano⟩; *also* : to sound in performance ⟨the organ is ~*ing*⟩ **8 :** to cause to emit sounds ⟨~ a radio⟩ **9 :** to act in a dramatic medium; *also* : to act in the character of ⟨~ the hero⟩ **10 :** GAMBLE **11 :** to behave in a specified way ⟨~ safe⟩; *also* : COOPERATE ⟨~ along with him⟩ **12 :** to deal with; *also* : EMPHASIZE ⟨~ up her good qualities⟩ **13 :** to perform for amusement ⟨~ a trick⟩ **14 :** WREAK **15 :** to contend with in a game; *also* : to fill (a certain position) on a team **16 :** to make wagers on ⟨~ the races⟩ **17 :** WIELD, PLY **18 :** to keep in action — **play·er** *n*

play·act·ing \ˈplā-ˌak-tiŋ\ *n* **1 :** performance in theatrical productions **2 :** insincere or artificial behavior

play·back \-ˌbak\ *n* : an act of reproducing a sound recording — **play back** *vb*

play·bill \-ˌbil\ *n* : a poster advertising the performance of a play

play·book \-ˌbu̇k\ *n* : a notebook containing diagrammed football plays

play·boy \-ˌbȯi\ *n* : a man whose chief interest is the pursuit of pleasure

play·go·er \-ˌgō-ər\ *n* : a person who frequently attends plays

play·ground \-ˌgrau̇nd\ *n* : an area used for games and play esp. by children

play·house \-ˌhau̇s\ *n* **1 :** THEATER **2 :** a small house for children to play in

playing card *n* : any of a set of 24 to 78 cards marked to show its rank and suit and used to play a game of cards

play·let \ˈplā-lət\ *n* : a short play

play·mate \-ˌmāt\ *n* : a companion in play

play·off \-ˌȯf\ *n* : a contest or series of contests to break a tie or determine a championship

play·pen \-ˌpen\ *n* : a portable enclosure in which a young child may play

play·suit \-ˌsüt\ *n* : a sports and play outfit for women and children

play·thing \-ˌthiŋ\ *n* : TOY

play·wright \-ˌrīt\ *n* : a writer of plays

pla·za \ˈpla-zə, ˈplä-\ *n* [Sp, fr. L *platea* broad street] **1 :** a public square in a city or town **2 :** a shopping center

PLC *abbr, Brit* public limited company

plea \ˈplē\ *n* **1 :** a defendant's answer in law to a charge or indictment **2 :** something alleged as an excuse **3 :** ENTREATY, APPEAL

plead \ˈplēd\ *vb* **plead·ed** *or* **pled** \ˈpled\; **plead·ing 1 :** to argue before a court or authority ⟨~ a case⟩ **2 :** to answer to a charge or indictment ⟨~ guilty⟩ **3 :** to argue for or against something ⟨~ for acquittal⟩ **4 :** to appeal earnestly ⟨~*s* for help⟩ **5 :** to offer as a plea (as in defense) ⟨~*ed* illness⟩ — **plead·er** *n*

pleas·ant \ˈplez-ᵊnt\ *adj* **1 :** giving pleasure : AGREEABLE ⟨a ~ experience⟩ **2 :** marked by pleasing behavior or appearance ⟨a ~ person⟩ — **pleas·ant·ly** *adv* — **pleas·ant·ness** *n*

pleas·ant·ry \-ᵊn-trē\ *n, pl* **-ries :** a pleasant and casual act or speech

¹**please** \ˈplēz\ *vb* **pleased; pleas·ing 1 :** to give pleasure or satisfaction to **2 :** LIKE ⟨do as you ~⟩ **3 :** to be the will or pleasure of ⟨may it ~ his Majesty⟩

²**please** *adv* — used as a function word to express politeness or emphasis in a request ⟨~ come in⟩

pleas·ing *adj* : giving pleasure — **pleas·ing·ly** *adv*

plea·sur·able \ˈple-zhə-rə-bəl\ *adj* : PLEASANT, GRATIFYING — **plea·sur·ably** \-blē\ *adv*

plea·sure \ˈple-zhər\ *n* **1 :** DESIRE, INCLINATION ⟨await your ~⟩ **2 :** a state of gratification : ENJOYMENT **3 :** a source of delight or joy

¹**pleat** \ˈplēt\ *vb* **1 :** FOLD; *esp* : to arrange in pleats **2 :** BRAID

²**pleat** *n* : a fold (as in cloth) made by doubling material over on itself

plebe \ˈplēb\ *n* : a freshman at a military or naval academy

¹**ple·be·ian** \pli-ˈbē-ən\ *n* **1 :** a member of the Roman plebs **2 :** one of the common people

²**plebeian** *adj* **1 :** of or relating to plebeians **2 :** COMMON, VULGAR

pleb·i·scite \ˈple-bə-ˌsīt, -sət\ *n* : a vote of the people (as of a country) on a proposal submitted to them

plebs \ˈplebz\ *n, pl* **ple·bes** \ˈplē-bēz\ **1 :** the general populace **2 :** the common people of ancient Rome

plec·trum \ˈplek-trəm\ *n, pl* **plec·tra** \-trə\ *or* **plec·trums** [L] : ³PICK 3

¹**pledge** \ˈplej\ *n* **1 :** something given as security for the performance of an act **2 :** the state of being held as a security or guaranty **3 :** TOAST 3 **4 :** PROMISE, VOW

²**pledge** *vb* **pledged; pledg·ing 1 :** to deposit as a pledge **2 :** TOAST 3 : to bind by a pledge : PLIGHT **4 :** PROMISE

Pleis·to·cene \ˈplī-stə-ˌsēn\ *adj* : of, relating to, or being the earlier epoch of the Quaternary — **Pleistocene** *n*

ple·na·ry \ˈplē-nə-rē, ˈple-\ *adj* **1 :** FULL ⟨~ power⟩ **2 :** including all entitled to attend ⟨~ session⟩

pleni·po·ten·tia·ry \ˌple-nə-pə-ˈten-chə-rē, -ˈten-chē-ˌer-ē\ *n, pl* **-ries :** a diplomatic agent having full authority — **plenipotentiary** *adj*

plen·i·tude \ˈple-nə-ˌtüd, -ˌtyüd\ *n* **1 :** COMPLETENESS **2 :** ABUNDANCE

plen·te·ous \ˈplen-tē-əs\ *adj* **1 :** FRUITFUL **2 :** existing in plenty

plen·ti·ful \ˈplen-ti-fəl\ *adj* **1 :** containing or yielding plenty **2 :** ABUNDANT — **plen·ti·ful·ly** *adv*

plen·ty \ˈplen-tē\ *n* : a more than adequate number or amount

ple·num \ˈple-nəm, ˈplē-\ *n, pl* **-nums** *or* **-na** \-nə\ : a general assembly of all members esp. of a legislative body

pleth·o·ra \ˈple-thə-rə\ *n* : an excessive quantity or fullness; *also* : PROFUSION

pleu·ri·sy \ˈplu̇r-ə-sē\ *n* : inflammation of the membrane that lines the chest and covers the lungs

plex·us \ˈplek-səs\ *n, pl* **plex·us·es** \-sə-səz\ : an interlacing network esp. of blood vessels or nerves

pli·able \ˈplī-ə-bəl\ *adj* **1 :** FLEXIBLE **2 :** yielding easily to others **syn** plastic, pliant, ductile, malleable, adaptable — **pli·abil·i·ty** \ˌplī-ə-ˈbi-lə-tē\ *n*

pli·ant \ˈplī-ənt\ *adj* **1 :** FLEXIBLE **2 :** easily influenced : PLIABLE — **pli·an·cy** \-ən-sē\ *n*

pli·ers \ˈplī-ərz\ *n pl* : small pincers for bending or cutting wire or handling small objects

¹**plight** \ˈplīt\ *vb* : to put or give in pledge : ENGAGE

²**plight** *n* : an unfortunate, difficult, or precarious situation

plinth \ˈplinth\ *n* : the lowest part of the base of an architectural column

Plio·cene \ˈplī-ə-ˌsēn\ *adj* : of, relating to, or being the latest epoch of the Tertiary — **Pliocene** *n*

PLO *abbr* Palestine Liberation Organization

plod \ˈpläd\ *vb* **plod·ded; plod·ding 1 :** to walk heavily or slowly : TRUDGE **2 :** to work laboriously and monotonously : DRUDGE — **plod·der** *n* — **plod·ding·ly** *adv*

plop \ˈpläp\ *vb* **plopped; plop·ping 1 :** to fall or move with a sound like that of something dropping into water **2** : to set, drop, or throw heavily — **plop** *n*

¹plot \'plät\ *n* **1** : a small area of ground **2** : a ground plan (as of an area) **3** : the main story (as of a book or movie) **4** : a secret scheme : INTRIGUE

²plot *vb* **plot·ted; plot·ting** **1** : to make a plot or plan of **2** : to mark on or as if on a chart **3** : to plan or contrive esp. secretly — **plot·ter** *n*

plo·ver \'plə-vər, 'plō-\ *n, pl* **plover** *or* **plovers** : any of a family of shore-inhabiting birds that differ from the sandpipers in having shorter stouter bills

¹plow *or* **plough** \'plaú\ *n* **1** : an implement used to cut, lift, turn over, and partly break up soil **2** : a device (as a snowplow) operating like a plow

²plow *or* **plough** *vb* **1** : to open, break up, or work with a plow **2** : to move through like a plow ⟨a ship ∼ing the waves⟩ **3** : to proceed laboriously — **plow·able** *adj* — **plow·er** *n*

plow·boy \'plaú-,bòi\ *n* : a boy who leads the horse drawing a plow

plow·man \-mən, -,man\ *n* **1** : a man who guides a plow **2** : a farm laborer

plow·share \-,sher\ *n* : a part of a plow that cuts the earth

ploy \'plói\ *n* : a tactic intended to embarrass or frustrate an opponent

¹pluck \'plək\ *vb* **1** : to pull off or out : PICK; *also* : to pull something from **2** : to play (an instrument) by pulling the strings **3** : TUG, TWITCH

²pluck *n* **1** : an act or instance of plucking **2** : SPIRIT, COURAGE

plucky \'plə-kē\ *adj* **pluck·i·er; -est** : COURAGEOUS, SPIRITED

¹plug \'pləg\ *n* **1** : STOPPER; *also* : an obstructing mass **2** : a cake of tobacco **3** : a poor or worn-out horse **4** : SPARK PLUG **5** : a lure with several hooks used in fishing **6** : a device on the end of a cord for making an electrical connection **7** : a piece of favorable publicity

²plug *vb* **plugged; plug·ging** **1** : to stop, make tight, or secure by inserting a plug **2** : HIT, SHOOT **3** : to publicize insistently **4** : PLOD, DRUDGE

plum \'pləm\ *n* [ME, fr. OE *plūme*, modif. of L *prunum* plum, fr. Gk *proumnon*] **1** : a smooth-skinned juicy fruit borne by trees related to the peach and cherry; *also* : a tree bearing plums **2** : a raisin when used in desserts (as puddings) **3** : something excellent; *esp* : something desirable given in return for a favor

plum·age \'plü-mij\ *n* : the feathers of a bird — **plum·aged** \-mijd\ *adj*

¹plumb \'pləm\ *n* : a weight on the end of a line (**plumb line**) used esp. by builders to show vertical direction

²plumb *adv* **1** : VERTICALLY **2** : COMPLETELY **3** : EXACTLY; *also* : IMMEDIATELY

³plumb *vb* : to sound, adjust, or test with a plumb ⟨∼ the depth of a well⟩

⁴plumb *adj* **1** : VERTICAL **2** : COMPLETE

plumb·er \'plə-mər\ *n* : a worker who fits or repairs pipes and fixtures

plumb·ing \'plə-miŋ\ *n* : a system of pipes in a building for supplying and carrying off water

¹plume \'plüm\ *n* : FEATHER; *esp* : a large, conspicuous, or showy feather — **plumed** \'plümd\ *adj* — **plumy** \'plü-mē\ *adj*

²plume *vb* **plumed; plum·ing** **1** : to provide or deck with feathers **2** : to indulge (oneself) in pride

¹plum·met \'plə-mət\ *n* : PLUMB; *also* : PLUMB LINE

²plummet *vb* : to drop or plunge straight down

¹plump \'pləmp\ *vb* **1** : to drop or fall suddenly or heavily **2** : to favor something strongly ⟨∼ing for change⟩

²plump *n* : a sudden heavy fall or blow; *also* : the sound made by it

³plump *adv* **1** : straight down; *also* : straight ahead **2** : UNQUALIFIEDLY

⁴plump *adj* : having a full rounded usu. pleasing form **syn** fleshy, stout, roly-poly, rotund — **plump·ness** *n*

¹plun·der \'plən-dər\ *vb* : to take the goods of by force or wrongfully : PILLAGE — **plun·der·er** *n*

²plunder *n* : something taken by force or theft : LOOT

¹plunge \'plənj\ *vb* **plunged; plung·ing** **1** : IMMERSE, SUBMERGE **2** : to enter or cause to enter a state or course of action suddenly or violently ⟨∼ into war⟩ **3** : to cast oneself into or as if into water **4** : to gamble heavily and recklessly **5** : to descend suddenly

²plunge *n* : a sudden dive, leap, or rush

plung·er \'plən-jər\ *n* **1** : one that plunges **2** : a sliding piece driven by or against fluid pressure : PISTON **3** : a rubber cup on a handle pushed against an opening to free a waste outlet of an obstruction

plunk \'pləŋk\ *vb* **1** : to make or cause to make a hollow metallic sound **2** : to drop heavily or suddenly — **plunk** *n*

plu·per·fect \(,)plü-'pər-fikt\ *adj* [ME *pluperfyth*, modif. of LL *plusquamperfectus*, lit., more than perfect] : of, relating to, or constituting a verb tense that denotes an action or state as completed at or before a past time spoken of — **pluperfect** *n*

plu·ral \'plür-əl\ *adj* [ME, fr. MF & L; MF *plurel*, fr. L *pluralis*, fr. *plur-*, *plus* more] : of, relating to, or constituting a word form used to denote more than one — **plural** *n*

plu·ral·i·ty \plù-'ra-lə-tē\ *n, pl* **-ties** **1** : the state of being plural **2** : an excess of votes over those cast for an opposing candidate **3** : the greatest number of votes cast when not a majority

plu·ral·ize \'plür-ə-,līz\ *vb* **-ized; -iz·ing** : to make plural or express in the plural form — **plu·ral·i·za·tion** \,plür-ə-lə-'zā-shən\ *n*

¹plus \'pləs\ *adj* [L, more] **1** : mathematically positive **2** : having or being in addition to what is anticipated **3** : falling high in a specified range ⟨a grade of B ∼⟩

²plus *n, pl* **plus·es** \'plə-səz\ *also* **plus·ses** **1** : a sign + (**plus sign**) used in mathematics to indicate addition or a positive quantity **2** : an added quantity; *also* : a positive quality **3** : SURPLUS

³plus *prep* **1** : increased by : with the addition of ⟨3 ∼ 4⟩ **2** : BESIDES

⁴plus *conj* : AND ⟨soup ∼ salad and bread⟩

¹plush \'pləsh\ *n* : a fabric with a pile longer and less dense than velvet pile — **plushy** *adj*

²plush *adj* : notably luxurious — **plush·ly** *adv* — **plush·ness** *n*

Plu·to \'plü-tō\ *n* : the planet farthest from the sun — see PLANET table

plu·toc·ra·cy \plü-'tä-krə-sē\ *n, pl* **-cies** **1** : government by the wealthy **2** : a controlling class of the wealthy — **plu·to·crat** \'plü-tə-,krat\ *n* — **plu·to·crat·ic** \,plü-tə-'kra-tik\ *adj*

plu·to·ni·um \plü-'tō-nē-əm\ *n* : a radioactive chemical element formed by the decay of neptunium — see ELEMENT table

plu·vi·al \'plü-vē-əl\ *adj* **1** : of or relating to rain **2** : characterized by abundant rain

¹ply \'plī\ *vb* **plied; ply·ing** **1** : to use, practice, or work diligently ⟨∼ a trade⟩ **2** : to keep supplying something to ⟨*plied* them with liquor⟩ **3** : to go or travel regularly esp. by sea

²ply *n, pl* **plies** : one of the folds, thicknesses, or strands of which something (as plywood or yarn) is made

³ply *vb* **plied; ply·ing** : to twist together ⟨∼ yarns⟩

Plym·outh Rock \'pli-məth-\ *n* : any of an American breed of medium-sized single-combed domestic fowls

ply·wood \'plī-,wúd\ *n* : material made of thin sheets of wood glued and pressed together

pm *abbr* premium

Pm *symbol* promethium

PM *abbr* **1** paymaster **2** police magistrate **3** postmaster

4 post meridiem — often not cap. and often punctuated **5** postmortem **6** prime minister **7** provost marshal

pmk *abbr* postmark

PMS *abbr* premenstrual syndrome

pmt *abbr* payment

pneu·mat·ic \nù-'ma-tik, nyù-\ *adj* **1** : of, relating to, or using air or wind **2** : moved by air pressure **3** : filled with compressed air — **pneu·mat·i·cal·ly** \-ti-k(ə-)lē\ *adv*

pneu·mo·co·ni·o·sis \nü-mō-ˌkō-nē-'ō-səs, ˌnyü-\ *n* : a disease of the lungs caused by habitual inhalation of irritant mineral or metallic particles

pneu·mo·nia \nù-'mō-nyə, nyù-\ *n* : an inflammatory disease of the lungs

Po *symbol* polonium

PO *abbr* **1** petty officer **2** post office

¹poach \'pōch\ *vb* [ME *pochen*, fr. MF *pocher*, fr. OF *pochier*, lit., to put into a bag, fr. *poche* bag, pocket, of Gmc origin] : to cook (as an egg or fish) in simmering liquid

²poach *vb* : to hunt or fish unlawfully — **poach·er** *n*

POB *abbr* post office box

pock \'päk\ *n* : a small swelling on the skin (as in smallpox); *also* : a spot suggesting this

¹pock·et \'pä-kət\ *n* **1** : a small bag open at the top or side inserted in a garment **2** : supply of money : MEANS **3** : RECEPTACLE, CONTAINER **4** : a small isolated area or group **5** : a small body of ore — **pock·et·ful** *n*

²pocket *vb* **1** : to put in or as if in a pocket **2** : STEAL

³pocket *adj* **1** : small enough to fit in a pocket; *also* : SMALL, MINIATURE **2** : carried in or paid from one's own pocket

¹pock·et·book \-ˌbùk\ *n* **1** : PURSE; *also* : HANDBAG **2** : financial resources

²pocketbook *adj* : relating to money

pocket gopher *n* : GOPHER 2

pock·et·knife \'pä-kət-ˌnīf\ *n* : a knife with a folding blade to be carried in the pocket

pocket veto *n* : an indirect veto of a legislative bill by an executive through retention of the bill unsigned until after adjournment of the legislature

pock·mark \'päk-ˌmärk\ *n* : a pit or scar caused by smallpox or acne — **pock·marked** \-ˌmärkt\ *adj*

po·co \'pō-kō, 'pò-\ *adv* [It, little, fr. L *paucus*] : SOMEWHAT — used to qualify a direction in music 〈~ allegro〉

po·co a po·co \ˌpō-kō-ä-'pō-kō, ˌpò-kō-ä-'pò-\ *adv* : little by little — used as a direction in music

pod \'päd\ *n* **1** : a dry fruit (as of a pea) that splits open when ripe **2** : an external streamlined compartment (as for a jet engine) on an airplane **3** : a compartment (as for personnel, a power unit, or an instrument) on a ship or craft

POD *abbr* pay on delivery

po·di·a·try \pə-'dī-ə-trē, pō-\ *n* : the medical care and treatment of the human foot — **po·di·a·trist** \pə-'dī-ə-trist, pō-\ *n*

po·di·um \'pō-dē-əm\ *n, pl* **podiums** *or* **po·dia** \-dē-ə\ **1** : a dais esp. for an orchestral conductor **2** : LECTERN

POE *abbr* port of entry

po·em \'pō-əm\ *n* : a composition in verse

po·esy \'pō-ə-zē\ *n* : POETRY

po·et \'pō-ət\ *n* [ME, fr. OF *poete*, fr. L *poeta*, fr. Gk *poiētēs* maker, poet, fr. *poiein* to make] : a writer of poetry; *also* : a creative artist of great sensitivity

po·et·as·ter \'pō-ə-ˌtas-tər\ *n* : an inferior poet

po·et·ess \'pō-ə-təs\ *n* : a girl or woman who is a poet

poetic justice *n* : an outcome in which vice is punished and virtue rewarded usu. in a manner peculiarly or ironically appropriate

po·et·ry \'pō-ə-trē\ *n* **1** : metrical writing **2** : POEMS — **po·et·ic** \pō-'e-tik\ *or* **po·et·i·cal** \-ti-kəl\ *adj*

po·grom \'pō-grəm, pō-'gräm\ *n* [Yiddish, fr. Russ, lit.,

devastation] : an organized massacre of helpless people and esp. of Jews

poi \'pòi\ *n, pl* **poi** *or* **pois** : a Hawaiian food of taro root cooked, pounded, and kneaded to a paste and often allowed to ferment

poi·gnant \'pòi-nyənt\ *adj* **1** : painfully affecting the feelings 〈~ grief〉 **2** : deeply moving 〈~ scene〉 — **poignan·cy** \-nyən-sē\ *n*

poin·ci·ana \ˌpòin-sē-'a-nə\ *n* : any of several ornamental tropical leguminous trees or shrubs with bright orange or red flowers

poin·set·tia \pòin-'se-tē-ə\ *n* : any of several showy tropical American spurges with usu. scarlet bracts around their small greenish flowers

¹point \'pòint\ *n* **1** : an individual detail; *also* : the most important essential **2** : PURPOSE **3** : a geometric element that has position but no size **4** : a particular place : LOCALITY **5** : a particular stage or degree **6** : a sharp end : TIP **7** : a projecting piece of land **8** : a punctuation mark; *esp* : PERIOD **9** : DECIMAL POINT **10** : one of the divisions of the compass **11** : a unit of counting (as in a game score) — **point·less** *adj* — **beside the point** : IRRELEVANT — **to the point** : RELEVANT, PERTINENT

²point *vb* **1** : to furnish with a point : SHARPEN **2** : PUNCTUATE **3** : to separate (a decimal fraction) from an integer by a decimal point — usu. used with *off* **4** : to indicate the position of esp. by extending a finger **5** : to direct attention to 〈~ out an error〉 **6** : AIM, DIRECT **7** : to lie extended, aimed, or turned in a particular direction : FACE, LOOK

point–blank \'pòint-'blaŋk\ *adj* **1** : so close to the target that a missile fired will travel in a straight line to the mark **2** : DIRECT, BLUNT — **point–blank** *adv*

point·ed \'pòin-təd\ *adj* **1** : having a point **2** : being to the point : DIRECT **3** : aimed at a particular person or group; *also* : CONSPICUOUS, MARKED — **point·ed·ly** *adv*

point·er \'pòin-tər\ *n* **1** : one that points out : INDICATOR **2** : a large short-haired hunting dog **3** : HINT, TIP

poin·til·lism \'pwan-tē-ˌyi-zəm, 'pòint-ᵊl-ˌi-zəm\ *n* [F *pointillisme*, fr. *pointiller* to stipple, fr. *point* point] : the theory or practice in painting of applying small strokes or dots of color to a surface so that from a distance they blend together — **poin·til·list** *also* **poin·til·liste** \ˌpwan-tē-'yēst, 'pòint-ᵊl-ist\ *n or adj*

point of no return : a critical point at which turning back or reversal is not possible

point of view : a position from which something is considered or evaluated

¹poise \'pòiz\ *n* **1** : BALANCE **2** : self-possessed calmness; *also* : a particular way of carrying oneself

²poise *vb* **poised; pois·ing** : BALANCE

poi·sha \'pòi-shə\ *n, pl* **poisha** : the paisa of Bangladesh

¹poi·son \'pòiz-ᵊn\ *n* [ME, fr. OF, drink, poisonous drink, poison, fr. L *potion-, potio* drink] : a substance that through its chemical action can injure or kill — **poison·ous** \-ᵊn-əs\ *adj*

²poison *vb* **1** : to injure or kill with poison **2** : to treat or taint with poison **3** : to affect destructively : CORRUPT 〈~ed her mind〉 — **poi·son·er** *n*

poison hemlock *n* : a large branching poisonous herb with finely divided leaves and white flowers that is related to the carrot

poison ivy *n* **1** : a usu. climbing plant related to the sumacs that has leaves composed of three shiny leaflets and produces an irritating oil causing a usu. intensely itching skin rash; *also* : any of several related plants **2** : a skin rash caused by poison ivy

☞ For illustration, see next page.

\ə\abut \ᵊ\kitten \ər\further \a\ash \ā\ace \ä\mop, mar
\aù\out \ch\chin \e\bet \ē\easy \g\go \i\hit \ī\ice \j\job
\ŋ\sing \ō\go \ò\law \òi\boy \th\thin \th\the \ü\loot \ù\foot
\y\yet \zh\vision *see also* Pronunciation Symbols page

poison ivy

poison oak *n* : any of several shrubby plants closely related to poison ivy and having similar properties

poison sumac *n* : a smooth American swamp shrub with pinnate leaves, greenish flowers, greenish white berries, and irritating properties like the related poison ivy

¹poke \'pōk\ *n* : BAG, SACK

²poke *vb* **poked; pok·ing 1** : PROD; *also* : to stir up by prodding **2** : to make a prodding or jabbing movement esp. repeatedly **3** : HIT, PUNCH **4** : to thrust forward obtrusively **5** : RUMMAGE **6** : MEDDLE, PRY **7** : DAWDLE — **poke fun at** : RIDICULE, MOCK

³poke *n* : a quick thrust; *also* : PUNCH

¹pok·er \'pō-kər\ *n* : a metal rod for stirring a fire

²po·ker \'pō-kər\ *n* : any of several card games in which the player with the highest hand at the end of the betting wins

poker: hands in descending value: *1* five of a kind, *2* royal flush, *3* straight flush, *4* four of a kind, *5* full house, *6* flush, *7* straight, *8* three of a kind, *9* two pairs, *10* one pair

poke·weed \'pōk-ˌwēd\ *n* : a coarse American perennial herb with clusters of white flowers and dark purple juicy berries

poky *or* **pok·ey** \'pō-kē\ *adj* **pok·i·er; -est 1** : small and cramped **2** : SHABBY, DULL **3** : annoyingly slow

pol \'päl\ *n* : POLITICIAN

po·lar \'pō-lər\ *adj* **1** : of or relating to a geographical pole **2** : of or relating to a pole (as of a magnet)

polar bear *n* : a large creamy-white bear that inhabits arctic regions

Po·lar·is \pə-'lar-əs\ *n* : NORTH STAR

po·lar·i·ty \pō-'lar-ə-tē\ *n, pl* **-ties** : the condition of having poles and esp. magnetic or electrical poles

po·lar·i·za·tion \ˌpō-lə-rə-'zā-shən\ *n* **1** : the action of polarizing : the state of being polarized **2** : concentration about opposing extremes

po·lar·ize \'pō-lə-ˌrīz\ *vb* **-ized; -iz·ing 1** : to cause (light waves) to vibrate in a definite way **2** : to give physical polarity to **3** : to break up into opposing groups

polar bear

pol·der \'pōl-dər, 'päl-\ *n* [D] : a tract of low land reclaimed from the sea

¹pole \'pōl\ *n* : a long slender piece of wood or metal ⟨telephone ~⟩

²pole *vb* **poled; pol·ing** : to impel or push with a pole

³pole *n* **1** : either end of an axis esp. of the earth **2** : either of the terminals of an electric device (as a battery or generator) **3** : one of two or more regions in a magnetized body at which the magnetism is concentrated — **pole·ward** \'pōl-wərd\ *adj or adv*

Pole \'pōl\ *n* : a native or inhabitant of Poland

¹pole·ax \'pōl-ˌaks\ *n* : a battle-ax with a short handle

²poleax *vb* : to attack or fell with or as if with a poleax

pole·cat \'pōl-ˌkat\ *n, pl* **polecats** *or* **polecat 1** : a European carnivorous mammal of which the ferret is considered a domesticated variety **2** : SKUNK

po·lem·ic \pə-'le-mik\ *n* : the art or practice of disputation — usu. used in pl. — **po·lem·i·cal** \-mi-kəl\ *also* **po·lem·ic** \-mik\ *adj* — **po·lem·i·cist** \-sist\ *n*

pole·star \'pōl-ˌstär\ *n* **1** : NORTH STAR **2** : a directing principle : GUIDE

pole vault *n* : a field contest in which each contestant uses a pole to vault for height over a crossbar — **pole-vault** *vb* — **pole–vault·er** *n*

¹po·lice \pə-'lēs\ *vb* **po·liced; po·lic·ing 1** : to control, regulate, or keep in order esp. by use of police ⟨~ a highway⟩ **2** : to make clean and put in order

²police *n, pl* **police** [MF, government, fr. LL *politia*, fr. Gk *politeia*, fr. *politēs* citizen, fr. *polis* city, state] **1** : the department of government that keeps public order and safety and enforces the laws; *also* : the members of this department **2** : a private organization resembling a police force; *also* : its members **3** : military personnel detailed to clean and put in order

po·lice·man \-mən\ *n* : POLICE OFFICER

police officer *n* : a member of a police force

police state *n* : a state characterized by repressive, arbitrary, totalitarian rule by means of secret police

po·lice·wom·an \pə-'lēs-ˌwu̇-mən\ *n* : a woman who is a police officer

¹pol·i·cy \'pä-lə-sē\ *n, pl* **-cies** : a definite course or method of action selected to guide and determine present and future decisions

²policy *n, pl* **-cies** : a writing whereby a contract of insurance is made

pol·i·cy·hold·er \'pä-lə-sē-ˌhōl-dər\ *n* : one granted an insurance policy

po·lio \'pō-lē-ˌō\ *n* : POLIOMYELITIS — **polio** *adj*

po·lio·my·eli·tis \-ˌmī-ə-'lī-təs\ *n* : an acute virus disease marked by inflammation of the nerve cells of the spinal cord

¹pol·ish \'pä-lish\ *vb* **1** : to make smooth and glossy usu. by rubbing **2** : to refine or improve in manners, condition, or style

²polish *n* **1** : a smooth glossy surface : LUSTER **2** : REFINEMENT, CULTURE **3** : the action or process of polishing **4** : a preparation used to produce a gloss

Pol·ish \'pō-lish\ *n* : the Slavic language of the Poles — **Polish** *adj*

polit *abbr* political; politician

po·lit·bu·ro \'pä-lət-ˌbyùr-ō, 'pō-, pə-'lit-\ n [Russ *politbyuro*] : the principal policy-making committee of a Communist party

po·lite \pə-'līt\ adj **po·lit·er; -est 1** : REFINED, CULTIVATED ⟨∼ society⟩ **2** : marked by correct social conduct : COURTEOUS; *also* : CONSIDERATE, TACTFUL — **po·lite·ly** adv — **po·lite·ness** n

po·li·tesse \ˌpä-li-'tes\ n [F] : formal politeness

pol·i·tic \'pä-lə-ˌtik\ adj **1** : wise in promoting a policy ⟨a ∼ statesman⟩ **2** : shrewdly tactful ⟨a ∼ move⟩

po·lit·i·cal \pə-'li-ti-kəl\ adj **1** : of or relating to government or politics **2** : involving or charged or concerned with acts against a government or a political system ⟨∼ prisoners⟩ — **po·lit·i·cal·ly** \-k(ə-)lē\ adv

politically correct adj : conforming to a belief that language and practices which could offend sensibilities (as in matters of sex or race) should be eliminated

pol·i·ti·cian \ˌpä-lə-'ti-shən\ n : a person actively engaged in government or politics

pol·i·tick \'pä-lə-ˌtik\ vb : to engage in political discussion or activity

po·lit·i·co \pə-'li-ti-ˌkō\ n, pl **-cos** also **-coes** : POLITICIAN

pol·i·tics \'pä-lə-ˌtiks\ n sing or pl **1** : the art or science of government, of guiding or influencing governmental policy, or of winning and holding control over a government **2** : political affairs or business; *esp* : competition between groups or individuals for power and leadership **3** : political opinions

pol·i·ty \'pä-lə-tē\ n, pl **-ties** : a politically organized unit; *also* : the form or constitution of such a unit

pol·ka \'pōl-kə, 'pō-kə\ n [Czech, fr. *Polka* Polish woman, fem. of *Polák* Pole] : a lively couple dance of Bohemian origin; *also* : music for this dance — **polka** vb

pol·ka dot \'pō-kə-ˌdät\ n : a dot in a pattern of regularly distributed dots — **polka–dot** or **polka–dot·ted** \-ˌdä-təd\ adj

¹poll \'pōl\ n **1** : HEAD **2** : the casting and recording of votes; *also* : the total vote cast **3** : the place where votes are cast — usu. used in pl. **4** : a questioning of persons to obtain information or opinions to be analyzed

²poll vb **1** : to cut off or shorten a growth or part of : CLIP, SHEAR **2** : to receive and record the votes of **3** : to receive (as votes) in an election **4** : to question in a poll

pol·lack or **pol·lock** \'pä-lək\ n, pl **pollack** or **pollock** : an important Atlantic food fish that is related to the cods; *also* : a related food fish of the north Pacific

pol·len \'pä-lən\ n [NL, fr. L, fine flour] : a mass of male spores of a seed plant usu. appearing as a yellow dust

pol·li·na·tion \ˌpä-lə-'nā-shən\ n : the carrying of pollen to the female part of a plant to fertilize the seed — **pol·li·nate** \'pä-lə-ˌnāt\ vb — **pol·li·na·tor** \-ˌnā-tər\ n

poll·ster \'pōl-stər\ n : one that conducts a poll or compiles data obtained by a poll

poll tax n : a tax of a fixed amount per person levied on adults

pol·lute \pə-'lüt\ vb **pol·lut·ed; pol·lut·ing** : to make impure; *esp* : to contaminate (an environment) esp. with man-made waste — **pol·lut·ant** \-'lüt-ᵊnt\ n — **pol·lut·er** n — **pol·lu·tion** \-'lü-shən\ n

pol·ly·wog or **pol·li·wog** \'pä-lē-ˌwäg\ n : TADPOLE

po·lo \'pō-lō\ n : a game played by two teams on horseback using long-handled mallets to drive a wooden ball

po·lo·ni·um \pə-'lō-nē-əm\ n [NL, fr. ML *Polonia* Poland, birthplace of its discoverer, Mme. Curie] : a radioactive metallic chemical element — see ELEMENT table

pol·ter·geist \'pōl-tər-ˌgīst\ n [G, fr. *poltern* to knock + *Geist* spirit] : a noisy usu. mischievous ghost held to be responsible for unexplained noises

pol·troon \päl-'trün\ n : COWARD

poly- comb form **1** : many : several ⟨*poly*syllabic⟩ **2** : polymeric ⟨*poly*ester⟩

poly·chlo·ri·nat·ed bi·phe·nyl \ˌpä-li-'klōr-ə-ˌnā-təd-ˌbī-'fen-ᵊl, -'fēn-\ n : any of several industrial compounds that are poisonous environmental pollutants

poly·clin·ic \ˌpä-li-'kli-nik\ n : a clinic or hospital treating diseases of many sorts

poly·es·ter \'pä-lē-ˌes-tər\ n : a polymer composed of ester groups used esp. in making fibers or plastics

poly·eth·yl·ene \ˌpä-lē-'e-thə-ˌlēn\ n : a lightweight plastic resistant to chemicals and moisture and used chiefly in packaging

po·lyg·a·my \pə-'li-gə-mē\ n : the practice of having more than one wife or husband at one time — **po·lyg·a·mist** \-mist\ n — **po·lyg·a·mous** \-məs\ adj

poly·glot \'pä-li-ˌglät\ adj **1** : speaking or writing several languages **2** : containing or made up of several languages — **polyglot** n

poly·gon \'pä-li-ˌgän\ n : a closed plane figure bounded by straight lines — **po·lyg·o·nal** \pə-'li-gən-ᵊl\ adj

poly·graph \'pä-li-ˌgraf\ n : an instrument for recording variations of several bodily functions (as blood pressure) simultaneously — **po·lyg·ra·pher** \pə-'li-grə-fər, 'pä-li-ˌgra-fər\ n

poly·he·dron \ˌpä-li-'hē-drən\ n : a solid formed by plane faces that are polygons — **poly·he·dral** \-drəl\ adj

poly·math \'pä-li-ˌmath\ n : a person of encyclopedic learning

poly·mer \'pä-lə-mər\ n : a chemical compound formed by union of small molecules and usu. consisting of repeating structural units — **poly·mer·ic** \ˌpä-lə-'mer-ik\ adj

po·lym·er·i·za·tion \pə-ˌli-mə-rə-'zā-shən\ n : a chemical reaction in which two or more small molecules combine to form polymers — **po·lym·er·ize** \pə-'li-mə-ˌrīz\ vb

Poly·ne·sian \ˌpä-lə-'nē-zhən\ n **1** : a member of any of the indigenous peoples of Polynesia **2** : a group of Austronesian languages spoken in Polynesia — **Polynesian** adj

poly·no·mi·al \ˌpä-lə-'nō-mē-əl\ n : an algebraic expression having one or more terms each of which consists of a constant multiplied by one or more variables raised to a nonnegative integral power — **polynomial** adj

pol·yp \'pä-ləp\ n **1** : an invertebrate animal (as a coral) that is a coelenterate having a hollow cylindrical body closed at one end **2** : a projecting mass of swollen and hypertrophied or tumorous membrane ⟨a rectal ∼⟩

po·lyph·o·ny \pə-'li-fə-nē\ n : music consisting of two or more melodically independent but harmonizing voice parts — **poly·phon·ic** \ˌpä-li-'fä-nik\ adj

poly·pro·pyl·ene \ˌpä-lē-'prō-pə-ˌlēn\ n : any of various polymer plastics or fibers

poly·sty·rene \ˌpä-lē-'stīr-ˌēn\ n : a rigid transparent nonconducting thermoplastic used esp. in molded products and foams

poly·syl·lab·ic \-sə-'la-bik\ adj **1** : having more than three syllables **2** : characterized by polysyllabic words

poly·syl·la·ble \'pä-li-ˌsi-lə-bəl\ n : a polysyllabic word

poly·tech·nic \ˌpä-li-'tek-nik\ adj : of, relating to, or instructing in many technical arts or applied sciences

poly·the·ism \'pä-li-thē-ˌi-zəm\ n : belief in or worship of many gods — **poly·the·ist** \-ˌthē-ist\ adj or n — **poly·the·is·tic** \ˌpä-li-thē-'is-tik\ adj

poly·un·sat·u·rat·ed \ˌpä-lē-ˌən-'sa-chə-ˌrā-təd\ adj : having many double or triple bonds in a molecule — used esp. of an oil or fatty acid

poly·ure·thane \ˌpä-lē-'yùr-ə-ˌthān\ n : any of various polymers used esp. in foams and in resins (as for coatings)

\ə\abut \ᵊ\kitten \ər\further \a\ash \ā\ace \ä\mop, mar
\aù\out \ch\chin \e\bet \ē\easy \g\go \i\hit \ī\ice \j\job
\ŋ\sing \ō\go \ò\law \òi\boy \th\thin \t̶h̶\the \ü\loot \ù\foot
\y\yet \zh\vision *see also* Pronunciation Symbols page

poly·vi·nyl \ˌpä-li-ˈvīn-ᵊl\ *adj* : of, relating to, or being a polymerized vinyl compound, resin, or plastic — often used in combination

pome·gran·ate \ˈpä-mə-ˌgra-nət\ *n* [ME *poumgrenet*, fr. MF *pomme grenate*, lit., seedy apple] : a tropical reddish fruit with many seeds and an edible crimson pulp; *also* : the tree that bears it

¹**pom·mel** \ˈpə-məl, ˈpä-\ *n* **1** : the knob on the hilt of a sword **2** : the knoblike bulge at the front and top of a saddlebow

²**pom·mel** \ˈpə-məl\ *vb* **-meled** *or* **-melled; -mel·ing** *or* **-mel·ling** : PUMMEL

pomp \ˈpämp\ *n* **1** : brilliant display : SPLENDOR **2** : OSTENTATION

pom·pa·dour \ˈpäm-pə-ˌdȯr\ *n* : a style of dressing the hair high over the forehead

pom·pa·no \ˈpäm-pə-ˌnō, ˈpəm-\ *n, pl* **-no** *or* **-nos** : a New World fish esp. of warmer Atlantic coasts

pom–pom \ˈpäm-ˌpäm\ *n* **1** : an ornamental ball or tuft used on a cap or costume **2** : a fluffy ball flourished by cheerleaders

pom·pon \ˈpäm-ˌpän\ *n* **1** : POM-POM **2** : a chrysanthemum or dahlia with small rounded flower heads

pomp·ous \ˈpäm-pəs\ *adj* **1** : suggestive of pomp; *esp* : OSTENTATIOUS **2** : pretentiously dignified **3** : excessively elevated or ornate **syn** arrogant, magisterial, self-important — **pom·pos·i·ty** \päm-ˈpä-sə-tē\ *n* — **pomp·ous·ly** *adv*

pon·cho \ˈpän-chō\ *n, pl* **ponchos** [AmerSp, fr. Araucanian (American Indian language of Chile)] **1** : a blanket with a slit in the middle for the head so that it can be worn as a garment **2** : a waterproof garment resembling a poncho

pond \ˈpänd\ *n* : a small body of water

pon·der \ˈpän-dər\ *vb* **pon·dered; pon·der·ing 1** : to weigh in the mind **2** : to consider carefully

pon·der·o·sa pine \ˈpän-də-ˌrō-sə-, -zə-\ *n* : a tall pine of western No. America with long needles; *also* : its strong reddish wood

pon·der·ous \ˈpän-də-rəs\ *adj* **1** : of very great weight **2** : UNWIELDY, CLUMSY ⟨a ~ weapon⟩ **3** : oppressively dull ⟨a ~ speech⟩ **syn** cumbrous, cumbersome, weighty

pone \ˈpōn\ *n, Southern & Midland* : an oval-shaped cornmeal cake; *also* : corn bread in the form of pones

pon·iard \ˈpän-yərd\ *n* : DAGGER

pon·tiff \ˈpän-təf\ *n* : POPE — **pon·tif·i·cal** \pän-ˈti-fi-kəl\ *adj*

¹**pon·tif·i·cate** \pän-ˈti-fi-kət, -fə-ˌkāt\ *n* : the state, office, or term of office of a pontiff

²**pon·tif·i·cate** \pän-ˈti-fə-ˌkāt\ *vb* **-cat·ed; -cat·ing** : to deliver dogmatic opinions

pon·toon \pän-ˈtün\ *n* **1** : a flat-bottomed boat **2** : a boat or float used in building a floating temporary bridge **3** : a float of a seaplane

po·ny \ˈpō-nē\ *n, pl* **ponies** : a small horse

po·ny·tail \-ˌtāl\ *n* : a style of arranging hair to resemble the tail of a pony

pooch \ˈpüch\ *n* : DOG

poo·dle \ˈpüd-ᵊl\ *n* [G *Pudel*, short for *Pudelhund*, fr. *pudeln* to splash + *Hund* dog] : a dog of any of three breeds of active intelligent heavy-coated solid-colored dogs

pooh–pooh \ˈpü-ˈpü\ *also* **pooh** \ˈpü\ *vb* **1** : to express contempt or impatience **2** : DERIDE, SCORN

¹**pool** \ˈpül\ *n* **1** : a small deep body of usu. fresh water **2** : a small body of standing liquid **3** : SWIMMING POOL

²**pool** *vb* : to form a pool

³**pool** *n* **1** : all the money bet on the result of a particular event **2** : any of several games of billiards played on a table having six pockets **3** : the amount contributed by the participants in a joint venture **4** : a combination between competing firms for mutual profit **5** : a readily available supply

⁴**pool** *vb* : to combine (as resources) in a common fund or effort

¹**poop** \ˈpüp\ *n* : an enclosed superstructure at the stern of a ship

²**poop** *n, slang* : INFORMATION

poop deck *n* : a partial deck above a ship's main afterdeck

poor \ˈpu̇r\ *adj* **1** : lacking material possessions ⟨~ people⟩ **2** : less than adequate : MEAGER ⟨~ crop⟩ **3** : arousing pity ⟨you ~ thing⟩ **4** : inferior in quality or value **5** : UNPRODUCTIVE, BARREN ⟨~ soil⟩ **6** : fairly unsatisfactory ⟨~ prospects⟩; *also* : UNFAVORABLE ⟨~ opinion⟩ — **poor·ly** *adv*

poor boy \ˈpō-ˌbȯi, ˈpȯr-\ *n* : SUBMARINE 2

poor·house \ˈpu̇r-ˌhau̇s\ *n* : a publicly supported home for needy or dependent persons

poor–mouth \-ˌmau̇th, -ˌmau̇th\ *vb* : to plead poverty as a defense or excuse

¹**pop** \ˈpäp\ *vb* **popped; pop·ping 1** : to go, come, enter, or issue forth suddenly or quickly ⟨~ into bed⟩ **2** : to put or thrust suddenly ⟨~ questions⟩ **3** : to burst or cause to burst with a sharp sound; *also* : to make a sharp sound **4** : to protrude from the sockets **5** : SHOOT **6** : to hit a pop-up

²**pop** *n* **1** : a sharp explosive sound **2** : SHOT **3** : SODA POP

³**pop** *n* : FATHER

⁴**pop** *adj* **1** : POPULAR ⟨~ music⟩ **2** : of or relating to pop music ⟨~ singer⟩ **3** : of or relating to the popular culture disseminated through the mass media ⟨~ psychology⟩ **4** : of, relating to, or imitating pop art ⟨~ painter⟩

⁵**pop** *n* : pop music or culture; *also* : POP ART

⁶**pop** *abbr* population

pop art *n* : art in which commonplace objects (as comic strips or soup cans) are used as subject matter — **pop artist** *n*

pop·corn \ˈpäp-ˌkȯrn\ *n* : an Indian corn whose kernels burst open into a white starchy mass when heated; *also* : the burst kernels

pope \ˈpōp\ *n, often cap* : the head of the Roman Catholic Church

pop–eyed \ˈpäp-ˌīd\ *adj* : having eyes that bulge (as from disease)

pop fly *n* : POP-UP

pop·gun \ˈpäp-ˌgən\ *n* : a toy gun for shooting pellets with compressed air

pop·in·jay \ˈpä-pən-ˌjā\ *n* [ME *papejay* parrot, fr. MF *papegai, papejai*, fr. Ar *babghā'*] : a strutting supercilious person

pop·lar \ˈpä-plər\ *n* **1** : any of a genus of slender quick-growing trees (as a cottonwood) related to the willows **2** : the wood of a poplar

pop·lin \ˈpä-plən\ *n* : a strong plain-woven fabric with crosswise ribs

pop·over \ˈpäp-ˌō-vər\ *n* : a hollow muffin made from a thin batter rich in egg

pop·per \ˈpä-pər\ *n* : a utensil for popping corn

pop·py \ˈpä-pē\ *n, pl* **poppies** : any of a genus of herbs with showy flowers including one that yields opium

pop·py·cock \-ˌkäk\ *n* : empty talk or writing : NONSENSE

pop·u·lace \ˈpä-pyə-ləs\ *n* **1** : the common people **2** : POPULATION

pop·u·lar \ˈpä-pyə-lər\ *adj* **1** : of or relating to the general public ⟨~ government⟩ **2** : suited to the tastes of the general public ⟨~ style⟩ **3** : INEXPENSIVE ⟨~ rates⟩ **4** : frequently encountered or widely accepted ⟨~ notion⟩ **5** : commonly liked or approved ⟨~ teacher⟩ — **pop·u·lar·i·ty** \ˌpä-pyə-ˈlar-ə-tē\ *n* — **pop·u·lar·ize** \ˈpä-pyə-lə-ˌrīz\ *vb* — **pop·u·lar·ly** *adv*

pop·u·late \ˈpä-pyə-ˌlāt\ *vb* **-lat·ed; -lat·ing 1** : to have a place in : INHABIT **2** : PEOPLE

pop·u·la·tion \ˌpä-pyə-ˈlā-shən\ *n* **1** : the people or number of people in an area **2** : the organisms inhabiting a particular locality **3** : a group of individuals or items from which samples are taken for statistical measurement

pop·u·la·tion explosion *n* : a pyramiding of numbers of a biological population; *esp* : the recent great increase in human numbers resulting from increased survival and exponential population growth

pop·u·list \'pä-pyə-list\ *n* : a believer in or advocate of the rights, wisdom, or virtues of the common people — **pop·u·lism** \-ˌli-zəm\ *n*

pop·u·lous \'pä-pyə-ləs\ *adj* 1 : densely populated; *also* : having a large population 2 : CROWDED — **pop·u·lous·ness** *n*

pop–up \'pəp-ˌəp\ *n* : a short high fly in baseball

por·ce·lain \'pȯr-sə-lən\ *n* : a fine-grained translucent ceramic ware

porch \'pȯrch\ *n* : a covered entrance usu. with a separate roof

por·cine \'pȯr-ˌsīn\ *adj* : of, relating to, or suggesting swine

por·cu·pine \'pȯr-kyə-ˌpīn\ *n* [ME *porkepin*, fr. MF *porc espin*, fr. It *porcospino*, fr. L *porcus* pig + *spina* spine, prickle] : any of various mammals having stiff sharp spines mingled with their hair

¹pore \'pȯr\ *vb* **pored; por·ing** 1 : to read studiously or attentively ⟨~ over a book⟩ 2 : PONDER, REFLECT

²pore *n* : a tiny hole or space (as in the skin or soil) — **pored** \'pȯrd\ *adj*

pork \'pȯrk\ *n* : the flesh of swine dressed for use as food

pork barrel *n* : government projects or appropriations yielding rich patronage benefits

pork·er \'pȯr-kər\ *n* : HOG; *esp* : a young pig suitable for use as fresh pork

por·nog·ra·phy \pȯr-'nä-grə-fē\ *n* : the depiction of erotic behavior intended to cause sexual excitement — **por·no·graph·ic** \ˌpȯr-nə-'gra-fik\ *adj*

po·rous \'pȯr-əs\ *adj* 1 : full of pores 2 : permeable to fluids : ABSORPTIVE — **po·ros·i·ty** \pə-'rä-sə-tē\ *n*

por·phy·ry \'pȯr-fə-rē\ *n, pl* **-ries** : a rock consisting of feldspar crystals embedded in a compact fine-grained base material — **por·phy·rit·ic** \ˌpȯr-fə-'ri-tik\ *adj*

por·poise \'pȯr-pəs\ *n* [ME *porpoys*, fr. MF *porpois*, fr. ML *porcopiscis*, fr. L *porcus* pig + *piscis* fish] : any of a family of small gregarious toothed whales; *also* : DOLPHIN 1

por·ridge \'pȯr-ij\ *n* : a soft food made by boiling meal of grains or legumes in milk or water

por·rin·ger \'pȯr-ən-jər\ *n* : a low one-handled metal bowl or cup

¹port \'pȯrt\ *n* 1 : HARBOR 2 : a city with a harbor 3 : AIRPORT

²port *n* 1 : an inlet or outlet (as in an engine) for a fluid 2 : PORTHOLE

³port *vb* : to turn or put a helm to the left

⁴port *n* : the left side of a ship or airplane looking forward — **port** *adj*

⁵port *n* : a sweet fortified wine

por·ta·ble \'pȯr-tə-bəl\ *adj* : capable of being carried — **portable** *n*

¹por·tage \'pȯr-tij, pȯr-'täzh\ *n* [ME, fr. MF, fr. *porter* to carry] : the carrying of boats and goods overland between navigable bodies of water; *also* : a route for such carrying

²portage *vb* **por·taged; por·tag·ing** : to carry gear over a portage

por·tal \'pȯrt-ᵊl\ *n* : DOOR, ENTRANCE; *esp* : a grand or imposing one

portal–to–portal *adj* : of or relating to the time spent by a worker in traveling from the entrance to an employer's property to the worker's actual job site (as in a mine)

port·cul·lis \pȯrt-'kə-ləs\ *n* : a grating at the gateway of

a castle or fortress that can be let down to stop entrance

porte co·chere \ˌpȯrt-kō-'sher\ *n* [F *porte cochère*, lit., coach door] : a roofed structure extending from the entrance of a building over an adjacent driveway and sheltering those getting in or out of vehicles

por·tend \pȯr-'tend\ *vb* 1 : to give a sign or warning of beforehand 2 : INDICATE, SIGNIFY **syn** augur, prognosticate, foretell, predict, forecast, prophesy

por·tent \'pȯr-ˌtent\ *n* 1 : something that foreshadows a coming event : OMEN 2 : MARVEL, PRODIGY

por·ten·tous \pȯr-'ten-təs\ *adj* 1 : of, relating to, or constituting a portent 2 : PRODIGIOUS 3 : self-consciously solemn : POMPOUS

¹por·ter \'pȯr-tər\ *n, chiefly Brit* : DOORKEEPER

²porter *n* 1 : a person who carries burdens; *esp* : one employed (as at a terminal) to carry baggage 2 : an attendant in a railroad car 3 : a dark heavy ale

por·ter·house \'pȯr-tər-ˌhaus\ *n* : a choice beefsteak with a large tenderloin

port·fo·lio \pȯrt-'fō-lē-ˌō\ *n, pl* **-li·os** 1 : a portable case for papers or drawings 2 : the office and functions of a minister of state 3 : the securities held by an investor

port·hole \'pȯrt-ˌhōl\ *n* : an opening (as a window) in the side of a ship or aircraft

por·ti·co \'pȯr-ti-ˌkō\ *n, pl* **-coes** *or* **-cos** [It] : a row of columns supporting a roof around or at the entrance of a building

¹por·tion \'pȯr-shən\ *n* 1 : one's part or share ⟨a ~ of food⟩ 2 : DOWRY 3 : an individual's lot 4 : a part of a whole ⟨a ~ of the sky⟩

²portion *vb* 1 : to divide into portions 2 : to allot to as a portion

port·land cement \'pȯrt-lənd-\ *n* : a cement made by calcining and grinding a mixture of clay and limestone

port·ly \'pȯrt-lē\ *adj* **port·li·er; -est** : somewhat stout

port·man·teau \pȯrt-'man-ˌtō\ *n, pl* **-teaus** *or* **-teaux** \-ˌtōz\ [MF *portemanteau*, fr. *porter* to carry + *manteau* mantle, fr. L *mantellum*] : a large traveling bag

port of call : an intermediate port where ships customarily stop for supplies, repairs, or transshipment of cargo

port of entry 1 : a place where foreign goods may be cleared through a customhouse 2 : a place where an alien may enter a country

por·trait \'pȯr-trət, -ˌträt\ *n* : a picture (as a painting or photograph) of a person usu. showing the face

por·trait·ist \-trə-tist\ *n* : a maker of portraits

por·trai·ture \'pȯr-trə-ˌchur\ *n* : the practice or art of making portraits

por·tray \pȯr-'trā\ *vb* 1 : to make a picture of : DEPICT 2 : to describe in words 3 : to play the role of — **por·tray·al** *n*

Por·tu·guese \'pȯr-chə-ˌgēz, -ˌgēs; ˌpȯr-chə-'gēz, -'gēs\ *n, pl* **Portuguese** 1 : a native or inhabitant of Portugal 2 : the language of Portugal and Brazil — **Portuguese** *adj*

Portuguese man–of–war *n* : any of several large colonial marine invertebrate animals related to the jellyfishes and having a large sac by which the colony floats at the surface

por·tu·la·ca \ˌpȯr-chə-'la-kə\ *n* : a tropical succulent herb cultivated for its showy flowers

pos *abbr* 1 position 2 positive

¹pose \'pōz\ *vb* **posed; pos·ing** 1 : to assume or cause to assume a posture usu. for artistic purposes 2 : to set forth : PROPOSE ⟨~ a question⟩ 3 : to affect an attitude or character

\ə\abut \ᵊ\kitten \ər\further \a\ash \ā\ace \ä\mop, mar \au̇\out \ch\chin \e\bet \ē\easy \g\go \i\hit \ī\ice \j\job \ŋ\sing \ō\go \ȯ\law \ȯi\boy \th\thin \th\the \ü\loot \u̇\foot \y\yet \zh\vision *see also* Pronunciation Symbols page

²pose *n* **1** : a sustained posture; *esp* : one assumed by a model **2** : an attitude assumed for effect : PRETENSE

¹pos·er \'pō-zər\ *n* : a puzzling question

²poser *n* : a person who poses

po·seur \pō-'zər\ *n* [F, lit., poser] : an affected or insincere person

posh \'päsh\ *adj* : FASHIONABLE

pos·it \'pä-zət\ *vb* : to assume the existence of : POSTULATE

po·si·tion \pə-'zi-shən\ *n* **1** : an arranging in order **2** : the stand taken on a question **3** : the point or area occupied by something : SITUATION **4** : a certain arrangement of bodily parts ⟨exercise in a sitting ∼⟩ **5** : RANK, STATUS **6** : EMPLOYMENT, JOB — **position** *vb*

¹pos·i·tive \'pä-zə-tiv\ *adj* **1** : expressed definitely ⟨her answer was a ∼ *no*⟩ **2** : CONFIDENT, CERTAIN **3** : of, relating to, or constituting the degree of grammatical comparison that denotes no increase in quality, quantity, or relation **4** : not fictitious : REAL **5** : active and effective in function ⟨∼ leadership⟩ **6** : having the light and shade as existing in the original subject ⟨a ∼ photograph⟩ **7** : numerically greater than zero ⟨a ∼ number⟩ **8** : being, relating to, or charged with electricity of which the proton is the elementary unit **9** : AFFIRMATIVE ⟨a ∼ response⟩ — **pos·i·tive·ly** *adv* — **pos·i·tive·ness** *n*

²positive *n* **1** : the positive degree or a positive form in a language **2** : a positive photograph

pos·i·tron \'pä-zə-,trän\ *n* : a positively charged particle having the same mass and magnitude of charge as the electron

poss *abbr* possessive

pos·se \'pä-sē\ *n* [ML *posse comitatus*, lit., power or authority of the county] : a body of persons organized to assist a sheriff in an emergency

pos·sess \pə-'zes\ *vb* **1** : to have as property : OWN **2** : to have as an attribute, knowledge, or skill **3** : to enter into and control firmly ⟨∼*ed* by a devil⟩ — **pos·ses·sor** \-'ze-sər\ *n*

pos·ses·sion \-'ze-shən\ *n* **1** : control or occupancy of property **2** : OWNERSHIP **3** : something owned : PROPERTY **4** : domination by something (as an evil spirit, a passion, or an idea) **5** : SELF-CONTROL

pos·ses·sive \pə-'ze-siv\ *adj* **1** : of, relating to, or constituting a grammatical case denoting ownership **2** : showing the desire to possess ⟨a ∼ nature⟩ — **possessive** *n* — **pos·ses·sive·ness** *n*

pos·si·ble \'pä-sə-bəl\ *adj* **1** : being within the limits of ability, capacity, or realization **2** : being something that may or may not occur ⟨∼ dangers⟩ **3** : able or fitted to become ⟨a ∼ site for a bridge⟩ — **pos·si·bil·i·ty** \,pä-sə-'bi-lə-tē\ *n* — **pos·si·bly** \'pä-sə-blē\ *adv*

pos·sum \'pä-səm\ *n* : OPOSSUM

¹post \'pōst\ *n* **1** : an upright piece of timber or metal serving esp. as a support : PILLAR **2** : a pole or stake set up as a mark or indicator

²post *vb* **1** : to affix to a usual place (as a wall) for public notices **2** : to publish or announce by or as if by a public notice ⟨∼ grades⟩ **3** : to forbid (property) to trespassers by putting up a notice **4** : SCORE

³post *n* **1** *obs* : COURIER **2** *chiefly Brit* : ¹MAIL; *also* : POST OFFICE

⁴post *vb* **1** : to ride or travel with haste : HURRY **2** : MAIL ⟨∼ a letter⟩ **3** : to enter in a ledger **4** : INFORM ⟨kept him ∼*ed* on new developments⟩

⁵post *n* **1** : the place at which a soldier is stationed; *esp* : a sentry's beat or station **2** : a station or task to which a person is assigned **3** : the place at which a body of troops is stationed : CAMP **4** : OFFICE, POSITION **5** : a trading settlement or station

⁶post *vb* **1** : to station in a given place **2** : to put up (as bond)

post·age \'pōs-tij\ *n* : the fee for postal service; *also* : stamps representing this fee

post·al \'pōst-ᵊl\ *adj* : of or relating to the mails or the post office

postal card *n* : POSTCARD

postal service *n* : a government agency or department handling the transmission of mail

post·card \'pōst-,kärd\ *n* : a card on which a message may be written for mailing without an envelope

post chaise *n* : a 4-wheeled closed carriage for two to four persons

post·con·so·nan·tal \,pōst-,kän-sə-'nant-ᵊl\ *adj* : immediately following a consonant

post·date \,pōst-'dāt\ *vb* : to date with a date later than that of execution ⟨∼ a check⟩

post·doc·tor·al \-'däk-tə-rəl\ *also* **post·doc·tor·ate** \-tə-rət\ *adj* : of, relating to, or engaged in advanced academic or professional work beyond a doctor's degree

post·er \'pō-stər\ *n* : a bill or placard for posting often in a public place

¹pos·te·ri·or \pō-'stir-ē-ər, pä-\ *adj* **1** : later in time **2** : situated behind

²pos·te·ri·or \pä-'stir-ē-ər, pō-\ *n* : the hinder bodily parts; *esp* : BUTTOCKS

pos·ter·i·ty \pä-'ster-ə-tē\ *n* **1** : the descendants from one ancestor **2** : all future generations

pos·tern \'pōs-tərn, 'päs-\ *n* **1** : a back door or gate **2** : a private or side entrance

post exchange *n* : a store at a military post that sells to military personnel and authorized civilians

post·grad·u·ate \(,)pōst-'gra-jə-wət\ *adj* : of or relating to studies beyond the bachelor's degree — **postgraduate** *n*

post·haste \'pōst-'hāst\ *adv* : with all possible speed

post·hole \-,hōl\ *n* : a hole for a post and esp. a fence post

post·hu·mous \'päs-chə-məs\ *adj* **1** : born after the death of the father **2** : published after the death of the author — **post·hu·mous·ly** *adv*

post·hyp·not·ic \,pōst-hip-'nä-tik\ *adj* : of, relating to, or characteristic of the period following a hypnotic trance

pos·til·ion *or* **pos·til·lion** \pō-'stil-yən\ *n* : a rider on the left-hand horse of a pair drawing a coach

Post·im·pres·sion·ism \,pōst-im-'pre-shə-,ni-zəm\ *n* : a late 19th century French theory or practice of art that stresses variously volume, picture structure, or expressionism

post·lude \'pōst-,lüd\ *n* : an organ solo played at the end of a church service

post·man \-mən, -,man\ *n* : MAILMAN

post·mark \-,märk\ *n* : an official postal marking on a piece of mail; *esp* : the mark canceling the postage stamp — **postmark** *vb*

post·mas·ter \-,mas-tər\ *n* : a person who has charge of a post office

postmaster general *n, pl* **postmasters general** : an official in charge of a national postal service

post me·ri·di·em \,pōst-mə-'ri-dē-əm\ *adj* [L] : being after noon

post·mis·tress \'pōst-,mis-trəs\ *n* : a woman in charge of a post office

¹post·mor·tem \,pōst-'mor-təm\ *adj* [L *post mortem* after death] **1** : done, occurring, or collected after death **2** : following the event

²postmortem *n* **1** : an analysis or discussion of an event after it is over **2** : AUTOPSY

post·na·sal drip \'pōst-,nā-zəl-\ *n* : flow of mucous secretion from the posterior part of the nasal cavity onto the wall of the pharynx

post·na·tal \(,)pōst-'nāt-ᵊl\ *adj* : occurring or being after birth; *esp* : of or relating to a newborn infant

post office *n* **1** : POSTAL SERVICE **2** : a local branch of a post office department

post·op·er·a·tive \(,)pōst-'ä-prə-tiv, -pə-,rā-\ *adj* : following or having undergone a surgical operation ⟨~ care⟩

post·paid \'pōst-'pād\ *adv* : with the postage paid by the sender and not chargeable to the receiver

post·par·tum \(,)pōst-'pär-təm\ *adj* [NL *post partum* after birth] : following parturition — **postpartum** *adv*

post·pone \pōst-'pōn\ *vb* **post·poned; post·pon·ing** : to put off to a later time — **post·pone·ment** *n*

post road *n* : a road over which mail is carried

post·script \'pōst-,skript\ *n* : a note added esp. to a completed letter

post time *n* : the designated time for the start of a horse race

pos·tu·lant \'päs-chə-lənt\ *n* : a probationary candidate for membership in a religious order

¹pos·tu·late \'päs-chə-,lāt\ *vb* **-lat·ed; -lat·ing** : to assume as true

²pos·tu·late \'päs-chə-lət, -,lāt\ *n* : a proposition taken for granted as true esp. as a basis for a chain of reasoning

¹pos·ture \'päs-chər\ *n* **1** : the position or bearing of the body or one of its parts **2** : STATE, CONDITION **3** : ATTITUDE

²posture *vb* **pos·tured; pos·tur·ing** : to strike a pose esp. for effect

post·war \'pōst-'wȯr\ *adj* : of or relating to the period after a war

po·sy \'pō-zē\ *n, pl* **posies 1** : a brief sentiment : MOTTO **2** : a bunch of flowers; *also* : FLOWER

¹pot \'pät\ *n* **1** : a rounded container used chiefly for domestic purposes **2** : the total of the bets at stake at one time **3** : RUIN ⟨go to ~⟩ — **pot·ful** *n*

²pot *vb* **pot·ted; pot·ting 1** : to preserve or place in a pot **2** : SHOOT

³pot *n* : MARIJUANA

po·ta·ble \'pō-tə-bəl\ *adj* : suitable for drinking — **po·ta·bil·i·ty** \,pō-tə-'bi-lə-tē\ *n*

po·tage \pȯ-'täzh\ *n* : a thick soup

pot·ash \'pät-,ash\ *n* [sing. of *pot ashes*] : potassium or any of its various compounds esp. as used in agriculture

po·tas·si·um \pə-'ta-sē-əm\ *n* : a silver-white soft metallic chemical element that occurs abundantly in nature — see ELEMENT table

potassium bromide *n* : a crystalline salt used as a sedative and in photography

potassium carbonate *n* : a white salt used in making glass and soap

potassium nitrate *n* : a soluble salt used in making gunpowder, as a fertilizer, and in medicine

po·ta·tion \pō-'tā-shən\ *n* : a usu. alcoholic drink; *also* : the act of drinking

po·ta·to \pə-'tā-tō\ *n, pl* **-toes** : the edible starchy tuber of a plant related to the tomato; *also* : this plant

potato beetle *n* : COLORADO POTATO BEETLE

potato bug *n* : COLORADO POTATO BEETLE

pot·bel·ly \'pät-,be-lē\ *n* : a protruding abdomen — **pot·bel·lied** \-,lēd\ *adj*

pot·boil·er \-,bȯi-lər\ *n* : a usu. inferior work of art or literature produced chiefly for profit

po·tent \'pōt-ᵊnt\ *adj* **1** : having authority or influence : POWERFUL **2** : chemically or medicinally effective **3** : able to copulate — used esp. of the male **syn** forceful, forcible, mighty, puissant — **po·ten·cy** \-ᵊn-sē\ *n*

po·ten·tate \'pōt-ᵊn-,tāt\ *n* : one who wields controlling power : RULER

¹po·ten·tial \pə-'ten-chəl\ *adj* : existing in possibility : capable of becoming actual ⟨a ~ champion⟩ **syn** dormant, latent, quiescent — **po·ten·ti·al·i·ty** \pə-,ten-chē-'a-lə-tē\ *n* — **po·ten·tial·ly** \-'ten-chə-lē\ *adv*

²potential *n* **1** : something that can develop or become actual ⟨a ~ for violence⟩ **2** : the work required to move a unit positive charge from infinity to a point in question; *also* : POTENTIAL DIFFERENCE

potential difference *n* : the difference in potential between two points that represents the work involved in the transfer of a unit quantity of electricity from one point to the other

potential energy *n* : the energy an object has because of its position or the arrangement of its parts

po·ten·ti·ate \pə-'ten-chē-,āt\ *vb* **-at·ed; -at·ing** : to make potent; *esp* : to augment the activity of (as a drug) synergistically — **po·ten·ti·a·tion** \-,ten-chē-'ā-shən\ *n*

pot·head \'pät-,hed\ *n* : a person who smokes marijuana

poth·er \'pä-thər\ *n* : a noisy disturbance; *also* : FUSS

pot·herb \'pät-,ərb, -,hərb\ *n* : an herb whose leaves or stems are boiled for greens or used to season food

pot·hole \'pät-,hōl\ *n* : a large pit or hole (as in a road surface)

pot·hook \-,hùk\ *n* : an S-shaped hook for hanging pots and kettles over an open fire

po·tion \'pō-shən\ *n* : a mixture of liquids (as liquor or medicine)

pot·luck \'pät-'lək\ *n* : the regular meal available to a guest for whom no special preparations have been made

pot·pie \-'pī\ *n* : pastry-covered meat and vegetables cooked in a deep dish

pot·pour·ri \,pō-pù-'rē\ *n* [F *pot pourri*, lit., rotten pot] **1** : a mixture of flowers, herbs, and spices used for scent **2** : a miscellaneous collection

pot·sherd \'pät-,shərd\ *n* : a pottery fragment

pot·shot \-,shät\ *n* **1** : a shot taken from ambush or at a random or easy target **2** : a critical remark made in a random or sporadic manner

pot·tage \'pä-tij\ *n* : a thick soup of vegetables and often meat

¹pot·ter \'pä-tər\ *n* : one that makes pottery

²potter *vb* : PUTTER

pot·tery \'pä-tə-rē\ *n, pl* **-ter·ies 1** : a place where earthen pots and dishes are made **2** : the art of the potter **3** : dishes, pots, and vases made from clay

¹pouch \'paùch\ *n* **1** : a small bag (as for tobacco) carried on the person **2** : a bag for storing or transporting goods ⟨mail ~⟩ ⟨diplomatic ~⟩ **3** : an anatomical sac; *esp* : one for carrying the young on the abdomen of a female marsupial (as a kangaroo)

²pouch *vb* : to put or form into or as if into a pouch

poult \'pōlt\ *n* : a young fowl; *esp* : a young turkey

poul·ter·er \'pōl-tər-ər\ *n* : one that deals in poultry

poul·tice \'pōl-təs\ *n* : a soft usu. heated and medicated mass spread on cloth and applied to a sore or injury — **poultice** *vb*

poul·try \'pōl-trē\ *n* : domesticated birds kept for eggs or meat — **poul·try·man** \-mən\ *n*

pounce \'paùns\ *vb* **pounced; pounc·ing** : to spring or swoop upon and seize something

¹pound \'paùnd\ *n, pl* **pounds** *also* **pound 1** : a unit of avoirdupois, troy, and apothecaries' weight — see WEIGHT table **2** — see MONEY table

²pound *n* : a public enclosure where stray animals are kept

³pound *vb* **1** : to crush to a powder or pulp by beating **2** : to strike or beat heavily or repeatedly **3** : DRILL 1 **4** : to move or move along heavily

pound·age \'paùn-dij\ *n* : POUNDS; *also* : weight in pounds

pound cake *n* : a rich cake made with a large proportion of eggs and shortening

pound–fool·ish \'paùnd-'fü-lish\ *adj* : imprudent in dealing with large sums or large matters

pour \'pȯr\ *vb* **1** : to flow or cause to flow in a stream

---

\ə\abut \ᵊ\kitten \ər\further \a\ash \ā\ace \ä\mop, mar
\aù\out \ch\chin \e\bet \ē\easy \g\go \i\hit \ī\ice \j\job
\ŋ\sing \ō\go \ȯ\law \ȯi\boy \th\thin \t̲h̲\the \ü\loot \ù\foot
\y\yet \zh\vision *see also* Pronunciation Symbols page

or flood 2 : to rain hard 3 : to supply freely and copiously

pour·boire \pùr-ˈbwär\ *n* [F, fr. *pour boire* for drinking] : TIP, GRATUITY

pout \ˈpaùt\ *vb* : to show displeasure by thrusting out the lips; *also* : to look sullen — **pout** *n*

pov·er·ty \ˈpä-vər-tē\ *n* [ME *poverte*, fr. OF *poverté*, fr. L *paupertat-*, *paupertas*, fr. *pauper* poor] 1 : lack of money or material possessions : WANT 2 : poor quality (as of soil)

poverty line *n* : a level of personal or family income below which one is classified as poor according to government standards

pov·er·ty–strick·en \ˈpä-vər-tē-ˌstri-kən\ *adj* : very poor : DESTITUTE

POW \ˌpē-(ˌ)ō-ˈdə-bəl-(ˌ)yü\ *n* : PRISONER OF WAR

¹**pow·der** \ˈpaù-dər\ *n* [ME *poudre*, fr. OF, fr. L *pulver-*, *pulvis* dust] 1 : dry material made up of fine particles; *also* : a usu. medicinal or cosmetic preparation in this form 2 : a solid explosive (as gunpowder) — **pow·dery** *adj*

²**powder** *vb* 1 : to sprinkle or cover with or as if with powder 2 : to reduce to powder

powder room *n* : a rest room for women

¹**pow·er** \ˈpaù-ər\ *n* 1 : the ability to act or produce an effect 2 : a position of ascendancy over others : AUTHORITY 3 : one that has control or authority; *esp* : a sovereign state 4 : physical might; *also* : mental or moral vigor 5 : the number of times as indicated by an exponent a number is to be multiplied by itself; *also* : the product itself 6 : force or energy used to do work; *also* : the time rate at which work is done or energy transferred 7 : MAGNIFICATION 2 — **pow·er·ful** \-fəl\ *adj* — **pow·er·ful·ly** *adv* — **pow·er·less** *adj*

²**power** *vb* : to supply with power and esp. motive power

pow·er·boat \-ˌbōt\ *n* : MOTORBOAT

pow·er·house \ˈpaù-ər-ˌhaùs\ *n* 1 : POWER PLANT 1 2 : one having great drive, energy, or ability

power plant *n* 1 : a building in which electric power is generated 2 : an engine and related parts supplying the motive power of a self-propelled vehicle

pow·wow \ˈpaù-ˌwaù\ *n* 1 : a No. American Indian ceremony (as for victory in war) 2 : a meeting for discussion : CONFERENCE

pox \ˈpäks\ *n, pl* **pox** *or* **pox·es** : any of various diseases (as smallpox or syphilis) marked by a rash on the skin

pp *abbr* 1 pages 2 pianissimo

PP *abbr* 1 parcel post 2 past participle 3 postpaid 4 prepaid

ppd *abbr* 1 postpaid 2 prepaid

PPS *abbr* [L *post postscriptum*] an additional postscript

ppt *abbr* precipitate

PQ *abbr* Province of Quebec

pr *abbr* 1 pair 2 price

Pr *symbol* praseodymium

PR *abbr* 1 payroll 2 public relations 3 Puerto Rico

prac·ti·ca·ble \ˈprak-ti-kə-bəl\ *adj* : capable of being put into practice, done, or accomplished — **prac·ti·ca·bil·i·ty** \ˌprak-ti-kə-ˈbi-lə-tē\ *n*

prac·ti·cal \ˈprak-ti-kəl\ *adj* 1 : of, relating to, or shown in practice ⟨∼ questions⟩ 2 : VIRTUAL ⟨∼ control⟩ 3 : capable of being put to use ⟨a ∼ knowledge of French⟩ 4 : inclined to action as opposed to speculation ⟨a ∼ person⟩ 5 : qualified by practice ⟨a good ∼ mechanic⟩ — **prac·ti·cal·i·ty** \ˌprak-ti-ˈka-lə-tē\ *n* — **prac·ti·cal·ly** \-k(ə-)lē\ *adv*

practical joke *n* : a prank intended to trick or embarrass someone or cause physical discomfort

practical nurse *n* : a professional nurse without all of the qualifications of a registered nurse; *esp* : LICENSED PRACTICAL NURSE

¹**prac·tice** *or* **prac·tise** \ˈprak-təs\ *vb* **prac·ticed** *or* **prac·tised; prac·tic·ing** *or* **prac·tis·ing** 1 : CARRY OUT, APPLY

⟨∼ what you preach⟩ 2 : to perform or work at repeatedly so as to become proficient ⟨∼ tennis strokes⟩ 3 : to do or perform customarily ⟨∼ politeness⟩ 4 : to be professionally engaged in ⟨∼ law⟩

²**practice** *also* **practise** *n* 1 : actual performance or application 2 : customary action : HABIT 3 : systematic exercise for proficiency 4 : the exercise of a profession; *also* : a professional business

prac·ti·tion·er \prak-ˈti-shə-nər\ *n* : one who practices a profession

prae·tor \ˈprē-tər\ *n* : an ancient Roman magistrate ranking below a consul — **prae·to·ri·an** \prē-ˈtōr-ē-ən, -ˈtor-\ *adj*

prag·mat·ic \prag-ˈma-tik\ *also* **prag·mat·i·cal** \-ti-kəl\ *adj* 1 : of or relating to practical affairs 2 : concerned with the practical consequences of actions or beliefs — **pragmatic** *n* — **prag·mat·i·cal·ly** \-ti-k(ə-)lē\ *adv*

prag·ma·tism \ˈprag-mə-ˌti-zəm\ *n* : a practical approach to problems and affairs

prai·rie \ˈprer-ē\ *n* : a broad tract of level or rolling grassland

prairie dog *n* : an American burrowing black-tailed rodent related to the squirrels and living in colonies

prairie schooner *n* : a covered wagon used by pioneers in cross-country travel

praise \ˈprāz\ *vb* **praised; prais·ing** 1 : to express approval of : COMMEND 2 : to glorify (a divinity or a saint) esp. in song — **praise** *n*

praise·wor·thy \-ˌwər-thē\ *adj* : LAUDABLE

pra·line \ˈprä-ˌlēn, ˈprā-\ *n* [F] : a confection of nuts and sugar

pram \ˈpram\ *n, chiefly Brit* : PERAMBULATOR

prance \ˈprans\ *vb* **pranced; pranc·ing** 1 : to spring from the hind legs ⟨a *prancing* horse⟩ 2 : SWAGGER; *also* : CAPER — **prance** *n* — **pranc·er** *n*

prank \ˈpraŋk\ *n* : a playful or mildly mischievous act : TRICK

prank·ster \ˈpraŋk-stər\ *n* : a person who plays pranks

pra·seo·dym·i·um \ˌprā-zē-ō-ˈdi-mē-əm\ *n* : a yellowish white metallic chemical element — see ELEMENT table

prate \ˈprāt\ *vb* **prat·ed; prat·ing** : to talk long and idly : chatter foolishly

prat·fall \ˈprat-ˌfol\ *n* 1 : a fall on the buttocks 2 : a humiliating blunder

¹**prat·tle** \ˈprat-ᵊl\ *vb* **prat·tled; prat·tling** : PRATE, BABBLE

²**prattle** *n* : trifling or childish talk

prawn \ˈpron\ *n* : any of numerous edible shrimplike crustaceans; *also* : SHRIMP 1

pray \ˈprā\ *vb* 1 : ENTREAT, IMPLORE 2 : to ask earnestly for something 3 : to address God or a god esp. with supplication

prayer \ˈprar\ *n* 1 : a supplication or expression addressed to God or a god; *also* : a set order of words used in praying 2 : an earnest request or wish 3 : the act or practice of praying to God or a god 4 : a religious service consisting chiefly of prayers — often used in pl. 5 : something prayed for 6 : a slight chance

prayer book *n* : a book containing prayers and often directions for worship

prayer·ful \ˈprar-fəl\ *adj* 1 : DEVOUT 2 : EARNEST — **prayer·ful·ly** *adv*

praying mantis *n* : MANTIS

PRC *abbr* People's Republic of China

preach \ˈprēch\ *vb* 1 : to deliver a sermon 2 : to set forth in a sermon 3 : to advocate earnestly — **preach·er** *n* — **preach·ment** *n*

pre·ad·o·les·cence \ˈprē-ˌad-ᵊl-ˈes-ᵊns\ *n* : the period of human development just preceding adolescence — **pre·ad·o·les·cent** \-ᵊnt\ *adj or n*

pre·am·ble \ˈprē-ˌam-bəl\ *n* [ME, fr. MF *preambule*, fr. ML *preambulum*, fr. LL, neut. of *praeambulus* walking in front of, fr. L *prae* in front of + *ambulare* to

walk] : an introductory part ⟨the ∼ to a constitution⟩
pre·ar·range \ˌprē-ə-ˈrānj\ *vb* : to arrange beforehand — **pre·ar·range·ment** *n*
pre·as·signed \ˌprē-ə-ˈsīnd\ *adj* : assigned beforehand
prec *abbr* preceding
Pre·cam·bri·an \ˈprē-ˈkam-brē-ən, -ˈkām-\ *adj* : of, relating to, or being the era that is earliest in geologic history and is characterized esp. by the appearance of single-celled organisms — **Precambrian** *n*
pre·can·cel \(ˌ)prē-ˈkan-səl\ *vb* : to cancel (a postage stamp) in advance of use — **precancel** *n* — **pre·can·cel·la·tion** \ˌprē-ˌkan-sə-ˈlā-shən\ *n*
pre·can·cer·ous \(ˌ)prē-ˈkan-sə-rəs\ *adj* : likely to become cancerous
pre·car·i·ous \pri-ˈkar-ē-əs\ *adj* : dependent on uncertain conditions : dangerously insecure : UNSTABLE ⟨a ∼ foothold⟩ ⟨∼ prosperity⟩ **syn** delicate, sensitive, ticklish, touchy, tricky — **pre·car·i·ous·ly** *adv* — **pre·car·i·ous·ness** *n*
pre·cau·tion \pri-ˈko-shən\ *n* : a measure taken beforehand to prevent harm or secure good — **pre·cau·tion·ary** \-shə-ˌner-ē\ *adj*
pre·cede \pri-ˈsēd\ *vb* **pre·ced·ed; pre·ced·ing** : to be, go, or come ahead or in front of (as in rank or time)
pre·ce·dence \ˈpre-sə-dəns, pri-ˈsēd-ᵊns\ *n* **1** : the act or fact of preceding **2** : consideration based on order of importance : PRIORITY
¹**prec·e·dent** \pri-ˈsēd-ᵊnt, ˈpre-sə-dənt\ *adj* : prior in time, order, or significance
²**prec·e·dent** \ˈpre-sə-dənt\ *n* : something said or done that may serve to authorize or justify further words or acts of the same or a similar kind
pre·ced·ing \pri-ˈsē-diŋ\ *adj* : that precedes **syn** antecedent, foregoing, prior, former, anterior
pre·cen·tor \pri-ˈsen-tər\ *n* : a leader of the singing of a choir or congregation
pre·cept \ˈprē-ˌsept\ *n* : a command or principle intended as a general rule of action or conduct
pre·cep·tor \pri-ˈsep-tər, ˈprē-ˌsep-\ *n* : TUTOR
pre·ces·sion \prē-ˈse-shən\ *n* : a slow gyration of the rotation axis of a spinning body (as the earth) — **pre·cess** \prē-ˈses\ *vb* — **pre·ces·sion·al** \-ˈse-shə-nəl\ *adj*
pre·cinct \ˈprē-ˌsiŋkt\ *n* **1** : an administrative subdivision (as of a city) : DISTRICT ⟨police ∼⟩ ⟨electoral ∼⟩ **2** : an enclosure bounded by the limits of a building or place — often used in pl. **3** *pl* : ENVIRONS
pre·ci·os·i·ty \ˌpre-shē-ˈä-sə-tē\ *n*, *pl* **-ties** : fastidious refinement
pre·cious \ˈpre-shəs\ *adj* **1** : of great value ⟨∼ jewels⟩ **2** : greatly cherished : DEAR ⟨∼ memories⟩ **3** : AFFECTED ⟨∼ language⟩
prec·i·pice \ˈpre-sə-pəs\ *n* : a steep cliff
pre·cip·i·tan·cy \pri-ˈsi-pə-tən-sē\ *n* : undue hastiness or suddenness
¹**pre·cip·i·tate** \pri-ˈsi-pə-ˌtāt\ *vb* **-tat·ed; -tat·ing** [L *praecipitare*, fr. *praecipit-, praeceps* headlong, fr. *prae* in front of + *caput* head] **1** : to throw violently **2** : to throw down **3** : to cause to happen quickly or abruptly ⟨∼ a quarrel⟩ **4** : to cause to separate from solution or suspension **5** : to fall as rain, snow, or hail **syn** speed, accelerate, quicken, hasten, hurry
²**pre·cip·i·tate** \pri-ˈsi-pə-tət, -ˌtāt\ *n* : the solid matter that separates from a solution or suspension
³**pre·cip·i·tate** \pri-ˈsi-pə-tət\ *adj* **1** : showing extreme or unwise haste : RASH **2** : falling with steep descent; *also* : PRECIPITOUS — **pre·cip·i·tate·ly** *adv* — **pre·cip·i·tate·ness** *n*
pre·cip·i·ta·tion \pri-ˌsi-pə-ˈtā-shən\ *n* **1** : rash haste **2** : the process of precipitating or forming a precipitate **3** : water that falls to earth esp. as rain or snow; *also* : the quantity of this water
pre·cip·i·tous \pri-ˈsi-pə-təs\ *adj* **1** : PRECIPITATE **2** : having the character of a precipice : very steep ⟨a ∼ slope⟩;

also : containing precipices ⟨∼ trails⟩ — **pre·cip·i·tous·ly** *adv*
pré·cis \prā-ˈsē\ *n*, *pl* **pré·cis** \-ˈsēz\ [F] : a concise summary of essentials
pre·cise \pri-ˈsīs\ *adj* **1** : exactly defined or stated : DEFINITE **2** : highly accurate : EXACT **3** : conforming strictly to a standard : SCRUPULOUS — **pre·cise·ly** *adv* — **pre·cise·ness** *n*
pre·ci·sion \pri-ˈsi-zhən\ *n* : the quality or state of being precise
pre·clude \pri-ˈklüd\ *vb* **pre·clud·ed; pre·clud·ing** : to make impossible : BAR, PREVENT
pre·co·cious \pri-ˈkō-shəs\ *adj* [L *praecoc-, praecox*, lit., ripening early, fr. *prae-* ahead + *coquere* to cook] : early in development and esp. in mental development — **pre·co·cious·ly** *adv* — **pre·coc·i·ty** \pri-ˈkä-sə-tē\ *n*
pre·con·ceive \ˌprē-kən-ˈsēv\ *vb* : to form an opinion of beforehand — **pre·con·cep·tion** \-ˈsep-shən\ *n*
pre·con·cert·ed \-ˈsər-təd\ *adj* : arranged or agreed on in advance
pre·con·di·tion \-ˈdi-shən\ *vb* : to put in proper or desired condition or frame of mind in advance
pre·cook \ˌprē-ˈkük\ *vb* : to cook partially or entirely before final cooking or reheating
pre·cur·sor \pri-ˈkər-sər\ *n* : one that precedes and indicates the approach of another : FORERUNNER
pred *abbr* predicate
pre·da·ceous *or* **pre·da·cious** \pri-ˈdā-shəs\ *adj* : living by preying on others : PREDATORY
pre·date \ˈprē-ˈdāt\ *vb* : ANTEDATE
pre·da·tion \pri-ˈdā-shən\ *n* **1** : the act of preying or plundering **2** : a mode of life in which food is primarily obtained by killing and consuming animals
pred·a·tor \ˈpre-də-tər\ *n* : an animal that lives by predation
pred·a·to·ry \ˈpre-də-ˌtōr-ē\ *adj* **1** : of or relating to plunder ⟨∼ warfare⟩ **2** : disposed to exploit others **3** : preying upon other animals
pre·de·cease \ˌprē-di-ˈsēs\ *vb* **-ceased; -ceas·ing** : to die before another person
pre·de·ces·sor \ˈpre-də-ˌse-sər, ˈprē-\ *n* : a previous holder of a position to which another has succeeded
pre·des·ig·nate \(ˌ)prē-ˈde-zig-ˌnāt\ *vb* : to designate beforehand
pre·des·ti·na·tion \ˌprē-ˌdes-tə-ˈnā-shən\ *n* : the act of foreordaining to an earthly lot or eternal destiny by divine decree; *also* : the state of being so foreordained — **pre·des·ti·nate** \prē-ˈdes-tə-ˌnāt\ *vb*
pre·des·tine \prē-ˈdes-tən\ *vb* : to settle beforehand : FOREORDAIN
pre·de·ter·mine \ˌprē-di-ˈtər-mən\ *vb* : to determine beforehand
pred·i·ca·ble \ˈpre-di-kə-bəl\ *adj* : capable of being predicated or affirmed
pre·dic·a·ment \pri-ˈdi-kə-mənt\ *n* : a difficult or trying situation **syn** dilemma, pickle, quagmire, jam
¹**pred·i·cate** \ˈpre-di-kət\ *n* : the part of a sentence or clause that expresses what is said of the subject
²**pred·i·cate** \ˈpre-də-ˌkāt\ *vb* **-cat·ed; -cat·ing** **1** : AFFIRM **2** : to assert to be a quality or attribute **3** : FOUND, BASE — **pred·i·ca·tion** \ˌpre-də-ˈkā-shən\ *n*
pre·dict \pri-ˈdikt\ *vb* : to declare in advance — **pre·dict·abil·i·ty** \-ˌdik-tə-ˈbi-lə-tē\ *n* — **pre·dict·able** \-ˈdik-tə-bəl\ *adj* — **pre·dict·ably** \-blē\ *adv* — **pre·dic·tion** \-ˈdik-shən\ *n*
pre·di·gest \ˌprē-dī-ˈjest\ *vb* : to simplify for easy use; *also* : to subject to artificial or natural partial digestion

---

\ə\abut \ᵊ\kitten \ər\further \a\ash \ā\ace \ä\mop, mar \aú\out \ch\chin \e\bet \ē\easy \g\go \i\hit \ī\ice \j\job \ŋ\sing \ō\go \ó\law \ói\boy \th\thin \th̲\the \ü\loot \ú\foot \y\yet \zh\vision *see also* Pronunciation Symbols page

pre·di·lec·tion \₁pre-də-ˈlek-shən, ₁prē-\ *n* : an established preference for something

pre·dis·pose \₁prē-di-ˈspōz\ *vb* : to incline in advance : make susceptible — **pre·dis·po·si·tion** \₁prē-₁dis-pə-ˈzi-shən\ *n*

pre·dom·i·nant \pri-ˈdä-mə-nənt\ *adj* : greater in importance, strength, influence, or authority — **pre·dom·i·nance** \-nəns\ *n*

pre·dom·i·nant·ly \-nənt-lē\ *adv* : for the most part : MAINLY

pre·dom·i·nate \pri-ˈdä-mə-₁nāt\ *vb* : to be superior esp. in power or numbers : PREVAIL

pree·mie \ˈprē-mē\ *n* : a premature baby

pre·em·i·nent \prē-ˈe-mə-nənt\ *adj* : having highest rank : OUTSTANDING — **pre·em·i·nence** \-nəns\ *n* — **pre·em·i·nent·ly** *adv*

pre·empt \prē-ˈempt\ *vb* **1** : to settle upon (public land) with the right to purchase before others; *also* : to take by such right **2** : to seize upon before someone else can **3** : to take the place of **syn** usurp, confiscate, appropriate, expropriate — **pre·emp·tion** \-ˈemp-shən\ *n*

pre·emp·tive \prē-ˈemp-tiv\ *adj* : marked by the seizing of the initiative : initiated by oneself ⟨~ attack⟩

preen \ˈprēn\ *vb* **1** : to dress or smooth up : PRIMP **2** : to trim or dress with the bill — used of a bird **3** : to pride (oneself) for achievement

pre·ex·ist \₁prē-ig-ˈzist\ *vb* : to exist before — **pre·ex·is·tence** \-ˈzis-təns\ *n* — **pre·ex·is·tent** \-tənt\ *adj*

pref *abbr* **1** preface **2** preference **3** preferred **4** prefix

pre·fab \(₁)prē-ˈfab, ˈprē-₁fab\ *n* : a prefabricated structure

pre·fab·ri·cate \(₁)prē-ˈfa-brə-₁kāt\ *vb* : to manufacture the parts of (a structure) beforehand for later assembly — **pre·fab·ri·ca·tion** \₁prē-₁fa-bri-ˈkā-shən\ *n*

¹**pref·ace** \ˈpre-fəs\ *n* : the introductory remarks of a speaker or writer — **pref·a·to·ry** \ˈpre-fə-₁tōr-ē\ *adj*

²**preface** *vb* **pref·aced; pref·ac·ing** : to introduce with a preface

pre·fect \ˈprē-₁fekt\ *n* **1** : a high official; *esp* : a chief officer or magistrate **2** : a student monitor

pre·fec·ture \ˈprē-₁fek-chər\ *n* : the office, term, or residence of a prefect

pre·fer \pri-ˈfər\ *vb* **pre·ferred; pre·fer·ring 1** : PROMOTE **2** : to like better **3** : to bring (as a charge) against a person — **pref·er·a·ble** \ˈpre-fə-rə-bəl\ *adj* — **pref·er·a·bly** \-blē\ *adv*

pref·er·ence \ˈpre-frəns, -fə-rəns\ *n* **1** : a special liking for one thing over another **2** : CHOICE, SELECTION — **pref·er·en·tial** \₁pre-fə-ˈren-chəl\ *adj*

pre·fer·ment \pri-ˈfər-mənt\ *n* : PROMOTION, ADVANCEMENT

preferred stock *n* : stock guaranteed priority by a corporation's charter in the payment of dividends and usu. in the distribution of assets

pre·fig·ure \prē-ˈfi-gyər\ *vb* **1** : FORESHADOW **2** : to imagine beforehand

¹**pre·fix** \ˈprē-₁fiks, prē-ˈfiks\ *vb* : to place before ⟨~ a title to a name⟩

²**pre·fix** \ˈprē-₁fiks\ *n* : an affix occurring at the beginning of a word

pre·flight \₁prē-ˈflīt\ *adj* : preparing for or preliminary to flight

pre·form \(₁)prē-ˈfȯrm, ˈprē-₁fȯrm\ *vb* : to form or shape beforehand

preg·na·ble \ˈpreg-nə-bəl\ *adj* : vulnerable to capture ⟨a ~ fort⟩

preg·nant \ˈpreg-nənt\ *adj* **1** : containing unborn young within the body **2** : rich in significance : MEANINGFUL — **preg·nan·cy** \-nən-sē\ *n*

pre·heat \prē-ˈhēt\ *vb* : to heat beforehand; *esp* : to heat (an oven) to a designated temperature before using

pre·hen·sile \prē-ˈhen-səl, -₁sīl\ *adj* : adapted for grasping esp. by wrapping around ⟨a monkey with a ~ tail⟩

pre·his·tor·ic \₁prē-his-ˈtȯr-ik\ *or* **pre·his·tor·i·cal** \-i-kəl\ *adj* : of, relating to, or existing in the period before written history began

pre·judge \(₁)prē-ˈjəj\ *vb* : to judge before full hearing or examination

¹**prej·u·dice** \ˈpre-jə-dəs\ *n* **1** : DAMAGE; *esp* : detriment to one's rights or claims **2** : an opinion made without adequate basis — **prej·u·di·cial** \₁pre-jə-ˈdi-shəl\ *adj*

²**prejudice** *vb* **-diced; -dic·ing 1** : to damage by a judgment or action esp. at law **2** : to cause to have prejudice

prel·ate \ˈpre-lət\ *n* : an ecclesiastic (as a bishop) of high rank — **prel·a·cy** \-lə-sē\ *n*

pre·launch \ˈprē-ˈlȯnch\ *adj* : preparing for or preliminary to launch

pre·lim \ˈprē-₁lim, pri-ˈlim\ *n or adj* : PRELIMINARY

¹**pre·lim·i·nary** \pri-ˈli-mə-₁ner-ē\ *n, pl* **-nar·ies** : something that precedes or introduces the main business or event

²**preliminary** *adj* : preceding the main discourse or business

pre·lude \ˈprel-₁yüd; ˈpre-₁lüd, ˈprā-\ *n* **1** : an introductory performance or event **2** : a musical section or movement introducing the main theme; *also* : an organ solo played at the beginning of a church service

prem *abbr* premium

pre·mar·i·tal \(₁)prē-ˈmar-ət-ᵊl\ *adj* : existing or occurring before marriage

pre·ma·ture \₁prē-mə-tùr, -ˈtyùr, -ˈchùr\ *adj* : happening, coming, born, or done before the usual or proper time — **pre·ma·ture·ly** *adv*

¹**pre·med** \₁prē-ˈmed\ *n* : a premedical student or course of study

²**premed** *adj* : PREMEDICAL

pre·med·i·cal \(₁)prē-ˈme-di-kəl\ *adj* : preceding and preparing for the professional study of medicine

pre·med·i·tate \pri-ˈme-də-₁tāt\ *vb* : to consider and plan beforehand — **pre·med·i·ta·tion** \-₁me-də-ˈtā-shən\ *n*

pre·men·stru·al \(₁)prē-ˈmen-strə-wəl\ *adj* : of, relating to, or occurring in the period just before menstruation

premenstrual syndrome *n* : a varying group of symptoms manifested by some women prior to menstruation

pre·mie *var of* PREEMIE

¹**pre·mier** \pri-ˈmir, -ˈmyir, ˈprē-mē-ər\ *adj* [ME *primier,* fr. MF *premier* first, chief, fr. L *primarius* of the first rank] : first in rank or importance : CHIEF; *also* : first in time : EARLIEST

²**premier** *n* : PRIME MINISTER — **pre·mier·ship** *n*

¹**pre·miere** \pri-ˈmyer, -ˈmir\ *n* : a first performance

²**premiere** *or* **pre·mier** *same as* ¹PREMIERE\ *vb* **pre·miered; pre·mier·ing** : to give or receive a first public performance

prem·ise \ˈpre-məs\ *n* **1** : a statement of fact or a supposition made or implied as a basis of argument **2** *pl* : a piece of land with the structures on it; *also* : the place of business of an enterprise

pre·mi·um \ˈprē-mē-əm\ *n* [L *praemium* booty, reward, fr. *prae* before + *emere* to take, buy] **1** : REWARD, PRIZE **2** : a sum over and above the stated value **3** : something paid over and above a fixed wage or price **4** : something given with a purchase **5** : the sum paid for a contract of insurance **6** : an unusually high value

pre·mix \₁prē-ˈmiks\ *vb* : to mix before use

¹**pre·mo·lar** \(₁)prē-ˈmō-lər\ *adj* : situated in front of or preceding the molar teeth

²**premolar** *n* : any of the double-pointed grinding teeth which are located between the canines and the true molars and of which there are two on each side of each human jaw

pre·mo·ni·tion \₁prē-mə-ˈni-shən, ₁pre-\ *n* **1** : previous warning **2** : PRESENTIMENT — **pre·mon·i·to·ry** \pri-ˈmä-nə-₁tōr-ē\ *adj*

pre·na·tal \'prē-'nāt-ªl\ *adj* : occurring, existing, or taking place before birth

pre·oc·cu·pa·tion \prē-ä-kyə-'pā-shən\ *n* : complete absorption of the mind or interests; *also* : something that causes such absorption

pre·oc·cu·pied \prē-'ä-kyə-ıpīd\ *adj* **1** : lost in thought; *also* : absorbed in some preoccupation **2** : already occupied **syn** abstracted, absent, absentminded

pre·oc·cu·py \-ıpī\ *vb* **1** : to occupy the attention of beforehand **2** : to take possession of before another

pre·op·er·a·tive \(ı)prē-'ä-prə-tiv, -pə-ırā-\ *adj* : occurring before a surgical operation

pre·or·dain \ıprē-òr-'dān\ *vb* : FOREORDAIN

pre—owned \(ı)prē-'ōnd\ *adj* : SECONDHAND

prep *abbr* **1** preparatory **2** preposition

pre·pack·age \(ı)prē-'pa-kij\ *vb* : to package (as food) before offering for sale to the customer

preparatory school *n* **1** : a usu. private school preparing students primarily for college **2** *Brit* : a private elementary school preparing students primarily for public schools

pre·pare \pri-'par\ *vb* **pre·pared; pre·par·ing** **1** : to make or get ready ⟨∼ dinner⟩ ⟨∼ a student for college⟩ **2** : to get ready beforehand **3** : to put together : COMPOUND ⟨∼ a prescription⟩ — **prep·a·ra·tion** \ıpre-pə-'rā-shən\ *n* — **pre·pa·ra·to·ry** \pri-'par-ə-ıtōr-ē\ *adj*

pre·pared·ness \pri-'par-əd-nəs\ *n* : a state of adequate preparation

pre·pay \(ı)prē-'pā\ *vb* **-paid** \-'pād\; **-pay·ing** : to pay or pay the charge on in advance

pre·pon·der·ant \pri-'pän-də-rənt\ *adj* : having greater weight, force, influence, or frequency — **pre·pon·der·ance** \-rəns\ *n* — **pre·pon·der·ant·ly** *adv*

pre·pon·der·ate \pri-'pän-də-ırāt\ *vb* **-at·ed; -at·ing** [L *praeponderare*, fr. *prae-* ahead + *ponder-, pondus* weight] : to exceed in weight, force, influence, or frequency : PREDOMINATE

prep·o·si·tion \ıpre-pə-'zi-shən\ *n* : a word that combines with a noun or pronoun to form a phrase — **prep·o·si·tion·al** \-'zi-shə-nəl\ *adj*

pre·pos·sess \ıprē-pə-'zes\ *vb* **1** : to cause to be preoccupied **2** : to influence beforehand esp. favorably

pre·pos·sess·ing *adj* : tending to create a favorable impression ⟨a ∼ manner⟩

pre·pos·ses·sion \-'ze-shən\ *n* **1** : PREJUDICE **2** : an exclusive concern with one idea or object

pre·pos·ter·ous \pri-'päs-tə-rəs\ *adj* : contrary to nature or reason : ABSURD

prep·py *or* **prep·pie** \'pre-pē\ *n, pl* **preppies 1** : a student at or a graduate of a preparatory school **2** : a person deemed to dress or behave like a preppy

pre·puce \'prē-ıpyüs\ *n* : FORESKIN

pre·quel \'prē-kwəl\ *n* : a literary or dramatic work whose story precedes that of an earlier work

pre·re·cord·ed \(ı)prē-ri-'kòr-dəd\ *adj* : recorded for later broadcast

pre·req·ui·site \prē-'re-kwə-zət\ *n* : something required beforehand or for the end in view — **prerequisite** *adj*

pre·rog·a·tive \pri-'rä-gə-tiv\ *n* : an exclusive or special right, power, or privilege

pres *abbr* **1** present **2** president

¹pres·age \'pre-sij\ *n* **1** : something that foreshadows a future event : OMEN **2** : FOREBODING

²pre·sage \'pre-sij, pri-'sāj\ *vb* **pre·saged; pre·sag·ing 1** : to give an omen or warning of : FORESHADOW **2** : FORETELL, PREDICT

pres·by·opia \ıprez-bē-'ō-pē-ə\ *n* : a visual condition in which loss of elasticity of the lens of the eye causes defective accommodation and inability to focus sharply for near vision — **pres·by·opic** \-'ō-pik, -'ä-\ *adj or n*

pres·by·ter \'prez-bə-tər\ *n* **1** : PRIEST, MINISTER **2** : an elder in a Presbyterian church

¹Pres·by·te·ri·an \ıprez-bə-'tir-ē-ən\ *n* : a member of a Presbyterian church

²Presbyterian *adj* **1** *often not cap* : characterized by a graded system of representative ecclesiastical bodies (as presbyteries) exercising legislative and judicial powers **2** : of or relating to a group of Protestant Christian bodies that are presbyterian in government — **Pres·by·te·ri·an·ism** \-ə-ıni-zəm\ *n*

pres·by·tery \'prez-bə-ıter-ē\ *n, pl* **-ter·ies 1** : the part of a church reserved for the officiating clergy **2** : a ruling body in Presbyterian churches consisting of the ministers and representative elders of a district

¹pre·school \'prē-ıskül\ *adj* : of or relating to the period in a child's life from infancy to the age of five or six — **pre·school·er** \-ıskü-lər\ *n*

²preschool *n* : NURSERY SCHOOL

pre·science \'pre-shəns, 'prē-\ *n* : foreknowledge of events; *also* : FORESIGHT — **pre·scient** \-shənt, -shē-ənt\ *adj*

pre·scribe \pri-'skrīb\ *vb* **pre·scribed; pre·scrib·ing 1** : to lay down as a guide or rule of action **2** : to direct the use of (as a medicine) as a remedy

pre·scrip·tion \pri-'skrip-shən\ *n* **1** : the action of prescribing rules or directions **2** : a written direction for the preparation and use of a medicine; *also* : a medicine prescribed

pres·ence \'prez-ªns\ *n* **1** : the fact or condition of being present **2** : the space immediately around a person **3** : one that is present **4** : the bearing of a person; *esp* : stately bearing

¹pres·ent \'prez-ªnt\ *n* : something presented : GIFT

²pre·sent \pri-'zent\ *vb* **1** : to bring into the presence or acquaintance of : INTRODUCE **2** : to bring before the public ⟨∼ a play⟩ **3** : to make a gift to **4** : to give formally **5** : to lay (as a charge) before a court for inquiry **6** : to aim or direct (as a weapon) so as to face in a particular direction — **pre·sent·able** *adj* — **pre·sen·ta·tion** \ıprē-ızen-'tā-shən, ıprez-ªn-\ *n* — **pre·sent·ment** \pri-'zent-mənt\ *n*

³pres·ent \'prez-ªnt\ *adj* **1** : now existing or in progress ⟨∼ conditions⟩ **2** : being in view or at hand ⟨∼ at the meeting⟩ **3** : under consideration ⟨the ∼ problem⟩ **4** : of, relating to, or constituting a verb tense that expresses present time or the time of speaking

⁴pres·ent \'prez-ªnt\ *n* **1** *pl* : the present legal document **2** : the present tense; *also* : a verb form in it **3** : the present time

pres·ent—day \'prez-ªnt-'dā\ *adj* : now existing or occurring : CURRENT

pre·sen·ti·ment \pri-'zen-tə-mənt\ *n* : a feeling that something is about to happen : PREMONITION

pres·ent·ly \'prez-ªnt-lē\ *adv* **1** : SOON **2** : NOW

present participle *n* : a participle that typically expresses present action and that in English is formed with the suffix *-ing* and is used in the formation of the progressive tenses

¹pre·serve \pri-'zərv\ *vb* **pre·served; pre·serv·ing 1** : to keep safe : GUARD, PROTECT **2** : to keep from decaying; *esp* : to process food (as by canning or pickling) to prevent spoilage **3** : MAINTAIN ⟨∼ silence⟩ — **pres·er·va·tion** \ıpre-zər-'vā-shən\ *n* — **pre·ser·va·tive** \pri-'zər-və-tiv\ *adj or n* — **pre·serv·er** *n*

²preserve *n* **1** : preserved fruit — often used in pl. **2** : an area for the protection of natural resources (as animals)

pre·set \(ı)prē-'set\ *vb* **-set; -set·ting** : to set beforehand

pre·shrunk \-'shrəŋk\ *adj* : subjected to a shrinking process during manufacture usu. to reduce later shrinking

pre·side \pri-'zīd\ *vb* **pre·sid·ed; pre·sid·ing** [L *prae-*

\ə\abut \ª\kitten \ər\further \a\ash \ā\ace \ä\mop, mar \au̇\out \ch\chin \e\bet \ē\easy \g\go \i\hit \ī\ice \j\job \ŋ\sing \ō\go \ò\law \òi\boy \th\thin \t͟h\the \ü\loot \u̇\foot \y\yet \zh\vision *see also* Pronunciation Symbols page *sidēre* to guard, preside over, fr. *prae* in front of + *sedēre* to sit] **1** : to exercise guidance or control **2** : to occupy the place of authority; *esp* : to act as chairman

pres·i·dent \\'pre-zə-dənt\ *n* **1** : one chosen to preside ⟨∼ of the assembly⟩ **2** : the chief officer of an organization (as a corporation or society) **3** : an elected official serving as both chief of state and chief political executive; *also* : a chief of state often with only minimal political powers — **pres·i·den·cy** \-dən-sē\ *n* — **pres·i·den·tial** \\,pre-zə-'den-chəl\ *adj*

pre·si·dio \pri-'sē-dē-,ō, -'si-\ *n, pl* **-di·os** [Sp] : a military post or fortified settlement in areas currently or orig. under Spanish control

pre·sid·i·um \pri-'si-dē-əm\ *n, pl* **-ia** \-dē-ə\ *or* **-iums** [Russ *prezidium*, fr. L *praesidium* garrison] : a permanent executive committee that acts for a larger body in a Communist country

¹pre·soak \(,)prē-'sōk\ *vb* : to soak beforehand

²pre·soak \\'prē-,sōk\ *n* **1** : an instance of presoaking **2** : a preparation used in presoaking clothes

pre·sort \(,)prē-'sȯrt\ *vb* : to sort (mail) by zip code usu. before delivery to a post office

¹press \\'pres\ *n* **1** : a crowded condition : THRONG **2** : a machine for exerting pressure **3** : CLOSET, CUPBOARD **4** : PRESSURE **5** : the properly creased condition of a freshly pressed garment **6** : PRINTING PRESS; *also* : the act or the process of printing **7** : a printing or publishing establishment **8** : the media (as newspapers and magazines) of public news and comment; *also* : persons (as reporters) employed in these media **9** : comment in newspapers and periodicals

²press *vb* **1** : to bear down upon : push steadily against **2** : ASSAIL, COMPEL **3** : to squeeze out the juice or contents of ⟨∼ grapes⟩ **4** : to squeeze to a desired density, shape, or smoothness; *esp* : IRON **5** : to try hard to persuade : URGE **6** : to follow through : PROSECUTE **7** : CROWD **8** : to force one's way **9** : to require haste or speed in action — **press·er** *n*

press agent *n* : an agent employed to establish and maintain good public relations through publicity

press·ing *adj* : URGENT

press·man \\'pres-mən, -,man\ *n* : the operator of a press and esp. a printing press

press·room \-,rüm, -,ru̇m\ *n* **1** : a room in a printing plant containing the printing presses **2** : a room for the use of reporters

¹pres·sure \\'pre-shər\ *n* **1** : the burden of physical or mental distress **2** : the action of pressing; *esp* : the application of force to something by something else in direct contact with it **3** : the force exerted over a surface divided by its area **4** : the stress or urgency of matters demanding attention

²pressure *vb* **pres·sured; pres·sur·ing** : to apply pressure to

pressure group *n* : a group that seeks to influence governmental policy but not to elect candidates to office

pressure suit *n* : an inflatable suit for high-altitude flight or spaceflight to protect the body from low pressure

pres·sur·ize \\'pre-shə-,rīz\ *vb* **-ized; -iz·ing 1** : to maintain higher pressure within than without; *esp* : to maintain normal atmospheric pressure within (as an airplane cabin) during high-altitude flight or spaceflight **2** : to apply pressure to **3** : to design to withstand pressure — **pres·sur·i·za·tion** \,pre-shə-rə-'zā-shən\ *n*

pres·ti·dig·i·ta·tion \,pres-tə-,di-jə-'tā-shən\ *n* : SLEIGHT OF HAND

pres·tige \pres-'tēzh, -'tēj\ *n* [F, fr. MF, conjuror's trick, illusion, fr. LL *praestigium*, fr. L *praestigiae*, pl., conjuror's tricks, fr. *praestringere* to graze, blunt, constrict, fr. *prae-* in front of + *stringere* to bind tight] : standing or estimation in the eyes of people : REPUTATION **syn** influence, authority, weight, cachet — **pres·ti·gious** \-'ti-jəs, -'tē-\ *adj*

pres·to \\'pres-tō\ *adv or adj* [It] **1** : suddenly as if by magic : IMMEDIATELY **2** : at a rapid tempo — used as a direction in music

pre·stress \(,)prē-'stres\ *vb* : to introduce internal stresses into (as a structural beam) to counteract later load stresses

pre·sum·ably \pri-'zü-mə-blē\ *adv* : by reasonable assumption

pre·sume \pri-'züm\ *vb* **pre·sumed; pre·sum·ing 1** : to take upon oneself without leave or warrant : DARE **2** : to take for granted : ASSUME **3** : to act or behave with undue boldness — **pre·sum·able** \-'zü-mə-bəl\ *adj*

pre·sump·tion \pri-'zəmp-shən\ *n* **1** : presumptuous attitude or conduct : AUDACITY **2** : an attitude or belief dictated by probability; *also* : the grounds lending probability to a belief — **pre·sump·tive** \-tiv\ *adj*

pre·sump·tu·ous \pri-'zəmp-chə-wəs\ *adj* : overstepping due bounds : taking liberties — **pre·sump·tu·ous·ly** *adv*

pre·sup·pose \,prē-sə-'pōz\ *vb* **1** : to suppose beforehand **2** : to require beforehand as a necessary condition — **pre·sup·po·si·tion** \(,)prē-,sə-pə-'zi-shən\ *n*

pre·teen \\'prē-'tēn\ *n* : a boy or girl not yet 13 years old — **preteen** *adj*

pre·tend \pri-'tend\ *vb* **1** : PROFESS ⟨doesn't ∼ to be scientific⟩ **2** : FEIGN ⟨∼ to be angry⟩ **3** : to lay claim ⟨∼ to a throne⟩ — **pre·tend·er** *n*

pre·tense *or* **pre·tence** \\'prē-,tens, pri-'tens\ *n* **1** : CLAIM; *esp* : one not supported by fact **2** : mere display ⟨show **3** : an attempt to attain a certain condition ⟨made a ∼ at discipline⟩ **4** : false show : PRETEXT — **pre·ten·sion** \pri-'ten-chən\ *n*

pre·ten·tious \pri-'ten-chəs\ *adj* **1** : making or possessing usu. unjustified claims (as to excellence) ⟨a ∼ literary style⟩ **2** : making demands on one's ability or means : AMBITIOUS ⟨too ∼ an undertaking⟩ — **pre·ten·tious·ly** *adv* — **pre·ten·tious·ness** *n*

pret·er·it *or* **pret·er·ite** \\'pre-tə-rət\ *adj* : PAST **3** — **pret·er·it** *n*

pre·ter·nat·u·ral \,prē-tər-'na-chə-rəl\ *adj* **1** : exceeding what is natural **2** : inexplicable by ordinary means — **pre·ter·nat·u·ral·ly** *adv*

pre·text \\'prē-,tekst\ *n* : a purpose stated or assumed to cloak the real intention or state of affairs

pret·ti·fy \\'pri-ti-,fī\ *vb* **-fied; -fy·ing** : to make pretty — **pret·ti·fi·ca·tion** \,pri-ti-fə-'kā-shən\ *n*

¹pret·ty \\'pri-tē\ *adj* **pret·ti·er; -est** [ME *praty, pretty*, fr. OE *prættig* tricky, fr. *prætt* trick] **1** : pleasing by delicacy or grace : having conventionally accepted elements of beauty ⟨∼ flowers⟩ **2** : MISERABLE, TERRIBLE ⟨a ∼ state of affairs⟩ **3** : moderately large ⟨a ∼ profit⟩ **syn** comely, fair, beautiful, attractive, lovely — **pret·ti·ly** \-tə-lē\ *adv* — **pret·ti·ness** \-tē-nəs\ *n*

²pretty *adv* : in some degree : MODERATELY

³pretty *vb* **pret·tied; pret·ty·ing** : to make pretty

pret·zel \\'pret-səl\ *n* [G *Brezel*, ultim. fr. L *brachiatus* having branches like arms, fr. *brachium* arm] : a brittle or chewy glazed usu. salted slender bread often shaped like a loose knot

prev *abbr* previous; previously

pre·vail \pri-'vāl\ *vb* **1** : to win mastery : TRIUMPH **2** : to be or become effective : SUCCEED **3** : to urge successfully ⟨∼ed upon her to sing⟩ **4** : to be frequent : PREDOMINATE — **pre·vail·ing·ly** *adv*

prev·a·lent \\'pre-və-lənt\ *adj* : generally or widely existent : WIDESPREAD — **prev·a·lence** \-ləns\ *n*

pre·var·i·cate \pri-'var-ə-,kāt\ *vb* **-cat·ed; -cat·ing** : to deviate from the truth : EQUIVOCATE — **pre·var·i·ca·tion** \-,var-ə-'kā-shən\ *n* — **pre·var·i·ca·tor** \-'var-ə-,kā-tər\ *n*

pre·vent \pri-'vent\ *vb* **1** : to keep from happening or existing ⟨steps to ∼ war⟩ **2** : to hold back : HINDER, STOP ⟨∼ us from going⟩ — **pre·vent·able** *also* **pre·vent·ible**

\-ˈven-tə-bəl\ *adj* — **pre·ven·tion** \-ˈven-chən\ *n* — **pre·ven·tive** \-ˈven-tiv\ *adj or n* — **pre·ven·ta·tive** \-ˈven-tə-tiv\ *adj or n*

pre·ver·bal \ˌprē-ˈvər-bəl\ *adj* : having not yet acquired the faculty of speech

¹**pre·view** \ˈprē-ˌvyü\ *vb* : to see or discuss beforehand; *esp* : to view or show in advance of public presentation

²**preview** *n* **1** : an advance showing or viewing **2** *also* **pre·vue** \-ˌvyü\ : a showing of snatches from a motion picture advertised for future appearance **3** : FORETASTE

pre·vi·ous \ˈprē-vē-əs\ *adj* : going before : EARLIER, FORMER **syn** foregoing, prior, preceding, antecedent — **pre·vi·ous·ly** *adv*

pre·vi·sion \prē-ˈvi-zhən\ *n* **1** : FORESIGHT, PRESCIENCE **2** : FORECAST, PREDICTION

pre·war \ˈprē-ˈwȯr\ *adj* : occurring or existing before a war

¹**prey** \ˈprā\ *n, pl* **prey** *also* **preys 1** : an animal taken for food by a predator; *also* : VICTIM **2** : the act or habit of preying

²**prey** *vb* **1** : to raid for booty **2** : to seize and devour prey **3** : to have a harmful or wearing effect

prf *abbr* proof

¹**price** \ˈprīs\ *n* **1** *archaic* : VALUE **2** : the amount of money paid or asked for the sale of a specified thing; *also* : the cost at which something is obtained

²**price** *vb* **priced; pric·ing 1** : to set a price on **2** : to ask the price of **3** : to drive by raising prices ⟨*priced* themselves out of the market⟩

price–fix·ing \ˈprīs-ˌfik-siŋ\ *n* : the setting of prices artificially (as by producers or government)

price·less \-ləs\ *adj* : having a value beyond any price : INVALUABLE **syn** precious, costly, expensive

price support *n* : artificial maintenance of prices of a commodity at a level usu. fixed through government action

price war *n* : a period of commercial competition in which prices are repeatedly cut by the competitors

pric·ey *also* **pricy** \ˈprī-sē\ *adj* **pric·i·er; -est** : EXPENSIVE

¹**prick** \ˈprik\ *n* **1** : a mark or small wound made by a pointed instrument **2** : something sharp or pointed **3** : an instance of pricking; *also* : a sensation of being pricked

²**prick** *vb* **1** : to pierce slightly with a sharp point; *also* : to have or cause a pricking sensation **2** : to affect with anguish or remorse ⟨∼s his conscience⟩ **3** : to outline with punctures ⟨∼ out a pattern⟩ **4** : to stand or cause to stand erect ⟨the dog's ears ∼ed up at the sound⟩ **syn** punch, puncture, perforate, bore, drill

prick·er \ˈpri-kər\ *n* : BRIAR; *also* : THORN

¹**prick·le** \ˈpri-kəl\ *n* **1** : a small sharp process (as on a plant) **2** : a slight stinging pain — **prick·ly** \ˈpri-klē\ *adj*

²**prickle** *vb* **prick·led; prick·ling 1** : to prick lightly **2** : TINGLE

prickly heat *n* : a red cutaneous eruption with intense itching and tingling caused by inflammation around the ducts of the sweat glands

prickly pear *n* : any of numerous cacti with usu. yellow flowers and prickly flat or rounded joints; *also* : the sweet pulpy pear-shaped edible fruit of various prickly pears

¹**pride** \ˈprīd\ *n* **1** : CONCEIT **2** : justifiable self-respect **3** : elation over an act or possession **4** : haughty behavior : DISDAIN **5** : ostentatious display — **pride·ful** *adj*

²**pride** *vb* **prid·ed; prid·ing** : to indulge (as oneself) in pride

priest \ˈprēst\ *n* [ME *preist*, fr. OE *prēost*, ultim. fr. LL *presbyter* elder, priest, fr. Gk *presbyteros*, fr. compar. of *presbys* old man, elder] : a person having authority to perform the sacred rites of a religion; *esp* : a member of the Anglican, Eastern, or Roman Catholic clergy ranking below a bishop and above a deacon — **priest·hood** *n* — **priest·li·ness** *n* — **priest·ly** *adj*

priest·ess \ˈprēs-təs\ *n* : a woman authorized to perform the sacred rites of a religion

prig \ˈprig\ *n* : one who irritates by rigid or pointed observance of proprieties — **prig·gish** \ˈpri-gish\ *adj* — **prig·gish·ly** *adv*

¹**prim** \ˈprim\ *adj* **prim·mer; prim·mest** : stiffly formal and precise — **prim·ly** *adv* — **prim·ness** *n*

²**prim** *abbr* **1** primary **2** primitive

pri·ma·cy \ˈprī-mə-sē\ *n* **1** : the state of being first (as in rank) **2** : the office, rank, or character of an ecclesiastical primate

pri·ma don·na \ˌpri-mə-ˈdä-nə\ *n, pl* **prima donnas** [It, lit., first lady] **1** : a principal female singer (as in an opera company) **2** : an extremely sensitive, vain, or undisciplined person

pri·ma fa·cie \ˈprī-mə-ˈfā-shə, -sē, -shē\ *adj or adv* [L, at first view] **1** : based on immediate impression : APPARENT **2** : SELF-EVIDENT

pri·mal \ˈprī-məl\ *adj* **1** : ORIGINAL, PRIMITIVE **2** : first in importance

pri·mar·i·ly \prī-ˈmer-ə-lē\ *adv* **1** : FUNDAMENTALLY **2** : ORIGINALLY

¹**pri·ma·ry** \ˈprī-ˌmer-ē, -mə-rē\ *adj* **1** : first in order of time or development; *also* : PREPARATORY **2** : of first rank or importance; *also* : FUNDAMENTAL **3** : not derived from or dependent on something else ⟨∼ sources⟩

²**primary** *n, pl* **-ries** : a preliminary election in which voters nominate or express a preference among candidates usu. of their own party

primary color *n* : any of a set of colors from which all other colors may be derived

primary school *n* **1** : a school usu. including grades 1-3 and sometimes kindergarten **2** : ELEMENTARY SCHOOL

pri·mate \ˈprī-ˌmāt or esp for 1 -mət\ *n* **1** *often cap* : the highest-ranking bishop of a province or nation **2** : any of an order of mammals including humans, apes, and monkeys

¹**prime** \ˈprīm\ *n* **1** : the earliest stage of something; *esp* : SPRINGTIME **2** : the most active, thriving, or successful stage or period (as of one's life) **3** : the best individual; *also* : the best part of something **4** : any integer other than 0, +1, or −1 that is not divisible without remainder by any integer except +1, −1, and plus or minus itself; *esp* : any such integer that is positive

²**prime** *adj* **1** : standing first (as in time, rank, significance, or quality) ⟨∼ requisite⟩ **2** : of, relating to, or being a number that is prime

³**prime** *vb* **primed; prim·ing 1** : FILL, LOAD **2** : to lay a preparatory coating upon (as in painting) **3** : to put in working condition **4** : to instruct beforehand : COACH

prime meridian *n* : the meridian of 0° longitude which runs through Greenwich, England, and from which other longitudes are reckoned east and west

prime minister *n* **1** : the chief minister of a ruler or state **2** : the chief executive of a parliamentary government

¹**prim·er** \ˈpri-mər\ *n* **1** : a small book for teaching children to read **2** : a small introductory book on a subject

²**prim·er** \ˈprī-mər\ *n* **1** : one that primes **2** : a device for igniting an explosive **3** : material for priming a surface

prime rate *n* : an interest rate announced by a bank to be the lowest available to its most credit-worthy customers

prime time *n* **1** : the time period when the television or radio audience is largest; *also* : prime-time television **2** : the choicest or busiest time

pri·me·val \prī-ˈmē-vəl\ *adj* : of or relating to the earliest ages : PRIMITIVE

¹**prim·i·tive** \ˈpri-mə-tiv\ *adj* **1** : ORIGINAL, PRIMARY **2**

\ə\abut \ᵊ\kitten \ər\further \a\ash \ā\ace \ä\mop, mar \aù\out \ch\chin \e\bet \ē\easy \g\go \i\hit \ī\ice \j\job \ŋ\sing \ō\go \ò\law \òi\boy \th\thin \th\the \ü\loot \ù\foot \y\yet \zh\vision *see also* Pronunciation Symbols page

: of, relating to, or characteristic of an early stage of development 3 : ELEMENTAL, NATURAL 4 : of, relating to, or produced by a tribal people or culture 5 : SELF-TAUGHT; *also* : produced by a self-taught artist — **prim·i·tive·ly** *adv* — **prim·i·tive·ness** *n* — **prim·i·tiv·i·ty** \ˌpri-mə-ˈti-və-tē\ *n*

²primitive *n* 1 : something primitive 2 : a primitive artist 3 : a member of a primitive people

prim·i·tiv·ism \ˈpri-mə-ti-ˌvi-zəm\ *n* 1 : belief in the superiority of a simple way of life close to nature 2 : the style of art of primitive peoples or primitive artists

pri·mo·gen·i·tor \ˌprī-mō-ˈje-nə-tər\ *n* : ANCESTOR, FOREFATHER

pri·mo·gen·i·ture \-ˈje-nə-ˌchùr\ *n* 1 : the state of being the firstborn of a family 2 : an exclusive right of inheritance belonging to the eldest son

pri·mor·di·al \prī-ˈmòr-dē-əl\ *adj* : first created or developed : existing in its original state : PRIMEVAL

primp \ˈprimp\ *vb* : to dress in a careful or finicky manner

prim·rose \ˈprim-ˌrōz\ *n* : any of a genus of perennial herbs with large leaves arranged at the base of the stem and clusters of showy flowers on leafless stalks

prin *abbr* 1 principal 2 principle

prince \ˈprins\ *n* [ME, fr. OF, fr. L *princeps* leader, initiator, fr. *primus* first + *capere* to take] 1 : MONARCH, KING 2 : a male member of a royal family; *esp* : a son of the monarch 3 : a person of high standing (as in a class) — **prince·dom** \-dəm\ *n* — **prince·ly** *adj*

prince·ling \-liŋ\ *n* : a petty prince

prin·cess \ˈprin-səs, -ˌses\ *n* 1 : a female member of a royal family 2 : the consort of a prince

¹prin·ci·pal \ˈprin-sə-pəl\ *adj* : most important — **prin·ci·pal·ly** *adv*

²principal *n* 1 : a leading person (as in a play) 2 : the chief officer of an educational institution 3 : the person from whom an agent's authority derives 4 : a capital sum placed at interest or used as a fund

prin·ci·pal·i·ty \ˌprin-sə-ˈpa-lə-tē\ *n, pl* **-ties** : the position, territory, or jurisdiction of a prince

principal parts *n pl* : the inflected forms of a verb

prin·ci·ple \ˈprin-sə-pəl\ *n* 1 : a general or fundamental law, doctrine, or assumption 2 : a rule or code of conduct; *also* : devotion to such a code 3 : the laws or facts of nature underlying the working of an artificial device 4 : a primary source : ORIGIN; *also* : an underlying faculty or endowment 5 : the active part (as of a drug)

prin·ci·pled \-pəld\ *adj* : exhibiting, based on, or characterized by principle ⟨high-*principled*⟩

prink \ˈpriŋk\ *vb* : PRIMP

¹print \ˈprint\ *n* 1 : a mark made by pressure 2 : something stamped with an impression 3 : printed state or form 4 : printed matter 5 : a copy made by printing 6 : cloth with a pattern applied by printing

²print *vb* 1 : to stamp (as a mark) in or on something 2 : to produce impressions of (as from type) 3 : to write in letters like those of printer's type 4 : to make (a positive picture) from a photographic negative

print·able \ˈprin-tə-bəl\ *adj* 1 : capable of being printed or of being printed from 2 : worthy or fit to be published

print·er \ˈprin-tər\ *n* : one that prints; *esp* : a device that produces printout

print·ing *n* 1 : reproduction in printed form 2 : the art, practice, or business of a printer 3 : IMPRESSION 5

printing press *n* : a machine that produces printed copies

print·out \ˈprint-ˌaùt\ *n* : a printed output produced by a computer — **print out** *vb*

¹pri·or \ˈprī-ər\ *n* : the superior ranking next to the abbot or abbess of a religious house

²pri·or *adj* 1 : earlier in time or order 2 : taking precedence logically or in importance — **pri·or·i·ty** \prī-ˈòr-ə-tē\ *n*

pri·or·ess \ˈprī-ə-rəs\ *n* : a nun corresponding in rank to a prior

pri·or·i·tize \prī-ˈòr-ə-ˌtīz, ˈprī-ə-rə-ˌtīz\ *vb* **-tized; -tiz·ing** : to list or rate in order of priority

prior to *prep* : in advance of : BEFORE

pri·o·ry \ˈprī-ə-rē\ *n, pl* **-ries** : a religious house under a prior or prioress

prise *chiefly Brit var of* ⁵PRIZE

prism \ˈpri-zəm\ *n* [LL *prisma*, fr. Gk, lit., anything sawed, fr. *priein* to saw] 1 : a solid whose sides are parallelograms and whose ends are parallel and alike in shape and size 2 : a usu. 3-sided transparent object that refracts light so that it breaks up into rainbow colors — **pris·mat·ic** \priz-ˈma-tik\ *adj*

pris·on \ˈpriz-ᵊn\ *n* : a place or state of confinement esp. for criminals

pris·on·er \ˈpriz-ᵊn-ər\ *n* : a person deprived of his liberty; *esp* : one on trial or in prison

prisoner of war : a person captured in war

pris·sy \ˈpri-sē\ *adj* **pris·si·er; -est** : being overly prim and precise : PRIGGISH — **pris·si·ness** \-sē-nəs\ *n*

pris·tine \ˈpris-ˌtēn, pri-ˈstēn\ *adj* 1 : PRIMITIVE 2 : having the purity of its original state : UNSPOILED

prith·ee \ˈpri-thē\ *interj, archaic* — used to express a wish or request

pri·va·cy \ˈprī-və-sē\ *n, pl* **-cies** 1 : the quality or state of being apart from others 2 : SECRECY

¹pri·vate \ˈprī-vət\ *adj* 1 : belonging to or intended for a particular individual or group ⟨∼ property⟩ 2 : restricted to the individual : PERSONAL ⟨∼ opinion⟩ 3 : carried on by the individual independently ⟨∼ study⟩ 4 : not holding public office ⟨a ∼ citizen⟩ 5 : withdrawn from company or observation ⟨a ∼ place⟩ 6 : not known publicly — **pri·vate·ly** *adv*

²private *n* : an enlisted man of the lowest rank in the marine corps or of one of the two lowest ranks in the army — **in private** : not openly or in public

pri·va·teer \ˌprī-və-ˈtir\ *n* : an armed private ship licensed to attack enemy shipping; *also* : a sailor on such a ship

private first class *n* : an enlisted man ranking next below a corporal in the army and next below a lance corporal in the marine corps

pri·va·tion \prī-ˈvā-shən\ *n* 1 : DEPRIVATION 1 2 : the state of being deprived; *esp* : lack of what is needed for existence

priv·et \ˈpri-vət\ *n* : a nearly evergreen shrub related to the olive and widely used for hedges

¹priv·i·lege \ˈpriv-lij, ˈpri-və-\ *n* [ME, fr. OF, fr. L *privilegium* law for or against a private person, fr. *privus* private + *leg-, lex* law] : a right or immunity granted as an advantage or favor esp. to some and not others

²privilege *vb* **-leged; -leg·ing** : to grant a privilege to

priv·i·leged *adj* 1 : having or enjoying one or more privileges ⟨∼ classes⟩ 2 : not subject to disclosure in a court of law ⟨a ∼ communication⟩

¹privy \ˈpri-vē\ *adj* 1 : PERSONAL, PRIVATE 2 : SECRET 3 : admitted as one sharing in a secret ⟨∼ to the conspiracy⟩ — **priv·i·ly** \ˈpri-və-lē\ *adv*

²privy *n, pl* **priv·ies** : TOILET; *esp* : OUTHOUSE

¹prize \ˈprīz\ *n* 1 : something offered or striven for in competition or in contests of chance 2 : something exceptionally desirable

²prize *adj* 1 : awarded or worthy of a prize ⟨a ∼ essay⟩; *also* : awarded as a prize ⟨a ∼ medal⟩ 2 : OUTSTANDING

³prize *vb* **prized; priz·ing** : to value highly : ESTEEM

⁴prize *n* : property (as a ship) lawfully captured in time of war

⁵prize *vb* **prized; priz·ing** : PRY

prize·fight \ˈprīz-ˌfīt\ *n* : a professional boxing match — **prize·fight·er** *n* — **prize·fight·ing** *n*

prize·win·ner \-ˌwi-nər\ *n* : a winner of a prize — **prize-win·ning** *adj*

¹**pro** \ˈprō\ *n, pl* **pros** : a favorable argument, person, or position

²**pro** *adv* : in favor : FOR

³**pro** *n or adj* : PROFESSIONAL

PRO *abbr* public relations officer

prob *abbr* **1** probable; probably **2** problem

prob·a·bil·i·ty \ˌprä-bə-ˈbi-lə-tē\ *n, pl* **-ties 1** : the quality or state of being probable **2** : something probable **3** : a measure of how often a particular event will occur if something (as tossing a coin) is done repeatedly which results in any of a number of possible events

prob·a·ble \ˈprä-bə-bəl\ *adj* **1** : apparently or presumably true ⟨a ~ hypothesis⟩ **2** : likely to be or become true or real ⟨a ~ result⟩ — **prob·a·bly** \-bə-blē\ *adv*

¹**pro·bate** \ˈprō-ˌbāt\ *n* : the judicial determination of the validity of a will

²**pro·bate** *vb* **pro·bat·ed; pro·bat·ing** : to establish (a will) by probate as genuine and valid

pro·ba·tion \prō-ˈbā-shən\ *n* **1** : subjection of an individual to a period of testing and trial to ascertain fitness (as for a job) **2** : the action of giving a convicted offender freedom during good behavior under the supervision of a probation officer — **pro·ba·tion·ary** \-shə-ˌner-ē\ *adj*

pro·ba·tion·er \-shə-nər\ *n* **1** : a person (as a newly admitted student nurse) whose fitness is being tested during a trial period **2** : a convicted offender on probation

pro·ba·tive \ˈprō-bə-tiv\ *adj* **1** : serving to test or try **2** : serving to prove

¹**probe** \ˈprōb\ *n* **1** : a slender instrument for examining a cavity (as a wound) **2** : an information-gathering device sent into outer space **3** : a penetrating investigation **syn** inquiry, inquest, research, inquisition

²**probe** *vb* **probed; prob·ing 1** : to examine with a probe **2** : to investigate thoroughly

pro·bi·ty \ˈprō-bə-tē\ *n* : UPRIGHTNESS, HONESTY

prob·lem \ˈprä-bləm\ *n* **1** : a question raised for consideration or solution **2** : an intricate unsettled question **3** : a source of perplexity or vexation — **problem** *adj*

prob·lem·at·ic \ˌprä-blə-ˈma-tik\ *or* **prob·lem·at·i·cal** \-ti-kəl\ *adj* **1** : difficult to solve or decide : PUZZLING **2** : DUBIOUS, QUESTIONABLE

pro·bos·cis \prə-ˈbä-səs, -ˈbäs-kəs\ *n, pl* **-bos·cis·es** *also* **-bos·ci·des** \-ˈbä-sə-ˌdez\ [L, fr. Gk *proboskis*, fr. *pro-* before + *boskein* to feed] : a long flexible snout (as the trunk of an elephant)

proc *abbr* proceedings

pro·caine \ˈprō-ˌkān\ *n* : a drug used esp. as a local anesthetic

pro·ce·dure \prə-ˈsē-jər\ *n* **1** : a particular way of doing something ⟨democratic ~⟩ **2** : a series of steps followed in a regular order ⟨surgical ~⟩ — **pro·ce·dur·al** \-ˈsē-jə-rəl\ *adj*

pro·ceed \prō-ˈsēd\ *vb* **1** : to come forth : ISSUE **2** : to go on in an orderly way; *also* : CONTINUE **3** : to begin and carry on an action **4** : to take legal action **5** : to go forward : ADVANCE

pro·ceed·ing *n* **1** : PROCEDURE **2** *pl* : DOINGS **3** *pl* : legal action **4** : TRANSACTION **5** *pl* : an official record of things said or done

pro·ceeds \ˈprō-ˌsēdz\ *n pl* : the total amount or the profit arising from a business deal : RETURN

¹**pro·cess** \ˈprä-ˌses, ˈprō-\ *n, pl* **pro·cess·es** \-ˌse-səz, -sə-səz, -sə-ˌsēz\ **1** : PROGRESS, ADVANCE **2** : something going on : PROCEEDING **3** : a natural phenomenon marked by gradual changes that lead toward a particular result ⟨the ~ of growth⟩ **4** : a series of actions or operations directed toward a particular result ⟨a manufacturing ~⟩ **5** : legal action **6** : a mandate issued by a court; *esp* : SUMMONS **7** : a projecting part of an organism or organic structure

²**process** *vb* : to subject to a special process

pro·ces·sion \prə-ˈse-shən\ *n* : a group of individuals moving along in an orderly often ceremonial way

pro·ces·sion·al \-ˈse-shə-nəl\ *n* **1** : music for a procession **2** : a ceremonial procession

pro·ces·sor \ˈprä-ˌse-sər, ˈprō-\ *n* **1** : one that processes **2** : the part of a computer that operates on data

pro–choice \(ˌ)prō-ˈchȯis\ *adj* : favoring the legalization of abortion

pro·claim \prō-ˈklām\ *vb* : to make known publicly : DECLARE

proc·la·ma·tion \ˌprä-klə-ˈmā-shən\ *n* : an official public announcement

pro·cliv·i·ty \prō-ˈkli-və-tē\ *n, pl* **-ties** : an inherent inclination esp. toward something objectionable

pro·con·sul \-ˈkän-səl\ *n* **1** : a governor or military commander of an ancient Roman province **2** : an administrator in a modern colony or occupied area — **pro·con·su·lar** \-sə-lər\ *adj*

pro·cras·ti·nate \prə-ˈkras-tə-ˌnāt, prō-\ *vb* **-nat·ed; -nat·ing** [L *procrastinare*, fr. *pro-* forward + *crastinus* of tomorrow, fr. *cras* tomorrow] : to put off usu. habitually doing something that should be done **syn** dawdle, delay — **pro·cras·ti·na·tion** \-ˌkras-tə-ˈnā-shən\ *n* — **pro·cras·ti·na·tor** \-ˈkras-tə-ˌnā-tər\ *n*

pro·cre·ate \ˈprō-krē-ˌāt\ *vb* **-at·ed; -at·ing** : to beget or bring forth offspring **syn** reproduce, breed, generate, propagate — **pro·cre·ation** \ˌprō-krē-ˈā-shən\ *n* — **pro·cre·ative** \ˈprō-krē-ˌā-tiv\ *adj* — **pro·cre·ator** \-ˌā-tər\ *n*

pro·crus·te·an \prə-ˈkrəs-tē-ən\ *adj, often cap* [fr. *Procrustes*, villain of Greek mythology who made victims fit his bed by stretching them or cutting off their legs] : marked by arbitrary often ruthless disregard of individual differences or special circumstances

proc·tor \ˈpräk-tər\ *n* : one appointed to supervise students (as at an examination) — **proctor** *vb* — **proc·to·ri·al** \präk-ˈtȯr-ē-əl\ *adj*

proc·u·ra·tor \ˈprä-kyə-ˌrā-tər\ *n* : a Roman provincial administrator

pro·cure \prə-ˈkyu̇r\ *vb* **pro·cured; pro·cur·ing 1** : to get possession of : OBTAIN **2** : to make women available for promiscuous sexual intercourse **3** : ACHIEVE **syn** secure, acquire, gain, win, earn — **pro·cur·able** \-ˈkyu̇r-ə-bəl\ *adj* — **pro·cure·ment** *n* — **pro·cur·er** *n*

¹**prod** \ˈpräd\ *vb* **prod·ded; prod·ding 1** : to thrust a pointed instrument into : GOAD **2** : INCITE, STIR — **prod** *n*

²**prod** *abbr* product; production

prod·i·gal \ˈprä-di-gəl\ *adj* **1** : recklessly extravagant; *also* : LUXURIANT **2** : WASTEFUL, LAVISH **syn** profuse, lush, opulent — **prodigal** *n* — **prod·i·gal·i·ty** \ˌprä-də-ˈga-lə-tē\ *n*

pro·di·gious \prə-ˈdi-jəs\ *adj* **1** : exciting wonder **2** : extraordinary in size or degree : ENORMOUS **syn** monstrous, tremendous, stupendous, monumental — **pro·di·gious·ly** *adv*

prod·i·gy \ˈprä-də-jē\ *n, pl* **-gies 1** : something extraordinary : WONDER **2** : a highly talented child

¹**pro·duce** \prə-ˈdüs, -ˈdyüs\ *vb* **pro·duced; pro·duc·ing 1** : to present to view : EXHIBIT **2** : to give birth or rise to : YIELD **3** : EXTEND, PROLONG **4** : to give being or form to : BRING ABOUT, MAKE; *esp* : MANUFACTURE **5** : to cause to accrue ⟨~ a profit⟩

²**pro·duce** \ˈprä-(ˌ)düs, ˈprō- *also* -(ˌ)dyüs\ *n* : PRODUCT **2**; *also* : agricultural products and esp. fresh fruits and vegetables

pro·duc·er \prə-ˈdü-sər, prō-, -ˈdyü-\ *n* **1** : one that pro-

\ə\abut \ᵊ\kitten \ər\further \a\ash \ā\ace \ä\mop, mar
\au̇\out \ch\chin \e\bet \ē\easy \g\go \i\hit \ī\ice \j\job
\ŋ\sing \ō\go \ȯ\law \ȯi\boy \th\thin \t̲h̲\the \ü\loot \u̇\foot
\y\yet \zh\vision *see also* Pronunciation Symbols page

duces **2** : a person who supervises or finances a play, a movie, or a radio or television program

prod·uct \'prä-(₁)dəkt\ *n* **1** : the number resulting from multiplication **2** : something produced

pro·duc·tion \prə-'dək-shən\ *n* **1** : something produced : PRODUCT **2** : the act or process of producing — **pro·duc·tive** \-'dək-tiv\ *adj* — **pro·duc·tive·ness** *n* — **pro·duc·tiv·i·ty** \(₁)prō-₁dək-'ti-və-tē, ₁prä-(₁)dək-\ *n*

pro·em \'prō-₁em\ *n* **1** : preliminary comment : PREFACE **2** : PRELUDE

prof *abbr* **1** professional **2** professor

¹pro·fane \prō-'fān\ *vb* **pro·faned; pro·fan·ing** **1** : to treat (something sacred) with irreverence or contempt **2** : to debase by an unworthy use — **prof·a·na·tion** \₁prä-fə-'nā-shən\ *n*

²profane *adj* [ME *prophane,* fr. MF, fr. L *profanus,* fr. *pro-* before + *fanum* temple] **1** : not concerned with religion : SECULAR **2** : not holy because unconsecrated, impure, or defiled **3** : serving to debase what is holy : IRREVERENT ⟨∼ language⟩ — **pro·fane·ly** *adv* — **pro·fane·ness** *n*

pro·fan·i·ty \prō-'fa-nə-tē\ *n, pl* **-ties** **1** : the quality or state of being profane **2** : the use of profane language **3** : profane language

pro·fess \prə-'fes\ *vb* **1** : to declare or admit openly : AFFIRM **2** : to declare in words only : PRETEND **3** : to confess one's faith in **4** : to practice or claim to be versed in (a calling or occupation) — **pro·fess·ed·ly** \-'fe-səd-lē\ *adv*

pro·fes·sion \prə-'fe-shən\ *n* **1** : an open declaration or avowal of a belief or opinion **2** : a calling requiring specialized knowledge and often long academic preparation **3** : the whole body of persons engaged in a calling

¹pro·fes·sion·al \prə-'fe-shə-nəl\ *adj* **1** : of, relating to, or characteristic of a profession **2** : engaged in one of the professions **3** : participating for gain in an activity often engaged in by amateurs — **pro·fes·sion·al·ly** *adv*

²professional *n* : one that engages in an activity professionally

pro·fes·sion·al·ism \-nə-₁li-zəm\ *n* **1** : the conduct, aims, or qualities that characterize or mark a profession or a professional person **2** : the following of a profession (as athletics) for gain or livelihood

pro·fes·sion·al·ize \-nə-₁līz\ *vb* **-ized; -iz·ing** : to give a professional nature to

pro·fes·sor \prə-'fe-sər\ *n* : a teacher at a university or college; *esp* : a faculty member of the highest academic rank — **pro·fes·so·ri·al** \₁prō-fə-'sōr-ē-əl, ₁prä-\ *adj* — **pro·fes·sor·ship** *n*

prof·fer \'prä-fər\ *vb* **prof·fered; prof·fer·ing** : to present for acceptance : OFFER — **proffer** *n*

pro·fi·cient \prə-'fi-shənt\ *adj* : well advanced in an art, occupation, or branch of knowledge **syn** adept, skillful, expert, masterful, masterly — **pro·fi·cien·cy** \-shən-sē\ *n* — **proficient** *n* — **pro·fi·cient·ly** *adv*

¹pro·file \'prō-₁fīl\ *n* [It *profilo,* fr. *profilare* to draw in outline, fr. *pro-* forward (fr. L) + *filare* to spin, fr. LL, fr. L *filum* thread] **1** : a representation of something in outline; *esp* : a human head seen in side view **2** : a concise biographical sketch **3** : degree or level of public exposure ⟨keep a low ∼⟩

²profile *vb* **pro·filed; pro·fil·ing** : to write or draw a profile of

¹prof·it \'prä-fət\ *n* **1** : a valuable return : GAIN **2** : the excess of the selling price of goods over their cost — **prof·it·less** *adj*

²profit *vb* **1** : to be of use : BENEFIT **2** : to derive benefit : GAIN — **prof·it·able** \'prä-fə-tə-bəl\ *adj* — **prof·it·ably** \-blē\ *adv*

prof·i·teer \₁prä-fə-'tir\ *n* : one who makes what is considered an unreasonable profit — **profiteer** *vb*

prof·li·gate \'prä-fli-gət, -flə-₁gāt\ *adj* **1** : completely given up to dissipation and licentiousness **2** : wildly ex-

travagant — **prof·li·ga·cy** \-gə-sē\ *n* — **profligate** *n* — **prof·li·gate·ly** *adv*

pro for·ma \(₁)prō-'fòr-mə\ *adj* : done or existing as a matter of form

pro·found \prə-'faùnd, prō-\ *adj* **1** : marked by intellectual depth or insight ⟨a ∼ thought⟩ **2** : coming from or reaching to a depth ⟨a ∼ sigh⟩ **3** : deeply felt : INTENSE ⟨∼ sympathy⟩ — **pro·found·ly** *adv* — **pro·fun·di·ty** \-'fən-də-tē\ *n*

pro·fuse \prə-'fyüs, prō-\ *adj* : pouring forth liberally : ABUNDANT **syn** lavish, prodigal, luxuriant, exuberant — **pro·fuse·ly** *adv* — **pro·fu·sion** \-'fyü-zhən\ *n*

prog *abbr* program

pro·gen·i·tor \prō-'je-nə-tər\ *n* **1** : a direct ancestor : FOREFATHER **2** : ORIGINATOR, PRECURSOR

prog·e·ny \'prä-jə-nē\ *n, pl* **-nies** : OFFSPRING, CHILDREN, DESCENDANTS

pro·ges·ter·one \prō-'jes-tə-₁rōn\ *n* : a female hormone that causes the uterus to undergo changes so as to provide a suitable environment for a fertilized egg

prog·na·thous \'präg-nə-thəs\ *adj* : having the jaws projecting beyond the upper part of the face

prog·no·sis \präg-'nō-səs\ *n, pl* **-no·ses** \-₁sēz\ **1** : the prospect of recovery from disease **2** : FORECAST

¹prog·nos·tic \präg-'näs-tik\ *n* **1** : PORTENT **2** : PROPHECY

²prognostic *adj* : of, relating to, or serving as ground for prognostication or a prognosis

prog·nos·ti·cate \präg-'näs-tə-₁kāt\ *vb* **-cat·ed; -cat·ing** : to foretell from signs or symptoms — **prog·nos·ti·ca·tion** \-₁näs-tə-'kā-shən\ *n* — **prog·nos·ti·ca·tor** \-'näs-tə-₁kā-tər\ *n*

¹pro·gram \'prō-₁gram, -grəm\ *n* **1** : a brief outline of the order to be pursued or the subjects included (as in a public entertainment); *also* : PERFORMANCE **2** : a plan of procedure **3** : coded instructions for a computer — **pro·gram·mat·ic** \₁prō-grə-'ma-tik\ *adj*

²program *also* **programme** *vb* **-grammed** *or* **-gramed; -gram·ming** *or* **-gram·ing** **1** : to enter in a program **2** : to provide (as a computer) with a program — **pro·gram·ma·bil·i·ty** \(₁)prō-₁gra-mə-'bi-lə-tē\ *n* — **pro·gram·ma·ble** \'prō-₁gra-mə-bəl\ *adj* — **pro·gram·mer** *also* **pro·gram·er** \'prō-₁gra-mər, -grə-\ *n*

programme *chiefly Brit var of* PROGRAM

programmed instruction *n* : instruction through information given in small steps with each requiring a correct response by the learner before going on to the next step

pro·gram·ming *or* **pro·gram·ing** *n* **1** : the process of instructing or learning by means of an instruction program **2** : the process of preparing an instruction program

¹prog·ress \'prä-grəs, -₁gres\ *n* **1** : a forward movement : ADVANCE **2** : a gradual betterment

²pro·gress \prə-'gres\ *vb* **1** : to move forward : PROCEED **2** : to develop to a more advanced stage : IMPROVE

pro·gres·sion \prə-'gre-shən\ *n* **1** : an act of progressing : ADVANCE **2** : a continuous and connected series

¹pro·gres·sive \prə-'gre-siv\ *adj* **1** : of, relating to, or characterized by progress ⟨a ∼ city⟩ **2** : moving forward or onward : ADVANCING **3** : increasing in extent or severity ⟨a ∼ disease⟩ **4** *often cap* : of or relating to political Progressives **5** : of, relating to, or constituting a verb form that expresses action in progress at the time of speaking or a time spoken of — **pro·gres·sive·ly** *adv*

²progressive *n* **1** : one that is progressive **2** : a person believing in moderate political change and social improvement by government action; *esp, cap* : a member of a Progressive Party in the U.S.

pro·hib·it \prō-'hi-bət\ *vb* **1** : to forbid by authority **2** : to prevent from doing something

pro·hi·bi·tion \₁prō-ə-'bi-shən\ *n* **1** : the act of prohibiting **2** : the forbidding by law of the sale or manufacture of alcoholic beverages — **pro·hi·bi·tion·ist** \-'bi-shə-nist\ *n* — **pro·hib·i·tive** \prō-ʰhi-bə-tiv\ *adj* — **pro·hib·i·tive·ly** *adv* — **pro·hib·i·to·ry** \-ʰhi-bə-ˌtōr-ē\ *adj*

[1]**proj·ect** \ʰprä-ˌjekt, -ˌjikt\ *n* **1** : a specific plan or design : SCHEME **2** : a planned undertaking ⟨a research ∼⟩

[2]**pro·ject** \prə-ʰjekt\ *vb* **1** : to devise in the mind : DESIGN **2** : to throw forward **3** : PROTRUDE **4** : to cause (light or shadow) to fall into space or (an image) to fall on a surface ⟨∼ a beam of light⟩ **5** : to attribute (a thought, feeling, or personal characteristic) to a person, group, or object — **pro·jec·tion** \-ʰjek-shən\ *n*

pro·jec·tile \prə-ʰjekt-ᵊl, -ʰjek-tīl\ *n* **1** : a body hurled or projected by external force; *esp* : a missile for a firearm **2** : a self-propelling weapon

pro·jec·tion·ist \prə-ʰjek-shə-nist\ *n* : one that operates a motion-picture projector or television equipment

pro·jec·tor \-ʰjek-tər\ *n* : one that projects; *esp* : a device for projecting pictures on a screen

pro·le·gom·e·non \ˌprō-li-ʰgä-mə-ˌnän, -nən\ *n, pl* **-e·na** \-nə\ : prefatory remarks

pro·le·tar·i·an \ˌprō-lə-ʰter-ē-ən\ *n* : a member of the proletariat — **proletarian** *adj*

pro·le·tar·i·at \-ē-ət\ *n* : the laboring class; *esp* : industrial workers who sell their labor to live

pro–life \(ˌ)prō-ʰlīf\ *n* : ANTIABORTION

pro·lif·er·ate \prə-ʰli-fə-ˌrāt\ *vb* **-at·ed; -at·ing** : to grow or increase by rapid production of new units (as cells or offspring) — **pro·lif·er·a·tion** \-ˌli-fə-ʰrā-shən\ *n*

pro·lif·ic \prə-ʰli-fik\ *adj* **1** : producing young or fruit abundantly **2** : marked by abundant inventiveness or productivity ⟨a ∼ writer⟩ — **pro·lif·i·cal·ly** \-fik(ə-)lē\ *adv*

pro·lix \prō-ʰliks, ʰprō-ˌliks\ *adj* : VERBOSE **syn** wordy, diffuse, redundant — **pro·lix·i·ty** \prō-ʰlik-sə-tē\ *n*

pro·logue *also* **pro·log** \ʰprō-ˌlȯg, -ˌläg\ *n* : PREFACE ⟨∼ of a play⟩

pro·long \prə-ʰlȯŋ\ *vb* **1** : to lengthen in time : CONTINUE ⟨∼ a meeting⟩ **2** : to lengthen in extent or range **syn** protract, extend, elongate, stretch — **pro·lon·ga·tion** \ˌprō-ˌlȯŋ-ʰgā-shən\ *n*

prom \ʰpräm\ *n* : a formal dance given by a high school or college class

[1]**prom·e·nade** \ˌprä-mə-ʰnäd, -ʰnäd\ *vb* **-nad·ed; -nad·ing** **1** : to take a promenade **2** : to walk about in or on

[2]**promenade** *n* [F, fr. *promener* to take for a walk, fr. L *prominare* to drive forward] **1** : a place for strolling **2** : a leisurely walk for pleasure or display **3** : an opening grand march at a formal ball

pro·me·thi·um \prə-ʰmē-thē-əm\ *n* : a metallic chemical element obtained from uranium or neodymium — see ELEMENT table

prom·i·nence \ʰprä-mə-nəns\ *n* **1** : something prominent **2** : the quality, state, or fact of being prominent or conspicuous **3** : a mass of cloudlike gas that arises from the sun's chromosphere

prom·i·nent \-nənt\ *adj* **1** : jutting out : PROJECTING **2** : readily noticeable : CONSPICUOUS **3** : DISTINGUISHED, EMINENT **syn** remarkable, outstanding, striking, salient — **prom·i·nent·ly** *adv*

pro·mis·cu·ous \prə-ʰmis-kyə-wəs\ *adj* **1** : consisting of various sorts and kinds : MIXED **2** : not restricted to one class or person **3** : having a number of sexual partners **syn** miscellaneous, assorted, heterogeneous, motley, varied — **pro·mis·cu·i·ty** \ˌprä-mis-ʰkyü-ə-tē, ˌprō-ˌmis-\ *n* — **pro·mis·cu·ous·ly** *adv* — **pro·mis·cu·ous·ness** *n*

[1]**prom·ise** \ʰprä-məs\ *n* **1** : a pledge to do or not to do something specified **2** : ground for expectation of success or improvement **3** : something promised

[2]**promise** *vb* **prom·ised; prom·is·ing** **1** : to engage to do, bring about, or provide ⟨∼ help⟩ **2** : to suggest beforehand ⟨dark clouds ∼ rain⟩ **3** : to give ground for expectation ⟨it ∼s to be a good game⟩

prom·is·ing *adj* : likely to succeed or yield good results — **prom·is·ing·ly** *adv*

prom·is·so·ry \ʰprä-mə-ˌsōr-ē\ *adj* : containing a promise

prom·on·to·ry \ʰprä-mən-ˌtōr-ē\ *n, pl* **-ries** : a point of land jutting into the sea : HEADLAND

pro·mote \prə-ʰmōt\ *vb* **pro·mot·ed; pro·mot·ing** **1** : to advance in station, rank, or honor **2** : to contribute to the growth or prosperity of : FURTHER **3** : LAUNCH — **pro·mo·tion** \-ʰmō-shən\ *n* — **pro·mo·tion·al** \-shə-nəl\ *adj*

pro·mot·er \-ʰmō-tər\ *n* : one that promotes; *esp* : one that assumes the financial responsibilities of a sports event

[1]**prompt** \ʰprämpt\ *vb* **1** : INCITE **2** : to assist (one acting or reciting) by suggesting the next words **3** : INSPIRE, URGE — **prompt·er** *n*

[2]**prompt** *adj* **1** : being ready and quick to act; *also* : PUNCTUAL **2** : performed readily or immediately ⟨∼ service⟩ — **prompt·ly** *adv* — **prompt·ness** *n*

prompt·book \-ˌbŭk\ *n* : a copy of a play with directions for performance used by a theater prompter

promp·ti·tude \ʰprämp-tə-ˌtüd, -ˌtyüd\ *n* : the quality or habit of being prompt : PROMPTNESS

pro·mul·gate \ʰprä-məl-ˌgāt; prō-ʰməl-\ *vb* **-gat·ed; -gat·ing** : to make known or put into force by open declaration — **prom·ul·ga·tion** \ˌprä-məl-ʰgā-shən, ˌprō-(ˌ)məl-\ *n*

pron *abbr* **1** pronoun **2** pronounced **3** pronunciation

prone \ʰprōn\ *adj* **1** : having a tendency or inclination : DISPOSED **2** : lying face downward; *also* : lying flat or prostrate **syn** subject, exposed, open, liable, susceptible — **prone·ness** *n*

prong \ʰprȯŋ\ *n* : one of the sharp points of a fork : TINE; *also* : a slender projecting part (as of an antler) — **pronged** \ʰprȯŋd\ *adj*

prong·horn \ʰprȯŋ-ˌhȯrn\ *n, pl* **pronghorn** *also* **prong·horns** : a ruminant mammal of treeless parts of western No. America that resembles an antelope

pronghorn

pro·noun \ʰprō-ˌnaủn\ *n* : a word used as a substitute for a noun

pro·nounce \prə-ʰnaủns\ *vb* **pro·nounced; pro·nounc·ing** **1** : to utter officially or as an opinion ⟨∼ sentence⟩ **2** : to employ the organs of speech in order to produce ⟨∼ a word⟩; *esp* : to say or speak correctly ⟨she can't ∼ his name⟩ — **pro·nounce·able** *adj* — **pro·nun·ci·a·tion** \-ˌnən-sē-ʰā-shən\ *n*

pro·nounced *adj* : strongly marked : DECIDED

\ə\abut \ᵊ\kitten \ər\further \a\ash \ā\ace \ä\mop, mar
\aủ\out \ch\chin \e\bet \ē\easy \g\go \i\hit \ī\ice \j\job
\ŋ\sing \ō\go \ȯ\law \ȯi\boy \th\thin \th\the \ü\loot \ủ\foot
\y\yet \zh\vision *see also* Pronunciation Symbols page

pro·nounce·ment \prə-'naùns-mənt\ n : a formal declaration of opinion; *also* : ANNOUNCEMENT

pron·to \'prän-ˌtō\ *adv* [Sp, fr. L *promptus* prompt] : QUICKLY

pro·nu·clear \'prō-'nü-klē-ər, -'nyü-\ *adj* : supporting the use of nuclear-powered electric generating stations

pro·nun·ci·a·men·to \prō-ˌnən-sē-ə-'men-tō\ n, pl **-tos** or **-toes** : PROCLAMATION, MANIFESTO

¹proof \'prüf\ n 1 : the evidence that compels acceptance by the mind of a truth or fact 2 : a process or operation that establishes validity or truth : TEST 3 : a trial impression (as from type) 4 : a trial print from a photographic negative 5 : alcoholic content (as of a beverage) indicated by a number that is twice the percent by volume of alcohol present ⟨whiskey of 90 ∼ is 45% alcohol⟩

²proof *adj* 1 : successful in resisting or repelling ⟨∼ against tampering⟩ ⟨water*proof*⟩ 2 : of standard strength or quality or alcoholic content

proof·read \-ˌrēd\ vb : to read and mark corrections in — **proof·read·er** n

¹prop \'präp\ n : something that props

²prop vb **propped; prop·ping** 1 : to support by placing something under or against 2 : SUSTAIN, STRENGTHEN

³prop n : PROPERTY 4

⁴prop n : PROPELLER

⁵prop *abbr* 1 property 2 proposition 3 proprietor

pro·pa·gan·da \ˌprä-pə-'gan-də, ˌprō-\ n [NL, fr. *Congregatio de propaganda fide* Congregation for propagating the faith, organization established by Pope Gregory XV] : the spreading of ideas or information to further or damage a cause; *also* : ideas or allegations spread for such a purpose — **pro·pa·gan·dist** \-dist\ n

pro·pa·gan·dize \-ˌdīz\ vb **-dized; -diz·ing** : to subject to or carry on propaganda

prop·a·gate \'prä-pə-ˌgāt\ vb **-gat·ed; -gat·ing** 1 : to reproduce or cause to reproduce biologically : MULTIPLY 2 : to cause to spread — **prop·a·ga·tion** \ˌprä-pə-'gā-shən\ n

pro·pane \'prō-ˌpān\ n : a heavy flammable gas found in petroleum and natural gas and used esp. as a fuel

pro·pel \prə-'pel\ vb **pro·pelled; pro·pel·ling** : to drive forward or onward **syn** push, shove, thrust

pro·pel·lant *also* **pro·pel·lent** \-'pe-lənt\ n : something (as a fuel) that propels — **propellant** *or* **propellent** *adj*

pro·pel·ler \prə-'pe-lər\ n : a device consisting of a hub fitted with blades that is used to propel a vehicle (as a motorboat or an airplane)

pro·pen·si·ty \prə-'pen-sə-tē\ n, pl **-ties** : an often intense natural inclination or preference

¹prop·er \'prä-pər\ *adj* 1 : referring to one individual only ⟨∼ noun⟩ 2 : belonging characteristically to a species or individual : PECULIAR 3 : very satisfactory : EXCELLENT 4 : strictly limited to a specified thing ⟨the city ∼⟩ 5 : CORRECT ⟨the ∼ way to proceed⟩ 6 : strictly decorous : GENTEEL 7 : marked by suitability or rightness ⟨∼ punishment⟩ **syn** meet, appropriate, fitting, seemly — **prop·er·ly** *adv*

²proper n : the parts of the Mass that vary according to the liturgical calendar

prop·er·tied \'prä-pər-tēd\ *adj* : owning property and esp. much property

prop·er·ty \'prä-pər-tē\ n, pl **-ties** 1 : a quality peculiar to an individual or thing 2 : something owned; *esp* : a piece of real estate 3 : OWNERSHIP 4 : an article or object used in a play or motion picture other than painted scenery and actor's costumes

proph·e·cy *also* **proph·e·sy** \'prä-fə-sē\ n, pl **-cies** *also*

PROOFREADERS' MARKS

ℰ or ૪ or ૭	delete; take it out	ℓc	set in lowercase ⟨lowercase⟩
ℭ	close up; print as one word	*ital*	set in italic ⟨*italic*⟩
ℬ̃	delete and close up	*rom*	set in roman ⟨roman⟩
∧ or > or ⅄	caret; insert here ⟨something⟩	*bf*	set in boldface ⟨**boldface**⟩
#	insert a space	= or -/ or ≗ or /H/	hyphen
eg#	space evenly where indicated	⅟ₙ or *en* or /N/	en dash ⟨1965–72⟩
stet	let marked text stand as set	⅟ₘ or *em* or /M/	em — or long — dash
tr	transpose; change order the	∨	superscript or superior ⟨²as in πr²⟩
/	used to separate two or more marks and often as a concluding stroke at the end of an insertion	∧	subscript or inferior ⟨₂as in H₂O⟩
⌊	set farther to the left	↕ or ⅄	centered ⟨⊙for a centered dot in p · q⟩
⌋	set farther to the right	⋌	comma
⌒	set æ or fl as ligatures æ or fl	⋎	apostrophe
⸗	straighten alignment	⊙	period
‖	straighten or align	; or ;/	semicolon
✗	imperfect or broken character	: or ⊙	colon
⊓	indent or insert em quad space	⸌⸍ or ⋎⋎	quotation marks
¶	begin a new paragraph	(/)	parentheses
⒮ⓟ	spell out ⟨set 5 lbs. as five pounds⟩	⌊/⌋	brackets
cap	set in capitals ⟨CAPITALS⟩	*ok/?*	query to author: has this been set as intended?
sm cap or *s.c.*	set in small capitals ⟨SMALL CAPITALS⟩	*wf*	wrong font; a character of the wrong size or esp. style

-sies 1 : an inspired utterance of a prophet **2** : PREDIC-
TION
proph·e·sy \-ˌsī\ *vb* **-sied; -sy·ing 1** : to speak or utter by
divine inspiration **2** : PREDICT — **proph·e·si·er** *n*
proph·et \ˈprä-fət\ *n* [ME *prophete*, fr. OF, fr. L *prophe-
ta*, fr. Gk *prophētēs*, fr. *pro* for + *phanai* to speak] **1**
: one who utters divinely inspired revelations **2** : one
who foretells future events
proph·et·ess \ˈprä-fə-təs\ *n* : a woman who is a prophet
pro·phet·ic \prə-ˈfe-tik\ *or* **pro·phet·i·cal** \-ti-kəl\ *adj*
: of, relating to, or characteristic of a prophet or prophecy — **pro·phet·i·cal·ly** \-ti-k(ə-)lē\ *adv*
Proph·ets \ˈprä-fəts\ *n pl* — see BIBLE table
¹**pro·phy·lac·tic** \ˌprō-fə-ˈlak-tik, ˌprä-\ *adj* **1** : preventing
or guarding from disease **2** : PREVENTIVE
²**prophylactic** *n* : something prophylactic; *esp* : a device
(as a condom) for preventing venereal infection or conception
pro·phy·lax·is \-ˈlak-səs\ *n*, *pl* **-lax·es** \-ˈlak-ˌsēz\
: measures designed to preserve health and prevent the
spread of disease
pro·pin·qui·ty \prə-ˈpiŋ-kwə-tē\ *n* **1** : KINSHIP **2** : nearness in place or time : PROXIMITY
pro·pi·ti·ate \prō-ˈpi-shē-ˌāt\ *vb* **-at·ed; -at·ing** : to gain
or regain the favor of : APPEASE — **pro·pi·ti·a·tion** \-ˌpi-
shē-ˈā-shən\ *n* — **pro·pi·tia·to·ry** \-ˈpi-shē-ə-ˌtōr-ē\ *adj*
pro·pi·tious \prə-ˈpi-shəs\ *adj* **1** : favorably disposed ⟨∼
deities⟩ **2** : being of good omen ⟨∼ circumstances⟩
prop·man \ˈpräp-ˌman\ *n* : one who is in charge of stage
properties
pro·po·nent \prə-ˈpō-nənt\ *n* : one who argues in favor
of something
¹**pro·por·tion** \prə-ˈpōr-shən\ *n* **1** : BALANCE, SYMMETRY
2 : SHARE, QUOTA **3** : the relation of one part to another
or to the whole with respect to magnitude, quantity, or
degree : RATIO **4** : SIZE, DEGREE — **in proportion** : PRO-
PORTIONAL
²**proportion** *vb* **-tioned; -tion·ing 1** : to adjust (a part or
thing) in size relative to other parts or things **2** : to
make the parts of harmonious
pro·por·tion·al \prə-ˈpōr-shə-nəl\ *adj* : corresponding in
size, degree, or intensity; *also* : having the same or a
constant ratio — **pro·por·tion·al·ly** *adv*
pro·por·tion·ate \prə-ˈpōr-shə-nət\ *adj* : PROPORTIONAL
— **pro·por·tion·ate·ly** *adv*
¹**pro·pose** \prə-ˈpōz\ *vb* **pro·posed; pro·pos·ing 1** : PLAN,
INTEND ⟨∼s to buy a house⟩ **2** : to make an offer of marriage **3** : to offer for consideration : SUGGEST ⟨∼ a pol-
icy⟩ — **pro·pos·al** \-ˈpō-zəl\ *n* — **pro·pos·er** *n*
¹**prop·o·si·tion** \ˌprä-pə-ˈzi-shən\ *n* **1** : something proposed for consideration : PROPOSAL **2** : a request for
sexual intercourse **3** : a statement of something to be
discussed, proved, or explained **4** : SITUATION, AFFAIR
⟨a tough ∼⟩ — **prop·o·si·tion·al** \-ˈzi-shə-nəl\ *adj*
²**proposition** *vb* **-tioned; -tion·ing** : to make a proposal
to; *esp* : to suggest sexual intercourse to
pro·pound \prə-ˈpaùnd\ *vb* : to set forth for consideration ⟨∼ a doctrine⟩
pro·pri·e·tary \prə-ˈprī-ə-ˌter-ē\ *adj* **1** : of, relating to,
or characteristic of a proprietor ⟨∼ rights⟩ **2** : made and
sold by one with the sole right to do so ⟨∼ medicines⟩
pro·pri·e·tor \prə-ˈprī-ə-tər\ *n* : OWNER — **pro·pri·
e·tor·ship** *n*
pro·pri·e·tress \-ˈprī-ə-trəs\ *n* : a woman who is a proprietor
pro·pri·e·ty \prə-ˈprī-ə-tē\ *n*, *pl* **-ties 1** : the standard of
what is socially acceptable in conduct or speech **2** *pl*
: the customs of polite society
pro·pul·sion \prə-ˈpəl-shən\ *n* **1** : the action or process
of propelling **2** : something that propels — **pro·pul·
sive** \-siv\ *adj*
pro ra·ta \(ˌ)prō-ˈrä-tə, -ˈrä-\ *adv* : in proportion to the
share of each : PROPORTIONATELY

pro·rate \(ˌ)prō-ˈrāt\ *vb* **pro·rat·ed; pro·rat·ing** : to di-
vide, distribute, or assess proportionately
pro·rogue \prə-ˈrōg\ *vb* **pro·rogued; pro·rogu·ing** : to
suspend or end a session of (a legislative body) — **pro·
ro·ga·tion** \ˌprō-rō-ˈgā-shən\ *n*
pros *pl of* PRO
pro·sa·ic \prō-ˈzā-ik\ *adj* : lacking imagination or excitement : DULL
pro·sce·ni·um \prō-ˈsē-nē-əm\ *n* **1** : the part of a stage
in front of the curtain **2** : the wall containing the arch
that frames the stage
pro·scribe \prō-ˈskrīb\ *vb* **pro·scribed; pro·scrib·ing 1**
: OUTLAW **2** : to condemn or forbid as harmful — **pro·
scrip·tion** \-ˈskrip-shən\ *n*
prose \ˈprōz\ *n* [ME, fr. MF, fr. L *prosa*, fr. fem. of *pror-
sus, prosus*, straightforward, being in prose, alter. of
proversus, pp. of *provertere* to turn forward] : the ordinary language people use in speaking or writing
pros·e·cute \ˈprä-si-ˌkyüt\ *vb* **-cut·ed; -cut·ing 1** : to follow to the end ⟨∼ an investigation⟩ **2** : to seek legal punishment of ⟨∼ a forger⟩ — **pros·e·cu·tion** \ˌprä-si-ˈkyü-
shən\ *n* — **pros·e·cu·tor** \ˈprä-si-ˌkyü-tər\ *n*
¹**pros·e·lyte** \ˈprä-sə-ˌlīt\ *n* : a new convert to a religion,
belief, or party — **pros·e·ly·tism** \-ˌlī-ˌti-zəm\ *n*
²**proselyte** *vb* **-lyt·ed; -lyt·ing** : PROSELYTIZE
pros·e·ly·tize \ˈprä-sə-lə-ˌtīz\ *vb* **-tized; -tiz·ing 1** : to induce someone to convert to one's faith **2** : to recruit
someone to join one's party, institution, or cause
pros·o·dy \ˈprä-sə-dē, -zə-\ *n*, *pl* **-dies** : the study of ver-
sification and esp. of metrical structure
¹**pros·pect** \ˈprä-ˌspekt\ *n* **1** : an extensive view; *also*
: OUTLOOK **2** : the act of looking forward **3** : a mental
vision of something to come **4** : something that is await-
ed or expected : POSSIBILITY **5** : a potential buyer or
customer; *also* : a likely candidate — **pro·spec·tive**
\prə-ˈspek-tiv, ˈprä-ˌspek-\ *adj* — **pro·spec·tive·ly** *adv*
²**pros·pect** \ˈprä-ˌspekt\ *vb* : to explore esp. for mineral
deposits — **pros·pec·tor** \-ˌspek-tər, prä-ˈspek-\ *n*
pro·spec·tus \prə-ˈspek-təs\ *n* : a preliminary statement
that describes an enterprise and is distributed to prospective buyers or participants
pros·per \ˈpräs-pər\ *vb* **pros·pered; pros·per·ing** : SUC-
CEED; *esp* : to achieve economic success
pros·per·i·ty \präs-ˈper-ə-tē\ *n* : thriving condition
: SUCCESS; *esp* : economic well-being
pros·per·ous \ˈpräs-pə-rəs\ *adj* **1** : FAVORABLE ⟨∼
winds⟩ **2** : marked by success or economic well-
being ⟨a ∼ business⟩
pros·tate \ˈpräs-ˌtāt\ *n* : PROSTATE GLAND — **pros·tat-
ic** \prä-ˈsta-tik\ *adj*
prostate gland *n* : a glandular body about the base of the
male urethra that produces a secretion which is a major
part of the fluid ejaculated during an orgasm
pros·ta·ti·tis \ˌpräs-tə-ˈtī-təs\ *n* : inflammation of the
prostate gland
pros·the·sis \präs-ˈthē-səs, ˈpräs-thə-\ *n*, *pl* **-the·ses**
\-ˌsēz\ : an artificial replacement for a missing body
part — **pros·thet·ic** \präs-ˈthe-tik\ *adj*
pros·thet·ics \-ˈthe-tiks\ *n pl* : the surgical or dental specialty concerned with the design, construction, and fitting of prostheses
¹**pros·ti·tute** \ˈpräs-tə-ˌtüt, -ˌtyüt\ *vb* **-tut·ed; -tut·ing 1**
: to offer indiscriminately for sexual activity esp. for
money **2** : to devote to corrupt or unworthy purposes
— **pros·ti·tu·tion** \ˌpräs-tə-ˈtü-shən, -ˈtyü-\ *n*
²**prostitute** *n* : one who engages in sexual activities for
money
¹**pros·trate** \ˈprä-ˌsträt\ *adj* **1** : stretched out with face on

\ə\abut \ᵊ\kitten \ər\further \a\ash \ā\ace \ä\mop, mar
\aù\out \ch\chin \e\bet \ē\easy \g\go \i\hit \ī\ice \j\job
\ŋ\sing \ō\go \ò\law \òi\boy \th\thin \t̲h̲\the \ü\loot \ù\foot
\y\yet \zh\vision *see also* Pronunciation Symbols page

the ground in adoration or submission **2** : lying flat **3** : completely overcome ⟨∼ with a cold⟩

²**prostrate** *vb* **pros·trat·ed; pros·trat·ing 1** : to throw or put into a prostrate position **2** : to reduce to a weak or powerless condition — **pros·tra·tion** \prä-ˈstrā-shən\ *n*

prosy \ˈprō-zē\ *adj* **pros·i·er; -est 1** : PROSAIC **2** : TEDIOUS

Prot *abbr* Protestant

prot·ac·tin·i·um \ˌprō-ˌtak-ˈti-nē-əm\ *n* : a metallic radioactive chemical element of relatively short life — see ELEMENT table

pro·tag·o·nist \prō-ˈta-gə-nist\ *n* **1** : the principal character in a drama or story **2** : a leader or supporter of a cause

pro·te·an \ˈprō-tē-ən\ *adj* : able to assume different shapes or roles

pro·tect \prə-ˈtekt\ *vb* : to shield from injury : GUARD

pro·tec·tion \prə-ˈtek-shən\ *n* **1** : the act of protecting : the state of being protected **2** : one that protects ⟨wear a helmet as a ∼⟩ **3** : the supervision or support of one that is smaller and weaker **4** : the freeing of producers from foreign competition in their home market by high duties on foreign competitive goods — **pro·tec·tive** \-ˈtek-tiv\ *adj*

pro·tec·tion·ist \-shə-nist\ *n* : an advocate of government economic protection for domestic producers through restrictions on foreign competitors — **pro·tec·tion·ism** \-shə-ˌni-zəm\ *n*

pro·tec·tor \prə-ˈtek-tər\ *n* **1** : one that protects : GUARDIAN **2** : a device used to prevent injury : GUARD **3** : REGENT 1

pro·tec·tor·ate \-tə-rət\ *n* **1** : government by a protector **2** : the relationship of superior authority assumed by one state over a dependent one; *also* : the dependent political unit in such a relationship

pro·té·gé \ˈprō-tə-ˌzhā\ *n* [F] : one who is protected, trained, or guided by an influential person

pro·tein \ˈprō-ˌtēn\ *n* [F *protéine*, fr. LGk *prōteios* primary, fr. Gk *prōtos* first] : any of numerous complex nitrogen-containing substances that consist of chains of amino acids, are present in all living cells, and are an essential part of the human diet

pro tem \prō-ˈtem\ *adv* : PRO TEMPORE

pro tem·po·re \prō-ˈtem-pə-rē\ *adv* [L] : for the time being

Pro·te·ro·zo·ic \ˌprä-tə-rə-ˈzō-ik, ˌprō-\ *adj* : of, relating to, or being the eon of geologic history between the Archean and the Phanerozoic — **Proterozoic** *n*

¹**pro·test** \ˈprō-ˌtest\ *n* **1** : the act of protesting; *esp* : an organized public demonstration of disapproval **2** : a complaint or objection against an idea, an act, or a course of action

²**pro·test** \prō-ˈtest\ *vb* **1** : to assert positively : make solemn declaration of ⟨∼s his innocence⟩ **2** : to object strongly : make a protest against ⟨∼ a ruling⟩ — **pro·tes·ta·tion** \ˌprä-təs-ˈtā-shən\ *n* — **pro·test·er** *or* **pro·tes·tor** \-tər\ *n*

Prot·es·tant \ˈprä-təs-tənt, *3 also* prə-ˈtes-\ *n* **1** : a member or adherent of one of the Christian churches deriving from the Reformation **2** : a Christian not of a Catholic or Orthodox church **3** *not cap* : one who makes a protest — **Prot·es·tant·ism** \ˈprä-təs-tən-ˌti-zəm\ *n*

pro·tha·la·mi·on \ˌprō-thə-ˈlā-mē-ən\ *or* **pro·tha·la·mi·um** \-mē-əm\ *n, pl* **-mia** \-mē-ə\ : a song in celebration of a marriage

pro·to·col \ˈprō-tə-ˌkȯl\ *n* [MF *prothocole*, fr. ML *protocollum*, fr. LGk *prōtokollon* first sheet of a papyrus roll bearing data of manufacture, fr. Gk *prōtos* first + *kollan* to glue together, fr. *kolla* glue] **1** : an original draft or record **2** : a preliminary memorandum of diplomatic negotiation **3** : a code of diplomatic or military etiquette

pro·ton \ˈprō-ˌtän\ *n* [Gk *prōton*, neut. of *prōtos* first] : a

positively charged atomic particle present in all atomic nuclei — **pro·ton·ic** \-ˈtä-nik\ *adj*

pro·to·plasm \ˈprō-tə-ˌpla-zəm\ *n* : the complex colloidal largely protein substance of living plant and animal cells — **pro·to·plas·mic** \ˌprō-tə-ˈplaz-mik\ *adj*

pro·to·type \ˈprō-tə-ˌtīp\ *n* : an original model : ARCHETYPE

pro·to·zo·an \ˌprō-tə-ˈzō-ən\ *n* : any of a phylum or subkingdom of unicellular lower invertebrate animals that include some pathogenic parasites of humans and domestic animals — **protozoan** *adj*

pro·tract \prō-ˈtrakt\ *vb* : to prolong in time or space **syn** extend, lengthen, elongate, stretch

pro·trac·tor \-ˈtrak-tər\ *n* : an instrument for drawing and measuring angles

pro·trude \prō-ˈtrüd\ *vb* **pro·trud·ed; pro·trud·ing** : to stick out or cause to stick out : jut out — **pro·tru·sion** \-ˈtrü-zhən\ *n*

pro·tu·ber·ance \prō-ˈtü-bə-rəns, -ˈtyü-\ *n* : something that protrudes

pro·tu·ber·ant \-rənt\ *adj* : extending beyond the surrounding surface in a bulge

proud \ˈpraud\ *adj* **1** : having or showing excessive self-esteem : HAUGHTY **2** : highly pleased : EXULTANT **3** : having proper self-respect ⟨too ∼ to beg⟩ **4** : GLORIOUS ⟨a ∼ occasion⟩ **5** : SPIRITED ⟨a ∼ steed⟩ **syn** arrogant, insolent, overbearing, disdainful — **proud·ly** *adv*

prov *abbr* **1** province; provincial **2** provisional

Prov *abbr* Proverbs

prove \ˈprüv\ *vb* **proved; proved** *or* **prov·en** \ˈprü-vən\; **prov·ing 1** : to test by experiment or by a standard **2** : to establish the truth of by argument or evidence **3** : to show to be correct, valid, or genuine **4** : to turn out esp. after trial or test ⟨the car *proved* to be a good choice⟩ — **prov·able** \ˈprü-və-bəl\ *adj*

prov·e·nance \ˈprä-və-nəns\ *n* : ORIGIN, SOURCE

Pro·ven·çal \ˌprō-vän-ˈsäl, ˌprä-vən-\ *n* **1** : a native or inhabitant of Provence **2** : a Romance language spoken in southern France — **Provençal** *adj*

prov·en·der \ˈprä-vən-dər\ *n* **1** : dry food for domestic animals : FEED **2** : FOOD, VICTUALS

prov·e·nience \prə-ˈvē-nyəns\ *n* : ORIGIN, SOURCE

prov·erb \ˈprä-ˌvərb\ *n* : a pithy popular saying : ADAGE

pro·ver·bi·al \prə-ˈvər-bē-əl\ *adj* **1** : of, relating to, or resembling a proverb **2** : commonly spoken of

Proverbs *n* — see BIBLE table

pro·vide \prə-ˈvīd\ *vb* **pro·vid·ed; pro·vid·ing** [ME, fr. L *providēre*, lit., to see ahead, fr. *pro-* forward + *vidēre* to see] **1** : to take measures beforehand ⟨∼ against inflation⟩ **2** : to make a proviso or stipulation **3** : to supply what is needed ⟨∼ for a family⟩ **4** : EQUIP **5** : to supply for use : YIELD — **pro·vid·er** *n*

pro·vid·ed *conj* : on condition that : IF

prov·i·dence \ˈprä-və-dəns\ *n* **1** *often cap* : divine guidance or care **2** *cap* : GOD 1 **3** : the quality or state of being provident

prov·i·dent \-dənt\ *adj* **1** : making provision for the future : PRUDENT **2** : FRUGAL — **prov·i·dent·ly** *adv*

prov·i·den·tial \ˌprä-və-ˈden-chəl\ *adj* **1** : of, relating to, or determined by Providence **2** : OPPORTUNE, LUCKY

pro·vid·ing *conj* : PROVIDED

prov·ince \ˈprä-vəns\ *n* **1** : an administrative district or division of a country **2** *pl* : all of a country except the metropolises **3** : proper business or scope : SPHERE

pro·vin·cial \prə-ˈvin-chəl\ *adj* **1** : of or relating to a province **2** : limited in outlook : NARROW ⟨∼ ideas⟩ — **pro·vin·cial·ism** \-chə-ˌli-zəm\ *n*

proving ground *n* : a place for scientific experimentation or testing

¹**pro·vi·sion** \prə-ˈvi-zhən\ *n* **1** : the act or process of providing; *also* : a measure taken beforehand **2** : a stock of needed supplies; *esp* : a stock of food — usu. used in pl. **3** : PROVISO

²**provision** *vb* : to supply with provisions

pro·vi·sion·al \-'vi-zhə-nəl\ *adj* : provided for a temporary need : CONDITIONAL — **pro·vi·sion·al·ly** *adv*

pro·vi·so \prə-'vī-zō\ *n, pl* **-sos** *or* **-soes** [ME, fr. ML *proviso quod* provided that] : an article or clause that introduces a condition : STIPULATION

prov·o·ca·tion \ˌprä-və-'kā-shən\ *n* **1** : the act of provoking **2** : something that provokes

pro·voc·a·tive \prə-'vä-kə-tiv\ *adj* : serving to provoke or excite

pro·voke \prə-'vōk\ *vb* **pro·voked; pro·vok·ing 1** : to incite to anger : INCENSE **2** : to call forth : EVOKE ⟨a remark that *provoked* laughter⟩ **3** : to stir up on purpose ⟨~ an argument⟩ **syn** irritate, exasperate, aggravate, inflame, rile, pique — **pro·vok·er** *n*

pro·vo·lo·ne \ˌprō-və-'lō-nē\ *n* : a usu. firm pliant often smoked Italian cheese

pro·vost \'prō-ˌvōst, 'prä-vəst\ *n* : a high official : DIGNITARY; *esp* : a high-ranking university administrative officer

pro·vost mar·shal \'prō-ˌvō-'mär-shəl\ *n* : an officer who supervises the military police of a command

prow \'praù\ *n* : the bow of a ship

prow·ess \'praù-əs\ *n* **1** : military valor and skill **2** : extraordinary ability

prowl \'praùl\ *vb* : to roam about stealthily — **prowl** *n* — **prowl·er** *n*

prox·i·mal \'präk-sə-məl\ *adj* **1** : next to or nearest the point of attachment or origin; *esp* : located toward the center of the body **2** : of, relating to, or being the mesial and distal surfaces of a tooth — **prox·i·mal·ly** *adv*

prox·i·mate \'präk-sə-mət\ *adj* **1** : DIRECT ⟨the ~ cause⟩ **2** : very near

prox·im·i·ty \präk-'si-mə-tē\ *n* : NEARNESS

prox·i·mo \'präk-sə-ˌmō\ *adj* [L *proximo mense* in the next month] : of or occurring in the next month after the present

proxy \'präk-sē\ *n, pl* **prox·ies** : the authority or power to act for another; *also* : a document giving such authorization — **proxy** *adj*

prude \'prüd\ *n* : a person who shows or affects extreme modesty — **prud·ery** \'prü-də-rē\ *n* — **prud·ish** *adj* — **prud·ish·ly** *adv*

pru·dent \'prüd-ᵊnt\ *adj* **1** : shrewd in the management of practical affairs **2** : CAUTIOUS, DISCREET **3** : PROVIDENT, FRUGAL **syn** judicious, foresighted, sensible, sane — **pru·dence** \-ᵊns\ *n* — **pru·den·tial** \prü-'den-chəl\ *adj* — **pru·dent·ly** *adv*

¹**prune** \'prün\ *n* : a dried plum

²**prune** *vb* **pruned; prun·ing** : to cut off unwanted parts (as of a tree)

pru·ri·ent \'prur-ē-ənt\ *adj* : LASCIVIOUS; *also* : exciting to lasciviousness — **pru·ri·ence** \-ē-əns\ *n*

¹**pry** \'prī\ *vb* **pried; pry·ing** : to look closely or inquisitively; *esp* : SNOOP

²**pry** *vb* **pried; pry·ing 1** : to raise, move, or pull apart with a pry or lever **2** : to detach or open with difficulty

³**pry** *n* : a tool for prying

Ps *or* **Psa** *abbr* Psalms

PS *abbr* **1** [L *postscriptum*] postscript **2** public school

PSA *abbr* public service announcement

psalm \'säm, 'sälm\ *n, often cap* [ME, fr. OE *psealm*, fr. LL *psalmus*, fr. Gk *psalmos*, lit., twanging of a harp, fr. *psallein* to pluck, play a stringed instrument] : a sacred song or poem; *esp* : one of the hymns collected in the Book of Psalms — **psalm·ist** *n*

psalm·o·dy \'sä-mə-dē, 'säl-\ *n* : the singing of psalms in worship

Psalms *n* — see BIBLE table

Psal·ter \'sȯl-tər\ *n* : the Book of Psalms; *also* : a collection of the Psalms arranged for devotional use

pseud *abbr* pseudonym; pseudonymous

pseu·do \'sü-dō\ *adj* : SPURIOUS, SHAM

pseu·do·nym \'sü-də-ˌnim\ *n* : a fictitious name — **pseu·don·y·mous** \sü-'dä-nə-məs\ *adj*

PSG *abbr* platoon sergeant

¹**psi** \'sī, 'psī\ *n* : the 23d letter of the Greek alphabet — Ψ or ψ

²**psi** *abbr* pounds per square inch

pso·ri·a·sis \sə-'rī-ə-səs\ *n* : a chronic skin disease characterized by red patches covered with white scales

PST *abbr* Pacific standard time

¹**psych** *also* **psyche** \'sīk\ *vb* **psyched; psych·ing 1** : OUTWIT, OUTGUESS; *also* : to analyze beforehand **2** : INTIMIDATE; *also* : to prepare oneself psychologically ⟨get *psyched* up for the game⟩

²**psych** *abbr* psychology

psy·che \'sī-kē\ *n* : SOUL, SELF; *also* : MIND

psy·che·del·ic \ˌsī-kə-'de-lik\ *adj* **1** : of, relating to, or causing abnormal psychic effects ⟨~ drugs⟩ **2** : relating to the taking of psychedelic drugs ⟨~ experience⟩ **3** : imitating, suggestive of, or reproducing the effects of psychedelic drugs ⟨~ art⟩ ⟨~ colors⟩ — **psychedelic** *n* — **psy·che·del·i·cal·ly** \-li-k(ə-)lē\ *adv*

psy·chi·a·try \sə-'kī-ə-trē, sī-\ *n* : a branch of medicine dealing with mental, emotional, and behavioral disorders — **psy·chi·at·ric** \ˌsī-kē-'a-trik\ *adj* — **psy·chi·a·trist** \sə-'kī-ə-trist, sī-\ *n*

¹**psy·chic** \'sī-kik\ *also* **psy·chi·cal** \-ki-kəl\ *adj* **1** : of or relating to the psyche **2** : lying outside the sphere of physical science **3** : sensitive to nonphysical or supernatural forces — **psy·chi·cal·ly** \-k(ə-)lē\ *adv*

²**psychic** *n* : a person apparently sensitive to nonphysical forces; *also* : MEDIUM 6

psy·cho \'sī-kō\ *n, pl* **psychos** : a mentally disturbed person — **psycho** *adj*

psy·cho·ac·tive \ˌsī-kō-'ak-tiv\ *adj* : affecting the mind or behavior

psy·cho·anal·y·sis \ˌsī-kō-ə-'na-lə-səs\ *n* : a method of dealing with psychic disorders by having the patient talk freely about personal experiences and esp. about early childhood and dreams — **psy·cho·an·a·lyst** \-'an-ᵊl-ist\ *n* — **psy·cho·an·a·lyt·ic** \-ˌan-ᵊl-'i-tik\ *adj* — **psy·cho·an·a·lyze** \-'an-ᵊl-ˌīz\ *vb*

psy·cho·dra·ma \ˌsī-kə-'drä-mə, -'dra-\ *n* **1** : an extemporized dramatization designed to afford catharsis for one or more of the participants from whose life the plot is taken **2** : a dramatic event or story with psychological overtones

psy·cho·gen·ic \-'je-nik\ *adj* : originating in the mind or in mental or emotional conflict

psychol *abbr* psychologist; psychology

psy·chol·o·gy \sī-'kä-lə-jē\ *n, pl* **-gies 1** : the science of mind and behavior **2** : the mental and behavioral characteristics of an individual or group — **psy·cho·log·i·cal** \ˌsī-kə-'lä-ji-kəl\ *adj* — **psy·cho·log·i·cal·ly** \-ji-k(ə-)lē\ *adv* — **psy·chol·o·gist** \sī-'kä-lə-jist\ *n*

psy·cho·path \'sī-kō-ˌpath\ *n* : a mentally ill or unstable person; *esp* : one who has not lost contact with reality but who engages in abnormally aggressive and seriously irresponsible behavior with little or no feeling of guilt — **psy·cho·path·ic** \ˌsī-kə-'pa-thik\ *adj*

psy·cho·sex·u·al \ˌsī-kō-'sek-shə-wəl\ *adj* **1** : of or relating to the mental, emotional, and behavioral aspects of sexual development **2** : of or relating to the physiological psychology of sex

psy·cho·sis \sī-'kō-səs\ *n, pl* **-cho·ses** \-ˌsēz\ : a serious mental illness (as schizophrenia) marked by loss of or greatly lessened ability to test whether what one is thinking and feeling about the real world is really true

psy·cho·so·mat·ic \ˌsī-kō-sə-'ma-tik\ *adj* : of, relating

\ə\abut \ᵊ\kitten \ər\further \a\ash \ā\ace \ä\mop, mar
\aù\out \ch\chin \e\bet \ē\easy \g\go \i\hit \ī\ice \j\job
\ŋ\sing \ō\go \ȯ\law \ȯi\boy \th\thin \t͟h\the \ü\loot \ù\foot
\y\yet \zh\vision *see also* Pronunciation Symbols page

to, involving, or concerned with bodily symptoms caused by mental or emotional disturbance

psy·cho·ther·a·py \ˌsī-kō-ˈther-ə-pē\ *n* : treatment of mental or emotional disorder or of related bodily ills by psychological means — **psy·cho·ther·a·pist** \-pist\ *n*

psy·chot·ic \sī-ˈkä-tik\ *adj* : of or relating to psychosis ⟨∼ behavior⟩ — **psychotic** *n*

psy·cho·tro·pic \ˌsī-kə-ˈtrō-pik\ *adj* : acting on the mind ⟨∼ drugs⟩

pt *abbr* 1 part 2 payment 3 pint 4 point 5 port

Pt *symbol* platinum

PT *abbr* 1 Pacific time 2 part-time 3 physical therapy 4 physical training

PTA *abbr* Parent-Teacher Association

ptar·mi·gan \ˈtär-mi-gən\ *n*, *pl* **-gan** *or* **-gans** : any of various grouses of northern regions with completely feathered feet

PT boat \(ˌ)pē-ˈtē-\ *n* [*patrol torpedo*] : a small fast patrol craft usu. armed with torpedoes

pte *abbr*, *Brit* private

ptg *abbr* printing

PTO *abbr* 1 Parent-Teacher Organization 2 please turn over

Pto·le·ma·ic \ˌtä-lə-ˈmā-ik\ *adj* : of or relating to the astronomy of Ptolemy of Alexandria

pto·maine \ˈtō-ˌmān\ *n* : any of various chemical substances formed by bacteria in decaying matter (as meat) and including a few poisonous ones

PTV *abbr* public television

Pu *symbol* plutonium

¹**pub** \ˈpəb\ *n*, *chiefly Brit* 1 : PUBLIC HOUSE 2 2 : TAVERN

²**pub** *abbr* 1 public 2 publication 3 published; publisher; publishing

pu·ber·ty \ˈpyü-bər-tē\ *n* : the condition of being or period of becoming first capable of reproducing sexually — **pu·ber·tal** \-bərt-ᵊl\ *adj*

pu·bes \ˈpyü-bēz\ *n*, *pl* **pubes** 1 : the hair that appears upon the lower middle region of the abdomen at puberty 2 : the pubic region

pu·bes·cence \pyü-ˈbes-ᵊns\ *n* 1 : the quality or state of being pubescent 2 : a pubescent covering or surface

pu·bes·cent \-ᵊnt\ *adj* 1 : arriving at or having reached puberty 2 : covered with fine soft short hairs

pu·bic \ˈpyü-bik\ *adj* : of, relating to, or situated near the pubes or the pubis

pu·bis \ˈpyü-bəs\ *n*, *pl* **pu·bes** \-bēz\ : the ventral and anterior of the three principal bones composing either half of the pelvis

publ *abbr* 1 publication 2 published; publisher

¹**pub·lic** \ˈpə-blik\ *adj* 1 : exposed to general view ⟨the story became ∼⟩ 2 : of, relating to, or affecting the people as a whole ⟨∼ opinion⟩ 3 : CIVIC, GOVERNMENTAL ⟨∼ expenditures⟩ 4 : of, relating to, or serving the community ⟨∼ officials⟩ 5 : not private : SOCIAL ⟨∼ morality⟩ 6 : open to all ⟨∼ library⟩ 7 : well known : PROMINENT ⟨∼ figures⟩ — **pub·lic·ly** *adv*

²**public** *n* 1 : the people as a whole : POPULACE 2 : a group of people having common interests

pub·li·can \ˈpə-bli-kən\ *n* 1 : a Jewish tax collector for the ancient Romans 2 *chiefly Brit* : the licensee of a pub

pub·li·ca·tion \ˌpə-blə-ˈkā-shən\ *n* 1 : the act or process of publishing 2 : a published work

public house *n* 1 : INN 2 *chiefly Brit* : a licensed saloon or bar

pub·li·cist \ˈpə-blə-sist\ *n* : one that publicizes; *esp* : PRESS AGENT

pub·lic·i·ty \(ˌ)pə-ˈbli-sə-tē\ *n* 1 : information with news value issued to gain public attention or support 2 : public attention or acclaim

pub·li·cize \ˈpə-blə-ˌsīz\ *vb* **-cized; -ciz·ing** : to bring to public attention : ADVERTISE

public relations *n sing or pl* : the business of fostering public goodwill toward a person, firm, or institution;

also : the degree of goodwill and understanding achieved

public school *n* 1 : an endowed secondary boarding school in Great Britain offering a classical curriculum and preparation for the universities or public service 2 : a free tax-supported school controlled by a local governmental authority

public–spirited *adj* : motivated by devotion to the general or national welfare

public television *n* : television supported by public funds and private contributions rather than by commercials

public works *n pl* : works (as schools or highways) constructed with public funds for public use

pub·lish \ˈpə-blish\ *vb* 1 : to make generally known : announce publicly 2 : to produce or release literature, information, musical scores or sometimes recordings, or art for sale to the public — **pub·lish·er** *n*

¹**puck** \ˈpək\ *n* : a mischievous sprite — **puck·ish** *adj* — **puck·ish·ly** *adv*

²**puck** *n* : a disk used in ice hockey

¹**puck·er** \ˈpə-kər\ *vb* **puck·ered; puck·er·ing** : to contract into folds or wrinkles

²**pucker** *n* : FOLD, WRINKLE

pud·ding \ˈpu̇-diŋ\ *n* : a soft, spongy, or thick creamy dessert

pud·dle \ˈpəd-ᵊl\ *n* : a very small pool of usu. dirty or muddy water

pu·den·dum \pyü-ˈden-dəm\ *n*, *pl* **-da** \-də\ [NL, fr. L *pudēre* to be ashamed] : the human external genital organs esp. of a woman

pudgy \ˈpə-jē\ *adj* **pudg·i·er; -est** : being short and plump : CHUBBY

pueb·lo \ˈpwe-blō, pü-ˈe-\ *n*, *pl* **-los** [Sp, village, lit., people, fr. L *populus*] 1 : an American Indian village of Arizona or New Mexico that consists of flat-roofed stone or adobe houses joined in groups sometimes several stories high 2 *cap* : a member of a group of American Indian peoples of the southwestern U.S.

pu·er·ile \ˈpyu̇-ə-rəl\ *adj* : CHILDISH, SILLY — **pu·er·il·i·ty** \ˌpyü-ə-ˈri-lə-tē\ *n*

pu·er·per·al \pyü-ˈər-pə-rəl\ *adj* : of, relating to, or occurring during childbirth or the period immediately following ⟨∼ infection⟩ ⟨∼ depression⟩

puerperal fever *n* : an abnormal condition that results from infection of the placental site following childbirth or abortion

Puer·to Ri·can \ˌpȯr-tə-ˈrē-kən, ˌpwer-\ *n* : a native or inhabitant of Puerto Rico — **Puerto Rican** *adj*

¹**puff** \ˈpəf\ *vb* 1 : to blow in short gusts 2 : PANT 3 : to emit small whiffs or clouds 4 : BLUSTER, BRAG 5 : INFLATE, SWELL 6 : to make proud or conceited 7 : to praise extravagantly

²**puff** *n* 1 : a short discharge (as of air or smoke); *also* : a slight explosive sound accompanying it 2 : a light fluffy pastry 3 : a slight swelling 4 : a fluffy mass; *also* : a small pad for applying cosmetic powder 5 : a laudatory notice or review — **puffy** *adj*

puff·ball \ˈpəf-ˌbȯl\ *n* : any of various globe-shaped and often edible fungi

puf·fin \ˈpə-fən\ *n* : any of several seabirds having a short neck and a deep grooved parti-colored bill

¹**pug** \ˈpəg\ *n* 1 : any of a breed of small stocky short-haired dogs with a wrinkled face 2 : a close coil of hair

²**pug** *n* : ¹BOXER

pu·gi·lism \ˈpyü-jə-ˌli-zəm\ *n* : BOXING — **pu·gi·list** \-list\ *n* — **pu·gi·lis·tic** \ˌpyü-jə-ˈlis-tik\ *adj*

pug·na·cious \ˌpəg-ˈnā-shəs\ *adj* : having a quarrelsome or combative nature **syn** belligerent, bellicose, contentious, truculent — **pug·nac·i·ty** \-ˈna-sə-tē\ *n*

puis·sance \ˈpwi-səns, ˈpyü-ə-\ *n* : POWER, STRENGTH — **puis·sant** \-sənt\ *adj*

puke \ˈpyük\ *vb* **puked; puk·ing** : VOMIT — **puke** *n*

puk·ka \ˈpə-kə\ *adj* [Hindi *pakkā* cooked, ripe, solid, fr.

pug

Skt *pakva*] : GENUINE, AUTHENTIC; *also* : FIRST‑CLASS, COMPLETE

pul \'pül\ *n*, *pl* **puls** \'pülz\ *or* **pul** — see *afghani* at MONEY table

pu·la \'pü-lə, 'pyü-\ *n*, *pl* **pula** — see MONEY table

pul·chri·tude \'pəl-krə-ˌtüd, -ˌtyüd\ *n* : BEAUTY — **pul·chri·tu·di·nous** \ˌpəl-krə-'tüd-ᵊn-əs, -'tyüd-\ *adj*

pule \'pyül\ *vb* **puled; pul·ing** : WHINE, WHIMPER

¹pull \'pùl\ *vb* **1** : to exert force so as to draw (something) toward the force; *also* : MOVE ⟨∼ out of a driveway⟩ **2** : PLUCK; *also* : EXTRACT ⟨∼ a tooth⟩ **3** : STRETCH, STRAIN ⟨∼ a tendon⟩ **4** : to draw apart : TEAR **5** : to make (as a proof) by printing **6** : REMOVE **7** : DRAW ⟨∼ a gun⟩ **8** : to carry out esp. with daring ⟨∼ a robbery⟩ **9** : PERPETRATE, COMMIT **10** : ATTRACT **11** : to express strong sympathy — **pull·er** *n*

²pull *n* **1** : the act or an instance of pulling **2** : the effort expended in moving **3** : ADVANTAGE; *esp* : special influence **4** : a device for pulling something or for operating by pulling **5** : a force that attracts or compels **6** : an injury from abnormal straining or stretching ⟨a muscle ∼⟩

pull·back \'pùl-ˌbak\ *n* : an orderly withdrawal of troops

pul·let \'pù-lət\ *n* : a young hen esp. of the domestic chicken when less than a year old

pul·ley \'pù-lē\ *n*, *pl* **pulleys** : a wheel used to transmit power by means of a belt, rope, or chain; *esp* : one with a grooved rim that forms part of a tackle for hoisting or for changing the direction of a force

Pull·man \'pùl-mən\ *n* : a railroad passenger car with comfortable furnishings esp. for night travel

pull off *vb* : to accomplish successfully

pull·out \'pùl-ˌaùt\ *n* : PULLBACK

pull·over \'pùl-ˌō-vər\ *adj* : put on by being pulled over the head ⟨∼ sweater⟩ — **pull·over** *n*

pull–up \'pùl-ˌəp\ *n* : CHIN-UP

pull up *vb* : to bring or come to an often abrupt halt : STOP

pul·mo·nary \'pùl-mə-ˌner-ē, 'pəl-\ *adj* : of, relating to, or carried on by the lungs ⟨the ∼ circulation⟩

pulp \'pəlp\ *n* **1** : the soft juicy or fleshy part of a fruit or vegetable **2** : a soft moist mass **3** : the soft sensitive tissue that fills the central cavity of a tooth **4** : a material (as from wood) used in making paper **5** : a magazine using cheap paper and often dealing with sensational material — **pulpy** *adj*

pul·pit \'pùl-ˌpit\ *n* : a raised platform or high reading desk used in preaching or conducting a worship service

pulp·wood \'pəlp-ˌwùd\ *n* : wood used in making pulp for paper

pul·sar \'pəl-ˌsär\ *n* : a celestial source of pulsating electromagnetic radiation (as radio waves)

pul·sate \'pəl-ˌsāt\ *vb* **pul·sat·ed; pul·sat·ing** : to expand and contract rhythmically : BEAT — **pul·sa·tion** \ˌpəl-'sā-shən\ *n*

pulse \'pəls\ *n* **1** : the regular throbbing in the arteries caused by the contractions of the heart **2** : rhythmical beating, vibrating, or sounding **3** : a brief change in electrical current or voltage — **pulse** *vb*

pul·ver·ize \'pəl-və-ˌrīz\ *vb* **-ized; -iz·ing 1** : to reduce (as by crushing or grinding) or be reduced to very small particles **2** : DEMOLISH

pu·ma \'pü-mə, 'pyü-\ *n*, *pl* **pumas** *also* **puma** : COUGAR

pum·ice \'pə-məs\ *n* : a light porous volcanic glass used esp. for smoothing and polishing

pum·mel \'pə-məl\ *vb* **-meled** *also* **-melled; -mel·ing** *also* **-mel·ling** : POUND, BEAT

¹pump \'pəmp\ *n* : a device for raising, transferring, or compressing fluids esp. by suction or pressure

²pump *vb* **1** : to raise (as water) with a pump **2** : to draw fluid from with a pump; *also* : to fill by means of a pump ⟨∼ up a tire⟩ **3** : to force or propel in the manner of a pump — **pump·er** *n*

³pump *n* : a low shoe that grips the foot chiefly at the toe and heel

pum·per·nick·el \'pəm-pər-ˌni-kəl\ *n* : a dark rye bread

pump·kin \'pəmp-kən, 'pəŋ-kən\ *n* : the large usu. orange fruit of a vine of the gourd family that is widely used as food; *also* : this vine

pun \'pən\ *n* : the humorous use of a word in a way that suggests two or more interpretations — **pun** *vb*

¹punch \'pənch\ *vb* **1** : PROD, POKE; *also* : DRIVE, HERD ⟨∼ing cattle⟩ **2** : to strike with the fist **3** : to emboss, perforate, or make with a punch **4** : to operate, produce, or enter (as data) by or as if by punching — **punch·er** *n*

²punch *n* **1** : a quick blow with or as if with the fist **2** : effective energy or forcefulness

³punch *n* : a tool for piercing, stamping, cutting, or forming

⁴punch *n* [perh. fr. Hindi *pāc* five, fr. Skt *pañca*; fr. the number of ingredients] : a drink usu. composed of wine or alcoholic liquor and nonalcoholic beverages; *also* : a drink composed of nonalcoholic beverages

punched card \'pəncht-\ *n* : a card with holes punched in particular positions to represent data

pun·cheon \'pən-chən\ *n* : a large cask

punch line *n* : the sentence or phrase in a joke that makes the point

punchy \'pən-chē\ *adj* **punch·i·er; -est 1** : having punch : FORCEFUL **2** : DAZED, CONFUSED

punc·til·io \ˌpəŋk-'ti-lē-ˌō\ *n*, *pl* **-i·os 1** : a nice detail of conduct in a ceremony or in observance of a code **2** : careful observance of forms (as in social conduct)

punc·til·i·ous \ˌpəŋk-'ti-lē-əs\ *adj* : marked by precise accordance with codes or conventions **syn** meticulous, scrupulous, careful, punctual

punc·tu·al \'pəŋk-chə-wəl\ *adj* : being on time : PROMPT — **punc·tu·al·i·ty** \ˌpəŋk-chə-'wa-lə-tē\ *n* — **punc·tu·al·ly** *adv*

punc·tu·ate \'pəŋk-chə-ˌwāt\ *vb* **-at·ed; -at·ing 1** : to mark or divide (written matter) with punctuation marks **2** : to break into at intervals **3** : EMPHASIZE

punc·tu·a·tion \ˌpəŋk-chə-'wā-shən\ *n* : the act, practice, or system of inserting standardized marks in written matter to clarify the meaning and separate structural units

¹punc·ture \'pəŋk-chər\ *n* **1** : an act of puncturing **2** : a small hole or wound made by puncturing

²puncture *vb* **punc·tured; punc·tur·ing 1** : to make a hole in : PIERCE **2** : to make useless as if by a puncture

pun·dit \'pən-dət\ *n* **1** : a learned person : TEACHER **2** : AUTHORITY, CRITIC

pun·gent \'pən-jənt\ *adj* **1** : having a sharp incisive qual-

\ə\abut \ᵊ\kitten \ər\further \a\ash \ā\ace \ä\mop, mar \aù\out \ch\chin \e\bet \ē\easy \g\go \i\hit \ī\ice \j\job \ŋ\sing \ō\go \ò\law \òi\boy \th\thin \th\the \ü\loot \ù\foot \y\yet \zh\vision *see also* Pronunciation Symbols page

ity : CAUSTIC ⟨a ∼ editorial⟩ **2** : causing a sharp or irritating sensation; *esp* : ACRID ⟨∼ smell of burning leaves⟩ — **pun·gen·cy** \-jən-sē\ *n* — **pun·gent·ly** *adv*

pun·ish \'pə-nish\ *vb* **1** : to impose a penalty on for a fault or crime ⟨∼ an offender⟩ **2** : to inflict a penalty for ⟨∼ treason with death⟩ **3** : to inflict injury on : HURT **syn** chastise, castigate, chasten, discipline, correct — **pun·ish·able** *adj*

pun·ish·ment *n* **1** : retributive suffering, pain, or loss : PENALTY **2** : rough treatment

pu·ni·tive \'pyü-nə-tiv\ *adj* : inflicting, involving, or aiming at punishment

¹punk \'pəŋk\ *n* **1** : a young inexperienced person **2** : a petty hoodlum

²punk *adj* : very poor : INFERIOR

³punk *n* : dry crumbly wood useful for tinder; *also* : a substance made from fungi for use as tinder

pun·kin \'pəŋ-kən\ *var of* PUMPKIN

pun·ster \'pən-stər\ *n* : one who is given to punning

¹punt \'pənt\ *n* : a long narrow flat-bottomed boat with square ends

²punt *vb* : to propel (as a punt) with a pole

³punt *vb* : to kick a football or soccer ball dropped from the hands before it touches the ground

⁴punt *n* : the act or an instance of punting a ball

pu·ny \'pyü-nē\ *adj* **pu·ni·er; -est** [MF *puisné* younger, lit., born afterward, fr. *puis* afterward (fr. L *post*) + *né* born, fr. L *natus*] : slight in power, size, or importance : WEAK

pup \'pəp\ *n* : a young dog; *also* : one of the young of some other animals

pu·pa \'pyü-pə\ *n, pl* **pu·pae** \-(ˌ)pē\ *or* **pupas** [NL, fr. L *pupa* doll] : a form of some insects (as a bee, moth, or beetle) between the larva and the adult that usu. has a protective covering (as a cocoon) — **pu·pal** \-pəl\ *adj*

¹pu·pil \'pyü-pəl\ *n* **1** : a child or young person in school or in the charge of a tutor **2** : DISCIPLE

²pupil *n* : the dark central opening of the iris of the eye

pup·pet \'pə-pət\ *n* [ME *popet*, fr. MF *poupette*, ultim. fr. L *pupa* doll] **1** : a small figure of a person or animal moved by hand or by strings or wires **2** : DOLL **3** : one whose acts are controlled by an outside force or influence

pup·pe·teer \ˌpə-pə-'tir\ *n* : one who manipulates puppets

pup·py \'pə-pē\ *n, pl* **puppies** : a young domestic dog

pur·blind \'pər-ˌblīnd\ *adj* **1** : partly blind **2** : lacking in insight : OBTUSE

¹pur·chase \'pər-chəs\ *vb* **pur·chased; pur·chas·ing** : to obtain by paying money or its equivalent : BUY — **pur·chas·able** \-chə-sə-bəl\ *adj* — **pur·chas·er** *n*

²purchase *n* **1** : an act or instance of purchasing **2** : something purchased **3** : a secure hold or grasp; *also* : advantageous leverage

pur·dah \'pər-də\ *n* : seclusion of women from public observation among Muslims and some Hindus esp. in India; *also* : a state of seclusion

pure \'pyür\ *adj* **pur·er; pur·est 1** : unmixed with any other matter : free from taint ⟨∼ gold⟩ ⟨∼ water⟩ **2** : SHEER, ABSOLUTE ⟨∼ nonsense⟩ **3** : ABSTRACT, THEORETICAL ⟨∼ mathematics⟩ **4** : free from what vitiates, weakens, or pollutes ⟨speaks a ∼ French⟩ **5** : free from moral fault : INNOCENT **6** : CHASTE, CONTINENT — **pure·ly** *adv*

pure–blood·ed \-ˌblə-dəd\ *or* **pure–blood** \-ˌbləd\ *adj* : FULL-BLOODED — **pure·blood** *n*

pure·bred \-'bred\ *adj* : bred from members of a recognized breed, strain, or kind without crossbreeding over many generations — **pure·bred** \-ˌbred\ *n*

¹pu·ree \pyù-'rā, -'rē\ *n* [F *purée*, fr. MF, fr. fem. of *puré*, pp. of *purer* to purify, strain, fr. L *purare* to purify] : a paste or thick liquid suspension usu. made from

finely ground cooked food; *also* : a thick soup made of pureed vegetables

²puree *vb* **pu·reed; pu·ree·ing** : to make a puree of

pur·ga·tion \ˌpər-'gā-shən\ *n* : the act or result of purging

¹pur·ga·tive \'pər-gə-tiv\ *adj* : purging or tending to purge

²purgative *n* : a strong laxative : CATHARTIC

pur·ga·to·ry \'pər-gə-ˌtōr-ē\ *n, pl* **-ries 1** : an intermediate state after death for expiatory purification **2** : a place or state of temporary punishment — **pur·ga·tor·i·al** \ˌpər-gə-'tōr-ē-əl\ *adj*

¹purge \'pərj\ *vb* **purged; purg·ing 1** : to cleanse or purify esp. from sin **2** : to have or cause strong and usu. repeated emptying of the bowels **3** : to get rid of ⟨the leaders had been *purged*⟩

²purge *n* **1** : something that purges, *esp* : PURGATIVE **2** : an act or result of purging; *esp* : a ridding of persons regarded as treacherous or disloyal

pu·ri·fy \'pyür-ə-ˌfī\ *vb* **-fied; -fy·ing** : to make or become pure — **pu·ri·fi·ca·tion** \ˌpyür-ə-fə-'kā-shən\ *n* — **pu·ri·fi·ca·to·ry** \pyü-'ri-fi-kə-ˌtōr-ē\ *adj* — **pu·ri·fi·er** *n*

Pu·rim \'pür-(ˌ)im\ *n* : a Jewish holiday celebrated in February or March in commemoration of the deliverance of the Jews from the massacre plotted by Haman

pu·rine \'pyür-ˌēn\ *n* : any of a group of bases including several (as adenine or guanine) that are constituents of DNA or RNA

pur·ism \'pyür-ˌi-zəm\ *n* : rigid adherence to or insistence on purity or nicety esp. in use of words — **pur·ist** \-ist\ *n* — **pu·ris·tic** \pyü-'ris-tik\ *adj*

pu·ri·tan \'pyür-ət-ᵊn\ *n* **1** *cap* : a member of a 16th and 17th century Protestant group in England and New England opposing the ceremonies and government of the Church of England **2** : one who practices or preaches a stricter or professedly purer moral code than that which prevails — **pu·ri·tan·i·cal** \ˌpyür-ə-'ta-ni-kəl\ *adj* — **pu·ri·tan·i·cal·ly** *adv*

pu·ri·ty \'pyür-ə-tē\ *n* : the quality or state of being pure

¹purl \'pərl\ *vb* : to knit in purl stitch

²purl *n* : a stitch in knitting

³purl *n* : a gentle murmur or movement (as of purling water)

⁴purl *vb* **1** : EDDY, SWIRL **2** : to make a soft murmuring sound

pur·lieu \'pər-lü, 'pərl-yü\ *n* **1** : an outlying district : SUBURB **2** *pl* : ENVIRONS

pur·loin \(ˌ)pər-'lȯin, 'pər-ˌlȯin\ *vb* : STEAL, FILCH

¹pur·ple \'pər-pəl\ *adj* **pur·pler; pur·plest 1** : of the color purple **2** : highly rhetorical ⟨a ∼ passage⟩ **3** : PROFANE ⟨∼ language⟩ — **pur·plish** *adj*

²purple *n* **1** : a bluish red color **2** : a purple robe emblematic esp. of regal rank or authority

¹pur·port \'pər-ˌpōrt\ *n* : meaning conveyed or implied; *also* : GIST

²pur·port \(ˌ)pər-'pōrt\ *vb* : to convey or profess outwardly as the meaning or intention : CLAIM — **pur·port·ed·ly** \-'pōr-təd-lē\ *adv*

¹pur·pose \'pər-pəs\ *n* **1** : an object or result aimed at : INTENTION **2** : RESOLUTION, DETERMINATION — **pur·pose·ful** \-fəl\ *adj* — **pur·pose·ful·ly** *adv* — **pur·pose·less** *adj* — **pur·pose·ly** *adv*

²purpose *vb* **pur·posed; pur·pos·ing** : to propose as an aim to oneself

purr \'pər\ *n* : a low murmur typical of a contented cat — **purr** *vb*

¹purse \'pərs\ *n* **1** : a receptacle (as a pouch) to carry money and often other small objects in **2** : RESOURCES **3** : a sum of money offered as a prize or present

²purse *vb* **pursed; purs·ing** : PUCKER

purs·er \'pər-sər\ *n* : an official on a ship who keeps accounts and attends to the comfort of passengers

purs·lane \'pər-slən, -ˌslān\ *n* : a fleshy-leaved weedy trailing plant with tiny yellow flowers that is sometimes used in salads

pur·su·ance \pər-'sü-əns\ *n* : the act of carrying out or into effect

pur·su·ant to \-'sü-ənt-\ *prep* : in carrying out : ACCORDING TO

pur·sue \pər-'sü\ *vb* **pur·sued; pur·su·ing 1** : to follow in order to overtake or overcome : CHASE **2** : to seek to accomplish ⟨∼ a goal⟩ **3** : to proceed along ⟨∼ a course⟩ **4** : to engage in ⟨∼ a career⟩ — **pur·su·er** *n*

pur·suit \pər-'süt\ *n* **1** : the act of pursuing **2** : OCCUPATION, BUSINESS

pu·ru·lent \'pyùr-ə-lənt, -yə-\ *adj* : containing or accompanied by pus ⟨a ∼ discharge⟩ — **pu·ru·lence** \-ləns\ *n*

pur·vey \(ˌ)pər-'vā\ *vb* **pur·veyed; pur·vey·ing** : to supply (as provisions) usu. as a business — **pur·vey·ance** \-əns\ *n* — **pur·vey·or** \-ər\ *n*

pur·view \'pər-ˌvyü\ *n* **1** : the range or limit esp. of authority, responsibility, or intention **2** : range of vision, understanding, or cognizance

pus \'pəs\ *n* : thick yellowish white fluid matter (as in a boil) formed at a place of inflammation and infection (as an abscess) and containing germs, blood cells, and tissue debris

¹push \'pùsh\ *vb* [ME *pusshen*, fr. OF *poulser* to beat, push, fr. L *pulsare*, fr. *pellere* to drive, strike] **1** : to press against with force in order to drive or impel **2** : to thrust forward, downward, or outward **3** : to urge on : press forward **4** : to cause to increase ⟨∼ prices to record levels⟩ **5** : to urge or press the advancement, adoption, or practice of; *esp* : to make aggressive efforts to sell **6** : to engage in the illicit sale of narcotics

²push *n* **1** : a vigorous effort : DRIVE **2** : an act of pushing : SHOVE **3** : vigorous enterprise : ENERGY

push–button *adj* **1** : operated or done by means of push buttons **2** : using or dependent on complex and more or less automatic mechanisms ⟨∼ warfare⟩

push button *n* : a small button or knob that when pushed operates something esp. by closing an electric circuit

push·cart \'pùsh-ˌkärt\ *n* : a cart or barrow pushed by hand

push·er \'pù-shər\ *n* : one that pushes; *esp* : one that pushes illegal drugs

push·over \-ˌō-vər\ *n* **1** : an opponent easy to defeat **2** : SUCKER **3** : something easily accomplished

push–up \-ˌəp\ *n* : a conditioning exercise performed in a prone position by raising and lowering the body with the straightening and bending of the arms while keeping the back straight and supporting the body on the hands and toes

pushy \'pù-shē\ *adj* **push·i·er; -est** : aggressive often to an objectionable degree

pu·sil·lan·i·mous \ˌpyü-sə-'la-nə-məs\ *adj* [LL *pusillanimis*, fr. L *pusillus* very small (dim. of *pusus* boy) + *animus* spirit] : contemptibly timid : COWARDLY — **pu·sil·la·nim·i·ty** \ˌpyü-sə-lə-'ni-mə-tē\ *n*

¹puss \'pùs\ *n* : CAT

²puss *n* : FACE

¹pussy \'pù-sē\ *n, pl* **puss·ies** : CAT

²pus·sy \'pə-sē\ *adj* **pus·si·er; -est** : full of or resembling pus

pussy·cat \'pù-sē-ˌkat\ *n* : CAT

pussy·foot \-ˌfùt\ *vb* **1** : to tread or move warily or stealthily **2** : to refrain from committing oneself

pussy willow \'pù-sē-\ *n* : a willow having large silky catkins

pus·tule \'pəs-chül\ *n* : a pus-filled pimple

put \'pùt\ *vb* **put; put·ting 1** : to bring into a specified position : PLACE ⟨∼ the book on the table⟩ **2** : SEND, THRUST **3** : to throw with an upward pushing motion ⟨∼ the shot⟩ **4** : to bring into a specified state ⟨∼ the plan into effect⟩ **5** : SUBJECT ⟨∼ traitors to death⟩ **6** : IMPOSE **7** : to set before one for decision ⟨∼ the question⟩ **8**

: EXPRESS, STATE **9** : TRANSLATE, ADAPT **10** : APPLY, ASSIGN ⟨∼ them to work⟩ **11** : ESTIMATE ⟨∼ the number at 20⟩ **12** : ATTACH, ATTRIBUTE ⟨∼ a high value on it⟩ **13** : to take a specified course ⟨the ship ∼ out to sea⟩

pu·ta·tive \'pyü-tə-tiv\ *adj* **1** : commonly accepted **2** : assumed to exist or to have existed

put–down \'pùt-ˌdaùn\ *n* : a belittling remark

put in *vb* **1** : to come in with : INTERPOSE ⟨*put in* a good word for me⟩ **2** : to spend time at some occupation or job ⟨*put in* eight hours at the office⟩

put off *vb* : POSTPONE, DELAY

¹put–on \'pùt-ˌȯn, -ˌän\ *adj* : PRETENDED, ASSUMED

²put–on *n* **1** : a deliberate act of misleading someone **2** : PARODY, SPOOF

put·out \'pùt-ˌaùt\ *n* : the retiring of a base runner or batter in baseball

put out *vb* **1** : EXTINGUISH **2** : ANNOY; *also* : INCONVENIENCE **3** : to cause to be out (as in baseball)

pu·tre·fy \'pyü-trə-ˌfī\ *vb* **-fied; -fy·ing** : to make or become putrid : ROT — **pu·tre·fac·tion** \ˌpyü-trə-'fak-shən\ *n* — **pu·tre·fac·tive** \-tiv\ *adj*

pu·tres·cent \pyü-'tres-ᵊnt\ *adj* : becoming putrid : ROTTING — **pu·tres·cence** \-ᵊns\ *n*

pu·trid \'pyü-trəd\ *adj* **1** : ROTTEN, DECAYED **2** : VILE, CORRUPT — **pu·trid·i·ty** \pyü-'tri-də-tē\ *n*

putsch \'pùch\ *n* [G] : a secretly plotted and suddenly executed attempt to overthrow a government

putt \'pət\ *n* : a golf stroke made on the green to cause the ball to roll into the hole — **putt** *vb*

put·tee \ˌpə-'tē, 'pə-tē\ *n* [Hindi *paṭṭī* strip of cloth] **1** : a cloth strip wrapped around the lower leg **2** : a leather legging

¹put·ter \'pù-tər\ *n* : one that puts

²putt·er \'pə-tər\ *n* **1** : a golf club used in putting **2** : one that putts

³put·ter \'pə-tər\ *vb* **1** : to move or act aimlessly or idly **2** : TINKER

put·ty \'pə-tē\ *n, pl* **putties** [F *potée* potter's glaze, lit., potful, fr. OF, fr. *pot* pot] **1** : a doughlike cement used esp. to fasten glass in sashes **2** : one who is easily manipulated — **putty** *vb*

put up *vb* **1** : SHEATHE **2** : to prepare so as to preserve for later use **3** : to offer for public sale ⟨*put* the house *up* for auction⟩ **4** : ACCOMMODATE, LODGE **5** : BUILD **6** : to engage in ⟨*put up* a struggle⟩ **7** : CONTRIBUTE, PAY — **put up with** : TOLERATE **?**

¹puz·zle \'pə-zəl\ *vb* **puz·zled; puz·zling 1** : to bewilder mentally : PERPLEX **2** : to solve with difficulty or ingenuity ⟨∼ out a riddle⟩ **3** : to be in a quandary ⟨∼ over what to do⟩ **4** : to attempt a solution of a puzzle ⟨∼ over a person's words⟩ **syn** mystify, bewilder, nonplus, confound — **puz·zle·ment** *n* — **puz·zler** *n*

²puzzle *n* : something that puzzles **2** : a question, problem, or contrivance designed for testing ingenuity

PVC *abbr* polyvinyl chloride

pvt *abbr* private

PW *abbr* prisoner of war

pwt *abbr* pennyweight

PX *abbr* post exchange

pya \pē-'ä\ *n* — see *kyat* at MONEY table

pyg·my \'pig-mē\ *n, pl* **pygmies** [ME *pigmei*, fr. L *pygmaeus* of a pygmy, dwarfish, fr. Gk *pygmaios*, fr. *pygmē* fist, measure of length] **1** *cap* : any of a small people of equatorial Africa **2** : DWARF — **pygmy** *adj*

py·ja·mas \pə-'jä-məz\ *chiefly Brit var of* PAJAMAS

py·lon \'pī-ˌlän, -lən\ *n* **1** : a usu. massive gateway; *esp* : an Egyptian one flanked by flat-topped pyramids **2** : a

---

\ə\abut \ᵊ\kitten \ər\further \a\ash \ā\ace \ä\mop, mar \aù\out \ch\chin \e\bet \ē\easy \g\go \i\hit \ī\ice \j\job \ŋ\sing \ō\go \ȯ\law \ȯi\boy \th\thin \th\the \ü\loot \ù\foot \y\yet \zh\vision *see also* Pronunciation Symbols page tower that supports wires over a long span **3** : a post or tower marking the course in an airplane race

py·or·rhea \ˌpī-ə-ˈrē-ə\ *n* : an inflammation with pus of the sockets of the teeth

¹pyr·a·mid \ˈpir-ə-ˌmid\ *n* **1** : a massive structure with a square base and four triangular faces meeting at a point **2** : a geometrical solid having a polygon for its base and three or more triangles for its sides that meet at a point to form the top — **py·ra·mi·dal** \pə-ˈra-məd-ᵊl, ˌpir-ə-ˈmid-\ *adj*

²pyramid *vb* **1** : to build up in the form of a pyramid : heap up **2** : to increase rapidly on a broadening base

pyre \ˈpīr\ *n* : a combustible heap for burning a dead body as a funeral rite

py·re·thrum \pī-ˈrē-thrəm\ *n* : an insecticide made from the dried heads of any of several Old World chrysanthemums

py·rim·i·dine \pī-ˈri-mə-ˌdēn\ *n* : any of a group of bases including several (as cytosine, thymine, or uracil) that are constituents of DNA or RNA

py·rite \ˈpī-ˌrīt\ *n* : a mineral containing sulfur and iron that is brass-yellow in color

py·rol·y·sis \pī-ˈrä-lə-səs\ *n* : chemical change caused by the action of heat

py·ro·ma·nia \ˌpī-rō-ˈmā-nē-ə\ *n* : an irresistible impulse to start fires — **py·ro·ma·ni·ac** \-nē-ˌak\ *n*

py·ro·tech·nics \ˌpī-rə-ˈtek-niks\ *n pl* **1** : a display of fireworks **2** : a spectacular display (as of extreme virtuosity) — **py·ro·tech·nic** \-nik\ *also* **py·ro·tech·ni·cal** \-ni-kəl\ *adj*

Pyr·rhic \ˈpir-ik\ *adj* : achieved at excessive cost ⟨a ∼ victory⟩; *also* : costly to the point of outweighing expected benefits

Py·thag·o·re·an theorem \pī-ˌtha-gə-ˈrē-ən-\ *n* : a theorem in geometry: the square of the length of the hypotenuse of a right triangle equals the sum of the squares of the lengths of the other two sides

py·thon \ˈpī-ˌthän, -thən\ *n* [L, monstrous serpent killed by the god Apollo, fr. Gk *Pythōn*] : a large snake (as a boa) that squeezes and suffocates its prey; *esp* : any of the large Old World snakes that include the largest snakes living at the present time

pyx \ˈpiks\ *n* : a small case used to carry the Eucharist to the sick

Q

¹q \ˈkyü\ *n, pl* **q's** *or* **qs** \ˈkyüz\ *often cap* : the 17th letter of the English alphabet

²q *abbr, often cap* **1** quart **2** quarto **3** queen **4** query **5** question

QB *abbr* quarterback

QED *abbr* [L *quod erat demonstrandum*] which was to be demonstrated

qin·tar \kin-ˈtär\ *n, pl* **qin·dar·ka** \kin-ˈdär-kə\ *or* **qin·tar** — see *lek* at MONEY table

qi·vi·ut \ˈkē-vē-ˌüt\ *n* [Inuit] : the wool of the undercoat of the musk ox

Qld *abbr* Queensland

QM *abbr* quartermaster

QMC *abbr* quartermaster corps

QMG *abbr* quartermaster general

qq v *abbr* [L *quae vide*] which (*pl*) see

qr *abbr* quarter

qt *abbr* **1** quantity **2** quart

q.t. \ˌkyü-ˈtē\ *n, often cap Q&T* : QUIET — usu. used in the phrase *on the q.t.*

qto *abbr* quarto

qty *abbr* quantity

qu *or* **ques** *abbr* question

¹quack \ˈkwak\ *vb* : to make the characteristic cry of a duck

²quack *n* : a sound made by quacking

³quack *n* **1** : CHARLATAN **2** : a pretender to medical skill syn faker, impostor, mountebank — **quack** *adj* — **quack·ery** \ˈkwa-kə-rē\ *n* — **quack·ish** *adj*

¹quad \ˈkwäd\ *n* : QUADRANGLE

²quad *n* : QUADRUPLET

³quad *abbr* quadrant

quad·ran·gle \ˈkwä-ˌdraŋ-gəl\ *n* **1** : QUADRILATERAL **2** : a 4-sided courtyard or enclosure — **quad·ran·gu·lar** \kwä-ˈdraŋ-gyə-lər\ *adj*

quad·rant \ˈkwä-drənt\ *n* **1** : one quarter of a circle : an arc of 90° **2** : any of the four quarters into which something is divided by two lines intersecting each other at right angles

qua·drat·ic \kwä-ˈdra-tik\ *adj* : having or being a term in which the variable (as *x*) is squared but containing no term in which the variable is raised to a higher power than a square ⟨a ∼ equation⟩ — **quadratic** *n*

qua·dren·ni·al \kwä-ˈdre-nē-əl\ *adj* **1** : consisting of or lasting for four years **2** : occurring every four years

qua·dren·ni·um \-nē-əm\ *n, pl* **-ni·ums** *or* **-nia** \-nē-ə\ : a period of four years

¹quad·ri·lat·er·al \ˌkwä-drə-ˈla-tə-rəl\ *n* : a polygon of four sides

²quadrilateral *adj* : having four sides

qua·drille \kwä-ˈdril, kə-\ *n* : a square dance made up of five or six figures in various rhythms

quad·ri·par·tite \ˌkwä-drə-ˈpär-ˌtīt\ *adj* **1** : consisting of four parts **2** : shared by four parties or persons

qua·driv·i·um \kwä-ˈdri-vē-əm\ *n* : the four liberal arts of arithmetic, music, geometry, and astronomy in a medieval university

quad·ru·ped \ˈkwä-drə-ˌped\ *n* : an animal having four feet — **qua·dru·pe·dal** \kwä-ˈdrü-pəd-ᵊl, ˌkwä-drə-ˈped-\ *adj*

¹qua·dru·ple \kwä-ˈdrü-pəl, -ˈdrə-; ˈkwä-drə-\ *vb* **qua·dru·pled; qua·dru·pling** : to make or become four times as great or as many

²quadruple *adj* : FOURFOLD

qua·dru·plet \kwä-ˈdrə-plət, -ˈdrü-; ˈkwä-drə-\ *n* **1** : one of four offspring born at one birth **2** : a group of four of a kind

¹qua·dru·pli·cate \kwä-ˈdrü-pli-kət\ *adj* **1** : repeated four times **2** : FOURTH

²qua·dru·pli·cate \-plə-ˌkāt\ *vb* **-cat·ed; -cat·ing 1** : QUADRUPLE **2** : to prepare in quadruplicate — **qua·dru·pli·ca·tion** \-ˌdrü-plə-ˈkā-shən\ *n*

³qua·dru·pli·cate \-ˈdrü-pli-kət\ *n* **1** : four copies all alike ⟨typed in ∼⟩ **2** : one of four like things

quaff \ˈkwäf, ˈkwaf\ *vb* : to drink deeply or repeatedly — **quaff** *n*

quag·mire \ˈkwag-ˌmīr, ˈkwäg-\ *n* **1** : soft miry land that yields under the foot **2** : PREDICAMENT

qua·hog \ˈkō-ˌhòg, ˈkwò-, ˈkwō-, -ˌhäg\ *n* : a round thick-shelled edible No. American clam

quai \ˈkā\ *n* : QUAY

¹quail \ˈkwāl\ *n, pl* **quail** *or* **quails** [ME *quaille*, fr. MF, fr. ML *quaccula*, of imit. origin] : any of numerous small short-winged plump game birds (as a bobwhite) related to the domestic chicken

²quail *vb* [ME, to grow feeble, fr. MD *quelen*] : to lose heart : COWER **syn** recoil, shrink, flinch, wince, blanch

quaint \'kwānt\ *adj* : unusual or different in character or appearance; *esp* : pleasingly old-fashioned or unfamiliar **syn** odd, queer, curious, strange — **quaint·ly** *adv* — **quaint·ness** *n*

¹quake \'kwāk\ *vb* **quaked; quak·ing 1** : to shake usu. from shock or instability **2** : to tremble usu. from cold or fear

²quake *n* : a shaking or trembling; *esp* : EARTHQUAKE

Quak·er \'kwā-kər\ *n* : FRIEND 5

qual *abbr* quality

qual·i·fi·ca·tion \ˌkwä-lə-fə-'kā-shən\ *n* **1** : LIMITATION, MODIFICATION **2** : a special skill that fits a person for some work or position **3** : REQUIREMENT

qual·i·fied \'kwä-lə-ˌfīd\ *adj* **1** : fitted for a given purpose or job **2** : limited in some way

qual·i·fi·er \'kwä-lə-ˌfī-ər\ *n* **1** : one that satisfies requirements **2** : a word or word group that limits the meaning of another word or word group

qual·i·fy \'kwä-lə-ˌfī\ *vb* **-fied; -fy·ing 1** : to reduce from a general to a particular form : MODIFY **2** : to make less harsh **3** : to limit the meaning of (as a noun) **4** : to fit by skill or training for some purpose **5** : to give or have a legal right to do something **6** : to demonstrate the necessary ability ⟨∼ for the finals⟩ **syn** moderate, temper

qual·i·ta·tive \'kwä-lə-ˌtā-tiv\ *adj* : of, relating to, or involving quality — **qual·i·ta·tive·ly** *adv*

¹qual·i·ty \'kwä-lə-tē\ *n, pl* **-ties 1** : peculiar and essential character : NATURE **2** : degree of excellence **3** : high social status **4** : a distinguishing attribute

²quality *adj* : being of high quality

qualm \'kwäm, 'kwälm\ *n* **1** : a sudden attack (as of nausea) **2** : a sudden feeling of doubt, fear, or uneasiness esp. in not following one's conscience or better judgment

qualm·ish \'kwä-mish, 'kwäl-\ *adj* **1** : feeling qualms : NAUSEATED **2** : overly scrupulous : SQUEAMISH **3** : of, relating to, or producing qualms

quan·da·ry \'kwän-drē\ *n, pl* **-ries** : a state of perplexity or doubt

quan·ti·ta·tive \'kwän-tə-ˌtā-tiv\ *adj* : of, relating to, or involving quantity — **quan·ti·ta·tive·ly** *adv*

quan·ti·ty \'kwän-tə-tē\ *n, pl* **-ties 1** : AMOUNT, NUMBER **2** : a considerable amount

quan·tize \'kwän-ˌtīz\ *vb* **quan·tized; quan·tiz·ing** : to subdivide (as energy) into small units

quan·tum \'kwän-təm\ *n, pl* **quan·ta** \-tə\ [L, neut. of *quantus* how much] **1** : QUANTITY, AMOUNT **2** : an elemental unit of energy

quantum mechanics *n sing or pl* : a theory of matter based on the concept of possession of wave properties by elementary particles — **quantum mechanical** *adj* — **quantum mechanically** *adv*

quantum theory *n* : a theory in physics based on the idea that radiant energy (as light) is composed of small separate packets of energy

quar *abbr* quarterly

quar·an·tine \'kwȯr-ən-ˌtēn\ *n* [modif. of It *quarantena*, lit., period of forty days, fr. *quaranta* forty, fr. L *quadraginta*] **1** : a period during which a ship suspected of carrying contagious disease is forbidden contact with the shore **2** : a restraint on the movements of persons or goods to prevent the spread of pests or disease **3** : a place or period of quarantine **4** : a state of enforced isolation — **quarantine** *vb*

quark \'kwȯrk, 'kwärk\ *n* : a hypothetical elementary particle that carries a fractional charge and is held to be a constituent of heavier particles (as protons and neutrons)

¹quar·rel \'kwȯr-əl\ *n* **1** : a ground of dispute **2** : a verbal clash : CONFLICT — **quar·rel·some** \-səm\ *adj*

²quarrel *vb* **-reled** *or* **-relled; -rel·ing** *or* **-rel·ling 1** : to find fault **2** : to dispute angrily : WRANGLE

¹quar·ry \'kwȯr-ē\ *n, pl* **quarries** [ME *querre* entrails of game given to the hounds, fr. MF *cuiree*] **1** : game hunted with hawks **2** : PREY

²quarry *n, pl* **quarries** [ME *quarey*, alter. of *quarrere*, fr. MF *quarriere*, fr. (assumed) OF *quarre* squared stone, fr. L *quadrum* square] : an open excavation usu. for obtaining building stone or limestone — **quarry** *vb*

quart \'kwȯrt\ *n* — see WEIGHT table

¹quar·ter \'kwȯr-tər\ *n* **1** : one of four equal parts **2** : a fourth of a dollar; *also* : a coin of this value **3** : a district of a city **4** *pl* : LODGINGS ⟨moved into new ∼s⟩ **5** : MERCY, CLEMENCY ⟨gave no ∼⟩ **6** : a fourth part of the moon's period

²quarter *vb* **1** : to divide into four equal parts **2** : to provide with shelter

¹quar·ter·back \-ˌbak\ *n* : a football player who calls the signals and directs the offensive play for the team

²quarterback *vb* **1** : to direct the offensive play of a football team **2** : LEAD, BOSS

quar·ter·deck \-ˌdek\ *n* : the stern area of a ship's upper deck

quarter horse *n* : any of a breed of compact muscular saddle horses characterized by great endurance and by high speed for short distances

quarter horse

¹quar·ter·ly \'kwȯr-tər-lē\ *adv* : at 3-month intervals

²quarterly *adj* : occurring, issued, or payable at 3-month intervals

³quarterly *n, pl* **-lies** : a periodical published four times a year

quar·ter·mas·ter \-ˌmas-tər\ *n* **1** : a petty officer who attends to a ship's helm, binnacle, and signals **2** : an army officer who provides clothing and subsistence for troops

quar·ter·staff \-ˌstaf\ *n, pl* **-staves** \-ˌstavz, -ˌstāvz\ : a long stout staff formerly used as a weapon

quar·tet *also* **quar·tette** \kwȯr-'tet\ *n* **1** : a musical composition for four instruments or voices **2** : a group of four and esp. of four musicians

quar·to \'kwȯr-tō\ *n, pl* **quartos 1** : the size of a piece of paper cut four from a sheet **2** : a book printed on quarto pages

quartz \'kwȯrts\ *n* : a common often transparent crystalline mineral that is a form of silica

quartz·ite \'kwȯrt-ˌsīt\ *n* : a compact granular rock composed of quartz and derived from sandstone

qua·sar \'kwā-ˌzär, -ˌsär\ *n* : any of a class of extremely distant starlike celestial objects

¹quash \'kwäsh, 'kwȯsh\ *vb* : to suppress or extinguish summarily and completely : QUELL

²quash *vb* : to set aside by judicial action

\ə\abut \ᵊ\kitten \ər\further \a\ash \ā\ace \ä\mop, mar
\au̇\out \ch\chin \e\bet \ē\easy \g\go \i\hit \ī\ice \j\job
\ŋ\sing \ō\go \ȯ\law \ȯi\boy \th\thin \th̲\the \ü\loot \u̇\foot
\y\yet \zh\vision *see also* Pronunciation Symbols page

qua·si \\'kwä-ˌzī, -ˌsī; 'kwä-zē, -sē\\ *adj* : being in some sense or degree ⟨a ∼ corporation⟩

quasi- *comb form* [L, as if, as it were, approximately, fr. *quam* as + *si* if] : in some sense or degree ⟨*quasi*-historical⟩

Qua·ter·na·ry \\'kwä-tər-ˌner-ē, kwə-'tər-nə-rē\\ *adj* : of, relating to, or being the geologic period from the end of the Tertiary to the present — **Quaternary** *n*

qua·train \\'kwä-ˌtrān\\ *n* : a unit of four lines of verse

qua·tre·foil \\'ka-tər-ˌfȯil, 'ka-trə-\\ *n* : a stylized figure often of a flower with four petals

qua·ver \\'kwä-vər\\ *vb* **1** : TREMBLE, SHAKE **2** : TRILL **3** : to speak in tremulous tones **syn** shudder, quake, twitter, quiver, shiver — **quaver** *n*

quay \\'kē, 'kwā, 'kā\\ *n* : WHARF

Que *abbr* Quebec

quean \\'kwēn\\ *n* : PROSTITUTE

quea·sy \\'kwē-zē\\ *adj* **quea·si·er; -est** : NAUSEATED — **quea·si·ly** \\-zə-lē\\ *adv* — **quea·si·ness** \\-zē-nəs\\ *n*

queen \\'kwēn\\ *n* **1** : the wife or widow of a king **2** : a female monarch **3** : a woman notable for rank, power, or attractiveness **4** : the most powerful piece in the game of chess **5** : a playing card bearing the figure of a queen **6** : a fertile female of a social insect (as a bee or termite) — **queen·ly** *adj*

Queen Anne's lace \\-'anz-\\ *n* : a widely naturalized Eurasian herb from which the cultivated carrot originated

queen consort *n*, *pl* **queens consort** : the wife of a reigning king

queen mother *n* : a dowager queen who is mother of the reigning sovereign

queen-size *adj* : having dimensions of approximately 60 inches by 80 inches ⟨∼ bed⟩; *also* : of a size that fits a queen-size bed

¹queer \\'kwir\\ *adj* **1** : differing from the usual or normal : PECULIAR, STRANGE **2** : COUNTERFEIT **syn** weird, bizarre, eccentric, curious — **queer** *n* — **queer·ly** *adv* — **queer·ness** *n*

²queer *vb* : to spoil the effect of : DISRUPT ⟨∼ed our plans⟩

quell \\'kwel\\ *vb* **1** : to put an end to by force ⟨∼ a riot⟩ **2** : CALM, PACIFY

quench \\'kwench\\ *vb* **1** : PUT OUT, EXTINGUISH **2** : SUBDUE **3** : SLAKE, SATISFY ⟨∼ed his thirst⟩ — **quench·able** *adj* — **quench·er** *n* — **quench·less** *adj*

quer·u·lous \\'kwer-ə-ləs, -yə-\\ *adj* **1** : constantly complaining **2** : FRETFUL, WHINING **syn** petulant, pettish, irritable, peevish, huffy — **quer·u·lous·ly** *adv* — **quer·u·lous·ness** *n*

que·ry \\'kwir-ē, 'kwer-\\ *n*, *pl* **queries** : QUESTION — **query** *vb*

quest \\'kwest\\ *n* : SEARCH — **quest** *vb*

¹ques·tion \\'kwes-chən\\ *n* **1** : an interrogative expression : QUERY **2** : a subject for debate; *also* : a proposition to be voted on **3** : INQUIRY **4** : DISPUTE

²question *vb* **1** : to ask questions **2** : DOUBT, DISPUTE **3** : to subject to analysis : EXAMINE **syn** interrogate, quiz, query — **ques·tion·er** *n*

ques·tion·able \\'kwes-chə-nə-bəl\\ *adj* **1** : not certain or exact : DOUBTFUL **2** : not believed to be true, sound, or moral **syn** dubious, problematical, moot, debatable — **ques·tion·ably** \\-blē\\ *adv*

question mark *n* : a punctuation mark ? used esp. at the end of a sentence to indicate a direct question

ques·tion·naire \\ˌkwes-chə-'nar\\ *n* : a set of questions for obtaining information

quet·zal \\ket-'säl, -'sal\\ *n*, *pl* **quetzals** *or* **quet·za·les** \\-'sä-läs, -'sa-\\ **1** : a Central American bird with brilliant plumage **2** *pl* **quetzales** — see MONEY table

¹queue \\'kyü\\ *n* [F, lit., tail, fr. L *cauda, coda*] **1** : a braid of hair usu. worn hanging at the back of the head **2** : a waiting line (as of persons)

²queue *vb* **queued; queu·ing** *or* **queue·ing** : to line up in a queue

quib·ble \\'kwi-bəl\\ *n* **1** : an evasion of or shifting from the point at issue **2** : a minor objection or criticism — **quibble** *vb* — **quib·bler** *n*

¹quick \\'kwik\\ *adj* **1** : LIVING **2** : RAPID, SPEEDY ⟨∼ steps⟩ **3** : prompt to understand, think, or perceive : ALERT **4** : easily aroused ⟨a ∼ temper⟩ **5** : turning or bending sharply ⟨a ∼ turn in the road⟩ **syn** fleet, fast, hasty, expeditious — **quick** *adv* — **quick·ly** *adv* — **quick·ness** *n*

²quick *n* **1** : a sensitive area of living flesh **2** : a vital part : HEART

quick bread *n* : a bread made with a leavening agent that permits immediate baking of the dough or batter

quick·en \\'kwi-kən\\ *vb* **1** : to come to life : REVIVE **2** : AROUSE, STIMULATE **3** : to increase in speed : HASTEN **4** : to show vitality (as by growing or moving) **syn** animate, enliven, liven, vivify

quick–freeze \\'kwik-'frēz\\ *vb* **-froze** \\-'frōz\\; **-fro·zen** \\-'frōz-ᵊn\\; **-freez·ing** : to freeze (food) for preservation so rapidly that the natural juices and flavor are not lost

quick·ie \\'kwi-kē\\ *n* : something hurriedly done or made

quick·lime \\'kwik-ˌlīm\\ *n* : ¹LIME

quick·sand \\-ˌsand\\ *n* : a deep mass of loose sand mixed with water

quick·sil·ver \\-ˌsil-vər\\ *n* : MERCURY 1

quick·step \\-ˌstep\\ *n* : a spirited march tune or dance

quick–wit·ted \\'kwik-'wi-təd\\ *adj* : mentally alert **syn** clever, bright, smart, intelligent

quid \\'kwid\\ *n* : a lump of something chewable ⟨a ∼ of tobacco⟩

quid pro quo \\ˌkwid-ˌprō-'kwō\\ *n* [NL, something for something] : something given or received for something else

qui·es·cent \\kwī-'es-ᵊnt\\ *adj* : being at rest : QUIET **syn** latent, dormant, potential — **qui·es·cence** \\-ᵊns\\ *n*

¹qui·et \\'kwī-ət\\ *n* : REPOSE

²quiet *adj* **1** : marked by little motion or activity : CALM **2** : GENTLE, MILD ⟨a ∼ disposition⟩ **3** : enjoyed in peace and relaxation ⟨a ∼ cup of tea⟩ **4** : free from noise or uproar **5** : not showy : MODEST ⟨∼ clothes⟩ **6** : SECLUDED ⟨a ∼ nook⟩ — **quiet** *adv* — **qui·et·ly** *adv* — **qui·et·ness** *n*

³quiet *vb* **1** : CALM, PACIFY **2** : to become quiet ⟨∼ down⟩

qui·etude \\'kwī-ə-ˌtüd, -ˌtyüd\\ *n* : QUIETNESS, REPOSE

qui·etus \\kwī-'ē-təs\\ *n* [ME *quietus est*, fr. ML, he is quit, formula of discharge from obligation] **1** : final settlement (as of a debt) **2** : DEATH

quill \\'kwil\\ *n* **1** : a large stiff feather; *also* : the hollow tubular part of a feather **2** : one of the hollow sharp spines of a hedgehog or porcupine **3** : a pen made from a feather

¹quilt \\'kwilt\\ *n* : a padded bed coverlet

²quilt *vb* **1** : to fill, pad, or line like a quilt **2** : to stitch or sew in layers with padding in between **3** : to make quilts

quince \\'kwins\\ *n* : a hard yellow applelike fruit; *also* : a tree related to the roses that bears this fruit

qui·nine \\'kwī-ˌnīn\\ *n* : a bitter white drug obtained from cinchona bark and used esp. in treating malaria

quint \\'kwint\\ *n* : QUINTUPLET

quin·tal \\'kwint-ᵊl, 'kant-\\ *n* : HUNDREDWEIGHT

quin·tes·sence \\kwin-'tes-ᵊns\\ *n* **1** : the purest essence of something **2** : the most typical example — **quint·es·sen·tial** \\ˌkwin-tə-'sen-chəl\\ *adj* — **quin·tes·sen·tial·ly** *adv*

quin·tet *also* **quin·tette** \\kwin-'tet\\ *n* **1** : a musical composition for five instruments or voices **2** : a group of five and esp. of five musicians

¹quin·tu·ple \\kwin-'tü-pəl, -'tyü-, -'tə-\\ *adj* **1** : having five units or members **2** : being five times as great or as many — **quintuple** *n*

²quintuple *vb* **quin·tu·pled; quin·tu·pling** : to make or become five times as great or as many

quin·tu·plet \kwin-'tə-plət, -'tü-, -'tyü-\ *n* **1** : a group of five of a kind **2** : one of five offspring born at one birth

¹quin·tu·pli·cate \kwin-'tü-pli-kət, -tyü-\ *adj* **1** : repeated five times **2** : FIFTH

²quintuplicate *n* **1** : one of five like things **2** : five copies all alike ⟨typed in ∼⟩

³quin·tu·pli·cate \-plə-ˌkāt\ *vb* **-cat·ed; -cat·ing 1** : QUIN-TUPLE **2** : to provide in quintuplicate

¹quip \'kwip\ *n* : a clever remark : GIBE

²quip *vb* **quipped; quip·ping 1** : to make quips : GIBE **2** : to jest or gibe at

quire \'kwīr\ *n* : a set of 24 or sometimes 25 sheets of paper of the same size and quality

quirk \'kwərk\ *n* : a peculiarity of action or behavior — **quirky** *adj*

quirt \'kwərt\ *n* : a riding whip with a short handle and a rawhide lash

quis·ling \'kwiz-liŋ\ *n* [Vidkun *Quisling* †1945 Norw. politician who collaborated with the Nazis] : one who helps the invaders of one's own country

quit \'kwit\ *vb* **quit** *also* **quit·ted; quit·ting 1** : CONDUCT, BEHAVE ⟨∼ themselves well⟩ **2** : to depart from : LEAVE; *also* : to bring to an end **3** : to give up for good ⟨∼ smoking⟩ ⟨∼ my job⟩ **syn** acquit, comport, deport, demean — **quit·ter** *n*

quite \'kwīt\ *adv* **1** : COMPLETELY, WHOLLY **2** : to an extreme : POSITIVELY **3** : to a considerable extent : RATHER

quits \'kwits\ *adj* : even or equal with another ⟨call it ∼⟩

quit·tance \'kwit-ᵊns\ *n* : REQUITAL

¹quiv·er \'kwi-vər\ *n* : a case for carrying arrows

²quiver *vb* **quiv·ered; quiv·er·ing** : to shake with a slight trembling motion **syn** shiver, shudder, quaver, quake, tremble — **quiv·er·ing·ly** *adv*

³quiver *n* : the act or action of quivering : TREMOR

qui vive \kē-'vēv\ *n* [F *qui-vive,* fr. *qui vive?* long live who?, challenge of a French sentry] : ALERT ⟨on the *qui vive* for prowlers⟩

quix·ot·ic \kwik-'sä-tik\ *adj* [fr. Don *Quixote,* hero of the novel *Don Quixote de la Mancha* by Cervantes] : foolishly impractical esp. in the pursuit of ideals — **quix·ot·i·cal·ly** \-ti-kə-lē\ *adv*

¹quiz \'kwiz\ *n, pl* **quiz·zes 1** : an eccentric person **2** : PRACTICAL JOKE **3** : a short oral or written test

²quiz *vb* **quizzed; quiz·zing 1** : MOCK **2** : to look at inquisitively **3** : to question closely **syn** ask, interrogate, query

quiz·zi·cal \'kwi-zi-kəl\ *adj* **1** : comically quaint **2** : mildly teasing or mocking **3** : expressive of puzzlement, curiosity, or disbelief

quoit \'kwāt, 'kwȯit, 'kȯit\ *n* **1** : a flattened ring of iron or circle of rope used in a throwing game **2** *pl* : a game in which quoits are thrown at an upright pin in an attempt to ring the pin

quon·dam \'kwän-dəm, -ˌdam\ *adj* [L, at one time, formerly, fr. *quom, cum* when] : FORMER

quo·rum \'kwȯr-əm\ *n* : the number of members required to be present for business to be legally transacted

quot *abbr* quotation

quo·ta \'kwō-tə\ *n* : a proportional part esp. when assigned : SHARE

quot·able \'kwō-tə-bəl\ *adj* : fit for or worth quoting — **quot·abil·i·ty** \-ˈbi-lə-tē\ *n*

quo·ta·tion \kwō-'tā-shən\ *n* **1** : the act or process of quoting **2** : the price currently bid or offered for something **3** : something that is quoted

quotation mark *n* : one of a pair of punctuation marks " " or ' ' used esp. to indicate the beginning and end of a quotation in which exact phraseology is directly cited

quote \'kwōt\ *vb* **quot·ed; quot·ing** [ML *quotare* to mark the number of, number references, fr. L *quotus* of what number or quantity, fr. *quot* how many, (as) many as] **1** : to speak or write a passage from another usu. with acknowledgment; *also* : to repeat a passage in substantiation or illustration **2** : to state the market price of a commodity, stock, or bond **3** : to inform a hearer or reader that matter following is quoted — **quote** *n*

quoth \'kwōth\ *vb past* [ME, past of *quethen* to say, fr. OE *cwethan*] *archaic* : SAID — usu. used in the 1st and 3d persons with the subject following

quo·tid·i·an \kwō-'ti-dē-ən\ *adj* **1** : DAILY **2** : COMMON-PLACE, ORDINARY

quo·tient \'kwō-shənt\ *n* : the number obtained by dividing one number by another

qv *abbr* [L *quod vide*] which see

qy *abbr* query

R

¹r \'är\ *n, pl* **r's** *or* **rs** \'ärz\ *often cap* : the 18th letter of the English alphabet

²r *abbr, often cap* **1** rabbi **2** radius **3** rare **4** Republican **5** rerun **6** resistance **7** right **8** river **9** roentgen **10** rook **11** run

Ra *symbol* radium

RA *abbr* **1** regular army **2** Royal Academy

¹rab·bet \'ra-bət\ *n* : a groove in the edge or face of a surface (as a board) esp. to receive another piece

²rabbet *vb* : to cut a rabbet in; *also* : to join by means of a rabbet

rab·bi \'ra-ˌbī\ *n* [LL, fr. Gk *rhabbi,* fr. Heb *rabbī* my master, fr. *rabh* master + *-ī* my] **1** : MASTER, TEACHER — used by Jews as a term of address **2** : a Jew trained and ordained for professional religious leadership — **rab·bin·ic** \rə-'bi-nik\ *or* **rab·bin·i·cal** \-ni-kəl\ *adj*

rab·bin·ate \'ra-bə-nət, -ˌnāt\ *n* **1** : the office of a rabbi **2** : the whole body of rabbis

rab·bit \'ra-bət\ *n, pl* **rabbit** *or* **rabbits** : any of various long-eared burrowing mammals distinguished from the related hares by being blind, naked, and helpless at birth; *also* : the pelt of a rabbit

rabbit ears *n* : an indoor V-shaped television antenna

rabble \'ra-bəl\ *n* **1** : MOB 2 **2** : the lowest class of people

rab·ble–rous·er \'ra-bəl-ˌraù-zər\ *n* : one that stirs up (as to hatred or violence) the masses of the people

Ra·bi \'rä-bē\ *n* [Ar *rabī'*] **1** : the 3d month of the Islamic year **2** : the 4th month of the Islamic year

ra·bid \'ra-bəd\ *adj* **1** : VIOLENT, FURIOUS **2** : being fanatical or extreme **3** : affected with rabies — **ra·bid·ly** *adv*

ra·bies \'rā-bēz\ *n, pl* **rabies** [NL, fr. L, madness] : an acute deadly virus disease of the nervous system transmitted by the bite of an affected animal

rac·coon \ra-'kün\ *n, pl* **raccoon** *or* **raccoons** : a gray No. American chiefly tree-dwelling mammal with a black mask, a bushy ringed tail, and nocturnal habits; *also* : its pelt

¹race \'rās\ *n* **1** : a strong current of running water; *also*

\ə\abut \ᵊ\kitten \ər\further \a\ash \ā\ace \ä\mop, mar
\aù\out \ch\chin \e\bet \ē\easy \g\go \i\hit \ī\ice \j\job
\ŋ\sing \ō\go \ȯ\law \ȯi\boy \th\thin \t͟h\the \ü\loot \ù\foot
\y\yet \zh\vision *see also* Pronunciation Symbols page

: its channel **2** : an onward course (as of time or life) **3** : a contest of speed **4** : a contest for a desired end (as election to office)

²**race** vb **raced; rac·ing 1** : to run in a race **2** : to run swiftly : RUSH **3** : to engage in a race with **4** : to drive or ride at high speed — **rac·er** n

³**race** n **1** : a family, tribe, people, or nation of the same stock; also : MANKIND **2** : a group of individuals within a biological species able to breed together — **ra·cial** \ˈrā-shəl\ adj — **ra·cial·ly** adv

race·course \ˈrās-ˌkōrs\ n : a course for racing

race·horse \-ˌhȯrs\ n : a horse bred or kept for racing

ra·ceme \rā-ˈsēm\ n [L racemus bunch of grapes] : a flower cluster with flowers borne along a stem and blooming from the base toward the tip — **rac·e·mose** \ˈra-sə-ˌmōs\ adj

race·track \ˈrās-ˌtrak\ n : a usu. oval course on which races are run

race·way \-ˌwā\ n **1** : a channel for a current of water **2** : RACECOURSE

ra·cial·ism \ˈrā-shə-ˌli-zəm\ n : RACISM — **ra·cial·ist** \-list\ n — **ra·cial·is·tic** \ˌrā-shə-ˈlis-tik\ adj

racing form n : a paper giving data about racehorses for use by bettors

rac·ism \ˈrā-ˌsi-zəm\ n : a belief that some races are by nature superior to others; also : discrimination based on such belief — **rac·ist** \-sist\ n

¹**rack** \ˈrak\ n **1** : an instrument of torture on which a body is stretched **2** : a framework on or in which something may be placed (as for display or storage) **3** : a bar with teeth on one side to mesh with a pinion or worm gear

²**rack** vb **1** : to torture on or as if on a rack **2** : to stretch or strain by force **3** : TORMENT **4** : to place on or in a rack

¹**rack·et** also **rac·quet** \ˈra-kət\ n [MF raquette, ultim. fr. Ar rāḥah palm of the hand] : a light bat made of netting stretched in an oval open frame having a handle and used for striking a ball or shuttlecock

²**racket** n **1** : confused noise : DIN **2** : a fraudulent or dishonest scheme or activity

³**racket** vb : to make a racket

rack·e·teer \ˌra-kə-ˈtir\ n : a person who obtains money by an illegal enterprise usu. involving intimidation — **rack·e·teer·ing** n

rack up vb : ACCUMULATE, GAIN

ra·con·teur \ˌra-ˌkän-ˈtər\ n : one good at telling anecdotes

racy \ˈrā-sē\ adj **rac·i·er; -est 1** : full of zest **2** : PUNGENT, SPICY **3** : RISQUÉ, SUGGESTIVE — **rac·i·ly** \ˈrā-sə-lē\ adv — **rac·i·ness** \-sē-nəs\ n

rad abbr **1** radical **2** radio **3** radius

ra·dar \ˈrā-ˌdär\ n [radio detecting and ranging] : a device that emits radio waves for detecting and locating an object by the reflection of the radio waves and that may use this reflection to determine the object's direction and speed

ra·dar·scope \ˈrā-ˌdär-ˌskōp\ n : a visual display for a radar receiver

¹**ra·di·al** \ˈrā-dē-əl\ adj : arranged or having parts arranged like rays around a common center ⟨the ∼ form of a starfish⟩ — **ra·di·al·ly** adv

²**radial** n : a pneumatic tire with cords laid perpendicular to the center line

radial engine n : an internal combustion engine with cylinders arranged radially like the spokes of a wheel

ra·di·ant \ˈrā-dē-ənt\ adj **1** : SHINING, GLOWING **2** : beaming with happiness **3** : transmitted by radiation **syn** brilliant, bright, luminous, lustrous — **ra·di·ance** \-əns\ n — **ra·di·ant·ly** adv

radiant energy n : energy traveling as electromagnetic waves

ra·di·ate \ˈrā-dē-ˌāt\ vb **-at·ed; -at·ing 1** : to send out

rays : SHINE, GLOW **2** : to issue in or as if in rays ⟨light ∼s⟩ **3** : to spread around as from a center — **ra·di·a·tion** \ˌrā-dē-ˈā-shən\ n

radiation sickness n : sickness that results from exposure to radiation and is commonly marked by fatigue, nausea, vomiting, loss of teeth and hair, and in more severe cases by damage to blood-forming tissue

ra·di·a·tor \ˈrā-dē-ˌā-tər\ n : any of various devices (as a set of pipes or tubes) for transferring heat from a fluid within to an area or object outside

¹**rad·i·cal** \ˈra-di-kəl\ adj [ME, fr. LL radicalis, fr. L radic-, radix root] **1** : FUNDAMENTAL, EXTREME, THOROUGHGOING **2** : of or relating to radicals in politics — **rad·i·cal·ism** \-kə-ˌli-zəm\ n — **rad·i·cal·ly** adv

²**radical** n **1** : a person who favors rapid and sweeping changes in laws and methods of government **2** : a group of atoms considered as a unit that remains unchanged during reactions **3** : a mathematical expression indicating a root by means of a radical sign; also : RADICAL SIGN

rad·i·cal·ize \-kə-ˌlīz\ vb **-ized; -iz·ing** : to make radical esp. in politics — **rad·i·cal·i·za·tion** \ˌra-di-kə-lə-ˈzā-shən\ n

radical sign n : the sign √ placed before a mathematical expression to indicate that its root is to be taken

radii pl of RADIUS

¹**ra·dio** \ˈrā-dē-ˌō\ n, pl **ra·di·os 1** : the wireless transmission or reception of signals using electromagnetic waves **2** : a radio receiving set **3** : the radio broadcasting industry — **radio** adj

²**radio** vb : to communicate or send a message to by radio

ra·dio·ac·tiv·i·ty \ˌrā-dē-ō-ˌak-ˈti-və-tē\ n : the property that some elements or isotopes have of spontaneously emitting energetic particles by the disintegration of their atomic nuclei — **ra·dio·ac·tive** \-ˈak-tiv\ adj

radio astronomy n : astronomy dealing with radio waves received from outside the earth's atmosphere

ra·dio·car·bon \ˌrā-dē-ō-ˈkär-bən\ n : CARBON 14

radio frequency n : an electromagnetic wave frequency intermediate between audio frequencies and infrared frequencies used esp. in radio and television transmission

ra·dio·gram \ˈrā-dē-ō-ˌgram\ n : a message transmitted by radio

ra·dio·graph \-ˌgraf\ n : a photograph made by some form of radiation other than light; esp : an X-ray photograph — **radiograph** vb — **ra·dio·graph·ic** \ˌrā-dē-ō-ˈgra-fik\ adj — **ra·dio·graph·i·cal·ly** \-fi-k(ə-)lē\ adv — **ra·di·og·ra·phy** \ˌrā-dē-ˈä-grə-fē\ n

ra·dio·iso·tope \ˌrā-dē-ō-ˈī-sə-ˌtōp\ n : a radioactive isotope

ra·di·ol·o·gy \ˌrā-dē-ˈä-lə-jē\ n : the use of radiant energy (as X rays and radium radiations) in medicine — **ra·di·ol·o·gist** \-jist\ n

ra·dio·man \ˈrā-dē-ō-ˌman\ n : a radio operator or technician

ra·di·om·e·ter \ˌrā-dē-ˈä-mə-tər\ n : an instrument for measuring the intensity of radiant energy — **ra·dio·met·ric** \ˌrā-dē-ō-ˈme-trik\ adj — **ra·di·om·e·try** \-mə-trē\ n

ra·dio·phone \ˈrā-dē-ə-ˌfōn\ n : RADIOTELEPHONE

ra·dio·sonde \ˈrā-dē-ō-ˌsänd\ n : a small radio transmitter carried aloft (as by balloon) and used to transmit meteorological data

ra·dio·tele·phone \ˌrā-dē-ō-ˈte-lə-ˌfōn\ n : a telephone that uses radio waves wholly or partly instead of connecting wires — **ra·dio·te·le·pho·ny** \-tə-ˈle-fə-nē, -ˈte-lə-ˌfō-nē\ n

radio telescope n : a radio receiver-antenna combination used for observation in radio astronomy

ra·dio·ther·a·py \ˌrā-dē-ō-ˈther-ə-pē\ n : the treatment of disease by means of radiation (as X rays) — **radiotherapist** \-pist\ n

rad·ish \'ra-dish\ *n* [ME, alter. of OE *rædic*, fr. L *radic-*, *radix* root, radish] : a pungent fleshy root usu. eaten raw; *also* : a plant related to the mustards that produces this root

ra·di·um \'rā-dē-əm\ *n* : a very radioactive metallic chemical element that is used in the treatment of cancer — see ELEMENT table

ra·di·us \'rā-dē-əs\ *n, pl* **ra·dii** \-ē-ˌī\ *also* **ra·di·us·es 1** : a straight line extending from the center of a circle or a sphere to the circumference or surface; *also* : the length of a radius **2** : the bone on the thumb side of the human forearm **3** : a circular area defined by the length of its radius **syn** range, reach, scope, compass

RADM *abbr* rear admiral

ra·don \'rā-ˌdän\ *n* : a heavy radioactive gaseous chemical element — see ELEMENT table

RAF *abbr* Royal Air Force

raf·fia \'ra-fē-ə\ *n* : fiber used esp. for making baskets and hats that is obtained from the stalks of the leaves of a Madagascar palm (**raffia palm**)

raff·ish \'ra-fish\ *adj* : jaunty or sporty esp. in a flashy or vulgar manner — **raff·ish·ly** *adv* — **raff·ish·ness** *n*

¹raf·fle \'ra-fəl\ *vb* **raf·fled; raf·fling** : to dispose of by a raffle

²raffle *n* : a lottery in which the prize is won by one of a number of persons buying chances

¹raft \'raft\ *n* **1** : a number of logs or timbers fastened together to form a float **2** : a flat structure for support or transportation on water

²raft *vb* **1** : to travel or transport by raft **2** : to make into a raft

³raft *n* : a large amount or number

raf·ter \'raf-tər\ *n* : any of the parallel beams that support a roof

¹rag \'rag\ *n* **1** : a waste piece of cloth **2** : NEWSPAPER

²rag *n* : a composition in ragtime

ra·ga \'rä-gə\ *n* **1** : a traditional melodic pattern or mode in Indian music **2** : an improvisation based on a raga

rag·a·muf·fin \'ra-gə-ˌmə-fən\ *n* [ME *Ragamuffyn*, name for a ragged, oafish person] : a ragged dirty person

¹rage \'rāj\ *n* **1** : violent and uncontrolled anger **2** : VOGUE, FASHION

²rage *vb* **raged; rag·ing 1** : to be furiously angry : RAVE **2** : to continue out of control (the fire *raged*)

rag·ged \'ra-gəd\ *adj* **1** : TORN, TATTERED; *also* : wearing tattered clothes **2** : done in an uneven way (a ~ performance) — **rag·ged·ly** *adv* — **rag·ged·ness** *n*

rag·lan \'ra-glən\ *n* : an overcoat with sleeves (**raglan sleeves**) sewn in with seams slanting from neck to underarm

ra·gout \ra-'gü\ *n* [F *ragoût*, fr. *ragoûter* to revive the taste, fr. *re-* + *a-* to (fr. L *ad-*) + *goût* taste, fr. L *gustus*] : a highly seasoned meat stew with vegetables

rag·pick·er \'rag-ˌpi-kər\ *n* : one who collects rags and refuse for a living

rag·time \-ˌtīm\ *n* : music in which there is more or less continuous syncopation in the melody

rag·top \'rag-ˌtäp\ *n* : CONVERTIBLE

rag·weed \-ˌwēd\ *n* : any of several chiefly No. American weedy composite herbs with allergenic pollen

¹raid \'rād\ *n* : a sudden usu. surprise attack or invasion : FORAY

²raid *vb* : to make a raid on — **raid·er** *n*

¹rail \'rāl\ *n* [ME *raile*, fr. MF *reille* ruler, bar, fr. L *regula* ruler, fr. *regere* to keep straight, direct, rule] **1** : a bar extending from one support to another as a guard or barrier **2** : a bar of steel forming a track for wheeled vehicles **3** : RAILROAD

²rail *vb* : to provide with a railing

³rail *n, pl* **rail** *or* **rails** : any of numerous small wading birds often hunted as game birds

⁴rail *vb* [ME, fr. MF *railler* to mock, fr. OProv *ralhar* to babble, joke] : to complain angrily : SCOLD, REVILE — **rail·er** *n*

rail·ing \'rā-liŋ\ *n* : a barrier of rails

rail·lery \'rā-lə-rē\ *n, pl* **-ler·ies** : good-natured ridicule : BANTER

¹rail·road \'rāl-ˌrōd\ *n* : a permanent road with rails fixed to ties providing a track for cars; *also* : such a road and its assets constituting a property

²railroad *vb* **1** : to put through (as a law) too hastily **2** : to convict hastily or with insufficient or improper evidence **3** : to send by rail **4** : to work on a railroad — **rail·road·er** *n* — **rail·road·ing** *n*

rail·way \-ˌwā\ *n* : RAILROAD

rai·ment \'rā-mənt\ *n* : CLOTHING

¹rain \'rān\ *n* **1** : water falling in drops from the clouds **2** : a shower of objects (a ~ of bullets) — **rainy** *adj*

²rain *vb* **1** : to send down rain **2** : to fall as or like rain **3** : to pour down

rain·bow \-ˌbō\ *n* : an arc or circle of colors formed by the refraction and reflection of the sun's rays in rain, spray, or mist

rainbow trout *n* : a large stout-bodied fish of western No. America closely related to the salmons of the Pacific and usu. having red or pink stripes with black dots along its sides

rain check *n* **1** : a ticket stub good for a later performance when the scheduled one is rained out **2** : an assurance of a deferred extension of an offer

rain·coat \'rān-ˌkōt\ *n* : a waterproof or water-repellent coat

rain·drop \-ˌdräp\ *n* : a drop of rain

rain·fall \-ˌföl\ *n* **1** : amount of precipitation measured by depth **2** : a fall of rain

rain forest *n* : a tropical woodland having an annual rainfall of at least 100 inches (254 centimeters) and marked by lofty broad-leaved evergreen trees forming a continuous canopy

rain·mak·ing \'rān-ˌmā-kiŋ\ *n* : the action or process of producing or attempting to produce rain by artificial means — **rain·mak·er** *n*

rain out *vb* : to interrupt or prevent by rain

rain·storm \'rān-ˌstörm\ *n* : a storm of or with rain

rain·wa·ter \-ˌwö-tər, -ˌwä-\ *n* : water fallen as rain

¹raise \'rāz\ *vb* **raised; rais·ing 1** : to cause or help to rise : LIFT (~ a window) **2** : AWAKEN, AROUSE (enough to ~ the dead) **3** : BUILD, ERECT (~ a monument) **4** : PROMOTE (was *raised* to captain) **5** : END (~ a siege) **6** : COLLECT (~ money) **7** : BREED, GROW (~ cattle) (~ corn); *also* : BRING UP (~ a family) **8** : PROVOKE (~ a laugh) **9** : to bring to notice (~ an objection) **10** : INCREASE (~ prices); *also* : to bet more than **11** : to make light and spongy (~ dough) **12** : to multiply a quantity by itself a specified number of times **13** : to cause to form (~ a blister) **syn** lift, hoist, boost, elevate — **rais·er** *n*

²raise *n* : an increase in amount (as of a bid or bet); *also* : an increase in pay

rai·sin \'rā-zᵊn\ *n* [ME, fr. MF, grape, fr. L *racemus* cluster of grapes or berries] : a grape dried for food

rai·son d'être \ˌrā-ˌzōⁿ-'detrᵊ\ *n* : reason or justification for existence

ra·ja *or* **ra·jah** \'rä-jə\ *n* [Hindi *rājā*, fr. Skt *rājan* king] : an Indian prince

Ra·jab \rə-'jab\ *n* [Ar] : the 7th month of the Islamic year

¹rake \'rāk\ *n* : a long-handled garden tool having a crossbar with prongs

²rake *vb* **raked; rak·ing 1** : to gather, loosen, or smooth with or as if with a rake **2 :** to sweep the length of (as a trench or ship) with gunfire

³**rake** *n* **:** inclination from either perpendicular or horizontal **:** SLANT

⁴**rake** *n* **:** a dissolute man **:** LIBERTINE

rake–off \'rāk-ˌȯf\ *n* **:** a percentage or cut taken

¹**rak·ish** \'rā-kish\ *adj* **:** DISSOLUTE — **rak·ish·ly** *adv* — **rak·ish·ness** *n*

²**rakish** *adj* **1 :** having a trim appearance indicative of speed ⟨a ∼ sloop⟩ **2 :** JAUNTY, SPORTY ⟨∼ clothes⟩ — **rak·ish·ly** *adv* — **rak·ish·ness** *n*

¹**ral·ly** \'ra-lē\ *vb* **ral·lied; ral·ly·ing 1 :** to bring together for a common purpose; *also* **:** to bring back to order ⟨a leader ∼*ing* his forces⟩ **2 :** to arouse to activity or from depression or weakness **3 :** to make a comeback **syn** stir, rouse, awaken, waken, kindle

²**rally** *n, pl* **rallies 1 :** an act of rallying **2 :** a mass meeting to arouse enthusiasm **3 :** a competitive automobile event run over public roads

³**rally** *vb* **ral·lied; ral·ly·ing :** BANTER

¹**ram** \'ram\ *n* **1 :** a male sheep **2 :** BATTERING RAM

²**ram** *vb* **rammed; ram·ming 1 :** to force or drive in or through **2 :** CRAM, CROWD **3 :** to strike against violently

RAM \'ram\ *n* **:** RANDOM-ACCESS MEMORY

Ra·ma·dan \'rä-mə-ˌdän, ˌrä-mə-ˈdän\ *n* [Ar *Ramaḍān*] **:** the 9th month of the Islamic year observed as sacred with fasting practiced daily from dawn to sunset

¹**ram·ble** \'ram-bəl\ *vb* **ram·bled; ram·bling :** to go about aimlessly **:** ROAM, WANDER

²**ramble** *n* **:** a leisurely excursion; *esp* **:** an aimless walk

ram·bler \'ram-blər\ *n* **1 :** a person who rambles **2 :** any of various climbing roses with large clusters of small often double flowers

ram·bunc·tious \ram-ˈbəŋk-shəs\ *adj* **:** UNRULY

ra·mie \'rā-mē, 'ra-\ *n* **:** a strong lustrous bast fiber from an Asian nettle

ram·i·fi·ca·tion \ˌra-mə-fə-ˈkā-shən\ *n* **1 :** the act or process of branching **2 :** CONSEQUENCE, OUTGROWTH

ram·i·fy \'ra-mə-ˌfī\ *vb* **-fied; -fy·ing :** to branch out

ramp \'ramp\ *n* **:** a sloping passage or roadway connecting different levels

¹**ram·page** \'ram-ˌpāj, (ˌ)ram-ˈpāj\ *vb* **ram·paged; ram·pag·ing :** to rush about wildly

²**ram·page** \'ram-ˌpāj\ *n* **:** a course of violent or riotous action or behavior — **ram·pa·geous** \ram-ˈpā-jəs\ *adj*

ram·pant \'ram-pənt\ *adj* **:** unchecked in growth or spread **:** RIFE ⟨fear was ∼ in the town⟩ — **ram·pan·cy** \-pən-sē\ *n* — **ram·pant·ly** *adv*

ram·part \'ram-ˌpärt\ *n* **1 :** a protective barrier **2 :** a broad embankment raised as a fortification

¹**ram·rod** \'ram-ˌräd\ *n* **1 :** a rod used to ram a charge into a muzzle-loading gun **2 :** a cleaning rod for small arms **3 :** BOSS, OVERSEER

²**ramrod** *adj* **:** marked by rigidity or severity

³**ramrod** *vb* **:** to direct, supervise, and control

ram·shack·le \'ram-ˌsha-kəl\ *adj* **:** RICKETY, TUMBLE-DOWN

ran *past of* RUN

¹**ranch** \'ranch\ *n* [MexSp *rancho* small ranch, fr. Sp, camp, hut & Sp dial., small farm, fr. Old Spanish *ranchear* (*se*) to take up quarters, fr. MF (*se*) *ranger* to take up a position, fr. *ranger* to set in a row] **1 :** an establishment for the raising and grazing of livestock (as cattle, sheep, or horses) **2 :** a large farm devoted to a specialty **3 :** RANCH HOUSE 2

²**ranch** *vb* **:** to live or work on a ranch — **ranch·er** *n*

ranch house *n* **1 :** the main house on a ranch **2 :** a one-story house typically with a low-pitched roof

ran·cho \'ran-chō, 'rän-\ *n, pl* **ranchos :** RANCH 1

ran·cid \'ran-səd\ *adj* **1 :** having a rank smell or taste **2 :** ROTTEN, SPOILED — **ran·cid·i·ty** \ran-ˈsi-də-tē\ *n*

ran·cor \'raŋ-kər\ *n* **:** bitter deep-seated ill will **syn** an-

tagonism, animosity, antipathy, enmity, hostility — **ran·cor·ous** *adj*

ran·cour *Brit var of* RANCOR

rand \'rand, 'ränd, 'ränt\ *n, pl* **rand** — see MONEY table

R & B *abbr* rhythm and blues

R and D *n* **:** research and development

ran·dom \'ran-dəm\ *adj* **:** CHANCE, HAPHAZARD — **ran·dom·ly** *adv* — **ran·dom·ness** *n*

random–access *adj* **:** allowing access to stored data in any order the user desires

random–access memory *n* **:** a computer memory that provides the main internal storage for programs and data

ran·dom·ize \'ran-də-ˌmīz\ *vb* **-ized; -iz·ing :** to select, assign, or arrange in a random way — **ran·dom·i·za·tion** \ˌran-də-mə-ˈzā-shən\ *n*

R and R *abbr* rest and recreation; rest and recuperation

rang *past of* RING

¹**range** \'rānj\ *n* **1 :** a series of things in a row **2 :** a cooking stove having an oven and a flat top with burners **3 :** open land where animals (as livestock) may roam and graze **4 :** the act of ranging about **5 :** the distance a weapon will shoot or is to be shot **6 :** a place where shooting is practiced **7 :** the space or extent included, covered, or used **:** SCOPE **8 :** a variation within limits **syn** reach, compass, radius, circle

²**range** *vb* **ranged; rang·ing 1 :** to set in a row or in proper order **2 :** to set in place among others of the same kind **3 :** to roam over or through **:** EXPLORE **4 :** to roam at large or freely **5 :** to correspond in direction or line **6 :** to vary within limits **7 :** to find the range of an object by instrument (as radar)

rang·er \'rān-jər\ *n* **1 :** FOREST RANGER **2 :** a member of a body of troops who range over a region **3 :** an expert in close-range fighting and raiding tactics

rangy \'rān-jē\ *adj* **rang·i·er; -est :** being long-limbed and slender — **rang·i·ness** \'rān-jē-nəs\ *n*

ra·ni *or* **ra·nee** \rä-ˈnē, 'rä-ˌnē\ *n* **:** a raja's wife

¹**rank** \'raŋk\ *adj* **1 :** strong and vigorous and usu. coarse in growth ⟨∼ weeds⟩ **2 :** unpleasantly strong-smelling — **rank·ly** *adv* — **rank·ness** *n*

²**rank** *n* **1 :** ROW **2 :** a line of soldiers ranged side by side **3** *pl* **:** the body of enlisted personnel ⟨rose from the ∼s⟩ **4 :** an orderly arrangement **5 :** CLASS, DIVISION **6 :** a grade of official standing (as in an army) **7 :** position in a group **8 :** superior position

³**rank** *vb* **1 :** to arrange in lines or in regular formation **2 :** RATE **3 :** to rate above (as in official standing) **4 :** to take or have a relative position

rank and file *n* **:** the general membership of a body as contrasted with its leaders

rank·ing \'raŋ-kiŋ\ *adj* **1 :** having a high position **:** FOREMOST **2 :** being next to the chairman in seniority

ran·kle \'raŋ-kəl\ *vb* **ran·kled; ran·kling** [ME *ranclen* to fester, fr. MF *rancler*, fr. OF *draoncler, raoncler*, fr. *draoncle, raoncle* festering sore, fr. (assumed) VL *dracunculus*, fr. L, dim. of *draco* serpent] **:** to cause anger, irritation, or bitterness

ran·sack \'ran-ˌsak\ *vb* **:** to search thoroughly; *esp* **:** to search through and rob

¹**ran·som** \'ran-səm\ *n* [ME *ransoun*, fr. OF *rançon*, fr. L *redemption-, redemptio* act of buying back, fr. *redimere* to buy back, redeem] **1 :** something paid or demanded for the freedom of a captive **2 :** the act of ransoming

²**ransom** *vb* **:** to free from captivity or punishment by paying a price — **ran·som·er** *n*

rant \'rant\ *vb* **1 :** to talk loudly and wildly **2 :** to scold violently — **rant·er** *n* — **rant·ing·ly** *adv*

¹**rap** \'rap\ *n* **1 :** a sharp blow **2 :** a sharp rebuke **3 :** a negative often undeserved reputation ⟨a bum ∼⟩ **4 :** responsibility for or consequences of an action ⟨take the ∼⟩

RANKS OF THE UNITED STATES ARMED FORCES

ARMY	MARINES	NAVY	AIR FORCE	COAST GUARD
general of the army		fleet admiral	general of the air force	
general	general	admiral	general	admiral or commandant
lieutenant general	lieutenant general	vice admiral	lieutenant general	vice admiral
major general	major general	rear admiral	major general	rear admiral
brigadier general	brigadier general	commodore	brigadier general	commodore
colonel	colonel	captain	colonel	captain
lieutenant colonel	lieutenant colonel	commander	lieutenant colonel	commander
major	major	lieutenant commander	major	lieutenant commander
captain	captain	lieutenant	captain	lieutenant
first lieutenant	first lieutenant	lieutenant, j.g.	first lieutenant	lieutenant, j.g.
second lieutenant	second lieutenant	ensign	second lieutenant	ensign
chief warrant officer, W-4	chief warrant officer, W-4	chief warrant officer, W-4	chief warrant officer, W-4	chief warrant officer, W-4
chief warrant officer, W-3	chief warrant officer, W-3	warrant officer, W-3	chief warrant officer, W-3	warrant officer, W-3
chief warrant officer, W-2	chief warrant officer, W-2	warrant officer, W-2	chief warrant officer, W-2	warrant officer, W-2
warrant officer, W-1	warrant officer, W-1	warrant officer, W-1	warrant officer, W-1	warrant officer, W-1
sergeant major of the army	sergeant major of the marine corps	master chief petty officer of the navy	chief master sergeant of the air force	master chief petty officer of the coast guard
command sergeant major	sergeant major or master gunnery sergeant	master chief petty officer	chief master sergeant	master chief petty officer
first sergeant or master sergeant	first sergeant or master sergeant	senior chief petty officer	senior master sergeant	senior chief petty officer
platoon sergeant or sergeant first class or specialist 7	gunnery sergeant	chief petty officer	master sergeant	chief petty officer
staff sergeant or specialist 6	staff sergeant	petty officer first class	technical sergeant	petty officer first class
sergeant or specialist 5	sergeant	petty officer second class	staff sergeant	petty officer second class
corporal or specialist 4	corporal	petty officer third class	sergeant	petty officer third class
private first class	lance corporal	seaman	airman first class	seaman
private, E-2	private first class	seaman apprentice	airman	seaman apprentice
private, E-1	private	seaman recruit	airman basic	seaman recruit

²**rap** *vb* **rapped; rap·ping 1** : to strike sharply : KNOCK **2** : to utter sharply **3** : to criticize sharply

³**rap** *vb* **rapped; rap·ping 1** : to talk freely and frankly **2** : to perform rap music

⁴**rap** *n* **1** : TALK, CONVERSATION **2** : a rhythmic chanting of usu. rhymed couplets to a musical accompaniment; *also* : a piece so performed

ra·pa·cious \rə-ˈpā-shəs\ *adj* **1** : excessively greedy or covetous **2** : living on prey **3** : RAVENOUS **2** — **ra·pa·cious·ly** *adv* — **ra·pa·cious·ness** *n* — **ra·pac·i·ty** \-ˈpa-sə-tē\ *n*

¹**rape** \ˈrāp\ *n* : a European herb related to the mustards that is grown as a forage crop and for its seeds (**rape-seed** \-ˌsēd\)

²**rape** *vb* **raped; rap·ing** : to commit rape on — **rap-er** *n* — **rap·ist** \ˈrā-pist\ *n*

³**rape** *n* **1** : a carrying away by force **2** : sexual intercourse by a man with a woman without her consent and chiefly by force or deception; *also* : unlawful sexual intercourse of any kind by force or threat

¹**rap·id** \ˈra-pəd\ *adj* [L *rapidus* strong-flowing, rapid, fr. *rapere* to seize, carry away] : very fast : SWIFT **syn** fleet, quick, speedy — **ra·pid·i·ty** \rə-ˈpi-də-tē\ *n* — **rap·id·ly** *adv*

²**rapid** *n* : a place in a stream where the current flows very fast usu. over obstructions — usu. used in pl.

rapid eye movement *n* : rapid conjugate movement of the eyes associated with REM sleep

rapid transit *n* : fast passenger transportation (as by subway) in cities

ra·pi·er \ˈrā-pē-ər\ *n* : a straight 2-edged sword with a narrow pointed blade

rapier

rap·ine \\'ra-pən, -ˌpīn\\ *n* : PILLAGE, PLUNDER

rap·pel \\rə-'pel, ra-\\ *vb* **-pelled; -pel·ling** : to descend (as from a cliff) by sliding down a rope

rap·pen \\'rä-pən\\ *n, pl* **rappen** : the centime of Switzerland

rap·port \\ra-'pōr\\ *n* : RELATION; *esp* : relation characterized by harmony

rap·proche·ment \\ˌra-ˌprōsh-'mäⁿ, ra-'prōsh-ˌmäⁿ\\ *n* : the establishment of or a state of having cordial relations

rap·scal·lion \\rap-'skal-yən\\ *n* : RASCAL, SCAMP

rapt \\'rapt\\ *adj* **1** : carried away with emotion **2** : ABSORBED, ENGROSSED — **rapt·ly** \\'rapt-lē\\ *adv* — **rapt·ness** *n*

rap·ture \\'rap-chər\\ *n* : spiritual or emotional ecstasy — **rap·tur·ous** \\-chə-rəs\\ *adj* — **rap·tur·ous·ly** *adv*

rapture of the deep : NITROGEN NARCOSIS

ra·ra avis \\ˌrar-ə-'ā-vəs\\ *n* [L, rare bird] : a rare person or thing : RARITY

¹rare \\'rar\\ *adj* **rar·er; rar·est 1** : not thick or dense : THIN ⟨∼ air⟩ **2** : unusually fine : EXCELLENT, SPLENDID **3** : seldom met with — **rare·ly** *adv* — **rare·ness** *n* — **rar·i·ty** \\'rar-ə-tē\\ *n*

²rare *adj* **rar·er; rar·est** : cooked so that the inside is still red ⟨∼ beef⟩

rare·bit \\'rar-bət\\ *n* : WELSH RABBIT

rar·efac·tion \\ˌrar-ə-'fak-shən\\ *n* **1** : the action or process of rarefying **2** : the state of being rarefied

rar·e·fy *also* **rar·i·fy** \\'rar-ə-ˌfī\\ *vb* **-fied; -fy·ing** : to make or become rare, thin, or less dense

rar·ing \\'rar-ən, -iŋ\\ *adj* : full of enthusiasm or eagerness ⟨∼ to go⟩

ras·cal \\'ras-kəl\\ *n* **1** : a mean or dishonest person **2** : a mischievous person — **ras·cal·i·ty** \\ras-'ka-lə-tē\\ *n* — **ras·cal·ly** \\'ras-kə-lē\\ *adj*

¹rash \\'rash\\ *adj* : having or showing little regard for consequences : too hasty in decision, action, or speech : RECKLESS **syn** daring, foolhardy, adventurous, venturesome — **rash·ly** *adv* — **rash·ness** *n*

²rash *n* : an eruption on the body

rash·er \\'ra-shər\\ *n* : a thin slice of bacon or ham broiled or fried; *also* : a portion consisting of several such slices

¹rasp \\'rasp\\ *vb* **1** : to rub with or as if with a rough file **2** : to grate harshly on (as one's nerves) **3** : to speak in a grating tone

²rasp *n* : a coarse file with cutting points instead of ridges

rasp·ber·ry \\'raz-ˌber-ē, -bə-rē\\ *n* **1** : any of various edible usu. black or red berries produced by some brambles; *also* : such a bramble **2** : a sound of contempt made by protruding the tongue through the lips and expelling air forcibly

¹rat \\'rat\\ *n* **1** : any of numerous rodents larger than the related mice **2** : a contemptible person; *esp* : one that betrays friends or associates

²rat *vb* **rat·ted; rat·ting 1** : to betray or inform on one's associates **2** : to hunt or catch rats

rat cheese *n* : CHEDDAR

ratch·et \\'ra-chət\\ *n* : a device that consists of a bar or wheel having slanted teeth into which a pawl drops so as to allow motion in only one direction

ratchet wheel *n* : a toothed wheel held in position or turned by a pawl

¹rate \\'rāt\\ *vb* **rat·ed; rat·ing** : to scold violently

²rate *n* **1** : quantity, amount, or degree measured by some standard **2** : an amount (as of payment) measured by its relation to some other amount (as of time) **3** : a charge, payment, or price fixed according to a ratio, scale, or standard ⟨tax ∼⟩ **4** : RANK, CLASS

³rate *vb* **rat·ed; rat·ing 1** : ESTIMATE **2** : CONSIDER, REGARD **3** : to settle the relative rank or class of **4** : to be classed : RANK **5** : to have a right to : DESERVE **6** : to be of consequence — **rat·er** *n*

rath·er \\'ra-thər, 'rä-, 'rə-\\ *adv* [ME, fr. OE *hrathor*, compar. of *hrathe* quickly] **1** : more properly **2** : PREFERABLY **3** : more correctly speaking **4** : to the contrary : INSTEAD **5** : SOMEWHAT

raths·kel·ler \\'rät-ˌske-lər, 'rat-\\ *n* [obs. G (now *Ratskeller*), city-hall basement restaurant, fr. *Rat* council + *Keller* cellar] : a usu. basement tavern or restaurant

rat·i·fy \\'ra-tə-ˌfī\\ *vb* **-fied; -fy·ing** : to approve and accept formally — **rat·i·fi·ca·tion** \\ˌra-tə-fə-'kā-shən\\ *n*

rat·ing \\'rā-tiŋ\\ *n* **1** : a classification according to grade : RANK **2** *Brit* : a naval enlisted man **3** : an estimate of the credit standing and business responsibility of a person or firm

ra·tio \\'rā-shō, -shē-ō\\ *n, pl* **ra·tios 1** : the indicated quotient of two numbers or mathematical expressions **2** : the relationship in number, quantity, or degree between two or more things

ra·ti·o·ci·na·tion \\ˌra-tē-ˌōs-ᵊn-'ā-shən, -shē-, -ˌäs-\\ *n* : exact thinking : REASONING — **ra·ti·o·ci·nate** \\-'ōs-ᵊn-ˌāt, -'äs-\\ *vb* — **ra·ti·o·ci·na·tive** \\-'ōs-ᵊn-ˌā-tiv, -'äs-\\ *adj* — **ra·ti·o·ci·na·tor** \\-'ōs-ᵊn-ˌā-tər, -'äs-\\ *n*

¹ra·tion \\'ra-shən, 'rä-\\ *n* **1** : a food allowance for one day **2** : FOOD, PROVISIONS, DIET — usu. used in pl. **3** : SHARE, ALLOTMENT

²ration *vb* **1** : to supply with or allot as rations **2** : to use or allot sparingly **syn** apportion, portion, prorate, parcel

¹ra·tio·nal \\'ra-shə-nəl\\ *adj* **1** : having reason or understanding **2** : of or relating to reason **3** : relating to, consisting of, or being one or more rational numbers — **ra·tio·nal·ly** *adv*

²rational *n* : RATIONAL NUMBER

ra·tio·nale \\ˌra-shə-'nal\\ *n* **1** : an explanation of principles controlling belief or practice **2** : an underlying reason

ra·tio·nal·ism \\'ra-shə-nə-ˌli-zəm\\ *n* : the practice of guiding one's actions and opinions solely by what seems reasonable — **ra·tio·nal·ist** \\-list\\ *n* — **rationalist** *or* **ra·tio·nal·is·tic** \\ˌra-shə-nə-'lis-tik\\ *adj*

ra·tio·nal·i·ty \\ˌra-shə-'na-lə-tē\\ *n, pl* **-ties** : the quality or state of being rational

ra·tio·nal·ize \\'ra-shə-nə-ˌlīz\\ *vb* **-ized; -iz·ing 1** : to make (something irrational) appear rational or reasonable **2** : to provide a natural explanation of (as a myth) **3** : to justify (as one's behavior or weaknesses) esp. to oneself **4** : to find plausible but untrue reasons for conduct — **ra·tio·nal·i·za·tion** \\ˌra-shə-nə-lə-'zā-shən\\ *n*

rational number *n* : an integer or the quotient of an integer divided by a nonzero integer

rat race *n* : strenuous, tiresome, and usu. competitive activity or rush

rat·tan \\ra-'tan, rə-\\ *n* : a cane or switch made from one of the long stems of an Asian climbing palm; *also* : this palm

rat·ter \\'ra-tər\\ *n* : a rat-catching dog or cat

¹rat·tle \\'rat-ᵊl\\ *vb* **rat·tled; rat·tling 1** : to make or cause to make a series of clattering sounds **2** : to move with a clattering sound **3** : to say or do in a brisk lively fashion ⟨∼ off the answers⟩ **4** : CONFUSE, UPSET ⟨∼ a witness⟩

²rattle *n* **1** : a toy that produces a rattle when shaken **2** : a series of clattering and knocking sounds **3** : a rattling organ at the end of a rattlesnake's tail

rat·tler \\'rat-lər\\ *n* : RATTLESNAKE

rat·tle·snake \\'rat-ᵊl-ˌsnāk\\ *n* : any of various American pit vipers with a rattle at the end of the tail

rat·tle·trap \\'rat-ᵊl-ˌtrap\\ *n* : something (as an old car) rickety and full of rattles

rat·tling \\'rat-liŋ\\ *adj* **1** : LIVELY, BRISK **2** : FIRST-RATE, SPLENDID

rat·trap \\'rat-ˌtrap\\ *n* **1** : a trap for rats **2** : a dilapidated building

rattlesnake

rat·ty \'ra-tē\ *adj* **rat·ti·er; -est 1** : infested with rats **2** : of, relating to, or suggestive of rats **3** : SHABBY

rau·cous \'rȯ-kəs\ *adj* **1** : HARSH, HOARSE, STRIDENT **2** : boisterously disorderly — **rau·cous·ly** *adv* — **rau·cous·ness** *n*

raun·chy \'rȯn-chē, 'rän-\ *adj* **raun·chi·er; -est 1** : SLOVENLY, DIRTY **2** : OBSCENE, SMUTTY — **raun·chi·ness** \-chē-nəs\ *n*

¹rav·age \'ra-vij\ *n* [F] : an act or result of ravaging : DEVASTATION

²ravage *vb* **rav·aged; rav·ag·ing** : to lay waste : DEVASTATE — **rav·ag·er** *n*

¹rave \'rāv\ *vb* **raved; rav·ing** [ME *raven*] **1** : to talk wildly in or as if in delirium : STORM, RAGE **2** : to talk with extreme enthusiasm

²rave *n* **1** : an act or instance of raving **2** : an extravagantly favorable criticism

¹rav·el \'ra-vəl\ *vb* **-eled** *or* **-elled; -el·ing** *or* **-el·ling 1** : UNRAVEL, UNTWIST **2** : TANGLE, CONFUSE

²ravel *n* **1** : something tangled **2** : something raveled out; *esp* : a loose thread

¹ra·ven \'rā-vən\ *n* : a large black bird related to the crow

²raven *adj* : black and glossy like a raven's feathers

³rav·en \'ra-vən\ *vb* **rav·ened; rav·en·ing 1** : to devour greedily **2** : DESPOIL, PLUNDER **3** : PREY

rav·en·ous \'ra-və-nəs\ *adj* **1** : RAPACIOUS, VORACIOUS **2** : eager for food : very hungry — **rav·en·ous·ly** *adv* — **rav·en·ous·ness** *n*

ra·vine \rə-'vēn\ *n* : a small narrow steep-sided valley larger than a gully

rav·i·o·li \ˌra-vē-'ō-lē\ *n* [It., fr. It dial., pl. of *raviolo*, lit., little turnip, dim. of *rava* turnip, fr. L *rapa*] : small cases of dough with a savory filling (as of meat or cheese)

rav·ish \'ra-vish\ *vb* **1** : to seize and take away by violence **2** : to overcome with emotion and esp. with joy or delight **3** : RAPE — **rav·ish·er** *n* — **rav·ish·ment** *n*

¹raw \'rȯ\ *adj* **raw·er** \'rȯ-ər\; **raw·est** \'rȯ-əst\ **1** : not cooked **2** : changed little from the original form : not processed ⟨∼ materials⟩ **3** : having the surface abraded or irritated ⟨a ∼ sore⟩ **4** : not trained or experienced ⟨∼ recruits⟩ **5** : VULGAR, COARSE **6** : disagreeably cold and damp ⟨a ∼ day⟩ **7** : UNFAIR ⟨∼ deal⟩ — **raw·ness** *n*

²raw *n* : a raw place or state; *esp* : NUDITY

raw·boned \'rȯ-bōnd\ *adj* **1** : LEAN, GAUNT **2** : having a heavy frame that seems to have little flesh

raw·hide \'rȯ-hīd\ *n* : the untanned skin of cattle; *also* : a whip made of this

¹ray \'rā\ *n* : any of an order of large flat catilaginous fishes that have the eyes on the upper surface and the hind end of the body slender and taillike

²ray *n* [ME, fr. MF *rai*, fr. L *radius* rod, ray] **1** : any of the lines of light that appear to radiate from a bright object **2** : a thin beam of radiant energy (as light) **3** : light from a beam **4** : a thin line like a beam of light **5** : an animal or plant structure resembling a ray **6** : a tiny bit : PARTICLE ⟨a ∼ of hope⟩

ray·on \'rā-ˌän\ *n* : a fiber made from cellulose; *also* : a yarn, thread, or fabric made from such fibers

raze \'rāz\ *vb* **razed; raz·ing 1** : to scrape, cut, or shave off **2** : to destroy to the ground : DEMOLISH

ra·zor \'rā-zər\ *n* : a sharp cutting instrument used to shave off hair

ra·zor–backed \'rā-zər-ˌbakt\ *or* **ra·zor·back** \-ˌbak\ *adj* : having a sharp narrow back ⟨∼ horse⟩

razor clam *n* : any of a family of marine bivalve mollusks having a long narrow curved thin shell

¹razz \'raz\ *n* : RASPBERRY 2

²razz *vb* : RIDICULE, TEASE

Rb *symbol* rubidium

RBC *abbr* red blood cells; red blood count

RBI \ˌär-(ˌ)bē-'ī, 'ri-bē\ *n, pl* **RBIs** *or* **RBI** [run *b*atted *in*] : a run in baseball that is driven in by a batter

RC *abbr* **1** Red Cross **2** Roman Catholic

RCAF *abbr* Royal Canadian Air Force

RCMP *abbr* Royal Canadian Mounted Police

RCN *abbr* Royal Canadian Navy

rct *abbr* recruit

rd *abbr* **1** road **2** rod **3** round

RD *abbr* rural delivery

RDA *abbr* recommended daily allowance; recommended dietary allowance

re \'rā, 'rē\ *prep* : with regard to

Re *symbol* rhenium

re- \rē, ˌrē, 'rē\ *prefix* **1** : again : for a second time **2** : anew : in a new or different form **3** : back : backward

reabsorb	reassess
reacquire	reassessment
reactivate	reassign
reactivation	reassignment
readdress	reassume
readjust	reattach
readjustment	reattachment
readmission	reattain
readmit	reattempt
reaffirm	reauthorization
reaffirmation	reauthorize
realign	reawaken
realignment	rebaptism
reallocate	rebaptize
reallocation	rebid
reanalysis	rebind
reanalyze	reboil
reanimate	rebroadcast
reanimation	reburial
reannex	rebury
reannexation	recalculate
reappear	recalculation
reappearance	rechannel
reapplication	recharge
reapply	rechargeable
reappoint	recharter
reappointment	recheck
reapportion	rechristen
reapportionment	reclassification
reappraisal	reclassify
reappraise	recoin
rearm	recolonization
rearmament	recolonize
rearouse	recolor
rearrange	recombine
rearrangement	recommence
rearrest	recommission
reascend	recommit
reassemble	recompile
reassembly	recompose
reassert	recomputation

\ə\abut \ᵊ\kitten \ər\further \a\ash \ā\ace \ä\mop, mar \au̇\out \ch\chin \e\bet \ē\easy \g\go \i\hit \ī\ice \j\job \ŋ\sing \ō\go \ȯ\law \ȯi\boy \th\thin \th\the \ü\loot \u̇\foot \y\yet \zh\vision *see also* Pronunciation Symbols page

recompute
reconceive
reconcentrate
reconception
recondensation
recondense
reconfirm
reconfirmation
reconnect
reconquer
reconquest
reconsecrate
reconsecration
recontact
recontaminate
recontamination
reconvene
reconvert
recook
recopy
recross
recrystallize
recut
redecorate
redecoration
rededicate
rededication
redefine
redefinition
redeposit
redesign
redetermination
redetermine
redevelop
redevelopment
redirect
rediscount
rediscover
rediscovery
redissolve
redistill
redistillation
redraft
redraw
reecho
reedit
reelect
reelection
reemerge
reemergence
reemphasis
reemphasize
reemploy
reemployment
reenact
reenactment
reenergize
reenlist
reenlistment
reenter
reequip
reestablish
reestablishment
reevaluate
reevaluation
reexamination
reexamine
reexport
refashion
refight
refigure
refinish
refit

refix
refloat
refold
reforge
reformulate
reformulation
refortify
refound
refreeze
refuel
refurnish
regain
regather
regild
regive
regrade
regrind
regrow
regrowth
rehandle
rehear
reheat
rehouse
reimpose
reimposition
reincorporate
reinsert
reinsertion
reintegrate
reinterpret
reinterpretation
reintroduce
reintroduction
reinvention
reinvest
reinvestment
reinvigorate
reinvigoration
reissue
rejudge
rekindle
reknit
relaunch
relearn
relight
reline
reload
remanufacture
remap
remarriage
remarry
rematch
remelt
remigration
remix
remold
rename
renegotiate
renegotiation
renominate
renomination
renumber
reoccupy
reoccur
reopen
reorder
reorganization
reorganize
reorient
reorientation
repack
repaint
repass

repeople
rephotograph
rephrase
replant
repopulate
reprice
reprocess
reprogram
republication
republish
repurchase
reradiate
reread
rereading
rerecord
reroute
reschedule
rescore
rescreen
reseal
reseed
resell
reset
resettle
resettlement
resew
reshow
resocialization
resow
respell
restaff
restart
restate
restatement
restock
restrengthen

restructure
restudy
restuff
restyle
resubmit
resummon
resupply
resurface
resurvey
resynthesis
resynthesize
retaste
retell
retest
retool
retrain
retransmission
retransmit
retrial
reunification
reunify
reunite
reusable
reuse
revaluate
revaluation
revalue
revisit
rewarm
rewash
reweave
rewed
reweigh
rewire
rezone

[1]**reach** \\'rēch\\ *vb* **1** : to stretch out **2** : to touch or attempt to touch or seize **3** : to extend to **4** : to communicate with **5** : to arrive at **syn** gain, realize, achieve, attain — **reach·able** *adj* — **reach·er** *n*

[2]**reach** *n* **1** : an unbroken stretch of a river **2** : the act of reaching **3** : a reachable distance; *also* : ability to reach **4** : a range of knowledge or comprehension

re·act \\rē-'akt\\ *vb* **1** : to exert a return or counteracting influence **2** : to have or show a reaction **3** : to act in opposition to a force or influence **4** : to move or tend in a reverse direction **5** : to undergo chemical reaction

re·ac·tant \\rē-'ak-tənt\\ *n* : a chemically reacting substance

re·ac·tion \\rē-'ak-shən\\ *n* **1** : the act or process of reacting **2** : a counter tendency; *esp* : a tendency toward a former esp. outmoded political or social order or policy **3** : bodily, mental, or emotional response to a stimulus **4** : chemical change **5** : a process involving change in atomic nuclei

re·ac·tion·ary \\rē-'ak-shə-ˌner-ē\\ *adj* : relating to, marked by, or favoring esp. political reaction — **reactionary** *n*

re·ac·tive \\rē-'ak-tiv\\ *adj* : reacting or tending to react

re·ac·tor \\rē-'ak-tər\\ *n* **1** : one that reacts **2** : a device for the controlled release of nuclear energy

[1]**read** \\'rēd\\ *vb* **read** \\'red\\; **read·ing 1** : to understand language by interpreting written symbols for speech sounds **2** : to utter aloud written or printed words **3** : to learn by observing ⟨∼ nature's signs⟩ **4** : to study by a course of reading ⟨∼s law⟩ **5** : to discover the meaning of ⟨∼ the clues⟩ **6** : to recognize or interpret as if by reading **7** : to attribute (a meaning) to something ⟨∼ guilt in his manner⟩ **8** : INDICATE ⟨thermometer ∼s 10°⟩ **9** : to consist in phrasing or meaning ⟨the two versions ∼ differently⟩ — **read·abil·i·ty** \\ˌrē-də-'bi-lə-tē\\ *n* — **read·able** \\'rē-də-bəl\\ *adj* — **read·ably** \\-blē\\ *adv* — **read·er** *n*

²**read** \'red\ *adj* : informed by reading ⟨widely ∼⟩

read·er·ship \'rē-dər-ˌship\ *n* : the mass or a particular group of readers

read·ing *n* **1** : something read or for reading **2** : a particular version **3** : data indicated by an instrument ⟨thermometer ∼⟩ **4** : a particular interpretation (as of a law) **5** : a particular performance (as of a musical work) **6** : an indication of a certain state of affairs

read–only memory *n* : a computer memory that contains special-purpose information (as a program) which cannot be altered

read·out \'rēd-ˌaut\ *n* : the process of removing information from an automatic device (as a computer) and displaying it in an understandable form; *also* : the information removed from such a device

read out *vb* **1** : to read aloud **2** : to expel from an organization

¹**ready** \'re-dē\ *adj* **read·i·er; -est 1** : prepared for use or action **2** : likely to do something indicated; *also* : willingly disposed : INCLINED **3** : spontaneously prompt ⟨her ∼ wit⟩ **4** : immediately available ⟨∼ cash⟩ — **read·i·ly** \'re-də-lē\ *adv* — **read·i·ness** \-dē-nəs\ *n* — **at the ready** : ready for immediate use

²**ready** *vb* **read·ied; ready·ing** : to make ready : PREPARE

ready–made \ˌre-dē-'mād\ *adj* : already made up for general sale : not specially made — **ready–made** *n*

ready room *n* : a room in which pilots are briefed and await orders

re·agent \rē-'ā-jənt\ *n* : a substance that takes part in or brings about a particular chemical reaction

¹**re·al** \'rēl\ *adj* [ME, real, relating to things (in law), fr. MF, fr. ML & LL; ML *realis* relating to things (in law), fr. LL, real, fr. L *res* thing, fact] **1** : of or relating to fixed or immovable things (as land) ⟨∼ property⟩ **2** : not artificial : GENUINE; *also* : not imaginary — **re·al·ness** *n* — **for real 1** : in earnest **2** : GENUINE

²**real** *adv* : VERY

real estate *n* : property in buildings and land

re·al·ism \'rē-ə-ˌli-zəm\ *n* **1** : the disposition to face facts and to deal with them practically **2** : true and faithful portrayal of nature and of people in art or literature — **re·al·ist** \-list\ *adj or n* — **re·al·is·tic** \ˌrē-ə-'lis-tik\ *adj* — **re·al·is·ti·cal·ly** \-ti-k(ə-)lē\ *adv*

re·al·i·ty \rē-'a-lə-tē\ *n, pl* **-ties 1** : the quality or state of being real **2** : something real **3** : the totality of real things and events

re·al·ize \'rē-ə-ˌlīz\ *vb* **-ized; -iz·ing 1** : to make actual : ACCOMPLISH **2** : to convert into money ⟨∼ assets⟩ **3** : OBTAIN, GAIN ⟨∼ a profit⟩ **4** : to be aware of : UNDERSTAND — **re·al·iz·able** *adj* — **re·al·i·za·tion** \ˌrē-ə-lə-'zā-shən\ *n*

re·al·ly \'rē-lē, 'ri-\ *adv* : in truth : in fact : ACTUALLY

realm \'relm\ *n* **1** : KINGDOM **2** : SPHERE, DOMAIN

real number *n* : any of the numbers (as −2, 3, ⅞, .25, π) that are rational or irrational

re·al·po·li·tik \rā-'äl-ˌpō-li-ˌtēk\ *n* [G] : politics based on practical and material factors rather than on theoretical or ethical objectives

real time *n* : the actual time during which something takes place — **real–time** *adj*

re·al·ty \'rēl-tē\ *n* : REAL ESTATE

¹**ream** \'rēm\ *n* [ME *reme*, fr. MF *raime*, fr. Ar *rizmah*, lit., bundle] : a quantity of paper that is variously 480, 500, or 516 sheets

²**ream** *vb* : to enlarge, shape, or clear with a reamer

ream·er \'rē-mər\ *n* : a tool with cutting edges that is used to enlarge or shape a hole

reap \'rēp\ *vb* **1** : to cut or clear with a scythe, sickle, or machine **2** : to gather by or as if by cutting : HARVEST ⟨∼ a reward⟩ — **reap·er** *n*

¹**rear** \'rir\ *vb* **1** : to erect by building **2** : to set or raise upright **3** : to breed and raise for use or market ⟨∼ livestock⟩ **4** : BRING UP, FOSTER **5** : to lift or rise up; *esp* : to rise on the hind legs

²**rear** *n* **1** : the unit (as of an army) or area farthest from the enemy **2** : BACK; *also* : the position at the back of something

³**rear** *adj* : being at the back

rear admiral *n* : a commissioned officer in the navy or coast guard ranking next below a vice admiral

¹**rear·ward** \'rir-wərd\ *adj* **1** : being at or toward the rear **2** : directed toward the rear

²**rear·ward** *also* **rear·wards** \-wərdz\ *adv* : at or toward the rear

reas *abbr* reasonable

¹**rea·son** \'rēz-ᵊn\ *n* [ME *resoun*, fr. OF *raison*, fr. L *ration-, ratio* reason, computation] **1** : a statement offered in explanation or justification **2** : GROUND, CAUSE **3** : the power to think : INTELLECT **4** : a sane or sound mind **5** : due exercise of the faculty of logical thought

²**reason** *vb* **1** : to talk with another to cause a change of mind **2** : to use the faculty of reason : THINK **3** : to discover or formulate by the use of reason — **rea·son·er** *n* — **rea·son·ing** *n*

rea·son·able \'rēz-ᵊn-ə-bəl\ *adj* **1** : being within the bounds of reason : not extreme **2** : INEXPENSIVE **3** : able to reason : RATIONAL — **rea·son·able·ness** *n* — **rea·son·ably** \-blē\ *adv*

re·as·sure \ˌrē-ə-'shur\ *vb* **1** : to assure again **2** : to restore confidence to : free from fear — **re·as·sur·ance** \-'shur-əns\ *n* — **re·as·sur·ing·ly** *adv*

¹**re·bate** \'rē-ˌbāt\ *vb* **re·bat·ed; re·bat·ing** : to make or give a rebate

²**rebate** *n* : a return of part of a payment **syn** deduction, abatement, discount

³**re·bate** \'ra-bət, 'rē-ˌbāt\ *chiefly Brit var of* RABBET

¹**reb·el** \'re-bəl\ *adj* [ME, fr. OF *rebelle*, fr. L *rebellis*, fr. *re-* + *bellum* war] : of or relating to rebels

²**rebel** *n* : one that rebels against authority

³**re·bel** \ri-'bel\ *vb* **re·belled; re·bel·ling 1** : to resist the authority of one's government **2** : to act in or show disobedience **3** : to feel or exhibit anger or revulsion

re·bel·lion \ri-'bel-yən\ *n* : resistance to authority; *esp* : defiance against a government through uprising or revolt

re·bel·lious \-yəs\ *adj* **1** : given to or engaged in rebellion **2** : inclined to resist authority — **re·bel·lious·ly** *adv* — **re·bel·lious·ness** *n*

re·birth \ˌrē-'bərth\ *n* **1** : a new or 2d birth **2** : RENAISSANCE, REVIVAL

re·born \-'bȯrn\ *adj* : born again : REGENERATED, REVIVED

¹**re·bound** \ˌrē-'baund, 'rē-ˌbaund\ *vb* **1** : to spring back on or as if on striking another body **2** : to recover from a setback or frustration

²**re·bound** \'rē-ˌbaund\ *n* **1** : the action of rebounding **2** : a rebounding ball **3** : a reaction to setback or frustration

re·buff \ri-'bəf\ *vb* : to reject or criticize sharply : SNUB — **rebuff** *n*

re·build \(ˌ)rē-'bild\ *vb* **-built** \-'bilt\; **-build·ing 1** : REPAIR, RECONSTRUCT; *also* : REMODEL **2** : to build again

¹**re·buke** \ri-'byük\ *vb* **re·buked; re·buk·ing** : to reprimand sharply : REPROVE

²**rebuke** *n* : a sharp reprimand

re·bus \'rē-bəs\ *n* [L, by things, abl. pl. of *res* thing] : a representation of syllables or words by means of pictures; *also* : a riddle composed of such pictures

re·but \ri-'bət\ *vb* **re·but·ted; re·but·ting** : to refute esp.

formally (as in debate) by evidence and arguments **syn** disprove, controvert, confute — **re·but·ter** *n*

re·but·tal \ri-'bət-ᵊl\ *n* : the act of rebutting

rec *abbr* **1** receipt **2** record; recording **3** recreation

re·cal·ci·trant \ri-'kal-sə-trənt\ *adj* [LL *recalcitrant-, recalcitrans,* prp. of *recalcitrare* to be stubbornly disobedient, fr. L, to kick back, fr. *re-* back, again + *calcitrare* to kick, fr. *calc-, calx* heel] **1** : stubbornly resisting authority **2** : resistant to handling or treatment **syn** refractory, headstrong, willful, unruly, ungovernable — **re·cal·ci·trance** \-trəns\ *n*

¹re·call \ri-'kȯl\ *vb* **1** : to call back **2** : REMEMBER, RECOLLECT **3** : REVOKE, CANCEL

²re·call \ri-'kȯl, 'rē-ˌkȯl\ *n* **1** : a summons to return **2** : the procedure of removing an official by popular vote **3** : remembrance of things learned or experienced **4** : the act of revoking **5** : a call by a manufacturer for the return of a product that may be defective or contaminated

re·cant \ri-'kant\ *vb* : to take back (something one has said) publicly : make an open confession of error — **re·can·ta·tion** \ˌrē-ˌkan-'tā-shən\ *n*

¹re·cap \'rē-ˌkap, rē-'kap\ *vb* **re·capped; re·cap·ping** : RECAPITULATE — **re·cap** \'rē-ˌkap\ *n*

²recap *vb* **re·capped; re·cap·ping** : RETREAD — **re·cap** \'rē-ˌkap\ *n*

re·ca·pit·u·late \ˌrē-kə-'pi-chə-ˌlāt\ *vb* **-lat·ed; -lat·ing** : to restate briefly : SUMMARIZE — **re·ca·pit·u·la·tion** \-ˌpi-chə-'lā-shən\ *n*

re·cap·ture \(ˌ)rē-'kap-chər\ *vb* **1** : to capture again **2** : to experience again ⟨∼ happy times⟩

re·cast \(ˌ)rē-'kast\ *vb* **1** : to cast again **2** : REVISE, REMODEL ⟨∼ a sentence⟩

recd *abbr* received

re·cede \ri-'sēd\ *vb* **re·ced·ed; re·ced·ing 1** : to move back or away **2** : to slant backward **3** : DIMINISH, CONTRACT

¹re·ceipt \ri-'sēt\ *n* **1** : RECIPE **2** : the act of receiving **3** : something received — usu. used in pl. **4** : a written acknowledgment of something received

²receipt *vb* **1** : to give a receipt for **2** : to mark as paid

re·ceiv·able \ri-'sē-və-bəl\ *adj* **1** : capable of being received; *esp* : acceptable as legal ⟨∼ certificates⟩ **2** : subject to call for payment ⟨notes ∼⟩

re·ceive \ri-'sēv\ *vb* **re·ceived; re·ceiv·ing 1** : to take in or accept (as something sent or paid) : come into possession of : GET **2** : CONTAIN, HOLD **3** : to permit to enter : GREET, WELCOME **4** : to be at home to visitors **5** : to accept as true or authoritative **6** : to be the subject of : UNDERGO, EXPERIENCE ⟨∼ a shock⟩ **7** : to change incoming radio waves into sounds or pictures

re·ceiv·er \ri-'sē-vər\ *n* **1** : one that receives **2** : a person legally appointed to receive and have charge of property or money involved in a lawsuit **3** : a device for converting electromagnetic waves or signals into audio or visual form ⟨telephone ∼⟩

re·ceiv·er·ship \-ˌship\ *n* **1** : the office or function of a receiver **2** : the condition of being in the hands of a receiver

re·cen·cy \'rēs-ᵊn-sē\ *n* : RECENTNESS

re·cent \'rēs-ᵊnt\ *adj* **1** : of the present time or time just past ⟨∼ history⟩ **2** : having lately come into existence : NEW, FRESH **3** *cap* : HOLOCENE — **re·cent·ly** *adv* — **re·cent·ness** *n*

re·cep·ta·cle \ri-'sep-ti-kəl\ *n* **1** : something used to receive and hold something else : CONTAINER **2** : the enlarged end of a flower stalk upon which the parts of the flower grow **3** : an electrical fitting containing the live parts of a circuit

re·cep·tion \ri-'sep-shən\ *n* **1** : the act of receiving **2** : a social gathering at which guests are formally welcomed

re·cep·tion·ist \ri-'sep-shə-nist\ *n* : a person employed to greet callers

re·cep·tive \ri-'sep-tiv\ *adj* : able or inclined to receive; *esp* : open and responsive to ideas, impressions, or suggestions — **re·cep·tive·ly** *adv* — **re·cep·tive·ness** *n* — **re·cep·tiv·i·ty** \ˌrē-ˌsep-'ti-və-tē\ *n*

re·cep·tor \ri-'sep-tər\ *n* **1** : one that receives; *esp* : SENSE ORGAN **2** : a chemical group or molecule in the outer cell membrane or in the cell interior that has an affinity for a specific chemical group, molecule, or virus

¹re·cess \'rē-ˌses, ri-'ses\ *n* **1** : a secret or secluded place **2** : an indentation in a line or surface (as an alcove in a room) **3** : a suspension of business or procedure for rest or relaxation

²recess *vb* **1** : to put into a recess **2** : to make a recess in **3** : to interrupt for a recess **4** : to take a recess

re·ces·sion \ri-'se-shən\ *n* **1** : the act of receding : WITHDRAWAL **2** : a departing procession (as at the end of a church service) **3** : a period of reduced economic activity

re·ces·sion·al \ri-'se-shə-nəl\ *n* **1** : a hymn or musical piece at the conclusion of a service or program **2** : RECESSION 2

¹re·ces·sive \ri-'se-siv\ *adj* **1** : tending to recede **2** : producing or being a bodily characteristic that is masked or not expressed when a contrasting dominant gene or trait is present ⟨∼ genes⟩ ⟨∼ traits⟩

²recessive *n* : a recessive characteristic or gene; *also* : an individual that has one or more recessive characteristics

re·cher·ché \rə-ˌsher-'shā, -'sheər-ˌshā\ *adj* [F] **1** : CHOICE, RARE **2** : excessively refined

re·cid·i·vism \ri-'si-də-ˌvi-zəm\ *n* : a tendency to relapse into a previous condition; *esp* : relapse into criminal behavior — **re·cid·i·vist** \-vist\ *n*

recip *abbr* reciprocal; reciprocity

rec·i·pe \'re-sə-(ˌ)pē\ *n* [L, take, imperative of *recipere* to take, receive, fr. *re-* back + *capere* to take] **1** : a set of instructions for making something from various ingredients **2** : a method of procedure : FORMULA

re·cip·i·ent \ri-'si-pē-ənt\ *n* : one that receives

¹re·cip·ro·cal \ri-'si-prə-kəl\ *adj* **1** : inversely related **2** : MUTUAL, SHARED **3** : serving to reciprocate **4** : mutually corresponding — **re·cip·ro·cal·ly** *adv*

²reciprocal *n* **1** : something in a reciprocal relationship to another **2** : one of a pair of numbers (as ⅔, 3⁄2) whose product is one

re·cip·ro·cate \-ˌkāt\ *vb* **-cat·ed; -cat·ing 1** : to move backward and forward alternately **2** : to give and take mutually **3** : to make a return for something done or given — **re·cip·ro·ca·tion** \-ˌsi-prə-'kā-shən\ *n*

rec·i·proc·i·ty \ˌre-sə-'prä-sə-tē\ *n, pl* **-ties 1** : the quality or state of being reciprocal **2** : mutual exchange of privileges (as trade advantages between countries)

re·cit·al \ri-'sīt-ᵊl\ *n* **1** : an act or instance of reciting : ACCOUNT **2** : a public reading or recitation ⟨a poetry ∼⟩ **3** : a concert given by a musician, dancer, or dance troupe **4** : a public exhibition of skill given by music or dance pupils — **re·cit·al·ist** \-ᵊl-ist\ *n*

rec·i·ta·tion \ˌre-sə-'tā-shən\ *n* **1** : RECITING, RECITAL **2** : delivery before an audience usu. of something memorized **3** : a classroom exercise in which pupils answer questions on a lesson they have studied

re·cite \ri-'sīt\ *vb* **re·cit·ed; re·cit·ing 1** : to repeat verbatim (as something memorized) **2** : to recount in some detail : RELATE **3** : to reply to a teacher's questions on a lesson — **re·cit·er** *n*

reck·less \'re-kləs\ *adj* : lacking caution : RASH **syn** hasty, brash, hotheaded, thoughtless — **reck·less·ly** *adv* — **reck·less·ness** *n*

reck·on \'re-kən\ *vb* **1** : COUNT, CALCULATE, COMPUTE **2** : CONSIDER, REGARD **3** *chiefly dial* : THINK, SUPPOSE, GUESS

reck·on·ing *n* **1** : an act or instance of reckoning ⟨2 : a settling of accounts ⟨day of ∼⟩

re·claim \ri-ˈklām\ *vb* **1** : to recall from wrong conduct : REFORM **2** : to change from an undesirable to a desired condition ⟨∼ marshy land⟩ **3** : to obtain from a waste product or by-product **4** : to demand or obtain the return of — **re·claim·able** *adj* — **rec·la·ma·tion** \ˌre-klə-ˈmā-shən\ *n*

re·cline \ri-ˈklīn\ *vb* **re·clined; re·clin·ing 1** : to lean or incline backward **2** : to lie down : REST

re·clin·er \ri-ˈklī-nər\ *n* : a chair with an adjustable back and footrest

re·cluse \ˈre-ˌklüs, ri-ˈklüs\ *n* : a person who leads a secluded or solitary life : HERMIT

rec·og·ni·tion \ˌre-kəg-ˈni-shən\ *n* **1** : the act of recognizing : the state of being recognized : ACKNOWLEDGMENT **2** : special notice or attention

re·cog·ni·zance \ri-ˈkäg-nə-zəns\ *n* : a promise recorded before a court or magistrate to do something (as to appear in court or to keep the peace) usu. under penalty of a money forfeiture

rec·og·nize \ˈre-kəg-ˌnīz\ *vb* **-nized; -niz·ing 1** : to acknowledge (as a speaker in a meeting) as one entitled to be heard at the time **2** : to acknowledge the existence or the independence of (a country or government) **3** : to take notice of **4** : to acknowledge with appreciation **5** : to acknowledge acquaintance with **6** : to identify as previously known **7** : to perceive clearly : REALIZE — **rec·og·niz·able** \ˈre-kəg-ˌnī-zə-bəl\ *adj* — **rec·og·niz·ably** \-blē\ *adv*

¹re·coil \ri-ˈkȯil\ *vb* **1** : to draw back : RETREAT **2** : to spring back to or as if to a starting point **syn** shrink, flinch, wince, quail, blanch

²re·coil \ˈrē-ˌkȯil, ri-ˈkȯil\ *n* : the action of recoiling (as by a gun or spring)

re·coil·less \-ˌkȯil-ləs, -ˈkȯil-\ *adj* : venting expanding propellant gas before recoil is produced ⟨∼ gun⟩

rec·ol·lect \ˌre-kə-ˈlekt\ *vb* : to recall to mind : REMEMBER **syn** recall, remind, reminisce, bethink

rec·ol·lec·tion \ˌre-kə-ˈlek-shən\ *n* **1** : the act or power of recollecting **2** : something recollected

re·com·bi·nant DNA \(ˌ)rē-ˈkäm-bə-nənt-\ *n* : genetically engineered DNA prepared in vitro by joining together DNA fragments usu. from more than one species of organism

rec·om·mend \ˌre-kə-ˈmend\ *vb* **1** : to present as deserving of acceptance or trial **2** : to give in charge : COMMIT **3** : to make acceptable **4** : ADVISE, COUNSEL — **rec·om·mend·able** \-ˈmen-də-bəl\ *adj*

rec·om·men·da·tion \ˌre-kə-mən-ˈdā-shən\ *n* **1** : the act of recommending **2** : something recommended **3** : something that recommends

¹rec·om·pense \ˈre-kəm-ˌpens\ *vb* **-pensed; -pens·ing 1** : to give compensation to : pay for **2** : to return in kind : REQUITE **syn** reimburse, indemnify, repay, compensate

²recompense *n* : COMPENSATION

rec·on·cile \ˈre-kən-ˌsīl\ *vb* **-ciled; -cil·ing 1** : to cause to be friendly or harmonious again **2** : ADJUST, SETTLE ⟨∼ differences⟩ **3** : to bring to submission or acceptance **syn** conform, accommodate, harmonize, coordinate — **rec·on·cil·able** *adj* — **rec·on·cile·ment** *n* — **rec·on·cil·er** *n*

rec·on·cil·i·a·tion \ˌre-kən-ˌsi-lē-ˈā-shən\ *n* **1** : the action of reconciling **2** : the Roman Catholic sacrament of penance

re·con·dite \ˈre-kən-ˌdīt\ *adj* **1** : hard to understand : PROFOUND, ABSTRUSE **2** : little known : OBSCURE

re·con·di·tion \ˌrē-kən-ˈdi-shən\ *vb* **1** : to restore to good condition (as by replacing parts) **2** : to condition anew

re·con·nais·sance \ri-ˈkä-nə-zəns, -səns\ *n* [F, lit., recognition] : a preliminary survey of an area; *esp* : an exploratory military survey of enemy territory

re·con·noi·ter *or* **re·con·noi·tre** \ˌrē-kə-ˈnȯi-tər, ˌre-\ *vb* **-noi·tered** *or* **-noi·tred; -noi·ter·ing** *or* **-noi·tring** : to make a reconnaissance of : engage in reconnaissance

re·con·sid·er \ˌrē-kən-ˈsi-dər\ *vb* : to consider again with a view to changing or reversing — **re·con·sid·er·a·tion** \-ˌsi-də-ˈrā-shən\ *n*

re·con·sti·tute \ˌrē-ˈkän-stə-ˌtüt, -ˌtyüt\ *vb* : to restore to a former condition by adding water ⟨∼ powdered milk⟩

re·con·struct \ˌrē-kən-ˈstrəkt\ *vb* : to construct again : REBUILD

re·con·struc·tion \ˌrē-kən-ˈstrək-shən\ *n* **1** : the action of reconstructing : the state of being reconstructed **2** *often cap* : the reorganization and reestablishment of the seceded states in the Union after the American Civil War **3** : something reconstructed

¹re·cord \ri-ˈkȯrd\ *vb* **1** : to set down in writing **2** : to register permanently **3** : INDICATE, READ **4** : to give evidence of **5** : to cause (as sound or visual images) to be registered (as on magnetic tape) in a form that permits reproduction

²rec·ord \ˈre-kərd\ *n* **1** : the act of being recorded **2** : a written account of proceedings **3** : known facts about a person; *also* : a collection of items of information (as in a database) treated as a unit **4** : an attested top performance **5** : something on which sound or visual images have been recorded

re·cord·er \ri-ˈkȯr-dər\ *n* **1** : a judge in some city courts **2** : one who records transactions officially **3** : a recording device **4** : a wind instrument with a whistle mouthpiece and eight fingerholes

re·cord·ing *n* : RECORD 5

re·cord·ist \ri-ˈkȯr-dist\ *n* : one who records sound esp. on film

¹re·count \ri-ˈkaunt\ *vb* : to relate in detail : TELL **syn** recite, rehearse, narrate, describe, state, report

²re·count \ˈrē-ˌkaunt, (ˌ)rē-ˈkaunt\ *vb* : to count again

³re·count \ˈrē-ˌkaunt, (ˌ)rē-ˈkaunt\ *n* : a second or fresh count

re·coup \ri-ˈküp\ *vb* : to get an equivalent or compensation for : make up for something lost

re·course \ˈrē-ˌkȯrs, ri-ˈkȯrs\ *n* **1** : a turning to someone or something for assistance or protection **2** : a source of aid : RESORT

re·cov·er \ri-ˈkə-vər\ *vb* **-ered; -er·ing 1** : to get back again : REGAIN, RETRIEVE **2** : to regain normal health, poise, or status **3** : to make up for : RECOUP ⟨∼ed all his losses⟩ **4** : RECLAIM ⟨∼ land from the sea⟩ **5** : to obtain a legal judgment in one's favor — **re·cov·er·able** *adj* — **re·cov·ery** \-ˈkə-və-rē\ *n*

re·cov·er \ˌrē-ˈkə-vər\ *vb* : to cover again

¹rec·re·ant \ˈre-krē-ənt\ *adj* [ME, fr. MF, fr. prp. of *recroire* to renounce one's cause in a trial by battle, fr. *re*-back + *croire* to believe, fr. L *credere*] **1** : COWARDLY **2** : UNFAITHFUL

²recreant *n* **1** : COWARD **2** : DESERTER

rec·re·ate \ˈre-krē-ˌāt\ *vb* **-at·ed; -at·ing 1** : to give new life or freshness to **2** : to take recreation — **rec·re·ative** \-ˌā-tiv\ *adj*

re·cre·ate \ˌrē-krē-ˈāt\ *vb* : to create again — **re·cre·ation** \-ˈā-shən\ *n* — **re·cre·ative** \-ˈā-tiv\ *adj*

rec·re·ation \ˌre-krē-ˈā-shən\ *n* : a refreshing of strength or spirits after work; *also* : a means of refreshment **syn** diversion, entertainment, amusement — **rec·re·ation·al** \-shə-nəl\ *adj*

recreational vehicle *n* : a vehicle designed for recreational use (as camping)

re·crim·i·na·tion \ri-ˌkri-mə-ˈnā-shən\ *n* : a retaliatory

\ə\abut \ᵊ\kitten \ər\further \a\ash \ā\ace \ä\mop, mar
\au\out \ch\chin \e\bet \ē\easy \g\go \i\hit \ī\ice \j\job
\ŋ\sing \ō\go \ȯ\law \ȯi\boy \th\thin \t̲h̲\the \ü\loot \u̇\foot
\y\yet \zh\vision *see also* Pronunciation Symbols page

accusation — **re·crim·i·nate** \-'kri-mə-nāt\ *vb* — **re·crim·i·na·to·ry** \-'kri-mə-nə-ˌtōr-ē\ *adj*

re·cru·des·cence \ˌrē-krü-'des-ᵊns\ *n* : a renewal or breaking out again esp. of something unhealthful or dangerous

¹**re·cruit** \ri-'krüt\ *vb* **1** : to form or strengthen with new members ⟨∼ an army⟩ **2** : to enlist as a member of an armed service **3** : to secure the services of **4** : to seek to enroll **5** : to restore or increase in health or vigor ⟨resting to ∼ his strength⟩ — **re·cruit·er** *n* — **re·cruit·ment** *n*

²**recruit** *n* [F *recrute, recrue* fresh growth, new levy of soldiers, fr. MF, fr. *recroistre* to grow up again, fr. L *recrescere*] : a newcomer to an activity or field; *esp* : a newly enlisted member of the armed forces

rec sec *abbr* recording secretary

rect *abbr* **1** receipt **2** rectangle; rectangular **3** rectified

rec·tal \'rekt-ᵊl\ *adj* : of or relating to the rectum — **rec·tal·ly** *adv*

rect·an·gle \'rek-ˌtaŋ-gəl\ *n* : a 4-sided figure with four right angles; *esp* : one with adjacent sides of unequal length — **rect·an·gu·lar** \rek-'taŋ-gyə-lər\ *adj*

rec·ti·fi·er \'rek-tə-ˌfī-ər\ *n* : one that rectifies; *esp* : a device for converting alternating current into direct current

rec·ti·fy \'rek-tə-ˌfī\ *vb* **-fied; -fy·ing** : to make or set right : CORRECT **syn** emend, amend, mend, right — **rec·ti·fi·ca·tion** \ˌrek-tə-fə-'kā-shən\ *n*

rec·ti·lin·ear \ˌrek-tə-'li-nē-ər\ *adj* **1** : moving in a straight line ⟨∼ motion⟩ **2** : characterized by straight lines

rec·ti·tude \'rek-tə-ˌtüd, -ˌtyüd\ *n* **1** : moral integrity **2** : correctness of procedure **syn** virtue, goodness, morality, probity

rec·to \'rek-tō\ *n, pl* **rectos** : a right-hand page

rec·tor \'rek-tər\ *n* **1** : a priest or minister in charge of a parish **2** : the head of a university or school — **rec·to·ri·al** \rek-'tōr-ē-əl\ *adj*

rec·to·ry \'rek-tə-rē\ *n, pl* **-ries** : the residence of a rector or a parish priest

rec·tum \'rek-təm\ *n, pl* **rectums** *or* **rec·ta** \-tə\ [ME, fr. ML, fr. *rectum intestinum*, lit., straight intestine] : the last part of the intestine joining the colon and anus

re·cum·bent \ri-'kəm-bənt\ *adj* : lying down : RECLINING

re·cu·per·ate \ri-'kü-pə-ˌrāt-, -'kyü-\ *vb* **-at·ed; -at·ing** : to get back (as health or strength) : RECOVER — **re·cu·per·a·tion** \-ˌkü-pə-'rā-shən, -ˌkyü-\ *n* — **re·cu·per·a·tive** \-'kü-pə-ˌrā-tiv, -'kyü-\ *adj*

re·cur \ri-'kər\ *vb* **re·curred; re·cur·ring 1** : to go or come back in thought or discussion **2** : to occur or appear again esp. after an interval : occur time after time — **re·cur·rence** \-'kər-əns\ *n* — **re·cur·rent** \-ənt\ *adj*

re·cy·cle \rē-'sī-kəl\ *vb* **1** : to pass again through a cycle of changes or treatment **2** : to process (as liquid body waste, glass, or cans) in order to regain materials for human use — **re·cy·cla·ble** \-k(ə)lə-bəl\ *adj* — **recycle** *n*

¹**red** \'red\ *adj* **red·der; red·dest 1** : of the color red **2** : endorsing radical social or political change esp. by force **3** *often cap* : of or relating to the former U.S.S.R. or its allies — **red·ly** *adv* — **red·ness** *n*

²**red** *n* **1** : the color of blood or of the ruby **2** : a revolutionary in politics **3** *cap* : COMMUNIST **4** : the condition of showing a loss ⟨in the ∼⟩

re·dact \ri-'dakt\ *vb* **1** : to put in writing : FRAME **2** : EDIT — **re·dac·tor** \-'dak-tər\ *n*

re·dac·tion \-'dak-shən\ *n* **1** : an act or instance of redacting **2** : EDITION

red alga *n* : any of a group of reddish usu. marine algae

red blood cell *n* : any of the hemoglobin-containing cells that carry oxygen from the lungs to the tissues and are responsible for the red color of vertebrate blood

red·breast \'red-ˌbrest\ *n* : ROBIN

red–carpet *adj* : marked by ceremonial courtesy

red cedar *n* : an American juniper with fragrant close-grained red wood; *also* : its wood

red clover *n* : a Eurasian clover with globe-shaped heads of reddish flowers widely cultivated for hay and forage

red·coat \'red-ˌkōt\ *n* : a British soldier esp. during the Revolutionary War

red·den \'red-ᵊn\ *vb* : to make or become red or reddish : FLUSH, BLUSH

red·dish \'re-dish\ *adj* : tinged with red — **red·dish·ness** *n*

re·deem \ri-'dēm\ *vb* [ME *redemen*, modif. of MF *redimer*, fr. L *redimere*, fr. *re-, red-* re- + *emere* to take, buy] **1** : to recover (property) by discharging an obligation **2** : to ransom, free, or rescue by paying a price **3** : to free from the consequences of sin **4** : to remove the obligation of by payment ⟨the government ∼s savings bonds⟩; *also* : to convert into something of value **5** : to make good (a promise) by performing : FULFILL **6** : to atone for — **re·deem·able** *adj* — **re·deem·er** *n*

re·demp·tion \ri-'demp-shən\ *n* : the act of redeeming : the state of being redeemed — **re·demp·tive** \-tiv\ *adj* — **re·demp·to·ry** \-tə-rē\ *adj*

re·de·ploy \ˌrē-di-'ploi\ *vb* **1** : to transfer from one area or activity to another **2** : to relocate men or equipment — **re·de·ploy·ment** *n*

red–eye \'red-ˌī\ *n* **1** : cheap whiskey **2** : a late night or overnight flight

red fox *n* : a fox with orange-red to reddish brown fur

red fox

red giant *n* : a very large star with a relatively low surface temperature

red–hand·ed \'red-'han-dəd\ *adv or adj* : in the act of committing a misdeed

red·head \-ˌhed\ *n* : a person having red hair — **red·head·ed** \-ˌhe-dəd\ *adj*

red herring *n* : a diversion intended to distract attention from the real issue

red–hot \'red-'hät\ *adj* **1** : extremely hot; *esp* : glowing with heat **2** : EXCITED, FURIOUS **3** : very new ⟨∼ news⟩

re·dial \'rē-ˌdīl\ *n* : a telephone function that automatically repeats the dialing of the last number called — **redial** *vb*

re·dis·trib·ute \ˌrē-də-'stri-byüt\ *vb* **1** : to alter the distribution of **2** : to spread to other areas — **re·dis·tri·bu·tion** \(ˌ)rē-ˌdis-trə-'byü-shən\ *n*

re·dis·trict \ˌrē-'dis-(ˌ)trikt\ *vb* : to organize into new territorial and esp. political divisions

red–let·ter \'red-ˌle-tər\ *adj* : of special significance : MEMORABLE

red–light district *n* : a district with many houses of prostitution

re·do \(ˌ)rē-'dü\ *vb* : to do over or again; *esp* : REDECORATE

red oak *n* : any of numerous American oaks with leaves usu. having spiny-tipped lobes and acorns that take two years to mature; *also* : the wood of a red oak

red·o·lent \'red-ᵊl-ənt\ *adj* **1** : FRAGRANT, AROMATIC **2** : having a specified fragrance ⟨a room ∼ of cooked cabbage⟩ **3** : REMINISCENT, SUGGESTIVE — **red·o·lence** \-əns\ *n* — **red·o·lent·ly** *adv*

re·dou·ble \(ˌ)rē-ˈdə-bəl\ *vb* : to make twice as great in size or amount; *also* : INTENSIFY

re·doubt \ri-ˈdaùt\ *n* [F *redoute*, fr. It *ridotto*, fr. ML *reductus* secret place, fr. L, withdrawn, fr. *reducere* to lead back, fr. *re-* back + *ducere* to lead] : a small usu. temporary fortification

re·doubt·able \ri-ˈdaù-tə-bəl\ *adj* [ME *redoutable*, fr. MF, fr. *redouter* to dread, fr. *re-* re- + *douter* to doubt] : arousing dread or fear : FORMIDABLE

re·dound \ri-ˈdaùnd\ *vb* **1** : to have an effect **2** : to become added or transferred : ACCRUE

red pepper *n* : CAYENNE PEPPER

¹re·dress \ri-ˈdres\ *vb* **1** : to set right : REMEDY **2** : COMPENSATE **3** : to remove the cause of (a grievance) **4** : AVENGE

²re·dress *n* **1** : relief from distress **2** : means or possibility of seeking a remedy **3** : compensation for loss or injury **4** : an act or instance of redressing

red·shift \ˈred-ˈshift\ *n* : displacement of the spectrum of a heavenly body toward longer wavelength

red snapper *n* : any of various reddish fishes including several food fishes

red spider *n* : SPIDER MITE

red squirrel *n* : a common American squirrel with the upper parts chiefly red

red–tailed hawk \ˈred-ˌtāld-\ *n* : a common rodent–eating hawk of eastern No. America with a rather short typically reddish tail

red tape *n* [fr. the red tape formerly used to bind legal documents in England] : official routine or procedure marked by excessive complexity which results in delay or inaction

red tide *n* : seawater discolored by the presence of large numbers of dinoflagellates which produce a toxin that renders infected shellfish poisonous

re·duce \ri-ˈdüs, -ˈdyüs\ *vb* **re·duced; re·duc·ing 1** : LESSEN **2** : to bring to a specified state or condition ⟨*reduced* them to tears⟩ **3** : to put in a lower rank or grade **4** : CONQUER ⟨∼ a fort⟩ **5** : to bring into a certain order or classification **6** : to correct (as a fracture) by restoration of displaced parts **7** : to lessen one's weight **syn** decrease, diminish, abate, dwindle, recede — **re·duc·er** *n* — **re·duc·ible** \-ˈdü-sə-bəl, -ˈdyü-\ *adj*

re·duc·tion \ri-ˈdək-shən\ *n* **1** : the act of reducing : the state of being reduced **2** : something made by reducing **3** : the amount taken off in reducing something

re·dun·dan·cy \ri-ˈdən-dən-sē\ *n, pl* **-cies 1** : the quality or state of being redundant : SUPERFLUITY **2** : something redundant or in excess **3** : the use of surplus words

re·dun·dant \-dənt\ *adj* : exceeding what is needed or normal : SUPERFLUOUS; *esp* : using more words than necessary — **re·dun·dant·ly** *adv*

red–winged blackbird \ˈred-ˌwiŋd-\ *n* : a No. American blackbird of which the adult male is black with a patch of bright scarlet on the wings

red·wood \ˈred-ˌwùd\ *n* : a tall coniferous timber tree esp. of coastal California; *also* : its durable wood

reed \ˈrēd\ *n* **1** : any of various tall slender grasses of wet areas; *also* : a stem or growth of reed **2** : a musical instrument made from the hollow stem of a reed **3** : an elastic tongue of cane, wood, or metal by which tones are produced in organ pipes and certain other wind instruments — **reedy** *adj*

re·ed·u·cate \(ˌ)rē-ˈe-jə-ˌkāt\ *vb* : to train again; *esp* : to rehabilitate through education — **re·ed·u·ca·tion** *n*

¹reef \ˈrēf\ *n* **1** : a part of a sail taken in or let out in regulating the sail's size **2** : reduction in sail area by reefing

²reef *vb* : to reduce the area of a sail by rolling or folding part of it

³reef *n* : a ridge of rocks, sand or coral at or near the surface of the water

reef·er \ˈrē-fər\ *n* : a marijuana cigarette

¹reek \ˈrēk\ *n* : a strong or disagreeable fume or odor

²reek *vb* **1** : to give off or become permeated with a strong or offensive odor **2** : to give a strong impression of some constituent quality ⟨an excuse that ∼*ed* of falsehood⟩ — **reek·er** *n* — **reeky** \ˈrē-kē\ *adj*

¹reel \ˈrēl\ *n* : a revolvable device on which something flexible (as film or tape) is wound; *also* : a quantity of something wound on such a device

²reel *vb* **1** : to wind on or as if on a reel **2** : to pull or draw (as a fish) by reeling a line — **reel·able** *adj* — **reel·er** *n*

³reel *vb* **1** : WHIRL; *also* : to be giddy **2** : to waver or fall back (as from a blow) **3** : to walk or move unsteadily

⁴reel *n* : a reeling motion

⁵reel *n* : a lively Scottish dance or its music

reel off *vb* : to tell or recite rapidly and easily ⟨*reeled off* the right answers⟩

re·en·try \rē-ˈen-trē\ *n* **1** : a second or new entry **2** : the action of reentering the earth's atmosphere from space

reeve \ˈrēv\ *vb* **rove** \ˈrōv\ *or* **reeved; reev·ing** : to pass (as a rope) through a hole in a block or cleat

¹ref \ˈref\ *n* : REFEREE 2

²ref *abbr* **1** reference **2** referred **3** reformed **4** refunding

re·fec·tion \ri-ˈfek-shən\ *n* **1** : refreshment esp. after hunger or fatigue **2** : food and drink together : REPAST

re·fec·to·ry \ri-ˈfek-tə-rē\ *n, pl* **-ries** : a dining hall (as in a monastery or college)

re·fer \ri-ˈfər\ *vb* **re·ferred; re·fer·ring 1** : to assign to a certain source, cause, or relationship **2** : to direct or send to some person or place (as for information or help) **3** : to submit to someone else for consideration or action **4** : to have recourse (as for information or aid) **5** : to have connection : RELATE **6** : to direct attention : speak of : MENTION, ALLUDE **syn** recur, repair, resort, apply, go, turn — **re·fer·able** \ˈre-fə-rə-bəl, ri-ˈfər-ə-\ *adj*

¹ref·er·ee \ˌre-fə-ˈrē\ *n* **1** : a person to whom an issue esp. in law is referred for investigation or settlement **2** : an umpire in certain games

²referee *vb* **-eed; -ee·ing** : to act as referee

ref·er·ence \ˈre-frəns, -fə-rəns\ *n* **1** : the act of referring **2** : RELATION, RESPECT **3** : ALLUSION, MENTION **4** : something that refers a reader to another passage or book **5** : consultation esp. for obtaining information ⟨books for ∼⟩ **6** : a person of whom inquiries as to character or ability can be made **7** : a written recommendation of a person for employment

ref·er·en·dum \ˌre-fə-ˈren-dəm\ *n, pl* **-da** \-də\ *or* **-dums** : the submitting of legislative measures to the voters for approval or rejection; *also* : a vote on a measure so submitted

ref·er·ent \ˈre-frənt, -fə-rənt\ *n* : one that refers or is referred to; *esp* : the thing a word stands for — **referent** *adj*

re·fer·ral \ri-ˈfər-əl\ *n* **1** : the act or an instance of referring **2** : one that is referred

¹re·fill \ˌrē-ˈfil\ *vb* : to fill again : REPLENISH — **re·fill·able** *adj*

²re·fill \ˈrē-ˌfil\ *n* : a new or fresh supply of something

re·fi·nance \ˌrē-fə-ˈnans, (ˌ)rē-ˈfī-nans\ *vb* : to renew or reorganize the financing of

re·fine \ri-ˈfīn\ *vb* **re·fined; re·fin·ing 1** : to free from impurities or waste matter **2** : IMPROVE, PERFECT **3** : to free or become free of what is coarse or uncouth **4** : to make improvements by introducing subtle changes — **re·fin·er** *n*

\ə\abut \ᵊ\kitten \ər\further \a\ash \ā\ace \ä\mop, mar \aù\out \ch\chin \e\bet \ē\easy \g\go \i\hit \ī\ice \j\job \ŋ\sing \ō\go \ò\law \òi\boy \th\thin \t̲h̲\the \ü\loot \ù\foot \y\yet \zh\vision *see also* Pronunciation Symbols page

re·fined \ri-ˈfīnd\ *adj* **1** : freed from impurities **2** : CULTURED, CULTIVATED **3** : SUBTLE

re·fine·ment \ri-ˈfīn-mənt\ *n* **1** : the action of refining **2** : the quality or state of being refined **3** : a refined feature or method; *also* : something intended to improve or perfect

re·fin·ery \ri-ˈfī-nə-rē\ *n, pl* **-er·ies** : a building and equipment for refining metals, oil, or sugar

refl *abbr* reflex; reflexive

re·flect \ri-ˈflekt\ *vb* [ME, fr. L *reflectere* to bend back, fr. *re-* back + *flectere* to bend] **1** : to bend or cast back (as light, heat, or sound) **2** : to give back a likeness or image of as a mirror does **3** : to bring as a result ⟨∼ed credit on him⟩ **4** : to cast reproach or blame ⟨their bad conduct ∼ed on their training⟩ **5** : PONDER, MEDITATE — **re·flec·tion** \-ˈflek-shən\ *n* — **re·flec·tive** \-tiv\ *adj* — **re·flec·tiv·ity** \(ˌ)rē-ˌflek-ˈti-və-tē\ *n*

re·flec·tor \ri-ˈflek-tər\ *n* : one that reflects; *esp* : a polished surface for reflecting radiation (as light)

¹**re·flex** \ˈrē-ˌfleks\ *n* **1** : an automatic and usu. inborn response to a stimulus not involving higher mental centers **2** *pl* : the power of acting or responding with enough speed ⟨an athlete with great ∼es⟩

²**reflex** *adj* **1** : bent or directed back **2** : of, relating to, or produced by a reflex — **re·flex·ly** *adv*

re·flex·ion *chiefly Brit var of* REFLECTION

¹**re·flex·ive** \ri-ˈflek-siv\ *adj* : of or relating to an action directed back upon the doer or the grammatical subject ⟨a ∼ verb⟩ ⟨the ∼ pronoun *himself*⟩ — **re·flex·ive·ly** *adv* — **re·flex·ive·ness** *n*

²**reflexive** *n* : a reflexive verb or pronoun

re·fo·cus \(ˌ)rē-ˈfō-kəs\ *vb* **1** : to focus again **2** : to change the emphasis or direction of ⟨∼ed her life⟩

re·for·es·ta·tion \ˌrē-ˌfȯr-ə-ˈstā-shən\ *n* : the action of renewing forest cover by planting seeds or young trees — **re·for·est** \rē-ˈfȯr-əst\ *vb*

¹**re·form** \ri-ˈfȯrm\ *vb* **1** : to make better or improve by removal of faults **2** : to correct or improve one's own character or habits **syn** correct, rectify, emend, remedy, redress, revise — **re·form·able** *adj* — **re·for·ma·tive** \-ˈfȯr-mə-tiv\ *adj*

²**reform** *n* : improvement or correction of what is corrupt or defective

re–form \ˌrē-ˈfȯrm\ *vb* : to form again

ref·or·ma·tion \ˌre-fər-ˈmā-shən\ *n* **1** : the act of reforming : the state of being reformed **2** *cap* : a 16th century religious movement marked by the establishment of the Protestant churches

¹**re·for·ma·to·ry** \ri-ˈfȯr-mə-ˌtōr-ē\ *adj* : aiming at or tending toward reformation : REFORMATIVE

²**reformatory** *n, pl* **-ries** : a penal institution for reforming esp. young or first offenders

re·form·er \ri-ˈfȯr-mər\ *n* **1** : one that works for or urges reform **2** *cap* : a leader of the Protestant Reformation

refr *abbr* refraction

re·fract \ri-ˈfrakt\ *vb* [L *refractus*, pp. of *refringere* to break open, break up, fr. *re-* back + *frangere* to break] : to subject to refraction

re·frac·tion \ri-ˈfrak-shən\ *n* : the bending of a ray (as of light) when it passes obliquely from one medium into another in which its speed is different — **re·frac·tive** \-tiv\ *adj*

re·frac·to·ry \ri-ˈfrak-tə-rē\ *adj* **1** : OBSTINATE, STUBBORN, UNMANAGEABLE **2** : capable of enduring high temperature ⟨∼ bricks⟩ **syn** recalcitrant, intractable, ungovernable, unruly, headstrong, willful — **re·frac·to·ri·ness** \ri-ˈfrak-tə-rē-nəs\ *n* — **refractory** *n*

¹**re·frain** \ri-ˈfrān\ *vb* : to hold oneself back : FORBEAR — **re·frain·ment** *n*

²**refrain** *n* : a phrase or verse recurring regularly in a poem or song

re·fresh \ri-ˈfresh\ *vb* **1** : to make or become fresh or fresher **2** : to revive by or as if by renewal of supplies

⟨∼ one's memory⟩ **3** : to freshen up **4** : to supply or take refreshment **syn** restore, rejuvenate, renovate, refurbish — **re·fresh·er** *n* — **re·fresh·ing·ly** *adv*

re·fresh·ment \-mənt\ *n* **1** : the act of refreshing : the state of being refreshed **2** : something that refreshes **3** *pl* : a light meal; *also* : assorted light foods

re·fried beans \ˈrē-ˌfrīd-\ *n pl* : beans cooked with seasonings, fried, then mashed and fried again

refrig *abbr* refrigerating; refrigeration

re·frig·er·ate \ri-ˈfri-jə-ˌrāt\ *vb* **-at·ed; -at·ing** : to make cool; *esp* : to chill or freeze (food) for preservation — **re·frig·er·ant** \-jə-rənt\ *adj or n* — **re·frig·er·a·tion** \-ˌfri-jə-ˈrā-shən\ *n* — **re·frig·er·a·tor** \-ˈfri-jə-ˌrā-tər\ *n*

ref·uge \ˈre-ˌfyüj\ *n* **1** : shelter or protection from danger or distress **2** : a place that provides protection

ref·u·gee \ˌre-fyù-ˈjē\ *n* : one who flees for safety esp. to a foreign country

re·ful·gence \ri-ˈfül-jəns, -ˈfəl-\ *n* : a radiant or resplendent quality or state — **re·ful·gent** \-jənt\ *adj*

¹**re·fund** \ri-ˈfənd, ˈrē-ˌfənd\ *vb* : to give or put back (money) : REPAY — **re·fund·able** *adj*

²**re·fund** \ˈrē-ˌfənd\ *n* **1** : the act of refunding **2** : a sum refunded

re·fur·bish \ri-ˈfər-bish\ *vb* : to brighten or freshen up : RENOVATE

¹**re·fuse** \ri-ˈfyüz\ *vb* **re·fused; re·fus·ing 1** : to decline to accept : REJECT **2** : to decline to do, give, or grant : DENY — **re·fus·al** \-ˈfyü-zəl\ *n*

²**ref·use** \ˈre-ˌfyüs, -ˌfyüz\ *n* : rejected or worthless matter : RUBBISH, TRASH

re·fute \ri-ˈfyüt\ *vb* **re·fut·ed; re·fut·ing** [L *refutare* to check, suppress, refute] : to prove to be false by argument or evidence — **ref·u·ta·tion** \ˌre-fyù-ˈtā-shən\ *n* — **re·fut·er** *n*

¹**reg** \ˈreg\ *n* : REGULATION

²**reg** *abbr* **1** region **2** register; registered; registration **3** regular

re·gal \ˈrē-gəl\ *adj* **1** : of, relating to, or befitting a king : ROYAL **2** : STATELY, SPLENDID — **re·gal·ly** *adv*

re·gale \ri-ˈgāl\ *vb* **re·galed; re·gal·ing 1** : to entertain richly or agreeably **2** : to give pleasure or amusement to **syn** gratify, delight, please, rejoice, gladden

re·ga·lia \ri-ˈgāl-yə\ *n pl* **1** : the emblems, symbols, or paraphernalia of royalty (as the crown and scepter) **2** : the insignia of an office or order **3** : special costume : FINERY

¹**re·gard** \ri-ˈgärd\ *n* **1** : CONSIDERATION, HEED; *also* : CARE, CONCERN **2** : GAZE, GLANCE, LOOK **3** : RESPECT, ESTEEM **4** *pl* : friendly greetings implying respect and esteem **5** : an aspect to be considered : PARTICULAR — **re·gard·ful** *adj* — **re·gard·less** *adj*

²**regard** *vb* **1** : to think of : CONSIDER **2** : to pay attention to **3** : to show respect for : HEED **4** : to hold in high esteem : care for **5** : to look at : gaze upon **6** *archaic* : to relate to

re·gard·ing *prep* : CONCERNING

regardless of \ri-ˈgärd-ləs-\ *prep* : in spite of

re·gat·ta \ri-ˈgä-tə, -ˈga-\ *n* : a boat race or a series of boat races

regd *abbr* registered

re·gen·cy \ˈrē-jən-sē\ *n, pl* **-cies 1** : the office or government of a regent or body of regents **2** : a body of regents **3** : the period during which a regent governs

re·gen·er·a·cy \ri-ˈje-nə-rə-sē\ *n* : the state of being regenerated

¹**re·gen·er·ate** \ri-ˈje-nə-rət\ *adj* **1** : formed or created again **2** : spiritually reborn or converted

²**re·gen·er·ate** \ri-ˈje-nə-ˌrāt\ *vb* **1** : to subject to spiritual renewal **2** : to reform completely **3** : to replace (a body part) by a new growth of tissue **4** : to give new life to : REVIVE — **re·gen·er·a·tion** \-ˌje-nə-ˈrā-shən\ *n* — **re·gen·er·a·tive** \-ˈje-nə-ˌrā-tiv\ *adj* — **re·gen·er·a·tor** \-ˌrā-tər\ *n*

re·gent \'rē-jənt\ *n* **1** : a person who rules during the childhood, absence, or incapacity of the sovereign **2** : a member of a governing board (as of a state university) — **regent** *adj*

reg·gae \'re-͵gā\ *n* : popular music of Jamaican origin that combines native styles with elements of rock and soul music

reg·i·cide \'re-jə-͵sīd\ *n* **1** : one who murders a king **2** : murder of a king

re·gime *also* **ré·gime** \rā-'zhēm, ri-\ *n* **1** : REGIMEN **2** : a form or system of government **3** : a government in power; *also* : a period of rule

reg·i·men \'re-jə-mən\ *n* **1** : a systematic course of treatment or training ⟨a strict dietary ∼⟩ **2** : GOVERNMENT

¹reg·i·ment \'re-jə-mənt\ *n* : a military unit consisting usu. of a number of battalions — **reg·i·men·tal** \͵re-jə-'ment-təl\ *adj*

²reg·i·ment \'re-jə-͵ment\ *vb* : to organize rigidly esp. for regulation or central control; *also* : to subject to order or uniformity — **reg·i·men·ta·tion** \͵re-jə-mən-'tā-shən\ *n*

reg·i·men·tals \͵re-jə-'men-təlz\ *n pl* **1** : a regimental uniform **2** : military dress

re·gion \'rē-jən\ *n* [ME, fr. MF, fr. L *region-, regio,* fr. *regere* to rule] : an often indefinitely defined part or area

re·gion·al \'rē-jə-nəl\ *adj* **1** : affecting a particular region : LOCALIZED **2** : of, relating to, characteristic of, or serving a region — **re·gion·al·ly** *adv*

¹reg·is·ter \'re-jə-stər\ *n* **1** : a record of items or details; *also* : a book or system for keeping such a record **2** : the range of a voice or instrument **3** : a device to regulate ventilation or heating **4** : an automatic device recording a number or quantity

²register *vb* **-tered; -ter·ing** **1** : to enter in a register (as in a list of guests) **2** : to record automatically **3** : to secure special care for (mail matter) by paying additional postage **4** : to convey an impression of : EXPRESS **5** : to make or adjust so as to correspond exactly

registered nurse *n* : a graduate trained nurse who has been licensed to practice by a state authority after passing qualifying examinations

reg·is·trant \'re-jə-strənt\ *n* : one that registers or is registered

reg·is·trar \-͵strär\ *n* : an official recorder or keeper of records (as at an educational institution)

reg·is·tra·tion \͵re-jə-'strā-shən\ *n* **1** : the act of registering **2** : an entry in a register **3** : the number of persons registered : ENROLLMENT **4** : a document certifying an act of registering

reg·is·try \'re-jə-strē\ *n, pl* **-tries 1** : ENROLLMENT, REGISTRATION **2** : a place of registration **3** : an official record book or an entry in one

reg·nant \'reg-nənt\ *adj* **1** : REIGNING **2** : DOMINANT **3** : of common or widespread occurrence

¹re·gress \'rē-͵gres\ *n* **1** : an act or the privilege of going or coming back **2** : RETROGRESSION

²re·gress \ri-'gres\ *vb* : to go or cause to go back or to a lower level — **re·gres·sive** *adj* — **re·gres·sor** \-'gre-sər\ *n*

re·gres·sion \ri-'gre-shən\ *n* : the act or an instance of regressing; *esp* : reversion to an earlier mental or behavioral level

¹re·gret \ri-'gret\ *vb* **re·gret·ted; re·gret·ting 1** : to mourn the loss or death of **2** : to be very sorry for **3** : to experience regret — **re·gret·ta·ble** \-'gre-tə-bəl\ *adj* — **re·gret·ter** *n*

²regret *n* **1** : sorrow caused by something beyond one's power to remedy **2** : an expression of sorrow **3** *pl* : a note politely declining an invitation — **re·gret·ful** \-fəl\ *adj* — **re·gret·ful·ly** *adv*

re·gret·ta·bly \-'gre-tə-blē\ *adv* **1** : to a regrettable extent **2** : it is to be regretted

re·group \(͵)rē-'grüp\ *vb* : to form into a new grouping

regt *abbr* regiment

¹reg·u·lar \'re-gyə-lər\ *adj* [ME *reguler,* fr. MF, fr. LL *regularis* regular, fr L, of a bar, fr. *regula* rule, straightedge, fr. *regere* to keep straight, rule] **1** : belonging to a religious order **2** : made, built, or arranged according to a rule, standard, or type; *also* : even or symmetrical in form or structure **3** : having all sides of equal length and all angles of equal size **4** : ORDERLY, METHODICAL ⟨∼ habits⟩; *also* : not varying : STEADY ⟨a ∼ pace⟩ **5** : made, selected, or conducted according to rule or custom **6** : properly qualified ⟨not a ∼ lawyer⟩ **7** : conforming to the normal or usual manner or inflection **8** : of, relating to, or constituting the permanent standing military force of a state — **reg·u·lar·i·ty** \͵re-gyə-'lar-ə-tē\ *n* — **reg·u·lar·ize** \'re-gyə-lə-͵rīz\ *vb* — **reg·u·lar·ly** *adv*

²regular *n* **1** : one that is regular (as in attendance) **2** : a member of the regular clergy **3** : a soldier in a regular army **4** : a player on an athletic team who is usu. in the starting lineup

reg·u·late \'re-gyə-͵lāt\ *vb* **-lat·ed; -lat·ing 1** : to govern or direct according to rule : CONTROL **2** : to bring under the control of law or authority **3** : to put in good order **4** : to fix or adjust the time, amount, degree, or rate of — **reg·u·la·tive** \-͵lā-tiv\ *adj* — **reg·u·la·tor** \-͵lā-tər\ *n* — **reg·u·la·to·ry** \-lə-͵tōr-ē\ *adj*

reg·u·la·tion \͵re-gyə-'lā-shən\ *n* **1** : the act of regulating : the state of being regulated **2** : a rule dealing with details of procedure **3** : an order issued by an executive authority of a government and having the force of law

re·gur·gi·tate \rē-'gər-jə-͵tāt\ *vb* **-tat·ed; -tat·ing** [ML *regurgitare,* fr. L *re-* re- + LL *gurgitare* to engulf, fr. L *gurgit-, gurges* whirlpool] : to throw or be thrown back, up, or out ⟨∼ food⟩ — **re·gur·gi·ta·tion** \-͵gər-jə-'tā-shən\ *n*

re·hab \'rē-͵hab\ *n* **1** : REHABILITATION **2** : a rehabilitated building — **rehab** *vb*

re·ha·bil·i·tate \͵rē-hə-'bi-lə-͵tāt, ͵rē-ə-\ *vb* **-tat·ed; -tat·ing 1** : to restore to a former capacity, rank, or right : REINSTATE **2** : to restore to good condition or health — **re·ha·bil·i·ta·tion** \-͵bi-lə-'tā-shən\ *n* — **re·ha·bil·i·ta·tive** \-͵tā-tiv\ *adj*

re·hash \rē-'hash\ *vb* : to present again in another form without real change or improvement — **rehash** *n*

re·hear·ing \͵rē-'hir-iŋ\ *n* : a second or new hearing by the same tribunal

re·hears·al \ri-'hər-səl\ *n* **1** : something told again : RECITAL **2** : a private performance or practice session preparatory to a public appearance

re·hearse \ri-'hərs\ *vb* **re·hearsed; re·hears·ing 1** : to say again : REPEAT **2** : to recount in order : ENUMERATE; *also* : RELATE 1 **3** : to give a rehearsal of **4** : to train by rehearsal **5** : to engage in a rehearsal — **re·hears·er** *n*

¹reign \'rān\ *n* **1** : the authority or rule of a sovereign **2** : the time during which a sovereign rules

²reign *vb* **1** : to rule as a sovereign **2** : to be predominant or prevalent

re·im·burse \͵rē-əm-'bərs\ *vb* **-bursed; -burs·ing** [*re-* re- + obs. E *imburse* to put in the pocket, pay, fr. ML *imbursare* to put into a purse, fr. L *in-* in- + ML *bursa* purse, fr. LL, hide of an ox, fr. Gk *byrsa*] : to pay back : make restitution : REPAY **syn** indemnify, recompense, requite, compensate — **re·im·burs·able** *adj* — **re·im·burse·ment** *n*

¹rein \'rān\ *n* **1** : a strap fastened to a bit by which a rider or driver controls an animal **2** : a restraining influence

---

\ə\abut \ᵊ\kitten \ər\further \a\ash \ā\ace \ä\mop, mar
\aü\out \ch\chin \e\bet \ē\easy \g\go \i\hit \ī\ice \j\job
\ŋ\sing \ō\go \ȯ\law \ȯi\boy \th\thin \th̲\the \ü\loot \ u̇\foot
\y\yet \zh\vision *see also* Pronunciation Symbols page

: CHECK **3** : controlling or guiding power **4** : complete freedom — usu. used in the phrase *give rein to*

²rein *vb* : to check or direct by reins

re·in·car·na·tion \ˌrē-(ˌ)in-(ˌ)kär-ˈnā-shən\ *n* : rebirth of the soul in a new body — **re·in·car·nate** \ˌrē-in-ˈkär-ˌnāt\ *vb*

rein·deer \ˈrān-ˌdir\ *n* [ME *reindere*, fr. ON *hreinn* reindeer + ME *deer*] : CARIBOU — used esp. for the Old World caribou

reindeer moss *n* : a gray, erect, tufted, and much-branched edible lichen of northern regions that is an important food of reindeer

re·in·fec·tion \ˌrē-in-ˈfek-shən\ *n* : infection following another infection of the same type

re·in·force \ˌrē-ən-ˈfōrs\ *vb* **1** : to strengthen with additional forces ⟨~ our troops⟩ **2** : to strengthen with new force, aid, material, or support — **re·in·force·ment** *n* — **re·in·forc·er** *n*

re·in·state \ˌrē-in-ˈstāt\ *vb* **-stat·ed; -stat·ing** : to restore to a former position, condition, or capacity — **re·in·state·ment** *n*

re·in·vent \ˌrē-in-ˈvent\ *vb* **1** : to make as if for the first time something already invented ⟨~ the wheel⟩ **2** : to remake completely

re·it·er·ate \rē-ˈi-tə-ˌrāt\ *vb* **-at·ed; -at·ing** : to state or do over again or repeatedly — **re·it·er·a·tion** \-ˌi-tə-ˈrā-shən\ *n*

¹re·ject \ri-ˈjekt\ *vb* **1** : to refuse to accept, consider, use, or submit to **2** : to refuse to hear, receive, or admit : REPEL **3** : to rebuff or withhold love from **4** : to throw out esp. as useless or unsatisfactory **5** : to subject to the immunological process of sloughing off (foreign tissue) — **re·jec·tion** \-ˈjek-shən\ *n*

²re·ject \ˈrē-ˌjekt\ *n* : a rejected person or thing

re·joice \ri-ˈjois\ *vb* **re·joiced; re·joic·ing 1** : to give joy to : GLADDEN **2** : to feel joy or great delight — **re·joic·er** *n*

re·join \(ˌ)rē-ˈjoin *for 1,* ri- *for 2*\ *vb* **1** : to join again **2** : to say in answer (as to a plaintiff's plea in court) : REPLY

re·join·der \ri-ˈjoin-dər\ *n* : REPLY; *esp* : an answer to a reply

re·ju·ve·nate \ri-ˈjü-və-ˌnāt\ *vb* **-nat·ed; -nat·ing** : to make young or youthful again : give new vigor to **syn** renew, refresh, renovate, restore — **re·ju·ve·na·tion** \-ˌjü-və-ˈnā-shən\ *n*

rel *abbr* **1** relating; relative **2** religion; religious

¹re·lapse \ri-ˈlaps, ˈrē-ˌlaps\ *n* **1** : the act or process of backsliding or worsening **2** : a recurrence of illness after a period of improvement

²re·lapse \ri-ˈlaps\ *vb* **re·lapsed; re·laps·ing** : to slip or fall back into a former worse state (as of illness)

re·late \ri-ˈlāt\ *vb* **re·lat·ed; re·lat·ing 1** : to give an account of : TELL, NARRATE **2** : to show or establish logical or causal connection between **3** : to have relationship or connection **4** : to have or establish relationship ⟨the way a child ~*s* to a teacher⟩ **5** : to respond favorably — **re·lat·able** *adj* — **re·lat·er** *or* **re·la·tor** \-ˈlā-tər\ *n*

re·lat·ed *adj* **1** : connected by some understood relationship **2** : connected through membership in the same family — **re·lat·ed·ness** *n*

re·la·tion \ri-ˈlā-shən\ *n* **1** : NARRATION, ACCOUNT **2** : CONNECTION, RELATIONSHIP **3** : connection by blood or marriage; *also* : RELATIVE **4** : REFERENCE, RESPECT ⟨in ~ to⟩ **5** : the state of being mutually interested or involved (as in social or commercial matters) **6** *pl* : DEALINGS, AFFAIRS **7** *pl* : SEXUAL INTERCOURSE — **re·la·tion·al** \-shə-nəl\ *adj*

re·la·tion·ship \-ˌship\ *n* : the state of being related or interrelated

¹rel·a·tive \ˈre-lə-tiv\ *n* **1** : a word referring grammatically to an antecedent **2** : a thing having a relation to or a dependence upon another thing **3** : a person connected with another by blood or marriage

²relative *adj* **1** : introducing a subordinate clause qualifying an expressed or implied antecedent ⟨~ pronoun⟩; *also* : introduced by such a connective ⟨~ clause⟩ **2** : PERTINENT, RELEVANT **3** : not absolute or independent **4** : COMPARATIVE **4** : expressed as the ratio of the specified quantity to the total magnitude or to the mean of all quantities involved **syn** dependent, contingent, conditional — **rel·a·tive·ly** *adv* — **rel·a·tive·ness** *n*

relative humidity *n* : the ratio of the amount of water vapor actually present in the air to the greatest amount possible at the same temperature

rel·a·tiv·is·tic \ˌre-lə-ti-ˈvis-tik\ *adj* **1** : of, relating to, or characterized by relativity **2** : moving at a velocity that is a significant fraction of the speed of light so that effects predicted by the theory of relativity become evident ⟨a ~ electron⟩ — **rel·a·tiv·is·ti·cal·ly** \-ti-k(ə-)lē\ *adv*

rel·a·tiv·i·ty \ˌre-lə-ˈti-və-tē\ *n, pl* **-ties 1** : the quality or state of being relative **2** : a theory in physics that considers mass and energy to be equivalent and that predicts changes in mass, dimension, and time which are related to speed but are noticeable esp. at speeds approaching that of light

re·lax \ri-ˈlaks\ *vb* **1** : to make or become less firm, tense, or rigid **2** : to make less severe or strict **3** : to seek rest or recreation — **re·lax·er** *n*

¹re·lax·ant \ri-ˈlak-sənt\ *adj* : of, relating to, or producing relaxation

²relaxant *n* : a relaxing agent; *esp* : a drug that induces muscular relaxation

re·lax·ation \ˌrē-ˌlak-ˈsā-shən\ *n* **1** : the act of relaxing or state of being relaxed : a lessening of tension **2** : DIVERSION, RECREATION

¹re·lay \ˈrē-ˌlā\ *n* **1** : a fresh supply (as of horses or men) arranged beforehand to relieve others **2** : a race between teams in which each team member covers a specified part of a course **3** : an electromagnetic device in which the opening or closing of one circuit activates another device (as a switch in another circuit) **4** : the act of passing along by stages

²re·lay \ˈrē-ˌlā, ri-ˈlā\ *vb* **re·layed; re·lay·ing 1** : to place in or provide with relays **2** : to pass along by relays **3** : to control or operate by a relay

³re·lay \(ˌ)rē-ˈlā\ *vb* **-laid** \-ˈlād\; **-lay·ing** : to lay again

¹re·lease \ri-ˈlēs\ *vb* **re·leased; re·leas·ing 1** : to set free from confinement or restraint; *also* : DISMISS **2** : to relieve from something that oppresses, confines, or burdens **3** : RELINQUISH ⟨~ a claim⟩ **4** : to permit publication, performance, exhibition, or sale of; *also* : to make available to the public **syn** emancipate, discharge, free, liberate

²release *n* **1** : relief or deliverance from sorrow, suffering, or trouble **2** : discharge from an obligation or responsibility **3** : an act of setting free : the state of being freed **4** : a document effecting a legal release **5** : a releasing for performance or publication; *also* : the matter released (as to the press) **6** : a device for holding or releasing a mechanism as required

rel·e·gate \ˈre-lə-ˌgāt\ *vb* **-gat·ed; -gat·ing 1** : to send into exile : BANISH **2** : to remove or dismiss to some less prominent position **3** : to assign to a particular class or sphere **4** : to submit to someone or something for appropriate action : DELEGATE **syn** commit, entrust, consign, commend — **rel·e·ga·tion** \ˌre-lə-ˈgā-shən\ *n*

re·lent \ri-ˈlent\ *vb* **1** : to become less stern, severe, or harsh **2** : SLACKEN

re·lent·less \-ləs\ *adj* : showing or promising no abatement of severity, intensity, or pace ⟨~ pressure⟩ — **re·lent·less·ly** *adv* — **re·lent·less·ness** *n*

rel·e·vance \ˈre-lə-vəns\ *n* : relation to the matter at hand; *also* : practical and esp. social applicability

rel·e·van·cy \-vən-sē\ *n* : RELEVANCE
rel·e·vant \'re-lə-vənt\ *adj* : bearing on the matter at hand : PERTINENT **syn** germane, material, applicable, apropos — **rel·e·vant·ly** *adv*
re·li·able \ri-'lī-ə-bəl\ *adj* : fit to be trusted or relied on : DEPENDABLE, TRUSTWORTHY — **re·li·abil·i·ty** \-ˌlī-ə-'bi-lə-tē\ *n* — **re·li·able·ness** *n* — **re·li·ably** \-'lī-ə-blē\ *adv*
re·li·ance \ri-'lī-əns\ *n* 1 : the act of relying 2 : the state of being reliant 3 : one relied on
re·li·ant \ri-'lī-ənt\ *adj* : having reliance on someone or something : DEPENDENT
rel·ic \'re-lik\ *n* 1 : an object venerated because of its association with a saint or martyr 2 : SOUVENIR, MEMENTO 3 *pl* : REMAINS, RUINS 4 : a remaining trace : VESTIGE
rel·ict \'re-likt\ *n* : WIDOW
re·lief \ri-'lēf\ *n* 1 : removal or lightening of something oppressive, painful, or distressing 2 : WELFARE 2 3 : military assistance to an endangered post or force 4 : release from a post or from performance of a duty; *also* : one that takes the place of another on duty 5 : legal remedy or redress 6 : projection of figures or ornaments from the background (as in sculpture) 7 : the elevations of a land surface
relief pitcher *n* : a baseball pitcher who takes over for another during a game
re·lieve \ri-'lēv\ *vb* **re·lieved; re·liev·ing** 1 : to free partly or wholly from a burden or from distress 2 : to bring about the removal or alleviation of : MITIGATE 3 : to release from a post or duty; *also* : to take the place of 4 : to break the monotony of 5 : to discharge the bladder or bowels of (oneself) **syn** alleviate, lighten, assuage, allay — **re·liev·er** *n*
relig *abbr* religion
re·li·gion \ri-'li-jən\ *n* 1 : the service and worship of God or the supernatural 2 : devotion to a religious faith 3 : a personal set or institutionalized system of religious beliefs, attitudes, and practices 4 : a cause, principle, or belief held to with faith and ardor — **re·li·gion·ist** *n*
¹**re·li·gious** \ri-'li-jəs\ *adj* 1 : relating or devoted to an acknowledged ultimate reality or deity 2 : of or relating to religious beliefs or observances 3 : scrupulously and conscientiously faithful 4 : FERVENT, ZEALOUS — **re·li·gious·ly** *adv*
²**religious** *n, pl* **religious** : a member of a religious order under monastic vows
re·lin·quish \ri-'liŋ-kwish, -'lin-\ *vb* 1 : to withdraw or retreat from : ABANDON, QUIT 2 : GIVE UP ⟨~ a title⟩ 3 : to let go of : RELEASE **syn** yield, leave, resign, surrender, cede, waive — **re·lin·quish·ment** *n*
rel·i·quary \'re-lə-ˌkwer-ē\ *n, pl* **-quar·ies** : a container for religious relics
¹**rel·ish** \'re-lish\ *n* [ME *reles* taste, fr. OF, something left behind, release, fr. *relessier* to relax, release, fr. L *relaxare*] 1 : characteristic flavor : SAVOR 2 : keen enjoyment or delight in something : GUSTO 3 : APPETITE, INCLINATION 4 : a highly seasoned sauce (as of pickles) eaten with other food to add flavor
²**relish** *vb* 1 : to add relish to 2 : to take pleasure in : ENJOY 3 : to eat with pleasure — **rel·ish·able** *adj*
re·live \(ˌ)rē-'liv\ *vb* : to live again or over again; *esp* : to experience again in the imagination
re·lo·cate \(ˌ)rē-'lō-ˌkāt, ˌrē-lō-'kāt\ *vb* 1 : to locate again 2 : to move to a new location — **re·lo·ca·tion** \ˌrē-lō-'kā-shən\ *n*
re·luc·tant \ri-'lək-tənt\ *adj* : feeling or showing aversion, hesitation or unwillingness ⟨~ to get involved⟩ **syn** disinclined, indisposed, hesitant, loath, averse — **re·luc·tance** \-təns\ — **re·luc·tant·ly** *adv*
re·ly \ri-'lī\ *vb* **re·lied; re·ly·ing** [ME *relien* to rally, fr. MF *relier* to connect, rally, fr. L *religare* to tie back, fr. *re-* back + *ligare* to tie] : to place faith or confidence : DEPEND

REM \'rem\ *n* : RAPID EYE MOVEMENT
re·main \ri-'mān\ *vb* 1 : to be left after others have been removed, subtracted, or destroyed 2 : to be something yet to be shown, done, or treated ⟨it ~s to be seen⟩ 3 : to stay after others have gone 4 : to continue unchanged
re·main·der \ri-'mān-dər\ *n* 1 : that which is left over : a remaining group, part, or trace 2 : the number left after a subtraction 3 : the number that is left over from the dividend after division and that is less than the divisor 4 : a book sold at a reduced price by the publisher after sales have slowed **syn** leavings, rest, balance, remnant, residue
re·mains \-'mānz\ *n pl* 1 : a remaining part or trace ⟨the ~ of a meal⟩ 2 : a dead body
¹**re·make** \(ˌ)rē-'māk\ *vb* **-made** \-'mād\; **-mak·ing** : to make anew or in a different form
²**re·make** \'rē-ˌmāk\ *n* : one that is remade; *esp* : a new version of a motion picture
re·mand \ri-'mand\ *vb* : to order back; *esp* : to return to custody pending trial or for further detention
¹**re·mark** \ri-'märk\ *n* 1 : the act of remarking : OBSERVATION, NOTICE 2 : a passing observation or comment
²**remark** *vb* 1 : to take notice of : OBSERVE 2 : to express as an observation or comment : SAY
re·mark·able \ri-'mär-kə-bəl\ *adj* : worthy of being or likely to be noticed : UNUSUAL, EXTRAORDINARY, NOTEWORTHY — **re·mark·able·ness** *n*
re·mark·ably \ri-'mär-kə-blē\ *adv* 1 : in a remarkable manner 2 : as is remarkable
re·me·di·a·ble \ri-'mē-dē-ə-bəl\ *adj* : capable of being remedied
re·me·di·al \ri-'mē-dē-əl\ *adj* : intended to remedy or improve
¹**rem·e·dy** \'re-mə-dē\ *n, pl* **-dies** 1 : a medicine or treatment that cures or relieves a disease or condition 2 : something that corrects or counteracts an evil or compensates for a loss
²**remedy** *vb* **-died; -dy·ing** : to provide or serve as a remedy for
re·mem·ber \ri-'mem-bər\ *vb* **-bered; -ber·ing** 1 : to bring to mind or think of again : RECOLLECT 2 : to keep from forgetting : keep in mind 3 : to convey greetings from 4 : COMMEMORATE
re·mem·brance \-brəns\ *n* 1 : an act of remembering : RECOLLECTION 2 : the ability to remember : MEMORY 3 : the period over which one's memory extends 4 : a memory of a person, thing, or event 5 : something that serves to bring to mind : REMINDER 6 : a greeting or gift recalling or expressing friendship or affection
re·mind \ri-'mīnd\ *vb* : to put in mind of something : cause to remember — **re·mind·er** *n*
rem·i·nisce \ˌre-mə-'nis\ *vb* **-nisced; -nisc·ing** : to indulge in reminiscence
rem·i·nis·cence \-'nis-ᵊns\ *n* 1 : a recalling or telling of a past experience 2 : an account of a memorable experience
rem·i·nis·cent \-ᵊnt\ *adj* 1 : of or relating to reminiscence 2 : marked by or given to reminiscence 3 : serving to remind : SUGGESTIVE — **rem·i·nis·cent·ly** *adv*
re·miss \ri-'mis\ *adj* 1 : negligent or careless in the performance of work or duty 2 : showing neglect or inattention **syn** lax, neglectful, delinquent, derelict — **re·miss·ly** *adv* — **re·miss·ness** *n*
re·mis·sion \ri-'mi-shən\ *n* 1 : the act or process of remitting 2 : a state or period during which something is remitted
re·mit \ri-'mit\ *vb* **re·mit·ted; re·mit·ting** 1 : FORGIVE,

PARDON **2** : to give or gain relief from (as pain) **3** : to refer for consideration, report, or decision **4** : to refrain from exacting or enforcing (as a penalty) **5** : to send (money) in payment of a bill

re·mit·tal \ri-'mit-ᵊl\ *n* : REMISSION

re·mit·tance \ri-'mit-ᵊns\ *n* **1** : a sum of money remitted **2** : transmittal of money (as to a distant place)

rem·nant \'rem-nənt\ *n* **1** : a usu. small part or trace remaining **2** : an unsold or unused end of fabrics that are sold by the yard

re·mod·el \rē-'mäd-ᵊl\ *vb* : to alter the structure of : MAKE OVER

re·mon·strance \ri-'män-strəns\ *n* : an act or instance of remonstrating

re·mon·strant \-strənt\ *adj* : vigorously objecting or opposing — **remonstrant** *n* — **re·mon·strant·ly** *adv*

re·mon·strate \ri-'män-ˌstrāt\ *vb* **-strat·ed; -strat·ing** : to plead in opposition to something : speak in protest or reproof **syn** expostulate, object, protest — **re·mon·stra·tion** \ri-ˌmän-'strā- shən, ˌre-mən-\ *n* — **re·mon·stra·tor** \ri-'män-ˌstrā-tər\ *n*

rem·o·ra \'re-mə-rə\ *n* : any of a family of marine bony fishes with sucking organs on the head by which they cling esp. to other fishes

re·morse \ri-'mȯrs\ *n* [ME, fr. MF *remors,* fr. ML *remorsus,* fr. LL, act of biting again, fr. L *remordēre* to bite again, fr. *re-* again + *mordēre* to bite] : a gnawing distress arising from a sense of guilt for past wrongs **syn** penitence, repentance, contrition — **re·morse·ful** *adj*

re·morse·less \-ləs\ *adj* **1** : MERCILESS **2** : PERSISTENT, RELENTLESS

¹**re·mote** \ri-'mōt\ *adj* **re·mot·er; -est 1** : far off in place or time : not near **2** : not closely related : DISTANT **3** : located out of the way : SECLUDED **4** : acting, acted on, or controlled indirectly or from a distance **5** : small in degree : SLIGHT ⟨a ∼ chance⟩ **6** : distant in manner — **re·mote·ly** *adv* — **re·mote·ness** *n*

²**remote** *n* **1** : a radio or television program or a portion of a program originating outside the studio **2** : REMOTE CONTROL **2**

remote control *n* **1** : control (as by radio signal) of operation from a point at some distance removed **2** : a device or mechanism for controlling something from a distance

¹**re·mount** \(ˌ)rē-'maůnt\ *vb* **1** : to mount again **2** : to furnish remounts to

²**re·mount** \'rē-ˌmaůnt\ *n* : a fresh horse to replace one disabled or exhausted

¹**re·move** \ri-'müv\ *vb* **re·moved; re·mov·ing 1** : to move from one place to another : TRANSFER **2** : to move by lifting or taking off or away **3** : DISMISS, DISCHARGE **4** : to get rid of : ELIMINATE ⟨∼ a fire hazard⟩ **5** : to change one's residence or location **6** : to go away : DEPART **7** : to be capable of being removed — **re·mov·able** *adj* — **re·mov·al** \-'mü-vəl\ *n* — **re·mov·er** *n*

²**remove** *n* **1** : a transfer from one location to another : MOVE **2** : a degree or stage of separation

REM sleep *n* : a state of sleep associated esp. with rapid eye movements and dreaming and occurring approximately at 90-minute intervals

re·mu·ner·ate \ri-'myü-nə-ˌrāt\ *vb* **-at·ed; -at·ing** : to pay an equivalent for or to : RECOMPENSE — **re·mu·ner·a·tor** \-ˌrā-tər\ *n*

re·mu·ner·a·tion \ri-ˌmyü-nə-'rā-shən\ *n* : COMPENSATION, PAYMENT

re·mu·ner·a·tive \ri-'myü-nə-rə-tiv, -ˌrā-\ *adj* : serving to remunerate : GAINFUL

re·nais·sance \ˌre-nə-'säns, -'zäns\ *n* **1** *cap* : the cultural revival and beginnings of modern science in Europe in the 14th-17th centuries; *also* : the period of the Renaissance **2** *often cap* : a movement or period of vigorous artistic and intellectual activity **3** : REBIRTH, REVIVAL

re·nal \'rēn-ᵊl\ *adj* : of, relating to, or located in or near the kidneys

re·na·scence \ri-'nas-ᵊns, -'nās-\ *n, often cap* : RENAISSANCE

rend \'rend\ *vb* **rent** \'rent\; **rend·ing 1** : to remove by violence : WREST **2** : to tear forcibly apart : SPLIT

ren·der \'ren-dər\ *vb* **1** : to extract (as lard) by heating **2** : to give to another; *also* : YIELD **3** : to give in return **4** : to do (a service) for another ⟨∼ aid⟩ **5** : to cause to be or become : MAKE **6** : to reproduce or represent by artistic or verbal means **7** : TRANSLATE ⟨∼ into English⟩

¹**ren·dez·vous** \'rän-di-ˌvü, -dā-\ *n, pl* **ren·dez·vous** \-ˌvüz\ [MF, fr. *rendez vous* present yourselves] **1** : a place appointed for a meeting; *also* : a meeting at an appointed place **2** : a place of popular resort **3** : the process of bringing two spacecraft together

²**rendezvous** *vb* **-voused** \-ˌvüd\; **-vous·ing** \-ˌvü-iŋ\; **-vouses** \-ˌvüz\ : to come or bring together at a rendezvous

ren·di·tion \ren-'di-shən\ *n* : an act or a result of rendering ⟨first ∼ of the work into English⟩

ren·e·gade \'re-ni-ˌgād\ *n* [Sp *renegado,* fr. ML *renegatus,* fr. pp. of *renegare* to deny, fr. L *re-* re- + *negare* to deny] : a deserter from one faith, cause, principle, or party for another

re·nege \ri-'nig, -'neg, -'nēg, -'nāg\ *vb* **re·neged; re·neg·ing 1** : to go back on a promise or commitment **2** : to fail to follow suit when able in a card game in violation of the rules — **re·neg·er** *n*

re·new \ri-'nü, -'nyü\ *vb* **1** : to make or become new, fresh, or strong again **2** : to restore to existence : RECREATE, REVIVE **3** : to make or do again : REPEAT ⟨∼ a complaint⟩ **4** : to begin again : RESUME ⟨∼ed his efforts⟩ **5** : REPLACE ⟨∼ the lining of a coat⟩ **6** : to grant or obtain an extension of or on ⟨∼ a lease⟩ ⟨∼ a subscription⟩ — **re·new·er** *n*

re·new·able \ri-'nü-ə-bəl, -'nyü-\ *adj* **1** : capable of being renewed **2** : capable of being replaced by natural ecological cycles or sound management procedures ⟨∼ resources⟩

re·new·al \ri-'nü-əl, -'nyü-\ *n* **1** : the act of renewing : the state of being renewed **2** : something renewed

ren·net \'re-nət\ *n* **1** : the contents of the stomach of an unweaned animal (as a calf) or the lining membrane of the stomach used for curdling milk **2** : rennin or a substitute used to curdle milk

ren·nin \'re-nən\ *n* : a stomach enzyme that coagulates casein and is used commercially to curdle milk in the making of cheese

re·nounce \ri-'naůns\ *vb* **re·nounced; re·nounc·ing 1** : to give up, refuse, or resign usu. by formal declaration **2** : to refuse further to follow, obey, or recognize : REPUDIATE — **re·nounce·ment** *n*

ren·o·vate \'re-nə-ˌvāt\ *vb* **-vat·ed; -vat·ing 1** : to make like new again : put in good condition : REPAIR **2** : to restore to vigor or activity — **ren·o·va·tion** \ˌre-nə-'vā-shən\ *n* — **ren·o·va·tor** \'re-nə-ˌvā-tər\ *n*

re·nown \ri-'naůn\ *n* : a state of being widely acclaimed and honored : FAME, CELEBRITY **syn** honor, glory, reputation, repute — **re·nowned** \-'naůnd\ *adj*

¹**rent** \'rent\ *n* **1** : money or the amount of money paid or due at intervals for the use of another's property **2** : property rented or for rent

²**rent** *vb* **1** : to give possession and use of in return for rent **2** : to take and hold under an agreement to pay rent **3** : to be for rent ⟨∼s for $100 a month⟩ — **rent·er** *n*

³**rent** *n* **1** : a tear in cloth **2** : a split in a party or organized group : SCHISM

¹**rent·al** \'ren-tᵊl\ *n* **1** : an amount paid or collected as rent **2** : something that is rented **3** : an act of renting

²**rental** *adj* : of or relating to rent

re·nun·ci·a·tion \ri-ˌnən-sē-'ā-shən\ *n* : the act of renouncing : REPUDIATION

rep *abbr* **1** repair **2** repeat **3** report; reporter **4** representative **5** republic

Rep *abbr* Republican

re·pack·age \(ˌ)rē-ˈpa-kij\ *vb* : to package again or anew; *esp* : to put into a more attractive form

¹re·pair \ri-ˈpar\ *vb* [ME, fr. MF *repairier* to go back to one's country, fr. LL *repatriare*, fr. L *re-* re- + *patria* native country] : to make one's way : GO ⟨~ed to the drawing room⟩

²repair *vb* [ME, fr. MF *reparer*, fr. L *reparare*, fr. *re-* re- + *parare* to prepare] **1** : to restore to good condition : FIX **2** : to restore to a healthy state **3** : REMEDY ⟨~ a wrong⟩ — **re·pair·er** *n* — **re·pair·man** \-ˌman\ *n*

³repair *n* **1** : a result of repairing **2** : an act of repairing **3** : condition with respect to need of repairing ⟨in bad ~⟩

rep·a·ra·tion \ˌre-pə-ˈrā-shən\ *n* **1** : the act of making amends for a wrong **2** : amends made for a wrong; *esp* : money paid by a defeated nation in compensation for damages caused during hostilities — usu. used in pl. **syn** redress, restitution, indemnity

re·par·a·tive \ri-ˈpar-ə-tiv\ *adj* **1** : of, relating to, or effecting repairs **2** : serving to make amends

rep·ar·tee \ˌre-pər-ˈtē\ *n* **1** : a witty reply **2** : a succession of clever replies; *also* : skill in making such replies

re·past \ri-ˈpast, ˈrē-ˌpast\ *n* : a supply of food and drink served as a meal

re·pa·tri·ate \rē-ˈpā-trē-ˌāt\ *vb* **-at·ed; -at·ing** : to send or bring back to the country of origin or citizenship ⟨~ prisoners of war⟩ — **re·pa·tri·ate** \-trē-ət, -trē-ˌāt\ *n* — **re·pa·tri·a·tion** \-ˌpā-trē-ˈā-shən\ *n*

re·pay \rē-ˈpā\ *vb* **-paid** \-ˈpād\; **-pay·ing 1** : to pay back : REFUND **2** : to give or do in return or requital **3** : to make a return payment to : RECOMPENSE, REQUITE **syn** remunerate, compensate, reimburse, indemnify — **re·pay·able** *adj* — **re·pay·ment** *n*

re·peal \ri-ˈpēl\ *vb* : to annul by authoritative and esp. legislative action — **repeal** *n* — **re·peal·er** *n*

¹re·peat \ri-ˈpēt\ *vb* **1** : to say again **2** : to do again **3** : to say over from memory — **re·peat·able** *adj* — **re·peat·er** *n*

²re·peat \ri-ˈpēt, ˈrē-ˌpēt\ *n* **1** : the act of repeating **2** : something repeated or to be repeated (as a radio or television program)

re·peat·ed \ri-ˈpē-təd\ *adj* : done or recurring again and again : FREQUENT — **re·peat·ed·ly** *adv*

re·pel \ri-ˈpel\ *vb* **re·pelled; re·pel·ling 1** : to drive away : REPULSE **2** : to fight against : RESIST **3** : to turn away : REJECT **4** : to cause aversion in : DISGUST

¹re·pel·lent *also* **re·pel·lant** \ri-ˈpe-lənt\ *adj* **1** : tending to drive away ⟨a mosquito-*repellent* spray⟩ **2** : causing disgust

²repellent *also* **repellant** *n* : something that repels; *esp* : a substance that repels insects

re·pent \ri-ˈpent\ *vb* **1** : to turn from sin and resolve to reform one's life **2** : to feel sorry for (something done) : REGRET — **re·pen·tance** \ri-ˈpent-ᵊns\ *n* — **re·pen·tant** \-ᵊnt\ *adj*

re·per·cus·sion \ˌrē-pər-ˈkə-shən, ˌre-\ *n* **1** : REVERBERATION **2** : a reciprocal action or effect **3** : a widespread, indirect, or unforeseen effect of something done or said

rep·er·toire \ˈre-pər-ˌtwär\ *n* [F] **1** : a list of plays, operas, pieces, or parts which a company or performer is prepared to present **2** : a list of the skills or devices possessed by a person or needed in his occupation

rep·er·to·ry \ˈre-pər-ˌtōr-ē\ *n, pl* **-ries 1** : REPOSITORY **2** : REPERTOIRE **3** : a company that presents its repertoire in the course of one season at one theater

rep·e·ti·tion \ˌre-pə-ˈti-shən\ *n* **1** : the act or an instance of repeating **2** : the fact of being repeated

rep·e·ti·tious \-ˈti-shəs\ *adj* : marked by repetition; *esp* : tediously repeating — **rep·e·ti·tious·ly** *adv* — **rep·e·ti·tious·ness** *n*

re·pet·i·tive \ri-ˈpe-ti-tiv\ *adj* : REPETITIOUS — **re·pet·i·tive·ly** *adv* — **re·pet·i·tive·ness** *n*

re·pine \ri-ˈpīn\ *vb* **re·pined; re·pin·ing 1** : to feel or express discontent or dejection **2** : to long for something

repl *abbr* replace; replacement

re·place \ri-ˈplās\ *vb* **1** : to restore to a former place or position **2** : to take the place of : SUPPLANT **3** : to put something new in the place of — **re·place·able** *adj* — **re·plac·er** *n*

re·place·ment \ri-ˈplās-mənt\ *n* **1** : the act of replacing : the state of being replaced **2** : one that replaces another esp. in a job or function

¹re·play \(ˌ)rē-ˈplā\ *vb* : to play again or over

²re·play \ˈrē-ˌplā\ *n* **1** : an act or instance of replaying **2** : the playing of a tape (as a videotape)

re·plen·ish \ri-ˈple-nish\ *vb* : to fill or build up again : stock or supply anew — **re·plen·ish·ment** *n*

re·plete \ri-ˈplēt\ *adj* **1** : fully provided **2** : FULL; *esp* : full of food — **re·plete·ness** *n*

re·ple·tion \ri-ˈple-shən\ *n* : the state of being replete

rep·li·ca \ˈre-pli-kə\ *n* [It, repetition, fr. *replicare* to repeat, fr. LL, fr. L, to fold back, fr. *re-* back + *plicare* to fold] **1** : an exact reproduction (as of a painting) executed by the original artist **2** : a copy exact in all details : DUPLICATE

¹rep·li·cate \ˈre-plə-ˌkāt\ *vb* **-cat·ed; -cat·ing** : DUPLICATE, REPEAT

²rep·li·cate \-pli-kət\ *n* : one of several identical experiments or procedures

rep·li·ca·tion \ˌre-plə-ˈkā-shən\ *n* **1** : ANSWER, REPLY **2** : precise copying or reproduction; *also* : an act or process of this

¹re·ply \ri-ˈplī\ *vb* **re·plied; re·ply·ing** : to say or do in answer : RESPOND

²reply *n, pl* **replies** : ANSWER, RESPONSE

¹re·port \ri-ˈpōrt\ *n* [ME, fr. MF, fr. OF, fr. *reporter* to report, fr. L *reportare*, fr. *re-* back + *portare* to carry] **1** : common talk : RUMOR **2** : FAME, REPUTATION **3** : a usu. detailed account or statement **4** : an explosive noise

²report *vb* **1** : to give an account of : RELATE, TELL **2** : to serve as carrier of (a message) **3** : to prepare or present (as an account of an event) for a newspaper or a broadcast **4** : to make a charge of misconduct against **5** : to present oneself (as for work) **6** : to make known to the authorities ⟨~ a fire⟩ **7** : to return or present (as a matter referred to a committee) with conclusions and recommendations — **re·port·able** *adj*

re·port·age \ri-ˈpōr-tij, *esp for 2* ˌre-pər-ˈtäzh, ˌre-ˌpȯr-ˈ\ *n* [F] **1** : the act or process of reporting news **2** : writing intended to give an account of observed or documented events

report card *n* : a periodic report on a student's grades

re·port·ed·ly \ri-ˈpōr-təd-lē\ *adv* : according to report

re·port·er \ri-ˈpōr-tər\ *n* : one that reports; *esp* : a person who gathers and reports news for a news medium — **re·por·to·ri·al** \ˌre-pər-ˈtōr-ē-əl\ *adj*

¹re·pose \ri-ˈpōz\ *vb* **re·posed; re·pos·ing 1** : to lay at rest **2** : to lie at rest **3** : to lie dead **4** : to take a rest **5** : to rest for support : LIE

²repose *n* **1** : a state of resting (as after exertion); *esp* : SLEEP **2** : eternal or heavenly rest **3** : CALM, PEACE **4** : cessation or absence of activity, movement, or animation **5** : composure of manner : POISE — **re·pose·ful** *adj*

³repose *vb* **re·posed; re·pos·ing 1** : to place (as trust) in someone or something **2** : to place for control, management, or use

re·pos·i·to·ry \ri-ˈpä-zə-ˌtōr-ē\ *n, pl* **-ries 1** : a place

\ə\abut \ᵊ\kitten \ər\further \a\ash \ā\ace \ä\mop, mar \aů\out \ch\chin \e\bet \ē\easy \g\go \i\hit \ī\ice \j\job \ŋ\sing \ō\go \ȯ\law \ȯi\boy \th\thin \t̲h̲\the \ü\loot \u̇\foot \y\yet \zh\vision *see also* Pronunciation Symbols page where something is deposited or stored **2** : a person to whom something is entrusted

re·pos·sess \ˌrē-pə-ˈzes\ *vb* **1** : to regain possession of **2** : to take possession of in default of the payment of installments due — **re·pos·ses·sion** \-ˈze-shən\ *n*

rep·re·hend \ˌre-pri-ˈhend\ *vb* : to express disapproval of : CENSURE **syn** criticize, condemn, denounce, blame, pan — **rep·re·hen·sion** \-ˈhen-chən\ *n*

rep·re·hen·si·ble \-ˈhen-sə-bəl\ *adj* : deserving blame or censure : CULPABLE — **rep·re·hen·si·bly** \-blē\ *adv*

rep·re·sent \ˌre-pri-ˈzent\ *vb* **1** : to present a picture or a likeness of : PORTRAY, DEPICT **2** : to serve as a sign or symbol of **3** : to act the role of **4** : to stand in the place of : act or speak for **5** : to be a member or example of : TYPIFY **6** : to serve as an elected representative of **7** : to describe as having a specified quality or character **8** : to state with the purpose of affecting judgment or action

rep·re·sen·ta·tion \ˌre-pri-ˌzen-ˈtā-shən\ *n* **1** : the act of representing **2** : one (as a picture or image) that represents something else **3** : the state of being represented in a legislative body; *also* : the body of persons representing a constituency **4** : a usu. formal statement made to effect a change

¹rep·re·sen·ta·tive \ˌre-pri-ˈzen-tə-tiv\ *adj* **1** : serving to represent **2** : standing or acting for another **3** : founded on the principle of representation : carried on by elected representatives ⟨∼ government⟩ — **rep·re·sen·ta·tive·ly** *adv* — **rep·re·sen·ta·tive·ness** *n*

²representative *n* **1** : a typical example of a group, class, or quality **2** : one that represents another; *esp* : one representing a district in a legislative body usu. as a member of a lower house

re·press \ri-ˈpres\ *vb* **1** : CURB, SUBDUE **2** : RESTRAIN, SUPPRESS **3** : to exclude from consciousness — **re·pres·sion** \-ˈpre-shən\ *n* — **re·pres·sive** \-ˈpre-siv\ *adj*

¹re·prieve \ri-ˈprēv\ *vb* **re·prieved; re·priev·ing 1** : to delay the punishment or execution of **2** : to give temporary relief to

²reprieve *n* **1** : the act of reprieving : the state of being reprieved **2** : a formal temporary suspension of a sentence esp. of death **3** : a temporary respite

¹rep·ri·mand \ˈre-prə-ˌmand\ *n* : a severe or formal reproof

²reprimand *vb* : to reprove severely or formally

¹re·print \(ˌ)rē-ˈprint\ *vb* : to print again

²re·print \ˈrē-ˌprint\ *n* : a reproduction of printed matter

re·pri·sal \ri-ˈprī-zəl\ *n* : an act in retaliation for something done by another

re·prise \ri-ˈprēz\ *n* : a recurrence, renewal, or resumption of an action; *also* : a musical repetition

¹re·proach \ri-ˈprōch\ *n* **1** : an expression of disapproval **2** : DISGRACE, DISCREDIT **3** : the act of reproaching : REBUKE **4** : a cause or occasion of blame or disgrace — **re·proach·ful** \-fəl\ *adj* — **re·proach·ful·ly** *adv* — **re·proach·ful·ness** *n*

²reproach *vb* **1** : CENSURE, REBUKE **2** : to cast discredit on **syn** chide, admonish, reprove, reprimand — **re·proach·able** *adj*

rep·ro·bate \ˈre-prə-ˌbāt\ *n* **1** : a person foreordained to damnation **2** : a thoroughly bad person : SCOUNDREL — **reprobate** *adj*

rep·ro·ba·tion \ˌre-prə-ˈbā-shən\ *n* : strong disapproval : CONDEMNATION

re·pro·duce \ˌrē-prə-ˈdüs, -ˈdyüs\ *vb* **1** : to produce again or anew **2** : to produce offspring — **re·pro·duc·ible** \-ˈdü-sə-bəl, -ˈdyü-\ *adj* — **re·pro·duc·tion** \-ˈdək-shən\ *n* — **re·pro·duc·tive** \-ˈdək-tiv\ *adj*

re·proof \ri-ˈprüf\ *n* : blame or censure for a fault

re·prove \ri-ˈprüv\ *vb* **re·proved; re·prov·ing 1** : to administer a rebuke to **2** : to express disapproval of **syn** reprimand, admonish, reproach, chide — **re·prov·er** *n*

rept *abbr* report

rep·tile \ˈrep-təl, -ˌtīl\ *n* [ME *reptil*, fr. MF or LL; MF *reptile*, fr. LL *reptile*, fr. L *repere* to crawl] : any of a large class of air-breathing scaly vertebrates including snakes, lizards, alligators, turtles, and extinct related forms (as dinosaurs) — **rep·til·i·an** \rep-ˈti-lē-ən\ *adj or n*

re·pub·lic \ri-ˈpə-blik\ *n* [F *république*, fr. MF *republique*, fr. L *respublica*, fr. *res* thing, wealth + *publica*, fem. of *publicus* public] **1** : a government having a chief of state who is not a monarch and is usu. a president; *also* : a nation or other political unit having such a government **2** : a government in which supreme power is held by the citizens entitled to vote and is exercised by elected officers and representatives governing according to law; *also* : a nation or other political unit having such a form of government

¹re·pub·li·can \-bli-kən\ *adj* **1** : of, relating to, or resembling a republic **2** : favoring or supporting a republic **3** *cap* : of, relating to, or constituting one of the two major political parties in the U.S. evolving in the mid-19th century — **re·pub·li·can·ism** *n, often cap*

²republican *n* **1** : one that favors or supports a republican form of government **2** *cap* : a member of a republican party and esp. of the Republican party of the U.S.

re·pu·di·ate \ri-ˈpyü-dē-ˌāt\ *vb* **-at·ed; -at·ing** [L *repudiare* to cast off, divorce, fr. *repudium* divorce] **1** : to cast off : DISOWN **2** : to refuse to have anything to do with : refuse to acknowledge, accept, or pay ⟨∼ a charge⟩ ⟨∼ a debt⟩ **syn** spurn, reject, decline — **re·pu·di·a·tion** \-ˌpyü-dē-ˈā-shən\ *n* — **re·pu·di·a·tor** \-ˈpyü-dē-ˌā-tər\ *n*

re·pug·nance \ri-ˈpəg-nəns\ *n* **1** : the quality or fact of being contradictory or inconsistent **2** : strong dislike, distaste, or antagonism

re·pug·nant \-nənt\ *adj* **1** : marked by repugnance **2** : contrary to a person's tastes or principles : exciting distaste or aversion **syn** repellent, abhorrent, distasteful, obnoxious, revolting, loathsome — **re·pug·nant·ly** *adv*

¹re·pulse \ri-ˈpəls\ *vb* **re·pulsed; re·puls·ing 1** : to drive or beat back : REPEL **2** : to repel by discourtesy or denial : REBUFF **3** : to cause a feeling of repulsion in : DISGUST

²repulse *n* **1** : REBUFF, REJECTION **2** : the action of repelling an attacker : the fact of being repelled

re·pul·sion \ri-ˈpəl-shən\ *n* **1** : the action of repulsing : the state of being repulsed **2** : the force with which bodies, particles, or like forces repel one another **3** : a feeling of aversion

re·pul·sive \-siv\ *adj* **1** : serving or tending to repel or reject **2** : arousing aversion or disgust **syn** repugnant, revolting, loathsome, noisome — **re·pul·sive·ly** *adv* — **re·pul·sive·ness** *n*

rep·u·ta·ble \ˈre-pyə-tə-bəl\ *adj* : having a good reputation : ESTIMABLE — **rep·u·ta·bly** \-blē\ *adv*

rep·u·ta·tion \ˌre-pyü-ˈtā-shən\ *n* **1** : overall quality or character as seen or judged by people in general **2** : place in public esteem or regard

¹re·pute \ri-ˈpyüt\ *vb* **re·put·ed; re·put·ing** : CONSIDER, ACCOUNT

²repute *n* **1** : REPUTATION **2** : the state of being favorably known or spoken of

re·put·ed \ri-ˈpyü-təd\ *adj* **1** : REPUTABLE **2** : according to reputation : SUPPOSED — **re·put·ed·ly** *adv*

req *abbr* **1** request **2** require; required **3** requisition

¹re·quest \ri-ˈkwest\ *n* **1** : an act or instance of asking for something **2** : a thing asked for **3** : the condition of being asked for ⟨available on ∼⟩

²request *vb* **1** : to make a request to or of **2** : to ask for — **re·quest·er** *n*

re·qui·em \ˈre-kwē-əm, ˈrā-\ *n* [ME, fr. L (first word of the requiem mass), acc. of *requies* rest, fr. *quies* quiet, rest] **1** : a mass for a dead person; *also* : a musical setting for this **2** : a musical service or hymn in honor of the dead

re·quire \ri-'kwīr\ *vb* **re·quired; re·quir·ing 1** : to demand as necessary or essential **2** : COMMAND, ORDER

re·quire·ment \-mənt\ *n* **1** : something (as a condition or quality) required ⟨entrance ~s⟩ **2** : NECESSITY

req·ui·site \'re-kwə-zət\ *adj* : REQUIRED, NECESSARY — **requisite** *n*

req·ui·si·tion \,re-kwə-'zi-shən\ *n* **1** : formal application or demand (as for supplies) **2** : the state of being in demand or use — **requisition** *vb*

re·quite \ri-'kwīt\ *vb* **re·quit·ed; re·quit·ing 1** : to make return for : REPAY **2** : to make retaliation for : AVENGE **3** : to make return to — **re·quit·al** \-'kwīt-ᵊl\ *n*

rere·dos \'rer-ə-,däs\ *n* : a usu. ornamental wood or stone screen or partition wall behind an altar

re·run \'rē-,rən, (,)rē-'rən\ *n* : the act or an instance of running again or anew; *esp* : a showing of a motion picture or television program after its first run — **re·run** \(,)rē-'rən\ *vb*

res *abbr* **1** research **2** reservation; reserve **3** reservoir **4** residence; resident **5** resolution

re·sale \'rē-,sāl, (,)rē-'sāl\ *n* : the act of selling again usu. to a new party — **re·sal·able** \(,)rē-'sā-lə-bəl\ *adj*

re·scind \ri-'sind\ *vb* : REPEAL, CANCEL, ANNUL — **re·scis·sion** \-'si-zhən\ *n*

re·script \'rē-,skript\ *n* : an official or authoritative order or decree

res·cue \'res-kyü\ *vb* **res·cued; res·cu·ing** [ME, fr. MF *rescourre*, fr. OF, fr. *re-* re- + *escourre* to shake out, fr. L *excutere*] : to free from danger, harm, or confinement — **rescue** *n* — **res·cu·er** *n*

re·search \ri-'sərch, 'rē-,sərch\ *n* **1** : careful or diligent search **2** : studious inquiry or examination aimed at the discovery and interpretation of new knowledge **3** : the collecting of information about a particular subject — **research** *vb* — **re·search·er** *n*

re·sec·tion \ri-'sek-shən\ *n* : the surgical removal of part of an organ or structure

re·sem·blance \ri-'zem-bləns\ *n* : the quality or state of resembling

re·sem·ble \ri-'zem-bəl\ *vb* **-bled; -bling** : to be like or similar to

re·sent \ri-'zent\ *vb* : to feel or exhibit annoyance or indignation at — **re·sent·ful** \-fəl\ *adj* — **re·sent·ful·ly** *adv* — **re·sent·ment** *n*

re·ser·pine \ri-'sər-,pēn, -pən\ *n* : a drug used in treating high blood pressure and nervous tension

res·er·va·tion \,re-zər-'vā-shən\ *n* **1** : an act of reserving **2** : something (as a room in a hotel) arranged for in advance **3** : something reserved; *esp* : a tract of public land set aside for special use **4** : a limiting condition

¹re·serve \ri-'zərv\ *vb* **re·served; re·serv·ing 1** : to store for future or special use **2** : to hold back for oneself **3** : to set aside or arrange to have set aside or held for special use

²reserve *n* **1** : something reserved : STOCK, STORE **2** : a military force withheld from action for later use — usu. used in pl. **3** : the military forces of a country not part of the regular services; *also* : RESERVIST **4** : a tract set apart : RESERVATION **5** : an act of reserving **6** : restraint or caution in one's words or bearing **7** : money or its equivalent kept in hand or set apart to meet liabilities

re·served \ri-'zərvd\ *adj* **1** : restrained in words and actions **2** : set aside for future or special use — **re·serv·ed·ly** \-'zər-vəd-lē\ *adv* — **re·serv·ed·ness** \-vəd-nəs\ *n*

re·serv·ist \ri-'zər-vist\ *n* : a member of a military reserve

res·er·voir \'re-zə-,vwär, -zər-, -,vwor\ *n* [F] : a place where something is kept in store; *esp* : an artificial lake where water is collected as a water supply

re·shuf·fle \rē-'shə-fəl\ *vb* **1** : to shuffle again **2** : to re-

organize usu. by redistribution of existing elements — **reshuffle** *n*

re·side \ri-'zīd\ *vb* **re·sid·ed; re·sid·ing 1** : to make one's home : DWELL **2** : to be present as a quality or vested as a right

res·i·dence \'re-zə-dəns\ *n* **1** : the act or fact of residing in a place as a dweller or in discharge of a duty or an obligation **2** : the place where one actually lives **3** : a building used as a home : DWELLING **4** : the period of living in a place

res·i·den·cy \'re-zə-dən-sē\ *n, pl* **-cies 1** : the residence of or the territory under a diplomatic resident **2** : a period of advanced training in a medical specialty

¹res·i·dent \-dənt\ *adj* **1** : RESIDING **2** : being in residence **3** : not migratory

²resident *n* **1** : one who resides in a place **2** : a diplomatic representative with governing powers (as in a protectorate) **3** : a physician serving a residency

res·i·den·tial \,re-zə-'den-chəl\ *adj* **1** : used as a residence or by residents **2** : occupied by or restricted to residences — **res·i·den·tial·ly** *adv*

¹re·sid·u·al \ri-'zi-jə-wəl\ *adj* : being a residue or remainder

²residual *n* **1** : a residual product or substance **2** : a payment (as to an actor or writer) for each rerun after an initial showing (as of a taped TV show)

re·sid·u·ary \ri-'zi-jə-,wer-ē\ *adj* : of, relating to, or constituting a residue esp. of an estate

res·i·due \'re-zə-,dü, -,dyü\ *n* : a part remaining after another part has been taken away : REMAINDER

re·sid·u·um \ri-'zi-jə-wəm\ *n, pl* **re·sid·ua** \-jə-wə\ [L] **1** : something remaining or residual after certain deductions are made **2** : a residual product

re·sign \ri-'zīn\ *vb* [ME, fr. MF *resigner*, fr. L *resignare*, lit., to unseal, cancel, fr. *signare* to sign, seal] **1** : to give up deliberately (as one's position) esp. by a formal act **2** : to give (oneself) over to grief or despair) without resistance — **re·sign·ed·ly** \-'zī-nəd-lē\ *adv*

re–sign \(,)rē-'sīn\ *vb* : to sign again

res·ig·na·tion \,re-zig-'nā-shən\ *n* **1** : an act or instance of resigning; *also* : a formal notification of such an act **2** : the quality or state of being resigned

re·sil·ience \ri-'zil-yəns\ *n* **1** : the ability of a body to regain its original size and shape after being compressed, bent, or stretched **2** : an ability to recover from or adjust easily to change or misfortune

re·sil·ien·cy \-yən-sē\ *n* : RESILIENCE

re·sil·ient \-yənt\ *adj* : marked by resilience

res·in \'rez-ᵊn\ *n* : any of various substances obtained from the gum or sap of some trees and used esp. in varnishes, plastics, and medicine; *also* : a comparable synthetic product — **res·in·ous** *adj*

¹re·sist \ri-'zist\ *vb* **1** : to fight against : OPPOSE ⟨~ aggression⟩ **2** : to withstand the force or effect of ⟨~ disease⟩ *syn* combat, repel — **re·sist·ible** \-'zis-tə-bəl\ *adj* — **re·sist·less** *adj*

²resist *n* : something (as a coating) that resists or prevents a particular action

re·sis·tance \ri-'zis-təns\ *n* **1** : the act or an instance of resisting : OPPOSITION **2** : the power or capacity to resist; *esp* : the inherent ability of an organism to resist harmful influences (as disease or infection) **3** : the opposition offered by a body to the passage through it of a steady electric current

re·sis·tant \-tənt\ *adj* : giving or capable of resistance

re·sis·tor \ri-'zis-tər\ *n* : a device used to provide resistance to the flow of an electric current in a circuit

res·o·lute \'re-zə-,lüt\ *adj* : firmly determined in purpose

\ə\abut \ᵊ\kitten \ər\further \a\ash \ā\ace \ä\mop, mar \au̇\out \ch\chin \e\bet \ē\easy \g\go \i\hit \ī\ice \j\job \ŋ\sing \ō\go \ȯ\law \ȯi\boy \th\thin \th\the \ü\loot \u̇\foot \y\yet \zh\vision *see also* Pronunciation Symbols page

: RESOLVED **syn** steadfast, staunch, faithful, true, loyal — **res·o·lute·ly** *adv* — **res·o·lute·ness** *n*

res·o·lu·tion \ˌre-zə-ˈlü-shən\ *n* **1** : the act or process of resolving **2** : the action of solving; *also* : SOLUTION **3** : the quality of being resolute : FIRMNESS, DETERMINATION **4** : a formal statement expressing the opinion, will, or intent of a body of persons

¹re·solve \ri-ˈzälv\ *vb* **re·solved; re·solv·ing 1** : to break up into constituent parts : ANALYZE **2** : to distinguish between or make visible adjacent parts of **3** : to find an answer to : SOLVE **4** : DETERMINE, DECIDE **5** : to make or pass a formal resolution — **re·solv·able** *adj*

²resolve *n* **1** : fixity of purpose **2** : something resolved

res·o·nance \ˈre-zə-nəns\ *n* **1** : the quality or state of being resonant **2** : a reinforcement of sound in a vibrating body caused by waves from another body vibrating at nearly the same rate

res·o·nant \-nənt\ *adj* **1** : continuing to sound : RESOUNDING **2** : relating to or exhibiting resonance **3** : intensified and enriched by or as if by resonance — **res·o·nant·ly** *adv*

res·o·nate \-ˌnāt\ *vb* **-nat·ed; -nat·ing 1** : to produce or exhibit resonance **2** : REVERBERATE, RESOUND

res·o·na·tor \-ˌnā-tər\ *n* : something that resounds or exhibits resonance

re·sorp·tion \rē-ˈsȯrp-shən, -ˈzȯrp-\ *n* : the action or process of breaking down and assimilating something (as a tooth or an embryo)

¹re·sort \ri-ˈzȯrt\ *n* [ME, fr. MF, resource, recourse, fr. *resortir* to rebound, resort, fr. OF, fr. *sortir* to escape, sally] **1** : one looked to for help : REFUGE **2** : RECOURSE **3** : frequent or general visiting ⟨place of ∼⟩ **4** : a frequently visited place : HAUNT **5** : a place providing recreation esp. to vacationers

²resort *vb* **1** : to go often or habitually **2** : to have recourse ⟨∼ed to violence⟩

re·sound \ri-ˈzaund\ *vb* **1** : to become filled with sound : REVERBERATE, RING **2** : to sound loudly

re·sound·ing *adj* **1** : RESONATING, RESONANT **2** : impressively sonorous ⟨∼ name⟩ **3** : EMPHATIC, UNEQUIVOCAL ⟨a ∼ success⟩ — **re·sound·ing·ly** *adv*

re·source \ˈrē-ˌsȯrs, ri-ˈsȯrs\ *n* [F *ressource,* fr. OF *ressourse* relief, resource, fr. *resourdre* to relieve, lit., to rise again, fr. L *resurgere,* fr. *re-* again + *surgere* to rise] **1** : a source of supply or support — usu. used in pl. **2** *pl* : available funds **3** : a possibility of relief or recovery **4** : a means of spending leisure time **5** : ability to meet and handle situations — **re·source·ful** \ri-ˈsȯrs-fəl\ *adj* — **re·source·ful·ness** *n*

resp *abbr* respective; respectively

¹re·spect \ri-ˈspekt\ *n* **1** : relation to something usu. specified : REGARD ⟨in ∼ to⟩ **2** : high or special regard : ESTEEM **3** *pl* : an expression of respect or deference **4** : DETAIL, PARTICULAR — **re·spect·ful** \-fəl\ *adj* — **re·spect·ful·ly** *adv* — **re·spect·ful·ness** *n*

²respect *vb* **1** : to consider deserving of high regard : ESTEEM **2** : to refrain from interfering with ⟨∼ another's privacy⟩ **3** : to have reference to : CONCERN — **re·spect·er** *n*

re·spect·able \ri-ˈspek-tə-bəl\ *adj* **1** : worthy of respect : ESTIMABLE **2** : decent or correct in conduct : PROPER **3** : fair in size, quantity, or quality : MODERATE, TOLERABLE **4** : fit to be seen : PRESENTABLE — **re·spect·a·bil·i·ty** \-ˌspek-tə-ˈbi-lə-tē\ *n* — **re·spect·ably** \-ˈspek-tə-blē\ *adv*

re·spect·ing *prep* : with regard to

re·spec·tive \-tiv\ *adj* : PARTICULAR, SEPARATE ⟨returned to their ∼ homes⟩

re·spec·tive·ly \-lē\ *adv* **1** : as relating to each **2** : each in the order given

res·pi·ra·tion \ˌres-pə-ˈrā-shən\ *n* **1** : an act or the process of breathing **2** : the physical and chemical processes (as breathing and oxidation) by which a living thing obtains oxygen and eliminates waste gases (as carbon dioxide) — **re·spi·ra·to·ry** \ˈres-pə-rə-ˌtōr-ē, ri-ˈspī-rə-\ *adj* — **re·spire** \ri-ˈspīr\ *vb*

res·pi·ra·tor \ˈres-pə-ˌrā-tər\ *n* **1** : a device covering the mouth or nose esp. to prevent inhaling harmful vapors **2** : a device for artificial respiration

re·spite \ˈres-pət\ *n* **1** : a temporary delay **2** : an interval of rest or relief

re·splen·dent \ri-ˈsplen-dənt\ *adj* : shining brilliantly : gloriously bright : SPLENDID — **re·splen·dence** \-dəns\ *n* — **re·splen·dent·ly** *adv*

re·spond \ri-ˈspänd\ *vb* **1** : ANSWER, REPLY **2** : REACT ⟨∼ed to a call for help⟩ **3** : to show favorable reaction ⟨∼ to medication⟩ — **re·spond·er** *n*

re·spon·dent \ri-ˈspän-dənt\ *n* : one who responds; *esp* : one who answers in various legal proceedings — **respondent** *adj*

re·sponse \ri-ˈspäns\ *n* **1** : an act of responding **2** : something constituting a reply or a reaction

re·spon·si·bil·i·ty \ri-ˌspän-sə-ˈbi-lə-tē\ *n, pl* **-ties 1** : the quality or state of being responsible **2** : something for which one is responsible

re·spon·si·ble \ri-ˈspän-sə-bəl\ *adj* **1** : liable to be called upon to answer for one's acts or decisions : ANSWERABLE **2** : able to fulfill one's obligations : RELIABLE, TRUSTWORTHY **3** : able to choose for oneself between right and wrong **4** : involving accountability or important duties ⟨∼ position⟩ — **re·spon·si·ble·ness** *n* — **re·spon·si·bly** \-blē\ *adv*

re·spon·sive \-siv\ *adj* **1** : RESPONDING **2** : quick to respond : SENSITIVE **3** : using responses ⟨∼ readings⟩ — **re·spon·sive·ly** *adv* — **re·spon·sive·ness** *n*

¹rest \ˈrest\ *n* **1** : REPOSE, SLEEP **2** : freedom from work or activity **3** : a state of motionlessness or inactivity **4** : a place of shelter or lodging **5** : a silence in music equivalent in duration to a note of the same value; *also* : a character indicating this **6** : something used as a support — **rest·ful** \-fəl\ *adj* — **rest·ful·ly** *adv*

rest 5

²rest *vb* **1** : to get rest by lying down; *esp* : SLEEP **2** : to cease from action or motion **3** : to give rest to : set at rest **4** : to sit or lie fixed or supported **5** : to place on or against a support **6** : to remain based or founded **7** : to cause to be firmly fixed : GROUND **8** : to remain for action : DEPEND

³rest *n* : something left over

res·tau·rant \ˈres-trənt, -tə-ˌränt\ *n* [F, fr. prp. of *restaurer* to restore, fr. L *restaurare*] : a public eating place

res·tau·ra·teur \ˌres-tə-rə-ˈtər\ *also* **res·tau·ran·teur** \-ˌrän-\ *n* : the operator or proprietor of a restaurant

rest home *n* : an establishment that gives care for the aged or convalescent

res·ti·tu·tion \ˌres-tə-ˈtü-shən, -ˈtyü-\ *n* : the act of restoring : the state of being restored; *esp* : restoration of something to its rightful owner **syn** amends, redress, reparation, indemnity, compensation

res·tive \ˈres-tiv\ *adj* [ME, fr. MF *restif,* fr. *rester* to stop behind, remain, fr. L *restare,* fr. *re-* back + *stare* to stand] **1** : BALKY **2** : UNEASY, FIDGETY **syn** restless, impatient, nervous — **res·tive·ly** *adv* — **res·tive·ness** *n*

rest·less \ˈrest-ləs\ *adj* **1** : lacking or denying rest ⟨a ∼ night⟩ **2** : never resting or settled : always moving ⟨the ∼ sea⟩ **3** : marked by or showing unrest esp. of mind ⟨∼ pacing back and forth⟩ **syn** restive, impatient, nervous, fidgety — **rest·less·ly** *adv* — **rest·less·ness** *n*

re·stor·able \ri-'stōr-ə-bəl\ *adj* : fit for restoring or reclaiming

res·to·ra·tion \ˌres-tə-'rā-shən\ *n* **1** : an act of restoring : the state of being restored **2** : something (as a building) that has been restored

re·stor·ative \ri-'stōr-ə-tiv\ *n* : something that restores esp. to consciousness or health — **restorative** *adj*

re·store \ri-'stōr\ *vb* **re·stored; re·stor·ing 1** : to give back : RETURN **2** : to put back into use or service **3** : to put or bring back into a former or original state **4** : to put again in possession of something — **re·stor·er** *n*

re·strain \ri-'strān\ *vb* **1** : to prevent from doing something **2** : to limit, restrict, or keep under control : CURB **3** : to place under restraint or arrest — **re·strain·able** *adj* — **re·strain·er** *n*

re·strained \ri-'strānd\ *adj* : marked by restraint : DISCIPLINED — **re·strain·ed·ly** \-'strā-nəd-lē\ *adv*

restraining order *n* : a legal order directing one person to stay away from another

re·straint \ri-'strānt\ *n* **1** : an act of restraining : the state of being restrained **2** : a restraining force, agency, or device **3** : deprivation or limitation of liberty : CONFINEMENT **4** : control over one's feelings : RESERVE

re·strict \ri-'strikt\ *vb* **1** : to confine within bounds : LIMIT **2** : to place under restriction as to use — **re·stric·tive** *adj* — **re·stric·tive·ly** *adv*

re·stric·tion \ri-'strik-shən\ *n* **1** : something (as a law or rule) that restricts **2** : an act of restricting : the state of being restricted

rest room *n* : a room or suite of rooms that includes sinks and toilets

¹**re·sult** \ri-'zəlt\ *vb* [ME, fr. ML *resultare,* fr. L, to rebound, fr. *re-* re- + *saltare* to leap] : to come about as an effect or consequence — **re·sul·tant** \-'zəlt-ᵊnt\ *adj or n*

²**result** *n* **1** : something that results : EFFECT, CONSEQUENCE **2** : beneficial or discernible effect **3** : something obtained by calculation or investigation

re·sume \ri-'züm\ *vb* **re·sumed; re·sum·ing 1** : to take or assume again **2** : to return to or begin again after interruption **3** : to take back to oneself — **re·sump·tion** \-'zəmp-shən\ *n*

ré·su·mé *or* **re·su·me** *or* **re·su·mé** \'re-zə-ˌmā, ˌre-zə-'mā\ *n* [F *résumé*] : SUMMARY; *esp* : a short account of one's career and qualifications usu. prepared by a job applicant

re·sur·gence \ri-'sər-jəns\ *n* : a rising again into life, activity, or prominence — **re·sur·gent** \-jənt\ *adj*

res·ur·rect \ˌre-zə-'rekt\ *vb* **1** : to raise from the dead **2** : to bring to attention or use again

res·ur·rec·tion \ˌre-zə-'rek-shən\ *n* **1** *cap* : the rising of Christ from the dead **2** *often cap* : the rising to life of all human dead before the final judgment **3** : REVIVAL

re·sus·ci·tate \ri-'sə-sə-ˌtāt\ *vb* **-tat·ed; -tat·ing** : to revive from apparent death or unconsciousness; *also* : REVITALIZE — **re·sus·ci·ta·tion** \ri-ˌsə-sə-'tā-shən, ˌrē-\ *n* — **re·sus·ci·ta·tor** \-ˌtā-tər\ *n*

ret *abbr* **1** retain **2** retired **3** return

¹**re·tail** \'rē-ˌtāl, *esp for 2 also* ri-'tāl\ *vb* **1** : to sell in small quantities directly to the ultimate consumer **2** : to tell in detail or to one person after another — **re·tail·er** *n*

²**re·tail** \'rē-ˌtāl\ *n* : the sale of goods in small amounts to ultimate consumers — **retail** *adj or adv*

re·tain \ri-'tān\ *vb* **1** : to hold in possession or use **2** : to engage (as a lawyer) by paying a fee in advance **3** : to keep in a fixed place or position **syn** detain, withhold, reserve

¹**re·tain·er** \ri-'tā-nər\ *n* **1** : one that retains **2** : a servant in a wealthy household; *also* : EMPLOYEE

²**retainer** *n* : a fee paid to secure services (as of a lawyer)

¹**re·take** \(ˌ)rē-'tāk\ *vb* **-took** \-'tùk\; **-tak·en** \-'tā-kən\; **-tak·ing 1** : to take or seize again **2** : to photograph again

²**re·take** \'rē-ˌtāk\ *n* : a second photographing of a motion-picture scene

re·tal·i·ate \ri-'ta-lē-ˌāt\ *vb* **-at·ed; -at·ing** : to return like for like; *esp* : to get revenge — **re·tal·i·a·tion** \-ˌta-lē-'ā-shən\ *n* — **re·tal·ia·to·ry** \-'tal-yə-ˌtōr-ē\ *adj*

re·tard \ri-'tärd\ *vb* : to hold back : delay the progress of **syn** slow, slacken, detain — **re·tar·da·tion** \ˌrē-ˌtär-'dā-shən, ri-\ *n* — **re·tard·er** *n*

re·tard·ed *adj* : slow or limited in intellectual, emotional, or academic progress ⟨a ~ child⟩

retch \'rech\ *vb* : to try to vomit; *also* : VOMIT

re·ten·tion \ri-'ten-chən\ *n* **1** : the act of retaining : the state of being retained **2** : the power of retaining esp. in the mind : RETENTIVENESS

re·ten·tive \-'ten-tiv\ *adj* : having the power of retaining; *esp* : retaining knowledge easily — **re·ten·tive·ness** *n*

re·think \(ˌ)rē-'thiŋk\ *vb* **-thought** \-'thȯt\; **-think·ing** : to think about again : RECONSIDER

ret·i·cent \'re-tə-sənt\ *adj* **1** : tending not to talk or give out information : RELUCTANT **syn** reserved, taciturn, closemouthed — **ret·i·cence** \-səns\ *n* — **ret·i·cent·ly** *adv*

ret·i·na \'ret-ᵊn-ə\ *n, pl* **retinas** *or* **ret·i·nae** \-ᵊn-ˌē\ : the sensory membrane lining the eye that receives the image formed by the lens — **ret·i·nal** \'ret-ᵊn-əl\ *adj*

ret·i·nue \'ret-ᵊn-ü, -ˌyü\ *n* : the body of attendants or followers of a distinguished person

re·tire \ri-'tīr\ *vb* **re·tired; re·tir·ing 1** : RETREAT **2** : to withdraw esp. for privacy **3** : to withdraw from one's occupation or position : conclude one's career **4** : to go to bed **5** : to cause to be out in baseball — **re·tire·ment** *n*

re·tired \ri-'tīrd\ *adj* **1** : SECLUDED, QUIET **2** : withdrawn from active duty or from one's career

re·tir·ee \ri-ˌtī-'rē\ *n* : a person who has retired from a career

re·tir·ing *adj* : SHY, RESERVED

¹**re·tort** \ri-'tȯrt\ *vb* [L *retortus,* pp. of *retorquēre,* lit., to twist back, hurl back, fr. *re-* back + *torquēre* to twist] **1** : to say in reply : answer back usu. sharply **2** : to answer (an argument) by a counter argument **3** : RETALIATE

²**retort** *n* : a quick, witty, or cutting reply

³**re·tort** \ri-'tȯrt, 'rē-ˌtȯrt\ *n* [MF *retorte,* fr. ML *retorta,* fr. L, fem. of *retortus,* pp. of *retorquēre* to twist back; fr. its shape] : a vessel in which substances are distilled or broken up by heat

re·touch \(ˌ)rē-'təch\ *vb* : TOUCH UP; *esp* : to change (as a photographic negative) in order to produce a more desirable appearance

re·trace \(ˌ)rē-'trās\ *vb* : to go over again or in a reverse direction ⟨*retraced* his steps⟩

re·tract \ri-'trakt\ *vb* **1** : to draw back or in **2** : to withdraw (as a charge or promise) : DISAVOW — **re·tract·able** *adj* — **re·trac·tion** \-'trak-shən\ *n*

re·trac·tile \ri-'trakt-ᵊl, -'trak-ˌtīl\ *adj* : capable of being drawn back or in ⟨~ claws⟩

¹**re·tread** \(ˌ)rē-'tred\ *vb* **re·tread·ed; re·tread·ing** : to put a new tread on (a worn tire)

²**re·tread** \'rē-ˌtred\ *n* **1** : a retreaded tire **2** : one pressed into service again; *also* : REMAKE

¹**re·treat** \ri-'trēt\ *n* **1** : an act of withdrawing esp. from something dangerous, difficult, or disagreeable **2** : a military signal for withdrawal; *also* : a military flag-lowering ceremony **3** : a place of privacy or safety : REFUGE **4** : a period of group withdrawal for prayer, meditation, and study

\ə\abut \ᵊ\kitten \ər\further \a\ash \ā\ace \ä\mop, mar \au̇\out \ch\chin \e\bet \ē\easy \g\go \i\hit \ī\ice \j\job \ŋ\sing \ō\go \ȯ\law \ȯi\boy \th\thin \th̲\the \ü\loot \u̇\foot \y\yet \zh\vision *see also* Pronunciation Symbols page

²**retreat** *vb* **1** : to make a retreat : WITHDRAW **2** : to slope backward

re·trench \ri-'trench\ *vb* [obs. F *retrencher* (now *retrancher*), fr. MF *retrenchier*, fr. *re-* + *trenchier* to cut] **1** : to cut down or pare away : REDUCE, CURTAIL **2** : to cut down expenses : ECONOMIZE — **re·trench·ment** *n*

ret·ri·bu·tion \ˌre-trə-'byü-shən\ *n* : something administered or exacted in recompense; *esp* : PUNISHMENT syn reprisal, vengeance, revenge, retaliation — **re·trib·u·tive** \ri-'tri-byə-tiv\ *adj* — **re·trib·u·to·ry** \-byə-ˌtōr-ē\ *adj*

re·trieve \ri-'trēv\ *vb* **re·trieved; re·triev·ing 1** : to search about for and bring in (killed or wounded game) **2** : RECOVER, RESTORE — **re·triev·able** *adj* — **re·triev·al** \-'trē-vəl\ *n*

re·triev·er \ri-'trē-vər\ *n* : one that retrieves; *esp* : a dog of any of several breeds used esp. for retrieving game

ret·ro·ac·tive \ˌre-trō-'ak-tiv\ *adj* : made effective as of a date prior to enactment ⟨a ~ pay raise⟩ — **ret·ro·ac·tive·ly** *adv*

ret·ro·fit \'re-tro-ˌfit, ˌre-trō-'fit\ *vb* : to furnish (as an aircraft) with newly available equipment — **ret·ro·fit** \'re-tro-ˌfit\ *n*

¹**ret·ro·grade** \'re-trə-ˌgrād\ *adj* **1** : moving or tending backward **2** : tending toward or resulting in a worse condition

²**retrograde** *vb* **1** : RETREAT **2** : DETERIORATE, DEGENERATE

ret·ro·gres·sion \ˌre-trə-'gre-shən\ *n* : return to a former and less complex level of development or organization — **ret·ro·gress** \ˌre-trə-'gres\ *vb* — **ret·ro·gres·sive** \ˌre-trə-'gre-siv\ *adj*

ret·ro·rock·et \'re-trō-ˌrä-kət\ *n* : an auxiliary rocket engine (as on a spacecraft) used to slow forward motion

ret·ro·spect \'re-trə-ˌspekt\ *n* : a review of past events — **ret·ro·spec·tion** \ˌre-trə-'spek-shən\ *n* — **ret·ro·spec·tive** \-'spek-tiv\ *adj* — **ret·ro·spec·tive·ly** *adv*

ret·ro·vi·rus \'re-trō-ˌvī-rəs\ *n* : any of a group of RNA-containing viruses (as HIV) that make DNA using RNA instead of the reverse

¹**re·turn** \ri-'tərn\ *vb* **1** : to go or come back **2** : to pass, give, or send back to an earlier possessor **3** : to put back to or in a former place or state **4** : REPLY, ANSWER **5** : to report esp. officially **6** : to elect to office **7** : to bring in (as profit) : YIELD **8** : to give or perform in return — **re·turn·er** *n*

²**return** *n* **1** : an act of coming or going back to or from a former place or state **2** : RECURRENCE **3** : a report of the results of balloting **4** : a formal statement of taxable income **5** : the profit from labor, investment, or business : YIELD **6** : the act of returning something **7** : something that returns or is returned; *also* : a means for conveying something (as water) back to its starting point **8** : something given in repayment or reciprocation; *also* : ANSWER, RETORT **9** : an answering play — **return** *adj*

¹**re·turn·able** \ri-'tər-nə-bəl\ *adj* : capable of being returned (as for reuse or recycling); *also* : permitted to be returned

²**returnable** *n* : a returnable beverage container

re·turn·ee \ri-ˌtər-'nē\ *n* : one who returns

re·union \rē-'yü-nyən\ *n* **1** : an act of reuniting : the state of being reunited **2** : a meeting of persons after separation

¹**rev** \'rev\ *n* : a revolution of a motor

²**rev** *vb* **revved; rev·ving** : to increase the revolutions per minute of (a motor)

³**rev** *abbr* **1** revenue **2** reverse **3** review; reviewed **4** revised; revision **5** revolution

Rev *abbr* **1** Revelation **2** Reverend

re·vamp \(ˌ)rē-'vamp\ *vb* : RECONSTRUCT, REVISE; *also* : RENOVATE

re·vanche \rə-'vänⁿsh\ *n* [F] : REVENGE; *esp* : a usu. political policy designed to recover lost territory or status

re·veal \ri-'vēl\ *vb* **1** : to make known **2** : to show plainly : open up to view

rev·eil·le \'re-və-lē\ *n* [modif. of F *réveillez*, imper. pl. of *réveiller* to awaken, fr. *eveiller* to awaken, fr. (assumed) VL *exvigilare*, fr. L *vigilare* to keep watch, stay awake] : a military signal sounded at about sunrise

¹**rev·el** \'re-vəl\ *vb* **-eled** *or* **-elled; -el·ing** *or* **-el·ling 1** : to take part in a revel **2** : to take great pleasure or satisfaction — **rev·el·er** *or* **rev·el·ler** *n* — **rev·el·ry** \-vəl-rē\ *n*

²**revel** *n* : a usu. wild party or celebration

rev·e·la·tion \ˌre-və-'lā-shən\ *n* **1** : an act of revealing **2** : something revealed; *esp* : an enlightening or astonishing disclosure

Revelation *n* — see BIBLE table

¹**re·venge** \ri-'venj\ *vb* **re·venged; re·veng·ing** : to inflict harm or injury in return for (a wrong) : AVENGE — **re·veng·er** *n*

²**revenge** *n* **1** : a desire for revenge **2** : an act or instance of retaliation to get even **3** : an opportunity for getting satisfaction syn vengeance, retribution, reprisal — **re·venge·ful** *adj*

rev·e·nue \'re-və-ˌnü, -ˌnyü\ *n* [ME, fr. MF, fr. *revenir* to return, fr. L *revenire*, fr. *re-* back + *venire* to come] **1** : investment income **2** : money collected by a government (as through taxes)

rev·e·nu·er \'re-və-ˌnü-ər, -ˌnyü-\ *n* : a revenue officer or boat

re·verb \ri-'vərb, 're-ˌvərb\ *n* : an electronically produced echo effect in recorded music; *also* : a device for producing reverb

re·ver·ber·ate \ri-'vər-bə-ˌrāt\ *vb* **-at·ed; -at·ing 1** : REFLECT ⟨~ light or heat⟩ **2** : to resound in or as if in a series of echoes — **re·ver·ber·a·tion** \-ˌvər-bə-'rā-shən\ *n*

re·vere \ri-'vir\ *vb* **re·vered; re·ver·ing** : to show honor and devotion to : VENERATE syn reverence, worship, adore

¹**rev·er·ence** \'re-vrəns, -və-rəns\ *n* **1** : honor or respect felt or shown **2** : a gesture (as a bow or curtsy) of respect

²**reverence** *vb* **-enced; -enc·ing** : to regard or treat with reverence

¹**rev·er·end** \'re-vrənd, -və-rənd\ *adj* **1** : worthy of reverence : REVERED **2** : being a member of the clergy — used as a title

²**reverend** *n* : a member of the clergy

rev·er·ent \'re-vrənt, -və-rənt\ *adj* : expressing reverence — **rev·er·ent·ly** *adv*

rev·er·en·tial \ˌre-və-'ren-chəl\ *adj* : REVERENT

rev·er·ie *also* **rev·ery** \'re-və-rē\ *n, pl* **-er·ies 1** : DAYDREAM **2** : the state of being lost in thought

re·ver·sal \ri-'vər-səl\ *n* : an act or process of reversing

¹**re·verse** \ri-'vərs\ *adj* **1** : opposite to a previous or normal condition ⟨in ~ order⟩ **2** : acting or working in a manner opposite the usual **3** : bringing about reverse movement ⟨~ gear⟩ — **re·verse·ly** *adv*

²**reverse** *vb* **re·versed; re·vers·ing 1** : to turn upside down or completely about in position or direction **2** : to set aside or change (as a legal decision) **3** : to change to the contrary ⟨~ a policy⟩ **4** : to go or cause to go in the opposite direction **5** : to put (as a car) in reverse — **re·vers·ible** \-'vər-sə-bəl\ *adj*

³**reverse** *n* **1** : something contrary to something else : OPPOSITE **2** : an act or instance of reversing; *esp* : a change for the worse **3** : the back of something **4** : a gear that reverses something

re·ver·sion \ri-'vər-zhən\ *n* **1** : the right of succession or future possession (as to a title or property) **2** : return toward some former or ancestral condition; *also* : a product of this — **re·ver·sion·ary** \-zhə-ˌner-ē\ *adj*

re·vert \ri-'vərt\ *vb* **1** : to come or go back ⟨∼ed to savagery⟩ **2** : to return to a proprietor or his or her heirs **3** : to return to an ancestral type

¹re·view \ri-'vyü\ *n* **1** : an act of revising **2** : a formal military inspection **3** : a general survey **4** : INSPECTION, EXAMINATION; *esp* : REEXAMINATION **5** : a critical evaluation (as of a book) **6** : a magazine devoted to reviews and essays **7** : a renewed study of previously studied material **8** : REVUE

²re·view \ri-'vyü, *1 also* 're-\ *vb* **1** : to examine or study again; *esp* : to reexamine judicially **2** : to hold a review of ⟨∼ troops⟩ **3** : to write a critical examination of ⟨∼ a novel⟩ **4** : to look back over ⟨∼ed her accomplishments⟩ **5** : to study material again

re·view·er \ri-'vyü-ər\ *n* : one that reviews; *esp* : a writer of critical reviews

re·vile \ri-'vīl\ *vb* **re·viled; re·vil·ing** : to abuse verbally : rail at **syn** vituperate, berate, rate, upbraid, scold — **re·vile·ment** *n* — **re·vil·er** *n*

re·vise \ri-'vīz\ *vb* **re·vised; re·vis·ing 1** : to look over something written in order to correct or improve **2** : to make a new version of — **re·vis·able** *adj* — **re·vise** *n* — **re·vis·er** *or* **re·vi·sor** \-'vī-zər\ *n* — **re·vi·sion** \-'vizhən\ *n*

re·vi·tal·ize \₁rē-'vīt-ᵊl-₁īz\ *vb* **-ized; -iz·ing** : to give new life or vigor to — **re·vi·tal·i·za·tion** \(₁)rē-₁vīt-ᵊl-ə-'zā-shən\ *n*

re·viv·al \ri-'vī-vəl\ *n* **1** : an act of reviving : the state of being revived **2** : a new publication or presentation (as of a book or play) **3** : an evangelistic meeting or series of meetings

re·vive \ri-'vīv\ *vb* **re·vived; re·viv·ing 1** : to bring back to life consciousness, or activity : make or become fresh or strong again **2** : to bring back into use — **re·viv·er** *n*

re·viv·i·fy \rē-'vi-və-₁fī\ *vb* : REVIVE — **re·viv·i·fi·ca·tion** \-₁vi-və-fə-'kā-shən\ *n*

re·vo·ca·ble \'re-və-kə-bəl *also* ri-'vō-kə-bəl\ *adj* : capable of being revoked

re·vo·ca·tion \₁re-və-'kā-shən\ *n* : an act or instance of revoking

re·voke \ri-'vōk\ *vb* **re·voked; re·vok·ing 1** : to annul by recalling or taking back : REPEAL, RESCIND **2** : RENEGE **2** — **re·vok·er** *n*

¹re·volt \ri-'vōlt\ *vb* **1** : to throw off allegiance to a ruler or government : REBEL **2** : to experience disgust or shock **3** : to turn or cause to turn away with disgust or abhorrence — **re·volt·er** *n*

²revolt *n* : REBELLION, INSURRECTION

re·volt·ing *adj* : extremely offensive — **re·volt·ing·ly** *adv*

rev·o·lu·tion \₁re-və-'lü-shən\ *n* **1** : the action by a heavenly body of going round in an orbit **2** : ROTATION **3** : a sudden, radical, or complete change; *esp* : the overthrow or renunciation of one ruler or government and substitution of another by the governed

¹rev·o·lu·tion·ary \-shə-₁ner-ē\ *adj* **1** : of or relating to revolution **2** : tending to or promoting revolution **3** : constituting or bringing about a major change

²revolutionary *n, pl* **-ar·ies** : one who takes part in a revolution or who advocates revolutionary doctrines

rev·o·lu·tion·ise *Brit var of* REVOLUTIONIZE

rev·o·lu·tion·ist \₁re-və-'lü-shə-nist\ *n* : REVOLUTIONARY — **revolutionist** *adj*

rev·o·lu·tion·ize \-₁nīz\ *vb* **-ized; -iz·ing** : to change fundamentally or completely : make revolutionary — **rev·o·lu·tion·iz·er** *n*

re·volve \ri-'välv\ *vb* **re·volved; re·volv·ing 1** : to turn over in the mind : reflect upon : PONDER **2** : to move in an orbit; *also* : ROTATE — **re·volv·able** *adj*

re·volv·er \ri-'väl-vər\ *n* : a pistol with a revolving cylinder of several chambers

re·vue \ri-'vyü\ *n* : a theatrical production consisting typically of brief often satirical sketches and songs

re·vul·sion \ri-'vəl-shən\ *n* **1** : a strong sudden reaction or change of feeling **2** : a feeling of complete distaste or repugnance

revved *past and past part of* REV

revving *pres part of* REV

¹re·ward \ri-'wȯrd\ *vb* **1** : to give a reward to or for **2** : RECOMPENSE

²reward *n* **1** : something given in return for good or evil done or received; *esp* : something given or offered for some service or attainment **2** : a stimulus that is administered to an organism after a response and that increases the probability of occurrence of the response **syn** premium, prize, award

¹re·wind \(₁)rē-'wīnd\ *vb* **-wound; -win·ding 1** : to wind again **2** : to reverse the winding of (as film)

²re·wind \'rē-₁wīnd\ *n* **1** : something that rewinds **2** : an act of rewinding

re·work \(₁)rē-'wərk\ *vb* **1** : REVISE **2** : to reprocess for further use

¹re·write \(₁)rē-'rīt\ *vb* **-wrote; -writ·ten; -writ·ing** : to make a revision of : REVISE

²re·write \'rē-₁rīt\ *n* : an instance or a piece of rewriting

RF *abbr* radio frequency

RFD *abbr* rural free delivery

Rh *symbol* rhodium

RH *abbr* right hand

rhap·so·dy \'rap-sə-dē\ *n, pl* **-dies** [L *rhapsodia* portion of an epic poem adapted for recitation, fr. Gk *rhapsōidia* recitation of selections from epic poetry, fr. *rhaptein* to sew, stitch together + *aidein* to sing] **1** : an expression of extravagant praise or ecstasy **2** : an instrumental composition of irregular form — **rhap·sod·ic** \rap-'sä-dik\ *adj* — **rhap·sod·i·cal·ly** \-di-k(ə-)lē\ *adv* — **rhap·so·dize** \'rap-sə-₁dīz\ *vb*

rhea \'rē-ə\ *n* : either of two large flightless 3-toed So. American birds that resemble but are smaller than the African ostrich

rhe·ni·um \'rē-nē-əm\ *n* : a rare heavy hard metallic chemical element — see ELEMENT table

rheo·stat \'rē-ə-₁stat\ *n* : a resistor for regulating an electric current by means of variable resistances — **rheo·stat·ic** \₁rē-ə-'sta-tik\ *adj*

rhe·sus monkey \'rē-səs-\ *n* : a pale brown Indian monkey often used in medical research

rhet·o·ric \'re-tə-rik\ *n* [ME *rethorik*, fr. MF *rethorique*, fr. L *rhetorica*, fr. Gk *rhētorikē*, lit., art of oratory, fr. *rhētōr* public speaker, fr. *eirein* to speak] : the art of speaking or writing effectively — **rhe·tor·i·cal** \ri-'tȯr-i-kəl\ *adj* — **rhet·o·ri·cian** \₁re-tə-'ri-shən\ *n*

rheum \'rüm\ *n* : a watery discharge from the mucous membranes esp. of the eyes or nose — **rheumy** *adj*

rheu·mat·ic fever \rü-'ma-tik-\ *n* : an acute disease chiefly of children and young adults that is characterized by fever, by inflammation and pain in and around the joints, and by inflammation of the membranes surrounding the heart and the heart valves

rheu·ma·tism \'rü-mə-₁ti-zəm, 'rü-\ *n* : any of various conditions marked by stiffness, pain, or swelling in muscles or joints — **rheu·mat·ic** \rü-'ma-tik\ *adj*

rheu·ma·toid arthritis \-₁tȯid-\ *n* : a progressive constitutional disease characterized by inflammation and swelling of joint structures

Rh factor \ˌär-'āch-\ *n* [*rhesus* monkey (in which it was first detected)] : any of one or more inherited substances in red blood cells that may cause dangerous reactions in some infants or in transfusions

---

\ə\abut \ᵊ\kitten \ər\further \a\ash \ā\ace \ä\mop, mar
\au̇\out \ch\chin \e\bet \ē\easy \g\go \i\hit \ī\ice \j\job
\ŋ\sing \ō\go \ȯ\law \ȯi\boy \th\thin \th̲\the \ü\loot \u̇\foot
\y\yet \zh\vision   *see also* Pronunciation Symbols page

rhine·stone \\'rīn-ˌstōn\ *n* : a colorless imitation stone of high luster made of glass, paste, or gem quartz

rhi·no \\'rī-nō\ *n, pl* **rhino** *or* **rhinos** : RHINOCEROS

rhi·noc·er·os \rī-'nä-sə-rəs\ *n, pl* **-noc·er·os·es** *or* **-noc·er·os** *or* **-noc·eri** \-'nä-sə-ˌrī\ [ME *rinoceros,* fr. L *rhinoceros,* fr. Gk *rhinokerōs,* fr. *rhin-, rhis* nose + *keras* horn] : any of a family of large thick-skinned mammals of Africa and Asia with one or two upright horns of keratin on the snout and three toes on each foot

rhi·zome \\'rī-ˌzōm\ *n* : a fleshy, rootlike, and usu. horizontal underground plant stem that forms shoots above and roots below — **rhi·zom·a·tous** \rī-'zä-mə-təs\ *adj*

Rh–neg·a·tive \ˌär-ˌāch-'ne-gə-tiv\ *adj* : lacking Rh factors in the red blood cells

rho \\'rō\ *n* : the 17th letter of the Greek alphabet — P or ρ

rho·di·um \\'rō-dē-əm\ *n* : a hard ductile metallic chemical element — see ELEMENT table

rho·do·den·dron \ˌrō-də-'den-drən\ *n* : any of a genus of shrubs or trees of the heath family with clusters of large bright flowers

rhom·boid \\'räm-ˌboid\ *n* : a parallelogram with unequal adjacent sides and angles that are not right angles — **rhomboid** *or* **rhom·boi·dal** \räm-'boid-ᵊl\ *adj*

rhom·bus \\'räm-bəs\ *n, pl* **rhom·bus·es** *or* **rhom·bi** \-ˌbī\ : a parallelogram having all four sides equal

rhombus

Rh–pos·i·tive \ˌär-ˌāch-'pä-zə-tiv\ *adj* : containing one or more Rh factors in the red blood cells

rhu·barb \\'rü-ˌbärb\ *n* [ME *rubarbe,* fr. MF *reubarbe,* fr. ML *reubarbarum,* alter. of *rha barbarum,* lit., barbarian rhubarb] : a garden plant related to the buckwheat having leaves with thick juicy edible pink and red stems

¹rhyme \\'rīm\ *n* **1** : a composition in verse that rhymes; *also* : POETRY **2** : correspondence in terminal sounds (as of two lines of verse)

²rhyme *vb* **rhymed; rhym·ing** **1** : to make rhymes; *also* : to write poetry **2** : to have rhymes : be in rhyme

rhythm \\'ri-thəm\ *n* **1** : regular rise and fall in the flow of sound in speech **2** : a movement or activity in which some action or element recurs regularly — **rhyth·mic** \\'rith-mik\ *or* **rhyth·mi·cal** \-mi-kəl\ *adj* — **rhyth·mi·cal·ly** \-k(ə-)lē\ *adv*

rhythm and blues *n* : popular music based on blues and black folk music

rhythm method *n* : birth control by refraining from sexual intercourse during the time when ovulation is most likely to occur

RI *abbr* Rhode Island

ri·al \rē-'ȯl, -'äl\ *n* — see MONEY table

¹rib \\'rib\ *n* **1** : any of the series of curved bones of the chest of most vertebrates that are joined to the backbone in pairs and help to support the body wall and protect the organs inside **2** : something resembling a rib in shape or function **3** : any of the parallel ridges in a knitted or woven fabric

²rib *vb* **ribbed; rib·bing** **1** : to furnish or strengthen with ribs **2** : to form ridges in knitting or weaving

³rib *vb* **ribbed; rib·bing** : to poke fun at : TEASE — **rib·ber** *n*

rib·ald \\'ri-bəld\ *adj* : coarse or indecent esp. in language ⟨~ jokes⟩ — **rib·ald·ry** \-bəl-drē\ *n*

rib·and \\'ri-bənd\ *n* : RIBBON

rib·bon \\'ri-bən\ *n* **1** : a narrow fabric typically of silk or velvet used for trimming and for badges **2** : a strip of inked cloth (as in a typewriter) **3** : TATTER, SHRED ⟨torn to ~s⟩

ri·bo·fla·vin \ˌrī-bə-'flā-vən, 'rī-bə-ˌflā-vən\ *n* : a growth-promoting vitamin of the vitamin B complex occurring in milk and liver

ri·bo·nu·cle·ic acid \ˌrī-bō-nù-ˌklē-ik-, -nyù-, -ˌklā-\ *n* : RNA

ri·bose \\'rī-ˌbōs\ *n* : a sugar with five carbon atoms and five oxygen atoms in each molecule that is part of RNA

ri·bo·some \\'rī-bə-ˌsōm\ *n* : any of the RNA-rich cytoplasmic granules in a cell that are sites of protein synthesis — **ri·bo·som·al** \ˌrī-bə-'sō-məl\ *adj*

rice \\'rīs\ *n* : the starchy seeds of an annual grass that are cooked and used for food; *also* : this widely cultivated grass of warm wet areas

rich \\'rich\ *adj* **1** : possessing or controlling great wealth : WEALTHY **2** : COSTLY, VALUABLE **3** : deep and pleasing in color or tone **4** : ABUNDANT **5** : containing much sugar, fat, or seasoning; *also* : high in combustible content **6** : FRUITFUL, FERTILE — **rich·ly** *adv* — **rich·ness** *n*

rich·es \\'ri-chəz\ *n pl* [ME, sing. or pl., fr. *richesse,* lit., richness, fr. OF, fr. *riche* rich] : things that make one rich : WEALTH

Rich·ter scale \\'rik-tər-\ *n* : a scale for expressing the magnitude of a seismic disturbance (as an earthquake) in terms of the energy dissipated in it

rick \\'rik\ *n* : a large stack (as of hay) in the open air

rick·ets \\'ri-kəts\ *n* : a childhood deficiency disease marked esp. by soft deformed bones and caused by inadequate sunlight or inadequate vitamin D

rick·ett·sia \ri-'ket-sē-ə\ *n, pl* **-si·as** *or* **-si·ae** \-sē-ˌē\ : any of a group of rod-shaped bacteria that cause various diseases (as typhus)

rick·ety \\'ri-kə-tē\ *adj* **1** : affected with rickets **2** : SHAKY; *also* : in unsound physical condition

rick·sha *or* **rick·shaw** \\'rik-ˌshò\ *n* : a small covered 2-wheeled carriage pulled by one person and used orig. in Japan

¹ric·o·chet \\'ri-kə-ˌshā, *Brit also* -ˌshet\ *n* : a bouncing off at an angle (as of a bullet off a wall); *also* : an object that ricochets

²ricochet *vb* **-cheted** \-ˌshād\ *or* **-chet·ted** \-ˌshe-təd\; **-chet·ing** \-ˌshā-iŋ\ *or* **-chet·ting** \-ˌshe-tiŋ\ : to skip with or as if with glancing rebounds

rid \\'rid\ *vb* **rid** *also* **rid·ded; rid·ding** : to make free : CLEAR, RELIEVE — **rid·dance** \\'rid-ᵊns\ *n*

rid·den \\'rid-ᵊn\ *adj* **1** : harassed, oppressed, or obsessed by ⟨debt-*ridden*⟩ **2** : excessively full of or supplied with ⟨slum-*ridden*⟩

¹rid·dle \\'rid-ᵊl\ *n* : a puzzling question to be solved or answered by guessing

²riddle *vb* **rid·dled; rid·dling** **1** : EXPLAIN, SOLVE **2** : to speak in riddles

³riddle *n* : a coarse sieve

⁴riddle *vb* **rid·dled; rid·dling** **1** : to sift with a riddle **2** : to pierce with many holes **3** : PERMEATE

¹ride \\'rīd\ *vb* **rode** \\'rōd\; **rid·den** \\'rid-ᵊn\; **rid·ing** **1** : to go on an animal's back or in a conveyance (as a boat, car, or airplane); *also* : to sit on and control so as to be carried along ⟨~ a bicycle⟩ **2** : to float or move on water ⟨~ at anchor⟩; *also* : to move like a floating object **3** : to bear along : CARRY ⟨*rode* her on their shoulders⟩ **4** : to travel over a surface ⟨car ~s well⟩ **5** : to proceed over on horseback **6** : to torment by nagging or teasing

²ride *n* **1** : an act of riding; *esp* : a trip on horseback or by vehicle **2** : a way (as a road or path) suitable for riding **3** : a mechanical device (as a merry-go-round) for riding on **4** : a means of transportation

rid·er \\'rī-dər\\ *n* **1** : one that rides **2** : an addition to a document often attached on a separate piece of paper **3** : a clause dealing with an unrelated matter attached to a legislative bill during passage — **rid·er·less** *adj*

¹ridge \\'rij\\ *n* **1** : a range of hills **2** : a raised line or strip **3** : the line made where two sloping surfaces (as of a roof) meet — **ridgy** *adj*

²ridge *vb* **ridged; ridg·ing 1** : to form into a ridge **2** : to extend in ridges

¹rid·i·cule \\'ri-də-ˌkyül\\ *n* : the act of exposing to laughter : DERISION

²ridicule *vb* **-culed; -cul·ing** : to laugh at or make fun of mockingly or contemptuously **syn** deride, taunt, twit, mock

ri·dic·u·lous \\rə-'di-kyə-ləs\\ *adj* : arousing or deserving ridicule : ABSURD, PREPOSTEROUS **syn** laughable, ludicrous, farcical, risible — **ri·dic·u·lous·ly** *adv* — **ri·dic·u·lous·ness** *n*

ri·el \\rē-'el\\ *n* — see MONEY table

RIF *abbr* reduction in force

rife \\'rīf\\ *adj* : WIDESPREAD, PREVALENT, ABOUNDING — **rife** *adv* — **rife·ly** *adv*

riff \\'rif\\ *n* : a repeated phrase in jazz typically supporting a solo improvisation; *also* : a piece based on such a phrase — **riff** *vb*

riff·raff \\'rif-ˌraf\\ *n* [ME *riffe raffe*, fr. *rif and raf* every single one, fr. MF *rif et raf* completely] **1** : RABBLE **2** : REFUSE, RUBBISH

¹ri·fle \\'rī-fəl\\ *vb* **ri·fled; ri·fling** : to ransack esp. with the intent to steal — **ri·fler** *n*

²rifle *vb* **ri·fled; ri·fling** : to cut spiral grooves into the bore of ⟨*rifled* pipe⟩ — **rifling** *n*

³rifle *n* **1** : a shoulder weapon with a rifled bore **2** *pl* : soldiers armed with rifles — **ri·fle·man** \\-fəl-mən\\ *n*

rift \\'rift\\ *n* **1** : CLEFT, FISSURE **2** : FAULT 6 **3** : ESTRANGEMENT, SEPARATION — **rift** *vb*

¹rig \\'rig\\ *vb* **rigged; rig·ging 1** : to fit out (as a ship) with rigging **2** : CLOTHE, DRESS **3** : EQUIP **4** : to set up esp. as a makeshift ⟨∼ up a shelter⟩

²rig *n* **1** : the distinctive shape, number, and arrangement of sails and masts of a ship **2** : a carriage with its horse **3** : CLOTHING, DRESS **4** : EQUIPMENT

³rig *vb* **rigged; rig·ging 1** : to manipulate or control esp. by deceptive or dishonest means **2** : to fix in advance for a desired result — **rig·ger** *n*

rig·ging \\'ri-giŋ, -gən\\ *n* **1** : the ropes and chains that hold and move masts, sails, and spars of a ship **2** : a network (as in theater scenery) used for support and manipulation

¹right \\'rīt\\ *adj* **1** : RIGHTEOUS, UPRIGHT **2** : JUST, PROPER **3** : conforming to truth or fact : CORRECT **4** : APPROPRIATE, SUITABLE **5** : STRAIGHT ⟨a ∼ line⟩ **6** : GENUINE, REAL **7** : of, relating to, or being the side of the body which is away from the heart and on which the hand is stronger and more skilled in most persons **8** : located nearer to the right hand; *esp* : being on the right when facing in the same direction as the observer **9** : made to be placed or worn outward ⟨∼ side of a rug⟩ **10** : NORMAL, SOUND ⟨not in her ∼ mind⟩ **syn** correct, accurate, exact, precise, nice — **right·ness** *n*

²right *n* **1** : qualities that constitute what is correct, just, proper, or honorable **2** : something (as a power or privilege) to which one has a just or lawful claim **3** : just action or decision : the cause of justice **4** : the side or part that is on or toward the right side **5** *cap* : political conservatives **6** *often cap* : a conservative position — **right·ward** \\-wərd\\ *adj*

³right *adv* **1** : according to what is right ⟨live ∼⟩ **2** : EXACTLY, PRECISELY ⟨∼ here and now⟩ **3** : DIRECTLY ⟨went ∼ home⟩ **4** : according to fact or truth ⟨guess ∼⟩ **5** : all the way : COMPLETELY ⟨∼ to the end⟩ **6** : IMMEDIATELY

⟨∼ after lunch⟩ **7** : QUITE, VERY ⟨∼ nice weather⟩ **8** : on or to the right ⟨looked ∼ and left⟩

⁴right *vb* **1** : to relieve from wrong **2** : to adjust or restore to a proper state or position **3** : to bring or restore to an upright position **4** : to become upright — **right·er** *n*

right angle *n* : an angle whose measure is 90° : an angle whose sides are perpendicular to each other — **right-an·gled** \\'rīt-'aŋ-gəld\\ *or* **right-an·gle** \\-gəl\\ *adj*

right circular cone *n* : CONE 2

righ·teous \\'rī-chəs\\ *adj* : acting or being in accordance with what is just, honorable, and free from guilt or wrong : UPRIGHT **syn** virtuous, noble, moral, ethical — **righ·teous·ly** *adv* — **righ·teous·ness** *n*

right·ful \\'rīt-fəl\\ *adj* **1** : JUST; *also* : FITTING **2** : having or held by a legally just claim — **right·ful·ly** *adv* — **right·ful·ness** *n*

right-hand \\'rīt-ˌhand\\ *adj* **1** : situated on the right **2** : RIGHT-HANDED **3** : chiefly relied on ⟨his ∼ man⟩

right-hand·ed \\-'han-dəd\\ *adj* **1** : using the right hand habitually or better than the left **2** : designed for or done with the right hand **3** : CLOCKWISE ⟨a ∼ twist⟩ — **right-handed** *adv* — **right-hand·ed·ly** *adv* — **right-hand·ed·ness** *n*

right·ly \\'rīt-lē\\ *adv* **1** : FAIRLY, JUSTLY **2** : PROPERLY **3** : CORRECTLY, EXACTLY

right-of-way *n, pl* **rights-of-way 1** : a legal right of passage over another person's ground **2** : the area over which a right-of-way exists **3** : the land on which a public road is built **4** : the land occupied by a railroad **5** : the land used by a public utility **6** : the right of traffic to take precedence over other traffic

right on *interj* — used to express agreement or give encouragement

right-to-life *adj* : ANTIABORTION — **right-to-lifer** *n*

right triangle *n* : a triangle having one right angle

rig·id \\'ri-jəd\\ *adj* **1** : lacking flexibility **2** : strictly observed **syn** severe, stern, rigorous, stringent — **rigid·i·ty** \\rə-'ji-də-tē\\ *n* — **rig·id·ly** *adv*

rig·ma·role \\'ri-gə-mə-ˌrōl\\ *n* [alter. of obs. *ragman roll* long list, catalog] **1** : confused or senseless talk **2** : a complex and ritualistic procedure

rig·or \\'ri-gər\\ *n* **1** : the quality of being inflexible or unyielding : STRICTNESS **2** : HARSHNESS, SEVERITY **3** : a tremor caused by a chill **4** : strict precision : EXACTNESS — **rig·or·ous** *adj* — **rig·or·ous·ly** *adv*

rig·or mor·tis \\ˌri-gər-'mor-təs\\ *n* [NL, stiffness of death] : temporary rigidity of muscles occurring after death

rig·our *chiefly Brit var of* RIGOR

rile \\'rīl\\ *vb* **riled; ril·ing 1** : to make angry **2** : ROIL 1

rill \\'ril\\ *n* : a very small brook

¹rim \\'rim\\ *n* **1** : the outer part of a wheel **2** : an outer edge esp. of something curved : BORDER, MARGIN

²rim *vb* **rimmed; rim·ming 1** : to serve as a rim for : BORDER **2** : to run around the rim of

¹rime \\'rīm\\ *n* **1** : FROST **2** — **rimy** \\'rī-mē\\ *adj*

²rime *var of* RHYME

rind \\'rīnd\\ *n* : a usu. hard or tough outer layer ⟨lemon ∼⟩

¹ring \\'riŋ\\ *n* **1** : a circular band worn as an ornament or token or used for holding or fastening ⟨wedding ∼⟩ ⟨key ∼⟩ **2** : something circular in shape ⟨smoke ∼⟩ **3** : a place for contest or display ⟨boxing ∼⟩; *also* : PRIZEFIGHTING **4** : ANNUAL RING **5** : a group of people who work together for selfish or dishonest purposes — **ring·like** \\'riŋ-ˌlīk\\ *adj*

²ring *vb* **ringed; ring·ing** \\'riŋ-iŋ\\ **1** : ENCIRCLE **2** : to

\\ə\\abut \\ᵊ\\kitten \\ər\\further \\a\\ash \\ā\\ace \\ä\\mop, mar \\aú\\out \\ch\\chin \\e\\bet \\ē\\easy \\g\\go \\i\\hit \\ī\\ice \\j\\job \\ŋ\\sing \\ō\\go \\ò\\law \\òi\\boy \\th\\thin \\t͟h\\the \\ü\\loot \\ú\\foot \\y\\yet \\zh\\vision *see also* Pronunciation Symbols page throw a ring over (a mark) in a game (as quoits) **3** : to move in a ring or spirally

³**ring** *vb* **rang** \'raŋ\; **rung** \'rəŋ\; **ring·ing** \'riŋ-iŋ\ **1** : to sound resonantly when struck; *also* : to feel as if filled with such sound **2** : to cause to make a clear metallic sound by striking **3** : to announce or call by or as if by striking a bell ⟨∼ an alarm⟩ **4** : to repeat loudly and persistently **5** : to summon esp. by a bell ⟨∼ for the butler⟩

⁴**ring** *n* **1** : a set of bells **2** : the clear resonant sound of vibrating metal **3** : resonant tone : SONORITY **4** : a sound or character expressive of a particular quality **5** : an act or instance of ringing; *esp* : a telephone call

¹**ring·er** \'riŋ-ər\ *n* **1** : one that sounds by ringing **2** : one that enters a competition under false representations **3** : one that closely resembles another

²**ringer** *n* : one that encircles or puts a ring around

ring finger *n* : the third finger of the left hand counting the forefinger as one

ring·git \'riŋ-git\ *n* — see MONEY table

ring·lead·er \'riŋ-₁lē-dər\ *n* : a leader esp. of a group of troublemakers

ring·let \-lət\ *n* : a long curl

ring·mas·ter \-₁mas-tər\ *n* : one in charge of performances in a circus ring

ring up *vb* **1** : to total and record esp. by means of a cash register **2** : ACHIEVE ⟨*rang up* many triumphs⟩

ring·worm \'riŋ-₁wərm\ *n* : any of several contagious skin diseases caused by fungi and marked by ring‐ shaped discolored patches

rink \'riŋk\ *n* : a level extent of ice marked off for skating or various games; *also* : a similar surface (as of wood) marked off or enclosed for a sport or game ⟨roller-skating ∼⟩

¹**rinse** \'rins\ *vb* **rinsed; rins·ing** [ME *rincen*, fr. MF *rincer*, fr. (assumed) VL *recentiare*, fr. L *recent-, recens* fresh, recent] **1** : to wash lightly or in water only **2** : to cleanse (as of soap) with clear water **3** : to treat (hair) with a rinse — **rins·er** *n*

²**rinse** *n* **1** : an act of rinsing **2** : a liquid used for rinsing **3** : a solution that temporarily tints hair

ri·ot \'rī-ət\ *n* **1** *archaic* : disorderly behavior **2** : disturbance of the public peace; *esp* : a violent public disorder **3** : random or disorderly profusion ⟨a ∼ of color⟩ **4** : one that is wildly amusing ⟨the comedy is a ∼⟩ — **riot** *vb* — **ri·ot·er** *n* — **ri·ot·ous** *adj*

¹**rip** \'rip\ *vb* **ripped; rip·ping 1** : to cut or tear open **2** : to saw or split (wood) with the grain — **rip·per** *n*

²**rip** *n* : a rent made by ripping

RIP *abbr* [L *requiescat in pace*] may he rest in peace, may she rest in peace; [L *requiescant in pace*] may they rest in peace

ri·par·i·an \rə-'per-ē-ən\ *adj* : of or relating to the bank of a stream, river, or lake

rip cord *n* : a cord that is pulled to release the pilot parachute which lifts a main parachute out of its container

ripe \'rīp\ *adj* **rip·er; rip·est 1** : fully grown and developed : MATURE ⟨∼ fruit⟩ **2** : fully prepared for some use or object : READY — **ripe·ly** *adv* — **ripe·ness** *n*

rip·en \'rī-pən\ *vb* **rip·ened; rip·en·ing 1** : to grow or make ripe **2** : to bring to completeness or perfection; *also* : to age or cure (cheese) to develop characteristic flavor, odor, body, texture, and color

rip–off \'rip-₁òf\ *n* **1** : an act of stealing : THEFT **2** : a cheap imitation — **rip off** *vb*

ri·poste \ri-'pōst\ *n* [F, modif. of It *risposta*, lit., answer] **1** : a fencer's return thrust after a parry **2** : a retaliatory maneuver or response; *esp* : a quick retort — **riposte** *vb*

rip·ple \'ri-pəl\ *vb* **rip·pled; rip·pling 1** : to become lightly ruffled on the surface **2** : to make a sound like that of rippling water — **ripple** *n*

rip·saw \'rip-₁sò\ *n* : a coarse-toothed saw used to cut wood in the direction of the grain

rip·stop \-₁stäp\ *adj* : being a fabric woven in such a way that small tears do not spread ⟨∼ nylon⟩ — **ripstop** *n*

¹**rise** \'rīz\ *vb* **rose** \'rōz\; **ris·en** \'riz-ᵊn\; **ris·ing 1** : to get up from sitting, kneeling, or lying **2** : to get up from sleep or from one's bed **3** : to return from death **4** : to take up arms **5** : to end a session : ADJOURN **6** : to appear above the horizon **7** : to move upward : ASCEND **8** : to extend above other objects **9** : to attain a higher level or rank **10** : to increase in quantity or in intensity **11** : to come into being : HAPPEN, BEGIN, ORIGINATE

²**rise** *n* **1** : a spot higher than surrounding ground **2** : an upward slope **3** : an act of rising : a state of being risen **4** : BEGINNING, ORIGIN **5** : the elevation of one point above another **6** : an increase in amount, number, or volume **7** : an angry reaction

ris·er \'rī-zər\ *n* **1** : one that rises **2** : the upright part between stair treads

ris·i·bil·i·ty \₁ri-zə-'bi-lə-tē\ *n, pl* **-ties** : the ability or inclination to laugh — often used in pl.

ris·i·ble \'ri-zə-bəl\ *adj* **1** : able or inclined to laugh **2** : arousing laughter; *esp* : amusingly ridiculous

¹**risk** \'risk\ *n* : exposure to possible loss or injury : DANGER, PERIL — **risk·i·ness** \'ris-kē-nəs\ *n* — **risky** *adj*

²**risk** *vb* **1** : to expose to danger ⟨∼*ed* his life⟩ **2** : to incur the danger of

ris·qué \ris-'kā\ *adj* [F] : verging on impropriety or indecency

ri·tard \ri-'tärd\ *adv or adj* : with a gradual slackening in tempo — used as a direction in music

rite \'rīt\ *n* **1** : a set form for conducting a ceremony **2** : the liturgy of a church **3** : a ceremonial act or action

rit·u·al \'ri-chə-wəl\ *n* **1** : the established form esp. for a religious ceremony **2** : a system of rites **3** : a ceremonial act or action **4** : a customarily repeated act or series of acts — **ritual** *adj* — **rit·u·al·ism** \-wə-₁li-zəm\ *n* — **rit·u·al·is·tic** \₁ri-chə-wə-'lis-tik\ *adj* — **rit·u·al·is·ti·cal·ly** \-ti-k(ə-)lē\ *adv* — **rit·u·al·ly** *adv*

riv *abbr* river

¹**ri·val** \'rī-vəl\ *n* [MF or L; MF, fr. L *rivalis* one using the same stream as another, rival in love, fr. *rivalis* of a stream, fr. *rivus* stream] **1** : one of two or more trying to get what only one can have **2** : one striving for competitive advantage **3** : one that equals another esp. in desired qualities : MATCH, PEER

²**rival** *adj* : COMPETING

³**rival** *vb* **-valed** *or* **-valled; -val·ing** *or* **-val·ling 1** : to be in competition with **2** : to try to equal or excel **3** : to have qualities that approach or equal another's

ri·val·ry \'rī-vəl-rē\ *n, pl* **-ries** : COMPETITION

rive \'rīv\ *vb* **rived** \'rīvd\; **riv·en** \'ri-vən\ *also* **rived; riv·ing 1** : SPLIT, REND **2** : SHATTER

riv·er \'ri-vər\ *n* **1** : a natural stream larger than a brook **2** : a large stream or flow

riv·er·bank \-₁baŋk\ *n* : the bank of a river

riv·er·bed \-₁bed\ *n* : the channel occupied by a river

riv·er·boat \-₁bōt\ *n* : a boat for use on a river

riv·er·front \-₁frənt\ *n* : the land or area along a river

riv·er·side \-₁sīd\ *n* : the side or bank of a river

¹**riv·et** \'ri-vət\ *n* : a metal bolt with a head at one end used to join parts by being put through holes in them and then being flattened on the plain end to make another head

²**rivet** *vb* : to fasten with or as if with a rivet — **riv·et·er** *n*

riv·u·let \'ri-vyə-lət, -və-\ *n* : a small stream

ri·yal \rē-'äl, -'al\ *n* — see MONEY table

rm *abbr* **1** ream **2** room

Rn *symbol* radon

¹**RN** \ˌär-'en\ *n* : REGISTERED NURSE

²**RN** *abbr* Royal Navy

RNA \ˌär-(ˌ)en-'ā\ *n* : any of various nucleic acids (as messenger RNA) that are found esp. in the cytoplasm of cells, have ribose as the 5-carbon sugar, and are as-

sociated with the control of cellular chemical activities
rnd *abbr* round
¹**roach** \'rōch\ *n, pl* **roach** *also* **roach·es** : any of various
bony fishes related to the carp; *also* : any of several
sunfishes
²**roach** *n* **1** : COCKROACH **2** : the butt of a marijuana cigarette
road \'rōd\ *n* **1** : ROADSTEAD — often used in pl. **2** : an
open way for vehicles, persons, and animals : HIGHWAY
3 : ROUTE, PATH **4** : a series of scheduled visits (as
games or performances) in several locations or the
travel necessary to make these visits ⟨the team is on the
∼⟩
road·bed \'rōd-ˌbed\ *n* **1** : the foundation of a road or
railroad **2** : the part of the surface of a road on which
vehicles travel
road·block \-ˌbläk\ *n* **1** : a barricade on the road ⟨a police
∼⟩ **2** : an obstruction to progress
road·ie \'rō-dē\ *n* : one who works for traveling entertainers
road·kill \'rōd-ˌkil\ *n* : an animal that has been killed on
a road by a motor vehicle
road·run·ner \-ˌrə-nər\ *n* : a largely terrestrial bird of
the southwestern U.S. and Mexico that is a speedy runner
road·side \'rōd-ˌsīd\ *n* : the strip of land along a road —
roadside *adj*
road·stead \-ˌsted\ *n* : an anchorage for ships usu. less
sheltered than a harbor
road·ster \'rōd-stər\ *n* **1** : a driving horse **2** : an open automobile that seats two
road·way \-ˌwā\ *n* : ROAD; *esp* : ROADBED
road·work \-ˌwərk\ *n* **1** : work done in constructing or
repairing roads **2** : conditioning for an athletic contest
(as a boxing match) consisting mainly of long runs
roam \'rōm\ *vb* **1** : WANDER, ROVE **2** : to range or wander
over or about
¹**roan** \'rōn\ *adj* : of dark color (as black, red, or brown)
sprinkled with white ⟨a ∼ horse⟩
²**roan** *n* : an animal (as a horse) with a roan coat; *also* : its
color
¹**roar** \'rōr\ *vb* **1** : to utter a full loud prolonged sound **2**
: to make a loud confused sound (as of wind or waves)
— **roar·er** *n*
²**roar** *n* : a sound of roaring
¹**roast** \'rōst\ *vb* **1** : to cook by dry heat (as before a fire
or in an oven) **2** : to criticize severely or kiddingly
²**roast** *n* **1** : a piece of meat suitable for roasting **2** : an
outing at which food is roasted ⟨corn ∼⟩ **3** : severe criticism or kidding
³**roast** *adj* : ROASTED
roast·er \'rō-stər\ *n* **1** : one that roasts **2** : a device for
roasting **3** : something suitable for roasting
rob \'räb\ *vb* **robbed; rob·bing 1** : to steal from **2** : to
deprive of something due or expected **3** : to commit
robbery — **rob·ber** *n*
robber fly *n* : any of a family of predaceous flies
rob·bery \'rä-bə-rē\ *n, pl* **-ber·ies** : the act or practice of
robbing; *esp* : theft of something from a person by use
of violence or threat
¹**robe** \'rōb\ *n* **1** : a long flowing outer garment; *esp* : one
used for ceremonial occasions **2** : a wrap or covering
for the lower body (as for sitting outdoors)
²**robe** *vb* **robed; rob·ing 1** : to clothe with or as if with a
robe **2** : DRESS
rob·in \'rä-bən\ *n* **1** : a small chiefly European thrush
with a somewhat orange face and breast **2** : a large No.
American thrush with a grayish back, a streaked
throat, and a chiefly dull reddish breast
ro·bot \'rō-ˌbät, -bət\ *n* [Czech, fr. *robota* compulsory
labor] **1** : a machine that looks and acts like a human
being **2** : an efficient but insensitive person **3** : a device

that automatically performs esp. repetitive tasks **4**
: something guided by automatic controls — **ro·bot·
ic** \rō-ˈbä-tik\ *adj*
ro·bot·ics \rō-ˈbä-tiks\ *n* : technology dealing with the
design, construction, and operation of robots
ro·bust \rō-ˈbəst, ˈrō-(ˌ)bəst\ *adj* [L *robustus* oaken,
strong, fr. *robur* oak, strength] : strong and vigorously
healthy — **ro·bust·ly** *adv* — **ro·bust·ness** *n*
ROC *abbr* Republic of China (Taiwan)
¹**rock** \'räk\ *vb* **1** : to move back and forth in or as if in
a cradle **2** : to sway or cause to sway back and forth
²**rock** *n* **1** : a rocking movement **2** : popular music usu.
played on electric instruments and characterized by a
strong beat and much repetition
³**rock** *n* **1** : a mass of stony material; *also* : broken pieces
of stone **2** : solid mineral deposits **3** : something like a
rock in firmness **4** : GEM; *esp* : DIAMOND — **rock** *adj* —
rock·like *adj* — **rocky** *adj*
rock and roll *n* : ²ROCK 2
rock·bound \'räk-ˌbaund\ *adj* : fringed or covered with
rocks
rock·er \'rä-kər\ *n* **1** : one of the curved pieces on which
something (as a chair or cradle) rocks **2** : a chair that
rocks on rockers **3** : a device that works with a rocking
motion **4** : a rock performer, song, or enthusiast
¹**rock·et** \'rä-kət\ *n* [It *rocchetta*, lit., small distaff] **1** : a
firework that is propelled through the air by the dis-
charge of gases produced by a burning substance **2** : a
jet engine that operates on the same principle as a firework rocket but carries the oxygen needed for burning
its fuel **3** : a rocket-propelled bomb or missile
²**rocket** *vb* **1** : to convey by means of a rocket **2** : to rise
abruptly and rapidly
rock·et·ry \'rä-kə-trē\ *n* : the study or use of rockets
rocket ship *n* : a rocket-propelled spacecraft
rock·fall \'räk-ˌfol\ *n* : a mass of falling or fallen rocks
rock·fish \-ˌfish\ *n* : any of various market bony fishes
that live among rocks or on rocky bottoms
rock salt *n* : common salt in rocklike masses or large
crystals
Rocky Mountain sheep *n* : BIGHORN
ro·co·co \rə-ˈkō-kō\ *adj* [F, irreg. fr. *rocaille* style of ornament, lit., stone debris] : of or relating to an artistic
style esp. of the 18th century marked by fanciful
curved forms and elaborate ornamentation — **rococo** *n*
rod \'räd\ *n* **1** : a straight slender stick **2** : a stick or hun-
dle of twigs used in punishing a person; *also* : PUNISH-
MENT **3** : a staff borne to show rank **4** — see WEIGHT
table **5** : any of the rod-shaped receptor cells of the retina that are sensitive to faint light **6** *slang* : HANDGUN
rode *past of* RIDE
ro·dent \'rōd-ᵊnt\ *n* [ultim. fr. L *rodent-, rodens,* prp. of
rodere to gnaw] : any of an order of relatively small
mammals (as mice, squirrels, and beavers) with sharp
front teeth used for gnawing
ro·deo \'rō-dē-ˌō, rə-ˈdā-ō\ *n, pl* **ro·de·os** [Sp, fr. *rodear*
to surround, fr. *rueda* wheel, fr. L *rota*] **1** : ROUNDUP 1
2 : a public performance featuring cowboy skills (as riding and roping)
¹**roe** \'rō\ *n, pl* **roe** *or* **roes** : DOE
²**roe** *n* : the eggs of a fish esp. while bound together in a
mass
roe·buck \'rō-ˌbək\ *n, pl* **roebuck** *or* **roebucks** : a male
roe deer
roe deer *n* : either of two small nimble European or
Asian deers
☞ For illustration, see next page.

\ə\abut \ᵊ\kitten \ər\further \a\ash \ā\ace \ä\mop, mar
\aù\out \ch\chin \e\bet \ē\easy \g\go \i\hit \ī\ice \j\job
\ŋ\sing \ō\go \ò\law \òi\boy \th\thin \th\the \ü\loot \ù\foot
\y\yet \zh\vision *see also* Pronunciation Symbols page

roe deer

roent·gen \\'rent-gən, 'rənt-, -jən\\ *n* : the international unit of measurement for X rays and gamma rays

rog·er \\'rä-jər\\ *interj* — used esp. in radio and signaling to indicate that a message has been received and understood

rogue \\'rōg\\ *n* **1** : a dishonest person : SCOUNDREL **2** : a mischievous person : SCAMP — **rogu·ery** \\'rō-gə-rē\\ *n* — **rogu·ish** *adj* — **rogu·ish·ly** *adv* — **rogu·ish·ness** *n*

roil \\'rȯil, *for 2 also* 'rīl\\ *vb* **1** : to make cloudy or muddy by stirring up **2** : RILE 1 — **roily** \\'rȯi-lē\\ *adj*

rois·ter \\'rȯi-stər\\ *vb* **rois·tered; rois·ter·ing** : to engage in noisy revelry : CAROUSE — **rois·ter·er** *n* — **rois·ter·ous** \\-stə-rəs\\ *adj*

ROK *abbr* Republic of Korea (South Korea)

role *also* **rôle** \\'rōl\\ *n* **1** : an assigned or assumed character; *also* : a part played (as by an actor) **2** : FUNCTION

role model *n* : a person whose behavior in a particular role is imitated by others

¹roll \\'rōl\\ *n* **1** : a document containing an official record **2** : an official list of names **3** : something (as a bun) that is rolled up or rounded as if rolled **4** : something that rolls : ROLLER

²roll *vb* **1** : to move by turning over and over **2** : to press with a roller **3** : to move on wheels **4** : to sound with a full reverberating tone **5** : to make a continuous beating sound (as on a drum) **6** : to utter with a trill **7** : to move onward as if by completing a revolution ⟨years ∼*ed* by⟩ **8** : to flow or seem to flow in a continuous stream or with a rising and falling motion ⟨the river ∼*ed* on⟩ **9** : to swing or sway from side to side **10** : to shape or become shaped in rounded form

³roll *n* **1** : a sound produced by rapid strokes on a drum **2** : a heavy reverberating sound **3** : a rolling movement or action **4** : a swaying movement (as of a ship) **5** : SOMERSAULT

roll·back \\'rōl-ˌbak\\ *n* : the act or an instance of rolling back

roll back *vb* **1** : to reduce (as a commodity price) on a national scale **2** : to cause to withdraw : push back

roll bar *n* : an overhead metal bar on an automobile designed to protect riders in case the automobile overturns

roll call *n* : the act or an instance of calling off a list of names (as of soldiers); *also* : a time for a roll call

roll·er \\'rō-lər\\ *n* **1** : a revolving cylinder used for moving, pressing, shaping, applying, or smoothing something **2** : a rod on which something is rolled up **3** : a long heavy ocean wave

roll·er coast·er \\'rō-lər-ˌkō-stər\\ *n* : an amusement ride consisting of an elevated railway having sharp curves and steep slopes

roller skate *n* : a skate with wheels instead of a runner — **roller–skate** *vb* — **roller skater** *n*

rol·lick \\'rä-lik\\ *vb* : ROMP, FROLIC

rol·lick·ing *adj* : full of fun and good spirits

roly–poly \\ˌrō-lē-'pō-lē\\ *adj* : ROTUND

Rom *abbr* **1** Roman **2** Romance **3** Romania; Romanian **4** Romans

ROM \\'räm\\ *n* : READ-ONLY MEMORY

ro·maine \\rō-'mān\\ *n* [F, lit., Roman] : a garden lettuce with a tall loose head of long crisp leaves

¹Ro·man \\'rō-mən\\ *n* **1** : a native or resident of Rome **2** *not cap* : roman letters or type

²Roman *adj* **1** : of or relating to Rome or the Romans and esp. the ancient Romans **2** *not cap* : relating to type in which the letters are upright (as in this definition) **3** : of or relating to the Roman Catholic Church

Roman candle *n* : a cylindrical firework that discharges balls of fire

Roman Catholic *adj* : of, relating to, or being a Christian church led by the pope and having a liturgy centered in the Mass — **Roman Catholicism** *n*

¹ro·mance \\rō-'mans, 'rō-ˌmans\\ *n* [ME *romauns*, fr. OF *romans* French, something written in French, tale in verse, fr. ML *Romanice* in a vernacular language, ultim. fr. L *Romanus* Roman] **1** : a medieval tale of knightly adventure **2** : a prose narrative dealing with heroic or mysterious events set in a remote time or place **3** : a love story **4** : a romantic attachment or episode between lovers — **ro·manc·er** *n*

²romance *vb* **ro·manced; ro·manc·ing 1** : to exaggerate or invent detail or incident **2** : to have romantic fancies **3** : to carry on a romantic episode with

Ro·mance \\rō-'mans, 'rō-ˌmans\\ *adj* : of or relating to any of several languages developed from Latin

Ro·ma·nian \\rù-'mā-nē-ən, rō-, -nyən\\ *n* **1** : a native or inhabitant of Romania **2** : the language of the Romanians

Roman numeral *n* : a numeral in a system of notation that is based on the ancient Roman system

Ro·ma·no \\rō-'mä-nō\\ *n* : a hard Italian cheese that is sharper than Parmesan

Ro·mans \\'rō-mənz\\ *n* — see BIBLE table

¹ro·man·tic \\rō-'man-tik\\ *n* : a romantic person; *esp* : a romantic writer, composer, or artist

²romantic *adj* **1** : IMAGINARY **2** : VISIONARY **3** : having an imaginative or emotional appeal **4** : of, relating to, or having the characteristics of romanticism — **ro·man·ti·cal·ly** \\-ti-k(ə-)lē\\ *adv*

ro·man·ti·cism \\rō-'man-tə-ˌsi-zəm\\ *n, often cap* : a literary movement (as in early 19th century England) marked esp. by emphasis on the imagination and the emotions and by the use of autobiographical material — **ro·man·ti·cist** \\-sist\\ *n, often cap*

romp \\'rämp\\ *vb* **1** : to play actively and noisily **2** : to win a contest easily — **romp** *n*

romp·er \\'räm-pər\\ *n* **1** : one that romps **2** : a child's one-piece garment with the lower part shaped like bloomers — usu. used in pl.

rood \\'rüd\\ *n* : CROSS, CRUCIFIX

¹roof \\'rüf, 'rùf\\ *n, pl* **roofs** \\'rüfs, 'rùfs; 'rüvz, 'rùvz\\ **1** : the upper covering part of a building **2** : something suggesting a roof of a building — **roofed** \\'rüft, 'rùft\\ *adj* — **roof·ing** *n* — **roof·less** *adj*

²roof *vb* : to cover with a roof

roof·top \\-ˌtäp\\ *n* : a roof esp. of a house

¹rook \\'rùk\\ *n* : a common Old World bird resembling the related crow

²rook *vb* : CHEAT, SWINDLE

³rook *n* : a chess piece that can move parallel to the sides of the board across any number of unoccupied squares

rook·ery \\'rù-kə-rē\\ *n, pl* **-er·ies** : a breeding ground or haunt of gregarious birds or mammals; *also* : a colony of such birds or mammals

rook·ie \\'rù-kē\\ *n* : BEGINNER, RECRUIT; *esp* : a first-year player in a professional sport

¹room \\'rüm, 'rùm\\ *n* **1** : an extent of space occupied by or sufficient or available for something **2** : a partitioned part of a building : CHAMBER; *also* : the people in a room **3** : OPPORTUNITY, CHANCE ⟨∼ to develop his talents⟩ — **room·ful** *n* — **roomy** *adj*

²**room** *vb* : to occupy lodgings : LODGE — **room·er** *n*

room·ette \rü-'met, rü-\ *n* : a small private room on a railroad sleeping car

room·mate \'rüm-₁māt, 'rùm-\ *n* : one of two or more persons sharing the same room or dwelling

¹**roost** \'rüst\ *n* : a support on which or a place where birds perch

²**roost** *vb* : to settle on or as if on a roost

roost·er \'rüs-tər, 'rùs-\ *n* : an adult male domestic chicken : COCK

¹**root** \'rüt, 'rùt\ *n* **1** : the leafless usu. underground part of a seed plant that functions in absorption, aeration, and storage or as a means of anchorage; *also* : an underground plant part esp. when fleshy and edible **2** : something (as the basal part of a tooth or hair) resembling a root **3** : SOURCE, ORIGIN **4** : the essential core : HEART ⟨get to the ∼ of the matter⟩ **5** : a number that when taken as a factor an indicated number of times gives a specified number **6** : the lower part **7** : a word or part of a word from which other words are formed — **root·less** *adj* — **root·like** *adj*

²**root** *vb* **1** : to form roots **2** : to fix or become fixed by or as if by roots : ESTABLISH **3** : UPROOT

³**root** *vb* **1** : to turn up or dig with the snout ⟨pigs ∼ing⟩ **2** : to poke or dig around (as in search of something)

⁴**root** \'rüt\ *vb* **1** : to applaud or encourage noisily : CHEER **2** : to wish success or lend support to — **root·er** *n*

root beer *n* : a sweetened carbonated beverage flavored with extracts of roots and herbs

root·let \'rüt-lət, 'rùt-\ *n* : a small root

root·stock \-₁stäk\ *n* : an underground part of a plant that resembles a rhizome

¹**rope** \'rōp\ *n* **1** : a large strong cord made of strands of fiber **2** : a hangman's noose **3** : a thick string (as of pearls) made by twisting or braiding

²**rope** *vb* **roped; rop·ing 1** : to bind, tie, or fasten together with a rope **2** : to separate or divide by means of a rope **3** : LASSO

Ror·schach test \'ròr-₁shäk-\ *n* : a psychological test in which a subject interprets ink-blot designs in terms that reveal intellectual and emotional factors

ro·sa·ry \'rō-zə-rē\ *n, pl* **-ries 1** *often cap* : a Roman Catholic devotion consisting of meditation on sacred mysteries during recitation of Hail Marys **2** : a string of beads used in praying

¹**rose** *past of* RISE

²**rose** \'rōz\ *n* **1** : any of a genus of usu. prickly often climbing shrubs with divided leaves and bright often fragrant flowers; *also* : one of these flowers **2** : something resembling a rose in form **3** : a moderate purplish red color — **rose** *adj*

ro·sé \rō-'zā\ *n* [F] : a light pink wine

ro·se·ate \'rō-zē-ət, -zē-₁āt\ *adj* **1** : resembling a rose esp. in color **2** : OPTIMISTIC ⟨a ∼ view of the future⟩

rose·bud \'rōz-₁bəd\ *n* : the flower of a rose when it is at most partly open

rose·bush \-₁bùsh\ *n* : a shrubby rose

rose·mary \'rōz-₁mer-ē\ *n, pl* **-mar·ies** [ME *rosmarine*, fr. L *rosmarinus*, fr. *ros* dew + *marinus* of the sea, fr. *mare* sea] : a fragrant shrubby Old World mint; *also* : its leaves used as a seasoning

ro·sette \rō-'zet\ *n* [F] **1** : a usu. small badge or ornament of ribbon gathered in the shape of a rose **2** : a circular ornament filled with representations of leaves

rose·wa·ter \'rōz-₁wò-tər, -₁wä-\ *n* : a watery solution of the fragrant constituents of the rose used as a perfume

rose·wood \-₁wùd\ *n* : any of various tropical trees with dark red wood streaked with black; *also* : this wood

Rosh Ha·sha·nah \₁räsh-hə-'shä-nə, ₁rōsh-, -'shō-\ *n*

[Heb *rōsh hashshānāh*, lit., beginning of the year] : the Jewish New Year observed as a religious holiday in September or October

ros·in \'räz-ᵊn\ *n* : a brittle resin obtained esp. from pine trees and used esp. in varnishes and on violin bows

ros·ter \'räs-tər\ *n* **1** : a list of personnel; *also* : the persons listed on a roster **2** : an itemized list

ros·trum \'räs-trəm\ *n, pl* **rostrums** *or* **ros·tra** \-trə\ [L *Rostra*, pl., a platform for speakers in the Roman Forum decorated with the beaks of captured ships, fr. pl. of *rostrum* beak, ship's beak, fr. *rodere* to gnaw] : a stage or platform for public speaking

rosy \'rō-zē\ *adj* **ros·i·er; -est 1** : of the color rose **2** : HOPEFUL, PROMISING — **ros·i·ly** \'rō-zə-lē\ *adv* — **ros·i·ness** \-zē-nəs\ *n*

¹**rot** \'rät\ *vb* **rot·ted; rot·ting** : to undergo decomposition : DECAY

²**rot** *n* **1** : DECAY **2** : any of various diseases of plants or animals in which tissue breaks down **3** : NONSENSE

¹**ro·ta·ry** \'rō-tə-rē\ *adj* **1** : turning on an axis like a wheel **2** : having a rotating part

²**rotary** *n, pl* **-ries 1** : a rotary machine **2** : a one-way circular road junction

ro·tate \'rō-₁tāt\ *vb* **ro·tat·ed; ro·tat·ing 1** : to turn or cause to turn about an axis or a center : REVOLVE **2** : to alternate in a series **syn** turn, circle, spin, whirl, twirl — **ro·ta·tion** \rō-'tā-shən\ *n* — **ro·ta·tor** \'rō-₁tā-tər\ *n* — **ro·ta·to·ry** \'rō-tə-₁tōr-ē\ *adj*

ROTC *abbr* Reserve Officers' Training Corps

rote \'rōt\ *n* **1** : repetition from memory often without attention to meaning **2** : fixed routine or repetition — **rote** *adj*

ro·tis·ser·ie \rō-'ti-sə-rē\ *n* [F] **1** : a restaurant specializing in broiled and barbecued meats **2** : an appliance fitted with a spit on which food is rotated before or over a source of heat

ro·to·gra·vure \₁rō-tə-grə-'vyùr\ *n* : PHOTOGRAVURE

ro·tor \'rō-tər\ *n* **1** : a part that rotates; *esp* : the rotating part of an electrical machine **2** : a system of rotating horizontal blades for supporting a helicopter

ro·to·till·er \'rō-tō-₁ti-lər\ *n* : an engine-powered machine with rotating blades used to lift and turn over soil

rot·ten \'rät-ᵊn\ *adj* **1** : having rotted **2** : CORRUPT **3** : extremely unpleasant or inferior — **rot·ten·ness** *n*

rot·ten·stone \'rät-ᵊn-₁stōn\ *n* : a decomposed siliceous limestone used for polishing

ro·tund \rō-'tənd\ *adj* : rounded out **syn** plump, chubby, portly, stout — **ro·tun·di·ty** \-'tən-də-tē\ *n*

ro·tun·da \rō-'tən-də\ *n* **1** : a round building; *esp* : one covered by a dome **2** : a large round room

rou·ble \'rü-bəl\ *var of* RUBLE

roué \rü-'ā\ *n* [F, lit., broken on the wheel, fr. pp. of *rouer* to break on the wheel, fr. ML *rotare*, fr. L, to rotate; fr. the feeling that such a person deserves this punishment] : a man devoted to a life of sensual pleasure : RAKE

rouge \'rüzh, 'rüj\ *n* [F, lit., red] : a cosmetic used to give a red color to cheeks and lips — **rouge** *vb*

¹**rough** \'rəf\ *adj* **rough·er; rough·est 1** : uneven in surface : not smooth **2** : SHAGGY **3** : not calm : TURBULENT, TEMPESTUOUS **4** : marked by harshness or violence **5** : DIFFICULT, TRYING **6** : coarse or rugged in character or appearance **7** : marked by lack of refinement **8** : CRUDE, UNFINISHED **9** : done or made hastily or tentatively — **rough·ly** *adv* — **rough·ness** *n*

²**rough** *n* **1** : uneven ground covered with high grass esp. along a golf fairway **2** : a crude, unfinished, or prelim-

inary state; *also* : something in such a state **3** : ROWDY, TOUGH

³**rough** *vb* **1** : ROUGHEN **2** : MANHANDLE **3** : to make or shape roughly esp. in a preliminary way — **rough·er** *n*

rough·age \'rə-fij\ *n* : FIBER 2; *also* : food containing much indigestible material acting as fiber

rough–and–ready \,rə-fən-'re-dē\ *adj* : rude or unpolished in nature, method, or manner but effective in action or use

rough–and–tum·ble \-'təm-bəl\ *n* : rough unrestrained fighting or struggling — **rough–and–tumble** *adj*

rough·en \'rə-fən\ *vb* **rough·ened; rough·en·ing** : to make or become rough

rough–hewn \'rəf-'hyün\ *adj* **1** : being rough and unfinished 〈~ beams〉 **2** : lacking smooth manners or social grace — **rough–hew** \-'hyü\ *vb*

rough·house \'rəf-,hau̇s\ *vb* **rough·housed; rough·hous·ing** : to participate in rough noisy behavior — **roughhouse** *n*

rough·neck \'rəf-,nek\ *n* **1** : ROWDY, TOUGH **2** : a worker on a crew drilling oil wells

rough·shod \'rəf-,shäd\ *adv* : with no consideration for the wishes or feelings of others 〈rode ~ over the opposition〉

rou·lette \rü-'let\ *n* [F, lit., small wheel] **1** : a gambling game in which a whirling wheel is used **2** : a wheel or disk with teeth around the outside

¹**round** \'rau̇nd\ *adj* **1** : having every part of the surface or circumference the same distance from the center **2** : CYLINDRICAL **3** : COMPLETE, FULL **4** : approximately correct; *esp* : exact only to a specific decimal or place 〈~ numbers〉 **5** : liberal or ample in size or amount **6** : BLUNT, OUTSPOKEN **7** : moving in or forming a circle **8** : having curves rather than angles — **round·ish** *adj* — **round·ness** *n*

²**round** *prep or adv* : AROUND

³**round** *n* **1** : something round (as a circle, globe, or ring) **2** : a curved or rounded part (as a rung of a ladder) **3** : an indirect path or course; *also* : a regularly covered route (as of a security guard) **4** : a series or cycle of recurring actions or events **5** : one shot fired by a soldier or a gun; *also* : ammunition for one shot **6** : a period of time or a unit of play in a game or contest **7** : a cut of meat (as beef) esp. between the rump and the lower leg — **in the round 1** : FREESTANDING **2** : with a center stage surrounded by an audience 〈theater *in the round*〉

⁴**round** *vb* **1** : to make or become round **2** : to go or pass around or part way around **3** : COMPLETE, FINISH **4** : to become plump or shapely **5** : to express as a round number — often used with *off* **6** : to follow a winding course : BEND

¹**round·about** \'rau̇n-də-,bau̇t\ *adj* : INDIRECT, CIRCUITOUS

²**roundabout** *n, Brit* : MERRY-GO-ROUND

roun·de·lay \'rau̇n-də-,lā\ *n* **1** : a simple song with a refrain **2** : a poem with a recurring refrain

round·house \'rau̇nd-,hau̇s\ *n* **1** : a circular building for housing and repairing locomotives **2** : a blow with the hand made with a wide swing

round·ly \'rau̇nd-lē\ *adv* **1** : in a complete manner; *also* : WIDELY **2** : in a blunt way **3** : with vigor

round–shoul·dered \-,shōl-dərd\ *adj* : having the shoulders stooping or rounded

Round Table *n* : the large round table of King Arthur and his knights

round–trip *n* : a trip to a place and back

round–up \'rau̇n-,dəp\ *n* **1** : the gathering together of cattle on the range by riding around them and driving them in; *also* : the ranch hands and horses engaged in a roundup **2** : a gathering in of scattered persons or things **3** : SUMMARY 〈news ~〉 — **round up** *vb*

round·worm \-,wərm\ *n* : NEMATODE

rouse \'rau̇z\ *vb* **roused; rous·ing** **1** : to excite to activity : stir up **2** : to wake from sleep — **rous·er** *n*

roust·about \'rau̇s-tə-,bau̇t\ *n* : one who does heavy unskilled labor (as on a dock or in an oil field)

¹**rout** \'rau̇t\ *n* **1** : MOB 1, 2 **2** : DISTURBANCE **3** : a fashionable gathering

²**rout** *vb* **1** : RUMMAGE **2** : to gouge out **3** : to expel by force

³**rout** *n* **1** : a state of wild confusion or disorderly retreat **2** : a disastrous defeat

⁴**rout** *vb* **1** : to put to flight **2** : to defeat decisively

¹**route** \'rüt, 'rau̇t\ *n* **1** : a traveled way **2** : CHANNEL **3** : a line of travel

²**route** *vb* **rout·ed; rout·ing** : to send by a selected route : DIRECT

route·man \-mən, -,man\ *n* : one who sells and makes deliveries on an assigned route

rout·er \'rau̇-tər\ *n* : a machine with a revolving spindle and cutter for shaping a surface (as of wood)

rou·tine \rü-'tēn\ *n* [F, fr. MF, fr. *route* traveled way] **1** : a regular course of procedure **2** : an often repeated speech or formula **3** : a part fully worked out 〈a comedy ~〉 **4** : a set of computer instructions that will perform a certain task — **routine** *adj* — **rou·tine·ly** *adv* — **rou·tin·ize** \-'tē-,nīz\ *vb*

¹**rove** \'rōv\ *vb* **roved; rov·ing** : to wander over or through — **rov·er** *n*

²**rove** *past and past part of* REEVE

¹**row** \'rō\ *vb* **1** : to propel a boat with oars **2** : to transport in a rowboat **3** : to pull an oar in a crew — **row·er** \'rō-ər\ *n*

²**row** *n* : an act or instance of rowing

³**row** *n* **1** : a number of objects in an orderly sequence **2** : WAY, STREET

⁴**row** \'rau̇\ *n* : a noisy quarrel

⁵**row** \'rau̇\ *vb* : to engage in a row

row·boat \'rō-,bōt\ *n* : a small boat designed to be rowed

row·dy \'rau̇-dē\ *adj* **row·di·er; -est** : coarse or boisterous in behavior : ROUGH — **row·di·ness** \'rau̇-dē-nəs\ *n* — **rowdy** *n* — **row·dy·ish** *adj* — **row·dy·ism** *n*

row·el \'rau̇-əl\ *n* : a small pointed wheel on a rider's spur — **rowel** *vb*

¹**roy·al** \'rȯi-əl\ *adj* **1** : of or relating to a sovereign : REGAL **2** : fit for a king or queen 〈a ~ welcome〉 — **roy·al·ly** *adv*

²**royal** *n* : a person of royal blood

royal flush *n* : a straight flush having an ace as the highest card

roy·al·ist \'rȯi-ə-list\ *n* : an adherent of a king or of monarchical government

roy·al·ty \'rȯi-əl-tē\ *n, pl* **-ties** **1** : the state of being royal **2** : royal persons **3** : a share of a product or profit (as of a mine or oil well) claimed by the owner for allowing another person to use the property **4** : a payment made to an author or composer for each copy of a work sold or to an inventor for each article sold under a patent

RP *abbr* **1** relief pitcher **2** Republic of the Philippines

rpm *abbr* revolutions per minute

rps *abbr* revolutions per second

rpt *abbr* **1** repeat **2** report

RR *abbr* **1** railroad **2** rural route

RS *abbr* **1** recording secretary **2** revised statutes **3** right side **4** Royal Society

RSV *abbr* Revised Standard Version

RSVP *abbr* [F *répondez s'il vous plaît*] please reply

rt *abbr* **1** right **2** route

RT *abbr* **1** radiotelephone **2** round-trip

rte *abbr* route

Ru *symbol* ruthenium

¹**rub** \'rəb\ *vb* **rubbed; rub·bing** **1** : to use pressure and friction on a body or object **2** : to fret or chafe with friction **3** : to scour, polish, erase, or smear by pressure and friction

²**rub** *n* **1** : DIFFICULTY, OBSTRUCTION **2** : something grating to the feelings

¹**rub·ber** \'rə-bər\ *n* **1** : one that rubs **2** : ERASER **3** : a flexible waterproof elastic substance made from the milky juice esp. of a So. American tropical tree or made synthetically; *also* : something made of this material — **rubber** *adj* — **rub·ber·ize** \'rə-bə-ˌrīz\ *vb* — **rub·bery** *adj*

²**rubber** *n* **1** : a contest that consists of an odd number of games and is won by the side that takes a majority **2** : an extra game played to decide a tie

¹**rub·ber·neck** \-ˌnek\ *n* **1** : an idly or overly inquisitive person **2** : a person on a guided tour

²**rubberneck** *vb* : to look about, stare, or listen with excessive curiosity — **rub·ber·neck·er** *n*

rub·bish \'rə-bish\ *n* **1** : useless waste or rejected matter : TRASH **2** : something worthless or nonsensical

rub·ble \'rə-bəl\ *n* : broken fragments esp. of a destroyed building

ru·bel·la \rü-'be-lə\ *n* : GERMAN MEASLES

ru·bi·cund \'rü-bi-(ˌ)kənd\ *adj* : RED, RUDDY

ru·bid·i·um \rü-'bi-dē-əm\ *n* : a soft silvery metallic chemical element — see ELEMENT table

ru·ble \'rü-bəl\ *n* — see MONEY table

ru·bric \'rü-brik\ *n* [ME *rubrike* red ocher, heading in red letters of part of a book, fr. MF *rubrique*, fr. L *rubrica*, fr. *ruber* red] **1** : HEADING, TITLE; *also* : CLASS, CATEGORY **2** : a rule esp. for the conduct of a religious service

ru·by \'rü-bē\ *n, pl* **rubies** : a clear red precious stone — **ruby** *adj*

ru·by–throat·ed hummingbird \'rü-bē-ˌthrō-təd-\ *n* : a bright green and whitish hummingbird of eastern No. America with a red throat in the male

ruck·us \'rə-kəs\ *n* : ROW, DISTURBANCE

rud·der \'rə-dər\ *n* : a movable flat piece attached vertically at the rear of a ship or aircraft for steering

rud·dy \'rə-dē\ *adj* **rud·di·er; -est** : REDDISH; *esp* : of a healthy reddish complexion — **rud·di·ness** \'rə-dē-nəs\ *n*

rude \'rüd\ *adj* **rud·er; rud·est** **1** : roughly made : CRUDE **2** : UNDEVELOPED, PRIMITIVE **3** : IMPOLITE **4** : UNSKILLED — **rude·ly** *adv* — **rude·ness** *n*

ru·di·ment \'rü-də-mənt\ *n* **1** : an elementary principle or basic skill — usu. used in pl. **2** : something not fully developed — usu. used in pl. — **ru·di·men·ta·ry** \ˌrü-də-'men-tə-rē\ *adj*

¹**rue** \'rü\ *n* : REGRET, SORROW — **rue·ful** \-fəl\ *adj* — **rue·ful·ly** *adv* — **rue·ful·ness** *n*

²**rue** *vb* **rued; ru·ing** : to feel regret, remorse, or penitence for

³**rue** *n* : a European strong-scented woody herb with bitter-tasting leaves

ruff \'rəf\ *n* **1** : a large round pleated collar worn about 1600 **2** : a fringe of long hair or feathers around the neck of an animal — **ruffed** \'rəft\ *adj*

ruf·fi·an \'rə-fē-ən\ *n* : a brutal person — **ruf·fi·an·ly** *adj*

¹**ruf·fle** \'rə-fəl\ *vb* **ruf·fled; ruf·fling** **1** : to roughen the surface of **2** : IRRITATE, VEX **3** : to erect (as hair or feathers) in or like a ruff **4** : to flip through (as pages) **5** : to draw into or provide with plaits or folds

²**ruffle** *n* **1** : a strip of fabric gathered or pleated on one edge **2** : RUFF **2** **3** : RIPPLE — **ruf·fly** \'rə-fə-lē, -flē\ *adj*

RU 486 \ˈär-ˌyü-ˌfōr-ˌā-tē-'siks\ *n* : a drug taken orally to induce abortion esp. early in pregnancy

rug \'rəg\ *n* **1** : a covering for the legs, lap, and feet **2** : a piece of heavy fabric usu. with a nap or pile used as a floor covering

rug·by \'rəg-bē\ *n, often cap* [*Rugby* School, Rugby, England, where it was first played] : a football game in which play is continuous and interference and forward passing are not permitted

rug·ged \'rə-gəd\ *adj* **1** : having a rough uneven surface **2** : TURBULENT, STORMY **3** : HARSH, STERN **4** : ROBUST, STURDY — **rug·ged·ize** \'rə-gə-ˌdīz\ *vb* — **rug·ged·ly** *adv* — **rug·ged·ness** *n*

¹**ru·in** \'rü-ən\ *n* **1** : complete collapse or destruction **2** : the remains of something destroyed — usu. used in pl. **3** : a cause of destruction **4** : the action of destroying

²**ruin** *vb* **1** : DESTROY **2** : to damage beyond repair **3** : BANKRUPT

ru·in·ation \ˌrü-ə-'nā-shən\ *n* : RUIN, DESTRUCTION

ru·in·ous \'rü-ə-nəs\ *adj* **1** : RUINED, DILAPIDATED **2** : causing ruin — **ru·in·ous·ly** *adv*

¹**rule** \'rül\ *n* **1** : a guide or principle for governing action : REGULATION **2** : the usual way of doing something **3** : the exercise of authority or control : GOVERNMENT **4** : RULER **2**

²**rule** *vb* **ruled; rul·ing** **1** : CONTROL; *also* : GOVERN **2** : to be supreme or outstanding in **3** : to give or state as a considered decision **4** : to mark on paper with or as if with a ruler

rul·er \'rü-lər\ *n* **1** : SOVEREIGN **2** : a straight strip of material (as wood or metal) marked off in units and used for measuring or as a straightedge

rum \'rəm\ *n* **1** : an alcoholic liquor made from molasses or sugarcane **2** : alcoholic liquor

Ru·ma·nian \rü-'mā-nē-ən, -nyən\ *n* : ROMANIAN — **Rumanian** *adj*

rum·ba \'rəm-bə, 'rüm-\ *n* : a dance of Cuban origin marked by strong rhythmic movements

¹**rum·ble** \'rəm-bəl\ *vb* **rum·bled; rum·bling** : to make a low heavy rolling sound; *also* : to move along with such a sound — **rum·bler** *n*

²**rumble** *n* **1** : a low heavy rolling sound **2** : a street fight esp. among gangs

rumble seat *n* : a folding seat in the back of an automobile that is not covered by the top

rum·bling \'rəm-bliŋ\ *n* **1** : RUMBLE **2** : widespread talk or complaints — usu. used in pl.

ru·men \'rü-mən\ *n, pl* **ru·mi·na** \-mə-nə\ *or* **rumens** : the large first compartment of the stomach of a ruminant (as a cow)

¹**ru·mi·nant** \'rü-mə-nənt\ *n* : a ruminant mammal

²**ruminant** *adj* **1** : chewing the cud; *also* : of or relating to a group of hoofed mammals (as cattle, deer, and camels) that chew the cud and have a complex usu. 4-chambered stomach **2** : MEDITATIVE

ru·mi·nate \'rü-mə-ˌnāt\ *vb* **-nat·ed; -nat·ing** [L *ruminari* to chew the cud, muse upon, fr. *rumin-, rumen* first stomach chamber of a ruminant] **1** : MEDITATE, MUSE **2** : to chew the cud — **ru·mi·na·tion** \ˌrü-mə-'nā-shən\ *n*

¹**rum·mage** \'rə-mij\ *vb* **rum·maged; rum·mag·ing** : to search thoroughly — **rum·mag·er** *n*

²**rummage** *n* **1** : a miscellaneous collection **2** : an act of rummaging

rum·my \'rə-mē\ *n* : any of several card games for two or more players

ru·mor \'rü-mər\ *n* **1** : common talk **2** : a statement or report current but not authenticated — **rumor** *vb*

ru·mour *chiefly Brit var of* RUMOR

rump \'rəmp\ *n* **1** : the rear part of an animal; *also* : a cut of meat (as beef) behind the upper sirloin **2** : a small or inferior remnant (as of a group)

rum·ple \'rəm-pəl\ *vb* **rum·pled; rum·pling** : TOUSLE, MUSS, WRINKLE — **rumple** *n* — **rum·ply** \'rəm-pə-lē\ *adj*

rum·pus \'rəm-pəs\ *n* : DISTURBANCE, RUCKUS

rumpus room *n* : a room usu. in the basement of a home that is used for games, parties, and recreation

---

\ə\abut \ᵊ\kitten \ər\further \a\ash \ā\ace \ä\mop, mar
\au̇\out \ch\chin \e\bet \ē\easy \g\go \i\hit \ī\ice \j\job
\ŋ\sing \ō\go \ȯ\law \oi̇\boy \th\thin \t̲h̲\the \ü\loot \u̇\foot
\y\yet \zh\vision *see also* Pronunciation Symbols page

¹**run** \'rən\ *vb* **ran** \'ran\; **run**; **run·ning 1** : to go faster than a walk **2** : to take to flight : FLEE **3** : to go without restraint ⟨let chickens ∼ loose⟩ **4** : to go rapidly or hurriedly : HASTEN, RUSH **5** : to make a quick or casual trip or visit **6** : to contend in a race; *esp* : to enter an election **7** : to put forward as a candidate for office **8** : to move on or as if on wheels : pass or slide freely **9** : to go back and forth : PLY **10** : to move in large numbers esp. to a spawning ground ⟨shad are *running*⟩ **11** : FUNCTION, OPERATE ⟨left the motor *running*⟩ **12** : to continue in force ⟨two years to ∼⟩ **13** : to flow rapidly or under pressure : MELT, FUSE, DISSOLVE; *also* : DISCHARGE **7** ⟨my nose is *running*⟩ **14** : to tend to produce or to recur ⟨family ∼s to blonds⟩ **15** : to take a certain direction **16** : to be worded or written **17** : to be current ⟨rumors *running* wild⟩ **18** : to cause to run **19** : TRACE ⟨∼ down a rumor⟩ **20** : to perform or bring about by running **21** : to cause to pass ⟨∼ a wire from the antenna⟩ **22** : to cause to collide **23** : SMUGGLE **24** : MANAGE, CONDUCT, OPERATE ⟨∼ a business⟩ **25** : INCUR ⟨∼ a risk⟩ **26** : to permit to accumulate before settling ⟨∼ up a bill⟩

²**run** *n* **1** : an act or the action of running **2** : a migration of fish; *also* : the migrating fish **3** : a score in baseball **4** : BROOK, CREEK **5** : a continuous series esp. of similar things **6** : persistent heavy demands from depositors, creditors, or customers **7** : the quantity of work turned out in a continuous operation; *also* : a period of operation (as of a machine or plant) **8** : the usual or normal kind ⟨the ordinary ∼ of students⟩ **9** : the distance covered in continuous travel or sailing **10** : a regular course or trip **11** : freedom of movement in a place or area ⟨has the ∼ of the house⟩ **12** : an enclosure for animals **13** : an inclined course (as for skiing) **14** : a lengthwise ravel (as in a stocking) — **run·less** *adj*

run·about \'rə-nə-ˌbau̇t\ *n* : a light wagon, automobile, or motorboat

run·a·gate \'rə-nə-ˌgāt\ *n* **1** : VAGABOND **2** : FUGITIVE

run·around \'rə-nə-ˌrau̇nd\ *n* : evasive or delaying action esp. in response to a request

¹**run·away** \'rə-nə-ˌwā\ *n* **1** : one that runs away : FUGITIVE **2** : the act of running away out of control; *also* : something (as a horse) that is running out of control

²**runaway** *adj* **1** : FUGITIVE **2** : won by a long lead; *also* : extremely successful **3** : subject to uncontrolled changes ⟨∼ inflation⟩ **4** : operating out of control ⟨a ∼ locomotive⟩

run·down \'rən-ˌdau̇n\ *n* : an item-by-item report or review : SUMMARY

run–down \'rən-'dau̇n\ *adj* **1** : EXHAUSTED, WORN-OUT ⟨that ∼ feeling⟩ **2** : being in poor repair ⟨a ∼ farm⟩

run down *vb* **1** : to collide with and knock down **2** : to chase until exhausted or captured **3** : to find by search **4** : DISPARAGE **5** : to cease to operate for lack of motive power **6** : to decline in physical condition

rune \'rün\ *n* **1** : any of the characters of any of several alphabets formerly used by the Germanic peoples **2** : MYSTERY, MAGIC **3** : a poem esp. in Finnish or Old Norse — **ru·nic** \'rü-nik\ *adj*

¹**rung** *past part of* RING

²**rung** \'rəŋ\ *n* **1** : a rounded crosspiece between the legs of a chair **2** : one of the crosspieces of a ladder

run–in \'rən-ˌin\ *n* **1** : ALTERCATION, QUARREL **2** : something run in

run in *vb* **1** : to insert as additional matter **2** : to arrest esp. for a minor offense **3** : to pay a casual visit

run·nel \'rən-ᵊl\ *n* : BROOK, STREAMLET

run·ner \'rə-nər\ *n* **1** : one that runs **2** : BASE RUNNER **3** : BALLCARRIER **4** : a thin piece or part on which something (as a sled or an ice skate) slides **5** : the support of a drawer or a sliding door **6** : a horizontal branch from the base of a plant that produces new plants **7** : a plant producing runners **8** : a long narrow carpet **9** : a narrow decorative cloth cover for a table or dresser top

run·ner–up \'rə-nər-ˌəp\ *n, pl* **runners–up** *also* **runner–ups** : the competitor in a contest who finishes second

¹**run·ning** *adj* **1** : FLOWING **2** : FLUID, RUNNY **3** : CONTINUOUS, INCESSANT **4** : measured in a straight line ⟨cost per ∼ foot⟩ **5** : of or relating to an act of running **6** : made or trained for running ⟨∼ horse⟩ ⟨∼ shoes⟩

²**running** *adv* : in succession

running light *n* : any of the lights carried by a vehicle (as a ship) at night

run·ny \'rə-nē\ *adj* : having a tendency to run ⟨a ∼ dough⟩ ⟨a ∼ nose⟩

run·off \'rən-ˌȯf\ *n* : a final contest (as an election) to a previous indecisive contest

run–of–the–mill *adj* : not outstanding : AVERAGE

run on *vb* **1** : to talk at length **2** : to continue (matter in type) without a break or a new paragraph **3** : to place or add (as an entry in a dictionary) at the end of a paragraphed item — **run–on** \'rən-ˌȯn, -ˌän\ *n*

runt \'rənt\ *n* : an unusually small person or animal : DWARF — **runty** *adj*

run·way \'rən-ˌwā\ *n* **1** : a beaten path made by animals; *also* : a passage for animals **2** : a paved strip of ground for the landing and takeoff of aircraft **3** : a narrow platform from a stage into an auditorium **4** : a support (as a track) on which something runs

ru·pee \rü-'pē, 'rü-ˌpē\ *n* — see MONEY table

ru·pi·ah \rü-'pē-ə\ *n, pl* **rupiah** *or* **rupiahs** — see MONEY table

¹**rup·ture** \'rəp-chər\ *n* : a breaking or tearing apart; *also* : HERNIA

²**rupture** *vb* **rup·tured; rup·tur·ing** : to cause or undergo rupture

ru·ral \'ru̇r-əl\ *adj* : of or relating to the country, country people, or agriculture

ruse \'rüs, 'rüz\ *n* : a wily subterfuge : TRICK, ARTIFICE

¹**rush** \'rəsh\ *n* : any of various often tufted and hollow-stemmed grasslike marsh plants — **rushy** *adj*

²**rush** *vb* [ME *russhen*, fr. MF *ruser* to put to flight, deceive, fr. L *recusare* to refuse] **1** : to move forward or act with too great haste or eagerness or without preparation **2** : to perform in a short time or at high speed **3** : ATTACK, CHARGE — **rush·er** *n*

³**rush** *n* **1** : a violent forward motion **2** : unusual demand or activity **3** : a crowding of people to one place **4** : a running play in football **5** : a sudden feeling of pleasure

⁴**rush** *adj* : requiring or marked by special speed or urgency ⟨∼ orders⟩

rush hour *n* : a time when the amount of traffic or business is at a peak

rusk \'rəsk\ *n* : a sweet or plain bread baked, sliced, and baked again until dry and crisp

Russ *abbr* Russia; Russian

rus·set \'rə-sət\ *n* **1** : a coarse reddish brown cloth **2** : a reddish brown or yellowish brown color **3** : a baking potato — **russet** *adj*

Rus·sian \'rə-shən\ *n* **1** : a native or inhabitant of Russia **2** : a Slavic language of the Russian people — **Russian** *adj*

rust \'rəst\ *n* **1** : a reddish coating formed on iron when it is exposed to esp. moist air **2** : any of numerous plant diseases characterized by usu. reddish spots; *also* : a fungus causing rust **3** : a reddish brown color — **rust** *vb* — **rusty** *adj*

¹**rus·tic** \'rəs-tik\ *adj* : of, relating to, or suitable for the country or country people — **rus·ti·cal·ly** \-ti-k(ə-)lē\ *adv* — **rus·tic·i·ty** \ˌrəs-'ti-sə-tē\ *n*

²**rustic** *n* : a rustic person

rus·ti·cate \'rəs-ti-ˌkāt\ *vb* **-cat·ed; -cat·ing** : to go into or reside in the country — **rus·ti·ca·tion** \ˌrəs-ti-'kā-shən\ *n*

¹**rus·tle** \'rə-səl\ *vb* **rus·tled; rus·tling 1** : to make or cause a rustle **2** : to cause to rustle ⟨∼ a newspaper⟩ **3** : to act or move with energy or speed; *also* : to procure

in this way **4** : to forage food **5** : to steal cattle from the range — **rus·tler** *n*

²rustle *n* : a quick series of small sounds ⟨∼ of leaves⟩

¹rut \'rət\ *n* : state or period of sexual excitement esp. in male deer — **rut** *vb*

²rut *n* **1** : a track worn by wheels or by habitual passage of something **2** : a usual or fixed routine

ru·ta·ba·ga \ˌrü-tə-'bā-gə, ˌrü-\ *n* : a turnip with a large yellowish root

Ruth \'rüth\ *n* — see BIBLE table

ru·the·ni·um \rü-'thē-nē-əm\ *n* : a hard brittle metallic chemical element — see ELEMENT table

ruth·less \'rüth-ləs\ *adj* [fr. *ruth* compassion, pity, fr.

ME *ruthe*, fr. *ruen* to rue, fr. OE *hrēowan*] : having no pity : MERCILESS, CRUEL — **ruth·less·ly** *adv* — **ruth·less·ness** *n*

¹RV \ˌär-'vē\ *n* : RECREATIONAL VEHICLE

²RV *abbr* Revised Version

R–value \'är-ˌval-yü\ *n* : a measure of resistance to the flow of heat through a substance (as insulation)

RW *abbr* **1** right worshipful **2** right worthy

rwy *or* **ry** *abbr* railway

-ry \rē\ *n suffix* : -ERY ⟨bigot*ry*⟩

rye \'rī\ *n* **1** : a hardy annual grass grown for grain or as a cover crop; *also* : its seed **2** : a whiskey distilled from a rye mash

S

¹s \'es\ *n, pl* **s's** *or* **ss** \'e-səz\ *often cap* : the 19th letter of the English alphabet

²s *abbr, often cap* **1** saint **2** second **3** senate **4** series **5** shilling **6** singular **7** small **8** son **9** south; southern

¹-s \s *after sounds* f, k, k, p, t, th; əz *after sounds* ch, j, s, sh, z, zh; z *after other sounds*\ *n pl suffix* — used to form the plural of most nouns that do not end in *s*, *z*, *sh*, *ch*, or postconsonantal *y* ⟨head*s*⟩ ⟨book*s*⟩ ⟨boy*s*⟩ ⟨belief*s*⟩, to form the plural of proper nouns that end in postconsonantal *y* ⟨Mary*s*⟩, and with or without a preceding apostrophe to form the plural of abbreviations, numbers, letters, and symbols used as nouns ⟨MC*s*⟩ ⟨4*s*⟩ ⟨+#*s*⟩ ⟨B'*s*⟩

²-s *adv suffix* — used to form adverbs denoting usual or repeated action or state ⟨works night*s*⟩

³-s *vb suffix* — used to form the third person singular present of most verbs that do not end in *s*, *z*, *sh*, *ch*, or postconsonantal *y* ⟨fall*s*⟩ ⟨take*s*⟩ ⟨play*s*⟩

S *symbol* sulfur

SA *abbr* **1** Salvation Army **2** seaman apprentice **3** sex appeal **4** [L *sine anno* without year] without date **5** South Africa **6** South America **7** subject to approval

Sab·bath \'sa-bəth\ *n* [ME *sabat*, fr. OF & OE, fr. L *sabbatum*, fr. Gk *sabbaton*, fr. Heb *shabbāth*, lit., rest] **1** : the 7th day of the week observed as a day of worship by Jews and some Christians **2** : Sunday observed among Christians as a day of worship

sab·bat·i·cal \sə-'ba-ti-kəl\ *n* : a leave often with pay granted (as to a college professor) usu. every 7th year for rest, travel, or research

sa·ber *or* **sa·bre** \'sā-bər\ *n* [F *sabre*] : a cavalry sword with a curved blade and thick back

saber saw *n* : a portable electric saw with a pointed reciprocating blade

sa·ble \'sā-bəl\ *n, pl* **sables** **1** : the color black **2** *pl* : mourning garments **3** : a dark brown mammal chiefly of northern Asia related to the weasels; *also* : its fur or pelt

¹sab·o·tage \'sa-bə-ˌtäzh\ *n* [F] **1** : deliberate destruction of an employer's property or hindering of production by workers **2** : destructive or hampering action by enemy agents or sympathizers in time of war

²sabotage *vb* **-taged; -tag·ing** : to practice sabotage on : WRECK

sab·o·teur \ˌsa-bə-'tər\ *n* : a person who practices sabotage

sac \'sak\ *n* : a pouch in an animal or plant often containing a fluid

SAC *abbr* Strategic Air Command

sac·cha·rin \'sa-kə-rən\ *n* : a white crystalline compound used as an artificial calorie-free sweetener

sac·cha·rine \'sa-kə-rən\ *adj* : nauseatingly sweet ⟨∼ poetry⟩

sac·er·do·tal \ˌsa-sər-'dōt-əl, -kər-\ *adj* : PRIESTLY

sac·er·do·tal·ism \-əl-ˌi-zəm\ *n* : a religious belief emphasizing the powers of priests as essential mediators between God and man

sa·chem \'sā-chəm\ *n* : a No. American Indian chief

sa·chet \sa-'shā\ *n* [F, fr. OF, dim. of *sac* bag] : a small bag filled with perfumed powder for scenting clothes

¹sack \'sak\ *n* **1** : a usu. rectangular-shaped bag (as of paper or burlap) **2** : a loose jacket or short coat

²sack *vb* : DISMISS, FIRE

³sack *n* [modif. of MF *sec* dry, fr. L *siccus*] : a white wine popular in England in the 16th and 17th centuries

⁴sack *vb* : to plunder a captured town

sack·cloth \-ˌklȯth\ *n* : a rough garment worn as a sign of penitence

sac·ra·ment \'sa-krə-mənt\ *n* **1** : a formal religious act or rite; *esp* : one (as baptism or the Eucharist) held to have been instituted by Christ **2** : the elements of the Eucharist — **sac·ra·men·tal** \ˌsa-krə-'ment-əl\ *adj*

sa·cred \'sā-krəd\ *adj* **1** : set apart for the service or worship of deity **2** : devoted exclusively to one service or use **3** : worthy of veneration or reverence **4** : of or relating to religion : RELIGIOUS **syn** blessed, divine, hallowed, holy, sanctified — **sa·cred·ly** *adv* — **sa·cred·ness** *n*

sacred cow *n* : one that is often unreasonably immune from criticism

¹sac·ri·fice \'sa-krə-ˌfīs\ *n* **1** : the offering of something precious to deity **2** : something offered in sacrifice **3** : LOSS, DEPRIVATION **4** : a bunt allowing a base runner to advance while the batter is put out; *also* : a fly ball allowing a runner to score after the catch — **sac·ri·fi·cial** \ˌsa-krə-'fi-shəl\ *adj* — **sac·ri·fi·cial·ly** *adv*

²sac·ri·fice *vb* **-ficed; -fic·ing** **1** : to offer up or kill as a sacrifice **2** : to accept the loss or destruction of for an end, cause, or ideal **3** : to make a sacrifice in baseball

sac·ri·lege \'sa-krə-lij\ *n* [ME, fr. OF, fr. L *sacrilegium*, fr. *sacrilegus* one who steals sacred things, fr. *sacr-*, *sacer* sacred + *legere* to gather, steal] **1** : violation of something consecrated to God **2** : gross irreverence toward a hallowed person, place, or thing — **sac·ri·le·gious** \ˌsa-krə-'li-jəs, -'lē-\ *adj* — **sac·ri·le·gious·ly** *adv*

sac·ris·tan \'sa-krə-stən\ *n* **1** : a church officer in charge of the sacristy **2** : SEXTON

sac·ris·ty \'sa-krə-stē\ *n, pl* **-ties** : VESTRY

\ə\abut \ᵊ\kitten \ər\further \a\ash \ā\ace \ä\mop, mar \aù\out \ch\chin \e\bet \ē\easy \g\go \i\hit \ī\ice \j\job \ŋ\sing \ō\go \ȯ\law \ȯi\boy \th\thin \t̲h̲\the \ü\loot \ù\foot \y\yet \zh\vision *see also* Pronunciation Symbols page

sac·ro·il·i·ac \ˌsa-krō-ˈi-lē-ˌak\ *n* : the joint between the upper part of the hipbone and the sacrum

sac·ro·sanct \ˈsa-krō-ˌsaŋkt\ *adj* : SACRED, INVIOLABLE

sa·crum \ˈsa-krəm, ˈsā-\ *n, pl* **sa·cra** \ˈsa-krə, ˈsā-\ : the part of the vertebral column that is directly connected with or forms a part of the pelvis and in humans consists of five fused vertebrae

sad \ˈsad\ *adj* **sad·der; sad·dest 1** : GRIEVING, MOURNFUL, DOWNCAST **2** : causing sorrow **3** : DULL, SOMBER — **sad·ly** *adv* — **sad·ness** *n*

sad·den \ˈsad-ᵊn\ *vb* : to make sad

¹sad·dle \ˈsad-ᵊl\ *n* **1** : a usu. padded leather-covered seat (as for a rider on horseback) **2** : the upper back portion of a carcass (as of mutton)

saddle 1

²saddle *vb* **sad·dled; sad·dling 1** : to put a saddle on **2** : OPPRESS, BURDEN

sad·dle·bow \ˈsad-ᵊl-ˌbō\ *n* : the arch in the front of a saddle

saddle horse *n* : a horse suited for or trained for riding

Sad·du·cee \ˈsa-jə-ˌsē, ˈsa-dyə-\ *n* : a member of an ancient Jewish sect consisting of a ruling class of priests and rejecting certain doctrines — **Sad·du·ce·an** \ˌsa-jə-ˈsē-ən, ˌsa-dyə-\ *adj*

sad·iron \ˈsa-ˌdi-ərn\ *n* : a flatiron with a removable handle

sa·dism \ˈsā-ˌdi-zəm, ˈsa-\ *n* : a sexual perversion in which gratification is obtained by inflicting physical or mental pain on others — **sa·dist** \ˈsā-dist, ˈsa-\ *n* — **sa·dis·tic** \sə-ˈdis-tik\ *adj* — **sa·dis·ti·cal·ly** \-ti-k(ə-)lē\ *adv*

SAE *abbr* **1** self-addressed envelope **2** Society of Automotive Engineers **3** stamped addressed envelope

Sa·far \sə-ˈfär\ *n* [Ar ṣafar] : the 2d month of the Islamic year

sa·fa·ri \sə-ˈfär-ē, -ˈfar-\ *n* [Ar safarī of a trip] **1** : a hunting expedition esp. in eastern Africa **2** : JOURNEY, TRIP

¹safe \ˈsāf\ *adj* **saf·er; saf·est 1** : free from harm or risk **2** : affording safety; *also* : secure from danger or loss **3** : RELIABLE — **safe·ly** *adv*

²safe *n* : a container for keeping articles (as valuables) safe

safe—con·duct \-ˈkän-(ˌ)dəkt\ *n* : a pass permitting a person to go through enemy lines

¹safe·guard \-ˌgärd\ *n* : a measure or device for preventing accident

²safeguard *vb* : to provide a safeguard for : PROTECT

safe·keep·ing \ˈsāf-ˈkē-piŋ\ *n* : a keeping or being kept in safety

safe sex *n* : sexual activity and esp. sexual intercourse in which various measures (as the use of latex condoms) are taken to avoid disease (as AIDS) transmitted by sexual contact

safe·ty \ˈsāf-tē\ *n, pl* **safeties 1** : freedom from danger : SECURITY **2** : a protective device **3** : a football play in which the ball is downed by the offensive team behind

its own goal line **4** : a defensive football back in the deepest position — **safety** *adj*

safety glass *n* : shatter-resistant material formed of two sheets of glass with a sheet of clear plastic between them

safety match *n* : a match that ignites only when struck on a special surface

saf·flow·er \ˈsa-ˌflau̇-ər\ *n* : a widely grown Old World herb related to the daisies that has large orange or red flower heads yielding a dyestuff and seeds rich in edible oil

saf·fron \ˈsa-frən\ *n* : a deep orange powder from the flower of a crocus used to color and flavor foods

sag \ˈsag\ *vb* **sagged; sag·ging 1** : to droop or settle from or as if from pressure **2** : to lose firmness or vigor — **sag** *n*

sa·ga \ˈsä-gə\ *n* [ON] : a narrative of heroic deeds; *esp* : one recorded in Iceland in the 12th and 13th centuries

sa·ga·cious \sə-ˈgā-shəs\ *adj* : of keen mind : SHREWD — **sa·gac·i·ty** \-ˈga-sə-tē\ *n*

sag·a·more \ˈsa-gə-ˌmȯr\ *n* : a subordinate No. American Indian chief

¹sage \ˈsāj\ *adj* [ME, fr. OF, fr. (assumed) VL *sapius*, fr. L *sapere* to taste, have good taste, be wise] : WISE, PRUDENT — **sage·ly** *adv*

²sage *n* : one who is distinguished for wisdom

³sage *n* [ME, fr. MF *sauge*, fr. L *salvia*, fr. *salvus* healthy; fr. its use as a medicinal herb] **1** : a mint with leaves used in flavoring **2** : SAGEBRUSH

sage·brush \ˈsāj-ˌbrəsh\ *n* : any of several low shrubby No. American composite plants; *esp* : one of the western U.S. with a sagelike odor

Sag·it·tar·i·us \ˌsa-jə-ˈter-ē-əs\ *n* [L, lit., archer] **1** : a zodiacal constellation between Scorpio and Capricorn usu. pictured as a centaur archer **2** : the 9th sign of the zodiac in astrology; *also* : one born under this sign

sa·go \ˈsā-gō\ *n, pl* **sagos** : a dry granulated starch esp. from the pith of various tropical palms (**sago palm**)

sa·gua·ro \sə-ˈwär-ə, -ˈgwär-, -ō\ *n, pl* **-ros** [MexSp] : a desert cactus of the southwestern U.S. and Mexico with a tall columnar simple or sparsely branched trunk of up to 60 feet (18 meters)

said *past and past part of* SAY

¹sail \ˈsāl\ *n* **1** : a piece of fabric by means of which the wind is used to propel a ship **2** : a sailing ship **3** : something resembling a sail **4** : a trip on a sailboat

²sail *vb* **1** : to travel on a sailing ship **2** : to pass over in a ship **3** : to manage or direct the course of a ship **4** : to move with ease, grace, or nonchalance

sail·board \ˈsāl-ˌbȯrd\ *n* : a modified surfboard having a mast and sailed by a standing person

sail·boat \-ˌbōt\ *n* : a boat propelled primarily by sail

sail·cloth \-ˌklȯth\ *n* : a heavy canvas used for sails, tents, or upholstery

sail·fish \-ˌfish\ *n* : any of a genus of large marine bony fishes with a large dorsal fin that are related to marlins

sail·ing *n* : the sport of handling or riding in a sailboat

sail·or \ˈsā-lər\ *n* : one that sails; *esp* : a member of a ship's crew

sail·plane \ˈsāl-ˌplān\ *n* : a glider designed to rise in an upward air current

saint \ˈsānt, *before a name* (ˌ)sānt *or* sənt\ *n* **1** : one officially recognized as preeminent for holiness **2** : one of the spirits of the departed in heaven **3** : a holy or godly person — **saint·ed** \-ˈsān-təd\ *adj* — **saint·hood** \-ˌhu̇d\ *n*

Saint Ber·nard \-bər-ˈnärd\ *n* : any of a Swiss alpine breed of tall powerful working dogs used esp. formerly in aiding lost travelers

saint·ly \ˈsānt-lē\ *adj* : relating to, resembling, or befitting a saint — **saint·li·ness** \-lē-nəs\ *n*

Saint Val·en·tine's Day \-ˈva-lən-ˌtīnz-\ *n* : February 14

Saint Bernard

observed in honor of St. Valentine and as a time for exchanging valentines

¹sake \'sāk\ *n* **1** : END, PURPOSE **2** : personal or social welfare, safety, or well-being

²sa·ke *or* **sa·ki** \'sä-kē\ *n* : a Japanese alcoholic beverage of fermented rice

sa·laam \sə-'läm\ *n* [Ar *salām*, lit., peace] **1** : a salutation or ceremonial greeting in the East **2** : an obeisance performed by bowing very low and placing the right palm on the forehead — **salaam** *vb*

sa·la·cious \sə-'lā-shəs\ *adj* **1** : arousing sexual desire or imagination **2** : LUSTFUL — **sa·la·cious·ly** *adv* — **sa·la·cious·ness** *n*

sal·ad \'sa-ləd\ *n* : a cold dish (as of lettuce, vegetables, fish, eggs, or fruit) served with dressing

sal·a·man·der \'sa-lə-ˌman-dər\ *n* : any of numerous amphibians that look like lizards but have scaleless usu. smooth moist skin

sa·la·mi \sə-'lä-mē\ *n* [It] : a highly seasoned sausage of pork and beef

sal·a·ry \'sa-lə-rē\ *n, pl* **-ries** [ME *salarie*, fr. L *salarium* pension, salary, fr. neut. of *salarius* of salt, fr. *sal* salt] : payment made at regular intervals for services

sale \'sāl\ *n* **1** : transfer of ownership of property from one person to another in return for money **2** : ready market : DEMAND **3** : AUCTION **4** : a selling of goods at bargain prices — **sal·able** *or* **sale·able** \'sā-lə-bəl\ *adj*

sales·girl \'sālz-ˌgərl\ *n* : SALESWOMAN

sales·man \-mən\ *n* : a person who sells in a store or to outside customers — **sales·man·ship** *n*

sales·per·son \-ˌpər-sən\ *n* : a salesman or saleswoman

sales·wom·an \-ˌwu̇-mən\ *n* : a woman who sells merchandise

sal·i·cyl·ic acid \ˌsa-lə-'si-lik-\ *n* : a crystalline organic acid used in the form of its salts and other derivatives to relieve pain and fever

¹sa·lient \'sāl-yənt, 'sā-lē-ənt\ *adj* : jutting forward beyond a line; *also* : PROMINENT **syn** conspicuous, striking, noticeable

²salient *n* : a projecting part in a line of defense

¹sa·line \'sā-ˌlēn, -ˌlīn\ *adj* : consisting of or containing salt : SALTY — **sa·lin·i·ty** \sā-'li-nə-tē, sə-\ *n*

²saline *n* **1** : a metallic salt esp. with a purgative action **2** : a saline solution

sa·li·va \sə-'lī-və\ *n* : a liquid secreted into the mouth that helps digestion — **sal·i·vary** \'sa-lə-ˌver-ē\ *adj*

sal·i·vate \'sa-lə-ˌvāt\ *vb* **-vat·ed; -vat·ing** : to produce saliva esp. in excess — **sal·i·va·tion** \ˌsa-lə-'vā-shən\ *n*

sal·low \'sa-lō\ *adj* : of a yellowish sickly color ⟨a ∼ face⟩

sal·ly \'sa-lē\ *n, pl* **sallies** **1** : a rushing attack on besiegers by troops of a besieged place **2** : a witty remark or retort **3** : a brief excursion — **sally** *vb*

salm·on \'sa-mən\ *n, pl* **salmon** *also* **salmons** **1** : any of several bony fishes with pinkish flesh used for food that

are related to the trouts **2** : a strong yellowish pink color or

sal·mo·nel·la \ˌsal-mə-'ne-lə\ *n, pl* **-nel·lae** \-'ne-(ˌ)lē, -ˌlī\ *or* **-nellas** *or* **-nella** : any of a genus of rod-shaped bacteria that cause various illnesses (as food poisoning)

sa·lon \sə-'län, 'sa-ˌlän, sa-'lōⁿ\ *n* [F] : an elegant drawing room; *also* : a fashionable shop ⟨beauty ∼⟩

sa·loon \sə-'lün\ *n* **1** : a large public cabin on a ship **2** : a place where liquors are sold and drunk : BARROOM **3** *Brit* : SEDAN 2

sal·sa \'sȯl-sə, 'säl-\ *n* : a spicy sauce of tomatoes, onions, and hot peppers

sal soda \ˌsal-'sō-də\ *n* : SODIUM CARBONATE

¹salt \'sȯlt\ *n* **1** : a white crystalline substance that consists of sodium and chlorine and is used in seasoning foods **2** : a saltlike cathartic substance (as Epsom salts) **3** : a compound formed usu. by action of an acid on metal **4** : SAILOR — **salt·i·ness** \'sȯl-tē-nəs\ *n* — **salty** \'sȯl-tē\ *adj*

²salt *vb* : to preserve, season, or feed with salt

³salt *adj* : preserved or treated with salt; *also* : SALTY

SALT *abbr* Strategic Arms Limitation Talks

salt away *vb* : to lay away safely : SAVE

salt·box \'sȯlt-ˌbäks\ *n* : a frame dwelling with two stories in front and one behind and a long sloping roof

salt·cel·lar \-ˌse-lər\ *n* : a small container for holding salt at the table

sal·tine \sȯl-'tēn\ *n* : a thin crisp cracker sprinkled with salt

salt lick *n* : LICK 5

salt·pe·ter \'sȯlt-'pē-tər\ *n* [ME *salt petre*, alter. of *salpetre*, fr. MF, fr. ML *sal petrae*, lit., salt of the rock] **1** : POTASSIUM NITRATE **2** : SODIUM NITRATE

salt·wa·ter \-ˌwȯ-tər, -ˌwä-\ *adj* : of, relating to, or living in salt water

sa·lu·bri·ous \sə-'lü-brē-əs\ *adj* : favorable to health

sal·u·tary \'sal-yə-ˌter-ē\ *adj* : health-giving; *also* : BENEFICIAL

sal·u·ta·tion \ˌsal-yə-'tā-shən\ *n* : an expression of greeting, goodwill, or courtesy usu. by word or gesture

sa·lu·ta·to·ri·an \sə-ˌlü-tə-'tȯr-ē-ən\ *n* : the student having the 2nd highest rank in a graduating class who delivers the salutatory address

sa·lu·ta·to·ry \sə-'lü-tə-ˌtȯr-ē\ *adj* : relating to or being the welcoming oration delivered at an academic commencement

¹sa·lute \sə-'lüt\ *vb* **sa·lut·ed; sa·lut·ing** **1** : GREET **2** : to honor by special ceremonies **3** : to show respect to (a superior officer) by a formal position of hand, rifle, or sword

²salute *n* **1** : GREETING **2** : the formal position assumed in saluting a superior

¹sal·vage \'sal-vij\ *n* **1** : money paid for saving a ship, its cargo, or passengers when the ship is wrecked or in danger **2** : the saving of a ship **3** : the saving of possessions in danger of being lost **4** : things saved from loss or destruction (as by a wreck or fire)

²salvage *vb* **sal·vaged; sal·vag·ing** : to rescue from destruction

sal·va·tion \sal-'vā-shən\ *n* **1** : the saving of a person from sin or its consequences esp. in the life after death **2** : the saving from danger, difficulty, or evil **3** : something that saves

¹salve \'sav, 'sàv\ *n* **1** : a medicinal substance applied to the skin **2** : a soothing influence

²salve *vb* **salved; salv·ing** : EASE, SOOTHE

sal·ver \'sal-vər\ *n* [F *salve*, fr. Sp *salva* sampling of food to detect poison, tray, fr. *salvar* to save, sample

---

\ə\abut \ᵊ\kitten \ər\further \a\ash \ā\ace \ä\mop, mar
\au̇\out \ch\chin \e\bet \ē\easy \g\go \i\hit \ī\ice \j\job
\ŋ\sing \ō\go \ȯ\law \ȯi\boy \th\thin \t͟h\the \ü\loot \u̇\foot
\y\yet \zh\vision *see also* Pronunciation Symbols page

food to detect poison, fr. LL *salvare* to save, fr. L *salvus* safe] : a small serving tray

sal·vo \'sal-vō\ *n, pl* **salvos** *or* **salvoes** : a simultaneous discharge of guns

Sam *or* **Saml** *abbr* Samuel

SAM \'sam, ¡es-¡ā-'em\ *n* [*surface-to-air* *m*issile] : a guided missile for use against aircraft by ground units

sa·mar·i·um \sə-'mer-ē-əm\ *n* : a gray lustrous metallic chemical element — see ELEMENT table

¹same \'sām\ *adj* **1** : being the one referred to : not different **2** : SIMILAR — **same·ness** *n*

²same *pron* : the same one or ones

³same *adv* : in the same manner

Sa·mo·an \sə-'mō-ən\ *n* : a native or inhabitant of Samoa — **Samoan** *adj*

sam·o·var \'sa-mə-¡vär\ *n* [Russ, fr. *samo-* self + *varit'* to boil] : an urn with a spigot at the base used esp. in Russia to boil water for tea

sam·pan \'sam-¡pan\ *n* : a flat-bottomed skiff of the Far East usu. propelled by two short oars

¹sam·ple \'sam-pəl\ *n* : a representative piece, item, or set of individuals that shows the quality or nature of the whole from which it was taken : EXAMPLE, SPECIMEN

²sample *vb* **sam·pled; sam·pling** : to judge the quality of by a sample

sam·pler \'sam-plər\ *n* : a piece of needlework; *esp* : one testing skill in embroidering

Sam·u·el \'sam-yə-wəl\ *n* — see BIBLE table

sam·u·rai \'sa-mə-¡rī, 'sam-yə-¡\ *n, pl* **samurai** : a member of a Japanese feudal warrior class practicing a chivalric code

san·a·to·ri·um \¡sa-nə-'tōr-ē-əm\ *n, pl* **-riums** *or* **-ria** \-ē-ə\ **1** : a health resort **2** : an establishment for the care esp. of convalescents or the chronically ill

sanc·ti·fy \'saŋk-tə-¡fī\ *vb* **-fied; -fy·ing 1** : to make holy : CONSECRATE **2** : to free from sin — **sanc·ti·fi·ca·tion** \¡saŋk-tə-fə-'kā-shən\ *n*

sanc·ti·mo·nious \¡saŋk-tə-'mō-nē-əs\ *adj* : hypocritically pious — **sanc·ti·mo·nious·ly** *adv*

¹sanc·tion \'saŋk-shən\ *n* **1** : authoritative approval **2** : a measure (as a threat or fine) designed to enforce a law or standard ⟨economic ∼s⟩

²sanction *vb* : to give approval to : RATIFY **syn** endorse, accredit, certify, approve

sanc·ti·ty \'saŋk-tə-tē\ *n, pl* **-ties 1** : GODLINESS **2** : SACREDNESS

sanc·tu·ary \'saŋk-chə-¡wer-ē\ *n, pl* **-ar·ies 1** : a consecrated place (as the part of a church in which the altar is placed) **2** : a place of refuge ⟨bird ∼⟩

sanc·tum \'saŋk-təm\ *n, pl* **sanctums** *also* **sanc·ta** \-tə\ : a private office or study : DEN ⟨an editor's ∼⟩

¹sand \'sand\ *n* : loose particles of hard broken rock — **sandy** *adj*

²sand *vb* **1** : to cover or fill with sand **2** : to scour, smooth, or polish with an abrasive (as sandpaper) — **sand·er** *n*

san·dal \'sand-əl\ *n* : a shoe consisting of a sole strapped to the foot; *also* : a low or open slipper or rubber overshoe

san·dal·wood \-¡wùd\ *n* : the fragrant yellowish heartwood of a parasitic tree of southern Asia that is much used in ornamental carving and cabinetwork; *also* : the tree

sand·bag \'sand-¡bag\ *n* : a bag filled with sand and used in fortifications, as ballast, or as a weapon

sand·bank \-¡baŋk\ *n* : a deposit of sand (as in a bar or shoal)

sand·bar \-¡bär\ *n* : a ridge of sand formed in water by tides or currents

sand·blast \-¡blast\ *vb* : to treat with a stream of sand blown (as for cleaning stone) by compressed air — **sand·blast·er** *n*

sand dollar *n* : any of numerous flat circular sea urchins chiefly of sandy bottoms in shallow water

S & H *abbr* shipping and handling

sand·hog \'sand-¡hòg, -¡häg\ *n* : a laborer who builds underwater tunnels

sand·lot \-¡lät\ *n* : a vacant lot esp. when used for the unorganized sports of children — **sand·lot** *adj* — **sand·lot·ter** *n*

sand·man \-¡man\ *n* : the genie of folklore who makes children sleepy

sand·pa·per \-¡pā-pər\ *n* : paper with abrasive (as sand) glued on one side used in smoothing and polishing surfaces — **sandpaper** *vb*

sand·pip·er \-¡pī-pər\ *n* : any of numerous shorebirds with a soft-tipped bill longer than that of the related plovers

sand·stone \-¡stōn\ *n* : rock made of sand united by a natural cement

sand·storm \-¡stòrm\ *n* : a windstorm that drives clouds of sand

sand trap *n* : a hazard on a golf course consisting of a hollow containing sand

¹sand·wich \'sand-(¡)wich\ *n* [after John Montagu, 4th Earl of *Sandwich* †1792 Eng. diplomat] **1** : two or more slices of bread with a layer (as of meat or cheese) spread between them **2** : something resembling a sandwich

²sandwich *vb* : to squeeze or crowd in

sane \'sān\ *adj* **san·er; san·est** : mentally sound and healthy; *also* : SENSIBLE, RATIONAL — **sane·ly** *adv*

sang *past of* SING

sang·froid \'sän-'frwä\ *n* [F *sang-froid*, lit., cold blood] : self-possession or an imperturbable state esp. under strain

san·gui·nary \'saŋ-gwə-¡ner-ē\ *adj* : BLOODY ⟨∼ battle⟩

san·guine \'saŋ-gwən\ *adj* **1** : RUDDY **2** : CHEERFUL, HOPEFUL

sanit *abbr* sanitary; sanitation

san·i·tar·i·an \¡sa-nə-'ter-ē-ən\ *n* : a specialist in sanitation and public health

san·i·tar·i·um \¡sa-nə-'ter-ē-əm\ *n, pl* **-i·ums** *or* **-ia** \-ē-ə\ : SANATORIUM

san·i·tary \'sa-nə-¡ter-ē\ *adj* **1** : of or relating to health : HYGIENIC **2** : free from filth or infective matter

sanitary napkin *n* : a disposable absorbent pad used to absorb uterine flow (as during menstruation)

san·i·ta·tion \¡sa-nə-'tā-shən\ *n* : the act or process of making sanitary; *also* : protection of health by maintenance of sanitary conditions

san·i·tize \'sa-nə-¡tīz\ *vb* **-tized; -tiz·ing 1** : to make sanitary **2** : to make more acceptable by removing unpleasant features

san·i·ty \'sa-nə-tē\ *n* : soundness of mind

sank *past of* SINK

sans \'sanz\ *prep* : WITHOUT

San·skrit \'san-¡skrit\ *n* : an ancient language that is the classical language of India and of Hinduism — **Sanskrit** *adj*

San·ta Ana \¡san-tə-'a-nə\ *n* [*Santa Ana* Mountains in southern Calif.] : a hot dry wind from the north, northeast, or east in southern California

¹sap \'sap\ *n* **1** : a vital fluid; *esp* : a watery fluid that circulates through a vascular plant **2** : a foolish gullible person — **sap·less** *adj*

²sap *vb* **sapped; sap·ping 1** : UNDERMINE **2** : to weaken gradually

sap·id \'sa-pəd\ *adj* : FLAVORFUL

sa·pi·ent \'sā-pē-ənt, 'sa-\ *adj* : WISE, DISCERNING — **sa·pi·ence** \-əns\ *n*

sap·ling \'sa-pliŋ\ *n* : a young tree

sap·phire \'sa-¡fīr\ *n* : a hard transparent usu. rich blue gem

sap·py \'sa-pē\ *adj* **sap·pi·er; -est 1** : full of sap **2** : overly sentimental **3** : SILLY, FOOLISH

sap·ro·phyte \'sa-prə-¡fīt\ *n* : a living thing and esp. a plant living on dead or decaying organic matter — **sap·ro·phyt·ic** \ˌsa-prə-ˈfi-tik\ adj

sap·suck·er \ˈsap-ˌse-kər\ n : any of a genus of small No. American woodpeckers

sap·wood \-ˌwu̇d\ n : the younger active and usu. lighter and softer outer layer of wood (as of a tree trunk)

sar·casm \ˈsär-ˌka-zəm\ n 1 : a cutting or contemptuous remark 2 : ironic criticism or reproach — **sar·cas·tic** \sär-ˈkas-tik\ adj — **sar·cas·ti·cal·ly** \-ti-k(ə-)lē\ adv

sar·co·ma \sär-ˈkō-mə\ n, pl **-mas** also **-ma·ta** \-mə-tə\ : a malignant tumor esp. of connective tissue, bone, cartilage, or striated muscle

sar·coph·a·gus \sär-ˈkä-fə-gəs\ n, pl **-gi** \-ˌgī, -ˌjī\ also **-gus·es** [L sarcophagus (lapis) limestone used for coffins, fr. Gk (lithos) sarkophagos, lit., flesh-eating stone, fr. sark-, sarx flesh + phagein to eat] : a large stone coffin

sar·dine \sär-ˈdēn\ n, pl **sardines** also **sardine** : a young or small fish preserved for use as food

sar·don·ic \sär-ˈdä-nik\ adj : disdainfully or skeptically humorous : derisively mocking **syn** ironic, satiric, sarcastic — **sar·don·i·cal·ly** \-ni-k(ə-)lē\ adv

sa·ri also **sa·ree** \ˈsär-ē\ n [Hindi sāṛī] : a garment worn by women in southern Asia that consists of a long cloth draped around the body and head or shoulder

sa·rong \sə-ˈrȯŋ, -ˈräŋ\ n : a loose garment wrapped around the body and worn by men and women of the Malay archipelago and the Pacific islands

sar·sa·pa·ril·la \ˌsas-ə-pə-ˈri-lə, ˌsärs-\ n 1 : the dried roots of a tropical American smilax used esp. for flavoring; also : the plant 2 : a sweetened carbonated beverage flavored with sassafras and an oil from a birch

sar·to·ri·al \sär-ˈtȯr-ē-əl\ adj : of or relating to a tailor or tailored clothes — **sar·to·ri·al·ly** adv

SASE abbr self-addressed stamped envelope

¹**sash** \ˈsash\ n : a broad band worn around the waist or over the shoulder

²**sash** n, pl **sash** also **sash·es** : a frame for panes of glass in a door or window; also : the movable part of a window

sa·shay \sa-ˈshā\ vb 1 : WALK, GLIDE, GO 2 : to strut or move about in an ostentatious manner 3 : to proceed in a diagonal or sideways manner

Sask abbr Saskatchewan

Sas·quatch \ˈsas-ˌkwach, -ˌkwäch\ n [Halkomelem (American Indian language of British Columbia) sésq̓əc] : a large hairy humanlike creature reported to exist in the northwestern U.S. and western Canada

sas·sa·fras \ˈsa-sə-ˌfras\ n [Sp sasafrás] : a No. American tree related to the laurel; also : its carcinogenic dried root bark

sassy \ˈsa-sē\ adj **sass·i·er; -est** : SAUCY

¹**sat** past and past part of SIT

²**sat** abbr saturate; saturated; saturation

Sat abbr Saturday

Sa·tan \ˈsāt-ᵊn\ n : DEVIL

sa·tang \sə-ˈtäŋ\ n, pl **satang** or **satangs** — see baht at MONEY table

sa·tan·ic \sə-ˈta-nik, sā-\ adj 1 : of or characteristic of Satan 2 : extremely malicious or wicked — **sa·tan·i·cal·ly** \-ni-k(ə-)lē\ adv

satch·el \ˈsa-chəl\ n : SUITCASE

sate \ˈsāt\ vb **sat·ed; sat·ing** : to satisfy to the full; also : SURFEIT, GLUT

sa·teen \sa-ˈtēn, sə-\ n : a cotton cloth finished to resemble satin

sat·el·lite \ˈsat-ᵊl-ˌīt\ n [F, fr. L satelles attendant] 1 : an obsequious follower of a distinguished person : TOADY 2 : a celestial body that orbits a larger body 3 : a manufactured object that orbits a celestial body

sa·ti·ate \ˈsā-shē-ˌāt\ vb **-at·ed; -at·ing** : to satisfy fully or to excess

sa·ti·ety \sə-ˈtī-ə-tē\ n : fullness to the point of excess

sat·in \ˈsat-ᵊn\ n : a fabric (as of silk) with a glossy surface — **sat·iny** adj

sat·in·wood \ˈsat-ᵊn-ˌwu̇d\ n : a hard yellowish brown wood of satiny luster; also : a tree yielding this wood

sat·ire \ˈsa-ˌtīr\ n : biting wit, irony, or sarcasm used to expose vice or folly; also : a literary work having these qualities — **sa·tir·ic** \sə-ˈtir-ik\ or **sa·tir·i·cal** \-i-kəl\ adj — **sa·tir·i·cal·ly** adv — **sat·i·rist** \ˈsa-tə-rist\ n — **sat·i·rize** \-tə-ˌrīz\ vb

sat·is·fac·tion \ˌsa-təs-ˈfak-shən\ n 1 : payment through penance of punishment incurred by sin 2 : CONTENTMENT, GRATIFICATION 3 : reparation for an insult 4 : settlement of a claim

sat·is·fac·to·ry \-ˈfak-tə-rē\ adj : giving satisfaction : ADEQUATE — **sat·is·fac·to·ri·ly** \-ˈfak-tə-rə-lē\ adv

sat·is·fy \ˈsa-təs-ˌfī\ vb **-fied; -fy·ing** 1 : to answer or discharge (a claim) in full 2 : to make happy : GRATIFY 3 : to pay what is due to 4 : CONVINCE 5 : to meet the requirements of — **sat·is·fy·ing·ly** adv

sa·trap \ˈsā-ˌtrap, ˈsa-\ n [ME, fr. L satrapes, fr. Gk satrapēs, fr. OPer khshathrapāvan, lit., protector of the dominion] : a petty prince : a subordinate ruler

sat·u·rate \ˈsa-chə-ˌrāt\ vb **-rat·ed; -rat·ing** 1 : to soak thoroughly 2 : to treat or charge with something to the point where no more can be absorbed, dissolved, or retained — **sat·u·ra·ble** \ˈsa-chə-rə-bəl\ adj — **sat·u·ra·tion** \ˌsa-chə-ˈrā-shən\ n

Sat·ur·day \ˈsa-tər-dē, -ˌdā\ n : the 7th day of the week

Saturday night special n : a cheap easily concealed handgun

Sat·urn \ˈsa-tərn\ n : the planet 6th in order from the sun — see PLANET table

sat·ur·nine \ˈsa-tər-ˌnīn\ adj : SULLEN, SARDONIC

sa·tyr \ˈsā-tər\ n 1 often cap : a woodland deity in Greek mythology having certain characteristics of a horse or goat 2 : a lecherous man

¹**sauce** \ˈsȯs, 3 usu ˈsas\ n 1 : a fluid dressing or topping for food 2 : stewed fruit 3 : IMPUDENCE

²**sauce** \ˈsȯs, 2 usu ˈsas\ vb **sauced; sauc·ing** 1 : to put sauce on; also : to add zest to 2 : to be impudent to

sauce·pan \ˈsȯs-ˌpan\ n : a small deep cooking pan with a handle

sau·cer \ˈsȯ-sər\ n : a rounded shallow dish for use under a cup

saucy \ˈsa-sē, ˈsȯ-\ adj **sauc·i·er; -est** : IMPUDENT, PERT — **sauc·i·ly** \-sə-lē\ adv — **sauc·i·ness** \-sē-nəs\ n

Sau·di \ˈsau̇-dē, ˈsȯ-; sä-ˈü-dē\ n : SAUDI ARABIAN — **Saudi** adj

Saudi Arabian n : a native or inhabitant of Saudi Arabia — **Saudi Arabian** adj

sau·er·kraut \ˈsau̇-ər-ˌkrau̇t\ n [G, fr. sauer sour + Kraut greens] : finely cut cabbage fermented in brine

sau·na \ˈsau̇-nə\ n 1 : a Finnish steam bath in which the steam is provided by water thrown on hot stones 2 : a dry heat bath; also : a room or cabinet used for such a bath

saun·ter \ˈsȯn-tər, ˈsän-\ vb : STROLL

sau·ro·pod \ˈsȯr-ə-ˌpäd\ n : any of a suborder of plant-eating dinosaurs (as a brontosaurus) with a long neck and tail and a small head — **sauropod** adj

sau·sage \ˈsȯ-sij\ n [ultim. fr. LL salsicia, fr. L salsus salted] : minced and highly seasoned meat (as pork) usu. enclosed in a tubular casing

S Aust abbr South Australia

sau·té \sȯ-ˈtā, sō-\ vb **sau·téed** or **sau·téd; sau·té·ing** [F] : to fry lightly in a little fat — **sauté** n

sau·terne \sō-ˈtərn, sȯ-\ n, often cap : a usu. semisweet American white wine

---

\ə\abut \ᵊ\kitten \ər\further \a\ash \ā\ace \ä\mop, mar
\au̇\out \ch\chin \e\bet \ē\easy \g\go \i\hit \ī\ice \j\job
\ŋ\sing \ō\go \ȯ\law \ȯi\boy \th\thin \t̶h̶\the \ü\loot \u̇\foot
\y\yet \zh\vision   see also Pronunciation Symbols page

¹**sav·age** \'sa-vij\ *adj* [ME *sauvage*, fr. MF, fr. ML *salvaticus*, alter. of L *silvaticus* of the woods, wild, fr. *silva* wood, forest] **1** : WILD, UNTAMED **2** : UNCIVILIZED, BARBAROUS **3** : CRUEL, FIERCE — **sav·age·ly** *adv* — **sav·age·ness** *n* — **sav·age·ry** \-rē\ *n*

²**savage** *n* **1** : a member of a primitive human society **2** : a rude, unmannerly, or brutal person

sa·van·na *or* **sa·van·nah** \sə-'va-nə\ *n* [Sp *zavana*] : grassland containing scattered trees

sa·vant \sa-'vänt, sə-, 'sa-vənt\ *n* : a learned person : SCHOLAR

¹**save** \'sāv\ *vb* **saved; sav·ing 1** : to redeem from sin **2** : to rescue from danger **3** : to preserve or guard from destruction or loss **4** : to put aside as a store or reserve — **sav·er** *n*

²**save** *n* : a play that prevents an opponent from scoring or winning

³**save** *prep* : EXCEPT

⁴**save** *conj* : BUT

savings and loan association *n* : a cooperative association that holds savings of members in the form of dividend-bearing shares and that invests chiefly in mortgage loans

savings bank *n* : a bank that holds funds of individual depositors in interest-bearing accounts and makes long-term investments (as mortgage loans)

savings bond *n* : a registered U.S. bond issued in denominations of $50 to $10,000

sav·ior *or* **sav·iour** \'sāv-yər\ *n* **1** : one who saves **2** *cap* : Jesus Christ

sa·voir faire \₁sav-₁wär-'far\ *n* [F *savoir-faire*, lit., knowing how to do] : sureness in social behavior

¹**sa·vor** *also* **sa·vour** \'sā-vər\ *n* **1** : the taste and odor of something **2** : a special flavor or quality — **sa·vory** *adj*

²**savor** *also* **savour** *vb* **1** : to have a specified taste, smell, or quality **2** : to taste with pleasure

sa·vo·ry \'sā-və-rē\ *n, pl* **-ries** : either of two aromatic mints used in cooking

¹**sav·vy** \'sa-vē\ *vb* **sav·vied; sav·vy·ing** : UNDERSTAND, COMPREHEND

²**savvy** *n* : practical know-how ⟨political ∼⟩ — **savvy** *adj*

¹**saw** *past of* SEE

²**saw** \'so\ *n* : a cutting tool with a blade having a line of teeth along its edge

³**saw** *vb* **sawed** \'sod\; **sawed** *or* **sawn** \'son\; **saw·ing** : to cut or shape with or as if with a saw — **saw·yer** \-yər\ *n*

⁴**saw** *n* : a common saying : MAXIM

saw·dust \'so-(₁)dəst\ *n* : fine particles made by a saw in cutting

saw·fly \-₁flī\ *n* : any of numerous insects belonging to the same order as bees and wasps and including many whose larvae are plant-feeding pests

saw·horse \-₁hors\ *n* : a rack on which wood is rested while being sawed by hand

saw·mill \-₁mil\ *n* : a mill for sawing logs

saw palmetto *n* : any of several shrubby palms with spiny-toothed petioles

sax \'saks\ *n* : SAXOPHONE

sax·i·frage \'sak-sə-frij, -₁frāj\ *n* [ME, fr. MF, fr. LL *saxifraga*, fr. L, fem. of *saxifragus*, breaking rocks] : any of a genus of plants with showy flowers and usu. with leaves growing in tufts close to the ground

sax·o·phone \'sak-sə-₁fōn\ *n* : a musical instrument having a conical metal tube with a reed mouthpiece and finger keys — **sax·o·phon·ist** \-₁fō-nist\ *n*

¹**say** \'sā\ *vb* **said** \'sed\; **say·ing; says** \'sez\ **1** : to express in words ⟨∼ what you mean⟩ **2** : to state as opinion or belief **3** : PRONOUNCE; *also* : RECITE, REPEAT ⟨∼ your prayers⟩ **4** : INDICATE ⟨the clock ∼s noon⟩

²**say** *n, pl* **says** \'sāz\ **1** : an expression of opinion **2** : power of decision

say·ing *n* : a commonly repeated statement

say–so \'sā-(₁)sō\ *n* : an esp. authoritative assertion or decision; *also* : the right to decide

sb *abbr* substantive

Sb *symbol* [L *stibium*] antimony

SB *abbr* [NL *scientiae baccalaureus*] bachelor of science

SBA *abbr* Small Business Administration

sc *abbr* **1** scale **2** scene **3** science

Sc *symbol* scandium

SC *abbr* **1** South Carolina **2** supreme court

¹**scab** \'skab\ *n* **1** : scabies of domestic animals **2** : a protective crust over a sore or wound **3** : a worker who replaces a striker or works under conditions not authorized by a union **4** : any of various bacterial or fungus plant diseases marked by crusted spots on stems or leaves — **scab·by** *adj*

²**scab** *vb* **scabbed; scab·bing 1** : to become covered with a scab **2** : to work as a scab

scab·bard \'ska-bərd\ *n* : a sheath for the blade of a weapon (as a sword)

sca·bies \'skā-bēz\ *n* [L] : contagious itch or mange caused by mites living as parasites under the skin

sca·brous \'ska-brəs, 'skā-\ *adj* **1** : DIFFICULT, KNOTTY **2** : rough to the touch : SCALY, SCURFY ⟨a ∼ leaf⟩ **3** : dealing with suggestive, indecent, or scandalous themes; *also* : SQUALID

scad \'skad\ *n* : a large number or quantity — usu. used in pl.

scaf·fold \'ska-fəld, -₁fōld\ *n* **1** : a raised platform for workers to sit or stand on **2** : a platform on which a criminal is executed (as by hanging)

scaf·fold·ing *n* : a system of scaffolds; *also* : materials for scaffolds

scal·a·wag \'ska-li-₁wag\ *n* : RASCAL

¹**scald** \'skold\ *vb* **1** : to burn with or as if with hot liquid or steam **2** : to heat to just below the boiling point

²**scald** *n* : a burn caused by scalding

¹**scale** \'skāl\ *n* **1** : either pan of a balance **2** : BALANCE — usu. used in pl. **3** : a weighing instrument

²**scale** *vb* **scaled; scal·ing** : WEIGH

³**scale** *n* **1** : one of the small thin plates that cover the body esp. of a fish or reptile **2** : a thin plate or flake **3** : a thin coating, layer, or incrustation **4** : SCALE INSECT — **scaled** \'skāld\ *adj* — **scale·less** \'skāl-ləs\ *adj* — **scaly** *adj*

⁴**scale** *vb* **scaled; scal·ing** : to strip of scales

⁵**scale** *n* [ME, fr. LL *scala* ladder, staircase, fr. L *scalae*, pl., stairs, rungs, ladder] **1** : something divided into regular spaces as a help in drawing or measuring **2** : a graduated series **3** : the size of a sample (as a model) in proportion to the size of the actual thing **4** : a standard of estimation or judgment **5** : a series of musical tones going up or down in pitch according to a specified scheme

⁶**scale** *vb* **scaled; scal·ing 1** : to climb by or as if by a ladder **2** : to arrange in a graded series

scale insect *n* : any of numerous small insects with wingless scale-covered females that are related to aphids and live and are often pests on plants

scale·pan \'skāl-₁pan\ *n* : SCALE 1

scal·lion \'skal-yən\ *n* [ultim. fr. L *ascalonia (caepa)* onion of Ascalon (seaport in Palestine)] : an onion without an enlarged bulb

¹**scal·lop** \'skä-ləp, 'ska-\ *n* **1** : any of numerous marine bivalve mollusks with radially ridged shells; *also* : a large edible muscle of this mollusk **2** : one of a continuous series of rounded projections forming an edge

²**scallop** *vb* **1** : to bake in a casserole ⟨∼ed potatoes⟩ **2** : to shape, cut, or finish in scallops ⟨∼ed edges⟩

¹**scalp** \'skalp\ *n* : the part of the skin and flesh of the head usu. covered with hair

²**scalp** *vb* **1** : to remove the scalp from **2** : to resell at greatly increased prices ⟨∼ tickets⟩ — **scalp·er** *n*

scal·pel \'skal-pəl\ *n* : a small straight knife with a thin blade used esp. in surgery

scam \'skam\ *n* : a fraudulent or deceptive act or operation

scamp \'skamp\ *n* : RASCAL

scam·per \'skam-pər\ *vb* : to run nimbly and playfully — **scamper** *n*

scam·pi \'skam-pē\ *n, pl* **scampi** [It] : SHRIMP; *esp* : large shrimp prepared with a garlic-flavored sauce

¹**scan** \'skan\ *vb* **scanned; scan·ning 1** : to read (verses) so as to show metrical structure **2** : to examine closely **3** : to examine with a sensing device esp. to obtain information **4** : to make a scan of (as the human body) — **scan·ner** *n*

²**scan** *n* **1** : the act or process of scanning **2** : a picture of the distribution of radioactive material in something; *also* : an image of a bodily part produced (as by computer) by combining radiographic data obtained from several angles or sections

Scand *abbr* Scandinavia; Scandinavian

scan·dal \'skand-ᵊl\ *n* [ME, fr. LL *scandalum* stumbling block, offense, fr. Gk *skandalon*] **1** : DISGRACE, DISHONOR **2** : malicious gossip : SLANDER — **scan·dal·ize** *vb* — **scan·dal·ous** *adj* — **scan·dal·ous·ly** *adv*

scan·dal·mon·ger \-ˌmən-gər, -ˌmän-\ *n* : a person who circulates scandal

Scan·di·na·vian \ˌskan-də-'nā-vē-ən\ *n* : a native or inhabitant of Scandinavia — **Scandinavian** *adj*

scan·di·um \'skan-dē-əm\ *n* : a white metallic chemical element — see ELEMENT table

¹**scant** \'skant\ *adj* **1** : barely sufficient **2** : having scarcely enough **syn** scanty, skimpy, meager, sparse, exiguous

²**scant** *vb* **1** : SKIMP **2** : STINT

scant·ling \'skant-liŋ\ *n* : a small piece of lumber (as an upright in a house)

scanty \'skan-tē\ *adj* **scant·i·er; -est** : barely sufficient : SCANT — **scant·i·ly** \'skan-tə-lē\ *adv* — **scant·i·ness** \-tē-nəs\ *n*

scape·goat \'skāp-ˌgōt\ *n* : one that bears the blame for others

scape·grace \-ˌgrās\ *n* [*scape* (escape)] : an incorrigible rascal

scap·u·la \'ska-pyə-lə\ *n, pl* **-lae** \-ˌlē\ *or* **-las** [L] : SHOULDER BLADE

scap·u·lar \-lər\ *n* : a pair of small cloth squares worn on the breast and back under the clothing esp. for religious purposes

scar \'skär\ *n* : a mark left after injured tissue has healed — **scar** *vb*

scar·ab \'skar-əb\ *n* [MF *scarabee*, fr. L *scarabaeus*] : any of a family of large stout beetles; *also* : an ornament (as a gem) representing such a beetle

scarce \'skers\ *adj* **scarc·er; scarc·est 1** : deficient in quantity or number : not plentiful **2** : intentionally absent ⟨made himself ∼ at inspection time⟩ — **scar·ci·ty** \'sker-sə-tē\ *n*

scarce·ly \-lē\ *adv* **1** : BARELY **2** : almost not **3** : very probably not

¹**scare** \'sker\ *vb* **scared; scar·ing** : FRIGHTEN, STARTLE

²**scare** *n* : FRIGHT — **scary** *adj*

scare·crow \'sker-ˌkrō\ *n* : a crude figure set up to scare birds away from crops

¹**scarf** \'skärf\ *n, pl* **scarves** \'skärvz\ *or* **scarfs 1** : a broad band (as of cloth) worn about the shoulders, around the neck, over the head, or about the waist **2** : a long narrow cloth cover for a table or dresser top

²**scarf** *vb* [alter. of earlier *scoff* eat greedily] : to eat greedily

scar·i·fy \'skar-ə-ˌfī\ *vb* **-fied; -fy·ing 1** : to make scratches or small cuts in ⟨∼ skin for vaccination⟩ ⟨∼ seeds to help them germinate⟩ **2** : to lacerate the feelings of **3** : to break up and loosen the surface of (as a road) — **scar·i·fi·ca·tion** \ˌskar-ə-fə-'kā-shən\ *n*

scar·let \'skär-lət\ *n* : a bright red color — **scarlet** *adj*

scarlet fever *n* : an acute contagious disease marked by fever, sore throat, and red rash and caused by certain streptococci

scarp \'skärp\ *n* : a line of cliffs produced by faulting or erosion

scath·ing \'skā-thiŋ\ *adj* : bitterly severe ⟨a ∼ condemnation⟩

scat·o·log·i·cal \ˌska-tə-'lä-ji-kəl\ *adj* : concerned with obscene matters

scat·ter \'ska-tər\ *vb* **1** : to distribute or strew about irregularly **2** : DISPERSE

scat·ter·brain \'ska-tər-ˌbrān\ *n* : a silly careless person — **scat·ter·brained** \-ˌbrānd\ *adj*

scav·enge \'ska-vənj\ *vb* **scav·enged; scav·eng·ing** : to work or function as a scavenger

scav·en·ger \'ska-vən-jər\ *n* [alter. of earlier *scavager*, fr. ME *skawager* customs collector, fr. *skawage* customs, fr. OF *escauwage* inspection] : a person or animal that collects, eats, or disposes of refuse or waste

sce·nar·io \sə-'nar-ē-ˌō\ *n, pl* **-i·os** : the plot or outline of a dramatic work; *also* : an account of a possible action

scene \'sēn\ *n* [MF, stage, fr. L *scena, scaena* stage, scene, prob. fr. Etruscan, fr. Gk *skēnē* temporary shelter, tent, building forming the background for a dramatic performance, stage] **1** : a division of one act of a play **2** : a single situation or sequence in a play or motion picture **3** : a stage setting **4** : VIEW, PROSPECT **5** : the place of an occurrence or action **6** : a display of strong feeling and esp. anger **7** : a sphere of activity ⟨the fashion ∼⟩ — **sce·nic** \'sē-nik\ *adj*

scen·ery \'sē-nə-rē\ *n, pl* **-er·ies 1** : the painted scenes or hangings and accessories used on a theater stage **2** : a picturesque view or landscape

¹**scent** \'sent\ *n* **1** : ODOR, SMELL **2** : sense of smell **3** : course of pursuit : TRACK **4** : PERFUME 2 — **scent·ed** \'sen-təd\ *adj* — **scent·less** *adj*

²**scent** *vb* **1** : SMELL **2** : to imbue or fill with odor

scep·ter \'sep-tər\ *n* : a staff borne by a sovereign as an emblem of authority

scep·tic \'skep-tik\ *var of* SKEPTIC

scep·tre *Brit var of* SCEPTER

sch *abbr* school

¹**sched·ule** \'ske-jül, *esp Brit* 'she-dyül\ *n* **1** : a list of items or details **2** : TIMETABLE

²**schedule** *vb* **sched·uled; sched·ul·ing 1** : to make a schedule of; *also* : to enter on a schedule **2** : to appoint, assign, or designate for a fixed time

sche·mat·ic \ski-'ma-tik\ *adj* : of or relating to a scheme or diagram : DIAGRAMMATIC — **schematic** *n* — **sche·mat·i·cal·ly** \-ti-k(ə-)lē\ *adv*

¹**scheme** \'skēm\ *n* **1** : a plan for doing something; *esp* : a crafty plot **2** : a systematic design

²**scheme** *vb* **schemed; schem·ing** : to form a plot : INTRIGUE — **schem·er** *n*

Schick test \'shik-\ *n* : a serological test for susceptibility to diphtheria

schil·ling \'shi-liŋ\ *n* — see MONEY table

schism \'si-zəm, 'ski-\ *n* **1** : DIVISION, SPLIT; *also* : DISCORD, DISSENSION **2** : a formal division in or separation from a religious body

schis·mat·ic \siz-'ma-tik, ski-\ *n* : one who creates or takes part in schism — **schismatic** *adj*

schist \'shist\ *n* : a metamorphic crystalline rock

schizo·phre·nia \ˌskit-sə-'frē-nē-ə\ *n* [NL, fr. Gk *schizein* to split + *phrēn* diaphragm, mind] : a psychotic mental illness that is characterized by a twisted view of the real world, by a greatly reduced ability to carry

---

\ə\abut \ᵊ\kitten \ər\further \a\ash \ā\ace \ä\mop, mar \au̇\out \ch\chin \e\bet \ē\easy \g\go \i\hit \ī\ice \j\job \ŋ\sing \ō\go \o\law \oi̇\boy \th\thin \t̲h̲\the \ü\loot \u̇\foot \y\yet \zh\vision *see also* Pronunciation Symbols page out one's daily tasks, and by abnormal ways of thinking, feeling, and behaving — **schiz·oid** \'skit-ˌsȯid\ *adj or n* — **schizo·phren·ic** \ˌskit-sə-'fre-nik\ *adj or n*

schle·miel \shlə-'mēl\ *n* : an unlucky bungler : CHUMP

schlepp *or* **schlep** \'shlep\ *vb* [Yiddish *shlepn*] **1** : DRAG, HAUL **2** : to move slowly or awkwardly

schlock \'shläk\ *or* **schlocky** \'shlä-kē\ *adj* : of low quality or value — **schlock** *n*

schmaltz *also* **schmalz** \'shmȯlts, 'shmälts\ *n* [Yiddish *shmalts*, lit., rendered fat] : sentimental or florid music or art — **schmaltzy** *adj*

schnau·zer \'shnaùt-sər, 'shnaù-zər\ *n* [G, fr. *Schnauze* snout] : a dog of any of three breeds that are characterized by a wiry coat, long head, small ears, heavy eyebrows, and long hair on the muzzle

schol·ar \'skä-lər\ *n* **1** : STUDENT, PUPIL **2** : a learned person : SAVANT — **schol·ar·ly** *adj*

schol·ar·ship \-ˌship\ *n* **1** : the qualities or learning of a scholar **2** : money awarded to a student to help pay for further education

scho·las·tic \skə-'las-tik\ *adj* : of or relating to schools, scholars, or scholarship

¹school \'skül\ *n* **1** : an institution for teaching and learning; *also* : the pupils in attendance **2** : a body of persons of like opinions or beliefs ⟨the radical ∼⟩

²school *vb* : TEACH, TRAIN, DRILL

³school *n* : a large number of one kind of water animal swimming and feeding together

school·boy \-ˌbȯi\ *n* : a boy attending school

school·fel·low \-ˌfe-lō\ *n* : SCHOOLMATE

school·girl \-ˌgərl\ *n* : a girl attending school

school·house \-ˌhaùs\ *n* : a building used as a school

school·marm \-ˌmärm\ *or* **school·ma'am** \-ˌmäm, -ˌmam\ *n* **1** : a woman schoolteacher **2** : a person who exhibits characteristics popularly attributed to schoolteachers

school·mas·ter \-ˌmas-tər\ *n* : a male schoolteacher

school·mate \-ˌmāt\ *n* : a school companion

school·mis·tress \-ˌmis-trəs\ *n* : a woman schoolteacher

school·room \-ˌrüm, -ˌrùm\ *n* : CLASSROOM

school·teach·er \-ˌtē-chər\ *n* : one who teaches in a school

schoo·ner \'skü-nər\ *n* : a fore-and-aft rigged sailing ship

schooner

schuss \'shùs, 'shüs\ *vb* [G *Schuss*, n., lit., shot] : to ski down a slope at high speed — **schuss** *n*

sci *abbr* science; scientific

sci·at·i·ca \sī-'a-ti-kə\ *n* : pain in the region of the hips or along the course of the nerve at the back of the thigh

sci·ence \'sī-əns\ *n* [ME, fr. MF, fr. L *scientia*, fr. *scient-, sciens* having knowledge, fr. prp. of *scire* to know] **1** : an area of knowledge that is an object of study; *esp* : NATURAL SCIENCE **2** : knowledge covering general truths or the operation of general laws especially as obtained and tested through the scientific method

— **sci·en·tif·ic** \ˌsī-ən-'ti-fik\ *adj* — **sci·en·tif·i·cal·ly** \-fi-k(ə-)lē\ *adv* — **sci·en·tist** \'sī-ən-tist\ *n*

science fiction *n* : fiction dealing principally with the impact of actual or imagined science on society or individuals

scientific method *n* : the rules and methods for the pursuit of knowledge involving the finding and stating of a problem, the collection of facts through observation and experiment, and the making and testing of ideas that need to be proven right or wrong

scim·i·tar \'si-mə-tər\ *n* : a curved sword used chiefly by Arabs and Turks

scin·til·la \sin-'ti-lə\ *n* : SPARK, TRACE

scin·til·late \'sint-ᵊl-ˌāt\ *vb* **-lat·ed; -lat·ing** : SPARKLE, GLEAM — **scin·til·la·tion** \ˌsint-ᵊl-'ā-shən\ *n*

sci·on \'sī-ən\ *n* **1** : a shoot of a plant joined to a stock in grafting **2** : DESCENDANT

scis·sors \'si-zərz\ *n pl* : a cutting instrument like shears but usu. smaller

scissors kick *n* : a swimming kick in which the legs move like scissors

scle·ro·sis \sklə-'rō-səs\ *n* : abnormal hardening of tissue (as of an artery); *also* : a disease characterized by this — **scle·rot·ic** \-'rä-tik\ *adj*

scoff \'skäf\ *vb* : MOCK, JEER — **scoff·er** *n*

scoff·law \-ˌlȯ\ *n* : a contemptuous law violator

¹scold \'skōld\ *n* : a person who scolds

²scold *vb* : to censure severely or angrily

sconce \'skäns\ *n* : a candlestick or an electric light fixture fastened to a wall

scone \'skōn, 'skän\ *n* : a biscuit (as of oatmeal) baked on a griddle

¹scoop \'sküp\ *n* **1** : a large shovel; *also* : a utensil with a shovellike or rounded end **2** : an act of scooping **3** : information of immediate interest

²scoop *vb* **1** : to take out or up or empty with or as if with a scoop **2** : to make hollow **3** : to report a news item in advance of

scoot \'sküt\ *vb* : to move swiftly

scoot·er \'skü-tər\ *n* **1** : a child's vehicle consisting of a narrow board mounted between two wheels tandem with an upright steering handle attached to the front wheel **2** : MOTOR SCOOTER

¹scope \'skōp\ *n* [It *scopo* purpose, goal, fr. Gk *skopos*] **1** : space or opportunity for action or thought **2** : extent covered : RANGE

²scope *n* : an instrument (as a microscope or radarscope) for viewing

scorch \'skȯrch\ *vb* : to burn the surface of; *also* : to dry or shrivel with heat ⟨∼ed lawns⟩

¹score \'skōr\ *n, pl* **scores 1** *or pl* **score** : TWENTY **2** : CUT, SCRATCH, SLASH **3** : a record of points made (as in a game) **4** : DEBT **5** : REASON, GROUND **6** : the music of a composition or arrangement with different parts indicated **7** : success in obtaining something (as drugs) esp. illegally

²score *vb* **scored; scor·ing 1** : RECORD **2** : to keep score in a game **3** : to mark with lines, grooves, scratches, or notches **4** : to gain or tally in or as if in a game ⟨*scored* a point⟩ **5** : to assign a grade or score to ⟨∼ the tests⟩ **6** : to compose a score for **7** : SUCCEED — **score·less** *adj* — **scor·er** *n*

¹scorn \'skȯrn\ *n* : an emotion involving both anger and disgust : CONTEMPT — **scorn·ful** \-fəl\ *adj* — **scorn·ful·ly** *adv*

²scorn *vb* : to hold in contempt : DISDAIN — **scorn·er** *n*

Scor·pio \'skȯr-pē-ˌō\ *n* [L, lit., scorpion] **1** : a zodiacal constellation between Libra and Sagittarius usu. pictured as a scorpion **2** : the 8th sign of the zodiac in astrology; *also* : one born under this sign

scor·pi·on \'skȯr-pē-ən\ *n* : any of an order of arthropods related to the spiders that have a poisonous stinger at the tip of a long jointed tail

scorpion

¹Scot \'skät\ *n* : a native or inhabitant of Scotland

²Scot *abbr* Scotland; Scottish

Scotch \'skäch\ *n* **1** : SCOTS **2** **Scotch** *pl* : the people of Scotland **3** : a whiskey distilled in Scotland esp. from malted barley — **Scotch** *adj* — **Scotch·man** \-mən\ *n* — **Scotch·wom·an** \-ˌwu̇-mən\ *n*

Scotch pine *n* : a pine that is naturalized in the U.S. from northern Europe and Asia and is a valuable timber tree

Scotch terrier *n* : SCOTTISH TERRIER

scot–free \'skät-'frē\ *adj* : free from obligation, harm, or penalty

Scots \'skäts\ *n* : the English language of Scotland

Scots·man \'skäts-mən\ *n* : SCOT

Scots·wom·an \-ˌwu̇-mən\ *n* : a woman who is a Scot

Scot·tie \'skä-tē\ *n* : SCOTTISH TERRIER

Scot·tish \'skä-tish\ *adj* : of, relating to, or characteristic of Scotland, Scots, or the Scots

Scottish terrier *n* : any of an old Scottish breed of terrier with short legs, a large head with small erect ears, a broad deep chest, and a thick rough coat

scoun·drel \'skau̇n-drəl\ *n* : a disreputable person : VILLAIN

¹scour \'skau̇r\ *vb* **1** : to rub (as with a gritty substance) in order to clean **2** : to cleanse by or as if by rubbing

²scour *vb* **1** : to move rapidly through : RUSH **2** : to examine thoroughly

¹scourge \'skərj\ *n* **1** : LASH, WHIP **2** : PUNISHMENT; *also* : a cause of affliction (as a plague)

²scourge *vb* **scourged; scourg·ing 1** : LASH, FLOG **2** : to punish severely

¹scout \'skau̇t\ *vb* [ME, fr. MF *escouter* to listen, fr. L *auscultare*] **1** : to look around : RECONNOITER **2** : to inspect or observe to get information

²scout *n* **1** : a person sent out to get information; *also* : a soldier, airplane, or ship sent out to reconnoiter **2** : BOY SCOUT **3** : GIRL SCOUT — **scout·mas·ter** \-ˌmas-tər\ *n*

³scout *vb* : SCORN, SCOFF

scow \'skau̇\ *n* : a large flat-bottomed boat with square ends

scowl \'skau̇l\ *vb* : to make a frowning expression of displeasure — **scowl** *n*

SCPO *abbr* senior chief petty officer

scrab·ble \'skra-bəl\ *vb* **scrab·bled; scrab·bling 1** : SCRAPE, SCRATCH **2** : CLAMBER, SCRAMBLE **3** : to work hard and long **4** : SCRIBBLE — **scrabble** *n* — **scrab·bler** *n*

scrag·gly \'skra-glē\ *adj* : IRREGULAR; *also* : RAGGED, UNKEMPT

scram \'skram\ *vb* **scrammed; scram·ming** : to go away at once

scram·ble \'skram-bəl\ *vb* **scram·bled; scram·bling 1** : to clamber clumsily around **2** : to struggle for or as if for possession of something **3** : to spread irregularly **4** : to mix together **5** : to cook (eggs) by stirring during frying — **scramble** *n*

¹scrap \'skrap\ *n* **1** : FRAGMENT, PIECE **2** : discarded material : REFUSE

²scrap *vb* **scrapped; scrap·ping 1** : to make into scrap ⟨~ a battleship⟩ **2** : to get rid of as useless

³scrap *n* : FIGHT

⁴scrap *vb* **scrapped; scrap·ping** : FIGHT, QUARREL — **scrap·per** *n*

scrap·book \'skrap-ˌbu̇k\ *n* : a blank book in which mementos are kept

¹scrape \'skrāp\ *vb* **scraped; scrap·ing 1** : to remove by drawing a knife over; *also* : to clean or smooth by rubbing off the covering **2** : to damage or injure the surface of by contact with something rough **3** : to draw across a surface with a grating sound **4** : to get together (money) by strict economy **5** : to get along with difficulty — **scrap·er** *n*

²scrape *n* **1** : the act or the effect of scraping **2** : a bow accompanied by a drawing back of the foot **3** : an unpleasant predicament

¹scrap·py \'skra-pē\ *adj* **scrap·pi·er; -est** : DISCONNECTED, FRAGMENTARY

²scrappy *adj* **scrap·pi·er; -est 1** : QUARRELSOME **2** : having an aggressive and determined spirit

¹scratch \'skrach\ *vb* **1** : to scrape, dig, or rub with or as if with claws or nails ⟨a dog ~*ing* at the door⟩ ⟨~*ed* my arm⟩ **2** : SCRAPE **3** ⟨~*ed* his nails across the blackboard⟩ **3** : SCRAPE **4 4** : to cancel or erase by or as if by drawing a line through **5** : to withdraw from a contest — **scratchy** *adj*

²scratch *n* **1** : a mark or injury made by or as if by scratching; *also* : a sound so made **2** : the starting line in a race **3** : a point at the beginning of a project at which nothing has been done ahead of time ⟨built from ~⟩

³scratch *adj* **1** : made as or used for a trial attempt ⟨~ paper⟩ **2** : made or done by chance ⟨a ~ hit⟩

scrawl \'skrȯl\ *vb* : to write hastily and carelessly — **scrawl** *n*

scraw·ny \'skrȯ-nē\ *adj* **scraw·ni·er; -est** : very thin : SKINNY

¹scream \'skrēm\ *vb* : to cry out loudly and shrilly

²scream *n* : a loud shrill cry

scream·ing *adj* : so striking as to attract notice as if by screaming ⟨~ headlines⟩

screech \'skrēch\ *vb* : SHRIEK — **screech** *n* — **screechy** \'skrē-chē\ *adj*

¹screen \'skrēn\ *n* **1** : a device or partition used to hide, restrain, protect, or decorate ⟨a window ~⟩; *also* : something that shelters, protects, or conceals **2** : a sieve or perforated material for separating finer from coarser parts (as of sand) **3** : a surface on which an image is made to appear (as in television) **4** : the motion-picture industry

²screen *vb* **1** : to shield with or as if with a screen **2** : to separate with or as if with a screen **3** : to present (as a motion picture) on the screen

screen·ing \'skrē-niŋ\ *n* **1** : metal or plastic mesh (as for window screens) **2** : a showing of a motion picture

¹screw \'skrü\ *n* [ME, fr. MF *escroe* female screw, nut, fr. ML *scrofa*, fr. L, sow] **1** : a machine consisting of a solid cylinder with a spiral groove around it and a corresponding hollow cylinder into which it fits **2** : a naillike metal piece with a spiral groove and a head with a slot that is inserted into material by rotating and is used to fasten pieces of solid material together **3** : PROPELLER

²screw *vb* **1** : to fasten or close by means of a screw **2** : to operate or adjust by means of a screw **3** : to move or cause to move spirally; *also* : to close or set in position by such an action

screw·ball \'skrü-ˌbȯl\ *n* **1** : a baseball pitch breaking in a direction opposite to a curve **2** : a whimsical, eccentric, or crazy person

screw·driv·er \-ˌdrī-vər\ n **1** : a tool for turning screws **2** : a drink made of vodka and orange juice

screw·worm \ˈskrü-ˌwərm\ n : an American blowfly of warm regions whose larva matures in wounds or sores of mammals and may cause disease or death; *esp* : its larva

screwy \ˈskrü-ē\ *adj* **screw·i·er; -est 1** : crazily absurd, eccentric, or unusual **2** : CRAZY, INSANE

scrib·ble \ˈskri-bəl\ *vb* **scrib·bled; scrib·bling** : to write hastily or carelessly — **scribble** *n* — **scrib·bler** *n*

scribe \ˈskrīb\ n **1** : a scholar of Jewish law in New Testament times **2** : a person whose business is the copying of writing **3** : JOURNALIST

scrim \ˈskrim\ n : a light loosely woven cotton or linen cloth

scrim·mage \ˈskri-mij\ n : the play between two football teams beginning with the snap of the ball; *also* : practice play between two teams — **scrimmage** *vb*

scrimp \ˈskrimp\ *vb* : to economize greatly ⟨∼ and save⟩

scrim·shaw \ˈskrim-ˌshȯ\ n : carved or engraved articles made orig. by American whalers usu. from baleen or whale ivory — **scrimshaw** *vb*

scrip \ˈskrip\ n **1** : a certificate showing its holder is entitled to something (as stock or land) **2** : paper money issued for temporary use in an emergency

¹script \ˈskript\ n **1** : written matter (as lines for a play or broadcast) **2** : HANDWRITING

²script *abbr* scripture

scrip·ture \ˈskrip-chər\ n **1** *cap* : the books of the Bible — often used in pl. **2** : the sacred writings of a religion — **scrip·tur·al** \ˈskrip-chə-rəl\ *adj* — **scrip·tur·al·ly** *adv*

scriv·en·er \ˈskri-və-nər\ n : SCRIBE, COPYIST, WRITER

scrod \ˈskräd\ n : a young fish (as a cod or haddock); *esp* : one split and boned for cooking

scrof·u·la \ˈskrȯ-fyə-lə\ n : tuberculosis of lymph nodes esp. in the neck

¹scroll \ˈskrōl\ n : a roll of paper or parchment for writing a document; *also* : a spiral or coiled ornamental form suggesting a loosely or partly rolled scroll

²scroll *vb* : to move or cause to move text or graphics up, down, or across a display screen

scroll saw n : JIGSAW

scro·tum \ˈskrō-təm\ n, *pl* **scro·ta** \-tə\ *or* **scrotums** [L] : a pouch that in most male mammals contains the testes

scrounge \ˈskraunj\ *vb* **scrounged; scroung·ing** : to collect by or as if by foraging

¹scrub \ˈskrəb\ n **1** : a thick growth of stunted trees or shrubs; *also* : an area of land covered with scrub **2** : an inferior domestic animal **3** : a person of insignificant size or standing **4** : a player not on the first team — **scrub** *adj* — **scrub·by** *adj*

²scrub *vb* **scrubbed; scrub·bing 1** : to clean or wash by rubbing ⟨∼ clothes⟩ ⟨∼ out a spot⟩ **2** : CANCEL

³scrub n : an act or instance of scrubbing ⟨gave the clothes a good ∼⟩

scrub·ber \ˈskrə-bər\ n : one that scrubs; *esp* : an apparatus for removing impurities esp. from gases

scruff \ˈskrəf\ n : the loose skin of the back of the neck : NAPE

scruffy \ˈskrə-fē\ *adj* **scruff·i·er; -est** : UNKEMPT, SLOVENLY

scrump·tious \ˈskrəmp-shəs\ *adj* : DELIGHTFUL, EXCELLENT; *esp* : DELICIOUS — **scrump·tious·ly** *adv*

¹scru·ple \ˈskrü-pəl\ n [ME *scrupul*, MF *scrupule*, fr. L *scrupulus*, dim. of *scrupus* source of uneasiness, lit., sharp stone] **1** : a point of conscience or honor **2** : hesitation due to ethical considerations

²scruple *vb* **scru·pled; scru·pling** : to be reluctant on grounds of conscience : HESITATE

scru·pu·lous \ˈskrü-pyə-ləs\ *adj* **1** : having moral integrity **2** : PAINSTAKING — **scru·pu·lous·ly** *adv* — **scru·pu·lous·ness** *n*

scru·ti·nize \ˈskrüt-ə-ˌnīz\ *vb* **-nized; -niz·ing** : to examine closely

scru·ti·ny \ˈskrüt-ᵊn-ē\ n, *pl* **-nies** [L *scrutinium*, fr. *scrutari* to search, examine, prob. fr. *scruta* trash] : a careful looking over **syn** inspection, examination, analysis

scu·ba \ˈskü-bə\ n [self-contained underwater breathing apparatus] : an apparatus for breathing while swimming underwater

scuba diver n : one who swims underwater with the aid of scuba gear

¹scud \ˈskəd\ *vb* **scud·ded; scud·ding** : to move speedily

²scud n : light clouds driven by the wind

¹scuff \ˈskəf\ *vb* **1** : to scrape the feet while walking : SHUFFLE **2** : to scratch or become scratched or worn away

²scuff n **1** : a mark or injury caused by scuffing **2** : a flat-soled slipper without heel strap

scuf·fle \ˈskə-fəl\ *vb* **scuf·fled; scuf·fling 1** : to struggle confusedly at close quarters **2** : to shuffle one's feet — **scuffle** *n*

¹scull \ˈskəl\ n **1** : an oar for use in sculling; *also* : one of a pair of short oars for a single oarsman **2** : a racing shell propelled by one or two persons using sculls

²scull *vb* : to propel (a boat) by an oar over the stern

scul·lery \ˈskə-lə-rē\ n, *pl* **-ler·ies** [ME, department of household in charge of dishes, fr. MF *escuelerie*, fr. *escuelle* bowl, fr. L *scutella* drinking bowl] : a small room near the kitchen used for cleaning dishes, cooking utensils, and vegetables

scul·lion \ˈskəl-yən\ n [ME *sculion*, fr. MF *escouillon* dishcloth, alter. of *escouvillon*, fr. *escouve* broom, fr. L *scopae*, lit., twigs bound together] : a kitchen helper

sculpt \ˈskəlpt\ *vb* : CARVE, SCULPTURE

sculp·tor \ˈskəlp-tər\ n : a person who produces works of sculpture

¹sculp·ture \ˈskəlp-chər\ n : the act, process, or art of carving or molding material (as stone, wood, or plastic); *also* : work produced this way — **sculp·tur·al** \ˈskəlp-chə-rəl\ *adj*

²sculpture *vb* **sculp·tured; sculp·tur·ing** : to form or alter as or as if a work of sculpture

scum \ˈskəm\ n **1** : a slimy or filmy covering on the surface of a liquid **2** : waste matter **3** : RABBLE

scup·per \ˈskə-pər\ n : an opening in the side of a ship through which water on deck is drained overboard

scurf \ˈskərf\ n : thin dry scales of skin (as dandruff); *also* : a scaly deposit or covering — **scurfy** \ˈskər-fē\ *adj*

scur·ri·lous \ˈskər-ə-ləs\ *adj* : coarsely jesting : OBSCENE, VULGAR

scur·ry \ˈskər-ē\ *vb* **scur·ried; scur·ry·ing** : SCAMPER

¹scur·vy \ˈskər-vē\ n : a disease marked by spongy gums, loosened teeth, and bleeding under the skin and caused by lack of vitamin C

²scurvy *adj* : MEAN, CONTEMPTIBLE — **scur·vi·ly** \ˈskər-və-lē\ *adv*

scutch·eon \ˈskə-chən\ n : ESCUTCHEON

¹scut·tle \ˈskət-ᵊl\ n : a pail for carrying coal

²scuttle n : a small opening with a lid esp. in the deck, side, or bottom of a ship

³scuttle *vb* **scut·tled; scut·tling** : to cut a hole in the deck, side, or bottom of (a ship) in order to sink

⁴scuttle *vb* **scut·tled; scut·tling** : SCURRY, SCAMPER

scut·tle·butt \ˈskət-ᵊl-ˌbət\ n : GOSSIP

scythe \ˈsīth\ n : an implement for mowing (as grass or grain) by hand — **scythe** *vb*

SD *abbr* **1** South Dakota **2** special delivery

S Dak *abbr* South Dakota

SDI *abbr* Strategic Defense Initiative

Se *symbol* selenium

SE *abbr* southeast

sea \\'sē\ *n* **1** : a large body of salt water **2** : OCEAN **3** : rough water; *also* : a large wave **4** : something likened to the sea esp. in vastness — **sea** *adj* — **at sea** : LOST, BEWILDERED

sea anemone *n* : any of numerous coelenterate polyps whose form, bright and varied colors, and cluster of tentacles superficially resemble a flower

sea·bird \\'sē-ıbərd\ *n* : a bird (as a gull) frequenting the open ocean

sea·board \-ıbōrd\ *n* : SEACOAST; *also* : the land bordering a coast

sea·coast \-ıkōst\ *n* : the shore of the sea

sea·far·er \-ıfar-ər\ *n* : SEAMAN

sea·far·ing \-ıfar-iŋ\ *n* : the use of the sea for travel or transportation — **seafaring** *adj*

sea·food \-ıfüd\ *n* : edible marine fish and shellfish

sea·go·ing \-ıgō-iŋ\ *adj* : OCEANGOING

sea horse *n* : any of a genus of small marine fishes with the head and forepart of the body sharply flexed like the head and neck of a horse

¹seal \\'sēl\ *n, pl* **seals** *also* **seal** **1** : any of numerous large carnivorous sea mammals occurring chiefly in cold regions and having limbs adapted for swimming **2** : the pelt of a seal

²seal *vb* : to hunt seals

³seal *n* **1** : GUARANTEE, PLEDGE **2** : a device having a raised design that can be stamped on clay or wax; *also* : the impression made by stamping with such a device **3** : something that seals or closes up ⟨safety ∼⟩

⁴seal *vb* **1** : to affix a seal to; *also* : AUTHENTICATE **2** : to fasten with or as if with a seal to prevent tampering **3** : to close or make secure against access, leakage, or passage **4** : to determine irrevocably ⟨∼ed his fate⟩

sea–lane \\'sē-ılān\ *n* : an established sea route

seal·ant \\'sē-lənt\ *n* : a sealing agent

seal·er \\'sē-lər\ *n* : a coat applied to prevent subsequent coats of paint or varnish from sinking in

sea level *n* : the level of the surface of the sea esp. at its mean midway between mean high and low water

sea lion *n* : any of several large Pacific seals with external ears

seal·skin \\'sēl-ıskin\ *n* **1** : ¹SEAL **2** : a garment of sealskin

¹seam \\'sēm\ *n* **1** : the line of junction of two edges and esp. of edges of fabric sewn together **2** : a layer of mineral matter **3** : WRINKLE — **seam·less** *adj*

²seam *vb* **1** : to join by or as if by sewing **2** : WRINKLE, FURROW

sea·man \\'sē-mən\ *n* **1** : one who assists in the handling of ships : MARINER **2** : an enlisted man in the navy ranking next below a petty officer third class

seaman apprentice *n* : an enlisted man in the navy ranking next below a seaman

seaman recruit *n* : an enlisted man of the lowest rank in the navy

sea·man·ship \\'sē-mən-ıship\ *n* : the art or skill of handling a ship

sea·mount \\'sē-ımaùnt\ *n* : an underwater mountain

seam·stress \\'sēm-strəs\ *n* : a woman who does sewing

seamy \\'sē-mē\ *adj* **seam·i·er; -est** **1** : UNPLEASANT **2** : DEGRADED, SORDID

sé·ance \\'sā-ıäns\ *n* [F] : a meeting to receive communications from spirits

sea·plane \\'sē-ıplān\ *n* : an airplane that can take off from and land on water

sea·port \-ıpōrt\ *n* : a port for oceangoing ships

sear \\'sir\ *vb* **1** : WITHER **2** : to burn or scorch esp. on the surface; *also* : BRAND — **sear** *n*

¹search \\'sərch\ *vb* [ME *cerchen*, fr. MF *cerchier* to go about, survey, search, fr. LL *circare* to go about, fr. L *circum* round about] **1** : to look through in trying to find something **2** : SEEK **3** : PROBE — **search·er** *n*

²search *n* : the act of searching

search·light \-ılīt\ *n* : an apparatus for projecting a powerful beam of light; *also* : the light projected

sea·scape \\'sē-ıskāp\ *n* **1** : a view of the sea **2** : a picture representing a scene at or of the sea

sea·shell \\'sē-ıshel\ *n* : the shell of a marine animal and esp. a mollusk

sea·shore \-ıshōr\ *n* : the shore of a sea

sea·sick \-ısik\ *adj* : nauseated by or as if by the motion of a ship — **sea·sick·ness** *n*

sea·side \\'sē-ısīd\ *n* : SEASHORE

¹sea·son \\'sē-zən\ *n* [ME, fr. OF *saison*, fr. L *sation-, satio* action of sowing, fr. *serere* to sow] **1** : one of the divisions of the year (as spring or summer) **2** : a special period ⟨the Easter ∼⟩ — **sea·son·al** \-zə-nəl\ *adj* — **sea·son·al·ly** *adv*

²season *vb* **1** : to make pleasant to the taste by use of salt, pepper, or spices **2** : to make (as by aging or drying) suitable for use **3** : to accustom or habituate to something (as hardship) **syn** harden, inure, acclimatize, toughen — **sea·son·er** *n*

sea·son·able \\'sē-zə-nə-bəl\ *adj* : occurring at a good or proper time **syn** timely, propitious, opportune — **sea·son·ably** \-blē\ *adv*

sea·son·ing *n* : something that seasons : CONDIMENT

¹seat \\'sēt\ *n* **1** : a chair, bench, or stool for sitting on **2** : a place which serves as a capital or center

²seat *vb* **1** : to place in or on a seat **2** : to provide seats for

seat belt *n* : straps designed to hold a person in a seat

SEATO \\'sē-ıtō\ *abbr* Southeast Asia Treaty Organization

seat–of–the–pants *adj* : employing or based on personal experience, judgment, and effort rather than technological aids ⟨∼ navigation⟩

sea urchin *n* : any of numerous spiny marine echinoderms having thin brittle globular shells

sea·wall \\'sē-ıwòl\ *n* : an embankment to protect the shore from erosion

¹sea·ward \\'sē-wərd\ *n* : the direction or side away from land and toward the open sea

²seaward *also* **sea·wards** \-wərdz\ *adv* : toward the sea

³seaward *adj* **1** : directed or situated toward the sea **2** : coming from the sea

sea·wa·ter \\'sē-ıwò-tər, -ıwä-\ *n* : water in or from the sea

sea·way \-ıwā\ *n* : an inland waterway that admits ocean shipping

sea·weed \-ıwēd\ *n* : a marine alga (as a kelp); *also* : a mass of marine algae

sea·wor·thy \-ıwər-thē\ *adj* : fit for a sea voyage ⟨a ∼ ship⟩

se·ba·ceous \si-'bā-shəs\ *adj* : of, relating to, or secreting fatty material

sec *abbr* **1** second; secondary **2** secretary **3** section **4** [L *secundum*] according to

SEC *abbr* Securities and Exchange Commission

se·cede \si-'sēd\ *vb* **se·ced·ed; se·ced·ing** : to withdraw from an organized body and esp. from a political body

se·ces·sion \si-'se-shən\ *n* : the act of seceding — **se·ces·sion·ist** *n*

se·clude \si-'klüd\ *vb* **se·clud·ed; se·clud·ing** : to keep or shut away from others

se·clu·sion \si-'klü-zhən\ *n* : the act of secluding : the state of being secluded — **se·clu·sive** \-siv\ *adj*

¹sec·ond \\'se-kənd\ *adj* [ME, fr. OF, fr. L *secundus* second, following, favorable, fr. *sequi* to follow] **1** : being number two in a countable series **2** : next after the first

3 : ALTERNATE ⟨every ~ year⟩ — **second** or **sec·ond·ly** adv

²**second** n **1 :** one that is second **2 :** one who assists another (as in a duel) **3 :** an inferior or flawed article (as of merchandise) **4 :** the second forward gear in a motor vehicle

³**second** n [ME secunde, fr. ML secunda, fr. L, fem. of secundus second; fr. its being the second division of a unit into 60 parts, as a minute is the first] **1 :** the 60th part of a minute of time or angular measure **2 :** an instant of time

⁴**second** vb **1 :** to encourage or give support to **2 :** to act as a second to **3 :** to support (a motion) by adding one's voice to that of a proposer

¹**sec·ond·ary** \'se-kən-ˌder-ē\ adj **1 :** second in rank, value, or occurrence : LESSER **2 :** belonging to a second or later stage of development **3 :** coming after the primary or elementary ⟨~ schools⟩ **syn** subordinate, collateral, dependent

²**secondary** n, pl **-ar·ies :** the defensive backfield of a football team

secondary sex characteristic n **:** a physical characteristic that appears in members of one sex at puberty or in seasonal breeders at breeding season and is not directly concerned with reproduction

second fiddle n **:** one that plays a supporting or subservient role

sec·ond–guess \ˌse-kənd-'ges\ vb **1 :** to think out other strategies or explanations for after the event **2 :** to seek to anticipate or predict

sec·ond·hand \-'hand\ adj **1 :** not original **2 :** not new : USED ⟨~ clothes⟩ **3 :** dealing in used goods

second lieutenant n **:** a commissioned officer (as in the army) ranking next below a first lieutenant

sec·ond–rate \ˌse-kənd-'rāt\ adj **:** INFERIOR

second–story man n **:** a burglar who enters by an upstairs window

sec·ond–string \'se-kənd-'striŋ\ adj **:** being a substitute (as on a team)

se·cre·cy \'sē-krə-sē\ n, pl **-cies 1 :** the habit or practice of being secretive **2 :** the condition of being hidden or concealed

¹**se·cret** \'sē-krət\ adj **1 :** HIDDEN, CONCEALED ⟨a ~ staircase⟩ **2 :** COVERT, STEALTHY; also **:** engaged in detecting or spying ⟨a ~ agent⟩ **3 :** kept from general knowledge — **se·cret·ly** adv

²**secret** n **1 :** MYSTERY **2 :** something kept from the knowledge of others

sec·re·tar·i·at \ˌse-krə-'ter-ē-ət\ n **1 :** the office of a secretary **2 :** the secretarial staff in an office **3 :** the administrative department of a governmental organization ⟨the UN ~⟩

sec·re·tary \'se-krə-ˌter-ē\ n, pl **-tar·ies 1 :** a person employed to handle records, correspondence, and routine work for another person **2 :** an officer of a corporation or business who is in charge of correspondence and records **3 :** an official at the head of a department of government **4 :** a writing desk — **sec·re·tari·al** \ˌse-krə-'ter-ē-əl\ adj — **sec·re·tary·ship** \'se-krə-ˌter-ē-ˌship\ n

¹**se·crete** \si-'krēt\ vb **se·cret·ed; se·cret·ing :** to form and give off (a secretion)

²**se·crete** \si-'krēt, 'sē-krət\ vb **se·cret·ed; se·cret·ing : HIDE, CONCEAL

se·cre·tion \si-'krē-shən\ n **1 :** the process of secreting something **2 :** a product of glandular activity; esp **:** one (as a hormone) useful in the organism **3 :** the act of hiding something — **se·cre·to·ry** \'sē-krə-ˌtōr-ē\ adj

se·cre·tive \'sē-krə-tiv, si-'krē-\ adj **:** tending to keep secrets or to act secretly — **se·cre·tive·ly** adv — **se·cre·tive·ness** n

¹**sect** \'sekt\ n **1 :** a dissenting religious body **2 :** a religious denomination **3 :** a group adhering to a distinctive doctrine or to a leader

²**sect** abbr section; sectional

¹**sec·tar·i·an** \sek-'ter-ē-ən\ adj **1 :** of or relating to a sect or sectarian **2 :** limited in character or scope — **sec·tar·i·an·ism** n

²**sectarian** n **1 :** an adherent of a sect **2 :** a narrow or bigoted person

sec·ta·ry \'sek-tə-rē\ n, pl **-ries :** a member of a sect

¹**sec·tion** \'sek-shən\ n **1 :** a part cut off or separated **2 :** a distinct part **3 :** the appearance that a thing has or would have if cut straight through

²**section** vb **1 :** to separate or become separated into sections **2 :** to represent in sections

sec·tion·al \'sek-shə-nəl\ adj **1 :** of, relating to, or characteristic of a section **2 :** local or regional rather than general in character **3 :** divided into sections — **sec·tion·al·ism** n

sec·tor \'sek-tər\ n **1 :** a part of a circle between two radii **2 :** an area assigned to a military leader to defend **3 :** a subdivision of society

sec·u·lar \'se-kyə-lər\ adj **1 :** not sacred or ecclesiastical **2 :** not bound by monastic vows ⟨a ~ priest⟩

sec·u·lar·ism \'se-kyə-lə-ˌri-zəm\ n **:** indifference to or exclusion of religion — **sec·u·lar·ist** \-rist\ n — **secu·larist** or **sec·u·lar·is·tic** \ˌse-kyə-lə-'ris-tik\ adj

sec·u·lar·ize \'se-kyə-lə-ˌrīz\ vb **-ized; -iz·ing 1 :** to make secular **2 :** to transfer from ecclesiastical to civil or lay use, possession, or control — **sec·u·lar·i·za·tion** \ˌse-kyə-lə-rə-'zā-shən\ n — **sec·u·lar·iz·er** \'se-kyə-lə-ˌrī-zər\ n

¹**se·cure** \si-'kyùr\ adj **se·cur·er; -est** [L securus safe, secure, fr. se without + cura care] **1 :** easy in mind : free from fear **2 :** free from danger or risk of loss : SAFE **3 :** CERTAIN, SURE — **se·cure·ly** adv

²**secure** vb **se·cured; se·cur·ing 1 :** to make safe : GUARD **2 :** to assure payment of by giving a pledge or collateral **3 :** to fasten safely ⟨~ a door⟩ **4 :** GET, ACQUIRE

se·cu·ri·ty \si-'kyùr-ə-tē\ n, pl **-ties 1 :** SAFETY **2 :** freedom from worry **3 :** something given as pledge of payment ⟨a ~ deposit⟩ **4** pl **:** bond or stock certificates **5 :** PROTECTION

secy abbr secretary

se·dan \si-'dan\ n **1 :** a covered chair borne on poles by two men **2 :** an automobile seating four or more people and usu. having a permanent top

¹**se·date** \si-'dāt\ adj **:** quiet and dignified in behavior **syn** staid, sober, serious, solemn — **se·date·ly** adv

²**sedate** vb **se·dat·ed; se·dat·ing :** to dose with sedatives — **se·da·tion** \si-'dā-shən\ n

¹**sed·a·tive** \'se-də-tiv\ adj **:** serving or tending to relieve tension

²**sedative** n **:** a sedative drug

sed·en·tary \'sed-ᵊn-ˌter-ē\ adj **:** characterized by or requiring much sitting

sedge \'sej\ n **:** any of a family of plants esp. of marshy areas that differ from the related grasses esp. in having solid stems — **sedgy** \'se-jē\ adj

sed·i·ment \'se-də-mənt\ n **1 :** the material that settles to the bottom of a liquid **2 :** material (as stones and sand) deposited by water, wind, or a glacier — **sed·i·men·ta·ry** \ˌse-də-'men-tə-rē\ adj — **sed·i·men·ta·tion** \-mən-'tā-shən, -ˌmen-\ n

se·di·tion \si-'di-shən\ n **:** the causing of discontent, insurrection, or resistance against a government — **se·di·tious** \-shəs\ adj

se·duce \si-'düs, -'dyüs\ vb **se·duced; se·duc·ing 1 :** to persuade to disobedience or disloyalty **2 :** to lead astray **3 :** to entice to sexual intercourse **syn** tempt, entice, inveigle, lure — **se·duc·er** n — **se·duc·tion** \-'dək-shən\ n — **se·duc·tive** \-tiv\ adj

sed·u·lous \'se-jə-ləs\ adj [L sedulus, fr. sedulo sincerely, diligently, fr. se without + dolus guile] **:** DILIGENT, PAINSTAKING

¹**see** \'sē\ vb **saw** \'sò\; **seen** \'sēn\; **see·ing 1 :** to perceive

by the eye; *also* : to have the power of sight **2** : EXPE-RIENCE **3** : UNDERSTAND **4** : to make sure ⟨∼ that order is kept⟩ **5** : to meet with **6** : to keep company with esp. in dating **7** : ACCOMPANY, ESCORT **syn** behold, descry, espy, view, observe, note, discern

²**see** *n* : the authority or jurisdiction of a bishop

¹**seed** \'sēd\ *n, pl* **seed** *or* **seeds 1** : the grains of plants used for sowing **2** : a ripened ovule of a flowering plant that may develop into a new plant; *also* : a plant struc-ture (as a spore or small dry fruit) capable of producing a new plant **3** : DESCENDANTS **4** : SOURCE, ORIGIN — **seed·less** *adj* — **go to seed** *or* **run to seed 1** : to develop seed **2** : DECAY

²**seed** *vb* **1** : SOW, PLANT ⟨∼ land to grass⟩ **2** : to bear or shed seeds **3** : to remove seeds from — **seed·er** *n*

seed·bed \-,bed\ *n* : soil or a bed of soil prepared for planting seed

seed·ling \'sēd-liŋ\ *n* **1** : a young plant grown from seed **2** : a young tree before it becomes a sapling

seed·time \'sēd-,tīm\ *n* : the season for sowing

seedy \'sē-dē\ *adj* **seed·i·er; -est 1** : containing or full of seeds **2** : SHABBY

seek \'sēk\ *vb* **sought** \'sȯt\; **seek·ing 1** : to search for **2** : to try to reach or obtain **3** : ATTEMPT — **seek·er** *n*

seem \'sēm\ *vb* **1** : to appear to the observation or un-derstanding **2** : to give the impression of being : APPEAR

seem·ing *adj* : outwardly apparent — **seem·ing·ly** *adv*

seem·ly \'sēm-lē\ *adj* **seem·li·er; -est 1** : conventionally proper **2** : FIT

seep \'sēp\ *vb* : to flow or pass slowly through fine pores or cracks — **seep·age** \'sē-pij\ *n*

seer \'sir\ *n* : a person who foresees or predicts events : PROPHET

seer·suck·er \'sir-,sə-kər\ *n* [Hindi *śīrśaker*, fr. Per *shīr= o-shakar*, lit., milk and sugar] : a light fabric of linen, cotton, or rayon usu. striped and slightly puckered

see·saw \'sē-,sȯ\ *n* **1** : a contest in which now one side now the other has the lead **2** : a children's sport of rid-ing up and down on the ends of a plank supported in the middle; *also* : the plank so used — **seesaw** *vb*

seethe \'sēth\ *vb* **seethed; seeth·ing** [archaic *seethe* boil] : to become violently agitated

seg·ment \'seg-mənt\ *n* **1** : a division of a thing : SECTION **2** : a part cut off from a geometrical figure (as a circle) by one or more points, lines, or planes — **seg·ment-ed** \-,men-təd\ *adj*

seg·re·gate \'se-gri-,gāt\ *vb* **-gat·ed; -gat·ing** [L *segre-gare*, fr. *se-* apart + *greg-, grex* herd, flock] : to cut off from others; *esp* : to separate by races — **seg·re·ga-tion** \,se-gri-'gā-shən\ *n*

seg·re·ga·tion·ist \,se-gri-'gā-shə-nist\ *n* : one who be-lieves in or practices the segregation of races

sei·gneur \sān-'yər\ *n, often cap* [MF, fr. ML *senior*, fr. L, adj., elder] : a feudal lord

¹**seine** \'sān\ *n* : a large weighted fishing net

²**seine** *vb* **seined; sein·ing** : to fish or catch with a seine — **sein·er** *n*

seis·mic \'sīz-mik, 'sīs-\ *adj* : of, relating to, resembling, or caused by an earthquake — **seis·mi·cal·ly** \-mik-(ə-)lē\ *adv* — **seis·mic·i·ty** \sīz-'mi-sə-tē, sīs-\ *n*

seis·mo·gram \'sīz-mə-,gram, 'sīs-\ *n* : the record of an earth tremor made by a seismograph

seis·mo·graph \-,graf\ *n* : an apparatus to measure and record seismic vibrations — **seis·mo·graph·ic** \,sīz-mə-'gra-fik, ,sīs-\ *adj* — **seis·mog·ra·phy** \sīz-'mä-grə-fē, sīs-\ *n*

seis·mol·o·gy \sīz-'mä-lə-jē, sīs-\ *n* : a science that deals with earthquakes — **seis·mo·log·i·cal** \,sīz-mə-'lä-ji-kəl, ,sīs-\ *adj* — **seis·mol·o·gist** \sīz-'mä-lə-jist, sīs-\ *n*

seis·mom·e·ter \sīz-'mä-mə-tər, sīs-\ *n* : a seismograph measuring the actual movement of the ground

seize \'sēz\ *vb* **seized; seiz·ing 1** : to lay hold of or take possession of by force **2** : ARREST **3** : UNDERSTAND **4** : to

attack or overwhelm physically : AFFLICT **syn** take, grasp, clutch, snatch, grab

sei·zure \'sē-zhər\ *n* **1** : the act of seizing : the state of being seized **2** : a sudden attack (as of disease)

sel *abbr* select; selected; selection

sel·dom \'sel-dəm\ *adv* : not often : RARELY

¹**se·lect** \sə-'lekt\ *adj* **1** : CHOSEN, PICKED; *also* : CHOICE **2** : judicious or restrictive in choice : DISCRIMINATING

²**select** *vb* : to choose from a number or group : pick out

se·lec·tion \sə-'lek-shən\ *n* **1** : the act or process of se-lecting **2** : something selected : CHOICE **3** : a natural or artificial process that tends to favor the survival and re-production of individuals with certain traits but not those with others

se·lec·tive \sə-'lek-tiv\ *adj* : of or relating to selection : selecting or tending to select ⟨∼ shoppers⟩

selective service *n* : a system for calling men up for mil-itary service : DRAFT

se·lect·man \si-'lekt-,man, -mən\ *n* : one of a board of officials elected in towns of most New England states to administer town affairs

se·le·ni·um \sə-'lē-nē-əm\ *n* : a nonmetallic chemical el-ement — see ELEMENT table

self \'self\ *n, pl* **selves** \'selvz\ **1** : the essential person distinct from all other persons in identity **2** : a partic-ular side of a person's character **3** : personal interest : SELFISHNESS

self- *comb form* **1** : oneself : itself **2** : of oneself or itself **3** : by oneself or itself; *also* : automatic **4** : to, for, or toward oneself

self-abasement	self-deception
self-absorbed	self-defeating
self-absorption	self-definition
self-accusation	self-delusion
self-acting	self-denial
self-addressed	self-denying
self-adjusting	self-deprecating
self-administer	self-deprecation
self-advancement	self-depreciation
self-aggrandizement	self-despair
self-aggrandizing	self-destruct
self-analysis	self-destruction
self-appointed	self-destructive
self-asserting	self-determination
self-assertion	self-discipline
self-assertive	self-distrust
self-assurance	self-doubt
self-assured	self-educated
self-awareness	self-employed
self-betrayal	self-employment
self-closing	self-esteem
self-conceit	self-examination
self-concern	self-explaining
self-condemned	self-explanatory
self-confessed	self-expression
self-confidence	self-forgetful
self-confident	self-giving
self-congratulation	self-governing
self-congratulatory	self-government
self-constituted	self-hate
self-contradiction	self-help
self-contradictory	self-hypnosis
self-control	self-identity
self-correcting	self-image
self-created	self-importance
self-criticism	self-important
self-cultivation	self-imposed
self-deceit	self-improvement

\ə\abut \ᵊ\kitten \ər\further \a\ash \ā\ace \ä\mop, mar \au̇\out \ch\chin \e\bet \ē\easy \g\go \i\hit \ī\ice \j\job \ŋ\sing \ō\go \ȯ\law \ȯi\boy \th\thin \t͟h\the \ü\loot \u̇\foot \y\yet \zh\vision *see also* Pronunciation Symbols page

self-incrimination
self-induced
self-indulgence
self-indulgent
self-inflicted
self-interest
self-knowledge
self-limiting
self-love
self-lubricating
self-luminous
self-operating
self-perception
self-perpetuating
self-pity
self-portrait
self-possessed
self-possession
self-preservation
self-proclaimed
self-propelled
self-propelling
self-protection
self-realization
self-referential

self-regard
self-reliance
self-reliant
self-reproach
self-respect
self-respecting
self-restraint
self-revelation
self-rule
self-sacrifice
self-sacrificing
self-satisfaction
self-satisfied
self-service
self-serving
self-starting
self-styled
self-sufficiency
self-sufficient
self-supporting
self-sustaining
self-taught
self-torment
self-winding
self-worth

self–cen·tered \'self-'sen-tərd\ *adj* : concerned only with one's own self — **self–cen·tered·ness** *n*

self–com·posed \₁self-kəm-'pōzd\ *adj* : having control over one's emotions

self–con·scious \'self-'kän-chəs\ *adj* : uncomfortably conscious of oneself as an object of observation by others — **self–con·scious·ly** *adv* — **self–con·scious·ness** *n*

self–con·tained \₁self-kən-'tānd\ *adj* 1 : complete in itself 2 : showing self-control; *also* : reserved in manner

self–de·fense \'self-di-'fens\ *n* 1 : a plea of justification for the use of force or for homicide 2 : the act of defending oneself, one's property, or a close relative

self–ef·fac·ing \-ə-'fā-siŋ\ *adj* : RETIRING, SHY

self–ev·i·dent \₁self-'e-və-dənt\ *adj* : evident without proof or reasoning

self–fer·til·iza·tion \₁self-₁fərt-ᵊl-ə-'zā-shən\ *n* : fertilization of a plant or animal by its own pollen or sperm

self–ful·fill·ing \₁self-fül-'fi-liŋ\ *adj* : becoming real or true by virtue of having been predicted or expected ⟨a ∼ prophecy⟩

self·ish \'sel-fish\ *adj* : concerned with one's own welfare excessively or without regard for others — **self·ish·ly** *adv* — **self·ish·ness** *n*

self·less \'self-ləs\ *adj* : UNSELFISH — **self·less·ness** *n*

self–made \'self-'mād\ *adj* : having achieved success or prominence by one's own efforts ⟨a ∼ man⟩

self–pol·li·na·tion \₁self-₁pä-lə-'nā-shən\ *n* : pollination of a flower by its own pollen or sometimes by pollen from another flower on the same plant

self–reg·u·lat·ing \'self-'re-gyə-₁lā-tiŋ\ *adj* : AUTOMATIC

self–righ·teous \'self-'rī-chəs\ *adj* : strongly convinced of one's own righteousness — **self–righ·teous·ly** *adv*

self·same \'self-₁sām\ *adj* : precisely the same : IDENTICAL

self–seal·ing \'self-'sē-liŋ\ *adj* : capable of sealing itself (as after puncture)

self–seek·ing \'self-'sē-kiŋ\ *adj* : seeking only to further one's own interests — **self–seeking** *n*

self–start·er \-'stär-tər\ *n* : a person who has initiative

self–will \'self-'wil\ *n* : OBSTINACY

sell \'sel\ *vb* **sold** \'sōld\; **sell·ing** 1 : to transfer (property) in return for money or something else of value 2 : to deal in as a business 3 : to be sold ⟨cars are ∼ing well⟩ — **sell·er** *n*

sell out *vb* 1 : to dispose of entirely by sale; *esp* : to sell one's business 2 : BETRAY — **sell·out** \'sel-₁aüt\ *n*

selt·zer \'selt-sər\ *n* [modif. of G *Selterser (Wasser)* wa-

ter of Selters, fr. Nieder *Selters,* Germany] : artificially carbonated water

sel·vage *or* **sel·vedge** \'sel-vij\ *n* : the edge of a woven fabric so formed as to prevent raveling

selves *pl of* SELF

sem *abbr* 1 semicolon 2 seminar 3 seminary

se·man·tic \si-'man-tik\ *also* **se·man·ti·cal** \-ti-kəl\ *adj* : of or relating to meaning in language

se·man·tics \si-'man-tiks\ *n sing or pl* : the study of meanings in language

sema·phore \'se-mə-₁fōr\ *n* 1 : a visual signaling apparatus with movable arms 2 : signaling by hand-held flags

semaphore 2: alphabet; 3 positions following Z: error, end of word, numerals follow; numerals 1,2,3,4,5,6,7,8,9,0 same as A through J

sem·blance \'sem-bləns\ *n* 1 : outward appearance 2 : IMAGE, LIKENESS

se·men \'sē-mən\ *n* [NL, fr. L, seed] : a sticky whitish fluid of the male reproductive tract that contains the sperm

se·mes·ter \sə-'mes-tər\ *n* [G, fr. L *semestris* half= yearly, fr. *sex* six + *mensis* month] 1 : half a year 2 : one of the two terms into which many colleges divide the school year

semi- \'se-mi, -₁mī\ *prefix* 1 : precisely half of 2 : half in quantity or value; *also* : half of or occurring halfway through a specified period 3 : partly : incompletely 4 : partial : incomplete 5 : having some of the characteristics of

semiannual
semiarid
semicentennial
semicircle
semicircular
semicivilized
semiclassical
semiconscious
semidarkness
semidivine
semiformal
semigloss
semi–independent
semiliquid
semiliterate
semimonthly

semiofficial
semipermanent
semipolitical
semiprecious
semiprivate
semiprofessional
semireligious
semiretired
semiskilled
semisoft
semisolid
semisweet
semitransparent
semiweekly
semiyearly

semi \'se-₁mī\ *n, pl* **sem·is** : SEMITRAILER

semi·au·to·mat·ic \₁se-mē-₁ȯ-tə-'ma-tik\ *adj, of a firearm* : reloading by mechanical means but requiring release and another press of the trigger to fire again

semi·co·lon \'se-mi-₁kō-lən\ *n* : a punctuation mark ; used esp. to separate major sentence elements

semi·con·duc·tor \₁se-mi-kən-'dək-tər\ *n* : a substance whose electrical conductivity is between that of a conductor and an insulator — **semi·con·duct·ing** *adj*

[1]**semi·fi·nal** \ˌse-mi-ˈfīn-ᵊl\ *adj* : being next to the last in an elimination tournament

[2]**semi·fi·nal** \ˈse-mi-ˌfīn-ᵊl\ *n* : a semifinal round or match — **semi·fi·nal·ist** \-ist\ *n*

semi·lu·nar \-ˈlü-nər\ *adj* : shaped like a crescent

sem·i·nal \ˈse-mən-ᵊl\ *adj* **1** : of, relating to, or consisting of seed or semen **2** : containing or contributing the seeds of later development : CREATIVE, ORIGINAL — **sem·i·nal·ly** *adv*

sem·i·nar \ˈse-mə-ˌnär\ *n* **1** : a course of study pursued by a group of advanced students doing original research under a professor **2** : CONFERENCE

sem·i·nary \ˈse-mə-ˌner-ē\ *n, pl* **-nar·ies** [ME, seedbed, nursery, fr. L *seminarium*, fr. *semen* seed] : an educational institution; *esp* : one that gives theological training — **sem·i·nar·i·an** \ˌse-mə-ˈner-ē-ən\ *n*

Sem·i·nole \ˈse-mə-ˌnōl\ *n, pl* **Semi·noles** *or* **Seminole** : a member of an American Indian people of Florida

semi·per·me·able \ˌse-mi-ˈpər-mē-ə-bəl\ *adj* : partially but not freely or wholly permeable; *esp* : permeable to some usu. small molecules but not to other usu. larger particles ⟨a ∼ membrane⟩ — **semi·per·me·abil·i·ty** \-ˌpər-mē-ə-ˈbi-lə-tē\ *n*

Sem·ite \ˈse-ˌmīt\ *n* : a member of any of a group of peoples (as the Hebrews or Arabs) of southwestern Asia — **Se·mit·ic** \sə-ˈmi-tik\ *adj*

semi·trail·er \ˈse-mi-ˌtrā-lər, -ˌmī-\ *n* : a freight trailer that when attached is supported at its forward end by the truck tractor; *also* : a semitrailer with attached tractor

semp·stress \ˈsemp-strəs\ *var of* SEAMSTRESS

[1]**sen** \ˈsen\ *n, pl* **sen** — see *yen* at MONEY table

[2]**sen** *n, pl* **sen** — see *dollar, ringgit, rupiah* at MONEY table

[3]**sen** *n, pl* **sen** — see *riel* at MONEY table

[4]**sen** *abbr* **1** senate; senator **2** senior

sen·ate \ˈse-nət\ *n* : the second of two chambers of a legislature

sen·a·tor \ˈse-nə-tər\ *n* : a member of a senate — **sen·a·to·ri·al** \ˌse-nə-ˈtȯr-ē-əl\ *adj*

send \ˈsend\ *vb* **sent** \ˈsent\; **send·ing 1** : to cause to go **2** : EMIT **3** : to propel or drive esp. with force **4** : to put or bring into a certain condition — **send·er** *n*

send–off \ˈsend-ˌȯf\ *n* : a demonstration of goodwill and enthusiasm at the start of a new venture (as a trip)

se·ne \ˈsā-(ˌ)nā\ *n, pl* **sene** — see *tala* at MONEY table

Sen·e·ca \ˈse-ni-kə\ *n, pl* **Seneca** *or* **Senecas** : a member of an American Indian people of western New York

Sen·e·ga·lese \ˌse-ni-gə-ˈlēz, -ˈlēs\ *n, pl* **Senegalese** : a native or inhabitant of Senegal — **Senegalese** *adj*

se·nes·cence \si-ˈnes-ᵊns\ *n* : the state of being old; *also* : the process of becoming old — **se·nes·cent** \-ᵊnt\ *adj*

se·nile \ˈsē-ˌnīl, ˈse-\ *adj* : OLD, AGED; *esp* : exhibiting a loss of mental ability associated with old age — **se·nil·i·ty** \si-ˈni-lə-tē\ *n*

[1]**se·nior** \ˈsē-nyər\ *n* **1** : a person older or of higher rank than another **2** : a member of the graduating class of a high school or college

[2]**senior** *adj* [ME, fr. L, older, elder, compar. of *senex* old] **1** : ELDER **2** : more advanced in dignity or rank **3** : belonging to the final year of a school or college course

senior chief petty officer *n* : a petty officer in the navy or coast guard ranking next below a master chief petty officer

senior citizen *n* : an elderly person; *esp* : one who has retired

senior high school *n* : a school usu. including grades 10 to 12

se·nior·i·ty \sēn-ˈyȯr-ə-tē\ *n* **1** : the quality or state of being senior **2** : a privileged status owing to length of continuous service

senior master sergeant *n* : a noncommissioned officer in

the air force ranking next below a chief master sergeant

sen·i·ti \ˈse-nə-tē\ *n, pl* **seniti** — see *pa'anga* at MONEY table

sen·na \ˈse-nə\ *n* **1** : CASSIA 2; *esp* : one used medicinally **2** : the dried leaflets or pods of a cassia used as a purgative

sen·sa·tion \sen-ˈsā-shən\ *n* **1** : awareness (as of noise or heat) or a mental process (as seeing or hearing) due to stimulation of a sense organ; *also* : an indefinite bodily feeling **2** : a condition of excitement; *also* : the thing that causes this condition

sen·sa·tion·al \-shə-nəl\ *adj* **1** : of or relating to sensation or the senses **2** : arousing an intense and usu. superficial interest or emotional reaction — **sen·sa·tion·al·ly** *adv*

sen·sa·tion·al·ism \-nə-ˌli-zəm\ *n* : the use or effect of sensational subject matter or treatment — **sen·sa·tion·al·ist** \-nə-list\ *adj or n* — **sen·sa·tion·al·is·tic** \-ˌsā-shə-nə-ˈlis-tik\ *adj*

sen·sa·tion·al·ize \-nə-ˌlīz\ *vb* **-ized; -iz·ing** : to present in a sensational manner

[1]**sense** \ˈsens\ *n* **1** : semantic content : MEANING **2** : the faculty of perceiving by means of sense organs; *also* : a bodily function or mechanism (as sight, hearing, or smell) basically involving a stimulus and a sense organ **3** : SENSATION, AWARENESS **4** : INTELLIGENCE, JUDGMENT **5** : OPINION ⟨the ∼ of the meeting⟩ — **sense·less** *adj* — **sense·less·ly** *adv*

[2]**sense** *vb* **sensed; sens·ing 1** : to be or become aware of ⟨∼ danger⟩; *also* : to perceive by the senses **2** : to detect (as radiation) automatically

sense organ *n* : a bodily structure (as an eye or ear) that receives stimuli (as heat or light) which excite nerve cells to send information to the brain

sen·si·bil·i·ty \ˌsen-sə-ˈbi-lə-tē\ *n, pl* **-ties** : delicacy of feeling : SENSITIVITY

sen·si·ble \ˈsen-sə-bəl\ *adj* **1** : capable of being perceived by the senses or the mind; *also* : capable of receiving sense impressions **2** : AWARE, CONSCIOUS **3** : REASONABLE, RATIONAL — **sen·si·bly** \-blē\ *adv*

sen·si·tive \ˈsen-sə-tiv\ *adj* **1** : subject to excitation by or responsive to stimuli **2** : having power of feeling **3** : of such a nature as to be easily affected **4** : TOUCHY ⟨a ∼ issue⟩ — **sen·si·tive·ness** *n* — **sen·si·tiv·i·ty** \ˌsen-sə-ˈti-və-tē\ *n*

sensitive plant *n* : any of several mimosas with leaves that fold or droop when touched

sen·si·tize \ˈsen-sə-ˌtīz\ *vb* **-tized; -tiz·ing** : to make or become sensitive or hypersensitive — **sen·si·ti·za·tion** \ˌsen-sə-tə-ˈzā-shən\ *n*

sen·sor \ˈsen-ˌsȯr, -sər\ *n* : a device that responds to a physical stimulus

sen·so·ry \ˈsen-sə-rē\ *adj* : of or relating to sensation or the senses

sen·su·al \ˈsen-shə-wəl\ *adj* **1** : relating to gratification of the senses **2** : devoted to the pleasures of the senses — **sen·su·al·ist** *n* — **sen·su·al·i·ty** \ˌsen-shə-ˈwa-lə-tē\ *n* — **sen·su·al·ly** *adv*

sen·su·ous \ˈsen-shə-wəs\ *adj* **1** : relating to the senses or to things that can be perceived by the senses **2** : VOLUPTUOUS — **sen·su·ous·ly** *adv* — **sen·su·ous·ness** *n*

sent *past and past part of* SEND

sen·te \ˈsen-tē\ *n, pl* **li·cen·te** *or* **li·sen·te** \li-ˈsen-tē\ — see *loti* at MONEY table

[1]**sen·tence** \ˈsent-ᵊns, -ᵊnz\ *n* [ME, fr. MF, fr. L *sententia*, lit., feeling, opinion, fr. *sentire* to feel] **1** : the punishment set by a court **2** : a grammatically self-contained

\ə\abut \ᵊ\kitten \ər\further \a\ash \ā\ace \ä\mop, mar \aú\out \ch\chin \e\bet \ē\easy \g\go \i\hit \ī\ice \j\job \ŋ\sing \ō\go \ȯ\law \ȯi\boy \th\thin \th\the \ü\loot \ù\foot \y\yet \zh\vision *see also* Pronunciation Symbols page speech unit that expresses an assertion, a question, a command, a wish, or an exclamation

²**sen·tence** *vb* **sen·tenced; sen·tenc·ing** : to impose a sentence on

sen·ten·tious \sen-'ten-chəs\ *adj* : using wise sayings or proverbs; *also* : using pompous language

sen·tient \'sen-chənt, -chē-ənt\ *adj* : capable of feeling : having perception

sen·ti·ment \'sen-tə-mənt\ *n* 1 : FEELING; *also* : thought and judgment influenced by feeling : emotional attitude 2 : OPINION, NOTION

sen·ti·men·tal \ˌsen-tə-'ment-ᵊl\ *adj* 1 : influenced by tender feelings 2 : affecting the emotions **syn** bathetic, maudlin, mawkish, mushy — **sen·ti·men·tal·ism** *n* — **sen·ti·men·tal·ist** *n* — **sen·ti·men·tal·i·ty** \-ˌmen-'ta-lə-tē, -mən-\ *n* — **sen·ti·men·tal·ly** *adv*

sen·ti·men·tal·ize \-'ment-ᵊl-ˌīz\ *vb* **-ized; -iz·ing** 1 : to indulge in sentiment 2 : to look upon or imbue with sentiment — **sen·ti·men·tal·i·za·tion** \-ˌment-ᵊl-ə-'zā-shən\ *n*

sen·ti·mo \sen-'tē-(ˌ)mō\ *n, pl* **-mos** — see *peso* at MONEY table

sen·ti·nel \'sent-ᵊn-əl\ *n* [MF *sentinelle*, fr. It *sentinella*, fr. *sentina* vigilance, fr. *sentire* to perceive, fr. L] : one that watches or guards

sen·try \'sen-trē\ *n, pl* **sentries** : SENTINEL, GUARD

sep *abbr* separate, separated

Sep *abbr* September

SEP *abbr* simplified employee pension

se·pal \'sē-pəl, 'se-\ *n* : one of the modified leaves comprising a flower calyx

sep·a·ra·ble \'se-pə-rə-bəl\ *adj* : capable of being separated

¹**sep·a·rate** \'se-pə-ˌrāt\ *vb* **-rat·ed; -rat·ing** 1 : to set or keep apart : DISCONNECT, SEVER 2 : to keep apart by something intervening 3 : to cease to be together : PART

²**sep·a·rate** \'se-prət, -pə-rət\ *adj* 1 : not connected 2 : divided from each other 3 : SINGLE, PARTICULAR ⟨the ~ pieces of the puzzle⟩ — **sep·a·rate·ly** *adv*

³**sep·a·rate** *n* : an article of dress designed to be worn interchangeably with others to form various combinations

sep·a·ra·tion \ˌse-pə-'rā-shən\ *n* 1 : the act or process of separating : the state of being separated 2 : a point, line, means, or area of division 3 : a formal separating of a married couple by agreement but without divorce

sep·a·rat·ist \'se-prə-tist, 'se-pə-ˌrā-\ *n* : an advocate of separation (as from a political body) — **sep·a·rat·ism** \'se-prə-ˌti-zəm\ *n*

sep·a·ra·tive \'se-pə-ˌrā-tiv, 'se-prə-tiv\ *adj* : tending toward, causing, or expressing separation

sep·a·ra·tor \'se-pə-ˌrā-tər\ *n* : one that separates; *esp* : a device for separating cream from milk

se·pia \'sē-pē-ə\ *n* : a brownish gray to dark brown color

sep·sis \'sep-səs\ *n, pl* **sep·ses** \'sep-ˌsēz\ : a toxic condition due to spread of bacteria or their products in the body

Sept *abbr* September

Sep·tem·ber \sep-'tem-bər\ *n* [ME *Septembre*, fr. OF & OE, both fr. L *September* (seventh month), fr. *septem* seven] : the 9th month of the year having 30 days

sep·tic \'sep-tik\ *adj* 1 : PUTREFACTIVE 2 : relating to or characteristic of sepsis

sep·ti·ce·mia \ˌsep-tə-'sē-mē-ə\ *n* : BLOOD POISONING

septic tank *n* : a tank in which sewage is disintegrated by bacteria

sep·tu·a·ge·nar·i·an \sep-ˌtü-ə-jə-'ner-ē-ən, -ˌtyü-\ *n* : a person whose age is in the seventies — **septuagenarian** *adj*

Sep·tu·a·gint \sep-'tü-ə-jənt, -'tyü-\ *n* : a Greek version of the Old Testament prepared in the 3d and 2d centuries B.C. by Jewish scholars

sep·tum \'sep-təm\ *n, pl* **sep·ta** \-tə\ : a dividing wall or membrane esp. between bodily spaces or masses of soft tissue

se·pul·chral \sə-'pəl-krəl\ *adj* 1 : relating to burial or the grave 2 : GLOOMY

¹**sep·ul·chre** *or* **sep·ul·cher** \'se-pəl-kər\ *n* : a burial vault : TOMB

²**sepulchre** *or* **sepulcher** *vb* **-chred** *or* **-chered; -chring** *or* **-cher·ing** : BURY, ENTOMB

sep·ul·ture \'se-pəl-ˌchür\ *n* 1 : BURIAL 2 : SEPULCHRE

seq *abbr* [L *sequens, sequentes, sequentia*] the following

seqq *abbr* [L *sequentia*] the following ones

se·quel \'sē-kwəl\ *n* 1 : logical consequence 2 : a literary or cinematic work continuing a story begun in a preceding one

se·quence \'sē-kwəns\ *n* 1 : SERIES 2 : chronological order of events 3 : RESULT, SEQUEL **syn** succession, chain, progression, train — **se·quen·tial** \si-'kwen-chəl\ *adj* — **se·quen·tial·ly** *adv*

se·quent \'sē-kwənt\ *adj* 1 : SUCCEEDING, CONSECUTIVE 2 : RESULTANT

se·ques·ter \si-'kwes-tər\ *vb* : to set apart : SEGREGATE

se·ques·trate \'sē-kwəs-ˌtrāt, si-'kwes-\ *vb* **-trat·ed; -trat·ing** : SEQUESTER — **se·ques·tra·tion** \ˌsē-kwəs-'trā-shən, ˌse-\ *n*

se·quin \'sē-kwən\ *n* 1 : an old gold coin of Turkey and Italy 2 : a small metal or plastic plate used for ornamentation esp. on clothing

se·quoia \si-'kwoi-ə\ *n* : either of two huge California coniferous trees

ser *abbr* 1 serial 2 series

sera *pl of* SERUM

se·ra·glio \sə-'ral-yō\ *n, pl* **-glios** [It *serraglio*] : HAREM

se·ra·pe \sə-'rä-pē\ *n* : a colorful woolen shawl worn over the shoulders esp. by Mexican men

ser·aph \'ser-əf\ *n, pl* **ser·a·phim** \-ə-ˌfim, -ˌfēm\ *or* **ser·aphs** : one of the 6-winged angels standing in the presence of God

ser·a·phim \'ser-ə-ˌfim, -ˌfēm\ *n pl* 1 : the highest order of angels 2 *sing, pl* **seraphim** : SERAPH — **se·raph·ic** \sə-'ra-fik\ *adj*

Serb \'sərb\ *n* : a native or inhabitant of Serbia

Ser·bo–Cro·a·tian \ˌsər-(ˌ)bō-krō-'ā-shən\ *n* : a Slavic language spoken in Croatia, Bosnia and Herzegovina, Serbia, and Montenegro

sere \'sir\ *adj* : DRY, WITHERED

¹**ser·e·nade** \ˌser-ə-'nād\ *n* [F, fr. It *serenata*, fr. *sereno* clear, calm (of weather)] : music sung or played as a compliment esp. outdoors at night for a woman being courted

²**serenade** *vb* **-nad·ed; -nad·ing** : to entertain with or perform a serenade

ser·en·dip·i·ty \ˌser-ən-'di-pə-tē\ *n* [fr. its possession by the heroes of the Persian fairy tale *The Three Princes of Serendip*] : the gift of finding valuable or agreeable things not sought for — **ser·en·dip·i·tous** \-təs\ *adj*

se·rene \sə-'rēn\ *adj* 1 : CLEAR ⟨~ skies⟩ 2 : QUIET, CALM **syn** tranquil, peaceful, placid — **se·rene·ly** *adv* — **se·ren·i·ty** \sə-'re-nə-tē\ *n*

serf \'sərf\ *n* : a member of a servile class bound to the land and subject to the will of the landowner — **serf·dom** \-dəm\ *n*

serg *or* **sergt** *abbr* sergeant

serge \'sərj\ *n* : a twilled woolen cloth

ser·geant \'sär-jənt\ *n* [ME, servant, attendant, sergeant, fr. OF *sergent, serjant,* fr. L *servient-, serviens,* prp. of *servire* to serve] 1 : a noncommissioned officer (as in the army) ranking next below a staff sergeant 2 : an officer in a police force

sergeant first class *n* : a noncommissioned officer in the army ranking next below a master sergeant

sergeant major *n, pl* **sergeants major** *or* **sergeant majors** 1 : a senior staff noncommissioned officer in the army or marine corps serving as advisor in matters related to enlisted personnel **2** : a noncommissioned officer in the marine corps ranking above a first sergeant

[1]se·ri·al \'sir-ē-əl\ *adj* **1** : appearing in parts that follow regularly ⟨a ~ story⟩ **2** : effecting a series of similar acts over a period of time ⟨a ~ killer⟩; *also* : occurring in such a series — **se·ri·al·ly** *adv*

[2]serial *n* : a serial story or other writing — **se·ri·al·ist** \-ə-list\ *n*

se·ries \'sir-ēz\ *n, pl* **series** : a number of things or events arranged in order and connected by being alike in some way **syn** succession, progression, sequence, chain, train, string

seri·graph \'ser-ə-ˌgraf\ *n* : an original silk-screen print — **se·rig·ra·pher** \sə-'ri-grə-fər\ *n* — **se·rig·ra·phy** \-fē\ *n*

se·ri·ous \'sir-ē-əs\ *adj* **1** : thoughtful or subdued in appearance or manner : SOBER **2** : requiring much thought or work **3** : EARNEST, DEVOTED **4** : DANGEROUS, HARMFUL **5** : excessive or impressive in quantity or degree ⟨making ~ money⟩ **syn** grave, sedate, staid — **se·ri·ous·ly** *adv* — **se·ri·ous·ness** *n*

ser·mon \'sər-mən\ *n* [ME, fr. OF, fr. ML *sermon, sermo,* fr. L, speech, conversation, fr. *serere* to link together] **1** : a religious discourse esp. as part of a worship service **2** : a lecture on conduct or duty

se·rol·o·gy \sə-'rä-lə-jē\ *n* : a science dealing with serums and esp. their reactions and properties — **se·ro·log·i·cal** \ˌsir-ə-'lä-ji-kəl\ *or* **se·ro·log·ic** \-jik\ *adj*

se·rous \'sir-əs\ *adj* : of, relating to, resembling, or producing serum; *esp* : of thin watery constitution

ser·pent \'sər-pənt\ *n* : SNAKE

[1]ser·pen·tine \'sər-pən-ˌtēn, -ˌtīn\ *adj* **1** : SLY, CRAFTY **2** : WINDING, TURNING

[2]ser·pen·tine \-ˌtēn\ *n* : a dull-green mineral having a mottled appearance

ser·rate \'ser-ˌāt\ *adj* : having a saw-toothed edge ⟨a ~ leaf⟩

ser·ried \'ser-ēd\ *adj* : DENSE

se·rum \'sir-əm\ *n, pl* **serums** *or* **se·ra** \-ə\ [L, whey, wheylike fluid] : the clear yellowish antibody-containing fluid that can be separated from blood when it clots; *also* : a preparation of animal serum containing specific antibodies and used to prevent or cure disease

serv *abbr* service

ser·vant \'sər-vənt\ *n* : one that serves others; *esp* : a person employed for domestic or personal work

[1]serve \'sərv\ *vb* **served; serv·ing** **1** : to work as a servant **2** : to render obedience and worship to (God) **3** : to comply with the commands or demands of **4** : to work through or perform a term of service (as in the army) **5** : PUT IN ⟨*served* five years in jail⟩ **6** : to be of use : ANSWER ⟨pine boughs *served* for a bed⟩ **7** : BENEFIT **8** : to prove adequate or satisfactory for ⟨a pie that ~s eight people⟩ **9** : to make ready and pass out ⟨~ drinks⟩ **10** : to furnish or supply with something ⟨one power company *serving* the whole state⟩ **11** : to wait on ⟨~ a customer⟩ **12** : to treat or act toward in a specified way **13** : to put the ball in play (as in tennis) — **serv·er** *n*

[2]serve *n* : the act of serving a ball (as in tennis)

[1]ser·vice \'sər-vəs\ *n* **1** : the occupation of a servant **2** : HELP, BENEFIT **3** : a meeting for worship; *also* : a form followed in worship or in a ceremony ⟨burial ~⟩ **4** : the act, fact, or means of serving **5** : performance of official or professional duties **6** : SERVE **7** : a set of dishes or silverware **8** : a branch of public employment; *also* : the persons in it ⟨civil ~⟩ **9** : military or naval duty

[2]service *vb* **ser·viced; ser·vic·ing** : to do maintenance or repair work on or for

ser·vice·able \'sər-və-sə-bəl\ *adj* : prepared for service : USEFUL, USABLE

ser·vice·man \'sər-vəs-ˌman, -mən\ *n* **1** : a male member

of the armed forces **2** : a man employed to repair or maintain equipment

service station *n* : a retail station for servicing motor vehicles

ser·vice·wom·an \'sər-vəs-ˌwu̇-mən\ *n* : a female member of the armed forces

ser·vile \'sər-vəl, -ˌvīl\ *adj* **1** : befitting a slave or servant **2** : behaving like a slave : SUBMISSIVE — **ser·vil·i·ty** \ˌsər-'vi-lə-tē\ *n*

serv·ing \'sər-viŋ\ *n* : HELPING

ser·vi·tor \'sər-və-tər\ *n* : a male servant

ser·vi·tude \'sər-və-ˌtüd, -ˌtyüd\ *n* : SLAVERY, BONDAGE

ser·vo \'sər-vō\ *n, pl* **servos** **1** : SERVOMOTOR **2** : SERVOMECHANISM

ser·vo·mech·a·nism \'sər-vō-ˌme-kə-ˌni-zəm\ *n* : a device for automatically correcting the performance of a mechanism

ser·vo·mo·tor \-ˌmō-tər\ *n* : a mechanism that supplements a primary control

ses·a·me \'se-sə-mē\ *n* : a widely cultivated annual herb of warm regions; *also* : its seeds that yield an edible oil (**sesame oil**) and are used in flavoring

ses·qui·cen·ten·ni·al \ˌses-kwi-sen-'te-nē-əl\ *n* [L *sesqui-* one and a half, half again] : a 150th anniversary or its celebration — **sesquicentennial** *adj*

ses·qui·pe·da·lian \ˌses-kwə-pə-'dāl-yən\ *adj* **1** : having many syllables : LONG **2** : using long words

ses·sile \'se-sil, -səl\ *adj* : permanently attached and not free to move about

ses·sion \'se-shən\ *n* **1** : a meeting or series of meetings of a body (as a court or legislature) for the transaction of business **2** : a meeting or period devoted to a particular activity

[1]set \'set\ *vb* **set; set·ting** **1** : to cause to sit **2** : PLACE **3** : ARRANGE, ADJUST **4** : to cause to be or do **5** : SETTLE, DECREE **6** : to fix in a frame **7** : to fix at a certain amount **8** : WAGER, STAKE **9** : to make or become fast or rigid **10** : to adapt (as words) to something (as music) **11** : to become fixed or firm or solid **12** : to be suitable : FIT **13** : BROOD **14** : to have a certain direction **15** : to pass below the horizon **16** : to defeat in bridge **17** : to arrange (type) for printing — **set about** : to begin to do — **set forth** : to begin a trip — **set off 1** : to start out on a course or a trip **2** : to cause to explode — **set out** : to begin a trip or undertaking — **set sail** : to begin a voyage — **set upon** : to attack usu. with violence

[2]set *n* **1** : a setting or a being set **2** : DIRECTION, COURSE; *also* : TENDENCY **3** : FORM, BUILD **4** : the fit of something (as a coat) **5** : an artificial setting for the scene of a play or motion picture **6** : a group of tennis games in which one side wins at least six **7** : a group of persons or things of the same kind or having a common characteristic usu. classed together **8** : a collection of things and esp. of mathematical elements (as numbers or points) **9** : an electronic apparatus ⟨a television ~⟩

[3]set *adj* **1** : DELIBERATE, INTENT **2** : fixed by authority or custom **3** : RIGID **4** : PERSISTENT

set·back \'set-ˌbak\ *n* : a temporary defeat : REVERSE

set back *vb* **1** : HINDER, DELAY; *also* : REVERSE **2** : COST

set piece 1 : a composition (as in literature or music) executed in fixed or ideal form often with brilliant effect **2** : a scene, depiction, speech, or event obviously designed to have an imposing effect

set·screw \'set-ˌskrü\ *n* : a screw screwed through one part tightly upon or into another part to prevent relative movement

set·tee \se-'tē\ *n* : a bench or sofa with a back and arms

set·ter \'se-tər\ *n* : a large long-coated hunting dog

\ə\abut \ᵊ\kitten \ər\further \a\ash \ā\ace \ä\mop, mar
\au̇\out \ch\chin \e\bet \ē\easy \g\go \i\hit \ī\ice \j\job
\ŋ\sing \ō\go \ȯ\law \ȯi\boy \th\thin \t͟h\the \ü\loot \u̇\foot
\y\yet \zh\vision *see also* Pronunciation Symbols page

set·ting \'se-tiŋ\ *n* **1** : the frame in which a gem is set **2** : the time, place, and circumstances in which something occurs or develops; *also* : SCENERY **3** : music written for a text (as of a poem) **4** : the eggs that a fowl sits on for hatching at one time

set·tle \'set-ᵊl\ *vb* **set·tled; set·tling** [ME *settlen* to seat, bring to rest, come to rest, fr. OE *setlan,* fr. *setl* seat] **1** : to place so as to stay **2** : to establish in residence; *also* : COLONIZE **3** : to make compact **4** : QUIET, CALM **5** : to establish or secure permanently **6** : to direct one's efforts **7** : to fix by agreement **8** : to give legally **9** : ADJUST, ARRANGE **10** : DECIDE, DETERMINE **11** : to make a final disposition of ⟨∼ an account⟩ **12** : to come to rest **13** : to reach an agreement on **14** : to sink gradually to a lower level **15** : to become clear by depositing sediment — **set·tler** *n*

set·tle·ment \'set-ᵊl-mənt\ *n* **1** : the act or process of settling **2** : BESTOWAL ⟨a marriage ∼⟩ **3** : payment or adjustment of an account **4** : COLONY **5** : a small village **6** : an institution providing various community services esp. to large city populations **7** : adjustment of doubts and differences

set–to \'set-₁tü\ *n, pl* **set–tos** : FIGHT

set·up \'set-₁əp\ *n* **1** : the manner or act of arranging **2** : glass, ice, and nonalcoholic beverage for mixing served to patrons who supply their own liquor **3** : something (as a plot) that has been constructed or contrived; *also* : FRAME-UP

set up *vb* **1** : to place in position; *also* : ASSEMBLE **2** : CAUSE **3** : FOUND, ESTABLISH **4** : FRAME **5**

sev·en \'se-vən\ *n* **1** : one more than six **2** : the 7th in a set or series **3** : something having seven units — **seven** *adj or pron* — **sev·enth** \-vənth\ *adj or adv or n*

sev·en·teen \₁se-vən-'tēn\ *n* : one more than 16 — **seventeen** *adj or pron* — **sev·en·teenth** \-'tēnth\ *adj or n*

seventeen–year locust *n* : a cicada of the U.S. that has in the North a life of 17 years and in the South of 13 years of which most is spent underground as a nymph and only a few weeks as a winged adult

sev·en·ty \'se-vən-tē\ *n, pl* **-ties** : seven times 10 — **sev·en·ti·eth** \-tē-əth\ *adj or n* — **seventy** *adj or pron*

sev·en·ty–eight \₁se-vən-tē-'āt\ *n* : a phonograph record designed to be played at 78 revolutions per minute

sev·er \'se-vər\ *vb* **sev·ered; sev·er·ing** : DIVIDE; *esp* : to separate by or as if by cutting — **sev·er·ance** \'sev-rəns, 'se-və-\ *n*

sev·er·al \'sev-rəl, 'se-və-\ *adj* [ME, fr. MF, fr. ML *separalis,* fr. L *separ* separate, fr. *separare* to separate] **1** : INDIVIDUAL, DISTINCT ⟨federal union of the ∼ states⟩ **2** : consisting of an indefinite number but yet not very many — **sev·er·al·ly** *adv*

severance pay *n* : extra pay given an employee upon termination of employment

se·vere \sə-'vir\ *adj* **se·ver·er; -est 1** : marked by strictness or sternness : AUSTERE **2** : strict in discipline **3** : causing distress and esp. physical discomfort or pain ⟨∼ weather⟩ ⟨a ∼ wound⟩ **4** : hard to endure ⟨∼ trials⟩ **5** : SERIOUS ⟨∼ depression⟩ **syn** stern, ascetic, astringent — **se·vere·ly** *adv* — **se·ver·i·ty** \-'ver-ə-tē\ *n*

sew \'sō\ *vb* **sewed; sewn** \'sōn\ *or* **sewed; sew·ing 1** : to unite or fasten by stitches **2** : to engage in sewing

sew·age \'sü-ij\ *n* : waste materials carried off by sewers

¹sew·er \'sō-ər\ *n* : one that sews

²sew·er \'sü-ər\ *n* : an artificial pipe or channel to carry off waste matter

sew·er·age \'sü-ə-rij\ *n* **1** : a system of sewers **2** : SEWAGE

sew·ing *n* **1** : the activity of one who sews **2** : material that has been or is to be sewed

sex \'seks\ *n* **1** : either of the two major forms that occur in many living things and are designated male or female according to their role in reproduction; *also* : the qualities by which these sexes are differentiated and which directly or indirectly function in reproduction involving

two parents **2** : sexual activity or behavior; *also* : SEXUAL INTERCOURSE — **sexed** \'sekst\ *adj* — **sex·less** *adj*

sex·a·ge·nar·i·an \₁sek-sə-jə-'ner-ē-ən\ *n* : a person whose age is in the sixties — **sexagenarian** *adj*

sex cell *n* : an egg cell or sperm cell

sex chromosome *n* : one of usu. a pair of chromosomes that are usu. similar in one sex but different in the other sex and are concerned with the inheritance of sex

sex hormone *n* : a hormone (as from the gonads or adrenal cortex) that affects the growth or function of the reproductive organs or the development of secondary sex characteristics

sex·ism \'sek-₁si-zəm\ *n* : prejudice or discrimination based on sex; *esp* : discrimination against women — **sex·ist** \'sek-sist\ *adj or n*

sex·pot \'seks-₁pät\ *n* : a conspicuously sexy woman

sex symbol *n* : a usu. renowned person (as an entertainer) noted and admired for conspicuous attractiveness

sex·tant \'sek-stənt\ *n* [NL *sextant-, sextans* sixth part of a circle, fr. L, sixth part, fr. *sextus* sixth] : a navigational instrument for determining latitude

sex·tet \sek-'stet\ *n* **1** : a musical composition for six voices or instruments; *also* : the performers of such a composition **2** : a group or set of six

sex·ton \'sek-stən\ *n* : one who takes care of church property

sex·u·al \'sek-shə-wəl\ *adj* : of, relating to, or involving sex or the sexes ⟨a ∼ spore⟩ ⟨∼ relations⟩ — **sex·u·al·i·ty** \₁sek-shə-'wa-lə-tē\ *n* — **sex·u·al·ly** \'sek-shə-wə-lē\ *adv*

sexual intercourse *n* **1** : intercourse between a male and a female in which the penis is inserted into the vagina **2** : intercourse between individuals involving genital contact other than insertion of the penis into the vagina

sexually transmitted disease *n* : a disease (as syphilis, gonorrhea, AIDS, or the genital form of herpes simplex) that is caused by a microorganism or virus usu. or both transmitted by direct sexual contact

sexual relations *n pl* : SEXUAL INTERCOURSE

sexy \'sek-sē\ *adj* **sex·i·er; -est** : sexually suggestive or stimulating : EROTIC

SF *abbr* **1** sacrifice fly **2** science fiction

SFC *abbr* sergeant first class

SG *abbr* **1** senior grade **2** sergeant **3** solicitor general **4** surgeon general

sgd *abbr* signed

Sgt *abbr* sergeant

Sgt Maj *abbr* sergeant major

sh *abbr* share

Sha'·ban \shə-'bän\ *n* [Ar *sha'bān*] : the 8th month of the Islamic year

shab·by \'sha-bē\ *adj* **shab·bi·er; -est 1** : dressed in worn clothes **2** : threadbare and faded from wear **3** : DESPICABLE, MEAN; *also* : UNFAIR ⟨∼ treatment⟩ — **shab·bi·ly** \'sha-bə-lē\ *adv* — **shab·bi·ness** \-bē-nəs\ *n*

shack \'shak\ *n* : HUT, SHANTY

¹shack·le \'sha-kəl\ *n* **1** : something (as a manacle or fetter) that confines the legs or arms **2** : a check on free action made as if by fetters **3** : a device for making something fast or secure

²shackle *vb* **shack·led; shack·ling** : to bind or fasten with shackles

shad \'shad\ *n, pl* **shad** : any of several sea fishes related to the herrings that swim up rivers to spawn and include some important food fishes

¹shade \'shād\ *n* **1** : partial obscurity **2** : space sheltered from the light esp. of the sun **3** : PHANTOM **4** : something that shelters from or intercepts light or heat; *also, pl* : SUNGLASSES **5** : a dark color or a variety of a color **6** : a small difference

²shade *vb* **shad·ed; shad·ing 1** : to shelter from light and heat **2** : DARKEN, OBSCURE **3** : to mark with degrees of light or color **4** : to show slight differences esp. in color or meaning

shad·ing *n* : the color and lines representing darkness or shadow in a drawing or painting

¹shad·ow \'sha-dō\ *n* **1** : partial darkness in a space from which light rays are cut off **2** : SHELTER **3** : shade cast upon a surface by something intercepting rays from a light ⟨the ∼ of a tree⟩ **4** : PHANTOM **5** : a shaded portion of a picture **6** : a small portion or degree : TRACE ⟨a ∼ of doubt⟩ **7** : a source of gloom or unhappiness — **shad·owy** *adj*

²shadow *vb* **1** : to cast a shadow on **2** : to represent faintly or vaguely **3** : to follow and watch closely : TRAIL

shad·ow·box \'sha-dō-ˌbäks\ *vb* : to box with an imaginary opponent esp. for training

shady \'shā-dē\ *adj* **shad·i·er; -est 1** : affording shade **2** : of questionable honesty or reputation

¹shaft \'shaft\ *n, pl* **shafts 1** : the long handle of a spear or lance **2** : SPEAR, LANCE **3** *or pl* **shaves** \'shavz\ : POLE; *esp* : one of two poles between which a horse is hitched to pull a vehicle **4** : something (as a column) long and slender **5** : a bar to support a rotating piece or to transmit power by rotation **6** : an inclined opening in the ground (as for finding or mining ore) **7** : a vertical opening (as for an elevator) through the floors of a building **8** : harsh or unfair treatment — usu. used with *the*

²shaft *vb* **1** : to fit with a shaft **2** : to treat unfairly or harshly

shag \'shag\ *n* : a shaggy tangled mass or covering (as of wool) : long coarse or matted fiber, nap, or pile

shag·gy \'sha-gē\ *adj* **shag·gi·er; -est 1** : rough with or as if with long hair or wool **2** : tangled or rough in surface

shah \'shä, 'shȯ\ *n, often cap* : a sovereign of Iran until 1979

Shak *abbr* Shakespeare

¹shake \'shāk\ *vb* **shook** \'shu̇k\; **shak·en** \'shā-kən\; **shak·ing 1** : to move or cause to move jerkily or irregularly **2** : BRANDISH, WAVE ⟨*shaking* his fist⟩ **3** : to disturb emotionally ⟨*shaken* by her death⟩ **4** : WEAKEN ⟨*shook* his faith⟩ **5** : to bring or come into a certain position, condition, or arrangement by or as if by moving jerkily **6** : to clasp (hands) in greeting or as a sign of goodwill or agreement **syn** tremble, quake, quaver, shiver, quiver — **shak·able** \'shā-kə-bəl\ *adj*

²shake *n* **1** : the act or a result of shaking **2** : DEAL, TREATMENT ⟨a fair ∼⟩

shake·down \'shāk-ˌdau̇n\ *n* **1** : an improvised bed **2** : EXTORTION **3** : a process or period of adjustment **4** : a test (as of a new ship or airplane) under operating conditions

shake down *vb* **1** : to take up temporary quarters **2** : to occupy a makeshift bed **3** : to become accustomed esp. to new surroundings or duties **4** : to settle down **5** : to give a shakedown test to **6** : to obtain money from in a deceitful or illegal manner **7** : to bring about a reduction of

shak·er \'shā-kər\ *n* **1** : one that shakes ⟨pepper ∼⟩ **2** *cap* : a member of a religious sect founded in England in 1747

shake–up \'shāk-ˌəp\ *n* : an extensive often drastic reorganization

shaky \'shā-kē\ *adj* **shak·i·er; -est** : UNSOUND, WEAK — **shak·i·ly** \'shā-kə-lē\ *adv* — **shak·i·ness** \-kē-nəs\ *n*

shale \'shāl\ *n* : a finely layered rock formed from clay, mud, or silt

shall \shəl, 'shal\ *vb, past* **should** \shəd, 'shu̇d\; *pres sing & pl* **shall** — used as an auxiliary to express a command, what seems inevitable or likely in the future, simple futurity, or determination

shal·lop \'sha-ləp\ *n* : a light open boat

shal·lot \shə-'lät, 'sha-lət\ *n* [modif. of F *échalote*] **1** : a small clustered bulb that is used in seasoning and is produced by a perennial herb belonging to a subspecies of the onion; *also* : this herb **2** : GREEN ONION

¹shal·low \'sha-lō\ *adj* **1** : not deep **2** : not intellectually profound

²shallow *n* : a shallow place in a body of water — usu. used in pl.

¹sham \'sham\ *n* **1** : an ornamental covering for a pillow **2** : COUNTERFEIT, IMITATION **3** : a person who shams

²sham *vb* **shammed; sham·ming** : FEIGN, PRETEND — **sham·mer** *n*

³sham *adj* : not genuine : FALSE, FEIGNED

sha·man \'shä-mən, 'shā-\ *n* [ultim. fr. Evenki (a language of Siberia) *šamán*] : a priest or priestess who uses magic to cure the sick, to divine the hidden, and to control events

sham·ble \'sham-bəl\ *vb* **sham·bled; sham·bling** : to shuffle along — **sham·ble** *n*

sham·bles \'sham-bəlz\ *n* **1** : a scene of great slaughter **2** : a scene or state of great destruction or disorder; *also* : MESS

¹shame \'shām\ *n* **1** : a painful sense of having done something wrong, improper, or immodest **2** : DISGRACE, DISHONOR **3** : a cause of feeling shame **4** : something to be regretted ⟨it's a ∼ you'll miss the party⟩ — **shame·ful** \-fəl\ *adj* — **shame·ful·ly** *adv* — **shame·less** *adj* — **shame·less·ly** *adv*

²shame *vb* **shamed; sham·ing 1** : DISGRACE **2** : to make ashamed

shame·faced \'shām-ˌfāst\ *adj* : ASHAMED, ABASHED — **shame·faced·ly** \-ˌfā-səd-lē, -ˌfāst-lē\ *adv*

¹sham·poo \sham-'pü\ *vb* [Hindi *cāpo*, imper. of *cāpnā* to press, shampoo] : to wash (as the hair) with soap and water or with a special preparation; *also* : to clean (as a rug) similarly

²shampoo *n, pl* **shampoos 1** : the act or an instance of shampooing **2** : a preparation for use in shampooing

sham·rock \'sham-ˌräk\ *n* [Ir *seamróg*, dim. of *seamar* clover] : a plant of folk legend with leaves composed of three leaflets that is associated with St. Patrick and Ireland

shang·hai \shaŋ-'hī\ *vb* **shang·haied; shang·hai·ing** [*Shanghai*, China] : to force aboard a ship for service as a sailor; *also* : to trick or force into an undesirable position

Shan·gri–la \ˌshaŋ-gri-'lä\ *n* [*Shangri-La*, imaginary land depicted in the novel *Lost Horizon* (1933) by James Hilton] : a remote idyllic hideaway

shank \'shaŋk\ *n* **1** : the part of the leg between the knee and the human ankle or a corresponding part of a quadruped **2** : a cut of meat from the leg **3** : the narrow part of the sole of a shoe beneath the instep **4** : the part of a tool or instrument (as a key or anchor) connecting the functioning part with a part by which it is held or moved

shan·tung \ˌshan-'təŋ\ *n* : a fabric in plain weave having a slightly irregular surface

shan·ty \'shan-tē\ *n, pl* **shanties** [prob. fr. CanF *chantier* lumber camp, hut, fr. F, gantry, fr. L *cantherius* rafter, trellis] : a small roughly built shelter or dwelling

¹shape \'shāp\ *vb* **shaped; shap·ing 1** : to form esp. in a particular shape **2** : DESIGN **3** : ADAPT, ADJUST **4** : REGULATE **syn** make, fashion, fabricate, manufacture, frame, mold

²shape *n* **1** : APPEARANCE **2** : surface configuration : FORM **3** : bodily contour apart from the head and face : FIGURE **4** : PHANTOM **5** : CONDITION — **shaped** \'shāpt\ *adj*

shape·less \'shā-pləs\ *adj* **1** : having no definite shape **2** : not shapely — **shape·less·ly** *adv* — **shape·less·ness** *n*

\ə\abut \ˈə\kitten \ər\further \a\ash \ā\ace \ä\mop, mar \au̇\out \ch\chin \e\bet \ē\easy \g\go \i\hit \ī\ice \j\job \ŋ\sing \ō\go \ȯ\law \ȯi\boy \th\thin \t̲h̲\the \ü\loot \u̇\foot \y\yet \zh\vision *see also* Pronunciation Symbols page shape·ly \ˈshā-plē\ adj shape·li·er; -est : having a pleasing shape — shape·li·ness n

shard \ˈshärd\ also sherd \ˈshərd\ n : a broken piece : FRAGMENT

¹share \ˈshar\ n : PLOWSHARE

²share n 1 : a portion belonging to one person or group 2 : any of the equal interests into which the capital stock of a corporation is divided

³share vb shared; shar·ing 1 : APPORTION 2 : to use or enjoy with others 3 : PARTICIPATE — shar·er n

share·crop·per \-ˌkrä-pər\ n : a farmer who works another's land in return for a share of the crop — share·crop vb

share·hold·er \-ˌhōl-dər\ n : STOCKHOLDER

¹shark \ˈshärk\ n : any of various active, usu. predaceous, and mostly large marine cartilaginous fishes

²shark n : a greedy crafty person

shark·skin \-ˌskin\ n 1 : the hide of a shark or leather made from it 2 : a fabric (as of cotton or rayon) woven from strands of many fine threads and having a sleek appearance and silky feel

¹sharp \ˈshärp\ adj 1 : having a thin cutting edge or fine point : not dull or blunt 2 : COLD, NIPPING ⟨a ∼ wind⟩ 3 : keen in intellect, perception, or attention 4 : BRISK, ENERGETIC 5 : IRRITABLE ⟨a ∼ temper⟩ 6 : causing intense distress ⟨a ∼ pain⟩ 7 : HARSH, CUTTING ⟨a ∼ rebuke⟩ 8 : affecting the senses as if cutting or piercing ⟨a ∼ sound⟩ ⟨a ∼ smell⟩ 9 : not smooth or rounded ⟨∼ features⟩ 10 : involving an abrupt or extreme change ⟨a ∼ turn⟩ 11 : CLEAR, DISTINCT ⟨mountains in ∼ relief⟩; also : easy to perceive ⟨a ∼ contrast⟩ 12 : higher than the true pitch; also : raised by a half step 13 : STYLISH ⟨a ∼ dresser⟩ syn keen, acute, quick-witted, penetrative — sharp·ly adv — sharp·ness n

²sharp adv 1 : in a sharp manner 2 : EXACTLY, PRECISELY ⟨left at 8 ∼⟩

³sharp n 1 : a sharp edge or point 2 : a character ♯ which indicates that a specified note is to be raised by a half step; also : the resulting note 3 : SHARPER

⁴sharp vb : to raise in pitch by a half step

sharp·en \ˈshär-pən\ vb : to make or become sharp — sharp·en·er n

sharp·er \ˈshär-pər\ n : SWINDLER; esp : a cheating gambler

sharp·ie or sharpy \ˈshär-pē\ n, pl sharp·ies 1 : SHARPER 2 : a person who is exceptionally keen or alert

sharp·shoot·er \ˈshärp-ˌshü-tər\ n : a good marksman — sharp·shoot·ing n

shat·ter \ˈsha-tər\ vb : to dash or burst into fragments — shat·ter·proof \ˈsha-tər-ˌprüf\ adj

¹shave \ˈshāv\ vb shaved; shaved or shav·en \ˈshā-vən\; shav·ing 1 : to slice in thin pieces 2 : to make bare or smooth by cutting the hair from 3 : to cut or pare off by the sliding movement of a razor 4 : to skim along or near the surface of

²shave n 1 : any of various tools for cutting thin slices 2 : an act or process of shaving

shav·er \ˈshā-vər\ n 1 : an electric razor 2 : BOY, YOUNGSTER

shaves pl of SHAFT

shav·ing n 1 : the act of one that shaves 2 : something shaved off

shawl \ˈshȯl\ n : a square or oblong piece of fabric used esp. by women as a loose covering for the head or shoulders

Shaw·nee \shȯ-ˈnē, shä-\ n, pl Shawnee or Shawnees : a member of an American Indian people orig. of the central Ohio valley; also : their language

Shaw·wal \shə-ˈwäl\ n [Ar shawwāl] : the 10th month of the Islamic year

shd abbr should

she \ˈshē\ pron : that female one ⟨who is ∼⟩; also : that one regarded as feminine ⟨∼'s a fine ship⟩

sheaf \ˈshēf\ n, pl sheaves \ˈshēvz\ 1 : a bundle of stalks and ears of grain 2 : a group of things bound together

¹shear \ˈshir\ vb sheared; sheared or shorn \ˈshȯrn\; shear·ing 1 : to cut the hair or wool from : CLIP, TRIM 2 : to deprive by or as if by cutting 3 : to cut or break sharply

²shear n 1 : any of various cutting tools that consist of two blades fastened together so that the edges slide one by the other — usu. used in pl. 2 chiefly Brit : the act, an instance, or the result of shearing 3 : an action or stress caused by applied forces that causes two parts of a body to slide on each other

sheath \ˈshēth\ n, pl sheaths \ˈshēthz, ˈshēths\ 1 : a case for a blade (as of a knife); also : an anatomical covering suggesting such a case 2 : a close-fitting dress usu. worn without a belt

sheathe \ˈshēth\ also sheath \ˈshēth\ vb sheathed; sheath·ing 1 : to put into a sheath 2 : to cover with something that guards or protects

sheath·ing \ˈshē-thiŋ, -thiŋ\ n : material used to sheathe something; esp : the first covering of boards or of waterproof material on the outside wall of a frame house or on a timber roof

sheave \ˈshiv, ˈshēv\ n : a grooved wheel or pulley (as on a pulley block)

she·bang \shi-ˈbaŋ\ n : CONTRIVANCE, AFFAIR, CONCERN ⟨sold the whole ∼⟩

She·bat \shə-ˈbät, -ˈvät\ n [Heb shĕbhāt] : the 5th month of the civil year or the 11th month of the ecclesiastical year in the Jewish calendar

¹shed \ˈshed\ vb shed; shed·ding 1 : to cause to flow from a cut or wound ⟨∼ blood⟩ 2 : to pour down in drops ⟨∼ tears⟩ 3 : to give out (as light) : DIFFUSE 4 : to throw off (as a natural covering) : DISCARD

²shed n : a slight structure built for shelter or storage

sheen \ˈshēn\ n : a subdued luster

sheep \ˈshēp\ n, pl sheep 1 : any of various cud-chewing mammals that are stockier than the related goats and lack a beard in the male; esp : one raised for meat or for its wool or skin 2 : a timid or defenseless person 3 : SHEEPSKIN

sheep dog n : a dog used to tend, drive, or guard sheep

sheep·fold \ˈshēp-ˌfōld\ n : a pen or shelter for sheep

sheep·herd·er \-ˌhər-dər\ n : a worker in charge of sheep esp. on open range — sheep·herd·ing n

sheep·ish \ˈshē-pish\ adj : BASHFUL, TIMID; esp : embarrassed by consciousness of a fault — sheep·ish·ly adv

sheep·skin \ˈshēp-ˌskin\ n 1 : the hide of a sheep or leather prepared from it; also : PARCHMENT 2 : DIPLOMA

¹sheer \ˈshir\ vb : to turn from a course

²sheer adj 1 : very thin or transparent 2 : UNQUALIFIED ⟨∼ folly⟩ 3 : very steep syn pure, simple, absolute, unadulterated, unmitigated — sheer adv

¹sheet \ˈshēt\ n 1 : a broad piece of cloth (as for a bed); also : SAIL 1 2 : a single piece of paper 3 : a broad flat surface ⟨a ∼ of ice⟩ 4 : something broad and long and relatively thin

²sheet n : a rope used to trim a sail

sheet·ing \ˈshē-tiŋ\ n : material in the form of sheets or suitable for forming into sheets

sheikh or sheik \ˈshēk, ˈshāk\ n : an Arab chief — sheikh·dom or sheik·dom \-dəm\ n

shek·el \ˈshe-kəl\ n — see MONEY table

shelf \ˈshelf\ n, pl shelves \ˈshelvz\ 1 : a thin flat usu. long and narrow structure fastened horizontally (as on a wall) above the floor to hold things 2 : something (as a sandbar) that suggests a shelf

shelf life n : the period of storage time during which a material will remain useful

¹shell \ˈshel\ n 1 : a hard or tough often thin outer covering of an animal (as a beetle, turtle, or mollusk) or of an egg or a seed or fruit (as a nut); also : something that resembles a shell ⟨a pastry ∼⟩ 2 : a light narrow racing

boat propelled by oarsmen **3** : a case holding an explosive and designed to be fired from a cannon; *also* : a case holding the charge of powder and shot or bullet for small arms **4** : a plain usu. sleeveless blouse or sweater — **shelled** \'sheld\ *adj* — **shelly** \'she-lē\ *adj*

²**shell** *vb* **1** : to remove from a shell or husk **2** : BOMBARD — **shell·er** *n*

¹**shel·lac** \shə-'lak\ *n* **1** : a purified lac **2** : lac dissolved in alcohol and used as a wood filler or finish

²**shellac** *vb* **shel·lacked; shel·lack·ing 1** : to coat or treat with shellac **2** : to defeat decisively

shel·lack·ing *n* : a sound drubbing

shell bean *n* : a bean grown esp. for its edible seeds; *also* : its edible seed

shell·fish \-ˌfish\ *n* : an invertebrate water animal (as an oyster or lobster) with a shell

shell out *vb* : PAY

shell shock *n* : a psychological and nervous disorder of soldiers resulting from traumatic experience in combat — **shell–shocked** \'shel-ˌshäkt\ *adj*

¹**shel·ter** \'shel-tər\ *n* : something that gives protection : REFUGE

²**shelter** *vb* **shel·tered; shel·ter·ing** : to give protection or refuge to

shelve \'shelv\ *vb* **shelved; shelv·ing 1** : to slope gradually **2** : to store on shelves **3** : to dismiss from service or use **4** : to put aside : DEFER ⟨∼ a proposal⟩

shelv·ing \'shel-viŋ\ *n* : material for shelves; *also* : SHELVES

she·nan·i·gan \shə-'na-ni-gən\ *n* **1** : an underhand trick **2** : questionable conduct — usu. used in pl. **3** : high= spirited or mischievous activity — usu. used in pl.

¹**shep·herd** \'she-pərd\ *n* **1** : one who tends sheep **2** : GERMAN SHEPHERD

²**shepherd** *vb* : to tend as or in the manner of a shepherd

shep·herd·ess \'she-pər-dəs\ *n* : a woman who tends sheep

sheq·el \'she-kəl\ *n, pl* **sheq·a·lim** \she-'kä-lim\ *var of* SHEKEL

sher·bet \'shər-bət\ *n* [Turk *şerbet,* fr. Per *sharbat,* fr. Ar *sharbah* drink] **1** : a drink of sweetened diluted fruit juice **2** *or* **sher·bert** \-bərt\ : a frozen dessert of fruit juices, sugar, milk or water, and egg whites or gelatin

sherd *var of* SHARD

sher·iff \'sher-əf\ *n* [ME *shirreve,* fr. OE *scīrgerēfa,* lit., shire reeve (local official)] : a county officer charged with the execution of the law and the preservation of order

sher·ry \'sher-ē\ *n, pl* **sherries** [alter. of earlier *sherris* (taken as pl.), fr. *Xeres* (now *Jerez*), Spain] : a fortified wine with a nutty flavor

Shet·land pony \'shet-lənd-\ *n* : any of a breed of small stocky shaggy hardy ponies

shew \'shō\ *Brit var of* SHOW

shi·at·su *also* **shi·at·zu** \shē-'ät-sü\ *n* [short for Jp *shi-atsuryōhō*] : a finger massage of those bodily areas used in acupuncture

shib·bo·leth \'shi-bə-ləth\ *n* [Heb *shibbōleth* stream; fr. the use of this word as a test to distinguish the men of Gilead from members of the tribe of Ephraim, who pronounced it *sibbōleth* (Judges 12:5, 6)] **1** : CATCHWORD 2 **2** : language that is a criterion for distinguishing members of a group

¹**shield** \'shēld\ *n* **1** : a broad piece of defensive armor carried on the arm **2** : something that protects or hides

²**shield** *vb* : to protect or hide with a shield **syn** protect, guard, safeguard

shier *comparative of* SHY

shiest *superlative of* SHY

¹**shift** \'shift\ *vb* **1** : EXCHANGE, REPLACE **2** : to change place, position, or direction : MOVE; *also* : to change gears **3** : GET BY, MANAGE

²**shift** *n* **1** : SCHEME, TRICK **2** : a woman's slip or loose=

fitting dress **3** : a change in direction, emphasis, or attitude **4** : a group working together alternating with other groups **5** : TRANSFER **6** : GEARSHIFT

shift·less \'shift-ləs\ *adj* : LAZY, INEFFICIENT — **shift·less·ness** *n*

shifty \'shif-tē\ *adj* **shift·i·er; -est 1** : TRICKY; *also* : ELUSIVE **2** : indicative of a tricky nature ⟨∼ eyes⟩

shih tzu \'shēd-ˌzü, 'shēt-ˌsü\ *n, pl* **shih tzus** *also* **shih tzu** *often cap* S&T : any of a breed of small short= legged dogs of Chinese origin that have a short muzzle and a long dense coat

shill \'shil\ *n* : one who acts as a decoy (as for a pitchman) — **shill** *vb*

shil·le·lagh *also* **shil·la·lah** \shə-'lā-lē\ *n* [*Shillelagh,* town in Ireland] : CUDGEL, CLUB

shil·ling \'shi-liŋ\ *n* — see MONEY TABLE

shilly–shally \'shi-lē-ˌsha-lē\ *vb* **shilly–shall·ied; shilly–shally·ing 1** : to show hesitation or lack of decisiveness **2** : to waste time

shim \'shim\ *n* : a thin often tapered piece of wood, metal, or stone used (as in leveling) to fill in space

shim·mer \'shi-mər\ *vb* : to shine waveringly or tremulously : GLIMMER **syn** flash, gleam, glint, sparkle, glitter — **shimmer** *n* — **shim·mery** *adj*

shim·my \'shi-mē\ *n, pl* **shimmies** : an abnormal vibration esp. in the front wheels of a motor vehicle — **shimmy** *vb*

¹**shin** \'shin\ *n* : the front part of the leg below the knee

²**shin** *vb* **shinned; shin·ning** : to climb (as a pole) by gripping alternately with arms or hands and legs

shin·bone \'shin-ˌbōn\ *n* : TIBIA

¹**shine** \'shīn\ *vb* **shone** \'shōn\ *or* **shined; shin·ing 1** : to give or cause to give light **2** : GLEAM, GLITTER **3** : to be eminent, conspicuous, or distinguished ⟨gave her a chance to ∼⟩ **4** : POLISH ⟨∼ your shoes⟩

²**shine** *n* **1** : BRIGHTNESS, RADIANCE **2** : LUSTER, BRILLIANCE **3** : fair weather : SUNSHINE ⟨rain or ∼⟩ **4** : LIKING, FANCY ⟨took a ∼ to them⟩ **5** : a polish given to shoes

shin·er \'shī-nər\ *n* **1** : a small silvery fish; *esp* : any of numerous small freshwater American fishes related to the carp **2** : a discoloration of the skin around the eye due to bruising

¹**shin·gle** \'shiŋ-gəl\ *n* **1** : a small thin piece of building material used in overlapping rows for covering a roof or outside wall **2** : a small sign

²**shingle** *vb* **shin·gled; shin·gling** : to cover with shingles

³**shingle** *n* : a beach strewn with gravel; *also* : coarse gravel (as on a beach)

shin·gles \'shiŋ-gəlz\ *n* : an acute inflammation of the spinal and cranial nerves caused by reactivation of the chicken pox virus and associated with eruptions and pain along the course of the affected nerves

shin·ny \'shi-nē\ *vb* **shin·nied; shin·ny·ing** : SHIN

shin·splints \'shin-ˌsplints\ *n sing or pl* : a condition marked by pain and sometimes tenderness and swelling in the shin caused by repeated small injuries to muscles and associated tissue esp. from running

Shin·to \'shin-ˌtō\ *n* : the indigenous religion of Japan consisting esp. in reverence of the spirits of natural forces and imperial ancestors — **Shin·to·ism** *n* — **Shin·to·ist** *n or adj*

shiny \'shī-nē\ *adj* **shin·i·er; -est** : BRIGHT, RADIANT; *also* : POLISHED

¹**ship** \'ship\ *n* **1** : a large oceangoing boat **2** : a ship's officers and crew **3** : AIRSHIP, AIRCRAFT, SPACECRAFT

²**ship** *vb* **shipped; ship·ping 1** : to put or receive on board a ship for transportation **2** : to have transported by a

---

\ə\abut \ᵊ\kitten \ər\further \a\ash \ā\ace \ä\mop, mar
\au̇\out \ch\chin \e\bet \ē\easy \g\go \i\hit \ī\ice \j\job
\ŋ\sing \ō\go \ȯ\law \ȯi\boy \th\thin \t̲h̲\the \ü\loot \u̇\foot
\y\yet \zh\vision   *see also* Pronunciation Symbols page

carrier **3** : to take or draw into a boat ⟨∼ oars⟩ ⟨∼ water⟩ **4** : to engage to serve on a ship — **ship·per** *n*

-ship \ˈship\ *n suffix* **1** : state : condition : quality ⟨friend*ship*⟩ **2** : office : dignity : profession ⟨lord*ship*⟩ ⟨clerk*ship*⟩ **3** : art : skill ⟨horseman*ship*⟩ **4** : something showing, exhibiting, or embodying a quality or state ⟨town*ship*⟩ **5** : one entitled to a (specified) rank, title, or appellation ⟨his Lord*ship*⟩ **6** : the body of persons engaged in a specified activity ⟨reader*ship*⟩

ship·board \ˈship-ˌbōrd\ *n* : SHIP

ship·build·er \-ˌbil-dər\ *n* : one who designs or builds ships

ship·fit·ter \-ˌfi-tər\ *n* **1** : one who constructs ships **2** : a naval enlisted man who works as a plumber

ship·mate \-ˌmāt\ *n* : a fellow sailor

ship·ment \-mənt\ *n* : the process of shipping; *also* : the goods shipped

ship·ping *n* **1** : SHIPS; *esp* : ships in one port or belonging to one country **2** : transportation of goods

ship·shape \ˈship-ˌshāp\ *adj* : TRIM, TIDY

ship·worm \-ˌwərm\ *n* : any of various wormlike marine clams that burrow in wood and damage wooden ships and wharves

¹ship·wreck \-ˌrek\ *n* **1** : a wrecked ship **2** : destruction or loss of a ship **3** : total loss or failure : RUIN

²shipwreck *vb* : to cause or meet disaster at sea through destruction or foundering

ship·wright \ˈship-ˌrīt\ *n* : a carpenter skilled in ship construction and repair

ship·yard \-ˌyärd\ *n* : a place where ships are built or repaired

shire \ˈshīr, *in place-name compounds* ˌshir, shər\ *n* : a county in Great Britain

shirk \ˈshərk\ *vb* : to avoid performing (duty or work) — **shirk·er** *n*

shirr \ˈshər\ *vb* **1** : to make shirring in **2** : to bake (eggs removed from the shell) until set

shirr·ing \ˈshər-iŋ\ *n* : a decorative gathering in cloth made by drawing up parallel lines of stitches

shirring

shirt \ˈshərt\ *n* **1** : a loose cloth garment usu. having a collar, sleeves, a front opening, and a tail long enough to be tucked inside trousers or a skirt **2** : UNDERSHIRT — **shirt·less** *adj*

shirt·ing \ˈshir-tiŋ\ *n* : cloth suitable for making shirts

shish ke·bab \ˈshish-kə-ˌbäb\ *n* [Turk *şiş kebabı*, fr. *şiş* spit + *kebap* roast meat] : kabob cooked on skewers

shiv \ˈshiv\ *n*, *slang* : KNIFE

¹shiv·er \ˈshi-vər\ *vb* : TREMBLE, QUIVER **syn** shudder, quaver, shake, quake

²shiver *n* : an instance of shivering — **shiv·ery** *adj*

¹shoal \ˈshōl\ *n* **1** : SHALLOW **2** : a sandbank or bar creating a shallow

²shoal *n* : a large group (as of fish)

shoat \ˈshōt\ *n* : a weaned young pig

¹shock \ˈshäk\ *n* : a pile of sheaves of grain or cornstalks set up in a field

²shock *n* [MF *choc*, fr. *choquer* to strike against] **1** : a sharp impact or violent shake or jar **2** : a sudden violent mental or emotional disturbance **3** : a state of bodily collapse caused esp. by crushing wounds, blood loss,

or burns **4** : the effect of a charge of electricity passing through the body **5** : an attack of stroke or heart disease **6** : SHOCK ABSORBER — **shock·proof** \-ˌprüf\ *adj*

³shock *vb* **1** : to strike with surprise, horror, or disgust **2** : to subject to the action of an electrical discharge

⁴shock *n* : a thick bushy mass (as of hair)

shock absorber *n* : any of several devices for absorbing the energy of sudden shocks in machinery

shock·er \ˈshä-kər\ *n* : one that shocks; *esp* : a sensational work of fiction or drama

shock·ing *adj* : extremely startling and offensive — **shock·ing·ly** *adv*

shock therapy *n* : the treatment of mental disorder by induction of coma or convulsions by drugs or electricity

shock wave *n* : a wave formed by the sudden violent compression of the medium through which it travels

¹shod·dy \ˈshä-dē\ *n* **1** : wool reclaimed from old rags; *also* : a fabric made from it **2** : inferior or imitation material

²shoddy *adj* **shod·di·er; -est** **1** : made of shoddy **2** : poorly done or made — **shod·di·ly** \ˈshä-də-lē\ *adv* — **shod·di·ness** \-dē-nəs\ *n*

¹shoe \ˈshü\ *n* **1** : a covering for the human foot **2** : HORSE-SHOE **3** : the part of a brake that presses on the wheel

²shoe *vb* **shod** \ˈshäd\ *also* **shoed** \ˈshüd\; **shoe·ing** : to put a shoe or shoes on

shoe·lace \ˈshü-ˌlās\ *n* : a lace or string for fastening a shoe

shoe·mak·er \-ˌmā-kər\ *n* : one who makes or repairs shoes

shoe·string \-ˌstriŋ\ *n* **1** : SHOELACE **2** : a small sum of money

sho·gun \ˈshō-gən\ *n* [Jp *shōgun* general] : any of a line of military governors ruling Japan until the revolution of 1867–68

shone *past and past part of* SHINE

shook *past of* SHAKE

shook–up \(ˌ)shùk-ˈəp\ *adj* : nervously upset : AGITATED

¹shoot \ˈshüt\ *vb* **shot** \ˈshät\; **shoot·ing** **1** : to drive (as an arrow or bullet) forward quickly or forcibly **2** : to hit, kill, or wound with a missile **3** : to cause a missile to be driven forth or forth from ⟨∼ a gun⟩ **4** : to send forth (as a ray of light) **5** : to thrust forward or out **6** : to pass rapidly along ⟨∼ the rapids⟩ **7** : PHOTOGRAPH, FILM **8** : to move swiftly : DART **9** : to grow by or as if by sending out shoots; *also* : MATURE, DEVELOP — **shoot·er** *n*

²shoot *n* **1** : a plant stem with its leaves and branches esp. when not yet mature **2** : an act of shooting **3** : a shooting match

shooting iron *n* : FIREARM

shooting star *n* : METEOR 2

shoot up *vb* : to inject a narcotic into a vein

¹shop \ˈshäp\ *n* [ME *shoppe*, fr. OE *sceoppa* booth] **1** : a place where things are made or worked on : FACTORY, MILL **2** : a retail store ⟨dress ∼⟩

²shop *vb* **shopped; shop·ping** : to visit stores for purchasing or examining goods — **shop·per** *n*

shop·keep·er \ˈshäp-ˌkē-pər\ *n* : a retail merchant

shop·lift \-ˌlift\ *vb* : to steal goods on display from a store — **shop·lift·er** *n*

shop·talk \-ˌtók\ *n* : talk about one's business or special interests

shop·worn \-ˌwōrn\ *adj* : soiled or frayed from much handling in a store

¹shore \ˈshōr\ *n* : land along the edge of a body of water — **shore·less** *adj*

²shore *vb* **shored; shor·ing** : to give support to : BRACE

³shore *n* : ¹PROP

shore·bird \-ˌbərd\ *n* : any of a suborder of birds (as the plovers and sandpipers) mostly found along the seashore

shore patrol *n* : a branch of a navy that exercises guard and police functions

shor·ing \\'shōr-iŋ\\ *n* : a group of things that shore something up

shorn *past part of* SHEAR

¹**short** \\'shȯrt\\ *adj* **1** : not long or tall **2** : not great in distance **3** : brief in time **4** : not coming up to standard or to an expected amount **5** : CURT, ABRUPT **6** : insufficiently supplied **7** : made with shortening : FLAKY **8** : consisting of or relating to a sale of securities or commodities that the seller does not possess or has not contracted for at the time of the sale ⟨~ sale⟩ — **short·ness** *n*

²**short** *adv* **1** : ABRUPTLY, CURTLY **2** : at some point before a goal aimed at

³**short** *n* **1** : something shorter than normal or standard **2** *pl* : drawers or trousers of less than knee length **3** : SHORT CIRCUIT

⁴**short** *vb* : SHORT-CIRCUIT

short·age \\'shȯr-tij\\ *n* : LACK, DEFICIT

short·cake \\'shȯrt-ˌkāk\\ *n* : a dessert consisting of short biscuit spread with sweetened fruit

short·change \-'chānj\\ *vb* : to cheat esp. by giving less than the correct amount of change

short circuit *n* : a connection made between points in an electric circuit where current is not intended to flow — **short–circuit** *vb*

short·com·ing \\'shȯrt-ˌkə-miŋ\\ *n* : FAULT 1, FAILING

short·cut \-ˌkət\\ *n* **1** : a route more direct than that usu. taken **2** : a quicker way of doing something

short·en \\'shȯrt-ᵊn\\ *vb* : to make or become short **syn** curtail, abbreviate, abridge, retrench

short·en·ing \\'shȯrt-ᵊn-iŋ\\ *n* : a substance (as lard or butter) that makes pastry tender and flaky

short·hand \\'shȯrt-ˌhand\\ *n* : a method of writing rapidly by using symbols and abbreviations for letters, words, or phrases : STENOGRAPHY

short·hand·ed \\ˌshȯrt-'han-dəd\\ *adj* : short of the needed number of people

short·horn \\'shȯrt-ˌhȯrn\\ *n, often cap* : any of a breed of red, roan, or white cattle of English origin

short hundredweight *n* — see WEIGHT table

short–lived \\'shȯrt-ˌlivd, -ˈlīvd\\ *adj* : of short life or duration

short·ly \\'shȯrt-lē\\ *adv* **1** : in a few words **2** : in a short time : SOON

short order *n* : an order for food that can be quickly cooked

short shrift *n* **1** : a brief respite from death **2** : little consideration

short·sight·ed \\'shȯrt-ˌsī-təd\\ *adj* **1** : NEARSIGHTED **2** : lacking foresight — **short·sight·ed·ness** *n*

short·stop \-ˌstäp\\ *n* : a baseball player defending the area between second and third base

short story *n* : a short work of fiction usu. dealing with a few characters and a single event

short–tem·pered \ˌshȯrt-'tem-pərd\\ *adj* : having a quick temper

short–term \\'shȯrt-ˌtərm\\ *adj* **1** : occurring over or involving a relatively short period of time **2** : of or relating to a financial transaction based on a term usu. of less than a year

short ton *n* — see WEIGHT table

short·wave \\'shȯrt-ˌwāv\\ *n* : a radio wave with a wavelength between 10 and 100 meters

Sho·sho·ne *or* **Sho·sho·ni** \shə-'shō-nē\\ *n, pl* **Shoshones** *or* **Shoshoni** : a member of an American Indian people orig. ranging through California, Idaho, Nevada, Utah, and Wyoming

¹**shot** \\'shät\\ *n* **1** : an act of shooting **2** : a stroke or throw in some games **3** : something that is shot : MISSILE, PROJECTILE; *esp* : small pellets forming a charge for a shotgun **4** : a metal sphere that is thrown for distance in the

shot put 5 : RANGE, REACH **6** : MARKSMAN **7** : a single photographic exposure **8** : a single sequence of a motion picture or a television program made by one camera **9** : an injection (as of medicine) into the body **10** : a small serving of undiluted liquor

²**shot** *past and past part of* SHOOT

shot·gun \\'shät-ˌgən\\ *n* : a gun with a smooth bore used to fire shot at short range

shot put *n* : a field event in which a shot is heaved for distance

should \\'shùd, shəd\\ *past of* SHALL — used as an auxiliary to express condition, obligation or propriety, probability, or futurity from a point of view in the past

¹**shoul·der** \\'shōl-dər\\ *n* **1** : the part of the body of a person or animal where the arm or foreleg joins the body **2** : either edge of a roadway **3** : a rounded or sloping part (as of a bottle) where the neck joins the body

²**shoulder** *vb* **1** : to push or thrust with the shoulder **2** : to bear on the shoulder **3** : to take the responsibility of

shoulder belt *n* : an automobile safety belt worn across the torso and over the shoulder

shoulder blade *n* : a flat triangular bone at the back of each shoulder

shout \\'shaùt\\ *vb* : to utter a sudden loud cry — **shout** *n*

shove \\'shəv\\ *vb* **shoved; shov·ing** : to push along, aside, or away — **shove** *n*

¹**shov·el** \\'shə-vəl\\ *n* **1** : a broad long-handled scoop used to lift and throw material **2** : the amount a shovel will hold

²**shovel** *vb* **-eled** *or* **-elled; -el·ing** *or* **-el·ling** **1** : to take up and throw with a shovel **2** : to dig or clean out with a shovel

¹**show** \\'shō\\ *vb* **showed** \\'shōd\\; **shown** \\'shōn\\ *or* **showed; show·ing** **1** : to cause or permit to be seen : EXHIBIT ⟨~ anger⟩ **2** : CONFER, BESTOW ⟨~ mercy⟩ **3** : REVEAL, DISCLOSE ⟨~ed courage in battle⟩ **4** : INSTRUCT ⟨~ me how⟩ **5** : PROVE ⟨~s he was guilty⟩ **6** : APPEAR **7** : to be noticeable **8** : to be third in a horse race

²**show** *n* **1** : a demonstrative display **2** : outward appearance ⟨a ~ of resistance⟩ **3** : SPECTACLE **4** : a theatrical presentation **5** : a radio or television program **6** : third place in a horse race

¹**show·case** \\'shō-ˌkās\\ *n* : a cabinet for displaying items (as in a store)

²**showcase** *vb* **show·cased; show·cas·ing** : EXHIBIT

show·down \\'shō-ˌdaùn\\ *n* : a decisive confrontation or contest; *esp* : the showing of poker hands to determine the winner of a pot

¹**show·er** \\'shaù-ər\\ *n* **1** : a brief fall of rain **2** : a party given by friends who bring gifts **3** : a bath in which water is showered on the person; *also* : a facility (as a stall) for such a bath — **show·ery** *adj*

²**shower** *vb* **1** : to rain or fall in a shower **2** : to bathe in a shower

show·man \\'shō-mən\\ *n* : one having a gift for dramatization and visual effectiveness — **show·man·ship** *n*

show–off \\'shō-ˌȯf\\ *n* : one that seeks to attract attention by conspicuous behavior

show off *vb* **1** : to display proudly **2** : to act as a show-off

show·piece \\'shō-ˌpēs\\ *n* : an outstanding example used for exhibition

show·place \-ˌplās\\ *n* : an estate or building that is a showpiece

show up *vb* : ARRIVE

showy \\'shō-ē\\ *adj* **show·i·er; -est** : superficially impres-

---

\ə\abut \ᵊ\kitten \ər\further \a\ash \ā\ace \ä\mop, mar
\aù\out \ch\chin \e\bet \ē\easy \g\go \i\hit \ī\ice \j\job
\ŋ\sing \ō\go \ȯ\law \ȯi\boy \th\thin \t͟h\the \ü\loot \ù\foot
\y\yet \zh\vision *see also* Pronunciation Symbols page

sive or striking — **show·i·ly** \\'shō-ə-lē\\ *adv* — **show·i·ness** \\-ē-nəs\\ *n*

shpt *abbr* shipment

shrap·nel \\'shrap-nəl\\ *n, pl* **shrapnel** : bomb, mine, or shell fragments

¹**shred** \\'shred\\ *n* : a narrow strip cut or torn off : a small fragment

²**shred** *vb* **shred·ded; shred·ding** : to cut or tear into shreds

shrew \\'shrü\\ *n* 1 : any of a family of very small mammals with velvety fur that are related to the moles 2 : a scolding woman

shrewd \\'shrüd\\ *adj* : CLEVER, ASTUTE — **shrewd·ly** *adv* — **shrewd·ness** *n*

shrew·ish \\'shrü-ish\\ *adj* : having an irritable disposition : ILL-TEMPERED

shriek \\'shrēk\\ *n* : a shrill cry : SCREAM, YELL — **shriek** *vb*

shrift \\'shrift\\ *n, archaic* : the act of shriving

shrike \\'shrīk\\ *n* : any of numerous usu. largely grayish or brownish birds that often impale their usu. insect prey upon thorns before devouring it

¹**shrill** \\'shril\\ *vb* : to make a high-pitched piercing sound

²**shrill** *adj* : high-pitched : PIERCING ⟨~ whistle⟩ — **shril·ly** *adv*

shrimp \\'shrimp\\ *n, pl* **shrimps** *or* **shrimp** 1 : any of various small marine crustaceans related to the lobsters 2 : a small or puny person

shrine \\'shrīn\\ *n* [ME, receptacle for the relics of a saint, fr. OE *scrīn*, fr. L *scrinium* case, chest] 1 : the tomb of a saint; *also* : a place where devotion is paid to a saint or deity 2 : a place or object hallowed by its associations

¹**shrink** \\'shriŋk\\ *vb* **shrank** \\'shraŋk\\ *also* **shrunk** \\'shrəŋk\\; **shrunk** *or* **shrunk·en** \\'shrəŋ-kən\\; **shrink·ing** 1 : to draw back or away 2 : to become smaller or more compact 3 : to lessen in value **syn** contract, constrict, compress, condense — **shrink·able** *adj*

²**shrink** *n* : a clinical psychiatrist or psychologist

shrink·age \\'shriŋ-kij\\ *n* 1 : the act of shrinking 2 : the amount lost by shrinkage

shrive \\'shrīv\\ *vb* **shrived** *or* **shrove** \\'shrōv\\; **shriv·en** \\'shri-vən\\ *or* **shrived** [ME, fr. OE *scrīfan* to prescribe, allot, shrive, fr. L *scribere* to write] : to minister the sacrament of penance to

shriv·el \\'shri-vəl\\ *vb* **-eled** *or* **-elled; -el·ing** *or* **-el·ling** : to shrink and draw into wrinkles : DWINDLE

¹**shroud** \\'shraud\\ *n* 1 : something that covers or screens 2 : a cloth placed over a dead body 3 : any of the ropes leading from the masthead of a ship to the side to support the mast

²**shroud** *vb* : to veil or screen from view

shrub \\'shrəb\\ *n* : a low usu. several-stemmed woody plant — **shrub·by** *adj*

shrub·bery \\'shrə-bə-rē\\ *n, pl* **-ber·ies** : a planting or growth of shrubs

shrug \\'shrəg\\ *vb* **shrugged; shrug·ging** : to hunch (the shoulders) up to express aloofness, indifference, or uncertainty — **shrug** *n*

shrug off *vb* 1 : to brush aside : MINIMIZE 2 : to shake off 3 : to remove (a garment) by wriggling out

¹**shuck** \\'shək\\ *n* : SHELL, HUSK

²**shuck** *vb* : to strip of shucks

shud·der \\'shə-dər\\ *vb* : TREMBLE, QUAKE — **shudder** *n*

shuf·fle \\'shə-fəl\\ *vb* **shuf·fled; shuf·fling** 1 : to mix in a disorderly mass 2 : to rearrange the order of (cards in a pack) by mixing two parts of the pack together 3 : to shift from place to place 4 : to move with a sliding or dragging gait 5 : to dance in a slow lagging manner — **shuffle** *n*

shuf·fle·board \\'shə-fəl-ˌbōrd\\ *n* : a game in which players use long-handled cues to shove disks into scoring areas marked on a smooth surface

shun \\'shən\\ *vb* **shunned; shun·ning** : to avoid deliberately or habitually **syn** evade, elude, escape, duck

¹**shunt** \\'shənt\\ *vb* [ME, to flinch] : to turn off to one side; *esp* : to switch (a train) from one track to another

²**shunt** *n* 1 : a method or device for turning or thrusting aside 2 : a conductor joining two points in an electrical circuit forming an alternate path through which a portion of the current may pass

shut \\'shət\\ *vb* **shut; shut·ting** 1 : CLOSE 2 : to forbid entrance into 3 : to lock up 4 : to fold together ⟨~ a penknife⟩ 5 : to cease or suspend activity ⟨~ down an assembly line⟩

shut·down \\-ˌdaun\\ *n* : a temporary cessation of activity (as in a factory)

shut-in \\'shət-ˌin\\ *n* : an invalid confined to home, a room, or bed

shut·out \\'shət-ˌaut\\ *n* : a game or contest in which one side fails to score

shut out *vb* 1 : EXCLUDE 2 : to prevent (an opponent) from scoring in a game or contest

shut·ter \\'shə-tər\\ *n* 1 : a movable cover for a door or window : BLIND 2 : the part of a camera that opens and closes to expose the film

shut·ter·bug \\'shə-tər-ˌbəg\\ *n* : a photography enthusiast

¹**shut·tle** \\'shət-ᵊl\\ *n* 1 : an instrument used in weaving for passing the horizontal threads between the vertical threads 2 : a vehicle traveling back and forth over a short route ⟨a ~ bus⟩ 3 : SPACE SHUTTLE

²**shuttle** *vb* **shut·tled; shut·tling** : to move back and forth frequently

shut·tle·cock \\'shət-ᵊl-ˌkäk\\ *n* : a light conical object (as of cork or plastic) used in badminton

shut up *vb* : to cease or cause to cease talking

¹**shy** \\'shī\\ *adj* **shi·er** *or* **shy·er** \\'shī-ər\\; **shi·est** *or* **shy·est** \\'shī-əst\\ 1 : easily frightened : TIMID 2 : WARY 3 : BASHFUL 4 : DEFICIENT, LACKING — **shy·ly** *adv* — **shy·ness** *n*

²**shy** *vb* **shied; shy·ing** 1 : to show a dislike : RECOIL 2 : to start suddenly aside through fright ⟨the horse *shied*⟩

shy·ster \\'shīs-tər\\ *n* : an unscrupulous lawyer or politician

Si *symbol* silicon

Si·a·mese \\ˌsī-ə-ˈmēz, -ˈmēs\\ *n, pl* **Sia·mese** : THAI — **Siamese** *adj*

Siamese twin *n* [fr. Chang †1874 and Eng †1874 twins born in Siam with bodies united] : one of a pair of twins with bodies joined together at birth

¹**sib·i·lant** \\'si-bə-lənt\\ *adj* : having, containing, or producing the sound of or a sound resembling that of the *s* or the *sh* in *sash* — **sib·i·lant·ly** *adv*

²**sibilant** *n* : a sibilant speech sound (as English \\s\\, \\z\\, \\sh\\, \\zh\\, \\ch\\ (=tsh)\\, or \\j\\ (=dzh)\\)

sib·ling \\'si-bliŋ\\ *n* : a brother or sister considered irrespective of sex; *also* : one of two or more offspring having one common parent

sib·yl \\'si-bəl\\ *n, often cap* : PROPHETESS — **sib·yl·line** \\-bə-ˌlīn, -ˌlēn\\ *adj*

sic \\'sik, ˈsēk\\ *adv* : intentionally so written — used after a printed word or passage to indicate that it exactly reproduces an original ⟨said he seed [~] it all⟩

sick \\'sik\\ *adj* 1 : not in good health : ILL; *also* : of, relating to, or intended for use in sickness ⟨~ pay⟩ 2 : NAUSEATED 3 : DISGUSTED 4 : PINING 5 : MACABRE, SADISTIC ⟨~ jokes⟩ — **sick·ly** *adj*

sick·bed \\'sik-ˌbed\\ *n* : a bed on which one lies sick

sick·en \\'si-kən\\ *vb* : to make or become sick — **sick·en·ing·ly** *adv*

sick·le \\'si-kəl\\ *n* : a cutting tool consisting of a curved metal blade with a short handle

sickle–cell anemia *n* : an inherited anemia in which red blood cells tend to become crescent-shaped and cannot carry oxygen properly and which occurs esp. in individuals of African, Mediterranean, or southwest Asian ancestry

sick·ness \'sik-nəs\ n 1 : ill health; *also* : a specific disease 2 : NAUSEA

side \'sīd\ n 1 : the right or left part of the trunk of a body 2 : a place away from a central point or line 3 : a border of an object; *esp* : one of the longer borders as contrasted with an end 4 : an outer surface of an object 5 : a position regarded as opposite to another 6 : a body of contestants — **side** *adj*

side·arm \-ˌärm\ *adj* : made with a sideways sweep of the arm — **sidearm** *adv*

side arm n : a weapon worn at the side or in the belt

side·bar \'sīd-ˌbär\ n : a short news story accompanying a major story and presenting related information

side·board \-ˌbōrd\ n : a piece of dining-room furniture for holding articles of table service

side·burns \-ˌbərnz\ n pl : whiskers on the side of the face in front of the ears

side by side *adv* 1 : beside one another 2 : in the same place, time, or circumstance — **side–by–side** *adj*

side·car \-ˌkär\ n : a one-wheeled passenger car attached to the side of a motorcycle

side effect n : a secondary and usu. adverse effect (as of a drug)

side·kick \'sīd-ˌkik\ n : PAL, PARTNER

¹**side·long** \'sīd-ˌlȯŋ\ *adv* : in the direction of or along the side : OBLIQUELY

²**sidelong** *adj* : directed to one side ⟨~ look⟩

side·man \'sīd-ˌman\ n : a member of a jazz or swing orchestra

side·piece \-ˌpēs\ n : a piece forming or contained in the side of something

si·de·re·al \sī-ˈdir-ē-əl, sə-\ *adj* [L *sidereus,* fr. *sider-, sidas* star, constellation] 1 : of or relating to the stars 2 : measured by the apparent motion of the stars

side·sad·dle \'sīd-ˌsad-ᵊl\ n : a saddle for women on which the rider sits with both legs on the same side of the horse — **sidesaddle** *adv*

side·show \'sīd-ˌshō\ n 1 : a minor show offered in addition to a main exhibition (as of a circus) 2 : an incidental diversion

side·step \-ˌstep\ *vb* 1 : to step aside 2 : AVOID, EVADE

side·stroke \-ˌstrōk\ n : a swimming stroke which is executed on the side and in which the arms are swept backward and downward and the legs do a scissors kick

side·swipe \-ˌswīp\ *vb* : to strike with a glancing blow along the side — **sideswipe** n

¹**side·track** \-ˌtrak\ n : SIDING 1

²**sidetrack** *vb* 1 : to switch from a main railroad line to a siding 2 : to turn aside from a purpose

side·walk \'sīd-ˌwȯk\ n : a paved walk at the side of a road or street

side·wall \-ˌwȯl\ n 1 : a wall forming the side of something 2 : the side of an automobile tire

side·ways \-ˌwāz\ *adv or adj* 1 : from the side 2 : with one side to the front 3 : to, toward, or at one side

side·wind·er \-ˌwīn-dər\ n : a small pale-colored desert rattlesnake of the southwestern U.S.

sid·ing \'sī-diŋ\ n 1 : a short railroad track connected with the main track 2 : material (as boards) covering the outside of frame buildings

si·dle \'sīd-ᵊl\ *vb* **si·dled; si·dling** : to move sideways or with one side foremost

SIDS *abbr* sudden infant death syndrome

siege \'sēj\ n 1 : the placing of an army around or before a fortified place to force its surrender 2 : a persistent attack (as of illness)

sie·mens \'sē-mənz, 'zē-\ n : a unit of conductance equivalent to one ampere per volt

si·er·ra \sē-ˈer-ə\ n [Sp, lit., saw, fr. L *serra*] : a range of mountains esp. with jagged peaks

si·es·ta \sē-ˈes-tə\ n [Sp, fr. L *sexta (hora)* noon, lit., sixth hour] : a midday rest or nap

sieve \'siv\ n : a utensil with meshes or holes to separate finer particles from coarser or solids from liquids

sift \'sift\ *vb* 1 : to pass through a sieve 2 : to separate with or as if with a sieve 3 : to examine carefully 4 : to scatter by or as if by passing through a sieve — **sift·er** n

sig *abbr* 1 signal 2 signature

sigh \'sī\ *vb* 1 : to let out a deep audible breath (as in weariness or sorrow) 2 : GRIEVE, YEARN — **sigh** n

¹**sight** \'sīt\ n 1 : something seen or worth seeing 2 : the process or power of seeing; *esp* : the sense of which the eye is the receptor and by which qualities of appearance (as position, shape, and color) are perceived 3 : INSPECTION 4 : a device (as a small bead on a gun barrel) that aids the eye in aiming 5 : VIEW, GLIMPSE 6 : the range of vision — **sight·less** *adj*

²**sight** *vb* 1 : to get sight of 2 : to aim by means of a sight

sight·ed \'sī-təd\ *adj* : having sight

sight·ly \-lē\ *adj* : pleasing to the sight

sight-see·ing \'sīt-ˌsē-iŋ\ *adj* : engaged in or used for seeing sights of interest — **sight·seer** \-ˌsē-ər\ n

sig·ma \'sig-mə\ n : the 18th letter of the Greek alphabet — Σ or σ or ς

¹**sign** \'sīn\ n 1 : a gesture expressing a command, wish, or thought 2 : SYMBOL 3 : a notice publicly displayed for advertising purposes or for giving direction or warning 4 : OMEN, PORTENT 5 : TRACE, VESTIGE

²**sign** *vb* 1 : to mark with a sign 2 : to represent by a sign 3 : to make a sign or signal 4 : to write one's name on in token of assent or obligation 5 : to assign legally 6 : to use sign language — **sign·er** n

¹**sig·nal** \'sig-nəl\ n 1 : a sign agreed on as the start of some joint action 2 : a sign giving warning or notice of something 3 : the message, sound, or image transmitted in electronic communication (as radio)

²**signal** *vb* **-naled** *or* **-nalled; -nal·ing** *or* **-nal·ling** 1 : to notify by a signal 2 : to communicate by signals

³**signal** *adj* : DISTINGUISHED ⟨a ~ honor⟩ — **sig·nal·ly** *adv*

sig·nal·ize \'sig-nə-ˌlīz\ *vb* **-ized; -iz·ing** : to point out or make conspicuous — **sig·nal·i·za·tion** \ˌsig-nə-lə-ˈzā-shən\ n

sig·nal·man \'sig-nəl-mən, -ˌman\ n : a person who signals or works with signals

sig·na·to·ry \'sig-nə-ˌtȯr-ē\ n, pl **-ries** : a person or government that signs jointly with others — **signatory** *adj*

sig·na·ture \'sig-nə-ˌchu̇r\ n 1 : the name of a person written by himself or herself 2 : the sign placed after the clef to indicate the key or the meter of a piece of music

sign·board \'sīn-ˌbōrd\ n : a board bearing a sign or notice

sig·net \'sig-nət\ n : a small intaglio seal (as in a ring)

sig·nif·i·cance \sig-ˈni-fi-kəns\ n 1 : something signified : MEANING 2 : SUGGESTIVENESS 3 : CONSEQUENCE, IMPORTANCE

sig·nif·i·cant \-kənt\ *adj* 1 : having meaning; *esp* : having a hidden or special meaning 2 : having or likely to have considerable influence or effect : IMPORTANT — **sig·nif·i·cant·ly** *adv*

sig·ni·fy \'sig-nə-ˌfī\ *vb* **-fied; -fy·ing** 1 : to show by a sign 2 : MEAN, IMPORT 3 : to have significance — **sig·ni·fi·ca·tion** \ˌsig-nə-fə-ˈkā-shən\ n

sign in *vb* : to make a record of arrival (as by signing a register)

sign language n : a formal system of hand gestures used for communication (as by the deaf)

\ə\abut \ᵊ\kitten \ər\further \a\ash \ā\ace \ä\mop, mar
\au̇\out \ch\chin \e\bet \ē\easy \g\go \i\hit \ī\ice \j\job
\ŋ\sing \ō\go \ȯ\law \ȯi\boy \th\thin \t̲h̲\the \ü\loot \u̇\foot
\y\yet \zh\vision *see also* Pronunciation Symbols page

sign off *vb* : to announce the end (as of a program or broadcast)

sign of the cross : a gesture of the hand forming a cross (as to invoke divine blessing)

sign on *vb* **1** : ENLIST **2** : to announce the start of broadcasting for the day

sign out *vb* : to make a record of departure (as by signing a register)

sign·post \'sīn-ˌpōst\ *n* : a post bearing a sign

Sikh \'sēk\ *n* : an adherent of a religion of India marked by rejection of caste — **Sikh·ism** *n*

si·lage \'sī-lij\ *n* : fodder fermented (as in a silo) to produce a rich moist animal feed

¹**si·lence** \'sī-ləns\ *n* **1** : the state of being silent **2** : STILLNESS **3** : SECRECY

²**silence** *vb* **si·lenced; si·lenc·ing 1** : to reduce to silence : STILL **2** : to cause to cease hostile firing or criticism

si·lenc·er \'sī-lən-sər\ *n* : a device for muffling the noise of a gunshot

si·lent \'sī-lənt\ *adj* **1** : not speaking : MUTE; *also* : TACITURN **2** : STILL, QUIET **3** : performed or borne without utterance **syn** reticent, reserved, closemouthed, close — **si·lent·ly** *adv*

¹**sil·hou·ette** \ˌsil-ə-'wet\ *n* [F] **1** : a representation of the outlines of an object filled in with black or some other uniform color **2** : OUTLINE ⟨∼ of a ship⟩

²**silhouette** *vb* **-ett·ed; -ett·ing** : to represent by a silhouette; *also* : to show against a light background

sil·i·ca \'si-li-kə\ *n* : a mineral that consists of silicon and oxygen

sil·i·cate \'si-lə-ˌkāt, 'si-li-kət\ *n* : a chemical salt that consists of a metal combined with silicon and oxygen

si·li·ceous *or* **si·li·cious** \sə-'li-shəs\ *adj* : of, relating to, or containing silica or a silicate

sil·i·con \'si-li-kən, 'si-lə-ˌkän\ *n* : a nonmetallic chemical element that occurs in combination as the most abundant element next to oxygen in the earth's crust and is used esp. in electronics — see ELEMENT table

sil·i·cone \'si-lə-ˌkōn\ *n* : an organic silicon compound used esp. for lubricants and varnishes

sil·i·co·sis \ˌsi-lə-'kō-səs\ *n* : a lung disease caused by prolonged inhaling of silica dusts

silk \'silk\ *n* **1** : a fine strong lustrous protein fiber produced by insect larvae usu. for their cocoons; *esp* : one from moth larvae (**silk·worms** \-ˌwərmz\) used for cloth **2** : thread or cloth made from silk — **silk·en** \'sil-kən\ *adj* — **silky** *adj*

silk screen *n* : a stencil process in which coloring matter is forced through the meshes of a prepared silk or organdy screen; *also* : a print made by this process — **silk–screen** *vb*

sill \'sil\ *n* : a heavy crosspiece (as of wood or stone) that forms the bottom member of a window frame or a doorway; *also* : a horizontal supporting piece at the base of a structure

sil·ly \'si-lē\ *adj* **sil·li·er; -est** [ME *sely, silly* happy, innocent, pitiable, feeble, fr. OE *sǣlig*] : FOOLISH, ABSURD, STUPID — **sil·li·ness** *n*

si·lo \'sī-lō\ *n, pl* **silos** [Sp] **1** : a trench, pit, or esp. a tall cylinder for making and storing silage **2** : an underground structure for housing a guided missile

¹**silt** \'silt\ *n* **1** : fine earth; *esp* : particles of such soil floating in rivers, ponds, or lakes **2** : a deposit (as by a river) of silt — **silty** *adj*

²**silt** *vb* : to obstruct or cover with silt — **silt·ation** \sil-'tā-shən\ *n*

Si·lu·ri·an \sī-'lùr-ē-ən\ *adj* : of, relating to, or being the period of the Paleozoic era between the Ordovician and the Devonian marked by the appearance of the first land plants — **Silurian** *n*

¹**sil·ver** \'sil-vər\ *n* **1** : a white ductile metallic chemical element that takes a high polish and is a better conductor of heat and electricity than any other substance —

see ELEMENT table **2** : coin made of silver **3** : FLATWARE **4** : a grayish white color — **sil·very** *adj*

²**silver** *adj* **1** : relating to, made of, or coated with silver **2** : SILVERY

³**silver** *vb* **sil·vered; sil·ver·ing** : to coat with or as if with silver — **sil·ver·er** *n*

silver bromide *n* : a light-sensitive compound used esp. in photography

sil·ver·fish \'sil-vər-ˌfish\ *n* : any of various small wingless insects found in houses and sometimes injurious esp. to sized paper and starched clothes

silver iodide *n* : a light-sensitive compound used in photography, rainmaking, and medicine

silver maple *n* : a No. American maple with deeply cut leaves that are green above and silvery white below

silver nitrate *n* : a soluble compound used in photography and as an antiseptic

sil·ver·ware \'sil-vər-ˌwar\ *n* : FLATWARE

sim·i·an \'si-mē-ən\ *n* : MONKEY, APE — **simian** *adj*

sim·i·lar \'si-mə-lər\ *adj* : marked by correspondence or resemblance **syn** alike, akin, comparable, parallel — **sim·i·lar·i·ty** \ˌsi-mə-'lar-ə-tē\ *n* — **sim·i·lar·ly** *adv*

sim·i·le \'si-mə-(ˌ)lē\ *n* [ME, fr. L, likeness, comparison, fr. neut. of *similis* like, similar] : a figure of speech in which two dissimilar things are compared by the use of *like* or *as* (as in "cheeks like roses")

si·mil·i·tude \sə-'mi-lə-ˌtüd, -ˌtyüd\ *n* : LIKENESS, RESEMBLANCE

sim·mer \'si-mər\ *vb* **sim·mered; sim·mer·ing 1** : to stew at or just below the boiling point **2** : to be on the point of bursting out with violence or emotional disturbance — **simmer** *n*

si·mo·nize \'sī-mə-ˌnīz\ *vb* **-nized; -niz·ing** : to polish with or as if with wax

si·mo·ny \'sī-mə-nē, 'si-\ *n* [ME *symonie*, fr. LL *simonia*, fr. *Simon* Magus sorcerer of Samaria in Acts 8:9–24] : the buying or selling of a church office

sim·pa·ti·co \sim-'pä-ti-ˌkō, -'pa-\ *adj* : CONGENIAL, LIKABLE

sim·per \'sim-pər\ *vb* : to smile in a silly manner — **simper** *n*

sim·ple \'sim-pəl\ *adj* **sim·pler** \-pə-lər\; **sim·plest** \-pə-ləst\ [ME, fr. OF, plain, uncomplicated, artless, fr. L *simplus, simplex,* lit., single; L *simplus* fr. *sim-* one + *-plus* multiplied by; L *simplex* fr. *sim-* + *-plex* -fold] **1** : free from dishonesty or vanity : INNOCENT **2** : free from ostentation **3** : of humble origin or modest position **4** : STUPID **5** : not complex : PLAIN ⟨a ∼ melody⟩ ⟨∼ directions⟩ **6** : lacking education, experience, or intelligence **7** : developing from a single ovary ⟨a ∼ fruit⟩ **syn** easy, facile, light, effortless — **sim·ple·ness** *n* — **sim·ply** *adv*

simple interest *n* : interest paid or computed on the original principal only of a loan or on the amount of an account

sim·ple·ton \'sim-pəl-tən\ *n* : FOOL

sim·plic·i·ty \sim-'pli-sə-tē\ *n* **1** : lack of complication : CLEARNESS **2** : CANDOR, ARTLESSNESS **3** : plainness in manners or way of life **4** : SILLINESS, FOLLY

sim·pli·fy \'sim-plə-ˌfī\ *vb* **-fied; -fy·ing** : to make less complex — **sim·pli·fi·ca·tion** \ˌsim-plə-fə-'kā-shən\ *n*

sim·plis·tic \sim-'plis-tik\ *adj* : excessively simple : tending to overlook complexities ⟨a ∼ solution⟩

sim·u·late \'sim-yə-ˌlāt\ *vb* **-lat·ed; -lat·ing** : to give or create the effect or appearance of : IMITATE; *also* : to make a simulation of — **sim·u·la·tor** \'sim-yə-ˌlā-tər\ *n*

sim·u·la·tion \ˌsim-yə-'lā-shən\ *n* **1** : the act or process of simulating **2** : an object that is not genuine **3** : the imitation by one system or process of the way in which another system or process works

si·mul·ta·ne·ous \ˌsī-məl-'tā-nē-əs, ˌsi-\ *adj* : occurring or operating at the same time — **si·mul·ta·ne·ous·ly** *adv* — **si·mul·ta·ne·ous·ness** *n*

¹**sin** \'sin\ *n* **1** : an offense esp. against God **2** : FAULT **3** : a weakened state of human nature in which the self is estranged from God — **sin·less** *adj*

²**sin** *vb* **sinned; sin·ning** : to commit a sin — **sin·ner** *n*

¹**since** \'sins\ *adv* **1** : from a past time until now **2** : backward in time : AGO **3** : after a time in the past

²**since** *conj* **1** : from the time when **2** : seeing that : BECAUSE

³**since** *prep* **1** : in the period after ⟨changes made ∼ the war⟩ **2** : continuously from ⟨has been here ∼ 1980⟩

sin·cere \sin-'sir\ *adj* **sin·cer·er; sin·cer·est** **1** : free from hypocrisy : HONEST **2** : GENUINE, REAL — **sin·cere·ly** *adv* — **sin·cer·i·ty** \-'ser-ə-tē\ *n*

si·ne·cure \'sī-ni-ˌkyu̇r, 'si-\ *n* : a paying job that requires little or no work

si·ne die \ˌsī-ni-'dī-ˌē, ˌsi-nā-'dē-ˌā\ *adv* [L, without day] : INDEFINITELY

si·ne qua non \ˌsi-ni-ˌkwä-'nän, -'nōn\ *n, pl* **sine qua nons** *also* **sine qui·bus non** \-ˌkwi-(ˌ)bu̇s-\ [LL, without which not] : something indispensable or essential

sin·ew \'sin-yü\ *n* **1** : TENDON **2** : physical strength — **sin·ewy** *adj*

sin·ful \'sin-fəl\ *adj* : marked by or full of sin : WICKED — **sin·ful·ly** *adv* — **sin·ful·ness** *n*

¹**sing** \'siŋ\ *vb* **sang** \'saŋ\ *or* **sung** \'səŋ\; **sung; sing·ing** **1** : to produce musical tones with the voice; *also* : to utter with musical tones **2** : to make a prolonged shrill sound ⟨locusts ∼*ing*⟩ **3** : to produce harmonious sustained sounds ⟨birds ∼*ing*⟩ **4** : CHANT, INTONE **5** : to write poetry; *also* : to celebrate in song or verse **6** : to give information or evidence — **sing·er** *n*

²**sing** *abbr* singular

Sin·ga·por·ean \ˌsiŋ-ə-'pōr-ē-ən\ *n* : a native or inhabitant of Singapore — **Singaporean** *adj*

singe \'sinj\ *vb* **singed; singe·ing** : to scorch lightly the outside of; *esp* : to remove the hair or down from (a plucked fowl) with flame

¹**sin·gle** \'siŋ-gəl\ *adj* **1** : UNMARRIED **2** : being alone : being the only one **3** : having only one feature or part **4** : made for one person **syn** sole, unique, lone, solitary, separate, particular — **sin·gle·ness** *n* — **sin·gly** *adv*

²**single** *vb* **sin·gled; sin·gling** **1** : to select (one) from a group **2** : to hit a single

³**single** *n* **1** : a separate person or thing; *also* : an unmarried person **2** : a hit in baseball that enables the batter to reach first base **3** *pl* : a tennis match with one player on each side

single bond *n* : a chemical bond in which one pair of electrons is shared by two atoms in a molecule

single–lens reflex *n* : a camera having a single lens that forms an image which is reflected to the viewfinder or recorded on film

sin·gle·tree \-ˌtrē\ *n* : WHIFFLETREE

sin·gu·lar \'siŋ-gyə-lər\ *adj* **1** : of, relating to, or constituting a word form denoting one person, thing, or instance **2** : OUTSTANDING, EXCEPTIONAL **3** : of unusual quality **4** : ODD, PECULIAR — **singular** *n* — **sin·gu·lar·i·ty** \ˌsiŋ-gyə-'lar-ə-tē\ *n* — **sin·gu·lar·ly** *adv*

sin·is·ter \'si-nəs-tər\ *adj* [ME, fr. L, on the left side, inauspicious] **1** : singularly evil or productive of evil **2** : accompanied by or leading to disaster **syn** baleful, malign, malefic, maleficent

¹**sink** \'siŋk\ *vb* **sank** \'saŋk\ *or* **sunk** \'səŋk\; **sunk; sink·ing 1** : SUBMERGE **2** : to descend lower and lower **3** : to grow less in volume or height **4** : to slope downward **5** : to penetrate downward **6** : to fail in health or strength **7** : LAPSE, DEGENERATE **8** : to cause (a ship) to descend to the bottom **9** : to make (a hole or shaft) by digging, boring, or cutting **10** : INVEST — **sink·able** *adj*

²**sink** *n* **1** : DRAIN, SEWER **2** : a basin connected with a drain **3** : an extensive depression in the land surface

sink·er \'siŋ-kər\ *n* : a weight for sinking a fishing line or net

sink·hole \'siŋk-ˌhōl\ *n* : a hollow place in which drainage collects

sin tax *n* : a tax on substances or activities considered sinful or harmful

sin·u·ous \'sin-yə-wəs\ *adj* : bending in and out : WINDING — **sin·u·os·i·ty** \ˌsin-yə-'wä-sə-tē\ *n*

si·nus \'sī-nəs\ *n* [ME, fr. ML, fr. L, curve, hollow] **1** : any of several cavities of the skull usu. connecting with the nostrils **2** : a space forming a channel (as for the passage of blood)

si·nus·itis \ˌsī-nə-'sī-təs\ *n* : inflammation of a sinus of the skull

Sioux \'sü\ *n, pl* **Sioux** *same or* \'süz\ [F] : DAKOTA

sip \'sip\ *vb* **sipped; sip·ping** : to drink in small quantities — **sip** *n*

¹**si·phon** \'sī-fən\ *n* **1** : a bent tube through which a liquid can be transferred by means of air pressure up and over the edge of one container and into another container placed at a lower level **2** *usu* **sy·phon** : a bottle that ejects soda water through a tube when a valve is opened

siphon 1

²**siphon** *vb* **si·phoned; si·phon·ing** : to draw off by means of a siphon

sir \'sər\ *n* [ME *sire* sire, fr. OF, fr. L *senior,* compar. of *senex* old, old man] **1** : a man of rank or position — used as a title before the given name of a knight or baronet **2** — used as a usu. respectful form of address

Si·rach \'sī-rak, sə-'räk\ *n* — see BIBLE table

¹**sire** \'sīr\ *n* **1** : FATHER; *also, archaic* : FOREFATHER **2** *archaic* : LORD — used as a form of address and a title **3** : the male parent of an animal (as a horse or dog)

²**sire** *vb* **sired; sir·ing** : BEGET

si·ren \'sī-rən\ *n* **1** : a seductive or alluring woman **2** : an electrically operated device for producing a loud shrill warning sound — **siren** *adj*

sir·loin \'sər-ˌlȯin\ *n* [alter. of earlier *surloin,* modif. of MF *surlonge,* fr. *sur* over (fr. L *super*) + *longe* loin] : a cut of beef taken from the part in front of the round

sirup *var of* SYRUP

si·sal \'sī-səl, -zəl\ *n* : a strong cordage fiber from an agave; *also* : this agave

sis·sy \'si-sē\ *n, pl* **sissies** : an effeminate boy or man; *also* : a timid or cowardly person

sis·ter \'sis-tər\ *n* **1** : a female having one or both parents in common with another individual **2** : a member of a religious order of women : NUN **3** *chiefly Brit* : NURSE **4** : a woman regarded as a comrade — **sis·ter·ly** *adj*

sis·ter·hood \-ˌhu̇d\ *n* **1** : the state of being a sister **2** : a community or society of sisters **3** : the solidarity of women based on shared conditions

sis·ter–in–law \'sis-tə-rən-ˌlȯ\ *n, pl* **sisters–in–law** : the sister of one's spouse; *also* : the wife of one's brother

sit \'sit\ *vb* **sat** \'sat\; **sit·ting 1** : to rest upon the buttocks or haunches **2** : ROOST, PERCH **3** : to occupy a seat **4** : to hold a session **5** : to cover eggs for hatching : BROOD **6** : to pose for a portrait **7** : to remain quiet or inactive **8** : FIT **9** : to cause (oneself) to be seated **10** : to place in position **11** : to keep one's seat on ⟨~ a horse⟩ **12** : BABY-SIT — **sit·ter** *n*

si·tar \si-'tär\ *n* [Hindi *sitār*] : an Indian lute with a long neck and a varying number of strings

sit·com \'sit-ˌkäm\ *n* : SITUATION COMEDY

site \'sīt\ *n* : LOCATION

sit–in \'sit-ˌin\ *n* : an act of sitting in the seats or on the floor of an establishment as a means of organized protest

sit·u·at·ed \'si-chə-ˌwā-təd\ *adj* : LOCATED, PLACED

sit·u·a·tion \ˌsi-chə-'wā-shən\ *n* **1** : LOCATION, SITE **2** : JOB **3** : CONDITION, CIRCUMSTANCES

situation comedy *n* : a radio or television comedy series that involves a continuing cast of characters in a succession of episodes

sit–up \'sit-ˌəp\ *n* : an exercise performed from a supine position by raising the trunk to a sitting position without lifting the feet and returning to the original position

Si·van \'si-vən\ *n* [Heb *Sīwān*] : the 9th month of the civil year or the 3d month of the ecclesiastical year in the Jewish calendar

six \'siks\ *n* **1** : one more than five **2** : the 6th in a set or series **3** : something having six units — **six** *adj or pron* — **sixth** \'siksth\ *adj or adv or n*

six–gun \'siks-ˌgən\ *n* : a 6-chambered revolver

six–pack \-ˌpak\ *n* : six bottles or cans (as of beer) packaged and purchased together; *also* : the contents of a six-pack

six·pence \-pəns, *US also* -ˌpens\ *n* : the sum of six pence; *also* : an English silver coin of this value

six–shoot·er \'siks-ˌshü-tər\ *n* : SIX-GUN

six·teen \ˌsiks-'tēn\ *n* : one more than 15 — **sixteen** *adj or pron* — **six·teenth** \-'tēnth\ *adj or n*

six·ty \'siks-tē\ *n*, *pl* **sixties** : six times 10 — **six·ti·eth** \'siks-tē-əth\ *adj or n* — **sixty** *adj or pron*

siz·able *or* **size·able** \'sī-zə-bəl\ *adj* : quite large — **sizably** \-blē\ *adv*

¹size \'sīz\ *n* : physical extent or bulk : DIMENSIONS; *also* : considerable proportions — **sized** \'sīzd\ *adj*

²size *vb* **sized**; **siz·ing 1** : to grade or classify according to size **2** : to form a judgment of ⟨~ up the situation⟩

³size *n* : a gluey material used for filling the pores in paper, plaster, or textiles — **siz·ing** *n*

⁴size *vb* **sized**; **siz·ing** : to cover, stiffen, or glaze with size

siz·zle \'si-zəl\ *vb* **siz·zled**; **siz·zling** : to fry or shrivel up with a hissing sound — **sizzle** *n*

SJ *abbr* Society of Jesus

SK *abbr* Saskatchewan

ska \'skä\ *n* : popular music of Jamaican origin combining traditional Caribbean rhythms and jazz

¹skate \'skāt\ *n*, *pl* **skates** *also* **skate** : any of a family of rays with thick broad winglike fins

²skate *n* **1** : a metal frame and runner attached to a shoe and used for gliding over ice **2** : ROLLER SKATE — **skate** *vb* — **skat·er** *n*

skate·board \'skāt-ˌbōrd\ *n* : a short board mounted on small wheels — **skate·board·er** *n* — **skate·board·ing** *n*

skeet \'skēt\ *n* : trapshooting in which clay targets are thrown in such a way that their angle of flight simulates that of a flushed game bird

skein \'skān\ *n* : a loosely twisted quantity of yarn or thread wound on a reel

skel·e·ton \'ske-lə-ᵗn\ *n* **1** : a usu. bony supporting framework of an animal body **2** : a bare minimum **3** : FRAMEWORK — **skel·e·tal** \-lət-ᵊl\ *adj*

skep·tic \'skep-tik\ *n* **1** : one who believes in skepticism

2 : a person disposed to skepticism esp. regarding religion — **skep·ti·cal** \-ti-kəl\ *adj*

skep·ti·cism \'skep-tə-ˌsi-zəm\ *n* **1** : a doubting state of mind **2** : a doctrine that certainty of knowledge cannot be attained **3** : doubt concerning religion

sketch \'skech\ *n* **1** : a rough drawing or outline **2** : a short or light literary composition (as a story or essay); *also* : a short comedy piece — **sketch** *vb* — **sketchy** *adj*

¹skew \'skyü\ *vb* : TWIST, SWERVE

²skew *n* : SLANT

skew·er \'skyü-ər\ *n* : a long pin for holding small pieces of meat and vegetables for broiling — **skewer** *vb*

¹ski \'skē\ *n*, *pl* **skis** [Norw, fr. ON *skīth* stick of wood, ski] : one of a pair of long strips (as of wood, metal or plastic) curving upward in front that are used for gliding over snow or water

²ski *vb* **skied** \'skēd\; **ski·ing** : to glide on skis — **ski·er** *n*

¹skid \'skid\ *n* **1** : a plank for supporting something above the ground **2** : a device placed under a wheel to prevent turning **3** : a timber or rail over or on which something is slid or rolled **4** : the act of skidding **5** : a runner on the landing gear of an aircraft **6** : ²PALLET

²skid *vb* **skid·ded**; **skid·ding 1** : to slide without rotating ⟨a *skidding* wheel⟩ **2** : to slide sideways on the road ⟨the car *skidded* on ice⟩ **3** : SLIDE, SLIP

skid row *n* : a district of cheap saloons frequented by vagrants and alcoholics

skiff \'skif\ *n* : a small boat

ski jump *n* : a jump made by a person wearing skis; *also* : a course or track prepared for such jumping — **ski jump** *vb* — **ski jumper** *n*

skil·ful *chiefly Brit var of* SKILLFUL

ski lift *n* : a mechanical device (as a chairlift) for carrying skiers up a long slope

skill \'skil\ *n* **1** : ability to use one's knowledge effectively in doing something **2** : developed or acquired ability **syn** art, craft, cunning, dexterity, expertise, know-how — **skilled** \'skild\ *adj*

skil·let \'ski-lət\ *n* : a frying pan

skill·ful \'skil-fəl\ *adj* **1** : having or displaying skill : EXPERT **2** : accomplished with skill — **skill·ful·ly** *adv* — **skill·ful·ness** *n*

¹skim \'skim\ *vb* **skimmed**; **skim·ming 1** : to take off from the top of a liquid; *also* : to remove (scum or cream) from ⟨~ milk⟩ **2** : to read rapidly and superficially **3** : to pass swiftly over — **skim·mer** *n*

²skim *adj* : having the cream removed

skimp \'skimp\ *vb* : to give insufficient attention, effort, or funds; *also* : to save by skimping

skimpy \'skim-pē\ *adj* **skimp·i·er**; **-est** : deficient in supply or execution

¹skin \'skin\ *n* **1** : the outer limiting layer of an animal body; *also* : the usu. thin tough tissue of which this is made **2** : an outer or surface layer (as a rind or peel) — **skin·less** *adj* — **skinned** *adj*

²skin *vb* **skinned**; **skin·ning** : to free from skin : remove the skin of

³skin *adj* : devoted to showing nudes ⟨~ magazines⟩

skin diving *n* : the sport of swimming under water with a face mask and flippers and esp. without a portable breathing device — **skin–dive** *vb* — **skin diver** *n*

skin·flint \'skin-ˌflint\ *n* : a very stingy person

skin graft *n* : a piece of skin taken from one area to replace skin in another area — **skin grafting** *n*

¹skin·ny \'ski-nē\ *adj* **skin·ni·er**; **-est 1** : resembling skin **2** : very thin

²skinny *n* : inside information

skin·ny–dip·ping \-ˌdi-piŋ\ *n* : swimming in the nude

skin·tight \'skin-'tīt\ *adj* : closely fitted to the figure

¹skip \'skip\ *vb* **skipped**; **skip·ping 1** : to move with leaps and bounds **2** : to leap lightly over **3** : to pass from point to point (as in reading) disregarding what is in between **4** : to pass over without notice or mention

²**skip** *n* : a light bouncing step; *also* : a gait of alternate hops and steps

skip·jack \'skip-ˌjak\ *n* : a small sailboat with vertical sides and a bottom similar to a flat V

skip·per \'ski-pər\ *n* [ME, fr. MD *schipper*, fr. *schip* ship] : the master of a ship; *also* : the manager of a baseball team — **skipper** *vb*

skir·mish \'skər-mish\ *n* : a minor engagement in war; *also* : a minor dispute or contest — **skirmish** *vb*

¹**skirt** \'skərt\ *n* : a free-hanging garment or part of a garment extending from the waist down

²**skirt** *vb* **1** : to pass around the outer edge of **2** : BORDER **3** : EVADE

skit \'skit\ *n* : a brief dramatic sketch

ski tow *n* : SKI LIFT

skit·ter \'ski-tər\ *vb* : to glide or skip lightly or quickly : skim along a surface

skit·tish \'ski-tish\ *adj* **1** : CAPRICIOUS **2** : easily frightened ⟨a ∼ horse⟩; *also* : WARY

ski·wear \'skē-ˌwar\ *n* : clothing suitable for wear while skiing

skosh \'skōsh\ *n* [Jp *sukoshi*] : a small amount : BIT

skul·dug·gery *or* **skull·dug·gery** \ˌskəl-'də-gə-rē\ *n*, *pl* **-ger·ies** : underhanded or unscrupulous behavior

skulk \'skəlk\ *vb* : to move furtively : SNEAK, LURK — **skulk·er** *n*

skull \'skəl\ *n* : the skeleton of the head of a vertebrate that protects the brain and supports the jaws

skull and crossbones *n*, *pl* **skulls and crossbones** : a depiction of a human skull over crossbones usu. indicating a danger

skull·cap \'skəl-ˌkap\ *n* : a close-fitting brimless cap

¹**skunk** \'skəŋk\ *n*, *pl* **skunks** *also* **skunk 1** : any of various New World mammals related to the weasels that can forcibly eject an ill-smelling fluid when startled **2** : a contemptible person

²**skunk** *vb* : to defeat decisively; *esp* : to shut out in a game

skunk cabbage *n* : either of two No. American perennial herbs related to the arums that occur in shaded wet to swampy areas and have a fetid odor suggestive of a skunk

sky \'skī\ *n*, *pl* **skies 1** : the upper air **2** : HEAVEN — **sky·ey** \'skī-ē\ *adj*

sky·cap \-ˌkap\ *n* : a person employed to carry luggage at an airport

sky·div·ing \-ˌdī-viŋ\ *n* : the sport of jumping from an airplane and executing various body maneuvers before opening a parachute — **sky diver** *n*

sky·jack \-ˌjak\ *vb* : to commandeer an airplane in flight by threat of violence — **sky·jack·er** *n* — **sky·jack·ing** *n*

¹**sky·lark** \-ˌlärk\ *n* : a European lark noted for singing in steep upward flight

²**skylark** *vb* : FROLIC, SPORT

sky·light \'skī-ˌlīt\ *n* : a window in a roof or ceiling — **sky·light·ed** \-ˌlī-təd\ *adj*

sky·line \-ˌlīn\ *n* **1** : HORIZON **2** : an outline against the sky

¹**sky·rock·et** \-ˌrä-kət\ *n* : ROCKET 1

²**skyrocket** *vb* : ROCKET 2

sky·scrap·er \-ˌskrā-pər\ *n* : a very tall building

sky·walk \-ˌwok\ *n* : an aerial walkway connecting two buildings

sky·ward \-wərd\ *adv* : toward the sky

sky·writ·ing \-ˌrī-tiŋ\ *n* : writing in the sky formed by smoke emitted from an airplane — **sky·writ·er** *n*

slab \'slab\ *n* : a thick flat piece or slice

¹**slack** \'slak\ *adj* **1** : CARELESS, NEGLIGENT **2** : SLUGGISH, LISTLESS **3** : not taut : LOOSE **4** : not busy or active **syn** lax, remiss, neglectful, delinquent, derelict — **slack·ly** *adv* — **slack·ness** *n*

²**slack** *vb* **1** : to make or become slack : LOOSEN, RELAX **2** : SLAKE 2

³**slack** *n* **1** : cessation of movement or flow : LETUP **2** : a part that hangs loose without strain ⟨∼ of a rope⟩ **3** : trousers esp. for casual wear — usu. used in pl.

slack·en \'sla-kən\ *vb* : to make or become slack

slack·er \'sla-kər\ *n* : one that shirks work or evades military duty

slag \'slag\ *n* : the waste left after the melting of ores and the separation of metal from them

slain *past part of* SLAY

slake \'slāk, *for 2 also* 'slak\ *vb* **slaked; slak·ing 1** : to relieve or satisfy with or as if with refreshing drink ⟨∼ thirst⟩ **2** : to cause (lime) to crumble by mixture with water

sla·lom \'slä-ləm\ *n* [Norw *slalåm*, lit., sloping track] : skiing in a zigzag course between obstacles

¹**slam** \'slam\ *n* : the winning of every trick or of all tricks but one in bridge

²**slam** *n* : a heavy jarring impact : BANG

³**slam** *vb* **slammed; slam·ming 1** : to shut violently and noisily **2** : to throw or strike with a loud impact

slam·mer \'sla-mər\ *n* : JAIL, PRISON

¹**slan·der** \'slan-dər\ *vb* : to utter slander against : DEFAME — **slan·der·er** *n*

²**slander** *n* [ME *sclaundre*, *slaundre*, fr. OF *esclandre*, fr. LL *scandalum* stumbling block, offense] : a false report maliciously uttered and tending to injure the reputation of a person — **slan·der·ous** *adj*

slang \'slaŋ\ *n* : an informal nonstandard vocabulary composed typically of invented words, arbitrarily changed words, and extravagant figures of speech — **slangy** *adj*

¹**slant** \'slant\ *n* **1** : a sloping direction, line, or plane **2** : a particular or personal viewpoint — **slant** *adj* — **slant·wise** \-ˌwīz\ *adv or adj*

²**slant** *vb* **1** : SLOPE **2** : to interpret or present in accordance with a special viewpoint or bias **syn** incline, lean, list, tilt, heel — **slant·ing·ly** *adv*

slap \'slap\ *vb* **slapped; slap·ping 1** : to strike sharply with the open hand **2** : REBUFF, INSULT — **slap** *n*

slap·stick \-ˌstik\ *n* : comedy stressing horseplay

¹**slash** \'slash\ *vb* **1** : to cut with sweeping strokes **2** : to cut slits in (a garment) **3** : to reduce sharply

²**slash** *n* **1** : GASH **2** : an ornamental slit in a garment

slat \'slat\ *n* : a thin narrow flat strip

¹**slate** \'slāt\ *n* **1** : a dense fine-grained rock that splits into thin layers **2** : a roofing tile or a writing tablet made from this rock **3** : a written or unwritten record ⟨start with a clean ∼⟩ **4** : a list of candidates for election

²**slate** *vb* **slat·ed; slat·ing 1** : to cover with slate **2** : to designate for action or appointment

slath·er \'sla-thər\ *vb* : to spread with or on thickly or lavishly

slat·tern \'sla-tərn\ *n* : a slovenly woman — **slat·tern·ly** *adj*

¹**slaugh·ter** \'slo-tər\ *n* **1** : the butchering of livestock for market **2** : great destruction of lives esp. in battle

²**slaughter** *vb* **1** : to kill (animals) for food : BUTCHER **2** : to kill in large numbers or in a bloody way : MASSACRE

slaugh·ter·house \-ˌhaus\ *n* : an establishment where animals are butchered

Slav \'släv, 'slav\ *n* : a person speaking a Slavic language

¹**slave** \'slāv\ *n* [ME *sclave*, fr. OF or ML; OF *esclave*, fr. ML *sclavus*, fr. *Sclavus* Slav; fr. the enslavement of Slavs in eastern Europe in the Middle Ages] **1** : a per-

---

\ə\abut \ᵊ\kitten \ər\further \a\ash \ā\ace \ä\mop, mar \au̇\out \ch\chin \e\bet \ē\easy \g\go \i\hit \ī\ice \j\job \ŋ\sing \ō\go \ȯ\law \oi\boy \th\thin \th̲\the \ü\loot \u̇\foot \y\yet \zh\vision *see also* Pronunciation Symbols page son held in servitude as property **2** : a device (as the printer of a computer) that is directly responsive to another — **slave** *adj*

²**slave** *vb* **slaved; slav·ing** : to work like a slave : DRUDGE

¹**sla·ver** \'slā-vər, 'slā-\ *n* : SLOBBER — **slaver** *vb*

²**slav·er** \'slā-vər\ *n* : a ship or a person engaged in transporting slaves

slav·ery \'slāv-rē, 'slā-və-\ *n* **1** : wearisome drudgery **2** : the condition of being a slave **3** : the practice of owning slaves **syn** servitude, bondage, enslavement

¹**Slav·ic** \'slä-vik, 'slā-\ *n* : a branch of the Indo-European language family including various languages (as Russian or Polish) of eastern Europe

²**Slavic** *adj* : of or relating to the Slavs or their languages

slav·ish \'slā-vish\ *adj* **1** : SERVILE **2** : obeying or imitating with no freedom of judgment or choice — **slav·ish·ly** *adv*

slaw \'slò\ *n* : COLESLAW

slay \'slā\ *vb* **slew** \'slü\; **slain** \'slān\; **slay·ing** : KILL — **slay·er** *n*

sleaze \'slēz\ *n* : a sleazy quality, appearance, or behavior

slea·zy \'slē-zē\ *adj* **slea·zi·er; -est 1** : FLIMSY, SHODDY **2** : marked by cheapness of character or quality

¹**sled** \'sled\ *n* : a vehicle usu. on runners adapted esp. for sliding on snow

²**sled** *vb* **sled·ded, sled·ding** : to ride or carry on a sled

¹**sledge** \'slej\ *n* : SLEDGEHAMMER

²**sledge** *n* : a strong heavy sled

sledge·ham·mer \'slej-ˌha-mər\ *n* : a large heavy hammer wielded with both hands — **sledgehammer** *adj or vb*

¹**sleek** \'slēk\ *vb* **1** : to make smooth or glossy **2** : to gloss over

²**sleek** *adj* : having a smooth well-groomed look

¹**sleep** \'slēp\ *n* **1** : the natural periodic suspension of consciousness during which bodily powers are restored **2** : a state (as death or coma) suggesting sleep — **sleep·less** *adj* — **sleep·less·ness** *n*

²**sleep** *vb* **slept** \'slept\; **sleep·ing 1** : to rest or be in a state of sleep; *also* : to spend in sleep **2** : to have sexual intercourse — usu. used with *with* **3** : to provide sleeping space for

sleep·er \'slē-pər\ *n* **1** : one that sleeps **2** : a horizontal beam to support something on or near ground level **3** : SLEEPING CAR **4** : someone or something unpromising or unnoticed that suddenly attains prominence or value

sleeping bag *n* : a warmly lined bag for sleeping esp. outdoors

sleeping car *n* : a railroad car with berths for sleeping

sleeping pill *n* : a drug in tablet or capsule form taken to induce sleep

sleeping sickness *n* : a serious disease of tropical Africa that is marked by fever, lethargy, tremors, and loss of weight and is caused by protozoans transmitted by the tsetse fly

sleep·walk·er \'slēp-ˌwò-kər\ *n* : one that walks while or as if while asleep — **sleep·walk** \-ˌwòk\ *vb*

sleepy \'slē-pē\ *adj* **sleep·i·er; -est 1** : ready for sleep **2** : quietly inactive — **sleep·i·ly** \'slē-pə-lē\ *adv* — **sleep·i·ness** \-pē-nəs\ *n*

sleet \'slēt\ *n* : frozen or partly frozen rain — **sleet** *vb* — **sleety** *adj*

sleeve \'slēv\ *n* **1** : a part of a garment covering an arm **2** : a tubular part designed to fit over another part — **sleeve·less** *adj*

¹**sleigh** \'slā\ *n* : an open usu. horse-drawn vehicle on runners for use on snow or ice

²**sleigh** *vb* : to drive or travel in a sleigh

sleight \'slīt\ *n* **1** : TRICK **2** : DEXTERITY

sleight of hand : a trick requiring skillful manual manipulation

slen·der \'slen-dər\ *adj* **1** : SLIM, THIN **2** : WEAK, SLIGHT **3** : MEAGER, INADEQUATE

slen·der·ize \-də-ˌrīz\ *vb* **-ized; -iz·ing** : to make slender

sleuth \'slüth\ *n* [short for *sleuthhound* bloodhound, fr. ME, fr. *sleuth* track of an animal or person, fr. ON *slōth*] : DETECTIVE

¹**slew** \'slü\ *past of* SLAY

²**slew** *vb* : TURN, VEER, SKID

¹**slice** \'slīs\ *vb* **sliced; slic·ing 1** : to cut a slice from; *also* : to cut into slices **2** : to hit (a ball) so that a slice results

²**slice** *n* **1** : a thin flat piece cut from something **2** : a flight of a ball (as in golf) that curves in the direction of the dominant hand of the player hitting it

¹**slick** \'slik\ *vb* : to make smooth or sleek

²**slick** *adj* **1** : very smooth : SLIPPERY **2** : CLEVER, SMART

³**slick** *n* **1** : a smooth patch of water covered with a film of oil **2** : a popular magazine printed on coated paper

slick·er \'sli-kər\ *n* **1** : a long loose raincoat **2** : a sly tricky person **3** : a city dweller esp. of natty appearance or sophisticated mannerisms

¹**slide** \'slīd\ *vb* **slid** \'slid\; **slid·ing** \'slī-diŋ\ **1** : to move smoothly along a surface **2** : to fall by a loss of support **3** : to pass unobtrusively **4** : to move or pass smoothly; *also* : to pass unnoticed ⟨let it ∼ by⟩ **5** : to fall or dive toward a base in baseball

²**slide** *n* **1** : an act or instance of sliding **2** : something (as a cover or fastener) that operates by sliding **3** : a fall of a mass of earth or snow down a hillside **4** : a surface on which something slides **5** : a glass plate on which a specimen is mounted for examination under a microscope **6** : a small transparent photograph that can be projected on a screen

slid·er \'slī-dər\ *n* **1** : one that slides **2** : a baseball pitch that looks like a fastball but curves slightly

slide rule *n* : a manual device for calculation consisting of a ruler and a movable middle piece graduated with logarithmic scales

slier *comparative of* SLY

sliest *superlative of* SLY

¹**slight** \'slīt\ *adj* **1** : SLENDER; *also* : FRAIL **2** : UNIMPORTANT **3** : SCANTY, MEAGER — **slight·ly** *adv*

²**slight** *vb* **1** : to treat as unimportant **2** : to ignore discourteously **3** : to perform or attend to carelessly

³**slight** *n* : a humiliating discourtesy

¹**slim** \'slim\ *adj* **slim·mer; slim·mest** [D, bad, inferior, fr. MD, *slimp* crooked, bad] **1** : SLENDER, SLIGHT, THIN **2** : SCANTY, MEAGER

²**slim** *vb* **slimmed; slim·ming** : to make or become slender

slime \'slīm\ *n* **1** : sticky mud **2** : a slippery substance (as on the skin of a slug or catfish) — **slimy** *adj*

¹**sling** \'sliŋ\ *vb* **slung** \'sləŋ\; **sling·ing 1** : to throw forcibly : FLING **2** : to hurl with or as if with a sling

²**sling** *n* **1** : a short strap with strings attached for hurling stones or shot **2** : something (as a rope or chain) used to hoist, lower, support, or carry; *esp* : a bandage hanging from the neck to support an arm or hand

sling·shot \'sliŋ-ˌshät\ *n* : a forked stick with elastic bands for shooting small stones or shot

slink \'sliŋk\ *vb* **slunk** \'sləŋk\ *also* **slinked** \'sliŋkt\; **slink·ing 1** : to move stealthily or furtively **2** : to move sinuously — **slinky** *adj*

¹**slip** \'slip\ *vb* **slipped; slip·ping 1** : to escape quietly or secretly **2** : to slide along or cause to slide along smoothly **3** : to make a mistake **4** : to pass unnoticed or undone **5** : to fall off from a standard or level

²**slip** *n* **1** : a ramp for repairing ships **2** : a ship's berth between two piers **3** : secret or hurried departure, escape, or evasion **4** : BLUNDER **5** : a sudden mishap **6** : a woman's one-piece garment worn under a dress **7** : PILLOWCASE

³**slip** *n* **1** : a shoot or twig from a plant for planting or

grafting **2** : a long narrow strip; *esp* : one of paper used for a record ⟨deposit ∿⟩

⁴**slip** *vb* **slipped; slip·ping** : to take slips from (a plant)

slip·knot \'slip-ˌnät\ *n* : a knot that slips along the rope around which it is made

slipped disk *n* : a protrusion of one of the disks of cartilage between vertebrae with pressure on spinal nerves resulting esp. in low back pain

slip·per \'sli-pər\ *n* : a light low shoe that may be easily slipped on and off

slip·pery \'sli-pə-rē\ *adj* **slip·per·i·er; -est 1** : icy, wet, smooth, or greasy enough to cause one to fall or lose one's hold **2** : not to be trusted : TRICKY — **slip·per·i·ness** *n*

slip·shod \'slip-ˈshäd\ *adj* : SLOVENLY, CARELESS ⟨∿ work⟩

slip·stream \'slip-ˌstrēm\ *n* : a stream (as of air) driven aft by a propeller

slip·up \'slip-ˌəp\ *n* **1** : MISTAKE **2** : ACCIDENT

¹**slit** \'slit\ *vb* **slit; slit·ting 1** : SLASH **2** : to cut off or away

²**slit** *n* : a long narrow cut or opening

slith·er \'sli-thər\ *vb* : to slip or glide along like a snake — **slith·ery** *adj*

sliv·er \'sli-vər\ *n* : SPLINTER

slob \'släb\ *n* : a slovenly or boorish person

slob·ber \'slä-bər\ *vb* **slob·bered; slob·ber·ing** : to dribble saliva — **slobber** *n*

sloe \'slō\ *n* : the fruit of the blackthorn

slog \'släg\ *vb* **slogged; slog·ging 1** : to hit hard : BEAT **2** : to work hard and steadily

slo·gan \'slo-gən\ *n* [alter. of earlier *slogorn*, fr. ScGael *sluagh-ghairm*, fr. *sluagh* army, host + *gairm* cry] : a word or phrase expressing the spirit or aim of a party, group, or cause

sloop \'slüp\ *n* : a single-masted sailboat with a jib and a fore-and-aft mainsail

¹**slop** \'släp\ *n* **1** : thin tasteless drink or liquid food — usu. used in pl. **2** : food waste for animal feed : SWILL **3** : excreted body waste — usu. used in pl.

²**slop** *vb* **slopped; slop·ping 1** : SPILL **2** : to feed with slop ⟨∿ hogs⟩

¹**slope** \'slōp\ *vb* **sloped; slop·ing** : SLANT, INCLINE

²**slope** *n* **1** : upward or downward slant or degree of slant **2** : ground that forms an incline **3** : the part of a landmass draining into a particular ocean

slop·py \'slä-pē\ *adj* **slop·pi·er; -est 1** : MUDDY, SLUSHY **2** : SLOVENLY, MESSY

slosh \'släsh\ *vb* **1** : to flounder through or splash about in or with water, mud, or slush **2** : to move with a splashing motion

slot \'slät\ *n* **1** : a long narrow opening or groove **2** : a position in a sequence

slot car *n* : an electric toy racing car that runs on a grooved track

sloth \'slòth\ *n, pl* **sloths** \'slòths, 'slòthz\ **1** : LAZINESS, INDOLENCE **2** : any of several slow-moving plant-eating arboreal mammals of So. and Central America — **sloth·ful** *adj*

slot machine *n* **1** : a machine whose operation is begun by dropping a coin into a slot **2** : a coin-operated gambling machine that pays off according to the matching of symbols on wheels spun by a handle

¹**slouch** \'slauch\ *n* **1** : a lazy or incompetent person **2** : a loose or drooping gait or posture

²**slouch** *vb* : to walk, stand, or sit with a slouch : SLUMP

¹**slough** \'slü, *2 usu* 'slau\ *n* **1** : a wet and marshy or muddy place (as a swamp) **2** : a discouraged state of mind

²**slough** \'sləf\ *also* **sluff** *n* : something that has been or may be shed or cast off

³**slough** \'sləf\ *also* **sluff** *vb* : to cast off

Slo·vak \'slō-ˌväk, -ˌvak\ *n* : a member of a Slavic people of Slovakia — **Slovak** *adj* — **Slo·va·ki·an** \slō-ˈvä-kē-ən, -ˈva-\ *adj or n*

sloth 2

slov·en \'slə-vən\ *n* [ME *sloveyn* rascal, perh. fr. D dial. *sloovin* woman of low character] : an untidy person

Slo·vene \'slō-ˌvēn\ *n* : a member of a Slavic people living largely in Slovenia — **Slovene** *adj* — **Slo·ve·nian** \slō-ˈvē-nē-ən\ *adj or n*

slov·en·ly \'slə-vən-lē\ *adj* **1** : untidy in dress or person **2** : lazily or carelessly done : SLIPSHOD

¹**slow** \'slō\ *adj* **1** : SLUGGISH; *also* : dull in mind : STUPID **2** : moving, flowing, or proceeding at less than the usual speed **3** : taking more than the usual time **4** : registering behind the correct time **5** : not lively : BORING **syn** dilatory, laggard, deliberate, leisurely — **slow** *adv* — **slow·ly** *adv* — **slow·ness** *n*

²**slow** *vb* **1** : to make slow : hold back **2** : to go slower

slow motion *n* : motion-picture action photographed so as to appear much slower than normal — **slow–motion** *adj*

SLR *abbr* single-lens reflex

sludge \'sləj\ *n* : a slushy mass : OOZE; *esp* : solid matter produced by sewage treatment processes

slue *var of* ²SLEW

¹**slug** \'sləg\ *n* **1** : a small mass of metal; *esp* : BULLET **2** : a metal disk for use (as in a slot machine) in place of a coin **3** : any of numerous wormlike mollusks related to the snails **4** : a quantity of liquor drunk

²**slug** *vb* **slugged; slug·ging** : to strike forcibly and heavily — **slug·ger** *n*

slug·gard \'slə-gərd\ *n* : a lazy person

slug·gish \'slə-gish\ *adj* **1** : SLOTHFUL, LAZY **2** : slow in movement or flow **3** : STAGNANT, DULL — **slug·gish·ly** *adv* — **slug·gish·ness** *n*

¹**sluice** \'slüs\ *n* **1** : an artificial passage for water with a gate for controlling the flow; *also* : the gate so used **2** : a channel that carries off surplus water **3** : an inclined trough or flume for washing ore or floating logs

²**sluice** *vb* **sluiced; sluic·ing 1** : to draw off through a sluice **2** : to wash with running water : FLUSH

¹**slum** \'sləm\ *n* : a thickly populated area marked by poverty and dirty or deteriorated houses

²**slum** *vb* **slummed; slum·ming** : to visit slums esp. out of curiosity; *also* : to go somewhere or do something that might be considered beneath one's station

¹**slum·ber** \'sləm-bər\ *vb* **slum·bered; slum·ber·ing 1** : DOZE; *also* : SLEEP **2** : to be in a sluggish or torpid state

²**slumber** *n* : SLEEP

slum·ber·ous \'sləm-bə-rəs\ *or* **slum·brous** \-brəs\ *adj* **1** : SLUMBERING, SLEEPY **2** : PEACEFUL, INACTIVE

slum·lord \'sləm-ˌlòrd\ *n* : a landlord who receives unusually large profits from substandard properties

\ə\abut \ᵊ\kitten \ər\further \a\ash \ā\ace \ä\mop, mar \au̇\out \ch\chin \e\bet \ē\easy \g\go \i\hit \ī\ice \j\job \ŋ\sing \ō\go \ȯ\law \ȯi\boy \th\thin \t̵h\the \ü\loot \u̇\foot \y\yet \zh\vision *see also* Pronunciation Symbols page

slump \\'sləmp\ *vb* **1 :** to sink down suddenly : COLLAPSE **2 :** SLOUCH **3 :** to decline sharply — **slump** *n*

slung *past and past part of* SLING

slunk *past and past part of* SLINK

¹slur \\'slər\ *vb* **slurred; slur·ring 1 :** to slide or slip over without due mention or emphasis **2 :** to perform two or more successive notes of different pitch in a smooth or connected way

²slur *n* **:** a curved line connecting notes to be slurred; *also* **:** a group of slurred notes

³slur *n* **:** a slighting remark : ASPERSION

slurp \\'slərp\ *vb* **:** to eat or drink noisily — **slurp** *n*

slur·ry \\'slər-ē\ *n, pl* **slur·ries :** a watery mixture of insoluble matter

slush \\'sləsh\ *n* **1 :** partly melted or watery snow **2 :** soft mud — **slushy** *adj*

slut \\'slət\ *n* **1 :** a slovenly woman **2 :** a lewd woman — **slut·tish** *adj*

sly \\'slī\ *adj* **sli·er** *also* **sly·er** \\'slī-ər\; **sli·est** *also* **sly·est** \\'slī-əst\ **1 :** CRAFTY, CUNNING **2 :** SECRETIVE, FURTIVE **3 :** ROGUISH **syn** tricky, wily, artful, foxy, guileful — **sly·ly** *adv* — **sly·ness** *n*

sm *abbr* small

Sm *symbol* samarium

SM *abbr* sergeant major

SMA *abbr* sergeant major of the army

¹smack \\'smak\ *n* **:** characteristic flavor; *also* **:** a slight trace

²smack *vb* **1 :** to have a taste **2 :** to have a trace or suggestion

³smack *vb* **1 :** to move (the lips) so as to make a sharp noise **2 :** to kiss or slap with a loud noise

⁴smack *n* **1 :** a sharp noise made by the lips **2 :** a noisy slap

⁵smack *adv* **:** squarely and sharply

⁶smack *n* **:** a sailing ship used in fishing

⁷smack *n, slang* **:** HEROIN

SMaj *abbr* sergeant major

¹small \\'smȯl\ *adj* **1 :** little in size or amount **2 :** operating on a limited scale **3 :** little or close to zero (as in number or value) **4 :** made up of little things **5 :** TRIFLING, UNIMPORTANT **6 :** MEAN, PETTY **syn** diminutive, petite, wee, tiny, minute — **small·ish** *adj* — **small·ness** *n*

²small *n* **:** a small part or product ⟨the ∼ of the back⟩

small capital *n* **:** a letter having the form of but smaller than a capital letter (as in THESE WORDS)

small·pox \\'smȯl-ˌpäks\ *n* **:** a contagious virus disease of humans formerly common but now eradicated

small–time \\'smȯl-ˈtīm\ *adj* **:** insignificant in performance and standing : MINOR — **small–tim·er** *n*

¹smart \\'smärt\ *vb* **1 :** to cause or feel a stinging pain **2 :** to feel or endure distress — **smart** *n*

²smart *adj* **1 :** making one smart ⟨a ∼ blow⟩ **2 :** mentally quick : BRIGHT **3 :** WITTY, CLEVER **4 :** STYLISH **5 :** being a guided missile **6 :** containing a microprocessor for limited computing capability ⟨∼ terminal⟩ **syn** knowing, quick-witted, intelligent, brainy, sharp — **smart·ly** *adv* — **smart·ness** *n*

smart al·eck \\'smärt-ˌa-lik\ *n* **:** a person given to obnoxious cleverness

¹smash \\'smash\ *n* **1 :** a smashing blow **2 :** a hard, overhand stroke in tennis **3 :** the act or sound of smashing **4 :** collision of vehicles : CRASH **5 :** COLLAPSE, RUIN; *esp* **:** BANKRUPTCY **6 :** a striking success : HIT — **smash** *adj*

²smash *vb* **1 :** to break or be broken into pieces **2 :** to move forward with force and shattering effect **3 :** to destroy utterly : WRECK

smat·ter·ing \\'sma-tə-riŋ\ *n* **1 :** superficial knowledge **2 :** a small scattered number or amount

¹smear \\'smir\ *n* **1 :** a spot left by an oily or sticky substance **2 :** material smeared on a surface (as of a microscope slide)

²smear *vb* **1 :** to overspread esp. with something oily or sticky **2 :** SMUDGE, SOIL **3 :** to injure by slander or insults

¹smell \\'smel\ *vb* **smelled** \\'smeld\ *or* **smelt** \\'smelt\; **smell·ing 1 :** to perceive the odor of by sense organs of the nose; *also* **:** to detect or seek with or as if with these organs **2 :** to have or give off an odor

²smell *n* **1 :** ODOR, SCENT **2 :** the process or power of perceiving odor; *also* **:** the special sense by which one perceives odor **3 :** an act of smelling — **smelly** *adj*

smelling salts *n pl* **:** an aromatic preparation used as a stimulant and restorative (as to relieve faintness)

¹smelt \\'smelt\ *n, pl* **smelts** *or* **smelt :** any of a family of small food fishes of coastal or fresh waters that are related to the trouts and salmons

²smelt *vb* **:** to melt or fuse (ore) in order to separate the metal; *also* **:** REFINE

smelt·er \\'smel-tər\ *n* **1 :** one that smelts **2 :** an establishment for smelting

smid·gen *also* **smid·geon** *or* **smid·gin** \\'smi-jən\ *n* **:** a small amount : BIT

smi·lax \\'smī-ˌlaks\ *n* **1 :** any of various mostly climbing and prickly plants related to the lilies **2 :** an ornamental plant related to the asparagus

¹smile \\'smīl\ *vb* **smiled; smil·ing 1 :** to look with a smile **2 :** to be favorable **3 :** to express by a smile

²smile *n* **:** a change of facial expression to express amusement, pleasure, or affection

smirch \\'smərch\ *vb* **1 :** to make dirty or stained **2 :** to bring disgrace on — **smirch** *n*

smirk \\'smərk\ *vb* **:** to wear a self-conscious or conceited smile : SIMPER — **smirk** *n*

smite \\'smīt\ *vb* **smote** \\'smōt\; **smit·ten** \\'smit-ᵊn\ *or* **smote; smit·ing** \\'smī-tiŋ\ **1 :** to strike heavily; *also* **:** to kill by striking **2 :** to affect as if by a heavy blow

smith \\'smith\ *n* **:** a worker in metals; *esp* **:** BLACKSMITH

smith·er·eens \ˌsmi-thə-'rēnz\ *n pl* [perh. fr. Ir *smidiríní*] **:** FRAGMENTS, BITS

smithy \\'smi-thē\ *n, pl* **smith·ies :** a smith's workshop

¹smock \\'smäk\ *n* **:** a loose garment worn over other clothes as a protection

²smock *vb* **:** to gather (cloth) in regularly spaced tucks — **smock·ing** *n*

smog \\'smäg, 'smȯg\ *n* [blend of *smoke* and *fog*] **:** a thick haze caused by the action of sunlight on air polluted by smoke and automobile exhaust fumes — **smog·gy** *adj*

¹smoke \\'smōk\ *n* **1 :** the gas from burning material (as coal, wood, or tobacco) in which are suspended particles of soot **2 :** a mass or column of smoke **3 :** something (as a cigarette) to smoke; *also* **:** the act of smoking — **smoke·less** *adj* — **smoky** *adj*

²smoke *vb* **smoked; smok·ing 1 :** to emit smoke **2 :** to inhale and exhale the fumes of burning tobacco; *also* **:** to use in smoking ⟨∼ a pipe⟩ **3 :** to stupefy or drive away by smoke **4 :** to discolor with smoke **5 :** to cure (as meat) with smoke — **smok·er** *n*

smoke detector *n* **:** an alarm that sounds automatically when it detects smoke

smoke jumper *n* **:** a forest firefighter who parachutes to locations otherwise difficult to reach

smoke·stack \\'smōk-ˌstak\ *n* **:** a pipe or funnel through which smoke and gases are discharged

smol·der *or* **smoul·der** \\'smōl-dər\ *vb* **smol·dered** *or* **smoul·dered; smol·der·ing** *or* **smoul·der·ing 1 :** to burn and smoke without flame **2 :** to burn inwardly — **smolder** *n*

smooch \\'smüch\ *vb* **:** KISS, PET — **smooch** *n*

¹smooth \\'smüth\ *adj* **1 :** not rough or uneven **2 :** not jarring or jolting **3 :** BLAND, MILD **4 :** fluent in speech and agreeable in manner — **smooth·ly** *adv* — **smooth·ness** *n*

²smooth *vb* **1 :** to make smooth **2 :** to free from trouble or difficulty

smooth muscle *n* **:** muscle with no cross striations that is typical of visceral organs (as the stomach and bladder) and is not under voluntary control

smor·gas·bord \'smȯr-gəs-ˌbȯrd\ *n* [Sw *smörgåsbord*, fr. *smörgås* open sandwich + *bord* table] : a luncheon or supper buffet consisting of many foods

smote *past and past part of* SMITE

¹smoth·er \'smə-thər\ *n* **1** : thick stifling smoke **2** : a dense cloud (as of fog or dust) **3** : a confused multitude of things

²smother *vb* **smoth·ered; smoth·er·ing 1** : to be overcome by or die from lack of air **2** : to kill by depriving of air **3** : SUPPRESS **4** : to cover thickly

SMSgt *abbr* senior master sergeant

¹smudge \'sməj\ *vb* **smudged; smudg·ing** : to soil or blur by rubbing or smearing

²smudge *n* : a dirty or blurred spot — **smudgy** *adj*

smug \'sməg\ *adj* **smug·ger; smug·gest** : conscious of one's virtue and importance : SELF-SATISFIED — **smug·ly** *adv* — **smug·ness** *n*

smug·gle \'smə-gəl\ *vb* **smug·gled; smug·gling 1** : to import or export secretly, illegally, or without paying the duties required by law **2** : to convey secretly — **smug·gler** \'smə-glər\ *n*

smut \'smət\ *n* **1** : something (as soot) that smudges; *also* : SMUDGE, SPOT **2** : any of various destructive diseases of plants caused by fungi; *also* : a fungus causing smut **3** : indecent language or matter — **smut·ty** *adj*

smutch \'sməch\ *n* : SMUDGE

Sn *symbol* [L. *stannum*] tin

SN *abbr* seaman

snack \'snak\ *n* : a light meal : BITE

snaf·fle \'sna-fəl\ *n* : a simple jointed bit for a horse's bridle

¹snag \'snag\ *n* **1** : a stump or piece of a tree esp. when under water **2** : an unexpected difficulty **syn** obstacle, obstruction, impediment, bar

²snag *vb* **snagged; snag·ging 1** : to become caught on or as if on a snag **2** : to seize quickly : SNATCH

snail \'snāl\ *n* : any of numerous small gastropod mollusks with a spiral shell into which they can withdraw

snake \'snāk\ *n* **1** : any of numerous long-bodied limbless reptiles : SERPENT **2** : a treacherous person **3** : something that resembles a snake — **snaky** *adj*

snake·bite \-ˌbīt\ *n* : the bite of a snake and esp. a venomous snake

¹snap \'snap\ *vb* **snapped; snapping 1** : to grasp or slash at something with the teeth **2** : to get or buy quickly **3** : to utter sharp or angry words **4** : to break suddenly with a sharp sound **5** : to give a sharp cracking noise **6** : to throw with a quick motion **7** : FLASH ⟨her eyes *snapped*⟩ **8** : to put a football into play — **snap·per** *n* — **snap·pish** *adj* — **snap·py** *adj*

²snap *n* **1** : the act of snapping **2** : something very easy to do : CINCH **3** : a short period of cold weather **4** : a catch or fastening that closes with a click **5** : a thin brittle cookie **6** : ENERGY, VIM; *also* : smartness of movement **7** : the putting of the ball into play in football

snap bean *n* : a bean grown primarily for its young tender pods that are usu. broken in pieces for cooking

snap·drag·on \'snap-ˌdra-gən\ *n* : any of a genus of herbs with long spikes of showy flowers

snapping turtle *n* : either of two large American turtles with powerful jaws and a strong musky odor

snap·shot \'snap-ˌshät\ *n* : a photograph taken usu. with an inexpensive hand-held camera

snare \'snar\ *n* : a trap often consisting of a noose for catching birds or mammals — **snare** *vb*

¹snarl \'snärl\ *vb* : to cause to become knotted and intertwined

²snarl *n* : TANGLE

³snarl *vb* : to growl angrily or threateningly

⁴snarl *n* : an angry ill-tempered growl

¹snatch \'snach\ *vb* **1** : to try to grasp something suddenly

2 : to seize or take away suddenly **syn** clutch, seize, grab, nab

²snatch *n* **1** : a short period **2** : an act of snatching **3** : something brief or fragmentary ⟨∼es of song⟩

¹sneak \'snēk\ *vb* **sneaked** \'snēkt\ *or* **snuck** \'snək\; **sneak·ing** : to move, act, or take in a furtive manner — **sneak·ing·ly** *adv*

²sneak *n* **1** : one who acts in a furtive or shifty manner **2** : a stealthy or furtive move or escape — **sneak·i·ly** \'snē-kə-lē\ *adv* — **sneaky** *adj*

sneak·er \'snē-kər\ *n* : a sports shoe with a pliable rubber sole

sneer \'snir\ *vb* : to show scorn or contempt by curling the lip or by a jeering tone — **sneer** *n*

sneeze \'snēz\ *vb* **sneezed; sneez·ing** : to force the breath out suddenly and violently as a reflex act — **sneeze** *n*

SNF *abbr* skilled nursing facility

snick·er \'sni-kər\ *n* : a partly suppressed laugh — **snicker** *vb*

snide \'snīd\ *adj* **1** : MEAN, LOW ⟨a ∼ trick⟩ **2** : slyly disparaging ⟨a ∼ remark⟩

sniff \'snif\ *vb* **1** : to draw air audibly up the nose esp. for smelling **2** : to show disdain or scorn **3** : to detect by or as if by smelling — **sniff** *n*

snif·fle \'sni-fəl\ *n* **1** *pl* : a head cold marked by nasal discharge **2** : SNUFFLE — **sniffle** *vb*

¹snip \'snip\ *n* **1** : a fragment snipped off **2** : a simple stroke of the scissors or shears

²snip *vb* **snipped; snip·ping** : to cut off by bits : CLIP; *also* : to remove by cutting off

¹snipe \'snīp\ *n, pl* **snipes** *or* **snipe** : any of several long-billed game birds esp. of marshy areas that belong to the same family as the sandpipers

²snipe *vb* **sniped; snip·ing** : to shoot at an exposed enemy from a concealed position — **snip·er** *n*

snip·py \'sni-pē\ *adj* **snip·pi·er; -est** : CURT, SNAPPISH

snips \'snips\ *n pl* : hand shears used esp. for cutting sheet metal ⟨tin ∼⟩

snitch \'snich\ *vb* **1** : INFORM, TATTLE **2** : PILFER, SNATCH

sniv·el \'sni-vəl\ *vb* **-eled** *or* **-elled; -el·ing** *or* **-el·ling 1** : to have a running nose; *also* : SNUFFLE **2** : to whine in a snuffling manner — **snivel** *n*

snob \'snäb\ *n* : one who seeks association with persons of higher social position and looks down on those considered inferior — **snob·bish** *adj* — **snob·bish·ly** *adv* — **snob·bish·ness** *n*

snob·bery \'snä-bə-rē\ *n, pl* **-ber·ies** : snobbish conduct

¹snoop \'snüp\ *vb* [D *snoepen* to buy or eat on the sly] : to pry in a furtive or meddlesome way

²snoop *n* : a prying meddlesome person

snooty \'snü-tē\ *adj* **snoot·i·er; -est** : DISDAINFUL, SNOBBISH

snooze \'snüz\ *vb* **snoozed; snooz·ing** : to take a nap : DOZE — **snooze** *n*

snore \'snȯr\ *vb* **snored; snor·ing** : to breathe with a rough hoarse noise while sleeping — **snore** *n*

snor·kel \'snȯr-kəl\ *n* [G *Schnorchel*] : a tube projecting above the water used by swimmers for breathing with the face under water — **snorkel** *vb*

snort \'snȯrt\ *vb* **1** : to force air violently and noisily through the nose ⟨his horse ∼ed⟩ **2** : INHALE — **snort** *n*

snot \'snät\ *n* : nasal mucus

snout \'snaut\ *n* **1** : a long projecting muzzle (as of a pig) **2** : a usu. large or grotesque nose

¹snow \'snō\ *n* **1** : crystals of ice formed from water vapor in the air **2** : a descent or shower of snow crystals

\ə\abut \ᵊ\kitten \ər\further \a\ash \ā\ace \ä\mop, mar \au̇\out \ch\chin \e\bet \ē\easy \g\go \i\hit \ī\ice \j\job \ŋ\sing \ō\go \ȯ\law \ȯi\boy \th\thin \ṯh\the \ü\loot \u̇\foot \y\yet \zh\vision *see also* Pronunciation Symbols page

²**snow** *vb* **1** : to fall or cause to fall in or as snow **2** : to cover or shut in with or as if with snow

¹**snow·ball** \'snō-ˌbȯl\ *n* : a round mass of snow pressed into shape in the hand for throwing

²**snowball** *vb* **1** : to throw snowballs at **2** : to increase or expand at a rapidly accelerating rate

snow·bank \-ˌbaŋk\ *n* : a mound or slope of snow

snow·belt \-ˌbelt\ *n, often cap* : a region that receives an appreciable amount of annual snowfall

snow·blow·er \-ˌblō-ər\ *n* : a machine in which a rotating spiral blade picks up and propels snow aside

snow·drift \-ˌdrift\ *n* : a bank of drifted snow

snow·drop \-ˌdräp\ *n* : a plant with narrow leaves and a nodding white flower that blooms early in the spring

snow·fall \-ˌfȯl\ *n* : a fall of snow

snow fence *n* : a fence across the path of prevailing winds to protect something (as a road) from drifting snow

snow·field \'snō-ˌfēld\ *n* : a mass of perennial snow at the head of a glacier

snow·mo·bile \'snō-mō-ˌbēl\ *n* : any of various automotive vehicles for travel on snow — **snow·mo·bil·er** \-ˌbē-lər\ *n* — **snow·mo·bil·ing** \-liŋ\ *n*

snow pea *n* : a cultivated pea with flat edible pods

snow·plow \'snō-ˌplau̇\ *n* **1** : a device for clearing away snow **2** : a skiing maneuver in which the heels of both skis are slid outward for slowing down or stopping

¹**snow·shoe** \-ˌshü\ *n* : a light frame of wood strung with thongs that is attached to a shoe or boot to prevent sinking down into soft snow

²**snowshoe** *vb* **snow·shoed; snow·shoe·ing** : to travel on snowshoes

snow·storm \-ˌstȯrm\ *n* : a storm of falling snow

snow thrower *n* : SNOWBLOWER

snowy \'snō-ē\ *adj* **snow·i·er; -est 1** : marked by snow **2** : white as snow

snub \'snəb\ *vb* **snubbed; snub·bing** : to treat with disdain : SLIGHT — **snub** *n*

snub–nosed \'snəb-ˌnōzd\ *adj* : having a nose slightly turned up at the end

snuck *past and past part of* SNEAK

¹**snuff** \'snəf\ *vb* **1** : to pinch off the charred end of (a candle) **2** : to put out (a candle) — **snuff·er** *n*

²**snuff** *vb* **1** : to draw forcibly into or through the nose **2** : SMELL

³**snuff** *n* : SNIFF

⁴**snuff** *n* : pulverized tobacco

snuf·fle \'snə-fəl\ *vb* **snuf·fled; snuf·fling 1** : to snuff or sniff audibly and repeatedly **2** : to breathe with a sniffing sound — **snuf·fle** *n*

snug \'snəg\ *adj* **snug·ger; snug·gest 1** : fitting closely and comfortably **2** : CONCEALED — **snug·ly** *adv* — **snug·ness** *n*

snug·gle \'snə-gəl\ *vb* **snug·gled; snug·gling** : to curl up or draw close comfortably : NESTLE

¹**so** \'sō\ *adv* **1** : in the manner indicated **2** : in the same way **3** : THUS **4** : FINALLY **5** : to the extent indicated **6** : THEREFORE

²**so** *conj* : for that reason ⟨he wanted it, ∼ he took it⟩

³**so** *pron* **1** : the same ⟨became chairman and remained ∼⟩ **2** : approximately that ⟨a dozen or ∼⟩

⁴**so** *abbr* south; southern

SO *abbr* strikeout

¹**soak** \'sōk\ *vb* **1** : to remain in a liquid **2** : WET, SATURATE **3** : to draw in by or as if by absorption **syn** drench, steep, impregnate

²**soak** *n* **1** : the act of soaking **2** : the liquid in which something is soaked **3** : DRUNKARD

soap \'sōp\ *n* : a cleansing substance made usu. by action of alkali on fat — **soap** *vb* — **soapy** *adj*

soap opera *n* [fr. its sponsorship by soap manufacturers] : a radio or television daytime serial drama

soap·stone \'sōp-ˌstōn\ *n* : a soft talc-containing stone with a soapy feel

soar \'sōr\ *vb* : to fly upward or at a height on or as if on wings

sob \'säb\ *vb* **sobbed; sob·bing** : to weep with convulsive heavings of the chest or contractions of the throat — **sob** *n*

so·ber \'sō-bər\ *adj* **so·ber·er** \-bər-ər\; **so·ber·est** \-bə-rəst\ **1** : temperate in the use of liquor **2** : not drunk **3** : serious or grave in mood or disposition **4** : having a quiet tone or color **syn** solemn, earnest, staid, sedate — **so·ber·ly** *adv* — **so·ber·ness** *n*

so·bri·ety \sō-ˈbrī-ə-tē\ *n* : the quality or state of being sober

so·bri·quet \'sō-bri-ˌkā, -ˌket\ *n* [F] : NICKNAME

soc *abbr* **1** social; society **2** sociology

so–called \'sō-ˈkȯld\ *adj* : commonly but often inaccurately so termed

soc·cer \'sä-kər\ *n* [by shortening & alter. fr. *association football*] : a game played on a field by two teams with a round inflated ball advanced by kicking

¹**so·cia·ble** \'sō-shə-bəl\ *adj* **1** : liking companionship : FRIENDLY **2** : characterized by pleasant social relations **syn** gracious, cordial, affable, genial — **so·cia·bil·i·ty** \ˌsō-shə-ˈbi-lə-tē\ *n* — **so·cia·bly** \'sō-shə-blē\ *adv*

²**sociable** *n* : SOCIAL

¹**so·cial** \'sō-shəl\ *adj* **1** : marked by pleasant companionship with one's friends **2** : naturally living and breeding in organized communities ⟨∼ insects⟩ **3** : of or relating to human society ⟨∼ institutions⟩ **4** : of, relating to, or based on rank in a particular society ⟨∼ circles⟩; *also* : of or relating to fashionable society — **so·cial·ly** *adv*

²**social** *n* : a social gathering

social disease *n* : VENEREAL DISEASE

so·cial·ism \'sō-shə-ˌli-zəm\ *n* : any of various social systems based on shared or government ownership and administration of the means of production and distribution of goods — **so·cial·ist** \'sō-shə-list\ *n or adj* — **so·cial·is·tic** \ˌsō-shə-ˈlis-tik\ *adj*

so·cial·ite \'sō-shə-ˌlīt\ *n* : a person prominent in fashionable society

so·cial·ize \'sō-shə-ˌlīz\ *vb* **-ized; -iz·ing 1** : to regulate according to the theory and practice of socialism **2** : to adapt to social needs or uses **3** : to participate actively in a social gathering — **so·cial·i·za·tion** \ˌso-shə-lə-ˈzā-shən\ *n*

social science *n* : a science (as economics or political science) dealing with a particular aspect of human society — **social scientist** *n*

social security *n, often cap both Ss* : a U.S. government program established in 1935 to include old-age and survivors insurance, contributions to state unemployment insurance, and old-age assistance

social work *n* : services, activities, or methods providing social services esp. to the economically underprivileged and socially maladjusted — **social worker** *n*

so·ci·e·ty \sə-ˈsī-ə-tē\ *n, pl* **-ties** [MF *societé*, fr. L *societat-, societas*, fr. *socius* companion] **1** : COMPANIONSHIP **2** : a voluntary association of persons for common ends **3** : a part of a community bound together by common interests and standards; *esp* : the group or set of fashionable people

so·cio·eco·nom·ic \ˌsō-sē-ō-ˌe-kə-ˈnä-mik, ˌsō-shē-, -ˌē-kə-\ *adj* : of, relating to, or involving both social and economic factors

sociol *abbr* sociologist; sociology

so·ci·ol·o·gy \ˌsō-sē-ˈä-lə-jē, ˌsō-shē-\ *n* : the science of society, social institutions, and social relationships — **so·cio·log·i·cal** \ˌsō-sē-ə-ˈlä-ji-kəl, ˌsō-shē-\ *adj* — **so·ci·ol·o·gist** \-ˈä-lə-jist\ *n*

¹**sock** \'säk\ *n, pl* **socks** *or* **sox** \'säks\ : a stocking with a short leg

²**sock** *vb* : to hit, strike, or apply forcefully

³**sock** *n* : a vigorous blow : PUNCH

sock·et \'sä-kət\ *n* : an opening or hollow that forms a holder for something

socket wrench *n* : a wrench usu. in the form of a bar and removable socket made to fit a bolt or nut

¹**sod** \'säd\ *n* : TURF 1

²**sod** *vb* **sod·ded; sod·ding** : to cover with sod

so·da \'sō-də\ *n* **1** : SODIUM CARBONATE **2** : SODIUM BICARBONATE **3** : SODIUM **4** : SODA WATER **5** : SODA POP **6** : a sweet drink of soda water, flavoring, and often ice cream

soda pop *n* : a carbonated, sweetened, and flavored soft drink

soda water *n* : a beverage of water charged with carbon dioxide

sod·den \'säd-ᵊn\ *adj* **1** : lacking spirit : DULLED **2** : SOAKED, DRENCHED **3** : heavy or doughy from being improperly cooked ⟨~ biscuits⟩

so·di·um \'sō-dē-əm\ *n* : a soft waxy silver white metallic chemical element occurring in nature in combined form (as in salt) — see ELEMENT table

sodium bicarbonate *n* : a white weakly alkaline salt used esp. in baking powders, fire extinguishers, and medicine

sodium carbonate *n* : a carbonate of sodium used esp. in washing and bleaching textiles

sodium chloride *n* : SALT 1

sodium fluoride *n* : a salt used chiefly in tiny amounts to prevent tooth decay

sodium hydroxide *n* : a white brittle caustic substance used in making soap and rayon and in bleaching

sodium nitrate *n* : a crystalline salt used as a fertilizer and in curing meat

sodium thiosulfate *n* : a hygroscopic crystalline salt used as a photographic fixing agent

sod·omy \'sä-də-mē\ *n* **1** : sexual intercourse with a member of the same sex or with an animal **2** : noncoital and esp. anal or oral sexual intercourse with a member of the opposite sex — **sod·om·ize** \'sä-də-₁mīz\ *vb*

so·ev·er \sō-'e-vər\ *adv* **1** : in any degree or manner ⟨how bad ~⟩ **2** : at all : of any kind ⟨any help ~⟩

so·fa \'sō-fə\ *n* [Ar *ṣuffah* long bench] : a couch usu. with upholstered back and arms

soft \'soft\ *adj* **1** : not hard or rough : NONVIOLENT **2** : RESTFUL, GENTLE, SOOTHING **3** : emotionally susceptible **4** : not prepared to endure hardship **5** : not containing certain salts that prevent lathering ⟨~ water⟩ **6** : occurring at such a speed as to avoid destructive impact ⟨~ landing of a spacecraft on the moon⟩ **7** : BIODEGRADABLE ⟨a ~ detergent⟩ **8** : not alcoholic ⟨~ drinks⟩ **9** : less detrimental than a hard narcotic ⟨~ drugs⟩ — **soft** *adv* — **soft·ness** *n*

soft·ball \'soft-₁bol\ *n* : a game similar to baseball played with a ball larger and softer than a baseball; *also* : the ball used in this game

soft·bound \-₁baund\ *adj* : not bound in hard covers ⟨~ books⟩

soft coal *n* : BITUMINOUS COAL

soft·en \'so-fən\ *vb* : to make or become soft — **soft·en·er** *n*

soft palate *n* : the fold at the back of the hard palate that partially separates the mouth and the pharynx

soft·ware \'soft-₁war\ *n* : the entire set of programs, procedures, and related documentation associated with a system; *esp* : computer programs

soft·wood \-₁wud\ *n* **1** : the wood of a coniferous tree as compared to that of a broad-leaved deciduous tree **2** : a tree that yields softwood — **softwood** *adj*

sog·gy \'sä-gē\ *adj* **sog·gi·er; -est** : heavy with water or moisture — **sog·gi·ly** \'sä-gə-lē\ *adv* — **sog·gi·ness** \-gē-nəs\ *n*

soi·gné *or* **soi·gnée** \swän-'yä\ *adj* : elegantly maintained; *esp* : WELL-GROOMED

¹**soil** \'soil\ *vb* **1** : CORRUPT, POLLUTE **2** : to make or become dirty **3** : STAIN, DISGRACE

²**soil** *n* **1** : STAIN, DEFILEMENT **2** : EXCREMENT, WASTE

³**soil** *n* **1** : firm land : EARTH **2** : the upper layer of earth in which plants grow **3** : COUNTRY, REGION

soi·ree *or* **soi·rée** \swä-'rā\ *n* [F *soirée* evening period, evening party, fr. MF, fr. *soir* evening, fr. L *sero* at a late hour] : an evening party

so·journ \'sō-jərn, sō-'jərn\ *vb* : to dwell in a place temporarily — **so·journ** *n* — **so·journ·er** *n*

¹**sol** \'säl, 'sōl\ *n* — see MONEY table

²**sol** *n* : a fluid colloidal system

³**sol** *abbr* **1** solicitor **2** soluble **3** solution

Sol \'säl\ *n* : SUN

¹**sol·ace** \'sä-ləs\ *n* : COMFORT

²**solace** *vb* **so·laced; so·lac·ing** : to give solace to : CONSOLE

so·lar \'sō-lər\ *adj* **1** : of, derived from, or relating to the sun **2** : measured by the earth's course in relation to the sun ⟨the ~ year⟩ **3** : operated by or using the sun's light or heat ⟨~ energy⟩

solar cell *n* : a photoelectric cell that converts light into electrical energy and is used as a power source

solar collector *n* : a device for the absorption of solar radiation for the heating of water or buildings or the production of electricity

solar flare *n* : a sudden temporary outburst of energy from a small area of the sun's surface

so·lar·i·um \sō-'lar-ē-əm\ *n, pl* **-ia** \-ē-ə\ *also* **-i·ums** : a room exposed to the sun; *esp* : a room (as in a hospital) for exposure of the body to sunshine

solar plexus *n* : the general area of the stomach below the sternum

solar system *n* : the sun together with the group of celestial bodies that revolve around it

solar wind *n* : plasma continuously ejected from the sun's surface

sold *past and past part of* SELL

sol·der \'sä-dər, 'so-\ *n* : a metallic alloy used when melted to mend or join metallic surfaces — **solder** *vb*

soldering iron *n* : a metal device for applying heat in soldering

¹**sol·dier** \'sōl-jər\ *n* [ME *soudier*, fr. MF, fr. *soulde* pay, fr. LL *solidus* a Roman coin, fr. L, solid] : a person in military service; *esp* : an enlisted man or woman — **sol·dier·ly** *adj or adv*

²**soldier** *vb* **sol·diered; sol·dier·ing 1** : to serve as a soldier **2** : to pretend to work while actually doing nothing

soldier of fortune : ADVENTURER 2

sol·diery \'sōl-jə-rē\ *n* : a body of soldiers

¹**sole** \'sōl\ *n* : any of various flatfishes marketed for food

²**sole** *n* **1** : the undersurface of the foot **2** : the bottom of a shoe

³**sole** *vb* **soled; sol·ing** : to furnish (a shoe) with a sole

⁴**sole** *adj* : SINGLE, ONLY — **sole·ly** \'sōl-lē\ *adv*

so·le·cism \'sä-lə-₁si-zəm, 'sō-\ *n* **1** : a mistake in grammar **2** : a breach of etiquette

sol·emn \'sä-ləm\ *adj* **1** : marked by or observed with full religious ceremony **2** : FORMAL, CEREMONIOUS **3** : highly serious **4** : GRAVE, SOMBER, GLOOMY — **so·lem·ni·ty** \sə-'lem-nə-tē\ *n* — **sol·emn·ly** \'sä-ləm-lē\ *adv*

sol·em·nize \'sä-ləm-₁nīz\ *vb* **-nized; -niz·ing 1** : to observe or honor with solemnity **2** : to celebrate (a marriage) with religious rites — **sol·em·ni·za·tion** \₁sä-ləm-nə-'zā-shən\ *n*

so·le·noid \'sō-lə-₁noid, 'sä-\ *n* : a coil of wire usu. in cy-

---

lindrical form that when carrying a current acts like a magnet

so·lic·it \sə-ˈli-sət\ *vb* **1** : ENTREAT, BEG **2** : to approach with a request or plea **3** : TEMPT, LURE — **so·lic·i·ta·tion** \-ˌli-sə-ˈtā-shən\ *n*

so·lic·i·tor \sə-ˈli-sə-tər\ *n* **1** : one that solicits **2** : LAWYER; *esp* : a legal official of a city or state

so·lic·i·tous \sə-ˈli-sə-təs\ *adj* **1** : WORRIED, CONCERNED **2** : EAGER, WILLING **syn** avid, impatient, keen, anxious — **so·lic·i·tous·ly** *adv*

so·lic·i·tude \sə-ˈli-sə-ˌtüd, -ˌtyüd\ *n* : CONCERN, ANXIETY

¹sol·id \ˈsä-ləd\ *adj* **1** : not hollow; *also* : written as one word without a hyphen ⟨a ∼ compound⟩ **2** : having, involving, or dealing with three dimensions or with solids ⟨∼ geometry⟩ **3** : not loose or spongy : COMPACT ⟨a ∼ mass of rock⟩; *also* : neither gaseous nor liquid : HARD, RIGID ⟨∼ ice⟩ **4** : of good substantial quality or kind ⟨∼ comfort⟩ **5** : thoroughly dependable : RELIABLE ⟨a ∼ citizen⟩; *also* : serious in purpose or character ⟨∼ reading⟩ **6** : UNANIMOUS, UNITED ⟨∼ for pay increases⟩ **7** : of one substance or character — **solid** *adv* — **so·lid·i·ty** \sə-ˈli-də-tē\ *n* — **sol·id·ly** *adv* — **sol·id·ness** *n*

²solid *n* **1** : a geometrical figure (as a cube or sphere) having three dimensions **2** : a solid substance

sol·i·dar·i·ty \ˌsä-lə-ˈdar-ə-tē\ *n* : unity based on shared interests, objectives, or standards

so·lid·i·fy \sə-ˈli-də-ˌfī\ *vb* **-fied; -fy·ing** : to make or become solid — **so·lid·i·fi·ca·tion** \-ˌli-də-fə-ˈkā-shən\ *n*

solid–state *adj* **1** : relating to the structure and properties of solid material **2** : using semiconductor devices rather than vacuum tubes

so·lil·o·quize \sə-ˈli-lə-ˌkwīz\ *vb* **-quized; -quiz·ing** : to talk to oneself : utter a soliloquy

so·lil·o·quy \sə-ˈli-lə-kwē\ *n, pl* **-quies** [LL *soliloquium,* fr. L *solus* alone + *loqui* to speak] **1** : the act of talking to oneself **2** : a dramatic monologue that represents unspoken reflections by a character

sol·i·taire \ˈsä-lə-ˌtar\ *n* **1** : a single gem (as a diamond) set alone **2** : a card game for one person

sol·i·tary \ˈsä-lə-ˌter-ē\ *adj* **1** : being or living apart from others **2** : LONELY, SECLUDED **3** : SOLE, ONLY

sol·i·tude \ˈsä-lə-ˌtüd, -ˌtyüd\ *n* **1** : the state of being alone : SECLUSION **2** : a lonely place

soln *abbr* solution

¹so·lo \ˈsō-lō\ *n, pl* **solos** [It, fr. *solo* alone, fr. L *solus*] **1** : a piece of music for a single voice or instrument with or without accompaniment **2** : an action in which there is only one performer — **solo** *adj or vb* — **so·lo·ist** *n*

²solo *adv* : without a companion : ALONE

so·lon \ˈsō-lən\ *n* **1** : a wise and skillful lawgiver **2** : a member of a legislative body

sol·stice \ˈsäl-stəs, ˈsōl-\ *n* [ME, fr. OF, fr. L *solstitium,* fr. *sol* sun + *-stit-, -stes* standing] : the time of the year when the sun is farthest north of the equator (**summer solstice**) about June 22 or farthest south (**winter solstice**) about Dec. 22 — **sol·sti·tial** \säl-ˈsti-shəl, sōl-\ *adj*

sol·u·ble \ˈsäl-yə-bəl\ *adj* **1** : capable of being dissolved in or as if in a liquid **2** : capable of being solved or explained — **sol·u·bil·i·ty** \ˌsäl-yə-ˈbi-lə-tē\ *n*

sol·ute \ˈsäl-ˌyüt\ *n* : a dissolved substance

so·lu·tion \sə-ˈlü-shən\ *n* **1** : an action or process of solving a problem; *also* : an answer to a problem **2** : an act or the process by which one substance is homogeneously mixed with another usu. liquid substance; *also* : a mixture thus formed

solve \ˈsälv\ *vb* **solved; solv·ing** : to find the answer to or a solution for — **solv·able** *adj*

sol·ven·cy \ˈsäl-vən-sē\ *n* : the condition of being solvent

¹sol·vent \-vənt\ *adj* **1** : able or sufficient to pay all legal debts **2** : dissolving or able to dissolve

²solvent *n* : a usu. liquid substance capable of dissolving or dispersing one or more other substances

So·ma·lian \sō-ˈmäl-yən\ *n* : a native or inhabitant of Somalia — **Somalian** *adj*

so·mat·ic \sō-ˈma-tik\ *adj* : of, relating to, or affecting the body in contrast to the mind or the sex cells and their precursors

som·ber *or* **som·bre** \ˈsäm-bər\ *adj* **1** : DARK, GLOOMY **2** : GRAVE, MELANCHOLY — **som·ber·ly** *adv*

som·bre·ro \səm-ˈbrer-ō\ *n, pl* **-ros** [Sp, fr. *sombra* shade] : a broad-brimmed felt hat worn esp. in the Southwest and in Mexico

sombrero

¹some \ˈsəm\ *adj* **1** : one unspecified ⟨∼ man called⟩ **2** : an unspecified or indefinite number of ⟨∼ berries are ripe⟩ **3** : at least a few or a little ⟨∼ years ago⟩

²some *pron* : a certain number or amount ⟨∼ of the berries are ripe⟩ ⟨∼ of it is missing⟩

¹-some \səm\ *adj suffix* : characterized by a (specified) thing, quality, state, or action ⟨awe*some*⟩ ⟨burden*some*⟩

²-some *n suffix* : a group of (so many) members and esp. persons ⟨four*some*⟩

¹some·body \ˈsəm-ˌbä-dē, -bə-\ *pron* : some person

²somebody *n* : a person of importance

some·day \ˈsəm-ˌdā\ *adv* : at some future time

some·how \-ˌhaù\ *adv* : by some means

some·one \-(ˌ)wən\ *pron* : some person

som·er·sault \ˈsə-mər-ˌsòlt\ *n* [MF *sombresaut* leap, ultim. fr. L *super* over + *saltus* leap, fr. *salire* to jump] : a leap or roll in which a person turns heels over head — **somersault** *vb*

som·er·set \-ˌset\ *n or vb* : SOMERSAULT

some·thing \ˈsəm-thiŋ\ *pron* : some undetermined or unspecified thing

some·time \-ˌtīm\ *adv* **1** : at a future time **2** : at an unknown or unnamed time

some·times \-ˌtīmz\ *adv* : OCCASIONALLY

¹some·what \-ˌhwät, -ˌhwət\ *pron* : SOMETHING

²somewhat *adv* : in some degree

some·where \-ˌhwer\ *adv* : in, at, or to an unknown or unnamed place

som·nam·bu·lism \säm-ˈnam-byə-ˌli-zəm\ *n* : performance of motor acts (as walking) during sleep; *also* : an abnormal condition of sleep characterized by this — **som·nam·bu·list** \-list\ *n*

som·no·lent \ˈsäm-nə-lənt\ *adj* : SLEEPY, DROWSY — **som·no·lence** \-ləns\ *n*

son \ˈsən\ *n* **1** : a male offspring or descendant **2** *cap* : Jesus Christ **3** : a person deriving from a particular source (as a country, race, or school)

so·nar \ˈsō-ˌnär\ *n* [*so*und *na*vigation *a*nd *r*anging] : a method or device for detecting and locating submerged objects (as submarines) by sound waves

so·na·ta \sə-ˈnä-tə\ *n* [It] : an instrumental composition with three or four movements differing in rhythm and mood but related in key

son·a·ti·na \ˌsä-nə-ˈtē-nə\ *n* [It, dim. of *sonata*] : a short usu. simplified sonata

song \ˈsȯŋ\ *n* **1** : vocal music; *also* : a short composition of words and music **2** : poetic composition **3** : a distinctive or characteristic sound (as of a bird) **4** : a small amount ⟨sold for a ∼⟩

song·bird \ˈsȯŋ-ˌbərd\ *n* : a bird that utters a series of musical tones

Song of Sol·o·mon \-ˈsä-lə-mən\ *n* — see BIBLE table

Song of Songs *n* — see BIBLE table

song·ster \ˈsȯŋ-stər\ *n* : one that sings

song·stress \-strəs\ *n* : a female singer

son·ic \ˈsä-nik\ *adj* : of or relating to sound waves or the speed of sound

sonic boom *n* : an explosive sound produced by an aircraft traveling at supersonic speed

son–in–law \ˈsən-ən-ˌlȯ\ *n, pl* **sons–in–law** : the husband of one's daughter

son·net \ˈsä-nət\ *n* : a poem of 14 lines usu. in iambic pentameter with a definite rhyme scheme

so·no·rous \sə-ˈnȯr-əs, ˈsä-nə-rəs\ *adj* **1** : giving out sound when struck **2** : loud, deep, or rich in sound : RESONANT **3** : high-sounding : IMPRESSIVE — **so·nor·i·ty** \sə-ˈnȯr-ə-tē\ *n*

soon \ˈsün\ *adv* **1** : before long **2** : PROMPTLY, QUICKLY **3** *archaic* : EARLY **4** : WILLINGLY, READILY

soot \ˈsut, ˈsət, ˈsüt\ *n* : a fine black powder consisting chiefly of carbon that is formed when something burns and that colors smoke — **sooty** *adj*

sooth \ˈsüth\ *n, archaic* : TRUTH

soothe \ˈsüth\ *vb* **soothed; sooth·ing 1** : to please by flattery or attention **2** : to calm down : COMFORT — **sooth·er** *n* — **sooth·ing·ly** *adv*

sooth·say·er \ˈsüth-ˌsā-ər\ *n* : one who foretells events — **sooth·say·ing** *n*

¹sop \ˈsäp\ *n* : a conciliatory bribe, gift, or concession

²sop *vb* **sopped; sop·ping 1** : to steep or dip in or as if in a liquid **2** : to wet thoroughly : SOAK; *also* : to mop up (a liquid)

SOP *abbr* standard operating procedure; standing operating procedure

soph *abbr* sophomore

soph·ism \ˈsä-ˌfi-zəm\ *n* **1** : an argument correct in form but embodying a subtle fallacy **2** : SOPHISTRY

soph·ist \ˈsä-fist\ *n* : PHILOSOPHER; *esp* : a captious or fallacious reasoner

so·phis·tic \sä-ˈfis-tik, sə-\ *or* **so·phis·ti·cal** \-ti-kəl\ *adj* : of or characteristic of sophists or sophistry **syn** fallacious, illogical, unreasonable, specious

so·phis·ti·cat·ed \sə-ˈfis-tə-ˌkā-təd\ *adj* **1** : COMPLEX ⟨∼ instruments⟩ **2** : made worldly-wise by wide experience **3** : intellectually appealing ⟨∼ novel⟩ — **so·phis·ti·ca·tion** \-ˌfis-tə-ˈkā-shən\ *n*

soph·ist·ry \ˈsä-fə-strē\ *n* : subtly deceptive reasoning or argument

soph·o·more \ˈsäf-ˌmȯr, ˈsä-fə-\ *n* : a student in the second year of high school or college

soph·o·mor·ic \ˌsäf-ˈmȯr-ik, ˌsä-fə-\ *adj* **1** : being overconfident of knowledge but poorly informed and immature **2** : of, relating to, or characteristic of a sophomore ⟨a ∼ prank⟩

So·pho·ni·as \ˌsä-fə-ˈnī-əs, ˌsō-\ *n* : ZEPHANIAH

sop·o·rif·ic \ˌsä-pə-ˈri-fik\ *adj* **1** : causing sleep or drowsiness **2** : LETHARGIC

so·pra·no \sə-ˈpra-nō, -ˈprä-\ *n, pl* **-nos** [It, fr. *sopra* above, fr. L *supra*] **1** : the highest singing voice; *also* : a singer with this voice **2** : the highest part in a 4-part chorus — **soprano** *adj*

sor·bet \sȯr-ˈbā\ *n* : a fruit-flavored ice served for dessert or between courses as a palate refresher

sor·cery \ˈsȯr-sə-rē\ *n* [ME *sorcerie*, fr. OF, fr. *sorcier* sorcerer, fr. (assumed) VL *sortiarius*, fr. L *sort-, sors* chance, lot] : the use of magic : WITCHCRAFT — **sor·cer·er** \-rər\ *n* — **sor·cer·ess** \-rəs\ *n*

sor·did \ˈsȯr-dəd\ *adj* **1** : marked by baseness or grossness : VILE **2** : DIRTY, SQUALID — **sor·did·ly** *adv* — **sor·did·ness** *n*

¹sore \ˈsȯr\ *adj* **sor·er; sor·est 1** : causing pain or distress ⟨a ∼ bruise⟩ **2** : painfully sensitive ⟨∼ muscles⟩ **3** : SEVERE, INTENSE **4** : IRRITATED, ANGRY — **sore·ly** *adv* — **sore·ness** *n*

²sore *n* **1** : a sore spot on the body; *esp* : one (as an ulcer) with the tissues broken and usu. infected **2** : a source of pain or vexation

sore·head \ˈsȯr-ˌhed, ˈsȯr-\ *n* : a person easily angered or discontented

sore throat *n* : painful throat due to inflammation

sor·ghum \ˈsȯr-gəm\ *n* : a tall variable Old World tropical grass grown widely for its edible seed, for forage, or for its sweet juice which yields a syrup

so·ror·i·ty \sə-ˈrȯr-ə-tē\ *n, pl* **-ties** [ML *sororitas* sisterhood, fr. L *soror* sister] : a club of girls or women esp. at a college

¹sor·rel \ˈsȯr-əl\ *n* : a brownish orange to light brown color; *also* : a sorrel-colored animal (as a horse)

²sorrel *n* : any of various herbs having a sour juice

sor·row \ˈsär-ō\ *n* **1** : deep distress, sadness, or regret; *also* : resultant unhappy or unpleasant state **2** : a cause of grief or sadness **3** : a display of grief or sadness — **sor·row** *vb* — **sor·row·ful** \-fəl\ *adj* — **sor·row·ful·ly** \-f(ə-)lē\ *adv*

sor·ry \ˈsär-ē\ *adj* **sor·ri·er; -est 1** : feeling sorrow, regret, or penitence **2** : MOURNFUL, SAD **3** : causing sorrow, pity, or scorn : WRETCHED

¹sort \ˈsȯrt\ *n* **1** : a group of persons or things that have similar characteristics : CLASS **2** : WAY, MANNER **3** : QUALITY, NATURE **4** : an instance of sorting — **out of sorts 1** : somewhat ill **2** : GROUCHY, IRRITABLE

²sort *vb* **1** : to put in a certain place according to kind, class, or nature **2** : to be in accord : AGREE — **sort·er** *n*

sor·tie \ˈsȯr-tē, sȯr-ˈtē\ *n* **1** : a sudden issuing of troops from a defensive position against the enemy **2** : one mission or attack by one airplane

sort of *adv* : to a moderate degree

SOS \ˌes-(ˌ)ō-ˈes\ *n* : a call or request for help or rescue

so–so \ˈsō-ˈsō\ *adv or adj* : PASSABLY

sot \ˈsät\ *n* : a habitual drunkard — **sot·tish** *adj* — **sot·tish·ly** *adv*

souf·flé \sü-ˈflā\ *n* [F, fr. *soufflé*, pp. of *souffler* to blow, puff up, fr. L *sufflare*, fr. *sub-* up + *flare* to blow] : a spongy dish made light in baking by stiffly beaten egg whites

sough \ˈsau̇, ˈsəf\ *vb* : to make a moaning or sighing sound — **sough** *n*

sought *past and past part of* SEEK

¹soul \ˈsōl\ *n* **1** : the immaterial essence of an individual life **2** : the spiritual principle embodied in human beings or the universe **3** : an active or essential part **4** : the moral and emotional nature of human beings **5** : spiritual or moral force **6** : PERSON ⟨a kindly ∼⟩ **7** : a strong, positive feeling (as of intense sensitivity and emotional fervor) conveyed esp. by black American performers; *also* : NEGRITUDE — **souled** \ˈsōld\ *adj* — **soul·less** \ˈsōl-ləs\ *adj*

²soul *adj* **1** : of, relating to, or characteristic of black Americans or their culture ⟨∼ food⟩ ⟨∼ music⟩ **2** : designed for or controlled by blacks ⟨∼ radio stations⟩

soul brother *n* : a black male

\ə\abut \ᵊ\kitten \ər\further \a\ash \ā\ace \ä\mop, mar \au̇\out \ch\chin \e\bet \ē\easy \g\go \i\hit \ī\ice \j\job \ŋ\sing \ō\go \ȯ\law \ȯi\boy \th\thin \th\the \ü\loot \u̇\foot \y\yet \zh\vision *see also* Pronunciation Symbols page

soul·ful \'sōl-fəl\ *adj* : full of or expressing deep feeling — **soul·ful·ly** *adv*

¹**sound** \'saund\ *adj* **1** : not diseased or sickly **2** : free from flaw or defect **3** : FIRM, STRONG **4** : free from error or fallacy : RIGHT **5** : LEGAL, VALID **6** : THOROUGH **7** : UNDISTURBED ⟨∼ sleep⟩ **8** : showing good judgment — **sound·ly** *adv* — **sound·ness** *n*

²**sound** *n* **1** : the sensation of hearing; *also* : mechanical energy transmitted by longitudinal pressure waves (**sound waves**) (as in air) that is the stimulus to hearing **2** : something heard : NOISE, TONE; *also* : hearing distance : EARSHOT **3** : a musical style — **sound·less** *adj* — **sound·less·ly** *adv* — **sound·proof** \-ˌprüf\ *adj or vb*

³**sound** *vb* **1** : to make or cause to make a sound **2** : to order or proclaim by a sound ⟨∼ the alarm⟩ **3** : to convey a certain impression : SEEM **4** : to examine the condition of by causing to give out sounds — **sound·able** \'saun-də-bəl\ *adj*

⁴**sound** *n* : a long passage of water wider than a strait often connecting two larger bodies of water ⟨Puget ∼⟩

⁵**sound** *vb* **1** : to measure the depth of (water) esp. by a weighted line dropped from the surface : FATHOM **2** : PROBE **3** : to dive down suddenly ⟨the hooked fish ∼ed⟩ — **sound·ing** *n*

sound·er \'saun-dər\ *n* : one that sounds; *esp* : a device for making soundings

sound·stage \'saund-ˌstāj\ *n* : the part of a motion-picture studio in which a production is filmed

soup \'süp\ *n* **1** : a liquid food with stock as its base and often containing pieces of solid food **2** : something having the consistency of soup **3** : an unfortunate predicament ⟨in the ∼⟩

soup·çon \süp-'sōⁿ\ *n* [F, lit., suspicion] : a little bit : ¹TRACE 2

soup up *vb* : to increase the power of

soupy \'sü-pē\ *adj* **soup·i·er; -est 1** : having the consistency of soup **2** : densely foggy or cloudy

¹**sour** \'saur\ *adj* **1** : having an acid or tart taste ⟨∼ as vinegar⟩ **2** : SPOILED, PUTRID ⟨a ∼ odor⟩ **3** : UNPLEASANT, DISAGREEABLE ⟨∼ disposition⟩ — **sour·ish** *adj* — **sour·ly** *adv* — **sour·ness** *n*

²**sour** *vb* : to become or make sour

source \'sōrs\ *n* **1** : ORIGIN, BEGINNING **2** : a supplier of information **3** : the beginning of a stream of water

¹**souse** \'saus\ *vb* **soused; sous·ing 1** : PICKLE **2** : to plunge into a liquid **3** : DRENCH **4** : to make drunk

²**souse** *n* **1** : something (as pigs' feet) steeped in pickle **2** : a soaking in liquid **3** : DRUNKARD

¹**south** \'sauth\ *adv* : to or toward the south; *also* : into a state of decline

²**south** *adj* **1** : situated toward or at the south **2** : coming from the south

³**south** *n* **1** : the direction to the right of one facing east **2** : the compass point directly opposite to north **3** *cap* : regions or countries south of a specified or implied point; *esp* : the southeastern part of the U.S. — **south·er·ly** \'sə-thər-lē\ *adj or adv* — **south·ern** \'sə-thərn\ *adj* — **South·ern·er** *n* — **south·ern·most** \-ˌmōst\ *adj* — **south·ward** \'sauth-wərd\ *adv or adj* — **southwards** \-wərdz\ *adv*

South African *n* : a native or inhabitant of the Republic of South Africa — **South African** *adj*

south·east \saù-'thēst, *naut* saù-'ēst\ *n* **1** : the general direction between south and east **2** : the compass point midway between south and east **3** *cap* : regions or countries southeast of a specified or implied point — **southeast** *adj or adv* — **south·east·er·ly** *adv or adj* — **south·east·ern** \-'ēs-tərn\ *adj*

south·paw \'sauth-ˌpo\ *n* : a left-handed person; *esp* : a left-handed baseball pitcher — **southpaw** *adj*

south pole *n, often cap S&P* : the southernmost point of the earth

south·west \sauth-'west, *naut* saù-'west\ *n* **1** : the gen-

eral direction between south and west **2** : the compass point midway between south and west **3** *cap* : regions or countries southwest of a specified or implied point — **southwest** *adj or adv* — **south·west·er·ly** *adv or adj* — **south·west·ern** \-'wes-tərn\ *adj*

sou·ve·nir \ˌsü-və-'nir\ *n* [F] : something serving as a reminder

sou'·west·er \saù-'wes-tər\ *n* : a long waterproof coat worn in storms at sea; *also* : a waterproof hat

¹**sov·er·eign** \'sä-vrən, -və-rən\ *n* **1** : one possessing the supreme power and authority in a state **2** : a gold coin of the United Kingdom

²**sovereign** *adj* **1** : EXCELLENT, FINE **2** : supreme in power or authority **3** : CHIEF, HIGHEST **4** : having independent authority

sov·er·eign·ty \-tē\ *n, pl* **-ties 1** : supremacy in rule or power **2** : power to govern without external control **3** : the supreme political power in a state

so·vi·et \'sō-vē-ˌet, 'sä-, -ət\ *n* **1** : an elected governmental council in a Communist country **2** *pl, cap* : the people and esp. the leaders of the U.S.S.R. — **soviet** *adj, often cap* — **so·vi·et·ize** *vb, often cap*

¹**sow** \'saù\ *n* : an adult female swine

²**sow** \'sō\ *vb* **sowed; sown** \'sōn\ *or* **sowed; sow·ing 1** : to plant seed esp. by scattering **2** : to strew with seed **3** : to scatter abroad — **sow·er** \'sō-ər\ *n*

sow bug \'saù-\ *n* : WOOD LOUSE

sox *pl of* SOCK

soy \'soi\ *n* : a sauce made from soybeans fermented in brine

soy·bean \'soi-ˌbēn\ *n* : an Asian legume widely grown for forage and for its edible seeds that yield a valuable oil (**soybean oil**); *also* : its seed

sp *abbr* **1** special **2** species **3** specimen **4** spelling **5** spirit

Sp *abbr* Spain

SP *abbr* **1** shore patrol; shore patrolman **2** shore police **3** specialist

spa \'spä\ *n* [*Spa*, watering place in Belgium] **1** : a resort with mineral springs **2** : a health and fitness facility **3** : a hot tub with a whirlpool device

¹**space** \'spās\ *n* **1** : a period of time **2** : some small measurable distance, area, or volume **3** : the limitless area in which all things exist and move **4** : an empty place **5** : the region beyond the earth's atmosphere **6** : a definite place (as a seat on a train or ship)

²**space** *vb* **spaced; spac·ing** : to place at intervals — **spac·er** *n*

space–age \'spās-ˌāj\ *adj* : of or relating to the age of space exploration

space·craft \-ˌkraft\ *n* : a vehicle for travel beyond the earth's atmosphere

space·flight \-ˌflīt\ *n* : flight beyond the earth's atmosphere

space heater *n* : a usu. portable device for heating a relatively small area

space·man \'spās-ˌman, -mən\ *n* : one who travels outside the earth's atmosphere

space·ship \-ˌship\ *n* : a vehicle used for space travel

space shuttle *n* : a reusable spacecraft designed to transport people and cargo between earth and space

space station *n* : a large artificial satellite serving as a base (as for scientific observation)

space suit *n* : a suit equipped to make life in space possible for its wearer

space walk *n* : a period of activity outside a spacecraft by an astronaut in space — **space·walk** \'spās-ˌwok\ *vb* — **space·walk·er** *n*

spa·cious \'spā-shəs\ *adj* : very large in extent : ROOMY **syn** commodious, capacious, ample — **spa·cious·ly** *adv* — **spa·cious·ness** *n*

¹**spade** \'spād\ *n* : a shovel with a blade for digging — **spade·ful** *n*

²**spade** *vb* **spad·ed; spad·ing** : to dig with a spade — **spad·er** *n*

³**spade** *n* : any of a suit of playing cards marked with a black figure resembling an inverted heart with a short stem at the bottom

spa·dix \'spā-diks\ *n, pl* **spa·di·ces** \'spā-də-ˌsēz\ : a floral spike with a fleshy or succulent axis usu. enclosed in a spathe

spa·ghet·ti \spə-'ge-tē\ *n* [It, fr. pl. of *spaghetto,* dim. of *spago* cord, string] : thin solid pasta strings

¹**span** \'span\ *n* **1** : an English unit of length equal to nine inches (about 23 centimeters) **2** : a limited portion of time **3** : the spread (as of an arch) from one support to another

²**span** *vb* **spanned; span·ning 1** : MEASURE **2** : to extend across

³**span** *n* : a pair of animals (as mules) driven together

Span *abbr* Spanish

span·dex \'span-ˌdeks\ *n* : any of various elastic synthetic textile fibers

span·gle \'spaŋ-gəl\ *n* : a small disk of shining metal or plastic used esp. on a dress for ornament — **spangle** *vb*

Span·glish \'spaŋ-glish\ *n* : a combination of Spanish and English

Span·iard \'span-yərd\ *n* : a native or inhabitant of Spain

span·iel \'span-yəl\ *n* [ME *spaniell,* fr. MF *espaignol,* lit., Spaniard] : a dog of any of several breeds of mostly small and short-legged dogs usu. with long wavy hair and large drooping ears

spaniel

Span·ish \'spa-nish\ *n* **1** : the chief language of Spain and of the countries colonized by the Spanish **2 Spanish** *pl* : the people of Spain — **Spanish** *adj*

Spanish American *n* : a resident of the U.S. whose native language is Spanish; *also* : a native or inhabitant of one of the countries of America in which Spanish is the national language — **Spanish–American** *adj*

Spanish fly *n* : a preparation of dried green European beetles noted as an aphrodisiac with often highly toxic side effects but not in reputable medical use

Spanish moss *n* : a plant related to the pineapple that grows in pendent tufts of grayish green filaments on trees from the southern U.S. to Argentina

Spanish rice *n* : rice cooked with onions, green peppers, and tomatoes

spank \'spaŋk\ *vb* : to hit on the buttocks with the open hand — **spank** *n*

spank·ing \'spaŋ-kiŋ\ *adj* : BRISK, LIVELY ⟨∼ breeze⟩ — **spanking** *adv*

span·ner \'span-ər\ *n, chiefly Brit* : WRENCH

¹**spar** \'spär\ *n* **1** : a stout pole **2** : a rounded wood or metal piece (as a mast, yard, boom, or gaff) for supporting sail rigging

²**spar** *vb* **sparred; spar·ring** : to box for practice without serious hitting; *also* : SKIRMISH, WRANGLE

¹**spare** \'spar\ *vb* **spared; spar·ing 1** : to refrain from punishing or injuring : show mercy to ⟨∼d the prisoners⟩ **2** : to exempt from something ⟨∼ me the trouble⟩ **3** : to get along without ⟨can't ∼ a dime⟩ **4** : to use frugally or rarely ⟨don't ∼ the syrup⟩

²**spare** *adj* **spar·er; spar·est 1** : held in reserve **2** : SUPERFLUOUS **3** : not liberal or profuse **4** : LEAN, THIN **5** : SCANTY **syn** meager, sparse, skimpy, exiguous, scant — **spare·ness** *n*

³**spare** *n* **1** : a duplicate kept in reserve; *esp* : a spare tire **2** : the knocking down of all the bowling pins with the first two balls

spar·ing \'spar-iŋ\ *adj* : SAVING, FRUGAL **syn** thrifty, economical, provident — **spar·ing·ly** *adv*

¹**spark** \'spärk\ *n* **1** : a small particle of a burning substance or a hot glowing particle struck from a mass (as by steel on flint) **2** : a short bright flash of electricity between two points **3** : SPARKLE **4** : a particle capable of being kindled or developed : GERM

²**spark** *vb* **1** : to emit or produce sparks **2** : to stir to activity : INCITE

³**spark** *vb* : WOO, COURT

¹**spar·kle** \'spär-kəl\ *vb* **spar·kled; spar·kling 1** : FLASH, GLEAM **2** : to perform brilliantly **3** : EFFERVESCE — **spar·kler** *n*

²**sparkle** *n* **1** : GLEAM **2** : ANIMATION

spark plug *n* **1** : a device that produces a spark to ignite the fuel mixture in an engine cylinder **2** : one that begins something or drives something forward

spar·row \'spar-ō\ *n* : any of several small dull-colored singing birds

sparse \'spärs\ *adj* **spars·er; spars·est** : thinly scattered : SCANTY **syn** meager, spare, skimpy, exiguous, scant — **sparse·ly** *adv* — **sparse·ness** *n*

spasm \'spa-zəm\ *n* **1** : a sudden involuntary and abnormal muscular contraction **2** : a sudden, violent, and temporary effort, feeling, or outburst

spas·mod·ic \spaz-'mä-dik\ *adj* **1** : relating to or affected or characterized by spasm ⟨∼ movements⟩; *also* : resembling a spasm **2** : INTERMITTENT — **spas·mod·i·cal·ly** \-di-k(ə-)lē\ *adv*

spas·tic \'spas-tik\ *adj* : of, relating to, marked by, or affected with muscular spasm ⟨∼ paralysis⟩ — **spastic** *n*

¹**spat** \'spat\ *past and past part of* SPIT

²**spat** *n, pl* **spat** *or* **spats** : a young bivalve mollusk (as an oyster)

³**spat** *n* : a gaiter covering instep and ankle

spat

⁴**spat** *n* : a brief petty quarrel : DISPUTE

⁵**spat** *vb* **spat·ted; spat·ting** : to quarrel briefly

spate \'spāt\ *n* : a sudden outburst

spathe \'spā<u>th</u>\ *n* : a sheathing bract or pair of bracts enclosing an inflorescence (as of the calla lily) and esp. a spadix on the same axis

spa·tial \'spā-shəl\ *adj* : of or relating to space — **spa·tial·ly** *adv*

spat·ter \'spa-tər\ *vb* **1** : to splash with drops of liquid **2** : to sprinkle around — **spatter** *n*

spat·u·la \'spa-chə-lə\ *n* : a flexible knifelike implement for scooping, spreading, or mixing soft substances

spav·in \'spa-vən\ *n* : a bony enlargement of the hock of a horse — **spav·ined** \-vənd\ *adj*

¹**spawn** \'spȯn\ *vb* [ME, fr. OF *espandre* to spread out, expand, fr. L *expandere*, fr. *ex-* out + *pandere* to spread] **1** : to produce eggs or offspring esp. in large numbers **2** : GENERATE — **spawn·er** *n*

²**spawn** *n* **1** : the eggs of water animals (as fishes or oysters) that lay many small eggs **2** : offspring esp. when produced in great quantities

spay \'spā\ *vb* **spayed; spay·ing** : to remove the ovaries of (a female animal)

SPCA *abbr* Society for the Prevention of Cruelty to Animals

SPCC *abbr* Society for the Prevention of Cruelty to Children

speak \'spēk\ *vb* **spoke** \'spōk\; **spo·ken** \'spō-kən\; **speak·ing 1** : to utter words **2** : to express orally **3** : to mention in speech or writing **4** : to address an audience **5** : to use or be able to use (a language) in talking

speak·easy \'spēk-ˌē-zē\ *n, pl* **-eas·ies** : an illicit drinking place

speak·er \'spē-kər\ *n* **1** : one that speaks **2** : the presiding officer of a deliberative assembly **3** : LOUDSPEAKER

¹**spear** \'spir\ *n* **1** : a long-shafted weapon with a sharp point for thrusting or throwing **2** : a sharp-pointed instrument with barbs used in spearing fish — **spear·man** \-mən\ *n*

²**spear** *vb* : to strike or pierce with or as if with a spear — **spear·er** *n*

³**spear** *n* : a usu. young blade, shoot, or sprout (as of asparagus)

spear·head \-ˌhed\ *n* : a leading force, element, or influence — **spearhead** *vb*

spear·mint \-ˌmint\ *n* : a common highly aromatic garden mint

spec *abbr* **1** special **2** specifically

spe·cial \'spe-shəl\ *adj* **1** : UNCOMMON, NOTEWORTHY **2** : particularly favored **3** : INDIVIDUAL, UNIQUE **4** : EXTRA, ADDITIONAL **5** : confined to or designed for a definite field of action, purpose, or occasion — **special** *n*

special delivery *n* : delivery of mail by messenger for an extra fee

special effects *n pl* : images in a television or film production added after filming is completed to enhance believability

Special Forces *n pl* : a branch of the army composed of soldiers specially trained in guerrilla warfare

spe·cial·ist \'spe-shə-list\ *n* **1** : a person who specializes in a particular branch of learning or activity **2** : any of four enlisted ranks in the army corresponding to the grades of corporal through sergeant first class

spe·cial·ize \'spe-shə-ˌlīz\ *vb* **-ized; -iz·ing** : to concentrate one's efforts in a special activity or field; *also* : to change in an adaptive manner — **spe·cial·i·za·tion** \ˌspe-shə-lə-ˈzā-shən\ *n*

spe·cial·ly \'spe-shə-lē\ *adv* **1** : in a special manner **2** : for a special purpose : in particular

spe·cial·ty \'spe-shəl-tē\ *n, pl* **-ties 1** : a particular quality or detail **2** : a product of a special kind or of special excellence **3** : something (as a discipline) in which one specializes

spe·cie \'spē-shē, -sē\ *n* : money in coin

spe·cies \'spē-shēz, -sēz\ *n, pl* **spe·cies** [ME, fr. L, appearance, kind, species, fr. *specere* to look] **1** : SORT, KIND **2** : a category of biological classification ranking just below the genus or subgenus and comprising closely related organisms potentially able to breed with one another

specif *abbr* specific; specifically

¹**spe·cif·ic** \spi-ˈsi-fik\ *adj* **1** : having a unique effect or influence or reacting in only one way or with only one thing ⟨∼ antibodies⟩ ⟨∼ enzymes⟩ **2** : DEFINITE, EXACT **3** : of, relating to, or constituting a species — **spe·cif·i·cal·ly** \-fi-k(ə-)lē\ *adv*

²**specific** *n* : something specific : DETAIL, PARTICULAR — usu. used in pl.

spec·i·fi·ca·tion \ˌspe-sə-fə-ˈkā-shən\ *n* **1** : the act or process of specifying **2** : a description of work to be done and materials to be used (as in building) — usu. used in pl.

specific gravity *n* : the ratio of the density of a substance to the density of some substance (as water) taken as a standard when both densities are obtained by weighing in air

spec·i·fy \'spe-sə-ˌfī\ *vb* **-fied; -fy·ing** : to mention or name explicitly

spec·i·men \'spe-sə-mən\ *n* : an item or part typical of a group or whole

spe·cious \'spē-shəs\ *adj* : seeming to be genuine, correct, or beautiful but not really so ⟨∼ reasoning⟩

speck \'spek\ *n* **1** : a small spot or blemish **2** : a small particle — **speck** *vb*

speck·le \'spe-kəl\ *n* : a little speck — **speck·le** *vb*

¹**specs** \'speks\ *n pl* : GLASSES

²**specs** *n pl* : SPECIFICATIONS

spec·ta·cle \'spek-ti-kəl\ *n* **1** : an unusual or impressive public display **2** *pl* : GLASSES — **spec·ta·cled** \-kəld\ *adj*

spec·tac·u·lar \spek-ˈta-kyə-lər\ *adj* : exciting to see : SENSATIONAL

spec·ta·tor \'spek-ˌtā-tər\ *n* : a person who looks on (as at a sports event) **syn** observer, witness, bystander, onlooker, eyewitness

spec·ter *or* **spec·tre** \'spek-tər\ *n* : a visible disembodied spirit : GHOST

spec·tral \'spek-trəl\ *adj* **1** : of, relating to, or resembling a specter **2** : of, relating to, or made by a spectrum

spec·tro·gram \'spek-trə-ˌgram\ *n* : a photograph or diagram of a spectrum

spec·tro·graph \-ˌgraf\ *n* : an instrument for dispersing radiation into a spectrum and photographing or mapping the spectrum — **spec·tro·graph·ic** \ˌspek-trə-ˈgra-fik\ *adj* — **spec·tro·graph·i·cal·ly** \-fi-k(ə-)lē\ *adv*

spec·trom·e·ter \spek-ˈträ-mə-tər\ *n* : an instrument for measuring spectra — **spec·tro·met·ric** \ˌspek-trə-ˈme-trik\ *adj* — **spec·trom·e·try** \spek-ˈträ-mə-trē\ *n*

spec·tro·scope \'spek-trə-ˌskōp\ *n* : an instrument that produces spectra esp. of visible electromagnetic radiation — **spec·tro·scop·ic** \ˌspek-trə-ˈskä-pik\ *adj* — **spec·tro·scop·i·cal·ly** \-pi-k(ə-)lē\ *adv* — **spec·tros·co·pist** \spek-ˈträs-kə-pist\ *n* — **spec·tros·co·py** \-pē\ *n*

spec·trum \'spek-trəm\ *n, pl* **spec·tra** \-trə\ *or* **spectrums** [NL, fr. L, appearance, fr. *specere* to look] **1** : a series of colors formed when a beam of white light is dispersed (as by a prism) so that its parts are arranged in the order of their wavelengths **2** : a series of radiations arranged in regular order **3** : a continuous sequence or range ⟨a wide ∼ of political opinions⟩

spec·u·late \'spe-kyə-ˌlāt\ *vb* **-lat·ed; -lat·ing** [L *speculari* to spy out, examine, fr. *specula* watchtower, fr. *specere* to look, look at] **1** : to think or wonder about a subject **2** : to take a business risk in hope of gain **syn** reason, think, deliberate, cogitate — **spec·u·la·tion** \ˌspe-kyə-ˈlā-shən\ *n* — **spec·u·la·tive** \'spe-kyə-lā-tiv\ *adj* — **spec·u·la·tive·ly** *adv* — **spec·u·la·tor** \-ˌlā-tər\ *n*

speech \'spēch\ *n* **1** : the act of speaking **2** : TALK, CONVERSATION **3** : a public talk or lecture **4** : LANGUAGE, DIALECT **5** : an individual manner of speaking **6** : the power of speaking — **speech·less** *adj*

¹**speed** \'spēd\ *n* **1** *archaic* : SUCCESS **2** : SWIFTNESS, RAPIDITY **3** : rate of motion or performance **4** : a transmission gear (as of a bicycle) **5** : METHAMPHETAMINE; *also* : a related drug **syn** haste, hurry, dispatch, celerity — **speed·i·ly** \'spē-də-lē\ *adv* — **speedy** *adj*

²**speed** *vb* **sped** \'sped\ *or* **speed·ed; speed·ing 1** *archaic* : PROSPER; *also* : GET ALONG, FARE **2** : to go fast; *esp* : to go at an excessive or illegal speed **3** : to cause to go faster — **speed·er** *n*

speed·boat \-ˌbōt\ *n* : a fast motorboat

speed bump *n* : a low raised ridge across a roadway (as in a parking lot) to limit vehicle speed

speed·om·e·ter \spi-'dä-mə-tər\ *n* : an instrument for indicating speed

speed·up \'spēd-ˌəp\ *n* : ACCELERATION

speed·way \-ˌwā\ *n* : a racecourse for motor vehicles

speed·well \'spēd-ˌwel\ *n* : a low creeping plant that bears spikes of small usu. bluish flowers and is related to the snapdragon

¹**spell** \'spel\ *vb* **spelled** \'speld, 'spelt\; **spell·ing 1** : to name, write, or print in order the letters of a word **2** : MEAN

²**spell** *n* [ME, talk, tale, fr. OE] **1** : a magic formula : INCANTATION **2** : a controlling influence

³**spell** *n* **1** : one's turn at work or duty **2** : a stretch of a specified kind of weather **3** : a period of bodily or mental distress or disorder : ATTACK

⁴**spell** *vb* **spelled** \'speld\; **spell·ing** : to take the place of for a time in work or duty : RELIEVE

spell·bind·er \-ˌbīn-dər\ *n* : a speaker of compelling eloquence

spell·bound \-ˌbaund\ *adj* : held by or as if by a spell : FASCINATED

spell·er \'spe-lər\ *n* **1** : one who spells words **2** : a book with exercises for teaching spelling

spelt *chiefly Brit past and past part of* SPELL

spe·lunk·er \spi-'lən-kər, 'spē-ˌlən-kər\ *n* [L *spelunca* cave, fr. Gk *spēlynx*] : one who makes a hobby of exploring caves — **spe·lunk·ing** *n*

spend \'spend\ *vb* **spent** \'spent\; **spend·ing 1** : to pay out : EXPEND **2** : WEAR OUT, EXHAUST; *also* : to consume wastefully **3** : to cause or permit to elapse : PASS — **spend·er** *n*

spend·thrift \'spend-ˌthrift\ *n* : one who spends wastefully or recklessly

spent \'spent\ *adj* : drained of energy

sperm \'spərm\ *n, pl* **sperm** *or* **sperms 1** : SEMEN **2** : a male gamete

sper·ma·to·zo·on \(ˌ)spər-ˌma-tə-'zō-ˌän, -'zō-ən\ *n, pl* **-zoa** \-'zō-ə\ : a motile male gamete of an animal usu. with a rounded or elongated head and a long posterior flagellum

sperm cell *n* : SPERM 2

sper·mi·cide \'spər-mə-ˌsīd\ *n* : a preparation or substance used to kill sperm — **sper·mi·cid·al** \ˌspər-mə-'sī-dəl\ *adj*

sperm whale *n* : a whale with conical teeth, no whalebone, and a large fluid-containing cavity in the head

spew \'spyü\ *vb* : VOMIT

SPF *abbr* sun protection factor

sp gr *abbr* specific gravity

sphag·num \'sfag-nəm\ *n* : any of a genus of atypical mosses that grow in wet acid areas where their remains become compacted with other plant debris to form peat; *also* : a mass of these mosses

sphere \'sfir\ *n* [ME *spere* globe, celestial sphere, fr. MF *espere*, fr. L *sphaera*, fr. Gk *sphaira*, lit., ball] **1** : a globe-shaped body : BALL **2** : a celestial body **3** : a solid figure so shaped that every point on its surface is an equal distance from the center **4** : range of action or influence — **spher·i·cal** \'sfir-i-kəl, 'sfer-\ *adj* — **spher·i·cal·ly** \-i-k(ə-)lē\ *adv*

spher·oid \'sfir-ˌoid, 'sfer-\ *n* : a figure similar to a sphere but not perfectly round — **sphe·roi·dal** \sfir-'oi-dəl\ *adj*

sphinc·ter \'sfiŋk-tər\ *n* : a muscular ring that closes a bodily opening

sphinx \'sfiŋks\ *n, pl* **sphinx·es** *or* **sphin·ges** \'sfin-ˌjēz\ **1** : a winged monster in Greek mythology having a woman's head and a lion's body and noted for killing anyone unable to answer its riddle **2** : an enigmatic or mysterious person **3** : an ancient Egyptian image having the body of a lion and the head of a man, ram, or hawk

spice \'spīs\ *n* **1** : any of various aromatic plant products (as pepper or nutmeg) used to season or flavor foods **2** : something that adds interest and relish — **spice** *vb* — **spicy** *adj*

spick–and–span *or* **spic–and–span** \ˌspik-ənd-'span\ *adj* : quite new; *also* : spotlessly clean

spic·ule \'spi-kyül\ *n* : a slender pointed body esp. of calcium or silica ⟨sponge ∼s⟩

spi·der \'spī-dər\ *n* **1** : any of an order of arachnids that have a 2-part body, eight legs, and two or more pairs of abdominal organs for spinning threads of silk used esp. in making webs for catching prey **2** : a cast-iron frying pan — **spi·dery** *adj*

spider mite *n* : any of several small web spinning mites that attack forage and crop plants

spider plant *n* : a houseplant of the lily family having long green leaves usu. striped with white and producing tufts of small plants on long hanging stems

spi·der·web \'spī-dər-ˌweb\ *n* : the web spun by a spider

spiel \'spēl\ *vb* : to talk in a fast, smooth, and usu. colorful manner — **spiel** *n*

spig·ot \'spi-gət, -kət\ *n* : FAUCET

¹**spike** \'spīk\ *n* **1** : a very large nail **2** : any of various pointed projections (as on the sole of a shoe to prevent slipping) — **spiky** *adj*

²**spike** *vb* **spiked; spik·ing 1** : to fasten with spikes **2** : to put an end to : QUASH ⟨∼ a rumor⟩ **3** : to pierce with or impale on a spike **4** : to add alcoholic liquor to (a drink)

³**spike** *n* **1** : an ear of grain **2** : a long cluster of usu. stemless flowers

¹**spill** \'spil\ *vb* **spilled** \'spild, 'spilt\ *also* **spilt** \'spilt\; **spill·ing 1** : to cause or allow to fall, flow, or run out esp. unintentionally **2** : to cause (blood) to flow **3** : to run out or over with resulting loss or waste **4** : to let out : DIVULGE — **spill·able** *adj*

²**spill** *n* **1** : an act of spilling; *also* : a fall from a horse or vehicle or an erect position **2** : something spilled

spill·way \-ˌwā\ *n* : a passage for surplus water to run over or around an obstruction (as a dam)

¹**spin** \'spin\ *vb* **spun** \'spən\; **spin·ning 1** : to draw out (fiber) and twist into thread; *also* : to form (thread) by such means **2** : to form thread by extruding a sticky quickly hardening fluid; *also* : to construct from such thread ⟨spiders ∼ their webs⟩ **3** : to produce slowly and by degrees ⟨∼ a story⟩ **4** : TWIRL **5** : WHIRL, REEL ⟨my head is *spinning*⟩ **6** : to move rapidly along — **spinner** *n*

²**spin** *n* **1** : a rapid rotating motion **2** : an excursion in a wheeled vehicle

spin·ach \'spi-nich\ *n* : a dark green herb grown for its edible leaves

---

\ə\abut \ᵊ\kitten \ər\further \a\ash \ā\ace \ä\mop, mar
\au\out \ch\chin \e\bet \ē\easy \g\go \i\hit \ī\ice \j\job
\ŋ\sing \ō\go \o\law \oi\boy \th\thin \th\the \ü\loot \u\foot
\y\yet \zh\vision *see also* Pronunciation Symbols page

spi·nal \'spīn-ᵊl\ *adj* : of or relating to the backbone or spinal cord — **spi·nal·ly** *adv*

spinal column *n* : BACKBONE

spinal cord *n* : the thick cord of nervous tissue that extends from the brain along the back in the cavity of the backbone and carries nerve impulses to and from the brain

spinal nerve *n* : any of the paired nerves which arise from the spinal cord and pass to various parts of the body and of which there are normally 31 pairs in human beings

spin·dle \'spind-ᵊl\ *n* **1** : a round tapering stick or rod by which fibers are twisted in spinning **2** : a turned part of a piece of furniture ⟨the ∼s of a chair⟩ **3** : a slender pin or rod which turns or on which something else turns

spin·dling \'spind-liŋ\ *adj* : SPINDLY

spin·dly \'spind-lē\ *adj* : being long or tall and thin and usu. weak

spin·drift \'spin-₁drift\ *n* : spray blown from waves

spine \'spīn\ *n* **1** : BACKBONE **2** : a stiff sharp process esp. on a plant or animal **3** : the part of a book where the pages are attached — **spine·less** *adj* — **spiny** *adj*

spi·nel \spə-'nel\ *n* : a hard crystalline mineral of variable color used as a gem

spin·et \'spi-nət\ *n* **1** : an early harpsichord having a single keyboard and only one string for each note **2** : a small upright piano

spin·na·ker \'spi-ni-kər\ *n* : a large triangular sail set on a long light pole

spinning jen·ny \-'je-nē\ *n* : an early multiple-spindle machine for spinning wool or cotton

spinning wheel *n* : a small machine for spinning thread or yarn in which a large wheel drives a single spindle

spin-off \'spin-₁óf\ *n* **1** : a usu. useful by-product **2** : something (as a TV show) derived from an earlier work — **spin off** *vb*

spin·ster \'spin-stər\ *n* : an unmarried woman past the common age for marrying — **spin·ster·hood** \-₁hùd\ *n*

spiny lobster *n* : any of several edible crustaceans differing from the related lobster in lacking the large front claws and in having a very spiny carapace

¹spi·ral \'spī-rəl\ *adj* : winding or coiling around a center or axis and usu. getting closer to or farther away from it — **spi·ral·ly** *adv*

²spiral *n* **1** : something that has a spiral form; *also* : a single turn in a spiral object **2** : a continuously spreading and accelerating increase or decrease

³spiral *vb* **-raled** *or* **-ralled; -ral·ing** *or* **-ral·ling 1** : to move and esp. to rise or fall in a spiral course **2** : to form into a spiral

spi·rant \'spī-rənt\ *n* : a consonant (as \f\, \s\, \sh\) uttered with decided friction of the breath against some part of the oral passage — **spirant** *adj*

spire \'spīr\ *n* **1** : a slender tapering stalk (as of grass) **2** : a pointed tip (as of an antler) **3** : STEEPLE — **spiry** *adj*

spi·rea *or* **spi·raea** \spī-'rē-ə\ *n* : any of a genus of shrubs related to the roses with dense clusters of small white or pink flowers

¹spir·it \'spir-ət\ *n* [ME, fr. OF or L; OF, fr. L *spiritus,* lit., breath, fr. *spirare* to blow, breathe] **1** : a life-giving force; *also* : the animating principle : SOUL **2** *cap* : HOLY SPIRIT **3** : SPECTER, GHOST **4** : PERSON **5** : DISPOSITION, MOOD **6** : VIVACITY, ARDOR **7** : essential or real meaning : INTENT **8** : distilled alcoholic liquor **9** : LOYALTY ⟨school ∼⟩ — **spir·it·less** *adj*

²spirit *vb* : to carry off secretly or mysteriously

spir·it·ed \'spir-ə-təd\ *adj* **1** : ANIMATED, LIVELY **2** : COURAGEOUS

¹spir·i·tu·al \'spir-i-chəl, -chə-wəl\ *adj* **1** : of, relating to, consisting of, or affecting the spirit : INCORPOREAL **2** : of or relating to sacred matters **3** : ecclesiastical rather than lay or temporal — **spir·i·tu·al·i·ty** \₁spir-i-chə-

'wa-lə-tē\ *n* — **spir·i·tu·al·ize** \'spir-i-chə-₁līz, -chə-wə-\ *vb* — **spir·i·tu·al·ly** *adv*

²spiritual *n* : a religious song originating among blacks of the southern U.S.

spir·i·tu·al·ism \'spir-i-chə-₁li-zəm, -chə-wə-\ *n* : a belief that spirits of the dead communicate with the living usu. through a medium — **spir·i·tu·al·ist** \-list\ *n, often cap* — **spir·i·tu·al·is·tic** \₁spir-i-chə-'lis-tik, -chə-wə-\ *adj*

spir·i·tu·ous \'spir-i-chəs, -chə-wəs; 'spir-ə-təs\ *adj* : containing alcohol

spi·ro·chete *also* **spi·ro·chaete** \'spī-rə-₁kēt\ *n* : any of an order of spirally undulating bacteria including those causing syphilis and Lyme disease

spirt *var of* SPURT

¹spit \'spit\ *n* **1** : a thin pointed rod for holding meat over a fire **2** : a point of land that runs out into the water

²spit *vb* **spit·ted; spit·ting** : to pierce with or as if with a spit

³spit *vb* **spit** *or* **spat** \'spat\; **spit·ting 1** : to eject (saliva) from the mouth **2** : to express by or as if by spitting **3** : to rain or snow lightly

⁴spit *n* **1** : SALIVA **2** : perfect likeness ⟨∼ and image of his father⟩

spit·ball \'spit-₁ból\ *n* **1** : paper chewed and rolled into a ball to be thrown as a missile **2** : a baseball pitch delivered after the ball has been moistened with saliva or sweat

¹spite \'spīt\ *n* : ill will with a wish to annoy, anger, or frustrate : petty malice **syn** malignity, spleen, grudge, malevolence — **spite·ful** \-fəl\ *adj* — **spite·ful·ly** *adv* — **spite·ful·ness** *n* — **in spite of** : in defiance or contempt of : NOTWITHSTANDING

²spite *vb* **spit·ed; spit·ing** : to treat maliciously : ANNOY, OFFEND

spit·tle \'spit-ᵊl\ *n* : SALIVA

spit·tle·bug \-₁bəg\ *n* : any of a family of leaping insects with froth-secreting larvae that are related to aphids

spit·toon \spi-'tün\ *n* : a receptacle for spit

splash \'splash\ *vb* **1** : to dash a liquid about **2** : to scatter a liquid on : SPATTER **3** : to fall or strike with a splashing noise **syn** sprinkle, bespatter, douse, splatter — **splash** *n*

splash·down \'splash-₁daùn\ *n* : the landing of a manned spacecraft in the ocean — **splash down** *vb*

splat·ter \'spla-tər\ *vb* : SPATTER — **splatter** *n*

¹splay \'splā\ *vb* : to spread outward or apart — **splay** *n*

²splay *adj* **1** : spread out : turned outward **2** : AWKWARD, CLUMSY

spleen \'splēn\ *n* **1** : a vascular organ located near the stomach in most vertebrates that is concerned esp. with the filtration and storage of blood, destruction of red blood cells, and production of lymphocytes **2** : SPITE, MALICE **syn** malignity, grudge, malevolence, ill will, spitefulness

splen·did \'splen-dəd\ *adj* [L *splendidus,* fr. *splendēre* to shine] **1** : SHINING, BRILLIANT **2** : SHOWY, GORGEOUS **3** : ILLUSTRIOUS **4** : EXCELLENT **syn** resplendent, glorious, sublime, superb — **splen·did·ly** *adv*

splen·dor \'splen-dər\ *n* **1** : BRILLIANCE **2** : POMP, MAGNIFICENCE

splen·dour *chiefly Brit var of* SPLENDOR

sple·net·ic \spli-'ne-tik\ *adj* : marked by bad temper or spite

splen·ic \'sple-nik\ *adj* : of, relating to, or located in the spleen

splice \'splīs\ *vb* **spliced; splic·ing 1** : to unite (as two ropes) by weaving the strands together **2** : to unite (as two lengths of film) by connecting the ends together — **splice** *n*

splint \'splint\ *n* **1** : a thin strip of wood interwoven with others to make something (as a basket) **2** : material or a device used to protect and keep in place an injured body part (as a broken arm)

¹**splin·ter** \'splin-tər\ *n* : a thin piece of something split off lengthwise : SLIVER

²**splinter** *vb* : to split into splinters

split \'split\ *vb* **split; split·ting 1** : to divide lengthwise or along a grain or seam **2** : to burst or break in pieces **3** : to divide into parts or sections **4** : LEAVE **syn** rend, cleave, rip, tear — **split** *n*

split–lev·el \'split-'le-vəl\ *n* : a house divided so that the floor in one part is about halfway between two floors in the other

split personality *n* : SCHIZOPHRENIA; *also* : MULTIPLE PERSONALITY

split·ting *adj* : causing a piercing sensation ⟨∼ headache⟩

splotch \'spläch\ *n* : BLOTCH

splurge \'splərj\ *vb* **splurged; splurging** : to spend more than usual esp. on oneself — **splurge** *n*

splut·ter \'splə-tər\ *n* : SPUTTER — **splutter** *vb*

¹**spoil** \'spȯil\ *n* : PLUNDER ⟨∼s of war⟩

²**spoil** *vb* **spoiled** \'spȯild, 'spȯilt\ *or* **spoilt** \'spȯilt\; **spoil·ing 1** : ROB, PILLAGE **2** : to damage seriously : RUIN **3** : to impair the quality or effect of **4** : to damage the disposition of by pampering; *also* : INDULGE, CODDLE **5** : DECAY, ROT **6** : to have an eager desire ⟨∼ing for a fight⟩ **syn** injure, harm, hurt, mar — **spoil·age** \'spȯi-lij\ *n*

spoil·er \'spȯi-lər\ *n* **1** : one that spoils **2** : a device (as on an airplane or automobile) used to disrupt airflow and decrease lift

spoil·sport \'spȯil-ˌspȯrt\ *n* : one who spoils the fun of others

¹**spoke** \'spōk\ *past & archaic past part of* SPEAK

²**spoke** *n* : any of the rods extending from the hub of a wheel to the rim

spo·ken \'spō-kən\ *past part of* SPEAK

spokes·man \'spōks-mən\ *n* : a person who speaks as the representative of another or others

spokes·per·son \-ˌpər-sən\ *n* : SPOKESMAN

spokes·wom·an \-ˌwu̇-mən\ *n* : a woman who speaks as the representative of another or others

spo·li·a·tion \ˌspō-lē-'ā-shən\ *n* : the act of plundering : the state of being plundered

¹**sponge** \'spənj\ *n* **1** : an elastic porous water-absorbing mass of fibers that forms the skeleton of various primitive sea animals; *also* : any of a phylum of chiefly marine sea animals that are the source of natural sponges **2** : a spongelike or porous mass or material — **spongy** \'spən-jē\ *adj*

²**sponge** *vb* **sponged; spong·ing 1** : to bathe or wipe with a sponge **2** : to live at another's expense **3** : to gather sponges — **spong·er** *n*

sponge cake *n* : a light cake made without shortening

sponge rubber *n* : a cellular rubber resembling natural sponge

spon·sor \'spän-sər\ *n* [LL, fr. L, guarantor, surety, fr. *spondēre* to promise] **1** : one who takes the responsibility for some other person or thing : SURETY **2** : GODPARENT **3** : a business firm that pays the cost of a radio or television program usu. in return for advertising time during its course — **sponsor** *vb* — **spon·sor·ship** *n*

spon·ta·ne·ous \spän-'tā-nē-əs\ *adj* [LL *spontaneus*, fr. L *sponte* of one's free will, voluntarily] **1** : done or produced freely or naturally **2** : acting or taking place without external force or cause **syn** impulsive, instinctive, automatic, unpremeditated — **spon·ta·ne·ity** \ˌspän-tə-'nē-ə-tē, -'nā-\ *n* — **spon·ta·ne·ous·ly** *adv*

spontaneous combustion *n* : a bursting into flame of material through heat produced within itself by chemical action (as oxidation)

spoof \'spüf\ *vb* **1** : DECEIVE, HOAX **2** : to make good-natured fun of — **spoof** *n*

¹**spook** \'spük\ *n* : GHOST, APPARITION — **spooky** *adj*

²**spook** *vb* : FRIGHTEN

spool \'spül\ *n* : a cylinder on which flexible material (as thread) is wound

spoon \'spün\ *n* [ME, fr. OE *spōn* splinter, chip] **1** : an eating or cooking implement consisting of a small shallow bowl with a handle **2** : a metal piece used on a fishing line as a lure — **spoon** *vb* — **spoon·ful** *n*

spoon·bill \'spün-ˌbil\ *n* : any of several wading birds related to the ibises that have a bill with a broad flat tip

spoon–feed \-ˌfēd\ *vb* **-fed** \-ˌfed\; **-feed·ing** : to feed by means of a spoon

spoor \'spu̇r, 'spȯr\ *n* : a track, a trail, a scent, or droppings esp. of a wild animal

spo·rad·ic \spə-'ra-dik\ *adj* : occurring now and then **syn** occasional, rare, scarce, infrequent, uncommon — **spo·rad·i·cal·ly** \-di-k(ə-)lē\ *adv*

spore \'spȯr\ *n* : a primitive usu. one-celled often environmentally resistant dormant or reproductive body produced by plants and some microorganisms

¹**sport** \'spȯrt\ *vb* [ME, to divert, disport, short for *disporten*, fr. MF *desporter*, fr. *des-* (fr. L *dis-* apart) + *porter* to carry, fr. L *portare*] **1** : to amuse oneself : FROLIC **2** : SHOW OFF **1** — **sport·ive** *adj*

²**sport** *n* **1** : a source of diversion : PASTIME **2** : physical activity engaged in for pleasure **3** : JEST **4** : MOCKERY ⟨make ∼ of his efforts⟩ **5** : BUTT, LAUGHINGSTOCK **6** : one who accepts results cheerfully whether favorable or not **7** : an individual exhibiting marked deviation from its normal type esp. as a result of mutation **syn** play, frolic, fun, recreation — **sporty** *adj*

³**sport** *or* **sports** *adj* : of, relating to, or suitable for sport or casual wear ⟨∼ coats⟩

sport fish *n* : a fish noted for the sport it affords anglers

sports·cast \'spȯrts-ˌkast\ *n* : a broadcast dealing with sports events — **sports·cast·er** \-ˌkas-tər\ *n*

sports·man \'spȯrts-mən\ *n* **1** : a person who engages in sports (as in hunting or fishing) **2** : one who plays fairly and wins or loses gracefully — **sports·man·like** \-ˌlīk\ *adj* — **sports·man·ship** *n*

sports·wom·an \-ˌwu̇-mən\ *n* : a woman who engages in sports

sports·writ·er \-ˌrī-tər\ *n* : one who writes about sports esp. for a newspaper — **sports·writ·ing** *n*

¹**spot** \'spät\ *n* **1** : STAIN, BLEMISH **2** : a small part different (as in color) from the main part **3** : LOCATION, SITE — **spot·less** *adj* — **spot·less·ly** *adv* — **on the spot 1** : at the place of action **2** : in difficulty or danger

²**spot** *vb* **spot·ted; spot·ting 1** : to mark or disfigure with spots **2** : to pick out : RECOGNIZE, IDENTIFY

³**spot** *adj* **1** : being, done, or originating on the spot ⟨a ∼ broadcast⟩ **2** : paid upon delivery **3** : made at random or at a few key points ⟨a ∼ check⟩

spot–check \'spät-ˌchek\ *vb* : to make a spot check of

spot·light \-ˌlīt\ *n* **1** : a circle of brilliant light projected upon a particular area, person, or object (as on a stage); *also* : the device that produces this light **2** : public notice — **spotlight** *vb*

spotted owl *n* : a rare large dark brown dark-eyed owl of humid old growth forests and thickly wooded canyons from British Columbia to southern California and central Mexico

spot·ter \'spä-tər\ *n* **1** : one that keeps watch : OBSERVER **2** : one that removes spots

spot·ty \'spä-tē\ *adj* **spot·ti·er; -est** : uneven in quality; *also* : sparsely distributed ⟨∼ attendance⟩

\ə\abut \ᵊ\kitten \ər\further \a\ash \ā\ace \ä\mop, mar
\au̇\out \ch\chin \e\bet \ē\easy \g\go \i\hit \ī\ice \j\job
\ŋ\sing \ō\go \ȯ\law \ȯi\boy \th\thin \t̶h̶\the \ü\loot \u̇\foot
\y\yet \zh\vision *see also* Pronunciation Symbols page

spou·sal \'spaù-zəl, -səl\ *n* : MARRIAGE 2, WEDDING — usu. used in pl. — **spou·sal** \'spaù-zəl, -səl\ *adj*

spouse \'spaùs\ *n* : one's husband or wife

¹spout \'spaùt\ *vb* **1** : to eject or issue forth forcibly and freely ⟨wells ∼*ing* oil⟩ **2** : to speak pompously

²spout *n* **1** : a pipe or hole through which liquid spouts **2** : a jet of liquid; *esp* : WATERSPOUT 2

spp *abbr, pl* species

¹sprain \'sprān\ *n* : a sudden or severe twisting of a joint with stretching or tearing of ligaments; *also* : a sprained condition

²sprain *vb* : to subject to sprain

sprat \'sprat\ *n* **1** : a small European herring **2** : a young herring

sprawl \'spról\ *vb* **1** : to lie or sit with limbs spread out awkwardly **2** : to spread out irregularly — **sprawl** *n*

¹spray \'sprā\ *n* : a usu. flowering branch; *also* : a decorative arrangement of flowers and foliage

²spray *n* **1** : liquid flying in small drops like water blown from a wave **2** : a jet of fine vapor (as from an atomizer) **3** : an instrument (as an atomizer) for scattering fine liquid

³spray *vb* **1** : to scatter or let fall in a spray **2** : to discharge spray on or into — **spray·er** *n*

spray can *n* : a pressurized container from which aerosols are sprayed

spray gun *n* : a device for spraying liquids (as paint or insecticide)

¹spread \'spred\ *vb* **spread; spread·ing 1** : to scatter over a surface **2** : to flatten out : open out **3** : to distribute over a period of time or among many persons **4** : to cover something with ⟨∼ rugs on the floor⟩ **5** : to prepare for a meal ⟨∼ a table⟩ **6** : to pass on from person to person **7** : to stretch, force, or push apart — **spread·er** *n*

²spread *n* **1** : the act or process of spreading **2** : EXPANSE, EXTENT **3** : a prominent display in a periodical **4** : a food to be spread on bread or crackers **5** : a cloth cover for a bed **6** : distance between two points : GAP

spread·sheet \'spred-₁shēt\ *n* : an accounting program for a computer

spree \'sprē\ *n* : an unrestrained outburst ⟨buying ∼⟩; *esp* : a drinking bout

sprig \'sprig\ *n* : a small shoot or twig

spright·ly \'sprīt-lē\ *adj* **spright·li·er; -est** : LIVELY, SPIRITED **syn** animated, vivacious, gay — **spright·li·ness** *n*

¹spring \'spriŋ\ *vb* **sprang** \'spraŋ\ *or* **sprung** \'sprəŋ\; **sprung; spring·ing 1** : to move suddenly upward or forward **2** : to grow quickly ⟨weeds *sprang* up overnight⟩ **3** : to come from by birth or descent **4** : to move quickly by elastic force **5** : WARP **6** : to develop (a leak) through the seams **7** : to cause to close suddenly ⟨∼ a trap⟩ **8** : to make known suddenly ⟨∼ a surprise⟩ **9** : to make lame : STRAIN

²spring *n* **1** : a source of supply; *esp* : an issuing of water from the ground **2** : SOURCE, ORIGIN; *also* : MOTIVE **3** : the season between winter and summer **4** : an elastic body or device that recovers its original shape when it is released after being distorted **5** : the act or an instance of leaping up or forward **6** : RESILIENCE — **springy** *adj*

spring·board \'spriŋ-₁bórd\ *n* : a springy board used in jumping or vaulting or for diving

spring fever *n* : a lazy or restless feeling often associated with the onset of spring

spring tide *n* : a tide of greater-than-average range that occurs at each new moon and full moon

spring·time \'spriŋ-₁tīm\ *n* : the season of spring

¹sprin·kle \'spriŋ-kəl\ *vb* **sprin·kled; sprin·kling** : to scatter in small drops or particles — **sprin·kler** *n*

²sprinkle *n* : a light rainfall

sprin·kling *n* : SMATTERING

¹sprint \'sprint\ *vb* : to run at top speed esp. for a short distance — **sprint·er** *n*

²sprint *n* **1** : a short run at top speed **2** : a short distance race

sprite \'sprīt\ *n* **1** : GHOST, SPIRIT **2** : ELF, FAIRY

spritz *vb* : SPRAY

sprock·et \'sprä-kət\ *n* : a toothed wheel whose teeth engage the links of a chain

¹sprout \'spraùt\ *vb* : to send out new growth ⟨∼*ing* seeds⟩

²sprout *n* : a usu. young and growing plant shoot (as from a seed)

¹spruce \'sprüs\ *vb* **spruced; spruc·ing** : to make or become spruce

²spruce *adj* **spruc·er; spruc·est** : neat and smart in appearance **syn** stylish, fashionable, modish, dapper, natty

³spruce *n* : any of a genus of evergreen pyramid= shaped trees related to the pines and having soft light wood; *also* : the wood of a spruce

sprung *past and past part of* SPRING

spry \'sprī\ *adj* **spri·er** *or* **spry·er** \'sprī-ər\; **spri·est** *or* **spry·est** \'sprī-əst\ : NIMBLE, ACTIVE **syn** agile, brisk, lively, sprightly

spud \'spəd\ *n* **1** : a sharp narrow spade **2** : POTATO

spume \'spyüm\ *n* : frothy matter on liquids : FOAM — **spumy** \'spyü-mē\ *adj*

spu·mo·ni *also* **spu·mo·ne** \spù-'mō-nē\ *n* [It *spumone*, fr. *spuma* foam] : ice cream in layers of different colors, flavors, and textures often with candied fruits and nuts

spun *past and past part of* SPIN

spun glass *n* : FIBERGLASS

spunk \'spəŋk\ *n* [fr. *spunk* tinder, fr. ScGael *spong* sponge, tinder, fr. L *spongia* sponge] : PLUCK, COURAGE — **spunky** *adj*

¹spur \'spər\ *n* **1** : a pointed device fastened to a rider's boot and used to urge on a horse **2** : something that urges to action **3** : a stiff sharp spine (as on the leg of a cock); *also* : a hollow projecting appendage of a flower (as a columbine) **4** : a ridge extending sideways from a mountain **5** : a branch of railroad track extending from the main line **syn** goad, motive, impulse, incentive, inducement — **spurred** \'spərd\ *adj* — **on the spur of the moment** : on hasty impulse

²spur *vb* **spurred; spur·ring 1** : to urge a horse on with spurs **2** : INCITE

spurge \'spərj\ *n* : any of a genus of herbs and woody plants with bitter milky juice

spu·ri·ous \'spyùr-ē-əs\ *adj* [LL *spurius* false, fr. L, of illegitimate birth, fr. *spurius*, n., bastard] : not genuine : FALSE

spurn \'spərn\ *vb* **1** : to kick away or trample on **2** : to reject with disdain

¹spurt \'spərt\ *vb* : to gush out : SPOUT

²spurt *n* : a sudden gushing or spouting

³spurt *n* **1** : a sudden brief burst of effort or speed **2** : a sharp increase of activity ⟨∼ in sales⟩

⁴spurt *vb* : to make a spurt

sput·ter \'spə-tər\ *vb* **1** : to spit small scattered particles : SPLUTTER **2** : to utter words hastily or explosively in excitement or confusion **3** : to make small popping sounds — **sputter** *n*

spu·tum \'spyü-təm\ *n, pl* **spu·ta** \-tə\ [L] : material that is spit or coughed up and consists of saliva and mucus

¹spy \'spī\ *vb* **spied; spy·ing 1** : to watch or search for information secretly : act as a spy **2** : to get a momentary or quick glimpse of : SEE

²spy *n, pl* **spies 1** : one who secretly watches others **2** : a secret agent who tries to get information for one country in the territory of an enemy

spy·glass \'spī-₁glas\ *n* : a small telescope

sq *abbr* **1** squadron **2** square

squab \'skwäb\ *n, pl* **squabs** *or* **squab** : a young bird and esp. a pigeon

squab·ble \'skwä-bəl\ *n* : a noisy altercation : WRANGLE **syn** quarrel, spat, row, tiff — **squabble** *vb*

squad \'skwäd\ *n* **1** : a small organized group of military personnel **2** : a small group engaged in a common effort
squad car *n* : a police car connected by two-way radio with headquarters
squad·ron \'skwä-drən\ *n* : any of several units of military organization
squal·id \'skwä-ləd\ *adj* **1** : filthy or degraded through neglect or poverty **2** : SORDID, DEBASED **syn** nasty, foul, dirty, grubby
squall \'skwȯl\ *n* : a sudden violent gust of wind often with rain or snow — **squally** *adj*
squa·lor \'skwä-lər\ *n* : the quality or state of being squalid
squan·der \'skwän-dər\ *vb* : to spend wastefully or foolishly
¹square \'skwar\ *n* **1** : an instrument used to lay out or test right angles **2** : a rectangle with all four sides equal **3** : something square **4** : the product of a number multiplied by itself **5** : an area bounded by four streets **6** : an open area in a city where streets meet **7** : a highly conventional person
²square *adj* **squar·er; squar·est** **1** : having four equal sides and four right angles **2** : forming a right angle ⟨cut a ∼ corner⟩ **3** : multiplied by itself : SQUARED ⟨x^2 is the symbol for x ∼⟩ **4** : being a unit of square measure equal to a square each side of which measures one unit ⟨a ∼ foot⟩ **5** : being of a specified length in each of two dimensions ⟨an area 10 feet ∼⟩ **6** : exactly adjusted **7** : JUST, FAIR ⟨a ∼ deal⟩ **8** : leaving no balance ⟨make accounts ∼⟩ **9** : SUBSTANTIAL ⟨a ∼ meal⟩ **10** : highly conservative or conventional — **square·ly** *adv*
³square *vb* **squared; squar·ing** **1** : to form with four equal sides and right angles or with flat surfaces ⟨∼ a timber⟩ **2** : to multiply (a number) by itself **3** : CONFORM, AGREE **4** : BALANCE, SETTLE ⟨∼ an account⟩
square dance *n* : a dance for four couples arranged to form a square
square measure *n* : a unit or system of units for measuring area — see METRIC SYSTEM table, WEIGHT table
square–rigged \'skwar-ˌrigd\ *adj* : having the chief sails extended on yards that are fastened to the masts horizontally and at their center
square–rig·ger \-ˌri-gər\ *n* : a square-rigged craft
square root *n* : either of the two numbers whose squares are equal to a given number ⟨the *square root* of 9 is +3 or −3⟩
¹squash \'skwäsh, 'skwȯsh\ *vb* **1** : to beat or press into a pulp or flat mass **2** : QUASH, SUPPRESS
²squash *n* **1** : the impact of something soft and heavy; *also* : the sound of such impact **2** : a crushed mass **3** : a game played on a 4-wall court with a racket and rubber ball
³squash *n, pl* **squash·es** *or* **squash** : a fruit of any of various plants related to the gourds that is used esp. as a vegetable; *also* : a plant and esp. a vine bearing squashes
squash racquets *n* : SQUASH 3
¹squat \'skwät\ *vb* **squat·ted; squat·ting** **1** : to sit down upon the hams or heels **2** : to settle on land without right or title; *also* : to settle on public land with a view to acquiring title — **squat·ter** *n*
²squat *n* : the act or posture of squatting
³squat *adj* **squat·ter; squat·test** : low to the ground; *also* : short and thick in stature **syn** thickset, stocky, heavyset, stubby
squaw \'skwȯ\ *n* : an American Indian woman
squawk \'skwȯk\ *n* : a harsh loud cry; *also* : a noisy protest — **squawk** *vb*
squeak \'skwēk\ *vb* **1** : to utter or speak in a weak shrill tone **2** : to make a thin high-pitched sound — **squeak** *n* — **squeaky** *adj*
¹squeal \'skwēl\ *vb* **1** : to make a shrill sound or cry **2** : to betray a secret or turn informer **3** : COMPLAIN, PROTEST

²squeal *n* : a shrill sharp cry or noise
squea·mish \'skwē-mish\ *adj* **1** : easily nauseated; *also* : NAUSEATED **2** : easily disgusted **syn** fussy, nice, dainty, fastidious, persnickety — **squea·mish·ness** *n*
squee·gee \'skwē-ˌjē\ *n* : a blade set crosswise on a handle and used for spreading or wiping liquid on, across, or off a surface — **squeegee** *vb*
¹squeeze \'skwēz\ *vb* **squeezed; squeez·ing** **1** : to exert pressure on the opposite sides or parts of **2** : to obtain by pressure ⟨∼ juice from a lemon⟩ **3** : to force, thrust, or cause to pass by pressure — **squeez·er** *n*
²squeeze *n* **1** : an act of squeezing **2** : a quantity squeezed out
squeeze bottle *n* : a flexible plastic bottle that dispenses its contents when it is squeezed
squelch \'skwelch\ *vb* **1** : to suppress completely : CRUSH **2** : to move in soft mud — **squelch** *n*
squib \'skwib\ *n* : a brief witty writing or speech
squid \'skwid\ *n, pl* **squid** *or* **squids** : any of an order of long-bodied sea mollusks having eight arms and two longer tentacles and usu. a slender internal shell
squint \'skwint\ *vb* **1** : to look or aim obliquely **2** : to look or peer with the eyes partly closed **3** : to be cross-eyed — **squint** *n or adj*
¹squire \'skwīr\ *n* [ME *squier*, fr. OF *esquier*, fr. LL *scutarius*, fr. L *scutum* shield] **1** : an armor-bearer of a knight **2** : a man gallantly devoted to a lady **3** : a member of the British gentry ranking below a knight and above a gentleman; *also* : a prominent landowner **4** : a local magistrate
²squire *vb* **squired; squir·ing** : to attend as a squire or escort
squirm \'skwərm\ *vb* : to twist about like a worm : WRIGGLE
¹squir·rel \'skwər-əl\ *n, pl* **squirrels** *also* **squirrel** [ME *squirel*, fr. MF *esquireul*, fr. (assumed) VL *scuriolus*, dim. of *scurius*, alter. of L *sciurus*, fr. Gk *skiouros*, prob. fr. *skia* shadow + *oura* tail] : any of various rodents usu. with a long bushy tail and strong hind legs; *also* : the fur of a squirrel
²squirrel *vb* **-reled** *or* **-relled; -rel·ing** *or* **-rel·ling** : to store up for future use
¹squirt \'skwərt\ *vb* : to eject liquid in a thin spurt
²squirt *n* **1** : an instrument (as a syringe) for squirting **2** : a small forcible jet of liquid
¹Sr *abbr* **1** senior **2** sister
²Sr *symbol* strontium
SR *abbr* seaman recruit
¹SRO \ˌes-(ˌ)är-'ō\ *n* [*single-room occupancy*] : a house or apartment building in which low-income tenants live in single rooms
²SRO *abbr* standing room only
SS *abbr* **1** saints **2** Social Security **3** steamship **4** sworn statement
SSA *abbr* Social Security Administration
SSE *abbr* south-southeast
SSG *or* **SSgt** *abbr* staff sergeant
SSI *abbr* supplemental security income
SSM *abbr* staff sergeant major
SSN *abbr* Social Security Number
ssp *abbr* subspecies
SSR *abbr* Soviet Socialist Republic
SSS *abbr* Selective Service System
SST \ˌes-(ˌ)es-'tē\ *n* [*supersonic transport*] : a supersonic passenger airplane
SSW *abbr* south-southwest
st *abbr* **1** stanza **2** state **3** stitch **4** stone **5** street
St *abbr* saint

\ə\abut \ᵊ\kitten \ər\further \a\ash \ā\ace \ä\mop, mar
\au̇\out \ch\chin \e\bet \ē\easy \g\go \i\hit \ī\ice \j\job
\ŋ\sing \ō\go \ȯ\law \ȯi\boy \th\thin \t̲h̲\the \ü\loot \u̇\foot
\y\yet \zh\vision *see also* Pronunciation Symbols page

ST *abbr* **1** short ton **2** standard time

-st — see -EST

sta *abbr* station; stationary

¹**stab** \'stab\ *n* **1** : a wound produced by a pointed weapon **2** : a quick thrust; *also* : a brief attempt

²**stab** *vb* **stabbed; stab·bing** : to pierce or wound with or as if with a pointed weapon; *also* : THRUST, DRIVE

sta·bile \'stā-₁bēl\ *n* : an abstract sculpture or construction similar to a mobile but made to be stationary

sta·bi·lize \'stā-bə-₁līz\ *vb* **-lized; -liz·ing 1** : to make stable **2** : to hold steady ⟨∼ prices⟩ — **sta·bi·li·za·tion** \₁stā-bə-lə-'zā-shən\ *n* — **sta·bi·liz·er** \'stā-bə-₁lī-zər\ *n*

¹**sta·ble** \'stā-bəl\ *n* : a building in which domestic animals are sheltered and fed — **sta·ble·man** \-mən, -₁man\ *n*

²**stable** *vb* **sta·bled; sta·bling** : to put or keep in a stable

³**stable** *adj* **sta·bler; sta·blest 1** : firmly established; *also* : mentally and emotionally healthy **2** : steady in purpose : CONSTANT **3** : DURABLE, ENDURING **4** : resistant to chemical or physical change **syn** lasting, permanent, perpetual, perdurable — **sta·bil·i·ty** \stə-'bi-lə-tē\ *n*

stac·ca·to \stə-'kä-tō\ *adj or adv* [It] : cut short so as not to sound connected ⟨∼ notes⟩

¹**stack** \'stak\ *n* **1** : a large pile (as of hay or grain) **2** : an orderly pile (as of poker chips) **3** : a large quantity **4** : a vertical pipe : SMOKESTACK **5** : a rack with shelves for storing books

²**stack** *vb* **1** : to pile up **2** : to arrange (cards) secretly for cheating

stack up *vb* : MEASURE UP

sta·di·um \'stā-dē-əm\ *n, pl* **-dia** \-dē-ə\ *or* **-di·ums** : a structure with tiers of seats for spectators built around a field for sports events

¹**staff** \'staf\ *n, pl* **staffs** \'stafs, 'stavz\ *or* **staves** \'stavz, 'stāvz\ **1** : a pole, stick, rod, or bar used for supporting, for measuring, or as a symbol of authority; *also* : CLUB, CUDGEL **2** : something that sustains ⟨bread is the ∼ of life⟩ **3** : the five horizontal lines on which music is written **4** : a body of assistants to an executive **5** : a group of officers holding no command but having duties concerned with planning and managing

²**staff** *vb* : to supply with a staff or with workers

staff·er \'sta-fər\ *n* : a member of a staff (as of a newspaper)

staff sergeant *n* : a noncommissioned officer ranking in the army next below a sergeant first class, in the air force next below a technical sergeant, and in the marine corps next below a gunnery sergeant

¹**stag** \'stag\ *n, pl* **stags** *or* **stag** : an adult male of various large deer

²**stag** *adj* : restricted to or intended for men ⟨a ∼ party⟩ ⟨∼ movies⟩

³**stag** *adv* : unaccompanied by a date

¹**stage** \'stāj\ *n* **1** : a raised platform on which an orator may speak or a play may be presented **2** : the acting profession : THEATER **3** : the scene of a notable action or event **4** : a station or resting place on a traveled road **5** : STAGECOACH **6** : a degree of advance in an undertaking, process, or development **7** : a propulsion unit in a rocket — **stagy** \'stā-jē\ *adj*

²**stage** *vb* **staged; stag·ing** : to produce or perform on or as if on a stage — **stage·able** *adj*

stage·coach \'stāj-₁kōch\ *n* : a horse-drawn coach that runs regularly between stations

stag·fla·tion \₁stag-'flā-shən\ *n* : inflation with stagnant economic activity and high unemployment

¹**stag·ger** \'sta-gər\ *vb* **1** : to reel from side to side : TOTTER **2** : to begin to doubt : WAVER **3** : to cause to reel or waver **4** : to arrange in overlapping or alternating positions or times ⟨∼ working hours⟩ **5** : ASTONISH — **stag·ger·ing·ly** *adv*

²**stagger** *n* **1** *sing or pl* : an abnormal condition of domestic mammals and birds associated with damage to the central nervous system and marked by lack of coordi-

nation and a reeling unsteady gait **2** : a reeling or unsteady gait or stance

stag·ing \'stā-jiŋ\ *n* **1** : SCAFFOLDING **2** : the assembling of troops and matériel in transit in a particular place

stag·nant \'stag-nənt\ *adj* **1** : not flowing : MOTIONLESS ⟨∼ water in a pond⟩ **2** : DULL, INACTIVE ⟨∼ business⟩

stag·nate \'stag-₁nāt\ *vb* **stag·nat·ed; stag·nat·ing** : to be or become stagnant — **stag·na·tion** \stag-'nā-shən\ *n*

staid \'stād\ *adj* : SOBER, SEDATE **syn** grave, serious, earnest

¹**stain** \'stān\ *vb* **1** : DISCOLOR, SOIL **2** : TAINT, CORRUPT **3** : DISGRACE **4** : to color (as wood, paper, or cloth) by processes affecting the material itself

²**stain** *n* **1** : a small soiled or discolored area **2** : a taint of guilt : STIGMA **3** : a preparation (as a dye or pigment) used in staining — **stain·less** *adj*

stainless steel *n* : steel alloyed with chromium that is highly resistant to stain, rust, and corrosion

stair \'star\ *n* **1** : a series of steps or flights of steps for passing from one level to another — often used in pl. **2** : one step of a stairway

stair·case \-₁kās\ *n* : a flight of steps with their supporting framework, casing, and balusters

stair·way \-₁wā\ *n* : one or more flights of stairs with connecting landings

stair·well \-₁wel\ *n* : a vertical shaft in which stairs are located

¹**stake** \'stāk\ *n* **1** : a pointed piece of material (as of wood) driven into the ground as a marker or a support **2** : a post to which a person is bound for death by burning; *also* : such a death **3** : something that is staked for gain or loss **4** : the prize in a contest

²**stake** *vb* **staked; stak·ing 1** : to mark the limits of by or as if by stakes **2** : to tie to a stake **3** : to support or secure with stakes **4** : BET, WAGER

stake·out \'stāk-₁aut\ *n* : a surveillance by police (as of a suspected criminal)

sta·lac·tite \stə-'lak-₁tīt\ *n* [NL *stalactites,* fr. Gk *stalaktos* dripping] : an icicle-shaped deposit hanging from the roof or sides of a cavern

sta·lag·mite \stə-'lag-₁mīt\ *n* [NL *stalagmites,* fr. Gk *stalagma* drop *or stalagmos* dripping] : a deposit resembling an inverted stalactite rising from the floor of a cavern

stale \'stāl\ *adj* **stal·er; stal·est 1** : having lost good taste and quality from age ⟨∼ bread⟩ **2** : used or heard so often as to be dull ⟨∼ news⟩ **3** : not as strong or effective as before ⟨∼ from lack of practice⟩ — **stale·ness** *n*

stale·mate \'stāl-₁māt\ *n* : a drawn contest : DEADLOCK — **stalemate** *vb*

¹**stalk** \'stok\ *n* : a plant stem; *also* : any slender usu. upright supporting or connecting part — **stalked** \'stokt\ *adj*

²**stalk** *vb* **1** : to pursue (game) stealthily **2** : to walk stiffly or haughtily

¹**stall** \'stol\ *n* **1** : a compartment in a stable or barn for one animal **2** : a booth or counter where articles may be displayed for sale **3** : a seat in a church choir; *also* : a church pew **4** *chiefly Brit* : a front orchestra seat in a theater

²**stall** *vb* : to bring or come to a standstill unintentionally ⟨∼ an engine⟩

³**stall** *n* : the condition of an airfoil or aircraft in which lift is lost and the airfoil or aircraft tends to drop

⁴**stall** *n* [alter. of *stale* lure] : a ruse to deceive or delay

⁵**stall** *vb* : to hold off, divert, or delay by evasion or deception

stal·lion \'stal-yən\ *n* : a male horse

stal·wart \'stol-wərt\ *adj* : STOUT, STRONG; *also* : BRAVE, VALIANT

sta·men \'stā-mən\ *n* : an organ of a flower that produces pollen

stam·i·na \'sta-mə-nə\ *n* [L, pl. of *stamen* warp, thread of life spun by the Fates] : VIGOR, ENDURANCE

sta·mi·nate \'stā-mə-nət, 'sta-mə-, -ˌnāt\ *adj* **1** : having or producing stamens **2** : having stamens but no pistils

stam·mer \'sta-mər\ *vb* : to hesitate or stumble in speaking — **stammer** *n* — **stam·mer·er** *n*

¹stamp \'stamp; *for 2 also* 'stämp *or* 'stòmp\ *vb* **1** : to pound or crush with a heavy instrument **2** : to strike or beat with the bottom of the foot **3** : IMPRESS, IMPRINT **4** : to cut out or indent with a stamp or die **5** : to attach a postage stamp to

²stamp *n* **1** : a device or instrument for stamping **2** : the mark made by stamping; *also* : a distinctive mark or quality **3** : the act of stamping **4** : a stamped or printed paper affixed to show that a charge has been paid ⟨postage ∼⟩ ⟨tax ∼⟩

¹stam·pede \stam-'pēd\ *n* : a wild headlong rush or flight esp. of frightened animals

²stampede *vb* **stam·ped·ed; stam·ped·ing** **1** : to flee or cause to flee in panic **2** : to act or cause to act together suddenly and heedlessly

stance \'stans\ *n* : a way of standing

¹stanch \'stònch, 'stänch\ *vb* : to check the flowing of (as blood); *also* : to cease flowing or bleeding

²stanch *var of* ²STAUNCH

stan·chion \'stan-chən\ *n* : an upright bar, post, or support

¹stand \'stand\ *vb* **stood** \'stùd\; **stand·ing** **1** : to take or be at rest in an upright or firm position **2** : to assume a specified position **3** : to remain stationary or unchanged **4** : to be steadfast **5** : to act in resistance ⟨∼ against a foe⟩ **6** : to maintain a relative position or rank **7** : to gather slowly and remain ⟨tears *stood* in her eyes⟩ **8** : to set upright **9** : ENDURE, TOLERATE ⟨I won't ∼ for that⟩ **10** : to submit to ⟨∼ trial⟩ — **stand pat** : to oppose or resist change

²stand *n* **1** : an act of standing, staying, or resisting **2** : a stop made to give a performance **3** : POSITION, VIEWPOINT **4** : a place taken by a witness to testify in court **5** *pl* : tiered seats for spectators **6** : a raised platform (as for speakers) **7** : a structure for a small retail business **8** : a structure for supporting or holding something upright ⟨music ∼⟩ **9** : a group of plants growing in a continuous area

stand–alone \'stan-də-ˌlōn\ *adj* : SELF-CONTAINED; *esp* : capable of operation independent of a computer system

stan·dard \'stan-dərd\ *n* **1** : a figure adopted as an emblem by a people **2** : the personal flag of a ruler; *also* : FLAG **3** : something set up as a rule for measuring or as a model to be followed **4** : an upright support ⟨lamp ∼⟩ — **standard** *adj*

stan·dard–bear·er \-ˌbar-ər\ *n* : the leader of a cause

standard deviation *n* : a measure of dispersion in a set of data

stan·dard·ize \'stan-dər-ˌdīz\ *vb* **-ized; -iz·ing** : to make standard or uniform — **stan·dard·i·za·tion** \ˌstan-dər-də-'zā-shən\ *n*

standard of living : the necessities, comforts, and luxuries that a person or group is accustomed to

standard time *n* : the time established by law or by general usage over a region or country

☞ For table, see next page.

¹stand·by \'stand-ˌbī\ *n, pl* **stand·bys** \-ˌbīz\ **1** : one that can be relied on **2** : a substitute in reserve — **on standby** : ready or available for immediate action or use

²standby *adj* **1** : ready for use **2** : relating to airline travel in which the passenger must wait for an available unreserved seat — **standby** *adv*

stand–in \'stan-ˌdin\ *n* **1** : someone employed to occupy an actor's place while lights and camera are readied **2** : SUBSTITUTE

¹stand·ing \'stan-diŋ\ *adj* **1** : ERECT **2** : not flowing : STAG-

NANT **3** : remaining at the same level or amount for an indefinite period ⟨∼ offer⟩ **4** : PERMANENT **5** : done from a standing position ⟨a ∼ jump⟩

²standing *n* **1** : length of service; *also* : relative position in society or in a profession : RANK **2** : DURATION

stand·off \'stan-ˌdòf\ *n* : TIE, DRAW

stand·off·ish \stan-'dò-fish\ *adj* : somewhat cold and reserved

stand·out \'stan-ˌdaùt\ *n* : something conspicuously excellent

stand·pipe \'stand-ˌpīp\ *n* : a high vertical pipe or reservoir for water used to produce a uniform pressure

stand·point \-ˌpòint\ *n* : a position from which objects or principles are judged

stand·still \-ˌstil\ *n* : a state of rest

stand–up \'stan-dəp\ *adj* : done or performing in a standing position ⟨a ∼ comic⟩ ⟨∼ comedy⟩

stank \'staŋk\ *past of* STINK

stan·za \'stan-zə\ *n* [It] : a group of lines forming a division of a poem

sta·pes \'stā-ˌpēz\ *n, pl* **stapes** *or* **sta·pe·des** \'stā-pə-ˌdēz\ : the small innermost bone of the ear of mammals

staph \'staf\ *n* : STAPHYLOCOCCUS

staph·y·lo·coc·cus \ˌsta-fə-lō-'kä-kəs\ *n, pl* **-coc·ci** \-'kä-ˌkī, -'käk-ˌsī\ : any of various spherical bacteria including some pathogens of skin and mucous membranes — **staph·y·lo·coc·cal** \-'kä-kəl\ *adj*

¹sta·ple \'stā-pəl\ *n* : a U-shaped piece of metal or wire with sharp points to be driven into a surface or through thin layers (as paper) for attaching or holding together — **staple** *vb* — **sta·pler** *n*

²staple *n* **1** : a chief commodity or product **2** : a chief part of something ⟨a ∼ of their diet⟩ **3** : unmanufactured or raw material **4** : a textile fiber suitable for spinning into yarn

³staple *adj* **1** : regularly produced in large quantities **2** : PRINCIPAL, MAIN

¹star \'stär\ *n* **1** : a celestial body that appears as a fixed point of light; *esp* : such a body that is gaseous, self=luminous, and of great mass **2** : a planet or configuration of planets that is held in astrology to influence one's fortune — usu. used in pl. **3** *obs* : DESTINY, FORTUNE **4** : a conventional figure representing a star; *esp* : ASTERISK **5** : an actor or actress playing the leading role **6** : a brilliant performer — **star·dom** \'stär-dəm\ *n* — **star·less** *adj* — **star·like** *adj* — **star·ry** *adj*

☞ For table, see page 531.

²star *vb* **starred; star·ring** **1** : to adorn with stars **2** : to mark with an asterisk **3** : to play the leading role

star·board \'stär-bərd\ *n* [ME *sterbord*, fr. OE *stēorbord*, fr. *stēor*- steering oar + *bord* ship's side] : the right side of a ship or airplane looking forward — **starboard** *adj*

¹starch \'stärch\ *vb* : to stiffen with or as if with starch

²starch *n* : a complex carbohydrate that is stored in plants, is an important foodstuff, and is used in adhesives and sizes, in laundering, and in pharmacy — **starchy** *adj*

stare \'star\ *vb* **stared; star·ing** : to look fixedly with wide-open eyes — **stare** *n* — **star·er** *n*

star·fish \'stär-ˌfish\ *n* : any of a class of echinoderms usu. having five arms arranged around a central disk and feeding largely on mollusks

star fruit *n* : CARAMBOLA 1

¹stark \'stärk\ *adj* **1** : rigid as if in death; *also* : STRICT **2** *archaic* : STRONG, ROBUST **3** : SHEER, UTTER **4** : BARREN, DESOLATE ⟨∼ landscape⟩; *also* : UNADORNED ⟨∼ realism⟩ **5** : sharply delineated — **stark·ly** *adv*

\ə\abut \ᵊ\kitten \ər\further \a\ash \ā\ace \ä\mop, mar \aù\out \ch\chin \e\bet \ē\easy \g\go \i\hit \ī\ice \j\job \ŋ\sing \ō\go \ò\law \òi\boy \th\thin \t͟h\the \ü\loot \ù\foot \y\yet \zh\vision *see also* Pronunciation Symbols page

STANDARD TIME IN 102 PLACES THROUGHOUT THE WORLD WHEN IT IS 12:00 NOON AT NEW YORK

CITY	TIME	CITY	TIME
Adelaide, Australia	2:30 A.M. next day	London, England	5:00 P.M.
Alexandria, Egypt	7:00 P.M.	Los Angeles, California	9:00 A.M.
[1]Amsterdam, Netherlands	6:00 P.M.	[1]Madrid, Spain	6:00 P.M.
Anchorage, Alaska	8:00 A.M.	Manila, Philippines	1:00 A.M. next day
Asunción, Paraguay	1:00 P.M.	Mecca, Saudi Arabia	8:00 P.M.
Athens, Greece	7:00 P.M.	Melbourne, Australia	3:00 A.M. next day
Auckland, New Zealand	5:00 A.M. next day	Mexico City, Mexico	11:00 A.M.
Baghdad, Iraq	8:00 P.M.	Miami, Florida	12:00 NOON
Bangkok, Thailand	12:00 MIDNIGHT	Montevideo, Uruguay	2:00 P.M.
Beijing, China	1:00 A.M. next day	Montreal, Quebec	12:00 NOON
Belgrade, Yugoslavia	6:00 P.M.	[1]Moscow, Russia	8:00 P.M.
Berlin, Germany	6:00 P.M.	Nairobi, Kenya	8:00 P.M.
Bogotá, Colombia	12:00 NOON	New Delhi, India	10:30 P.M.
Bombay, India	10:30 P.M.	Nome, Alaska	8:00 A.M.
Boston, Massachusetts	12:00 NOON	Oslo, Norway	6:00 P.M.
[1]Brussels, Belgium	6:00 P.M.	Ottawa, Ontario	12:00 NOON
Bucharest, Romania	7:00 P.M.	Panama City, Panama	12:00 NOON
Budapest, Hungary	6:00 P.M.	[1]Paris, France	6:00 P.M.
[1]Buenos Aires, Argentina	2:00 P.M.	Perth, Australia	1:00 A.M. next day
Cairo, Egypt	7:00 P.M.	Philadelphia, Pennsylvania	12:00 NOON
Calcutta, India	10:30 P.M.	Prague, Czech Republic	6:00 P.M.
Cape Town, Republic of So. Africa	7:00 P.M.	Quito, Ecuador	12:00 NOON
		Regina, Saskatchewan	11:00 A.M.
Caracas, Venezuela	1:00 P.M.	Reykjavik, Iceland	4:00 P.M.
[1]Casablanca, Morocco	6:00 P.M.	Rio de Janeiro, Brazil	2:00 P.M.
Chicago, Illinois	11:00 A.M.	Rome, Italy	6:00 P.M.
Colombo, Sri Lanka	10:30 P.M.	Saint John's, Newfoundland	1:30 P.M.
Copenhagen, Denmark	6:00 P.M.		
Denver, Colorado	10:00 A.M.	Saint Louis, Missouri	11:00 A.M.
Detroit, Michigan	12:00 NOON	Saint Petersburg, Russia	8:00 P.M.
Dublin, Ireland	5:00 P.M.	San Francisco, California	9:00 A.M.
Edmonton, Alberta	10:00 A.M.	San Juan, Puerto Rico	1:00 P.M.
Geneva, Switzerland	6:00 P.M.	Santiago, Chile	1:00 P.M.
Glasgow, Scotland	5:00 P.M.	São Paulo, Brazil	2:00 P.M.
Halifax, Nova Scotia	1:00 P.M.	Seattle, Washington	9:00 A.M.
Havana, Cuba	12:00 NOON	Seoul, South Korea	2:00 A.M. next day
Helsinki, Finland	7:00 P.M.	Shanghai, China	1:00 A.M. next day
Ho Chi Minh City, Vietnam	12:00 MIDNIGHT	Singapore	1:00 A.M. next day
		Sofia, Bulgaria	7:00 P.M.
Hong Kong	1:00 A.M. next day	Stockholm, Sweden	6:00 P.M.
Honolulu, Hawaii	7:00 A.M.	Sydney, Australia	3:00 A.M. next day
Houston, Texas	11:00 A.M.	Tehran, Iran	8:30 P.M.
Istanbul, Turkey	7:00 P.M.	Tokyo, Japan	2:00 A.M. next day
Jakarta, Indonesia	12:00 MIDNIGHT	Toronto, Ontario	12:00 NOON
Jerusalem, Israel	7:00 P.M.	Vancouver, British Columbia	9:00 A.M.
Johannesburg, Republic of So. Africa	7:00 P.M.		
		Vienna, Austria	6:00 P.M.
Juneau, Alaska	8:00 A.M.	[1]Vladivostok, Russia	3:00 A.M. next day
Karachi, Pakistan	10:00 P.M.	Warsaw, Poland	6:00 P.M.
Kiev, Ukraine	7:00 P.M.	Washington, D.C.	12:00 NOON
Kuala Lumpur, Malaysia	1:00 A.M. next day	Wellington, New Zealand	5:00 A.M. next day
Lagos, Nigeria	6:00 P.M.	Winnipeg, Manitoba	11:00 A.M.
La Paz, Bolivia	1:00 P.M.	Yangon, Myanmar	11:30 P.M.
Lima, Peru	12:00 NOON		

[1]Time is one hour in advance of the standard meridian.

---

²**stark** *adv* : WHOLLY, ABSOLUTELY ⟨∼ naked⟩
star·light \'stär-ˌlīt\ *n* : the light given by the stars
star·ling \'stär-liŋ\ *n* : a dark brown or in summer glossy greenish black European bird related to the crows that is naturalized nearly worldwide and often considered a pest
¹**start** \'stärt\ *vb* **1** : to give an involuntary twitch or jerk (as from surprise) **2** : BEGIN, COMMENCE **3** : to set going **4** : to enter or cause to enter a game or contest; *also* : to be in the starting lineup — **start·er** *n*

²**start** *n* **1** : a sudden involuntary motion : LEAP **2** : a spasmodic and brief effort or action **3** : BEGINNING; *also* : the place of beginning
star·tle \'stärt-ᵊl\ *vb* **star·tled; star·tling** : to frighten or surprise suddenly : cause to start
star·tling *adj* : causing sudden fear, surprise, or anxiety
starve \'stärv\ *vb* **starved; starv·ing** [ME *sterven*, fr. OE *steorfan*] **1** : to die or cause to die from hunger **2** : to suffer extreme hunger or deprivation ⟨*starving* for affection⟩ **3** : to subdue by famine — **star·va·tion** \stär-'vā-shən\ *n*

FIFTY IMPORTANT STARS

NAME & PRONUNCIATION	CONSTELLATION[1]	
Achernar \'ak-ər-ˌnär, 'ä-kər-\	α	Eridani
Albireo \al-'bir-ē-ˌō\	β	Cygni
Alcor \'al-ˌkȯr\	80	Ursae Majoris
Alcyone \al-'sī-ə-(ˌ)nē\	η	Tauri
Aldebaran \al-'deb-ə-rən\	α	Tauri
Algenib \al-'jen-əb, -'jēn-\	γ	Pegasi
Algol \'al-ˌgäl, -ˌgȯl\	β	Persei
Alioth \'al-ē-ˌäth, -ˌȯth\	ε	Ursae Majoris
Alkaid \al-'kīd, -'kād\	η	Ursae Majoris
Almach \'al-ˌmak\	γ	Andromedae
Alphard \'al-ˌfärd\	α	Hydrae
Alphecca \al-'fek-ə\	α	Corona Borealis
Alpheratz \al-'fer- əts\	α	Andromedae or δ Pegasi
Altair \al-'tīr, -'tar\	α	Aquilae
Antares \an-'tar-ēz\	α	Scorpii
Arcturus \ärk-'t(y)ur-əs\	α	Boötis
Bellatrix \bə-'lā-triks\	γ	Orionis
Betelgeuse \'bet-əl-ˌjüz, 'bēt-\	α	Orionis
Canopus \kə-'nō-pəs\	α	Carinae
Capella \kə-'pel-ə\	α	Aurigae
Castor \'kas-tər\	α	Geminorum
Deneb \'den-ˌeb, -əb\	α	Cygni
Deneb Kaitos \'den-ˌeb-'kīt-əs, -əb-, -'kāt-, -ˌäs\	β	Ceti
Denebola \də-'neb-ə-lə\	β	Leonis
Dubhe \'dü-bə, 'də-\	α	Ursae Majoris
Elnath \'el-ˌnath\	β	Tauri
Fomalhaut \'fō-məl-ˌhȯt\	α	Piscis Austrni
Hamal \'ham-əl\	α	Arietis
Markab \'mär-ˌkab\	α	Pegasi
Megrez \'mē-ˌgrez, 'meg-ˌrez\	δ	Ursae Majoris
Menkar \'men-ˌkär\	α	Ceti
Merak \'mē-ˌrak\	β	Ursae Majoris
Mira \'mī-rə\	o	Ceti
Mirach \'mī-ˌrak\	β	Andromedae
Mirfak \'mir-ˌfak\	α	Persei
Mizar \'mī-ˌzär\	ζ	Ursae Majoris
Phecda \'fek-də\	γ	Ursae Majoris
Polaris \pō-'lar-əs\	α	Ursae Minoris
Pollux \'päl-əks\	β	Geminorum
Procyon \'prō-sē-ˌän\	α	Canis Minoris
Rasalgethi \ˌras-əl-'jet-ē, -'jeth-\	α	Herculis
Rasalhague \ˌras-əl-'häg-wē\	α	Ophiuchi
Regulus \'reg-yə-ləs\	α	Leonis
Rigel \'rī-jel, -gəl\	β	Orionis
Scheat \shē-'at, -'ät; 'shē-ˌat, -ˌät\	β	Pegasi
Schedar \'shed-ər\	α	Cassiopeiae
Sirius \'sir-ē-əs\	α	Canis Majoris
Spica \'spī-kə\	α	Virginis
Thuban \'th(y)ü-ˌban\	α	Draconis
Vega \'veg-ə, 'vā-gə\	α	Lyrae

[1] The Greek letter indicates relative brightness of the star within the constellation: α (the first letter of the Greek alphabet) indicates the brightest; β (the second letter) indicates the second brightest, etc. (See Greek Alphabet table at GREEK.) Alcor is the 80th brightest star in the constellation Ursae Majoris.

---

starve·ling \'stärv-liŋ\ n : one that is thin from lack of nourishment

stash \'stash\ vb : to store in a secret place for future use — **stash** n

stat abbr 1 [L statim] immediately 2 statute

[1]**state** \'stāt\ n [ME stat, fr. OF & L; OF estat, fr. L status, fr. stare to stand] 1 : mode or condition of being

⟨the four ∼s of matter⟩ 2 : condition of mind 3 : social position 4 : a body of people occupying a territory and organized under one government; also : the government of such a body of people 5 : one of the constituent units of a nation having a federal government — **state·hood** \-ˌhud\ n

[2]**state** vb **stat·ed; stat·ing 1** : FIX ⟨stated intervals⟩ **2** : to express in words

state·craft \'stāt-ˌkraft\ n : the art of conducting state affairs

state·house \-ˌhaus\ n : the building in which a state legislature meets

state·ly \'stāt-lē\ adj **state·li·er; -est 1** : having lofty dignity : HAUGHTY **2** : IMPRESSIVE, MAJESTIC **syn** magnificent, imposing, august — **state·li·ness** n

state·ment \'stāt-mənt\ n **1** : the act or result of presenting in words **2** : a summary of a financial account

state·room \'stāt-ˌrüm, -ˌrum\ n : a private room on a ship or railroad car

state·side \'stāt-ˌsīd\ adj : of or relating to the U.S. as regarded from outside its continental limits — **stateside** adv

states·man \'stāts-mən\ n : a person engaged in fixing the policies and conducting the affairs of a government; esp : one wise and skilled in such matters — **states-man·like** adj — **states·man·ship** n

[1]**stat·ic** \'sta-tik\ adj **1** : acting by mere weight without motion ⟨∼ pressure⟩ **2** : relating to bodies at rest or forces in equilibrium **3** : not moving : not active **4** : of or relating to stationary charges of electricity **5** : of, relating to, or caused by radio static

[2]**static** n : noise produced in a radio or television receiver by atmospheric or other electrical disturbances

[1]**sta·tion** \'stā-shən\ n **1** : the place where a person or thing stands or is assigned to remain **2** : a regular stopping place on a transportation route : DEPOT **3** : a place where a fleet is assigned for duty **4** : a stock farm or ranch esp. in Australia or New Zealand **5** : social standing **6** : a complete assemblage of radio or television equipment for sending or receiving

[2]**station** vb : to assign to a station

sta·tion·ary \'stā-shə-ˌner-ē\ adj **1** : fixed in a station, course, or mode **2** : unchanging in condition

stationary front n : the boundary between two air masses neither of which is advancing

station break n : a pause in a radio or television broadcast to announce the identity of the network or station

sta·tio·ner \'stā-shə-nər\ n : one that sells stationery

sta·tio·nery \'stā-shə-ˌner-ē\ n : materials (as paper, pens, or ink) for writing; esp : letter paper with envelopes

station wagon n : an automobile having a passenger compartment which extends to the back of the vehicle and no trunk

sta·tis·tic \stə-'tis-tik\ n **1** : a single term or datum in a collection of statistics **2** : a quantity (as the mean) that is computed from a sample

sta·tis·tics \-tiks\ n sing or pl [G Statistik study of political facts and figures, fr. NL statisticus of politics, fr. L status state] : a branch of mathematics dealing with the collection, analysis, and interpretation of masses of numerical data; also : a collection of such numerical data — **sta·tis·ti·cal** \-ti-kəl\ adj — **sta·tis·ti·cal·ly** \-ti-k(ə-)lē\ adv — **stat·is·ti·cian** \ˌsta-tə-'sti-shən\ n

stat·u·ary \'sta-chə-ˌwer-ē\ n, pl **-ar·ies 1** : the art of making statues **2** : STATUES

stat·ue \'sta-chü\ n : a likeness (as of a person or animal)

\ə\abut \ə̇\kitten \ər\further \a\ash \ā\ace \ä\mop, mar \au̇\out \ch\chin \e\bet \ē\easy \g\go \i\hit \ī\ice \j\job \ŋ\sing \ō\go \ȯ\law \ȯi\boy \th\thin \th\the \ü\loot \u̇\foot \y\yet \zh\vision see also Pronunciation Symbols page sculptured, modeled, or cast in a solid substance

stat·u·esque \ˌsta-chə-'wesk\ *adj* : tall and shapely

stat·u·ette \ˌsta-chə-'wet\ *n* : a small statue

stat·ure \'sta-chər\ *n* **1** : natural height (as of a person) **2** : quality or status gained (as by achievement)

sta·tus \'stā-təs, 'sta-\ *n* **1** : the condition of a person in the eyes of others or of the law **2** : state of affairs

sta·tus quo \-'kwō\ *n* [L, state in which] : the existing state of affairs

stat·ute \'sta-chüt\ *n* : a law enacted by a legislative body

stat·u·to·ry \'sta-chə-ˌtōr-ē\ *adj* : imposed by statute : LAWFUL

statutory rape *n* : sexual intercourse with a person who is below the statutory age of consent

¹staunch \'stónch\ *var of* ¹STANCH

²staunch *adj* **1** : WATERTIGHT ⟨a ~ ship⟩ **2** : FIRM, STRONG; *also* : STEADFAST, LOYAL **syn** resolute, constant, true, faithful — **staunch·ly** *adv*

¹stave \'stāv\ *n* **1** : CUDGEL, STAFF **2** : any of several narrow strips of wood placed edge to edge to make something (as a barrel) **3** : STANZA

²stave *vb* **staved** *or* **stove** \'stōv\; **stav·ing 1** : to break in the staves of; *also* : to break a hole in **2** : to drive or thrust away ⟨~ off trouble⟩

staves *pl of* STAFF

¹stay \'stā\ *n* **1** : a strong rope or wire used to support a mast **2** : ¹GUY

²stay *vb* **stayed** \'stād\ *also* **staid** \'stād\; **stay·ing 1** : PAUSE, WAIT **2** : REMAIN **3** : to stand firm **4** : LIVE, DWELL **5** : DELAY, POSTPONE **6** : to last out (as a race) **7** : STOP, CHECK **8** : to satisfy (as hunger) for a time **syn** remain, abide, linger, tarry

³stay *n* **1** : STOP, HALT **2** : a residence or sojourn in a place

⁴stay *n* **1** : PROP, SUPPORT **2** : CORSET — usu. used in pl.

⁵stay *vb* : to hold up : PROP

staying power *n* : STAMINA

stbd *abbr* starboard

std *abbr* standard

STD \ˌes-(ˌ)tē-'dē\ *n* : SEXUALLY TRANSMITTED DISEASE

Ste *abbr* [F *sainte*] saint (female)

stead \'sted\ *n* **1** : ADVANTAGE ⟨stood him in good ~⟩ **2** : the place or function ordinarily occupied or carried out by another ⟨acted in her brother's ~⟩

stead·fast \'sted-ˌfast\ *adj* **1** : firmly fixed in place **2** : not subject to change **3** : firm in belief, determination, or adherence : LOYAL **syn** resolute, true, faithful, staunch — **stead·fast·ly** *adv* — **stead·fast·ness** *n*

¹steady \'ste-dē\ *adj* **steadi·er; -est 1** : direct or sure in movement; *also* : CALM **2** : FIRM; FIXED **3** : STABLE **4** : CONSTANT, RESOLUTE **5** : REGULAR **6** : RELIABLE, SOBER **syn** uniform, even — **steadi·ly** \-də-lē\ *adv* — **steadi·ness** \-dē-nəs\ *n* — **steady** *adv*

²steady *vb* **stead·ied; steady·ing** : to make or become steady

steak \'stāk\ *n* : a slice of meat and esp. beef; *also* : a slice of a large fish

¹steal \'stēl\ *vb* **stole** \'stōl\; **sto·len** \'stō-lən\; **steal·ing 1** : to take and carry away without right or permission **2** : to come or go secretly or gradually **3** : to get for oneself slyly or by skill and daring ⟨~ a kiss⟩ ⟨~ the ball in basketball⟩ **4** : to gain or attempt to gain a base in baseball by running without the aid of a hit or an error **syn** pilfer, filch, purloin, swipe

²steal *n* **1** : an act of stealing **2** : BARGAIN

stealth \'stelth\ *n* **1** : secret or unobtrusive procedure **2** : an aircraft design intended to produce a weak radar return

stealthy \'stel-thē\ *adj* **stealth·i·er; -est** : done by stealth : FURTIVE, SLY **syn** secret, covert, clandestine, surreptitious, underhanded — **stealth·i·ly** \'stel-thə-lē\ *adv*

¹steam \'stēm\ *n* **1** : the vapor into which water is changed when heated to the boiling point **2** : water va-

por when compressed so that it supplies heat and power **3** : POWER, FORCE, ENERGY — **steamy** *adj*

²steam *vb* **1** : to pass off as vapor **2** : to emit vapor **3** : to move by or as if by the agency of steam — **steam·er** *n*

steam·boat \'stēm-ˌbōt\ *n* : a boat driven by steam

steam engine *n* : a reciprocating engine having a piston driven by steam

steam·fit·ter \'stēm-ˌfi-tər\ *n* : a worker who puts in or repairs equipment (as steam pipes) for heating, ventilating, or refrigerating systems

steam·roll·er \-ˌrō-lər\ *n* : a machine for compacting roads or pavements — **steam·roll·er** *also* **steam·roll** \-ˌrōl\ *vb*

steam·ship \-ˌship\ *n* : a ship driven by steam

steed \'stēd\ *n* : HORSE

¹steel \'stēl\ *n* **1** : iron treated with intense heat and mixed with carbon to make it hard and tough **2** : an article made of steel **3** : a quality (as hardness of mind) that suggests steel — **steel** *adj* — **steely** *adj*

²steel *vb* : to fill with courage or determination

steel wool *n* : long fine steel shavings used esp. for cleaning and polishing

¹steep \'stēp\ *adj* **1** : having a very sharp slope : PRECIPITOUS **2** : too great or too high ⟨~ prices⟩ — **steep·ly** *adv* — **steep·ness** *n*

²steep *n* : a steep slope

³steep *vb* **1** : to soak in a liquid; *esp* : to extract the essence of by soaking ⟨~ tea⟩ **2** : SATURATE ⟨~ed in learning⟩

stee·ple \'stē-pəl\ *n* : a tall tapering structure built on top of a church tower; *also* : a church tower

stee·ple·chase \-ˌchās\ *n* [fr. the use of church steeples as landmarks to guide the riders] : a horse race across country; *also* : a race over a course obstructed by hurdles

¹steer \'stir\ *n* : a male bovine animal castrated before sexual maturity and usu. raised for beef

²steer *vb* **1** : to direct the course of (as by a rudder or wheel) **2** : GUIDE, CONTROL **3** : to pursue a course of action **4** : to be subject to guidance or direction — **steers·man** \'stirz-mən\ *n*

steer·age \'stir-ij\ *n* **1** : DIRECTION, GUIDANCE **2** : a section in a passenger ship for passengers paying the lowest fares

stego·sau·rus \ˌste-gə-'sòr-əs\ *n* : any of a genus of plant-eating armored dinosaurs with a series of bony plates along the backbone

stein \'stīn\ *n* : an earthenware mug

stel·lar \'ste-lər\ *adj* : of or relating to stars : resembling a star

¹stem \'stem\ *n* **1** : the main stalk of a plant; *also* : a plant part that supports another part (as a leaf or fruit) **2** : the bow of a ship **3** : a line of ancestry : STOCK **4** : that part of an inflected word which remains unchanged throughout a given inflection **5** : something resembling the stem of a plant — **stem·less** *adj* — **stemmed** \'stemd\ *adj*

²stem *vb* **stemmed; stem·ming** : to have a specified source : DERIVE

³stem *vb* **stemmed; stem·ming** : to make headway against ⟨~ the tide⟩

⁴stem *vb* **stemmed; stem·ming** : to stop or check by or as if by damming

stench \'stench\ *n* : STINK

sten·cil \'sten-səl\ *n* [ME *stanselen* to ornament with sparkling colors, fr. MF *estanceler*, fr. *estancele* spark, fr. (assumed) VL *stincilla*, alter. of L *scintilla*] : an impervious material (as metal or paper) perforated with lettering or a design through which a substance (as ink or paint) is applied to a surface to be printed — **stencil** *vb*

ste·nog·ra·phy \stə-'nä-grə-fē\ *n* : the art or process of writing in shorthand — **ste·nog·ra·pher** \-fər\ *n* — **steno·graph·ic** \ˌste-nə-ˈgra-fik\ *adj*

sten·to·ri·an \sten-ˈtōr-ē-ən\ *adj* : extremely loud and powerful

¹step \ˈstep\ *n* **1** : a rest for the foot in ascending or descending : STAIR **2** : an advance made by raising one foot and putting it down elsewhere **3** : manner of walking **4** : a small space or distance **5** : a degree, rank, or plane in a series **6** : a sequential measure leading to a result

²step *vb* **stepped; step·ping 1** : to advance or recede by steps **2** : to go on foot : WALK **3** : to move along briskly **4** : to press down with the foot **5** : to measure by steps **6** : to construct or arrange in or as if in steps

step·broth·er \ˈstep-ˌbrə-<u>th</u>ər\ *n* : the son of one's stepparent by a former marriage

step·child \-ˌchīld\ *n* : a child of one's husband or wife by a former marriage

step·daugh·ter \-ˌdȯ-tər\ *n* : a daughter of one's wife or husband by a former marriage

step down *vb* **1** : RETIRE, RESIGN **2** : to lower (a voltage) by means of a transformer

step·fa·ther \-ˌfä-<u>th</u>ər\ *n* : the husband of one's mother by a subsequent marriage

step·lad·der \ˈstep-ˌla-dər\ *n* : a light portable set of steps in a hinged frame

step·moth·er \-ˌmə-<u>th</u>ər\ *n* : the wife of one's father by a subsequent marriage

step·par·ent \-ˌpar-ənt\ *n* : one's stepfather or stepmother

steppe \ˈstep\ *n* [Russ *step'*] : dry level grass-covered treeless land in regions of wide temperature range esp. in southeastern Europe and Asia

step·sis·ter \ˈstep-ˌsis-tər\ *n* : the daughter of one's stepparent by a former marriage

step·son \-ˌsən\ *n* : a son of one's wife or husband by a former marriage

step up *vb* **1** : to increase (a voltage) by means of a transformer **2** : INCREASE, ACCELERATE **3** : to come forward — **step–up** \ˈstep-ˌəp\ *n*

ster *abbr* sterling

ste·reo \ˈster-ē-ˌō, ˈstir-\ *n, pl* **ste·re·os 1** : stereophonic reproduction **2** : a stereophonic sound system — **stereo** *adj*

ste·reo·phon·ic \ˌster-ē-ə-ˈfä-nik, ˌstir-\ *adj* : of or relating to sound reproduction designed to create the effect of listening to the original — **ste·reo·phon·i·cal·ly** \-ˈfä-ni-k(ə-)lē\ *adv*

ster·e·o·scope \ˈster-ē-ə-ˌskōp, ˈstir-\ *n* [Gk *stereos* solid + *-skopion* means for viewing] : an optical instrument that blends two slightly different pictures of the same subject to give the effect of depth

ste·reo·scop·ic \ˌster-ē-ə-ˈskä-pik, ˌstir-\ *adj* **1** : of or relating to the stereoscope **2** : characterized by the seeing of objects in three dimensions ⟨∼ vision⟩ — **ste·reo·scop·i·cal·ly** \-ˈskä-pi-k(ə-)lē\ *adv* — **ste·re·os·co·py** \ˌster-ē-ˈäs-kə-pē, ˌstir-\ *n*

ste·reo·type \ˈster-ē-ə-ˌtīp, ˈstir-\ *n* **1** : a metal printing plate cast from a mold made from set type **2** : something agreeing with a pattern; *esp* : an idea that many people have about a thing or a group and that may often be untrue or only partly true — **stereotype** *vb* — **ste·reo·typ·i·cal** \ˌster-ē-ə-ˈti-pi-kəl\ *adj* — **ste·reo·typ·i·cal·ly** \-pi-k(ə-)lē\ *adv*

ste·reo·typed \-ˌtīpt\ *adj* : lacking originality or individuality **syn** trite, clichéd, commonplace, hackneyed, stale, threadbare

ster·ile \ˈster-əl\ *adj* **1** : unable to bear fruit, crops, or offspring **2** : free from living things and esp. germs — **ste·ril·i·ty** \stə-ˈri-lə-tē\ *n*

ster·il·ize \ˈster-ə-ˌlīz\ *vb* **-ized; -iz·ing** : to make sterile; *esp* : to free from germs — **ster·il·i·za·tion** \ˌster-ə-lə-ˈzā-shən\ *n* — **ster·il·iz·er** \ˈster-ə-ˌlī-zər\ *n*

¹ster·ling \ˈstər-liŋ\ *n* **1** : British money **2** : sterling silver

²sterling *adj* **1** : of, relating to, or calculated in terms of British sterling **2** : having a fixed standard of purity represented by an alloy of 925 parts of silver with 75 parts of copper **3** : made of sterling silver **4** : EXCELLENT

¹stern \ˈstərn\ *adj* **1** : SEVERE, AUSTERE **2** : STOUT, STURDY ⟨∼ resolve⟩ — **stern·ly** *adv* — **stern·ness** *n*

²stern *n* : the rear end of a boat

ster·num \ˈstər-nəm\ *n, pl* **sternums** *or* **ster·na** \-nə\ : a long flat bone or cartilage at the center front of the chest connecting the ribs of the two sides

ste·roid \ˈstir-ˌȯid\ *n* : any of numerous compounds including various hormones (as anabolic steroids) and sugar derivatives — **steroid** *or* **ste·roi·dal** \stə-ˈrȯid-ᵊl\ *adj*

stetho·scope \ˈste-thə-ˌskōp\ *n* : an instrument used to detect and listen to sounds produced in the body

ste·ve·dore \ˈstē-və-ˌdōr\ *n* [Sp *estibador*, fr. *estibar* to pack, fr. L *stipare* to press together] : one who works at loading and unloading ships

¹stew \ˈstü, ˈstyü\ *n* **1** : a dish of stewed meat and vegetables served in gravy **2** : a state of agitation, worry, or resentment

²stew *vb* **1** : to boil slowly : SIMMER **2** : to be in a state of agitation, worry, or resentment

stew·ard \ˈstü-ərd, ˈstyü-\ *n* [ME, fr. OE *stīweard*, fr. *stī, stig* hall, sty + *weard* ward] **1** : one employed on a large estate to manage domestic concerns **2** : one who supervises the provision and distribution of food (as on a ship); *also* : an employee on a ship or airplane who serves passengers **3** : one actively concerned with the direction of the affairs of an organization — **stew·ard·ship** *n*

stew·ard·ess \ˈstü-ər-dəs, ˈstyü-\ *n* : a woman who is a steward esp. on an airplane

stg *abbr* sterling

¹stick \ˈstik\ *n* **1** : a cut or broken branch or twig; *also* : a long slender piece of wood **2** : ROD, STAFF **3** : something resembling a stick **4** : a dull uninteresting person **5** *pl* : remote usu. rural areas

²stick *vb* **stuck** \ˈstək\; **stick·ing 1** : STAB, PRICK **2** : IMPALE **3** : ATTACH, FASTEN **4** : to thrust or project in some direction or manner **5** : to be unable to proceed or move freely **6** : to hold fast by or as if by gluing : ADHERE **7** : to hold to something firmly or closely : CLING **8** : to become jammed or blocked

stick·er \ˈsti-kər\ *n* : one that sticks (as a bur) or causes sticking (as glue); *esp* : an adhesive label

stick insect *n* : any of various usu. wingless insects with a long round body resembling a stick

stick·ler \ˈsti-klər, -kə-lər\ *n* : one who insists on exactness or completeness

stick shift *n* : a manually operated automobile gearshift usu. mounted on the floor

stick–to–it·ive·ness \stik-ˈtü-ə-tiv-nəs\ *n* : dogged perseverance : TENACITY

stick up *vb* : to rob at gunpoint — **stick·up** \ˈstik-ˌəp\ *n*

sticky \ˈsti-kē\ *adj* **stick·i·er; -est 1** : ADHESIVE **2** : VISCOUS, GLUEY **3** : tending to stick ⟨∼ valve⟩ **4** : DIFFICULT

¹stiff \ˈstif\ *adj* **1** : not pliant : RIGID **2** : not limber ⟨∼ joints⟩; *also* : TENSE, TAUT **3** : not flowing or working easily ⟨∼ paste⟩ **4** : not natural and easy : FORMAL **5** : STRONG, FORCEFUL ⟨∼ breeze⟩ **6** : HARSH, SEVERE **syn** inflexible, inelastic — **stiff·ly** *adv* — **stiff·ness** *n*

²stiff *vb* : to refuse to pay or tip

stiff·en \ˈsti-fən\ *vb* : to make or become stiff — **stiff·en·er** *n*

\ə\abut \ᵊ\kitten \ər**further** \a\ash \ā\ace \ä\mop, mar \aủ\out \ch\chin \e\bet \ē\easy \g\go \i\hit \ī\ice \j\job \ŋ\sing \ō\go \ȯ\law \ȯi\boy \th\thin \<u>th</u>\the \ü\loot \ủ\foot \y\yet \zh\vision *see also* Pronunciation Symbols page

stiff–necked \'stif-'nekt\ *adj* : STUBBORN, HAUGHTY
sti·fle \'stī-fəl\ *vb* **sti·fled; sti·fling 1** : to kill by depriving of or die from lack of oxygen or air : SMOTHER **2** : to keep in check by effort : SUPPRESS ⟨∼ a sneeze⟩ — **sti·fling·ly** *adv*
stig·ma \'stig-mə\ *n, pl* **stig·ma·ta** \stig-'mä-tə, 'stig-mə-tə\ *or* **stigmas** [L] **1** : a mark of disgrace or discredit **2** *pl* : bodily marks resembling the wounds of the crucified Christ **3** : the upper part of the pistil of a flower that receives the pollen in fertilization — **stig·mat·ic** \stig-'ma-tik\ *adj*
stig·ma·tize \'stig-mə-ˌtīz\ *vb* **-tized; -tiz·ing 1** : to mark with a stigma **2** : to characterize as disgraceful
stile \'stīl\ *n* : steps used for crossing a fence or wall
sti·let·to \stə-'le-tō\ *n, pl* **-tos** *or* **-toes** [It, dim. of *stilo* stylus, dagger] : a slender dagger
¹still \'stil\ *adj* **1** : MOTIONLESS **2** : making no sound : SILENT — **still·ness** *n*
²still *vb* : to make or become still
³still *adv* **1** : without motion ⟨sit ∼⟩ **2** : up to and during this or that time **3** : in spite of that : NEVERTHELESS **4** : EVEN ⟨ran ∼ faster⟩ **5** : BESIDES, YET
⁴still *n* **1** : STILLNESS, SILENCE **2** : a static photograph esp. from a motion picture
⁵still *n* **1** : DISTILLERY **2** : apparatus used in distillation
still·birth \'stil-ˌbərth\ *n* : the birth of a dead fetus
still·born \-'bȯrn\ *adj* : born dead
still life *n, pl* **still lifes** : a picture of inanimate objects
stilt \'stilt\ *n* : one of a pair of poles for walking with each having a step or loop for the foot to elevate the wearer above the ground; *also* : a polelike support of a structure above ground or water level
stilt·ed \'stil-təd\ *adj* : not easy and natural ⟨∼ language⟩
Stil·ton \'stilt-ᵊn\ *n* : a blue cheese of English origin
stim·u·lant \'sti-myə-lənt\ *n* **1** : an agent (as a drug) that temporarily increases the activity of an organism or any of its parts **2** : STIMULUS **3** : an alcoholic beverage — **stimulant** *adj*
stim·u·late \-ˌlāt\ *vb* **-lat·ed; -lat·ing** : to make active or more active : ANIMATE, AROUSE **syn** excite, provoke, motivate, quicken — **stim·u·la·tion** \ˌsti-myə-'lā-shən\ *n* — **stim·u·la·tive** \'sti-myə-ˌlā-tiv\ *adj*
stim·u·lus \'sti-myə-ləs\ *n, pl* **-li** \-ˌlī\ [L] **1** : something that moves to activity **2** : an agent that directly influences the activity of a living organism or one of its parts
¹sting \'stiŋ\ *vb* **stung** \'stəŋ\; **sting·ing 1** : to prick painfully esp. with a sharp or poisonous process **2** : to cause to suffer acutely — **sting·er** *n*
²sting *n* **1** : an act of stinging; *also* : a resultant wound, sore, or pain **2** : a pointed often venom-bearing organ (as of a bee) : STINGER **3** : an elaborate confidence game; *esp* : one worked by undercover police to trap criminals
stin·gy \'stin-jē\ *adj* **stin·gi·er; -est** : not generous : giving or spending as little as possible — **stin·gi·ness** *n*
stink \'stiŋk\ *vb* **stank** \'staŋk\ *or* **stunk** \'stəŋk\; **stunk; stink·ing** : to give forth a strong and offensive smell; *also* : to be extremely bad in quality or repute — **stink** *n* — **stink·er** *n*
stink·bug \'stiŋk-ˌbəg\ *n* : any of various true bugs that emit a disagreeable odor
¹stint \'stint\ *vb* **1** : to be sparing or frugal **2** : to cut short in amount
²stint *n* **1** : an assigned amount of work **2** : RESTRAINT, LIMITATION **3** : a period of time spent at a particular activity
sti·pend \'stī-ˌpend, -pənd\ *n* [ME, alter. of *stipendy,* fr. L *stipendium,* fr. *stips* gift + *pendere* to weigh, pay] : a fixed sum of money paid periodically for services or to defray expenses
stip·ple \'sti-pəl\ *vb* **stip·pled; stip·pling 1** : to engrave by means of dots and light strokes **2** : to apply (as paint or ink) with small short touches — **stipple** *n*

stip·u·late \'sti-pyə-ˌlāt\ *vb* **-lat·ed; -lat·ing** : to make an agreement; *esp* : to make a special demand for something as a condition in an agreement — **stip·u·la·tion** \ˌsti-pyə-'lā-shən\ *n*
¹stir \'stər\ *vb* **stirred; stir·ring 1** : to move slightly **2** : AROUSE, EXCITE **3** : to mix, dissolve, or make by continued circular movement ⟨∼ eggs into cake batter⟩ **4** : to move to activity (as by pushing, beating, or prodding)
²stir *n* **1** : a state of agitation or activity **2** : an act of stirring
stir–fry \'stər-ˌfrī\ *vb* : to fry quickly over high heat while stirring continuously — **stir–fry** *n*
stir·ring \'stər-iŋ\ *adj* **1** : ACTIVE, BUSTLING **2** : ROUSING, INSPIRING
stir·rup \'stər-əp\ *n* [ME *stirop,* fr. OE *stigrāp,* lit., mounting rope] **1** : a light frame hung from a saddle to support the rider's foot **2** : STAPES
¹stitch \'stich\ *n* **1** : a sudden sharp pain esp. in the side **2** : one of the series of loops formed by or over a needle in sewing
²stitch *vb* **1** : to fasten or join with stitches **2** : to decorate with stitches **3** : SEW
stk *abbr* stock
stoat \'stōt\ *n, pl* **stoats** *also* **stoat** : the common Old and New World ermine esp. in its brown summer coat
¹stock \'stäk\ *n* **1** *archaic* : a block of wood **2** : a stupid person **3** : a wooden part of a thing serving as its support, frame, or handle **4** *pl* : a device for publicly punishing offenders consisting of a wooden frame with holes in which the feet and hands can be locked **5** : the original from which others derive; *also* : a group having a common origin : FAMILY **6** : LIVESTOCK **7** : a supply of goods **8** : the ownership element in a corporation divided to give the owners an interest and usu. voting power **9** : a company of actors playing at a particular theater and presenting a series of plays **10** : liquid in which meat, fish, or vegetables have been simmered that is used as a basis for soup, gravy, or sauce

stocks 4

²stock *vb* : to provide with stock
³stock *adj* : kept regularly for sale or use; *also* : commonly used : STANDARD
stock·ade \stä-'kād\ *n* [Sp *estacada,* fr. *estaca* stake, pale] : an enclosure (as of posts and stakes) for defense or confinement
stock·bro·ker \-ˌbrō-kər\ *n* : one who executes orders to buy and sell securities
stock car *n* : a racing car that is similar to a regular car
stock exchange *n* : a place where the buying and selling of securities is conducted
stock·hold·er \'stäk-ˌhōl-dər\ *n* : one who owns corporate stock
stock·i·nette *or* **stock·i·net** \ˌstä-kə-'net\ *n* : an elastic knitted fabric used esp. for infants' wear and bandages

stock·ing \'stä-kiŋ\ *n* : a close-fitting knitted covering for the foot and leg

stock market *n* **1** : STOCK EXCHANGE **2** : a market for stocks

stock·pile \'stäk-ˌpīl\ *n* : a reserve supply esp. of something essential — **stockpile** *vb*

stocky \'stä-kē\ *adj* **stock·i·er; -est** : being short and relatively thick : STURDY **syn** thickset, squat, heavyset, stubby

stock·yard \'stäk-ˌyärd\ *n* : a yard for stock; *esp* : one for livestock about to be slaughtered or shipped

stodgy \'stä-jē\ *adj* **stodg·i·er; -est 1** : HEAVY, DULL **2** : extremely old-fashioned

¹sto·ic \'stō-ik\ *n* [ME, fr. L *stoicus,* fr. Gk *stōïkos,* lit., of the portico, fr. *Stoa (Poikilē)* the Painted Portico, portico at Athens where the philosopher Zeno taught] : one who suffers without complaining

²stoic *or* **sto·i·cal** \-i-kəl\ *adj* : not affected by passion or feeling; *esp* : showing indifference to pain **syn** impassive, phlegmatic, apathetic, stolid — **sto·ical·ly** \-i-k(ə-)lē\ *adv* — **sto·icism** \'stō-ə-ˌsi-zəm\ *n*

stoke \'stōk\ *vb* **stoked; stok·ing 1** : to stir up a fire **2** : to tend and supply fuel to a furnace — **stok·er** *n*

STOL *abbr* short takeoff and landing

¹stole \'stōl\ *past of* STEAL

²stole *n* **1** : a long narrow band worn round the neck by some clergymen **2** : a long wide scarf or similar covering worn by women

stolen *past part of* STEAL

stol·id \'stä-ləd\ *adj* : not easily aroused or excited : showing little or no emotion **syn** phlegmatic, apathetic, impassive, stoic — **sto·lid·i·ty** \stä-'li-də-tē\ *n* — **stol·id·ly** *adv*

sto·lon \'stō-lən, -ˌlän\ *n* : RUNNER 6

¹stom·ach \'stə-mək\ *n* **1** : a saclike digestive organ of a vertebrate into which food goes from the mouth by way of the throat and which opens below into the intestine **2** : a cavity in an invertebrate animal that is analogous to a stomach **3** : ABDOMEN **4** : desire for food caused by hunger : APPETITE **5** : INCLINATION, DESIRE

²stomach *vb* : to bear without open resentment : put up with

stom·ach·ache \-ˌāk\ *n* : pain in or in the region of the stomach

stom·ach·er \'stə-mi-kər, -chər\ *n* : the front of a bodice often appearing between the laces of an outer garment (as in 16th century costume)

stomp \'stämp, 'stȯmp\ *vb* : STAMP — **stomp** *n*

¹stone \'stōn\ *n* **1** : hardened earth or mineral matter : ROCK **2** : a small piece of rock **3** : a precious stone : GEM **4** : CALCULUS 3 **5** : a hard stony seed (as of a date) or one (as of a plum) with a stony covering **6** *pl usu* **stone** : a British unit of weight equal to 14 pounds — **stony** *also* **ston·ey** \'stō-nē\ *adj*

²stone *vb* **stoned; ston·ing 1** : to pelt or kill with stones **2** : to remove the stones of (a fruit)

Stone Age *n* : the first known period of prehistoric human culture characterized by the use of stone tools

stoned \'stōnd\ *adj* **1** : DRUNK **2** : being under the influence of a drug

stone·wall \'stōn-ˌwȯl\ *vb* : to refuse to comply or cooperate with

stone·washed \'stōn-ˌwȯsht, -ˌwäsht\ *adj* : having been washed with stones during manufacture to create a softer fabric ⟨∼ jeans⟩

stood *past and past part of* STAND

stooge \'stüj\ *n* **1** : a person who plays a subordinate or compliant role to a principal **2** : STRAIGHT MAN

stool \'stül\ *n* **1** : a seat usu. without back or arms **2** : FOOTSTOOL **3** : a seat used while urinating or defecating **4** : a discharge of fecal matter

stool pigeon *n* : DECOY, INFORMER

¹stoop \'stüp\ *vb* **1** : to bend forward and downward **2** : CONDESCEND **3** : to lower oneself morally

²stoop *n* **1** : an act of bending forward **2** : a bent position of head and shoulders

³stoop *n* : a porch or platform at a house door

¹stop \'stäp\ *vb* **stopped; stop·ping 1** : to close (an opening) by filling or covering closely **2** : BLOCK, HALT **3** : to cease to go on **4** : to bring activity or operation to an end **5** : STAY, TARRY **syn** quit, discontinue, desist, cease

²stop *n* **1** : END, CESSATION **2** : a set of organ pipes of one tone quality; *also* : a control knob for such a set **3** : OBSTRUCTION **4** : PLUG, STOPPER **5** : an act of stopping : CHECK **6** : a delay in a journey : STAY **7** : a place for stopping **8** *chiefly Brit* : any of several punctuation marks

stop·gap \'stäp-ˌgap\ *n* : something that serves as a temporary expedient

stop·light \-ˌlīt\ *n* : TRAFFIC LIGHT

stop·over \'stäp-ˌō-vər\ *n* **1** : a stop at an intermediate point in one's journey **2** : a stopping place on a journey

stop·page \'stä-pij\ *n* : the act of stopping : the state of being stopped

stop·per \'stä-pər\ *n* : something (as a cork) for sealing an opening

stop·watch \'stäp-ˌwäch\ *n* : a watch that can be started or stopped at will for exact timing

stor·age \'stȯr-ij\ *n* **1** : space for storing; *also* : cost of storing **2** : MEMORY 6 **3** : the act of storing; *esp* : the safekeeping of goods (as in a warehouse)

storage battery *n* : a group of connected rechargeable electrochemical cells used to provide electric current

¹store \'stȯr\ *vb* **stored; stor·ing 1** : to place or leave in a safe location for preservation or future use **2** : to provide esp. for a future need

²store *n* **1** : something accumulated and kept for future use **2** : a large or ample quantity **3** : STOREHOUSE **4** : a retail business establishment

store·house \-ˌhaus\ *n* : a building for storing goods or supplies; *also* : an abundant source or supply

store·keep·er \-ˌkē-pər\ *n* : one who operates a retail store

store·room \-ˌrüm, -ˌrum\ *n* : a room for storing goods or supplies

sto·ried \'stȯr-ēd\ *adj* : celebrated in story or history

stork \'stȯrk\ *n* : any of various large stout-billed Old World wading birds related to the herons and ibises

¹storm \'stȯrm\ *n* **1** : a heavy fall of rain, snow, or hail with high wind; *also* : the high wind accompanying such a fall **2** : a violent outbreak or disturbance **3** : a mass attack on a defended position — **storm·i·ly** \'stȯr-mə-lē\ *adv* — **storm·i·ness** \-mē-nəs\ *n* — **stormy** *adj*

²storm *vb* **1** : to blow with violence; *also* : to rain, snow, or hail heavily **2** : to make a mass attack against **3** : to be violently angry : RAGE **4** : to rush along furiously

¹sto·ry \'stȯr-ē\ *n, pl* **stories 1** : NARRATIVE, ACCOUNT **2** : REPORT, STATEMENT **3** : ANECDOTE **4** : SHORT STORY **5** : LIE, FALSEHOOD **6** : a news article or broadcast **syn** untruth, tale, canard

²story *also* **sto·rey** \'stȯr-ē\ *n, pl* **stories** *also* **storeys** : a floor of a building or the space between two adjacent floor levels

sto·ry·tell·er \-ˌte-lər\ *n* : a teller of stories

sto·tin·ka \stō-'tiŋ-kə\ *n, pl* **-tin·ki** \-kē\ — see *lev* at MONEY table

¹stout \'staut\ *adj* **1** : BRAVE **2** : FIRM **3** : STURDY **4** : STAUNCH, ENDURING **5** : SOLID **6** : FORCEFUL, VIOLENT

---

7 : BULKY, THICKSET **syn** fleshy, fat, portly, corpulent, obese, plump — **stout·ly** *adv* — **stout·ness** *n*

²stout *n* : a dark heavy ale

¹stove \'stōv\ *n* : an apparatus that burns fuel or uses electricity to provide heat (as for cooking or heating)

²stove *past and past part of* STAVE

stow \'stō\ *vb* **1** : HIDE, STORE **2** : to pack in a compact mass

stow·away \'stō-ə-ˌwā\ *n* : one who hides on a vehicle to ride free

STP *abbr* standard temperature and pressure

strad·dle \'strad-ᵊl\ *vb* **strad·dled; strad·dling 1** : to stand, sit, or walk with legs spread apart **2** : to favor or seem to favor two apparently opposite sides — **strad·dle** *n*

strafe \'strāf\ *vb* **strafed; straf·ing** [G *Gott strafe England* may God punish England, propaganda slogan during World War I] : to fire upon with machine guns from a low-flying airplane

strag·gle \'stra-gəl\ *vb* **strag·gled; strag·gling 1** : to wander from the direct course : ROVE, STRAY **2** : to become separated from others of the same kind — **straggler** *n* — **strag·gly** \'stra-g(ə-)lē\ *adj*

¹straight \'strāt\ *adj* **1** : free from curves, bends, angles, or irregularities **2** : not wandering from the main point or proper course ⟨∼ thinking⟩ **3** : HONEST, UPRIGHT **4** : having the elements in correct order **5** : UNMIXED, UNDILUTED ⟨∼ whiskey⟩ **6** : CONVENTIONAL, SQUARE; *also* : HETEROSEXUAL

²straight *adv* : in a straight manner

³straight *n* **1** : a straight line, course, or arrangement **2** : the part of a racetrack between the last turn and the finish **3** : a sequence of five cards in a poker hand

straight–arm \'strāt-ˌärm\ *n* : an act of warding off a football tackler with the arm fully extended — **straight–arm** *vb*

straight·away \'strā-tə-ˌwā\ *n* : a straight stretch (as at a racetrack)

straight·edge \'strāt-ˌej\ *n* : a piece of material with a straight edge for testing straight lines and surfaces or drawing straight lines

straight·en \'strāt-ᵊn\ *vb* : to make or become straight

straight flush *n* : a poker hand containing five cards of the same suit in sequence

straight·for·ward \strāt-'for-wərd\ *adj* **1** : FRANK, CANDID, HONEST **2** : proceeding in a straight course or manner

straight man *n* : an entertainer who feeds lines to a comedian

straight·way \'strāt-'wā, -ˌwā\ *adv* : IMMEDIATELY

¹strain \'strān\ *n* [ME *streen* progeny, lineage, fr. OE *strēon* gain, acquisition] **1** : LINEAGE, ANCESTRY **2** : a group (as of people or plants) of presumed common ancestry **3** : an inherited or inherent character or quality ⟨a ∼ of madness in the family⟩ **4** : STREAK, TRACE **5** : MELODY **6** : the general style or tone

²strain *vb* [ME, fr. MF *estraindre*, fr. L *stringere* to bind or draw tight, press together] **1** : to draw taut **2** : to exert to the utmost **3** : to strive violently **4** : to injure by improper or excessive use **5** : to filter or remove by filtering **6** : to stretch beyond a proper limit — **strain·er** *n*

³strain *n* **1** : excessive tension or exertion (as of body or mind) **2** : bodily injury from excessive tension, effort, or use; *esp* : one in which muscles or ligaments are unduly stretched usu. from a wrench or twist **3** : deformation of a material body under the action of applied forces

¹strait \'strāt\ *adj* [ME, fr. OF *estreit*, fr. L *strictus* strait, strict] **1** *archaic* : STRICT **2** *archaic* : NARROW **3** *archaic* : CONSTRICTED **4** : DIFFICULT, STRAITENED

²strait *n* **1** : a narrow channel connecting two bodies of water **2** *pl* : DISTRESS

strait·en \'strāt-ᵊn\ *vb* **1** : to hem in : CONFINE **2** : to make distressing or difficult

strait·jack·et *also* **straight·jack·et** \'strāt-ˌja-kət\ *n* : a cover or garment of strong material (as canvas) used to bind the body and esp. the arms closely in restraining a violent prisoner or patient — **straitjacket** *vb*

strait·laced *or* **straight·laced** \-'lāst\ *adj* : strict in manners, morals or opinion

¹strand \'strand\ *n* : SHORE, BEACH

²strand *vb* **1** : to run, drift, or drive upon the shore ⟨a ∼ed ship⟩ **2** : to place or leave in a helpless position

³strand *n* **1** : one of the fibers twisted or plaited together into a cord, rope, or cable; *also* : a cord, rope, or cable made up of such fibers **2** : a twisted or plaited ropelike mass ⟨a ∼ of pearls⟩ — **strand·ed** \'stran-dəd\ *adj*

strange \'strānj\ *adj* **strang·er; strang·est** [ME, fr. OF *estrange*, fr. L *extraneus*, lit., external, fr. *extra* outside] **1** : of external origin, kind, or character **2** : NEW, UNFAMILIAR **3** : DISTANT 6 **4** : UNACCUSTOMED, INEXPERIENCED **syn** singular, peculiar, eccentric, erratic, odd, queer, quaint, curious — **strange·ly** *adv* — **strangeness** *n*

strang·er \'strān-jər\ *n* **1** : FOREIGNER **2** : INTRUDER **3** : a person with whom one is unacquainted

stran·gle \'straŋ-gəl\ *vb* **stran·gled; stran·gling 1** : to choke to death : THROTTLE **2** : STIFLE, SUPPRESS — **stran·gler** *n*

stran·gu·late \'straŋ-gyə-ˌlāt\ *vb* **-lat·ed; -lat·ing 1** : STRANGLE, CONSTRICT **2** : to become so constricted as to stop circulation

stran·gu·la·tion \ˌstraŋ-gyə-'lā-shən\ *n* : the act or process of strangling or strangulating; *also* : the state of being strangled or strangulated

¹strap \'strap\ *n* : a narrow strip of flexible material used esp. for fastening, holding together, or wrapping

²strap *vb* **strapped; strap·ping 1** : to secure with a strap **2** : BIND, CONSTRICT **3** : to flog with a strap **4** : STROP

strap·less \-ləs\ *adj* : having no straps; *esp* : having no shoulder straps

¹strap·ping \'stra-piŋ\ *adj* : LARGE, STRONG, HUSKY

²strap·ping *n* : material for a strap

strat·a·gem \'stra-tə-jəm, -ˌjem\ *n* **1** : a trick to deceive or outwit the enemy; *also* : a deceptive scheme **2** : skill in deception

strat·e·gy \'stra-tə-jē\ *n, pl* **-gies** [Gk *stratēgia* generalship, fr. *stratēgos* general, fr. *stratos* camp, army + *agein* to lead] **1** : the science and art of military command aimed at meeting the enemy under conditions advantageous to one's own force **2** : a careful plan or method esp. for achieving an end — **stra·te·gic** \strə-'tē-jik\ *adj* — **strat·e·gist** \'stra-tə-jist\ *n*

strat·i·fy \'stra-tə-ˌfī\ *vb* **-fied; -fy·ing** : to form or arrange in layers — **strat·i·fi·ca·tion** \ˌstra-tə-fə-'kā-shən\ *n*

stra·tig·ra·phy \strə-'ti-grə-fē\ *n* : geology that deals with rock strata — **strati·graph·ic** \ˌstra-tə-'gra-fik\ *adj*

strato·sphere \'stra-tə-ˌsfir\ *n* : the part of the earth's atmosphere between about 7 miles (11 kilometers) and 31 miles (50 kilometers) above the earth — **strato·spher·ic** \ˌstra-tə-'sfir-ik, -'sfer-\ *adj*

stra·tum \'strā-təm, 'stra-\ *n, pl* **stra·ta** \'strā-tə, 'stra-\ [NL, fr. L, spread, bed, fr. neut. of *stratus*, pp. of *sternere* to spread out] **1** : a bed, layer, or sheetlike mass (as of one kind of rock lying between layers of other kinds of rock) **2** : a level of culture; *also* : a group of people representing one stage in cultural development

¹straw \'strȯ\ *n* **1** : stalks of grain after threshing; *also* : a single coarse dry stem (as of a grass) **2** : a thing of small worth : TRIFLE **3** : a tube (as of paper or plastic) for sucking up a beverage

²straw *adj* **1** : made of straw **2** : having no real force or validity ⟨a ∼ vote⟩

straw·ber·ry \'strȯ-ˌber-ē, -bə-rē\ *n* : an edible juicy usu. red pulpy fruit of any of serveral low herbs with white flowers and long slender runners; *also* : one of these herbs

strawberry

straw boss *n* : a foreman of a small group of workers
straw·flow·er \'strȯ-ˌflaů-ər\ *n* : any of several plants whose flowers can be dried with little loss of form or color
¹**stray** \'strā\ *n* **1** : a domestic animal wandering at large or lost **2** : WAIF
²**stray** *vb* **1** : to wander or roam without purpose **2** : DEVIATE
³**stray** *adj* **1** : having strayed : separated from the group or the main body **2** : occurring at random ⟨~ remarks⟩
¹**streak** \'strēk\ *n* **1** : a line or mark of a different color or texture from its background **2** : a narrow band of light; *also* : a lightning bolt **3** : a slight admixture : TRACE **4** : a brief run (as of luck); *also* : an unbroken series
²**streak** *vb* **1** : to form streaks in or on **2** : to move very swiftly
¹**stream** \'strēm\ *n* **1** : a body of water (as a river) flowing on the earth; *also* : any body of flowing fluid (as water or gas) **2** : a continuous procession ⟨a ~ of traffic⟩
²**stream** *vb* **1** : to flow in or as if in a stream **2** : to pour out streams of liquid **3** : to trail out in length **4** : to move forward in a steady stream
stream·bed \'strēm-ˌbed\ *n* : the channel occupied by a stream
stream·er \'strē-mər\ *n* **1** : a long narrow ribbonlike flag **2** : a long ribbon on a dress or hat **3** : a newspaper headline that runs across the entire sheet **4** *pl* : AURORA
stream·let \'strēm-lət\ *n* : a small stream
stream·lined \-ˌlīnd\ *adj* **1** : made with contours to reduce resistance to motion through water or air **2** : SIMPLIFIED **3** : MODERNIZED — **streamline** *vb*
street \'strēt\ *n* [ME *strete*, fr. OE *strēt*, fr. LL *strata* paved road, fr. L, fem. of *stratus*, pp. of *sternere* to spread out] **1** : a thoroughfare esp. in a city, town, or village **2** : the occupants of the houses on a street
street·car \-ˌkȧr\ *n* : a passenger vehicle running on rails on city streets
street railway *n* : a company operating streetcars or buses
street·walk·er \'strēt-ˌwȯ-kər\ *n* : PROSTITUTE
strength \'strenth\ *n* **1** : the quality of being strong : ability to do or endure : POWER **2** : TOUGHNESS, SOLIDITY **3** : power to resist attack **4** : INTENSITY **5** : force as measured in numbers ⟨the ~ of an army⟩
strength·en \'stren-thən\ *vb* : to make or become stronger — **strength·en·er** *n*
stren·u·ous \'stren-yə-wəs\ *adj* **1** : VIGOROUS, ENERGETIC **2** : requiring energy or stamina — **stren·u·ous·ly** *adv*

strep \'strep\ *n* : STREPTOCOCCUS
strep throat *n* : an inflammatory sore throat caused by streptococci and marked by fever, prostration, and toxemia
strep·to·coc·cus \ˌstrep-tə-'kä-kəs\ *n, pl* **-coc·ci** \-'kä-ˌkī, -'käk-ˌsī, -'kä-ˌkē, -'käk-ˌsē\ : any of various spherical bacteria that usu. grow in chains and include some causing serious diseases — **strep·to·coc·cal** \-kəl\ *adj*
strep·to·my·cin \-'mīs-ᵊn\ *n* : an antibiotic produced by soil bacteria and used esp. in treating tuberculosis
¹**stress** \'stres\ *n* **1** : PRESSURE, STRAIN; *esp* : a force that tends to distort a body **2** : a factor that induces bodily or mental tension; *also* : a state induced by such a stress **3** : EMPHASIS **4** : relative prominence of sound **5** : ACCENT; *also* : any syllable carrying the accent — **stress·ful** \'stres-fəl\ *adj*
²**stress** *vb* **1** : to put pressure or strain on **2** : to put emphasis on : ACCENT
¹**stretch** \'strech\ *vb* **1** : to spread or reach out : EXTEND **2** : to draw out in length or breadth : EXPAND **3** : to make tense : STRAIN **4** : EXAGGERATE **5** : to become extended without breaking ⟨rubber ~es easily⟩
²**stretch** *n* **1** : an act of extending or drawing out beyond ordinary or normal limits **2** : a continuous extent in length, area, or time **3** : the extent to which something may be stretched **4** : either of the straight sides of a racecourse
³**stretch** *adj* : easily stretched ⟨~ pants⟩
stretch·er \'stre-chər\ *n* **1** : one that stretches **2** : a device for carrying a sick, injured, or dead person
strew \'strü\ *vb* **strewed; strewed** *or* **strewn** \'strün\; **strew·ing 1** : to spread by scattering **2** : to cover by or as if by scattering something over or on **3** : DISSEMINATE
stria \'strī-ə\ *n, pl* **stri·ae** \'strī-ˌē\ **1** : STRIATION 3 **2** : a stripe or line (as in the skin)
stri·at·ed muscle \'strī-ˌā-təd-\ *n* : muscle tissue made up of long thin cells with many nuclei and alternate light and dark stripes that includes esp. the muscle of the heart and muscle that moves the vertebrate skeleton and is mostly under voluntary control
stri·a·tion \strī-'ā-shən\ *n* **1** : the state of being marked with stripes or lines **2** : arrangement of striations or striae **3** : a minute groove, scratch, or channel esp. when one of a parallel series
strick·en \'stri-kən\ *adj* **1** : afflicted by or as if by disease, misfortune, or sorrow **2** : WOUNDED
strict \'strikt\ *adj* **1** : allowing no evasion or escape : RIGOROUS ⟨~ discipline⟩ **2** : ACCURATE, PRECISE **syn** stringent, rigid — **strict·ly** *adv* — **strict·ness** *n*
stric·ture \'strik-chər\ *n* **1** : an abnormal narrowing of a bodily passage; *also* : the narrowed part **2** : hostile criticism : a critical remark
¹**stride** \'strīd\ *vb* **strode** \'strōd\; **strid·den** \'strid-ᵊn\; **strid·ing** : to walk or run with long regular steps — **strid·er** *n*
²**stride** *n* **1** : a long step **2** : a stage of progress **3** : manner of striding : GAIT
stri·dent \'strīd-ᵊnt\ *adj* : harsh sounding : GRATING, SHRILL
strife \'strīf\ *n* : CONFLICT, FIGHT, STRUGGLE **syn** discord, contention, dissension
¹**strike** \'strīk\ *vb* **struck** \'strək\; **struck** *also* **stricken** \'stri-kən\; **strik·ing 1** : to take a course : GO ⟨*struck* off through the brush⟩ **2** : to touch or hit sharply; *also* : to deliver a blow **3** : to produce by or as if by a blow ⟨*struck* terror in the foe⟩ **4** : to lower (as a flag or sail) **5** : to collide with; *also* : to injure or destroy by colli-

sion 6 : DELETE, CANCEL 7 : to produce by impressing ⟨*struck* a medal⟩; *also* : COIN ⟨∼ a new cent⟩ 8 : to cause to sound ⟨∼ a bell⟩ 9 : to afflict suddenly : lay low ⟨*stricken* with a high fever⟩ 10 : to appear to; *also* : to appear to as remarkable : IMPRESS 11 : to reach by reckoning ⟨∼ an average⟩ 12 : to stop work in order to obtain a change in conditions of employment 13 : to cause (a match) to ignite by rubbing 14 : to come upon ⟨∼ gold⟩ 15 : TAKE ON, ASSUME ⟨∼ a pose⟩ — **strik·er** *n*

²**strike** *n* 1 : an act or instance of striking 2 : a sudden discovery of rich ore or oil deposits 3 : a pitched baseball that is swung at but not hit 4 : the knocking down of all the bowling pins with the 1st ball 5 : a military attack

strike·break·er \-ˌbrā-kər\ *n* : a person hired to replace a striking worker

strike·out \-ˌaut\ *n* : an out in baseball as a result of a batter's being charged with three strikes

strike out *vb* 1 : to enter upon a course of action 2 : to start out vigorously 3 : to make an out in baseball by a strikeout

strike up *vb* 1 : to begin or cause to begin to sing or play 2 : BEGIN

strike zone *n* : the area over home plate through which a pitched baseball must pass to be called a strike

strik·ing \ˈstrī-kiŋ\ *adj* : attracting attention : very noticeable **syn** arresting, salient, conspicuous, outstanding, remarkable, prominent — **strik·ing·ly** *adv*

¹**string** \ˈstriŋ\ *n* 1 : a line usu. composed of twisted threads 2 : a series of things arranged as if strung on a cord 3 : a plant fiber (as a leaf vein) 4 *pl* : the stringed instruments of an orchestra **syn** succession, progression, sequence, chain, train

²**string** *vb* **strung** \ˈstrəŋ\; **string·ing** 1 : to provide with strings ⟨∼ a racket⟩ 2 : to make tense 3 : to thread on or as if on a string ⟨∼ pearls⟩ 4 : to hang, tie, or fasten by a string 5 : to take the strings out of ⟨∼ beans⟩ 6 : to extend like a string

string bean *n* : a bean of one of the older varieties of kidney bean that have stringy fibers on the lines of separation of the pods; *also* : SNAP BEAN

stringed \ˈstriŋd\ *adj* 1 : having strings ⟨∼ instruments⟩ 2 : produced by strings

strin·gen·cy \ˈstrin-jən-sē\ *n* 1 : STRICTNESS, SEVERITY 2 : SCARCITY ⟨∼ of money⟩ — **strin·gent** \-jənt\ *adj*

string·er \ˈstriŋ-ər\ *n* 1 : a long horizontal member in a framed structure or a bridge 2 : a news correspondent paid by the amount of copy

stringy \ˈstriŋ-ē\ *adj* **string·i·er; -est** 1 : resembling string esp. in tough, fibrous, or disordered quality ⟨∼ meat⟩ ⟨∼ hair⟩ 2 : lean and sinewy in build

¹**strip** \ˈstrip\ *vb* **stripped** \ˈstript\ *also* **stript; strip·ping** 1 : to take the covering or clothing from 2 : to take off one's clothes 3 : to pull or tear off 4 : to make bare or clear (as by cutting or grazing) 5 : PLUNDER, PILLAGE **syn** divest, denude, deprive, dismantle — **strip·per** *n*

²**strip** *n* 1 : a long narrow flat piece 2 : AIRSTRIP

¹**stripe** \ˈstrīp\ *vb* **striped** \ˈstrīpt\; **strip·ing** : to make stripes on

²**stripe** *n* 1 : a line or long narrow division having a different color from the background 2 : a strip of braid (as on a sleeve) indicating military rank or length of service 3 : TYPE, CHARACTER — **striped** \ˈstrīpt, ˈstrī-pəd\ *adj*

striped bass *n* : a large marine bony fish of the Atlantic and Pacific coasts of the U.S. that is an excellent food and sport fish

strip·ling \ˈstri-pliŋ\ *n* : YOUTH, LAD

strip mine *n* : a mine that is worked from the earth's surface by the stripping of the topsoil — **strip–mine** *vb*

strip·tease \ˈstrip-ˌtēz\ *n* : a burlesque act in which a performer removes clothing piece by piece — **strip·teas·er** *n*

strive \ˈstrīv\ *vb* **strove** \ˈstrōv\ *also* **strived** \ˈstrīvd\;

striv·en \ˈstri-vən\ *or* **strived; striv·ing** 1 : to make effort : labor hard 2 : to struggle in opposition : CONTEND **syn** endeavor, attempt, try, assay

strobe \ˈstrōb\ *n* 1 : STROBOSCOPE 2 : a device for high-speed intermittent illumination (as in photography)

stro·bo·scope \ˈstrō-bə-ˌskōp\ *n* : an instrument for studying rapid motion by means of a rapidly flashing light

strode *past of* STRIDE

¹**stroke** \ˈstrōk\ *vb* **stroked; strok·ing** 1 : to rub gently 2 : to flatter in a manner designed to persuade

²**stroke** *n* 1 : the act of striking : BLOW, KNOCK 2 : a sudden action or process producing an impact ⟨∼ of lightning⟩; *also* : an unexpected result 3 : sudden weakening or loss of consciousness or the power to move or feel caused by rupture or obstruction (as by a clot) of an artery of the brain 4 : one of a series of movements against air or water to get through or over it ⟨the ∼ of a bird's wing⟩ 5 : a rower who sets the pace for a crew 6 : a vigorous effort 7 : the sound of striking (as of a clock) 8 : a single movement with or as if with a tool or implement (as a pen)

stroll \ˈstrōl\ *vb* : to walk in a leisurely or idle manner — **stroll** *n* — **stroll·er** *n*

strong \ˈstrȯŋ\ *adj* **stron·ger** \ˈstrȯŋ-gər\; **stron·gest** \ˈstrȯŋ-gəst\ 1 : POWERFUL, VIGOROUS 2 : HEALTHY, ROBUST 3 : of a specified number ⟨an army 10 thousand ∼⟩ 4 : not mild or weak 5 : VIOLENT ⟨∼ wind⟩ 6 : ZEALOUS 7 : not easily broken 8 : FIRM, SOLID **syn** stout, sturdy, stalwart, tough — **strong·ly** *adv*

strong–arm \ˈstrȯŋ-ˌärm\ *adj* : having or using undue force ⟨∼ methods⟩

strong force *n* : the physical force responsible for binding together nucleons in the atomic nucleus

strong·hold \-ˌhōld\ *n* : a fortified place : FORTRESS

strong·man \-ˌman\ *n* : one who leads or controls by force of will and character or by military strength

stron·tium \ˈsträn-chē-əm, ˈsträn-tē-əm\ *n* : a soft malleable metallic chemical element — see ELEMENT table

¹**strop** \ˈsträp\ *n* : STRAP; *esp* : one for sharpening a razor

²**strop** *vb* **stropped; strop·ping** : to sharpen a razor on a strop

stro·phe \ˈstrō-fē\ *n* [Gk *strophē*, lit., act of turning] : a division of a poem — **stroph·ic** \ˈsträ-fik\ *adj*

strove *past of* STRIVE

struck *past and past part of* STRIKE

¹**struc·ture** \ˈstrək-chər\ *n* [ME, fr. L *structura*, fr. *structus*, pp. of *struere* to heap up, build] 1 : the action of building : CONSTRUCTION 2 : something built (as a house or a dam); *also* : something made up of interdependent parts in a definite pattern of organization 3 : arrangement or relationship of elements (as particles, parts, or organs) in a substance, body, or system — **struc·tur·al** *adj*

²**structure** *vb* **struc·tured; struc·tur·ing** : to make into a structure

stru·del \ˈstrüd-ᵊl, ˈshtrüd-\ *n* [G, lit., whirlpool] : a pastry made of a thin sheet of dough rolled up with filling and baked ⟨apple ∼⟩

¹**strug·gle** \ˈstrə-gəl\ *vb* **strug·gled; strug·gling** 1 : to make strenuous efforts against opposition : STRIVE 2 : to proceed with difficulty or with great effort **syn** endeavor, attempt, try, assay

²**struggle** *n* 1 : CONTEST, STRIFE 2 : a violent effort or exertion

strum \ˈstrəm\ *vb* **strummed; strum·ming** : to play on a stringed instrument by brushing the strings with the fingers ⟨∼ a guitar⟩

strum·pet \ˈstrəm-pət\ *n* : PROSTITUTE

strung \ˈstrəŋ\ *past and past part of* STRING

¹**strut** \ˈstrət\ *vb* **strut·ted; strut·ting** : to walk with an affectedly proud gait

²**strut** *n* **1** : a bar or rod for resisting lengthwise pressure **2** : a haughty or pompous gait

strych·nine \'strik-ₙnīn, -nən, -ₙnēn\ *n* : a bitter poisonous plant alkaloid used as a poison (as for rats) and medicinally as a stimulant to the central nervous system

¹**stub** \'stəb\ *n* **1** : STUMP 2 **2** : a short blunt end **3** : a small part of each leaf (as of a checkbook) kept as a memorandum of the items on the detached part

²**stub** *vb* **stubbed; stub·bing** : to strike (as one's toe) against something

stub·ble \'stə-bəl\ *n* **1** : the cut stem ends of herbs and esp. grasses left in the soil after harvest **2** : a rough surface or growth resembling stubble — **stub·bly** \-b(ə-)lē\ *adj*

stub·born \'stə-bərn\ *adj* **1** : FIRM, DETERMINED **2** : done or continued in a willful, unreasonable, or persistent manner **3** : not easily controlled or remedied ⟨a ∼ cold⟩ — **stub·born·ly** *adv* — **stub·born·ness** *n*

stub·by \'stə-bē\ *adj* : short, blunt, and thick like a stub

stuc·co \'stə-kō\ *n, pl* **stuccos** *or* **stuccoes** [It] : plaster for coating exterior walls — **stuc·coed** \'stə-kōd\ *adj*

stuck *past and past part of* STICK

stuck–up \'stək-'əp\ *adj* : CONCEITED

¹**stud** \'stəd\ *n* : a male animal and esp. a horse (**stud·horse** \-ₙhȯrs\) kept for breeding

²**stud** *n* **1** : one of the smaller uprights in a building to which the wall materials are fastened **2** : a removable device like a button used as a fastener or ornament ⟨shirt ∼s⟩ **3** : a projecting nail, pin, or rod

³**stud** *vb* **stud·ded; stud·ding 1** : to supply with or adorn with studs **2** : DOT

⁴**stud** *abbr* student

stud·book \'stəd-ₙbùk\ *n* : an official record of the pedigree of purebred animals (as horses or dogs)

stud·ding \'stə-diŋ\ *n* : the studs in a building or wall

stu·dent \'stüd-ᵊnt, 'styüd-\ *n* : SCHOLAR, PUPIL; *esp* : one who attends a school

stud·ied \'stə-dēd\ *adj* : INTENTIONAL ⟨a ∼ insult⟩ **syn** deliberate, considered, premeditated, designed

stu·dio \'stü-dē-ₙō, 'styü-\ *n, pl* **-dios 1** : a place where an artist works; *also* : a place for the study of an art **2** : a place where motion pictures are made **3** : a place equipped for the transmission of radio or television programs

stu·di·ous \'stü-dē-əs, 'styü-\ *adj* : devoted to study — **stu·di·ous·ly** *adv*

¹**study** \'stə-dē\ *n, pl* **stud·ies 1** : the use of the mind to gain knowledge **2** : the act or process of learning about something **3** : careful examination **4** : INTENT, PURPOSE **5** : a branch of learning **6** : a room esp. for reading and writing

²**study** *vb* **stud·ied; study·ing 1** : to engage in study or the study of **2** : to consider attentively or in detail **syn** consider, contemplate, weigh

¹**stuff** \'stəf\ *n* **1** : personal property **2** : raw material **3** : a finished textile fabric; *esp* : a worsted fabric **4** : writing, talk, or ideas of little or transitory worth **5** : an unspecified material substance or aggregate of matter **6** : fundamental material **7** : special knowledge or capability

²**stuff** *vb* **1** : to fill by packing things in : CRAM **2** : to eat greedily : GORGE **3** : to prepare (as meat) by filling with a stuffing **4** : to fill (as a cushion) with a soft material **5** : to stop up : PLUG

stuffed shirt \'stəft-\ *n* : a smug, conceited, and usu. pompous and inflexibly conservative person

stuff·ing *n* : material used to fill tightly; *esp* : a mixture of bread crumbs and spices used to stuff meat and poultry

stuffy \'stə-fē\ *adj* **stuff·i·er; -est 1** : STODGY **2** : lacking fresh air : CLOSE; *also* : blocked up ⟨a ∼ nose⟩

stul·ti·fy \'stəl-tə-ₙfī\ *vb* **-fied; -fy·ing 1** : to cause to appear foolish or stupid **2** : to impair, invalidate, or make

ineffective **3** : to have a dulling effect on — **stul·ti·fi·ca·tion** \ₙstəl-tə-fə-'kā-shən\ *n*

stum·ble \'stəm-bəl\ *vb* **stum·bled; stum·bling 1** : to blunder morally **2** : to trip in walking or running **3** : to walk unsteadily; *also* : to speak or act in a blundering or clumsy manner **4** : to happen by chance — **stumble** *n*

stumbling block *n* : an obstacle to belief, understanding, or progress

¹**stump** \'stəmp\ *n* **1** : the base of a bodily part (as a leg or tooth) left after the rest is removed **2** : the part of a plant and esp. a tree remaining with the root after the trunk is cut off **3** : a place or occasion for political public speaking — **stumpy** *adj*

²**stump** *vb* **1** : BAFFLE, PERPLEX **2** : to clear (land) of stumps **3** : to tour (a region) making political speeches **4** : to walk clumsily and heavily

stun \'stən\ *vb* **stunned; stun·ning 1** : to make senseless or dizzy by or as if by a blow **2** : BEWILDER, STUPEFY

stung *past and past part of* STING

stunk *past and past part of* STINK

stun·ning *adj* **1** : causing astonishment or disbelief **2** : strikingly beautiful — **stun·ning·ly** *adv*

¹**stunt** \'stənt\ *vb* : to hinder the normal growth or progress of

²**stunt** *n* : an unusual or spectacular feat

stu·pe·fy \'stü-pə-ₙfī, 'styü-\ *vb* **-fied; -fy·ing 1** : to make stupid, groggy, or insensible **2** : ASTONISH — **stu·pe·fac·tion** \ₙstü-pə-'fak-shən, ₙstyü-\ *n*

stu·pen·dous \stù-'pen-dəs, styü-\ *adj* : causing astonishment esp. because of great size or height **syn** tremendous, prodigious, monumental, monstrous — **stu·pen·dous·ly** *adv*

stu·pid \'stü-pəd, 'styü-\ *adj* [MF *stupide*, fr. L *stupidus*, fr. *stupēre* to be numb, be astonished] **1** : very dull in mind **2** : showing or resulting from dullness of mind — **stu·pid·i·ty** \stù-'pi-də-tē, styü-\ *n* — **stu·pid·ly** *adv*

stu·por \'stü-pər, 'styü-\ *n* **1** : a condition of greatly dulled or completely suspended sense or feeling **2** : a state of extreme apathy or torpor often following stress or shock — **stu·por·ous** *adj*

stur·dy \'stər-dē\ *adj* **stur·di·er; -est** [ME, brave, stubborn, fr. OF *estourdi* stunned, fr. pp. of *estourdir* to stun] **1** : RESOLUTE, UNYIELDING **2** : STRONG, ROBUST **syn** stout, stalwart, tough, tenacious — **stur·di·ly** \-də-lē\ *adv* — **stur·di·ness** \-dē-nəs\ *n*

stur·geon \'stər-jən\ *n* : any of a family of large bony fishes including some whose roe is made into caviar

sturgeon

stut·ter \'stə-tər\ *vb* : to speak with involuntary disruption or blocking of sounds — **stutter** *n*

¹**sty** \'stī\ *n, pl* **sties** : a pen or housing for swine

²**sty** *or* **stye** *n, pl* **sties** *or* **styes** : an inflamed swelling of a skin gland on the edge of an eyelid

¹**style** \'stīl\ *n* **1** : mode of address : TITLE **2** : a way of speaking or writing; *esp* : one characteristic of an individual, period, school, or nation ⟨ornate ∼⟩ **3** : manner or method of acting, making, or performing; *also* : a distinctive or characteristic manner **4** : a slender pointed instrument or process; *esp* : STYLUS **5** : a fashionable

---

\ə\abut \ᵊ\kitten \ər\further \a\ash \ā\ace \ä\mop, mar \aù\out \ch\chin \e\bet \ē\easy \g\go \i\hit \ī\ice \j\job \ŋ\sing \ō\go \ò\law \òi\boy \th\thin \t̲h̲\the \ü\loot \ù\foot \y\yet \zh\vision *see also* Pronunciation Symbols page

manner or mode **6** : overall excellence, skill, or grace in performance, manner, or appearance **7** : the custom followed in spelling, capitalization, punctuation, and typography — **sty·lis·tic** \stī-ˈlis-tik\ adj

²**style** vb **styled; styl·ing 1** : NAME, DESIGNATE **2** : to make or design in accord with a prevailing mode

styl·ing \ˈstī-liŋ\ n : the way in which something is styled

styl·ish \ˈstī-lish\ adj : conforming to current fashion **syn** modish, smart, chic — **styl·ish·ly** adv — **styl·ish·ness** n

styl·ist \ˈstī-list\ n **1** : one (as a writer) noted for a distinctive style **2** : a developer or designer of styles

styl·ize \ˈstī-ˌlīz, ˈstī-ə-\ vb **styl·ized; styl·iz·ing** : to conform to a style; esp : to represent or design according to a pattern or style rather than according to nature or tradition

sty·lus \ˈstī-ləs\ n, pl **sty·li** \ˈstī-ˌlī\ also **sty·lus·es** \ˈstī-lə-səz\ [L stylus, stilus spike, stylus] **1** : a pointed implement used by the ancients for writing on wax **2** : a phonograph needle

sty·mie \ˈstī-mē\ vb **sty·mied; sty·mie·ing** : BLOCK, FRUSTRATE

styp·tic \ˈstip-tik\ adj : tending to check bleeding — **styptic** n

suave \ˈswäv\ adj [MF, pleasant, sweet, fr. L suavis] : persuasively pleasing : smoothly agreeable **syn** urbane, smooth, bland — **suave·ly** adv — **sua·vi·ty** \ˈswä-və-tē\ n

¹**sub** \ˈsəb\ n : SUBSTITUTE — **sub** vb

²**sub** n : SUBMARINE

³**sub** abbr **1** subtract **2** suburb

sub- \ˈsəb\ prefix **1** : under : beneath **2** : subordinate : secondary **3** : subordinate portion of : subdivision of **4** : with repetition of a process described in a simple verb so as to form, stress, or deal with subordinate parts or relations **5** : somewhat **6** : falling nearly in the category of : bordering on

subacute	subliterate
subagency	subminimal
subagent	subminimum
subaqueous	suboptimal
subarctic	suborder
subarea	subparagraph
subatmospheric	subparallel
subaverage	subphylum
subbasement	subplot
subcategory	subpopulation
subcellular	subproblem
subchapter	subprofessional
subclass	subprogram
subclassify	subregion
subcommittee	subroutine
subcontract	subsection
subcontractor	subsense
subculture	subsoil
subcutaneous	subspecies
subdiscipline	substage
subentry	substation
subfamily	subsystem
subfield	subteen
subfreezing	subthreshold
subgenre	subtopic
subgenus	subtotal
subgroup	subtreasury
subhead	subtype
subheading	subunit
subhuman	subvariety
subkingdom	subvisible
sublethal	subzero

sub·al·pine \ˌsəb-ˈal-ˌpīn\ adj **1** : of or relating to the region about the foot and lower slopes of the Alps **2** : of, relating to, or inhabiting high upland slopes esp. just below the timberline

sub·al·tern \sə-ˈból-tərn\ n : SUBORDINATE; esp : a junior officer (as in the British army)

sub·as·sem·bly \ˌsəb-ə-ˈsem-blē\ n : an assembled unit to be incorporated with other units in a finished product

sub·atom·ic \ˌsəb-ə-ˈtä-mik\ adj : of or relating to the inside of the atom or to particles smaller than atoms

sub·clin·i·cal \ˌsəb-ˈkli-ni-kəl\ adj : not detectable by the usual clinical tests ⟨a ∼ infection⟩

sub·com·pact \ˈsəb-ˈkäm-ˌpakt\ n : an automobile smaller than a compact

¹**sub·con·scious** \ˌsəb-ˈkän-chəs, ˈsəb-\ adj : existing in the mind without entering conscious awareness — **sub·con·scious·ly** adv — **sub·con·scious·ness** n

²**subconscious** n : mental activities just below the threshold of consciousness

sub·con·ti·nent \ˌsəb-ˈkänt-ᵊn-ənt\ n : a major subdivision of a continent — **sub·con·ti·nen·tal** \ˌsəb-ˌkänt-ᵊn-ˈent- ᵊl\ adj

sub·di·vide \ˌsəb-də-ˈvīd, ˈsəb-də-ˌvīd\ vb : to divide the parts of into more parts; esp : to divide (a tract of land) into building lots — **sub·di·vi·sion** \-ˈvi-zhən, -ˌvi-\ n

sub·duc·tion \səb-ˈdək-shən\ n : the descent of the edge of one crustal plate beneath the edge of an adjacent plate

sub·due \səb-ˈdü, -ˈdyü\ vb **sub·dued; sub·du·ing 1** : to bring into subjection : VANQUISH **2** : to bring under control : CURB **3** : to reduce the intensity of

subj abbr **1** subject **2** subjunctive

¹**sub·ject** \ˈsəb-jikt\ n [ME, fr. MF, fr. L subjectus one under authority & subjectum subject of a proposition, fr. subicere to subject, lit., to throw under, fr. sub- under + jacere to throw] **1** : a person under the authority of another **2** : a person subject to a sovereign **3** : an individual that is studied or experimented on **4** : the person or thing discussed or treated : TOPIC, THEME **5** : a word or word group denoting that of which something is predicated

²**subject** adj **1** : being under the power or rule of another **2** : LIABLE, EXPOSED ⟨∼ to floods⟩ **3** : dependent on some act or condition ⟨appointment ∼ to senate approval⟩ **syn** subordinate, secondary, tributary, collateral, dependent

³**sub·ject** \səb-ˈjekt\ vb **1** : to bring under control : CONQUER **2** : to make liable **3** : to cause to undergo or endure — **sub·jec·tion** \-ˈjek-shən\ n

sub·jec·tive \(ˌ)səb-ˈjek-tiv\ adj **1** : of, relating to, or constituting a subject **2** : of, relating to, or arising within in one's self or mind in contrast to what is outside : PERSONAL — **sub·jec·tive·ly** adv — **sub·jec·tiv·i·ty** \-ˌjek-ˈti-və-tē\ n

subject matter n : matter presented for consideration, discussion, or study

sub·join \(ˌ)səb-ˈjóin\ vb : APPEND

sub ju·di·ce \(ˌ)süb-ˈyü-di-ˌkā, ˈsəb-ˈjü-də-(ˌ)sē\ adv [L] : before a judge or court : not yet legally decided

sub·ju·gate \ˈsəb-ji-ˌgāt\ vb **-gat·ed; -gat·ing** : CONQUER, SUBDUE; also : ENSLAVE **syn** reduce, overcome, overthrow, vanquish, defeat, beat — **sub·ju·ga·tion** \ˌsəb-ji-ˈgā-shən\ n

sub·junc·tive \səb-ˈjəŋk-tiv\ adj : of, relating to, or constituting a verb form that represents an act or state as contingent or possible or viewed emotionally (as with desire) ⟨the ∼ mood⟩ — **subjunctive** n

sub·lease \ˈsəb-ˈlēs, -ˌlēs\ n : a lease by a lessee of part or all of leased premises to another person with the original lessee retaining some right under the original lease — **sublease** vb

¹**sub·let** \ˈsəb-ˈlet\ vb **-let; -let·ting** : to let all or a part of (a leased property) to another; also : to rent (a property) from a lessee

²**sublet** \-ˌlet\ *n* : property and esp. housing obtained by or available through a sublease

sub·li·mate \ˈsə-blə-ˌmāt\ *vb* **-mat·ed; -mat·ing 1** : SUBLIME **2** : to direct the expression of (as a desire or impulse) from a primitive to a more socially and culturally acceptable form — **sub·li·ma·tion** \ˌsə-blə-ˈmā-shən\ *n*

¹**sub·lime** \sə-ˈblīm\ *vb* **sub·limed; sub·lim·ing** : to pass or cause to pass directly from the solid to the vapor state

²**sublime** *adj* **1** : EXALTED, NOBLE **2** : having awe-inspiring beauty or grandeur **syn** glorious, splendid, superb, resplendent, gorgeous — **sub·lime·ly** *adv* — **sub·lim·i·ty** \-ˈbli-mə-tē\ *n*

sub·lim·i·nal \(ˌ)səb-ˈli-mən-ᵊl, ˈsəb-\ *adj* **1** : inadequate to produce a sensation or mental awareness ⟨∼ stimuli⟩ **2** : existing or functioning below the threshold of consciousness ⟨the ∼ mind⟩ ⟨∼ advertising⟩

sub·ma·chine gun \ˌsəb-mə-ˈshēn-ˌgən\ *n* : an automatic firearm fired from the shoulder or hip

¹**sub·ma·rine** \ˈsəb-mə-ˌrēn, ˌsəb-mə-ˈrēn\ *adj* : UNDERWATER; *esp* : UNDERSEA

²**submarine** *n* **1** : a naval vessel designed to operate underwater **2** : a large sandwich made from a long split roll with any of a variety of fillings

sub·merge \səb-ˈmərj\ *vb* **sub·merged; sub·merg·ing 1** : to put or plunge under the surface of water **2** : INUNDATE — **sub·mer·gence** \-ˈmər-jəns\ *n*

sub·merse \səb-ˈmərs\ *vb* **sub·mersed; sub·mers·ing** : SUBMERGE — **sub·mer·sion** \-ˈmər-zhən\ *n*

¹**sub·mers·ible** \səb-ˈmər-sə-bəl\ *adj* : capable of being submerged

²**submersible** *n* : something that is submersible; *esp* : a small underwater craft used for deep-sea research

sub·mi·cro·sco·pic \ˌsəb-ˌmī-krə-ˈskä-pik\ *adj* : too small to be seen in an ordinary light microscope

sub·min·ia·ture \ˌsəb-ˈmi-nē-ə-ˌchùr, ˈsəb-, -ˈmi-ni-ˌchùr, -chər\ *adj* : very small

sub·mit \səb-ˈmit\ *vb* **sub·mit·ted; sub·mit·ting 1** : to commit to the discretion or decision of another or of others **2** : YIELD, SURRENDER **3** : to put forward as an opinion — **sub·mis·sion** \-ˈmi-shən\ *n* — **sub·mis·sive** \-ˈmi-siv\ *adj*

sub·nor·mal \ˌsəb-ˈnòr-məl\ *adj* : falling below what is normal; *also* : having less of something and esp. intelligence than is normal — **sub·nor·mal·i·ty** \ˌsəb-nòr-ˈma-lə-tē\ *n*

sub·or·bit·al \ˌsəb-ˈòr-bət-ᵊl, ˈsəb-\ *adj* : being or involving less than one orbit

¹**sub·or·di·nate** \sə-ˈbòrd-ᵊn-ət\ *adj* **1** : of lower class or rank **2** : INFERIOR **3** : submissive to authority **4** : subordinated to other elements in a sentence : DEPENDENT ⟨∼ clause⟩ **syn** secondary, subject, tributary, collateral

²**subordinate** *n* : one that is subordinate

³**sub·or·di·nate** \sə-ˈbòrd-ᵊn-ˌāt\ *vb* **-nat·ed; -nat·ing 1** : to place in a lower rank or class **2** : SUBDUE — **sub·or·di·na·tion** \-ˌbòrd-ᵊn-ˈā-shən\ *n*

sub·orn \sə-ˈbòrn\ *vb* **1** : to induce secretly to do an unlawful thing **2** : to induce to commit perjury — **sub·or·na·tion** \ˌsə-ˌbòr-ˈnā-shən\ *n*

¹**sub·poe·na** \sə-ˈpē-nə\ *n* [ME *suppena,* fr. L *sub poena* under penalty] : a writ commanding the person named in it to attend court under penalty for failure to do so

²**subpoena** *vb* **-naed; -na·ing** : to summon with a subpoena

sub—Sa·ha·ran \ˌsəb-sə-ˈhar-ən\ *adj* : of, relating to, or being the part of Africa south of the Sahara

sub·scribe \səb-ˈskrīb\ *vb* **sub·scribed; sub·scrib·ing 1** : to sign one's name to a document **2** : to give consent by or as if by signing one's name **3** : to promise to contribute by signing one's name with the amount promised **4** : to place an order by signing **5** : to receive a periodical or service regularly on order **6** : FAVOR, AP-

PROVE **syn** agree, acquiesce, assent, accede — **sub·scrib·er** *n*

sub·script \ˈsəb-ˌskript\ *n* : a symbol (as a letter or number) immediately below or below and to the right or left of another written character — **subscript** *adj*

sub·scrip·tion \səb-ˈskrip-shən\ *n* **1** : the act of subscribing : SIGNATURE **2** : a purchase by signed order

sub·se·quent \ˈsəb-si-kwənt, -sə-ˌkwent\ *adj* : following after : SUCCEEDING — **sub·se·quent·ly** *adv*

sub·ser·vi·ence \səb-ˈsər-vē-əns\ *n* **1** : a subordinate place or condition **2** : SERVILITY — **sub·ser·vi·en·cy** \-ən-sē\ *n* — **sub·ser·vi·ent** \-ənt\ *adj*

sub·set \ˈsəb-ˌset\ *n* : a set each of whose elements is an element of an inclusive set

sub·side \səb-ˈsīd\ *vb* **sub·sid·ed; sub·sid·ing** [L *subsidere,* fr. *sub-* under + *sidere* to sit down, sink] **1** : to settle to the bottom of a liquid **2** : to tend downward : DESCEND **3** : SINK, SUBMERGE **4** : to become quiet and tranquil **syn** abate, wane, moderate, slacken — **sub·sid·ence** \səb-ˈsīd-ᵊns, ˈsəb-sə-dəns\ *n*

¹**sub·sid·iary** \səb-ˈsi-dē-ˌer-ē\ *adj* **1** : furnishing aid or support **2** : of secondary importance **3** : of or relating to a subsidy **syn** auxiliary, contributory, subservient, accessory

²**subsidiary** *n, pl* **-iar·ies** : one that is subsidiary; *esp* : a company controlled by another

sub·si·dize \ˈsəb-sə-ˌdīz\ *vb* **-dized; -diz·ing** : to aid or furnish with a subsidy

sub·si·dy \ˈsəb-sə-dē\ *n, pl* **-dies** [ME, fr. L *subsidium* reserve troops, support, assistance, fr. *sub-* near + *sedēre* to sit] : a gift of public money to a private person or company or to another government

sub·sist \səb-ˈsist\ *vb* **1** : EXIST, PERSIST **2** : to have the means (as food and clothing) of maintaining life; *esp* : to nourish oneself

sub·sis·tence \səb-ˈsis-təns\ *n* **1** : EXISTENCE **2** : means of subsisting : the minimum (as of food and clothing) necessary to support life

sub·son·ic \ˌsəb-ˈsä-nik, ˈsəb-\ *adj* : being or relating to a speed less than that of sound; *also* : moving at such a speed

sub·species \ˈsəb-ˌspē-shēz, -sēz\ *n* : a subdivision of a species; *esp* : a category in biological classification ranking just below a species that designates a geographic population genetically distinct from other such populations and potentially able to breed with them where its range overlaps theirs

sub·stance \ˈsəb-stəns\ *n* **1** : essential nature : ESSENCE ⟨divine ∼⟩; *also* : the fundamental or essential part or quality ⟨the ∼ of the speech⟩ **2** : physical material from which something is made or which has discrete existence; *also* : matter of particular or definite chemical constitution **3** : material possessions : PROPERTY, WEALTH

substance abuse *n* : excessive use of a drug (as alcohol or cocaine) : use of a drug without medical justification

sub·stan·dard \ˌsəb-ˈstan-dərd\ *adj* : falling short of a standard or norm

sub·stan·tial \səb-ˈstan-chəl\ *adj* **1** : existing as or in substance : MATERIAL; *also* : not illusory : REAL **2** : IMPORTANT, ESSENTIAL **3** : NOURISHING, SATISFYING ⟨∼ meal⟩ **4** : having means : WELL-TO-DO **5** : CONSIDERABLE ⟨∼ profit⟩ **6** : STRONG, FIRM — **sub·stan·tial·ly** *adv*

sub·stan·ti·ate \səb-ˈstan-chē-ˌāt\ *vb* **-at·ed; -at·ing 1** : to give substance or body to **2** : VERIFY, PROVE — **sub·stan·ti·a·tion** \-ˌstan-chē-ˈā-shən\ *n*

sub·stan·tive \ˈsəb-stən-tiv\ *n* : NOUN; *also* : a word or phrase used as a noun

---

\ə\abut \ᵊ\kitten \ər\further \a\ash \ā\ace \ä\mop, mar
\aù\out \ch\chin \e\bet \ē\easy \g\go \i\hit \ī\ice \j\job
\ŋ\sing \ō\go \ò\law \òi\boy \th\thin \t̲h̲\the \ü\loot \ù\foot
\y\yet \zh\vision *see also* Pronunciation Symbols page

¹**sub·sti·tute** \'səb-stə-ˌtüt, -ˌtyüt\ n : a person or thing replacing another — **substitute** adj

²**substitute** vb **-tut·ed; -tut·ing 1 :** to put or use in the place of another **2 :** to serve as a substitute — **sub·sti·tu·tion** \ˌsəb-stə-'tü-shən, -'tyü-\ n

sub·strate \'səb-ˌstrāt\ n **1 :** the base on which a plant or animal lives **2 :** a substance acted upon (as by an enzyme)

sub·stra·tum \'səb-ˌstrā-təm, -ˌstra-\ n, pl **-stra·ta** \-tə\ : the layer or structure (as subsoil) lying underneath

sub·struc·ture \'səb-ˌstrək-chər\ n : FOUNDATION, GROUNDWORK

sub·sur·face \'səb-ˌsər-fəs\ n : earth material near the surface of the ground — **subsurface** adj

sub·ter·fuge \'səb-tər-ˌfyüj\ n : a trick or device used in order to conceal, escape, or evade **syn** fraud, deception, trickery

sub·ter·ra·nean \ˌsəb-tə-'rā-nē-ən\ adj **1 :** lying or being underground **2 :** SECRET, HIDDEN

sub·tile \'sət-ᵊl\ adj **sub·til·er** \'sət-lər, -ᵊl-ər\; **sub·til·est** \'sət-ləst, -ᵊl-əst\ : SUBTLE

sub·ti·tle \'səb-ˌtīt-ᵊl\ n **1 :** a secondary or explanatory title (as of a book) **2 :** printed matter projected on a motion-picture screen during or between the scenes

sub·tle \'sət-ᵊl\ adj **sub·tler** \'sət-ᵊl-ər\; **sub·tlest** \'sət-ᵊl-əst\ **1 :** hardly noticeable ⟨∼ differences⟩ **2 :** SHREWD, PERCEPTIVE **3 :** CLEVER, SLY — **sub·tle·ty** \-tē\ n — **sub·tly** \'sət-ᵊl-ē\ adv

sub·tract \səb-'trakt\ vb : to take away (as one part or number) from another; also : to perform the operation of deducting one number from another — **sub·trac·tion** \-'trak-shən\ n

sub·tra·hend \'səb-trə-ˌhend\ n : a number that is to be subtracted from another

sub·trop·i·cal \ˌsəb-'trä-pi-kəl, 'səb-\ also **sub·trop·ic** \-pik\ adj : of, relating to, or being regions bordering on the tropical zone — **sub·trop·ics** \-piks\ n pl

sub·urb \'sə-ˌbərb\ n **1 :** an outlying part of a city; also : a small community adjacent to a city **2** pl : a residential area adjacent to a city — **sub·ur·ban** \sə-'bər-bən\ adj or n — **sub·ur·ban·ite** \sə-'bər-bə-ˌnīt\ n

sub·ur·bia \sə-'bər-bē-ə\ n **1 :** SUBURBS **2 :** suburban people or customs

sub·ven·tion \səb-'ven-chən\ n : SUBSIDY, ENDOWMENT

sub·vert \səb-'vərt\ vb **1 :** OVERTHROW, RUIN **2 :** CORRUPT — **sub·ver·sion** \-'vər-zhən\ n — **sub·ver·sive** \-'vər-siv\ adj

sub·way \'səb-ˌwā\ n : an underground way; esp : an underground electric railway

suc·ceed \sək-'sēd\ vb **1 :** to follow next in order or next after another; esp : to inherit sovereignty, rank, title, or property **2 :** to attain a desired object or end : be successful

suc·cess \sək-'ses\ n **1 :** favorable or desired outcome **2** : the gaining of wealth and fame **3 :** one that succeeds — **suc·cess·ful** \-fəl\ adj — **suc·cess·ful·ly** adv

suc·ces·sion \sək-'se-shən\ n **1 :** the order, act, or right of succeeding to a property, title, or throne **2 :** the act or process of following in order **3 :** a series of persons or things that follow one after another **syn** progression, sequence, chain, train, string

suc·ces·sive \sək-'se-siv\ adj : following in order : CONSECUTIVE — **suc·ces·sive·ly** adv

suc·ces·sor \sək-'se-sər\ n : one that succeeds (as to a throne, title, estate, or office)

suc·cinct \(ˌ)sək-'siŋkt, sə-'siŋkt\ adj : BRIEF, CONCISE **syn** terse, laconic, summary, curt, short — **suc·cinct·ly** adv — **suc·cinct·ness** n

suc·cor \'sə-kər\ n [ME succur, fr. earlier sucurs, taken as pl., fr. OF sucors, fr. ML succursus, fr. L succurrere to run up, run to help] : AID, HELP, RELIEF — **succor** vb

suc·co·tash \'sə-kə-ˌtash\ n [Narraganset (American Indian language of Rhode Island) msíckquatash boiled

corn kernels] : beans and corn kernels cooked together

suc·cour chiefly Brit var of SUCCOR

¹**suc·cu·lent** \'sə-kyə-lənt\ adj **:** full of juice : JUICY; also : having fleshy tissues that conserve moisture ⟨∼ plants⟩ — **suc·cu·lence** \-ləns\ n

²**succulent** n : a succulent plant (as a cactus)

suc·cumb \sə-'kəm\ vb **1 :** to yield to superior strength or force or overpowering appeal or desire **2 :** DIE **syn** submit, capitulate, relent, defer

¹**such** \'səch, 'sich\ adj **1 :** of this or that kind **2 :** having a quality just specified or to be specified

²**such** pron **1 :** such a one or ones ⟨he's a star, and acted as ∼⟩ **2 :** that or those similar or related thereto ⟨boards and nails and ∼⟩

³**such** adv : to that degree : so

such·like \'səch-ˌlīk\ adj : SIMILAR

¹**suck** \'sək\ vb **1 :** to draw in liquid and esp. mother's milk with the mouth **2 :** to draw liquid from by action of the mouth ⟨∼ an orange⟩ **3 :** to take in or up or remove by or as if by suction

²**suck** n **1 :** a sucking movement or force **2 :** the act of sucking

suck·er \'sə-kər\ n **1 :** one that sucks **2 :** a part of an animal's body used for sucking or for clinging **3 :** a fish with thick soft lips for sucking in food **4 :** a shoot from the roots or lower part of a plant **5 :** a person easily deceived **6** — used as a generalized term of reference

suck·le \'sə-kəl\ vb **suck·led; suck·ling :** to give or draw milk from the breast or udder; also : NURTURE

suck·ling \'sə-kliŋ\ n : a young unweaned mammal

su·cre \'sü-(ˌ)krā\ n — see MONEY table

su·crose \'sü-ˌkrōs, -ˌkrōz\ n : a sweet sugar obtained commercially esp. from sugarcane or sugar beets

suc·tion \'sək-shən\ n **1 :** the act of sucking **2 :** the act or process of drawing something (as liquid or dust) into a space (as in a vacuum cleaner or a pump) by partially exhausting the air in the space — **suc·tion·al** \-shə-nəl\ adj

suction cup n : a cup-shaped device in which a partial vacuum is produced when applied to a surface

Su·da·nese \ˌsüd-ᵊn-'ēz, -'ēs\ n : a native or inhabitant of Sudan — **Sudanese** adj

sud·den \'səd-ᵊn\ adj [ME sodain, fr. MF, fr. L subitaneus, fr. subitus sudden, fr. pp. of subire to come up] **1 :** happening or coming unexpectedly ⟨∼ shower⟩; also : changing angle or character all at once ⟨∼ turn⟩ ⟨∼ descent⟩ **2 :** HASTY, RASH ⟨∼ decision⟩ **3 :** made or brought about in a short time : PROMPT ⟨∼ cure⟩ **syn** precipitate, headlong, impetuous — **sud·den·ly** adv — **sud·den·ness** n

sudden infant death syndrome n : death due to unknown causes of an apparently healthy infant usu. before one year of age and esp. during sleep

suds \'sədz\ n pl : soapy water esp. when frothy — **sudsy** \'səd-zē\ adj

sue \'sü\ vb **sued; su·ing 1 :** PETITION, SOLICIT **2 :** to seek justice or right by bringing legal action

suede or **suède** \'swād\ n [F gants de Suède Swedish gloves] **1 :** leather with a napped surface **2 :** a fabric with a suedelike nap

su·et \'sü-ət\ n : the hard fat from beef and mutton that yields tallow

suff abbr **1** sufficient **2** suffix

suf·fer \'sə-fər\ vb **suf·fered; suf·fer·ing 1 :** to feel or endure pain **2 :** EXPERIENCE, UNDERGO **3 :** to bear loss, damage, or injury **4 :** ALLOW, PERMIT **syn** endure, abide, tolerate, stand, brook, stomach — **suf·fer·able** \'sə-fə-rə-bəl\ adj — **suf·fer·er** n

suf·fer·ance \'sə-frəns, -fə-rəns\ n **1 :** consent or approval implied by lack of interference or resistance **2 :** ENDURANCE, PATIENCE

suf·fer·ing \'sə-friŋ, -fə-riŋ\ n : PAIN, MISERY, HARDSHIP

suf·fice \sə-'fīs\ vb **suf·ficed; suf·fic·ing 1 :** to satisfy a need : be sufficient **2** : to be capable or competent

suf·fi·cien·cy \sə-ˈfi-shən-sē\ *n* **1** : a sufficient quantity to meet one's needs **2** : ADEQUACY

suf·fi·cient \sə-ˈfi-shənt\ *adj* : adequate to accomplish a purpose or meet a need — **suf·fi·cient·ly** *adv*

¹suf·fix \ˈsə-ˌfiks\ *n* : an affix occurring at the end of a word

²suf·fix \ˈsə-fiks, (ˌ)sə-ˈfiks\ *vb* : to attach as a suffix — **suf·fix·a·tion** \ˌsə-ˌfik-ˈsā-shən\ *n*

suf·fo·cate \ˈsə-fə-ˌkāt\ *vb* **-cat·ed; -cat·ing** : STIFLE, SMOTHER, CHOKE — **suf·fo·cat·ing·ly** *adv* — **suf·fo·ca·tion** \ˌsə-fə-ˈkā-shən\ *n*

suf·fra·gan \ˈsə-fri-gən\ *n* : an assistant bishop; *esp* : one not having the right of succession — **suffragan** *adj*

suf·frage \ˈsə-frij\ *n* [L *suffragium*] **1** : VOTE **2** : the right to vote : FRANCHISE

suf·frag·ette \ˌsə-fri-ˈjet\ *n* : a woman who advocates suffrage for women

suf·frag·ist \ˈsəf-ri-jist\ *n* : one who advocates extension of the suffrage esp. to women

suf·fuse \sə-ˈfyüz\ *vb* **suf·fused; suf·fus·ing** : to spread over or through in the manner of a fluid or light **syn** infuse, imbue, ingrain, steep — **suf·fu·sion** \-ˈfyü-zhən\ *n*

¹sug·ar \ˈshu̇-gər\ *n* **1** : a sweet substance that is colorless or white when pure and is chiefly sucrose from sugarcane or sugar beets **2** : a water-soluble compound (as glucose) similar to sucrose — **sug·ary** *adj*

²sugar *vb* **sug·ared; sug·ar·ing 1** : to mix, cover, or sprinkle with sugar **2** : SWEETEN ⟨∼ advice with flattery⟩ **3** : to form sugar ⟨a syrup that ∼s⟩ **4** : GRANULATE

sugar beet *n* : a large beet with a white root from which sugar is made

sug·ar·cane \ˈshu̇-gər-ˌkān\ *n* : a tall grass widely grown in warm regions for the sugar in its stalks

sugar daddy *n* **1** : a well-to-do usu. older man who supports or spends lavishly on a mistress or girlfriend **2** : a generous benefactor of a cause

sugar maple *n* : a maple with a sweet sap; *esp* : one of eastern No. America with sap that is the chief source of maple syrup and maple sugar

sugar pea *n* : SNOW PEA

sug·ar·plum \ˈshu̇-gər-ˌpləm\ *n* : a small ball of candy

sug·gest \səg-ˈjest, sə-\ *vb* **1** : to put (as a thought, plan, or desire) into a person's mind **2** : to remind or evoke by association of ideas **syn** imply, hint, intimate, insinuate, connote

sug·gest·i·ble \səg-ˈjes-tə-bəl, sə-\ *adj* : easily influenced by suggestion

sug·ges·tion \-ˈjes-chən\ *n* **1** : an act or instance of suggesting; *also* : something suggested **2** : a slight indication

sug·ges·tive \-ˈjes-tiv\ *adj* : tending to suggest something; *esp* : suggesting something improper or indecent — **sug·ges·tive·ly** *adv* — **sug·ges·tive·ness** *n*

sui·cide \ˈsü-ə-ˌsīd\ *n* **1** : the act of killing oneself purposely **2** : one that commits or attempts suicide — **sui·cid·al** \ˌsü-ə-ˈsīd-ᵊl\ *adj*

sui ge·ner·is \ˌsü-ˌī-ˈje-nə-rəs, ˌsü-ē-\ *adj* [L, of its own kind] : being in a class by itself : UNIQUE

¹suit \ˈsüt\ *n* **1** : an action in court to recover a right or claim **2** : an act of suing or entreating; *esp* : COURTSHIP **3** : a number of things used together ⟨∼ of clothes⟩ **4** : one of the four sets of playing cards in a pack

²suit *vb* **1** : to be appropriate or fitting **2** : to be becoming to **3** : to meet the needs or desires of : PLEASE

suit·able \ˈsü-tə-bəl\ *adj* : FITTING, PROPER, APPROPRIATE **syn** fit, meet, apt, happy — **suit·abil·i·ty** \ˌsü-tə-ˈbi-lə-tē\ *n* — **suit·able·ness** \ˈsü-tə-bəl-nəs\ *n* — **suit·ably** \-tə-blē\ *adv*

suit·case \ˈsüt-ˌkās\ *n* : a bag or case carried by hand and designed to hold a traveler's clothing and personal articles

suite \ˈswēt, *for 4 also* ˈsüt\ *n* **1** : RETINUE **2** : a group of

rooms occupied as a unit **3** : a modern instrumental composition in several movements of different character; *also* : a long orchestral concert arrangement in suite form of material drawn from a longer work **4** : a set of matched furniture for a room

suit·ing \ˈsü-tiŋ\ *n* : fabric for suits of clothes

suit·or \ˈsü-tər\ *n* **1** : one who sues or petitions **2** : one who seeks to marry a woman

su·ki·ya·ki \ˌskē-ˈyä-kē, ˌsu̇-kē-ˈyä-\ *n* : thin slices of meat, bean curd, and vegetables cooked in soy sauce and sugar

sul·fa drug \ˈsəl-fə-\ *n* : any of various synthetic organic bacteria-inhibiting drugs

sul·fate \ˈsəl-ˌfāt\ *n* : a salt or ester of sulfuric acid

sul·fide \ˈsəl-ˌfīd\ *n* : a compound of sulfur

sul·fur *also* **sul·phur** \ˈsəl-fər\ *n* : a nonmetallic chemical element used esp. in the chemical and paper industries and in vulcanizing rubber — see ELEMENT table

sulfur di·ox·ide \-dī-ˈäk-ˌsīd\ *n* : a heavy pungent toxic gas that is used esp. in bleaching, as a preservative, and as a refrigerant, and is a major air pollutant

sul·fu·ric \ˌsəl-ˈfyu̇r-ik\ *adj* : of, relating to, or containing sulfur

sulfuric acid *or* **sul·phu·ric acid** \ˌsəl-ˈfyu̇r-ik-\ *n* : a heavy corrosive oily strong acid

sul·fu·rous *also* **sul·phu·rous** \ˈsəl-fə-rəs, -fyə-, *also esp for 1* ˌsəl-ˈfyu̇r-əs\ *adj* **1** : of, relating to, or containing sulfur **2** : of or relating to brimstone or the fire of hell : INFERNAL **3** : FIERY, INFLAMED ⟨∼ sermons⟩

¹sulk \ˈsəlk\ *vb* : to be or become moodily silent or irritable

²sulk *n* : a sulky mood or spell

¹sulky \ˈsəl-kē\ *adj* : inclined to sulk : MOROSE, MOODY **syn** surly, glum, sullen, gloomy — **sulk·i·ly** \ˈsəl-kə-lē\ *adv* — **sulk·i·ness** \-kē-nəs\ *n*

²sulky *n, pl* **sulkies** : a light 2-wheeled horse-drawn vehicle with a seat for the driver and usu. no body

sul·len \ˈsə-lən\ *adj* **1** : gloomily silent : MOROSE **2** : DISMAL, GLOOMY ⟨a ∼ sky⟩ **syn** glum, surly, dour, saturnine — **sul·len·ly** *adv* — **sul·len·ness** *n*

sul·ly \ˈsə-lē\ *vb* **sul·lied; sul·ly·ing** : SOIL, SMIRCH, DEFILE

sul·tan \ˈsəlt-ᵊn\ *n* : a sovereign esp. of a Muslim state — **sul·tan·ate** \-ˌāt\ *n*

sul·ta·na \ˌsəl-ˈta-nə\ *n* **1** : a female member of a sultan's family **2** : a pale seedless grape; *also* : a raisin of this grape

sul·try \ˈsəl-trē\ *adj* **sul·tri·er; -est** [obs. E *sulter* to swelter, alter. of E *swelter*] : very hot and moist : SWELTERING; *also* : exciting sexual desire

¹sum \ˈsəm\ *n* [ME *summe*, fr. OF, fr. L *summa*, fr. fem. of *summus* highest] **1** : a quantity of money **2** : the whole amount **3** : GIST **4** : the result obtained by adding numbers **5** : a problem in arithmetic

²sum *vb* **summed; sum·ming** : to find the sum of by adding or counting

su·mac *also* **su·mach** \ˈsü-ˌmak, ˈshü-\ *n* : any of a genus of trees, shrubs, and woody vines with feathery compound leaves and spikes of red or whitish berries ☞ For illustration, see next page.

sum·ma·rize \ˈsə-mə-ˌrīz\ *vb* **-rized; -riz·ing** : to tell in a summary

¹sum·ma·ry \ˈsə-mə-rē\ *adj* **1** : covering the main points briefly : CONCISE **2** : done without delay or formality ⟨∼ punishment⟩ **syn** terse, succinct, laconic — **sum·mar·i·ly** \(ˌ)sə-ˈmer-ə-lē, ˈsə-mə-rə-lē\ *adv*

²sum·ma·ry *n, pl* **-ries** : a concise statement of the main points

---

\ə\abut \ᵊ\kitten \ər\further \a\ash \ā\ace \ä\mop, mar
\au̇\out \ch\chin \e\bet \ē\easy \g\go \i\hit \ī\ice \j\job
\ŋ\sing \ō\go \ȯ\law \ȯi\boy \th\thin \th̲\the \ü\loot \u̇\foot
\y\yet \zh\vision *see also* Pronunciation Symbols page

sumac

sum·ma·tion \(ˌ)sə-ˈmā-shən\ *n* : a summing up; *esp* : a speech in court summing up the arguments in a case

sum·mer \ˈsə-mər\ *n* : the season of the year in a region in which the sun shines most directly : the warmest period of the year — **sum·mery** *adj*

sum·mer·house \ˈsə-mər-ˌhaús\ *n* : a covered structure in a garden or park to provide a shady retreat

summer squash *n* : any of various garden squashes (as zucchini) used as a vegetable while immature

sum·mit \ˈsə-mət\ *n* **1** : the highest point **2** : a conference of highest-level officials

sum·mon \ˈsə-mən\ *vb* [ME *somonen*, fr. OF *somondre*, fr. (assumed) VL *summonere*, alter. of L *summonēre* to remind secretly] **1** : to call to a meeting : CONVOKE **2** : to send for; *also* : to order to appear in court **3** : to evoke esp. by an act of the will ⟨∼ up courage⟩ — **sum·mon·er** *n*

sum·mons \ˈsə-mənz\ *n, pl* **sum·mons·es 1** : an authoritative call to appear at a designated place or to attend to a duty **2** : a warning or citation to appear in court at a specified time to answer charges

sump·tu·ous \ˈsəmp-shə-wəs, -chə-\ *adj* : LAVISH, LUXURIOUS

sum up *vb* : SUMMARIZE

¹**sun** \ˈsən\ *n* **1** : the shining celestial body around which the earth and other planets revolve and from which they receive light and heat **2** : a celestial body like the sun **3** : SUNSHINE — **sun·less** *adj* — **sun·ny** *adj*

²**sun** *vb* **sunned; sun·ning 1** : to expose to or as if to the rays of the sun **2** : to sun oneself

Sun *abbr* Sunday

sun·bath \ˈsən-ˌbath, -ˌbáth\ *n* : an exposure to sunlight or a sunlamp — **sun·bathe** \-ˌbāth\ *vb*

sun·beam \-ˌbēm\ *n* : a ray of sunlight

sun·block \ˈsən-ˌbläk\ *n* : a preparation for blocking out more of the sun's rays than a sunscreen

sun·bon·net \-ˌbä-nət\ *n* : a bonnet with a wide brim to shield the face and neck from the sun

¹**sun·burn** \-ˌbərn\ *vb* **-burned** \-ˌbərnd\ *or* **-burnt** \-ˌbərnt\; **-burn·ing** : to cause or become affected with sunburn

²**sunburn** *n* : a skin inflammation caused by overexposure to sunlight

sun·dae \ˈsən-(ˌ)dā, -dē\ *n* : ice cream served with topping

Sun·day \ˈsən-dē, -ˌdā\ *n* : the 1st day of the week : the Christian Sabbath

sun·der \ˈsən-dər\ *vb* : to force apart **syn** sever, part, disjoin, disunite

sun·di·al \-ˌdī(-ə)l\ *n* : a device for showing the time of day from the shadow cast on a plate by an object with a straight edge

sun·down \-ˌdaún\ *n* : SUNSET 2

sun·dries \ˈsən-drēz\ *n pl* : various small articles or items

sun·dry \ˈsən-drē\ *adj* : SEVERAL, DIVERS, VARIOUS

sun·fish \ˈsən-ˌfish\ *n* **1** : a huge marine fish with a deep flattened body **2** : any of numerous often brightly colored American freshwater fishes related to the perches and usu. having the body flattened from side to side

sun·flow·er \-ˌflaú-ər\ *n* : any of a genus of tall New World plants related to the daisies and often grown for the oil-rich seeds of their yellow-petaled dark-centered flower heads

sung *past and past part of* SING

sun·glasses \ˈsən-ˌgla-səz\ *n pl* : glasses to protect the eyes from the sun

sunk *past and past part of* SINK

sunk·en \ˈsəŋ-kən\ *adj* **1** : SUBMERGED **2** : fallen in : HOLLOW ⟨∼ cheeks⟩ **3** : lying in a depression ⟨∼ garden⟩; *also* : constructed below the general floor level ⟨∼ living room⟩

sun·lamp \ˈsən-ˌlamp\ *n* : an electric lamp designed to emit radiation of wavelengths from ultraviolet to infrared

sun·light \-ˌlīt\ *n* : SUNSHINE

sun·lit \-ˌlit\ *adj* : lighted by or as if by the sun

sun·rise \-ˌrīz\ *n* **1** : the apparent rising of the sun above the horizon **2** : the time at which the sun rises

sun·roof \-ˌrüf, -ˌrúf\ *n* : a panel in an automobile roof that can be opened

sun·screen \-ˌskrēn\ *n* : a substance used in suntan preparations to protect the skin

sun·set \-ˌset\ *n* **1** : the apparent descent of the sun below the horizon **2** : the time at which the sun sets

sun·shade \ˈsən-ˌshād\ *n* : something (as a parasol or awning) used as a protection from the sun's rays

sun·shine \-ˌshīn\ *n* : the direct light of the sun — **sun·shiny** *adj*

sun·spot \-ˌspät\ *n* : any of the dark spots that appear from time to time on the sun's surface

sun·stroke \-ˌstrōk\ *n* : heatstroke caused by direct exposure to the sun

sun·tan \-ˌtan\ *n* : a browning of the skin from exposure to the sun's rays

sun·up \-ˌəp\ *n* : SUNRISE 2

¹**sup** \ˈsəp\ *vb* **supped; sup·ping** : to take or drink in swallows or gulps

²**sup** *n* : a mouthful esp. of liquor or broth; *also* : a small quantity of liquid

³**sup** *vb* **supped; sup·ping 1** : to eat the evening meal **2** : to make one's supper ⟨*supped* on roast beef⟩

⁴**sup** *abbr* **1** superior **2** supplement; supplementary **3** supply **4** supra

¹**su·per** \ˈsü-pər\ *n* : SUPERINTENDENT

²**super** *adj* **1** : very fine : EXCELLENT **2** : EXTREME, EXCESSIVE

super- \ˌsü-pər\ *prefix* **1** : over and above : higher in quantity, quality, or degree than : more than **2** : in addition : extra **3** : exceeding a norm **4** : in excessive degree or intensity **5** : surpassing all or most others of its kind **6** : situated above, on, or at the top of **7** : next above or higher **8** : more inclusive than **9** : superior in status or position

superabsorbent
superachiever
superagency
superblock
superbomb
supercity
superclean
superexpensive
superfine
superheat
superheavy
superhero

superhuman
superhumanly
superindividual
superliner
superman
supermom
supernormal
superpatriot
superpatriotic
superpatriotism
superpremium
superrich

supersalesman
supersecret
supersize
supersized
supersmart
supersophisticated
superspy
superstar
superstate

superstore
superstratum
superstrength
superstrong
supersubtle
supersystem
supertanker
superthin
superwoman

su·per·abun·dant \ˌsü-pər-ə-ˈbən-dənt\ adj : more than ample — **su·per·abun·dance** \-dəns\ n

su·per·an·nu·ate \ˌsü-pər-ˈan-yə-ˌwāt\ vb **-at·ed; -at·ing 1** : to make out-of-date **2** : to retire and pension because of age or infirmity — **su·per·an·nu·at·ed** adj

su·perb \su̇-ˈpərb\ adj [L superbus excellent, proud, fr. super above] : marked to the highest degree by excellence, brilliance, or competence **syn** resplendent, glorious, gorgeous, sublime — **su·perb·ly** adv

su·per·charg·er \ˈsü-pər-ˌchär-jər\ n : a device for increasing the amount of air supplied to an internal combustion engine

su·per·cil·ious \ˌsü-pər-ˈsi-lē-əs\ adj [L superciliosus, fr. supercilium eyebrow, haughtiness] : haughtily contemptuous **syn** disdainful, overbearing, arrogant, lordly, superior

su·per·com·pu·ter \ˈsü-pər-kəm-ˌpyü-tər\ n : a large very fast mainframe

su·per·con·duc·tiv·i·ty \ˌsü-pər-ˌkän-ˌdək-ˈti-və-tē\ n : a complete disappearance of electrical resistance in a substance esp. at very low temperatures — **su·per·con·duc·tive** \-kən-ˈdək-tiv\ adj — **su·per·con·duc·tor** \-ˈdək-tər\ n

su·per·con·ti·nent \ˈsü-pər-ˌkänt-ᵊn-ənt\ n : a former large continent from which other continents are held to have broken off and drifted away

su·per·ego \ˌsü-pər-ˈē-gō\ n : the one of the three divisions of the psyche in psychoanalytic theory that functions to reward and punish through a system of moral attitudes, conscience, and a sense of guilt

su·per·fi·cial \ˌsü-pər-ˈfi-shəl\ adj **1** : of or relating to the surface or appearance only **2** : not thorough : SHALLOW — **su·per·fi·ci·al·i·ty** \-ˌfi-shē-ˈa-lə-tē\ n — **su·per·fi·cial·ly** adv

su·per·flu·ous \su̇-ˈpər-flə-wəs\ adj : exceeding what is sufficient or necessary : SURPLUS **syn** extra, spare, supernumerary — **su·per·flu·i·ty** \ˌsü-pər-ˈflü-ə-tē\ n

su·per·high·way \ˌsü-pər-ˈhī-ˌwā\ n : a broad highway designed for high-speed traffic

su·per·im·pose \-im-ˈpōz\ vb : to lay (one thing) over or above something else

su·per·in·tend \ˌsü-pə-rin-ˈtend\ vb : to have or exercise the charge and oversight of : DIRECT — **su·per·in·ten·dence** \-ˈten-dəns\ n — **su·per·in·ten·den·cy** \-dən-sē\ n — **su·per·in·ten·dent** \-dənt\ n

¹su·pe·ri·or \su̇-ˈpir-ē-ər\ adj **1** : situated higher up, over, or near the top; also : higher in rank or numbers **2** : of greater value or importance **3** : courageously indifferent (as to pain or misfortune) **4** : better than most others of its kind **5** : ARROGANT, HAUGHTY — **su·pe·ri·or·i·ty** \-ˌpir-ē-ˈȯr-ə-tē\ n

²superior n **1** : one who is above another in rank, office, or station; esp : the head of a religious house or order **2** : one higher in quality or merit **3** : SUPERSCRIPT

¹su·per·la·tive \su̇-ˈpər-lə-tiv\ adj **1** : of, relating to, or constituting the degree of grammatical comparison that denotes an extreme or unsurpassed level or extent **2** : surpassing others : SUPREME **syn** peerless, incomparable, superb — **su·per·la·tive·ly** adv

²superlative n **1** : the superlative degree or a superlative form in a language **2** : the utmost degree : ACME

su·per·mar·ket \ˈsü-pər-ˌmär-kət\ n : a self-service retail market selling foods and household merchandise

su·per·nal \su̇-ˈpər-nəl\ adj **1** : being or coming from on high **2** : of heavenly or spiritual character

su·per·nat·u·ral \ˌsü-pər-ˈna-chə-rəl\ adj : of or relating to phenomena beyond or outside of nature; esp : relating to or attributed to a divinity, ghost, or devil — **su·per·nat·u·ral·ly** adv

su·per·no·va \ˌsü-pər-ˈnō-və\ n : the explosion of a very large star

¹su·per·nu·mer·ary \-ˈnü-mə-ˌrer-ē, -ˈnyü-\ adj : exceeding the usual or required number : EXTRA **syn** surplus, superfluous, spare

²supernumerary n, pl **-ar·ies** : an extra person or thing; esp : an actor hired for a nonspeaking part

su·per·pose \ˌsü-pər-ˈpōz\ vb **-posed; -pos·ing** : SUPERIMPOSE — **su·per·po·si·tion** \-pə-ˈzi-shən\ n

su·per·pow·er \ˈsü-pər-ˌpau̇-ər\ n **1** : excessive or superior power **2** : one of a few politically and militarily dominant nations

su·per·sat·u·rat·ed \-ˈsa-chə-ˌrā-təd\ adj : containing an amount of a substance greater than that required for saturation

su·per·scribe \ˈsü-pər-ˌskrīb, ˌsü-pər-ˈskrīb\ vb **-scribed; -scrib·ing** : to write on the top or outside : ADDRESS — **su·per·scrip·tion** \ˌsü-pər-ˈskrip-shən\ n

su·per·script \ˈsü-pər-ˌskript\ n : a symbol (as a numeral or letter) written immediately above or above and to one side of another character

su·per·sede \ˌsü-pər-ˈsēd\ vb **-sed·ed; -sed·ing** [MF superseder to refrain from, fr. L supersedēre to be superior to, refrain from, fr. super- above + sedēre to sit] : to take the place of : REPLACE

su·per·son·ic \-ˈsä-nik\ adj **1** : ULTRASONIC **2** : being or relating to speeds from one to five times the speed of sound; also : capable of moving at such a speed ⟨a ~ airplane⟩

su·per·sti·tion \ˌsü-pər-ˈsti-shən\ n **1** : beliefs or practices resulting from ignorance, fear of the unknown, or trust in magic or chance **2** : an unreasoning fear of nature, the unknown, or God resulting from superstition — **su·per·sti·tious** \-shəs\ adj

su·per·struc·ture \ˈsü-pər-ˌstrək-chər\ n : something built on a base or as a vertical extension

su·per·vene \ˌsü-pər-ˈvēn\ vb **-vened; -ven·ing** : to occur as something additional or unexpected

su·per·vise \ˈsü-pər-ˌvīz\ vb **-vised; -vis·ing** : OVERSEE, SUPERINTEND — **su·per·vi·sion** \ˌsü-pər-ˈvi-zhən\ n — **su·per·vi·sor** \ˈsü-pər-ˌvī-zər\ n — **su·per·vi·so·ry** \ˌsü-pər-ˈvī-zə-rē\ adj

su·pine \su̇-ˈpīn\ adj **1** : lying on the back or with the face upward **2** : LETHARGIC, SLUGGISH; also : ABJECT **syn** inactive, inert, passive, idle

supp or **suppl** abbr supplement; supplementary

sup·per \ˈsə-pər\ n : the evening meal esp. when dinner is taken at midday — **sup·per·time** \-ˌtīm\ n

sup·plant \sə-ˈplant\ vb **1** : to take the place of (another) esp. by force or trickery **2** : REPLACE

sup·ple \ˈsə-pəl\ adj **sup·pler; sup·plest 1** : COMPLIANT, ADAPTABLE **2** : capable of bending without breaking or creasing : LIMBER **syn** resilient, elastic, flexible

¹sup·ple·ment \ˈsə-plə-mənt\ n **1** : something that supplies a want or makes an addition **2** : a continuation (as of a book) containing corrections or additional material — **sup·ple·men·tal** \ˌsə-plə-ˈment-ᵊl\ adj — **sup·ple·men·ta·ry** \-ˈmen-tə-rē\ adj

²sup·ple·ment \ˈsə-plə-ˌment\ vb : to fill up the deficiencies of : add to

sup·pli·ant \ˈsə-plē-ənt\ n : one who supplicates : PETITIONER, PLEADER

\ə\abut \ᵊ\kitten \ər\further \a\ash \ā\ace \ä\mop, mar \au̇\out \ch\chin \e\bet \ē\easy \g\go \i\hit \ī\ice \j\job \ŋ\sing \ō\go \ȯ\law \ȯi\boy \th\thin \th\the \ü\loot \u̇\foot \y\yet \zh\vision see also Pronunciation Symbols page

sup·pli·cant \'sə-pli-kənt\ *n* : SUPPLIANT

sup·pli·cate \'sə-plə-ˌkāt\ *vb* **-cat·ed; -cat·ing 1** : to make a humble entreaty; *esp* : to pray to God **2** : to ask earnestly and humbly : BESEECH **syn** implore, beg, entreat, plead — **sup·pli·ca·tion** \ˌsə-plə-'kā-shən\ *n*

¹**sup·ply** \sə-'plī\ *vb* **sup·plied; sup·ply·ing** [ME *supplien*, fr. MF *soupleier*, fr. L *supplēre* to fill up, supplement, supply, fr. *sub-* under, up to + *plēre* to fill] **1** : to add as a supplement **2** : to satisfy the needs of **3** : FURNISH, PROVIDE — **sup·pli·er** *n*

²**supply** *n, pl* **supplies 1** : the quantity or amount (as of a commodity) needed or available; *also* : PROVISIONS, STORES — usu. used in pl. **2** : the act or process of filling a want or need : PROVISION **3** : the quantities of goods or services offered for sale at a particular time or at one price

sup·ply–side \sə-'plī-ˌsīd\ *adj* : of, relating to, or being an economic theory that recommends the reduction of tax rates to expand economic activity

¹**sup·port** \sə-'pōrt\ *vb* **1** : BEAR, TOLERATE **2** : to take sides with : BACK, ASSIST **3** : to provide with food, clothing, and shelter **4** : to hold up or serve as a foundation for **syn** uphold, advocate, champion — **sup·port·able** *adj* — **sup·port·er** *n*

²**support** *n* **1** : the act of supporting : the state of being supported **2** : one that supports : PROP, BASE

support group *n* : a group of people with common experiences and concerns who provide emotional and moral support for one another

sup·pose \sə-'pōz\ *vb* **sup·posed; sup·pos·ing 1** : to assume to be true (as for the sake of argument) **2** : EXPECT ⟨I am *supposed* to go⟩ **3** : to think probable — **sup·pos·al** *n*

sup·posed \sə-'pōzd, -'pō-zəd\ *adj* : BELIEVED; *also* : mistakenly believed — **sup·pos·ed·ly** \-'pō-zəd-lē, -'pōzd-lē\ *adv*

sup·pos·ing *conj* : if by way of hypothesis : on the assumption that

sup·po·si·tion \ˌsə-pə-'zi-shən\ *n* **1** : something that is supposed : HYPOTHESIS **2** : the act of supposing

sup·pos·i·to·ry \sə-'pä-zə-ˌtōr-ē\ *n, pl* **-ries** [ML *suppositorium*, fr. LL, neut. of *suppositorius* placed beneath] : a small easily melted mass of usu. medicated material for insertion (as into the rectum)

sup·press \sə-'pres\ *vb* **1** : to put down by authority or force : SUBDUE ⟨~ a revolt⟩ **2** : to keep from being known; *also* : to stop the publication or circulation of **3** : to hold back : REPRESS ⟨~ anger⟩ ⟨~ a cough⟩ — **sup·press·ible** \-'pre-sə-bəl\ *adj* — **sup·pres·sion** \-'pre-shən\ *n*

sup·pres·sant \sə-'pres-ᵊnt\ *n* : an agent (as a drug) suppressing rather than eliminating something (a cough ~)

sup·pu·rate \'sə-pyə-ˌrāt\ *vb* **-rat·ed; -rat·ing** : to form or give off pus — **sup·pu·ra·tion** \ˌsə-pyə-'rā-shən\ *n*

su·pra \'sü-prə, -ˌprä\ *adv* : earlier in this writing : ABOVE

su·pra·na·tion·al \ˌsü-prə-'na-shə-nəl, -ˌprä-\ *adj* : going beyond national boundaries, authority, or interests ⟨~ organizations⟩

su·prem·a·cist \sú-'pre-mə-sist\ *n* : an advocate of group supremacy

su·prem·a·cy \sú-'pre-mə-sē\ *n, pl* **-cies** : supreme rank, power, or authority

su·preme \sú-'prēm\ *adj* [L *supremus*, superl. of *superus* upper, fr. *super* over, above] **1** : highest in rank or authority **2** : highest in degree or quality ⟨~ among poets⟩ **3** : ULTIMATE ⟨the ~ sacrifice⟩ **syn** superlative, surpassing, peerless, incomparable — **su·preme·ly** *adv* — **su·preme·ness** *n*

Supreme Being *n* : GOD 1

supreme court *n* : the highest court in a political unit (as the U.S. or one of its states)

supt *abbr* superintendent

sur·cease \'sər-ˌsēs\ *n* : CESSATION, RESPITE

¹**sur·charge** \'sər-ˌchärj\ *vb* **1** : to fill to excess : OVERLOAD **2** : to apply a surcharge to (postage stamps)

²**surcharge** *n* **1** : an extra fee or cost **2** : an excessive load or burden **3** : something officially printed on a postage stamp esp. to change its value

sur·cin·gle \'sər-ˌsiŋ-gəl\ *n* : a band put around a horse's body to make something (as a saddle) fast

¹**sure** \'shùr\ *adj* **sur·er; sur·est** [ME, fr. MF *sur*, fr. L *securus* secure] **1** : firmly established **2** : TRUSTWORTHY, RELIABLE **3** : CONFIDENT **4** : not to be disputed : UNDOUBTED **5** : bound to happen **6** : careful to remember or attend to something ⟨be ~ to lock the door⟩ **syn** certain, cocksure, positive — **sure·ness** *n*

²**sure** *adv* : SURELY

sure·fire \'shùr-'fīr\ *adj* : certain to get results : DEPENDABLE

sure·ly \'shùr-lē\ *adv* **1** : in a sure manner **2** : without doubt **3** : INDEED, REALLY

sure·ty \'shùr-ə-tē\ *n, pl* **-ties 1** : SURENESS, CERTAINTY **2** : something that makes sure : GUARANTEE **3** : one who is a guarantor for another person

¹**surf** \'sərf\ *n* **1** : waves that break upon the shore; *also* : the sound or foam of breaking waves

²**surf** *vb* : to ride the surf (as on a surfboard) — **surf·er** *n* — **surf·ing** *n*

¹**sur·face** \'sər-fəs\ *n* **1** : the outside of an object or body **2** : outward aspect or appearance — **surface** *adj*

²**surface** *vb* **sur·faced; sur·fac·ing 1** : to give a surface to : make smooth **2** : to rise to the surface

surf·board \'sərf-ˌbōrd\ *n* : a buoyant board used in surfing

¹**sur·feit** \'sər-fət\ *n* **1** : EXCESS, SUPERABUNDANCE **2** : excessive indulgence (as in food or drink) **3** : disgust caused by excess

²**surfeit** *vb* : to feed, supply, or indulge to the point of surfeit : CLOY

surg *abbr* surgeon; surgery; surgical

¹**surge** \'sərj\ *vb* **surged; surg·ing 1** : to rise and fall actively : TOSS **2** : to move in waves **3** : to rise suddenly to an excessive or abnormal value

²**surge** *n* **1** : a sweeping onward like a wave of the sea ⟨~ of emotion⟩ **2** : a large billow **3** : a transient sudden increase of current or voltage in an electrical circuit

sur·geon \'sər-jən\ *n* : a physician who specializes in surgery

sur·gery \'sər-jə-rē\ *n, pl* **-ger·ies** [ME *surgerie*, fr. OF *cirurgie, surgerie*, fr. L *chirurgia*, fr. Gk *cheirourgia*, fr. *cheirourgos* surgeon, fr. *cheirourgos* doing by hand, fr. *cheir* hand + *ergon* work] **1** : a branch of medicine concerned with the correction of physical defects, the repair of injuries, and the treatment of disease esp. by operations **2** : a room or area where surgery is performed **3** : the work done by a surgeon

sur·gi·cal \'sər-ji-kəl\ *adj* : of, relating to, or associated with surgeons or surgery — **sur·gi·cal·ly** \-k(ə-)lē\ *adv*

sur·ly \'sər-lē\ *adj* **sur·li·er; -est** [alter. of ME *sirly* lordly, imperious, fr. *sir*] : having a rude unfriendly disposition **syn** morose, glum, sullen, sulky, gloomy — **sur·li·ness** \-lē-nəs\ *n*

sur·mise \sər-'mīz\ *vb* **sur·mised; sur·mis·ing** : GUESS **syn** conjecture, presume, suppose — **surmise** *n*

sur·mount \sər-'maùnt\ *vb* **1** : to prevail over : OVERCOME **2** : to get to or lie at the top of

sur·name \'sər-ˌnām\ *n* **1** : NICKNAME **2** : the name borne in common by members of a family

sur·pass \sər-'pas\ *vb* **1** : to be superior to in quality, degree, or performance : EXCEL **2** : to go beyond the reach or powers of **syn** transcend, outdo, outstrip, exceed — **sur·pass·ing·ly** *adv*

sur·plice \'sər-pləs\ *n* : a loose white outer garment worn at church services

sur·plus \'sər-(ˌ)pləs\ *n* **1** : quantity left over : EXCESS **2**

: the excess of assets over liabilities **syn** superfluity, overabundance, surfeit

¹**sur·prise** \sər-ˈprīz\ *n* **1** : an attack made without warning **2** : a taking unawares **3** : something that surprises **4** : AMAZEMENT, ASTONISHMENT

²**surprise** *also* **sur·prize** *vb* **sur·prised; sur·pris·ing 1** : to come upon and attack unexpectedly **2** : to take unawares **3** : AMAZE **4** : to cause astonishment or surprise **syn** astonish, astound, dumbfound — **sur·pris·ing** *adj*

sur·pris·ing·ly \-ˈprī-ziŋ-lē\ *adv* **1** : in a surprising manner or degree **2** : it is surprising that

sur·re·al \sə-ˈrē-əl, -ˈrēl\ *adj* **1** : having the intense irrational reality of a dream **2** : of or relating to surrealism

sur·re·al·ism \sə-ˈrē-ə-ˌli-zəm\ *n* : art, literature, or theater characterized by fantastic or incongruous imagery or effects produced by unnatural juxtapositions and combinations — **sur·re·al·ist** \-list\ *n or adj* — **sur·re·al·is·tic** \sə-ˌrē-ə-ˈlis-tik\ *adj* — **sur·re·al·is·ti·cal·ly** \-ti-k(ə-)lē\ *adv*

¹**sur·ren·der** \sə-ˈren-dər\ *vb* **-dered; -der·ing 1** : to yield to the power of another : give up under compulsion **2** : RELINQUISH

²**surrender** *n* : the act of giving up or yielding oneself or the possession of something to another

sur·rep·ti·tious \ˌsər-əp-ˈti-shəs\ *adj* : done, made, or acquired by stealth : CLANDESTINE **syn** underhand, covert, furtive — **sur·rep·ti·tious·ly** *adv*

sur·rey \ˈsər-ē\ *n, pl* **surreys** : a 2-seated horse⹀drawn carriage

surrey

sur·ro·ga·cy \ˈsər-ə-gə-sē\ *n* : SURROGATE MOTHERHOOD

sur·ro·gate \ˈsər-ə-ˌgāt, -gət\ *n* **1** : DEPUTY, SUBSTITUTE **2** : a law officer in some states with authority in the probate of wills, the settlement of estates, and the appointment of guardians **3** : SURROGATE MOTHER

surrogate mother *n* : a woman who becomes pregnant (as by surgical implantation of a fertilized egg) in order to carry the fetus for another woman — **surrogate motherhood** *n*

sur·round \sə-ˈraund\ *vb* **1** : to enclose on all sides : ENCIRCLE **2** : to enclose so as to cut off retreat or escape

sur·round·ings \sə-ˈraun-diŋz\ *n pl* : conditions by which one is surrounded

sur·tax \ˈsər-ˌtaks\ *n* : an additional tax over and above a normal tax

sur·tout \(ˌ)sər-ˈtü\ *n* [F, fr. *sur* over (fr. L *super*) + *tout* all, fr. L *totus* whole] : a man's long close-fitting overcoat

surv *abbr* survey; surveying; surveyor

sur·veil·lance \sər-ˈvā-ləns\ *n* [F] : close watch; *also* : SUPERVISION

¹**sur·vey** \sər-ˈvā\ *vb* **sur·veyed; sur·vey·ing 1** : to look over and examine closely **2** : to find and represent the contours, measurements, and position of a part of the earth's surface (as a tract of land) **3** : to view or study

something as a whole **syn** scrutinize, examine, inspect, study — **sur·vey·or** \-ər\ *n*

²**sur·vey** \ˈsər-ˌvā\ *n, pl* **surveys** : the act or an instance of surveying; *also* : something that is surveyed

sur·vive \sər-ˈvīv\ *vb* **sur·vived; sur·viv·ing 1** : to remain alive or existent **2** : OUTLIVE, OUTLAST — **sur·viv·al** *n* — **sur·vi·vor** \-ˈvī-vər\ *n*

sus·cep·ti·ble \sə-ˈsep-tə-bəl\ *adj* **1** : of such a nature as to permit ⟨words ∼ of being misunderstood⟩ **2** : having little resistance to a stimulus or agency ⟨∼ to colds⟩ **3** : IMPRESSIONABLE, RESPONSIVE **syn** sensitive, subject, exposed, prone, liable, open — **sus·cep·ti·bil·i·ty** \-ˌsep-tə-ˈbi-lə-tē\ *n*

su·shi \ˈsü-shē\ *n* [Jp] : cold rice formed into various shapes and garnished esp. with bits of raw fish or seafood

¹**sus·pect** \ˈsəs-ˌpekt, sə-ˈspekt\ *adj* : regarded with suspicion; *also* : QUESTIONABLE

²**sus·pect** \ˈsəs-ˌpekt\ *n* : one who is suspected (as of a crime)

³**sus·pect** \sə-ˈspekt\ *vb* **1** : to have doubts of : MISTRUST **2** : to imagine to be guilty without proof **3** : SURMISE

sus·pend \sə-ˈspend\ *vb* **1** : to bar temporarily from a privilege, office, or function **2** : to stop temporarily : make inactive for a time **3** : to withhold ⟨judgment⟩ for a time **4** : HANG; *esp* : to hang so as to be free except at one point **5** : to keep from falling or sinking by some invisible support

sus·pend·er \sə-ˈspen-dər\ *n* : one of two supporting straps which pass over the shoulders and to which the trousers are fastened

sus·pense \sə-ˈspens\ *n* **1** : SUSPENSION **2** : mental uncertainty : ANXIETY **3** : excitement as to an outcome — **sus·pense·ful** *adj*

sus·pen·sion \sə-ˈspen-chən\ *n* **1** : the act of suspending : the state or period of being suspended **2** : the state of a substance when its particles are mixed with but undissolved in a fluid or solid; *also* : a substance in this state **3** : something suspended **4** : a device by which something is suspended

sus·pen·so·ry \sə-ˈspen-sə-rē\ *adj* **1** : SUSPENDED; *also* : fitted or serving to suspend something **2** : temporarily leaving undetermined

sus·pi·cion \sə-ˈspi-shən\ *n* **1** : the act or an instance of suspecting something wrong without proof **2** : TRACE, SOUPÇON **syn** mistrust, uncertainty, doubt, skepticism

sus·pi·cious \sə-ˈspi-shəs\ *adj* **1** : open to or arousing suspicion **2** : inclined to suspect **3** : showing suspicion — **sus·pi·cious·ly** *adv*

sus·tain \sə-ˈstān\ *vb* **1** : to provide with nourishment **2** : to keep going : PROLONG ⟨∼ed effort⟩ **3** : to hold up : PROP **4** : to hold up under : ENDURE **5** : SUFFER ⟨∼ a broken arm⟩ **6** : to support as true, legal, or valid **7** : PROVE, CORROBORATE — **sus·tain·able** \səs-ˈtā-nə-bəl\ *adj*

sus·te·nance \ˈsəs-tə-nəns\ *n* **1** : FOOD, NOURISHMENT **2** : a supplying with the necessities of life **3** : something that sustains or supports

su·ture \ˈsü-chər\ *n* **1** : material or a stitch for sewing a wound together **2** : a seam or line along which two things or parts are joined by or as if by sewing

su·zer·ain \ˈsü-zə-rən, -ˌrān\ *n* [F] **1** : a feudal lord **2** : a nation that has political control over the foreign relations of another nation — **su·zer·ain·ty** \-tē\ *n*

svc *or* **svce** *abbr* service

svelte \ˈsfelt\ *adj* [F, fr. It *svelto*, fr. pp. of *svellere* to pluck out, modif. of L *evellere*, fr. *e-* out + *vellere* to pluck] : SLENDER, LITHE

\ə\abut \ᵊ\kitten \ər\further \a\ash \ā\ace \ä\mop, mar
\aù\out \ch\chin \e\bet \ē\easy \g\go \i\hit \ī\ice \j\job
\ŋ\sing \ō\go \ò\law \òi\boy \th\thin \ṯh\the \ü\loot \ù\foot
\y\yet \zh\vision *see also* Pronunciation Symbols page

svgs *abbr* savings

SW *abbr* **1** shortwave **2** southwest

¹**swab** \'swäb\ *n* **1** : MOP **2** : a wad of absorbent material esp. for applying medicine or for cleaning; *also* : a sample taken with a swab **3** : SAILOR

²**swab** *vb* **swabbed; swab·bing** : to use a swab on : MOP

swad·dle \'swäd-°l\ *vb* **swad·dled; swad·dling 1** : to bind (an infant) in bands of cloth **2** : to wrap up : SWATHE

swaddling clothes *n pl* : bands of cloth wrapped around an infant

swag \'swag\ *n* : stolen goods : LOOT

swag·ger \'swa-gər\ *vb* **1** : to walk with a conceited swing or strut **2** : BOAST, BRAG — **swagger** *n*

Swa·hi·li \swä-'hē-lē\ *n* : a language that is a trade and governmental language over much of East Africa and the Congo region

swain \'swān\ *n* [ME *swein* boy, servant, fr. ON *sveinn*] **1** : RUSTIC; *esp* : SHEPHERD **2** : ADMIRER, SUITOR

SWAK *abbr* sealed with a kiss

¹**swal·low** \'swä-lō\ *n* : any of numerous small long-winged migratory birds that often have a deeply forked tail

²**swallow** *vb* **1** : to take into the stomach through the throat **2** : to envelop or take in as if by swallowing **3** : to accept or believe without question, protest, or anger

³**swallow** *n* **1** : an act of swallowing **2** : an amount that can be swallowed at one time

swal·low·tail \'swä-lō-ˌtāl\ *n* **1** : a deeply forked and tapering tail like that of a swallow **2** : TAILCOAT **3** : any of various large butterflies with the border of each hind wing usu. drawn out into a process resembling a tail — **swal·low–tailed** \-ˌtāld\ *adj*

swam *past of* SWIM

swa·mi \'swä-mē\ *n* [Hindi *svāmī*, fr. Skt *svāmin* owner, lord] : a Hindu ascetic or religious teacher

¹**swamp** \'swämp\ *n* : a spongy wetland — **swamp** *adj* — **swampy** *adj*

²**swamp** *vb* **1** : to fill or become filled with or as if with water **2** : OVERWHELM **3**

swamp·land \-ˌland\ *n* : SWAMP

swan \'swän\ *n, pl* **swans** *also* **swan** : any of various heavy-bodied long-necked mostly pure white swimming birds related to the geese

¹**swank** \'swaŋk\ *or* **swanky** \'swaŋ-kē\ *adj* **swank·er** *or* **swank·i·er; -est** : showily smart and dashing; *also* : fashionably elegant

²**swank** *n* **1** : PRETENTIOUSNESS **2** : ELEGANCE

swans·down \'swänz-ˌdaůn\ *n* **1** : the very soft down of a swan used esp. for trimming **2** : a soft thick cotton flannel

swan song *n* : a farewell appearance, act, or pronouncement

swap \'swäp\ *vb* **swapped; swap·ping** : TRADE, EXCHANGE — **swap** *n*

sward \'swȯrd\ *n* : the grassy surface of land

¹**swarm** \'swȯrm\ *n* **1** : a great number of honeybees leaving together from a hive with a queen to start a new colony; *also* : a hive of bees **2** : a large crowd

²**swarm** *vb* **1** : to form in a swarm and depart from a hive **2** : to throng together : gather in great numbers

swart \'swȯrt\ *adj* : SWARTHY

swar·thy \'swȯr-thē, -thē\ *adj* **swar·thi·er; -est** : dark in color or complexion : dark-skinned

swash \'swäsh\ *vb* : to move about with a splashing sound — **swash** *n*

swash·buck·ler \-ˌbə-klər\ *n* : a swaggering or daring soldier or adventurer — **swash·buck·ling** *adj*

swas·ti·ka \'swäs-ti-kə\ *n* [Skt *svastika*, fr. *svasti* well-being, fr. *su-* well + *as-* to be] : a symbol or ornament in the form of a cross with the ends of the arms bent at right angles

swat \'swät\ *vb* **swat·ted; swat·ting** : to hit sharply ⟨~ a fly⟩ ⟨~ a ball⟩ — **swat** *n* — **swat·ter** *n*

SWAT *abbr* Special Weapons and Tactics

swatch \'swäch\ *n* : a sample piece (as of fabric) or a collection of samples

swath \'swäth, 'swȯth\ *or* **swathe** \'swäth, 'swȯth, 'swäth\ *n* [ME, fr. OE *swæth* footstep, trace] **1** : a row of cut grass or grain **2** : the sweep of a scythe or mowing machine or the path cut in mowing

swathe \'swäth, 'swȯth, 'swäth\ *vb* **swathed; swath·ing** : to bind or wrap with or as if with a bandage

¹**sway** \'swā\ *n* **1** : a gentle swinging from side to side **2** : controlling influence or power : DOMINION

²**sway** *vb* **1** : to swing gently from side to side **2** : RULE, GOVERN **3** : to cause to swing from side to side **4** : BEND, SWERVE; *also* : INFLUENCE **syn** oscillate, fluctuate, vibrate, waver

sway·backed \'swā-ˌbakt\ *also* **sway·back** \-ˌbak\ *adj* : having an abnormally sagging back ⟨a ~ mare⟩ — **swayback** *n*

swear \'swar\ *vb* **swore** \'swȯr\; **sworn** \'swȯrn\; **swear·ing 1** : to make a solemn statement or promise under oath **2** : to assert or promise emphatically or earnestly **3** : to administer an oath to **4** : to bind by or as if by an oath **5** : to use profane or obscene language — **swear·er** *n*

swear in *vb* : to induct into office by administration of an oath

sweat \'swet\ *vb* **sweat** *or* **sweat·ed; sweat·ing 1** : to excrete salty moisture from glands of the skin : PERSPIRE **2** : to form drops of moisture on the surface **3** : to work so that one sweats : TOIL **4** : to cause to sweat **5** : to draw out or get rid of by or as if by sweating **6** : to make a person overwork — **sweat** *n* — **sweaty** *adj*

sweat·er \'swe-tər\ *n* **1** : one that sweats **2** : a knitted or crocheted jacket or pullover

sweat·shirt \'swet-ˌshərt\ *n* : a loose collarless pullover usu. of heavy cotton jersey

sweat·shop \'swet-ˌshäp\ *n* : a shop or factory in which workers are employed for long hours at low wages and under unhealthy conditions

Swed *abbr* Sweden

swede \'swēd\ *n* **1** *cap* : a native or inhabitant of Sweden **2** *chiefly Brit* : RUTABAGA

Swed·ish \'swē-dish\ *n* **1** : the language of Sweden **2** **Swedish** *pl* : the people of Sweden — **Swedish** *adj*

¹**sweep** \'swēp\ *vb* **swept** \'swept\; **sweep·ing 1** : to remove or clean by or as if by brushing **2** : to destroy completely; *also* : to remove or take with a single swift movement **3** : to remove from sight or consideration **4** : to move over with speed and force ⟨the tide *swept* over the shore⟩ **5** : to win an overwhelming victory in; *also* : to win all the games or contests of **6** : to move or extend in a wide curve — **sweep·er** *n*

²**sweep** *n* **1** : something (as a long oar) that operates with a sweeping motion **2** : a clearing off or away **3** : a winning of all the contests or prizes in a competition **4** : a sweeping movement **5** : CURVE, BEND **6** : RANGE, SCOPE

sweep·ing *adj* : EXTENSIVE ⟨~ reforms⟩; *also* : indiscriminately inclusive ⟨~ generalities⟩

sweep·ings \'swē-piŋz\ *n pl* : things collected by sweeping

sweep–sec·ond hand \'swēp-ˌse-kənd-\ *n* : a hand marking seconds on a timepiece

sweep·stakes \'swēp-ˌstāks\ *also* **sweep·stake** \-ˌstāk\ *n, pl* **sweepstakes 1** : a race or contest in which the entire prize may go to the winner **2** : any of various lotteries

¹**sweet** \'swēt\ *adj* **1** : being or causing the one of the four basic taste sensations that is caused esp. by table sugar and is identified esp. by the taste buds at the front of the tongue; *also* : pleasing to the taste **2** : AGREEABLE **3** : pleasing to a sense other than taste ⟨a ~ smell⟩ ⟨~ music⟩ **4** : not stale or spoiled : WHOLESOME ⟨~ milk⟩ **5** : not salted ⟨~ butter⟩ — **sweet·ish** *adj* — **sweet·ly** *adv* — **sweet·ness** *n*

²**sweet** *n* **1** : something sweet : CANDY **2** : DARLING
sweet·bread \'swēt-ˌbred\ *n* : the pancreas or thymus of an animal (as a calf or lamb) used for food
sweet·bri·er *also* **sweet·bri·ar** \-ˌbrī-ər\ *n* : a thorny Old World rose with fragrant white to deep pink flowers
sweet clover *n* : any of a genus of erect legumes widely grown for soil improvement or hay
sweet corn *n* : an Indian corn with kernels rich in sugar and cooked as a vegetable while immature
sweet·en \'swēt-ᵊn\ *vb* **sweet·ened; sweet·en·ing** : to make sweet — **sweet·en·er** *n* — **sweet·en·ing** *n*
sweet·heart \'swēt-ˌhärt\ *n* : one who is loved
sweet·meat \-ˌmēt\ *n* : CANDY
sweet pea *n* : a garden plant of the legume family with climbing stems and fragrant flowers of many colors; *also* : its flower
sweet pepper *n* : a large mild thick-walled fruit of a pepper; *also* : a plant related to the potato that bears sweet peppers
sweet potato *n* : a tropical vine related to the morning glory; *also* : its sweet yellow edible root
sweet–talk \'swēt-ˌtȯk\ *vb* : FLATTER, COAX — **sweet talk** *n*
sweet tooth *n* : a craving or fondness for sweet food
sweet wil·liam \ˌswēt-'wil-yəm\ *n, often cap W* : a widely cultivated Old World pink with small white to deep red or purple flowers often showily spotted, banded, or mottled
¹**swell** \'swel\ *vb* **swelled; swelled** *or* **swol·len** \'swō-lən\; **swell·ing 1** : to grow big or make bigger **2** : to expand or distend abnormally or excessively ⟨a *swollen* joint⟩; *also* : BULGE **3** : to fill or be filled with emotion (as pride) **syn** expand, amplify, distend, inflate, dilate — **swell·ing** *n*
²**swell** *n* **1** : a long crestless wave or series of waves in the open sea **2** : the condition of being protuberant **3** : a person dressed in the height of fashion; *also* : a person of high social position
³**swell** *adj* **1** : STYLISH; *also* : socially prominent **2** : EXCELLENT
swelled head *n* : an exaggerated opinion of oneself : SELF-CONCEIT
swell·head \'swel-ˌhed\ *n* : one who has a swelled head — **swell·head·ed** \-ˌhe-dəd\ *adj*
swel·ter \'swel-tər\ *vb* [ME *sweltren,* fr. *swelten* to die, be overcome by heat, fr. OE *sweltan* to die] **1** : to be faint or oppressed with the heat **2** : to become exceedingly hot
swept *past and past part of* SWEEP
swerve \'swərv\ *vb* **swerved; swerv·ing** : to move abruptly aside from a straight line or course — **swerve** *n*
¹**swift** \'swift\ *adj* **1** : moving or capable of moving with great speed **2** : occurring suddenly **3** : READY, ALERT — **swift·ly** *adv* — **swift·ness** *n*
²**swift** *n* : any of numerous small insect-eating birds with long narrow wings
swig \'swig\ *vb* **swigged; swig·ging** : to drink in long drafts — **swig** *n*
¹**swill** \'swil\ *vb* **1** : to swallow greedily : GUZZLE **2** : to feed (as hogs) on swill
²**swill** *n* **1** : food for animals composed of edible refuse mixed with liquid **2** : GARBAGE
¹**swim** \'swim\ *vb* **swam** \'swam\; **swum** \'swəm\; **swim·ming 1** : to propel oneself along in water by natural means (as by hands and legs, by tail, or by fins) **2** : to glide smoothly along **3** : FLOAT **4** : to be covered with or as if with a liquid **5** : to be dizzy ⟨his head *swam*⟩ **6** : to cross or go over by swimming — **swim·mer** *n*
²**swim** *n* **1** : an act of swimming **2** : the main current of activity ⟨in the ∼⟩
swim·ming *n* : the action, art, or sport of swimming and diving

swimming pool *n* : a tank (as of concrete or plastic) designed for swimming
swim·suit \'swim-ˌsüt\ *n* : a suit for swimming or bathing
swin·dle \'swin-dᵊl\ *vb* **swin·dled; swin·dling** [fr. *swindler,* fr. G *Schwindler* giddy person, fr. *schwindeln* to be dizzy] : CHEAT, DEFRAUD — **swindle** *n* — **swin·dler** *n*
swine \'swīn\ *n, pl* **swine 1** : any of a family of stout short-legged hoofed mammals with bristly skin and a long flexible snout; *esp* : one widely raised as a meat animal **2** : a contemptible person — **swin·ish** *adj*
¹**swing** \'swiŋ\ *vb* **swung** \'swəŋ\; **swing·ing 1** : to move or cause to move rapidly in an arc **2** : to sway or cause to sway back and forth **3** : to hang so as to move freely back and forth or in a curve **4** : to be executed by hanging **5** : to move or turn on a hinge or pivot **6** : to manage or handle successfully **7** : to march or walk with free swaying movements **8** : to have a steady pulsing rhythm; *also* : to play swing music **9** : to be lively and up-to-date; *also* : to engage freely in sex **syn** wield, manipulate, ply, maneuver — **swing·er** *n* — **swing·ing** *adj*
²**swing** *n* **1** : the act of swinging **2** : a swinging blow, movement, or rhythm **3** : the distance through which something swings : FLUCTUATION **4** : progression of an activity or process ⟨in full ∼⟩ **5** : a seat suspended by a rope or chain for swinging back and forth for pleasure **6** : jazz music played esp. by a large band and marked by a steady lively rhythm, simple harmony, and a basic melody often submerged in improvisation
³**swing** *adj* **1** : of or relating to swing music **2** : that may swing often decisively either way (as on an issue) ⟨∼ voters⟩
¹**swipe** \'swīp\ *n* : a strong sweeping blow
²**swipe** *vb* **swiped; swip·ing 1** : to strike or wipe with a sweeping motion **2** : PILFER, SNATCH
swirl \'swərl\ *vb* : to move or cause to move with a whirling motion — **swirl** *n* — **swirly** \'swər-lē\ *adj*
swish \'swish\ *n* **1** : a prolonged hissing sound **2** : a light sweeping or brushing sound — **swish** *vb*
Swiss \'swis\ *n* **1** *pl* **Swiss** : a native or inhabitant of Switzerland **2** : a hard cheese with large holes
Swiss chard *n* : a beet having large leaves and succulent stalks often cooked as a vegetable
¹**switch** \'swich\ *n* **1** : a slender flexible whip, rod, or twig **2** : a blow with a switch **3** : a shift from one thing to another; *also* : change from the usual **4** : a device for adjusting the rails of a track so that a locomotive or train may be turned from one track to another; *also* : a railroad siding **5** : a device for making, breaking, or changing the connections in an electrical circuit **6** : a heavy strand of hair often used in addition to a person's own hair for some coiffures
²**switch** *vb* **1** : to punish or urge on with a switch **2** : WHISK ⟨a cow ∼*ing* her tail⟩ **3** : to shift or turn by operating a switch **4** : CHANGE, EXCHANGE
switch·back \'swich-ˌbak\ *n* : a zigzag road, trail, or section of railroad tracks for climbing a steep hill
switch·blade \-ˌblād\ *n* : a pocket-knife with a spring-operated blade
switch·board \-ˌbȯrd\ *n* : a panel for controlling the operation of a number of electric circuits; *esp* : one used to make and break telephone connections
switch–hit·ter \-'hi-tər\ *n* : a baseball player who bats either right-handed or left-handed — **switch–hit** \-'hit\ *vb*
switch·man \'swich-mən\ *n* : one who attends a railroad switch
Switz *abbr* Switzerland

\ə\abut \ᵊ\kitten \ər\further \a\ash \ā\ace \ä\mop, mar
\au̇\out \ch\chin \e\bet \ē\easy \g\go \i\hit \ī\ice \j\job
\ŋ\sing \ō\go \ȯ\law \ȯi\boy \th\thin \th̲\the \ü\loot \u̇\foot
\y\yet \zh\vision *see also* Pronunciation Symbols page

¹**swiv·el** \'swi-vəl\ *n* : a device joining two parts so that one or both can turn freely

²**swivel** *vb* **-eled** *or* **-elled; -el·ing** *or* **-el·ling** : to swing or turn on or as if on a swivel

swiv·et \'swi-vət\ *n* : an agitated state

swiz·zle stick \'swi-zəl-\ *n* : a stick used to stir mixed drinks

swollen *past part of* SWELL

swoon \'swün\ *vb* : FAINT — **swoon** *n*

swoop \'swüp\ *vb* : to move with a sweep ⟨the eagle ∼*ed* down on its prey⟩ — **swoop** *n*

swop *chiefly Brit var of* SWAP

sword \'sȯrd\ *n* **1** : a weapon with a long blade for cutting or thrusting **2** : the use of force

sword·fish \-ˌfish\ *n* : a very large ocean fish used for food that has the upper jaw prolonged into a long swordlike beak

swordfish

sword·play \-ˌplā\ *n* : the art or skill of wielding a sword

swords·man \'sȯrdz-mən\ *n* : one skilled in swordplay; *esp* : FENCER

sword·tail \'sȯrd-ˌtāl\ *n* : a small brightly marked Central American fish

swore *past of* SWEAR

sworn *past part of* SWEAR

swum *past part of* SWIM

swung *past and past part of* SWING

syb·a·rite \'si-bə-ˌrīt\ *n* : a lover of luxury : VOLUPTUARY — **syb·a·rit·ic** \ˌsi-bə-'ri-tik\ *adj*

syc·a·more \'si-kə-ˌmȯr\ *n* : a large spreading tree of eastern and central No. America that has light brown flaky bark and small round fruits hanging on long stalks

sy·co·phant \'si-kə-fənt\ *n* : a servile flatterer — **syc·o·phan·tic** \ˌsi-kə-'fan-tik\ *adj*

syl *or* **syll** *abbr* syllable

syl·lab·i·ca·tion \sə-ˌla-bə-'kā-shən\ *n* : the division of words into syllables

syl·lab·i·fy \sə-'la-bə-ˌfī\ *vb* **-fied; -fy·ing** : to form or divide into syllables — **syl·lab·i·fi·ca·tion** \-ˌla-bə-fə-'kā-shən\ *n*

syl·la·ble \'si-lə-bəl\ *n* [ME, fr. MF *sillabe*, fr. L *syllaba*, fr. Gk *syllabē*, fr. *syllambanein* to gather together, fr. *syn* with + *lambanein* to take] : a unit of spoken language consisting of an uninterrupted utterance and forming either a whole word (as *cat*) or a commonly recognized division of a word (as *syl* in *syl-la-ble*); *also* : one or more letters representing such a unit — **syl·lab·ic** \sə-'la-bik\ *adj*

syl·la·bus \'si-lə-bəs\ *n, pl* **-bi** \-ˌbī\ *or* **-bus·es** : a summary containing the heads or main topics of a speech, book, or course of study

syl·lo·gism \'si-lə-ˌji-zəm\ *n* : a logical scheme of a formal argument consisting of a major and a minor premise and a conclusion which must logically be true if the premises are true — **syl·lo·gis·tic** \ˌsi-lə-'jis-tik\ *adj*

sylph \'silf\ *n* **1** : an imaginary being inhabiting the air **2** : a slender graceful woman

syl·van \'sil-vən\ *adj* **1** : living or located in a wooded area; *also* : of, relating to, or characteristic of forest **2** : abounding in woods or trees

sym *abbr* **1** symbol **2** symmetrical

sym·bi·o·sis \ˌsim-ˌbī-'ō-səs, -bē-\ *n, pl* **-o·ses** \-ˌsēz\ : the living together in close association of two dissimilar organisms esp. when mutually beneficial — **sym·bi·ot·ic** \-'ä-tik\ *adj*

sym·bol \'sim-bəl\ *n* **1** : something that stands for something else; *esp* : something concrete that represents or suggests another thing that cannot in itself be pictured ⟨the lion is a ∼ of bravery⟩ **2** : a letter, character, or sign used in writing or printing to represent operations, quantities, elements, sounds, or other ideas — **sym·bol·ic** \sim-'bä-lik\ *also* **sym·bol·i·cal** \-li-kəl\ *adj* — **sym·bol·i·cal·ly** \-k(ə-)lē\ *adv*

sym·bol·ism \'sim-bə-ˌli-zəm\ *n* : representation of abstract or intangible things by means of symbols

sym·bol·ize \'sim-bə-ˌlīz\ *vb* **-ized; -iz·ing 1** : to serve as a symbol of **2** : to represent by symbols — **sym·bol·i·za·tion** \ˌsim-bə-lə-'zā-shən\ *n*

sym·me·try \'si-mə-trē\ *n, pl* **-tries 1** : an arrangement marked by regularity and balanced proportions **2** : correspondence in size, shape, and position of parts that are on opposite sides of a dividing line or center — **sym·met·ri·cal** \sə-'me-tri-kəl\ *or* **sym·met·ric** \sə-'me-trik\ *adj* — **sym·met·ri·cal·ly** \-k(ə-)lē\ *adv*

sympathetic nervous system *n* : the part of the autonomic nervous system that is concerned esp. with preparing the body to react to situations of stress or emergency and that tends to decrease the tone and contractility of muscle not under direct voluntary control, increase the activity of the heart and the blood pressure, and cause the contraction of blood vessels

sym·pa·thize \'sim-pə-ˌthīz\ *vb* **-thized; -thiz·ing** : to feel or show sympathy — **sym·pa·thiz·er** *n*

sym·pa·thy \'sim-pə-thē\ *n, pl* **-thies 1** : a relationship between persons or things wherein whatever affects one similarly affects the other **2** : harmony of interests and aims **3** : FAVOR, SUPPORT **4** : the capacity for entering into and sharing the feelings or interests of another; *also* : COMPASSION, PITY **5** : an expression of sorrow for another's loss, grief, or misfortune — **sym·pa·thet·ic** \ˌsim-pə-'the-tik\ *adj* — **sym·pa·thet·i·cal·ly** \-ti-k(ə-)lē\ *adv*

sym·pho·ny \'sim-fə-nē\ *n, pl* **-nies 1** : harmony of sounds **2** : a large and complex composition for a full orchestra **3** : a large orchestra of a kind that plays symphonies — **sym·phon·ic** \sim-'fä-nik\ *adj*

sym·po·sium \sim-'pō-zē-əm\ *n, pl* **-sia** \-zē-ə\ *or* **-siums** : a conference at which a particular topic is discussed by various speakers; *also* : a collection of opinions about a subject

symp·tom \'simp-təm\ *n* [LL *symptoma*, fr. Gk *symptōma* happening, attribute, symptom, fr. *sympiptein* to happen, fr. *syn* with + *piptein* to fall] **1** : something that indicates the presence of disease or abnormality; *esp* : something (as a headache) that can be sensed only by the individual affected **2** : SIGN, INDICATION — **symp·tom·at·ic** \ˌsimp-tə-'ma-tik\ *adj*

syn *abbr* synonym; synonymous; synonymy

syn·a·gogue *or* **syn·a·gog** \'si-nə-ˌgäg\ *n* [ME *synagoge*, fr. OF, fr. LL *synagoga*, fr. Gk *synagōgē* assembly, synagogue, fr. *synagein* to bring together] **1** : a Jewish congregation **2** : the house of worship of a Jewish congregation

syn·apse \'si-ˌnaps, sə-'naps\ *n* : the point at which a nervous impulse passes from one neuron to another

¹**sync** *also* **synch** \'siŋk\ *vb* **synced** *also* **synched** \'siŋkt\; **sync·ing** *also* **synch·ing** \'siŋ-kiŋ\ : SYNCHRONIZE

²**sync** *also* **synch** *n* : SYNCHRONIZATION, SYNCHRONISM — **sync** *adj*

syn·chro·nize \'siŋ-krə-ˌnīz, 'sin-\ *vb* **-nized; -niz·ing 1** : to occur or cause to occur at the same instant **2** : to represent, arrange, or tabulate according to dates or time **3** : to cause to agree in time **4** : to make synchronous in operation — **syn·chro·nism** \-ˌni-zəm\ *n* —

syn·chro·ni·za·tion \ˌsiŋ-krə-nə-ˈzā-shən, ˌsin-\ *n* — **syn·chro·niz·er** *n*

syn·chro·nous \ˈsiŋ-krə-nəs, ˈsin-\ *adj* **1** : happening at the same time : CONCURRENT **2** : working, moving, or occurring together at the same rate and at the proper time

syn·co·pa·tion \ˌsiŋ-kə-ˈpā-shən, ˌsin-\ *n* : a shifting of the regular musical accent : occurrence of accented notes on the weak beat — **syn·co·pate** \ˈsiŋ-kə-ˌpāt, ˈsin-\ *vb*

syn·co·pe \ˈsiŋ-kə-(ˌ)pē, ˈsin-\ *n* : the loss of one or more sounds or letters in the interior of a word (as in *fo'c'sle* for *forecastle*)

¹syn·di·cate \ˈsin-di-kət\ *n* **1** : a group of persons who combine to carry out a financial or industrial undertaking **2** : a loose association of racketeers **3** : a business concern that sells materials for publication in many newspapers and periodicals at the same time

²syn·di·cate \-də-ˌkāt\ *vb* **-cat·ed; -cat·ing** **1** : to combine into or manage as a syndicate **2** : to publish through a syndicate — **syn·di·ca·tion** \ˌsin-də-ˈkā-shən\ *n*

syn·drome \ˈsin-ˌdrōm\ *n* : a group of signs and symptoms that occur together and characterize a particular abnormality

syn·er·gism \ˈsin-ər-ˌji-zəm\ *n* : interaction of discrete agencies (as industrial firms), agents (as drugs), or conditions such that the total effect is greater than the sum of the individual effects — **syn·er·gist** \-jist\ *n* — **syn·er·gis·tic** \ˌsi-nər-ˈjis-tik\ *adj* — **syn·er·gis·ti·cal·ly** \-ti-k(ə-)lē\ *adv*

syn·fuel \ˈsin-ˌfyül\ *n* [*synthetic*] : a fuel derived esp. from a fossil fuel

syn·od \ˈsi-nəd\ *n* : COUNCIL, ASSEMBLY; *esp* : a religious governing body — **syn·od·al** \-nəd-ᵊl, -ˌnäd-ᵊl\ *adj* — **syn·od·ic** \-dik\ *or* **syn·od·i·cal** \sə-ˈnä-di-kəl\ *adj*

syn·onym \ˈsi-nə-ˌnim\ *n* : one of two or more words in the same language which have the same or very nearly the same meaning — **syn·on·y·mous** \sə-ˈnä-nə-məs\ *adj* — **syn·on·y·my** \-mē\ *n*

syn·op·sis \sə-ˈnäp-səs\ *n*, *pl* **-op·ses** \-ˌsēz\ : a condensed statement or outline (as of a treatise) : ABSTRACT

syn·op·tic \sə-ˈnäp-tik\ *also* **syn·op·ti·cal** \-ti-kəl\ *adj* : characterized by or affording a comprehensive view

syn·tax \ˈsin-ˌtaks\ *n* : the way in which words are put together to form phrases, clauses, or sentences — **syn·tac·tic** \sin-ˈtak-tik\ *or* **syn·tac·ti·cal** \-ti-kəl\ *adj*

syn·the·sis \ˈsin-thə-səs\ *n*, *pl* **-the·ses** \-ˌsēz\ : the combination of parts or elements into a whole; *esp* : the production of a substance by union of chemically simpler substances — **syn·the·size** \-ˌsīz\ *vb* — **syn·the·siz·er** *n*

syn·thet·ic \sin-ˈthe-tik\ *adj* : produced artificially esp. by chemical means; *also* : not genuine — **synthetic** *n* — **syn·thet·i·cal·ly** \-ti-k(ə-)lē\ *adv*

syph·i·lis \ˈsi-fə-ləs\ *n* [NL, fr. *Syphilus*, hero of the poem *Syphilis sive Morbus Gallicus* (*Syphilis or the French disease*) (1530) by Girolamo Fracastoro †1553 Ital. physician] : an infectious usu. venereal disease caused by a spirochete — **syph·i·lit·ic** \ˌsi-fə-ˈli-tik\ *adj or n*

sy·phon *var of* SIPHON

Syr·i·an \ˈsir-ē-ən\ *n* : a native or inhabitant of Syria — **Syrian** *adj*

¹sy·ringe \sə-ˈrinj\ *n* : a device used esp. for injecting liquids into or withdrawing them from the body

²syringe *vb* **sy·ringed; sy·ring·ing** : to flush or cleanse with or as if with a syringe

syr·up \ˈsər-əp, ˈsir-əp\ *n* **1** : a thick sticky solution of sugar and water often flavored or medicated **2** : the concentrated juice of a fruit or plant — **syr·upy** *adj*

syst *abbr* system

sys·tem \ˈsis-təm\ *n* **1** : a group of units so combined as to form a whole and to operate in unison **2** : the body as a functioning whole; *also* : a group of bodily organs (as the nervous system) that together carry on some vital function **3** : a definite scheme or method of procedure or classification **4** : regular method or order — **sys·tem·at·ic** \ˌsis-tə-ˈma-tik\ *also* **sys·tem·at·i·cal** \-ti-kəl\ *adj* — **sys·tem·at·i·cal·ly** \-k(ə-)lē\ *adv*

sys·tem·atize \ˈsis-tə-mə-ˌtīz\ *vb* **-atized; -atiz·ing** : to make into a system : arrange methodically

¹sys·tem·ic \sis-ˈte-mik\ *adj* **1** : of, relating to, or affecting the whole body ⟨∼ disease⟩ **2** : of, relating to, or being a pesticide that when absorbed into the sap or bloodstream makes the entire plant or animal toxic to a pest (as an insect or fungus)

²systemic *n* : a systemic pesticide

systemic lupus erythematosus *n* : a systemic disease esp. of women characterized by fever, skin rash, and arthritis, often by anemia, by small hemorrhages of the skin and mucous membranes, and in serious cases by involvement of various internal organs

sys·tem·ize \ˈsis-tə-ˌmīz\ *vb* **-ized; -iz·ing** : SYSTEMATIZE

systems analyst *n* : a person who studies a procedure or business to determine its goals or purposes and to discover the best ways to accomplish them — **systems analysis** *n*

sys·to·le \ˈsis-tə-(ˌ)lē\ *n* : a rhythmically recurrent contraction of the heart — **sys·tol·ic** \sis-ˈtä-lik\ *adj*

T

¹t \ˈtē\ *n, pl* **t's** *or* **ts** \ˈtēz\ *often cap* : the 20th letter of the English alphabet

²t *abbr, often cap* **1** metric ton **2** tablespoon **3** teaspoon **4** temperature **5** ton **6** transitive **7** troy **8** true

T *abbr* **1** toddler **2** T-shirt

Ta *symbol* tantalum

TA *abbr* teaching assistant

¹tab \ˈtab\ *n* **1** : a short projecting flap, loop, or tag; *also* : a small insert or addition **2** : close surveillance : WATCH ⟨keep ∼s on him⟩ **3** : BILL, CHECK

²tab *vb* **tabbed; tab·bing** : DESIGNATE

tab·by \ˈta-bē\ *n, pl* **tabbies** : a usu. striped or mottled domestic cat; *also* : a female domestic cat

tab·er·na·cle \ˈta-bər-ˌna-kəl\ *n* [ME, fr. OF, fr. LL *tabernaculum*, fr. L, tent, fr. *taberna* hut] **1** *often cap* : a tent sanctuary used by the Israelites during the Exodus **2** : a receptacle for the consecrated elements of the Eucharist **3** : a house of worship

¹ta·ble \ˈtā-bəl\ *n* **1** : a flat slab or plaque : TABLET **2** : a piece of furniture consisting of a smooth flat top fixed on legs **3** : a supply of food : BOARD, FARE **4** : a group of people assembled at or as if at a table **5** : an orderly arrangement of data usu. in rows and columns **6** : a short list ⟨∼ of contents⟩ — **ta·ble·top** \-ˌtäp\ *n*

²table *vb* **ta·bled; ta·bling** **1** *Brit* : to place on the agenda

---

\ə\abut \ᵊ\kitten \ər\further \a\ash \ā\ace \ä\mop, mar \au̇\out \ch\chin \e\bet \ē\easy \g\go \i\hit \ī\ice \j\job \ŋ\sing \ō\go \ȯ\law \ȯi\boy \th\thin \t͟h\the \ü\loot \u̇\foot \y\yet \zh\vision *see also* Pronunciation Symbols page

2 : to remove (a parliamentary motion) from consideration indefinitely

tab·leau \'ta-ˌblō\ *n, pl* **tab·leaux** \-ˌblōz\ *also* **tableaus** [F] : a scene or event usu. presented on a stage by costumed participants who remain silent and motionless

ta·ble·cloth \'tā-bəl-ˌklȯth\ *n* : a covering spread over a dining table before the table is set

ta·ble d'hôte \ˌtä-bəl-'dōt\ *n* [F, lit., host's table] : a complete meal of several courses offered at a fixed price

ta·ble·land \'tā-bəl-ˌland\ *n* : PLATEAU

ta·ble·spoon \-ˌspün\ *n* **1** : a large spoon used esp. for serving **2** : a unit of measure equal to ½ fluid ounce (15 milliliters)

ta·ble·spoon·ful \-ˌfül\ *n, pl* **-spoonfuls** \-ˌfülz\ *also* **-spoons·ful** \-ˌspünz-ˌfül\ : TABLESPOON 2

tab·let \'ta-blət\ *n* **1** : a flat slab suited for or bearing an inscription **2** : a collection of sheets of paper glued together at one edge **3** : a compressed or molded block of material; *esp* : a usu. disk-shaped medicated mass

table tennis *n* : a game resembling tennis played on a tabletop with wooden paddles and a small hollow plastic ball

ta·ble·ware \'tā-bəl-ˌwar\ *n* : utensils (as of china or silver) for table use

¹tab·loid \'ta-ˌblȯid\ *adj* : condensed into small scope

²tabloid *n* : a newspaper marked by small pages, condensation of the news, and usu. many photographs; *esp* : one characterized by sensationalism

¹ta·boo *also* **ta·bu** \tə-'bü, ta-\ *adj* [Tongan (a Polynesian language) *tabu*] : prohibited by a taboo

²taboo *also* **tabu** *n, pl* **taboos** *also* **tabus** **1** : a prohibition against touching, saying, or doing something for fear of immediate harm from a supernatural force **2** : a prohibition imposed by social custom

ta·bor *also* **ta·bour** \'tā-bər\ *n* : a small drum used to accompany a pipe or fife played by the same person

tab·u·lar \'ta-byə-lər\ *adj* **1** : having a flat surface **2** : arranged in a table; *esp* : set up in rows and columns **3** : computed by means of a table

tab·u·late \-ˌlāt\ *vb* **-lat·ed; -lat·ing** : to put into tabular form — **tab·u·la·tion** \ˌta-byə-'lā-shən\ *n* — **tab·u·la·tor** \'ta-byə-ˌlā-tər\ *n*

TAC \'tak\ *abbr* Tactical Air Command

tach \'tak\ *n* : TACHOMETER

ta·chom·e·ter \ta-'kä-mə-tər, tə-\ *n* [ultim. fr. Gk *tachos* speed] : a device to indicate speed of rotation

tachy·car·dia \ˌta-ki-'kär-dē-ə\ *n* : relatively rapid heart action

tachy·on \'ta-kē-ˌän\ *n* : a hypothetical particle held to travel faster than light

tac·it \'ta-sət\ *adj* [F or L; F *tacite*, fr. L *tacitus* silent, fr. *tacēre* to be silent] **1** : expressed without words or speech **2** : implied or indicated but not actually expressed ⟨~ consent⟩ — **tac·it·ly** *adv* — **tac·it·ness** *n*

tac·i·turn \'ta-sə-ˌtərn\ *adj* : disinclined to talk **syn** uncommunicative, reserved, reticent, closemouthed — **tac·i·tur·ni·ty** \ˌta-sə-'tər-nə-tē\ *n*

¹tack \'tak\ *vb* **1** : to fasten with tacks; *also* : to add on **2** : to change the direction of (a sailing ship) from one tack to another **3** : to follow a zigzag course

²tack *n* **1** : a small sharp nail with a broad flat head **2** : the direction toward the wind that a ship is sailing ⟨starboard ~⟩; *also* : the run of a ship on one tack **3** : a change of course from one tack to another **4** : a zigzag course **5** : a course of action

³tack *n* : gear for harnessing a horse

¹tack·le \'ta-kəl, *naut often* 'tā-\ *n* **1** : GEAR, APPARATUS, EQUIPMENT **2** : the rigging of a ship **3** : an arrangement of ropes and pulleys for hoisting or pulling heavy objects **4** : the act or an instance of tackling; *also* : a football lineman playing between guard and end

²tackle *vb* **tack·led; tack·ling** **1** : to attach and secure

with or as if with tackle **2** : to seize, grapple with, or throw down with the intention of subduing or stopping **3** : to set about dealing with ⟨~ a problem⟩ — **tack·ler** *n*

¹tacky \'ta-kē\ *adj* **tack·i·er; -est** : sticky to the touch

²tacky *adj* **tack·i·er; -est** **1** : SHABBY, SEEDY **2** : marked by lack of style or good taste; *also* : cheaply showy

ta·co \'tä-kō\ *n, pl* **tacos** \-kōz\ [MexSp] : a usu. fried tortilla rolled up with or folded over a filling

tact \'takt\ *n* [F, sense of touch, fr. L *tactus*, fr. *tangere* to touch] : a keen sense of what to do or say to keep good relations with others — **tact·ful** \-fəl\ *adj* — **tact·ful·ly** *adv* — **tact·less** *adj* — **tact·less·ly** *adv*

tac·tic \'tak-tik\ *n* : a planned action for accomplishing an end

tac·tics \'tak-tiks\ *n sing or pl* **1** : the science of maneuvering forces in combat **2** : the skill of using available means to reach an end — **tac·ti·cal** \-ti-kəl\ *adj* — **tac·ti·cian** \tak-'ti-shən\ *n*

tac·tile \'takt-ᵊl, 'tak-ˌtīl\ *adj* : of, relating to, or perceptible through the sense of touch

tad·pole \'tad-ˌpōl\ *n* [ME *taddepol*, fr. *tode* toad + *polle* head] : an aquatic larva of a frog or toad that has a tail and gills

tae kwon do \'tī-'kwän-'dō\ *n* : a Korean martial art resembling karate

taf·fe·ta \'ta-fə-tə\ *n* : a crisp lustrous fabric (as of silk or rayon)

taff·rail \'taf-ˌrāl, -rəl\ *n* : the rail around a ship's stern

taf·fy \'ta-fē\ *n, pl* **taffies** : a candy usu. of molasses or brown sugar stretched until porous and light-colored

¹tag \'tag\ *n* **1** : a metal or plastic binding on an end of a shoelace **2** : a piece of hanging or attached material **3** : a hackneyed quotation or saying **4** : a descriptive or identifying epithet

²tag *vb* **tagged; tag·ging** **1** : to provide or mark with or as if with a tag; *esp* : IDENTIFY **2** : to attach as an addition **3** : to follow closely and persistently ⟨~s along everywhere we go⟩ **4** : to hold responsible for something

³tag *n* : a game in which one player chases others and tries to touch one of them

⁴tag *vb* **tagged; tag·ging** **1** : to touch in or as if in a game of tag **2** : SELECT

TAG *abbr* the adjutant general

tag sale *n* : GARAGE SALE

Ta·hi·tian \tə-'hē-shən\ *n* **1** : a native or inhabitant of Tahiti **2** : the Polynesian language of the Tahitians — **Tahitian** *adj*

tai·ga \'tī-gə\ *n* [Russ *taĭga*] : a swampy coniferous subarctic forest extending south from the tundra

¹tail \'tāl\ *n* **1** : the rear end or a process extending from the rear end of an animal **2** : something resembling an animal's tail **3** *pl* : full evening dress for men **4** : the back, last, lower, or inferior part of something; *esp* : the reverse of a coin **5** : one who follows or keeps watch on someone — **tailed** \'tāld\ *adj* — **tail·less** \'tāl-ləs\ *adj*

²tail *vb* : FOLLOW; *esp* : to follow for the purpose of surveillance

tail·coat \-'kōt\ *n* : a coat with tails; *esp* : a man's full-dress coat with two long tapering skirts at the back

¹tail·gate \-ˌgāt\ *n* : a board or gate at the back end of a vehicle that can be let down (as for loading)

²tailgate *vb* **tail·gat·ed; tail·gat·ing** **1** : to drive dangerously close behind another vehicle **2** : to hold a tailgate picnic

³tailgate *adj* : relating to or being a picnic set up on the tailgate esp. of a station wagon

tail·light \-ˌlīt\ *n* : a usu. red warning light mounted at the rear of a vehicle

¹tai·lor \'tā-lər\ *n* [ME *taillour*, fr. OF *tailleur*, fr. *taillier* to cut, fr. LL *taliare*, fr. L *talea* twig, cutting] : a person whose occupation is making or altering garments

²tailor *vb* **1** : to make or fashion as the work of a tailor **2** : to make or adapt to suit a special purpose

tail pipe *n* : an outlet by which the exhaust gases are removed from an engine (as of an automobile)

tail·spin \'tāl-ˌspin\ *n* : a rapid descent or downward spiral

tail wind *n* : a wind blowing in the same general direction as a course of movement (as of an aircraft)

¹taint \'tānt\ *vb* **1** : CORRUPT, CONTAMINATE **2** : to affect or become affected with something bad (as putrefaction)

²taint *n* : a contaminating mark or influence

Tai·wan·ese \ˌtī-wə-'nēz, -'nēs\ *n* : a native or inhabitant of Taiwan — **Taiwanese** *adj*

ta·ka \'tä-kə\ *n* — see MONEY table

¹take \'tāk\ *vb* **took** \'tùk\; **tak·en** \'tā-kən\; **tak·ing 1** : to get into one's hands or possession : GRASP, SEIZE **2** : CAPTURE; *also* : DEFEAT **3** : to obtain or secure for use **4** : to catch or attack through the effect of a sudden force or influence ⟨*taken* ill⟩ **5** : CAPTIVATE, DELIGHT **6** : to bring into a relation ⟨∼ a wife⟩ **7** : REMOVE, SUBTRACT **8** : to pick out : CHOOSE **9** : ASSUME, UNDERTAKE **10** : RECEIVE, ACCEPT **11** : to use for transportation ⟨∼ a bus⟩ **12** : to become impregnated with : ABSORB ⟨∼s a dye⟩ **13** : to receive into one's body (as by swallowing) ⟨∼ a pill⟩ **14** : ENDURE, UNDERGO **15** : to lead, carry, or cause to go along to another place **16** : NEED, REQUIRE **17** : to obtain as the result of a special procedure ⟨∼ a snapshot⟩ **18** : to undertake and do, make, or perform ⟨∼ a walk⟩ **19** : to take effect : ACT, OPERATE **syn** grab, clutch, snatch, seize, nab, grapple — **tak·er** *n* — **take advantage of 1** : to profit by **2** : EXPLOIT — **take after** : RESEMBLE — **take care** : to be careful — **take care of** : to care for : attend to — **take effect** : to become operative — **take exception** : OBJECT — **take for** : to suppose to be; *esp* : to mistake for — **take place** : HAPPEN — **take to 1** : to go to **2** : to apply or devote oneself to **3** : to conceive a liking for

²take *n* **1** : the number or quantity taken; *also* : PROCEEDS, RECEIPTS **2** : an act or the action of taking **3** : a television or movie scene filmed or taped at one time; *also* : a sound recording made at one time **4** : a distinct or personal point of view

take·off \'tā-ˌkòf\ *n* **1** : IMITATION; *esp* : PARODY **2** : an act or instance of taking off

take off *vb* **1** : REMOVE **2** : DEDUCT **3** : to set out : go away **4** : to leave the surface; *esp* : to begin flight

take on *vb* **1** : to begin to perform or deal with; *also* : to contend with as an opponent **2** : ENGAGE, HIRE **3** : to assume or acquire as or as if one's own **4** : to make an unusual show of one's feelings esp. of grief or anger

take over *vb* : to assume control or possession of or responsibility for — **take·over** \'tā-ˌkō-vər\ *n*

take up *vb* **1** : PICK UP **2** : to begin to occupy **3** : to absorb or incorporate into itself ⟨plants *taking up* nutrients⟩ **4** : to begin to engage in ⟨*took up* jogging⟩ **5** : to make tighter or shorter ⟨*take up* the slack⟩

tak·ings \'tā-kiŋz\ *n pl* : receipts esp. of money

ta·la \'tä-lə\ *n, pl* tala — see MONEY table

talc \'talk\ *n* : a soft mineral with a soapy feel used esp. in making toilet powder (**tal·cum powder** \'tal-kəm-\)

tale \'tāl\ *n* **1** : a relation of a series of events **2** : a report of a confidential matter **3** : idle talk; *esp* : harmful gossip **4** : a usu. imaginative narrative **5** : FALSEHOOD **6** : COUNT, TALLY

tal·ent \'ta-lənt\ *n* **1** : an ancient unit of weight and value **2** : the natural endowments of a person **3** : a special often creative or artistic aptitude **4** : mental power : ABILITY **5** : a person of talent **syn** genius, gift, faculty, aptitude, knack — **tal·ent·ed** *adj*

ta·ler \'tä-lər\ *n* : any of numerous silver coins issued by German states from the 15th to the 19th centuries

tales·man \'tālz-mən\ *n* : a person summoned for jury duty

tal·is·man \'ta-ləs-mən, -ləz-\ *n, pl* **-mans** [F *talisman* or Sp *talismán* or It *talismano,* fr. Ar *ṭilsam,* fr. MGk *telesma,* fr. Gk, consecration, fr. *telein* to initiate into the mysteries, complete, fr. *telos* end] : an object thought to act as a charm

¹talk \'tòk\ *vb* **1** : to express in speech : utter words : SPEAK **2** : DISCUSS ⟨∼ business⟩ **3** : to influence or cause by talking ⟨∼*ed* him into going⟩ **4** : to use (a language) for communicating **5** : CONVERSE **6** : to reveal confidential information; *also* : GOSSIP **7** : to give a talk : LECTURE — **talk·er** *n* — **talk back** : to answer impertinently

²talk *n* **1** : the act of talking **2** : a way of speaking **3** : a formal discussion **4** : REPORT, RUMOR **5** : the topic of comment or gossip ⟨the ∼ of the town⟩ **6** : an informal address or lecture

talk·ative \'tò-kə-tiv\ *adj* : given to talking **syn** loquacious, chatty, gabby, garrulous — **talk·ative·ly** *adv* — **talk·ative·ness** *n*

talk·ing-to \'tò-kiŋ-ˌtü\ *n* : REPRIMAND, REPROOF

tall \'tòl\ *adj* **1** : high in stature; *also* : of a specified height ⟨six feet ∼⟩ **2** : LARGE, FORMIDABLE ⟨a ∼ order⟩ **3** : UNBELIEVABLE, IMPROBABLE ⟨a ∼ story⟩ — **tall·ness** *n*

tal·low \'ta-lō\ *n* : a hard white fat rendered usu. from cattle or sheep tissues and used esp. in candles

¹tal·ly \'ta-lē\ *n, pl* **tallies** [ME *talye,* fr. ML *talea,* fr. L, twig, cutting] **1** : a device for visibly recording or accounting esp. business transactions **2** : a recorded account **3** : a corresponding part; *also* : CORRESPONDENCE

²tally *vb* **tal·lied; tal·ly·ing 1** : to mark on or as if on a tally **2** : to make a count of : RECKON; *also* : SCORE **3** : CORRESPOND, MATCH **syn** square, accord, harmonize, conform, jibe

tal·ly·ho \ˌta-lē-'hō\ *n, pl* **-hos** : a call of a huntsman at sight of the fox

Tal·mud \'täl-ˌmùd, 'tal-məd\ *n* [Late Heb *talmūdh,* lit., instruction] : the authoritative body of Jewish tradition — **Tal·mu·dic** \tal-'mü-dik, -'myü-, -'mə-; täl-'mù-\ *adj* — **Tal·mud·ist** \'täl-ˌmù-dist, 'tal-mə-\ *n*

tal·on \'ta-lən\ *n* : the claw of an animal and esp. of a bird of prey

ta·lus \'tā-ləs, 'ta-\ *n* : rock debris at the base of a cliff

tam \'tam\ *n* : TAM-O'-SHANTER

ta·ma·le \tə-'mä-lē\ *n* [MexSp *tamales,* pl. of *tamal* tamale, fr. Nahuatl (American Indian language) *tamalli* steamed cornmeal dough] : ground meat seasoned with chili, rolled in cornmeal dough, wrapped in corn husks, and steamed

tam·a·rack \'ta-mə-ˌrak\ *n* : a larch of northern No. America; *also* : its hard resinous wood

tam·a·rind \'ta-mə-rənd, -ˌrind\ *n* [Sp & Pg *tamarindo,* fr. Ar *tamr hindī,* lit., Indian date] : a tropical tree of the legume family with hard yellowish wood and feathery leaves; *also* : its acid fruit

tam·ba·la \täm-'bä-lə\ *n, pl* **-la** *or* **-las** — see *kwacha* at MONEY table

tam·bou·rine \ˌtam-bə-'rēn\ *n* : a small shallow drum with loose disks at the sides played by shaking or striking with the hand

¹tame \'tām\ *adj* **tam·er; tam·est 1** : reduced from a state of native wildness esp. so as to be useful to humans : DOMESTICATED **2** : made docile : SUBDUED **3** : lacking spirit or interest : INSIPID **syn** submissive, domestic, domesticated — **tame·ly** *adv* — **tame·ness** *n*

²tame *vb* **tamed; tam·ing 1** : to make or become tame;

\ə\abut \ᵊ\kitten \ər\further \a\ash \ā\ace \ä\mop, mar
\au̇\out \ch\chin \e\bet \ē\easy \g\go \i\hit \ī\ice \j\job
\ŋ\sing \ō\go \ò\law \ói\boy \th\thin \th̲\the \ü\loot \u̇\foot
\y\yet \zh\vision *see also* Pronunciation Symbols page

also : to subject (land) to cultivation **2** : HUMBLE, SUB-DUE — **tam·able** *or* **tame·able** \'tā-mə-bəl\ *adj* — **tame·less** *adj* — **tam·er** *n*

Tam·muz \'tä-ˌmu̇z\ *n* [Heb *Tammūz*] : the 10th month of the civil year or the 4th month of the ecclesiastical year in the Jewish calendar

tam-o'–shan·ter \'ta-mə-ˌshan-tər\ *n* [fr. poem *Tam o' Shanter* (1790) by Robert Burns †1796 Scot. poet] : a Scottish woolen cap with a wide flat circular crown and usu. a pompon in the center

tamp \'tamp\ *vb* : to drive down or in by a series of light blows

tam·per \'tam-pər\ *vb* **1** : to carry on underhand nego-tiations (as by bribery) ⟨∼ with a witness⟩ **2** : to inter-fere so as to weaken or change for the worse ⟨∼ with a document⟩ **3** : to try foolish or dangerous experiments

tam·pon \'tam-ˌpän\ *n* [F, lit., plug] : a plug (as of cotton) introduced into a body cavity usu. to absorb se-cretions (as from menstruation) or to arrest bleeding

¹**tan** \'tan\ *vb* **tanned; tan·ning 1** : to change (hide) into leather esp. by soaking in a liquid containing tannin **2** : to make or become brown (as by exposure to the sun) **3** : WHIP, THRASH

²**tan** *n* **1** : a brown skin color induced by sun or weather **2** : a light yellowish brown color

³**tan** *abbr* tangent

tan·a·ger \'ta-ni-jər\ *n* : any of numerous American birds that are often brightly colored

tan·bark \'tan-ˌbärk\ *n* : bark (as of oak or sumac) that is rich in tannin and used in tanning

¹**tan·dem** \'tan-dəm\ *n* [L, at last, at length (taken to mean "lengthwise"), fr. *tam* so] **1** : a 2-seated carriage with horses hitched tandem; *also* : its team **2** : a bicycle for two persons sitting one behind the other — **in tan-dem** : in a tandem arrangement

²**tandem** *adv* : one behind another

³**tandem** *adj* **1** : consisting of things arranged one behind the other **2** : working in conjunction with each other

tang \'taŋ\ *n* **1** : a part in a tool that connects the blade with the handle **2** : a sharp distinctive flavor; *also* : a pungent odor — **tangy** *adj*

¹**tan·gent** \'tan-jənt\ *adj* [L *tangent-, tangens,* prp. of *tangere* to touch] : TOUCHING; *esp* : touching a circle or sphere at only one point

²**tangent** *n* **1** : a tangent line, curve, or surface **2** : an abrupt change of course — **tan·gen·tial** \tan-'jen-chəl\ *adj*

tan·ger·ine \'tan-jə-ˌrēn, ˌtan-jə-'rēn\ *n* : a deep orange loose-skinned citrus fruit; *also* : a tree that bears tan-gerines

¹**tan·gi·ble** \'tan-jə-bəl\ *adj* **1** : perceptible esp. by the sense of touch : PALPABLE **2** : substantially real : MA-TERIAL ⟨∼ rewards⟩ **3** : capable of being appraised syn appreciable, perceptible, sensible, discernible — **tan-gi·bil·i·ty** \ˌtan-jə-'bi-lə-tē\ *n*

²**tangible** *n* : something tangible; *esp* : a tangible asset

¹**tan·gle** \'tan-gəl\ *vb* **tan·gled; tan·gling 1** : to involve so as to hamper or embarrass; *also* : ENTRAP **2** : to unite or knit together in intricate confusion : ENTANGLE

²**tangle** *n* **1** : a tangled twisted mass **2** : a confusedly com-plicated state : MUDDLE

tan·go \'taŋ-gō\ *n, pl* **tangos** : a dance of Latin-American origin — **tango** *vb*

tank \'taŋk\ *n* **1** : a large artificial receptacle for liquids **2** : a heavily armed and armored combat vehicle that moves on tracks — **tank·ful** *n*

tan·kard \'taŋ-kərd\ *n* : a tall one-handled drinking ves-sel

tank·er \'taŋ-kər\ *n* : a vehicle equipped for transporting a liquid

tank top *n* : a sleeveless collarless pullover shirt with shoulder straps

tank town *n* : a small town

tan·ner \'ta-nər\ *n* : one that tans hides

tan·nery \'ta-nə-rē\ *n, pl* **-ner·ies** : a place where tanning is carried on

tan·nic acid \'ta-nik-\ *n* : TANNIN

tan·nin \'ta-nən\ *n* : any of various plant substances used esp. in tanning and dyeing, in inks, and as astrin-gents

tan·sy \'tan-zē\ *n, pl* **tansies** [ME *tanesey,* fr. MF *tane-sie,* fr. ML *athanasia,* fr. Gk, immortality, fr. *athanatos* immortal, fr. *a-* not + *thanatos* death] : a common weedy herb related to the daisies with an aromatic odor and bitter-tasting finely divided leaves

tan·ta·lise *Brit var of* TANTALIZE

tan·ta·lize \'tan-tə-ˌlīz\ *vb* **-lized; -liz·ing** [fr. *Tantalus,* king of Greek myth punished in Hades by having to stand up to his chin in water that receded as he bent to drink] : to tease or torment by presenting something de-sirable but keeping it out of reach — **tan·ta·liz·er** *n* — **tan·ta·liz·ing·ly** *adv*

tan·ta·lum \'tan-tə-ləm\ *n* : a hard ductile metallic chem-ical element — see ELEMENT table

tan·ta·mount \'tan-tə-ˌmau̇nt\ *adj* : equivalent in value or meaning

tan·trum \'tan-trəm\ *n* : a fit of bad temper

Tan·za·ni·an \ˌtan-zə-'nē-ən\ *n* : a native or inhabitant of Tanzania — **Tanzanian** *adj*

Tao·ism \'tau̇-ˌi-zəm, 'dau̇-\ *n* : a Chinese mystical phi-losophy; *also* : a religion developed from Taoist philos-ophy and Buddhism — **Tao·ist** \-ist\ *adj or n*

¹**tap** \'tap\ *n* **1** : FAUCET, COCK **2** : liquor drawn through a tap **3** : the removing of fluid from a container or cavity by tapping **4** : a tool for forming an internal screw thread **5** : a point in an electric circuit where a connec-tion may be made

²**tap** *vb* **tapped; tap·ping 1** : to release or cause to flow by piercing or by drawing a plug from a container or cavity **2** : to pierce so as to let out or draw off a fluid **3** : to draw from ⟨∼ resources⟩ **4** : to cut in on (a tel-ephone wire) to get information; *also* : to cut in (an electrical circuit) on another circuit **5** : to form an in-ternal screw thread in by means of a tap **6** : to connect (as a gas or water main) with a local supply — **tap-per** *n*

³**tap** *vb* **tapped; tap·ping 1** : to rap lightly **2** : to bring about by repeated light blows **3** : SELECT; *esp* : to elect to membership

⁴**tap** *n* **1** : a light blow or stroke; *also* : its sound **2** : a small metal plate for the sole or heel of a shoe

¹**tape** \'tāp\ *n* **1** : a narrow band of woven fabric **2** : a nar-row flexible strip; *esp* : MAGNETIC TAPE

²**tape** *vb* **taped; tap·ing 1** : to fasten or support with tape **2** : to record on magnetic tape

tape deck *n* : a device used to play back magnetic tapes that usu. has to be connected to an audio system

tape measure *n* : a tape marked off in units (as inches) for measuring

¹**ta·per** \'tā-pər\ *n* **1** : a slender wax candle; *also* : a long waxed wick **2** : a gradual lessening of thickness or width in a long object

²**taper** *vb* **ta·pered; ta·per·ing 1** : to make or become gradually smaller toward one end **2** : to diminish grad-ually

tape–re·cord \ˌtā-pri-'kȯrd\ *vb* : to make a recording of on magnetic tape — **tape recorder** *n* — **tape recording** *n*

tap·es·try \'ta-pə-strē\ *n, pl* **-tries** : a heavy reversible textile that has designs or pictures woven into it and is used esp. as a wall hanging

tape·worm \'tāp-ˌwərm\ *n* : any of a class of long flat segmented worms parasitic in vertebrate intestines

tap·i·o·ca \ˌta-pē-'ō-kə\ *n* : a usu. granular preparation of cassava starch used esp. in puddings; *also* : a dish (as pudding) that contains tapioca

ta·pir \'tā-pər\ *n, pl* **tapir** *or* **tapirs** : any of a genus of large harmless hoofed mammals of tropical America and Asia from Myanmar to Sumatra

tapir

tap·pet \'ta-pət\ *n* : a lever or projection moved by some other piece (as a cam) or intended to move something else

tap·room \'tap-ˌrüm, -ˌrùm\ *n* : BARROOM

tap·root \-ˌrüt, -ˌrùt\ *n* : a large main root growing straight down and giving off small side roots

taps \'taps\ *n sing or pl* : the last bugle call at night blown as a signal that lights are to be put out; *also* : a similar call blown at military funerals and memorial services

tap·ster \'tap-stər\ *n* : BARTENDER

¹tar \'tär\ *n* **1** : a thick dark sticky liquid distilled from organic material (as wood or coal) **2** : SAILOR, SEAMAN

²tar *vb* **tarred; tar·ring** : to cover or smear with or as if with tar

tar·an·tel·la \ˌtar-ən-'te-lə\ *n* : a lively folk dance of southern Italy in 6/8 time

ta·ran·tu·la \tə-'ran-chə-lə, -tə-lə\ *n, pl* **tarantulas** *also* **ta·ran·tu·lae** \-'ran-chə-ˌlē, -tə-ˌlē\ : any of a family of large hairy American spiders with a sharp bite that is not very poisonous to human beings

tar·dy \'tär-dē\ *adj* **tar·di·er; -est** **1** : moving slowly : SLUGGISH **2** : LATE **syn** behindhand, overdue, belated — **tar·di·ly** \-də-lē\ *adv* — **tar·di·ness** \-dē-nəs\ *n*

¹tare \'tar\ *n* : a weed of grainfields

²tare *n* : a deduction from the gross weight of a substance and its container made in allowance for the weight of the container — **tare** *vb*

¹tar·get \'tär-gət\ *n* [ME, fr. MF *targette*, dim. of *targe* light shield, of Gmc origin] **1** : a mark to shoot at **2** : an object of ridicule or criticism **3** : a goal to be achieved

²target *vb* : to make a target of

tar·iff \'tar-əf\ *n* [It *tariffa*, fr. Ar *taʿrīf* notification] **1** : a schedule of duties imposed by a government esp. on imported goods; *also* : a duty or rate of duty imposed in such a schedule **2** : a schedule of rates or charges

tar·mac \'tär-ˌmak\ *n* : a surface paved with crushed stone covered with tar

tarn \'tärn\ *n* : a small mountain lake

tar·nish \'tär-nish\ *vb* : to make or become dull or discolored — **tarnish** *n*

ta·ro \'tär-ō, 'tar-\ *n, pl* **taros** : a tropical plant related to the arums that is grown for its edible starchy fleshy root; *also* : this root

tar·ot \'tar-ō\ *n* : one of a set of usu. 78 playing cards used esp. for fortune-telling

tar·pau·lin \tär-'pò-lən, 'tär-pə-\ *n* : a piece of material (as durable plastic) used for protecting exposed objects

tar·pon \'tär-pən\ *n, pl* **tarpon** *or* **tarpons** : a large silvery bony fish often caught for sport in the warm coastal waters of the Atlantic esp. off Florida

tar·ra·gon \'tar-ə-gən\ *n* : a small widely cultivated perennial wormwood with pungent leaves used as a flavoring; *also* : its leaves

¹tar·ry \'tar-ē\ *vb* **tar·ried; tar·ry·ing** **1** : to be tardy : DELAY; *esp* : to be slow in leaving **2** : to stay in or at a place : SOJOURN **syn** remain, wait, linger, abide

²tar·ry \'tär-ē\ *adj* : of, resembling, or smeared with tar

tar sand *n* : sand or sandstone that is naturally soaked with the heavy sticky portions of petroleum

tar·sus \'tär-səs\ *n, pl* **tar·si** \-ˌsī\ [NL] : the part of a vertebrate foot between the metatarsus and the leg; *also* : the small bones that support this part — **tar·sal** \-səl\ *adj or n*

¹tart \'tärt\ *adj* **1** : agreeably sharp to the taste : PUNGENT **2** : BITING, CAUSTIC — **tart·ly** *adv* — **tart·ness** *n*

²tart *n* **1** : a small pie or pastry shell containing jelly, custard, or fruit **2** : PROSTITUTE

tar·tan \'tärt-ᵊn\ *n* : a twilled woolen fabric with a plaid design of Scottish origin consisting of stripes of varying width and color usu. patterned to designate a distinctive clan

tar·tar \'tär-tər\ *n* **1** : a substance in the juice of grapes deposited (as in wine casks) as a reddish crust or sediment **2** : a hard crust of saliva, food debris, and calcium salts on the teeth

tar·tar sauce *or* **tar·tare sauce** \'tär-tər-\ *n* : mayonnaise with chopped pickles, olives, or capers

¹task \'task\ *n* [ME *taske*, fr. OF *tasque*, fr. ML *tasca* tax or service imposed by a feudal superior, fr. *taxare* to tax] : a piece of assigned work **syn** job, duty, chore, stint, assignment

²task *vb* : to oppress with great labor

task force *n* : a temporary grouping to accomplish a particular objective

task·mas·ter \'task-ˌmas-tər\ *n* : one that imposes a task or burdens another with labor

¹tas·sel \'ta-səl, 'tä-\ *n* **1** : a hanging ornament made of a bunch of cords of even length fastened at one end **2** : something suggesting a tassel; *esp* : a male flower cluster of Indian corn

²tassel *vb* **-seled** *or* **-selled; -sel·ing** *or* **-sel·ling** : to adorn with or put forth tassels

¹taste \'tāst\ *vb* **tast·ed; tast·ing** **1** : EXPERIENCE, UNDERGO **2** : to try or determine the flavor of by taking a bit into the mouth **3** : to eat or drink esp. in small quantities : SAMPLE **4** : to have a specific flavor

²taste *n* **1** : a small amount tasted **2** : BIT; *esp* : a sample of experience **3** : the special sense that identifies sweet, sour, bitter, or salty qualities and is mediated by receptors in the taste buds of the tongue **4** : a quality perceptible to the sense of taste; *also* : a complex sensation involving true taste, smell, and touch **5** : individual preference **6** : critical judgment, discernment, or appreciation; *also* : aesthetic quality **syn** tang, relish, flavor, savor — **taste·ful** \-fəl\ *adj* — **taste·ful·ly** *adv* — **taste·less** *adj* — **taste·less·ly** *adv* — **tast·er** *n*

taste bud *n* : a sense organ mediating the sensation of taste

tasty \'tā-stē\ *adj* **tast·i·er; -est** : pleasing to the taste : SAVORY **syn** palatable, appetizing, toothsome, flavorsome — **tast·i·ness** \'tā-stē-nəs\ *n*

tat \'tat\ *vb* **tat·ted; tat·ting** : to work at or make by tatting

¹tat·ter \'ta-tər\ *vb* : to make or become ragged

²tatter *n* **1** : a part torn and left hanging **2** *pl* : tattered clothing

tat·ter·de·ma·lion \ˌta-tər-di-'māl-yən\ *n* : one that is ragged or disreputable

tat·ter·sall \'ta-tər-ˌsòl, -səl\ *n* : a pattern of colored lines forming squares on solid background; *also* : a fabric in a tattersall pattern

---

\ə\abut \ᵊ\kitten \ər\further \a\ash \ā\ace \ä\mop, mar \aù\out \ch\chin \e\bet \ē\easy \g\go \i\hit \ī\ice \j\job \ŋ\sing \ō\go \ò\law \òi\boy \th\thin \th̶\the \ü\loot \ù\foot \y\yet \zh\vision *see also* Pronunciation Symbols page

tat·ting \'ta-tiŋ\ *n* : a delicate handmade lace formed usu. by looping and knotting with a single thread and a small shuttle; *also* : the act or process of making such lace

tat·tle \'tat-ᵊl\ *vb* **tat·tled; tat·tling 1** : CHATTER, PRATE **2** : to tell secrets; *also* : to inform against another — **tat·tler** *n*

tat·tle·tale \'tat-ᵊl-ₜtāl\ *n* : one that tattles : INFORMER

¹tat·too \ta-'tü\ *n, pl* **tattoos** [alter. of earlier *taptoo*, fr. D *taptoe*, fr. the phrase *tap toe!* taps shut!] **1** : a call sounded before taps as notice to go to quarters **2** : a rapid rhythmic rapping

²tattoo *vb* : to mark (the skin) with tattoos

³tattoo *n, pl* **tattoos** [Tahitian *tatau*] : an indelible figure fixed upon the body esp. by insertion of pigment under the skin

tau \'taù, 'tò\ *n* : the 19th letter of the Greek alphabet— T or τ

taught *past and past part of* TEACH

¹taunt \'tònt\ *n* : a sarcastic challenge or insult

²taunt *vb* : to reproach or challenge in a mocking manner : jeer at **syn** mock, deride, ridicule, twit — **taunt·er** *n*

taupe \'tōp\ *n* : a brownish gray

Tau·rus \'tòr-əs\ *n* [L, lit., bull] **1** : a zodiacal constellation between Aries and Gemini usu. pictured as a bull **2** : the 2d sign of the zodiac in astrology; *also* : one born under this sign

taut \'tòt\ *adj* **1** : tightly drawn : not slack **2** : extremely nervous : TENSE **3** : TRIM, TIDY ⟨a ∼ ship⟩ — **taut·ly** *adv* — **taut·ness** *n*

tau·tol·o·gy \tò-'tä-lə-jē\ *n, pl* **-gies** : needless repetition of an idea, statement, or word; *also* : an instance of such repetition — **tau·to·log·i·cal** \ₜtòt-ᵊl-ə-ji-kəl\ *adj* — **tau·to·log·i·cal·ly** \-ji-k(ə-)lē\ *adv* — **tau·tol·o·gous** \tò-'tä-lə-gəs\ *adj* — **tau·tol·o·gous·ly** *adv*

tav·ern \'ta-vərn\ *n* [ME *taverne*, fr. OF, fr. L *taberna* hut, shop] **1** : an establishment where alcoholic liquors are sold to be drunk on the premises **2** : INN

taw \'tò\ *n* **1** : a marble used as a shooter **2** : the line from which players shoot at marbles

taw·dry \'tò-drē\ *adj* **taw·dri·er; -est** [*tawdry lace* a tie of lace for the neck, fr. *St. Audrey* (St. Etheldreda) †679 queen of Northumbria] : cheap and gaudy in appearance and quality **syn** garish, flashy, chintzy, meretricious — **taw·dri·ly** *adv*

taw·ny \'tò-nē\ *adj* **taw·ni·er; -est** : of a brownish orange color

¹tax \'taks\ *vb* **1** : to levy a tax on **2** : CHARGE, ACCUSE **3** : to put under pressure — **tax·able** \'tak-sə-bəl\ *adj* — **tax·a·tion** \tak-'sā-shən\ *n*

²tax *n* **1** : a charge usu. of money imposed by authority on persons or property for public purposes **2** : a heavy charge : STRAIN

¹taxi \'tak-sē\ *n, pl* **tax·is** \-sēz\ *also* **tax·ies** : TAXICAB; *also* : a similarly operated boat or aircraft

²taxi *vb* **tax·ied; taxi·ing** *or* **taxy·ing; tax·is** *or* **tax·ies 1** : to move along the ground or on the water under an aircraft's own power when starting or after a landing **2** : to go by taxicab

taxi·cab \'tak-sē-ₜkab\ *n* : an automobile that carries passengers for a fare usu. based on the distance traveled

taxi·der·my \'tak-sə-ₜdər-mē\ *n* : the skill or occupation of preparing, stuffing, and mounting skins of animals — **taxi·der·mist** \-mist\ *n*

tax·on·o·my \tak-'sä-nə-mē\ *n* : classification esp. of animals or plants according to natural relationships — **tax·o·nom·ic** \ₜtak-sə-'nä-mik\ *adj* — **tax·on·o·mist** \tak-'sä-nə-mist\ *n*

tax·pay·er \'taks-ₜpā-ər\ *n* : one who pays or is liable for a tax — **tax·pay·ing** *adj*

Tay–Sachs disease \'tā-'saks-\ *n* : a hereditary disorder caused by the absence of an enzyme needed to break down fatty material, marked by buildup of lipids in nervous tissue, and causing death in childhood

tb *abbr* tablespoon; tablespoonful

Tb *symbol* terbium

TB \ₜtē-'bē\ *n* : TUBERCULOSIS

TBA *abbr, often not cap* to be announced

T–bar \'tē-ₜbär\ *n* : a ski lift with a series of T= shaped bars

tbs *or* **tbsp** *abbr* tablespoon; tablespoonful

Tc *symbol* technetium

TC *abbr* teachers college

T cell *n* : any of several lymphocytes (as a helper T cell) specialized esp. for activity in and control of immunity and the immune response

TD *abbr* **1** touchdown **2** Treasury Department

TDD *abbr* telecommunications device for the deaf

TDY *abbr* temporary duty

Te *symbol* tellurium

tea \'tē\ *n* **1** : the cured leaves and leaf buds of a shrub grown chiefly in China, Japan, India, and Sri Lanka; *also* : this shrub **2** : a drink made by steeping tea in boiling water **3** : refreshments usu. including tea served in late afternoon; *also* : a reception at which tea is served

teach \'tēch\ *vb* **taught** \'tòt\; **teach·ing 1** : to cause to know something : act as a teacher **2** : to show how ⟨∼ a child to swim⟩ **3** : to make to know the disagreeable consequences of an action **4** : to guide the studies of **5** : to impart the knowledge of ⟨∼ algebra⟩ — **teach·able** *adj* — **teach·er** *n*

teach·ing *n* **1** : the act, practice, or profession of a teacher **2** : something taught; *esp* : DOCTRINE

tea·cup \'tē-ₜkəp\ *n* : a small cup used with a saucer for hot beverages

teak \'tēk\ *n* : the hard durable yellowish brown wood of a tall East Indian timber tree related to the vervains; *also* : this tree

tea·ket·tle \'tē-ₜket-ᵊl\ *n* : a covered kettle with a handle and spout for boiling water

teal \'tēl\ *n, pl* **teal** *or* **teals 1** : any of various small short= necked wild ducks **2** : a dark greenish blue color

teal 1

¹team \'tēm\ *n* [ME *teme*, fr. OE *tēam* offspring, lineage, group of draft animals] **1** : two or more draft animals harnessed to the same vehicle or implement **2** : a number of persons associated in work or activity; *esp* : a group on one side in a match

²team *vb* **1** : to haul with or drive a team **2** : to form a team : join forces

³team *adj* : of or performed by a team; *also* : marked by devotion to teamwork ⟨a ∼ player⟩

team·mate \-ₜmāt\ *n* : a fellow member of a team

team·ster \'tēm-stər\ *n* : one that drives a team or truck

team·work \-ₜwərk\ *n* : the work or activity of a number of persons acting in close association as members of a unit

tea·pot \'tē-ₜpät\ *n* : a vessel with a spout for brewing and serving tea

¹tear \'tir\ *n* : a drop of the salty liquid that moistens the eye and inner side of the eyelids; *also, pl* : an act of weeping or grieving — **tear·ful** \-fəl\ *adj* — **tear·ful·ly** *adv*

²**tear** \'tir\ *vb* : to fill with or shed tears ⟨eyes ∼*ing* in the wind⟩

³**tear** \'tar\ *vb* **tore** \'tōr\; **torn** \'tōrn\; **tear·ing** **1** : to separate parts of or pull apart by force : REND **2** : LACERATE **3** : to disrupt by the pull of contrary forces **4** : to remove by force : WRENCH **5** : to move or act with violence, haste, or force **syn** rip, split, cleave, rend

⁴**tear** \'tar\ *n* **1** : the act of tearing **2** : a hole or flaw made by tearing : RENT

tear gas \'tir-\ *n* : a substance that on dispersion in the atmosphere blinds the eyes with tears — **tear gas** *vb*

tear·jerk·er \'tir-₁jər-kər\ *n* : an extravagantly pathetic story, song, play, movie, or broadcast

¹**tease** \'tēz\ *vb* **teased; teas·ing** **1** : to disentangle and lay parallel by combing or carding ⟨∼ wool⟩ **2** : to scratch the surface of (cloth) so as to raise a nap **3** : to annoy persistently esp. in fun by goading, coaxing, or tantalizing **4** : to comb (hair) by taking a strand and pushing the short hairs toward the scalp with the comb **syn** harass, worry, pester, annoy

²**tease** *n* **1** : the act of teasing or state of being teased **2** : one that teases

tea·sel \'tē-zəl\ *n* : a prickly herb or its flower head covered with stiff bracts and used to raise the nap on cloth; *also* : an artificial device used for this purpose

tea·spoon \'tē-₁spün\ *n* **1** : a small spoon suitable for stirring beverages **2** : a unit of measure equal to ⅙ fluid ounce (5 milliliters)

tea·spoon·ful \-₁fül\ *n, pl* **-spoonfuls** *also* **-spoons·ful** \-₁spünz-₁fül\ : TEASPOON 2

teat \'tit, 'tēt\ *n* : the protuberance through which milk is drawn from an udder or breast

Te·bet \tā-'vāt, -'vāth; 'tā-vəs\ *n* [Heb *Tēbhēth*] : the 4th month of the civil year or the 10th month of the ecclesiastical year in the Jewish calendar

tech *abbr* **1** technical; technically; technician **2** technological; technology

tech·ne·tium \tek-'nē-shē-əm\ *n* : a metallic chemical element produced in certain nuclear reactions — see ELEMENT table

tech·nic \'tek-nik, tek-'nēk\ *n* : TECHNIQUE 1

tech·ni·cal \'tek-ni-kəl\ *adj* [Gk *technikos* of art, skillful, fr. *technē* art, craft, skill] **1** : having special knowledge esp. of a mechanical or scientific subject ⟨∼ experts⟩ **2** : of or relating to a particular and esp. a practical or scientific subject ⟨∼ training⟩ **3** : according to a strict interpretation of the rules **4** : of or relating to technique — **tech·ni·cal·ly** \-k(ə-)lē\ *adv*

tech·ni·cal·i·ty \₁tek-nə-'ka-lə-tē\ *n, pl* **-ties** **1** : a detail meaningful only to a specialist **2** : the quality or state of being technical

technical sergeant *n* : a noncommissioned officer in the air force ranking next below a master sergeant

tech·ni·cian \tek-'ni-shən\ *n* : a person who has acquired the technique of a specialized skill or subject

tech·nique \tek-'nēk\ *n* [F] **1** : the manner in which technical details are treated or basic physical movements are used **2** : technical methods

tech·noc·ra·cy \tek-'nä-krə-sē\ *n* : management of society by technical experts — **tech·no·crat** \'tek-nə-₁krat\ *n* — **tech·no·crat·ic** \₁tek-nə-'kra-tik\ *adj*

tech·nol·o·gy \tek-'nä-lə-jē\ *n, pl* **-gies** : ENGINEERING; *also* : a manner of accomplishing a task using technical methods or knowledge — **tech·no·log·i·cal** \₁tek-nə-'lä-ji-kəl\ *adj*

tec·ton·ics \tek-'tä-niks\ *n sing or pl* **1** : geological structural features **2** : geology dealing esp. with the faulting and folding of a planet or moon — **tec·ton·ic** \-nik\ *adj*

ted·dy bear \'te-dē-₁bar\ *n* [*Teddy* Roosevelt; fr. a cartoon depicting the president sparing the life of a bear cub while hunting] : a stuffed toy bear

te·dious \'tē-dē-əs\ *adj* : tiresome because of length or dullness **syn** boring, tiring, irksome — **te·dious·ly** *adv* — **te·dious·ness** *n*

te·di·um \'tē-dē-əm\ *n* : TEDIOUSNESS; *also* : BOREDOM

¹**tee** \'tē\ *n* : a small mound or peg on which a golf ball is placed to be hit at the beginning of play on a hole; *also* : the area from which the ball is hit to begin play

²**tee** *vb* **teed; tee·ing** : to place (a ball) on a tee

teem \'tēm\ *vb* : to become filled to overflowing : ABOUND **syn** swarm, crawl, flow

teen *adj* : TEENAGE

teen·age \'tē-₁nāj\ *or* **teen·aged** \-₁nājd\ *adj* : of, being, or relating to people in their teens — **teen·ag·er** \-₁nā-jər\ *n*

teens \'tēnz\ *n pl* : the numbers 13 to 19 inclusive; *esp* : the years 13 to 19 in a person's life

tee·ny \'tē-nē\ *adj* **tee·ni·er; -est** : TINY

tee·pee *var of* TEPEE

tee shirt *var of* T-SHIRT

tee·ter \'tē-tər\ *vb* **1** : to move unsteadily **2** : SEESAW — **teeter** *n*

teeth *pl of* TOOTH

teethe \'tēth\ *vb* **teethed; teeth·ing** : to grow teeth : cut one's teeth

teeth·ing *n* : growth of the first set of teeth through the gums with its accompanying phenomena

tee·to·tal \'tē-'tōt-°l, -₁tōt-\ *adj* : of or relating to the practice of complete abstinence from alcoholic drinks — **tee·to·tal·er** *or* **tee·to·tal·ler** \-'tōt-°l-ər\ *n* — **tee·to·tal·ism** \-°l-₁i-zəm\ *n*

TEFL *abbr* teaching English as a foreign language

tek·tite \'tek-₁tīt\ *n* : a glassy body of probably meteoric origin

tel *abbr* **1** telegram **2** telegraph **3** telephone

tele·cast \'te-li-₁kast\ *vb* **-cast** *also* **-cast·ed; -cast·ing** : to broadcast by television — **telecast** *n* — **tele·cast·er** *n*

tele·com·mu·ni·ca·tion \₁te-li-kə-₁myü- nə-'kā-shən\ *n* : communication at a distance (as by telephone or radio)

tele·con·fer·ence \'te-li-₁kän-fə-rəns\ *n* : a conference among people remote from one another held using telecommunications — **tele·con·fer·enc·ing** *n*

teleg *abbr* telegraphy

tele·ge·nic \₁te-lə-'je-nik, -'jē-\ *adj* : markedly attractive to television viewers

tele·gram \'te-lə-₁gram\ *n* : a message sent by telegraph

¹**tele·graph** \-₁graf\ *n* : an electric apparatus or system for sending messages by a code over wires — **tele·graph·ic** \₁te-lə-'gra-fik\ *adj*

²**telegraph** *vb* : to send or communicate by or as if by telegraph — **te·leg·ra·pher** \tə-'le-grə-fər\ *n*

te·leg·ra·phy \tə-'le-grə-fē\ *n* : the use or operation of a telegraph apparatus or system

tele·mar·ket·ing \₁te-lə-'mär-kə-tiŋ\ *n* : the marketing of goods or services by telephone — **tele·mar·ket·er** \-tər\ *n*

te·lem·e·try \tə-'le-mə-trē\ *n* : the transmission esp. by radio of measurements made by automatic instruments to a distant station — **te·le·me·ter** \'te-lə-₁mē-tər\ *n*

te·lep·a·thy \tə-'le-pə-thē\ *n* : apparent communication from one mind to another by extrasensory means — **tele·path·ic** \₁te-lə-'pa-thik\ *adj* — **tele·path·i·cal·ly** \-thi-k(ə-)lē\ *adv*

¹**tele·phone** \'te-lə-₁fōn\ *n* : an instrument for sending and receiving sounds over long distances by electricity

²**telephone** *vb* **-phoned; -phon·ing** **1** : to send or commu-

---

\ə\abut \ᵊ\kitten \ər\further \a\ash \ā\ace \ä\mop, mar
\au̇\out \ch\chin \e\bet \ē\easy \g\go \i\hit \ī\ice \j\job
\ŋ\sing \ō\go \ȯ\law \oi\boy \th\thin \th\the \ü\loot \u̇\foot
\y\yet \zh\vision *see also* Pronunciation Symbols page

nicate by telephone **2** : to speak to (a person) by telephone — **te·le·phon·er** *n*

te·le·pho·ny \tə-'le-fə-nē, 'te-lə-ˌfō-\ *n* : use or operation of apparatus for transmission of sounds between distant points — **tel·e·phon·ic** \ˌte-lə-'fä-nik\ *adj*

tele·pho·to \ˌte-lə-'fō-tō\ *adj* : being a camera lens giving a large image of a distant object — **tele·pho·tog·ra·phy** \-fə-'tä-grə-fē\ *n*

tele·play \'te-li-ˌplā\ *n* : a play written for television

tele·print·er \'te-lə-ˌprin-tər\ *n* : TELETYPEWRITER

¹tele·scope \'te-lə-ˌskōp\ *n* **1** : a cylindrical instrument equipped with lenses or mirrors for viewing distant objects **2** : RADIO TELESCOPE

²telescope *vb* **-scoped; -scop·ing 1** : to slide or pass or cause to slide or pass one within another like the sections of a collapsible hand telescope **2** : COMPRESS, CONDENSE

tele·scop·ic \ˌte-lə-'skä-pik\ *adj* **1** : of or relating to a telescope **2** : seen only by a telescope **3** : able to discern objects at a distance **4** : having parts that telescope — **tele·scop·i·cal·ly** \-pi-k(ə-)lē\ *adv*

tele·text \'te-lə-ˌtekst\ *n* : a system for broadcasting text over a television signal and displaying it on a decoder-equipped television

tele·thon \'te-lə-ˌthän\ *n* : a long television program usu. to solicit funds for a charity

tele·type·writ·er \ˌte-lə-'tīp-ˌrī-tər\ *n* : a printing device resembling a typewriter used to send and receive signals over telephone lines

tele·vise \'te-lə-ˌvīz\ *vb* **-vised; -vis·ing** : to broadcast by television

tele·vi·sion \'te-lə-ˌvi-zhən\ *n* [F *télévision*, fr. Gk *tēle* far, at a distance + F *vision* vision] : a system for transmitting images and sound by converting them into electrical or radio waves which are converted back into images and sound by a receiver; *also* : a television receiving set

tell \'tel\ *vb* **told** \'tōld\; **tell·ing 1** : COUNT, ENUMERATE **2** : to relate in detail : NARRATE **3** : SAY, UTTER **4** : to make known : REVEAL **5** : to report to : INFORM **6** : ORDER, DIRECT **7** : to find out by observing **8** : to have a marked effect **9** : to serve as evidence **syn** disclose, discover, betray

tell·er \'te-lər\ *n* **1** : one that relates : NARRATOR **2** : one that counts **3** : a bank employee handling money received or paid out

tell·ing \'te-liŋ\ *adj* : producing a marked effect : EFFECTIVE **syn** cogent, convincing, sound

tell off *vb* : REPRIMAND, SCOLD

tell·tale \'tel-ˌtāl\ *n* **1** : INFORMER, TATTLETALE **2** : something that serves to disclose : INDICATION — **telltale** *adj*

tel·lu·ri·um \tə-'lùr-ē-əm\ *n* : a chemical element used esp. in alloys — see ELEMENT table

tem·blor \'tem-blər\ *n* [Sp, lit., trembling] : EARTHQUAKE

te·mer·i·ty \tə-'mer-ə-tē\ *n, pl* **-ties** : rash or presumptuous daring : BOLDNESS **syn** audacity, effrontery, gall, nerve, cheek

¹temp \'temp\ *n* **1** : TEMPERATURE **2** : a temporary worker

²temp *abbr* temporary

¹tem·per \'tem-pər\ *vb* **1** : to dilute or soften by the addition of something else ⟨~ justice with mercy⟩ **2** : to bring (as steel) to a desired hardness by reheating and cooling **3** : to toughen (glass) by gradual heating and cooling **4** : TOUGHEN **5** : TUNE

²temper *n* **1** : characteristic tone : TENDENCY **2** : the hardness or toughness of a substance ⟨~ of a knife blade⟩ **3** : a characteristic frame of mind : DISPOSITION **4** : calmness of mind : COMPOSURE **5** : state of feeling or frame of mind at a particular time **6** : heat of mind or emotion **syn** temperament, character, personality, makeup — **tem·pered** \'tem-pərd\ *adj*

tem·pera \'tem-pə-rə\ *n* [It] : a painting process using an

albuminous or colloidal medium as a vehicle; *also* : a painting done in tempera

tem·per·a·ment \'tem-prə-mənt, -pər-mənt\ *n* **1** : characteristic or habitual inclination or mode of emotional response : DISPOSITION ⟨nervous ~⟩ **2** : excessive sensitiveness or irritability **syn** character, personality, nature, makeup — **tem·per·a·men·tal** \ˌtem-prə-'ment-ᵊl, -pər-'ment-\ *adj*

tem·per·ance \'tem-prəns, -pə-rəns\ *n* : habitual moderation in the indulgence of the appetites or passions; *esp* : moderation in or abstinence from the use of intoxicating drink

tem·per·ate \'tem-prət, -pə-rət\ *adj* **1** : not extreme or excessive : MILD **2** : moderate in indulgence of appetite or desire **3** : moderate in the use of intoxicating liquors **4** : having a moderate climate **syn** sober, continent, abstemious

temperate zone *n, often cap T&Z* : the region between the tropic of Cancer and the arctic circle or between the tropic of Capricorn and the antarctic circle

tem·per·a·ture \'tem-pər-ˌchùr, -prə-ˌchùr, -chər\ *n* **1** : degree of hotness or coldness of something (as air, water, or the body) as shown by a thermometer **2** : FEVER

tem·pest \'tem-pəst\ *n* [ME, fr. OF *tempeste*, ultim. fr. L *tempestas* season, weather, storm, fr. *tempus* time] : a violent storm

tem·pes·tu·ous \tem-'pes-chə-wəs\ *adj* : of, involving, or resembling a tempest : STORMY — **tem·pes·tu·ous·ly** *adv* — **tem·pes·tu·ous·ness** *n*

tem·plate *also* **tem·plet** \'tem-plət\ *n* : a gauge, mold, or pattern that functions as a guide to the form or structure of something being made

¹tem·ple \'tem-pəl\ *n* **1** : an edifice for the worship of a deity **2** : a place devoted to a special or exalted purpose

²temple *n* : the flattened space on each side of the forehead esp. of humans

tem·po \'tem-pō\ *n, pl* **tem·pi** \-(ˌ)pē\ *or* **tempos** [It, lit., time] **1** : the rate of speed of a musical piece or passage **2** : rate of motion or activity : PACE

¹tem·po·ral \'tem-pə-rəl\ *adj* **1** : of, relating to, or limited by time ⟨~ and spatial bounds⟩ **2** : of or relating to earthly life or secular concerns ⟨~ power⟩

²temporal *adj* : of or relating to the temples or the sides of the skull

¹tem·po·rary \'tem-pə-ˌrer-ē\ *adj* : lasting for a time only : TRANSITORY **syn** transient, ephemeral, momentary, impermanent — **tem·po·rar·i·ly** \ˌtem-pə-'rer-ə-lē\ *adv*

²temporary *n, pl* **-rar·ies** : one serving for a limited time

tem·po·rize \'tem-pə-ˌrīz\ *vb* **-rized; -riz·ing 1** : to adapt one's actions to the time or the dominant opinion : COMPROMISE **2** : to draw out matters so as to gain time — **tem·po·riz·er** *n*

tempt \'tempt\ *vb* **1** : to entice to do wrong by promise of pleasure or gain **2** : PROVOKE **3** : to risk the dangers of **4** : to induce to do something : INCITE **syn** inveigle, decoy, seduce, lure — **tempt·er** *n* — **tempt·ing·ly** *adv*

temp·ta·tion \temp-'tā-shən\ *n* **1** : the act of tempting : the state of being tempted **2** : something that tempts

tempt·ress \'temp-trəs\ *n* : a woman who tempts

ten \'ten\ *n* **1** : one more than nine **2** : the 10th in a set or series **3** : something having 10 units — **ten** *adj or pron* — **tenth** \'tenth\ *adj or adv or n*

ten·a·ble \'te-nə-bəl\ *adj* : capable of being held, maintained, or defended — **ten·a·bil·i·ty** \ˌte-nə-'bi-lə-tē\ *n*

te·na·cious \tə-'nā-shəs\ *adj* **1** : not easily pulled apart : COHESIVE, TOUGH ⟨a ~ metal⟩ **2** : holding fast ⟨~ of his rights⟩ **3** : RETENTIVE ⟨a ~ memory⟩ — **te·na·cious·ly** *adv* — **te·nac·i·ty** \tə-'na-sə-tē\ *n*

ten·an·cy \'te-nən-sē\ *n, pl* **-cies** : the temporary possession or occupancy of something (as a house) that belongs to another; *also* : the period of a tenant's occupancy

ten·ant \'te-nənt\ *n* **1** : one who rents or leases (as a house) from a landlord **2** : DWELLER, OCCUPANT — **ten-ant** *vb* — **ten·ant·less** *adj*

tenant farmer *n* : a farmer who works land owned by another and pays rent either in cash or in shares of produce

ten·ant·ry \'te-nən-trē\ *n, pl* **-ries** : the body of tenants esp. on a great estate

Ten Commandments *n pl* : the commandments of God given to Moses on Mount Sinai

¹tend \'tend\ *vb* **1** : to apply oneself ⟨∼ to your affairs⟩ **2** : to take care of ⟨∼ a plant⟩ **3** : to manage the operations of ⟨∼ a machine⟩

²tend *vb* **1** : to move or develop one's course in a particular direction **2** : to show an inclination or tendency

ten·den·cy \'ten-dən-sē\ *n, pl* **-cies 1** : DRIFT, TREND **2** : a proneness to or readiness for a particular kind of thought or action : PROPENSITY **syn** bent, leaning, disposition, inclination

ten·den·tious \ten-'den-chəs\ *adj* : marked by a tendency in favor of a particular point of view : BIASED — **ten·den·tious·ly** *adv* — **ten·den·tious·ness** *n*

¹ten·der \'ten-dər\ *adj* **1** : having a soft texture : easily broken, chewed, or cut **2** : physically weak : DELICATE; *also* : IMMATURE **3** : expressing or responsive to love or sympathy : LOVING, COMPASSIONATE **4** : SENSITIVE, TOUCHY **syn** sympathetic, warm, warmhearted — **ten·der·ly** *adv* — **ten·der·ness** *n*

²tender *n* **1** : an offer or proposal made for acceptance; *esp* : an offer of a bid for a contract **2** : something (as money) that may be offered in payment

³tender *vb* : to present for acceptance

⁴tend·er \'ten-dər\ *n* **1** : one that tends or takes care **2** : a boat carrying passengers and freight to a larger ship **3** : a car attached to a steam locomotive for carrying fuel and water

ten·der·foot \'ten-dər-ˌfut\ *n, pl* **-feet** \-ˌfēt\ *also* **-foots** \-ˌfuts\ **1** : one not hardened to frontier or rough outdoor life **2** : an inexperienced beginner

ten·der·heart·ed \ˌten-dər-'här-təd\ *adj* : easily moved to love, pity, or sorrow

ten·der·ize \'ten-də-ˌrīz\ *vb* **-ized; -iz·ing** : to make (meat) tender — **ten·der·iz·er** \'ten-də-ˌrī-zər\ *n*

ten·der·loin \'ten-dər-ˌloin\ *n* **1** : a tender strip of beef or pork from near the backbone **2** : a district of a city largely devoted to vice

ten·di·ni·tis *or* **ten·don·itis** \ˌten-də-'nī-təs\ *n* : inflammation of a tendon

ten·don \'ten-dən\ *n* : a tough cord of dense white fibrous tissue uniting a muscle with another part (as a bone) — **ten·di·nous** \-də-nəs\ *adj*

ten·dril \'ten-drəl\ *n* : a slender coiling organ by which some climbing plants attach themselves to a support

ten·e·brous \'te-nə-brəs\ *adj* : shut off from the light : GLOOMY, OBSCURE

ten·e·ment \'te-nə-mənt\ *n* **1** : a house used as a dwelling **2** : a building divided into apartments for rent to families; *esp* : one meeting only minimum standards of safety and comfort **3** : APARTMENT, FLAT

te·net \'te-nət\ *n* [L, he holds, fr. *tenēre* to hold] : one of the principles or doctrines held in common by members of a group (as a church or profession) **syn** doctrine, dogma, belief

ten·fold \'ten-ˌfōld, -'fōld\ *adj* : being 10 times as great or as many — **ten·fold** \-'fōld\ *adv*

ten–gallon hat *n* : a wide-brimmed hat with a large soft crown

Tenn *abbr* Tennessee

ten·nis \'te-nəs\ *n* : a game played with a ball and racket on a court divided by a net

ten·on \'te-nən\ *n* : a projecting part in a piece of material (as wood) for insertion into a mortise to make a joint

ten·or \'te-nər\ *n* **1** : the general drift of something spo-

ken or written **2** : the highest natural adult male voice; *also* : a singer having this voice **3** : a continuing in a course, movement, or activity ⟨the ∼ of my life⟩

ten·our *chiefly Brit var of* TENOR

ten·pen·ny \'ten-ˌpe-nē\ *adj* : amounting to, worth, or costing 10 pennies

tenpenny nail *n* : a nail three inches (about 7.6 centimeters) long

ten-pin \'ten-ˌpin\ *n* : a bottle-shaped bowling pin set in groups of 10 and bowled at in a game (**tenpins**)

¹tense \'tens\ *n* [ME *tens* time, tense, fr. MF, fr. L *tempus*] : distinction of form of a verb to indicate the time of the action or state

²tense *adj* **tens·er; tens·est** [L *tensus*, fr. pp. of *tendere* to stretch] **1** : stretched tight : TAUT **2** : feeling or showing nervous tension **syn** stiff, rigid, inflexible — **tense·ly** *adv* — **tense·ness** *n* — **ten·si·ty** \'ten-sə-tē\ *n*

³tense *vb* **tensed; tens·ing** : to make or become tense

ten·sile \'ten-səl, -ˌsīl\ *adj* : of or relating to tension ⟨∼ strength⟩

ten·sion \'ten-chən\ *n* **1** : the act of straining or stretching; *also* : the condition of being strained or stretched **2** : a state of mental unrest often with signs of bodily stress **3** : a state of latent hostility or opposition

ten–speed \'ten-ˌspēd\ *n* : a bicycle with a derailleur having 10 possible combinations of gears

¹tent \'tent\ *n* **1** : a collapsible shelter of material stretched and supported by poles **2** : a canopy placed over the head and shoulders to retain vapors or oxygen given for medical reasons

²tent *vb* **1** : to lodge in tents **2** : to cover with or as if with a tent

ten·ta·cle \'ten-ti-kəl\ *n* : any of various long flexible projections about the head or mouth (as of an insect, mollusk, or fish) — **ten·ta·cled** \-kəld\ *adj* — **ten·tac·u·lar** \ten-'ta-kyə-lər\ *adj*

ten·ta·tive \'ten-tə-tiv\ *adj* **1** : not fully worked out or developed ⟨∼ plans⟩ **2** : HESITANT, UNCERTAIN ⟨a ∼ smile⟩ — **ten·ta·tive·ly** *adv*

ten·u·ous \'ten-yə-wəs\ *adj* **1** : not dense : RARE ⟨a ∼ fluid⟩ **2** : not thick : SLENDER ⟨a ∼ rope⟩ **3** : having little substance : FLIMSY, WEAK ⟨∼ influences⟩ **4** : lacking stability : SHAKY ⟨∼ reasoning⟩ — **te·nu·i·ty** \te-'nü-ə-tē, tə-, -'nyü-\ *n* — **ten·u·ous·ly** *adv* — **ten·u·ous·ness** *n*

ten·ure \'ten-yər\ *n* : the act, right, manner, or period of holding something (as a landed property, an office, or a position)

ten·ured \'ten-yərd\ *adj* : having tenure ⟨∼ faculty members⟩

te·o·sin·te \ˌtā-ō-'sin-tē\ *n* : a tall annual grass of Mexico and Central America closely related to maize

te·pee \'tē-(ˌ)pē\ *n* [Dakota *tʰípi*, fr. *tʰi-* to dwell] : an American Indian conical tent usu. of skins

tep·id \'te-pəd\ *adj* **1** : moderately warm : LUKEWARM **2** : HALFHEARTED

te·qui·la \tə-'kē-lə, tā-\ *n* : a Mexican liquor made from mescal

ter *abbr* **1** terrace **2** territory

ter·bi·um \'tər-bē-əm\ *n* : a metallic chemical element — see ELEMENT table

ter·cen·te·na·ry \ˌtər-sen-'te-nə-rē, tər-'sent-ᵊn-ˌer-ē\ *n, pl* **-ries** : a 300th anniversary or its celebration — **tercentenary** *adj*

ter·cen·ten·ni·al \ˌtər-ˌsen-'te-nē-əl\ *adj or n* : TERCENTENARY

te·re·do \tə-'rē-dō, -'rā-\ *n, pl* **teredos** *or* **te·red·i·nes** \-'red-ᵊn-ˌēz\ [L] : SHIPWORM

\ə\abut \ᵊ\kitten \ər\further \a\ash \ā\ace \ä\mop, mar \au̇\out \ch\chin \e\bet \ē\easy \g\go \i\hit \ī\ice \j\job \ŋ\sing \ō\go \ȯ\law \ȯi\boy \th\thin \t͟h\the \ü\loot \u̇\foot \y\yet \zh\vision *see also* Pronunciation Symbols page

¹**term** \ˈtərm\ *n* 1 : END, TERMINATION 2 : DURATION; *esp* : a period of time fixed esp. by law or custom 3 : a mathematical expression connected with another by a plus or minus sign; *also* : an element (as a numerator) of a fraction or proportion 4 : a word or expression that has a precise meaning in some uses or is limited to a particular subject or field 5 *pl* : PROVISIONS, CONDITIONS ⟨∼s of a contract⟩ 6 *pl* : mutual relationship ⟨on good ∼s⟩ 7 : AGREEMENT, CONCORD

²**term** *vb* : to apply a term to : CALL

ter·ma·gant \ˈtər-mə-gənt\ *n* : an overbearing or nagging woman : SHREW

¹**ter·mi·nal** \ˈtər-mən-ᵊl\ *adj* 1 : of, relating to, or forming an end, limit, or terminus 2 : being or being in the final stages of a fatal disease ⟨a ∼ patient⟩ ⟨∼ illness⟩ **syn** final, concluding, last, latest — **ter·mi·nal·ly** *adv*

²**terminal** *n* 1 : EXTREMITY, END 2 : a device at the end of a wire or on electrical equipment for making a connection 3 : either end of a transportation line (as a railroad) with its offices and freight and passenger stations; *also* : a freight or passenger station 4 : a device (as in a computer system) for data entry and display

ter·mi·nate \ˈtər-mə-ˌnāt\ *vb* **-nat·ed; -nat·ing** : to bring or come to an end **syn** conclude, finish, complete — **ter·mi·na·ble** \-nə-bəl\ *adj* — **ter·mi·na·tion** \ˌtər-mə-ˈnā-shən\ *n* — **ter·mi·na·tor** \ˈtər-mə-ˌnā-tər\ *n*

ter·mi·nol·o·gy \ˌtər-mə-ˈnä-lə-jē\ *n, pl* **-gies** : the technical or special terms used in a business, art, science, or special subject

ter·mi·nus \ˈtər-mə-nəs\ *n, pl* **-ni** \-ˌnī\ *or* **-nus·es** [L] 1 : final goal : END 2 : either end of a transportation line or travel route; *also* : the station or city at such a place

ter·mite \ˈtər-ˌmīt\ *n* : any of numerous pale soft-bodied social insects that feed on wood

tern \ˈtərn\ *n* : any of various chiefly marine birds with narrow wings and often a forked tail

ter·na·ry \ˈtər-nə-rē\ *adj* 1 : of, relating to, or proceeding by threes 2 : having three elements or parts

terr *abbr* territory

¹**ter·race** \ˈter-əs\ *n* 1 : a flat roof or open platform 2 : a level area next to a building 3 : an embankment with level top 4 : a bank or ridge on a slope to conserve moisture and soil 5 : a row of houses on raised land; *also* : a street with such a row of houses 6 : a strip of park in the middle of a street

²**terrace** *vb* **ter·raced; ter·rac·ing** : to form into a terrace or supply with terraces

ter·ra-cot·ta \ˌter-ə-ˈkä-tə\ *n* [It *terra cotta,* lit., baked earth] : a reddish brown earthenware

terra fir·ma \-ˈfər-mə\ *n* [NL] : solid ground

ter·rain \tə-ˈrān\ *n* : the surface features of an area of land ⟨a rough ∼⟩

ter·ra in·cog·ni·ta \ˈter-ə-ˌin-ˌkäg-ˈnē-tə\ *n, pl* **ter·rae in·cog·ni·tae** \ˈter-ˌī-ˌin-ˌkäg-ˈnē-tī\ [L] : an unexplored area or field of knowledge

ter·ra·pin \ˈter-ə-pən\ *n* : any of various turtles of fresh or brackish water

ter·rar·i·um \tə-ˈrar-ē-əm\ *n, pl* **-ia** \-ē-ə\ *or* **-i·ums** : a usu. transparent enclosure for keeping or raising small plants and animals indoors

ter·res·tri·al \tə-ˈres-trē-əl\ *adj* 1 : of or relating to the earth or its inhabitants 2 : living or growing on land ⟨∼ plants⟩ **syn** mundane, earthly, worldly

ter·ri·ble \ˈter-ə-bəl\ *adj* 1 : exciting terror : FEARFUL, DREADFUL ⟨∼ weapons⟩ 2 : hard to bear : DISTRESSING ⟨a ∼ situation⟩ 3 : extreme in degree : INTENSE ⟨∼ heat⟩ 4 : of very poor quality : AWFUL ⟨a ∼ play⟩ **syn** frightful, horrible, shocking, appalling — **ter·ri·bly** \-blē\ *adv*

ter·ri·er \ˈter-ē-ər\ *n* [F (*chien*) *terrier,* lit., earth dog, fr. *terrier* of earth, fr. ML *terrarius,* fr. L *terra* earth] : any of various usu. small dogs orig. used by hunters to drive small game animals from their holes

ter·rif·ic \tə-ˈri-fik\ *adj* 1 : exciting terror 2 : EXTRAORDINARY, ASTOUNDING ⟨∼ speed⟩ 3 : unusually good ⟨makes ∼ chili⟩

ter·ri·fy \ˈter-ə-ˌfī\ *vb* **-fied; -fy·ing** : to fill with terror : FRIGHTEN **syn** scare, terrorize, startle, alarm — **ter·ri·fy·ing·ly** *adv*

ter·ri·to·ry \ˈter-ə-ˌtōr-ē\ *n, pl* **-ries** 1 : a geographical area belonging to or under the authority of a governmental authority 2 : a part of the U.S. not included within any state but organized with a separate legislature 3 : REGION, DISTRICT; *also* : a region in which one feels at home 4 : a field of knowledge or interest 5 : an assigned area 6 : an area occupied and defended by one or a group of animals — **ter·ri·to·ri·al** \ˌter-ə-ˈtōr-ē-əl\ *adj*

ter·ror \ˈter-ər\ *n* 1 : a state of intense fear : FRIGHT 2 : one that inspires fear **syn** panic, consternation, dread, alarm, dismay, horror, trepidation

ter·ror·ism \ˈter-ər-ˌi-zəm\ *n* : the systematic use of terror esp. as a means of coercion — **ter·ror·ist** \-ist\ *adj or n*

ter·ror·ize \ˈter-ər-ˌīz\ *vb* **-ized; -iz·ing** 1 : to fill with terror : SCARE 2 : to coerce by threat or violence **syn** terrify, frighten, alarm, startle

ter·ry \ˈter-ē\ *n, pl* **terries** : an absorbent fabric with a loose pile of uncut loops

terse \ˈtərs\ *adj* **ters·er; ters·est** [L *tersus* clean, neat, fr. pp. of *tergēre* to wipe off] : effectively brief : CONCISE — **terse·ly** *adv* — **terse·ness** *n*

ter·tia·ry \ˈtər-shē-ˌer-ē\ *adj* 1 : of third rank, importance, or value 2 *cap* : of, relating to, or being the earlier period of the Cenozoic era 3 : occurring in or being the third stage

Tertiary *n* : the Tertiary period

TESL *abbr* teaching English as a second language

TESOL *abbr* Teachers of English to Speakers of Other Languages

¹**test** \ˈtest\ *n* [ME, vessel in which metals were assayed, fr. MF, fr. L *testum* earthen vessel] 1 : a critical examination or evaluation : TRIAL 2 : a means or result of testing

²**test** *vb* 1 : to put to test : TRY, EXAMINE 2 : to undergo or score on tests

tes·ta·ment \ˈtes-tə-mənt\ *n* 1 *cap* : either of two main divisions of the Bible 2 : EVIDENCE, WITNESS 3 : CREDO 4 : the legal instructions for the disposition of one's property after death : WILL — **tes·ta·men·ta·ry** \ˌtes-tə-ˈmen-tə-rē\ *adj*

tes·tate \ˈtes-ˌtāt, -tət\ *adj* : having left a valid will

tes·ta·tor \ˈtes-ˌtā-tər, tes-ˈtā-\ *n* : a person who dies leaving a valid will

tes·ta·trix \tes-ˈtā-triks\ *n* : a female testator

¹**tes·ter** \ˈtēs-tər, ˈtes-\ *n* : a canopy over a bed, pulpit, or altar

²**test·er** \ˈtes-tər\ *n* : one that tests

tes·ti·cle \ˈtes-ti-kəl\ *n* : TESTIS; *esp* : one of a higher mammal usu. with its enclosing structures

tes·ti·fy \ˈtes-tə-ˌfī\ *vb* **-fied; -fy·ing** 1 : to make a statement based on personal knowledge or belief : bear witness 2 : to serve as evidence or proof

tes·ti·mo·ni·al \ˌtes-tə-ˈmō-nē-əl\ *n* 1 : a statement testifying to benefits received; *also* : a character reference 2 : an expression of appreciation : TRIBUTE — **testimonial** *adj*

tes·ti·mo·ny \ˈtes-tə-ˌmō-nē\ *n, pl* **-nies** 1 : evidence based on observation or knowledge 2 : an outward sign : SYMBOL 3 : a solemn declaration made by a witness under oath esp. in a court **syn** evidence, confirmation, proof, testament

tes·tis \ˈtes-təs\ *n, pl* **tes·tes** \ˈtes-ˌtēz\ [L, witness, testis] : a typically paired male reproductive gland that produces sperm and in most mammals is contained within the scrotum at sexual maturity

tes·tos·ter·one \te-ˈstäs-tə-ˌrōn\ *n* : a male sex hormone causing development of the male reproductive system and secondary sex characteristics

test tube *n* : a glass tube closed at one end and used esp. in chemistry and biology

tes·ty \ˈtes-tē\ *adj* **tes·ti·er; -est** [ME *testif*, fr. Anglo= French (the French of medieval England), headstrong, fr. OF *teste* head, fr. LL *testa* skull, fr. L, shell] : easily annoyed; *also* : marked by ill humor

tet·a·nus \ˈtet-ᵊn-əs\ *n* : an infectious disease caused by bacterial poisons and marked by muscle stiffness and spasms esp. of the jaws — **tet·a·nal** \-ᵊl\ *adj*

tetchy \ˈte-chē\ *adj* **tetchi·er; -est** : irritably or peevishly sensitive

¹tête–à–tête \ˈtāt-ˌtāt\ *n* [F, lit., head to head] : a private conversation between two persons

²tête–à–tête \ˌtāt-ə-ˈtāt\ *adv* : in private

³tête–à–tête \ˈtāt-ə-ˌtāt\ *adj* : being face-to-face : PRIVATE

¹teth·er \ˈte-thər\ *n* **1** : something (as a rope) by which an animal is fastened **2** : the limit of one's strength or resources

²tether *vb* : to fasten or restrain by or as if by a tether

tet·ra·eth·yl lead \ˌte-trə-ˈe-thəl-\ *n* : a heavy oily poisonous liquid used as an antiknock agent in gasoline

tet·ra·he·dron \-ˈhē-drən\ *n, pl* **-drons** *or* **-dra** \-drə\ : a polyhedron that has four faces — **tet·ra·he·dral** \-drəl\ *adj*

tet·ra·hy·dro·can·nab·i·nol \ˌhī-drə-kə-ˈna-bə-ˌnȯl, -ˌnōl\ *n* : THC

te·tram·e·ter \te-ˈtra-mə-tər\ *n* : a line of verse consisting of four metrical feet

Teu·ton·ic \tü-ˈtä-nik, tyü-\ *adj* : GERMANIC

Tex *abbr* Texas

text \ˈtekst\ *n* **1** : the actual words of an author's work **2** : the main body of printed or written matter on a page **3** : a scriptural passage chosen as the subject esp. of a sermon **4** : THEME, TOPIC **5** : TEXTBOOK — **tex·tu·al** \ˈteks-chə-wəl\ *adj*

text·book \ˈtekst-ˌbu̇k\ *n* : a book used in the study of a subject

tex·tile \ˈtek-ˌstīl, ˈtekst-ᵊl\ *n* : CLOTH; *esp* : a woven or knit cloth

tex·ture \ˈteks-chər\ *n* **1** : the visual or tactile surface characteristics and appearance of something ⟨a coarse ∼⟩ **2** : essential part **3** : basic scheme or structure : FABRIC **4** : overall structure

TGIF *abbr* thank God it's Friday

¹Th *abbr* Thursday

²Th *symbol* thorium

¹-th — see ¹-ETH

²-th *or* **-eth** *adj suffix* — used in forming ordinal numbers ⟨hundred*th*⟩

³-th *n suffix* **1** : act or process **2** : state or condition ⟨dear*th*⟩

Thai \ˈtī\ *n, pl* **Thai** *or* **Thais** **1** : a native or inhabitant of Thailand **2** : the official language of Thailand — **Thai** *adj*

thal·a·mus \ˈtha-lə-məs\ *n, pl* **-mi** \-ˌmī\ [NL] : a subdivision of the brain that serves as a relay station to and from the cerebral cortex and functions in arousal and the integration of sensory information

thal·li·um \ˈtha-lē-əm\ *n* : a poisonous metallic chemical element — see ELEMENT table

¹than \ˈthən, ˈthan\ *conj* **1** — used after a comparative adjective or adverb to introduce the second part of a comparison expressing inequality ⟨older ∼ I am⟩ **2** — used after *other* or a word of similar meaning to express a difference of kind, manner, or identity ⟨adults other ∼ parents⟩

²than *prep* : in comparison with ⟨older ∼ me⟩

thane \ˈthān\ *n* **1** : a free retainer of an Anglo-Saxon lord **2** : a Scottish feudal lord

thank \ˈthaŋk\ *vb* : to express gratitude to ⟨∼ed them for the present⟩

thank·ful \ˈthaŋk-fəl\ *adj* **1** : conscious of benefit received **2** : expressive of thanks **3** : GLAD — **thank·ful·ness** *n*

thank·ful·ly \-fə-lē\ *adv* **1** : in a thankful manner **2** : as makes one thankful

thank·less \ˈthaŋ-kləs\ *adj* **1** : UNGRATEFUL **2** : UNAPPRECIATED

thanks \ˈthaŋks\ *n pl* : an expression of gratitude

thanks·giv·ing \thaŋks-ˈgi-viŋ\ *n* **1** : the act of giving thanks **2** : a prayer expressing gratitude **3** *cap* : the 4th Thursday in November observed as a legal holiday for giving thanks for divine goodness

¹that \ˈthat, thət\ *pron, pl* **those** \ˈthōz\ **1** : the one indicated, mentioned, or understood ⟨∼ is my house⟩ **2** : the one farther away or first mentioned ⟨this is an elm, ∼'s a maple⟩ **3** : what has been indicated or mentioned ⟨after ∼, we left⟩ **4** : the one or ones : IT, THEY ⟨those who wish to leave may do so⟩

²that \thət, ˈthat\ *conj* **1** : the following, namely ⟨he said ∼ he would⟩; *also* : which is, namely ⟨there's a chance ∼ it may fail⟩ **2** : to this end or purpose ⟨shouted ∼ all might hear⟩ **3** : as to result in the following, namely ⟨so heavy ∼ it can't be moved⟩ **4** : for this reason, namely : BECAUSE ⟨we're glad ∼ you came⟩

³that *adj, pl* **those** **1** : being the one mentioned, indicated, or understood ⟨∼ boy⟩ ⟨those people⟩ **2** : being the one farther away or less immediately under discussion ⟨this chair or ∼ one⟩

⁴that \thət, ˈthat\ *pron* **1** : WHO, WHOM, WHICH ⟨the man ∼ saw you⟩ ⟨the man ∼ you saw⟩ ⟨the money ∼ was spent⟩ **2** : in, on, or at which ⟨the way ∼ he drives⟩ ⟨the day ∼ it rained⟩

⁵that \ˈthat\ *adv* : to such an extent or degree ⟨I like it, but not ∼ much⟩

¹thatch \ˈthach\ *vb* : to cover with or as if with thatch — **thatch·er** *n*

²thatch *n* **1** : plant material (as straw) for use as roofing **2** : a mat of grass clippings accumulated next to the soil on a lawn **3** : a covering of or as if of thatch ⟨a ∼ of white hair⟩

thaw \ˈthȯ\ *vb* **1** : to melt or cause to melt **2** : to become so warm as to melt ice or snow **3** : to abandon aloofness or hostility — **thaw** *n*

THC \ˌtē-(ˌ)āch-ˈsē\ *n* [*t*etra*h*ydro*c*annabinol] : a physiologically active chemical from hemp plant resin that is the chief intoxicant in marijuana

¹the \thə, *before vowel sounds usu* thē\ *definite article* **1** : that in particular **2** — used before adjectives functioning as nouns ⟨a word to ∼ wise⟩

²the *adv* **1** : to what extent ⟨∼ sooner, the better⟩ **2** : to that extent ⟨the sooner, ∼ better⟩

theat *abbr* theater; theatrical

the·ater *or* **the·atre** \ˈthē-ə-tər\ *n* [ME *theatre*, fr. MF, fr. L *theatrum*, fr. Gk *theatron*, fr. *theasthai* to view, fr. *thea* act of seeing] **1** : a building for dramatic performances; *also* : a building or area for showing motion pictures **2** : a place of enactment of significant events ⟨∼ of war⟩ **3** : a place (as a lecture room) resembling a theater **4** : dramatic literature or performance

theater–in–the–round *n* : a theater with the stage in the center of the auditorium

the·at·ri·cal \thē-ˈa-tri-kəl\ *also* **the·at·ric** \-trik\ *adj* **1** : of or relating to the theater **2** : marked by artificiality of emotion : HISTRIONIC **3** : marked by extravagant display : SHOWY

the·at·ri·cals \-kəlz\ *n pl* : the performance of plays

\ə\abut \ᵊ\kitten \ər\further \a\ash \ā\ace \ä\mop, mar \au̇\out \ch\chin \e\bet \ē\easy \g\go \i\hit \ī\ice \j\job \ŋ\sing \ō\go \ȯ\law \ȯi\boy \th\thin \t͟h\the \ü\loot \u̇\foot \y\yet \zh\vision *see also* Pronunciation Symbols page

the·at·rics \thē-'a-triks\ *n pl* **1** : THEATRICALS **2** : staged or contrived effects

the·be \'thä-bā\ *n, pl* **thebe** — see *pula* at MONEY table

thee \'thē\ *pron, archaic objective case of* THOU

theft \'theft\ *n* : the act of stealing

thegn \'thān\ *n* : THANE 1

their \thər, 'ther\ *adj* : of or relating to them or themselves

theirs \'therz\ *pron* : their one : their ones

the·ism \'thē-ˌi-zəm\ *n* : belief in the existence of a god or gods — **the·ist** \-ist\ *n or adj* — **the·is·tic** \thē-'is-tik\ *adj*

them \thəm, 'them\ *pron, objective case of* THEY

theme \'thēm\ *n* **1** : a subject or topic of discourse or of artistic representation **2** : a written exercise : COMPOSITION **3** : a melodic subject of a musical composition or movement — **the·mat·ic** \thi-'ma-tik\ *adj*

them·selves \thəm-'selvz, them-\ *pron pl* : THEY, THEM — used reflexively, for emphasis, or in absolute constructions ⟨they govern ∼⟩ ⟨they ∼ came⟩ ⟨∼ busy, they sent me⟩

¹then \'then\ *adv* **1** : at that time **2** : soon after that : NEXT **3** : in addition : BESIDES **4** : in that case **5** : CONSEQUENTLY

²then *n* : that time ⟨since ∼⟩

³then *adj* : existing or acting at that time ⟨the ∼ attorney general⟩

thence \'thens, 'thens\ *adv* **1** : from that place **2** *archaic* : THENCEFORTH **3** : from that fact : THEREFROM

thence·forth \-ˌfōrth\ *adv* : from that time forward : THEREAFTER

thence·for·ward \thens-'fòr-wərd, thens-\ *also* **thence·for·wards** \-wərdz\ *adv* : onward from that place or time

the·oc·ra·cy \thē-'ä-krə-sē\ *n, pl* **-cies** **1** : government by officials regarded as divinely inspired **2** : a state governed by a theocracy — **the·o·crat·ic** \ˌthē-ə-'kra-tik\ *adj*

theol *abbr* theological; theology

the·ol·o·gy \thē-'ä-lə-jē\ *n, pl* **-gies** **1** : the study of religious faith, practice, and experience; *esp* : the study of God and of God's relation to the world **2** : a theory or system of theology — **the·o·lo·gian** \ˌthē-ə-'lō-jən\ *n* — **the·o·log·i·cal** \-'lä-ji-kəl\ *adj*

the·o·rem \'thē-ə-rəm, 'thir-əm\ *n* **1** : a statement esp. in mathematics that has been or is to be proved **2** : an idea accepted or proposed as a demonstrable truth : PROPOSITION

the·o·ret·i·cal \ˌthē-ə-'re-ti-kəl\ *also* **the·o·ret·ic** \-tik\ *adj* **1** : relating to or having the character of theory **2** : existing only in theory : HYPOTHETICAL — **the·o·ret·i·cal·ly** \-ti-k(ə-)lē\ *adv*

the·o·rize \'thē-ə-ˌrīz\ *vb* **-rized; -riz·ing** : to form a theory : SPECULATE — **the·o·rist** \-rist\ *n*

the·o·ry \'thē-ə-rē, 'thir-ē\ *n, pl* **-ries** **1** : abstract thought **2** : the general principles of a subject **3** : a plausible or scientifically acceptable general principle offered to explain observed facts **4** : HYPOTHESIS, CONJECTURE

theory of games : GAME THEORY

the·os·o·phy \thē-'ä-sə-fē\ *n* : belief about God and the world held to be based on mystical insight — **theo·soph·i·cal** \ˌthē-ə-'sä-fi-kəl\ *adj* — **the·os·o·phist** \thē-'ä-sə-fist\ *n*

ther·a·peu·tic \ˌther-ə-'pyü-tik\ *adj* [Gk *therapeutikos*, fr. *therapeuein* to attend, treat, fr. *theraps* attendant] : of, relating to, or dealing with healing and esp. with remedies for diseases — **ther·a·peu·ti·cal·ly** \-ti-k(ə-)lē\ *adv*

ther·a·peu·tics \ˌther-ə-'pyü-tiks\ *n* : a branch of medical or dental science dealing with the use of remedies

ther·a·py \'ther-ə-pē\ *n, pl* **-pies** : treatment of bodily, mental, or behavioral disorders — **ther·a·pist** \-pist\ *n*

¹there \'thar, 'ther\ *adv* **1** : in or at that place — often used interjectionally **2** : to or into that place : THITHER **3** : in that matter or respect

²there \'thar, 'ther, thər\ *pron* — used as a function word to introduce a sentence or clause ⟨∼'s a pen here⟩

³there \'thar, 'ther\ *n* **1** : that place ⟨get away from ∼⟩ **2** : that point ⟨you take it from ∼⟩

there·abouts \ˌthar-ə-'baùts, ˌther-; 'thar-ə-ˌbaùts, 'ther-\ *or* **there·about** \-'baùt, -ˌbaùt\ *adv* **1** : near that place or time **2** : near that number, degree, or quantity

there·af·ter \thar-'af-tər, ther-\ *adv* : after that : AFTERWARD

there·at \-'at\ *adv* **1** : at that place **2** : at that occurrence : on that account

there·by \thar-'bī, ther-, 'thar-ˌbī, 'ther-ˌbī\ *adv* **1** : by that : by that means **2** : connected with or with reference to that

there·for \thar-'fòr, ther-\ *adv* : for or in return for that

there·fore \'thar-ˌfōr, 'ther-\ *adv* : for that reason : CONSEQUENTLY

there·from \thar-'frəm, ther-\ *adv* : from that or it

there·in \thar-'in, ther-\ *adv* **1** : in or into that place, time, or thing **2** : in that respect

there·of \-'əv, -'äv\ *adv* **1** : of that or it **2** : from that : THEREFROM

there·on \-'òn, -'än\ *adv* **1** : on that **2** *archaic* : THEREUPON 3

there·to \thar-'tü, ther-\ *adv* : to that

there·un·to \thar-'ən-(ˌ)tü, ˌthar-ən-'tü, ˌther-\ *adv, archaic* : THERETO

there·upon \'thar-ə-ˌpòn, 'ther-, -ˌpän; ˌthar-ə-'pòn, -'pän, ˌther-\ *adv* **1** : on that matter **2** : THEREFORE **3** : immediately after that : at once

there·with \thar-'with, ther-, -'with\ *adv* **1** : with that **2** *archaic* : THEREUPON, FORTHWITH

there·with·al \'thar-wi-ˌthòl, 'ther-, -ˌthòl\ *adv* **1** *archaic* : BESIDES **2** : THEREWITH

therm *abbr* thermometer

ther·mal \'thər-məl\ *adj* **1** : of, relating to, or caused by heat **2** : designed to prevent the loss of body heat ⟨∼ underwear⟩ — **ther·mal·ly** *adv*

thermal pollution *n* : the discharge of heated liquid (as waste water from a factory) into natural waters at a temperature harmful to the environment

therm·is·tor \'thər-ˌmis-tər\ *n* : an electrical resistor whose resistance varies sharply with temperature

ther·mo·cline \'thər-mə-ˌklīn\ *n* : the region in a thermally stratified body of water that separates warmer surface water from cold deep water

ther·mo·cou·ple \'thər-mə-ˌkə-pəl\ *n* : a device for measuring temperature by measuring the temperature-dependent potential difference created at the junction of two dissimilar metals

ther·mo·dy·nam·ics \ˌthər-mə-dī-'na-miks\ *n* : physics that deals with the mechanical action or relations of heat — **ther·mo·dy·nam·ic** \-mik\ *adj* — **ther·mo·dy·nam·i·cal·ly** \-mi-k(ə-)lē\ *adv*

ther·mom·e·ter \thər-'mä-mə-tər\ *n* [F *thermomètre*, fr. Gk *thermē* heat + *metron* measure] : an instrument for measuring temperature typically by the rise or fall of a liquid (as mercury) in a thin glass tube — **ther·mo·met·ric** \ˌthər-mə-'me-trik\ *adj* — **ther·mo·met·ri·cal·ly** \-tri-k(ə-)lē\ *adv*

ther·mo·nu·cle·ar \ˌthər-mō-'nü-klē-ər, -'nyü-\ *adj* **1** : of or relating to changes in the nucleus of atoms of low atomic weight (as hydrogen) that require a very high temperature (as in the hydrogen bomb) **2** : utilizing or relating to a thermonuclear bomb ⟨∼ war⟩

ther·mo·plas·tic \ˌthər-mə-'plas-tik\ *adj* : capable of softening when heated and of hardening again when cooled ⟨∼ resins⟩ — **thermoplastic** *n*

ther·mos \'thər-məs\ *n* : a cylindrical container with a vacuum between an inner and an outer wall used to keep liquids hot or cold

ther·mo·sphere \'thər-mə-ˌsfir\ *n* : the part of the earth's atmosphere that lies above the mesosphere and that is characterized by steadily increasing temperature with height

ther·mo·stat \'thər-mə-ˌstat\ *n* : a device that automatically controls temperature — **ther·mo·stat·ic** \ˌthər-mə-'sta-tik\ *adj* — **ther·mo·stat·i·cal·ly** \-ti-k(ə-)lē\ *adv*

the·sau·rus \thi-'sȯr-əs\ *n, pl* **-sau·ri** \-'sȯr-ˌī\ *or* **-sau·rus·es** \-'sȯr-ə-səz\ [NL, fr. L, treasure, collection, fr. Gk *thēsauros*] : a book of words and their synonyms — **the·sau·ral** \-'sȯr-əl\ *adj*

these *pl of* THIS

the·sis \'thē-səs\ *n, pl* **the·ses** \'thē-ˌsēz\ **1** : a proposition that a person advances and offers to maintain by argument **2** : an essay embodying results of original research; *esp* : one written for an academic degree

¹**thes·pi·an** \'thes-pē-ən\ *adj, often cap* [fr. *Thespis*, 6th cent. B.C. Greek poet and reputed originator of tragedy] : relating to the drama : DRAMATIC

²**thespian** *n* : ACTOR

Thess *abbr* Thessalonians

Thes·sa·lo·nians \ˌthe-sə-'lō-nyənz, -nē-ənz\ *n* — see BIBLE table

the·ta \'thā-tə\ *n* : the 8th letter of the Greek alphabet — Θ or θ

thew \'thü, 'thyü\ *n* : MUSCLE, SINEW — usu. used in pl.

they \'thā\ *pron* **1** : those individuals under discussion : the ones previously mentioned or referred to **2** : unspecified persons : PEOPLE

thi·a·mine \'thī-ə-mən, -ˌmēn\ *also* **thi·a·min** \-mən\ *n* : a vitamin of the vitamin B complex essential to normal metabolism and nerve function

¹**thick** \'thik\ *adj* **1** : having relatively great depth or extent from one surface to its opposite ⟨a ~ plank⟩; *also* : heavily built : THICKSET **2** : densely massed : CROWDED; *also* : FREQUENT, NUMEROUS **3** : dense or viscous in consistency ⟨~ syrup⟩ **4** : marked by haze, fog, or mist ⟨~ weather⟩ **5** : measuring in thickness ⟨one meter ~⟩ **6** : imperfectly articulated : INDISTINCT ⟨~ speech⟩ **7** : STUPID, OBTUSE **8** : associated on close terms : INTIMATE **9** : EXCESSIVE **syn** compact, close, tight — **thick·ly** *adv*

²**thick** *n* **1** : the most crowded or active part **2** : the part of greatest thickness

thick·en \'thi-kən\ *vb* : to make or become thick — **thick·en·er** *n*

thick·et \'thi-kət\ *n* : a dense growth of bushes or small trees

thick·ness \-nəs\ *n* **1** : the smallest of three dimensions ⟨length, width, and ~⟩ **2** : the quality or state of being thick **3** : LAYER, SHEET ⟨a single ~ of canvas⟩

thick·set \'thik-'set\ *adj* **1** : closely placed or planted **2** : having a thick body : BURLY

thick–skinned \-'skind\ *adj* **1** : having a thick skin **2** : not easily bothered by criticism or insult

thief \'thēf\ *n, pl* **thieves** \'thēvz\ : one that steals esp. secretly

thieve \'thēv\ *vb* **thieved; thiev·ing** : STEAL, ROB **syn** filch, pilfer, purloin, swipe

thiev·ery \'thē-və-rē\ *n, pl* **-er·ies** : the act of stealing : THEFT

thigh \'thī\ *n* : the part of the vertebrate hind limb between the knee and the hip

thigh·bone \'thī-ˌbōn\ *n* : FEMUR

thim·ble \'thim-bəl\ *n* : a cap or guard worn on the finger to push the needle in sewing — **thim·ble·ful** *n*

¹**thin** \'thin\ *adj* **thin·ner; thin·nest** **1** : having little extent from one surface through to its opposite : not thick : SLENDER **2** : not closely set or placed : SPARSE ⟨~ hair⟩ **3** : not dense or not dense enough : more fluid or rarefied than normal ⟨~ air⟩ ⟨~ syrup⟩ **4** : lacking sub-

stance, fullness, or strength ⟨~ broth⟩ **5** : FLIMSY — **thin·ly** *adv* — **thin·ness** *n*

²**thin** *vb* **thinned; thin·ning** : to make or become thin

thine \'thīn\ *pron, archaic* : one or the ones belonging to thee

thing \'thiŋ\ *n* **1** : a matter of concern : AFFAIR ⟨~s to do⟩ **2** *pl* : state of affairs ⟨~s are improving⟩ **3** : EVENT, CIRCUMSTANCE ⟨the crime was a terrible ~⟩ **4** : DEED, ACT ⟨expected great ~s of him⟩ **5** : a distinct entity : OBJECT **6** : an inanimate object distinguished from a living being **7** *pl* : POSSESSIONS, EFFECTS **8** : an article of clothing **9** : DETAIL, POINT **10** : IDEA, NOTION **11** : something one likes to do : SPECIALTY ⟨doing her ~⟩

think \'thiŋk\ *vb* **thought** \'thȯt\; **think·ing** **1** : to form or have in the mind **2** : to have as an opinion : BELIEVE **3** : to reflect on : PONDER **4** : to call to mind : REMEMBER **5** : REASON **6** : to form a mental picture of : IMAGINE **7** : to devise by thinking ⟨*thought* up a plan to escape⟩ **syn** conceive, fancy, realize, envisage — **think·er** *n*

think tank *n* : an institute, corporation, or group organized for interdisciplinary research (as in technological or social problems)

thin·ner \'thi-nər\ *n* : a volatile liquid (as turpentine) used to thin paint

thin–skinned \'thin-'skind\ *adj* **1** : having a thin skin **2** : extremely sensitive to criticism or insult

¹**third** \'thərd\ *adj* : next after the second — **third** *or* **third·ly** *adv*

²**third** *n* **1** : one of three equal parts of something **2** : one that is number three in a countable series **3** : the 3d forward gear in an automotive vehicle

third degree *n* : the subjection of a prisoner to mental or physical torture to force a confession

third dimension *n* **1** : thickness, depth, or apparent thickness or depth that confers solidity on an object **2** : a quality that confers reality — **third–dimensional** *adj*

third world *n, often cap T&W* : the aggregate of the underdeveloped nations of the world

¹**thirst** \'thərst\ *n* **1** : a feeling of dryness in the mouth and throat associated with a desire to drink; *also* : a bodily condition producing this **2** : an ardent desire : CRAVING ⟨a ~ for knowledge⟩ — **thirsty** *adj*

²**thirst** *vb* **1** : to need drink : suffer thirst **2** : to have a strong desire : CRAVE

thir·teen \ˌthər-'tēn\ *n* : one more than 12 — **thirteen** *adj or pron* — **thir·teenth** \-'tēnth\ *adj or n*

thir·ty \'thər-tē\ *n, pl* **thirties** : three times 10 — **thir·ti·eth** \-tē-əth\ *adj or n* — **thirty** *adj or pron*

¹**this** \'this\ *pron, pl* **these** \'thēz\ **1** : the one close or closest in time or space ⟨~ is your book⟩ **2** : what is in the present or under immediate observation or discussion ⟨~ is a mess⟩; *also* : what is happening or being done now ⟨after ~ we'll leave⟩

²**this** *adj, pl* **these** **1** : being the one near, present, just mentioned, or more immediately under observation ⟨~ book⟩ **2** : constituting the immediate past or future ⟨friends all *these* years⟩

³**this** *adv* : to such an extent or degree ⟨we need a book about ~ big⟩

this·tle \'thi-səl\ *n* : any of various tall prickly composite plants with often showy heads of tightly packed tubular flowers

this·tle·down \-ˌdau̇n\ *n* : the down from the ripe flower head of a thistle

¹**thith·er** \'thi-thər\ *adv* : to that place

²**thither** *adj* : being on the farther side

thith·er·ward \-wərd\ *adv* : toward that place : THITHER

thole \'thōl\ *n* : a pin set in the gunwale of a boat to hold an oar in place

thong \'thȯŋ\ *n* **1** : a strip esp. of leather or hide **2** : a sandal held on the foot by a thong between the toes

tho·rax \'thȯr-,aks\ *n*, *pl* **tho·rax·es** *or* **tho·ra·ces** \'thōr-ə-,sēz\ **1** : the part of the body of a mammal between the neck and the abdomen; *also* : its cavity containing the heart and lungs **2** : the middle of the three main divisions of the body of an insect — **tho·rac·ic** \thə-'ra-sik\ *adj*

tho·ri·um \'thōr-ē-əm\ *n* : a radioactive metallic chemical element — see ELEMENT table

thorn \'thȯrn\ *n* **1** : a woody plant bearing sharp processes **2** : a sharp rigid plant process that is usu. a modified leafless branch **3** : something that causes distress — **thorny** *adj*

thor·ough \'thər-ō\ *adj* **1** : COMPLETE, EXHAUSTIVE ⟨a ∼ search⟩ **2** : very careful : PAINSTAKING ⟨a ∼ scholar⟩ **3** : having full mastery — **thor·ough·ly** *adv* — **thor·ough·ness** *n*

¹thor·ough·bred \'thər-ə-,bred\ *adj* **1** : bred from the best blood through a long line **2** *cap* : of or relating to the Thoroughbred breed of horses **3** : marked by high-spirited grace

²thoroughbred *n* **1** *cap* : any of an English breed of light speedy horses kept chiefly for racing **2** : one (as a pedigreed animal) of excellent quality

Thoroughbred 1

thor·ough·fare \-,far\ *n* : a public road or street

thor·ough·go·ing \,thər-ə-'gō-iŋ\ *adj* : marked by thoroughness or zeal

thorp \'thȯrp\ *n*, *archaic* : VILLAGE

those *pl of* THAT

¹thou \'thaü\ *pron*, *archaic* : the person addressed

²thou \'thaü\ *n*, *pl* **thou** : a thousand of something (as dollars)

¹though \'thō\ *conj* **1** : despite the fact that ⟨∼ the odds are hopeless, they fight on⟩ **2** : granting that ⟨∼ it may look bad, still, all is not lost⟩

²though *adv* : HOWEVER, NEVERTHELESS ⟨not for long, ∼⟩

¹thought \'thȯt\ *past and past part of* THINK

²thought *n* **1** : the process of thinking **2** : serious consideration : REGARD **3** : reasoning power **4** : the power to imagine : CONCEPTION **5** : IDEA, NOTION **6** : OPINION, BELIEF

thought·ful \'thȯt-fəl\ *adj* **1** : absorbed in thought **2** : marked by careful thinking ⟨a ∼ essay⟩ **3** : considerate of others ⟨a ∼ host⟩ — **thought·ful·ly** *adv* — **thought·ful·ness** *n*

thought·less \-ləs\ *adj* **1** : insufficiently alert : CARELESS ⟨a ∼ worker⟩ **2** : RECKLESS ⟨a ∼ act⟩ **3** : lacking concern for others : INCONSIDERATE ⟨∼ remarks⟩ — **thought·less·ly** *adv* — **thought·less·ness** *n*

thou·sand \'thaüz-ᵊnd\ *n*, *pl* **thousands** *or* **thousand** : 10 times 100 — **thousand** *adj* — **thou·sandth** \-ᵊnth\ *adj or n*

thousands place *n* : the place four to the left of the decimal point in an Arabic number

thrall \'thrȯl\ *n* **1** : SLAVE, BONDMAN **2** : a state of servitude — **thrall·dom** *or* **thral·dom** \'thrȯl-dəm\ *n*

thrash \'thrash\ *vb* **1 2** : THRESH **1 2** : BEAT, WHIP; *also* : DEFEAT **3** : to move about violently **4** : to go over again and again ⟨∼ over the matter⟩; *also* : to hammer out ⟨∼ out a plan⟩

¹thrash·er \'thra-shər\ *n* : one that thrashes or threshes

²thrasher *n* : any of various long-tailed American songbirds related to the mockingbird

¹thread \'thred\ *n* **1** : a thin continuous strand of spun and twisted textile fibers **2** : something resembling a textile thread **3** : the ridge or groove that winds around a screw **4** : a train of thought **5** : a continuing element

²thread *vb* **1** : to pass a thread through the eye of (a needle) **2** : to pass (as film) through something **3** : to make one's way through or between **4** : to put together on a thread ⟨∼ beads⟩ **5** : to form a screw thread on or in

thread·bare \-,bar\ *adj* **1** : having the nap worn off so that the thread shows : SHABBY **2** : TRITE

thready \'thre-dē\ *adj* **1** : consisting of or bearing fibers of filaments ⟨a ∼ bark⟩ **2** : lacking in fullness, body, or vigor

threat \'thret\ *n* **1** : an expression of intent to do harm **2** : one that threatens

threat·en \'thret-ᵊn\ *vb* **1** : to utter threats against **2** : to give signs or warning of : PORTEND **3** : to hang over as a threat : MENACE — **threat·en·ing·ly** *adv*

threat·ened *adj* : having an uncertain chance of continued survival; *esp* : likely to become an endangered species

three \'thrē\ *n* **1** : one more than two **2** : the 3d in a set or series **3** : something having three units — **three** *adj or pron*

3-D \'thrē-'dē\ *n* : three-dimensional form

three–dimensional *adj* **1** : relating to or having three dimensions **2** : giving the illusion of varying distances ⟨a ∼ picture⟩

three·fold \'thrē-,fōld, -'fōld\ *adj* **1** : having three parts : TRIPLE **2** : being three times as great or as many — **three·fold** \-'fōld\ *adv*

three·pence \'thre-pəns, 'thri-, 'thrə-, *US also* 'thrē-pens\ *n* **1** *pl* **threepence** *or* **three·penc·es** : a coin worth three pennies **2** : the sum of three British pennies

three·score \'thrē-'skōr\ *adj* : being three times twenty : SIXTY

three·some \'thrē-səm\ *n* : a group of three persons or things

thren·o·dy \'thre-nə-dē\ *n*, *pl* **-dies** : a song of lamentation : ELEGY

thresh \'thrash, 'thresh\ *vb* **1** : to separate (as grain from straw) mechanically **2** : THRASH — **thresh·er** *n*

thresh·old \'thresh-,hōld\ *n* **1** : the sill of a door **2** : a point or place of beginning or entering : OUTSET **3** : a point at which a physiological or psychological effect begins to be produced

threw *past of* THROW

thrice \'thrīs\ *adv* **1** : three times **2** : in a threefold manner or degree

thrift \'thrift\ *n* [ME, fr. ON, prosperity, fr. *thrīfask* to thrive] : careful management esp. of money : FRUGALITY — **thrift·i·ly** \'thrif-tə-lē\ *adv* — **thrift·less** *adj* — **thrifty** *adj*

thrill \'thril\ *vb* [ME *thirlen*, *thrillen* to pierce, fr. OE *thyrlian*, fr. *thyrel* hole, fr. *thurh* through] **1** : to have or cause to have sudden sharp feeling of excitement; *also* : TINGLE, SHIVER **2** : TREMBLE, VIBRATE — **thrill** *n* — **thrill·er** *n* — **thrill·ing·ly** *adv*

thrive \'thrīv\ *vb* **throve** \'thrōv\ *or* **thrived; thriv·en**

\\'thri-vən\ *also* **thrived; thriv·ing 1** : to grow luxuriantly : FLOURISH **2** : to gain in wealth or possessions : PROSPER

throat \\'thrōt\ *n* : the part of the neck in front of the spinal column; *also* : the passage through it to the stomach and lungs — **throat·ed** *adj*

throaty \\'thrō-tē\ *adj* **throat·i·er; -est 1** : uttered or produced from low in the throat ⟨a ∼ voice⟩ **2** : heavy, thick, or deep as if from the throat ⟨∼ notes of a horn⟩ — **throat·i·ly** \-tə-lē\ *adv* — **throat·i·ness** \-tē-nəs\ *n*

¹throb \\'thräb\ *vb* **throbbed; throb·bing** : to pulsate or pound esp. with abnormal force or rapidity : BEAT, VIBRATE

²throb *n* : BEAT, PULSE

throe \\'thrō\ *n* **1** : PANG, SPASM **2** *pl* : a hard or painful struggle

throm·bo·sis \thräm-'bō-səs\ *n, pl* **-bo·ses** \-ˌsēz\ : the formation or presence of a clot in a blood vessel — **throm·bot·ic** \-'bä-tik\ *adj*

throm·bus \\'thräm-bəs\ *n, pl* **throm·bi** \-ˌbī\ : a clot of blood formed within a blood vessel and remaining attached to its place of origin

throne \\'thrōn\ *n* **1** : the chair of state of a sovereign or high dignitary **2** : royal power : SOVEREIGNTY

¹throng \\'thrȯŋ\ *n* **1** : MULTITUDE **2** : a crowding together of many persons

²throng *vb* **thronged; throng·ing** : CROWD

¹throt·tle \\'thrät-ᵊl\ *vb* **throt·tled; throt·tling** [ME *throtlen,* fr. *throte* throat] **1** : CHOKE, STRANGLE **2** : SUPPRESS **3** : to reduce the speed of (an engine) by closing the throttle — **throt·tler** *n*

²throttle *n* : a valve regulating the flow of steam or fuel to an engine; *also* : the lever controlling this valve

¹through \\'thrü\ *prep* **1** : into at one side and out at the other side of ⟨go ∼ the door⟩ **2** : by way of ⟨entered ∼ a skylight⟩ **3** : in the midst of ⟨a path ∼ the trees⟩ **4** : by means of ⟨succeeded ∼ hard work⟩ **5** : over the whole of ⟨rumors swept ∼ the office⟩ **6** : during the whole of ⟨∼ the night⟩ **7** : to and including ⟨Monday ∼ Friday⟩

²through *adv* **1** : from one end or side to the other **2** : from beginning to end : to completion ⟨see it ∼⟩ **3** : to the core : THOROUGHLY ⟨he was wet ∼⟩ **4** : into the open : OUT ⟨break ∼⟩

³through *adj* **1** : permitting free passage ⟨a ∼ street⟩ **2** : going from point of origin to destination without change or transfer ⟨a ∼ train⟩ **3** : coming from or going to points outside a local area ⟨∼ traffic⟩ **4** : FINISHED ⟨∼ with the job⟩

¹through·out \thrü-'aȯt\ *adv* **1** : EVERYWHERE **2** : from beginning to end

²throughout *prep* **1** : in or to every part of **2** : during the whole period of

through·put \\'thrü-ˌpu̇t\ *n* : OUTPUT, PRODUCTION ⟨the ∼ of a computer⟩

throve *past of* THRIVE

¹throw \\'thrō\ *vb* **threw** \\'thrü\; **thrown** \\'thrōn\; **throw·ing 1** : to propel through the air esp. with a forward motion of the hand and arm ⟨∼ a ball⟩ **2** : to cause to fall or fall off **3** : to put suddenly in a certain position or condition ⟨∼ into panic⟩ **4** : to put on or take off hastily ⟨∼ on a coat⟩ **5** : to lose intentionally ⟨∼ a game⟩ **6** : to move (a lever) so as to connect or disconnect parts of something (as a clutch) **7** : to act as host for ⟨∼ a party⟩ **syn** toss, fling, pitch, sling — **throw·er** *n*

²throw *n* **1** : an act of throwing, hurling, or flinging; *also* : CAST **2** : the distance a missile may be thrown **3** : a light coverlet **4** : a woman's scarf or light wrap

throw·away \\'thrō-ə-ˌwā\ *n* : something that is or is designed to be thrown away esp. after one use

throw·back \-ˌbak\ *n* : reversion to an earlier type or phase; *also* : an instance or product of this

throw up *vb* **1** : to build hurriedly **2** : VOMIT

thrum \\'thrəm\ *vb* **thrummed; thrum·ming** : to play or pluck a stringed instrument idly : STRUM

thrush \\'thrəsh\ *n* : any of numerous small or medium-sized songbirds that are mostly of a plain color often with spotted underparts

¹thrust \\'thrəst\ *vb* **thrust; thrust·ing 1** : to push or drive with force : SHOVE **2** : STAB, PIERCE **3** : INTERJECT **4** : to press the acceptance of upon someone

²thrust *n* **1** : a lunge with a pointed weapon **2** : ATTACK **3** : the pressure of one part of a construction against another (as of an arch against an abutment) **4** : the force produced by a propeller or jet or rocket engine that drives a vehicle (as an aircraft) forward **5** : a violent push : SHOVE

thrust·er *also* **thrust·or** \\'thrəs-tər\ *n* : one that thrusts; *esp* : a rocket engine

thru·way \\'thrü-ˌwā\ *n* : EXPRESSWAY

¹thud \\'thəd\ *n* **1** : BLOW **2** : a dull sound

²thud *vb* **thud·ded; thud·ding** : to move or strike so as to make a thud

thug \\'thəg\ *n* [Hindi *ṭhag,* lit., thief] : a brutal ruffian or assassin — **thug·gish** *adj*

thu·li·um \\'thü-lē-əm, 'thyü-\ *n* : a rare metallic chemical element — see ELEMENT table

¹thumb \\'thəm\ *n* **1** : the short thick first digit of the human hand or a corresponding digit of a lower animal **2** : the part of a glove or mitten that covers the thumb

²thumb *vb* **1** : to leaf through (pages) with the thumb **2** : to wear or soil with the thumb by frequent handling **3** : to request or obtain (a ride) in a passing automobile by signaling with the thumb

¹thumb·nail \\'thəm-ˌnāl\ *n* : the nail of the thumb

²thumbnail *adj* : BRIEF, CONCISE ⟨a ∼ description⟩

thumb·print \-ˌprint\ *n* : an impression made by the thumb

thumb·screw \-ˌskrü\ *n* **1** : a screw with a head that may be turned by the thumb and forefinger **2** : a device of torture for squeezing the thumb

thumb·tack \-ˌtak\ *n* : a tack with a broad flat head for pressing with one's thumb into a board or wall

¹thump \\'thəmp\ *vb* **1** : to strike with or as if with something thick or heavy so as to cause a dull sound **2** : POUND

²thump *n* : a blow with or as if with something blunt or heavy; *also* : the sound made by such a blow

¹thun·der \\'thən-dər\ *n* **1** : the sound following a flash of lightning; *also* : a noise like such a sound **2** : a loud utterance or threat

²thunder *vb* **1** : to produce thunder **2** : ROAR, SHOUT

thun·der·bolt \-ˌbōlt\ *n* : a flash of lightning with its accompanying thunder

thun·der·clap \-ˌklap\ *n* : a crash of thunder

thun·der·cloud \-ˌklau̇d\ *n* : a dark storm cloud producing lightning and thunder

thun·der·head \-ˌhed\ *n* : a large cumulus cloud often appearing before a thunderstorm

thun·der·ous \\'thən-də-rəs\ *adj* : producing thunder; *also* : making a noise like thunder — **thun·der·ous·ly** *adv*

thun·der·show·er \\'thən-dər-ˌshau̇-ər\ *n* : a shower accompanied by thunder and lightning

thun·der·storm \-ˌstȯrm\ *n* : a storm accompanied by thunder and lightning

thun·der·struck \-ˌstrək\ *adj* : stunned as if struck by a thunderbolt

Thurs *or* **Thu** *abbr* Thursday

Thurs·day \\'thərz-dē, -ˌdā\ *n* [ME, fr. OE *thursdæg,* fr.

\ə\abut \ᵊ\kitten \ər\further \a\ash \ā\ace \ä\mop, mar
\au̇\out \ch\chin \e\bet \ē\easy \g\go \i\hit \ī\ice \j\job
\ŋ\sing \ō\go \ȯ\law \ȯi\boy \th\thin \tẖ\the \ü\loot \u̇\foot
\y\yet \zh\vision *see also* Pronunciation Symbols page

ON *thōrsdagr,* lit., day of Thor (Norse god)] : the 5th day of the week

thus \ˈthəs\ *adv* **1** : in this or that manner **2** : to this degree or extent : so **3** : because of this or that : HENCE

¹thwack \ˈthwak\ *vb* : to strike with or as if with something flat or heavy

²thwack *n* : a heavy blow : WHACK

¹thwart \ˈthwȯrt\ *vb* **1** : FOIL, BAFFLE **2** : BLOCK, DEFEAT *syn* balk, outwit, frustrate

²thwart \ˈthwȯrt, *naut often* ˈthȯrt\ *adv* : ATHWART

³thwart *adj* : situated or placed across something else

⁴thwart \ˈthwȯrt\ *n* : a rower's seat extending across a boat

thy \ˈthī\ *adj, archaic* : of, relating to, or done by or to thee or thyself

thyme \ˈtīm, ˈthīm\ *n* [ME, fr. MF *thym,* fr. L *thymum,* fr. Gk *thymon,* prob. fr. *thyein* to make a burnt offering, sacrifice] : a garden mint with aromatic leaves used esp. in seasoning; *also* : its leaves so used

thy·mine \ˈthī-ˌmēn\ *n* : a pyrimidine base that is one of the four bases coding genetic information in the molecular chain of DNA

thy·mus \ˈthī-məs\ *n* : a glandular organ of the neck region that is composed largely of lymphoid tissue, functions esp. in the development of the immune system, and tends to atrophy in the adult

thy·ris·tor \thī-ˈris-tər\ *n* : a semiconductor device that acts as a switch, rectifier, or voltage regulator

thy·roid \ˈthī-ˌrȯid\ *also* **thy·roi·dal** \thī-ˈrȯid-ᵊl\ *adj* [NL *thyroides,* fr. Gk *thyreoeidēs* shield-shaped, thyroid, fr. *thyreos* shield shaped like a door, fr. *thyra* door] : of, relating to, or being a large endocrine gland that lies at the base of the neck and produces several iodine-containing hormones that affect growth, development, and metabolism — **thyroid** *n*

thy·rox·ine *or* **thy·rox·in** \thī-ˈräk-ˌsēn, -sən\ *n* : an iodine-containing hormone that is produced by the thyroid gland, increases metabolic rate, and is used to treat thyroid disorders

thy·self \thī-ˈself\ *pron, archaic* : YOURSELF

Ti *symbol* titanium

ti·ara \tē-ˈar-ə, -ˈer-, -ˈär-\ *n* **1** : the pope's triple crown **2** : a decorative headband or semicircle for formal wear by women

Ti·bet·an \tə-ˈbet-ᵊn\ *n* : a native or inhabitant of Tibet — **Tibetan** *adj*

tib·ia \ˈti-bē-ə\ *n, pl* **-i·ae** \-bē-ˌē\ *also* **-i·as** [L] : the inner of the two bones of the vertebrate hind limb between the knee and the ankle

tic \ˈtik\ *n* : a local and habitual twitching of muscles esp. of the face

ti·cal \ti-ˈkäl, ˈti-kəl\ *n, pl* **ticals** *or* **tical** : BAHT

¹tick \ˈtik\ *n* : any of a large group of small blood-sucking arachnids

²tick *n* : the fabric case of a mattress or pillow; *also* : a mattress consisting of a tick and its filling

³tick *n* **1** : a light rhythmic audible tap or beat **2** : a small mark used to draw attention to or check something

⁴tick *vb* **1** : to make the sound of a tick or series of ticks **2** : to mark, count, or announce by or as if by ticking beats **3** : to mark or check with a tick **4** : to function as an operating mechanism : RUN

⁵tick *n* : CREDIT; *also* : a credit account

tick·er \ˈti-kər\ *n* **1** : something (as a watch) that ticks **2** : a telegraph instrument that prints information (as stock prices) on paper tape **3** *slang* : HEART

ticker tape *n* : the paper ribbon on which a telegraphic ticker prints

¹tick·et \ˈti-kət\ *n* [MF *etiquet, estiquette* notice attached to something, fr. *estiquier* to attach, fr. MD *steken* to stick] **1** : CERTIFICATE, LICENSE, PERMIT; *esp* : a certificate or token showing that a fare or admission fee has

been paid **2** : TAG, LABEL **3** : SLATE 4 **4** : a summons issued to a traffic offender

²ticket *vb* **1** : to attach a ticket to **2** : to furnish or serve with a ticket

tick·ing \ˈti-kiŋ\ *n* : a strong fabric used in upholstering and as a mattress covering

tick·le \ˈti-kəl\ *vb* **tick·led; tick·ling 1** : to excite or stir up agreeably : PLEASE, AMUSE **2** : to have a tingling sensation **3** : to touch (as a body part) lightly so as to cause uneasiness, laughter, or spasmodic movements — **tickle** *n*

tick·lish \-kə-lish\ *adj* **1** : OVERSENSITIVE, TOUCHY **2** : UNSTABLE ⟨a ∼ foothold⟩ **3** : requiring delicate handling ⟨∼ subject⟩ **4** : sensitive to tickling — **tick·lish·ly** *adv* — **tick·lish·ness** *n*

tid·al wave \ˈtīd-ᵊl-\ *n* **1** : an unusually high sea wave that sometimes follows an earthquake **2** : an unusual rise of water alongshore due to strong winds

tid·bit \ˈtid-ˌbit\ *n* : a choice morsel

¹tide \ˈtīd\ *n* [ME, time, fr. OE *tīd*] **1** : the alternate rising and falling of the surface of the ocean **2** : something that fluctuates like the tides of the sea — **tid·al** \ˈtīd-ᵊl\ *adj*

²tide *vb* **tid·ed; tid·ing** : to carry through or help along as if by the tide ⟨a loan to ∼ us over⟩

tide·land \ˈtīd-ˌland, -lənd\ *n* **1** : land overflowed during flood tide **2** : land under the ocean within a nation's territorial waters — often used in pl.

tide·wa·ter \-ˌwȯ-tər, -ˌwä-\ *n* **1** : water overflowing land at flood tide **2** : low-lying coastal land

tid·ings \ˈtī-diŋz\ *n pl* : NEWS, MESSAGE

¹ti·dy \ˈtī-dē\ *adj* **ti·di·er; -est 1** : well ordered and cared for : NEAT **2** : LARGE, SUBSTANTIAL ⟨a ∼ sum⟩ — **ti·di·ness** \ˈtī-dē-nəs\ *n*

²tidy *vb* **ti·died; ti·dy·ing 1** : to put in order **2** : to make things tidy

³tidy *n, pl* **tidies** : a decorated covering used to protect the back or arms of a chair from wear or soil

¹tie \ˈtī\ *n* **1** : a line, ribbon, or cord used for fastening, uniting, or closing **2** : a structural element (as a beam or rod) holding two pieces together **3** : one of the cross supports to which railroad rails are fastened **4** : a connecting link : BOND ⟨family ∼s⟩ **5** : an equality in number (as of votes or scores); *also* : an undecided or deadlocked contest **6** : NECKTIE

²tie *vb* **tied; ty·ing** *or* **tie·ing 1** : to fasten, attach, or close by means of a tie **2** : to bring together firmly : UNITE **3** : to form a knot or bow in ⟨∼ a scarf⟩ **4** : to restrain from freedom of action : CONSTRAIN **5** : to make or have an equal score with

tie·back \ˈtī-ˌbak\ *n* : a decorative strip for draping a curtain to the side of a window

tie–dye·ing \ˈtī-ˌdī-iŋ\ *n* : a method of producing patterns in textiles by tying parts of the fabric so that they will not absorb the dye — **tie–dyed** \-ˌdīd\ *adj*

tie–in \ˈtī-ˌin\ *n* : CONNECTION

tier \ˈtir\ *n* : ROW, LAYER; *esp* : one of two or more rows arranged one above another — **tiered** \ˈtird\ *adj*

tie–rod \ˈtī-ˌräd\ *n* : a rod used as a connecting member or brace

tie–up \-ˌəp\ *n* **1** : a slowing or stopping of traffic or business **2** : CONNECTION

tiff \ˈtif\ *n* : a petty quarrel — **tiff** *vb*

Tif·fa·ny \ˈti-fə-nē\ *adj* : made of pieces of stained glass ⟨a ∼ lamp⟩

ti·ger \ˈtī-gər\ *n* : a very large tawny black-striped Asian cat — **ti·ger·ish** *adj*

¹tight \ˈtīt\ *adj* **1** : so close in structure as to prevent passage of a liquid or gas **2** : strongly fixed or held : SECURE **3** : TAUT **4** : fitting usu. too closely ⟨∼ shoes⟩ **5** : set close together : COMPACT ⟨a ∼ formation⟩ **6** : DIFFICULT, TRYING ⟨get in a ∼ spot⟩ **7** : STINGY, MISERLY **8** : evenly contested : CLOSE **9** : INTOXICATED **10** : low in

tiger

supply : hard to get ⟨money is ∼⟩ — **tight·ly** *adv* — **tight·ness** *n*

²tight *adv* **1** : TIGHTLY, FIRMLY **2** : SOUNDLY ⟨sleep ∼⟩

tight·en \'tīt-ᵊn\ *vb* : to make or become tight

tight-fist·ed \'tīt-'fis-təd\ *adj* : STINGY

tight·rope \-ˌrōp\ *n* : a taut rope or wire for acrobats to perform on

tights \'tīts\ *n pl* : skintight garments covering the body esp. below the waist; *also, Brit* : PANTY HOSE

tight·wad \'tīt-ˌwäd\ *n* : a stingy person

ti·gress \'tī-grəs\ *n* : a female tiger

til·de \'til-də\ *n* [Sp, fr. ML *titulus* tittle] : a mark ˜ placed esp. over the letter *n* (as in Spanish *señor* sir) to denote the sound \nʸ\ or over vowels (as in Portuguese *irmã* sister) to indicate nasal quality

¹tile \'tīl\ *n* **1** : a flat or curved piece of fired clay, stone, or concrete used for roofs, floors, or walls; *also* : a pipe of earthenware or concrete used for a drain **2** : a thin piece (as of linoleum) used for covering walls or floors — **til·ing** \'tī-liŋ\ *n*

²tile *vb* **tiled; til·ing** : to cover with tiles — **til·er** *n*

¹till \'til\ *prep or conj* : UNTIL

²till *vb* : to work by plowing, sowing, and raising crops : CULTIVATE — **till·able** *adj*

³till *n* : DRAWER; *esp* : a money drawer in a store or bank

till·age \'ti-lij\ *n* **1** : the work of tilling land **2** : cultivated land

¹til·ler \'ti-lər\ *n* [OE *telgor, telgra* twig, shoot] : a sprout or stalk esp. from the base or lower part of a plant

²till·er \'ti-lər\ *n* : one that tills

³til·ler \'ti-lər\ *n* [ME *tiler* stock of a crossbow, fr. MF *telier*, lit., beam of a loom, fr. ML *telarium*, fr. L *tela* web] : a lever used for turning a boat's rudder from side to side

¹tilt \'tilt\ *n* **1** : a contest in which two combatants charging usu. with lances try to unhorse each other : JOUST; *also* : a tournament of tilts **2** : a verbal contest **3** : SLANT, TIP

²tilt *vb* **1** : to move or shift so as to incline : TIP **2** : to engage in or as if in combat with lances : JOUST, ATTACK

tilth \'tilth\ *n* **1** : TILLAGE 2 **2** : the state of a soil esp. in relation to the suitability of its particle size and structure for growing crops

Tim *abbr* Timothy

tim·ber \'tim-bər\ *n* [ME, fr. OE, building, wood] **1** : growing trees or their wood — often used interjectionally to warn of a falling tree **2** : wood for use in making something **3** : a usu. large squared or dressed piece of wood

tim·bered \'tim-bərd\ *adj* : having walls framed by exposed timbers

tim·ber·land \'tim-bər-ˌland\ *n* : wooded land

tim·ber·line \'tim-bər-ˌlīn\ *n* : the upper limit of tree growth in mountains or high latitudes

timber rattlesnake *n* : a widely distributed rattlesnake of the eastern U.S.

timber wolf *n* : GRAY WOLF

tim·bre *also* **tim·ber** \'tam-bər, 'tim-\ *n* [F, fr. MF, bell struck by a hammer, fr. OF, drum, fr. MGk *tymbanon*

kettledrum, fr. Gk *tympanon*] : the distinctive quality given to a sound by its overtones

tim·brel \'tim-brəl\ *n* : a small hand drum or tambourine

¹time \'tīm\ *n* **1** : a period during which an action, process, or condition exists or continues ⟨gone a long ∼⟩ **2** : LEISURE ⟨found ∼ to read⟩ **3** : a point or period when something occurs : OCCASION ⟨the last ∼ we met⟩ **4** : a set or customary moment or hour for something to occur ⟨arrived on ∼⟩ **5** : AGE, ERA **6** : state of affairs : CONDITIONS ⟨hard ∼s⟩ **7** : a rate of speed : TEMPO **8** : a moment, hour, day, or year as indicated by a clock or calendar ⟨what ∼ is it⟩ **9** : a system of reckoning time ⟨solar ∼⟩ **10** : one of a series of recurring instances; *also, pl* : added or accumulated quantities or examples ⟨five ∼s greater⟩ **11** : a person's experience during a particular period ⟨had a good ∼⟩ **12** : the hours or days of one's work; *also* : an hourly pay rate ⟨straight ∼⟩ **13** : TIME-OUT

²time *vb* **timed; tim·ing** **1** : to arrange or set the time of : SCHEDULE ⟨∼s his calls conveniently⟩ **2** : to set the tempo or duration of ⟨∼ a performance⟩ **3** : to cause to keep time with **4** : to determine or record the time, duration, or rate of ⟨∼ a sprinter⟩ — **tim·er** *n*

time bomb *n* **1** : a bomb so made as to explode at a predetermined time **2** : something with a potentially dangerous delayed reaction

time clock *n* : a clock that records the time workers arrive and depart

time frame *n* : a period of time esp. with respect to some action or project

time–hon·ored \'tīm-ˌä-nərd\ *adj* : honored because of age or long usage

time·keep·er \-ˌkē-pər\ *n* **1** : a clerk who keeps records of the time worked by employees **2** : one appointed to mark and announce the time in an athletic game or contest

time·less \-ləs\ *adj* **1** : ETERNAL **2** : not limited or affected by time ⟨∼ works of art⟩ — **time·less·ly** *adv* — **time·less·ness** *n*

time·ly \-lē\ *adj* **time·li·er; -est** **1** : coming early or at the right time ⟨a ∼ arrival⟩ **2** : appropriate to the time ⟨a ∼ book⟩ — **time·li·ness** *n*

time–out \'tīm-'aut\ *n* : a brief suspension of activity esp. in an athletic game

time·piece \-ˌpēs\ *n* : a device (as a clock) to show the passage of time

times \'tīmz\ *prep* : multiplied by ⟨2 ∼ 2 is 4⟩

time–shar·ing \'tīm-ˌsher-iŋ\ *n* **1** : simultaneous use of a computer by many users **2** : joint onwership or rental of a vacation lodging by several persons with each taking turns using the place

times sign *n* : the symbol × used to indicate multiplication

time·ta·ble \'tīm-ˌtā-bəl\ *n* **1** : a table of the departure and arrival times (as of trains) **2** : a schedule showing a planned order or sequence

time warp *n* : an anomaly, discontinuity, or suspension held to occur in the progress of time

time·worn \-ˌwōrn\ *adj* **1** : worn by time **2** : HACKNEYED, STALE

time zone *n* : a geographical region within which the same standard time is used

☞ For illustration, see next page.

tim·id \'ti-məd\ *adj* : lacking in courage or self-confidence : FEARFUL — **ti·mid·i·ty** \tə-'mi-də-tē\ *n* — **tim·id·ly** *adv*

tim·o·rous \'ti-mə-rəs\ *adj* : of a timid disposition : AFRAID — **tim·o·rous·ly** *adv* — **tim·o·rous·ness** *n*

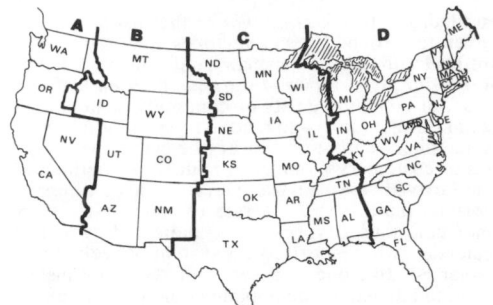

time zone: *A* Pacific time, *B* mountain time, *C* central time, *D* eastern time

tim·o·thy \'ti-mə-thē\ *n* : a grass with long cylindrical spikes widely grown for hay

Tim·o·thy \'ti-mə-thē\ *n* — see BIBLE table

tim·pa·ni \'tim-pə-nē\ *n sing or pl* [It] : a set of kettle-drums played by one performer in an orchestra — **tim·pa·nist** \-nist\ *n*

¹tin \'tin\ *n* **1** : a soft white crystalline metallic chemical element malleable at ordinary temperatures that is used esp. in solders and alloys — see ELEMENT table **2** : a container (as a can) made of metal (as tinplate)

²tin *vb* **tinned; tin·ning 1** : to cover or plate with tin **2** : to pack in tins

TIN *abbr* taxpayer identification number

tinct \'tiŋkt\ *n* : TINCTURE, TINGE

¹tinc·ture \'tiŋk-chər\ *n* **1** *archaic* : a substance that colors **2** : a slight admixture : TRACE **3** : an alcoholic solution of a medicinal substance **syn** touch, suggestion, suspicion, tinge

²tincture *vb* **tinc·tured; tinc·tur·ing 1** : COLOR, TINGE **2** : AFFECT

tin·der \'tin-dər\ *n* **1** : a very flammable substance used as kindling **2** : something serving to incite or inflame

tin·der·box \'tin-dər-ˌbäks\ *n* **1** : a metal box for holding tinder and usu. flint and steel for striking a spark **2** : a highly flammable object or place

tine \'tīn\ *n* : a slender pointed part (as of a fork or an antler) : PRONG

tin·foil \'tin-ˌfȯil\ *n* : a thin metal sheeting usu. of aluminum or tin-lead alloy

¹tinge \'tinj\ *vb* **tinged; tinge·ing** *or* **ting·ing 1** : to color slightly : TINT **2** : to affect or modify esp. with a slight odor or taste

²tinge *n* : a slight coloring, flavor, or quality : TRACE **syn** touch, suggestion, suspicion, tincture, soupçon

tin·gle \'tiŋ-gəl\ *vb* **tin·gled; tin·gling 1** : to feel a prickling or thrilling sensation **2** : TINKLE — **tingle** *n*

¹tin·ker \'tiŋ-kər\ *n* **1** : a usu. itinerant mender of household utensils **2** : an unskillful mender : BUNGLER

²tinker *vb* : to repair or adjust something in an unskillful or experimental manner — **tin·ker·er** *n*

¹tin·kle \'tiŋ-kəl\ *vb* **tin·kled; tin·kling** : to make or cause to make a tinkle

²tinkle *n* : a series of short high ringing or clinking sounds

tin·ny \'ti-nē\ *adj* **tin·ni·er; -est 1** : abounding in or yielding tin **2** : resembling tin; *also* : LIGHT, CHEAP **3** : thin in tone ⟨a ~ voice⟩ — **tin·ni·ly** \-nə-lē\ *adv* — **tin·ni·ness** \-nē-nəs\ *n*

tin·plate \'tin-'plāt\ *n* : thin sheet iron or steel coated with tin — **tin–plate** *vb*

tin·sel \'tin-səl\ *n* [MF *etincelle* spark, glitter] **1** : a thread, strip, or sheet of metal, paper, or plastic used to produce a glittering appearance **2** : something superficially attractive but of little worth

tin·smith \'tin-ˌsmith\ *n* : one that works with sheet metal (as tinplate)

¹tint \'tint\ *n* **1** : a slight or pale coloration : HUE **2** : any of various shades of a color

²tint *vb* : to impart a tint to : COLOR

tin·tin·nab·u·la·tion \ˌtin-tə-ˌna-byə-'lā-shən\ *n* **1** : the ringing of bells **2** : a tingling sound as if of bells

tin·ware \'tin-ˌwar\ *n* : articles and esp. utensils made of tinplate

ti·ny \'tī-nē\ *adj* **ti·ni·er; -est** : very small : MINUTE **syn** miniature, diminutive, wee, lilliputian

¹tip \'tip\ *vb* **tipped; tip·ping 1** : OVERTURN, UPSET **2** : LEAN, SLANT; *also* : to raise and tilt forward ⟨tipped his hat⟩

²tip *n* : the act or an instance of tipping

³tip *vb* **tipped; tip·ping 1** : to furnish with a tip **2** : to cover or adorn the tip of

⁴tip *n* **1** : the usu. pointed end of something **2** : a small piece or part serving as an end, cap, or point

⁵tip *n* : a light touch or blow

⁶tip *vb* **tipped; tip·ping** : to strike lightly : TAP

⁷tip *n* : a piece of advice or expert or confidential information : HINT

⁸tip *vb* **tipped; tip·ping** : to impart a piece of information about or to

⁹tip *vb* **tipped; tip·ping** : to give a gratuity to

¹⁰tip *n* : a gift or small sum given for a service performed or anticipated

tip–off \'tip-ˌȯf\ *n* : WARNING, TIP

tip·pet \'ti-pət\ *n* : a long scarf or shoulder cape

tip·ple \'ti-pəl\ *vb* **tip·pled; tip·pling** : to drink intoxicating liquor esp. habitually or excessively — **tipple** *n* — **tip·pler** *n*

tip·ster \'tip-stər\ *n* : a person who gives or sells tips esp. for gambling

tip·sy \'tip-sē\ *adj* **tip·si·er; -est** : unsteady or foolish from the effects of alcohol — **tip·si·ly** \-sə-lē\ *adv*

¹tip·toe \'tip-ˌtō\ *n* : the position of being balanced on the balls of the feet and toes with the heels raised; *also* : the ends of the toes

²tiptoe *adv or adj* : on or as if on tiptoe

³tiptoe *vb* **tip·toed; tip·toe·ing** : to walk or proceed on or as if on tiptoe

¹tip–top \'tip-'täp\ *n* : the highest point

²tip–top *adj* : EXCELLENT, FIRST-RATE

ti·rade \'tī-ˌrād\ *n* [F, shot, tirade, fr. MF, fr. It *tirata*, fr. *tirare* to draw, shoot] : a prolonged speech of abuse or condemnation

¹tire \'tīr\ *vb* **tired; tir·ing 1** : to make or become weary : FATIGUE **2** : to wear out the patience of : BORE

²tire *n* **1** : a metal hoop that forms the tread of a wheel **2** : a rubber cushion usu. containing compressed air that encircles a wheel (as of a bike)

tired \'tīrd\ *adj* **1** : WEARY, FATIGUED **2** : HACKNEYED — **tired·ness** *n*

tire·less \'tīr-ləs\ *adj* : not tiring : UNTIRING, INDEFATIGABLE — **tire·less·ly** *adv* — **tire·less·ness** *n*

tire·some \-səm\ *adj* : tending to bore : WEARISOME, TEDIOUS — **tire·some·ly** *adv* — **tire·some·ness** *n*

tiro *chiefly Brit var of* TYRO

Tish·ri \'tish-rē\ *n* [Heb *tishrī*] : the 1st month of the civil year or the 7th month of the ecclesiastical year in the Jewish calendar

tis·sue \'ti-shü\ *n* [ME *tissu*, a rich fabric, fr. OF, fr. *tistre* to weave, fr. L *texere*] **1** : a fine lightweight often sheer fabric **2** : NETWORK, WEB **3** : a soft absorbent paper **4** : a mass or layer of cells forming a basic structural material of an animal or plant

¹tit \'tit\ *n* : TEAT

²tit *n* : TITMOUSE

Tit *abbr* Titus

ti·tan \'tīt-ᵊn\ *n* **1** *cap* : one of a family of giants overthrown by the gods of ancient Greece **2** : one gigantic in size or power

ti·tan·ic \tī-'ta-nik\ *adj* : enormous in size, force, or power **syn** immense, gigantic, giant, colossal, mammoth

ti·ta·ni·um \tī-'tā-nē-əm\ *n* : a gray light strong metallic chemical element used esp. in alloys — see ELEMENT table

tit·bit \'tit-ˌbit\ *var of* TIDBIT

tithe \'tīth\ *n* : a 10th part paid or given esp. for the support of a church — **tithe** *vb* — **tith·er** *n*

tit·il·late \'tit-ᵊl-ˌāt\ *vb* **-lat·ed; -lat·ing 1** : to excite pleasurably **2** : TICKLE — **tit·il·la·tion** \ˌtit-ᵊl-'ā-shən\ *n*

tit·i·vate *or* **tit·ti·vate** \'ti-tə-ˌvāt\ *vb* **-vat·ed; -vat·ing** : to dress up : spruce up — **tit·i·va·tion** \ˌti-tə-'vā-shən\ *n*

ti·tle \'tīt-ᵊl\ *n* **1** : CLAIM, RIGHT; *esp* : a legal right to the ownership of property **2** : the distinguishing name esp. of an artistic production (as a book) **3** : an appellation of honor, rank, or office **4** : CHAMPIONSHIP **syn** designation, denomination, appellation

ti·tled \'tīt-ᵊld\ *adj* : having a title esp. of nobility

title page *n* : a page of a book bearing the title and usu. the names of the author and publisher

tit·mouse \'tit-ˌmaus\ *n, pl* **tit·mice** \-ˌmīs\ : any of numerous small long-tailed insect-eating birds

ti·tra·tion \tī-'trā-shən\ *n* : a process of finding the concentration of a solution (as of an acid) by adding small portions of a second solution of known concentration (as of a base) to a fixed amount of the first until an expected change (as in color) occurs

tit·ter \'ti-tər\ *vb* : to laugh in an affected or in a nervous or half-suppressed manner : GIGGLE — **titter** *n*

tit·tle \'tit-ᵊl\ *n* : a tiny piece : JOT

tit·tle–tat·tle \'tit-ᵊl-ˌtat-ᵊl\ *n* : idle talk : GOSSIP — **tittle–tattle** *vb*

tit·u·lar \'ti-chə-lər\ *adj* **1** : existing in title only : NOMINAL (~ ruler) **2** : of, relating to, or bearing a title (~ role)

Ti·tus \'tī-təs\ *n* — see BIBLE table

tiz·zy \'ti-zē\ *n, pl* **tizzies** : a highly excited and distracted state of mind

tk *abbr* **1** tank **2** truck

TKO \ˌtē-ˌkā-'ō\ *n* [*technical knock*out] : the termination of a boxing match when a boxer is declared unable to continue the fight

tkt *abbr* ticket

Tl *symbol* thallium

TLC *abbr* tender loving care

T lymphocyte *n* : T CELL

Tm *symbol* thulium

TM *abbr* trademark

T-man \'tē-ˌman\ *n* : a special agent of the U.S. Treasury Department

tn *abbr* **1** ton **2** town

TN *abbr* Tennessee

tng *abbr* training

tnpk *abbr* turnpike

TNT \ˌtē-(ˌ)en-'tē\ *n* : a flammable toxic compound used as a high explosive

¹to \tə, 'tü\ *prep* **1** : in the direction of and reaching (drove ~ town) **2** : in the direction of : TOWARD **3** : ON, AGAINST (apply salve ~ a burn) **4** : as far as (can pay up ~ a dollar) **5** : so as to become or bring about (beaten ~ death) (broken ~ pieces) **6** : BEFORE (it's five minutes ~ six) **7** : UNTIL (from May ~ December) **8** : fitting or being a part of : FOR (key ~ the lock) **9** : with the accompaniment of (sing ~ the music) **10** : in relation or comparison with (similar ~ that one) (won 10 ~ 6) **11** : in accordance with (add salt ~ taste) **12** : within the range of (~ my knowledge) **13** : contained, occurring, or included in (two pints ~ a quart) **14** : as regards (agreeable ~ everyone) **15** : affecting as the receiver or

beneficiary (whispered ~ her) (gave it ~ me) **16** : for no one except (a room ~ myself) **17** : into the action of (we got ~ talking) **18** — used for marking the following verb as an infinitive (wants ~ go) and often used by itself at the end of a clause in place of an infinitive suggested by the preceding context (goes to town whenever he wants ~) (can leave if you'd like ~)

²to \'tü\ *adv* **1** : in a direction toward (run ~ and fro) **2** : into contact esp. with the frame of a door (the door slammed ~) **3** : to the matter in hand (fell ~ and ate heartily) **4** : to a state of consciousness or awareness (came ~ hours after the accident)

TO *abbr* turn over

toad \'tōd\ *n* : any of numerous tailless leaping amphibians differing typically from the related frogs in having a shorter stockier build, rough dry warty skin, and less aquatic habits

toad

toad·stool \-ˌstül\ *n* : MUSHROOM; *esp* : one that is poisonous or inedible

toady \'tō-dē\ *n, pl* **toad·ies** : a person who flatters in the hope of gaining favors : SYCOPHANT — **toady** *vb*

to–and–fro \ˌtü-ən-'frō\ *adj* : forward and backward — **to–and–fro** *n*

¹toast \'tōst\ *vb* **1** : to warm thoroughly **2** : to make (as bread) crisp, hot, and brown by heat **3** : to become toasted

²toast *n* **1** : sliced toasted bread **2** : someone or something in whose honor persons drink **3** : an act of drinking in honor of a toast

³toast *vb* : to propose or drink to as a toast

toast·er \'tō-stər\ *n* : an electrical appliance for toasting

toaster oven *n* : a portable electrical appliance that bakes, broils, and toasts

toast·mas·ter \'tōst-ˌmas-tər\ *n* : a person who presides at a banquet and introduces the after-dinner speakers

toast·mis·tress \-ˌmis-trəs\ *n* : a woman who acts as toastmaster

Tob *abbr* Tobit

to·bac·co \tə-'ba-kō\ *n, pl* **-cos** [Sp *tabaco*] **1** : a tall broad-leaved herb related to the potato; *also* : its leaves prepared for smoking or chewing or as snuff **2** : manufactured tobacco products; *also* : smoking as a practice

to·bac·co·nist \tə-'ba-kə-nist\ *n* : a dealer in tobacco

To·bi·as \tō-'bī-əs\ *n* : TOBIT

To·bit \'tō-bət\ *n* — see BIBLE table

¹to·bog·gan \tə-'bä-gən\ *n* : a long flat-bottomed light sled made of thin boards curved up at one end

²toboggan *vb* **1** : to coast on or as if on a toboggan **2** : to decline suddenly (as in value) — **to·bog·gan·er** *n*

\ə\abut \ᵊ\kitten \ər\further \a\ash \ā\ace \ä\mop, mar
\aú\out \ch\chin \e\bet \ē\easy \g\go \i\hit \ī\ice \j\job
\ŋ\sing \ō\go \ó\law \ói\boy \th\thin \th\the \ü\loot \ú\foot
\y\yet \zh\vision *see also* Pronunciation Symbols page

toc·sin \'täk-sən\ *n* **1** : an alarm bell **2** : a warning signal

¹to·day \tə-'dā\ *adv* **1** : on or for this day **2** : at the present time

²today *n* : the present day, time, or age

tod·dle \'täd-ᵊl\ *vb* **tod·dled; tod·dling** : to walk with short tottering steps in the manner of a young child — **toddle** *n* — **tod·dler** *n*

tod·dy \'tä-dē\ *n, pl* **toddies** [Hindi *tārī* juice of a palm, fr. *tār* a palm, fr. Skt *tāla*] : a drink made of liquor, sugar, spices, and hot water

to–do \tə-'dü\ *n, pl* **to–dos** \-'düz\ : BUSTLE, STIR, FUSS

¹toe \'tō\ *n* **1** : one of the jointed parts of the front end of a vertebrate's foot **2** : the front part of a foot or hoof

²toe *vb* **toed; toe·ing** : to touch, reach, or drive with the toes

toea \'tȯi-ə\ *n* — see *kina* at MONEY table

toe·hold \'tō-ˌhōld\ *n* **1** : a place of support for the toes **2** : a slight footing

toe·nail \'tō-ˌnāl\ *n* : a nail of a toe

tof·fee *or* **tof·fy** \'tȯ-fē, 'tä-\ *n, pl* **toffees** *or* **toffies** : candy of brittle but tender texture made by boiling sugar and butter together

to·fu \'tō-(ˌ)fü\ *n* [Jp *tōfu*] : a soft vegetable cheese made from soybeans

tog \'täg, 'tȯg\ *vb* **togged; tog·ging** : to put togs on : DRESS

to·ga \'tō-gə\ *n* : the loose outer garment worn in public by citizens of ancient Rome — **to·gaed** \-gəd\ *adj*

¹to·geth·er \tə-'ge-thər\ *adv* **1** : in or into one place or group **2** : in or into contact or association ⟨mix ∼⟩ **3** : at one time : SIMULTANEOUSLY ⟨talk and work ∼⟩ **4** : in succession ⟨for days ∼⟩ **5** : in or into harmony or coherence ⟨get ∼ on a plan⟩ **6** : as a group : JOINTLY — **to·geth·er·ness** *n*

²together *adj* : composed in mind or manner

tog·gery \'tä-gə-rē, 'tȯ-\ *n* : CLOTHING

tog·gle switch \'tä-gəl-\ *n* : an electric switch operated by pushing a projecting lever through a small arc

To·go·lese \ˌtō-gə-'lēz, -'lēs\ *n* : a native or inhabitant of Togo — **Togolese** *adj*

togs \'tägz, 'tȯgz\ *n pl* : CLOTHING; *esp* : clothes for a specified use ⟨riding ∼⟩

¹toil \'tȯil\ *n* **1** : laborious effort **2** : long fatiguing labor : DRUDGERY — **toil·ful** \-fəl\ *adj* — **toil·some** *adj*

²toil *vb* [ME, to argue, struggle, fr. OF *toeillier* to stir, disturb, dispute, fr. L *tudiculare* to crush, grind, fr. *tudicula* machine for crushing olives, dim. of *tudes* hammer] **1** : to work hard and long **2** : to proceed with great effort : PLOD — **toil·er** *n*

³toil *n* [ME *toile* cloth, net, fr. L *tela* cloth on a loom] : NET, TRAP — usu. used in pl.

toi·let \'tȯi-lət\ *n* **1** : the act or process of dressing and grooming oneself **2** : BATHROOM **3** : a fixture for use in urinating and defecating; *esp* : one consisting essentially of a water-flushed bowl and seat — **toilet** *vb*

toi·let·ry \'tȯi-lə-trē\ *n, pl* **-ries** : an article or preparation used in making one's toilet — usu. used in pl.

toi·lette \twä-'let\ *n* **1** : TOILET 1 **2** : formal attire; *also* : a particular costume

toilet training *n* : the process of training a child to control bladder and bowel movements and to use the toilet — **toilet train** *vb*

toil·worn \'tȯil-ˌwȯrn\ *adj* : showing the effects of toil

To·kay \tō-'kā\ *n* : naturally sweet wine from Hungary

toke \'tōk\ *n, slang* : a puff on a marijuana cigarette or pipe

¹to·ken \'tō-kən\ *n* **1** : an outward sign **2** : SYMBOL, EMBLEM **3** : SOUVENIR, KEEPSAKE **4** : a small part representing the whole **5** : a piece resembling a coin issued as money or for use by a particular group on specified terms

²token *adj* **1** : done or given as a token esp. in partial ful-

fillment of an obligation **2** : representing only a symbolic effort : MINIMAL, PERFUNCTORY

to·ken·ism \'tō-kə-ˌni-zəm\ *n* : the policy or practice of making only a symbolic effort (as to desegregate)

told *past and past part of* TELL

tole \'tōl\ *n* : sheet metal and esp. tinplate for use in domestic and ornamental wares

tol·er·a·ble \'tä-lə-rə-bəl\ *adj* **1** : capable of being borne or endured **2** : moderately good : PASSABLE — **tol·er·a·bly** \-blē\ *adv*

tol·er·ance \'tä-lə-rəns\ *n* **1** : the act or practice of tolerating; *esp* : sympathy or indulgence for beliefs or practices differing from one's own **2** : the allowable deviation from a standard (as of size) **3** : the body's ability to become less responsive over time to something (as a drug) — **tol·er·ant** *adj* — **tol·er·ant·ly** *adv*

tol·er·ate \'tä-lə-ˌrāt\ *vb* **-at·ed; -at·ing** **1** : to exhibit physiological tolerance for (as a drug) **2** : to allow to be or to be done without hindrance **syn** abide, bear, suffer, stand, brook — **tol·er·a·tion** \ˌtä-lə-'rā-shən\ *n*

¹toll \'tōl\ *n* **1** : a tax paid for a privilege (as for passing over a bridge) **2** : a charge for a service (as for a long-distance telephone call) **3** : the cost in life, health, loss, or suffering

²toll *vb* **1** : to cause the slow regular sounding of (a bell) esp. by pulling a rope **2** : to give signal of : SOUND **3** : to sound with slow measured strokes **4** : to announce by tolling

³toll *n* : the sound of a tolling bell

toll·booth \'tōl-ˌbüth\ *n* : a booth where tolls are paid

toll·gate \-ˌgāt\ *n* : a point where vehicles stop to pay a toll

toll·house \-ˌhaus\ *n* : a house or booth where tolls are paid

tol·u·ene \'täl-yə-ˌwēn\ *n* : a liquid hydrocarbon used esp. as a solvent

tom \'täm\ *n* : the male of various animals (as a cat or turkey)

¹tom·a·hawk \'tä-mə-ˌhȯk\ *n* : a light ax used as a missile and as a hand weapon esp. by No. American Indians

²tomahawk *vb* : to strike or kill with a tomahawk

to·ma·to \tə-'mā-tō, -'mä-\ *n, pl* **-toes** : a usu. large, rounded, and red or yellow pulpy edible berry of a widely grown tropical herb related to the potato; *also* : this herb

tomb \'tüm\ *n* **1** : a place of burial : GRAVE **2** : a house, chamber, or vault for the dead — **tomb** *vb*

tom·boy \'täm-ˌbȯi\ *n* : a girl who behaves in a manner usu. considered boyish — **tom·boy·ish** *adj*

tomb·stone \'tüm-ˌstōn\ *n* : a stone marking a grave

tom·cat \'täm-ˌkat\ *n* : a male domestic cat

Tom Col·lins \'täm-'kä-lənz\ *n* : a tall iced drink with a base of gin

tome \'tōm\ *n* : BOOK; *esp* : a large or weighty one

tom·fool·ery \täm-'fü-lə-rē\ *n* : playful or foolish behavior

tom·my gun \'tä-mē-ˌgən\ *n* : SUBMACHINE GUN — **tommy–gun** *vb*

to·mog·ra·phy \tō-'mä-grə-fē\ *n* : a method of producing a three-dimensional image of the internal structures of a solid object (as the human body or the earth) — **to·mo·graph·ic** \ˌtō-mə-'gra-fik\ *adj*

to·mor·row \tə-'mär-ō\ *adv* : on or for the day after today — **tomorrow** *n*

tom·tit \'täm-ˌtit, täm-'tit\ *n* : any of various small active birds

tom–tom \'täm-ˌtäm\ *n* : a small-headed drum beaten with the hands

ton \'tən\ *n, pl* **tons** *also* **ton** **1** — see WEIGHT table **2** : a unit equal to the volume of a long ton weight of seawater used in reckoning the displacement of ships and equal to 35 cubic feet

to·nal·i·ty \tō-'na-lə-tē\ *n, pl* **-ties** : tonal quality

¹**tone** \'tōn\ *n* [ME, fr. L *tonus* tension, tone, fr. Gk *tonos*, lit., act of stretching; fr. the dependence of the pitch of a musical string on its tension] **1** : vocal or musical sound; *esp* : sound quality **2** : a sound of definite pitch **3** : WHOLE STEP **4** : accent or inflection expressive of an emotion **5** : the pitch of a word often used to express differences of meaning **6** : style or manner of expression **7** : color quality; *also* : SHADE, TINT **8** : the effect in painting of light and shade together with color **9** : healthy and vigorous condition of a living body or bodily part; *also* : the state of partial contraction characteristic of normal muscle **10** : general character, quality, or trend **syn** atmosphere, feeling, mood, vein — **ton·al** \'tōn-ᵊl\ *adj*

²**tone** *vb* **toned; ton·ing 1** : to give a particular intonation or inflection to **2** : to impart tone to **3** : SOFTEN, MELLOW **4** : to harmonize in color : BLEND

tone·arm *n* : the movable part of a record player that carries the pickup and the needle

tong \'täŋ, 'tȯŋ\ *n* : a Chinese secret society in the U.S.

tongs \'täŋz, 'tȯŋz\ *n pl* : a grasping device consisting of two pieces joined at one end by a pivot or hinged like scissors — **tong** *vb*

¹**tongue** \'təŋ\ *n* **1** : a fleshy movable process of the floor of the mouth used in tasting and in taking and swallowing food and in humans as a speech organ **2** : the flesh of a tongue (as of the ox) used as food **3** : the power of communication **4** : LANGUAGE 1 **5** : manner or quality of utterance; *also* : intended meaning **6** : ecstatic usu. unintelligible utterance accompanying religious excitation — usu. used in pl. **7** : something resembling an animal's tongue esp. in being elongated and fastened at one end only — **tongued** \'təŋd\ *adj* — **tongue·less** *adj*

²**tongue** *vb* **tongued; tongu·ing 1** : to touch or lick with the tongue **2** : to articulate notes on a wind instrument

tongue–in–cheek *adj* : characterized by insincerity, irony, or whimsical exaggeration — **tongue in cheek** *adv*

tongue–lash \'təŋ-ˌlash\ *vb* : CHIDE, REPROVE — **tongue–lash·ing** \-iŋ\ *n*

tongue–tied \-ˌtīd\ *adj* : unable or disinclined to speak clearly or freely (as from shyness or a tongue impairment)

tongue twister *n* : an utterance that is difficult to articulate because of a succession of similar consonants

¹**ton·ic** \'tä-nik\ *adj* **1** : of, relating to, or producing a healthy physical or mental condition : INVIGORATING **2** : relating to or based on the 1st tone of a scale — **ton·ic·i·ty** \tō-ˈni-sə-tē\ *n*

²**tonic** *n* **1** : something that invigorates, restores, or refreshes **2** : the 1st degree of a musical scale

tonic water *n* : a carbonated beverage flavored with a bit of quinine, lemon, and lime

¹**to·night** \tə-ˈnīt\ *adv* : on this present night or the coming night

²**tonight** *n* : the present or the coming night

ton·nage \'tə-nij\ *n* **1** : a duty on ships based on tons carried **2** : ships in terms of the number of tons registered or carried **3** : total weight in tons shipped, carried, or mined

ton·sil \'tän-səl\ *n* : either of a pair of oval masses of lymphoid tissue that lie one on each side of the throat at the back of the mouth

ton·sil·lec·to·my \ˌtän-sə-ˈlek-tə-mē\ *n, pl* **-mies** : the surgical removal of the tonsils

ton·sil·li·tis \-ˈlī-təs\ *n* : inflammation of the tonsils

ton·so·ri·al \tän-ˈsȯr-ē-əl\ *adj* : of or relating to a barber or a barber's work

ton·sure \'tän-chər\ *n* [ME, fr. ML *tonsura*, fr. L, act of shearing, fr. *tonsus*, pp. of *tondēre* to shear] **1** : the rite of admission to the clerical state by the clipping or shaving of the head **2** : the shaven crown or patch worn by clerics (as monks) — **tonsure** *vb*

too \'tü\ *adv* **1** : in addition : ALSO **2** : EXCESSIVELY **3** : to such a degree as to be regrettable **4** : VERY

took *past of* TAKE

¹**tool** \'tül\ *n* **1** : a hand instrument that aids in accomplishing a task **2** : the cutting or shaping part in a machine; *also* : a machine for shaping metal in any way **3** : something used in doing a job ⟨a scholar's books are his ∼s⟩; *also* : a means to an end **4** : a person used by another : DUPE **5** *pl* : natural ability

²**tool** *vb* **1** : to shape, form, or finish with a tool; *esp* : to letter or decorate (as a book cover) by means of hand tools **2** : to equip a plant or industry with machines and tools for production **3** : DRIVE, RIDE ⟨∼ing along at 60⟩

¹**toot** \'tüt\ *vb* **1** : to sound or cause to sound in short blasts **2** : to blow an instrument (as a horn) — **toot·er** *n*

²**toot** *n* : a short blast (as on a horn)

tooth \'tüth\ *n, pl* **teeth** \'tēth\ **1** : one of the hard bony structures borne esp. on the jaws of vertebrates and used for seizing and chewing food and as weapons; *also* : a hard sharp structure esp. around the mouth of an invertebrate **2** : something resembling an animal's tooth **3** : any of the projections on the edge of a wheel that fits into corresponding projections on another wheel — **toothed** \'tütht\ *adj* — **tooth·less** *adj*

tooth·ache \'tüth-ˌāk\ *n* : pain in or about a tooth

tooth·brush \-ˌbrəsh\ *n* : a brush for cleaning the teeth

tooth·paste \-ˌpāst\ *n* : a paste for cleaning the teeth

tooth·pick \-ˌpik\ *n* : a pointed instrument for removing food particles caught between the teeth

tooth powder *n* : a powder for cleaning the teeth

tooth·some \'tüth-səm\ *adj* **1** : AGREEABLE, ATTRACTIVE **2** : pleasing to the taste : DELICIOUS **syn** palatable, appetizing, savory, tasty

toothy \'tü-thē\ *adj* **tooth·i·er; -est** : having or showing prominent teeth

¹**top** \'täp\ *n* **1** : the highest part, point, or level of something **2** : the stalks and leaves of a plant with edible roots ⟨beet ∼s⟩ **3** : the upper end, edge, or surface ⟨the ∼ of a page⟩ **4** : an upper piece, lid, or covering **5** : the highest degree, pitch, or rank

²**top** *vb* **topped; top·ping 1** : to remove or trim the top of : PRUNE ⟨∼ a tree⟩ **2** : to cover with a top or on the top : CROWN, CAP **3** : to be superior to : EXCEL, SURPASS **4** : to go over the top of **5** : to strike (a ball) above the center **6** : to make an end or conclusion ⟨∼ off a meal with coffee⟩

³**top** *adj* **1** : of, relating to, or being at the top : HIGHEST **2** : CHIEF

⁴**top** *n* : a child's toy that has a tapering point on which it is made to spin

to·paz \'tō-ˌpaz\ *n* : a hard silicate of aluminum; *esp* : a yellow transparent topaz used as a gem

top·coat \'täp-ˌkōt\ *n* **1** : a lightweight overcoat **2** : a protective coating (as of paint)

top dollar *n* : the highest amount being paid for a commodity or service

top–dress \-ˌdres\ *vb* : to apply material to (as land) without working it in; *esp* : to scatter fertilizer over

top·dress·ing \-ˌdre-siŋ\ *n* : a material used to top-dress soil

top·flight \'täp-ˈflīt\ *adj* : of, relating to, or being the highest level of excellence or rank — **top flight** *n*

top hat *n* : a tall-crowned hat usu. of beaver or silk

top–heavy \'täp-ˌhe-vē\ *adj* : having the top part too heavy for the lower part

top·ic \'tä-pik\ *n* **1** : a heading in an outlined argument **2** : the subject of a discourse or a section of it : THEME

\ə\abut \ᵊ\kitten \ər\further \a\ash \ā\ace \ä\mop, mar \aů\out \ch\chin \e\bet \ē\easy \g\go \i\hit \ī\ice \j\job \ŋ\sing \ō\go \ȯ\law \ȯi\boy \th\thin \t̲h̲\the \ü\loot \ů\foot \y\yet \zh\vision *see also* Pronunciation Symbols page

top·i·cal \-pi-kəl\ *adj* **1** : designed to be applied to or to work on a part (as of the body) **2** : of, relating to, or arranged by topics ⟨a ∼ outline⟩ **3** : relating to current or local events — **top·i·cal·ly** \-k(ə-)lē\ *adv*

top·knot \'täp-ˌnät\ *n* **1** : an ornament (as a knot of ribbons) forming a headdress **2** : a crest of feathers or tuft of hair on the top of the head

top·less \-ləs\ *adj* **1** : wearing no clothing on the upper body **2** : featuring topless waitresses or entertainers

top·mast \'täp-ˌmast, -məst\ *n* : the 2d mast above a ship's deck

top·most \'täp-ˌmōst\ *adj* : highest of all : UPPERMOST

top–notch \-'näch\ *adj* : of the highest quality : FIRST=RATE

to·pog·ra·phy \tə-'pä-grə-fē\ *n* **1** : the art of showing in detail on a map or chart the physical features of a place or region **2** : the outline of the form of a place showing its relief and the position of features (as rivers, roads, or cities) — **to·pog·ra·pher** \-fər\ *n* — **top·o·graph·ic** \ˌtä-pə-'gra-fik\ *or* **top·o·graph·i·cal** \-fi-kəl\ *adj*

top·ping \'tä-piŋ\ *n* : a food served on top of another to make it look or taste better

top·ple \'tä-pəl\ *vb* **top·pled; top·pling** **1** : to fall from or as if from being top-heavy **2** : to push over : OVERTURN; *also* : OVERTHROW

tops \'täps\ *adj* : topmost in quality or importance ⟨∼ in his field⟩

top·sail \'täp-ˌsāl, -səl\ *also* **top·s'l** \-səl\ *n* : the sail next above the lowest sail on a mast in a square-rigged ship

top secret *adj* : demanding complete secrecy among those concerned

top·side \'täp-'sīd\ *adv or adj* **1** : to or on the top or surface **2** : on deck

top·sides \-'sīdz\ *n pl* : the top portion of the outer surface of a ship on each side above the waterline

top·soil \'täp-ˌsȯil\ *n* : surface soil usu. including the organic layer in which plants have most of their roots

top·sy–tur·vy \ˌtäp-sē-'tər-vē\ *adv* **1** : in utter confusion **2** : UPSIDE DOWN — **topsy–turvy** *adj*

toque \'tōk\ *n* : a woman's small hat without a brim

tor \'tȯr\ *n* : a high craggy hill

To·rah \'tōr-ə\ *n* **1** : a scroll of the first five books of the Old Testament used in a synagogue; *also* : these five books **2** : the body of divine knowledge and law found in the Jewish scriptures and tradition

¹**torch** \'tȯrch\ *n* **1** : a flaming light made of something that burns brightly and usu. carried in the hand **2** : something that resembles a torch in giving light, heat, or guidance **3** *chiefly Brit* : FLASHLIGHT **4** : a portable burner for producing a hot flame

²**torch** *vb* : to set fire to

torch·bear·er \'tȯrch-ˌbar-ər\ *n* : one who carries a torch; *also* : one in the forefront (as of a political campaign)

torch·light \-ˌlīt\ *n* : light given by torches

torch song *n* : a popular sentimental song of unrequited love

tore *past of* TEAR

to·re·ador \'tȯr-ē-ə-ˌdȯr\ *n* : TORERO

to·re·ro \tə-'rer-ō\ *n, pl* **-ros** [Sp] : BULLFIGHTER

¹**tor·ment** \'tȯr-ˌment\ *n* **1** : extreme pain or anguish of body or mind **2** : a source of vexation or pain

²**tor·ment** \tȯr-'ment\ *vb* **1** : to cause severe suffering of body or mind to **2** : DISTORT, TWIST **syn** rack, afflict, try, torture — **tor·men·tor** \-'men-tər\ *n*

torn *past part of* TEAR

tor·na·do \tȯr-'nā-dō\ *n, pl* **-does** *or* **-dos** [modif of Sp *tronada* thunderstorm, fr. *tronar* to thunder, fr. L *tonare*] : a violent destructive whirling wind accompanied by a funnel-shaped cloud that moves over a narrow path

¹**tor·pe·do** \tȯr-'pē-dō\ *n, pl* **-does** : a thin cylindrical self=propelled underwater weapon

²**torpedo** *vb* **tor·pe·doed; tor·pe·do·ing** : to hit or destroy with or as if with a torpedo

torpedo boat *n* : a small very fast boat for firing torpedoes

tor·pid \'tȯr-pəd\ *adj* **1** : having lost motion or the power of exertion : DORMANT **2** : SLUGGISH **3** : lacking vigor : DULL — **tor·pid·i·ty** \tȯr-'pi-də-tē\ *n*

tor·por \'tȯr-pər\ *n* **1** : DULLNESS, APATHY **2** : extreme sluggishness : STAGNATION **syn** stupor, lethargy, languor, lassitude

¹**torque** \'tȯrk\ *n* : a force that produces or tends to produce rotation or torsion

²**torque** *vb* **torqued; torqu·ing** : to impart torque to : cause to twist (as about an axis)

tor·rent \'tȯr-ənt\ *n* [F, fr. L *torrent-, torrens*, fr. *torrent-, torrens* burning, seething, rushing, fr. prp. of *torrēre* to parch, burn] **1** : a tumultuous outburst **2** : a rushing stream (as of water)

tor·ren·tial \tȯ-'ren-chəl\ *adj* : relating to or resembling a torrent ⟨∼ rains⟩

tor·rid \'tȯr-əd\ *adj* **1** : parched with heat esp. of the sun : HOT **2** : ARDENT

torrid zone *n* : the region of the earth between the tropic of Cancer and the tropic of Capricorn

tor·sion \'tȯr-shən\ *n* **1** : a wrenching by which one part of a body is under pressure to turn about a longitudinal axis while the other part is held fast or is under pressure to turn in the opposite direction **2** : a twisting of a bodily organ or part on its own axis — **tor·sion·al** \'tȯr-shə-nəl\ *adj* — **tor·sion·al·ly** *adv*

tor·so \'tȯr-sō\ *n, pl* **torsos** *or* **tor·si** \'tȯr-ˌsē\ [It, lit., stalk] : the trunk of the human body

tort \'tȯrt\ *n* : a wrongful act which does not involve a breach of contract and for which the injured party can recover damages in a civil action

tor·ti·lla \tȯr-'tē-ə\ *n* : a round thin cake of unleavened cornmeal or wheat flour bread

tor·toise \'tȯr-təs\ *n* : TURTLE; *esp* : any of a family of land turtles

tor·toise·shell \-ˌshel\ *n* : the mottled horny substance of the shell of some turtles used in inlaying and in making various ornamental articles — **tortoiseshell** *adj*

tor·to·ni \tȯr-'tō-nē\ *n* : rich ice cream often made with minced almonds and chopped cherries and flavored with rum

tor·tu·ous \'tȯr-chə-wəs\ *adj* **1** : marked by twists or turns : WINDING **2** : DEVIOUS, TRICKY

¹**tor·ture** \'tȯr-chər\ *n* **1** : anguish of body or mind **2** : the infliction of severe pain esp. to punish or coerce

²**torture** *vb* **tor·tured; tor·tur·ing** **1** : to cause intense suffering to : TORMENT **2** : to punish or coerce by inflicting severe pain **3** : TWIST, DISTORT **syn** rack, harrow, afflict, try — **tor·tur·er** \-'men-tər\ *n*

To·ry \'tȯr-ē\ *n, pl* **Tories** **1** : a member of a chiefly 18th century British party upholding the established church and the traditional political structure **2** : an American supporter of the British during the American Revolution **3** *often not cap* : an extreme conservative — **Tory** *adj*

¹**toss** \'tȯs, 'täs\ *vb* **1** : to fling to and fro or up and down **2** : to throw with a quick light motion; *also* : BANDY **3** : to fling or lift with a sudden motion ⟨∼ed her head angrily⟩ **4** : to move restlessly or turbulently ⟨∼es on the waves⟩ **5** : to twist and turn repeatedly **6** : FLOUNCE **7** : to accomplish readily ⟨∼ off an article⟩ **8** : to decide an issue by flipping a coin

²**toss** *n* : an act or instance of tossing; *esp* : TOSS-UP 1

toss–up \-ˌəp\ *n* **1** : a deciding by flipping a coin **2** : an even chance (as about an aim) **3** : something that offers no clear basis for choice

¹**tot** \'tät\ *n* **1** : a small child **2** : a small drink of alcoholic liquor : SHOT

²**tot** *vb* **tot·ted; tot·ting** : to add up

³tot *abbr* total

¹to·tal \'tōt-ᵊl\ *adj* **1** : making up a whole : ENTIRE ⟨~ amount⟩ **2** : COMPLETE, UTTER ⟨a ~ failure⟩ **3** : involving a complete and unified effort esp. to achieve a desired effect — **to·tal·ly** *adv*

²total *n* **1** : SUM **4 2** : the entire amount **syn** aggregate, whole, gross, totality

³total *vb* **to·taled** *or* **to·talled; to·tal·ing** *or* **to·tal·ling 1** : to add up : COMPUTE **2** : to amount to : NUMBER **3** : to make a total wreck of (a car)

to·tal·i·tar·i·an \tō-ˌta-lə-'ter-ē-ən\ *adj* : of, relating to, or advocating a political regime based on subordination of the individual to the state and strict control of all aspects of life esp. by coercive measures — **totalitarian** *n* — **to·tal·i·tar·i·an·ism** \-ē-ə-ˌni-zəm\ *n*

to·tal·i·ty \tō-'ta-lə-tē\ *n, pl* **-ties 1** : an aggregate amount : SUM, WHOLE **2** : ENTIRETY, WHOLENESS

to·tal·iza·tor *or* **to·tal·isa·tor** \'tōt-ᵊl-ə-ˌzā-tər\ *n* : a machine for registering and indicating the number of bets and the odds on a horse or dog race

¹tote \'tōt\ *vb* **tot·ed; tot·ing** : CARRY

²tote *vb* **tot·ed; tot·ing** : ADD, TOTAL — usu. used with *up*

to·tem \'tō-təm\ *n* : an object (as an animal or plant) serving as the emblem of a family or clan and often as a reminder of its ancestry; *also* : something usu. carved or painted to represent such an object

totem pole *n* : a pole that is carved with a series of totems and is erected before the houses of some northwest American Indians

tot·ter \'tä-tər\ *vb* **1** : to tremble or rock as if about to fall : SWAY **2** : to move unsteadily : STAGGER

tou·can \'tü-ˌkan\ *n* : any of a family of fruit-eating birds of tropical America with brilliant coloring and a very large beak

¹touch \'təch\ *vb* **1** : to bring a bodily part (as the hand) into contact with so as to feel **2** : to be or cause to be in contact **3** : to strike or push lightly esp. with the hand or foot **4** : DISTURB, HARM **5** : to make use of ⟨never ~es alcohol⟩ **6** : to induce to give or lend **7** : to get to : REACH **8** : to refer to in passing : MENTION **9** : to affect the interest of : CONCERN **10** : to leave a mark on; *also* : BLEMISH **11** : to move to sympathetic feeling **12** : to come close : VERGE **13** : to have a bearing : RELATE **14** : to make a usu. brief or incidental stop in port **syn** affect, influence, impress, strike, sway

²touch *n* **1** : a light stroke or tap **2** : the act or fact of touching or being touched **3** : the sense by which pressure or traction on the skin or mucous membrane is perceived; *also* : a particular sensation conveyed by this sense **4** : mental or moral sensitiveness : TACT **5** : a small quantity : HINT ⟨a ~ of spring in the air⟩ **6** : a manner of striking or touching esp. the keys of a keyboard instrument **7** : an improving detail ⟨add a few ~es to the painting⟩ **8** : distinctive manner or skill ⟨the ~ of a master⟩ **9** : the state of being in contact ⟨keep in ~⟩ **syn** suggestion, suspicion, tincture, tinge

touch·down \'təch-ˌdaún\ *n* : the act of scoring six points in American football by being lawfully in possession of the ball on, above, or behind an opponent's goal line

tou·ché \tü-'shā\ *interj* [F] — used to acknowledge a hit in fencing or the success of an argument, an accusation, or a witty point

touch football *n* : football in which touching is substituted for tackling

touch·ing *adj* : capable of stirring emotions **syn** moving, impressive, poignant, affecting

touch off *vb* **1** : to describe with precision **2** : to start by or as if by touching with fire

touch·stone \'təch-ˌstōn\ *n* : a test or criterion of genuineness or quality **syn** standard, gauge, benchmark, yardstick

touch up *vb* : to improve or perfect by small additional strokes or alterations — **touch–up** \'təch-ˌəp\ *n*

touchy \'tə-chē\ *adj* **touch·i·er; -est 1** : easily offended : PEEVISH **2** : calling for tact in treatment ⟨a ~ subject⟩ **syn** irascible, cranky, cross, tetchy, testy

¹tough \'təf\ *adj* **1** : strong or firm in texture but flexible and not brittle **2** : not easily chewed **3** : characterized by severity and determination ⟨a ~ policy⟩ **4** : capable of enduring strain or hardship : ROBUST **5** : hard to influence : STUBBORN **6** : difficult to accomplish, resolve, or cope with ⟨a ~ problem⟩ **7** : ROWDYISH **syn** tenacious, stout, sturdy, stalwart — **tough·ly** *adv* — **tough·ness** *n*

²tough *n* : a tough person : ROWDY

tough·en \'tə-fən\ *vb* **tough·ened; tough·en·ing** : to make or become tough

tou·pee \tü-'pā\ *n* [F *toupet* forelock] : a small wig for a bald spot

¹tour \'tùr, *1 is also* 'taùr\ *n* **1** : one's turn : SHIFT **2** : a journey in which one returns to the starting point

²tour *vb* : to make a tour

tour de force \ˌtùr-də-'fōrs\ *n, pl* **tours de force** *same*\ [F] : a feat of strength, skill, or ingenuity

tour·ist \'tùr-ist\ *n* : one that makes a tour for pleasure or culture

tourist class *n* : economy accommodations (as on a ship)

tour·ma·line \'tùr-mə-lən, -ˌlēn\ *n* : a mineral that when transparent is valued as a gem

tour·na·ment \'tùr-nə-mənt, 'tər-\ *n* **1** : a medieval sport in which mounted armored knights contended with blunted lances or swords **2** : a championship series of games or athletic contests

tour·ney \-nē\ *n, pl* **tourneys** : TOURNAMENT

tour·ni·quet \'tùr-ni-kət, 'tər-\ *n* : a device (as a tight bandage) for stopping bleeding or blood flow

tou·sle \'taù-zəl\ *vb* **tou·sled; tou·sling** : to disorder by rough handling : DISHEVEL, MUSS

tout \'taùt, *2 is also* 'tüt\ *vb* **1** : to give a tip or solicit bets on a racehorse **2** : to praise or publicize loudly — **tout** *n*

¹tow \'tō\ *vb* : to draw or pull along behind

²tow *n* **1** : an act of towing or condition of being towed **2** : something (as a barge) that is towed

³tow *n* : short or broken fiber (as of flax or hemp) used esp. for yarn, twine, or stuffing

to·ward \'tōrd, 'tō-ərd, tə-'wórd\ *or* **to·wards** \'tōrdz, 'tō-ərdz, tə-'wórdz\ *prep* **1** : in the direction of ⟨heading ~ the river⟩ **2** : along a course leading to ⟨efforts ~ reconciliation⟩ **3** : in regard to ⟨tolerance ~ minorities⟩ **4** : so as to face ⟨turn the chair ~ the window⟩ **5** : close upon ⟨it was getting along ~ sundown⟩ **6** : for part payment of ⟨here's $100 ~ your tuition⟩

tow·boat \'tō-ˌbōt\ *n* : TUGBOAT

tow·el \'taù-əl\ *n* : an absorbent cloth or paper for wiping or drying

tow·el·ing *or* **tow·el·ling** *n* : a cotton or linen fabric for making towels

¹tow·er \'taù-ər\ *n* **1** : a tall structure either isolated or built upon a larger structure ⟨an observation ~⟩ **2** : a towering citadel — **tow·ered** *adj*

²tower *vb* : to reach or rise to a great height

tow·er·ing *adj* **1** : LOFTY ⟨~ pines⟩ **2** : reaching high intensity ⟨a ~ rage⟩ **3** : EXCESSIVE ⟨~ ambition⟩

tow·head \'tō-ˌhed\ *n* : a person having whitish blond hair — **tow·head·ed** \-ˌhe-dəd\ *adj*

to·whee \'tō-hē, 'tō-(ˌ)ē, tō-'hē\ *n* : a common finch of eastern No. America having the male black, white, and reddish; *also* : any of several closely related finches

---

\ə\abut \ᵊ\kitten \ər\further \a\ash \ā\ace \ä\mop, mar
\aú\out \ch\chin \e\bet \ē\easy \g\go \i\hit \ī\ice \j\job
\ŋ\sing \ō\go \ò\law \òi\boy \th\thin \th\the \ü\loot \ù\foot
\y\yet \zh\vision *see also* Pronunciation Symbols page

to wit *adv* : NAMELY

town \'taün\ *n* **1** : a compactly settled area usu. larger than a village but smaller than a city **2** : CITY **3** : the inhabitants of a town **4** : a New England territorial and political unit usu. containing both rural and urban areas; *also* : a New England community in which matters of local government are decided by a general assembly (**town meeting**) of qualified voters

town house *n* **1** : the city residence of a person having a country home **2** : a single-family house of two or sometimes three stories connected to another house by a common wall

town·ie *or* **towny** \'taü-nē\ *n*, *pl* **townies** : a permanent resident of a town as distinguished from a member of another group

towns·folk \'taünz-ıfōk\ *n pl* : TOWNSPEOPLE

town·ship \'taün-ıship\ *n* **1** : TOWN 4 **2** : a unit of local government in some states **3** : an unorganized subdivision of a county; *also* : an administrative division **4** : a division of territory in surveys of U.S. public land containing 36 square miles **5** : an area in the Republic of South Africa segregated for occupation by persons of non-European descent

towns·man \'taünz-mən\ *n* **1** : a native or resident of a town or city **2** : a fellow citizen of a town

towns·peo·ple \-ıpē-pəl\ *n pl* **1** : the inhabitants of a town or city **2** : town-bred persons

towns·wom·an \-ıwu̇-mən\ *n* **1** : a woman who is a native or resident of a town or city **2** : a woman who is a fellow citizen of a town

tow·path \'tō-ıpath, -ıpȧth\ *n* : a path (as along a canal) traveled esp. by draft animals towing boats

tow truck *n* : a truck equipped for towing disabled vehicles

tox·emia \täk-'sē-mē-ə\ *n* : a bodily disorder associated with the presence of toxic substances in the blood

tox·ic \'täk-sik\ *adj* [LL *toxicus*, fr. L *toxicum* poison, fr. Gk *toxikon* arrow poison, fr. neut. of *toxikos* of a bow, fr. *toxon* bow, arrow] : of, relating to, or caused by poison or a toxin : POISONOUS — **tox·ic·i·ty** \täk-'si-sə-tē\ *n*

tox·i·col·o·gy \ıtäk-sə-'kä-lə-jē\ *n* : a science that deals with poisons and esp. with problems of their use and control — **tox·i·co·log·i·cal** \-'lä-ji-kəl\ *or* **tox·i·co·log·ic** \ıtäk-si-kə-'lä-jik\ *adj* — **tox·i·col·o·gist** \-'kä-lə-jist\ *n*

toxic shock syndrome *n* : an acute disease associated with the presence of a bacterium that is characterized by fever, diarrhea, nausea, diffuse erythema, and shock and occurs esp. in menstruating females using tampons

tox·in \'täk-sən\ *n* : a poisonous substance produced by metabolic activities of a living organism that is usu. unstable, very toxic when introduced into the tissues, and usu. capable of inducing antibodies

¹toy \'tȯi\ *n* **1** : something trifling **2** : a small ornament : BAUBLE **3** : something for a child to play with

²toy *vb* **1** : to deal with something lightly : TRIFLE **2** : FLIRT **3** : to amuse oneself as if with a plaything

³toy *adj* **1** : DIMINUTIVE **2** : designed for use as a toy

tp *abbr* **1** title page **2** township

tpk *or* **tpke** *abbr* turnpike

tr *abbr* **1** translated; translation; translator **2** transpose **3** troop

¹trace \'trās\ *n* **1** : a mark (as a footprint or track) left by something that has passed **2** : a minute or barely detectable amount

²trace *vb* **traced; trac·ing 1** : to mark out : SKETCH **2** : to form (as letters) carefully **3** : to copy (a drawing) by marking lines on transparent paper laid over the drawing to be copied **4** : to follow the trail of : track down **5** : to study out and follow the development of — **trace·able** *adj*

³trace *n* : either of two lines of a harness for fastening a draft animal to a vehicle

trac·er \'trā-sər\ *n* **1** : one that traces **2** : ammunition containing a chemical to mark the flight of projectiles by a trail of smoke or fire

trac·ery \'trā-sə-rē\ *n*, *pl* **-er·ies** : ornamental work having a design with branching or interlacing lines

tra·chea \'trā-kē-ə\ *n*, *pl* **-che·ae** \-kē-ıē\ *also* **-che·as** : the main tube by which air enters the lungs of vertebrates : WINDPIPE — **tra·che·al** \-kē-əl\ *adj*

tra·che·ot·o·my \ıtrā-kē-'ä-tə-mē\ *n*, *pl* **-mies** : the surgical operation of cutting into the trachea esp. through the skin

trac·ing *n* **1** : the act of one that traces **2** : something that is traced **3** : a graphic record made by an instrument for measuring vibrations or pulsations

¹track \'trak\ *n* **1** : a mark left in passing **2** : PATH, ROUTE, TRAIL **3** : a course laid out for racing; *also* : track-and-field sports **4** : one of a series of paths along which material (as music) is recorded (as on magnetic tape) **5** : the course along which something moves; *esp* : a way made by two parallel lines of metal rails **6** : awareness of a fact or progression (lost ∼ of time) **7** : either of two endless metal belts on which a vehicle (as a bulldozer) travels

²track *vb* **1** : to follow the tracks or traces of : TRAIL **2** : to observe the moving path of (as a missile) **3** : to make tracks on **4** : to carry (as mud) on the feet and deposit — **track·er** *n*

track·age \'tra-kij\ *n* : lines of railway track

track–and–field *adj* : of or relating to athletic contests held on a running track or on the adjacent field

¹tract \'trakt\ *n* **1** : an area without precise boundaries (huge ∼s of land) **2** : a defined area of land **3** : a system of body parts or organs that act together to perform some function (the digestive ∼)

²tract *n* : a pamphlet of political or religious propaganda

trac·ta·ble \'trak-tə-bəl\ *adj* : easily controlled : DOCILE **syn** amenable, obedient, biddable

tract house *n* : any of many similar houses built on a tract of land

trac·tion \'trak-shən\ *n* **1** : the act of drawing : the state of being drawn **2** : the drawing of a vehicle by motive power; *also* : the particular form of motive power used **3** : the adhesive friction of a body on a surface on which it moves **4** : a pulling force applied to a skeletal structure (as a broken bone) by using a special device; *also* : a state of tension created by such a pulling force (a leg in ∼) — **trac·tion·al** \-shə-nəl\ *adj* — **trac·tive** \'trak-tiv\ *adj*

trac·tor \'trak-tər\ *n* **1** : an automotive vehicle used esp. for drawing farm equipment **2** : a truck for hauling a trailer

¹trade \'trād\ *n* **1** : one's regular business or work : OCCUPATION **2** : an occupation requiring manual or mechanical skill **3** : the persons engaged in a business or industry **4** : the business of buying and selling or bartering commodities **5** : an act of trading : TRANSACTION

²trade *vb* **trad·ed; trad·ing 1** : to give in exchange for another commodity : BARTER **2** : to engage in the exchange, purchase, or sale of goods **3** : to deal regularly as a customer — **trade on** : EXPLOIT (*trades on* his family name)

trade–in \'trād-ıin\ *n* : an item of merchandise traded in

trade in *vb* : to turn in as part payment for a purchase

¹trade·mark \'trād-ımärk\ *n* : a device (as a word or mark) that points distinctly to the origin or ownership of merchandise to which it is applied and that is legally reserved for the exclusive use of the owner; *also* : something that identifies a person or thing

²trademark *vb* : to secure the trademark rights for

trade name *n* : a name that is given by a manufacturer or merchant to a product to distinguish it as made or sold by him and that may be used and protected as a trademark

trad·er \'trā-dər\ *n* **1** : a person whose business is buying or selling **2** : a ship engaged in trade

trades·man \'trādz-mən\ *n* **1** : one who runs a retail store : SHOPKEEPER **2** : CRAFTSMAN

trades·peo·ple \-ˌpē-pəl\ *n pl* : people engaged in trade

trade union *n* : LABOR UNION

trade wind *n* : a wind blowing almost constantly in one direction

trading stamp *n* : a printed stamp given as a premium to a retail customer that when accumulated may be redeemed for merchandise

tra·di·tion \trə-'di-shən\ *n* **1** : an inherited, established, or customary pattern of thought or action **2** : the handing down of beliefs and customs by word of mouth or by example without written instruction; *also* : a belief or custom thus handed down — **tra·di·tion·al** \-'di-shə-nəl\ *adj* — **tra·di·tion·al·ly** *adv*

tra·duce \trə-'düs, -'dyüs\ *vb* **tra·duced; tra·duc·ing** : to lower the reputation of : DEFAME, SLANDER **syn** malign, libel, calumniate — **tra·duc·er** *n*

¹traf·fic \'tra-fik\ *n* **1** : the business of bartering or buying and selling **2** : communication or dealings between individuals or groups **3** : the movement (as of vehicles) along a route; *also* : the vehicles, people, ships, or planes moving along a route **4** : the passengers or cargo carried by a transportation system

²traffic *vb* **traf·ficked; traf·fick·ing** : to carry on traffic — **traf·fick·er** *n*

traffic circle *n* : ROTARY 2

traffic light *n* : an electrically operated visual signal for controlling traffic

tra·ge·di·an \trə-'jē-dē-ən\ *n* **1** : a writer of tragedies **2** : an actor who plays tragic roles

tra·ge·di·enne \trə-ˌjē-dē-'en\ *n* [F] : an actress who plays tragic roles

trag·e·dy \'tra-jə-dē\ *n, pl* **-dies** [ME *tragedie*, fr. MF, fr. L *tragoedia*, fr. Gk *tragōidia*, fr. *tragos* goat + *aeidein* to sing] **1** : a serious drama with a sorrowful or disastrous conclusion **2** : a disastrous event : CALAMITY; *also* : MISFORTUNE **3** : tragic quality or element ⟨the ~ of life⟩

trag·ic \'tra-jik\ *also* **trag·i·cal** \-ji-kəl\ *adj* **1** : of, relating to, or expressive of tragedy **2** : appropriate to tragedy **3** : LAMENTABLE, UNFORTUNATE — **trag·i·cal·ly** \-ji-k(ə-)lē\ *adv*

¹trail \'trāl\ *vb* **1** : to hang down so as to drag along or sweep the ground **2** : to draw or drag along behind **3** : to extend over a surface in a straggling manner **4** : to lag behind **5** : to follow the track of : PURSUE **6** : DWINDLE ⟨her voice ~ed off⟩

²trail *n* **1** : something that trails or is trailed ⟨a ~ of smoke⟩ **2** : a trace or mark left by something that has passed or been drawn along : SCENT, TRACK ⟨a ~ of blood⟩ **3** : a beaten path; *also* : a marked path through woods

trail bike *n* : a small motorcycle for off-road use

trail·blaz·er \-ˌblā-zər\ *n* : PATHFINDER, PIONEER — **trail·blaz·ing** *adj or n*

trail·er \'trā-lər\ *n* **1** : one that trails; *esp* : a creeping plant (as an ivy) **2** : a vehicle that is hauled by another (as a tractor) **3** : a vehicle equipped to serve wherever parked as a dwelling or place of business

trailing arbutus *n* : a trailing spring-flowering plant of the heath family with fragrant pink or white flowers; *also* : its flower

¹train \'trān\ *n* **1** : a part of a gown that trails behind the wearer **2** : RETINUE **3** : a moving file of persons, vehicles, or animals **4** : a connected series ⟨a ~ of thought⟩ **5** : AFTERMATH **6** : a connected line of railroad cars usu. hauled by a locomotive **syn** succession, sequence, procession, chain

²train *vb* **1** : to cause to grow as desired ⟨~ a vine on a trellis⟩ **2** : to form by instruction, discipline, or drill **3** : to make or become prepared (as by exercise) for a test of skill **4** : to aim or point at an object ⟨~ guns on a fort⟩ **syn** discipline, school, educate, instruct — **train·er** *n*

train·ee \trā-'nē\ *n* : one who is being trained esp. for a job

train·ing *n* **1** : the act, process, or method of one who trains **2** : the skill, knowledge, or experience gained by one who trains

train·man \-mən\ *n* : a member of a train crew

traipse \'trāps\ *vb* **traipsed; traips·ing** : TRAMP, WALK

trait \'trāt\ *n* **1** : a distinguishing quality (as of personality) : PECULIARITY **2** : an inherited characteristic

trai·tor \'trā-tər\ *n* [ME *traitre*, fr. OF, fr. L *traditor*, fr. *tradere* to hand over, deliver, betray, fr. *trans-* across + *dare* to give] **1** : one who betrays another's trust or is false to an obligation **2** : one who commits treason — **trai·tor·ous** *adj*

tra·jec·to·ry \trə-'jek-tə-rē\ *n, pl* **-ries** : the curve that a body (as a planet in its orbit) describes in space

tram \'tram\ *n* **1** : a boxlike car running on a railway (**tram·way** \-ˌwā\) in a mine **2** *chiefly Brit* : STREETCAR **3** : an overhead cable car

¹tram·mel \'tra-məl\ *n* [ME *tramayle*, a kind of net, fr. MF *tremail*, fr. LL *tremaculum*, fr. L *tres* three + *macula* mesh, spot] : something impeding activity, progress, or freedom

²trammel *vb* **-meled** *or* **-melled; -mel·ing** *or* **-mel·ling** **1** : to catch and hold in or as if in a net **2** : HAMPER **syn** clog, fetter, shackle, hobble

¹tramp \'tramp, *1 & 3 are also* 'trämp, 'trómp\ *vb* **1** : to walk, tread, or step heavily **2** : to walk about or through; *also* : HIKE **3** : to tread on forcibly and repeatedly

²tramp \'tramp, *5 is also* 'trämp, 'trómp\ *n* **1** : a foot traveler **2** : a begging or thieving vagrant **3** : an immoral woman; *esp* : PROSTITUTE **4** : a walking trip : HIKE **5** : the succession of sounds made by the beating of feet on a road **6** : a ship that does not follow a regular course but takes cargo to any port

tram·ple \'tram-pəl\ *vb* **tram·pled; tram·pling** **1** : to tread heavily so as to bruise, crush, or injure **2** : to inflict injury or destruction **3** : to press down or crush by or as if by treading — **trample** *n* — **tram·pler** *n*

tram·po·line \ˌtram-pə-'lēn, 'tram-pə-ˌlēn\ *n* [It *trampolino* springboard] : a resilient sheet or web (as of nylon) supported by springs in a metal frame and used as a springboard in tumbling — **tram·po·lin·ist** \-nist\ *n*

trance \'trans\ *n* [ME, fr. MF *transe*, fr. *transir* to pass away, swoon, fr. L *transire* to pass, pass away, fr. *trans-* across + *ire* to go] **1** : a living state in which the vital bodily and mental activities slow down greatly **2** : a sleeplike state (as of deep hypnosis) **3** : a state of very deep absorption

tran·quil \'traŋ-kwəl, 'tran-\ *adj* : free from agitation or disturbance : QUIET **syn** serene, placid, peaceful — **tran·quil·i·ty** *or* **tran·quil·li·ty** \tran-'kwi-lə-tē, traŋ-\ *n* — **tran·quil·ly** *adv*

tran·quil·ize *also* **tran·quil·lize** \'traŋ-kwə-ˌlīz, 'tran-\ *vb* **-ized** *also* **-lized; -iz·ing** *also* **-liz·ing** : to make or become tranquil; *esp* : to relieve of mental tension and anxiety by means of drugs

tran·quil·iz·er *also* **tran·quil·liz·er** \-ˌlī-zər\ *n* : a drug used to relieve mental disturbance (as tension and anxiety)

\ə\abut \ᵊ\kitten \ər\further \a\ash \ā\ace \ä\mop, mar \aú\out \ch\chin \e\bet \ē\easy \g\go \i\hit \ī\ice \j\job \ŋ\sing \ō\go \ó\law \ói\boy \th\thin \t̲h̲\the \ü\loot \ú\foot \y\yet \zh\vision *see also* Pronunciation Symbols page

trans *abbr* **1** transaction **2** transitive **3** translated; translation; translator **4** transmission **5** transportation **6** transverse

trans·act \tran-ˈzakt, -ˈsakt\ *vb* : CARRY OUT, PERFORM; *also* : CONDUCT

trans·ac·tion \-ˈzak-shən, -ˈsak-\ *n* **1** : something transacted; *esp* : a business deal **2** : an act or process of transacting **3** *pl* : the records of the proceedings of a society or organization

trans·at·lan·tic \ˌtrans-ət-ˈlan-tik, ˌtranz-\ *adj* : crossing or extending across or situated beyond the Atlantic Ocean

trans·ax·le \trans-ˈak-səl\ *n* : a unit combining the transmission and the front axle of a front-wheel-drive automobile

trans·ceiv·er \tran-ˈsē-vər\ *n* : a radio transmitter= receiver that uses many of the same components for both transmission and reception

tran·scend \tran-ˈsend\ *vb* **1** : to rise above the limits of **2** : SURPASS **syn** exceed, outdo, outshine, outstrip

tran·scen·dent \-ˈsen-dənt\ *adj* **1** : exceeding usual limits : SURPASSING **2** : transcending material existence **syn** superlative, supreme, peerless, incomparable

tran·scen·den·tal \ˌtran-ˌsen-ˈdent-ᵊl, -sən-\ *adj* **1** : TRANSCENDENT 2 **2** : of, relating to, or characteristic of transcendentalism; *also* : ABSTRUSE

tran·scen·den·tal·ism \-ᵊl-ˌi-zəm\ *n* : a philosophy holding that ultimate reality is unknowable or asserting the primacy of the spiritual over the material and empirical — **tran·scen·den·tal·ist** \-ᵊl-ist\ *adj or n*

trans·con·ti·nen·tal \ˌtrans-ˌkänt-ᵊn-ˈent-ᵊl\ *adj* : extending or going across a continent

tran·scribe \trans-ˈkrīb\ *vb* **tran·scribed; tran·scrib·ing 1** : to write a copy of **2** : to make a copy of (dictated or recorded matter) in longhand or on a typewriter **3** : to represent (speech sounds) by means of phonetic symbols; *also* : to make a musical transcription of

tran·script \ˈtran-ˌskript\ *n* **1** : a written, printed, or typed copy **2** : an official copy esp. of a student's educational record

tran·scrip·tion \tran-ˈskrip-shən\ *n* **1** : an act or process of transcribing **2** : COPY, TRANSCRIPT **3** : an arrangement of a musical composition for some instrument or voice other than the original

tran·scrip·tion·ist \-shə-nist\ *n* : one that transcribes; *esp* : a typist who transcribes medical reports

trans·der·mal \trans-ˈdər-məl, ˈtranz-\ *adj* : relating to, being, or supplying a medication in a form for absorption through the skin ⟨∼ nicotine patch⟩

trans·duc·er \trans-ˈdü-sər, tranz-, -ˈdyü-\ *n* : a device that is actuated by power from one system and supplies power usu. in another form to a second system

tran·sept \ˈtran-ˌsept\ *n* : the part of a cruciform church that crosses at right angles to the greatest length; *also* : either of the projecting ends

¹**trans·fer** \trans-ˈfər, ˈtrans-ˌfər\ *vb* **trans·ferred; trans·fer·ring 1** : to pass or cause to pass from one person, place, or situation to another : TRANSPORT, TRANSMIT **2** : to make over the possession of : CONVEY **3** : to print or copy from one surface to another by contact **4** : to change from one vehicle or transportation line to another — **trans·fer·able** \trans-ˈfər-ə-bəl\ *adj* — **trans·fer·al** \-əl\ *n*

²**trans·fer** \ˈtrans-ˌfər\ *n* **1** : conveyance of right, title, or interest in property from one person to another **2** : an act or process of transferring **3** : one that transfers or is transferred **4** : a ticket entitling a passenger to continue a trip on another route

trans·fer·ence \trans-ˈfər-əns\ *n* : an act, process, or instance of transferring

trans·fig·ure \trans-ˈfi-gyər\ *vb* **-ured; -ur·ing 1** : to change the form or appearance of **2** : EXALT, GLORIFY — **trans·fig·u·ra·tion** \ˌtrans-ˌfi-gyə-ˈrā-shən, -gə-\ *n*

trans·fix \trans-ˈfiks\ *vb* **1** : to pierce through with or as if with a pointed weapon **2** : to hold motionless by or as if by piercing

trans·form \trans-ˈfórm\ *vb* : to change in structure, appearance, or character **syn** transmute, transfigure, transmogrify — **trans·for·ma·tion** \ˌtrans-fər-ˈmā-shən\ *n*

trans·form·er \trans-ˈfór-mər\ *n* : one that transforms; *esp* : a device for converting variations of current in one circuit into variations of voltage and current in another circuit

trans·fuse \trans-ˈfyüz\ *vb* **trans·fused; trans·fus·ing 1** : to cause to pass from one to another **2** : to diffuse into or through **3** : to transfer (as blood) into a vein of a person or animal — **trans·fu·sion** \-ˈfyü-zhən\ *n*

trans·gress \trans-ˈgres, tranz-\ *vb* [F *transgresser*, fr. L *transgressus*, pp. of *transgredi* to step beyond or across, fr. *trans-* across + *gradi* to step] **1** : to go beyond the limits set by ⟨∼ the divine law⟩ **2** : to go beyond : EXCEED **3** : SIN — **trans·gres·sion** \-ˈgre-shən\ *n* — **trans·gres·sor** \-ˈgre-sər\ *n*

¹**tran·sient** \ˈtran-shənt; -sē-ənt, -shē-, -zē-\ *adj* **1** : not lasting long : SHORT-LIVED **2** : passing through a place with only a brief stay **syn** transitory, passing, momentary, fleeting — **tran·sient·ly** *adv*

²**transient** *n* : one that is transient; *esp* : a transient guest

tran·sis·tor \tran-ˈzis-tər, -ˈsis-\ *n* [*transfer* + re*sistor*; fr. its transferring an electrical signal across a resistor] **1** : a small electronic semiconductor device used in electronic equipment **2** : a radio having transistors

tran·sis·tor·ized \-tə-ˌrīzd\ *adj* : having or using transistors

tran·sit \ˈtran-sət, -zət\ *n* **1** : a passing through, across, or over : PASSAGE **2** : conveyance of persons or things from one place to another **3** : usu. local transportation esp. of people by public conveyance **4** : a surveyor's instrument for measuring angles

tran·si·tion \tran-ˈsi-shən, -ˈzi-\ *n* : passage from one state, place, stage, or subject to another : CHANGE — **tran·si·tion·al** \-ˈsi-shə-nəl, ˈzi-\ *adj*

tran·si·tive \ˈtran-sə-tiv, -zə-\ *adj* **1** : having or containing an object required to complete the meaning **2** : TRANSITIONAL — **tran·si·tive·ly** *adv* — **tran·si·tive·ness** *n* — **tran·si·tiv·i·ty** \ˌtran-sə-ˈti-və-tē, -zə-\ *n*

tran·si·to·ry \ˈtran-sə-ˌtōr-ē, -zə-\ *adj* : of brief duration : SHORT-LIVED, TEMPORARY **syn** transient, passing, momentary, fleeting

transl *abbr* translated; translation

trans·late \trans-ˈlāt, tranz-\ *vb* **trans·lat·ed; trans·lat·ing 1** : to change from one place, state, or form to another **2** : to convey to heaven without death **3** : to turn into one's own or another language — **trans·lat·able** *adj* — **trans·la·tion** \-ˈlā-shən\ *n* — **trans·la·tor** \-ˈlā-tər\ *n*

trans·lit·er·ate \trans-ˈli-tə-ˌrāt, tranz-\ *vb* **-at·ed; -at·ing** : to represent or spell in the characters of another alphabet — **trans·lit·er·a·tion** \ˌtrans-ˌli-tə-ˈrā-shən, ˌtranz-\ *n*

trans·lu·cent \trans-ˈlüs-ᵊnt, tranz-\ *adj* : not transparent but clear enough to allow light to pass through — **trans·lu·cence** \-ᵊns\ *n* — **trans·lu·cen·cy** \-ᵊn-sē\ *n* — **trans·lu·cent·ly** *adv*

trans·mi·grate \-ˈmī-ˌgrāt\ *vb* : to pass at death from one body or being to another — **trans·mi·gra·tion** \ˌtrans-ˌmī-ˈgrā-shən, ˌtranz-\ *n* — **trans·mi·gra·to·ry** \trans-ˈmī-grə-ˌtōr-ē\ *adj*

trans·mis·sion \-ˈmi-shən\ *n* **1** : an act or process of transmitting **2** : the passage of radio waves between transmitting stations and receiving stations **3** : the gears by which power is transmitted from the engine of an automobile to the axle that propels the vehicle **4** : something transmitted

trans·mit \-ˈmit\ *vb* **trans·mit·ted; trans·mit·ting 1** : to transfer from one person or place to another : FORWARD **2** : to pass on by or as if by inheritance **3** : to cause or allow to spread abroad or to another ⟨∼ a disease⟩ **4** : to cause (as light, electricity, or force) to pass through space or a medium **5** : to send out (radio or television signals) **syn** convey, communicate, impart — **trans-mis-si-ble** \-¦mi-sə-bəl\ *adj* — **trans-mit-ta-ble** \-¦mi-tə-bəl\ *adj* — **trans-mit-tal** \-¦mit-ᵊl\ *n*

trans-mit-ter \-¦mi-tər\ *n* : one that transmits; *esp* : an apparatus for transmitting telegraph, radio, or television signals

trans-mog-ri-fy \trans-¦mä-grə-₁fī, tranz-\ *vb* **-fied; -fy-ing** : to change or alter often with grotesque or humorous effect — **trans-mog-ri-fi-ca-tion** \-₁mä-grə-fə-¦kā-shən\ *n*

trans-mute \-¦myüt\ *vb* **trans-muted; trans-mut-ing** : to change or alter in form, appearance, or nature **syn** transform, convert, transfigure, metamorphose — **trans-mu-ta-tion** \₁trans-myü-¦tā-shən, ₁tranz-\ *n*

trans-na-tion-al \ ¦na-shə-nəl\ *adj* : extending beyond national boundaries

trans-oce-an-ic \₁trans-₁ō-shē-¦a-nik, ₁tranz-\ *adj* **1** : lying or dwelling beyond the ocean **2** : crossing or extending across the ocean

tran-som \¦tran-səm\ *n* **1** : a piece (as a crossbar in the frame of a window or door) that lies crosswise in a structure **2** : a window above an opening (as a door) built on and often hinged to a horizontal crossbar

tran-son-ic *also* **trans-son-ic** \trans-¦sä-nik\ *adj* : being or relating to speeds near that of sound in air or about 741 miles (1185 kilometers) per hour

trans-pa-cif-ic \₁trans-pə-¦si-fik\ *adj* : crossing, extending across, or situated beyond the Pacific Ocean

trans-par-ent \trans-¦par-ənt\ *adj* **1** : clear enough to be seen through **2** : SHEER, DIAPHANOUS ⟨a ∼ fabric⟩ **3** : readily understood : CLEAR; *also* : easily detected ⟨a ∼ lie⟩ **syn** lucid, translucent, lucent — **trans-par-en-cy** \-ən-sē\ *n* — **trans-par-ent-ly** *adv*

tran-spire \trans-¦pīr\ *vb* **trans-pired; trans-pir-ing** [MF *transpirer*, fr. L *trans-* across + *spirare* to breathe] **1** : to pass or give off (as water vapor) through pores or a membrane **2** : to become known **3** : to take place : HAPPEN — **tran-spi-ra-tion** \₁trans-pə-¦rā-shən\ *n*

¹**trans-plant** \trans-¦plant\ *vb* **1** : to dig up and plant elsewhere **2** : to remove from one place and settle or introduce elsewhere : TRANSPORT **3** : to transfer (an organ or tissue) from one part or individual to another — **trans-plan-ta-tion** \₁trans-₁plan-¦tā-shən\ *n*

²**trans-plant** \¦trans-₁plant\ *n* **1** : a person or thing transplanted **2** : the act or process of transplanting

trans-po-lar \trans-¦pō-lər\ *adj* : going or extending across either of the polar regions

transponder \tran-¦spän-dər\ *n* [*transmitter* + re*spond*er] : a radio or radar set that upon receiving a certain signal emits a signal of its own and that is used esp. for the identification and location of objects

¹**trans-port** \trans-¦pōrt\ *vb* **1** : to convey from one place to another : CARRY **2** : to carry away by strong emotion : ENRAPTURE **3** : to send to a penal colony overseas **syn** bear, ferry — **trans-por-ta-tion** \₁trans-pər-¦tā-shən\ *n* — **trans-port-er** *n*

²**trans-port** \¦trans-₁pōrt\ *n* **1** : an act of transporting **2** : strong or intensely pleasurable emotion ⟨∼s of joy⟩ **3** : a ship used in transporting troops or supplies; *also* : a vehicle (as a truck or plane) used to transport persons or goods

trans-pose \trans-¦pōz\ *vb* **trans-posed; trans-pos-ing 1** : to change the position or sequence of ⟨∼ the letters in a word⟩ **2** : to write or perform (a musical composition) in a different key — **trans-po-si-tion** \₁trans-pə-¦zi-shən\ *n*

trans-sex-u-al \(₁)trans-¦sek-shə-wəl\ *n* : a person with a psychological urge to belong to the opposite sex that may be carried to the point of undergoing surgery to modify the sex organs to mimic the opposite sex

trans-ship \tran-¦ship, trans-\ *vb* : to transfer for further transportation from one ship or conveyance to another — **trans-ship-ment** *n*

tran-sub-stan-ti-a-tion \₁tran-səb-₁stan-chē-¦ā-shən\ *n* : the change in the eucharistic elements from the substance of bread and wine to the substance of the body of Christ with only the appearances of bread and wine remaining

trans-verse \trans-¦vərs, tranz-\ *adj* : lying across : set crosswise — **transverse** \¦trans-₁vərs, ¦tranz-\ *n* — **trans-verse-ly** *adv*

trans-ves-tite \trans-¦ves-₁tīt, tranz-\ *n* : a person and esp. a male who adopts the dress and often the behavior of the opposite sex — **transvestite** *adj* — **trans-ves-tism** \-₁ti-zəm\ *n*

¹**trap** \¦trap\ *n* **1** : a device for catching animals **2** : something by which one is caught unawares; *also* : a situation from which escape is difficult or impossible **3** : a machine for throwing clay pigeons into the air; *also* : SAND TRAP **4** : a light one-horse carriage on springs **5** : a device to allow some one thing to pass through while keeping other things out ⟨a ∼ in a drainpipe⟩ **6** *pl* : a group of percussion instruments (as in a dance orchestra)

²**trap** *vb* **trapped; trap-ping 1** : to catch in or as if in a trap; *also* : CONFINE **2** : to provide or set (a place) with traps **3** : to set traps for animals esp. as a business **syn** snare, entrap, ensnare, bag, lure, decoy — **trap-per** *n*

trap-door \¦trap-¦dōr\ *n* : a lifting or sliding door covering an opening in a floor or roof

tra-peze \tra-¦pēz\ *n* : a gymnastic apparatus consisting of a horizontal bar suspended by two parallel ropes

trap-e-zoid \¦tra-pə-₁zȯid\ *n* [NL *trapezōides*, fr. Gk *trapezoeidēs* trapezoidal, fr. *trapeza* table, fr. *tra-* four + *peza* foot] : a plane 4-sided figure with two and only two sides parallel — **trap-e-zoi-dal** \₁tra-pə-¦zȯid-ᵊl\ *adj*

trap-pings \¦tra-piŋz\ *n pl* **1** : CAPARISON 1 **2** : outward decoration or dress; *also* : outward sign ⟨∼ of success⟩

traps \¦traps\ *n pl* : personal belongings : LUGGAGE

trap-shoot-ing \¦trap-₁shü-tiŋ\ *n* : shooting at clay pigeons sprung from a trap into the air away from the shooter

¹**trash** \¦trash\ *n* **1** : something of little worth : RUBBISH **2** : a worthless person; *also* : such persons as a group : RIFFRAFF — **trashy** *adj*

²**trash** *vb* **1** : VANDALIZE, DESTROY **2** : ATTACK **3** : SPOIL, RUIN **4** : to criticize or disparage harshly

trau-ma \¦trau̇-mə, ¦trȯ-\ *n, pl* **traumas** *also* **trau-ma-ta** \-mə-tə\ [Gk] : a bodily or mental injury usu. caused by an external agent; *also* : a cause of trauma — **trau-mat-ic** \trə-¦ma-tik, trȯ-, trau̇-\ *adj*

¹**tra-vail** \trə-¦vāl, ¦tra-₁vāl\ *n* **1** : painful work or exertion : TOIL **2** : AGONY, TORMENT **3** : CHILDBIRTH, LABOR

²**travail** *vb* : to labor hard : TOIL

¹**trav-el** \¦tra-vəl\ *vb* **-eled** *or* **-elled; -el-ing** *or* **-el-ling** [ME *travailen* to labor, journey, fr. OF *travaillier* to torture, labor, fr. (assumed) VL *trepaliare* to torture, fr. LL *trepalium* instrument of torture] **1** : to go on or as if on a trip or tour : JOURNEY **2** : to move as if by traveling ⟨news ∼s fast⟩ **3** : ASSOCIATE **4** : to go from place to place as a sales representative **5** : to move from point to point ⟨light waves ∼ very fast⟩ **6** : to journey over or through ⟨∼ing the highways⟩ — **trav-el-er** *or* **trav-el-ler** *n*

\ə\abut \ᵊ\kitten \ər\further \a\ash \ā\ace \ä\mop, mar
\au̇\out \ch\chin \e\bet \ē\easy \g\go \i\hit \ī\ice \j\job
\ŋ\sing \ō\go \ȯ\law \ȯi\boy \th\thin \th̲\the \ü\loot \u̇\foot
\y\yet \zh\vision *see also* Pronunciation Symbols page

²**travel** *n* **1** : the act of traveling : PASSAGE **2** : JOURNEY, TRIP — often used in pl. **3** : the number traveling : TRAFFIC **4** : the motion of a piece of machinery and esp. when to and fro

traveler's check *n* : a check paid for in advance that is signed when bought and signed again when cashed

traveling bag *n* : SUITCASE

trav·el·ogue *or* **trav·el·og** \'tra-və-ˌlóg, -ˌläg\ *n* : a usu. illustrated lecture on travel

¹**tra·verse** \'tra-vərs\ *n* : something that crosses or lies across

²**tra·verse** \trə-'vərs, tra-'vərs *or* 'tra-vərs\ *vb* **tra·versed; tra·vers·ing 1** : to go or travel across or over **2** : to move or pass along or through **3** : to extend over **4** : SWIVEL

³**tra·verse** \'tra-ˌvərs\ *adj* : TRANSVERSE

trav·er·tine \'tra-vər-ˌtēn, -tən\ *n* : a crystalline mineral formed by deposition from spring waters

¹**trav·es·ty** \'tra-və-stē\ *vb* **-tied; -ty·ing** : to make a travesty of

²**travesty** *n, pl* **-ties** [obs. E *travesty* disguised, parodied, fr. F *travesti*, pp. of *travestir* to disguise, fr. It *travestire*, fr. *tra-* across (fr. L *trans-*) + *vestire* to dress] : an imitation that makes crude fun of something; *also* : an inferior imitation

¹**trawl** \'tról\ *vb* : to fish or catch with a trawl — **trawl·er** *n*

²**trawl** *n* **1** : a large conical net dragged along the sea bottom in fishing **2** : a long heavy fishing line equipped with many hooks in series

tray \'trā\ *n* : an open receptacle with flat bottom and low rim for holding, carrying, or exhibiting articles

treach·er·ous \'tre-chə-rəs\ *adj* **1** : characterized by treachery **2** : UNTRUSTWORTHY, UNRELIABLE **3** : providing insecure footing or support **syn** traitorous, faithless, false, disloyal — **treach·er·ous·ly** *adv*

treach·ery \'tre-chə-rē\ *n, pl* **-er·ies** : violation of allegiance or trust

trea·cle \'trē-kəl\ *n* [ME *triacle* a medicinal compound, fr. MF, fr. L *theriaca*, fr. Gk *thēriakē* antidote against a poisonous bite, fr. *thērion* wild animal] *chiefly Brit* : MOLASSES — **treacly** \-k(ə-)lē\ *adj*

¹**tread** \'tred\ *vb* **trod** \'träd\; **trod·den** \'träd-ᵊn\ *or* **trod; tread·ing 1** : to step or walk on or over **2** : to move on foot : WALK; *also* : DANCE **3** : to beat or press with the feet

²**tread** *n* **1** : a mark made by or as if by treading **2** : the manner or sound of stepping **3** : the part of a wheel that makes contact with a road **4** : the horizontal part of a step

trea·dle \'tred-ᵊl\ *n* : a lever device pressed by the foot to drive a machine — **treadle** *vb*

tread·mill \'tred-ˌmil\ *n* **1** : a mill worked by persons who tread on steps around the edge of a wheel or by animals that walk on an endless belt **2** : a device with an endless belt on which a person walks or runs in place **3** : a wearisome routine

treas *abbr* treasurer; treasury

trea·son \'trēz-ᵊn\ *n* : the offense of attempting to overthrow the government of one's country or of assisting its enemies in war — **trea·son·able** \-ᵊn-ə-bəl\ *adj* — **trea·son·ous** \-ᵊn-əs\ *adj*

¹**trea·sure** \'tre-zhər, 'trā-\ *n* **1** : wealth stored up or held in reserve **2** : something of great value

²**treasure** *vb* **trea·sured; trea·sur·ing 1** : HOARD **2** : to keep as precious : CHERISH **syn** prize, value, appreciate, esteem

trea·sur·er *n* : an officer of a club, business, or government who has charge of money taken in and paid out

treasure trove \-ˌtrōv\ *n* **1** : treasure of unknown ownership found buried or hidden **2** : a valuable discovery

trea·sury \'tre-zhə-rē, 'trā-\ *n, pl* **-sur·ies 1** : a place in which stores of wealth are kept **2** : the place where collected funds are stored and paid out **3** *cap* : a governmental department in charge of finances

¹**treat** \'trēt\ *vb* **1** : NEGOTIATE **2** : to deal with esp. in writing; *also* : HANDLE **3** : to pay for the food or entertainment of **4** : to behave or act toward ⟨∼ them well⟩ **5** : to regard in a specified manner ⟨∼ as inferiors⟩ **6** : to give medical or surgical care to **7** : to subject to some action ⟨∼ soil with lime⟩

²**treat** *n* **1** : an entertainment given free to those invited **2** : a source of joy or amusement

trea·tise \'trē-təs\ *n* : a systematic written exposition or argument

treat·ment \'trēt-mənt\ *n* : the act or manner or an instance of treating someone or something; *also* : a substance or method used in treating

trea·ty \'trē-tē\ *n, pl* **treaties** : an agreement made by negotiation or diplomacy esp. between two or more states or governments

¹**tre·ble** \'tre-bəl\ *n* **1** : the highest of the four voice parts in vocal music : SOPRANO **2** : a high-pitched or shrill voice or sound **3** : the upper half of the musical pitch range

²**treble** *adj* **1** : triple in number or amount **2** : relating to or having the range of a musical treble **3** : high‑pitched : SHRILL — **tre·bly** *adv*

³**treble** *vb* **tre·bled; tre·bling** : to make or become three times the size, amount, or number

¹**tree** \'trē\ *n* **1** : a woody perennial plant usu. with a single main stem and a head of branches and leaves at the top **2** : a piece of wood adapted to a particular use ⟨a shoe ∼⟩ **3** : something resembling a tree ⟨a genealogical ∼⟩ — **tree·less** *adj*

²**tree** *vb* **treed; tree·ing** : to drive to or up a tree ⟨∼ a raccoon⟩

tree farm *n* : an area of forest land managed to ensure continuous commercial production

tree line *n* : TIMBERLINE

tree of heaven : a Chinese ailanthus that is widely grown as a shade and ornamental tree

tree surgery *n* : operative treatment of diseased trees esp. for control of decay — **tree surgeon** *n*

tre·foil \'trē-ˌfóil, 'tre-\ *n* **1** : an herb (as clover) with leaves with three leaflets **2** : a decorative design with three leaflike parts

¹**trek** \'trek\ *vb* **trekked; trek·king 1** *chiefly southern Africa* : to travel or migrate by ox wagon **2** : to make one's way arduously

²**trek** *n chiefly southern Africa* **1** : a migration esp. of settlers by ox wagon **2** : a slow or difficult journey

¹**trel·lis** \'tre-ləs\ *n* [ME *trelis*, fr. MF *treliz* fabric of coarse weave, trellis, fr. (assumed) VL *trilicius* woven with triple thread, fr. L *tres* three + *licium* thread] : a frame of latticework used esp. for climbing plants

²**trellis** *vb* : to provide with a trellis; *esp* : to train (as a vine) on a trellis

trem·a·tode \'tre-mə-ˌtōd\ *n* : any of a class of parasitic worms

¹**trem·ble** \'trem-bəl\ *vb* **trem·bled; trem·bling 1** : to shake involuntarily (as with fear or cold) : SHIVER **2** : to move, sound, pass, or come to pass as if shaken or tremulous **3** : to be affected with fear or doubt

²**tremble** *n* : a spell of shaking or quivering

tre·men·dous \tri-'men-dəs\ *adj* **1** : causing dread, awe, or terror : TERRIFYING **2** : unusually large, powerful, great, or excellent **syn** stupendous, monumental, monstrous — **tre·men·dous·ly** *adv*

trem·o·lo \'tre-mə-ˌlō\ *n, pl* **-los** [It] : a rapid fluttering of a tone or alternating tones

trem·or \'tre-mər\ *n* **1** : a trembling or shaking esp. from weakness, emotional stress, or disease **2** : a quivering motion of the earth (as during an earthquake)

trem·u·lous \'trem-yə-ləs\ *adj* **1** : marked by trembling or tremors : QUIVERING **2** : TIMOROUS, TIMID — **trem-u·lous·ly** *adv*

¹trench \'trench\ *n* [ME *trenche* track cut through a wood, fr. MF, act of cutting, fr. *trenchier* to cut, prob. fr. (assumed) VL *trinicare* to cut in three, fr. L *trini* three each] **1** : a long narrow cut in the ground : DITCH; *esp* : a ditch protected by banks of earth and used to shelter soldiers **2** *pl* : a place or situation likened to trench warfare **3** : a long narrow steep-sided depression in the ocean floor

²trench *vb* **1** : to cut or dig trenches in **2** : to protect (troops) with trenches **3** : to come close : VERGE

tren·chant \'tren-chənt\ *adj* **1** : vigorously effective; *also* : CAUSTIC **2** : sharply perceptive : KEEN **3** : CLEAR=CUT, DISTINCT

tren·cher \'tren-chər\ *n* : a wooden platter for serving food

tren·cher·man \'tren-chər-mən\ *n* : a hearty eater

trench foot *n* : a painful foot disorder resembling frostbite and resulting from exposure to cold and wet

trench mouth *n* : a progressive painful disease of the mouth and adjacent parts that is marked by ulceration and associated with a great increase in certain bacteria normally present in the mouth

¹trend \'trend\ *vb* **1** : to have or take a general direction : TEND **2** : to show a tendency : INCLINE

²trend *n* **1** : a general direction taken (as by a stream or mountain range) **2** : a prevailing tendency : DRIFT **3** : a current style or preference : VOGUE

trendy \'tren-dē\ *adj* **trend·i·er; -est** : very fashionable; *also* : marked by superficial or faddish appeal or taste

trep·i·da·tion \ˌtre-pə-'dā-shən\ *n* : nervous agitation : APPREHENSION **syn** horror, terror, panic, consternation, dread, fright, dismay

¹tres·pass \'tres-pəs, -ˌpas\ *n* **1** : SIN, OFFENSE **2** : unlawful entry on someone else's land **syn** transgression, violation, infraction, infringement

²trespass *vb* **1** : to commit an offense : ERR, SIN **2** : INTRUDE, ENCROACH; *esp* : to enter unlawfully upon the land of another — **tres·pass·er** *n*

tress \'tres\ *n* : a long lock of hair — usu. used in pl.

tres·tle *also* **tres·sel** \'tre-səl\ *n* **1** : a supporting framework consisting esp. of a horizontal piece with spreading legs at each end **2** : a braced framework of timbers, piles, or steel for carrying a road or railroad over a depression

trey \'trā\ *n, pl* **treys** : a card or the side of a die with three spots

tri·ad \'trī-ˌad, -əd\ *n* : a union or group of three usu. closely related persons or things

tri·age \trē-'äzh, 'trē-ˌäzh\ *n* [F, sorting] : the sorting of and allocation of treatment to patients and esp. battle or disaster victims according to a system of priorities designed to maximize the number of survivors

tri·al \'trī-əl\ *n* **1** : the action or process of trying or putting to the proof : TEST **2** : the hearing and judgment of a matter in issue before a competent tribunal **3** : a source of vexation or annoyance **4** : an experiment to test quality, value, or usefulness **5** : EFFORT, ATTEMPT **syn** cross, ordeal, tribulation, affliction — **trial** *adj*

tri·an·gle \'trī-ˌaŋ-gəl\ *n* **1** : a plane figure that has three sides and three angles : a polygon having three sides **2**

: something shaped like a triangle — **tri·an·gu·lar** \trī-'aŋ-gyə-lər\ *adj* — **tri·an·gu·lar·ly** *adv*

tri·an·gu·la·tion \(ˌ)trī-ˌaŋ-gyə-'lā-shən\ *n* : a method using trigonometry to find the location of a point using bearings from two fixed points a known distance apart — **tri·an·gu·late** \trī-'aŋ-gyə-ˌlāt\ *vb*

Tri·as·sic \trī-'a-sik\ *adj* : of, relating to, or being the earliest period of the Mesozoic era marked by the first appearance of the dinosaurs — **Triassic** *n*

trib *abbr* tributary

tribe \'trīb\ *n* **1** : a social group comprising numerous families, clans, or generations **2** : a group of persons having a common character, occupation, or interest **3** : a group of related plants or animals ⟨the cat ∼⟩ — **trib·al** \'trī-bəl\ *adj*

tribes·man \'trībz-mən\ *n* : a member of a tribe

trib·u·la·tion \ˌtri-byə-'lā-shən\ *n* [ME *tribulacion*, fr. OF, fr. L *tribulatio*, fr. *tribulare* to press, oppress, fr. *tribulum* drag used in threshing] : distress or suffering resulting from oppression or persecution; *also* : a trying experience **syn** trial, affliction, cross, ordeal

tri·bu·nal \trī-'byün-ᵊl, tri-\ *n* **1** : the seat of a judge **2** : a court of justice **3** : something that decides or determines ⟨the ∼ of public opinion⟩

tri·bune \'tri-ˌbyün, tri-'byün\ *n* **1** : an official in ancient Rome with the function of protecting the interests of plebeian citizens from the patricians **2** : a defender of the people

¹trib·u·tary \'tri-byə-ˌter-ē\ *adj* **1** : paying tribute : SUBJECT **2** : flowing into a larger stream or a lake **syn** subordinate, secondary, dependent

²tributary *n, pl* **-tar·ies 1** : a ruler or state that pays tribute **2** : a tributary stream

trib·ute \'tri-(ˌ)byüt, -byət\ *n* **1** : a payment by one ruler or nation to another as an act of submission or price of protection **2** : a usu. excessive tax, rental, or levy exacted by a sovereign or superior **3** : a gift or service showing respect, gratitude, or affection; *also* : PRAISE **syn** eulogy, citation, encomium, panegyric

trice \'trīs\ *n* : INSTANT, MOMENT

tri·ceps \'trī-ˌseps\ *n, pl* **triceps** : a large muscle along the back of the upper arm that is attached at its upper end by three main parts and acts to extend the forearm at the elbow joint

tri·cer·a·tops \(ˌ)trī-'ser-ə-ˌtäps\ *n, pl* **-tops** *also* **-tops·es** [NL, fr. Gk *tri-* three + *kerat-, keras* horn + *ōps* face] : any of a genus of large plant-eating Cretaceous dinosaurs with three horns, a bony crest on the neck, and hoofed toes

tri·chi·na \tri-'kī-nə\ *n, pl* **-nae** \-(ˌ)nē\ *also* **-nas** : a small slender nematode worm that in the larval state is parasitic in the voluntary muscles of flesh-eating mammals (as the hog and humans)

trich·i·no·sis \ˌtri-kə-'nō-səs\ *n* : infestation with or disease caused by trichinae and marked esp. by pain, fever, and swelling

¹trick \'trik\ *n* **1** : a crafty procedure meant to deceive **2** : a mischievous action : PRANK **3** : a childish action **4** : a deceptive or ingenious feat designed to puzzle or amuse **5** : PECULIARITY, MANNERISM **6** : a quick or artful way of getting a result : KNACK **7** : the cards played in one round of a card game **8** : a tour of duty : SHIFT **syn** ruse, maneuver, artifice, wile, feint

²trick *vb* **1** : to deceive by cunning or artifice : CHEAT **2** : to dress ornately

trick·ery \'tri-kə-rē\ *n* : deception by tricks and stratagems

triangle 1: *1* equilateral, *2* isosceles, *3* right triangle

trick·le \'tri-kəl\ vb **trick·led; trick·ling** 1 : to run or fall in drops 2 : to flow in a thin gentle stream — **trickle** n
trick·ster \'trik-stər\ n : one who tricks or cheats
tricky \'tri-kē\ adj **trick·i·er; -est** 1 : inclined to trickery 2 : requiring skill or caution ⟨a ~ situation to handle⟩ 3 : UNRELIABLE ⟨a ~ lock⟩
tri·col·or \'trī-ˌkə-lər\ n : a flag of three colors ⟨the French ~⟩
tri·cy·cle \'trī-(ˌ)si-kəl\ n : a 3-wheeled vehicle usu. propelled by pedals
tri·dent \'trīd-ᵊnt\ n [L trident-, tridens, fr. tri- three + dent-, dens tooth] : a 3-pronged spear
tried \'trīd\ adj 1 : found trustworthy through testing 2 : subjected to trials
tri·en·ni·al \trī-'e-nē-əl\ adj 1 : occurring or being done every three years 2 : lasting for three years — **triennial** n
¹**tri·fle** \'trī-fəl\ n : something of little value or importance
²**trifle** vb **tri·fled; tri·fling** 1 : to talk in a jesting or mocking manner 2 : to treat someone or something as unimportant 3 : DALLY, FLIRT 4 : to handle idly : TOY — **tri·fler** n
tri·fling \'trī-fliŋ\ adj 1 : FRIVOLOUS 2 : TRIVIAL, INSIGNIFICANT **syn** petty, paltry, measly, inconsequential
tri·fo·cals \trī-'fō-kəlz\ n pl : eyeglasses with lenses having one part for close focus, one for intermediate focus, and one for distant focus
tri·fo·li·ate \trī-'fō-lē-ət\ adj : having three leaves or leaflets
¹**trig** \'trig\ adj : stylishly trim : SMART
²**trig** n : TRIGONOMETRY
¹**trig·ger** \'tri-gər\ n [alter. of earlier tricker, fr. D trekker, fr. MD trecker one that pulls, fr. trecken to pull] : a movable lever that activates a device when it is squeezed; esp : the part of a firearm lock moved by the finger to fire a gun — **trigger** adj — **trig·gered** adj
²**trigger** vb 1 : to fire by pulling a trigger 2 : to initiate, actuate, or set off as if by a trigger
tri·glyc·er·ide n : any of a group of fats and oils that are derived from glycerol and fatty acids and are widespread in animal tissue
trig·o·nom·e·try \ˌtri-gə-'nä-mə-trē\ n : the branch of mathematics dealing with the properties of triangles and esp. with finding unknown angles or sides given the size or length of some angles or sides — **trig·o·no·met·ric** \-nə-'me-trik\ also **trig·o·no·met·ri·cal** \-tri-kəl\ adj
trike \'trīk\ n : TRICYCLE
¹**trill** \'tril\ n 1 : the alternation of two musical tones a scale degree apart 2 : WARBLE 3 : the rapid vibration of one speech organ against another (as of the tip of the tongue against the teeth)
²**trill** vb : to utter as or with a trill
tril·lion \'tril-yən\ n 1 : a thousand billions 2 Brit : a million billions — **trillion** adj — **tril·lionth** \-yənth\ adj or n
tril·li·um \'tri-lē-əm\ n : any of a genus of herbs of the lily family with an erect stem bearing a whorl of three leaves and a large solitary usu. spring-blooming flower with three petals
tril·o·gy \'tri-lə-jē\ n, pl **-gies** : a series of three dramas or literary or musical compositions that are closely related and develop one theme
¹**trim** \'trim\ vb **trimmed; trim·ming** [OE trymian, trymman to strengthen, arrange, fr. trum strong, firm] 1 : to put ornaments on : ADORN 2 : to defeat esp. resoundingly 3 : to make trim, neat, regular, or less bulky by or as if by cutting ⟨~ a beard⟩ ⟨~ a budget⟩ 4 : to cause (a boat) to assume a desired position in the water by arrangement of the load; also : to adjust (as a submarine or airplane) esp. for horizontal motion 5 : to adjust (a sail) to a desired position 6 : to change one's views for safety or expediency — **trim·ly** adv — **trim·mer** n — **trim·ness** n

²**trim** adj **trim·mer; trim·mest** : showing neatness, good order, or compactness ⟨a ~ figure⟩ **syn** tidy, trig, smart, spruce, shipshape
³**trim** n 1 : good condition : FITNESS 2 : material used for ornament or trimming; esp : the woodwork in the finish of a house esp. around doors and windows 3 : the position of a ship or boat esp. with reference to the horizontal; also : the relation between the plane of a sail and the direction of a ship 4 : the position of an airplane at which it will continue in level flight with no adjustments to the controls 5 : something that is trimmed off
tri·ma·ran \'trī-mə-ˌran, ˌtrī-mə-'ran\ n : a sailboat with three hulls
tri·mes·ter \trī-'mes-tər, 'trī-ˌmes-tər\ n 1 : a period of three or about three months (as in pregnancy) 2 : one of three terms into which an academic year is sometimes divided
trim·e·ter \'tri-mə-tər\ n : a line of verse consisting of three metrical feet
trim·ming \'tri-miŋ\ n 1 : DEFEAT 2 : the action of one that trims 3 : something that trims, ornaments, or completes
tri·month·ly \trī-'mənth-lē\ adj : occurring every three months
trine \'trīn\ adj : THREEFOLD, TRIPLE
Trin·i·da·di·an \ˌtri-nə-'dā-dē-ən, -'da-\ n : a native or inhabitant of the island of Trinidad — **Trinidadian** adj
Trin·i·tar·i·an \ˌtri-nə-'ter-ē-ən\ n : a believer in the doctrine of the Trinity — **Trin·i·tar·i·an·ism** \-ē-ə-ˌni-zəm\ n
Trin·i·ty \'tri-nə-tē\ n 1 : the unity of Father, Son, and Holy Spirit as three persons in one Godhead 2 not cap : TRIAD
trin·ket \'triŋ-kət\ n 1 : a small ornament (as a jewel or ring) 2 : TRIFLE
trio \'trē-ō\ n, pl **tri·os** 1 : a musical composition for three voices or three instruments 2 : the performers of a trio 3 : a group or set of three
¹**trip** \'trip\ vb **tripped; trip·ping** 1 : to move with light quick steps 2 : to catch the foot against something so as to stumble or cause to stumble 3 : to make a mistake : SLIP; also : to detect in a misstep : EXPOSE 4 : to release (as a spring or switch) by moving a catch; also : ACTIVATE 5 : to get high on a drug and esp. a hallucinatory drug
²**trip** n 1 : JOURNEY, VOYAGE 2 : a quick light step 3 : a false step : STUMBLE; also : ERROR 4 : the action of tripping mechanically; also : a device for tripping 5 : an intense drug-induced hallucinatory experience 6 : absorption in an attitude or state of mind ⟨an ego ~⟩
tri·par·tite \trī-'pär-ˌtīt\ adj 1 : divided into three parts 2 : having three corresponding parts or copies 3 : made between three parties ⟨a ~ treaty⟩
tripe \'trīp\ n 1 : stomach tissue of a ruminant and esp. an ox used as food 2 : something poor, worthless, or offensive : TRASH
¹**tri·ple** \'tri-pəl\ vb **tri·pled; tri·pling** 1 : to make or become three times as great or as many 2 : to hit a triple
²**triple** n 1 : a triple quantity 2 : a group of three 3 : a hit in baseball that lets the batter reach third base
³**triple** adj 1 : being three times as great or as many 2 : having three units or members 3 : repeated three times
triple bond n : a chemical bond in which three pairs of electrons are shared by two atoms in a molecule
triple point n : the condition of temperature and pressure under which the gaseous, liquid, and solid forms of a substance can exist in equilibrium
trip·let \'tri-plət\ n 1 : a unit of three lines of verse 2 : a group of three of a kind 3 : one of three offspring born at one birth
tri·plex \'tri-ˌpleks, 'trī-\ adj : THREEFOLD, TRIPLE

¹trip·li·cate \'tri-pli-kət\ *adj* : made in three identical copies

²trip·li·cate \-plə-ˌkāt\ *vb* **-cat·ed; -cat·ing 1** : TRIPLE **2** : to provide three copies of ⟨∼ a document⟩

³trip·li·cate \-pli-kət\ *n* : three copies all alike — used with *in* ⟨typed in ∼⟩

tri·ply \'tri-plē, 'tri-pə-lē\ *adv* : in a triple degree, amount, or manner

tri·pod \'trī-ˌpäd\ *n* : something (as a caldron, stool, or camera stand) that rests on three legs — **tripod** *or* **tri·po·dal** \'tri-pəd-ᵊl, 'trī-ˌpäd-\ *adj*

trip·tych \'trip-tik\ *n* : a picture or carving in three panels side by side

tri·reme \'trī-ˌrēm\ *n* : an ancient galley having three banks of oars

tri·sect \'trī-ˌsekt, trī-'sekt\ *vb* : to divide into three usu. equal parts — **tri·sec·tion** \'trī-ˌsek-shən\ *n*

trite \'trīt\ *adj* **trit·er; trit·est** [L *tritus,* fr. pp. of *terere* to rub, wear away] : used so commonly that the novelty is worn off : STALE **syn** hackneyed, stereotyped, commonplace, clichéd

tri·ti·um \'tri-tē-əm, 'tri-shē-\ *n* : a radioactive form of hydrogen with atoms of three times the mass of ordinary hydrogen atoms

tri·ton \'trīt-ᵊn\ *n* : any of various large marine gastropod mollusks with a heavy elongated conical shell; *also* : the shell of a triton

trit·u·rate \'tri-chə-ˌrāt\ *vb* **-rat·ed; -rat·ing** : to rub or grind to a fine powder

¹tri·umph \'trī-əmf\ *n, pl* **tri·umphs 1** : the joy or exultation of victory or success **2** : VICTORY, CONQUEST — **tri·um·phal** \trī-'əm-fəl\ *adj*

²triumph *vb* **1** : to obtain victory : PREVAIL **2** : to celebrate victory or success exultantly — **tri·um·phant** \trī-'əm-fənt\ *adj* — **tri·um·phant·ly** *adv*

tri·um·vir \trī-'əm-vər\ *n, pl* **-virs** *also* **-vi·ri** \-və-ˌrī\ : a member of a triumvirate

tri·um·vi·rate \-və-rət\ *n* : a ruling body of three persons

tri·une \'trī-ˌün, -ˌyün\ *adj, often cap* : being three in one ⟨the ∼ God⟩

triv·et \'tri-vət\ *n* **1** : a 3-legged stand : TRIPOD **2** : a usu. metal stand with short feet for use under a hot dish

triv·ia \'tri-vē-ə\ *n sing or pl* : unimportant matters : TRIFLES

triv·i·al \'tri-vē-əl\ *adj* [L *trivialis* found everywhere, commonplace, fr. *trivium* crossroads, fr. *tri-* three + *via* way] : of little importance — **triv·i·al·i·ty** \ˌtri-vē-'a-lə-tē\ *n*

triv·i·um \'tri-vē-əm\ *n, pl* **triv·ia** \-vē-ə\ : the three liberal arts of grammar, rhetoric, and logic in a medieval university

tri·week·ly \trī-'wē-klē\ *adj* **1** : occurring or appearing three times a week **2** : occurring or appearing every three weeks — **triweekly** *adv*

tro·che \'trō-kē\ *n* : a medicinal lozenge

tro·chee \'trō-(ˌ)kē\ *n* : a metrical foot of one accented syllable followed by one unaccented syllable — **tro·cha·ic** \trō-'kā-ik\ *adj*

trod *past and past part of* TREAD

trodden *past part of* TREAD

troi·ka \'troi-kə\ *n* [Russ *troĭka,* fr. *troe* three] : a group of three; *esp* : an administrative or ruling body of three

Tro·jan War \'trō-jən-\ *n* : a 10-year war between ancient Greeks and the people of Troy

¹troll \'trōl\ *vb* **1** : to sing the parts of (a song) in succession **2** : to fish by trailing a lure or baited hook from a moving boat **3** : to sing or play jovially

²troll *n* : a lure used in trolling; *also* : the line with its lure

³troll *n* : a dwarf or giant in Scandinavian folklore inhabiting caves or hills

trol·ley *also* **trol·ly** \'trä-lē\ *n, pl* **trolleys** *also* **trollies 1** : a device (as a grooved wheel on the end of a pole) to carry current from a wire to an electrically driven ve-

hicle **2** : a streetcar powered electrically through a trolley **3** : a wheeled carriage running on an overhead rail or track

trol·ley·bus \'trä-lē-ˌbəs\ *n* : a bus powered electrically through a trolley

trolley car *n* : TROLLEY 2

trol·lop \'trä-ləp\ *n* : a disreputable woman; *esp* : one who engages in sex promiscuously

trom·bone \träm-'bōn, 'träm-ˌbōn\ *n* [It, lit., big trumpet, fr. *tromba* trumpet] : a brass wind instrument that consists of a long metal tube with two turns and a flaring end and that usu. has a movable slide to vary the pitch — **trom·bon·ist** \-'bō-nist, -ˌbō-\ *n*

trombone

tromp \'trämp, 'trȯmp\ *vb* **1** : TRAMP, MARCH **2** : to stamp with the foot **3** : DEFEAT

¹troop \'trüp\ *n* **1** : a cavalry unit corresponding to an infantry company **2** *pl* : armed forces : SOLDIERS **3** : a collection of people or things **4** : a unit of Girl Scouts or Boy Scouts under an adult leader

²troop *vb* : to move or gather in crowds

troop·er \'trü-pər\ *n* **1** : an enlisted cavalryman; *also* : a cavalry horse **2** : a mounted or a state police officer

troop·ship \'trüp-ˌship\ *n* : a ship for carrying troops

trope \'trōp\ *n* : a word or expression used in a figurative sense

tro·phy \'trō-fē\ *n, pl* **trophies** : something gained or given in conquest or victory esp. when preserved or mounted as a memorial

trop·ic \'trä-pik\ *n* [ME *tropik,* fr. L *tropicus* of the solstice, fr. Gk *tropikos,* fr. *tropē* turn] **1** : either of the two parallels of latitude approximately 23½ degrees north (**tropic of Can·cer** \-'kan-sər\) or south (**tropic of Cap·ri·corn** \-'ka-prə-ˌkȯrn\) of the equator where the sun is directly overhead when it reaches its most northerly or southerly point in the sky **2** *pl, often cap* : the region lying between the tropics — **trop·i·cal** \-pi-kəl\ *or* **tropic** *adj*

tro·pism \'trō-ˌpi-zəm\ *n* : an automatic movement by an organism in response to a source of stimulation; *also* : a reflex reaction involving this

tro·po·sphere \'trō-pə-ˌsfir, 'trä-\ *n* : the part of the atmosphere between the earth's surface and the stratosphere in which most weather changes occur — **tro·po·spher·ic** \ˌtrō-pə-'sfir-ik, ˌträ-, -'sfer-\ *adj*

¹trot \'trät\ *n* **1** : a moderately fast gait of a 4-footed animal (as a horse) in which the legs move in diagonal pairs **2** : a human jogging gait between a walk and a run

²trot *vb* **trot·ted; trot·ting 1** : to ride, drive, or go at a trot **2** : to proceed briskly : HURRY — **trot·ter** *n*

troth \'träth, 'trȯth, 'trōth\ *n* **1** : pledged faithfulness **2** : one's pledged word; *also* : BETROTHAL

trou·ba·dour \'trü-bə-ˌdȯr\ *n* [F, fr. OProv *trobador,* fr. *trobar* to compose] : any of a class of poet-musicians flourishing esp. in southern France and northern Italy during the 11th, 12th, and 13th centuries

¹trou·ble \'trə-bəl\ *vb* **trou·bled; trou·bling 1** : to agitate mentally or spiritually : DISTURB, WORRY **2** : to produce physical disorder in : AFFLICT **3** : to put to inconvenience **4** : RUFFLE ⟨∼ the waters⟩ **5** : to make an effort

---

\ə\abut \ᵊ\kitten \ər\further \a\ash \ā\ace \ä\mop, mar
\aú\out \ch\chin \e\bet \ē\easy \g\go \i\hit \ī\ice \j\job
\ŋ\sing \ō\go \ȯ\law \ȯi\boy \th\thin \t͟h\the \ü\loot \ú\foot
\y\yet \zh\vision *see also* Pronunciation Symbols page

syn distress, ail, upset — **trou·ble·some** *adj* — **trou·ble·some·ly** *adv* — **trou·blous** \-bə-ləs\ *adj*

²**trouble** *n* **1** : the quality or state of being troubled esp. mentally **2** : an instance of distress or annoyance **3** : DISEASE, AILMENT ⟨heart ∼⟩ **4** : EXERTION, PAINS ⟨took the ∼ to phone⟩ **5** : a cause of disturbance or distress

trou·ble·mak·er \-ˌmā-kər\ *n* : a person who causes trouble

trou·ble·shoot·er \-ˌshü-tər\ *n* **1** : a worker employed to locate trouble and make repairs in equipment **2** : an expert in resolving disputes or problems — **trou·ble·shoot** *vb*

trough \ˈtròf, ˈtròth, *by bakers often* ˈtrō\ *n, pl* **troughs** \ˈtròfs, ˈtròvz; ˈtròths, ˈtróthz; ˈtròz\ **1** : a long shallow open boxlike container esp. for water or feed for livestock **2** : a gutter along the eaves of a house **3** : a long channel or depression (as between waves or hills) **4** : an elongated area of low barometric pressure

trounce \ˈtraùns\ *vb* **trounced; trounc·ing** **1** : to thrash or punish severely **2** : to defeat decisively

troupe \ˈtrüp\ *n* : COMPANY; *esp* : a group of performers on the stage — **troup·er** *n*

trou·sers \ˈtraù-zərz\ *n pl* [alter. of earlier *trouse,* fr. ScGael *triubhas*] : an outer garment covering each leg separately and usu. extending from the waist to the ankle — **trouser** *adj*

trous·seau \ˈtrü-sō, trü-ˈsō\ *n, pl* **trousseaux** \-sōz, -ˈsōz\ *or* **trousseaus** [F] : the personal outfit of a bride

trout \ˈtraùt\ *n, pl* **trout** *also* **trouts** [ME, fr. OE *trūht,* fr. LL *tructa,* a fish with sharp teeth, fr. Gk *trōktēs,* lit., gnawer] : any of various mostly freshwater food and game fishes usu. smaller than the related salmons

trow \ˈtrō\ *vb, archaic* : THINK, SUPPOSE

trow·el \ˈtraù-əl\ *n* **1** : a hand tool used for spreading, shaping, or smoothing loose or plastic material (as mortar or plaster) **2** : a small flat or scooplike implement used in gardening — **trowel** *vb*

troy \ˈtrói\ *adj* : expressed in troy weight ⟨∼ ounce⟩

troy weight *n* : a system of weights based on a pound of 12 ounces and an ounce of 480 grains (31 grams) — see WEIGHT table

tru·ant \ˈtrü-ənt\ *n* [ME, vagabond, idler, fr. OF, vagrant] : a student who stays out of school without permission — **tru·an·cy** \-ən-sē\ *n* — **truant** *adj*

truce \ˈtrüs\ *n* **1** : ARMISTICE **2** : a respite esp. from something unpleasant

¹**truck** \ˈtrək\ *vb* **1** : EXCHANGE, BARTER **2** : to have dealings : TRAFFIC

²**truck** *n* **1** : BARTER **2** : small goods or merchandise; *esp* : vegetables grown for market **3** : DEALINGS

³**truck** *n* **1** : a wheeled vehicle (as a strong heavy automobile) designed for carrying heavy articles or hauling a trailer **2** : a swiveling frame with springs and one or more pairs of wheels used to carry and guide one end of a locomotive or railroad car

⁴**truck** *vb* **1** : to transport on a truck **2** : to be employed in driving a truck — **truck·er** *n*

truck farm *n* : a farm growing vegetables for market — **truck farmer** *n*

truck·le \ˈtrə-kəl\ *vb* **truck·led; truck·ling** : to yield slavishly to the will of another : SUBMIT **syn** fawn, toady, cringe, cower

truc·u·lent \ˈtrə-kyə-lənt\ *adj* **1** : feeling or showing ferocity : SAVAGE **2** : aggressively self-assertive : PUGNACIOUS — **truc·u·lence** \-ləns\ *n* — **truc·u·len·cy** \-lən-sē\ *n* — **truc·u·lent·ly** *adv*

trudge \ˈtrəj\ *vb* **trudged; trudg·ing** : to walk or march steadily and usu. laboriously

¹**true** \ˈtrü\ *adj* **tru·er; tru·est** **1** : STEADFAST, LOYAL **2** : agreeing with facts or reality ⟨a ∼ description⟩ **3** : CONSISTENT ⟨∼ to expectations⟩ **4** : properly so called ⟨∼ love⟩ **5** : RIGHTFUL ⟨∼ and lawful king⟩ **6** : conform-

able to a standard or pattern; *also* : placed or formed accurately **syn** constant, staunch, resolute, steadfast

²**true** *adv* **1** : TRUTHFULLY **2** : ACCURATELY ⟨the bullet flew straight and ∼⟩; *also* : without variation from type ⟨breed ∼⟩

³**true** *n* **1** : TRUTH, REALITY — usu. used with *the* **2** : the state of being accurate (as in alignment) ⟨out of ∼⟩

⁴**true** *vb* **trued; tru·ing** *also* **tru·ing** : to bring or restore to a desired precision

true–blue *adj* : marked by unswerving loyalty

true bug *n* : BUG 2

true·heart·ed \ˈtrü-ˈhär-təd\ *adj* : FAITHFUL, LOYAL

truf·fle \ˈtrə-fəl, ˈtrü-\ *n* **1** : the usu. dark and wrinkled edible fruit of any of several European underground fungi; *also* : one of these fungi **2** : a candy made of chocolate, butter, and sugar shaped into balls and coated with cocoa

tru·ism \ˈtrü-ˌi-zəm\ *n* : an undoubted or self-evident truth **syn** commonplace, platitude, bromide, cliché

tru·ly \ˈtrü-lē\ *adv* **1** : in all sincerity **2** : in agreement with fact **3** : ACCURATELY **4** : in a proper or suitable manner

¹**trump** \ˈtrəmp\ *n* : TRUMPET

²**trump** *n* : a card of a designated suit any of whose cards will win over a card that is not of this suit; *also* : the suit itself — often used in pl.

³**trump** *vb* : to take with a trump

trumped–up \ˈtrəmpt-ˈəp\ *adj* : fraudulently concocted : SPURIOUS

trum·pery \ˈtrəm-pə-rē\ *n* **1** : NONSENSE **2** : trivial articles : JUNK

¹**trum·pet** \ˈtrəm-pət\ *n* **1** : a wind instrument consisting of a long curved metal tube flaring at one end and with a cup-shaped mouthpiece at the other **2** : something that resembles a trumpet or its tonal quality **3** : a funnel-shaped instrument for collecting, directing, or intensifying sound

²**trumpet** *vb* **1** : to blow a trumpet **2** : to proclaim on or as if on a trumpet — **trum·pet·er** *n*

¹**trun·cate** \ˈtrəŋ-ˌkāt, ˈtrən-\ *adj* : having the end square or blunt

²**truncate** *vb* **trun·cat·ed; trun·cat·ing** : to shorten by or as if by cutting : LOP — **trun·ca·tion** \ˌtrəŋ-ˈkā-shən\ *n*

trun·cheon \ˈtrən-chən\ *n* : a police officer's club

trun·dle \ˈtrənd-ᵊl\ *vb* **trun·dled; trun·dling** : to roll along : WHEEL

trundle bed *n* : a low bed that can be stored under a higher bed

trunk \ˈtrəŋk\ *n* **1** : the main stem of a tree **2** : the body of a person or animal apart from the head and limbs **3** : the main or central part of something **4** : a box or chest used to hold usu. clothes or personal effects (as of a traveler); *also* : the enclosed luggage space in the rear of an automobile **5** : the long muscular nose of an elephant **6** *pl* : men's shorts worn chiefly for sports **7** : a usu. major channel or passage

trunk line *n* : a system handling long-distance through traffic

¹**truss** \ˈtrəs\ *vb* **1** : to secure tightly : BIND **2** : to arrange for cooking by binding close the wings or legs of (a fowl) **3** : to support, strengthen, or stiffen by or as if by a truss

²**truss** *n* **1** : a collection of structural parts (as beams) forming a rigid framework (as in bridge or building construction) **2** : a device worn to reduce a hernia by pressure

¹**trust** \ˈtrəst\ *n* **1** : assured reliance on the character, strength, or truth of someone or something **2** : a basis of reliance, faith, or hope **3** : confident hope **4** : financial credit **5** : a property interest held by one person for the benefit of another **6** : a combination of firms formed by a legal agreement; *esp* : one that reduces competition **7** : something entrusted to one to be cared for in

the interest of another **8** : CARE, CUSTODY **syn** confidence, dependence, faith, reliance
²trust *vb* **1** : to place confidence : DEPEND **2** : to be confident : HOPE **3** : ENTRUST **4** : to permit to stay or go or to do something without fear or misgiving **5** : to rely on or on the truth of : BELIEVE **6** : to extend credit to
trust·ee \ˌtrəs-ˈtē\ *n* **1** : a person to whom property is legally committed in trust **2** : a country charged with the supervision of a trust territory
trust·ee·ship \ˌtrəs-ˈtē-ˌship\ *n* **1** : the office or function of a trustee **2** : supervisory control by one or more nations over a trust territory
trust·ful \ˈtrəst-fəl\ *adj* : full of trust : CONFIDING — **trust·ful·ly** *adv* — **trust·ful·ness** *n*
trust territory *n* : a non-self-governing territory placed under a supervisory authority by the Trusteeship Council of the United Nations
trust·wor·thy \-ˌwər-thē\ *adj* : worthy of confidence : DEPENDABLE **syn** trusty, tried, reliable — **trust·wor·thi·ness** *n*
¹trusty \ˈtrəs-tē\ *adj* **trust·i·er; -est** : TRUSTWORTHY, DEPENDABLE
²trusty \ˈtrəs-tē, ˌtrəs-ˈtē\ *n, pl* **trust·ies** : a trusted person; *esp* : a convict considered trustworthy and allowed special privileges
truth \ˈtrüth\ *n, pl* **truths** \ˈtrüthz, ˈtrüths\ **1** : TRUTHFULNESS, HONESTY **2** : the real state of things : FACT **3** : the body of real events or facts : ACTUALITY **4** : a true or accepted statement or proposition ⟨the ∼s of science⟩ **5** : agreement with fact or reality : CORRECTNESS **syn** veracity, verity
truth·ful \ˈtrüth-fəl\ *adj* : telling or disposed to tell the truth — **truth·ful·ly** *adv* — **truth·ful·ness** *n*
truth serum *n* : a drug held to induce a subject under questioning to talk freely
¹try \ˈtrī\ *vb* **tried; try·ing 1** : to examine or investigate judicially **2** : to conduct the trial of **3** : to put to test or trial **4** : to subject to strain, affliction, or annoyance **5** : to extract or clarify (as lard) by melting **6** : to make an effort to do something : ATTEMPT, ENDEAVOR **syn** essay, assay, strive, struggle
²try *n, pl* **tries** : an experimental trial
try·ing *adj* : severely straining the powers of endurance
try on *vb* : to put on (a garment) to test the fit and looks
try out *vb* : to participate in competition esp. for a position on an athletic team or a part in a play — **try·out** \ˈtrī-ˌaůt\ *n*
tryst \ˈtrist\ *n* **1** : an agreement (as between lovers) to meet **2** : an appointed meeting or meeting place — **tryst** *vb* — **tryst·er** *n*
tsar \ˈzär, ˈtsär, ˈsär\ *var of* CZAR
tset·se fly \ˈtset-sē-, ˈtsēt-, ˈtet-, ˈtēt-, ˈset-, ˈsēt-\ *n* : any of several sub-Saharan African dipteran flies including the vector of sleeping sickness
TSgt *abbr* technical sergeant
T–shirt \ˈtē-ˌshərt\ *n* : a collarless short-sleeved or sleeveless cotton undershirt; *also* : an outer shirt of similar design — **T–shirt·ed** \-ˌshər-təd\ *adj*
tsp *abbr* teaspoon; teaspoonful
T square *n* : a ruler with a crosspiece at one end for making parallel lines
tsu·na·mi \sů-ˈnä-mē, tsů-\ *n* [Jp] : a tidal wave caused by an underwater earthquake or volcanic eruption
TT *abbr* Trust Territories
TTY *abbr* teletypewriter
Tu *abbr* Tuesday
tub \ˈtəb\ *n* **1** : a wide low bucketlike vessel **2** : BATHTUB; *also* : BATH **3** : the amount that a tub will hold
tu·ba \ˈtü-bə, ˈtyü-\ *n* : a large low-pitched brass wind instrument
tub·al \ˈtü-bəl, ˈtyü-\ *adj* : of, relating to, or involving a tube and esp. a fallopian tube
tube \ˈtüb, ˈtyüb\ *n* **1** : any of various usu. cylindrical

structures or devices; *esp* : one to convey fluids **2** : a slender hollow anatomical part (as a fallopian tube) functioning as a channel in a plant or animal body : DUCT **3** : a soft round container from which a paste is squeezed **4** : a tunnel for vehicular or rail travel **5** : INNER TUBE **6** : ELECTRON TUBE **7** : TELEVISION — **tubed** *adj* — **tube·less** *adj*
tu·ber \ˈtü-bər, ˈtyü-\ *n* : a short fleshy usu. underground stem (as of a potato plant) bearing minute scale-like leaves each with a bud at its base
tu·ber·cle \ˈtü-bər-kəl, ˈtyü-\ *n* **1** : a small knobby prominence or outgrowth esp. on an animal or plant **2** : a small abnormal lump in an organ or on the skin; *esp* : one caused by tuberculosis
tubercle bacillus *n* : a bacterium that is the cause of tuberculosis
tu·ber·cu·lar \tü-ˈbər-kyə-lər, tyü-\ *adj* **1** : TUBERCULOUS **2** : of, resembling, or being a tubercle
tu·ber·cu·lin \tü-ˈbər-kyə-lən, tyü-\ *n* : a sterile liquid extracted from the tubercle bacillus and used in the diagnosis of tuberculosis esp. in children and cattle
tu·ber·cu·lo·sis \tü-ˌbər-kyə-ˈlō-səs, tyü-\ *n, pl* **-lo·ses** \-ˌsēz\ : a communicable bacterial disease typically marked by wasting, fever, and formation of cheesy tubercles often in the lungs — **tu·ber·cu·lous** \-ˈbər-kyə-ləs\ *adj*
tube·rose \ˈtüb-ˌrōz, ˈtyüb-\ *n* : a bulbous herb related to the agaves and often grown for its spike of fragrant waxy-white flowers
tu·ber·ous \ˈtü-bə-rəs, ˈtyü-\ *adj* : of, resembling, or being a tuber
tub·ing \ˈtü-biŋ, ˈtyü-\ *n* **1** : material in the form of a tube; *also* : a length of tube **2** : a series or system of tubes
tu·bu·lar \ˈtü-byə-lər, ˈtyü-\ *adj* : having the form of or consisting of a tube; *also* : made with tubes
tu·bule \ˈtü-byül, ˈtyü-\ *n* : a small tube
¹tuck \ˈtək\ *n* **1** : a fold stitched into cloth to shorten, decorate, or control fullness **2** : a cosmetic surgical operation for the removal of excess skin or fat ⟨a tummy ∼⟩
²tuck *vb* **1** : to pull up into a fold ⟨∼ed up her skirt⟩ **2** : to make tucks in **3** : to put into a snug often concealing place ⟨∼ a book under the arm⟩ **4** : to secure in place by pushing the edges under ⟨∼ in a blanket⟩ **5** : to cover by tucking in bedclothes
tuck·er \ˈtə-kər\ *vb* **tuck·ered; tuck·er·ing** : EXHAUST, FATIGUE
Tues *or* **Tue** *abbr* Tuesday
Tues·day \ˈtüz-dē, ˈtyüz-, -dā\ *n* : the 3d day of the week
tu·fa \ˈtü-fə, ˈtyü-\ *n* : a porous rock formed as a deposit from springs or streams
tuff \ˈtəf\ *n* : a rock composed of volcanic detritus
¹tuft \ˈtəft\ *n* **1** : a small cluster of long flexible outgrowths (as hairs); *also* : a bunch of soft fluffy threads cut off short and used as ornament **2** : CLUMP, CLUSTER — **tuft·ed** *adj*
²tuft *vb* **1** : to provide or adorn with a tuft **2** : to make (as a mattress) firm by stitching at intervals and sewing on tufts — **tuft·er** *n*
¹tug \ˈtəg\ *vb* **tugged; tug·ging 1** : to pull hard **2** : to struggle in opposition : CONTEND **3** : to move by pulling hard : HAUL **4** : to tow with a tugboat
²tug *n* **1** : a harness trace **2** : an act of tugging : PULL **3** : a straining effort **4** : a struggle between opposing people or forces **5** : TUGBOAT
tug·boat \-ˌbōt\ *n* : a strongly built boat used for towing or pushing
tug–of–war \ˌtəg-əv-ˈwór\ *n, pl* **tugs–of–war 1** : a strug-

\ə\abut \ʔ\kitten \ər\further \a\ash \ā\ace \ä\mop, mar
\aů\out \ch\chin \e\bet \ē\easy \g\go \i\hit \ī\ice \j\job
\ŋ\sing \ō\go \ó\law \ói\boy \th\thin \th\the \ü\loot \ů\foot
\y\yet \zh\vision *see also* Pronunciation Symbols page

gle for supremacy **2** : an athletic contest in which two teams pull against each other at opposite ends of a rope

tu·grik *or* **tu·ghrik** \'tü-grik\ *n* — see MONEY table

tu·ition \tü-'i-shən, tyü-\ *n* : money paid for instruction ⟨college ∼⟩

tu·la·re·mia \ˌtü-lə-'rē-mē-ə, ˌtyü-\ *n* : an infectious bacterial disease esp. of wild rabbits, rodents, humans, and some domestic animals that in humans is marked by symptoms (as fever) of toxemia

tu·lip \'tü-ləp, 'tyü-\ *n* [NL *tulipa*, fr. Turk *tülbent* turban] : any of a genus of Eurasian bulbous herbs related to the lilies and grown for their large showy erect cup-shaped flowers; *also* : a flower or bulb of a tulip

tulip tree *n* : a tall American timber tree with greenish tulip-shaped flowers and soft white wood that is related to the magnolias

tulle \'tül\ *n* : a sheer often stiffened silk, rayon, or nylon net ⟨a veil of ∼⟩

¹**tum·ble** \'təm-bəl\ *vb* **tum·bled; tum·bling** [ME, fr. *tumben* to dance, fr. OE *tumbian*] **1** : to fall or cause to fall suddenly and helplessly **2** : to fall into ruin **3** : to perform gymnastic feats of rolling and turning **4** : to roll over and over : TOSS **5** : to issue forth hurriedly and confusedly **6** : to come into understand **7** : to throw together in a confused mass

²**tumble** *n* **1** : a disorderly state **2** : an act or instance of tumbling

tum·ble·down \'təm-bəl-'daùn\ *adj* : DILAPIDATED, RAMSHACKLE

tum·bler \'təm-blər\ *n* **1** : one that tumbles; *esp* : ACROBAT **2** : a drinking glass without foot or stem **3** : a movable obstruction in a lock that must be adjusted to a particular position (as by a key) before the bolt can be thrown

tum·ble·weed \'təm-bəl-ˌwēd\ *n* : a plant that breaks away from its roots in autumn and is driven about by the wind

tum·brel *or* **tum·bril** \'təm-brəl\ *n* **1** : CART **2** : a vehicle carrying condemned persons (as during the French Revolution) to a place of execution

tu·mid \'tü-məd, 'tyü-\ *adj* **1** : SWOLLEN, DISTENDED **2** : BOMBASTIC, TURGID

tum·my \'tə-mē\ *n, pl* **tummies** : BELLY, ABDOMEN, STOMACH

tu·mor \'tü-mər, 'tyü-\ *n* : an abnormal and functionless mass of tissue that is not inflammatory and arises from preexistent tissue — **tu·mor·ous** *adj*

tu·mour *chiefly Brit var of* TUMOR

tu·mult \'tü-ˌməlt, 'tyü-\ *n* **1** : UPROAR **2** : violent agitation of mind or feelings

tu·mul·tu·ous \tü-'məl-chə-wəs, tyü-, -chəs\ *adj* **1** : marked by tumult **2** : tending to incite a tumult **3** : marked by violent upheaval

tun \'tən\ *n* : a large cask

tu·na \'tü-nə, 'tyü-\ *n, pl* **tuna** *or* **tunas** [Sp] : any of several mostly large marine fishes related to the mackerels and caught for food and sport; *also* : the flesh of a tuna

tuna

tun·able \'tü-nə-bəl, 'tyü-\ *adj* : capable of being tuned — **tun·abil·i·ty** \ˌtü-nə-'bi-lə-tē, ˌtyü-\ *n*

tun·dra \'tən-drə\ *n* [Russ] : a treeless plain of arctic and subarctic regions

¹**tune** \'tün, 'tyün\ *n* **1** : a succession of pleasing musical tones : MELODY **2** : correct musical pitch **3** : harmonious relationship : AGREEMENT ⟨in ∼ with the times⟩ **4** : general attitude ⟨changed his ∼⟩ **5** : AMOUNT, EXTENT ⟨in debt to the ∼ of millions⟩

²**tune** *vb* **tuned; tun·ing** **1** : to adjust in musical pitch **2** : to bring or come into harmony : ATTUNE **3** : to put in good working order **4** : to adjust a radio or television receiver so as to receive a broadcast **5** : to adjust the frequency of the output of (a device) to a chosen frequency — **tun·er** *n*

tune·ful \-fəl\ *adj* : MELODIOUS, MUSICAL — **tune·ful·ly** *adv* — **tune·ful·ness** *n*

tune·less \-ləs\ *adj* **1** : UNMELODIOUS **2** : not producing music — **tune·less·ly** *adv*

tune-up \'tün-ˌəp, 'tyün-\ *n* : an adjustment to ensure efficient functioning ⟨an engine ∼⟩

tung·sten \'təŋ-stən\ *n* [Sw, fr. *tung* heavy + *sten* stone] : a white hard heavy ductile metallic chemical element used esp. for electrical purposes and in alloys — see ELEMENT table

tu·nic \'tü-nik, 'tyü-\ *n* **1** : a usu. knee-length belted under or outer garment worn by ancient Greeks and Romans **2** : a hip-length or longer blouse or jacket

tuning fork *n* : a 2-pronged metal implement that gives a fixed tone when struck and is useful for tuning musical instruments

Tu·ni·sian \tü-'nē-zhən, tyü-, -'ni-\ *n* : a native or inhabitant of Tunisia — **Tunisian** *adj*

¹**tun·nel** \'tən-ᵊl\ *n* : an enclosed passage (as a tube or conduit); *esp* : one underground (as in a mine)

²**tunnel** *vb* **-neled** *or* **-nelled; -nel·ing** *or* **-nel·ling** : to make a tunnel through or under

tun·ny \'tə-nē\ *n, pl* **tunnies** *also* **tunny** : TUNA

tuque \'tük, 'tyük\ *n* [CanF] : a warm knitted cone-shaped cap

tur·ban \'tər-bən\ *n* **1** : a headdress worn esp. by Muslims and made of a cap around which is wound a long cloth **2** : a headdress resembling a turban; *esp* : a woman's close-fitting hat without a brim

tur·bid \'tər-bəd\ *adj* [L *turbidus* confused, turbid, fr. *turba* confusion, crowd] **1** : cloudy or discolored by suspended particles ⟨a ∼ stream⟩ **2** : CONFUSED, MUDDLED — **tur·bid·i·ty** \ˌtər-'bi-də-tē\ *n*

tur·bine \'tər-bən, -ˌbīn\ *n* [F, fr. L *turbin-, turbo* top, whirlwind, whirl] : an engine whose central driveshaft is fitted with curved vanes spun by the pressure of water, steam, or gas

tur·bo·fan \-ˌfan\ *n* : a jet engine having a fan driven by a turbine for supplying air for combustion

tur·bo·jet \-ˌjet\ *n* : an airplane powered by a jet engine (**turbojet engine**) having a turbine-driven air compressor supplying compressed air to the combustion chamber

tur·bo·prop \-ˌpräp\ *n* : an airplane powered by a jet engine (**turboprop engine**) having a turbine-driven propeller

tur·bot \'tər-bət\ *n, pl* **turbot** *also* **turbots** : a European flatfish that is a popular food fish; *also* : any of several similar flatfishes

tur·bu·lence \'tər-byə-ləns\ *n* : the quality or state of being turbulent

tur·bu·lent \-lənt\ *adj* **1** : causing violence or disturbance **2** : marked by agitation or tumult : TEMPESTUOUS — **tur·bu·lent·ly** *adv*

tu·reen \tə-'rēn, tyù-\ *n* [F *terrine*, fr. MF, fr. fem. of *terrin* of earth] : a deep bowl from which foods (as soup) are served at table

¹**turf** \'tərf\ *n, pl* **turfs** \'tərfs\ *also* **turves** \'tərvz\ **1** : the upper layer of soil bound by grass and roots into a close mat; *also* : a piece of this **2** : an artificial substitute for turf (as on a playing field) **3** : a piece of peat dried for fuel **4** : a track or course for horse racing; *also* : horse racing as a sport or business

²**turf** *vb* : to cover with turf

tur·gid \'tər-jəd\ *adj* 1 : being in a swollen state 2 : excessively embellished in style or language : BOMBASTIC — **tur·gid·i·ty** \ₜtər-'ji-də-tē\ *n*

Turk \'tərk\ *n* : a native or inhabitant of Turkey

tur·key \'tər-kē\ *n, pl* **turkeys** [*Turkey,* country in western Asia and southeastern Europe; fr. confusion with the guinea fowl, supposed to be imported from Turkish territory] : a large American bird related to the domestic chicken and widely raised for food; *also* : its flesh

turkey buzzard *n* : TURKEY VULTURE

turkey vulture *n* : an American vulture with a red head and whitish bill

Turk·ish \'tər-kish\ *n* : the language of Turkey — **Turkish** *adj*

tur·mer·ic \'tər-mə-rik\ *n* : a spice or dyestuff obtained from the large aromatic deep-yellow rhizome of an East Indian perennial herb related to the ginger; *also* : this herb

tur·moil \'tər-ₜmȯil\ *n* : an extremely confused or agitated condition

¹**turn** \'tərn\ *vb* 1 : to move or cause to move around an axis or center : ROTATE, REVOLVE ⟨∼ a wheel⟩ 2 : to effect a desired end by turning something ⟨∼ the oven on⟩ 3 : WRENCH ⟨∼ an ankle⟩ 4 : to change or cause to change position by moving through an arc of a circle ⟨∼ed her chair to the fire⟩ 5 : to cause to move around a center so as to show another side of ⟨∼ a page⟩ 6 : to revolve mentally : PONDER 7 : to become dizzy : REEL 8 : to reverse the sides or surfaces of ⟨∼ a pancake⟩ 9 : UPSET, DISORDER ⟨things were ∼ed topsy-turvy⟩ 10 : to set in another esp. contrary direction 11 : to change one's course or direction 12 : to go around ⟨∼ a corner⟩ 13 : BECOME ⟨my hair ∼ed gray⟩ ⟨∼ed twenty-one⟩ 14 : to direct toward or away from something; *also* : DEVOTE, APPLY 15 : to have recourse 16 : to become or make hostile 17 : to cause to become of a specified nature or appearance ⟨∼s the leaves yellow⟩ 18 : to make or become spoiled : SOUR 19 : to pass from one state to another ⟨water ∼s to ice⟩ 20 : CONVERT, TRANSFORM 21 : TRANSLATE, PARAPHRASE 22 : to give a rounded form to; *esp* : to shape by means of a lathe 23 : to gain by passing in trade ⟨∼ a quick profit⟩ — **turn color** 1 : BLUSH 2 : to become pale — **turn loose** : to set free

²**turn** *n* 1 : a turning about a center or axis : REVOLUTION, ROTATION 2 : the action or an act of giving or taking a different direction ⟨make a left ∼⟩ 3 : a change of course or tendency ⟨a ∼ for the better⟩ 4 : a place at which something turns : BEND, CURVE 5 : a short walk or trip round about ⟨take a ∼ around the block⟩ 6 : an act affecting another ⟨did him a good ∼⟩ 7 : a place, time, or opportunity accorded in a scheduled order ⟨waited his ∼ in line⟩ 8 : a period of duty : SHIFT 9 : a short act esp. in a variety show 10 : a special purpose or requirement ⟨the job serves his ∼⟩ 11 : a skillful fashioning ⟨neat ∼ of phrase⟩ 12 : a single round (as of rope passed around an object) 13 : natural or special aptitude 14 : a usu. sudden and brief disorder of body or spirits; *esp* : a spell of nervous shock or faintness

turn·about \'tər-nə-ₜbau̇t\ *n* 1 : a reversal of direction, trend, or policy 2 : RETALIATION

turn·buck·le \'tərn-ₜbə-kəl\ *n* : a link with a screw thread at one or both ends for tightening a rod or stay

turn·coat \-ₜkōt\ *n* : one who switches to an opposing side or party : TRAITOR

turn down *vb* : to decline to accept : REJECT — **turndown** \'tərn-ₜdau̇n\ *n*

turn·er \'tər-nər\ *n* 1 : one that turns or is used for turning 2 : one that forms articles with a lathe

turn·ery \'tər-nə-rē\ *n, pl* **-er·ies** : the work, products, or shop of a turner

turn in *vb* 1 : to deliver up 2 : to inform on 3 : to acquit oneself of ⟨*turn in* a good job⟩ 4 : to go to bed

turn·ing *n* 1 : the act or course of one that turns 2 : a place of a change of direction

tur·nip \'tər-nəp\ *n* 1 : a garden herb related to the cabbage with a thick edible usu. white root 2 : RUTABAGA 3 : the root of a turnip

turn·key \'tərn-ₜkē\ *n, pl* **turnkeys** : one who has charge of a prison's keys

turn·off \'tərn-ₜȯf\ *n* : a place for turning off esp. from an expressway

turn off *vb* 1 : to deviate from a straight course or a main road 2 : to stop the functioning or flow of 3 : to cause to lose interest; *also* : to evoke a negative feeling in

turn on *vb* 1 : to cause to flow, function, or operate 2 : to get high or cause to get high as a result of using a drug (as marijuana) 3 : EXCITE, STIMULATE

turn·out \'tərn-ₜau̇t\ *n* 1 : an act of turning out 2 : the number of people who participate or attend an event 3 : a widened place in a highway for vehicles to pass or park 4 : manner of dress 5 : net yield : OUTPUT

turn out *vb* 1 : EXPEL, EVICT 2 : PRODUCE 3 : to come forth and assemble 4 : to get out of bed 5 : to prove to be in the end

¹**turn·over** \'tər-ₜnō-vər\ *n* 1 : UPSET 2 : SHIFT, REVERSAL 3 : a filled pastry made by turning half of the crust over the other half 4 : the volume of business done 5 : movement (as of goods or people) into, through, and out of a place 6 : the number of persons hired within a period to replace those leaving or dropped 7 : an instance of a team's losing possession of the ball esp. through error

²**turnover** *adj* : capable of being turned over

turn over *vb* : TRANSFER ⟨*turn* the job *over* to her⟩

turn·pike \'tərn-ₜpīk\ *n* [ME *turnepike* revolving frame bearing spikes and serving as a barrier, fr. *turnen* to turn + *pike*] 1 : TOLLGATE; *also* : an expressway on which tolls are charged 2 : a main road

turn·stile \-ₜstīl\ *n* : a post with arms pivoted on the top set in a passageway so that persons can pass through only on foot one by one

turn·ta·ble \-ₜtā-bəl\ *n* : a circular platform that revolves (as for turning a locomotive or a phonograph record)

turn to *vb* : to apply oneself to work

turn up *vb* 1 : to come to light or bring to light : DISCOVER, APPEAR 2 : to arrive at an appointed time or place 3 : to happen unexpectedly

tur·pen·tine \'tər-pən-ₜtīn\ *n* 1 : a mixture of oil and resin obtained from various cone-bearing trees (as pines) 2 : an oil distilled from turpentine or pine wood and used as a solvent and paint thinner

tur·pi·tude \'tər-pə-ₜtüd, -ₜtyüd\ *n* : inherent baseness : DEPRAVITY

tur·quoise *also* **tur·quois** \'tər-ₜkȯiz, -ₜkwȯiz\ *n* [ME *turkeis, turcas,* fr. MF *turquoyse,* fr. fem. of *turquoys* Turkish, fr. OF, fr. *Turc* Turk] 1 : a blue, bluish green, or greenish gray mineral that is valued as a gem 2 : a light greenish blue color

tur·ret \'tər-ət\ *n* 1 : a little tower often at an angle of a larger structure and merely ornamental 2 : a low usu. revolving structure (as on a tank or warship) in which one or more guns are mounted

¹**tur·tle** \'tərt-ᵊl\ *n, archaic* : TURTLEDOVE

²**turtle** *n, pl* **turtles** *also* **turtle** : any of an order of horny= beaked land, freshwater, or sea reptiles with the trunk enclosed in a bony shell

tur·tle·dove \'tərt-ᵊl-ₜdəv\ *n* : any of several small pigeons noted for plaintive cooing

tur·tle·neck \-ₜnek\ *n* : a high close-fitting turnover collar (as on a sweater); *also* : a sweater or shirt with a turtleneck — **tur·tle·necked** \-ₜnekt\ *adj*

\ə\abut \ᵊ\kitten \ər\further \a\ash \ā\ace \ä\mop, mar \au̇\out \ch\chin \e\bet \ē\easy \g\go \i\hit \ī\ice \j\job \ŋ\sing \ō\go \ȯ\law \ȯi\boy \th\thin \th̲\the \ü\loot \u̇\foot \y\yet \zh\vision *see also* Pronunciation Symbols page

turves pl of TURF

Tus·ca·ro·ra \ˌtəs-kə-ˈrōr-ə\ n, pl **Tuscarora** or **Tusca-roras** : a member of an American Indian people of No. Carolina and later of New York and Ontario

tusk \ˈtəsk\ n : a long enlarged protruding tooth (as of an elephant, walrus, or boar) used esp. to dig up food or as a weapon — **tusked** \ˈtəskt\ adj

tusk·er \ˈtəs-kər\ n : an animal with tusks; esp : a male elephant with two normally developed tusks

¹**tus·sle** \ˈtə-səl\ n 1 : a physical struggle : SCUFFLE 2 : an intense argument, controversy, or struggle

²**tussle** vb **tus·sled; tus·sling** : to struggle roughly

tus·sock \ˈtə-sək\ n : a dense tuft esp. of grass or sedge; also : a hummock in a marsh or bog bound together by roots — **tus·socky** adj

tu·te·lage \ˈtüt-ᵊl-ij, ˈtyüt-\ n 1 : an act of guarding or protecting 2 : the state of being under a guardian or tutor 3 : instruction esp. of an individual

tu·te·lary \ˈtüt-ᵊl-ˌer-ē, ˈtyüt-\ adj : acting as a guardian ⟨∼ deity⟩

¹**tu·tor** \ˈtü-tər, ˈtyü-\ n 1 : a person charged with the instruction and guidance of another 2 : a private teacher

²**tutor** vb 1 : to have the guardianship of 2 : to teach or guide individually : COACH ⟨∼ed her in Latin⟩ 3 : to receive instruction esp. privately

tu·to·ri·al \tü-ˈtōr-ē-əl, tyü-\ n : a class conducted by a tutor for one student or a small number of students

tut·ti \ˈtü-tē, ˈtù-, -ˌtē\ adj or adv [It, pl. of tutto all] : with all voices and instruments playing together — used as a direction in music

tut·ti-frut·ti \ˌtü-ti-ˈfrü-tē, ˌtù-\ n [It, lit., all fruits] : a confection or ice cream containing chopped usu. candied fruits

tux·e·do \ˌtək-ˈsē-dō\ n, pl **-dos** or **-does** [Tuxedo Park, N.Y.] 1 : a usu. black or blackish blue jacket 2 : semiformal evening clothes for men

TV \ˈtē-ˈvē\ n : TELEVISION

TVA abbr Tennessee Valley Authority

TV dinner n : a frozen packaged dinner that needs only heating before serving

twad·dle \ˈtwäd-ᵊl\ n : silly idle talk : DRIVEL — **twaddle** vb

twain \ˈtwān\ n 1 : TWO 2 : PAIR

¹**twang** \ˈtwaŋ\ n 1 : a harsh quick ringing sound like that of a plucked bowstring 2 : nasal speech or resonance 3 : the characteristic speech of a region

²**twang** vb **twanged; twang·ing** 1 : to sound or cause to sound with a twang 2 : to speak with a nasal twang

tweak \ˈtwēk\ vb : to pinch and pull with a sudden jerk and twitch — **tweak** n

tweed \ˈtwēd\ n 1 : a rough woolen fabric made usu. in twill weaves 2 pl : tweed clothing; esp : a tweed suit

tweedy \ˈtwē-dē\ adj **tweed·i·er; -est** 1 : of or resembling tweed 2 : given to wearing tweeds 3 : suggestive of the outdoors in taste or habits

tween \ˈtwēn\ prep : BETWEEN

tweet \ˈtwēt\ n : a chirping note — **tweet** vb

tweet·er \ˈtwē-tər\ n : a small loudspeaker that reproduces sounds of high pitch

twee·zers \ˈtwē-zərz\ n pl [obs. E tweeze, n., case for small implements, short for obs. E etweese, fr. pl. of obs. E etwee, fr. F étui] : a small pincerlike implement held between the thumb and forefinger for grasping something

twelve \ˈtwelv\ n 1 : one more than 11 2 : the 12th in a set or series 3 : something having 12 units — **twelfth** \ˈtwelfth\ adj or n — **twelve** adj or pron

twelve·month \-ˌmənth\ n : YEAR

twen·ty \ˈtwen-tē\ n, pl **twenties** : two times 10 — **twen-ti·eth** \-tē-əth\ adj or n — **twenty** adj or pron

twenty-twenty or **20/20** \ˌtwen-tē-ˈtwen-tē\ adj : characterized by a visual capacity for seeing detail that is normal for the human eye ⟨∼ vision⟩

twice \ˈtwīs\ adv 1 : on two occasions 2 : two times ⟨∼ two is four⟩

¹**twid·dle** \ˈtwid-ᵊl\ vb **twid·dled; twid·dling** 1 : to be busy with trifles; also : to play idly with something 2 : to rotate lightly or idly

²**twiddle** n : TURN, TWIST

twig \ˈtwig\ n : a small branch — **twig·gy** adj

twi·light \ˈtwī-ˌlīt\ n 1 : the light from the sky between full night and sunrise or between sunset and full night 2 : a state of imperfect clarity; also : a period of decline

twilight zone n 1 : TWILIGHT 2; also : an area just beyond ordinary legal or ethical limits 2 : a world of fantasy or unreality

twill \ˈtwil\ n [ME twyll, fr. OE twilic having a double thread, part trans. of L bilic-, bilix, fr. bi- two + licium thread] 1 : a fabric with a twill weave 2 : a textile weave that gives an appearance of diagonal lines

twilled \ˈtwild\ adj : made with a twill weave

¹**twin** \ˈtwin\ n 1 : either of two offspring produced at a birth 2 : one of two persons or things closely related to or resembling each other

²**twin** vb **twinned; twin·ning** 1 : to be coupled with another 2 : to bring forth twins

³**twin** adj 1 : born with one another or as a pair at one birth ⟨∼ brother⟩ ⟨∼ girls⟩ 2 : made up of two similar or related members or parts 3 : being one of a pair ⟨∼ city⟩

¹**twine** \ˈtwīn\ n 1 : a strong thread of two or three strands twisted together 2 : an act of entwining or interlacing — **twiny** adj

²**twine** vb **twined; twin·ing** 1 : to twist together; also : to form by twisting 2 : INTERLACE, WEAVE 3 : to coil about a support 4 : to stretch or move in a sinuous manner — **twin·er** n

¹**twinge** \ˈtwinj\ vb **twinged; twing·ing** or **twinge·ing** : to affect with or feel a sharp sudden pain

²**twinge** n : a sudden sharp stab (as of pain or distress)

¹**twin·kle** \ˈtwiŋ-kəl\ vb **twin·kled; twin·kling** 1 : to shine or cause to shine with a flickering or sparkling light 2 : to appear bright with merriment 3 : to flutter or flit rapidly — **twin·kler** n

²**twinkle** n 1 : a wink of the eyelids; also : the duration of a wink 2 : an intermittent radiance 3 : a rapid flashing motion — **twin·kly** \ˈtwiŋ-klē\ adj

twin·kling \ˈtwiŋ-kliŋ\ n : the time required for a wink : INSTANT

¹**twirl** \ˈtwərl\ vb : to turn or cause to turn rapidly ⟨∼ a baton⟩ **syn** revolve, rotate, circle, spin, swirl, pirouette — **twirl·er** n

²**twirl** n 1 : an act of twirling 2 : COIL, WHORL — **twirly** \ˈtwər-lē\ adj

¹**twist** \ˈtwist\ vb 1 : to unite by winding one thread or strand round another 2 : WREATHE, TWINE 3 : to turn so as to hurt ⟨∼ed her ankle⟩ 4 : to twirl into spiral shape 5 : to subject (as a shaft) to torsion 6 : to turn from the true form or meaning 7 : to pull off or break by torsion 8 : to follow a winding course 9 : to turn around

²**twist** n 1 : something formed by twisting or winding 2 : an act of twisting : the state of being twisted 3 : a spiral turn or curve; also : SPIN 4 : a turning aside 5 : ECCENTRICITY 6 : a distortion of meaning 7 : an unexpected turn or development 8 : DEVICE, TRICK 9 : a variant approach or method

twist·er \ˈtwis-tər\ n 1 : one that twists; esp : a ball with a forward and spinning motion 2 : TORNADO; also : WATERSPOUT 2

¹**twit** \ˈtwit\ n : FOOL

²**twit** vb **twit·ted; twit·ting** : to ridicule as a fault; also : TAUNT **syn** deride, mock, razz

¹**twitch** \ˈtwich\ vb 1 : to move or pull with a sudden motion : JERK 2 : to move jerkily : QUIVER

²**twitch** n 1 : an act or movement of twitching 2 : a short sharp contraction of muscle fibers

¹twit·ter \'twi-tər\ *vb* **1** : to make a succession of chirping noises **2** : to talk in a chattering fashion **3** : to tremble with agitation : FLUTTER

²twitter *n* **1** : a slight agitation of the nerves **2** : a small tremulous intermittent noise (as made by a swallow) **3** : a light chattering

twixt \'twikst\ *prep* : BETWEEN

two \'tü\ *n, pl* **twos 1** : one more than one **2** : the second in a set or series **3** : something having two units — **two** *adj or pron*

two cents *n* **1** : a sum or object of very small value **2** *or* **two cents worth** : an opinion offered on a topic under discussion

two–faced \'tü-ˌfāst\ *adj* **1** : DOUBLE-DEALING, FALSE **2** : having two faces

two·fold \'tü-ˌfōld, -'fōld\ *adj* **1** : having two units or members **2** : being twice as much or as many — **two·fold** \-'fōld\ *adv*

2,4–D \ˌtü-ˌfōr-'dē\ *n* : an irritant compound used esp. as a weed killer

2,4,5–T \-ˌfīv-'tē\ *n* : an irritant compound used esp. as an herbicide and defoliant

two·pence \'tə-pəns, *US also* 'tü-ˌpens\ *n* : the sum of two pence

two·pen·ny \'tə-pə-nē, *US also* 'tü-ˌpe-nē\ *adj* : of the value of or costing twopence

two–ply \'tü-ˌplī\ *adj* **1** : woven as a double cloth **2** : consisting of two strands or thicknesses

two·some \'tü-səm\ *n* **1** : a group of two persons or things : COUPLE **2** : a golf match between two players

two–step \'tü-ˌstep\ *n* : a ballroom dance performed with a sliding step in march or polka time; *also* : a piece of music for this dance — **two–step** *vb*

two–time \'tü-ˌtīm\ *vb* : to betray (a spouse or lover) by secret lovemaking with another — **two–tim·er** *n*

two–way *adj* : involving two elements or allowing movement or use in two directions or manners

2WD *abbr* two-wheel drive

twp *abbr* township

TWX *abbr* teletypewriter exchange

TX *abbr* Texas

-ty *n suffix* : quality : condition : degree ⟨real*ty*⟩

ty·coon \tī-'kün\ *n* [Jp *taikun*] **1** : a masterful leader (as in politics) **2** : a powerful businessman or industrialist

tying *pres part of* TIE

tyke \'tīk\ *n* : a small child

tym·pan·ic membrane \tim-'pa-nik-\ *n* : EARDRUM

tym·pa·num \'tim-pə-nəm\ *n, pl* **-na** \-nə\ *also* **-nums** : EARDRUM; *also* : MIDDLE EAR — **tym·pan·ic** \tim-'pa-nik\ *adj*

¹type \'tīp\ *n* [ME, fr. LL *typus*, fr. L & Gk; L *typus* image, fr. Gk *typos* blow, impression, model, fr. *typtein* to strike, beat] **1** : a person, thing, or event that foreshadows another to come : TOKEN, SYMBOL **2** : MODEL, EXAMPLE **3** : a distinctive stamp, mark, or sign : EMBLEM **4** : rectangular blocks usu. of metal each having a face so shaped as to produce a character when printed **5** : the letters or characters printed from or as if from type **6** : general character or form common to a number of individuals and setting them off as a distinguishable class ⟨horses of draft ∼⟩ **7** : a class, kind, or group set apart by common characteristics ⟨a seedless ∼ of orange⟩; *also* : something distinguishable as a variety ⟨reactions of this ∼⟩ **syn** sort, nature, character, description

²type *vb* **typed; typ·ing 1** : to represent beforehand as a type **2** : to produce a copy of; *also* : REPRESENT, TYPIFY **3** : to write with a typewriter **4** : to identify as belonging to a type **5** : TYPECAST

type·cast \-ˌkast\ *vb* **-cast; -cast·ing 1** : to cast (an actor) in a part calling for characteristics possessed by the actor **2** : to cast repeatedly in the same type of role

type·face \-ˌfās\ *n* : all type of a single design

type·script \'tīp-ˌskript\ *n* : typewritten matter

type·set \-ˌset\ *vb* **-set; -set·ting** : to set in type : COMPOSE — **type·set·ter** *n*

type·write \-ˌrīt\ *vb* **-wrote** \-ˌrōt\; **-writ·ten** \-ˌrit-ᵊn\ : TYPE 3

type·writ·er \-ˌrī-tər\ *n* **1** : a machine for writing in characters similar to those produced by printers' type by means of types striking a ribbon to transfer ink or carbon impressions onto paper **2** : TYPIST

type·writ·ing \-ˌrī-tiŋ\ *n* : the use of a typewriter ⟨teach ∼⟩; *also* : writing produced with a typewriter

¹ty·phoid \'tī-ˌfȯid, tī-'fȯid\ *adj* : of, relating to, or being a communicable bacterial disease (**typhoid fever**) marked by fever, diarrhea, prostration, and intestinal inflammation

²typhoid *n* : TYPHOID FEVER

ty·phoon \tī-'fün\ *n* : a tropical cyclone in the region of the Philippines or the China sea

ty·phus \'tī-fəs\ *n* : a severe infectious disease transmitted esp. by body lice, caused by a rickettsia, and marked by high fever, stupor and delirium, intense headache, and a dark red rash

typ·i·cal \'ti-pi-kəl\ *adj* **1** : being or having the nature of a type **2** : exhibiting the essential characteristics of a group **3** : conforming to a type — **typ·i·cal·i·ty** \ˌti-pə-'ka-lə-tō\ *n* **typ·i·cal·ness** *n*

typ·i·cal·ly \-pi-k(ə-)lē\ *adv* **1** : in a typical manner **2** : in typical circumstances

typ·i·fy \'ti-pə-ˌfī\ *vb* **-fied; -fy·ing 1** : to represent by an image, form, model, or resemblance **2** : to embody the essential or common characteristics of

typ·ist \'tī-pist\ *n* : one who operates a typewriter

ty·po \'tī-pō\ *n, pl* **typos** : an error in typing or in setting type

ty·pog·ra·pher \tī-'pä-grə-fər\ *n* : one who designs or arranges printing

ty·pog·ra·phy \tī-'pä-grə-fē\ *n* : the art of printing with type; *also* : the style, arrangement, or appearance of printed matter — **ty·po·graph·ic** \ˌtī-pə-'gra-fik\ *or* **ty·po·graph·i·cal** \-fi-kəl\ *adj* — **ty·po·graph·i·cal·ly** *adv*

ty·ran·ni·cal \tə-'ra-ni-kəl, tī-\ *also* **ty·ran·nic** \-nik\ *adj* : of or relating to a tyrant : DESPOTIC **syn** arbitrary, absolute, autocratic — **ty·ran·ni·cal·ly** \-ni-k(ə-)lē\ *adv*

tyr·an·nize \'tir-ə-ˌnīz\ *vb* **-nized; -niz·ing** : to act as a tyrant : rule with unjust severity — **tyr·an·niz·er** *n*

ty·ran·no·saur \tə-'ra-nə-ˌsȯr\ *n* : a very large American flesh-eating dinosaur of the Cretaceous that had small forelegs and walked on its hind legs

ty·ran·no·sau·rus \tə-ˌra-nə-'sȯr-əs\ *n* : TYRANNOSAUR

tyr·an·nous \'tir-ə-nəs\ *adj* : TYRANNICAL — **tyr·an·nous·ly** *adv*

tyr·an·ny \'tir-ə-nē\ *n, pl* **-nies 1** : oppressive power **2** : the rule or authority of a tyrant : government in which absolute power is vested in a single ruler **3** : a tyrannical act

ty·rant \'tī-rənt\ *n* **1** : an absolute ruler : DESPOT **2** : a ruler who governs oppressively or brutally **3** : one who uses authority or power harshly

tyre *chiefly Brit var of* TIRE

ty·ro \'tī-rō\ *n, pl* **tyros** [ML, fr. L *tiro* young soldier, tyro] : a beginner in learning : NOVICE

tzar \'zär, 'tsär, 'sär\ *var of* CZAR

U

¹**u** \'yü\ *n, pl* **u's** *or* **us** \'yüz\ *often cap* : the 21st letter of the English alphabet
²**u** *abbr, often cap* unit
¹**U** \'yü\ *adj* : characteristic of the upper classes
²**U** *abbr* 1 [abbr. of *Union of Orthodox Hebrew Congregations*] kosher certification — often enclosed in a circle 2 university 3 unsatisfactory
³**U** *symbol* uranium
UAE *abbr* United Arab Emirates
UAR *abbr* United Arab Republic
UAW *abbr* United Automobile Workers
ubiq·ui·tous \yü-'bi-kwə-təs\ *adj* : existing or being everywhere at the same time : OMNIPRESENT — **ubiq·ui·tous·ly** *adv* — **ubiq·ui·ty** \-kwə-tē\ *n*
U–boat \'yü-ˌbōt\ *n* [trans. of G *U-boot*, short for *Unterseeboot*, lit., undersea boat] : a German submarine
UC *abbr* uppercase
ud·der \'ə-dər\ *n* : an organ (as of a cow) consisting of two or more milk glands enclosed in a large hanging sac and each provided with a nipple
UFO \ˌyü-(ˌ)ef-'ō\ *n, pl* **UFO's** *or* **UFOs** \-'ōz\ : an unidentified flying object; *esp* : FLYING SAUCER
Ugan·dan \ü-'gan-dən, yü-, -'gän-\ *n* : a native or inhabitant of Uganda — **Ugandan** *adj*
ug·ly \'ə-glē\ *adj* **ug·li·er; -est** [ME, fr. ON *ugligr*, fr. *uggr* fear] 1 : FRIGHTFUL, DIRE 2 : offensive to the sight : HIDEOUS 3 : offensive or unpleasant to any sense 4 : morally objectionable : REPULSIVE 5 : likely to cause inconvenience or discomfort 6 : SURLY, QUARRELSOME ⟨an ∼ disposition⟩ — **ug·li·ness** \-glē-nəs\ *n*
UHF *abbr* ultrahigh frequency
UK *abbr* United Kingdom
ukase \yü-'kās, -'kāz\ *n* [F & Russ; F, fr. Russ *ukaz*, fr. *ukazat'* to show, order] : an edict esp. of a Russian emperor or government
Ukrai·ni·an \yü-'krā-nē-ən\ *n* : a native or inhabitant of Ukraine — **Ukrainian** *adj*
uku·le·le *also* **uke·le·le** \ˌyü-kə-'lā-lē\ *n* [Hawaiian *'ukulele*, fr. *'uku* flea + *lele* jumping] : a small usu. 4-stringed guitar popularized in Hawaii
ul·cer \'əl-sər\ *n* 1 : an open eroded sore of skin or mucous membrane often discharging pus 2 : something that festers and corrupts like an open sore — **ul·cer·ous** *adj*
ul·cer·ate \'əl-sə-ˌrāt\ *vb* **-at·ed; -at·ing** : to become affected with an ulcer — **ul·cer·ative** \'əl-sə-ˌrā-tiv\ *adj*
ul·cer·ation \ˌəl-sə-'rā-shən\ *n* 1 : the process of forming or state of having an ulcer 2 : ULCER 1
ul·na \'əl-nə\ *n* : the bone on the little-finger side of the human forearm; *also* : a corresponding bone of the forelimb of vertebrates above fishes
ul·ster \'əl-stər\ *n* : a long loose overcoat
ult *abbr* 1 ultimate 2 ultimo
ul·te·ri·or \ˌəl-'tir-ē-ər\ *adj* 1 : lying farther away : more remote 2 : situated beyond or on the farther side 3 : going beyond what is openly said or shown : HIDDEN ⟨∼ motives⟩
¹**ul·ti·mate** \'əl-tə-mət\ *adj* 1 : most remote in space or time : FARTHEST 2 : last in a progression : FINAL 3 : the best or most extreme of its kind 4 : arrived at as the last resort 5 : FUNDAMENTAL, ABSOLUTE, SUPREME ⟨∼ reality⟩ 6 : incapable of further analysis or division : ELEMENTAL 7 : MAXIMUM **syn** concluding, eventual, latest, terminal — **ul·ti·mate·ly** *adv*
²**ultimate** *n* : something ultimate
ul·ti·ma·tum \ˌəl-tə-'mā-təm, -'mä-\ *n, pl* **-tums** *or* **-ta**

\-tə\ : a final condition or demand whose rejection will bring about a resort to forceful action
ul·ti·mo \'əl-tə-ˌmō\ *adj* [L *ultimo mense* in the last month] : of or occurring in the month preceding the present
¹**ul·tra** \'əl-trə\ *adj* : going beyond others or beyond due limits : EXTREME
²**ultra** *n* : EXTREMIST
ul·tra·con·ser·va·tive \-kən-'sər-və-tiv\ *adj* : extremely conservative
ul·tra·high frequency \-'hī-\ *n* : a radio frequency between 300 and 3000 megahertz
¹**ul·tra·light** \'əl-trə-ˌlīt\ *adj* : extremely light esp. in weight
²**ultralight** *n* : a very light recreational aircraft typically carrying only one person
ul·tra·ma·rine \ˌəl-trə-mə-'rēn\ *n* 1 : a deep blue pigment 2 : a very bright deep blue color
ul·tra·mi·cro·scop·ic \-ˌmī-krə-'skä-pik\ *adj* : too small to be seen with an ordinary microscope
ul·tra·mod·ern \-'mä-dərn\ *adj* : extremely or excessively modern in idea, style, or tendency
ul·tra·mon·tane \-'män-ˌtān, -ˌmän-'tān\ *adj* 1 : of or relating to countries or peoples beyond the mountains (as the Alps) 2 : favoring greater or absolute supremacy of papal authority in the Roman Catholic Church — **ultramontane** *n, often cap* — **ul·tra·mon·tan·ism** \-'mänt-ᵊn-ˌi-zəm\ *n*
ul·tra·pure \-'pyùr\ *adj* : of the utmost purity
ul·tra·short \-'shòrt\ *adj* 1 : having a wavelength below 10 meters 2 : very short in duration
ul·tra·son·ic \ˌəl-trə-'sä-nik\ *adj* : having a frequency too high to be heard by the human ear — **ul·tra·son·i·cal·ly** \-ni-k(ə-)lē\ *adv*
ul·tra·son·ics \-'sä-niks\ *n sing or pl* 1 : ultrasonic vibrations 2 : the science of ultrasonic phenomena
ul·tra·sound \-ˌsaùnd\ *n* 1 : ultrasonic vibrations 2 : the diagnostic or therapeutic use of ultrasound to form a two-dimensional image of internal body structures 3 : a diagnostic examination using ultrasound
ul·tra·vi·o·let \-'vī-ə-lət\ *adj* : having a wavelength shorter than those of visible light and longer than those of X rays ⟨∼ radiation⟩; *also* : producing or employing ultraviolet radiation — **ultraviolet** *n*
ul·tra vi·res \ˌəl-trə-'vī-rēz\ *adv or adj* [NL, lit., beyond power] : beyond the scope of legal power or authority
ul·u·late \'əl-yə-ˌlāt\ *vb* **-lat·ed; -lat·ing** : HOWL, WAIL
um·bel \'əm-bəl\ *n* : a flat-topped or rounded flower cluster in which the individual flower stalks all arise near one point on the main stem
um·ber \'əm-bər\ *n* : a brown earthy substance valued as a pigment either in its raw state or burnt — **umber** *adj*
umbilical cord *n* : a cord containing blood vessels that connects the navel of a fetus with the placenta of its mother
um·bi·li·cus \ˌəm-'bi-li-kəs, ˌəm-bə-'lī-\ *n, pl* **um·bi·li·ci** \ˌəm-'bi-lə-ˌkī; ˌəm-bə-'lī-ˌkī, -ˌsī\ *or* **um·bi·li·cus·es** : NAVEL — **um·bil·i·cal** \ˌəm-'bi-li-kəl\ *adj*
um·bra \'əm-brə\ *n, pl* **umbras** *or* **um·brae** \-(ˌ)brē, -ˌbrī\ 1 : SHADE, SHADOW 2 : the conical part of the shadow of a celestial body from which the sun's light is completely blocked
um·brage \'əm-brij\ *n* 1 : SHADE; *also* : FOLIAGE 2 : RESENTMENT, OFFENSE ⟨take ∼ at a remark⟩
um·brel·la \ˌəm-'bre-lə\ *n* 1 : a collapsible shade for pro-

tection against weather consisting of fabric stretched over hinged ribs radiating from a center pole **2** : something that resembles an umbrella in shape or purpose

umi·ak \'ü-mē-ₐak\ *n* : an open Eskimo boat made of a wooden frame covered with skins

umiak

um·pire \'əm-ₚpīr\ *n* [ME *oumpere,* alter. of *noumpere* (the phrase *a noumpere* being understood as *an oumpere*), fr. MF *nomper* not equal, not paired, fr. *non* not + *per* equal, fr. L *par*] **1** : one having authority to decide finally a controversy or question between parties **2** : an official in a sport who rules on plays — **umpire** *vb*

ump·teen \'əmp-ₜtēn\ *adj* : very many : indefinitely numerous — **ump·teenth** \-ₜtēnth\ *adj*

UN *abbr* United Nations

un- \ₚən, 'ən\ *prefix* **1** : not : IN-, NON- **2** : opposite of : contrary to

unabashed	unashamed
unabated	unasked
unabsorbed	unassertive
unabsorbent	unassisted
unacademic	unathletic
unaccented	unattainable
unacceptable	unattended
unacclimatized	unattested
unaccommodating	unattractive
unaccredited	unauthentic
unacknowledged	unauthorized
unacquainted	unavailable
unadapted	unavowed
unadjusted	unawakened
unadorned	unbaked
unadventurous	unbaptized
unadvertised	unbeloved
unaesthetic	unbleached
unaffiliated	unblemished
unafraid	unblinking
unaggressive	unbound
unaided	unbranched
unalike	unbranded
unaltered	unbreakable
unambiguous	unbridgeable
unambiguously	unbruised
unambitious	unbrushed
unanchored	unbudging
unannounced	unburied
unanswerable	unburned
unanswered	uncanceled
unanticipated	uncanonical
unapologetic	uncap
unapparent	uncapitalized
unappealing	uncared–for
unappeased	uncataloged
unappetizing	uncaught
unappreciated	uncensored
unappreciative	uncensured
unapproachable	unchallenged
unappropriated	unchangeable
unapproved	unchanged
unarguable	unchanging
unarguably	unchaperoned
unarmored	uncharacteristic
unartistic	unchaste

unchastely	undated
unchasteness	undecided
unchastity	undecipherable
unchecked	undeclared
unchivalrous	undecorated
unchristened	undefeated
unclad	undefended
unclaimed	undefiled
unclassified	undefinable
uncleaned	undefined
unclear	undemanding
uncleared	undemocratic
unclouded	undenominational
uncluttered	undependable
uncoated	undeserved
uncollected	undeserving
uncolored	undesired
uncombed	undetected
uncombined	undetermined
uncomely	undeterred
uncomic	undeveloped
uncommercial	undifferentiated
uncompensated	undigested
uncomplaining	undignified
uncompleted	undiluted
uncomplicated	undiminished
uncomplimentary	undimmed
uncompounded	undiplomatic
uncomprehending	undirected
unconcealed	undisciplined
unconfined	undisclosed
unconfirmed	undiscovered
unconformable	undiscriminating
uncongenial	undisguised
unconnected	undismayed
unconquered	undisputed
unconsecrated	undissolved
unconsidered	undistinguished
unconsolidated	undistributed
unconstrained	undisturbed
unconsumed	undivided
unconsummated	undocumented
uncontaminated	undogmatic
uncontested	undomesticated
uncontrolled	undone
uncontroversial	undoubled
unconverted	undramatic
unconvincing	undraped
uncooked	undreamed
uncooperative	undressed
uncoordinated	undrinkable
uncorrected	undulled
uncorroborated	undutiful
uncountable	undyed
uncreative	uneager
uncredited	uneatable
uncropped	uneaten
uncrowded	uneconomic
uncrowned	uneconomical
uncrystallized	unedifying
uncultivated	unedited
uncultured	uneducated
uncured	unembarrassed
uncurious	unemotional
uncurtained	unemphatic
uncustomary	unenclosed
undamaged	unencumbered
undamped	unendurable

\ə\abut \ᵊ\kitten \ər\further \a\ash \ā\ace \ä\mop, mar
\au̇\out \ch\chin \e\bet \ē\easy \g\go \i\hit \ī\ice \j\job
\ŋ\sing \ō\go \ȯ\law \ȯi\boy \th\thin \t͟h\the \ü\loot \u̇\foot
\y\yet \zh\vision *see also* Pronunciation Symbols page

unenforceable
unenforced
unenlightened
unenterprising
unenthusiastic
unenviable
unequipped
unessential
unethical
unexamined
unexcelled
unexceptional
unexcited
unexciting
unexpired
unexplained
unexploded
unexplored
unexposed
unexpressed
unexpurgated
unfading
unfaltering
unfashionable
unfashionably
unfathomable
unfavorable
unfavorably
unfeasible
unfeminine
unfenced
unfermented
unfertilized
unfilled
unfiltered
unfitted
unflagging
unflattering
unflavored
unfocused
unfolded
unforced
unforeseeable
unforeseen
unforgivable
unforgiving
unformulated
unfortified
unframed
unfree
unfulfilled
unfunded
unfunny
unfurnished
unfussy
ungentle
ungentlemanly
ungerminated
unglamorous
unglazed
ungoverned
ungraceful
ungracefully
ungraded
ungrammatical
unground
ungrudging
unguided
unhackneyed
unhampered
unhardened
unharmed
unharvested

unhatched
unhealed
unhealthful
unheated
unheeded
unhelpful
unheralded
unheroic
unhesitating
unhindered
unhistorical
unhonored
unhoused
unhurried
unhurt
unhygienic
unidentifiable
unidentified
unidiomatic
unimaginable
unimaginative
unimpaired
unimpassioned
unimpeded
unimportant
unimposing
unimpressed
unimpressive
unimproved
unincorporated
uninfected
uninfluenced
uninformative
uninformed
uninhabitable
uninhabited
uninitiated
uninjured
uninspired
uninstructed
uninstructive
uninsured
unintended
unintentional
unintentionally
uninteresting
uninvited
uninviting
unjointed
unjustifiable
unjustified
unkept
unknowable
unknowledgeable
unlabeled
unladylike
unlamented
unleavened
unlicensed
unlighted
unlikable
unlimited
unlined
unlit
unliterary
unlivable
unlovable
unloved
unloving
unmade
unmalicious
unmanageable
unmanned

unmapped
unmarked
unmarketable
unmarred
unmarried
unmasculine
unmatched
unmeant
unmeasurable
unmeasured
unmelodious
unmentioned
unmerited
unmilitary
unmilled
unmixed
unmodified
unmolested
unmotivated
unmounted
unmovable
unmoved
unmusical
unnameable
unnamed
unnecessary
unneeded
unnewsworthy
unnoticeable
unnoticed
unobjectionable
unobservant
unobserved
unobstructed
unobtainable
unofficial
unofficially
unopened
unopposed
unoriginal
unorthodox
unorthodoxy
unostentatious
unowned
unpaged
unpaid
unpainted
unpaired
unpalatable
unpardonable
unpasteurized
unpatriotic
unpaved
unpeeled
unperceived
unperceptive
unperformed
unpersuaded
unpersuasive
unperturbed
unplanned
unplanted
unpleasing
unplowed
unpoetic
unpolished
unpolitical
unpolluted
unposed
unpractical
unpredictable
unpredictability
unprejudiced

unpremeditated
unprepared
unpreparedness
unprepossessing
unpressed
unpretending
unpretty
unprivileged
unprocessed
unproductive
unprofessed
unprofessional
unprogrammed
unprogressive
unpromising
unprompted
unpronounceable
unpropitious
unprotected
unproven
unprovided
unprovoked
unpublished
unpunished
unquenchable
unquestioned
unraised
unrated
unratified
unreachable
unreadable
unready
unrealistic
unrealized
unrecognizable
unrecognized
unrecorded
unrecoverable
unredeemable
unrefined
unreflecting
unreflective
unregistered
unregulated
unrehearsed
unrelated
unreliable
unrelieved
unremarkable
unremembered
unremovable
unrepentant
unreported
unrepresentative
unrepresented
unrepressed
unresistant
unresisting
unresolved
unresponsive
unresponsiveness
unrestful
unrestricted
unreturnable
unrewarding
unrhymed
unrhythmic
unripened
unromantic
unromantically
unsafe
unsaid
unsalable

unsalted
unsanctioned
unsanitary
unsatisfactory
unsatisfied
unscented
unscheduled
unscholarly
unsealed
unseasoned
unseaworthy
unsegmented
unself–conscious
unself–consciously
unsensational
unsentimental
unserious
unserviceable
unsexual
unshaded
unshakable
unshaken
unshapely
unshaven
unshorn
unsifted
unsigned
unsinkable
unsmiling
unsociable
unsoiled
unsold
unsoldierly
unsolicited
unsolvable
unsolved
unsorted
unspecified
unspectacular
unspent
unspiritual
unspoiled
unspoken
unsportsmanlike
unstained
unstated
unsterile
unstructured
unstylish
unsubdued
unsubstantiated
unsubtle
unsuccessful
unsuccessfully
unsuitable
unsuited
unsullied
unsupervised
unsupportable
unsupported
unsure
unsurpassed
unsurprising
unsurprisingly
unsuspected
unsuspecting

unsuspicious
unsweetened
unsymmetrical
unsympathetic
unsystematic
untactful
untainted
untalented
untamed
untanned
untapped
untarnished
untaxed
unteachable
untenable
untenanted
untended
untested
unthrifty
untidy
untilled
untitled
untraceable
untraditional
untrained
untrammeled
untranslatable
untranslated
untraveled
untraversed
untreated
untrimmed
untrod
untroubled
untrustworthy
untruthful
untypical
unusable
unvaried
unvarying
unventilated
unverifiable
unverified
unversed
unvisited
unwanted
unwarranted
unwary
unwashed
unwavering
unweaned
unwearable
unwearied
unweathered
unwed
unwelcome
unwilling
unwillingly
unwillingness
unwomanly
unworkable
unworn
unworried
unwounded
unwoven

un·able \ˌən-'ā-bəl\ *adj* **1 :** not able **2 :** UNQUALIFIED, IN-
COMPETENT
un·abridged \ˌən-ə-'brijd\ *adj* **1 :** not abridged ⟨an ~
edition of Shakespeare⟩ **2 :** complete of its class : not
based on one larger ⟨an ~ dictionary⟩
un·ac·com·pa·nied \ˌən-ə-'kəm-pə-nēd\ *adj* **:** not ac-

companied; *esp* **:** being without instrumental accompaniment
un·ac·count·able \ˌən-ə-'kaùn-tə-bəl\ *adj* **1 :** not to be
accounted for **:** INEXPLICABLE **2 :** not responsible **— un·
ac·count·ably** \-blē\ *adv*
un·ac·count·ed \-'kaùn-təd\ *adj* **:** not accounted ⟨the
loss was ~ for⟩
un·ac·cus·tomed \ˌən-ə-'kəs-təmd\ *adj* **1 :** not customary **:** not usual or common **2 :** not accustomed or habituated ⟨~ to noise⟩
un·adul·ter·at·ed \ˌən-ə-'dəl-tə-ˌrā-təd\ *adj* **:** PURE, UN-
MIXED **syn** absolute, sheer, simple, unalloyed, undiluted, unmitigated
un·af·fect·ed \ˌən-ə-'fek-təd\ *adj* **1 :** not influenced or
changed mentally, physically, or chemically **2 :** free
from affectation **:** NATURAL, GENUINE **— un·af·fect·
ed·ly** *adv*
un·alien·able \-'āl-yə-nə-bəl, -'ā-lē-ə-\ *adj* **:** INALIENA-
BLE
un·aligned \ˌən-ə-'līnd\ *adj* **:** not associated with any
one of competing international blocs ⟨~ nations⟩
un·al·loyed \ˌən-ə-'lòid\ *adj* **:** UNMIXED, UNQUALIFIED,
PURE ⟨~ happiness⟩
un·al·ter·able \ˌən-'òl-tə-rə-bəl\ *adj* **:** not capable of being altered or changed **— un·al·ter·ably** \-blē\ *adv*
un–Amer·i·can \ˌən-ə-'mer-ə-kən\ *adj* **:** not characteristic of or consistent with American customs or principles
unan·i·mous \yù-'na-nə-məs\ *adj* [L *unanimus,* fr. *unus*
one + *animus* mind] **1 :** being of one mind **:** AGREEING
2 : formed with or indicating the agreement of all **—
una·nim·i·ty** \ˌyü-nə-'ni-mə-tē\ *n* **— unan·i·mous·ly**
adv
un·arm \ˌən-'ärm\ *vb* **:** DISARM
un·armed \-'ärmd\ *adj* **:** not armed or armored
un·as·sail·able \ˌən-ə-'sā-lə-bəl\ *adj* **:** not liable to
doubt, attack, or question
un·as·sum·ing \ˌən-ə-'sü-miɳ\ *adj* **:** MODEST, RETIRING
syn humble, lowly, meek
un·at·tached \ˌən-ə-'tacht\ *adj* **1 :** not married or engaged **2 :** not joined or united
un·avail·ing \ˌən-ə-'vā-liɳ\ *adj* **:** being of no avail **— un·
avail·ing·ly** *adv*
un·avoid·able \ˌən-ə-'vòi-də-bəl\ *adj* **:** not avoidable
: INEVITABLE **syn** certain, ineluctable, inescapable, necessary **— un·avoid·ably** \-blē\ *adv*
¹un·aware \ˌən-ə-'war\ *adv* **:** UNAWARES
²unaware *adj* **:** not aware **:** IGNORANT **— un·aware·ness**
n
un·awares \-'warz\ *adv* **1 :** without knowing **:** UNINTEN-
TIONALLY **2 :** without warning **:** by surprise ⟨taken ~⟩
un·bal·anced \ˌən-'ba-lənst\ *adj* **1 :** not in a state of balance **2 :** mentally disordered **3 :** not adjusted so as to
make credits equal to debits
un·bar \-'bär\ *vb* **:** UNBOLT, OPEN
un·bear·able \ˌən-'bar-ə-bəl\ *adj* **:** greater than can be
borne ⟨~ pain⟩ **syn** insufferable, insupportable, intol-
erable, unendurable, unsupportable **— un·bear·ably**
\-blē\ *adv*
un·beat·able \-'bē-tə-bəl\ *adj* **:** not capable of being defeated **syn** indomitable, invincible, invulnerable, unconquerable
un·beat·en \-'bēt-ᵊn\ *adj* **1 :** not pounded, beaten, or
whipped **2 :** UNTROD **3 :** UNDEFEATED
un·be·com·ing \ˌən-bi-'kə-miɳ\ *adj* **:** not becoming **:** UN-
SUITABLE, IMPROPER **syn** indecorous, indecent, indeli-
cate, unseemly **— un·be·com·ing·ly** *adv*
un·be·knownst \ˌən-bi-'nōnst\ *also* **un·be·known**

\ə\abut \ᵊ\kitten \ər\further \a\ash \ā\ace \ä\mop, mar
\aù\out \ch\chin \e\bet \ē\easy \g\go \i\hit \ī\ice \j\job
\ɳ\sing \ō\go \ò\law \òi\boy \th\thin \t̲h̲\the \ü\loot \ù\foot
\y\yet \zh\vision *see also* Pronunciation Symbols page

\-'nōn\ *adj* : happening without one's knowledge

un·be·lief \ˌən-bə-'lēf\ *n* : the withholding or absence of belief : DOUBT — **un·be·liev·ing** \-'lē-viŋ\ *adj*

un·be·liev·able \-'lē-və-bəl\ *adj* : too improbable for belief; *also* : of such a superlative degree as to be hard to believe ⟨an ~ catch for a touchdown⟩ **syn** inconceivable, unimaginable, unthinkable — **un·be·liev·ably** \-blē\ *adv*

un·be·liev·er \-'lē-vər\ *n* **1** : DOUBTER **2** : INFIDEL

un·bend \-'bend\ *vb* **-bent** \-'bent\; **-bend·ing 1** : to free from being bent : make or become straight **2** : UNTIE **3** : to make or become less stiff or more affable : RELAX

un·bend·ing *adj* : formal and distant in manner : INFLEXIBLE

un·bi·ased \ˌən-'bī-əst\ *adj* : free from bias; *esp* : UNPREJUDICED **syn** disinterested, dispassionate, impartial, nondiscriminatory, nonpartisan, objective, uncolored

un·bid·den \-'bid-ᵊn\ *also* **un·bid** \-'bid\ *adj* : not bidden : UNASKED

un·bind \-'bīnd\ *vb* **-bound** \-'baund\; **-bind·ing 1** : to remove bindings from : UNTIE **2** : RELEASE

un·blessed *also* **un·blest** \ˌən-'blest\ *adj* **1** : not blessed **2** : EVIL

un·block \-'bläk\ *vb* : to free from being blocked

un·blush·ing \-'blə-shiŋ\ *adj* **1** : not blushing **2** : SHAMELESS — **un·blush·ing·ly** *adv*

un·bod·ied \-'bä-dēd\ *adj* **1** : having no body; *also* : DISEMBODIED **2** : FORMLESS

un·bolt \ˌən-'bōlt\ *vb* : to open or unfasten by withdrawing a bolt

un·bolt·ed \-'bōl-təd\ *adj* : not fastened by bolts

un·born \-'born\ *adj* : not yet born

un·bos·om \-'bu̇-zəm, -'bü-\ *vb* **1** : DISCLOSE, REVEAL **2** : to disclose the thoughts or feelings of oneself

un·bound·ed \-'baun-dəd\ *adj* : having no bounds or limits ⟨~ enthusiasm⟩ **syn** boundless, endless, immeasurable, limitless, measureless, unlimited

un·bowed \ˌən-'baud\ *adj* **1** : not bowed down **2** : UNSUBDUED

un·bri·dled \-'brīd-ᵊld\ *adj* **1** : UNRESTRAINED **2** : not confined by a bridle

un·bro·ken \-'brō-kən\ *adj* **1** : not damaged **2** : not subdued or tamed **3** : not interrupted : CONTINUOUS

un·buck·le \-'bə-kəl\ *vb* : to loose the buckle of : UNFASTEN ⟨~ a belt⟩

un·bur·den \-'bərd-ᵊn\ *vb* **1** : to free or relieve from a burden **2** : to relieve oneself of (as cares or worries)

un·but·ton \-'bət-ᵊn\ *vb* : to unfasten the buttons of ⟨~ your coat⟩

un·called–for \ˌən-'kȯld-ˌfȯr\ *adj* : not called for, needed, or wanted

un·can·ny \-'ka-nē\ *adj* **1** : GHOSTLY, MYSTERIOUS, EERIE **2** : suggesting superhuman or supernatural powers **syn** spooky, unearthly, weird — **un·can·ni·ly** \-'kan-ᵊl-ē\ *adv*

un·ceas·ing \-'sē-siŋ\ *adj* : never ceasing **syn** ceaseless, continuous, endless, interminable, unending, unremitting — **un·ceas·ing·ly** *adv*

un·cer·e·mo·ni·ous \ˌən-ˌser-ə-'mō-nē-əs\ *adj* : acting without or lacking ordinary courtesy : ABRUPT — **un·cer·e·mo·ni·ous·ly** *adv*

un·cer·tain \ˌən-'sərt-ᵊn\ *adj* **1** : not determined or fixed ⟨an ~ quantity⟩ **2** : subject to chance or change : not dependable ⟨~ weather⟩ **3** : not definitely known **4** : not sure ⟨~ of the truth⟩ — **un·cer·tain·ly** *adv*

un·cer·tain·ty \-ᵊn-tē\ *n* **1** : lack of certainty : DOUBT **2** : something that is uncertain **syn** concern, doubt, dubiety, incertitude, skepticism, suspicion

un·chain \ˌən-'chān\ *vb* : to free by or as if by removing a chain

un·charged \ˌən-'chärjd\ *adj* : having no electrical charge

un·char·i·ta·ble \-'char-ə-tə-bəl\ *adj* : not charitable;

esp : severe in judging others — **un·char·i·ta·ble·ness** *n* — **un·char·i·ta·bly** \-blē\ *adv*

un·chart·ed \-'chär-təd\ *adj* **1** : not recorded on a map, chart, or plan **2** : UNKNOWN

un·chris·tian \-'kris-chən\ *adj* **1** : not of the Christian faith **2** : contrary to the Christian spirit

un·churched \-'chərcht\ *adj* : not belonging to or connected with a church

un·cial \'ən-shəl, -chəl; 'ən-sē-əl\ *adj* : relating to or written in a form of script with rounded letters used esp. in early Greek and Latin manuscripts — **uncial** *n*

un·cir·cu·lat·ed \ˌən-'sər-kyə-ˌlā-təd\ *adj* : issued for use as money but kept out of circulation

un·cir·cum·cised \ˌən-'sər-kəm-ˌsīzd\ *adj* : not circumcised; *also* : HEATHEN

un·civ·il \ˌən-'si-vəl\ *adj* **1** : not civilized : BARBAROUS **2** : DISCOURTEOUS, ILL-MANNERED, IMPOLITE

un·civ·i·lized \-'si-və-ˌlīzd\ *adj* **1** : not civilized : BARBAROUS **2** : remote from civilization : WILD

un·clasp \-'klasp\ *vb* : to open by or as if by loosing the clasp

un·cle \'əŋ-kəl\ *n* [ME, fr. OF, fr. L *avunculus* mother's brother] : the brother of one's father or mother; *also* : the husband of one's aunt

un·clean \ˌən-'klēn\ *adj* **1** : morally or spiritually impure **2** : prohibited by ritual law for use or contact **3** : DIRTY, SOILED — **un·clean·li·ness** \-lē-nəs\ *n* — **un·clean·ly** *adj* — **un·clean·ness** *n*

un·clench \-'klench\ *vb* : to open from a clenched position : RELAX

Uncle Tom \-'täm\ *n* [fr. *Uncle Tom*, faithful slave in Harriet Beecher Stowe's novel *Uncle Tom's Cabin* (1851-52)] : a black eager to win the approval of whites

un·cloak \ˌən-'klōk\ *vb* **1** : to remove a cloak or cover from **2** : UNMASK, REVEAL

un·clog \-'kläg\ *vb* : to remove an obstruction from

un·close \-'klōz\ *vb* : OPEN — **un·closed** \-'klōzd\ *adj*

un·clothe \-'klōth\ *vb* : to strip of clothes or a covering — **un·clothed** \-'klōthd\ *adj*

un·coil \ˌən-'kȯil\ *vb* : to release or become released from a coiled state

un·com·fort·able \ˌən-'kəmf-tə-bəl, -'kəm-fər-tə-\ *adj* **1** : causing discomfort **2** : feeling discomfort — **un·com·fort·ably** *adv*

un·com·mit·ted \ˌən-kə-'mi-təd\ *adj* : not committed; *esp* : not pledged to a particular belief, allegiance, or program

un·com·mon \ˌən-'kä-mən\ *adj* **1** : not ordinarily encountered : UNUSUAL, RARE **2** : REMARKABLE, EXCEPTIONAL **syn** extraordinary, phenomenal, singular, unique — **un·com·mon·ly** *adv*

un·com·mu·ni·ca·tive \ˌən-kə-'myü-nə-ˌkā-tiv, -ni-kə-\ *adj* : not inclined to talk or impart information : RESERVED **syn** closemouthed, reticent, silent, taciturn

un·com·pro·mis·ing \ˌən-'käm-prə-ˌmī-ziŋ\ *adj* : not making or accepting a compromise : UNYIELDING **syn** adamant, inflexible, obdurate, rigid, unbending

un·con·cern \ˌən-kən-'sərn\ *n* **1** : lack of care or interest : INDIFFERENCE **2** : freedom from excessive concern

un·con·cerned \-'sərnd\ *adj* **1** : not having any part or interest **2** : not anxious or upset : free of worry **syn** aloof, detached, incurious, remote, uncurious, uninterested — **un·con·cern·ed·ly** \-'sər-nəd-lē\ *adv*

un·con·di·tion·al \ˌən-kən-'di-shə-nəl\ *adj* : not limited in any way — **un·con·di·tion·al·ly** *adv*

un·con·di·tioned \-'di-shənd\ *adj* **1** : not subject to conditions **2** : not acquired or learned : NATURAL ⟨~ responses⟩ **3** : producing an unconditioned response ⟨~ stimuli⟩

un·con·quer·able \ˌən-'käŋ-kə-rə-bəl\ *adj* : incapable of being conquered or overcome : INDOMITABLE

un·con·scio·na·ble \-'kän-shə-nə-bəl\ *adj* **1** : not guided or controlled by conscience **2** : not in accordance with what is right or just **syn** unreasonable, undue, unjustifiable, unwarrantable, unwarranted — **un·con·scio·na·bly** \-blē\ *adv*

¹un·con·scious \ən-ˈkän-chəs, -shəs\ *adj* **1** : not knowing or perceiving : not aware **2** : not done consciously or on purpose **3** : having lost consciousness **4** : of or relating to the unconscious — **un·con·scious·ly** *adv* — **un·con·scious·ness** *n*

²unconscious *n* : the part of one's mental life of which one is not ordinarily aware but which is often a powerful force in controlling behavior

un·con·sti·tu·tion·al \ˌən-ˌkän-stə-ˈtü-shə-nəl, -ˈtyü-\ *adj* : not according to or consistent with the constitution of a state or society — **un·con·sti·tu·tion·al·i·ty** \-tü-shə-ˈna-lə-tē, -ˈtyü-\ *n* — **un·con·sti·tu·tion·al·ly** \-ˈtü-shə-nə-lē, -ˈtyü-\ *adv*

un·con·trol·la·ble \ˌən-kən-ˈtrō-lə-bəl\ *adj* : incapable of being controlled : UNGOVERNABLE — **un·con·trol·la·bly** \-blē\ *adv*

un·con·ven·tion·al \-ˈven-chə-nəl\ *adj* : not conventional : being out of the ordinary — **un·con·ven·tion·al·i·ty** \-ˌven-chə-ˈna-lə-tē\ *n* — **un·con·ven·tion·al·ly** \-ˈven-chə-nə-lē\ *adv*

un·cork \ˌən-ˈkórk\ *vb* **1** : to draw a cork from **2** : to release from a sealed or pent-up state; *also* : to let go

un·count·ed \-ˈkaün-təd\ *adj* **1** : not counted **2** : INNUMERABLE

un·cou·ple \-ˈkə-pəl\ *vb* : DISCONNECT

un·couth \-ˈküth\ *adj* [ME, unfamiliar, fr. OE *uncūth*, fr. *un-* + *cūth* known] **1** : strange, awkward, and clumsy in shape or appearance **2** : vulgar in conduct or speech : RUDE **syn** discourteous, ill-mannered, impolite, ungracious, unmannered, unmannerly

un·cov·er \-ˈkə-vər\ *vb* **1** : to make known : DISCLOSE, REVEAL **2** : to expose to view by removing some covering **3** : to take the cover from **4** : to remove the hat from; *also* : to take off the hat as a token of respect — **un·covered** *adj*

un·crit·i·cal \ˌən-ˈkri-ti-kəl\ *adj* **1** : not critical : lacking in discrimination **2** : showing lack or improper use of critical standards or procedures — **un·crit·i·cal·ly** \-k(ə-)lē\ *adv*

un·cross \-ˈkrós\ *vb* : to change from a crossed position ⟨~ed his legs⟩

unc·tion \ˈəŋk-shən\ *n* **1** : the act of anointing as a rite of consecration or healing **2** : exaggerated or insincere earnestness of language or manner

unc·tu·ous \ˈəŋk-chə-wəs\ *adj* [ME, fr. MF or ML; MF *unctueux*, fr. ML *unctuosus*, fr. L *unctus* act of anointing, fr. *unguere* to anoint] **1** : FATTY, OILY **2** : insincerely smooth in speech and manner — **unc·tu·ous·ly** *adv*

un·curl \ˌən-ˈkərl\ *vb* : to make or become straightened out from a curled or coiled position

un·cut \ˌən-ˈkət\ *adj* **1** : not cut down or into **2** : not shaped by cutting ⟨an ~ diamond⟩ **3** : not having the folds of the leaves slit ⟨an ~ book⟩ **4** : not abridged or curtailed ⟨the ~ version of the film⟩ **5** : not diluted ⟨~ heroin⟩

un·daunt·ed \-ˈdón-təd\ *adj* : not daunted : not discouraged or dismayed **syn** bold, brave, dauntless, fearless, intrepid, valiant — **un·daunt·ed·ly** *adv*

un·de·ceive \ˌən-di-ˈsēv\ *vb* : to free from deception, illusion, or error

un·de·mon·stra·tive \ˌən-di-ˈmän-strə-tiv\ *adj* : restrained in expression of feeling : RESERVED

un·de·ni·able \ˌən-di-ˈnī-ə-bəl\ *adj* **1** : plainly true : INCONTESTABLE **2** : unquestionably excellent or genuine **syn** incontrovertible, indisputable, indubitable, unquestionable — **un·de·ni·ably** \-blē\ *adv*

¹un·der \ˈən-dər\ *adv* **1** : in or into a position below or beneath something **2** : below some quantity, level, or limit ⟨$10 or ~⟩ **3** : in or into a condition of subjection,

subordination, or unconsciousness ⟨the ether put him ~⟩

²un·der \ˌən-dər, ˈən-\ *prep* **1** : lower than and overhung, surmounted, or sheltered by ⟨~ a tree⟩ **2** : subject to the authority or guidance of ⟨served ~ him⟩ ⟨was ~ contract⟩ **3** : subject to the action or effect of ⟨~ the influence of alcohol⟩ **4** : within the division or grouping of ⟨items ~ this heading⟩ **5** : less or lower than ⟨as in size, amount, or rank⟩ ⟨earns ~ $5000⟩

³under \ˈən-dər\ *adj* **1** : lying below, beneath, or on the ventral side **2** : facing or protruding downward **3** : SUBORDINATE **4** : lower than usual, proper, or desired in amount, quality, or degree

un·der·achiev·er \ˌən-dər-ə-ˈchē-vər\ *n* : one who performs below an expected level of proficiency

un·der·act \-ˈakt\ *vb* : to perform feebly or with restraint

un·der·ac·tive \-ˈak-tiv\ *adj* : characterized by abnormally low activity ⟨~ glands⟩ — **un·der·ac·tiv·i·ty** \ˌak-ˈti-və-tē\ *n*

un·der·age \-ˈāj\ *adj* : of less than mature or legal age

un·der·arm \-ˈärm\ *adj* **1** : UNDERHAND 2 ⟨an ~ throw⟩ **2** : placed under or on the underside of the arms ⟨~ seams⟩ — **underarm** *adv or n*

un·der·bel·ly \ˈən-dər-ˌbe-lē\ *n* **1** : the underside of a body or mass **2** : a vulnerable area

un·der·bid \ˌən-dər-ˈbid\ *vb* **-bid; -bid·ding 1** : to bid less than another **2** : to bid too low

un·der·body \ˈən-dər-ˌbä-dē\ *n* : the lower parts of the body of a vehicle

un·der·bred \ˌən-dər-ˈbred\ *adj* : marked by lack of good breeding

un·der·brush \ˈən-dər-ˌbrəsh\ *n* : shrubs, bushes, or small trees growing beneath large trees

un·der·car·riage \-ˌkar-ij\ *n* **1** : a supporting framework ⟨as of an automobile⟩ **2** *chiefly Brit* : the landing gear of an airplane

un·der·charge \ˌən-dər-ˈchärj\ *vb* : to charge ⟨as a person⟩ too little — **undercharge** \ˈən-dər-ˌchärj\ *n*

un·der·class·man \ˌən-dər-ˈklas-mən\ *n* : a member of the freshman or sophomore class

un·der·clothes \ˈən-dər-ˌklōthz\ *n pl* : UNDERWEAR

un·der·cloth·ing \-ˌklō-thiŋ\ *n* : UNDERWEAR

un·der·coat \-ˌkōt\ *n* **1** : a coat worn under another **2** : a growth of short hair or fur partly concealed by the longer and usu. coarser hairs of a mammal **3** : a coat of paint under another

un·der·coat·ing \-ˌkō-tiŋ\ *n* : a special waterproof coating applied to the underside of a vehicle

un·der·cov·er \ˌən-dər-ˈkə-vər\ *adj* : acting or executed in secret; *esp* : employed or engaged in secret investigation ⟨an ~ agent⟩

un·der·croft \ˈən-dər-ˌkróft\ *n* [ME, fr. *under* + *crofte* crypt, fr. MD, fr. ML *crupta*, fr. L *crypta*] : a vaulted chamber under a church

un·der·cur·rent \-ˌkər-ənt\ *n* **1** : a current below the surface **2** : a hidden tendency of feeling or opinion

un·der·cut \ˌən-dər-ˈkət\ *vb* **-cut; -cut·ting 1** : to cut away the underpart of **2** : to offer to sell or to work at a lower rate than **3** : to strike ⟨the ball⟩ obliquely downward so as to give a backward spin or elevation to the shot — **un·der·cut** \ˈən-dər-ˌkət\ *n*

un·der·de·vel·oped \ˌən-dər-di-ˈve-ləpt\ *adj* **1** : not normally or adequately developed ⟨~ muscles⟩ **2** : having a relatively low level of economic development ⟨the ~ nations⟩

un·der·dog \ˈən-dər-ˌdóg\ *n* : the loser or predicted loser in a struggle

---

\ə\abut \ᵊ\kitten \ər\further \a\ash \ā\ace \ä\mop, mar
\aú\out \ch\chin \e\bet \ē\easy \g\go \i\hit \ī\ice \j\job
\ŋ\sing \ō\go \ò\law \òi\boy \th\thin \t̲h̲\the \ü\loot \ú\foot
\y\yet \zh\vision *see also* Pronunciation Symbols page

un·der·done \ˌən-dər-ˈdən\ *adj* : not thoroughly done or cooked : RARE

un·der·draw·ers \ˈən-dər-ˌdrȯrz, -ˌdrȯ-ərz\ *n pl* : UNDERPANTS

un·der·em·pha·size \ˌən-dər-ˈem-fə-sīz\ *vb* : to emphasize inadequately — **un·der·em·pha·sis** \-səs\ *n*

un·der·em·ployed \-im-ˈplȯid\ *adj* : having less than full-time or adequate employment

un·der·es·ti·mate \-ˈes-tə-ˌmāt\ *vb* : to set too low a value on

un·der·ex·pose \-ik-ˈspōz\ *vb* : to expose (a photographic plate or film) for less time than is needed — **un·der·ex·po·sure** \-ˈspō-zhər\ *n*

un·der·feed \ˌən-dər-ˈfēd\ *vb* **-fed** \-ˈfed\; **-feed·ing** : to feed with too little food

un·der·foot \-ˈfut\ *adv* **1** : under the feet ⟨flowers trampled ∼⟩ **2** : close about one's feet : in the way

un·der·fur \ˈən-dər-ˌfər\ *n* : an undercoat of fur esp. when thick and soft

un·der·gar·ment \-ˌgär-mənt\ *n* : a garment to be worn under another

un·der·gird \ˌən-dər-ˈgərd\ *vb* : to brace up : STRENGTHEN

un·der·go \ˌən-dər-ˈgō\ *vb* **-went** \-ˈwent\; **-gone** \-ˈgȯn, -ˈgän\; **-go·ing** **1** : to submit to : ENDURE **2** : to go through : EXPERIENCE

un·der·grad \ˈən-dər-ˌgrad\ *n* : UNDERGRADUATE

un·der·grad·u·ate \ˌən-dər-ˈgra-jə-wət, -jə-ˌwāt\ *n* : a student at a university or college who has not taken a first degree

¹un·der·ground \ˌən-dər-ˈgraund\ *adv* **1** : beneath the surface of the earth **2** : in or into hiding or secret operation

²un·der·ground \ˈən-dər-ˌgraund\ *n* **1** : a space under the surface of the ground; *esp* : SUBWAY **2** : a secret political movement or group; *esp* : an organized body working in secret to overthrow a government or an occupying power **3** : an avant-garde group or movement that operates outside the establishment

³underground \ˈən-dər-ˌgraund\ *adj* **1** : being, growing, operating, or located below the surface of the ground ⟨∼ stems⟩ **2** : conducted by secret means **3** : produced or published by the underground ⟨∼ publications⟩; *also* : of or relating to the avant-garde underground

un·der·growth \ˈən-dər-ˌgrōth\ *n* : low growth (as of herbs and shrubs) on the floor of a forest

¹un·der·hand \ˈən-dər-ˌhand\ *adv* **1** : in an underhanded or secret manner **2** : with an underhand motion

²underhand *adj* **1** : UNDERHANDED **2** : made with the hand kept below the level of the shoulder

¹un·der·hand·ed \ˌən-dər-ˈhan-dəd\ *adv* : UNDERHAND

²underhanded *adj* : marked by secrecy and deception — **un·der·hand·ed·ly** *adv* — **un·der·hand·ed·ness** *n*

un·der·lie \-ˈlī\ *vb* **-lay** \-ˈlā\; **-lain** \-ˈlān\; **-ly·ing** \-ˈlī-iŋ\ **1** : to lie or be situated under **2** : to be at the basis of : form the foundation of : SUPPORT

un·der·line \ˈən-dər-ˌlīn\ *vb* **1** : to draw a line under **2** : EMPHASIZE, STRESS — **underline** *n*

un·der·ling \ˈən-dər-liŋ\ *n* : SUBORDINATE, INFERIOR

un·der·lip \ˌən-dər-ˈlip\ *n* : the lower lip

un·der·ly·ing \ˌən-dər-ˌlī-iŋ\ *adj* **1** : lying under or below **2** : FUNDAMENTAL, BASIC ⟨∼ principles⟩

un·der·mine \-ˈmīn\ *vb* **1** : to excavate beneath **2** : to weaken or wear away secretly or gradually

un·der·most \ˈən-dər-ˌmōst\ *adj* : lowest in relative position — **undermost** *adv*

¹un·der·neath \ˌən-dər-ˈnēth\ *prep* **1** : directly under **2** : under subjection to

²underneath *adv* **1** : below a surface or object : BENEATH **2** : on the lower side

un·der·nour·ished \ˌən-dər-ˈnər-isht\ *adj* : supplied with insufficient nourishment — **un·der·nour·ish·ment** \-ˈnər-ish-mənt\ *n*

un·der·pants \ˈən-dər-ˌpants\ *n pl* : a usu. short undergarment for the lower trunk : DRAWERS

un·der·part \-ˌpärt\ *n* : a part lying on the lower side esp. of a bird or mammal

un·der·pass \-ˌpas\ *n* : a crossing of a highway and another way (as a road) at different levels; *also* : the lower level

un·der·pay \ˌən-dər-ˈpā\ *vb* : to pay too little

un·der·pin·ning \ˈən-dər-ˌpi-niŋ\ *n* : the material and construction (as a foundation) used for support of a structure — **un·der·pin** \ˌən-dər-ˈpin\ *vb*

un·der·play \ˌən-dər-ˈplā\ *vb* : to treat or handle with restraint; *esp* : to play a role in with subdued force

un·der·pop·u·lat·ed \ˌən-dər-ˈpä-pyə-ˌlā-təd\ *adj* : having a lower than normal or desirable density of population

un·der·priv·i·leged \-ˈpriv-lijd, -ˈpri-və-lijd\ *adj* : having fewer esp. economic and social privileges than others

un·der·pro·duc·tion \ˌən-dər-prə-ˈdək-shən\ *n* : the production of less than enough to satisfy the demand or of less than the usual supply

un·der·rate \-ˈrāt\ *vb* : to rate or value too low

un·der·rep·re·sent·ed \-ˌre-pri-ˈzen-təd\ *adj* : inadequately represented

un·der·score \ˈən-dər-ˌskōr\ *vb* **1** : to draw a line under : UNDERLINE **2** : EMPHASIZE — **underscore** *n*

¹un·der·sea \ˌən-dər-ˈsē\ *adj* : being, carried on, or used beneath the surface of the sea

²undersea *or* **un·der·seas** \-ˈsēz\ *adv* : beneath the surface of the sea

un·der·sec·re·tary \ˌən-dər-ˈse-krə-ˌter-ē\ *n* : a secretary immediately subordinate to a principal secretary ⟨∼ of state⟩

un·der·sell \-ˈsel\ *vb* **-sold** \-ˈsōld\; **-sell·ing** : to sell articles cheaper than

un·der·sexed \-ˈsekst\ *adj* : deficient in sexual desire

un·der·shirt \ˈən-dər-ˌshərt\ *n* : a collarless undergarment with or without sleeves

un·der·shoot \ˌən-dər-ˈshüt\ *vb* **-shot** \-ˈshät\; **-shoot·ing** **1** : to shoot short of or below (a target) **2** : to fall short of (a runway) in landing an airplane

un·der·shorts \ˈən-dər-ˌshȯrts\ *n pl* : SHORT 2

un·der·shot \ˈən-dər-ˌshät\ *adj* **1** : moved by water passing beneath ⟨an ∼ waterwheel⟩ **2** : having the lower front teeth projecting beyond the upper when the mouth is closed

un·der·side \ˈən-dər-ˌsīd, ˌən-dər-ˈsīd\ *n* : the side or surface lying underneath

un·der·signed \ˈən-dər-ˌsīnd\ *n, pl* **undersigned** : one whose name is signed at the end of a document

un·der·sized \ˌən-dər-ˈsīzd\ *also* **un·der·size** \-ˈsīz\ *adj* : of a size less than is common, proper, or normal

un·der·skirt \ˈən-dər-ˌskərt\ *n* : a skirt worn under an outer skirt; *esp* : PETTICOAT

un·der·staffed \ˌən-dər-ˈstaft\ *adj* : inadequately staffed

un·der·stand \ˌən-dər-ˈstand\ *vb* **-stood** \-ˈstud\; **-stand·ing** **1** : to grasp the meaning of : COMPREHEND **2** : to have thorough or technical acquaintance with or expertness in ⟨∼ finance⟩ **3** : to have reason to believe ⟨I ∼ you are leaving tomorrow⟩ **4** : INTERPRET ⟨we ∼ this to be a refusal⟩ **5** : to have a sympathetic attitude **6** : to accept as settled ⟨it is *understood* that he will pay the expenses⟩ — **un·der·stand·able** \-ˈstan-də-bəl\ *adj*

un·der·stand·ably \-blē\ *adv* : as can be easily understood

¹un·der·stand·ing \ˌən-dər-ˈstan-diŋ\ *n* **1** : knowledge and ability to judge : INTELLIGENCE ⟨a person of ∼⟩ **2** : agreement of opinion or feeling **3** : a mutual agreement informally or tacitly entered into

²understanding *adj* : endowed with understanding : TOLERANT, SYMPATHETIC

un·der·state \ˌən-dər-ˈstāt\ *vb* **1** : to represent as less than is the case **2** : to state with restraint esp. for effect — **un·der·state·ment** *n*

un·der·stood \ˌən-dər-ˈstu̇d\ *adj* **1** : agreed upon **2** : IMPLICIT

un·der·sto·ry \ˈən-dər-ˌstōr-ē, -ˌstȯr-\ *n* : the vegetative layer between the top layer of a forest and the ground cover

un·der·study \ˈən-dər-ˌstə-dē, ˌən-dər-ˈstə-dē\ *vb* : to study another actor's part in order to substitute in an emergency — **understudy** \ˈən-dər-ˌstə-dē\ *n*

un·der·sur·face \ˈən-dər-ˌsər-fəs\ *n* : UNDERSIDE

un·der·take \ˌən-dər-ˈtāk\ *vb* **-took** \-ˈtu̇k\; **-tak·en** \-ˈtā-kən\; **-tak·ing 1** : to take upon oneself : set about ⟨∼ a task⟩ **2** : to put oneself under obligation **3** : GUARANTEE, PROMISE

un·der·tak·er \ˈən-dər-ˌtā-kər\ *n* : one whose business is to prepare the dead for burial and to arrange and manage funerals

un·der·tak·ing \ˈən-dər-ˌtā-kiŋ, ˌən-dər-ˈtā-kiŋ; *2 is* ˈən-dər-ˌtā-kiŋ *only*\ *n* **1** : the act of one who undertakes or engages in any project **2** : the business of an undertaker **3** : something undertaken **4** : PROMISE, GUARANTEE

under–the–counter *adj* : UNLAWFUL, ILLICIT ⟨∼ sale of drugs⟩

un·der·tone \ˈən-dər-ˌtōn\ *n* **1** : a low or subdued tone or utterance **2** : a subdued color (as seen through and modifying another color)

un·der·tow \-ˌtō\ *n* : the current beneath the surface that flows seaward when waves are breaking upon the shore

un·der·trick \-ˌtrik\ *n* : a trick by which a declarer in bridge falls short of making the contract

un·der·val·ue \ˌən-dər-ˈval-yü\ *vb* **1** : to value or estimate below the real worth **2** : to esteem lightly

un·der·wa·ter \ˌən-dər-ˈwȯ-tər, -ˈwä-\ *adj* : lying, growing, worn, or operating below the surface of the water — **un·der·wa·ter** *adv*

under way \-ˈwā\ *adv* **1** : into motion from a standstill **2** : in progress

un·der·wear \ˈən-dər-ˌwar\ *n* : clothing or a garment worn next to the skin and under other clothing

un·der·weight \ˌən-dər-ˈwāt\ *n* : weight below what is normal, average, or necessary — **underweight** *adj*

un·der·world \ˈən-dər-ˌwərld\ *n* **1** : the place of departed souls : HADES **2** : the side of the world opposite to one **3** : the world of organized crime

un·der·write \ˈən-dər-ˌrīt, ˌən-dər-ˈrīt\ *vb* **-wrote** \-ˌrōt, -ˈrōt\; **-writ·ten** \-ˌrit-ᵊn, -ˈrit-ᵊn\; **-writ·ing 1** : to write under or at the end of something else **2** : to set one's name to an insurance policy and thereby become answerable for a designated loss or damage **3** : to subscribe to : agree to **4** : to guarantee financial support of — **un·der·writ·er** *n*

un·de·sign·ing \ˌən-di-ˈzī-niŋ\ *adj* : having no artful, ulterior, or fraudulent purpose : SINCERE

un·de·sir·able \-ˈzī-rə-bəl\ *adj* : not desirable — **undesirable** *n*

un·de·vi·at·ing \ˌən-ˈdē-vē-ˌā-tiŋ\ *adj* : keeping a true course

un·dies \ˈən-dēz\ *n pl* : UNDERWEAR; *esp* : women's underwear

un·do \ˌən-ˈdü\ *vb* **-did** \-ˈdid\; **-done** \-ˈdən\; **-do·ing 1** : to make or become unfastened or loosened : OPEN **2** : to make null or as if not done : REVERSE **3** : to bring to ruin; *also* : UPSET

un·do·ing *n* : a cause of ruin

un·doubt·ed \-ˈdau̇-təd\ *adj* : not doubted or called into question : CERTAIN — **un·doubt·ed·ly** *adv*

¹**un·dress** \ˌən-ˈdres\ *vb* : to remove the clothes or covering of : STRIP, DISROBE

²**undress** *n* **1** : informal dress; *esp* : a loose robe or dressing gown **2** : ordinary dress **3** : NUDITY

un·due \-ˈdü, -ˈdyü\ *adj* **1** : not due **2** : exceeding or violating propriety or fitness : EXCESSIVE

un·du·lant \ˈən-jə-lənt, ˈən-də-, -dyə-\ *adj* : UNDULATING

undulant fever *n* : a human disease caused by bacteria from infected domestic animals or their products and marked by intermittent fever, pain and swelling in the joints, and great weakness

un·du·late \-ˌlāt\ *vb* **-lated; -lating** [LL *undula* small wave, fr. L *unda* wave] **1** : to have a wavelike motion or appearance **2** : to rise and fall in pitch or volume

un·du·la·tion \ˌən-jə-ˈlā-shən, ˌən-də-, -dyə-\ *n* **1** : wavy or wavelike motion **2** : pulsation of sound **3** : a wavy appearance or outline — **un·du·la·to·ry** \ˈən-jə-lə-ˌtōr-ē, ˈən-də-, -dyə-\ *adj*

un·du·ly \ˌən-ˈdü-lē, ˈən-, -ˈdyü-\ *adv* : in an undue manner; *esp* : EXCESSIVELY

un·dy·ing \-ˈdī-iŋ\ *adj* : not dying : IMMORTAL, PERPETUAL

un·earned \-ˈərnd\ *adj* : not earned by labor, service, or skill ⟨∼ income⟩

un·earth \ˌən-ˈərth\ *vb* **1** : to dig up out of or as if out of the earth ⟨∼ buried treasure⟩ **2** : to bring to light : DISCOVER ⟨∼ a secret⟩

un·earth·ly \-lē\ *adj* **1** : not of or belonging to the earth **2** : SUPERNATURAL, WEIRD; *also* : ABSURD

un·easy \ˌən-ˈē-zē\ *adj* **1** : AWKWARD, EMBARRASSED ⟨∼ among strangers⟩ **2** : disturbed by pain or worry; *also* : RESTLESS **3** : UNSTABLE ⟨an ∼ truce⟩ — **un·eas·i·ly** \-ˈē-zə-lē\ *adv* — **un·eas·i·ness** \-ˈē-zē-nəs\ *n*

un·em·ployed \ˌən-im-ˈplȯid\ *adj* : not being used; *also* : having no job

un·em·ploy·ment \-ˈplȯi-mənt\ *n* **1** : lack of employment **2** : money paid at regular intervals (as by a government agency) to an unemployed person

un·end·ing \ˌən-ˈen-diŋ\ *adj* : having no ending : ENDLESS

un·equal \ˌən-ˈē-kwəl\ *adj* **1** : not alike (as in size, amount, number, or value) **2** : not uniform : VARIABLE **3** : badly balanced or matched **4** : INADEQUATE, INSUFFICIENT ⟨∼ to the task⟩ — **un·equal·ly** *adv*

un·equaled *or* **un·equalled** \-kwəld\ *adj* : not equaled : UNPARALLELED

un·equiv·o·cal \ˌən-i-ˈkwi-və-kəl\ *adj* : leaving no doubt : CLEAR — **un·equiv·o·cal·ly** *adv*

un·err·ing \ˌən-ˈer-iŋ, ˌən-ˈər-\ *adj* : making no errors : CERTAIN, UNFAILING — **un·err·ing·ly** *adv*

UNES·CO \yu̇-ˈnes-kō\ *abbr* United Nations Educational, Scientific, and Cultural Organization

un·even \ˌən-ˈē-vən\ *adj* **1** : ODD 3 **2** : not even : not level or smooth : RUGGED, RAGGED **3** : IRREGULAR; *also* : varying in quality — **un·even·ly** *adv* — **un·even·ness** *n*

un·event·ful \ˌən-i-ˈvent-fəl\ *adj* : lacking interesting or noteworthy incidents — **un·event·ful·ly** *adv*

un·ex·am·pled \ˌən-ig-ˈzam-pəld\ *adj* : UNPRECEDENTED, UNPARALLELED

un·ex·cep·tion·able \ˌən-ik-ˈsep-shə-nə-bəl\ *adj* : not open to exception or objection : beyond reproach

un·ex·pect·ed \ˌən-ik-ˈspek-təd\ *adj* : not expected : UNFORESEEN — **un·ex·pect·ed·ly** *adv*

un·fail·ing \ˌən-ˈfā-liŋ\ *adj* **1** : not failing, flagging, or waning : CONSTANT **2** : INEXHAUSTIBLE **3** : INFALLIBLE, SURE — **un·fail·ing·ly** *adv*

un·fair \-ˈfar\ *adj* **1** : marked by injustice, partiality, or deception : UNJUST **2** : not equitable in business dealings — **un·fair·ly** *adv* — **un·fair·ness** *n*

un·faith·ful \ˌən-ˈfāth-fəl\ *adj* **1** : not observant of vows, allegiance, or duty : DISLOYAL **2** : INACCURATE, UN-

\ə\abut \ᵊ\kitten \ər\further \a\ash \ā\ace \ä\mop, mar \au̇\out \ch\chin \e\bet \ē\easy \g\go \i\hit \ī\ice \j\job \ŋ\sing \ō\go \o\law \oi\boy \th\thin \t̲h̲\the \ü\loot \u̇\foot \y\yet \zh\vision *see also* Pronunciation Symbols page

TRUSTWORTHY — **un·faith·ful·ly** *adv* — **un·faith·ful·ness** *n*

un·fa·mil·iar \ˌən-fə-ˈmil-yər\ *adj* 1 : not well-known : STRANGE ⟨an ∼ place⟩ 2 : not well acquainted ⟨∼ with the subject⟩ — **un·fa·mil·iar·i·ty** \-ˌmi-lē-ˈar-, -ˈyar-\ *n*

un·fas·ten \ˌən-ˈfas-ᵊn\ *vb* : to make or become loose : UNDO, DETACH

un·feel·ing \-ˈfē-liŋ\ *adj* 1 : lacking feeling : INSENSATE 2 : HARDHEARTED, CRUEL — **un·feel·ing·ly** *adv*

un·feigned \-ˈfānd\ *adj* : not feigned : not hypocritical : GENUINE

un·fet·ter \-ˈfe-tər\ *vb* 1 : to free from fetters 2 : LIBERATE

un·fil·ial \ˌən-ˈfi-lē-əl, -ˈfil-yəl\ *adj* : not observing the obligations of a child to a parent : UNDUTIFUL

un·fin·ished \ˌən-ˈfi-nisht\ *adj* 1 : not brought to an end 2 : being in a rough or unpolished state

¹**un·fit** \-ˈfit\ *adj* : not fit or suitable; *esp* : physically or mentally unsound — **un·fit·ness** *n*

²**unfit** *vb* : DISABLE, DISQUALIFY

un·fix \-ˈfiks\ *vb* 1 : to loosen from a fastening : DETACH 2 : UNSETTLE

un·flap·pa·ble \-ˈfla-pə-bəl\ *adj* : not easily upset or panicked — **un·flap·pa·bly** *adv*

un·fledged \ˌən-ˈflejd\ *adj* : not feathered or ready for flight; *also* : IMMATURE, CALLOW

un·flinch·ing \-ˈflin-chiŋ\ *adj* : not flinching or shrinking : STEADFAST — **un·flinch·ing·ly** *adv*

un·fold \-ˈfōld\ *vb* 1 : to open the folds of : open up 2 : to lay open to view : DISCLOSE 3 : BLOSSOM, DEVELOP

un·for·get·ta·ble \ˌən-fər-ˈge-tə-bəl\ *adj* : incapable of being forgotten — **un·for·get·ta·bly** \-blē\ *adv*

un·formed \-ˈfȯrmd\ *adj* : not regularly formed or ordered : UNDEVELOPED

un·for·tu·nate \-ˈfȯr-chə-nət\ *adj* 1 : not fortunate : UNLUCKY 2 : attended with misfortune 3 : UNSUITABLE — **unfortunate** *n*

un·for·tu·nate·ly \-nət-lē\ *adv* 1 : in an unfortunate manner 2 : it is unfortunate

un·found·ed \ˌən-ˈfau̇n-dəd\ *adj* : lacking a sound basis : GROUNDLESS

un·freeze \-ˈfrēz\ *vb* **-froze** \-ˈfrōz\; **-fro·zen** \-ˈfrōz-ᵊn\; **-freez·ing** 1 : to cause to thaw 2 : to remove from a freeze ⟨∼ prices⟩

un·fre·quent·ed \ˌən-frē-ˈkwen-təd; ˌən-ˈfrē-kwən-\ *adj* : seldom visited or traveled over

un·friend·ly \ˌən-ˈfrend-lē\ *adj* 1 : not friendly or kind : HOSTILE 2 : UNFAVORABLE — **un·friend·li·ness** \-lē-nəs\ *n*

un·frock \-ˈfräk\ *vb* : DEFROCK

un·fruit·ful \-ˈfrüt-fəl\ *adj* 1 : not producing fruit or offspring : BARREN 2 : yielding no valuable result : UNPROFITABLE — **un·fruit·ful·ness** *n*

un·furl \-ˈfərl\ *vb* : to loose from a furled state : UNFOLD

un·gain·ly \-ˈgān-lē\ *adj* [*un-* + obs. *gainly* proper, becoming, fr. *gain* direct, handy, fr. ME *geyn,* fr. OE *gēn,* fr. ON *gegn*] : CLUMSY, AWKWARD — **un·gain·li·ness** \-lē-nəs\ *n*

un·gen·er·ous \ˌən-ˈje-nə-rəs\ *adj* : not generous or liberal : STINGY

un·glued \ˌən-ˈglüd\ *adj* : UPSET, DISORDERED

un·god·ly \ˌən-ˈgäd-lē, -ˈgȯd-\ *adj* 1 : IMPIOUS, IRRELIGIOUS 2 : SINFUL, WICKED 3 : OUTRAGEOUS ⟨an ∼ hour⟩ — **un·god·li·ness** \-lē-nəs\ *n*

un·gov·ern·able \-ˈgə-vər-nə-bəl\ *adj* : not capable of being governed, guided, or restrained : UNRULY

un·gra·cious \-ˈgrā-shəs\ *adj* 1 : not courteous : RUDE 2 : not pleasing : DISAGREEABLE

un·grate·ful \ˌən-ˈgrāt-fəl\ *adj* 1 : not thankful for favors 2 : DISAGREEABLE; *also* : THANKLESS — **un·grate·ful·ly** *adv* — **un·grate·ful·ness** *n*

un·guard·ed \-ˈgär-dəd\ *adj* 1 : UNPROTECTED 2 : DIRECT, INCAUTIOUS ⟨∼ remarks⟩

un·guent \ˈəŋ-gwənt, ˈən-\ *n* : a soothing or healing salve : OINTMENT

¹**un·gu·late** \ˈəŋ-gyə-lət, ˈən-, -ˌlāt\ *adj* [LL *ungulatus,* fr. L *ungula* hoof, fr. *unguis* nail, hoof] : having hoofs

²**ungulate** *n* : a hoofed mammal (as a cow, horse, or rhinoceros)

Unh *symbol* unnilhexium

un·hal·lowed \ˌən-ˈha-lōd\ *adj* 1 : not consecrated : UNHOLY 2 : IMPIOUS, PROFANE 3 : contrary to accepted standards : IMMORAL

un·hand \ˌən-ˈhand\ *vb* : to remove the hand from : let go

un·hand·some \-ˈhan-səm\ *adj* 1 : not beautiful or handsome : HOMELY 2 : UNBECOMING 3 : DISCOURTEOUS, RUDE

un·handy \-ˈhan-dē\ *adj* : INCONVENIENT; *also* : AWKWARD

un·hap·py \-ˈha-pē\ *adj* 1 : UNLUCKY, UNFORTUNATE 2 : SAD, MISERABLE 3 : INAPPROPRIATE — **un·hap·pi·ly** \-ˈha-pə-lē\ *adv* — **un·hap·pi·ness** \-pē-nəs\ *n*

un·har·ness \-ˈhär-nəs\ *vb* : to remove the harness from (as a horse)

un·healthy \-ˈhel-thē\ *adj* 1 : not conducive to health : UNWHOLESOME 2 : SICKLY, DISEASED

un·heard \-ˈhərd\ *adj* 1 : not heard 2 : not granted a hearing

unheard–of *adj* : previously unknown; *esp* : UNPRECEDENTED

un·hinge \ˌən-ˈhinj\ *vb* 1 : to take from the hinges 2 : to make unstable esp. mentally

un·hitch \-ˈhich\ *vb* : UNFASTEN, LOOSE

un·ho·ly \-ˈhō-lē\ *adj* : not holy : PROFANE, WICKED — **un·ho·li·ness** \-lē-nəs\ *n*

un·hook \-ˈhu̇k\ *vb* : to loose from a hook

un·horse \-ˈhȯrs\ *vb* : to dislodge from or as if from a horse

uni·cam·er·al \ˌyü-ni-ˈka-mə-rəl\ *adj* : having a single legislative house or chamber

UNI·CEF \ˈyü-nə-ˌsef\ *abbr* [United Nations International Children's Emergency Fund, its former name] United Nations Children's Fund

uni·cel·lu·lar \ˌyü-ni-ˈsel-yə-lər\ *adj* : having or consisting of a single cell

uni·corn \ˈyü-nə-ˌkȯrn\ *n* [ME *unicorne,* fr. OF, fr. LL *unicornis,* fr. L, having one horn, fr. *unus* one + *cornu* horn] : a mythical animal with one horn in the middle of the forehead

uni·cy·cle \ˈyü-ni-ˌsī-kəl\ *n* : a vehicle that has a single wheel and is usu. propelled by pedals

uni·di·rec·tion·al \ˌyü-ni-də-ˈrek-shə-nəl, -dī-\ *adj* : having, moving in, or responsive in a single direction

uni·fi·ca·tion \ˌyü-nə-fə-ˈkā-shən\ *n* : the act, process, or result of unifying : the state of being unified

¹**uni·form** \ˈyü-nə-ˌfȯrm\ *adj* 1 : not varying 2 : of the same form with others ⟨∼ procedures⟩ — **uni·form·ly** *adv*

²**uniform** *vb* : to clothe with a uniform

³**uniform** *n* : distinctive dress worn by members of a particular group (as an army or a police force)

uni·for·mi·ty \ˌyü-nə-ˈfȯr-mə-tē\ *n, pl* **-ties** : the state of being uniform

uni·fy \ˈyü-nə-ˌfī\ *vb* **-fied; -fy·ing** : to make into a coherent whole : UNITE

uni·lat·er·al \ˌyü-nə-ˈla-tə-rəl\ *adj* : of, having, affecting, or done by one side only — **uni·lat·er·al·ly** *adv*

un·im·peach·able \ˌən-im-ˈpē-chə-bəl\ *adj* : not liable to accusation : BLAMELESS, IRREPROACHABLE

un·in·hib·it·ed \ˌən-in-ˈhi-bə-təd\ *adj* : free from inhibition; *also* : boisterously informal — **un·in·hib·it·ed·ly** *adv*

un·in·tel·li·gent \-ˈte-lə-jənt\ *adj* : lacking intelligence

un·in·tel·li·gi·ble \-jə-bəl\ *adj* : not intelligible : OBSCURE — **un·in·tel·li·gi·bly** \-blē\ *adv*

un·in·ter·est·ed \ˌən-ˈin-trəs-təd, -tə-rəs-, -tə-ˌres-\ *adj* : not interested : not having the mind or feelings engaged or aroused

un·in·ter·rupt·ed \ˌən-ˌin-tə-ˈrəp-təd\ *adj* : not interrupted : CONTINUOUS

union \ˈyü-nyən\ *n* **1** : an act or instance of uniting two or more things into one : the state of being so united : COMBINATION, JUNCTION **2** : a uniting in marriage **3** : something formed by a combining of parts or members; *esp* : a confederation of independent individuals (as nations or persons) for some common purpose **4** : an organization of workers (as a labor union or a trade union) formed to advance its members' interests esp. in respect to wages and working conditions **5** : a device emblematic of union used on or as a national flag; *also* : the upper inner corner of a flag **6** : a device for connecting parts (as of a machine); *esp* : a coupling for pipes

union·ism \ˈyü-nyə-ˌni-zəm\ *n* **1** : the principle or policy of forming or adhering to a union; *esp*, *cap* : adherence to the policy of a firm federal union before or during the U.S. Civil War **2** : the principles or system of trade unions — **union·ist** *n*

union·ize \ˈyü-nyə-ˌnīz\ *vb* **-ized; -iz·ing** : to form into or cause to join a labor union — **union·i·za·tion** \ˌyü-nyə-nə-ˈzā-shən\ *n*

union jack *n* **1** : a flag consisting of the part of a national flag that signifies union **2** *cap U&J* : the national flag of the United Kingdom

unique \yu̇-ˈnēk\ *adj* **1** : being the only one of its kind : SINGLE, SOLE **2** : very unusual : NOTABLE — **unique·ly** *adv* — **unique·ness** *n*

uni·sex \ˈyü-nə-ˌseks\ *adj* : not distinguishable as male or female; *also* : suitable or designed for both males and females — **unisex** *n*

uni·sex·u·al \ˌyü-nə-ˈsek-shə-wəl\ *adj* **1** : having only male or only female sex organs **2** : UNISEX

uni·son \ˈyü-nə-sən, -zən\ *n* [MF, fr. ML *unisonus* having the same sound, fr. L *unus* one + *sonus* sound] **1** : sameness or identity in musical pitch **2** : the condition of being tuned or sounded at the same pitch or in octaves ⟨sing in ∼⟩ **3** : harmonious agreement or union : ACCORD

unit \ˈyü-nət\ *n* **1** : the smallest whole number greater than zero : ONE **2** : a definite amount or quantity used as a standard of measurement **3** : a single thing, person, or group that is a constituent of a whole; *also* : a part of a military establishment that has a prescribed organization — **unit** *adj*

Uni·tar·i·an \ˌyü-nə-ˈter-ē-ən\ *n* : a member of a religious denomination stressing individual freedom of belief — **Uni·tar·i·an·ism** *n*

uni·tary \ˈyü-nə-ˌter-ē\ *adj* **1** : of or relating to a unit **2** : not divided — **uni·tar·i·ly** \ˌyü-nə-ˈter-ə-lē\ *adv*

unite \yu̇-ˈnīt\ *vb* **unit·ed; unit·ing 1** : to put or join together so as to make one : COMBINE, COALESCE **2** : to join by a legal or moral bond; *also* : to join in interest or fellowship **3** : AMALGAMATE, CONSOLIDATE **4** : to act in concert

unit·ed \yu̇-ˈnī-təd\ *adj* **1** : made one : COMBINED **2** : relating to or produced by joint action **3** : being in agreement : HARMONIOUS

unit·ize \ˈyü-nə-ˌtīz\ *vb* **-ized; -iz·ing 1** : to form into or convert into a unit **2** : to divide into units

uni·ty \ˈyü-nə-tē\ *n*, *pl* **-ties 1** : the quality or state of being or being made one : ONENESS **2** : a definite quantity or combination of quantities taken as one or for which 1 is made to stand in calculation **3** : CONCORD, ACCORD, HARMONY **4** : continuity without change ⟨∼ of purpose⟩ **5** : reference of all the parts of a literary or artistic composition to a single main idea **6** : totality of related parts **syn** solidarity, union, integrity

univ *abbr* **1** universal **2** university

uni·valve \ˈyü-ni-ˌvalv\ *n* : a mollusk having a shell with only one piece; *esp* : GASTROPOD — **univalve** *adj*

uni·ver·sal \ˌyü-nə-ˈvər-səl\ *adj* **1** : including, covering, or affecting the whole without limit or exception : UNLIMITED, GENERAL ⟨a ∼ rule⟩ **2** : present or occurring everywhere **3** : used or for use among all ⟨a ∼ language⟩ — **uni·ver·sal·ly** *adv*

uni·ver·sal·i·ty \-vər-ˈsa-lə-tē\ *n* : the quality or state of being universal

uni·ver·sal·ize \-ˈvər-sə-ˌlīz\ *vb* **-ized; -iz·ing** : to make universal : GENERALIZE — **uni·ver·sal·i·za·tion** \-ˌvər-sə-lə-ˈzā-shən\ *n*

universal joint *n* : a shaft coupling for transmitting rotation from one shaft to another not in a straight line with it

universal joint

Universal Product Code *n* : a combination of a bar code and numbers by which a scanner can identify a product and usu. assign a price

uni·verse \ˈyü-nə-ˌvərs\ *n* [L *universum*, fr. neut. of *universus* entire, whole, fr. *unus* one + *versus* turned toward, fr. pp. of *vertere* to turn] : the whole body of things observed or assumed : COSMOS

uni·ver·si·ty \ˌyü-nə-ˈvər-sə-tē\ *n*, *pl* **-ties** : an institution of higher learning authorized to confer degrees in various special fields (as theology, law, and medicine) as well as in the arts and sciences generally

un·just \ˌən-ˈjəst\ *adj* : characterized by injustice — **un·just·ly** *adv*

un·kempt \-ˈkempt\ *adj* **1** : lacking order or neatness; *also* : ROUGH, UNPOLISHED **2** : not combed : DISHEVELED

un·kind \-ˈkīnd\ *adj* : not kind or sympathetic ⟨an ∼ remark⟩ — **un·kind·ly** *adv* — **un·kind·ness** *n*

un·kind·ly \-ˈkīnd-lē\ *adj* : UNKIND — **un·kind·li·ness** *n*

un·know·ing \ˌən-ˈnō-iŋ\ *adj* : not knowing — **un·know·ing·ly** *adv*

un·known \-ˈnōn\ *adj* : not known or not well-known — **unknown** *n*

un·lace \ˌən-ˈlās\ *vb* : to loose by undoing a lace

un·lade \-ˈlād\ *vb* **-lad·ed; -laded** *or* **-lad·en** \-ˈlād-ᵊn\; **-lad·ing** : to take the load or cargo from : UNLOAD

un·latch \-ˈlach\ *vb* **1** : to open or loose by lifting the latch **2** : to become loosed or opened

un·law·ful \ˌən-ˈlȯ-fəl\ *adj* **1** : not lawful : ILLEGAL **2** : ILLEGITIMATE — **un·law·ful·ly** *adv*

un·lead·ed \-ˈle-dəd\ *adj* : not treated or mixed with lead or lead compounds

un·learn \-ˈlərn\ *vb* : to put out of one's knowledge or memory; *also* : to discard the habit of

un·learned \-ˈlər-nəd *for 1*; -ˈlərnd *for 2*\ *adj* **1** : UNEDUCATED, ILLITERATE **2** : not gained by study or training

un·leash \-ˈlēsh\ *vb* : to free from or as if from a leash : let loose

un·less \ən-ˈles, ˈən-ˌles\ *conj* : except on condition that ⟨won't go ∼ you do⟩

\ə\abut \ᵊ\kitten \ər\further \a\ash \ā\ace \ä\mop, mar \au̇\out \ch\chin \e\bet \ē\easy \g\go \i\hit \ī\ice \j\job \ŋ\sing \ō\go \ȯ\law \ȯi\boy \th\thin \ṯh\the \ü\loot \u̇\foot \y\yet \zh\vision *see also* Pronunciation Symbols page

un·let·tered \ˌən-ˈle-tərd\ *adj* : not educated : ILLITER-ATE

¹un·like \-ˈlīk\ *adj* **1** : not like : DISSIMILAR, DIFFERENT **2** : UNEQUAL — **un·like·ness** *n*

²unlike *prep* **1** : different from ⟨she's quite ∼ her sister⟩ **2** : unusual for ⟨it's ∼ you to be late⟩ **3** : differently from ⟨behaves ∼ his brother⟩

un·like·li·hood \ˌən-ˈlī-klē-ˌhůd\ *n* : IMPROBABILITY

un·like·ly \-ˈlī-klē\ *adj* **1** : not likely : IMPROBABLE **2** : likely to fail

un·lim·ber \ˌən-ˈlim-bər\ *vb* : to get ready for action

un·list·ed \ˌən-ˈlis-təd\ *adj* **1** : not appearing on a list; *esp* : not appearing in a telephone book **2** : not listed on a stock exchange

un·load \-ˈlōd\ *vb* **1** : to take away or off : REMOVE ⟨∼ cargo from a hold⟩; *also* : to get rid of **2** : to take a load from ⟨∼ the ship⟩; *also* : to relieve or set free : UNBUR-DEN ⟨∼ one's mind of worries⟩ **3** : to draw the charge from ⟨∼*ed* the gun⟩ **4** : to sell in volume

un·lock \-ˈläk\ *vb* **1** : to open or unfasten through release of a lock **2** : RELEASE ⟨∼ a flood of emotions⟩ **3** : DIS-CLOSE, REVEAL ⟨∼ nature's secrets⟩

un·looked–for \-ˈlůkt-ˌfôr\ *adj* : UNEXPECTED

un·loose \ˌən-ˈlüs\ *vb* : to relax the strain of : set free; *also* : UNTIE

un·loos·en \-ˈlüs-ᵊn\ *vb* : UNLOOSE

un·love·ly \-ˈləv-lē\ *adj* : having no charm or appeal : not amiable

un·luck·i·ly \-ˈlə-kə-lē\ *adv* : UNFORTUNATELY

un·lucky \-ˈlə-kē\ *adj* **1** : UNFORTUNATE, ILL-FATED **2** : likely to bring misfortune : INAUSPICIOUS **3** : REGRET-TABLE

un·man \ˌən-ˈman\ *vb* **1** : to deprive of manly courage **2** : CASTRATE

un·man·ly \-ˈman-lē\ *adj* : not manly : COWARDLY; *also* : EFFEMINATE

un·man·ner·ly \-ˈma-nər-lē\ *adj* : RUDE, IMPOLITE — **un·mannerly** *adv*

un·mask \ˌən-ˈmask\ *vb* **1** : to strip of a mask or a dis-guise : EXPOSE **2** : to remove one's mask

un·mean·ing \-ˈmē-niŋ\ *adj* : having no meaning : SENSE-LESS

un·me·di·at·ed \ˌən-ˈmē-dē-ˌā-təd\ *adj* : not mediated : not communicated or transformed by an intervening agency

un·meet \-ˈmēt\ *adj* : not meet or fit : UNSUITABLE, IM-PROPER

un·men·tion·able \-ˈmen-chə-nə-bəl\ *adj* : not fit or proper to be talked about

un·mer·ci·ful \-ˈmər-si-fəl\ *adj* : not merciful : CRUEL, MERCILESS — **un·mer·ci·ful·ly** *adv*

un·mind·ful \-ˈmīnd-fəl\ *adj* : not mindful : CARELESS, UNAWARE

un·mis·tak·able \ˌən-mə-ˈstā-kə-bəl\ *adj* : not capable of being mistaken or misunderstood : CLEAR, OBVIOUS — **un·mis·tak·ably** \-blē\ *adv*

un·mit·i·gat·ed \ˌən-ˈmi-tə-ˌgā-təd\ *adj* **1** : not softened or lessened **2** : ABSOLUTE, DOWNRIGHT ⟨an ∼ liar⟩

un·moor \-ˈmůr\ *vb* : to loose from or as if from moor-ings

un·mor·al \-ˈmôr-əl\ *adj* : having no moral perception or quality : AMORAL — **un·mo·ral·i·ty** \ˌən-mə-ˈra-lə-tē\ *n*

un·muz·zle \-ˈmə-zəl\ *vb* : to remove a muzzle from

un·nat·u·ral \ˌən-ˈna-chə-rəl\ *adj* : contrary to or acting contrary to nature or natural instincts; *also* : ABNORMAL — **un·nat·u·ral·ly** *adv* — **un·nat·u·ral·ness** *n*

un·nec·es·sar·i·ly \ˌən-ˈne-sə-ˈser-ə-lē\ *adv* **1** : not by necessity **2** : to an unnecessary degree ⟨∼ harsh⟩

un·nerve \ˌən-ˈnərv\ *vb* : to deprive of courage, strength, or steadiness; *also* : UPSET

un·nil·hex·i·um \ˌyün-ᵊl-ˈhek-sē-əm\ *n* [NL, fr. *unnil-*(fr. L *unus* one + *nil* zero) + Gk *hex* six + NL *-ium*]

: the chemical element of atomic number 106 — see EL-EMENT table

un·nil·pen·ti·um \-ˈpen-tē-əm\ *n* : the chemical element of atomic number 105 — see ELEMENT table

un·nil·qua·di·um \-ˈkwä-dē-əm\ *n* : the chemical ele-ment of atomic number 104 — see ELEMENT table

un·num·bered \ˌən-ˈnəm-bərd\ *adj* : not numbered or counted : INNUMERABLE

un·ob·tru·sive \ˌən-əb-ˈtrü-siv\ *adj* : not obtrusive or forward : not bold : INCONSPICUOUS — **un·ob·tru·sive·ly** *adv*

un·oc·cu·pied \ˌən-ˈä-kyə-ˌpīd\ *adj* **1** : not busy : UNEM-PLOYED **2** : not occupied : EMPTY, VACANT

un·or·ga·nized \-ˈôr-gə-ˌnīzd\ *adj* **1** : not formed or brought into an integrated or ordered whole **2** : not or-ganized into unions ⟨∼ labor⟩

Unp *symbol* unnilpentium

un·pack \ˌən-ˈpak\ *vb* **1** : to separate and remove things packed **2** : to open and remove the contents of

un·par·al·leled \ˌən-ˈpar-ə-ˌleld\ *adj* : having no paral-lel; *esp* : having no equal or match

un·par·lia·men·ta·ry \ˌən-ˌpär-lə-ˈmen-tə-rē\ *adj* : con-trary to parliamentary practice

un·peg \ˌən-ˈpeg\ *vb* **1** : to remove a peg from **2** : to un-fasten by or as if by removing a peg

un·per·son \ˈən-ˌpərs-ᵊn, -ˌpərs-\ *n* : a person who usu. for political or ideological reasons is removed from rec-ognition or consideration

un·pile \ˌən-ˈpīl\ *vb* : to take or disentangle from a pile

un·pin \-ˈpin\ *vb* : to remove a pin from : UNFASTEN

un·pleas·ant \-ˈplez-ᵊnt\ *adj* : not pleasant : DISAGREE-ABLE — **un·pleas·ant·ly** *adv* — **un·pleas·ant·ness** *n*

un·plug \ˌən-ˈpləg\ *vb* **1** : UNCLOG **2** : to remove (a plug) from a receptacle; *also* : to disconnect from an electric circuit by removing a plug

un·plumbed \-ˈpləmd\ *adj* **1** : not tested or measured with a plumb line **2** : not thoroughly explored

un·pop·u·lar \ˌən-ˈpä-pyə-lər\ *adj* : not popular : looked upon or received unfavorably — **un·pop·u·lar·i·ty** \ˌən-ˌpä-pyə-ˈlar-ə-tē\

un·prec·e·dent·ed \ˌən-ˈpre-sə-ˌden-təd\ *adj* : having no precedent : NOVEL

un·pre·ten·tious \ˌən-pri-ˈten-chəs\ *adj* : not pretentious : MODEST

un·prin·ci·pled \ˌən-ˈprin-sə-pəld\ *adj* : lacking sound or honorable principles : UNSCRUPULOUS

un·print·able \-ˈprin-tə-bəl\ *adj* : unfit to be printed

un·prof·it·able \ˌən-ˈprä-fə-tə-bəl\ *adj* : not profitable : USELESS, VAIN

Unq *symbol* unnilquadium

un·qual·i·fied \ˌən-ˈkwä-lə-ˌfīd\ *adj* **1** : not having req-uisite qualifications **2** : not modified or restricted by reservations : COMPLETE — **un·qual·i·fied·ly** \-ˌfī-əd-lē\ *adv*

un·ques·tion·able \-ˈkwes-chə-nə-bəl\ *adj* : not ques-tionable : INDISPUTABLE — **un·ques·tion·ably** \-blē\ *adv*

un·ques·tion·ing \-chə-niŋ\ *adj* : not questioning : ac-cepting without examination or hesitation — **un·ques-tion·ing·ly** *adv*

un·qui·et \-ˈkwī-ət\ *adj* **1** : not quiet : AGITATED, DIS-TURBED **2** : physically, emotionally, or mentally restless : UNEASY

un·quote \ˈən-ˌkwōt\ *n* — used orally to indicate the end of a direct quotation

un·rav·el \ˌən-ˈra-vəl\ *vb* **1** : to separate the threads of **2** : SOLVE ⟨∼ a mystery⟩ **3** : to become unraveled

un·read \-ˈred\ *adj* **1** : not read; *also* : left unexamined **2** : lacking the benefits or the experience of reading

un·re·al \-ˈrēl\ *adj* : lacking in reality, substance, or gen-uineness — **un·re·al·i·ty** \ˌən-rē-ˈa-lə-tē\ *n*

un·rea·son·able \-ˈrēz-ᵊn-ə-bəl\ *adj* **1** : not governed by or acting according to reason; *also* : not conformable to reason : ABSURD **2** : exceeding the bounds of reason or moderation — **un·rea·son·able·ness** *n* — **un·rea·son·ably** *adv*

un·rea·soned \-'rēz-ᵊnd\ *adj* : not based on reason or reasoning

un·rea·son·ing \-'rēz-ᵊn-iŋ\ *adj* : not using or showing the use of reason as a guide or control

un·re·con·struct·ed \ˌən-ˌrē-kən-'strək-təd\ *adj* : not reconciled to some political, economic, or social change; *esp* : holding stubbornly to a particular belief, view, place, or style

un·reel \ˌən-'rēl\ *vb* **1** : to unwind from or as if from a reel **2** : to perform successfully

un·re·gen·er·ate \ˌən-ri-'je-nə-rət\ *adj* : not regenerated or reformed

un·re·lent·ing \-'len-tiŋ\ *adj* **1** : not yielding in determination : STERN ⟨∼ leader⟩ **2** : not letting up or weakening in vigor or pace : CONSTANT — **un·re·lent·ing·ly** *adv*

un·re·mit·ting \-'mi-tiŋ\ *adj* : CONTINUOUS, INCESSANT, PERSEVERING — **un·re·mit·ting·ly** *adv*

un·re·quit·ed \ˌən-ri-'kwī-təd\ *adj* : not requited : not reciprocated or returned in kind ⟨∼ love⟩

un·re·served \-'zərvd\ *adj* **1** : not limited or partial ⟨∼ enthusiasm⟩ **2** : not cautious or reticent : FRANK, OPEN **3** : not set aside for special use — **un·re·serv·ed·ly** \-'zər-vəd-lē\ *adv*

un·rest \ˌən-'rest\ *n* : a disturbed or uneasy state : TURMOIL

un·re·strained \ˌən-ri-'strānd\ *adj* **1** : IMMODERATE, UNCONTROLLED **2** : SPONTANEOUS

un·re·straint \-ri-'strānt\ *n* : lack of restraint

un·rid·dle \ˌən-'rid-ᵊl\ *vb* : to find the explanation of : SOLVE

un·righ·teous \-'rī-chəs\ *adj* **1** : SINFUL, WICKED **2** : UNJUST — **un·righ·teous·ness** *n*

un·ripe \-'rīp\ *adj* : not ripe : IMMATURE

un·ri·valed *or* **un·ri·valled** \ˌən-'rī-vəld\ *adj* : having no rival : SUPREME

un·robe \-'rōb\ *vb* : DISROBE, UNDRESS

un·roll \-'rōl\ *vb* **1** : to unwind a roll of : open out **2** : DISPLAY, DISCLOSE **3** : to become unrolled or spread out

un·roof \-'rüf, -'rùf\ *vb* : to strip off the roof or covering of

un·ruf·fled \ˌən-'rə-fəld\ *adj* **1** : not agitated or upset **2** : not ruffled : SMOOTH ⟨∼ water⟩

un·ruly \-'rü-lē\ *adj* [ME *unreuly*, fr. *un-* + *reuly* disciplined, fr. *reule* rule, fr. OF, tr. L *regula* straightedge, rule, fr. *regere* to direct] : not submissive to rule or restraint : TURBULENT ⟨∼ passions⟩ — **un·rul·i·ness** \-'rü-lē-nəs\ *n*

un·sad·dle \ˌən-'sad-ᵊl\ *vb* **1** : to remove the saddle from a horse **2** : UNHORSE

un·sat·u·rat·ed \-'sa-chə-ˌrā-təd\ *adj* **1** : capable of absorbing or dissolving more of something **2** : containing double or triple bonds between carbon atoms ⟨∼ fats or oils⟩ — **un·sat·u·rate** \-rət\ *n*

un·saved \ˌən-'sāvd\ *adj* : not saved; *esp* : not rescued from eternal punishment

un·sa·vory \-'sā-və-rē\ *adj* **1** : TASTELESS **2** : unpleasant to taste or smell **3** : morally offensive

un·say \-'sā\ *vb* **-said** \-'sed\; **-say·ing** : to take back (something said) : RETRACT, WITHDRAW

un·scathed \-'skāthd\ *adj* : wholly unharmed : not injured

un·schooled \-'sküld\ *adj* : not schooled : UNTAUGHT, UNTRAINED

un·sci·en·tif·ic \ˌən-ˌsī-ən-'ti-fik\ *adj* : not scientific : not in accord with the principles and methods of science

un·scram·ble \ˌən-'skram-bəl\ *vb* **1** : RESOLVE, CLARIFY **2** : to restore (as a radio message) to intelligible form

un·screw \-'skrü\ *vb* **1** : to draw the screws from **2** : to loosen by turning

un·scru·pu·lous \-'skrü-pyə-ləs\ *adj* : not scrupulous : UNPRINCIPLED — **un·scru·pu·lous·ly** *adv* — **un·scru·pu·lous·ness** *n*

un·seal \-'sēl\ *vb* : to break or remove the seal of : OPEN

un·search·able \-'sər-chə-bəl\ *adj* : not capable of being searched or explored

un·sea·son·able \-'sēz-ᵊn-ə-bəl\ *adj* : not seasonable : happening or coming at the wrong time : UNTIMELY — **un·sea·son·ably** \-blē\ *adv*

un·seat \-'sēt\ *vb* **1** : to throw from one's seat esp. on horseback **2** : to remove from political office

un·seem·ly \-'sēm-lē\ *adj* : not according with established standards of good form or taste; *also* : not suitable — **un·seem·li·ness** *n*

un·seen \ˌən-'sēn\ *adj* : not seen : INVISIBLE

un·seg·re·gat·ed \-'se-gri-ˌgā-təd\ *adj* : not segregated; *esp* : free from racial segregation

un·self·ish \-'sel-fish\ *adj* : not selfish : GENEROUS — **un·self·ish·ly** *adv* — **un·self·ish·ness** *n*

un·set·tle \ˌən-'set-ᵊl\ *vb* : to move or loosen from a settled position : DISPLACE, DISTURB

un·set·tled \-'set-ᵊld\ *adj* **1** : not settled : not fixed (as in position or character) **2** : not calm : DISTURBED **3** : not decided in mind : UNDETERMINED **4** : not paid ⟨∼ accounts⟩ **5** : not occupied by settlers

un·shack·le \-'sha-kəl\ *vb* : to free from shackles

un·shaped \-'shāpt\ *adj* : not shaped; *esp* : not being in finished, final, or perfect form ⟨∼ ideas⟩ ⟨∼ timber⟩

un·sheathe \ˌən-'shēth\ *vb* : to draw from or as if from a sheath

un·ship \-'ship\ *vb* **1** : to remove from a ship **2** : to remove or become removed from position ⟨∼ an oar⟩

un·shod \ˌən-'shäd\ *adj* : not wearing or provided with shoes

un·sight·ly \ˌən-'sīt-lē\ *adj* : unpleasant to the sight : UGLY

un·skilled \-'skild\ *adj* **1** : not skilled; *esp* : not skilled in a specified branch of work **2** : not requiring skill

un·skill·ful \-'skil-fəl\ *adj* : lacking in skill or proficiency — **un·skill·ful·ly** *adv*

un·sling \-'sliŋ\ *vb* **-slung** \-'sləŋ\; **-sling·ing** : to remove from being slung

un·snap \-'snap\ *vb* : to loosen or free by or as if by undoing a snap

un·snarl \-'snärl\ *vb* : to remove snarls from : UNTANGLE

un·so·phis·ti·cat·ed \ˌən-sə-'fis-tə-ˌkā-təd\ *adj* **1** : not worldly-wise : lacking sophistication **2** : SIMPLE

un·sought \ˌən-'sot\ *adj* : not sought : not searched for or asked for : not obtained by effort ⟨∼ honors⟩

un·sound \-'saùnd\ *adj* **1** : not healthy or whole; *also* : not mentally normal **2** : not valid **3** : not firmly made or fixed — **un·sound·ly** *adv* — **un·sound·ness** *n*

un·spar·ing \-'spar-iŋ\ *adj* **1** : HARD, RUTHLESS **2** : not frugal : LIBERAL, PROFUSE

un·speak·able \-'spē-kə-bəl\ *adj* **1** : impossible to express in words **2** : extremely bad — **un·speak·ably** \-blē\ *adv*

un·spot·ted \-'spä-təd\ *adj* : not spotted or stained; *esp* : free from moral stain

un·sprung \-'sprəŋ\ *adj* : not sprung; *esp* : not equipped with springs

un·sta·ble \-'stā-bəl\ *adj* **1** : not stable **2** : FICKLE, VACILLATING; *also* : lacking effective emotional control **3** : readily changing (as by decomposing) in chemical or physical composition or in biological activity ⟨an ∼ atomic nucleus⟩

un·steady \ˌən-'ste-dē\ *adj* : not steady : UNSTABLE —

\ə\abut \ᵊ\kitten \ər\further \a\ash \ā\ace \ä\mop, mar \aù\out \ch\chin \e\bet \ē\easy \g\go \i\hit \ī\ice \j\job \ŋ\sing \ō\go \ò\law \òi\boy \th\thin \t͟h\the \ü\loot \ù\foot \y\yet \zh\vision *see also* Pronunciation Symbols page

un·stead·i·ly \-'sted-ᵊl-ē\ adv — **un·stead·i·ness** \-'ste-dē-nəs\ n

un·stint·ing \-'stin-tiŋ\ adj 1 : not restricting or holding back 2 : giving or being given freely or generously ⟨∼ praise⟩

un·stop \-'stäp\ vb 1 : UNCLOG 2 : to remove a stopper from

un·stop·pa·ble \,ən-'stä-pə-bəl\ adj : incapable of being stopped

un·strap \-'strap\ vb : to remove or loose a strap from

un·stressed \,ən-'strest\ adj : not stressed; esp : not bearing a stress or accent

un·strung \-'strəŋ\ adj 1 : having the strings loose or detached 2 : nervously tired or anxious

un·stud·ied \-'stə-dēd\ adj 1 : not acquired by study 2 : NATURAL, UNFORCED ⟨moved with ∼ grace⟩

un·sub·stan·tial \,ən-səb-'stan-chəl\ adj : INSUBSTANTIAL

un·sung \,ən-'səŋ\ adj 1 : not sung 2 : not celebrated in song or verse ⟨∼ heroes⟩

un·swerv·ing \,ən-'swer-viŋ\ adj 1 : not swerving or turning aside 2 : STEADY

un·tan·gle \-'taŋ-gəl\ vb 1 : DISENTANGLE 2 : to straighten out : RESOLVE ⟨∼ a problem⟩

un·taught \-'tȯt\ adj 1 : not instructed or taught : IGNORANT 2 : NATURAL, SPONTANEOUS ⟨∼ kindness⟩

un·think·able \-'thiŋ-kə-bəl\ adj : not to be thought of or considered as possible ⟨∼ cruelty⟩

un·think·ing \,ən-'thiŋ-kiŋ\ adj : not thinking; esp : THOUGHTLESS, HEEDLESS — **un·think·ing·ly** adv

un·thought \,ən-'thȯt\ adj : not anticipated : UNEXPECTED — often used with of ⟨unthought-of development⟩

un·tie \-'tī\ vb **-tied; -ty·ing** or **-tie·ing** 1 : to free from something that ties, fastens, or restrains : UNBIND 2 : DISENTANGLE, RESOLVE 3 : to become loosened or unbound

¹**un·til** \,ən-'til\ prep : up to the time of ⟨worked ∼ 5 o'clock⟩

²**until** conj 1 : up to the time that ⟨wait ∼ he calls⟩ 2 : to the point or degree that ⟨ran ∼ she was breathless⟩

¹**un·time·ly** \,ən-'tīm-lē\ adv : at an inopportune time : UNSEASONABLY; also : PREMATURELY

²**untimely** adj : PREMATURE ⟨∼ death⟩; also : INOPPORTUNE, UNSEASONABLE

un·tir·ing \,ən-'tī-riŋ\ adj : not becoming tired : INDEFATIGABLE — **un·tir·ing·ly** adv

un·to \'ən-,tü\ prep : TO

un·told \,ən-'tōld\ adj 1 : not counted : VAST, NUMBERLESS 2 : not told : not revealed

¹**un·touch·able** \,ən-'tə-chə-bəl\ adj : forbidden to the touch

²**untouchable** n : a member of the lowest social class in India having in traditional Hindu belief the quality of defiling by contact a member of a higher caste

un·touched \,ən-'təcht\ adj 1 : not subjected to touching 2 : not described or dealt with 3 : not tasted 4 : being in a primeval state or condition 5 : UNAFFECTED

un·to·ward \,ən-'tōrd, -'tō-ərd, ,ən-tə-'wȯrd\ adj 1 : difficult to manage : STUBBORN, WILLFUL ⟨an ∼ child⟩ 2 : INCONVENIENT, TROUBLESOME ⟨an ∼ encounter⟩

un·tried \,ən-'trīd\ adj : not tested or proved by experience or trial; also : not tried in court

un·true \-'trü\ adj 1 : not faithful : DISLOYAL 2 : not according with a standard of correctness 3 : FALSE

un·truth \,ən-'trüth, 'ən-,trüth\ n 1 : lack of truthfulness 2 : FALSEHOOD

un·tune \-'tün, -'tyün\ vb 1 : to put out of tune 2 : DISARRANGE, DISCOMPOSE

un·tu·tored \-'tü-tərd, -'tyü-\ adj : UNTAUGHT, UNLEARNED, IGNORANT

un·twine \-'twīn\ vb : UNWIND, DISENTANGLE

un·twist \,ən-'twist\ vb 1 : to separate the twisted parts of : UNTWINE 2 : to become untwined

un·used \-'yüst, -'yüzd for 1; -'yüzd for 2\ adj 1 : UNACCUSTOMED 2 : not used

un·usu·al \-'yü-zhə-wəl\ adj : not usual : UNCOMMON, RARE — **un·usu·al·ly** adv

un·ut·ter·able \-'ə-tə-rə-bəl\ adj : being beyond the powers of description : INEXPRESSIBLE — **un·ut·ter·ably** \-blē\ adv

un·var·nished \-'vär-nisht\ adj 1 : not varnished 2 : not embellished : PLAIN ⟨the ∼ truth⟩

un·veil \,ən-'vāl\ vb 1 : to remove a veil or covering from : DISCLOSE 2 : to remove a veil : reveal oneself

un·voiced \-'vȯist\ adj 1 : not verbally expressed : UNSPOKEN 2 : VOICELESS 2

un·war·rant·able \-'wȯr-ən-tə-bəl\ adj : not justifiable : INEXCUSABLE — **un·war·rant·ably** \-blē\ adv

un·weave \-'wēv\ vb **-wove** \-'wōv\; **-wo·ven** \-'wō-vən\; **-weav·ing** : DISENTANGLE, RAVEL

un·well \,ən-'wel\ adj : SICK, AILING

un·whole·some \-'hōl-səm\ adj 1 : harmful to physical, mental, or moral well-being 2 : CORRUPT, UNSOUND; also : offensive to the senses : LOATHSOME

un·wieldy \-'wēl-dē\ adj : not easily managed, handled, or used (as because of bulk, weight, or complexity) : AWKWARD ⟨an ∼ tool⟩

un·wind \-'wīnd\ vb **-wound** \-'waùnd\; **-wind·ing** 1 : to undo something that is wound : loose from coils 2 : to become unwound : be capable of being unwound 3 : RELAX

un·wise \,ən-'wīz\ adj : not wise : FOOLISH — **un·wise·ly** adv

un·wit·ting \-'wi-tiŋ\ adj 1 : not knowing : UNAWARE 2 : not intended : INADVERTENT ⟨∼ mistake⟩ — **un·wit·ting·ly** adv

un·wont·ed \-'wȯn-təd, -'wōn-\ adj 1 : RARE, UNUSUAL 2 : not accustomed by experience — **un·wont·ed·ly** adv

un·world·ly \-'wərld-lē\ adj 1 : not of this world; esp : SPIRITUAL 2 : NAIVE 3 : not swayed by worldly considerations — **un·world·li·ness** \-lē-nəs\ n

un·wor·thy \,ən-'wər-thē\ adj 1 : BASE, DISHONORABLE 2 : not meritorious : not worthy : UNDESERVING 3 : not deserved : UNMERITED ⟨∼ treatment⟩ — **un·wor·thi·ly** \-thə-lē\ adv — **un·wor·thi·ness** \-thē-nəs\ n

un·wrap \-'rap\ vb : to remove the wrapping from : DISCLOSE

un·writ·ten \-'rit-ᵊn\ adj 1 : not in writing : ORAL, TRADITIONAL ⟨an ∼ law⟩ 2 : containing no writing : BLANK

un·yield·ing \,ən-'yēl-diŋ\ adj 1 : characterized by lack of softness or flexibility 2 : characterized by firmness or obduracy

un·yoke \-'yōk\ vb : to remove a yoke from; also : SEPARATE, DISCONNECT

un·zip \-'zip\ vb : to zip open : open by means of a zipper

¹**up** \'əp\ adv 1 : in or to a higher position or level; esp : away from the center of the earth 2 : from beneath a surface (as ground or water) 3 : from below the horizon 4 : in or into an upright position; esp : out of bed 5 : with greater intensity ⟨speak ∼⟩ 6 : in or into a better or more advanced state or a state of greater intensity or activity ⟨stir ∼ a fire⟩ 7 : into existence, evidence, or knowledge ⟨the missing book turned ∼⟩ 8 : into consideration ⟨brought the matter ∼⟩ 9 : to or at bat 10 : into possession or custody ⟨gave himself ∼⟩ 11 : ENTIRELY, COMPLETELY ⟨eat it ∼⟩ 12 — used for emphasis ⟨clean ∼ a room⟩ 13 : ASIDE, BY ⟨lay ∼ supplies⟩ 14 : so as to arrive or approach ⟨ran ∼ the path⟩ 15 : in a direction opposite to down 16 : in or into parts ⟨tear ∼ paper⟩ 17 : to a stop ⟨pull ∼ at the curb⟩ 18 : for each side ⟨the score was 15 ∼⟩

²**up** adj 1 : risen above the horizon ⟨the sun is ∼⟩ 2 : being out of bed ⟨∼ by 6 o'clock⟩ 3 : relatively high ⟨prices are ∼⟩ 4 : RAISED, LIFTED ⟨windows are ∼⟩ 5 : BUILT,

CONSTRUCTED ⟨the house is ∼⟩ **6** : grown above a surface ⟨the corn is ∼⟩ **7** : moving, inclining, or directed upward **8** : marked by agitation, excitement, or activity **9** : READY; *esp* : highly prepared **10** : going on : taking place ⟨find out what is ∼⟩ **11** : EXPIRED, ENDED ⟨the time is ∼⟩ **12** : well informed ⟨∼ on the news⟩ **13** : being ahead or in advance of an opponent ⟨one hole ∼ in a match⟩ **14** : presented for or being under consideration **15** : charged before a court ⟨∼ for robbery⟩

³up *prep* **1** : to, toward, or at a higher point of ⟨∼ a ladder⟩ **2** : to or toward the source of ⟨∼ the river⟩ **3** : to or toward the northern part of ⟨∼ the coast⟩ **4** : to or toward the interior of ⟨traveling ∼ the country⟩ **5** : ALONG ⟨walk ∼ the street⟩

⁴up *n* **1** : an upward course or slope **2** : a period or state of prosperity or success ⟨he had his ∼s and downs⟩

⁵up *vb* upped \'əpt\ *or in* 2 up; upped; up·ping; ups *or in* 2 up **1** : to rise from a lying or sitting position **2** : to act abruptly or surprisingly ⟨she *upped* and left home⟩ **3** : to move or cause to move upward ⟨*upped* the prices⟩

Upa·ni·shad \ü-'pän-i-ˌshäd\ *n* : one of a set of Vedic philosophical treatises

¹up·beat \'əp-ˌbēt\ *n* : an unaccented beat in a musical measure; *esp* : the last beat of the measure

²upbeat *adj* : OPTIMISTIC, CHEERFUL

up·braid \ˌəp-'brād\ *vb* : to criticize, reproach, or scold severely

up·bring·ing \'əp-ˌbriŋ-iŋ\ *n* : the process of bringing up and training

UPC *abbr* Universal Product Code

up·chuck \'əp-ˌchək\ *vb* : VOMIT

up·com·ing \'əp-ˌkə-miŋ\ *adj* : FORTHCOMING, APPROACHING

up–coun·try \'əp-ˌkən-trē\ *adj* : of or relating to the interior of a country or a region — **up–country** \'əp-'kən-\ *adv*

up·date \ˌəp-'dāt\ *vb* : to bring up to date — **update** \'əp-ˌdāt\ *n*

up·draft \'əp-ˌdraft, -ˌdráft\ *n* : an upward movement of gas (as air)

up·end \ˌəp-'end\ *vb* : to set, stand, or rise on end; *also* : OVERTURN

up–front \'əp-ˌfrənt, ˌəp-'frənt\ *adj* **1** : HONEST, CANDID **2** : ADVANCE ⟨∼ payment⟩

up front *adv* : in advance ⟨paid *up front*⟩

¹up·grade \'əp-ˌgrād\ *n* **1** : an upward grade or slope **2** : INCREASE, RISE

²up·grade \'əp-ˌgrād, ˌəp-'grad\ *vb* : to raise to a higher grade or position; *esp* : to advance to a job requiring a higher level of skill

up·growth \'əp-ˌgrōth\ *n* : the process of growing upward : DEVELOPMENT; *also* : a product or result of this

up·heav·al \ˌəp-'hē-vəl\ *n* **1** : the action or an instance of uplifting esp. of part of the earth's crust **2** : a violent agitation or change

¹up·hill \'əp-'hil\ *adv* : upward on a hill or incline; *also* : against difficulties

²up·hill \-ˌhil\ *adj* **1** : situated on elevated ground **2** : ASCENDING **3** : DIFFICULT, LABORIOUS

up·hold \ˌəp-'hōld\ *vb* -held \-'held\; -hold·ing **1** : to give support to **2** : to support against an opponent **3** : to keep elevated — **up·hold·er** *n*

up·hol·ster \ˌəp-'hōl-stər\ *vb* : to furnish with or as if with upholstery — **up·hol·ster·er** *n*

up·hol·stery \-stə-rē\ *n, pl* -ster·ies [ME *upholdester* upholsterer, fr. *upholden* to uphold, fr. *up* + *holden* to hold] : materials (as fabrics, padding, and springs) used to make a soft covering esp. for a seat

UPI *abbr* United Press International

up·keep \'əp-ˌkēp\ *n* : the act or cost of keeping up or maintaining; *also* : the state of being maintained

up·land \'əp-lənd, -ˌland\ *n* : high land esp. at some distance from the sea — **upland** *adj*

¹up·lift \ˌəp-'lift\ *vb* **1** : to lift or raise up : ELEVATE **2** : to improve the condition of esp. morally, socially, or intellectually

²up·lift \'əp-ˌlift\ *n* **1** : a lifting up; *esp* : an upheaval of the earth's surface **2** : moral or social improvement; *also* : a movement to make such improvement

up·mar·ket \ˌəp-'mär-kət\ *adj* : appealing to wealthy consumers

up·most \'əp-ˌmōst\ *adj* : UPPERMOST

up·on \ə-'pòn, -'pän\ *prep* : ON

¹up·per \'ə-pər\ *adj* **1** : higher in physical position, rank, or order **2** : constituting the smaller and more restricted branch of a bicameral legislature **3** *cap* : being a later part or formation of a specific geological period **4** : being toward the interior ⟨the ∼ Amazon⟩ **5** : NORTHERN ⟨∼ New York State⟩

²upper *n* : one that is upper; *esp* : the parts of a shoe or boot above the sole

up·per·case \ˌə-pər-'kās\ *adj* : CAPITAL 1 — **uppercase** *n*

upper class *n* : a social class occupying a position above the middle class and having the highest status in a society — **upper–class** *adj*

up·per·class·man \ˌə-pər-'klas-mən\ *n* : a junior or senior in a college or high school

upper crust *n* : the highest social class or group; *esp* : the highest circle of the upper class

up·per·cut \'ə-pər-ˌkət\ *n* : a short swinging punch delivered (as in boxing) in an upward direction usu. with a bent arm

upper hand *n* : MASTERY, ADVANTAGE

up·per·most \'ə-pər-ˌmōst\ *adv* : in or into the highest or most prominent position — **uppermost** *adj*

up·pish \'ə-pish\ *adj* : UPPITY

up·pi·ty \'ə-pə-tē\ *adj* : ARROGANT, PRESUMPTUOUS

up·raise \ˌəp-'rāz\ *vb* : to lift up : ELEVATE

¹up·right \'əp-ˌrīt\ *adj* **1** : PERPENDICULAR, VERTICAL **2** : erect in carriage or posture **3** : morally correct : JUST — **upright** *adv* — **up·right·ly** *adv* — **up·right·ness** *n*

²upright *n* **1** : the state of being upright : a vertical position **2** : something that stands upright

upright piano *n* : a piano whose strings run vertically

up·ris·ing \'əp-ˌrī-ziŋ\ *n* : INSURRECTION, REVOLT, REBELLION

up·riv·er \'əp-'ri-vər\ *adv or adj* : toward or at a point nearer the source of a river

up·roar \'əp-ˌrȯr\ *n* [D *oproer*, fr. MD, fr. *op* *up* + *roer* motion] : a state of commotion, excitement, or violent disturbance

up·roar·i·ous \ˌəp-'rȯr-ē-əs\ *adj* **1** : marked by uproar **2** : extremely funny — **up·roar·i·ous·ly** *adv*

up·root \ˌəp-'rüt, -'rùt\ *vb* : to remove by or as if by pulling up by the roots

¹up·set \ˌəp-'set\ *vb* -set; -set·ting **1** : to force or be forced out of the usual upright, level, or proper position **2** : to disturb emotionally : WORRY; *also* : to make somewhat ill **3** : UNSETTLE, DISARRANGE **4** : to defeat unexpectedly

²up·set \'əp-ˌset\ *n* **1** : an upsetting or being upset; *esp* : a minor illness **2** : a derangement of plans or ideas **3** : an unexpected defeat

³up·set \(ˌ)əp-'set\ *adj* : emotionally disturbed or agitated

up·shot \'əp-ˌshät\ *n* : the final result

¹up·side \'əp-ˌsīd\ *n* : the upper side

²up·side \ˌəp-'sīd\ *prep* : up on or against the side of ⟨knocked him ∼ the head⟩

up·side down \ˌəp-ˌsīd-'daùn\ *adv* **1** : with the upper and

---

\ə\abut \ᵊ\kitten \ər\further \a\ash \ā\ace \ä\mop, mar
\aù\out \ch\chin \e\bet \ē\easy \g\go \i\hit \ī\ice \j\job
\ŋ\sing \ō\go \ò\law \ȯi\boy \th\thin \t̲h̲\the \ü\loot \ù\foot
\y\yet \zh\vision *see also* Pronunciation Symbols page

the lower parts reversed in position **2** : in or into confusion or disorder — **upside–down** *adj*

up·si·lon \'üp-sə-ˌlän, 'yüp-, 'əp-\ *n* : the 20th letter of the Greek alphabet — Y or *υ*

¹**up·stage** \'əp-ˈstāj\ *adv or adj* : toward or at the rear of a theatrical stage

²**up·stage** \ˌəp-ˈstāj\ *vb* : to draw attention away from (as an actor)

¹**up·stairs** \ˌəp-ˈstarz\ *adv* **1** : up the stairs : to or on a higher floor **2** : to or at a higher position

²**up·stairs** \'əp-ˈstarz\ *adj* : situated above the stairs esp. on an upper floor ⟨∼ bedroom⟩

³**up·stairs** \'əp-ˈstarz, 'əp-ˌstarz\ *n sing or pl* : the part of a building above the ground floor

up·stand·ing \ˌəp-ˈstan-diŋ, 'əp-\ *adj* **1** : ERECT **2** : STRAIGHTFORWARD, HONEST

¹**up·start** \ˌəp-ˈstärt\ *vb* : to jump up suddenly

²**up·start** \'əp-ˌstärt\ *n* : one that has risen suddenly; *esp* : one that claims more personal importance than is warranted — **up·start** \-ˈstärt\ *adj*

up·state \'əp-ˈstāt\ *adj* : of, relating to, or characteristic of a part of a state away from a large city and esp. to the north — **upstate** *adv* — **upstate** *n*

up·stream \'əp-ˈstrēm\ *adv* : at or toward the source of a stream — **upstream** *adj*

up·stroke \'əp-ˌstrōk\ *n* : an upward stroke (as of a pen)

up·surge \-ˌsərj\ *n* : a rapid or sudden rise

up·swept \'əp-ˌswept\ *adj* : swept upward ⟨∼ hairdo⟩

up·swing \'əp-ˌswiŋ\ *n* : an upward swing; *esp* : a marked increase or rise (as in activity)

up·take \'əp-ˌtāk\ *n* **1** : UNDERSTANDING, COMPREHENSION ⟨quick on the ∼⟩ **2** : the process or an instance of absorbing and incorporating esp. into a living organism

up·thrust \'əp-ˌthrəst\ *n* : an upward thrust (as of the earth's crust) — **upthrust** *vb*

up·tight \'əp-ˈtīt\ *adj* **1** : TENSE, NERVOUS, UNEASY; *also* : ANGRY, INDIGNANT **2** : rigidly conventional

up–to–date *adj* **1** : extending up to the present time **2** : abreast of the times : MODERN — **up–to–date·ness** *n*

up·town \'əp-ˌtaùn\ *n* : the upper part of a town or city; *esp* : the residential district — **up·town** \'əp-ˈtaùn\ *adj or adv*

¹**up·turn** \'əp-ˌtərn, ˌəp-ˈtərn\ *vb* **1** : to turn (as earth) up or over **2** : to turn or direct upward

²**up·turn** \'əp-ˌtərn\ *n* : an upward turn esp. toward better conditions or higher prices

¹**up·ward** \'əp-wərd\ *or* **up·wards** \-wərdz\ *adv* **1** : in a direction from lower to higher **2** : toward a higher or better condition **3** : toward a greater amount or higher number, degree, or rate

²**upward** *adj* : directed or moving toward or situated in a higher place or level : ASCENDING — **up·ward·ly** *adv*

upwards of *also* **upward of** *adv* : more than : in excess of ⟨they cost *upwards of* $25 each⟩

up·well \ˌəp-ˈwel\ *vb* : to move or flow upward

up·well·ing \-ˈwe-liŋ\ *n* : a rising or an appearance of rising to the surface and flowing outward; *esp* : the movement of deep cold usu. nutrient-rich ocean water to the surface

up·wind \'əp-ˈwind\ *adv or adj* : in the direction from which the wind is blowing

ura·cil \'yùr-ə-ˌsil\ *n* : a pyrimidine base that is one of the four bases coding genetic information in the molecular chain of RNA

ura·ni·um \yù-ˈrā-nē-əm\ *n* : a silvery heavy radioactive metallic chemical element used as a source of atomic energy — see ELEMENT table

Ura·nus \'yùr-ə-nəs, yù-ˈrā-\ *n* [LL, the sky personified as a god, fr. Gk *Ouranos*, fr. *ouranos* sky, heaven] : the planet 7th in order from the sun — see PLANET table

ur·ban \'ər-bən\ *adj* : of, relating to, characteristic of, or constituting a city

ur·bane \ˌər-ˈbān\ *adj* [L *urbanus* urban, urbane, fr.

urbs city] : very polite and polished in manner : SUAVE

ur·ban·ite \'ər-bə-ˌnīt\ *n* : a person who lives in a city

ur·ban·i·ty \ˌər-ˈba-nə-tē\ *n, pl* **-ties** : the quality or state of being urbane

ur·ban·ize \'ər-bə-ˌnīz\ *vb* **-ized; -iz·ing** : to cause to take on urban characteristics — **ur·ban·i·za·tion** \ˌər-bə-nə-ˈzā-shən\ *n*

urban renewal *n* : a construction program to replace or restore substandard buildings in an urban area

ur·chin \'ər-chən\ *n* [ME, hedgehog, fr. MF *herichon*, ultim. fr. L *ericius*] : a pert or mischievous youngster

Ur·du \'ùr-dü, 'ər-\ *n* [Hindi *urdū*, fr. Per *zabān-e-urdū= e-muallā* language of the Exalted Comp (the imperial bazaar in Delhi)] : an official language of Pakistan that is widely used by Muslims in urban areas of India

urea \yù-ˈrē-ə\ *n* : a soluble nitrogenous compound that is the chief solid constituent of mammalian urine

ure·mia \yù-ˈrē-mē-ə\ *n* : accumulation in the blood of materials normally passed off in the urine resulting in a poisoned condition — **ure·mic** \-mik\ *adj*

ure·ter \'yùr-ə-tər\ *n* : a duct that carries the urine from a kidney to the bladder

ure·thra \yù-ˈrē-thrə\ *n, pl* **-thras** *or* **-thrae** \-(ˌ)thrē\ : the canal that in most mammals carries off the urine from the bladder and in the male also serves to carry semen from the body — **ure·thral** \-thrəl\ *adj*

ure·thri·tis \ˌyùr-i-ˈthrī-təs\ *n* : inflammation of the urethra

¹**urge** \'ərj\ *vb* **urged; urging** **1** : to present, advocate, or demand earnestly **2** : to try to persuade or sway ⟨∼ a guest to stay⟩ **3** : to serve as a motive or reason for **4** : to impress or impel to some course or activity ⟨the dog *urged* the sheep onward⟩

²**urge** *n* **1** : the act or process of urging **2** : a force or impulse that urges or drives

ur·gent \'ər-jənt\ *adj* **1** : calling for immediate attention : PRESSING **2** : urging insistently — **ur·gen·cy** \-jən-sē\ *n* — **ur·gent·ly** *adv*

uric \'yùr-ik\ *adj* : of, relating to, or found in urine

uric acid *n* : a nearly insoluble acid that is the chief nitrogenous excretory product of birds but is present in only small amounts in mammalian urine

uri·nal \'yùr-ən-ᵊl\ *n* **1** : a receptacle for urine **2** : a place for urinating

uri·nal·y·sis \ˌyùr-ə-ˈna-lə-səs\ *n* : chemical analysis of urine

uri·nary \'yùr-ə-ˌner-ē\ *adj* **1** : relating to, occurring in, or being organs for the formation and discharge of urine **2** : of, relating to, or for urine

urinary bladder *n* : a membranous sac in many vertebrates that serves for the temporary retention of urine and discharges by the urethra

uri·nate \'yùr-ə-ˌnāt\ *vb* **-nat·ed; -nat·ing** : to release or give off urine — **uri·na·tion** \ˌyùr-ə-ˈnā-shən\ *n*

urine \'yùr-ən\ *n* : a waste material from the kidneys that is usu. a yellowish watery liquid in mammals but is semisolid in birds and reptiles

urn \'ərn\ *n* **1** : a vessel that typically has the form of a vase on a pedestal and often is used to hold the ashes of the dead **2** : a closed vessel usu. with a spout for serving a hot beverage

uro·gen·i·tal \ˌyùr-ō-ˈje-nət-ᵊl\ *adj* : of, relating to, or being the excretory and reproductive organs or functions

urol·o·gy \yù-ˈrä-lə-jē\ *n* : a branch of medical science dealing with the urinary or urogenital tract and its disorders — **uro·log·ic** \ˌyùr-ə-ˈlä-jik\ *or* **uro·log·i·cal** \-ji-kəl\ *adj* — **urol·o·gist** \yù-ˈrä-lə-jist\ *n*

Ur·sa Ma·jor \ˌər-sə-ˈmā-jər\ *n* [L, lit., greater bear] : the northern constellation that contains the stars which form the Big Dipper

Ursa Mi·nor \-ˈmī-nər\ *n* [L, lit., lesser bear] : the constellation including the north pole of the heavens and the stars that form the Little Dipper with the North Star at the tip of the handle

ur·sine \'ər-ˌsīn\ *adj* : of, relating to, or resembling a bear

ur·ti·car·ia \ˌər-tə-'kar-ē-ə\ *n* [NL, fr. L *urtica* nettle] : HIVES

Uru·guay·an \ˌür-ə-'gwī-ən, ˌyùr-ə-'gwā-\ *n* : a native or inhabitant of Uruguay — **Uruguayan** *adj*

us \'əs\ *pron, objective case of* WE

US *abbr* United States

USA *abbr* **1** United States Army **2** United States of America

us·able *also* **use·able** \'yü-zə-bəl\ *adj* : suitable or fit for use — **us·abil·i·ty** \ˌyü-zə-'bi-lə-tē\ *n*

USAF *abbr* United States Air Force

us·age \'yü-sij, -zij\ *n* **1** : habitual or customary practice or procedure **2** : the way in which words and phrases are actually used **3** : the action or mode of using **4** : manner of treating

USCG *abbr* United States Coast Guard

USDA *abbr* United States Department of Agriculture

¹**use** \'yüs\ *n* **1** : the act or practice of using or employing something : EMPLOYMENT, APPLICATION **2** : the fact or state of being used **3** : the way of using **4** : USAGE, CUSTOM **5** : the privilege or benefit of using something **6** : the ability or power to use something (as a limb) **7** : the legal enjoyment of property that consists in its employment, occupation, or exercise; *also* : the benefit or profit esp. from property held in trust **8** : USEFULNESS, UTILITY; *also* : the end served : OBJECT, FUNCTION **9** : the occasion or need to employ (he had no more ~ for it) **10** : ESTEEM, LIKING (had no ~ for modern art)

²**use** \'yüz\ *vb* **used** \'yüzd; *"used to" usu* 'yüs-tə\; **us·ing 1** : to put into action or service : EMPLOY **2** : to consume or take (as drugs) regularly **3** : UTILIZE (~ tact); *also* : MANIPULATE (*used* his friends to get ahead) **4** : to expend or consume by putting to use **5** : to behave toward : TREAT (*used* the horse cruelly) **6** : to benefit from (house could ~ a coat of paint) **7** — used in the past with *to* to indicate a former practice, fact, or state (we *used* to work harder) — **us·er** *n*

used \'yüzd\ *adj* **1** : having been used by another : SECONDHAND (~ cars) **2** : ACCUSTOMED, HABITUATED (~ to the heat)

use·ful \'yüs-fəl\ *adj* : capable of being put to use : ADVANTAGEOUS; *esp* : serviceable for a beneficial end — **use·ful·ly** *adv* — **use·ful·ness** *n*

use·less \-ləs\ *adj* : having or being of no use : WORTHLESS — **use·less·ly** *adv* — **use·less·ness** *n*

USES *abbr* United States Employment Service

use up *vb* : to consume completely

¹**ush·er** \'ə-shər\ *n* [ME *ussher*, fr. MF *ussier*, fr. (assumed) VL *ustiarius* doorkeeper, fr. L *ostium, ustium* door, mouth of a river] **1** : an officer who walks before a person of rank **2** : one who escorts people to their seats (as in a church or theater)

²**usher** *vb* **1** : to conduct to a place **2** : to precede as an usher, forerunner, or harbinger **3** : INAUGURATE, INTRODUCE (~ in a new era)

ush·er·ette \ˌə-shə-'ret\ *n* : a girl or woman who is an usher (as in a theater)

USIA *abbr* United States Information Agency

USMC *abbr* United States Marine Corps

USN *abbr* United States Navy

USO *abbr* United Service Organizations

USP *abbr* United States Pharmacopeia

USPS *abbr* United States Postal Service

USS *abbr* United States ship

USSR *abbr* Union of Soviet Socialist Republics

usu *abbr* usual; usually

usu·al \'yü-zhə-wəl\ *adj* **1** : accordant with usage, custom, or habit : NORMAL **2** : commonly or ordinarily used **3** : ORDINARY **syn** customary, habitual, accustomed,

routine — **usu·al·ly** \'yü-zhə-wə-lē, 'yü-zhə-lē\ *adv*

usu·fruct \'yü-zə-ˌfrəkt\ *n* [L *ususfructus*, fr. *usus et fructus* use and enjoyment] : the legal right to use and enjoy the benefits and profits of something belonging to another

usu·rer \'yü-zhər-ər\ *n* : one that lends money esp. at an exorbitant rate

usu·ri·ous \yü-'zhùr-ē-əs\ *adj* : practicing, involving, or constituting usury (a ~ rate of interest)

usurp \yü-'sərp, -'zərp\ *vb* [ME, fr. MF *usurper*, fr. L *usurpare*, lit., to take possession of without legal claim, fr. *usu* (abl. of *usus* use) + *rapere* to seize] : to seize and hold by force or without right (~ a throne) — **usurpation** \ˌyü-sər-'pā-shən, -zər-\ *n* — **usurp·er** \yü-'sər-pər, -'zər-\ *n*

usu·ry \'yü-zhə-rē\ *n, pl* **-ries 1** : the lending of money with an interest charge for its use **2** : an excessive rate or amount of interest charged; *esp* : interest above an established legal rate

UT *abbr* Utah

Ute \'yüt\ *n, pl* **Ute** *or* **Utes** : a member of an American Indian people orig. ranging through Utah, Colorado, Arizona, and New Mexico

uten·sil \yü-'ten-səl\ *n* [ME, vessels for domestic use, fr. MF *utensile*, fr. L *utensilia*, fr. neut. pl. of *utensilis* useful, fr. *uti* to use] **1** : an instrument or vessel used in a household and esp. a kitchen **2** : a useful tool

uter·ine tube \'yü-tə-ˌrīn-, -rən\ *n* : FALLOPIAN TUBE

uter·us \'yü-tə-rəs\ *n, pl* **uteri** \'yü-tə-ˌrī\ *also* **uter·us·es** : the muscular organ of a female mammal. in which the young develop before birth — **uter·ine** \-ˌrīn, -rən\ *adj*

utile \'yüt-ʾl, 'yü-ˌtīl\ *adj* : USEFUL

¹**util·i·tar·i·an** \yù-ˌti-lə-'ter-ē-ən\ *n* : a person who believes in utilitarianism

²**utilitarian** *adj* **1** : of or relating to utilitarianism **2** : of or relating to utility : aiming at usefulness rather than beauty; *also* : serving a useful purpose

util·i·tar·i·an·ism \-ē-ə-ˌni-zəm\ *n* : a theory that the greatest good for the greatest number should be the main consideration in making a choice of actions

¹**util·i·ty** \yü-'ti-lə-tē\ *n, pl* **-ties 1** : USEFULNESS **2** : something useful or designed for use **3** : a business organization performing a public service and subject to special governmental regulation **4** : a public service or a commodity (as electricity or water) provided by a public utility; *also* : equipment to provide such or a similar service

²**utility** *adj* **1** : capable of serving esp. as a substitute in various uses or positions (a ~ outfielder) (a ~ knife) **2** : being of a usable but poor quality (~ beef)

uti·lize \'yüt-ʾl-ˌīz\ *vb* **-lized; -liz·ing** : to make use of : turn to profitable account or use — **uti·li·za·tion** \ˌyüt-ʾl-ə-'zā-shən\ *n*

ut·most \'ət-ˌmōst\ *adj* **1** : situated at the farthest or most distant point : EXTREME **2** : of the greatest or highest degree, quantity, number, or amount — **utmost** *n*

uto·pia \yü-'tō-pē-ə\ *n* [*Utopia*, imaginary island described in Sir Thomas More's *Utopia*, fr. Gk *ou* not, no + *topos* place] **1** *often cap* : a place of ideal perfection esp. in laws, government, and social conditions **2** : an impractical scheme for social improvement

¹**uto·pi·an** \-pē-ən\ *adj, often cap* **1** : of, relating to, or resembling a utopia **2** : proposing ideal social and political schemes that are impractical **3** : VISIONARY

²**utopian** *n* **1** : a believer in the perfectibility of human society **2** : one that proposes or advocates utopian schemes

\ə\abut \ᵊ\kitten \ər\further \a\ash \ā\ace \ä\mop, mar \aù\out \ch\chin \e\bet \ē\easy \g\go \i\hit \ī\ice \j\job \ŋ\sing \ō\go \ò\law \òi\boy \th\thin \th\the \ü\loot \ù\foot \y\yet \zh\vision *see also* Pronunciation Symbols page

¹ut·ter \\'ə-tər\ *adj* [ME, remote, fr. OE *ūtera* outer, compar. adj. fr. *ūt* out, adv.] : ABSOLUTE, TOTAL ⟨∼ ruin⟩ — **ut·ter·ly** *adv*

²utter *vb* [ME *uttren*, fr. *utter* outside, adv., fr. OE *ūtor*, compar. of *ūt* out] **1** : to send forth as a sound : express in usu. spoken words : PRONOUNCE, SPEAK **2** : to put (as currency) into circulation — **ut·ter·er** *n*

ut·ter·ance \\'ə-tə-rəns\ *n* **1** : something uttered; *esp* : an oral or written statement **2** : the action of uttering with the voice : SPEECH **3** : power, style, or manner of speaking

ut·ter·most \\'ə-tər-ˌmōst\ *adj* : EXTREME, UTMOST ⟨the ∼ parts of the earth⟩ — **uttermost** *n*

U–turn \\'yü-ˌtərn\ *n* : a turn resembling the letter U; *esp* : a 180-degree turn made by a vehicle in a road

UV *abbr* ultraviolet

uvu·la \\'yü-vyə-lə\ *n, pl* **-las** *or* **-lae** \-ˌlē, -ˌlī\ : the fleshy lobe hanging at the back of the roof of the mouth — **uvu·lar** \-lər\ *adj*

UW *abbr* underwriter

ux·o·ri·ous \ˌək-'sōr-ē-əs, ˌəg-'zōr-\ *adj* : excessively devoted or submissive to a wife

V

¹v \\'vē\ *n, pl* **v's** *or* **vs** \\'vēz\ *often cap* : the 22d letter of the English alphabet

²v *abbr, often cap* **1** vector **2** velocity **3** verb **4** verse **5** versus **6** very **7** victory **8** vide **9** voice **10** voltage **11** volume **12** vowel

V *symbol* **1** vanadium **2** volt

Va *abbr* Virginia

VA *abbr* **1** Veterans Administration **2** vice admiral **3** Virginia

va·can·cy \\'vā-kən-sē\ *n, pl* **-cies 1** : a vacating esp. of an office, position, or piece of property **2** : a vacant office, position, or tenancy; *also* : the period during which it stands vacant **3** : empty space : VOID **4** : the state of being vacant

va·cant \\'vā-kənt\ *adj* **1** : not occupied ⟨∼ seat⟩ ⟨∼ room⟩ **2** : EMPTY ⟨∼ space⟩ **3** : free from business or care ⟨a few ∼ hours⟩ **4** : devoid of thought, reflection, or expression ⟨a ∼ smile⟩ — **va·cant·ly** *adv*

va·cate \\'vā-ˌkāt\ *vb* **va·cat·ed; va·cat·ing 1** : to make void : ANNUL **2** : to make vacant (as an office or house); *also* : to give up the occupancy of

¹va·ca·tion \vā-'kā-shən, və-\ *n* : a period of rest from work : HOLIDAY

²vacation *vb* : to take or spend a vacation — **va·ca·tion·er** *n*

va·ca·tion·ist \-shə-nist\ *n* : a person taking a vacation

va·ca·tion·land \-shən-ˌland\ *n* : an area with recreational attractions and facilities for vacationists

vac·ci·nate \\'vak-sə-ˌnāt\ *vb* **-nat·ed; -nat·ing** : to administer a vaccine to usu. by injection; *also* : to produce immunity to smallpox by inoculating (a person) with the related cowpox virus

vac·ci·na·tion \ˌvak-sə-'nā-shən\ *n* **1** : the act of vaccinating **2** : the scar left by vaccinating

vac·cine \vak-'sēn, 'vak-ˌsēn\ *n* [L *vaccinus* of or from cows, fr. *vacca* cow; so called from the derivation of smallpox vaccine from cows] : material (as a preparation of killed or weakened virus or bacteria) used in vaccinating to induce immunity to a disease

vac·cin·ia \vak-'si-nē-ə\ *n* : COWPOX

vac·il·late \\'va-sə-ˌlāt\ *vb* **-lat·ed; -lat·ing 1** : SWAY, TOTTER; *also* : FLUCTUATE **2** : to incline first to one course or opinion and then to another : WAVER — **vac·il·la·tion** \ˌva-sə-'lā-shən\ *n*

va·cu·ity \va-'kyü-ə-tē\ *n, pl* **-ities 1** : an empty space **2** : the state, fact, or quality of being vacuous **3** : something that is vacuous

vac·u·ole \\'va-kyə-ˌwōl\ *n* : a usu. fluid-filled cavity esp. in the cytoplasm of an individual cell — **vac·u·o·lar** \ˌva-kyə-'wō-lər, -ˌlär\ *adj*

vac·u·ous \\'va-kyə-wəs\ *adj* **1** : EMPTY, VACANT, BLANK **2** : DULL, STUPID, INANE — **vac·u·ous·ly** *adv* — **vac·u·ous·ness** *n*

¹vac·u·um \\'va-(ˌ)kyüm, -kyəm\ *n, pl* **vacuums** *or* **vac-**

ua \-kyə-wə\ [L, fr. neut. of *vacuus* empty] **1** : a space entirely empty of matter **2** : a space from which most of the air has been removed (as by a pump) **3** : VOID, GAP **4** : VACUUM CLEANER — **vacuum** *adj*

²vacuum *vb* : to use a vacuum device (as a vacuum cleaner) on

vacuum bottle *n* : THERMOS

vacuum cleaner *n* : a household appliance for cleaning (as floors or rugs) by suction

vacuum–packed *adj* : having much of the air removed before being hermetically sealed

vacuum tube *n* : an electron tube from which most of the air has been removed

va·de me·cum \ˌvā-dē-'mē-kəm, ˌvä-dē-'mä-\ *n, pl* **vade mecums** [L, go with me] : something (as a handbook or manual) carried as a constant companion

VADM *abbr* vice admiral

¹vag·a·bond \\'va-gə-ˌbänd\ *adj* **1** : WANDERING, HOMELESS **2** : of, characteristic of, or leading the life of a vagrant or tramp **3** : leading an unsettled or irresponsible life

²vagabond *n* : one leading a vagabond life; *esp* : TRAMP

va·gar·i·ous \vā-'ger-ē-əs\ *adj* : marked by vagaries : CAPRICIOUS — **va·gar·i·ous·ly** *adv*

va·ga·ry \\'vā-gə-rē, və-'ger-ē\ *n, pl* **-ries** : an odd or eccentric idea or action : WHIM, CAPRICE

va·gi·na \və-'jī-nə\ *n, pl* **-nae** \-(ˌ)nē\ *or* **-nas** [L, lit., sheath] : a canal that leads from the uterus to the external opening of the female sex organs — **vag·i·nal** \\'va-jən-ᵊl\ *adj*

vag·i·ni·tis \ˌva-jə-'nī-təs\ *n* : inflammation of the vagina

va·gran·cy \\'vā-grən-sē\ *n, pl* **-cies 1** : the quality or state of being vagrant; *also* : a vagrant act or notion **2** : the offense of being a vagrant

¹va·grant \\'vā-grənt\ *n* : a person who has no job and wanders from place to place

²vagrant *adj* **1** : of, relating to, or characteristic of a vagrant **2** : following no fixed course : RANDOM, CAPRICIOUS ⟨∼ thoughts⟩ — **va·grant·ly** *adv*

vague \\'vāg\ *adj* **vagu·er; vagu·est** [MF, fr. L *vagus*, lit., wandering] **1** : not clear, definite, or distinct **2** : not clearly felt or analyzed ⟨a ∼ unrest⟩ **syn** obscure, dark, enigmatic, ambiguous, equivocal — **vague·ly** *adv* — **vague·ness** *n*

vain \\'vān\ *adj* [ME, fr. MF, fr. L *vanus* empty, vain] **1** : of no real value : IDLE, WORTHLESS **2** : FUTILE, UNSUCCESSFUL **3** : proud of one's looks or abilities **syn** conceited, narcissistic, vainglorious — **vain·ly** *adv*

vain·glo·ri·ous \ˌvān-'glōr-ē-əs\ *adj* : marked by vainglory : BOASTFUL

vain·glo·ry \\'vān-ˌglōr-ē\ *n* **1** : excessive or ostentatious pride esp. in one's own achievements **2** : vain display : VANITY

val *abbr* value; valued

va·lance \\'va-ləns, 'vā-\ *n* **1** : drapery hanging from an edge (as of an altar, table, or bed) **2** : a drapery or a decorative frame across the top of a window

vale \\'vāl\ *n* : VALLEY, DALE

vale·dic·tion \\va-lə-'dik-shən\ *n* [L *valedicere* to say farewell, fr. *vale* farewell + *dicere* to say] : an act or utterance of leave-taking : FAREWELL

vale·dic·to·ri·an \-ˌdik-'tōr-ē-ən\ *n* : the student usu. of the highest rank in a graduating class who delivers the valedictory address at commencement

vale·dic·to·ry \-'dik-tə-rē\ *adj* : bidding farewell : delivered as a valediction ⟨a ~ address⟩ — **valedictory** *n*

va·lence \\'vā-ləns\ *n* [LL *valentia* power, capacity, fr. L *valēre* to be strong] : the combining power of an atom as shown by the number of its electrons that are lost, gained, or shared in the formation of chemical bonds

Va·len·ci·ennes \və-ˌlen-sē-'en, ˌva-lən-sē-, -'enz\ *n* : a fine handmade lace

val·en·tine \\'va-lən-ˌtīn\ *n* : a sweetheart chosen or complimented on St. Valentine's Day; *also* : a greeting card sent on this day

Valentine's Day *also* **Valentine Day** *n* : SAINT VALENTINE'S DAY

¹**va·let** \\'va-lət, -(ˌ)lā; va-'lā\ *n* **1** : a male servant who takes care of a man's clothes and performs personal services **2** : an attendant in a hotel who performs personal services for customers

²**valet** *vb* : to serve as a valet

val·e·tu·di·nar·i·an \ˌva-lə-ˌtüd-ᵊn-'er-ē-ən, -ˌtyüd-\ *n* : a person of a weak or sickly constitution; *esp* : one whose chief concern is being or becoming an invalid — **val·e·tu·di·nar·i·an·ism** \-ē-ə-ˌni-zəm\ *n*

val·iant \\'val-yənt\ *adj* : having or showing valor : BRAVE, HEROIC **syn** valorous, doughty, courageous, bold, audacious, dauntless, undaunted, intrepid — **valiant·ly** *adv*

val·id \\'va-ləd\ *adj* **1** : having legal force ⟨a ~ contract⟩ **2** : founded on truth or fact : capable of being justified or defended ⟨sound ⟨a ~ argument⟩ ⟨~ reasons⟩ — **va·lid·i·ty** \və-'li-də-tē\ *n* — **val·id·ly** *adv*

val·i·date \\'va-lə-ˌdāt\ *vb* **-dat·ed; -dat·ing 1** : to make legally valid **2** : to confirm the validity of **3** : VERIFY — **val·i·da·tion** \ˌva-lə-'dā-shən\ *n*

va·lise \və-'lēs\ *n* [F] : SUITCASE

val·ley \\'va-lē\ *n, pl* **valleys** : a long depression between ranges of hills or mountains

val·or \\'va-lər\ *n* [ME, fr. MF *valour*, fr. ML *valor* value, valor, fr. L *valēre* to be strong] ; personal bravery **syn** heroism, prowess, gallantry — **val·or·ous** \\'va-lə-rəs\ *adj*

val·o·ri·za·tion \ˌva-lə-rə-'zā-shən\ *n* : the support of commodity prices by any of various forms of government subsidy — **val·o·rize** \\'va-lə-ˌrīz\ *vb*

val·our *chiefly Brit var of* VALOR

valse \\'väls\ *n* [F] : WALTZ; *esp* : a concert waltz

¹**valu·able** \\'val-yə-bəl, -yə-wə-bəl\ *adj* **1** : having money value **2** : having great money value **3** : of great use or service **syn** invaluable, priceless, costly, expensive, dear, precious

²**valuable** *n* : a usu. personal possession of considerable value ⟨their ~s were stolen⟩

val·u·ate \\'val-yə-ˌwāt\ *vb* **-at·ed; -at·ing** : to place a value on : APPRAISE — **val·u·a·tor** \-ˌwā-tər\ *n*

val·u·a·tion \ˌval-yə-'wā-shən\ *n* **1** : the act or process of valuing; *esp* : appraisal of property **2** : the estimated or determined market value of a thing

¹**val·ue** \\'val-yü\ *n* **1** : a fair return or equivalent in money, goods, or services for something exchanged **2** : the monetary worth of a thing; *also* : relative worth, utility, or importance ⟨nothing of ~ to say⟩ **3** : an assigned or computed numerical quantity ⟨the ~ of *x* in an equation⟩ **4** : relative lightness or darkness of a color : LUMINOSITY **5** : the relative length of a tone or note **6**

: something (as a principle or ideal) intrinsically valuable or desirable ⟨human rather than material ~s⟩ — **val·ue·less** *adj*

²**value** *vb* **val·ued; valu·ing 1** : to estimate the monetary worth of : APPRAISE **2** : to rate in usefulness, importance, or general worth **3** : to consider or rate highly : PRIZE, ESTEEM — **val·u·er** *n*

val·ue–add·ed tax *n* : an incremental excise tax that is levied on the value added at each stage of the processing of a raw material or the production and distribution of a commodity

valve \\'valv\ *n* **1** : a structure (as in a vein) that temporarily closes a passage or that permits movement in one direction only **2** : a device by which the flow of a fluid material may be regulated by a movable part; *also* : the movable part of such a device **3** : a device in a brass wind instrument for quickly varying the tube length in order to change the fundamental tone by some definite interval **4** : one of the separate usu. hinged pieces of which the shell of some animals and esp. bivalve mollusks consists **5** : one of the pieces into which a ripe seed capsule or pod separates — **valved** \\'valvd\ *adj* **valve·less** *adj*

val·vu·lar \\'val-vyə-lər\ *adj* : of, relating to, or affecting a valve esp. of the heart ⟨~ heart disease⟩

va·moose \və-'müs, va-\ *vb* **va·moosed; va·moos·ing** [Sp *vamos* let us go] : to leave or go away quickly

¹**vamp** \\'vamp\ *vb* **1** : to provide with a new vamp **2** : to patch up with a new part **3** : INVENT, IMPROVISE ⟨~ up an excuse⟩

²**vamp** *n* **1** : the part of a boot or shoe upper covering esp. the front part of the foot **2** : a short introductory musical passage often repeated

³**vamp** *n* : a woman who uses her charm or wiles to seduce and exploit men

⁴**vamp** *vb* : to practice seductive wiles on

vam·pire \\'vam-ˌpīr\ *n* **1** : a night-wandering bloodsucking ghost **2** : a person who preys on other people; *esp* : a woman who exploits and ruins her lover **3** : VAMPIRE BAT

vampire bat *n* : any of various bats of Central and South America that feed on the blood of animals; *also* : any of several other bats that do not feed on blood but are sometimes reputed to do so

¹**van** \\'van\ *n* : VANGUARD

²**van** *n* : a usu. enclosed wagon or motortruck for moving goods or animals; *also* : a versatile enclosed box-like motor vehicle

va·na·di·um \və-'nā-dē-əm\ *n* : a soft grayish ductile metallic chemical element used esp. to form alloys — see ELEMENT table

Van Al·len belt \van-'a-lən-\ *n* : a belt of intense radiation in the magnetosphere composed of charged particles trapped by earth's magnetic field

van·dal \\'vand-ᵊl\ *n* **1** *cap* : a member of a Germanic people who sacked Rome in A.D. 455 **2** : a person who willfully mars or destroys property

van·dal·ise *Brit var of* VANDALIZE

van·dal·ism \-ˌi-zəm\ *n* : willful or malicious destruction or defacement of public or private property

van·dal·ize \-ˌīz\ *vb* **-ized; -iz·ing** : to subject to vandalism : DAMAGE

Van·dyke \van-'dīk\ *n* : a trim pointed beard

vane \\'vān\ *n* [ME, fr. OE *fana* banner] **1** : a movable device attached to a high object for showing wind direction **2** : a thin flat or curved object that is rotated about an axis by a flow of fluid or that rotates to cause

---

\ə\abut \ᵊ\kitten \ər\further \a\ash \ā\ace \ä\mop, mar \aù\out \ch\chin \e\bet \ē\easy \g\go \i\hit \ī\ice \j\job \ŋ\sing \ō\go \ò\law \òi\boy \th\thin \th\the \ü\loot \ù\foot \y\yet \zh\vision *see also* Pronunciation Symbols page

a fluid to flow or that redirects a flow of fluid ⟨the ~s of a windmill⟩

van·guard \'van-ˌgärd\ n 1 : the troops moving at the front of an army 2 : the forefront of an action or movement

va·nil·la \və-'ni-lə\ n [NL, genus name, fr. Sp *vainilla* vanilla (plant and fruit), dim. of *vaina* sheath, fr. L *vagina*] : a flavoring extract obtained from the long bean-like pods (**vanilla beans**) of a tropical American climbing orchid or made synthetically; *also* : this orchid

van·ish \'va-nish\ vb : to pass from sight or existence : disappear completely — **van·ish·er** n

van·i·ty \'va-nə-tē\ n, pl **-ties** 1 : something that is vain, empty, or useless 2 : the quality or fact of being useless or futile : FUTILITY 3 : undue pride in oneself or one's appearance : CONCEIT 4 : a small case for cosmetics : COMPACT

vanity plate n : an automobile license plate bearing distinctive letters or numbers designated by the owner

van·quish \'vaŋ-kwish, 'van-\ vb 1 : to overcome in battle or in a contest 2 : to gain mastery over (as an emotion)

van·tage \'van-tij\ n 1 : superiority in a contest 2 : a position giving a strategic advantage or a commanding perspective

va·pid \'va-pəd, 'vā-\ adj : lacking spirit, liveliness, or zest : FLAT, INSIPID — **va·pid·i·ty** \va-'pi-də-tē\ n — **vap·id·ly** adv — **vap·id·ness** n

va·por \'vā-pər\ n 1 : fine separated particles (as fog or smoke) floating in the air and clouding it 2 : a substance in the gaseous state; *esp* : one that is liquid under ordinary conditions 3 : something insubstantial or fleeting 4 pl : a depressed or hysterical nervous condition

va·por·ing \'vā-pə-riŋ\ n : an idle, boastful, or high-flown expression or speech — usu. used in pl.

va·por·ise *Brit var of* VAPORIZE

va·por·ize \'vā-pə-ˌrīz\ vb **-ized; -iz·ing** : to convert into vapor — **va·por·i·za·tion** \ˌvā-pə-rə-'zā-shən\ n

va·por·iz·er \-ˌrī-zər\ n : a device that vaporizes something (as a medicated liquid)

vapor lock n : an interruption of flow of a fluid (as fuel in an engine) caused by the formation of vapor in the feeding system

va·por·ous \'vā-pə-rəs\ adj 1 : full of vapors : FOGGY, MISTY 2 : UNSUBSTANTIAL, VAGUE — **va·por·ous·ly** adv — **va·por·ous·ness** n

va·pory \'vā-pə-rē\ adj : MISTY

va·pour *chiefly Brit var of* VAPOR

va·que·ro \vä-'ker-ō\ n, pl **-ros** [Sp, fr. *vaca* cow, fr. L *vacca*] : a ranch hand : COWBOY

var abbr 1 variable 2 variant; variation 3 variety 4 various

¹**var·i·able** \'ver-ē-ə-bəl\ adj 1 : able or apt to vary : CHANGEABLE 2 : FICKLE 3 : not true to type : ABERRANT ⟨a ~ wheat⟩ — **var·i·abil·i·ty** \ˌver-ē-ə-'bi-lə-tē, ˌvar-\ n — **var·i·ably** \-blē\ adv

²**variable** n 1 : a quantity that may take on any of a set of values; *also* : a mathematical symbol representing a variable 2 : something that is variable

var·i·ance \'ver-ē-əns\ n 1 : variation or a degree of variation : DEVIATION 2 : DISAGREEMENT, DISPUTE 3 : a license to do something contrary to the usual rule ⟨a zoning ~⟩ 4 : the square of the standard deviation **syn** discord, contention, dissension, strife, conflict

¹**var·i·ant** \'ver-ē-ənt\ adj 1 : differing from others of its kind or class 2 : varying usu. slightly from the standard or type

²**variant** n 1 : one that exhibits variation from a type or norm 2 : one of two or more different spellings or pronunciations of a word

var·i·a·tion \ˌver-ē-'ā-shən\ n 1 : the act, process, or an instance of varying : a change in form, position, or con-

dition : MODIFICATION, ALTERATION 2 : extent of change or difference 3 : divergence in the characteristics of an organism from those typical or usual for its group; *also* : one exhibiting such variation 4 : repetition of a musical theme with modifications in rhythm, tune, harmony, or key

vari·col·ored \'ver-i-ˌkə-lərd\ adj : having various colors : VARIEGATED

var·i·cose \'var-ə-ˌkōs\ adj : abnormally swollen and dilated ⟨~ veins⟩ — **var·i·cos·i·ty** \ˌvar-ə-'kä-sə-tē\ n

var·ied \'ver-ēd\ adj 1 : having many forms or types : DIVERSE 2 : VARIEGATED — **var·ied·ly** adv

var·ie·gat·ed \'ver-ē-ə-ˌgā-təd\ adj 1 : having patches, stripes, or marks of different colors ⟨~ flowers⟩ 2 : VARIED 1 — **var·ie·gate** \-ˌgāt\ vb — **var·ie·ga·tion** \ˌver-ē-ə-'gā-shən\ n

¹**va·ri·etal** \və-'rī-ət-ᵊl\ adj : of or relating to a variety; *esp* : of, relating to, or producing a varietal

²**varietal** n : a wine bearing the name of the principal grape from which it is made

va·ri·ety \və-'rī-ə-tē\ n, pl **-et·ies** 1 : the state of being varied or various : DIVERSITY 2 : a collection of different things : ASSORTMENT 3 : something varying from others of the same general kind 4 : any of various groups of plants or animals within a species distinguished by characteristics insufficient to separate species : SUBSPECIES 5 : entertainment such as is given in a stage presentation comprising a series of performances (as songs, dances, or acrobatic acts)

var·i·o·rum \ˌver-ē-'ōr-əm\ n : an edition or text of a work containing notes by various persons or variant readings of the text

var·i·ous \'ver-ē-əs\ adj 1 : VARICOLORED 2 : of differing kinds : MULTIFARIOUS 3 : UNLIKE ⟨animals as ~ as the jaguar and the sloth⟩ 4 : having a number of different aspects 5 : NUMEROUS, MANY 6 : INDIVIDUAL, SEPARATE **syn** divergent, disparate, different, dissimilar, diverse, unlike — **var·i·ous·ly** adv

var·let \'vär-lət\ n 1 : ATTENDANT 2 : SCOUNDREL, KNAVE

var·mint \'vär-mənt\ n [alter. of *vermin*] 1 : an animal considered a pest; *esp* : one classed as vermin and unprotected by game law 2 : a contemptible person : RASCAL

¹**var·nish** \'vär-nish\ n 1 : a liquid preparation that is spread on a surface and dries into a hard glossy coating; *also* : the glaze of this coating 2 : something suggesting varnish by its gloss 3 : outside show : deceptive or superficial appearance

²**varnish** vb 1 : to cover with varnish 2 : to cover or conceal with something that gives a fair appearance : GLOSS

var·si·ty \'vär-sə-tē\ n, pl **-ties** [by shortening & alter. of *university*] 1 Brit : UNIVERSITY 2 : the principal team representing a college, school, or club

vary \'ver-ē\ vb **var·ied; vary·ing** 1 : ALTER, CHANGE 2 : to make or be of different kinds : introduce or have variety : DIVERSIFY, DIFFER 3 : DEVIATE, SWERVE 4 : to change in bodily structure or function away from what is usual for members of a group

vas·cu·lar \'vas-kyə-lər\ adj [NL *vascularis,* fr. L *vasculum* small vessel, dim. of *vas* vase, vessel] : of or relating to a channel or system of channels for the conveyance of a body fluid (as blood or sap); *also* : supplied with or containing such vessels and esp. blood vessels

vascular plant n : a plant having a specialized system for carrying fluids that includes xylem and phloem

vase \'vās, 'vāz\ n : a usu. round vessel of greater depth than width used chiefly for ornament or for flowers

va·sec·to·my \və-'sek-tə-mē, vā-'zek-\ n, pl **-mies** : surgical excision of all or part of the sperm-carrying ducts of the testis usu. to induce sterility

va·so·con·stric·tion \ˌvas-ō-kən-'strik-shən, ˌvāz-\ n : narrowing of the interior diameter of blood vessels

va·so·con·stric·tor \-tər\ *n* : an agent (as a nerve fiber or a drug) that initiates or induces vasoconstriction

vas·sal \ˈva-səl\ *n* **1** : a person under the protection of a feudal lord to whom he owes homage and loyalty : a feudal tenant **2** : one occupying a dependent or subordinate position — **vassal** *adj*

vas·sal·age \-sə-lij\ *n* **1** : the state of being a vassal **2** : the homage and loyalty due from a vassal **3** : SERVITUDE, SUBJECTION

¹vast \ˈvast\ *adj* : very great in size, amount, degree, intensity, or esp. extent **syn** enormous, huge, gigantic, colossal, mammoth — **vast·ly** *adv* — **vast·ness** *n*

²vast *n* : a great expanse : IMMENSITY

vasty \ˈvas-tē\ *adj* : VAST, IMMENSE

vat \ˈvat\ *n* : a large vessel (as a tub or barrel) esp. for holding liquids in manufacturing processes

VAT *abbr* value-added tax

vat·ic \ˈva-tik\ *adj* : PROPHETIC, ORACULAR

Vat·i·can \ˈva-ti-kən\ *n* **1** : the papal headquarters in Rome **2** : the papal government

vaude·ville \ˈvȯd-vəl, ˈväd-, ˈvōd-, -ˌvil\ *n* [F, fr. MF, satirical song, alter. of *vaudevire*, fr. *vau-de-Vire* valley of Vire, town in northwest France where such songs were composed] : a stage entertainment consisting of unrelated acts (as of acrobats, comedians, dancers, or singers)

¹vault \ˈvȯlt\ *n* **1** : an arched masonry structure usu. forming a ceiling or roof; *also* : something (as the sky) resembling a vault **2** : a room or space covered by a vault esp. when underground **3** : a room or compartment for the safekeeping of valuables **4** : a burial chamber; *also* : a usu. metal or concrete case in which a casket is enclosed at burial — **vaulty** *adj*

²vault *vb* : to form or cover with a vault

³vault *vb* : to leap vigorously esp. by aid of the hands or a pole — **vault·er** *n*

⁴vault *n* : an act of vaulting : LEAP

vault·ed *adj* **1** : built in the form of a vault : ARCHED **2** : covered with a vault

vault·ing *adj* : reaching for the heights ⟨∼ ambition⟩

vaunt \ˈvȯnt\ *vb* [ME, fr. MF *vanter*, fr. LL *vanitare*, ultim. fr. L *vanus* vain] : BRAG, BOAST — **vaunt** *n*

vaunt·ed *adj* : much praised or boasted of

vb *abbr* verb; verbal

VCR \ˌvē-(ˌ)sē-ˈär\ *n* [*video*cassette *r*ecorder] : a videotape recorder that uses videocassettes

VD *abbr* venereal disease

VDT *abbr* video display terminal

Ve·adar \ˈvā-ˌä-ˌdär, ˈvä-ə-\ *n* [Heb *wĕ-Adhār*, the second Adar] : the intercalary month of the Jewish calendar following Adar in leap years

veal \ˈvēl\ *n* : the flesh of a young calf

vec·tor \ˈvek-tər\ *n* **1** : a quantity that has magnitude and direction **2** : an organism (as a fly or tick) that transmits disease germs

Ve·da \ˈvā-də\ *n* [Skt., lit., knowledge] : any of a class of Hindu sacred writings — **Ve·dic** \ˈvā-dik\ *adj*

Ve·dan·ta \vā-ˈdän-tə, və-, -ˈdan-\ *n* : an orthodox Hindu philosophy based on the Upanishads

vee·jay \ˈvē-ˌjā\ *n* : an announcer of a program featuring music videos

veep \ˈvēp\ *n* : VICE PRESIDENT

veer \ˈvir\ *vb* : to shift from one direction or course to another **syn** turn, avert, deflect, divert — **veer** *n*

veg·an \ˈvē-gən, ˈvā-; ˈve-jən, -ˌjan\ *n* : a strict vegetarian who consumes no animal food or dairy products — **veg·an·ism** \ˈvē-gə-ˌni-zəm, ˈvā-, ˈve-\ *n*

¹veg·e·ta·ble \ˈvej-tə-bəl, ˈve-jə-\ *adj* [ME, fr. ML *vegetabilis* vegetative, fr. *vegetare* to grow, fr. L, to animate, fr. *vegetus* lively, fr. *vegēre* to enliven] **1** : of, relating to, or growing like plants ⟨the ∼ kingdom⟩ **2** : made or obtained from plants ⟨∼ oils⟩ **3** : suggesting that of a plant (as in inertness) ⟨a ∼ existence⟩

²vegetable *n* **1** : PLANT 1 **2** : a usu. herbaceous plant grown for an edible part that is usu. eaten as part of a meal; *also* : such an edible part

veg·e·tal \ˈve-jət-əl\ *adj* **1** : VEGETABLE **2** : VEGETATIVE

veg·e·tar·i·an \ˌve-jə-ˈter-ē-ən\ *n* : one that believes in or practices living on a diet of vegetables, fruits, grains, nuts, and sometimes animal products (as milk and cheese) — **vegetarian** *adj* — **veg·e·tar·i·an·ism** \-ē-ə-ˌni-zəm\ *n*

veg·e·tate \ˈve-jə-ˌtāt\ *vb* **-tat·ed; -tat·ing** : to live or grow in the manner of a plant; *esp* : to lead a dull inert life

veg·e·ta·tion \ˌve-jə-ˈtā-shən\ *n* **1** : the act or process of vegetating; *also* : inert existence **2** : plant life or cover (as of an area) — **veg·e·ta·tion·al** \-shə-nəl\ *adj*

veg·e·ta·tive \ˈve-jə-ˌtā-tiv\ *adj* **1** : of or relating to nutrition and growth esp. as contrasted with reproduction **2** : of, relating to, or composed of vegetation **3** : VEGETABLE 3

veg out \ˈvej-\ *vb* **vegged out; vegging out** [short for *vegetate*] : to spend time idly or passively

ve·he·ment \ˈvē-ə-mənt\ *adj* **1** : marked by great force or energy **2** : marked by strong feeling or expression : PASSIONATE, FERVID — **ve·he·mence** \-məns\ *n* — **ve·he·ment·ly** *adv*

ve·hi·cle \ˈvē-ə-kəl, ˈvē-ˌhi-\ *n* **1** : a medium by which a thing is applied or administered ⟨linseed oil is a ∼ for pigments⟩ **2** : a medium through or by means of which something is conveyed or expressed **3** : a means of transporting persons or goods **syn** instrument, agent, agency, organ, channel — **ve·hic·u·lar** \vē-ˈhi-kyə-lər\ *adj*

¹veil \ˈvāl\ *n* **1** : a piece of often sheer or diaphanous material used to screen or curtain something or to cover the head or face **2** : the state of becoming a nun ⟨take the ∼⟩ **3** : something that hides or obscures like a veil

²veil *vb* : to cover with or as if with a veil : wear a veil

¹vein \ˈvān\ *n* **1** : a fissure in rock filled with mineral matter; *also* : a bed of useful mineral matter **2** : any of the tubular branching vessels that carry blood from the capillaries toward the heart **3** : any of the bundles of vascular vessels forming the framework of a leaf **4** : any of the thickened ribs that stiffen the wings of an insect **5** : something (as a wavy variegation in marble) suggesting veins **6** : a distinctive style of expression **7** : a distinctive element or quality : STRAIN **8** : MOOD, HUMOR — **veined** \ˈvānd\ *adj*

²vein *vb* : to pattern with or as if with veins — **vein·ing** *n*

vel *abbr* velocity

ve·lar \ˈvē-lər\ *adj* : of or relating to a velum and esp. that of the soft palate

veld *or* **veldt** \ˈvelt, ˈfelt\ *n* [Afrikaans *veld*, fr. D, field] : an open grassland esp. in southern Africa usu. with few shrubs or trees

vel·lum \ˈve-ləm\ *n* [ME *velim*, fr. MF *veelin*, fr. *veelin*, adj., of a calf, fr. *veel* calf] **1** : a fine-grained lambskin, kidskin, or calfskin prepared for writing on or for binding books **2** : a strong cream-colored paper — **vellum** *adj*

ve·loc·i·pede \və-ˈlä-sə-ˌpēd\ *n* : an early bicycle

ve·loc·i·ty \və-ˈlä-sə-tē\ *n, pl* **-ties** : quickness of motion : SPEED ⟨the ∼ of light⟩

ve·lour *or* **ve·lours** \və-ˈlu̇r\ *n, pl* **velours** \-ˈlu̇rz\ : any of various textile fabrics with pile like that of velvet

ve·lum \ˈvē-ləm\ *n, pl* **ve·la** \-lə\ : a membranous body part (as the soft palate) resembling a veil

vel·vet \ˈvel-vət\ *n* [ME *veluet, velvet*, fr. MF *velu* shag-

---

\ə\abut \ᵊ\kitten \ər\further \a\ash \ā\ace \ä\mop, mar
\au̇\out \ch\chin \e\bet \ē\easy \g\go \i\hit \ī\ice \j\job
\ŋ\sing \ō\go \ȯ\law \ȯi\boy \th\thin \t͟h\the \ü\loot \u̇\foot
\y\yet \zh\vision *see also* Pronunciation Symbols page

gy, ultim. fr. L *villus* shaggy hair] **1** : a fabric having a short soft dense warp pile **2** : something resembling or suggesting velvet (as in softness or luster) **3** : the soft skin covering the growing antlers of deer — **velvet** *adj* — **velvety** *adj*

vel·ve·teen \ˌvel-və-ˈtēn\ *n* **1** : a fabric woven usu. of cotton in imitation of velvet **2** *pl* : clothes made of velveteen

Ven *abbr* venerable

ve·nal \ˈvēn-ᵊl\ *adj* : capable of being bought or bribed : MERCENARY, CORRUPT — **ve·nal·i·ty** \vi-ˈnal-ə-tē\ *n* — **ve·nal·ly** \ˈvēn-ᵊl-ē\ *adv*

ve·na·tion \ve-ˈnā-shən, vē-\ *n* : an arrangement or system of veins ⟨the ∼ of the hand⟩ ⟨leaf ∼⟩

venation

vend \ˈvend\ *vb* : SELL; *esp* : to sell as a hawker or peddler — **vend·ible** *adj*

vend·ee \ven-ˈdē\ *n* : one to whom a thing is sold : BUYER

ven·det·ta \ven-ˈde-tə\ *n* : a feud marked by acts of revenge

vending machine *n* : a coin-operated machine for selling merchandise

ven·dor \ˈven-dər, *for 1 also* ven-ˈdȯr\ *n* **1** : one that vends : SELLER **2** : VENDING MACHINE

¹**ve·neer** \və-ˈnir\ *n* [G *Furnier*, fr. *furnieren* to veneer, fr. F *fournir* to furnish] **1** : a thin usu. superficial layer of material ⟨brick ∼⟩; *esp* : a thin layer of fine wood glued over a cheaper wood **2** : superficial display : GLOSS

²**veneer** *vb* : to overlay with a veneer

ven·er·a·ble \ˈve-nə-rə-bəl\ *adj* **1** : deserving to be venerated — often used as a religious title **2** : made sacred by association

ven·er·ate \ˈve-nə-ˌrāt\ *vb* **-at·ed; -at·ing** : to regard with reverential respect **syn** adore, revere, reverence, worship — **ven·er·a·tion** \ˌve-nə-ˈrā-shən\ *n*

ve·ne·re·al \və-ˈnir-ē-əl\ *adj* : of or relating to sexual intercourse or to diseases transmitted by it ⟨a ∼ infection⟩

venereal disease *n* : a contagious disease (as gonorrhea or syphilis) usu. acquired by having sexual intercourse with someone who already has it

ve·ne·tian blind \və-ˈnē-shən-\ *n* : a blind having thin horizontal parallel slats that can be adjusted to admit a desired amount of light

Ven·e·zue·lan \ˌve-nə-ˈzwā-lən\ *n* : a native or inhabitant of Venezuela — **Venezuelan** *adj*

ven·geance \ˈven-jəns\ *n* : punishment inflicted in retaliation for an injury or offense : REVENGE

venge·ful \ˈvenj-fəl\ *adj* : filled with a desire for revenge : VINDICTIVE — **venge·ful·ly** *adv*

ve·nial \ˈvē-nē-əl\ *adj* : capable of being forgiven : EXCUSABLE ⟨∼ sin⟩

ve·ni·re \və-ˈnī-rē\ *n* : a panel from which a jury is drawn

ve·ni·re fa·ci·as \-ˈfā-shē-əs\ *n* [ME, fr. ML, you should cause to come] : a writ summoning persons to appear in court to serve as jurors

ve·ni·re·man \və-ˈnī-rē-mən, -ˈnir-ē-\ *n* : a member of a venire

ven·i·son \ˈven-ə-sən, -zən\ *n, pl* **venisons** *also* **venison** [ME, fr. OF *veneison* hunting, game, fr. L *venatio*, fr. *venari* to hunt, pursue] : the edible flesh of a deer

ven·om \ˈven-əm\ *n* [ME *venim, venom*, fr. OF *venim*, ultim. fr. L *venenum* magic charm, drug, poison] **1** : poisonous material secreted by some animals (as snakes, spiders, or bees) and transmitted usu. by biting or stinging **2** : ILL WILL, MALEVOLENCE

ven·om·ous \ˈve-nə-məs\ *adj* **1** : full of venom : POISONOUS **2** : SPITEFUL, MALEVOLENT **3** : secreting and using venom ⟨∼ snakes⟩ — **ven·om·ous·ly** *adv*

ve·nous \ˈvē-nəs\ *adj* **1** : of, relating to, or full of veins **2** : being purplish red oxygen-deficient blood rich in carbon dioxide that is present in most veins

¹**vent** \ˈvent\ *vb* **1** : to provide with a vent **2** : to serve as a vent for **3** : EXPEL, DISCHARGE **4** : to give vigorous or emotional expression to

²**vent** *n* **1** : an opportunity or way of escape or passage : OUTLET **2** : an opening for the escape of a gas or liquid or for the relief of pressure

³**vent** *n* : a slit in a garment esp. in the lower part of a seam (as of a jacket or skirt)

ven·ti·late \ˈvent-ᵊl-ˌāt\ *vb* **-lat·ed; -lat·ing 1** : to discuss freely and openly ⟨∼ a question⟩ **2** : to give vent to ⟨∼ one's grievances⟩ **3** : to cause fresh air to circulate through (as a room or mine) so as to replace foul air **4** : to provide with a vent or outlet **syn** express, vent, air, utter, voice, broach — **ven·ti·la·tor** \-ᵊl-ˌā-tər\ *n*

ven·ti·la·tion \ˌvent-ᵊl-ˈā-shən\ *n* **1** : the act or process of ventilating **2** : circulation of air (as in a room) **3** : a system or means of providing fresh air

ven·tral \ˈven-trəl\ *adj* **1** : of or relating to the belly : ABDOMINAL **2** : of, relating to, or located on or near the surface of the body that in humans is the front but in most other animals is the lower surface — **ven·tral·ly** *adv*

ven·tri·cle \ˈven-tri-kəl\ *n* **1** : a chamber of the heart that receives blood from the atrium of the same side and pumps it into the arteries **2** : any of the communicating cavities of the brain that are continuous with the central canal of the spinal cord

ven·tril·o·quism \ven-ˈtri-lə-ˌkwi-zəm\ *n* [LL *ventriloquus* ventriloquist, fr. L *venter* belly + *loqui* to speak; fr. the belief that the voice is produced from the ventriloquist's stomach] : the production of the voice in such a manner that the sound appears to come from a source other than the speaker — **ven·tril·o·quist** \-kwist\ *n*

ven·tril·o·quy \-kwē\ *n* : VENTRILOQUISM

¹**ven·ture** \ˈven-chər\ *vb* **ven·tured; ven·tur·ing 1** : to expose to hazard : RISK **2** : to undertake the risks of : BRAVE **3** : to offer at the risk of rebuff, rejection, or censure ⟨∼ an opinion⟩ **4** : to proceed despite danger : DARE

²**venture** *n* **1** : an undertaking involving chance or risk; *esp* : a speculative business enterprise **2** : something risked in a speculative venture : STAKE

ven·ture·some \ˈven-chər-səm\ *adj* **1** : involving risk : DANGEROUS, HAZARDOUS **2** : inclined to venture : BOLD, DARING **syn** adventurous, venturous, rash, reckless, foolhardy — **ven·ture·some·ly** *adv* — **ven·ture·some·ness** *n*

ven·tur·ous \ˈven-chə-rəs\ *adj* : VENTURESOME — **ven·tur·ous·ly** *adv* — **ven·tur·ous·ness** *n*

ven·ue \ˈven-yü\ *n* : the place in which the alleged events from which a legal action arises took place; *also* : the place from which the jury is taken and where the trial is held

Ve·nus \\'vē-nəs\ *n* : the planet 2d in order from the sun — see PLANET table

Ve·nu·sian \vi-'nü-zhən, -'nyü-\ *adj* : of or relating to the planet Venus

Ve·nus's–fly·trap \\'vē-nə-səz-'flī-ˌtrap\ *or* **Venus fly-trap** *n* : an insect-eating plant of the Carolina coast that has the leaf tip modified into an insect trap

ve·ra·cious \və-'rā-shəs\ *adj* **1** : TRUTHFUL, HONEST **2** : TRUE, ACCURATE — **ve·ra·cious·ly** *adv*

ve·rac·i·ty \və-'ra-sə-tē\ *n, pl* **-ties 1** : devotion to truth : TRUTHFULNESS **2** : conformity with fact : ACCURACY **3** : something true

ve·ran·da *or* **ve·ran·dah** \və-'ran-də\ *n* : a long open usu. roofed porch

verb \\'vərb\ *n* : a word that is the grammatical center of a predicate and expresses an act, occurrence, or mode of being

¹ver·bal \\'vər-bəl\ *adj* **1** : of, relating to, or consisting of words; *esp* : having to do with words rather than with the ideas to be conveyed **2** : expressed in usu. spoken words : not written : ORAL ⟨a ∼ contract⟩ **3** : of, relating to, or formed from a verb **4** : LITERAL, VERBATIM — **ver·bal·ly** *adv*

²verbal *n* : a word that combines characteristics of a verb with those of a noun or adjective

verbal auxiliary *n* : an auxiliary verb

ver·bal·ize \\'vər-bə-ˌlīz\ *vb* **-ized; -iz·ing 1** : to speak or write in wordy or empty fashion **2** : to express something in words : describe verbally **3** : to convert into a verb — **ver·bal·i·za·tion** \ˌvər-bə-lə-'zā-shən\ *n*

verbal noun *n* : a noun derived directly from a verb or verb stem and in some uses having the sense and constructions of a verb

ver·ba·tim \(ˌ)vər-'bā-təm\ *adv or adj* : in the same words : word for word

ver·be·na \(ˌ)vər-'bē-nə\ *n* : VERVAIN; *esp* : any of several garden plants of hybrid origin with showy spikes of bright often fragrant flowers

ver·biage \\'vər-bē-ij, -bij\ *n* **1** : superfluity of words usu. of little or obscure content **2** : DICTION, WORDING

ver·bose \(ˌ)vər-'bōs\ *adj* : using more words than are needed : WORDY **syn** prolix, diffuse, redundant, windy — **ver·bos·i·ty** \-'bä-sə-tē\ *n*

ver·bo·ten \vər-'bōt-ᵊn, fər-\ *adj* [G] : forbidden usu. by dictate

ver·dant \\'vərd-ᵊnt\ *adj* : green with growing plants — **ver·dant·ly** *adv*

ver·dict \\'vər-(ˌ)dikt\ *n* [alter. of ME *verdit*, fr. Anglo-French (the French of medieval England), fr. OF *ver* true (fr. L *verus*) + *dit* saying, dictum, fr. L *dictum*, fr. *dicere* to say] **1** : the finding or decision of a jury **2** : DECISION, JUDGMENT

ver·di·gris \\'vər-də-ˌgrēs, -ˌgris\ *n* : a green or bluish deposit that forms on copper, brass, or bronze surfaces

ver·dure \\'vər-jər\ *n* : the greenness of growing vegetation; *also* : such vegetation

¹verge \\'vərj\ *n* **1** : a staff carried as an emblem of authority or office **2** : something that borders or bounds : EDGE, MARGIN **3** : BRINK, THRESHOLD

²verge *vb* **verged; verg·ing 1** : to be contiguous **2** : to be on the verge

³verge *vb* **verged; verg·ing 1** : to move or extend in some direction or toward some condition : INCLINE **2** : to be in transition or change

verg·er \\'vər-jər\ *n* **1** *chiefly Brit* : an attendant who carries a verge (as before a bishop) **2** : SEXTON

ve·rid·i·cal \və-'ri-di-kəl\ *adj* **1** : TRUTHFUL **2** : not illusory : GENUINE

ver·i·fy \\'ver-ə-ˌfī\ *vb* **-fied; -fy·ing 1** : to confirm in law by oath **2** : to establish the truth, accuracy, or reality of **syn** authenticate, corroborate, substantiate, validate — **ver·i·fi·able** *adj* — **ver·i·fi·ca·tion** \ˌver-ə-fə-'kā-shən\ *n*

ver·i·ly \\'ver-ə-lē\ *adv* **1** : in very truth : CERTAINLY **2** : TRULY, CONFIDENTLY

veri·si·mil·i·tude \ˌver-ə-sə-'mi-lə-ˌtüd, -ˌtyüd\ *n* : the quality or state of appearing to be true

ver·i·ta·ble \\'ver-ə-tə-bəl\ *adj* : ACTUAL, GENUINE, TRUE — **ver·i·ta·bly** *adv*

ver·i·ty \\'ver-ə-tē\ *n, pl* **-ties 1** : the quality or state of being true or real : TRUTH, REALITY **2** : something (as a statement) that is true **3** : HONESTY, VERACITY

ver·meil *n* [MF] **1** \\'vər-məl, -ˌmāl\ : VERMILION **2** \ver-'mā\ : gilded silver

ver·mi·cel·li \ˌvər-mə-'che-lē, -'se-\ *n* [It, fr. pl. of *vermicello*, dim. of *verme* worm] : a pasta made in thinner strings than spaghetti

ver·mic·u·lite \vər-'mi-kyə-ˌlīt\ *n* : any of various lightweight water-absorbent minerals derived from mica

ver·mi·form appendix \\'vər-mə-ˌform-\ *n* : APPENDIX 2

ver·mil·ion *also* **ver·mil·lion** \vər-'mil-yən\ *n* : a bright reddish orange color; *also* : any of various red pigments

ver·min \\'vər-mən\ *n, pl* **vermin 1** : small common harmful or objectionable animals (as lice or mice) that are difficult to get rid of **2** : birds and mammals that prey on game — **ver·min·ous** *adj*

ver·mouth \vər-'müth\ *n* [F *vermout*, fr. G *Wermut* wormwood] : a dry or sweet wine flavored with herbs and often used in mixed drinks

¹ver·nac·u·lar \vər-'na-kyə-lər\ *adj* [L *vernaculus* native, fr. *verna* slave born in the master's house, native] **1** : of, relating to, or being a language or dialect native to a region or country rather than a literary, cultured, or foreign language **2** : of, relating to, or being the normal spoken form of a language **3** : applied to a plant or animal in common speech as distinguished from biological nomenclature ⟨∼ names⟩

²vernacular *n* **1** : a vernacular language **2** : the mode of expression of a group or class **3** : a vernacular name of a plant or animal

ver·nal \\'vərn-ᵊl\ *adj* : of, relating to, or occurring in the spring

ver·ni·er \\'vər-nē-ər\ *n* : a short scale made to slide along the divisions of a graduated instrument to indicate parts of divisions

ve·ron·i·ca \və-'rä-ni-kə\ *n* : SPEEDWELL

ver·sa·tile \\'vər-sət-ᵊl\ *adj* : turning with ease from one thing or position to another; *esp* : having many aptitudes — **ver·sa·til·i·ty** \ˌvər-sə-'ti-lə-tē\ *n*

¹verse \\'vərs\ *n* **1** : a line of poetry; *also* : STANZA **2** : metrical writing distinguished from poetry esp. by its lower level of intensity **3** : POETRY **4** : POEM **5** : one of the short divisions of a chapter in the Bible

²verse *vb* **versed; vers·ing** : to familiarize by experience, study, or practice ⟨well *versed* in the theater⟩

ver·si·cle \\'vər-si-kəl\ *n* : a verse or sentence said or sung by a leader in public worship and followed by a response from the people

ver·si·fi·ca·tion \ˌvər-sə-fə-'kā-shən\ *n* **1** : the making of verses **2** : metrical structure

ver·si·fy \\'vər-sə-ˌfī\ *vb* **-fied; -fy·ing 1** : to write verse **2** : to turn into verse — **ver·si·fi·er** \-ˌfī-ər\ *n*

ver·sion \\'vər-zhən\ *n* **1** : TRANSLATION; *esp* : a translation of the Bible **2** : an account or description from a particular point of view esp. as contrasted with another **3** : a form or variant of a type or original

vers li·bre \ˌver-'lēbrᵊ\ *n, pl* **vers li·bres** *same*\ [F] : FREE VERSE

ver·so \\'vər-sō\ *n, pl* **versos** : a left-hand page

ver·sus \\'vər-səs\ *prep* **1** : AGAINST 1 ⟨the champion ∼

the challenger⟩ **2** : in contrast or as an alternative to ⟨free trade ∼ protection⟩

vert *abbr* vertical

ver·te·bra \'vər-tə-brə\ *n, pl* **-brae** \-ˌbrā, -ˌ(ˌ)brē\ *or* **-bras** [L] : one of the segments of bone or cartilage making up the backbone

ver·te·bral \(ˌ)vər-'tē-brəl, 'vər-tə-\ *adj* : of, relating to, or made up of vertebrae : SPINAL

vertebral column *n* : BACKBONE

¹ver·te·brate \'vər-tə-brət, -ˌbrāt\ *adj* **1** : having a backbone **2** : of or relating to the vertebrates

²vertebrate *n* : any of a large group of animals (as mammals, birds, reptiles, amphibians, or fishes) that have a backbone or in some primitive forms (as a lamprey) a flexible rod of cells and that have a tubular nervous system arranged along the back and divided into a brain and spinal cord

ver·tex \'vər-ˌteks\ *n, pl* **ver·ti·ces** \'vər-tə-ˌsēz\ *also* **ver·tex·es** [L *vertex, vortex* whirl, whirlpool, top of the head, summit, fr. *vertere* to turn] **1** : the point opposite to and farthest from the base of a geometrical figure **2** : the point where the sides of an angle or three or more edges of a polyhedron (as a cube) meet **3** : the highest point : TOP, SUMMIT

ver·ti·cal \'vər-ti-kəl\ *adj* **1** : of, relating to, or located at the vertex : directly overhead **2** : rising perpendicularly from a level surface : UPRIGHT — **vertical** *n* — **ver·ti·cal·i·ty** \ˌvər-tə-'ka-lə-tē\ *n* — **ver·ti·cal·ly** \-k(ə-)lē\ *adv*

ver·tig·i·nous \(ˌ)vər-'ti-jə-nəs\ *adj* : marked by, affected with, or tending to cause dizziness

ver·ti·go \'vər-ti-ˌgō\ *n, pl* **-goes** *or* **-gos** : DIZZINESS, GIDDINESS

ver·vain \'vər-ˌvān\ *n* : any of a genus of chiefly American herbs or low woody plants with often showy heads or spikes of tubular flowers

verve \'vərv\ *n* : liveliness of imagination; *also* : VIVACITY

¹very \'ver-ē\ *adj* **veri·er; -est** [ME *verray, verry,* fr. OF *verai,* ultim. fr. L *verax* truthful, fr. *verus* true] **1** : EXACT, PRECISE ⟨the ∼ heart of the city⟩ **2** : exactly suitable ⟨the ∼ tool for the job⟩ **3** : ABSOLUTE, UTTER ⟨the *veriest* nonsense⟩ **4** — used as an intensive esp. to emphasize identity ⟨before my ∼ eyes⟩ **5** : MERE, BARE ⟨the ∼ idea scared him⟩ **6** : SELFSAME, IDENTICAL ⟨the ∼ man I saw⟩

²very *adv* **1** : in actual fact : TRULY **2** : to a high degree : EXTREMELY

very high frequency *n* : a radio frequency of between 30 and 300 megahertz

ves·i·cant \'ve-si-kənt\ *n* : an agent that causes blistering — **vesicant** *adj*

ves·i·cle \'ve-si-kəl\ *n* : a membranous and usu. fluid=filled cavity in a plant or animal; *also* : BLISTER — **ve·sic·u·lar** \və-'si-kyə-lər\ *adj*

¹ves·per \'ves-pər\ *n* **1** *cap, archaic* : EVENING STAR **2** : a vesper bell **3** *archaic* : EVENING, EVENTIDE

²vesper *adj* : of or relating to vespers or the evening

ves·pers \-pərz\ *n pl, often cap* : a late afternoon or evening worship service

ves·sel \'ve-səl\ *n* **1** : a container (as a barrel, bottle, bowl, or cup) for holding something **2** : a person held to be the recipient of a quality (as grace) **3** : a craft bigger than a rowboat **4** : a tube in which a body fluid (as blood or sap) is contained and circulated

¹vest \'vest\ *vb* **1** : to place or give into the possession or discretion of some person or authority **2** : to grant or endow with a particular authority, right, or property **3** : to become legally vested **4** : to clothe with or as if with a garment; *esp* : to garb in ecclesiastical vestments

²vest *n* **1** : a man's sleeveless garment for the upper body usu. worn under a suit coat; *also* : a similar garment for women **2** *chiefly Brit* : a man's sleeveless undershirt **3**

: a front piece of a dress resembling the front of a vest

¹ves·tal \'vest-əl\ *adj* : CHASTE

²vestal *n* : VESTAL VIRGIN

vestal virgin *n* **1** : a virgin consecrated to the Roman goddess Vesta and to the service of watching the sacred fire perpetually and kept burning on her altar **2** : a chaste woman

vest·ed *adj* : fully and unconditionally guaranteed as a legal right, benefit, or privilege

vested interest *n* : an interest (as in an existing political, economic, or social arrangement) to which the holder has a strong commitment; *also* : one (as a corporation) having a vested interest

ves·ti·bule \'ves-tə-ˌbyül\ *n* **1** : any of various bodily cavities forming or suggesting an entrance to some other cavity or space **2** : a passage or room between the outer door and the interior of a building — **ves·tib·u·lar** \ve-'sti-byə-lər\ *adj*

ves·tige \'ves-tij\ *n* [F, fr. L *vestigium* footprint, track, vestige] : a trace or visible sign left by something lost or vanished; *also* : a minute remaining amount — **ves·ti·gial** \ve-'sti-jē-əl, -jəl\ *adj* — **ves·ti·gial·ly** *adv*

vest·ing \'ves-tiŋ\ *n* : the conveying to an employee of inalienable rights to share in a pension fund; *also* : the right so conveyed

vest·ment \'vest-mənt\ *n* **1** : an outer garment; *esp* : a ceremonial or official robe **2** *pl* : CLOTHING, GARB **3** : a garment or insignia worn by a clergyman when officiating or assisting at a religious service

vest–pocket *adj* : very small ⟨a ∼ park⟩

ves·try \'ves-trē\ *n, pl* **vestries 1** : a room in a church for vestments, altar linens, and sacred vessels **2** : a room used for church meetings and classes **3** : a body administering the temporal affairs of an Episcopal parish

ves·try·man \-mən\ *n* : a member of a vestry

ves·ture \'ves-chər\ *n* **1** : a covering garment **2** : CLOTHING, APPAREL

¹vet \'vet\ *n* : VETERINARIAN

²vet *adj or n* : VETERAN

vetch \'vech\ *n* : any of a genus of twining herbs related to the garden pea including some grown for fodder and green manure

vet·er·an \'ve-trən, -tə-rən\ *n* [L *veteranus,* fr. *veteranus* old, of long experience, fr. *veter-, vetus* old] **1** : an old soldier of long service **2** : a former member of the armed forces **3** : a person of long experience in an occupation or skill — **veteran** *adj*

Veterans Day *n* : November 11 observed as a legal holiday in commemoration of the end of hostilities in 1918 and 1945

vet·er·i·nar·i·an \ˌve-trə-'ner-ē-ən, ˌve-tə-rə-\ *n* : one qualified and authorized to practice veterinary medicine

¹vet·er·i·nary \'ve-trə-ˌner-ē, 've-tə-rə-\ *adj* : of, relating to, or being the medical care of animals and esp. domestic animals

²veterinary *n, pl* **-nar·ies** : VETERINARIAN

¹ve·to \'vē-tō\ *n, pl* **vetoes** [L, I forbid] **1** : an authoritative prohibition **2** : a power of one part of a government to forbid the carrying out of projects attempted by another part; *esp* : a power vested in a chief executive to prevent the carrying out of measures adopted by a legislature **3** : the exercise of the power of veto

²veto *vb* **1** : FORBID, PROHIBIT **2** : to refuse assent to ⟨a legislative bill⟩ so as to prevent enactment or cause reconsideration — **ve·to·er** *n*

vex \'veks\ *vb* **vexed** *also* **vext; vex·ing 1** : to bring trouble, distress, or agitation to **2** : to annoy continually with little irritations

vex·a·tion \vek-'sā-shən\ *n* **1** : the act of vexing **2** : the quality or state of being vexed : IRRITATION **3** : a cause of trouble or annoyance

vex·a·tious \-shəs\ *adj* **1** : causing vexation : ANNOYING

2 : full of distress or annoyance : TROUBLED — **vex-a·tious·ly** *adv* — **vex·a·tious·ness** *n*

vexed \'vekst\ *adj* : fully debated or discussed ⟨a ∼ question⟩

VF *abbr* **1** video frequency **2** visual field

VFD *abbr* volunteer fire department

VFW *abbr* Veterans of Foreign Wars

VG *abbr* **1** very good **2** vicar-general

VHF *abbr* very high frequency

VI *abbr* Virgin Islands

via \'vī-ə, 'vē-ə\ *prep* **1** : by way of **2** : by means of

vi·a·ble \'vī-ə-bəl\ *adj* **1** : capable of living; *esp* : capable of surviving outside the mother's womb without artificial support ⟨a ∼ fetus⟩ **2** : capable of growing and developing ⟨∼ seeds⟩ **3** : capable of being put into practice : WORKABLE **4** : having a reasonable chance of succeeding ⟨a ∼ candidate⟩ — **vi·a·bil·i·ty** \ˌvī-ə-'bi-lə-tē\ *n* — **vi·a·bly** \'vī-ə-blē\ *adv*

via·duct \'vī-ə-ˌdəkt\ *n* : a long elevated roadway usu. consisting of a series of short spans supported on arches, piers, or columns

viaduct

vi·al \'vī-əl\ *n* : a small vessel for liquids

vi·and \'vī-ənd\ *n* : an article of food

vi·at·i·cum \vī-'a-ti-kəm, vē-\ *n, pl* **-cums** *or* **-ca** \-kə\ **1** : the Christian Eucharist given to a person in danger of death **2** : an allowance esp. in money for traveling needs and expenses

vibes \'vībz\ *n pl* **1** : VIBRAPHONE **2** : VIBRATIONS

vi·brant \'vī-brənt\ *adj* **1** : VIBRATING, PULSATING **2** : pulsating with vigor or activity **3** : readily set in vibration : RESPONSIVE **4** : sounding from vibration — **vi·bran·cy** \-brən-sē\ *n*

vi·bra·phone \'vī-brə-ˌfōn\ *n* : a percussion instrument like the xylophone but with metal bars and motor-driven resonators

vi·brate \'vī-ˌbrāt\ *vb* **vi·brat·ed; vi·brat·ing** **1** : OSCILLATE **2** : to set in vibration **3** : to be in vibration **4** : WAVER, FLUCTUATE **5** : to respond sympathetically : THRILL

vi·bra·tion \vī-'brā-shən\ *n* **1** : a rapid to-and-fro motion of the particles of an elastic body or medium (as a stretched cord) that produces sound **2** : an act of vibrating : a state of being vibrated : OSCILLATION **3** : a trembling motion **4** : VACILLATION **5** : a feeling or impression that someone or something gives off — usu. used in pl. ⟨good ∼s⟩ — **vi·bra·tion·al** \-shə-nəl\ *adj*

vi·bra·to \vi-'brä-tō\ *n, pl* **-tos** [It] : a slightly tremulous effect imparted to vocal or instrumental music

vi·bra·tor \'vī-ˌbrā-tər\ *n* : one that vibrates or causes vibration; *esp* : a vibrating electrical device used in massage or for sexual stimulation

vi·bra·to·ry \'vī-brə-ˌtōr-ē\ *adj* : consisting of, capable of, or causing vibration

vi·bur·num \vī-'bər-nəm\ *n* : any of a genus of widely distributed shrubs or trees related to the honeysuckle and bearing small usu. white flowers in broad clusters

vic *abbr* vicinity

Vic *abbr* Victoria

vic·ar \'vi-kər\ *n* **1** : an administrative deputy **2** : a minister in charge of a church who serves under the authority of another minister — **vi·car·i·ate** \vī-'ker-ē-ət\ *n*

vic·ar·age \'vi-kə-rij\ *n* : a vicar's home

vicar–general *n, pl* **vicars–general** : an administrative deputy (as of a Roman Catholic or Anglican bishop)

vic·ar·i·ous \vī-'ker-ē-əs, -'kar-\ *adj* **1** : acting for another **2** : done or suffered by one person on behalf of another or others ⟨a ∼ sacrifice⟩ **3** : sharing in someone else's experience through the use of the imagination or sympathetic feelings — **vic·ar·i·ous·ly** *adv* — **vi·car·i·ous·ness** *n*

¹**vice** \'vīs\ *n* **1** : DEPRAVITY, WICKEDNESS **2** : a moral fault or failing **3** : a habitual usu. trivial fault **4** : an undesirable behavior pattern in a domestic animal

²**vice** *chiefly Brit var of* VISE

³**vi·ce** \'vī-sē\ *prep* : in the place of; *also* : rather than

vice admiral *n* : a commissioned officer in the navy or coast guard ranking above a rear admiral

vice·ge·rent \'vīs-'jir-ənt\ *n* : an administrative deputy of a king or magistrate — **vice·ge·ren·cy** \-ən-sē\ *n*

vi·cen·ni·al \vī-'se-nē-əl\ *adj* : occurring once every 20 years

vice presidency *n* : the office of vice president

vice president *n* **1** : an officer ranking next to a president and usu. empowered to act for the president during an absence or disability **2** : any of several of a president's deputies

vice·re·gal \'vīs-'rē-gəl\ *adj* : of or relating to a viceroy

vice·roy \'vīs-ˌrȯi\ *n* : the governor of a country or province who rules as representative of the sovereign — **vice·roy·al·ty** \-əl-tē\ *n*

vice ver·sa \ˌvī-si-'vər-sə, 'vīs-'vər-\ *adv* : with the order reversed

vi·chys·soise \ˌvi-shē-'swäz, ˌvē-\ *n* [F] : a soup made esp. from leeks or onions and potatoes, cream, and chicken stock and usu. served cold

vic·i·nage \'vis-ᵊn-ij\ *n* : a neighboring or surrounding district : VICINITY

vi·cin·i·ty \və-'si-nə-tē\ *n, pl* **-ties** [MF *vicinité*, fr. L *vicinitas*, fr. *vicinus* neighboring, fr. *vicus* row of houses, village] **1** : NEARNESS, PROXIMITY **2** : a surrounding area : NEIGHBORHOOD

vi·cious \'vi-shəs\ *adj* **1** : having the quality of vice : WICKED, DEPRAVED **2** : DEFECTIVE, FAULTY; *also* : INVALID **3** : IMPURE, FOUL **4** : having a savage disposition; *also* : marked by violence or ferocity **5** : MALICIOUS, SPITEFUL **6** : worsened by internal causes that augment each other ⟨∼ wage-price spiral⟩ — **vi·cious·ly** *adv* — **vi·cious·ness** *n*

vi·cis·si·tude \və-'si-sə-ˌtüd, vī-, -ˌtyüd\ *n* : an irregular, unexpected, or surprising change

vic·tim \'vik-təm\ *n* **1** : a living being offered as a sacrifice in a religious rite **2** : an individual injured or killed (as by disease or accident) **3** : a person cheated, fooled, or injured ⟨a ∼ of circumstances⟩

vic·tim·ize \'vik-tə-ˌmīz\ *vb* **-ized; -iz·ing** : to make a victim of — **vic·tim·i·za·tion** \ˌvik-tə-mə-'zā-shən\ *n* — **vic·tim·iz·er** \'vik-tə-ˌmī-zər\ *n*

vic·tim·less *adj* : having no victim ⟨considered gambling to be a ∼ crime⟩

vic·tor \'vik-tər\ *n* : WINNER, CONQUEROR

\ə\abut \ᵊ\kitten \ər\further \a\ash \ā\ace \ä\mop, mar \au̇\out \ch\chin \e\bet \ē\easy \g\go \i\hit \ī\ice \j\job \ŋ\sing \ō\go \ȯ\law \ȯi\boy \th\thin \t͟h\the \ü\loot \u̇\foot \y\yet \zh\vision *see also* Pronunciation Symbols page

vic·to·ria \vik-ˈtȯr-ē-ə\ *n* : a low 4-wheeled carriage with a folding top and a raised driver's seat in front

¹Vic·to·ri·an \vik-ˈtȯr-ē-ən\ *adj* **1** : of or relating to the reign of Queen Victoria of England or the art, letters, or tastes of her time **2** : typical of the standards, attitudes, or conduct of the age of Victoria esp. when considered prudish or narrow

²Victorian *n* **1** : a person and esp. an author of the Victorian period **2** : a typically large ornate house built during Queen Victoria's reign

vic·to·ri·ous \vik-ˈtȯr-ē-əs\ *adj* **1** : having won a victory **2** : of, relating to, or characteristic of victory — **vic·to·ri·ous·ly** *adv*

vic·to·ry \ˈvik-tə-rē\ *n, pl* **-ries 1** : the overcoming of an enemy or an antagonist **2** : achievement of mastery or success in a struggle or endeavor

¹vict·ual \ˈvit-ᵊl\ *n* **1** : food fit for humans **2** *pl* : food supplies

²victual *vb* **-ualed** *or* **-ualled; -ual·ing** *or* **-ual·ling 1** : to supply with food **2** : to store up provisions

vict·ual·ler *or* **vict·ual·er** \ˈvit-ᵊl-ər\ *n* : one that supplies provisions (as to an army or a ship)

vi·cu·ña *or* **vi·cu·na** \vi-ˈkün-yə, vī-; vī-ˈkü-nə, -ˈkyü-\ *n* **1** : a So. American wild mammal related to the llama and alpaca; *also* : its wool **2** : a soft fabric woven from the wool of the vicuña; *also* : a sheep's wool imitation of this

vi·de \ˈvī-dē, ˈvē-ˌdā\ *vb imper* [L] : SEE — used to direct a reader to another item

vi·de·li·cet \və-ˈde-lə-ˌset, vī-; vi-ˈdā-li-ˌket\ *adv* [ME, fr. L, fr. *vidēre* to see + *licet* it is permitted] : that is to say : NAMELY

¹vid·eo \ˈvi-dē-ˌō\ *n* **1** : TELEVISION **2** : VIDEOTAPE **3** : a videotaped performance ⟨music ∼s⟩

²video *adj* **1** : relating to or used in transmission or reception of the television image **2** : relating to or being images on a television screen or computer display ⟨a ∼ terminal⟩

vid·eo·cas·sette \ˌvi-dē-ō-kə-ˈset\ *n* **1** : a case containing videotape for use with a VCR **2** : a recording (as of a movie) on a videocassette

videocassette recorder *n* : VCR

vid·eo·disc *or* **vid·eo·disk** \ˈvi-dē-ō-ˌdisk\ *n* **1** : a disc similar in appearance and use to a phonograph record on which programs have been recorded for playback on a television set; *also* : OPTICAL DISK **2** : a recording (as of a movie) on a videodisc

video game *n* : an electronic game played on a video screen

vid·eo·phone \ˈvid-ē-ə-ˌfōn\ *n* : a telephone for transmitting both audio and video signals

¹vid·eo·tape \ˈvid-ē-ō-ˌtāp\ *n* : a recording of visual images and sound made on magnetic tape; *also* : the magnetic tape used for such a recording

²videotape *vb* : to make a videotape of

videotape recorder *n* : a device for recording and playing back videotapes

vie \ˈvī\ *vb* **vied; vy·ing** \ˈvī-iŋ\ : to compete for superiority : CONTEND — **vi·er** \ˈvī-ər\ *n*

Viet·cong \vē-ˈet-ˈkäŋ, ˌvē-ət-, -ˈkȯŋ\ *n, pl* **Vietcong** : a guerrilla soldier of the Vietnamese communist movement

Viet·nam·ese \vē-ˌet-nə-ˈmēz, ˌvē-ət-, -ˈmēs\ *n, pl* **Vietnamese** : a native or inhabitant of Vietnam — **Vietnamese** *adj*

¹view \ˈvyü\ *n* **1** : the act of seeing or examining : INSPECTION; *also* : SURVEY **2** : a way of looking at or regarding something **3** : ESTIMATE, JUDGMENT ⟨stated his ∼s⟩ **4** : a sight (as of a landscape) regarded for its pictorial quality **5** : extent or range of vision ⟨within ∼⟩ **6** : OBJECT, PURPOSE ⟨done with a ∼ to promotion⟩ **7** : a picture of a scene

²view *vb* **1** : to look at attentively : EXAMINE **2** : SEE,

WATCH **3** : to examine mentally : CONSIDER — **view·er** *n*

view·er·ship \ˈvyü-ər-ˌship\ *n* : a television audience esp. with respect to size or makeup

view·find·er \ˈvyü-ˌfīn-dər\ *n* : a device on a camera for showing the view to be included in the picture

view·point \-ˌpȯint\ *n* : POINT OF VIEW, STANDPOINT

vi·ges·i·mal \vī-ˈje-sə-məl\ *adj* : based on the number 20

vig·il \ˈvi-jəl\ *n* **1** : a religious observance formerly held on the night before a religious feast **2** : the day before a religious feast observed as a day of spiritual preparation **3** : evening or nocturnal devotions or prayers — usu. used in pl. **4** : an act or a time of keeping awake when sleep is customary; *esp* : WATCH 1

vig·i·lance \ˈvi-jə-ləns\ *n* : the quality or state of being vigilant

vigilance committee *n* : a committee of vigilantes

vig·i·lant \ˈvi-jə-lənt\ *adj* : alertly watchful esp. to avoid danger — **vig·i·lant·ly** *adv*

vig·i·lan·te \ˌvi-jə-ˈlan-tē\ *n* : a member of a volunteer committee organized to suppress and punish crime summarily (as when the processes of law appear inadequate); *also* : a self-appointed doer of justice — **vig·i·lan·tism** \-ˈlan-ˌti-zəm\ *n*

¹vi·gnette \vin-ˈyet\ *n* [F, fr. MF *vignete,* fr. dim. of *vigne* vine] **1** : a small decorative design **2** : a picture (as an engraving or a photograph) that shades off gradually into the surrounding ground **3** : a short descriptive literary sketch

²vignette *vb* **vi·gnett·ed; vi·gnett·ing 1** : to finish (as a photograph) in the manner of a vignette **2** : to describe briefly

vig·or \ˈvi-gər\ *n* **1** : active strength or energy of body or mind **2** : INTENSITY, FORCE

vig·or·ous \ˈvi-gə-rəs\ *adj* **1** : having vigor : ROBUST **2** : done with force and energy — **vig·or·ous·ly** *adv* — **vig·or·ous·ness** *n*

vig·our *chiefly Brit var of* VIGOR

Vi·king \ˈvī-kiŋ\ *n* [ON *vīkingr*] : any of the pirate Norsemen who raided or invaded the coasts of Europe in the 8th to 10th centuries

vil *abbr* village

vile \ˈvīl\ *adj* **vil·er; vil·est 1** : morally despicable **2** : physically repulsive : FOUL **3** : of little worth **4** : DEGRADING, IGNOMINIOUS **5** : utterly bad or contemptible ⟨∼ weather⟩ — **vile·ly** \ˈvīl-lē\ *adv* — **vile·ness** *n*

vil·i·fy \ˈvi-lə-ˌfī\ *vb* **-fied; -fy·ing** : to blacken the character of with abusive language : DEFAME **syn** malign, calumniate, slander, libel, traduce — **vil·i·fi·ca·tion** \ˌvi-lə-fə-ˈkā-shən\ *n* — **vil·i·fi·er** \ˈvi-lə-ˌfī-ər\ *n*

vil·la \ˈvi-lə\ *n* **1** : a country estate **2** : the rural or suburban residence of a wealthy person

vil·lage \ˈvi-lij\ *n* **1** : a settlement usu. larger than a hamlet and smaller than a town **2** : an incorporated minor municipality **3** : the people of a village

vil·lag·er \ˈvi-li-jər\ *n* : an inhabitant of a village

vil·lain \ˈvi-lən\ *n* **1** : VILLEIN **2** : an evil person : SCOUNDREL

vil·lain·ess \-lə-nəs\ *n* : a woman who is a villain

vil·lain·ous \-lə-nəs\ *adj* **1** : befitting a villain : WICKED, EVIL **2** : highly objectionable : DETESTABLE **syn** vicious, iniquitous, nefarious, infamous, corrupt, degenerate — **vil·lain·ous·ly** *adv* — **vil·lain·ous·ness** *n*

vil·lainy \-lə-nē\ *n, pl* **-lain·ies 1** : villainous conduct; *also* : a villainous act **2** : villainous character or nature

vil·lein \ˈvi-lən, -ˌlān\ *n* **1** : a free villager of Anglo-Saxon times **2** : an unfree peasant having the status of a slave to a feudal lord

vil·len·age \ˈvil-ə-nij\ *n* **1** : the holding of land at the will of a feudal lord **2** : the status of a villein

vil·lous \ˈvi-ləs\ *adj* : covered with fine hairs or villi

vil·lus \ˈvi-ləs\ *n, pl* **vil·li** \-ˌlī, -(ˌ)lē\ : a slender usu. vascular process; *esp* : one of the tiny projections of the mucous membrane of the small intestine that function in the absorption of food

vim \\'vim\\ *n* : robust energy and enthusiasm : VITALITY

VIN *abbr* vehicle identification number

vin·ai·grette \\ˌvin-i-'gret\\ *n* [F] : a sauce made typically of oil and vinegar, onions, parsley, and herbs

vin·ci·ble \\'vin-sə-bəl\\ *adj* : capable of being overcome or subdued

vin·di·cate \\'vin-də-ˌkāt\\ *vb* **-cat·ed; -cat·ing** **1** : AVENGE **2** : EXONERATE, ABSOLVE **3** : CONFIRM, SUBSTANTIATE **4** : to provide defense for : JUSTIFY **5** : to maintain a right to : ASSERT — **vin·di·ca·tor** \\-ˌkā-tər\\ *n*

vin·di·ca·tion \\ˌvin-də-'kā-shən\\ *n* : a vindicating or being vindicated; *esp* : justification against denial or censure : DEFENSE

vin·dic·tive \\vin-'dik-tiv\\ *adj* **1** : disposed to revenge **2** : intended for or involving revenge **3** : VICIOUS, SPITEFUL — **vin·dic·tive·ly** *adv* — **vin·dic·tive·ness** *n*

vine \\'vīn\\ *n* [ME, fr. OF *vigne*, fr. L *vinea* vine, vineyard, fr. fem. of *vineus* of wine, fr. *vinum* wine] **1** : GRAPE 2 **2** : a plant whose stem requires support and which climbs (as by tendrils) or trails along the ground; *also* : the stem of such a plant

vin·e·gar \\'vi-ni-gər\\ *n* [ME *vinegre*, fr. OF *vinaigre*, fr. *vin* wine + *aigre* keen, sour] : a sour liquid obtained by fermentation (as of cider, wine, or malt) and used in cookery and pickling

vin·e·gary \\-gə-rē\\ *adj* **1** : resembling vinegar : SOUR **2** : disagreeable in manner or disposition : CRABBED

vine·yard \\'vin-yərd\\ *n* **1** : a field of grapevines esp. to produce grapes for wine production **2** : a sphere of activity : field of endeavor

vi·nous \\'vī-nəs\\ *adj* **1** : of, relating to, or made with wine ⟨∼ medications⟩ **2** : showing the effects of the use of wine ⟨∼ bloodshot eyes⟩

¹**vin·tage** \\'vin-tij\\ *n* **1** : a season's yield of grapes or wine **2** : WINE; *esp* : a usu. superior wine which comes from a single year **3** : the act or period of gathering grapes or making wine **4** : a period of origin ⟨clothes of 1890 ∼⟩

²**vintage** *adj* **1** : of, relating to, or produced in a particular vintage **2** : of old, recognized, and enduring interest, importance, or quality : CLASSIC ⟨∼ cars⟩ **3** : of the best and most characteristic — used with a proper noun

vint·ner \\'vint-nər\\ *n* : a dealer in wines

vi·nyl \\'vīn-ᵊl\\ *n* **1** : a chemical derived from ethylene by the removal of one hydrogen atom **2** : a polymer of a vinyl compound or a product (as a textile fiber) made from one

vinyl chloride *n* : a flammable gaseous carcinogenic compound used esp. to make vinyl resins

vi·ol \\'vī-əl\\ *n* : a bowed stringed instrument chiefly of the 16th and 17th centuries having a fretted neck and usu. six strings

¹**vi·o·la** \\vī-'ō-lə\\ *n* : VIOLET 1; *esp* : any of various hybrid garden plants with white, yellow, purple, or variously colored flowers that resemble but are smaller than the related pansies

²**vi·o·la** \\vē-'ō-lə\\ *n* : an instrument of the violin family slightly larger and tuned lower than a violin — **vi·o·list** \\-list\\ *n*

vi·o·la·ble \\'vī-ə-lə-bəl\\ *adj* : capable of being violated

vi·o·late \\'vī-ə-ˌlāt\\ *vb* **-lat·ed; -lat·ing** **1** : BREAK, DISREGARD ⟨∼ a law⟩ ⟨∼ a frontier⟩ **2** : RAPE **3** : PROFANE, DESECRATE **4** : INTERRUPT, DISTURB ⟨*violated* his privacy⟩ — **vi·o·la·tor** \\-ˌlā-tər\\ *n*

vi·o·la·tion \\ˌvī-ə-'lā-shən\\ *n* : an act or instance of violating : the state of being violated **syn** breach, infraction, trespass, infringement, transgression

vi·o·lence \\'vī-ləns, 'vī-ə-\\ *n* **1** : exertion of physical force so as to injure or abuse **2** : injury by or as if by infringement or profanation **3** : intense or furious often destructive action or force **4** : vehement feeling or ex-

pression : INTENSITY **5** : jarring quality : DISCORDANCE **syn** compulsion, coercion, duress, constraint

vi·o·lent \\-lənt\\ *adj* **1** : marked by extreme force or sudden intense activity **2** : caused by or showing strong feeling ⟨∼ words⟩ **3** : EXTREME, INTENSE **4** : emotionally agitated to the point of loss of self-control **5** : caused by force : not natural ⟨∼ death⟩ — **vi·o·lent·ly** *adv*

vi·o·let \\'vī-ə-lət\\ *n* **1** : any of a genus of chiefly herbs usu. with heart-shaped leaves and both aerial and underground flowers; *esp* : one with small usu. solid-colored flowers **2** : a reddish blue color

vi·o·lin \\ˌvī-ə-'lin\\ *n* : a bowed stringed instrument with four strings that has a shallow body, a fingerboard without frets, and a curved bridge — **vi·o·lin·ist** \\-'li-nist\\ *n*

violin

vi·o·lon·cel·lo \\ˌvī-ə-lən-'che-lō\\ *n* [It] : CELLO — **vi·o·lon·cel·list** \\-list\\ *n*

VIP \\ˌvē-ˌī-'pē\\ *n, pl* **VIPs** \\-'pēz\\ [*very important person*] : a person of great influence or prestige; *esp* : a high official with special privileges

vi·per \\'vī-pər\\ *n* **1** : a common stout-bodied Eurasian venomous snake having a bite only rarely fatal to humans; *also* : any snake (as a pit viper) of the same family as the viper **2** : any venomous or reputedly venomous snake **3** : a vicious or treacherous person — **vi·per·ine** \\-pə-ˌrīn\\ *adj*

vi·ra·go \\və-'rä-gō, -'rā-\\ *n, pl* **-goes** *or* **-gos** [ME, fr. L, strong or heroic woman, fr. *vir* man] **1** : a loud overbearing woman **2** : a woman of great strength and courage

vi·ral \\'vī-rəl\\ *adj* : of, relating to, or caused by a virus

vir·eo \\'vir-ē-ˌō\\ *n, pl* **-e·os** [L, a small bird, fr. *virēre* to be green] : any of various small insect-eating American songbirds mostly olive green and grayish in color

¹**vir·gin** \\'vər-jən\\ *n* **1** : an unmarried woman devoted to religion **2** : an unmarried girl or woman **3** *cap* : the mother of Jesus **4** : a person who has not had sexual intercourse

²**virgin** *adj* **1** : free from stain : PURE, SPOTLESS **2** : CHASTE **3** : befitting a virgin : MODEST **4** : FRESH, UNSPOILED; *esp* : not altered by human activity ⟨∼ forest⟩ **5** : INITIAL, FIRST

¹**vir·gin·al** \\'vər-jən-ᵊl\\ *adj* : of, relating to, or characteristic of a virgin or virginity — **vir·gin·al·ly** *adv*

²**virginal** *n* : a small rectangular spinet without legs popular in the 16th and 17th centuries

Vir·gin·ia creeper \\vər-'jin-yə-\\ *n* : a No. American vine related to the grapes that has leaves with five leaflets and bluish black berries

Virginia reel *n* : an American country-dance

vir·gin·i·ty \vər-ˈji-nə-tē\ *n, pl* **-ties 1** : the quality or state of being virgin; *esp* : MAIDENHOOD **2** : the unmarried life : CELIBACY

Vir·go \ˈvər-ˌgō\ *n* [L, lit., virgin] **1** : a zodiacal constellation between Leo and Libra usu. pictured as a young woman **2** : the 6th sign of the zodiac in astrology; *also* : one born under this sign

vir·gule \ˈvər-gyül\ *n* : a mark / used typically to denote "or" (as in *and/or*) or "per" (as in *feet/second*)

vir·i·des·cent \ˌvir-ə-ˈdes-ᵊnt\ *adj* : slightly green : GREENISH

vir·ile \ˈvir-əl\ *adj* **1** : having the nature, powers, or qualities of a man **2** : MASCULINE, MALE **3** : MASTERFUL, FORCEFUL — **vi·ril·i·ty** \və-ˈri-lə-tē\ *n*

vi·ri·on \ˈvī-rē-ˌän, ˈvir-ē-\ *n* : a complete virus particle consisting of an RNA or DNA core with a protein coat

vi·rol·o·gy \vī-ˈrä-lə-jē\ *n* : a branch of science that deals with viruses — **vi·rol·o·gist** \-jist\ *n*

vir·tu \ˌvər-ˈtü, vir-\ *n* [It *virtù*, lit., virtue] **1** : a love of or taste for objects of art **2** : objects of art (as curios and antiques)

vir·tu·al \ˈvər-chə-wəl\ *adj* : being in essence or in effect though not formally recognized or admitted ⟨a ∼ dictator⟩

vir·tu·al·ly \ˈvər-chə-wə-lē\ *adv* **1** : almost entirely : NEARLY **2** : for all practical purposes

vir·tue \ˈvər-chü\ *n* [ME *virtu*, fr. OF, fr. L *virtus* strength, manliness, virtue, fr. *vir* man] **1** : conformity to a standard of right : MORALITY **2** : a particular moral excellence **3** : manly strength or courage : VALOR **4** : a commendable quality : MERIT **5** : active power to accomplish a given effect : POTENCY, EFFICACY **6** : chastity esp. in a woman

vir·tu·os·i·ty \ˌvər-chə-ˈwä-sə-tē\ *n, pl* **-ties** : great technical skill in the practice of a fine art

vir·tu·o·so \ˌvər-chə-ˈwō-sō, -zō\ *n, pl* **-sos** *or* **-si** \-sē, -zē\ [It] **1** : one skilled in or having a taste for the fine arts **2** : one who excels in the technique of an art; *esp* : a highly skilled musical performer **syn** expert, adept, artist, doyen, master — **virtuoso** *adj*

vir·tu·ous \ˈvər-chə-wəs\ *adj* **1** : having or showing virtue and esp. moral virtue **2** : CHASTE — **vir·tu·ous·ly** *adv*

vir·u·lent \ˈvir-ə-lənt, ˈvir-yə-\ *adj* **1** : highly infectious ⟨a ∼ germ⟩; *also* : marked by a rapid, severe, and often deadly course ⟨a ∼ disease⟩ **2** : extremely poisonous or venomous : NOXIOUS **3** : full of malice : MALIGNANT — **vir·u·lence** \-ləns\ *n* — **vir·u·lent·ly** *adv*

vi·rus \ˈvī-rəs\ *n* [L, venom, poisonous emanation] **1** : any of a large group of submicroscopic infectious agents that have an outside coat of protein around a core of RNA or DNA, that can grow and multiply only in living cells, and that cause important diseases in human beings, lower animals, and plants; *also* : a disease caused by a virus **2** : something (as a corrupting influence) that poisons the mind or spirit **3** : a computer program usu. hidden within another program that reproduces itself and inserts the copies into other programs and that usu. performs a malicious action (as destroying data)

vis *abbr* **1** visibility **2** visual

¹vi·sa \ˈvē-zə, -sə\ *n* [F] **1** : an endorsement by the proper authorities on a passport to show that it has been examined and the bearer may proceed **2** : a signature by a superior official signifying approval of a document

²visa *vb* **vi·saed** \-zəd, -səd\; **vi·sa·ing** \-zə-iŋ, -sə-\ : to give a visa to (a passport)

vis·age \ˈvi-zij\ *n* : the face or countenance of a person or sometimes an animal; *also* : LOOK, APPEARANCE

¹vis–à–vis \ˌvēz-ə-ˈvē, ˌvēs-\ *prep* [F, lit., face-to-face] **1**

: face-to-face with : OPPOSITE **2** : in relation to **3** : as compared with

²vis–à–vis *n, pl* **vis–à–vis** \same *or* -ˈvēz\ **1** : one that is face-to-face with another **2** : ESCORT **3** : COUNTERPART **4** : TÊTE-À-TÊTE

³vis–à–vis *adv* : in company : TOGETHER

viscera *pl of* VISCUS

vis·cer·al \ˈvi-sə-rəl\ *adj* **1** : felt in or as if in the viscera **2** : not intellectual : INSTINCTIVE **3** : of or relating to the viscera — **vis·cer·al·ly** *adv*

vis·cid \ˈvi-səd\ *adj* : VISCOUS — **vis·cid·i·ty** \vi-ˈsi-də-tē\ *n*

vis·cos·i·ty \vis-ˈkä-sə-tē\ *n, pl* **-ties** : the quality of being viscous; *esp* : the property of resistance to flow in a fluid

vis·count \ˈvī-ˌkaünt\ *n* : a member of the British peerage ranking below an earl and above a baron

vis·count·ess \-ˌkaün-təs\ *n* **1** : the wife or widow of a viscount **2** : a woman who holds the rank of viscount in her own right

vis·cous \ˈvis-kəs\ *adj* [ME *viscouse*, fr. LL *viscosus* full of birdlime, viscous, fr. L *viscum* mistletoe, birdlime] **1** : having the sticky consistency of glue **2** : having or characterized by viscosity

vis·cus \ˈvis-kəs\ *n, pl* **vis·cera** \ˈvi-sə-rə\ : an internal organ of the body; *esp* : one (as the heart or liver) located in the cavity of the trunk

vise \ˈvīs\ *n* [MF *vis* something winding, fr. L *vitis* vine] : a tool with two jaws for holding work that typically close with a screw or lever

vis·i·bil·i·ty \ˌvi-zə-ˈbi-lə-tē\ *n, pl* **-ties 1** : the quality, condition, or degree of being visible **2** : the degree of clearness of the atmosphere

vis·i·ble \ˈvi-zə-bəl\ *adj* : capable of being seen ⟨∼ stars⟩; *also* : MANIFEST, APPARENT ⟨has no ∼ means of support⟩ — **vis·i·bly** \-blē\ *adv*

¹vi·sion \ˈvi-zhən\ *n* **1** : something seen otherwise than by ordinary sight (as in a dream or trance) **2** : a vivid picture created by the imagination **3** : the act or power of imagination **4** : unusual wisdom in foreseeing what is going to happen **5** : the act or power of seeing : SIGHT **6** : something seen; *esp* : a lovely sight

²vision *vb* : IMAGINE, ENVISION

¹vi·sion·ary \ˈvi-zhə-ˌner-ē\ *adj* **1** : of the nature of a vision : ILLUSORY, UNREAL **2** : not practical : UTOPIAN **3** : seeing or likely to see visions : given to dreaming or imagining **syn** imaginary, fantastic, chimerical, quixotic

²visionary *n, pl* **-ar·ies 1** : one whose ideas or projects are impractical : DREAMER **2** : one who sees visions

¹vis·it \ˈvi-zət\ *vb* **1** : to go to see in order to comfort or help **2** : to call on either as an act of courtesy or friendship **3** : to dwell with for a time as a guest **4** : to come to or upon as a reward, affliction, or punishment **5** : INFLICT **6** : to make a visit or regular or frequent visits **7** : CHAT, CONVERSE — **vis·it·able** *adj*

²visit *n* **1** : a short stay : CALL **2** : a brief residence as a guest **3** : a journey to and stay at a place **4** : a formal or professional call (as by a doctor)

vis·i·tant \ˈvi-zə-tənt\ *n* : VISITOR

vis·i·ta·tion \ˌvi-zə-ˈtā-shən\ *n* **1** : VISIT; *esp* : an official visit **2** : a special dispensation of divine favor or wrath; *also* : a severe trial

visiting nurse *n* : a nurse employed to visit sick persons or perform public health services in a community

vis·i·tor \ˈvi-zə-tər\ *n* : one that visits

vi·sor \ˈvī-zər\ *n* **1** : the front piece of a helmet; *esp* : a movable upper piece **2** : VIZARD **3** : a projecting part (as on a cap) to shade the eyes — **vi·sored** \-zərd\ *adj*

vis·ta \ˈvis-tə\ *n* **1** : a distant view through or along an avenue or opening **2** : an extensive mental view over a series of years or events

VISTA *abbr* Volunteers in Service to America

¹vi·su·al \ˈvi-zhə-wəl\ *adj* **1** : of, relating to, or used in vision ⟨∼ organs⟩ **2** : perceived by vision ⟨a ∼ impression⟩ **3** : VISIBLE **4** : done by sight only ⟨∼ navigation⟩ **5** : of or relating to instruction by means of sight ⟨∼ aids⟩ — **vi·su·al·ly** adv

²**visual** n : something (as a picture, chart, or film) that appeals to the sight and is used for illustration, demonstration, or promotion — usu. used in pl.

vi·su·al·ize \'vi-zhə-wə-ˌlīz\ vb **-ized; -iz·ing** : to make visible; esp : to form a mental image of — **vi·su·al·i·za·tion** \ˌvi-zhə-wə-lə-'zā-shən\ n — **vi·su·al·iz·er** n

vi·ta \'vē-tə, 'vī-\ n, pl **vi·tae** \'vē-ˌtī, 'vī-tē\ [L, lit., life] : a brief autobiographical sketch

vi·tal \'vīt-əl\ adj **1** : concerned with or necessary to the maintenance of life **2** : full of life and vigor : ANIMATED **3** : of, relating to, or characteristic of life or living beings **4** : FATAL, MORTAL ⟨∼ wound⟩ **5** : FUNDAMENTAL, INDISPENSABLE — **vi·tal·ly** adv

vi·tal·i·ty \vī-'ta-lə-tē\ n, pl **-ties 1** : the property distinguishing the living from the nonliving **2** : mental and physical vigor **3** : enduring quality **4** : ANIMATION, LIVELINESS

vi·tal·ize \'vīt-əl-ˌīz\ vb **-ized; -iz·ing** : to impart life or vigor to : ANIMATE — **vi·tal·i·za·tion** \ˌvīt-əl-ə-'zā-shən\ n

vi·tals \'vīt-əlz\ n pl **1** : vital organs (as the heart and brain) **2** : essential parts

vital signs n pl : the pulse rate, respiratory rate, body temperature, and often blood pressure of a person

vital statistics n pl : statistics dealing with births, deaths, marriages, health, and disease

vi·ta·min \'vī-tə-mən\ n : any of various organic substances that are essential in tiny amounts to the nutrition of most animals and some plants and are mostly obtained from foods

vitamin A n : any of several vitamins (as from egg yolk or fish-liver oils) required esp. for good vision

vitamin B n **1** : VITAMIN B COMPLEX **2** or **vitamin B₁** : THIAMINE

vitamin B complex n : a group of vitamins that are found widely in foods and are essential for normal function of certain enzymes and for growth

vitamin B₆ \-'bē-'siks\ n : any of several compounds that are considered essential to vertebrate nutrition

vitamin B₁₂ \-'bē-'twelv\ n : a complex cobalt-containing compound that occurs esp. in liver and is essential to normal blood formation, neural function, and growth; also : any of several compounds of similar action

vitamin C n : a vitamin found esp. in fruits and vegetables that is needed by the body to prevent scurvy

vitamin D n : any or all of several vitamins that are needed for normal bone and tooth structure and are found esp. in fish-liver oils, egg yolk, and milk or are produced by the body in response to ultraviolet light

vitamin E n : any of various oily fat-soluble liquid vitamins whose absence in the body is associated with such ailments as infertility, the breakdown of muscles, and vascular problems and which are found esp. in leaves and in seed germ oils

vitamin K n [Dan koagulation coagulation] : any of several vitamins needed for blood to clot properly

vi·ti·ate \'vi-shē-ˌāt\ vb **-at·ed; -at·ing 1** : CONTAMINATE, POLLUTE; also : DEBASE, PERVERT **2** : to make legally ineffective : INVALIDATE — **vi·ti·a·tion** \ˌvi-shē-'ā-shən\ n — **vi·ti·a·tor** \'vi-shē-ˌā-tər\ n

vi·ti·cul·ture \'vi-tə-ˌkəl-chər\ n : the growing of grapes — **vi·ti·cul·tur·al** \ˌvi-tə-'kəl-chə-rəl\ adj — **vi·ti·cul·tur·ist** \-rist\ n

vit·re·ous \'vi-trē-əs\ adj **1** : of, relating to, or resembling glass : GLASSY ⟨∼ rocks⟩ **2** : of, relating to, or being the clear colorless transparent jelly (**vitreous humor**) behind the lens in the eyeball

vit·ri·ol \'vi-trē-əl\ n : something resembling acid in be-

ing caustic, corrosive, or biting — **vit·ri·ol·ic** \ˌvi-trē-'ä-lik\ adj

vit·tles \'vit-əlz\ n pl : VICTUALS

vi·tu·per·ate \vī-'tü-pə-ˌrāt, və-, -'tyü-\ vb **-at·ed; -at·ing** : to abuse in words : SCOLD syn revile, berate, rate, upbraid, rail, lash — **vi·tu·per·a·tive** \-'tü-pə-rə-tiv, -'tyü-, -ˌrā-\ adj — **vi·tu·per·a·tive·ly** adv

vi·tu·per·a·tion \(ˌ)vī-tü-pə-'rā-shən, və-, -tyü-\ n : lengthy harsh criticism or abuse

vi·va \'vē-və\ interj [It & Sp, long live] — used to express goodwill or approval

vi·va·ce \vē-'vä-chä\ adv or adj [It] : in a brisk spirited manner — used as a direction in music

vi·va·cious \və-'vā-shəs, vī-\ adj : lively in temper, conduct, or spirit : SPRIGHTLY — **vi·va·cious·ly** adv — **vi·va·cious·ness** n

vi·vac·i·ty \-'va-sə-tē\ n : the quality or state of being vivacious

vi·va vo·ce \ˌvī-və-'vō-sē, ˌvē-və-'vō-ˌchä\ adj [ML, with the living voice] : expressed or conducted by word of mouth : ORAL — **viva voce** adv

viv·id \'vi-vəd\ adj **1** : having the appearance of vigorous life **2** : BRILLIANT, INTENSE ⟨a ∼ red⟩ **3** : producing a strong impression on the senses; esp : producing distinct mental pictures ⟨a ∼ description⟩ — **viv·id·ly** adv — **viv·id·ness** n

viv·i·fy \'vi-və-ˌfī\ vb **-fied; -fy·ing 1** : to put life into : ANIMATE **2** : to make vivid — **viv·i·fi·ca·tion** \ˌvi-və-fə-'kā-shən\ n — **viv·i·fi·er** n

vi·vip·a·rous \vī-'vi-pə-rəs, və-\ adj : producing living young from within the body rather than from eggs — **vi·vi·par·i·ty** \ˌvī-və-'par-ə-tē, ˌvi-\ n

vivi·sec·tion \ˌvi-və-'sek-shən, 'vi-və-ˌsek-\ n : the cutting of or operation on a living animal; also : animal experimentation esp. if causing distress to the subject

vix·en \'vik-sən\ n **1** : an ill-tempered scolding woman **2** : a female fox

viz abbr videlicet

viz·ard \'vi-zərd\ n : a mask for disguise or protection

vi·zier \və-'zir\ n : a high executive officer of many Muslim countries

VJ abbr veejay

VOA abbr Voice of America

voc abbr **1** vocational **2** vocative

vocab abbr vocabulary

vo·ca·ble \'vō-kə-bəl\ n : TERM, NAME; esp : a word as such without regard to its meaning

vo·cab·u·lary \vō-'ka-byə-ˌler-ē\ n, pl **-lar·ies 1** : a list or collection of words usu. alphabetically arranged and defined or explained : LEXICON **2** : a stock of words in a language used by a class or individual or in relation to a subject

vocabulary entry n : a word (as the noun book), hyphened or open compound (as the verb cross-refer or the noun boric acid), word element (as the affix -an), abbreviation (as agt), verbalized symbol (as Na), or term (as master of ceremonies) entered alphabetically in a dictionary for the purpose of definition or identification or expressly included as an inflected form (as the noun mice or the verb saw) or as a derived form (as the noun godlessness or the adverb globally) or related phrase (as in spite of) run on at its base word and usu. set in a type (as boldface) readily distinguishable from that of the lightface running text which defines, explains, or identifies the entry

¹**vo·cal** \'vō-kəl\ adj **1** : uttered by the voice : ORAL **2** : relating to, composed or arranged for, or sung by the human voice ⟨∼ music⟩ **3** : given to expressing oneself

---

\ə\abut \ʼ\kitten \ər\further \a\ash \ā\ace \ä\mop, mar \aú\out \ch\chin \e\bet \ē\easy \g\go \i\hit \ī\ice \j\job \ŋ\sing \ō\go \ò\law \òi\boy \th\thin \tẖ\the \ü\loot \ù\foot \y\yet \zh\vision see also Pronunciation Symbols page freely or insistently : OUTSPOKEN **4** : of or relating to the voice

²vocal *n* **1** : a vocal sound **2** : a vocal composition or its performance

vocal cords *n pl* : either of two pairs of elastic folds of mucous membrane that project into the cavity of the larynx and function in the production of vocal sounds

vo·cal·ic \vō-ˈka-lik\ *adj* : of, relating to, or functioning as a vowel

vo·cal·ist \ˈvō-kə-list\ *n* : SINGER

vo·cal·ize \-ˌlīz\ *vb* **-ized; -iz·ing 1** : to give vocal expression to : UTTER; *esp* : SING **2** : to make voiced rather than voiceless — **vo·cal·iz·er** *n*

vo·ca·tion \vō-ˈkā-shən\ *n* **1** : a summons or strong inclination to a particular state or course of action ⟨religious ∼⟩ **2** : regular employment : OCCUPATION, PROFESSION — **vo·ca·tion·al** \-shə-nəl\ *adj*

vo·ca·tion·al·ism \-shə-nə-ˌli-zəm\ *n* : emphasis on vocational training in education

voc·a·tive \ˈvä-kə-tiv\ *adj* : of, relating to, or constituting a grammatical case marking the one addressed — **vocative** *n*

vo·cif·er·ate \vō-ˈsi-fə-ˌrāt\ *vb* **-at·ed; -at·ing** [L *vociferari*, fr. *voc-*, *vox* voice + *ferre* to bear] : to cry out loudly : CLAMOR, SHOUT — **vo·cif·er·a·tion** \-ˌsi-fə-ˈrā-shən\ *n*

vo·cif·er·ous \vō-ˈsi-fə-rəs\ *adj* : making or given to loud outcry — **vo·cif·er·ous·ly** *adv* — **vo·cif·er·ous·ness** *n*

vod·ka \ˈväd-kə\ *n* [Russ, fr. *voda* water] : a colorless liquor distilled from a mash

vogue \ˈvōg\ *n* [MF, action of rowing, course, fashion, fr. It *voga*, fr. *vogare* to row] **1** : popular acceptance or favor : POPULARITY **2** : a period of popularity **3** : one that is in fashion at a particular time **syn** mode, fad, rage, craze, trend, fashion

vogu·ish \ˈvō-gish\ *adj* **1** : FASHIONABLE, SMART **2** : suddenly or temporarily popular

¹voice \ˈvȯis\ *n* **1** : sound produced through the mouth by vertebrates and esp. by human beings in speaking or shouting **2** : musical sound produced by the vocal cords : the power to produce such sound; *also* : one of the melodic parts in a vocal or instrumental composition **3** : the vocal organs as a means of tone production ⟨train the ∼⟩ **4** : sound produced by vibration of the vocal cords as heard in vowels and some consonants **5** : the power of speaking **6** : a sound suggesting a voice ⟨the ∼ of the sea⟩ **7** : an instrument or medium of expression **8** : a choice, opinion, or wish openly expressed; *also* : right of expression **9** : distinction of form of a verb to indicate the relation of the subject to the action expressed by the verb

²voice *vb* **voiced; voic·ing** : to give voice or expression to : UTTER ⟨∼ a complaint⟩ **syn** express, vent, air, ventilate

voice box *n* : LARYNX

voiced \ˈvȯist\ *adj* **1** : having a voice ⟨soft-*voiced*⟩ **2** : uttered with voice ⟨a ∼ consonant⟩ — **voiced·ness** \ˈvȯist-nəs, ˈvȯi-səd-nəs\ *n*

voice·less \ˈvȯis-ləs\ *adj* **1** : having no voice **2** : not pronounced with voice — **voice·less·ly** *adv* — **voice·less·ness** *n*

voice mail *n* : an electronic communication system in which spoken messages are recorded for later playback to the intended recipient

voice–over *n* : the voice in a film or television program of a person who is heard but not seen or not seen talking

voice·print \ˈvȯis-ˌprint\ *n* : an individually distinctive pattern of voice characteristics that is spectrographically produced

¹void \ˈvȯid\ *adj* **1** : UNOCCUPIED, VACANT **2** : containing nothing : EMPTY **3** : LACKING, DEVOID ⟨proposals ∼ of

sense⟩ **4** : VAIN, USELESS **5** : of no legal force or effect : NULL

²void *n* **1** : empty space : EMPTINESS, VACUUM **2** : a feeling of want or hollowness

³void *vb* **1** : to make or leave empty; *also* : VACATE, LEAVE **2** : DISCHARGE, EMIT ⟨∼ urine⟩ **3** : to render void : ANNUL, NULLIFY ⟨∼ a contract⟩ — **void·able** *adj* — **void·er** *n*

voi·là \vwä-ˈlä\ *interj* [F] — used to call attention or to express satisfaction or approval

voile \ˈvȯil\ *n* : a sheer fabric used for women's clothing and curtains

vol *abbr* **1** volume **2** volunteer

vol·a·tile \ˈvä-lət-ᵊl\ *adj* **1** : readily becoming a vapor at a relatively low temperature ⟨a ∼ liquid⟩ **2** : likely to change suddenly ⟨a ∼ temper⟩ — **vol·a·til·i·ty** \ˌvä-lə-ˈti-lə-tē\ *n* — **vol·a·til·ize** \ˈvä-lət-ᵊl-ˌīz\ *vb*

vol·ca·nic \väl-ˈka-nik\ *adj* **1** : of, relating to, or produced by a volcano **2** : explosively violent

vol·ca·nism \ˈväl-kə-ˌni-zəm\ *n* : volcanic action or activity

vol·ca·no \väl-ˈkā-nō\ *n*, *pl* **-noes** *or* **-nos** [It *vulcano*, fr. L *Volcanus*, *Vulcanus* Roman god of fire and metalworking] : an opening in the earth's crust from which molten rock and steam issue; *also* : a hill or mountain composed of the ejected material

vol·ca·nol·o·gy \ˌväl-kə-ˈnä-lə-jē\ *n* : a branch of geology that deals with volcanic phenomena — **vol·ca·nol·o·gist** \-kə-ˈnä-lə-jist\ *n*

vole \ˈvōl\ *n* : any of various small rodents that are closely related to the lemmings and muskrats

vo·li·tion \vō-ˈli-shən\ *n* **1** : the act or the power of making a choice or decision : WILL **2** : a choice or decision made — **vo·li·tion·al** \-ˈli-shə-nəl\ *adj*

¹vol·ley \ˈvä-lē\ *n*, *pl* **volleys 1** : a flight of missiles (as arrows) **2** : simultaneous discharge of a number of missile weapons **3** : an act of volleying **4** : a burst of many things at once ⟨a ∼ of angry letters⟩

²volley *vb* **vol·leyed; vol·ley·ing 1** : to discharge or become discharged in or as if in a volley **2** : to hit an object of play in the air before it touches the ground

vol·ley·ball \-ˌbȯl\ *n* : a game played by volleying an inflated ball over a net; *also* : the ball used in this game

volt \ˈvōlt\ *n* : the meter-kilogram-second unit of electrical potential difference and electromotive force equal to the difference in potential between two points in a wire carrying a constant current of one ampere when the power dissipated between the points is equal to one watt

volt·age \ˈvōl-tij\ *n* : potential difference measured in volts

vol·ta·ic \väl-ˈtā-ik, vōl-\ *adj* : of, relating to, or producing direct electric current by chemical action

volte–face \ˌvȯlt-ˈfäs, ˌvȯl-tə-\ *n* : a reversal in policy : ABOUT-FACE

volt·me·ter \ˈvōlt-ˌmē-tər\ *n* : an instrument for measuring in volts the difference in potential between different points of an electrical circuit

vol·u·ble \ˈväl-yə-bəl\ *adj* : fluent and smooth in speech : GLIB **syn** garrulous, loquacious, talkative — **vol·u·bil·i·ty** \ˌväl-yə-ˈbi-lə-tē\ *n* — **vol·u·bly** \ˈväl-yə-blē\ *adv*

vol·ume \ˈväl-yəm\ *n* [ME, fr. MF, fr. L *volumen* roll, scroll, fr. *volvere* to roll] **1** : a series of printed sheets bound typically in book form; *also* : an arbitrary number of issues of a periodical **2** : space occupied as measured by cubic units ⟨the ∼ of a cylinder⟩ **3** : sufficient matter to fill a book ⟨her glance spoke ∼s⟩ **4** : AMOUNT ⟨increasing ∼ of business⟩ **5** : the degree of loudness of a sound **syn** body, bulk, mass

vo·lu·mi·nous \və-ˈlü-mə-nəs\ *adj* : having or marked by great volume or bulk : LARGE — **vo·lu·mi·nous·ly** *adv* — **vo·lu·mi·nous·ness** *n*

VOLUME FORMULAS

FIGURE	FORMULA	MEANING OF LETTERS
cube	$V = a^3$	a = length of one edge
rectangular solid	$V = lwh$	l = length of base; w = width of base; h = height
pyramid	$V = \dfrac{Ah}{3}$	A = area of base; h = height
cylinder	$V = \pi r^2 h$	π = 3.1416; r = radius of the base; h = height
cone	$V = \dfrac{\pi r^2 h}{3}$	π = 3.1416; r = radius of the base; h = height
sphere	$V = \dfrac{4\pi r^3}{3}$	π = 3.1416; r = radius

¹vol·un·tary \'vä-lən-ıter-ē\ *adj* **1** : done, made, or given freely and without compulsion ⟨a ∼ sacrifice⟩ **2** : done on purpose : INTENTIONAL ⟨∼ manslaughter⟩ **3** : of, relating to, or regulated by the will ⟨∼ behavior⟩ **4** : having power of free choice **5** : provided or supported by voluntary action ⟨a ∼ organization⟩ **syn** deliberate, willful, willing, witting — **vol·un·tar·i·ly** \ˌvä-lən-'ter-ə-lē\ *adv*

²voluntary *n, pl* **-tar·ies** : an organ solo played in a religious service

voluntary muscle *n* : muscle (as most striated muscle) under voluntary control

¹vol·un·teer \ˌvä-lən-'tir\ *n* **1** : a person who voluntarily undertakes a service or duty **2** : a plant growing spontaneously esp. from seeds lost from a previous crop

²volunteer *vb* **1** : to offer or give voluntarily **2** : to offer oneself as a volunteer

vo·lup·tu·ary \və-'ləp-chə-ˌwer-ē\ *n, pl* **-ar·ies** : a person whose chief interest in life is the indulgence of sensual appetites

vo·lup·tuous \-chə-wəs\ *adj* **1** : giving sensual gratification **2** : given to or spent in enjoyment of luxury or pleasure **syn** luxurious, epicurean, sensuous — **vo·lup·tuous·ly** *adv* — **vo·lup·tuous·ness** *n*

vo·lute \və-'lüt\ *n* : a spiral or scroll-shaped decoration

¹vom·it \'vä-mət\ *n* : an act or instance of throwing up the contents of the stomach through the mouth; *also* : the matter thrown up

²vomit *vb* **1** : to throw up the contents of the stomach through the mouth **2** : to belch forth : GUSH

voo·doo \'vü-dü\ *n, pl* **voodoos 1** : a religion that is derived from African polytheism and is practiced chiefly in Haiti **2** : a person who deals in spells and necromancy; *also* : ¹SPELL 1 **3** : a charm used in voodoo — **voo·doo** *adj*

voo·doo·ism \-ˌi-zəm\ *n* **1** : VOODOO 1 **2** : the practice of witchcraft

vo·ra·cious \vȯ-'rā-shəs, və-\ *adj* **1** : having a huge appetite : RAVENOUS **2** : very eager ⟨a ∼ reader⟩ **syn** gluttonous, ravening, rapacious — **vo·ra·cious·ly** *adv* — **vo·ra·cious·ness** *n* — **vo·rac·i·ty** \-'ra-sə-tē\ *n*

vor·tex \'vȯr-ˌteks\ *n, pl* **vor·ti·ces** \'vȯr-tə-ˌsēz\ *also* **vor·tex·es** \'vȯr-ˌtek-səz\ : WHIRLPOOL; *also* : something resembling a whirlpool

vo·ta·ry \'vō-tə-rē\ *n, pl* **-ries 1** : ENTHUSIAST, DEVOTEE; *also* : a devoted adherent or admirer **2** : a devout or zealous worshiper

¹vote \'vōt\ *n* [ME, fr. L *votum* vow, wish, fr. *vovēre* to vow] **1** : a choice or opinion of a person or body of persons expressed usu. by a ballot, spoken word, or raised hand; *also* : the ballot, word, or gesture used to express a choice or opinion **2** : the decision reached by voting **3** : the right of suffrage **4** : a group of voters with some common characteristics ⟨the big city ∼⟩ — **vote·less** *adj*

²vote *vb* **vot·ed; vot·ing 1** : to cast a vote **2** : to elect, decide, pass, defeat, grant, or make legal by a vote **3** : to declare by general agreement **4** : to offer as a suggestion : PROPOSE **5** : to cause to vote esp. in a given way — **vot·er** *n*

vo·tive \'vō-tiv\ *adj* : consisting of or expressing a vow, wish, or desire

vou *abbr* voucher

vouch \'vau̇ch\ *vb* **1** : PROVE, SUBSTANTIATE **2** : to verify by examining documentary evidence **3** : to give a guarantee **4** : to supply supporting evidence or testimony; *also* : to give personal assurance

vouch·er \'vau̇-chər\ *n* **1** : an act of vouching **2** : one that vouches for another **3** : a documentary record of a business transaction **4** : a written affidavit or authorization **5** : a form indicating a credit against future purchases or expenditures

vouch·safe \vau̇ch-'sāf\ *vb* **vouch·safed; vouch·saf·ing** : to grant or give as or as if a privilege or a special favor — **vouch·safe·ment** *n*

¹vow \'vau̇\ *n* : a solemn promise or statement; *esp* : one by which a person is bound to an act, service, or condition ⟨marriage ∼s⟩

²vow *vb* **1** : to make a vow or as a vow **2** : to bind or commit by a vow — **vow·er** *n*

vow·el \'vau̇-əl\ *n* **1** : a speech sound produced without obstruction or friction in the mouth **2** : a letter representing such a sound

vox po·pu·li \'väks-'pä-pyə-ˌlī\ *n* [L, voice of the people] : popular sentiment

¹voy·age \'vȯi-ij\ *n* [ME, fr. OF *voiage*, fr. LL *viaticum*, fr. L, traveling money, fr. neut. of *viaticus* of a journey, fr. *via* way] : a journey esp. by water from one place or country to another

²voyage *vb* **voy·aged; voy·ag·ing** : to take or make a voyage — **voy·ag·er** *n*

voya·geur \ˌvȯi-ə-'zhər, ˌvwä-yä-\ *n* [CanF] : a person employed by a fur company to transport goods to and from remote stations esp. in the Canadian Northwest

voy·eur \vwä-'yər, vȯi-'ər\ *n* : one who habitually seeks sexual stimulation by visual means — **voy·eur·ism** \-ˌi-zəm\ *n*

VP *abbr* **1** verb phrase **2** vice president

vs *abbr* **1** verse **2** versus

vss *abbr* **1** verses **2** versions

V/STOL *abbr* vertical or short takeoff and landing

Vt *or* **VT** *abbr* Vermont

VTOL *abbr* vertical takeoff and landing

VTR *abbr* videotape recorder

vul·ca·nize \'vəl-kə-ˌnīz\ *vb* **-nized; -niz·ing** : to treat rubber or rubberlike material chemically to give useful properties (as elasticity and strength)

Vulg *abbr* Vulgate

vul·gar \'vəl-gər\ *adj* [ME, fr. L *vulgaris* of the mob, vulgar, fr. *vulgus* mob, common people] **1** : VERNACULAR ⟨the ∼ tongue⟩ **2** : of or relating to the common people : GENERAL, COMMON **3** : lacking cultivation or refinement : BOORISH; *also* : offensive to good taste or refined feelings **syn** gross, obscene, ribald, dirty, indecent, profane — **vul·gar·ly** *adv*

vul·gar·i·an \ˌvəl-'gar-ē-ən\ *n* : a vulgar person

vul·gar·ism \'vəl-gə-ˌri-zəm\ *n* **1** : VULGARITY **2** : a word or expression originated or used chiefly by illiterate persons **3** : a coarse expression : OBSCENITY

vul·gar·i·ty \ˌvəl-'gar-ə-tē\ *n, pl* **-ties 1** : something vulgar **2** : the quality or state of being vulgar

---

\ə\abut \ˀ\kitten \ər\further \a\ash \ā\ace \ä\mop, mar
\au̇\out \ch\chin \e\bet \ē\easy \g\go \i\hit \ī\ice \j\job
\ŋ\sing \ō\go \ȯ\law \ȯi\boy \th\thin \t̲h̲\the \ü\loot \u̇\foot
\y\yet \zh\vision *see also* Pronunciation Symbols page

vul·gar·ize \\'vəl-gə-ˌrīz\\ *vb* **-ized; -iz·ing** : to make vulgar — **vul·gar·i·za·tion** \\ˌvəl-gə-rə-'zā-shən\\ *n* — **vul·gar·iz·er** \\'vəl-gə-ˌrī-zər\\ *n*

Vul·gate \\'vəl-ˌgāt\\ *n* [ML *vulgata,* fr. LL *vulgata editio* edition in general circulation] : a Latin version of the Bible used by the Roman Catholic Church

vul·ner·a·ble \\'vəl-nə-rə-bəl\\ *adj* **1** : capable of being wounded : susceptible to wounds **2** : open to attack **3** : liable to increased penalties in contract bridge — **vul·ner·a·bil·i·ty** \\ˌvəl-nə-rə-'bi-lə-tē\\ *n* — **vul·ner·a·bly** \\'vəl-nə-rə-blē\\ *adv*

vul·pine \\'vəl-ˌpīn\\ *adj* : of, relating to, or resembling a fox esp. in cunning

vul·ture \\'vəl-chər\\ *n* **1** : any of various large birds (as a turkey vulture) related to the hawks, eagles, and falcons but having weaker claws and the head usu. naked and living chiefly on carrion **2** : a rapacious person

vul·va \\'vəl-və\\ *n, pl* **vul·vae** \\-ˌvē\\ [NL, fr. L, womb, female genitals] : the external parts of the female genital organs

vv *abbr* **1** verses **2** vice versa

vying *pres part of* VIE

W

¹w \\'də-bəl-(ˌ)yü\\ *n, pl* **w's** *or* **ws** *often cap* : the 23d letter of the English alphabet

²w *abbr, often cap* **1** water **2** watt **3** week **4** weight **5** west; western **6** wide; width **7** wife **8** with

W *symbol* [G *Wolfram*] tungsten

WA *abbr* **1** Washington **2** Western Australia

wacky \\'wa-kē\\ *adj* **wack·i·er; -est** : ECCENTRIC, CRAZY

¹wad \\'wäd\\ *n* **1** : a little mass, bundle, or tuft ⟨∼s of clay⟩ **2** : a soft mass of usu. light fibrous material **3** : a pliable plug (as of felt) used to retain a powder charge (as in a cartridge) **4** : a considerable amount (as of money) **5** : a roll of paper money

²wad *vb* **wad·ded; wad·ding 1** : to push a wad into ⟨∼ a gun⟩ **2** : to form into a wad **3** : to hold in by a wad ⟨∼ a bullet in a gun⟩ **4** : to stuff or line with a wad : PAD

wad·ding \\'wä-diŋ\\ *n* **1** : WADS; *also* : material for making wads **2** : a soft mass or sheet of short loose fibers used for stuffing or padding

wad·dle \\'wäd-ᵊl\\ *vb* **wad·dled; wad·dling** : to walk with short steps swaying from side to side like a duck — **waddle** *n*

wade \\'wād\\ *vb* **wad·ed; wad·ing 1** : to step in or through a medium (as water) more resistant than air **2** : to move or go with difficulty or labor and often with determination ⟨∼ through a dull book⟩ — **wad·able** *or* **wade·able** \\'wā-də-bəl\\ *adj* — **wade** *n*

wad·er \\'wā-dər\\ *n* **1** : one that wades **2** : SHOREBIRD; *also* : WADING BIRD **3** *pl* : a waterproof garment consisting of pants with attached boots for wading

wa·di \\'wä-dē\\ *n* [Ar *wādiy*] : a streambed of southwest Asia and northern Africa that is dry except in the rainy season

wading bird *n* : any of an order of long-legged birds (as sandpipers, cranes, or herons) that wade in water in search of food

wa·fer \\'wā-fər\\ *n* **1** : a thin crisp cake or cracker **2** : a thin round piece of unleavened bread used in the Eucharist **3** : something (as a piece of candy) that resembles a wafer

waf·fle \\'wä-fəl\\ *n* : a soft but crisped cake of batter cooked in a special hinged metal utensil (**waffle iron**)

¹waft \\'wäft, 'waft\\ *vb* : to cause to move or go lightly by or as if by the impulse of wind or waves

²waft *n* **1** : a slight breeze : PUFF **2** : the act of waving

¹wag \\'wag\\ *vb* **wagged; wag·ging 1** : to sway or swing shortly from side to side or to-and-fro ⟨the dog *wagged* his tail⟩ **2** : to move in chatter or gossip ⟨scandal caused tongues to ∼⟩

²wag *n* : an act of wagging : a wagging movement

³wag *n* : WIT, JOKER

¹wage \\'wāj\\ *n* **1** : payment for labor or services usu. according to contract **2** *pl* : RECOMPENSE, REWARD

²wage *vb* **waged; wag·ing 1** : to engage in : CARRY ON ⟨∼ a war⟩ **2** : to be in process of being waged

¹wa·ger \\'wā-jər\\ *n* **1** : BET, STAKE **2** : something on which bets are laid : GAMBLE

²wager *vb* : BET — **wa·ger·er** *n*

wag·gery \\'wa-gə-rē\\ *n, pl* **-ger·ies 1** : mischievous merriment : PLEASANTRY **2** : JEST, TRICK

wag·gish \\'wa-gish\\ *adj* **1** : resembling or characteristic of a wag : MISCHIEVOUS **2** : SPORTIVE, HUMOROUS

wag·gle \\'wa-gəl\\ *vb* **wag·gled; wag·gling** : to move backward and forward or from side to side : WAG — **waggle** *n*

wag·on *chiefly Brit var of* WAGON

wag·on \\'wa-gən\\ *n* **1** : a 4-wheeled vehicle; *esp* : one drawn by animals and used for freight or merchandise **2** : PADDY WAGON **3** : a child's 4-wheeled cart **4** : STATION WAGON

wag·on·er \\'wa-gə-nər\\ *n* : the driver of a wagon

wag·on·ette \\ˌwa-gə-'net\\ *n* : a light wagon with two facing seats along the sides behind a cross seat in front

wa·gon–lit \\ˌvä-gōⁿ-'lē\\ *n, pl* **wagons–lits** *or* **wagon–lits** *same or* -'lēz\\ [F, fr. *wagon* railroad car + *lit* bed] : a railroad sleeping car

wagon train *n* : a column of wagons traveling overland

wag·tail \\'wag-ˌtāl\\ *n* : any of various slender-bodied mostly Old World birds with a long tail that jerks up and down

wa·hi·ne \\wä-'hē-nä\\ *n* **1** : a Polynesian woman **2** : a female surfer

wa·hoo \\'wä-ˌhü\\ *n, pl* **wahoos** : a large vigorous food and sport fish related to the mackerel and found in warm seas

waif \\'wāf\\ *n* **1** : something found without an owner and esp. by chance **2** : a stray person or animal; *esp* : a homeless child

wail \\'wāl\\ *vb* **1** : LAMENT, WEEP **2** : to make a sound suggestive of a mournful cry **3** : COMPLAIN — **wail** *n*

wail·ful \\-fəl\\ *adj* : SORROWFUL, MOURNFUL **syn** melancholy, doleful, lugubrious, lamentable, plaintive, woeful — **wail·ful·ly** *adv*

wain \\'wān\\ *n* : a usu. large heavy farm wagon

wain·scot \\'wān-skət, -ˌskōt, -ˌskät\\ *n* **1** : a usu. paneled wooden lining of an interior wall of a room **2** : the lower part of an interior wall when finished differently from the rest — **wainscot** *vb*

wain·scot·ing *or* **wain·scot·ting** \\-ˌskō-tiŋ, -ˌskä-, -skə-\\ *n* : material for a wainscot; *also* : WAINSCOT

waist \\'wāst\\ *n* **1** : the narrowed part of the body between the chest and hips **2** : a part resembling the human waist esp. in narrowness or central position ⟨the ∼ of a ship⟩ **3** : a garment or part of a garment (as a blouse or bodice) for the upper part of the body

waist·band \\-ˌband\\ *n* : a band (as on trousers or a skirt) that fits around the waist

waist·coat \\'wes-kət, 'wāst-ˌkōt\\ *n, chiefly Brit* : VEST

waist·line \\'wāst-ˌlīn\\ *n* **1** : a line around the waist at its narrowest part; *also* : the length of this **2** : the line at which the bodice and skirt of a dress meet

¹**wait** \'wāt\ *vb* **1** : to remain inactive in readiness or expectation : AWAIT ⟨~ for orders⟩ **2** : to delay serving (a meal) **3** : to act as attendant or servant ⟨~ on customers⟩ **4** : to attend as a waiter : SERVE ⟨~ tables⟩ ⟨~ at a banquet⟩ **5** : to be ready

²**wait** *n* **1** : a position of concealment usu. with intent to attack or surprise ⟨lie in ~⟩ **2** : an act or period of waiting

wait·er \'wā-tər\ *n* **1** : one that waits on another; *esp* : a person who waits tables **2** : TRAY

waiting game *n* : a strategy in which one or more participants withhold action in the hope of an opportunity for more effective action later

waiting room *n* : a room (as at a doctor's office) for the use of persons who are waiting

wait·per·son \'wāt-ˌpər-sən\ *n* : a waiter or waitress

wait·ress \'wā-trəs\ *n* : a woman who waits tables

waive \'wāv\ *vb* **waived; waiv·ing** [ME *weiven*, fr. OF *weyver*, fr. *waif* lost, unclaimed] **1** : to give up claim to ⟨*waived* his right to a trial⟩ **2** : POSTPONE

waiv·er \'wā-vər\ *n* : the act of waiving right, claim, or privilege; *also* : a document containing a declaration of such an act

¹**wake** \'wāk\ *vb* **woke** \'wōk\ *also* **waked** \'wākt\; **wo·ken** \'wō-kən\ *also* **waked** *or* **woke; wak·ing 1** : to be or remain awake; *esp* : to keep watch (as over a corpse) **2** : AWAKE, AWAKEN ⟨the baby *woke* up early⟩

²**wake** *n* **1** : the state of being awake **2** : a watch held over the body of a dead person prior to burial

³**wake** *n* : the track left by a ship in the water; *also* : a track left behind

wake·ful \'wāk-fəl\ *adj* : not sleeping or able to sleep : SLEEPLESS, ALERT — **wake·ful·ness** *n*

wak·en \'wā-kən\ *vb* : WAKE

wake–rob·in \'wāk-ˌrä-bən\ *n* : TRILLIUM

wak·ing \'wā-kiŋ\ *adj* : passed in a conscious or alert state ⟨every ~ hour⟩

wale \'wāl\ *n* : a ridge esp. on cloth; *also* : the texture esp. of a fabric

¹**walk** \'wȯk\ *vb* [partly fr. ME *walken*, fr. OE *wealcan* to roll, toss and partly fr. ME *walkien*, fr. OE *wealcian* to roll up, muffle up] **1** : to move or cause to move on foot usu. at a natural unhurried gait ⟨~ to town⟩ ⟨~ a horse⟩ **2** : to pass over, through, or along by walking ⟨~ the streets⟩ **3** : to perform or accomplish by walking ⟨~ guard⟩ **4** : to follow a course of action or way of life ⟨~ humbly in the sight of God⟩ **5** : WALK OUT **6** : to receive a base on balls; *also* : to give a base on balls to — **walk·er** *n*

²**walk** *n* **1** : a going on foot ⟨go for a ~⟩ **2** : a place, path, or course for walking **3** : distance to be walked ⟨a quarter-mile ~ from here⟩ **4** : manner of living : CONDUCT, BEHAVIOR **5** : social or economic status ⟨various ~s of life⟩ **6** : manner of walking : GAIT; *esp* : a slow 4-beat gait of a horse **7** : BASE ON BALLS

walk·away \'wȯ-kə-ˌwā\ *n* : an easily won contest

walk·ie-talk·ie \ˌwȯ-kē-'tȯ-kē\ *n* : a small portable radio transmitting and receiving set

¹**walk–in** \'wȯk-ˌin\ *adj* : large enough to be walked into ⟨a ~ refrigerator⟩

²**walk–in** *n* **1** : an easy election victory **2** : one that walks in

walking papers *n pl* : DISMISSAL, DISCHARGE

walking stick *n* **1** : a stick used in walking **2** *usu* **walking·stick** : STICK INSECT; *esp* : one common in parts of the U.S.

walk–on \'wȯk-ˌȯn, -ˌän\ *n* : a small part in a dramatic production

walk·out \-ˌau̇t\ *n* **1** : a labor strike **2** : the action of leaving a meeting or organization as an expression of disapproval

walking stick 2

walk out *vb* **1** : to leave suddenly often as an expression of disapproval **2** : to go on strike

walk·over \-ˌō-vər\ *n* : a one-sided contest : an easy victory

walk–up \'wȯk-ˌəp\ *n* : a building or apartment house without an elevator — **walk–up** *adj*

walk·way \-ˌwā\ *n* : a passage for walking

¹**wall** \'wȯl\ *n* [ME, fr. OE *weall*, fr. L *vallum* rampart, fr. *vallus* stake, palisade] **1** : a structure (as of stone or brick) intended for defense or security or for enclosing something **2** : one of the upright enclosing parts of a building or room **3** : the inside surface of a cavity or container ⟨the ~ of a boiler⟩ **4** : something like a wall in appearance, function, or effect ⟨a tariff ~⟩ — **walled** \'wȯld\ *adj*

²**wall** *vb* **1** : to provide, separate, or surround with or as if with a wall ⟨~ in a garden⟩ **2** : to close (an opening) with or as if with a wall ⟨~ up a door⟩

wal·la·by \'wä-lə-bē\ *n, pl* **wallabies** *also* **wallaby** : any of various small or medium-sized kangaroos

wall·board \'wȯl-ˌbȯrd\ *n* : a structural material (as of wood pulp or plaster) made in large sheets and used for sheathing interior walls and ceilings

wal·let \'wä-lət\ *n* **1** : a bag or sack for carrying things on a journey **2** : a pocketbook with compartments (as for personal papers and usu. unfolded money) : BILLFOLD

wall·eye \'wȯ-ˌlī\ *n* **1** : an eye with a whitish iris or an opaque white cornea **2** : a large vigorous No. American food and sport fish related to the perches — **wall·eyed** \-ˌlīd\ *adj*

wall·flow·er \'wȯl-ˌflau̇-ər\ *n* **1** : any of several Old World plants related to the mustards; *esp* : one with showy fragrant flowers **2** : a person who usu. from shyness or unpopularity remains alone (as at a dance)

Wal·loon \wä-'lün\ *n* : a member of a people of southern and southeastern Belgium and adjacent parts of France — **Walloon** *adj*

¹**wal·lop** \'wä-ləp\ *vb* [ME *walopen* to gallop, fr. OF *waloper*] **1** : to beat soundly : TROUNCE **2** : to hit hard : SOCK **syn** batter, beat, lambaste, pound, pummel, thrash

²**wallop** *n* **1** : a powerful blow or impact **2** : the ability to hit hard **3** : emotional, sensory, or psychological force : IMPACT

wal·lop·ing \'wä-lə-piŋ\ *adj* **1** : LARGE, WHOPPING **2** : exceptionally fine or impressive

¹**wal·low** \'wä-lō\ *vb* **1** : to roll oneself about sluggishly in or as if in deep mud ⟨hogs ~*ing* in the mire⟩ **2** : to indulge oneself excessively ⟨~ in luxury⟩ **3** : to become or remain helpless ⟨~ in ignorance⟩ **syn** bask, indulge, luxuriate, revel, welter

²**wallow** *n* : a muddy or dust-filled area where animals wallow

wall·pa·per \'wȯl-ˌpā-pər\ *n* : decorative paper for the walls of a room — **wallpaper** *vb*

wall–to–wall adj **1** : covering the entire floor ⟨wall-to-wall carpeting⟩ **2** : covering or filling one entire space or time ⟨crowds of wall-to-wall people⟩

wal·nut \'wȯl-(ˌ)nət\ n [ME walnot, fr. OE wealhhnutu, lit., foreign nut, fr. Wealh Welshman, foreigner + hnutu nut] **1** : a nut with a furrowed usu. rough shell and an adherent husk from any of a genus of trees related to the hickories; esp : the large edible nut of a Eurasian tree **2** : a tree that bears walnuts **3** : the usu. reddish to dark brown wood of a walnut used esp. in cabinetwork and veneers

wal·rus \'wȯl-rəs, 'wäl-\ n, pl **walrus** or **wal·rus·es** : a large mammal of northern seas related to the seals and having ivory tusks

¹waltz \'wȯlts\ n **1** : a gliding dance done to music having three beats to the measure **2** : music for or suitable for waltzing

²waltz vb [G Walzer, fr. walzen to roll, dance] **1** : to dance a waltz **2** : to move or advance easily, successfully, or conspicuously ⟨he ∼ed off with the championship⟩

wam·ble \'wäm-bəl\ vb **wam·bled; wam·bling** : to progress unsteadily or with a lurching shambling gait

wam·pum \'wäm-pəm\ n [short for wampumpeag, fr. Massachuset (a North American Indian language) wampompeag, fr. wampan white + api string + -ag, pl. suffix] **1** : beads made of shells strung in strands, belts, or sashes and used by No. American Indians as money and ornaments **2** slang : MONEY

wan \'wän\ adj **wan·ner; wan·nest 1** : SICKLY, PALLID; also : FEEBLE **2** : DIM, FAINT **3** : LANGUID ⟨a ∼ smile⟩ **syn** ashen, blanched, doughy, livid, pale, waxen — **wan·ly** adv — **wan·ness** n

wand \'wänd\ n **1** : a slender staff carried in a procession **2** : the staff of a fairy, diviner, or magician

wan·der \'wän-dər\ vb **1** : to move about aimlessly or without a fixed course or goal : RAMBLE **2** : to go astray in conduct or thought; esp : to become delirious **syn** gad, gallivant, meander, range, roam, rove — **wan·der·er** n

wandering Jew n : either of two trailing or creeping plants cultivated for their showy and often white-striped foliage

wan·der·lust \'wän-dər-ˌləst\ n : strong longing for or impulse toward wandering

¹wane \'wän\ vb **waned; wan·ing 1** : to grow gradually smaller or less ⟨the moon ∼s⟩ ⟨his strength waned⟩ **2** : to lose power, prosperity, or influence **3** : to draw near an end ⟨summer is waning⟩ **syn** abate, ebb, moderate, relent, slacken, subside

²wane n : a waning (as in size or power); also : a period in which something is waning

wan·gle \'waŋ-gəl\ vb **wan·gled; wan·gling 1** : to obtain by sly or devious means; also : to use trickery or questionable means to achieve an end **2** : MANIPULATE; also : FINAGLE

wan·na·be \'wä-nə-ˌbē\ n : a person who wants or aspires to be someone or something else or who tries to look or act like someone else

¹want \'wȯnt, 'wänt\ vb **1** : to fail to possess : LACK ⟨they ∼ the necessities of life⟩ **2** : to feel or suffer the need of **3** : NEED, REQUIRE ⟨the house ∼s painting⟩ **4** : to desire earnestly : WISH

²want n **1** : a lack of a required or usual amount : SHORTAGE **2** : dire need : DESTITUTION **3** : something wanted : DESIRE **4** : personal defect : FAULT

¹want·ing \'wȯn-tiŋ, 'wän-\ adj **1** : not present or in evidence : ABSENT **2** : falling below standards or expectations **3** : lacking in ability or capacity : DEFICIENT ⟨∼ in common sense⟩

²wanting prep **1** : LESS, MINUS ⟨a month ∼ two days⟩ **2** : WITHOUT ⟨a book ∼ a cover⟩

¹wan·ton \'wȯnt-ᵊn, 'wänt-\ adj [ME, undisciplined, fr. wan- deficient, wrong + towen, pp. of teen to draw,

train, discipline] **1** : UNCHASTE, LEWD, LUSTFUL; also : SENSUAL **2** : having no regard for justice or for other persons' feelings, rights, or safety : MERCILESS, INHUMANE ⟨∼cruelty⟩ **3** : having no just cause ⟨a ∼ attack⟩ — **wan·ton·ly** adv — **wan·ton·ness** n

²wanton n : a wanton individual; esp : a lewd or immoral person

³wanton vb **1** : to be wanton : act wantonly **2** : to pass or waste wantonly

wa·pi·ti \'wä-pə-tē\ n, pl **wapiti** or **wapitis** : ELK 2

¹war \'wȯr\ n **1** : a state or period of usu. open and declared armed fighting between states or nations **2** : the art or science of warfare **3** : a state of hostility, conflict, or antagonism **4** : a struggle between opposing forces or for a particular end ⟨∼ against disease⟩ — **war·less** \-ləs\ adj

²war vb **warred; war·ring** : to engage in warfare : be in conflict

³war abbr warrant

¹war·ble \'wȯr-bəl\ n **1** : a melodious succession of low pleasing sounds **2** : a musical trill

²warble vb **war·bled; war·bling 1** : to sing or utter in a trilling manner or with variations **2** : to express by or as if by warbling

³warble n : a swelling under the hide esp. of the back of cattle, horses, and wild mammals caused by the maggot of a fly (**warble fly**); also : its maggot

war·bler \'wȯr-blər\ n **1** : SONGSTER **2** : any of various small slender-billed Old World singing birds related to the thrushes and noted for their song **3** : any of numerous small bright-colored American insect-eating birds with a usu. weak and unmusical song

war·bon·net \'wȯr-ˌbä-nət\ n : a feathered American Indian ceremonial headdress

war cry n **1** : a cry used by fighters in war **2** : a slogan used esp. to rally people to a cause

¹ward \'wȯrd\ n **1** : a guarding or being under guard or guardianship; esp : CUSTODY **2** : a body of guards **3** : a division of a prison **4** : a division in a hospital **5** : a division of a city for electoral or administrative purposes **6** : a person (as a child) under the protection of a guardian or a law court **7** : a person or body of persons under the protection or tutelage of a government **8** : a means of defense : PROTECTION

²ward vb : to turn aside : DEFLECT — usu. used with off ⟨∼ off a blow⟩

¹-ward \wərd\ also **-wards** \wərdz\ adj suffix **1** : that moves, tends, faces, or is directed toward ⟨windward⟩ **2** : that occurs or is situated in the direction of ⟨seaward⟩

²-ward or **-wards** adv suffix **1** : in a (specified) direction ⟨upwards⟩ ⟨afterward⟩ **2** : toward a (specified) point, position, or area ⟨skyward⟩

war dance n : a dance performed (as by American Indians) before going to war or in celebration of victory

war·den \'wȯrd-ᵊn\ n **1** : GUARDIAN, KEEPER **2** : the governor of a town, district, or fortress **3** : an official charged with special supervisory or enforcement duties ⟨game ∼⟩ ⟨air raid ∼⟩ **4** : an official in charge of the operation of a prison **5** : one of two ranking lay officers of an Episcopal parish **6** : any of various British college officials

ward·er \'wȯr-dər\ n : WATCHMAN, WARDEN

ward heel·er \-ˌhē-lər\ n : a local worker for a political boss

ward·robe \'wȯr-ˌdrōb\ n [ME warderobe, fr. OF, fr. warder to guard + robe robe] **1** : a room or closet where clothes are kept; also : CLOTHESPRESS **2** : a collection of wearing apparel ⟨his summer ∼⟩

ward·room \-ˌdrüm, -ˌdrum\ n : the dining area for officers aboard a warship

ward·ship \'wȯrd-ˌship\ n **1** : GUARDIANSHIP **2** : the state of being under care of a guardian

ware \'war\ *n* **1** : manufactured articles or products of art or craft : GOODS ⟨glass*ware*⟩ **2** : an article of merchandise ⟨a peddler hawking his ~s⟩ **3** : items (as dishes) of fired clay : POTTERY

ware·house \-ₐhaὐs\ *n* : a place for the storage of merchandise or commodities : STOREHOUSE — **warehouse** *vb* — **ware·house·man** \-mən\ *n* — **ware·hous·er** \-ₐhaὐ-zər, -sər\ *n*

ware·room \'war-ₐrüm, -ₐrὐm\ *n* : a room in which goods are exhibited for sale

war·fare \'wȯr-ₐfar\ *n* **1** : military operations between enemies : WAR; *also* : an activity undertaken by one country to weaken or destroy another ⟨economic ~⟩ **2** : STRUGGLE, CONFLICT

war·fa·rin \'wȯr-fə-rən\ *n* : an anticoagulant compound used as a rodent poison and in medicine

war·head \'wȯr-ₐhed\ *n* : the section of a missile containing the charge

war·horse \-ₐhȯrs\ *n* **1** : a horse for use in war **2** : a veteran soldier or public person (as a politician)

war·like \-ₐlīk\ *adj* **1** : fond of war ⟨~ peoples⟩ **2** : of, relating to, or useful in war : MILITARY, MARTIAL ⟨~ supplies⟩ **3** : befitting or characteristic of war or of soldiers ⟨~ attitudes⟩

war·lock \-ₐläk\ *n* [ME *warloghe,* fr. OE *wǣrloga* one that breaks faith, the Devil, fr. *wǣr* faith, troth + *-loga* (fr. *lēogan* to lie)] : SORCERER, WIZARD

war·lord \-ₐlȯrd\ *n* **1** : a high military leader **2** : a military commander exercising local civil power by force ⟨former Chinese ~s⟩

¹**warm** \'wȯrm\ *adj* **1** : having or giving out heat to a moderate or adequate degree ⟨~ milk⟩ ⟨a ~ stove⟩ **2** : serving to retain heat ⟨~ clothes⟩ **3** : feeling or inducing sensations of heat ⟨~ from exercise⟩ ⟨a ~ climb⟩ **4** : showing or marked by strong feeling : ARDENT ⟨~ support⟩ **5** : marked by tense excitement or hot anger ⟨a ~ campaign⟩ **6** : giving a pleasant impression of warmth, cheerfulness, or friendliness ⟨~ colors⟩ ⟨a ~ tone of voice⟩ **7** : marked by or tending toward injury, distress, or pain ⟨made things ~ for the enemy⟩ **8** : newly made : FRESH ⟨a ~ scent⟩ **9** : near to a goal ⟨getting ~ in a search⟩ — **warm·ly** *adv*

²**warm** *vb* **1** : to make or become warm **2** : to give a feeling of warmth or vitality to **3** : to experience feelings of affection or pleasure ⟨she ~ed to her guest⟩ **4** : to reheat for eating ⟨~ed over the roast⟩ **5** : to make ready for operation or performance by preliminary exercise or operation ⟨~ up the motor⟩ **6** : to become increasingly ardent, interested, or competent ⟨the speaker ~ed to his topic⟩ — **warm·er** *n*

warm–blood·ed \-ˈblə-dəd\ *adj* : able to maintain a relatively high and constant body temperature relatively independent of that of the surroundings

warmed–over \'wȯrmd-ˈō-vər\ *adj* **1** : REHEATED ⟨~ cabbage⟩ **2** : not fresh or new ⟨~ ideas⟩

warm front *n* : an advancing edge of a warm air mass

warm·heart·ed \'wȯrm-ˈhär-təd\ *adj* : marked by warmth of feeling : CORDIAL — **warm·heart·ed·ness** *n*

warming pan *n* : a long-handled covered pan filled with live coals and formerly used to warm a bed

war·mon·ger \'wȯr-ₐmən-gər, -ₐmäŋ-\ *n* : one who urges or attempts to stir up war

warmth \'wȯrmth\ *n* **1** : the quality or state of being warm **2** : ZEAL, ARDOR, FERVOR

warm up *vb* : to engage in exercise or practice esp. before entering a game or contest — **warm–up** \'wȯrm-ₐəp\ *n*

¹**warn** \'wȯrn\ *vb* **1** : to put on guard : CAUTION; *also* : ADMONISH, COUNSEL **2** : to notify esp. in advance : INFORM **3** : to order to go or keep away

¹**warn·ing** \'wȯr-niŋ\ *n* **1** : the act of warning : the state of being warned **2** : something that warns or serves to warn

²**warning** *adj* : serving as an alarm, signal, summons, or admonition ⟨~ bell⟩ — **warn·ing·ly** *adv*

¹**warp** \'wȯrp\ *n* **1** : the lengthwise threads on a loom or in a woven fabric **2** : a twist out of a true plane or straight line ⟨a ~ in a board⟩

²**warp** *vb* [ME, fr. OE *weorpan* to throw] **1** : to turn or twist out of shape; *also* : to become so twisted **2** : to lead astray : PERVERT; *also* : FALSIFY, DISTORT

war paint *n* : paint put on the face and body by American Indians as a sign of going to war

war·path \'wȯr-ₐpath, -ₐpȧth\ *n* : the course taken by a party of American Indians going on a hostile expedition — **on the warpath** : ready to fight or argue

war·plane \-ₐplān\ *n* : a military airplane; *esp* : one armed for combat

¹**war·rant** \'wȯr-ənt, 'wär-\ *n* **1** : AUTHORIZATION; *also* : JUSTIFICATION, GROUND **2** : evidence (as a document) of authorization; *esp* : a legal writ authorizing an officer to take action (as in making an arrest, seizure, or search) **3** : a certificate of appointment issued to an officer of lower rank than a commissioned officer

²**warrant** *vb* **1** : to guarantee security or immunity to : SECURE **2** : to declare or maintain positively ⟨I ~ this is so⟩ **3** : to assure (a person) of the truth of what is said **4** : to guarantee to be as it appears or as it is represented ⟨~ goods as of the first quality⟩ **5** : SANCTION, AUTHORIZE **6** : to give proof of : ATTEST; *also* : GUARANTEE **7** : JUSTIFY ⟨his need ~s the expenditure⟩

warrant officer *n* **1** : an officer in the armed forces ranking next below a commissioned officer **2** : a commissioned officer ranking below an ensign in the navy or coast guard and below a second lieutenant in the marine corps

war·ran·ty \'wȯr-ən-tē, 'wär-\ *n, pl* **-ties** : an expressed or implied statement that some situation or thing is as it appears to be or is represented to be; *esp* : a usu. written guarantee of the integrity of a product and of the maker's responsibility for the repair or replacement of defective parts

war·ren \'wȯr-ən, 'wär-\ *n* **1** : an area where rabbits breed; *also* : a structure where rabbits are bred or kept **2** : a crowded tenement or district

war·rior \'wȯr-yər, 'wȯr-ē-ər, 'wär-\ *n* : a man engaged or experienced in warfare

war·ship \'wȯr-ₐship\ *n* : a naval vessel

wart \'wȯrt\ *n* **1** : a small usu. horny projecting growth on the skin; *esp* : one caused by a virus **2** : a protuberance resembling a wart (as on a plant) — **warty** *adj*

wart·hog \'wȯrt-ₐhȯg, -ₐhäg\ *n* : a wild African hog which has large tusks and the males of which have two pairs of rough warty protuberances below the eyes

war·time \'wȯr-ₐtīm\ *n* : a period during which a war is in progress

wary \'war-ē\ *adj* **war·i·er; -est** : very cautious; *esp* : careful in guarding against danger or deception

was *past 1st & 3d sing of* BE

¹**wash** \'wȯsh, 'wäsh\ *vb* **1** : to clean with water and usu. soap or detergent ⟨~ clothes⟩ ⟨~ your hands⟩ **2** : to wet thoroughly : DRENCH **3** : to flow along the border of ⟨waves ~ the shore⟩ **4** : to pour or flow in a stream or current **5** : to move or remove by or as if by the action of water **6** : to cover or daub lightly with a liquid (as whitewash) **7** : to run water over (as gravel or ore) in order to separate valuable matter from refuse ⟨~ sand for gold⟩ **8** : to undergo laundering ⟨a dress that doesn't ~ well⟩ **9** : to stand a test ⟨that story will not ~⟩ **10** : to be worn away by water

²**wash** *n* **1** : the act or process or an instance of washing

\ə\abut \ᵊ\kitten \ər\further \a\ash \ā\ace \ä\mop, mar
\aὐ\out \ch\chin \e\bet \ē\easy \g\go \i\hit \ī\ice \j\job
\ŋ\sing \ō\go \ȯ\law \ȯi\boy \th\thin \th̲\the \ü\loot \ὐ\foot
\y\yet \zh\vision *see also* Pronunciation Symbols page

or being washed **2 :** articles to be washed or being washed **3 :** the flow or action of a mass of water (as a wave) **4 :** erosion by waves (as of the sea) **5** *West* **:** the dry bed of a stream **6 :** worthless esp. liquid waste : RE- FUSE, SWILL **7 :** a thin coat of paint (as watercolor) **8 :** a disturbance in the air caused by the passage of a wing or propeller

³wash *adj* **:** WASHABLE

Wash *abbr* Washington

wash·able \'wȯ-shə-bəl, 'wä-\ *adj* **:** capable of being washed without damage

wash–and–wear *adj* **:** of, relating to, or being a fabric or garment that needs little or no ironing after washing

wash·ba·sin \'wȯsh-ˌbās-ᵊn, 'wäsh-\ *n* **:** WASHBOWL

wash·board \-ˌbȯrd\ *n* **:** a grooved board to scrub clothes on

wash·bowl \-ˌbōl\ *n* **:** a large bowl for water for washing hands and face

wash·cloth \-ˌklȯth\ *n* **:** a cloth used for washing one's face and body

washed–out \'wȯsht-'aut, 'wäsht-\ *adj* **1 :** faded in color **2 :** EXHAUSTED ⟨felt ∼ after working all night⟩

washed–up \-'əp\ *adj* **:** no longer successful, popular, skillful, or needed

wash·er \'wȯ-shər, 'wä-\ *n* **1 :** a ring or perforated plate used around a bolt or screw to ensure tightness or re- lieve friction **2 :** one that washes; *esp* **:** a machine for washing

wash·er·wom·an \-ˌwu-mən\ *n* **:** a woman whose occu- pation is washing clothes

wash·house \'wȯsh-ˌhaus, 'wäsh-\ *n* **:** a house or build- ing for washing clothes

wash·ing \'wȯ-shiŋ, 'wä-\ *n* **1 :** material obtained by washing **2 :** articles washed or to be washed

washing soda *n* **:** SODIUM CARBONATE

Wash·ing·ton's Birthday \'wȯ-shiŋ-tənz-, 'wä-\ *n* **:** the 3d Monday in February observed as a legal holiday

wash·out \'wȯsh-ˌaut, 'wäsh-\ *n* **1 :** the washing away of earth (as from a road); *also* **:** a place where earth is washed away **2 :** a complete failure

wash·room \-ˌrüm, -ˌrum\ *n* **:** BATHROOM

wash·stand \-ˌstand\ *n* **1 :** a stand holding articles need- ed for washing face and hands **2 :** LAVATORY 1

wash·tub \-ˌtəb\ *n* **:** a tub for washing or soaking clothes

wash·wom·an \'wȯsh-ˌwu-mən, 'wäsh-\ *n* **:** WASHER- WOMAN

washy \'wȯ-shē, 'wä-\ *adj* **wash·i·er; -est 1 :** WEAK, WA- TERY **2 :** PALLID **3 :** lacking in vigor, individuality, or definiteness

wasp \'wäsp, 'wȯsp\ *n* **:** any of numerous social or sol- itary winged insects related to the bees and ants with biting mouthparts and in females and workers an often formidable sting

WASP *or* **Wasp** *n* [*white Anglo-Saxon Protestant*] **:** an American of northern European and esp. British ances- try and of Protestant background

wasp·ish \'wäs-pish, 'wȯs-\ *adj* **1 :** SNAPPISH, IRRITABLE **2 :** resembling a wasp in form; *esp* **:** slightly built **syn** fractious, fretful, huffy, peevish, petulant, querulous

wasp waist *n* **:** a very slender waist

¹was·sail \'wä-səl, wä-'sāl\ *n* [ME *wæs hæil*, fr. ON *ves heill* be well] **1 :** an early English toast to someone's health **2 :** a hot drink made with wine, beer, or cider, spices, sugar, and usu. baked apples and traditionally served at Christmas **3 :** riotous drinking : REVELRY

²wassail *vb* **1 :** CAROUSE **2 :** to drink to the health of — **was·sail·er** *n*

Was·ser·mann test \'wä-sər-mən-, 'vä-\ *n* **:** a blood test for infection with syphilis

wast·age \'wā-stij\ *n* **:** WASTE 3

¹waste \'wāst\ *n* **1 :** a sparsely settled or barren region : DESERT; *also* **:** uncultivated land **2 :** the act or an in- stance of wasting : the state of being wasted **3 :** gradual

loss or decrease by use, wear, or decay **4 :** material left over, rejected, or thrown away; *also* **:** an unwanted by- product of a manufacturing or chemical process **5 :** re- fuse (as garbage) that accumulates about habitations **6 :** material (as feces) produced but not used by a living organism — **waste·ful** \-fəl\ *adj* — **waste·ful·ly** *adv* — **waste·ful·ness** *n*

²waste *vb* **wast·ed; wast·ing 1 :** DEVASTATE **2 :** to wear away or diminish gradually : CONSUME **3 :** to spend or use carelessly or uselessly : SQUANDER **4 :** to lose or cause to lose weight, strength, or energy ⟨*wasting* away from fever⟩ **5 :** to become diminished in bulk or sub- stance : DWINDLE **syn** depredate, desolate, despoil, rav- age, spoil, strip — **wast·er** *n*

³waste *adj* **1 :** being wild and uninhabited : BARREN, DES- OLATE; *also* **:** UNCULTIVATED **2 :** being in a ruined con- dition **3 :** discarded as worthless after being used ⟨∼ water⟩ **4 :** excreted from or stored in inert form in a liv- ing organism as a by-product of vital activity ⟨∼ matter from birds⟩

waste·bas·ket \'wāst-ˌbas-kət\ *n* **:** a receptacle for refuse

waste·land \-ˌland, -lənd\ *n* **:** land that is barren or unfit for cultivation

waste·pa·per \-'pā-pər\ *n* **:** paper thrown away as used, not needed, or not fit for use

wast·rel \'wā-strəl\ *n* **:** one that wastes : SPENDTHRIFT

¹watch \'wäch, 'wȯch\ *vb* **1 :** to be or stay awake inten- tionally : keep vigil ⟨∼ed by the patient's bedside⟩ ⟨∼ and pray⟩ **2 :** to be on the lookout for danger : be on one's guard **3 :** to keep guard ⟨∼ outside the door⟩ **4 :** OBSERVE ⟨∼ a game⟩ **5 :** to keep in view so as to pre- vent harm or warn of danger ⟨∼ a brush fire carefully⟩ **6 :** to keep oneself informed about ⟨∼ his progress⟩ **7 :** to lie in wait for esp. so as to take advantage of ⟨∼ed her opportunity⟩ — **watch·er** *n*

²watch *n* **1 :** the act of keeping awake to guard, protect, or attend; *also* **:** a state of alert and continuous atten- tion **2 :** a public weather alert ⟨tornado ∼⟩ **3 :** close ob- servation **4 :** LOOKOUT, WATCHMAN, GUARD **5 :** a period during which a part of a ship's crew is on duty; *also* **:** the part of a crew on duty during a watch **6 :** a port- able timepiece carried on the person

watch·band \'wäch-ˌband, 'wȯch-\ *n* **:** the bracelet or strap of a wristwatch

watch·dog \-ˌdȯg\ *n* **1 :** a dog kept to guard property **2 :** one that guards or protects

watch·ful \-fəl\ *adj* **:** steadily attentive and alert esp. to danger : VIGILANT — **watch·ful·ly** *adv* — **watch·ful·ness** *n*

watch·mak·er \-ˌmā-kər\ *n* **:** one that makes or repairs watches — **watch·mak·ing** \-ˌmā-kiŋ\ *n*

watch·man \-mən\ *n* **:** a person assigned to watch : GUARD

watch night *n* **:** a devotional service lasting until after midnight esp. on New Year's Eve

watch·tow·er \'wäch-ˌtau-ər, 'wȯch-\ *n* **:** a tower for a lookout

watch·word \-ˌwərd\ *n* **1 :** a secret word used as a signal or sign of recognition **2 :** a word or motto used as a slo- gan or rallying cry

¹wa·ter \'wȯ-tər, 'wä-\ *n* **1 :** the liquid that descends as rain and forms rivers, lakes, and seas **2 :** a natural min- eral water — usu. used in pl. **3** *pl* **:** the water occupying or flowing in a particular bed; *also* **:** a band of seawater bordering on and under the control of a country ⟨sailing Canadian ∼s⟩ **4 :** any of various liquids containing or resembling water; *esp* **:** a watery fluid (as tears, urine, or sap) formed or circulating in a living organism **5 :** a specified degree of thoroughness or completeness ⟨a scoundrel of the first ∼⟩

²water *vb* **1 :** to supply with or get or take water ⟨∼ hors- es⟩ ⟨the ship ∼ed at each port⟩ **2 :** to treat (as cloth) so as to give a lustrous appearance in wavy lines **3 :** to dilute by or as if by adding water to **4** : to form or secrete water or watery matter ⟨her eyes ∼ed⟩ ⟨my mouth ∼ed⟩

water bed *n* : a bed whose mattress is a watertight bag filled with water

wa·ter·borne \-ˌbōrn\ *adj* : supported or carried by water

water buffalo *n* : a common oxlike often domesticated Asian bovine

water buffalo

water chestnut *n* : a whitish crunchy vegetable used esp. in Chinese cooking that is the peeled tuber of a widely cultivated Asian sedge; *also* : the tuber or the sedge itself

water closet *n* : a compartment or room with a toilet bowl : BATHROOM; *also* : a toilet bowl along with its accessories

wa·ter·col·or \ˈwȯ-tər-ˌkə-lər\ *n* **1** : a paint whose liquid part is water **2** : the art of painting with watercolors **3** : a picture made with watercolors

wa·ter·course \-ˌkōrs\ *n* : a stream of water; *also* : the bed of a stream

wa·ter·craft \-ˌkraft\ *n* : a craft for water transport : SHIP, BOAT

wa·ter·cress \-ˌkres\ *n* : a perennial European cress with white flowers that is naturalized in the U.S. and is used esp. in salads

wa·ter·fall \-ˌfȯl\ *n* : a very steep descent of the water of a stream

wa·ter·fowl \ˈwȯ-tər-ˌfaul, ˈwä-\ *n* **1** : a bird that frequents water **2 waterfowl** *pl* : wild ducks and geese hunted as game

wa·ter·front \-ˌfrənt\ *n* : land or a section of a town fronting or abutting on a body of water

water gap *n* : a pass in a mountain ridge through which a stream runs

water glass *n* : a drinking glass

water hyacinth *n* : a showy floating aquatic plant of tropical America that often clogs waterways (as in the southern U.S.)

watering place *n* : a resort that features mineral springs or bathing

water lily *n* : any of various aquatic plants with floating roundish leaves and showy solitary flowers

wa·ter·line \ˈwȯ-tər-ˌlīn, ˈwä-\ *n* : a line that marks the level of the surface of water on something (as a ship or the shore)

wa·ter·logged \-ˌlȯgd, -ˌlägd\ *adj* : so filled or soaked with water as to be heavy or unmanageable ⟨a ∼ boat⟩

wa·ter·loo \ˌwȯ-tər-ˈlü, ˌwä-\ *n, pl* **-loos** [*Waterloo*, Belgium, scene of Napoleon's defeat in 1815] : a decisive or final defeat or setback

¹wa·ter·mark \ˈwȯ-tər-ˌmärk, ˈwä-\ *n* **1** : a mark indicating height to which water has risen **2** : a marking in paper visible when the paper is held up to the light

²watermark *vb* : to mark (paper) with a watermark

wa·ter·mel·on \-ˌme-lən\ *n* : a large roundish or oblong fruit with sweet juicy usu. red pulp; *also* : a widely grown African vine related to the squashes that produces watermelons

water moccasin *n* : a venomous pit viper chiefly of the southeastern U.S. that is related to the copperhead

water ou·zel \-ˈü-zəl\ *n* : DIPPER 1

water pipe *n* : a pipe for smoking that has a long flexible tube whereby the smoke is cooled by passing through water

water polo *n* : a team game played in a swimming pool with a ball resembling a soccer ball

wa·ter·pow·er \ˈwȯ-tər-ˌpau̇-ər, ˈwä-\ *n* : the power of moving water used to run machinery

¹wa·ter·proof \ˈwȯ-tər-ˌprüf, ˈwä-\ *adj* : not letting water through; *esp* : covered or treated with a material to prevent permeation by water — **wa·ter·proof·ing** *n*

²waterproof *n* **1** : a waterproof fabric **2** *chiefly Brit* : RAINCOAT

³waterproof *vb* : to make waterproof

wa·ter–re·pel·lent \ˌwȯ-tər-ri-ˈpe-lənt, ˌwä-\ *adj* : treated with a finish that is resistant to water penetration

wa·ter–re·sis·tant \-ri-ˈzis-tənt\ *adj* : WATER-REPELLENT

wa·ter·shed \ˈwȯ-tər-ˌshed, ˈwä-\ *n* **1** : a dividing ridge between two drainage areas **2** : the region or area drained by a particular body of water

wa·ter·side \-ˌsīd\ *n* : the land bordering a body of water

water ski *n* : a ski used on water when the wearer is towed — **wa·ter–ski** *vb* — **wa·ter–ski·er** \-ˌskē-ər\ *n*

wa·ter·spout \ˈwȯ-tər-ˌspau̇t, ˈwä-\ *n* **1** : a pipe for carrying water from a roof **2** : a funnel-shaped cloud extending from a cloud down to a spray torn up by whirling winds from an ocean or lake

water strider *n* : any of various long-legged bugs that move about swiftly on the surface of water

water table *n* : the upper limit of the portion of the ground wholly saturated with water

wa·ter·tight \ˌwȯ-tər-ˈtīt, ˌwä-\ *adj* **1** : constructed so as to keep water out **2** : allowing no possibility for doubt or uncertainty ⟨a ∼ case against the accused⟩

wa·ter·way \ˈwȯ-tər-ˌwā, ˈwä-\ *n* : a navigable body of water

wa·ter·wheel \-ˌhwēl\ *n* : a wheel made to turn by water flowing against it

water wings *n pl* : an air-filled device to give support to a person's body esp. when learning to swim

wa·ter·works \ˈwȯ-tər-ˌwərks, ˈwä-\ *n pl* : a system for supplying water (as to a city)

wa·tery \ˈwȯ-tə-rē, ˈwä-\ *adj* **1** : containing, full of, or giving out water ⟨∼ clouds⟩ **2** : being like water : THIN, WEAK ⟨∼ lemonade⟩; *also* : being soft and soggy ⟨∼ turnips⟩

WATS \ˈwäts\ *abbr* Wide-Area Telecommunications Service

watt \ˈwät\ *n* [James *Watt* †1819 Scottish engineer and inventor] : the metric unit of power equal to the work done at the rate of one joule per second or to the power produced by a current of one ampere across a potential difference of one volt

watt·age \ˈwä-tij\ *n* : amount of power expressed in watts

wat·tle \ˈwät-ᵊl\ *n* **1** : a framework of rods with flexible branches or reeds interlaced used esp. formerly in building; *also* : material for this framework **2** : a naked fleshy process hanging usu. from the head or neck (as of a bird) — **wat·tled** \-ᵊld\ *adj*

W Aust *abbr* Western Australia

¹wave \ˈwāv\ *vb* **waved; wav·ing 1** : FLUTTER ⟨flags *wav*-

\ə\abut \ᵊ\kitten \ər\further \a\ash \ā\ace \ä\mop, mar \au̇\out \ch\chin \e\bet \ē\easy \g\go \i\hit \ī\ice \j\job \ŋ\sing \ō\go \ȯ\law \ȯi\boy \th\thin \t̲h̲\the \ü\loot \u̇\foot \y\yet \zh\vision *see also* Pronunciation Symbols page

ing in the breeze⟩ **2** : to motion with the hands or with something held in them in signal or salute **3** : to become moved or brandished to-and-fro; *also* : BRANDISH, FLOURISH ⟨∼ a sword⟩ **4** : to move before the wind with a wavelike motion ⟨fields of *waving* grain⟩ **5** : to curve up and down like a wave : UNDULATE

²**wave** *n* **1** : a moving ridge or swell on the surface of water **2** : a wavelike formation or shape ⟨a ∼ in the hair⟩ **3** : the action or process of making wavy or curly **4** : a waving motion; *esp* : a signal made by waving something **5** : FLOW, GUSH ⟨a ∼ of anger swept over her⟩ **6** : a peak of activity ⟨a ∼ of selling⟩ **7** : a disturbance that transfers energy progressively from point to point in a medium ⟨light travels in ∼s⟩ ⟨a sound ∼⟩ **8** : a period of hot or cold weather — **wave·like** *adj*

wave·length \ˈwāv-ˌleŋth\ *n* **1** : the distance in the line of advance of a wave from any one point (as a crest) to the next corresponding point **2** : a line of thought that reveals a common understanding

wave·let \-lət\ *n* : a little wave : RIPPLE

wa·ver \ˈwā-vər\ *vb* **1** : to fluctuate in opinion, allegiance, or direction **2** : REEL, TOTTER; *also* : QUIVER, FLICKER ⟨∼*ing* flames⟩ **3** : FALTER **4** : to give an unsteady sound : QUAVER **syn** falter, hesitate, shilly-shally, vacillate — **waver** *n* — **wa·ver·er** *n* — **wa·ver·ing·ly** *adv*

wavy \ˈwā-vē\ *adj* **wav·i·er; -est** : having waves : moving in waves

¹**wax** \ˈwaks\ *n* **1** : a yellowish plastic substance secreted by bees for constructing the honeycomb **2** : any of various substances like beeswax

²**wax** *vb* : to treat or rub with wax

³**wax** *vb* **1** : to increase in size, numbers, strength, volume, or duration **2** : to increase in apparent size ⟨the moon ∼*es* toward the full⟩ **3** : to take on a quality or state : BECOME ⟨∼*ed* indignant⟩ ⟨the party ∼*ed* merry⟩

wax bean *n* : a kidney bean with pods that turn creamy yellow to bright yellow when mature enough to use as snap beans

wax·en \ˈwak-sən\ *adj* **1** : made of or covered with wax **2** : resembling wax (as in color or consistency)

wax myrtle *n* : any of a genus of shrubs or trees with aromatic leaves; *esp* : an evergreen shrub of the eastern U.S. that produces small hard berries with a thick coating of white wax used for candles

wax·wing \ˈwaks-ˌwiŋ\ *n* : any of a genus of chiefly brown to gray singing birds with a showy crest and red waxy material on the tips of some wing feathers

wax·work \-ˌwərk\ *n* **1** : an effigy usu. of a person in wax **2** *pl* : an exhibition of wax figures

waxy \ˈwak-sē\ *adj* **wax·i·er; -est 1** : made of or full of wax **2** : WAXEN 2

way \ˈwā\ *n* **1** : a thoroughfare for travel or passage : ROAD, PATH, STREET **2** : ROUTE **3** : a course of action ⟨chose the easy ∼⟩; *also* : opportunity, capability, or fact of doing as one pleases ⟨always had your own ∼⟩ **4** : a possible course : POSSIBILITY ⟨no two ∼s about it⟩ **5** : METHOD, MODE ⟨this ∼ of thinking⟩ ⟨a new ∼ of painting⟩ **6** : FEATURE, RESPECT ⟨a good worker in many ∼s⟩ **7** : the usual or characteristic state of affairs ⟨as is the ∼ with old people⟩; *also* : individual characteristic or peculiarity ⟨used to her ∼s⟩ **8** : DISTANCE ⟨a short ∼ from here⟩ ⟨a long ∼ from success⟩ **9** : progress along a course ⟨working my ∼ through college⟩ **10** : something having direction : LOCALITY ⟨out our ∼⟩ **11** : STATE, CONDITION ⟨the ∼ things are⟩ **12** *pl* : an inclined structure upon which a ship is built or is supported in launching **13** : CATEGORY, KIND ⟨get what you need in the ∼ of supplies⟩ **14** : motion or speed of a boat through the water — **by the way** : by way of interjection or digression — **by way of 1** : for the purpose of ⟨*by way of* illustration⟩ **2** : by the route through : VIA

— **out of the way 1** : WRONG, IMPROPER **2** : SECLUDED, REMOTE

way·bill \ˈwā-ˌbil\ *n* : a paper that accompanies a freight shipment and gives details of goods, route, and charges

way·far·er \ˈwā-ˌfar-ər\ *n* : a traveler esp. on foot — **way·far·ing** \-ˌfar-iŋ\ *adj*

way·lay \ˈwā-ˌlā\ *vb* **-laid** \-ˌlād\; **-lay·ing** : to lie in wait for or attack from ambush

way–out \ˈwā-ˈaüt\ *adj* : FAR-OUT

-ways \ˌwāz\ *adv suffix* : in (such) a way, course, direction, or manner ⟨side*ways*⟩

ways and means *n pl* : methods and resources esp. for raising revenues needed by a state; *also* : a legislative committee concerned with this function

way·side \ˈwā-ˌsīd\ *n* : the side of or land adjacent to a road or path

way station *n* : an intermediate station on a line of travel (as a railroad)

way·ward \ˈwā-wərd\ *adj* [ME, short for *awayward* turned away, fr. *away*, adv. + *-ward* directed toward] **1** : following one's own capricious or wanton inclinations ⟨∼ children⟩ **2** : UNPREDICTABLE, IRREGULAR ⟨a ∼ act⟩

WBC *abbr* white blood cells

WC *abbr* **1** water closet **2** without charge

WCTU *abbr* Women's Christian Temperance Union

we \ˈwē\ *pron* **1** — used of a group that includes the speaker or writer **2** — used for the singular *I* by a monarch, editor, or writer

weak \ˈwēk\ *adj* **1** : lacking strength or vigor : FEEBLE **2** : not able to sustain or resist much weight, pressure, or strain **3** : deficient in vigor of mind or character; *also* : resulting from or indicative of such deficiency ⟨a ∼ policy⟩ ⟨a ∼ will⟩ ⟨*weak*-minded⟩ **4** : not supported by truth or logic ⟨a ∼ argument⟩ **5** : lacking skill or proficiency; *also* : indicative of a lack of skill or aptitude **6** : lacking vigor of expression or effect **7** : of less than usual strength ⟨∼ tea⟩ **8** : not having or exerting authority ⟨∼ government⟩; *also* : INEFFECTIVE, IMPOTENT **9** : of, relating to, or constituting a verb or verb conjugation that forms the past tense and past participle by adding *-ed* or *-d* or *-t* — **weak·ly** *adv*

weak·en \ˈwē-kən\ *vb* : to make or become weak **syn** enfeeble, debilitate, undermine, sap, cripple, disable

weak·fish \ˈwēk-ˌfish\ *n* [obs. D *weekvis*, fr. D *week* soft + *vis* fish; fr. its tender flesh] : a common marine fish of the Atlantic coast of the U.S. caught for food and sport; *also* : any of several related food fishes

weak force *n* : the physical force responsible for particle decay processes in radioactivity

weak–kneed \ˈwēk-ˈnēd\ *adj* : lacking willpower or resolution

weak·ling \ˈwē-kliŋ\ *n* : a person who is physically, mentally, or morally weak

weak·ly \ˈwē-klē\ *adj* : FEEBLE, WEAK

weak·ness \ˈwēk-nəs\ *n* **1** : the quality or state of being weak; *also* : an instance or period of being weak ⟨in a moment of ∼ he agreed to go⟩ **2** : FAULT, DEFECT **3** : an object of special desire or fondness ⟨chocolate is her ∼⟩

¹**weal** \ˈwēl\ *n* : WELL-BEING, PROSPERITY

²**weal** *n* : WELT

weald \ˈwēld\ *n* [The *Weald*, wooded district in England, fr. ME *Weeld* the Weald, fr. OE *weald* forest] **1** : FOREST **2** : WOLD

wealth \ˈwelth\ *n* [ME *welthe* welfare, prosperity, fr. *wele* weal] **1** : abundance of possessions or resources : AFFLUENCE, RICHES **2** : abundant supply : PROFUSION ⟨a ∼ of detail⟩ **3** : all property that has a money or an exchange value; *also* : all objects or resources that have economic value **syn** fortune, property, substance, worth

wealthy \'wel-thē\ *adj* **wealth·i·er; -est** : having wealth : RICH

wean \'wēn\ *vb* **1** : to accustom (a young mammal) to take food by means other than nursing **2** : to free from a source of dependence; *also* : to free from a usu. unwholesome habit or interest

weap·on \'we-pən\ *n* **1** : something (as a gun, knife, or club) used to injure, defeat, or destroy **2** : a means of contending against another — **weap·on·less** \-ləs\ *adj*

weap·on·ry \-rē\ *n* : WEAPONS

¹wear \'war\ *vb* **wore** \'wōr\; **worn** \'wōrn\; **wear·ing 1** : to use as an article of clothing or adornment ⟨~ a coat⟩ ⟨~s earrings⟩; *also* : to carry on the person ⟨~ a gun⟩ **2** : EXHIBIT, PRESENT ⟨~ a smile⟩ **3** : to impair, diminish, or decay by use or by scraping or rubbing ⟨clothes *worn* to shreds⟩; *also* : to produce gradually by friction, rubbing, or wasting away ⟨~ a hole in the rug⟩ **4** : to exhaust or lessen the strength of : WEARY, FATIGUE ⟨*worn* by care and toil⟩ **5** : to endure use : last under use or the passage of time ⟨this cloth ~s well⟩ **6** : to diminish or fail with the passage of time ⟨the day ~s on⟩ ⟨the effect of the drug *wore* off⟩ **7** : to grow or become by attrition, use, or age ⟨the coin was *worn* thin⟩ — **wear·able** \'war-ə-bəl\ *adj* — **wear·er** *n*

²wear *n* **1** : the act of wearing : the state of being worn ⟨clothes for everyday ~⟩ **2** : clothing usu. of a particular kind or for a special occasion or use ⟨children's ~⟩ **3** : wearing or lasting quality ⟨the coat still has lots of ~ in it⟩ **4** : the result of wearing or use : impairment due to use ⟨the suit shows ~⟩

wear and tear *n* : the loss, injury, or stress to which something is subjected in the course of use; *esp* : normal depreciation

wear down *vb* : to weary and overcome by persistent resistance or pressure

wea·ri·some \'wir-ē-səm\ *adj* : causing weariness : TIRESOME — **wea·ri·some·ly** *adv* — **wea·ri·some·ness** *n*

wear out *vb* **1** : TIRE **2** : to make or become useless by wear

¹wea·ry \'wir-ē\ *adj* **wea·ri·er; -est 1** : worn out in strength, energy, or freshness **2** : expressing or characteristic of weariness ⟨a ~ sigh⟩ **3** : having one's patience, tolerance, or pleasure exhausted ⟨~ of war⟩ — **wea·ri·ly** \'wir-ə-lē\ *adv* — **wea·ri·ness** \-ē-nəs\ *n*

²weary *vb* **wea·ried; wea·ry·ing** : to become or make weary : TIRE

¹wea·sel \'wē-zəl\ *n, pl* **weasels** : any of various small slender flesh-eating mammals related to the minks

weasel

²weasel *vb* **wea·seled; wea·sel·ing 1** : to use weasel words : EQUIVOCATE **2** : to escape from or evade a situation or obligation — often used with *out*

weasel word *n* [fr. the weasel's reputed habit of sucking the contents out of an egg while leaving the shell superficially intact] : a word used to avoid a direct or forthright statement or position

¹weath·er \'we-thər\ *n* **1** : the state of the atmosphere with respect to heat or cold, wetness or dryness, calm or storm, clearness or cloudiness **2** : a particular and

esp. a disagreeable atmospheric state : RAIN, STORM

²weather *vb* **1** : to expose to or endure the action of weather; *also* : to alter (as in color or texture) by such exposure **2** : to bear up against successfully ⟨~ a storm⟩ ⟨~ troubles⟩

³weather *adj* : WINDWARD

weath·er–beat·en \'we-thər-ˌbēt-ᵊn\ *adj* : worn or damaged by exposure to the weather; *also* : toughened or tanned by the weather ⟨~ face⟩

weath·er·cock \-ˌkäk\ *n* : a weather vane shaped like a rooster

weath·er·ing \'we-thə-riŋ\ *n* : the action of the weather in altering the color, texture, composition, or form of exposed objects; *also* : alteration thus effected

weath·er·ize \'we-thə-ˌrīz\ *vb* **-ized; -iz·ing** : to make (as a house) better protected against winter weather (as by adding insulation)

weath·er·man \-ˌman\ *n* : one who reports and forecasts the weather : METEOROLOGIST

weath·er·per·son \-ˌpər-sən\ *n* : a person who reports and forecasts the weather : METEOROLOGIST

weath·er·proof \'we-thər-ˌprüf\ *adj* : able to withstand exposure to weather — **weatherproof** *vb*

weather stripping *n* : material used to seal a door or window at the edges

weather vane *n* : VANE 1

weath·er·worn \'we-thər-ˌwōrn\ *adj* : worn by exposure to the weather

¹weave \'wēv\ *vb* **wove** \'wōv\ *or* **weaved; wo·ven** \'wō-vən\ *or* **weaved; weav·ing 1** : to form by interlacing strands of material; *esp* : to make on a loom by interlacing warp and filling threads ⟨~ cloth⟩ **2** : to interlace (as threads) into a fabric and esp. cloth **3** : SPIN 2 **4** : to make as if by weaving together parts **5** : to insert as a part : work in **6** : to move in a winding or zigzag course esp. to avoid obstacles ⟨we *wove* our way through the crowd⟩ — **weav·er** *n*

²weave *n* : something woven; *also* : a pattern or method of weaving ⟨a loose ~⟩

¹web \'web\ *n* **1** : a fabric on a loom or coming from a loom **2** : COBWEB; *also* : SNARE, ENTANGLEMENT ⟨caught in a ~ of deceit⟩ **3** : an animal or plant membrane; *esp* : one uniting the toes (as in many birds) **4** : NETWORK ⟨a ~ of highways⟩ **5** : the series of barbs on each side of the shaft of a feather — **webbed** \'webd\ *adj*

²web *vb* **webbed; web·bing 1** : to make a web **2** : to cover or provide with webs or a network **3** : ENTANGLE, ENSNARE

web·bing \'we-biŋ\ *n* : a strong closely woven tape designed for bearing weight and used esp. for straps, harness, or upholstery

web–foot·ed \'web-ˈfu̇-təd\ *adj* : having webbed feet

wed \'wed\ *vb* **wed·ded** *also* **wed; wed·ding 1** : to take, give, enter into, or join in marriage : MARRY **2** : to unite firmly

Wed *abbr* Wednesday

wed·ding \'we-diŋ\ *n* **1** : a marriage ceremony usu. with accompanying festivities : NUPTIALS **2** : a joining in close association **3** : a wedding anniversary or its celebration

¹wedge \'wej\ *n* **1** : a piece of wood or metal that tapers to a thin edge and is used to split logs or rocks or to raise heavy weights **2** : something (as an action or policy) that serves to open up a way for a breach, change, or intrusion **3** : a wedge-shaped object or part ⟨a ~ of pie⟩

²wedge *vb* **wedged; wedg·ing 1** : to hold firm by or as if by driving in a wedge **2** : to force (something) into a narrow space

wed·lock \'wed-ˌläk\ *n* [ME *wedlok*, fr. OE *wedlāc* marriage bond, fr. *wedd* pledge + *-lāc*, suffix denoting activity] : the state of being married : MARRIAGE, MATRIMONY

Wednes·day \'wenz-dē, -(ˌ)dā\ *n* [ME, fr. OE *wōdnesdæg*, lit., day of Woden (supreme god of the pagan Anglo-Saxons)] : the 4th day of the week

wee \'wē\ *adj* [ME *we*, fr. *we*, n., little bit, fr. OE *wæge* weight] **1** : very small : TINY **2** : very early ⟨∼ hours of the morning⟩

¹weed \'wēd\ *n* : a plant that tends to grow thickly where it is not wanted and to choke out more desirable plants

²weed *vb* **1** : to clear of or remove weeds or something harmful, inferior, or superfluous ⟨∼ a garden⟩ **2** : to get rid of ⟨∼ out the troublemakers⟩ — **weed·er** *n*

³weed *n* : mourning clothes — usu. used in pl. ⟨widow's ∼s⟩

weedy \'wē-dē\ *adj* **1** : full of weeds **2** : resembling a weed esp. in vigor of growth or spread **3** : noticeably lean and scrawny : LANKY

week \'wēk\ *n* **1** : seven successive days; *esp* : a calendar period of seven days beginning with Sunday and ending with Saturday **2** : the working or school days of the calendar week

week·day \'wēk-ˌdā\ *n* : a day of the week except Sunday or sometimes except Saturday and Sunday

¹week·end \-ˌend\ *n* : the period between the close of one working or business or school week and the beginning of the next

²weekend *vb* : to spend the weekend

¹week·ly \'wē-klē\ *adj* **1** : occurring, appearing, or done every week **2** : computed in terms of one week — **weekly** *adv*

²weekly *n, pl* **weeklies** : a weekly publication

ween \'wēn\ *vb, archaic* : SUPPOSE 3

wee·ny \'wē-nē\ *also* **ween·sy** \'wēn-sē\ *adj* : exceptionally small

weep \'wēp\ *vb* **wept** \'wept\; **weep·ing 1** : to express emotion and esp. sorrow by shedding tears : BEWAIL, CRY **2** : to give off fluid slowly : OOZE — **weep·er** *n*

weep·ing *adj* **1** : TEARFUL **2** : having slender drooping branches

weeping willow *n* : a willow with slender drooping branches

weepy \'wē-pē\ *adj* : inclined to weep

wee·vil \'wē-vəl\ *n* : any of a large group of mostly small beetles with a long head usu. curved into a snout and larvae that feed esp. in fruits or seeds — **wee·vily** *or* **wee·vil·ly** \'wē-və-lē\ *adj*

weft \'weft\ *n* **1** : a filling thread or yarn in weaving **2** : WEB, FABRIC; *also* : something woven

¹weigh \'wā\ *vb* [ME *weyen*, fr. OE *wegan* to move, carry, weigh] **1** : to find the heaviness of **2** : to have weight or a specified weight **3** : to consider carefully : PONDER **4** : to merit consideration as important : COUNT ⟨evidence ∼ing against him⟩ **5** : to raise before sailing ⟨∼ anchor⟩ **6** : to press down with or as if with a heavy weight

²weigh *n* [alter. of *way*] : WAY — used in the phrase *under weigh*

¹weight \'wāt\ *n* **1** : the amount that something weighs; *also* : the standard amount that something should weigh **2** : a quantity or object weighing a usu. specified amount **3** : a unit (as a pound or kilogram) of weight or mass; *also* : a system of such units **4** : a heavy object for holding or pressing something down; *also* : a heavy object for throwing or lifting in an athletic contest **5** : a mental or emotional burden **6** : IMPORTANCE; *also* : INFLUENCE ⟨threw his ∼ around⟩ **7** : overpowering force **8** : relative thickness (as of a textile) ⟨summer-*weight*

clothes⟩ **syn** significance, moment, consequence, import, authority, prestige, credit

²weight *vb* **1** : to load with or as if with a weight **2** : to oppress with a burden ⟨∼ed down with cares⟩

weight·less \'wāt-ləs\ *adj* : having little weight : lacking apparent gravitational pull — **weight·less·ly** *adv* — **weight·less·ness** *n*

weighty \'wā-tē\ *adj* **weight·i·er; -est 1** : of much importance or consequence : MOMENTOUS, SERIOUS ⟨∼ problems⟩ **2** : SOLEMN ⟨a ∼ manner⟩ **3** : HEAVY **4** : POWERFUL, TELLING ⟨∼ arguments⟩

weir \'war, 'wir\ *n* **1** : a fence set in a waterway for catching fish **2** : a dam in a stream to raise the water level or divert its flow

weird \'wird\ *adj* [ME *wird, werd* fate, destiny, fr. OE *wyrd*] **1** : MAGICAL **2** : UNEARTHLY, MYSTERIOUS **3** : ODD, UNUSUAL **syn** eerie, uncanny, spooky — **weird·ly** *adv* — **weird·ness** *n*

weirdo \'wir-(ˌ)dō\ *n, pl* **weird·os** : a person who is extraordinarily strange or eccentric

Welch \'welch\ *var of* WELSH

¹wel·come \'wel-kəm\ *vb* **wel·comed; wel·com·ing 1** : to greet cordially or courteously **2** : to accept, meet, or face with pleasure ⟨he ∼s criticism⟩

²welcome *adj* **1** : received gladly into one's presence ⟨a ∼ visitor⟩ **2** : giving pleasure : PLEASING ⟨∼ news⟩ **3** : willingly permitted or admitted ⟨all are ∼ to use the books⟩ **4** — used in the phrase "You're welcome" as a reply to an expression of thanks

³welcome *n* **1** : a cordial greeting or reception **2** : the state of being welcome ⟨overstayed their ∼⟩

¹weld \'weld\ *vb* **1** : to unite (metal or plastic parts) either by heating and allowing the parts to flow together or by hammering or pressing together **2** : to unite closely or intimately ⟨∼ed together in friendship⟩ — **weld·er** *n*

²weld *n* **1** : a welded joint **2** : union by welding

wel·fare \'wel-ˌfar\ *n* **1** : the state of doing well esp. in respect to happiness, well-being, or prosperity **2** : aid in the form of money or necessities for those in need; *also* : the agency through which the aid is given

welfare state *n* : a nation or state that assumes primary responsibility for the individual and social welfare of its citizens

wel·kin \'wel-kən\ *n* : SKY; *also* : AIR

¹well \'wel\ *n* **1** : a spring with its pool : FOUNTAIN; *also* : a source of supply ⟨a ∼ of information⟩ **2** : a hole sunk in the earth to obtain a natural deposit (as of water, oil, or gas) **3** : an open space (as for a staircase) extending vertically through floors of a structure **4** : something suggesting a well

²well *vb* : to rise up and flow out

³well *adv* **bet·ter** \'be-tər\; **best** \'best\ **1** : in a good or proper manner : RIGHTLY; *also* : EXCELLENTLY, SKILLFULLY **2** : SATISFACTORILY, FORTUNATELY ⟨the party turned out ∼⟩ **3** : ABUNDANTLY ⟨eat ∼⟩ **4** : with reason or courtesy : PROPERLY ⟨I cannot ∼ refuse⟩ **5** : COMPLETELY, FULLY, QUITE ⟨∼ worth the price⟩ ⟨*well*-hidden⟩ **6** : INTIMATELY, CLOSELY ⟨I know him ∼⟩ **7** : CONSIDERABLY, FAR ⟨∼ over a million⟩ ⟨∼ ahead⟩ **8** : without trouble or difficulty ⟨we could ∼ have gone⟩ **9** : EXACTLY, DEFINITELY ⟨remember it ∼⟩

⁴well *adj* **1** : PROSPEROUS; *also* : being in satisfactory condition or circumstances **2** : SATISFACTORY, PLEASING ⟨all is ∼⟩ **3** : ADVISABLE, DESIRABLE ⟨it is not ∼ to anger him⟩ **4** : free or recovered from ill health : HEALTHY **5** : FORTUNATE ⟨it is ∼ that this has happened⟩

well–ad·just·ed \ˌwel-ə-'jəs-təd\ *adj* : WELL-BALANCED 2

well–ad·vised \-əd-'vīzd\ *adj* **1** : PRUDENT **2** : resulting from, based on, or showing careful deliberation or wise counsel ⟨∼ plans⟩

well–ap·point·ed \-ə-'pȯin-təd\ *adj* : properly fitted out

well–ba·lanced \'wel-'ba-lənst\ *adj* **1** : nicely or evenly

WEIGHTS AND MEASURES[1]

UNIT	ABBREVIATION OR SYMBOL	EQUIVALENT IN OTHER U.S. UNITS	METRIC EQUIVALENT
WEIGHT			
avoirdupois (ordinary commodities)			
ton			
short ton		20 short hundredweight, 2000 pounds	0.907 metric ton
long ton		20 long hundredweight, 2240 pounds	1.016 metric tons
hundredweight	cwt		
short hundredweight		100 pounds, 0.05 short ton	45.359 kilograms
long hundredweight		112 pounds, 0.05 long ton	50.802 kilograms
pound	lb or lb avdp also #	16 ounces, 7000 grains (1.215 apothecaries' or troy pound)	0.454 kilogram
ounce	oz or oz avdp	16 drams, 437.5 grains (0.911 apothecaries' or troy ounce)	28.350 grams
dram	dr or dr avdp	27.344 grains, 0.0625 ounce	1.772 grams
grain	gr	0.037 dram, 0.002286 ounce (1.0 apothecaries' or troy grain)	0.0648 gram
troy (precious metals, jewels)			
pound	lb t	12 ounces, 240 pennyweight, 5760 grains (0.823 avoirdupois pound, 1.0 apothecaries' pound)	0.373 kilogram
ounce	oz t	20 pennyweight, 480 grains (1.097 avoirdupois ounce, 1.0 apothecaries' ounce)	31.103 grams
pennyweight	dwt also pwt	24 grains, 0.05 ounce	1.555 grams
grain	gr	0.042 pennyweight, 0.002083 ounce (1.0 avoirdupois or apothecaries' grain)	0.0648 gram
apothecaries' (drugs)			
pound	lb ap	12 ounces, 5760 grains (0.822 avoirdupois pound, 1.0 troy pound)	0.373 kilogram
ounce	oz ap or ʒ	8 drams, 480 grains (1.097 avoirdupois ounce, 1.0 troy ounce)	31.103 grams
dram	dr ap or ʒ	0.125 ounce, 60 grains	3.888 grams
grain	gr	0.0166 dram, 0.002083 ounce (1.0 avoirdupois or troy grain)	0.0648 gram
CAPACITY			
U.S. liquid measure			
gallon	gal	4 quarts (231 cubic inches)	3.785 liters
quart	qt	2 pints (57.75 cubic inches)	0.946 liter
pint	pt	4 gills (28.875 cubic inches)	0.473 liter
gill	gi	4 fluid ounces (7.219 cubic inches)	118.294 milliliters
fluid ounce	fl oz or fʒ	8 fluid drams (1.805 cubic inches)	29.573 milliliters
fluid dram	fl dr or fʒ	60 minims (0.226 cubic inch)	3.697 milliliters
minim	min or ♏	1/60 fluid dram (0.003760 cubic inch)	0.061610 milliliter
U.S. dry measure			
bushel	bu	4 pecks (2150.42 cubic inches)	35.239 liters
peck	pk	8 quarts (537.605 cubic inches)	8.810 liters
quart	qt	2 pints (67.201 cubic inches)	1.101 liters
pint	pt	1/2 quart (33.600 cubic inches)	0.551 liter
LENGTH			
mile	mi	5280 feet, 320 rods, 1760 yards	1.609 kilometers
rod	rd	5.50 yards, 16.5 feet	5.029 meters
yard	yd	3 feet, 36 inches	0.9144 meter
foot	ft or '	12 inches, 0.333 yard	30.48 centimeters
inch	in or "	0.083 foot, 0.028 yard	2.54 centimeters
AREA			
square mile	sq mi or mi^2	640 acre, 102,400 square rods	2.590 square kilometers
acre		4840 square yards, 43,560 square feet	4047 square meters
square rod	sq rd or rd^2	30.25 square yards, 0.00625 acre	25.293 square meters
square yard	sq yd or yd^2	1296 square inches, 9 square feet	0.836 square meter
square foot	sq ft or ft^2	144 square inches, 0.111 square yard	0.093 square meter
square inch	sq in or in^2	0.0069 square foot, 0.00077 square yard	6.452 square centimeters
VOLUME			
cubic yard	cu yd or yd^3	27 cubic feet, 46,656 cubic inches	0.765 cubic meter
cubic foot	cu ft or ft^3	1728 cubic inches, 0.0370 cubic yard	0.028 cubic meter
cubic inch	cu in or in^3	0.00058 cubic foot, 0.000021 cubic yard	16.387 cubic centimeters

[1]For U.S. equivalents of metric units see Metric System table

balanced or arranged **2** : emotionally or psychologically untroubled

well–be·ing \-ˈbē-iŋ\ *n* : the state of being happy, healthy, or prosperous

well·born \-ˈbȯrn\ *adj* : born of noble or wealthy lineage

well–bred \-ˈbred\ *adj* : having or indicating good breeding : REFINED

well–de·fined \-di-ˈfīnd\ *adj* : having clearly distinguishable limits or boundaries

well–dis·posed \-di-ˈspōzd\ *adj* : disposed to be friendly, favorable, or sympathetic

well–done \ˈwel-ˈdən\ *adj* **1** : rightly or properly performed **2** : cooked thoroughly

well–fa·vored \-ˈfā-vərd\ *adj* : GOOD-LOOKING, HANDSOME

well–fixed \-ˈfikst\ *adj* : WELL-HEELED

well–found·ed \-ˈfau̇n-dəd\ *adj* : based on good reasons

well–groomed \-ˈgrümd, -ˈgru̇md\ *adj* : neatly dressed or cared for

well–ground·ed \-ˈgrau̇n-dəd\ *adj* **1** : having a firm foundation **2** : WELL-FOUNDED

well·head \-ˌhed\ *n* **1** : the source of a spring or a stream **2** : principal source **3** : the top of or a structure built over a well

well–heeled \-ˈhēld\ *adj* : financially well-off

well–known \-ˈnōn\ *adj* : fully or widely known

well–mean·ing \-ˈmē-niŋ\ *adj* : having or based on good intentions

well·ness \-nəs\ *n* : good health esp. as an actively sought goal ⟨∼ clinics⟩ ⟨lifestyles that promote ∼⟩

well–nigh \-ˈnī\ *adv* : ALMOST, NEARLY

well–off \-ˈȯf\ *adj* : being in good condition or circumstances; *esp* : WELL-TO-DO

well–or·dered \-ˈȯr-dərd\ *adj* : having an orderly procedure or arrangement

well–read \-ˈred\ *adj* : well informed through reading

well–round·ed \-ˈrau̇n-dəd\ *adj* **1** : broadly trained, educated, and experienced **2** : COMPREHENSIVE ⟨a ∼ program of activities⟩

well–spo·ken \ˈwel-ˈspō-kən\ *adj* **1** : speaking well and esp. courteously **2** : spoken with propriety ⟨∼ words⟩

well·spring \-ˌspriŋ\ *n* : a source of continuous supply

well–timed \-ˈtīmd\ *adj* : TIMELY

well–to–do \ˌwel-tə-ˈdü\ *adj* : having more than adequate financial resources : PROSPEROUS

well–turned \ˈwel-ˈtərnd\ *adj* **1** : pleasingly shaped ⟨a ∼ ankle⟩ **2** : pleasingly expressed ⟨a ∼ phrase⟩

well–wish·er \ˈwel-ˌwi-shər\ *n* : one that wishes well to another — **well–wish·ing** *adj or n*

welsh \ˈwelsh, ˈwelch\ *vb* **1** : to avoid payment **2** : to break one's word ⟨∼ed on his promises⟩

Welsh \ˈwelsh\ *n* **1 Welsh** *pl* : the people of Wales **2** : the Celtic language of Wales — **Welsh** *adj* — **Welsh·man** \-mən\ *n*

Welsh cor·gi \-ˈkȯr-gē\ *n* [W *corgi*, fr. *cor* dwarf + *ci* dog] : a short-legged long-backed dog with foxy head of either of two breeds of Welsh origin

Welsh rabbit *n* : melted often seasoned cheese served over toast or crackers

Welsh rare·bit \-ˈrar-bət\ *n* : WELSH RABBIT

¹welt \ˈwelt\ *n* **1** : the narrow strip of leather between a shoe upper and sole to which other parts are stitched **2** : a doubled edge, strip, insert, or seam for ornament or reinforcement **3** : a ridge or lump raised on the skin usu. by a blow; *also* : a heavy blow

²welt *vb* **1** : to furnish with a welt **2** : to hit hard

¹wel·ter \ˈwel-tər\ *vb* **1** : WRITHE, TOSS; *also* : WALLOW **2** : to rise and fall or toss about in or with waves **3** : to become deeply sunk, soaked, or involved **4** : to be in turmoil

²welter *n* **1** : TURMOIL **2** : a chaotic mass or jumble

wel·ter·weight \ˈwel-tər-ˌwāt\ *n* : a boxer weighing more than 135 but not over 147 pounds

wen \ˈwen\ *n* : an abnormal growth or a cyst protruding from a surface esp. of the skin

wench \ˈwench\ *n* [ME *wenche*, short for *wenchel* child, fr. OE *wencel*] **1** : a young woman **2** : a female servant

wend \ˈwend\ *vb* : to direct one's course : proceed on (one's way)

went *past of* GO

wept *past and past part of* WEEP

were *past 2d sing, past pl, or past subjunctive of* BE

were·wolf \ˈwer-ˌwu̇lf, ˈwir-, ˈwər-\ *n, pl* **were·wolves** \-ˌwu̇lvz\ [ME, fr. OE *werwulf*, fr. *wer* man + *wulf* wolf] : a person transformed into a wolf or capable of assuming a wolf's form

wes·kit \ˈwes-kət\ *n* : VEST 1

¹west \ˈwest\ *adv* : to or toward the west

²west *adj* **1** : situated toward or at the west **2** : coming from the west

³west *n* **1** : the general direction of sunset **2** : the compass point directly opposite to east **3** *cap* : regions or countries west of a specified or implied point **4** *cap* : Europe and the Americas — **west·er·ly** \ˈwes-tər-lē\ *adv or adj* — **west·ward** *adv or adj* — **west·wards** *adv*

¹west·ern \ˈwes-tərn\ *adj* **1** : lying toward or coming from the west **2** *cap* : of, relating to, or characteristic of a region conventionally designated West **3** *cap* : of or relating to the Roman Catholic or Protestant segment of Christianity — **West·ern·er** *n*

²western *n, often cap* : a novel, story, film, or radio or television show about life in the western U.S. during the latter half of the 19th century

west·ern·ize \ˈwes-tər-ˌnīz\ *vb* **-ized; -iz·ing** : to give western characteristics to

¹wet \ˈwet\ *adj* **wet·ter; wet·test 1** : consisting of or covered or soaked with liquid (as water) **2** : RAINY **3** : not dry ⟨∼ paint⟩ **4** : permitting or advocating the manufacture and sale of alcoholic beverages ⟨a ∼ town⟩ ⟨a ∼ candidate⟩ **syn** damp, dank, moist, humid — **wet·ly** *adv* — **wet·ness** *n*

²wet *n* **1** : WATER; *also* : WETNESS, MOISTURE **2** : rainy weather : RAIN **3** : an advocate of a wet liquor policy

³wet *vb* **wet** *or* **wet·ted; wet·ting** : to make or become wet

wet blanket *n* : one that quenches or dampens enthusiasm or pleasure

weth·er \ˈwe-thər\ *n* : a castrated male sheep or goat

wet·land \ˈwet-ˌland, -lənd\ *n* : land or areas (as swamps) containing much soil moisture — usu. used in pl.

wet nurse *n* : a woman who cares for and suckles children not her own

wet suit *n* : a rubber suit for swimmers that acts to retain body heat by keeping a layer of water against the body as insulation

wh *abbr* **1** which **2** white

¹whack \ˈhwak\ *vb* **1** : to strike with a smart or resounding blow **2** : to cut with or as if with a whack

²whack *n* **1** : a smart or resounding blow; *also* : the sound of such a blow **2** : PORTION, SHARE **3** : CONDITION, STATE ⟨the machine is out of ∼⟩ **4** : an opportunity or attempt to do something : CHANCE **5** : a single action or occasion ⟨made three pies at a ∼⟩

¹whale \ˈhwāl\ *n, pl* **whales 1** *or pl* **whale** : CETACEAN; *esp* : one (as a sperm whale or killer whale) of large size **2** : a person or thing impressive in size or quality ⟨a ∼ of a story⟩

²whale *vb* **whaled; whal·ing** : to fish or hunt for whales

³whale *vb* **whaled; whal·ing 1** : THRASH **2** : to strike or hit vigorously

whale·boat \-ˌbōt\ *n* : a long narrow rowboat originally used by whalers

whale·bone \-ˌbōn\ *n* : BALEEN

whal·er \ˈhwā-lər\ *n* **1** : a person or ship that hunts whales **2** : WHALEBOAT

wham·my \ˈhwa-mē\ *n, pl* **wham·mies** : JINX, HEX

wharf \\'hwȯrf\\ *n, pl* **wharves** \\'hwȯrvz\\ *also* **wharfs** : a structure alongside which ships lie to load and unload

[1]**what** \\'hwät, 'hwət\\ *pron* **1** — used to inquire about the identity or nature of a being, an object, or some matter or situation ⟨∼ is he, a salesman⟩ ⟨∼'s that⟩ ⟨∼ happened⟩ **2** : that which ⟨I know ∼ you want⟩ **3** : WHATEVER 1 ⟨take ∼ you want⟩

[2]**what** *adv* **1** : in what respect : HOW ⟨∼ does he care⟩ **2** — used with *with* to introduce a prepositional phrase that expresses cause ⟨kept busy ∼ with school and work⟩

[3]**what** *adj* **1** — used to inquire about the identity or nature of a person, object, or matter ⟨∼ books do you read⟩ **2** : how remarkable or surprising ⟨∼ an idea⟩ **3** : WHATEVER

[1]**what·ev·er** \\hwät-'e-vər\\ *pron* **1** : anything or everything that ⟨does ∼ he wants to⟩ **2** : no matter what ⟨∼ you do, don't cheat⟩ **3** : WHAT 1 — used as an intensive ⟨∼ do you mean⟩

[2]**whatever** *adj* : of any kind at all ⟨no food ∼⟩

[1]**what·not** \\'hwät-ˌnät\\ *pron* : any of various other things that might also be mentioned ⟨needles, pins, and ∼⟩

[2]**whatnot** *n* : a light open set of shelves for small ornaments

what·so·ev·er \\ˌhwät-sō-'e-vər\\ *pron or adj* : WHATEVER

wheal \\'hwēl\\ *n* : a rapidly formed flat slightly raised itching or burning patch on the skin; *also* : WELT

wheat \\'hwēt\\ *n* : a cereal grain that yields a fine white flour and is the chief breadstuff of temperate regions; *also* : any of several grasses yielding wheat — **wheat·en** *adj*

wheat germ *n* : the vitamin-rich wheat embryo separated in milling

whee·dle \\'hwēd-ᵊl\\ *vb* **whee·dled; whee·dling 1** : to entice by flattery **2** : to gain or get by wheedling

[1]**wheel** \\'hwēl\\ *n* **1** : a disk or circular frame that turns on a central axis **2** : a device whose main part is a wheel **3** : something resembling a wheel in shape or motion **4** : a curving or circular movement **5** : machinery that imparts motion : moving power ⟨the ∼s of government⟩ **6** : a person of importance **7** *pl, slang* : AUTOMOBILE — **wheeled** \\'hwēld\\ *adj* — **wheel·less** *adj*

[2]**wheel** *vb* **1** : ROTATE, REVOLVE **2** : to change direction as if turning on a pivot **3** : to convey or move on wheels or in a vehicle

wheel·bar·row \\-ˌbar-ō\\ *n* : a vehicle with handles and usu. one wheel for carrying small loads

wheel·base \\-ˌbās\\ *n* : the distance in inches between the front and rear axles of an automotive vehicle

wheel·chair \\-ˌcher\\ *n* : a chair mounted on wheels esp. for the use of disabled persons

wheel·er \\'hwē-lər\\ *n* **1** : one that wheels **2** : WHEELHORSE **3** : something that has wheels — used in combination ⟨a side-*wheeler*⟩

wheel·er–deal·er \\ˌhwē-lər-'dē-lər\\ *n* : a shrewd operator esp. in business or politics

wheel·horse \\'hwēl-ˌhȯrs\\ *n* **1** : a horse in a position nearest the front wheels of a wagon **2** : a steady and effective worker esp. in a political body

wheel·house \\-ˌhaús\\ *n* : PILOTHOUSE

wheel–thrown \\'hwēl-ˌthrōn\\ *adj* : made on a potter's wheel

wheel·wright \\-ˌrīt\\ *n* : a maker and repairer of wheels and wheeled vehicles

[1]**wheeze** \\'hwēz\\ *vb* **wheezed; wheez·ing** : to breathe with difficulty usu. with a whistling sound

[2]**wheeze** *n* **1** : a sound of wheezing **2** : an often repeated and well-known joke **3** : a trite saying

wheezy \\'hwē-zē\\ *adj* **wheez·i·er; -est 1** : inclined to wheeze **2** : having a wheezing sound — **wheez·i·ly** \\-zə-lē\\ *adv* — **wheez·i·ness** \\-zē-nəs\\ *n*

whelk \\'hwelk\\ *n* : a large sea snail; *esp* : one much used as food in Europe

whelm \\'hwelm\\ *vb* : to overcome or engulf completely : OVERWHELM

[1]**whelp** \\'hwelp\\ *n* : any of the young of various carnivorous mammals (as a dog)

[2]**whelp** *vb* : to give birth to (whelps); *also* : bring forth young

[1]**when** \\'hwen\\ *adv* **1** : at what time ⟨∼ will you return⟩ **2** : at or during which time ⟨a time ∼ things were better⟩

[2]**when** *conj* **1** : at or during the time that ⟨leave ∼ I do⟩ **2** : every time that ⟨they all clapped ∼ he sang⟩ **3** : in the event that : IF ⟨disqualified ∼ you cheat⟩ **4** : ALTHOUGH ⟨quit politics ∼ he might have had a great career in it⟩

[3]**when** *pron* : what or which time ⟨since ∼ have you been the boss⟩

[4]**when** *n* : the time of a happening

whence \\'hwens\\ *adv or conj* : from what place, source, or cause

when·ev·er \\hwe-'ne-vər, hwə-\\ *conj or adv* : at whatever time

when·so·ev·er \\'hwen-sō-ˌe-vər\\ *conj* : at whatever time

[1]**where** \\'hwer\\ *adv* **1** : at, in, or to what place ⟨∼ is it⟩ ⟨∼ will we go⟩ **2** : at, in, or to what situation, position, direction, circumstances, or respect ⟨∼ does this road lead⟩

[2]**where** *conj* **1** : at, in, or to what place ⟨knows ∼ the house is⟩ **2** : at, in, or to what situation, position, direction, circumstances, or respect ⟨shows ∼ the road leads⟩ **3** : WHEREVER ⟨goes ∼ she likes⟩ **4** : at, in, or to which place ⟨the town ∼ we live⟩ **5** : at, in, or to the place at, in, or to which ⟨stay ∼ you are⟩ **6** : in a case, situation, or respect in which ⟨outstanding ∼ endurance is called for⟩

[3]**where** *n* : PLACE, LOCATION ⟨the ∼ and how of the accident⟩

[1]**where·abouts** \\-ə-ˌbaúts\\ *also* **where·about** \\-ˌbaút\\ *adv* : about where : near what place ⟨∼ does he live⟩

[2]**whereabouts** *n sing or pl* : the place where a person or thing is ⟨his present ∼ are unknown⟩

where·as \\hwer-'az\\ *conj* **1** : while on the contrary; *also* : ALTHOUGH **2** : in view of the fact that : SINCE

where·at \\-'at\\ *conj* **1** : at or toward which **2** : in consequence of which : WHEREUPON

where·by \\-'bī\\ *conj* : by, through, or in accordance with which ⟨the means ∼ we achieved our goals⟩

[1]**where·fore** \\'hwer-ˌfȯr\\ *adv* **1** : for what reason or purpose : WHY. **2** : THEREFORE

[2]**wherefore** *n* : an answer or statement giving an explanation : REASON

[1]**where·in** \\hwer-'in\\ *adv* : in what : in what respect ⟨∼ was I wrong⟩

[2]**wherein** *conj* **1** : in which : WHERE ⟨the city ∼ we live⟩ **2** : during which **3** : in what way : HOW ⟨showed me ∼ I was wrong⟩

where·of \\-'ȯv, -'äv\\ *conj* **1** : of what ⟨knows ∼ he speaks⟩ **2** : of which or whom ⟨books ∼ the best are lost⟩

where·on \\-'ȯn, -'än\\ *conj* : on which ⟨the base ∼ it rests⟩

where·so·ev·er \\'hwer-sō-ˌe-vər\\ *conj* : WHEREVER

where·to \\'hwer-ˌtü\\ *conj* : to which

where·up·on \\'hwer-ə-ˌpȯn, -ˌpän\\ *conj* **1** : on which **2** : closely following and in consequence of which

[1]**wher·ev·er** \\hwer-'e-vər\\ *adv* : where in the world ⟨∼ did he get that tie⟩

[2]**wherever** *conj* **1** : at, in, or to whatever place **2** : in any circumstance in which

---

\\ə\\abut \\ᵊ\\kitten \\ər\\further \\a\\ash \\ā\\ace \\ä\\mop, mar \\aú\\out \\ch\\chin \\e\\bet \\ē\\easy \\g\\go \\i\\hit \\ī\\ice \\j\\job \\ŋ\\sing \\ō\\go \\ȯ\\law \\ȯi\\boy \\th\\thin \\t͟h\\the \\ü\\loot \\ú\\foot \\y\\yet \\zh\\vision *see also* Pronunciation Symbols page

where·with \'hwer-ˌwith, -ˌwith\ *conj* : with or by means of which

where·with·al \'hwer-wi-ˌthȯl, -ˌthȯl\ *n* : MEANS, RESOURCES; *esp* : MONEY

wher·ry \'hwer-ē\ *n, pl* **wherries** : a long light rowboat sharp at both ends

whet \'hwet\ *vb* **whet·ted; whet·ting** 1 : to sharpen by rubbing on or with something abrasive (as a whetstone) 2 : to make keen : STIMULATE ⟨~ the appetite⟩

wheth·er \'hwe-thər\ *conj* 1 : if it is or was true that ⟨ask ~ he is going⟩ 2 : if it is or was better ⟨uncertain ~ to go or stay⟩ 3 : whichever is or was the case, namely that ⟨~ we succeed or fail, we must try⟩ 4 : EITHER ⟨turned out well ~ by accident or design⟩

whet·stone \'hwet-ˌstōn\ *n* : a stone for sharpening blades

whey \'hwā\ *n* : the watery part of milk that separates after the milk sours and thickens

¹**which** \'hwich\ *adj* 1 : being what one or ones out of a group ⟨~ shirt should I wear⟩ 2 : WHICHEVER

²**which** *pron* 1 : which one or ones ⟨~ is yours⟩ ⟨~ are his⟩ ⟨it's in May or June, I'm not sure ~⟩ 2 : WHICHEVER ⟨we have all kinds; take ~ you like⟩ 3 — used to introduce a relative clause and to serve as a substitute therein for the noun modified by the clause ⟨the money ~ is coming to me⟩

¹**which·ev·er** \hwich-'e-vər\ *adj* : no matter which ⟨~ way you go⟩

²**whichever** *pron* : whatever one or ones

which·so·ev·er \ˌhwich-sō-'e-vər\ *pron or adj* : WHICHEVER

whick·er \'hwi-kər\ *vb* : NEIGH, WHINNY — **whicker** *n*

¹**whiff** \'hwif\ *n* 1 : a quick puff or slight gust (as of air) 2 : an inhalation of odor, gas, or smoke 3 : a slight trace 4 : STRIKEOUT

²**whiff** *vb* 1 : to expel, puff out, or blow away in or as if in whiffs 2 : to inhale an odor 3 : STRIKE OUT 3

whif·fle·tree \'hwi-fəl-(ˌ)trē\ *n* : the pivoted swinging bar to which the traces of a harness are fastened

Whig \'hwig\ *n* [short for *Whiggamore*, member of a Scottish group that marched to Edinburgh in 1648 to oppose the court party] 1 : a member or supporter of a British political group of the late 17th through early 19th centuries seeking to limit royal authority and increase parliamentary power 2 : an American favoring independence from Great Britain during the American Revolution 3 : a member or supporter of an American political party formed about 1834 to oppose the Democrats

¹**while** \'hwīl\ *n* 1 : a period of time ⟨stay a ~⟩ 2 : the time and effort used : TROUBLE ⟨worth your ~⟩

²**while** *conj* 1 : during the time that ⟨she called ~ you were out⟩ 2 : AS LONG AS ⟨~ there's life there's hope⟩ 3 : ALTHOUGH ⟨~ he's respected, he's not liked⟩

³**while** *vb* **whiled; whil·ing** : to cause to pass esp. pleasantly ⟨~ away an hour⟩

¹**whi·lom** \'hwī-ləm\ *adv* [ME, lit., at times, fr. OE *hwīlum,* dat. pl. of *hwīl* time, while] *archaic* : FORMERLY

²**whilom** *adj* : FORMER ⟨his ~ friends⟩

whilst \'hwīlst\ *conj, chiefly Brit* : WHILE

whim \'hwim\ *n* : a sudden wish, desire, or change of mind

whim·per \'hwim-pər\ *vb* : to make a low whining plaintive or broken sound — **whimper** *n*

whim·si·cal \'hwim-zi-kəl\ *adj* 1 : full of whims : CAPRICIOUS 2 : resulting from or characterized by whim or caprice : ERRATIC — **whim·si·cal·i·ty** \ˌhwim-zə-'ka-lə-tē\ *n* — **whim·si·cal·ly** \'hwim-zi-k(ə-)lē\ *adv*

whim·sy *or* **whim·sey** \'hwim-zē\ *n, pl* **whimsies** *or* **whimseys** 1 : WHIM, CAPRICE 2 : a fanciful or fantastic device, object, or creation esp. in writing or art

whine \'hwīn\ *vb* **whined; whin·ing** [ME, fr. OE *hwīnan* to whiz] 1 : to utter a usu. high-pitched plaintive or distressed cry; *also* : to make a sound similar to such a cry 2 : to complain with or as if with a whine — **whine** *n* — **whin·er** *n* — **whiny** *also* **whin·ey** \'hwī-nē\ *adj*

¹**whin·ny** \'hwi-nē\ *vb* **whin·nied; whin·ny·ing** : to neigh usu. in a low or gentle manner

²**whinny** *n, pl* **whinnies** : NEIGH

¹**whip** \'hwip\ *vb* **whipped; whip·ping** 1 : to move, snatch, or jerk quickly or forcefully ⟨~ out a gun⟩ 2 : to strike with a slender lithe implement (as a lash) esp. as a punishment; *also* : SPANK 3 : to drive or urge on by or as if by using a whip 4 : to bind or wrap (as a rope or rod) with cord in order to protect and strengthen; *also* : to wind or wrap around something 5 : DEFEAT 6 : to stir up : INCITE ⟨~ up enthusiasm⟩ 7 : to produce in a hurry ⟨~ up a meal⟩ 8 : to beat (as eggs or cream) into a froth 9 : to proceed nimbly or briskly; *also* : to flap about forcefully ⟨flags *whipping* in the wind⟩ — **whip·per** *n* — **whip into shape** : to bring forcefully to a desired state or condition

²**whip** *n* 1 : a flexible instrument used for whipping 2 : a stroke or cut with or as if with a whip 3 : a dessert made by whipping a portion of the ingredients ⟨prune ~⟩ 4 : a person who handles a whip 5 : a member of a legislative body appointed by a party to enforce party discipline 6 : a whipping or thrashing motion

whip·cord \-ˌkȯrd\ *n* 1 : a thin tough braided cord 2 : a strong cloth with fine diagonal cords or ribs

whip hand *n* : positive control : ADVANTAGE

whip·lash \'hwip-ˌlash\ *n* 1 : the lash of a whip 2 : injury resulting from a sudden sharp movement of the neck and head (as of a person in a vehicle that is struck from the rear)

whip·per·snap·per \'hwi-pər-ˌsna-pər\ *n* : a small, insignificant, or presumptuous person

whip·pet \'hwi-pət\ *n* : any of a breed of small swift slender dogs that are used for racing

whipping boy *n* : SCAPEGOAT

whip·ple·tree \'hwi-pəl-(ˌ)trē\ *n* : WHIFFLETREE

whip·poor·will \'hwi-pər-ˌwil\ *n* : an American insect-eating bird with dull variegated plumage whose call at nightfall and just before dawn is suggestive of its name

whippoorwill

whip·saw \'hwip-ˌsȯ\ *vb* : to beset with two or more adverse conditions or situations at once

¹**whir** *also* **whirr** \'hwər\ *vb* **whirred; whir·ring** : to move, fly, or revolve with a whir

²**whir** *also* **whirr** *n* : a continuous fluttering or vibratory sound made by something in rapid motion

¹**whirl** \'hwərl\ *vb* 1 : to move or drive in a circle or curve esp. with force or speed 2 : to turn or cause to turn rapidly in circles 3 : to turn abruptly : WHEEL 4 : to move or go quickly 5 : to become dizzy or giddy : REEL

²**whirl** *n* 1 : a rapid rotating or circling movement; *also* : something whirling 2 : COMMOTION, BUSTLE ⟨the social ~⟩ 3 : a state of mental confusion 4 : TRY ⟨gave it a ~⟩

whirl·i·gig \'hwər-li-ˌgig\ *n* [ME *whirlegigg,* fr. *whirlen* to whirl + *gigg* top] 1 : a child's toy having a whirling motion **2** : something that continuously whirls or changes

whirl·pool \'hwərl-ˌpül\ *n* : water moving rapidly in a circle so as to produce a depression in the center into which floating objects may be drawn

whirl·wind \-ˌwind\ *n* **1** : a small whirling windstorm **2** : a confused rush **3** : a violent or destructive force

whirly·bird \'hwər-lē-ˌbərd\ *n* : HELICOPTER

¹whish \'hwish\ *vb* : to move with a whish or swishing sound

²whish *n* : a rushing sound : SWISH

¹whisk \'hwisk\ *n* **1** : a quick light sweeping or brushing motion **2** : a usu. wire kitchen implement for beating food by hand **3** : WHISK BROOM

²whisk *vb* **1** : to move nimbly and quickly **2** : to move or convey briskly ⟨∼ed the children off to bed⟩ **3** : to beat or whip lightly ⟨∼ eggs⟩ **4** : to brush or wipe off lightly ⟨∼ a coat⟩

whisk broom *n* : a small broom with a short handle used esp. as a clothes brush

whis·ker \'hwis-kər\ *n* **1** : one hair of the beard **2** *pl* : the part of the beard that grows on the sides of the face or on the chin **3** : one of the long bristles or hairs growing near the mouth of an animal (as a cat or mouse) — **whis·kered** \-kərd\ *adj*

whis·key *or* **whis·ky** \'hwis-kē\ *n, pl* **whiskeys** *or* **whiskies** [Ir *uisce beathadh* & ScGael *uisge beatha*, lit., water of life] : a liquor distilled from the fermented mash of grain (as rye, corn, or barley)

¹whis·per \'hwis-pər\ *vb* **1** : to speak very low or under the breath; *also* : to tell or utter by whispering ⟨∼ a secret⟩ **2** : to make a low rustling sound ⟨∼ing leaves⟩

²whisper *n* **1** : something communicated by or as if by whispering : HINT, RUMOR **2** : an act or instance of whispering

whist \'hwist\ *n* : a card game played by four players in two partnerships with a deck of 52 cards

¹whis·tle \'hwi-səl\ *n* **1** : a device by which a shrill sound is produced ⟨steam ∼⟩ ⟨tin ∼⟩ **2** : a shrill clear sound made by forcing breath out or air in through the puckered lips **3** : the sound or signal produced by a whistle or as if by whistling **4** : the shrill clear note of an animal (as a bird)

²whistle *vb* **whis·tled; whis·tling 1** : to utter a shrill clear sound by blowing or drawing air through the puckered lips **2** : to utter a shrill note or call resembling a whistle **3** : to make a shrill clear sound esp. by rapid movements ⟨the wind *whistled*⟩ **4** : to blow or sound a whistle **5** : to signal or call by a whistle **6** : to produce, utter, or express by whistling ⟨∼ a tune⟩ — **whis·tler** *n*

whis·tle–blow·er \'hwi-səl-ˌblō-ər\ *n* : INFORMER

whis·tle–stop \-ˌstäp\ *n* : a brief personal appearance by a political candidate orig. on the rear platform of a touring train

whit \'hwit\ *n* [prob. alter. of ME *wiht, wight* creature, thing, fr. OE *wiht*] : the smallest part or particle : BIT

¹white \'hwīt\ *adj* **whit·er; whit·est 1** : free from color **2** : of the color of new snow or milk; *esp* : of the color white **3** : light or pallid in color ⟨lips ∼ with fear⟩ **4** : SILVERY; *also* : made of silver **5** : of, relating to, or being a member of a group or race characterized by light-colored skin **6** : free from spot or blemish : PURE, INNOCENT **7** : BLANK **2** ⟨∼ space in printed matter⟩ **8** : not intended to cause harm ⟨a ∼ lie⟩ **9** : wearing white ⟨∼ friars⟩ **10** : marked by snow ⟨∼ Christmas⟩ **11** : consisting of a wide range of frequencies ⟨∼ light⟩ — **white·ness** \-nəs\ *n* — **whit·ish** \'hwī-tish\ *adj*

²white *n* **1** : the color of maximal lightness that characterizes objects which both reflect and transmit light : the opposite of black **2** : a white or light-colored part or thing ⟨the ∼ of an egg⟩; *also, pl* : white garments **3** : the light-colored pieces in a 2-player board game; *also* : the person by whom these are played **4** : one that is or ap-

proaches the color white **5** : a person of a light-skinned race

white ant *n* : TERMITE

white blood cell *n* : a colorless blood cell (as a lymphocyte) that does not contain hemoglobin but does have a nucleus

white–bread \'hwīt-'bred\ *adj* : being, typical of, or having qualities (as blandness) associated with the white middle class

white·cap \'hwīt-ˌkap\ *n* : a wave crest breaking into white foam

white chocolate *n* : a whitish chocolate candy

white–col·lar \'hwīt-'kä-lər\ *adj* : of, relating to, or constituting the class of salaried workers whose duties do not require the wearing of work clothes or protective clothing

white dwarf *n* : a small very dense whitish star of low luminosity

white elephant *n* **1** : an Indian elephant of a pale color that is sometimes venerated in India, Sri Lanka, Thailand, and Myanmar **2** : something requiring much care and expense and giving little profit or enjoyment

white feather *n* [fr. the superstition that a white feather in the plumage of a gamecock is a mark of a poor fighter] : a mark or symbol of cowardice

white·fish \'hwīt-ˌfish\ *n* : any of various freshwater food fishes related to the salmons and trouts

white flag *n* : a flag of pure white used to signify truce or surrender

white gold *n* : a pale alloy of gold resembling platinum in appearance

white goods *n pl* : white fabrics or articles (as sheets or towels) typically made of cotton or linen

White·hall \'hwīt-ˌhòl\ *n* : the British government

white·head \-ˌhed\ *n* : a small whitish lump in the skin due to retention of secretion in an oil gland duct

white heat *n* : a temperature higher than red heat at which a body becomes brightly incandescent

white–hot *adj* **1** : being at or radiating white heat **2** : FERVID

White House \-ˌhaus\ *n* **1** : the executive department of the U.S. government **2** : a residence of the president of the U.S.

white lead *n* : a heavy white poisonous carbonate of lead used esp. as a pigment in exterior paints

white matter *n* : whitish nerve tissue that consists largely of nerve-cell processes enclosed in a fatty material and that lies under the gray matter of the brain and spinal cord or is collected into nerves

whit·en \'hwīt-ᵊn\ *vb* : to make or become white **syn** blanch, bleach — **whit·en·er** *n*

white pine *n* : a tall-growing pine of eastern No. America with needles in clusters of five; *also* : its wood

white sale *n* : a sale on white goods

white shark *n* : GREAT WHITE SHARK

white slave *n* : a woman or girl held unwillingly for purposes of prostitution — **white slavery** *n*

white·tail \'hwīt-ˌtāl\ *n* : WHITE-TAILED DEER

white–tailed deer *n* : a No. American deer with a rather long tail white on the underside the males of which have forward-arching antlers

white·wall \'hwīt-ˌwòl\ *n* : an automobile tire having a white band on the sidewall

¹white·wash \-ˌwòsh, -ˌwäsh\ *vb* **1** : to whiten with whitewash **2** : to clear of a charge of wrongdoing by offering excuses, hiding facts, or conducting a perfunctory investigation **3** : SHUT OUT **2**

²whitewash *n* **1** : a liquid mixture (as of lime and water)

\ə\abut \ᵊ\kitten \ər\further \a\ash \ā\ace \ä\mop, mar \aù\out \ch\chin \e\bet \ē\easy \g\go \i\hit \ī\ice \j\job \ŋ\sing \ō\go \ò\law \òi\boy \th\thin \t̲h̲\the \ü\loot \ù\foot \y\yet \zh\vision *see also* Pronunciation Symbols page

for whitening a surface **2** : a clearing of wrongdoing by whitewashing

white·wood \-ˌwu̇d\ *n* : any of various trees and esp. a tulip tree having light-colored wood; *also* : such wood

¹whith·er \ˈhwi-t͟hər\ *adv* **1** : to what place **2** : to what situation, position, degree, or end ⟨∼ will this drive him⟩

²whither *conj* **1** : to the place at, in, or to which; *also* : to which place **2** : to whatever place

whith·er·so·ev·er \ˌhwi-t͟hər-sō-ˈe-vər\ *conj* : to whatever place

¹whit·ing \ˈhwī-tiŋ\ *n* : any of several usu. light or silvery food fishes (as a hake) found mostly near seacoasts

²whiting *n* : calcium carbonate in powdered form used esp. as a pigment and in putty

whit·low \ˈhwit-ˌlō\ *n* : a deep inflammation of a finger or toe with pus formation

Whit·sun·day \ˈhwit-ˈsən-dē, -sən-ˌdā\ *n* [ME *Whitsonday*, fr. OE *hwīta sunnandæg*, lit., white Sunday; prob. fr. the custom of wearing white robes by those newly baptized at this season] : PENTECOST

whit·tle \ˈhwit-ᵊl\ *vb* **whit·tled**; **whit·tling 1** : to pare or cut off chips from the surface of (wood) with a knife; *also* : to cut or shape by such paring **2** : to reduce as if by paring down ⟨∼ down expenses⟩

¹whiz *or* **whizz** \ˈhwiz\ *vb* **whizzed**; **whiz·zing** : to hum, whir, or hiss like a speeding object (as an arrow or ball) passing through air

²whiz *or* **whizz** *n, pl* **whiz·zes** : a hissing, buzzing, or whizzing sound

³whiz *n, pl* **whiz·zes** : WIZARD 2

who \ˈhü\ *pron* **1** : what or which person or persons ⟨∼ did it⟩ ⟨∼ is he⟩ ⟨∼ are they⟩ **2** : the person or persons that ⟨knows ∼ did it⟩ **3** — used to introduce a relative clause and to serve as a substitute therein for the substantive modified by the clause ⟨the man ∼ lives there is rich⟩

WHO *abbr* World Health Organization

whoa \ˈwō, ˈhwō, ˈhō\ *vb imper* — a command to an animal to stand still

who·dun·it *also* **who·dun·nit** \hü-ˈdə-nət\ *n* : a detective or mystery story

who·ev·er \hü-ˈe-vər\ *pron* : whatever person : no matter who

¹whole \ˈhōl\ *adj* [ME *hool* healthy, unhurt, entire, fr. OE *hāl*] **1** : being in healthy or sound condition : free from defect or damage **2** : having all its proper parts or elements ⟨∼ milk⟩ **3** : constituting the total sum of : ENTIRE ⟨owns the ∼ island⟩ **4** : each or all of the ⟨the ∼ family⟩ **5** : not scattered or divided : CONCENTRATED ⟨gave me his ∼ attention⟩ **6** : seemingly complete or total ⟨the ∼ idea is to help, not hinder⟩ **syn** perfect, intact, sound — **whole·ness** *n*

²whole *n* **1** : a complete amount or sum **2** : something whole or entire — **on the whole 1** : in view of all the circumstances or conditions **2** : in general

whole·heart·ed \ˈhōl-ˈhär-təd\ *adj* : undivided in purpose, enthusiasm, or will : HEARTY, ZESTFUL, SINCERE

whole note *n* : a musical note equal to one measure of four beats

whole number *n* : any of the set of nonnegative integers; *also* : INTEGER

¹whole·sale \ˈhōl-ˌsāl\ *n* : the sale of goods in quantity usu. for resale by a retail merchant

²wholesale *adj* **1** : performed on a large scale without discrimination ⟨∼ slaughter⟩ **2** : of, relating to, or engaged in wholesaling — **wholesale** *adv*

³wholesale *vb* **whole·saled**; **whole·sal·ing** : to sell at wholesale — **whole·sal·er** *n*

whole·some \ˈhōl-səm\ *adj* **1** : promoting mental, spiritual, or bodily health or well-being ⟨a ∼ environment⟩ **2** : sound in body, mind, or morals : HEALTHY **3** : PRUDENT ⟨∼ respect for the law⟩ — **whole·some·ness** *n*

whole step *n* : a musical interval comprising two half steps (as C–D or F♯–G♯)

whole wheat *adj* : made of ground entire wheat kernels

whol·ly \ˈhōl-lē\ *adv* **1** : COMPLETELY, TOTALLY **2** : SOLELY, EXCLUSIVELY

whom \ˈhüm\ *pron, objective case of* WHO

whom·ev·er \hü-ˈme-vər\ *pron, objective case of* WHOEVER

whom·so·ev·er \ˌhüm-sō-ˈe-vər\ *pron, objective case of* WHOSOEVER

¹whoop \ˈhwu̇p, ˈhwùp, ˈhüp, ˈhu̇p\ *vb* **1** : to shout or call loudly and vigorously **2** : to make the characteristic whoop of whooping cough **3** : to go or pass with a loud noise **4** : to utter or express with a whoop; *also* : to urge, drive, or cheer with a whoop

²whoop *n* **1** : a whooping sound or utterance : SHOUT, HOOT **2** : a crowing intake of breath after a fit of coughing in whooping cough

whooping cough *n* : an infectious bacterial disease esp. of children marked by convulsive coughing fits often followed by a shrill gasping intake of breath

whooping crane *n* : a large white nearly extinct No. American crane noted for its loud whooping call

whooping crane

whoop·la \ˈhwu̇p-ˌlä, ˈhwu̇p-\ *n* **1** : HOOPLA **2** : boisterous merrymaking

whop·per \ˈhwä-pər\ *n* : something unusually large or extreme of its kind; *esp* : a monstrous lie

whop·ping \ˈhwä-piŋ\ *adj* : extremely large

whore \ˈhȯr\ *n* : PROSTITUTE

whorl \ˈhwȯrl, ˈhwərl\ *n* **1** : a group of parts (as leaves or petals) encircling an axis and esp. a plant stem **2** : something that whirls or coils around a center : COIL, SPIRAL **3** : one of the turns of a snail shell

whorled \ˈhwȯrld, ˈhwərld\ *adj* : having or arranged in whorls

¹whose \ˈhüz\ *adj* : of or relating to whom or which esp. as possessor or possessors, agent or agents, or object or objects of an action ⟨asked ∼ bag it was⟩

²whose *pron* : whose one or ones ⟨∼ is this car⟩ ⟨∼ are those books⟩

who·so \ˈhü-ˌsō\ *pron* : WHOEVER

who·so·ev·er \ˌhü-sō-ˈe-vər\ *pron* : WHOEVER

whs *or* **whse** *abbr* warehouse

whsle *abbr* wholesale

¹why \ˈhwī\ *adv* : for what reason, cause, or purpose ⟨∼ did you do it?⟩

²why *conj* **1** : the cause, reason, or purpose for which ⟨that is ∼ you did it⟩ **2** : for which : on account of which ⟨knows the reason ∼ you did it⟩

³why *n, pl* **whys** : REASON, CAUSE ⟨the ∼s of racial prejudice⟩

⁴why \ˈwī, ˈhwī\ *interj* — used to express surprise, hesitation, approval, disapproval, or impatience ⟨∼, here's what I was looking for⟩

WI *abbr* **1** West Indies **2** Wisconsin

WIA *abbr* wounded in action

wick \ˈwik\ *n* : a loosely bound bundle of soft fibers that draws up oil, tallow, or wax to be burned in a candle, oil lamp, or stove

wick·ed \'wi-kəd\ *adj* **1** : morally bad : EVIL, SINFUL **2** : FIERCE, VICIOUS **3** : ROGUISH ⟨a ~ glance⟩ **4** : REPUGNANT, VILE ⟨a ~ odor⟩ **5** : HARMFUL, DANGEROUS ⟨a ~ attack⟩ **6** : impressively excellent ⟨throws a ~ fastball⟩ — **wick·ed·ly** *adv* — **wick·ed·ness** *n*

wick·er \'wi-kər\ *n* **1** : a small pliant branch (as an osier or a withe) **2** : WICKERWORK — **wicker** *adj*

wick·er·work \-ˌwərk\ *n* : work made of osiers, twigs, or rods : BASKETRY

wick·et \'wi-kət\ *n* **1** : a small gate or door; *esp* : one forming a part of or placed near a larger one **2** : a window-like opening usu. with a grille or grate (as at a ticket office) **3** : a set of three upright rods topped by two crosspieces bowled at in cricket **4** : an arch or hoop in croquet

wick·i·up \'wi-kē-ˌəp\ *n* : a hut used by nomadic Indians of the western and southwestern U.S. with a usu. oval base and a rough frame covered with reed mats, grass, or brushwood

wid *abbr* widow, widower

¹wide \'wīd\ *adj* **wider; wid·est 1** : covering a vast area **2** : measured across or at right angles to the length **3** : not narrow : BROAD; *also* : ROOMY **4** : opened to full width ⟨eyes ~ with wonder⟩ **5** : not limited : EXTENSIVE ⟨~ experience⟩ **6** : far from the goal, mark, or truth ⟨a ~ guess⟩ — **wide·ly** *adv*

²wide *adv* **wid·er; wid·est 1** : over a great distance or extent : WIDELY ⟨searched far and ~⟩ **2** : over a specified distance, area, or extent **3** : so as to leave a wide space between ⟨~ apart⟩ **4** : so as to clear by a considerable distance ⟨ran ~ around left end⟩ **5** : COMPLETELY, FULLY ⟨opened her eyes ~⟩

wide–awake \ˌwīd-ə-ˈwāk\ *adj* : fully awake; *also* : KNOWING, ALERT

wide–body \'wīd-ˌbä-dē\ *n* : a large jet aircraft

wide–eyed \'wīd-ˈīd\ *adj* **1** : having the eyes wide open esp. with wonder or astonishment **2** : NAIVE

wide·mouthed \-ˈmau̇thd, -ˈmau̇tht\ *adj* **1** : having one's mouth opened wide (as in awe) **2** : having a wide mouth ⟨~ jars⟩

wid·en \'wīd-ᵊn\ *vb* : to increase in width, scope, or extent

wide·spread \'wīd-ˈspred\ *adj* **1** : widely scattered or prevalent **2** : widely extended or spread out ⟨~ wings⟩

¹wid·ow \'wi-dō\ *n* : a woman who has lost her husband by death and has not married again — **wid·ow·hood** *n*

²widow *vb* : to cause to become a widow or widower

wid·ow·er \'wi-də-wər\ *n* : a man who has lost his wife by death and has not married again

width \'width\ *n* **1** : a distance from side to side : the measurement taken at right angles to the length : BREADTH **2** : largeness of extent or scope; *also* : FULLNESS **3** : a measured and cut piece of material ⟨a ~ of calico⟩

wield \'wēld\ *vb* **1** : to use or handle esp. effectively ⟨~ a broom⟩ **2** : to exert authority by means of : EMPLOY ⟨~ influence⟩ — **wield·er** *n*

wie·ner \'wē-nər\ *n* [short for *wienerwurst*, fr. G, lit., Vienna sausage] : FRANKFURTER

wife \'wīf\ *n, pl* **wives** \'wīvz\ **1** *dial* : WOMAN **2** : a woman acting in a specified capacity — used in combination **3** : a female partner in a marriage — **wife·hood** *n* — **wife·less** *adj* — **wife·ly** *adj*

wig \'wig\ *n* [short for *periwig*, fr. MF *perruque*, fr. It *parrucca, perrucca* hair, wig] : a manufactured covering of natural or synthetic hair for the head; *also* : TOUPEE

wi·geon *or* **wid·geon** \'wi-jən\ *n, pl* **wigeon** *or* **wigeons** *or* **widgeon** *or* **widgeons** : any of several medium-sized freshwater ducks

wig·gle \'wi-gəl\ *vb* **wig·gled; wig·gling 1** : to move to

and fro with quick jerky or shaking movements : JIGGLE **2** : WRIGGLE — **wiggle** *n*

wig·gler \'wi-glər, -gə-lər\ *n* **1** : a larva or pupa of a mosquito **2** : one that wiggles

wig·gly \'wi-glē, -gə-lē\ *adj* **1** : tending to wiggle ⟨a ~ worm⟩ **2** : WAVY ⟨~ lines⟩

wight \'wīt\ *n* : a living being : CREATURE

wig·let \'wi-glət\ *n* : a small wig used esp. to enhance a hairstyle

¹wig·wag \'wig-ˌwag\ *vb* **1** : to signal by or as if by a flag or light waved according to a code **2** : to make or cause to make a signal (as with the hand or arm)

²wigwag *n* : the art or practice of wigwagging

wig·wam \'wig-ˌwäm\ *n* : a hut of the Indians of the eastern U.S. having typically an arched framework of poles overlaid with bark, rush mats, or hides

¹wild \'wīld\ *adj* **1** : living in a state of nature and not ordinarily tamed ⟨~ ducks⟩ **2** : growing or produced without human aid or care ⟨~ honey⟩ ⟨~ plants⟩ **3** : WASTE, DESOLATE ⟨~ country⟩ **4** : UNCONTROLLED, UNRESTRAINED, UNRULY ⟨~ passions⟩ ⟨a ~ young stallion⟩ **5** : TURBULENT, STORMY ⟨a ~ night⟩ **6** : EXTRAVAGANT, FANTASTIC, CRAZY ⟨~ ideas⟩ **7** : indicative of strong passion, desire, or emotion ⟨a ~ stare⟩ **8** : UNCIVILIZED, SAVAGE **9** : deviating from the natural or expected course : ERRATIC ⟨a ~ throw⟩ **10** : having a denomination determined by the holder ⟨deuces ~⟩ — **wild·ly** *adv* — **wild·ness** *n*

²wild *adv* **1** : WILDLY **2** : without regulation or control ⟨running ~⟩

³wild *n* **1** : WILDERNESS **2** : a natural or undomesticated state or existence

wild boar *n* : an Old World wild hog from which most domestic swine have been derived

wild carrot *n* : QUEEN ANNE'S LACE

¹wild·cat \'wīld-ˌkat\ *n, pl* **wildcats 1** : any of various small or medium-sized cats (as a lynx or ocelot) **2** : a quick-tempered hard-fighting person

²wildcat *adj* **1** : not sound or safe ⟨~ schemes⟩ **2** : initiated by a group of workers without formal union approval ⟨~ strike⟩

³wildcat *vb* **wild·cat·ted; wild·cat·ting** : to drill an oil or gas well in a region not known to be productive

wil·de·beest \'wil-də-ˌbēst\ *n, pl* **wildebeests** *also* **wildebeest** [Afrikaans *wildebees*, fr. *wilde* wild + *bees* ox] : GNU

wil·der·ness \'wil-dər-nəs\ *n* [ME, fr. *wildern* wild, fr. OE *wilddēoren* of wild beasts] : an uncultivated and uninhabited region

wild·fire \'wīld-ˌfīr\ *n* : an uncontrollable fire — **like wildfire** : very rapidly

wild·fowl \-ˌfau̇l\ *n* : a bird and esp. a waterfowl (as a wild duck or goose) hunted as game

wild–goose chase *n* : the pursuit of something unattainable

wild·life \'wīld-ˌlīf\ *n* : nonhuman living things and esp. wild animals living in their natural environment

wild oat *n* **1** : any of several wild grasses **2** *pl* : offenses and indiscretions attributed to youthful exuberance — usu. used in the phrase *sow one's wild oats*

wild rice *n* : a No. American aquatic grass; *also* : its edible seed

wild·wood \'wīld-ˌwu̇d\ *n* : a wood unaltered or unfrequented by humans

¹wile \'wīl\ *n* **1** : a trick or stratagem intended to ensnare or deceive; *also* : a playful trick **2** : TRICKERY, GUILE

²wile *vb* **wiled; wil·ing** : LURE, ENTICE

¹will \'wil\ *vb, past* **would** \'wu̇d\; *pres sing & pl* **will 1**

\ə\abut \ᵊ\kitten \ər\further \a\ash \ā\ace \ä\mop, mar \au̇\out \ch\chin \e\bet \ē\easy \g\go \i\hit \ī\ice \j\job \ŋ\sing \ō\go \ȯ\law \ȯi\boy \th\thin \th\the \ü\loot \u̇\foot \y\yet \zh\vision *see also* Pronunciation Symbols page

: WISH, DESIRE ⟨call it what you ∼⟩ **2** — used as an auxiliary verb to express (1) desire, willingness, or in negative constructions refusal ⟨∼ you have another⟩ ⟨he *won't* do it⟩, (2) customary or habitual action ⟨∼ get angry over nothing⟩, (3) simple futurity ⟨tomorrow we ∼ go shopping⟩, (4) capability or sufficiency ⟨the back seat ∼ hold three⟩, (5) determination or willfulness ⟨I ∼ go despite them⟩, (6) probability ⟨that ∼ be the mailman⟩, (7) inevitability ⟨accidents ∼ happen⟩, or (8) a command ⟨you ∼ do as I say⟩

²will *n* **1** : wish or desire often combined with determination ⟨the ∼ to win⟩ **2** : something desired; *esp* : a choice or determination of one having authority or power **3** : the act, process, or experience of willing : VOLITION **4** : the mental powers manifested as wishing, choosing, desiring, or intending **5** : a disposition to act according to principles or ends **6** : power of controlling one's own actions or emotions ⟨a leader of iron ∼⟩ **7** : a legal document in which a person declares to whom his or her possessions are to go after death

³will *vb* **1** : to dispose of by or as if by a will : BEQUEATH **2** : to determine by an act of choice; *also* : DECREE, ORDAIN **3** : INTEND, PURPOSE; *also* : CHOOSE

will·ful *or* **wil·ful** \'wil-fəl\ *adj* **1** : governed by will without regard to reason : OBSTINATE **2** : INTENTIONAL ⟨∼ murder⟩ — **will·ful·ly** *adv*

wil·lies \'wi-lēz\ *n pl* : a fit of nervousness : JITTERS — used with *the*

will·ing \'wi-liŋ\ *adj* **1** : inclined or favorably disposed in mind : READY ⟨∼ to go⟩ **2** : prompt to act or respond ⟨∼ workers⟩ **3** : done, borne, or accepted voluntarily or without reluctance **4** : of or relating to the will : VOLITIONAL — **will·ing·ly** *adv* — **will·ing·ness** *n*

wil·li·waw \'wi-lē-ˌwȯ\ *n* : a sudden violent gust of cold land air common along mountainous coasts of high latitudes

will-o'-the-wisp \ˌwil-ə-thə-'wisp\ *n* **1** : a light that appears at night over marshy grounds **2** : a misleading or elusive goal or hope

wil·low \'wi-lō\ *n* **1** : any of a genus of quick-growing shrubs and trees with tough pliable shoots **2** : an object made of willow wood

wil·low·ware \-ˌwar\ *n* : dinnerware that is usu. blue and white and that is decorated with a story-telling design featuring a large willow tree by a little bridge

wil·lowy \'wi-lə-wē\ *adj* : PLIANT; *also* : gracefully tall and slender

will·pow·er \'wil-ˌpau̇-ər\ *n* : energetic determination : RESOLUTENESS

wil·ly-nil·ly \ˌwi-lē-'ni-lē\ *adv or adj* [alter. of *will I nill I* or *will ye nill ye* or *will he nill he*; *nill* fr. archaic *nill* to be unwilling, fr. ME *nilen*, fr. OE *nyllan*, fr. *ne* not + *wyllan* to wish] : without regard for one's choice : by compulsion ⟨they rushed us along ∼⟩

¹wilt \'wilt\ *vb* **1** : to lose or cause to lose freshness and become limp esp. from lack of water : DROOP **2** : to grow weak or faint : LANGUISH

²wilt *n* : any of various plant disorders marked by wilting and often shriveling

wily \'wī-lē\ *adj* **wil·i·er; -est** : full of guile : TRICKY — **wil·i·ness** \-lē-nəs\ *n*

wimp \'wimp\ *n* : a weak, cowardly, or ineffectual person — **wimpy** \'wim-pē\ *adj*

¹wim·ple \'wim-pəl\ *n* : a cloth covering worn over the head and around the neck and chin by women esp. in the late medieval period and by some nuns

²wimple *vb* **wim·pled; wim·pling 1** : to cover with or as if with a wimple **2** : to ripple or cause to ripple

¹win \'win\ *vb* **won** \'wən\; **win·ning** [ME *winnen*, fr. OE *winnan* to struggle] **1** : to get possession of esp. by effort : GAIN; *also* : to obtain by work : EARN **2** : to gain in or as if in battle or contest; *also* : to be the victor in

⟨*won* the war⟩ **3** : to solicit and gain the favor of; *esp* : to induce to accept oneself in marriage

²win *n* : VICTORY; *esp* : 1st place at the finish (as of a horse race)

wince \'wins\ *vb* **winced; winc·ing** : to shrink back involuntarily (as from pain) : FLINCH — **wince** *n*

winch \'winch\ *n* : a machine that has a drum on which is wound a rope or cable for hauling or hoisting — **winch** *vb*

¹wind \'wind\ *n* **1** : a movement of the air **2** : a prevailing force or influence : TENDENCY, TREND **3** : BREATH ⟨he had the ∼ knocked out of him⟩ **4** : gas produced in the stomach or intestines **5** : something insubstantial; *esp* : idle words **6** : air carrying a scent (as of game) **7** : INTIMATION ⟨they got ∼ of our plans⟩ **8** : WIND INSTRUMENTS; *also*, *pl* : players of wind instruments

²wind *vb* **1** : to get a scent of ⟨the dogs ∼*ed* the game⟩ **2** : to cause to be out of breath ⟨he was ∼*ed* from the climb⟩ **3** : to allow (as a horse) to rest so as to recover breath

³wind \'wīnd, 'wind\ *vb* **wind·ed** \'wīn-dəd, 'win-\ *or* **wound** \'wau̇nd\; **wind·ing** : to sound by blowing ⟨∼ a horn⟩

⁴wind \'wīnd\ *vb* **wound** \'wau̇nd\ *also* **wind·ed; wind·ing 1** : ENTANGLE, INVOLVE **2** : to introduce stealthily : INSINUATE **3** : to encircle or cover with something pliable : WRAP, COIL, TWINE ⟨∼ a bobbin⟩ **4** : to hoist or haul by a rope or chain and a winch **5** : to tighten the spring of; *also* : CRANK **6** : to raise to a high level (as of excitement) **7** : to cause to move in a curving line or path **8** : to have a curving course or shape ⟨a river ∼*ing* through the valley⟩ **9** : to move or lie so as to encircle

⁵wind \'wīnd\ *n* : COIL, TURN

wind·age \'win-dij\ *n* : the influence of the wind in deflecting the course of a projectile through the air; *also* : the amount of such deflection

wind·bag \'wind-ˌbag\ *n* : an overly talkative person

wind·blown \-ˌblōn\ *adj* : blown by the wind; *also* : having the appearance of being blown by the wind

wind·break \-ˌbrāk\ *n* : a growth of trees or shrubs serving to break the force of the wind; *also* : a shelter from the wind

wind·break·er \-ˌbrā-kər\ *n* : a light jacket made of material that can resist the wind

wind–bro·ken \-ˌbrō-kən\ *adj* : having the power of breathing impaired by disease — used of a horse

wind·burned \-ˌbərnd\ *adj* : irritated and inflamed by exposure to the wind — **wind·burn** \-ˌbərn\ *n*

wind·chill \-ˌchil\ *n* : a still-air temperature that would have the same cooling effect on exposed human skin as a given combination of temperature and wind speed

windchill factor *n* : WINDCHILL

wind·er \'wīn-dər\ *n* : one that winds

wind·fall \'wind-ˌfȯl\ *n* **1** : something (as a tree or fruit) blown down by the wind **2** : an unexpected or sudden gift, gain, or advantage

wind·flow·er \-ˌflau̇-ər\ *n* : ANEMONE

¹wind·ing \'wīn-diŋ\ *n* : material (as wire) wound or coiled about an object

²winding *adj* **1** : having a pronounced curve or spiral ⟨∼ stairs⟩ **2** : having a course that winds ⟨a ∼ road⟩

wind·ing–sheet \-ˌshēt\ *n* : SHROUD

wind instrument *n* : a musical instrument (as a flute or horn) sounded by wind and esp. by the breath

wind·jam·mer \'wind-ˌja-mər\ *n* : a sailing ship; *also* : one of its crew

wind·lass \'wind-ləs\ *n* [ME *wyndlas*, alter. of *wyndas*, fr. ON *vindāss*, fr. *vinda* to wind + *āss* pole] : a winch used esp. on ships for hoisting or hauling

wind·mill \'wind-ˌmil\ *n* : a mill or machine worked by the wind turning sails or vanes that radiate from a central shaft

win·dow \'win-dō\ *n* [ME *windowe*, fr. ON *vindauga*, fr.

vindr wind + *auga* eye] **1** : an opening in the wall of a building to let in light and air; *also* : the framework with fittings that closes such an opening **2** : WINDOWPANE **3** : an opening resembling or suggesting that of a window in a building **4** : an interval of time during which certain conditions or an opportunity exists **5** : an area of a computer display on which different information may be displayed independently — **win·dow·less** *adj*

window box *n* : a box for growing plants in or by a window

window dressing *n* **1** : display of merchandise in a store window **2** : a showing made to create a deceptively favorable impression

win·dow·pane \'win-dō-ˌpān\ *n* : a pane in a window

win·dow–shop \-ˌshäp\ *vb* : to look at the displays in store windows without going inside the stores to make purchases — **win·dow–shop·per** *n*

win·dow·sill \-ˌsil\ *n* : the horizontal member at the bottom of a window

wind·pipe \'wind-ˌpīp\ *n* : the passage for the breath from the larynx to the lungs

wind·proof \-'prüf\ *adj* : impervious to wind ⟨a ∼ jacket⟩

wind·row \'wind-ˌrō\ *n* **1** : hay raked up into a row to dry **2** : a row of something (as dry leaves) swept up by or as if by the wind

wind shear *n* : a radical shift in wind speed and direction that occurs over a very short distance

wind·shield \'wind-ˌshēld\ *n* : a transparent screen (as of glass) in front of the occupants of a vehicle

wind sock *n* : an open-ended truncated cloth cone mounted in an elevated position to indicate wind direction

wind·storm \-ˌstȯrm\ *n* : a storm with high wind and little or no rain

wind·surf·ing \-ˌsər-fiŋ\ *n* : the sport or activity of riding a sailboard — **wind·surf** \-ˌsərf\ *vb* — **wind·surf·er** *n*

wind·swept \'wind-ˌswept\ *adj* : swept by or as if by wind ⟨∼ plains⟩

wind tunnel *n* : an enclosed passage through which air is blown to investigate air flow around an object

wind–up \'wīn-ˌdəp\ *n* **1** : CONCLUSION, FINISH **2** : a series of regular and distinctive motions made by a pitcher preliminary to delivering a pitch

wind up *vb* **1** : to bring or come to a conclusion : END **2** : to put in order for the purpose of bringing to an end **3** : to arrive in a place, situation, or condition at the end or as a result of a course of action ⟨*wound up* as paupers⟩ **4** : to make a pitching windup

¹**wind·ward** \'win-dwərd\ *n* : the side or direction from which the wind is blowing

²**windward** *adj* : being in or facing the direction from which the wind is blowing

windy \'win-dē\ *adj* **wind·i·er; -est 1** : having wind : exposed to winds ⟨a ∼ day⟩ ⟨a ∼ prairie⟩ **2** : STORMY **3** : FLATULENT **4** : indulging in or characterized by useless talk : VERBOSE

¹**wine** \'wīn\ *n* **1** : fermented grape juice used as a beverage **2** : the usu. fermented juice of a plant product (as fruit) used as a beverage ⟨rice ∼⟩

²**wine** *vb* **wined; win·ing** : to treat to or drink wine

wine cellar *n* : a room for storing wines; *also* : a stock of wines

wine·grow·er \-ˌgrō-ər\ *n* : one that cultivates a vineyard and makes wine

wine·press \-ˌpres\ *n* : a vat in which juice is pressed from grapes

¹**wing** \'wiŋ\ *n* **1** : one of the movable feathered or membranous paired appendages by means of which a bird, bat, or insect flies **2** : something suggesting a wing : an airfoil that develops the lift which supports an aircraft in flight **3** : a plant or animal appendage or part likened to a wing **4** : a turned-back or extended edge on

an article of clothing **5** : a means of flight or rapid progress **6** : the act or manner of flying : FLIGHT **7** *pl* : the area at the side of the stage out of sight **8** : one of the positions or players on either side of a center position or line **9** : either of two opposing groups within an organization : FACTION **10** : a unit in military aviation consisting of two or more squadrons — **wing·less** *adj* — **on the wing** : in flight : FLYING — **under one's wing** : in one's charge or care

²**wing** *vb* **1** : to fit with wings; *also* : to enable to fly easily **2** : to pass through in flight : FLY ⟨∼ the air⟩ ⟨swallows ∼*ing* southward⟩ **3** : to let fly : DISPATCH **4** : to wound in the wing ⟨∼ a bird⟩; *also* : to wound without killing **5** : to perform without preparation : IMPROVISE ⟨∼*ing* it⟩

wing·ding \'wiŋ-ˌdiŋ\ *n* : a wild, lively, or lavish party

winged \'wiŋd, 'wiŋ-əd, *in compounds* 'wiŋd\ *adj* **1** : having wings esp. of a specified character **2** : soaring with or as if with wings : ELEVATED **3** : SWIFT, RAPID

wing·span \'wiŋ-ˌspan\ *n* : the distance between the tips of a pair of wings

wing·spread \-ˌspred\ *n* : the spread of the wings; *esp* : the distance between the tips of the fully extended wings of a winged animal

¹**wink** \'wiŋk\ *vb* **1** : to close and open one eye quickly as a signal or hint **2** : to close and open the eyes quickly : BLINK **3** : to avoid seeing or noticing something ⟨∼ at a traffic violation⟩ **4** : TWINKLE, FLICKER — **wink·er** \'wiŋ-kər\ *n*

²**wink** *n* **1** : a brief period of sleep : NAP **2** : an act of winking; *esp* : a hint or sign given by winking **3** : INSTANT ⟨dries in a ∼⟩

win·ner \'wi-nər\ *n* : one that wins

¹**win·ning** \'wi-niŋ\ *n* **1** : VICTORY **2** : something won; *esp* : money won at gambling ⟨large ∼s⟩

²**winning** *adj* **1** : successful esp. in competition **2** : ATTRACTIVE, CHARMING

win·now \'wi-nō\ *vb* **1** : to remove (as chaff) by a current of air; *also* : to free (as grain) from waste in this manner **2** : to sort or separate as if by winnowing

wino \'wī-nō\ *n, pl* **win·os** : one who is addicted to drinking wine

win·some \'win-səm\ *adj* [ME *winsum,* fr. OE *wynsum,* fr. *wynn* joy] **1** : generally pleasing and engaging **2** : CHEERFUL, GAY — **win·some·ly** *adv* — **win·some·ness** *n*

¹**win·ter** \'win-tər\ *n* : the season of the year in any region in which the noonday sun shines most obliquely : the coldest period of the year

²**winter** *adj* : sown in autumn for harvesting in the following spring or summer ⟨∼ wheat⟩

win·ter·green \'win-tər-ˌgrēn\ *n* **1** : a low evergreen plant of the heath family with white bell-shaped flowers and spicy red berries **2** : an aromatic oil from the common wintergreen or its flavor or something flavored with it

win·ter·ize \'win-tə-ˌrīz\ *vb* **-ized; -iz·ing** : to make ready for winter

win·ter–kill \'win-tər-ˌkil\ *vb* : to kill or die by exposure to winter weather

winter squash *n* : any of various hard-shelled squashes that keep well in storage

win·ter·tide \-ˌtīd\ *n* : WINTER

win·ter·time \-ˌtīm\ *n* : WINTER

win·try \'win-trē\ *also* **win·tery** \'win-tə-rē\ *adj* **win·tri·er; -est 1** : of, relating to, or characteristic of winter ⟨∼ weather⟩ **2** : CHILLING, CHEERLESS ⟨a ∼ welcome⟩

¹**wipe** \'wīp\ *vb* **wiped; wip·ing 1** : to clean or dry by rubbing ⟨∼ dishes⟩ **2** : to remove by or as if by rubbing ⟨∼

\ə\abut \ᵊ\kitten \ər\further \a\ash \ā\ace \ä\mop, mar
\au̇\out \ch\chin \e\bet \ē\easy \g\go \i\hit \ī\ice \j\job
\ŋ\sing \ō\go \ȯ\law \ȯi\boy \th\thin \t͟h\the \ü\loot \u̇\foot
\y\yet \zh\vision *see also* Pronunciation Symbols page

away tears⟩ **3** : to erase completely : OBLITERATE **4** : to pass or draw over a surface ⟨*wiped* his hand across his face⟩ — **wip·er** *n*

²**wipe** *n* **1** : an act or instance of wiping; *also* : BLOW, STRIKE, SWIPE **2** : something used for wiping

wipe out *vb* : to destroy completely

¹**wire** \ˈwīr\ *n* **1** : metal in the form of a thread or slender rod; *also* : a thread or rod of metal **2** : hidden or secret influences controlling the action of a person or organization — usu. used in pl. ⟨pull ∼*s*⟩ **3** : a line of wire for conducting electric current **4** : a telegraph or telephone wire or system **5** : TELEGRAM, CABLEGRAM **6** : the finish line of a race

²**wire** *vb* **wired; wir·ing 1** : to provide or equip with wire ⟨∼ a house⟩ **2** : to bind, string, or mount with wire **3** : to send or send word to by telegraph

wire·hair \ˈwīr-ˌhar\ *n* : a wirehaired dog or cat

wire·haired \-ˈhard\ *adj* : having a stiff wiry outer coat of hair

¹**wire·less** \-ləs\ *adj* **1** : having no wire or wires **2** *chiefly Brit* : RADIO

²**wireless** *n* **1** : wireless telegraphy **2** *chiefly Brit* : RADIO

wire–pull·er \-ˌpu̇-lər\ *n* : one who uses secret or underhanded means to influence the acts of a person or organization — **wire–pull·ing** *n*

wire service *n* : a news agency that sends out syndicated news copy to subscribers by wire or satellite

wire·tap \-ˌtap\ *n* : the act or an instance of tapping a telephone or telegraph wire to get information; *also* : an electrical connection used for such tapping — **wiretap** *vb* — **wire·tap·per** \-ˌta-pər\ *n*

wire·worm \-ˌwərm\ *n* : any of various slender hard‗ coated beetle larvae esp. destructive to plant roots

wir·ing \ˈwīr-iŋ\ *n* : a system of wires

wiry \ˈwīr-ē\ *adj* **wir·i·er** \ˈwī-rē-ər\; **-est 1** : made of or resembling wire **2** : slender yet strong and sinewy — **wir·i·ness** \ˈwī-rē-nəs\ *n*

Wis *or* **Wisc** *abbr* Wisconsin

Wisd *abbr* Wisdom

wis·dom \ˈwiz-dəm\ *n* [ME, fr. OE *wīsdom*, fr. *wīs* wise] **1** : accumulated philosophic or scientific learning : KNOWLEDGE; *also* : INSIGHT **2** : good sense : JUDGMENT **3** : a wise attitude or course of action

Wisdom *n* — see BIBLE table

wisdom of Sol·o·mon \-ˈsä-lə-mən\ — see BIBLE table

wisdom tooth *n* : the last tooth of the full set on each half of each human jaw

¹**wise** \ˈwīz\ *n* : WAY, MANNER, FASHION ⟨in no ∼⟩ ⟨in this ∼⟩

²**wise** *adj* **wis·er; wis·est 1** : having wisdom : SAGE **2** : having or showing good sense or good judgment **3** : aware of what is going on : KNOWING; *also* : CRAFTY, SHREWD **4** : possessing inside information — **wise·ly** *adv*

-wise \-ˌwīz\ *adv comb form* : in the manner or direction of ⟨slant*wise*⟩

wise·acre \ˈwī-ˌzā-kər\ *n* [MD *wijssegger* soothsayer] : SMART ALECK

¹**wise·crack** \ˈwīz-ˌkrak\ *n* : a clever, smart, or flippant remark

²**wisecrack** *vb* : to make a wisecrack

¹**wish** \ˈwish\ *vb* **1** : to have a desire : long for ⟨∼ you were here⟩ ⟨∼ for a puppy⟩ **2** : to form or express a wish concerning ⟨∼*ed* him a happy birthday⟩ **3** : BID ⟨he ∼*ed* me good morning⟩ **4** : to request by expressing a desire ⟨I ∼ you to go now⟩

²**wish** *n* **1** : an act or instance of wishing or desire : WANT; *also* : GOAL **2** : an expressed will or desire

wish·bone \-ˌbōn\ *n* : a forked bone in front of the breastbone in most birds

wish·ful \ˈwish-fəl\ *adj* **1** : expressive of a wish; *also* : having a wish **2** : according with wishes rather than fact ⟨∼ thinking⟩

wishy–washy \ˈwi-shē-ˌwȯ-shē, -ˌwä-\ *adj* : WEAK, INSIPID; *also* : morally feeble

wisp \ˈwisp\ *n* **1** : a small handful (as of hay or straw) **2** : a thin strand, strip, or fragment ⟨a ∼ of hair⟩; *also* : a thready streak ⟨a ∼ of smoke⟩ **3** : something frail, slight, or fleeting ⟨a ∼ of a smile⟩ — **wispy** *adj*

wis·te·ria \wis-ˈtir-ē-ə\ *or* **wis·tar·ia** \-ˈtir-ē-ə -ˈter-\ *n* : any of a genus of chiefly Asian mostly woody vines related to the peas and widely grown for their long showy clusters of blue, white, purple, or rose flowers

wist·ful \ˈwist-fəl\ *adj* : feeling or showing a timid desire — **wist·ful·ly** *adv* — **wist·ful·ness** *n*

wit \ˈwit\ *n* **1** : reasoning power : INTELLIGENCE **2** : mental soundness : SANITY — usu. used in pl. **3** : RESOURCEFULNESS, INGENUITY; *esp* : quickness and cleverness in handling words and ideas **4** : a talent for making clever remarks; *also* : a person noted for making witty remarks — **wit·ted** \ˈwi-təd\ *adj* — **at one's wit's end** : at a loss for a means of solving a problem

¹**witch** \ˈwich\ *n* **1** : a person believed to have magic power; *esp* : SORCERESS **2** : an ugly old woman : HAG **3** : a charming or alluring girl or woman

²**witch** *vb* : BEWITCH

witch·craft \ˈwich-ˌkraft\ *n* : the power or practices of a witch : SORCERY

witch doctor *n* : a person in a primitive society who uses magic to treat sickness and to fight off evil spirits

witch·ery \ˈwi-chə-rē\ *n, pl* **-er·ies 1** : SORCERY **2** : FASCINATION, CHARM

witch·grass \ˈwich-ˌgras\ *n* : any of several grasses that are weeds in cultivated areas

witch ha·zel \ˈwich-ˌhā-zəl\ *n* **1** : a shrub of eastern No. America bearing small yellow flowers in the fall **2** : a soothing alcoholic lotion made from witch hazel bark

witch–hunt \ˈwich-ˌhənt\ *n* **1** : a searching out and persecution of persons accused of witchcraft **2** : the searching out and deliberate harassment esp. of political opponents

witch·ing \ˈwi-chiŋ\ *adj* : of, relating to, or suitable for sorcery or supernatural occurrences

with \ˈwith, ˈwith\ *prep* **1** : AGAINST ⟨a fight ∼ his brother⟩ **2** : FROM ⟨parting ∼ friends⟩ **3** : in mutual relation to ⟨talk ∼ a friend⟩ **4** : in the company of ⟨went there ∼ her⟩ **5** : AS REGARDS, TOWARD ⟨is patient ∼ children⟩ **6** : compared to ⟨on equal terms ∼ another⟩ **7** : in support of ⟨I'm ∼ you all the way⟩ **8** : in the presence of : CONTAINING ⟨tea ∼ sugar⟩ **9** : in the opinion of : as judged by ⟨their arguments had weight ∼ her⟩ **10** : BECAUSE OF, THROUGH ⟨pale ∼ anger⟩; *also* : by means of ⟨hit him ∼ a club⟩ **11** : in a manner indicating ⟨work ∼ a will⟩ **12** : GIVEN, GRANTED ⟨∼ your permission I'll leave⟩ **13** : HAVING ⟨came ∼ good news⟩ ⟨stood there ∼ his mouth open⟩ **14** : at the time of : right after ⟨∼ that we left⟩ **15** : DESPITE ⟨∼ all her cleverness, she failed⟩ **16** : in the direction of ⟨swim ∼ the tide⟩

with·al \wi-ˈthȯl, -ˈthȯl\ *adv* **1** : together with this : BESIDES **2** : on the other hand : NEVERTHELESS

with·draw \with-ˈdrȯ, with-\ *vb* **-drew** \-ˈdrü\; **-drawn** \-ˈdrȯn\; **-draw·ing** \-ˈdrȯ-iŋ\ **1** : to take back or away : REMOVE **2** : to call back (as from consideration); *also* : RETRACT **3** : to go away : RETREAT, LEAVE **4** : to terminate one's participation in or use of something

with·draw·al \-ˈdrȯ-əl\ *n* **1** : an act or instance of withdrawing **2** : the discontinuance of the use or administration of a drug and esp. an addicting drug; *also* : the period following such discontinuance marked by often painful physiological and psychological symptoms **3** : a pathological retreat from the real world (as in some schizophrenic states)

with·drawn \with-ˈdrȯn\ *adj* **1** : ISOLATED, SECLUDED **2** : socially detached and unresponsive

withe \ˈwith\ *n* : a slender flexible twig or branch

with·er \ˈwi-thər\ *vb* **1** : to shrivel from or as if from loss of bodily moisture and esp. sap **2** : to lose or cause to lose vitality, force, or freshness **3** : to cause to feel shriveled ⟨∼ed him with a glance⟩

with·ers \'wi-thərz\ *n pl* : the ridge between the shoulder bones of a horse; *also* : the corresponding part in other 4-footed animals

with·hold \with-'hōld, with-\ *vb* **-held** \-'held\; **-hold·ing 1** : to hold back : RESTRAIN; *also* : RETAIN **2** : to refrain from granting, giving, or allowing ⟨∼ permission⟩ ⟨∼ names⟩

withholding tax *n* : a tax on income withheld at the source

¹with·in \wi-'thin, -'thin-\ *adv* **1** : in or into the interior : INSIDE **2** : inside oneself : INWARDLY

²within *prep* **1** : inside the limits or influence of ⟨∼ call⟩ **2** : in the limits or compass of ⟨∼ a mile⟩ **3** : in or to the inner part of ⟨∼ the room⟩

with–it \'wi-thət, -thət\ *adj* : socially or culturally up-to-date

¹with·out \wi-'thaút, -'thaút\ *prep* **1** : OUTSIDE **2** : LACKING ⟨∼ hope⟩; *also* : not accompanied by or showing ⟨spoke ∼ thinking⟩

²without *adv* **1** : on the outside : EXTERNALLY **2** : with something lacking or absent ⟨has learned to do ∼⟩

with·stand \with-'stand, with-\ *vb* **-stood** \-'stúd\; **-stand·ing** : to stand against : RESIST; *esp* : to oppose (as an attack) successfully

wit·less \'wit-ləs\ *adj* : lacking wit or understanding : FOOLISH — **wit·less·ly** *adv* — **wit·less·ness** *n*

¹wit·ness \'wit-nəs\ *n* [ME *witnesse*, fr. OE *witnes* knowledge, testimony, witness, fr. *wit* mind, intelligence] **1** : TESTIMONY ⟨bear ∼ to the fact⟩ **2** : one that gives evidence; *esp* : one who testifies in a cause or before a court **3** : one present at a transaction so as to be able to testify that it has taken place **4** : one who has personal knowledge or experience of something **5** : something serving as evidence or proof : SIGN

²witness *vb* **1** : to bear witness : TESTIFY **2** : to act as legal witness of **3** : to furnish proof of : BETOKEN **4** : to be a witness of **5** : to be the scene of ⟨this region has ∼ed many wars⟩

wit·ti·cism \'wi-tə-ˌsi-zəm\ *n* : a witty saying or phrase

wit·ting \'wi-tiŋ\ *adj* : done knowingly : INTENTIONAL — **wit·ting·ly** *adv*

wit·ty \'wi-tē\ *adj* **wit·ti·er**; **-est** : marked by or full of wit : AMUSING ⟨a ∼ writer⟩ ⟨a ∼ remark⟩ **syn** humorous, facetious, jocular, jocose — **wit·ti·ly** \-tə-lē\ *adv* — **wit·ti·ness** \-tē-nəs\ *n*

wive \'wīv\ *vb* **wived**; **wiv·ing** : to take a wife

wives *pl of* WIFE

wiz·ard \'wi-zərd\ *n* [ME *wysard* wise man, fr. *wys* wise] **1** : MAGICIAN, SORCERER **2** : a very clever or skillful person ⟨a ∼ at chess⟩

wiz·ard·ry \'wi-zər-drē\ *n, pl* **-ries 1** : magic skill : SORCERY **2** : great skill or cleverness in an activity

wiz·en \'wiz-ᵊn, 'wēz-\ *vb* : to become or cause to become dry, shrunken, or wrinkled

wk *abbr* **1** week **2** work

WL *abbr* wavelength

wmk *abbr* watermark

WNW *abbr* west-northwest

WO *abbr* warrant officer

w/o *abbr* without

woad \'wōd\ *n* : a European herb related to the mustards; *also* : a blue dyestuff made from its leaves

wob·ble \'wä-bəl\ *vb* **wob·bled**; **wob·bling 1** : to move or cause to move with an irregular rocking or side-to-side motion **2** : TREMBLE, QUAVER **3** : WAVER, VACILLATE — **wobble** *n* — **wob·bly** \-bə-lē\ *adj*

woe \'wō\ *n* **1** : deep suffering from misfortune, affliction, or grief **2** : TROUBLE, MISFORTUNE ⟨economic ∼s⟩

woe·be·gone \'wō-bi-ˌgȯn\ *adj* : exhibiting woe, sorrow, or misery; *also* : being in a sorry condition

woe·ful *also* **wo·ful** \'wō-fəl\ *adj* **1** : full of woe : AFFLICTED **2** : involving, bringing, or relating to woe **3** : DEPLORABLE — **woe·ful·ly** *adv*

wok \'wäk\ *n* : a bowl-shaped cooking utensil used esp. in stir-frying

woke *past of* WAKE

woken *past part of* WAKE

wold \'wōld\ *n* : an upland plain or stretch of rolling land without woods

¹wolf \'wúlf\ *n, pl* **wolves** \'wúlvz\ **1** : any of several large erect-eared bushy-tailed doglike predatory mammals that live and hunt in packs; *esp* : GRAY WOLF **2** : a fierce or destructive person — **wolf·ish** *adj*

²wolf *vb* : to eat greedily : DEVOUR

wolf·hound \-ˌhaúnd\ *n* : any of several large dogs orig. used in hunting wolves

wol·fram \'wúl-frəm\ *n* : TUNGSTEN

wol·ver·ine \ˌwúl-və-'rēn\ *n, pl* **wolverines** *also* **wolverine** : a dark shaggy-coated flesh-eating mammal of northern forests and associated tundra that is related to the weasels

wom·an \'wú-mən\ *n, pl* **wom·en** \'wi-mən\ [ME, fr. OE *wīfman*, fr. *wīf* woman, wife + *man* human being, man] **1** : an adult female person **2** : WOMANKIND **3** : feminine nature : WOMANLINESS **4** : a female servant or attendant

wom·an·hood \'wú-mən-ˌhúd\ *n* **1** : the state of being a woman : the distinguishing qualities of a woman or of womankind **2** : WOMEN, WOMANKIND

wom·an·ish \'wú-mə-nish\ *adj* **1** : of, relating to, or characteristic of a woman **2** : suitable to a woman rather than to a man : EFFEMINATE

wom·an·kind \'wú-mən-ˌkīnd\ *n* : the females of the human race : WOMEN

wom·an·like \-ˌlīk\ *adj* : WOMANLY

wom·an·ly \-lē\ *adj* : having qualities characteristic of a woman — **wom·an·li·ness** \-lē-nəs\ *n*

woman suffrage *n* : possession and exercise of suffrage by women

womb \'wüm\ *n* **1** : UTERUS **2** : a place where something is generated

wom·bat \'wäm-ˌbat\ *n* : any of several stocky burrowing Australian marsupials that resemble small bears

wom·en·folk \'wi-mən-ˌfōk\ *also* **wom·en·folks** \-ˌfōks\ *n pl* : WOMEN

¹won \'wən\ *past and past part of* WIN

²won \'wȯn\ *n, pl* **won** — see MONEY table

¹won·der \'wən-dər\ *n* **1** : a cause of astonishment or surprise : MARVEL; *also* : MIRACLE **2** : the quality of exciting wonder ⟨the charm and ∼ of the scene⟩ **3** : a feeling (as of awed astonishment or uncertainty) aroused by something extraordinary or affecting

²wonder *vb* **1** : to feel surprise or amazement **2** : to feel curiosity or doubt

wonder drug *n* : MIRACLE DRUG

won·der·ful \'wən-dər-fəl\ *adj* **1** : exciting wonder : MARVELOUS, ASTONISHING **2** : unusually good : ADMIRABLE — **won·der·ful·ly** \-f(ə-)lē\ *adv* — **won·der·ful·ness** *n*

won·der·land \-ˌland, -lənd\ *n* **1** : an imaginary place of delicate beauty or magical charm **2** : a place that excites admiration or wonder

won·der·ment \-mənt\ *n* **1** : ASTONISHMENT, SURPRISE **2** : a cause of or occasion for wonder **3** : curiosity about something

won·drous \'wən-drəs\ *adj* : WONDERFUL, MARVELOUS — **won·drous·ly** *adv* — **won·drous·ness** *n*

¹wont \'wȯnt, 'wōnt\ *adj* [ME *woned*, *wont*, fr. pp. of *wonen* to dwell, be used to, fr. OE *wunian*] **1** : ACCUSTOMED, USED ⟨as we are ∼ to do⟩ **2** : INCLINED, APT

\ə\abut \ᵊ\kitten \ər\further \a\ash \ā\ace \ä\mop, mar
\aú\out \ch\chin \e\bet \ē\easy \g\go \i\hit \ī\ice \j\job
\ŋ\sing \ō\go \ȯ\law \ȯi\boy \th\thin \th\the \ü\loot \ú\foot
\y\yet \zh\vision *see also* Pronunciation Symbols page

²**wont** n : CUSTOM, USAGE, HABIT ⟨according to her ∼⟩
won't \'wōnt\ : will not
wont·ed \'wȯn-təd, 'wōn-\ adj : ACCUSTOMED, CUSTOM-
ARY ⟨his ∼ courtesy⟩
woo \'wü\ vb **1** : to try to gain the love of : COURT **2** : SO-
LICIT, ENTREAT **3** : to try to gain or bring about ⟨∼ public favor⟩ — **woo·er** n
¹**wood** \'wud\ n **1** : a dense growth of trees usu. larger
than a grove and smaller than a forest — often used in
pl. **2** : a hard fibrous substance that is basically xylem
and forms the bulk of trees and shrubs beneath the
bark; also : this material fit or prepared for some use
(as burning or building) **3** : something made of wood
²**wood** adj **1** : WOODEN **2** : suitable for holding, cutting, or
working with wood **3** or **woods** \'wudz\ : living or growing in woods
³**wood** vb **1** : to supply or load with wood esp. for fuel **2**
: to cover with a growth of trees
wood alcohol n : METHANOL
wood·bine \'wud-,bīn\ n : any of several honeysuckles;
also : VIRGINIA CREEPER
wood·block \-,bläk\ n : WOODCUT
wood·chop·per \-,chä-pər\ n : one engaged esp. in chopping down trees
wood·chuck \-,chək\ n : a thickset grizzled marmot of
Alaska, Canada, and the northeastern U.S.
wood·cock \'wud-,käk\ n, pl **woodcocks** : a brown eastern No. American game bird with a short neck and long
bill that is related to the snipe; also : a related and similar Old World bird
wood·craft \-,kraft\ n **1** : skill and practice in matters relating to the woods and esp. in how to take care of oneself in them **2** : skill in shaping or constructing articles
from wood
wood·cut \-,kət\ n **1** : a relief printing surface engraved
on a block of wood **2** : a print from a woodcut
wood·cut·ter \-,kə-tər\ n : a person who cuts wood
wood·ed \'wu-dəd\ adj : covered with woods or trees ⟨∼
slopes⟩
wood·en \'wud-ᵊn\ adj **1** : made of wood **2** : lacking flexibility : awkwardly stiff — **wood·en·ly** adv — **wood-
en·ness** n
wood·en·ware \'wud-ᵊn-,war\ n : articles made of wood
for domestic use
wood·land \'wud-lənd, -,land\ n : land covered with
trees : FOREST — **woodland** adj
wood·lot \'wud-,lät\ n : a restricted area of woodland
usu. privately kept to meet fuel and timber needs ⟨a
farm ∼⟩
wood louse n : any of various small flat crustaceans that
live esp. in ground litter and under stones and bark
wood·man \'wud-mən\ n : WOODSMAN
wood·note \-,nōt\ n : verbal expression that is natural
and artless
wood nymph n : a nymph living in the woods
wood·peck·er \'wud-,pe-kər\ n : any of numerous usu.
brightly marked climbing birds with stiff spiny tail
feathers and a chisellike bill used to drill into trees for
insects
wood·pile \-,pīl\ n : a pile of wood and esp. firewood
wood·shed \-,shed\ n : a shed for storing wood and esp.
firewood
woods·man \'wudz-mən\ n : a person who frequents or
works in the woods; esp : one skilled in woodcraft
woodsy \'wud-zē\ adj : relating to or suggestive of
woods
wood·wind \'wud-,wind\ n : one of a group of wind instruments including flutes, clarinets, oboes, bassoons,
and sometimes saxophones
wood·work \-,wərk\ n : work made of wood; esp : interior fittings (as moldings or stairways) of wood
woody \'wu-dē\ adj **wood·i·er**; **-est 1** : abounding or
overgrown with woods **2** : of or containing wood or

wood fibers **3** : characteristic or suggestive of wood —
wood·i·ness \'wu-dē-nəs\ n
woof \'wuf\ n [alter. of ME oof, fr. OE ōwef, fr. ō- (fr.
on on) + wefan to weave] **1** : WEFT 1 **2** : a woven fabric;
also : its texture
woof·er \'wu-fər\ n : a loudspeaker that reproduces
sounds of low pitch
wool \'wul\ n **1** : the soft wavy or curly hair of some
mammals and esp. the domestic sheep; also : something (as a textile or garment) made of wool **2** : material
that resembles a mass of wool — **wooled** \'wuld\ adj
¹**wool·en** or **wool·len** \'wu-lən\ adj **1** : made of wool **2** : of
or relating to the manufacture or sale of woolen prod-
ucts ⟨∼ mills⟩
²**woolen** or **woollen** n **1** : a fabric made of wool **2** : garments of woolen fabric — usu. used in pl.
wool·gath·er·ing \-,ga-thə-rin\ n : idle daydreaming
¹**wool·ly** also **wooly** \'wu-lē\ adj **wool·li·er**; **-est 1** : of, relating to, or bearing wool **2** : consisting of or resembling
wool **3** : mentally confused ⟨∼ thinking⟩ **4** : marked by
a lack of order or restraint ⟨the wild and ∼ West⟩
²**wool·ly** also **wool·ie** or **wooly** \'wu-lē\ n, pl **wool·lies** : a
garment made from wool; esp : underclothing of knit-
ted wool — usu. used in pl.
woolly bear n : any of numerous very hairy moth caterpillars
woo·zy \'wu-zē\ adj **woo·zi·er**; **-est 1** : BEFUDDLED **2**
: somewhat dizzy, nauseated, or weak — **woo·zi·ness**
\'wu-zē-nəs\ n
¹**word** \'wərd\ n **1** : something that is said; esp : a brief
remark **2** : a speech sound or series of speech sounds
that communicates a meaning; also : a graphic representation of such a sound or series of sounds **3** : ORDER,
COMMAND **4** often cap : the 2d person of the Trinity;
also : GOSPEL **5** : NEWS, INFORMATION **6** : PROMISE **7** pl
: QUARREL, DISPUTE **8** : a verbal signal : PASSWORD —
word·less adj
²**word** vb : to express in words : PHRASE
word·age \'wər-dij\ n **1** : WORDS **2** : number of words **3**
: WORDING
word·book \'wərd-,buk\ n : VOCABULARY, DICTIONARY
word·ing \'wər-din\ n : verbal expression : PHRASEOLO-
GY
word of mouth : oral communication
word·play \'wərd-,plā\ n : verbal wit
word processing n : the production of typewritten documents with automated and usu. computerized text=
editing equipment — **word process** vb
word processor n : a keyboard-operated terminal for use
in word processing; also : software to perform word
processing
wordy \'wər-dē\ adj **word·i·er**; **-est** : using many words
: VERBOSE **syn** prolix, diffuse, redundant — **word·i-
ness** \-dē-nəs\ n
wore past of WEAR
¹**work** \'wərk\ n **1** : TOIL, LABOR; also : EMPLOYMENT ⟨out
of ∼⟩ **2** : TASK, JOB ⟨have ∼ to do⟩ **3** : the energy used
when a force is applied over a given distance **4** : DEED,
ACHIEVEMENT **5** : a fortified structure **6** pl : engineering
structures **7** pl : a place where industrial labor is done
: PLANT, FACTORY **8** pl : the moving parts of a mechanism **9** : something produced by mental effort or physical labor; esp : an artistic production (as a book or
needlework) **10** : WORKMANSHIP ⟨careless ∼⟩ **11** : material in the process of manufacture **12** pl : everything
possessed, available, or belonging ⟨the whole ∼s went
overboard⟩; also : drastic treatment ⟨gave him the ∼s⟩
syn occupation, employment, business, pursuit, calling
— **in the works** : in process of preparation
²**work** adj **1** : used for work ⟨∼ elephants⟩ **2** : suitable or
styled for wear while working ⟨∼ clothes⟩
³**work** vb **worked** \'wərkt\ or **wrought** \'ròt\; **work·ing 1**
: to bring to pass : EFFECT **2** : to fashion or create a use-

ful or desired product through labor or exertion **3** : to prepare for use (as by kneading) **4** : to bring into a desired form by a manufacturing process ⟨∼ cold steel⟩ **5** : to set or keep in operation : OPERATE ⟨a pump ∼ed by hand⟩ **6** : to solve by reasoning or calculation ⟨∼ out a problem⟩ **7** : to cause to toil or labor ⟨∼ed the men hard⟩; *also* : to make use of ⟨∼ a mine⟩ **8** : to pay for with labor or service ⟨∼ off a debt⟩ **9** : to bring or get into some position or condition by stages ⟨the stream ∼ed itself clear⟩ ⟨the knot ∼ed loose⟩ **10** : CONTRIVE, ARRANGE ⟨∼ it so you can leave early⟩ **11** : to practice trickery or cajolery on ⟨∼ed the management for a free ticket⟩ **12** : EXCITE, PROVOKE ⟨∼ed himself into a rage⟩ **13** : to exert oneself physically or mentally; *esp* : to perform work regularly for wages **14** : to function according to plan or design **15** : to produce a desired effect : SUCCEED ⟨the plan ∼ed⟩ **16** : to make way slowly and with difficulty ⟨he ∼ed forward through the crowd⟩ **17** : to permit of being worked ⟨this wood ∼s easily⟩ **18** : to be in restless motion; *also* : FERMENT 1 — **work on 1** : AFFECT **2** : to try to influence or persuade — **work upon** : to have effect upon : operate on : INFLUENCE

work·able \ˈwər-kə-bəl\ *adj* **1** : capable of being worked **2** : PRACTICABLE, FEASIBLE — **work·able·ness** *n*
work·a·day \ˈwər-kə-ˌdā\ *adj* **1** : relating to or suited for working days **2** : PROSAIC, ORDINARY
work·a·hol·ic \ˌwər-kə-ˈhȯ-lik, -ˈhä-\ *n* : a compulsive worker
work·bench \-ˌbench\ *n* : a bench on which work esp. of mechanics, machinists, and carpenters is performed
work·book \-ˌbu̇k\ *n* **1** : a worker's manual **2** : a student's book of problems to be answered directly on the pages
work·day \ˈwərk-ˌdā\ *n* **1** : a day on which work is done as distinguished from a day off **2** : the period of time in a day when work is performed
work·er \ˈwər-kər\ *n* **1** : one that works; *esp* : a person who works for wages **2** : any of the sexually undeveloped individuals of a colony of social insects (as bees, ants, or termites) that perform the work of the community
worker's compensation *n* : a system of insurance that reimburses an employer for damages paid to an employee who was injured while working
work ethic *n* : belief in work as a moral good
work farm *n* : a farm on which persons guilty of minor law violations are confined
work·horse \ˈwərk-ˌhȯrs\ *n* **1** : a horse used for hard work **2** : a person who does most of the work of a group task **3** : a strong useful machine or vehicle
work·house \-ˌhau̇s\ *n* **1** *Brit* : POORHOUSE **2** : a house of correction for persons guilty of minor law violations
¹work·ing \ˈwər-kiŋ\ *n* **1** : manner of functioning — usu. used in pl. **2** *pl* : an excavation made in mining or tunneling
²working *adj* **1** : engaged in work ⟨a ∼ journalist⟩ **2** : adequate to allow work to be done ⟨a ∼ majority⟩ ⟨a ∼ knowledge of French⟩ **3** : adopted or assumed to help further work or activity ⟨a ∼ model of the car⟩ **4** : spent at work ⟨∼ life⟩
work·ing·man \ˈwər-kiŋ-ˌman\ *n* : WORKER 1
work·man \ˈwərk-mən\ *n* **1** : WORKER 1 **2** : ARTISAN, CRAFTSMAN
work·man·like \-ˌlīk\ *adj* : worthy of a good workman : SKILLFUL
work·man·ship \-ˌship\ *n* : the art or skill of a workman : CRAFTSMANSHIP; *also* : the quality of a piece of work ⟨a vase of exquisite ∼⟩
work·out \ˈwərk-ˌau̇t\ *n* **1** : a practice or exercise to test or improve one's fitness, ability, or performance **2** : a test or trial to determine ability or capacity or suitability
work out *vb* **1** : to bring about esp. by resolving diffi-

culties **2** : DEVELOP, ELABORATE **3** : to prove effective, practicable, or suitable **4** : to amount to a total or calculated figure — used with *at* **5** : to engage in a workout
work·room \ˈwərk-ˌrüm, -ˌru̇m\ *n* : a room used for work
work·shop \-ˌshäp\ *n* **1** : a shop where manufacturing or handicrafts are carried on **2** : a seminar emphasizing exchange of ideas and practical methods
work·sta·tion \-ˌstā-shən\ *n* : an area with equipment for the performance of a specialized task; *also* : an intelligent terminal or personal computer usu. connected to a computer network
world \ˈwərld\ *n* [ME, fr. OE *woruld* human existence, this world, age, fr. a prehistoric compound whose first constituent is represented by OE *wer* man and whose second constituent is akin to OE *eald* old] **1** : the earth with its inhabitants and all things upon it **2** : people in general : MANKIND **3** : human affairs ⟨withdraw from the ∼⟩ **4** : UNIVERSE, CREATION **5** : a state of existence : scene of life and action ⟨the ∼ of the future⟩ **6** : a distinctive class of persons or their sphere of interest ⟨the musical ∼⟩ **7** : a part or section of the earth or its inhabitants by itself **8** : a great number or quantity ⟨a ∼ of troubles⟩ **9** : a celestial body
world–beat·er \-ˌbē-tər\ *n* : one that excels all others of its kind : CHAMPION
world·ling \-liŋ\ *n* : a person absorbed in the concerns of the present world
world·ly \-lē\ *adj* **1** : of, relating to, or devoted to this world and its pursuits rather than to religion or spiritual affairs **2** : WORLDLY-WISE, SOPHISTICATED — **world·li·ness** \-lē-nəs\ *n*
world·ly–wise \-ˌwīz\ *adj* : possessing a practical and often shrewd understanding of human affairs
world·wide \ˈwərld-ˈwīd\ *adj* : extended throughout the entire world — **worldwide** *adv*
¹worm \ˈwərm\ *n* **1** : any of various small long usu. naked and soft-bodied round or flat invertebrate animals (as an earthworm, nematode, tapeworm, or maggot) **2** : a human being who is an object of contempt, loathing, or pity : WRETCH **3** : something that inwardly torments or devours **4** *pl* : infestation with or disease caused by parasitic worms **5** : a spiral or wormlike thing (as the thread of a screw) — **wormy** *adj*
²worm *vb* **1** : to move or cause to move or proceed slowly and deviously **2** : to insinuate or introduce (oneself) by devious or subtle means **3** : to obtain or extract by artful or insidious pleading, asking, or persuading ⟨∼ed the truth out of him⟩ **4** : to treat (an animal) with a drug to destroy or expel parasitic worms
worm–eat·en \ˈwərm-ˌēt-ᵊn\ *adj* : eaten or burrowed by worms
worm gear *n* : a mechanical linkage consisting of a short rotating screw whose threads mesh with the teeth of a gear wheel
worm·hole \ˈwərm-ˌhōl\ *n* : a hole or passage burrowed by a worm
worm·wood \-ˌwu̇d\ *n* **1** : any of a genus of aromatic woody plants (as a sagebrush); *esp* : one of Europe used in absinthe **2** : something bitter or grievous : BITTERNESS
worn *past part of* WEAR
worn–out \ˈwōrn-ˈau̇t\ *adj* : exhausted or used up by or as if by wear
wor·ri·some \ˈwər-ē-səm\ *adj* **1** : causing distress or worry **2** : inclined to worry or fret
¹wor·ry \ˈwər-ē\ *vb* **wor·ried; wor·ry·ing** **1** : to shake and mangle with the teeth ⟨a terrier ∼ing a rat⟩ **2** : to

make anxious or upset ⟨her poor health *worries* me⟩ **3** : to feel or express great care or anxiety : FRET — **wor·ri·er** *n*

²**worry** *n, pl* **worries 1** : ANXIETY **2** : a cause of anxiety : TROUBLE

wor·ry·wart \'wər-ē-ˌwȯrt\ *n* : one who is inclined to worry unduly

¹**worse** \'wərs\ *adj, comparative of* BAD *or of* ILL **1** : bad or evil in a greater degree : less good **2** : more unfavorable, unpleasant, or painful; *also* : SICKER

²**worse** *n* **1** : one that is worse **2** : a greater degree of ill or badness ⟨a turn for the ∼⟩

³**worse** *adv, comparative of* BAD *or of* ILL : in a worse manner : to a worse extent or degree

wors·en \'wərs-ᵊn\ *vb* : to make or become worse

¹**wor·ship** \'wər-shəp\ *n* [ME *worshipe* worthiness, respect, reverence paid to a divine being, fr. OE *weorthscipe* worthiness, respect, fr. *weorth* worthy, worth + *-scipe* -ship, suffix denoting quality or condition] **1** *chiefly Brit* : a person of importance — used as a title for officials **2** : reverence toward a divine being or supernatural power; *also* : the expression of such reverence **3** : extravagant respect or admiration or devotion ⟨∼ of the dollar⟩

²**worship** *vb* **-shiped** *or* **-shipped; -ship·ing** *or* **-ship·ping 1** : to honor or reverence as a divine being or supernatural power **2** : IDOLIZE **3** : to perform or take part in worship — **wor·ship·er** *or* **wor·ship·per** *n*

wor·ship·ful \'wər-shəp-fəl\ *adj* **1** *archaic* : NOTABLE, DISTINGUISHED **2** *chiefly Brit* — used as a title for various persons or groups of rank or distinction **3** : VENERATING, WORSHIPING

¹**worst** \'wərst\ *adj, superlative of* BAD *or of* ILL **1** : most bad, evil, ill, or corrupt **2** : most unfavorable, unpleasant, or painful; *also* : most unsuitable, faulty, or unattractive **3** : least skillful or efficient

²**worst** *adv, superlative of* ILL *or of* BAD *or* BADLY **1** : to the extreme degree of badness or inferiority : in the worst manner **2** : MOST ⟨those who need help ∼⟩

³**worst** *n* : one that is worst

⁴**worst** *vb* : DEFEAT

wor·sted \'wu̇s-təd, 'wər-stəd\ *n* [ME, fr. *Worsted* (now *Worstead*), England] : a smooth compact yarn made from long wool fibers; *also* : a fabric made from such yarn

wort \'wərt, 'wȯrt\ *n* : a solution obtained by infusion from malt and fermented to form beer

¹**worth** \'wərth\ *n* **1** : monetary value; *also* : the equivalent of a specified amount or figure ⟨$5 ∼ of gas⟩ **2** : the value of something measured by its qualities **3** : MERIT, EXCELLENCE

²**worth** *prep* **1** : equal in value to; *also* : having possessions or income equal to **2** : deserving of ⟨well ∼ the effort⟩

worth·less \'wərth-ləs\ *adj* **1** : lacking worth : VALUELESS; *also* : USELESS **2** : LOW, DESPICABLE — **worth·less·ness** *n*

worth·while \'wərth-'hwīl\ *adj* : being worth the time or effort spent

¹**wor·thy** \'wər-thē\ *adj* **wor·thi·er; -est 1** : having worth or value : ESTIMABLE **2** : HONORABLE, MERITORIOUS **3** : having sufficient worth ⟨∼ of the honor⟩ — **wor·thi·ly** \'wər-thə-lē\ *adv* — **wor·thi·ness** \-thē-nəs\ *n*

²**worthy** *n, pl* **worthies** : a worthy person

would \'wu̇d\ *past of* WILL **1** *archaic* : wish for : WANT **2** : strongly desire : WISH ⟨I ∼ I were young again⟩ **3** — used as an auxiliary to express (1) preference ⟨∼ rather run than fight⟩, (2) wish, desire, or intent ⟨those who ∼ forbid gambling⟩, (3) habitual action ⟨we ∼ meet often for lunch⟩, (4) a contingency or possibility ⟨if he were coming, he ∼ be here by now⟩, (5) probability ⟨∼ have won if he hadn't tripped⟩, or (6) a request ⟨∼ you help us⟩ **4** : COULD **5** : SHOULD

would–be \'wu̇d-ˌbē\ *adj* : desiring or pretending to be ⟨a ∼ artist⟩

¹**wound** \'wünd\ *n* **1** : an injury involving cutting or breaking of bodily tissue (as by violence, accident, or surgery) **2** : an injury or hurt to feelings or reputation

²**wound** *vb* : to inflict a wound to or in

³**wound** \'wau̇nd\ *past and past part of* WIND

wove *past of* WEAVE

woven *past part of* WEAVE

¹**wow** \'wau̇\ *n* : a striking success : HIT

²**wow** *vb* : to arouse enthusiastic approval

WP *abbr* word processing; word processor

WPM *abbr* words per minute

wpn *abbr* weapon

wrack \'rak\ *n* [ME, fr. OE *wræc* misery, punishment, something driven by the sea] : violent or total destruction

wraith \'rāth\ *n, pl* **wraiths** \'rāths, 'rā*th*z\ **1** : GHOST, SPECTER **2** : an insubstantial appearance : SHADOW

¹**wran·gle** \'raŋ-gəl\ *vb* **wran·gled; wran·gling 1** : to quarrel angrily or peevishly : BICKER **2** : ARGUE **3** : to obtain by persistent arguing **4** : to herd and care for (livestock) on the range — **wran·gler** *n*

²**wrangle** *n* : an angry, noisy, or prolonged dispute; *also* : CONTROVERSY

¹**wrap** \'rap\ *vb* **wrapped; wrap·ping 1** : to cover esp. by winding or folding **2** : to envelop and secure for transportation or storage **3** : to enclose wholly : ENFOLD **4** : to coil, fold, draw, or twine about something **5** : SURROUND, ENVELOP ⟨*wrapped* in mystery⟩ **6** : INVOLVE, ENGROSS ⟨*wrapped* up in a hobby⟩ **7** : to complete filming or videotaping

²**wrap** *n* **1** : WRAPPER, WRAPPING **2** : an article of clothing that may be wrapped around a person **3** *pl* : SECRECY ⟨kept under ∼s⟩ **4** : completion of filming or videotaping

wrap·around \'ra-pə-ˌrau̇nd\ *n* : a garment (as a dress) adjusted to the figure by wrapping around

wrap·per \'ra-pər\ *n* **1** : that in which something is wrapped **2** : one that wraps **3** : an article of clothing worn wrapped around the body

wrap·ping \'ra-piŋ\ *n* : something used to wrap an object : WRAPPER

wrap–up \'rap-ˌəp\ *n* : SUMMARY

wrap up *vb* **1** : SUMMARIZE, SUM UP **2** : to bring to a usu. successful conclusion

wrasse \'ras\ *n* : any of a large family of usu. brightly colored marine fishes including many food fishes

wrath \'rath\ *n* **1** : violent anger : RAGE **2** : divine punishment **syn** indignation, ire, fury, anger

wrath·ful \-fəl\ *adj* **1** : filled with wrath : very angry **2** : showing, marked by, or arising from anger — **wrath·ful·ly** *adv* — **wrath·ful·ness** *n*

wreak \'rēk\ *vb* **1** : to exact as a punishment : INFLICT ⟨∼ vengeance on an enemy⟩ **2** : to give free scope or rein to ⟨∼ed his wrath⟩ **3** : BRING ABOUT, CAUSE ⟨∼ havoc⟩

wreath \'rēth\ *n, pl* **wreaths** \'rēthz, 'rēths\ : something (as boughs or flowers) intertwined into a circular shape

wreathe \'rēth\ *vb* **wreathed; wreath·ing 1** : to shape or take on the shape of a wreath **2** : to crown, decorate, or cover with or as if with a wreath ⟨a face *wreathed* in smiles⟩

¹**wreck** \'rek\ *n* **1** : something (as goods) cast up on the land by the sea after a shipwreck **2** : SHIPWRECK **3** : the action of breaking up or destroying something **4** : broken remains (as of a vehicle after a crash) **5** : something disabled or in a state of ruin; *also* : an individual broken in health or strength

²**wreck** *vb* **1** : SHIPWRECK **2** : to ruin or damage by breaking up : involve in disaster or ruin

wreck·age \'re-kij\ *n* **1** : the act of wrecking : the state of being wrecked : RUIN **2** : the remains of a wreck

wreck·er \'re-kər\ *n* **1** : one that searches for or works upon the wrecks of ships **2** : TOW TRUCK **3** : one that wrecks; *esp* : one whose work is the demolition of buildings

wren \'ren\ *n* : any of a family of small mostly brown singing birds with short wings and often a tail that points upward

¹wrench \'rench\ *vb* **1** : to move with a violent twist **2** : to pull, strain, or tighten with violent twisting or force **3** : to injure or disable by a violent twisting or straining **4** : to snatch forcibly : WREST

²wrench *n* **1** : a forcible twisting; *also* : an injury (as to one's ankle) by twisting **2** : a tool for holding, twisting, or turning (as nuts or bolts)

¹wrest \'rest\ *vb* **1** : to pull or move by a forcible twisting movement **2** : to gain with difficulty by or as if by force or violence ⟨∼ control of the government from the dictator⟩

²wrest *n* : a forcible twist : WRENCH

¹wres·tle \'re-səl, 'ra-\ *vb* **wres·tled; wres·tling 1** : to scuffle with and try to throw down an opponent **2** : to compete against in wrestling **3** : to struggle for control (as of something difficult) ⟨∼ with a problem⟩ — **wres·tler** \'res-lər, 'ras-\ *n*

²wrestle *n* : the action or an instance of wrestling : STRUGGLE

wres·tling \'res-liŋ\ *n* : the sport in which two opponents wrestle each other

wretch \'rech\ *n* [ME *wrecche*, fr. OE *wrecca* outcast, exile] **1** : a miserable unhappy person **2** : a base, despicable, or vile person

wretch·ed \'re-chəd\ *adj* **1** : deeply afflicted, dejected, or distressed : MISERABLE **2** : WOEFUL, GRIEVOUS ⟨a ∼ accident⟩ **3** : DESPICABLE ⟨a ∼ trick⟩ **4** : poor in quality or ability : INFERIOR ⟨∼ workmanship⟩ — **wretch·ed·ly** *adv* — **wretch·ed·ness** *n*

wrig·gle \'ri-gəl\ *vb* **wrig·gled; wrig·gling 1** : to twist or move to and fro like a worm : SQUIRM ⟨*wriggled* in his chair⟩ ⟨∼ your toes⟩; *also* : to move along by twisting and turning ⟨a snake *wriggled* along the path⟩ **2** : to extricate oneself as if by wriggling ⟨∼ out of difficulty⟩ — **wriggle** *n*

wrig·gler *n* **1** : one that wriggles **2** : WIGGLER 1

wring \'riŋ\ *vb* **wrung** \'rəŋ\; **wring·ing** \'riŋ-iŋ\ **1** : to squeeze or twist esp. so as to make dry or to extract moisture or liquid ⟨∼ wet clothes⟩ **2** : to get by or as if by twisting or pressing ⟨∼ the truth out of him⟩ **3** : to twist so as to strain or sprain : CONTORT ⟨∼ his neck⟩ **4** : to twist together as a sign of anguish ⟨*wrung* her hands⟩ **5** : to affect painfully as if by wringing : TORMENT ⟨her plight *wrung* my heart⟩

wring·er \'riŋ-ər\ *n* : one that wrings; *esp* : a device for squeezing out liquid or moisture ⟨clothes ∼⟩

¹wrin·kle \'riŋ-kəl\ *n* **1** : a crease or small fold on a surface (as in the skin or in cloth) **2** : a clever or new method, trick, or idea — **wrin·kly** \-k(ə-)lē\ *adj*

²wrinkle *vb* **wrin·kled; wrin·kling** : to develop or cause to develop wrinkles

wrist \'rist\ *n* : the joint or region between the hand and the arm; *also* : a corresponding part in a lower animal

wrist·band \-ˌband\ *n* : a band or the part of a sleeve encircling the wrist

wrist·let \-lət\ *n* : WRISTBAND; *esp* : a close-fitting knitted band attached to the top of a glove or the end of a sleeve

wrist·watch \-ˌwäch\ *n* : a small watch attached to a bracelet or strap to fasten about the wrist

writ \'rit\ *n* **1** : something written **2** : a written legal order signed by a court officer

write \'rīt\ *vb* **wrote** \'rōt\; **writ·ten** \'rit-ᵊn\ *also* **writ** \'rit\; **writ·ing** \'rī-tiŋ\ [ME, fr. OE *wrītan* to scratch, draw, inscribe] **1** : to form characters, letters, or words on a surface ⟨learn to read and ∼⟩ **2** : to form the letters

or the words of ⟨∼ your name⟩ ⟨∼ a check⟩ **3** : to put down on paper : express in writing **4** : to make up and set down for others to read ⟨∼ a book⟩ ⟨∼ music⟩ **5** : to write a letter to **6** : to communicate by letter : CORRESPOND

write–in \'rīt-ˌin\ *n* : a vote cast by writing in the name of a candidate; *also* : a candidate whose name is written in

write in *vb* : to insert (a name not listed on a ballot) in an appropriate space; *also* : to cast (a vote) in this manner

write off *vb* **1** : to reduce the estimated value of : DEPRECIATE **2** : CANCEL ⟨*write off* a bad debt⟩

writ·er \'rī-tər\ *n* : one that writes esp. as a business or occupation : AUTHOR

writer's cramp *n* : a painful spasmodic cramp of muscles of the hand or fingers brought on by excessive writing

write–up \'rīt-ˌəp\ *n* : a written account (as in a newspaper); *esp* : a flattering article

writhe \'rīth\ *vb* **writhed; writh·ing 1** : to twist and turn this way and that ⟨∼ in pain⟩ **2** : to suffer with shame or confusion

writ·ing *n* **1** : the act of one that writes; *also* : HANDWRITING **2** : something that is written or printed **3** : a style or form of composition **4** : the occupation of a writer

wrnt *abbr* warrant

¹wrong \'röŋ\ *n* **1** : an injurious, unfair, or unjust act **2** : a violation of the legal rights of another person **3** : something that is wrong : wrong principles, practices, or conduct ⟨know right from ∼⟩ **4** : the state, position, or fact of being wrong

²wrong *adj* **wrong·er** \'röŋ-ər\; **wrong·est** \'röŋ-əst\ **1** : SINFUL, IMMORAL **2** : not right according to a standard or code : IMPROPER **3** : INCORRECT ⟨a ∼ solution⟩ **4** : UNSATISFACTORY **5** : UNSUITABLE, INAPPROPRIATE **6** : constituting a surface that is considered the back, bottom, inside, or reverse of something ⟨iron only on the ∼ side of the fabric⟩ **syn** false, erroneous, incorrect, inaccurate, untrue — **wrong·ly** *adv*

³wrong *adv* **1** : INCORRECTLY **2** : in a wrong direction, manner, or relation

⁴wrong *vb* **wronged; wrong·ing** \'röŋ-iŋ\ **1** : to do wrong to : INJURE, HARM **2** : to treat unjustly : DISHONOR, MALIGN **syn** oppress, persecute, aggrieve

wrong·do·er \'röŋ-ˌdü-ər\ *n* : a person who does wrong and esp. moral wrong — **wrong·do·ing** \-ˌdü-iŋ\ *n*

wrong·ful \'röŋ-fəl\ *adj* **1** : WRONG, UNJUST **2** : UNLAWFUL — **wrong·ful·ly** *adv* — **wrong·ful·ness** *n*

wrong·head·ed \-'he-dəd\ *adj* : stubborn in clinging to wrong opinion or principle — **wrong·head·ed·ly** *adv* — **wrong·head·ed·ness** *n*

wrote *past of* WRITE

wroth \'röth, 'rȯth\ *adj* : filled with wrath : ANGRY

wrought \'rȯt\ *adj* [ME, fr. pp. of *worken* to work] **1** : FASHIONED, FORMED ⟨carefully ∼ essays⟩ **2** : ORNAMENTED **3** : beaten into shape by tools : HAMMERED ⟨∼ metals⟩ **4** : deeply stirred : EXCITED ⟨gets easily ∼ up⟩

wrought iron *n* : a commercial form of iron that is tough, malleable, and relatively soft — **wrought–iron** *adj*

wrung *past and past part of* WRING

wry \'rī\ *adj* **wry·er** \'rī-ər\; **wry·est** \'rī-əst\ **1** : having a bent or twisted shape ⟨a ∼ smile⟩; *esp* : turned abnormally to one side : CONTORTED ⟨a ∼ neck⟩ **2** : cleverly and often ironically humorous — **wry·ly** *adv* — **wry·ness** *n*

\ə\abut \ᵊ\kitten \ər\further \a\ash \ā\ace \ä\mop, mar \au̇\out \ch\chin \e\bet \ē\easy \g\go \i\hit \ī\ice \j\job \ŋ\sing \ō\go \ȯ\law \ȯi\boy \th\thin \t͟h\the \ü\loot \u̇\foot \y\yet \zh\vision *see also* Pronunciation Symbols page

wry·neck \'rī-ˌnek\ *n* **1** : either of two Old World wood-peckers that differ from typical woodpeckers in having a peculiar manner of twisting the head and neck **2** : an abnormal twisting of the neck and head to one side caused by muscle spasms
WSW *abbr* west-southwest
wt *abbr* weight
wurst \'wərst, 'würst\ *n* : SAUSAGE

WV *or* **W Va** *abbr* West Virginia
WW *abbr* World War
w/w *abbr* wall-to-wall
WY *or* **Wyo** *abbr* Wyoming
WYS·I·WYG \'wi-zē-ˌwig\ *adj* [*what you see is what you get*] : of, relating to, or being a computer display that shows a document exactly as it will appear when printed out

X

¹**x** \'eks\ *n, pl* **x's** *or* **xs** \'ek-səz\ *often cap* **1** : the 24th letter of the English alphabet **2** : an unknown quantity
²**x** *vb* **x-ed** *also* **x'd** *or* **xed** \'ekst\; **x-ing** *or* **x'ing** \'ek-siŋ\ : to cancel or obliterate with a series of *x*'s — usu. used with *out*
³**x** *abbr* **1** ex **2** experimental
⁴**x** *symbol* **1** times ⟨3 *x* 2 is 6⟩ **2** by ⟨a 3 *x* 5 index card⟩ **3** *often cap* power of magnification
Xan·a·du \'za-nə-ˌdü, -ˌdyü\ *n* [fr. *Xanadu*, locality in *Kubla Khan* (1798), poem by Eng. poet Samuel Taylor Coleridge †1834] : an idyllic, exotic, or luxurious place
Xan·thip·pe \zan-'thi-pē, -'ti-\ *or* **Xan·tip·pe** \-'ti-pē\ *n* [Gk *Xanthippē*, shrewish wife of Socrates] : an ill-tempered woman
x–ax·is \'eks-ˌak-səs\ *n* : the axis of a graph or of a system of coordinates in a plane parallel to which abscissas are measured
X–C *abbr* cross-country
X chromosome *n* : a sex chromosome that usually occurs paired in each female cell and single in each male cell in organisms (as human beings) in which the male normally has two unlike sex chromosomes
Xe *symbol* xenon
xe·non \'zē-ˌnän, 'ze-\ *n* [Gk, neut. of *xenos* strange] : a heavy gaseous chemical element occurring in minute quantities in air — see ELEMENT table
xe·no·pho·bia \ˌze-nə-'fō-bē-ə, ˌzē-\ *n* : fear and hatred of strangers or foreigners or of what is strange or foreign — **xe·no·phobe** \'ze-nə-ˌfōb, 'zē-\ *n* — **xe·no·pho·bic** \ˌze-nə-'fō-bik, ˌzē-\ *adj*
xe·ric \'zir-ik, 'zer-\ *adj* : characterized by or requiring only a small amount of moisture ⟨a ∼ habitat⟩
xe·rog·ra·phy \zə-'rä-grə-fē\ *n* : a process for copying printed matter by the action of light on an electrically

charged surface in which the latent image usu. is developed with a powder — **xe·ro·graph·ic** \ˌzir-ə-'gra-fik\ *adj*
xe·ro·phyte \'zir-ə-ˌfīt\ *n* : a plant adapted for growth with a limited water supply — **xe·ro·phyt·ic** \ˌzir-ə-'fi-tik\ *adj*
xi \'zī, 'ksī\ *n* : the 14th letter of the Greek alphabet — Ξ or ξ
XL *abbr* **1** extra large **2** extra long
Xmas \'kris-məs *also* 'eks-məs\ *n* [*X* (symbol for *Christ*, fr. the Gk letter chi (X), initial of *Christos* Christ) + *-mas* (in *Christmas*)] : CHRISTMAS
XO *abbr* executive officer
x–ra·di·a·tion \ˌeks-ˌrā-dē-'ā-shən\ *n, often cap* **1** : exposure to X rays **2** : radiation consisting of X rays
x–ray \'eks-ˌrā\ *vb, often cap* : to examine, treat, or photograph with X rays
X ray \'eks-ˌrā\ *n* **1** : a radiation of the same nature as light rays but of extremely short wavelength that is able to penetrate through various thicknesses of solids and to act on photographic film **2** : a photograph taken with X rays — **X–ray** *adj*
XS *abbr* extra small
xu \'sü\ *n, pl* **xu** — see *dong* at MONEY table
xy·lem \'zī-ləm, -ˌlem\ *n* : a woody tissue of vascular plants that transports water and dissolved materials upward, functions in support and storage, and lies central to the phloem
xy·lo·phone \'zī-lə-ˌfōn\ *n* [Gk *xylon* wood + *phōnē* voice, sound] : a musical instrument consisting of a series of wooden bars graduated in length to produce the musical scale, supported on belts of straw or felt, and sounded by striking with two small wooden hammers — **xy·lo·phon·ist** \-ˌfō-nist\ *n*

Y

¹**y** \'wī\ *n, pl* **y's** *or* **ys** \'wīz\ *often cap* : the 25th letter of the English alphabet
²**y** *abbr* **1** yard **2** year
¹**Y** \'wī\ *n* : YMCA, YWCA
²**Y** *symbol* yttrium
¹**-y** *also* **-ey** \ē\ *adj suffix* **1** : characterized by : full of ⟨dirt*y*⟩ ⟨clay*ey*⟩ **2** : having the character of : composed of ⟨icy⟩ **3** : like : like that of ⟨home*y*⟩ ⟨wintr*y*⟩ ⟨stag*y*⟩ **4** : tending or inclined to ⟨sleep*y*⟩ ⟨chatt*y*⟩ **5** : giving occasion for (specified) action ⟨tear*y*⟩ **6** : performing (specified) action ⟨curl*y*⟩
²**-y** \ē\ *n suffix, pl* **-ies 1** : state : condition : quality ⟨beggar*y*⟩ **2** : activity, place of business, or goods dealt with ⟨laundr*y*⟩ **3** : whole body or group ⟨soldier*y*⟩
³**-y** *n suffix, pl* **-ies** : instance of a (specified) action ⟨entreat*y*⟩ ⟨inquir*y*⟩

YA *abbr* young adult
¹**yacht** \'yät\ *n* [obs. D *jaght*, fr. Middle Low German *jacht*, short for *jachtschip*, lit., hunting ship] : a usu. large recreational watercraft
²**yacht** *vb* : to race or cruise in a yacht
yacht·ing *n* : the sport of racing or cruising in a yacht
yachts·man \'yäts-mən\ *n* : a person who owns or sails a yacht
ya·hoo \'yā-hü, 'yä-\ *n, pl* **yahoos** [fr. *Yahoo*, one of a race of brutes having the form of men in Jonathan Swift's *Gulliver's Travels*] : a boorish, crass, or stupid person
Yah·weh \'yä-ˌwā\ *also* **Yah·veh** \-ˌvä\ *n* : GOD 1 — used esp. by the Hebrews
¹**yak** \'yak\ *n, pl* **yaks** *also* **yak** : a large long-haired wild or domesticated ox of Tibet and adjacent Asian uplands

yak

²**yak** also **yack** \\'yak\ n : persistent or voluble talk — **yak** also **yack** vb

yam \\'yam\ n 1 : the edible starchy root of a twining vine that largely replaces the potato as food in the tropics; also : a plant that produces yams 2 : a usu. deep orange sweet potato

yam·mer \\'ya-mər\ vb [ME yameren, alter. of yomeren to murmur, be sad, fr. OE gēomrian] 1 : WHIMPER 2 : CHATTER — **yammer** n

¹**yank** \\'yaŋk\ n : a strong sudden pull : JERK

²**yank** vb : to pull with a quick vigorous movement

Yank \\'yaŋk\ n : YANKEE

Yan·kee \\'yaŋ-kē\ n 1 : a native or inhabitant of New England; also : a native or inhabitant of the northern U.S. 2 : AMERICAN 2

yan·qui \\'yäŋ-kē\ n, often cap [Sp] : a citizen of the U.S. as distinguished from a Latin American

¹**yap** \\'yap\ vb **yapped; yap·ping** 1 : BARK, YELP 2 : GAB

²**yap** n 1 : a quick sharp bark 2 : CHATTER

¹**yard** \\'yärd\ n [ME, fr. OE geard enclosure, yard] 1 : a small enclosed area open to the sky and adjacent to a building 2 : the grounds of a building 3 : the grounds surrounding a house usu. covered with grass 4 : an enclosure for livestock 5 : an area set aside for a particular business or activity 6 : a system of railroad tracks for storing cars and making up trains

²**yard** n [ME yarde, fr. OE gierd twig, measure, yard] 1 — see WEIGHT table 2 : a long spar tapered toward the ends that supports and spreads the head of a sail — **the whole nine yards** : all of a set of circumstances, conditions, or details

yard·age \\'yär-dij\ n : an aggregate number of yards; also : the length, extent, or volume of something as measured in yards

yard·arm \\'yärd-ˌärm\ n : either end of the yard of a square-rigged ship

yard·man \-mən, -ˌman\ n : a person employed in or about a yard

yard·mas·ter \-ˌmas-tər\ n : the person in charge of a railroad yard

yard·stick \-ˌstik\ n 1 : a graduated measuring stick three feet long 2 : a standard for making a critical judgment : CRITERION syn gauge, touchstone, benchmark, measure

yar·mul·ke also **yar·mel·ke** \\'yä-mə-kə, 'yär-, -məl-\ n : a skullcap worn esp. by Jewish males in the synagogue and the home

yarn \\'yärn\ n 1 : a continuous often plied strand composed of fibers or filaments and used in weaving and knitting to form cloth 2 : STORY; esp : a tall tale

yar·row \\'yar-ō\ n : a strong-scented herb related to the daisies that has white or pink flowers in flat clusters

yaw \\'yȯ\ vb : to deviate erratically from a course ⟨the ship ∼ed in the heavy seas⟩ — **yaw** n

yawl \\'yȯl\ n : a 2-masted sailboat with the shorter mast aft of the rudder

¹**yawn** \\'yȯn\ vb : to open wide; esp : to open the mouth wide usu. as an involuntary reaction to fatigue or boredom — **yawn·er** n

²**yawn** n : a deep usu. involuntary intake of breath through the wide-open mouth

yawp or **yaup** \\'yȯp\ vb 1 : to make a raucous noise : SQUAWK 2 : CLAMOR, COMPLAIN — **yawp·er** n

yaws \\'yȯz\ n pl : an infectious tropical disease caused by a spirochete closely resembling the causative agent of syphilis

y–ax·is \\'wī-ˌak-səs\ n : the axis of a graph or of a system of coordinates in a plane parallel to which the ordinates are measured

Yb symbol ytterbium

YB abbr yearbook

Y chromosome n : a sex chromosome that is characteristic of male cells in organisms (as humans) in which the male typically has two unlike sex chromosomes

yd abbr yard

¹**ye** \\'yē\ pron : YOU 1

²**ye** \yē, yə, originally same as THE\ definite article, archaic : THE — used by early printers to represent the manuscript word þe (the)

¹**yea** \\'yā\ adv 1 : YES — used in oral voting 2 : INDEED, TRULY

²**yea** n : an affirmative vote; also : a person casting such a vote

year \\'yir\ n 1 : the period of about 365¼ solar days required for one revolution of the earth around the sun 2 : a cycle of 365 or 366 days beginning with January 1; also : a calendar year specified usu. by a number 3 pl : a time of special significance ⟨their glory ∼s⟩ 4 pl : AGE ⟨advanced in ∼s⟩ 5 : a period of time other than a calendar year ⟨the school ∼⟩

☞ For table, see next page.

year·book \-ˌbùk\ n 1 : a book published annually esp. as a report 2 : a school publication recording the history and activities of a graduating class

year·ling \\'yir-liŋ, 'yər-lən\ n 1 : one that is a year old 2 : a racehorse between January 1st of the year after the year in which it was born and the next January 1st

year·long \\'yir-'lȯŋ\ adj : lasting through a year

¹**year·ly** \\'yir-lē\ adj : ANNUAL

²**yearly** adv : every year

yearn \\'yərn\ vb 1 : to feel a longing or craving 2 : to feel tenderness or compassion syn long, pine, hanker, hunger, thirst

yearn·ing n : a tender or urgent longing

year–round \\'yir-'raùnd\ adj : effective, employed, or operating for the full year : not seasonal ⟨a ∼ resort⟩

yeast \\'yēst\ n 1 : a surface froth or a sediment in sugary liquids (as fruit juices) that consists largely of cells of a tiny fungus and is used in making alcoholic liquors and as a leaven in baking 2 : a commercial product containing yeast plants in a moist or dry medium 3 : a minute one-celled fungus present and functionally active in yeast that reproduces by budding; also : any of several similar fungi 4 archaic : the foam of waves : SPUME 5 : something that causes ferment or activity

yeasty \\'yē-stē\ adj **yeast·i·er; -est** 1 : of, relating to, or resembling yeast 2 : UNSETTLED 3 : full of vitality; also : FRIVOLOUS

yegg \\'yeg\ n : one that breaks open safes to steal; also : ROBBER

¹**yell** \\'yel\ vb : to utter a loud cry or scream : SHOUT

²**yell** n 1 : SHOUT 2 : a cheer used esp. to encourage an athletic team (as at a college)

¹**yel·low** \\'ye-lō\ adj 1 : of the color yellow 2 : having a yellow complexion or skin 3 : SENSATIONAL ⟨∼ journalism⟩ 4 : COWARDLY — **yel·low·ish** \\'ye-lə-wish\ adj

²**yellow** n 1 : a color between green and orange in the spectrum : the color of ripe lemons or sunflowers 2 : something yellow; esp : the yolk of an egg 3 pl : any

---

\ə\abut \ᵊ\kitten \ər\further \a\ash \ā\ace \ä\mop, mar \aù\out \ch\chin \e\bet \ē\easy \g\go \i\hit \ī\ice \j\job \ŋ\sing \ō\go \ȯ\law \ȯi\boy \th\thin \th̲\the \ü\loot \ù\foot \y\yet \zh\vision see also Pronunciation Symbols page

YEARS OF THREE OF THE PRINCIPAL CALENDARS

CALENDAR	GREGORIAN	JEWISH	MUSLIM
YEAR CHRONOLOGY	From Roman year 754, the year immediately following the birth of Christ as placed by Dionysus Exiguus in the 753d year of Rome	From the Creation as fixed at 3761 B.C.	From the year of the Hegira, A.D. 622
YEAR BEGINS	Ten days after the winter solstice	First new moon after the autumnal equinox. The postexilic year began in the spring with the month Nisan, this now being sometimes called the ecclesiastical year	Retrogresses through the seasons; the year 1 began on Friday, July 16
NUMBER OF DAYS	365 (common years) 366 (leap years)	defective 353 (common years) 383 (leap years) regular 354 (common years) 384 (leap years) perfect *or* abundant 355 (common years) 385 (leap years) (There is no regular pattern for defective, regular, and perfect years; adjustments are made so that certain holidays will fall on proper days of the week)	354 (common years) 355 (leap years)
LEAP YEARS	Every fourth year but only those centesimal years divisible by 400	The 3d, 6th, 8th, 11th, 14th, 17th, and 19th years of each 19-year cycle	The 2d, 5th, 7th, 10th, 13th, 16th, 18th, 21st, 24th, 26th, and 29th years of each 30-year cycle

of several plant diseases marked by stunted growth and yellowing of foliage

³**yellow** *vb* : to make or turn yellow

yellow birch *n* : a No. American birch with thin lustrous gray or yellow bark; *also* : its strong hard wood

yellow fever *n* : an acute destructive virus disease marked by prostration, jaundice, fever, and often hemorrhage and transmitted by a mosquito

yellow jack *n* : YELLOW FEVER

yellow jacket *n* : any of various small social wasps having the body barred with bright yellow

yelp \ˈyelp\ *vb* [ME, to boast, cry out, fr. OE *gielpan* to boast, exult] : to utter a sharp quick shrill cry — **yelp** *n*

Ye·me·ni \ˈye-mə-nē\ *n* : YEMENITE — **Yemeni** *adj*

Ye·men·ite \ˈye-mə-ˌnīt\ *n* : a native or inhabitant of Yemen — **Yemenite** *adj*

¹**yen** \ˈyen\ *n, pl* **yen** — see MONEY table

²**yen** *n* [obs. E argot *yen-yen* craving for opium, fr. Chin (Guangdong dial.) *yīn-yáhn*, fr. *yīn* opium + *yáhn* craving] : a strong desire : LONGING

yeo·man \ˈyō-mən\ *n* **1** : an attendant or officer in a royal or noble household **2** : a naval petty officer who performs clerical duties **3** : a person who owns and cultivates a small farm; *esp* : one of a class of English freeholders below the gentry

yeo·man·ry \-rē\ *n* : the body of yeomen and esp. of small landed proprietors

-yer — see -ER

¹**yes** \ˈyes\ *adv* — used as a function word esp. to express assent or agreement or to introduce a more emphatic or explicit phrase

²**yes** *n* : an affirmative reply

ye·shi·va *or* **ye·shi·vah** \yə-ˈshē-və\ *n, pl* **yeshivas** *or* **ye·shi·voth** \-ˌshē-ˈvōt, -ˈvōth\ : a Jewish school esp. for religious instruction

yes–man \ˈyes-ˌman\ *n* : a person who endorses uncritically every opinion or proposal of a superior

¹**yes·ter·day** \ˈyes-tər-dē, -ˌdā\ *adv* **1** : on the day preceding today **2** : only a short time ago

²**yesterday** *n* **1** : the day last past **2** : time not long past

yes·ter·year \ˈyes-tər-ˌyir\ *n* **1** : last year **2** : the recent past

¹**yet** \ˈyet\ *adv* **1** : in addition : BESIDES; *also* : EVEN 6 **2** : up to now; *also* : STILL **3** : so soon as now ⟨not time to go ∼⟩ **4** : EVENTUALLY **5** : NEVERTHELESS, HOWEVER

²**yet** *conj* : but nevertheless : BUT

ye·ti \ˈye-tē, ˈyā-\ *n* [Tibetan] : ABOMINABLE SNOWMAN

yew \ˈyü\ *n* **1** : any of a genus of evergreen trees and shrubs with dark stiff poisonous needles and fleshy fruits **2** : the wood of a yew; *esp* : that of an Old World yew

Yid·dish \ˈyi-dish\ *n* [Yiddish *yidish*, short for *yidish daytsh*, lit., Jewish German] : a language derived from medieval German and spoken by Jews esp. of eastern European origin — **Yiddish** *adj*

¹**yield** \ˈyēld\ *vb* **1** : to give as fitting, owed, or required **2** : GIVE UP; *esp* : to give up possession of on claim or demand **3** : to bear as a natural product **4** : PRODUCE, SUPPLY **5** : to bring in : RETURN **6** : to give way (as to force or influence) **7** : to give place **syn** relinquish, cede, waive, surrender

²**yield** *n* : something yielded; *esp* : the amount or quantity produced or returned

yield·ing \ˈyēl-diŋ\ *adj* **1** : not rigid or stiff : FLEXIBLE **2** : SUBMISSIVE, COMPLIANT

yikes \'yīks\ *interj* — used to express fear or astonishment

yip \'yip\ *vb* **yipped; yip·ping** : YAP

YMCA \ˌwī-ˌem-(ˌ)sē-'ā\ *n* : Young Men's Christian Association

YMHA \ˌwī-ˌem-ˌāch-'ā\ *n* : Young Men's Hebrew Association

yo \'yō\ *interj* — used to call attention, indicate attentiveness, or express affirmation

YOB *abbr* year of birth

yo·del \'yōd-ᵊl\ *vb* **yo·deled** *or* **yo·delled; yo·del·ing** *or* **yo·del·ling** : to sing by suddenly changing from chest voice to falsetto and back; *also* : to shout or call in this manner — **yodel** *n* — **yo·del·er** *n*

yo·ga \'yō-gə\ *n* [Skt., lit., yoking, fr. *yunakti* he yokes] **1** *cap* : a Hindu theistic philosophy teaching the suppression of all activity of body, mind, and will in order that the self may realize its distinction from them and attain liberation **2** : a system of exercises for attaining bodily or mental control and well-being

yo·gi \'yō-gē\ *also* **yo·gin** \-gən, -ˌgin\ *n* **1** : a person who practices yoga **2** *cap* : an adherent of Yoga philosophy

yo·gurt *also* **yo·ghurt** \'yō-gərt\ *n* [Turk *yoğurt*] : a soured slightly acid often flavored semisolid milk food made of skimmed cow's milk and milk solids to which cultures of bacteria have been added

¹yoke \'yōk\ *n, pl* **yokes 1** : a wooden bar or frame by which two draft animals (as oxen) are coupled at the heads or necks for working together; *also* : a frame fitted to a person's shoulders to carry a load in two equal portions **2** : a clamp that embraces two parts to hold or unite them in position **3** *pl usu* **yoke** : two animals yoked together **4** : SERVITUDE, BONDAGE **5** : TIE, LINK ⟨the ∼ of matrimony⟩ **6** : a fitted or shaped piece esp. at the shoulder of a garment **syn** couple, pair, brace

yoke 1

²yoke *vb* **yoked; yok·ing 1** : to put a yoke on : couple with a yoke **2** : to attach a draft animal to ⟨∼ a plow⟩ **3** : JOIN; *esp* : MARRY

yo·kel \'yō-kəl\ *n* : a naive or gullible country person

yolk \'yōk\ *n* **1** : the yellow rounded inner mass of the egg of a bird or reptile **2** : the stored food material of an egg consisting chiefly of proteins, lecithin, and cholesterol — **yolked** \'yōkt\ *adj*

Yom Kip·pur \ˌyōm-ki-'pùr, ˌyäm-, -'ki-pər\ *n* [Heb *yōm kippūr*, lit., day of atonement] : a Jewish holiday observed in September or October with fasting and prayer as a day of atonement

¹yon \'yän\ *adj* : YONDER

²yon *adv* **1** : YONDER **2** : THITHER ⟨ran hither and ∼⟩

¹yon·der \'yän-dər\ *adv* : at or to that place

²yonder *adj* **1** : more distant ⟨the ∼ side of the river⟩ **2** : being at a distance within view ⟨∼ hills⟩

yore \'yōr\ *n* [ME, fr. *yore*, adv., long ago, fr. OE *geāra*, fr. *gēar* year] : time long past ⟨in days of ∼⟩

York·ie \'yòr-kē\ *n* : YORKSHIRE TERRIER

York·shire terrier \'yòrk-ˌshir-, -shər-\ *n* : any of a breed of compact toy terriers with long straight silky hair

you \'yü\ *pron* **1** : the person or persons addressed ⟨∼ are a nice person⟩ ⟨∼ are nice people⟩ **2** : ONE 2 ⟨∼ turn this knob to open it⟩

¹young \'yəŋ\ *adj* **youn·ger** \'yəŋ-gər\; **youn·gest** \'yəŋ-gəst\ **1** : being in the first or an early stage of life, growth, or development **2** : having little experience **3** : recently come into being **4** : YOUTHFUL **5** *cap* : belonging to or representing a new or revived usu. political group or movement — **young·ish** \'yəŋ-ish\ *adj*

²young *n, pl* **young** : young persons; *also* : young animals

young·ling \'yəŋ-liŋ\ *n* : one that is young — **youngling** *adj*

young·ster \-stər\ *n* **1** : a young person **2** : CHILD

your \'yùr, 'yòr, yər\ *adj* : of or relating to you or yourself

yours \'yùrz, 'yòrz\ *pron* : one or the ones belonging to you

your·self \yər-'self\ *pron, pl* **yourselves** \-'selvz\ : YOU — used reflexively, for emphasis, or in absolute constructions ⟨you'll hurt ∼⟩ ⟨do it ∼⟩

youth \'yüth\ *n, pl* **youths** \'yüthz, 'yüths\ **1** : the period of life between childhood and maturity **2** : a young man; *also* : young persons **3** : YOUTHFULNESS

youth·ful \'yüth-fəl\ *adj* **1** : of, relating to, or appropriate to youth **2** : being young and not yet mature **3** : FRESH, VIGOROUS — **youth·ful·ly** *adv* — **youth·ful·ness** *n*

youth hostel *n* : HOSTEL 2

yowl \'yaùl\ *vb* : to utter a loud long mournful cry : WAIL — **yowl** *n*

yo–yo \'yō-(ˌ)yō\ *n, pl* **yo–yos** : a thick grooved double disk with a string attached to its center which is made to fall and rise to the hand by unwinding and rewinding on the string

yr *abbr* **1** year **2** your

yrbk *abbr* yearbook

YT *abbr* Yukon Territory

yt·ter·bi·um \i-'tər-bē-əm\ *n* : a rare metallic chemical element — see ELEMENT table

yt·tri·um \'i-trē-əm\ *n* : a rare metallic chemical element — see ELEMENT table

yu·an \'yü-ən, yù-'än\ *n, pl* **yuan 1** — see MONEY table **2** : the dollar of the Republic of China (Taiwan)

yuc·ca \'yə-kə\ *n* : any of a genus of plants related to the agaves that grow esp. in warm dry regions and bear large clusters of white cup-shaped flowers atop a long stiff stalk

yuck \'yək\ *interj* — used to express rejection or disgust

Yu·go·slav \ˌyü-gō-'släv, -'slav\ *n* : a native or inhabitant of Yugoslavia — **Yugoslav** *adj* — **Yu·go·sla·vi·an** \-'slä-vē-ən\ *adj or n*

yule \'yül\ *n, often cap* : CHRISTMAS

Yule log *n* : a large log formerly put onthe hearth on Christmas Eve as the foundation of the fire

yule·tide \'yül-ˌtīd\ *n, often cap* : CHRISTMASTIDE

yum·my \'yə-mē\ *adj* **yum·mi·er; -est** : highly attractive or pleasing

yup·pie \'yə-pē\ *n* [prob. fr. *young urban professional* + *-ie* (as in hippie)] : a young college-educated adult employed in a well-paying profession and living and working in or near a large city

yurt \'yùrt\ *n* : a light round tent of skins or felt stretched over a lattice framework used by pastoral peoples of inner Asia

YWCA \ˌwī-ˌdə-bəl-yü-(ˌ)sē-'ā\ *n* : Young Women's Christian Association

YWHA \-ˌāch-'ā\ *n* : Young Women's Hebrew Association

Z

¹**z** \ˈzē\ *n, pl* **z's** *or* **zs** *often cap* : the 26th letter of the English alphabet

²**z** *abbr* **1** zero **2** zone

Z *symbol* atomic number

Zach *abbr* Zacharias

Zach·a·ri·as \ˌza-kə-ˈrī-əs\ *n* : ZECHARIAH

zaire \ˈzīr, zä-ˈir\ *n, pl* **zaires** *or* **zaire** — see MONEY table

Zair·ian \zä-ˈir-ē-ən\ *n* : a native or inhabitant of Zaire — **Zairian** *adj*

Zam·bi·an \ˈzam-bē-ən\ *n* : a native or inhabitant of Zambia — **Zambian** *adj*

¹**za·ny** \ˈzā-nē\ *n, pl* **zanies** [It *zanni*, a traditional masked clown, fr. It dial. *Zanni*, nickname for It *Giovanni* John] **1** : CLOWN, BUFFOON **2** : a silly or foolish person

²**zany** *adj* **za·ni·er; -est 1** : characteristic of a zany **2** : CRAZY, FOOLISH — **za·ni·ly** \ˈzā-nə-lē, ˈzān-əl-ē\ *adv* — **za·ni·ness** \ˈzā-nē-nəs\ *n*

zap \ˈzap\ *vb* **zapped; zap·ping 1** : DESTROY, KILL **2** : to irradiate esp. with microwaves

zeal \ˈzēl\ *n* : eager and ardent interest in the pursuit of something • FERVOR **syn** enthusiasm, passion, ardor

zeal·ot \ˈze-lət\ *n* : a zealous person; *esp* : a fanatical partisan **syn** enthusiast, bigot

zeal·ous \ˈze-ləs\ *adj* : filled with, characterized by, or due to zeal — **zeal·ous·ly** *adv* — **zeal·ous·ness** *n*

ze·bra \ˈzē-brə\ *n, pl* **zebras** *also* **zebra** : any of several African mammals related to the horse but conspicuously striped with black or brown and white or buff

ze·bu \ˈzē-bü, -byü\ *n* : an ox of any of various breeds developed in India that have a large fleshy hump over the shoulders, a dewlap, drooping ears, and marked resistance to heat and to insect attack

zebu

Zech *abbr* Zechariah

Zech·a·ri·ah \ˌze-kə-ˈrī-ə\ *n* — see BIBLE table

zed \ˈzed\ *n, chiefly Brit* : the letter *z*

zeit·geist \ˈtsīt-ˌgīst, ˈzīt-\ *n* [G, fr. *Zeit* time + *Geist* spirit] : the general intellectual, moral, and cultural state of an era

Zen \ˈzen\ *n* : a Japanese Buddhist sect that teaches self-discipline, meditation, and attainment of enlightenment through direct intuitive insight

ze·na·na \zə-ˈnä-nə\ *n* : HAREM

ze·nith \ˈzē-nəth\ *n* **1** : the point in the heavens directly overhead **2** : the highest point • ACME **syn** culmination, pinnacle, apex

ze·o·lite \ˈzē-ə-ˌlīt\ *n* : any of various feldsparlike silicates used esp. as water softeners

Zeph *abbr* Zephaniah

Zeph·a·ni·ah \ˌze-fə-ˈnī-ə\ *n* — see BIBLE table

zeph·yr \ˈze-fər\ *n* : a breeze from the west; *also* : a gentle breeze

zep·pe·lin \ˈze-plən, -pə-lən\ *n* [Count Ferdinand von *Zeppelin* †1917 Ger. airship manufacturer] : a cylindrical rigid blimplike airship

¹**ze·ro** \ˈzē-rō, ˈzir-ō\ *n, pl* **zeros** *also* **zeroes** [ultim. fr. Ar *ṣifr*] **1** : the numerical symbol 0 **2** : the number represented by the symbol 0 **3** : the point at which the graduated degrees or measurements on a scale (as of a thermometer) begin **4** : the lowest point

²**zero** *adj* **1** : of, relating to, or being a zero **2** : having no magnitude or quantity **3** : ABSENT, LACKING; *esp* : having no modified inflectional form

³**zero** *vb* : to adjust the sights of a firearm to hit the point aimed at ⟨∼ in⟩

zero hour *n* : the time at which an event (as a military operation) is scheduled to begin

zest \ˈzest\ *n* **1** : a quality of enhancing enjoyment • PIQUANCY **2** : keen enjoyment • GUSTO — **zest·ful** \-fəl\ *adj* — **zest·ful·ly** *adv* — **zest·ful·ness** *n*

ze·ta \ˈzā-tə, ˈzē-\ *n* : the 6th letter of the Greek alphabet — Z or ζ

zi·do·vu·dine \zi-ˈdō-vyü-ˌdēn\ *n* : AZT

¹**zig·zag** \ˈzig-ˌzag\ *n* : one of a series of short sharp turns, angles, or alterations in a course; *also* : something marked by such a series

²**zigzag** *adv* : in or by a zigzag path

³**zigzag** *adj* : having short sharp turns or angles

⁴**zigzag** *vb* **zig·zagged; zig·zag·ging** : to form into or proceed along a zigzag

zil·lion \ˈzil-yən\ *n* : a large indeterminate number

Zim·ba·bwe·an \zim-ˈbä-bwē-ən\ *n* : a native or inhabitant of Zimbabwe — **Zimbabwean** *adj*

zinc \ˈziŋk\ *n* : a bluish white crystalline metallic chemical element that is commonly found in minerals and is used esp. as a protective coating for iron and steel — see ELEMENT table

zinc ointment *n* : ZINC OXIDE OINTMENT

zinc oxide *n* : a white solid used esp. as a pigment, in compounding rubber, and in ointments

zinc oxide ointment *n* : an ointment containing zinc oxide and used for skin disorders

zing \ˈziŋ\ *n* **1** : a shrill humming noise **2** : VITALITY **4** — **zing** *vb*

zing·er \ˈziŋ-ər\ *n* : a pointed witty remark or retort

zin·nia \ˈzi-nē-ə, ˈzēn-yə\ *n* : any of a small genus of tropical American herbs related to the daisies and widely grown for their showy long-lasting flower heads

Zi·on \ˈzī-ən\ *n* **1** : the Jewish people **2** : the Jewish homeland as a symbol of Judaism or of Jewish national aspiration **3** : HEAVEN **4** : UTOPIA

Zi·on·ism \ˈzī-ə-ˌni-zəm\ *n* : an international movement orig. for the establishment of a Jewish national or religious community in Palestine and later for the support of modern Israel — **Zi·on·ist** \-nist\ *adj or n*

¹**zip** \ˈzip\ *vb* **zipped; zip·ping** : to move, act, or function with speed or vigor

²**zip** *n* **1** : a sudden sharp hissing sound **2** : ENERGY, VIM

³**zip** *n* : NOTHING, ZERO

⁴**zip** *vb* **zipped; zip·ping** : to close or open with a zipper

zip code *n, often cap Z&I&P* [*z*one *i*mprovement *p*lan]

: a number that identifies each postal delivery area in the U.S.

zip·per \'zi-pər\ *n* : a fastener consisting of two rows of metal or plastic teeth on strips of tape and a sliding piece that closes an opening by drawing the teeth together

zip·py \'zi-pē\ *adj* **zip·pi·er; -est** : BRISK, SNAPPY

zir·con \'zər-ˌkän\ *n* : a zirconium-containing mineral transparent varieties of which are used as gems

zir·co·ni·um \ˌzər-'kō-nē-əm\ *n* : a gray corrosion-resistant metallic chemical element used esp. in alloys and ceramics — see ELEMENT table

zit \'zit\ *n* : PIMPLE

zith·er \'zi-thər, -thər\ *n* : a musical instrument having 30 to 40 strings played with plectrum and fingers

zi·ti \'zē-tē\ *n, pl* **ziti** [It] : medium-size tubular pasta

zlo·ty \'zlȯ-tē\ *n, pl* **zlo·tys** \-tēz\ *or* **zloty** — see MONEY table

Zn *symbol* zinc

zo·di·ac \'zō-dē-ˌak\ *n* [ME, fr. MF *zodiaque*, fr. L *zodiacus*, fr. Gk *zōidiakos*, fr. *zōidion* carved figure, sign of the zodiac, fr. dim. of *zōion* living being, figure] **1** : an imaginary belt in the heavens that encompasses the paths of most of the planets and that is divided into 12 constellations or signs **2** : a figure representing the signs of the zodiac and their symbols — **zo·di·a·cal** \zō-'dī-ə-kəl\ *adj*

SIGNS OF THE ZODIAC

NUMBER	NAME	SYMBOL	SUN ENTERS	
1	Aries the Ram	♈	March	21
2	Taurus the Bull	♉	April	20
3	Gemini the Twins	♊	May	21
4	Cancer the Crab	♋	June	22
5	Leo the Lion	♌	July	23
6	Virgo the Virgin	♍	August	23
7	Libra the Balance	♎	September	23
8	Scorpio the Scorpion	♏	October	24
9	Sagittarius the Archer	♐	November	22
10	Capricorn the Goat	♑	December	22
11	Aquarius the Water Bearer	♒	January	20
12	Pisces the Fishes	♓	February	19

zom·bie *also* **zom·bi** \'zäm-bē\ *n* : a person who is believed to have died and been brought back to life without speech or free will

zon·al \'zōn-ᵊl\ *adj* : of, relating to, or having the form of a zone — **zon·al·ly** *adv*

¹zone \'zōn\ *n* [ME, fr. L *zona* belt, zone, fr. Gk *zōnē*] **1** : any of five great divisions of the earth's surface made according to latitude and temperature and including the torrid zone about the equator, the two temperate zones lying between the torrid zone and the polar circles, and the two frigid zones lying between the polar circles and the poles **2** : an encircling band or girdle ⟨a ~ of trees⟩ **3** : a section of an area or territory created for a particular purpose ⟨business ~⟩ ⟨postal ~⟩

²zone *vb* **zoned; zon·ing 1** : ENCIRCLE **2** : to arrange in or mark off into zones; *esp* : to divide (as a city) into sections reserved for different purposes

zonked \'zäŋkt\ *adj* : being or acting as if under the influence of alcohol or a drug : HIGH

zoo \'zü\ *n, pl* **zoos** : a zoological garden or collection of living animals usu. for public display

zoo·ge·og·ra·phy \ˌzō-ə-jē-'ä-grə-fē\ *n* : a branch of biogeography concerned with the geographical distribution of animals — **zoo·ge·og·ra·pher** \-fər\ *n* — **zoo·geo·graph·ic** \-ˌjē-ə-'gra-fik\ *also* **zoo·geo·graph·i·cal** \-fi-kəl\ *adj*

zoo·keep·er \'zü-ˌkē-pər\ *n* : a person who cares for animals in a zoo

zool *abbr* zoological; zoology

zoological garden *n* : a garden or park where wild animals are kept for exhibition

zo·ol·o·gy \zō-'ä-lə-jē\ *n* : a branch of biology that deals with the classification and the properties and vital phenomena of animals — **zo·o·log·i·cal** \ˌzō-ə-'lä-ji-kəl\ *adj* — **zo·ol·o·gist** \zō-'ä-lə-jist\ *n*

zoom \'züm\ *vb* **1** : to move with a loud hum or buzz **2** : to gain altitude quickly **3** : to focus a camera or microscope using a special lens that permits the apparent distance of the object to be varied — **zoom** *n*

zoom lens *n* : a camera lens in which the image size can be varied continuously while the image remains in focus

zoo·mor·phic \ˌzō-ə-'mȯr-fik\ *adj* **1** : having the form of an animal **2** : of, relating to, or being the representation of a deity in the form or with the attributes of an animal

zoo·plank·ton \ˌzō-ə-'plaŋk-tən, -ˌtän\ *n* : animal life of the plankton

zoo·spore \'zō-ə-ˌspȯr\ *n* : a motile spore

zoot suit \'züt-\ *n* : a flashy suit of extreme cut typically consisting of a thigh-length jacket with wide padded shoulders and trousers that are wide at the top and narrow at the bottom — **zoot-suit·er** \-ˌsü-tər\ *n*

Zo·ro·as·tri·an·ism \ˌzōr-ə-'was-trē-ə-ˌni-zəm\ *n* : a religion founded by the Persian prophet Zoroaster — **Zo·ro·as·tri·an** \-trē-ən\ *adj or n*

Zou·ave \zü-'äv\ *n* : a member of a French infantry unit orig. composed of Algerians wearing a brilliant uniform and conducting a quick spirited drill; *also* : a member of a military unit modeled on the Zouaves

zounds \'zaündz\ *interj* [euphemism for *God's wounds*] — used as a mild oath

zoy·sia \'zȯi-shə, -zhə, -sē-ə, -zē-ə\ *n* : any of a genus of creeping perennial grasses having fine wiry leaves and including some used as lawn grasses

ZPG *abbr* zero population growth

Zr *symbol* zirconium

zuc·chet·to \zü-'ke-tō, tsü-\ *n, pl* **-tos** [It] : a small round skullcap worn by Roman Catholic ecclesiastics

zuc·chi·ni \zù-'kē-nē\ *n, pl* **-ni** *or* **-nis** [It] : a summer squash of bushy growth with smooth cylindrical dark green fruits; *also* : its fruit

Zu·lu \'zü-ˌlü\ *n, pl* **Zulu** *or* **Zulus** : a member of a Bantu-speaking people of South Africa; *also* : the Bantu language of the Zulus

Zu·ni \'zü-nē\ *or* **Zu·ñi** \-nyē\ *n, pl* **Zuni** *or* **Zunis** *or* **Zuñi** *or* **Zuñis** : a member of an American Indian people of western New Mexico; *also* : the language of the Zuni people

zwie·back \'swē-ˌbak, 'swī-, 'zwē-, 'zwī-, -ˌbäk\ *n* [G, lit., twice baked, fr. *zwie-* twice + *backen* to bake] : a usu. sweetened bread that is baked and then sliced and toasted until dry and crisp

Zwing·li·an \'zwiŋ-glē-ən, 'swiŋ-, -lē-; 'tsfiŋ-lē-\ *adj* : of or relating to the Swiss religious reformer Ulrich Zwingli or his teachings — **Zwinglian** *n*

zy·gote \'zī-ˌgōt\ *n* : a cell formed by the union of two sexual cells; *also* : the developing individual produced from such a cell — **zy·got·ic** \zī-'gä-tik\ *adj*

Common English Given Names

The following vocabulary presents given names that are most frequent in English use. The list is not exhaustive either of the names themselves or the variant spellings of those names which are entered. Compound or double names and surnames used as given names are not entered except in cases where long-continued or common use gives them an independent character.

Besides the pronunciations of the names, the list usually provides at least one of the following kinds of information at each entry: (1) etymology, indicating the language source but not the original form of the name, and (2) meaning where known or ascertainable with reasonable certainty.

Names of Men

Aar·on \'ar-ən, 'er-\ [Heb]
Abra·ham \'ā-brə-₁ham\ [Heb]
Ad·am \'ad-əm\ [Heb] man
Ad·di·son \'ad-ə-sən\ [fr. a surname]
Adolph \'ad-₁älf, 'ā-₁dälf\ [Gmc] noble wolf, *i.e.,* noble hero
Adri·an \'ā-drē-ən\ [L] of Hadria, ancient town in central Italy
Al \'al\ *dim of* ALAN, ALBERT, etc.
Al·an \'al-ən\ [Celt]
Al·bert \'al-bərt\ [Gmc] illustrious through nobility
Al·den \'ȯl-dən\ [OE] old friend
Al·ex \'al-iks\ *or* **Al·ec** \'al-ik\ *dim of* ALEXANDER
Al·ex·an·der \₁al-ig-'zan-dər\ [Gk] a defender of men
Al·fred \'al-frəd, -fərd\ [OE] elf counsel, *i.e.,* good counsel
Al·len *or* **Al·lan** *or* **Al·lyn** \'al-ən\ *var of* ALAN
Al·ton \'ȯlt-ᵊn, 'alt-\ [prob. fr. a surname]
Al·va *or* **Al·vah** \'al-və\ [Heb]
Al·vin \'al-vən\ [Gmc]
Amos \'ā-məs\ [Heb]
An·dre \'än-(₁)drā\ [F] *var of* ANDREW
An·drew \'an-(₁)drü\ [Gk] manly
An·dy \'an-dē\ *dim of* ANDREW
An·ge·lo \'an-jə-₁lō\ [It, fr. Gk] angel, messenger
An·gus \'aŋ-gəs\ [Celt]
An·tho·ny \'an(t)-thə-nē, *chiefly Brit* 'an-tə-\ [L]
An·ton \'ant-ᵊn, 'an-₁tän\ [G & Slav] *var of* ANTHONY
An·to·nio \an-'tō-nē-₁ō\ [It] *var of* ANTHONY
Ar·chi·bald \'är-chə-₁bȯld, -bəld\ [Gmc]
Ar·chie \'är-chē\ *dim of* ARCHIBALD
Ar·den \'ärd-ᵊn\ [prob. fr. a surname]
Ar·len *or* **Ar·lin** \'är-lən\ [prob. fr. a surname]
Ar·lo \'är-(₁)lō\
Ar·mand \'är-₁mänd, -mənd\ [F] *var of* HERMAN
Arne \'ärn\ [Scand] eagle
Ar·nold \'ärn-ᵊld\ [Gmc] power of an eagle
Art \'ärt\ *dim of* ARTHUR
Ar·thur \'är-thər\ [prob. L]
Au·brey \'ȯ-brē\ [Gmc] elf ruler
Au·gust \'ȯ-gəst\ [L] August, majestic
Aus·tin \'ȯs-tən, 'äs-\ *alter of* Augustine

Bai·ley \'bā-lē\ [fr. a surname]
Bar·clay \'bär-klē\ [fr. a surname]
Bar·net *or* **Bar·nett** \bär-'net\ [fr. a surname]
Bar·ney \'bär-nē\ *dim of* BERNARD
Bar·rett \'bar-ət\ [fr. a surname]
Bar·ry *or* **Bar·rie** \'bar-ē\ [Ir]
Bart \'bärt\ *dim of* Bartholomew
Bar·ton \'bärt-ᵊn\ [fr. a surname]

Ba·sil \'baz-əl, 'bäs-, 'bās-, 'bāz-\ [Gk] kingly, royal
Ben \'ben\ *or* **Ben·nie** *or* **Ben·ny** \'ben-ē\ *dim of* BENJAMIN
Ben·e·dict \'ben-ə-₁dikt\ [L] blessed
Ben·ja·min \'benj-(ə-)mən\ [Heb] son of the right hand
Ben·nett \'ben-ət\ [OF] *var of* BENEDICT
Ben·ton \'bent-ᵊn\ [fr. a surname]
Ber·nard \'bər-nərd, (₁)bər-'närd\ *or* **Bern·hard** \'bərn-₁härd\ [Gmc] bold as a bear
Ber·nie \'bər-nē\ *dim of* BERNARD
Bert *or* **Burt** \'bərt\ *dim of* BERTRAM, ALBERT, etc.
Ber·tram \'bər-trəm\ [Gmc] bright raven
Bill \'bil\ *or* **Bil·ly** *or* **Bil·lie** \'bil-ē\ *dim of* WILLIAM
Blaine \'blān\ [fr. a surname]
Blair \'bla(ə)r, 'ble(ə)r\ [fr. a surname]
Bob·by \'bäb-ē\ *or* **Bob** \'bäb\ *dim of* ROBERT
Bo·ris \'bōr-əs, 'bȯr-, 'bär-\ [Russ]
Boyd \'bȯid\ [fr. a surname]
Brad·ford \'brad-fərd\ [fr. a surname]
Brad·ley \'brad-lē\ [fr. a surname]
Bran·don \'bran-dən\ [fr. a surname]
Bren·dan \'bren-dən\ [Celt]
Brent \'brent\ [fr. a surname]
Brett *or* **Bret** \'bret\ [IrGael]
Bri·an *or* **Bry·an** \'brī-ən\ [Celt]
Brooks \'brüks\ [fr. a surname]
Bruce \'brüs\ [fr. a surname]
Bru·no \'brü-(₁)nō\ [It, fr. Gmc] brown
Bryce *or* **Brice** \'brīs\ [fr. a surname]
Bud·dy \'bəd-ē\ [prob. alter. of *brother*]
Bu·ford \'byü-fərd\ [fr. a surname]
Burke \'bərk\ [fr. a surname]
Bur·ton \'bərt-ᵊn\ [fr. a surname]
By·ron \'bī-rən\ [fr. a surname]

Cal·vin \'kal-vən\ [fr. a surname]
Cam·er·on \'kam-(ə-)rən\ [fr. a surname]
Carl \'kär(-ə)l\ *var of* KARL
Car·los \'kär-ləs, -₁lōs\ [Sp] *var of* CHARLES
Carl·ton *or* **Carle·ton** \'kär(-ə)l-tən, 'kärlt-ᵊn\ [fr. a surname]
Car·lyle \kär-'lī(ə)l, 'kär-₁\ [fr. a surname]
Car·men \'kär-mən\ [Sp, fr. L] song
Car·roll \'kar-əl\ [fr. a surname]
Car·son \'kärs-ᵊn\ [fr. a surname]
Car·ter \'kärt-ər\ [fr. a surname]
Cary *or* **Car·ey** \'ka(ə)r-ē, 'ke(ə)r-ē\ [fr. a surname]
Ce·cil \'sē-səl, 'ses-əl\ [L]
Chad \'chad\ [Gmc]

\ə\abut \ᵊ\kitten \ər\further \a\ash \ā\ace \ä\mop, mar \aù\out \ch\chin \e\bet \ē\easy \g\go \i\hit \ī\ice \j\job \ŋ\sing \ō\go \ȯ\law \ȯi\boy \th\thin \t͟h\the \ü\loot \ù\foot \y\yet \zh\vision *see also* Pronunciation Symbols page

Charles \\'chär(-ə)lz\ [Gmc] man of the common people
Ches·ter \\'ches-tər\ [fr. a surname]
Chris \\'kris\ *dim of* CHRISTOPHER
Chris·tian \\'kris(h)-chən\ [Gk] Christian (the believer)
Chris·to·pher \\'kris-tə-fər\ [Gk] Christ bearer
Clar·ence \\'klar-ən(t)s\ [fr. the English dukedom]
Clark *or* **Clarke** \\'klärk\ [fr. a surname]
Claude *or* **Claud** \\'klȯd\ [L]
Clay \\'klā\ *dim of* CLAYTON
Clay·ton \\'klāt-ᵊn\ [fr. a surname]
Clem \\'klem\ *dim of* CLEMENT
Clem·ent \\'klem-ənt\ [L] mild, merciful
Clif·ford \\'klif-ərd\ [fr. a surname]
Clif·ton \\'klif-tən\ [fr. a surname]
Clint \\'klint\ *dim of* CLINTON
Clin·ton \\'klint-ᵊn\ [fr. a surname]
Clyde \\'klīd\ [fr. a surname]
Cole \\'kōl\ [fr. a surname]
Co·lin \\'käl-ən, 'kō-lən\ *or* **Col·lin** \\'käl-ən\ *dim of* NICH-OLAS
Con·rad \\'kän-₁rad, -rəd\ [Gmc] bold counsel
Con·stan·tine \\'kän(t)-stən-₁tēn, -₁tīn\ [L]
Cor·ey \\'kȯr-ē\ [fr. a surname]
Cor·ne·lius \kȯr-'nēl-yəs\ [L]
Craig \\'krāg\ [fr. a surname]
Cur·tis \\'kərt-əs\ [OF] courteous
Cyr·il \\'sir-əl\ [Gk] lordly
Cy·rus \\'sī-rəs\ [OPer]

Dale \\'dā(ə)l\ [fr. a surname]
Dal·las \\'dal-əs\ [fr. a surname]
Dal·ton \\'dȯlt-ᵊn\ [fr. a surname]
Dan \\'dan\ [Heb] judge
Da·na \\'dā-nə\ [fr. a surname]
Dan·iel \\'dan-yəl *also* 'dan-ᵊl\ [Heb] God has judged
Dan·ny \\'dan-ē\ *dim of* DANIEL
Dar·old \\'dar-əld\ *perh alter of* DARRELL
Dar·rell *or* **Dar·rel** *or* **Dar·ryl** *or* **Dar·yl** \\'dar-əl\ [fr. a surname]
Dar·win \\'där-wən\ [fr. a surname]
Dave \\'dāv\ *dim of* DAVID
Da·vid \\'dā-vəd\ [Heb] beloved
Da·vis \\'dā-vəs\ [fr. a surname]
Dean *or* **Deane** \\'dēn\ [fr. a surname]
Del·a·no \\'del-ə-₁nō\ [fr. a surname]
Del·bert \\'del-bərt\ *dim of* Adalbert
Del·mar \\'del-mər, -₁mär\ *or* **Del·mer** \-mər\ [fr. a surname]
Den·nis *or* **Den·is** \\'den-əs\ [OF, fr. Gk] belonging to Dionysus, god of wine
Den·ny \\'den-ē\ *dim of* DENNIS
Den·ton \\'dent-ᵊn\ [fr. a surname]
Der·ek \\'der-ik\ [Middle Dutch, fr. Gmc] ruler of the people
Dew·ey \\'d(y)ü-ē\ [fr. a surname]
De·witt \di-'wit\ [fr. a surname]
Dex·ter \\'dek-stər\ [L] on the right hand, fortunate
Dick \\'dik\ *dim of* RICHARD
Dirk \\'dərk\ [Dutch] *var of* DEREK
Dom·i·nic *or* **Dom·i·nick** \\'däm-ə-(₁)nik\ [L] belonging to the Lord
Don *or* **Donn** \\'dän\ *dim of* DONALD
Don·al \\'dän-ᵊl\ *var of* DONALD
Don·ald \\'dän-ᵊld\ [ScGael] world ruler
Don·nie \\'dän-ē\ *dim of* DON
Don·o·van \\'dän-ə-vən, 'dən-\ [fr. a surname]
Doug \\'dəg\ *dim of* DOUGLAS
Doug·las *or* **Doug·lass** \\'dəg-ləs\ [fr. a surname]
Duane \dü-'ān, 'dwän\ [fr. a surname]
Dud·ley \\'dəd-lē\ [fr. a surname]
Dun·can \\'dəŋ-kən\ [ScGael] brown head
Dur·ward \\'dər-wərd\ [fr. a surname]
Dwayne *or* **Dwaine** \\'dwān\ [fr. a surname]

Dwight \\'dwīt\ [fr. a surname]
Dy·lan \\'dil-ən\ [W]

Earl *or* **Earle** \\'ər(-ə)l\ [OE] warrior, noble
Ed \\'ed\ *dim of* EDWARD, EDGAR, etc.
Ed·die *or* **Ed·dy** \\'ed-ē\ *dim of* ED
Ed·gar \\'ed-gər\ [OE] spear of wealth
Ed·mund *or* **Ed·mond** \\'ed-mənd\ [OE] protector of wealth
Ed·son \\'ed-sən\ [fr. a surname]
Ed·ward \\'ed-wərd\ [OE] guardian of wealth
Ed·win \\'ed-wən\ [OE] friend of wealth
El·bert \\'el-bərt\ *var of* ALBERT
Eli \\'ē-₁lī\ [Heb] high
E·li·as \i-'lī-əs\ [Gk] *var of* Elijah
El·liott *or* **El·liot** *or* **El·iot** \\'el-ē-ət, 'el-yət\ [fr. a surname]
El·lis \\'el-əs\ *var of* ELIAS
Ells·worth \\'elz-(₁)wərth\ [fr. a surname]
El·mer \\'el-mər\ [fr. a surname]
El·mo \\'el-(₁)mō\ [It, fr. Gk] lovable
El·ton \\'elt-ᵊn\ [fr. a surname]
El·vin \\'el-vən\ [fr. a surname]
El·wood *or* **Ell·wood** \\'el-₁wůd\ [fr. a surname]
Em·man·u·el *or* **Eman·u·el** \i-'man-yə(-wə)l\ [Heb] God with us
Em·er·son \\'em-ər-sən\ [fr. a surname]
Emil \\'ā-məl\ *or* **Emile** \ā-'mē(ə)l\ [L]
Em·mett \\'em-ət\ [fr. a surname]
Em·o·ry *or* **Em·ery** \\'em-(ə-)rē\ [Gmc]
Er·ic *or* **Er·ich** *or* **Er·ik** \\'er-ik\ [Scand]
Er·nest *or* **Ear·nest** \\'ər-nəst\ [G] earnestness
Er·nie \\'ər-nē\ *dim of* ERNEST
Ernst \\'ərn(t)st, 'e(ə)rn(t)st\ [G] *var of* ERNEST
Er·rol \\'er-əl\ [prob. fr. a surname]
Ethan \\'ē-thən\ [Heb] strength
Eu·gene \yů-'jēn, 'yü-₁\ [Gk] wellborn
Ev·an \\'ev-ən\ [W] *var of* JOHN
Ev·er·ett \\'ev-(ə-)rət\ [fr. a surname]

Fe·lix \\'fē-liks\ [L] happy, prosperous
Fer·di·nand \\'fərd-ᵊn-₁and\ [Gmc]
Fer·nan·do \fər-'nan-(₁)dō\ [Sp] *var of* FERDINAND
Fletch·er \\'flech-ər\ [fr. a surname]
Floyd \\'flȯid\ [fr. a surname]
For·rest *or* **For·est** \\'fȯr-əst, 'fär-\ [fr. a surname]
Fos·ter \\'fȯs-tər, 'fäs-\ [fr. a surname]
Fran·cis \\'fran(t)-səs\ [OIt & OF] Frenchman
Fran·cis·co \fran-'sis-(₁)kō\ [Sp] *var of* FRANCIS
Frank \\'fraŋk\ [Gmc] freeman, Frank
Frank·lin *or* **Frank·lyn** \\'fraŋ-klən\ [fr. a surname]
Fred \\'fred\ *dim of* FREDERICK, ALFRED
Fred·die \\'fred-ē\ *dim of* FREDERICK
Fred·er·ick *or* **Fred·er·ic** *or* **Fred·rick** *or* **Fred·ric** \\'fred-(ə-)rik\ [Gmc] peaceful ruler
Free·man \\'frē-mən\ [fr. a surname]
Fritz \\'frits\ [G] *dim of* Friedrich

Ga·bri·el \\'gā-brē-əl\ [Heb] man of God
Gar·land \\'gär-lənd\ [fr. a surname]
Gar·rett \\'gar-ət\ [fr. a surname]
Garth \\'gärth\ [fr. a surname]
Gary \\'gar-ē, 'ger-ē\ *or* **Gar·ry** \\'gar-\ [prob. fr. a surname]
Gay·lord \\'gā-₁lȯ(ə)rd\ [fr. a surname]
Gene \\'jēn\ *dim of* EUGENE
Geof·frey \\'jef-rē\ [OF, fr. Gmc]
George \\'jȯ(ə)rj\ [Gk] of or relating to a farmer
Ger·ald \\'jer-əld\ [Gmc] spear dominion
Ge·rard \jə-'rärd, *chiefly Brit* 'jer-₁ärd, -ərd\ *or* **Ger·hard** \\'ge(ə)r-₁härd\ [Gmc] strong with the spear
Ger·ry \\'jer-ē\ *var of* JERRY

Gil·bert \\'gil-bərt\\ [Gmc] *prob* illustrious through hostages
Giles \\'jī(ə)lz\\ [OF, fr. LL]
Glenn *or* **Glen** \\'glen\\ [fr. a surname]
Gor·don \\'gȯrd-ᵊn\\ [fr. a surname]
Gra·ham \\'grā-əm, 'gra(-ə)m\\ [fr. a surname]
Grant \\'grant\\ [fr. a surname]
Gran·ville \\'gran-ˌvil\\ [fr. a surname]
Gray \\'grā\\ [fr. a surname]
Gregg *or* **Greg** \\'greg\\ *dim of* GREGORY
Greg·o·ry \\'greg-(ə-)rē\\ [LGk] vigilant
Gro·ver \\'grō-vər\\ [fr. a surname]
Gus \\'gəs\\ *dim of* Gustav *or* Augustus
Guy \\'gī\\ [OF, fr. Gmc]

Hal \\'hal\\ *dim of* HENRY
Hall \\'hȯl\\ [fr. a surname]
Ham·il·ton \\'ham-əl-tən, -əlt-ᵊn\\ [fr. a surname]
Hans \\'hanz, 'hän(t)s\\ [G] *dim of* Johannes
Har·lan \\'här-lən\\ *or* **Har·land** \\-lənd\\ [fr. a surname]
Har·ley \\'här-lē\\ [fr. a surname]
Har·low \\'här-(ˌ)lō\\ [fr. a surname]
Har·mon \\'här-mən\\ [fr. a surname]
Har·old \\'har-əld\\ [OE] army dominion
Har·ris \\'har-əs\\ [fr. a surname]
Har·ri·son \\'har-ə-sən\\ [fr. a surname]
Har·ry \\'har-ē\\ *dim of* HENRY
Har·vey \\'här-vē\\ [fr. a surname]
Hec·tor \\'hek-tər\\ [Gk] holding fast
Hel·mut \\'hel-mət, -ˌmüt\\ [G] helmet courage
Hen·ry \\'hen-rē\\ [Gmc] ruler of the home
Her·bert \\'hər-bərt\\ [Gmc] illustrious by reason of an army
Her·man *or* **Her·mann** \\'hər-mən\\ [Gmc] warrior
Her·schel *or* **Her·shel** \\'hər-shəl\\ [fr. a surname]
Hi·ram \\'hī-rəm\\ [Phoenician]
Ho·bart \\'hō-bərt, -ˌbärt\\ [fr. a surname]
Hol·lis \\'häl-əs\\ [fr. a surname]
Ho·mer \\'hō-mər\\ [Gk]
Hor·ace \\'hȯr-əs, 'här-\\ [L]
How·ard \\'haů(-ə)rd\\ [fr. a surname]
How·ell \\'haů(-ə)l\\ [W]
Hu·bert \\'hyü-bərt\\ [Gmc] bright in spirit
Hud·son \\'həd-sən\\ [fr. a surname]
Hugh \\'hyü\\ *or* **Hu·go** \\'hyü-(ˌ)gō\\ [Gmc] *prob* mind, spirit

Ian \\'ē-ən\\ [ScGael] *var of* JOHN
Ira \\'ī-rə\\ [Heb]
Ir·ving \\'ər-viŋ\\ *or* **Ir·vin** \\-vən\\ [fr. a surname]
Ir·win \\'ər-wən\\ [fr. a surname]
Isaac \\'ī-zik, -zək\\ [Heb] he laughs
Ivan \\'ī-vən\\ [Russ] *var of* JOHN

Jack \\'jak\\ *dim of* JOHN
Jack·son \\'jak-sən\\ [fr. a surname]
Ja·cob \\'jā-kəb, -kəp\\ [Heb] one who supplants
Jacques *or* **Jacque** \\'zhäk\\ [F] *var of* JAMES
Jake \\'jāk\\ *dim of* JACOB
James \\'jāmz\\ [OF, fr. LL *Jacobus*] *var of* JACOB
Ja·mie \\'jā-mē\\ *dim of* JAMES
Jan \\'jan\\ [Dutch & LG] *var of* JOHN
Jar·ed \\'jar-əd, 'jer-\\ [Heb] descent
Ja·son \\'jās-ᵊn\\ [Gk]
Jay \\'jā\\ [prob. fr. a surname]
Jed \\'jed\\ *dim of* Jedidiah
Jef·frey *or* **Jeff·ery** *or* **Jef·fry** \\'jef-(ə-)rē\\ *var of* GEOFFREY
Jer·ald *or* **Jer·old** *or* **Jer·rold** \\'jer-əld\\ *var of* GERALD
Jer·e·my \\'jer-ə-mē\\ *or* **Jer·e·mi·ah** \\ˌjer-ə-'mī-ə\\ [Heb] *prob* Yahweh exalts
Je·rome \\jə-'rōm, *Brit also* 'jer-əm\\ [Gk] bearing a holy name
Jer·ry *or* **Jere** \\'jer-ē\\ *dim of* GERALD

Jes·se \\'jes-ē\\ [Heb]
Jim \\'jim\\ *or* **Jim·my** *or* **Jim·mie** \\'jim-ē\\ *dim of* JAMES
Jo·dy \\'jō-dē\\ *perh alter of* JOSEPH
Joe \\'jō\\ *dim of* JOSEPH
Jo·el \\'jō-əl\\ [Heb] Yahweh is God
John \\'jän\\ [Heb] Yahweh is gracious
Jon \\'jän\\ *var of* JOHN
Jo·nah \\'jō-nə\\ [Heb]
Jon·a·than \\'jän-ə-thən\\ [Heb] Yahweh has given
Jor·dan \\'jȯrd-ᵊn\\ [fr. a surname]
Jo·seph *or* **Josef** \\'jō-zəf *also* -səf\\ [Heb] he shall add
Josh·u·a \\'jäsh-(ə-)wə\\ [Heb] Yahweh saves
Judd \\'jəd\\ [fr. a surname]
Jud·son \\'jəd-sən\\ [fr. a surname]
Jules \\'jülz\\ [F] *var of* JULIUS
Ju·lian *or* **Ju·lien** \\'jül-yən\\ [L] sprung from or belonging to Julius
Ju·lius \\'jül-yəs\\ *or* **Ju·lio** \\-(ˌ)yō\\ [L]
Jus·tin \\'jəs-tən\\ *or* **Jus·tus** \\-təs\\ [L] just

Karl \\'kär(-ə)l\\ [G & Scand] *var of* CHARLES
Keith \\'kēth\\ [fr. a surname]
Kel·ly \\'kel-ē\\ [fr. a surname]
Ken \\'ken\\ *dim of* KENNETH
Ken·dall \\'ken-dᵊl\\ [fr. a surname]
Ken·neth \\'ken-əth\\ [ScGael]
Kent \\'kent\\ [prob. fr. a surname]
Ken·ton \\'kent-ᵊn\\ [fr. a surname]
Ker·mit \\'kər-mət\\ [prob. fr. a surname]
Ker·ry \\'ker-ē\\ [prob. fr. the county of Ireland]
Kev·in \\'kev-ən\\ [OIr]
Kir·by \\'kər-bē\\ [fr. a surname]
Kirk \\'kərk\\ [fr. a surname]
Klaus \\'klaůs, 'klȯs\\ [G] *dim of* Nikolaus
Kurt \\'kərt, 'ků(ə)rt\\ [G] *dim of* CONRAD
Kyle \\'kī(ə)l\\ [Celt]

La·mar \\lə-'mär\\ [fr. a surname]
Lance \\'lan(t)s\\ *dim of* Lancelot
Lane \\'lān\\ [fr. a surname]
Lan·ny \\'lan-ē\\ *prob dim of* LAWRENCE
Lar·ry \\'lar-ē\\ *dim of* LAWRENCE
Lars \\'lärz\\ [Sw] *var of* LAWRENCE
Law·rence *or* **Lau·rence** \\'lȯr-ən(t)s, 'lär-\\ [L] of Laurentum, ancient city in central Italy
Lee *or* **Leigh** \\'lē\\ [fr. a surname]
Leigh·ton *or* **Lay·ton** \\'lāt-ᵊn\\ [fr. a surname]
Le·land \\'lē-lənd\\ [fr. a surname]
Len \\'len\\ *dim of* LEONARD
Leo \\'le-(ˌ)ō\\ [L] lion
Le·on \\'lē-ˌän, -ən\\ [Sp] *var of* LEO
Leon·ard \\'len-ərd\\ [G] strong or brave as a lion
Le·roy \\li-'rȯi, 'lē-ˌrȯi\\ [OF] royal
Les·lie \\'les-lē, 'lez-\\ [fr. a surname]
Les·ter \\'les-tər\\ [fr. a surname]
Lew·is \\'lü-əs\\ *var of* LOUIS
Li·am \\'lē-əm\\ [Ir]
Lin·coln \\'liŋ-kən\\ [fr. a surname]
Li·o·nel \\'lī-ən-ᵊl, -ə-ˌnel\\ [OF] young lion
Lloyd *or* **Loyd** \\'lȯid\\ [W] gray
Lo·gan \\'lō-gən\\ [fr. a surname]
Lon \\'län\\ *dim of* Alonzo
Lon·nie *or* **Lon·ny** \\'län-ē\\ *dim of* LON
Lo·ren \\'lȯr-ən, 'lȯr-\\ *dim of* Lorenzo
Lou·ie \\'lü-ē\\ *var of* LOUIS
Lou·is *or* **Lu·is** \\'lü-əs, 'lü-ē\\ [Gmc] famous warrior
Low·ell \\'lō-əl\\ [fr. a surname]
Lu·cian \\'lü-shən\\ [Gk]

\\ə\\abut \\ᵊ\\kitten \\ər\\further \\a\\ash \\ā\\ace \\ä\\mop, mar
\\aů\\out \\ch\\chin \\e\\bet \\ē\\easy \\g\\go \\i\\hit \\ī\\ice \\j\\job
\\ŋ\\sing \\ō\\go \\ȯ\\law \\ȯi\\boy \\th\\thin \\ <u>th</u> \\the \\ü\\loot \\ů\\foot
\\y\\yet \\zh\\vision *see also* Pronunciation Symbols page

Lud·wig \ˈləd-(ˌ)wig, ˈlüd-\ [G] *var of* LOUIS
Luke \ˈlük\ [Gk] *prob dim of* LUCIUS
Lu·ther \ˈlü-thər\ [fr. a surname]
Lyle \ˈlī(ə)l\ [fr. a surname]
Ly·man \ˈlī-mən\ [fr. a surname]
Lynn \ˈlin\ [fr. a surname]

Mack *or* **Mac** \ˈmak\ [fr. surnames beginning with *Mc* or *Mac*, fr. Gael *mac* son]
Mal·colm \ˈmal-kəm\ [ScGael] servant of (St.) Columba (6th cent. Irish missionary)
Man·fred \ˈman-frəd\ [Gmc] peace among men
Man·u·el \ˈman-yə(-wə)l\ [Sp & Pg] *var of* EMMANUEL
Mar·cus \ˈmär-kəs\ [L]
Ma·rio \ˈmär-ē-ˌō\ [It] *var of* MARIUS
Mar·i·on \ˈmer-ē-ən, ˈmar-\ [fr. a surname]
Mark *or* **Marc** \ˈmärk\ *var of* MARCUS
Mar·lin \ˈmär-lən\ [prob. fr. a surname]
Mar·shall *or* **Mar·shal** \ˈmär-shəl\ [fr. a surname]
Mar·tin \ˈmärt-ᵊn\ [LL] of Mars
Mar·vin \ˈmär-vən\ [prob. fr. a surname]
Ma·son \ˈmās-ᵊn\ [fr. a surname]
Matt \ˈmat\ *dim of* MATTHEW
Mat·thew \ˈmath-(ˌ)yü *also* ˈmath-(ˌ)ü\ [Heb] gift of Yahweh
Mau·rice \ˈmȯr-əs, ˈmär-; mȯ-ˈrēs\ [LL] *prob* Moorish
Max \ˈmaks\ *dim of* MAXIMILIAN
Max·well \ˈmak-ˌswel, -swəl\ [fr. a surname]
May·nard \ˈmā-nərd\ [Gmc] bold in strength
Mel·ville \ˈmel-ˌvil\ [fr. a surname]
Mel·vin *or* **Mel·vyn** \ˈmel-vən\ [prob. fr. a surname]
Mer·e·dith \ˈmer-əd-əth\ [W]
Merle \ˈmər(-ə)l\ [F] blackbird
Mer·lin *or* **Mer·lyn** \ˈmər-lən\ [Celt]
Mer·rill \ˈmer-əl\ [fr. a surname]
Mi·chael \ˈmī-kəl\ [Heb] who is like God?
Mick·ey \ˈmik-ē\ *dim of* MICHAEL
Mike \ˈmīk\ *dim of* MICHAEL
Mi·lan \ˈmī-lən\ [prob. fr. the city in Italy]
Miles *or* **Myles** \ˈmī(ə)lz\ [Gmc]
Mil·ford \ˈmil-fərd\ [fr. a surname]
Mil·lard \ˈmil-ərd, mil-ˈärd\ [fr. a surname]
Mi·lo \ˈmī-(ˌ)lō\ [prob. L]
Mil·ton \ˈmilt-ᵊn\ [fr. a surname]
Mitch·ell \ˈmich-əl\ [fr. a surname]
Mon·roe \mən-ˈrō, ˈmən-ˌ\ [fr. a surname]
Mon·te *or* **Mon·ty** \ˈmänt-ē\ *dim of* MONTAGUE
Mor·gan \ˈmȯr-gən\ [W] *prob* dweller on the sea
Mor·ris \ˈmȯr-əs, ˈmär-\ *var of* MAURICE
Mor·ton \ˈmȯrt-ᵊn\ [fr. a surname]
Mur·ray \ˈmər-ē, ˈmə-rē\ [fr. a surname]
My·ron \ˈmī-rən\ [Gk]

Na·than \ˈnā-thən\ [Heb] given, gift
Na·than·iel \nə-ˈthan-yəl\ [Heb] gift of God
Ned \ˈned\ *dim of* EDWARD, EDWIN
Neil *or* **Neal** \ˈnē(ə)l\ [Celt]
Nel·son \ˈnel-sən\ [fr. a surname]
Nev·ille \ˈnev-əl\ [fr. a surname]
Nev·in \ˈnev-ən\ [fr. a surname]
New·ell \ˈn(y)ü-əl\ [fr. a surname]
New·ton \ˈn(y)üt-ᵊn\ [fr. a surname]
Nich·o·las \ˈnik-(ə-)ləs\ [Gk] victorious among the people
Nick \ˈnik\ *dim of* NICHOLAS
Niles \ˈnī(ə)lz\ [fr. a surname]
Nils \ˈnils, ˈnē(ə)ls\ [Scand]
No·ah \ˈnō-ə\ [Heb] rest
No·el \ˈnō-əl\ [F, fr. L] Christmas
No·lan \ˈnō-lən\ [fr. a surname]
Nor·man \ˈnȯr-mən\ [Gmc] Norseman, Norman
Nor·ris \ˈnȯr-əs, ˈnär-\ [fr. a surname]
Nor·ton \ˈnȯrt-ᵊn\ [fr. a surname]

Ol·i·ver \ˈäl-ə-vər\ [OF]
Ol·lie \ˈäl-ē\ *dim of* OLIVER
Or·lan·do \ȯr-ˈlan-(ˌ)dō\ [It] *var of* ROLAND
Or·rin \ˈȯr-ən, ˈär-\ *or* **Orin** *or* **Oren** \ˈȯr-, ˈär-, ˈōr-\ [prob. fr. a surname]
Or·ville *or* **Or·val** \ˈȯr-vəl\ [prob. fr. a surname]
Os·car \ˈäs-kər\ [OE] spear of a deity
Otis \ˈōt-əs\ [fr. a surname]
Ot·to \ˈät-(ˌ)ō\ [Gmc]
Ow·en \ˈō-ən\ [OW]

Palm·er \ˈpäm-ər, ˈpäl-mər\ [fr. a surname]
Par·ker \ˈpär-kər\ [fr. a surname]
Pat \ˈpat\ *dim of* PATRICK
Pat·rick \ˈpa-trik\ [L] patrician
Paul \ˈpȯl\ [L] little
Pe·dro \ˈpē-(ˌ)drō, ˈpā-\ [Sp] *var of* PETER
Per·cy \ˈpər-sē\ [fr. a surname]
Per·ry \ˈper-ē\ [fr. a surname]
Pete \ˈpēt\ *dim of* PETER
Pe·ter \ˈpēt-ər\ [Gk] rock
Phil \ˈfil\ *dim of* PHILIP
Phil·ip *or* **Phil·lip** \ˈfil-əp\ [Gk] lover of horses
Pierre \pē-ˈe(ə)r\ [F] *var of* PETER
Por·ter \ˈpȯrt-ər, ˈpȯrt-\ [fr. a surname]
Pres·ton \ˈpres-tən\ [fr. a surname]

Quen·tin \ˈkwent-ᵊn\ [LL] of or relating to the fifth

Ra·fa·el *or* **Ra·pha·el** \ˈraf-ē-əl, ˈrä-fē-\ [Heb] God has healed
Ra·leigh \ˈrȯl-ē, ˈräl-\ [fr. a surname]
Ralph \ˈralf, *Brit also* ˈrāf\ [Gmc] wolf in counsel
Ra·mon \rə-ˈmōn, ˈrä-mən\ [Sp] *var of* RAYMOND
Ran·dall *or* **Ran·dal** \ˈran-dᵊl\ *var of* RANDOLPH
Ran·dolph \ˈran-ˌdälf\ [Gmc] shield wolf
Ran·dy \ˈran-dē\ *dim of* RANDOLPH
Ray \ˈrā\ *dim of* RAYMOND
Ray·mond \ˈrā-mənd\ [Gmc] wise protection
Reed *or* **Reid** \ˈrēd\ [fr. a surname]
Reg·gie \ˈrej-ē\ *dim of* REGINALD
Reg·i·nald \ˈrej-ən-ᵊld\ [Gmc] wise dominion
Re·gis \ˈrē-jəs\ [fr. a proper name]
Re·ne \ren-(ˌ)ā, rə-ˈnā, ˈrä-nē, ˈrē-nē\ [F, fr. L] reborn
Reu·ben *or* **Ru·ben** \ˈrü-bən\ [Heb]
Rex \ˈreks\ [L] king
Reyn·old \ˈren-ᵊld\ *var of* REGINALD
Rich·ard \ˈrich-ərd\ [Gmc] strong in rule
Rob·ert \ˈräb-ərt\ [Gmc] bright in fame
Ro·ber·to \rə-ˈbert-(ˌ)ō, rō-, -ˈbert-\ [Sp & It] *var of* ROBERT
Rob·in \ˈräb-ən\ *dim of* ROBERT
Rod·er·ick \ˈräd-(ə-)rik\ [Gmc] famous ruler
Rod·ney \ˈräd-nē\ [fr. a surname]
Rog·er *or* **Rod·ger** \ˈräj-ər\ [Gmc] famous spear
Rog·ers \ˈräj-ərz\ [fr. a surname]
Ro·land \ˈrō-lənd\ *or* **Rol·land** \ˈräl-ənd\ *or* **Row·land** \ˈrō-lənd\ [Gmc] famous land
Rolf \ˈrälf\ *var of* RUDOLPH
Rol·lin \ˈräl-ən\ *var of* ROLAND
Ron \ˈrän\ *dim of* RONALD
Ron·al \ˈrän-ᵊl\ *var of* RONALD
Ron·ald \ˈrän-ᵊld\ [ON] *var of* REGINALD
Ron·nie *or* **Ron·ny** \ˈrän-ē\ *dim of* RONALD
Ros·coe \ˈräs-(ˌ)kō, ˈrȯs-\ [fr. a surname]
Ross \ˈrȯs\ [fr. a surname]
Roy \ˈrȯi\ [ScGael]
Roy·al \ˈrȯi(-ə)l\ [prob. fr. a surname]
Royce \ˈrȯis\ [fr. a surname]
Ru·dolph *or* **Ru·dolf** \ˈrü-ˌdälf\ [Gmc] famous wolf
Ru·dy \ˈrüd-ē\ *dim of* RUDOLPH
Ru·fus \ˈrü-fəs\ [L] red, red-haired
Ru·pert \ˈrü-pərt\ *var of* ROBERT

Rus·sell or **Rus·sel** \\'rəs-əl\ [fr. a surname]
Ry·an \\'rī-ən\ [IrGael]

Sal·va·tore \\'sal-və-ˌtō(ə)r, -ˌtò(ə)r; ˌsal-və-'tòr-ē, -'tòr-\ [It] savior
Sam \\'sam\ dim of SAMUEL
Sam·my or **Sam·mie** \\'sam-ē\ dim of SAM
Sam·u·el \\'sam-yə(-wə)l\ [Heb] name of God
San·ford \\'san-fərd\ [fr. a surname]
Saul \\'sòl\ [Heb] asked for
Scott \\'skät\ [fr. a surname]
Sean \\'shòn\ [Ir] var of JOHN
Seth \\'seth\ [Heb]
Sey·mour \\'sē-ˌmō(ə)r, -ˌmò(ə)r\ [fr. a surname]
Shel·by \\'shel-bē\ [fr. a surname]
Shel·don \\'shel-dən\ [fr. a surname]
Sher·i·dan \\'sher-əd-ᵊn\ [fr. a surname]
Sher·man \\'shər-mən\ [fr. a surname]
Sher·win \\'shər-wən\ [fr. a surname]
Sher·wood \\'shər-ˌwùd, 'she(ə)r-\ [fr. a surname]
Sid·ney or **Syd·ney** \\'sid-nē\ [fr. a surname]
Sieg·fried \\'sig-ˌfrēd, 'sēg-\ [Gmc] victorious peace
Sig·mund \\'sig-mənd\ [Gmc] victorious protection
Si·mon \\'sī-mən\ [Heb]
Sol·o·mon \\'säl-ə-mən\ [Heb] peaceable
Spen·cer \\'spen(t)-sər\ [fr. a surname]
Sta·cy or **Sta·cey** \\'stā-sē\ [ML]
Stan \\'stan\ dim of STANLEY
Stan·ford \\'stan-fərd\ [fr. a surname]
Stan·ley \\'stan-lē\ [fr. a surname]
Stan·ton \\'stant-ᵊn\ [fr. a surname]
Ste·fan \\'stef-ən, -ˌän\ [Pol] var of STEPHEN
Ste·phen or **Ste·ven** or **Ste·phan** \\'stē-vən\ [Gk] crown
Ster·ling \\'stər-liŋ\ [fr. a surname]
Steve \\'stēv\ dim of STEVEN
Stu·art or **Stew·art** \\'st(y)ü-ərt, 'st(y)ü-(ə)rt\ [fr. a surname]
Syl·ves·ter \sil-'ves-tər\ [L] woodsy, of the woods

Tay·lor \\'tā-lər\ [fr. a surname]
Ted \\'ted\ or **Ted·dy** \\'ted-ē\ dim of EDWARD, THEODORE
Ter·ence or **Ter·rance** or **Ter·rence** \\'ter-ən(t)s\ [L]
Ter·rell or **Ter·rill** \\'ter-əl\ [fr. a surname]
Ter·ry \\'ter-ē\ dim of TERENCE
Thad \\'thad\ dim of THADDEUS
Thad·de·us \\'thad-ē-əs\ [Gk]
The·o·dore \\'thē-ə-ˌdō(ə)r, -ˌdò(ə)r, -əd-ər\ [Gk] gift of God
Thom·as \\'täm-əs\ [Aram] twin
Thur·man \\'thər-mən\ [fr. a surname]
Tim \\'tim\ dim of TIMOTHY
Tim·o·thy \\'tim-ə-thē\ [Gk] revering God
To·by \\'tō-bē\ dim of TOBIAS
Todd \\'täd\ [prob. fr. a surname]
Tom \\'täm\ or **Tom·my** or **Tom·mie** \\'täm-ē\ dim of THOMAS
To·ny \\'tō-nē\ dim of ANTHONY
Tra·cy \\'trā-sē\ [fr. a surname]
Trav·is \\'trav-əs\ [fr. a surname]
Trent \\'trent\ [fr. a surname]
Tre·vor \\'trev-ər\ [Celt]
Troy \\'tròi\ [prob. fr. a surname]
Tru·man \\'trü-mən\ [fr. a surname]
Ty·ler \\'tī-lər\ [fr. a surname]
Ty·rone \\'tī-ˌrōn, tī-'; tir-'ōn\ [prob. fr. the county in Ireland]

Val \\'val\ dim of VALENTINE
Van \\'van\ [fr. surnames beginning with Van, fr. Dutch van of]
Vance \\'van(t)s\ [fr. a surname]
Vaughn \\'vòn, 'vän\ [fr. a surname]
Verne or **Vern** \\'vərn\ prob alter of VERNON

Ver·non \\'vər-nən\ [prob. fr. a surname]
Vic·tor \\'vik-tər\ [L] conqueror
Vin·cent \\'vin(t)-sənt\ [LL] of or relating to the conquering one
Vir·gil \\'vər-jəl\ [L]

Wade \\'wād\ [fr. a surname]
Wal·lace or **Wal·lis** \\'wäl-əs\ [fr. a surname]
Walt \\'wòlt\ dim of WALTER
Wal·ter \\'wòl-tər\ [Gmc] army of dominion
Wal·ton \\'wòlt-ᵊn\ [fr. a surname]
Ward \\'wò(ə)rd\ [fr. a surname]
War·ner \\'wòr-nər\ [fr. a surname]
War·ren \\'wòr-ən, 'wär-\ [fr. a surname]
Wayne \\'wān\ [fr. a surname]
Wel·don \\'wel-dən\ [fr. a surname]
Wen·dell \\'wen-dᵊl\ [fr. a surname]
Wer·ner \\'wər-nər, 'we(ə)r-\ [Gmc] army of the Varini, a Germanic people
Wes·ley \\'wes-lē also 'wez-\ [fr. a surname]
Wil·bur or **Wil·ber** \\'wil-bər\ [fr. a surname]
Wi·ley or **Wy·lie** \\'wī-lē\ [fr. a surname]
Wil·ford \\'wil-fərd\ [fr. a surname]
Wil·fred \\'wil-frəd\ [OE] desired peace
Will \\'wil\ or **Wil·lie** \-ē\ dim of WILLIAM
Wil·lard \\'wil-ərd\ [fr. a surname]
Wil·liam \\'wil-yəm\ [Gmc] desired helmet
Wil·lis \\'wil-əs\ [fr. a surname]
Wil·mer \\'wil-mər\ [fr. a surname]
Wil·son \\'wil-sən\ [fr. a surname]
Wil·ton \\'wilt-ᵊn\ [fr. a surname]
Win·field \\'win-ˌfēld\ [fr. a surname]
Win·fred \\'win-frəd\ [OE] prob joyous peace
Win·ston \\'win(t)-stən\ [fr. a surname]
Win·ton \\'wint-ᵊn\ [fr. a surname]
Wood·row \\'wùd-(ˌ)rō\ [fr. a surname]
Wy·att \\'wī-ət\ [fr. a surname]

Yale \\'yā(ə)l\ [fr. a surname]

Zach·a·ry \\'zak-ə-rē\ dim of ZACHARIAH
Zane \\'zān\ [fr. a surname]

Names of Women

Ab·by \\'ab-ē\ dim of ABIGAIL
Ab·i·gail \\'ab-ə-ˌgāl\ [Heb] prob source of joy
Ada \\'ād-ə\ [Heb] prob ornament
Ad·di·son \\'ad-ə-sən\ [fr. a surname]
Ad·e·laide \\'ad-ᵊl-ˌād\ [Gmc] of noble rank
Adele \ə-'del\ [Gmc] noble
Adri·enne \\'ā-drē-ˌen, -ən\ [F] fem of ADRIEN
Ag·nes \\'ag-nəs\ [LL]
Ai·leen \ī-'lēn\ [IrGael] var of HELEN
Al·ber·ta \al-'bərt-ə\ fem of ALBERT
Al·ex·an·dra \ˌal-ig-'zan-drə\ [Gk] fem of ALEXANDER
Alex·is \ə-'lek-səs\ [Gk]
Al·ice or **Al·yce** \\'al-əs\ [OF] var of ADELAIDE
Ali·cia \ə-'lish-ə\ [ML] var of ADELAIDE
Al·i·son or **Al·li·son** \\'al-ə-sən\ [OF] dim of ALICE
Al·ma \\'al-mə\ [L] nourishing, cherishing
Al·va \\'al-və\ [Sp, fr. L] white
Aman·da \ə-'man-də\ [L] worthy to be loved
Am·ber \\'am-bər\ [E]
Ame·lia \ə-'mēl-yə\ [Gmc]

\ə\abut \ᵊ\kitten \ər\further \a\ash \ā\ace \ä\mop, mar
\aù\out \ch\chin \e\bet \ē\easy \g\go \i\hit \ī\ice \j\job
\ŋ\sing \ō\go \ò\law \òi\boy \th\thin \t̲h̲\the \ü\loot \ù\foot
\y\yet \zh\vision see also Pronunciation Symbols page

Amy \'ā-mē\ [L] beloved
An·as·ta·sia \ˌan-ə-'stā-zh(ē-)ə\ [LGk] of the Resurrection
An·drea \'an-drē-ə, an-'drā-ə\ *fem of* ANDREW
An·ge·la \'an-jə-lə\ [It, fr. Gk] angel
An·gel·i·ca \an-'jel-i-kə\ *var of* ANGELA
An·ge·line \'an-jə-ˌlīn, -ˌlēn\ *dim of* ANGELA
Ani·ta \ə-'nēt-ə\ [Sp] *dim of* ANN
Ann *or* **Anne** \'an\ *or* **An·na** \'an-ə\ [Heb] grace
An·na·belle \'an-ə-ˌbel\ *prob var of* MABEL
An·nette \a-'net, ə-\ *or* **An·net·ta** \-'net-ə\ [F] *dim of* ANN
An·nie \'an-ē\ *dim of* ANN
An·toi·nette \ˌan-t(w)ə-'net\ [F] *dim of* ANTONIA
April \'ā-prəl\ [E] April (the month)
Ar·dell *or* **Ar·delle** \är-'del\ *var of* ADELE
Ar·leen *or* **Ar·leen** *or* **Ar·line** \är-'lēn\
Ash·ley \'ash-lē\ [OE] ash-tree meadow
As·trid \'as-trəd\ [Scand] beautiful as a deity
Au·dra \'o-drə\ *var of* AUDREY
Au·drey \'o-drē\ [OE] noble strength

Ba·bette \ba-'bet\ [F] *dim of* ELIZABETH
Bar·ba·ra \'bär-b(ə-)rə\ [Gk] foreign
Be·atrice \'bē-ə-trəs\ [It, fr. ML] she that makes happy
Becky \'bek-ē\ *dim of* REBECCA
Ber·na·dette \ˌbər-nə-'det\ [F] *fem of* BERNARD
Ber·na·dine \'bər-nə-ˌdēn\ *fem of* BERNARD
Ber·nice \(ˌ)bər-'nēs, 'bər-nəs\ [Gk] bringing victory
Ber·tha \'bər-thə\ [Gmc] bright
Ber·yl \'ber-əl\ [Gk] beryl (the mineral)
Bes·sie \'bes-ē\ *dim of* ELIZABETH
Beth \'beth\ *dim of* ELIZABETH
Bet·sey *or* **Bet·sey** \'bet-sē\ *dim of* ELIZABETH
Bet·ty *or* **Bet·te** *or* **Bet·tye** *or* **Bet·tie** \'bet-ē\ *dim of* ELIZABETH
Beu·lah \'byü-lə\ [Heb] married
Bev·er·ly *or* **Bev·er·ley** \'bev-ər-lē\ [prob. fr. a surname]
Bil·lie \'bil-ē\ *fem of* BILLY
Blair \'ble(ə)r\ [fr. a surname]
Blake \'blāk\ [fr. a surname]
Blanche \'blanch\ [OF, fr. Gmc] white
Bob·bie \'bäb-ē\ *dim of* ROBERTA
Bo·ni·ta \bə-'nēt-ə\ [Sp] pretty
Bon·nie \'bän-ē\ [ME] pretty
Bran·dy \'bran-dē\ [E]
Bren·da \'bren-də\ [Scand]
Bri·gitte \'brij-ət, brə-'jit\ [G] *var of* BRIDGET
Brit·tany \'brit-ᵊn-ē\ [E]
Brooke \'brŭk\ [OE] brook

Cait·lin \'kāt-lin\ [Ir] *var of* CATHERINE
Ca·mil·la \kə-'mil-ə\ [L] freeborn girl attendant at a sacrifice
Ca·mille \kə-'mē(ə)l\ [F] *var of* CAMILLA
Can·da·ce \'kan-dəs, kan-'dā-sē\ [Gk]
Car·la \'kär-lə\ [It] *fem of* Carlo
Car·lene \kär-'lēn\ *var of* CARLA
Car·lot·ta \kär-'lät-ə\ [It] *var of* CHARLOTTE
Car·men \'kär-mən\ *or* **Car·mine** \kär-'mēn, 'kär-mən\ [Sp, fr. L] song
Car·ol *or* **Car·ole** *or* **Car·yl** \'kar-əl\ *dim of* CAROLYN
Car·o·lyn \'kar-ə-lən\ *or* **Car·o·line** \-lən, -ˌlīn\ [It] *fem of* CHARLES
Car·rie \'kar-ē\ *dim of* CAROLINE
Cath·er·ine *or* **Cath·a·rine** \'kath-(ə-)rən\ [LGk]
Cath·leen \kath-'lēn\ [IrGael] *var of* CATHERINE
Cath·ryn \'kath-rən\ *var of* CATHERINE
Cathy *or* **Cath·ie** \'kath-ē\ *dim of* CATHERINE
Ce·cile \sə-'sē(ə)l\ *var of* CECILIA
Ce·ci·lia \sə-'sēl-yə, -'sil-\ *or* **Ce·ce·lia** \-'sēl-\ [L] *fem of* CECIL
Ce·leste \sə-'lest\ [L] heavenly
Ce·lia \'sēl-yə\ *dim of* CECILIA

Char·lene \shär-'lēn\ *fem of* CHARLES
Char·lotte \'shär-lət\ [F] *fem dim of* CHARLES
Cher·ie \'sher-ē\ [F] dear
Cher·ry \'cher-ē\ [E] cherry
Cher·yl \'cher-əl, 'sher-\ *prob var of* CHERRY
Chloe \'klō-ē\ [Gk] young verdure
Chris·tie \'kris-tē\ *dim of* CHRISTINE
Chris·tine \kris-'tēn\ *or* **Chris·ti·na** \-'tē-nə\ [Gk] Christian
Cin·dy \'sin-dē\ *dim of* LUCINDA
Claire *or* **Clare** \'kla(ə)r, 'kle(ə)r\ *var of* CLARA
Clara \'klar-ə\ [L] bright
Cla·rice \'klar-əs, klə-'rēs\ *dim of* CLARA
Clau·dette \klo-'det\ [F] *fem of* CLAUDE
Clau·dia \'klod-ē-ə\ [L] *fem of* CLAUDE
Clau·dine \klo-'dēn\ [F] *fem of* CLAUDE
Cleo \'klē-(ˌ)ō\ *dim of* Cleopatra
Co·lette \kä-'let\ [OF] *fem dim of* NICHOLAS
Col·leen \kä-'lēn\ [IrGael] girl
Con·nie \'kän-ē\ *dim of* CONSTANCE
Con·stance \'kän(t)-stən(t)s\ [L] constancy
Co·ra \'kor-ə, 'kor-\ [Gk] maiden
Cor·ey \'kor-ē\ [Ir]
Co·rinne *or* **Cor·rine** \kə-'rin, -'rēn\ [Gk] *dim of* CORA
Cor·ne·lia \kor-'nēl-yə\ [L] *fem of* CORNELIUS
Court·ney \'kō(ə)rt-nē, 'ko(ə)rt-\ [OE] of the court
Crys·tal \'kris-tᵊl\ [E]
Cyn·thia \'sin(t)-thē-ə\ [Gk] she of Mount Cynthus on the island of Delos

Dai·sy \'dā-zē\ [E] daisy
Dale \'dā(ə)l\ [E] valley
Da·na \'dā-nə\ [fr. a surname]
Dan·ielle \dăn-'yel\ [F] *fem of* DANIEL
Daph·ne \'daf-nē\ [Gk] laurel
Dar·la \'där-lə\ [deriv. of *darling*]
Dar·lene \där-'lēn\ [deriv. of *darling*]
Dawn \'don, 'dän\ [E] dawn
De·an·na \dē-'an-ə\ *or* **De·anne** \-'an\ *var of* DIANA
Deb·bie *or* **Deb·by** \'deb-ē\ *dim of* DEBORAH
Deb·o·rah *or* **Deb·o·ra** \'deb-(ə-)rə\ [Heb] bee
Deb·ra \'deb-rə\ *var of* DEBORAH
Dee \'dē\ *prob dim of* EDITH
Deir·dre \'di(ə)r-drē, 'de(ə)r-\ [IrGael]
De·lia \'dēl-yə\ [Gk] she of Delos (i.e. the goddess Artemis)
Del·la \'del-ə\ *dim of* ADELAIDE, DELIA
De·lo·res \də-'lor-əs, -'lor-\ *var of* DOLORES
De·na *or* **Dee·na** \'dē-nə\ *dim of* GERALDINE
De·nise \də-'nēz, -'nēs\ [F] *fem of* DENIS
Di·ana *or* **Di·an·na** \dī-'an-ə\ [L]
Di·ane *or* **Di·anne** *or* **Di·an** *or* **Di·ann** \dī-'an\ [F] *var of* DIANA
Di·na *or* **Di·nah** \'dī-nə\ [Heb] judged
Dix·ie \'dik-sē\ [E] *prob* Dixie (nickname for the southern states of the U.S.)
Do·lo·res \də-'lor-əs, -'lor-\ [Sp, fr. L] sorrows (i.e. those of the Virgin Mary)
Don·na \'dän-ə\ *or* **Do·na** \'dän-ə, 'dō-nə\ [It, fr. L] lady
Do·ra \'dor-ə, 'dor-\ *dim of* THEODORA, Eudora
Do·reen \do-'rēn, də-\ [IrGael]
Do·ris \'dor-əs, 'där-\ [Gk] *prob* Dorian (a member of an ancient Hellenic race)
Dor·o·thy \'dor-ə-thē, 'där-\ *or* **Dor·o·thea** \ˌdor-ə-'thē-ə, ˌdär-\ [LGk] goddess of gifts
Dot·tie *or* **Dot·ty** \'dät-ē\ *dim of* DOROTHY

Edith *or* **Edythe** \'ēd-əth\ [OE]
Ed·na \'ed-nə\ [Aram]
Ed·wi·na \e-'dwē-nə, -'dwin-ə\ *fem of* EDWIN
Ef·fie \'ef-ē\ *dim of* Euphemia
Ei·leen \ī-'lēn\ [IrGael] *var of* HELEN
Elaine \i-'lān\ [OF] *var of* HELEN

El·ea·nor or **El·i·nor** or **El·ea·nore** \\'el-ə-nər, -ˌnȯ(ə)r, -ˌnō(ə)r\\ [OProv] var of HELEN
Ele·na \\'el-ə-nə, ə-'lē-nə\\ [It] var of HELEN
Elise \ə-'lēz, -'lēs\\ [F] var of ELIZABETH
Eliz·a·beth or **Elis·a·beth** \i-'liz-ə-bəth\\ [Heb] God has sworn
El·la \\'el-ə\\ [OF]
El·len or **El·lyn** \\'el-ən\\ var of HELEN
El·o·ise \\'el-ə-ˌwēz, ˌel-ə-'\\ [OF, fr. Gmc]
El·sa \\'el-sə\\ [G] dim of ELIZABETH
El·sie \\'el-sē\\ dim of ELIZABETH
El·va \\'el-və\\ [Gmc] elf
Em·i·ly or **Em·i·lie** \\'em-(ə-)lē\\ [L] fem of EMIL
Em·ma \\'em-ə\\ [Gmc] var of ERMA
Enid \\'ē-nəd\\ [W]
Er·i·ka \\'er-i-kə\\ fem of ERIC
Er·in \\'er-ən\\ [IrGael]
Er·ma \\'ər-mə\\ [Gmc]
Er·nes·tine \\'ər-nə-ˌstēn\\ fem of ERNEST
Es·telle \e-'stel\ or **Es·tel·la** \e-'stel-ə\\ [OProv, fr. L] star
Es·ther \\'es-tər\\ [prob. fr. Per] prob star
Eth·el \\'eth-əl\\ [OE] noble
Et·ta \\'et-ə\\ dim of HENRIETTA
Eu·ge·nia \yü-'jēn-yə\ or **Eu·ge·nie** \-'jē-nē\\ fem of EUGENE
Eu·nice \\'yü-nəs\\ [Gk] having (i.e. bringing) happy victory
Eva \\'ē-və\\ var of EVE
Evan·ge·line \i-'van-jə-lən, -ˌlēn, -ˌlīn\\ [Gk] bringing good news
Eve \\'ēv\\ [Heb] life, living
Ev·e·lyn \\'ev-(ə-)lən, chiefly Brit 'ēv-\\ [OF, fr. Gmc]

Faith \\'fāth\\ [E] faith
Faye or **Fay** \\'fā\\ dim of FAITH
Fe·lice \fə-'lēs\\ [L] happiness
Fern or **Ferne** \\'fərn\\ [E] fern
Flo·ra \\'flōr-ə, 'flȯr-\\ [L] goddess of flowers
Flor·ence \\'flȯr-ən(t)s, 'flär-\\ [L] bloom, prosperity
Fran·ces \\'fran(t)-səs, -səz\\ fem of FRANCIS
Fran·cine \fran-'sēn\\ [F] prob dim of FRANCES
Fre·da or **Frie·da** \\'frēd-ə\\ dim of WINIFRED
Fred·er·ic·ka or **Fred·er·i·ca** \ˌfred-(ə-)'rē-kə, -'rik-ə\\ fem of FREDERICK

Gail or **Gayle** or **Gale** \\'gā(ə)l\\ dim of ABIGAIL
Gay \\'gā\\ [E] gay
Ge·ne·va \jə-'nē-və\\ var of GENEVIEVE
Gen·e·vieve \\'jen-ə-ˌvēv\\ [prob. fr. Celt]
George·ann \ˌjȯr-'jan\\ [George + Ann]
Geor·gette \jȯr-'jet\\ fem of GEORGE
Geor·gia \\'jȯr-jə\\ fem of GEORGE
Geor·gi·na \jȯr-'jē-nə\\ fem of GEORGE
Ger·al·dine \\'jer-əl-ˌdēn\\ fem of GERALD
Ger·trude \\'gər-ˌtrüd\\ [Gmc] spear strength
Gil·li·an \\'jil-ē-ən\\ var of JULIANA
Gin·ger \\'jin-jər\\ [E] ginger
Gi·sela \jə-'sel-ə, -'zel-\\ [Gmc] pledge
Gi·selle \jə-'zel\\ var of GISELA
Glad·ys \\'glad-əs\\ [W]
Glen·da \\'glen-də\\ prob var of GLENNA
Glen·na \\'glen-ə\\ fem of GLENN
Glo·ria \\'glōr-ē-ə, 'glȯr-\\ [L] glory
Grace \\'grās\\ [L] favor, grace
Gre·ta \\'grēt-ə, 'gret-\\ dim of MARGARET
Gretch·en \\'grech-ən\\ [G] dim of MARGARET
Gwen \\'gwen\\ dim of GWENDOLYN
Gwen·do·lyn \\'gwen-də-lən\\ [W]

Han·nah \\'han-ə\\ [Heb] var of ANN
Har·ri·et or **Har·ri·ett** or **Har·ri·ette** \\'har-ē-ət\\ var of HENRIETTA
Hat·tie \\'hat-ē\\ dim of HARRIET

Ha·zel \\'hā-zəl\\ [E] hazel
Heath·er \\'heth-ər\\ [ME] heather (the shrub)
Hei·di \\'hīd-ē\\ [G] dim of ADELAIDE
He·laine \hə-'lān\\ var of HELEN
Hel·en \\'hel-ən\ or **He·le·na** \\'hel-ə-nə, hə-'lē-nə\\ [Gk]
He·lene \hə-'lēn\\ [F] var of HELEN
Hel·ga \\'hel-gə\\ [Scand] holy
Hen·ri·et·ta \ˌhen-rē-'et-ə\\ [MF] fem of HENRY
Her·mine \\'hər-ˌmēn\\ [G] prob fem of HERMAN
Hes·ter \\'hes-tər\\ var of ESTHER
Hil·ary or **Hil·la·ry** \\'hil-ə-rē\\ [L] cheerful
Hil·da \\'hil-də\\ [OE] battle
Hil·de·gard or **Hil·de·garde** \\'hil-də-ˌgärd\\ [Gmc] prob battle enclosure
Hol·ly \\'häl-ē\\ [E] holly
Hope \\'hōp\\ [E] hope

Ida \\'īd-ə\\ [Gmc]
Ilene \ī-'lēn\\ var of EILEEN
Imo·gene \\'im-ə-ˌjēn, 'ī-mə-\\
Ina \\'ī-nə\\
Inez \ī-'nez, 'ī-nəz\\ [Sp] var of AGNES
In·grid \\'iŋ-grəd\\ [Scand] beautiful as Ing (an ancient Germanic god)
Irene \ī-'rēn\\ [Gk] peace
Iris \\'ī-rəs\\ [Gk] rainbow
Ir·ma \\'ər-mə\\ var of ERMA
Is·a·bel or **Is·a·belle** \\'iz-ə-ˌbel\\ [OProv] var of ELIZABETH

Jack·ie or **Jacky** \\'jak-ē\\ dim of JACQUELINE
Jac·que·line or **Jac·que·lyn** or **Jac·que·lin** \\'jak-(w)ə-lən, -ˌlēn\\ [OF] fem of JACOB
Ja·mie \\'jā-mē\\ fem of JAMES
Jan \\'jan\\ dim of JANET
Jane or **Jayne** \\'jān\\ [OF] var of JOAN
Ja·net or **Ja·nette** \\'jan-ət, jə-'net\\ dim of JANE
Ja·nice \\'jan-əs, jə-'nēs\ or **Jan·is** \\'jan-əs\\ prob dim of JANE
Ja·nie \\'jā-nē\\ dim of JANE
Jean or **Jeanne** \\'jēn\\ [OF] var of JOAN
Jea·nette or **Jean·nette** \jə-'net\\ [F] dim of JEANNE
Jean·ie or **Jean·ie** \\'jē-nē\\ dim of JEAN
Jean·nine or **Jea·nine** \jə-'nēn\\ [F] dim of JEANNE
Jen·nie or **Jen·ny** \\'jen-ē\\ dim of JANE
Jen·ni·fer \\'jen-ə-fər\\ [Celt]
Jer·al·dine \\'jer-əl-ˌdēn\\ var of GERALDINE
Jer·i·lyn \\'jer-ə-lən\\ var of GERALDINE
Jer·ry or **Jeri** or **Jer·rie** \\'jer-ē\\ dim of GERALDINE
Jes·si·ca \\'jes-i-kə\\ [prob. Heb]
Jes·sie \\'jes-ē\\ [Sc] dim of JANET
Jew·el or **Jew·ell** \\'jü(-ə)l, 'jü(-ə)l\\ [E] jewel
Jill \\'jil\\ dim of JULIANA
Jo \\'jō\\ dim of JOSEPHINE
Joan or **Joann** or **Joanne** \\'jō(-ə)n, jō-'an\\ [Gk] fem of JOHN
Jo·an·na \jō-'an-ə\ or **Jo·han·na** \-'(h)an-ə\\ var of JOAN
Joc·e·lyn \\'jäs-(ə-)lən\\ [OF, fr. Gmc]
Jo·dy or **Jo·die** \\'jō-dē\\ alter of JUDITH
Jo·lene \jō-'lēn\\ prob dim of JO
Jo·se·phine \\'jō-zə-ˌfēn also 'jō-sə-\\ fem of JOSEPH
Joy \\'jȯi\\ [E] joy
Joyce \\'jȯis\\ [OF]
Jua·ni·ta \wä-'nēt-ə\\ [Sp] fem dim of JOHN
Ju·dith \\'jüd-əth\\ [Heb] Jewess
Ju·dy or **Ju·di** or **Ju·die** \\'jüd-ē\\ dim of JUDITH
Ju·lia \\'jül-yə\\ [L] fem of JULIUS
Ju·li·ana \ˌjül-ē-'an-ə\\ [LL] fem of JULIAN

\ə\abut \ᵊ\kitten \ər\further \a\ash \ā\ace \ä\mop, mar
\aú\out \ch\chin \e\bet \ē\easy \g\go \i\hit \ī\ice \j\job
\ŋ\sing \ō\go \ȯ\law \ȯi\boy \th\thin \t͟h\the \ü\loot \ u\foot
\y\yet \zh\vision see also Pronunciation Symbols page

Ju·li·anne or **Ju·li·ann** \ˌjü-lē-ˈan, jül-ˈyan\ var of JULI-
ANA
Ju·lie \ˈjü-lē\ [MF] var of JULIA
Ju·liet \ˈjül-yət, -ē-ˌet, -ē-ət; ˌjül-ē-ˈet, jül-ˈyet, ˈjül-ˌyet\
[It] dim of JULIA
June \ˈjün\ [E] June (the month)
Jus·tine \ˌjəs-ˈtēn\ [F] fem of JUSTIN

Ka·ra \ˈkär-ə, ˈkar-ə\ var of CATHERINE
Kar·en or **Kar·in** or **Kaa·ren** \ˈkar-ən, ˈkär-\ [Scand] var
of CATHERINE
Kar·la \ˈkär-lə\ var of CARLA
Kar·ol \ˈkar-əl\ var of CAROL
Kar·o·lyn \ˈkar-ə-lən\ var of CAROLYN
Kate \ˈkāt\ dim of CATHERINE
Kath·er·ine or **Kath·a·rine** or **Kath·ryn** \ˈkath-(ə-)rən\
var of CATHERINE
Kath·leen \kath-ˈlēn\ [IrGael] var of CATHERINE
Kathy \ˈkath-ē\ dim of CATHERINE
Ka·tie \ˈkāt-ē\ dim of KATE
Kay or **Kaye** \ˈkā\ dim of CATHERINE
Kel·ly \ˈkel-ē\ [fr. a surname]
Ker·ry \ˈker-ē\ [prob. fr. the county of Ireland]
Kim \ˈkim\ prob dim of KIMBERLY
Kim·ber·ly \ˈkim-bər-lē\ [OE]
Kit·ty \ˈkit-ē\ dim of CATHERINE
Kris·tin \ˈkris-tən\ [Scand] var of CHRISTINE
Kris·tine \kris-ˈtēn\ var of CHRISTINE

La·na \ˈlan-ə, ˈlän-ə, ˈlā-nə\
Lau·ra \ˈlȯr-ə, ˈlär-\ [ML] prob fem dim of LAWRENCE
Lau·rel \ˈlȯr-əl, ˈlär-\ [E] laurel
Lau·ren \ˈlȯr-ən, ˈlär-\ var of LAURA
Lau·rie \ˈlȯr-ē, ˈlär-\ dim of LAURA
La·verne or **La·vern** \lə-ˈvərn\
Le·ah \ˈlē-ə\ [Heb] prob wild cow
Le·anne \lē-ˈan\ [prob. fr. Lee + Ann]
Lee \ˈlē\ [fr. a surname]
Leigh \ˈlē\ var of LEE
Lei·la or **Le·la** \ˈlē-lə\ [Per] dark as night
Le·lia \ˈlēl-yə\ [L]
Le·na \ˈlē-nə\ [G] dim of HELENA. Magdalena
Le·nore \lə-ˈnō(ə)r, -ˈnȯ(ə)r\ or **Le·no·ra** \lə-ˈnōr-ə,
-ˈnȯr-\ var of LEONORA
Le·o·na \lē-ˈō-nə\ fem of LEON
Le·o·no·ra \ˌlē-ə-ˈnōr-ə, -ˈnȯr-\ var of ELEANOR
Les·lie or **Les·ley** \ˈles-lē also ˈlez-\ [fr. a surname]
Le·ti·tia \li-ˈtish-ə, -ˈtē-shə\ [L] gladness
Lib·by \ˈlib-ē\ dim of ELIZABETH
Li·la \ˈlī-lə\ var of LEILA
Lil·lian \ˈlil-yən, ˈlil-ē-ən\ prob dim of ELIZABETH
Lil·lie \ˈlil-ē\ var of LILLIAN
Lily \ˈlil-ē\ [E] lily
Lin·da or **Lyn·da** \ˈlin-də\ dim of MELINDA. Belinda
Lind·sey or **Lind·say** \ˈlin-zē\ [OE] linden isle
Li·sa \ˈlī-zə, ˈlē-\ dim of ELIZABETH
Lo·is \ˈlō-əs\ [Gk]
Lo·la \ˈlō-lə\ [Sp] dim of DOLORES
Lon·na \ˈlän-ə\ fem of LON
Lo·ra \ˈlōr-ə, ˈlȯr-\ var of LAURA
Lo·re·lei \ˈlōr-ə-ˌlī, ˈlȯr-\ [G]
Lo·rene \lȯ-ˈrēn\ dim of LORA
Lo·ret·ta \lə-ˈret-ə, lȯ-\ [ML] var of Lauretta
Lo·ri \ˈlōr-ē, ˈlȯr-\ var of LAURA
Lor·na \ˈlȯr-nə\
Lor·raine or **Lo·raine** \lə-ˈrān, lȯ-\ [prob. fr. Lorraine,
region in northeast France]
Lou \ˈlü\ dim of LOUISE
Lou·ise \lu̇-ˈēz\ or **Lou·i·sa** \-ˈē-zə\ fem of LOUIS
Lu·anne \lü-ˈan\ [Lu- + Anne]
Lu·cille or **Lu·cile** \lü-ˈsē(ə)l\ [L] prob dim of LUCIA
Lu·cin·da \lü-ˈsin-də\ [L] var of LUCY
Lu·cre·tia \lü-ˈkrē-shə\ [L]

Lu·cy \ˈlü-sē\ or **Lu·cia** \ˈlü-shə\ [L] fem of Lucius
Lu·el·la \lü-ˈel-ə\ [prob. fr. Lou (dim. of Louise) + Ella]
Lyd·ia \ˈlid-ē-ə\ [Gk] woman of Lydia, ancient country
in Asia Minor
Ly·nette \lə-ˈnet\ [W]
Lynne or **Lynn** \ˈlin\ dim of CAROLYN. JACQUELYN. etc.

Ma·bel \ˈmā-bəl\ [L] lovable
Mac·ken·zie \mə-ˈken-zē\ [fr. a surname]
Mad·e·line or **Mad·e·leine** or **Mad·e·lyn** \ˈmad-ᵊl-ən\
[Gk] woman of Magdala, ancient town in northern Pal-
estine
Madge \ˈmaj\ dim of MARGARET
Mal·lory \ˈmal-(ə-)rē\ [fr. a surname]
Ma·mie \ˈmā-mē\ dim of MARGARET
Ma·ra \ˈmär-ə\ var of MARY
Mar·cel·la \mär-ˈsel-ə\ [L] fem of Marcellus
Mar·cia \ˈmär-shə\ [L] fem of MARCUS
Mar·ga·ret \ˈmär-g(ə-)rət\ [Gk] pearl
Mar·gery \ˈmärj-(ə-)rē\ [OF] var of MARGARET
Mar·gie \ˈmär-jē\ dim of MARGARET
Mar·go \ˈmär-(ˌ)gō\ var of MARGOT
Mar·got \ˈmär-(ˌ)gō, -gət\ var of MARGARET
Mar·gue·rite \ˌmär-g(y)ə-ˈrēt\ [OF] var of MARGARET
Ma·ria \mə-ˈrē-ə also -ˈrī-\ var of MARY
Mar·i·an \ˈmer-ē-ən, ˈmar-\ var of MARIANNE
Mar·i·anne \ˌmer-ē-ˈan, ˌmar-\ or **Mar·i·an·na** \-ˈan-ə\
[F] dim of MARY
Ma·rie \mə-ˈrē\ [OF] var of MARY
Mar·i·et·ta \ˌmer-ē-ˈet-ə, ˌmar-\ dim of MARY
Mar·i·lee \ˈmer-ə-(ˌ)lē, ˈmar-\ [prob. fr. Mary + Lee]
Mar·i·lyn or **Mar·i·lynn** or **Mar·y·lyn** \ˈmer-ə-lən,
ˈmar-\ [prob. fr. Mary + -lyn]
Ma·ri·na \mə-ˈrē-nə\ [LGk]
Mar·i·on \ˈmer-ē-ən, ˈmar-\ var of MARY
Mar·jo·rie or **Mar·jo·ry** \ˈmärj-(ə-)rē\ var of MARGERY
Mar·la \ˈmär-lə\ prob dim of MARLENE
Mar·lene \mär-ˈlēn(-ə), -ˈlā-nə\ [G] dim of Magdalene
Mar·lyn \ˈmär-lən\ prob var of MARLENE
Mar·sha \ˈmär-shə\ var of MARCIA
Mar·ta \ˈmärt-ə\ [It] var of MARTHA
Mar·tha \ˈmär-thə\ [Aram] lady
Mar·va \ˈmär-və\ prob fem of MARVIN
Mary \ˈme(ə)r-ē, ˈmā-rē\ [Gk, fr. Heb]
Mary·ann or **Mary·anne** \ˌmer-ē-ˈan, ˌmā-rē-\ [Mary +
Ann]
Mary·el·len \ˌmer-ē-ˈel-ən, ˌmā-rē-\ [Mary + Ellen]
Mar·y·lon \ˈmer-ə-lən, ˈmar-\ var of MARILYN
Maude \ˈmȯd\ [OF] var of Matilda
Mau·reen or **Mau·rine** \mȯ-ˈrēn\ [Ir] dim of MARY
Max·ine \mak-ˈsēn\ [F] fem dim of Maximilian
May or **Mae** \ˈmā\ dim of MARY
Me·gan \ˈmeg-ən, ˈmē-gən\ [Ir]
Mel·a·nie \ˈmel-ə-nē\ [Gk] blackness
Mel·ba \ˈmel-bə\ [E] woman of Melbourne, Australia
Me·lin·da \mə-ˈlin-də\ prob alter of Belinda
Me·lis·sa \mə-ˈlis-ə\ [Gk] bee
Mel·va \ˈmel-və\ prob fem of MELVIN
Mer·e·dith \ˈmer-əd-əth\ [W]
Merle \ˈmər(-ə)l\ [F] blackbird
Mer·ri·ly \ˈmer-ə-lē\ alter of MARILEE
Mer·ry \ˈmer-ē\ [E] merry
Mia \ˈmē-ə\ [It]
Mi·chele or **Mi·chelle** \mi-ˈshel\ [F] fem of MICHAEL
Mil·dred \ˈmil-drəd\ [OE] gentle strength
Mil·li·cent \ˈmil-ə-sənt\ [Gmc]
Mil·lie \ˈmil-ē\ dim of MILDRED
Min·nie \ˈmin-ē\ [Sc] dim of MARY
Mir·an·da \mə-ˈran-də\ [L] admirable
Mir·i·am \ˈmir-ē-əm\ [Heb] var of MARY
Mit·zi \ˈmit-sē\ prob dim of MARGARET
Mol·ly or **Mol·lie** \ˈmäl-ē\ dim of MARY
Mo·na \ˈmō-nə\ [IrGael]

Mon·i·ca \\'män-i-kə\ [LL]
Mu·ri·el \\'myu̇r-ē-əl\ [prob. Celt]
My·ra \\'mī-rə\
Myr·na \\'mər-nə\
Myr·tle \\'mərt-ᵊl\ [Gk] myrtle

Na·dine \nā-'dēn, nə-\ [F, fr. Russ] hope
Nan \\'nan\ dim of ANN
Nan·cy \\'nan(t)-sē\ dim of ANN
Nan·nette or Na·nette \na-'net, nə-\ [F] dim of ANN
Na·o·mi \nā-'ō-mē\ [Heb] pleasant
Nat·a·lie \\'nat-ᵊl-ē\ [LL] of or relating to Christmas
Nel·lie \\'nel-ē\ or Nell \\'nel\ dim of ELLEN, HELEN, ELEANOR
Net·tie \\'net-ē\ [Sc] dim of JANET
Ni·cole \nē-'kōl\ [F] fem of NICHOLAS
Ni·na \\'nē-nə\ [Russ] dim of ANN
Ni·ta \\'nēt-ə\ [Sp] dim of JUANITA
No·na \\'nō-nə\ [L] ninth
No·ra \\'nōr-ə, 'nȯr-\ dim of LEONORA, ELEANOR, Honora
No·reen \nȯ-'rēn\ [IrGael] dim of NORA
Nor·ma \\'nȯr-mə\ [It]

Ol·ga \\'äl-gə, 'ōl-\ [Russ] var of HELGA
Ol·ive \\'äl-iv, -əv\ or O·liv·ia \ə-'liv-ē-ə, ō-\ [L] olive
Opal \\'ō-pəl\ [E] opal

Pam \\'pam\ dim of PAMELA
Pa·me·la \\'pam-ə-lə; pə-'mē-lə, pa-\
Pa·tri·cia \pə-'trish-ə, -'trē-shə\ [L] fem of PATRICK
Pat·sy \\'pat-sē\ dim of PATRICIA
Pat·ty or Pat·ti or Pat·tie \\'pat-ē\ dim of PATRICIA
Pau·la \\'pȯ-lə\ [L] fem of PAUL
Pau·lette \pȯ-'let\ fem dim of PAUL
Pau·line \pȯ-'lēn\ fem dim of PAUL
Pearl \\'pər(-ə)l\ [E] pearl
Peg·gy \\'peg-ē\ dim of MARGARET
Pe·nel·o·pe \pə-'nel-ə-pē\ [Gk]
Pen·ny \\'pen-ē\ dim of PENELOPE
Phoe·be \\'fē-bē\ [Gk] shining
Phyl·lis \\'fil-əs\ [Gk] green leaf
Pol·ly \\'päl-ē\ dim of MARY
Por·tia \\'pōr-shə, 'pȯr-\ [L]
Pris·cil·la \prə-'sil-ə\ [L]
Pru·dence \\'prüd-ᵊn(t)s\ [E] prudence

Ra·chel \\'rā-chəl\ [Heb] ewe
Rae \\'rā\ dim of RACHEL
Ra·mo·na \rə-'mō-nə\ [Sp] fem of RAMON
Re·ba \\'rē-bə\ dim of REBECCA
Re·bec·ca \ri-'bek-ə\ [Heb]
Re·gi·na \ri-'jē-nə, -'jī-\ [L] queen
Re·nee \rə-'nā, 'ren-(,)ā, 'rā-nē, 'rē-nē\ [F] reborn
Rhea \\'rē-ə\ [Gk]
Rho·da \\'rōd-ə\ [Gk] rose
Ri·ta \\'rēt-ə\ [It] dim of MARGARET
Ro·ber·ta \rə-'bərt-ə, rō-\ fem of ROBERT
Rob·in or Rob·yn \\'räb-ən\ [E] robin
Ro·chelle \rō-'shel\ [prob. fr. a surname]
Ro·na or Rho·na \\'rō-nə\
Ron·da \\'rän-də\ var of Rhonda
Ron·nie \\'rän-ē\ dim of VERONICA
Ro·sa·lie \\'rō-zə-(,)lē, 'räz-ə-\ [L] festival of roses
Ro·sa·lind \\'räz-(ə-)lənd, 'rō-zə-lənd\ [Sp]
Rose \\'rōz\ or Ro·sa \\'rō-zə\ [L] rose
Rose·anne \rō-'zan\ [Rose + Anne]
Rose·mary \\'rōz-,mer-ē\ or Rose·ma·rie \,rōz-mə-'rē\ [E] rosemary
Ro·set·ta \rō-'zet-ə\ dim of ROSE
Ros·lyn \\'räz-lən\ or Ro·sa·lyn or Ro·se·lyn \\'räz-(ə-)lən, 'rō-zə-lən\ var of ROSALIND
Ro·we·na \rə-'wē-nə\ [perh. fr. OE]
Rox·anne \räk-'san\ [OPer]
Ru·by \\'rü-bē\ [E] ruby
Ruth \\'rüth\ [Heb]

Ruth·ann \rü-'than\ [Ruth + Ann]

Sa·bra \\'sā-brə\ dim of Sabrina
Sa·die \\'sād-ē\ dim of SARA
Sal·ly or Sal·lie \\'sal-ē\ dim of SARA
Sa·man·tha \sə-'man-thə\ [Aram]
San·dra \\'san-drə, 'sän-\ dim of ALEXANDRA
San·dy \\'san-dē\ dim of ALEXANDRA
Sar·ah or Sara \\'ser-ə, 'sar-ə, 'sā-rə\ [Heb] princess
Sara·lee \\'ser-ə-(,)lē, 'sar-\ [prob. fr. Sara + Lee]
Saun·dra \\'sȯn-drə, 'sän-\ var of SANDRA
Sel·ma \\'sel-mə\ [Sw] fem dim of Anselm
Shari \\'sha(ə)r-ē, 'she(ə)r-\ dim of SHARON
Shar·lene \shär-'lēn\ var of CHARLENE
Shar·on or Shar·ron \\'shar-ən, 'sher-\ [Heb]
Shei·la \\'shē-lə\ [IrGael] var of CECILIA
She·lia \\'shēl-yə\ var of SHEILA
Shel·ley \\'shel-ē\ [fr. a surname]
Sher·rill or Sher·yl \\'sher-əl\ [prob. fr. a surname]
Sher·ry or Sher·rie or Sheri \\'sher-ē\
Shir·ley \\'shər-lē\ [fr. a surname]
Sig·rid \\'sig-rəd\ [Scand] beautiful as victory
Son·dra \\'sän-drə\ var of SANDRA
So·nia or So·nya or So·nja \\'sō-nyə, 'sȯ-\ [Russ] dim of SOPHIA
So·phia \sə-'fē-ə, -'fī-\ or So·phie \\'sō-fē\ [Gk] wisdom
Sta·cy or Sta·cey \\'stā-sē\ dim of ANASTASIA
Stel·la \\'stel-ə\ [L] star
Steph·a·nie \\'stef-ə-nē\ fem of STEPHEN
Sue \\'sü\ or Su·sie \\'sü-zē\ dim of SUSAN
Su·el·len \sü-'el-ən\ [Sue + Ellen]
Su·san or Su·zan \\'süz-ᵊn\ dim of SUSANNA
Su·san·na or Su·san·nah \sü-'zan-ə\ [Heb] lily
Su·zanne or Su·sanne or Su·zann \sü-'zan\ [F] var of SUSAN
Syb·il \\'sib-əl\ [Gk] sibyl
Syl·via \\'sil-vē-ə\ [L] she of the forest

Ta·mara \tə-'mar-ə\ [prob. fr. Georgian (language of the Republic of Georgia)]
Tan·ya \\'tan-yə\ [Russ] dim of TATIANA
Ta·ra \\'tär-ə\ [IrGael]
Tat·i·ana \,tät-ē-'än-ə\ [Russ]
Te·re·sa \tə-'rē-sə\ var of THERESA
Ter·ry or Ter·ri \\'ter-ē\ dim of THERESA
Thel·ma \\'thel-mə\
The·o·do·ra \,thē-ə-'dōr-ə, -'dȯr-\ [LGk] fem of THEODORE
The·re·sa or Te·re·sa \tə-'rē-sə\ [LL]
The·rese \tə-'rēs\ var of THERESA
Tif·fa·ny \\'tif-ə-nē\ [Gk]
Ti·na \\'tē-nə\ dim of CHRISTINA
To·by \\'tō-bē\
To·ni \\'tō-nē\ dim of Antonia
Tra·cy \\'trā-sē\ [fr. a surname]
Tru·dy \\'trüd-ē\ dim of GERTRUDE

Ur·su·la \\'ər-sə-lə\ [LL] little she-bear

Val·er·ie \\'val-ə-rē\ [L] prob strong
Van·es·sa \və-'nes-ə\
Vel·ma \\'vel-mə\
Ve·ra \\'vir-ə\ [Russ] faith
Ver·na \\'vər-nə\ prob fem of VERNON
Ve·ron·i·ca \və-'rän-i-kə\ [LL]
Vicki or Vicky or Vick·ie \\'vik-ē\ dim of VICTORIA
Vic·to·ria \vik-'tōr-ē-ə, -'tȯr-\ [L] victory
Vi·da \\'vēd-ə, 'vīd-\ fem dim of DAVID
Vi·o·la \vī-'ō-lə, vē-'ō-, 'vī-ə-, 'vē-ə-\ [L] violet

\ə\abut \ᵊ\kitten \ər\further \a\ash \ā\ace \ä\mop, mar
\au̇\out \ch\chin \e\bet \ē\easy \g\go \i\hit \ī\ice \j\job
\ŋ\sing \ō\go \ȯ\law \ȯi\boy \th\thin \t͟h\the \ü\loot \u̇\foot
\y\yet \zh\vision see also Pronunciation Symbols page

Vi·o·let \'vī-ə-lət\ [OF, fr. L] violet
Vir·gin·ia \vər-'jin-yə, -'jin-ē-ə\ [L]
Viv·i·an \'viv-ē-ən\ [LL]

Wan·da \'wän-də\ [Pol]
Wen·dy \'wen-dē\
Whit·ney \'hwit-nē, 'wit-\ [OE]
Wil·da \'wil-də\ *var of* WILLA

Wil·la \'wil-ə\ *or* **Wil·lie** \'wil-ē\ *prob fem dim of* WILLIAM
Wil·ma \'wil-mə\ *prob fem dim of* WILLIAM
Win·i·fred \'win-ə-frəd\ [W]

Yvette \i-'vet\ [F]
Yvonne \i-'vän\ [F]

Zel·da \'zel-də\ *dim of* Griselda

Foreign Words and Phrases

ab·eunt stu·dia in mo·res \ˈä-be-ˌůnt-ˈstü-dē-ˌä-in-ˈmō-ˌräs\ [L] : practices zealously pursued pass into habits

à bien·tôt \à-byaⁿ-tō\ [F] : so long

ab in·cu·na·bu·lis \ˌäb-ˌiŋ-ků-ˈnä-bů-ˌlēs\ [L] : from the cradle : from infancy

à bon chat, bon rat \à-bōⁿ-ˈshà-bōⁿ-ˈrà\ [F] : to a good cat, a good rat : retaliation in kind

à bouche ou·ver·te \à-bü-shü-vert\ [F] : with open mouth : eagerly : uncritically

ab ovo us·que ad ma·la \àb-ˈō-vō-ˌůs-kwe-ˌàd-ˈmä-là\ [L] : from egg to apples : from soup to nuts : from beginning to end

à bras ou·verts \à-brà-zü-ver\ [F] : with open arms : cordially

ab·sit in·vi·dia \ˈäb-ˌsit-in-ˈwi-dē-ˌä\ [L] : let there be no envy or ill will

ab uno dis·ce om·nes \äb-ˈü-nō-ˌdis-ke-ˈóm-ˌnäs\ [L] : from one learn to know all

ab ur·be con·di·ta \äb-ˈůr-be-ˈkòn-di-ˌtä\ [L] : from the founding of the city (Rome, founded 753 B.C.) — used by the Romans in reckoning dates

ab·usus non tol·lit usum \ˈä-ˌbü-sůs-ˌnōn-ˌtò-lit-ˈü-sům\ [L] : abuse does not take away use, i.e., is not an argument against proper use

à compte \à-kōⁿt\ [F] : on account

à coup sûr \à-kü-sՠr\ [F] : with sure stroke : surely

acte gra·tuit \àk-tə-grà-twˈē\ [F] : gratuitous impulsive act

ad ar·bi·tri·um \ˌad-är-ˈbi-trē-ům\ [L] : at will : arbitrarily

ad as·tra per as·pe·ra \ad-ˈas-trə-ˌpər-ˈas-pə-rə\ [L] : to the stars by hard ways — motto of Kansas

ad ex·tre·mum \ˌad-ik-ˈstrē-məm\ [L] : to the extreme : at last

ad ka·len·das Grae·cas \ˌäd-kä-ˈlen-däs-ˈgrī-ˌkäs\ [L] : at the Greek calends : never (since the Greeks had no calends)

ad ma·jo·rem Dei glo·ri·am \ˌäd-mä-ˈyōr-ˌem-ˈde-ˌē-ˈglór-ē-ˌäm\ [L] : to the greater glory of God — motto of the Society of Jesus

ad pa·tres \äd-ˈpä-ˌträs\ [L] : (gathered) to his fathers : deceased

ad re·fe·ren·dum \ˌäd-ˌre-fe-ˈren-dům\ [L] : for reference : for further consideration by one having the authority to make a final decision

à droite \à-drwät\ [F] : to or on the right hand

ad un·guem \äd-ˈůŋ-ˌgwem\ [L] : to the fingernail : to a nicety : exactly (from the use of the fingernail to test the smoothness of marble)

ad utrum·que pa·ra·tus \ˌäd-ù-ˈtrům-kwe-pä-ˈrä-tůs\ [L] : prepared for either (event)

ad vi·vum \äd-ˈwē-wům\ [L] : to the life

ae·gri som·nia \ˈī-grē-ˈsóm-nē-ˌä\ [L] : a sick man's dreams

ae·quam ser·va·re men·tem \ˈī-ˌkwäm-ser-ˈwä-rä-ˈmen-ˌtem\ [L] : to preserve a calm mind

ae·quo ani·mo \ˈī-ˌkwō-ˈä-ni-ˌmō\ [L] : with even mind : calmly

ae·re per·en·ni·us \ˈī-rä-pe-ˈre-nē-ˌůs\ [L] : more lasting than bronze

à gauche \à-gōsh\ [F] : to or on the left hand

age quod agis \ˈä-ge-ˌkwód-ˈä-gis\ [L] : do what you are doing : to the business at hand

à grands frais \à-grän-fre\ [F] : at great expense

à huis clos \à-wˈē-klō\ [F] : with closed doors

aide-toi, le ciel t'ai·dera \ed-twà-lə-ˈsyel-te-drà\ [F] : help yourself (and) heaven will help you

aî·né \e-nā\ [F] : elder : senior (masc.)

aî·née \e-nā\ [F] : elder : senior (fem.)

à l'aban·don \à-là-bäⁿ-dōⁿ\ [F] : carelessly : in disorder

à la belle étoile \à-là-bel-ä-twàl\ [F] : under the beautiful star : in the open air at night

à la bonne heure \à-là-bò-nœr\ [F] : at a good time : well and good : all right

à la fran·çaise \à-là-fräⁿ-sez\ [F] : in the French manner

à l'amé·ri·caine \à-là-mä-rē-ken\ [F] : in the American manner : of the American kind

à l'an·glaise \à-läⁿ-glez\ [F] : in the English manner

à la page \à-là-päzh\ [F] : at the page : up-to-the-minute

à la russe \à-là-rՠes\ [F] : in the Russian manner

alea jac·ta est \ˈä-lē-ˌä-ˌyäk-tä-ˈest\ [L] : the die is cast

à l'im·pro·viste \à-laⁿ-prò-vēst\ [F] : unexpectedly

ali·quan·do bo·nus dor·mi·tat Ho·me·rus \ˈä-li-ˌkwän-dō-ˈbò-nůs-dòr-ˈmē-tät-hō-ˈmer-ůs\ [L] : sometimes (even) good Homer nods

alis vo·lat pro·pri·is \ˈä-ˌlēs-ˈwò-ˌlät-ˈprō-prē-ˌēs\ [L] : she flies with her own wings — motto of Oregon

al-ki \ˈal-ˌkī\ [Chinook Jargon] : by and by — motto of Washington

alo·ha oe \à-ˈlō-hä-ˈói, -ˈō-ē\ [Hawaiian] : love to you : greetings : farewell

al·ter idem \ˈòl-tər-ˈī-ˌdem, ˌäl-ter-ˈē-\ [L] : second self

a max·i·mis ad mi·ni·ma \ä-ˈmäk-si-ˌmēs-ˌäd-ˈmi-ni-ˌmä\ [L] : from the greatest to the least

ami·cus hu·ma·ni ge·ne·ris \ä-ˈmē-kůs-hü-ˈmä-nē-ˈge-ne-ris\ [L] : friend of the human race

ami·cus us·que ad aras \-ˌůs-kwe-ˌäd-ˈär-ˌäs\ [L] : a friend as far as to the altars, i.e., except in what is contrary to one's religion; *also* : a friend to the last extremity

ami de cour \à-mē-də-kůr\ [F] : court friend : insincere friend

amor pa·tri·ae \ˈä-ˌmór-ˈpä-trē-ˌī\ [L] : love of one's country

amor vin·cit om·nia \ˈä-ˌmór-ˈwiŋ-kit-ˈóm-nē-ä\ [L] : love conquers all things

an·cienne no·blesse \äⁿ-syen-nò-bles\ [F] : old-time nobility : the French nobility before the Revolution of 1789

an·guis in her·ba \ˈäŋ-gwis-in-ˈher-ˌbä\ [L] : snake in the grass

ani·mal bi·pes im·plu·me \ˈä-ni-ˌmäl-ˈbi-ˌpäs-im-ˈplü-me\ [L] : two-legged animal without feathers (i.e., the human race)

ani·mis opi·bus·que pa·ra·ti \ˈä-ni-ˌmēs-ˌò-pi-ˈbůs-kwe-pä-ˈrä-tē\ [L] : prepared in mind and resources — one of the mottoes of South Carolina

an·no ae·ta·tis su·ae \ˈä-nō-ī-ˌtä-tis-ˈsü-ˌī\ [L] : in the (specified) year of his or her age

an·no mun·di \ˈä-nō-ˈmůn-dē\ [L] : in the year of the world — used in reckoning dates from the supposed pe-

\ə\abut \ᵊ\kitten \ər\further \a\ash \ā\ace \ä\mop, mar \aů\out \ch\chin \e\bet \ē\easy \g\go \i\hit \ī\ice \j\job \ŋ\sing \ō\go \ò\law \ói\boy \th\thin \t̲h̲\the \ü\loot \ů\foot \y\yet \zh\vision *see also* Pronunciation Symbols page riod of the creation of the world, esp. as fixed by James Ussher at 4004 B.C. or by the Jews at 3761 B.C.

an·no ur·bis con·di·tae \'ä-nō-'ùr-bis-'kòn-di-ˌtī\ [L] : in the year of the founded city (Rome, founded 753 B.C.)

an·nu·it coep·tis \'ä-nù-ˌwit-'kòip-ˌtēs\ [L] : He (God) has approved our beginnings — motto on the reverse of the Great Seal of the United States

à peu près \à-pœ-pre\ [F] : nearly : approximately

à pied \à-pyā\ [F] : on foot

après moi le dé·luge \à-pre-mwà-lə-dā-lᵫzh\ *or* **après nous le déluge** \-à-pre-nü-\ [F] : after me the deluge — attributed to Louis XV

à pro·pos de bottes \à-prə-pō-də-bòt\ [F] : apropos of boots — used to change the subject

à pro·pos de rien \-ryaⁿ\ [F] : apropos of nothing

aqua et ig·ni in·ter·dic·tus \'äk-wä-et-'ig-nē-ˌin-ter-'dik-tùs\ [L] : forbidden to be furnished with water and fire : outlawed

Ar·ca·des am·bo \'är-kä-ˌdes-'äm-bō\ [L] : both Arcadians : two persons of like occupations or tastes; *also* : two rascals

ar·rec·tis au·ri·bus \à-'rek-ˌtēs-'aù-ri-ˌbùs\ [L] : with ears pricked up : attentively

ar·ri·ve·der·ci \à-ˌrē-ve-'der-chē\ [It] : till we meet again : farewell

ars est ce·la·re ar·tem \'ärs-ˌest-kā-'lär-ā-'är-ˌtem\ [L] : it is (true) art to conceal art

ars lon·ga, vi·ta bre·vis \'ärs-'lòŋ-ˌgä-'wē-ˌtä-'bre-wis\ [L] : art is long, life is short

a ter·go \ä-'ter-(ˌ)gō\ [L] : from behind

à tort et à tra·vers \à-tòr-ā-à-trà-ver\ [F] : wrong and crosswise : at random : without rhyme or reason

au bout de son la·tin \ō-bü-də-sōⁿ-là-taⁿ\ [F] : at the end of one's Latin : at the end of one's mental resources

au con·traire \ō-kōⁿ-trer\ [F] : on the contrary

au·de·mus ju·ra nos·tra de·fen·de·re \aù-'dā-mùs-'yùr-ä-ˌnò-strä-dā-'fen-de-rā\ [L] : we dare defend our rights — motto of Alabama

au·den·tes for·tu·na ju·vat \aù-'den-ˌtäs-fòr-'tü-nä-'yù-ˌwät\ [L] : fortune favors the bold

au·di al·ter·am par·tem \'aù-dē-'äl-te-ˌräm-'pär-ˌtem\ [L] : hear the other side

au fait \ō-fet, -fe\ [F] : to the point : fully competent : fully informed : socially correct

au fond \ō-fōⁿ\ [F] : at bottom : fundamentally

au grand sé·rieux \ō-grän-sā-ryœ\ [F] : in all seriousness

au pays des aveugles les borgnes sont rois \ō-pā-ē-dā-zà-vœgl°-lā-bórnʸ-ə-sōⁿ-rwä\ [F] : in the country of the blind the one-eyed men are kings

au·rea me·di·o·cri·tas \'aù-rē-ä-ˌme-dē-'ò-kri-ˌtäs\ [L] : the golden mean

au reste \ō-rest\ [F] : for the rest : besides

aus·si·tôt dit, aus·si·tôt fait \ō-sē-tō-dē-ō-sē-tō-fe\ [F] : no sooner said than done

aut Cae·sar aut ni·hil \'aùt-'kī-sär-ˌaùt-'ni-ˌhil\ [L] : either a Caesar or nothing

aut Caesar aut nul·lus \-'nù-lùs\ [L] : either a Caesar or a nobody

au·tres temps, au·tres mœurs \ō-trə-täⁿ-ō-trə-mœrs\ [F] : other times, other customs

aut vin·ce·re aut mo·ri \ˌaùt-'wiŋ-ke-rā-ˌaùt-'mò-ˌrē\ [L] : either to conquer or to die

aux armes \ō-zàrm\ [F] : to arms

avant la lettre \à-vän-là-letrᵉ\ [F] : before the letter : before a (specified) name existed

ave at·que va·le \'ä-ˌwā-ˌàt-kwe-'wä-ˌlā\ [L] : hail and farewell

à vo·tre san·té \à-vòt-sän-tā, -vò-trə-\ [F] : to your health — used as a toast

beaux yeux \bō-zyᴒ\ [F] : beautiful eyes : beauty of face

bel·la fi·gu·ra \'bel-lä-fē-'gü-rä\ [It] : fine appearance or impression

belle laide \bel-led\ [F] : beautiful ugly woman : a woman who is attractive though not conventionally beautiful

bien en·ten·du \byaⁿ-nän-tän-dᵫ\ [F] : well understood : of course

bien–pen·sant \byaⁿ-pän-säⁿ\ [F] : right-minded : one who holds orthodox views

bien·sé·ance \byaⁿ-sā-äⁿs\ [F] : propriety

bis dat qui ci·to dat \'bis-ˌdät-kwē-'ki-tō-ˌdät\ [L] : he or she gives twice who gives promptly

bon ap·pé·tit \bò-nà-pā-tē\ [F] : good appetite : enjoy your meal

bon gré, mal gré \'bōⁿ-ˌgrā-'màl-ˌgrā\ [F] : whether with good grace or bad : willy-nilly

bo·nis avi·bus \'bò-ˌnēs-'ä-wi-ˌbùs\ [L] : under good auspices

bon·jour \bōⁿ-zhür\ [F] : good day : good morning

bonne foi \bòn-fwä\ [F] : good faith

bon·soir \bōⁿ-swàr\ [F] : good evening

bru·tum ful·men \'brü-tùm-'fùl-men\ [L] : insensible thunderbolt : a futile threat or display of force

buon gior·no \bwòn-'jòr-nō\ [It] : good day

ca·dit quae·stio \'kä-dit-'kwī-stē-ˌō\ [L] : the question drops : the argument collapses

cau·sa si·ne qua non \'kaù-ˌsä-ˌsi-nā-kwä-'nōn\ [L] : an indispensable cause or condition

ça va sans dire \sà-và-sän-dēr\ [F] : it goes without saying

ca·ve ca·nem \'kä-wā-'kä-ˌnem\ [L] : beware the dog

ce·dant ar·ma to·gae \'kā-ˌdänt-'är-mə-'tō-ˌgi\ [L] : let arms yield to the toga : let military power give way to civil power — motto of Wyoming

ce n'est que le pre·mier pas qui coûte \snek-lə-prə-myā-pä-kē-küt\ [F] : it is only the first step that costs

c'est–à–dire \se-tà-dēr\ [F] : that is to say : namely

c'est au·tre chose \se-tōt-shōz, -tō-trə-\ [F] : that's a different thing

c'est la guerre \se-là-ger\ [F] : that's war : it cannot be helped

c'est la vie \se-là-vē\ [F] : that's life : that's how things happen

c'est plus qu'un crime, c'est une faute \se-plᵫ-kœⁿ-krēm-se-tᵫn-fōt\ [F] : it is worse than a crime, it is a blunder

ce·te·ra de·sunt \'kā-te-ˌrä-'dā-ˌsùnt\ [L] : the rest is missing

cha·cun à son goût \shà-kœⁿ-nà-sōⁿ-gü\ [F] : everyone to his or her taste

châ·teau en Es·pagne \shä-tō-äⁿ-nes-pánʸ\ [F] : castle in Spain : a visionary project

cher·chez la femme \sher-shā-là-fàm\ [F] : look for the woman

che sa·rà, sa·rà \ˌkā-sä-ˌrä-sä-'rä\ [It] : what will be, will be

che·val de ba·taille \shə-vàl-də-bá-täʸ\ [F] : war-horse : argument constantly relied on : favorite subject

co·gi·to, er·go sum \'kō-gi-ˌtō-ˌer-gō-'sùm\ [L] : I think, therefore I exist

co·mé·die hu·maine \kò-mā-dē-ᵫ-men\ [F] : human comedy : the whole variety of human life

comme ci, comme ça \kòm-sē-kòm-sà\ [F] : so-so

com·pa·gnon de voy·age \kōⁿ-pà-nʸōⁿ-də-vwä-yàzh\ [F] : traveling companion

compte ren·du \kōⁿt-rän-dᵫ\ [F] : report (as of proceedings in an investigation)

con·cor·dia dis·cors \kòn-'kòr-dē-ä-'dis-ˌkòrs\ [L] : discordant harmony

cor·rup·tio op·ti·mi pes·si·ma \kò-'rùp-tē-ˌō-'äp-ti-ˌmē-'pe-si-ˌmä\ [L] : the corruption of the best is the worst of all

coup de maî·tre \küd-metrᵉ, kü-də-\ [F] : masterstroke

coup d'es·sai \kü-dā-se\ [F] : experiment : trial

coûte que coûte \küt-kə-küt\ [F] : cost what it may

cre·do quia ab·sur·dum est \\'krā-dō-ˌ'kwē-ä-ˌ'ap-ˌ'sùr-dùm-ˌ'est\\ [L] : I believe it because it is absurd

cres·cit eun·do \\'kres-kit-ˌ'eùn-dō\\ [L] : it grows as it goes — motto of New Mexico

crise de nerfs *or* **crise des nerfs** \\krēz-də-ner\\ [F] : crisis of nerves : nervous collapse : hysterical fit

crux cri·ti·co·rum \\'krùks-ˌ'kri-ti-ˌ'kôr-ùm\\ [L] : crux of critics

cu·jus re·gio, ej·us re·li·gio \\'kü-yùs-ˌ're-gē-ˌō-'e-yùs-re-ˌ'li-gē-ˌō\\ [L] : whose region, his or her religion : subjects are to accept the religion of their ruler

cum gra·no sa·lis \\kùm-ˌ'grä-nō-ˌ'sä-lis\\ [L] : with a grain of salt

cur·sus ho·no·rum \\'kùr-sùs-hò-ˌ'nō-rùm\\ [L] : course of honors : succession of offices of increasing importance

cus·tos mo·rum \\'kùs-tōs-ˌ'môr-ùm\\ [L] : guardian of manners or morals : censor

d'ac·cord \\dä-kôr\\ [F] : in accord : agreed

dame d'hon·neur \\dám-dò-nœr\\ [F] : lady-in-waiting

dam·nant quod non in·tel·li·gunt \\'däm-nänt-ˌkwòd-'nōn-in-ˌ'te-li-ˌgùnt\\ [L] : they condemn what they do not understand

de bonne grâce \\də-bòn-gräs\\ [F] : with good grace : willingly

de gus·ti·bus non est dis·pu·tan·dum \\dä-ˌ'gùs-ti-ˌbùs-ˌ'nōn-ˌest-ˌdis-pù-'tän-ˌdùm\\ [L] : there is no disputing about tastes

Dei gra·tia \\'dē-ˌē-ˌ'grä-tē-ˌä\\ [L] : by the grace of God

de in·te·gro \\dä-ˌ'in-te-ˌgrō\\ [L] : anew : afresh

de l'au·dace, en·core de l'au·dace, et tou·jours de l'au·dace \\də-lō-dás-äⁿ-kôr-də-lō-dás-ā-tü-zhür-də-lō-dás\\ [F] : audacity, more audacity, and ever more audacity

de·len·da est Car·tha·go \\dā-ˌ'len-dä-ˌest-kär-'tä-gō\\ [L] : Carthage must be destroyed

de·li·ne·a·vit \\dā-ˌlē-nä-'ä-wit\\ [L] : he or she drew it

de mal en pis \\də-má-läⁿ-pē\\ [F] : from bad to worse

de mi·ni·mis non cu·rat lex \\dā-ˌ'mi-ni-ˌmēs-ˌnōn-ˌkü-ˌrät-'leks\\ [L] : the law takes no account of trifles

de mor·tu·is nil ni·si bo·num \\dā-ˌ'mòr-tù-ˌwēs-ˌnēl-ˌni-sē-'bò-nùm\\ [L] : of the dead (say) nothing but good

de nos jours \\də-nō-zhür\\ [F] : of our time : contemporary — used postpositively esp. after a proper name

Deo fa·ven·te \\dā-ō-fä-'ven-tä\\ [L] : with God's favor

Deo gra·ti·as \\ˌdā-ō-'grä-tē-ˌäs\\ [L] : thanks (be) to God

de pro·fun·dis \\dā-prō-'fùn-dēs\\ [L] : out of the depths

der Geist der stets ver·neint \\dər-ˌ'gīst-dər-ˌshtäts-fer-'nīnt\\ [G] : the spirit that ever denies — applied originally to Mephistopheles

de·si·pe·re in lo·co \\dā-'si-pe-rä-in-'lò-kō\\ [L] : to indulge in trifling at the proper time

Deus vult \\'dā-ùs-'wùlt\\ [L] : God wills it — rallying cry of the First Crusade

di·es fau·stus \\'dē-ˌäs-ˌ'faù-stùs\\ [L] : lucky day

dies in·fau·stus \\-ˌ'in-ˌfaù-stùs\\ [L] : unlucky day

dies irae \\-ˌ'ē-ˌrī\\ [L] : day of wrath — used of the Judgment Day

Dieu et mon droit \\dyœ-ā-mòⁿ-drwä\\ [F] : God and my right — motto on the British royal arms

Dieu vous garde \\dyœ-vü-gárd\\ [F] : God keep you

di·ri·go \\'dē-ri-ˌgō\\ [L] : I direct — motto of Maine

dis ali·ter vi·sum \\'dēs-ˌ'ä-li-ˌter-'wē-ˌsùm\\ [L] : the Gods decreed otherwise

di·tat De·us \\'dē-ˌtät-'dā-ˌùs\\ [L] : God enriches — motto of Arizona

di·vi·de et im·pe·ra \\'dē-wi-ˌde-ˌet-'im-pe-ˌrä\\ [L] : divide and rule

do·cen·do dis·ci·mus \\dò-ˌken-dō-'dis-ki-ˌmùs\\ [L] : we learn by teaching

Do·mi·ne di·ri·ge nos \\'dò-mi-ˌne-ˌ'dē-ri-ge-ˌnōs\\ [L] : Lord, direct us — motto of the City of London

Do·mi·nus vo·bis·cum \\'dò-mi-ˌnùs-wō-ˌbēs-ˌkùm\\ [L] : the Lord be with you

dul·ce et de·co·rum est pro pa·tria mo·ri \\'dùl-ˌkä-et-

de-ˌ'kôr-ùm-ˌest-prō-ˌ'pä-trē-ˌä-ˌ'mò-ˌrē\\ [L] : it is sweet and seemly to die for one's country

dum spi·ro, spe·ro \\dùm-ˌ'spē-rō-ˌ'spä-rō\\ [L] : while I breathe I hope — one of the mottoes of South Carolina

dum vi·vi·mus vi·va·mus \\dùm-ˌ'wē-wē-ˌmùs-wē-ˌ'wä-mùs\\ [L] : while we live, let us live

d'un certain âge \\dœⁿ-ser-te-nàzh\\ [F] : of a certain age : no longer young

dux fe·mi·na fac·ti \\'dùks-ˌ'fā-mi-nä-'fäk-ˌtē\\ [L] : a woman was leader of the exploit

ec·ce sig·num \\'e-ke-ˌ'sig-ˌnùm\\ [L] : behold the sign : look at the proof

e con·tra·rio \\ˌā-kòn-'trär-ē-ˌō\\ [L] : on the contrary

écra·sez l'in·fâme \\ā-krä-zä-laⁿ-fäm\\ [F] : crush the infamous thing

eheu fu·ga·ces la·bun·tur an·ni \\'ā-ˌheù-fü-ˌ'gä-ˌkäs-lä-ˌbùn-ˌtùr-'än-ˌē\\ [L] : alas! the fleeting years glide on

ein' fes·te Burg ist un·ser Gott \\īn-ˌfes-tə-ˌ'bùrk-ist-ˌùn-zər-ˌ'gòt\\ [G] : a mighty fortress is our God

em·bar·ras de ri·chesses *or* **embarras de ri·chesse** \\äⁿ-bä-rä-də-rē-shes\\ [F] : embarrassing surplus of riches : confusing abundance

em·bar·ras de choix \\äⁿ-bä-rä-də-shwà\\ *or* **embarras du choix** \\-dü͞e-shwä\\ [F] : embarrassing variety of choice

en ami \\äⁿ-nà-mē\\ [F] : as a friend

en ef·fet \\äⁿ-nā-fe\\ [F] : in fact : indeed

en fa·mille \\äⁿ-fä-mēy\\ [F] : in or with one's family : at home : informally

en·fant ché·ri \\äⁿ-fäⁿ-shä-rē\\ [F] : loved or pampered child : one that is highly favored

en·fant gâ·té \\äⁿ-fäⁿ-gä-tā\\ [F] : spoiled child

en·fants per·dus \\äⁿ-fäⁿ-per-dü͞e\\ [F] : lost children : soldiers sent to a dangerous post

en·fin \\äⁿ-faⁿ\\ [F] : in conclusion : in a word

en gar·çon \\äⁿ-gár-sōⁿ\\ [F] : as or like a bachelor

en garde \\äⁿ-gárd\\ [F] : on guard

en pan·tou·fles \\äⁿ-päⁿ-tüfl^ə\\ [F] : in slippers : at ease : informally

en plein air \\äⁿ-ple-ner\\ [F] : in the open air

en plein jour \\äⁿ-plaⁿ-zhür\\ [F] : in broad day

en règle \\äⁿ-regl^ə\\ [F] : in order : in due form

en re·tard \\äⁿ-rə-tàr\\ [F] : behind time : late

en re·traite \\äⁿ-rə-tret\\ [F] : in retreat : in retirement

en re·vanche \\äⁿ-rə-väⁿsh\\ [F] : in return : in compensation

en se·condes noces \\äⁿ-sə-gōⁿd-nòs\\ [F] : in a second marriage

en·se pe·tit pla·ci·dam sub li·ber·ta·te qui·e·tem \\'en-se-ˌ'pe-tit-ˌ'plä-ki-ˌdäm-sùb-ˌ'lē-ber-ˌtä-te-kwē-ˌ'ä-ˌtem\\ [L] : with the sword she seeks calm repose under liberty : by the sword we seek peace, but peace only under liberty — motto of Massachusetts

eo ip·so \\ˌā-ō-ˌ'ip-(ˌ)sō\\ [L] : by that itself : by that fact alone

épa·ter le bour·geois \\ā-pà-tā-lə-bür-zhwà\\ [F] : to shock the middle classes

e plu·ri·bus unum \\ˌē-ˌ'plùr-ə-bəs-ˌ'yü-nəm, ˌā-ˌ'plùr-i-bùs-ˌ'ü-nùm\\ [L] : one out of many — used on the Great Seal of the U.S. and on several U.S. coins

ep·pur si muo·ve \\äp-ˌ'pür-sē-ˌ'mwò-vä\\ [It] : and yet it does move — attributed to Galileo after recanting his assertion of the earth's motion

Erin go bragh \\'er-ən-gə-ˌ'brò, -gō-ˌ'brä\\ [Ir *go brách* or *go bráth*, lit., till doomsday] : Ireland forever

er·ra·re hu·ma·num est \\e-ˌ'rär-e-hü-ˌ'mä-nùm-ˌest\\ [L] : to err is human

es·prit de l'es·ca·lier \\es-prēd-les-kà-lyā\\ *or* **es·prit**

---

d'es·ca·lier \-prē-des-\ [F] : staircase wit : repartee thought of only too late

es·se quam vi·de·ri \'e-sā-ₐkwäm-wi-'dā-rē\ [L] : to be rather than to seem — motto of North Carolina

est mo·dus in re·bus \est-'mò-ₐdùs-in-'rä-ₐbùs\ [L] : there is a proper measure in things, i.e., the golden mean should always be observed

es·to per·pe·tua \'es-ₐtō-per-'pe-tù-ₐwä\ [L] : may she endure forever — motto of Idaho

et hoc ge·nus om·ne \et-'hòk-ₐge-nùs-'òm-ne\ *or* **et id genus omne** \et-ₐid-\ [L] : and everything of this kind

et in Ar·ca·dia ego \ₐet-in-är-'kä-dē-ä-'e-gō\ [L] : I too (lived) in Arcadia

et sic de si·mi·li·bus \et-'sēk-dā-si-'mi-li-ₐbùs\ [L] : and so of like things

et tu Bru·te \et-'tü-'brü-te\ [L] : thou too, Brutus — exclamation attributed to Julius Caesar on seeing his friend Brutus among his assassins

eu·re·ka \yù-'rē-kə\ [Gk] : I have found it — motto of California

Ewig–Weib·li·che \ₐā-vik̲-'vīp-li-k̲ə\ [G] : eternal feminine

ex·al·té \eg-zàl-tā\ [F] : emotionally excited or elated : fanatic

ex ani·mo \eks-'ä-ni-ₐmō\ [L] : from the heart : sincerely

ex·cel·si·or \ik-'sel-sē-ər, eks-'kel-sē-ₐòr\ [L] : still higher — motto of New York

ex·cep·tio pro·bat re·gu·lam de re·bus non ex·cep·tis \eks-'kep-tē-ₐō-'prō-bät-'rä-gù-ₐläm-dā-'rä-ₐbùs-'nōn-eks-'kep-ₐtēs\ [L] : an exception establishes the rule as to things not excepted

ex·cep·tis ex·ci·pi·en·dis \eks-'kep-ₐtēs-eks-ₐki-pē-'en-ₐdēs\ [L] : with the proper or necessary exceptions

ex·i·tus ac·ta pro·bat \'ek-si-ₐtùs-'äk-tä-'prò-ₐbät\ [L] : the outcome justifies the deed

ex li·bris \eks-'lē-bris\ [L] : from the books of — used on bookplates

ex me·ro mo·tu \ₐeks-'mer-ō-'mō-tü\ [L] : out of mere impulse : of one's own accord

ex ne·ces·si·ta·te rei \ₐeks-ne-ₐke-si-'tä-te-'rä-ₐē\ [L] : from the necessity of the case

ex ni·hi·lo ni·hil fit \eks-'ni-hi-ₐlō-'ni-ₐhil-'fit\ [L] : from nothing nothing is produced

ex pe·de Her·cu·lem \eks-'pe-de-'her-kù-ₐlem\ [L] : from the foot (we may judge of the size of) Hercules : from a part we may judge of the whole

ex·per·to cre·de \eks-'per-tō-'krä-de\ *or* **experto cre·di·te** \-'krä-di-ₐte\ [L] : believe one who has had experience

ex un·gue le·o·nem \eks-'ùŋ-gwe-le-'ò-ₐnem\ [L] : from the claw (we may judge of) the lion : from a part we may judge of the whole

ex vi ter·mi·ni \eks-'wē-'ter-mi-ₐnē\ [L] : from the force of the term

fa·ci·le prin·ceps \'fä-ki-le-'priŋ-ₐkeps\ [L] : easily first

fa·ci·lis de·scen·sus Aver·no \'fä-ki-ₐlis-dā-'skän-ₐsùs-ä-'wer-nō\ *or* **facilis descensus Aver·ni** \-(ₐ)nē\ [L] : the descent to Avernus is easy : the road to evil is easy

fa·çon de par·ler \fä-sōⁿ-də-pàr-lā\ [F] : manner of speaking : figurative or conventional expression

faire suivre \fer-swʸēvrᵊ\ [F] : have forwarded : please forward

fas est et ab ho·ste do·ce·ri \ₐfäs-'est-et-äb-'hò-ste-dò-'kä-(ₐ)rē\ [L] : it is right to learn even from an enemy

Fa·ta vi·am in·ve·ni·ent \'fä-tä-'wē-ₐäm-in-'we-nē-ₐent\ [L] : the Fates will find a way

fat·ti mas·chii, pa·ro·le fe·mi·ne \'fät-tē-'mäs-ₐkē-pä-'rò-lā-'fä-mē-ₐnā\ [It] : deeds are males, words are females : deeds are more effective than words — motto of Maryland, where it is generally interpreted as meaning "manly deeds, womanly words"

faux bon·homme \fō-bò-nòm\ [F] : pretended good fellow

faux–naïf \fœ-nà-ēf\ [F] : spuriously or affectedly childlike : artfully simple

fe·lix cul·pa \'fä-liks-'kùl-pä\ [L] : fortunate fault — used esp. of original sin in relation to the consequent coming of Christ

femme de cham·bre \fäm-də-shäⁿbrᵊ\ [F] : chambermaid : lady's maid

fe·sti·na len·te \fe-'stē-nä-'len-ₐtä\ [L] : make haste slowly

feux d'ar·ti·fice \fœ-dàr-tē-fēs\ [F] : fireworks : display of wit

fi·at ex·pe·ri·men·tum in cor·po·re vi·li \'fē-ät-ek-ₐsper-ē-'men-ₐtùm-in-'kòr-pò-re-'wē-lē\ [L] : let experiment be made on a worthless body

fi·at ju·sti·tia, ru·at cae·lum \'fē-ät-yùs-'ti-tē-ä-'rù-ät-'kī-ₐlùm\ [L] : let justice be done though the heavens fall

fi·at lux \'fē-ₐät-'lùks\ [L] : let there be light

Fi·dei De·fen·sor \'fi-de-ₐē-dā-'fän-ₐsòr\ [L] : Defender of the Faith — a title of the sovereigns of England

fi·dus Acha·tes \ₐfē-dùs-ä-'kä-ₐtäs\ [L] : faithful Achates : trusty friend

fille de cham·bre \fēy-də-shäⁿbrᵊ\ [F] : lady's maid

fille d'hon·neur \fēy-dò-nœr\ [F] : maid of honor

fils \fēs\ [F] : son — used orig. after French and now also after other family names to distinguish a son from his father

fi·nem re·spi·ce \'fē-nem-'rä-spi-ₐke\ [L] : consider the end

fi·nis co·ro·nat opus \ₐfē-nis-kò-'rō-ₐnät-'ō-ₐpùs\ [L] : the end crowns the work

flo·re·at \'flō-rē-ₐät\ [L] : may (he, she, or it) flourish — usu. followed by a name

fluc·tu·at nec mer·gi·tur \'flùk-tù-ₐwät-ₐnek-'mer-gi-ₐtùr\ [L] : it is tossed by the waves but does not sink — motto of Paris

fo·lie de gran·deur *or* **fo·lie des gran·deurs** \fò-lē-də-gräⁿ-dœr\ [F] : delusion of greatness : megalomania

force de frappe \fòrs-də-fràp\ [F] : military striking force esp. with nuclear weapons

fors·an et haec olim me·mi·nis·se ju·va·bit \'fòr-ₐsän-ₐet-'hīk-ₐō-lim-ₐme-mi-'ni-se-yù-'wä-bit\ [L] : perhaps this too will be a pleasure to look back on one day

for·tes for·tu·na ju·vat \'fòr-ₐtäs-fòr-'tü-nä-'yù-ₐwät\ [L] : fortune favors the brave

fron·ti nul·la fi·des \'fròn-tē-'nù-lä-'fi-ₐdäs\ [L] : no reliance can be placed on appearance

fu·it Ili·um \'fù-it-'i-lē-ùm\ [L] : Troy has been (i.e., is no more)

fu·ror lo·quen·di \'für-ₐòr-lò-'kwen-(ₐ)dē\ [L] : rage for speaking

furor po·e·ti·cus \-pò-'ā-ti-kùs\ [L] : poetic frenzy

furor scri·ben·di \-skrē-'ben-(ₐ)dē\ [L] : rage for writing

Gal·li·ce \'gä-li-ₐke\ [L] : in French : after the French manner

gar·çon d'hon·neur \gàr-sōⁿ-dò-nœr\ [F] : bridegroom's attendant

garde du corps \gàrd-dū̄e-kòr\ [F] : bodyguard

gar·dez la foi \gàr-dā-là-fwä\ [F] : keep faith

gau·de·a·mus igi·tur \ₐgaù-dē-'ä-mùs-'i-gi-ₐtùr\ [L] : let us then be merry

gens d'é·glise \zhäⁿ-dā-glēz\ [F] : church people : clergy

gens de guerre \zhäⁿ-də-ger\ [F] : military people : soldiery

gens du monde \zhäⁿ-dū̄e-mōⁿd\ [F] : people of the world : fashionable people

gno·thi se·au·ton \'gnō-thē-ₐse-aù-'tòn\ [Gk] : know thyself

grand monde \gräⁿ-mōⁿd\ [F] : great world : high society

gros·so mo·do \'gròs-(ₐ)sō-'mō-(ₐ)dō\ [It] : roughly

guerre à ou·trance \ger-à-ü-träⁿs\ [F] : war to the uttermost

gu·ten Tag \'güt-ᵊn-'täk\ [G] : good day
has·ta la vis·ta \̩äs-tä-lä-'vēs-tä\ [Sp] : good-bye
haut goût \ō-gü\ [F] : high flavor : slight taint of decay
hic et nunc \'hēk-et-'nu̇ŋk\ [L] : here and now
hic et ubi·que \'hēk-et-u̇-'bē-kwe\ [L] : here and every-where
hic ja·cet \hik-'jä-sət, hēk-'yä-ket\ [L] : here lies — used preceding a name on a tombstone
hinc il·lae la·cri·mae \'hiŋk-'i-̩lī-'lä-kri-̩mī\ [L] : hence those tears
hoc age \hōk-'äg-e\ [L] : do this : apply yourself to what you are about
hoc opus, hic la·bor est \̩hōk-'ò-̩pu̇s-̩hēk-'lä-̩bòr-'est\ [L] : this is the hard work, this is the toil
homme d'af·faires \òm-dà-fer\ [F] : man of business : business agent
homme d'es·prit \-des-prē\ [F] : man of wit
homme moyen sen·suel \òm-mwà-yaⁿ-sän-swʸel\ [F] : the average nonintellectual man
ho·mo sum: hu·ma·ni nil a me ali·e·num pu·to \'hò-mō-̩su̇m-hü-'mä-nē-'nēl-ä-̩mā-̩ä-lē-'ä-nu̇m-'pu̇-tō\[L] : I am a human being: I regard nothing of human concern as foreign to my interests
ho·ni soit qui mal y pense \ò-nē-swá-kē̩ mál-ē-päⁿs\ [F] : shamed be he who thinks evil of it — motto of the Order of the Garter
hu·ma·num est er·ra·re \hü-'mä-nu̇m-̩est-e-'rär-e\ [L] : to err is human
ich dien \ik-'dēn\ [G] : I serve — motto of the Prince of Wales
ici on parle fran·cais \ē-sē-ōⁿ-párl-fräⁿ-se\ [F] : French is spoken here
idées re·çues \ē-dā-rə-s ̄œ\ [F] : received ideas : conventional opinions
id est \id-'est\ [L] : that is
ig·no·ran·tia ju·ris ne·mi·nem ex·cu·sat \̩ig-nə-'rän-tē-ä-̩'yu̇r-is-'nä-mi-̩nem-eks-'kü-̩sät\ [L] : ignorance of the law excuses no one
ig·no·tum per ig·no·ti·us \ig-'nō-tu̇m-̩per-ig-'nō-tē-̩u̇s\ [L] : (explaining) the unknown by means of the more unknown
il faut cul·ti·ver no·tre jar·din \ēl-fō-k ̄œl-tē-vä-nòt-zhàr-daⁿ, -nò-trə-zhàr-\ [F] : we must cultivate our garden : we must tend to our own affairs
in ae·ter·num \̩in-ī-'ter-̩nu̇m\ [L] : forever
in du·bio \in-'du̇b-ē-̩ō\ [L] : in doubt : undetermined
in fu·tu·ro \̩in-fu̇-'tu̇r-ō\ [L] : in the future
in hoc sig·no vin·ces \̩in-̩hok-'sig-nō-'wiŋ-̩kās\ [L] : by this sign (the Cross) you will conquer
in li·mi·ne \in-'lē-mi-̩ne\ [L] : on the threshold : at the beginning
in om·nia pa·ra·tus \in-'òm-nē-ä-pä-'rä-̩tu̇s\ [L] : ready for all things
in par·ti·bus in·fi·de·li·um \in-'pär-ti-̩bu̇s-̩in-fə-'dä-lē-̩u̇m\ [L] : in the regions of the infidels — used of a titular bishop having no diocesan jurisdiction, usu. in non-Christian countries
in prae·sen·ti \̩in-prī-'sen-̩tē\ [L] : at the present time
in sae·cu·la sae·cu·lo·rum \in-'sī-ku̇-̩lä-̩sī-ku̇-'lōr-u̇m, -'sä-ku̇-̩lä-sä-\ [L] : for ages of ages : forever and ever
insh·al·lah \̩in-shä-'lä\ [Ar] : if Allah wills : God willing
in sta·tu quo an·te bel·lum \in-'stä-tü-kwō-'än-te-'be-lu̇m\ [L] : in the same state as before the war
in·te·ger vi·tae sce·le·ris·que pu·rus \'in-te-gər-'wē-̩tī-̩iske-le-'ris-kwe-'pü-ru̇s\ [L] : upright of life and free from wickedness
in·ter nos \̩in-tər-'nōs\ [L] : between ourselves
in·tra mu·ros \̩in-trä-'mü-̩rōs\ [L] : within the walls
in usum Del·phi·ni \in-'ü-su̇m-del-'fē- nē\ [L] : for the use of the Dauphin : expurgated
in utrum·que pa·ra·tus \̩in-ü-'trùm-kwe-pä-'rä-̩tu̇s\ [L] : prepared for either (event)
in·ve·nit \in-'wā-nit\ [L] : he or she devised it

in vi·no ve·ri·tas \in-'wē-nō-'wā-ri-̩täs\ [L] : there is truth in wine
in·vi·ta Mi·ner·va \in-'wē-̩tä-mi-'ner-̩wä\ [L] : Minerva being unwilling : without natural talent or inspiration
ip·sis·si·ma ver·ba \ip-'si-si-̩mä-'wer-̩bä\ [L] : the very words
ira fu·ror bre·vis est \'ē-rä-'für-̩òr-'bre-wis-'est\ [L] : anger is a brief madness
j'ac·cuse \zhà-k ̄œz\ [F] : I accuse : bitter denunciation
jac·ta alea est \'yäk-tä-'ä-lē-̩ä-'est\ [L] : the die is cast
j'adoube \zhà-düb\ [F] : I adjust — used in chess when touching a piece without intending to move it
ja·nu·is clau·sis \̩yä-nü-̩wēs-'klau̇-̩sēs\ [L] : behind closed doors
je main·tien·drai \zhə-maⁿ-tyaⁿ-drā\ [F] : I will maintain — motto of the Netherlands
jeu de mots \zhœ̄-də-mō\ [F] : play on words : pun
Jo·an·nes est no·men eius \yō-'ä-näs-est-'nō-men-'ä-yùs\ [L] : John is his name — motto of Puerto Rico
jo·lie laide \zhò-lē-led\ [F] : good-looking ugly woman : woman who is attractive though not conventionally pretty
jour·nal in·time \zhür-nàl-aⁿ-tēm\ [F] : intimate journal : private diary
jus di·vi·num \'yüs-di-'wē-̩nu̇m\ [L] : divine law
jus·ti·tia om·ni·bus \'yu̇s-'ti-tē-ä-'òm-ni-̩bu̇s\ [L] : justice for all — motto of the District of Columbia
j'y suis, j'y reste \zhē-sw ̄ē-zhē-rest\ [F] : here I am, here I remain
la belle dame sans mer·ci \là-bel-dàm-säⁿ-mer-sē\ [F] : the beautiful lady without mercy
la·bo·ra·re est ora·re \̩lä-bō-'rär-ä-̩est-'ō-̩rär-ā\ [L] : to work is to pray
la·bor om·nia vin·cit \'lä-̩bòr-̩òm-nē-̩ä-'wiŋ-kit\ [L] : labor conquers all things — motto of Oklahoma
la·cri·mae re·rum \'lä-kri-̩mī-'rä-̩rùm\ [L] : tears for things : pity for misfortune; also : tears in things : tragedy in life
lais·sez–al·ler or lais·ser–al·ler \le-sä-à-lā\ [F] : letting go : lack of restraint
lap·sus ca·la·mi \'läp-sùs-'kä-lä-̩mē\ [L] : slip of the pen
lap·sus lin·guae \-'liŋ-̩gwī\ [L] : slip of the tongue
la reine le veut \là-ren-lə-v ̄œ\ [F] : the queen wills it
la·scia·te ogni spe·ran·za, voi ch'en·tra·te \läsh-'shä-tä-̩ō-nʸē-spä-'rän-tsä ̩vō-ē-kän-'trä-tä\ [It] : abandon all hope, ye who enter
lau·da·tor tem·po·ris ac·ti \lau̇-'dä-̩tòr-̩tem-pò-ris-'äk-̩tē\ [L] : one who praises past times
laus Deo \lau̇s-'dä-ō\ [L] : praise (be) to God
Le·bens·welt \'lä-bəns-̩velt\ [G] : life world : world of lived experience
le cœur a ses rai·sons que la rai·son ne con·naît point \lə-kœr-à-sā-re-zōⁿk-là-re-zōⁿ-nə-kò-ne-pwaⁿ\ [F] : the heart has its reasons that reason knows nothing of
le roi est mort, vive le roi \lə-rwä-e-mòr-vēv-lə-rwä\ [F] : the king is dead, long live the king
le roi le veut \-lə-v ̄œ\ [F] : the king wills it
le roi s'avi·se·ra \-sá-vēz-rà\ [F] : the king will consider
le style, c'est l'homme \lə-stēl-se-lòm\ [F] : the style is the man
l'état, c'est moi \lā-tà-se-mwà\ [F] : the state, it is I
l'étoile du nord \lā-twàl-d ̄œ-nòr\ [F] : the star of the north — motto of Minnesota
Lie·der·kranz \'lē-dər-̩kränts\ [G] : wreath of songs : German singing society
lit·tera scrip·ta ma·net \'li-te-̩rä-'skrip-tä-'mä-net\ [L] : the written letter abides

---

\ə\abut \ᵊ\kitten \ər\further \a\ash \ā\ace \ä\mop, mar
\au̇\out \ch\chin \e\bet \ē\easy \g\go \i\hit \ī\ice \j\job
\ŋ\sing \ō\go \ò\law \òi\boy \th\thin \t͟h\the \ü\loot \u̇\foot
\y\yet \zh\vision *see also* Pronunciation Symbols page

lo·cus in quo \ˈlȯ-kùs-in-ˈkwō\ [L] : place in which

l'union fait la force \l͞ē-nyōⁿ-fe-là-fȯrs\ [F] : union makes strength — motto of Belgium

lu·sus na·tu·rae \ˈlü-sùs-nä-ˈtùr-ē, -ˈtùr-ˌī\ [L] : freak of nature

ma foi \mà-fwä\ [F] : my faith! : indeed

mag·na est ve·ri·tas et prae·va·le·bit \ˈmäg-nä-ˌest-ˈwä-ri-ˌtäs-et-ˌprī-wä-ˈlä-bit\ [L] : truth is mighty and will prevail

mag·ni no·mi·nis um·bra \ˈmäg-nē-ˈnō-mi-nis-ˈùm-brä\ [L] : the shadow of a great name

ma·ha·lo \ˈmä-hä-lō\ [Hawaiian] : thank you

mai·son de san·té \mä-zōⁿ-də-sän-tä\ [F] : private hospital : asylum

ma·lade ima·gi·naire \mà-làd-ē-mà-zhē-ner\ [F] : imaginary invalid : hypochondriac

ma·lis avi·bus \ˈmä-ˌlēs-ˈä-wi-ˌbùs\ [L] : under evil auspices

ma·no a ma·no \ˈmä-nō-ä-ˈmä-nō\ [Sp] : hand to hand : in direct competition or confrontation

man spricht Deutsch \ˌmän-ˌshpri̱kt-ˈdȯich\ [G] : German spoken

ma·riage de con·ve·nance \mà-ryäzh-də-kōⁿv-näⁿs\ [F] : marriage of convenience

mau·vaise honte \mȯ-vez-ōⁿt\ [F] : bad shame : bashfulness

mau·vais quart d'heure \mȯ-ve-kàr-dœr\ [F] : bad quarter hour : an uncomfortable though brief experience

me·dio tu·tis·si·mus ibis \ˈme-dē-ˌō-tü-ˈti-si-mùs-ˈē-bis\ [L] : you will go most safely by the middle course

me ju·di·ce \mä-ˈyü-di-ke\ [L] : I being judge : in my judgment

mens sa·na in cor·po·re sa·no \ˈmäns-ˈsä-nä-in-ˈkȯr-pȯ-re-ˈsä-nō\ [L] : a sound mind in a sound body

me·um et tu·um \ˈmē-ùm-ˌet-ˈtü-ùm, ˈmä-ùm-\ [L] : mine and thine : distinction of private property

mi·ra·bi·le vi·su \mi-ˈrä-bi-lä-ˈwē-sü\ [L] : wonderful to behold

mi·ra·bi·lia \ˌmir-ä-ˈbi-lē-ä\ [L] : wonders : miracles

mœurs \mœr, mœrs\ [F] : mores : attitudes, customs, and manners of a society

mo·le ru·it sua \ˈmō-le-ˈrù-it-ˈsù-ä\ [L] : it collapses from its own bigness

monde \mōⁿd\ [F] : world : fashionable world : society

mon·ta·ni sem·per li·be·ri \mȯn-ˈtä-nē-ˈsem-per-ˈlē-be-ˌrē\ [L] : mountaineers are always free — motto of West Virginia

mo·nu·men·tum ae·re per·en·ni·us \ˌmȯ-nù-ˈmen-tùm-ˌī-re-pe-ˈre-nē-ùs\ [L] : a monument more lasting than bronze — used of an immortal work of art or literature

mo·ri·tu·ri te sa·lu·ta·mus \ˌmȯr-i-ˈtùr-ē-ˌtä-sä-lù-ˈtä-mùs\ or **morituri te sa·lu·tant** \-ˈsä-lù-ˌtänt\ [L] : we (or those) who are about to die salute thee

mul·tum in par·vo \ˈmùl-tùm-in-ˈpär-vō\ [L] : much in little

mu·ta·to no·mi·ne de te fa·bu·la nar·ra·tur \mü-ˈtä-tō-ˈnō-mi-ne-ˌdä-ˈtä-ˈfä-bù-lä-nä-ˈrä-ˌtùr\ [L] : with the name changed the story applies to you

my·ster·i·um tre·men·dum \mi-ˈster-ē-ˌùm-tre-ˈmen-dùm\ [L] : overwhelming mystery

na·tu·ram ex·pel·las fur·ca, ta·men us·que re·cur·ret \nä-ˈräm-ek-ˌspe-läs-ˈfür-kä-ˌtä-men-ˈùs-kwe-re-ˈkùr-et\ [L] : you may drive nature out with a pitchfork, but she will keep coming back

na·tu·ra non fa·cit sal·tum \nä-ˈtü-rä-ˌnōn-ˈfä-kit-ˈsäl-ˌtùm\ [L] : nature makes no leap

ne ce·de ma·lis \nä-ˈkä-de-ˈmä-ˌlēs\ [L] : yield not to misfortunes

ne·mo me im·pu·ne la·ces·sit \ˈnä-mō-ˈmä-im-ˈpü-nä-lä-ˈke-sit\ [L] : no one attacks me with impunity — motto of Scotland and of the Order of the Thistle

ne quid ni·mis \ˌnä-ˌkwid-ˈni-mis\ [L] : not anything in excess

n'est—ce pas? \nes-pä\ [F] : isn't it so?

nicht wahr? \ni̱kt-ˈvär\ [G] : not true? : isn't it so?

nil ad·mi·ra·ri \ˈnēl-ˌäd-mi-ˈrär-ē\ [L] : to be excited by nothing : equanimity

nil de·spe·ran·dum \ˈnēl-ˌdā-spä-ˈrän-dùm\ [L] : never despair

nil si·ne nu·mi·ne \ˈnēl-ˌsi-nä-ˈnü-mi-ne\ [L] : nothing without the divine will — motto of Colorado

n'im·porte \naⁿ-pȯrt\ [F] : it's no matter

no·lens vo·lens \ˈnō-ˌlenz-ˈvō-ˌlenz\ [L] : unwilling (or) willing : willy-nilly

non om·nia pos·su·mus om·nes \nōn-ˈȯm-nē-ä-ˌpȯ-sù-mùs-ˈȯm-ˌnäs\ [L] : we can't all (do) all things

non om·nis mo·ri·ar \nōn-ˈȯm-nis-ˈmȯr-ē-ˌär\ [L] : I shall not wholly die

non sans droict \nōⁿ-sän-drwä\ [OF] : not without right — motto on Shakespeare's coat of arms

non sum qua·lis eram \nōn-ˌsùm-ˈkwä-lis-ˈer-ˌäm\ [L] : I am not what I used to be

nos·ce te ip·sum \ˈnȯs-ke-ˌtä-ˈip-ˌsùm\ [L] : know thyself

nos·tal·gie de la boue \nȯs-tàl-zhē-də-là-bü\ [F] : yearning for the mud : attraction to what is unworthy, crude, or degrading

nous avons chan·gé tout ce·la \nü-zà-vōⁿ-shäⁿ-zhä-tü-sə-là\ [F] : we have changed all that

nous ver·rons ce que nous ver·rons \nü-ve-rōⁿ-sə-kə-nü-ve-rōⁿ\ [F] : we shall see what we shall see

no·vus ho·mo \ˈnȯ-wùs-ˈhȯ-mō\ [L] : new man : man newly ennobled : upstart

no·vus or·do se·clo·rum \-ˈȯr-ˌdō-sä-ˈklȯr-ùm\ [L] : a new cycle of the ages — motto on the reverse of the Great Seal of the United States

nu·gae \ˈnü-ˌgī\ [L] : trifles

nuit blanche \nwʸē-bläⁿsh\ [F] : white night : a sleepless night

nyet \ˈnyet\ [Russ] : no

ob·iit \ˈȯ-bē-ˌit\ [L] : he or she died

ob·scu·rum per ob·scu·ri·us \ȯb-ˈskyùr-ùm-ˌper-ȯb-ˈskyùr-ē-ùs\ [L] : (explaining) the obscure by means of the more obscure

ode·rint dum me·tu·ant \ˈō-de-ˌrint-ˌdùm-ˈme-tù-ˌwänt\ [L] : let them hate, so long as they fear

odi et amo \ˈō-ˌdē-et-ˈä-(ˌ)mō\ [L] : I hate and I love

omer·tà \ȯ-ˈmer-tä\ [It] : submission : code chiefly among members of the criminal underworld that enjoins private vengeance and the refusal to give information to outsiders (as the police)

om·ne ig·no·tum pro mag·ni·fi·co \ˈȯm-ne-ig-ˈnō-ˌtùm-prō-mäg-ˈni-fi-ˌkō\ [L] : everything unknown (is taken) as grand : the unknown tends to be exaggerated in importance or difficulty

om·nia mu·tan·tur, nos et mu·ta·mur in il·lis \ˈȯm-nē-ä-mü-ˈtän-ˌtùr-ˌnōs-ˌet-mü-ˈtä-mùr-in-ˈi-ˌlēs\ [L] : all things are changing, and we are changing with them

om·nia vin·cit amor \ˈȯm-nē-ä-ˈwiŋ-kit-ˈä-ˌmȯr\ [L] : love conquers all

onus pro·ban·di \ˈō-nùs-prō-ˈban-ˌdī, -dē\ [L] : burden of proof

ora pro no·bis \ˈō-rä-prō-ˈnō-ˌbēs\ [L] : pray for us

ore ro·tun·do \ˈȯr-ä-rō-ˈtùn-dō\ [L] : with round mouth : eloquently

oro y pla·ta \ˈȯr-ō-ē-ˈplä-tä\ [Sp] : gold and silver — motto of Montana

o tem·pora! o mo·res! \ō-ˈtem-pȯ-rä-ō-ˈmō-ˌräs\ [L] : oh the times! oh the manners!

oti·um cum dig·ni·ta·te \ˈō-tē-ùm-kùm-ˌdig-ni-ˈtä-te\ [L] : leisure with dignity

où sont les neiges d'an·tan? \ü-sōⁿ-lä-nezh-däⁿ-täⁿ\ [F] : where are the snows of yesteryear?

outre—mer \ütrᵊ-mer\ [F] : overseas : distant lands

pal·li·da Mors \ˈpa-li-də-ˈmȯrz\ [L] : pale Death

pa·nem et cir·cen·ses \ˈpän-ˌem-et-kir-ˈkän-ˌsäs\ [L] : bread and circuses : provision of the means of life and recreation by government to appease discontent

pan·ta rhei \ˌpän-ˌtä-ˈrä\ [Gk] : all things are in flux

par avance \pär-à-väⁿs\ [F] : in advance : by anticipation

par avion \pär-à-vyōⁿ\ [F] : by airplane — used on airmail

par ex·em·ple \pär-äg-zänplᵃ\ [F] : for example

pars pro to·to \ˈpärs-ˌprō-ˈtō-(ˌ)tō\ [L] : part (taken) for the whole

par·tu·ri·unt mon·tes, nas·ce·tur ri·di·cu·lus mus \pär-ˈtùr-ē-ˌùnt-ˈmȯn-ˌtās-näs-ˈkä-ˌtùr-ri-ˈdi-kù-lùs-ˈmüs\ [L] : the mountains are in labor, and a ridiculous mouse will be brought forth

pa·ter pa·tri·ae \ˈpä-ˌter-ˈpä-trē-ˌī\ [L] : father of his country

pau·cis ver·bis \ˈpaù-ˌkēs-ˈwer-ˌbēs\ [L] : in a few words

pax vo·bis·cum \ˈpäks-vō-ˈbēs-ˌkùm\ [L] : peace (be) with you

peine forte et dure \pen-fȯr-tā-dᵫr\ [F] : strong and hard punishment : torture

per an·gus·ta ad au·gus·ta \per-ˈän-ˌgùs-tä-äd-ˈaù-ˌgùs-tä\ [L] : through difficulties to honors

père \per\ [F] : father — used orig. after French and now also after other family names to distinguish a father from his son

per·eant qui an·te nos nos·tra dix·e·runt \ˈper-e-ˌänt-kwē-ˌän-te-ˈnōs-ˈnòs-trä-dēk-ˈsā-ˌrùnt\ [L] : may they perish who have expressed our bright ideas before us

per·fide Al·bion \per-fēd-àl-byōⁿ\ [F] : perfidious Albion (England)

peu à peu \pœ-à-pœ\ [F] : little by little

peu de chose \pœ-də-shōz\ [F] : a trifle

pièce d'oc·ca·sion \pyes-dò-kä-zyōⁿ\ [F] : piece for a special occasion

pinx·it \ˈpiŋk-sit\ [L] : he or she painted it

place aux dames \plås-ō-dàm\ [F] : (make) room for the ladies

ple·no ju·re \ˈplā-nō-ˈyùr-e\ [L] : with full right

plus ça change, plus c'est la même chose \plᵫ-sà-shäⁿzh-plᵫ-se-là-mem-shōz\ [F] : the more that changes, the more it's the same thing — often shortened to *plus ça change*

plus roy·a·liste que le roi \plᵫ-rwà-yà-lēst-kəl-rwà\ [F] : more royalist than the king

po·cas pa·la·bras \ˈpō-käs-pä-ˈlä vräs\ [Sp] : few words

po·eta nas·ci·tur, non fit \pò-ˈä-tä-ˈnäs-ki-ˌtùr-nōn-ˈfit\ [L] : a poet is born, not made

pol·li·ce ver·so \ˈpò-li-ke-ˈver-sō\ [L] : with thumb turned : with a gesture or expression of condemnation

post hoc, er·go prop·ter hoc \ˈpòst-ˌhōk-ˌer-gō-ˈpròp-ter-ˌhōk\ [L] : after this, therefore on account of it (a fallacy of argument)

post ob·itum \ˈpòst-ˈò-bi-ˌtùm\ [L] : after death

pour ac·quit \pür-à-kē\ [F] : received payment

pour le mé·rite \pür-lə-mā-rēt\ [F] : for merit

pri·mum non no·ce·re \ˌprē-mùm-ˌnōn-nò-ˈkä-re\ [L] : the first thing (is) to do no harm

pro aris et fo·cis \prō-ˈä-ˌrēs-et-ˈfò-ˌkēs\ [L] : for altars and firesides

pro bo·no pu·bli·co \prō-ˈbò-nō-ˈpü-bli-ˌkō\ [L] : for the public good

pro hac vi·ce \prō-ˈhäk-ˈwi-ke\ [L] : for this occasion

pro pa·tria \prō-ˈpä-trē-ä\ [L] : for one's country

pro re·ge, le·ge, et gre·ge \prō-ˈrä-ˌge-ˈlä-ˌge-et-ˈgre-ˌge\ [L] : for the king, the law, and the people

pro re na·ta \ˌprō-ˈrä-ˈnä-tä\ [L] : for an occasion that has arisen : as needed — used in medical prescriptions

quand même \kän-mem\ [F] : even so : all the same

quan·tum mu·ta·tus ab il·lo \ˈkwän-tùm-mü-ˈtä-tis-äb-ˈi-lō\ [L] : how changed from what he once was

quan·tum suf·fi·cit \ˈkwän-tùm-ˈsə-fi-ˌkit\ [L] : as much as suffices : a sufficient quantity — used chiefly in medical prescriptions

¿quién sa·be? \kyän-ˈsä-vā\ [Sp] : who knows?

qui fa·cit per ali·um fa·cit per se \kwē-ˈfä-kit-ˌper-ˈä-lē-ˌùm-ˈfä-kit-ˌper-ˈsä\ [L] : he who does (something) through another does it through himself

quis cus·to·di·et ip·sos cus·to·des? \ˌkwis-kùs-ˈtō-dē-ˌet-ip-ˌsōs-kùs-ˈtō-ˌdäs\ [L] : who will keep the keepers themselves?

qui s'ex·cuse s'ac·cuse \kē-sek-skᵫz-sà-kᵫz\ [F] : he who excuses himself accuses himself

quis se·pa·ra·bit? \ˌkwis-ˌsä-pä-ˈrä-bit\ [L] : who shall separate (us)? — motto of the Order of St. Patrick

qui trans·tu·lit sus·ti·net \kwē-ˈträns-tù-ˌlit-ˈsùs-ti-ˌnet\ [L] : He who transplanted sustains (us) — motto of Connecticut

qui va là? \kē-vá-là\ [F] : who goes there?

quo·ad hoc \ˌkwò-ˌäd-ˈhōk\ [L] : as far as this : to this extent

quod erat de·mon·stran·dum \ˌkwòd-ˈer-ˌät-ˌde-mòn-ˈsträn-dùm\ [L] : which was to be proved

quod erat fa·ci·en·dum \-ˌfä-kē-ˈen-ˌdùm\ [L] : which was to be done

quod sem·per, quod ubi·que, quod ab om·ni·bus \ˌkwòd-ˈsem-ˌper-kwòd-ˈù-bi-ˌkwä-ˌkwòd-äb-ˈòm-ni-ˌbùs\ [L] : what (has been held) always, everywhere, by everybody

quod vi·de \kwòd-ˈwi-ˌde\ [L] : which see

quo·rum pars mag·na fui \ˈkwòr-ùm-ˌpärs-ˈmäg-nə-ˈfù-ē\ [L] : in which I played a great part

quos de·us vult per·de·re pri·us de·men·tat \kwōs-ˈde-ùs-ˌwùlt-ˈper-de-ˌre-ˈprē-ùs-dä-ˈmen-ˌtät\ [L] : those whom a god wishes to destroy he first drives mad

quot ho·mi·nes, tot sen·ten·ti·ae \kwòt-ˈhò-mi-ˌnäs-ˌtòt-sen-ˈten-tē-ˌī\ [L] : there are as many opinions as there are men

quo va·dis? \kwō-ˈvä-dis, -ˈwä-\ [L] : whither are you going?

rai·son d'état \re-zōⁿ-dā-tà\ [F] : reason of state

re·cu·ler pour mieux sau·ter \rə-kᵫ-lä-pür-myœ-sō-tā\ [F] : to draw back in order to make a better jump

reg·nat po·pu·lus \ˈreg-ˌnät-ˈpò-pù-ˌlùs\ [L] : the people rule — motto of Arkansas

re in·fec·ta \ˈrä-in-ˈfek-ˌtä\ [L] : the business being unfinished : without accomplishing one's purpose

re·li·gio lo·ci \re-ˈli-gē-ˌō-ˈlò-ˌkē\ [L] : religious sanctity of a place

rem acu te·ti·gis·ti \ˌrem-ˈä-ˌkü-ˌte-ti-ˈgis-tē\ [L] : you have touched the point with a needle : you have hit the nail on the head

ré·pon·dez s'il vous plaît \rā-pōⁿ-dā-sēl-vü-ple\ [F] : reply, if you please

re·qui·es·cat in pa·ce \ˌre-kwē-ˈes-ˌkät-in-ˈpä-ˌke, ˌrā-kwē-ˈes-ˌkät-in-ˈpä-ˌchä\ [L] : may he or she rest in peace — used on tombstones

re·spi·ce fi·nem \ˈrä-spi-ˌke-ˈfē-ˌnem\ [L] : look to the end : consider the outcome

re·sur·gam \re-ˈsùr-ˌgäm\ [L] : I shall rise again

re·te·nue \rət-nᵫ\ [F] : self-restraint : reserve

re·ve·nons à nos mou·tons \rəv-nōⁿ-à-nō-mü-tōⁿ\ [F] : let us return to our sheep : let us get back to the subject

ruse de guerre \rᵫz-də-ger\ [F] : war stratagem

rus in ur·be \ˈrüs-in-ˈùr-ˌbe\ [L] : country in the city

sae·va in·dig·na·tio \ˈsī-wä-ˌin-dig-ˈnä-tē-ō\ [L] : fierce indignation

---

\ə\abut \ᵊ\kitten \ər\further \a\ash \ā\ace \ä\mop, mar
\aù\out \ch\chin \e\bet \ē\easy \g\go \i\hit \ī\ice \j\job
\ŋ\sing \ō\go \ò\law \òi\boy \th\thin \t̲h̲\the \ü\loot \ù\foot
\y\yet \zh\vision *see also* Pronunciation Symbols page

sal At·ti·cum \\'sal-'a-ti-kəm\ [L] : Attic salt : wit

salle à man·ger \sàl-á-män-zhä\ [F] : dining room

sa·lon des re·fu·sés \sà-lón-dā-rə-fǖ-zä\ [F] : salon of the refused : exhibition of art that has been rejected by an official body

sa·lus po·pu·li su·pre·ma lex es·to \'säl-üs-'pò-pù-,lē-sù-'prä-mä-,leks-'es-tō\ [L] : let the welfare of the people be the supreme law — motto of Missouri

sanc·ta sim·pli·ci·tas \,säŋk-tä-sim-'pli-ki-,täs\ [L] : holy simplicity — often used ironically in reference to another's naïveté

sans doute \sän-'düt\ [F] : without doubt

sans gêne \sän-zhen\ [F] : without embarrassment or constraint

sans peur et sans re·proche \sän-pœr-ā-sän-rə-prósh\ [F] : without fear and without reproach

sans sou·ci \sän-sü-sē\ [F] : without worry

sa·yo·na·ra \,sä-yō-'när-ä\ [Jp] : good-bye

sculp·sit \'skülp-sit\ [L] : he or she carved it

scu·to bo·nae vo·lun·ta·tis tu·ae co·ro·nas·ti nos \'skü-,tō-,bò-,nī-,vó-lùn-'tä-tis-'tù-,ī-,kòr-ō-'näs-tē-'nōs\ [L] : Thou hast crowned us with the shield of Thy good will — a motto on the Great Seal of Maryland

se·cun·dum ar·tem \se-'kùn-dùm-'är-,tem\ [L] : according to the art : according to the accepted practice of a profession or trade

secundum na·tu·ram \-nä-'tü-,räm\ [L] : according to nature : naturally

se de·fen·den·do \'sā-,dā-,fen-'den-dō\ [L] : in self=defense

se ha·bla es·pa·ñol \sā-,äb-lä-,äs-pä-'nʸól\ [Sp] : Spanish spoken

sem·per ea·dem \'sem-,per-'e-ä-,dem\ [L] : always the same (fem.) — motto of Queen Elizabeth I

sem·per fi·de·lis \'sem-pər-fi-'dä-lis\ [L] : always faithful — motto of the U.S. Marine Corps

sem·per idem \'sem-,per-'ē-,dem\ [L] : always the same (masc.)

sem·per pa·ra·tus \,sem-pər-pä-'rä-təs\ [L] : always prepared — motto of the U.S. Coast Guard

se non è ve·ro, è ben tro·va·to \sā-,nōn-e-'vä-rō-e-,ben-trō-'vä-tō\ [It] : even if it is not true, it is well conceived

sic itur ad as·tra \,sēk-'i-,tùr-,äd-'äs-trä\ [L] : thus one goes to the stars : such is the way to immortality

sic sem·per ty·ran·nis \,sik-'sem-pər-ti-'ra-nis\ [L] : thus ever to tyrants — motto of Virginia

sic trans·it glo·ria mun·di \,sēk-'trän-sit-'glōr-ē-ä-'mùn-dē\ [L] : so passes away the glory of the world

si jeu·nesse sa·vait, si vieil·lesse pou·vait! \sē-zhœ-ness-sä-ve-sē-vye-yes-pü-ve\ [F] : if youth only knew, if age only could!

si·lent le·ges in·ter ar·ma \'si-,lent-'lā-,gäs-,in-ter-'är-mä\ [L] : the laws are silent in the midst of arms

s'il vous plaît \sēl-vü-ple\ [F] : if you please

si·mi·lia si·mi·li·bus cu·ran·tur \si-'mi-lē-ä-si-'mi-li-bùs-kü-'rän-,tùr\ [L] : like is cured by like

si·mi·lis si·mi·li gau·det \'si-mi-lis-'si-mi-lē-,gaù-,det\ [L] : like takes pleasure in like

si mo·nu·men·tum re·qui·ris, cir·cum·spi·ce \,sē-,mò-nù-'men-tùm-re-'kwē-ris-kir-'kùm-spi-ke\ [L] : if you seek his monument, look around — epitaph of Sir Christopher Wren in St. Paul's, London, of which he was architect

sim·pliste \san-plēst\ [F] : simplistic : overly simple or naive

si quae·ris pen·in·su·lam amoe·nam, cir·cum·spi·ce \sē-'kwī-ris-pä-'nin-sù-,läm-ä-'mòi-,näm-kir-'kùm-spi-ke\ [L] : if you seek a beautiful peninsula, look around — motto of Michigan

sis·te vi·a·tor \'sis-te-wē-'ä-,tòr\ [L] : stop, traveler — used on Roman roadside tombs

si vis pa·cem, pa·ra bel·lum \,sē-'wēs-'pä-,kem-,pä-rä-'be-,lùm\ [L] : if you wish peace, prepare for war

sol·vi·tur am·bu·lan·do \'sòl-wi-,tùr-,äm-bù-'län-dō\ [L] : it is solved by walking : the problem is solved by a practical experiment

splen·di·de men·dax \'splen-di-,dä-'men-,däks\ [L] : nobly untruthful

spo·lia opi·ma \'spò-lē-ä-ō-'pē-mä\ [L] : rich spoils : the arms taken by the victorious from the vanquished general

sta·tus in quo \'stä-tùs-,in-'kwō\ [L] : state in which : the existing state

status quo an·te bel·lum \-kwō-,än-te-'be-lùm\ [L] : the state existing before the war

sua·vi·ter in mo·do, for·ti·ter in re \'swä-wi-,ter-in-'mò-dō-'fòr-ti-,ter-in-'rä\ [L] : gently in manner, strongly in deed

sub ver·bo \,sùb-'wer-bō\ or **sub vo·ce** \,sùb-'wō-ke\ [L] : under the word — introducing a cross-reference in a dictionary or index

sunt la·cri·mae re·rum \,sùnt-,lä-kri-,mī-'rä-rùm\ [L] : there are tears for things : tears attend trials

suo ju·re \,sù-ō-'yùr-e\ [L] : in his or her own right

suo lo·co \-'lò-kō\ [L] : in its proper place

suo Mar·te \-'mär-te\ [L] : by one's own exertions

su·um cui·que \,sù-ùm-'kwi-kwe\ [L] : to each his own

tant mieux \täⁿ-myœ\ [F] : so much the better

tant pis \-pē\ [F] : so much the worse : too bad

tem·po·ra mu·tan·tur, nos et mu·ta·mur in il·lis \'tem-pò-rä-mü-'tän-,tùr-'nōs-,et-mü-'tä-mùr-in-'i-,lēs\ [L] : the times are changing, and we are changing with them

tem·pus edax re·rum \'tem-pùs-,e-,däks-'rä-rùm\ [L] : time, that devours all things

tem·pus fu·git \'tem-pəs-'fyü-jət, 'tem-pùs-'fü-git\ [L] : time flies

ti·meo Da·na·os et do·na fe·ren·tes \'ti-mē-,ō-'dä-nä-,ōs-,et-,dō-nä-fe-'ren-,täs\ [L] : I fear the Greeks even when they bring gifts

to·ti·dem ver·bis \'tò-ti-,dem-'wer-,bēs\ [L] : in so many words

to·tis vi·ri·bus \'tō-,tēs-'wē-ri-,bùs\ [L] : with all one's might

to·to cae·lo \'tō-tō-'kī-lō\ or **toto coe·lo** \-'kòi-lō\ [L] : by the whole extent of the heavens : diametrically

tou·jours per·drix \tü-zhür-per-drē\ [F] : always partridge : too much of a good thing

tour d'ho·ri·zon \tür-dò-rē-zōⁿ\ [F] : circuit of the horizon : general survey

tous frais faits \tü-fre-fe\ [F] : all expenses defrayed

tout à fait \tü-tà-fe\ [F] : altogether : quite

tout au con·traire \tü-tō-kōⁿ-trer\ [F] : quite the contrary

tout à vous \tü-tà-vü\ [F] : wholly yours : at your service

tout bien ou rien \tü-byäⁿ-nü-ryäⁿ\ [F] : everything well (done) or nothing (attempted)

tout com·pren·dre c'est tout par·don·ner \tü-kōⁿ-prän-drə-se-tü-pàr-dò-nä\ [F] : to understand all is to forgive all

tout court \tü-kür\ [F] : quite short : and nothing more : simply : just; also : brusquely

tout de même \tüt-mem\ [F] : all the same : nevertheless

tout de suite \tüt-swʸēt\ [F] : immediately; also : all at once : consecutively

tout en·sem·ble \tü-tän-sänblᵊ\ [F] : all together : general effect

tout est per·du fors l'hon·neur \tü-te-per-dǖē-fòr-lò-nœr\ or **tout est perdu hors l'honneur** \-dǖē-ór-\ [F] : all is lost save honor

tout le monde \tül-mōⁿd\ [F] : all the world : everybody

tra·hi·son des clercs \trà-ē-zòⁿ-dā-klerk\ [F] : treason of the intellectuals

tranche de vie \träⁿsh-də-vē\ [F] : slice of life

trist·esse \trē-stes\ [F] : melancholy

tru·di·tur di·es die \'trü-di-ı‌tùr-'di-ıas-'di-ıā\ [L] : day is pushed forth by day : one day hurries on another

tu·e·bor \tù-'ā-ıbòr\ [L] : I will defend — a motto on the Great Seal of Michigan

ua mau ke ea o ka ai·na i ka po·no \ù-ä-'mä-ù-ke-'e-ä-ō-kä-'ä-ē-nä-ıē-kä-'pō-nō\ [Hawaiian] : the life of the land is established in righteousness — motto of Hawaii

über alles [G] : above everything else

ue·ber·mensch \'ū̄e-bər-ımensh\ [G] : superman

ul·ti·ma ra·tio re·gum \'ùl-ti-mä-ırä-tē-ō-'rä-gùm\ [L] : the final argument of kings, i.e., war

und so wei·ter \ıùnt-zō-'vī-tər\ [G] : and so on

uno ani·mo \'ü-nō-'ä-ni-ımō\ [L] : with one mind : unanimously

ur·bi et or·bi \'ùr-bē-ıet-'òr-bē\ [L] : to the city (Rome) and the world : to everyone

uti·le dul·ci \'ü-ti-le-'dùl-ıkē\ [L] : the useful with the agreeable

ut in·fra \ùt-'in-frä\ [L] : as below

ut su·pra \ùt-'sü-prä\ [L] : as above

va·de re·tro me, Sa·ta·na \'wä-de-'rä-trō-ımä-'sä-tä-ınä\ [L] : get thee behind me, Satan

vae vic·tis \wī-'wik-ıtēs\ [L] : woe to the vanquished

va·ria lec·tio \'wär-ē-ä-'lek-tē-ıō\ *pl* **va·ri·ae lec·ti·o·nes** \'wär-ē-ī-ılek-tē-ō-ınäs\ [L] : variant reading

va·ri·um et mu·ta·bi·le sem·per fe·mi·na \'wär-ē-ùm-ıet-mü-'tä-bi-le-'sem-ıper-ıfā-mi-nä\ [L] : woman is ever a fickle and changeable thing

ve·di Na·po·li e poi mo·ri \'vā-dē-'nä-pō-lē-ä-ıpò-ē-'mò-rē\ [It] : see Naples and then die

ve·ni, vi·di, vi·ci \'wā-nē-'wē-dē-'wē- kē\ [L] : I came, I saw, I conquered

ven·tre à terre \vä‌n-trà-ter\ [F] : belly to the ground : at very great speed

ver·ba·tim ac lit·te·ra·tim \wer-'bä-tim-ıäk-ıli-te-'rä-tim\ [L] : word for word and letter for letter

ver·bum sat sa·pi·en·ti est \'wer-bùm-'sät-ısä-pē-'en-tē-'est\ [L] : a word to the wise is sufficient

vieux jeu \vyȫ-zhȫ\ [F] : old game : old hat

vin·cit om·nia ve·ri·tas \'wiŋ-ket-'óm-nē-ä-'wä-ri-ıtäs\ [L] : truth conquers all things

vin·cu·lum ma·tri·mo·nii \'wiŋ-kù-lùm-ımä-tri-'mō-nē-ıē\ [L] : bond of marriage

vin du pays \va‌n-dūe-pä-ē\ *or* **vin de pays** \va‌n-də-\ [F] : wine of the locality

vir·gi·ni·bus pu·e·ris·que \wir-'gi-ni-bùs-ıpù-e-'rēs-kwe\ [L] : for girls and boys

vir·go in·tac·ta \'vīr-ıgō-in-'täk-tä\ [L] : untouched virgin

vir·tu·te et ar·mis \wir-'tü-te-ıet-'är-mēs\ [L] : by valor and arms — motto of Mississippi

vis me·di·ca·trix na·tu·rae \'wēs-ıme-di-'kä-triks-nä-'tü-ırī\ [L] : the healing power of nature

vive la dif·fé·rence \vēv-lä-dē-fä-rä‌ns\ [F] : long live the difference (between the sexes)

vive la reine \vēv-là-ren\ [F] : long live the queen

vive le roi \vēv-lə-rwä\ [F] : long live the king

vix·e·re for·tes an·te Aga·mem·no·na \wik-'sä-re-'fòr-ıtäs-ıän-te-ıä-gä-'mem-nò-ınä\ [L] : brave men lived before Agamemnon

vogue la ga·lère \vòg-là-gà-ler\ [F] : let the galley be kept rowing : keep on, whatever may happen

voi·là tout \vwà-là-tü\ [F] : that's all

vox et prae·te·rea ni·hil \'wòks-et-prī-'ter-e-ä-'ni-ıhil\ [L] : voice and nothing more

vox po·pu·li vox Dei \'wòks-'pò-pù-ılē-'wòks-'de-ē\ [L] : the voice of the people is the voice of God

Wan·der·jahr \'vän-dər-ıyär\ [G] : year of wandering

wie geht's? \vē-'gāts\ [G] : how goes it?

wun·der·bar \'vùn-dər-ıbär\ [G] : wonderful

Biographical, Biblical, and Mythological Names

This section is a listing of the names of important figures from recorded history, biblical tradition, classical mythology, popular legend, and current events. Figures from the Bible, myth, or legend are clearly identified as such. In cases where figures have alternate names, they are entered under the name by which they are best known. The part of the name shown in boldface type is either the family name or the common shorter name for that figure. The dates following the name or pronunciation are the birth and death dates. Other dates in the entry refer to the dates of a particular office, honor, or achievement. Italicized names within an entry refer to a person's nickname, original name, title, or other name.

Aar·on \\'ar-ən, 'er-\\ brother of Moses and first high priest of the Hebrews in the Bible

Abel \\'ā-bəl\\ son of Adam and Eve and brother of Cain in the Bible

Abra·ham \\'ā-brə-ˌham\\ patriarch and founder of the Hebrew people in the Bible

Achil·les \\ə-'kil-ēz\\ Greek hero in the Trojan War in mythology

Ad·am \\'ad-əm\\ the first man in the Bible

Ad·ams \\'ad-əmz\\ Abigail 1744–1818 American writer; wife of John Adams

Adams John 1735–1826 2d president of the U.S. (1797–1801)

Adams John Quin·cy \\'kwin-zē, 'kwin(t)-sē\\ 1767–1848 6th president of the U.S. (1825–29); son of John and Abigail Adams

Adams Samuel 1722–1803 patriot in the American Revolutionary War

Ad·dams \\'ad-əmz\\ Jane 1860–1935 American social worker; Nobel Prize winner (1931)

Ado·nis \\ə-'dän-əs, -'dō-nəs\\ beautiful youth in Greek mythology who is loved by Aphrodite

Ae·ne·as \\i-'nē-əs\\ Trojan hero in Greek and Roman mythology

Ae·o·lus \\'ē-ə-ləs\\ god of the winds in Greek mythology

Aes·chy·lus \\'es-kə-ləs, 'ēs-\\ 525–456 B.C. Greek dramatist

Aes·cu·la·pi·us \\ˌes-kyə-'lā-pē-əs\\ god of medicine in Roman mythology — compare ASCLEPIUS

Ae·sop \\'ē-ˌsäp, -səp\\ legendary Greek writer of fables

Ag·a·mem·non \\ˌag-ə-'mem-ˌnän, -nən\\ leader of the Greeks during the Trojan War in Greek mythology

Ag·nes \\'ag-nəs\\ Saint died 304 A.D. Christian martyr

Ahab \\'ā-ˌhab\\ king of Israel in the 9th century B.C. and husband of Jezebel

Ajax \\'ā-ˌjaks\\ hero in Greek mythology who kills himself because the armor of Achilles is awarded to Odysseus during the Trojan War

Alad·din \\ə-'lad-ᵊn\\ youth in the *Arabian Nights' Entertainments* who comes into possession of a magic lamp and ring

Al·cott \\'ȯl-kət, 'al-, -ˌkät\\ Louisa May 1832–1888 American author

Al·ex·an·der \\ˌal-ig-'zan-der, ˌel-\\ name of eight popes: especially **VI** (Rodrigo Lanzol y Borja) 1431–1503 (pope 1492–1503)

Alexander III of Macedon 356–323 B.C. *the Great* king (336–323)

Al·fred \\'al-frəd, -fərd\\ 849–899 *the Great* king of the West Saxons (871–899)

Ali Ba·ba \\ˌal-ē-'bäb-ə\\ a woodcutter in the *Arabian Nights' Entertainments* who enters the cave of the Forty Thieves by using the password *Sesame*

Al·len \\'al-ən\\ Ethan 1738–1789 American Revolutionary soldier

Amerigo Vespucci — see VESPUCCI

Am·herst \\'am-(ˌ)ərst\\ Jeffrey 1717–1797 *Baron Amherst* British general in America

Amund·sen \\'äm-ən-sən\\ Roald 1872–1928 Norwegian explorer and discoverer of the South Pole (1911)

An·a·ni·as \\ˌan-ə-'nī-əs\\ early Christian struck dead for lying

An·der·sen \\'an-dər-sən\\ Hans Christian 1805–1875 Danish writer of fairy tales

An·der·son \\'an-dər-sən\\ Marian 1897–1993 American contralto

Anne \\'an\\ 1665–1714 queen of Great Britain (1702–14)

An·tho·ny \\'an(t)-thə-nē\\ Susan Brownell 1820–1906 American suffragist

An·tig·o·ne \\an-'tig-ə-nē\\ daughter of Oedipus and Jocasta in Greek mythology

An·to·ni·us \\an-'tō-nē-əs\\ Marcus *about* 82–30 B.C. *Mark* or *Marc An·to·ny* or *An·tho·ny* \\'an(t)-thə-nē, *chiefly British* 'an-tə-nē\\ Roman general

Aph·ro·di·te \\ˌaf-rə-'dīt-ē\\ goddess of love and beauty in Greek mythology — compare VENUS

Apol·lo \\ə-'päl-ō\\ god of sunlight, prophecy, music, and poetry in Greek and Roman mythology

Aqui·nas \\ə-'kwī-nəs\\ Saint Thomas 1224 (or 1225)–1274 Italian theologian

Ar·chi·me·des \\ˌär-kə-'mēd-ēz\\ *about* 287–212 B.C. Greek mathematician

Ares \\'a(ə)r-ēz, 'e(ə)r-\\ god of war in Greek mythology — compare MARS

Ar·is·toph·a·nes \\ˌar-ə-'stäf-ə-ˌnēz\\ *about* 450– *about* 388 B.C. Greek dramatist

Ar·is·tot·le \\'ar-ə-ˌstät-ᵊl\\ 384–322 B.C. Greek philosopher

Arm·strong \\'ärm-ˌstrȯŋ\\ Louis 1901–1971 *Satch·mo* \\'sach-ˌmō\\ American jazz musician

Armstrong Neil Alden 1930– American astronaut and first man on the moon (1969)

Ar·nold \\'ärn-ᵊld\\ Benedict 1741–1801 American Revolutionary general and traitor

Ar·te·mis \\'ärt-ə-məs\\ goddess of the moon, wild ani-

\\ə\\abut \\ᵊ\\kitten \\ər\\further \\a\\ash \\ā\\ace \\ä\\mop, mar
\\au̇\\out \\ch\\chin \\e\\bet \\ē\\easy \\g\\go \\i\\hit \\ī\\ice \\j\\job
\\ŋ\\sing \\ō\\go \\ȯ\\law \\ȯi\\boy \\th\\thin \\t̲h̲\\the \\ü\\loot \\u̇\\foot
\\y\\yet \\zh\\vision *see also* Pronunciation Symbols page

mals, and hunting in Greek mythology — compare DI-ANA

Ar·thur \'är-thər\ legendary king of the Britons whose story is based on traditions of a 6th century military leader — **Ar·thu·ri·an** \är-'th(y)ùr-ē-ən\ adj

Arthur Chester Alan 1829–1886 21st president of the U.S. (1881–85)

As·cle·pi·us \ə-'sklē-pē-əs\ god of medicine in Greek mythology — compare AESCULAPIUS

As·tor \'as-tər\ John Jacob 1763–1848 American (German-born) fur trader and capitalist

Athe·na \ə-'thē-nə\ or **Athe·ne** \-nē\ goddess of wisdom in Greek mythology — compare MINERVA

At·las \'at-ləs\ Titan in Greek mythology forced to bear the heavens on his shoulders

At·ti·la \ə-'til-ə, 'at-ºl-ə\ 406?–453 A.D. the Scourge of God king of the Huns

At·tucks \'at-əks\ Crispus 1723?–1770 American patriot; one of five men killed in Boston Massacre

Au·du·bon \'ȯd-ə-ˌbän, -bən\ John James 1785–1851 American (Haitian-born) artist and naturalist

Au·gus·tine \'ȯ-gə-ˌstēn; ȯ-'gəs-tən, ə-\ Saint 354–430 A.D. church father; bishop of Hippo (396–430)

Au·gus·tus \ȯ-'gəs-təs, ə-\ or **Augustus Caesar** or **Oc·ta·vi·an** \äk-'tā-vē-ən\ 63 B.C.–14 A.D. 1st Roman emperor (27 B.C.–14 A.D.)

Aus·ten \'ȯs-tən, 'äs-\ Jane 1775–1817 English author

Bac·chus \'bak-əs\ — see DIONYSUS

Bach \'bäk̲, 'bäk\ Johann Sebastian 1685–1750 German composer and organist

Ba·con \'bā-kən\ Francis 1561–1626 English philosopher and author

Ba·den–Pow·ell \ˌbād-ºn-'pō-əl\ Robert Stephenson Smyth 1857–1941 English founder of Boy Scout movement

Baf·fin \'baf-ən\ William about 1584–1622 English navigator

Bal·boa, de \bal-'bō-ə\ Vasco Núñez 1475–1519 Spanish explorer and discoverer of Pacific Ocean (1513)

Bal·ti·more \'bȯl-tə-ˌmō(ə)r, -ˌmȯ(ə)r\ Lord — see George CALVERT

Bal·zac, de \'bȯl-ˌzak, 'bal-\ Honoré 1799–1850 French author

Ba·rab·bas \bə-'rab-əs\ prisoner released in preference to Jesus at the demand of the multitude

Bar·num \'bär-nəm\ Phineas Taylor 1810–1891 American show-business manager

Bar·rie \'bar-ē\ Sir James Matthew 1860–1937 Scottish author

Bar·thol·di \bär-'täl-dē, -'tȯl-, -'thäl-, -'thȯl-\ Frédéric-Auguste 1834–1904 French sculptor who designed the Statue of Liberty

Bar·ton \'bärt-ºn\ Clara 1821–1912 founder of American Red Cross Society

Beau·re·gard \'bōr-ə-ˌgärd, 'bȯr-\ Pierre Gustave Toutant 1818–1893 American Confederate general

Beck·et, à \ə-'bek-ət, ä-\ Saint Thomas about 1118–1170 archbishop of Canterbury (1162–1170)

Bee·tho·ven \'bā-ˌtō-vən\ Ludwig van 1770–1827 German composer

Bell \'bel\ Alexander Graham 1847–1922 American (Scottish-born) inventor of the telephone

Ben·e·dict \'ben-ə-ˌdikt\ name of 15 popes: especially **XIV** (Prospero Lambertini) 1675–1758 (pope 1740–58); **XV** (Giacomo della Chiesa) 1854–1922 (pope 1914–22)

Be·nét \bə-'nā\ Stephen Vincent 1898–1943 American author

Ben·ja·min \'benj-(ə-)mən\ youngest son of Jacob and ancestor of one of the 12 tribes of Israel in the Bible

Ben·ton \'bent-ºn\ Thomas Hart 1889–1975 American painter

Be·o·wulf \'bā-ə-ˌwùlf\ legendary warrior and hero of the Old English poem Beowulf

Be·ring \'bi(ə)r-iŋ, 'be(ə)r-\ Vitus 1681–1741 Danish navigator; discovered Bering strait and Bering sea

Ber·lin \(ˌ)bər-'lin\ Irving 1888–1989 American (Russian-born) composer

Ber·ni·ni \bər-'nē-nē\ Gian Lorenzo 1598–1680 Italian sculptor, architect, and painter

Bes·se·mer \'bes-ə-mər\ Sir Henry 1813–1898 English engineer and inventor

Be·thune \bə-'th(y)ün\ Mary 1875–1955 née McLeod American educator

Bi·zet \bē-'zā\ Alexandre-César-Léopold 1838–1875 called Georges French composer

Black Hawk \'blak-ˌhȯk\ 1767–1838 American Indian chief

Black·well \'blak-ˌwel, -wəl\ Elizabeth 1821–1910 American (English-born) physician

Blake \'blāk\ William 1757–1827 English poet and artist

Bloom·er \'blü-mər\ Amelia Jenks 1818–1894 American social reformer

Boc·cac·cio \bō-'käch-(ē-ˌ)ō\ Giovanni 1313–1375 Italian author

Bohr \'bō(ə)r, 'bȯ(ə)r\ Niels 1885–1962 Danish physicist

Bo·leyn \bù-'lin, 'bùl-ən\ Anne 1507?–1536 2d wife of Henry VIII and mother of Elizabeth I of England

Bo·lí·var Si·món \sē-ˌmōn-bə-'lē-ˌvär, ˌsī-mən-'bäl-ə-vər\ 1783–1830 South American liberator

Bon·i·face \'bän-ə-fəs, -ˌfās\ name of nine popes: especially **VIII** (Benedetto Caetani) about 1235 (or 1240)–1303 (pope 1294–1303)

Boone \'bün\ Daniel 1734–1820 American pioneer

Booth \'büth\ John Wilkes 1838–1865 assassin of Abraham Lincoln

Bo·re·as \'bōr-ē-əs, 'bȯr-\ god of the north wind in Greek mythology

Bot·ti·cel·li \ˌbät-ə-'chel-ē\ Sandro 1445–1510 Italian painter

Bow·ie \'bü-ə, 'bō-\ James 1796–1836 hero of Texas revolution

Boyle \'bȯi(ə)l\ Robert 1627–1691 English physicist and chemist

Brad·bury \'brad-ˌber-ē, -b(ə-)rē\ Ray Douglas 1920– American author

Brad·dock \'brad-ək\ Edward 1695–1755 British general in America

Brad·ford \'brad-fərd\ William 1590–1657 Pilgrim leader

Brad·street \'brad-ˌstrēt\ Anne about 1612–1672 American poet

Bra·dy \'brād-ē\ Mathew B. 1823?–1896 American photographer

Brah·ma \'bräm-ə\ creator god of the Hindu sacred triad — compare SIVA, VISHNU

Brahms \'brämz\ Johannes 1833–1897 German composer

Braille \'brā(ə)l, 'brī\ Louis 1809–1852 French blind teacher of the blind

Braun \'braùn\ Wernher von 1912–1977 American (German-born) engineer

Brezh·nev \'brezh-ˌnef\ Leonid Ilyich 1906–1982 Russian politician; 1st secretary of Communist party (1964–82); president of the U.S.S.R. (1960–64; 1977–82)

Brid·ger \'brij-ər\ James 1804–1881 American pioneer and scout

Bron·të \'bränt-ē, 'brän-ˌtā\ family of English writers: Charlotte 1816–1855 and her sisters Emily 1818–1848 and Anne 1820–1849

Brooks \'brùks\ Gwendolyn Elizabeth 1917– American poet

Brown \'braùn\ John Old Brown of Osa·wat·o·mie \ˌō-sə-'wät- ə-mē\ 1800–1859 American abolitionist

Brow·ning \'braù-niŋ\ Elizabeth Barrett 1806–1861 English poet; wife of Robert

Browning Robert 1812–1889 English poet; husband of Elizabeth

Bru·tus \'brüt-əs\ Marcus Junius 85–42 B.C. Roman politician; one of Julius Caesar's assassins

Bry·an \'brī-ən\ William Jennings 1860–1925 American lawyer and politician

Bu·chan·an \byü-'kan-ən, bə-\ James 1791–1868 15th president of the U.S. (1857–61)

Buck \'bək\ Pearl 1892–1973 American author; Nobel Prize winner (1938)

Buddha — see GAUTAMA BUDDHA

Buffalo Bill — see William Frederick CODY

Bun·yan \'bən-yən\ John 1628–1688 English preacher and author

Bur·bank \'bər-₁baŋk\ Luther 1849–1926 American horticulturist

Bur·goyne \(₁)bər-'goin, 'bər-₁goin\ John 1722–1792 British general in America

Burns \'bərnz\ Robert 1759–1796 Scottish poet

Burn·side \'bərn-₁sīd\ Ambrose Everett 1824–1881 American general

Burr \'bər\ Aaron 1756–1836 vice president of the U.S. (1801–05)

Bush \'bůsh\ George Herbert Walker 1924–   41st president of the U.S. (1989–93)

By·ron \'bī-rən\ Lord 1788–1824 *George Gordon Byron* English poet

Cab·ot \'kab-ət\ John *about* 1450–*about* 1499 Italian navigator; explored coast of North America for England

Cabot Sebastian 1476?–1557 English navigator; son of John Cabot

Ca·bri·ni \kə-'brē-nē\ Saint Frances Xavier 1850–1917 *Mother Cabrini* first American (Italian-born) saint (1946)

Cae·sar \'sē-zər\ Gaius Julius 100–44 B.C. Roman general, political leader, and writer

Cain \'kān\ brother of Abel in the Bible

Cal·houn \kal-'hün\ John Caldwell 1782–1850 vice president of the U.S. (1825–32)

Ca·lig·u·la \kə-'lig-yə-lə\ 12–41 A.D. *Gaius Caesar* Roman emperor (37–41)

Cal·li·ope \kə-'lī-ə-₁pē\ muse of heroic poetry in Greek mythology

Cal·vert \'kal-vərt\ George 1580?–1632 1st Baron *Baltimore* English colonist in America

Cal·vin \'kal-vən\ John 1509–1564 French theologian and reformer

Ca·nute \kə-'n(y)üt\ *died* 1035 *the Great* king of England (1016–35); of Denmark (1018–35); of Norway (1028–35)

Car·ne·gie \'kär-nə-gē, kär-'neg-ē\ Andrew 1835–1919 American (Scottish-born) industrialist and philanthropist

Carroll Lewis — see Charles Lutwidge DODGSON

Car·son \'kärs-ᵊn\ Christopher 1809–1868 *Kit* American soldier and guide

Carson Rachel Louise 1907–1964 American scientist

Car·ter \'kärt-ər\ James Earl, Jr. 1924–   *Jimmy* 39th president of the U.S. (1977–81)

Car·tier \kär-'tyā, 'kärt-ē-₁ā\ Jacques 1491–1557 French navigator; discovered Saint Lawrence river

Ca·ru·so \kə-'rü-sō, -zō\ En·ri·co \en-'rē-kō\ 1873–1921 Italian tenor

Car·ver \'kär-vər\ George Washington *about* 1864–1943 American botanist

Ca·sa·no·va \₁kaz-ə-'nō-və, ₁kas-\ Giovanni Giacomo 1725–1798 Italian adventurer

Cas·san·dra \kə-'san-drə\ daughter of Priam in Greek mythology who is endowed with the gift of prophecy but fated never to be believed

Cas·satt \kə-'sat\ Mary 1845–1926 American painter

Cas·tro \'kas-trō, 'käs-\ **(Ruz)** \'rüs\ Fi·del \fē-'del\ 1926–   Cuban premier (1959–)

Cath·er \'kath-ər\ Willa Sibert 1873–1947 American author

Cath·er·ine \'kath-(ə-)rən\ name of 1st, 5th, and 6th wives of Henry VIII of England: Catherine of Aragon 1485–1536; Catherine Howard 1520?–1542; Catherine Parr 1512–1548

Catherine I 1684–1727 wife of Peter the Great; empress of Russia (1725–27)

Catherine II 1729–1796 *the Great* empress of Russia (1762–96)

Cav·en·dish \'kav-ən-(₁)dish\ Henry 1731–1810 English scientist

Ce·ci·lia \sə-'sēl-yə, -'sil-\ Saint 2d or 3d century A.D. Roman martyr; patron saint of music

Ce·res \'si(ə)r-₁ēz\ the goddess of agriculture in Roman mythology — compare DEMETER

Cer·van·tes \sər-'van-₁tēz\ Miguel de 1547–1616 Spanish author

Cé·zanne \sā-'zan\ Paul 1839–1906 French painter

Cha·gall \shə-'gäl, -'gal\ Marc 1887–1985 Russian painter

Cham·plain \(')sham-'plān\ Samuel de *about* 1567–1635 French explorer in America; founder of Quebec

Chap·lin \'chap-lən\ Sir Charles Spencer 1889–1977 British actor and producer

Chap·man \'chap-mən\ John 1774–1845 *Johnny Appleseed* \'ap-əl-₁sēd\ American pioneer

Char·le·magne \'shär-lə-₁mān\ 742–814 A.D. *Charles the Great* or *Charles I* Frankish king (768–814); emperor of the West (800–814)

Charles \'chär(-ə)lz\ name of 10 kings of France: especially **I** 823–877 A.D. (reigned 840–77) *the Bald*; Holy Roman emperor as *Charles II* (875–77); **IV** 1294–1328 (reigned 1322–28) *the Fair*; **V** 1337–1380 (reigned 1364–80) *the Wise*; **VI** 1368–1422 (reigned 1380–1422) *the Mad* or *the Beloved*; **VII** 1403–1461 (reigned 1422–61) *the Victorious*; **IX** 1550–1574 (reigned 1560–74); **X** 1757–1836 (reigned 1824–30)

Charles name of two kings of Great Britain: **I** 1600–1649 (reigned 1625–49) *Charles Stuart*; **II** 1630–1685 (reigned 1660–85) son of Charles I

Charles V 1500–1558 Holy Roman emperor (1519–56); king of Spain as *Charles I* (1516–56)

Charles Edward Stuart 1720–1788 *the Young Pretender*; *(Bonnie) Prince Charlie* English prince

Charles Mar·tel \mär-'tel\ *about* 688–741 A.D. Frankish ruler (719–41); grandfather of Charlemagne

Cha·ryb·dis \kə-'rib-dəs, shə-, chə-\ a whirlpool off the coast of Sicily personified in Greek mythology as a female monster

Chau·cer \'cho-sər\ Geoffrey *about* 1342–1400 English poet

Che·khov \'chek-₁óf, -₁óv\ Anton Pavlovich 1860–1904 Russian author

Cheops — see KHUFU

Ches·ter·ton \'ches-tərt-ᵊn\ Gilbert Keith 1874–1936 English author

Cho·pin \'shō-₁pan\ Frédéric François 1810–1849 Polish pianist and composer

Chou En-lai \'jō-'en-'lī\ 1898–1976 Chinese Communist politician; premier (1949–76)

Christ Jesus — see JESUS

Chris·tie \'kris-tē\ Agatha 1890–1976 English author

Chur·chill \'chər-₁chil, 'chərch-₁hil\ Sir Winston Leonard Spencer 1874–1965 British prime minister (1940–45; 1951–55)

Clark \'klärk\ George Rogers 1752–1818 American soldier and pioneer

---

\ə\abut \ᵊ\kitten \ər\further \a\ash \ā\ace \ä\mop, mar
\aů\out \ch\chin \e\bet \ē\easy \g\go \i\hit \ī\ice \j\job
\ŋ\sing \ō\go \ó\law \ói\boy \th\thin \t͟h\the \ü\loot \ů\foot
\y\yet \zh\vision *see also* Pronunciation Symbols page

Clark William 1770–1838 American explorer

Clay \'klā\ Henry 1777–1852 American politician and orator

Clem·ens \'klem-ənz\ Samuel Langhorne 1835–1910 pseudonym *Mark Twain* \'twān\ American author

Cle·o·pa·tra \ˌklē-ə-'pa-trə, -'pä-, -'pä-\ 69–30 B.C. queen of Egypt (51–30)

Cleve·land \'klēv-lənd\ (Stephen) Grover 1837–1908 22d and 24th president of the U.S. (1885–89; 1893–97)

Clin·ton \'klin-tᵊn\ William Jefferson 1946–   42d president of the U.S.(1993–   )

Cly·tem·nes·tra \ˌklīt-əm-'nes- trə\ wife of Agamemnon in Greek mythology

Cobb \'käb\ Tyrus Raymond 1886–1961 *Ty* American baseball player

Co·chise \kō-'chēs\ 1812?–1874 Apache Indian chief

Co·dy \'kōd-ē\ William Frederick 1846–1917 *Buffalo Bill* American hunter, guide, and entertainer

Co·han \'kō-ˌhan\ George Michael 1878–1942 American actor and composer

Cole·ridge \'kōl-rij, 'kō-lə-rij\ Samuel Taylor 1772–1834 English poet

Co·lette \kȯ-'let\ Sidonie-Gabrielle 1873–1954 French author

Co·lum·bus \kə-'ləm-bəs\ Christopher 1451–1506 Italian navigator; discovered America for Spain (1492)

Con·fu·cius \kən-'fyü-shəs\ 551–479 B.C. Chinese philosopher

Con·rad \'kän-ˌrad\ Joseph 1857–1924 British (Ukrainian-born of Polish parents) author

Con·sta·ble \'kən(t)-stə-bəl, 'kän(t)-\ John 1776–1837 English painter

Con·stan·tine \'kän(t)-stən-ˌtēn, -ˌtīn\ *died* 337 A.D. *the Great* Roman emperor (306–37)

Cook \'kùk\ Captain James 1728–1779 English navigator

Coo·lidge \'kü-lij\ (John) Calvin 1872–1933 30th president of the U.S. (1923–29)

Coo·per \'kü-pər, 'kùp-ər\ James Fen·i·more \'fen-ə-ˌmō(ə)r, -ˌmȯ(ə)r\ 1789–1851 American author

Co·per·ni·cus \kō-'pər-ni-kəs\ Nicolaus 1473–1543 Polish astronomer

Cop·land \'kō-plənd\ Aaron 1900–1990 American composer

Cop·ley \'käp-lē\ John Sin·gle·ton \'siŋ-gəl-tən\ 1738–1815 American portrait painter

Corn·wal·lis \kȯrn-'wäl-əs\ 1st Marquis 1738–1805 *Charles Cornwallis* British general in America

Co·ro·na·do \ˌkȯr-ə-'näd-ō, ˌkär-\ Francisco Vásquez de *about* 1510–1554 Spanish explorer of southwestern U.S.

Cor·tés \kȯr-'tez, 'kȯr-ˌtez\ Hernán *or* Hernando 1485–1547 Spanish conqueror of Mexico

Cous·teau \kü-'stō\ Jacques-Yves 1910–   French marine explorer

Crane \'krān\ Stephen 1871–1900 American author

Crazy Horse \'krā-zē-ˌhȯrs\ 1842–1877 Sioux Indian chief

Crock·ett \'kräk-ət\ David 1786–1836 *Davy* American pioneer

Crom·well \'kräm-ˌwel, 'krəm-, -wəl\ Oliver 1599–1658 English general and political leader; lord protector of England (1653–58)

Cro·nus \'krō-nəs, 'krän-əs\ a Titan in Greek mythology overthrown by his son Zeus

Cum·mings \'kəm-iŋz\ Edward Estlin 1894–1962 known as *e. e. cummings* American poet

Cu·pid \'kyü-pəd\ god of love in Roman mythology — compare EROS

Cu·rie \kyù-'rē, 'kyù(ə)r-ē\ Marie 1867–1934 French (Polish-born) chemist; Nobel Prize winner (1903–1911)

Curie Pierre 1859–1906 French chemist; Nobel Prize winner (1903)

Cus·ter \'kəs-tər\ George Armstrong 1839–1876 American general

Cy·ra·no de Ber·ge·rac \ˌsir-ə-ˌnō-də-'ber-zhə-ˌrak\ Savinien de 1619–1655 French poet and soldier

Dae·da·lus \'ded-ᵊl-əs, 'dēd-\ builder in Greek mythology of the Cretan labyrinth and inventor of wings by which he and his son Icarus escape from it

Dal·ton \'dȯlt-ᵊn\ John 1766–1844 English chemist and physicist

Da·na \'dā-nə\ Richard Henry 1815–1882 American author

Dan·iel \'dan-yəl\ a prophet in the Bible who is held captive in Babylon and delivered by God from a den of lions

Dan·te \'dän-tā, 'dan-, -tē\ 1265–1321 Italian poet

Dare \'da(ə)r, 'de(ə)r\ Virginia 1587–? first child born in America of English parents

Da·ri·us I \də-'rī-əs\ 550–486 B.C. *the Great* king of Persia (522–486)

Dar·row \'dar-ō\ Clarence Seward 1857–1938 American lawyer

Dar·win \'där-wən\ Charles Robert 1809–1882 English naturalist

Da·vid \'dā-vəd\ a youth in the Bible who slays Goliath and succeeds Saul as king of Israel

Da·vis \'dā-vəs\ Jefferson 1808–1889 president of the Confederate States of America (1861–65)

Dawes \'dȯz\ William 1745–1799 American patriot

Debs \'debz\ Eugene Victor 1855–1926 American socialist

De·bus·sy \ˌdeb-yù-'sē, ˌdāb-; də-'byü-sē\ (Achille) Claude 1862–1918 French composer

De·ca·tur \di-'kāt-ər\ Stephen 1779–1820 American naval officer

De·foe \di-'fō\ Daniel 1660–1731 English author

De·gas \də-'gä\ (Hilaire-Germain-) Edgar 1834–1917 French painter

de Gaulle \di-'gōl, -'gȯl\ Charles-André-Joseph-Marie 1890–1970 French general; president of Fifth Republic (1958–69)

De·li·lah \di-'lī-lə\ mistress and betrayer of Samson in the Bible

De·me·ter \di-'mēt-ər\ goddess of agriculture in Greek mythology — compare CERES

de Mille \də-'mil\ Agnes George 1909?–1993 American dancer and choreographer

Des·cartes \dā-'kärt\ René 1596–1650 French mathematician and philosopher

de So·to \di-'sōt-ō\ Hernando 1496 (or 1499 or 1500)–1542 Spanish explorer in America

Dew·ey \'d(y)ü-ē\ George 1837–1917 American admiral

Dewey John 1859–1952 American philosopher and educator

Dewey Melvil 1851–1931 American librarian

Di·ana \dī-'an-ə\ goddess of the forest and of childbirth in ancient Italian mythology who was identified with Artemis by the Romans

Dick·ens \'dik-ənz\ Charles John Huffam 1812–1870 pseudonym *Boz* \'bäz, 'bōz\ English author

Dick·in·son \'dik-ən-sən\ Emily Elizabeth 1830–1886 American poet

Di·do \'dīd-ō\ legendary queen of Carthage who falls in love with Aeneas and kills herself when he leaves her

Di·o·ny·sus \ˌdī-ə-'nī -səs, -'nē-\ god of wine and ecstasy in Greek mythology — **Di·o·ny·sian** \ˌdī-ə-'nizh-ē-ən\ *adj*

Dis·ney \'diz-nē\ Walter Elias 1901–1966 American film producer

Dis·rae·li \diz-'rā-lē\ Benjamin 1804–1881 1st Earl of *Bea·cons·field* \'bē-kənz-ˌfēld\ British prime minister (1868; 1874–80)

Dix \'diks\ Dorothea Lynde 1802–1887 American social reformer

Dodg·son \'däj-sən, 'däd-\ Charles Lut·widge \'lət-wij\ 1832–1898 pseudonym *Lewis Car·roll* \'kar-əl\ English author and mathematician

Donne \'dən\ John 1572–1631 English poet and minister

Don Qui·xote \ˌdän-kē-'(h)ōt-ē, ˌdän-; dän-'kwik-sət\ the idealistic and impractical hero of Cervantes' *Don Quixote*

Dos·to·yev·ski\ˌdäs-tə-'yef-skē, -'yev-\Fyodor Mikhaylovich 1821–1881 Russian novelist

Doug·las \'dəg-ləs\ Stephen Arnold 1813–1861 American politician

Doug·lass \'dəg-ləs\ Frederick 1817–1895 American abolitionist

Doyle \'dȯi(ə)l\ Sir Arthur Co·nan \'kō-nən\ 1859–1930 British physician, novelist, and detective-story writer

Drake \'drāk\ Sir Francis 1540 (or 1543)–1596 English navigator and admiral

Drei·ser \'drī-sər, -zər\ Theodore 1871–1945 American author

Du Bois \d(y)ü-'bȯis\ William Edward Burghardt 1868–1963 American educator and writer

Du·mas \d(y)ü-'mä, 'd(y)ü-ˌmä\ Alexandre 1802–1870 *Dumas père* \'pe(ə)r\ French author

Dumas Alexandre 1824–1895 *Dumas fils* \'fēs\ French author

Dun·can \'dən-kən\ Isadora 1877–1927 American dancer

Dü·rer \'d(y)ùr-ər\ Albrecht 1471–1528 German painter and engraver

Ea·kins \'ā-kənz\ Thomas 1844–1916 American artist

Ear·hart \'e(ə)r-ˌhärt, 'i(ə)r-\ Amelia 1897–1937 American aviator

Ed·dy \'ed-ē\ Mary Baker 1821–1910 American founder of the Christian Science Church

Ed·i·son \'ed-ə-sən\ Thomas Alva 1847–1931 American inventor

Ed·ward \'ed-wərd\ name of eight post-Norman kings of England: **I** 1239–1307 (reigned 1272–1307) *Longshanks*; **II** 1284–1327 (reigned 1307–27); **III** 1312–1377 (reigned 1327–77); **IV** 1442–1483 (reigned 1461–70; 1471–83); **V** 1470–1483 (reigned 1483); **VI** 1537–1553 (reigned 1547–53) son of Henry VIII and Jane Seymour; **VII** 1841–1910 (reigned 1901–10) *Albert Edward* son of Queen Victoria; **VIII** 1894–1972 (reigned 1936; abdicated) *Duke of Windsor* son of George V

Ein·stein \'īn-ˌstīn\ Albert 1879–1955 American (German-born) physicist; Nobel Prize winner (1921)

Ei·sen·how·er \'īz-ᵊn-ˌhaù-(ə)r\ Dwight David 1890–1969 American general; 34th president of the U.S. (1953–61)

Elec·tra \i-'lek-trə\ sister of Orestes in Greek mythology who with her brother avenges their father's murder

Eli·jah \i-'lī-jə\ Hebrew prophet of the 9th century B.C.

El·iot \'el-ē-ət, 'el-yət\ George 1819–1880 pseudonym of *Mary Ann Evans* English author

Eliot Thomas Stearns 1888–1965 British (American-born) poet and critic

Eliz·a·beth I \i-'liz-ə-bəth\ 1533–1603 daughter of Henry VIII and Anne Boleyn; queen of England (1558–1603)

Elizabeth II 1926–   queen of the United Kingdom (1952–   )

Em·er·son \'em-ər-sən\ Ralph Waldo 1803–1882 American essayist and poet

En·dym·i·on \en-'dim-ē-ən\ beautiful youth in Greek mythology loved by the goddess of the moon

Ep·i·cu·rus \ˌep-i-'kyùr-əs\ 341–270 B.C. Greek philosopher

Er·ik \'er-ik\ *the Red* 10th century Norwegian navigator; explored Greenland coast

Eriksson Leif — see LEIF ERIKSSON

Eros \'e(ə)r-ˌäs, 'i(ə)r-\ god of love in Greek mythology — compare CUPID

Esau \'ē-(ˌ)sȯ\ son of Isaac and Rebekah and elder twin brother of Jacob in the Bible

Es·ther \'es-tər\ Hebrew woman in the Bible who as the queen of Persia delivers her people from destruction

Eu·clid \'yü-kləd\ *flourished about* 300 B.C. Greek mathematician

Eu·rip·i·des \yù-'rip-ə-ˌdēz\ *about* 484–406 B.C. Greek dramatist

Eu·ro·pa \yù-'rō-pə\ a princess in Greek mythology who was carried off by Zeus disguised as a white bull

Eu·ryd·i·ce \yù-'rid-ə-sē\ the wife of Orpheus whom he attempts to bring back from Hades

Eve \'ēv\ the first woman in the Bible

Eze·kiel \i-'zē-kyəl, -kē-əl\ Hebrew prophet of the 6th century B.C.

Fahr·en·heit \'far-ən-ˌhīt, 'fär-\ Daniel Gabriel 1686–1736 German physicist

Far·a·day \'far-ə-ˌdā, -əd-ē\ Michael 1791–1867 English chemist and physicist

Far·ra·gut \'far-ə-gət\ David Glasgow 1801–1870 American admiral

Faulk·ner \'fȯk-nər\ William 1897–1962 American author; Nobel Prize winner (1949)

Faust \'faùst\ *or* **Fau·stus** \'faù-stəs, 'fȯ-\ a legendary German magician who sells his soul to the devil

Fawkes \'fȯks\ Guy 1570–1606 English conspirator

Fer·di·nand \'fərd-ᵊn-ˌand\ **II** of Aragon *or* **V** of Castile 1452–1516 *the Catholic* king of Castile (1474–1504); of Aragon (1479–1516); of Naples (1504–16); founder of the Spanish monarchy

Fer·mi \'fe(ə)r-mē\ Enrico 1901–1954 American (Italian-born) physicist; Nobel Prize winner (1938)

Fiel·ding \'fē(ə)l-diŋ\ Henry 1707–1754 English author

Fill·more \'fil-ˌmō(ə)r, -ˌmȯ(ə)r\ Millard 1800–1874 13th president of the U.S. (1850–53)

Fitz·ger·ald \fits-'jer-əld\ Francis Scott Key 1896–1940 American author

Flem·ing \'flem-iŋ\ Sir Alexander 1881–1955 British bacteriologist; Nobel Prize winner (1945)

Flo·ra \'flōr-ə, 'flȯr-\ goddess of flowers in Roman mythology

Flying Dutchman legendary Dutch mariner condemned to sail the seas until Judgment Day

Ford \'fō(ə)rd, 'fȯ(ə)rd\ Gerald Rudolph 1913–   38th president of the U.S. (1974–77)

Ford Henry 1863–1947 American automobile manufacturer

Fos·ter \'fȯs-tər, 'fäs-\ Stephen Collins 1826–1864 American songwriter

Francis \'fran(t)-səs\ **of As·si·si** \ə-'sis-ē, -'sē-zē, -'sē-sē, -'siz-ē\ Saint 1181 (or 1182)–1226 Italian friar; founder of Franciscan order

Frank·lin \'fraŋ-klən\ Benjamin 1706–1790 American patriot, author, and inventor

Fred·er·ick I \'fred-(ə-)rik\ *about* 1123–1190 *Frederick Bar·ba·ros·sa* \ˌbär-bə-'räs-ə, -'rȯs-\ Holy Roman emperor (1152–90)

Frederick II 1712–1786 *the Great* king of Prussia (1740–86)

Fré·mont \'frē-ˌmänt\ John Charles 1813–1890 American general and explorer

French \'french\ Daniel Chester 1850–1931 American sculptor

Freud \'frȯid\ Sigmund 1856–1939 Austrian neurologist; founder of psychoanalysis

Frig·ga \'frig-ə\ wife of Odin and goddess of married love and the hearth in Norse mythology

Frost \'frȯst\ Robert Lee 1874–1963 American poet

\ə\abut \ᵊ\kitten \ər\further \a\ash \ā\ace \ä\mop, mar
\aù\out \ch\chin \e\bet \ē\easy \g\go \i\hit \ī\ice \j\job
\ŋ\sing \ō\go \ȯ\law \ȯi\boy \th\thin \t͟h\the \ü\loot \ù\foot
\y\yet \zh\vision *see also* Pronunciation Symbols page

Ful·ler \'fül-ər\ (Richard) Buckminster 1895–1983 American engineer

Fuller (Sarah) Margaret 1810–1850 American author and reformer

Ful·ton \'fült-ᵊn\ Robert 1765–1815 American inventor

Ga·bri·el \'gā-brē-əl\ one of the four archangels named in Hebrew tradition — compare MICHAEL, RAPHAEL, URIEL

Ga·ga·rin \gə-'gär-ən\ Yu·ry \'yü(ə)r-ē\ Alekseyevich 1934–1968 Russian astronaut; first man in space

Gage \'gāj\ Thomas 1721–1787 British general in America

Gal·a·had \'gal-ə-ˌhad\ knight of the Round Table who finds the Holy Grail

Gal·a·tea \ˌgal-ə-'tē-ə\ a female figure sculpted by Pygmalion in Greek mythology and given life by Aphrodite in answer to the sculptor's prayer

Ga·len \'gā-lən\ 129–*about* 199 A.D. Greek physician and writer

Ga·li·lei \ˌgal-ə-'lā-ˌē\ Ga·li·leo \ˌgal-ə-'lē-ō, -'lā-\ 1564–1642 usually called *Galileo* Italian astronomer and physicist — **Gal·i·le·an** \ˌgal-ə-'lē-ən\ *adj*

Gall \'gòl\ 1840?–1894 Sioux Indian leader

Ga·ma, da \'gam-ə, 'gäm-\ Vasco *about* 1460–1524 Portuguese navigator

Gan·dhi \'gän-dē, 'gan-\ Mohandas Karamchand 1869–1948 *Ma·hat·ma* \mə-'hät-mə, -'hat-\ Indian leader

Gar·field \'gär-ˌfēld\ James Abram 1831–1881 20th president of the U.S. (1881)

Gar·i·bal·di \ˌgar-ə-'bòl-dē\ Giuseppe 1807–1882 Italian patriot

Gar·ri·son \'gar-ə-sən\ William Lloyd 1805–1879 American abolitionist

Gau·guin \gō-'gan\ (Eugène-Henri-) Paul 1848–1903 French painter

Gau·ta·ma Bud·dha \ˌgaùt-ə-mə-'büd-ə, -'bùd-\ *about* 563–*about* 483 B.C. The Buddha Indian philosopher; founder of Buddhism

Gen·ghis Khan \ˌjeŋ-gə-'skän, ˌgeŋ-\ *about* 1162–1227 Mongol conqueror

George \'jò(ə)rj\ name of six kings of Great Britain: **I** 1660–1727 (reigned 1714–27); **II** 1683–1760 (reigned 1727–60); **III** 1738–1820 (reigned 1760–1820); **IV** 1762–1830 (reigned 1820–30); **V** 1865–1936 (reigned 1910–36); **VI** 1895–1952 (reigned 1936–52)

Ge·ron·i·mo \jə-'rän-ə-ˌmō\ 1829–1909 Apache Indian leader

Gersh·win \'gərsh-wən\ George 1898–1937 American composer

Gid·e·on \'gid-ē-ən\ Hebrew hero in the Bible

Gil·bert \'gil-bərt\ Sir William Schwenck 1836–1911 English librettist and poet; collaborator with Sir Arthur Sullivan

Glad·stone \'glad-ˌstōn, *chiefly British* -stən\ William Ewart 1809–1898 British prime minister (1868–74; 1880–85; 1886; 1892–94)

Glenn \'glen\ John Herschel 1921–   American astronaut and politician; first American to orbit the earth (1962)

Go·di·va \gə-'dī-və\ an English gentlewoman who in legend rode naked through Coventry to save its citizens from a tax

Goe·thals \'gō-thəlz\ George Washington 1858–1928 American general and engineer

Goe·the \'gə(r)-tə\ Johann Wolfgang von 1749–1832 German author

Gogh, van \van-'gō, -'gäk, -'kòk\ Vincent Willem 1853–1890 Dutch painter

Go·li·ath \gə-'lī-əth\ Philistine giant who is killed by David in the Bible

Gom·pers \'gäm-pərz\ Samuel 1850–1924 American (British-born) labor leader

Good·year \'gùd-ˌyi(ə)r, 'gùj-ˌi(ə)r\ Charles 1800–1860 American inventor

Gor·gas \'gòr-gəs\ William Crawford 1854–1920 American army surgeon

Gra·ham \'grā-əm, 'gra(-ə)m\ Martha 1893–1991 American dancer and choreographer

Grant \'grant\ Ulysses 1822–1885 originally *Hiram Ulysses Grant* American general; 18th president of the U.S. (1869–77)

Gre·co, El \el-'grek-ō\ 1541–1614 *Doménikos Theotokópoulos* Spanish (Cretan-born) painter

Gree·ley \'grē-lē\ Horace 1811–1872 American journalist and politician

Greene \'grēn\ Graham 1904–1991 British novelist

Greene Nathanael 1742–1786 American Revolutionary general

Greg·o·ry \'greg-(ə-)rē\ name of 16 popes: especially **I** Saint *about* 540–604 *the Great* (pope 590–604); **VII** Saint *about* 1020–1085 (pope 1073–85); **XIII** 1502–1585 (pope 1572–85)

Grey \'grā\ Lady Jane 1537–1554 English noblewoman beheaded as a possible rival for the throne of Mary I

Grey Zane 1875–1939 American novelist

Grimm \'grim\ Jacob 1785–1863 and his brother Wilhelm 1786–1859 German philologists and folklorists

Guin·e·vere \'gwin-ə-ˌvi(ə)r\ wife of King Arthur and lover of Lancelot

Gu·ten·berg \'güt-ᵊn-ˌbərg\ Johannes *about* 1390–1468 German inventor of printing from movable type

Ha·des \'hād-ˌēz\ — see PLUTO

Ha·dri·an \'hā-drē-ən\ 76–138 A.D. Roman emperor (117–138)

Ha·gar \'hā-ˌgär, -gər\ mistress of Abraham and mother of Ishmael in the Bible

Hai·le Se·las·sie \ˌhī-lē-sə-'las-ē, -'läs-\ 1892–1975 emperor of Ethiopia (1930–36; 1941–74)

Hale \'hā(ə)l\ Edward Everett 1822–1909 American minister and author

Hale Nathan 1755–1776 American Revolutionary hero

Hal·ley \'hal-ē, 'hā-lē\ Edmond *or* Edmund 1656–1742 English astronomer

Hal·sey \'hòl-sē, -zē\ William Frederick 1882–1959 American admiral

Ham·il·ton \'ham-əl-tən\ Alexander 1755–1804 American political leader

Ham·mu·ra·bi \ˌham-ə-'räb-ē\ *or* **Ham·mu·ra·pi** \-'räp-ē\ *died* 1750 B.C. king of Babylon (1792–50)

Han·cock \'han-ˌkäk\ John 1737–1793 American Revolutionary patriot

Han·del \'han-dᵊl\ George Frideric 1685–1759 British (German-born) composer

Han·dy \'han-dē\ William Christopher 1873–1958 American blues musician

Han·ni·bal \'han-ə-bəl\ 247–183 B.C. Carthaginian general

Har·ding \'härd-iŋ\ Warren Gamaliel 1865–1923 29th president of the U.S. (1921–23)

Har·dy \'härd-ē\ Thomas 1840–1928 English author

Har·ri·son \'har-ə-sən\ Benjamin 1833–1901 23d president of the U.S. (1889–93); grandson of William Henry Harrison

Harte \'härt\ Francis Brett 1836–1902 known as *Bret* American author

Har·vey \'här-vē\ William 1578–1657 English physician and anatomist

Haw·thorne \'hò-ˌthò(ə)rn\ Nathaniel 1804–1864 American author

Hayes \'hāz\ Rutherford Birchard 1822–1893 19th president of the U.S. (1877–81)

Hearst \'hərst\ William Randolph 1863–1951 American newspaper publisher

Hec·tor \'hek-tər\ son of Priam and Trojan hero slain by Achilles in Greek mythology

Hec·u·ba \'hek-yə-bə\ wife of Priam in Greek mythology
Hel·en of Troy \hel-ə-nəv-'trói\ wife of Menelaus whose abduction by Paris in Greek mythology caused the Trojan War
He·li·os \'hē-lē-əs, -ōs\ god of the sun in Greek mythology
Hem·ing·way \'hem-iŋ-ˌwā\ Ernest Miller 1899–1961 American author; Nobel Prize winner (1954)
Hen·ry \'hen-rē\ name of eight kings of England: **I** 1068–1135 (reigned 1100–35); **II** 1133–1189 (reigned 1154–89); **III** 1207–1272 (reigned 1216–72); **IV** 1367–1413 (reigned 1399–1413); **V** 1387–1422 (reigned 1413–22); **VI** 1421–1471 (reigned 1422–61; 1470–71); **VII** 1457–1509 (reigned 1485–1509); **VIII** 1491–1547 (reigned 1509–47)
Henry name of 4 kings of France: **I** 1008–1060 (reigned 1031–60); **II** 1519–1559 (reigned 1547–59); **III** 1551–1589 (reigned 1574–89); **IV** 1553–1610 *Henry of Navarre* (reigned 1589–1610)
Henry O. — see William Sydney PORTER
Henry Patrick 1736–1799 American patriot and orator
He·phaes·tus \hi-'fes-təs, -'fēs-\ god of fire and of metalworking in Greek mythology — compare VULCAN
He·ra \'hir-ə, 'hē-rə\ sister and wife of Zeus and goddess of women and marriage in Greek mythology — compare JUNO
Her·cu·les \'hər-kyə-ˌlēz\ *or* **Her·a·cles** \'her-ə-ˌklēz\ hero in Greek mythology noted for his strength and for performing 12 labors imposed on him by Hera
Her·maph·ro·di·tus \(ˌ)hər-ˌmaf-rə-'dīt-əs\ son of Hermes and Aphrodite who in Greek mythology is joined with a nymph into one body
Her·mes \'hər-mēz\ god of commerce, eloquence, invention, travel, and theft who serves as herald and messenger of the other gods in Greek mythology
Her·od \'her-əd\ 73–4 B.C. *the Great* Roman king of Judea (37–4)
Herod An·ti·pas \'ant-ə-ˌpas, -pəs\ 21 B.C.–39 A.D. Roman governor of Galilee (4 B.C.–39 A.D.); son of Herod the Great
Hey·er·dahl \'hā-ər-ˌdäl, 'hī-\ Thor 1914– Norwegian explorer and author
Hi·a·wa·tha \ˌhī-ə-'wò-thə, ˌhē-ə-, -'wäth-ə\ legendary Indian chief
Hick·ok \'hik-ˌäk\ James Butler 1837–1876 *Wild Bill* American scout and United States marshal
Hil·ton \'hilt-ən\ James 1900–1954 English novelist
Hip·poc·ra·tes \hip-'äk-rə-ˌtēz\ *about* 460–*about* 377 B.C. *founder of medicine* Greek physician
Hi·ro·hi·to \ˌhir-ō-'hē-tō\ 1901–1989 emperor of Japan (1926–89)
Hit·ler \'hit-lər\ Adolf 1889–1945 German (Austrian-born) chancellor (1933–45)
Holmes \'hōmz, 'hōlmz\ Oliver Wendell 1809–1894 American physician and author
Holmes Oliver Wendell 1841–1935 American jurist; son of the preceding
Ho·mer \'hō-mər\ 9th–8th? century B.C. Greek epic poet — **Ho·mer·ic** \hō-'mer-ik\ *adj*
Homer Winslow 1836–1910 American painter
Hooke \'hùk\ Robert 1635–1703 English scientist
Hook·er \'hùk-ər\ Thomas 1586?–1647 English colonist; a founder of Connecticut
Hoo·ver \'hü-vər\ Herbert Clark 1874–1964 31st president of the U.S. (1929–33)
Hoover John Edgar 1895–1972 American criminologist; director of the Federal Bureau of Investigation (1924–72)
Hou·di·ni \hü-'dē-nē\ Harry 1874–1926 originally *Ehrich Weiss* American magician
Hous·ton \'(h)yü-stən\ Samuel 1793–1863 *Sam* American general; president of the Republic of Texas (1836–38; 1841–44)
Howe \'haù\ Elias 1819–1867 American inventor

Howe Julia 1819–1910 née *Ward* American suffragist and reformer
Hud·son \'həd-sən\ Henry *died* 1611 English navigator and explorer
Hughes \'hyüz *also* 'yüz\ (James) Langston 1902–1967 American author
Hus·sein I \hü-'sān\ 1935– king of Jordan (1952–)
Hutch·in·son \'həch-ə(n)-sən\ Anne 1591–1643 religious leader in America
Hutchinson Thomas 1711–1780 American colonial administrator
Hux·ley \'hək-slē\ Aldous Leonard 1894–1963 English author
Hy·men \'hī-mən\ god of marriage in Greek mythology
Ib·sen \'ib-sən, 'ip-\ Henrik 1828–1906 Norwegian dramatist and poet
Ic·a·rus \'ik-ə-rəs\ son of Daedalus who in Greek mythology falls into the sea when the wax of his artificial wings melts as he flies too near the sun
Ig·na·tius \ig-'nā-sh(ē-)əs\ *Saint Ignatius of Loy·o·la* \lòi-'ō-lə\ 1491–1556 Spanish soldier and priest; founded the Society of Jesus
In·no·cent \'in-ə-sənt\ name of 13 popes: especially **II** *died* 1143 (pope 1130–43); **III** 1160 (or 1161)–1216 (pope 1198–1216); **IV** *died* 1254 (pope 1243–54); **XI** 1611–1689 (pope 1676–89)
Ir·ving \'ər-viŋ\ Washington 1783–1859 American author
Isaac \'ī-zik, -zək\ son of Abraham and father of Jacob in the Bible
Is·a·bel·la I \ˌiz-ə-'bel-ə\ 1451–1504 queen of Castile (1474–1504) and of Aragon (1479–1504); wife of Ferdinand V of Castile
Isa·iah \ī-'zā-ə\ Hebrew prophet of the 8th century B.C.
Ish·ma·el \'ish-(ˌ)mā-əl, -mē-\ outcast son of Abraham and Hagar in the Bible
Ives \'īvz\ Charles Edward 1874–1954 American composer
Jack·son \'jak-sən\ Andrew 1767–1845 American general; 7th president of the U.S. (1829–37)
Jackson Thomas Jonathan 1824–1863 *Stonewall* American Confederate general
Ja·cob \'jā-kəb\ son of Isaac and Rebekah and younger twin brother of Esau in the Bible
James \'jāmz\ one of the 12 apostles in the Bible
James *the Less* one of the 12 apostles in the Bible
James name of two kings of Great Britain: **I** 1566–1625 (reigned 1603–25); king of Scotland as *James VI* (reigned 1567–1603); **II** 1633–1701 (reigned 1685–88)
James Henry 1843–1916 British (American-born) author
Ja·nus \'jā-nəs\ god of gates and doors and of beginnings and endings in Roman mythology who is usually pictured as having two opposite faces
Ja·son \'jās-ən\ hero in Greek mythology noted for his successful quest of the Golden Fleece
Jay \'jā\ John 1745–1829 American jurist and political leader; 1st chief justice of the U.S. Supreme Court (1789–95)
Jef·fer·son \'jef-ər-sən\ Thomas 1743–1826 3d president of the U.S. (1801–09) — **Jef·fer·so·nian** \ˌjef-ər-'sō-nē-ən, -nyən\ *adj*
Jer·e·mi·ah \ˌjer-ə-'mī-ə\ Hebrew prophet of the 6th and 7th centuries B.C.
Je·sus \'jē-zəs, -zəz\ *or* **Jesus Christ** \'krīst\ *or* **Christ** *Jesus about* 6 B.C.–*about* 30 A.D. source of the Christian religion and Savior in the Christian faith
Jez·e·bel \'jez-ə-ˌbel\ queen of Israel and wife of Ahab who was noted for her wickedness

---

\ə\abut \ˈə\kitten \ər\further \a\ash \ā\ace \ä\mop, mar \aù\out \ch\chin \e\bet \ē\easy \g\go \i\hit \ī\ice \j\job \ŋ\sing \ō\go \ò\law \òi\boy \th\thin \t̷h\the \ü\loot \ù\foot \y\yet \zh\vision *see also* Pronunciation Symbols page

Joan of Arc \jō-nə-'värk\ Saint *about* 1412–1431 *the Maid of Orleans* French national heroine

Job \'jōb\ man in the Bible who has many sufferings but keeps his faith

Jo·cas·ta \jō-'kas-tə\ queen of Thebes in Greek mythology who unknowingly marries her son Oedipus

John \'jän\ *the Baptist* prophet and baptizer of Jesus in the Bible

John one of the 12 apostles believed to be the author of the fourth Gospel, three Epistles, and the Book of Revelation

John name of 21 popes: especially **XXIII** 1881–1963 (pope 1958–63)

John 1167–1216 *John Lack·land* \'lak-ıland\ king of England (1199–1216)

John·son \'jän(t)-sən\ Andrew 1808–1875 17th president of the U.S. (1865–69)

Johnson Lyndon Baines 1908–1973 36th president of the U.S. (1963–69)

Johnson Samuel 1709–1784 *Dr. Johnson* English lexicographer and author

Jol·liet *or* **Jo·liet** \zhȯl-'yä, ıjō-lē-'et\ Louis 1645–1700 French explorer in America

Jo·nah \'jō-nə\ Hebrew prophet who in the Bible spends three days in the belly of a great fish

Jones \'jōnz\ John Paul 1747–1792 American (Scottish-born) naval officer

Jop·lin \'jäp-lən\ Scott 1868–1917 American pianist and composer

Jo·seph \'jō-zəf *also* -səf\ a son of Jacob in the Bible who rose to high office in Egypt after being sold into slavery by his brothers

Joseph *about* 1840–1904 Nez Percé Indian chief

Joseph *Saint* husband of Mary, the mother of Jesus, in the Bible

Josh·ua \'jäsh-(ə-)wə\ Hebrew leader in the Bible who succeeds Moses during the settlement of the Israelites in Canaan

Ju·dah \'jüd-ə\ son of Jacob and ancestor of one of the 12 tribes of Israel in the Bible

Ju·das \'jüd-əs\ *or* **Judas Is·car·i·ot** \-is-'kar-ē-ət\ one of the 12 apostles and the betrayer of Jesus in the Bible

Ju·no \'jü-nō\ the queen of heaven in Roman mythology, wife of Jupiter, and goddess of light, birth, women, and marriage — compare HERA

Ju·pi·ter \'jü-pət-ər\ the chief god in Roman mythology, husband of Juno, and the god of light, of the sky and weather, and of the state

Kalb \'kälp, 'kalb\ Johann 1721–1780 Baron *de Kalb* \di-'kalb\ German general in American Revolutionary army

Keats \'kēts\ John 1795–1821 English poet

Kel·ler \'kel-ər\ Helen Adams 1880–1968 American deaf and blind lecturer

Kel·vin \'kel-vən\ 1st Baron 1824–1907 *William Thomson* British mathematician and physicist

Ken·ne·dy \'ken-əd-ē\ John Fitzgerald 1917–1963 35th president of the U.S. (1961–63)

Kennedy Robert Francis 1925–1968 American politician; attorney general of the U.S. (1961–64); brother of John F. Kennedy

Ke·o·kuk \'kē-ə-ıkək\ 1788?–?1848 American Indian chief

Key \'kē\ Francis Scott 1779–1843 American lawyer; author of "The Star-Spangled Banner"

Khayyám Omar — see OMAR KHAYYÁM

Khru·shchev \krüsh-'(ch)ȯf, -'(ch)ȯv, -'(ch)ef\ Ni·ki·ta \nə-'kēt-ə\ Sergeyevich 1894–1971 premier of U.S.S.R. (1958–64)

Khu·fu \'kü-fü\ *or Greek* **Che·ops** \'kē-ıäps\ 26th century B.C. king of Egypt and pyramid builder

Kidd \'kid\ William *about* 1645–1701 *Captain Kidd* Scottish pirate

King \'kiŋ\ Martin Luther, Jr. 1929–1968 American minister and civil rights leader; Nobel Prize winner (1964)

Kip·ling \'kip-liŋ\ Rud·yard \'rəd-yərd, 'rəj-ərd\ 1865–1936 English author

Kis·sin·ger \'kis-ᵊn-jər\ Henry Alfred 1923– American (German-born) scholar and government official; U.S. secretary of state (1973–77); Nobel Prize winner (1973)

Knox \'näks\ John *about* 1514–1572 Scottish religious reformer

Koch \'kȯk, 'kȯk̲\ Robert 1843–1910 German bacteriologist; Nobel Prize winner (1905)

Koś·ciusz·ko \ıkäs-ē-'əs-ıkō, kȯsh-'chüsh-kō\ Tadeusz 1746–1817 Polish patriot and general in American Revolutionary army

Krish·na \'krish-nə\ god worshipped in later Hinduism

Kriss Kringle — see SANTA CLAUS

Ku·blai Khan \ıkü-blə-'kän, -ıblī-\ 1215–1294 founder of Mongol dynasty in China

La·fa·yette \ıläf-ē-'et, ılaf-\ Marquis de 1757–1834 French general in American Revolutionary army

La·ius \'lā-(y)əs, 'lī-əs\ king of Thebes who in Greek mythology is killed by his son Oedipus

Lan·ce·lot \'lan(t)-sə-ılät\ legendary knight of the Round Table and lover of Queen Guinevere

La Salle \lə-'sal\ Sieur de 1643–1687 French explorer in America

La·voi·sier \ləv-'wäz-ē-ıā\ Antoine-Laurent 1743–1794 French chemist

Law·rence \'lȯr-ən(t)s, 'lär-\ Thomas Edward 1888–1935 *Lawrence of Arabia* later surnamed *Shaw* British archaeologist, soldier, and author

Laz·a·rus \'laz-(ə-)rəs\ brother of Mary and Martha who in the Bible is raised by Jesus from the dead

Lazarus beggar in the biblical parable of the rich man and the beggar

Le·da \'lēd-ə\ a queen of Sparta in Greek mythology who is courted by Zeus in the form of a swan

Lee \'lē\ Ann 1736–1784 English mystic; founder of Shaker society in the U.S.

Lee Henry 1756–1818 *Light-Horse Harry* American general

Lee Robert Edward 1807–1870 American Confederate general

Leeu·wen·hoek \'lā-vən-ıhuk\ Antonie van 1632–1723 Dutch naturalist

Leif Er·iks·son \ılā-'ver-ik-sən, ılē-'fer-\ *or* **Er·ics·son** *flourished* 1000 Norwegian explorer; son of Erik the Red

Le·nin \'len-ən\ 1870–1924 originally *Vladimir Ilyich Ul·ya·nov* \ül-'yän-əf, -ıȯf, -ıȯv\ Russian Communist leader

Leo \'lē-ō\ name of 13 popes: especially **I** Saint *died* 461 (pope 440–61); **III** Saint *died* 816 (pope 795–816); **XIII** 1810–1903 (pope 1878–1903)

Le·o·nar·do da Vin·ci \ılē-ə-'närd-ıōd-ə-'vin-chē, ılā-, -'vēn-\ 1452–1519 Italian painter, sculptor, architect, and engineer

Lew·is \'lü-əs\ John Llewellyn 1880–1969 American labor leader

Lewis Meriwether 1774–1809 American explorer (with William Clark)

Lewis (Harry) Sinclair 1885–1951 American author; Nobel Prize winner (1930)

Lin·coln \'liŋ-kən\ Abraham 1809–1865 16th president of the U.S. (1861–65)

Lind·bergh \'lin(d)-ıbərg\ Charles Augustus 1902–1974 American aviator

Lin·nae·us \lə-'nē-əs, -'nā-\ Carolus 1707–1778 Swedish *Carl von Lin·né* \lə-'nā\ Swedish botanist

Lis·ter \'lis-tər\ Joseph 1827–1912 English surgeon

Liszt \'list\ Franz 1811–1886 Hungarian pianist and composer

Liv·ing·stone \\'liv-iŋ-stən\ David 1813–1873 Scottish explorer in Africa

Long·fel·low \\'lȯŋ-ˌfel-ō\ Henry Wads·worth \\'wädz-(ˌ)wərth\ 1807–1882 American poet

Lou·is \\'lü-ē, 'lü-əs\ name of 18 kings of France: especially **IX** Saint 1214–1270 (reigned 1226–70); **XI** 1423–1483 (reigned 1461–83); **XII** 1462–1515 (reigned 1498–1515); **XIII** 1601–1643 (reigned 1610–43); **XIV** 1638–1715 (reigned 1643–1715); **XV** 1710–1774 (reigned 1715–74); **XVI** 1754–1793 (reigned 1774–92; guillotined); **XVII** 1785–1795 (reigned in name 1793–95); **XVIII** 1755–1824 (reigned 1814–15; 1815–24)

Low \\'lō\ Juliette Gordon 1860–1927 American founder of the Girl Scouts

Low·ell \\'lō-əl\ Amy 1874–1925 American poet

Lowell James Russell 1819–1891 American author

Luke \\'lük\ physician and companion of the apostle Paul believed to be the author of the third Gospel and the Book of Acts

Lu·ther \\'lü-thər\ Martin 1483–1546 German Reformation leader

Ly·on \\'lī-ən\ Mary 1797–1849 American educator

Mac·Ar·thur \mə-'kär-thər\ Douglas 1880–1964 American general

Mc·Car·thy \mə-'kär-thē\ Joseph Raymond 1908–1957 American politician

Mc·Clel·lan \mə-'klel-ən\ George Brinton 1826–1885 American general

Mc·Cor·mick \mə-'kȯr-mik\ Cyrus Hall 1809–1884 American inventor

Mc·Kin·ley \mə-'kin-lē\ William 1843–1901 25th president of the U.S. (1897–1901)

Ma·cy \\'mā-sē\ Anne Sullivan 1866–1936 American educator; teacher of Helen Keller

Mad·i·son \\'mad-ə-sən\ James 1751–1836 4th president of the U.S. (1809–17)

Ma·gel·lan \mə-'jel-ən\ Ferdinand *about* 1480–1521 Portuguese navigator

Mal·colm X \ˌmal-kə-'meks\ 1925–1965 American civil rights leader

Ma·net \ma-'nā, mä-\ Édouard 1832–1883 French painter

Mann \\'man\ Horace 1796–1859 American educator

Mao Tse-tung \ˌmaȯ(d)-zə-'duŋ, ˌmaȯt-sə-\ 1893–1976 Chinese Communist; leader of People's Republic of China (1949–76)

Mar·co·ni \mär-'kō-nē\ Guglielmo 1874–1937 Italian physicist and inventor; Nobel Prize winner (1909)

Ma·rie An·toi·nette \mə-'rē-ˌan-t(w)ə-'net\ 1755–1793 wife of Louis XVI

Mar·i·on \\'mer-ē-ən, 'mar-ē-\ Francis 1732?–1795 *the Swamp Fox* American commander in Revolution

Mark \\'märk\ evangelist believed to be the author of the second Gospel

Mar·quette \mär-'ket\ Jacques 1637–1675 French-born Jesuit missionary and explorer in America

Mars \\'märz\ the god of war in Roman mythology

Mar·shall \\'mär-shəl\ George Catlett 1880–1959 American general and diplomat

Marshall John 1755–1835 American jurist; chief justice of the U.S. Supreme Court (1801–35)

Mar·tha \\'mär-thə\ sister of Lazarus and Mary and friend of Jesus in the Bible

Mar·tin \\'märt-ᵊn\ Saint *about* 316–397 *Martin of Tours* \-'tü(ə)r\ patron saint of France

Marx \\'märks\ Karl 1818–1883 German political philosopher and socialist

Mary \\'me(ə)r-ē, 'ma(ə)r-ē, 'mā-rē\ mother of Jesus

Mary sister of Lazarus and Martha in the Bible

Mary I 1516–1558 *Mary Tudor*; *Bloody Mary* queen of England (1553–58)

Mary II 1662–1694 joint British sovereign with William III (1689–94)

Mary Mag·da·lene \-'mag-də-ˌlən, -ˌlēn\ woman in the Bible who was healed of evil spirits by Jesus and who later saw the risen Christ

Mary Stuart 1542–1587 *Mary, Queen of Scots* queen of Scotland (1542–87)

Mas·sa·soit \ˌmas-ə-'sȯit\ *died* 1661 Indian chief in eastern Massachusetts

Math·er \\'math-ər, 'math-\ Cotton 1663–1728 American religious leader and author

Mather Increase 1639–1723 American minister and author; father of Cotton Mather

Mat·thew \\'math-yü\ apostle believed to be the author of the first Gospel

Mau·pas·sant \ˌmō-pə-'sänt\ (Henri-René-Albert-) Guy de 1850–1893 French short-story writer

Mead \\'mēd\ Margaret 1901–1978 American anthropologist

Meade \\'mēd\ George Gordon 1815–1872 American general

Mea·ny \\'mē-nē\ George 1894–1980 American labor leader

Me·dea \mə-'dē-ə\ woman with magic powers in Greek mythology who helps Jason to win the Golden Fleece and who kills her children when he leaves her

Me·di·ci, de' \\'med-ə-chē\ Catherine 1519–1589 French *Catherine de Médicis* \ˌmäd-ə-'sē(s)\ queen of Henry II of France

Me·ir \me-'i(ə)r\ Golda 1898–1978 prime minister of Israel (1969–74)

Mel·ville \\'mel-ˌvil\ Herman 1819–1891 American author

Men·del \\'men-dᵊl\ Gregor Johann 1822–1884 Austrian botanist

Men·e·la·us \ˌmen-ᵊl-'ā-əs\ king of Sparta, brother of Agamemnon, and husband of Helen of Troy in Greek mythology

Meph·is·toph·e·les \ˌmef-ə-'stäf-ə-ˌlēz\ chief devil in the Faust legend

Mer·ca·tor \(ˌ)mər-'kāt-ər\ Gerardus 1512–1594 Flemish mapmaker

Mer·cu·ry \\'mər-kyə-rē, -k(ə-)rē\ god of commerce, eloquence, travel, and theft who serves as herald and messenger of the other gods in Roman mythology

Mer·lin \\'mər-lən\ prophet and magician in the legend of King Arthur

Mi·chael \\'mī-kəl\ one of the four archangels named in Hebrew tradition — compare GABRIEL, RAPHAEL, URIEL

Mi·chel·an·ge·lo \ˌmī-kə-'lan-jə-ˌlō, ˌmik-ə-'lan-, ˌmē-kə-'län-\ 1475–1564 Italian sculptor, painter, architect, and poet

Mi·das \\'mīd-əs\ legendary king who was given the power to turn everything he touched into gold

Mil·lay \mil-'ā\ Edna St. Vincent 1892–1950 American poet

Mil·ler \\'mil-ər\ Arthur 1915– American author

Mil·ton \\'milt-ᵊn\ John 1608–1674 English poet

Mi·ner·va \mə-'nər-və\ goddess of wisdom in Roman mythology — compare ATHENA

Mi·no·taur \\'min-ə-ˌtȯ(ə)r, 'mī-nə-\ monster in Greek mythology shaped half like a man and half like a bull

Min·u·it \\'min-yə-wət\ Peter 1580–1638 Dutch colonial administrator in America

Mitch·ell \\'mich-əl\ Maria 1818–1889 American astronomer

Mo·lière \mōl-'ye(ə)r, 'mōl-ˌye(ə)r\ 1622–1673 originally *Jean-Baptiste Poquelin* French actor and dramatist

Mo·net \mō-'nā\ Claude 1840–1926 French painter

\ə\abut \ᵊ\kitten \ər\further \a\ash \ā\ace \ä\mop, mar
\aȯ\out \ch\chin \e\bet \ē\easy \g\go \i\hit \ī\ice \j\job
\ŋ\sing \ō\go \ȯ\law \ȯi\boy \th\thin \th\the \ü\loot \ù\foot
\y\yet \zh\vision *see also* Pronunciation Symbols page

Mon·roe \mən-ˈrō\ James 1758–1831 5th president of the U.S. (1817–25)

Mont·calm de Saint-Vé·ran \mänt-ˈkäm-də-ˌsan-vä-ˈrän, -ˈkälm-\ Marquis de 1712–1759 French field marshal in Canada

Mon·tes·so·ri \ˌmänt-ə-ˈsȯr-ē, -ˈsȯr-\ Maria 1870–1952 Italian physician and educator

Mon·te·zu·ma II \ˌmänt-ə-ˈzü-mə\ 1466–1520 last Aztec emperor of Mexico (1502–20)

Moore \ˈmȯ(ə)r, ˈmō(ə)r, ˈmù(ə)r\ Marianne Craig 1887–1972 American poet

More \ˈmō(ə)r, ˈmȯ(ə)r\ Sir Thomas 1478–1535 *Saint* English public official and author

Mor·gan \ˈmȯr-gən\ John Pierpont 1837–1913 American financier

Morse \ˈmȯ(ə)rs\ Samuel Finlcy Breese 1791–1872 American artist and inventor

Mo·ses \ˈmō-zəz *also* -zəs\ Hebrew prophet and lawgiver who in the Bible freed the Israelites from slavery in Egypt

Mott \ˈmät\ Lucretia 1793–1880 American reformer

Mo·zart \ˈmōt-ˌsärt\ Wolfgang Amadeus 1756–1791 Austrian composer

Mu·h·am·mad \mō-ˈham-əd, -ˈhäm- *also* mü-\ *about* 570–632 Arab prophet and founder of Islam

Mus·so·li·ni \ˌmü-sə-ˈlē-nē, ˌmùs-ə-\ Be·ni·to \bə-ˈnēt-ō\ 1883–1945 *Il Du·ce* \ēl-ˈdü-chā\ Italian fascist premier (1922–43)

Na·po·léon I \nə-ˈpōl-yən, -ˈpō-lē-ən\ *or* **Napoléon Bo·na·parte** \ˈbō-nə-ˌpärt\ 1769–1821 emperor of the French (1804–15) — **Na·po·le·on·ic** \nə-ˌpō-lē-ˈän-ik\ *adj*

Nar·cis·sus \när-ˈsis-əs\ a beautiful youth in Greek mythology who pines away for love of his own reflection and is then turned into the narcissus flower

Nash \ˈnash\ Ogden 1902–1971 American poet

Na·tion \ˈnā-shən\ Car·ry \ˈkar-ē\ Amelia 1846–1911 American social reformer

Neb·u·cha·drez·zar II \ˌneb-(y)ə-kə-ˈdrez-ər\ *also* **Neb·u·chad·nez·zar** \-kəd-ˈnez-\ *about* 630–562 B.C. Chaldean king of Babylon (605–562)

Neh·ru \ˈne(ə)r-ü, ˈnä-rü\ Ja·wa·har·lal \jə-ˈwä-hər-ˌläl\ 1889–1964 Indian nationalist; 1st prime minister (1947–64)

Nel·son \ˈnel-sən\ Horatio 1758–1805 Viscount *Nelson* British admiral

Nem·e·sis \ˈnem-ə-səs\ the goddess of reward and punishment in Greek mythology

Nep·tune \ˈnep-ˌt(y)ün\ the god of the sea in Roman mythology

Ne·ro \ˈnē-ˌrō, ˈni(ə)r-ō\ 37–68 A.D. Roman emperor (54–68)

New·ton \ˈn(y)üt-ᵊn\ Sir Isaac 1642–1727 English mathematician and physicist

Nich·o·las \ˈnik-(ə-)ləs\ Saint 4th century Christian bishop

Nicholas I 1796–1855 czar of Russia (1825–55)

Nicholas II 1868–1918 czar of Russia (1894–1917)

Night·in·gale \ˈnīt-ᵊn-ˌgāl, -iŋ-\ Florence 1820–1910 English nurse and philanthropist

Ni·ke \ˈnī-kē\ the goddess of victory in Greek mythology

Ni·o·be \ˈnī-ə-bē\ a daughter of Tantalus in Greek mythology who while weeping for her slain children is turned into a stone from which her tears continue to flow

Nix·on \ˈnik-sən\ Richard Mil·hous \ˈmil-ˌhaùs\ 1913–1994 37th president of the U.S. (1969–74)

No·ah \ˈnō-ə\ Old Testament builder of the ark in which he, his family, and living creatures of every kind survived the Flood

No·bel \nō-ˈbel\ Alfred Bernhard 1833–1896 Swedish manufacturer, inventor, and philanthropist

Oce·anus \ō-ˈsē-ə-nəs\ a Titan who rules over a great river encircling the earth in Greek mythology

Odin \ˈōd-ᵊn\ *or* **Wo·den** \ˈwōd-ᵊn\ god of war and patron of heroes in Norse mythology

Odys·seus \ō-ˈdis-ē-əs, -ˈdis-yəs, -ˈdish-əs, -ˈdish-üs\ *or* **Ulys·ses** \yü-ˈlis-ēz\ king of Ithaca and hero in Greek mythology who after the Trojan war wanders for 10 years before reaching home

Oe·di·pus \ˈed-ə-pəs, ˈēd-\ son of Laius and Jocasta who in Greek mythology kills his father and marries his mother not knowing their identity

Ogle·thorpe \ˈō-gəl-ˌthȯrp\ James Edward 1696–1785 English general and philanthropist; founder of Georgia

O'·Keeffe \ō-ˈkēf\ Georgia 1887–1986 American painter

Omar Khay·yám \ˌō-ˌmär-kī-ˈ(y)äm, ˌō-mər-, -ˈ(y)am\ 1048?–1122 Persian poet and astronomer

O'·Neill \ō-ˈnē(ə)l\ Eugene Gladstone 1888–1953 American dramatist; Nobel Prize winner (1936)

Or·pheus \ˈȯr-ˌfyüs, -fē-əs\ poet and musician in Greek mythology who almost rescues his wife Eurydice from Hades by charming Pluto and Persephone with his lyre

Or·well \ˈȯr-ˌwel, -wəl\ George 1903–1950 pseudonym of *Eric Blair* English author — **Or·well·ian** \ȯr-ˈwel-ē-ən\ *adj*

Osce·o·la \ˌäs-ē-ˈō-lə, ˌō-sē-\ *about* 1800–1838 Seminole Indian chief

Otis \ˈōt-əs\ James 1725–1783 American Revolutionary patriot

Ov·id \ˈäv-əd\ 43 B.C.–17 A.D.? Roman poet

Ow·en \ˈō-ən\ Robert 1771–1858 Welsh social reformer

Ow·ens \ˈō-ənz\ Jesse 1913–1980 originally *James Cleveland* American athlete

Paine \ˈpān\ Thomas 1737–1809 American (English-born) political philosopher and author

Pan \ˈpan\ god of forests, pastures, flocks, and shepherds in Greek mythology who is represented as having the legs, ears, and horns of a goat

Pan·do·ra \pan-ˈdōr-ə, -ˈdȯr-\ woman in Greek mythology who out of curiosity opened a box and let loose all of the evils that trouble humans

Par·is \ˈpar-əs\ son of Priam whose abduction of Helen of Troy in Greek mythology led to the Trojan War

Park·man \ˈpärk-mən\ Francis 1823–1893 American historian

Pas·cal \pas-ˈkal\ Blaise 1623–1662 French mathematician and philosopher

Pas·ter·nak \ˈpas-tər-ˌnak\ Boris Leonidovich 1890–1960 Russian author; Nobel Prize winner (1958)

Pas·teur \pas-ˈtər\ Louis 1822–1895 French chemist and microbiologist

Pat·rick \ˈpa-trik\ Saint 5th century apostle and patron saint of Ireland

Pat·ton \ˈpat-ᵊn\ George Smith 1885–1945 American general

Paul \ˈpȯl\ Saint *died between* 62 *and* 68 A.D. author of several New Testament epistles — **Pau·line** \ˈpȯ-ˌlīn\ *adj*

Paul name of six popes: especially **III** 1468–1549 (pope 1534–49); **V** 1552–1621 (pope 1605–21); **VI** 1897–1978 (pope 1963–78)

Paul Bun·yan \ˈpȯl-ˈbən-yən\ giant lumberjack in American folklore

Pau·ling \ˈpȯ-liŋ\ Linus Carl 1901–   American chemist; Nobel Prize winner (1954, 1962)

Pav·lov \ˈpäv-ˌlȯf, ˈpav-, -ˌlȯv\ Ivan Petrovich 1849–1936 Russian physiologist; Nobel Prize winner (1904)

Pa·vlo·va \ˈpav-lə-və, pav-ˈlō-və\ Anna 1882–1931 Russian ballerina

Pea·ry \ˈpi(ə)r-ē\ Robert Edwin 1856–1920 American arctic explorer

Pe·cos Bill \ˌpā-kəs-ˈbil\ a cowboy in American folklore known for his extraordinary feats

Peg·a·sus \ˈpeg-ə-səs\ winged horse in Greek mythology

Penn \'pen\ William 1644–1718 English Quaker; founder of Pennsylvania

Per·i·cles \'per-ə-ˌklēz\ *about* 495–429 B.C. Athenian political leader

Per·ry \'per-ē\ Matthew Calbraith 1794–1858 American commodore

Perry Oliver Hazard 1785–1819 American naval officer

Per·seph·o·ne \pər-'sef-ə-nē\ daughter of Zeus and Demeter who in Greek mythology is abducted by Pluto to rule with him over the underworld

Per·shing \'pər-shiŋ, -zhiŋ\ John Joseph 1860–1948 American general

Pe·ter \'pēt-ər\ Saint *died about* 64 A.D. *Si·mon Peter* \'sī-mən-\ one of the 12 apostles in the Bible

Peter I 1672–1725 *the Great* czar of Russia (1682–1725)

Phil·ip \'fil-əp\ one of the 12 apostles in the Bible

Philip 1639?–1676 American Indian chief

Philip name of six kings of France: espcially **II** *or* **Philip Augustus** 1165–1223 (reigned 1179–1223); **IV** 1268–1314 (reigned 1285–1314) *the Fair*; **VI** 1293–1350 (reigned 1328–50)

Philip name of five kings of Spain: especially **II** 1527–1598 (reigned 1556–98); **V** 1683–1746 (reigned 1700–46)

Philip II 382–336 B.C. king of Macedon (359–336); father of Alexander the Great

Pi·cas·so \pi-'käs-ō, -'kas-\ Pablo 1881–1973 Spanish painter and sculptor in France

Pick·ett \'pik-ət\ George Edward 1825–1875 American Confederate general

Pierce \'pi(ə)rs\ Franklin 1804–1869 14th president of the U.S. (1853–57)

Pi·late \'pī-lət\ Pon·tius \'pän-chəs, 'pən-chəs\ *died* after 36 A.D. Roman governor of Judea

Pitt \'pit\ William 1759–1806 English prime minister (1783–1801; 1804–6)

Pi·us \'pī-əs\ name of 12 popes: especially **VII** 1742–1823 (pope 1800–23); **IX** 1792–1878 (pope 1846–78); **X** 1835–1914 (pope 1903–14); **XI** 1857–1939 (pope 1922–39); **XII** 1876–1958 (pope 1939–58)

Pi·zar·ro \pə-'zär-ō\ Francisco *about* 1475–1541 Spanish conqueror of Peru

Pla·to \'plāt-ō\ *about* 428–348 (*or* 347) B.C. Greek philosopher

Plu·to \'plüt-ō\ god of the dead and the underworld in Greek mythology

Po·ca·hon·tas \ˌpō-kə-'hänt-əs\ *about* 1595–1617 American Indian princess

Poe \'pō\ Edgar Allan 1809–1849 American author

Polk \'pōk\ James Knox 1795–1849 11th president of the U.S. (1845–49)

Po·lo \'pō-lō\ Mar·co \'mär-kō\ 1254–1324 Venetian traveler

Poly·phe·mus \ˌpäl-ə-'fē-məs\ a Cyclops in Greek mythology who is blinded by Odysseus

Ponce de Le·ón \ˌpän(t)-sə-ˌdā-lē-'ōn, ˌpän(t)s-də-'lē-ən\ Juan 1460–1521 Spanish explorer and discoverer of Florida (1513)

Pon·ti·ac \'pänt-ē-ˌak\ *about* 1720–1769 American Indian chief

Por·ter \'pōrt-ər, 'pȯrt-\ Cole Albert 1891–1964 American composer and songwriter

Porter David Dixon 1813–1891 American admiral

Porter Katherine Anne 1890–1980 American author

Porter William Sydney 1862–1910 pseudonym *O. Henry* \(')ō-'hen-rē\ American author

Po·sei·don \pə-'sīd-ᵊn\ god of the sea in Greek mythology — compare NEPTUNE

Pot·ter \'pät-ər\ Beatrix 1866–1943 British author and illustrator

Pow·ha·tan \ˌpaù-ə-'tan, paù-'hat-ᵊn\ 1550?–1618 American Indian chief

Pri·am \'prī-əm, -ˌam\ king of Troy during the Trojan War in Greek mythology

Pro·me·theus \prə-'mē-th(y)üs, -thē-əs\ a Titan in Greek mythology who is punished by Zeus for stealing fire from heaven and giving it to human beings

Pro·teus \'prō-ˌt(y)üs, 'prōt-ē-əs\ sea god in Greek mythology who is capable of assuming different forms

Puc·ci·ni \pü-'chē-nē\ Giacomo 1858–1924 Italian composer

Pu·las·ki \pə-'las-kē, pyü-\ Kazimierz 1747–1779 Polish soldier in American Revolutionary army

Pu·lit·zer \'pul-ət-sər, 'pyü-lət-sər\ Joseph 1847–1911 American (Hungarian-born) journalist

Pyg·ma·lion \pig-'māl-yən, -'mā-lē-ən\ a sculptor in Greek mythology who falls in love with a statue which is then brought to life

Py·thag·o·ras \pə-'thag-ə-rəs, pī-\ *about* 580–*about* 500 B.C. Greek philosopher and mathematician

Ra \'rä, 'rȯ\ god of the sun and chief deity of ancient Egypt

Ra·leigh *or* **Ra·legh** \'rȯl-ē, 'räl- *also* 'ral-\ Sir Walter 1554–1618 English navigator and historian

Ram·ses \'ram-ˌsēz\ *or* **Ram·e·ses** \'ram-ə-ˌsēz\ name of 12 kings of Egypt: especially **II** (reigned 1304–1237 B.C.); **III** (reigned 1198–66 B.C.)

Ran·dolph \'ran-ˌdälf\ Asa Philip 1889–1979 American labor leader

Ra·pha·el \'raf-ē-əl, 'rā-fē-\ one of the four archangels named in Hebrew tradition — compare GABRIEL, MICHAEL, URIEL

Ra·pha·el \'raf-ē-əl, 'rā-fē-, 'räf-ē-\ 1483–1520 Italian painter

Ras·pu·tin \ra-'sp(y)üt-ᵊn, -'sput-\ Grigory Yefimovich 1872–1916 Russian mystic

Rea·gan \'rā-gən *also* 'rē-\ Ronald Wilson 1911– 40th president of the U.S. (1981–89)

Re·bek·ah *or* **Re·bec·ca** \ri-'bek-ə\ wife of Isaac in the Bible

Red Cloud \'red-ˌklaùd\ 1822–1909 American Indian chief

Reed \'rēd\ Walter 1851–1902 American army surgeon

Rem·brandt \'rem-ˌbrant *also* -ˌbränt\ 1606–1669 Dutch painter

Re·mus \'rē-məs\ son of Mars who in Roman mythology is killed by his twin brother Romulus

Re·noir \'ren-ˌwär, rən-'wär\ Pierre-Auguste 1841–1919 French painter

Re·vere \ri-'vi(ə)r\ Paul 1735–1818 American patriot and silversmith

Rich·ard \'rich-ərd\ name of three kings of England: **I** 1157–1199 (reigned 1189–99) *the Lion-Hearted*; **II** 1367–1400 (reigned 1377–99); **III** 1452–1485 (reigned 1483–85)

Rob·in Good·fel·low \ˌräb-ən-'gud-ˌfel-ō\ mischievous elf in English folklore

Rob·in·son \'räb-ən-sən\ Edwin Arlington 1869–1935 American poet

Rob·in·son Cru·soe \ˌräb-ə(n)-sən-'krü-sō\ a shipwrecked sailor in Daniel Defoe's *Robinson Crusoe* who lives for many years on a desert island

Ro·cham·beau \rō-ˌsham-'bō\ Comte de 1725–1807 French general in American Revolution

Rocke·fel·ler \'räk-i-ˌfel-ər, 'räk-ˌfel-\ John Davison father 1839–1937 and son 1874–1960 American oil magnates and philanthropists

Ro·ma·nov *or* **Ro·ma·noff** \rō-'män-əf, 'rō-mə-ˌnäf\ Michael 1596–1645 1st czar (1613–45) of Russian Romanov dynasty (1613–1917)

Rom·u·lus \'räm-yə-ləs\ son of Mars in Roman mythol-

\ə\abut \ᵊ\kitten \ər\further \a\ash \ā\ace \ä\mop, mar
\aù\out \ch\chin \e\bet \ē\easy \g\go \i\hit \ī\ice \j\job
\ŋ\sing \ō\go \ȯ\law \ȯi\boy \th\thin \t͟h\the \ü\loot \u̇\foot
\y\yet \zh\vision *see also* Pronunciation Symbols page

ogy who was the twin brother of Remus and the founder of Rome

Rönt·gen *or* **Roent·gen** \'rent-gən, 'rənt-, -jən\ Wilhelm Conrad 1845–1923 German physicist; Nobel Prize winner (1901)

Roo·se·velt \'rō-zə-vəlt (*Roosevelts' usual pronunciation*), -ˌvelt *also* 'rü-\ (Anna) Eleanor 1884–1962 American lecturer and writer; wife of Franklin Delano Roosevelt

Roosevelt Franklin Del·a·no \'del-ə-ˌnō\ 1882–1945 32d president of the U.S. (1933–45)

Roosevelt Theodore 1858–1919 26th president of the U.S. (1901–09); Nobel Prize winner (1906)

Ross \'rȯs\ Betsy 1752–1836 reputed maker of first American flag

Ros·si·ni \rȯ-'sē-nē, rə-\ Gioacchino Antonio 1792–1868 Italian composer

Ru·bens \'rü-bənz\ Peter Paul 1577–1640 Flemish painter

Rus·sell \'rəs-əl\ Bertrand Arthur William 1872–1970 English mathematician and philosopher; Nobel Prize winner (1950)

Ruth \'rüth\ woman in the Bible who was one of the ancestors of King David

Ruth George Herman 1895–1948 *Babe* American baseball player

Ruth·er·ford \'rəth-ə(r)-fərd, 'rəth-\ Ernest 1871–1937 1st Baron *Rutherford of Nelson* British physicist

Sa·bin \'sā-bin\ Albert Bruce 1906–1993 American physician

Sac·a·ga·wea \ˌsak-ə-jə-'wē-ə, -'wä-ə\ 1786?–1812 American Indian guide to Lewis and Clark

Sa·dat \sə-'dat, -'dät\ Anwar as- 1918–1981 president of Egypt (1970–81)

Saint Nicholas — see NICHOLAS, SANTA CLAUS

Sal·in·ger \'sal-ən-jər\ Jerome David 1919–   American author

Salk \'sȯk, 'sȯlk\ Jonas Edward 1914–   American physician

Sa·lo·me \sə-'lō-mē\ niece of Herod Antipas who in the Bible is given the head of John the Baptist as a reward for her dancing

Sa·mo·set \'sam-ə-ˌset, sə-'mäs-ət\ *died about* 1653 American Indian leader

Sam·son \'sam(p)-sən\ powerful Hebrew hero in the Bible who fought against the Philistines

Sam·u·el \'sam-yə(-wə)l\ Hebrew judge in the Bible who appointed Saul and then David king

Sand·burg \'san(d)-ˌbərg\ Carl 1878–1967 American author

San·ta Claus \'sant-ē-ˌklȯz, 'sant-ə-\ *or* **Saint Nich·o·las** \sänt-'nik-(ə-)ləs, sənt-\ *or* **Kriss Krin·gle** \'kris-'kriŋ-gəl\ a fat jolly old man in modern folklore who delivers presents to good children at Christmastime

Sap·pho \'saf-ō\ *flourished about* 610–*about* 580 B.C. Greek poet

Sa·rah \'ser-ə, 'sar-ə, 'sā-rə\ wife of Abraham and mother of Isaac in the Bible

Sar·gent \'sär-jənt\ John Singer 1856–1925 American painter

Sat·urn \'sat-ərn\ a god of agriculture in Roman mythology

Saul \'sȯl\ first king of Israel in the Bible

Saul *or* **Saul of Tar·sus** \-'tär-səs\ the apostle Paul

Sche·her·a·zade \shə-ˌher-ə-'zäd(-ə), -'zäd(-ē)\ fictional oriental queen and narrator of the tales in the *Arabian Nights' Entertainments*

Schu·bert \'shü-bərt, -ˌbərt\ Franz Peter 1797–1828 Austrian composer

Schweit·zer \'shwīt-sər, 'swīt-, 'shvīt-\ Albert 1875–1965 French Protestant minister, philosopher, physician, and music scholar; Nobel Prize winner (1952)

Scott \'skät\ Dred \'dred\ 1795?–1858 American slave

Scott Sir Walter 1771–1832 Scottish author

Scott Winfield 1786–1866 American general

Scyl·la \'sil-ə\ a nymph in Greek mythology who is changed into a monster and inhabits a cave opposite the whirlpool Charybdis off the coast of Sicily

Se·quoya \si-'kwȯi-ə\ *about* 1760–1843 Cherokee Indian leader

Ser·ra \'ser-ə\ Junípero 1713–1784 Spanish missionary in Mexico and California

Se·ton \'sēt-ᵊn\ Saint Elizabeth Ann Bayley 1774–1821 *Mother Seton* American religious leader

Sew·ard \'sü-ərd, 'sü-(ə)rd\ William Henry 1801–1872 American politician; secretary of state (1861–69)

Shake·speare \'shāk-ˌspi(ə)r\ William 1564–1616 English dramatist and poet

Shaw \'shȯ\ George Bernard 1856–1950 British author

Shel·ley \'shel-ē\ Mary Woll·stone·craft \'wȯl-stən-ˌkraft\ 1797–1851 English novelist; wife of Percy Bysshe Shelley

Shelley Percy Bysshe \'bish\ 1792–1822 English poet

Shep·ard \'shep-ərd\ Alan Bartlett 1923–   American astronaut; first American in space (1961)

Sher·i·dan \'sher-əd-ᵊn\ Philip Henry 1831–1888 American general

Sher·lock Holmes \'shər-ˌläk-'hōmz, -'hōlmz\ detective in stories by Sir Arthur Conan Doyle

Sher·man \'shər-mən\ John 1823–1900 American politician

Sherman William Tecumseh 1820–1891 American general

Sieg·fried \'sig-ˌfrēd, 'sēg-\ hero in Germanic legend who kills a dragon guarding a gold hoard

Si·mon \'sī-mən\ *or* **Simon the Zealot** one of the 12 apostles

Sind·bad the Sailor \'sin-ˌbad-\ citizen of Baghdad whose adventures are narrated in the *Arabian Nights' Entertainments*

Sis·y·phus \'sis-ə-fəs\ king of Corinth who in Greek mythology is condemned to roll a heavy stone up a hill in Hades only to have it roll down again as it nears the top

Sit·ting Bull \ˌsit-iŋ-'bùl\ *about* 1831–90 Sioux Indian leader

Si·va \'shiv-ə, 'siv-; 'shē-və, 'sē-\ god of destruction in the Hindu sacred triad — compare BRAHMA, VISHNU

Smith \'smith\ Bessie 1894 (or 1898)–1937 American blues singer

Smith John *about* 1580–1631 English colonist in America

Smith Joseph 1805–1844 American founder of the Mormon Church

Soc·ra·tes \'säk-rə-ˌtēz\ *about* 470–399 B.C. Greek philosopher

Sol·o·mon \'säl-ə-mən\ son of David and 10th-century B.C. king of Israel noted for his wisdom

Soph·o·cles \'säf-ə-ˌklēz\ *about* 496–406 B.C. Greek dramatist

Sou·sa \'sü-zə, 'sü-sə\ John Philip 1854–1932 American bandmaster and composer

Spar·ta·cus \'spärt-ə-kəs\ *died* 71 B.C. Roman slave and gladiator; leader of a slave rebellion

Sphinx \'sfiŋ(k)s\ monster in Greek mythology having a lion's body, wings, and the head and bust of a woman

Squan·to \'skwän-tō\ *died* 1622 Indian friend of the Pilgrims

Sta·lin \'stäl-ən, 'stal-, -ˌēn\ Joseph 1879–1953 Soviet leader

Stan·dish \'stan-dish\ Myles *or* Miles 1584?–1656 American colonist

Stan·ley \'stan-lē\ Sir Henry Morton 1841–1904 British explorer in Africa

Stan·ton \'stant-ᵊn\ Elizabeth Cady 1815–1902 American suffragist

Stein \'stīn\ Gertrude 1874–1946 American author

Stein·beck \'stīn-ˌbek\ John Ernst 1902–1968 American author; Nobel Prize winner (1962)

Steu·ben, von \'st(y)ü-bən, 'shtȯi-\ Baron Friedrich Wilhelm Ludolf Gerhard Augustin 1730–1794 Prussian-born general in American Revolution

Ste·ven·son \'stē-vən-sən\ Adlai Ewing 1900–1965 American politician

Stevenson Robert Louis Balfour 1850–1894 Scottish author

Stowe \'stō\ Harriet Elizabeth Beecher 1811–1896 American author

Stra·di·va·ri \ˌstrad-ə-'vär-ē, -'var-, -'ver-\ Antonio 1644–1737 Latin *Antonius Strad·i·var·i·us* \ˌstrad-ə-'var-ē-əs, -'ver-\ Italian violin maker

Strauss \'straus, 'shtraus\ Johann father 1804–1849 and his sons Johann 1825–1899 and Josef 1827–1870 Austrian composers

Stu·art \'st(y)ü-ərt, 'st(y)ù(-ə)rt\ — see CHARLES I, MARY STUART

Stuart Charles—CHARLES EDWARD STUART

Stuart Gilbert Charles 1755–1828 American painter

Stuart James Ewell Brown 1833–1864 *Jeb* American Confederate general

Stuy·ve·sant \'stī-və-sənt\ Peter *about* 1610–1672 Dutch colonial administrator in America

Sul·li·van \'səl-ə-vən\ Sir Arthur Seymour 1842–1900 English composer; collaborator with Sir William Gilbert

Sullivan Louis Henri 1856–1924 American architect

Sum·ner \'səm-nər\ Charles 1811–1874 American politician

Swift \'swift\ Jonathan 1667–1745 English author

Taft \'taft\ William Howard 1857–1930 27th president of the U.S. (1909–13); chief justice of the U.S. Supreme Court (1921–30)

Ta·ney \'tȯ-nē\ Roger Brooke 1777–1864 American jurist; chief justice of the U.S. Supreme Court (1836–64)

Tan·ta·lus \'tant-ᵊl-əs\ king in Greek mythology who is condemned to stand up to his chin in a pool of water in Hades and beneath fruit-laden boughs only to have the water or fruit go out of reach at each attempt to drink or eat

Tay·lor \'tā-lər\ Zachary 1784–1850 12th president of the U.S. (1849–50)

Tchai·kov·sky \chī-'kȯf-skē, chə-, -'kȯv-\ Pyotr Ilich 1840–1893 Russian composer

Te·cum·seh \tə-'kəm(p)-sə, -sē\ 1768–1813 Shawnee Indian chief

Ten·ny·son \'ten-ə-sən\ Alfred 1809–1892 known as *Alfred, Lord Tennyson* English poet

Te·re·sa \tə-'rā-zə, -'rē-sə\ **of Ávi·la** \'äv-i-lə\ Saint 1515–1582 Spanish nun and mystic

The·seus \'thē-ˌsüs, -sē-əs\ hero in Greek mythology who kills the Minotaur and conquers the Amazons

Thom·as \'täm-əs\ apostle in the Bible who demanded proof of Christ's resurrection

Thomas à Becket — see BECKET, À

Thor \'thȯ(ə)r\ god of thunder, weather, and crops in Norse mythology

Tho·reau \thə-'rō, thȯ-; 'thȯr-ō\ Henry David 1817–1862 American author

Thur·ber \'thər-bər\ James Grover 1894–1961 American author

Ti·be·ri·us \tī-'bir-ē-əs\ 42 B.C.–37 A.D. Roman emperor (14–37)

Tocque·ville \'tōk-ˌvil, 'tȯk-, 'täk-, -ˌvēl, -vəl\ Alexis Charles-Henri Clérel de 1805–1859 French politician and author

Tol·kien \'tȯl-ˌkēn, 'tōl-, 'täl-\ John Ronald Reuel 1892–1973 English author

Tol·stoy \tȯl-'stȯi, tōl-'stȯi, täl-'stȯi, 'tȯl-ˌstȯi, 'tōl-ˌstȯi, 'täl-ˌstȯi\ Count Lev Nikolayevich 1828–1910 Russian author

Tri·ton \'trīt-ᵊn\ sea god in Greek mythology who is half man and half fish

Trots·ky \'trät-skē, 'trȯt-\ Leon 1879–1940 originally *Lev Davidovich Bronstein* Russian Communist

Tru·man \'trü-mən\ Harry S 1884–1972 33d president of the U.S. (1945–53)

Truth \'trüth\ Sojourner 1797?–1883 American abolitionist

Tub·man \'təb-mən\ Harriet *about* 1820–1913 American abolitionist

Tut·ankh·a·men \ˌtü-ˌtaŋ-'käm-ən, -ˌtäŋ-\ *or* **Tut·ankh·a·ten** \-'kät-ᵊn\ *about* 1370–1352 B.C. king of Egypt (1361–1352 B.C.)

Twain Mark — see CLEMENS

Tweed \'twēd\ William Marcy 1823–1878 *Boss Tweed* American politician

Ty·ler \'tī-lər\ John 1790–1862 10th president of the U.S. (1841–45)

Ulysses — see ODYSSEUS

Ura·nus \'yùr-ə-nəs, yù-'rā-\ the sky personified as a god and father of the Titans in Greek mythology

Ur·ban \'ər-bən\ name of eight popes: especially **II** *about* 1035–1099 (pope 1088–99)

Uri·el \'yùr-ē-əl\ one of the four archangels named in Hebrew tradition — compare GABRIEL, MICHAEL, RAPHAEL

Val·en·tine \'val-ən-ˌtīn\ Saint 3d century Christian martyr

Van Bu·ren \van-'byùr-ən, vən-\ Martin 1782–1862 8th president of the U.S.(1837–41)

Van Dyck *or* **Van·dyke** \van-'dīk, vən-\ Sir Anthony 1599–1641 Flemish painter

Ve·láz·quez \və-'las-kəs\ Diego Rodríguez de Silva 1599–1660 Spanish painter

Ve·nus \'vē-nəs\ the goddess of love and beauty in Roman mythology — compare APHRODITE

Ver·di \'ve(ə)rd-ē\ Giuseppe Fortunio Francesco 1813–1901 Italian composer

Ver·meer \vər-'me(ə)r, -'mi(ə)r\ Jan 1632–1675 also called *Jan van der Meer van Delft* Dutch painter

Verne Jules \'jülz-'vərn\ 1828–1905 French author

Ves·puc·ci \ve-'spü-chē\ Ame·ri·go \ˌäm-ə-'rē-gō\ 1454–1512 Latin *Amer·i·cus Ves·pu·cius* \ə-'mer-ə-kəs-ˌves-'pyü-sh(ē-)əs\ Italian navigator for whom America was named

Vic·to·ria \vik-'tōr-ē-ə, -'tȯr-\ 1819–1901 *Alexandrina Victoria* queen of Great Britain (1837–1901)

Vinci, da Leonardo — see LEONARDO DA VINCI

Vir·gil *also* **Ver·gil** \'vər-jəl\ 70–19 B.C. Roman poet

Vish·nu \'vish-nü\ god of preservation in the Hindu sacred triad — compare BRAHMA, SIVA

Vol·ta \'vōl-tə, 'väl-, 'vȯl-\ Count Alessandro Giuseppe Antonio Anastasio 1745–1827 Italian physicist

Vol·taire \vōl-'ta(ə)r, vȯl-, väl-, -'te(ə)r\ 1694–1778 originally *François-Marie Arouet* French author

Vul·can \'vəl-kən\ the god of fire and metalworking in Roman mythology — compare HEPHAESTUS

Wag·ner \'väg-nər\ (Wilhelm) Ri·chard \'rik-ˌärt, 'rik-\ 1813–1883 German composer

War·ren \'wȯr-ən, 'wär-\ Earl 1891–1974 American jurist; chief justice of the U.S. Supreme Court (1953–69)

Wash·ing·ton \'wȯsh-iŋ-tən, 'wäsh-\ Book·er \'bùk-ər\ Tal·ia·ferro \'täl-ə-vər\ 1856–1915 American educator

Washington George 1732–1799 American general; 1st president of the U.S. (1789–97)

Watt \'wät\ James 1736–1819 Scottish inventor

Wayne \'wān\ Anthony 1745–1796 *Mad Anthony* American general

\ə\abut \ᵊ\kitten \ər\further \a\ash \ā\ace \ä\mop, mar \au\out \ch\chin \e\bet \ē\easy \g\go \i\hit \ī\ice \j\job \ŋ\sing \ō\go \ȯ\law \ȯi\boy \th\thin \t͟h\the \ü\loot \ù\foot \y\yet \zh\vision *see also* Pronunciation Symbols page

Web·ster \\'web-stər\\ Daniel 1782–1852 American politician

Webster Noah 1758–1843 American lexicographer

Wel·ling·ton \\'wel-iŋ-tən\\ 1st Duke of 1769–1852 *Arthur Wellesley*; *the Iron Duke* British general and politician

Wells \\'welz\\ Herbert George 1866–1946 English author and historian

Wes·ley \\'wes-lē, 'wez-\\ John 1703–1791 English founder of Methodism

Wes·ting·house \\'wes-tiŋ-ₘhaús\\ George 1846–1914 American inventor

Whar·ton \\'hwòrt-ᵊn, 'wòrt-\\ Edith Newbold 1862–1937 American author

Whis·tler \\'hwis-lər, 'wis-\\ James Abbott McNeill 1834–1903 American artist

Whit·man \\'hwit-mən, 'wit-\\ Walt 1819–1892 American poet

Whit·ney \\'hwit-nē, 'wit-\\ Eli 1765–1825 American inventor

Whit·ti·er \\'hwit-ē-ər, 'wit-\\ John Greenleaf 1807–1892 American poet

Wilde \\'wī(ə)ld\\ Oscar Fingal O'Flahertie Wills 1854–1900 Irish author

Wil·der \\'wīl-dər\\ Thornton Niven 1897–1975 American author

Wil·liam \\'wil-yəm\\ name of four kings of England: **I** *(the Conqueror) about* 1028–1087 (reigned 1066–87); **II** *(Rufus* \\'rü-fəs\\) *about* 1056–1100 (reigned 1087–1100); **III** 1650–1702 (reigned 1689–1702); **IV** 1765–1837 (reigned 1830–37)

Wil·liam Tell \\ₘwil-yəm-'tel\\ legendary Swiss patriot commanded to shoot an apple from his son's head

Wil·liams \\'wil-yəmz\\ Roger 1603?–1683 English colonist; founder of Rhode Island

Williams Tennessee 1911–1983 originally *Thomas Lanier Williams* American dramatist

Wil·son \\'wil-sən\\ (Thomas) Wood·row \\'wùd-ₘrō\\ 1856–1924 28th president of the U.S. (1913–21); Nobel Prize winner (1919)

Win·throp \\'win(t)-thrəp\\ John 1588–1649 1st governor of Massachusetts Bay Colony

Woden — see ODIN

Woolf \\'wùlf\\ Virginia 1882–1941 English author

Words·worth \\'wərdz-(ₒ)wərth\\ William 1770–1850 English poet

Wren \\'ren\\ Sir Christopher 1632–1723 English architect

Wright \\'rīt\\ Frank Lloyd 1867–1959 American architect

Wright Or·ville \\'òr-vəl\\ 1871–1948 and his brother Wilbur 1867–1912 American pioneers in aviation

Wright Richard 1908–1960 American author

Wy·eth \\'wī-əth\\ Andrew Newell 1917–　　American painter

Yeats \\'yāts\\ William Butler 1865–1939 Irish author

Young \\'yəŋ\\ Brig·ham \\'brig-əm\\ 1801–1877 American Mormon leader

Zech·a·ri·ah \\ₒzek-ə-'rī-ə\\ Hebrew prophet of the 6th century B.C.

Zeng·er \\'zeŋ-(g)ər\\ John Peter 1697–1746 American (German-born) journalist and printer

Zeph·y·rus \\'zef-ə-rəs\\ god of the west wind in Greek mythology

Zeus \\'züs\\ chief god, ruler of the sky and weather (as lightning and rain), and husband of Hera in Greek mythology

Geographical Names

This section contains definitions of current and historical place names likely to be of interest to the student. It adds to the general vocabulary by entering many adjectives and nouns formed from geographical names, such as **Florentine** at **Florence** and **Libyan** at **Libya**.

In the entries the letters N, E, S, and W singly or in combination indicate direction and are not part of a place name. They may represent either the name of the direction (as *north*) or the adjective derived from it (as *northern*); thus, west-northwest of Santiago appears as WNW of Santiago and southern California appears as S California. The only other special abbreviations used in this section are U.S. for United States, and U.S.S.R. for Union of Soviet Socialist Republics. All heights and distances are given in metric units.

Ab·er·deen \ˌab-ər-ˈdēn\ city NE Scotland in Grampian region — **Ab·er·do·ni·an** \-ˈdō-nē-ən\ *adj or n*

Ab·i·djan \ˌab-i-ˈjän\ city, capital of Ivory Coast

Abu Dha·bi \ˌäb-ü-ˈdäb-ē\ city, capital of United Arab Emirates

Abu·ja \ä-ˈbü-jä\ city, official capital of Nigeria

Ab·ys·sin·ia \ˌab-ə-ˈsin-ē-ə, -ˈsin-yə\ — see ETHIOPIA — **Ab·ys·sin·i·an** \-ē-ən, -yən\ *adj or n*

Aca·dia \ə-ˈkād-ē-ə\ *or French* **Aca·die** \à-kà-dē\ NOVA SCOTIA — an early name — **Aca·di·an** \-ē-ən\ *adj or n*

Aca·pul·co \ˌäk-ə-ˈpül-kō, ˌak-\ city S Mexico on the Pacific

Ac·cra \ə-ˈkrä\ city, capital of Ghana

Acon·ca·gua \ˌak-ən-ˈkäg-wə, ˌäk-, -əŋ-\ mountain 6960 meters W Argentina; highest in the Andes & in North America & South America

Ad·dis Aba·ba \ˌad-ə-ˈsab-ə-bə\ city, capital of Ethiopia

Ad·e·laide \ˈad-ᵊl-ˌād\ city, capital of South Australia

Aden \ˈäd-ᵊn, ˈād-, ˈad-\ city S Yemen; formerly capital of People's Democratic Republic of Yemen

Aden, Gulf of arm of Indian ocean between Yemen (Arabia) & Somalia (Africa)

Ad·i·ron·dack \ˌad-ə-ˈrän-ˌdak\ mountains NE New York; highest Mount Marcy 1629 meters

Ad·mi·ral·ty \ˈad-m(ə-)rəl-tē\ 1 island SE Alaska in N Alexander island group 2 islands W Pacific N of New Guinea; belong to Papua New Guinea

Adri·at·ic \ˌā-drē-ˈat-ik, ˌad-rē-\ sea arm of Mediterranean between Italy & Balkan peninsula

Ae·ge·an \i-ˈjē-ən\ sea arm of Mediterranean between Asia Minor & Greece

Af·ghan·i·stan \af-ˈgan-ə-ˌstan\ country W Asia E of Iran; capital, Kabul

Af·ri·ca \ˈaf-ri-kə\ continent S of Mediterranean

Aga·na \ə-ˈgän-yə\ town, capital of Guam

Ag·as·siz Lake \ˈag-ə-sē-\ prehistoric lake 1130 kilometers long in region consisting of present S Manitoba, E Saskatchewan, NW Minnesota, & E North Dakota

Agra \ˈäg-rə\ city N India

Aguas·ca·lien·tes \ˌäg-wə-sˌkäl-ˈyen-ˌtās\ city central Mexico, NE of Guadalajara

Agul·has, Cape \-ə-ˈgəl-əs\ cape Republic of South Africa in S Cape Province; most southerly point of Africa, at 34°50′ S latitude

Ahag·gar \ə-ˈhäg-ər, ˌä-hə-ˈgär\ mountains S Algeria in W central Sahara

Ah·mad·abad *or* **Ah·med·abad** \ˈäm-əd-ə-ˌbäd\ city W India

Ak·ron \ˈak-rən\ city NE Ohio

Al·a·bama \ˌal-ə-ˈbam-ə\ state SE U.S.; capital, Montgomery — **Al·a·bam·i·an** \-ˈbam-ē-ən\ *or* **Al·a·bam·an** \-ˈbam-ən\ *adj or n*

Alas·ka \ə-ˈlas-kə\ 1 peninsula SW Alaska SW of Cook inlet 2 state of U.S. in NW North America; capital, Juneau 3 mountain range S Alaska extending from Alaska peninsula to Yukon boundary — **Alas·kan** \-kən\ *adj or n*

Alaska, Gulf of inlet of Pacific off S Alaska between Alaska peninsula on W & Alexander island group on E

Al·ba·nia \al-ˈbā-nē-ə, -nyə\ country S Europe in Balkan peninsula on Adriatic; capital, Tirane

Al·ba·ny \ˈȯl-bə-nē\ city, capital of New York

Al·be·marle \ˈal-bə-ˌmärl\ inlet of Atlantic in NE North Carolina

Al·bert, Lake \-ˈal-bərt\ lake E Africa between Uganda & Zaire in course of Nile

Al·ber·ta \al-ˈbərt-ə\ province W Canada; capital, Edmonton — **Al·ber·tan** \-ˈbərt-ᵊn\ *adj or n*

Al·bu·quer·que \ˈal-b(y)ə-ˌkər-kē\ city central New Mexico

Al·ca·traz \ˈal-kə-ˌtraz\ island California in San Francisco Bay

Al·da·bra \ˈal-də-brə\ island NW Indian ocean N of Madagascar; belongs to Seychelles

Al·der·ney \ˈȯl-dər-nē\ island in English channel — see CHANNEL

Alep·po \ə-ˈlep-ō\ city N Syria

Aleu·tian \ə-ˈlü-shən\ islands SW Alaska extending 1930 kilometers W from Alaska peninsula

Al·ex·an·der \ˌal-ig-ˈzan-dər, ˌel-\ island group SE Alaska

Al·ex·an·dria \ˌal-ig-ˈzan-drē-ə, ˌel-\ 1 city N Virginia 2 city N Egypt on Mediterranean — **Al·ex·an·dri·an** \-drē-ən\ *adj or n*

Al·ge·ria \al-ˈjir-ē-ə\ country NW Africa on Mediterranean; capital, Algiers — **Al·ge·ri·an** \-ē-ən\ *adj or n*

Al·giers \al-ˈji(ə)rz\ city, capital of Algeria — **Al·ge·rine** \ˌal-jə-ˈrēn\ *adj or n*

Al·lah·abad \ˈal-ə-hə-ˌbad, -ˌbäd\ city N India

Al·le·ghe·ny \ˌal-ə-ˈgā-nē\ 1 river 523 kilometers long W Pennsylvania & SW New York 2 mountains of Appalachian system E U.S. in Pennsylvania, Maryland, Virginia, & West Virginia

Al·len·town \ˈal-ən-ˌtaŭn\ city E Pennsylvania

Al·ma–Ata \ˌal-mə-ə-ˈtä\ city, capital of Kazakhstan

Alps \ˈalps\ mountain system central Europe — see MONT BLANC

\ə\abut \ᵊ\kitten \ər\further \a\ash \ā\ace \ä\mop, mar \aŭ\out \ch\chin \e\bet \ē\easy \g\go \i\hit \ī\ice \j\job \ŋ\sing \ō\go \ȯ\law \ȯi\boy \th\thin \t͟h\the \ü\loot \ŭ\foot \y\yet \zh\vision *see also* Pronunciation Symbols page

Al·tai \'al-ˌtī\ mountain system central Asia between Mongolia & W China & between Kazakhstan & Russia; highest peak Tabun Bogdo 4653 meters

Ama·ga·sa·ki \ˌam-ə-gə-'säk-ē\ city Japan in W central Honshu

Am·a·ril·lo \ˌam-ə-'ril-ō, -'ril-ə\ city NW Texas

Am·a·zon \'am-ə-ˌzän, -zən\ river about 6275 kilometers long N South America flowing from Peruvian Andes into Atlantic in N Brazil

Amer·i·ca \ə-'mer-ə-kə\ **1** either continent (North America or South America) of western hemisphere **2** or **the Amer·i·cas** \-kəz\ lands of western hemisphere including North, Central, & South America & West Indies **3** UNITED STATES OF AMERICA

American Falls — see NIAGARA FALLS

American Samoa or **Eastern Samoa** islands SW central Pacific; capital, Pago Pago (on Tutuila island)

Am·man \a-'män, -'man\ city, capital of Jordan

Am·ster·dam \'am(p)-stər-ˌdam\ city, official capital of the Netherlands

Amur \ä-'mù(ə)r\ river 2865 kilometers long E Asia flowing into the Pacific & forming part of boundary between China & Russia

An·a·heim \'an-ə-ˌhīm\ city SW California E of Long Beach

An·a·to·lia \ˌan-ə-'tō-lē-ə, -'tōl-yə\ — see ASIA MINOR — **An·a·to·li·an** \-'tō-lē-ən, -'tōl-yən\ adj or n

An·chor·age \'aŋ-k(ə-)rij\ city S central Alaska

An·da·man \'an-də-mən, -ˌman\ **1** islands India in Bay of Bengal S of Myanmar & N of Nicobar islands **2** sea arm of Bay of Bengal S of Myanmar — **An·da·man·ese** \ˌan-də-mə-'nēz, -'nēs\ adj or n

An·des \'an-dēz\ mountain system W South America extending from Panama to Tierra del Fuego — see ACONCAGUA — **An·de·an** \'an-(ˌ)dē-ən, an-'dē-\ adj — **Andine** \'an-ˌdēn, -ˌdīn\ adj

An·dor·ra \an-'dór-ə, -där-ə\ country SW Europe in E Pyrenees between France & Spain; capital, Andorra la Vella — **An·dor·ran** \-ən\ adj or n

An·dros \'an-drəs\ island, largest of Bahamas

An·gel Falls \ˌän-jəl-\ waterfall 979 meters SE Venezuela; world's highest waterfall

Ang·kor \'aŋ-ˌkó(ə)r\ ruins of ancient city NW Cambodia

An·gle·sey \'aŋ-gəl-sē\ island NW Wales

An·go·la \aŋ-'gō-lə, an-\ country SW Africa S of mouth of Congo river; until 1975 a dependency of Portugal; capital, Luanda — **An·go·lan** \-lən\ adj or n

An·i·ak·chak Crater \ˌan-ē-'ak-ˌchak-\ volcano 1347 meters SW Alaska on Alaska peninsula; crater 10 kilometers in diameter

An·ka·ra \'aŋ-kə-rə, äŋ-\ city, capital of Turkey in N central Anatolia

An·nap·o·lis \ə-'nap-(ə-)ləs\ city, capital of Maryland

Ann Ar·bor \a-'när-bər\ city SE Michigan

An·shan \'än-'shän\ city NE China

An·ta·nan·a·ri·vo \ˌan-tə-ˌnan-ə-'rē-vō\ city, capital of Madagascar

Ant·arc·ti·ca \(')ant-'ärk-ti-kə, -'ärt-i-\ or **Ant·arc·tic continent** \-'ärk-tik-, -'ärt-ik-\ body of land around the South Pole; plateau covered by great ice cap

An·ti·gua \an-'tē-gə\ island West Indies in the Leewards E of Nevis; capital, Saint Johns; part of independent Antigua and Barbuda

Antigua and Barbuda country West Indies in the Leewards; capital, St. Johns

An·til·les \an-'til-ēz\ the West Indies except for the Bahamas — see GREATER ANTILLES, LESSER ANTILLES — **An·til·le·an** \-'til-ē-ən\ adj

An·trim \'an-trəm\ **1** district E Northern Ireland **2** town in Antrim district

Aorangi — see COOK, MOUNT

Ap·en·nines \'ap-ə-ˌnīnz\ mountain chain Italy extending length of the peninsula; highest point Monte Corno (NE of Rome) 2914 meters — **Ap·en·nine** \-ˌnīn\ adj

Apia \ə-'pē-ə\ town, capital of Western Samoa

Apo, Mount \-'äp-ō\ volcano Philippines in SE Mindanao 2594 meters; highest peak in the Philippines

Ap·pa·la·chia \ˌap-ə-'lā-chə, -'lach-ə, -'lā-shə\ region E U.S. including Appalachian mountains from S central New York to central Alabama

Ap·pa·la·chian \ˌap-ə-'lā-ch(ē-)ən, -'lach(-ē)-ən, -'lāsh(ē-)ən\ mountain system E North America extending from S Quebec to central Alabama — see MITCHELL, MOUNT

'Aqa·ba, Gulf of \-'äk-ə-bə, -'ak-\ arm of Red sea E of Sinai peninsula

Aquid·neck Island \ə-'kwid-ˌnek-\ or **Rhode Island** island SE Rhode Island in Narragansett Bay

Ara·bia \ə-'rā-bē-ə\ peninsula of SW Asia including Saudi Arabia, Yemen, Oman, & Persian Gulf States

Ara·bi·an \ə-'rā-bē-ən\ sea NW section of Indian ocean between Arabia & India

Ar·a·fu·ra \ˌar-ə-'fùr-ə\ sea between N Australia & W New Guinea

Ar·al sea \'ar-əl-\ or formerly **Lake Aral** lake W Asia between Kazakhstan & Uzbekistan

Ar·a·rat \'ar-ə-ˌrat\ mountain 5165 meters E Turkey near border of Iran

Arc·tic \'ärk-tik, 'ärt-ik\ **1** ocean N of Arctic circle **2** Arctic regions **3** island group N Canada in N & E Northwest Territories

Ar·da·bil or **Ar·de·bil** \ˌär-də-'bē(ə)l\ city NW Iran

Ards \'ärdz\ district E Northern Ireland

Ar·gen·ti·na \ˌär-jən-'tē-nə\ country S South America between the Andes & the Atlantic; capital, Buenos Aires — **Argentine** \'är-jən-ˌtēn, -ˌtīn\ adj or n — **Ar·gen·tin·ean** or **Ar·gen·tin·i·an** \ˌär-jən-'tin-ē-ən\ adj or n

Ar·gos \'är-ˌgäs, -gəs\ ancient Greek city & state S Greece

Ar·i·zo·na \ˌar-ə-'zō-nə\ state SW U.S.; capital, Phoenix — **Ar·i·zo·nan** \-nən\ or **Ar·i·zo·nian** \-nē-ən, -nyən\ adj or n

Ar·kan·sas \'är-kən-ˌsò; 1 is also är-'kan-zəs\ **1** river 2335 kilometers long SW central U.S. flowing SE into the Mississippi **2** state S central U.S.; capital, Little Rock — **Ar·kan·san** \är-'kan-zən\ adj or n

Ar·ling·ton \'är-liŋ-tən\ city N Texas

Ar·magh \är-'mä, 'är-ˌmä\ **1** district S Northern Ireland **2** town in Armagh district

Ar·me·nia \är-'mē-nē-ə, -nyə\ **1** region W Asia in mountainous area SE of Black sea & SW of Caspian sea divided between Iran, Turkey, & Armenia (country) **2** country E Europe; capital, Yerevan; a republic of U.S.S.R. 1936–91 — **Ar·me·ni·an** \-nē-ən, -nyən\ adj or n

Arn·hem Land \'är-nəm-\ region N Australia on N coast of Northern Territory

Ar·no \'är-nō\ river 225 kilometers long central Italy flowing through Florence

Aru·ba \ə-'rü-bə\ island Netherlands Antilles off coast of NW Venezuela

Ashkh·a·bad \'ash-kə-ˌbad, -ˌbäd\ city, capital of Turkmenistan

Asia \'ā-zhə, -shə\ continent of eastern hemisphere N of equator — see EURASIA

Asia Mi·nor \-'mī-nər\ or **Anatolia** peninsula in modern Turkey between Black sea on N & the Mediterranean on S

Asmara \az-'mär-ə, -'mar-ə\ city, capital of Eritrea

As·syr·ia \ə-'sir-ē-ə\ ancient empire W Asia extending along the middle Tigris & over foothills to the E — **As·syr·i·an** \-ən\ adj or n

Asun·ción \ə-ˌsün(t)-sē-ˈōn, (ˌ)ä-\ city, capital of Paraguay

As·wân \a-ˈswän, ä-\ city S Egypt on the Nile near site of **Aswân High Dam**

Ata·ca·ma \ˌat-ə-ˈkäm-ə\ desert N Chile

Atchaf·a·laya \(ə-ˌ)chaf-ə-ˈlī-ə\ river 362 kilometers long S Louisiana flowing S into Gulf of Mexico

Ath·a·bas·ca or **Ath·a·bas·ka** \ˌath-ə-ˈbas-kə\ river 1231 kilometers long NE Alberta flowing into Lake Athabasca

Athabasca, Lake lake W central Canada on Alberta–Saskatchewan border

Ath·ens \ˈath-ənz\ city, capital of Greece — **Athe·nian** \ə-ˈthē-nē-ən, -nyən\ adj or n

At·lan·ta \ət-ˈlant-ə, at-\ city, capital of Georgia

At·lan·tic \ət-ˈlant-ik, at-\ ocean separating North America & South America from Europe & Africa — **Atlantic** adj

At·las \ˈat-ləs\ mountains NW Africa extending from SW Morocco to N Tunisia

At·ti·ca \ˈat-i-kə\ ancient division & state E Greece; chief city Athens — **At·tic** \ˈat-ik\ adj

Auck·land \ˈȯ-klənd\ city N New Zealand on NW North island

Au·gus·ta \ȯ-ˈgəst-ə, ə-\ city, capital of Maine

Au·ro·ra \ə-ˈrȯr-ə, ȯ-, -ˈrȯr-\ city NE central Colorado

Aus·tin \ˈȯs-tən, ˈäs-\ city, capital of Texas

Aus·tral·asia \ˌȯs-trə-ˈlā-zhə, ˌäs-, -ˈlā-shə\ Australia, Tasmania, New Zealand, & Melanesia — **Aus·tral·asian** \-zhən, -shən\ adj or n

Aus·tra·lia \ȯ-ˈstrāl-yə, ä-, ə-\ **1** continent of eastern hemisphere SE of Asia **2** independent country in the Commonwealth including continent of Australia & island of Tasmania; capital, Canberra — **Aus·tra·lian** \-yən\ adj or n

Australian Alps mountain range SE Australia in E Victoria & SE New South Wales; part of Great Dividing range

Australian Capital Territory district SE Australia including two areas, one containing Canberra (capital of Australia) & the other on Jervis Bay; surrounded by New South Wales

Aus·tria \ˈȯs-trē-ə, ˈäs-\ country central Europe; capital, Vienna — **Aus·tri·an** \-ən\ adj or n

Aus·tria–Hun·ga·ry \-ˈhəŋ-gə-rē\ country 1867–1918 central Europe including Bohemia, Moravia, Bukovina, Transylvania, Galicia, and what are now Austria, Hungary, Slovenia, Croatia, & part of NE Italy — **Aus·tro–Hun·gar·i·an** \ˈȯs-(ˌ)trō-ˌhəŋ-ˈgar-ē-ən, ˈäs-, -ˈger-\ adj or n

Aus·tro·ne·sia \ˌȯs-trə-ˈnē-zhə, ˌäs-, -ˈnē-shə\ **1** islands of the S Pacific **2** area extending from Madagascar through Malay peninsula & island group to Hawaii & Easter island — **Aus·tro·ne·sian** \-zhən, -shən\ adj or n

Avon \ˈā-vən, ˈav-ən, in the U.S. also ˈā-ˌvän\ **1** river 155 kilometers long central England flowing WSW into the Severn **2** county SW England

Ayles·bury \ˈā(ə)lz-b(ə-)rē, in the U.S. also -ber-ē\ borough SE central England in Buckinghamshire

Ayr \ˈa(ə)r, ˈe(ə)r\ or **Ayr·shire** \-ˌshi(ə)r, -shər\ former county SW Scotland

Az·ca·po·tzal·co \ˌäs-kə-pət-ˈsäl-(ˌ)kō, ˌäz-gə-\ city central Mexico, NW of Mexico City

Azer·bai·jan \ˌaz-ər-bī-ˈjän, ˌäz-\ country SE Europe bordering on Caspian sea; capital, Baku; a republic of U.S.S.R. 1936–91

Azores \ˈā-ˌzō(ə)rz, -ˌzȯ(ə)rz; ə-ˈzō(ə)rz, -ˈzȯ(ə)rz\ islands N Atlantic belonging to Portugal & lying 1290 kilometers W of Portuguese coast — **Azor·e·an** or **Azor·i·an** \ā-ˈzōr-ē-ən, ə-, -ˈzȯr-\ adj or n

Bab·y·lon \ˈbab-ə-lən, -ˌlän\ ancient city, capital of Babylonia; site about 80 kilometers S of Baghdad near the

Euphrates — **Bab·y·lo·nian** \ˌbab-ə-ˈlō-nyən, -nē-ən\ adj or n

Bab·y·lo·nia \ˌbab-ə-ˈlō-nyə, -nē-ə\ ancient country W Asia in valley of lower Euphrates and Tigris rivers; capital, Babylon — **Bab·y·lo·nian** \-nyən, -nē-ən\ adj or n

Bac·tria \ˈbak-trē-ə\ ancient country W Asia in present NE Afghanistan — **Bac·tri·an** \-ən\ adj or n

Bad Lands barren region SW South Dakota & NW Nebraska

Baf·fin \ˈbaf-ən\ island NE Canada in Arctic island group N of Hudson strait

Baffin Bay inlet of the Atlantic between W Greenland & E Baffin island

Bagh·dad \ˈbag-ˌdad\ city, capital of Iraq on the Tigris

Ba·guio \ˌbäg-ē-ˈō\ city, summer capital of the Philippines in NW central Luzon

Ba·ha·mas \bə-ˈhäm-əz, by outsiders also -ˈhä-məz\ islands in N Atlantic SE of Florida; an independent member of the Commonwealth; capital, Nassau — **Ba·ha·mi·an** \-ˈhā-mē-ən, -ˈhäm-ē-ən\ or **Ba·ha·man** \-ˈhä-mən, -ˈhäm-ən\ adj or n

Bahia — see SALVADOR

Bah·rain \bä-ˈrān\ islands in Persian gulf off coast of Arabia; an independent country; capital, Manama

Bai·kal, Lake \-bī-ˈkȯl, -ˈkäl\ lake Russia, in mountains N of Mongolia

Ba·ja California \ˌbä-(ˌ)hä-\ peninsula NW Mexico W of Gulf of California

Ba·kers·field \ˈbā-kərz-ˌfēld\ city S California

Ba·ku \bä-ˈkü\ city, capital of Azerbaijan on W coast of Caspian sea

Bal·a·ton \ˈbal-ə-ˌtän, ˈbȯl-ə-ˌtōn\ lake W Hungary

Bal·boa Heights \(ˌ)bal-ˌbō-ə-\ town Panama; formerly the center of administration for Canal Zone

Ba·li \ˈbäl-ē\ island Indonesia off E end of Java — **Ba·li·nese** \ˌbäl-i-ˈnēz, ˌbal-, -ˈnēs\ adj or n

Bal·kan \ˈbȯl-kən\ **1** mountains N Bulgaria extending from Yugoslavia border to Black sea; highest about 2380 meters **2** peninsula SE Europe between Adriatic & Ionian seas on the W & Aegean & Black seas on the E

Bal·kans \ˈbȯl-kənz\ or **Balkan States** countries occupying the Balkan peninsula: Slovenia, Croatia, Bosnia and Herzegovina, Macedonia, Yugoslavia, Romania, Bulgaria, Albania, Greece, Turkey (in Europe)

Bal·ly·cas·tle \ˌbal-ē-ˈkas-əl\ town N Northern Ireland in Moyledistrict

Bal·ly·me·na \ˌbal-ē-ˈmē-nə\ district NE central Northern Ireland

Bal·ly·mon·ey \ˌbal-ē-ˈmən-ē\ district N central Northern Ireland

Bal·tic \ˈbȯl-tik\ sea arm of the Atlantic N Europe E of Scandinavian peninsula

Bal·ti·more \ˈbȯl-tə-ˌmō(ə)r, -ˌmȯ(ə)r; ˈbȯl-(tə-)mər\ city N central Maryland

Ba·ma·ko \ˌbäm-ə-ˈkō\ city, capital of Mali on the Niger

Ba·na·ras or **Be·na·res** \bə-ˈnär-əs, -ēz\ or **Va·ra·na·si** \və-ˈrän-ə-(ˌ)sē\ city N India

Ban·bridge \ban-ˈbrij\ district SE central Northern Ireland

Ban·dar Se·ri Be·ga·wan \ˌbən-dər-ˌser-ē-bə-ˈgä-wən\ town, capital of Brunei

Ban·dung \ˈbän-ˌduŋ\ city Indonesia in W Java SE of Djakarta

Ban·ga·lore \ˈbaŋ-gə-ˌlō(ə)r, -ˌlȯ(ə)r\ city S India W of Madras

Bang·kok \ˈbaŋ-ˌkäk, baŋ-ˈkäk\ city, capital of Thailand

Ban·gla·desh \ˌbäŋ-gle-ˈdesh, ˌbaŋ-, -ˈdäsh\ country S Asia E of India; formerly part of Pakistan; an independent state since 1971; capital, Dacca — see EAST PAKISTAN

Ban·gor \ˈbaŋ-ˌgó(ə)r, ˈban-ˌgó(ə)r, ˈbaŋ-gər\ city area E Northern Ireland in North Down district

Ban·gui \bäŋ-ˈgē\ city, capital of Central African Republic

Ban·jul \ˈbän-ˌjül\ or formerly **Bath·urst** \ˈbath-(ˌ)ərst\ city, capital of Gambia

Bao·tou or **Pao–t'ou** \ˈbaú-ˈtō\ city N China

Bar·ba·dos \bär-ˈbād-əs, -ōz, -äs, -ōs\ island West Indies in Lesser Antilles E of Windward Islands; an independent country in the Commonwealth since 1966; capital, Bridgetown — **Bar·ba·di·an** \-ˈbäd-ē-ən\ adj or n

Bar·bu·da \bär-ˈbüd-ə\ island West Indies; part of independent Antigua and Barbuda

Bar·ce·lo·na \ˌbär-sə-ˈlō-nə\ city NE Spain on the Mediterranean; chief city of Catalonia

Bar·king \ˈbär-kiŋ\ city area of E Greater London county, England

Bar·na·ul \ˌbär-nə-ˈül\ city S Russia

Bar·net \ˈbär-nət\ city area of N Greater London county, England

Bar·ran·qui·lla \ˌbar-ən-ˈkē-(y)ə\ city N Colombia

Barren Grounds treeless plains N Canada W of Hudson bay

Bar·row, Point \-ˈbar-ō\ most northerly point of Alaska & of United States at about 71°25′N latitude

Ba·si·lan \bä-ˈsē-ˌlän\ island S Philippines

Bas·il·don \ˈbaz-əl-dən\ town SE England in Essex county

Bass \ˈbas\ strait separating Tasmania & continent of Australia

Basse·terre \bas-ˈte(ə)r, bäs-\ seaport St. Kitts, capital of Saint Kitts-Nevis

Basutoland — see LESOTHO

Batavia — see JAKARTA

Bathurst — see BANJUL

Bat·on Rouge \ˌbat-ᵊn-ˈrüzh\ city, capital of Louisiana

Ba·var·ia \bə-ˈver-ē-ə, -ˈvar-\ or German **Bay·ern** \ˈbī-ərn\ state SE Germany bordering on Czech Republic & Austria — **Ba·var·i·an** \bə-ˈver-ē-ən, -ˈvar-\ adj or n

Ba·ya·mon \ˌbī-ə-ˈmōn\ city NE central Puerto Rico

Beau·fort \ˈbō-fərt\ sea consisting of part of Arctic ocean NE of Alaska & NW of Canada

Beau·mont \ˈbō-ˌmänt, bō-ˈmänt\ city SE Texas

Bech·u·a·na·land \ˌbech-(ə-)ˈwän-ə-ˌland\ **1** region S Africa N of Orange river **2** — see BOTSWANA — **Bech·u·a·na** \ˌbech-(ə-)ˈwän-ə\ adj or n

Bed·ford·shire \ˈbed-fərd-ˌshi(ə)r, -shər\ or **Bedford** county SE England

Bedloe's or **Bedloe** — see LIBERTY

Bei·jing \ˈbā-ˈjiŋ\ or **Pe·king** \ˈpē-ˈkiŋ, ˈpā-\ city, capital of China

Bei·rut \bā-ˈrüt\ city, capital of Lebanon

Be·la·rus \ˌbē-lə-ˈrüs, ˌbyel-ə-\ or **Bye·la·rus** \bē-ˌel-ə-, ˌbyel-ə-\ country central Europe; capital, Minsk

Be·lau \bə-ˈlaú\ or formerly **Pa·lau** \pə-ˈlaú\ island group W Pacific in the W Carolines

Be·lém \bə-ˈlem\ city N Brazil

Bel·fast \ˈbel-ˌfast, bel-ˈfast\ **1** district E Northern Ireland **2** city, capital of Northern Ireland in Antrim district

Belgian Congo — see ZAIRE

Bel·gium \ˈbel-jəm\ or French **Bel·gique** \bel-zhēk\ or Flemish **Bel·gië** \ˈbel-gē-ə\ county W Europe; capital, Brussels — **Bel·gian** \ˈbel-jən\ adj or n

Bel·grade \ˈbel-ˌgrād, -ˌgräd, -ˌgrad\ or **Beo·grad** \ˈbeú-ˌgräd\ city, capital of Yugoslavia on the Danube

Be·lize \bə-ˈlēz\ or formerly **British Honduras** country Central America on the Caribbean; capital, Belmopan

Bel·mo·pan \ˌbel-mō-ˈpan\ city, capital of Belize

Be·lo Ho·ri·zon·te \ˈbā-lō-ˌhór-ə-ˈzänt-ē, ˈbel-ō-, -ˌhär-\ city E Brazil N of Rio de Janeiro

Be·lo·rus·sia \ˌbel-ō-ˈrəsh-ə, ˌbyel-\ or **Bye·lo·rus·sia** \bē-ˌel-ō-, ˌbyel-ō-\ former republic of U.S.S.R.; became independent Belarus in 1991 — **Belorussian** adj or n

Benares — see BANARAS

Ben·gal \ben-ˈgól, beŋ-\ region S Asia including delta of Ganges & Brahmaputra rivers; divided between Bangladesh & India — **Ben·gal·ese** \ˌbeŋ-gə-ˈlēz, ˌben-, -ˈlēs\ adj or n

Bengal, Bay of arm of Indian ocean between India & Myanmar

Be·nin \bə-ˈnin, -ˈnēn; ˈben-ən\ or formerly **Da·ho·mey** \də-ˈhō-mē\ country W Africa on Gulf of Guinea; capital, Porto-Novo — **Ben·i·nese** \bə-ˌnin-ˈēz, -ˌnēn-; ˌben-i-ˈnēz, -ˈnēs\ adj or n

Ben Nev·is \ben-ˈnev-əs\ mountain 1343 meters W Scotland in the Grampians; highest in Great Britain

Ber·gen \ˈbər-gən, ˈbe(ə)r-\ city SW Norway

Be·ring \ˈbi(ə)r-iŋ, ˈbe(ə)r-\ **1** sea arm of the N Pacific between Alaska & NE Siberia **2** strait about 90 kilometers wide between North America (Alaska) and Asia (Russia)

Berke·ley \ˈbər-klē\ city W California on San Francisco Bay N of Oakland

Berk·shire \ˈbərk-ˌshi(ə)r, -shər, for 2 British usually -ˈbärk-\ **1** hills W Massachusetts; highest point Mount Greylock 1064 meters **2** county S England W of London

Ber·lin \(ˌ)bər-ˈlin\ city, official capital of Germany; divided 1945–90 into **East Berlin** (capital of East Germany) & **West Berlin** (city of West Germany lying within East Germany) — **Ber·lin·er** \-ˈlin-ər\ n

Ber·mu·da \(ˌ)bər-ˈmyüd-ə\ islands W Atlantic ESE of Cape Hatteras; a British colony; capital, Hamilton — **Ber·mu·dan** \-ˈmyüd-ᵊn\ or **Ber·mu·di·an** \-ˈmyüd-ē-ən\ adj or n

Bern or **Berne** \ˈbərn, ˈbe(ə)rn\ city, capital of Switzerland — **Ber·nese** \(ˌ)bər-ˈnēz, -ˈnēs\ adj or n

Bes·sa·ra·bia \ˌbes-ə-ˈrā-bē-ə\ region SE Europe now chiefly in Moldova — **Bes·sa·ra·bi·an** \-bē-ən\ adj or n

Beth·le·hem \ˈbeth-li-ˌhem, -lē-həm, -lē-əm\ town of ancient Palestine in Judea SW of Jerusalem in area occupied by Israel since 1967

Bev·er·ly Hills \ˌbev-ər-lē-ˈhilz\ city SW California within city of Los Angeles

Bex·ley \ˈbek-slē\ city area of E Greater London county, England

Bho·pal \bō-ˈpäl\ city N central India

Bhu·tan \bü-ˈtan, -ˈtän\ country S Asia in the Himalayas on NE border of India; capital, Thimbu — **Bhu·ta·nese** \ˌbüt-ᵊn-ˈēz, -ˈēs\ adj or n

Bi·ki·ni \bə-ˈkē-nē\ island W Pacific in Marshall islands

Bil·lings \ˈbil-iŋz\ city S central Montana; largest in state

Bi·lox·i \bə-ˈlək-sē, -ˈläk-\ city SE Mississippi on Gulf of Mexico

Bi·o·ko \bē-ˈō-kō\ or formerly **Fer·nan·do Po** \fər-ˌnan-(ˌ)dō-ˈpō\ or 1973–79 **Ma·cí·as Ngue·ma Bi·yo·go** \ˈmä-thē-ə-səŋ-ˈ(g)wä-mə-bi-ˈyō-(ˌ)gō\ island portion of Equatorial Guinea in Gulf of Guinea

Bir·ken·head \ˈbər-kən-ˌhed, ˌbər-kən-ˈhed\ city area NW England in Merseyside county

Bir·ming·ham \ˈbər-miŋ-ˌham, British usually -miŋ-əm\ **1** city N central Alabama **2** city W central England in West Midlands county

Bisayas — see VISAYAN

Bis·cay, Bay of \-ˈbis-ˌkā, -kē\ inlet of the Atlantic between W coast of France & N coast of Spain

Bish·kek \bish-ˈkek\ or 1926–91 **Frunze** \ˈfrün-zə\ city, capital of Kyrgyzstan

Bis·marck \ˈbiz-ˌmärk\ **1** city, capital of North Dakota

2 island group W Pacific N of E end of New Guinea

Bis·sau \bis-ˈau̇\ city, capital of Guinea-Bissau

Bi·thyn·ia \bə-ˈthin-ē-ə\ ancient country NW Asia Minor bordering on Sea of Marmara and Black sea — **Bi·thyn·i·an** \-ē-ən\ *adj or n*

Bit·ter·root Range \ˈbit-ə(r)-ˌrüt-, -ˌru̇t-\ range of the Rockies along Idaho-Montana boundary

Black·burn \ˈblak-(ˌ)bərn\ city area NW England in Lancashire

Black Forest forested mountain region SW Germany along E bank of the upper Rhine

Black hills mountains W South Dakota & NE Wyoming; highest Harney Peak 2207 meters

Black·pool \ˈblak-ˌpül\ city area NW England in Lancashire

Black sea *or ancient* **Pon·tus Eux·i·nus** \ˈpänt-əs-ˌyük-ˈsī-nəs\ *or* **Pon·tus** sea between Europe & Asia connected with Aegean sea through the Bosporus, Sea of Marmara, & Dardanelles

Blanc, Mont — see MONT BLANC

Bloem·fon·tein \ˈblüm-fən-ˌtān, -ˌfän-\ city Republic of South Africa, capital of Orange Free State & judicial capital of the country

Blue Ridge E range of the Applachians E U.S. extending from S Pennsylvania to N Georgia

Boe·o·tia \bē-ˈō-sh(ē-)ə\ ancient state E central Greece NW of Attica; chief ancient city, Thebes — **Boe·o·tian** \bē-ˈō-shən\ *adj or n*

Bo·go·tá \ˌbō-gə-ˈtò, -ˈtä\ city, capital of Colombia

Bo Hai *or* **Po Hai** \ˈbō-ˈhī\ *or* **Gulf of Chih·li** \ˈchē-lē, ˈjir-\ arm of Yellow Sea NE China

Bo·he·mia \bō-ˈhē-mē-ə\ region W Czech Republic; once a kingdom; chief city, Prague

Bo·hol \bō-ˈhól\ island S central Philippines

Boi·se \ˈbói-sē, -zē\ city, capital of Idaho

Bo·liv·ia \bə-ˈliv-ē-ə\ country W central South America; administrative capital, La Paz; constitutional capital, Sucre — **Bo·liv·i·an** \-ē-ən\ *adj or n*

Bol·ton \ˈbōlt-ᵊn\ *or in full* **Bolton–le–Moors** \-lə-ˌmü(ə)rz\ city area NW England in Greater Manchester county

Bom·bay \bäm-ˈbā\ city W India

Bonn \ˈbän, ˈbòn\ city, seat of government of Germany; formerly capital of West Germany

Boo·thia \ˈbü-thē-ə\ peninsula N Canada W of Baffin island; its N tip is most northerly point in North America except for islands

Bor·ders \ˈbòrd-ərz\ region SE Scotland; established 1975

Bor·neo \ˈbòr-nē-ˌō\ island Malay group SW of the Philippines; divided between Brunei, Indonesia, and Malaysia

Bos·nia \ˈbäz-nē-ə\ region S Europe; with Herzegovina forms independent **Bosnia and Her·ze·go·vi·na** \ˌhert-sə-gō-ˈvē-nə, ˌhərt-, -ˈgō-və-nə\; capital, Sarajevo — **Bos·ni·an** \-nē-ən\ *adj or n*

Bos·po·rus \ˈbäs-p(ə-)rəs\ *or ancient* **Bosporus Thra·ci·us** \-ˈthrā-sh(ē-)əs\ strait about 29 kilometers long between Turkey in Europe & Turkey in Asia connecting Sea of Marmara & Black sea

Bos·ton \ˈbò-stən\ city, capital of Massachusetts — **Bos·to·nian** \bò-ˈstō-nē-ən, -nyən\ *adj or n*

Bot·a·ny Bay \ˈbät-ᵊn-ē-, ˈbät-nē-\ inlet of S Pacific SE Australia in New South Wales S of Sydney

Both·nia, Gulf of \-ˈbäth-nē-ə\ arm of Baltic sea between Sweden & Finland

Bo·tswa·na \bät-ˈswän-ə\ country S Africa; formerly (as Bechuanaland) dependent on Britain; now an independent state; capital, Gaborone

Boul·der \ˈbōl-dər\ city N central Colorado

Boulder Dam — see HOOVER DAM

Bourne·mouth \ˈbō(ə)rn-məth, ˈbò(ə)rn-, ˈbu̇(ə)rn-\ town S England in Dorset county on English channel

Brad·ford \ˈbrad-fərd\ city N England in West Yorkshire

Brah·ma·pu·tra \ˌbräm-ə-ˈp(y)ü-trə\ river 2705 kilometers long S Asia flowing from the Himalayas in Tibet to Ganges delta

Bra·sí·lia \brə-ˈzil-yə\ city, capital of Brazil

Bra·ti·sla·va \ˌbrat-ə-ˈsläv-ə, ˌbrät-\ city on the Danube; capital of Slovakia

Bra·zil \brə-ˈzil\ country E & central South America; capital, Brasília — **Bra·zil·ian** \brə-ˈzil-yən\ *adj or n*

Braz·za·ville \ˈbraz-ə-ˌvil, ˈbräz-ə-ˌvēl\ city, capital of Congo on W bank of lower Congo river

Bre·men \ˈbrem-ən, ˈbrā-mən\ city NW Germany

Bren·ner \ˈbren-ər\ pass 1397 meters in the Alps between Austria & Italy

Brent \ˈbrent\ city area of W Greater London county, England

Bret·on, Cape \kāp-ˈbret-ᵊn, kə-ˈbret-, -ˈbrit-\ cape Canada; most easterly point of Cape Breton Island & of Nova Scotia

Bridge·port \ˈbrij-ˌpō(ə)rt, -ˌpu̇(ə)rt\ city SW Connecticut

Bridge·town \ˈbrij-ˌtau̇n\ city, capital of Barbados

Brigh·ton \ˈbrīt-ᵊn\ city area S England in East Sussex county on English channel

Bris·bane \ˈbriz-bən, -ˌbān\ city E Australia, capital of Queensland

Bris·tol \ˈbris-tᵊl\ **1** city SW England in Avon **2** channel between S Wales & SW England

Brit·ain \ˈbrit-ᵊn\ **1** the island of Great Britain **2** UNITED KINGDOM

British Columbia province W Canada on Pacific coast; capital, Victoria

British Commonwealth of Nations — see COMMONWEALTH, THE

British Guiana — see GUYANA

British Honduras — see BELIZE

British India the part of India formerly under direct British administration

British Indian Ocean Territory British colony in Indian ocean consisting of Chagos island group

British Isles island group W Europe consisting of Great Britain, Ireland, & nearby islands

British Virgin Islands E islands of Virgin islands group; a British possession

British West Indies islands of the West Indies belonging to the Commonwealth & including Jamaica, Trinidad and Tobago, & the Bahama & Cayman islands, Windward Islands, Leeward Islands, & British Virgin Islands

Brit·ta·ny \ˈbrit-ᵊn-ē\ region NW France SW of Normandy

Brom·ley \ˈbräm-lē\ city area of SE Greater London county, England

Bronx \ˈbräŋ(k)s\ *or* **The Bronx** section of New York City NE of Manhattan island

Brook·lyn \ˈbru̇k-lən\ section of New York City at SW end of Long Island

Brooks Range \ˈbru̇ks-\ mountains N Alaska

Browns·ville \ˈbrau̇nz-ˌvil, -vəl\ city S Texas on the Rio Grande

Bru·nei \brü-ˈnī, ˈbrü-ˌnī\ country NE Borneo; formerly under British authority; capital, Bandar Seri Begawan

Brus·sels \ˈbrəs-əlz\ city, capital of Belgium

Bu·cha·rest \ˈb(y)ü-kə-ˌrest\ city, capital of Romania

Buck·ing·ham·shire \ˈbək-iŋ-əm-ˌshi(ə)r, -shər, *in the* U.S. *also* -iŋ-ˌham-\ *or* **Buckingham** county SE central England

---

\ə\abut \ᵊ\kitten \ər\further \a\ash \ā\ace \ä\mop, mar
\au̇\out \ch\chin \e\bet \ē\easy \g\go \i\hit \ī\ice \j\job
\ŋ\sing \ō\go \ò\law \òi\boy \th\thin \t͟h\the \ü\loot \u̇\foot
\y\yet \zh\vision *see also* Pronunciation Symbols page

Bu·da·pest \\'büd-ə-ˌpest *also* ˈbyüd-, ˈbùd-, -ˌpesht\\ city, capital of Hungary

Bue·nos Ai·res \\ˌbwä-nə-ˈsa(ə)r-ēz, ˌbō-nə-, -ˈse(ə)r-, -ˈsī(ə)r-\\ city, capital of Argentina

Buf·fa·lo \\'bəf-ə-ˌlō\\ city W New York on Lake Erie

Bu·jum·bu·ra \\ˌbü-jəm-ˈbùr-ə\\ city, capital of Burundi

Bu·ko·vi·na \\ˌbü-kə-ˈvē-nə\\ region E central Europe in foothills of E Carpathians

Bul·gar·ia \\ˌbəl-ˈgar-ē-ə, bùl-, -ˈger-\\ country SE Europe on Black sea; capital, Sofia

Bull Run \\'bùl-ˈrən\\ stream NE Virginia

Bun·ker Hill \\ˌbəŋ-kər-\\ height in Boston, Massachusetts

Bur·gun·dy \\'bər-gən-dē\\ region E France — **Bur·gun·di·an** \\(ˌ)bər-ˈgən-dē-ən\\ *adj or n*

Bur·ki·na Fa·so \\bùr-ˈkē-nə-ˈfä-sō\\ *or formerly* **Upper Volta** \\-ˈvōl-tə, -ˈvòl-\\ country W Africa N of Ivory Coast, Ghana, & Togo; capital, Ouagadougou

Bur·ling·ton \\'bər-liŋ-tən\\ city NW Vermont; largest in state

Bur·ma \\'bər-mə\\ — see MYANMAR

Bu·run·di \\bù-ˈrün-dē\\ country E central Africa; capital, Bujumbura — see RUANDA-URUNDI

Bute \\'byüt\\ island SW Scotland in Firth of Clyde

Butte \\'byüt\\ city SW Montana

Byelarus — see BELARUS

Byelorussia — see BELORUSSIA

By·zan·tine Empire \\'biz-ᵊn-ˌtēn, ˈbīz-, -ˌtīn; bə-ˈzan-ˌtēn, -tīn, bī-\\ empire of SE and S Europe and W Asia from 4th to 15th century

By·zan·ti·um \\bə-ˈzan-sh(ē-)əm, -ˈzant-ē-əm\\ ancient city on site of modern Istanbul

Caer·nar·von \\kär-ˈnär-vən, kə(r)-\\ city area NW Wales in Gwynedd county

Cai·ro \\'kī-rō\\ city, capital of Egypt — **Cai·rene** \\kī-ˈrēn\\ *adj or n*

Ca·la·bria \\kə-ˈlā-brē-ə, -ˈläb-rē-\\ district of ancient Italy consisting of area forming heel of Italian peninsula — **Ca·la·bri·an** \\kə-ˈlā-brē-ən, -ˈläb-rē-\\ *adj or n*

Cal·cut·ta \\kal-ˈkət-ə\\ city E India on Hooghly river — **Cal·cut·tan** \\-ˈkət-ᵊn\\ *adj or n*

Cal·e·do·nia \\ˌkal-ə-ˈdō-nyə, -nē-ə\\ — see SCOTLAND — **Cal·e·do·nian** \\-nyən, -nē-ən\\ *adj or n*

Cal·ga·ry \\'kal-gə-rē\\ city SW Alberta, Canada

Ca·li \\'käl-ē\\ city W Colombia

Cal·i·for·nia \\ˌkal-ə-ˈfòr-nyə\\ state SW U.S.; capital, Sacramento — **Cal·i·for·nian** \\-nyən\\ *adj or n*

California, Gulf of arm of the Pacific NW Mexico

Cal·va·ry \\'kalv-(ə-)rē\\ place outside ancient Jerusalem where Christ was crucified

Cam·bay, Gulf of \\-kam-ˈbā\\ inlet of Arabian sea India N of Bombay

Cam·bo·dia \\kam-ˈbōd-ē-ə\\ *or* **Kam·pu·chea** \\ˌkam-pə-ˈchē-ə\\ *or 1970–75* **Khmer Republic** \\kə-ˈme(ə)r-\\ country SE Asia in S Indochina; capital, Phnom Penh

Cam·bria \\'kam-brē-ə\\ WALES — an old name

Cam·bridge \\'kām-brij\\ city E England in Cambridgeshire

Cam·bridge·shire \\'kām-brij-ˌshi(ə)r, -shər\\ *or* **Cambridge** county E England

Cam·den \\'kam-dən\\ city area of N Greater London county, England

Cam·er·oon *or French* **Cam·er·oun** \\ˌkam-ə-ˈrün\\ country W Africa; capital, Yaoundé — **Cam·er·oo·nian** \\-ˈrü-nē-ən, -rü-nyən\\ *adj or n*

Ca·mi·guin \\ˌkam-ə-ˈgēn\\ island Philippines, off N coast of Mindanao

Ca·naan \\'kā-nən\\ ancient region SW Asia; approximately the area later called Palestine — **Ca·naan·ite** \\'kā-nə-ˌnīt\\ *adj or n*

Can·a·da \\'kan-ə-də\\ country N North America; independent state in the Commonwealth; capital, Ottawa — **Ca·na·di·an** \\kə-ˈnād-ē-ən\\ *adj or n*

Canadian Falls — see NIAGARA FALLS

Canadian Shield — see LAURENTIAN HIGHLANDS

Canal Zone *or* **Panama Canal Zone** former strip of territory Panama leased to U.S. for Panama canal

Ca·nary \\kə-ˈne(ə)r-ē\\ islands in the Atlantic off NW coast of Africa belonging to Spain

Ca·nav·er·al, Cape \\-kə-ˈnav-(ə-)rəl\\ *or 1963–1973* **Cape Ken·ne·dy** \\-ˈken-ə-dē\\ cape E Florida in the Atlantic on Canaveral peninsula E of Indian river

Can·ber·ra \\'kan-b(ə-)rə, -ˌber-ə\\ city, capital of Australia in Australian Capital Territory

Can·on City \\ˌkan-yən\\ city S central Colorado on Arkansas river

Can·ter·bury \\'kant-ə(r)-ˌber-ē, -b(ə-)rē\\ **1** city SE Australia in E New South Wales **2** city SE England in Kent county

Canton — see GUANGZHOU

Cape Bret·on Island \\kāp-ˈbret-ᵊn-, kə-ˈbret-, -ˈbrit-\\ island NE Nova Scotia

Cape Horn — see HORN, CAPE

Cape of Good Hope 1 — see GOOD HOPE, CAPE OF **2** — see CAPE PROVINCE

Cape Province *or* **Cape of Good Hope** *or formerly* **Cape Colony** province S Republic of South Africa; capital, Cape Town

Cape Town \\'kāp-ˌtaùn\\ city Republic of South Africa, capital of Cape Province & legislative capital of the country

Cape Verde \\-ˈvərd\\ islands in the N Atlantic off W Africa; an independent country; capital, Praia; until 1975 belonged to Portugal

Cape York peninsula \\-ˈyò(ə)rk-\\ peninsula NE Australia in N Queensland

Ca·pri \\ka-ˈprē, kə-; ˈkäp-rē, ˈkap-\\ island Italy S of Bay of Naples

Ca·ra·cas \\kə-ˈrak-əs, -ˈräk-\\ city, capital of Venezuela

Car·diff \\'kärd-əf\\ city, capital of Wales in South Glamorgan county

Ca·rib·be·an \\ˌkar-ə-ˈbē-ən, kə-ˈrib-ē-\\ sea arm of the Atlantic; on N & E are the West Indies, on S is South America, & on W is Central America — **Caribbean** *adj*

Car·lisle \\kär-ˈlī(ə)l, kər-, ˈkär-ˌlī(ə)l\\ city NW England in Cumbria county

Carls·bad Caverns \\'kär(-ə)lz-ˌbad-\\ series of caves SE New Mexico

Car·mar·then \\kär-ˈmär-then, kə(r)-\\ port S Wales in Dyfed county

Car·o·li·na \\ˌkar-ə-ˈlī-nə\\ English colony on E coast of North America founded 1663 & divided 1729 into North Carolina & South Carolina (the **Carolinas**) — **Car·o·lin·i·an** \\-ˈlin-e-ən\\ *adj or n*

Ca·ro·li·na \\ˌkär-ə-ˈlē -nə\\ city NE Puerto Rico

Car·o·line \\'kar-ə-ˌlīn, -lən\\ islands W Pacific E of S Philippines; formerly part of Trust Territory of the Pacific Islands

Car·pa·thi·an \\kär-ˈpā-thē-ən\\ mountains E central Europe along boundary between Slovakia & Poland & in N & central Romania; highest Gerlachovka 2663 meters

Car·pen·tar·ia, Gulf of \\-ˌkär-pən-ˈter-ē-ə, -tar-\\ inlet of Arafura sea N of Australia

Car·rick·fer·gus \\ˌkar-ik-ˈfər-gəs\\ district E Northern Ireland

Car·son City \\'kärs-ᵊn-\\ city, capital of Nevada

Car·thage \\'kär-thij\\ ancient city N Africa NE of modern Tunis; capital of an empire that once included much of NW Africa, E Spain, & Sicily — **Car·tha·gin·ian** \\ˌkär-thə-ˈjin-yən, -ˈjin-ē-ən\\ *adj or n*

Ca·sa·blan·ca \\ˌkas-ə-ˈblaŋ-kə, ˌkaz-\\ city W Morocco on the Atlantic

Cas·cade Range \\(ˈ)kas-ˈkād-\\ mountains NW U.S. in Washington, Oregon, & N California — see RAINIER, MOUNT

Cas·per \\'kas-pər\\ city central Wyoming; largest in state

Cas·pi·an sea \\'kas-pē-ən-\ salt lake between Europe and Asia about 27 meters below sea level

Cas·tile \kas-'tē(ə)l\ *or in full* **Cas·ti·lla** \kà-'stē-yà\ region & ancient kingdom central & N Spain

Cast·le·reagh \\'kas-əl-rā\ district E Northern Ireland

Cas·tries \\'kas-ˌtrēz, -ˌtrēs\ seaport, capital of Saint Lucia

Cat·a·lo·nia \ˌkat-ᵊl-'ō-nyə, -nē-ə\ region NE Spain bordering on France & the Mediterranean; chief city, Barcelona — **Cat·a·lo·nian** \-'ō-nyən, -nē-ən\ *adj or n*

Ca·tan·dua·nes \ˌkät-ən-'dwän-əs\ island E Philippines

Ca·thay \kath-'ā\ an old name for China

Cats·kill \\'kat-ˌskil\ mountains in Appalachian system SE New York W of the Hudson

Cau·ca·sus \\'kò-kə-səs\ mountain system SE Europe between Black and Caspian seas in Russia, Georgia, Azerbaijan, & Armenia

Cay·enne \kī-'en, kā-\ city, capital of French Guiana

Cay·man \(')kā-'man, 'kā-mən\ islands West Indies NW of Jamaica; a British colony

Ce·bu \sā-'bü\ island E central Philippines

Ce·dar Rapids \\'sēd-ər-\ city E Iowa

Celebes — see SULAWESI

Cel·tic \\'kel-tik, 'sel-\ sea inlet of the Atlantic in British Isles SE of Ireland, SW of Wales, & W of Cornwall and Isles of Scilly county, England

Central region central Scotland; established 1975

Central African Republic country N central Africa; capital, Bangui

Central America narrow portion of North America from S border of Mexico to South America — **Central American** *adj or n*

Central Valley valley of Sacramento & San Joaquin rivers in California between Sierra Nevada & Coast ranges

Cey·lon \si-'län, sā-\ 1 island in Indian ocean off S India 2 — see SRI LANKA — **Cey·lon·ese** \ˌsā-lə-'nēz, ˌsē-lə-, ˌsel-ə-, -'nēs\ *adj or n*

Chad \'chad\ country N central Africa; capital, N'Djamena — **Chad·ian** \'chad-ē-ən\ *adj or n*

Chad, Lake shallow lake N central Africa at junction of boundaries of Chad, Niger, & Nigeria

Cha·gos \'chä-gəs\ island group central Indian ocean; forms British Indian Ocean Territory — see DIEGO GARCIA

Chal·dea \kal-'dē-ə\ ancient region SW Asia on Euphrates river & Persian gulf — **Chal·de·an** \-'dē-ən\ *adj or n* — **Chal·dee** \'kal-ˌdē\ *n*

Cham·pagne \sham-'pān\ region NE France

Champlain, Lake \sham-'plān\ lake between New York & Vermont extending N into Quebec

Chan·di·garh \'chən-dē-gər\ city N India N of Delhi

Chang \'chäŋ\ *or* **Yang·tze** \'yaŋ-'sē, 'yaŋ(k)t-'sē\ river 4990 kilometers long central China flowing into East China sea

Chang·chun \'chäŋ-'chùn\ city NE China

Chang·sha \'chäŋ-'shä\ city SE central China

Channel 1 — see SANTA BARBARA 2 islands in English channel including Jersey, Guernsey, & Alderney & belonging to United Kingdom

Charles \'chär(ə)lz\ river 76 kilometers long E Massachusetts flowing into Boston harbor

Charles, Cape cape E Virginia N of entrance to Chesapeake Bay

Charles·ton \'chärl-stən\ 1 seaport SE South Carolina 2 city, capital of West Virginia

Char·lotte \'shär-lət\ city S North Carolina

Charlotte Ama·lie \-'am-ə-lē\ city, capital of Virgin Islands of the U.S.; on Saint Thomas island

Char·lottes·ville \'shär-ləts-ˌvil, -vəl\ city central Virginia

Char·lotte·town \'shär-lət-ˌtaùn\ city, capital of Prince Edward Island, Canada

Chat·ta·noo·ga \ˌchat-ə-'nü-gə, ˌchat-ᵊn-'ü-\ city SE Tennessee

Chelms·ford \'chelm-sfərd, 'chem-\ city area SE England in Essex county

Che·lya·binsk \chel-'yä-bən(t)sk\ city W Russia, S of Sverdlovsk

Cheng·chou — see ZHENGZHOU

Cheng·du *or* **Ch'eng–tu** \'chəŋ-'dü\ city SW central China

Ches·a·peake \'ches-(ə-)ˌpēk\ city SE Virginia

Chesapeake Bay inlet of the Atlantic in Virginia & Maryland

Chesh·ire \'chesh-ər, 'chesh-ˌi(ə)r\ *or* **Ches·ter** \'chestər\ county W England bordering on Wales

Ches·ter \'ches-tər\ city NW England in Cheshire

Chev·i·ot \'chev-ē-ət, 'chē-vē-ət\ hills along English= Scottish border

Chey·enne \shī-'an, -'en\ city, capital of Wyoming

Chi·ba \'chē-bə\ city E Japan in Honshu on Tokyo Bay E of Tokyo

Chi·ca·go \shə-'käg-ō, -'kòg-\ city NE Illinois — **Chi·ca·go·an** \-'käg-ə-wən, -'kòg-\ *n*

Chi·chén It·zá \chə-ˌchen-ət-'sä\ ruined Mayan city SE Mexico in Yucatán

Chich·es·ter \'chich-ə-stər\ city S England in West Sussex county

Ch'i–ch'i–ha–erh — see QIQIHAR

Chihli, Gulf of — see BO HAI

Chi·le \'chil-ē\ country SW South America; capital, Santiago — **Chil·ean** \'chil-ē-ən, chə-'lā-ən\ *adj or n*

Chim·bo·ra·zo \ˌchim-bə-'räz-ō, ˌshim-\ mountain 6267 meters W central Ecuador

Chi·na \'chī-nə\ 1 *or in full* **People's Republic of China** country E Asia; capital, Beijing 2 *or officially* **Republic of China** — see TAIWAN 3 sea section of the W Pacific; divided at Taiwan strait into East China & South China seas

Chin–chou *or* **Chinchow** — see JINZHOU

Chit·ta·gong \'chit-ə-ˌgäŋ, -ˌgòŋ\ city SE Bangladesh on Bay of Bengal

Chong·qing *or* **Ch'ung–ch'ing** \'chùŋ-'chiŋ\ *or* **Chungking** \'chùŋ-'kiŋ\ city SW central China

Christ·church \'krīs(t)-ˌchərch\ city New Zealand on E coast of South island

Christ·mas \'kris-məs\ island E Indian ocean SW of Java; governed by Australia

Cin·cin·na·ti \ˌsin(t)-sə-'nat-ē, -'nat-ə\ city SW Ohio

Ciudad Trujillo — see SANTO DOMINGO

Cleve·land \'klēv-lənd\ 1 city NE Ohio 2 county N England N of North Yorkshire

Clwyd \'klüid\ county NE Wales; established 1974

Clyde \'klīd\ river 171 kilometers long SW Scotland flowing into **Firth of Clyde** (estuary)

Coast mountains mountain range W British Columbia, Canada; the N continuation of Cascade range

Coast ranges chain of mountain ranges W North America extending along Pacific coast W of Sierra Nevada & Cascade range & through Vancouver island into S Alaska to Kenai peninsula & Kodiak island

Cod, Cape \-'käd\ peninsula SE Massachusetts

Coim·ba·tore \ˌkòim-bə-'tō(ə)r, -'tò(ə)r\ city S India

Cole·raine \kōl-'rān, 'kōl-ˌran\ 1 county N Northern Ireland 2 port in Coleraine county

Co·logne \kə-'lōn\ city W Germany on the Rhine

Co·lom·bia \kə-'ləm-bē-ə\ country NW South America; capital, Bogotá — **Co·lom·bi·an** \-bē-ən\ *adj or n*

Co·lom·bo \kə-'ləm-bō\ city, capital of Sri Lanka

Col·o·ra·do \ˌkäl-ə-'rad-ō, -'räd-\ 1 river 2335 kilome-

\ə\abut \ᵊ\kitten \ər\further \a\ash \ā\ace \ä\mop, mar
\aù\out \ch\chin \e\bet \ē\easy \g\go \i\hit \ī\ice \j\job
\ŋ\sing \ō\go \ò\law \òi\boy \th\thin \t̲h̲\the \ü\loot \ù\foot
\y\yet \zh\vision *see also* Pronunciation Symbols page

ters long SW U.S. & NW Mexico flowing from N Colorado into Gulf of California **2** desert SE California **3** plateau region SW U.S. W of Rocky mountains **4** state W U.S.; capital, Denver — **Col·o·rad·an** \-ˈrad-ⁿn, -ˈräd-\ *or* **Co·lo·ra·do·an** \-ˈrad-ə-wən, -ˈräd-\ *adj or n*

Colorado Springs city central Colorado

Co·lum·bia \kə-ˈləm-bē-ə\ **1** river 2045 kilometers long SW Canada & NW U.S. flowing S & W from SE British Columbia into the Pacific **2** plateau in Columbia river basin in E Washington, E Oregon, & SW Idaho **3** city, capital of South Carolina **4** — see UNITED STATES OF AMERICA

Co·lum·bus \kə-ˈləm-bəs\ **1** city W Georgia **2** city, capital of Ohio

Com·mon·wealth, the \ˈkäm-ən-ˌwel(t)th\ *or* **Commonwealth of Nations** *or formerly* **British Commonwealth of Nations** the United Kingdom & most of the countries formerly dependent on it

Com·o·ro \ˈkäm-ə-ˌrō\ islands off SE Africa NW of Madagascar; formerly a French possession; an independent country (except for Mayotte Island remaining French) since 1975; capital, Moroni

Con·a·kry \ˈkän-ə-krē\ city, capital of Guinea

Con·cord \ˈkäŋ-kərd\ **1** city W California **2** city, capital of New Hampshire **3** town E Massachusetts NW of Boston

Con·go \ˈkäŋ-gō\ **1** *or* **Zaire** \ˈzī(ə)r, zä-ˈi(ə)r\ river 4830 kilometers long W Africa flowing into the Atlantic **2** — see ZAIRE **3** country W central Africa W of lower Congo river; capital, Brazzaville — **Con·go·lese** \ˌkäŋ-gə-ˈlēz, -ˈlēs\ *adj or n*

Con·nacht \ˈkän-ˌȯt\ province W Ireland

Con·nect·i·cut \kə-ˈnet-i-kət\ **1** river 655 kilometers long NE U.S. flowing S from N New Hampshire into Long Island Sound **2** state NE U.S.; capital, Hartford

Constantinople — see ISTANBUL

Con·ti·nen·tal Di·vide \ˌkänt-ⁿn-ˌent-ⁿl-di-ˈvīd\ line of highest points of land separating the waters flowing W from those flowing N or E and extending SSE from NW Canada across W U.S. through Mexico & Central America to South America where it joins the Andes mountains

Cook \ˈkùk\ **1** inlet of the Pacific S Alaska W of Kenai peninsula **2** islands S Pacific SW of Society islands belonging to New Zealand **3** strait New Zealand between North island & South island

Cook, Mount *or formerly* **Ao·rangi** \aù-ˈräŋ-ē\ mountain 3764 meters New Zealand in W central South island in Southern Alps; highest in New Zealand

Cooks·town \ˈkùk-ˌstaùn\ district central Northern Ireland

Co·pen·ha·gen \ˌkō-pən-ˈhā-gən, -ˈhäg-ən\ city, capital of Denmark

Cor·al \ˈkȯr-əl, ˈkär-\ sea arm of the W Pacific NE of Australia

Cór·do·ba \ˈkȯrd-ə-bə, -ə-və\ city N central Argentina

Cor·inth \ˈkȯr-ən(t)th, ˈkär-\ **1** region of ancient Greece **2** ancient city, its capital; site SW of present city of Corinth — **Co·rin·thi·an** \kə-ˈrin(t)-thē-ən\ *adj or n*

Corinth, Gulf of inlet of Ionian sea central Greece N of the Peloponnisos

Cork \ˈkȯ(ə)rk\ city S Ireland in Munster

Corn·wall \ˈkȯrn-ˌwȯl, -wəl\ area and once a county SW England

Cornwall and Isles of Scilly county SW England

Cor·pus Chris·ti \ˌkȯr-pə-ˈskris-tē\ city S Texas

Cor·reg·i·dor \kə-ˈreg-ə-ˌdȯ(ə)r\ island Philippines at entrance to Manila Bay

Cor·si·ca \ˈkȯr-si-kə\ island France in the Mediterranean N of Sardinia — **Cor·si·can** \ˈkȯr-si-kən\ *adj or n*

Cos·ta Ri·ca \ˌkäs-tə-ˈrē-kə, ˌkȯs-, ˌkōs-\ country Central America between Nicaragua & Panama; capital, San José — **Cos·ta Ri·can** \-ˈrē-kən\ *adj or n*

Cots·wold \ˈkät-ˌswōld\ hills SW central England

Cov·en·try \ˈkäv-ən-trē, ˈkəv-\ city central England in West Midlands county

Cow·pens \ˈkaù-ˌpenz\ town NW South Carolina

Craig·av·on \krā-ˈgav-ən\ district central Northern Ireland

Cra·ter \ˈkrāt-ər\ lake 589 meters deep SW Oregon in Cascade range — see MAZAMA, MOUNT

Crete \ˈkrēt\ island Greece in E Mediterranean — **Cre·tan** \ˈkrēt-ⁿn\ *adj or n*

Cri·mea \krī-ˈmē-ə, krə-\ peninsula SE Europe, extending into Black sea — **Cri·me·an** \krī-ˈmē-ən, krə-\ *adj*

Cro·atia \krō-ˈä-sh(ē-)ə\ country SE Europe; capital, Zagreb; a republic of Yugoslavia 1946-91

Croy·don \ˈkrȯid-ⁿn\ city area of S Greater London county, England

Cu·ba \ˈkyü-bə\ island in the West Indies; an independent country; capital, Havana — **Cu·ban** \-bən\ *adj or n*

Cum·ber·land \ˈkəm-bər-lənd\ river 1106 kilometers long S Kentucky & N Tennessee

Cumberland Gap pass through Cumberland plateau NE Tennessee

Cumberland plateau *or* **Cumberland mountains** mountain region E U.S.; part of S Appalachian mountains extending from S West Virginia to NE Alabama

Cum·bria \ˈkəm-brē-ə\ county NW England — **Cum·bri·an** \-ən\ *adj or n*

Cumbrian mountains NW England chiefly in Cumbria county

Cu·par \ˈkü-pər\ town E Scotland in Fife region

Cu·ri·ti·ba \ˌkùr-ə-ˈtē-bə\ city S Brazil SW of São Paulo

Cush \ˈkəsh, ˈkùsh\ ancient country NE Africa in upper Nile valley S of Egypt — **Cush·ite** \-ˌīt\ *n* — **Cush·it·ic** \ˌkəsh-ˈit-ik, kùsh-\ *adj*

Cuz·co \ˈkü-skō\ city S central Peru

Cymru — see WALES

Cy·prus \ˈsī-prəs\ island E Mediterranean S of Turkey; an independent country in the Commonwealth; capital, Nicosia — **Cyp·ri·ot** \ˈsip-rē-ət, -rē-ˌät\ *or* **Cyp·ri·ote** \-ˌōt, -ət\ *adj or n*

Cy·re·na·ica \ˌsir-ə-ˈnā-ə-kə, ˌsī-rə-\ ancient region N Africa on coast W of Egypt; capital, Cyrene — **Cy·re·na·i·can** \-kən\ *adj or n*

Czecho·slo·va·kia \ˌchek-ə-slō-ˈväk-ē-ə, -ˈvak-\ former country central Europe; capital, Prague; since January 1, 1993 divided into the independent states of the **Czech Republic** (capital, Prague) & **Slovakia** (capital, Bratislava) — **Czecho·slo·vak** \-ˈslō-ˌväk, -ˌvak\ *adj or n* — **Czecho·slo·va·ki·an** \-slō-ˈväk-ē-ən, -ˈvak-\ *adj or n*

Dac·ca *or* **Dha·ka** \ˈdak-ə, ˈdäk-ə\ city, capital of Bangladesh

Dahomey — see BENIN

Dairen — see LÜDA

Da·kar \ˈdak-ˌär, də-ˈkär\ city, capital of Senegal

Da·ko·ta Territory \də-ˈkōt-ə-\ territory 1861–89 NW U.S. divided 1889 into states of North Dakota & South Dakota (the **Da·ko·tas** \-əz\)

Dal·las \ˈdal-əs, -is\ city NE Texas

Dal·ma·tia \dal-ˈmā-sh(ē-)ə\ region W Balkan peninsula on the Adriatic — **Dal·ma·tian** \-shən\ *adj or n*

Da·mas·cus \də-ˈmas-kəs\ city, capital of Syria

Dan·ube \ˈdan-yüb\ river 2776 kilometers long S Europe flowing from SW Germany into Black sea — **Da·nu·bi·an** \da-ˈnyü-bē-ən\ *adj*

Dar·da·nelles \ˌdärd-ⁿn-ˈelz\ *or* **Hel·les·pont** \ˈhel-ə-ˌspänt\ strait NW Turkey connecting Sea of Marmara & the Aegean

Dar es Sa·laam \ˌdär-ˌes-sə-ˈläm\ city, capital of Tanzania

Dar·ling \ˈdär-liŋ\ river 1865 kilometers long SE Australia in Queensland & New South Wales flowing SW into the Murray

Dar·win \\'där-wən\ city Australia, capital of Northern Territory

Da·vao \'däv-ˌaū,dä-'vaū\ city S Philippines in E Mindanao on Davao Gulf

Dav·en·port \'dav-ən-ˌpō(ə)rt, -ˌpȯ(ə)rt\ city E Iowa

Da·vis \'dā-vəs\ strait between SW Greenland & E Baffin island connecting Baffin Bay & the Atlantic

Day·ton \'dāt-ᵊn\ city SW Ohio

Dead sea \'ded-\ salt lake between Israel & Jordan; 397 meters below sea level

Death Valley \'deth-\ dry valley E California & S Nevada containing lowest point in U.S. (86 meters below sea level)

Dec·can \'dek-ən, -ˌan\ plateau region S India

Del·a·ware \'del-ə-ˌwa(ə)r, -ˌwe(ə)r, -wər\ 1 river 476 kilometers long E U.S. flowing S from S New York into Delaware Bay 2 state E U.S.; capital, Dover — **Del·a·war·ean** or **Del·a·war·ian** \ˌdel-ə-'war-ē-ən, -'wer-\ adi or n

Delaware Bay inlet of the Atlantic between SW New Jersey & E Delaware

Del·hi \'del-ē\ city N India — see NEW DELHI

De·los \'dē-ˌläs\ island Greece — **De·lian** \'dē-lē-ən, 'dēl-yən\ adi or n

Del·phi \'del-ˌfī\ ancient town central Greece on S slope of Parnassus

Democratic Republic of the Congo — see ZAIRE

Denali — see MCKINLEY, MOUNT

Den·mark \'den-ˌmärk\ country N Europe occupying most of Jutland & neighboring islands; capital, Copenhagen

Den·ver \'den-vər\ city, capital of Colorado

Der·by \'där-bē, chiefly in the U.S. 'dər-bē\ city area N central England in Derbyshire

Der·by·shire \'där-bē-ˌshi(ə)r, -shər, U.S. also 'dər-\ or **Derby** county N central England

Der·ry \'der-ē\ or **Lon·don·der·ry** \ˌlən-dən-'der-ē; 'lən-dən-ˌder-ē, -d(ə-)rē\ 1 district NW Northern Ireland 2 seaport in Londonderry district

Des Moines \di-'mȯin\ city, capital of Iowa

De·troit \di-'trȯit\ 1 river 50 kilometers long between SE Michigan & Ontario connecting Lake Saint Clair & Lake Erie 2 city SE Michigan

Dev·on \'dev-ən\ or **De·von·shire** \-ˌshi(ə)r, -shər\ county SW England

Dhaka — see DACCA

Die·go Gar·cia \dē-ˌā-gō-ˌgär-'sē-ə\ island in Indian ocean; chief island of Chagos island group

Di·nar·ic Alps \də-ˌnar-ik-\ range of the E Alps in W Slovenia, W Croatia, Bosnia and Herzegovina, & Montenegro

District of Co·lum·bia \-kə-'ləm-bē-ə\ federal district E U.S. coextensive with city of Washington

Djakarta — see JAKARTA

Dji·bou·ti \jə-'büt-ē\ 1 country E Africa on Gulf of Aden 2 city, its capital

Dne·pro·pe·trovsk \'nep-(ˌ)rō-pə-'trȯfsk\ city E central Ukraine

Dodge City \'däj-\ city S Kansas on Arkansas river

Do·ha \'dō-hä\ city & port, capital of Qatar on Persian gulf

Dom·i·ni·ca \ˌdäm-ə-'nē-kə, də-'min-ə-kə\ island West Indies in the Leeward Islands; an independent country; capital, Roseau

Do·min·i·can Republic \də-ˌmin-i-kən-\ country West Indies in E Hispaniola; capital, Santo Domingo — **Do·min·i·can** \də-'min-i-kən\ adj or n

Don \'dän\ river 1930 kilometers long SW Russia

Do·netsk \də-'netsk\ city E Ukraine

Dor·ches·ter \'dȯr-chə-stər, -ˌches-tər\ city area S England in Dorset county

Dor·set \'dȯr-sət\ or **Dor·set·shire** \-ˌshi(ə)r, -shər\ county S England on English channel

Dort·mund \'dȯ(ə)rt-ˌmunt, -mənd\ city W Germany in the Ruhr

Dou·ro \'dōr-ü, 'dȯr-\ or Spanish **Due·ro** \'dwe(ə)r-ō\ or ancient **Du·ri·us** \'d(y)ùr-ē-əs\ river 780 kilometers long N Spain & N Portugal flowing into the Atlantic

Do·ver \'dō-vər\ city, capital of Delaware

Dover, Strait of channel between SE England & N France; the most easterly section of English channel

Down \'daùn\ district SE Northern Ireland

Down·pat·rick \daùn-'pa-trik\ city district E Northern Ireland in Down district

Dra·kens·berg \'dräk-ənz-ˌbərg\ mountain range E Republic of South Africa & Lesotho; highest peak Thabana Ntlenyana 3482 meters

Dres·den \'drez-dən\ city E Germany

Dub·lin \'dəb-lən\ or ancient **Eb·la·na** \'eb-lə-nə\ city, capital of Ireland in Leinster

Dud·ley \'dəd-lē\ city area W central England in West Midlands county

Duis·burg \'dü-əs-ˌbərg; 'd(y)üz-ˌbərg\ city W Germany at junction of Rhine & Ruhr rivers

Du·luth \də-'lüth\ city NE Minnesota

Dum·fries \ˌdəm-'frēs\ town S Scotland in Dumfries and Galloway region

Dumfries and Gal·lo·way \-'gal-ə-ˌwā\ region S Scotland; established 1975

Dun·dee \ˌdən-'dē\ city E Scotland in Tayside region

Dun·gan·non \dən-'gan-ən\ district W Northern Ireland

Dur·ban \'dər-bən\ city E Republic of South Africa in E Natal

Dur·ham \'dər-əm, 'də-rəm, 'dùr-əm\ 1 city N central North Carolina 2 county N England on North sea 3 city area in Durham county

Du·shan·be \d(y)ü-'sham-bə, -'shäm-\ city, capital of Tajikistan

Düs·sel·dorf \'d(y)üs-əl-ˌdȯrf\ city W Germany on the Rhine

Dutch East Indies — see NETHERLANDS EAST INDIES

Dy·fed \'dəv-ed, -əd\ county SW Wales; established 1974

Ea·ling \'ē-liŋ\ city area of W Greater London county, England

East An·glia \-aŋ-glē-ə\ region E England including Norfolk & Suffolk counties

East China sea — see CHINA

Eas·ter \'ē-stər\ island SE Pacific 3220 kilometers W of Chilean coast; belongs to Chile

Eastern Ghats \-'gȯts\ chain of low mountains SE India along coast

Eastern Roman Empire the Byzantine Empire from 395 to 474

Eastern Samoa — see AMERICAN SAMOA

East Germany the German Democratic Republic — see GERMANY

East Indies the Malay island group — **East Indian** adj or n

East London city S republic of south africa in SE Cape Province

East Pakistan the former E division of Pakistan consisting of E portion of Bengal; now the independent country of Bangladesh

East river strait SE New York connecting upper New York Bay & Long Island Sound & separating Manhattan island and Long Island

East Sus·sex \-'səs-iks, U.S. also -ˌeks\ county SE England

Eblana — see DUBLIN

Ebro \\ˈā-brō\ river 775 kilometers long NE Spain flowing into the Mediterranean

Ec·ua·dor \\ˈek-wə-ˌdȯ(ə)r\ country W South America; capital, Quito — **Ec·ua·dor·an** \\ˌek-wə-ˈdȯr-ən, -ˈdȯr-\ or **Ec·ua·dor·ean** or **Ec·ua·dor·ian** \-ē-ən\ adj or n

Ed·in·burgh \\ˈed-ᵊn-ˌbər-ə, -ˌbə-rə, -b(ə-)rə\ city, capital of Scotland, in Lothian region

Ed·mon·ton \\ˈed-mən-tən\ city, capital of Alberta, Canada

Edom \\ˈēd-əm\ ancient country SW Asia S of Judea & Dead sea — **Edom·ite** \\ˈēd-ə-ˌmīt\ n

Egypt \\ˈē-jəpt\ country NE Africa & Sinai peninsula of SW Asia bordering on Mediterranean & Red seas; capital, Cairo

Eire — see IRELAND

Elam \\ˈē-ləm\ ancient country SW Asia at head of Persian gulf E of Babylonia — **Elam·ite** \\ˈē-lə-ˌmīt\ n

Elbe \\ˈel-bə, ˈelb\ river 1160 kilometers long N Czech Republic & NE Germany flowing NW into North sea

El·bert, Mount \-ˈel-bərt\ mountain 4399 meters W central Colorado; highest in Colorado & the Rocky mountains

El·burz \el-ˈbu̇(ə)rz\ mountains N Iran

Eliz·a·beth \i-ˈliz-ə-bəth\ city NE New Jersey

Elles·mere \\ˈelz-ˌmi(ə)r\ island N Canada in Northwest Territories

Ellice — see TUVALU

El Paso \el-ˈpas-ō\ city W Texas on Rio Grande

El Sal·va·dor \el-ˈsal-və-ˌdȯ(ə)r, -ˌsal-və-ˈdȯ(ə)r\ country Central America bordering on the Pacific; capital, San Salvador

Ely, Isle of \-ˈē-lē\ district E England in Cambridgeshire

En·field \\ˈen-ˌfēld\ city area of N Greater London county, England

En·gland \\ˈiŋ-glənd also ˈiŋ-lənd\ country S Great Britain; a division of United Kingdom; capital, London

English channel arm of the Atlantic between S England & N France

En·nis·kil·len \ˌen-ə-ˈskil-ən\ city district SW Northern Ireland in Fermanagh district

Ephra·im \\ˈē-frē-əm\ 1 hilly region N Jordan E of Jordan river 2 — see ISRAEL — **Ephra·im·ite** \\ˈē-frē-ə-ˌmīt\ n

Equatorial Guinea or formerly **Spanish Guinea** country W Africa including Río Muni & Bioko; capital, Malabo

Erie \\ˈi(ə)r-ē\ 1 city NW Pennsylvania 2 canal New York between Hudson river at Albany & Lake Erie at Buffalo; built 1817–25; now superseded by New York State Barge Canal

Erie, Lake lake E central North America in U.S. & Canada; one of the Great Lakes

Er·in \\ˈer-ən\ poetic name of Ireland

Er·i·trea \ˌer-ə-ˈtrē-ə, -ˈtrā-\ country NE Africa; capital, Asmara — **Er·i·tre·an** \-ən\ adj or n

Española — see HISPANIOLA

Es·sen \\ˈes-ᵊn\ city W Germany in the Ruhr

Es·sex \\ˈes-iks\ county SE England on North sea

Es·to·nia \e-ˈstō-nē-ə, -nyə\ country E Europe on Baltic sea; capital, Tallinn; a republic of U.S.S.R. 1940–91

Ethi·o·pia \ˌē-thē-ˈō-pē-ə\ or **Ab·ys·sin·ia** \ˌab-ə-ˈsin-yə, -ˈsin-ē-ə\ country E Africa; capital, Addis Ababa — **Ethi·o·pi·an** \-ən\ adj or n

Et·na \\ˈet-nə\ volcano 3323 meters Italy in NE Sicily

Eto·bi·coke \et-ˈō-bi-ˌkō\ city Canada in SE Ontario

Etru·ria \i-ˈtrur-ē-ə\ ancient country central Italy

Eu·gene \yü-ˈjēn\ city W Oregon

Eu·phra·tes \yu̇-ˈfrāt-ēz\ river 2735 kilometers long SW Asia flowing from E Turkey & uniting with the Tigris to form the Shatt-al-Arab

Eur·asia \yu̇-ˈrā-zhə, -shə\ landmass consisting of Europe & Asia — **Eur·asian** \-zhən, -shən\ adj or n

Eu·rope \\ˈyu̇r-əp\ continent of the eastern hemisphere between Asia & the Atlantic

Ev·ans·ville \\ˈev-ənz-ˌvil\ city SW Indiana

Ev·er·est, Mount \-ˈev-(ə-)rəst\ mountain 8848 meters S Asia in the Himalayas on border between Nepal & Tibet; highest in the world

Ev·er·glades \\ˈev-ər-ˌglādz\ swamp region S Florida now partly drained

Ex·e·ter \\ˈek-sət-ər\ 1 town SE New Hampshire 2 city SW England in Devon county

Faer·oe or **Far·oe** \\ˈfa(ə)r-ō, ˈfe(ə)r-\ islands NE Atlantic NW of the Shetlands belonging to Denmark — **Faeroese** \ˌfar-ə-ˈwēz, ˌfer-, -ˈwēs\ adj or n

Fair·field \\ˈfa(ə)r-ˌfēld, ˈfe(ə)r-\ city SE Australia in E New South Wales

Fai·sa·la·bad \ˌfī-ˈsäl-ə-ˌbäd, -ˌsal-ə-ˈbad\ or formerly **Ly·all·pur** \lē-ˌäl-ˈpu̇(ə)r\ city NE Pakistan W of Lahore

Falk·land \\ˈfȯ(l)-klənd\ or Spanish **Is·las Mal·vi·nas** \ˌēz-läz-mäl-ˈvē-näs\ islands SW Atlantic E of S end of Argentina; a British colony; capital, Stanley

Far East the countries of E Asia & the Malay island group — usually thought to consist of the Asian countries bordering on the Pacific but sometimes including also India, Sri Lanka, Bangladesh, Tibet, & Myanmar — **Far Eastern** adj

Far·go \\ˈfär-gō\ city E North Dakota; largest in state

Fear, Cape \-ˈfi(ə)r\ cape SE North Carolina at mouth of Cape Fear river

Fer·man·agh \fər-ˈman-ə\ district SW Northern Ireland

Fernando Po — see BIOKO

Fez \\ˈfez\ city N central Morocco

Fife \\ˈfīf\ or **Fife·shire** \-ˌshi(ə)r, -shər\ region E Scotland

Fi·ji \\ˈfē-jē\ islands SW Pacific; an independent country in the Commonwealth; capital, Suva — **Fi·ji·an** \-jē-ən\ adj or n

Fin·land \\ˈfin-lənd\ country NE Europe; capital, Helsinki — **Fin·land·er** n

Flan·ders \\ˈflan-dərz\ region W Belgium & N France on North sea

Flat·tery, Cape \-ˈflat-ə-rē\ cape NW Washington at entrance to Strait of Juan de Fuca

Flint \\ˈflint\ city SE Michigan

Flor·ence \\ˈflȯr-ən(t)s, ˈflär-\ or Italian **Fi·ren·ze** \fē-ˈrent-sä\ or ancient **Flo·ren·tia** \flə-ˈren-chə, -chē-ə\ city central Italy — **Flor·en·tine** \\ˈflȯr-ən-ˌtēn, ˈflär-, -ˌtīn\ adj or n

Flor·i·da \\ˈflȯr-əd-ə, ˈflär-\ state SE U.S.; capital, Tallahassee — **Flo·rid·i·an** \flə-ˈrid-ē-ən\ or **Flor·i·dan** \\ˈflȯr-əd-ᵊn, ˈflär-\ adj or n

Florida, Straits of channel between Florida Keys on NW & Cuba & Bahamas on S & E connecting Gulf of Mexico & the Atlantic

Florida Keys chain of islands off S tip of Florida

Foochow — see FUZHOU

For·a·ker, Mount \-ˈfȯr-i-kər, -ˈfär-\ mountain 5304 meters S central Alaska in Alaska range

For·mo·sa \fȯr-ˈmō-sə, fər-, -zə\ — see TAIWAN — **For·mo·san** \-ˈmōs-ᵊn, -ˈmōz-\ adj or n

For·ta·le·za \ˌfȯrt-ᵊl-ˈä-zə\ city NE Brazil

Fort–de–France \ˌfȯrd-ə-ˈfräns\ city West Indies, capital of Martinique on W coast

Forth \\ˈfō(ə)rth, ˈfȯ(ə)rth\ river 183 kilometers long S central Scotland flowing E into North sea through **Firth of Forth**

Fort Knox \-ˈnäks\ military reservation N central Kentucky SSW of Louisville; location of U.S. Gold Bullion Depository

Fort Lau·der·dale \-ˈlȯd-ər-ˌdāl\ city SE Florida

Fort Wayne \-ˈwān\ city NE Indiana

Fort Worth \-ˈwərth\ city NE Texas

Fox \\ˈfäks\ islands SW Alaska in the E Aleutians

Foxe Basin \\ˈfäks-\ inlet of the Atlantic N Canada in E Northwest Territories W of Baffin island

France \\'fran(t)s\\ country W Europe between the English channel & the Mediterranean; capital, Paris
Frank·fort \\'fraŋk-fərt\\ city, capital of Kentucky
Frank·furt \\'fraŋk-fərt, 'fräŋ-₁fů(ə)rt\\ *or in full* **Frankfurt am Main** \\-(₁)äm-'mīn\\ *or* **Frankfort on the Main** city W Germany on Main river
Frank·lin \\'fraŋ-klən\\ former district N Canada in Northwest Territories including Arctic islands & Boothia & Melville peninsulas
Fra·ser \\'frā-zər, -zhər\\ river 1370 kilometers long Canada in S central British Columbia flowing into the Pacific
Fred·er·ic·ton \\'fred-(ə-)rik-tən\\ city, capital of New Brunswick, Canada
Free·town \\'frē-₁taůn\\ city, capital of Sierra Leone
Fre·mont \\'frē-mänt\\ city W California
French Guiana country N South America on the Atlantic; an overseas division of France; capital, Cayenne
French Indochina — see INDOCHINA
Fres·no \\'frez-nō\\ city S central California
Frunze — see BISHKEK
Fu·ji \\'f(y)ü-jē\\ *or* **Fu·ji·ya·ma** \\₁f(y)ü-jē-'(y)äm-ə\\ mountain 3776 meters Japan in S central Honshu; highest in Japan
Fu·ku·o·ka \\₁fü-kə-'wō-kə\\ city Japan in N Kyushu
Ful·ler·ton \\'fůl-ərt-ᵊn\\ city SW California
Fu·na·fu·ti \\₁f(y)ü-nə-'f(y)üt-ē\\ city, capital of Tuvalu
Fun·dy, Bay of \\-'fən-dē\\ inlet of the Atlantic SE Canada between New Brunswick & Nova Scotia
Fu·shun \\'fü-'shůn\\ city NE China E of Shenyang
Fu·zhou \\'fü-'jō\\ *or* **Foo·chow** \\'fü-'jō, -'chaů\\ city SE China
Ga·bon \\ga-'bōn\\ country W Africa on the equator; capital, Libreville — **Gab·o·nese** \\₁gab-ə-'nēz, -'nēs\\ *adj or n*
Ga·bo·rone \\₁gäb-ə-'rōn\\ city, capital of Botswana
Gads·den Purchase \\'gadz-dən-\\ area of land S of Gila river in present Arizona & New Mexico purchased 1853 by the U.S. from Mexico
Ga·la·pa·gos islands \\gə-'läp-ə-gəs, -'lap-\\ island group Ecuador in the Pacific 965 kilometers W of South America
Ga·la·tia \\gə-'lā-sh(ē-)ə\\ ancient country central Asia Minor in region around modern Ankara, Turkey — **Ga·la·tian** \\-shən\\ *adj or n*
Ga·li·cia \\gə-'lish-(ē-)ə\\ **1** region E central Europe now divided between Poland & Ukraine **2** region NW Spain on the Atlantic — **Ga·li·cian** \\-'lish-ən\\ *adj or n*
Gal·i·lee \\'gal-ə-₁lē\\ hilly region N Israel — **Gal·i·le·an** \\₁gal-ə-'lē-ən\\ *adj or n*
Galilee, Sea of *or* **Lake of Gen·nes·a·ret** \\-gə-'nəs-ə-₁ret, -rət\\ lake N Israel on Syrian border; crossed by Jordan river
Gal·lo·way \\'gal-ə-₁wā\\ district SW Scotland — see DUMFRIES AND GALLOWAY
Gam·bia \\'gam-bē-ə\\ country W Africa; capital, Banjul — **Gam·bi·an** \\-bē-ən\\ *adj or n*
Gan·ges \\'gan-₁jēz\\ river 2495 kilometers long N India flowing from the Himalayas SE & E to unite with the Brahmaputra & empty into Bay of Bengal through a vast delta — **Gan·get·ic** \\gan-'jet-ik\\ *adj*
Garden Grove city SW California
Gar·land \\'gär-lənd\\ city NE Texas
Ga·ronne \\gə-'rän, -'rōn\\ river 571 kilometers long SE France flowing NW
Gary \\'ga(ə)r-ē, 'ge(ə)r-ē\\ city NW Indiana on Lake Michigan
Gas·co·ny \\'gas-kə-nē\\ region SW France — **Gas·con** \\'gas-kən\\ *adj or n*
Gas·pé \\gas-'pā, 'gas-₁pā\\ peninsula SE Quebec E of mouth of the Saint Lawrence — **Gas·pe·sian** \\ga-'spē-zhən\\ *adj or n*
Gaul \\'gól\\ *or Latin* **Gal·lia** \\'gal-ē-ə\\ ancient country W

Europe chiefly consisting of region occupied by modern France & Belgium but at one time including also Po valley in N Italy
Ga·za Strip \\'gäz-ə-\\ district NE Sinai Peninsula on the Mediterranean
Gee·long \\jə-'lóŋ\\ city SE Australia in S Victoria
Ge·ne·va \\jə-'nē-və\\ city SW Switzerland on Lake of Geneva — **Ge·ne·van** \\-vən\\ *adj or n* — **Gen·e·vese** \\₁jen-ə-'vēz, -'vēs\\ *adj or n*
Geneva, Lake of lake on border between SW Switzerland & E France; crossed by the Rhone
Gen·oa \\'jen-ə-wə\\ *or Italian* **Ge·no·va** \\'je-nō-vä\\ city NW Italy — **Gen·o·ese** \\₁jen-ə-'wēz, -'wēs\\ *or* **Gen·o·vese** \\-ə-'vēz, -'vēs\\ *adj or n*
George·town \\'jó(ə)rj-₁taůn\\ **1** a W section of Washington, District of Columbia **2** city, capital of Guyana
Geor·gia \\'jór-jə\\ **1** state SE U.S.; capital, Atlanta **2** *or* **Republic of Georgia** country SE Europe on Black sea S of Caucasus mountains; capital, Tiflis; a republic of U.S.S.R. 1936–91 — **Georgian** *adj or n*
Georgia, Strait of channel Canada & U.S. between Vancouver Island & main part of British Columbia NW of Puget Sound
Georgian Bay inlet of Lake Huron in S Ontario
Ger·man·town \\'jər-mən-₁taůn\\ a NW section of Philadelphia, Pennsylvania
Ger·ma·ny \\'jərm-(ə-)nē\\ country central Europe bordering on North & Baltic seas; official capital, Berlin; divided 1946–90 into two independent states: the Federal Republic of Germany (capital, Bonn) & the German Democratic Republic (capital, East Berlin)
Get·tys·burg \\'get-ēz-₁bərg\\ town S Pennsylvania
Gha·na \\'gän-ə, 'gan-ə\\ *or formerly* **Gold Coast** country W Africa on Gulf of Guinea; an independent state in the Commonwealth; capital, Accra — **Gha·na·ian** \\gä-'nā-ən, ga-, -yən; -'nī-ən\\ *or* **Gha·ni·an** \\'gän-ē-ən, 'gän-yən, 'gan-\\ *adj or n*
Ghats \\'góts\\ two mountain chains S India — see EASTERN GHATS, WESTERN GHATS
Ghent \\'gent\\ city NW central Belgium
Gi·bral·tar \\jə-'bról-tər\\ British colony on S coast of Spain including Rock of Gibraltar
Gibraltar, Rock of cape on S coast of Spain in Gibraltar colony at E end of Strait of Gibraltar; highest point 426 meters
Gibraltar, Strait of passage between Spain & Africa connecting the Atlantic & the Mediterranean
Gi·la \\'hē-lə\\ river 1015 kilometers long SW New Mexico & S Arizona flowing W into the Colorado
Gil·bert and El·lice Islands \\'gil-bərt-ən(d)-'el-əs-\\ island group W Pacific; until 1976 a British colony; now divided into the independent states of Kiribati and Tuvalu
Gil·e·ad \\'gil-ē-əd\\ mountain region NE Palestine E of Jordan river; now in NW Jordan — **Gil·e·ad·ite** \\-ē-ə-₁dīt\\ *n*
Gi·za \\'gē-zə\\ city N Egypt on the Nile SW of Cairo
Gla·cier Bay \\glā-shər-\\ inlet SE Alaska at S end of Saint Elias range
Glas·gow \\'glas-kō, 'glas-gō, 'glaz-gō\\ city S central Scotland in Strathclyde region on the Clyde — **Glas·we·gian** \\glas-'wē-jən\\ *adj or n*
Glen·dale \\'glen-₁dāl\\ city S California NE of Los Angeles
Glouces·ter \\'gläs-tər, 'glós-\\ city area SW central England in Gloucestershire
Glouces·ter·shire \\'gläs-tər-₁shi(ə)r, 'glós-, -shər\\ *or* **Gloucester** county SW central England

---

\\ə\abut \\ᵊ\kitten \\ər\further \\a\ash \\ā\ace \\ä\mop, mar
\\aů\out \\ch\chin \\e\bet \\ē\easy \\g\go \\i\hit \\ī\ice \\j\job
\\ŋ\sing \\ō\go \\ó\law \\ói\boy \\th\thin \\t̲h̲\the \\ü\loot \\ů\foot
\\y\yet \\zh\vision *see also* Pronunciation Symbols page

Goa \\'gō-ə\\ district W India on Malabar coast belonging to Portugal before 1962
Goat Island island W New York in Niagara river — see NIAGARA FALLS
Go·bi \\'gō-bē\\ desert E central Asia in Mongolia & N China
Godt·haab \\'gȯt-ˌhȯb, 'gät-\\ town, capital of Greenland on SW coast
Godwin Austen — see K2
Go·lan Heights \\ˌgō-ˌlän-, -lən-\\ hilly region NE of Sea of Galilee
Gol·con·da \\gäl-'kän-də\\ ruined city central India W of Hyderabad
Gold Coast 1 — see GHANA **2** coast region W Africa on N shore of Gulf of Guinea E of Ivory Coast
Golden Gate strait W California
Good Hope, Cape of \\-ˌgu̇d-'hōp\\ cape S Republic of South Africa in SW Cape Province
Gor'kiy or **Gorky** — see NIZHNI NOVGOROD
Gram·pi·an \\'gram-pē-ən\\ **1** hills N central Scotland **2** region NE central Scotland; established 1975
Grand Banks shallow area in the W Atlantic SE of Newfoundland
Grand Canyon gorge of Colorado river NW Arizona
Grand Canyon of the Snake — see HELLS CANYON
Grande, Rio — see RIO GRANDE
Grand Rapids city SW Michigan
Great Australian Bight wide bay on S coast of Australia
Great Barrier Reef coral reef Australia off NE coast of Queensland
Great Basin region W U.S. between Sierra Nevada & Wasatch mountains including most of Nevada & parts of California, Idaho, Utah, Wyoming, and Oregon; has no drainage to ocean
Great Bear lake Canada in W Northwest Territories draining through Great Bear river into Mackenzie river
Great Brit·ain \\-'brit-ᵊn\\ **1** island W Europe NW of France consisting of England, Scotland, & Wales **2** UNITED KINGDOM
Great Dividing range mountain system E Australia & Tasmania extending S from Cape York peninsula — see KOSCIUSKO, MOUNT
Greater An·til·les \\-an-'til-ēz\\ group of islands of the West Indies including Cuba, Hispaniola, Jamaica, & Puerto Rico — see LESSER ANTILLES
Greater London county SE England consisting of City of London & 32 surrounding city areas
Greater Manchester county NW England including city of Manchester
Great Lakes chain of five lakes (Superior, Michigan, Huron, Erie, & Ontario) central North America in U.S. & Canada
Great Plains elevated plains region W central U.S. & W Canada E of the Rockies; extending from W Texas to NE British Columbia & NW Alberta
Great Rift valley \\-'rift-\\ basin SW Asia & E Africa extending with several breaks from valley of the Jordan S to central Mozambique
Great Salt lake N Utah having salty waters & no outlet
Great Slave lake NW Canada in S Northwest Territories drained by Mackenzie river
Great Smoky mountains between W North Carolina & E Tennessee; highest Clingmans Dome 2024 meters
Greece \\'grēs\\ country S Europe at S end of Balkan peninsula; capital, Athens
Green \\'grēn\\ **1** mountains E North America in the Appalachians extending from S Quebec S through Vermont into W Massachusetts **2** river 1175 kilometers long W U.S. flowing from W Wyoming S into the Colorado in SE Utah
Green Bay inlet of NW Lake Michigan 193 kilometers long in NW Michigan & NE Wisconsin
Green·land \\'grēn-lənd, -ˌland\\ island in the N Atlantic

off NE North America belonging to Denmark; capital, Godthaab
Greens·boro \\'grēnz-ˌbər-ə, -ˌbə-rə\\ city N central North Carolina
Green·wich \\'grin-ij, 'gren-, -ich\\ city area of SE Greater London county, England
Green·wich Village \\gren-ich-, ˌgrin-, -ij-\\ section of New York City in Manhattan on lower W side
Gre·na·da \\grə-'nād-ə\\ island West Indies in S Windward Islands; an independent country; capital, Saint George's
Gua·da·la·ja·ra \\ˌgwäd-ə-lə-'här-ə\\ city W central Mexico
Gua·dal·ca·nal \\ˌgwäd-ᵊl-kə-'nal, ˌgwäd-ə-kə-\\ island W Pacific in the SE Solomons
Gua·dal·qui·vir \\ˌgwäd-ᵊl-'kwiv-ər, -ki-'vi(ə)r\\ river 602 kilometers long S Spain flowing into the Atlantic
Gua·de·loupe \\'gwäd-ᵊl-ˌüp\\ two islands separated by a narrow channel in West Indies in central Leeward Islands; an overseas division of France
Gua·lla·ti·ri \\ˌgwä-yə-'tir-ē, ˌgwī-ə-\\ volcano 6060 meters N Chile; highest volcano in world
Guam \\'gwäm\\ island W Pacific in S Marianas belonging to U.S.; capital, Agana — **Gua·ma·ni·an** \\gwä-'mä-nē-ən\\ adj or n
Gua·na·ba·ra Bay \\ˌgwän-ə-'bar-ə, -'bär-\\ inlet of the Atlantic SE Brazil on which city of Rio de Janeiro is located
Guang·zhou \\'gwäŋ-'jō\\ or **Can·ton** \\'kan-ˌtän, kan-'\\ city SE China
Guan·tá·na·mo Bay \\gwän-'tän-ə-ˌmō\\ inlet of the Caribbean in SE Cuba; site of U.S. naval station
Gua·te·ma·la \\ˌgwät-ə-'mäl-ə\\ **1** country Central America **2** or **Guatemala City** city, its capital — **Gua·te·ma·lan** \\-'mäl-ən\\ adj or n
Gua·ya·quil \\ˌgwī-ə-'kē(ə)l, -'kil\\ city W Ecuador
Guern·sey \\'gərn-zē\\ island in English channel — see CHANNEL
Gui·a·na \\gē-'an-ə, -'än-ə; gī-'an-ə\\ region N South America on the Atlantic; includes Guyana, French Guiana, Suriname, & nearby parts of Brazil & Venezuela — **Gui·a·nan** \\-ən\\ adj or n
Guin·ea \\'gin-ē\\ **1** region W Africa on the Atlantic extending along coast from Gambia to Angola **2** country W Africa N of Sierra Leone & Liberia; capital, Conakry — **Guin·ean** \\'gin-ē-ən\\ adj or n
Guinea, Gulf of arm of the Atlantic W central Africa
Guin·ea–Bis·sau \\ˌgin-ē-bis-'au̇\\ country W Africa; an independent state since 1974; capital, Bissau
Gui·yang \\'gwē-'yäŋ\\ or **Kuei–yang** \\'gwā-'yäŋ\\ city S China
Gulf States states of U.S. bordering on Gulf of Mexico: Florida, Alabama, Mississippi, Louisiana, and Texas
Gulf Stream warm current of the Atlantic ocean flowing from Gulf of Mexico NE along coast of U.S. to Nantucket island and from there eastward
Guy·ana \\gī-'an-ə\\ or formerly **British Guiana** country N South America on the Atlantic; an independent state in the Commonwealth since 1970; capital, Georgetown
Gwent \\'gwent\\ county SE Wales; established 1974
Gwyn·edd \\'gwin-eth\\ county NW Wales; established 1974
Hack·ney \\'hak-nē\\ city area of N Greater London county, England
Hague, The \\thə-'hāg\\ city SW Netherlands; a capital of the Netherlands
Haidarabad — see HYDERABAD
Hai·kou \\'hī-'kō\\ city SE China
Hai·ti \\'hāt-ē\\ **1** — see HISPANIOLA **2** country West Indies in W Hispaniola; capital, Port-au-Prince — **Hai·tian** \\'hā-shən\\ adj or n
Ha·le·a·ka·la Crater \\ˌhäl-ē-ˌäk-ə-'lä\\ crater 829 meters

deep & 32 kilometers in circumference Hawaii in E Maui Island

Hal·i·fax \'hal-ə-ˌfaks\ city, capital of Nova Scotia, Canada

Ham·burg \'ham-ˌbərg, 'häm-ˌbu̇(ə)rg\ city N Germany on the Elbe — **Ham·burg·er** \-ˌbər-gər, -ˌbu̇r-\ n

Ham·il·ton \'ham-əl-tən, -əlt-ᵊn\ **1** city S Ontario, Canada **2** town, capital of Bermuda

Ham·mer·smith \'ham-ər-ˌsmith\ city area of SW Greater London county, England

Hamp·shire \'ham(p)-ˌshi(ə)r, -shər\ county S England on English channel

Hamp·ton \'ham(p)-tən\ city SE Virginia

Hampton Roads channel SE Virginia through which James river flows into Chesapeake Bay

Hang·zhou \'häŋ-'jō\ or **Hang·chow** \'haŋ-'chau̇, 'häŋ-'jō\ or **Hang–chou** \'häŋ-'jō\ city E China

Han·ni·bal \'han-ə-bəl\ city NE Missouri on the Mississippi river

Han·no·ver or **Han·o·ver** \'han-ˌō-vər, 'han-ə-vər; German hä-'nō-vər\ city N central Germany

Ha·noi \ha-'nȯi, hə-, hä-\ city, capital of Vietnam

Ha·ra·re \hə-'rä-rā\ or formerly **Salis·bury** \'sȯlz-ˌber-ē, -b(ə-)rē\ city, capital of Zimbabwe

Har·bin \'här-bən, här-'bin\ or **Ha–erh–pin** \'hä-'er-'bin\ city NE China

Har·in·gey \'har-iŋ-ˌgā\ city area of N Greater London county, England

Har·lem \'här-ləm\ section of New York City in N Manhattan

Har·ris·burg \'har-əs-ˌbərg\ city, capital of Pennsylvania

Har·row \'har-ō\ city area of NW Greater London county, England

Hart·ford \'härt-fərd\ city, capital of Connecticut

Hat·ter·as, Cape \-'hat-ə-rəs, -'ha-trəs\ cape, North Carolina on Cape Hatteras Island

Ha·vana \hə-'van-ə\ city, capital of Cuba

Hav·ant and **Wa·ter·loo** \'hav-ənt-ᵊn-ˌwȯt-ər-'lü, -ˌwät-\ town S England in Hampshire

Ha·ver·ing \'hāv-(ə-)riŋ\ city area of NE Greater London county, England

Ha·waii \hə-'wä-(y)ē, -'wī-, -'wȯ-\ **1** or **Ha·wai·ian Is·lands** or formerly **Sand·wich islands** \ˌsan-(ˌ)dwich-\ group of islands central Pacific belonging to U.S. **2** island, largest of the group **3** state of U.S. consisting of Hawaiian Islands except Midway; capital, Honolulu

Heb·ri·des \'heb-rə-ˌdēz\ islands W Scotland in the Atlantic consisting of **Outer Hebrides** (to W) and **Inner Hebrides** (to E) — see WESTERN ISLES — **Heb·ri·de·an** \ˌheb-rə-'dē-ən\ adj or n

Hel·e·na \'hel-ə-nə\ city, capital of Montana

Hellespont — see DARDANELLES

Hells Canyon \'helz-\ or **Grand Canyon of the Snake** canyon of Snake river on Idaho-Oregon boundary

Hel·sin·ki \'hel-ˌsiŋ-kē, hel-'siŋ-\ city, capital of Finland

Henry, Cape \-'hen-rē\ cape E Virginia S of entrance to Chesapeake Bay

Her·e·ford and Wor·ces·ter \'her-ə-fərd-ᵊn-'wu̇s-tər, in the U.S. also 'hər-fərd-\ county W England bordering on Wales

Hert·ford·shire \'här-fərd-ˌshi(ə)r, -shər, also 'härt-, in the U.S. also 'hərt-\ or **Hertford** county SE England

Hi·a·le·ah \ˌhī-ə-'lē-ə\ city SE Florida

Hi·ber·nia \hī-'bər-nē-ə\ — see IRELAND — **Hi·ber·ni·an** \-ən\ adj or n

Hi·ga·shi·ōsa·ka \hē-ˌgä-shē-ō-'säk-ə\ city Japan in S Honshu E of Osaka

High·land \'hī-lənd\ region NW Scotland

High·lands \'hī-lən(d)z\ the mountainous N part of Scotland lying N & W of the Lowlands

High Plains the Great Plains especially from Nebraska southward

Hil·ling·don \'hil-iŋ-dən\ city area of W Greater London county, England

Hi·ma·la·ya \ˌhim-ə-'lā-ə, hə-'mäl-(ə-)yə\ mountain system S Asia on border between India & Tibet & in Kashmir, Nepal, & Bhutan — see EVEREST, MOUNT — **Hi·ma·la·yan** \ˌhim-ə-'lā-ən, hə-'mäl-(ə-)yən\ adj

Hin·du Kush \ˌhin-(ˌ)dü-'ku̇sh, -'kəsh\ mountain range central Asia SW of the Pamirs on border of Kashmir & in Afghanistan

Hin·du·stan \ˌhin-(ˌ)dü-'stan, -də-, -'stän\ **1** region N India **2** the subcontinent of India **3** the country of India

Hi·ro·shi·ma \ˌhir-ə-'shē-mə, hə-'rō-shə-mə\ city Japan in SW Honshu on Inland sea

His·pan·io·la \ˌhis-pən-'yō-lə\ or Spanish **Es·pa·ño·la** \ˌes-ˌpän-'yō-lə\ or formerly **Hai·ti** \'hāt-ē\ island West Indies in Greater Antilles divided between Haiti on W & Dominican Republic on E

Ho·bart \'hō-ˌbärt\ city Australia, capital of Tasmania

Ho Chi Minh City \ˌhō-ˌchē-ˌmin-, -ˌshē-\ or formerly **Sai·gon** \sī-'gän, 'sī-ˌgän\ city S Vietnam

Hoh·hot \'hō-'hōt\ or **Hu·he·hot** \'hü-ˌhä-'hōt\ city N China, capital of Inner Mongolia

Hok·kai·do \hä-'kīd-ō\ island N Japan N of Honshu

Hol·land \'häl-ənd\ **1** county of Holy Roman Empire bordering on North sea & consisting of area now forming part of W Netherlands **2** — see NETHERLANDS — **Hol·land·er** \-ən-dər\ n

Hol·ly·wood \'häl-ē-ˌwu̇d\ **1** section of Los Angeles, California, NW of downtown district **2** city SE Florida

Holy Land PALESTINE

Holy Roman Empire empire consisting mainly of German and Italian territories and existing from the 9th or 10th century to 1806

Hon·du·ras \hän-'d(y)u̇r-əs\ country Central America; capital, Tegucigalpa — **Hon·du·ran** \-ən\ or **Hon·du·ra·ne·an** or **Hon·du·ra·ni·an** \ˌhän-d(y)ü-'rā-nē-ən\ adj or n

Hong Kong \'häŋ-ˌkäŋ, -'käŋ; 'hȯŋ-ˌkȯŋ, -'kȯŋ\ British colony on coast of SE China including Hong Kong Island & Kowloon peninsula; capital, Victoria

Ho·ni·a·ra \ˌhō-nē-'är-ə\ town, capital of Solomon Islands

Ho·no·lu·lu \ˌhän-ᵊl-'ü-lü, ˌhōn-ᵊl-\ city, capital of Hawaii on Oahu Island

Hon·shu \'hän-shü\ or **Hon·do** \'hän-dō\ island Japan; largest of the four chief islands

Hood, Mount \-'hu̇d\ mountain 3424 meters NW Oregon in Cascade Range

Hoo·ghly or **Hu·gli** \'hü-glē\ river 193 kilometers long E India flowing S into Bay of Bengal; most westerly channel of the Ganges in its delta

Hoo·ver Dam \ˌhü-vər-\ or **Boul·der Dam** \ˌbōl-dər-\ dam 221 meters high in Colorado river between Arizona & Nevada — see MEAD, LAKE

Horn, Cape \-'hȯ(ə)rn\ cape S Chile on an island in Tierra del Fuego; the most southerly point of South America at 55°59′ S latitude

Horseshoe Falls — see NIAGARA FALLS

Houns·low \'hau̇nz-ˌlō\ city area of SW Greater London county, England

Hous·ton \'(h)yü-stən\ city SE Texas

How·rah \'hau̇-rə\ city E India on Hooghly river opposite Calcutta

Huang or **Hwang** \'hwäŋ\ or **Yellow** river 4830 kilometers long N China flowing into Bo Hai

Hud·ders·field \'həd-ərz-ˌfēld\ city area N England in West Yorkshire NE of Manchester

Hud·son \'həd-sən\ **1** river 492 kilometers long E New

\ə\abut \ᵊ\kitten \ər\further \a\ash \ā\ace \ä\mop, mar
\au̇\out \ch\chin \e\bet \ē\easy \g\go \i\hit \ī\ice \j\job
\ŋ\sing \ō\go \ȯ\law \ȯi\boy \th\thin \th̲\the \ü\loot \u̇\foot
\y\yet \zh\vision *see also* Pronunciation Symbols page

York flowing S **2** bay inlet of the Atlantic in N Canada **3** strait NE Canada connecting Hudson bay & the Atlantic

Huhehot — see HOHHOT

Hull \'həl\ or **Kings·ton upon Hull** \'kiŋ(k)-stən-\ city N England in Humberside county

Hum·ber·side \'həm-bər-ˌsīd\ county E England

Hun·ga·ry \'həŋ-g(ə-)rē\ country central Europe; capital, Budapest

Hunt·ing·ton Beach \'hənt-iŋ-tən-\ city SW California

Hunts·ville \'hən(t)s-ˌvil, -vəl\ city N Alabama

Hu·ron, Lake \-ˈ(h)yùr-ən, -ˈ(h)yù(ə)r-ˌän\ lake E central North America in U.S. & Canada; one of the Great Lakes

Hy·der·abad \'hīd-(ə-)rə-ˌbad, -ˌbäd\ **1** or **Hai·dar·abad** city S central India **2** city SE Pakistan on the Indus

Iba·dan \i-ˈbäd-ᵊn, -ˈbad-\ city SW Nigeria

Ibe·ri·an \ī-ˈbir-ē-ən\ peninsula SW Europe occupied by Spain & Portugal

Ice·land \'ī-slənd, -ˌsland\ island SE of Greenland between Arctic & Atlantic oceans; capital, Reykjavik — **Ice·land·er** \-ˌslan-dər, -slən-dər\ n

Ida·ho \'īd-ə-ˌhō\ state NW U.S.; capital, Boise — **Ida·ho·an** \ˌīd-ə-ˈhō-ən\ adj or n

Igua·çu or Spanish **Igua·zú** \ˌē-gwə-ˈsü\ river 612 kilometers long S Brazil flowing W

IJs·sel or **Ijs·sel** \'ī-səl\ river 113 kilometers long E Netherlands flowing out of Rhine N into IJsselmeer

IJs·sel·meer \'ī-səl-ˈme(ə)r\ or **Lake Ijs·sel** freshwater lake N Netherlands separated from North sea by a dike; part of former Zuider Zee (inlet of North sea)

Ilium or **Ilion** — see TROY

Il·li·nois \ˌil-ə-ˈnȯi also -ˈnȯiz\ state N central U.S.; capital, Springfield — **Il·li·nois·an** \-ˈnȯi-ən, -ˈnȯiz-ᵊn\ adj or n

Il·lyr·ia \il-ˈir-ē-ə\ ancient country S Europe and Balkan peninsula on the Adriatic — **Il·lyr·i·an** \-ē-ən\ adj or n

Im·pe·ri·al Valley \im-ˈpir-ē-əl-\ valley SE corner of California & partly in Baja California, Mexico

In·chon \'in-ˌchän\ city South Korea on Yellow sea

In·de·pen·dence \ˌin-də-ˈpen-dən(t)s\ city W Missouri E of Kansas City

In·dia \'in-dē-ə\ **1** subcontinent S Asia S of the Himalayas between Bay of Bengal & Arabian sea **2** or **Bha·rat** \'bər-ət, ˈbə-rət\ country consisting of major portion of the subcontinent; an independent state in the Commonwealth; capital, New Delhi **3** or **Indian Empire** before 1947 those parts of the Indian subcontinent under British rule or protection

In·di·an \'in-dē-ən\ ocean E of Africa, S of Asia, W of Australia, & N of Antarctica

In·di·ana \ˌin-dē-ˈan-ə\ state E central U.S.; capital, Indianapolis — **In·di·an·an** \-ˈan-ən\ or **In·di·an·i·an** \-ˈan-ē-ən\ adj or n

In·di·a·nap·o·lis \ˌin-dē-ə-ˈnap-(ə-)ləs\ city, capital of Indiana

Indian river lagoon 266 kilometers long E Florida between main part of the state & coastal islands

Indian Territory former territory S U.S. in present state of Oklahoma

In·dies \'in-dēz\ **1** EAST INDIES **2** WEST INDIES

In·do·chi·na \'in-(ˌ)dō-ˈchī-nə\ **1** peninsula SE Asia including Myanmar, Malay peninsula, Thailand, Cambodia, Laos, & Vietnam **2** or **French Indochina** former country SE Asia consisting of area now forming Cambodia, Laos, & Vietnam — **In·do–Chi·nese** \-chī-ˈnēz, -ˈnēs\ adj or n

In·do·ne·sia \ˌin-də-ˈnē-zhə, -shə\ country SE Asia in Malay island group consisting of Sumatra, Java, S & E Borneo, Sulawesi, W New Guinea, & many smaller islands; capital, Jakarta — see NETHERLANDS EAST INDIES — **In·do·ne·sian** \-zhən, -shən\ adj or n

In·dore \in-ˈdō(ə)r, -ˈdȯ(ə)r\ city W central India

In·dus \'in-dəs\ river 2900 kilometers long S Asia flowing from Tibet NW & SSW through Pakistan into Arabian sea

In·gle·wood \'iŋ-gəl-ˌwùd\ city SW California

In·land \'in-ˌland, -lənd\ sea inlet of the Pacific in SW Japan between Honshu on N and Shikoku and Kyushu on S

Inner Hebrides — see HEBRIDES

Inner Mon·go·lia \-män-ˈgōl-yə, mäŋ-, -ˈgō-lē-ə\ region N China

Inside Passage or **Inland Passage** protected shipping route between Puget Sound, Washington, & Skagway, Alaska

In·ver·ness \ˌin-vər-ˈnes\ town NW Scotland in Highland region

Io·ni·an \ī-ˈō-nē-ən\ **1** sea arm of the Mediterranean between SE Italy & W Greece **2** islands W Greece in Ionian sea

Io·wa \'ī-ə-wə\ state N central U.S.; capital, Des Moines — **Io·wan** \-wən\ adj or n

Ips·wich \'ip-(ˌ)swich\ city area SE England in Suffolk county

Iran \i-ˈrän, -ˈran; ī-ˈran\ or formerly **Per·sia** \'pər-zhə\ country SW Asia; capital, Tehran — **Irani** \i-ˈrän-ē, -ˈran-\ adj or n — **Ira·nian** \ir-ˈā-nē-ən, -ˈan-ē-, -ˈän-ē-\ adj or n

Iraq \i-ˈräk, -ˈrak\ country SW Asia in Mesopotamia; capital, Baghdad — **Iraqi** \-ˈräk-ē, -ˈrak-\ adj or n

Ire·land \'ī(ə)r-lənd\ **1** or Latin **Hi·ber·nia** \hī-ˈbər-nē-ə\ island W Europe in the Atlantic; one of the British Isles **2** or **Irish Republic** or **Ei·re** \'ar-ə, ˈar-ē, ˈer-, ˈār-, ˈir-\ country occupying major portion of the island; capital, Dublin

Irish sea \'īr-ish-\ arm of the Atlantic between Great Britain & Ireland

Ir·kutsk \i(ə)r-ˈkütsk, ˌər-\ city S Russia near Lake Baikal

Ir·ra·wad·dy \ˌir-ə-ˈwäd-ē\ river 2175 kilometers long Myanmar flowing S into Bay of Bengal

Ir·tysh \i(ə)r-ˈtish, ˌər-\ river 3540 kilometers long central Asia flowing NW & N from Altai mountains in China, through Kazakhstan, and into W central Russia

Ir·ving \'ər-viŋ\ city NE Texas NW of Dallas

Is·fa·han \ˌis-fə-ˈhän, -ˈhan\ or formerly **Is·pa·han** \ˌis-pə-\ city W central Iran

Is·lam·abad \is-ˈläm-ə-ˌbäd, iz-ˈlam-ə-ˌbad\ city, capital of Pakistan

Isle of Man — see MAN, ISLE OF

Isle of Wight \-ˈwīt\ island and county S England in English channel

Isle Roy·ale \(ˈ)ī(ə)l-ˈrȯi(-ə)l\ island Michigan in Lake Superior

Isles of Scilly — see CORNWALL AND ISLES OF SCILLY; SCILLY

Is·ling·ton \'iz-liŋ-tən\ city area of N Greater London county, England

Is·ra·el \'iz-rē-əl, -rā-əl, -rəl\ **1** ancient kingdom Palestine consisting of lands occupied by the Hebrew people **2** or **Ephra·im** \'ē-frē-əm\ the N part of the Hebrew kingdom after about 933 B.C. **3** country SW Asia in Palestine; established 1948; capital, Jerusalem — **Is·rae·li** \iz-ˈrā-lē\ adj or n

Is·tan·bul \ˌis-təm-ˈbül, -ˌtäm-, -ˌtam-, -ˌtän-\ or formerly **Con·stan·ti·no·ple** \ˌkän-ˌstant-ᵊn-ˈō-pəl\ city NW Turkey on the Bosporus & Sea of Marmara; former capital of Turkey

Is·tria \'is-trē-ə\ peninsula in Croatia & Slovenia extending into the N Adriatic — **Is·tri·an** \-trē-ən\ adj or n

It·a·ly \'it-ᵊl-ē\ **1** peninsula 1225 kilometers long S Europe extending into the Mediterranean between Adriatic & Tyrrhenian seas **2** country including the peninsula of Italy, Sicily, & Sardinia; capital, Rome

Itas·ca, Lake \-ī-ˈtas-kə\ lake NW central Minnesota; source of the Mississippi

Ivory Coast country W Africa on Gulf of Guinea; capital, Abidjan

Iwo Ji·ma \ˌē-(ˌ)wō-ˈjē-mə\ island Japan in W Pacific about 1130 kilometers SSE of Tokyo

Ix·ta·pa·la·pa \ˌē-stə-pə-ˈläp-ə\ city S central Mexico SE of Mexico City

Izhevsk \ˈē-ˌzhefsk\ or 1985-87 **Usti·nov** \ˈüs-ti-ˌnóf, -ˌnóv\ city W Russia

Iz·mir \iz-ˈmi(ə)r\ or formerly **Smyr·na** \ˈsmər-nə\ city W Turkey

Jack·son \ˈjak-sən\ city, capital of Mississippi

Jack·son·ville \ˈjak-sən-ˌvil\ city NE Florida

Jai·pur \ˈjī-ˌpu̇(ə)r\ city NW India

Jakarta or **Dja·kar·ta** \jə-ˈkärt-ə\ city, capital of Indonesia in NW Java

Ja·mai·ca \jə-ˈmā-kə\ island West Indies in Greater Antilles; an independent country in the Commonwealth; capital, Kingston — **Ja·mai·can** \-kən\ adj or n

James \ˈjāmz\ 1 river 1145 kilometers long North Dakota and South Dakota flowing S into the Missouri 2 river 550 kilometers long Virginia flowing E into Chesapeake Bay

James Bay the S extension of Hudson bay between NE Ontario & W Quebec

James·town \ˈjām-ˌstȧun\ ruined village E Virginia on James river; first permanent English settlement in America (1607)

Jam·shed·pur \ˈjäm-ˌshed-ˌpu̇(ə)r\ city E India

Ja·pan \jə-ˈpan, ji-, ja-\ or Japanese **Nip·pon** \nip-ˈän\ country E Asia consisting of Honshu, Hokkaido, Kyushu, Shikoku, & other islands in the W Pacific; capital, Tokyo

Japan, Sea of arm of the Pacific between Japan & main part of Asia

Ja·va \ˈjäv-ə, ˈjav-ə\ island Indonesia SW of Borneo; chief city, Jakarta — **Ja·van** \-ən\ adj or n

Jef·fer·son City \ˈjef-ər-sən-\ city, capital of Missouri

Jer·sey \ˈjər-zē\ island in English channel — see CHANNEL — **Jer·sey·ite** \-zē-ˌīt\ n

Jersey City city NE New Jersey on Hudson river

Je·ru·sa·lem \jə-ˈrü-s(ə-)ləm, -ˈrüz-(ə-)ləm\ city NW of Dead sea divided 1948–67 between Israel & Jordan; capital of Israel since 1950 & formerly of ancient kingdom of Israel

Jid·da \ˈjid-ə\ city W Saudi Arabia on Red sea

Ji·lin \ˈjē-ˈlin\ or **Ki·rin** \ˈkē-ˈrin\ city NE China

Ji·nan or **Tsi·nan** \ˈjē-ˈnän\ city E China

Jin·zhou or **Chin–chou** or **Chin·chow** \ˈjin-ˈjō\ city NE China

Jo·han·nes·burg \jō-ˈhan-əs-ˌbərg, -ˈhän-\ city NE Republic of South Africa in S Transvaal province

Jor·dan \ˈjȯrd-ᵊn\ 1 river 320 kilometers long Israel & Jordan flowing S from Syria into Dead sea 2 country SW Asia in NW Arabia; capital, Amman — **Jor·da·ni·an** \jȯr-ˈdā-nē-ən\ adj or n

Juan de Fu·ca, Strait of \-ˌ(h)wän-də-ˈfyü-kə\ strait 160 kilometers long between Vancouver Island, British Columbia, & Olympic peninsula, Washington

Ju·dea or **Ju·daea** \ju̇-ˈdē-ə, -ˈdā-\ ancient region Palestine forming the S division (Judah) of the country under Persian, Greek, & Roman rule — **Ju·dean** \-ən\ adj or n

Ju·go·sla·via \ˌyü-gō-ˈsläv-ē-ə\ — see YUGOSLAVIA — **Ju·go·slav** \ˌyü-gō-ˈsläv, -ˈslav\ or **Ju·go·sla·vi·an** \-ˈsläv-ē-ən\ adj or n

Ju·neau \ˈjü-nō, jü-ˈnō\ city, capital of Alaska

Ju·ra \ˈju̇r-ə\ mountain range extending along boundary between France & Switzerland N of Lake of Geneva

Jut·land \ˈjət-lənd\ 1 peninsula N Europe extending into North sea & consisting of main part of Denmark & N portion of Germany 2 the main part of Denmark

Ka·bul \ˈkäb-əl, kä-ˈbül\ city, capital of Afghanistan

Ka Lae \kä-ˈlä-ä\ or **South Cape** or **South Point** most southerly point of Hawaii & of U.S.

Kal·a·ha·ri \ˌkal-ə-ˈhär-ē\ desert region S Africa N of Orange river in S Botswana & NW Republic of South Africa

Kalgan — see ZHANGJIAKOU

Ka·li·man·tan \ˌkal-ə-ˈman-ˌtan, ˌkäl-ə-ˈmän-ˌtän\ 1 BORNEO — its Indonesian name 2 the S & E portion of Borneo belonging to Indonesia; formerly part of Netherlands East Indies

Kam·chat·ka \kam-ˈchat-kə\ peninsula 1205 kilometers long E Russia

Kam·pa·la \käm-ˈpäl-ə\ city, capital of Uganda

Kampuchea — see CAMBODIA

Ka·no \ˈkän-ō\ city N central Nigeria

Kan·pur \ˈkän-ˌpu̇(ə)r\ city N India on the Ganges

Kan·sas \ˈkan-zəs\ state W central U.S.; capital, Topeka — **Kan·san** \-zən\ adj or n

Kansas City 1 city NE Kansas bordering on Kansas City, Missouri 2 city W Missouri

Kao·hsiung \ˈkau̇-shē-ˈu̇ŋ, ˈgau̇-\ city China in SW Taiwan

Ka·ra·chi \kə-ˈräch-ē\ city S Pakistan on Arabian sea

Ka·ra·gan·da \ˌkar-ə-gən-ˈdä\ city central Kazakhstan

Ka·re·lia \kə-ˈrē-lē-ə, -ˈrēl-yə\ region NE Europe in Finland & Russia — **Ka·re·lian** \-ˈrē-lē-ən, -ˈrēl-yən\ adj or n

Kar·roo \kə-ˈrü\ plateau region W Republic of South Africa W of Drakensberg mountains

Kash·mir \ˈkash-ˌmi(ə)r, ˈkazh-, kash-ˈmi(ə)r, kazh-ˈmi(ə)r\ region and former state N Indian subcontinent — **Kash·miri** \kash-ˈmi(ə)r-ē, kazh-\ adj or n

Ka·thi·a·war \ˌkät-ē-ə-ˈwär\ peninsula W India N of Gulf of Cambay

Kath·man·du or **Kat·man·du** \ˌkat-ˌman-ˈdü\ city, capital of Nepal

Kat·mai, Mount \-ˈkat-ˌmī\ volcano 2047 meters S Alaska on Alaska peninsula

Kat·te·gat \ˈkat-i-ˌgat\ arm of North sea between Sweden & E coast of Jutland peninsula of Denmark

Kau·ai \ˈkau̇-ˌī\ island Hawaii NW of Oahu

Ka·wa·sa·ki \ˌkä-wə-ˈsäk-ē\ city Japan in E Honshu S of Tokyo

Ka·zakh·stan \kə-ˌzak-ˈstan; kə-ˌzäk-ˈstän, ˌkä-\ country NW central Asia; capital, Alma-Ata; a republic (**Kazakh Soviet Socialist Republic** \kə-ˌzak-, -ˌzäk-\) of U.S.S.R. 1936–91

Ka·zan \kə-ˈzan, -ˈzän(-yə)\ city W Russia

Kee·wa·tin \kē-ˈwät-ᵊn\ former district N Canada in E Northwest Territories NW of Hudson bay

Ke·me·ro·vo \ˈkem-ə-rə-və, -ˌrō-və, -rə-ˌvō\ city S central Russia

Ke·nai \ˈkē-ˌnī\ peninsula S Alaska E of Cook inlet

Kennedy, Cape — see CANAVERAL, CAPE

Ken·sing·ton and Chel·sea \ˈken-ziŋ-tən-ən-ˈchel-sē, ˈken(t)-siŋ-\ city area of W Greater London county, England

Kent \ˈkent\ county SE England — **Kent·ish** \ˈkent-ish\ adj

Ken·tucky \kən-ˈtək-ē\ state E central U.S.; capital, Frankfort — **Ken·tuck·i·an** \-ē-ən\ adj or n

Ken·ya \ˈken-yə, ˈkēn-\ 1 mountain 5194 meters central Kenya 2 country E Africa S of Ethiopia; capital, Nairobi — **Ken·yan** \-yən\ adj or n

Key West \ˈkē-ˈwest\ city SW Florida on Key West island

Kha·ba·rovsk \kə-ˈbär-əfsk\ city SE Russia

Khar·kov \ˈkär-ˌkȯf, -ˌkȯv, -kəf\ city NE Ukraine

\ə\abut \ᵊ\kitten \ər\further \a\ash \ā\ace \ä\mop, mar
\au̇\out \ch\chin \e\bet \ē\easy \g\go \i\hit \ī\ice \j\job
\ŋ\sing \ō\go \ȯ\law \ȯi\boy \th\thin \t̲h̲\the \ü\loot \u̇\foot
\y\yet \zh\vision see also Pronunciation Symbols page

Khar·toum \kär-'tüm\ city, capital of Sudan

Khmer Republic — see CAMBODIA

Khy·ber \'kī-bər\ pass 53 kilometers long on border between Afghanistan & Pakistan

Ki·bo \'kē-bō\ mountain peak 5888 meters NE Tanzania; highest peak of Kilimanjaro & highest point in Africa

Kiel \'kē(ə)l\ canal 98 kilometers long N Germany across base of Jutland peninsula connecting Baltic sea & North sea

Ki·ev or Russian **Ki·yev** \'kē-₁(y)ef, -(y)ev, -(y)əf\ city, capital of Ukraine

Ki·ga·li \ki-'gäl-ē\ city, capital of Rwanda

Ki·lau·ea \₁kē-₁laủ-'ā-ə\ volcanic crater Hawaii on Hawaii island on E slope of Mauna Loa

Kil·i·man·ja·ro \₁kil-ə-mən-'jär-ō, -'jar-\ mountain NE Tanzania; highest in Africa — see KIBO

Kil·lar·ney, Lakes of \-kil-'är-nē\ three lakes SW Ireland

Kings·ton \'kiŋ-stən\ city, capital of Jamaica

Kingston upon Hull — see HULL

Kingston upon Thames \-'temz\ city area of SW Greater London county, England

Kings·town \'kiŋ-₁staủn\ seaport, capital of Saint Vincent and the Grenadines

Kin·sha·sa \kin-'shäs-ə\ city, capital of Zaire

Kirgiz Republic or **Kirghiz Republic** or **Kirghizia** — see KYRGYZSTAN

Ki·ri·bati \'kir-ə-₁bas\ island group W Pacific; an independent country; capital, Tarawa

Kirin — see JILIN

Kirk·wall \'kər-₁kwȯl\ town and port N Scotland in Orkney region

Ki·shi·nev \'kish-ə-₁nef, -nev\ city central Moldova; its capital

Ki·ta·kyu·shu \kē-'tä-kē-'ü-shü\ city Japan in N Kyushu

Kitch·e·ner \'kich-(ə-)nər\ city SE Ontario, Canada

Kit·ty Hawk \'kit-ē-₁hȯk\ village E North Carolina

Klon·dike \'klän-₁dīk\ region NW Canada in central Yukon Territory in valley of Klondike river

Knox·ville \'näks-₁vil, -vəl\ city E Tennessee

Ko·be \'kō-bē, -₁bā\ city Japan in S Honshu

Ko·di·ak \'kōd-ē-₁ak\ island S Alaska E of Alaska peninsula

Ko·la \'kō-lə\ peninsula NW Russia

Ko·rea \kə-'rē-ə, especially South kō-\ country E Asia between Yellow sea & Sea of Japan; capital, Seoul; divided after World War II at 38th parallel of latitude into independent countries of **North Korea** (capital, Pyongyang) & **South Korea** (capital, Seoul)

Kos·ci·us·ko, Mount \-₁käz-ē-'əs-kō\ mountain 2230 meters SE Australia in SE New South Wales; highest in Greater Dividing range & in Australia

Kow·loon \'kaủ-'lün\ **1** peninsula SE China in Hong Kong colony opposite Hong Kong island **2** city on Kowloon peninsula

Krak·a·toa \₁krak-ə-'tō-ə\ or **Krak·a·tau** \-'taủ\ island & volcano Indonesia between Sumatra & Java

Kra·kow \'kräk-₁aủ, 'krak-, 'kräk-, -ō, Polish 'kräk-₁üf\ city S Poland

Kras·no·dar \'kras-nə-₁där\ city SW Russia

Kras·no·yarsk \₁kras-nə-'yärsk\ city S central Russia

Kri·voy Rog \₁kriv-₁ȯi-'rȯg, -'rȯk\ city SE central Ukraine

K2 \'kā-'tü\ or **God·win Aus·ten** \₁gäd-wə-'nȯs-tən, -'näs-tən\ mountain 8611 meters N Kashmir in Karakoram range; second highest in the world

Kua·la Lum·pur \₁kwäl-ə-'lüm-₁pủ(ə)r, -'ləm-\ city, capital of Malaysia

Kuei-yang — see GUIYANG

Kun·lun \'kün-lün\ mountain system W China extending E from the Pamirs; highest peak Ulugh Muztagh 7724 meters

Kun·ming \'kün-'miŋ\ city S China

Kur·di·stan \₁kủr-də-'stan, ₁kər-, -'stän; 'kər-də-₁\ region SW Asia chiefly in E Turkey, NW Iran, & N Iraq

Ku·ril or **Ku·rile** \'kyủr-₁ēl, 'kủr-; kyủ-'rē(ə)l, kủ-\ islands Russia in W Pacific between Kamchatka peninsula & Hokkaido island

Ku·wait \kə-'wāt\ **1** country SW Asia in Arabia at head of Persian gulf **2** city, its capital — **Ku·waiti** \-'wāt-ē\ adj or n

Kuybyshev — see SAMARA

Kuz·netsk basin \kủz-'netsk-\ or **Kuz·bass** or **Kuz·bas** \'kủz-₁bas\ basin S central Russia

Kwa·ja·lein \'kwäj-ə-lən, -₁lān\ island W Pacific in Marshall islands

Kwang·ju \'gwäŋ-jü, 'kwäŋ-\ city SW South Korea

Kyo·to \kē-'ōt-ō\ city Japan in W central Honshu; formerly capital of Japan

Kyr·gyz·stan \₁kir-gi-'stan, -'stän; 'kir-gi-₁\ country W central Asia; capital, Bishkek; a republic (**Kir·giz Republic** or **Kir·ghiz Republic** \(₁)kir-'gēz-\ or **Kir·ghizia** \kir-'gē-zh(ē-)ə, -zē-ə\ of U.S.S.R. 1936–91

Kyu·shu \kē-'ü-shü\ island Japan S of W end of Honshu

Lab·ra·dor \'lab-rə-₁dȯ(ə)r\ **1** peninsula E Canada between Hudson bay & the Atlantic divided between Quebec & Newfoundland **2** the part of the peninsula belonging to Newfoundland — **Lab·ra·dor·ean** or **Lab·ra·dor·ian** \₁lab-rə-'dȯr-ē-ən, -'dōr-\ adj or n

Lac·ca·dive \'lak-ə-₁dēv, -₁dīv\ islands India in Arabian sea N of Maldive islands

Lac·e·dae·mon \₁las-ə-'dē-mən\ — see SPARTA — **Lac·e·dae·mo·nian** \₁las-əd-i-'mō-nē-ən, -nyən\ adj or n

La·co·nia \lə-'kō-nē-ə, -nyə\ ancient country S Greece in SE Peloponnisos; capital, Sparta — **La·co·nian** \-nē-ən, -nyən\ adj or n

La·gos \'lä-₁gäs\ city, former capital of Nigeria

La·hore \lə-'hō(ə)r, -'hȯ(ə)r\ city E Pakistan

Lake District region NW England in Cumbria county & NW Lancashire containing many lakes & mountains

Lake·hurst \'lāk-(₁)hərst\ town E New Jersey

Lake·wood \'lā-₁kwủd\ city central Colorado

Lam·beth \'lam-bəth, -₁beth\ city area of S Greater London county, England

La·nai \lə-'nī\ island Hawaii W of Maui

Lan·ca·shire \'laŋ-kə-₁shi(ə)r, -shər\ or **Lan·cas·ter** \'laŋ-kə-stər\ county NW England — **Lan·cas·tri·an** \laŋ-'kas-trē-ən, lan-\ adj or n

Lan·cas·ter \'laŋ-kə-stər; 'lan-₁kas-tər, 'laŋ-\ city area, capital of Lancashire, England

Land's End \'land(-)-'zend\ cape SW England; most westerly point of England, at 5°41′ W longitude

Lan·sing \'lan(t)-siŋ\ city, capital of Michigan

Lan·zhou or **Lan–chou** \'län-'jō\ city W China

Laos \'laủs, 'lä-₁äs, 'lä-ōs\ country SE Asia in Indochina NE of Thailand; capital, Vientiane

La Paz \lə-'paz, -'päz, -'päs\ city, administrative capital of Bolivia

Lap·land \'lap-₁land, -lənd\ region N Europe above the arctic circle in N Norway, N Sweden, N Finland, & Kola peninsula of Russia — **Lap·land·er** \-₁lan-dər, -lən-\ n

La·re·do \lə-'rā-(₁)dō\ city S Texas on the Rio Grande

Larne \'lärn\ district NE Northern Ireland

Las·sen Peak \'las-ᵊn-\ volcano 3187 meters N California at S end of Cascade Range

Las Ve·gas \läs-'vā-gəs\ city SE Nevada

Latin America 1 Spanish America and Brazil **2** all of the Americas S of the U.S. — **Latin–American** adj — **Latin American** n

Latin Quarter section of Paris, France S of the Seine

Lat·via \'lat-vē-ə\ country E Europe on Baltic sea; capital, Riga; a republic of U.S.S.R. 1940–91

Lau·ren·tian \lȯ-'ren-chən\ hills E Canada in S Quebec N of the Saint Lawrence on S edge of Laurentian Highlands

Laurentian Highlands or **Canadian Shield** plateau region E Canada & NE U.S. extending from Mackenzie basin E to Davis strait & S to S Quebec, S central Ontario, NE Minnesota, N Wisconsin, NW Michigan, and NE New York including the Adirondacks

La·val \lə-'val\ city S Quebec NW of Montreal

Law·rence \'lȯr-ən(t)s, 'lär-\ city NE corner of Massachusetts

Leb·a·non \'leb-ə-nən, -ˌnän\ **1** mountains Lebanon running parallel to coast; highest Dahr el Qadib 3088 meters **2** country SW Asia on the Mediterranean; capital, Beirut — **Leb·a·nese** \ˌleb-ə-'nēz, -'nēs\ adj or n

Leeds \'lēdz\ city N England in West Yorkshire

Lee·ward Islands \'lē-wərd-\ **1** islands Hawaii extending WNW from main islands of the group **2** islands S Pacific in W Society islands **3** islands West Indies in N Lesser Antilles extending from Virgin islands (on N) to Dominica (on S)

Le Ha·vre \lə-'hävrᵉ\ city N France on English channel

Leh·man Caves \'le-mən-\ limestone caverns E Nevada

Leices·ter \'les-tər\ city central England in Leicestershire ENE of Birmingham

Leices·ter·shire \'les-tər-ˌshi(ə)r, -shər\ or **Leicester** county central England

Lein·ster \'len(t)-stər\ province E Ireland

Leip·zig \'līp-sig, -sik\ city E Germany

Le·na \'lē-nə, 'lā-\ river 4830 kilometers long E Russia, flowing NE & N from mountains W of Lake Baikal into Arctic ocean

Leningrad — see SAINT PETERSBURG

Le·ón \lā-'ōn\ city central Mexico

Ler·wick \'lər-(')wik, 'lᵉ(ə)r\ town and port N Scotland in Shetland region

Le·so·tho \lə-'sō-tō, -'sü-(ˌ)tü\ country S Africa surrounded by Republic of South Africa; formerly British territory of **Ba·su·to·land** \bə-'süt-ə-ˌland\, now an independent country in the Commonwealth; capital, Maseru

Lesser An·til·les \-an-'til-ēz\ islands in the West Indies including Virgin Islands, Leeward Islands, & Windward Islands, Barbados, Trinidad, Tobago, & islands in the S Caribbean N of Venezuela — see GREATER ANTILLES

Le·vant \lə-'vant\ the countries bordering on the E Mediterranean — **Lev·an·tine** \'lev-ən-ˌtīn, -ˌtēn, lə-'van-\ adj or n

Lew·es \'lü-əs\ city area S England in East Sussex county

Lew·i·sham \'lü-ə-shəm\ city area of SE Greater London county, England

Lew·is with Har·ris \ˌlü-ə-swəth-'har-əs, -swəth-\ island NW Scotland in Outer Hebrides

Lex·ing·ton \'lek-siŋ-tən\ town NE Massachusetts

Lexington–Fayette \'lek-siŋ-tən-fā-'et\ city N central Kentucky

Ley·te \'lāt-ē\ island Philippines S of Samar

Lha·sa \'läs-ə, 'las-\ city SW China, capital of Tibet

Li·be·ria \lī-'bir-ē-ə\ country W Africa on the Atlantic; capital, Monrovia — **Li·be·ri·an** \-ē-ən\ adj or n

Lib·er·ty \'lib-ərt-ē\ or formerly **Bed·loe's** \'bed-ˌlōz\ or **Bed·loe** \-lō\ island SE New York; the Statue of Liberty is on it

Li·bre·ville \'lē-brə-ˌvil, -ˌvē(ə)l\ city, capital of Gabon

Lib·ya \'lib-ē-ə\ **1** the part of Africa N of the Sahara and just W of Egypt — an ancient name **2** northern Africa W of Egypt — an ancient name **3** country N Africa on the Mediterranean W of Egypt; capital, Tripoli — **Lib·y·an** \'lib-ē-ən\ adj or n

Libyan desert N Africa W of the Nile in Libya, Egypt, & Sudan

Liech·ten·stein \'lik-tən-ˌstīn, -ˌshtīn\ country W Europe between Austria & Switzerland; capital, Vaduz — **Liech·ten·stein·er** \-ˌstī-nər, -ˌshtī-\ n

Lif·fey \'lif-ē\ river 80 kilometers long E Ireland

Li·gu·ria \lə-'gyu̇r-ē-ə\ ancient region SW Europe — **Li·gu·ri·an** \-ē-ən\ adj or n

Ligurian sea arm of the Mediterranean N of Corsica

Li·lon·gwe \li-'lȯŋ-wā\ city, capital of Malawi

Li·ma \'lē-mə\ city, capital of Peru

Lim·a·vady \ˌlim-ə-'vad-ē\ district NW Northern Ireland

Lim·po·po \lim-'pō-pō\ river 1610 kilometers long Africa flowing from Transvaal into Indian ocean in Mozambique

Lin·coln \'liŋ-kən\ **1** city, capital of Nebraska **2** city E England in Lincolnshire

Lin·coln·shire \'liŋ-kən-ˌshi(ə)r, -shər\ or **Lincoln** county E England

Line \'līn\ islands Kiribati S of Hawaii; formerly divided between U.S. & United Kingdom

Lis·bon \'liz-bən\ or Portuguese **Lis·boa** \lēzh-'vō-ə\ city, capital of Portugal

Lis·burn \'liz-(ˌ)bərn\ district E Northern Ireland

Lith·u·a·nia \ˌlith-(y)ə-'wā-nē-ə, -nyə\ country E Europe; capital, Vilnius; a republic of U.S.S.R. 1940–91

Lit·tle Rock \'lit-ᵊl-ˌräk\ city, capital of Arkansas

Liv·er·pool \'liv-ər-ˌpül\ city NW England in Merseyside county

Li·vo·nia \lə-'vō-nē-ə, -nyə\ city SE Michigan

Lju·blja·na \lē-ˌü-blē-'än-ə\ city, capital of Slovenia

Llan·drin·dod Wells \hlan-'drin-ˌdȯd-, lan-\ town E Wales in Powys county

Lla·no Es·ta·ca·do \ˈlan-(ˌ)ō-ˌes-ta-'käd-ō, 'län-\ or **Staked Plain** \'stāk(t)-\ plateau region SE New Mexico & NW Texas

Lodz \'lüj, 'lädz\ city central Poland WSW of Warsaw

Lo·fo·ten \'lō-ˌfōt-ᵊn\ islands NW Norway

Lo·gan, Mount \-'lō-gən\ mountain 6050 meters NW Canada in Saint Elias range; highest in Canada & second highest in North America

Loire \lə-'wär\ river 1005 kilometers long central France flowing NW & W into Bay of Biscay

Lo·mé \lō-'mā\ city, capital of Togo

Lo·mond, Loch \-'lō-mənd\ lake S central Scotland

Lon·don \'lən-dən\ **1** city S Ontario, Canada **2** city, capital of England & of United Kingdom on the Thames; consists of **City of London** & Greater London county — **Lon·don·er** \-də-nər\ n

Londonderry — see DERRY

Long Beach city SW California S of Los Angeles

Long Island island 190 kilometers long SE New York S of Connecticut

Long Island Sound inlet of the Atlantic between Connecticut & Long Island, New York

Lon·gueuil \lȯŋ-'gā(ə)l\ city Canada in S Quebec E of Montreal

Lor·raine \lə-'rān, lȯ-\ region NE France

Los An·ge·les \lȯ-'san-jə-ləs also -'saŋ-g(ə-)ləs\ city SW California

Lo·thi·an \'lō-thē-ən\ region SE Scotland S of Firth of Forth; established 1975; includes Edinburgh

Lou·ise, Lake \-lü-'ēz\ lake SW Alberta, Canada

Lou·i·si·ana \lü-ˌē-zē-'an-ə, ˌlü-ə-zē-, ˌlü-zē-\ state S U.S.; capital, Baton Rouge — **Lou·i·si·an·ian** \-'an-ē-ən, -'an-yən\ or **Lou·i·si·an·an** \-'an-ən\ adj or n

Louisiana Purchase area W central U.S. between Rocky mountains & the Mississippi purchased 1803 from France

Lou·is·ville \'lü-i-ˌvil, -vəl\ city N Kentucky on the Ohio river

---

\ə\abut \ᵊ\kitten \ər\further \a\ash \ā\ace \ä\mop, mar
\au̇\out \ch\chin \e\bet \ē\easy \g\go \i\hit \ī\ice \j\job
\ŋ\sing \ō\go \ȯ\law \ȯi\boy \th\thin \t͟h\the \ü\loot \u̇\foot
\y\yet \zh\vision see also Pronunciation Symbols page

Low Countries region W Europe consisting of modern Belgium, Luxembourg, & the Netherlands

Lower 48 the continental states of the U.S. excluding Alaska

Low·lands \'lō-lən(d)z, -ₗlan(d)z\ the central & E part of Scotland

Lu·an·da \lü-'an-də\ city, capital of Angola

Lub·bock \'ləb-ək\ city NW Texas

Luck·now \'lək-ₗnaủ\ city N India

Lü·da or **Lü–ta** \'lü-'dä\ or **Dai·ren** \'dī-'ren\ city NE China

Lu·ray Caverns \'lü-ₗrā-, lü-'rā-\ series of caves N Virginia

Lu·sa·ka \lü-'säk-ə\ city, capital of Zambia

Lü·shun \'lü-'shủn\ or **Port Ar·thur** \-'är-thər\ city NE China

Lu·ton \'lüt-ᵊn\ city area SE central England in Bedfordshire

Lux·em·bourg or **Lux·em·burg** \'lək-səm-ₗbərg, 'lủk-səm-ₗbủ(ə)rg\ **1** country W Europe bordered by Belgium, France, & Germany **2** city, its capital — **Lux·em·bourg·er** \-ₗbər-gər, -ₗbủr-\ n — **Lux·em·bourg·ian** \ₗlək-səm-'bər-gē-ən, ₗlủk-səm-'bủr-\ adj

Lu·zon \lü-'zän\ island N Philippines

Lvov \lə-'vóf, -'vòv\ or Polish **Lwów** \lə-'vüf, -'vüv\ or Ukrainian **Lwiw** \lə-'vēf\ city W Ukraine

Lyallpur — see FAISALABAD

Lyd·ia \'lid-ē-ə\ ancient country W Asia Minor on the Aegean — **Lyd·i·an** \-ē-ən\ adj or n

Lynn \'lin\ city NE corner of Massachusetts

Ma·cao or Portuguese **Ma·cau** \mə-'kaủ\ **1** Portuguese territory on coast of SE China W of Hong Kong **2** city, its capital — **Mac·a·nese** \ₗmak-ə-'nēz, -'nēs\ n

Mac·e·do·nia \ₗmas-ə-'dō-nyə, -nē-ə\ **1** region S Europe in Balkan peninsula in NE Greece, the country of Macedonia, and SW Bulgaria including territory of ancient kingdom of Macedonia (**Mac·e·don** \'mas-əd-ən, -ə-ₗdän\) **2** country S central Balkan peninsula; capital, Skopje; a former republic of Yugoslavia — **Mac·e·do·nian** \ₗmas-ə-'dō-nyən, -nē-ən\ adj or n

Mac·gil·li·cud·dy's Reeks \mə-ₗgil-ə-ₗkəd-ēz-'rēks\ mountains SW Ireland; highest Carrantuo hill 1041 meters

Ma·chu Pic·chu \ₗmäch-ü-'pēk-chü\ site SE Peru of ancient Inca city

Macías Nguema Biyogo — see BIOKO

Mac·ken·zie \mə-'ken-zē\ **1** river 1800 kilometers long NW Canada flowing from Great Slave lake NW into Beaufort sea **2** former district NW Canada in W Northwest Territories in basin of Mackenzie river

Mack·i·nac, Straits of \-'mak-ə-ₗnak, -ₗnó\ channel N Michigan connecting Lake Huron & Lake Michigan

Mc·Kin·ley, Mount \mə-'kin-lē\ or **De·na·li** \də-'näl-ē\ mountain 6194 meters S central Alaska in Alaska range; highest in U.S. & North America

Ma·con \'mā-kən\ city central Georgia

Mad·a·gas·car \ₗmad-ə-'gas-kər\ or formerly **Mal·a·gasy Republic** \ₗmal-ə-gas-ē-\ island W Indian ocean off SE Africa; an independent country; capital, Antananarivo — **Mad·a·gas·can** \ₗmad-ə-'gas-kən\ adj or n

Ma·dei·ra \mə-'dir-ə, -'der-\ **1** river 3380 kilometers long W Brazil flowing NE into the Amazon **2** islands in the N Atlantic N of the Canary islands belonging to Portugal **3** island; chief of the Madeira group — **Ma·dei·ran** \-ən\ adj or n

Ma·di·nat ash Sha'b \mə-'dē-ₗnət-ash-'shab\ town S Yemen

Mad·i·son \'mad-ə-sən\ city, capital of Wisconsin

Ma·dras \mə-'dras, -'dräs\ city SE India

Ma·drid \mə-'drid\ city, capital of Spain

Ma·du·rai \ₗmäd-ə-'rī\ city S India

Magh·er·a·felt \'mär-ə-ₗfelt, 'ma̱k-ə-rə-ₗfelt\ district central Northern Ireland

Maid·stone \'mād-stən, -ₗstōn\ city district SE England in Kent county

Main \'mīn, 'mān\ river 490 kilometers long S central Germany flowing W into the Rhine

Maine \'mān\ state NE U.S.; capital, Augusta

Ma·jor·ca \mə-'jór-kə, -'yòr-\ or Spanish **Ma·llor·ca** \mə-'yòr-kä\ island Spain in W Mediterranean — **Ma·jor·can** \-'jòr-kən, -'yòr-\ adj or n

Mal·a·bar \'mal-ə-ₗbär\ coast region SW India on Arabian sea

Ma·la·bo \mä-'lä-bō\ city, capital of Equatorial Guinea

Ma·lac·ca, Strait of \-mə-'lak-ə, -'läk-\ channel between S Malay peninsula & island of Sumatra

Ma·la·wi \mə-'lä-wē, -'laủ-ē\ or formerly **Ny·asa·land** \nī-'as-ə-ₗland, nē-\ country SE Africa on Lake Nyasa; an independent state since 1964; capital, Lilongwe

Ma·lay \mə-'lā, 'mā-lā\ **1** island group SE Asia including Sumatra, Java, Borneo, Sulawesi, Moluccas, & Timor; usually thought to include the Philippines & sometimes New Guinea **2** peninsula about 1100 kilometers long SE Asia divided between Thailand and Malaysia (country)

Ma·laya \mə-'lä-ə, mä-\ **1** the Malay peninsula **2** former country SE Asia on Malay peninsula; since 1963 part of Malaysia — see MALAYSIA

Ma·lay·sia \mə-'lä-zh(ē-)ə, -sh(ē-)ə\ **1** the Malay island group **2** the Malay peninsula & Malay island group **3** country SE Asia, a union of Malaya, Sabah, Sarawak, & (until 1965) Singapore; capital, Kuala Lumpur — **Ma·lay·sian** \mə-'lä-zhən, -shən\ adj or n

Mal·dives \'mal-ₗdīvz, 'mól-\ islands in Indian ocean S of the Laccadives; formerly under British protection; since 1965 an independent country; capital, Male — **Mal·div·i·an** \mól-'div-ē-ən\ adj or n

Ma·li \'mäl-ē, 'mal-ē\ country W Africa; capital, Bamako — **Ma·li·an** \-ē-ən\ adj or n

Mal·ta \'mòl-tə\ islands in the Mediterranean S of Sicily; a former British colony; an independent country since 1964; capital, Valletta

Malvinas, Islas — see FALKLAND

Mam·moth Cave \ₗmam-əth-\ limestone caverns SW central Kentucky

Man, Isle of \-'man\ island British Isles in Irish sea; has own legislature & laws

Ma·na·gua \mə-'näg-wə\ city, capital of Nicaragua

Ma·na·ma \mə-'nam-ə\ city, capital of Bahrain

Man·ches·ter \'man-ₗches-tər, -chə-stər\ **1** city S central New Hampshire; largest in state **2** city NW England in Greater Manchester county

Man·chu·ria \man-'chủr-ē-ə\ region NE China S of the Amur — **Man·chu·ri·an** \man-'chủr-ē-ən\ adj or n

Man·hat·tan \man-'hat-ᵊn, mən-\ **1** island SE New York in New York City **2** section of New York City consisting chiefly of Manhattan island

Ma·nila \mə-'nil-ə\ city, capital of Philippines in W Luzon

Man·i·to·ba \ₗman-ə-'tō-bə\ province central Canada; capital, Winnipeg — **Man·i·to·ban** \-'tō-bən\ adj or n

Man·i·tou·lin \ₗman-ə-'tü-lən\ island 130 kilometers long S Ontario in Lake Huron

Ma·pu·to \mä-'pü-tō\ city, capital of Mozambique

Mar·a·cai·bo \ₗmar-ə-'kī-bō\ city NW Venezuela

Maracaibo, Lake extension of a gulf NW Venezuela

Mar·a·thon \'mar-ə-ₗthän, -thən\ plain E Greece NE of Athens

Mar·i·ana \ₗmar-ē-'an-ə, ₗmer-\ islands W Pacific N of Caroline islands; comprise Commonwealth of Northern Mariana Islands & Guam

Mariana Trench ocean trench W Pacific extending from SE of Guam to NW of Mariana islands; deepest in world

Ma·rin·du·que \ₗmar-ən-'dü-kā, ₗmär-\ island central Philippines

Maritime Provinces the Canadian provinces of New

Brunswick, Nova Scotia, & Prince Edward Island & sometimes thought to include Newfoundland

Ma·ri·u·pol \ˌmar-ē-ˈü-ˌpȯl\ *or* *1949–89* **Zhda·nov** \zhə-ˈdän-əf\ city E Ukraine

Mar·ma·ra, Sea of \-ˈmär-mə-rə\ sea NW Turkey connected with Black sea by the Bosporus & with Aegean sea by the Dardanelles

Marne \ˈmärn\ river 523 kilometers long NE France flowing W into the Seine

Mar·que·sas \mär-ˈkā-zəz, -zəs, -səz, -səs\ islands S Pacific — **Mar·que·san** \-zən, -sən\ *adj or n*

Mar·seilles \mär-ˈsā, -ˈsā(ə)lz\ *or* **Mar·seille** \mär-ˈsā\ *or ancient* **Mas·sil·ia** \mə-ˈsil-ē-ə\ city SE France

Mar·shall \ˈmär-shəl\ islands W Pacific E of the Carolines; formerly part of Trust Territory of the Pacific Islands

Mar·tha's Vineyard \ˌmär-thəz-\ island SE Massachusetts off SW coast of Cape Cod WNW of Nantucket

Mar·ti·nique \ˌmärt-ᵊn-ˈēk\ island West Indies in the Windward Islands; an overseas division of France; capital, Fort-de-France

Mary·land \ˈmer-ə-lənd\ state E U.S.; capital, Annapolis — **Mary·land·er** \-lən-dər, -ˌlan-\ *n*

Mas·ba·te \mäz-ˈbät-ē\ island central Philippines

Mas·e·ru \ˈmaz-ə-ˌrü\ city, capital of Lesotho

Mash·had \mə-ˈshad\ city NE Iran

Ma·son–Dix·on line \ˌmās-ᵊn-ˈdik-sən-\ boundary between Maryland & Pennsylvania; was in part boundary between free & slave states

Mas·sa·chu·setts \ˌmas(-ə)-ˈchü-səts, -zəts\ state NE U.S.; capital, Boston

Mat·a·be·le·land \ˌmat-ə-ˈbē-lē-ˌland\ region SW Zimbabwe

Mat·lock\ˈmat-ˌläk\ town N England in Derbyshire

Mat·ter·horn \ˈmat-ər-ˌhȯ(ə)rn, ˈmät-\ mountain 4478 meters on border between Switzerland & Italy

Maui \ˈmau̇-ē\ island Hawaii NW of Hawaii island

Mau·na Kea \ˌmau̇-nə-ˈkā-ə\ extinct volcano 4205 meters Hawaii in N central Hawaii island

Mau·na Loa \ˌmau̇-nə-ˈlō-ə\ volcano 4170 meters Hawaii in S central Hawaii island

Mau·re·ta·nia *or* **Mau·ri·ta·nia** \ˌmȯr-ə-ˈtā-nē-ə, ˌmär-, -nyə\ ancient country NW Africa in modern Morocco & W Algeria — **Mau·re·ta·ni·an** \-nē-ən, -nyən\ *adj or n*

Mauritania country NW Africa on the Atlantic N of Senegal river; capital, Nouakchott — **Mauritanian** *adj or n*

Mau·ri·tius \mȯ-ˈrish-(ē-)əs\ island in Indian ocean E of Madagascar; an independent country in the Commonwealth; capital, Port Louis — **Mau·ri·tian** \-ˈrish-ən\ *adj or n*

May, Cape \-ˈmā\ cape S New Jersey at entrance to Delaware Bay

Ma·yon, Mount \-mä-ˈyȯn\ volcano 2525 meters Philippines in SE Luzon

Ma·yotte Island \mä-ˈyät-\ island Comoro group — see COMORO

Ma·za·ma, Mount \-mə-ˈzäm-ə\ prehistoric mountain SW Oregon the collapse of whose top formed Crater lake

Mba·bane \em-bə-ˈbän\ city, capital of Swaziland

Mbi·ni \em-ˈbē-nē\ *or formerly* **Río Mu·ni** \ˌrē-ō-ˈmü-nē\ mainland portion of Equatorial Guinea

Mead, Lake \-ˈmēd\ reservoir NW Arizona & SE Nevada formed by Hoover Dam in Colorado river

Mec·ca \ˈmek-ə\ city W Saudi Arabia containing the Great Mosque of Islam

Me·dan \mā-ˈdän\ city Indonesia in N Sumatra

Me·de·llín \ˌmed-ᵊl-ˈēn, ˌmā-thə-ˈyēn\ city NW Colombia

Med·i·ter·ra·nean \ˌmed-ə-tə-ˈrā-nē-ən, -nyən\ sea 3750 kilometers long between Europe & Africa connecting with the Atlantic through Strait of Gibraltar

Me·kong \ˈmā-ˈkȯŋ, -ˈkäŋ\ river 4185 kilometers long SE Asia flowing from E Tibet S & SE into South China sea in S Vietnam

Mel·a·ne·sia \ˌmel-ə-ˈnē-zhə, -shə\ islands of the Pacific NE of Australia & S of Micronesia including Bismarck, the Solomons, Vanuatu, New Caledonia, & the Fijis

Mel·bourne \ˈmel-bərn\ city SE Australia, capital of Victoria

Me·los \ˈmē-ˌläs\ island Greece — **Me·li·an** \ˈmē-lē-ən\ *adj or n*

Mel·ville \ˈmel-ˌvil\ 1 island N Canada in N Northwest Territories 2 peninsula E Northwest Territories, Canada

Mem·phis \ˈmem(p)-fəs\ 1 city SW Tennessee 2 ancient city N Egypt S of modern Cairo

Men·do·ci·no, Cape \-ˌmen-də-ˈsē-nō\ cape NW California

Mer·cia \ˈmər-sh(ē-)ə\ ancient Anglo-Saxon kingdom central England — **Mer·cian** \ˈmər-shən\ *adj or n*

Mer·sey \ˈmər-zē\ river 110 kilometers long NW England flowing NW & W into Irish sea

Mer·sey·side \ˈmər-zē-ˌsīd\ county NW England; includes Liverpool

Mer·ton \ˈmərt-ᵊn\ city area of SW Greater London county, England

Me·sa \ˈmā-sə\ city S central Arizona

Me·sa·bi range \mə-ˈsäb-ē\ region NE Minnesota that contains iron ore

Mes·o·po·ta·mia \ˌmes-(ə-)pə-ˈtā-mē-ə, -myə\ 1 region SW Asia between Euphrates & Tigris rivers 2 the entire Tigris-Euphrates valley — **Mes·o·po·ta·mian** \-mē-ən, -myən\ *adj or n*

Meuse \ˈmyüz, ˈmə(r)z\ river 925 kilometers long W Europe flowing from NE France into North sea in the Netherlands

Mex·i·co \ˈmek-si-ˌkō\ 1 country S North America 2 *or* **Mexico City** city, its capital

Mexico, Gulf of inlet of the Atlantic SE North America

Mi·ami \mī-ˈam-ē, -ˈam-ə\ city SE Florida

Miami Beach city SE Florida

Mich·i·gan \ˈmish-i-gən\ state N central U.S.; capital, Lansing — **Mich·i·gan·der** \ˌmish-i-ˈgan-dər\ *n* — **Mich·i·gan·ite** \ˈmish-i-gə-ˌnīt\ *n*

Michigan, Lake lake N central U.S.; one of the Great Lakes

Mi·cro·ne·sia \ˌmī-krə-ˈnē-zhə, -shə\ islands of the W Pacific E of the Philippines & N of Melanesia including Caroline, Kiribati, Mariana, & Marshall groups — **Mi·cro·ne·sian** \-zhən, -shən\ *adj or n*

Middle East the countries of SW Asia & N Africa usually thought to include the countries extending from Libya on the W to Afghanistan on the E — **Middle Eastern** *or* **Mid·east·ern** \ˈmid-ˈē-stərn\ *adj*

Mid·dles·brough \ˈmid-ᵊlz-brə\ town N England in Cleveland county

Mid Gla·mor·gan \ˈmid-glə-ˈmȯr-gən\ county SE Wales; established 1974

Mid·i·an \ˈmid-ē-ən\ ancient region NW Arabia E of Gulf of ʿAqaba — **Mid·i·an·ite** \-ē-ə-ˌnīt\ *n*

Mid·lands \ˈmid-lən(d)z\ the central counties of England usually thought to consist of Bedfordshire, Buckinghamshire, Cambridgeshire, Derbyshire, Leicestershire, Lincolnshire, Northamptonshire, Nottinghamshire, Oxfordshire, Staffordshire, Warwickshire, West Midlands, & part of Hereford and Worcester

Mid·way \ˈmid-ˌwā\ islands central Pacific in Hawaiian group 2090 kilometers WNW of Honolulu belonging to U.S.; not included in state of Hawaii

---

\ə\abut \ᵊ\kitten \ər\further \a\ash \ā\ace \ä\mop, mar
\au̇\out \ch\chin \e\bet \ē\easy \g\go \i\hit \ī\ice \j\job
\ŋ\sing \ō\go \ȯ\law \ȯi\boy \th\thin \t͟h\the \ü\loot \u̇\foot
\y\yet \zh\vision *see also* Pronunciation Symbols page

Mid·west \ˌmid-ˈwest\ *or* **Middle West** region N central U.S. including area around Great Lakes & in upper Mississippi valley from Ohio on the E to North Dakota, South Dakota, Nebraska, & Kansas on the W — **Mid·wes·tern** \ˌmid-ˈwes-tərn\ *or* **Middle Western** *adj* — **Mid·wes·tern·er** \ˌmid-ˈwes-tə(r)-nər\ *or* **Middle Westerner** *n*

Mi·lan \mə-ˈlan, -ˈlän\ *or Italian* **Mi·la·no** \mi-ˈlän-ō\ city NW Italy — **Mil·a·nese** \ˌmil-ə-ˈnēz, -ˈnēs\ *adj or n*

Mil·wau·kee \mil-ˈwȯ-kē\ city SE Wisconsin

Mi·nas Basin \ˌmī-nəs-\ bay central Nova Scotia; NE extension of Bay of Fundy

Min·da·nao \ˌmin-də-ˈnä-ō, -ˈnaù\ island S Philippines

Min·do·ro \min-ˈdȯr-ō, -ˈdȯr-\ island central Philippines

Min·ne·ap·o·lis \ˌmin-ē-ˈap-(ə-)ləs\ city SE Minnesota

Min·ne·so·ta \ˌmin-ə-ˈsōt-ə\ state N central U.S.; capital, Saint Paul — **Min·ne·so·tan** \-ˈsōt-ᵊn\ *adj or n*

Mi·nor·ca \mə-ˈnȯr-kə\ island Spain in W Mediterranean — **Mi·nor·can** \mə-ˈnȯr-kən\ *adj or n*

Minsk \ˈmin(t)sk\ city, capital of Belarus

Mis·sis·sip·pi \ˌmis-(ə-)ˈsip-ē\ **1** river 3975 kilometers long central U.S. flowing into Gulf of Mexico — see ITASCA, LAKE **2** state S U.S.; capital, Jackson

Mis·sou·ri \mə-ˈzù(ə)r-ē, -ˈzùr-ə\ **1** river 4345 kilometers long W U.S. flowing from SW Montana to the Mississippi in E Missouri **2** state central U.S.; capital, Jefferson City — **Mis·sou·ri·an** \-ˈzùr-ē-ən\ *adj or n*

Mitch·ell, Mount \-ˈmich-əl\ mountain 2037 meters W North Carolina in the Appalachians; highest in U.S. E of the Mississippi

Mo·bile \mō-ˈbē(ə)l, ˈmō-ˌbēl\ city SW Alabama on Mobile Bay

Mo·des·to \mə-ˈdəs-tō\ city central California

Mog·a·di·shu \ˌmäg-ə-ˈdish-ü, -ˈdēsh-\ *or* **Mog·a·di·scio** \-ō\ city, capital of Somalia

Mo·hawk \ˈmō-ˌhȯk\ river E central New York flowing into the Hudson

Mo·ja·ve *or* **Mo·ha·ve** \mə-ˈhäv-ē\ desert S California SE of S end of Sierra Nevada

Mold \ˈmōld\ town NE Wales in Clwyd county

Mol·da·via \mäl-ˈdā-vē-ə, -vyə\ **1** region E Europe in NE Romania & Moldova **2** former republic of U.S.S.R. bordered by Ukraine, Black sea, & Romania; became independent (as Moldova) 1991 — **Mol·da·vian** \-vē-ən, -vyən\ *adj or n*

Mol·do·va \mäl-ˈdō-və, mȯl-\ country E Europe in E Moldavia region; capital, Kishinev

Mol·o·kai \ˌmäl-ə-ˈkī, ˌmō-lə-\ island Hawaii ESE of Oahu

Mo·luc·cas \mə-ˈlək-əz\ islands Indonesia E of Sulawesi — **Mo·luc·ca** \mə-ˈlək-ə\ *adj* — **Mo·luc·can** \-ən\ *adj or n*

Mo·na·co \ˈmän-ə-ˌkō *also* mə-ˈnäk-ō\ country W Europe on Mediterranean coast of France; capital, Monaco — **Mo·na·can** \ˈmän-ə-kən, mə-ˈnäk-ən\ *adj or n* — **Mon·e·gasque** \ˌmän-i-ˈgask\ *n*

Mon·go·lia \män-ˈgōl-yə, mäŋ-, -ˈgō-lē-ə\ **1** region E Asia E of Altai mountains; includes Gobi desert **2** country E Asia consisting of major portion of Mongolia region; capital Ulan Bator

Mo·non·ga·he·la \mə-ˌnäŋ-gə-ˈhē-lə, -ˌnäŋ-gə-, -ˈhā-lə\ river N West Virginia & SW Pennsylvania

Mon·ro·via \(ˌ)mən-ˈrō-vē-ə\ city, capital of Liberia

Mon·tana \män-ˈtan-ə\ state NW U.S.; capital, Helena — **Mon·tan·an** \-ən\ *adj or n*

Mont Blanc \ˈmōn-ˈbläŋ(k)\ mountain 4807 meters SE France on Italian border; highest in the Alps

Mon·te·ne·gro \ˌmän-tə-ˈnē-(ˌ)grō, -ˈnä-\ region SW Yugoslavia on the Adriatic sea

Mon·ter·rey \ˌmänt-ə-ˈrā\ city NE Mexico

Mon·te·vi·deo \ˌmänt-ə-və-ˈdā-ō, -ˈvid-ē-ˌō\ city, capital of Uruguay

Mont·gom·ery \(ˌ)mən(t)-ˈgəm-(ə-)rē, män(t)-, -ˈgäm-\ city, capital of Alabama

Mont·pe·lier \mänt-ˈpēl-yər, -ˈpil-\ city, capital of Vermont

Mont·re·al \ˌmän-trē-ˈȯl, ˌmən-\ city S Quebec, Canada on Montreal Island in the Saint Lawrence

Mont·ser·rat \ˌmän(t)-sə-ˈrat\ island West Indies in the Leeward Islands

Mo·ra·via \mə-ˈrā-vē-ə\ region E Czech Republic — **Mo·ra·vi·an** \mə-ˈrā-vē-ən\ *adj or n*

Mo·rea \mə-ˈrē-ə\ PELOPONNISOS — an old name — **Mo·re·an** \-ˈrē-ən\ *adj or n*

Mo·roc·co \mə-ˈräk-ō\ country NW Africa; a kingdom; capital, Rabat — **Mo·roc·can** \-ˈräk-ən\ *adj or n*

Mo·ro·ni \mȯ-ˈrō-nē\ city, capital of Comoro

Mos·cow \ˈmäs-ˌkaù, -kō\ *or Russian* **Mos·kva** \mäsk-ˈvä\ city, capital of Russia and formerly of U.S.S.R. and of Russian Soviet Federated Socialist Republic

Mourne \ˈmō(ə)rn, ˈmȯ(ə)rn\ district S Northern Ireland

Moyle \ˈmȯi(ə)l\ district N Northern Ireland

Mo·zam·bique \ˌmō-zəm-ˈbēk\ **1** channel SE Africa between Mozambique & Madagascar **2** country SE Africa; capital, Maputo

Mukden — see SHENYANG

Mul·tan \mùl-ˈtän\ city NE Pakistan SW of Lahore

Mu·nich \ˈmyü-nik\ *or German* **Mün·chen** \ˈm(y)ün-kən\ city S Germany in Bavaria

Mun·ster \ˈmən(t)-stər\ province S Ireland

Mur·cia \ˈmər-sh(ē-)ə\ region & ancient kingdom SE Spain — **Mur·cian** \-shən\ *adj or n*

Mur·ray \ˈmər-ē, ˈmə-rē\ river 1930 kilometers long SE Australia flowing W from E Victoria into Indian ocean in South Australia — see DARLING

Mur·rum·bidg·ee \ˌmər-əm-ˈbij-ē, ˌmə-rəm-\ river 1610 kilometers long SE Australia in New South Wales flowing W into the Murray

Mus·cat \ˈməs-ˌkat, -kət\ town E Arabia, capital of Oman

Muscovy \ˈməs-kə-vē\ principality from about 1280 to 15th century consisting of Moscow, Russia

Myan·mar \ˈmyän-ˌmär\ *or* **Myan·ma** \-ˌmä\ *or formerly* **Bur·ma** \ˈbər-mə\ country SE Asia; capital, Yangon

My·ce·nae \mī-ˈsē-nē\ ancient city S Greece in NE Peloponnisos

My·sore \mī-ˈsō(ə)r, -ˈsȯ(ə)r\ city S India

Nab·a·taea *or* **Nab·a·tea** \ˌnab-ə-ˈtē-ə\ ancient Arab kingdom SE of Palestine — **Nab·a·tae·an** *or* **Nab·a·te·an** \-ˈtē-ən\ *adj or n*

Na·goya \nə-ˈgȯi-ə, ˈnäg-ə-ˌyä\ city Japan in S central Honshu

Nag·pur \ˈnäg-ˌpù(ə)r\ city E central India

Nai·ro·bi \nī-ˈrō-bē\ city, capital of Kenya

Na·mib·ia \nə-ˈmib-ē-ə\ *or formerly* **South–West Africa** country SW Africa on the Atlantic; capital, Windhoek

Nan·chang \ˈnän-ˈjäŋ\ city SE China

Nan·jing \ˈnän-ˈjiŋ\ *or* **Nan·king** \ˈnan-ˈkiŋ, ˈnän-\ city E China

Nan·tuck·et \nan-ˈtək-ət\ island SE Massachusetts S of Cape Cod

Na·ples \ˈnā-pəlz\ *or Italian* **Na·po·li** \ˈnäp-ə-lē\ *or ancient* **Ne·ap·o·lis** \nē-ˈap-ə-ləs\ city S Italy on Bay of Naples — **Ne·a·pol·i·tan** \ˌnē-ə-ˈpäl-ət-ᵊn\ *adj or n*

Nar·ra·gan·sett Bay \ˌnar-ə-ˈgan(t)-sət\ inlet of the Atlantic SE Rhode Island

Nash·ville \ˈnash-ˌvil, -vəl\ city, capital of Tennessee

Nas·sau \ˈnas-ˌȯ\ city, capital of Bahamas on New Providence island

Na·tal \nə-ˈtal, -ˈtäl\ province E Republic of South Africa; capital, Pietermaritzburg

Na·u·ru \nä-ˈü-rü\ island W Pacific 42 kilometers S of the equator; formerly a shared British, New Zealand,

& Australian trust territory; an independent country in the Commonwealth since 1968

Naz·a·reth \\'naz-(ə-)rəth\ town of ancient Palestine in central Galilee; now a city of N Israel

N'Dja·me·na \en-'jäm-ə-nə\ city, capital of Chad

Neagh, Lough \läk-'nä\ lake Northern Ireland; largest in British Isles

Near East the countries of NE Africa & SW Asia — **Near Eastern** adj

Ne·bras·ka \nə-'bras-kə\ state central U.S.; capital, Lincoln — **Ne·bras·kan** \-kən\ adj or n

Neg·ev \'neg-₁ev\ desert region S Israel

Ne·gros \'nä-(₁)grōs\ island central Philippines

Ne·pal \nə-'pol, -'päl, -'pal\ country Asia on NE border of India in the Himalayas; a kingdom; capital, Kathmandu — **Nep·a·lese** \₁nep-ə-'lēz, -'lēs\ adj or n — **Ne·pali** \nə-'pol-ē, -'päl-, -'pal-\ adj or n

Ness, Loch \-'nes\ lake NW Scotland

Neth·er·lands \'neth-ər-lən(d)z\ 1 or Dutch **Ne·der·land** \'näd-ər-₁länt\ also **Holland** country NW Europe on North sea; a kingdom; capitals, Amsterdam and The Hague 2 LOW COUNTRIES — an historical usage — **Neth·er·land** \'neth-ər-lənd\ adj — **Neth·er·land·er** \-₁lan-dər, -lən-\ n — **Neth·er·land·ish** \-dish\ adj

Netherlands An·til·les \-an-'til-ēz\ islands of the West Indies belonging to the Netherlands

Netherlands East Indies or **Netherlands India** or **Dutch East Indies** former Dutch possessions in the East Indies including Indonesia

Ne·va \'nē-və, 'nä-\ river 65 kilometers long W Russia; flows through Saint Petersburg

Ne·vada \nə-'vad-ə, -'väd-ə\ state W U.S.; capital, Carson City — **Ne·vad·an** \-'vad-ᵊn, -'väd-ᵊn\ or **Ne·vad·i·an** \-'vad-ē-ən, -'väd-\ adj or n

Ne·vis \'nē-vəs\ island West Indies in the Leeward Islands — see SAINT KITTS

New Am·ster·dam \-'am(p)-stər-₁dam\ town founded 1625 on Manhattan island by the Dutch; renamed New York 1664 by the British

New·ark \'n(y)ü-ərk, 'n(y)ü-(-ə)rk\ city NE New Jersey

New Brit·ain \-'brit-ᵊn\ island W Pacific

New Bruns·wick \-'brənz-(₁)wik\ province SE Canada; capital, Fredericton

New Cal·e·do·nia \-₁kal-ə-'dō-nyə, -nē-ə\ island SW Pacific SW of Vanuatu; an overseas department of France; capital, Nouméa

New·cas·tle \'n(y)ü-₁kas-əl\ city SE Australia in E New South Wales

Newcastle or **New·cas·tle up·on Tyne** \n(y)ü-'kas-əl-ə-₁pòn-'tīn\ city N England in Tyne and Wear county

New Del·hi \-'del-ē\ city, capital of India S of Delhi

New England section of U.S. consisting of states of Maine, New Hampshire, Vermont, Massachusetts, Rhode Island, & Connecticut — **New En·gland·er** \-'iŋ-glən-dər also -'iŋ-lən-\ n

New·found·land \'n(y)ü-fən-(d)lənd, -₁(d)land; ₁n(y)ü-fən-'(d)land\ 1 island Canada in the Atlantic 2 province E Canada consisting of Newfoundland island & Labrador; capital, Saint John's — **New·found·land·er** \-(d)lən-dər, -'(d)lan-dər\ n

New France the possessions of France in North America before 1763

New Guin·ea \-'gin-ē\ 1 island W Pacific N of E Australia divided between West Irian & Papua New Guinea 2 the NE portion of the island of New Guinea together with some nearby islands; now part of Papua New Guinea — **New Guin·e·an** \-'gin-ē-ən\ adj or n

New·ham \'n(y)ü-əm\ city area of E Greater London county, England

New Hamp·shire \-'ham(p)-shər, -₁shi(ə)r\ state NE U.S.; capital, Concord — **New Hamp·shire·man** \-mən\ n — **New Hamp·shir·ite** \-₁īt\ n

New Ha·ven \-'hā-vən\ city S Connecticut

New Hebrides — see VANUATU

New Jer·sey \-'jər-zē\ state E U.S.; capital, Trenton — **New Jer·sey·ite** \-₁īt\ n

New Mex·i·co \-'mek-si-₁kō\ state SW U.S.; capital, Santa Fe — **New Mex·i·can** \-si-kən\ adj or n

New Neth·er·land \-'neth-ər-lənd\ former Dutch colony (1613–64) North America along Hudson & lower Delaware rivers; capital, New Amsterdam

New Or·leans \-'òr-lē-ənz, -'òrl-(y)ənz, -(₁)òr-'lēnz\ city SE Louisiana

New·port \'n(y)ü-₁pō(ə)rt, -₁pò(ə)rt\ 1 city area S England in Isle of Wight 2 city SE Wales in Gwent county

Newport News \n(y)ü-₁pòrt-'n(y)üz, -₁pòrt-, -pərt-\ city SE Virginia

New Prov·i·dence \-'präv-əd-ən(t)s, -ə-₁den(t)s\ island NW central Bahamas; chief town, Nassau

New·ry \'n(y)ü(ə)r-ē\ city district S Northern Ireland in Mourne district

New South Wales state SE Australia; capital, Sydney

New Spain former Spanish possessions in North America, Central America, West Indies, & the Philippines; capital, Mexico City

New Sweden former Swedish colony (1638–55) North America on W bank of Delaware river

New·town·ab·bey \₁n(y)üt-ᵊn-'ab-ē\ district E Northern Ireland

New·town·ards \₁n(y)üt-ᵊn-'ärdz\ city area E Northern Ireland in Ards district

Newtown Saint Bos·wells \-sənt-'bäz-wəlz, -sänt-\ village S Scotland in Borders region

New World the western hemisphere including North America and South America

New York \-'yó(ə)rk\ 1 state NE U.S.; capital, Albany 2 or **New York City** city SE New York — **New York·er** \-'yòr-kər\ n

New York State Barge Canal — see ERIE

New Zea·land \-'zē-lənd\ country SW Pacific ESE of Australia; an independent country in the Commonwealth; capital, Wellington — **New Zea·land·er** \-lən-dər\ n

Ni·ag·a·ra Falls \(₁)nī-'ag-(ə-)rə-\ falls New York & Ontario in **Niagara river** (58 kilometers long flowing N from Lake Erie into Lake Ontario); divided by Goat Island into Horseshoe Falls, or Canadian Falls (48 meters high, 917 meters wide) & American Falls (51 meters high, 323 meters wide)

Nia·mey \nē-'äm-ā, nyä-'mā\ city, capital of Niger

Ni·caea \nī-'sē-ə\ or **Nice** \'nīs\ ancient city W Bithynia; site at modern village in NW Turkey — **Ni·cae·an** \nī-'sē-ən\ adj or n — **Ni·cene** \'nī-₁sēn, nī-'sēn\ adj

Ni·ca·ra·gua \₁nik-ə-'räg-wə\ 1 lake 160 kilometers long S Nicaragua 2 country Central America; capital, Managua — **Ni·ca·ra·guan** \-wən\ adj or n

Nic·o·bar \'nik-ə-₁bär\ islands India in Bay of Bengal S of the Andamans — see ANDAMAN

Nic·o·sia \₁nik-ə-'sē-ə\ city, capital of Cyprus

Ni·ger \'nī-jər\ 1 river 4185 kilometers long W Africa flowing into Gulf of Guinea 2 country W Africa N of Nigeria; capital, Niamey

Ni·ge·ria \nī-'jir-ē-ə\ country W Africa on Gulf of Guinea; an independent state in the Commonwealth; official capital, Abuja — **Ni·ge·ri·an** \-ē-ən\ adj or n

Nii·hau \'nē-₁haù\ island Hawaii WSW of Kauai

Nile \'nī(ə)l\ river 6497 kilometers long E Africa flowing from Lake Victoria in Uganda N into the Mediterranean in Egypt

Nil·gi·ri \'nil-gə-rē\ hills S India

\ə\abut \ᵊ\kitten \ər\further \a\ash \ā\ace \ä\mop, mar \aù\out \ch\chin \e\bet \ē\easy \g\go \i\hit \ī\ice \j\job \ŋ\sing \ō\go \ò\law \òi\boy \th\thin \th\the \ü\loot \ù\foot \y\yet \zh\vision see also Pronunciation Symbols page

Nin·e·veh \\'nin-ə-və\ ancient city, capital of Assyria; ruins in Iraq on the Tigris

Nip·i·gon, Lake \\-'nip-ə-ˌgän\ lake Canada in W Ontario N of Lake Superior

Nip·pon \nip-'än\ — see JAPAN — **Nip·pon·ese** \ˌnip-ə-'nēz, -'nēs\ *adj or n*

Nizh·ni Nov·go·rod \ˌnizh-nē-'näv-gə-ˌräd, -'nòv-gə-rət\ *or 1932-89* **Gor'·kiy** *or* **Gor·ki** \\'gòr-kē\ city W Russia

Nome \\'nōm\ city W Alaska

Nor·folk\\'nòr-fək, *in the U.S. also* -ˌfòk\ **1** city SE Virginia **2** county E England on North sea

Nor·man·dy \\'nòr-mən-dē\ region NW France NE of Brittany

North 1 river estuary of the Hudson between NE New Jersey & SE New York **2** sea arm of the Atlantic E of Great Britain **3** island N New Zealand

North·al·ler·ton \nòr-'thal-ərt-ᵊn\ town N England in North Yorkshire

North America continent of western hemisphere NW of South America & N of the equator — **North American** *adj or n*

North·amp·ton \nòrth-'(h)am(p)-tən\ city area central England in Northamptonshire

North·amp·ton·shire \nòrth-'(h)am(p)-tən-ˌshi(ə)r, -shər\ *or* **Northampton** county central England

North Cape cape New Zealand at N end of North island

North Car·o·li·na \ˌkar-ə-'lī-nə\ state E U.S.; capital, Raleigh — **North Car·o·lin·ian** \-'lin-ē-ən, -'lin-yən\ *adj or n*

North Da·ko·ta \-də-'kōt-ə\ state N U.S.; capital, Bismarck — **North Da·ko·tan** \-'kōt-ᵊn\ *adj or n*

North Down district E Northern Ireland

Northern Cook \-'kùk\ islands S central Pacific N of Cook islands

Northern Ireland region N Ireland comprising 26 districts of Ulster; a division of United Kingdom; capital, Belfast

Northern Mar·i·ana Islands \-ˌmar-ē-'an-ə-, -ˌmer-\ islands W Pacific; a U.S. commonwealth since 1986

Northern Rhodesia — see ZAMBIA

Northern Territory territory N & central Australia; capital, Darwin

North Korea — see KOREA

North Slope region N Alaska between Brooks Range & Arctic ocean

North·um·ber·land \nòr-'thəm-bər-lənd\ county N England — **North·um·bri·an** \-'thəm-brē-ən\ *adj or n*

North·um·bria \nòr-'thəm-brē-ə\ ancient country Great Britain in what is now N England and S Scotland — **North·um·bri·an** \-brē-ən\ *adj or n*

North Vietnam — see VIETNAM

Northwest Territories territory N Canada consisting of the arctic islands, the mainland N of 60° between Yukon Territory & Hudson bay, & the islands in Hudson bay

North Yorkshire county N England

Nor·way \\'nò(ə)r-ˌwā\ country N Europe in Scandinavia; a kingdom; capital, Oslo

Nor·wich \\'nò(ə)r-(ˌ)wich\ 'nòr-ich, 'när-\ city E England in Norfolk county

Not·ting·ham \\'nät-iŋ-əm, *in the U.S. also* -ˌham\ city N central England in Nottinghamshire

Not·ting·ham·shire \\'nät-iŋ-əm-shi(ə)r, -shər, *in the U.S. also* -ˌham-\ *or* **Nottingham** county N central England

Nouak·chott \nù-'äk-ˌshät\ city, capital of Mauritania

Nou·méa \nü-'mā-ə\ city, capital of New Caledonia

No·va Sco·tia \ˌnō-və-'skō-shə\ province SE Canada; capital, Halifax — **No·va Sco·tian** \-'skō-shən\ *adj or n*

No·vo·kuz·netsk \ˌnō-(ˌ)vō-küz-'netsk\ city S Russia

No·vo·si·birsk \ˌnō-(ˌ)vō-sə-'bi(ə)rsk\ city S Russia

Nu·bia \\'n(y)ü-bē-ə\ region NE Africa in Nile valley in S Egypt & N Sudan — **Nu·bi·an** \-bē-ən\ *adj or n*

Nu·ku·a·lo·fa \ˌnü-kə-wə-'lò-fə\ seaport, capital of Tonga

Nu·mid·ia \n(y)ù-'mid-ē-ə\ ancient country N Africa E of Mauretania in modern Algeria — **Nu·mid·i·an** \-ē-ən\ *adj or n*

Ny·asa, Lake \-nī-'as-ə, -nē-\ lake SE Africa in Malawi, Mozambique, & Tanzania

Nyasaland — see MALAWI

Oa·hu \ə-'wä-hü\ island Hawaii; site of Honolulu

Oak·land \\'ō-klənd\ city W California on San Francisco Bay E of San Francisco

Oce·a·nia \ˌō-shē-'an-ē-ə, -'ä-nē-ə\ lands of the central & S Pacific: Micronesia, Melanesia, Polynesia including New Zealand, & sometimes Australia & Malay island group — **Oce·a·ni·an** \-'an-ē-ən, -'ä-nē-\ *adj or n*

Oder \\'ōd-ər\ *or* **Odra** \\'ò-drə\ river 906 kilometers long central Europe flowing from Silesia NW into Baltic sea; forms part of boundary between Poland & Germany

Odes·sa \ō-'des-ə\ city & port S Ukraine on Black sea

Ohio \ō-'hī-ō\ **1** river 1579 kilometers long E U.S. flowing from W Pennsylvania into the Mississippi **2** state E central U.S.; capital, Columbus — **Ohio·an** \ō-'hī-ə-wən\ *adj or n*

Oka·ya·ma \ˌō-kə-'yäm-ə\ city Japan in W Honshu on Inland sea

Okee·cho·bee, Lake \ˌō-kə-'chō-bē\ lake S central Florida

Oke·fe·no·kee \ˌō-kə-fə-'nō-kē\ swamp SE Georgia & NE Florida

Oki·na·wa \ˌō-kə-'nä-wə, -'naù-ə\ **1** islands Japan in central Ryukyus **2** island, chief of group — **Oki·na·wan** \-'nä-wən, -'naù-ən\ *adj or n*

Okla·ho·ma \ˌō-klə-'hō-mə\ state S U.S.; capital, Oklahoma City — **Okla·ho·man** \-mən\ *adj or n*

Oklahoma City city, capital of Oklahoma

Old·ham \\'ōl-dəm\ city NW England in Greater Manchester county

Old Point Comfort cape SE Virginia N of entrance to Hampton Roads

Ol·du·vai Gorge \\'ōl-də-ˌvī-\ canyon N Tanzania SE of Serengeti Plain; site of fossil beds

Old World the half of the earth to the east of the Atlantic ocean including Europe, Asia, and Africa; *esp* : the continent of Europe

Olym·pia \ə-'lim-pē-ə, ō-\ **1** city, capital of Washington **2** plain S Greece in NW Peloponnisos

Olym·pic \ə-'lim-pik, ō-\ mountains NW Washington on Olympic peninsula; highest Mt. Olympus 2428 meters

Olym·pus \ə-'lim-pəs, ō-\ mountains NE Greece

Omagh \\'ō-mə\ **1** district W Northern Ireland **2** town in Omagh district

Oma·ha \\'ō-mə-ˌhò, -ˌhä\ city E Nebraska

Oman \ō-'män, -'man\ country SW Asia in SE Arabia; a sultanate; capital, Muscat

Oman, Gulf of arm of Arabian sea between Oman & SE Iran

Omsk \\'òm(p)sk, 'äm(p)sk\ city S Russia

On·tar·io \än-'ter-ē-ˌō, -'tar-\ province E Canada; capital, Toronto — **On·tar·i·an** \-ē-ən\ *adj or n*

Ontario, Lake lake E central North America in U.S. & Canada; one of the Great Lakes

Or·ange \\'òr-inj, 'är-, -ənj\ river 2090 kilometers long S Africa flowing W from Drakensberg mountains into the Atlantic

Orange Free State province E central Republic of South Africa; capital, Bloemfontein

Or·e·gon \\'òr-i-gən, 'är-, -ˌgän\ state NW U.S.; capital, Salem — **Or·e·go·nian** \ˌòr-i-'gō-nē-ən, ˌär-, -nyən\ *adj or n*

Oregon Trail pioneer route to the Pacific Northwest about 3220 kilometers long from Missouri to Washington

Ori·no·co \ˌōr-ə-ˈnō-kō, ˌor-\ river 2575 kilometers long Venezuela flowing into the Atlantic
Ork·ney \ˈork-nē\ islands N Scotland forming a region
Or·lan·do \or-ˈlan-dō\ city central Florida
Osa·ka \ō-ˈsäk-ə\ city Japan in S Honshu
Osh·a·wa \ˈäsh-ə-ˌwä\ city SE Ontario, Canada on Lake Ontario ENE of Toronto
Os·lo \ˈäz-lō, ˈäs-\ city, capital of Norway
Ot·ta·wa \ˈät-ə-ˌwä, -wə, -ˌwo\ city, capital of Canada in SE Ontario on Ottawa river
Ottoman Empire \ˌät-ə-mən-\ former Turkish sultanate in SE Europe, W Asia, & N Africa
Oua·ga·dou·gou \ˌwäg-ə-ˈdü-ˌgü\ city, capital of Burkina Faso
Outer Hebrides — see HEBRIDES
Ox·ford \ˈäks-fərd\ city central England in Oxfordshire
Ox·ford·shire \ˈäks-fərd-ˌshi(ə)r, -shər\ or **Oxford** county central England
Ox·nard \ˈäk-ˌsnärd\ city SW California
Ozark plateau \ˈō-ˌzärk-\ or **Ozark mountains** eroded plateau N Arkansas, S Missouri, & NE Oklahoma with E extension into S Illinois
Pa·cif·ic \pə-ˈsif-ik\ ocean extending from arctic circle to the equator (North Pacific) and from the equator to the antarctic regions (South Pacific) & from W North America & W South America to E Asia & Australia — **Pacific** adj
Pacific Islands, Trust Territory of the grouping of islands in W Pacific formerly under U.S. administration: the Carolines & the Marshalls
Pa·dang \ˈpä-ˌdäŋ\ city Indonesia in W Sumatra
Pa·dre \ˈpäd-rē, ˈpad-\ island about 160 kilometers long S Texas in Gulf of Mexico
Pa·go Pa·go \ˌpäŋ-(g)ō-ˈpäŋ-(g)ō, ˌpäg-ō-ˈpäg-ō\ town, capital of American Samoa on Tutuila island
Painted Desert region N central Arizona
Pak·i·stan \ˈpak-i-ˌstan, ˌpäk-i-ˈstän\ country S Asia NW of India; until 1971 included also an eastern division E of India; capital, Islamabad — see EAST PAKISTAN — **Pak·i·stani** \-ˈstan-ē, -ˈstän-ē\ adj or n
Palau — see BELAU
Pa·la·wan \pə-ˈlä-wən, -ˌwän\ island W Philippines between South China & Sulu seas
Pa·lem·bang \ˌpäl-əm-ˈbäŋ\ city Indonesia in SE Sumatra
Pa·ler·mo \pə-ˈlər-mō, -ˈle(ə)r-\ city Italy, capital of Sicily
Pal·es·tine \ˈpal-ə-ˌstīn, -ˌstēn\ region SW Asia between Syrian Desert & the Mediterranean now divided between Israel & Jordan — **Pal·es·tin·ian** \ˌpal-ə-ˈstin-ē-ən, -ˈstin-yən\ adj or n
Pal·i·sades \ˌpal-ə-ˈsädz\ line of high cliffs 24 kilometers long on W bank of the Hudson in SE New York & NE New Jersey
Pa·mirs \pə-ˈmi(ə)rz\ or **Pa·mir** \pə-ˈmi(ə)r\ elevated mountainous region central Asia in E Tajikistan & on borders of China, India, Pakistan, & Afghanistan; many peaks over 6000 meters
Pam·li·co \ˈpam-li-ˌkō\ inlet of the Atlantic E North Carolina between main part of the state & offshore islands
Pam·pa \ˈpam-pə\ city NW Texas
Pan·a·ma \ˈpan-ə-ˌmä, -ˌmo, ˌpan-ə-ˈmä, -ˈmo\ **1** country S Central America **2** or **Panama City** city, its capital on the Pacific **3** canal 82 kilometers long Panama connecting Atlantic & Pacific oceans — **Pan·a·ma·ni·an** \ˌpan-ə-ˈmä-nē-ən\ adj or n
Panama, Isthmus of or formerly **Isthmus of Dar·i·en** \-ˌdar-ē-ˈen\ strip of land central Panama connecting North America & South America
Panama Canal Zone — see CANAL ZONE
Pa·nay \pə-ˈnī\ island central Philippines
Pao-t'ou — see BAOTOU
Pap·ua, Territory of \-ˈpap-yə-wə, -ˈpäp-ə-wə\ former

British territory consisting of SE New Guinea & off-shore islands; now part of Papua New Guinea
Papua New Guinea country combining former territories of Papua & New Guinea; formerly a United Nations trust territory governed by Australia; independent since 1975; capital, Port Moresby
Par·a·guay \ˈpar-ə-ˌgwī, -ˌgwä\ **1** river 2415 kilometers long central South America flowing from Brazil S into the Paraná in Paraguay **2** country central South America; capital, Asunción — **Par·a·guay·an** \ˌpar-ə-ˈgwī-ən, -ˈgwä-\ adj or n
Par·a·mar·i·bo \ˌpar-ə-ˈmar-ə-ˌbō\ city, capital of Suriname
Pa·ra·ná \ˌpar-ə-ˈnä\ river 3285 kilometers long central South America flowing S from Brazil into Argentina
Pa·ri·cu·tin \pə-ˈrē-kə-ˌtēn\ **1** former village Mexico **2** volcano on site of former village of Paricutín
Par·is \ˈpar-əs\ city, capital of France — **Pa·ri·sian** \pə-ˈrizh-ən, -ˈrēzh-\ adj or n
Par·nas·sus \pär-ˈnas-əs\ mountain central Greece
Par·os \ˈpar-ˌäs, ˈper-\ island Greece — **Par·i·an** \ˈpar-ē-ən, ˈper-\ adj
Par·ra·mat·ta \ˌpar-ə-ˈmat-ə\ city SE Australia in New South Wales NW of Sydney
Par·thia \ˈpär-thē-ə\ ancient country SW Asia in NE modern Iran — **Par·thi·an** \-thē-ən\ adj or n
Pas·a·de·na \ˌpas-ə-ˈdē-nə\ **1** city SW California E of Glendale **2** city SE Texas
Pat·a·go·nia \ˌpat-ə-ˈgō-nyə, -nē-ə\ region South America S of about 40° S latitude in S Argentina & S tip of Chile; sometimes thought to include Tierra del Fuego — **Pat·a·go·nian** \-nyən, -nē-ən\ adj or n
Pat·er·son \ˈpat-ər-sən\ city NE New Jersey
Pat·mos \ˈpat-məs\ island Greece SSW of Samos
Pat·na \ˈpət-nə\ city NE India on the Ganges
Pearl Harbor inlet Hawaii on S coast of Oahu W of Honolulu
Peking — see BEIJING
Pe·li·on \ˈpē-lē-ən\ mountain 1618 meters NE Greece
Pel·o·pon·ni·sos \ˌpel-ə-pə-ˈnē-səs\ peninsula forming S part of mainland of Greece
Pen·nine Chain \ˈpen-ˌīn-\ mountains N England; highest Cross Fell 893 meters
Penn·syl·va·nia \ˌpen(t)-səl-ˈvā-nyə, -nē-ə\ state E U.S.; capital, Harrisburg
People's Democratic Republic of Yemen — see YEMEN
People's Republic of China — see CHINA
Pe·o·ria \pē-ˈor-ē-ə, -ˈor-\ city N central Illinois
Per·ga·mum \ˈpər-gə-məm\ or **Per·ga·mus** \-məs\ ancient Greek kingdom including most of Asia Minor; at its height 263–133 B.C.; capital, Pergamum (in what is now W Turkey)
Perm \ˈpərm, ˈpe(ə)rm\ city W Russia
Pernambuco — see RECIFE
Persia — see IRAN
Per·sian \ˈpər-zhən\ gulf arm of Arabian sea between Iran & Arabia
Perth \ˈpərth\ city, capital of Western Australia
Pe·ru \pə-ˈrü\ country W South America; capital, Lima — **Pe·ru·vi·an** \pə-ˈrü-vē-ən\ adj or n
Pe·ter·bor·ough \ˈpēt-ər-ˌbər-ə, -ˌbə-rə, -b(ə-)rə\ city area central England in Cambridgeshire
Pe·tra \ˈpē-trə, ˈpe-trə\ ancient city NW Arabia; site in SW Jordan
Petrograd — see SAINT PETERSBURG
Phil·a·del·phia \ˌfil-ə-ˈdel-fyə, -fē-ə\ city SE Pennsylvania — **Phil·a·del·phian** \-fyən, -fē-ən\ adj or n
Phil·ip·pines \ˌfil-ə-ˌpēnz, ˈfil-ə-ˌpēnz\ island group ap-

\ə\abut \ᵊ\kitten \ər\further \a\ash \ā\ace \ä\mop, mar
\aů\out \ch\chin \e\bet \ē\easy \g\go \i\hit \ī\ice \j\job
\ŋ\sing \ō\go \o\law \oi\boy \th\thin \th\the \ü\loot \ů\foot
\y\yet \zh\vision *see also* Pronunciation Symbols page

proximately 800 kilometers off SE coast of Asia; an independent country; capital, Manila — **Phil·ip·pine** \-'pēn, -₁pēn\ *adj*

Phnom Penh \(pə-)'nŏm-'pen, (pə-)'näm-\ city, capital of Cambodia

Phoe·ni·cia \fi-'nish-(ē-)ə, -'nēsh-\ ancient country SW Asia on the Mediterranean in modern Syria & Lebanon

Phoe·nix \'fē-niks\ city, capital of Arizona

Phry·gia \'frij-(ē-)ə\ ancient country W central Asia Minor

Pied·mont \'pēd-₁mänt\ plateau region E U.S. E of the Appalachians between SE New York & NE Alabama — **Pied·mon·tese** \₁pēd-mən-'tēz, -(₁)män-, -'tēs\ *adj or n*

Pierre \'pi(ə)r\ city, capital of South Dakota

Pie·ter·mar·itz·burg \₁pēt-ər-'mar-əts-₁bərg\ city E Republic of South Africa, capital of Natal

Pikes Peak \'pīks-\ mountain 4301 meters E central Colorado in a range of the Rockies

Pin·dus \'pin-dəs\ mountains W Greece; highest point 2480 meters

Pi·sa \'pē-zə\ city W central Italy W of Florence

Pit·cairn \'pit-₁ka(ə)rn, -₁ke(ə)rn\ island S Pacific; a British colony

Pitts·burgh \'pits-₁bərg\ city SW Pennsylvania

Plac·id, Lake \-'plas-əd\ lake NE New York

Plym·outh \'plim-əth\ **1** town SE Massachusetts **2** city SW England in Devon county

Po \'pō\ river 673 kilometers N Italy flowing into the Adriatic

Po Hai — see BO HAI

Po·land \'pō-lənd\ country central Europe on Baltic sea; capital, Warsaw

Pol·y·ne·sia \₁päl-ə-'nē-zhə, -shə\ islands of the central & S Pacific including Hawaii, the Line, Tonga, Cook, & Samoa islands, & often New Zealand among others

Pom·er·a·nia \₁päm-ə-'rā-nē-ə, -nyə\ region N Europe on Baltic sea; formerly in Germany, now mostly in Poland

Pom·peii \päm-'pā, -'pā-₁ē\ ancient city S Italy SE of Naples destroyed 79 A.D. by eruption of Vesuvius — **Pom·pe·ian** \-'pā-ən\ *adj or n*

Po·na·pe \'pō-nə-₁pā\ island W Pacific in the E Carolines

Pon·ce \'pòn(t)-sä\ city S Puerto Rico

Pon·do·land \'pän-(₁)dō-₁land\ territory E Republic of South Africa

Pon·ta Del·ga·da \₁pän-tə-del-'gäd-ə, -'gad-\ city & port Portugal, largest in the Azores

Pont·char·train, Lake \'pän-chər-₁trān, -₁pän-chər-'trān\ lake SE Louisiana E of the Mississippi & N of New Orleans

Pon·tus \'pänt-əs\ **1** ancient country NE Asia Minor **2** *or* **Pontus Euxinus** — see BLACK SEA — **Pon·tic** \'pänt-ik\ *adj or n*

Poole \'pül\ city area S England in Dorset county on English Channel

Poo·na \'pü-nə\ city W India, ESE of Bombay

Po·po·ca·te·petl \₁pō-pə-₁kat-ə-'pet-əl\ volcano 5452 meters SE central Mexico

Port Arthur — see LÜSHUN

Port–au–Prince \₁pōrt-ō-'prin(t)s, ₁port-\ city, capital of Haiti

Port Jack·son \-'jak-sən\ inlet of S Pacific SE Australia in New South Wales; harbor of Sydney

Port·land \'pōrt-lənd, 'port-\ **1** city SW Maine; largest in state **2** city NW Oregon

Port Lou·is \-'lü-əs, -'lü-ē, -lü-'ē\ city, capital of Mauritius

Port Mores·by \-'mō(ə)rz-bē, -'mò(ə)rz-\ city, capital of Papua New Guinea

Pôr·to Ale·gre \₁pōrt-ō-ə-'leg-rə, ₁port-\ city S Brazil

Port of Spain city NW Trinidad, capital of Trinidad and Tobago

Por·to–No·vo \₁pōrt-ə-'nō-vō, ₁port-\ city, capital of Benin

Port Phil·lip Bay \-'fil-əp-\ inlet of S Pacific SE Australia in Victoria; harbor of Melbourne

Ports·mouth \'pōrt-sməth, 'port-\ **1** city SE Virginia **2** city S England in Hampshire

Por·tu·gal \'pōr-chi-gəl, 'por-\ country SW Europe; capital, Lisbon

Portuguese India former Portuguese possession on W coast of India; became part of India 1962

Po·to·mac \pə-'tō-mək, -mik\ river 462 kilometers long flowing from West Virginia into Chesapeake Bay & forming boundary between Maryland & Virginia

Pough·keep·sie \pə-'kip-sē, pō-\ city and river port SE New York on the Hudson

Po·wys \'pō-əs\ county E central Wales; established 1974

Prague \'präg\ *or Czech* **Pra·ha** \'prä-hä\ city, capital of Czech Republic & formerly of Czechoslovakia

Praia \'prī-ə\ town, capital of Cape Verde

Prairie Provinces the Canadian provinces of Alberta, Manitoba, & Saskatchewan

Pres·ton \'pres-tən\ city area NW England in Lancashire

Pre·to·ria \pri-'tōr-ē-ə, -'tòr-\ city Republic of South Africa, capital of Transvaal & administrative capital of the country

Prib·i·lof \'prib-ə-₁lòf\ islands Alaska in Bering sea

Prince Ed·ward Island \-₁ed-wərd-\ island SE Canada in Gulf of Saint Lawrence; a province; capital, Charlottetown

Prince Ru·pert's Land \-'rü-pərts-\ historical region N & W Canada consisting of drainage basin of Hudson bay granted 1670 by King Charles II to Hudson's Bay Company

Prince·ton \'prin(t)-stən\ town W central New Jersey

Prin·ci·pe \'prin(t)-sə-pə\ island W Africa in Gulf of Guinea — see SAO TOME AND PRINCIPE

Prom·on·to·ry \'präm-ən-₁tōr-ē, -₁tòr-\ locality NW Utah

Pro·vence \prə-'vän(t)s\ region SE France on the Mediterranean

Prov·i·dence \'präv-əd-ən(t)s, -ə-₁den(t)s\ city, capital of Rhode Island

Prus·sia \'prəsh-ə\ former kingdom &, later, state Germany; capital, Berlin — **Prus·sian** \-ən\ *adj or n*

Pueb·lo \pü-'eb-lō, 'pweb-, pyü-'eb-\ city SE central Colorado SSE of Colorado Springs

Puer·to Ri·co \₁pōrt-ə-'rē-kō, ₁port-, ₁pwert-\ island West Indies E of Hispaniola; a self-governing commonwealth associated with U.S.; capital, San Juan — **Puerto Ri·can** \-'rē-kən\ *adj or n*

Pu·get Sound \₁pyü-jət-\ arm of the Pacific W Washington

Pun·jab \₁pən-'jäb, -'jab, 'pen-₁jäb, -₁jab\ region in Pakistan & NW India in valley of the Indus

Pu·san \'pü-₁sän\ city SE South Korea

Pyong·yang \pē-'òŋ-₁yäŋ, pē-'əŋ-, -₁yaŋ\ city, capital of North Korea

Pyr·e·nees \'pir-ə-₁nēz\ mountains on French-Spanish border extending from Bay of Biscay to the Mediterranean; highest Pico de Aneto 3404 meters

Qa·tar \'kät-ər, 'gät-, 'gət-\ independent country E Arabia on peninsula extending into Persian gulf; capital, Doha

Qing·dao \'chiŋ-'daù\ *or* **Tsing·tao** \'chiŋ-'daù, '(t)siŋ-\ city & port E China

Qi·qi·har \'chē-'chē-'här\ *or* **Ch'i·ch'i·ha·erh** \'chē-'chē-'hä-'ər\ city NE China

Que·bec \kwi-'bek, ki-\ *or French* **Qué·bec** \kā-bek\ **1** province E Canada **2** city, its capital, on the Saint Lawrence

Queens \'kwēnz\ section of New York City on Long Island E of Brooklyn

Queens·land \'kwēnz-₁land, -lənd\ state NE Australia; capital, Brisbane — **Queens·land·er** \-ər\ *n*

Que·zon City \'kā-₁sòn-\ city Philippines in Luzon; formerly capital of the country

Qui·to \'kē-tō\ city, capital of Ecuador

Ra·bat \rə-'bät\ city, capital of Morocco

Rai·nier, Mount \rə-'ni(ə)r, -rā-\ mountain 4392 meters W central Washington; highest in Cascade Range

Rajasthan — see RAJPUTANA

Raj·pu·ta·na \₁räj-pə-'tän-ə\ *or* **Ra·ja·sthan** \'räj-ə-₁stän\ region NW India S of Punjab

Ra·leigh \'rò-lē, 'räl-ē\ city, capital of North Carolina

Rand — see WITWATERSRAND

Rand·wick \'ran-(₁)dwik\ city SE Australia in E New South Wales

Rangoon — see YANGON

Ra·wal·pin·di \₁rä-wəl-'pin-dē, raùl-'pin-, ròl-'pin-\ city NE Pakistan NNW of Lahore

Read·ing \'red-iŋ\ city area S England in Berkshire

Re·ci·fe \rə-'sē-fə\ *or formerly* **Per·nam·bu·co** \₁pər-nəm-'b(y)ü-kō, ₁per-nəm-'bü-\ city NE Brazil

Red \'red\ **1** river 1638 kilometers long flowing E on Oklahoma-Texas boundary & into the Atchafalaya & the Mississippi in Louisiana **2** sea between Arabia & NE Africa

Red·bridge \'red-(₁)brij\ city area of NE Greater London county, England

Re·gi·na \ri-'jī-nə\ city, capital of Saskatchewan, Canada

Re·no \'rē-nō\ city NW Nevada

Republic of China — see CHINA

Ré·union \rē-'yün-yən\ island W Indian ocean; an overseas division of France; capital Saint-Denis

Reyk·ja·vik \'rāk-(y)ə-₁vik, -₁vēk\ city, capital of Iceland

Rhine \'rīn\ river 1320 kilometers long W Europe flowing from SE Switzerland to North sea in the Netherlands — **Rhen·ish** \'ren-ish, 'rē-nish\ *adj or n*

Rhine·land \'rīn-₁land, -lənd\ *or German* **Rhein·land** \'rīn-₁länt\ the part of Germany W of the Rhine — **Rhine·land·er** \'rīn-₁lan-dər, -lən-\ *n*

Rhode Is·land \rō-'dī-lənd\ **1** *or officially* **Rhode Island and Providence Plantations** state NE U.S.; capital, Providence **2** — see AQUIDNECK ISLAND — **Rhode Is·land·er** \-lən-dər\ *n*

kho·de·sia \rō-'dē-zh(ē-)ə\ — see ZIMBABWE — **Rho·de·sian** \-zh(e-)ən\ *adj or n*

Rhone *or French* Rhône \'rōn\ *or ancient* **Rhod·a·nus** \'räd-ᵊn-əs\ river 800 kilometers long Switzerland & SE France

Rich·mond \'rich-mənd\ **1** — see STATEN ISLAND **2** city, capital of Virginia

Richmond upon Thames \-'temz\ city area of SW Greater London county, England

Ri·ga \'rē-gə\ city, capital of Latvia

Rio \'rē-ō\ RIO DE JANEIRO

Rio de Ja·nei·ro \'rē-ō-də-zhə-'ne(ə)r-ō, -₁dē-, -də-, -jə-'ne(ə)r-\ city SE Brazil on Guanabara Bay

Rio Grande \₁rē-(₁)ō-'grand(-ē)\ *or Mexican* **Rio Bra·vo** \-'bräv-ō\ river 3035 kilometers long SW U.S. forming part of U.S.-Mexico boundary & flowing into Gulf of Mexico

Río Muni — see MBINI

Riv·er·side \'riv-ər-₁sīd\ city S California

Riv·i·era \₁riv-ē-'er-ə\ coast region SE France & NW Italy

Ri·yadh \rē-'(y)äd\ city, capital of Saudi Arabia

Ro·a·noke \'rō-(ə-)₁nōk\ city W Virginia

Roanoke Island island North Carolina S of entrance to Albemarle sound

Rob·son, Mount \-'räb-sən\ mountain 3954 meters W Canada in E British Columbia; highest in the Canadian Rockies

Roch·es·ter \'räch-ə-stər, 'räch-₁es-tər\ city W New York

Rock·ford \'räk-fərd\ city N Illinois

Rocky \'räk-ē\ mountains W North America extending SE from N Alaska to central New Mexico — see ELBERT, MOUNT; ROBSON, MOUNT

Roman Empire the empire of ancient Rome

Ro·ma·nia \rō-'mā-nē-ə, -nyə\ *or* **Ru·ma·nia** \rù-\ country SE Europe on Black sea; capital, Bucharest

Rom·blon \räm-'blōn\ island group central Philippines

Rome \'rōm\ **1** *or Italian* **Ro·ma** \'rō-mä\ city, capital of Italy **2** the Roman Empire

Ro·sa·rio \rō-'zär-ē-₁ō, -'sär-\ city E central Argentina

Ro·seau \rō-'zō\ seaport, capital of Dominica

Ros·tov \rə-'stòf, -'stòv\ city SW Russia, on the Don

Ros·well \'räz-₁wel, -wəl\ city SE New Mexico

Ro·ta \'rōt-ə\ island W Pacific in Marianas

Rot·ter·dam \'rät-ər-₁dam\ city SW Netherlands

Ru·an·da–Urun·di \rù-'än-də-ù-'rün-dē\ former territory E central Africa bordering on Lake Tanganyika & administered by Belgium; divided into Burundi & Rwanda 1962

Ru·dolf, Lake \-'rü-₁dälf\ lake N Kenya in Great Rift valley

Ruhr \'rù(ə)r\ industrial district W Germany E of the Rhine in valley of Ruhr river

Rupert's Land PRINCE RUPERT'S LAND

Rush·more, Mount \-'rəsh-₁mō(ə)r, -₁mò(ə)r\ mountain 1890 meters W South Dakota in Black hills

Rus·sia \'rəsh-ə\ **1** former empire largely having the same boundaries as U.S.S.R.; capital, Petrograd (Saint Petersburg) **2** : UNION OF SOVIET SOCIALIST REPUBLICS **3** country E Europe & N Asia; capital, Moscow; a republic (**Russian Soviet Federated Socialist Republic** *or* **Soviet Russia**) of U.S.S.R. 1922-91

Ru·the·nia \rü-'thē-nyə, -nē-ə\ region W Ukraine W of the N Carpathians — **Ru·the·nian** \rü-'thē-nyən, -nē-ən\ *adj or n*

Ru·wen·zo·ri \₁rü-(w)ən-'zōr-ē, -'zòr-\ mountain group E central Africa between Uganda & Zaire; highest Mount Margherita 5019 meters

Rwan·da *or formerly* **Ru·an·da** \rù-'än-də\ country E central Africa, until 1962 part of Ruanda-Urundi trust territory; capital, Kigali — **Rwan·dan** \-dən\ *adj or n*

Ryu·kyu \rē-'(y)ü-k(y)ü\ islands W Pacific extending in an arc from Kyushu, Japan, to Taiwan, China; belong to Japan — **Ryu·kyu·an** \-₁(y)ü-'k(y)ü-ən\ *adj or n*

Saar \'sär, 'zär\ **1** river 135 kilometers long Europe flowing from E France to W Germany **2** *or* **Saar·land** \'sär-₁land, 'zär-\ district W Europe in valley of Saar river between France and Germany

Sa·bah \'säb-ə\ part of Malaysia in NE Borneo

Sac·ra·men·to \₁sak-rə-'ment-ō\ **1** river 615 kilometers long N California flowing S into Suisun Bay **2** city, capital of California

Sag·ue·nay \'sag-ə-₁nā, ₁sag-ə-'nā\ river 200 kilometers long Canada in S Quebec flowing E into the Saint Lawrence

Sa·ha·ra \sə-'har-ə, -'her-, -'här-\ desert region N Africa N of Sudan region extending from Atlantic coast to Red sea or, as sometimes thought, to the Nile — **Sa·ha·ran** \-ən\ *adj*

Sa·hel \'sa-hil, sə-'hil\ the S fringe of the Sahara

Saigon — see HO CHI MINH CITY

Saint Al·bans \-'òl-bənz\ city area SE England in Hertfordshire

Saint Cath·a·rines \-'kath-(ə-)rənz\ city Canada in SE Ontario

Saint Clair, Lake \-ˈklā(ə)r, -ˈkle(ə)r\ lake SE Michigan & SE Ontario connected by **Saint Clair river** (64 kilometers long) with Lake Huron & draining by Detroit river into Lake Erie

Saint Croix \sānt-ˈkròi, sənt-\ **1** river 120 kilometers long Canada & U.S. on border between New Brunswick & Maine **2** island West Indies; largest of Virgin Islands of the U.S.

Saint Eli·as, Mount \-ˌsānt-ᵊl-ˈī-əs\ mountain 5489 meters on Alaska-Canada boundary in **Saint Elias range**

Saint George's \-ˈjȯr-jəz\ town, capital of Grenada

Saint George's Channel channel British Isles between SW Wales & Ireland

Saint Gott·hard \sānt-ˈgät-ərd, -ˈgäth-, sənt-\ **1** pass S central Switzerland in Saint Gotthard range of the Alps **2** tunnel 15 kilometers long near the pass

Saint He·le·na \ˌsānt-ᵊl-ˈē-nə, ˌsānt-hə-ˈlē-\ island S Atlantic; a British colony

Saint Hel·ens \sānt-ˈhel-ənz, sənt-\ city area NW England in Merseyside county ENE of Liverpool

Saint Helens, Mount volcano S Washington

Saint John \sānt-ˈjän, sənt-\ city Canada in New Brunswick

Saint Johns \sānt-ˈjänz, sənt-\ city, capital of Antigua and Barbuda

Saint John's \sānt-ˈjänz, sənt-\ city, capital of Newfoundland, Canada

Saint Kitts \sānt-ˈkits\ *or* Saint Chris·to·pher \-ˈkris-tə-fər\ island West Indies in the Leeward Islands; with Nevis forms independent **Saint Kitts-Nevis**; capital Basseterre (on Saint Kitts)

Saint Law·rence \sānt-ˈlȯr-ən(t)s, sənt-, -ˈlär-\ **1** river 1225 kilometers long E Canada in Ontario & Quebec bordering on U.S. in New York & flowing from Lake Ontario NE into the **Gulf of Saint Lawrence** (inlet of the Atlantic) **2** seaway Canada &U.S. in & along the Saint Lawrence between Lake Ontario & Montreal

Saint Lou·is \sānt-ˈlü-əs, sənt-\ city E Missouri on the Mississippi

Saint Lu·cia \sānt-ˈlü-shə, sənt-\ island West Indies in the Windwards S of Martinique; an independent country; capital, Castries

Saint Paul \sānt-ˈpȯl\ city, capital of Minnesota

Saint Pe·ters·burg \-ˈpēt-ərz-ˌbərg\ **1** city W Florida **2** *or 1914–24* Pet·ro·grad \ˈpe-trə-ˌgrad, -ˌgräd\ *or 1924–91* Le·nin·grad \ˈlen-ən-ˌgrad, -ˌgräd\ city W Russia

Saint Thom·as \-ˈtäm-əs\ island West Indies, one of Virgin Islands of the U.S.; chief town, Charlotte Amalie

Saint Vin·cent \sānt-ˈvin(t)-sənt, sənt-\ island West Indies in the central Windward Islands; with N Grenadines forms independent **Saint Vincent and the Grenadines**; capital, Kingstown (on Saint Vincent)

Sai·pan \sī-ˈpan, -ˈpän; ˈsī-ˌpan, -ˌpän\ island W Pacific in S central Marianas

Sa·kai \(ˈ)sä-ˈkī\ city Japan in S Honshu

Sa·kha·lin \ˈsak-ə-ˌlēn, -lən; ˌsak-ə-ˈlēn\ island SE Russia W Pacific N of Hokkaido, Japan; until 1945 divided between Japan & U.S.S.R.

Sal·a·mis \ˈsal-ə-məs\ **1** ancient city Cyprus on E coast **2** island Greece off Attica

Sa·lem \ˈsā-ləm\ city, capital of Oregon

Sal·ford \ˈsȯl-fərd\ city area NW England in Greater Manchester county

Salisbury — see HARARE

Sa·lo·ni·ka \sə-ˈlän-i-kə, ˌsal-ə-ˈnē-kə\ *or* Thes·sa·lo·ni·ca \ˌthes-ə-lə-ˈnī-kə, -ˈlän-i-kə\ city N Greece in Macedonia

Sal·op \ˈsal-əp\ *or* Shrop·shire \ˈshräp-ˌshi(ə)r, -shər\ county W England bordering on Wales

Salt Lake City city, capital of Utah

Sal·va·dor \ˈsal-və-ˌdȯ(ə)r, ˌsal-və-ˈdȯ(ə)r\ *or* Ba·hia \bä-ˈē-ə\ city NE Brazil on the Atlantic — **Sal·va·dor-**

an \ˌsal-və-ˈdȯr-ən, -ˈdōr-\ *or* Sal·va·dor·ian \-ē-ən\ *adj or n*

Sal·ween \ˈsal-ˌwēn\ river 2815 kilometers long SE Asia flowing S

Sa·mar \ˈsäm-ˌär\ island central Philippines

Sa·ma·ra \sə-ˈmär-ə\ *or 1935–91* Kuy·by·shev \ˈkwē-bə-ˌshef, -ˌshev\ city W Russia, on the Volga

Sam·ni·um \ˈsam-nē-əm\ ancient country S central Italy — Sam·nite \ˈsam-ˌnīt\ *adj or n*

Sa·moa \sə-ˈmō-ə\ islands SW central Pacific N of Tonga islands; divided at longitude 171° W into American Samoa or Eastern Samoa & Western Samoa — Sa·mo·an \-ən\ *adj or n*

Sa·mos \ˈsā-ˌmäs\ island Greece in the Aegean off coast of Turkey — Sa·mi·an \-mē-ən\ *adj or n*

San·'a \ˈsan-ˌä, san-ˈä\ city SW Arabia, capital of Yemen & formerly of Yemen Arab Republic

San An·to·nio \ˌsan-ən-ˈtō-nē-ˌō\ city S Texas

San Ber·nar·di·no \ˌsan-ˌbər-nə(r)-ˈdē-nō\ city S California

San Di·ego \ˌsan-dē-ˈā-gō\ city SW California

Sand·wich \ˈsan-(ˌ)(d)wich\ town SE England

Sandwich islands — see HAWAII

San Fran·cis·co \ˌsan-frən-ˈsis-kō\ city W California on San Francisco Bay & Pacific ocean

San Joa·quin \ˌsan-wä-ˈkēn, -wȯ-\ river 563 kilometers long central California flowing NW into the Sacramento

San Jo·se \ˌsan-ə-ˈzā\ city W California SE of San Francisco

San Jo·sé \ˌsan-ə-ˈzā, -ō-ˈzā, -hō-ˈzā\ city, capital of Costa Rica

San Juan \san-ˈhwän, -ˈwän\ city, capital of Puerto Rico

San Ma·ri·no \ˌsan-mə-ˈrē-nō\ **1** country S Europe on Italian peninsula ENE of Florence near Adriatic sea **2** town, its capital

San Sal·va·dor \san-ˈsal-və-ˌdȯ(ə)r\ **1** island central Bahama islands **2** city, capital of El Salvador

San·ta Ana \ˌsant-ə-ˈan-ə\ city SW California ESE of Long Beach

San·ta Bar·ba·ra \-ˈbär-b(ə-)rə\ *or* Channel islands California in the Pacific off SW coast

San·ta Fe \ˌsant-ə-ˈfā\ city, capital of New Mexico

Santa Fe Trail pioneer route to the Southwest 1290 kilometers long used especially 1821–80 from vicinity of Kansas City, Missouri, to Santa Fe, New Mexico

San·ti·a·go \ˌsant-ē-ˈäg-ō, ˌsänt-\ city, capital of Chile

San·to Do·min·go \ˌsant-əd-ə-ˈmiŋ-gō\ *or formerly* Ci·u·dad Tru·ji·llo \ˌsē-ù-ˌthä-trü-ˈhē-(y)ō, ˌsē-ù-ˌdad-\ city, capital of Dominican Republic

São Pau·lo \ˌsä-ō-ˈpaù-lō\ city SE Brazil

São To·mé \ˌsä-ō-tō-ˈmā\ town, capital of Sao Tome and Principe

Sao Tome and Principe country W Africa; formerly a Portuguese colony; became independent 1975; capital São Tomé

Sap·po·ro \ˈsäp-ə-ˌrō; sə-ˈpōr-ō, -ˈpȯr-\ city Japan on W Hokkaido

Sa·ra·tov \sə-ˈrät-əf\ city W Russia, on the Volga

Sa·ra·wak \sə-ˈrä-(ˌ)wä(k), -ˌwak\ part of Malaysia in N Borneo

Sar·din·ia \sär-ˈdin-ē-ə, -ˈdin-yə\ island Italy in the Mediterranean S of Corsica — Sar·din·ian \-ˈdin-ē-ən, -ˈdin-yən\ *adj or n*

Sar·gas·so sea \sär-ˌgas-ō-\ area of nearly still water in the N Atlantic lying chiefly between 25°& 35° N latitude & 40°& 70° W longitude

Sas·katch·e·wan \sə-ˈskach-ə-wən, sa-, -ˌwän\ province W Canada; capital, Regina

Sas·ka·toon \ˌsas-kə-ˈtün\ city central Saskatchewan, Canada

Sau·di Ara·bia \ˌsaùd-ē-ə-ˈrā-bē-ə, ˌsȯd-ē-, sä-ˌüd-ē-\ country SW Asia occupying largest part of Arabian peninsula; a kingdom; capital, Riyadh — **Saudi** *adj or n* — **Saudi Arabian** *adj or n*

Sault Sainte Ma·rie canals \ˌsü-(ˌ)sänt-mə-ˈrē-\ *or* **Soo canals** \ˌsü-\ three ship canals, two in U.S. (Michigan) & one in Canada (Ontario), at rapids in river connecting Lake Superior & Lake Huron

Sa·vaii \sə-ˈvī-ˌē\ island, largest in Western Samoa

Sa·van·nah \sə-ˈvan-ə\ city E Georgia

Sa·voy \sə-ˈvȯi\ *or French* **Sa·voie** \sȧ-vwȧ\ region SE France SW of Switzerland bordering on Italy — **Sa·voy·ard** \sə-ˈvȯi-ˌärd, ˌsav-ˌȯi-ˈärd; ˌsav-ˌwä-ˈyär(d)\ *adj or n*

Sca·fell Pike \ˈskȯ-ˈfel-\ mountain 978 meters NW England in Cumbria county; highest in Cumbrian mountains & in England

Scan·di·na·via \ˌskan-də-ˈnā-vē-ə, -vyə\ **1** peninsula N Europe occupied by Norway & Sweden **2** Denmark, Norway, Sweden, & sometimes also Iceland & Finland — **Scan·di·na·vian** \-vē-ən, -vyən\ *adj or n*

Scar·bor·ough \ˈskär-ˌbər-ə, -b(ə-)rə\ city Canada in SE Ontario near Toronto

Scheldt \ˈskelt\ *or* **Schel·de** \ˈskel-də\ *or ancient* **Scal·dis** \ˈskal-dəs\ river 435 kilometers long W Europe flowing from N France through Belgium into North sea in Netherlands

Scil·ly \ˈsil-ē\ islands SW England off Land's End in Cornwall and Isles of Scilly county

Sco·tia \ˈskō-shə\ SCOTLAND — the Medieval Latin name

Scot·land \ˈskät-lənd\ *or Latin* **Cal·e·do·nia** \ˌkal-ə-ˈdō-nyə, -nē-ə\ country N Great Britain; a division of United Kingdom of Great Britain and Northern Ireland; capital, Edinburgh

Scyth·ia \ˈsith-ē-ə, ˈsith-\ ancient area of Europe & Asia N & NE of Black sea & E of Aral sea — **Scyth·i·an** \-ē-ən\ *adj or n*

Se·at·tle \sē-ˈat-ᵊl\ city W Washington

Seine \ˈsān, ˈsen\ river 773 kilometers long N France flowing NW into English channel

Sel·kirk \ˈsel-kərk\ range of the Rocky mountains SE British Columbia, Canada; highest peak, Mount Sir Donald 3390 meters

Se·ma·rang \sə-ˈmär-ˌäŋ\ city Indonesia in central Java

Sen·dai \(ˈ)sen-ˈdī\ city Japan in NE Honshu

Sen·e·ca Falls \ˈsen-i-kə-\ village N central New York

Sen·e·gal \ˌsen-i-ˈgȯl\ **1** river 1690 kilometers long W Africa flowing W into the Atlantic **2** country W Africa; capital, Dakar — **Sen·e·ga·lese** \ˌsen-i-gə-ˈlēz, -ˈlēs\ *adj or n*

Seoul \ˈsōl\ city, capital of South Korea

Ser·bia \ˈsər-bē-ə\ region in the Balkans comprising the largest part of Yugoslavia

Ser·en·ge·ti Plain \ˌser-ən-ˈget-ē\ area N Tanzania

Seven Hills the seven hills upon and about which was built the city of Rome

Sev·ern \ˈsev-ərn\ river 338 kilometers long Wales & England flowing from E central Wales into Bristol channel

Se·ville \sə-ˈvil\ *or Spanish* **Se·vi·lla** \sā-ˈvē-(y)ä\ city SW Spain

Sey·chelles \sā-ˈshel(z)\ islands W Indian ocean NE of Madagascar; formerly a British colony; became independent 1976; capital, Victoria

Shang·hai \shaŋ-ˈhī\ city E China

Shan·non \ˈshan-ən\ river 386 kilometers long W Ireland flowing S & W into the Atlantic

Shas·ta, Mount \ˈshas-tə\ mountain 4317 meters N California in Cascade Range

Shatt-al-Ar·ab \ˌshat-ˌal-ˈar-əb\ river 193 kilometers long SE Iraq formed by flowing together of Euphrates & Tigris rivers & flowing SE into Persian gulf

Shef·field \ˈshef-ˌēld\ city N England in South Yorkshire

Shen·an·do·ah Valley \ˌshen-ən-ˈdō-ə-, ˌshan-ə-ˈdō-ə-\

valley Virginia between the Allegheney & Blue Ridge mountains

Shen·yang \ˈshən-ˈyäŋ\ *or* **Muk·den** \ˈmùk-dən, ˈmək-; mùk-ˈden\ city NE China; chief city of Manchuria

Sher·brooke \ˈshər-ˌbrùk\ city Quebec, Canada E of Montreal

Sher·wood Forest \ˌshər-ˌwùd-\ ancient royal forest central England chiefly in Nottinghamshire

Shet·land \ˈshet-lənd\ **1** islands N Scotland NE of the Orkneys **2** *or* **Zet·land** \ˈzet-\ region consisting of the Shetland islands

Shi·jia·zhuang *or* **Shih·kia·chwang** \ˈshi(ə)r-jē-ˈäj-ˈwäŋ, ˈshē-jē-\ city NE China

Shi·ko·ku \shi-ˈkō-kü\ island S Japan E of Kyushu

Shreve·port \ˈshrēv-ˌpō(ə)rt, -ˌpȯ(ə)rt\ city NW Louisiana

Shrews·bury \ˈsh(r)üz-ˌber-ē, ˈshrōz-\ city area W England in Salop county

Shropshire — *see* SALOP

Siam — *see* THAILAND

Siam, Gulf of *or* **Gulf of Thailand** arm of South China sea between Indochina and Malay peninsula

Sian — *see* XI'AN

Si·be·ria \sī-ˈbir-ē-ə\ region N Asia in Russia between the Urals & the Pacific — **Si·be·ri·an** \-ē-ən\ *adj or n*

Sic·i·ly \ˈsis-(ə-)lē\ *or Italian* **Si·ci·lia** \sē-ˈchēl-yä\ island S Italy SW of toe of Italian peninsula; capital, Palermo — **Si·cil·ian** \sə-ˈsil-yən\ *adj or n*

Si·er·ra Le·one \sē-ˌer-ə-lē-ˈōn, ˌsir-ə-\ country W Africa on the Atlantic; capital, Freetown — **Si·er·ra Le·on·ean** \-ˈō-nē-ən\ *adj or n*

Si·er·ra Ma·dre \sē-ˌer-ə-ˈmäd-rē\ mountain system Mexico including **Sierra Madre Oc·ci·den·tal** \-ˌäk-sə-ˌden-ˈtäl\ range W of the central plateau, **Sierra Madre Ori·en·tal** \-ˌōr-ē-ˌen-ˈtäl, -ˌȯr-\ range E of the plateau, & **Sierra del Sur** \sē-ˌer-ə-ˈdel-ˈsü(ə)r\ range to the S

Sierra Ne·va·da \-nə-ˈvad-ə, -ˈväd-\ **1** mountain range E California & W Nevada — *see* WHITNEY, MOUNT **2** mountain range S Spain; highest peak Mulhacén 3477 meters, highest in Spain

Sik·kim \ˈsik-əm, -ˌim\ former country SE Asia on S slope of the Himalayas between Nepal & Bhutan; part of India (country) since 1975; capital, Gangtok

Si·le·sia \sī-ˈlē-zh(ē-)ə, -sh(ē-)ə, sə-\ region E central Europe in valley of the upper Oder; formerly chiefly in Germany now chiefly in E Czech Republic & SW Poland — **Si·le·sian** \-zh(ē-)ən, -sh(e-)ən\ *adj or n*

Sim·coe, Lake \-ˈsim-kō\ lake Canada in SE Ontario

Si·nai \ˈsī-ˌnī\ **1** mountain on Sinai peninsula where according to the Bible the Law was given to Moses **2** peninsula extension of continent of Asia NE Egypt between Red sea & the Mediterranean

Sin·ga·pore \ˈsiŋ-(g)ə-ˌpō(ə)r, -ˌpȯ(ə)r\ **1** island off S end of Malay peninsula; an independent country in the Commonwealth **2** city, its capital — **Sin·ga·por·ean** \ˌsiŋ-(g)ə-ˈpōr-ē-ən, -ˈpȯr-\ *adj or n*

Sinkiang Uighur — *see* XINJIANG UYGUR

Sioux Falls \ˈsü-\ city SE South Dakota; largest in state

Skag·ge·rak \ˈskag-ə-ˌrak\ arm of North sea between S Norway & N Denmark

Skag·way \ˈskag-wā\ city SE Alaska

Sla·vo·nia \slə-ˈvō-nē-ə, -nyə\ region E Croatia — **Sla·vo·ni·an** \-nē-ən, -nyən\ *adj or n*

Slo·va·kia \slō-ˈväk-ē-ə, -ˈvak-\ country central Europe; capital, Bratislava; formerly part of Czechoslovakia

Slo·ve·nia \slō-ˈvē-nē-ə, -nyə\ country S Europe; capital, Ljubljana; a republic of Yugoslavia 1946–91

Smyrna — *see* IZMIR

\ə\abut \ᵊ\kitten \ər\further \a\ash \ā\ace \ä\mop, mar
\aù\out \ch\chin \e\bet \ē\easy \g\go \i\hit \ī\ice \j\job
\ŋ\sing \ō\go \ȯ\law \ȯi\boy \th\thin \t̲h̲\the \ü\loot \ù\foot
\y\yet \zh\vision *see also* Pronunciation Symbols page

Snake \'snāk\ river NW U.S. flowing from NW Wyoming into the Columbia in SE Washington

Snow·don \'snōd-ᵊn\ massif 1085 meters NW Wales; highest point in Wales

Snow·do·nia \snō-'dō-nē-ə, -nyə\ mountainous district NW Wales in area around Snowdon

So·ci·e·ty \sə-'sī-ət-ē\ islands S Pacific; belong to France; chief island, Tahiti

So·fia \'sō-fē-ə, 'sò-, sō-'fē-\ city, capital of Bulgaria

So·ho \'sō-ıhō\ district of central London, England, in Westminster

So·li·hull \ısō-li-'həl\ city area central England in West Midlands county

Sol·o·mon \'säl-ə-mən\ 1 islands W Pacific E of New Guinea divided between Papua New Guinea & independent Solomon Islands (capital, Honiara) 2 sea arm of Coral sea W of the Solomons

So·ma·lia \sō-'mäl-ē-ə, sə-, -'mäl-yə\ country E Africa on Gulf of Aden & Indian ocean; capital, Mogadishu — **So·ma·li·an** \-'mäl-ē-ən, -'mäl-yən\ adj or n

So·ma·li·land \sō-'mäl-ē-ıland, sə-\ region E Africa consisting of Somalia, Djibouti, & part of E Ethiopia — **So·ma·li** \sō-'mäl-ē\ n

Som·er·set \'səm-ər-ıset, -sət\ or **Som·er·set·shire** \-ıshi(ə)r, -shər\ county SW England

So·nor·an \sə-'nōr-ən, -'nòr-\ or **Sonora** desert SW U.S. & NW Mexico

Soo canals — see SAULT SAINTE MARIE CANALS

South island S New Zealand

South Africa, Republic of country S Africa; formerly (as **Union of South Africa**) a British dominion; became independent 1961; administrative capital, Pretoria; legislative capital, Cape Town; judicial capital, Bloemfontein — **South African** adj or n

South America continent of western hemisphere SE of North America & chiefly S of the equator — **South American** adj or n

South·amp·ton \saùth-'(h)am(p)-tən\ city S England in Hampshire

South Australia state S Australia; capital, Adelaide — **South Australian** adj or n

South Bend \-'bend\ city N Indiana

South Cape or **South Point** — see KA LAE

South Car·o·li·na \-ıkar-ə-'lī-nə\ state SE U.S.; capital, Columbia — **South Car·o·lin·i·an** \-'lin-ē-ən, -'lin-yən\ adj or n

South China sea — see CHINA

South Da·ko·ta \-də-'kōt-ə\ state NW central U.S.; capital, Pierre — **South Da·ko·tan** \-'kōt-ᵊn\ adj or n

South·end on Sea \ısaù-ıthend-\ city area SE England in Essex county E of London

Southern Alps mountain range New Zealand in W South island extending almost the length of the island

Southern Rhodesia — see ZIMBABWE

South Gla·mor·gan \-glə-'mòr-gən\ county SE Wales; established 1974; includes Cardiff

South Korea — see KOREA

South seas the areas of the Atlantic, Indian, & Pacific oceans in the southern hemisphere

South Shields \-'shē(ə)l(d)z\ city N England in Tyne and Wear county

South Vietnam — see VIETNAM

South·wark \'səth-ərk, 'saùth-wərk\ city area of S Greater London county, England

South–West Africa territory SW Africa; under administration of Union (later Republic) of South Africa 1919–90 — see NAMIBIA

South Yorkshire county N England; includes Barnsley

Soviet Central Asia portion of central & SW Asia formerly belonging to U.S.S.R. & including Kirghiz Soviet Socialist Republic, Tadzhik Soviet Socialist Republic, Turkmen Soviet Socialist Republic, Uzbek Soviet Socialist Republic & sometimes Kazakhstan

Soviet Russia 1 — see RUSSIA **2** — see UNION OF SOVIET SOCIALIST REPUBLICS

Soviet Union — see UNION OF SOVIET SOCIALIST REPUBLICS

Spain \'spān\ country SW Europe in Iberian peninsula; a kingdom; capital, Madrid

Spanish America 1 the Spanish-speaking countries of America **2** the parts of America settled & formerly governed by the Spanish

Spanish Guinea — see EQUATORIAL GUINEA

Spanish Sahara — see WESTERN SAHARA

Spar·ta \'spärt-ə\ or **Lac·e·dae·mon** \ılas-ə-'dē-mən\ ancient city S Greece in Peloponnisos; capital of Laconia

Spo·kane \spō-'kan\ city E Washington

Spring·field \'spriŋ-ıfēld\ **1** city, capital of Illinois **2** city SW Massachusetts **3** city SW Missouri

Sri Lan·ka \(')srē-'läŋ-kə, (')shrē-\ or formerly **Cey·lon** \si-'län, sā-\ country having the same boundaries as island of Ceylon; an independent state in the Commonwealth; capital, Colombo

Sri·na·gar \sri-'nəg-ər\ city N India

Staked Plain — see LLANO ESTACADO

Staf·ford \'staf-ərd\ city area W central England in Staffordshire

Staf·ford·shire \'staf-ərd-ıshi(ə)r, -shər\ or **Stafford** county W central England

Stam·ford \'stam(p)-fərd\ city SW Connecticut

Stan·ley \'stan-lē\ town, capital of Falkland islands

Stat·en Island \'stat-ᵊn-\ **1** island SE New York SW of mouth of the Hudson **2** or formerly **Rich·mond** \'rich-mənd\ section of New York City including Staten Island

Sterling Heights city SE Michigan

Stir·ling \'stər-liŋ\ town central Scotland in Central region

Stock·holm \'stäk-ıhō(l)m\ city, capital of Sweden

Stock·port \'stäk-ıpō(ə)rt, -ıpò(ə)rt\ city area NW England in Greater Manchester county

Stock·ton \'stäk-tən\ city central California

Stoke on Trent \ıstō-ıkön-'trent, -ıkän-\ city central England in Staffordshire

Stone Mountain mountain 514 meters NW Georgia E of Atlanta

Stor·no·way \'stòr-nə-ıwā\ town NW Scotland in Western Isles region

Stra·bane \strə-'ban\ district W Northern Ireland

Strath·clyde \strath-'klīd\ region SW Scotland; established 1975; includes Glasgow

Strom·bo·li \'sträm-bə-lē\ volcano 927 meters Italy on Stromboli Island

Stutt·gart \'shtùt-ıgärt, 'stùt-, 'stət-\ city SW Germany

Styx \'stiks\ chief river of the underworld in Greek mythology

Süchow — see XUZHOU

Su·cre \'sü-krā\ city, constitutional capital of Bolivia

Su·dan \sü-'dan, -'dän\ **1** region N Africa S of the Sahara between the Atlantic & the upper Nile **2** country NE Africa S of Egypt; capital, Khartoum — **Su·da·nese** \ısüd-ᵊn-'ēz, -'ēs\ adj or n

Sud·bury \'səd-ıber-ē, -b(ə-)rē\ city SE Ontario, Canada

Su·ez \sü-'ez, 'sü-ıez\ canal 148 kilometers long NE Egypt across Isthmus of Suez

Suez, Gulf of arm of Red sea

Suez, Isthmus of isthmus NE Egypt between Mediterranean & Red seas connecting Africa &Asia

Suf·folk \'səf-ək\ county E England on North sea

Sui·sun Bay \sə-'sün-\ inlet of San Francisco Bay, W central California

Su·la·we·si \ısü-lə-'wä-sē\ or **Ce·le·bes** \'sel-ə-ıbēz, -'lē-bēz\ island Indonesia E of Borneo

Su·lu \'sü-lü\ **1** island group SW Philippines SW of Mindanao **2** sea W Philippines

Su·ma·tra \sù-'mä-trə\ island W Indonesia S of Malay peninsula — Su·ma·tran \-trən\ *adj or n*
Su·mer \'sü-mər\ the S division of ancient Babylonia — Su·me·ri·an \sü-'mer-ē-ən, -'mir-\ *adj or n*
Sun·da \'sün-də\ strait between Java & Sumatra
Sun·der·land \'sən-dər-lənd\ city area N England in Tyne and Wear county
Sun·ny·vale \'sən-ē-₁val\ city W California
Sun Valley resort center central Idaho
Su·pe·ri·or, Lake \-sù-'pir-ē-ər\ lake E central North America in U.S. & Canada; largest of the Great Lakes
Su·ra·ba·ja \₁sùr-ə-'bī-ə\ city Indonesia in NE Java
Su·ri·na·me \₁sùr-ə-'näm-ə\ *or* Su·ri·nam \'sùr-ə-₁nam, ₁sùr-ə-'näm\ country N South America between Guyana & French Guiana; formerly a territory of the Netherlands; became independent 1975; capital, Paramaribo
Sur·rey \'sər-ē, 'sə-rē\ **1** county SE England SW of London **2** city Canada in SW British Columbia
Sut·ton \'sət-ᵊn\ city area of S Greater London county, England
Su·va \'sü-və\ city, capital of Fiji on Viti Levu island
Sverdlovsk — *se* YEKATERINBURG
Swan·sea \'swän-zē\ city SE Wales in West Glamorgan county
Swa·zi·land \'swäz-ē-₁land\ country SE Africa between Transvaal & Mozambique; an independent kingdom; capital, Mbabane — Swa·zi \'swäz-ē\ *adj or n*
Swe·den \'swēd-ᵊn\ country N Europe on Scandinavian peninsula bordering on Baltic sea; a kingdom; capital, Stockholm
Swit·zer·land \'swit-sər-lənd\ country W Europe in the Alps; capital, Bern
Syd·ney \'sid-nē\ city SE Australia, capital of New South Wales
Syr·a·cuse \'sir-ə-₁kyüs, -kyüz\ city central New York
Syr·ia \'sir-ē-ə\ **1** ancient region SW Asia bordering on the Mediterranean **2** former area under administration of France (1920–44) including present Syria & Lebanon **3** country S of Turkey; capital, Damascus — Syr·i·an \'sir-ē-ən\ *adj or n*
Syrian Desert desert region between Mediterranean coast & the Euphrates in N Saudi Arabia, SE Syria, W Iraq, & NE Jordan
Ta·ble Bay harbor of Cape Town, Republic of South Africa
Ta·briz \tə-'brēz\ city NW Iran
Ta·co·ma \tə-'kō-mə\ city W Washington
Tae·gu \ta-'gü, tī-\ city South Korea NNW of Pusan
Tae·jon \ta-'jòn, tī-\ city South Korea NW of Taegu
Ta·gus \'tä-gəs\ *or Spanish* Ta·jo \'tä-hō\ *or Portuguese* Te·jo \'tä-zhü\ river 911 kilometers long Spain & Portugal flowing W into the Atlantic
Ta·hi·ti \tə-'hēt-ē\ island S Pacific in Society islands — Ta·hi·tian \-'hē-shən\ *adj or n*
Tai·chung \'tī-'chùŋ\ city China in W Taiwan
Tai·nan \'tī-'nän\ city China in SW Taiwan
Tai·pei \'tī-'pā, -'bā\ *or formerly* Tai·ho·ku \'tī-'hō-₁kü\ city, capital of (Nationalist) China in N Taiwan
Tai·wan \'tī-'wän\ *or* For·mo·sa \fòr-'mō-sə, fər-, -zə\ **1** island China off SE coast; since 1949 seat of government of (Nationalist) Republic of China; capital, Taipei **2** strait between Taiwan & main part of China connecting East China & South China seas — Tai·wan·ese \₁tī-wə-'nēz, -'nēs\ *adj or n*
Tai·yuan \'tī-yù-'än\ city N China
Ta·jik·i·stan \tä-₁jik-i-'stan, -'stän, -₁jik-i-₁, -₁jēk-\ country W central Asia bordering on China & Afghanistan; capital, Dushanbe; a republic (**Ta·dzhik Soviet Socialist Republic** \tä-'jik-, -'jēk-\ *or* **Ta·dzhik·i·stan** *same as* TAJIKISTAN\) of U.S.S.R. 1929–91
Ta·kli·ma·kan *or* Ta·kla Ma·kan \₁täk-lə-mə-'kän\ desert W China
Tal·la·has·see \₁tal-ə-'has-ē\ city, capital of Florida

Tal·linn \'tal-ən, 'täl-\ city, capital of Estonia
Tam·pa \'tam-pə\ city W Florida on Tampa Bay
Tan·gan·yi·ka \₁tan-gən-'yē-kə, ₁taŋ-gən-, -gə-'nē-\ former country E Africa S of Kenya; became part of Tanzania 1964
Tanganyika, Lake lake E Africa between Tanzania & Zaire
Tang·shan \'däŋ-'shän, 'täŋ-\ city NE China
Tan·za·nia \₁tan-zə-'nē-ə, ₁tàn-\ country E Africa on Indian ocean; formed 1964 by union of Tanganyika & Zanzibar; capital, Dar es Salaam — Tan·za·ni·an \-'nē-ən\ *adj or n*
Ta·ra·wa \tə-'rä-wə, 'tar-ə-₁wä\ island central Pacific, capital of Kiribati
Tar·lac \'tär-₁läk\ city Philippines in central Luzon
Tar·ry·town \'tar-ē-₁taùn\ village SE New York
Tar·sus \'tär-səs\ ancient city of S Asia Minor; now a city in S Turkey
Tash·kent \tash-'kent\ city, capital of Uzbekistan
Tas·man \'taz-mən\ sea consisting of the part of the S Pacific between SE Australia & New Zealand
Tas·ma·nia \taz-'mä-nē-ə, -nyə\ *or earlier* Van Die·men's Land \van-'dē-mənz-\ island SE Australia S of Victoria; a state; capital, Hobart — Tas·ma·nian \-nē-ən, -nyən\ *adj or n*
Ta·try \'tä-trē\ *or* Ta·tra \'tä-trə\ mountains N Slovakia & S Poland in central Carpathian mountains
Taun·ton \'tònt-ᵊn, 'tänt-, 'tant-\ city area SW England in Somerset county
Tay·side \'tä-₁sīd\ region E central Scotland; established 1975
Tbi·li·si \tə-'bil-ə-sē\ *or* Tif·lis \'tif-ləs, tə-'flēs\ city, capital of Republic of Georgia
Te·gu·ci·gal·pa \tə-₁gü-sə-'gal-pə\ city, capital of Honduras
Teh·ran \₁tā-'ran, -'rän\ city, capital of Iran; at foot of S slope of Elburz mountains
Tel Aviv \₁tel-ə-'vēv\ city W Israel
Tem·pe \'tem-'pē\ city S central Arizona
Ten·nes·see \₁ten-ə-'sē, 'ten-ə-₁sē\ **1** river 1049 kilometers long in Tennessee, N Alabama, & W Kentucky **2** state E central U.S.; capital, Nashville
Te·noch·ti·tlan \tä-₁nòch-tē-'tlän\ ancient name of Mexico City
Tex·as \'tek-səs, -siz\ state S U.S.; capital, Austin — Tex·an \-sən\ *adj or n*
Thai·land \'tī-₁land, -lənd\ *or formerly* Si·am \sī-'am\ country SE Asia on Gulf of Siam; capital, Bangkok — Thai·land·er \'tī-₁lan-dər, -lən-dər\ *n*
Thames \'temz\ river 338 kilometers long S England flowing E from the Cotswolds in Gloucestershire into the North sea
Thar \'tär\ desert E Pakistan & NW India (country) E of Indus river
Thebes \'thēbz\ **1** *or ancient* The·bae \'thē-bē\ ancient city S Egypt on the Nile **2** ancient city E Greece NNW of Athens on site of modern village of Thivai — The·ban \'thē-bən\ *adj or n*
Thes·sa·lo·ni·ca \₁thes-ə-lə-'nī-kə, -'län-i-kə\ — *see* SA·LONIKA — Thes·sa·lo·nian \-'lō-nē-ən, -'lō-nyən\ *adj or n*
Thim·bu \'thim-bü\ city, capital of Bhutan
Thousand islands Canada & U.S. in the Saint Lawrence in Ontario & New York
Thrace \'thrās\ *or ancient* Thra·cia \'thrā-sh(ē-)ə\ region SE Europe in Balkan peninsula N of the Aegean now divided between Greece & Turkey; in ancient

---

\ə\abut \ᵊ\kitten \ər\further \a\ash \ā\ace \ä\mop, mar
\aù\out \ch\chin \e\bet \ē\easy \g\go \i\hit \ī\ice \j\job
\ŋ\sing \ō\go \ò\law \òi\boy \th\thin \ṯẖ\the \ü\loot \ù\foot
\y\yet \zh\vision *see also* Pronunciation Symbols page

times extended N to the Danube — Thra·cian \\'thrā-shən\\ *adj or n*

Three Rivers *or* **Trois–Ri·vieres** \\.t(r)wä-riv-'ye(ə)r\\ city S Quebec, Canada

Thunder Bay city SW Ontario, Canada

Thur·rock \\'thər-ək, 'thə-rək\\ district SE England in Essex county

Tian·jin \\tē-'än-'jin\\ *or* **Tien·tsin** \\tē-'en(t)-'sin\\ city NE China SE of Beijing

Tian Shan *or* **Tien Shan** \\tē-'en-'shän, tē-'än-\\ mountain system central Asia extending NE from Pamirs

Ti·ber \\'tī-bər\\ *or Italian* **Te·ve·re** \\'tā-vā-rā\\ *or ancient* **Ti·ber·is** \\'tī-bə-rəs\\ river 360 kilometers long central Italy flowing through Rome into Tyrrhenian sea

Ti·bes·ti \\tə-'bes-tē\\ mountains N central Africa in central Sahara in NW Chad; highest 3415 meters

Ti·bet \\tə-'bet\\ region SW China on high plateau (average altitude 4875 meters) N of the Himalayas; capital, Lhasa

Tier·ra del Fue·go \\tē-'er-ə-,del-f(y)ù-'ā-gō\\ **1** island group off S South America **2** chief island of the group; divided between Argentina & Chile

Tiflis — see TBILISI

Ti·gris \\'tī-grəs\\ river 1850 kilometers long Turkey & Iraq flowing SSE & uniting with the Euphrates to form the Shatt-al-Arab

Ti·mor \\'tē-,mò(ə)r, tē-'mò(ə)r\\ island Indonesia SE of Sulawesi; W half formerly belonged to Netherlands, E half to Portugal

Ti·ra·ne *or* **Ti·ra·na** \\ti-'rän-ə\\ city, capital of Albania

Ti·rol *or* **Ty·rol** \\tə-'rōl; 'tī-,rōl, tī-'rōl; 'tir-əl\\ *or Italian* **Ti·ro·lo** \\tē-'rò-lō\\ region in E Alps in W Austria & NE Italy — **Ti·ro·le·an** \\tə-'rō-lē-ən, tī-; ,tir-ə-'lē-, ,tī-rə-'lē-\\ *or* **Tir·o·lese** \\,tir-ə-'lēz, ,tī-rə-, -'lēs\\ *adj or n*

Ti·ti·ca·ca, Lake \\-,tit-i-'käk-ə\\ lake on Bolivia-Peru boundary at altitude of 3810 meters

To·ba·go \\tə-'bā-gō\\ island West Indies NE of Trinidad; part of independent Trinidad and Tobago

To·go \\'tō-gō\\ country W Africa on Gulf of Guinea; capital, Lomé — **To·go·lese** \\,tō-gə-'lēz, -'lēs\\ *adj or n*

To·kyo \\'tō-kē-,ō\\ city, capital of Japan in SE Honshu on Tokyo Bay — **To·kyo·ite** \\'tō-kē-(,)ō-,īt\\ *n*

To·le·do \\tə-'lēd-ō, -'lēd-ə\\ city NW Ohio

Tol'·yat·ti \\tòl-'yät-ē\\ city W Russia; NW of Samara

Ton·ga \\'täŋ-(g)ə\\ islands SW Pacific E of Fiji islands; a kingdom in the Commonwealth; capital, Nukualofa — **Ton·gan** \\-(g)ən\\ *adj or n*

To·pe·ka \\tə-'pē-kə\\ city, capital of Kansas

Tor·bay \\(')tòr-'bā\\ town SW England in Devon county

To·ron·to \\tə-'ränt-ō, -'ränt-ə\\ city, capital of Ontario, Canada

Tor·rance \\'tòr-ən(t)s, 'tär-\\ city SW California

Tor·res \\'tòr-əs\\ strait between New Guinea & Cape York peninsula, Australia

Tower Hamlets city area of E Greater London county, England

To·yo·na·ka \\,tòi-ə-'näk-ə\\ city Japan on Honshu; a suburb of Osaka

Trans·vaal \\tran(t)s-'väl, tranz-\\ province NE Republic of South Africa; capital, Pretoria

Tran·syl·va·nia \\,tran(t)s-əl-'vā-nyə, -nē-ə\\ region W Romania — **Tran·syl·va·nian** \\-nyən, -nē-ən\\ *adj or n*

Transylvanian Alps a S extension of Carpathian mountains in central Romania

Tren·ton \\'trent-ᵊn\\ city, capital of New Jersey

Trin·i·dad \\'trin-ə-,dad\\ island West Indies off NE coast of Venezuela; with Tobago forms (since 1962) the independent country of **Trinidad and Tobago**; capital, Port of Spain — **Trin·i·da·di·an** \\,trin-ə-'dād-ē-ən, -'dad-\\ *adj or n*

Trip·o·li \\'trip-ə-lē\\ city, capital of Libya

Tris·tan da Cu·nha \\,tris-tən-də-'kü-nə, -nyə\\ island S

Atlantic, chief of the Tristan da Cunha islands belonging to British colony of Saint Helena

Tri·van·drum \\triv-'an-drəm\\ city S India

Tro·bri·and \\'trō-brē-,änd\\ islands SW Pacific in Solomon sea belonging to Papua New Guinea

Trois–Rivieres — see THREE RIVERS

Trow·bridge \\'trō-(,)brij\\ town S England in Wiltshire

Troy \\'tròi\\ *or* **Il·i·um** \\'il-ē-əm\\ *or* **Il·i·on** \\'il-ē-,än, -ē-ən\\ *or ancient* **Troia** \\'tròi-ə, 'trō-yə\\ *or* **Tro·ja** \\'trō-jə, -yə\\ ancient city NW Asia Minor SW of the Dardanelles

Truk \\'trək, 'trùk\\ islands W Pacific in central Carolines

Tru·ro \\'trù(ə)r-ō\\ city SW England in Cornwall and Isles of Scilly county

Trust Territory of the Pacific Islands — see PACIFIC ISLANDS, TRUST TERRITORY OF THE

Tsinan — see JINAN

Tsingtao — see QINGDAO

Tuc·son \\tü-'sän, 'tü-,sän\\ city SE Arizona

Tu·la \\'tü-lə\\ city W Russia S of Moscow

Tul·sa \\'təl-sə\\ city NE Oklahoma

Tu·nis \\'t(y)ü-nəs\\ city, capital of Tunisia

Tu·ni·sia \\t(y)ü-'nē-zh(ē-)ə, -'nizh-(ē-)ə\\ country N Africa on the Mediterranean E of Algeria; capital, Tunis — **Tu·ni·sian** \\-'nē-zh(ē-)ən, -'nizh-(ē-)ən\\ *adj or n*

Tu·rin \\'t(y)ü-rən, t(y)ù-'rin\\ city NW Italy on the Po

Tur·key \\'tər-kē\\ country W Asia & SE Europe between Mediterranean & Black seas; capital, Ankara

Turk·men·i·stan \\(,)tərk-,men-ə-'stan, -'stän; -'men-ə-,\\ country central Asia; capital, Ashkhabad; a republic (**Turk·men Soviet Socialist Republic** \\'tərk-mən-\\) of U.S.S.R. 1925–91 — **Turk·me·ni·an** \\,tərk-'mē-nē-ən\\ *adj*

Turks and Cai·cos \\,tərk-sən-'kā-kəs\\ two groups of islands West Indies at SE end of the Bahamas; a British colony

Tu·tu·ila \\,tüt-ə-'wē-lə\\ island S Pacific, chief of American Samoa group

Tu·va·lu \\tü-'väl-ü, -'vär-\\ *or formerly* **El·lice** \\'el-əs\\ islands W Pacific N of Fiji; an independent country in the Commonwealth; capital, Funafuti — see GILBERT AND ELLICE ISLANDS

Tyne and Wear \\'tī-nən-'(d)wi(ə)r\\ county N England; includes Newcastle

Tyre \\'tī(ə)r\\ ancient city, capital of Phoenicia; now a town of S Lebanon — **Tyr·i·an** \\'tir-ē-ən\\ *adj or n*

Tyrol — see TIROL — **Tyrolean** *adj or n* — **Tyrolese** *adj or n*

Tyr·rhe·ni·an \\tə-'rē-nē-ən\\ sea, part of the Mediterranean SW of Italy, N of Sicily, & E of Sardinia & Corsica

Ufa \\ü-'fä\\ city W Russia NE of Samara

Ugan·da \\yü-'gan-də, -'gän-, -'gän-\\ country E Africa N of Lake Victoria; an independent state in the Commonwealth; capital, Kampala — **Ugan·dan** \\-dən\\ *adj or n*

Ukraine \\yü-'krān, 'yü-,krān\\ *or* **the Ukraine** country E Europe on N coast of Black sea; capital, Kiev; a republic of U.S.S.R. 1923–91

Ulan Ba·tor \\,ü-,län-'bä-,tò (ə)r\\ city, capital of Mongolia

Ul·ster \\'əl-stər\\ **1** region N Ireland (island) consisting of Northern Ireland & N Ireland (country) **2** province N Ireland (country) **3** NORTHERN IRELAND

Um·bria \\'əm-brē-ə\\ region central Italy in the Apennines

Un·ga·va \\,ən-'gav-ə\\ **1** bay inlet of Hudson strait NE Canada **2** peninsula region NE Canada in N Quebec

Union of South Africa — see SOUTH AFRICA, REPUBLIC OF

Union of Soviet Socialist Republics *or* **Soviet Union** *or* **Soviet Russia** country 1922–91 E Europe & N Asia; a union of 15 now independent republics; capital, Moscow

United Arab Emir·ates \\-i-'mi(ə)r-əts, -,āts\\ country E Arabia on Persian Gulf; composed of seven emirates; capital, Abu Dhabi

Geographical Names 713

United Kingdom *or in full* United Kingdom of Great Britain and Northern Ireland country W Europe in British Isles consisting of England, Scotland, Wales, Northern Ireland, Channel islands, & Isle of Man; capital, London

United Nations international territory; a small area in New York City in E central Manhattan; seat of permanent headquarters of the United Nations

United States of America *or* United States country North America bordering on Atlantic, Pacific, & Arctic oceans & including Hawaii; capital, Washington

Upper Volta — see BURKINA FASO — Upper Vol·tan \-ˈvält-ᵊn, -ˈvōlt-, -ˈvȯlt-\ *adj or n*

Ural \ˈyu̇r-əl\ 1 mountains Russia & Kazakhstan extending about 2575 kilometers; usually thought of as dividing line between Europe & Asia; highest about 1830 meters 2 river 2255 kilometers long Russia & Kazakhstan flowing from S end of Ural mountains into Caspian sea

Uru·guay \ˈ(y)u̇r-ə-ˌgwī, ˈyu̇r-ə-ˌgwä\ 1 river 1577 kilometers long SE South America 2 country SE South America; capital, Montevideo — Uru·guay·an \ˌ(y)u̇r-ə-ˈgwī-ən, ˌyu̇r-ə-ˈgwä-\ *adj or n*

Ürüm·qi \ˈ(y)u̇r-ə-ˈgwī-ən, ˌyu̇r-ə-ˈgwä-\ *or* Urum·chi \u̇-ˈru̇m-chē, ˌu̇r-əm-ˈchē\ city NW China

Us·pa·lla·ta \ˌu̇-spə-ˈyät-ə, -ˈzhät-\ mountain pass 3840 meters S South America in the Andes between Argentina & Chile

Ustinov — see IZHEVSK

Utah \ˈyü-ˌtȯ, -ˌtä\ state W U.S.; capital, Salt Lake City — Utah·an \-ˌtȯ(-ə)n, -ˌtä(-ə)n\ *adj or n* — Utahn \-ˌtȯ(-ə)n, -ˌtä(-ə)n\ *n*

Uz·bek·i·stan \(ˌ)u̇z-ˌbek-i-ˈstan, -ˈstän; -ˈbek-i-ˌ\ country W central Asia between Aral sea & Afghanistan; capital, Tashkent; a republic (Uz·bek Soviet Socialist Republic \ˈu̇z-ˌbek, ˈəz-; u̇z-ˈ\) of U.S.S.R. 1924–91

Va·duz \vä-ˈdüts\ town, capital of Liechtenstein

Val·dez \val-ˈdēz\ town and port S Alaska

Va·len·cia \və-ˈlen-ch(ē-)ə, -ˈlen(t)-sē-ə\ 1 region & ancient kingdom E Spain 2 city, its capital, on the Mediterranean

Valley Forge locality SE Pennsylvania

Val·let·ta \və-ˈlet-ə\ city, capital of Malta

Van·cou·ver \van-ˈkü-vər\ 1 island W Canada in SW British Columbia 2 city SW British Columbia, Canada

Van Diemen's Land — see TASMANIA

Van·u·atu \ˌvan-ˌwä-ˈtü, ˌvän-, -ˈwä-ˌtü\ *or formerly* New Heb·ri·des \-ˈheb-rə-ˌdēz\ islands SW Pacific W of Fiji; formerly under shared British and French administration; became independent 1980; capital, Vila

Varanasi — see BANARAS

Vat·i·can City \ˌvat-i-kən-\ independent state within Rome, Italy; created 1929 as headquarters for the Pope

Ven·e·zu·e·la \ˌven-əz-(ə)-ˈwā-lə, -ˈwē-\ country N South America; capital, Caracas — Ven·e·zu·e·lan \-lən\ *adj or n*

Ven·ice \ˈven-əs\ *or Italian* Ve·ne·zia \və-ˈnet-sē-ə\ city N Italy on islands in Lagoon of Venice

Ve·ra·cruz \ˌver-ə-ˈkrüz, -ˈkrüs\ city E Mexico

Ver·mont \vər-ˈmänt\ state NE U.S.; capital, Montpelier — Ver·mont·er \-ər\ *n*

Ve·ro·na \və-ˈrō-nə\ city N Italy W of Venice

Ve·su·vi·us \və-ˈsü-vē-əs\ volcano about 1220 meters S Italy near Bay of Naples

Vicks·burg \ˈviks-ˌbərg\ city W Mississippi

Vic·to·ria \vik-ˈtōr-ē-ə, -ˈtȯr-\ 1 city, capital of British Columbia, Canada on Vancouver island 2 island N Canada in Arctic island group 3 state SE Australia; capital, Melbourne 4 city, capital of Hong Kong 5 seaport, capital of Seychelles — Vic·to·ri·an \-ē-ən\ *adj or n*

Victoria, Lake lake E Africa in Tanzania, Kenya, & Uganda

Vi·en·na \vē-ˈen-ə\ *or ancient* Vin·dob·o·na \vin-ˈdäb-

ə-nə\ *or* Vin·dob·na \-ˈdäb-nə\ city,capital of Austria on the Danube — Vi·en·nese \ˌvē-ə-ˈnēz, -ˈnēs\ *adj or n*

Vien·tiane \(ˈ)vyen-ˈtyän\ city, capital of Laos

Viet·nam \vē-ˈet-ˈnäm, vyet-, ˌvē-ət-, -ˈnam\ country SE Asia in Indochina; capital, Hanoi; established 1945–46 & divided 1954–75 at 17th parallel into the independent states of North Vietnam (capital, Hanoi) & South Vietnam (capital, Saigon)

Vi·la \ˈvē-lə\ city, capital of Vanuatu

Vil·ni·us \ˈvil-nē-əs\ *or Russian* Vil·na \ˈvil-nə\ *or* Vil·no \-nō\ city, capital of Lithuania

Vin·land \ˈvin-lənd\ a portion of the coast of North America visited and so called by Norse voyagers about 1000 A.D.; perhaps Newfoundland

Vir·gin·ia \vər-ˈjin-yə, -ˈjin-ē-ə\ state E U.S.; capital, Richmond — Vir·gin·ian \-yən, -ē-ən\ *adj or n*

Virginia Beach city SE Virginia

Virginia City village W Nevada

Vir·gin Islands \ˌvər-jən-\ island group West Indies E of Puerto Rico — see BRITISH VIRGIN ISLANDS; VIRGIN ISLANDS OF THE UNITED STATES

Virgin Islands of the United States the W islands of the Virgin Islands group; capital, Charlotte Amalie (on Saint Thomas)

Vi·sa·yan \və-ˈsī-ən\ *or* Bi·sa·yas \bə-ˈsī-əz\ islands central Philippines

Vish·a·kha·pat·nam \vi-ˌshäk-ə-ˈpət-nəm\ *or* Vis·a·kha·pat·nam \-ˌsä-\ city E India

Vis·tu·la \ˈvis(h)-chə-lə, ˈvis-tə-lə\ river 1015 kilometers long Poland flowing N from the Carpathians

Vi·ti Le·vu \ˌvēt-ē-ˈlev-ü\ island SW Pacific; largest of the Fiji group

Vlad·i·vos·tok \ˌvlad-ə-və-ˈstäk, -ˈväs-ˌtäk\ city & port SE Russia on Sea of Japan

Vol·ga \ˈväl-gə, ˈvȯl-, ˈvōl-\ river 3742 kilometers long W Russia; longest river in Europe

Vol·go·grad \ˈväl-gə-ˌgrad, ˈvȯl-, ˈvōl-\ city SW Russia, on the Volga

Vol·ta \ˈväl-tə, ˈvȯl-\ river 160 kilometers long Ghana flowing from Lake Volta (reservoir) into Gulf of Guinea

Vo·ro·nezh \və-ˈrȯ-nish\ city SW Russia

Vosges \ˈvōzh\ mountains NE France on W side of Rhine valley; highest 1423 meters

Wa·co \ˈwā-kō\ city central Texas

Wake \ˈwāk\ island N Pacific N of Marshall islands; belongs to U.S.

Wake·field \ˈwāk-ˌfēld\ city N England in West Yorkshire

Wa·la·chia *or* Wal·la·chia \wä-ˈlā-kē-ə\ region S Romania between Transylvanian Alps & the Danube

Wales \ˈwā(ə)lz\ *or Welsh* Cym·ru \ˈkəm-ˌrē\ principality SW Great Britain; a division of United Kingdom; capital, Cardiff

Wal·sall \ˈwȯl-ˌsȯl, -səl\ city area W central England in West Midlands county

Wal·tham Forest \ˌwȯl-thəm-\ city area of NE Greater London county, England

Wands·worth \ˈwän(d)z-(ˌ)wərth\ city area of SW Greater London county, England

War·ley \ˈwȯr-lē\ city area W central England in West Midlands county

War·ren \ˈwȯr-ən, ˈwär-\ city SE Michigan

War·saw \ˈwȯr-ˌsȯ\ *or Polish* War·sza·wa \vär-ˈshäv-ə\ city, capital of Poland

War·wick \ˈwär-ik\ city area central England in Warwickshire

War·wick·shire \ˈwär-ik-ˌshi(ə)r, -shər\ *or* Warwick- county central England

\ə\abut \ᵊ\kitten \ər\further \a\ash \ā\ace \ä\mop, mar \au̇\out \ch\chin \e\bet \ē\easy \g\go \i\hit \ī\ice \j\job \ŋ\sing \ō\go \ȯ\law \ȯi\boy \th\thin \th\the \ü\loot \u̇\foot \y\yet \zh\vision *see also* Pronunciation Symbols page

Wa·satch \'wȯ-₁sach\ range of the Rockies SE Idaho & N central Utah; highest Mount Timpanogos 3660 meters (in Utah)

Wash·ing·ton \'wȯsh-iŋ-tən, 'wȧsh-\ **1** state NW U.S.; capital, Olympia **2** city, capital of U.S.; having the same boundaries as District of Columbia — **Wash·ing·to·nian** \₁wȯsh-iŋ-'tō-nē-ən, ₁wȧsh-, -nyən\ *adj or n*

Washington, Mount mountain 1917 meters N New Hampshire; highest in White mountains

Wa·ter·bury \'wȯt-ə(r)-₁ber-ē, 'wȧt-\ city W central Connecticut

Wa·ver·ley \'wā-vər-lē\ city SE Australia in E New South Wales

Wei·mar Republic \'vī-₁mär-\ the German republic 1919–33

Wel·land \'wel-ənd\ canal 45 kilometers long SE Ontario connecting Lake Erie & Lake Ontario

Wel·ling·ton \'wel-iŋ-tən\ city, capital of New Zealand

Wes·sex \'wes-iks\ ancient kingdom S England; capital, Winchester

West Bank area Palestine W of Jordan river; occupied by Israel since 1967

West Brom·wich \-'brəm-ij, -'bräm-, -ich\ city area W central England in West Midlands county

Western Australia state W Australia; capital, Perth — **Western Australian** *adj or n*

Western Ghats \-'gȯts\ chain of low mountains SW India

Western Isles region W Scotland consisting of the Outer Hebrides; established 1975

Western Sahara *or* **Spanish Sahara** region NW Africa; occupied by Morocco

Western Samoa islands Samoa W of 171° W; an independent country in the Commonwealth since 1962; capital, Apia

West Germany the Federal Republic of Germany — see GERMANY

West Gla·mor·gan \-glə-'mȯr-gən\ county S Wales; established 1974

West Indies islands lying between SE North America & N South America & consisting of the Greater Antilles, Lesser Antilles, & Bahamas — **West Indian** *adj or n*

West Iri·an \-₁ir-ē-'än\ *or* **West New Guinea** territory of Indonesia consisting of W half of New Guinea

West Midlands county W central England; includes Birmingham

West·min·ster \'wes(t)-₁min(t)-stər\ *or* **City of Westminster** city area of W central Greater London county, England

West Pakistan the former W division of Pakistan now having the same boundaries as Pakistan

West·pha·lia \wes(t)-'fāl-yə, -'fā-lē-ə\ region W Germany E of the Rhine — **West·pha·lian** \-'fāl-yən, -'fā-lē-ən\ *adj or n*

West Point U.S. military post SE New York

West Quod·dy Head \-₁kwäd-ē-\ cape; most easterly point of Maine & of the Lower 48 states

West Sus·sex \-'səs-iks\ county SE England

West Virginia state E U.S.; capital, Charleston — **West Virginian** *adj or n*

West York·shire \-'yȯrk-₁shi(ə)r, -shər\ county NW England; includes Wakefield

White mountains N New Hampshire in the Appalachians — see WASHINGTON, MOUNT

White·horse \'hwīt-₁hȯ(ə)rs, 'wīt-\ city, capital of Yukon Territory, Canada

White sea sea inlet NW Russia

Whit·ney, Mount \-'hwit-nē, -'wit-\ mountain 4418 meters SE central California in Sierra Nevada; highest in U.S. outside of Alaska

Wich·i·ta \'wich-ə-₁tȯ\ city S Kansas

Wight, Isle of \-'wīt\ — see ISLE OF WIGHT

Wil·lem·stad \'vil-əm-₁stät\ city, capital of Netherlands Antilles

Wil·liams·burg \'wil-yəmz-₁bərg\ city SE Virginia

Wil·ming·ton \'wil-miŋ-tən\ city N Delaware; largest in state

Wilt·shire \'wilt-₁shi(ə)r, 'wil-chər, 'wilt-shər\ county S England

Win·ches·ter \'win-₁ches-tər, -chə-stər\ city area S England in Hampshire

Win·der·mere \'win-də(r)-₁mi(ə)r\ lake NW England in Lake District

Wind·hoek \'vint-₁hu̇k\ city, capital of Namibia

Wind·sor \'win-zər\ city S Ontario, Canada on Detroit river

Wind·ward Islands \'win-dwərd-\ islands West Indies in the S Lesser Antilles extending S from Martinique but not including Barbados, Tobago, or Trinidad

Win·ni·peg \'win-ə-₁peg\ city, capital of Manitoba, Canada

Winnipeg, Lake lake S central Manitoba, Canada

Win·ni·pe·sau·kee, Lake \-₁win-ə-pə-'sȯ-kē\ lake central New Hampshire

Win·ston–Sa·lem \₁win(t)-stən-'sā-ləm\ city N central North Carolina

Wis·con·sin \wis-'kän(t)-sən\ state N central U.S.; capital, Madison — **Wis·con·sin·ite** \-sə-₁nīt\ *n*

Wit·wa·ters·rand \'wit-₁wȯt-ərz-₁rand, -₁wät-, -₁ränd, -₁ränt\ *or* **Rand** \'rand, 'ränd, 'ränt\ ridge of gold-bearing rock NE Republic of South Africa in S Transvaal

Wol·lon·gong \'wu̇l-ən-₁gäŋ, -₁gȯŋ\ city SE Australia in E New South Wales S of Sydney

Wol·ver·hamp·ton \'wu̇l-vər-₁ham(p)-tən\ city area W central England in West Midlands county NW of Birmingham

Worces·ter \'wu̇s-tər\ **1** city E central Massachusetts **2** city W central England in Hereford and Worcester county

Wran·gell, Mount \'raŋ-gəl\ volcano 4317 meters S Alaska in Wrangell range

Wro·claw \'vrȯt-₁släf, -₁släv\ city SW Poland in Silesia

Wu·han \'wü-'hän\ city S China

Wu·sih *or* **Wu–hsi** \'wü-'shē\ city E China

Wy·o·ming \wī-'ō-miŋ\ state NW U.S.; capital, Cheyenne — **Wy·o·ming·ite** \-miŋ-₁īt\ *n*

Xi'·an *or* **Si·an** \'shē-'än\ cityE central China

Xin·jiang Uy·gur *or* **Sin·kiang Ui·ghur** \'shin-jē-'äŋ-'wē-gər\ region W China

Xu·zhou \'shü-'jō\ *or* **Sü·chow** \'shü-'jō, 'sü-; 'sü-'chau̇\ city E China

Yak·i·ma \'yak-ə-₁mȯ\ city S central Washington

Ya·lu \'yäl-ü\ river 480 kilometers long SE Manchuria & North Korea

Yan·gon \₁yän-'gȯn\ *or formerly* **Ran·goon** \ran-'gün, raŋ-\ city, capital of Myanmar

Yangtze — see CHANG

Yaoun·dé \yau̇n-'dā\ city, capital of Cameroon

Yap \'yap, 'yäp\ island W Pacific in the W Carolines

Ya·ro·slavl \₁yär-ə-'släv-əl\ city W Russia, NE of Moscow

Yaz·oo \ya-'zü, 'yaz-ü\ river W central Mississippi

Ye·ka·te·rin·burg \yi-'kat-ə-rən-₁bərg, -'kät-, -₁bərk\ *or* *1924–91* **Sverd·lovsk** \sverd-'lȯfsk\ city W Russia, in central Ural mountains

Yellow 1 — see HUANG **2** sea section of East China sea between N China, North Korea, & South Korea

Yel·low·knife \'yel-ə-₁nīf\ town, capital of Northwest Territories, Canada

Ye·men \'yem-ən\ country S Arabia bordering on Red sea & Gulf of Aden; capital, San'a; before 1990 divided into the independent states of **Yemen Arab Republic** (capital, San'a) & **People's Democratic Republic of Yemen** (capital, Aden) — **Ye·me·ni** \'yem-ə-nē\ *adj or n* — **Ye·men·ite** \-ə-₁nīt\ *n*

Yen·i·sey \ˌyen-ə-ˈsā\ river 4505 kilometers long central Russia, flowing N into Arctic ocean

Ye·re·van \ˌyer-ə-ˈvän\ city, capital of Armenia

Yo·ko·ha·ma \ˌyō-kə-ˈhäm-ə\ city Japan in SE Honshu on Tokyo Bay S of Tokyo

Yon·kers \ˈyäŋ-kərz\ city SE New York N of New York City

York \ˈyȯ(ə)rk\ city N England in North Yorkshire

York, Cape cape NE Australia in Queensland at N tip of Cape York peninsula

York·shire \ˈyȯrk-ˌshi(ə)r, -shər\ former county N England

Yo·sem·i·te Falls \yō-ˌsem-ət-ē-\ waterfall E California in Yosemite valley; includes two falls, the upper 436 meters & the lower 98 meters

Youngs·town \ˈyəŋ-ˌstau̇n\ city NE Ohio

Yu·ca·tán \ˌyü-kə-ˈtan, -ˈtän\ peninsula SE Mexico & N Central America including Belize& N Guatemala

Yu·go·sla·via or **Ju·go·sla·via** \ˌyü-gō-ˈsläv-ē-ə\ country S Europe including Serbia & Montenegro and formerly also Slovenia, Croatia, Bosnia and Herzegovina, & Macedonia; capital, Belgrade — **Yu·go·slav** \ˈyü-gō-ˌsläv, -ˌslav\ or **Yu·go·sla·vi·an** \-ˈsläv-ē-ən\ adj or n

Yu·kon \ˈyü-ˌkän\ **1** river 3185 kilometers long NW Canada & Alaska flowing into Bering sea **2** or **Yukon Territory** territory NW Canada; capital, Whitehorse

Yu·ma \ˈyü-mə\ city SW corner of Arizona on the Colorado

Za·greb \ˈzäg-ˌreb\ city, capital of Croatia

Zaire \zä-ˈi(ə)r also ˈzī(ə)r\ **1** river in Africa — see CONGO **2** or formerly **Democratic Republic of the Congo** or earlier **Belgian Congo** country central Africa consisting of most of Congo river basin E of lower Congo river; capital, Kinshasa

Zam·be·zi or **Zam·be·si** \zam-ˈbē-zē\ river 2655 kilometers long SE Africa flowing from NW Zambia into Mozambique channel

Zam·bia \ˈzam-bē-ə\ country S Africa N of the Zambezi; formerly (as **Northern Rhodesia**) dependent on Britain; became independent 1964; capital, Lusaka

Zan·zi·bar \ˈzan-zə-ˌbär\ island Tanzania off NE Tanganyika coast; formerly a sultanate; became independent 1963; united 1964 with Tanganyika forming Tanzania

Za·po·ro·zhye \ˌzäp-ə-ˈrȯ-zhə\ city SE Ukraine

Zetland — see SHETLAND

Zhang·jia·kou \ˈjäŋ-jē-ˈä-ˈkō\ or **Kal·gan** \ˈkal-ˈgan\ city NE China NW of Beijing

Zhdanov — see MARIUPOL

Zheng·zhou or **Cheng–chou** \ˈjəŋ-ˈjō\ city NE central China

Zim·ba·bwe \zim-ˈbäb-wē, -wā\ or formerly **Rhodesia** country S Africa S of Zambezi river; an independent state in the Commonwealth; capital, Harare

Zui·der Zee \ˌzīd-ər-ˈzā, -ˈzē\ former inlet of North sea N Netherlands — see IJSSELMEER

Zu·lu·land \ˈzü-(ˌ)lü-ˌland\ territory E Republic of South Africa in NE Natal on Indian ocean

Zu·rich \ˈzu̇(ə)r-ik\ city N Switzerland

Nations of the World

Name and Pronunciation	Population
Afghanistan \af-'ga-nə-ˌstan\	20,269,000
Albania \al-'bā-nē-ə\	3,422,000
Algeria \al-'jir-ē-ə\	27,029,000
Andorra \an-'dòr-ə\	61,900
Angola \aŋ-'gō-lə, an-\	10,916,000
Antigua and Barbuda \an-'tē-gə…bär-'bü-də\	66,000
Argentina \ˌär-jen-'tē-nə\	33,507,000
Armenia \är-'mē-nē-ə\	3,550,000
Australia \ò-'strāl-yə\	17,729,000
Austria \'òs-trē-ə\	7,938,000
Azerbaijan \ˌä-zər-ˌbī-'jän\	7,398,000
Bahamas \bə-'hä-məz\	266,000
Bahrain \bä-'rān\	486,000
Bangladesh \ˌbäŋ-glə-'desh, -'däsh\	115,075,000
Barbados \bär-'bā-dəs, -(ˌ)dōz, -(ˌ)däs\	260,000
Belarus \ˌbye-lə-'rüs\	10,353,000
Belgium \'bel-jəm\	10,072,000
Belize \bə-'lēz\	204,000
Benin \bə-'nin\	5,091,000
Bhutan \bü-'tan, -'tän\	1,546,000
Bolivia \bə-'li-vē-ə\	7,715,000
Bosnia and Herzegovina \'bäz-nē-ə…hert-sə-gō-'vē-nə, -'gō-və-nə\	4,422,000
Botswana \bät-'swä-nə\	1,406,000
Brazil \brə-'zil\	156,493,000
Brunei \brü-'nī\	275,000
Bulgaria \ˌbəl-'gar-ē-ə, -'gär-\	8,466,000
Burkina Faso \bùr-ˌkē-nə-'fä-sō\	9,780,000
Burundi \bù-'rün-dē\	5,665,000
Cambodia \kam-'bō-dē-ə\	9,287,000
Cameroon \ˌka-mə-'rün\	13,103,000
Canada \'ka-nə-də\	27,296,859
Cape Verde \ˌkāp-'vərd\	350,000
Central African Republic	2,998,000
Chad \'chad\	6,118,000
Chile \'chi-lē\	13,542,000
China, People's Republic of \-'chī-nə\	1,179,467,000
Colombia \kə-'ləm-bē-ə\	33,951,000
Comoro Islands \'kä-mə-ˌrō-\	516,000
Congo \'käŋ-go\	2,775,000
Costa Rica \ˌkäs-tə-'rē-kə\	3,199,000
Croatia \krō-'ā-shə\	4,821,000
Cuba \'kyü-bə\	10,892,000
Cyprus \'sī-prəs\	764,000
Czech Republic \'chek-\	10,332,000
Denmark \'den-ˌmärk\	5,187,000
Djibouti \jə-'bü-tē\	565,000
Dominica \ˌdä-mə-'nē-kə\	74,000
Dominican Republic \də-'mi-ni-kən-\	7,634,000
Ecuador \'e-kwə-ˌdòr\	10,985,000
Egypt \'ē-jəpt\	57,109,000
El Salvador \el-'sal-və-ˌdòr\	5,517,000
Equatorial Guinea \-'gi-nē\	377,000
Eritrea \ˌer-ə-'trā-ə\	3,317,611
Estonia \e-'stō-nē-ə\	1,536,000

Name and Pronunciation	Population
Ethiopia \ˌē-thē-'ō-pē-ə\	52,078,000
Fiji \'fē-(ˌ)jē\	762,000
Finland \'fin-lənd\	5,058,000
France \'frans\	57,690,000
Gabon \ga-'bōn\	1,280,000
Gambia \'gam-bē-ə\	1,033,000
Georgia \'jòr-jə\	5,493,000
Germany \'jər-mə-nē\	81,187,000
Ghana \'gä-nə\	15,636,000
Greece \'grēs\	10,310,000
Grenada \grə-'nā-də\	91,000
Guatemala \ˌgwä-tə-'mä-lə\	9,713,000
Guinea \'gi-nē\	7,418,000
Guinea-Bissau \-bi-'saù\	1,036,000
Guyana \gī-'a-nə\	755,000
Haiti \'hā-tē\	6,902,000
Honduras \hän-'dùr-əs\	5,148,000
Hungary \'həŋ-gə-rē\	10,296,000
Iceland \'īs-lənd, -ˌland\	264,000
India \'in-dē-ə\	896,567,000
Indonesia \ˌin-də-'nē-zhə\	188,216,000
Iran \i-'ran, -'rän\	60,768,000
Iraq \i-'räk, -'rak\	19,435,000
Ireland \'īr-lənd\	3,516,000
Israel \'iz-rē-əl\	5,451,000
Italy \'i-tə-lē\	57,235,000
Ivory Coast	13,459,000
Jamaica \jə-'mā-kə\	2,472,000
Japan \jə-'pan\	124,670,000
Jordan \'jòr-dən\	3,764,000
Kazakhstan \ˌkä-ˌzäk-'stän\	17,186,000
Kenya \'ken-yə, 'kēn-\	28,113,000
Kiribati \'kir-ə-ˌbas\	76,900
Kuwait \kə-'wāt\	1,433,000
Kyrgyzstan \ˌkir-gi-'stän\	4,526,000
Laos \'laùs, 'lä-ōs\	4,533,000
Latvia \'lat-vē-ə\	2,596,000
Lebanon \'le-bə-nən\	2,909,000
Lesotho \lə-'sü-ˌtü\	1,903,000
Liberia \lī-'bir-ē-ə\	2,844,000
Libya \'li-bē-ə\	4,573,000
Liechtenstein \'lik-tən-ˌshtīn\	30,100
Lithuania \ˌli-thə-'wā-nē-ə\	3,753,000
Luxembourg \'lək-səm-ˌbərg, 'lùk-səm-ˌbùrg\	392,000
Macedonia \ˌma-sə-'dō-nē-ə\	2,063,000
Madagascar \ˌma-də-'gas-kər\	13,255,000
Malawi \mə-'lä-wē\	10,581,000
Malaysia \mə-'lā-zhə\	19,077,000
Maldives \'mòl-ˌdēvz, -ˌdīvz\	237,000
Mali \'mä-lē\	8,646,000
Malta \'mòl-tə\	363,000
Mauritania \ˌmòr-ə-'tā-nē-ə\	2,171,000

\ə\abut \ᵊ\kitten \ər\further \a\ash \ā\ace \ä\mop, mar \aù\out \ch\chin \e\bet \ē\easy \g\go \i\hit \ī\ice \j\job \ŋ\sing \ō\go \ò\law \òi\boy \th\thin \t̲h̲\the \ü\loot \ù\foot \y\yet \zh\vision *see also* Pronunciation Symbols page

Name and Pronunciation	Population
Mauritius \mȯ-ˈri-shē-əs\	1,103,000
Mexico \ˈmek-si-ˌkō\	89,955,000
Moldova \mäl-ˈdō-və\	4,362,000
Monaco \ˈmä-nə-ˌkō\	30,500
Mongolia \män-ˈgōl-yə\	2,256,000
Morocco \mə-ˈrä-kō\	26,494,000
Mozambique \ˌmō-zəm-ˈbēk\	15,243,000
Myanmar \ˈmyän-ˌmär\	44,613,000
Namibia \na-ˈmi-bē-ə\	1,537,000
Nauru \nä-ˈü-(ˌ)rü\	10,000
Nepal \nə-ˈpȯl\	19,264,000
Netherlands \ˈne-thər-ləndz\	15,302,000
New Zealand \-ˈzē-lənd\	3,520,000
Nicaragua \ˌni-kə-ˈrä-gwə\	4,265,000
Niger \ˈnī-jər\	8,516,000
Nigeria \nī-ˈjir-ē-ə\	91,549,000
North Korea \-kə-ˈrē-ə\	22,646,000
Norway \ˈnȯr-ˌwā\	4,308,000
Oman \ō-ˈmän\	1,698,000
Pakistan \ˈpa-ki-ˌstan, ˌpä-ki-ˈstän\	127,962,000
Panama \ˈpa-nə-ˌmä\	2,563,000
Papua New Guinea \ˈpä-pə-wə-\	3,918,000
Paraguay \ˈpar-ə-ˌgwī, -ˌgwä\	4,613,000
Peru \pə-ˈrü\	22,916,000
Philippines \ˌfi-lə-ˈpēnz, ˈfi-lə-ˌpēnz\	64,954,000
Poland \ˈpō-lənd\	38,521,000
Portugal \ˈpōr-chi-gəl\	9,823,000
Qatar \ˈkä-tər\	539,000
Romania \rů-ˈmä-nē-ə\	22,789,000
Russia \ˈrə-shə\	148,000,000
Rwanda \rů-ˈän-də\	7,584,000
St. Kitts-Nevis \-ˈkits-ˈnē-vəs\	41,800
St. Lucia \-ˈlü-shə\	136,000
St. Vincent and the Grenadines \-ˈvin-sənt...ˌgre-nə-ˈdēnz\	109,000
San Marino \ˌsan-mə-ˈrē-nō\	24,100
Sao Tome and Principe \ˌsaů-tə-ˈmä...ˈprin-sə-pə\	125,000
Saudi Arabia \ˌsaů-dē-ə-ˈrä-bē-ə, ˌsä-ů-dē-\	17,419,000
Senegal \ˌse-ni-ˈgȯl\	7,899,000
Seychelles \sā-ˈchelz\	71,000
Sierra Leone \sē-ˌer-ə-lē-ˈōn\	4,491,000
Singapore \ˈsiŋ-ə-ˌpōr\	2,876,000
Slovakia \slō-ˈvä-kē-ə\	5,329,000
Slovenia \slō-ˈvē-nē-ə\	1,997,000
Solomon Islands \ˈsä-lə-mən-\	349,000

Name and Pronunciation	Population
Somalia \sō-ˈmä-lē-ə\	8,050,000
South Africa, Republic of	33,071,000
South Korea \-kə-ˈrē-ə\	44,042,000
Spain \ˈspān\	39,141,000
Sri Lanka \srē-ˈläŋ-kə, shrē-\	17,616,000
Sudan \sü-ˈdan\	25,000,000
Suriname \ˌsůr-ə-ˈnä-mə\	405,000
Swaziland \ˈswä-zē-ˌland\	814,000
Sweden \ˈswē-dən\	8,727,000
Switzerland \ˈswit-sər-lənd\	6,996,000
Syria \ˈsir-ē-ə\	13,398,000
Taiwan (Republic of China) \tī-ˈwän\	20,926,000
Tajikistan \tä-ˌji-ki-ˈstän\	5,705,000
Tanzania \ˌtan-zə-ˈnē-ə\	26,542,000
Thailand \ˈtī-ˌland, -lənd\	57,829,000
Togo \ˈtō-gō\	3,810,000
Tonga \ˈtäŋ-gə\	99,100
Trinidad and Tobago \ˈtrin-ə-ˌdad...tə-ˈbä-gō\	1,249,000
Tunisia \tü-ˈnē-zhə\	8,530,000
Turkey \ˈtər-kē\	59,869,000
Turkmenistan \ˌtərk-ˌme-nə-ˈstän\	4,294,000
Tuvalu \tü-ˈvä-lü\	9,500
Uganda \yü-ˈgan-də\	17,741,000
Ukraine \ˈyü-ˌkrān, ˌyü-ˈkrān\	52,344,000
United Arab Emirates	1,986,000
United Kingdom of Great Britain and Northern Ireland \-ˈbri-tən...ˈīr-lənd\	55,500,000
England \ˈiŋ-glənd\	46,161,000
Northern Ireland	1,583,000
Scotland \ˈskät-lənd\	4,957,000
Wales \ˈwālz\	2,799,000
United States of America \-ə-ˈmer-i-kə\	249,632,692
Uruguay \ˈür-ə-ˌgwī, ˈyůr-ə-ˌgwä\	3,149,000
Uzbekistan \ůz-ˌbe-ki-ˈstän\	21,901,000
Vanuatu \ˌvan-ˌwä-ˈtü\	160,000
Vatican City State \ˈva-ti-kən-\	1,800
Venezuela \ˌve-nə-ˈzwä-lə\	20,609,000
Vietnam \vē-ˈet-ˈnäm\	70,902,000
Western Samoa \-sə-ˈmō-ə\	163,000
Yemen \ˈye-mən\	12,519,000
Yugoslavia \ˌyü-gō-ˈslä-vē-ə\	10,561,000
Zaire \zä-ˈir\	42,473,000
Zambia \ˈzam-bē-ə\	8,504,000
Zimbabwe \zim-ˈbäb-wā\	10,123,000

Population of Places in the United States

Having 19,000 or More Inhabitants in 1990

A

Aberdeen, S. Dak.	24,927
Abilene, Tex.	106,654
Addison, Ill.	32,058
Adrian, Mich.	22,097
Agawam, Mass.	27,323
Agoura Hills, Calif.	20,390
Aiken, S.C.	19,872
Akron, Ohio	223,019
Alameda, Calif.	76,459
Alamogordo, N. Mex.	27,596
Albany, Ga.	78,122
Albany, N.Y.	101,082
Albany, Oreg.	29,462
Albuquerque, N. Mex.	384,736
Alexandria, La.	49,188
Alexandria, Va.	111,183
Alhambra, Calif.	82,106
Alice, Tex.	19,788
Allen Park, Mich.	31,092
Allentown, Pa.	105,090
Alliance, Ohio	23,376
Altamonte Springs, Fla.	34,879
Alton, Ill.	32,905
Altoona, Pa.	51,881
Altus, Okla.	21,910
Alvin, Tex.	19,220
Amarillo, Tex.	157,615
Ames, Iowa	47,198
Amherst, Mass.	35,228
Amsterdam, N.Y.	20,714
Anaheim, Calif.	266,406
Anchorage, Alaska	226,338
Anderson, Ind.	59,459
Anderson, S.C.	26,184
Andover, Mass.	29,151
Annapolis, Md.	33,187
Ann Arbor, Mich.	109,592
Anniston, Ala.	26,623
Antioch, Calif.	62,195
Appleton, Wis.	65,695
Apple Valley, Calif.	46,079
Apple Valley, Minn.	34,598
Arcadia, Calif.	48,290
Ardmore, Okla.	23,079
Arlington, Mass.	44,630
Arlington, Tex.	261,721
Arlington Heights, Ill.	75,460
Arvada, Colo.	89,235
Asheville, N.C.	61,607
Ashland, Ky.	23,622
Ashland, Ohio	20,079
Ashtabula, Ohio	21,633
Atascadero, Calif.	23,138
Athens, Ga.	45,734
Athens, Ohio	21,265
Atlanta, Ga.	394,017
Atlantic City, N.J.	37,986
Attleboro, Mass.	38,383
Atwater, Calif.	22,282
Auburn, Ala.	33,830
Auburn, Me.	24,309
Auburn, N.Y.	31,258
Auburn, Wash.	33,102
Augusta, Ga.	44,639
Augusta, Me.	21,325
Aurora, Colo.	222,103
Aurora, Ill.	99,581
Austin, Minn.	21,907
Austin, Tex.	465,622
Azusa, Calif.	41,333

B

Bakersfield, Calif.	174,820
Baldwin, Pa.	21,923
Baldwin Park, Calif.	69,330
Ballwin, Mo.	21,816
Baltimore, Md.	736,014
Bangor, Me.	33,181
Banning, Calif.	20,570
Barberton, Ohio	27,623
Barnstable, Mass.	40,949
Barstow, Calif.	21,472
Bartlesville, Okla.	34,256
Bartlett, Ill.	19,373
Bartlett, Tenn.	26,989
Baton Rouge, La.	219,531
Battle Creek, Mich.	53,540
Bay City, Mich.	38,936
Bayonne, N.J.	61,444
Baytown, Tex.	63,850
Beaumont, Tex.	114,323
Beavercreek, Ohio	33,626
Beaverton, Oreg.	53,310
Bedford, Tex.	43,762
Bell, Calif.	34,365
Belleville, Ill.	42,785
Belleville, N.J.	34,213
Bellevue, Nebr.	30,982
Bellevue, Wash.	86,874
Bellflower, Calif.	61,815
Bell Gardens, Calif.	42,355
Bellingham, Wash.	52,179
Bellwood, Ill.	20,241
Belmont, Calif.	24,127
Belmont, Mass.	24,720
Beloit, Wis.	35,573
Benbrook, Tex.	19,564
Bend, Oreg.	20,469
Benicia, Calif.	24,437
Berea, Ohio	19,051
Bergenfield, N.J.	24,458
Berkeley, Calif.	102,724
Berwyn, Ill.	45,426
Bessemer, Ala.	33,497
Bethany, Okla.	20,075

Bethel Park, Pa.	33,823
Bethesda, Md.	62,936
Bethlehem, Pa.	71,428
Bettendorf, Iowa	28,132
Beverly, Mass.	38,195
Beverly Hills, Calif.	31,971
Biddeford, Me.	20,710
Big Spring, Tex.	23,093
Billerica, Mass.	37,609
Billings, Mont.	81,151
Biloxi, Miss.	46,319
Binghamton, N.Y.	53,008
Birmingham, Ala.	265,968
Birmingham, Mich.	19,997
Bismarck, N. Dak.	49,256
Blacksburg, Va.	34,590
Blaine, Minn.	38,975
Bloomfield, N.J.	45,061
Bloomington, Ill.	51,972
Bloomington, Ind.	60,633
Bloomington, Minn.	86,335
Blue Island, Ill.	21,203
Blue Springs, Mo.	40,153
Blytheville, Ark.	22,906
Boca Raton, Fla.	61,492
Boise, Idaho	125,738
Bolingbrook, Ill.	40,843
Bossier City, La.	52,721
Boston, Mass.	574,283
Boulder, Colo.	83,312
Bountiful, Utah	36,659
Bowie, Md.	37,589
Bowling Green, Ky.	40,641
Bowling Green, Ohio	28,176
Boynton Beach, Fla.	46,194
Bozeman, Mont.	22,660
Bradenton, Fla.	43,779
Braintree, Mass.	33,836
Branford, Conn.	27,603
Brea, Calif.	32,873
Bremerton, Wash.	38,142
Bridgeport, Conn.	141,686
Bristol, Conn.	60,640
Bristol, R.I.	21,625
Bristol, Tenn.	23,421
Brockton, Mass.	92,788
Broken Arrow, Okla.	58,043
Brookfield, Wis.	35,184
Brookline, Mass.	54,718
Brooklyn Center, Minn.	28,887
Brooklyn Park, Minn.	56,381
Brook Park, Ohio	22,865
Broomfield, Colo.	24,638
Brownsville, Tex.	98,962
Brunswick, Me.	20,906
Brunswick, Ohio	28,230
Bryan, Tex.	55,002
Buena Park, Calif.	68,784
Buffalo, N.Y.	328,123
Buffalo Grove, Ill.	36,427
Bullhead City, Ariz.	21,951
Burbank, Calif.	93,643
Burbank, Ill.	27,600
Burlingame, Calif.	26,801
Burlington, Iowa	27,208
Burlington, Mass.	23,302
Burlington, N.C.	39,498
Burlington, Vt.	39,127
Burnsville, Minn.	51,288
Burton, Mich.	27,617
Butte, Mont.	33,336

C

Calumet City, Ill.	37,840
Camarillo, Calif.	52,303
Cambridge, Mass.	95,802
Camden, N.J.	87,492
Campbell, Calif.	36,048
Canton, Ohio	84,161
Cape Coral, Fla.	74,991
Cape Girardeau, Mo.	34,438
Carbondale, Ill.	27,033
Carlsbad, Calif.	63,126
Carlsbad, N. Mex.	24,952
Carmel, Ind.	25,380
Carol Stream, Ill.	31,716
Carpentersville, Ill.	23,049
Carrollton, Tex.	82,169
Carson, Calif.	83,995
Carson City, Nev.	40,443
Carteret, N.J.	19,025
Cary, N.C.	43,858
Casa Grande, Ariz.	19,082
Casper, Wyo.	46,742
Cathedral City, Calif.	30,085
Cedar Falls, Iowa	34,298
Cedar Hill, Tex.	19,976
Cedar Rapids, Iowa	108,751
Centerville, Ohio	21,082
Ceres, Calif.	26,314
Cerritos, Calif.	53,240
Champaign, Ill.	63,502
Chandler, Ariz.	90,533
Chapel Hill, N.C.	38,719
Charleston, Ill.	20,398
Charleston, S.C.	80,414
Charleston, W. Va.	57,287
Charlotte, N.C.	395,934
Charlottesville, Va.	40,341
Chattanooga, Tenn.	152,466
Chelmsford, Mass.	32,383
Chelsea, Mass.	28,710
Chesapeake, Va.	151,976
Cheshire, Conn.	25,684
Chester, Pa.	41,856
Chesterfield, Mo.	37,991
Cheyenne, Wyo.	50,008
Chicago, Ill.	2,783,726
Chicago Heights, Ill.	33,072
Chico, Calif.	40,079
Chicopee, Mass.	56,632
Chillicothe, Ohio	21,923
Chino, Calif.	59,682
Chula Vista, Calif.	135,163
Cicero, Ill.	67,436
Cincinnati, Ohio	364,040
Claremont, Calif.	32,503
Clarksdale, Miss.	19,717
Clarksville, Ind.	19,833
Clarksville, Tenn.	75,494
Clearfield, Utah	21,435
Clearwater, Fla.	98,784
Cleburne, Tex.	22,205
Cleveland, Ohio	505,616
Cleveland, Tenn.	30,354
Cleveland Heights, Ohio	54,052
Cliffside Park, N.J.	20,393
Clifton, N.J.	71,742
Clinton, Iowa	29,201
Clinton, Miss.	21,847
Clovis, Calif.	50,323
Clovis, N. Mex.	30,954
Coconut Creek, Fla.	27,485
Coeur d'Alene, Idaho	24,563

College Park, Ga.	20,457	Delano, Calif.	22,762
College Park, Md.	21,927	Delaware, Ohio	20,030
College Station, Tex.	52,456	Del City, Okla.	23,928
Collinsville, Ill.	22,446	Delray Beach, Fla.	47,181
Colorado Springs, Colo.	281,140	Del Rio, Tex.	30,705
Colton, Calif.	40,213	Denison, Tex.	21,505
Columbia, Mo.	69,101	Denton, Tex.	66,270
Columbia, S.C.	98,052	Denver, Colo.	467,610
Columbia, Tenn.	28,583	Derry, N.H.	29,603
Columbus, Ga.	179,278	Des Moines, Iowa	193,187
Columbus, Ind.	31,802	De Soto, Tex.	30,544
Columbus, Miss.	23,799	Des Plaines, Ill.	53,223
Columbus, Nebr.	19,480	Detroit, Mich.	1,027,974
Columbus, Ohio	632,910	Diamond Bar, Calif.	53,672
Compton, Calif.	90,454	Dodge City, Kans.	21,129
Concord, Calif.	111,348	Dolton, Ill.	23,930
Concord, N.H.	36,006	Dothan, Ala.	53,589
Concord, N.C.	27,347	Dover, Del.	27,630
Conroe, Tex.	27,610	Dover, N.H.	25,042
Conway, Ark.	26,481	Downers Grove, Ill.	46,858
Cookeville, Tenn.	21,744	Downey, Calif.	91,444
Coon Rapids, Minn.	52,978	Dracut, Mass.	25,594
Cooper City, Fla.	20,791	Duarte, Calif.	20,688
Copperas Cove, Tex.	24,079	Dublin, Calif.	23,229
Coral Gables, Fla.	40,091	Dubuque, Iowa	57,546
Coral Springs, Fla.	79,443	Duluth, Minn.	85,493
Corona, Calif.	76,095	Duncan, Okla.	21,732
Coronado, Calif.	26,540	Duncanville, Tex.	35,748
Corpus Christi, Tex.	257,453	Dunedin, Fla.	34,012
Corsicana, Tex.	22,911	Durham, N.C.	136,611
Cortland, N.Y.	19,801		
Corvallis, Oreg.	44,757	**E**	
Costa Mesa, Calif.	96,357	Eagan, Minn.	47,409
Cottage Grove, Minn.	22,935	Eagle Pass, Tex.	20,651
Council Bluffs, Iowa	54,315	East Chicago, Ind.	33,892
Coventry, R.I.	31,083	East Cleveland, Ohio	33,096
Covina, Calif.	43,207	East Detroit, Mich.	35,283
Covington, Ky.	43,264	East Hartford, Conn.	50,452
Cranston, R.I.	76,060	East Haven, Conn.	26,144
Crystal, Minn.	23,788	Eastlake, Ohio	21,161
Crystal Lake, Ill.	24,512	East Lansing, Mich.	50,677
Cudahy, Calif.	22,817	East Moline, Ill.	20,147
Culver City, Calif.	38,793	Easton, Mass.	19,807
Cumberland, Md.	23,706	Easton, Pa.	26,276
Cumberland, R.I.	29,038	East Orange, N.J.	73,552
Cupertino, Calif.	40,263	East Palo Alto, Calif.	23,451
Cuyahoga Falls, Ohio	48,950	East Peoria, Ill.	21,378
Cypress, Calif.	42,655	East Point, Ga.	34,402
		East Providence, R.I.	50,380
D		East Ridge, Tenn.	21,101
Dallas, Tex.	1,006,877	East St. Louis, Ill.	40,944
Dalton, Ga.	21,761	Eau Claire, Wis.	56,856
Daly City, Calif.	92,311	Eden Prairie, Minn.	39,311
Dana Point, Calif.	31,896	Edina, Minn.	46,070
Danbury, Conn.	65,585	Edinburg, Tex.	29,885
Danvers, Mass.	24,174	Edmond, Okla.	52,315
Danville, Calif.	31,306	Edmonds, Wash.	30,744
Danville, Ill.	33,828	El Cajon, Calif.	88,693
Danville, Va.	53,056	El Centro, Calif.	31,384
Dartmouth, Mass.	27,244	El Cerrito, Calif.	22,869
Davenport, Iowa	95,333	El Dorado, Ark.	23,146
Davie, Fla.	47,217	Elgin, Ill.	77,010
Davis, Calif.	46,209	Elizabeth, N.J.	110,002
Dayton, Ohio	182,044	Elk Grove Village, Ill.	33,429
Daytona Beach, Fla.	61,921	Elkhart, Ind.	43,627
Dearborn, Mich.	89,286	Elmhurst, Ill.	42,029
Dearborn Heights, Mich.	60,838	Elmira, N.Y.	33,724
Decatur, Ala.	48,761	El Monte, Calif.	106,209
Decatur, Ill.	83,885	Elmwood Park, Ill.	23,206
Dedham, Mass.	23,782	El Paso, Tex.	515,342
Deerfield Beach, Fla.	46,325	Elyria, Ohio	56,746
Deer Park, Tex.	27,652	Emporia, Kans.	25,512
De Kalb, Ill.	34,925	Encinitas, Calif.	55,386

Enfield, Conn.	45,532
Englewood, Colo.	29,387
Englewood, N.J.	24,850
Enid, Okla.	45,309
Enterprise, Ala.	20,123
Erie, Pa.	108,718
Escondido, Calif.	108,635
Euclid, Ohio	54,875
Eugene, Oreg.	112,669
Euless, Tex.	38,149
Eureka, Calif.	27,025
Evanston, Ill.	73,233
Evansville, Ind.	126,272
Everett, Mass.	35,701
Everett, Wash.	69,961
Evergreen Park, Ill.	20,874

F

Fairbanks, Alaska	30,843
Fairborn, Ohio	31,300
Fairfax, Va.	19,622
Fairfield, Calif.	77,211
Fairfield, Conn.	53,418
Fairfield, Ohio	39,729
Fair Lawn, N.J.	30,548
Fairmont, W. Va.	20,210
Fall River, Mass.	92,703
Falmouth, Mass.	27,960
Fargo, N. Dak.	74,111
Farmers Branch, Tex.	24,250
Farmington, N. Mex.	33,997
Farmington Hills, Mich.	74,652
Fayetteville, Ark.	42,099
Fayetteville, N.C.	75,695
Ferguson, Mo.	22,286
Ferndale, Mich.	25,084
Findlay, Ohio	35,703
Fitchburg, Mass.	41,194
Flagstaff, Ariz.	45,857
Flint, Mich.	140,761
Florence, Ala.	36,426
Florence, S.C.	29,813
Florissant, Mo.	51,206
Folsom, Calif.	29,802
Fond du Lac, Wis.	37,757
Fontana, Calif.	87,535
Fort Collins, Colo.	87,758
Fort Dodge, Iowa	25,894
Fort Lauderdale, Fla.	149,377
Fort Lee, N.J.	31,997
Fort Myers, Fla.	45,206
Fort Pierce, Fla.	36,830
Fort Smith, Ark.	72,798
Fort Walton Beach, Fla.	21,471
Fort Wayne, Ind.	173,072
Fort Worth, Tex.	447,619
Foster City, Calif.	28,176
Fountain Valley, Calif.	53,691
Framingham, Mass.	64,989
Frankfort, Ky.	25,968
Franklin, Mass.	22,095
Franklin, Tenn.	20,098
Franklin, Wis.	21,855
Frederick, Md.	40,148
Fredericksburg, Va.	19,027
Freeport, Ill.	25,840
Freeport, N.Y.	39,894
Fremont, Calif.	173,339
Fremont, Nebr.	23,680
Fresno, Calif.	354,202
Fridley, Minn.	28,335
Friendswood, Tex.	22,814
Fullerton, Calif.	114,144

G

Gadsden, Ala.	42,523
Gahanna, Ohio	27,791
Gainesville, Fla.	84,770
Gaithersburg, Md.	39,542
Galesburg, Ill.	33,530
Gallup, N. Mex.	19,154
Galveston, Tex.	59,070
Gardena, Calif.	49,847
Garden City, Kans.	24,097
Garden City, Mich.	31,846
Garden City, N.Y.	21,686
Garden Grove, Calif.	143,050
Gardner, Mass.	20,125
Garfield, N.J.	26,727
Garfield Heights, Ohio	31,739
Garland, Tex.	180,650
Gary, Ind.	116,646
Gastonia, N.C.	54,732
Germantown, Tenn.	32,893
Gilbert, Ariz.	29,188
Gilroy, Calif.	31,487
Gladstone, Mo.	26,243
Glastonbury, Conn.	27,901
Glen Cove, N.Y.	24,149
Glendale, Ariz.	148,134
Glendale, Calif.	180,038
Glendale Heights, Ill.	27,973
Glendora, Calif.	47,828
Glen Ellyn, Ill.	24,944
Glenview, Ill.	37,093
Gloucester, Mass.	28,716
Golden Valley, Minn.	20,971
Goldsboro, N.C.	40,709
Goose Creek, S.C.	24,692
Goshen, Ind.	23,797
Grand Forks, N. Dak.	49,425
Grand Island, Nebr.	39,386
Grand Junction, Colo.	29,034
Grand Prairie, Tex.	99,616
Grand Rapids, Mich.	189,126
Grandview, Mo.	24,967
Granite City, Ill.	32,862
Grapevine, Tex.	29,202
Great Falls, Mont.	55,097
Greeley, Colo.	60,536
Green Bay, Wis.	96,466
Greenbelt, Md.	21,096
Greenfield, Wis.	33,403
Greensboro, N.C.	183,521
Greenville, Miss.	45,226
Greenville, N.C.	44,972
Greenville, S.C.	58,282
Greenville, Tex.	23,071
Greenwich, Conn.	58,441
Greenwood, Ind.	26,265
Greenwood, S.C.	20,807
Gresham, Oreg.	68,235
Griffin, Ga.	21,347
Groton, Conn.	45,144
Grove City, Ohio	19,661
Guilford, Conn.	19,848
Gulfport, Miss.	40,775

H

Hackensack, N.J.	37,049
Hagerstown, Md.	35,445
Hallandale, Fla.	30,996
Haltom City, Tex.	32,856
Hamden, Conn.	52,434
Hamilton, Ohio	61,368
Hammond, Ind.	84,236

Hampton, Va.	133,793	Irvine, Calif.	110,330
Hanford, Calif.	30,897	Irving, Tex.	155,037
Hanover Park, Ill.	32,895	Ithaca, N.Y.	29,541
Harlingen, Tex.	48,735		
Harrisburg, Pa.	52,376	**J**	
Harrison, N.Y.	23,308	Jackson, Mich.	37,446
Harrisonburg, Va.	30,707	Jackson, Miss.	196,637
Hartford, Conn.	139,739	Jackson, Tenn.	48,949
Harvey, Ill.	29,771	Jacksonville, Ark.	29,101
Hastings, Nebr.	22,837	Jacksonville, Fla.	672,971
Hattiesburg, Miss.	41,882	Jacksonville, Ill.	19,324
Havelock, N.C.	20,268	Jacksonville, N.C.	30,013
Haverhill, Mass.	51,418	Jamestown, N.Y.	34,681
Hawthorne, Calif.	71,349	Janesville, Wis.	52,133
Hayward, Calif.	111,498	Jefferson City, Mo.	35,481
Hazel Park, Mich.	20,051	Jeffersontown, Ky.	23,221
Hazleton, Pa.	24,730	Jeffersonville, Ind.	21,841
Helena, Mont.	24,569	Jersey City, N.J.	228,537
Hemet, Calif.	36,094	Johnson City, Tenn.	49,381
Hempstead, N.Y.	49,453	Johnston, R.I.	26,542
Henderson, Ky.	25,945	Johnstown, Pa.	28,134
Henderson, Nev.	64,942	Joliet, Ill.	76,836
Hendersonville, Tenn.	32,188	Jonesboro, Ark.	46,535
Hesperia, Calif.	50,418	Joplin, Mo.	40,961
Hialeah, Fla.	188,004	Junction City, Kans.	20,604
Hickory, N.C.	28,301	Juneau, Alaska	26,751
Highland, Calif.	34,439	Jupiter, Fla.	24,986
Highland, Ind.	23,696		
Highland Park, Ill.	30,575	**K**	
Highland Park, Mich.	20,121	Kailua, Hawaii	36,818
High Point, N.C.	69,496	Kalamazoo, Mich.	80,277
Hillsboro, Oreg.	37,520	Kaneohe, Hawaii	35,448
Hilo, Hawaii	37,808	Kankakee, Ill.	27,575
Hilton Head Island, S.C.	23,694	Kannapolis, N.C.	29,696
Hinesville, Ga.	21,603	Kansas City, Kans.	149,767
Hingham, Mass.	19,821	Kansas City, Mo.	435,146
Hobart, Ind.	21,822	Kearney, Nebr.	24,396
Hobbs, N. Mex.	29,115	Kearny, N.J.	34,874
Hoboken, N.J.	33,397	Keene, N.H.	22,430
Hoffman Estates, Ill.	46,561	Keizer, Oreg.	21,884
Holland, Mich.	30,745	Kenner, La.	72,033
Hollister, Calif.	19,212	Kennewick, Wash.	42,155
Hollywood, Fla.	121,697	Kenosha, Wis.	80,352
Holyoke, Mass.	43,704	Kent, Ohio	28,835
Homestead, Fla.	26,866	Kent, Wash.	37,960
Homewood, Ala.	22,922	Kentwood, Mich.	37,826
Homewood, Ill.	19,278	Kettering, Ohio	60,569
Honolulu, Hawaii	365,272	Key West, Fla.	24,832
Hoover, Ala.	39,788	Killeen, Tex.	63,535
Hopewell, Va.	23,101	Kingsport, Tenn.	36,365
Hopkinsville, Ky.	29,809	Kingston, N.Y.	23,095
Hot Springs, Ark.	32,462	Kingsville, Tex.	25,276
Houma, La.	30,495	Kinston, N.C.	25,295
Houston, Tex.	1,630,553	Kirkland, Wash.	40,052
Huber Heights, Ohio	38,696	Kirkwood, Mo.	27,291
Huntington, W. Va.	54,844	Kissimmee, Fla.	30,050
Huntington Beach, Calif.	181,519	Knoxville, Tenn.	165,121
Huntington Park, Calif.	56,065	Kokomo, Ind.	44,962
Huntsville, Ala.	159,789		
Huntsville, Tex.	27,925	**L**	
Hurst, Tex.	33,574	La Cañada Flintridge, Calif.	19,378
Hutchinson, Kans.	39,308	Lacey, Wash.	19,279
		Lackawanna, N.Y.	20,585
I		La Crosse, Wis.	51,003
Idaho Falls, Idaho	43,929	Lafayette, Calif.	23,501
Imperial Beach, Calif.	26,512	Lafayette, Ind.	43,764
Independence, Mo.	112,301	Lafayette, La.	94,440
Indianapolis, Ind.	741,952	La Grange, Ga.	25,597
Indio, Calif.	36,793	Laguna Beach, Calif.	23,170
Inglewood, Calif.	109,602	Laguna Niguel, Calif.	44,400
Inkster, Mich.	30,772	La Habra, Calif.	51,266
Inver Grove Heights, Minn.	22,477	Lake Charles, La.	70,580
Iowa City, Iowa	59,738	Lake Havasu City, Ariz.	24,363

Lake Jackson, Tex.	22,776
Lakeland, Fla.	70,576
Lake Oswego, Oreg.	30,576
Lakeville, Minn.	24,854
Lakewood, Calif.	73,557
Lakewood, Colo.	126,481
Lakewood, Ohio	59,718
Lake Worth, Fla.	28,564
La Mesa, Calif.	52,931
La Mirada, Calif.	40,452
Lancaster, Calif.	97,291
Lancaster, Ohio	34,507
Lancaster, Pa.	55,551
Lancaster, Tex.	22,117
Lansing, Ill.	28,086
Lansing, Mich.	127,321
La Porte, Ind.	21,507
La Porte, Tex.	27,910
La Puente, Calif.	36,955
Laramie, Wyo.	26,687
Laredo, Tex.	122,899
Largo, Fla.	65,674
Las Cruces, N. Mex.	62,126
Las Vegas, Nev.	258,295
Lauderdale Lakes, Fla.	27,341
Lauderhill, Fla.	49,708
Laurel, Md.	19,438
La Verne, Calif.	30,897
Lawndale, Calif.	27,331
Lawrence, Ind.	26,763
Lawrence, Kans.	65,608
Lawrence, Mass.	70,207
Lawton, Okla.	80,561
Layton, Utah	41,784
League City, Tex.	30,159
Leavenworth, Kans.	38,495
Leawood, Kans.	19,693
Lebanon, Pa.	24,800
Lee's Summit, Mo.	46,418
Lemon Grove, Calif.	23,984
Lenexa, Kans.	34,034
Leominster, Mass.	38,145
Lewiston, Idaho	28,082
Lewiston, Me.	39,757
Lewisville, Tex.	46,521
Lexington, Ky.	225,366
Lexington, Mass.	28,974
Liberty, Mo.	20,459
Libertyville, Ill.	19,174
Lima, Ohio	45,549
Lincoln, Nebr.	191,972
Lincoln Park, Mich.	41,832
Linden, N.J.	36,701
Lindenhurst, N.Y.	26,879
Lisle, Ill.	19,512
Little Rock, Ark.	175,795
Littleton, Colo.	33,685
Livermore, Calif.	56,741
Livonia, Mich.	100,850
Lockport, N.Y.	24,426
Lodi, Calif.	51,874
Lodi, N.J.	22,355
Logan, Utah	32,762
Lombard, Ill.	39,408
Lomita, Calif.	19,382
Lompoc, Calif.	37,649
Long Beach, Calif.	429,433
Long Beach, N.Y.	33,510
Long Branch, N.J.	28,658
Longmont, Colo.	51,555
Longview, Tex.	70,311
Longview, Wash.	31,499
Lorain, Ohio	71,245

Los Altos, Calif.	26,303
Los Angeles, Calif.	3,485,398
Los Gatos, Calif.	27,357
Louisville, Ky.	269,063
Loveland, Colo.	37,352
Lowell, Mass.	103,439
Lubbock, Tex.	186,206
Lufkin, Tex.	30,206
Lynbrook, N.Y.	19,208
Lynchburg, Va.	66,049
Lynn, Mass.	81,245
Lynnwood, Wash.	28,695
Lynwood, Calif.	61,945

M

McAllen, Tex.	84,021
Machesney Park, Ill.	19,033
McKeesport, Pa.	26,016
McKinney, Tex.	21,283
Macomb, Ill.	19,952
Macon, Ga.	106,612
Madera, Calif.	29,281
Madison, Wis.	191,262
Madison Heights, Mich.	32,196
Malden, Mass.	53,884
Manassas, Va.	27,957
Manchester, Conn.	51,618
Manchester, N.H.	99,567
Manhattan, Kans.	37,712
Manhattan Beach, Calif.	32,063
Manitowoc, Wis.	32,520
Mankato, Minn.	31,477
Mansfield, Conn.	21,103
Mansfield, Ohio	50,627
Manteca, Calif.	40,773
Maple Grove, Minn.	38,736
Maple Heights, Ohio	27,089
Maplewood, Minn.	30,954
Marblehead, Mass.	19,971
Margate, Fla.	42,985
Marietta, Ga.	44,129
Marina, Calif.	26,436
Marion, Ind.	32,618
Marion, Iowa	20,403
Marion, Ohio	34,075
Marlborough, Mass.	31,813
Marquette, Mich.	21,977
Marshall, Tex.	23,682
Marshalltown, Iowa	25,178
Marshfield, Mass.	21,531
Marshfield, Wis.	19,291
Martinez, Calif.	31,808
Maryland Heights, Mo.	25,407
Maryville, Tenn.	19,208
Mason City, Iowa	29,040
Massillon, Ohio	31,007
Mayfield Heights, Ohio	19,847
Maywood, Calif.	27,850
Maywood, Ill.	27,139
Medford, Mass.	57,407
Medford, Oreg.	46,951
Melbourne, Fla.	59,646
Melrose, Mass.	28,150
Melrose Park, Ill.	20,859
Memphis, Tenn.	610,337
Menlo Park, Calif.	28,040
Menomonee Falls, Wis.	26,840
Mentor, Ohio	47,358
Merced, Calif.	56,216
Mercer Island, Wash.	20,816
Meriden, Conn.	59,479
Meridian, Miss.	41,036
Merrillville, Ind.	27,257

Mesa, Ariz.	288,091
Mesquite, Tex.	101,484
Methuen, Mass.	39,990
Miami, Fla.	358,548
Miami Beach, Fla.	92,639
Michigan City, Ind.	33,822
Middletown, Conn.	42,762
Middletown, N.Y.	24,160
Middletown, Ohio	46,022
Middletown, R.I.	19,460
Midland, Mich.	38,053
Midland, Tex.	89,443
Midwest City, Okla.	52,267
Milford, Conn.	49,938
Milford, Mass.	25,355
Mililani Town, Hawaii	29,359
Millbrae, Calif.	20,412
Millville, N.J.	25,992
Milpitas, Calif.	50,686
Milton, Mass.	25,725
Milwaukee, Wis.	628,088
Minneapolis, Minn.	368,383
Minnetonka, Minn.	48,370
Minot, N. Dak.	34,544
Miramar, Fla.	40,663
Mishawaka, Ind.	42,608
Mission, Tex.	28,653
Mission Viejo, Calif.	72,820
Missoula, Mont.	42,918
Missouri City, Tex.	36,176
Mobile, Ala.	196,278
Modesto, Calif.	164,730
Moline, Ill.	43,202
Monroe, La.	54,909
Monroe, Mich.	22,902
Monroeville, Pa.	29,169
Monrovia, Calif.	35,761
Montclair, Calif.	28,434
Montclair, N.J.	37,729
Montebello, Calif.	59,564
Monterey, Calif.	31,954
Monterey Park, Calif.	60,738
Montgomery, Ala.	187,106
Moore, Okla.	40,318
Moorhead, Minn.	32,295
Moorpark, Calif.	25,494
Moreno Valley, Calif.	118,779
Morgan Hill, Calif.	23,928
Morgantown, W. Va.	25,879
Morristown, Tenn.	21,385
Morton Grove, Ill.	22,408
Mountain Brook, Ala.	19,810
Mountain View, Calif.	67,460
Mountlake Terrace, Wash.	19,320
Mount Pleasant, Mich.	23,285
Mount Pleasant, S.C.	30,108
Mount Prospect, Ill.	53,170
Mount Vernon, N.Y.	67,153
Muncie, Ind.	71,035
Mundelein, Ill.	21,215
Munster, Ind.	19,949
Murfreesboro, Tenn.	44,922
Murray, Utah	31,282
Muscatine, Iowa	22,881
Muskegon, Mich.	40,283
Muskogee, Okla.	37,708
Myrtle Beach, S.C.	24,848

N

Nacogdoches, Tex.	30,872
Nampa, Idaho	28,365
Napa, Calif.	61,842
Naperville, Ill.	85,351

Naples, Fla.	19,505
Nashua, N.H.	79,662
Nashville, Tenn.	510,784
Natchez, Miss.	19,460
Natick, Mass.	30,510
National City, Calif.	54,249
Naugatuck, Conn.	30,625
Needham, Mass.	27,557
Neenah, Wis.	23,219
New Albany, Ind.	36,322
Newark, Calif.	37,861
Newark, Del.	25,098
Newark, N.J.	275,221
Newark, Ohio	44,389
New Bedford, Mass.	99,922
New Berlin, Wis.	33,592
New Braunfels, Tex.	27,334
New Brighton, Minn.	22,207
New Britain, Conn.	75,491
New Brunswick, N.J.	41,711
Newburgh, N.Y.	26,454
New Castle, Pa.	28,334
New Haven, Conn.	130,474
New Hope, Minn.	21,853
New Iberia, La.	31,828
Newington, Conn.	29,208
New London, Conn.	28,540
New Milford, Conn.	23,629
New Orleans, La.	496,938
Newport, R.I.	28,227
Newport Beach, Calif.	66,643
Newport News, Va.	170,045
New Rochelle, N.Y.	67,265
Newton, Mass.	82,585
Newtown, Conn.	20,779
New York City, N.Y.	7,322,564
Bronx	1,203,789
Brooklyn	2,300,664
Manhattan	1,487,536
Queens	1,951,598
Richmond	378,977
Niagara Falls, N.Y.	61,840
Niles, Ill.	28,284
Niles, Ohio	21,128
Nogales, Ariz.	19,489
Norco, Calif.	28,302
Norfolk, Nebr.	21,476
Norfolk, Va.	261,229
Normal, Ill.	40,023
Norman, Okla.	80,071
Norristown, Pa.	30,749
Northampton, Mass.	29,289
North Andover, Mass.	22,792
North Attleboro, Mass.	25,038
Northbrook, Ill.	32,308
North Charleston, S.C.	70,218
North Chicago, Ill.	34,978
Northglenn, Colo.	27,195
North Haven, Conn.	22,247
North Kingstown, R.I.	23,786
North Las Vegas, Nev.	47,707
North Lauderdale, Fla.	26,506
North Little Rock, Ark.	61,741
North Miami, Fla.	49,998
North Miami Beach, Fla.	35,359
North Olmsted, Ohio	34,204
North Platte, Nebr.	22,605
North Providence, R.I.	32,090
North Richland Hills, Tex.	45,895
North Ridgeville, Ohio	21,564
North Royalton, Ohio	23,197
North Tonawanda, N.Y.	34,989
Norton Shores, Mich.	21,755

Norwalk, Calif.	94,279
Norwalk, Conn.	78,331
Norwich, Conn.	37,391
Norwood, Mass.	28,700
Norwood, Ohio	23,674
Novato, Calif.	47,585
Novi, Mich.	32,998
Nutley, N.J.	27,099

O

Oak Creek, Wis.	19,513
Oak Forest, Ill.	26,203
Oakland, Calif.	372,242
Oakland Park, Fla.	26,326
Oak Lawn, Ill.	56,182
Oak Park, Ill.	53,648
Oak Park, Mich.	30,462
Oak Ridge, Tenn.	27,310
Ocala, Fla.	42,045
Oceanside, Calif.	128,398
Odessa, Tex.	89,699
Ogden, Utah	63,909
Oklahoma City, Okla.	444,719
Olathe, Kans.	63,352
Olympia, Wash.	33,840
Omaha, Nebr.	335,795
Ontario, Calif.	133,179
Opelika, Ala.	22,122
Orange, Calif.	110,658
Orange, N.J.	29,925
Orange, Tex.	19,381
Orem, Utah	67,561
Orlando, Fla.	164,693
Orland Park, Ill.	35,720
Ormond Beach, Fla.	29,721
Oshkosh, Wis.	55,006
Ossining, N.Y.	22,582
Oswego, N.Y.	19,195
Ottumwa, Iowa	24,488
Overland Park, Kans.	111,790
Owatonna, Minn.	19,386
Owensboro, Ky.	53,549
Oxnard, Calif.	142,216

P

Pacifica, Calif.	37,670
Paducah, Ky.	27,256
Palatine, Ill.	39,253
Palm Bay, Fla.	62,632
Palm Springs, Calif.	40,181
Palo Alto, Calif.	55,900
Pampa, Tex.	19,959
Panama City, Fla.	34,378
Paradise, Calif.	25,408
Paramount, Calif.	47,669
Paramus, N.J.	25,067
Paris, Tex.	24,699
Parkersburg, W. Va.	33,862
Park Forest, Ill.	24,646
Park Ridge, Ill.	36,175
Parma, Ohio	87,876
Parma Heights, Ohio	21,448
Pasadena, Calif.	119,363
Pasadena, Tex.	131,591
Pascagoula, Miss.	25,899
Pasco, Wash.	20,337
Passaic, N.J.	58,041
Paterson, N.J.	140,891
Pawtucket, R.I.	72,644
Peabody, Mass.	47,039
Peachtree City, Ga.	19,027
Pearl, Miss.	19,588
Pearl City, Hawaii	30,993

Peekskill, N.Y.	19,536
Pekin, Ill.	32,254
Pembroke Pines, Fla.	65,452
Pensacola, Fla.	58,165
Peoria, Ariz.	50,618
Peoria, Ill.	113,504
Perris, Calif.	21,460
Perth Amboy, N.J.	41,967
Petaluma, Calif.	43,184
Petersburg, Va.	38,386
Pharr, Tex.	32,921
Phenix City, Ala.	25,312
Philadelphia, Pa.	1,585,577
Phoenix, Ariz.	983,403
Pico Rivera, Calif.	59,177
Pine Bluff, Ark.	57,140
Pinellas Park, Fla.	43,426
Piqua, Ohio	20,612
Pittsburg, Calif.	47,564
Pittsburgh, Pa.	369,879
Pittsfield, Mass.	48,622
Placentia, Calif.	41,259
Plainfield, N.J.	46,567
Plainview, Tex.	21,700
Plano, Tex.	128,713
Plantation, Fla.	66,692
Plant City, Fla.	22,754
Plattsburgh, N.Y.	21,255
Pleasant Hill, Calif.	31,585
Pleasanton, Calif.	50,553
Plum, Pa.	25,609
Plymouth, Mass.	45,608
Plymouth, Minn.	50,889
Pocatello, Idaho	46,080
Pomona, Calif.	131,723
Pompano Beach, Fla.	72,411
Ponca City, Okla.	26,359
Pontiac, Mich.	71,166
Portage, Ind.	29,060
Portage, Mich.	41,042
Port Arthur, Tex.	58,724
Port Chester, N.Y.	24,728
Porterville, Calif.	29,563
Port Hueneme, Calif.	20,319
Port Huron, Mich.	33,694
Portland, Me.	64,358
Portland, Oreg.	437,319
Port Orange, Fla.	35,317
Port St. Lucie, Fla.	55,866
Portsmouth, N.H.	25,925
Portsmouth, Ohio	22,676
Portsmouth, Va.	103,907
Pottstown, Pa.	21,831
Poughkeepsie, N.Y.	28,844
Poway, Calif.	43,516
Prairie Village, Kans.	23,186
Prattville, Ala.	19,587
Prescott, Ariz.	26,455
Prichard, Ala.	34,311
Providence, R.I.	160,728
Provo, Utah	86,835
Pueblo, Colo.	98,640
Pullman, Wash.	23,478
Puyallup, Wash.	23,875

Q

Quincy, Ill.	39,681
Quincy, Mass.	84,985

R

Racine, Wis.	84,298
Radcliff, Ky.	19,772
Rahway, N.J.	25,325

Raleigh, N.C.	207,951
Rancho Cucamonga, Calif.	101,409
Rancho Palos Verdes, Calif.	41,659
Randolph, Mass.	30,093
Rapid City, S. Dak.	54,523
Raytown, Mo.	30,601
Reading, Mass.	22,539
Reading, Pa.	78,380
Redding, Calif.	66,462
Redlands, Calif.	60,394
Redmond, Wash.	35,800
Redondo Beach, Calif.	60,167
Redwood City, Calif.	66,072
Reno, Nev.	133,850
Renton, Wash.	41,688
Revere, Mass.	42,786
Reynoldsburg, Ohio	25,748
Rialto, Calif.	72,388
Richardson, Tex.	74,840
Richfield, Minn.	35,710
Richland, Wash.	32,315
Richmond, Calif.	87,425
Richmond, Ind.	38,705
Richmond, Ky.	21,155
Richmond, Va.	203,056
Ridgecrest, Calif.	27,725
Ridgefield, Conn.	20,919
Ridgewood, N.J.	24,152
Rio Rancho, N. Mex.	32,505
Riverside, Calif.	226,505
Riviera Beach, Fla.	27,639
Roanoke, Va.	96,397
Rochester, Minn.	70,745
Rochester, N.H.	26,630
Rochester, N.Y.	231,636
Rochester Hills, Mich.	61,766
Rockford, Ill.	139,426
Rock Hill, S.C.	41,643
Rock Island, Ill.	40,552
Rocklin, Calif.	19,033
Rock Springs, Wyo.	19,050
Rockville, Md.	44,835
Rockville Centre, N.Y.	24,727
Rocky Mount, N.C.	48,997
Rocky River, Ohio	20,410
Rogers, Ark.	24,692
Rohnert Park, Calif.	36,326
Rolling Meadows, Ill.	22,591
Rome, Ga.	30,326
Rome, N.Y.	44,350
Romulus, Mich.	22,897
Roselle, Ill.	20,819
Roselle, N.J.	20,314
Rosemead, Calif.	51,638
Rosenberg, Tex.	20,183
Roseville, Calif.	44,685
Roseville, Mich.	51,412
Roseville, Minn.	33,485
Roswell, Ga.	47,923
Roswell, N. Mex.	44,654
Round Rock, Tex.	30,923
Rowlett, Tex.	23,260
Roy, Utah	24,603
Royal Oak, Mich.	65,410
Russellville, Ark.	21,260
Ruston, La.	20,027

S

Sacramento, Calif.	369,365
Saginaw, Mich.	69,512
St. Charles, Ill.	22,501
St. Charles, Mo.	54,555
St. Clair Shores, Mich.	68,107
St. Cloud, Minn.	48,812
St. George, Utah	28,502
St. Joseph, Mo.	71,852
St. Louis, Mo.	396,685
St. Louis Park, Minn.	43,787
St. Paul, Minn.	272,235
St. Peters, Mo.	45,779
St. Petersburg, Fla.	238,629
Salem, Mass.	38,091
Salem, N.H.	25,746
Salem, Oreg.	107,786
Salem, Va.	23,756
Salina, Kans.	42,303
Salinas, Calif.	108,777
Salisbury, Md.	20,592
Salisbury, N.C.	23,087
Salt Lake City, Utah	159,936
San Angelo, Tex.	84,474
San Antonio, Tex.	935,933
San Benito, Tex.	20,125
San Bernardino, Calif.	164,164
San Bruno, Calif.	38,961
San Carlos, Calif.	26,167
San Clemente, Calif.	41,100
San Diego, Calif.	1,110,549
San Dimas, Calif.	32,397
Sandusky, Ohio	29,764
Sandy, Utah	75,058
San Fernando, Calif.	22,580
Sanford, Fla.	32,387
Sanford, Me.	20,463
San Francisco, Calif.	723,959
San Gabriel, Calif.	37,120
San Jose, Calif.	782,248
San Juan Capistrano, Calif.	26,183
San Leandro, Calif.	68,223
San Luis Obispo, Calif.	41,958
San Marcos, Calif.	38,974
San Marcos, Tex.	28,743
San Mateo, Calif.	85,486
San Pablo, Calif.	25,158
San Rafael, Calif.	48,404
San Ramon, Calif.	35,303
Santa Ana, Calif.	293,742
Santa Barbara, Calif.	85,571
Santa Clara, Calif.	93,613
Santa Clarita, Calif.	110,642
Santa Cruz, Calif.	49,040
Santa Fe, N. Mex.	55,859
Santa Maria, Calif.	61,284
Santa Monica, Calif.	86,905
Santa Paula, Calif.	25,062
Santa Rosa, Calif.	113,313
Santee, Calif.	52,902
Sarasota, Fla.	50,961
Saratoga, Calif.	28,061
Saratoga Springs, N.Y.	25,001
Saugus, Mass.	25,549
Savannah, Ga.	137,560
Sayreville, N.J.	34,986
Schaumburg, Ill.	68,586
Schenectady, N.Y.	65,566
Schererville, Ind.	19,926
Schofield Barracks, Hawaii	19,597
Scottsdale, Ariz.	130,069
Scranton, Pa.	81,805
Seal Beach, Calif.	25,098
Seaside, Calif.	38,901
Seattle, Wash.	516,259
Sedalia, Mo.	19,800
Selma, Ala.	23,755
Shaker Heights, Ohio	30,831
Shawnee, Kans.	37,993

Shawnee, Okla.	26,017
Sheboygan, Wis.	49,676
Shelton, Conn.	35,418
Sherman, Tex.	31,601
Shoreview, Minn.	24,587
Shreveport, La.	198,525
Shrewsbury, Mass.	24,146
Sierra Vista, Ariz.	32,983
Simi Valley, Calif.	100,217
Simsbury, Conn.	22,023
Sioux City, Iowa	80,505
Sioux Falls, S. Dak.	100,814
Skokie, Ill.	59,432
Slidell, La.	24,124
Smithfield, R.I.	19,163
Smyrna, Ga.	30,981
Socorro, Tex.	22,995
Somerville, Mass.	76,210
South Bend, Ind.	105,511
South El Monte, Calif.	20,850
South Euclid, Ohio	23,866
Southfield, Mich.	75,728
South Gate, Calif.	86,284
Southgate, Mich.	30,771
South Holland, Ill.	22,105
Southington, Conn.	38,518
South Kingstown, R.I.	24,631
South Lake Tahoe, Calif.	21,586
South Milwaukee, Wis.	20,958
South Pasadena, Calif.	23,936
South Plainfield, N.J.	20,489
South Portland, Me.	23,163
South St. Paul, Minn.	20,197
South San Francisco, Calif.	54,312
South Windsor, Conn.	22,090
Sparks, Nev.	53,367
Spartanburg, S.C.	43,467
Spokane, Wash.	177,196
Springdale, Ark.	29,941
Springfield, Ill.	105,227
Springfield, Mass.	156,983
Springfield, Mo.	140,494
Springfield, Ohio	70,487
Springfield, Oreg.	44,683
Spring Valley, N.Y.	21,802
Stamford, Conn.	108,056
Stanton, Calif.	30,491
State College, Pa.	38,923
Staunton, Va.	24,461
Sterling Heights, Mich.	117,810
Steubenville, Ohio	22,125
Stevens Point, Wis.	23,006
Stillwater, Okla.	36,676
Stockton, Calif.	210,943
Stoneham, Mass.	22,203
Stoughton, Mass.	26,777
Stow, Ohio	27,702
Stratford, Conn.	49,389
Streamwood, Ill.	30,987
Strongsville, Ohio	35,308
Suffolk, Va.	52,141
Sugar Land, Tex.	24,529
Suisun City, Calif.	22,686
Sulphur, La.	20,125
Summerville, S.C.	22,519
Summit, N.J.	19,757
Sumter, S.C.	41,943
Sunnyvale, Calif.	117,229
Sunrise, Fla.	64,407
Superior, Wis.	27,134
Syracuse, N.Y.	163,860

T

Tacoma, Wash.	176,664
Tallahassee, Fla.	124,773
Tamarac, Fla.	44,822
Tampa, Fla.	280,015
Taunton, Mass.	49,832
Taylor, Mich.	70,811
Temecula, Calif.	27,099
Tempe, Ariz.	141,865
Temple, Tex.	46,109
Temple City, Calif.	31,100
Terre Haute, Ind.	57,483
Tewksbury, Mass.	27,266
Texarkana, Ark.	22,631
Texarkana, Tex.	31,656
Texas City, Tex.	40,822
The Colony, Tex.	22,113
Thornton, Colo.	55,031
Thousand Oaks, Calif.	104,352
Tigard, Oreg.	29,344
Tinley Park, Ill.	37,121
Titusville, Fla.	39,394
Toledo, Ohio	332,943
Topeka, Kans.	119,883
Torrance, Calif.	133,107
Torrington, Conn.	33,687
Tracy, Calif.	33,558
Trenton, Mich.	20,586
Trenton, N.J.	88,675
Troy, Mich.	72,884
Troy, N.Y.	54,269
Troy, Ohio	19,478
Trumbull, Conn.	32,016
Tucson, Ariz.	405,390
Tulare, Calif.	33,249
Tulsa, Okla.	367,302
Tupelo, Miss.	30,685
Turlock, Calif.	42,198
Tuscaloosa, Ala.	77,759
Tustin, Calif.	50,689
Twin Falls, Idaho	27,591
Tyler, Tex.	75,450

U

Union City, Calif.	53,762
Union City, N.J.	58,012
University City, Mo.	40,087
University Park, Tex.	22,259
Upland, Calif.	63,374
Upper Arlington, Ohio	34,128
Urbana, Ill.	36,344
Urbandale, Iowa	23,500
Utica, N.Y.	68,637

V

Vacaville, Calif.	71,479
Valdosta, Ga.	39,806
Vallejo, Calif.	109,199
Valley Stream, N.Y.	33,946
Valparaiso, Ind.	24,414
Vancouver, Wash.	46,380
Ventura (San Buenaventura), Calif.	92,575
Vernon, Conn.	29,841
Vestavia Hills, Ala.	19,749
Vicksburg, Miss.	20,908
Victoria, Tex.	55,076
Victorville, Calif.	40,674
Villa Park, Ill.	22,253
Vincennes, Ind.	19,859
Vineland, N.J.	54,870
Virginia Beach, Va.	393,069
Visalia, Calif.	75,636

Vista, Calif.	71,872	West Springfield, Mass.	27,537
		West Valley City, Utah	86,976
W		West Warwick, R.I.	29,268
Waco, Tex.	103,590	Wethersfield, Conn.	25,651
Waipahu, Hawaii	31,435	Weymouth, Mass.	54,063
Wakefield, Mass.	24,825	Wheaton, Ill.	51,464
Walla Walla, Wash.	26,478	Wheat Ridge, Colo.	29,419
Wallingford, Conn.	40,822	Wheeling, Ill.	29,911
Walnut, Calif.	29,105	Wheeling, W. Va.	34,882
Walnut Creek, Calif.	60,569	White Bear Lake, Minn.	24,704
Walpole, Mass.	20,212	Whitehall, Ohio	20,572
Waltham, Mass.	57,878	White Plains, N.Y.	48,718
Wareham, Mass.	19,232	Whittier, Calif.	77,671
Warner Robins, Ga.	43,726	Wichita, Kans.	304,011
Warren, Mich.	144,864	Wichita Falls, Tex.	96,259
Warren, Ohio	50,793	Wilkes-Barre, Pa.	47,523
Warwick, R.I.	85,427	Wilkinsburg, Pa.	21,080
Washington, D.C.	609,909	Williamsport, Pa.	31,933
Watauga, Tex.	20,009	Willoughby, Ohio	20,510
Waterbury, Conn.	108,961	Wilmette, Ill.	26,690
Waterloo, Iowa	66,467	Wilmington, Del.	71,529
Watertown, Conn.	20,456	Wilmington, N.C.	55,530
Watertown, Mass.	33,284	Wilson, N.C.	36,930
Watertown, N.Y.	29,429	Winchester, Mass.	20,267
Watertown, Wis.	19,142	Winchester, Va.	21,947
Watsonville, Calif.	31,099	Windham, Conn.	22,039
Waukegan, Ill.	69,392	Windsor, Conn.	27,817
Waukesha, Wis.	56,958	Winona, Minn.	25,399
Wausau, Wis.	37,060	Winston-Salem, N.C.	143,485
Wauwatosa, Wis.	49,366	Winter Haven, Fla.	24,725
Wayne, Mich.	19,899	Winter Park, Fla.	22,242
Webster Groves, Mo.	22,987	Winter Springs, Fla.	22,151
Weirton, W. Va.	22,124	Woburn, Mass.	35,943
Wellesley, Mass.	26,615	Woodbury, Minn.	20,075
Wenatchee, Wash.	21,756	Woodland, Calif.	39,802
Weslaco, Tex.	21,877	Woodridge, Ill.	26,256
West Allis, Wis.	63,221	Woonsocket, R.I.	43,877
West Bend, Wis.	23,916	Wooster, Ohio	22,191
West Covina, Calif.	96,086	Worcester, Mass.	169,759
West Des Moines, Iowa	31,702	Wyandotte, Mich.	30,938
Westerly, R.I.	21,605	Wyoming, Mich.	63,891
Westerville, Ohio	30,269		
Westfield, Mass.	38,372	**X**	
Westfield, N.J.	28,870		
West Hartford, Conn.	60,110	Xenia, Ohio	24,664
West Haven, Conn.	54,021		
West Hollywood, Calif.	36,118	**Y**	
West Jordan, Utah	42,892	Yakima, Wash.	54,827
West Lafayette, Ind.	25,907	Yarmouth, Mass.	21,174
Westlake, Ohio	27,018	Yonkers, N.Y.	188,082
Westland, Mich.	84,724	Yorba Linda, Calif.	52,422
West Memphis, Ark.	28,259	York, Pa.	42,192
West Mifflin, Pa.	23,644	Youngstown, Ohio	95,732
Westminster, Calif.	78,118	Ypsilanti, Mich.	24,846
Westminster, Colo.	74,625	Yuba City, Calif.	27,437
Westmont, Ill.	21,228	Yucaipa, Calif.	32,824
West New York, N.J.	38,125	Yukon, Okla.	20,935
West Orange, N.J.	39,103	Yuma, Ariz.	54,923
West Palm Beach, Fla.	67,643		
Westport, Conn.	24,410	**Z**	
West Sacramento, Calif.	28,898	Zanesville, Ohio	26,778
West St. Paul, Minn.	19,248	Zion, Ill.	19,775

United States Facts
States, Territories, and Possessions

STATES

NAME, U.S. P.O. ABBR., and NICKNAME	AREA[1] sq.mi. (sq. km.)	rank	POPULATION 1990 census	rank	ADMITTED TO UNION[2] date	rank	CAPITAL	MOTTO
Alabama (AL) *Heart of Dixie*	51,705 (133,916)	29th	4,040,587	22d	1819	22d	Montgomery	We Dare Defend Our Rights
Alaska[3] (AK) *The Last Frontier*	591,004 (1,530,700)	1st	550,043	49th	1959	49th	Juneau	North to the Future
Arizona (AZ) *Grand Canyon State*	114,000 (295,260)	6th	3,665,228	24th	1912	48th	Phoenix	Ditat Deus (God Enriches)
Arkansas (AR) *Land of Opportunity*	53,187 (137,754)	27th	2,350,725	33d	1836	25th	Little Rock	Regnat Populus (The People Rule)
California (CA) *Golden State*	158,706 (411,048)	3d	29,760,020	1st	1850	31st	Sacramento	Eureka (I Have Found It)
Colorado (CO) *Centennial State*	104,247 (270,000)	8th	3,294,394	26th	1876	38th	Denver	Nil Sine Numine (Nothing Without the Divine Will)
Connecticut[2] (CT) *Constitution State, Nutmeg State*	5,018 (12,997)	48th	3,287,116	27th	1788	5th	Hartford	Qui Transtulit Sustinet (He Who Transplanted Sustains)
Delaware[2] (DE) *First State, Diamond State*	2,057 (5,328)	49th	666,168	46th	1787	1st	Dover	Liberty and Independence
Florida (FL) *Sunshine State*	58,664 (151,940)	22d	12,937,926	4th	1845	27th	Tallahassee	In God We Trust
Georgia[2] (GA) *Empire State of the South, Peach State*	58,910 (152,577)	21st	6,478,216	11th	1788	4th	Atlanta	Wisdom, Justice, Moderation
Hawaii[3] (HI) *Aloha State*	6,471 (16,760)	47th	1,108,229	41st	1959	50th	Honolulu	Ua Mau Ke Ea O Ka Aina I Ka Pono (The Life of the Land is Established in Righteousness)
Idaho (ID) *Gem State*	83,557 (216,413)	13th	1,006,749	42d	1890	43d	Boise	Esto Perpetua (May She Endure Forever)
Illinois (IL) *Prairie State*	56,400 (146,076)	24th	11,430,602	6th	1818	21st	Springfield	State Sovereignty–National Union

NAME, U.S. P.O. ABBR., and NICKNAME	AREA[1] sq.mi. (sq. km.)	rank	POPULATION 1990 census	rank	ADMITTED TO UNION[2] date	rank	CAPITAL	MOTTO
Indiana (IN) *Hoosier State*	36,291 (93,994)	38th	5,544,159	14th	1816	19th	Indianapolis	The Crossroads of America
Iowa (IA) *Hawkeye State*	56,275 (145,752)	25th	2,776,755	30th	1846	29th	Des Moines	Our Liberties We Prize and Our Rights We Will Maintain
Kansas (KS) *Sunflower State*	82,277 (213,097)	14th	2,477,574	32d	1861	34th	Topeka	Ad Astra per Aspera (To the Stars by Hard Ways)
Kentucky (KY) *Bluegrass State*	40,395 (104,623)	37th	3,685,296	23d	1792	15th	Frankfort	United We Stand, Divided We Fall
Louisiana (LA) *Pelican State*	48,523 (125,674)	31st	4,219,973	21st	1812	18th	Baton Rouge	Union, Justice, Confidence
Maine (ME) *Pine Tree State*	33,265 (86,156)	39th	1,227,928	38th	1820	23d	Augusta	Dirigo (I Direct)
Maryland[2] (MD) *Old Line State*	10,460 (27,091)	42d	4,781,468	19th	1788	7th	Annapolis	Fatti Maschii, Parole Femine (Manly Deeds, Womanly Words)
Massachusetts[2] (MA) *Bay State*	8,284 (21,456)	45th	6,016,425	13th	1788	6th	Boston	Ense Petit Placidam Sub Libertate Quietem (By the Sword We Seek Peace, but Peace Only Under Liberty)
Michigan (MI) *Wolverine State, Great Lakes State*	58,216 (150,779)	23d	9,295,297	8th	1837	26th	Lansing	Si Quaeris Peninsulam Amoenam Circumspice (If You Seek a Beautiful Peninsula, Look Around)
Minnesota (MN) *Gopher State, North Star State*	84,068 (217,736)	12th	4,375,099	20th	1858	32d	St. Paul	L'étoile du Nord (Star of the North)
Mississippi (MS) *Magnolia State*	47,689 (123,514)	32d	2,573,216	31st	1817	20th	Jackson	Virtute et Armis (By Valor and Arms)
Missouri (MO) *Show Me State*	69,697 (180,515)	19th	5,117,073	15th	1821	24th	Jefferson City	Salus Populi Suprema Lex Esto (Let the Welfare of the People Be the Supreme Law)
Montana (MT) *Treasure State*	147,046 (380,849)	4th	799,065	44th	1889	41st	Helena	Oro y Plata (Gold and Silver)
Nebraska (NE) *Cornhusker State*	77,355 (200,349)	15th	1,578,385	36th	1867	37th	Lincoln	Equality Before the Law
Nevada (NV) *Silver State*	110,561 (286,353)	7th	1,201,833	39th	1864	36th	Carson City	All For Our Country

NAME, U.S. P.O. ABBR., and NICKNAME	AREA[1]		POPULATION		ADMITTED TO UNION[2]		CAPITAL	MOTTO
	sq.mi. (sq. km.)	rank	1990 census	rank	date	rank		
New Hampshire[2] (NH) *Granite State*	9,279 (24,033)	44th	1,109,252	40th	1788	9th	Concord	Live Free Or Die
New Jersey[2] (NJ) *Garden State*	7,787 (20,168)	46th	7,730,188	9th	1787	3d	Trenton	Liberty and Prosperity
New Mexico (NM) *Land of Enchantment*	121,593 (314,926)	5th	1,515,069	37th	1912	47th	Santa Fe	Crescit Eundo (It Grows As It Goes)
New York[2] (NY) *Empire State*	49,576 (128,402)	30th	17,990,456	2d	1788	11th	Albany	Excelsior (Still Higher)
North Carolina[2] (NC) *Tar Heel State, Old North State*	52,669 (136,413)	28th	6,628,637	10th	1789	12th	Raleigh	To Be Rather Than To Seem
North Dakota (ND) *Flicker-tail State*	70,665 (183,022)	17th	638,800	47th	1889	39th	Bismarck	Liberty and Union, Now and Forever, One and Inseparable
Ohio (OH) *Buckeye State*	41,222 (106,765)	35th	10,847,115	7th	1803	17th	Columbus	
Oklahoma (OK) *Sooner State*	69,956 (181,186)	18th	3,145,585	28th	1907	46th	Oklahoma City	Labor Omnia Vin-cit (Labor Con-quers All Things)
Oregon (OR) *Beaver State*	97,073 (251,419)	10th	2,842,321	29th	1859	33d	Salem	Alis Volat Propriis (She Flies With Her Own Wings)
Pennsylvania[2] (PA) *Keystone State*	45,333 (117,412)	33d	11,881,643	5th	1787	2d	Harrisburg	Virtue, Liberty, and Independence
Rhode Island[2] (RI) *Ocean State, Little Rhody*	1,212 (3,139)	50th	1,003,464	43d	1790	13th	Providence	Hope
South Carolina[2] (SC) *Palmetto State*	31,113 (80,583)	40th	3,486,703	25th	1788	8th	Columbia	Dum Spiro, Spero (While I Breathe, I Hope)
South Dakota (SD) *Mount Rushmore State*	77,116 (199,730)	16th	696,004	45th	1889	40th	Pierre	Under God the People Rule
Tennessee (TN) *Volunteer State*	42,144 (109,153)	34th	4,877,185	17th	1796	16th	Nashville	Agriculture and Commerce
Texas (TX) *Lone Star State*	266,807 (691,030)	2d	16,986,510	3d	1845	28th	Austin	Friendship
Utah (UT) *Beehive State*	84,899 (219,888)	11th	1,722,850	35th	1896	45th	Salt Lake City	Industry
Vermont (VT) *Green Mountain State*	9,609 (24,887)	43d	562,758	48th	1791	14th	Montpelier	Freedom and Unity

NAME, U.S. P.O. ABBR., and NICKNAME	AREA[1] sq.mi. (sq. km.)	rank	POPULATION 1990 census	rank	ADMITTED TO UNION[2] date	rank	CAPITAL	MOTTO
Virginia[2] (VA) *Old Dominion*	40,767 (105,586)	36th	6,187,358	12th	1788	10th	Richmond	Sic Semper Tyrannis (Thus Ever to Tyrants)
Washington (WA) *Evergreen State*	68,192 (176,617)	20th	4,866,692	18th	1889	42d	Olympia	Alki (By and By)
West Virginia (WV) *Mountain State*	24,181 (62,629)	41st	1,793,477	34th	1863	35th	Charleston	Montani Semper Liberi (Mountaineers Are Always Free)
Wisconsin (WI) *Badger State*	56,154 (145,439)	26th	4,891,769	16th	1848	30th	Madison	Forward
Wyoming (WY) *Equality State, Cowboy State*	97,914 (253,597)	9th	453,588	50th	1890	44th	Cheyenne	Equal Rights
District of Columbia[4] (DC)	69 (179)		609,909				Washington	E Pluribus Unum (One Out of Many)

TERRITORIES AND POSSESSIONS

NAME and U.S. P.O. ABBR.	TOTAL AREA sq. mi.	sq. km.	POPULATION 1990 census	CAPITAL
American Samoa (AS)	77	199	46,773	Pago Pago
Guam (GU)	209	541	133,152	Agana
Puerto Rico[6] (PR)	3435	8897	3,522,037	San Juan
Virgin Islands of the United States (VI)	133	345	101,809	Charlotte Amalie
Other (Belau, Northern Mariana Islands, etc.)	367	951	63,982	

[1]Total land and inland water.
[2]Date of admission of the 13 original colonies is that of ratification of the Constitution.
[3]The Alaska Statehood Act was signed by the President July 7, 1958; the Hawaii Statehood Act, Mar. 18, 1959.
[4]Coextensive with the city of Washington.
[5]Total land and inland water; does not include 74,364 sq. mi. (192,603 sq. km.) of Great Lakes and other primary bodies of water, of which total the state of Michigan has 38,575 sq. mi. (99,909 sq. km.).
[6]Adopted constitution 1952 establishing it as a commonwealth with autonomy in internal affairs.

Population of Places in Canada

Having 21,500 or More Inhabitants in 1991

Place	Population	Place	Population
Ajax, Ont.	57,350	Lachine, Que.	35,266
Alma, Que.	25,910	Langley, B.C.	66,040
Ancaster, Ont.	21,988	LaSalle, Que.	73,804
Anjou, Que.	37,210	Laval, Que.	314,398
Aurora, Ont.	29,454	Lethbridge, Alta.	60,974
Aylmer, Que.	32,244	Lévis-Lauzon, Que.	39,452
Baie-Comeau, Que.	26,012	London, Ont.	303,165
Barrie, Ont.	62,728	Longueuil, Que.	129,874
Beauport, Que.	69,158	Lunenburg, N.S.	25,720
Belleville, Ont.	37,243	Maple Ridge, B.C.	48,422
Blainville, Que.	22,679	Markham, Ont.	153,811
Boucherville, Que.	33,796	Mascouche, Que.	25,828
Brampton, Ont.	234,445	Matsqui, B.C.	68,064
Brandon, Man.	38,567	Medicine Hat, Alta.	43,625
Brantford, Ont.	81,997	Milton, Ont.	32,075
Brockville, Ont.	21,582	Mission, B.C.	26,202
Brossard, Que.	64,793	Mississauga, Ont.	463,388
Burlington, Ont.	129,575	Moncton, N.B.	57,010
Burnaby, B.C.	158,858	Montreal, Que.	1,017,666
Caledon, Ont.	34,965	Montreal North, Que.	85,516
Calgary, Alta.	710,677	Moose Jaw, Sask.	33,593
Cambridge, Ont.	92,772	Mount Pearl, Nfld.	23,689
Cap-de-la-Madeleine, Que.	33,716	Nanaimo, B.C.	60,129
Charlesbourg, Que.	70,788	Nanticoke, Ont.	22,727
Châteauguay, Que.	39,833	Nepean, Ont.	107,627
Chatham, Ont.	43,557	Newcastle, Ont.	49,479
Chicoutimi, Que.	62,670	Newmarket, Ont.	45,474
Chilliwack, B.C.	49,531	New Westminster, B.C.	43,585
Coquitlam, B.C.	84,021	Niagara Falls, Ont.	75,399
Corner Brook, Nfld.	22,410	North Bay, Ont.	55,405
Cornwall, Ont.	47,137	North Vancouver, B.C.	38,436
Côte-St-Luc, Que.	28,700	North York, Ont.	562,564
Cumberland, Ont.	40,697	Oakville, Ont.	114,670
Dartmouth, N.S.	67,798	Orillia, Ont.	25,925
Delta, B.C.	88,978	Oshawa, Ont.	129,344
Dollard-des-Ormeaux, Que.	46,922	Ottawa, Ont.	313,987
Drummondville, Que.	35,462	Outremont, Que.	22,935
Dundas, Ont.	21,868	Owen Sound, Ont.	21,674
East York, Ont.	102,696	Penticton, B.C.	27,258
Edmonton, Alta.	616,741	Peterborough, Ont.	68,371
Etobicoke, Ont.	309,993	Pickering, Ont.	68,631
Flamborough, Ont.	29,616	Pierrefonds, Que.	48,735
Fort Erie, Ont.	26,006	Pointe-Claire, Que.	27,647
Fort McMurray, Alta.	34,706	Port Coquitlam, B.C.	36,773
Fredericton, N.B.	46,466	Prince Albert, Sask.	34,181
Gatineau, Que.	92,284	Prince George, B.C.	69,653
Georgina, Ont.	29,746	Quebec, Que.	167,517
Gloucester, Ont.	101,677	Red Deer, Alta.	58,134
Granby, Que.	42,804	Regina, Sask.	179,178
Grande Prairie, Alta.	28,271	Repentigny, Que.	49,630
Guelph, Ont.	87,976	Richmond Hill, Ont.	80,142
Halifax, N.S.	114,455	Rimouski, Que.	30,873
Halton Hills, Ont.	36,816	Rouyn-Noranda, Que.	26,448
Hamilton, Ont.	318,499	Saanich, B.C.	95,577
Hull, Que.	60,707	St. Albert, Alta.	42,146
Innisfil, Ont.	21,667	St-Bruno-de-Montarville, Que.	23,849
Jonquière, Que.	57,933	St. Catharines, Ont.	129,300
Kamloops, B.C.	67,057	Ste-Foy, Que.	71,133
Kanata, Ont.	37,344	Ste-Thérèse, Que.	24,158
Kelowna, B.C.	75,950	St. Eustache, Que.	37,278
Kingston, Ont.	56,597	St-Hubert, Que.	74,027
Kitchener, Ont.	168,282	St-Hyacinthe, Que.	39,292

St-Jean-sur-Richelieu, Que.	37,607	Thunder Bay, Ont.	113,946
St-Jerôme, Que.	23,384	Timmins, Ont.	47,461
Saint John, N.B.	74,969	Toronto, Ont.	635,395
St. John's, Nfld.	95,770	Trois-Rivières, Que.	49,426
St-Laurent, Que.	72,402	Val-d'Or, Que.	23,842
St-Léonard, Que.	73,120	Valley East, Ont.	21,939
St. Thomas, Ont.	29,990	Vancouver, B.C.	471,844
Salaberry-de-Valleyfield, Que.	27,598	Vaughan, Ont.	111,359
Sarnia-Clearwater, Ont.	74,376	Verdun, Que.	61,307
Saskatoon, Sask.	186,058	Vernon, B.C.	23,514
Sault Ste. Marie, Ont.	81,476	Victoria, B.C.	71,228
Scarborough, Ont.	524,598	Waterloo, Ont.	71,181
Sept-Iles, Que.	24,848	Welland, Ont.	47,914
Sherbrooke, Que.	76,429	West Vancouver, B.C.	38,783
Stoney Creek, Ont.	49,968	Whitby, Ont.	61,281
Stratford, Ont.	27,666	Windsor, Ont.	191,435
Sudbury, Ont.	92,884	Winnipeg, Man.	616,790
Surrey, B.C.	245,173	Woodstock, Ont.	30,075
Sydney, N.S.	26,063	York, Ont.	140,525
Terrebonne, Que.	39,678		

Population of Canada in 1991

Summary by Provinces and Territories

Alberta	2,545,553	Prince Edward Island	129,765
British Columbia	3,282,061	Quebec	6,895,963
Manitoba	1,091,942	Saskatchewan	988,928
New Brunswick	723,900	Yukon Territory	27,797
Newfoundland	568,474	Northwest Territories	57,649
Nova Scotia	899,942	TOTAL	27,296,859
Ontario	10,084,885		

Signs and Symbols

Astronomy

☉	the sun; Sunday	⊕, ⊖, or ♁	the earth
☽, ☾, or ☽	the moon; Monday	♂	Mars; Tuesday
●	new moon	♃	Jupiter; Thursday
☽, ☽, ☽, ☽	first quarter	♄ or ♄	Saturn; Saturday
○ or ☺	full moon	♁, ♅, or ♅	Uranus
☾, ☽, ☾, ☾	last quarter	♆, ♆, or ♆	Neptune
☿	Mercury; Wednesday	♇	Pluto
♀	Venus; Friday	☄	comet
		* or ✳	fixed star

Business

a/c	account ⟨in a/c with⟩	%	percent
@	at; each ⟨4 apples @ 5¢ = 20¢⟩	‰	per thousand
/ or ℈	per	$	dollars
c/o	care of	¢	cents
#	number if it precedes a numeral ⟨track #3⟩; pounds if it follows ⟨a 5# sack of sugar⟩	£	pounds
		/	shillings
℔	pound; pounds	©	copyrighted
		®	registered trademark

Mathematics

+	plus; positive ⟨a+b=c⟩—used also to indicate omitted figures or an approximation	<	is less than ⟨3<4⟩
		≧ or ≥	is greater than or equal to
		≦ or ≤	is less than or equal to
−	minus; negative	∝	varies directly as; is proportional to
±	plus or minus ⟨the square root of 4a² is ± 2a⟩	:	is to; the ratio of
		∴	therefore
×	multiplied by; times ⟨6×4=24⟩—also indicated by placing a dot between the factors ⟨6·4=24⟩ or by writing the factors one after the other, often enclosed in parentheses, without explicitly indicating multiplication ⟨(4)(5)(3)=60⟩ ⟨−4abc⟩	∞	infinity
		∠	angle; the angle ⟨∠ABC⟩
		∟	right angle ⟨∟ABC⟩
		⊥	the perpendicular; is perpendicular to ⟨AB⊥CD⟩
		∥	parallel; is parallel to ⟨AB ∥ CD⟩
÷ or :	divided by ⟨24÷6=4⟩—also indicated by writing the divisor under the dividend with a line between ⟨$\frac{24}{6}$=4⟩ or by writing the divisor after the dividend with an oblique line between ⟨3/8⟩	⊙ or ○	circle
		⌒	arc of a circle
		△	triangle
		□	square
		▭	rectangle
=	equals ⟨6+2=8⟩	√ or √	root—used without a figure to indicate a square root (as in √4=2) or with an index above the sign to indicate a higher degree (as in $\sqrt[3]{3}$, $\sqrt[5]{7}$);
≠ or ≠	is not equal to		
>	is greater than ⟨6>5⟩		

also denoted by a fractional index at the right of a number whose denominator expresses the degree of the root $\langle 3^{1/3} = \sqrt[3]{3} \rangle$

( ) parentheses ⎫ indicate that the quan-
[ ] brackets ⎬ tities enclosed by them
{ } braces ⎭ are to be taken together

s standard deviation of a sample taken from a population

σ standard deviation of a population

$\bar{x}$ arithmetic mean of a sample of a variable x

μ arithmetic mean of a population

μ_2 or σ^2 variance

π pi; the number $3.14159265+$; the ratio of the circumference of a circle to its diameter

$\degree$ degree $\langle 60° \rangle$

$'$ minute; foot $\langle 30' \rangle$—used also to distinguish between different values of the same variable or between different variables (as a', a'', a''', usually read a prime, a double prime, a triple prime)

$''$ second; inch $\langle 30'' \rangle$

$^{0,\ 1,\ 2,\ 3,}$ etc. —used as exponents placed above and at the right of an expression to indicate that it is raised to a power whose degree is indicated by the figure $\langle a^0$ equals $1 \rangle$ $\langle a^1$ equals $a \rangle$ $\langle a^2$ is the square of $a \rangle$

$^{-1,\ -2,\ -3,}$ etc. —used as exponents placed above and at the right of an expression to indicate that the reciprocal of the expression is raised to the power whose degree is indicated by the figure $\langle a^{-1}$ equals $1/a \rangle$ $\langle a^{-2}$ equals $1/a^2 \rangle$

$!$ factorial $\langle n! = n\ (n\text{-}1)(n\text{-}2) \ldots 1 \rangle$

n an unspecified number esp. when an integer

$\subset$ is included in, is a subset of

$\supset$ contains as a subset

$\in$ or ϵ is an element of

$\notin$ is not an element of

Medicine

$\overline{AA}$, $\overline{A}$, or āā of each

℞ take—used on prescriptions; prescription; treatment

☠ poison

Miscellaneous

& and

&c et cetera; and so forth

" or " ditto marks

/ virgule; used to mean "or" (as in *and/or*), "and/or" (as in *dead/wounded*), "per" (as in *feet/second*), indicates end of a line of verse; separates the figures of a date (4/8/74)

☞ index *or* fist

< derived from ⎫
> whence derived ⎬ used in linguistics
+ and ⎭

* hypothetical, ungrammatical

† died—used esp. in genealogies

✚ cross

✴ monogram from Greek XP signifying Christ

卐 swastika

✡ Judaism

† ankh

℣ versicle

℞ response

✶ —used in Roman Catholic and Anglican service books to divide each verse of a psalm, indicating where the response begins

✝ *or* + —used in some service books to indicate where the sign of the cross is to be made; also used by certain Roman Catholic and Anglican prelates as a sign of the cross preceding their signatures

LXX Septuagint

fl or *f*: relative aperture of a photographic lens

☢ civil defense

☮ peace

Reference marks

*	asterisk *or* star		§	section *or* numbered clause
†	dagger		‖	parallels
‡	double dagger		¶ *or* ℙ	paragraph

Stamps and stamp collecting

★ *or* *	unused
★★ *or* **	unused with original gum intact and never mounted with a stamp hinge
⊙ *or* ○ *or* 0	used
⊞	block of four or more
⊠	entire cover or card

Weather

H *or* Ⓗ	high pressure region		∞	haze
L *or* Ⓛ	low pressure region		●	hurricane
◎	calm		ϟ	tropical storm
○	clear		•	rain
◐	cloudy (partly)		✷	rain and snow
●	cloudy (completely overcast)		✼	frost
⤧	drifting or blowing snow		⇴	sandstorm or dust storm
❚	drizzle		▽	shower(s)
≡	fog		•̽	shower of rain
∿	freezing rain		▵̽	shower of hail
▲▲▲▲	cold front		△	sleet
⌒⌒⌒	warm front		✳	snow
⌒∿	stationary front		℞	thunderstorm
)(	funnel clouds		⌐∿∿	visibility reduced by smoke

A Handbook of Style

Punctuation

The English writing system uses punctuation marks to separate groups of words for meaning and emphasis; to convey an idea of the variations of pitch, volume, pauses, and intonations of speech; and to help avoid contextual ambiguity. The use of the standard English punctuation marks is discussed in the following pages; examples are provided to illustrate the general rules.

Apostrophe '

1. Indicates the possessive case of nouns and indefinite pronouns. The possessive case of almost all singular nouns may be formed by adding 's. Traditionally, however, only the apostrophe is added when the s would not be pronounced in normal speech. The possessive case of plural nouns ending in s or in an \s\ or \z\ sound is generally formed by adding an apostrophe only; the possessive of irregular plurals is formed by adding 's.

> her mother-in-law's car
>
> anyone's guess
>
> the boy's mother
>
> the boys' mothers
>
> Degas's drawings
>
> Knox's products
>
> Aristophanes' play
>
> for righteousness' sake
>
> the Stephenses' house
>
> children's laughter

2. Marks omission of letters in contracted words.

> didn't
>
> o'clock
>
> hang 'em up

3. Marks omission of digits in numbers.

> class of '83

4. Is often used to form plurals of letters, figures, punctuated abbreviations, symbols, and words referred to as words.

> Dot your *i*'s and cross your *t*'s.

> Two of the junior faculty have Ph.D's.
>
> She has trouble pronouncing her *the*'s.

Brackets [ ]

1. Set off interpolated editorial matter within quoted material.

> He wrote, "I ain't [sic] going."
>
> Vaulting ambition, which o'erleaps itself
> And falls on the other [side].
> —Shakespeare

2. Function as parentheses within parentheses.

> Bowman Act (22 Stat., ch. 4, § [or sec.] 4, p. 50)

3. Set off phonetic symbols and transcriptions.

> [t] in British *duty*
>
> the word is pronounced [ˈek-sə-jənt]

Colon :

1. Introduces a clause or phrase that explains, illustrates, amplifies, or restates what has gone before.

> The sentence was poorly constructed: it lacked both unity and coherence.

2. Directs attention to an appositive.

> He had only one pleasure: eating.

3. Introduces a series.

> Three abstained: England, France, and Belgium.

4. Introduces lengthy quoted material set off from the rest of a text by indentation but not by quotation marks.

> I quote from the text of Chapter One:

5. Separates elements in page references, in bibliographical and biblical citations, and in set formulas used to express ratios and time.

> *Journal of the American Medical Association*
> 48:356
>
> Stendhal, *Love* (New York: Penguin, 1975)
>
> John 4:10   a ratio of 3:5   8:30 a.m.

6. Separates titles and subtitles (as of books).

> *Battle Cry of Freedom: The Era of the Civil War*

7. Follows the salutation in formal correspondence.

> Dear Sir or Madam:
>
> Ladies and Gentlemen:

8. Punctuates headings in memorandums and formal correspondence.

> TO: VIA:
>
> SUBJECT: REFERENCE:

Comma   **,**

1. Separates main clauses joined by a coordinating conjunction (such as *and, but, or, nor,* or *for*) and sometimes short parallel clauses not joined by conjunctions.

> She knew very little about him, and he volunteered nothing.
>
> I came, I saw, I conquered.

2. Sets off an adverbial clause or a long adverbial phrase that precedes or interrupts the main clause.

> When she discovered the answer, she reported it to us.
>
> The report, after being read aloud, was put up for consideration.

3. Sets off transitional words and expressions (such as *on the contrary, on the other hand*), conjunctive adverbs (such as *consequently, furthermore, however*), and expressions that introduce an illustration or example (such as *namely, for example*).

> My partner, on the other hand, remains unconvinced.
>
> The regent's whim, however, threw the negotiations into chaos.
>
> She responded as completely as she could; that is, she answered each individual question specifically.

4. Sets off contrasting and opposing expressions within sentences.

> The cost is not $65.00, but $56.65.

> He changed his style, not his ethics.

5. Separates words, phrases, or clauses in series. (Many omit the comma before the conjunction introducing the last item in a series when no ambiguity results.)

> He was young, eager, and restless.
>
> It requires one to travel constantly, to have no private life, and to live on almost nothing.
>
> Be sure to pack a flashlight, a sweater and an extra pair of socks.

6. Separates coordinate adjectives modifying a noun. However, a comma is not used between two adjectives when the first modifies the combination of the second adjective and the word or phrase it modifies.

> The harsh, damp, piercing wind cut through his jacket.
>
> a low common denominator

7. Sets off parenthetical elements such as nonrestrictive clauses and phrases.

> Our guide, who wore a blue beret, was an experienced traveler.
>
> We visited Gettysburg, site of the famous battle.
>
> The book's author, Marie Jones, was an accomplished athlete.

8. Introduces a direct quotation, terminates a direct quotation that is neither a question nor an exclamation, and sets off split quotations. The comma is not used with quotations that are tightly integrated into the sentences in which they appear (e.g., as subject or predicate nominatives) or those that do not represent actual dialogue.

> Mary said, "I am leaving."
>
> "I am leaving," Mary said.
>
> "I am leaving," Mary said with determination, "even if you want me to stay."
>
> "The computer is down" was the reply she feared.
>
> The fact that he said he was about to "faint from hunger" doesn't mean he actually fainted.

9. Sets off words in direct address, absolute phrases, and mild interjections.

> You may go, John, if you wish.
>
> I fear their encounter, his temper being what it is.
>
> Ah, that's my idea of an excellent dinner.

10. Separates a tag question from the rest of the sentence.

> It's a fine day, isn't it?

11. Indicates the omission of a word or words used in a parallel construction earlier in the sentence. When the meaning of the sentence is quite clear without the comma, the comma is omitted.

> Common stocks are preferred by some investors; bonds, by others.
>
> He was in love with her and she with him.

12. Is used to avoid ambiguity that might arise from adjacent words.

To Mary, Jane was someone special.

13. Is used to to divide digits in numbers into groups of three; however, it is generally not used in pagination, in dates, or in street numbers, and sometimes not used in numbers with four digits.

Smithville, pop. 100,000

4,550 cars

but

page 1411   4507 Main St.

3600 rpm   the year 1983

14. Punctuates an inverted name.

Morton, William A.

15. Separates a surname from a following title or degree and often from the words "Junior" and "Senior" and their abbreviations.

Sandra H. Cobb, Vice President

Jesse Ginsburg, D.D.M.

16. Sets off geographical names (such as state or country from city), elements of dates, and addresses. When just the month and the year are given in a date, the comma is usually omitted.

Shreveport, Louisiana, is the site of a large air base.

On Sunday, June 23, 1940, he was wounded.

Number 10 Downing Street, London, is a famous address.

She began her career in April 1993 at a modest salary.

17. Follows the salutation in informal correspondence, and follows the complimentary close of a letter.

Dear Mark,

Affectionately,

Very truly yours,

Dash   —

1. Usually marks an abrupt change or break in the continuity of a sentence.

When in 1960 the stockpile was sold off—indeed, dumped as surplus—natural rubber sales were hard hit.—Barry Commoner.

2. Is sometimes used in place of commas or parentheses when special emphasis is required.

The presentations—and especially the one by Ms. Dow—impressed the audience.

3. Introduces a statement that explains, summarizes, or expands on what precedes it.

Oil, steel, and wheat—these are the sinews of industrialization.

The motion was then tabled—that is, removed indefinitely from consideration.

4. Often precedes the attribution of a quotation.

My foot is on my native heath. . .
—Sir Walter Scott

5. Sets off an interrupting clause or phrase. The dash takes the place of a comma that would ordinarily set off the clause, but an exclamation point or question mark is retained.

If we don't succeed—and the critics say we won't—then the whole project is in jeopardy.

They are demanding that everything—even the marshland!—be transferred to the new trust.

Your question—it was *your* question, wasn't it, Mr. Jones?—just can't be answered.

Ellipsis (or Suspension Points)   . . . .

1. Indicates the omission of one or more words within a quoted passage. When four dots are used, the ellipsis indicates the omission of one or more sentences within the passage or the omission of words at the end of a sentence. The first or the last of the four dots is a period.

In the little world in which children have their existence, . . . there is nothing so finely perceived and so finely felt as injustice.
—Charles Dickens

Security is mostly a superstition. . . . Avoiding danger is no safer in the long run than outright exposure. . . . Life is either a daring adventure or nothing.—Helen Keller

2. Usually indicates omission of one or more lines of poetry when ellipsis is extended the length of the line.

I think that I shall never see

A poem lovely as a tree

. . . .

Poems are made by fools like me,

But only God can make a tree.
—Joyce Kilmer

3. Indicates halting speech or an unfinished sentence in dialogue.

"I'd like to. . . that is. . . if you don't mind. . . ."

Exclamation Point   !

1. Ends an emphatic phrase or sentence.

Get out of here!

Her notorious ostentation—she flew her friends to Bangkok for her birthday parties!—was feasted on by the popular press.

2. Ends an emphatic interjection.

> Encore!
>
> All of this proves—at long last!—that we were right from the start.

Hyphen　　　-

The hyphen is often used between parts of a compound. The styling of such words varies; when in doubt, see the entry in the dictionary at its own place or in a list of undefined words at an individual prefix. For unentered compounds, advice will be found in *Webster's Standard American Style Manual* or a comparable guide.

1. Is often used between a prefix and root, especially whenever the root is capitalized, when two identical vowels come together, or when the resulting word could be confused with another identically spelled word.

> pre-Renaissance　　　co-opted
>
> anti-inflationary
>
> re-cover a sofa
>
> 　*but*
>
> recover from an illness

2. Is used in some compounds, especially those containing prepositions.

> president-elect　　　sister-in-law
>
> good-for-nothing　　over-the-counter
>
> falling-out　　　write-off

3. Is often used in compound modifiers in attributive position.

> traveling in a fast-moving van
>
> She has gray-green eyes.
>
> a come-as-you-are party

4. Suspends the first element of a hyphenated compound or a prefix (hyphenated or not) when the second element or base word is part of a following hyphenated compound or derived form.

> a six- or eight-cylinder engine
>
> pre- and postadolescent trauma

5. Marks division of a word at the end of a line.

> 　　　　　　　　　The ruling pas-
>
> sion of his life

6. Is used in writing out compound numbers between 21 and 99.

> thirty-four
>
> one hundred and thirty-eight

7. Is often used between the numerator and the denominator in writing out fractions, especially when they are used as modifiers. However, fractions used as nouns are often written as open compounds, especially when ei-

ther the numerator or the denominator already contains a hyphen.

> a two-thirds majority of the vote
>
> three fifths of her paycheck
>
> one seventy-second of an inch

8. Serves as an equivalent of *through* or (*up*) *to and including* when used between indicators of range such as numbers and dates. (In typeset material the longer en dash is used.)

> pages 40–98
>
> the years 1980–89

9. Serves as the equivalent of *to, and,* or *versus* in indicating linkage or opposition. (In typeset material the longer en dash is used.)

> the New York–Paris flight
>
> the Hardy–Weinberg law
>
> the Lincoln–Douglas Debates
>
> The final score was 7–2.

Hyphen, Double　　

Is used at the end-of-line division of a hyphenated compound to indicate that the compound is hyphenated and not closed.

> self⸗ [end of line] seeker
>
> 　*but*
>
> self- [end of line] same

Parentheses　　（　）

1. Enclose words, numbers, phrases, or clauses that provide examples, explanations, or supplementary material that does not essentially alter the meaning of the sentence.

> Three old destroyers (all now out of commission) will be scrapped.
>
> He has followed the fortunes of the modern renaissance (*al-Nahdad*) in the Arabic-speaking world.

2. Enclose numerals that confirm a written number in a text.

> Delivery will be made in thirty (30) days.

3. Enclose numbers or letters in a series.

> We must set forth (1) our long-term goals, (2) our immediate objectives, and (3) the means at our disposal.

4. Enclose abbreviations that follow their spelled-out forms or spelled-out forms that follow their abbreviations.

> a ruling by the Federal Communications Commission (FCC)

the manufacture and disposal of PVC (polyvinyl chloride)

5. Indicate alternative terms.

Please indicate the lecture(s) you would like to attend.

6. Enclose publication data in footnotes and endnotes.

Marguerite Yourcenar, *The Dark Brain of Piranesi and Other Essays* (New York: Farrar, Straus and Giroux, 1985), p. 9.

7. Are used with other punctuation marks in the following ways:

If the parenthetic expression is an independent sentence standing alone, its first word is capitalized and a period is included *inside* the last parenthesis. However, if the parenthetic expression, even if it could stand alone as a sentence, occurs within a sentence, it is uncapitalized and has no sentence period but may have an exclamation point, a question mark, a period for an abbreviation, or quotation marks within the closing parenthesis.

The discussion was held in the boardroom. (The results are still confidential.)

Although we liked the restaurant (their Italian food was the best), we seldom went there.

After waiting in line for an hour (why do we do these things?), we finally left.

Years ago, someone (I wish I could remember who!) told me about it.

What was once informally known as A.B.D. status is now often recognized by the degree of Master of Philosophy (M. Phil.).

He was depressed ("I must resign") and refused to do anything.

No punctuation mark should be placed directly before parenthetical material in a sentence; if a break is required, punctuation should be placed *after* the final parenthesis.

I'll get back to you tomorrow (Friday), when I have more details.

Period

1. Ends sentences or sentence fragments that are neither interrogatory nor exclamatory.

Not bad.

Give it your best.

I gave it my best.

He asked if she had given it her best.

2. Follows some abbreviations and contractions.

| Dr. | A.D. | ibid. | i.e. |
| Jr. | etc. | cont. | |

3. Is normally used with an individual's initials.

F. Scott Fitzgerald

T. S. Eliot

4. Is used after numerals and letters in vertical enumerations and outlines.

Required skills are:
1. Shorthand
2. Typing
3. Transcription
I. Objectives
  A. Economy
    1. low initial cost
    2. low maintenance cost
  B. Ease of operation

Question Mark   ?

1. Ends a direct question.

How did she do it?

"How did she do it?" he asked.

2. Ends a question that is part of a larger sentence, but not an indirect question.

How did she do it? was the question on each person's mind.

He wondered, Will it work?

He wondered whether it would work.

3. Indicates the writer's ignorance or uncertainty.

Geoffrey Chaucer, English poet (1342?–1400)

Quotation Marks, Double   "   "

1. Enclose direct quotations but not indirect quotations.

She said, "I am leaving."

She said that she was leaving.

2. Enclose words or phrases borrowed from others, words used in a special way, and words of marked informality when introduced into formal writing.

Much of the population in the hellish future he envisions is addicted to "derms," patches that deliver potent drug doses instantaneously through the skin.

He called himself "emperor," but he was really just a dictator.

He was arrested for smuggling "smack."

3. Enclose titles of poems, short stories, articles, lectures, chapters of books, short musical compositions, and radio and TV programs.

Robert Frost's "After Apple-Picking"

Cynthia Ozick's "Rosa"

The third chapter of *Treasure Island* is entitled "The Black Spot."

"All the Things You Are"

Debussy's "Clair de lune"

NBC's "Today Show"

4. Are used with other punctuation marks in the following ways:

The period and the comma fall *within* the quotation marks.

"I am leaving," she said.

It was unclear how she maintained such an estate on "a small annuity."

The colon and semicolon fall *outside* the quotation marks.

There was only one thing to do when he said, "I may not run": promise him a large campaign contribution.

He spoke of his "little cottage in the country"; he might better have called it a mansion.

The dash, the question mark, and the exclamation point fall *within* the quotation marks when they refer to the quoted matter only; they fall *outside* when they refer to the whole sentence.

"I can't see how—" he started to say.

He asked, "When did she leave?"

What is the meaning of "the open door"?

The sergeant shouted "Halt!"

Save us from his "mercy"!

5. Are not used with *yes* or *no* except in direct discourse.

She said yes to all our requests.

6. Are not used with lengthy quotations set off from the text.

He took the title for his biography of Thoreau from a passage in *Walden*:

I long ago lost a hound, a bay horse, and a turtledove, and am still on their trail. . . . I have met one or two who had heard the hound, and the tramp of the horse, and even seen the dove disappear behind a cloud, and they seemed as anxious to recover them as if they had lost them themselves.

However, the title *A Hound, a Bay Horse, and a Turtle-Dove* probably puzzled some readers.

Quotation Marks, Single   ' '

1. Enclose a quotation within a quotation in American usage. When both single and double quotation marks occur at the end of a sentence, the period typically falls within *both* sets of marks.

The witness said, "I distinctly heard him say, 'Don't be late,' and then heard the door close."

The witness said, "I distinctly heard him say, 'Don't be late.'"

2. Are sometimes used in place of double quotation marks especially in British usage. In this case a quotation within a quotation is set off by double quotation marks.

The witness said, 'I distinctly heard him say, "Don't be late," and then heard the door close.'

Semicolon   ;

1. Links independent clauses not joined by a coordinating conjunction.

Some people have the ability to write well; others do not.

2. Links clauses joined by a conjunctive adverb (such as *consequently, furthermore, however*).

Speeding is illegal; furthermore, it is very dangerous.

3. Often occurs before expressions that introduce expansions or series (such as *for example, for instance, that is, e.g.,* or *i.e.*).

As a manager she tried to do the best job she could; that is, to keep her project on schedule and under budget.

4. Separates phrases that contain commas.

The country's resources consist of large ore deposits; lumber, waterpower, and fertile soils; and a strong, rugged people.

Send copies to our offices in Portland, Maine; Springfield, Illinois; and Savannah, Georgia.

5. Is placed outside quotation marks and parentheses.

They again demanded "complete autonomy"; the demand was again rejected.

Virgule (or Slash)   /

1. Separates alternatives.

high-heat and/or high-speed applications

. . . sit hour after hour. . . and finally year after year in a catatonic/frenzied trance rewriting the Bible —William Saroyan

2. Replaces the word *to* or *and* between related terms that are compounded.

the fiscal year 1983/1984

in the May/June issue

3. Divides run-in lines of poetry.

Say, sages, what's the charm on earth/Can turn
death's dart aside?—Robert Burns

4. Divides elements in dates and divides numerators
and denominators in fractions.

offer expires 5/19/94

Fifteen and 44/100 dollars

5. Often represents *per* or *to* when used with units of
measure or to indicate the terms of a ratio.

9 ft/sec

risk/reward trade-off

6. Sets off phonemes of phonemic transcription.

/b/ as in *but*

Capitalization

Capitals are used for two broad purposes in English: they mark a beginning (as of a
sentence) and they signal a proper noun, pronoun, or adjective. The following principles,
each with examples, describe the most common uses of capital letters.

Beginnings

1. The first word of a sentence or sentence fragment is
capitalized.

The play lasted nearly three hours.

How are you feeling?

Bravo!

2. The first word of a sentence contained within parentheses is capitalized if it does not occur within another
sentence. The first word of a parenthetical sentence
within another sentence is not capitalized.

The discussion was held in the boardroom. (The
results are still confidential.)

Although we liked the restaurant (their Italian
food was the best), we seldom ate there.

After waiting in line for an hour (why do we do
these things?), we finally left.

3. The first word of a direct quotation is capitalized.
However, if the quotation is interrupted in the middle of
a sentence, the second part does not begin with a capital. When a quotation, whether a sentence fragment or
a complete sentence, is syntactically dependent on the
sentence in which it occurs, the quotation does not begin
with a capital.

The President said, "We have rejected this report
entirely."

"We have rejected this report entirely," the
President said, "and we will not comment on it
further."

The President made it clear that "there is no
room for compromise."

4. The first word of a sentence within a sentence is usually capitalized when it represents a direct question, a

motto or aphorism, or spoken or unspoken dialogue.
The first word following a colon may be either lowercased or capitalized if it introduces a complete sentence.
While the former is more usual, the latter is common
when the sentence is fairly lengthy and distinctly separate from the preceding clause.

That question, as Disraeli said, is this: Is man an
ape or an angel?

My first thought was, How can I avoid this
assignment?

The advantage of this particular system is clear:
it's inexpensive.

The situation is critical: This company

cannot hope to recoup the fourth-quarter losses
that were sustained in five operating divisions.

5. The first word of a line of poetry is traditionally capitalized; however, in much twentieth-century poetry the
line beginnings are lowercased.

The best lack all conviction, while the worst
Are full of passionate intensity.
—W. B. Yeats

6. The first words of run-in enumerations that form
complete sentences are capitalized, as are usually the
first words of vertical lists and enumerations. However,
enumerations of words or phrases run in with the introductory text are generally lowercased.

Do the following tasks at the end of the day:
1. Clear your desktop of papers. 2. Cover office
machines. 3. Straighten the contents of your
desk drawers, cabinets, and bookcases.

This is the agenda:
Call to order
Roll call
Minutes of the previous meeting
Treasurer's report

On the agenda will be (1) call to order, (2) roll call, (3) minutes of the previous meeting, (4) treasurer's report. . . .

7. The first word in an outline heading is capitalized.

I. Editorial tasks

II. Production responsibilities
A. Cost estimates
B. Bids

8. The first word of the salutation of a letter and the first word of a complimentary close are capitalized.

Dear Mary,

Ladies and Gentlemen:

Sincerely yours,

Proper Nouns, Pronouns, and Adjectives

Capitals are used with almost all proper nouns—that is, nouns that name particular persons, places, or things (including abstract entities), distinguishing them from others of the same class—and proper adjectives—that is, adjectives that take their meaning from what is named by the proper noun. The essential distinction in the use of capitals and lowercase letters at the beginnings of words lies in this individualizing significance of capitals as against the generalizing significance of lowercase. The following subject headings are in alphabetical order.

ARMED FORCES

1. Branches and units of the armed forces are capitalized, as are easily recognized short forms of full branch and unit designations. However, the words *army, navy,* etc., are lowercased when used in their plural forms or when they are not part of an official title.

United States Army

a contract with the Army

Corps of Engineers

a bridge built by the Engineers

allied armies

AWARDS

2. Names of awards and prizes are capitalized.

the Nobel Prize in Chemistry

Distinguished Service Cross

Academy Award

DERIVATIVES OF PROPER NAMES

3. Derivatives of proper names are capitalized when used in their primary sense. However, if the derived term has taken on a specialized meaning, it is usually not capitalized.

Roman customs

Shakespearean comedies

Edwardian era

but

quixotic

herculean

bohemian tastes

GEOGRAPHICAL REFERENCES

4. Divisions of the earth's surface and names of distinct areas, regions, places, or districts are capitalized, as are most derivative adjectives and some derivative nouns and verbs.

The Eastern Hemisphere

Midwest

Tropic of Cancer

Springfield, Massachusetts

the Middle Eastern situation

an Americanism

but

french fries

a japan finish

manila envelope

5. Popular names of localities are capitalized.

the Corn Belt	the Loop
The Big Apple	the Gold Coast
the Pacific Rim	

6. Words designating global, national, regional, or local political divisions are capitalized when they are essential elements of specific names. However, they are usually lowercased when they precede a proper name or stand alone. (In legal documents, these words are often capitalized regardless of position.)

the British Empire	Washington State
New York City	Ward 1
but	
the fall of the empire	the state of Washington
the city of New York	fires in three wards

7. Generic geographical terms (such as *lake, mountain, river, valley*) are capitalized if they are part of a specific proper name.

Hudson Bay	Long Island
Niagara Falls	Crater Lake
the Shenandoah	Valley

8. Generic terms preceding names are usually capitalized.

Lakes Michigan and Superior

Mounts Whitney and Rainier

9. Generic terms following names are usually lowercased, as are singular or plural generic terms that are used descriptively or alone.

the Himalaya and Andes mountains

the Atlantic coast of Labrador

the Hudson valley

the river valley

the valley

10. Compass points are capitalized when they refer to a geographical region or when they are part of a street name, but they are lowercased when they refer to simple direction.

> up North
>
> back East
>
> the Northwest
>
> West Columbus Avenue
>
> Park Avenue South
>
> > *but*
>
> west of the Rockies
>
> the east coast of Florida

11. Adjectives derived from compass points and nouns designating the inhabitants of some geographical regions are capitalized. When in doubt, see the entry in the dictionary.

> a Southern accent
>
> Northerners

12. Terms designating public places are capitalized if they are part of a proper name.

> Brooklyn Bridge
>
> Lincoln Park
>
> the St. Regis Hotel
>
> Independence Hall
>
> > *but*
>
> Wisconsin and Connecticut avenues
>
> the Plaza and St. Regis hotels

GOVERNMENTAL AND JUDICIAL BODIES

13. Full names of legislative, deliberative, executive, and administrative bodies are capitalized, as are short forms of these names. However, nonspecific noun and adjective references to them are usually lowercased.

> the U.S. House of Representatives
>
> the House
>
> the Federal Bureau of Investigation
>
> > *but*
>
> both houses of Congress
>
> a federal agency

14. Names of international courts, the U.S. Supreme Court, and other higher courts are capitalized. However, names of city and county courts are usually lowercased.

> The International Court of Arbitration
>
> the Supreme Court of the United States
>
> the Supreme Court
>
> the United States Court of Appeals for the Second Circuit
>
> the Michigan Court of Appeals

Lawton municipal court

Newark night court

HISTORICAL PERIODS AND EVENTS

15. Names of congresses, councils, and expositions are capitalized.

> the Yalta Conference
>
> the Republican National Convention

16. Names of historical events, some historical periods, and some cultural periods and movements are capitalized. When in doubt, consult the entry in the dictionary, especially for periods.

> the Boston Tea Party
>
> Renaissance
>
> Prohibition
>
> the Augustan Age
>
> the Enlightenment
>
> > *but*
>
> the space age
>
> neoclassicism

17. Numerical designations of historical time periods are capitalized when they are part of a proper name; otherwise they are lowercased.

> the Third Reich
>
> the Roaring Twenties
>
> > *but*
>
> the eighteenth century
>
> the eighties

18. Names of treaties, laws, and acts are capitalized.

> Treaty of Versailles
>
> The Clear Air Act of 1990

ORGANIZATIONS

19. Names of firms, corporations, schools, and organizations and their members are capitalized. However, common nouns occurring after the names of two or more organizations are lowercased. The word *the* at the beginning of such names is only capitalized when the full legal name is used.

> Thunder's Mouth Press
>
> University of Wisconsin
>
> European Community
>
> Rotary International
>
> Kiwanians
>
> American and United airlines

20. Words such as *group, division, department, office,* or *agency* that designate a corporate and organizational unit are capitalized only when used with its specific name.

> in the Editorial Department of Merriam-Webster
>
> > *but*

a notice to all department heads

PEOPLE

21. Names of persons are capitalized. However, the capitalization of particles such as *de, della, der, du, l', la, ten,* and *van* varies widely, especially in names of people in English-speaking countries.

Noah Webster   Werner Von Braun

W.E.B. Du Bois   Anthony Van Dyck

Daphne du Maurier

22. Titles preceding the name of a person and epithets used instead of a name are capitalized. However, titles following a name or used alone are usually lowercased.

President Roosevelt

Professor Kaiser

Queen Elizabeth

Old Hickory

the Iron Chancellor

but

Henry VIII, king of England

23. Corporate titles are capitalized when used with an individual's name; otherwise, they are lowercased.

Lisa Dominguez, Vice President

The sales manager called me.

24. Words of family relationship preceding or used in place of a person's name are capitalized; however, these words are lowercased if they are part of a noun phrase used in place of a name.

Cousin Julia

I know when Mother's birthday is.

but

I know when my mother's birthday is.

25. Words designating peoples, nationalities, religious groups, tribes, races, and languages are capitalized. Other terms used to refer to groups of people are often lowercased. Designations based on color are usually lowercased.

Canadians   Iroquois

Ibo   African-American

Latin   Indo-European

highlander (an inhabitant of a highland)

Highlander (an inhabitant of the Highlands of Scotland)

black   white

PERSONIFICATIONS

26. Personifications are capitalized.

She dwells with Beauty—Beauty, that must die;
And Joy, whose hand is ever at his lips
Bidding adieu.
                              —John Keats

obey the commands of Nature

PRONOUNS

27. The pronoun *I* is capitalized. For pronouns referring to the Deity, see rule 29 below.

. . . no one but I myself had yet printed any of my work.—Paul Bowles

RELIGIOUS TERMS

28. Words designating the Deity are capitalized.

An anthropomorphic, vengeful Jehovah became a spiritual, benevolent Supreme Being.
                              —A. R. Katz

29. Personal pronouns referring to the Deity are usually capitalized, even when they closely follow their antecedent. However, many writers never capitalize such pronouns.

All Thy works, O Lord, shall bless Thee.
          —*Oxford American Hymnal*

God's in his heaven—
All's right with the world!
                    —Robert Browning

30. Traditional designations of revered persons, such as prophets, apostles, and saints, are often capitalized.

our Lady

the Prophet

the Lawgiver

31. Names of religions, creeds and confessions, denominations, and religious orders are capitalized, as is the word *Church* when used as part of a proper name.

Judaism

Apostles' Creed

the Thirty-nine Articles of the Church of England

Society of Jesus

Hunt Memorial Church

but

the local Baptist church

32. Names for the Bible or parts, versions, or editions of it and names of other sacred books are capitalized but not italicized. Adjectives derived from the names of sacred books are irregularly capitalized or lowercased; when in doubt, see the entry in the dictionary.

Authorized   New English Bible
Version

Old Testament   Pentateuch

Apocrypha   Gospel of Saint
                    Mark

Talmud   Koran

biblical   Koranic

SCIENTIFIC TERMS

33. Names of planets and their satellites, asteroids, stars, constellations and groups of stars, and other unique celestial objects are capitalized. However, the

words *sun, earth*, and *moon* are usually lowercased unless they occur with other astronomical names.

Venus   Ganymede

Sirius   Pleiades

the Milky Way

enjoying the beauty of the moon

probes heading for the Moon and Mars

34. New Latin genus names in zoology and botany are capitalized; the second term in binomial scientific names, identifying the species, is not.

a cabbage butterfly *(Pieris rapae)*

a common buttercup *(Ranunculus acris)*

35. New Latin names of all groups above genus in zoology and botany (such as class or family) are capitalized; however, their derivative adjectives and nouns are not.

Gastropoda   *but*   gastropod

Cetacea   *but*   cetacean

36. Names of geological eras, periods, epochs, and strata and names of prehistoric divisions are capitalized.

Silurian period   Pleistocene epoch

Age of Reptiles   Neolithic age

SEASONS, MONTHS, DAYS

37. Names of months, days of the week, and holidays and holy days are capitalized.

January   Ramadan

Tuesday   Thanksgiving

Yom Kippur   Easter

38. Names of seasons are not capitalized except when personified.

last spring

the sweet breath of Spring

TITLES OF PRINTED MATTER AND WORKS OF ART

39. Words in titles are capitalized, with the exception of internal conjunctions, prepositions, and articles. In some publications, prepositions of five or more letters are capitalized also.

Of Mice and Men

"The Man Who Would Be King"

"To His Coy Mistress"

Slouching Toward Bethlehem

40. Capitalization of the titles of movies, plays, paintings, sculpture, and musical compositions follow similar conventions. For more details, see the Italicization section below.

41. Major sections of books, long articles, or reports are capitalized when they are referred to within the same material.

See the Appendix for further information.

The Introduction explains the scope of this book.

discussed later in Chapter 4

42. Nouns used with numbers or letters to designate major reference headings are capitalized. Nouns designating minor elements are typically lowercased.

Volume V

page 101

Table 3

note 10

TRADEMARKS

43. Registered trademarks and service marks are capitalized.

Express Mail   Orlon

Kleenex   Walkman

VEHICLES

44. Names of ships, aircraft, and spacecraft are capitalized.

Titanic

Lindbergh's *Spirit of St. Louis*

Apollo 13

Italicization

The following are usually italicized in print and underlined in manuscript and typescript.

1. Words and passages that are to be emphasized.

This was their fatal error: there *was* no cache of supplies in the now-abandoned depot.

2. Titles of books, magazines, newspapers, plays, long poems, movies, paintings, sculpture, and long musical compositions (but not musical compositions identified by the name of their genre).

Dickens's *Bleak House*

National Geographic

Christian Science Monitor

Shakespeare's *Othello*

Eliot's *The Waste Land*

the movie *Back to the Future*

Gainsborough's *Blue Boy*

Mozart's *Don Giovanni*

but

Schubert's Sonata in B-flat Major, D. 960

NOTE: In the plurals of such italicized titles, the *s* or *es* endings are usually in roman type.

hidden under a stack of *New Yorker*s

3. Names of ships, aircraft, and spacecraft.

Titanic

Lindbergh's *Spirit of St. Louis*

Apollo 13

4. Words, letters, and figures when referred to as such.

The *g* in *align* is silent.

The first *2* and the last *0* are barely legible.

5. Unfamiliar words when first introduced and defined in a text.

Heart failure is often accompanied by *edema*, an accumulation of fluid which tends to produce swelling of the lower extremities.

6. Foreign words and phrases that have not been naturalized in English. In general, any word entered in the main A–Z vocabulary of this dictionary need not be italicized.

c'est la vie

aere perennius

che sarà, sarà

sans peur et sans reproche

but

pasta   ad hoc   ex officio

7. New Latin scientific names of genera, species, subspecies, races, and varieties (but not groups of higher rank, such as phyla, classes, or orders) in botanical or zoological names.

a thick-shelled American clam *(Mercenaria mercenaria)*

a mallard *(Anas platyrhynchos)*

but

the family Hominidae

8. Case titles in legal citations, both in full and shortened form; "v" for "versus" is set in either roman or italic.

Jones v. *Ohio*   the *Jones* case

Smith et al v. Jones   *Jones*

Documentation of Sources

Writers and editors use various methods to indicate the source of a quotation or piece of information borrowed from another work. In works published for the general public and traditionally in scholarly works in the humanities, footnotes or endnotes have been preferred. In this system, sequential numbers within the text refer the reader to notes at the bottom of the page or at the end of the article, chapter, or book; these notes contain full bibliographical information of the works cited. In scholarly works in the social and natural sciences, and increasingly in the humanities as well, parenthetical references within the text refer the reader to an alphabetically arranged list of sources at the end of the work. The system of footnotes or endnotes is the more flexible, in that it allows for commentary on the work or subject and can also be used for brief peripheral discussions not tied to any specific work. However, style manuals tend to encourage the use of parenthetical references in addition to or instead of footnotes or endnotes, since for most kinds of material they are efficient and convenient for both writer and reader. In a carefully documented work, a bibliography or list of sources normally follows the entire text (including any endnotes) regardless of which system is used.

Though different publishers and journals have adopted slightly varying styles, the following examples illustrate standard styles for references, notes, and bibliographic entries. For more extensive treatment than can be provided here, *Webster's Standard American Style Manual*, *The Chicago Manual of Style*, *The MLA Style Manual*, or the *Publication Manual of the American Psychological Association* may be consulted.

Footnotes and Endnotes

Footnotes and endnotes are indicated by superscript Arabic numerals placed immediately after the material to be documented. The numbering is consecutive throughout an article or monograph; in a book, it usually starts over with each new chapter or section. Footnotes appear at the bottom of the page; endnotes, which take the same form as footnotes, are gathered at the end of the article, chapter, or book. Endnotes are generally preferred over footnotes by writers and publishers because they are easier to handle when preparing both manuscript and printed pages, though they can be less convenient for the reader. All of the examples shown reflect humanities citation style. All of the cited works appear again in the Lists of Sources section below.

Books

One author	[1]Elizabeth Bishop, *The Complete Poems: 1927–1979* (New York: Farrar, Straus & Giroux, 1983), 46.
Two or more authors	[2]Bert Holldobler and Edward O. Wilson, *The Ants* (Cambridge, Mass.: Belknap–Harvard Univ. Press, 1990), 119.
	[3]Randolph Quirk et al., *A Comprehensive Grammar of the English Language* (London: Longman, 1985), 135.
Edition and/or translation	[4]Arthur S. Banks, ed. *Political Handbook of the World: 1992* (Binghamton, N.Y.: CSA Publications, 1992), 293–95.
	[5]Simone de Beauvoir, *The Second Sex,* trans. and ed. H.M. Parshley (New York: Knopf, 1953; Random House, 1974), 446.
Second or later edition	[6]Albert C. Baugh and Thomas Cable, *A History of the English Language*, 3d ed. (Englewood Cliffs, N.J.: Prentice Hall, 1978), 14.
Article in a collection or festschrift	[7]Ernst Mayr, "Processes of Speciation in Animals," in *Mechanisms of Speciation*, ed. C. Barigozzi (New York: Alan R. Liss, 1982), 1–3.

Work in two or more volumes   [8]Ronald M. Nowak, *Walker's Mammals of the World*, 5th ed. (Baltimore: Johns Hopkins Univ. Press, 1991), 2:661.

Corporate author   [9]Commission of the Humanities. *The Humanities in American Life* (Berkeley: Univ. of California Press, 1980), 46.

Book lacking publication data   [10]*Photographic View Album of Cambridge* [England], n.p., n.d., n.pag.

Subsequent reference   [11]Baugh and Cable, 18–19.

Articles

Journal paginated consecutively throughout annual volume   [12]Stephen Jay Gould and Niles Eldredge, "Punctuated Equilibria: The Tempo and Mode of Evolution Reconsidered," *Paleobiology* 3 (1977): 121.

Journal paginated consecutively only within each issue   [13]Roseann Duenas Gonzalez, "Teaching Mexican American Students to Write: Capitalizing on the Culture," *English Journal* 71.7 (Nov. 1982): 22–24.

Monthly magazine   [14]John Lukacs, "The End of the Twentieth Century," *Harper's*, Jan. 1993: 40.

Weekly magazine   [15]Richard Preston, "A Reporter at Large: Crisis in the Hot Zone," *New Yorker*, 26 Oct. 1992: 58.

Newspaper   [16]William J. Broad, "Big Science Squeezes Small-Scale Researchers," *New York Times*, 29 Dec. 1992: C1.

Signed review   [17]George Steiner, review of *Oeuvres en Prose Complètes, Tome 3*, by Charles Péguy, *Times Literary Supplement*, 25 Dec. 1992: 3.

Parenthetical References

Parenthetical references are highly abbreviated bibliographical citations that appear within the text itself, enclosed in parentheses. Such references direct the reader to a detailed bibliography or list of sources at the end of the work, often removing the need for footnotes or endnotes. The parenthetical references usually include only the author's last name and a page reference. (In the social and natural sciences, the year of publication is included after the author's name, and the page number is often omitted.) Any element of the reference that is clear from the context may be omitted. To distinguish among cited works published by the same author, the author's name may be followed by the specific work's title, which is usually shortened. (If the author-date system is being used, a lowercase letter can be added after the year—e.g., 1992a, 1992b—to distinguish between works published in the same year.) Each of the following references is keyed to an entry in the Lists of Sources section below.

Humanities style   (Quirk et al., 135)
(Baugh and Cable, *History*, 14)
(Commission on the Humanities, 46)

Sciences style   (Mayr 1982, 1–3)
(Nowak 1991, 2:661)
(Gould and Eldredge 1977)

Lists of Sources

A bibliography or list of sources in alphabetical order usually appears at the end of the work. The following lists of cited works illustrate standard styles employed in, respectively, the humanities and the social and natural sciences. The principal differences between the two styles are these. In the sciences, (1) an initial is generally used instead of the author's first name, (2) the date is placed directly after the author's name, (3) all words in titles are lowercased except the first word and the first word of any subtitle as well as proper nouns and adjectives, and (4) article titles are not set off by quotation marks. (In some scientific publications, book and journal titles are not italicized.)

Humanities style

Baugh, Albert C., and Thomas Cable. *A History of the English Language.* 3d ed. Englewood Cliffs, N.J.: Prentice Hall, 1978.

Beauvoir, Simone de. *The Second Sex.* Trans. and ed. H. M. Parshley. New York: Alfred A. Knopf, 1953. Reprint. New York: Random House, 1974.

Bishop, Elizabeth. *The Complete Poems: 1927–1979.* New York: Farrar, Straus & Giroux, 1983.

Commission on the Humanities. *The Humanities in American Life.* Berkeley: University of California Press, 1980.

Gonzalez, Roseann Duenas. "Teaching Mexican American Students to Write: Capitalizing on the Culture." *English Journal* 71.7 (November 1982): 22–24.

Lukacs, John. "The End of the Twentieth Century." *Harper's,* January 1993: 39–58.

Photographic View Album of Cambridge [England]. N.d., n.p., n. pag.

Quirk, Randolph, Sidney Greenbaum, Geoffrey Leech, and Jan Svartvik. *A Comprehensive Grammar of the English Language.* London: Longman, 1985.

Steiner, George. Review of *Oeuvres en Prose Complètes, Tome 3,* by Charles Péguy. *Times Literary Supplement,* 25 December 1992: 3–4.

Sciences style

Banks, A. S., ed. 1992. *Political handbook of the world: 1992.* Binghamton, N.Y.: CSA Publications.

Broad, W. J. 1992. Big science squeezes small-scale researchers. *New York Times,* 29 Dec.: C1 +.

Gould, S. J., and N. Eldredge. 1977. Punctuated equilibria: The tempo and mode of evolution reconsidered. *Paleobiology* 3: 115–151.

Holldobler, B., and E. O. Wilson. 1990. *The ants.* Cambridge, Mass.: Belknap–Harvard Univ. Press.

Mayr, E. 1982. Processes of speciation in animals. In C. Barigozzi, ed., *Mechanisms of speciation.* New York: Alan R. Liss: 1–19.

Nowak, R.M. 1991. *Walker's mammals of the world.* 5th ed. 2 vols. Baltimore: Johns Hopkins Univ. Press.

Preston, R. 1992. A reporter at large: Crisis in the hot zone. *New Yorker,* 26 Oct.: 58–81.

Forms of Address

Since the relationship between correspondents affects the form of address used in letters, no rigid guidelines can be set down for all occasions; however, the following examples show a generally accepted form. When two or more salutations are shown for the same entry, the more formal comes first. In general, male and female names are used alternately. For any given entry, the form of address for the opposite sex can be easily determined. The female equivalent of "Sir" is "Madam" (or "Madame" when the addressee is foreign). The female equivalent of "Mr." when it immediately precedes a name is "Ms." (or "Mrs." or "Miss" if either is known to be preferred by the addressee). The male equivalent of "Madam" standing alone is "Sir." When "Madam" precedes another title, the male equivalent is "Mr." The male equivalent of "Ms." is "Mr."

Addressee	Form of Address	Salutation

Clerical and Religious Orders

Addressee	Form of Address	Salutation
abbot	The Right Reverend John R. Smith, O.S.B. Abbot of _____	Right Reverend and dear Father: Dear Father Abbot: Dear Father:
archbishop	The Most Reverend Archbishop of _____ *or* The Most Reverend John R. Smith Archbishop of _____	Your Excellency: (same) Dear Archbishop Smith:
bishop, Catholic	The Most Reverend John R. Smith Bishop of _____	Most Reverend Sir: Your Excellency: Dear Bishop Smith:
bishop, Episcopal	The Right Reverend John R. Smith Bishop of _____	Right Reverend Sir: Dear Bishop Smith:
bishop, Protestant (excluding Episcopal)	The Reverend John R. Smith *or* Bishop John R. Smith	Reverend Sir: Dear Bishop Smith:
brotherhood, Catholic, member of	Brother James, S.J.	Dear Brother James:
brotherhood, Catholic, superior of	Brother Michael, S.J., Superior	Dear Brother Michael:
cardinal	His Eminence John Cardinal Smith	Your Eminence: Dear Cardinal Smith:
clergy, Protestant	The Reverend Amelia R. Smith *or with a doctorate* The Reverend Dr. Amelia R. Smith *or* The Reverend Amelia R. Smith, D.D.	Dear Ms. Smith: *or* Dear Dr. Smith:
monsignor	The Reverend Monsignor John R. Smith *or* The Rev. Msgr. John R. Smith	Reverend and dear Monsignor Smith: Dear Monsignor Smith:

Addressee	Form of Address	Salutation
patriarch (of an Eastern church)	His Beatitude the Patriarch of _____	Most Reverend Lord: Your Beatitude:
pope	His Holiness Pope _____ *or* His Holiness the Pope	Your Holiness: Most Holy Father:
priest	The Reverend John R. Smith *or* The Reverend Father Smith	Reverend Father: Dear Father Smith: Dear Father:
rabbi	Rabbi Amelia R. Smith *or with a doctorate* Rabbi Amelia R. Smith, D.D.	Dear Rabbi Smith: *or* Dear Dr. Smith:
sisterhood, member of	Sister Mary Angelica, S.C.	Dear Sister Mary Angelica: Dear Sister:
sisterhood, superior of	The Reverend Mother Superior, S.C., Superior	Reverend Mother: Dear Reverend Mother:

College and University Officials

chancellor	Dr. Amelia R. Smith Chancellor	Dear Dr. Smith:
dean	Dean John R. Smith	Dear Dean Smith: Dear Dr. Smith:
president	President Amelia R. Smith *or* Dr. Amelia R. Smith	Dear President Smith: *or* Dear Dr. Smith:
professor, assistant or associate	Mr. John R. Smith Assistant/Associate Professor of _____ *or with a doctorate* Dr. John R. Smith Assistant/Associate Professor of _____	Dear Professor Smith: Dear Mr. Smith: *or* Dear Dr. Smith:
professor, full	Professor Amelia R. Smith *or* Dr. Amelia R. Smith	Dear Professor Smith: *or* Dear Dr. Smith:

Diplomats and Consular Officers

ambassador, American	The Honorable John R. Smith American Ambassador *or if in Canada or Latin America* The Ambassador of the United States of America	Sir: Dear Mr. Ambassador:
ambassador, foreign	Her Excellency Amelia R. Smith Ambassador of _____	Excellency: Dear Madame Ambassador:

Addressee	Form of Address	Salutation
chargé d'affaires, American	John R. Smith, Esq. American Chargé d'Affaires *or if in Canada or Latin America* The United States Chargé d'Affaires	Sir: Dear Mr. Smith:
chargé d'affaires, foreign	Ms. Amelia R. Smith Chargé d'Affaires of _____	Madame: Dear Ms. Smith:
consul, American	The American Consul *or if in Canada or Latin America* The Consul of the United States of America	Sir: Dear Sir:
	or if individual name is known John R. Smith, Esq. American Consul *or if in Canada or Latin America* John R. Smith, Esq. Consul of the United States of America	Sir: Dear Mr. Smith:
consul, foreign	The Consul of _____ *or if individual name is known* The Honorable Amelia R. Smith _____Consul *or* Consul of _____	Sir: Madame: Dear Ms. Smith:
secretary-general, U.N.	His Excellency John R. Smith Secretary-General of the United Nations	Excellency: Dear Mr. Secretary-General:

Foreign Heads of State or Government

premier	Her Excellency Amelia R. Smith Premier of _____	Excellency: Dear Madame Premier:
president	His Excellency John R. Smith President of _____	Excellency: Dear Mr. President:
prime minister	His Excellency Amelia R. Smith Prime Minister of _____	Excellency: Dear Madame Prime Minister:

Government Officials, Federal

attorney general	The Honorable John R. Smith Attorney General	Sir: Dear Mr. Attorney General:
cabinet officer (other than attorney general)	The Secretary of _____ *or* The Honorable Amelia R. Smith Secretary of _____	Madam: Dear Madam Secretary: Dear Ms. Smith:
chair of a committee or subcommittee, U.S. Congress	The Honorable John R. Smith Chairman, Committee on _____ United States Senate/House of Representatives	Dear Mr. Chairman: Dear Senator/Representative Smith:

Addressee	Form of Address	Salutation
commissioner	The Honorable Amelia R. Smith Commissioner	Dear Madam Commissioner: Dear Ms. Smith:
director of an agency	The Honorable John R. Smith Director	Dear Mr. Smith:
judge	The Honorable Amelia R. Smith Judge of the United States District Court of the _____ District of _____	Madam: Dear Judge Smith:
president	The President The White House *or* The Honorable John R. Smith President of the United States The White House	Mr. President: Dear Mr. President:
representative, U.S. Congress	The Honorable Amelia R. Smith United States House of Representatives *or for local address* The Honorable Amelia R. Smith Representative in Congress	Madam: Dear Representative Smith: Dear Ms. Smith:
senator, U.S. Senate	The Honorable John R. Smith United States Senator	Sir: Dear Senator Smith:
speaker, U.S. House of Representatives	The Honorable Speaker of the House of Representatives *or* The Honorable Amelia R. Smith Speaker of the House of Representatives	Madam: Dear Madam Speaker: Dear Ms. Smith:
supreme court, associate justice	Mr. Justice Smith The Supreme Court of the United States	Sir: Dear Justice Smith:
supreme court, chief justice	The Chief Justice of the United States The Supreme Court of the United States *or* The Chief Justice The Supreme Court	Madam: Dear Madam Chief Justice:
vice president	The Vice President of the United States United States Senate *or* The Honorable John R. Smith Vice President of the United States	Sir: Dear Mr. Vice President:

Government Officials, State and Local

alderman	— see COUNCIL MEMBER	
assemblyman	— see REPRESENTATIVE, STATE	
attorney, city (state's)	The Honorable Amelia R. Smith	Dear Ms. Smith:

Addressee Form of Address Salutation

Addressee	Form of Address	Salutation
clerk of a court	John R. Smith, Esq. Clerk of the Court of _____	Dear Mr. Smith:
council member	The Honorable Amelia R. Smith Councilwoman *or* Councilwoman Amelia R. Smith	Dear Ms. Smith: Dear Councilwoman Smith:
county clerk	The Honorable John R. Smith Clerk of _____ County	Dear Mr. Smith:
county treasurer	— see COUNTY CLERK	
delegate	— see REPRESENTATIVE. STATE	
governor	The Honorable Amelia R. Smith Governor of _____ *or in some states* Her Excellency, the Governor of _____	Madam: Dear Governor Smith:
judge, state or local court	The Honorable John R. Smith Judge of the _____ Court	Dear Judge Smith:
lieutenant governor	The Honorable Lieutenant Governor of _____ *or* The Honorable Amelia R. Smith Lieutenant Governor of _____	Madam: Dear Ms. Smith:
mayor	The Honorable John R. Smith Mayor of _____	Sir: Dear Mayor Smith:
representative, state	The Honorable Amelia R. Smith House of Representatives	Madam: Dear Ms. Smith:
secretary of state	The Honorable Secretary of State of _____ *or* The Honorable John R. Smith Secretary of State of _____	Sir: Dear Mr. Secretary:
selectman	— see COUNCIL MEMBER	
senate, state, president of	The Honorable Amelia R. Smith President of the Senate of the State of _____	Madam: Dear Senator Smith: Dear Ms. Smith:
senator, state	The Honorable John R. Smith The Senate of _____	Sir: Dear Senator Smith: Dear Mr. Smith:
speaker, state assembly (house of delegates, house of representatives)	The Honorable Amelia R. Smith Speaker of _____	Madam: Dear Ms. Smith:
supreme court, state, associate justice	The Honorable John R. Smith Associate Justice of the Supreme Court of _____	Sir: Dear Justice Smith:

Addressee	Form of Address	Salutation
supreme court, state, chief justice	The Honorable Amelia R. Smith Chief Justice of the Supreme Court of _____	Madam: Dear Madam Chief Justice:

Military Personnel

The first entry below describes the appropriate form of address for any member of the armed forces. The central column of the subsequent entries shows only the special rank abbreviations used by the different service branches. In actual practice, salutations will differ according to degree of formality. The most formal will often employ the address-ee's full title (as shown in the left column). The salutations listed below generally represent a level of formality between the highly formal and the familiar.

all ranks	*full or abbreviated rank + full name + comma + abbreviation for branch of service* (USA, USN, USAF, USMC, USCG) *Example:* First Lieutenant John R. Smith, USAF *or* 1LT John R. Smith, USAF	Dear Lieutenant Smith:
Admiral	*Navy, Coast Guard:* ADM	Dear Admiral Smith:
Fleet Admiral	*Navy:* FADM	(same)
Rear Admiral	*Navy, Coast Guard:* RADM	(same)
Vice Admiral	*Navy, Coast Guard:* VADM	(same)
Airman	*Air Force:* Amn	Dear Airman Smith:
Airman First Class	*Air Force:* A1C	(same)
Airman Basic	*Air Force:* AB	(same)
Captain	*Army:* CPT; *Navy, Coast Guard:* CAPT; *Air Force, Marine Corps:* Capt	Dear Captain Smith:
Colonel	*Army:* COL; *Air Force, Marine Corps:* Col	Dear Colonel Smith:
Lieutenant Colonel	*Army:* LTC; *Air Force, Marine Corps:* LtCol	(same)
Commander	*Navy, Coast Guard:* CDR	Dear Commander Smith:
Lieutenant Commander	*Navy, Coast Guard:* LCDR	(same)
Corporal	*Army:* CPL; *Marine Corps:* Cpl	Dear Corporal Smith:
Lance Corporal	*Marine Corps:* LCpl	(same)
Ensign	*Navy, Coast Guard:* ENS	Dear Ensign Smith:

Addressee   Form of Address   Salutation

Addressee	Form of Address	Salutation
General	*Army:* GEN; *Air Force, Marine Corps:* Gen	Dear General Smith:
Lieutenant General	*Army:* LTG; *Air Force, Marine Corps:* LtGen	(same)
Major General	*Army:* MG; *Air Force, Marine Corps:* MajGen	(same)
Brigadier General	*Army:* BG; *Air Force:* BGen; *Marine Corps:* BrigGen	(same)
Lieutenant	*Navy, Coast Guard:* LT	Dear Lieutenant Smith:
First Lieutenant	*Army:* 1LT; *Air Force, Marine Corps:* 1stLt	(same)
Second Lieutenant	*Army:* 2LT; *Air Force, Marine Corps:* 2ndLt	(same)
Lieutenant Junior Grade	*Navy, Coast Guard:* LTJG	Dear Mr./Ms. Smith:
Major	*Army:* MAJ; *Air Force, Marine Corps:* Maj	Dear Major Smith:
Petty Officer (1st, 2nd, 3rd Class)	*Navy, Coast Guard:* PO1, PO2, PO3	Dear Petty Officer Smith:
Chief Petty Officer	*Navy, Coast Guard:* CPO	Dear Chief Smith:
Master Chief Petty Officer	*Navy, Coast Guard:* MCPO	Dear Master Chief Smith:
Senior Chief Petty Officer	*Navy, Coast Guard:* SCPO	Dear Senior Chief Smith:
Private	*Army:* PVT; *Marine Corps:* Pvt	Dear Private Smith:
Private First Class	*Army, Marine Corps:* PFC	(same)
Seaman	*Navy, Coast Guard:* Seaman	Dear Seaman Smith:
Seaman Apprentice	*Navy, Coast Guard:* SA	(same)
Seaman Recruit	*Navy, Coast Guard:* SR	(same)
Sergeant	*Army:* SGT; *Air Force, Marine Corps:* Sgt	Dear Sergeant Smith:
Sergeant Major	*Army:* SGM; *Marine Corps:* SgtMaj	Dear Sergeant Major Smith:
Sergeant Major of the Army	*Army:* SMA	(same)
Sergeant Major of the Marine Corps	*Marine Corps:* SgtMaj	(same)

Addressee — Form of Address — Salutation

Addressee	Form of Address	Salutation
Command Sergeant Major	*Army:* CSM	(same)
Master Sergeant	*Army:* MSG; *Air Force, Marine Corps:* MSgt	Dear Sergeant Smith:
Chief Master Sergeant	*Air Foce:* CMSgt	(same)
Chief Master Sergeant of the Air Force	*Air Force:* CMSAF	(same)
Sergeant First Class	*Army:* SFC	(same)
First Sergeant	*Army:* 1SG; *Marine Corps:* 1stSgt	(same)
Staff Sergeant	*Army:* SSG; *Air Force, Marine Corps:* SSgt	(same)
Technical Sergeant	*Air Force:* TSgt	(same)
Gunnery Sergeant	*Marine Corps:* GySgt	(same)
Master Gunnery Sergeant	*Marine Corps:* MGySgt	(same)
Specialist	*Army:* SPC	Dear Specialist Smith:
Warrant Officer	*Army:* WO1, WO2; *Navy:* WO-1; *Air Force, Marine Corps:* WO	Dear Warrant Officer Smith:
Chief Warrant Officer	*Army:* CW2, CW3, CW4, CW5; *Navy, Coast Guard, Air Force:* CWO-2, CWO-3, CWO-4; *Marine Corps:* CWO2, CW03, CWO4	Dear Chief Warrant Officer Smith:

Miscellaneous Professional Ranks and Titles

attorney	Mr. John R. Smith Attorney-at-Law *or* John R. Smith, Esq.	Dear Mr. Smith:
certified public accountant	Amelia R. Smith, C.P.A.	Dear Ms. Smith:
dentist	John R. Smith, D.D.S. (*or* D.M.D.) (office address) *or* Dr. John R. Smith (home address)	Dear Dr. Smith:

Addressee	Form of Address	Salutation
physician	Amelia R. Smith, M.D. (office address) *or* Dr. Amelia R. Smith (home address)	Dear Dr. Smith:
veterinarian	John R. Smith, D.V.M. (office address) *or* Dr. John R. Smith (home address)	Dear Dr. Smith: